The National Hockey League Official Guide & Record Book 1992-93

Published by the National Hockey League.
Compiled by the NHL Communications Group
and the 24 NHL Club Public Relations Directors.

THE NATIONAL HOCKEY LEAGUE
Official Guide & Record Book/1992-93

Staff:
For the NHL: Michael Berger; Supervising Editor: Greg Inglis; Statistician: Benny Ercolani; Editorial Staff: Susan Elliott, Stu Hackel, David Keon, Michele Romanin.

Managing Editors: Ralph Dinger, James Duplacey

Contributing Editor: Igor Kuperman

European Editor: Tom Ratschunas

Contributors:
Bill Benswanger, Nonni Daly (Hockey East), Luca Del-Vita, Norm Dueck (WHL), Peter Fillman, Mel Foster, Manon Gagnon (QMJHL), John Garner (ECAC), Erik Haglund, Patrick Kelly (ECHL), Neil McDonald, Nathan McGregor, Mike Meyers (IHL), Herb Morell (OHL), Marc Nathan, NHL Broadcasters' Association, NHL Central Registry, Valentina Riazanova, Renato Rossi, Hellen M. Schroeder (AHL), John Spencer (WCHA), Steven Steinsaltz, Jeff Weiss (CCHA), Richard Zulewski, Peter Jagla.

Consulting Publisher: Dan Diamond

Photo Credits:
Historical and special event photos: Bruce Bennett, David Bier, New York Rangers, Rice Studio, Robert Shaver, Imperial Oil Turofsky Collection, Hockey Hall of Fame, Public Archives of Canada.

Current photos: Graig Abel, Toronto; Joe Angeles, St. Louis; Steve Babineau, Boston; Sol Benjamin, Chicago, Bruce Bennett, NY Islanders, Tony Biegun, Winnipeg, Denis Brodeur, Montreal; Mark Buckner, St. Louis; Denny Cavanaugh, Pittsburgh; Steve Crandall, New Jersey; Bill Cunningham, Vancouver; Willie Dagenais, Montreal; Bob Fisher, Montreal; Ray Grabowski, Chicago; John Hartman, Detroit; J. Henson Photographics, Washington; George Kalinsky, NY Rangers; Deborah King, Washington; Jim Mackey, Detroit; McElligott-Teckles Sports Focus Imaging, Ottawa; Bill McKeown, Edmonton; Jack Murray, Vancouver; Tim Parker, St. Louis; Photography Ink, Los Angeles; Andre Pichette, Quebec; Richard Pilling, New Jersey; Len Redkoles, Philadelphia; Wen Roberts, Los Angeles, Al Ruelle, Boston; Harry Scull, Jr., Buffalo; Don Smith, San Jose; Diane Sobolewski, Hartford; Gerry Thomas, Edmonton; Jim Turner, New Jersey; Brad Watson, Calgary; Westfile, Edmonton; Rocky Widner, San Jose; Bill Wippert, Buffalo.

Canadian representatives:
North 49 Books, 193 Bartley Drive, Toronto, Ontario M4A 1E6
416/750-7777; FAX 416/750-2049
NHL Publishing, 194 Dovercourt Road, Toronto, Ontario M6J 3C8
416/531-6535; FAX 416/531-3939

U.S. representatives: Triumph Books,
644 South Clark Street, Chicago, Illinois 60605 312/939-3330; FAX 312/663-3557

International representatives: Barkers Worldwide Publications,
155 Maybury Road, Woking, Surrey, England GU21 5JR
Tel. and FAX: 011/44/483/776-141

Typesetting: Caledon Data Management, Caledon, Ontario
Printing: The Alger Press Limited, Oshawa and Toronto

9 8 7 6 5 4 3 2 1
Digit on the right indicates the number of this printing.

ISBN 0-920445-21-7

The National Hockey League
1800 McGill College Ave., suite 2600, Montreal, Quebec H3A 3J6
650 Fifth Avenue, 33rd floor, New York, New York 10019-6108
75 International Boulevard, suite 300, Toronto, Ontario M9W 6L9

Table of Contents

Table of Contents *continued*

(1992-93 NHL Schedule begins inside front cover)

Introduction

Growth and Change

WELCOME TO *THE NHL OFFICIAL GUIDE & RECORD BOOK FOR 1992-93.* GROWTH AND CHANGE in the National Hockey League is reflected throughout this 61st edition of the game's most comprehensive statistical annual. The Ottawa Senators and Tampa Bay Lightning have been added to the club section at the beginning the book. Players drafted and signed as free agents by Ottawa can be found on page 65. Tampa Bay's roster is on page 87. Detailed career stats for these players are also included in the Player and Goaltender Registers which, in this year's biggest-ever 424-page edition, begin on page 221 for players and page 397 for goaltenders.

The Player and Goaltender Registers in this book reflect changes in professional hockey. In previous editions, we have added players drafted in the first three rounds of the previous year's entry draft. The increasing number of players from Eastern Europe now appearing on NHL rosters have a necessitated a change. Beginning with this year's Player and Goaltender Registers, players drafted in rounds four, five and six are added as well. In addition, a careful analysis of each club's free agent signings and list of protected players has resulted in numerous additions and deletions to the Registers. Together, these changes combine to produce our most comprehensive listing of those players and goaltenders that comprise the talent pool that supplies the NHL.

On pages seven, eight and nine, you will find a brief history of Stanley Cup play, published to mark the Centennial of the Stanley Cup trophy. It was Lord Stanley of Preston, Canada's sixth Governor General, who, in 1892, decided to donate a silver bowl to be awarded to Canada's hockey champion. In the intervening one hundred years, the game and the trophy have undergone significant changes, but winning the Cup has remained the game's ultimate achievement. The NHL will celebrate the Cup's 100th birthday throughout the 1992-93 season. In addition, the statistical record of Stanley Cup hockey begins on page 198 of this edition.

On page 176 are brief biographies of those players drafted in the first round of the 1992 Entry Draft along with photos of those players drafted first through sixth. Scores of games played between the Canadian and U.S. Olympic Teams and NHL clubs are found on page 111. Twenty-four regular-season games are scheduled for non-NHL cities in 1992-93. These games and their locations are included in the overall NHL Schedule that begins on the inside cover of this edition and are also listed in each team's schedule panel found in the book's Club Section that begins on page 13.

As always, our thanks to readers and members of the media who take the time to comment on the *Guide & Record Book.* Thanks as well to the people working in the communications departments of the NHL's member clubs and to their counterparts in the AHL, IHL, ECHL, junior leagues and college conferences.

Best wishes for an enjoyable Stanley Cup Centennial Season in 1992-93.

ACCURACY REMAINS THE *GUIDE & RECORD BOOK*'S TOP PRIORITY.
We appreciate comments and clarification from our readers. Please direct these to:

Michael Berger 40th floor, 1633 Broadway, New York, NY 10019 . . . or . . .
Greg Inglis 75 International Blvd., suite 300, Rexdale, Ontario M9W 6L9.

Your involvement makes a better book.

National Hockey League

Organized November 22, 1917

Board of Governors

BOARD OF GOVERNORS OFFICERS
Chairman – Bruce McNall
Chairman's Executive Committee –
Ronald Corey
Michael Ilitch
Peter Pocklington
Edward M. Snider
Secretary – David Zimmerman

Boston Bruins
(Boston Professional Hockey Association, Inc.)
Jeremy Jacobs – Governor
Harry Sinden – Alternate Governor
Louis Jacobs – Alternate Governor

Buffalo Sabres
(Niagara Frontier Hockey, L.P.)
Seymour H. Knox III – Governor
Gerry Meehan – Alternate Governor
Robert O. Swados – Alternate Governor
Seymour H. Knox IV – Alternate Governor

Calgary Flames
(Calgary Flames Hockey Club)
Harley N. Hotchkiss – Governor
Byron J. Seaman – Alternate Governor
William C. Hay – Alternate Governor

Chicago Blackhawks
(Chicago Blackhawk Hockey Team, Inc.)
William W. Wirtz – Governor
Arthur M. Wirtz Jr. – Alternate Governor
Thomas N. Ivan – Alternate Governor
Robert Pulford – Alternate Governor
W. Rockwell Wirtz – Alternate Governor
Gene Gozdecki – Alternate Governor

Detroit Red Wings
(Detroit Red Wings, Inc.)
Michael Ilitch – Governor
James Lites – Alternate Governor
Jim Devellano – Alternate Governor

Edmonton Oilers
(Edmonton Oilers Hockey Corp.)
Peter Pocklington – Governor
Glen Sather – Alternate Governor
Lorne J. Ruzicka – Alternate Governor

Hartford Whalers
(Hartford Whalers Hockey Club Limited Partnership)
Richard Gordon – Governor
Emile Francis – Alternate Governor

Los Angeles Kings
(L.A. Kings, Ltd.)
Bruce McNall – Governor
Rogatien Vachon – Alternate Governor
Roy Mlakar – Alternate Governor

Minnesota North Stars
(North Stars Hockey Club, Inc.)
Norman N. Green – Governor
Patrick T. Forciea – Alternate Governor
John W.G. Donahue – Alternate Governor

Montreal Canadiens
(Le Club de Hockey Canadien, Inc.)
Ronald Corey – Governor
Ron Bowman – Alternate Governor
Serge Savard – Alternate Governor

New Jersey Devils
(Meadowlanders, Inc.)
Dr. John J. McMullen – Governor
John C. Whitehead – Alternate Governor
Louis A. Lamoriello – Alternate Governor

New York Islanders
(Nassau Sports)
Steve Walsh – Governor
William A. Torrey – Alternate Governor
Jerome Grossman – Alternate Governor
Robert Rosenthal – Alternate Governor
Jack Krumpe – Alternate Governor

New York Rangers
(New York Rangers Hockey Club, a Division of Madison Square Garden Center, Inc.)
Stanley R. Jaffe – Governor
Kevin R. Billet – Alternate Governor
Robert Gutkowski – Alternate Governor
Neil Smith – Alternate Governor

Ottawa Senators
(Ottawa Senators Hockey Club)
Bruce M. Firestone – Governor
Rod Bryden – Alternate Governor
Randy J. Sexton – Alternate Governor

Philadelphia Flyers
(Philadelphia Flyers Limited Partnership)
Jay T. Snider – Governor
Edward M. Snider – Alternate Governor
Ron Ryan – Alternate Governor
Russ Farwell – Alternate Governor
Bob Clarke – Alternate Governor

Pittsburgh Penguins
(Pittsburgh Hockey Associates)
Howard Baldwin – Governor
Paul Martha – Alternate Governor
Craig Patrick – Alternate Governor
Morris Belzberg – Alternate Governor
Thomas V. Ruta – Alternate Governor

Quebec Nordiques
(Le Club de Hockey les Nordiques, Societe en Commandite)
Marcel Aubut – Governor
Pierre Page – Alternate Governor
Gilles Leger – Alternate Governor

St. Louis Blues
(St. Louis Blues Hockey Club, L.P.)
Michael F. Shanahan – Governor
Ron Caron – Alternate Governor
Jack Quinn – Alternate Governor
Thomas Guilfoil – Alternate Governor

San Jose Sharks
(San Jose Sharks)
George Gund – Governor
Gordon Gund – Alternate Governor
Art Savage – Alternate Governor
Irvin A. Leonard – Alternate Governor

Tampa Bay Lightning
(Lightning Partners, Ltd.)
David LeFevre – Governor
Phil Esposito – Alternate Governor
Mel Lowell – Alternate Governor

Toronto Maple Leafs
(Maple Leaf Gardens, Limited)
Steve Stavro – Governor
Cliff Fletcher – Alternate Governor
Brian Bellmore – Alternate Governor

Vancouver Canucks
(Vancouver Hockey Club, Ltd.)
Arthur R. Griffiths – Governor
Frank A. Griffiths – Alternate Governor
Frank W. Griffiths – Alternate Governor
Pat Quinn – Alternate Governor

Washington Capitals
(Washington Hockey Limited Partnership)
Abe Pollin – Governor
David R. Poile – Alternate Governor
Richard Patrick – Alternate Governor

Winnipeg Jets
(8 Jets Hockey Ventures, Inc.)
Barry Shenkarow – Governor
Michael A. Smith – Alternate Governor
Bill Davis – Alternate Governor

League Offices

MONTREAL
1800 McGill College Ave.
Suite 2600
Montreal, Que. H3A 3J6
Phone: 514/288-9220
FAX: 514/284-0300

NEW YORK
33rd Floor, 650 Fifth Avenue
New York, NY, 10019-6108
Phone: 212/398-1100
FAX: 212/245-8221

TORONTO
75 International Blvd., Suite 300
Rexdale, Ont., M9W 6L9
Phone: 416/798-0809
General FAX: 416/798-0819
Communications FAX: 416/798-0852

LEAGUE OFFICERS
President – Gil Stein
Vice-President, Finance and Treasurer – Ken Sawyer
Vice-President, Hockey Operations – Jim Gregory
Vice-President, Marketing – Steve Ryan

League Departments

MONTREAL

Administration
Phil Scheuer – Director
Steve Hatzepetros – Assistant Director
Nancy Starnino – Secretary
Robert Bouchard – Administrative Assistant

Central Registry
Garry Lovegrove – Director
Steve Pellegrini – Assistant
Madeleine Supino – Assistant
Audrey Harari – Assistant

Consulting Services
Brian F. O'Neill – Consultant
Madeleine Supino – Secretary

Information Systems
Mario Carangi – Director
Miranda Ishak – Assistant Director
Luc Coulombe – Assistant Director
Tony Borsellino – Programmer/Analyst
John Sullivan – Programmer/Analyst
Guylene Mercier – Programmer
Antonio Fusco – Programmer
Johanne Hinds – Operations
Chantal Biron – PC Development/Support

Finance
Joseph DeSousa – Controller
Rosa Troiano – Secretary
Olivia Pietrantonio – Assistant Controller
Donna Gillman – Accounting Supervisor
Jocelyne Comeau – Accountant
Brenda Tang – Accountant
Adelina Valela – Accounts Receivable

Pension
Yvon Chamberland – Director
Lynne Blagrave – Manager, Pension Administration
Mary Skiadopoulos – Controller, Pension
Susan Lee – Administrative Assistant
Vivianne Chen – Administrative Assistant

Office Services
Jean Huard – Administrative Assistant
Darrin Burke – Office Assistant
Marcia Golding – Receptionist

NEW YORK

President's Staff
Pat Honig – Assistant to the President
Elaine Maginley – Executive Assistant
Carol Stephens – Executive Secretary

Finance
Ken Sawyer – Vice-President, Finance and Treasurer
Dorian Comparato – Executive Secretary
Pat Cassell-Cooper – Assistant Controller

Legal Department
David Zimmerman – Associate General Counsel

Alumni Relations
Darcy Rota – Coordinator

Security
Frank Torpey – Director of Security

TORONTO

Jim Gregory – Vice-President, Hockey Operations
Bryan Lewis – Director of Officiating
Wally Harris – Assistant Director of Officiating
Will Norris – Coordinator of Development
Frank Bonello – Director of Central Scouting
John Andersen – Central Scouting Administration
Al Wiseman – Assistant Director of Security
Chris Edwards – Video Coordinator
David Keon – Administrative Assistant
Dorothy Reaves – Receptionist

Secretarial Staff
Mary Keenan, Jacqueline Rinaldi, Kelley Rosset

Officiating Supervisory Staff
Dave Newell, Matt Pavelich, Lou Maschio, Jim Christison, John D'Amico, Bob Nadin, Sam Sisco, Charlie Banfield, Ron Ego, Art Skov, Dutch Van Deelen

Central Scouting Staff
Tim Bernhardt, Rob Pulford, Pat Carmichael, Mike Donaldson, Gary Eggleston, Laurence Ferguson, Ralph Goldhirsch, Paul Goulet, Ron Harris, Tom Martin, Dan Reinisch, Jack Timmins, Barry Trapp, Rolland Faubert, Al Godfrey

Communications Group
Gary Meagher – Executive Director of Communications
Susan Elliott – Director of Information and Editorial Services
Benny Ercolani – Statistician/Information Officer
Greg Inglis – Information Officer
Michele Romanin – Communications Assistant

NHL Enterprises, Inc.

1633 Broadway
40th Floor
New York, NY 10019
Phone: 212/767-4600
FAX:212/767-4646

Steve Ryan – President
Lucia Ripi Benke – Assistant to the President

Legal
Richard Zahnd – Senior Vice President, General Counsel

Finance
Walter Luby – Controller
Mary C. McCarthy – Assistant Controller

Broadcast Services
Stu Hackel – Director of Broadcasting

Administration
Janet A. Meyers – Director
Andrew Crawford – Office Services Assistant

Retail Licensing
J. Robert Carey – Senior Vice President
Fred Scalera – General Manager
Brian Jennings – Regional Sales Manager, Eastern Region
Bill Tighe – Regional Sales Manager, Western Region
Ilene Kent – Licensing & Marketing Director – Collectibles
Judy Salsberg – Director, Non-Apparel Products
Ann Kiely – Special Projects Coordinator
Jim Haskins – Licensing Contract Manager

Promotional Licensing
Steve Flatow – Executive Director
Sarah Galvin – Director of Sponsor Services

Publishing
Michael A. Berger – General Manager

Event Marketing
Frank Supovitz – General Manager
Karen Hovsepian – Director
Maria Pace Buettel – Assistant Director, Special Events
Mindy Kopper – Coordinator
Maria Sutherland – Coordinator

Anniversaries
John Karr – Executive Director (612) 854-1069
John Halligan – Director of Communications

NHL Enterprises Canada, Inc.

75 International Blvd. Suite 301
Rexdale, Ont. M9W 6L9
Phone: 416/798-9388
FAX: 416/798-9395

Bob McLaughlin – Managing Director, Canadian Licensing

NHL All-Star Weekend

960 Sun Life Building
1155 Metcalfe Avenue
Montreal, Que. H3B 2W2
Phone: 514/879-1040
FAX: 514/879-1022

Ann Devney – Manager
Anne Grotefeld – Manager
Mike Santos – Manager

Hockey Hall of Fame and Museum

Exhibition Place
Toronto, Ont. M6K 3C3
Phone: 416/595-1345
FAX: 416/971-5828

Ian Morrison – Chairman
David Taylor – President
Phil Denyes – Director of Marketing and Communications
Jeff Denomme – Director of Finance and Operations
Sue Bolender – Sponsorship Coordinator
Ray Paquet – Director, Facility Systems and Exhibit Development
Philip Pritchard – Director of Information and Acquisitions
Andy Yemen – Retail and Merchandise Manager

National Hockey League Players' Association

One Dundas Street West
Suite 2406
Toronto, Ontario
M5G 1Z3
Phone: 416/408-4040
FAX: 416/408-3685

Bob Goodenow – Executive Director
Sam Simpson – Director of Operations
Ted Saskin – Director of Licensing
Ian Pulver – Associate Counsel
Michael Humes – Director of Special Projects

SPECIAL FEATURE

Stanley Cup Centennial, 1893-1993

"Inscribed with Dreams"

It was Lord Stanley of Preston, Canada's sixth Governor General, who altered the course of hockey history when, in the spring of 1892, he announced his decision to donate a challenge cup to be awarded to the champion hockey club in Canada. The Stanley Cup – a squat bowl-shaped trophy purchased for the equivalent of fifty dollars – was first awarded in 1893. The trophy and the game of hockey have both undergone considerable change in the ensuing one hundred years. Rules have changed and leagues have come and gone, but the allure of the Stanley Cup – now a glittering silver barrel almost three feet high – has remained the centerpoint of hockey.

The National Hockey League will celebrate the centennial of the Stanley Cup with special events throughout the 1992-93 season. The slogan for the Centennial season is "Inscribed with Dreams." It describes the very special relationship that has always existed between Lord Stanley's trophy and those who care about the game of hockey.

Here is a brief history of the Stanley Cup since 1893.

Lord Stanley's sons Arthur, standing, second from left, and Edward, seated, far left, were members of the Rideau Rebels, an Ottawa-based club that played in 1893, the first year the Stanley Cup was awarded.

1. The Beginning, 1893-1909

The Stanley Cup's early years reflected the wide-open character of Canada – a nation newly-formed. Early hockey was a slow game, played without substitutions by seven hard-rock players per team. This was the era of epic Stanley Cup challenges, as any team in the Dominion of Canada – if judged a worthy opponent by the Cup's trustees – could throw down the gauntlet and take on the defending champions. Playoff formats varied from single game to two-game, total-goals to best-of-three encounters. Though the game's first "big-time" clubs were located in Ottawa, Montreal, and Toronto,

One Hundred Years of Stanley Cup Hockey

continued

challenges were received and accepted from locations as diverse as Rat Portage (later Kenora), Ontario; Dawson City, Yukon and New Glasgow, Nova Scotia. "Ringers" – players paid under the table to strengthen amateur clubs – were a part of the game from the beginning until finally, at the end of the era, Stanley Cup hockey had evolved into a competition solely between professional clubs.

The famed Ottawa Silver Seven – hockey's first great dynasty team – salted the ice in their arena to slow down a faster rival in 1904. Early in 1905, a team of hardy gold miners from the Yukon challenged for the Cup and travelled by dogsled, boat, road and rail to Ottawa, only to be shellacked by lopsided scores. A 1906 dispute over the eligibility of two well-known "ringers" almost resulted in the Stanley Cup being pitched into Ontario's Lake of the Woods.

2. The Professional Leagues, 1910-1926

The Seattle Metropolitans defeated the Montreal Canadiens in 1917 to become the first U.S.-based Stanley Cup winner.

Hockey and the Stanley Cup literally grew up together in this era. Two dominant professional leagues were formed at the beginning of the period: The National Hockey Association in Eastern Canada and the Pacific Coast Hockey Association in the West. Contract-jumping was commonplace, as top players changed teams and leagues at the wave of a better offer. Lester and Frank Patrick – pioneer players, innovators and entrepreneurs – built Canada's first artificial ice rinks in Vancouver and Victoria. By 1914, the Stanley Cup's status as a challenge trophy had changed. Instead, it was awarded to the winner of a best-of-five showdown series between the champions of the NHA and PCHA. The Seattle Metropolitans won the Cup in 1917, becoming the first U.S.-based team to claim the trophy. The NHA reorganized as the NHL later that same year. By the mid-1920s, a Golden Age of Sports was underway in the U.S. Salaries and celebrity escalated, eventually pricing the PCHA out of existence. In a deal orchestrated by the Patricks, the PCHA's players were sold en masse to new NHL franchises playing in huge new sports complexes in major American cities. These new clubs in New York, Boston, Chicago, and Detroit established the NHL as the game's pre-eminent league.

Joe Malone and Marty Walsh had ten-goal games in Stanley Cup play during this era. The Duke of Gloucester amended his travel plans to witness two exhibition games between the Ottawa Senators and Vancouver Millionaires in 1912. The Hamilton Tigers, the NHL's top team in regular-season play in 1924-25, went on strike before the playoffs to demand extra pay for extra games played. The Tigers' players were suspended and the league's second and third-place teams played off for the NHL championship.

3. The NHL Takes the Cup, 1927-1942

The NHL's new Ottawa Senators have a distinguished Stanley Cup pedigree. Ottawa clubs were Stanley Cup powerhouses in the early days of hockey, winning the Cup in 1903, 1904, 1905, 1909, 1911, and four times in the 1920s. The Senators' last Cup win saw the club defeat Boston two out of four games with two games tied.

With the Cup now the exclusive property of the NHL, the league launched into an era of unprecedented expansion, operating with as many as ten teams in American and Canadian divisions. Tube skates, frequent substitutions, and modification of passing and offside rules sped up play. Forward combinations like the Bread Line in New York, the S-Line for the Montreal Maroons, and the Kraut Line in Boston emerged to capture fans' imaginations. A new medium – radio – delivered the NHL and its star players into homes across Canada, with audiences of more than a million households commonplace by the early 1930s. The Rangers, Red Wings, Bruins and Black Hawks won their first Stanley Cup championships.

The NHL's two longest overtime games occurred in the 1930s. Ken Doraty scored for Toronto after 164 minutes of play in 1933; Mud Bruneteau scored for Detroit after 176 minutes in 1938. The Chicago Blackhawks won the Cup with a line-up made up of an equal number of Canadian- and American-born players. In addition, an injury to their goaltender forced the Hawks to begin the Stanley Cup finals with a minor-league goaltender who was pressed into service just an hour before game time. In 1942, the Toronto Maple Leafs became the first club to rally from a 3-0 deficit in games to win the Stanley Cup four games to three.

Maurice Richard holds the career record for playoff overtime goals with six, including three in 1951.

4. The Golden Age Begins, 1943-55

The folding of the Montreal Maroons and the New York Americans left the NHL as a cozy six-team circuit that was to enjoy stability and prosperity for a quarter of a century. The center red line was introduced in 1943, opening up play by allowing forward passing up to the middle of the rink. This was the era of dynasty teams in the NHL as the Maple Leafs in the late 1940s, and the Red Wings in the early 1950s won clusters of Stanley Cups. The game's most glittering superstar, Rocket Richard, began his career in 1942-43, and soon became the NHL's first 50-goal scorer, its fiercest competitor, and number-one gate attraction. Detroit built a powerhouse team around another superstar winger, Gordie Howe. Rivalries between clubs and players ran deep as the 120 players in the NHL played tighter defensive hockey than at any other time in the 75-year history of the league. By the end of this era, *Hockey Night in Canada* was a staple of yet another new medium, television.

Richard scored five goals in one playoff game in 1944. The Maple Leafs became the first NHL team to win three consecutive Cups with wins in 1947, 1948, and 1949. They won again in 1951, in a five-game series against the Canadiens in which every game was decided in overtime. Toronto defenseman Bill Barilko scored the winner in game five, but never played again. Shortly after the playoffs, he was killed when a small plane carrying him on a fishing trip in Northern Ontario was lost. The Canadiens and Red Wings hooked up in successive seven-game finals in 1954 and 1955. The 1954 series ended on a freak deflection into the Montreal net in overtime of the final game. The 1955 series was preceeded by the Richard Riot, a rowdy disturbance sparked by the suspension of Rocket Richard for the balance of the season and playoffs.

5. The Flying Frenchmen, 1956-1967

The Montreal Canadiens broke through to dominate the NHL beginning in 1955-56. With new coach Toe Blake and an emerging superstar in Jean Béliveau, the Habs were unstoppable, pouring on the scoring power to win five consecutive Stanley Cups. Toronto won three times in the early 1960s, before the Habs won twice more. The two clubs hooked up in a Stanley Cup classic in 1967, with the veteran-laden Leafs winning in Canada's centennial year. Boom-Boom Geoffrion and Bobby Hull matched Richard's 50-goal mark before Hull broke the barrier with 54 goals in 1966. Bobby Orr – a prodigiously talented young defenseman who would have a lasting impact on the way the game is played – appeared in 1966.

Bobby Hull and Jack "Tex" Evans enjoy the afterglow of Chicago's Stanley Cup win in 1961.

The Canadiens won 20 of 25 final-series games from 1956 to 1960. In 1964, Toronto's Bob Baun scored a crucial goal and then played an additional full game with a cracked bone in his tightly-taped leg. Three years later, Toronto coach Punch Imlach instructed defenseman Allan Stanley to take a crucial last-minute faceoff against Jean Béliveau in the Leafs' end. Stanley hadn't taken a faceoff in five years, but won the draw, leading to an empty-net goal by George Armstrong that clinched the 1967 Cup for the Leafs.

6. The Great Expansion, 1968-1979

The NHL doubled in size to twelve teams in 1967, adding clubs in six American cities. Additional expansion followed. That, combined with competition for players from a rival league, resulted in a scrappy kind of hockey that was dominated by big, tough Boston Bruins teams in the early 1970s. The Philadelphia Flyers enjoyed great success, winning back-to-back titles in 1974 and 1975. The Montreal Canadiens, led by superstar winger Guy Lafleur trumped the Flyers' rugged game by building a team that combined size and speed. The Canadiens would hold the Cup from 1976 to 1979.

Orr's airborne overtime goal in 1970 brought Boston its first Cup in 29 seasons. Unheralded goaltender Ken Dryden stunned the Bruins in the playoffs the following year and went on to backstop the Canadiens to an upset Cup win. The 1974 finals between Buffalo and Philadelphia were interrupted by fog seeping from the ice in a very warm arena. Guy Lafleur ripped a pin-point shot past Boston goaltender Gilles Gilbert to force overtime in game seven of the 1979 semi-finals after the Bruins had been penalized for having too many men on the ice.

7. The Great One Cometh, 1980-1992

The turmoil between the NHL and its rival, the World Hockey Association ended in 1979 when four former-WHA teams joined the NHL, The resulting 21-team league would soon be dominated by the game's most gifted player, Wayne Gretzky, a scoring phenomenon tapped for stardom since the age of six. Gretzky made believers of those who thought that he would be intimidated in the NHL by demolishing the league's scoring records. The New York Islanders established a four-Cup dynasty to begin the decade, riding the marksmanship of Mike Bossy and efforts of a core of hard-working skilled players to the title from 1980 to 1983. Gretzky and the Oilers became champions in 1984 and would win the Cup in three of the next four seasons. The Oilers' trademark was speed and all-out offense. Gretzky's landmark trade to Los Angeles in 1988 initiated an era of parity in the league, but the emergence of the Pittsburgh Penguins, Cup winners in 1991 and 1992 on the strength of superstar Mario Lemieux's scoring prowess, suggests that the concept of dynasty hockey may still prove relevant in today's NHL. Pittsburgh's young Czech right winger, Jaromir Jagr, performed superbly in the finals, indicating that the recent influx of talented eastern European players into the NHL is already being felt in Stanley Cup play.

Despite player changes, the Edmonton Oilers won five of seven Stanley Cup championships between 1984 and 1990. This celebration occurred in 1988.

Excerpted from The Official National Hockey League Stanley Cup Centennial Book, *published in November of 1992 by McClelland and Stewart, Toronto. Hard cover, 288 pages, 250 photos, $40. Available at bookstores, NHL arenas, or by mail. To order, see page on page 420 of this book.*

Referees and Linesmen

BLAINE ANGUS . . . Referee . . . Born: Sept. 25, 1961 in Shawville, Que. . . . Hired by the NHL in 1991, Angus has been an NHL trainee since 1988 . . . refereed in the OHL and OHA last season . . . enjoys golf, running and carpentry in the off-season . . . is a registered x-ray technologist . . . resides in Barrie, Ontario with his wife and two children.

RON ASSELSTINE . . . Linesman . . . Born: Nov. 6, 1946 in Toronto, Ont. . . . First NHL Game: Oct. 10, 1979 . . . Total NHL Games: 1,034 . . . Worked 1,000th NHL game on January 4, 1992 at New Jersey. Ron is very active in his community as chairman of the "Make-A-Wish" Foundation and as an Ontario Provincial Police "Auxiliary" Officer. He is married and has two children.

WAYNE BONNEY . . . Linesman . . . Born: May 27, 1953 in Ottawa, Ont. . . . First NHL Game: Oct. 10, 1979 . . . Total NHL Games: 998 . . . Joined the NHL in 1979. Bonney worked the 1989 All-Star Game in Edmonton and the Stanley Cup Championship series in 1991 and 1992. He currently resides in Kirkland, Que., with his wife and daughter. He is an avid baseball player.

RYAN BOZAK . . . Linesman . . . Born: Jan. 3, 1947 in Swift Current, Sask. . . . First NHL Game: 1972 . . . Total NHL Games: 1,461 . . . Joined the NHL in 1972 and worked his 1,450th NHL game in 1991-92. He was selected to officiate in the 1983 NHL All-Star Game on Long Island. During the off-season he enjoys golf and tennis and resides in San Diego, CA. Bozak has two children.

GORD BROSEKER . . . Linesman . . . Born: July 8, 1950 in Baltimore, MD . . . First NHL Game: Jan 14, 1975 . . . Total NHL Games: 1,271 . . . Joined the NHL in 1973 and officiated in his 1,250th NHL game in 1991-92. Before beginning his officiating career, he played baseball in the Texas Rangers' organization. Broseker was selected to officiate in the 1991 Stanley Cup championship series. He currently resides in Richmond, VA, with his wife and daughter.

PIERRE CHAMPOUX . . . Linesman . . . Born: Apr. 18, 1963 in Ville St. Pierre, Que. . . . First NHL Game: Oct. 8, 1988 . . . Total NHL Games: 240 . . . Began officiating minor league games at the age of 12 in the Quebec pee wee league. Since then he has worked in two international competitions, having officiated in an exhibition game between the United States and Canada at the Forum and in Canada Cup 1987. During the off-season, Champoux enjoys golf, tennis and cycling. Champoux is single.

KEVIN COLLINS . . . Linesman . . . Born: Dec. 15,1950 in Springfield, MA . . . First NHL Game: Oct. 13, 1977 . . . Total NHL Games: 1,201 . . . Joined the NHL in 1971. He was selected to officiate in the 1988 NHL All-Star Game in St. Louis and officiated in the 1991 Stanley Cup championship series. Currently residing in Springfield, MA, Collins is married and has three children.

MICHAEL CVIK . . . Linesman . . . Born: July 6, 1962 in Calgary, Alta. . . . First NHL Game: Oct. 8, 1987 . . . Total NHL Games: 346 . . . The tallest of the officials at 6'9", began his officiating career in the AAHA in 1978. After working his way through the WHL, he joined the NHL in 1987. During the off-season, Mike is an instructor at the AAHA Development Camps and the WHL School of Officiating. He enjoys weightlifting, cycling, music, reading, yoga and golf. He is single.

PAT DAPUZZO . . . Linesman . . . Born: Dec. 29, 1958 in Hoboken, NJ . . . First NHL Game: Dec. 5, 1984 . . . Total NHL Games: 576 . . . Officiated in his first NHL game on Dec. 5, 1984, in Madison Square Garden. He worked six games in the 1991 Canada Cup. Pat resides in North Bergen, NJ and is single. He is an avid weightlifter and karate enthusiast.

BERNARD DEGRACE . . . Linesman . . . Born: May 1, 1967 in Lameque, N.B. . . . First NHL Game: Oct. 15, 1991 . . . Total NHL Games: 36 . . . Worked the 1992 Calder Cup Finals . . . During the off-season he enjoys golf, fishing, biking and travelling . . . He is single.

PAUL DEVORSKI . . . Referee . . . Born: Aug. 18, 1958 in Guelph, Ont. . . . Joined the NHL in 1987 . . . Total NHL Games: 73 . . . Devorski is a part owner of Gold's Gym in Guelph and enjoys golf, weightlifting and mountain biking. He is single.

SCOTT DRISCOLL . . . Linesman . . . Born: May 2, 1968 in Seaforth, Ont. . . . Hired by the NHL in 1991 . . . Began refereeing minor hockey at the age of 13 . . . Worked the 1992 OHL Finals . . . Enjoys playing several sports in the off-season . . . He is married.

MARK FAUCETTE . . . Referee . . . Born: June 9, 1958 in Springfield, MA . . . First NHL Game: 1985 . . . Total NHL Games: 200 . . . Joined the NHL in 1985. First playoff game was 6-5 overtime win by Los Angeles over Vancouver in 1991. He is single.

RON FINN . . . Linesman . . . Born: Dec. 1, 1940 in Toronto, Ont. . . . First NHL Game: October 11, 1969 . . . Total NHL Games: 1,766 . . . Has worked in more games than any other active official. . . . A resident of Brampton, Ont. He has worked in two All-Star Games including 1977 (Vancouver) and 1982 (Washington, D.C.). He also worked during Rendez-Vous '87 in Quebec City. Finn set an NHL playoff record for officials by working in his 252nd career playoff game on April 23, 1991. He is active in his community during the off-season, working with the Canadian Special Olympics and is an instructor at various officiating schools in Ontario. Ron is married and has four children.

KERRY FRASER . . . Referee . . . Born: June 30, 1952 in Sarnia, Ont. . . . Total NHL Games: 751 . . . After playing minor league hockey as a youngster, attended the NHL training camp for officials in 1972. Fraser has become one of the League's most experienced and respected referees, as proven by his selection to referee five Stanley Cup championship series (1985, 1986, 1989-91). During the off-season, Fraser assists in numerous charitable fundraisers, attends public speaking engagements to service clubs and works with amateur hockey officials' groups. Fraser enjoys sailing and golf. He is married and has seven children.

GERARD GAUTHIER . . . Linesman . . . Born: Sept. 5, 1948 in Montreal, Que. . . . First NHL Game: Oct. 16, 1971 . . . Total NHL Games: 1,598 . . . Attended his first NHL training camp in 1971 after two years in junior hockey. He has been selected to work at two NHL All-Star Games in his career; Los Angeles (1981) and Calgary (1985). In addition, he has worked in the 1984 Canada Cup and in three Stanley Cup Championship series — 1982, 1983 and 1992. On January 25, 1991, Gauthier became the fifth linesman in NHL history to reach 1,500 career games. During the off-season, Gauthier enjoys golfing and tennis. He is married and has two children.

TERRY GREGSON . . . Referee . . . Born: Nov. 7 1953 in Guelph, Ont. . . . First NHL Game: Dec. 19, 1981 . . . Total NHL Games: 623 . . . Joined the NHL in 1979. Gregson was selected to officiate his second career All-Star Game in 1991 at Chicago. Worked the 1992 Stanley Cup Championship. President of the National Hockey League Officials Association, Gregson is also Co-Chairman of the NHLOA's Children's Wish Foundation. During the off-season he is an avid traveller and participates in charity golf tournaments. Gregson is married.

SHANE HEYER . . . Referee . . . Born: Feb. 7,1964 in Summerland, B.C. . . . First NHL Game: Oct. 5, 1988 . . . Total NHL Games: 299 . . . Began officiating in Penticton, B.C., at the age of 10 and was invited to join the NHL program in 1988. In his first year of service, Heyer was selected to work in the December 31 game between the Los Angeles Kings and the Dynamo Riga club during Super Series '88-89. Heyer is single and enjoys softball, cycling and golf.

BOB HODGES . . . Linesman . . . Born: Aug. 16, 1944 in Hespeler, Ont. . . . First NHL Game: Oct. 14, 1972 . . . Total NHL Games: 1,425 . . . Hired by the NHL in 1972-73 season at the age of 28, Hodges is one of the NHL's senior officials. He has been chosen to work in the Stanley Cup Finals three times (1982, 1986 and 1987) and officiated at the All-Star Game in Calgary (1985) and Pittsburgh (1990). During the off-season he works with the Juvenile Diabetes Foundation and enjoys hunting, fishing and golf. Hodges is married and has two children.

RON HOGGARTH . . . Referee . . . Born: Apr. 12, 1948 in Barrie, Ont. . . . First NHL Game: Oct. 16, 1971 . . . Total NHL Games: 1,043 . . . Began officiating while still a student at McMaster University. He joined the NHL in 1971. Worked his 1,000th game December 21, 1991. During the summer, Hoggarth owns and operates KoHo pools in Barrie and is active in golf and tennis. He is married and has two daughters.

DAVE JACKSON . . . Referee . . . Born: Nov. 28, 1964 in Montreal, Que. . . . Total NHL Games: 9 . . . One of two officials to join the NHL in 1989, he was an NHL trainee at the age of 21. He made his first NHL appearance in the 1990-91 season. During the off-season, he enjoys golf, softball, biking and travelling. Jackson is married.

SWEDE KNOX . . . Linesman . . . Born: Mar. 2, 1948 in Edmonton, Alta. . . . First NHL Game: Oct. 14, 1972 . . . Total NHL Games: 1,554 . . . Joined the NHL in 1971. In 1982, he was selected to work in the NHL All-Star Game in Washington, D.C. He has also worked in five Stanley Cup championship series. Worked his 1,500th game October 26, 1991. A full-time resident of Edmonton, Swede is married and has two children. He enjoys squash and golf during the off-season.

DON KOHARSKI . . . Referee . . . Born: Dec. 2, 1955 in Halifax, N.S. . . . First NHL Game: Oct. 14, 1977 . . . Total NHL Games: 748 (163 as a linesman) . . . Hired as an official in the WHA at the age of 18. He joined the NHL in 1977 as a linesman, becoming a referee after 163 games. Koharski gained international experience in Canada Cup 1987 and has worked in six Stanley Cup Finals (1986-88, 1990-92). He refereed his first NHL All-Star Game in 1992. He is married and has two sons.

DENNIS LARUE . . . Referee . . . Born: July 14, 1959 in Savannah, GA . . . Total NHL Games: 9 . . . Attended the USA Hockey Referee Development Camp in 1983 and joined the NHL in 1988. He made his NHL debut on March 26, 1991. During the off-season he is involved in summer camp programs for children and in an instructor at the USA Hockey Referee Development Camp. He is an avid golfer. Dennis is married and has two children.

BRAD LAZAROWICH . . . Linesman . . . Born: Aug. 4, 1962 in Vancouver, B.C. . . . First NHL Game: Oct. 9, 1986 . . . Total NHL Games: 443 . . . Joined the NHL in 1986. During the off-season, Brad is employed by the Delta Corporation in the Water Works division and is an avid bicyclist, golfer and weightlifter. He is married and has a daughter.

DAN MAROUELLI . . . Referee . . . Born: July 16, 1955 in Edmonton, Alta. . . . First NHL Game: Nov. 2, 1984 . . . Total NHL Games: 477 . . . Began his officiating career at the age of 13 with the Knights of Columbus. He joined the NHL in 1982. During the summer, Marouelli works at a number of refereeing schools and owns a small construction business in addition to participating in many charity fundraising events. He is an avid golfer. Dan is married and has three children.

ROB MARTELL . . . Referee . . . Born: October 21, 1963 in Winnipeg, Man. . . . First NHL Game: Mar. 14, 1984 . . . Began officiating minor hockey at the age of 14 . . . During the off-season he is a volunteer with the Special Olympics . . . Enjoys golf and summer hockey . . . He is married.

DAN McCOURT . . . Linesman . . . Born: Aug. 14, 1954 in Falconbridge, Ont. . . . First NHL Game: Dec. 27, 1980 . . . Total NHL Games: 808 . . . Joined the NHL in 1979. . . . Worked the 1990 All-Star Game in Pittsburgh. During the off-season, he works with the Easter Seals Society. He enjoys golf, baseball, boating and water-skiing. McCourt is married and has two daughters.

BILL McCREARY . . . Referee . . . Born: Nov. 17, 1955 in Guelph, Ont. . . . First NHL Game: Nov. 3, 1984 . . . Total NHL Games: 493 . . . Joined the NHL in 1982. He was selected to referee the Red Army vs. Buffalo Sabres game on January 9 in Super Series '88-89. During the off-season, McCreary is active in charity events for the Make-a-Wish Foundation and Special Olympics and coaches minor baseball and hockey. He also enjoys hunting and fishing. He is married and has two sons and a daughter.

MIKE McGEOUGH . . . Referee . . . Born: June 20, 1957 in Regina, Sask. . . . Total NHL Games: 79 . . . Began his NHL career in 1987. During the off-season, McGeough enjoys golf and bicycling. He instructs at various refereeing schools. He is married and has three children.

RANDY MITTON . . . Linesman . . . Born: Sept. 22, 1950 in Fredericton, N.B. . . . First NHL Game: Dec. 26, 1973 . . . Total NHL Games: 1,361 . . . Became involved in NHL officiating in 1972 after working in the WHL and AHL for two years. He gained international experience as a linesman for the 1987 Canada Cup and was selected to officiate in the 1988 NHL All-Star Game in St. Louis. During the off-season, Mitton teaches at a number of officiating schools in Western Canada. He is married and has two children.

DENIS MOREL . . . Referee . . . Born: Dec. 13, 1948 in Quebec City, Que. . . . First NHL Game: Jan. 18, 1976 . . . Total NHL Games: 1,008 . . . Began officiating in Quebec minor leagues before joining the NHL in 1976. Morel has worked in two Stanley Cup Championship series — 1988 and 1989. Worked 1,000th game, March 14, 1992. During the summer, he is active in the Trois-Rivieres Special Olympics Program and hosts an annual charity golf tournament. He enjoys swimming and golf and is an avid reader. He is married and has two children.

JEAN MORIN . . . Linesman . . . Born: August 10, 1963 in Sorel, Que. . . . First NHL Game: Oct. 5, 1991 . . . Worked three games during the 1991-92 series between the U.S. or Canadian National Team and NHL teams . . . Enjoys golf, reading, softball and volleyball . . . He is married and has one child.

BRIAN MURPHY . . . Linesman . . . Born: Dec. 13, 1964 in Dover, NH . . . First NHL Game: Oct. 7, 1988 . . . Total NHL Games: 246 . . . Joined the League in 1988-89 after graduating from the University of New Hampshire with a degree in Business Administration. During his years at University, he worked in the NCAA officiating ranks, including the 1988 NCAA Division I National Championship Game in Lake Placid. During the off-season, Murphy works as a part-time accountant. Murphy is married.

DAN O'HALLORAN . . . Referee . . . Born: March 25, 1964 at Leamington, Ont. . . . Worked the 1992 IHL All-Star Game and the 1992 Turner Cup Finals . . . Enjoys playing golf . . . He is married and has one child.

MARK PARE . . . Linesman . . . Born: July 26, 1957 in Windsor, Ont. . . . First NHL Game: Oct. 11, 1979 . . . Total NHL Games: 1,015 . . . Joined the NHL in 1979 after working minor leagues in Windsor. Pare worked his 1,000th game in 1991-92. He made his NHL All-Star Game debut in 1992. He enjoys golfing. Pare is married and has two children.

JERRY PATEMAN . . . Linesman . . . Born: Jan. 12, 1958 in The Hague, Netherlands . . . First NHL Game: Nov. 10, 1982 . . . Total NHL Games: 427 . . . The only NHL official not born in North America, Pateman started refereeing minor hockey in Chatham, Ont. at the age of 14. He joined the NHL in 1982 and officiated in the 1991 All-Star Game in Chicago. During the summer, Pateman works part-time at a food products company and enjoys gardening, golf and baseball. Pateman now resides in Tecumseh, Ont. with his wife and two children.

LANCE ROBERTS . . . Referee . . . Born: May 28, 1957 in Edmonton, Alta. . . . Total NHL Games: 35 . . . Began his career at the age of 15 in the minor leagues of Alberta. Roberts takes college courses during the summer and also works with young offenders at a detention center. He is married with two daughters and enjoys golf and baseball.

RAY SCAPINELLO . . . Linesman . . . Born: Nov. 5, 1946 in Guelph, Ont. . . . First NHL Game in 1971 in Buffalo . . . Total NHL Games: 1,690. . . . Joined NHL in 1971 . . . Has worked three All-Star Games, 11 consecutive Stanley Cup Finals plus the Canada Cup, Challenge Cup and Rendez-Vous 87 . . . In the off-season, Ray is a two-handicap golfter and works with the "Make-A-Wish" chapter in Guelph . . . He is married and has a son.

DAN SCHACHTE . . . Linesman . . . Born: July 13, 1958 in Madison, WI . . . First NHL Game: October 8, 1982 . . . Total NHL Games: 739 . . . Joined the NHL in 1982. He was chosen to officiate in the 1991 All-Star Game in Chicago. Also worked in the 1991 Canada Cup. He enjoys hunting, fishing and boating. He is married and has two children.

LYLE SEITZ . . . Linesman . . . Born: Jan. 22, 1969 in Brooks, Alta. . . . Began officiating minor hockey at the age of 9 . . . Worked the 1991 WHL All-Star Game and the 1992 Memorial Cup Finals . . . Off-season activities include cattle and grain farming . . . Enjoys racquet sports, golf, cycling and weightlifting. He is single.

JAY SHARRERS . . . Linesman . . . Born: July 3, 1967 in New Westminster, B.C. . . . Joined the NHL in 1990 . . . Total NHL games: 117 . . . Has also worked Canadian college games and, in 1985-86, a tournament involving college teams from the U.S., Canada and Japan . . . Enjoys camping, fishing, baseball and golf. He is single.

ROB SHICK . . . Referee . . . Born: Dec. 4, 1957, in Port Alberni, B.C. . . . First NHL Game: Apr. 6, 1986 . . . Total NHL Games: 310 . . . Joined the NHL in 1984. He is married. Instructs at a referees' school in the off-season. Enjoys golf, fishing and travelling.

PAUL STEWART . . . Referee . . . Born: Mar. 21, 1955 in Boston, MA . . . First NHL Game: Mar. 27, 1987 . . . Total NHL Games: 312 . . . Joined the NHL in 1985. Shortly after joining the League, he was asked to officiate in the 1987 Canada Cup. Stewart is the only former NHL player on the active officiating staff. During the off-season, Stewart continues his graduate studies at Northeastern University and is employed in estate planning. Stewart is married and enjoys landscaping, gardening and golf.

LEON STICKLE . . . Linesman . . . Born: Apr. 20, 1948 in Toronto, Ont. . . . First NHL Game: Oct. 17, 1970 . . . Total NHL Games: 1,663 . . . Joined the NHL in 1969 after four years in the minor leagues. In his career, he has worked in three NHL All-Star Games (Montreal, 1975; Buffalo,1978 and Long Island, 1983). He also was selected as an official for the Canada Cup tournament in 1981 and 1984. He has worked in the Stanley Cup Finals six times (1977, 1978, 1980, 1981, 1984 and 1985). During the off-season, Stickle is active with the Ontario and Canadian Special Olympics and coaches minor league baseball. He also enjoys golf. He is married and has three children.

RICHARD TROTTIER . . . Referee . . . Born: Feb. 28, 1957 in Laval, Que. . . . Total NHL Games: 45 . . . During his career, he has served as the executive vice-president for the Quebec Esso Cup in 1987-88 and 1988-89 and has been the referee-in-chief for the Quebec Ice Hockey Federation since 1986. During the off-season, he enjoys golf, racquetball and badminton.

ANDY vanHELLEMOND . . . Referee . . . Born: Feb. 16, 1948 in Winnipeg, Man. . . . First NHL Game: Nov. 22, 1972 . . . Total NHL Games: 1,264 . . . Joined the NHL in 1971 and has become one of the senior NHL officials. He worked in the NHL All-Star contest in Calgary (1985) and Rendez-Vous '87 in Quebec City. He has been selected to work in the Stanley Cup Final series 16 consecutive years since 1977. During the off-season, vanHellemond enjoys golfing, gardening and baseball.

DON VAN MASSENHOVEN . . . Referee . . . Born: July 17, 1960 in London, Ont. . . . Began officiating at the age of 15 . . . Worked the 1990 Memorial Cup Final in Hamilton. Is a police officer in the off-season. He is married and has two children.

MARK VINES . . . Linesman . . . Born: Dec. 3, 1960 in Elmira, Ont. . . . First NHL Game: Oct. 13, 1984 . . . Total NHL Games: 636 . . . Joined the NHL in 1984. Worked the 1991 Canada Cup and at the 1992 NHL All-Star game in Philadelphia. He attends university during the off-season and is single.

STEPHEN WALKOM . . . Referee . . . Born: Aug. 8, 1963 in North Bay, Ontario. . . . NHL officiating trainee since 1989-90, working OHL and minor pro games . . . Has also worked Canadian college, Northern OHA, senior and junior B . . . Honors degree in Commerce from Laurentian U . . . Lives in Kitchener, Ont. . . . Enjoys running, cycling, racquet sports and sailing . . . Power-skating instructor.

MARK WHELER . . . Linesman . . . Born: Sept. 20, 1965 in North Battleford, Sask. . . . Began officiating at the age of 12. Worked the 1989 and 1992 Memorial Cup Finals. Enjoys playing golf, cycling and other outdoor activities. He is married.

NHL Attendance

Season	Regular Season Games	Regular Season Attendance	Playoffs Games	Playoffs Attendance	Total Attendance
1960-61	210	2,317,142	17	242,000	2,559,142
1961-62	210	2,435,424	18	277,000	2,712,424
1962-63	210	2,590,574	16	220,906	2,811,480
1963-64	210	2,732,642	21	309,149	3,041,791
1964-65	210	2,822,635	20	303,859	3,126,494
1965-66	210	2,941,164	16	249,000	3,190,184
1966-67	210	3,084,759	16	248,336	3,333,095
1967-68[1]	444	4,938,043	40	495,089	5,433,132
1968-69	456	5,550,613	33	431,739	5,982,352
1969-70	456	5,992,065	34	461,694	6,453,759
1970-71[2]	546	7,257,677	43	707,633	7,965,310
1971-72	546	7,609,368	36	582,666	8,192,034
1972-73[3]	624	8,575,651	38	624,637	9,200,288
1973-74	624	8,640,978	38	600,442	9,241,420
1974-75[4]	720	9,521,536	51	784,181	10,305,717
1975-76	720	9,103,761	48	726,279	9,830,040
1976-77	720	8,563,890	44	646,279	9,210,169
1977-78	720	8,526,564	45	686,634	9,213,198
1978-79	680	7,758,053	45	694,521	8,452,574
1979-80[5]	840	10,533,623	63	976,699	11,510,322
1980-81	840	10,726,198	68	966,390	11,692,588
1981-82	840	10,710,894	71	1,058,948	11,769,842
1982-83	840	11,020,610	66	1,088,222	12,028,832
1983-84	840	11,359,386	70	1,107,400	12,466,786
1984-85	840	11,633,730	70	1,107,500	12,741,230
1985-86	840	11,621,000	72	1,152,503	12,773,503
1986-87	840	11,855,880	87	1,383,967	13,239,847
1987-88	840	12,117,512	83	1,336,901	13,454,413
1988-89	840	12,417,969	83	1,327,214	13,745,183
1989-90	840	12,579,651	85	1,355,593	13,935,244
1990-91	840	12,343,897	92	1,442,203	13,786,100
1991-92[6]	880	12,769,676	86	1,327,920	14,097,596

[1] First expansion: Los Angeles, Pittsburgh, California (Cleveland), Philadelphia, St. Louis and Minnesota
[2] Second expansion: Buffalo and Vancouver
[3] Third expansion: Atlanta (Calgary) and New York Islanders
[4] Fourth expansion: Kansas City (Colorado, New Jersey) and Washington
[5] Fifth expansion: Edmonton, Hartford, Quebec and Winnipeg
[6] Sixth expansion: San Jose

League Presidents

Gil Stein

John A. Ziegler, Jr.

Clarence Campbell

Mervyn "Red" Dutton

Frank Calder

Gil Stein

President, 1992 to date

Gil Stein, for 15 years the National Hockey League's vice president and general counsel, was named president and chief executive officer of the NHL on October 1, 1992, succeeding John A. Ziegler, Jr.

A Philadelphia native, the 64-year-old Stein began working in professional hockey in 1972, when he was retained by the Philadelphia Flyers as general counsel and alternate governor for the club. Stein became executive vice president and chief executive officer of the Flyers in September of 1976. He served as president and governor of the Maine Mariners (the Flyers' American Hockey League affiliate) through the summer of 1977, and joined the NHL as vice president and general counsel in December of 1977.

A World War II veteran whose 18-month stint in the U.S. Army prolonged his undergraduate college career at Temple University from 1944 through 1949, Stein graduated from Boston University School of Law in 1952. In 1955 he became a regional director for the Pennsylvania Labor Relations Board, a position he held until becoming first deputy controller for the city of Philadelphia in 1958. Stein served in that capacity for a total of 12 years, interrupting his tenure to become deputy district attorney for Philadelphia during 1968 and 1969. He entered private practice in 1971 with Blank, Rome, Comisky & McCauley (where he remained until 1976), and served six months as executive director of the Philadelphia Housing Authority through 1972-73.

A long-time season ticket holder for both the New York Rangers and Philadelphia Flyers, Gil and his wife Barbara make their home in Villanova, PA. They have three children (sons Andrew and John, and daughter Holly Spinner) and two grandchildren (Samantha and Emily Spinner).

John A. Ziegler, Jr.

President, 1977 to 1992

John A. Ziegler, Jr. was born in Grosse Pointe, Michigan, on February 9, 1934.

He graduated from the University of Michigan in 1957, earning a bachelor of arts and *juris* doctor degrees. Upon graduation he joined the Detroit law firm of Dickinson, Wright, McKean and Cudlip and became a partner in the firm in 1964. In 1969 he left the firm and in September of 1970 he set up his own firm, Ziegler, Dykhouse & Wise. He continued as senior partner in the firm until assuming his position in September, 1977.

In 1959 he began to do legal work for Olympia Stadium, the Detroit Red Wings and Mr. Bruce Norris. He continued to serve these clients in various capacities until his election as president of the National Hockey League. In 1966 he joined the NHL Board of Governors as an alternate governor for the Detroit Red Wings and, as such, worked on many of the NHL's committees and was involved in various aspects of the League's litigation as well as relations and negotiations with the Players' Association.

In June of 1976, he succeeded William Wirtz as Chairman of the National Hockey League Board of Governors. He was inducted into the Hockey Hall of Fame as a Builder in June, 1987.

Clarence Campbell

President, 1946 to 1977

Clarence Campbell was a Rhodes Scholar who was born July 9, 1905 in Fleming, Saskatchewan. In 1926, a 20-year-old Campbell graduated from the University of Alberta with bachelor of arts and bachelor of law degrees.

Following his studies at Oxford, England, Campbell returned to Canada to begin his law practise. Forever active in sports, he also became an NHL referee, working 155 regular-season games and twelve Stanley Cup playoff contests through 1939 when he joined the Canadian Armed Forces for the duration of World War II.

On September 5, 1946, Campbell became the NHL's third president succeeding Mervyn "Red" Dutton. Within a year of his appointment, he established the NHL Players' Pension Plan which has since become the prototype for other professional sports leagues.

Campbell led the League through its greatest era of expansion in 1967 when the NHL doubled in size from six to twelve teams. In 1972, he also succeeded in breaking ground in a new era of international competition, when, for the first time in hockey history, Canada's finest NHL talent faced-off against the Soviet Union's elite in an eight-game challenge series.

Elected to the Hockey Hall of Fame in 1966, Campbell also received the Lester Patrick Trophy for "outstanding service to hockey in the United States" in 1972. He retired from the NHL in 1977, but continued to stay close to the League until his death in 1984.

Mervyn "Red" Dutton

President, 1943 to 1946

Born on July 23, 1898 in Russell, Manitoba, Mervyn "Red" Dutton succeeded Frank Calder as the second president of the NHL. For two seasons, 1943-44 and 1944-45, Dutton remained at the head of the League before resuming his career in private business. Most remembered for his rugged playing style, Dutton overcame severe war injuries to skate as a professional for over a decade. After anchoring the defense for Calgary in the Western Hockey League from 1921 to 1925, Dutton signed with the NHL's Montreal Maroons. He stayed with the Maroons through 1930 when he joined the New York Americans. In 1936, he took over coaching and managing that club and remained there until 1942 when the team disbanded.

Upon Frank Calder's death in 1943, Dutton became president of the NHL, a position he maintained until Clarence Campbell assumed the role in 1946. Dutton was elected to the Hockey Hall of Fame in 1958.

Frank Calder

President, 1917 to 1943

After an illustrious tenure as secretary of the National Hockey Association, Frank Calder was elected as the first president of the National Hockey League when the League was formed in 1917. He served in this capacity until his death on February 4, 1943.

Born in England in 1877, Calder came to Canada at the turn of the century as a school teacher, but turned to sports writing in 1909. His forthright writing style won him the attention and respect of Montreal Canadiens' owner George Kennedy whose support helped Calder to the position of NHL president.

For nearly 26 years, Calder worked hard to change the League from a small-time circuit to a grand international sports organization. Among his many achievements, Calder guided the NHL through its first expansion into the U.S., including the addition of the Boston Bruins in 1924 and the Chicago Blackhawks, Detroit Cougars and New York Rangers in 1926.

To commemorate his years of service, the League established the Calder Memorial Trophy to honor the rookie of the year at the conclusion of each season. Additionally, Calder was elected to the Hockey Hall of Fame in 1945 as one of its first inductees.

Boston Bruins

1991-92 Results: 36W-32L-12T 84PTS. Second, Adams Division

Ray Bourque, far right, earned his 13th consecutive All-Star berth in 1991-92. Vladimir Ruzicka, right, led the Bruins with 39 goals, including 18 on the power-play and six game-winners.

Schedule

	Home		Away
Oct.	Thur. 8 Hartford	Oct.	Thur. 15 San Jose
	Sat. 10 NY Islanders		Sat. 17 Los Angeles
	Mon. 12 Ottawa		Thur. 22 Calgary
	Thur. 29 Los Angeles		Fri. 23 Edmonton
	Sun. 25 Chicago		Sun. 25 Vancouver*
Nov.	Thur. 5 Quebec	Nov.	Wed. 11 Buffalo
	Sat. 7 NY Rangers		Mon. 16 Montreal
	Thur. 12 Calgary		Mon. 23 Ottawa
	Sat. 14 Toronto		Wed. 25 Washington
	Thur. 19 NY Islanders		Sat. 28 Hartford
	Sat. 21 Philadelphia		Mon. 30 Quebec
	Fri. 27 Hartford*	Dec.	Sat. 5 New Jersey
Dec.	Thu. 3 Montreal		Sun. 6 Philadelphia
	Thur. 10 Ottawa		Wed. 9 Buffalo
	Mon. 14 Buffalo		Sat. 12 Montreal
	Sat. 19 Washington		Fri. 18 Detroit
	Tues. 22 Tampa Bay		Sat. 26 Hartford
Jan.	Sat. 2 Hartford		Sun. 27 NY Rangers
	Thur. 7 Quebec		Tues. 29 Winnipeg
	Sat. 9 New Jersey		Thur. 31 Minnesota
	Tues. 12 Buffalo	Jan.	Tues. 5 Pittsburgh
	Thur. 14 Pittsburgh		Tues. 19 NY Islanders
	Sat. 16 Philadelphia		Thur. 21 Philadelphia
	Mon. 18 San Jose*		Mon. 25 Montreal
	Sat. 23 New Jersey		Tues. 26 Quebec
	Thur. 28 Winnipeg		Sat. 30 NY Islanders
Feb.	Tues. 2 Edmonton	Feb.	Wed. 3 Quebec
	Thur. 25 Minnesota		Mon. 8 Pittsburgh
	Sat. 27 Washington*		(at Atlanta)
Mar.	Mon. 1 Montreal		Tues. 9 St Louis
	Thur. 4 Vancouver		Thur. 11 Chicago
	Sat. 6 St Louis		Sun. 14 Tampa Bay
	Thur. 11 Montreal		Wed. 17 Montreal
	Sat. 13 Ottawa*		Sat. 20 Toronto
	Tues. 16 New Jersey	Mar.	Tues. 9 Pittsburgh
	(at Providence)		Mon. 15 NY Rangers
	Sat. 20 Detroit*		Thur. 18 Ottawa
	Mon. 22 Hartford		Wed. 24 Buffalo
	Thur. 25 Montreal		Tues. 30 Hartford
	Sat. 27 Pittsburgh*	Apr.	Sun. 4 Buffalo*
Apr.	Sat. 3 Buffalo*		Tues. 6 Quebec
	Thur. 8 Quebec		Sat. 10 Montreal
	Sun. 11 Ottawa		Wed. 14 Ottawa

* Denotes afternoon game.

Home Starting Times:

Weeknights	7:35 p.m.
Saturdays and Sundays	7:05 p.m.
Matinees	1:35 p.m.

Franchise date: November 1, 1924

69th NHL Season

Year-by-Year Record

		Home			Road			Overall							
Season	GP	W	L	T	W	L	T	W	L	T	GF	GA	Pts.	Finished	Playoff Result
1991-92	80	23	11	6	13	21	6	36	32	12	270	275	84	2nd, Adams Div.	Lost Conf. Championship
1990-91	80	26	9	5	18	15	7	44	24	12	299	264	100	1st, Adams Div.	Lost Conf. Championship
1989-90	80	23	13	4	23	12	5	46	25	9	289	232	101	1st, Adams Div.	Lost Final
1988-89	80	17	15	8	20	14	6	37	29	14	289	256	88	2nd, Adams Div.	Lost Div. Final
1987-88	80	24	13	3	20	17	3	44	30	6	300	251	94	2nd, Adams Div.	Lost Final
1986-87	80	25	11	4	14	23	3	39	34	7	301	276	85	3rd, Adams Div.	Lost Div. Semi-Final
1985-86	80	24	9	7	13	22	5	37	31	12	311	288	86	3rd, Adams Div.	Lost Div. Semi-Final
1984-85	80	21	15	4	15	19	6	36	34	10	303	287	82	4th, Adams Div.	Lost Div. Semi-Final
1983-84	80	25	12	3	24	13	3	49	25	6	336	261	104	1st, Adams Div.	Lost Div. Semi-Final
1982-83	80	28	6	6	22	14	4	50	20	10	327	228	110	1st, Adams Div.	Lost Conf. Championship
1981-82	80	24	12	4	10	15	6	43	27	10	323	285	96	2nd, Adams Div.	Lost Div. Final
1980-81	80	26	10	4	11	20	9	37	30	13	316	272	87	2nd, Adams Div.	Lost Prelim. Round
1979-80	80	27	9	4	19	12	9	46	21	13	310	234	105	2nd, Adams Div.	Lost Quarter-Final
1978-79	80	25	10	5	18	13	9	43	23	14	316	270	100	1st, Adams Div.	Lost Semi-Final
1977-78	80	29	6	5	22	12	6	51	18	11	333	218	113	1st, Adams Div.	Lost Final
1976-77	80	27	7	6	22	16	2	49	23	8	312	240	106	1st, Adams Div.	Lost Final
1975-76	80	27	5	8	21	10	9	48	15	17	313	237	113	1st, Adams Div.	Lost Semi-Final
1974-75	80	29	5	6	11	21	8	40	26	14	345	245	94	2nd, Adams Div.	Lost Prelim. Round
1973-74	78	33	4	2	19	13	7	52	17	9	349	221	113	1st, East Div.	Lost Final
1972-73	78	27	10	2	24	12	3	51	22	5	330	235	107	2nd, East Div.	Lost Quarter-Final
1971-72	**78**	28	4	7	26	9	4	**54**	**13**	**11**	**330**	**204**	**119**	**1st, East Div.**	**Won Stanley Cup**
1970-71	78	33	4	2	24	10	5	57	14	7	399	207	121	1st, East Div.	Lost Quarter-Final
1969-70	**76**	27	3	8	13	14	11	**40**	**17**	**19**	**277**	**216**	**99**	**2nd, East Div.**	**Won Stanley Cup**
1968-69	76	29	3	6	13	15	10	42	18	16	303	221	100	2nd, East Div.	Lost Semi-Final
1967-68	74	22	9	6	15	18	4	37	27	10	259	216	84	3rd, East Div.	Lost Quarter-Final
1966-67	70	10	21	4	7	22	6	17	43	10	182	253	44	6th,	Out of Playoffs
1965-66	70	15	17	3	6	26	3	21	43	6	174	275	48	5th,	Out of Playoffs
1964-65	70	12	17	6	9	26	0	21	43	6	166	253	48	6th,	Out of Playoffs
1963-64	70	13	15	7	5	25	5	18	40	12	170	212	48	6th,	Out of Playoffs
1962-63	70	7	18	10	7	21	7	14	39	17	198	281	45	6th,	Out of Playoffs
1961-62	70	9	22	4	6	25	4	15	47	8	177	306	38	6th,	Out of Playoffs
1960-61	70	13	17	5	2	25	8	15	42	13	176	254	43	6th,	Out of Playoffs
1959-60	70	21	11	3	7	23	5	28	34	8	220	241	64	5th,	Out of Playoffs
1958-59	70	21	11	3	11	18	6	32	29	9	205	215	73	2nd,	Lost Semi-Final
1957-58	70	15	14	6	12	14	9	27	28	15	199	194	69	4th,	Lost Final
1956-57	70	20	9	6	14	15	6	34	24	12	195	174	80	3rd,	Lost Final
1955-56	70	14	14	7	9	20	6	23	34	13	147	185	59	5th,	Out of Playoffs
1954-55	70	16	10	9	7	16	12	23	26	21	169	188	67	4th,	Lost Semi-Final
1953-54	70	22	8	5	10	20	5	32	28	10	177	181	74	4th,	Lost Semi-Final
1952-53	70	19	10	6	9	19	7	28	29	13	152	172	69	3rd,	Lost Final
1951-52	70	15	12	8	10	17	8	25	29	16	162	176	66	4th,	Lost Semi-Final
1950-51	70	13	12	10	9	18	8	22	30	18	178	197	62	4th,	Lost Semi-Final
1949-50	70	15	12	8	7	20	8	22	32	16	198	228	60	5th,	Out of Playoffs
1948-49	60	18	10	2	11	13	6	29	23	8	178	163	66	2nd,	Lost Semi-Final
1947-48	60	12	8	10	11	16	3	23	24	13	167	168	59	3rd,	Lost Semi-Final
1946-47	60	18	7	5	8	16	6	26	23	11	190	175	63	3rd,	Lost Semi-Final
1945-46	50	11	5	4	13	13	4	24	18	8	167	156	56	2nd,	Lost Final
1944-45	50	11	12	2	5	18	2	16	30	4	179	219	36	4th,	Lost Semi-Final
1943-44	50	15	8	2	4	18	3	19	26	5	223	268	43	5th,	Out of Playoffs
1942-43	50	17	3	5	7	14	4	24	17	9	195	176	57	2nd,	Lost Final
1941-42	48	17	4	3	8	13	3	25	17	6	160	118	56	3rd,	Lost Semi-Final
1940-41	**48**	15	4	5	12	4	8	**27**	**8**	**13**	**168**	**102**	**67**	**1st,**	**Won Stanley Cup**
1939-40	48	20	3	1	11	9	4	31	12	5	170	98	67	1st,	Lost Semi-Final
1938-39	**48**	20	2	2	16	8	0	**36**	**10**	**2**	**156**	**76**	**74**	**1st,**	**Won Stanley Cup**
1937-38	48	18	3	3	12	8	4	30	11	7	142	89	67	1st, Amn. Div.	Lost Semi-Final
1936-37	48	9	11	4	14	7	3	23	18	7	120	110	53	2nd, Amn. Div.	Lost Quarter-Final
1935-36	48	15	8	1	7	12	5	22	20	6	92	83	50	2nd, Amn. Div.	Lost Quarter-Final
1934-35	48	17	7	0	9	9	6	26	16	6	129	112	58	1st, Amn. Div.	Lost Semi-Final
1933-34	48	11	11	2	7	14	3	18	25	5	111	130	41	4th, Amn. Div.	Out of Playoffs
1932-33	48	20	2	3	5	13	5	25	15	8	124	88	58	1st, Amn. Div.	Lost Semi-Final
1931-32	48	11	10	3	4	11	9	15	21	12	122	117	42	4th, Amn. Div.	Out of Playoffs
1930-31	44	17	1	5	11	9	1	28	10	6	143	90	62	1st, Amn. Div.	Lost Semi-Final
1929-30	44	23	1	0	15	4	1	38	5	1	179	98	77	1st, Amn. Div.	Lost Final
1928-29	**44**	16	6	1	10	7	4	**26**	**13**	**5**	**89**	**52**	**57**	**1st, Amn. Div.**	**Won Stanley Cup**
1927-28	44	13	4	5	7	9	6	20	13	11	77	70	51	1st, Amn. Div.	Lost Semi-Final
1926-27	44	15	7	0	6	13	3	21	20	3	97	89	45	2nd, Amn. Div.	Lost Final
1925-26	36	10	7	1	7	8	3	17	15	4	92	85	38	4th,	Out of Playoffs
1924-25	30	3	12	0	3	12	0	6	24	0	49	119	12	6th,	Out of Playoffs

1992-93 Player Personnel

FORWARDS	HT	WT	S	Place of Birth	Date	1991-92 Club
BANKS, Darren	6-2	215	L	Toronto, Ont.	3/18/66	Salt Lake
CROMBIE, Chris	6-2	195	L	Hamilton, Ont.	4/2/72	London
DONATELLI, Clark	5-10	180	L	Providence, RI	11/22/67	Tm. USA
DONATO, Ted	5-10	170	L	Dedham, MA	4/28/69	Tm. USA-Boston
DOPITA, Jiri	6-4	215	L	Sumperk, Czech.	12/2/68	Olomouc
EVANS, Doug	5-9	185	L	Peterborough, Ont.	6/2/63	Wpg.-Monc.-Peoria
HEINZE, Steve	5-11	180	R	Lawrence, MA	1/30/70	Tm. USA-Boston
HUGHES, Brent	5-11	185	L	New Westminster, B.C.	4/5/66	Bos.-Balt.-Maine
JUNEAU, Joe	6-0	175	R	Pont-Rouge, Que.	1/5/68	Tm. Canada-Boston
KIMBLE, Darin	6-2	205	R	Lucky Lake, Sask.	11/22/68	St. Louis
KUMPEL, Mark	6-0	190	R	Wakefield, MA	3/7/61	Moncton
KVARTALNOV, Dmitri	5-11	180	L	Voskresensk, USSR	11/13/72	Riga HC
LAVIOLETTE, Peter	6-2	200	L	Norwood, MA	12/7/64	Binghamton
LEACH, Steve	5-11	200	R	Cambridge, MA	1/16/66	Boston
McKIM, Andrew	5-8	175	R	St. John, N.B.	7/6/70	St. John's
MISKOLCZI, Ted	6-3	180	R	Port Colborne, Ont.	8/5/70	Johnstown
MURRAY, Glen	6-2	200	R	Bridgewater, N.S.	11/1/72	Boston
NEELY, Cam	6-1	210	R	Comox, B.C.	6/6/65	Boston
OATES, Adam	5-11	190	R	Weston, Ont.	8/27/62	St. Louis-Boston
PANTALEYEV, Gregori	5-9	185	L	Gastello, USSR	11/13/72	Riga HC
PAVLOV, Eugene	6-2	195	L	St. Petersburg, Russia	1/22/71	SKA St. P.
POULIN, Dave	5-11	190	L	Timmins, Ont.	12/17/58	Boston
REID, Dave	6-1	205	L	Toronto, Ont.	5/15/64	Boston-Maine
RUZICKA, Vladimir	6-3	210	L	Most, Czechoslovakia	6/6/63	Boston
STUMPEL, Josef	6-1	190	R	Nitra, Czechoslovakia	6/20/72	Boston-Cologne
SWEENEY, Bob	6-3	200	R	Concord, MA	1/25/64	Boston-Maine
VESEY, Jim	6-1	200	R	Boston, MA	9/29/65	Boston-Maine
WINNES, Chris	6-0	170	R	Ridgefield, CT	2/12/68	Boston-Maine
ZHOLTOK, Sergei	6-0	185	L	Riga, Latvia	12/2/72	Riga HC
DEFENSEMEN						
ALLAIN, Rick	6-0	190	L	Guelph, Ont.	5/20/69	Maine
BEERS, Bob	6-2	200	R	Pittsburgh, PA	5/20/67	Boston-Maine
BOURQUE, Ray	5-11	210	L	Montreal, Que.	12/28/60	Boston
CHERUYAKOV, Denis	6-0	185	L	St. Petersburg, Russia	4/20/70	Riga HC
FEATHERSTONE, Glen	6-4	215	L	Toronto, Ont.	7/8/68	Boston
HUSCROFT, Jamie	6-2	200	R	Creston, B.C.	1/9/67	Utica
KRYS, Mark	6-0	185	R	Timmins, Ont.	5/29/69	Maine-Johnstown
MURPHY, Gord	6-2	195	R	Willowdale, Ont.	2/23/67	Philadelphia-Boston
OLSEN, Darryl	6-0	180	L	Calgary, Alta.	10/7/66	Calgary-Salt Lake
ROBERTS, Gord	6-0	190	L	Detroit, MI	10/2/57	Pittsburgh
SEHER, Kurt	6-1	180	L	Lethbridge, Alta.	4/15/73	Seattle
SHAW, David	6-2	204	R	St. Thomas, Ont.	5/25/64	NYR-Edm.-Min.
SWEENEY, Don	5-10	185	L	St. Stephen, N.B.	8/17/66	Boston
TILEY, Brad	6-1	185	L	Markdale, Ont.	7/5/71	Maine
WESLEY, Glen	6-1	195	L	Red Deer, Alta.	10/2/68	Boston
WIEMER, Jim	6-4	210	L	Sudbury, Ont.	1/9/61	Boston-Maine

GOALTENDERS	HT	WT	C	Place of Birth	Date	1991-92 Club
BAILEY, Scott	6-0	195	L	Calgary, Alta.	5/2/72	Spokane
BALES, Mike	6-1	180	L	Prince Albert, Sask.	8/6/71	Ohio St.
BLUE, John	5-10	185	L	Huntington Beach, CA	2/19/66	Maine
COUSINEAU, Marcel	5-10	175	L	Lachine, Que.	4/30/73	Beauport
LEMELIN, Reggie	5-11	170	L	Quebec City, Que.	11/19/54	Boston
MOOG, Andy	5-9	170	L	Penticton, B.C.	2/18/60	Boston
PARSON, Mike	6-0	170	L	Listowel, Ont.	3/12/70	Maine-Johnstown

General Managers' History

Arthur H. Ross, 1924-25 to 1953-54; Lynn Patrick, 1954-55 to 1964-65; Leighton "Hap" Emms, 1965-66 to 1966-67; Milt Schmidt, 1967-68 to 1971-72; Harry Sinden, 1972-73 to date.

Coaching History

Arthur H. Ross, 1924-25 to 1927-28; Cy Denneny, 1928-29; Arthur H. Ross, 1929-30 to 1933-34; Frank Patrick, 1934-35 to 1935-36; Arthur H. Ross, 1936-37 to 1938-39; Ralph (Cooney) Weiland, 1939-40 to 1940-41; Arthur H. Ross, 1941-42 to 1944-45; Aubrey V. (Dit) Clapper, 1945-46 to 1948-49; George (Buck) Boucher, 1949-50; Lynn Patrick, 1950-51 to 1953-54; Lynn Patrick and Milt Schmidt, 1954-55; Milt Schmidt, 1955-56 to 1960-61; Phil Watson, 1961-62; Phil Watson and Milt Schmidt, 1962-63; Milt Schmidt, 1963-64 to 1965-66; Harry Sinden, 1966-67 to 1969-70; Tom Johnson, 1970-71 to 1971-72; Tom Johnson and Bep Guidolin, 1972-73; Bep Guidolin, 1973-74; Don Cherry, 1974-75 to 1978-79; Fred Creighton and Harry Sinden, 1979-80; Gerry Cheevers, 1980-81 to 1983-84; Gerry Cheevers and Harry Sinden, 1984-85; Butch Goring, 1985-86; Butch Goring and Terry O'Reilly, 1986-87; Terry O'Reilly, 1987-88 to 1988-89; Mike Milbury, 1989-90 to 1990-91; Rick Bowness, 1991-92; Brian Sutter, 1992-93.

Retired Numbers

2	Eddie Shore	1926-1940
3	Lionel Hitchman	1925-1934
4	Bobby Orr	1966-1976
5	Dit Clapper	1927-1947
7	Phil Esposito	1967-1975
9	John Bucyk	1957-1978
15	Milt Schmidt	1936-1955

1991-92 Scoring

Regular Season

Pos	#	Player	Team	GP	G	A	Pts	+/-	PIM	PP	SH	GW	GT	S	%
C	12	Adam Oates	STL	54	10	59	69	4–	12	3	0	3	1	118	8.5
			BOS	26	10	20	30	5–	10	3	0	1	1	73	13.7
			TOTAL	80	20	79	99	9–	22	6	0	4	2	191	10.5
D	77	Ray Bourque	BOS	80	21	60	81	11	56	7	1	2	0	334	6.3
C	38	Vladimir Ruzicka	BOS	77	39	36	75	10–	48	18	0	6	3	228	17.1
R	27	Stephen Leach	BOS	78	31	29	60	8–	147	12	0	4	0	243	12.8
L	11	Bob Carpenter	BOS	60	25	23	48	3–	46	6	1	6	2	171	14.6
D	26	Glen Wesley	BOS	78	9	37	46	9–	54	4	0	1	0	211	4.3
L	18	Brent Ashton	WPG	7	1	0	1	3–	4	0	0	0	0	6	16.7
			BOS	61	17	22	39	4–	47	6	1	1	1	124	13.7
			TOTAL	68	18	22	40	7–	51	6	1	1	1	130	13.8
L	25	Andy Brickley	BOS	23	10	17	27	6	2	5	0	1	1	28	35.7
R	16	Peter Douris	BOS	54	10	13	23	9	10	0	0	1	0	107	9.3
C	20	Bob Sweeney	BOS	63	6	14	20	9–	103	0	1	1	0	70	8.6
C	49*	Joe Juneau	BOS	14	5	14	19	6	4	2	0	0	0	38	13.2
D	28	Gordon Murphy	PHI	31	2	8	10	4–	33	0	0	0	0	50	4.0
			BOS	42	3	6	9	2	51	0	0	0	1	82	3.7
			TOTAL	73	5	14	19	2–	84	0	0	0	1	132	3.8
C	10	Ken Hodge	BOS	42	6	11	17	8–	10	3	1	3	0	62	9.7
L	17	Dave Reid	BOS	43	7	7	14	5	27	2	1	0	0	70	10.0
D	32	Don Sweeney	BOS	75	3	11	14	9–	74	0	0	1	0	92	3.3
C	21	Barry Pederson	HFD	5	2	2	4	2–	0	1	0	0	0	6	33.3
			BOS	32	3	6	9	5–	8	1	0	0	0	41	7.3
			TOTAL	37	5	8	13	7–	8	2	0	0	0	47	10.6
R	8	Cam Neely	BOS	9	9	3	12	9	16	1	0	2	0	30	30.0
L	14	Jeff Lazaro	BOS	27	3	6	9	4	31	0	0	0	0	46	6.5
D	36	Jim Wiemer	BOS	47	1	8	9	10	84	0	0	0	0	60	1.7
L	29	Scott Arniel	BOS	29	5	3	8	5	20	0	0	1	0	34	14.7
C	19	Dave Poulin	BOS	18	4	4	8	2–	18	0	1	1	0	31	12.9
R	45*	Stephen Heinze	BOS	14	3	4	7	1–	6	0	0	2	0	29	10.3
D	47*	Gord Hynes	BOS	15	0	5	5	8	6	0	0	0	0	16	.0
D	22*	Bob Beers	BOS	31	0	5	5	13–	29	0	0	0	0	25	.0
R	44*	Glen Murray	BOS	5	3	1	4	2	0	1	0	0	0	20	15.0
R	40*	Chris Winnes	BOS	24	1	3	4	6–	6	0	0	0	0	20	5.0
L	39	Lou Crawford	BOS	19	2	1	3	6–	9	0	0	0	0	14	14.3
C	46*	Ted Donato	BOS	10	1	2	3	1–	8	0	0	0	0	13	7.7
G	35	Andy Moog	BOS	62	0	3	3	0	52	0	0	0	0	0	.0
L	42	Brent Hughes	BOS	8	1	1	2	1	38	0	0	1	0	10	10.0
R	34	Lyndon Byers	BOS	31	1	1	2	5–	129	0	0	0	0	12	8.3
R	42*	John Byce	BOS	3	1	0	1	1–	0	1	0	0	0	2	50.0
R	48*	Jozef Stumpel	BOS	4	1	0	1	1	0	0	0	0	0	3	33.3
R	51	Brian Dobbin	BOS	7	1	0	1	0	22	0	0	0	0	4	25.0
D	6	Glen Featherstone	BOS	7	1	0	1	2–	20	0	0	0	0	8	12.5
C	37*	Ralph Barahona	BOS	3	0	1	1	1	0	0	0	0	0	0	.0
R	49*	Shayne Stevenson	BOS	5	0	1	1	1	2	0	0	0	0	3	.0
G	1	Rejean Lemelin	BOS	8	0	1	1	0	2	0	0	0	0	0	.0
L	50*	Clark Donatelli	BOS	10	0	1	1	8–	22	0	0	0	0	7	.0
L	41	Dave Thomlinson	BOS	12	0	1	1	2–	17	0	0	0	0	12	.0
D	43*	Matt Hervey	BOS	16	0	1	1	5–	55	0	0	0	0	8	.0
D	23*	Jack Capuano	BOS	2	0	0	0	1–	0	0	0	0	0	1	.0
D	52	Petr Prajsler	BOS	3	0	0	0	1–	2	0	0	0	0	3	.0
L	39*	Matt Glennon	BOS	3	0	0	0	0	2	0	0	0	0	2	.0
R	54*	Jim Vesey	BOS	4	0	0	0	0	0	0	0	0	0	1	.0
L	31	Alan Stewart	N.J.	1	0	0	0	0	5	0	0	0	0	0	.0
			BOS	4	0	0	0	1–	17	0	0	0	0	1	.0
			TOTAL	5	0	0	0	1–	22	0	0	0	0	1	.0

Goaltending

No.	Goaltender	GPI	Mins	Avg	W	L	T	EN	SO	GA	SA	S%
31	Daniel Berthiaume	8	399	3.16	1	4	2	0	0	21	156	.865
35	Andy Moog	62	3640	3.23	28	22	9	7	1	196	1727	.887
1	Rejean Lemelin	8	407	3.39	5	1	0	0	0	23	210	.890
33	* Matt Delguidice	10	424	3.96	2	5	1	0	0	28	239	.883
	Totals	**80**	**4880**	**3.38**	**36**	**32**	**12**	**7**	**1**	**275**	**2339**	**.882**

Playoffs

Pos	#	Player	Team	GP	G	A	Pts	+/-	PIM	PP	SH	GW	GT	S	%
C	12	Adam Oates	BOS	15	5	14	19	6–	4	3	0	2	1	35	14.3
C	49*	Joe Juneau	BOS	15	4	8	12	3–	21	2	0	0	0	29	13.8
D	77	Ray Bourque	BOS	12	3	6	9	10–	12	2	0	0	0	51	5.9
C	46*	Ted Donato	BOS	15	3	4	7	0	4	0	0	1	1	20	15.0
L	17	Dave Reid	BOS	15	2	5	7	2	4	0	0	1	0	17	11.8
R	44*	Glen Murray	BOS	15	4	2	6	1–	10	1	0	0	0	19	21.1
C	19	Dave Poulin	BOS	15	3	3	6	2	22	1	0	1	0	24	12.5
D	26	Glen Wesley	BOS	15	2	4	6	3	16	0	0	0	0	35	5.7
R	16	Peter Douris	BOS	7	2	3	5	2	0	0	0	1	1	15	13.3
C	38	Vladimir Ruzicka	BOS	13	2	3	5	7–	2	2	0	0	0	16	12.5
R	27	Stephen Leach	BOS	15	4	0	4	2–	10	0	0	1	0	30	13.3
D	36	Jim Wiemer	BOS	15	1	3	4	3	14	0	0	1	0	28	3.6
D	47*	Gord Hynes	BOS	12	1	2	3	3–	6	0	0	0	0	7	14.3
R	45*	Stephen Heinze	BOS	7	0	3	3	3	17	0	0	0	0	6	.0
L	42	Brent Hughes	BOS	10	2	0	2	3–	20	0	0	0	0	5	40.0
C	20	Bob Sweeney	BOS	14	1	0	1	7–	25	0	1	0	0	24	4.2
D	28	Gordon Murphy	BOS	15	1	0	1	1–	12	0	0	0	0	28	3.6
L	11	Bob Carpenter	BOS	8	0	1	1	1–	6	0	0	0	0	13	.0
L	14	Jeff Lazaro	BOS	9	0	1	1	0	2	0	0	0	0	9	.0
G	35	Andy Moog	BOS	15	0	1	1	0	17	0	0	0	0	0	.0
D	22*	Bob Beers	BOS	1	0	0	0	0	0	0	0	0	0	0	.0
L	50*	Clark Donatelli	BOS	2	0	0	0	0	0	0	0	0	0	0	.0
R	34	Lyndon Byers	BOS	5	0	0	0	3–	12	0	0	0	0	2	.0
D	43*	Matt Hervey	BOS	5	0	0	0	1–	6	0	0	0	0	4	.0
D	32	Don Sweeney	BOS	15	0	0	0	3–	10	0	0	0	0	13	.0

Goaltending

No.	Goaltender	GPI	Mins	Avg	W	L	EN	SO	GA	SA	S%
35	Andy Moog	15	866	3.19	8	7	1	1	46	385	.881
1	Rejean Lemelin	2	54	3.33	0	0	1	0	3	23	.870
	Totals	**15**	**926**	**3.30**	**8**	**7**	**2**	**1**	**51**	**410**	**.876**

Club Records

Team

(Figures in brackets for season records are games played; records for fewest points, wins, ties, losses, goals, goals against are for 70 or more games)

Record		
Most Points	**121**	1970-71 (78)
Most Wins	**57**	1970-71 (78)
Most Ties	**21**	1954-55 (70)
Most Losses	**47**	1961-62 (70)
Most Goals	**399**	1970-71 (78)
Most Goals Against	**306**	1961-62 (70)
Fewest Points	**38**	1961-62 (70)
Fewest Wins	**14**	1962-63 (70)
Fewest Ties	**5**	1972-73 (78)
Fewest Losses	**13**	1971-72 (78)
Fewest Goals	**147**	1955-56 (70)
Fewest Goals Against	**172**	1952-53 (70)
Longest Winning Streak		
Over-all	**14**	Dec. 3/29-Jan. 9/30
Home	***20**	Dec. 3/29-Mar. 18/30
Away	**8**	Feb. 17-Mar. 8/72
Longest Undefeated Streak		
Over-all	**23**	Dec. 22/40-Feb. 23/41 (15 wins, 8 ties)
Home	**27**	Nov. 22/70-Mar. 20/71 (26 wins, 1 tie)
Away	**15**	Dec. 22/40-Mar. 16/41 (9 wins, 6 ties)
Longest Losing Streak		
Over-all	**11**	Dec. 3/24-Jan. 5/25
Home	***11**	Dec. 8/24-Feb. 17/25
Away	**14**	Dec. 27/64-Feb. 21/65
Longest Winless Streak		
Over-all	**20**	Jan. 28-Mar. 11/62 (16 losses, 4 ties)
Home	**11**	Dec. 8/24-Feb. 17/25 (11 losses)
Away	**14**	Three times
Most Shutouts, Season	**15**	1927-28 (44)
Most PIM, Season	**2,443**	1987-88 (80)
Most Goals, Game	**14**	Jan. 21/45 (NYR 3 at Bos. 14)

Individual

Record		
Most Seasons	**21**	John Bucyk
Most Games	**1,436**	John Bucyk
Most Goals, Career	**545**	John Bucyk
Most Assists, Career	**794**	John Bucyk
Most Points, Career	**1,339**	John Bucyk (545 goals, 794 assists)
Most PIM, Career	**2,095**	Terry O'Reilly
Most Shutouts, Career	**74**	Tiny Thompson
Longest Consecutive Games Streak	**418**	John Bucyk (Jan. 23/69-Mar. 2/75)
Most Goals, Season	**76**	Phil Esposito (1970-71)
Most Assists, Season	**102**	Bobby Orr (1970-71)
Most Points, Season	**152**	Phil Esposito (1970-71) (76 goals, 76 assists)
Most PIM, Season	**304**	Jay Miller (1987-88)
Most Points, Defenseman Season	***139**	Bobby Orr (1970-71) (37 goals, 102 assists)
Most Points, Center Season	**152**	Phil Esposito (1970-71) (76 goals, 76 assists)
Most Points, Right Wing Season	**105**	Ken Hodge (1970-71) (43 goals, 62 assists); Ken Hodge (1973-74) (50 goals, 55 assists); Rick Middleton (1983-84) (47 goals, 58 assists)
Most Points, Left Wing Season	**116**	John Bucyk (1970-71) (51 goals, 65 assists)
Most Points, Rookie Season	**92**	Barry Pederson (1981-82) (44 goals, 48 assists)
Most Shutouts, Season	**15**	Hal Winkler (1927-28)
Most Goals, Game	**4**	Several players
Most Assists, Game	**6**	Ken Hodge (Feb. 9/71); Bobby Orr (Jan. 1/73)
Most Points, Game	**7**	Bobby Orr (Nov. 15/73); Phil Esposito (Dec. 19/74); Barry Pederson (Apr. 4/82); Cam Neely (Oct. 16/88)

* NHL Record.

Captains' History

No Captain, 1924-25 to 1926-27; Lionel Hitchman, 1927-28 to 1930-31; George Owen, 1931-32; Dit Clapper, 1932-33 to 1937-38; Cooney Weiland, 1938-39; Dit Clapper, 1939-40 to 1945-46; Dit Clapper, John Crawford, 1946-47; John Crawford 1947-48 to 1949-50; Milt Schmidt, 1950-51 to 1953-54; Milt Schmidt, Ed Sanford, 1954-55; Fern Flaman, 1955-56 to 1960-61; Don McKenney, 1961-62, 1962-63; Leo Boivin, 1963-64 to 1965-66; John Bucyk, 1966-67; no captain, 1967-68 to 1972-73; John Bucyk, 1973-74 to 1976-77; Wayne Cashman, 1977-78 to 1982-83; Terry O'Reilly, 1983-84, 1984-85; Ray Bourque, Rick Middleton (co-captains) 1985-86 to 1987-88; Ray Bourque, 1988-89 to date.

All-time Record vs. Other Clubs

Regular Season

	At Home							On Road							Total						
	GP	W	L	T	GF	GA	PTS	GP	W	L	T	GF	GA	PTS	GP	W	L	T	GF	GA	PTS
Buffalo	76	45	22	9	320	236	99	75	24	37	14	241	287	62	151	69	59	23	561	523	161
Calgary	37	22	10	5	127	101	49	36	19	15	2	133	139	40	73	41	25	7	260	240	89
Chicago	274	159	83	32	997	770	350	276	92	140	44	738	890	228	550	251	223	76	1735	1660	578
Detroit	277	151	83	43	980	729	345	276	76	148	52	697	918	204	553	227	231	95	1677	1647	549
Edmonton	21	16	3	2	99	58	34	20	9	8	3	67	72	21	41	25	11	5	166	130	55
Hartford	48	33	11	4	201	126	70	48	19	22	7	171	176	45	96	52	33	11	372	302	115
Los Angeles	52	39	10	3	247	142	81	51	29	17	5	194	175	63	103	68	27	8	441	317	144
Minnesota	51	38	6	7	234	120	83	51	28	12	11	192	140	67	102	66	18	18	426	260	150
Montreal	302	138	112	52	890	814	328	301	82	175	44	690	1027	208	603	220	287	96	1580	1840	536
New Jersey	31	20	8	3	139	95	43	30	17	5	8	114	82	42	61	37	13	11	253	177	85
NY Islanders	36	19	9	8	140	103	46	37	19	15	3	126	120	41	73	38	24	11	266	223	87
NY Rangers	275	150	87	38	1005	767	336	278	103	121	54	774	844	260	553	253	208	92	1779	1611	598
Philadelphia	51	34	11	6	213	148	74	49	22	21	6	146	164	50	100	56	32	12	359	312	124
Pittsburgh	52	39	7	6	244	148	84	51	26	14	11	206	160	63	103	65	21	17	450	308	147
Quebec	48	25	15	8	195	151	58	48	28	16	4	216	184	60	96	53	31	12	411	335	118
St. Louis	49	32	10	7	220	133	71	50	21	20	9	174	159	51	99	53	30	16	394	292	122
San Jose	1	1	0	0	7	6	2	1	1	0	0	4	1	2	2	2	0	0	11	7	4
Toronto	278	151	80	47	923	747	349	278	86	146	46	722	945	218	556	237	226	93	1645	1687	567
Vancouver	41	34	3	4	188	90	72	42	21	13	8	178	141	50	83	55	16	12	366	231	122
Washington	32	19	9	4	133	91	42	33	17	8	8	129	99	42	65	36	17	12	262	190	84
Winnipeg	20	14	3	3	94	64	31	21	11	8	2	75	72	24	41	25	11	5	169	136	55
Defunct Clubs	164	112	39	13	525	306	237	164	79	67	18	496	440	176	328	191	106	31	1021	746	413
Totals	**2216**	**1291**	**621**	**304**	**8121**	**5945**	**2884**	**2216**	**829**	**1028**	**359**	**6483**	**7235**	**2017**	**4432**	**2120**	**1649**	**663**	**14604**	**13174**	**4903**

Playoffs

	Series	W	L	GP	W	L	T	GF	GA	Last Mtg.	Round	Result
Buffalo	5	5	0	29	19	10	0	120	94	1992	DSF	W 4-3
Chicago	6	5	1	22	16	5	1	97	63	1978	QF	W 4-0
Detroit	7	4	3	33	19	14	0	96	98	1957	SF	W 4-1
Edmonton	2	0	2	9	1	8	0	20	41	1990	F	L 1-4
Hartford	2	2	0	13	8	5	0	24	17	1991	DSF	W 4-2
Los Angeles	2	2	0	13	8	5	0	56	38	1977	QF	W 4-2
Minnesota	1	0	1	3	0	3	0	13	20	1981	PR	L 0-3
Montreal	27	6	21	132	48	84	0	317	410	1992	DF	W 4-0
New Jersey	1	1	0	7	4	3	0	30	19	1988	CF	W 4-3
NY Islanders	2	0	2	11	3	8	0	35	49	1983	CF	L 2-4
NY Rangers	9	6	3	42	22	18	2	114	104	1973	QF	L 1-4
Philadelphia	4	2	2	20	11	9	0	60	57	1978	SF	W 4-1
Pittsburgh	4	2	2	19	9	10	0	62	67	1992	CF	L 0-4
Quebec	2	1	1	11	6	5	0	37	36	1983	DSF	W 3-1
St. Louis	2	2	0	8	8	0	0	48	15	1972	SF	W 4-0
Toronto	13	5	8	62	30	31	1	153	150	1974	QF	W 4-0
Washington	1	1	0	4	4	0	0	15	6	1990	CF	W 4-0
Defunct Clubs	3	1	2	11	4	5	2	20	20			
Totals	**93**	**45**	**48**	**439**	**220**	**223**	**6**	**1333**	**1325**			

Playoff Results 1992-88

Year	Round	Opponent	Result	GF	GA
1992	CF	Pittsburgh	L 0-4	7	19
	DF	Montreal	W 4-0	14	8
	DSF	Buffalo	W 4-3	19	24
1991	CF	Pittsburgh	L 2-4	18	27
	DF	Montreal	W 4-3	18	18
	DSF	Hartford	W 4-2	24	17
1990	F	Edmonton	L 1-4	8	20
	CF	Washington	W 4-0	15	6
	DF	Montreal	W 4-1	16	12
	DSF	Hartford	W 4-3	23	21
1989	DF	Montreal	L 1-4	13	16
	DSF	Buffalo	W 4-1	16	14
1988	F	Edmonton	L 0-4	12	21
	CF	New Jersey	W 4-3	30	19
	DF	Montreal	W 4-1	15	10
	DSF	Buffalo	W 4-2	28	22

Abbreviations: Round: F – Final; **CF** – conference final; **DF** – division final; **DSF** – division semi-final; **SF** – semi-final; **QF** – quarter-final; **PR** – preliminary round. **GA** – goals against; **GF** – goals for.

1990-91 Results

Home				Away			
Oct.	3	NY Rangers	5-3	**Oct.**	7	NY Rangers	1-2
	5	NY Islanders	3-4		9	Buffalo	4-4
	12	Montreal	0-6		17	Vancouver	3-3
	31	Los Angeles	2-4		19	San Jose	4-1
Nov.	2	Detroit	4-1		24	St Louis	5-6
	7	Calgary	4-4		26	Minnesota	0-4
	9	New Jersey	4-0		27	Chicago	6-3
	14	Quebec	5-2	**Nov.**	4	NY Islanders	4-6
	23	Buffalo	7-4		5	Pittsburgh	5-5
	29	Montreal	5-4		16	Hartford	5-4
Dec.	1	Hartford	5-4		20	Buffalo	1-3
	5	Quebec	2-2		22	Washington	3-6
	7	Philadelphia	3-5		25	Montreal	3-4
	12	Montreal	5-2		27	NY Islanders	3-2
	14	Toronto	4-3	**Dec.**	8	NY Rangers	0-4
	19	Pittsburgh	4-6		10	Quebec	2-5
	21	Edmonton	6-3		22	Montreal	2-3
	26	Hartford	3-2		27	Buffalo	1-8
Jan.	2	Winnipeg	1-3		29	Winnipeg	6-3
	4	Buffalo	4-2		31	Detroit	5-3
	9	Quebec	5-4	**Jan.**	8	Montreal	2-3
	11	Philadelphia	5-1		15	Hartford	4-3
	16	Hartford	4-3		22	Toronto	5-2
	23	Montreal	1-3		25	Hartford	4-4
	27	Minnesota	3-2		28	Quebec	4-2
	30	Calgary	3-1	**Feb.**	4	Winnipeg	3-3
Feb.	1	Buffalo	2-2		6	Philadelphia	1-5
	8	New Jersey	4-6		13	St Louis	0-4
	9	Pittsburgh	6-3		17	Los Angeles	3-6
	27	Toronto	4-2		19	Calgary	4-6
	29	Washington	5-5		21	Edmonton	5-3
Mar.	5	Vancouver	2-2		23	Vancouver	1-2
	7	Chicago	1-2	**Mar.**	1	Washington	4-1
	15	Los Angeles	5-1		3	Hartford	0-4
	19	St Louis	1-4		8	Chicago	0-4
	21	Edmonton	3-4		11	Buffalo	3-6
	23	San Jose	7-6		14	Quebec	5-4
	28	Buffalo	4-3		26	New Jersey	2-4
Apr.	12	Quebec	1-1		31	Quebec	5-4
	13	Hartford	6-3	**Apr.**	15	Montreal	4-4

*Denotes afternoon game

Entry Draft Selections 1992-78

1992
Pick
16 Dmitri Kvartalnov
55 Sergei Zholtok
112 Scott Bailey
133 Jiri Dopita
136 Grigory Panteleyev
184 Kurt Seher
208 Mattias Timander
232 Chris Crombie
256 Denis Chervyakov
257 Evgeny Pavlov

1991
Pick
18 Glen Murray
40 Jozef Stumpel
62 Marcel Cousineau
84 Brad Tiley
106 Mariusz Czerkawski
150 Gary Golczewski
172 John Moser
194 Daniel Hodge
216 Steve Norton
238 Stephen Lombardi
260 Torsten Kienass

1990
Pick
21 Bryan Smolinski
63 Cameron Stewart
84 Jerome Buckley
105 Mike Bales
126 Mark Woolf
147 Jim Mackey
168 John Gruden
189 Darren Wetherill
210 Dean Capuano
231 Andy Bezeau
252 Ted Miskolczi

1989
Pick
17 Shayne Stevenson
38 Mike Parson
57 Wes Walz
80 Jackson Penney
101 Mark Montanari
122 Stephen Foster
143 Otto Hascak
164 Rick Allain
185 James Lavish
206 Geoff Simpson
227 David Franzosa

1988
Pick
18 Robert Cimetta
60 Stephen Heinze
81 Joe Juneau
102 Daniel Murphy
123 Derek Geary
165 Mark Krys
186 Jon Rohloff
228 Eric Reisman
249 Doug Jones

1987
Pick
3 Glen Wesley
14 Stephane Quintal
56 Todd Lalonde
67 Darwin McPherson
77 Matt Delguidice
98 Ted Donato
119 Matt Glennon
140 Rob Cheevers
161 Chris Winnes
182 Paul Ohman
203 Casey Jones
224 Eric Lemarque
245 Sean Gorman

1986
Pick
13 Craig Janney
34 Pekka Tirkkonen
76 Dean Hall
97 Matt Pesklewis
118 Garth Premak
139 Paul Beraldo
160 Brian Ferreira
181 Jeff Flaherty
202 Greg Hawgood
223 Staffan Malmqvist
244 Joel Gardner

1985
Pick
31 Alain Cote
52 Bill Ranford
73 Jaime Kelly
94 Steve Moore
115 Gord Hynes
136 Per Martinelle
157 Randy Burridge
178 Gord Cruickshank
199 Dave Buda
210 Bob Beers
220 John Byce
241 Marc West

1984
Pick
19 Dave Pasin
40 Ray Podloski
61 Jeff Cornelius
82 Robert Joyce
103 Mike Bishop
124 Randy Oswald
145 Mark Thietke
166 Don Sweeney
186 Kevin Heffernan
207 J.D. Urbanic
227 Bill Kopecky
248 Jim Newhouse

1983
Pick
21 Nevin Markwart
42 Greg Johnston
62 Greg Puhalski
82 Alain Larochelle
102 Allen Pederson
122 Terry Taillefer
142 Ian Armstrong
162 Francois Olivier
182 Harri Laurilla
202 Paul Fitzsimmons
222 Norm Foster
242 Greg Murphy

1982
Pick
1 Gord Kluzak
22 Brian Curran
39 Lyndon Byers
60 Dave Reid
102 Bob Nicholson
123 Bob Sweeney
144 John Meulenbroeks
165 Tony Fiore
186 Doug Kostynski
207 Tony Gilliard
228 Tommy Lehmann
249 Bruno Campese

1981
Pick
14 Normand Leveille
35 Luc Dufour
77 Scott McLellan
98 Joe Mantione
119 Bruce Milton
140 Mats Thelin
161 Armel Parisee
182 Don Sylvestri
203 Richard Bourque

1980
Pick
18 Barry Pederson
60 Tom Fergus
81 Steve Kasper
102 Randy Hillier
123 Steve Lyons
144 Tony McMurchy
165 Mike Moffat
186 Michael Thelven
207 Jens Ohling

1979
Pick
8 Ray Bourque
15 Brad McCrimmon
36 Doug Morrison
57 Keith Crowder
78 Larry Melnyk
99 Marco Baron
120 Mike Krushelnyski

1978
Pick
16 Al Secord
35 Graeme Nicolson
52 Brad Knelson
68 George Buat
85 Darryl MacLeod
102 Jeff Brubaker
119 Murray Skinner
136 Robert Hehir
153 Craig MacTavish

General Manager

SINDEN, HARRY JAMES
President and General Manager, Boston Bruins.
Born in Collins Bay, Ont., September 14, 1932.

Harry Sinden never played a game in the NHL but stepped into the Bruins' organization with an impressive coaching background in minor professional hockey and his continued excellence has earned him a place in the Hockey Hall of Fame as one of the true builders in hockey history. In 1965-66 as playing-coach of Oklahoma City Blazers in the CPHL, Sinden led the club to second place in the regular standings and then to eight straight playoff victories for the Jack Adams Trophy. After five years in OHA Senior hockey — including 1958 with the World Amateur Champion Whitby Dunlops — Sinden was named playing-coach in the old Eastern Professional League and its successor, the Central Professional League. Under his guidance, the Bruins of 1967-68 made the playoffs for the first time in nine seasons, finishing third in the East Division, and were nosed out of first place in 1968-69 by Montreal. In 1969-70, Sinden led the Bruins to their first Stanley Cup win since 1940-41. The following season he went into private business but returned to the hockey scene in the summer of 1972 when he was appointed coach of Team Canada. He moulded that group of NHL stars into a powerful unit and led them into an exciting eight-game series against the Soviet national team in September of 1972. Team Canada emerged the winner by a narrow margin with a record of four wins, three losses and one tie. Sinden then returned to the Bruins organization early in the 1972-73 season. Sinden took over as the Bruins' coach in February 1985, after replacing Gerry Cheevers. Boston finished 11-10-3 with Sinden behind the bench before being defeated by Montreal in five games in the Adams Division semi-finals.

NHL Coaching Record

		Regular Season					Playoffs			
Season	Team	Games	W	L	T	%	Games	W	L	%
1966-67	Boston	70	17	43	10	.314				
1967-68	Boston	74	37	27	10	.568	4	0	4	.000
1968-69	Boston	76	42	18	16	.658	10	6	4	.600
1969-70	Boston	76	40	17	19	.651	14	12	2	.857*
1979-80	Boston	10	4	6	0	.400	9	4	5	.444
1984-85	Boston	24	11	10	3	.521	5	2	3	.400
	NHL Totals	330	151	121	58	.545	42	24	18	.571

* Stanley Cup win.

Club Directory

Boston Garden
150 Causeway Street
Boston, Massachusetts 02114
Phone **617/227-3206**
FAX 617/523-7184
Capacity: 14,448

Executive
Owner and Governor .... Jeremy M. Jacobs
Alternative Governor .... Louis Jacobs
Alternative Governor, President and General Manager .... Harry Sinden
Vice President .... Tom Johnson
Ass't General Manager .... Mike Milbury
Assistant to the President .... Nate Greenberg
General Counsel .... Barbara Macon
Director of Administration .... Dale Hamilton
Administrative Assistant .... Carol Gould
Receptionist .... Karen Leonard

Coaching Staff
Coach .... Brian Sutter
Assistant Coach .... Tom McVie
Coach, Providence Bruins .... Mike O'Connell

Scouting Staff
Coordinator of Minor League Player Personnel/ Scouting .... Bob Tindall
Director of Player Evaluation .... Bart Bradley
Scouting Staff .... Jim Morrison (Ontario), Andre Lachapelle (Quebec), Don Saatzer (Minnesota), Joe Lyons (New England), Harvey Keck (Western Canada), Jean Ratelle (College & High School), Lars Waldner & Svenvake Svensson (Europe), Yuri Agureikin & Dmitry Yeryomin (CIS), Marcel Pelletier (Pro Consultant), Gordie Clark (Professional Leagues)

Communications Staff
Director of Media Relations .... Heidi Holland
Director of Community Relations, Marketing Services .... Sue Byrne
Public Relations Ass't .... Kevin Lyons
Director of Player & Alumni Community Relations .... John Bucyk
Administrative Assistant .... Mal Viola
Video Producer .... Joe Curnane

Medical and Training Staff
Athletic Trainer .... Jim Narrigan
Athletic Therapist .... Don Worden
Equipment Manager .... Ken Fleger
Assistant Equipment Manager .... Eric Anderson
Team Physicians .... Dr. Bertram Zarins, Dr. Ashby Moncure, Dr. John J. Boyle
Team Dentists .... Dr. John Kelly and Dr. Bruce Donoff
Team Psychologist .... Dr. Fred Neff

Ticketing and Finance Staff
Director of Ticket Operations .... Matt Brennan
Assistant Director of Ticket Operations .... Jim Foley
Receptionist .... Linda Bartlett
Controller .... Bob Vogel
Accounting Manager .... Richard McGlinchey
Accounts Payable .... Barbara Johnson

Television and Radio
Broadcasters (WSBK-TV 38) .... Fred Cusick and Derek Sanderson
Broadcasters (NESN) .... Fred Cusick, Derek Sanderson and Dave Shea
Broadcasters (Radio) .... Bob Wilson and John Bucyk
TV Channels .... New England Sports Network (NESN) and WSBK-TV 38
Radio Station .... WEEI (590 AM) and Bruins Radio Network

Seating Capacity 14,448
Dimensions of Rink .... 191 feet by 83 feet
Club Colors .... Gold, Black and White

Coach

SUTTER, BRIAN
Coach, Boston Bruins. Born in Viking, Alta., October 7, 1956.

Brian Sutter became the 20th coach in the history of the Boston Bruins, joining the organization after four successful seasons as head coach of the St. Louis Blues. Sutter, who received the Jack Adams Trophy as the NHL's Coach of the Year in 1990-91 after directing the Blues to a club-record 47 wins, led the Blues to an above-.500 record in three of his four seasons behind the St. Louis bench. A second round draft selection in 1976, Sutter spent his entire playing career with the Blues, and ranks second in franchise history in games (779), goals (303), assists (333) and points (636).

Coaching Record

		Regular Season					Playoffs			
Season	Team	Games	W	L	T	%	Games	W	L	%
1988-89	St. Louis (NHL)	80	33	35	12	.488	10	5	5	.500
1989-90	St. Louis (NHL)	80	37	34	9	.519	12	7	5	.583
1990-91	St. Louis (NHL)	80	47	22	11	.656	13	6	7	.462
1991-92	St. Louis (NHL)	80	36	33	11	.519	6	2	4	.333
	NHL Totals	320	153	124	43	.545	41	20	21	.488

Buffalo Sabres

1991-92 Results: 31W-37L-12T 74PTS. Third, Adams Division

Pat LaFontaine, who joined the Sabres from the NY Islanders, compiled 46 goals and 47 assists in only 57 games in 1991-92.

Schedule

Home				Away			
Oct.	Thur.	8	Quebec	**Oct.**	Sat.	10	Hartford
	Sun.	11	Montreal		Tues.	13	Pittsburgh
	Fri.	16	Tampa Bay		Sat.	17	Washington
	Wed.	21	Chicago		Wed.	28	Toronto
	Fri.	23	San Jose		Sat.	31	Ottawa
	Fri.	30	Ottawa	**Nov.**	Mon.	2	NY Rangers
Nov.	Wed.	11	Boston		Thur.	5	San Jose
	Fri.	13	Hartford		Sat.	7	Los Angeles
	Sat.	21	Minnesota		Sat.	14	NY Islanders
	Wed.	25	Quebec		Tues.	17	Pittsburgh
	Fri.	27	Ottawa		Wed.	18	New Jersey
Dec.	Fri.	4	NY Islanders		(at Hamilton)		
	Sun.	6	New Jersey		Sun.	22	Philadelphia
	Wed.	9	Boston		Sun.	29	Ottawa
	Fri.	11	Hartford		Mon.	30	Montreal
	Sun.	20	Toronto	**Dec.**	Mon.	7	Quebec
	Wed.	23	Washington		Sat.	12	Hartford
	Sun.	27	Pittsburgh*		Mon.	14	Boston
	Thur.	31	NY Rangers		Sat.	19	Montreal
Jan.	Sun.	3	St Louis	**Jan.**	Sat.	2	Ottawa
	Fri.	8	NY Islanders		Wed.	6	Hartford
	Sun.	10	Calgary		Tues.	12	Boston
	Fri.	22	Quebec		Fri.	15	Vancouver
	Wed.	27	Washington		Sun.	17	Edmonton
	Fri.	29	NY Rangers		Tues.	19	Calgary
	Sun.	31	Edmonton*		Sat.	23	Quebec
Feb.	Wed.	3	Hartford		Tues.	26	Philadelphia
	Fri.	12	Vancouver	**Feb.**	Mon.	8	Ottawa
	Sun.	14	Pittsburgh		Wed.	10	Winnipeg
	Wed.	24	Detroit		Wed.	17	Hartford
	Fri.	26	Montreal		Fri.	19	New Jersey
Mar.	Mon.	1	Vancouver		Sat.	27	Montreal
	(at Hamilton)			**Mar.**	Wed.	3	NY Rangers
	Fri.	5	Hartford		Wed.	10	Quebec
	Sun.	7	Winnipeg		Sat.	13	Hartford*
	Sun.	14	Los Angeles*		Tues.	16	St Louis
	Wed.	24	Boston		Sat.	20	Tampa Bay*
	Sun.	28	Ottawa		Mon.	22	Montreal
	Wed.	31	New Jersey		Thur.	25	Chicago
Apr.	Sun.	4	Boston*		Tues.	30	Washington
	Sun.	11	Quebec	**Apr.**	Sat.	3	Boston*
	Tues.	13	Montreal		Tues.	6	Minnesota
	Thur.	15	Philadelphia		Sat.	10	Detroit*

* Denotes afternoon game.

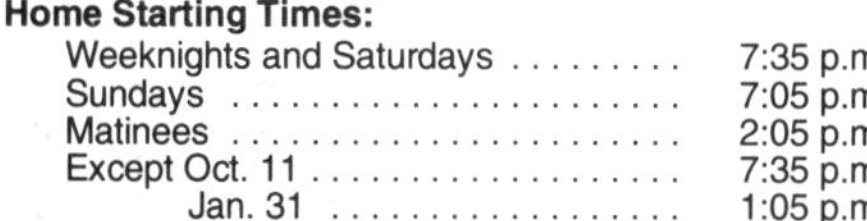

Home Starting Times:

Weeknights and Saturdays	7:35 p.m.
Sundays	7:05 p.m.
Matinees	2:05 p.m.
Except Oct. 11	7:35 p.m.
Jan. 31	1:05 p.m.

Franchise date: May 22, 1970

23rd NHL Season

Year-by-Year Record

		Home			Road			Overall							
Season	**GP**	**W**	**L**	**T**	**W**	**L**	**T**	**W**	**L**	**T**	**GF**	**GA**	**Pts.**	**Finished**	**Playoff Result**
1991-92	80	22	13	5	9	24	7	31	37	12	289	299	74	3rd, Adams Div.	Lost Div. Semi-Final
1990-91	80	15	13	12	16	17	7	31	30	19	292	278	81	3rd, Adams Div.	Lost Div. Semi-Final
1989-90	80	27	11	2	18	16	6	45	27	8	286	248	98	2nd, Adams Div.	Lost Div. Semi-Final
1988-89	80	25	12	3	13	23	4	38	35	7	291	299	83	3rd, Adams Div.	Lost Div. Semi-Final
1987-88	80	19	14	7	18	18	4	37	32	11	283	305	85	3rd, Adams Div.	Lost Div. Semi-Final
1986-87	80	18	18	4	10	26	4	28	44	8	280	308	64	5th, Adams Div.	Out of Playoffs
1985-86	80	23	16	1	14	21	5	37	37	6	296	291	80	5th, Adams Div.	Out of Playoffs
1984-85	80	23	10	7	15	18	7	38	28	14	290	237	90	3rd, Adams Div.	Lost Div. Semi-Final
1983-84	80	25	9	6	23	16	1	48	25	7	315	257	103	2nd, Adams Div.	Lost Div. Semi-Final
1982-83	80	25	7	8	13	22	5	38	29	13	318	285	89	3rd, Adams Div.	Lost Div. Final
1981-82	80	23	8	9	16	18	6	39	26	15	307	273	93	3rd, Adams Div.	Lost Div. Semi-Final
1980-81	80	21	7	12	18	13	9	39	20	21	327	250	99	1st, Adams Div.	Lost Quarter-Final
1979-80	80	27	5	8	20	12	8	47	17	16	318	201	110	1st, Adams Div.	Lost Semi-Final
1978-79	80	19	13	8	17	15	8	36	28	16	280	263	88	2nd, Adams Div.	Lost Prelim. Round
1977-78	80	25	7	8	19	12	9	44	19	17	288	215	105	2nd, Adams Div.	Lost Quarter-Final
1976-77	80	27	8	5	21	16	3	48	24	8	301	220	104	2nd, Adams Div.	Lost Quarter-Final
1975-76	80	28	7	5	18	14	8	46	21	13	339	240	105	2nd, Adams Div.	Lost Quarter-Final
1974-75	80	28	6	6	21	10	9	49	16	15	354	240	113	1st, Adams Div.	Lost Final
1973-74	78	23	10	6	9	24	6	32	34	12	242	250	76	5th, East Div.	Out of Playoffs
1972-73	78	30	6	3	7	21	11	37	27	14	257	219	88	4th, East Div.	Lost Quarter-Final
1971-72	78	11	19	9	5	24	10	16	43	19	203	289	51	6th, East Div.	Out of Playoffs
1970-71	78	16	13	10	8	26	5	24	39	15	217	291	63	5th, East Div.	Out of Playoffs

1992-93 Player Personnel

FORWARDS	HT	WT	S	Place of Birth	Date	1991-92 Club
AMBROZIAK, Peter	6-0	206	L	Toronto, Ont.	9/15/71	Rochester
ANDREYCHUK, Dave	6-3	225	R	Hamilton, Ont.	9/29/63	Buffalo
AUDETTE, Donald	5-8	175	R	Laval, Que.	9/23/69	Buffalo
BARKLEY, Mike	6-0	185	R	Port Alberni, B.C.	4/7/70	U. of Maine
BARNABY, Matthew	6-0	170	L	Ottawa, Ont.	5/4/73	Beauport
CIAVAGLIA, Peter	5-10	173	L	Albany, NY	7/15/69	Rochester
CIERNY, Jozef	6-2	176	L	Zvolen, Czech.	5/13/74	Zvolen
CLANCY, Chris	6-2	198	L	Kitchener, Ont.	11/28/72	Cornwall
CORKUM, Bob	6-2	212	R	Salisbury, MA	12/18/67	Rochester
DAWE, Jason	5-10	195	L	Scarborough, Ont.	5/29/73	Peterborough
DONNELLY, Gord	6-1	202	R	Montreal, Que.	4/5/62	Winnipeg-Buffalo
FRAWLEY, Dan	6-1	196	R	Sturg. Falls, Ont.	6/2/62	Rochester
GAGE, Jody	6-0	190	R	Toronto, Ont.	11/29/59	Rochester
GORDIJUK, Viktor	5-10	176	R	Moscow, USSR	4/11/70	Soviet Wings
HANNAN, Dave	5-10	185	L	Sudbury, Ont.	11/26/61	Toronto-Buffalo
HAWERCHUK, Dale	5-11	190	L	Toronto, Ont.	4/4/63	Buffalo
IOB, Tony	5-11	206	L	Renfrew, Ont.	1/2/71	Rochester
KHMYLEV, Yuri	6-1	189	R	Moscow, USSR	8/9/64	Soviet Wings
KOWALSKY, Rick	6-0	184	R	Simcoe, Ont.	3/20/72	Sault Ste. Marie
LAFONTAINE, Pat	5-10	177	R	St. Louis, MO	2/22/65	Buffalo
MacDONALD, Doug	6-0	192	L	Port Moody, B.C.	2/8/69	U. of Wisconsin
MAY, Brad	6-0	200	L	Toronto, Ont.	11/29/71	Buffalo
McLAUGHLIN, Mike	6-1	175	L	Longmeadow, MA	3/29/70	U. of Vermont
MOGILNY, Alexander	5-11	187	L	Khabarovsk, USSR	2/18/69	Buffalo
PATTERSON, Colin	6-2	195	R	Rexdale, Ont.	5/11/60	Buffalo
PRESLEY, Wayne	5-11	180	R	Detroit, MI	3/23/65	San Jose-Buffalo
RAY, Rob	6-0	203	L	Stirling, Ont.	6/8/68	Buffalo
RUBACHUK, Brad	5-11	185	L	Winnipeg, Man.	6/11/70	Rochester
RUSHFORTH, Paul	6-0	189	R	Prince George, B.C.	4/22/74	North Bay
SAVAGE, Joel	5-11	205	R	Surrey, B.C.	12/25/69	Rochester
SIMON, Todd	5-10	188	R	Toronto, Ont.	4/21/72	Niagara Falls
STEER, Jamie	5-11	180	R	Calgary, Alta.	2/24/69	Michigan Tech
THOMAS, Scott	6-2	195	R	Buffalo, NY	1/18/70	Clarkson
TILTGEN, Dean	5-11	175	L	Ponoka, Alta.	2/3/74	Tri-City
WINCH, Jason	6-1	215	L	Listowel, Ont.	5/23/71	Rochester
WOOD, Randy	6-0	195	L	Princeton, NJ	10/12/63	NY Islanders-Buffalo
YOUNG, Jason	5-10	197	L	Sudbury, Ont.	12/16/72	Sudbury
DEFENSEMEN						
ASTLEY, Mark	5-11	185	L	Calgary, Alta.	3/30/69	Lake Superior St.
BODGER, Doug	6-2	213	L	Chemainus, B.C.	6/18/66	Buffalo
BOUCHER, Philippe	6-2	188	R	St. Apollinaire, Que.	3/24/73	Laval
BROWN, Greg	6-0	185	R	Hartford, CT	3/7/68	Rochester
CARNEY, Keith	6-2	205	L	Providence, RI	2/3/70	Buffalo
COOPER, David	6-2	204	L	Ottawa, Ont.	11/2/73	Medicine Hat
DI VITA, David	6-2	195	L	St. Clair Shores, MI	2/3/69	Rochester
HOULDER, Bill	6-3	218	L	Thunder Bay, Ont.	3/11/67	Rochester
LEDYARD, Grant	6-2	195	L	Winnipeg, Man.	11/19/61	Buffalo
MATIKAINEN, Petri	6-0	185	L	Savonlinna, Finland	1/7/67	
MELANSON, Dean	5-11	211	R	Antigonish, N.S.	11/19/73	St. Hyacinthe
MOLLER, Randy	6-2	207	R	Red Deer, Alta.	8/23/63	NY Rangers-Buffalo
O'DONNELL, Sean	6-2	224	L	Ottawa, Ont.	10/13/71	Rochester
PASCALL, Brad	6-2	192	L	Coquitlan, B.C.	7/29/70	North Dakota
RAMSEY, Mike	6-3	195	L	Minneapolis, MN	12/3/60	Buffalo
SMEHLIK, Richard	6-3	208	L	Ostrava, Czech.	1/23/70	Vitkovice
SNELL, Chris	5-11	200	L	Regina, Sask.	5/12/71	Rochester
SUTTON, Ken	6-0	198	L	Edmonton, Alta.	5/11/69	Buffalo
SVOBODA, Petr	6-1	175	L	Most, Czech.	2/14/66	Montreal-Buffalo

GOALTENDERS	HT	WT	C	Place of Birth	Date	1991-92 Club
DRAPER, Tom	5-11	185	L	Outremont, Que.	11/20/66	Buffalo
HASEK, Dominik	5-11	168	R	Pardubice, Czech.	1/29/65	Chicago
MALARCHUK, Clint	6-0	185	L	Grande Prairie, Alta.	5/1/61	Buffalo
PUPPA, Daren	6-3	205	R	Kirkland Lake, Ont.	3/23/65	Buffalo
PYE, Bill	5-9	180	L	Canton, MI	4/9/69	Rochester

Coaching History

"Punch" Imlach, 1970-71; "Punch" Imlach, Floyd Smith and Joe Crozier, 1971-72; Joe Crozier, 1972-73 to 1973-74; Floyd Smith, 1974-75 to 1976-77; Marcel Pronovost, 1977-78; Marcel Pronovost and Bill Inglis, 1978-79; Scott Bowman, 1979-80; Roger Neilson, 1980-81; Jim Roberts and Scott Bowman, 1981-82; Scott Bowman 1982-83 to 1984-85; Jim Schoenfeld and Scott Bowman, 1985-86; Scott Bowman, Craig Ramsay and Ted Sator, 1986-87; Ted Sator, 1987-88 to 1988-89; Rick Dudley, 1989-90 to 1990-91; Rick Dudley and John Muckler, 1991-92; John Muckler, 1992-93.

Captains' History

Floyd Smith, 1970-71; Gerry Meehan, 1971-72 to 1973-74; Gerry Meehan and Jim Schoenfeld, 1974-75; Jim Schoenfeld, 1975-76 to 1976-77; Danny Gare, 1977-78 to 1980-81; Danny Gare and Gil Perreault, 1981-82; Gil Perreault, 1982-83 to 1985-86; Gil Perreault and Lindy Ruff, 1986-87; Lindy Ruff, 1987-88; Lindy Ruff and Mike Foligno, 1988-89; Mike Foligno, 1989-90. Mike Foligno and Mike Ramsey, 1990-91; Mike Ramsey, 1991-92 to date.

1991-92 Scoring

Regular Season

Pos #	Player	Team	GP	G	A	Pts	+/–	PIM	PP	SH	GW	GT	S	%
C 10	Dale Hawerchuk	BUF	77	23	75	98	22–	27	13	0	4	0	242	9.5
C 16	Pat Lafontaine	BUF	57	46	47	93	10	98	23	0	5	1	203	22.7
L 25	Dave Andreychuk	BUF	80	41	50	91	9–	71	28	0	2	2	337	12.2
R 89	Alexander Mogilny	BUF	67	39	45	84	7	73	15	0	2	0	236	16.5
R 28*	Donald Audette	BUF	63	31	17	48	1–	75	5	0	6	1	153	20.3
D 8	Doug Bodger	BUF	73	11	35	46	1	108	4	0	1	0	180	6.1
L 15	Randy Wood	NYI	8	2	2	4	3–	21	0	0	0	0	30	6.7
		BUF	70	20	16	36	9–	65	7	1	3	0	185	10.8
		TOTAL	78	22	18	40	12–	86	7	1	3	0	215	10.2
R 19	Tony Tanti	BUF	70	15	16	31	4–	100	6	1	0	1	133	11.3
D 7	Petr Svoboda	MTL	58	5	16	21	9	94	1	0	3	0	88	5.7
		BUF	13	1	6	7	8–	52	0	0	0	0	23	4.3
		TOTAL	71	6	22	28	1	146	1	0	3	0	111	5.4
R 18	Wayne Presley	S.J.	47	8	14	22	29–	76	3	0	0	0	114	7.0
		BUF	12	2	2	4	2	57	0	0	1	0	21	9.5
		TOTAL	59	10	16	26	27–	133	3	0	1	0	135	7.4
C 21	Christian Ruuttu	BUF	70	4	21	25	7–	76	0	2	1	0	108	3.7
D 3	Grant Ledyard	BUF	50	5	16	21	4–	45	0	0	0	0	87	5.7
D 41*	Ken Sutton	BUF	64	2	18	20	5	71	0	0	0	0	81	2.5
L 27*	Brad May	BUF	69	11	6	17	12–	309	1	0	3	0	82	13.4
D 5	Mike Ramsey	BUF	66	3	14	17	8	67	0	0	1	0	55	5.5
R 17	Colin Patterson	BUF	52	4	8	12	4–	30	0	2	0	0	33	12.1
D 24	Randy Moller	NYR	43	2	7	9	15–	78	0	0	1	0	44	4.5
		BUF	13	1	2	3	1	59	0	0	0	0	19	5.3
		TOTAL	56	3	9	12	14–	137	0	0	1	0	63	4.8
C 14	Dave Hannan	TOR	35	2	2	4	10–	16	0	1	0	0	24	8.3
		BUF	12	2	4	6	1	48	0	2	0	1	8	25.0
		TOTAL	47	4	6	10	9–	64	0	3	0	1	32	12.5
L 32	Rob Ray	BUF	63	5	3	8	9–	354	0	0	0	0	29	17.2
R 29*	Bob Corkum	BUF	20	2	4	6	9–	21	0	0	0	0	23	8.7
D 34	Gord Donnelly	WPG	4	0	0	0	5–	11	0	0	0	0	5	.0
		BUF	67	2	3	5	7–	305	0	0	1	0	25	8.0
		TOTAL	71	2	3	5	12–	316	0	0	1	0	30	6.7
D 44	Brad Miller	BUF	42	1	4	5	5–	192	0	0	0	0	30	3.3
R 22	Rick Vaive	BUF	20	1	3	4	2–	14	0	0	0	0	25	4.0
D 26*	Keith Carney	BUF	14	1	2	3	3–	18	1	0	0	0	17	5.9
G 35*	Tom Draper	BUF	26	0	2	2	0	2	0	0	0	0	0	.0
D 47	Bill Houlder	BUF	10	1	0	1	2–	8	0	0	0	0	18	5.6
R 14	Jody Gage	BUF	9	0	1	1	1–	2	0	0	0	0	9	.0
D 23	Randy Hillier	NYI	8	0	0	0	3–	11	0	0	0	0	5	.0
		BUF	28	0	1	1	14–	48	0	0	0	0	18	.0
		TOTAL	36	0	1	1	17–	59	0	0	0	0	23	.0
L 37	Lou Franceschetti	BUF	1	0	0	0	0	0	0	0	0	0	0	.0
G 1*	Dave Littman	BUF	1	0	0	0	0	0	0	0	0	0	0	.0
L 36*	Darcy Loewen	BUF	2	0	0	0	0	2	0	0	0	0	1	.0
C 12*	Pete Ciavaglia	BUF	2	0	0	0	1	0	0	0	0	0	1	.0
D 39	Brian Curran	BUF	3	0	0	0	0	14	0	0	0	0	1	.0
G 30	Clint Malarchuk	BUF	29	0	0	0	0	6	0	0	0	0	0	.0
G 31	Daren Puppa	BUF	33	0	0	0	0	2	0	0	0	0	0	.0

Goaltending

No.	Goaltender	GPI	Mins	Avg	W	L	T	EN	SO	GA	SA	S%
35	*Tom Draper	26	1403	3.21	10	9	5	2	1	75	712	.895
30	Clint Malarchuk	29	1639	3.73	10	13	3	1	0	102	903	.887
31	Daren Puppa	33	1757	3.89	11	14	4	1	0	114	932	.878
1	*Dave Littman	1	60	4.00	0	1	0	0	0	4	29	.862
	Totals	**80**	**4869**	**3.68**	**31**	**37**	**12**	**4**	**1**	**299**	**2580**	**.884**

Playoffs

Pos #	Player	Team	GP	G	A	Pts	+/–	PIM	PP	SH	GW	GT	S	%
C 16	Pat Lafontaine	BUF	7	8	3	11	0	4	5	1	1	0	27	29.6
C 10	Dale Hawerchuk	BUF	7	2	5	7	3	0	0	0	0	0	24	8.3
R 18	Wayne Presley	BUF	7	3	3	6	2	14	0	0	0	0	10	30.0
D 7	Petr Svoboda	BUF	7	1	4	5	0	6	0	1	0	0	12	8.3
L 27*	Brad May	BUF	7	1	4	5	3	2	0	0	1	0	18	5.6
L 25	Dave Andreychuk	BUF	7	1	3	4	0	12	0	0	0	0	27	3.7
D 8	Doug Bodger	BUF	7	2	1	3	1	2	2	0	1	0	11	18.2
L 15	Randy Wood	BUF	7	2	1	3	2	6	0	0	0	0	17	11.8
R 19	Tony Tanti	BUF	7	0	3	3	2	4	0	0	0	0	8	.0
D 26*	Keith Carney	BUF	7	0	3	3	0	0	0	0	0	0	6	.0
C 14	Dave Hannan	BUF	7	2	0	2	4–	2	2	0	0	0	9	22.2
R 89	Alexander Mogilny	BUF	2	0	2	2	1–	0	0	0	0	0	4	.0
D 5	Mike Ramsey	BUF	7	0	2	2	1	8	0	0	0	0	3	.0
D 41*	Ken Sutton	BUF	7	0	2	2	0	4	0	0	0	0	5	.0
R 29*	Bob Corkum	BUF	4	1	0	1	1–	0	1	0	0	0	9	11.1
R 17	Colin Patterson	BUF	5	1	0	1	2–	0	0	0	0	0	2	50.0
D 34	Gord Donnelly	BUF	6	0	1	1	0	0	0	0	0	0	0	.0
C 21	Christian Ruuttu	BUF	3	0	0	0	1–	6	0	0	0	0	1	.0
G 35*	Tom Draper	BUF	7	0	0	0	0	0	0	0	0	0	0	.0
D 24	Randy Moller	BUF	7	0	0	0	0	8	0	0	0	0	8	.0
L 32	Rob Ray	BUF	7	0	0	0	2–	2	0	0	0	0	0	.0

Goaltending

No.	Goaltender	GPI	Mins	Avg	W	L	EN	SO	GA	SA	S%
35	*Tom Draper	7	433	2.63	3	4	0	1	19	201	.905
	Totals	**7**	**433**	**2.63**	**3**	**4**	**0**	**1**	**19**	**201**	**.905**

General Managers' History

George "Punch" Imlach, 1970-71 to 1977-78; John Anderson (acting), 1978-79; Scott Bowman, 1979-80 to 1985-86; Scott Bowman and Gerry Meehan, 1986-87; Gerry Meehan, 1987-88 to date.

Retired Numbers

11	Gilbert Perreault	1970-1987

Club Records

Team

(Figures in brackets for season records are games played; records for fewest points, wins, ties, losses, goals, goals against are for 70 or more games)

Record		
Most Points	**113**	1974-75 (80)
Most Wins	**49**	1974-75 (80)
Most Ties	**21**	1980-81 (80)
Most Losses	**44**	1986-87 (80)
Most Goals	**354**	1974-75 (80)
Most Goals Against	**308**	1986-87 (80)
Fewest Points	**51**	1971-72 (78)
Fewest Wins	**16**	1971-72 (78)
Fewest Ties	**6**	1985-86 (80)
Fewest Losses	**16**	1974-75 (80)
Fewest Goals	**203**	1971-72 (78)
Fewest Goals Against	**201**	1979-80 (80)
Longest Winning Streak		
Over-all	**10**	Jan. 4-23/84
Home	**12**	Nov. 12/72-Jan. 7/73; Oct. 13-Dec. 10/89
Away	**10**	Dec. 10/83-Jan. 23/84
Longest Undefeated Streak		
Over-all	**14**	March 6-April 6/80 (8 wins, 6 ties)
Home	**21**	Oct. 8/72-Jan. 7/73 (18 wins, 3 ties)
Away	**10**	Dec. 10/83-Jan. 23/84 (10 wins)
Longest Losing Streak		
Over-all	**7**	Oct. 25-Nov. 8/70
Home	**5**	Feb. 15-Mar. 3/85; Dec. 29/89-Jan. 26/90
Away	**7**	Oct. 14-Nov. 7/70; Feb. 6-27/71
Longest Winless Streak		
Over-all	**12**	Nov. 23-Dec. 20/91 (8 losses, 4 ties)
Home	**12**	Jan. 27-Mar. 10/91 (7 losses, 5 ties)
Away	**23**	Oct. 30/71-Feb. 19/72 (15 losses, 8 ties)
Most Shutouts, Season	**7**	1974-75 (80)
Most PIM, Season	**2,712**	1991-92 (80)
Most Goals, Game	**14**	Jan. 21/75 (Wsh. 2 at Buf. 14); Mar. 19/81 (Tor. 4 at Buf. 14)

Individual

Record		
Most Seasons	**17**	Gilbert Perreault
Most Games	**1,191**	Gilbert Perreault
Most Goals, Career	**512**	Gilbert Perreault
Most Assists, Career	**814**	Gilbert Perreault
Most Points, Career	**1,326**	Gilbert Perreault
Most PIM, Career	**1,450**	Mike Foligno
Most Shutouts, Career	**14**	Don Edwards
Longest Consecutive Games Streak	**776**	Craig Ramsay (Mar. 27/73-Feb. 10/83)
Most Goals, Season	**56**	Danny Gare (1979-80)
Most Assists, Season	**75**	Dale Hawerchuk (1991-92)
Most Points, Season	**113**	Gilbert Perreault (1975-76) (44 goals, 69 assists)
Most PIM, Season	**354**	Rob Ray (1991-92)
Most Points, Defenseman Season	**81**	Phil Housley (1989-90) (21 goals, 60 assists)
Most Points, Center Season	**113**	Gilbert Perreault (1975-76) (44 goals, 69 assists)
Most Points, Right Wing Season	**100**	René Robert (1974-75) (40 goals, 60 assists)
Most Points, Left Wing Season	**95**	Richard Martin (1974-75) (52 goals, 43 assists)
Most Points, Rookie Season	**74**	Richard Martin (1971-72) (44 goals, 30 assists)
Most Shutouts, Season	**5**	Don Edwards (1977-78); Tom Barrasso (1984-85)
Most Goals, Game	**5**	Dave Andreychuk (Feb. 6/86)
Most Assists, Game	**5**	Gilbert Perreault (Feb. 1/76; Mar. 9/80; Jan. 4/84); Dale Hawerchuk (Jan. 15/92)
Most Points, Game	**7**	Gilbert Perreault (Feb. 1/76)

* NHL Record.

All-time Record vs. Other Clubs

Regular Season

	At Home							On Road							Total						
	GP	W	L	T	GF	GA	PTS	GP	W	L	T	GF	GA	PTS	GP	W	L	T	GF	GA	PTS
Boston	75	37	24	14	287	241	88	76	22	45	9	236	320	53	151	59	69	23	523	561	141
Calgary	36	20	12	4	149	110	44	36	13	13	10	125	132	36	72	33	25	14	274	242	80
Chicago	43	27	10	6	169	112	60	41	13	22	6	109	132	32	84	40	32	12	278	244	92
Detroit	43	30	6	7	195	111	67	45	17	23	5	137	168	39	88	47	29	12	332	279	106
Edmonton	21	9	8	4	90	84	22	20	3	15	2	51	91	8	41	12	23	6	141	175	30
Hartford	48	25	16	7	199	160	57	48	23	19	6	151	152	52	96	48	35	13	350	312	109
Los Angeles	43	21	14	8	179	137	50	44	20	16	8	155	150	48	87	41	30	16	334	287	98
Minnesota	43	23	10	10	162	115	56	44	19	19	6	139	139	44	87	42	29	16	301	254	100
Montreal	71	32	21	18	219	209	82	71	19	44	8	208	296	46	142	51	65	26	427	505	128
New Jersey	30	23	3	4	147	85	50	31	19	6	6	130	98	44	61	42	9	10	277	183	94
NY Islanders	37	20	13	4	128	107	44	37	17	14	6	108	106	40	74	37	27	10	236	213	84
NY Rangers	44	27	11	6	200	144	60	42	14	18	10	119	150	38	86	41	29	16	319	294	98
Philadelphia	41	21	14	6	148	122	48	43	9	27	7	110	161	25	84	30	41	13	258	283	73
Pittsburgh	43	22	7	14	196	117	58	44	15	17	12	158	169	42	87	37	24	26	354	286	100
Quebec	48	28	13	7	200	159	63	48	16	24	8	150	185	40	96	44	37	15	350	344	103
St. Louis	42	28	10	4	178	128	60	41	12	24	5	111	157	29	83	40	34	9	289	285	89
San Jose	2	1	1	0	7	9	2	1	0	1	0	4	5	0	3	1	2	0	11	14	2
Toronto	48	30	16	2	204	138	62	47	22	18	7	176	148	51	95	52	34	9	380	286	113
Vancouver	42	22	12	8	156	119	52	42	12	20	10	139	161	34	84	34	32	18	295	280	86
Washington	33	24	5	4	148	89	52	32	21	5	6	135	85	48	65	45	10	10	283	174	100
Winnipeg	20	17	1	2	96	52	36	20	10	8	2	74	66	22	40	27	9	4	170	118	58
Defunct Clubs	23	13	5	5	94	63	31	23	12	8	3	97	76	27	46	25	13	8	191	139	58
Totals	**876**	**500**	**232**	**144**	**3551**	**2611**	**1144**	**876**	**328**	**406**	**142**	**2822**	**3147**	**798**	**1752**	**828**	**638**	**286**	**6373**	**5758**	**1942**

Playoffs

	Series	W	L	GP	W	L	T	GF	GA	Last Mtg.	Round	Result
Boston	5	0	5	29	10	19	0	94	120	1992	DSF	L 3-4
Chicago	2	2	0	9	8	1	0	36	17	1980	QF	W 4-0
Minnesota	2	1	1	7	3	4	0	28	26	1981	QF	L 1-4
Montreal	5	2	3	27	13	14	0	82	98	1991	DSF	L 2-4
NY Islanders	3	0	3	16	4	12	0	45	59	1980	SF	L 2-4
NY Rangers	1	1	0	3	2	1	0	11	6	1978	PR	W 2-1
Philadelphia	2	0	2	11	3	8	0	23	35	1978	QF	L 1-4
Pittsburgh	1	0	1	3	1	2	0	9	9	1979	PR	L 1-2
Quebec	2	0	2	8	2	6	0	27	35	1985	DSF	L 2-3
St. Louis	1	1	0	3	2	1	0	7	8	1976	PR	W 2-1
Vancouver	2	2	0	7	6	1	0	28	14	1981	PR	W 3-0
Totals	**26**	**9**	**17**	**123**	**54**	**69**	**0**	**390**	**420**			

Playoff Results 1992-88

Year	Round	Opponent	Result	GF	GA
1992	DSF	Boston	L 3-4	24	19
1991	DSF	Montreal	L 2-4	24	29
1990	DSF	Montreal	L 2-4	13	17
1989	DSF	Boston	L 1-4	14	16
1988	DSF	Boston	L 2-4	22	28

Abbreviations: Round: F – Final; **CF** – conference final; **DF** – division final; **DSF** – division semi-final; **PR** – preliminary round. **GA** – goals against; **GF** – goals for.

1990-91 Results

Home				Away			
Oct.	4	Pittsburgh	4-5	**Oct.**	5	Washington	1-3
	9	Boston	4-4		12	Quebec	5-4
	13	Vancouver	1-3		16	Montreal	1-5
	18	Montreal	3-1		19	Hartford	1-4
	25	San Jose	3-1		30	Detroit	1-3
	27	Hartford	5-1	**Nov.**	2	Montreal	0-5
Nov.	1	Montreal	1-5		7	Philadelphia	2-5
	8	Philadelphia	4-3		12	San Jose	7-1
	20	Boston	3-1		14	Los Angeles	2-2
	22	Chicago	2-0		16	Calgary	5-4
	27	Quebec	4-4		23	Boston	4-7
	29	NY Rangers	4-5		30	Quebec	3-4
Dec.	8	Calgary	2-4	**Dec.**	4	Winnipeg	4-5
	11	St Louis	3-6		7	Hartford	6-6
	13	Hartford	4-8		14	Montreal	2-4
	18	Washington	2-2		21	Toronto	4-1
	20	Edmonton	4-4		23	Hartford	3-4
	27	Boston	8-1		28	New Jersey	0-3
	31	St Louis	4-3	**Jan.**	4	Boston	2-4
Jan.	3	NY Islanders	5-2		7	Philadelphia	5-5
	8	Quebec	4-2		14	NY Rangers	2-6
	10	Edmonton	8-2		15	New Jersey	8-8
	12	NY Rangers	6-3		21	St Louis	4-5
	26	Winnipeg*	5-2		23	Pittsburgh	5-4
	31	Montreal	5-3		25	Montreal*	4-3
Feb.	4	Washington	7-3		29	Detroit	4-4
	7	Minnesota	0-2	**Feb.**	1	Boston	2-2
	9	Los Angeles	4-5		11	Hartford	1-5
	12	Detroit	4-9		19	Vancouver	5-6
	14	San Jose	7-6		23	Edmonton	2-5
	16	Hartford	5-4		25	Calgary	5-3
Mar.	1	Chicago	1-3		29	Pittsburgh*	2-5
	6	New Jersey	5-4	**Mar.**	3	Quebec	4-4
	8	NY Islanders	2-6		14	NY Islanders*	1-4
	11	Boston	6-3		17	Minnesota	1-3
	15	Quebec	6-4		19	Los Angeles	8-2
	25	Toronto	5-2		22	Chicago	6-2
	29	Hartford	2-2		28	Boston*	3-4
Apr.	2	Montreal	3-1		31	Minnesota	3-5
	5	Quebec	3-4	**Apr.**	4	Quebec	3-7

*Denotes afternoon game

Entry Draft Selections 1992-78

1992
Pick
11 David Cooper
35 Jozef Cierny
59 Ondrej Steiner
80 Dean Melanson
83 Matthew Barnaby
107 Markus Ketterer
108 Yuri Khmylev
131 Paul Rushforth
179 Dean Tiltgen
203 Todd Simon
227 Rick Kowalsky
251 Chris Clancy

1991
Pick
13 Philippe Boucher
35 Jason Dawe
57 Jason Young
72 Peter Ambroziak
101 Steve Shields
123 Sean O'Donnell
124 Brian Holzinger
145 Chris Snell
162 Jiri Kuntos
189 Tony Iob
211 Spencer Meany
233 Mikhail Volkov
255 Michael Smith

1990
Pick
14 Brad May
82 Brian McCarthy
97 Richard Smehlik
100 Todd Bojcun
103 Brad Pascall
142 Viktor Gordiyuk
166 Milan Nedoma
187 Jason Winch
208 Sylvain Naud
229 Kenneth Martin
250 Brad Rubachuk

1989
Pick
14 Kevin Haller
56 John (Scott) Thomas
77 Doug MacDonald
98 Ken Sutton
107 Bill Pye
119 Mike Barkley
161 Derek Plante
183 Donald Audette
194 Mark Astley
203 John Nelson
224 Todd Henderson
245 Michael Bavis

1988
Pick
13 Joel Savage
55 Darcy Loewen
76 Keith E. Carney
89 Alexander Mogilny
97 Robert Ray
106 David Di Vita
118 Mike McLaughlin
139 Mike Griffith
160 Daniel Ruoho
181 Wade Flaherty
223 Thomas Nieman
244 Robert Wallwork

1987
Pick
1 Pierre Turgeon
22 Brad Miller
53 Andrew MacVicar
84 John Bradley
85 David Pergola
106 Chris Marshall
127 Paul Flanagan
148 Sean Dooley
153 Tim Roberts
169 Grant Tkachuk
190 Ian Herbers
211 David Littman
232 Allan MacIsaac

1986
Pick
5 Shawn Anderson
26 Greg Brown
47 Bob Corkum
56 Kevin Kerr
68 David Baseggio
89 Larry Rooney
110 Miguel Baldris
131 Mike Hartman
152 Francois Guay
173 Shawn Whitham
194 Kenton Rein
215 Troy Arndt

1985
Pick
14 Calle Johansson
35 Benoit Hogue
56 Keith Gretzky
77 Dave Moylan
98 Ken Priestlay
119 Joe Reekie
140 Petri Matikainen
161 Trent Kaese
182 Jiri Sejba
203 Boyd Sutton
224 Guy Larose
245 Ken Baumgartner

1984
Pick
18 Mikael Andersson
39 Doug Trapp
60 Ray Sheppard
81 Bob Halkidis
102 Joey Rampton
123 James Gasseau
144 Darcy Wakaluk
165 Orvar Stambert
206 Brian McKinnon
226 Grant Delcourt
247 Sean Baker

1983
Pick
5 Tom Barrasso
10 Normand Lacombe
11 Adam Creighton
31 John Tucker
34 Richard Hajdu
74 Daren Puppa
94 Jayson Meyer
114 Jim Hofford
134 Christian Ruutlu
154 Don McSween
174 Tim Hoover
194 Mark Ferner
214 Uwe Krupp
234 Marc Hamelin
235 Kermit Salfi

1982
Pick
6 Phil Housley
9 Paul Cyr
16 Dave Andreychuk
26 Mike Anderson
30 Jens Johansson
68 Timo Jutila
79 Jeff Hamilton
100 Bob Logan
111 Jeff Parker
121 Jacob Gustavsson
142 Allen Bishop
163 Claude Verret
184 Rob Norman
205 Mike Craig
226 Jim Plankers

1981
Pick
17 Jiri Dudacek
38 Hannu Virta
59 Jim Aldred
60 Colin Chisholm
80 Jeff Eatough
83 Anders Wikberg
101 Mauri Eivola
122 Ali Butorac
143 Heikki Leime
164 Gates Orlando
185 Venci Sebek
206 Warren Harper

1980
Pick
20 Steve Patrick
41 Mike Moller
56 Sean McKenna
62 Jay North
83 Jim Wiemer
104 Dirk Rueter
125 Daniel Naud
146 Jari Paavola
167 Randy Cunneyworth
188 Dave Beckon
209 John Bader

1979
Pick
11 Mike Ramsey
32 Lindy Ruff
53 Mark Robinson
55 Jacques Cloutier
74 Gilles Hamel
95 Alan Haworth
116 Rick Knickle

1978
Pick
13 Larry Playfair
32 Tony McKegney
49 Rob McClanahan
66 Mike Gazdic
82 Randy Ireland
99 Cam MacGregor
116 Dan Eastman
133 Eric Strobel
150 Eugene O'Sullivan

Coach

MUCKLER, JOHN
Coach, Buffalo Sabres. Born in Midland, Ont., April 3, 1934.

John Muckler, who joined the Buffalo organization in May of 1991 as Director of Hockey Operations, replaced Rick Dudley as Buffalo coach midway through the 1991-92 campaign and will return for a full season behind the bench in 1992-93. One of the NHL's most experienced coaches, Muckler has been named as Coach of the Year in three different leagues; the EHL, the AHL and the CHL. Muckler, who started his professional coaching career in 1959, joined the Edmonton Oilers in 1981 as coach of their Wichita farm affiliate and was eventually named as co-coach of the NHL squad in 1986. In 1988-89, he was hired as only the third coach in Oilers' history and promptly led the team to their fifth Stanley Cup championship. After taking over from Dudley, Muckler led the Sabres to a 22-22-8 record.

Coaching Record

		Regular Season					Playoffs			
Season	Team	Games	W	L	T	%	Games	W	L	%
1964-65	Long Island (EHL)	72	42	29	1	.590	15	11	4	.733
1965-66	Long Island (EHL)	72	46	23	3	.660	12	7	5	.583
1968-69	**Minnesota (NHL)**	**35**	**6**	**23**	**6**	**.257**	....	....	....	....
1971-72	Cleveland (AHL)	76	32	34	10	.487	6	2	4	.333
1972-73	*Cleveland (AHL)	76	23	44	9	.362	....	....	....	....
1973-74	Providence (AHL)	76	38	26	12	.579	15	9	6	.600
1974-75	Providence (AHL)	76	43	21	12	.645	6	2	4	.333
1975-76	Providence (AHL)	76	34	34	8	.500	3	0	3	.000
1976-77	Providence (AHL)	53	21	30	2	.415	....	....	....	....
1978-79	Dallas (CHL)	76	45	28	3	.612	9	8	1	.889
1981-82	Wichita (CHL)	80	44	33	3	.569	7	3	4	.423
1989-90	**Edmonton (NHL)**	**80**	**38**	**28**	**14**	**.563**	**22**	**16**	**6**	**.727****
1990-91	**Edmonton (NHL)**	**80**	**37**	**37**	**6**	**.500**	**18**	**9**	**9**	**.500**
1991-92	**Buffalo (NHL)**	**52**	**22**	**22**	**8**	**.500**	**7**	**3**	**4**	**.429**
	NHL Totals	**247**	**103**	**110**	**34**	**.486**	**47**	**28**	**19**	**.596**

* Club moved to Jacksonville during regular season. ** Stanley Cup Win.

Club Directory

Memorial Auditorium
Buffalo, NY 14202
Phone **716/856-7300**
Outside Buffalo: **800/333-PUCK**
GM FAX 716/856-7350
Capacity: 16,325

Board of Directors
Chairman of the Board and President .... Seymour H. Knox, III
Vice-Chairman of the Board and Counsel .... Robert O. Swados
Vice-Chairman of the Board .... Robert E. Rich, Jr.
Treasurer .... Joseph T.J. Stewart
Board of Directors......................... Edwin C. Andrews
Niagara Frontier Hockey, L.P. Peter C. Andrews
(includes above listed officers) George L. Collins, Jr. M.D.
John B. Fisher
John Houghton
Richard Rupp
Howard T. Saperston, Jr.
Paul A. Schoellkopf
George Strawbridge, Jr.
Consultant................................ Northrup R. Knox

Administration
Assistant to the President.................... Seymour H. Knox, IV
Senior Vice-President/Administration .... Mitchell Owen
Senior Vice-President/Finance................ Robert W. Pickel
Vice-President/Marketing..................... George Bergantz
Vice-President/General Manager.............. Gerry Meehan
Administrative Assistants:
General Manager .... Debbie Bonner
Finance .... Elaine Burzynski
President............................... Carol McHugh
Administration........................... Verna B. Wojcik
Controller .... Dan DiPofi
Director of Event Sales...................... Jeffrey Pickel
Ticket Manager............................ John Sinclair

Hockey Department
Director of Hockey Operations/Head Coach ..... John Muckler
Director of Player Personnel .... Don Luce
Assistant to the General Manager .... Craig Ramsay
Assistant Coach .... Don Lever
Assistant Coach .... John Tortorella
Director of Scouting .... Rudy Migay
Scouting Staff .... Don Barrie, Jack Bowman, Larry Carriere, Baris Janicek, Dennis McIvor, Paul Merritt, Mike Racicot, Frank Zywiec
Information Manager .... Ken Bass

Training/Medical
Head Athletic Trainer .... Jim Pizzutelli
Trainer.................................. Rip Simonick
Equipment Supervisor .... John Allaway
Club Doctor............................... John L. Butsch, M.D.
Orthopedic Consultant .... Peter James, M.D.
Club Dentist .... Donald DeRose, D.D.S.

Communications
Director of Communications................. Paul Wieland
Director of Public Relations .... Steve Rossi
Public Relations Assistant .... Bruce Wawrzyniak
Community Relations Assistant .... Mary Beth Romano

Sales & Marketing
Director of Sales........................... John Livsey
Advertising Sales Manager .... Bob Russell
Television Sales Manager .... Jim DiMino
Marketing Associates .... Jeff Hall, Tom Pokel
Director of Corporate Relations .... Larry Playfair
Director of Promotions .... Stan Makowski
Promotions Manager .... Matt Rabinowitz
Director of Amateur Hockey Development ...... John Mickler
Club Staff: Olive Anticola, Evelyn Battleson, Barb Blendowski, Dave Boldt, Robert M. Dahar, Cyndi Dyll, Jennifer Glowny, Birgid Haensel, Chris Ivansitz, Mary Jones, Mike Kaminska, Melissa Kreuzer, Sally Lippert, Gerry Magill, Jennifer Pawlowski, George Peddle, Anne Robillard, Cheryl Schoenthaler, Ann Seaman, Sue Smith
Manager/Sabreland .... Cliff Smith
Team Photographer .... Bill Wippert
Public Address Announcer.................. Milt Ellis
Music.................................... Dave Perry

Radio & TV
Radio Flagship Station .... WGR AM-550
Radio Play-by-Play Announcer .... Rick Jeanneret
TV Stations - Home .... Empire Sports Network
Away........................... WUTV Fox 29
TV Play-by-Play Announcer.................. John Gurtler

General Information
Dimensions of Rink......................... 193 feet by 84 feet
Location of Press Box....................... Suspended from ceiling on west side
Club Colors............................... Blue, Gold & White
Training Camp/Practice Site.................. Sabreland/Wheatfield, NY

General Manager

MEEHAN, GERARD MARCUS (GERRY)
General Manager, Buffalo Sabres. Born in Toronto, Ont., September 3, 1946.

Gerry Meehan became general manager of the Sabres midway through the 1986-87 season. He retired as a player in 1979 after ten NHL seasons as a center with six different clubs. He played in Buffalo from 1970 to 1974 and, after his playing career, remained in the Buffalo area, earning an undergraduate degree from Canisius College and a law degree from the University of Buffalo. He practiced law in Buffalo before accepting the post of assistant GM for the Sabres in 1984-85 when he became the first former Buffalo player to move into the club's front office.

Calgary Flames

1991-92 Results: 31W-37L-12T 74PTS. Fifth, Smythe Division

Schedule

Home

Oct. Tues. 6 Los Angeles
Thur. 8 Edmonton
Sat. 10 Toronto
Tues. 20 Los Angeles
Thur. 22 Boston
Fri. 30 Washington
Sat. 31 Minnesota
Nov. Mon. 2 Vancouver
Thur. 5 Ottawa
Thur. 19 Vancouver
Sat. 21 NY Islanders
Wed. 25 San Jose
Fri. 27 Tampa Bay
Sat. 28 Chicago
Dec. Wed. 2 Winnipeg
Fri. 4 St Louis
Mon. 7 Edmonton
Sat. 19 Los Angeles
Mon. 21 Edmonton
Thur. 31 Montreal
Jan. Sat. 2 Philadelphia
Tues. 5 Winnipeg
Tues. 19 Buffalo
Fri. 22 Winnipeg
Sat. 23 Pittsburgh
Tues. 26 Detroit
Feb. Wed. 10 San Jose
Fri. 12 Quebec
Sat. 13 Hartford
Tues. 16 Philadelphia (at Cincinnati)
Fri. 26 NY Rangers
Sat. 27 San Jose
Mar. Thur. 11 Detroit
Sat. 13 New Jersey
Sun. 14 Vancouver
Tues. 16 Chicago
Wed. 24 St Louis
Sun. 28 Toronto
Tues. 30 Winnipeg
Apr. Thur. 1 Minnesota
Fri. 9 Vancouver
Thur. 15 San Jose

Away

Oct. Tues. 13 Minnesota (at Saskatoon)
Thur. 15 Los Angeles
Sat. 17 San Jose
Sun. 25 Edmonton
Wed. 28 Winnipeg
Nov. Wed. 4 Vancouver
Sun. 8 Quebec*
Mon. 9 Montreal
Wed. 11 Hartford
Thur. 12 Boston
Sat. 14 Tampa Bay
Dec. Tues. 8 Edmonton
Fri. 11 Toronto
Sat. 12 Ottawa
Mon. 14 Detroit
Tues. 15 NY Rangers
Wed. 23 Winnipeg
Sun. 27 Edmonton
Jan. Thur. 7 St Louis
Sat. 9 Pittsburgh*
Sun. 10 Buffalo
Tues. 12 NY Islanders
Thur. 14 Philadelphia
Sat. 16 Minnesota
Thur. 28 Los Angeles
Sat. 30 San Jose
Feb. Tues. 2 Washington
Wed. 3 New Jersey
Wed. 17 Toronto
Fri. 19 Detroit
Sun. 21 Chicago*
Tues. 23 San Jose
Mar. Tues. 2 Los Angeles
Thur. 4 St Louis
Sat. 6 Tampa Bay
Sun. 21 Winnipeg*
Fri. 26 Vancouver
Apr. Sat. 3 San Jose*
Sun. 4 San Jose
Tues. 6 Los Angeles
Sun. 11 Vancouver*
Tues. 13 Edmonton

* Denotes afternoon game.

Home Starting Times:
Weeknights . . . . 7:35 p.m.
Saturdays, Sundays and Dec. 31 6:05 p.m.

Franchise date: June 24, 1980

21st NHL Season

Year-by-Year Record

Season	GP	Home W	Home L	Home T	Road W	Road L	Road T	Overall W	Overall L	Overall T	GF	GA	Pts.	Finished	Playoff Result
1991-92	80	19	14	7	12	23	5	31	37	12	296	305	74	5th, Smythe Div.	Out of Playoffs
1990-91	80	29	8	3	17	18	5	46	26	8	344	263	100	2nd, Smythe Div.	Lost Div. Semi-Final
1989-90	80	28	7	5	14	16	10	42	23	15	348	265	99	1st, Smythe Div.	Lost Div. Semi-Final
1988-89	**80**	**32**	**4**	**4**	**22**	**13**	**5**	**54**	**17**	**9**	**354**	**226**	**117**	**1st, Smythe Div.**	**Won Stanley Cup**
1987-88	80	26	11	3	22	12	6	48	23	9	397	305	105	1st, Smythe Div.	Lost Div. Final
1986-87	80	25	13	2	21	18	1	46	31	3	318	289	95	2nd, Smythe Div.	Lost Div. Semi-Final
1985-86	80	23	11	6	17	20	3	40	31	9	354	315	89	2nd, Smythe Div.	Lost Final
1984-85	80	23	11	6	18	16	6	41	27	12	363	302	94	3rd, Smythe Div.	Lost Div. Semi-Final
1983-84	80	22	11	7	12	21	7	34	32	14	311	314	82	2nd, Smythe Div.	Lost Div. Final
1982-83	80	21	12	7	11	22	7	32	34	14	321	317	78	2nd, Smythe Div.	Lost Div. Final
1981-82	80	20	11	9	9	23	8	29	34	17	334	345	75	3rd, Smythe Div.	Lost Div. Semi-Final
1980-81	80	25	5	10	14	22	4	39	27	14	329	298	92	3rd, Patrick Div.	Lost Semi-Final
1979-80	80	18	15	7	17	17	6	35	32	13	282	269	83	4th, Patrick Div.	Lost Prelim. Round
1978-79	80	25	11	4	16	20	4	41	31	8	327	280	90	4th, Patrick Div.	Lost Prelim. Round
1977-78	80	20	13	7	14	14	12	34	27	19	274	252	87	3rd, Patrick Div.	Lost Prelim. Round
1976-77	80	22	11	7	12	23	5	34	34	12	264	265	80	3rd, Patrick Div.	Lost Prelim. Round
1975-76	80	19	14	7	16	19	5	35	33	12	262	237	82	3rd, Patrick Div.	Lost Prelim. Round
1974-75	80	24	9	7	10	22	8	34	31	15	243	233	83	4th, Patrick Div.	Out of Playoffs
1973-74	78	17	15	7	13	19	7	30	34	14	214	238	74	4th, West Div.	Lost Quarter-Final
1972-73	78	16	16	7	9	22	8	25	38	15	191	239	65	7th, West Div.	Out of Playoffs

Robert Reichel had his finest NHL season with 20 goals and 34 assists for the Flames.

1992-93 Player Personnel

FORWARDS	HT	WT	S	Place of Birth	Date	1991-92 Club
BERUBE, Craig	6-1	205	L	Calahoo, Alta.	12/17/65	Toronto-Calgary
CHERNOMAZ, Rich	5-8	185	R	Selkirk, Man.	9/1/63	Salt Lake-Calgary
CLARK, Kerry	6-1	190	R	Kelvington, Sask.	8/21/68	Salt Lake
DEASLEY, Bryan	6-3	205	L	Toronto, Ont.	11/26/68	Salt Lake
FLEURY, Theoren	5-6	160	R	Oxbow, Sask.	6/29/68	Calgary
FORSLUND, Tomas	6-0	185	L	Falund, Sweden	11/24/68	Calgary-Salt Lake
GILLINGHAM, Todd	6-2	200	L	Labrador City, Nfld.	1/31/70	St. John's
GOMOLAYAKOV, Sergei	6-3	205	L	Chelyabinsk, USSR	1/19/70	Traktor
GREGOR, Colin	6-0	195	L	Grand Prairie, Alta.	7/29/70	Acadia U.
HARKINS, Todd	6-3	210	R	Cleveland, OH	10/8/68	Salt Lake-Calgary
HARRIS, Tim	6-2	190	R	Uxbridge, Ont.	10/16/67	Salt Lake
HEAPHY, Shawn	5-8	180	L	Sudbury, Ont.	1/27/68	Salt Lake
HOFFMAN, Matt	6-0	200	R	Saginaw, MI	7/6/71	Oshawa
KRUSE, Paul	6-0	202	L	Merritt, B.C.	3/15/70	Salt Lake-Calgary
LEEMAN, Gary	5-11	185	R	Toronto, Ont.	2/19/64	Toronto-Calgary
LINDBERG, Chris	6-1	185	L	Ft. Francis, Ont.	4/16/67	Cdn. National-Calgary
MAKAROV, Sergei	5-11	185	L	Chelyabinsk, USSR	6/19/58	Calgary
McCARTHY, Sandy	6-3	224	R	Toronto, Ont.	6/15/72	Laval
NIEUWENDYK, Joe	6-1	195	L	Oshawa, Ont.	9/10/66	Calgary
NIKOLIC, Alex	6-1	200	L	Sudbury, Ont.	3/1/70	Cornell
OTTO, Joel	6-4	220	R	Elk River, Man.	10/29/61	Calgary
POTAICHUK, Andrei	5-10	185	R	Moscow, USSR	8/18/70	Soviet Wings
RANHEIM, Paul	6-0	195	R	St. Louis, MO	1/25/66	Calgary
REICHEL, Robert	5-10	185	L	Most, Czechoslovakia	6/25/71	Calgary
ROBERTS, Gary	6-1	190	L	North York, Ont.	5/23/66	Calgary
ST. PIERRE, David	6-0	180	R	Montreal, Que.	3/22/72	Verdun
STERN, Ron	6-0	195	R	Ste. Agathe, Que.	1/11/67	Calgary
STILLMAN, Cory	6-0	180	L	Peterborough, Ont.	12/20/73	Windsor
STRUCH, David	5-10	180	L	Flin Flon, Man.	2/11/71	Salt Lake-Saskatoon
WILSON, Carey	6-2	205	R	Winnipeg, Man.	5/19/62	Calgary
YOUNG, C.J.	5-10	180	R	Waban, MA	1/1/68	Salt Lake-U.S. National
DEFENSEMEN						
BOUCHARD, Joel	6-0	180	L	Montreal, Que.	1/23/74	Verdun
DAHL, Kevin	5-11	190	R	Regina, Sask.	12/30/68	Cdn. National-Salt Lake
DIXON, Paul	5-11	175	L	Sunderland, England	4/8/73	Humberside
GODYNYUK, Alexander	6-0	207	L	Kiev, USSR	1/27/70	Toronto-Calgary
GRANT, Kevin	6-3	210	R	Toronto, Ont.	1/9/69	Salt Lake
GROLEAU, Francois	6-0	193	L	Longueuil, Que.	1/23/73	Shawinigan
GUY, Kevan	6-3	202	R	Edmonton, Alta.	7/16/65	Calgary-Salt Lake
JOHANSSON, Roger	6-3	190	L	Ljungby, Sweden	4/17/67	Leksand
MacINNIS, Al	6-2	196	R	Inverness, N.S.	7/11/63	Calgary
MARBLE, Evan	6-0	190	R	Eston, Sask.	4/9/72	Medicine Hat
MELROSE, Kevan	5-10	185	L	Calgary, Alta.	3/28/66	Salt Lake
MUSIL, Frank	6-3	215	L	Pardubice, Czech.	12/17/64	Calgary
PETIT, Michel	6-1	205	R	St. Malo, Que.	2/12/64	Toronto-Calgary
SMYTH, Greg	6-3	212	R	Oakville, Ont.	4/23/66	Quebec-Calgary
STOLK, Darren	6-4	205	L	Taber, Alta.	7/22/68	Salt Lake
SUTER, Gary	6-0	190	L	Madison, WI	6/24/64	Calgary
SVEHLA, Robert	5-11	190	R	Martin, Czechoslovakia	1/2/69	Dukla Trencin
WORTMAN, Kevin	6-0	200	R	Sagus, MA	2/22/69	Salt Lake
YAWNEY, Trent	6-3	195	L	Hudson Bay, Sask.	9/29/65	Calgary
YUDIN, Alexander	6-1	195	L	Minsk, USSR	4/1/69	Moscow Dynamo

GOALTENDERS	HT	WT	C	Place of Birth	Date	1991-92 Club
KIDD, Trevor	6-2	185	L	Dugald, Man.	3/29/72	Cdn. National-Calgary
MUZZATTI, Jason	6-1	190	L	Toronto, Ont.	2/3/70	Salt Lake
REESE, Jeff	5-9	170	L	Brantford, Ont.	3/24/66	Toronto-Calgary
SHARPLES, Scott	6-0	180	L	Montreal, Que.	3/1/68	Salt Lake-Calgary
TREFILOV, Andrei	6-0	180	L	Moscow, USSR	8/31/69	Moscow Dynamo
VERNON, Mike	5-9	170	L	Calgary, Alta.	2/24/63	Calgary

1991-92 Scoring

Regular Season

Pos	#	Player	Team	GP	G	A	Pts	+/-	PIM	PP	SH	GW	GT	S	%
L	10	Gary Roberts	CGY	76	53	37	90	32	207	15	0	2	3	196	27.0
D	2	Al Macinnis	CGY	72	20	57	77	13	83	11	0	0	1	304	6.6
C	14	Theoren Fleury	CGY	80	33	40	73	0	133	11	1	6	0	225	14.7
R	42	Sergei Makarov	CGY	68	22	48	70	14	60	6	0	2	0	83	26.5
C	25	Joe Nieuwendyk	CGY	69	22	34	56	1–	55	7	0	2	1	137	16.1
D	20	Gary Suter	CGY	70	12	43	55	1	128	4	0	0	0	189	6.3
C	26	Robert Reichel	CGY	77	20	34	54	1	32	8	0	3	0	181	11.0
L	28	Paul Ranheim	CGY	80	23	20	43	16	32	1	3	3	0	159	14.5
C	29	Joel Otto	CGY	78	13	21	34	10–	161	5	1	3	0	105	12.4
R	11	Gary Leeman	TOR	34	7	13	20	1–	44	3	0	0	0	91	7.7
			CGY	29	2	7	9	11–	27	1	0	0	0	50	4.0
			TOTAL	63	9	20	29	12–	71	4	0	0	0	141	6.4
D	7	Michel Petit	TOR	34	1	13	14	17–	85	1	0	1	0	61	1.6
			CGY	36	3	10	13	2	79	3	0	0	0	68	4.4
			TOTAL	70	4	23	27	15–	164	4	0	1	0	129	3.1
C	33	Carey Wilson	CGY	42	11	12	23	6–	37	4	2	2	0	74	14.9
R	22	Ronnie Stern	CGY	72	13	9	22	0	338	0	1	1	0	96	13.5
C	17	Marc Habscheid	CGY	46	7	11	18	11–	42	2	0	2	0	60	11.7
L	16	Craig Berube	TOR	40	5	7	12	2–	109	1	0	1	0	42	11.9
			CGY	36	1	4	5	3–	155	0	0	0	0	27	3.7
			TOTAL	76	6	11	17	5–	264	1	0	1	0	69	8.7
R	27*	Tomas Forslund	CGY	38	5	9	14	6–	12	0	0	1	0	48	10.4
D	18	Trent Yawney	CGY	47	4	9	13	5–	45	1	0	0	0	33	12.1
L	23	Nevin Markwart	BOS	18	3	6	9	2	44	0	0	0	0	12	25.0
			CGY	10	2	1	3	2–	25	0	0	0	0	4	50.0
			TOTAL	28	5	7	12	0	69	0	0	0	0	16	31.3
D	3	Frank Musil	CGY	78	4	8	12	12	103	1	1	0	0	71	5.6
D	21*	Alexander Godynyuk	TOR	31	3	6	9	12–	59	1	0	1	0	30	10.0
			CGY	6	0	1	1	2–	4	0	0	0	0	12	.0
			TOTAL	37	3	7	10	14–	63	1	0	1	0	42	7.1
D	55*	Mark Osiecki	CGY	50	2	7	9	4–	24	1	0	2	0	44	4.5
L	32*	Chris Lindberg	CGY	17	2	5	7	3	17	0	0	0	0	19	10.5
G	30	Mike Vernon	CGY	63	0	7	7	0	8	0	0	0	0	0	.0
L	12*	Paul Kruse	CGY	16	3	1	4	1	65	0	0	0	0	12	25.0
R	13*	Martin Simard	CGY	21	1	3	4	4–	119	1	0	0	0	11	9.1
R	19	Tim Hunter	CGY	30	1	3	4	2	167	0	0	0	0	19	5.3
D	6	Greg Smyth	QUE	29	0	2	2	10–	138	0	0	0	0	24	.0
			CGY	7	1	1	2	7	15	0	0	0	0	10	10.0
			TOTAL	36	1	3	4	3–	153	0	0	0	0	34	2.9
L	7	Tim Sweeney	CGY	11	1	2	3	0	4	0	0	1	0	16	6.3
D	15	Neil Sheehy	CGY	35	1	2	3	7–	119	0	0	0	0	19	5.3
C	21	Richard Zemlak	CGY	5	0	1	1	2–	42	0	0	0	0	4	.0
G	35	Jeff Reese	TOR	8	0	0	0	0	0	0	0	0	0	0	.0
			CGY	12	0	1	1	0	12	0	0	0	0	0	.0
			TOTAL	20	0	1	1	0	12	0	0	0	0	0	.0
D	4	Jim Kyte	CGY	21	0	1	1	2	107	0	0	0	0	13	.0
D	32*	Darryl Olsen	CGY	1	0	0	0	2–	0	0	0	0	0	3	.0
G	1*	Warren Sharples	CGY	1	0	0	0	0	0	0	0	0	0	0	.0
G	37*	Trevor Kidd	CGY	2	0	0	0	0	0	0	0	0	0	0	.0
D	5	Kevan Guy	CGY	3	0	0	0	2	2	0	0	0	0	3	.0
R	37*	Todd Harkins	CGY	5	0	0	0	2–	7	0	0	0	0	4	.0
R	16	Rich Chernomaz	CGY	11	0	0	0	9–	6	0	0	0	0	21	.0

Goaltending

No.	Goaltender	GPI	Mins	Avg	W	L	T	EN	SO	GA	SA	S%
30	Mike Vernon	63	3640	3.58	24	30	9	2	0	217	1853	.883
1	* Warren Sharples	1	65	3.69	0	0	1	0	0	4	40	.900
35	Jeff Reese	12	587	3.78	3	2	2	2	0	37	290	.872
37	* Trevor Kidd	2	120	4.00	1	1	0	1	0	8	56	.857
31	Rick Wamsley	9	457	4.46	3	4	0	0	0	34	226	.850
	Totals	**80**	**4879**	**3.75**	**31**	**37**	**12**	**5**	**0**	**305**	**2470**	**.877**

Coaching History

Bernie Geoffrion, 1972-73 to 1973-74; Bernie Geoffrion and Fred Creighton, 1974-75; Fred Creighton, 1975-76 to 1978-79; Al MacNeil, 1979-80 (Atlanta); 1980-81 to 1981-82 (Calgary); Bob Johnson, 1982-83 to 1986-87; Terry Crisp, 1987-88 to 1989-90; Doug Risebrough, 1990-91; Doug Risebrough and Guy Charron, 1991-92; Dave King, 1992-93.

Captains' History

Keith McCreary, 1972-73 to 1974-75; Pat Quinn, 1975-76, 1976-77; Tom Lysiak, 1977-78, 1978-79; Jean Pronovost, 1979-80; Brad Marsh, 1980-81; Phil Russell, 1981-82, 1982-83; Lanny McDonald, Doug Risebrough (co-captains), 1983-84; Lanny McDonald, Doug Risebrough, Jim Peplinski (tri-captains), 1984-85 to 1986-87; Lanny McDonald, Jim Peplinski (co-captains), 1987-88; Lanny McDonald, Jim Peplinski, Tim Hunter (tri-captains), 1988-89; Brad McCrimmon, 1989-90; Rotating, 1990-91 to date.

General Managers' History

Cliff Fletcher, 1972-73 to 1990-91. Doug Risebrough, 1991-92.

Retired Numbers

9 Lanny McDonald 1981-1989

Al MacInnis finished second in team scoring in 1991-92 with 20 goals and 57 assists.

Club Records

Team

(Figures in brackets for season records are games played; records for fewest points, wins, ties, losses, goals, goals against are for 70 or more games)

Record		
Most Points	117	1988-89 (80)
Most Wins	54	1988-89 (80)
Most Ties	19	1977-78 (80)
Most Losses	38	1972-73 (78)
Most Goals	397	1987-88 (80)
Most Goals Against	345	1981-82 (80)
Fewest Points	65	1972-73 (78)
Fewest Wins	25	1972-73 (78)
Fewest Ties	3	1986-87 (80)
Fewest Losses	17	1988-89 (80)
Fewest Goals	191	1972-73 (78)
Fewest Goals Against	226	1988-89 (80)
Longest Winning Streak		
Overall	10	Oct. 14-Nov. 3/78
Home	9	Oct. 17-Nov. 15/78 Jan. 3-Feb. 5/89 Mar. 3-Apr. 1/90 Feb. 21-Mar. 14/91
Away	7	Nov. 10-Dec. 4/88
Longest Undefeated Streak		
Over-all	13	Nov. 10-Dec. 8/88 (12 wins, 1 tie)
Home	18	Dec. 29/90-Mar. 14/91 (17 wins, 1 tie)
Away	9	Feb. 20-Mar. 21/88 (6 wins, 3 ties) Nov. 11-Dec. 16/90 (6 wins, 3 ties)
Longest Losing Streak		
Over-all	11	Dec. 14/85-Jan. 7/86
Home	4	Five times
Away	9	Dec. 1/85-Jan. 12/86
Longest Winless Streak		
Over-all	11	Dec. 14/85-Jan. 7/86 (11 losses)
Home	6	Nov. 25-Dec. 18/82 (5 losses, 1 tie)
Away	13	Feb. 3-Mar. 29/73 (10 losses, 3 ties)
Most Shutouts, Season	8	1974-75 (80)
Most PIM, Season	2,655	1991-92 (80)
Most Goals, Game	12	Mar. 21/75 (Van. 4 at Atl. 12) Feb. 22/90 (Tor. 2 at Cgy. 12)

Individual

Record		
Most Seasons	10	Jim Peplinski
Most Games	705	Jim Peplinski
Most Goals, Career	229	Kent Nilsson
Most Assists, Career	512	Al MacInnis
Most Points, Career	686	Al MacInnis (174 goals, 512 assists)
Most PIM, Career	2,405	Tim Hunter
Most Shutouts, Career	20	Dan Bouchard
Longest Consecutive Games Streak	257	Brad Marsh (Oct. 11/78-Nov. 10/81)
Most Goals, Season	66	Lanny McDonald (1982-83)
Most Assists, Season	82	Kent Nilsson (1980-81)
Most Points, Season	131	Kent Nilsson (1980-81) (49 goals, 82 assists)
Most PIM, Season	375	Tim Hunter (1988-89)
Most Points, Defenseman Season	103	Al MacInnis (1990-91) (28 goals, 75 assists)
Most Points, Center Season	131	Kent Nilsson (1980-81) (49 goals, 82 assists)
Most Points, Right Wing Season	110	Joe Mullen (1988-89) (51 goals, 59 assists)
Most Points, Left Wing Season	90	Gary Roberts (1991-92) (53 goals, 37 assists)
Most Points, Rookie Season	92	Joe Nieuwendyk (1987-88) (51 goals, 41 assists)
Most Shutouts, Season	5	Dan Bouchard (1973-74) Phil Myre (1974-75)
Most Goals, Game	5	Joe Nieuwendyk (Jan. 11/89)
Most Assists, Game	6	Guy Chouinard (Feb. 25/81) Gary Suter (Apr. 4/86)
Most Points, Game	7	Sergei Makarov (Feb. 25/90)

All-time Record vs. Other Clubs

Regular Season

	At Home							On Road							Total						
	GP	W	L	T	GF	GA	PTS	GP	W	L	T	GF	GA	PTS	GP	W	L	T	GF	GA	PTS
Boston	36	15	19	2	139	133	32	37	10	22	5	101	127	25	73	25	41	7	240	260	57
Buffalo	36	13	13	10	132	125	36	36	12	20	4	110	149	28	72	25	33	14	242	274	64
Chicago	39	20	12	7	135	117	47	38	12	17	9	118	139	33	77	32	29	16	253	256	80
Detroit	36	22	9	5	166	110	49	35	11	19	5	117	142	27	71	33	28	10	283	252	76
Edmonton	48	23	19	6	223	186	52	47	13	26	8	167	212	34	95	36	45	14	390	398	86
Hartford	20	15	4	1	110	71	31	20	10	7	3	80	69	23	40	25	11	4	190	140	54
Los Angeles	64	40	16	8	312	217	88	62	24	33	5	238	251	53	126	64	49	13	550	468	141
Minnesota	38	24	4	10	159	101	58	38	15	18	5	125	143	35	76	39	22	15	284	244	93
Montreal	35	10	20	5	113	127	25	36	10	20	6	88	127	26	71	20	40	11	201	254	51
New Jersey	34	26	4	4	166	88	56	35	22	10	3	136	99	47	69	48	14	7	302	187	103
NY Islanders	41	18	12	11	149	129	47	41	10	22	9	110	164	29	82	28	34	20	259	293	76
NY Rangers	41	24	10	7	188	126	55	42	18	19	5	153	155	41	83	42	29	12	341	281	96
Philadelphia	42	21	13	8	171	141	50	42	11	30	1	112	175	23	84	32	43	9	283	316	73
Pittsburgh	36	21	8	7	155	107	49	36	10	17	9	121	134	29	72	31	25	16	276	241	78
Quebec	21	12	4	5	98	68	29	20	9	7	4	81	84	22	41	21	11	9	179	152	51
St. Louis	38	20	15	3	138	109	43	39	18	15	6	129	140	42	77	38	30	9	267	249	85
San Jose	3	2	1	0	14	6	4	4	3	1	0	14	11	6	7	5	2	0	28	17	10
Toronto	38	23	11	4	178	129	50	36	15	14	7	145	144	37	74	38	25	11	323	273	87
Vancouver	64	44	11	9	289	179	97	65	28	24	13	220	235	69	129	72	35	22	509	414	166
Washington	30	21	5	4	136	72	46	31	12	15	4	111	119	28	61	33	20	8	247	191	74
Winnipeg	45	32	8	5	222	140	69	45	16	21	8	163	190	40	90	48	29	13	385	330	109
Defunct Clubs	13	8	4	1	51	34	17	13	7	3	3	43	33	17	26	15	7	4	94	67	34
Totals	**798**	**454**	**222**	**122**	**3444**	**2515**	**1030**	**798**	**296**	**380**	**122**	**2682**	**3042**	**714**	**1596**	**750**	**602**	**244**	**6126**	**5557**	**1744**

Playoffs

	Series	W	L	GP	W	L	T	GF	GA	Last Mtg.	Round	Result
Chicago	2	2	0	8	7	1	0	30	17	1989	CF	W 4-1
Detroit	1	0	1	2	0	2	0	5	8	1978	PR	L 0-2
Edmonton	5	1	4	30	11	19	0	96	132	1991	DSF	L 3-4
Los Angeles	5	2	3	20	11	9	0	74	72	1990	DSF	L 2-4
Minnesota	1	0	1	6	2	4	0	18	25	1981	SF	L 2-4
Montreal	2	1	1	11	5	6	0	32	31	1989	F	W 4-2
NY Rangers	1	0	1	4	1	3	0	8	14	1980	PR	L 1-3
Philadelphia	2	1	1	11	4	7	0	28	43	1981	QF	W 4-3
St. Louis	1	1	0	7	4	3	0	28	22	1986	CF	W 4-3
Toronto	1	0	1	2	0	2	0	5	9	1979	PR	L 0-2
Vancouver	4	3	1	18	10	8	0	62	57	1989	DSF	W 4-3
Winnipeg	3	1	2	13	6	7	0	43	45	1987	DSF	L 2-4
Totals	**28**	**12**	**16**	**132**	**61**	**71**	**0**	**439**	**475**			

Playoff Results 1992-88

Year	Round	Opponent	Result	GF	GA
1991	DSF	Edmonton	L 3-4	20	22
1990	DSF	Los Angeles	L 2-4	24	29
1989	**F**	**Montreal**	**W 4-2**	**19**	**16**
	CF	Chicago	W 4-1	15	8
	DF	Los Angeles	W 4-0	22	11
	DSF	Vancouver	W 4-3	26	20
1988	DF	Edmonton	L 0-4	11	18
	DSF	Los Angeles	W 4-1	30	18

Abbreviations: Round: F – Final; **CF** – conference final; **DF** – division final; **DSF** – division semi-final; **SF** – semi-final; **QF** – quarter-final; **PR** – preliminary round. **GA** – goals against; **GF** – goals for.

1991-92 Results

Home			Away		
Oct. 4	Edmonton	9-2	**Oct.** 6	Winnipeg	3-5
15	Minnesota	6-3	8	San Jose	3-4
17	Toronto	6-4	10	Los Angeles	7-1
30	New Jersey	2-5	12	Edmonton	1-3
Nov. 12	Detroit	4-5	19	Vancouver	2-5
14	Vancouver	2-2	22	Minnesota	4-2
16	Buffalo	4-5	24	Chicago	5-2
21	Vancouver	3-2	26	St Louis	2-2
25	Winnipeg	3-3	**Nov.** 1	Winnipeg	7-6
28	Los Angeles	5-3	4	NY Rangers	0-4
30	San Jose	1-2	6	Hartford	3-2
Dec. 14	Detroit	3-4	7	Boston	4-4
17	Winnipeg	7-4	9	Toronto	6-1
19	Quebec	5-5	22	Vancouver	5-6
28	Philadelphia	5-1	**Dec.** 3	Detroit	2-5
29	Los Angeles	6-2	5	New Jersey	3-6
31	Montreal	3-2	7	Montreal	1-5
Jan. 4	Edmonton	2-3	8	Buffalo	4-2
8	San Jose	10-3	10	Washington	1-4
10	Pittsburgh	7-5	21	Winnipeg	2-7
22	NY Rangers	4-4	23	Edmonton	3-5
27	Chicago	3-4	**Jan.** 5	Edmonton	3-2
Feb. 5	Quebec	5-3	13	Montreal	2-2
11	NY Islanders	1-3	14	Quebec	5-3
13	Washington	4-4	16	NY Rangers	4-6
19	Boston	6-4	24	San Jose	3-2
21	Los Angeles	9-7	25	Los Angeles	3-4
25	Buffalo	3-5	30	Boston	1-3
27	Philadelphia	0-3	**Feb.** 1	Washington	2-5
Mar. 3	Pittsburgh	3-6	2	NY Islanders	3-6
5	Toronto	5-5	7	Winnipeg	1-4
7	St Louis	5-1	15	St Louis	2-7
14	Vancouver	4-6	16	Chicago	5-5
16	Hartford	3-4	23	San Jose*	4-2
19	San Jose	3-1	**Mar.** 1	Vancouver*	0-11
24	Edmonton	4-4	10	Pittsburgh	2-5
26	Los Angeles	7-2	12	Philadelphia	4-5
28	Minnesota	4-3	21	Los Angeles*	2-5
31	Edmonton	5-2	**Apr.** 2	Vancouver	4-4
Apr. 5	Winnipeg	3-4	3	San Jose	4-3

*Denotes afternoon game

Entry Draft Selections 1992-78

1992
Pick
6 Cory Stillman
30 Chris O'Sullivan
54 Mathias Johansson
78 Robert Svehla
102 Sami Helenius
126 Ravil Yakubov
129 Joel Bouchard
150 Pavel Rajnoha
174 Ryan Mulhern
198 Brandon Carper
222 Jonas Hoglund
246 Andrei Potaichuk

1991
Pick
19 Niklas Sundblad
41 Francois Groleau
52 Sandy McCarthy
63 Brian Caruso
85 Steven Magnusson
107 Jerome Butler
129 Bobby Marshall
140 Matt Hoffman
151 Kelly Harper
173 David St. Pierre
195 David Struch
217 Sergei Zolotov
239 Marko Jantunen
261 Andrei Trefilov

1990
Pick
11 Trevor Kidd
26 Nicolas P. Perreault
32 Vesa Viitakoski
41 Etienne Belzile
62 Glen Mears
83 Paul Kruse
125 Chris Tschupp
146 Dmitri Frolov
167 Shawn Murray
188 Mike Murray
209 Rob Sumner
230 invalid claim
251 Leo Gudas

1989
Pick
24 Kent Manderville
42 Ted Drury
50 Veli-Pekka Kautonen
63 Corey Lyons
70 Robert Reichel
84 Ryan O'Leary
105 F. (Toby) Kearney
147 Alex Nikolic
168 Kevin Wortman
189 Sergei Gomolyako
210 Dan Sawyer
231 Alexander Yudin
252 Kenneth Kennholt

1988
Pick
21 Jason Muzzatti
42 Todd Harkins
84 Gary Socha
85 Thomas Forslund
90 Scott Matusovich
126 Jonas Bergqvist
147 Stefan Nilsson
168 Troy Kennedy
189 Brett Peterson
210 Guy Darveau
231 Dave Tretowicz
252 Sergei Priakhan

1987
Pick
19 Bryan Deasley
25 Stephane Matteau
40 Kevin Grant
61 Scott Mahoney
70 Tim Harris
103 Tim Corkery
124 Joe Aloi
145 Peter Ciavaglia
166 Theoren Fleury
187 Mark Osiecki
208 William Sedergren
229 Peter Hasselblad
250 Magnus Svensson

1986
Pick
16 George Pelawa
37 Brian Glynn
79 Tom Quinlan
100 Scott Bloom
121 John Parker
142 Rick Lessard
163 Mark Olsen
184 Warren Sharples
205 Doug Pickell
226 Anders Lindstrom
247 Antonin Stavjana

1985
Pick
17 Chris Biotti
27 Joe Nieuwendyk
38 Jeff Wenaas
59 Lane MacDonald
80 Roger Johansson
101 Esa Keskinen
122 Tim Sweeney
143 Stu Grimson
164 Nate Smith
185 Darryl Olsen
206 Peter Romberg
227 Alexander Koznevnikov
248 Bill Gregoire

1984
Pick
12 Gary Roberts
33 Ken Sabourin
38 Paul Ranheim
75 Petr Rosol
96 Joel Paunio
117 Brett Hull
138 Kevan Melrose
159 Jiri Hrdina
180 Gary Suter
200 Petr Rucka
221 Stefan Jonsson
241 Rudolf Suchanek

1983
Pick
13 Dan Quinn
51 Brian Bradley
55 Perry Berezan
66 John Bekkers
71 Kevan Guy
77 Bill Claviter
91 Igor Liba
111 Grant Blair
131 Jeff Hogg
151 Chris MacDonald
171 Rob Kivell
191 Tom Pratt
211 Jaroslav Benak
231 Sergei Makarov

1982
Pick
29 Dave Reierson
37 Richard Kromm
51 Jim Laing
65 Dave Meszaros
72 Mark Lamb
93 Lou Kiriakou
114 Jeff Vaive
118 Mats Kihlstrom
135 Brad Ramsden
156 Roy Myllari
177 Ted Pearson
198 Jim Uens
219 Rick Erdall
240 Dale Thompson

1981
Pick
15 Allan MacInnis
56 Mike Vernon
78 Peter Madach
99 Mario Simioni
120 Todd Hooey
141 Rick Heppner
162 Dale Degray
183 George Boudreau
204 Bruce Eakin

1980
Pick
13 Denis Cyr
31 Tony Curtale
32 Kevin LaVallee
39 Steve Konroyd
76 Marc Roy
97 Randy Turnbull
118 John Multan
139 Dave Newsom
160 Claude Drouin
181 Hakan Loob
202 Steve Fletcher

1979
Pick
12 Paul Reinhart
23 Mike Perovich
33 Pat Riggin
54 Tim Hunter
75 Jim Peplinski
96 Brad Kempthorne
117 Glenn Johnson

1978
Pick
11 Brad Marsh
47 Tim Bernhardt
64 Jim MacRae
80 Gord Wappel
97 Greg Meredith
114 Dave Hindmarch
131 Dave Morrison
148 Doug Todd
165 Mark Green
180 Robert Sullivan
196 Bernhard Englbrecht

Club Directory

Olympic Saddledome
P.O. Box 1540 Station M
Calgary, Alberta T2P 3B9
Phone **403/261-0475**
FAX 403/261-0470
Capacity: 20,214

Owners	Harley N. Hotchkiss, Norman L. Kwong, Sonia Scurfield, Byron J. Seaman, Daryl K. Seaman
Management	
President / Alternate Governor	W.C. (Bill) Hay
Vice-President, General Manager	Doug Risebrough
Vice-President, Business and Finance	Clare Rhyasen
Vice-President, Broadcasting	Leo Ornest
Vice-President, Marketing	Lanny McDonald
Hockey Club Personnel	
Director of Hockey Operations	Al MacNeil
Assistant General Manager	Al Coates
Head Coach	Dave King
Assistant Coaches	Guy Charron, Jamie Hislop
Goaltending Consultant	Glenn Hall
Assistant Coach – Development	Slavomir Lener
Salt Lake City Head Coach	Bob Francis
Chief Scout	Gerry Blair
Scouts	Ray Clearwater, Jiri Hrdina, Guy Lapointe, Ian McKenzie, Lou Reycroft
Pro Scouts	Gerry McNamara, Nick Polano
Scouting Staff	Ron Ferguson, Glen Giovanucci, David Mayville, Lars Normman, Larry Popein, Pekka Rautalkallio, Tom Thompson
Secretary to President and Finance	Yvette Mutcheson
Secretary to General Manager	June Yeates
Secretary to Head Coach and Hockey Operations	Brenda Koyich
Administration	
Controller	Lynne Tosh
Assistant Controller	Dorothy Stuart
Accounting Clerk	Lynn Horton
Receptionist	Karla Piper
Marketing	
Manager, Marketing and Advertising	Pat Halls
Assistant, VP Marketing	Judy Shupe
Retail Stores Manager	Mark Mason
Retail Operations Assistants	Mike Vassey, Linda Carrigan
Public Relations	
Director of Public Relations	Rick Skaggs
Assistant Public Relations Director	Mike Burke
Secretary to Public Relations and Broadcasting	Bernie Doenz
Ticketing	
Ticket Manager	Anne Marie Malarchuk
Assistant Ticket Manager	Linda Forrest
Medical/Training Staff	
Head Trainer	Jim (Bearcat) Murray
Physiotherapist and Fitness Coordinator	James Gattinger
Equipment Manager	Bobby Stewart
Director of Medicine	Dr. Terry Groves
Orthopedic Surgeon	Dr. Lowell Van Zuiden
Team Dentist	Dr. Bill Blair
Consulting	Dr. Hap Davis
Facility	
Home Ice	Olympic Saddledome
Capacity	20,214
Location of Press Boxes	Print – north side Radio – south side TV – concourse
Dimensions of Rink	200 feet by 85 feet

General Manager

RISEBROUGH, DOUG
General Manager, Calgary Flames. Born in Guelph, Ont., January 29, 1954.

Doug Risebrough enters his second full NHL season as general manager of the Calgary Flames. After ending his 14-year NHL playing career with the Flames in 1987, Risebrough was named an assistant coach with Calgary and joined Terry Crisp behind the bench. Risebrough was appointed head coach of the Flames on May 18, 1990 and on May 16, 1991, he also assumed the role of general manager. Late in the 1991-92 campaign he handed the coaching responsibilities over to Guy Charron for the balance of the season.

During his first season as an NHL head coach, Risebrough led the Flames to a fourth place overall finish in the NHL standings. Risebrough was Montreal's first selection, seventh overall, in the 1974 Amateur Draft. During his nine years with the Canadiens, he helped his club to four consecutive Stanley Cup championships between 1976 and 1979. He joined the Flames just prior to the start of the club's 1982 training camp. During his NHL career, his clubs have won five Stanley Cups (1976-1979 and 1989 with Calgary) and two Presidents' Trophies (1987-88 and 1988-89).

NHL Coaching Record

		Regular Season					Playoffs			
Season	**Team**	**Games**	**W**	**L**	**T**	**%**	**Games**	**W**	**L**	**%**
1990-91	Calgary	80	46	26	8	.625	7	3	4	.429
1991-92	Calgary	64	25	30	9	.461	....	....	....	....
	NHL Totals	**144**	**71**	**56**	**17**	**.522**	**7**	**3**	**4**	**.429**

Coach

KING, DAVE
Coach, Calgary Flames. Born in Saskatoon, Sask., December 22, 1947.

Dave King, who is entering his 21st season as a coach, brings a wealth of experience to the Calgary Flames' organization. Long respected for his outstanding contribution to the Canadian National Team program, King started his coaching career with the University of Saskatchewan in 1972-73, eventually moving on to the WHL before returning to Saskatchewan and leading the Huskies to the CIAU title in 1983. King first attracted nation-wide attention when he led the Canadian National Junior Team to the gold medal at the 1982 World Junior Championships. Since that time, he has directed the National and Olympic Teams in both the World Championships and the Olympics. Under his Guidance, Canada captured the silver medal at the 1992 Games, the country's first Olympic hockey medal since 1968.

Coaching Record

		World Championships					Olympics				
Year	**Team**	**Games**	**W**	**L**	**T**	**%**	**Games**	**W**	**L**	**T**	**%**
1984	Canadian National	....	....	....	....	....	7	4	3	0	.571
1987	Canadian National	10	3	5	2	.400	....	....	....	....	....
1988	Canadian National	....	....	....	....	....	8	5	2	1	.688
1989	Canadian National	10	7	3	0	.700	....	....	....	....	....
1990	Canadian National	10	6	3	1	.650	....	....	....	....	....
1991	Canadian National	10	5	2	3	.650	....	....	....	....	....
1992	Canadian National	6	2	3	1	.417	8	6	2	0	.750

Chicago Blackhawks

1991-92 Results: 36W-29L-15T 87PTS. Second, Norris Division

Schedule

	Home		Away
Oct.	Sun. 11 Tampa Bay	Oct.	Wed. 7 Tampa Bay
	Thur. 15 Edmonton		Sat. 10 St Louis
	Sun. 18 Vancouver		Sat. 17 Toronto
	Thur. 22 New Jersey		Wed. 21 Buffalo
	Sun. 25 Detroit		Sat. 31 Boston
	Thur. 29 Philadelphia	Nov.	Tues. 3 Washington
Nov.	Sun. 1 San Jose		(at Indianapolis)
	Thur. 5 Toronto		Sat. 7 Quebec*
	Sun. 8 Pittsburgh		Sat. 14 Minnesota*
	Thur. 12 St Louis		Tues. 17 Detroit
	Sun. 15 Minnesota		Thur. 19 Los Angeles
Dec.	Tues. 1 Los Angeles		Sat. 21 San Jose
	(at Milwaukee)		Mon. 23 Vancouver
	Thur. 3 Toronto		Fri. 27 Edmonton
	Sun. 6 Montreal		Sat. 28 Calgary
	Thur. 10 NY Islanders	Dec.	Sat. 5 Toronto
	Thur. 17 Winnipeg		Tues. 8 Detroit
	Sun. 20 Minnesota		Sat. 12 Minnesota
	Sat. 26 St Louis		Sat. 19 Philadelphia*
	Sun. 27 Detroit		Wed. 23 Ottawa
	Thur. 31 Tampa Bay		Tues. 29 Detroit
Jan.	Sun. 3 Winnipeg	Jan.	Sat. 2 Washington*
	Thur. 7 Edmonton		Sat. 9 St Louis
	Sun. 10 Los Angeles		Tues. 12 Minnesota
	Thur. 14 Minnesota		Sat. 16 Toronto
	Sun. 17 Toronto		Tues. 19 Winnipeg
	Thur. 21 Washington		Sat. 23 Hartford*
	Sun. 24 Vancouver		Wed. 27 Vancouver
Feb.	Thur. 11 Boston		Fri. 29 San Jose
	Sun. 14 Detroit		Sat. 30 Los Angeles
	Thur. 18 Los Angeles	Feb.	Wed. 3 Detroit
	Sun. 21 Calgary*		Sat. 13 Pittsburgh*
	Sun. 28 St Louis		Thur. 25 Tampa Bay
Mar.	Thur. 4 Quebec		Sat. 27 Detroit*
	Sun. 7 Ottawa*	Mar.	Fri. 5 New Jersey
	Thur. 11 NY Rangers		Sun. 14 Edmonton*
	Sun. 21 Tampa Bay		Tues. 16 Calgary
	Thur. 25 Buffalo		Sat. 20 Montreal
	Sun. 28 Hartford		Fri. 26 NY Rangers
Apr.	Thur. 1 Detroit	Apr	Sat. 3 St Louis
	Sun. 4 St Louis		Thur. 8 NY Islanders
	Sun. 11 Tampa Bay*		Sat. 10 Tampa Bay*
	Thur. 15 Toronto		Tues. 13 Minnesota

* Denotes afternoon game.

Home Starting Times:
All games .... 7:35 p.m.
Except Matinees .... 1:35 p.m.

Franchise date: September 25, 1926

67th NHL Season

Year-by-Year Record

		Home			Road			Overall							
Season	GP	W	L	T	W	L	T	W	L	T	GF	GA	Pts.	Finished	Playoff Result
1991-92	80	23	9	8	13	20	7	36	29	15	257	236	87	2nd, Norris Div.	Lost Final
1990-91	80	28	8	4	21	15	4	49	23	8	284	211	106	1st, Norris Div.	Lost Div. Semi-Final
1989-90	80	25	13	2	16	20	4	41	33	6	316	294	88	1st, Norris Div.	Lost Conf. Championship
1988-89	80	16	14	10	11	27	2	27	41	12	297	335	66	4th, Norris Div.	Lost Conf. Championship
1987-88	80	21	17	2	9	24	7	30	41	9	284	326	69	3rd, Norris Div.	Lost Div. Semi-Final
1986-87	80	18	13	9	11	24	5	29	37	14	290	310	72	3rd, Norris Div.	Lost Div. Semi-Final
1985-86	80	23	12	5	16	21	3	39	33	8	351	349	86	1st, Norris Div.	Lost Div. Semi-Final
1984-85	80	22	16	2	16	19	5	38	35	7	309	299	83	2nd, Norris Div.	Lost Conf. Championship
1983-84	80	25	13	2	5	29	6	30	42	8	277	311	68	4th, Norris Div.	Lost Div. Semi-Final
1982-83	80	29	8	3	18	15	7	47	23	10	338	268	104	1st, Norris Div.	Lost Conf. Championship
1981-82	80	20	13	7	10	25	5	30	38	12	332	363	72	4th, Norris Div.	Lost Conf. Championship
1980-81	80	21	11	8	10	22	8	31	33	16	304	315	78	2nd, Smythe Div.	Lost Prelim. Round
1979-80	80	21	12	7	13	15	12	34	27	19	241	250	87	1st, Smythe Div.	Lost Quarter-Final
1978-79	80	18	12	10	11	24	5	29	36	15	244	277	73	1st, Smythe Div.	Lost Quarter-Final
1977-78	80	20	9	11	12	20	8	32	29	19	230	220	83	1st, Smythe Div.	Lost Quarter-Final
1976-77	80	19	16	5	7	27	6	26	43	11	240	298	63	3rd, Smythe Div.	Lost Prelim. Round
1975-76	80	17	15	8	15	15	10	32	30	18	254	261	82	1st, Smythe Div.	Lost Quarter-Final
1974-75	80	24	12	4	13	23	4	37	35	8	268	241	82	3rd, Smythe Div.	Lost Quarter-Final
1973-74	78	20	6	13	21	8	10	41	14	23	272	164	105	2nd, West Div.	Lost Semi-Final
1972-73	78	26	9	4	16	18	5	42	27	9	284	225	93	1st, West Div.	Lost Final
1971-72	78	28	3	8	18	14	7	46	17	15	256	166	107	1st, West Div.	Lost Semi-Final
1970-71	78	30	6	3	19	14	6	49	20	9	277	184	107	1st, West Div.	Lost Final
1969-70	76	26	7	5	19	15	4	45	22	9	250	170	99	1st, East Div.	Lost Semi-Final
1968-69	76	20	14	4	14	19	5	34	33	9	280	246	77	6th, East Div.	Out of Playoffs
1967-68	74	20	13	4	12	13	12	32	26	16	212	222	80	4th, East Div.	Lost Semi-Final
1966-67	70	24	5	6	17	12	6	41	17	12	264	170	94	1st,	Lost Semi-Final
1965-66	70	21	8	6	16	17	2	37	25	8	240	187	82	2nd,	Lost Semi-Final
1964-65	70	20	13	2	14	15	6	34	28	8	224	176	76	3rd,	Lost Final
1963-64	70	26	4	5	10	18	7	36	22	12	218	169	84	2nd,	Lost Semi-Final
1962-63	70	17	9	9	15	12	8	32	21	17	194	178	81	2nd,	Lost Semi-Final
1961-62	70	20	10	5	11	16	8	31	26	13	217	186	75	3rd,	Lost Final
1960-61	**70**	20	6	9	9	18	8	**29**	**24**	**17**	**198**	**180**	**75**	**3rd,**	**Won Stanley Cup**
1959-60	70	18	11	6	10	18	7	28	29	13	191	180	69	3rd,	Lost Semi-Final
1958-59	70	14	12	9	14	17	4	28	29	13	197	208	69	3rd,	Lost Semi-Final
1957-58	70	15	17	3	9	22	4	24	39	7	163	202	55	5th,	Out of Playoffs
1956-57	70	12	15	8	4	24	7	16	39	15	169	225	47	6th,	Out of Playoffs
1955-56	70	9	19	7	10	20	5	19	39	12	155	216	50	6th,	Out of Playoffs
1954-55	70	6	21	8	7	19	9	13	40	17	161	235	43	6th,	Out of Playoffs
1953-54	70	8	21	6	4	30	1	12	51	7	133	242	31	6th,	Out of Playoffs
1952-53	70	14	11	10	13	17	5	27	28	15	169	175	69	4th,	Lost Semi-Final
1951-52	70	9	19	7	8	25	2	17	44	9	158	241	43	6th,	Out of Playoffs
1950-51	70	8	22	5	5	25	5	13	47	10	171	280	36	6th,	Out of Playoffs
1949-50	70	13	18	4	9	20	6	22	38	10	203	244	54	6th,	Out of Playoffs
1948-49	60	13	12	5	8	19	3	21	31	8	173	211	50	5th,	Out of Playoffs
1947-48	60	10	17	3	10	17	3	20	34	6	195	225	46	6th,	Out of Playoffs
1946-47	60	10	17	3	9	20	1	19	37	4	193	274	42	6th,	Out of Playoffs
1945-46	50	15	5	5	8	15	2	23	20	7	200	178	53	3rd,	Lost Semi-Final
1944-45	50	9	14	2	4	16	5	13	30	7	141	194	33	5th,	Out of Playoffs
1943-44	50	15	6	4	7	17	1	22	23	5	178	187	49	4th,	Lost Final
1942-43	50	14	3	8	3	15	7	17	18	15	179	180	49	5th,	Out of Playoffs
1941-42	48	15	8	1	7	15	2	22	23	3	145	155	47	4th,	Lost Quarter-Final
1940-41	48	11	10	3	5	15	4	16	25	7	112	139	39	5th,	Lost Semi-Final
1939-40	48	15	7	2	8	12	4	23	19	6	112	120	52	4th,	Lost Quarter-Final
1938-39	48	5	13	6	7	15	2	12	28	8	91	132	32	7th,	Out of Playoffs
1937-38	**48**	10	10	4	4	15	5	**14**	**25**	**9**	**97**	**139**	**37**	**3rd, Amn. Div.**	**Won Stanley Cup**
1936-37	48	8	13	3	6	14	4	14	27	7	99	131	35	4th, Amn. Div.	Out of Playoffs
1935-36	48	15	7	2	6	12	6	21	19	8	93	92	50	3rd, Amn. Div.	Lost Quarter-Final
1934-35	48	12	9	3	14	8	2	26	17	5	118	88	57	2nd, Amn. Div.	Lost Quarter-Final
1933-34	**48**	13	4	7	7	13	4	**20**	**17**	**11**	**88**	**83**	**51**	**2nd, Amn. Div.**	**Won Stanley Cup**
1932-33	48	12	7	5	4	13	7	16	20	12	88	101	44	4th, Amn. Div.	Out of Playoffs
1931-32	48	13	5	6	5	14	5	18	19	11	86	101	47	2nd, Amn. Div.	Lost Quarter-Final
1930-31	44	14	7	1	10	10	2	24	17	3	108	78	51	2nd, Amn. Div.	Lost Final
1929-30	44	12	9	1	9	9	4	21	18	5	117	111	47	2nd, Amn. Div.	Lost Quarter-Final
1928-29	44	3	13	6	4	16	2	7	29	8	33	85	22	5th, Amn. Div.	Out of Playoffs
1927-28	44	2	18	2	5	16	1	7	34	3	68	134	17	5th, Amn. Div.	Out of Playoffs
1926-27	44	12	8	2	7	14	1	19	22	3	115	116	41	3rd, Amn. Div.	Lost Quarter-Final

Coaching History

Pete Muldoon, 1926-27; Barney Stanley and Hugh Lehman, 1927-28; Herb Gardiner, 1928-29; Tom Shaughnessy and Bill Tobin, 1929-30; Dick Irvin, 1930-31; Dick Irvin and Bill Tobin, 1931-32; Godfrey Matheson, Emil Iverson and Tommy Gorman, 1932-33; Tommy Gorman, 1933-34; Clem Loughlin, 1934-35 to 1936-37; Bill Stewart, 1937-38; Bill Stewart and Paul Thompson, 1938-39; Paul Thompson, 1939-40 to 1943-44; Paul Thompson and Johnny Gottselig, 1944-45; Johnny Gottselig, 1945-46 to 1946-47; Johnny Gottselig and Charlie Conacher, 1947-48; Charlie Conacher, 1948-49 to 1949-50; Ebbie Goodfellow, 1950-51 to 1951-52; Sid Abel, 1952-53 to 1953-54; Frank Eddolls, 1954-55; Dick Irvin, 1955-56; Tommy Ivan, 1956-57; Tommy Ivan and Rudy Pilous, 1957-58; Rudy Pilous, 1958-59 to 1962-63; Billy Reay, 1963-64 to 1975-76; Billy Reay and Bill White, 1976-77; Bob Pulford, 1977-78 to 1978-79; Eddie Johnston, 1979-80; Keith Magnuson, 1980-81; Keith Magnuson and Bob Pulford, 1981-82; Orval Tessier, 1982-83 to 1983-84; Orval Tessier and Bob Pulford, 1984-85; Bob Pulford, 1985-86 to 1986-87; Bob Murdoch, 1987-88; Mike Keenan, 1988-89 to 1991-92; Darryl Sutter, 1992-93.

Captains' History

Dick Irvin, 1926-27 to 1928-29; Duke Dutkowski, 1929-30; Ty Arbour, 1930-31 Cy Wentworth, 1931-32; Helge Bostrom, 1932-33; Chuck Gardiner, 1933-34; no captain, 1934-35; Johnny Gottselig, 1935-36 to 1939-40; Earl Seibert, 1940-41, 1941-42; Doug Bentley, 1942-43, 1943-44; Clint Smith 1944-45; John Mariucci, 1945-46; Red Hamill, 1946-47; John Mariucci, 1947-48; Gaye Stewart, 1948-49; Doug Bentley, 1949-50; Jack Stewart, 1950-51, 1951-52; Bill Gadsby, 1952-53, 1953-54; Gus Mortson, 1954-55 to 1956-57; no captain, 1957-58; Eddie Litzenberger, 1958-59 to 1960-61; Pierre Pilote, 1961-62 to 1967-68, no captain, 1968-69; Pat Stapleton, 1969-70; no captain, 1970-71 to 1974-75; Stan Mikita, Pit Martin, 1975-76; Stan Mikita, Pit Martin, Keith Magnuson, 1976-77; Keith Magnuson, 1977-78, 1978-79; Keith Magnuson, Terry Ruskowski, 1979-80; Terry Ruskowski, 1980-81, 1981-82; Darryl Sutter, 1982-83 to 1986-87; Keith Brown, Troy Murray, Denis Savard, 1987-88; Dirk Graham, 1988-89 to date.

1992-93 Player Personnel

FORWARDS	HT	WT	S	Place of Birth	Date	1991-92 Club
ANDRIYEVSKI, Alexander	6-5	211	R	Minsk, USSR	8/10/68	Dynamo Moscow
BELANGER, Hugo	6-1	190	L	St. Herbert, Que.	5/28/70	Clarkson U.
BOYER, Zac	6-1	185	R	Inuvik, N.W.T.	10/25/71	Kamloops
BROWN, Rob	5-11	185	L	Kingston, Ont.	4/10/68	Hartford-Chicago
BYRAM, Shawn	6-2	204	L	Neepawa, Man.	9/12/68	Indianapolis-Chicago
CONN, Rob	6-2	200	R	Calgary, Alta.	9/3/68	Indianapolis-Chicago
DAM, Trevor	5-10	208	R	Scarborough, Ont.	4/20/70	Indianapolis
EGELAND, Tracy	6-1	180	R	Lethbridge, Alta.	8/20/70	Indianapolis
ELVENES, Stefan	6-1	183	L	Lund, Sweden	3/30/70	Rogle
GILBERT, Greg	6-1	191	L	Mississauga, Ont.	1/22/62	Chicago
GOULET, Michel	6-1	195	L	Peribonka, Que.	4/21/60	Chicago
GRAHAM, Dirk	5-11	190	R	Regina, Sask.	7/29/59	Chicago
GRIMSON, Stu	6-5	220	L	Kamloops, B.C.	5/20/65	Chicago-Indianapolis
HORACEK, Tony	6-4	215	L	Vancouver, B.C.	2/3/67	Philadelphia-Chicago
HOUSE, Bobby	6-1	200	R	Whitehorse, Yukon	1/7/73	Brandon
HRKAC, Tony	5-11	170	L	Thunder Bay, Ont.	7/7/63	San Jose-Chicago
HUDSON, Mike	6-1	185	L	Guelph, Ont.	2/6/67	Chicago
KIRTON, Scott	6-4	215	R	Penetanguishene, Ont.	10/4/71	U.N. Dakota
KLIMOVICH, Sergei	6-2	189	R	Novosibirsk, USSR	3/8/74	Dynamo Moscow
KRIVAKRASOV, Sergei	5-11	175	L	Angarsk, USSR	4/15/74	CSKA
LAFAYETTE, Justin	6-6	220	L	Vancouver, B.C.	1/23/70	Indianapolis
LARMER, Steve	5-10	189	L	Peterborough, Ont.	6/16/61	Chicago
LAUER, Brad	6-0	195	L	Humboldt, Sask.	10/27/66	NY Islanders-Chicago
LEMIEUX, Jocelyn	5-10	200	L	Mont-Laurier, Que.	11/18/67	Chicago
LESSARD, Owen	6-1	196	L	Sudbury, Ont.	1/11/70	Indianapolis
MacINTYRE, Andy	6-1	190	L	Thunder Bay, Ont.	4/16/74	Seattle-Saskatoon
MATTEAU, Stephane	6-3	195	L	Rouyn Noranda, Que.	9/2/69	Calgary-Chicago
MATTHEWS, Jamie	6-1	190	R	Amherst, N.S.	5/25/73	Sudbury
McAMMOND, Dean	5-11	185	L	Grand Cache, Alta.	6/15/73	Prince Albert-Chicago
NOONAN, Brian	6-1	180	R	Boston, MA	5/29/65	Chicago
POJAR, Jon	6-1	190	L	St. Paul, MN	5/5/70	St. Cloud State
PROKOPEC, Mike	6-1	175	R	Toronto, Ont.	5/17/74	Cornwall
ROENICK, Jeremy	6-0	170	R	Boston, MA	1/17/70	Chicago
ROLAND, Layne	6-1	215	R	Vernon, B.C.	2/6/74	Portland
RUUTTU, Christian	5-11	194	L	Lappeenranta, Finland	2/20/64	Finland
SAUNDERS, Matt	6-0	180	L	Ottawa, Ont.	7/17/70	Northeastern
SHANTZ, Jeff	6-0	184	R	Duchess, Alta.	10/10/73	Regina
St. JACQUES, Kevin	5-11	190	R	Edmonton, Alta.	2/25/71	Lethbridge
SUTTER, Brent	5-11	180	R	Viking, Alta.	6/10/62	NY Islanders-Chicago
TEPPER, Stephen	6-4	215	R	Santa Ana, CA	3/10/69	U. of Maine
TOPOROWSKI, Kerry	6-2	212	R	Prince Albert, Sask.	4/9/71	Indianapolis
TUCKER, Chris	5-11	183	L	White Plains, NY	2/9/72	U. of Wisconsin
WILLIAMS, Sean	6-1	182	L	Oshawa, Ont.	1/28/68	Indianapolis-Chicago
WOODCROFT, Craig	6-1	195	L	Toronto, Ont.	12/3/69	Indianapolis
DEFENSEMEN						
AUGER, Jacques	6-1	215	R	Levis, Que.	4/20/72	Hull
BANCROFT, Steve	6-1	214	L	Toronto, Ont.	10/6/70	Maine-Indianapolis
BENNETT, Adam	6-4	206	R	Georgetown, Ont.	3/30/71	Indianapolis-Chicago
BROWN, Keith	6-1	195	R	Cornerbrook, Nfld.	5/6/60	Chicago
BUSKAS, Rod	6-1	200	R	Wetaskiwin, Alta.	1/7/61	Los Angeles-Chicago
CHELIOS, Chris	6-1	192	R	Chicago, IL	1/25/62	Chicago
CLEARY, Joe	6-0	190	R	Buffalo, NY	1/17/70	Boston College
DROPPA, Ivan	6-3	209	L	Czechoslovakia	2/1/72	Kosice
DYKHUIS, Karl	6-3	200	L	Sept-Iles, Que.	7/8/72	Col. Francais-Chicago
HAKSTOL, Dave	6-1	200	R	Warberg, Alta.	7/30/68	Indianapolis
KRAVCHUK, Igor	6-1	200	L	VFA, USSR	9/13/66	Red Army-Chicago
KUCERA, Frantisek	6-2	205	R	Prague, Czech.	2/3/68	Chicago-Indianapolis
MARCHMENT, Bryan	6-1	198	L	Scarborough, Ont.	5/1/69	Chicago
RAYMOND, Richard	6-1	187	R	Sudbury, Ont.	4/4/74	Cornwall
RUSSELL, Cam	6-4	175	L	Halifax, N.S.	1/12/69	Indianapolis-Chicago
SIRKKA, Jeff	6-1	205	L	Copper Cliff, Ont.	6/17/68	Indianapolis
SKRYPEC, Gerry	5-11	186	L	Kitchener, Ont.	6/21/74	Ottawa
SMITH, Steve	6-4	215	L	Glasgow, Scotland	4/30/63	Chicago
SPEER, Michael	6-2	202	L	Toronto, Ont.	3/26/71	Indianapolis
TICHY, Milan	6-3	198	L	Plzen, Czech.	9/22/69	Indianapolis

GOALTENDERS	HT	WT	C	Place of Birth	Date	1991-92 Club
BELFOUR, Ed	5-11	182	L	Carman, Man.	4/21/65	Chicago
BELLEY, Roch	5-10	170	L	Hull, Que.	8/12/71	Indianapolis
LeBLANC, Ray	5-10	170	R	Fitchburg, MA	10/24/64	Indy-Team USA-Chi.
WAITE, Jim	6-0	163	L	Sherbrooke, Que.	4/15/69	Indy-Hershey-Chi.

Brent Sutter shows off the vintage jersey worn by the Blackhawks during the NHL's 75th Anniversary season.

1991-92 Scoring

Regular Season

Pos	#.	Player	Team	GP	G	A	Pts	+/–	PIM	PP	SH	GW	GT	S	%
C	27	Jeremy Roenick	CHI	80	53	50	103	23	98	22	3	13	0	234	22.6
R	28	Steve Larmer	CHI	80	29	45	74	10	65	11	2	3	0	292	9.9
L	16	Michel Goulet	CHI	75	22	41	63	20	69	9	0	4	0	176	12.5
C	12	Brent Sutter	NYI	8	4	6	10	5–	6	1	0	1	0	21	19.0
			CHI	61	18	32	50	5–	30	7	1	2	1	185	9.7
			TOTAL	69	22	38	60	10–	36	8	1	3	1	206	10.7
D	7	Chris Chelios	CHI	80	9	47	56	24	245	2	2	2	1	239	3.8
R	22	Rob Brown	HFD	42	16	15	31	14–	39	13	0	2	2	65	24.6
			CHI	25	5	11	16	1–	34	3	0	1	0	41	12.2
			TOTAL	67	21	26	47	15–	73	16	0	3	2	106	19.8
R	33	Dirk Graham	CHI	80	17	30	47	5–	89	6	1	1	0	222	7.7
R	10	Brian Noonan	CHI	65	19	12	31	9	81	4	0	0	2	154	12.3
D	5	Steve Smith	CHI	76	9	21	30	23	304	3	0	1	0	153	5.9
C	20	Mike Hudson	CHI	76	14	15	29	11–	92	2	1	2	0	97	14.4
D	4	Keith Brown	CHI	57	6	10	16	7	69	2	1	1	0	105	5.7
L	26	Jocelyn Lemieux	CHI	78	6	10	16	2–	80	0	0	1	0	103	5.8
D	2	Bryan Marchment	CHI	58	5	10	15	4–	168	2	0	0	0	55	9.1
C	11	Tony Hrkac	S.J.	22	2	10	12	2–	4	0	0	0	0	31	6.5
			CHI	18	1	2	3	4	6	0	0	0	0	22	4.5
			TOTAL	40	3	12	15	2	10	0	0	0	0	53	5.7
L	32	Stephane Matteau	CGY	4	1	0	1	2	19	0	0	0	0	7	14.3
			CHI	20	5	8	13	3	45	1	0	0	0	31	16.1
			TOTAL	24	6	8	14	5	64	1	0	0	0	38	15.8
D	6	Frantisek Kucera	CHI	61	3	10	13	3	36	1	0	1	0	82	3.7
L	14	Greg Gilbert	CHI	50	7	5	12	4–	35	0	0	1	0	45	15.6
L	44	Mike Peluso	CHI	63	6	3	9	1	408	2	0	0	0	32	18.8
L	34	Tony Horacek	PHI	34	1	3	4	9–	51	0	0	0	0	22	4.5
			CHI	12	1	4	5	2	21	0	0	0	0	10	10.0
			TOTAL	46	2	7	9	7–	72	0	0	0	0	32	6.3
D	3*	Igor Kravchuk	CHI	18	1	8	9	3–	4	0	0	1	0	40	2.5
C	15	Mike Stapleton	CHI	19	4	4	8	0	8	1	0	0	0	32	12.5
L	17	Dan Vincelette	CHI	29	3	5	8	6–	56	0	0	0	0	28	10.7
L	23	Stu Grimson	CHI	54	2	2	4	2–	234	0	0	0	0	23	8.7
D	19*	Karl Dykhuis	CHI	6	1	3	4	1–	4	1	0	0	0	12	8.3
D	25	Rod Buskas	L.A.	5	0	0	0	1–	11	0	0	0	0	1	.0
			CHI	42	0	4	4	12–	80	0	0	0	0	22	.0
			TOTAL	47	0	4	4	13–	91	0	0	0	0	23	.0
C	19*	Dean McAmmond	CHI	5	0	2	2	2–	0	0	0	0	0	4	.0
D	42*	Ryan McGill	CHI	9	0	2	2	1	20	0	0	0	0	15	.0
G	30	Ed Belfour	CHI	52	0	2	2	0	38	0	0	0	0	0	.0
R	11	Brad Lauer	NYI	8	1	0	1	2–	2	0	1	0	0	12	8.3
			CHI	6	0	0	0	3–	4	0	0	0	0	6	.0
			TOTAL	14	1	0	1	5–	6	0	1	0	0	18	5.6
G	29*	Jim Waite	CHI	17	0	1	1	0	0	0	0	0	0	0	.0
L	46*	Shawn Byram	CHI	1	0	0	0	0	0	0	0	0	0	1	.0
L	42	Jeff Jackson	CHI	1	0	0	0	0	2	0	0	0	0	0	.0
D	42	Rick Lanz	CHI	1	0	0	0	0	2	0	0	0	0	0	.0
G	50	Raymond Leblanc	CHI	1	0	0	0	0	0	0	0	0	0	0	.0
R	53*	Sean Williams	CHI	2	0	0	0	0	4	0	0	0	0	0	.0
R	42*	Rob Conn	CHI	2	0	0	0	1	2	0	0	0	0	3	.0
D	47*	Adam Bennett	CHI	5	0	0	0	1	12	0	0	0	0	6	.0
D	8*	Cam Russell	CHI	19	0	0	0	8–	34	0	0	0	0	9	.0
G	31*	Dominik Hasek	CHI	20	0	0	0	0	8	0	0	0	0	0	.0

Goaltending

No.	Goaltender	GPI	Mins	Avg	W	L	T	EN	SO	GA	SA	S%
50	Raymond Leblanc	1	60	1.00	1	0	0	0	0	1	22	.955
31	*Dominik Hasek	20	1014	2.60	10	4	1	0	1	44	413	.893
30	Ed Belfour	52	2928	2.70	21	18	10	4	5	132	1241	.894
29	*Jim Waite	17	877	3.69	4	7	4	1	0	54	347	.844
	Totals	**80**	**4884**	**2.90**	**36**	**29**	**15**	**5**	**6**	**236**	**2028**	**.884**

Playoffs

Pos	#	Player	Team	GP	G	A	Pts	+/–	PIM	PP	SH	GW	GT	S	%
C	27	Jeremy Roenick	CHI	18	12	10	22	11	12	4	0	3	1	56	21.4
D	7	Chris Chelios	CHI	18	6	15	21	19	37	3	0	1	0	54	11.1
R	28	Steve Larmer	CHI	18	8	7	15	9	6	3	0	0	0	69	11.6
R	10	Brian Noonan	CHI	18	6	9	15	3–	30	3	0	1	0	37	16.2
R	33	Dirk Graham	CHI	18	7	5	12	9	8	0	0	1	0	45	15.6
D	5	Steve Smith	CHI	18	1	11	12	12	16	1	0	0	0	37	2.7
L	32	Stephane Matteau	CHI	18	4	6	10	5	24	1	1	0	0	32	12.5
C	20	Mike Hudson	CHI	16	3	5	8	1	26	0	0	0	0	26	11.5
C	12	Brent Sutter	CHI	18	3	5	8	2–	22	1	0	1	0	41	7.3
D	3*	Igor Kravchuk	CHI	18	2	6	8	2–	8	1	0	0	0	48	4.2
D	4	Keith Brown	CHI	14	0	8	8	3–	18	0	0	0	0	20	.0
L	16	Michel Goulet	CHI	9	3	4	7	4	6	0	0	1	0	19	15.8
R	22	Rob Brown	CHI	8	2	4	6	1	4	1	0	0	0	8	25.0
L	26	Jocelyn Lemieux	CHI	18	3	1	4	0	33	0	0	2	0	32	9.4
L	14	Greg Gilbert	CHI	10	1	3	4	1	16	0	0	1	0	9	11.1
L	44	Mike Peluso	CHI	17	1	2	3	3–	8	0	0	1	0	4	25.0
R	15	Brad Lauer	CHI	7	1	1	2	2	2	0	0	0	0	9	11.1
D	8*	Cam Russell	CHI	12	0	2	2	2	2	0	0	0	0	7	.0
L	34	Tony Horacek	CHI	2	1	0	1	1	2	0	0	0	0	1	100.0
D	2	Bryan Marchment	CHI	16	1	0	1	0	36	0	0	0	0	11	9.1
D	25	Rod Buskas	CHI	6	0	1	1	3–	0	0	0	0	0	1	.0
L	23	Stu Grimson	CHI	14	0	1	1	1–	10	0	0	0	0	2	.0
C	11	Tony Hrkac	CHI	3	0	0	0	0	2	0	0	0	0	2	.0
C	19*	Dean McAmmond	CHI	3	0	0	0	1	2	0	0	0	0	1	.0
D	6	Frantisek Kucera	CHI	6	0	0	0	3–	0	0	0	0	0	4	.0

Goaltending

No.	Goaltender	GPI	Mins	Avg	W	L	EN	SO	GA	SA	S%
30	Ed Belfour	18	949	2.47	12	4	0	1	39	398	.902
31	*Dominik Hasek	3	158	3.04	0	2	1	0	8	70	.886
	Totals	**18**	**1106**	**2.60**	**12**	**6**	**1**	**1**	**48**	**469**	**.898**

Club Records

Team

(Figures in brackets for season records are games played; records for fewest points, wins, ties, losses, goals, goals against are for 70 or more games)

Record		
Most Points	107	1970-71 (78) 1971-72 (78)
Most Wins	49	1970-71 (78) 1990-91 (80)
Most Ties	23	1973-74 (78)
Most Losses	51	1953-54 (70)
Most Goals	351	1985-86 (80)
Most Goals Against	363	1981-82 (80)
Fewest Points	31	1953-54 (70)
Fewest Wins	12	1953-54 (70)
Fewest Ties	6	1989-90 (80)
Fewest Losses	14	1973-74 (78)
Fewest Goals	*133	1953-54 (70)
Fewest Goals Against	164	1973-74 (78)
Longest Winning Streak		
Over-all	8	Dec. 9-26/71 Jan. 4-21/81
Home	13	Nov. 11- Dec. 20/70
Away	7	Dec. 9-29/64
Longest Undefeated Streak		
Over-all	15	Jan. 14- Feb. 16/67 (12 wins, 3 ties)
Home	18	Oct. 11- Dec. 20/70 (16 wins, 2 ties)
Away	12	Oct. 29- Dec. 3/75 (6 wins, 9 ties)
Longest Losing Streak		
Over-all	13	Feb. 25- Oct. 11/51
Home	11	Feb. 8- Nov. 22/28
Away	17	Jan. 2- Oct. 7/54
Longest Winless Streak		
Over-all	21	Dec. 17/50- Jan. 28/51 (18 losses, 3 ties)
Home	*15	Dec. 16/28- Feb. 28/29 (11 losses, 4 ties)
Away	23	Dec. 19/50- Oct. 11/51 (15 losses, 8 ties)
Most Shutouts, Season	15	1969-70 (76)
Most PIM, Season	2,663	1991-92 (80)
Most Goals, Game	12	Jan. 30/69 (Chi. 12 at Phil. 0)

Individual

Record		
Most Seasons	22	Stan Mikita
Most Games	1,394	Stan Mikita
Most Goals, Career	604	Bobby Hull
Most Assists, Career	926	Stan Mikita
Most Points, Career	1,467	Stan Mikita (541 goals, 926 assists)
Most PIM, Career	1,442	Keith Magnuson
Most Shutouts, Career	74	Tony Esposito
Longest Consecutive Games Streak	800	Steve Larmer (1982-83 to present)
Most Goals, Season	58	Bobby Hull (1968-69)
Most Assists, Season	87	Denis Savard (81-82, 87-88)
Most Points, Season	131	Denis Savard (1987-88) (44 goals, 87 assists)
Most PIM, Season	408	Mike Peluso (1991-92)
Most Points, Defenseman Season	85	Doug Wilson (1981-82) (39 goals, 46 assists)
Most Points, Center, Season	131	Denis Savard (1987-88) (44 goals, 87 assists)
Most Points, Right Wing, Season	101	Steve Larmer (1990-91) (44 goals, 57 assists)
Most Points, Left Wing, Season	107	Bobby Hull (1968-69) (58 goals, 49 assists)
Most Points, Rookie, Season	90	Steve Larmer (1982-83) (43 goals, 47 assists)
Most Shutouts, Season	15	Tony Esposito (1969-70)
Most Goals, Game	5	Grant Mulvey (Feb. 3/82)
Most Assists, Game	6	Pat Stapleton (Mar. 30/69)
Most Points, Game	7	Max Bentley (Jan. 28/43) Grant Mulvey (Feb. 3/82)

* NHL Record.

General Managers' History

Major Frederic McLaughlin, 1926-27 to 1941-42; Bill Tobin, 1942-43 to 1953-54; Tommy Ivan, 1954-55 to 1976-77; Bob Pulford, 1977-78 to 1989-90; Mike Keenan, 1990-91 to date.

Retired Numbers

1	Glenn Hall	1957-1967
9	Bobby Hull	1957-1972
21	Stan Mikita	1958-1980
35	Tony Esposito	1969-1984

All-time Record vs. Other Clubs

Regular Season

	At Home							On Road							Total						
	GP	W	L	T	GF	GA	PTS	GP	W	L	T	GF	GA	PTS	GP	W	L	T	GF	GA	PTS
Boston	276	140	92	44	890	738	324	274	83	159	32	770	997	198	550	223	251	76	1660	1735	522
Buffalo	41	22	13	6	132	109	50	43	10	27	6	112	169	26	84	32	40	12	244	278	76
Calgary	38	17	12	9	139	118	43	39	12	20	7	117	135	31	77	29	32	16	256	253	74
Detroit	302	142	112	48	915	830	332	301	87	186	28	740	1038	202	603	229	298	76	1655	1868	534
Edmonton	20	11	7	2	90	90	24	21	6	14	1	74	105	13	41	17	21	3	164	195	37
Hartford	20	12	5	3	94	58	27	21	10	9	2	72	75	22	41	22	14	5	166	133	49
Los Angeles	50	26	17	7	195	151	59	50	23	22	5	174	175	51	100	49	39	12	369	326	110
Minnesota	81	53	18	10	344	215	116	81	33	37	11	275	290	77	162	86	55	21	619	505	193
Montreal	265	90	121	54	715	742	234	265	51	166	48	624	1026	150	530	141	287	102	1339	1768	384
New Jersey	37	23	8	6	157	105	52	36	14	15	7	112	111	35	73	37	23	13	269	216	87
NY Islanders	39	18	16	5	126	138	41	37	10	16	11	110	135	31	76	28	32	16	236	273	72
NY Rangers	276	125	109	42	846	768	292	277	106	117	54	780	823	266	553	231	226	96	1626	1591	558
Philadelphia	51	24	10	17	180	136	65	52	15	27	10	142	173	40	103	39	37	27	322	309	105
Pittsburgh	50	33	8	9	210	141	75	49	22	22	5	166	173	49	99	55	30	14	376	314	124
Quebec	21	13	7	1	88	69	27	20	8	8	4	81	85	20	41	21	15	5	169	154	47
St. Louis	84	51	22	11	343	259	113	82	27	40	15	259	289	69	166	78	62	26	602	548	182
San Jose	2	2	0	0	12	4	4	1	0	1	0	2	5	0	3	2	1	0	14	9	4
Toronto	292	147	106	39	903	759	333	293	86	157	50	751	1012	222	585	233	263	89	1654	1771	555
Vancouver	47	30	12	5	176	112	65	48	15	22	11	137	146	41	95	45	34	16	313	258	106
Washington	30	19	6	5	125	89	43	30	10	17	3	98	117	23	60	29	23	8	223	206	66
Winnipeg	22	15	4	3	114	71	33	23	9	11	3	87	96	21	45	24	15	6	201	167	54
Defunct Clubs	139	79	40	20	408	267	178	140	52	67	21	316	345	125	279	131	107	41	724	612	303
Totals	**2183**	**1092**	**745**	**346**	**7202**	**5969**	**2530**	**2183**	**689**	**1160**	**334**	**5999**	**7520**	**1712**	**4366**	**1781**	**1905**	**680**	**13201**	**13489**	**4242**

Playoffs

	Series	W	L	GP	W	L	T	GF	GA	Last Mtg.	Round	Result
Boston	6	1	5	22	5	16	1	63	97	1978	QF	L 0-4
Buffalo	2	0	2	9	1	8	0	17	36	1980	QF	L 0-4
Calgary	2	0	2	8	1	7	0	17	30	1989	CF	L 1-4
Detroit	13	8	5	64	37	27	0	198	177	1992	DF	W 4-0
Edmonton	4	1	3	20	8	12	0	77	102	1992	CF	W 4-0
Los Angeles	1	1	0	5	4	1	0	10	7	1974	QF	W 4-1
Minnesota	6	4	2	33	19	14	0	119	119	1991	DSF	L 2-4
Montreal	17	5	12	81	29	50	2	185	261	1976	QF	L 0-4
NY Islanders	2	0	2	6	0	6	0	6	21	1979	QF	L 0-4
NY Rangers	5	4	1	24	14	10	0	66	54	1973	SF	W 4-1
Philadelphia	1	1	0	4	4	0	0	20	8	1971	QF	W 4-0
Pittsburgh	2	1	1	8	4	4	0	24	23	1992	F	L 0-4
St. Louis	8	7	1	41	27	14	0	160	116	1992	DSF	W 4-2
Toronto	7	2	5	25	9	15	1	57	76	1986	DSF	L 0-3
Vancouver	1	0	1	5	1	4	0	13	18	1982	CF	L 1-4
Defunct Clubs	4	2	2	9	5	3	1	16	15			
Totals	**81**	**37**	**44**	**364**	**168**	**191**	**5**	**1048**	**1160**			

Playoff Results 1992-88

Year	Round	Opponent	Result	GF	GA
1992	F	Pittsburgh	L 0-4	10	15
	CF	Edmonton	W 4-0	21	8
	DF	Detroit	W 4-0	11	6
	DSF	St. Louis	W 4-2	23	19
1991	DSF	Minnesota	L 2-4	16	23
1990	CF	Edmonton	L 2-4	20	25
	DF	St. Louis	W 4-3	28	22
	DSF	Minnesota	W 4-3	21	18
1989	CF	Calgary	L 1-4	8	15
	DF	St. Louis	W 4-1	19	12
	DSF	Detroit	W 4-2	25	18
1988	DSF	St. Louis	L 4-1	17	21

Abbreviations: Round: F – Final; **CF** – conference final; **DF** – division final; **DSF** – division semi-final; **SF** – semi-final; **QF** – quarter-final; **PR** – preliminary round. **GA** – goals against; **GF** – goals for.

1991-92 Results

Home				Away			
Oct.	3	Detroit	3-3	**Oct.**	5	Minnesota	2-4
	6	New Jersey	2-4		12	Washington	7-2
	10	Vancouver	7-6		19	St Louis	4-4
	13	San Jose	7-3		22	Pittsburgh	4-4
	17	Edmonton	4-2		26	Hartford	4-2
	20	St Louis	1-4	**Nov.**	2	Minnesota	3-4
	24	Calgary	2-5		9	Montreal	2-4
	27	Boston	3-6		16	Toronto	2-2
	31	NY Islanders	4-3		19	Detroit	1-4
Nov.	3	Minnesota	4-4		22	Buffalo	0-2
	7	Quebec	4-2		27	Edmonton	2-6
	10	Hartford	3-0		29	Vancouver	2-5
	14	Toronto	3-0	**Dec.**	1	Winnipeg	2-3
	17	St Louis	5-1		7	NY Islanders	5-2
Dec.	5	Los Angeles	6-2		10	Detroit	3-5
	8	Minnesota	7-2		14	Philadelphia*	1-1
	15	Philadelphia	4-4		21	New Jersey	1-1
	19	Montreal	6-4		26	St Louis	1-3
	22	St Louis	5-2		31	Minnesota	2-6
	27	Winnipeg	3-3	**Jan.**	4	Toronto	4-2
	29	Detroit	4-6		10	Winnipeg	2-6
Jan.	2	NY Rangers	3-4		14	Philadelphia	1-1
	5	Minnesota	5-2		25	Minnesota*	2-0
	9	Toronto	2-0		27	Calgary	4-3
	12	Washington	4-2		29	Edmonton	4-3
	16	Toronto	4-0		30	Vancouver	1-4
	23	Quebec	4-2	**Feb.**	1	Los Angeles	0-2
Feb.	13	Los Angeles	2-2		5	San Jose	2-5
	16	Calgary	5-5		8	St Louis	3-1
	20	New Jersey	4-4		22	Detroit*	1-2
	23	St Louis	4-2		25	NY Rangers	1-4
	27	Detroit	4-2		29	Toronto	5-6
Mar.	5	NY Islanders	4-4	**Mar.**	1	Buffalo	3-1
	8	Boston*	4-0		7	Boston*	2-1
	10	San Jose	5-1		11	NY Rangers	1-7
	15	Pittsburgh	3-4		21	Toronto	3-1
	19	Minnesota	4-1		26	Quebec	5-4
	22	Buffalo	2-6		28	Hartford	3-1
	29	Toronto	5-1		31	Detroit	3-3
Apr.	5	Detroit	1-2	**Apr.**	4	St Louis	3-5

*Denotes afternoon game

Entry Draft Selections 1992-78

1992
Pick
12 Sergei Krivokrasov
36 Jeff Shantz
41 Sergei Klimovich
89 Andy MacIntyre
113 Tim Hogan
137 Gerry Skrypec
161 Mike Prokopec
185 Layne Roland
209 David Hymovitz
233 Richard Raymond

1991
Pick
22 Dean McAmmond
39 Michael Pomichter
44 Jamie Matthews
66 Bobby House
71 Igor Kravchuk
88 Zac Boyer
110 Maco Balkovec
112 Kevin St. Jacques
132 Jacques Auger
154 Scott Kirton
176 Roch Belley
198 Scott MacDonald
220 A. Andriyevsky
242 Mike Larkin
264 Scott Dean

1990
Pick
16 Karl Dykhuis
37 Ivan Droppa
79 Chris Tucker
121 Brett Stickney
124 Derek Edgerly
163 Hugo Belanger
184 Owen Lessard
205 Erik Peterson
226 Steve Dubinsky
247 Dino Grossi

1989
Pick
6 Adam Bennett
27 Michael Speer
48 Bob Kellogg
111 Tommi Pullola
132 Tracy Egeland
153 Milan Tichy
174 Jason Greyerbiehl
195 Matt Saunders
216 Mike Kozak
237 Michael Doneghey

1988
Pick
8 Jeremy Roenick
50 Trevor Dam
71 Stefan Elvenas
92 Joe Cleary
113 Justin Lafayette
134 Craig Woodcroft
155 Jon Pojar
176 Mathew Hentges
197 Daniel Maurice
218 Dirk Tenzer
239 Andreas Lupzig

1987
Pick
8 Jimmy Waite
29 Ryan McGill
50 Cam Russell
60 Mike Dagenais
92 Ulf Sandstrom
113 Mike McCormick
134 Stephen Tepper
155 John Reilly
176 Lance Werness
197 Dale Marquette
218 Bill Lacouture
239 Mike Lappin

1986
Pick
14 Everett Sanipass
35 Mark Kurzawski
77 Frantisek Kucera
98 Lonnie Loach
119 Mario Doyon
140 Mike Hudson
161 Marty Nanne
182 Geoff Benic
203 Glen Lowes
224 Chris Thayer
245 Sean Williams

1985
Pick
11 Dave Manson
53 Andy Helmuth
74 Dan Vincelette
87 Rick Herbert
95 Brad Belland
116 Jonas Heed
137 Victor Posa
158 John Reid
179 Richard LaPlante
200 Brad Hamilton
221 Ian Pound
242 Rick Braccia

1984
Pick
3 Ed Olczyk
45 Trent Yawney
66 Tommy Eriksson
90 Timo Lehkonen
101 Darin Sceviour
111 Chris Clifford
132 Mike Stapleton
153 Glen Greenough
174 Ralph DiFiorie
194 Joakim Persson
215 Bill Brown
224 David Mackey
235 Dan Williams

1983
Pick
18 Bruce Cassidy
39 Wayne Presley
59 Marc Bergevin
79 Tarek Howard
99 Kevin Robinson
115 Jari Torkki
119 Mark Lavarre
139 Scot Birnie
159 Kevin Paynter
179 Brian Noonan
199 Dominik Hasek
219 Steve Pepin

1982
Pick
7 Ken Yaremchuk
28 Rene Badeau
49 Tom McMurchy
70 Bill Watson
91 Brad Beck
112 Mark Hatcher
133 Jay Ness
154 Jeff Smith
175 Phil Patterson
196 Jim Camazzola
217 Mike James
238 Bob Andrea

1981
Pick
12 Tony Tanti
25 Kevin Griffin
54 Darrell Anholt
75 Perry Pelensky
96 Doug Chessell
117 Bill Schafhauser
138 Marc Centrone
159 Johan Mellstrom
180 John Benns
201 Sylvain Roy

1980
Pick
3 Denis Savard
15 Jerome Dupont
28 Steve Ludzik
30 Ken Solheim
36 Len Dawes
57 Troy Murray
58 Marcel Frere
67 Carey Wilson
78 Brian Shaw
99 Kevin Ginnell
120 Steve Larmer
141 Sean Simpson
162 Jim Ralph
183 Don Dietrich
204 Dan Frawley

1979
Pick
7 Keith Brown
28 Tim Trimper
49 Bill Gardner
70 Louis Begin
91 Lowell Loveday
112 Doug Crossman

1978
Pick
10 Tim Higgins
29 Doug Lecuyer
46 Rick Paterson
63 Brian Young
79 Mark Murphy
96 Dave Feamster
113 Dave Mancuso
130 Sandy Ross
147 Mark Locken
164 Glenn Van
179 Darryl Sutter

General Manager

KEENAN, MICHAEL (MIKE)
General Manager, Chicago Blackhawks.
Born in Toronto, Ont., October 21, 1949.

In his fourth season as coach of the Blackhawks, Mike Keenan guided his club to their first Stanley Cup Final in 19 years. After series victories over St. Louis, Detroit and Edmonton, Keenan's Blackhawks came up short against Pittsburgh in their attempt to bring the Stanley Cup to Chicago for the first time since 1961.

Keenan spent four years as head coach of the Philadelphia Flyers (1984-85 to 1987-88) before being hired by the Blackhawks on June 9, 1988. While with the Flyers, he led his team to the Stanley Cup Final twice in four years and distinguished himself as the first coach in League history to register 40-or-more wins in each of his first three seasons. Keenan was the head coach for Team Canada in the 1987 Canada Cup and led his club to a 2-1 series victory over the Soviet Union in the final.

NHL Coaching Record

		Regular Season					Playoffs			
Season	Team	Games	W	L	T	%	Games	W	L	%
1984-85	Philadelphia (NHL)	80	53	20	7	.706	19	12	7	.632
1985-86	Philadelphia (NHL)	80	53	23	4	.688	5	2	3	.400
1986-87	Philadelphia (NHL)	80	46	26	8	.625	26	15	11	.577
1987-88	Philadelphia (NHL)	80	38	33	9	.531	7	3	4	.429
1988-89	Chicago (NHL)	80	27	41	12	.413	16	9	7	.563
1989-90	Chicago (NHL)	80	41	33	6	.550	20	10	10	.500
1990-91	Chicago (NHL)	80	49	23	8	.663	6	2	4	.333
1991-92	Chicago (NHL)	80	36	29	15	.544	18	12	6	.667
	NHL Totals	**640**	**343**	**228**	**69**	**.590**	**117**	**65**	**52**	**.556**

Club Directory

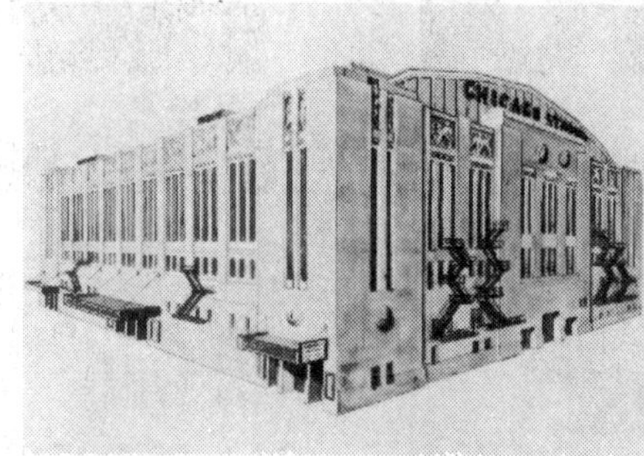

Chicago Stadium
1800 W. Madison St.
Chicago, IL 60612
Phone **312/783-5300**
FAX 312/733-5356
Capacity: 17,317

President	William W. Wirtz
Executive Vice-President	Arthur Michael Wirtz, Jr.
Vice-President & Assistant to the President	Thomas N. Ivan
Senior Vice-President	Robert J. Pulford
General Manager	Mike Keenan
Assistant General Manager	Jack Davison
Director of Player Personnel	Bob Murray
Head Coach	Darryl Sutter
Assistant Coach	Rich Preston
Assistant Coach	Paul Baxter
Chief Scout	Michel Dumas
Scouts	Jim Walker, Russ Houston, Dave Lucas, Jan Spieczny, Kerry Davison, Jim Pappin, Steve Lyons, Brian DeBruyn
Director of Team Services	Ed O'Brien
Executive Secretary	Cindy Bodnarchuk
Receptionist/Secretary	Vicki Littleton
Medical Staff	
Club Doctors	Louis W. Kolb, Howard Baim
Club Dentist	Robert Duresa
Head Trainer	Michael Gapski
Equipment Manager/Assistant Trainer	Randy Lacey, Lou Varga
Team Psychologist	Cal Botterill
Fitness Consultant	Mark Kling
Finance	
Controller	Robert Rinkus
Assistant to the Controller	Penny Swenson
Accounting Secretary	Pat Dema
Public Relations/Marketing	
Director of Marketing	Peter Wirtz
Director of Public Relations	Jim DeMaria
Asst. PR & Director of Community Relations	Tom Finks
Public Relations Secretary	Barbara Davidson
Ticketing	
Ticket Manager	John Stroth
Season Ticket Coordinator	Mildred Hornik
Switchboard Operators	Esther Cox, Mary Joiner
Team Photographer	Ray Grabowski
Organist	Frank Pellico
Soloist	Wayne Messmer
Public Address Announcer	Harvey Wittenberg
Executive Offices	Chicago Stadium
Home Ice	Chicago Stadium
Seating Capacity	17,317
Largest Hockey Crowd	20,960 on April 10, 1982 vs. Minnesota
Location of Press Box	West end of Stadium
Dimensions of Rink	185 feet by 85 feet
Ends of Rink	Plexi-glass extends above boards all around rink
Club Colors	Red, Black and White
Uniforms	Home - Base color white, trimmed with black and red; Away - Base color red trimmed with black and white
Radio Station	WLUP (AM 1000)
Television Station	SportsChannel
Broadcasters	Pat Foley, Dale Tallon

Coach

SUTTER, DARRYL JOHN
Coach, Chicago Blackhawks. Born in Viking, Alberta, August 19, 1958.

Darryl Sutter was appointed as the 29th coach in Chicago Blackhawks' history on June 11, 1992. Sutter, who spent his entire eight-year playing career with Chicago before injuries forced him to retire in 1987, served as an associate coach to Mike Keenan for the past two seasons. Following his retirement, Sutter spent a year as an assistant coach under Bob Murdoch before taking over the head coaching reins of the Blackhawks' top IHL farm affiliate in Saginaw. In his first season as head coach, Sutter led the squad to 46-26-10 record, the best in the league. When the Saginaw franchise was shifted to Indianapolis for the following season, Sutter guided the team to the IHL's Turner Cup championship, earning IHL coach of the year honors.

Coaching Record

		Regular Season					Playoffs			
Season	Team	Games	W	L	T	%	Games	W	L	%
1988-89	Saginaw (IHL)	82	46	26	10	.560	6	2	4	.333
1989-90	Indianapolis (IHL)	82	53	21	8	.646	14	12	2	.857

Detroit Red Wings

1991-92 Results: 43W-25L-12T 98PTS. First, Norris Division

Sergei Fedorov

Schedule

Home

Oct.	Thur.	15	Quebec
	Sat.	17	Edmonton
	Tues.	20	Winnipeg
	Wed.	28	San Jose
	Fri.	30	Toronto
Nov.	Wed.	4	Montreal
	Fri.	6	Hartford
	Fri.	13	Pittsburgh
	Tues.	17	Chicago
	Thur.	19	Winnipeg
	Mon.	23	Tampa Bay
	Wed.	25	St Louis
	Fri.	27	Los Angeles
	Mon.	30	Washington
Dec.	Thur.	3	Minnesota
	Tues.	8	Chicago
	Fri.	11	Philadelphia
	Mon.	14	Calgary
	Fri.	18	Boston
	Tues.	22	Toronto
	Tues.	29	Chicago
	Thur.	31	Ottawa
Jan.	Mon.	4	Toronto
	Fri.	8	Vancouver
	Mon.	11	St Louis
	Wed.	13	Tampa Bay
	Fri.	15	San Jose
	Tues.	19	NY Rangers
	Thur.	21	St Louis
Feb.	Wed.	3	Chicago
	Tues.	9	New Jersey
	Wed.	17	Tampa Bay
	Fri.	19	Calgary
	Sat.	27	Chicago*
Mar.	Fri.	5	Toronto
	Tues.	16	Washington (at Milwaukee)
	Thur.	18	Minnesota
	Tues.	23	NY Islanders
	Mon.	29	Los Angeles
Apr.	Sat.	3	Vancouver*
	Sat.	10	Buffalo*
	Thur.	15	Minnesota

Away

Oct.	Tues.	6	Winnipeg
	Thur.	8	Los Angeles
	Sat.	10	San Jose
	Thur.	22	Pittsburgh
	Sat.	24	St Louis
	Sun.	25	Chicago
	Sat.	31	Toronto
Nov.	Sat.	7	Montreal
	Wed.	11	Tampa Bay
	Sat.	14	Hartford
	Fri.	20	Washington
	Sat.	28	St Louis
Dec.	Wed.	2	NY Rangers
	Sat.	5	Tampa Bay
	Wed.	9	Toronto
	Tues.	15	Ottawa
	Sat.	19	Minnesota
	Sat.	26	Toronto
	Sun.	27	Chicago
Jan.	Sat.	2	Quebec
	Sun.	17	Philadelphia
	Sat.	23	St Louis
	Tues.	26	Calgary
	Wed.	27	Edmonton
	Sat.	30	Vancouver
Feb.	Thur.	11	Los Angeles
	Sat.	13	St Louis
	Sun.	14	Chicago
	Sun.	21	Minnesota*
	Mon.	22	Philadelphia (at Cleveland)
	Wed.	24	Buffalo
	Sun.	28	New Jersey
Mar.	Tues.	2	NY Islanders
	Sun.	7	Minnesota
	Wed.	10	Edmonton
	Thur.	11	Calgary
	Sun.	14	San Jose*
	Sat.	20	Boston*
	Sun.	21	Minnesota*
	Sat.	27	Tampa Bay
Apr.	Thur.	1	Chicago
	Thur.	8	Tampa Bay

* Denotes afternoon game.

Home Starting Times:

Weeknights and Saturdays	7:35 p.m.
Sundays	7:05 p.m.
Matinees	1:05 p.m.

Franchise date: September 25, 1926

67th NHL Season

Year-by-Year Record

		Home			Road			Overall							
Season	**GP**	**W**	**L**	**T**	**W**	**L**	**T**	**W**	**L**	**T**	**GF**	**GA**	**Pts.**	**Finished**	**Playoff Result**
1991-92	80	24	12	4	19	13	8	43	25	12	320	256	98	1st, Norris Div.	Lost Div. Final
1990-91	80	26	14	0	8	24	8	34	38	8	273	298	76	3rd, Norris Div.	Lost Div. Semi-Final
1989-90	80	20	14	6	8	24	8	28	38	14	288	323	70	5th, Norris Div.	Out of Playoffs
1988-89	80	20	14	6	14	20	6	34	34	12	313	316	80	1st, Norris Div.	Lost Div. Semi-Final
1987-88	80	24	10	6	17	18	5	41	28	11	322	269	93	1st, Norris Div.	Lost Conf. Championship
1986-87	80	20	14	6	14	22	4	34	36	10	260	274	78	2nd, Norris Div.	Lost Conf. Championship
1985-86	80	10	26	4	7	31	2	17	57	6	266	415	40	5th, Norris Div.	Out of Playoffs
1984-85	80	19	14	7	8	27	5	27	41	12	313	357	66	3rd, Norris Div.	Lost Div. Semi-Final
1983-84	80	18	20	2	13	22	5	31	42	7	298	323	69	3rd, Norris Div.	Lost Div. Semi-Final
1982-83	80	14	19	7	7	25	8	21	44	15	263	344	57	5th, Norris Div.	Out of Playoffs
1981-82	80	15	19	6	6	28	6	21	47	12	270	351	54	6th, Norris Div.	Out of Playoffs
1980-81	80	16	15	9	3	28	9	19	43	18	252	339	56	5th, Norris Div.	Out of Playoffs
1979-80	80	14	21	5	12	22	6	26	43	11	268	306	63	5th, Norris Div.	Out of Playoffs
1978-79	80	15	17	8	8	24	8	23	41	16	252	295	62	5th, Norris Div.	Out of Playoffs
1977-78	80	22	11	7	10	23	7	32	34	14	252	266	78	2nd, Norris Div.	Lost Quarter-Final
1976-77	80	12	22	6	4	33	3	16	55	9	183	309	41	5th, Norris Div.	Out of Playoffs
1975-76	80	17	15	8	9	29	2	26	44	10	226	300	62	4th, Norris Div.	Out of Playoffs
1974-75	80	17	17	6	6	28	6	23	45	12	259	335	58	4th, Norris Div.	Out of Playoffs
1973-74	78	21	12	6	8	27	4	29	39	10	255	319	68	6th, East Div.	Out of Playoffs
1972-73	78	22	12	5	15	17	7	37	29	12	265	243	86	5th, East Div.	Out of Playoffs
1971-72	78	25	11	3	8	24	7	33	35	10	261	262	76	5th, East Div.	Out of Playoffs
1970-71	78	17	15	7	5	30	4	22	45	11	209	308	55	7th, East Div.	Out of Playoffs
1969-70	76	20	11	7	20	10	8	40	21	15	246	199	95	3rd, East Div.	Lost Quarter-Final
1968-69	76	23	8	7	10	23	5	33	31	12	239	221	78	5th, East Div.	Out of Playoffs
1967-68	74	18	15	4	9	20	8	27	35	12	245	257	66	6th, East Div.	Out of Playoffs
1966-67	70	21	11	3	6	28	1	27	39	4	212	241	58	5th,	Out of Playoffs
1965-66	70	20	8	7	11	19	5	31	27	12	221	194	74	4th,	Lost Final
1964-65	70	25	7	3	15	16	4	40	23	7	224	175	87	1st,	Lost Semi-Final
1963-64	70	23	9	3	7	20	8	30	29	11	191	204	71	4th,	Lost Final
1962-63	70	19	10	6	13	15	7	32	25	13	200	194	77	4th,	Lost Final
1961-62	70	17	11	7	6	22	7	23	33	14	184	219	60	5th,	Out of Playoffs
1960-61	70	15	13	7	10	16	9	25	29	16	195	215	66	4th,	Lost Final
1959-60	70	18	14	3	8	15	12	26	29	15	186	197	67	4th,	Lost Semi-Final
1958-59	70	13	17	5	12	20	3	25	37	8	167	218	58	6th,	Out of Playoffs
1957-58	70	16	11	8	13	18	4	29	29	12	176	207	70	3rd,	Lost Semi-Final
1956-57	70	23	7	5	15	13	7	38	20	12	198	157	88	1st,	Lost Semi-Final
1955-56	70	21	6	8	9	18	8	30	24	16	183	148	76	2nd,	Lost Final
1954-55	**70**	25	5	5	17	12	6	**42**	**17**	**11**	**204**	**134**	**95**	**1st,**	**Won Stanley Cup**
1953-54	**70**	24	4	7	13	15	7	**37**	**19**	**14**	**191**	**132**	**88**	**1st,**	**Won Stanley Cup**
1952-53	70	20	5	10	16	11	8	36	16	18	222	133	90	1st,	Lost Semi-Final
1951-52	**70**	24	7	4	20	7	8	**44**	**14**	**12**	**215**	**133**	**100**	**1st,**	**Won Stanley Cup**
1950-51	70	25	3	7	19	10	6	44	13	13	236	139	101	1st,	Lost Semi-Final
1949-50	**70**	19	9	7	18	10	7	**37**	**19**	**14**	**229**	**164**	**88**	**1st,**	**Won Stanley Cup**
1948-49	60	21	6	3	13	13	4	34	19	7	195	145	75	1st,	Lost Final
1947-48	60	16	9	5	14	9	7	30	18	12	187	148	72	2nd,	Lost Final
1946-47	60	14	10	6	8	17	5	22	27	11	190	193	55	4th,	Lost Semi-Final
1945-46	50	16	5	4	4	15	6	20	20	10	146	159	50	4th,	Lost Semi-Final
1944-45	50	19	5	1	12	9	4	31	14	5	218	161	67	2nd,	Lost Final
1943-44	50	18	5	2	8	13	4	26	18	6	214	177	58	2nd,	Lost Semi-Final
1942-43	**50**	16	4	5	9	10	6	**25**	**14**	**11**	**169**	**124**	**61**	**1st,**	**Won Stanley Cup**
1941-42	48	14	7	3	5	18	1	19	25	4	140	147	42	5th,	Lost Final
1940-41	48	14	5	5	7	11	6	21	16	11	112	102	53	3rd,	Lost Final
1939-40	48	11	10	3	5	16	3	16	26	6	91	126	38	5th,	Lost Semi-Final
1938-39	48	14	8	2	4	16	4	18	24	6	107	128	42	5th,	Lost Semi-Final
1937-38	48	8	10	6	4	15	5	12	25	11	99	133	35	4th, Amn. Div.	Out of Playoffs
1936-37	**48**	14	5	5	11	9	4	**25**	**14**	**9**	**128**	**102**	**59**	**1st, Amn. Div.**	**Won Stanley Cup**
1935-36	**48**	14	5	5	10	11	3	**24**	**16**	**8**	**124**	**103**	**56**	**1st, Amn. Div.**	**Won Stanley Cup**
1934-35	48	11	8	5	8	14	2	19	22	7	127	114	45	4th, Amn. Div.	Out of Playoffs
1933-34	48	15	5	4	9	9	6	24	14	10	113	98	58	1st, Amn. Div.	Lost Final
1932-33*	48	17	3	4	8	12	4	25	15	8	111	93	58	2nd, Amn. Div.	Lost Semi-Final
1931-32	48	15	3	6	3	17	4	18	20	10	95	108	46	3rd, Amn. Div.	Lost Quarter-Final
1930-31**	44	10	7	5	6	14	2	16	21	7	102	105	39	4th, Amn. Div.	Out of Playoffs
1929-30	44	9	10	3	5	14	3	14	24	6	117	133	34	4th, Amn. Div.	Out of Playoffs
1928-29	44	11	6	5	8	10	4	19	16	9	72	63	47	3rd, Amn. Div.	Lost Quarter-Final
1927-28	44	9	10	3	10	9	3	19	19	6	88	79	44	4th, Amn. Div.	Out of Playoffs
1926-27***	44	6	15	1	6	13	3	12	28	4	76	105	28	5th, Amn. Div.	Out of Playoffs

* Team name changed to Red Wings. ** Team name changed to Falcons. *** Team named Cougars.

1992-93 Player Personnel

FORWARDS	HT	WT	S	Place of Birth	Date	1991-92 Club
AIVAZOFF, Micah	6-0	185	L	Powell River, B.C.	5/4/69	Adirondack
BERMINGHAM, Jim	6-3	201	L	Montreal, Que.	11/12/71	Laval
BOWEN, Curtis	6-1	190	L	Kenora, Ont.	3/24/74	Ottawa
BURR, Shawn	6-1	200	L	Sarnia, Ont.	7/1/66	Detroit
CARSON, Jimmy	6-0	200	R	Southfield, MI	7/20/68	Detroit
CASSELMAN, Mike	5-11	180	L	Morrisburg, Ont.	8/23/68	Toledo-Adirondack
CICCARELLI, Dino	5-10	175	R	Sarnia, Ont.	2/8/60	Washington
CLOUTIER, Sylvain	6-0	195	L	Mont-Laureir, Que.	2/13/74	Guelph
CROWDER, Troy	6-4	220	R	Sudbury, Ont.	5/3/68	Detroit
CROWE, Phil	6-2	220	L	Manton, Alta.	4/14/70	Col.-Tol.-Adi.
CUMMINS, Jim	6-2	200	R	Dearborn, MI	5/17/70	Adirondack-Detroit
DRAKE, Dallas	6-0	170	L	Trail, B.C.	2/4/69	Northern Mich.
FEDOROV, Sergei	6-1	191	L	Pskov, USSR	12/13/69	Detroit
FEDYK, Brent	6-0	195	R	Yorkton, Sask.	3/8/67	Detroit-Adirondack
FIRTH, Jason	5-11	175	L	Dartmouth, N.S.	3/29/71	North Bay
FLANAGAN, Dave	6-1	210	R	Charlottetown, P.E.I.	12/13/67	Toledo-Adirondack
GALLANT, Gerard	5-10	190	L	Summerside, P.E.I.	9/2/63	Detroit
HURD, Kelly	5-10	170	R	Castlegar, B.C.	5/13/68	Ft. Wayne-Adirondack
JUDSON, Rick	5-11	180	L	Toledo, OH	8/13/69	Ill.-Chicago
KENNEDY, Sheldon	5-10	175	R	Brandon, Man.	6/15/69	Detroit-Adirondack
KERR, Alan	5-11	195	R	Hazelton, B.C.	3/28/64	Detroit
KOCUR, Kory	5-11	185	R	Kelvington, Sask.	3/6/69	Ft. Wayne
KOZLOV, Vyacheslav	5-10	172	L	Voskresenski, USSR	5/3/72	CSKA-Detroit
LAPOINTE, Martin	5-11	200	R	Villa St. Pierre, Que.	9/12/73	Laval-Detroit
MacLELLAN, Brian	6-3	220	L	Guelph, Ont.	10/27/58	Detroit
McCARTY, Darren	6-1	214	R	Burnaby, B.C.	4/1/72	Belleville
McCAUGHEY, Brad	6-1	195	R	Ann Arbor, MI	6/10/66	Toledo-Adirondack
McDONALD, Jason	6-0	195	R	Charlottetown, P.E.I.	4/1/74	Owen Sound
MIDDENDORF, Max	6-4	210	R	Syracuse, NY	8/18/67	Cape Breton-Adi.
POTVIN, Marc	6-1	200	R	Ottawa, Ont.	1/29/67	Adirondack-Detroit
PRIMEAU, Keith	6-4	225	L	Toronto, Ont.	11/24/71	Detroit-Adirondack
PROBERT, Bob	6-3	225	L	Windsor, Ont.	6/5/65	Detroit
QUINNEY, Ken	5-10	186	R	Westminster, B.C.	5/23/65	Adirondack
SHEPPARD, Ray	6-1	190	R	Pembroke, Ont.	5/27/66	Detroit
SHUCHUK, Gary	5-10	185	R	Edmonton, Alta.	2/17/67	Adirondack
SILLINGER, Mike	5-10	191	R	Regina, Sask.	6/29/71	Adirondack-Detroit
SORENSON, Kelly	5-11	170	R	Newmarket, Ont.	6/11/70	Ferris St.
STAUBER, Pete	5-11	185	L	Duluth, MN	5/10/66	Adirondack-Toledo
TANCILL, Chris	5-10	185	L	Livonia, MI	2/7/68	Hfd.-Det.-Adi.
TOMLINSON, Kirk	5-11	190	L	Tottenham, Ont.	5/5/68	Adirondack
YSEBAERT, Paul	6-1	190	L	Sarnia, Ont.	5/15/66	Detroit
YZERMAN, Steve	5-11	185	R	Cranbrook, B.C.	5/9/65	Detroit
DEFENSEMEN						
ANGLEHART, Serge	6-2	189	R	Hull, Que.	4/18/70	Adirondack
BOUGHNER, Bob	5-11	201	R	Windsor, Ont.	3/8/71	Adirondack-Toledo
BURNS, Tony	6-1	195	L	Duluth, MN	9/18/71	St. Cloud St.-Toledo
CHIASSON, Steve	6-1	205	L	Barrie, Ont.	4/14/67	Detroit
DOLLAS, Bob	6-2	212	L	Montreal, Que.	1/31/65	Detroit-Adirondack
DUPUIS, Guy	6-2	199	R	Moncton, N.B.	5/10/70	Adirondack
KONSTANTINOV, Vlad.	5-11	185	R	Murmansk, USSR	3/19/67	Detroit
KRUPPKE, Gord	6-1	200	R	Slave Lake, Alta.	4/2/69	Adirondack
LIDSTROM, Nicklas	6-2	180	L	Vasteras, Sweden	4/28/70	Detroit
LUONGO, Chris	6-0	180	R	Detroit, MI	3/17/67	Adirondack
MALGUNAS, Stewart	5-11	190	L	Prince George, B.C.	4/21/70	Adirondack
McCORMACK, Brian	5-10	170	R	Bloomington, MN	11/11/69	Harvard
McCRIMMON, Brad	5-11	197	L	Dodsland, Sask.	3/29/59	Detroit
PUSHOR, Jamie	6-3	192	R	Lethbridge, Alta.	2/11/73	Lethbridge
RACINE, Yves	6-0	200	L	Matane, Que.	2/7/69	Detroit
SUHY, Andy	6-1	190	L	Detroit, MI	3/9/70	Western Mich.
WALKER, Jeff	6-4	190	L	Sudbury, Ont.	2/6/74	Peterborough
WILKIE, Bob	6-2	200	R	Calgary, Alta.	2/11/69	Adirondack
YORK, Jason	6-1	192	R	Ottawa, Ont.	5/20/70	Adirondack

GOALTENDERS	HT	WT	C	Place of Birth	Date	1991-92 Club
BESTER, Allan	5-7	155	L	Hamilton, Ont.	3/26/64	Detroit-Adirondack
CHEVELDAE, Tim	5-10	195	L	Melville, Sask.	2/15/68	Detroit
DENOMME, C.J.	5-11	180	L	London, Ont.	4/8/74	Kitchener
GAGNON, Dave	6-0	185	L	Windsor, Ont.	10/31/67	Toledo-Ft. Wayne
KING, Scott	6-1	185	L	Thunder Bay, Ont.	6/25/67	Det.-Adi.-Tol.
OSGOOD, Chris	5-9	156	L	Peace River, Alta.	11/26/72	Bra.-M. Hat-Sea.
RIENDEAU, Vincent	5-10	189	L	St. Hyacinthe, Que.	4/20/66	St. L.-Det.-Adi.
SCOTT, Greg	6-2	191	L	Brampton, Ont.	2/27/73	Niagara Falls

General Managers' History

Art Duncan, 1926-27; Jack Adams, 1927-28 to 1962-63; Sidney Abel, 1963-64 to 1969-70; Sidney Abel and Ned Harkness, 1970-71; Ned Harkness, 1971-72 to 1973-74; Alex Delvecchio, 1974-75 to 1975-76; Alex Delvecchio and Ted Lindsay, 1976-77; Ted Lindsay, 1977-78 to 1979-80; Jimmy Skinner, 1980-81 to 1981-82; Jim Devellano, 1982-83 to 1989-90; Bryan Murray, 1990-91 to date.

1991-92 Scoring

Regular Season

Pos	#	Player	Team	GP	G	A	Pts	+/–	PIM	PP	SH	GW	GT	S	%
C	19	Steve Yzerman	DET	79	45	58	103	26	64	9	8	9	0	295	15.3
C	91	Sergei Fedorov	DET	80	32	54	86	26	72	7	2	5	0	249	12.9
L	21	Paul Ysebaert	DET	79	35	40	75	44	55	3	4	3	1	211	16.6
C	12	Jimmy Carson	DET	80	34	35	69	17	30	11	0	3	0	150	22.7
R	26	Ray Sheppard	DET	74	36	26	62	7	27	11	1	4	1	178	20.2
D	5*	Nicklas Lidstrom	DET	80	11	49	60	36	22	5	0	1	1	168	6.5
L	11	Shawn Burr	DET	79	19	32	51	26	118	2	0	3	1	140	13.6
R	23	Kevin Miller	DET	80	20	26	46	6	53	3	1	4	0	130	15.4
R	24	Bob Probert	DET	63	20	24	44	16	276	8	0	1	0	96	20.8
L	17	Gerard Gallant	DET	69	14	22	36	16	187	4	0	1	1	116	12.1
D	3	Steve Chiasson	DET	62	10	24	34	22	136	5	0	2	1	143	7.0
D	16*	Vlad. Konstantinov	DET	79	8	26	34	25	172	1	0	2	0	108	7.4
D	2	Brad McCrimmon	DET	79	7	22	29	39	118	2	1	1	0	94	7.4
D	33	Yves Racine	DET	61	2	22	24	6–	94	1	0	0	0	103	1.9
L	55	Keith Primeau	DET	35	6	10	16	9	83	0	0	0	0	27	22.2
R	14	Brent Fedyk	DET	61	5	8	13	5–	42	0	0	1	0	60	8.3
R	28	Sheldon Kennedy	DET	27	3	8	11	2–	24	0	0	1	1	33	9.1
R	18	Alan Kerr	DET	58	3	8	11	1	133	0	0	1	0	41	7.3
D	29	Doug Crossman	DET	26	0	8	8	8	14	0	0	0	0	21	.0
D	20	Brad Marsh	DET	55	3	4	7	8	53	0	0	1	0	29	10.3
L	27	Brian Maclellan	DET	23	1	5	6	4	38	0	0	0	0	17	5.9
D	8	Bobby Dollas	DET	27	3	1	4	4	20	0	1	0	0	26	11.5
D	4	Bob McGill	S.J.	62	3	1	4	34–	70	0	1	1	0	56	5.4
			DET	12	0	0	0	3–	21	0	0	0	0	6	.0
			TOTAL	74	3	1	4	37–	91	0	1	1	0	62	4.8
G	32	Tim Cheveldae	DET	72	0	4	4	0	6	0	0	0	0	0	.0
C	13*	Vyacheslav Kozlov	DET	7	0	2	2	2–	2	0	0	0	0	9	.0
R	46*	Marc Potvin	DET	5	1	0	1	2–	52	0	0	0	0	4	25.0
D	36	Dennis Vial	DET	27	1	0	1	1	72	0	0	0	0	6	16.7
R	22*	Martin Lapointe	DET	4	0	1	1	2	5	0	0	0	0	2	.0
G	35	Allan Bester	DET	1	0	0	0	0	0	0	0	0	0	0	.0
G	31*	Scott King	DET	1	0	0	0	0	0	0	0	0	0	0	.0
R	47*	Jim Cummins	DET	1	0	0	0	0	7	0	0	0	0	0	.0
G	37	Vincent Riendeau	STL	3	0	0	0	0	0	0	0	0	0	0	.0
			DET	2	0	0	0	0	0	0	0	0	0	0	.0
			TOTAL	5	0	0	0	0	0	0	0	0	0	0	.0
R	25	Troy Crowder	DET	7	0	0	0	0	35	0	0	0	0	2	.0
G	34	Greg Millen	NYR	0	0	0	0	0	0	0	0	0	0	0	.0
			DET	10	0	0	0	0	0	0	0	0	0	0	.0
			TOTAL	10	0	0	0	0	0	0	0	0	0	0	.0
C	48*	Chris Tancill	HFD	10	0	0	0	6–	2	0	0	0	0	13	.0
			DET	1	0	0	0	0	0	0	0	0	0	0	.0
			TOTAL	11	0	0	0	6–	2	0	0	0	0	13	.0

Goaltending

No.	Goaltender	GPI	Mins	Avg	W	L	T	EN	SO	GA	SA	S%
37	Vincent Riendeau	2	87	1.38	2	0	0	0	0	2	31	.935
34	Greg Millen	10	487	2.71	3	2	3	2	0	22	212	.896
32	Tim Cheveldae	72	4236	3.20	38	23	9	1	2	226	1978	.886
31	* Scott King	1	16	3.75	0	0	0	0	0	1	5	.800
35	Allan Bester	1	31	3.87	0	0	0	0	0	2	9	.778
	Totals	**80**	**4870**	**3.15**	**43**	**25**	**12**	**3**	**3**	**256**	**2238**	**.886**

Tim Cheveldae and Vincent Riendeau shared a shutout vs Tor on Oct 25, 1991

Playoffs

Pos	#	Player	Team	GP	G	A	Pts	+/–	PIM	PP	SH	GW	GT	S	%
C	91	Sergei Fedorov	DET	11	5	5	10	2	8	1	2	1	1	27	18.5
R	26	Ray Sheppard	DET	11	6	2	8	1	4	3	0	0	0	27	22.2
C	19	Steve Yzerman	DET	11	3	5	8	3–	12	0	1	1	0	48	6.3
R	24	Bob Probert	DET	11	1	6	7	2	28	0	0	0	0	13	7.7
L	11	Shawn Burr	DET	11	1	5	6	4	10	0	0	0	0	20	5.0
D	3	Steve Chiasson	DET	11	1	5	6	6	12	1	0	0	0	30	3.3
C	12	Jimmy Carson	DET	11	2	3	5	0	0	0	0	0	0	20	10.0
C	15*	Mike Sillinger	DET	8	2	2	4	4	2	0	0	0	0	7	28.6
L	17	Gerard Gallant	DET	11	2	2	4	4–	25	0	0	1	0	8	25.0
D	33	Yves Racine	DET	11	2	1	3	0	10	1	0	1	1	19	10.5
D	5*	Nicklas Lidstrom	DET	11	1	2	3	5–	0	1	0	0	0	16	6.3
R	18	Alan Kerr	DET	9	2	0	2	1–	17	0	0	0	0	13	15.4
R	23	Kevin Miller	DET	9	0	2	2	4–	4	0	0	0	0	13	.0
L	21	Paul Ysebaert	DET	10	1	0	1	1–	10	0	0	0	0	24	4.2
D	8	Bobby Dollas	DET	2	0	1	1	1	0	0	0	0	0	3	.0
R	22*	Martin Lapointe	DET	3	0	1	1	0	4	0	0	0	0	4	.0
G	32	Tim Cheveldae	DET	11	0	1	1	0	6	0	0	0	0	0	.0
D	2	Brad McCrimmon	DET	11	0	1	1	4–	8	0	0	0	0	8	.0
D	16*	Vlad. Konstantinov	DET	11	0	1	1	5	16	0	0	0	0	10	.0
R	25	Troy Crowder	DET	1	0	0	0	0	0	0	0	0	0	0	.0
R	14	Brent Fedyk	DET	1	0	0	0	0	2	0	0	0	0	0	.0
R	46*	Marc Potvin	DET	1	0	0	0	0	0	0	0	0	0	0	.0
G	37	Vincent Riendeau	DET	2	0	0	0	0	0	0	0	0	0	0	.0
D	20	Brad Marsh	DET	3	0	0	0	1	0	0	0	0	0	1	.0
D	4	Bob McGill	DET	8	0	0	0	1–	14	0	0	0	0	6	.0
L	55	Keith Primeau	DET	11	0	0	0	1–	14	0	0	0	0	11	.0

Goaltending

No.	Goaltender	GPI	Mins	Avg	W	L	EN	SO	GA	SA	S%
32	Tim Cheveldae	11	597	2.51	3	7	1	2	25	277	.910
37	Vincent Riendeau	2	73	3.29	1	0	0	0	4	30	.867
	Totals	**11**	**677**	**2.66**	**4**	**7**	**1**	**2**	**30**	**308**	**.903**

Club Records

Team

(Figures in brackets for season records are games played; records for fewest points, wins, ties, losses, goals, goals against are for 70 or more games)

Record		
Most Points	101	1950-51 (70)
Most Wins	44	1950-51 (70) 1951-52 (70)
Most Ties	18	1952-53 (70) 1980-81 (80)
Most Losses	57	1985-86 (80)
Most Goals	322	1987-88 (80)
Most Goals Against	415	1985-86 (80)
Fewest Points	40	1985-86 (80)
Fewest Wins	16	1976-77 (80)
Fewest Ties	4	1966-67 (70)
Fewest Losses	13	1950-51 (70)
Fewest Goals	167	1958-59 (70)
Fewest Goals Against	132	1953-54 (70)
Longest Winning Streak		
Over-all	9	Mar. 3-21/51; Feb. 27-Mar. 20/55
Home	14	Jan. 21-Mar. 25/65
Away	5	Four times
Longest Undefeated Streak		
Over-all	15	Nov. 27-Dec. 28/52 (8 wins, 7 ties)
Home	18	Dec. 26/54-Mar. 20/55 (13 wins, 5 ties)
Away	15	Oct. 18-Dec. 20/51 (10 wins, 5 ties)
Longest Losing Streak		
Over-all	14	Feb. 24-Mar. 25/82
Home	7	Feb. 20-Mar. 25/82
Away	14	Oct. 19-Dec. 21/66
Longest Winless Streak		
Over-all	19	Feb. 26-Apr. 3/77 (18 losses, 1 tie)
Home	10	Dec. 11/85-Jan. 18/86 (9 losses, 1 tie)
Away	26	Dec. 15/76-Apr. 3/77 (23 losses, 3 ties)
Most Shutouts, Season	13	1953-54 (70)
Most. PIM, Season	2,393	1985-86 (80)
Most Goals, Game	15	Jan. 23/44 (NYR 0 at Det. 15)

Individual

Record		
Most Seasons	25	Gordie Howe
Most Games	1,687	Gordie Howe
Most Goals, Career	786	Gordie Howe
Most Assists, Career	1,023	Gordie Howe
Most Points, Career	1,809	Gordie Howe (786 goals, 1,023 assists)
Most PIM, Career	1,714	Joey Kocur
Most Shutouts, Career	85	Terry Sawchuk
Longest Consecutive Games Streak	548	Alex Delvecchio (Dec. 13/56-Nov. 11/64)
Most Goals, Season	65	Steve Yzerman (1988-89)
Most Assists, Season	90	Steve Yzerman (1988-89)
Most Points, Season	155	Steve Yzerman (1988-89) (65 goals, 90 assists)
Most PIM, Season	398	Bob Probert (1987-88)
Most Points, Defenseman Season	74	Reed Larson (1982-83) (22 goals, 52 assists)
Most Points, Center, Season	155	Steve Yzerman (1988-89) (65 goals, 90 assists)
Most Points, Right Wing, Season	103	Gordie Howe (1968-69) (44 goals, 59 assists)
Most Points, Left Wing, Season	105	John Ogrodnick (1984-85) (55 goals, 50 assists)
Most Points, Rookie, Season	87	Steve Yzerman (1983-84) (39 goals, 48 assists)
Most Shutouts, Season	12	Terry Sawchuk (1951-52; 1953-54; 1954-55) Glenn Hall (1955-56)
Most Goals, Game	6	Syd Howe (Feb. 3/44)
Most Assists, Game	*7	Billy Taylor (Mar. 16/47)
Most Points, Game	7	Carl Liscombe (Nov. 5/42) Don Grosso (Feb. 3/44) Billy Taylor (Mar. 16/47)

* NHL Record

Captains' History

Art Duncan, 1926-27; Reg Noble, 1927-28 to 1929-30; George Hay, 1930-31; Carson Cooper, 1931-32; Larry Aurie, 1932-33; Herbie Lewis, 1933-34; Ebbie Goodfellow, 1934-35; Doug Young, 1935-36 to 1937-38; Ebbie Goodfellow, 1938-39 to 1941-42; Sid Abel, 1942-43; Mud Bruneteau, Bill Hollett (co-captains), 1943-44; Bill Hollett, 1944-45; Bill Hollett, Sid Abel, 1945-46; Sid Abel, 1946-47 to 1951-52; Ted Lindsay, 1952-53 to 1955-56; Red Kelly, 1956-57, 1957-58; Gordie Howe, 1958-59 to 1961-62; Alex Delvecchio, 1962-63 to 1973-74; Marcel Dionne, 1974-75; Danny Grant, Terry Harper, 1975-76; Danny Grant, Dennis Polonich, 1976-77; Dan Maloney, Dennis Hextall, 1977-78; Dennis Hextall, Nick Libett, Paul Woods, 1978-79; Dale McCourt, 1979-80; Errol Thompson, Reed Larson, 1980-81; Reed Larson, 1981-82; Danny Gare, 1982-83 to 1985-86; Steve Yzerman, 1986-87 to date.

1991-92 Results

Home			Away		
Oct. 10	Montreal	1-4	**Oct.** 3	Chicago	3-3
15	Edmonton	3-1	5	Toronto	5-8
17	St Louis	6-3	12	Minnesota	2-3
23	Winnipeg	2-3	19	Quebec	6-1
25	Toronto	4-0	26	Toronto	1-6
28	Los Angeles	3-4	**Nov.** 2	Boston	1-4
30	Buffalo	3-1	8	Washington	5-4
Nov. 1	Hartford	8-5	12	Calgary	5-4
5	Minnesota	2-3	14	San Jose	3-3
7	St Louis	10-3	16	Los Angeles	5-3
19	Chicago	4-1	23	Minnesota	2-2
22	Minnesota	4-3	30	St Louis	3-7
25	Washington	5-4	**Dec.** 7	New Jersey	2-2
27	St Louis	6-4	14	Calgary	4-3
Dec. 3	Calgary	5-2	15	Edmonton	4-1
6	NY Rangers	6-5	17	Vancouver	1-2
10	Chicago	5-3	21	Los Angeles	5-2
12	Quebec	4-1	28	Toronto	5-4
31	Boston	3-5	29	Chicago	6-4
Jan. 3	Toronto	6-4	**Jan.** 4	St Louis	6-2
7	NY Islanders	2-5	14	NY Islanders	2-6
9	Minnesota	9-4	25	New Jersey	7-0
11	Edmonton	5-5	**Feb.** 1	Montreal	3-4
16	Pittsburgh	3-3	3	Pittsburgh	4-4
21	Philadelphia	7-3	9	NY Rangers	5-5
23	Vancouver	1-3	11	Toronto	3-4
29	Buffalo	4-4	12	Buffalo	9-4
31	New Jersey	3-6	23	Hartford*	4-0
Feb. 5	Washington	4-1	27	Chicago	2-4
7	Toronto	3-4	29	St Louis	3-2
15	San Jose	11-1	**Mar.** 7	Quebec	4-4
17	St Louis	5-3	8	Montreal	1-4
20	Toronto	3-2	12	St Louis	5-4
22	Chicago*	2-1	14	Minnesota*	1-4
Mar. 3	Winnipeg	3-4	15	Winnipeg*	1-1
5	Minnesota	2-4	17	San Jose	5-4
20	NY Rangers	2-4	22	Philadelphia	3-4
24	Pittsburgh	4-3	29	NY Islanders	6-2
28	Vancouver*	3-1	**Apr.** 4	Minnesota	7-4
31	Chicago	3-3	5	Chicago	2-1

*Denotes afternoon game

All-time Record vs. Other Clubs

Regular Season

	At Home							On Road							Total						
	GP	W	L	T	GF	GA	PTS	GP	W	L	T	GF	GA	PTS	GP	W	L	T	GF	GA	PTS
Boston	276	148	76	52	918	697	348	277	83	151	43	729	980	209	553	231	227	95	1647	1677	557
Buffalo	45	23	17	5	168	137	51	43	6	30	7	111	195	19	88	29	47	12	279	332	70
Calgary	35	19	11	5	142	117	43	36	9	22	5	110	166	23	71	28	33	10	252	283	66
Chicago	301	186	87	28	1038	740	400	302	112	142	48	830	915	272	603	298	229	76	1868	1655	672
Edmonton	21	7	12	2	81	100	16	20	6	11	3	85	107	15	41	13	23	5	166	207	31
Hartford	20	7	7	6	74	64	20	20	6	13	1	55	80	13	40	13	20	7	129	144	33
Los Angeles	55	23	25	7	220	204	53	56	14	32	10	167	238	38	111	37	57	17	387	442	91
Minnesota	76	36	28	12	300	262	84	77	21	43	13	221	303	55	153	57	71	25	521	565	139
Montreal	272	124	95	53	770	699	301	272	62	167	43	606	965	167	544	186	262	96	1376	1664	468
New Jersey	30	17	11	2	128	102	36	31	9	14	8	88	109	26	61	26	25	10	216	211	62
NY Islanders	35	18	15	2	127	118	38	36	13	21	2	103	144	28	71	31	36	4	230	262	66
NY Rangers	276	157	75	44	970	683	358	274	86	130	58	701	844	230	550	243	205	102	1671	1527	588
Philadelphia	49	22	18	9	174	163	53	49	10	29	10	141	200	30	98	32	47	19	315	363	83
Pittsburgh	56	35	10	11	221	158	81	55	13	38	4	156	242	30	111	48	48	15	377	400	111
Quebec	20	12	7	1	84	69	25	21	6	12	3	74	91	15	41	18	19	4	158	160	40
St. Louis	77	32	34	11	280	254	75	76	21	45	10	206	287	52	153	53	79	21	486	541	127
San Jose	1	1	0	0	11	1	2	2	1	0	1	8	7	3	3	2	0	1	19	8	5
Toronto	295	155	97	43	873	717	353	295	94	157	44	776	984	232	590	249	254	87	1649	1701	585
Vancouver	42	24	12	6	176	125	54	42	12	24	6	128	175	30	84	36	36	12	304	300	84
Washington	37	16	11	10	137	108	42	36	13	19	4	110	141	30	73	29	30	14	247	249	72
Winnipeg	23	11	9	3	91	88	25	22	7	7	8	70	74	22	45	18	16	11	161	162	47
Defunct Clubs	141	76	40	25	429	307	177	141	49	63	29	363	375	127	282	125	103	54	792	682	304
Totals	**2183**	**1149**	**697**	**337**	**7412**	**5913**	**2635**	**2183**	**653**	**1170**	**360**	**5838**	**7622**	**1666**	**4366**	**1802**	**1867**	**697**	**13250**	**13535**	**4301**

Playoffs

	Series	W	L	GP	W	L	T	GF	GA	Last Mtg.	Round	Result
Boston	7	3	4	33	14	19	0	98	96	1957	SF	L 1-4
**Calgary	1	1	0	2	2	0	0	8	5	1978	PR	W 2-0
Chicago	13	5	8	64	27	37	0	177	198	1992	DF	L 0-4
Edmonton	2	0	2	10	2	8	0	26	39	1988	CF	L 1-4
Minnesota	1	1	0	7	4	3	0	23	19	1992	DSF	W 4-3
Montreal	12	7	5	62	29	33	0	149	161	1978	QF	L 1-4
NY Rangers	5	4	1	23	13	10	0	57	49	1950	F	W 4-3
St. Louis	3	1	2	16	8	8	0	53	51	1991	DF	L 3-4
Toronto	22	11	11	110	56	54	0	291	287	1988	DSF	W 4-2
Defunct Clubs	4	3	1	10	7	2	1	21	13			
Totals	**70**	**36**	**34**	**337**	**162**	**174**	**1**	**903**	**918**			

Playoff Results 1992-88

Year	Round	Opponent	Result	GF	GA
1992	DF	Chicago	L 0-4	6	11
	DSF	Minnesota	W 4-3	23	19
1991	DSF	St. Louis	L 3-4	20	24
1989	DSF	Chicago	L 2-4	18	25
1988	CF	Edmonton	L 1-4	16	23
	DF	St. Louis	W 4-1	21	14
	DSF	Toronto	W 4-2	32	20

Abbreviations: Round: F – Final; **CF** – conference final; **DF** – division final; **DSF** – division semi-final; **SF** – semi-final; **QF** – quarter-final; **PR** – preliminary round. **GA** – goals against; **GF** – goals for.

Entry Draft Selections 1992-78

1992
Pick
22 Curtis Bowen
46 Darren McCarty
70 Sylvain Cloutier
118 Mike Sullivan
142 Jason MacDonald
166 Greg Scott
183 Justin Krall
189 C.J. Denomme
214 Jeff Walker
238 Daniel McGillis
262 Ryan Bach

1991
Pick
10 Martin Lapointe
32 Jamie Pushor
54 Chris Osgood
76 Michael Knuble
98 Dmitri Motkov
142 Igor Malykhin
186 Jim Bermingham
208 Jason Firth
230 Bart Turner
252 Andrew Miller

1990
Pick
3 Keith Primeau
45 Vyacheslav Kozlov
66 Stewart Malgunas
87 Tony Burns
108 Claude Barthe
129 Jason York
150 Wes McCauley
171 Anthony Gruba
192 Travis Tucker
213 Brett Larson
234 John Hendry

1989
Pick
11 Mike Sillinger
32 Bob Boughner
53 Nicklas Lidstrom
74 Sergei Fedorov
95 Shawn McCosh
116 Dallas Drake
137 Scott Zygulski
158 Andy Suhy
179 Bob Jones
200 Greg Bignell
204 Rick Judson
221 Vladimir Konstantinov
242 Joseph Frederick
246 Jason Glickman

1988
Pick
17 Kory Kocur
38 Serge Anglehart
47 Guy Dupuis
59 Petr Hrbek
80 Sheldon Kennedy
143 Kelly Hurd
164 Brian McCormack
185 Jody Praznik
206 Glen Goodall
227 Darren Colbourne
248 Donald Stone

1987
Pick
11 Yves Racine
32 Gordon Kruppke
41 Bob Wilkie
52 Dennis Holland
74 Mark Reimer
95 Radomir Brazda
116 Sean Clifford
137 Mike Gober
158 Kevin Scott
179 Mikko Haapakoski
200 Darin Bannister
221 Craig Quinlan
242 Tomas Jansson

1986
Pick
1 Joe Murphy
22 Adam Graves
43 Derek Mayer
64 Tim Cheveldae
85 Johan Garpenlov
106 Jay Stark
127 Per Djoos
148 Dean Morton
169 Marc Potvin
190 Scott King
211 Tom Bissett
232 Peter Ekroth

1985
Pick
8 Brent Fedyk
29 Jeff Sharples
50 Steve Chiasson
71 Mark Gowans
92 Chris Luongo
113 Randy McKay
134 Thomas Bjur
155 Mike Luckraft
176 Rob Schenna
197 Erik Hamalainen
218 Bo Svanberg
239 Mikael Lindman

1984
Pick
7 Shawn Burr
28 Doug Houda
49 Milan Chalupa
91 Mats Lundstrom
112 Randy Hansch
133 Stefan Larsson
152 Lars Karlsson
154 Urban Nordin
175 Bill Shibicky
195 Jay Rose
216 Tim Kaiser
236 Tom Nickolau

1983
Pick
4 Steve Yzerman
25 Lane Lambert
46 Bob Probert
68 David Korol
86 Petr Klima
88 Joey Kocur
106 Chris Pusey
126 Bob Pierson
146 Craig Butz
166 Dave Sikorski
186 Stuart Grimson
206 Jeff Frank
226 Charles Chiatto

1982
Pick
17 Murray Craven
23 Yves Courteau
44 Carmine Vani
66 Craig Coxe
86 Brad Shaw
107 Claude Vilgrain
128 Greg Hudas
149 Pat Lahey
170 Gary Cullen
191 Brent Meckling
212 Mike Stern
233 Shaun Reagan

1981
Pick
23 Claude Loiselle
44 Corrado Micalef
86 Larry Trader
107 Gerard Gallant
128 Greg Stefan
149 Rick Zombo
170 Don Leblanc
191 Robert Nordmark

1980
Pick
11 Mike Blaisdell
46 Mark Osborne
88 Mike Corrigan
109 Wayne Crawford
130 Mike Braun
151 John Beukeboom
172 Dave Miles
193 Brian Rorabeck

1979
Pick
3 Mike Foligno
45 Jody Gage
46 Boris Fistric
66 John Ogrodnick
87 Joe Paterson
108 Carmine Cirella

1978
Pick
9 Willie Huber
12 Brent Peterson
28 Glenn Hicks
31 Al Jensen
53 Doug Derkson
62 Bjorne Skaare
78 Ted Nolan
95 Sylvain Locas
112 Wes George
129 John Barrett
146 Jim Malazdrewicz
163 Geoff Shaw
178 Carl Van Harrewyn
194 Ladislav Svozil
208 Tom Bailey
219 Larry Lozinski
224 Randy Betty
226 Brian Crawley
228 Doug Feasby

Club Directory

Joe Louis Arena
600 Civic Center Drive
Detroit, Michigan 48226
Phone **(313) 567-7333**
FAX PR: (313) 567-0296
Capacity: 19,275

Owner/President	Mike Ilitch
Owner/Secretary-Treasurer	Marian Ilitch
Executive Vice-President	Jim Lites
General Counsel	Denise Ilitch Lites
Senior Vice-President	Jim Devellano
General Manager/Head Coach	Bryan Murray
Assistant General Manager	Doug MacLean
Administrative Assistant/Scouting Coordinator	Mike Abbamont
Assistant Coach	Dave Lewis
Goaltending Coach	Phil Myre
Pro Scouting Director	Dan Belisle
Amateur Scouting Director	Ken Holland
U.S. Scouting Director	Billy Dea
Western Hockey League Scout	Wayne Meier
Western U.S. Scout	Chris Coury
Eastern U.S. Scout	Mike Addesa
Ontario Scouts	Paul Crowley, Sam McMaster
Eastern Canada Scout	John Stanton
Maritimes Scout	Jim Clark
European Scouts	Hakan Andersson, Vladimir Havlug
Controller	Scott Fisher
Marketing Director	Jeff Cogen
Public Relations Director	Bill Jamieson
Advertising Sales Director	Terry Murphy
Strategic Sales Director	Len Perna
Broadcast Sales Director	Amy Goan
Public Relations Coordinator	Howard Berlin
Public Relations Assistants	Kathy Best, Marilyn Charbonneau
Box Office Manager	Bob Kerlin
Secretary to General Manager	Nancy Beard
Accounting Assistant	Cathy Witzke
Athletic Therapist/Strength & Conditioning	John Wharton
Athletic Trainer	Mark Brennan
Assistant Trainer	Tim Abbot
Team Physicians	Dr. John Finley, D.O., Dr. David Collon, M.D.
Team Dentist	Dr. C.J. Regula, D.M.D.
Team Ophthalmologist	Dr. Charles Slater, M.D.
Home Ice	Joe Louis Arena
Seating Capacity	19,275
Press Box & Radio-TV Booths	Jefferson Avenue side of arena, top of seats
Media Lounge	First-floor hallway near Red Wings' dressing room, Atwater Street side of arena
Rink Dimensions	200 feet by 85 feet; S.A.R. Plastic above boards
Uniforms	Home: Base color white, trimmed in red Road: Base color red, trimmed in white
Radio flagship station	WJR-AM (760)
TV stations	WKBD (Channel 50); PASS Cable; Special Order Sports
Radio announcers	Bruce Martyn, Paul Woods
TV announcers	Dave Strader, Mickey Redmond

Coach

MURRAY, BRYAN CLARENCE
Coach and General Manager, Detroit Red Wings.
Born in Shawville, Que., December 5, 1942.

Appointed coach and G.M. of the Red Wings in the summer of 1990, Bryan Murray guided the Red Wings to the best record in the Norris Division in 1991-92, compiling a 43-25-12 record, Detroit's best finish in 30 years.

A graduate of McGill, his first major coaching experience came in junior hockey when he took over the last-place Regina Pats and carried the team to the WHL championship in 1979-80. His one-year success in Regina translated into a professional coaching job in 1980-81 with the Capitals' AHL farm team, the Hershey Bears, whom he guided to their best season in over 40 years. That first-year effort netted him the Hockey News Minor League Coach-of-the-Year honors. Although he began the 1981-82 campaign in Hershey, Murray was promoted to Washington and the NHL on November 11, 1981.

Coaching Record

		Regular Season					Playoffs			
Season	Team	Games	W	L	T	%	Games	W	L	%
1979-80	Regina (WHL)	72	47	24	1	.660	22	16	6	.727
1980-81	Hershey (AHL)	80	47	24	9	.644	10	6	4	.600
1981-82	**Washington (NHL)**	**76**	**25**	**28**	**13**	**.477**	....	....	....	....
1982-83	**Washington (NHL)**	**80**	**39**	**25**	**16**	**.588**	**4**	**1**	**3**	**.250**
1983-84	**Washington (NHL)**	**80**	**48**	**27**	**5**	**.631**	**8**	**4**	**4**	**.500**
1984-85	**Washington (NHL)**	**80**	**46**	**25**	**9**	**.631**	**5**	**2**	**3**	**.400**
1985-86	**Washington (NHL)**	**80**	**50**	**23**	**7**	**.669**	**9**	**5**	**4**	**.556**
1986-87	**Washington (NHL)**	**80**	**38**	**32**	**10**	**.538**	**7**	**3**	**4**	**.429**
1987-88	**Washington (NHL)**	**80**	**38**	**33**	**9**	**.531**	**14**	**7**	**7**	**.500**
1988-89	**Washington (NHL)**	**80**	**41**	**29**	**10**	**.575**	**6**	**2**	**4**	**.333**
1989-90	**Washington (NHL)**	**46**	**18**	**24**	**4**	**.435**	....	....	....	....
1990-91	**Detroit (NHL)**	**80**	**34**	**38**	**8**	**.475**	**7**	**3**	**4**	**.429**
1991-92	**Detroit (NHL)**	**80**	**43**	**25**	**12**	**.613**	**11**	**4**	**7**	**.364**
	NHL Totals	**832**	**420**	**309**	**103**	**.567**	**71**	**31**	**40**	**.437**

Coaching History

Art Duncan, 1926-27; Jack Adams, 1927-28 to 1946-47; Tommy Ivan, 1947-48 to 1953-54; Jimmy Skinner, 1954-55 to 1956-57; Jimmy Skinner and Sid Abel, 1957-58; Sid Abel, 1958-59 to 1967-68; Bill Gadsby, 1968-69; Bill Gadsby and Sid Abel, 1969-70; Ned Harkness and Doug Barkley, 1970-71; Doug Barkley and John Wilson, 1971-72; John Wilson, 1972-73; Ted Garvin and Alex Delvecchio, 1973-74; Alex Delvecchio, 1974-75; Doug Barkley and Alex Delvecchio, 1975-76; Alex Delvecchio and Larry Wilson, 1976-77; Bobby Kromm, 1977-78 to 1978-79; Bobby Kromm and Ted Lindsay, 1979-80; Ted Lindsay and Wayne Maxner, 1980-81; Wayne Maxner and Billy Dea, 1981-82; Nick Polano, 1982-83 to 1984-85; Harry Neale and Brad Park, 1985-86; Jacques Demers, 1986-87 to 1989-90; Bryan Murray, 1990-91 to date.

Retired Numbers

6	Larry Aurie	1927-1939
7	Ted Lindsay	1944-57, 64-65
9	Gordie Howe	1946-1971
10	Alex Delvecchio	1951-1973

Edmonton Oilers

1991-92 Results: 36W-34L-10T 82PTS. Third, Smythe Division

Schedule

Home		Away	
Oct.	Tues. 6 Vancouver	**Oct.**	Thur. 8 Calgary
	Sun. 11 Toronto		Sat. 10 Vancouver
	Fri. 23 Boston		Wed. 14 Winnipeg
	Sun. 25 Calgary		Thur. 15 Chicago
	Wed. 28 Minnesota		Sat. 17 Detroit
	Sat. 31 Washington		Tues. 20 Tampa Bay
Nov.	Tues. 3 Ottawa	**Nov.**	Fri. 6 Winnipeg
	Wed. 18 Vancouver		Sat. 7 Minnesota
	Sun. 22 NY Islanders		Tues. 10 St Louis
	Wed. 25 Los Angeles		Thur. 12 San Jose
	Fri. 27 Chicago		Sat. 14 Los Angeles
	Sat. 28 Tampa Bay		Sat. 21 Vancouver
Dec.	Sat. 5 St Louis	**Dec.**	Tues. 1 San Jose
	Tues. 8 Calgary		Thur. 3 Vancouver
	Wed. 16 Vancouver		Mon. 7 Calgary
	Fri. 18 Los Angeles		Thur. 10 Minnesota
	Wed. 23 San Jose		Sat. 12 Tampa Bay
	Sun. 27 Calgary		Sun. 13 NY Islanders
	Tues. 29 Montreal		(at Oklahoma City)
Jan.	Sat. 2 Tampa Bay		Mon. 21 Calgary
	Sun. 3 Philadelphia		Thur. 31 Winnipeg*
	Wed. 13 Winnipeg	**Jan.**	Tues. 5 St Louis
	Fri. 15 Hartford		Thur. 7 Chicago
	Sun. 17 Buffalo		Sat. 9 Washington
	Tues. 19 Los Angeles		Sun. 10 Philadelphia
	Fri. 22 Pittsburgh		Sat. 23 Winnipeg
	Wed. 27 Detroit		Sun. 31 Buffalo*
Feb.	Fri. 12 San Jose	**Feb.**	Tues. 2 Boston
	Sun. 14 Quebec*		Wed. 3 Ottawa
	Sat. 27 NY Rangers		Tues. 9 Los Angeles
	Sun. 28 San Jose		Tues. 16 NY Islanders
Mar.	Thur. 4 Winnipeg		Thur. 18 Pittsburgh
	Wed. 10 Detroit		Sat. 20 Hartford*
	Fri. 12 New Jersey		Sun. 21 Montreal
	Sun. 14 Chicago*		Tues. 23 Quebec
	Sun. 21 Pittsburgh	**Mar.**	Sat. 6 Los Angeles
	(at Cleveland)		Sun. 7 San Jose
	Fri. 26 Los Angeles		Wed. 17 NY Rangers
	Sat. 27 Toronto		Thur. 18 New Jersey
	Wed. 31 Minnesota		Sat. 20 Toronto
Apr.	Sat. 3 Winnipeg	**Apr.**	Tues. 6 San Jose
	Sun. 11 Winnipeg*		Wed. 7 Vancouver
	Tues. 13 Calgary		Thur. 15 Winnipeg

* Denotes afternoon game.

Home Starting Times:

Weeknights	7:35 p.m.
Saturdays and Sundays	6:05 p.m.
Matinees	2:05 p.m.

Franchise date: June 22, 1979

14th NHL Season

Year-by-Year Record

Season	GP	Home W	Home L	Home T	Road W	Road L	Road T	Overall W	Overall L	Overall T	GF	GA	Pts.	Finished	Playoff Result
1991-92	80	22	13	5	14	21	5	36	34	10	295	297	82	3rd, Smythe Div.	Lost Conf. Championship
1990-91	80	22	15	3	15	22	3	37	37	6	272	272	80	3rd, Smythe Div.	Lost Conf. Championship
1989-90	**80**	**23**	**11**	**6**	**15**	**17**	**8**	**38**	**28**	**14**	**315**	**283**	**90**	**2nd, Smythe Div.**	**Won Stanley Cup**
1988-89	80	21	16	3	17	18	5	38	34	8	325	306	84	3rd, Smythe Div.	Lost Div. Semi-Final
1987-88	**80**	28	8	4	16	17	7	**44**	**25**	**11**	**363**	**288**	**99**	**2nd, Smythe Div.**	**Won Stanley Cup**
1986-87	**80**	29	6	5	21	18	1	**50**	**24**	**6**	**372**	**284**	**106**	**1st, Smythe Div.**	**Won Stanley Cup**
1985-86	80	32	6	2	24	11	5	56	17	7	426	310	119	1st, Smythe Div.	Lost Div. Final
1984-85	**80**	26	7	7	23	13	4	**49**	**20**	**11**	**401**	**298**	**109**	**1st, Smythe Div.**	**Won Stanley Cup**
1983-84	**80**	31	5	4	26	13	1	**57**	**18**	**5**	**446**	**314**	**119**	**1st, Smythe Div.**	**Won Stanley Cup**
1982-83	80	25	9	6	22	12	6	47	21	12	424	315	106	1st, Smythe Div.	Lost Final
1981-82	80	31	5	4	17	12	11	48	17	15	417	295	111	1st, Smythe Div.	Lost Div. Semi-Final
1980-81	80	17	13	10	12	22	6	29	35	16	328	327	74	4th, Smythe Div.	Lost Quarter-Final
1979-80	80	17	14	9	11	25	4	28	39	13	301	322	69	4th, Smythe Div.	Lost Prelim. Round

Bernie Nicholls had 49 points in 49 games for the Oilers in 1991-92.

1992-93 Player Personnel

FORWARDS	HT	WT	S	Place of Birth	Date	1991-92 Club
ALLISON, Scott	6-4	194	L	St. Boniface, Man.	4/22/72	Moose Jaw
ANTOS, Dean	5-11	175	L	Killam, Alta.	5/20/67	C. Breton-W.-Salem
BERANEK, Josef	6-2	185	L	Litvinov, Czech.	10/25/69	Edmonton
BLAIN, Joel	6-0	195	L	Malartic, Que.	10/12/61	Hull
BORGO, Richard	5-11	190	R	Thunder Bay, Ont.	9/25/70	Cape Breton
BREEN, George	6-2	200	R	Webster, MA	8/3/73	Providence
BUCHBERGER, Kelly	6-2	210	L	Langenburg, Sask.	12/2/66	Edmonton
CORSON, Shayne	6-0	201	L	Barrie, Ont.	8/13/66	Montreal
CROWLEY, Joe	6-2	195	L	Concord, MA	2/29/72	T.-Rivières-W.-Salem
CURRIE, Dan	6-2	195	L	Burlington, Ont.	3/15/68	Edm.-C. Breton
DeBRUSK, Louie	6-1	225	L	Cambridge, Ont.	3/19/71	Edm.-C. Breton
FISHER, Craig	6-3	180	L	Oshawa, Ont.	6/30/70	Cape Breton
GELINAS, Martin	5-11	195	L	Shawinigan, Que.	6/5/70	Edmonton
GIBSON, Steve	6-0	204	L	Listowel, Ont.	10/10/72	Windsor
GILCHRIST, Brent	5-11	181	L	Moose Jaw, Sask.	4/3/67	Montreal
HAAS, David	6-2	196	L	Toronto, Ont.	6/23/68	C. Breton-N. Haven
HULBIG, Joe	6-3	212	L	Norwood, MA	9/29/73	St. Sebastian's HS
KAPUSTA, Tomas	6-0	187	L	Zlin, Czech.	2/23/67	Cape Breton
KLIMA, Petr	6-0	190	L	Chaomutov, Czech.	12/23/64	Edmonton
MacTAVISH, Craig	6-1	195	L	London, Ont.	8/15/58	Edmonton
MALEY, David	6-2	195	L	Beaver Dam, WI	4/24/63	N. Jersey-Edm.
MALTBY, Kirk	6-0	180	R	Guelph, Ont.	12/22/72	Owen Sound
McDOUGALL, Bill	6-0	185	R	Mississauga, Ont.	8/10/66	Adiron.-C. Breton
MELLANBY, Scott	6-1	205	R	Montreal, Que.	6/11/66	Edmonton
MURPHY, Joe	6-1	190	L	London, Ont.	10/16/67	Edmonton
NICHOLLS, Bernie	6-1	185	R	Haliburton, Ont.	6/24/61	NYR-Edm.
PODEIN, Shjon	6-2	200	L	Rochester, MN	3/5/68	Cape Breton
RICE, Steve	6-0	215	R	Kitchener, Ont.	5/26/71	Edm.-C. Breton
RIIHIJARVI, Juha	6-3	196	R	Salla, Finland	12/15/69	JyP HT
SIMPSON, Craig	6-2	195	R	London, Ont.	2/15/67	Edmonton
THORNTON, Scott	6-2	200	L	London, Ont.	1/9/71	Edm.-C. Breton
TIKKANEN, Esa	6-1	200	L	Helsinki, Finland	1/25/65	Edmonton
VAN ALLEN, Shaun	6-1	200	L	Shaunavon, Sask.	8/29/67	Cape Breton
VUJTEK, Vladimir	6-0	190	L	Ostrava, Czech.	2/17/72	Montreal-Tri-City
WHITE, Peter	5-11	200	L	Montreal, Que.	3/15/69	Michigan State
WRIGHT, Tyler	5-11	170	R	Canora, Sask.	4/6/73	Swift Current
ZAVISHA, Brad	6-2	205	L	Hines Creek, Alta.	1/4/72	Portland-Lethbridge
DEFENSEMEN						
GLYNN, Brian	6-4	215	L	Iserlohn, W. Germany	11/23/67	Minnesota-Edmonton
HAWGOOD, Greg	5-10	190	L	Edmonton, Alta.	8/10/68	Edm.-C. Breton
JOSEPH, Chris	6-2	210	R	Burnaby, B.C.	10/10/69	Edm.-C. Breton
LAFORGE, Marc	6-2	210	L	Sudbury, Ont.	1/3/68	Cape Breton
LEGAULT, Alexandre	6-1	205	R	Chicoutimi, Que.	12/27/71	Beauport-W.-Salem
LEROUX, Francois	6-6	225	L	Ste-Adele, Que.	4/18/70	C. Breton-Edm.
LOWE, Kevin	6-2	195	L	Lachute, Que.	4/15/59	Edmonton
MACIVER, Norm	5-11	180	L	Thunder Bay, Ont.	9/8/64	Edmonton
MANSON, Dave	6-2	202	L	Prince Albert, Sask.	1/27/67	Edmonton
MARTINI, Darcy	6-4	220	L	Castlegar, B.C.	1/30/69	Michigan Tech
MUNI, Craig	6-3	200	L	Toronto, Ont.	7/19/62	Edmonton
RICHARDSON, Luke	6-4	210	L	Ottawa, Ont.	3/26/69	Edmonton
SMITH, Geoff	6-3	200	L	Edmonton, Alta.	3/7/69	Edmonton
WERENKA, Brad	6-2	205	L	Two Hills, Alta.	2/12/69	Cape Breton

GOALTENDERS	HT	WT	C	Place of Birth	Date	1991-92 Club
FOSTER, Norm	5-9	175	L	Vancouver, B.C.	2/10/65	Edm.-C. Breton
ING, Peter	6-2	175	L	Toronto, Ont.	4/28/69	Edm.-C. Breton
RANFORD, Bill	5-10	170	L	Brandon, Man.	12/14/66	Edmonton
TUGNUTT, Ron	5-11	155	L	Scarborough, Ont.	10/22/67	Que.-Halifax-Edm.
VERNER, Andrew	6-0	194	L	Weston, Ont.	11/20/72	Peterborough

General Managers' History

Glen Sather, 1979-80 to date.

Coaching History

Glen Sather, 1979-80; Bryan Watson and Glen Sather, 1980-81; Glen Sather, 1981-82 to 1988-89; John Muckler, 1989-90 to 1990-91; Ted Green, 1991-92 to date.

Captains' History

Ron Chipperfield, 1979-80; Lee Fogolin, 1980-81 to 1982-83; Wayne Gretzky, 1983-84 to 1987-88; Mark Messier, 1988-89 to 1990-91; Kevin Lowe, 1991-92.

Retired Numbers

3	Al Hamilton	1972-1980

1991-92 Scoring

Regular Season

Pos	#	Player	Team	GP	G	A	Pts	+/–	PIM	PP	SH	GW	GT	S	%
L	21	Vincent Damphousse	EDM	80	38	51	89	10	53	12	1	8	1	247	15.4
R	8	Joe Murphy	EDM	80	35	47	82	17	52	10	2	2	2	193	18.1
L	18	Craig Simpson	EDM	79	24	37	61	8	80	6	0	2	0	128	18.8
R	27	Scott Mellanby	EDM	80	23	27	50	5	197	7	0	5	0	159	14.5
C	9	Bernie Nicholls	NYR	1	0	0	0	1–	0	0	0	0	0	2	.0
			EDM	49	20	29	49	5	60	7	0	2	0	115	17.4
			TOTAL	50	20	29	49	4	60	7	0	2	0	117	17.1
D	24	Dave Manson	EDM	79	15	32	47	9	220	7	0	2	0	206	7.3
L	16	Kelly Buchberger	EDM	79	20	24	44	9	157	0	4	3	1	90	22.2
C	19	Anatoli Semenov	EDM	59	20	22	42	12	16	3	0	3	0	105	19.0
D	36	Norm Maciver	EDM	57	6	34	40	20	38	2	0	3	0	69	8.7
L	85	Petr Klima	EDM	57	21	13	34	18–	52	5	0	0	0	107	19.6
C	14	Craig MacTavish	EDM	80	12	18	30	1–	98	0	2	1	0	86	14.0
L	20	Martin Gelinas	EDM	68	11	18	29	14	62	1	0	0	0	94	11.7
L	10	Esa Tikkanen	EDM	40	12	16	28	8–	44	6	2	1	0	117	10.3
C	42*	Josef Beranek	EDM	58	12	16	28	2–	18	0	0	1	0	79	15.2
C	7	Mark Lamb	EDM	59	6	22	28	4	46	2	0	1	0	61	9.8
L	12	David Maley	N.J.	37	7	11	18	0	58	1	0	0	0	42	16.7
			EDM	23	3	6	9	8	46	0	0	1	0	31	9.7
			TOTAL	60	10	17	27	8	104	1	0	1	0	73	13.7
D	6	Brian Glynn	MIN	37	2	12	14	16–	24	0	0	0	1	53	3.8
			EDM	25	2	6	8	11	6	0	1	0	0	29	6.9
			TOTAL	62	4	18	22	5–	30	0	1	0	1	82	4.9
D	22	Luke Richardson	EDM	75	2	19	21	9–	118	0	0	0	0	85	2.4
D	25	Geoff Smith	EDM	74	2	16	18	5–	43	0	0	0	0	61	3.3
D	34	Greg Hawgood	EDM	20	2	11	13	19	22	0	0	0	0	24	8.3
D	4	Kevin Lowe	EDM	55	2	8	10	4–	107	0	0	0	0	33	6.1
D	28	Craig Muni	EDM	54	2	5	7	11	34	0	0	0	0	38	5.3
L	29*	Louie DeBrusk	EDM	25	2	1	3	4	124	0	0	1	0	7	28.6
G	1	Peter Ing	EDM	12	0	3	3	0	0	0	0	0	0	0	.0
G	30	Bill Ranford	EDM	67	0	3	3	0	4	0	0	0	0	0	.0
L	23*	Dan Currie	EDM	7	1	0	1	1–	0	0	0	0	0	3	33.3
C	17	Scott Thornton	EDM	15	0	1	1	6–	43	0	0	0	0	11	.0
R	15*	Steven Rice	EDM	3	0	0	0	2–	2	0	0	0	0	2	.0
D	35*	Francois Leroux	EDM	4	0	0	0	1–	7	0	0	0	0	0	.0
D	2	Chris Joseph	EDM	7	0	0	0	1–	8	0	0	0	0	5	.0
G	33	Norm Foster	EDM	10	0	0	0	0	2	0	0	0	0	0	.0
G	32	Ron Tugnutt	QUE	30	0	0	0	0	0	0	0	0	0	0	.0
			EDM	3	0	0	0	0	2	0	0	0	0	0	.0
			TOTAL	33	0	0	0	0	2	0	0	0	0	0	.0

Goaltending

No.	Goaltender	GPI	Mins	Avg	W	L	T	EN	SO	GA	SA	S%
33	Norm Foster	10	439	2.73	5	3	0	0	0	20	183	.891
30	Bill Ranford	67	3822	3.58	27	26	10	5	1	228	1971	.884
1	Peter Ing	12	463	4.28	3	4	0	1	0	33	252	.869
32	Ron Tugnutt	3	124	4.84	1	1	0	0	0	10	73	.863
	Totals	**80**	**4858**	**3.67**	**36**	**34**	**10**	**6**	**1**	**297**	**2485**	**.880**

Playoffs

Pos	#	Player	Team	GP	G	A	Pts	+/–	PIM	PP	SH	GW	GT	S	%
R	8	Joe Murphy	EDM	16	8	16	24	2	12	4	0	2	1	32	25.0
C	9	Bernie Nicholls	EDM	16	8	11	19	2	25	4	0	1	0	32	25.0
L	21	Vincent Damphousse	EDM	16	6	8	14	5	8	1	0	0	0	45	13.3
D	24	Dave Manson	EDM	16	3	9	12	2–	44	1	0	0	0	47	6.4
L	10	Esa Tikkanen	EDM	16	5	3	8	1–	8	1	0	1	0	37	13.5
D	6	Brian Glynn	EDM	16	4	1	5	1	12	1	0	1	0	13	30.8
L	85	Petr Klima	EDM	15	1	4	5	1–	8	0	0	0	0	22	4.5
L	16	Kelly Buchberger	EDM	16	1	4	5	2	32	0	0	0	0	12	8.3
D	22	Luke Richardson	EDM	16	0	5	5	2–	45	0	0	0	0	11	.0
D	2	Chris Joseph	EDM	5	1	3	4	2	2	0	0	0	0	6	16.7
L	20	Martin Gelinas	EDM	15	1	3	4	3–	10	0	0	0	0	15	6.7
C	14	Craig MacTavish	EDM	16	3	0	3	4	28	0	1	1	0	27	11.1
C	42*	Josef Beranek	EDM	12	2	1	3	6–	0	1	0	1	0	17	11.8
R	27	Scott Mellanby	EDM	16	2	1	3	3–	29	1	0	1	0	26	7.7
D	36	Norm Maciver	EDM	13	1	2	3	3	10	0	0	0	0	17	5.9
D	4	Kevin Lowe	EDM	11	0	3	3	2–	16	0	0	0	0	7	.0
D	34	Greg Hawgood	EDM	13	0	3	3	4–	23	0	0	0	0	19	.0
C	19	Anatoli Semenov	EDM	8	1	1	2	3	6	0	0	0	0	12	8.3
L	12	David Maley	EDM	10	1	1	2	4–	4	0	0	0	0	6	16.7
C	7	Mark Lamb	EDM	16	1	1	2	5–	10	0	0	0	0	13	7.7
D	25	Geoff Smith	EDM	5	0	1	1	2	6	0	0	0	0	5	.0
L	18	Craig Simpson	EDM	1	0	0	0	0	0	0	0	0	0	1	.0
C	17	Scott Thornton	EDM	1	0	0	0	1–	0	0	0	0	0	1	.0
G	32	Ron Tugnutt	EDM	2	0	0	0	0	0	0	0	0	0	0	.0
D	28	Craig Muni	EDM	3	0	0	0	4–	2	0	0	0	0	3	.0
G	30	Bill Ranford	EDM	16	0	0	0	0	0	0	0	0	0	0	.0

Goaltending

No.	Goaltender	GPI	Mins	Avg	W	L	EN	SO	GA	SA	S%
32	Ron Tugnutt	2	60	3.00	0	0	0	0	3	34	.912
30	Bill Ranford	16	909	3.37	8	8	0	2	51	484	.895
	Totals	**16**	**971**	**3.34**	**8**	**8**	**0**	**2**	**54**	**518**	**.896**

Club Records

Team

(Figures in brackets for season records are games played; records for fewest points, wins, ties, losses, goals, goals against are for 70 or more games)

Record		
Most Points	119	1983-84 (80) 1985-86 (80)
Most Wins	57	1983-84 (80)
Most Ties	16	1980-81 (80)
Most Losses	39	1979-80 (80)
Most Goals	*446	1983-84 (80)
Most Goals Against	327	1980-81 (80)
Fewest Points	69	1979-80 (80)
Fewest Wins	28	1979-80 (80)
Fewest Ties	5	1983-84 (80)
Fewest Losses	17	1981-82 (80) 1985-86 (80)
Fewest Goals	272	1990-91 (80)
Fewest Goals Against	272	1990-91 (80)
Longest Winning Streak		
Over-all	8	Five times
Home	8	Jan. 19/85-Feb. 22/85 Feb. 24-Apr. 2/86
Away	8	Dec. 9/86-Jan. 17/87
Longest Undefeated Streak		
Over-all	15	Oct. 11/84-Nov. 9/84 (12 wins, 3 ties)
Home	14	Nov. 15/89-Jan. 6/90 (11 wins, 3 ties)
Away	9	Jan. 17-Mar. 2/82 (6 wins, 3 ties) Nov. 23/82-Jan. 18/83 (7 wins, 2 ties)
Longest Losing Streak		
Over-all	9	Oct. 21-Nov. 10/90
Home	4	Twice
Away	9	Nov. 25-Dec. 30/80
Longest Winless Streak		
Over-all	9	Oct. 21-Nov. 10/90
Home	7	Oct. 24-Nov. 19/80 (3 losses, 4 ties)
Away	9	Nov. 25-Dec. 30/80 (9 losses)
Most Shutouts, Season	4	1987-88 (80)
Most PIM, Season	2,173	1987-88 (80)
Most Goals, Game	13	Nov. 19/83 (NJ 4 at Edm. 13) Nov. 8/85 (Van. 0 at Edm. 13)

Individual

Record		
Most Seasons	13	Kevin Lowe
Most Games	966	Kevin Lowe
Most Goals, Career	583	Wayne Gretzky
Most Assists, Career	1,086	Wayne Gretzky
Most Points, Career	1,669	Wayne Gretzky (583 goals, 1,086 assists)
Most PIM, Career	1,278	Kevin McClelland
Most Shutouts, Career	9	Grant Fuhr
Longest Consecutive Games Streak	478	Craig MacTavish (Oct. 11/86-Apr. 14/92)
Most Goals, Season	*92	Wayne Gretzky (1981-82)
Most Assists, Season	*163	Wayne Gretzky (1985-86)
Most Points, Season	*215	Wayne Gretzky (1985-86) (52 goals, 163 assists)
Most PIM, Season	286	Steve Smith (1987-88)
Most Points, Defenseman, Season	138	Paul Coffey (1985-86) (48 goals, 90 assists)
Most Points, Center, Season	*215	Wayne Gretzky (1985-86) (52 goals, 163 assists)
Most Points, Right Wing, Season	135	Jari Kurri (1984-85) (71 goals, 64 assists)
Most Points, Left Wing, Season	106	Mark Messier (1982-83) (48 goals, 58 assists)
Most Points, Rookie, Season	75	Jari Kurri (1980-81) (32 goals, 43 assists)
Most Shutouts, Season	4	Grant Fuhr (1987-88)
Most Goals, Game	5	Wayne Gretzky (Feb. 18/81, Dec. 30/81, Dec. 15/84, Dec. 6/87) Jari Kurri (Nov. 19/83) Pat Hughes (Feb. 3/84)
Most Assists, Game	*7	Wayne Gretzky (Feb. 15/80; Dec. 11/85; Feb. 14/86)
Most Points, Game	8	Wayne Gretzky (Nov. 19/83) Paul Coffey (Mar. 14/86) Wayne Gretzky (Jan. 4/84)

* NHL Record.

All-time Record vs. Other Clubs

Regular Season

	At Home							On Road							Total						
	GP	W	L	T	GF	GA	PTS	GP	W	L	T	GF	GA	PTS	GP	W	L	T	GF	GA	PTS
Boston	20	8	9	3	72	67	19	21	3	16	2	58	99	8	41	11	25	5	130	166	27
Buffalo	20	15	3	2	91	51	32	21	8	9	4	84	90	20	41	23	12	6	175	141	52
Calgary	47	26	13	8	212	167	60	48	19	23	6	186	223	44	95	45	36	14	398	390	104
Chicago	21	14	6	1	105	74	29	20	7	11	2	90	90	16	41	21	17	3	195	164	45
Detroit	20	11	6	3	107	85	25	21	12	7	2	100	81	26	41	23	13	5	207	166	51
Hartford	21	16	2	3	97	61	35	20	9	8	3	76	83	21	41	25	10	6	173	144	56
Los Angeles	48	27	10	11	257	190	65	47	20	18	9	221	204	49	95	47	28	20	478	394	114
Minnesota	20	13	1	6	104	64	32	21	11	6	4	81	78	26	41	24	7	10	185	142	58
Montreal	21	12	9	0	73	62	24	20	6	11	3	63	72	15	41	18	20	3	136	134	39
New Jersey	23	12	7	4	115	90	28	23	12	9	2	85	78	26	46	24	16	6	200	168	54
NY Islanders	21	13	5	3	83	64	29	20	5	8	7	85	84	17	41	18	13	10	168	148	46
NY Rangers	20	10	9	1	83	71	21	20	11	6	3	85	83	25	40	21	15	4	168	154	46
Philadelphia	20	12	5	3	78	60	27	21	5	15	1	65	97	11	41	17	20	4	143	157	38
Pittsburgh	20	16	3	1	114	70	33	21	11	9	1	102	82	23	41	27	12	2	216	152	56
Quebec	20	16	4	0	117	59	32	20	12	6	2	99	79	26	40	28	10	2	216	138	58
St. Louis	21	13	5	3	101	81	29	20	10	7	3	90	77	23	41	23	12	6	191	158	52
San Jose	4	3	0	1	22	11	7	3	0	3	0	7	17	0	7	3	3	1	29	28	7
Toronto	20	13	3	4	110	66	30	21	12	8	1	109	87	25	41	25	11	5	219	153	55
Vancouver	47	35	8	4	252	148	74	48	27	15	6	217	174	60	95	62	23	10	469	322	134
Washington	20	8	8	4	82	73	20	20	8	11	1	76	90	17	40	16	19	5	158	163	37
Winnipeg	46	31	12	3	218	150	65	44	25	15	4	213	179	54	90	56	27	7	431	329	119
Totals	**520**	**324**	**128**	**68**	**2493**	**1764**	**716**	**520**	**233**	**221**	**66**	**2192**	**2147**	**532**	**1040**	**557**	**349**	**134**	**4685**	**3911**	**1248**

Playoffs

	Series	W	L	GP	W	L	T	GF	GA	Last Mtg.	Round	Result
Boston	2	2	0	9	8	1	0	41	20	1990	F	W 4-1
Calgary	5	4	1	30	19	11	0	132	96	1991	DSF	W 4-3
Chicago	4	3	1	20	12	8	0	102	77	1992	CF	L 0-4
Detroit	2	2	0	10	8	2	0	39	26	1988	CF	W 4-1
Los Angeles	7	5	2	36	24	12	0	154	127	1992	DSF	W 4-2
Minnesota	2	1	1	9	5	4	0	36	30	1991	CF	L 1-4
Montreal	1	1	0	3	3	0	0	15	6	1981	PR	W 3-0
NY Islanders	3	1	2	15	6	9	0	47	58	1984	F	W 4-1
Philadelphia	3	2	1	15	8	7	0	49	44	1987	F	W 4-3
Vancouver	2	2	0	9	7	2	0	35	20	1992	DF	W 4-2
Winnipeg	6	6	0	26	22	4	0	120	75	1990	DSF	W 4-3
Totals	**37**	**29**	**8**	**180**	**120**	**60**	**0**	**770**	**579**			

Playoff Results 1992-88

Year	Round	Opponent	Result	GF	GA
1992	CF	Chicago	L 0-4	8	21
	DF	Vancouver	W 4-2	18	15
	DSF	Los Angeles	W 4-2	23	18
1991	CF	Minnesota	L 1-4	14	20
	DF	Los Angeles	W 4-2	21	20
	DSF	Calgary	W 4-3	22	20
1990	**F**	**Boston**	**W 4-1**	**20**	**8**
	CF	Chicago	W 4-2	25	20
	DF	Los Angeles	W 4-0	24	10
	DSF	Winnipeg	W 4-3	24	22
1989	DSF	Los Angeles	L 3-4	20	25
1988	**F**	**Boston**	**W 4-0**	**21**	**12**
	CF	Detroit	W 4-1	23	16
	DF	Calgary	W 4-0	18	11
	DSF	Winnipeg	W 4-1	25	17

Abbreviations: Round: F – Final; **CF** – conference final; **DF** – division final; **DSF** – division semi-final; **SF** – semi-final; **QF** – quarter-final; **PR** – preliminary round. **GA** – goals against; **GF** – goals for.

1991-92 Results

Home			Away		
Oct. 6	Los Angeles	2-2	**Oct.** 4	Calgary	2-9
12	Calgary	3-1	8	Los Angeles	3-6
23	Washington	5-6	10	St Louis	2-3
26	Vancouver	5-4	15	Detroit	1-3
30	St Louis	2-2	17	Chicago	2-4
Nov. 1	New Jersey	1-3	19	NY Islanders	4-2
6	NY Islanders	5-3	20	NY Rangers	4-3
23	Winnipeg	0-4	27	Vancouver	6-3
27	Chicago	6-2	**Nov.** 3	Vancouver*	2-7
29	San Jose	4-4	8	San Jose	2-6
Dec. 1	Vancouver*	7-0	9	Los Angeles	4-4
3	Pittsburgh	5-3	13	Pittsburgh	4-5
8	San Jose	3-1	14	Philadelphia	1-3
14	Winnipeg	7-5	16	Quebec	6-2
15	Detroit	1-4	18	Montreal	0-1
23	Calgary	5-3	**Dec.** 6	Winnipeg	4-4
28	Los Angeles	4-9	10	Vancouver	7-4
29	Montreal	1-3	12	San Jose	3-6
Jan. 5	Calgary	2-3	18	Toronto	7-5
15	Vancouver	3-5	20	Buffalo	4-4
21	San Jose	9-2	21	Boston	3-6
23	NY Rangers	1-3	**Jan.** 2	Los Angeles	3-5
29	Chicago	3-4	4	Calgary	3-2
31	Hartford	4-1	8	Winnipeg	2-5
Feb. 2	Quebec*	8-2	10	Buffalo	2-8
5	Montreal	2-1	11	Detroit	5-5
7	NY Islanders	4-2	13	Minnesota	7-4
19	Los Angeles	4-3	25	San Jose	2-5
21	Boston	3-5	28	Vancouver	5-3
23	Buffalo	5-2	**Feb.** 11	Minnesota	5-4
26	Winnipeg	6-1	13	Hartford	3-1
28	Philadelphia	4-2	15	Philadelphia*	5-8
Mar. 4	Toronto	2-5	16	Toronto	5-7
6	St Louis	5-3	**Mar.** 1	Winnipeg*	4-2
11	New Jersey	2-2	17	Pittsburgh	5-6
14	Hartford	3-1	19	New Jersey	5-3
27	Minnesota	5-3	21	Boston*	4-3
29	Los Angeles	2-2	22	Washington*	2-6
Apr. 3	Winnipeg	2-6	24	Calgary	4-4
5	San Jose*	6-4	31	Calgary	2-5

*Denotes afternoon game

Entry Draft Selections 1992-79

1992

Pick	
13	Joe Hulbig
37	Martin Reichel
61	Simon Roy
65	Kirk Maltby
96	Ralph Intranuovo
109	Joaquin Gage
157	Steve Gibson
181	Kyuin Shim
190	Colin Schmidt
205	Marko Tuomainen
253	Bryan Rasmussen

1991

Pick	
12	Tyler Wright
20	Martin Rucinsky
34	Andrew Verner
56	George Breen
78	Mario Nobili
93	Ryan Haggerty
144	David Oliver
166	Gary Kitching
210	Vegar Barlie
232	Evgeny Belosheikin
254	Juha Riihijarvi

1989

Pick	
17	Scott Allison
38	Alexandre Legault
59	Joe Crowley
67	Joel Blain
101	Greg Louder
122	Keijo Sailynoja
143	Mike Power
164	Roman Mejzlik
185	Richard Zemlicka
206	Petr Korinek
227	invalid claim
248	Sami Nuutinen

1989

Pick	
15	Jason Soules
36	Richard Borgo
78	Josef Beranek
92	Peter White
120	Anatoli Semenov
140	Davis Payne
141	Sergei Yashin
162	Darcy Martini
225	Roman Bozek

1988

Pick	
19	Francois Leroux
39	Petro Koivunen
53	Trevor Sim
61	Collin Bauer
82	Cam Brauer
103	Don Martin
124	Len Barrie
145	Mike Glover
166	Shjon Podein
187	Tom Cole
208	Vladimir Zubkov
229	Darin MacDonald
250	Tim Tisdale

1987

Pick	
21	Peter Soberlak
42	Brad Werenka
63	Geoff Smith
64	Peter Eriksson
105	Shaun Van Allen
126	Radek Toupal
147	Tomas Srsen
168	Age Ellingsen
189	Gavin Armstrong
210	Mike Tinkham
231	Jeff Pauletti
241	Jesper Duus
252	Igor Vyazmikin

1986

Pick	
21	Kim Issel
42	Jamie Nichols
63	Ron Shudra
84	Dan Currie
105	David Haas
126	Jim Ennis
147	Ivan Matulik
168	Nicolas Beaulieu
189	Mike Greenlay
210	Matt Lanza
231	Mojmir Bozik
252	Tony Hand

1985

Pick	
20	Scott Metcalfe
41	Todd Carnelley
62	Mike Ware
104	Tomas Kapusta
125	Brian Tessier
146	Shawn Tyers
167	Tony Fairfield
188	Kelly Buchberger
209	Mario Barbe
230	Peter Headon
251	John Haley

1984

Pick	
21	Selmar Odelein
42	Daryl Reaugh
63	Todd Norman
84	Rich Novak
105	Richard Lambert
106	Emanuel Viveiros
126	Ivan Dornic
147	Heikki Riihijarvi
168	Todd Ewen
209	Joel Curtis
229	Simon Wheeldon
250	Darren Gani

1983

Pick	
19	Jeff Beukeboom
40	Mike Golden
60	Mike Flanagan
80	Esa Tikkanen
120	Don Barber
140	Dale Derkatch
160	Ralph Vos
180	Dave Roach
200	Warren Yadlowski
220	John Miner
240	Steve Woodburn

1982

Pick	
20	Jim Playfair
41	Steve Graves
62	Brent Loney
83	Jaroslav Pouzar
104	Dwayne Boettger
125	Raimo Summanen
146	Brian Small
167	Dean Clark
188	Ian Wood
209	Grant Dion
230	Chris Smith
251	Jeff Crawford

1981

Pick	
8	Grant Fuhr
29	Todd Strueby
71	Paul Houck
92	Phil Drouillard
111	Steve Smith
113	Marc Habscheid
155	Mike Sturgeon
176	Miloslav Horava
197	Gord Sherven

1980

Pick	
6	Paul Coffey
48	Shawn Babcock
69	Jari Kurri
90	Walt Poddubny
111	Mike Winther
132	Andy Moog
153	Rob PolmanTuin
174	Lars-Gunnar Pettersson

1979

Pick	
21	Kevin Lowe
48	Mark Messier
69	Glenn Anderson
84	Maxwell Kostovich
105	Mike Toal
126	Blair Barnes

General Manager

SATHER, GLEN CAMERON
President and General Manager, Edmonton Oilers. Born in High River, Alta., Sept. 2, 1943.

A journeyman left-winger who played for six different teams during his nine-year NHL career, 49-year-old Glen Sather was one of the League's most successful coaches ever before relinquishing his coaching duties on June 12, 1989. He was the 1985-86 Jack Adams Award winner, led his club to four Stanley Cup championships and had a ten-year winning percentage of .629 (442-241-99). His 442 wins place him sixth on the all-time list in regular season wins. In addition, Sather led his team to 89 play-off victories, fourth on the all-time list. His .706 winning percentage in the playoffs ranks him first.

After closing out his NHL playing career in 1975-76 with an 80-113-193 scoring mark in 660 games, Sather jumped to the Oilers in the World Hockey Association, where he enjoyed his best and last season as a player with totals of 19-34-53 in 81 games. Midway through that 1976-77 campaign, on January 27, 1977, he also assumed the Edmonton coaching duties and led his team to the first of its 11 straight WHA and NHL playoff appearances. Three years later, when the club entered the NHL, Sather took on the added responsibilities of Oilers' president and general manager, which he currently maintains.

NHL Coaching Record

		Regular Season					Playoffs			
Season	Team	Games	W	L	T	%	Games	W	L	%
1979-80	Edmonton (NHL)	80	28	39	13	.431	3	0	3	.000
1980-81	Edmonton (NHL)	62	25	26	11	.492	9	5	4	.555
1981-82	Edmonton (NHL)	80	48	17	15	.694	5	2	3	.400
1982-83	Edmonton (NHL)	80	47	21	12	.663	16	11	5	.687
1983-84	Edmonton (NHL)	80	57	18	5	.744	19	15	4	.789*
1984-85	Edmonton (NHL)	80	49	20	11	.681	18	15	3	.833*
1985-86	Edmonton (NHL)	80	56	17	7	.744	10	6	4	.600
1986-87	Edmonton (NHL)	80	50	24	6	.663	21	16	5	.762*
1987-88	Edmonton (NHL)	80	44	25	11	.619	18	16	2	.889*
1988-89	Edmonton (NHL)	80	38	34	8	.538	7	3	4	.429
	NHL Totals	782	442	241	99	.629	126	89	37	.706

* Stanley Cup win.

Club Directory

Northlands Coliseum
Edmonton, Alberta T5B 4M9
Phone **403/474-8561**
Ticketing 403/471-2191
FAX 403/477-9625
Capacity: 17,313 (standing 190)

Owner/Governor	Peter Pocklington
Alternate Governor	Glen Sather
General Counsel	Bob Lloyd, Gary Frohlich
President/General Manager	Glen Sather
Exec. Vice-President/Assistant G.M.	Bruce MacGregor
Coach	Ted Green
Assistant Coaches	Ron Low, Kevin Primeau
Director of Player Personnel/Chief Scout	Barry Fraser
Administrative Assistant Hockey Operations	Kevin Prendergast
Scouting Staff	Ace Bailey, Ed Chadwick, Lorne Davis, Bob Freeman, Harry Howell, Curly Reeves, Jan Slepicka, Brad Smith
Executive Secretary	Betsy Dolinsky
Receptionist/Secretary	Pattie Zack
Medical and Training Staff	
Athletic Trainer/Therapist	Ken Lowe
Athletic Trainer	Barrie Stafford
Assistant Trainer	Lyle Kulchisky
Massage Therapist	Stewart Poirier
Team Medical Chief of Staff	Dr. Gordon Cameron
Team Orthopedic Surgeon / Director of Glen Sather Sports Medicine Clinic	Dr. David C. Reid
Team Physician	Dr. Don Groot
Team Dentists	Dr. Tony Sneazwell, Dr. Brian Nord
Fitness Consultant	Dr. Art Quinney
Physical Therapist Consultant	Dr. Dave Magee
Sports Psychologist	Dr. Murray Smith
Finance	
Vice-President, Finance	Werner Baum
Accountants	Ellie Merrick, Allison Coward, Jill Semple
Executive Secretary	Lisa Colby
Public Relations	
Director of Public Relations	Bill Tuele
Coordinator of Publications and Statistics	Steve Knowles
Director of Community Relations/Special Events	Trish Kerr
Public Relations Secretary	Fiona Liew
Marketing	
Director of Marketing	Stew MacDonald
Marketing Representative/Properties Mgr.	Darrell Holowaychuk
Marketing Representative	Brad MacGregor
Sales Representative	Dave Semenko
Marketing Secretary	Heather Hansch
Merchandising Clerks	Julia Sharman, Yvette Miller, Tina Scott
Warehouse Supervisor	Ray MacDonald
Warehouse Assistant	Jim Groff
Ticketing	
Director of Ticketing Operations	Sheila Stock
Ticketing Operations	Sheila McCaskill, Marcia Godwin, Marcella Kinsman
Retail Sales	
Manager – Champions Retail Store	Skip Krake
Team Administration Offices	Northlands Coliseum, Edmonton, Alta., Canada T5B 4M9
Seating Capacity	17,313 (with standing 17,503)
Location of Press Box	East Side at top (Radio/TV) West Side at top (Media)
Dimensions of Rink	200 feet by 85 feet
Ends of Rink	Herculite extends above boards around rink
Club Colours	Blue, Orange, White
Team Uniforms	Home - Base colour white, trimmed with blue and orange Away - Base colour blue, trimmed with white and orange
Training Camp Site	Northlands Coliseum, Edmonton, Alberta
Television Channel	CFRN (Channel 3, Cable 2) CBXT TV (Channel 5, Cable 4)
Radio Station	CFCW (790 AM)

Coach

GREEN, TED
Coach, Edmonton Oilers. Born in Eriksdale, Man., March 23, 1940.

Ted Green, who became the fourth coach of the Edmonton Oilers on June 27, 1991, led the Oilers to the conference finals for the third consecutive season. In his playing/coaching career, Green has played a vital role on twelve championship teams. A member of the Memorial Cup-winning Winnipeg Braves in 1959, Green established himself as a steady, "stay-at-home" defenseman in the NHL with the Boston Bruins, earning two All-Star berths and winning the Stanley Cup in 1972.

In 1973, Green joined the WHA, where he added three Avco Cup championship rings to his collection. After retiring as a player, Green coached the Carman Hornets to the Manitoba Intermediate championship. In 1981, Green joined the Oilers' organization as an assistant coach and has been a part of each of the Oilers' Stanley Cup victories. Green also served as an assistant coach for the Team Canada squad that captured the Canada Cup in 1984. Following a one-year sabbatical from the Oilers in 1986, Green rejoined the team in 1987 and was named co-coach in the 1989-90 season.

Coaching Record

		Regular Season					Playoffs			
Season	Team	Games	W	L	T	%	Games	W	L	%
1991-92	Edmonton (NHL)	80	36	34	10	.513	16	8	8	.500
	NHL Totals	80	36	34	10	.513	16	8	8	.500

Hartford Whalers

1991-92 Results: 26W-41L-13T 65PTS. Fourth, Adams Division

Schedule

	Home		Away
Oct.	Tues. 6 Montreal	**Oct.**	Thur. 8 Boston
	Sat. 10 Buffalo		Mon. 12 NY Rangers
	Wed. 14 Ottawa		Tues. 20 New Jersey
	Sat. 17 Pittsburgh		Thur. 22 Ottawa
	Wed. 28 New Jersey		Sat. 24 NY Islanders
	Sat. 31 Los Angeles	Nov.	Fri. 6 Detroit
Nov.	Tues. 3 Quebec		Fri. 13 Buffalo
	Sat. 7 Washington		Thur. 19 Ottawa
	Wed. 11 Calgary		Sat. 21 Quebec*
	Sat. 14 Detroit		Fri. 27 Boston*
	Wed. 18 St Louis	**Dec.**	Tues. 1 St Louis
	Wed. 25 Montreal		Thur. 3 San Jose
	Sat. 28 Boston		Sat. 5 Los Angeles
Dec.	Wed. 9 Ottawa		Fri. 11 Buffalo
	Sat. 12 Buffalo		Fri. 18 Washington
	Wed. 16 Washington		Mon. 21 Montreal
	Sat. 19 NY Rangers		Sun. 27 New Jersey
	Wed. 23 Tampa Bay	**Jan.**	Sat. 2 Boston
	Sat. 26 Boston		Wed. 13 Montreal
	Tues. 29 St Louis		Fri. 15 Edmonton
	(at Birmingham)		Sat. 16 Vancouver
	Thur. 31 Quebec		Mon. 18 Winnipeg
Jan.	Sun. 3 Minnesota		(at Saskatoon)
	Wed. 6 Buffalo		Sun. 24 Philadelphia
	Sat. 9 Quebec		Wed. 27 Montreal
	Sun. 10 Montreal		Thur. 28 Ottawa
	Thur. 21 San Jose	**Feb.**	Wed. 3 Buffalo
	Sat. 23 Chicago*		Fri. 12 Winnipeg
	Sat. 30 Winnipeg		Sat. 13 Calgary
Feb.	Wed. 17 Buffalo		Sat. 27 Quebec
	Sat. 20 Edmonton*	**Mar.**	Fri. 5 Buffalo
	Sun. 21 Pittsburgh*		Mon. 8 Quebec
	Wed. 24 Philadelphia		Wed. 10 Toronto
	Sun. 28 NY Islanders		Tues. 16 Tampa Bay
Mar.	Wed. 3 New Jersey		Fri. 19 Washington
	Sat. 6 Vancouver		Mon. 22 Boston
	Sat. 13 Buffalo*		Sat. 27 Minnesota
	Sun. 14 Philadelphia*		Sun. 28 Chicago
	Wed. 24 Montreal	**Apr.**	Thur. 1 Pittsburgh
	Tues. 30 Boston		Mon. 5 NY Rangers
Apr.	Sat. 3 Ottawa		Wed. 7 Ottawa
	Sun. 11 Toronto		Sat. 10 Quebec
	Wed. 14 NY Islanders		Thur. 15 NY Islanders

* Denotes afternoon game.

Pat Verbeek fired 22 goals for the Whalers in 1991-92.

Home Starting Times:

Weeknights and Saturdays	7:35 p.m.
Sundays	7:05 p.m.
Matinees	1:35 p.m.

Franchise date: June 22, 1979

14th NHL Season

Year-by-Year Record

		Home			Road			Overall							
Season	**GP**	**W**	**L**	**T**	**W**	**L**	**T**	**W**	**L**	**T**	**GF**	**GA**	**Pts.**	**Finished**	**Playoff Result**
1991-92	80	13	17	10	13	24	3	26	41	13	247	283	65	4th, Adams Div.	Lost Div. Semi-Final
1990-91	80	18	16	6	13	22	5	31	38	11	238	276	73	4th, Adams Div.	Lost Div. Semi-Final
1989-90	80	17	18	5	21	15	4	38	33	9	275	268	85	4th, Adams Div.	Lost Div. Semi-Final
1988-89	80	21	17	2	16	21	3	37	38	5	299	290	79	4th, Adams Div.	Lost Div. Semi-Final
1987-88	80	21	14	5	14	24	2	35	38	7	249	267	77	4th, Adams Div.	Lost Div. Semi-Final
1986-87	80	26	9	5	17	21	2	43	30	7	287	270	93	1st, Adams Div.	Lost Div. Semi-Final
1985-86	80	21	17	2	19	19	2	40	36	4	332	302	84	4th, Adams Div.	Lost Div. Final
1984-85	80	17	18	5	13	23	4	30	41	9	268	318	69	5th, Adams Div.	Out of Playoffs
1983-84	80	19	16	5	9	26	5	28	42	10	288	320	66	5th, Adams Div.	Out of Playoffs
1982-83	80	13	22	5	6	32	2	19	54	7	261	403	45	5th, Adams Div.	Out of Playoffs
1981-82	80	13	17	10	8	24	8	21	41	18	264	351	60	5th, Adams Div.	Out of Playoffs
1980-81	80	14	17	9	7	24	9	21	41	18	292	372	60	4th, Norris Div.	Out of Playoffs
1979-80	80	22	12	6	5	22	13	27	34	19	303	312	73	4th, Norris Div.	Lost Prelim. Round

1992-93 Player Personnel

FORWARDS	HT	WT	S	Place of Birth	Date	1991-92 Club
BELANGER, Ken	6-3	190	L	Sault Ste. Marie, Ont.	4/14/74	Ottawa
BRIGHT, Chris	6-0	187	L	Guelph, Ont.	10/14/70	Springfield-Louisville
BUCHANAN, Trevor	6-0	182	L	Ft. McMurray, Alta.	6/7/69	Louisville
CARUSO, Jamie	5-10	199	R	Toronto, Ont.	1/31/73	North Bay-Kitchener
CASSELS, Andrew	6-0	192	L	Bramalea, ONt.	7/23/69	Hartford
CHALIFOUX, Denis	5-8	165	R	Laval, Que.	2/21/71	Springfield
CRAVEN, Murray	6-2	185	L	Medicine Hat, Alta.	7/20/64	Philadelphia-Hartford
CULLEN, John	5-10	187	R	Puslinch, Ont.	8/2/64	Hartford
CUNNEYWORTH, Randy	6-0	180	L	Etobicoke, Ont.	5/10/61	Hartford
CYR, Paul	5-10	195	L	Port Alberni, B.C.	10/31/63	Hartford-Springfield
DANIELS, Scott	6-3	200	L	Prince Albert, B.C.	9/19/69	Springfield
DAY, Joe	5-11	180	L	Chicago, IL	5/11/68	Hartford-Springfield
EGELAND, Allan	5-11	165	L	Enchant, Alta.	1/31/73	Tacoma
ENS, Kelly	6-2	195	L	Saskatoon, Sask.	6/15/69	Springfield-Louisville
GILLIS, Paul	5-11	198	L	Toronto, Ont.	12/31/63	Chi.-Hfd.-Indianapolis
GOVEDARIS, Chris	6-0	200	L	Toronto, Ont.	2/2/70	Springfield
GREIG, Mark	5-11	190	R	High River, Alta.	1/28/70	Hartford-Springfield
GUAY, Paul	5-11	185	R	Providence, RI	9/2/63	Milwaukee
HARDING, Mike	5-8	181	L	Brantford, Ont.	6/19/73	Peterborough
JANSSENS, Mark	6-3	216	L	Surrey, B.C.	5/19/68	NYR-Minnesota
JOBE, Trevor	6-1	190	L	Lethbridge, Alta.	5/14/67	Nashville-Richmond
JOHNSON, Lance	6-3	195	L	Prince George, B.C.	1/16/73	Kamloops
KERR, Tim	6-3	230	R	WIndsor, Ont.	1/3/60	NY Rangers
KJENSTAD, Olaf	6-4	215	L	Ft. Saskatchewan, Alta.	9/6/72	Medicine Hat
KYPREOS, Nick	6-0	195	L	Toronto, Ont.	6/4/66	Washington
MATSOS, David	5-11	179	R	Burlington, Ont.	11/12/73	Sault Ste. Marie
McHUGH, Mike	5-10	190	L	Bowdoin, MA	8/16/65	Springfield
McKENZIE, Jim	6-3	210	L	Gull Lake, Sask.	11/3/69	Hartford
MORROW, Scott	6-1	181	L	Chicago, IL	6/18/69	U. of New Hampshire
NIECAR, Barry	6-3	200	L	Rama, Sask.	12/16/67	Raleigh-Phoenix
NAPOLITANO, Joseph	6-2	245	R	Pointe Claire, Que.	1/5/72	Victoriaville-Hull
NYLANDER, Mikael	5-11	176	L	Stockholm, Sweden	10/3/72	AIK Solna
PETROVICKY, Robert	5-11	172	L	Kosico, Czech.	10/26/73	Dukla Trencin
PETRUIC, Jeff	6-1	195	R	Avonlea, Sask.	5/19/74	Moose Jaw
PICARD, Michael	5-11	190	L	Beauport, Que.	11/7/69	Hartford-Springfield
PUOLIN, Patrick	6-1	208	L	Vanier, Que.	4/23/73	Hartford-St. Hyacinthe
POWERS, Jim	5-11	180	R	Springfield, MA	7/13/67	Raleigh
PURDIE, Dennis	5-10	185	R	Windsor, Ont.	11/27/72	London
REID, Jarrett	5-10	182	R	Sault Ste. Marie, Ont.	3/10/73	Sault Ste. Marie
RYCHEL, Warren	6-0	190	L	Tecumseh, Ont.	5/12/67	Moncton-Kalamazoo
SANDERSON, Geoff	6-0	185	L	Hay River, N.W.T.	2/1/72	Hartford
SICILIANO, Peter	6-2	224	L	Springfield, MA	12/9/68	Hampton Roads
SMYTH, Kevin	6-2	217	L	Banff, Alta.	11/22/73	Moose Jaw
STIENBURG, Trevor	6-1	200	R	Kingston, Ont.	5/13/66	New Haven
TOMLAK, Mike	6-3	205	L	Thunder Bay, Ont.	10/17/64	Hartford-Springfield
TOROPCHENKO, Leonid	6-4	235	L		8/28/68	Khimik Voskresensk
VERBEEK, Pat	5-9	190	R	Sarnia, Ont.	5/24/64	Hartford
WALKER, Todd	6-0	180	L	Ingleside, Ont.	4/14/74	Cornwall
WARE, Michael	6-5	216	R	York, Ont.	3/22/67	Did not play
YAKE, Terry	5-11	185	R	N. Westminster, B.C.	10/22/68	Hartford-Springfield
ZIMMER, Brad	6-1	195	L	Duysland, Alta.	2/18/73	Lethbridge
DEFENSEMEN						
AGNEW, Jim	6-1	190	L	Hartney, Man.	3/21/66	Vancouver
BEAULIEU, Corey	6-1	210	L	Winnipeg, Man.	9/9/69	Springfield-Louisville
BONNER, Craig	6-4	205	R	Edmonton, Alta.	5/20/72	Kamloops
BOUSQUET, Jarrett	6-2	197	L	Cranbrook, B.C.	8/16/73	Kamloops
BRAUER, Cam	6-3	200	L	Calgary, Alta.	1/4/70	Springfield-Louisville
BURT, Adam	6-0	190	L	Detroit, MI	1/15/69	Hartford
HAMRLIK, Martin	5-11	176	R	Zlin, Czech.	5/6/73	ZPS Zlin
HOUDA, Doug	6-2	200	R	Blairmore, Alta.	6/3/66	Hartford
HUMENJUK, Scott	6-0	190	R	Saskatoon, Sask.	9/10/69	Springfield-Louisville
JOHNSTON, Karl	6-0	190	L	Windsor, Ont.	8/11/67	Springfield
KECZMER, Dan	6-1	190	L	Mt. Clemens, MI	5/25/68	US Oly.-Hfd.-Springfield
KONROYD, Steve	6-1	195	L	Scarborough, Ont.	2/10/61	Chicago-Hartford
KRIVOKHIZHA, Yuri	6-2	225	L	Minsk, Belo-Russia	3/30/68	Dynamo Minsk
LADOUCEUR, Randy	6-2	220	L	Brockville, Ont.	6/30/60	Hartford
LAMONTHE, Carl	6-2	180	R	Montreal, Que.	10/7/73	Verdun
MATESOVICH, Scott	6-2	205	L	Southbury, CT	10/31/69	Yale
McBAIN, Jason	6-2	178	R	Ilion, NY	4/12/74	Lethbridge-Portland
McCOSH, Shayne	6-0	190	R	Oshawa, Ont.	6/5/69	Kitchener
PEDERSEN, Allen	6-3	210	L	Ft. Sask., Alta.	1/13/65	Minnesota
PERKINS, Darrin	6-2	210	R	New Norway, Alta.	3/26/73	Prince Albert
RICHARDS, Todd	6-0	190	R	Robbinsdale, MN	10/20/66	Hartford-Springfield
ROCHEFORT, Normand	6-1	214	L	Trois-Rivières, Que.	1/28/61	NY Rangers
STEVENS, John	6-1	195	L	Completon, N.B.	5/4/66	Hartford-Springfield
SUOMALAINEN, Jukka	6-5	198	L	Helsinki, Finland	4/20/66	Springfield
VAN IMPE, Darren	6-1	200	L	Saskatoon, Sask.	5/18/73	Prince Albert
WEINRICH, Eric	6-1	205	L	Roanoke, VA	12/19/66	New Jersey
YULE, Steve	6-0	210	R	Gleichen, Alta.	5/27/72	Kamloops
ZALAPSKI, Zarley	6-1	210	L	Edmonton, Alta.	4/22/68	Hartford

GOALTENDERS	HT	WT	C	Place of Birth	Date	1991-92 Club
BURKE, Sean	6-4	210	L	Windsor, Ont.	1/29/67	Cdn. Oly./San Diego
GOSSELIN, Mario	5-8	160	L	Thetford Mines, Que.	6/15/63	Springfield
LABBE, Jean-Francois	5-9	165	L	Sherbrooke, Que.	6/15/72	Trois-Rivières
LENARDUZZI, Mike	6-1	168	L	London, Ont.	9/14/72	S.S. Marie-Ott.-Sud.
MASSON, Dale	5-10	172	L	Edmonton, Alta.	1/18/73	Kamloops
PIETRANGELO, Frank	5-10	185	L	Niagara Falls, Ont.	12/17/64	Pittsburgh-Hartford
WHITMORE, Kay	5-11	175	L	Sudbury, Ont.	4/10/67	Hartford

1991-92 Scoring

Regular Season

Pos	#	Player	Team	GP	G	A	Pts	+/–	PIM	PP	SH	GW	GT	S	%
C	11	John Cullen	HFD	77	26	51	77	28–	141	10	0	4	0	172	15.1
L	12	Murray Craven	PHI	12	3	3	6	2	8	1	0	0	0	19	15.8
			HFD	61	24	30	54	4–	38	8	4	1	1	133	18.0
			TOTAL	73	27	33	60	2–	46	9	4	1	1	152	17.8
R	16	Pat Verbeek	HFD	76	22	35	57	16–	243	10	0	3	0	163	13.5
D	3	Zarley Zalapski	HFD	79	20	37	57	7–	120	4	0	3	1	230	8.7
L	34	Mikael Andersson	HFD	74	18	29	47	18	14	1	3	1	0	149	12.1
L	24	Bobby Holik	HFD	76	21	24	45	4	44	1	0	2	1	207	10.1
C	21	Andrew Cassels	HFD	67	11	30	41	3	18	2	2	3	0	99	11.1
C	8*	Geoff Sanderson	HFD	64	13	18	31	5	18	2	0	1	0	98	13.3
D	5	Steve Konroyd	CHI	49	2	14	16	4	65	0	0	0	0	70	2.9
			HFD	33	2	10	12	5–	32	1	0	0	0	56	3.6
			TOTAL	82	4	24	28	1–	97	1	0	0	0	126	3.2
D	32	Brad Shaw	HFD	62	3	22	25	1	44	0	0	0	0	101	3.0
D	6	Adam Burt	HFD	66	9	15	24	16–	93	4	0	1	0	89	10.1
D	25	Marc Bergevin	HFD	75	7	17	24	13–	64	4	1	1	0	96	7.3
R	26	Mark Hunter	HFD	63	10	13	23	8–	159	5	0	0	0	92	10.9
L	20	Yvon Corriveau	HFD	38	12	8	20	5	36	3	0	0	0	69	17.4
L	7	Randy Cunneyworth	HFD	39	7	10	17	5–	71	0	0	1	0	63	11.1
C	23*	James Black	HFD	30	4	6	10	4–	10	1	0	1	0	54	7.4
D	29	Randy Ladouceur	HFD	74	1	9	10	1–	127	0	0	0	0	59	1.7
D	27	Doug Houda	HFD	56	3	6	9	2–	125	1	0	1	0	40	7.5
L	47*	Michel Picard	HFD	25	3	5	8	2–	6	1	0	0	0	41	7.3
L	33	Jim Mckenzie	HFD	67	5	1	6	6–	87	0	0	0	1	34	14.7
R	17*	Mark Greig	HFD	17	0	5	5	7	6	0	0	0	0	18	.0
R	22	Ed Kastelic	HFD	25	1	3	4	4–	61	0	0	0	0	4	25.0
D	45	John Stevens	HFD	21	0	4	4	4–	19	0	0	0	0	13	.0
L	18	Paul Cyr	HFD	17	0	3	3	4–	19	0	0	0	0	20	.0
L	41*	Joe Day	HFD	24	0	3	3	2–	10	0	0	0	0	13	.0
R	36	Daniel Shank	HFD	13	2	0	2	4–	18	0	0	0	0	10	20.0
C	38*	Terry Yake	HFD	15	1	1	2	2–	4	0	0	0	0	12	8.3
C	44	Paul Gillis	CHI	2	0	0	0	3–	6	0	0	0	0	1	.0
			HFD	12	0	2	2	0	48	0	0	0	0	6	.0
			TOTAL	14	0	2	2	3–	54	0	0	0	0	7	.0
G	30	Peter Sidorkiewicz	HFD	35	0	1	1	0	2	0	0	0	0	0	.0
G	35	Kay Whitmore	HFD	45	0	1	1	0	16	0	0	0	0	0	.0
D	40	Jergus Baca	HFD	1	0	0	0	1–	0	0	0	0	0	1	.0
D	4*	Dan Keczmer	HFD	1	0	0	0	1–	0	0	0	0	0	2	.0
L	37*	Patrick Poulin	HFD	1	0	0	0	1–	2	0	0	0	0	0	.0
C	28	Mike Tomlak	HFD	6	0	0	0	2–	0	0	0	0	0	10	.0
D	46*	Todd Richards	HFD	6	0	0	0	2–	2	0	0	0	0	3	.0
G	40	Frank Pietrangelo	PIT	5	0	0	0	0	0	0	0	0	0	0	.0
			HFD	5	0	0	0	0	0	0	0	0	0	0	.0
			TOTAL	10	0	0	0	0	0	0	0	0	0	0	.0

Goaltending

No.	Goaltender	GPI	Mins	Avg	W	L	T	EN	SO	GA	SA	S%
40	Frank Pietrangelo	5	306	2.35	3	1	1	0	0	12	156	.923
30	Peter Sidorkiewicz	35	1995	3.34	9	19	6	3	2	111	940	.882
35	Kay Whitmore	45	2567	3.62	14	21	6	2	3	155	1292	.880
	Totals	**80**	**4878**	**3.48**	**26**	**41**	**13**	**5**	**5**	**283**	**2393**	**.882**

Playoffs

Pos	#	Player	Team	GP	G	A	Pts	+/–	PIM	PP	SH	GW	GT	S	%
L	12	Murray Craven	HFD	7	3	3	6	0	6	0	1	0	0	20	15.0
C	21	Andrew Cassels	HFD	7	2	4	6	1–	6	1	0	0	0	10	20.0
L	20	Yvon Corriveau	HFD	7	3	2	5	1–	18	2	0	1	1	17	17.6
D	3	Zarley Zalapski	HFD	7	2	3	5	1	6	0	0	0	0	25	8.0
L	7	Randy Cunneyworth	HFD	7	3	0	3	0	9	1	1	1	0	11	27.3
C	11	John Cullen	HFD	7	2	1	3	2–	12	1	0	1	0	18	11.1
L	37*	Patrick Poulin	HFD	7	2	1	3	2	0	1	0	0	0	3	66.7
D	46*	Todd Richards	HFD	5	0	3	3	2	4	0	0	0	0	8	.0
D	27	Doug Houda	HFD	6	0	2	2	2–	13	0	0	0	0	4	.0
L	34	Mikael Andersson	HFD	7	0	2	2	2–	6	0	0	0	0	10	.0
R	16	Pat Verbeek	HFD	7	0	2	2	1	12	0	0	0	0	15	.0
C	8*	Geoff Sanderson	HFD	7	1	0	1	1–	2	0	0	0	0	9	11.1
D	32	Brad Shaw	HFD	3	0	1	1	2–	4	0	0	0	0	9	.0
C	44	Paul Gillis	HFD	5	0	1	1	1	0	0	0	0	0	2	.0
L	24	Bobby Holik	HFD	7	0	1	1	2–	6	0	0	0	0	18	.0
D	5	Steve Konroyd	HFD	7	0	1	1	1–	2	0	0	0	0	16	.0
D	29	Randy Ladouceur	HFD	7	0	1	1	0	11	0	0	0	0	2	.0
G	35	Kay Whitmore	HFD	1	0	0	0	0	0	0	0	0	0	0	.0
D	6	Adam Burt	HFD	2	0	0	0	1–	0	0	0	0	0	0	.0
R	26	Mark Hunter	HFD	4	0	0	0	1	6	0	0	0	0	4	.0
D	25	Marc Bergevin	HFD	5	0	0	0	1	2	0	0	0	0	7	.0
R	36	Daniel Shank	HFD	5	0	0	0	0	22	0	0	0	0	0	.0
G	40	Frank Pietrangelo	HFD	7	0	0	0	0	0	0	0	0	0	0	.0

Goaltending

No.	Goaltender	GPI	Mins	Avg	W	L	EN	SO	GA	SA	S%
40	Frank Pietrangelo	7	425	2.68	3	4	1	0	19	244	.922
35	Kay Whitmore	1	19	3.16	0	0	0	0	1	5	.800
	Totals	**7**	**446**	**2.83**	**3**	**4**	**1**	**0**	**21**	**250**	**.916**

General Managers' History

Jack Kelly, 1979-80 to 1981-82; Emile Francis, 1982-83 to 1988-89; Ed Johnston, 1989-90 to 1991-92; Brian Burke, 1992-93.

Coaching History

Don Blackburn, 1979-80; Don Blackburn and Larry Pleau, 1980-81; Larry Pleau, 1981-82; Larry Kish and Larry Pleau and John Cuniff, 1982- 83; Jack "Tex" Evans, 1983-84 to 1986-87; Jack "Tex" Evans and Larry Pleau, 1987-88; Larry Pleau, 1988-89; Rick Ley, 1989-90 to 1990-91; Jim Roberts, 1991-92; Paul Holmgren, 1992-93.

Captains' History

Rick Ley, 1979-80; Rick Ley, Mark Howe and Mike Rogers, 1980-81. Dave Keon, 1981-82; Russ Anderson, 1982-83; Mark Johnson, 1983-84; Mark Johnson and Ron Francis, 1984-85; Ron Francis, 1985-86 to 1990-91; Randy Ladouceur, 1991-92.

Club Records

Team

(Figures in brackets for season records are games played; records for fewest points, wins, ties, losses, goals, goals against are for 70 or more games)

Record		
Most Points	93	1986-87 (80)
Most Wins	43	1986-87 (80)
Most Ties	19	1979-80 (80)
Most Losses	54	1982-83 (80)
Most Goals	332	1985-86 (80)
Most Goals Against	403	1982-83 (80)
Fewest Points	45	1982-83 (80)
Fewest Wins	19	1982-83 (80)
Fewest Ties	4	1985-86 (80)
Fewest Losses	30	1986-87 (80)
Fewest Goals	238	1990-91 (80)
Fewest Goals Against	267	1987-88 (80)
Longest Winning Streak		
Over-all	7	Mar. 16-29/85
Home	5	Mar. 17-29/85
Away	6	Nov. 10-Dec. 7/90
Longest Undefeated Streak		
Over-all	10	Jan. 20-Feb. 10/82 (6 wins, 4 ties)
Home	7	Mar. 15-Apr. 5/86 (5 wins, 2 ties)
Away	6	Jan. 23-Feb. 10/82 (3 wins, 3 ties) Nov. 30-Dec. 26/89 (5 wins, 1 tie) Nov. 10-Dec. 7/90
Longest Losing Streak		
Over-all	9	Feb. 19/83-Mar. 8/83
Home	6	Feb. 19/83-Mar. 12/83 Feb. 10-Mar. 3/85
Away	13	Dec. 18/82-Feb. 5/83
Longest Winless Streak		
Over-all	14	Jan. 4/92-Feb. 9/92 (8 losses, 6 ties)
Home	13	Jan. 15-Mar. 10/85 (11 losses, 2 ties)
Away	15	Nov. 11/79-Jan. 9/80 (11 losses, 4 ties)
Most Shutouts, Season	5	1986-87 (80)
Most PIM, Season	2,209	1990-91 (80)
Most Goals, Game	11	Feb. 12/84 (Edm. 0 at Hfd. 11) Oct. 19/85 (Mtl. 6 at Hfd. 11) Jan. 17/86 (Que. 6 at Hfd. 11) Mar. 15/86 (Chi. 4 at Hfd. 11)

Individual

Record		
Most Seasons	10	Ron Francis
Most Games	714	Ron Francis
Most Goals, Career	264	Ron Francis
Most Assists, Career	557	Ron Francis
Most Points, Career	821	Ron Francis (264 goals, 557 assists)
Most PIM, Career	1,368	Torrie Robertson
Most Shutouts, Career	13	Mike Liut
Longest Consecutive Games Streak	419	Dave Tippett (Mar. 3/84-Oct. 7/89)
Most Goals, Season	56	Blaine Stoughton (1979-80)
Most Assists, Season	69	Ron Francis (1989-90)
Most Points, Season	105	Mike Rogers (1979-80) (44 goals, 61 assists) (1980-81) (40 goals, 65 assists)
Most PIM, Season	358	Torrie Robertson (1985-86)
Most Points, Defenseman Season	69	Dave Babych (1985-86) (14 goals, 55 assists)
Most Points, Center, Season	105	Mike Rogers (1979-80) (44 goals, 61 assists) Mike Rogers (1980-81) (40 goals, 65 assists)
Most Points, Right Wing, Season	100	Blaine Stoughton (1979-80) (56 goals, 44 assists)
Most Points, Left Wing, Season	80	Pat Boutette (1980-81) (28 goals, 52 assists)
Most Points, Rookie, Season	72	Sylvain Turgeon (1983-84) (40 goals, 32 assists)
Most Shutouts, Season	4	Mike Liut (1986-87) Peter Sidorkiewicz (1988-89)
Most Goals, Game	4	Jordy Douglas (Feb. 3/80) Ron Francis (Feb. 12/84)
Most Assists, Game	6	Ron Francis (Mar. 5/87)
Most Points, Game	6	Paul Lawless (Jan. 4/87) Ron Francis (Mar. 5/87, Oct. 8/89)

Retired Numbers

2	Rick Ley	1979-1981
9	Gordie Howe	1979-1980
19	John McKenzie	1976-1979

1991-92 Results

Home			Away		
Oct. 8	Montreal	2-2	**Oct.** 5	Quebec	2-4
12	NY Rangers	5-2	14	Montreal	4-3
19	Buffalo	4-1	16	Winnipeg	3-2
23	San Jose	3-0	27	Buffalo	1-5
26	Chicago	2-4	**Nov.** 1	Detroit	5-8
30	Los Angeles	4-4	2	Pittsburgh	6-5
Nov. 6	Calgary	2-3	9	St Louis	4-3
12	Quebec	5-4	10	Chicago	0-3
14	Montreal	2-2	17	Toronto	3-1
16	Boston	4-5	22	New Jersey	2-8
23	Washington	2-3	25	Quebec	2-5
30	Montreal	3-2	27	Philadelphia	7-3
Dec. 4	Toronto	0-3	**Dec.** 1	Boston	4-5
7	Buffalo	6-6	13	Buffalo	8-4
14	NY Rangers	2-6	21	Montreal	2-3
17	NY Islanders	2-4	26	Boston	2-3
19	New Jersey	1-4	28	Quebec	1-4
23	Buffalo	4-3	**Jan.** 9	NY Islanders	1-2
29	NY Islanders	6-4	11	Montreal	2-3
Jan. 2	Quebec	4-1	16	Boston	3-4
4	Washington	2-2	26	Montreal*	1-3
15	Boston	3-4	31	Edmonton	1-4
21	Winnipeg	3-3	**Feb.** 1	Vancouver	4-4
25	Boston*	4-4	4	San Jose	5-6
28	Minnesota	3-4	6	Los Angeles	5-5
Feb. 9	Minnesota*	4-4	15	New Jersey*	1-4
11	Buffalo	5-1	16	Buffalo	4-5
13	Edmonton	1-3	27	Pittsburgh	8-4
19	Montreal	2-2	29	Minnesota*	5-4
22	Quebec*	4-0	**Mar.** 1	NY Rangers	4-9
23	Detroit*	0-4	9	Quebec	0-2
25	St Louis	2-5	13	Winnipeg	1-0
Mar. 3	Boston	4-0	14	Edmonton	1-3
5	Quebec	4-10	16	Calgary	4-3
7	Vancouver	1-5	18	Vancouver	2-3
11	Los Angeles	4-0	24	Washington	8-2
21	San Jose	4-5	26	St Louis	2-7
22	Pittsburgh	2-2	29	Buffalo	2-2
28	Chicago	1-3	**Apr.** 2	Philadelphia	4-3
Apr. 4	Philadelphia*	4-2	5	Boston	3-6

*Denotes afternoon game

All-time Record vs. Other Clubs

Regular Season

	At Home							On Road							Total						
	GP	W	L	T	GF	GA	PTS	GP	W	L	T	GF	GA	PTS	GP	W	L	T	GF	GA	PTS
Boston	48	22	19	7	176	171	51	48	11	33	4	126	201	26	96	33	52	11	302	372	77
Buffalo	48	19	23	6	152	151	44	48	16	25	7	160	199	39	96	35	48	13	312	350	83
Calgary	20	7	10	3	69	80	17	20	4	15	1	71	110	9	40	11	25	4	140	190	26
Chicago	21	9	10	2	75	72	20	20	5	12	3	58	94	13	41	14	22	5	133	166	33
Detroit	20	13	6	1	80	55	27	20	7	7	6	64	74	20	40	20	13	7	144	129	47
Edmonton	20	8	9	3	83	76	19	21	2	16	3	61	97	7	41	10	25	6	144	173	26
Los Angeles	21	12	6	3	88	83	27	20	6	11	3	80	87	15	41	18	17	6	168	170	42
Minnesota	21	9	11	1	76	79	19	20	8	11	1	69	87	17	41	17	22	2	145	166	36
Montreal	48	17	23	8	151	177	42	48	8	34	6	139	221	22	96	25	57	14	290	398	64
New Jersey	20	11	5	4	76	60	26	21	9	10	2	87	80	20	41	20	15	6	163	140	46
NY Islanders	21	8	10	3	70	83	19	20	6	12	2	51	78	14	41	14	22	5	121	161	33
NY Rangers	21	12	7	2	85	76	26	20	6	12	2	62	90	14	41	18	19	4	147	166	40
Philadelphia	20	9	7	4	85	82	22	21	6	14	1	59	87	13	41	15	21	5	144	169	35
Pittsburgh	20	12	7	1	92	78	25	21	9	9	3	91	92	21	41	21	16	4	183	170	46
Quebec	48	21	17	10	172	170	52	48	13	28	7	152	210	33	96	34	45	17	324	380	85
St. Louis	20	8	10	2	65	65	18	21	8	11	2	72	81	18	41	16	21	4	137	146	36
San Jose	2	1	1	0	7	5	2	1	0	1	0	5	6	0	3	1	2	0	12	11	2
Toronto	20	12	5	3	97	67	27	20	12	6	2	85	70	26	40	24	11	5	182	137	53
Vancouver	20	8	8	4	67	74	20	21	7	8	6	59	72	20	41	15	16	10	126	146	40
Washington	21	7	11	3	67	83	17	20	8	11	1	61	70	17	41	15	22	4	128	153	34
Winnipeg	20	10	5	5	85	65	25	21	10	11	0	73	74	20	41	20	16	5	158	139	45
Totals	**520**	**235**	**210**	**75**	**1918**	**1852**	**545**	**520**	**161**	**297**	**62**	**1685**	**2180**	**384**	**1040**	**396**	**507**	**137**	**3603**	**4032**	**929**

Playoffs

	Series	W	L	GP	W	L	T	GF	GA	Last Mtg.	Round	Result
Boston	2	0	2	13	5	8	0	38	47	1991	DSF	L 2-4
Montreal	5	0	5	27	8	19	0	70	96	1992	DSF	L 3-4
Quebec	2	1	1	9	5	4	0	35	34	1987	DSF	L 2-4
Totals	**9**	**1**	**8**	**49**	**18**	**31**	**0**	**143**	**177**			

Playoff Results 1992-88

Year	Round	Opponent	Result	GF	GA
1992	DSF	Montreal	L 3-4	18	21
1991	DSF	Boston	L 2-4	17	24
1990	DSF	Boston	L 3-4	21	23
1989	DSF	Montreal	L 0-4	11	18
1988	DSF	Montreal	L 2-4	20	23

Abbreviations: Round: F – Final; **CF** – conference final; **DF** – division final; **DSF** – division semi-final; **SF** – semi-final; **QF** – quarter-final; **PR** – preliminary round. **GA** – goals against; **GF** – goals for.

Entry Draft Selections 1992-79

1992
Pick
9 Robert Petrovicky
47 Andrei Nikolishin
57 Jan Vopat
79 Kevin Smyth
81 Jason McBain
143 Jarret Reid
153 Ken Belanger
177 Konstantin Korotkov
201 Greg Zwakman
225 Steven Halko
249 Joacim Esbjors

1991
Pick
9 Patrick Poulin
31 Martin Hamrlik
53 Todd Hall
59 Mikael Nylander
75 Jim Storm
119 Mike Harding
141 Brian Mueller
163 Steve Yule
185 Chris Belanger
207 Jason Currie
229 Mike Santonelli
251 Rob Peters

1990
Pick
15 Mark Greig
36 Geoff Sanderson
57 Mike Lenarduzzi
78 Chris Bright
120 Cory Keenan
141 Jergus Baca
162 Martin D'Orsonnens
183 Corey Osmak
204 Espen Knutsen
225 Tommie Eriksen
246 Denis Chalifoux

1989
Pick
10 Robert Holik
52 Blair Atcheynum
73 Jim McKenzie
94 James Black
115 Jerome Bechard
136 Scott Daniels
157 Raymond Saumier
178 Michel Picard
199 Trevor Buchanan
220 John Battice
241 Peter Kasowski

1988
Pick
11 Chris Govedaris
32 Barry Richter
74 Dean Dyer
95 Scott Morrow
116 Corey Beaulieu
137 Kerry Russell
158 Jim Burke
179 Mark Hirth
200 Wayde Bucsis
221 Rob White
242 Dan Slatalla

1987
Pick
18 Jody Hull
39 Adam Burt
81 Terry Yake
102 Marc Rousseau
123 Jeff St. Cyr
144 Greg Wolf
165 John Moore
186 Joe Day
228 Kevin Sullivan
249 Steve Laurin

1986
Pick
11 Scott Young
32 Marc Laforge
74 Brian Chapman
95 Bill Horn
116 Joe Quinn
137 Steve Torrel
158 Ron Hoover
179 Robert Glasgow
200 Sean Evoy
221 Cal Brown
242 Brian Verbeek

1985
Pick
5 Dana Murzyn
26 Kay Whitmore
68 Gary Callaghan
110 Shane Churla
131 Chris Brant
152 Brian Puhalsky
173 Greg Dornbach
194 Paul Tory
215 Jerry Pawlowski
236 Bruce Hill

1984
Pick
11 Sylvain Cote
110 Mike Millar
131 Mike Vellucci
173 John Devereaux
193 Brent Regan
214 Jim Culhane
234 Pete Abric

1983
Pick
2 Sylvain Turgeon
20 David Jensen
23 Ville Siren
61 Leif Carlsson
64 Dave MacLean
72 Ron Chyzowski
104 Brian Johnson
124 Joe Reekie
143 Chris Duperron
144 James Falle
164 Bill Fordy
193 Reine Karlsson
204 Allan Acton
224 Darcy Kaminski

1982
Pick
14 Paul Lawless
35 Mark Paterson
56 Kevin Dineen
67 Ulf Samuelsson
88 Ray Ferraro
109 Randy Gilhen
130 Jim Johannson
151 Mickey Kramptoich
172 Kevin Skilliter
214 Martin Linse
235 Randy Cameron

1981
Pick
4 Ron Francis
61 Paul MacDermid
67 Michael Hoffman
93 Bill Maguire
103 Dan Bourbonnais
130 John Mokosak
151 Denis Dore
172 Jeff Poeschl
193 Larry Power

1980
Pick
8 Fred Arthur
29 Michel Galarneau
50 Mickey Volcan
71 Kevin McClelland
92 Darren Jensen
113 Mario Cerri
134 Mike Martin
155 Brent Denat
176 Paul Fricker
197 Lorne Bokshowan

1979
Pick
18 Ray Allison
39 Stuart Smith
60 Don Nachbaur
81 Ray Neufeld
102 Mark Renaud
123 Dave McDonald

General Manager

BURKE, BRIAN
General Manager, Hartford Whalers. Born in Providence, RI, June 30, 1955.

Brian Burke became the fifth general manager of the Hartford Whalers on May 26, 1992, following a five-year term as the Vancouver Canucks' vice president and director of hockey operations. A native of Providence, RI, Burke captained the Providence College Friars in 1977 before turning professional with the AHL's Maine Mariners. A graduate of the Harvard University School of Law, Burke spent six years in active practice, during which time he became a player's agent, representing more than 45 clients. Hired by the Canucks in 1987, he played a prominent role in the Canucks' rise from a fourth-place club to a first-place squad and Stanley Cup contender.

Coach

HOLMGREN, PAUL
Coach, Hartford Whalers. Born in St. Paul, MN, December 2, 1955.

Paul Holmgren became the seventh man to be named coach of the Hartford Whalers, succeeding Jimmy Roberts, on June 15, 1992. A sixth round draft selection of the Philadelphia Flyers in 1975, Holmgren spent nine years with the team before finishing his career with the Minnesota North Stars in 1985. The next season, he was named as an assistant to Mike Keenan, spending three years in that role. In 1988, Holmgren became the first former-Flyer to be named as head-coach, serving in that capacity for four seasons. In Philadelphia, Holmgren compiled a 107-126-31 record before being replaced by Bill Dineen on December 4, 1991.

Coaching Record

		Regular Season					Playoffs			
Season	Team	Games	W	L	T	%	Games	W	L	%
1988-89	Philadelphia (NHL)	80	36	36	8	.500	19	10	9	.526
1989-90	Philadelphia (NHL)	80	30	39	11	.444	....	....	....	....
1990-91	Philadelphia (NHL)	80	33	37	10	.475	....	....	....	....
1991-92	Philadelphia (NHL)	24	8	14	2	.375	....	....	....	....
	NHL Totals	264	107	126	31	.464	19	10	9	.526

Club Directory

Hartford Whalers
242 Trumbull Street
Eighth Floor
Hartford, Connecticut 06103
Phone **203/728-3366**
GM FAX 203/493-2423
FAX 203/522-7707
Capacity: 15,635

Managing General Partner/Governor.......... Richard Gordon

Hockey Department
General Manager.......... Brian P. Burke
Assistant General Manager.......... Ken Schinkel
Assistant to the General Manager.......... Tom Rowe
Head Coach.......... Paul Holmgren
Assistant Coaches.......... Kevin McCarthy, Pierre Maguire
Strength and Conditioning Coach.......... Doug McKenney
Director of Pro Scouting.......... Kevin Maxwell
Pro Scout.......... Claude Larose
Amateur Scouting Staff.......... Leo Boivin, Bruce Haralson, Fred Gore, Willy Lindstrom, Roger Oxborough, Steve Rooney
Executive Secretary.......... Anne Sullivan
Secretary.......... Karen Stansfield
Medical Trainer.......... Frank "Bud" Gouvela
Equipment Manager.......... Skip Cunningham
Assistant Equipment Manager.......... Keith Parker
Assistant to Equipment Manager.......... Dave Nichols
Club Doctor.......... Dr. John Fulkerson
Club Dentist.......... Dr. Robert Hall

Administration
President/Alternate Governor.......... Emile Francis
Vice President of Finance & Administration.......... Michael J. Amendola
Vice President of Marketing & Sales.......... Rick Francis
Advertising Sales Manager.......... Richard Chmura
Director of Public Relations.......... John H. Forslund
Public Relations Assistant.......... Mary Lynn Gorman
Chief Statistician/Head Archivist.......... Frank Polnaszek
Ticket Sales Manager.......... Jim Baldwin
Ticket Office Supervisors.......... Mike Barnes, Chris O'Connor

General Information
Radio Play-by-Play.......... Chuck Kaiton
Radio Color, Home Games.......... Arnold Dean
Radio Color, Road Games.......... John Forslund
TV/Cable Play-by-Play.......... Rick Peckham
TV/Cable Commentator.......... Gerry Cheevers
Cable TV Outlet.......... SportsChannel - New England
Radio Network Flagship Station.......... WTIC-AM (1080)
Home Ice.......... Hartford Civic Center Veterans Memorial Coliseum
Dimensions of Rink.......... 200 feet by 85 feet

John Cullen led Hartford in scoring in 1991-92, scoring 26 goals and adding 51 assists.

Los Angeles Kings

1991-92 Results: 35W-31L-14T 84PTS. Second, Smythe Division

Year-by-Year Record

Season	GP	Home W	Home L	Home T	Road W	Road L	Road T	Overall W	Overall L	Overall T	GF	GA	Pts.	Finished		Playoff Result
1991-92	80	20	11	9	15	20	5	35	31	14	287	296	84	2nd,	Smythe Div.	Lost Div. Semi-Final
1990-91	80	26	9	5	20	15	5	46	24	10	340	254	102	1st,	Smythe Div.	Lost Div. Final
1989-90	80	21	16	3	13	23	4	34	39	7	338	337	75	4th,	Smythe Div.	Lost Div. Final
1988-89	80	25	12	3	17	19	4	42	31	7	376	335	91	2nd,	Smythe Div.	Lost Div. Final
1987-88	80	19	18	3	11	24	5	30	42	8	318	359	68	4th,	Smythe Div.	Lost Div. Semi-Final
1986-87	80	20	17	3	11	24	5	31	41	8	318	341	70	4th,	Smythe Div.	Lost Div. Semi-Final
1985-86	80	9	27	4	14	22	4	23	49	8	284	389	54	5th,	Smythe Div.	Out of Playoffs
1984-85	80	20	14	6	14	18	8	34	32	14	339	326	82	4th,	Smythe Div.	Lost Div. Semi-Final
1983-84	80	13	19	8	10	25	5	23	44	13	309	376	59	5th,	Smythe Div.	Out of Playoffs
1982-83	80	20	13	7	7	28	5	27	41	12	308	365	66	5th,	Smythe Div.	Out of Playoffs
1981-82	80	19	15	6	5	26	9	24	41	15	314	369	63	4th,	Smythe Div.	Lost Div. Final
1980-81	80	22	11	7	21	13	6	43	24	13	337	290	99	2nd,	Norris Div.	Lost Prelim. Round
1979-80	80	18	13	9	12	23	5	30	36	14	290	313	74	2nd,	Norris Div.	Lost Prelim. Round
1978-79	80	20	13	7	14	21	5	34	34	12	292	286	80	3rd,	Norris Div.	Lost Prelim. Round
1977-78	80	18	16	6	13	18	9	31	34	15	243	245	77	3rd,	Norris Div.	Lost Prelim. Round
1976-77	80	20	13	7	14	18	8	34	31	15	271	241	83	2nd,	Norris Div.	Lost Quarter-Final
1975-76	80	22	13	5	16	20	4	38	33	9	263	265	85	2nd,	Norris Div.	Lost Quarter-Final
1974-75	80	22	7	11	20	10	10	42	17	21	269	185	105	2nd,	Norris Div.	Lost Prelim. Round
1973-74	78	22	13	4	11	20	8	33	33	12	233	231	78	3rd,	West Div.	Lost Quarter-Final
1972-73	78	21	11	7	10	25	4	31	36	11	232	245	73	6th,	West Div.	Out of Playoffs
1971-72	78	14	23	2	6	26	7	20	49	9	206	305	49	7th,	West Div.	Out of Playoffs
1970-71	78	17	14	8	8	26	5	25	40	13	239	303	63	5th,	West Div.	Out of Playoffs
1969-70	76	12	22	4	2	30	6	14	52	10	168	290	38	6th,	West Div.	Out of Playoffs
1968-69	76	19	14	5	5	28	5	24	42	10	185	260	58	4th,	West Div.	Lost Semi-Final
1967-68	74	20	13	4	11	20	6	31	33	10	200	224	72	2nd,	West Div.	Lost Quarter-Final

Schedule

Home		Away	
Oct.	Thur. 8 Detroit	Oct.	Tues. 6 Calgary
	Sat. 10 Winnipeg		Tues. 20 Calgary
	Tues. 13 San Jose		Fri. 23 Winnipeg
	Thur. 15 Calgary		Sat. 24 Minnesota
	Sat. 17 Boston		Tues. 27 NY Islanders
Nov.	Thur. 5 New Jersey		Thur. 29 Boston
	Sat. 7 Buffalo		Sat. 31 Hartford
	Thur. 12 Vancouver	Nov.	Sun. 8 San Jose
	Sat. 14 Edmonton		Tues. 10 Winnipeg
	Thur. 19 Chicago		Mon. 16 Vancouver
	Sat. 21 Toronto		Tues. 17 San Jose
Dec.	Thur. 3 Pittsburgh		Wed. 25 Edmonton
	Sat. 5 Hartford		Fri. 27 Detroit
	Tues. 8 Montreal		Sat. 28 Toronto
	(at Phoenix)	Dec.	Tues. 1 Chicago
	Thur. 10 Quebec		(at Milwaukee)
	Sat. 12 St Louis		Fri. 18 Edmonton
	Tues. 15 Tampa Bay		Sat. 19 Calgary
	Tues. 22 Vancouver		Sat. 26 San Jose
	Tues. 29 Philadelphia		Thur. 31 Vancouver
Jan.	Sat. 2 Montreal	Jan.	Fri. 8 Winnipeg
	Wed. 6 Tampa Bay		Sun. 10 Chicago
	Sat. 16 Winnipeg		Tues. 12 Ottawa
	Thur. 21 Vancouver		Thur. 14 New Jersey
	Sat. 23 NY Rangers		Tues. 19 Edmonton
	Tues. 26 San Jose	Feb.	Tues. 2 Quebec
	Thur. 28 Calgary		Wed. 3 Montreal
	Sat. 30 Chicago		Wed. 17 Minnesota
Feb.	Tues. 9 Edmonton		Thur. 18 Chicago
	Thur. 11 Detroit		Sat. 20 Washington*
	Sat. 13 Washington		Mon. 22 Tampa Bay
	Mon. 15 Vancouver*		Thur. 25 St Louis
	Sat. 27 Toronto	Mar.	Tues. 9 NY Rangers
Mar.	Tues. 2 Calgary		Thur. 11 Pittsburgh
	Thur. 4 Ottawa		Sat. 13 Philadelphia*
	Sat. 6 Edmonton		Sun. 14 Buffalo*
	Tues. 16 Winnipeg		Wed. 24 Vancouver
	Thur. 18 NY Islanders		Fri. 26 Edmonton
	Sat. 20 St Louis		Sun. 28 Winnipeg*
Apr.	Sat. 3 Minnesota*		Mon. 29 Detroit
	Tues. 6 Calgary		Wed. 31 Toronto
	Thur. 8 San Jose	Apr.	Sat. 10 San Jose
	Thur. 15 Vancouver		Tues. 13 Vancouver

* Denotes afternoon game.

Home Starting Times:
All Games .... 7:35 p.m.
Except Matinees .... 1:05 p.m.

Franchise date: June 5, 1967

26th NHL Season

Tony Granato had his finest season in 1991-92, scoring 39 goals for the Los Angeles Kings.

1992-93 Player Personnel

FORWARDS	HT	WT	S	Place of Birth	Date	1991-92 Club
BERG, Bob	6-1	190	L	Beamsville, Ont.	7/2/70	Phoenix-Richmond
BJUGSTAD, Scott	6-1	185	L	St. Paul, MN	6/2/61	Los Angeles-Phoenix
BOGOYEVAC, Steve	6-0	175	R	Hollywood, CA	2/12/68	Alaska-Anch.
BREAULT, Frank	5-11	190	L	Acton Vale, Que.	11/5/67	Los Angeles-Phoenix
BRESLIN, Tim	6-0	180	L	Downers Grove, IL	12/8/67	Phoenix
BROWN, Kevin	6-1	212	R	Birmingham, Eng.	5/11/74	Belleville
CONACHER, Pat	5-8	190	L	Edmonton, Alta.	5/1/59	New Jersey-Utica
COUTURIER, Sylvain	6-2	205	L	Greenfield Park, Que.	4/23/68	Los Angeles-Phoenix
CROWE, Phil	6-2	220	R	Olds, Alta.	4/14/70	Columbus-Adirondack
DANYLUK, Cam	6-4	215	L	Ft. Saskatchewan, Alta.	9/6/72	Medicine Hat
DONNELLY, Mike	5-11	185	L	Livonia, MI	10/10/63	Los Angeles
FLANAGAN, Joe	6-0	185	R	Arlington, MA	3/5/69	N. Hampshire
GRANATO, Tony	5-10	185	R	Downers Grove, IL	7/25/64	Los Angeles
GRETZKY, Wayne	6-0	170	L	Brantford, Ont.	1/26/61	Los Angeles
HILLER, Jim	6-2	200	R	Port Alberni, B.C.	5/15/69	N. Michigan
KASTELIC, Ed	6-4	215	L	Toronto, Ont.	1/29/64	Hartford
KRAMER, Ted	6-0	190	R	Findlay, OH	10/29/69	Michigan
KUDELSKI, Bob	6-1	200	R	Springfield, MA	3/3/64	Los Angeles
KURRI, Jari	6-1	195	R	Helsinki, Fin.	5/18/60	Los Angeles
LANG, Robert	6-2	180	R	Teplice, Czech.	12/19/70	Litvinov-Czech. National
LARKIN, Jim	6-0	175	L	South Weymouth, MA	4/15/70	Vermont
LEVEQUE, Guy	5-11	166	R	Kingston, Ont.	2/28/72	Cornwall
LONGAUER, Michal	6-2	200	R	Banska, Czech.	2/26/72	Hull
McCOSH, Shawn	6-0	188	R	Oshawa, Ont.	6/5/69	Phoenix-Los Angeles
McINTYRE, John	6-1	175	L	Ravenwood, Ont.	4/29/69	Los Angeles
McSORLEY, Marty	6-1	225	R	Hamilton, Ont.	5/18/63	Los Angeles
MILLEN, Corey	5-7	168	R	Clouquet, MN	3/30/64	NYR-Bing.-L.A.
MILLER, Jay	6-2	210	L	Wellesley, MA	7/16/60	Los Angeles
PISIAK, Ryan	6-2	190	R	Swift Current, Sask.	5/12/74	Pr. Albert
REDMOND, Keith	6-3	208	L	Richmond Hill, Ont.	10/25/72	Bowling Green-Belleville-Detroit
ROBITAILLE, Luc	6-1	190	L	Montreal, Que.	2/17/66	Los Angeles
RYCHEL, Warren	6-0	190	L	Tecumseh, Ont.	5/12/67	Kalamazoo
SANDSTROM, Tomas	6-2	200	L	Jakobstad, Fin.	9/4/64	Los Angeles
SAUMIER, Marc	5-10	190	L	Hull, Que.	4/18/67	Phoenix
SCHMIDT, Chris	6-0	186	L	Regina, Sask.	6/4/72	Moose Jaw
SEGUIN, Brett	5-9	199	L	Rochester, NY	2/20/72	Ottawa
SEMCHUK, Brandy	6-1	187	R	Calgary, Alta.	9/22/71	Phoenix-Raleigh
SHEVALIER, Jeff	5-11	180	L	Mississauga, Ont.	3/14/74	North Bay
TAYLOR, Dave	6-0	195	R	Levack, Ont.	12/4/55	Los Angeles
VUKONICH, Mike	6-1	220	L	Duluth, MN	5/11/68	Phoenix
WHYTE, Sean	6-0	198	R	Sudbury, Ont.	5/4/70	Phoenix-Los Angeles
WILLIAMS, Darryl	5-11	185	L	Mt. Pearl, Nfld.	2/9/68	N. Hampshire-Phx.

DEFENSEMEN	HT	WT	S	Place of Birth	Date	1991-92 Club
AHOLA, Peter	6-3	205	L	Espoo, Fin.	5/14/68	Los Angeles-Phoenix
BLAKE, Rob	6-3	215	R	Simcoe, Ont.	12/10/69	Los Angeles
BOOTH, Derek	6-1	200	L	Niagara Falls, Ont.	7/19/70	Phoenix
CHAPDELAINE, Rene	6-1	195	R	Weyland, Sask.	9/27/66	Phoenix-Los Angeles
COFFEY, Paul	6-0	200	L	Weston, Ont.	6/1/61	Pittsburgh-Los Angeles
GAUL, Michael	6-1	197	R	Lachine, Que.	4/28/73	Laval
HOCKING, Justin	6-4	206	R	Coronation, Alta.	1/9/74	Spokane
HOLDEN, Paul	6-3	210	L	Kitchener, Ont.	3/15/70	Phoenix
HUDDY, Charlie	6-0	210	L	Oshawa, Ont.	6/2/59	Los Angeles
MacDONALD, Kevin	6-0	195	L	Prescott, Ont.	2/24/66	Phoenix
MAHER, Jim	6-1	205	L	Warren, MI	6/30/70	Ill.-Chicago-Phoenix
MASKARINEC, Martin	6-0	175	L	Liberec, Czech.	2/3/69	Sparta Prague
OLSSON, Mattias	6-1	183	L	Karlstad, Sweden	4/1/71	Farjestad
ROBISON, Jeff	6-1	183	L	Norwood, MA	6/3/70	Providence
RUARK, Mike	6-2	190	L	Calgary, Alta.	4/18/71	Phoenix
SNEDDON, Kevin	6-1	188	L	St. Catharines, Ont.	4/23/70	Harvard
STEWART, Dave	5-11	195	L	Norwood, Ont.	1/11/72	Kingston
SYDOR, Darryl	6-0	205	L	Edmonton, Alta.	5/13/72	Kamloops-L.A.
THOMPSON, Brent	6-2	190	L	Calgary, Alta.	1/9/71	Phoenix-Los Angeles
TRETOWICZ, Dave	5-11	195	L	Liverpool, NY	3/15/69	Phoenix-Team USA
WATTERS, Tim	5-11	185	L	Kamloops, B.C.	7/25/59	Los Angeles-Phoenix

GOALTENDERS	HT	WT	C	Place of Birth	Date	1991-92 Club
ALLAN, Sandy	6-0	175	L	Nassau, Bahamas	1/22/74	North Bay
AUSTIN, Darcy	5-10	185	L	Red Deer, Alta.	4/17/72	Lethbridge
BRATHWAITE, Fred	5-7	170	L	Nepean, Ont.	11/24/72	London-Oshawa
GILMOUR, Darryl	6-0	171	L	Winnipeg, Man.	2/13/67	Phoenix
GOVERDE, David	6-0	210	R	Toronto, Ont.	4/9/70	Phx.-N.H.-L.A.
HRUDEY, Kelly	5-10	189	L	Edmonton, Alta.	1/13/61	Los Angeles
JAKS, Pauli	6-0	194	L	Schaffhausen, Switz.	1/25/72	Ambri Piotta
STAUBER, Robb	5-11	180	L	Duluth, MN	11/25/67	Phoenix

1991-92 Scoring

Regular Season

Pos	#.	Player	Team	GP	G	A	Pts	+/–	PIM	PP	SH	GW	GT	S	%
C	99	Wayne Gretzky	L.A.	74	31	90	121	12–	34	12	2	2	1	215	14.4
L	20	Luc Robitaille	L.A.	80	44	63	107	4–	95	26	0	6	1	240	18.3
D	77	Paul Coffey	PIT	54	10	54	64	4	62	5	0	1	0	207	4.8
			L.A.	10	1	4	5	3–	25	0	0	0	0	25	4.0
			TOTAL	64	11	58	69	1	87	5	0	1	0	232	4.7
L	21	Tony Granato	L.A.	80	39	29	68	4	187	7	2	8	1	223	17.5
L	17	Jari Kurri	L.A.	73	23	37	60	24–	24	10	1	3	0	167	13.8
C	23	Corey Millen	NYR	11	1	4	5	1–	10	0	0	0	0	20	5.0
			L.A.	46	20	21	41	3	44	8	1	3	0	89	22.5
			TOTAL	57	21	25	46	2	54	8	1	3	0	109	19.3
L	11	Mike Donnelly	L.A.	80	29	16	45	5	20	0	1	4	0	197	14.7
C	37	Bob Kudelski	L.A.	80	22	21	43	15–	42	2	1	2	0	155	14.2
R	7	Tomas Sandstrom	L.A.	49	17	22	39	2–	70	5	0	4	0	147	11.6
R	18	Dave Taylor	L.A.	77	10	19	29	10	63	0	0	2	0	81	12.3
D	33	Marty McSorley	L.A.	71	7	22	29	13–	268	2	1	0	0	119	5.9
C	44	John Mcintyre	L.A.	73	5	19	24	0	100	0	0	1	0	40	12.5
D	22	Charlie Huddy	L.A.	56	4	19	23	10–	43	2	1	0	0	109	3.7
D	4	Rob Blake	L.A.	57	7	13	20	5–	102	5	0	0	0	131	5.3
D	26*	Peter Ahola	L.A.	71	7	12	19	12	101	0	0	0	1	74	9.5
D	19	Larry Robinson	L.A.	56	3	10	13	1	37	0	0	0	0	46	6.5
L	29	Jay Miller	L.A.	67	4	7	11	8–	249	0	0	0	0	32	12.5
L	14*	Kyosti Karjalainen	L.A.	28	1	8	9	4	12	0	0	0	0	20	5.0
D	5	Tim Watters	L.A.	37	0	7	7	2–	92	0	0	0	0	29	.0
L	8	Scott Bjugstad	L.A.	22	2	4	6	1–	10	0	0	0	0	25	8.0
D	40*	Darryl Sydor	L.A.	18	1	5	6	3–	22	0	0	0	0	18	5.6
D	56*	Brent Thompson	L.A.	27	0	5	5	7–	89	0	0	0	0	18	.0
C	12*	Sylvain Couturier	L.A.	14	3	1	4	3–	2	0	0	0	0	21	14.3
R	25	Jim Thomson	L.A.	45	1	2	3	1–	162	0	0	0	0	24	4.2
R	24*	Frank Breault	L.A.	6	1	0	1	0	30	0	0	0	0	6	16.7
G	43*	David Goverde	L.A.	2	0	1	1	0	0	0	0	0	0	0	.0
R	9	Ilkka Sinisalo	L.A.	3	0	1	1	0	2	0	0	0	0	3	.0
D	63*	Rene Chapdelaine	L.A.	16	0	1	1	0	10	0	0	0	0	6	.0
G	1	Steve Weeks	NYI	23	0	0	0	0	2	0	0	0	0	0	.0
			L.A.	7	0	1	1	0	0	0	0	0	0	0	.0
			TOTAL	30	0	1	1	0	2	0	0	0	0	0	.0
G	32	Kelly Hrudey	L.A.	60	0	1	1	0	12	0	0	0	0	0	.0
R	57*	Sean Whyte	L.A.	3	0	0	0	1–	0	0	0	0	0	0	.0
C	50*	Shawn McCosh	L.A.	4	0	0	0	0	4	0	0	0	0	2	.0

Goaltending

No.	Goaltender	GPI	Mins	Avg	W	L	T	EN	SO	GA	SA	S%
32	Kelly Hrudey	60	3509	3.37	26	17	13	4	1	197	1916	.897
36	Daniel Berthiaume	19	979	4.04	7	10	1	2	0	66	541	.878
1	Steve Weeks	7	252	4.05	1	3	0	1	0	17	136	.875
43	* David Goverde	2	120	4.50	1	1	0	0	0	9	63	.857
	Totals	**80**	**4874**	**3.64**	**35**	**31**	**14**	**7**	**1**	**296**	**2663**	**.889**

Playoffs

Pos	#	Player	Team	GP	G	A	Pts	+/–	PIM	PP	SH	GW	GT	S	%
D	77	Paul Coffey	L.A.	6	4	3	7	5–	2	3	0	0	0	28	14.3
L	20	Luc Robitaille	L.A.	6	3	4	7	1–	12	1	0	1	0	28	10.7
C	99	Wayne Gretzky	L.A.	6	2	5	7	3–	2	1	0	0	0	11	18.2
L	21	Tony Granato	L.A.	6	1	5	6	1	10	0	0	0	0	19	5.3
C	44	John Mcintyre	L.A.	6	0	4	4	2	12	0	0	0	0	0	.0
D	4	Rob Blake	L.A.	6	2	1	3	2	12	0	0	0	0	12	16.7
L	17	Jari Kurri	L.A.	4	1	2	3	1	4	1	0	0	0	10	10.0
R	7	Tomas Sandstrom	L.A.	6	0	3	3	2–	8	0	0	0	0	13	.0
L	29	Jay Miller	L.A.	5	1	1	2	2	12	0	0	0	0	3	33.3
D	22	Charlie Huddy	L.A.	6	1	1	2	2–	10	0	0	1	0	12	8.3
R	18	Dave Taylor	L.A.	6	1	1	2	0	20	0	0	0	0	5	20.0
L	11	Mike Donnelly	L.A.	6	1	0	1	2–	4	0	0	0	0	14	7.1
D	33	Marty McSorley	L.A.	6	1	0	1	1	21	0	0	0	0	10	10.0
L	14*	Kyosti Karjalainen	L.A.	3	0	1	1	0	2	0	0	0	0	2	.0
C	23	Corey Millen	L.A.	6	0	1	1	2–	6	0	0	0	0	6	.0
D	19	Larry Robinson	L.A.	2	0	0	0	2–	0	0	0	0	0	1	.0
D	56*	Brent Thompson	L.A.	4	0	0	0	1	4	0	0	0	0	2	.0
G	32	Kelly Hrudey	L.A.	6	0	0	0	0	0	0	0	0	0	0	.0
R	37	Bob Kudelski	L.A.	6	0	0	0	1–	0	0	0	0	0	5	.0
D	5	Tim Watters	L.A.	6	0	0	0	0	8	0	0	0	0	3	.0
D	26*	Peter Ahola	L.A.	6	0	0	0	4	2	0	0	0	0	8	.0

Goaltending

No.	Goaltender	GPI	Mins	Avg	W	L	EN	SO	GA	SA	S%
32	Kelly Hrudey	6	355	3.72	2	4	1	0	22	179	.877
	Totals	**6**	**360**	**3.83**	**2**	**4**	**1**	**0**	**23**	**180**	**.872**

General Managers' History

Larry Regan, 1967-68 to 1972-73; Larry Regan and Jake Milford, 1973-74; Jake Milford, 1974-75 to 1976-77; George Maguire, 1977-78 to 1982-83; George Maguire and Rogatien Vachon, 1983-84; Rogatien Vachon, 1984-85 to 1991-92; Nick Beverly, 1992-93.

Coaching History

Leonard "Red" Kelly, 1967-68 to 1968-69; Hal Laycoe and John Wilson, 1969-70; Larry Regan, 1970-71; Larry Regan and Fred Glover, 1971-72; Bob Pulford, 1972-73 to 1976-77; Ron Stewart, 1977-78; Bob Berry, 1978-79 to 1980-81; Parker MacDonald and Don Perry, 1981-82; Don Perry, 1982-83; Don Perry, Rogatien Vachon and Roger Neilson, 1983-84; Pat Quinn, 1984-85 to 1985-86; Pat Quinn and Mike Murphy 1986-87; Mike Murphy and Robbie Ftorek, 1987-88; Robbie Ftorek, 1988-89; Tom Webster, 1989-90 to 1991-92; Barry Melrose, 1992-93.

Captains' History

Bob Wall, 1967-68, 1968-69; Larry Cahan, 1969-70, 1970-71; Bob Pulford, 1971-72, 1972-73; Terry Harper, 1973-74, 1974-75; Mike Murphy, 1975-76 to 1980-81; Dave Lewis, 1981-82, 1982-83; Terry Ruskowski, 1983-84, 1984-85; Dave Taylor, 1985-86 to 1988-89; Wayne Gretzky, 1989-90 to date.

Club Records

Team

(Figures in brackets for season records are games played; records for fewest points, wins, ties, losses, goals, goals against are for 70 or more games)

Record		
Most Points	**105**	1974-75 (80)
Most Wins	**46**	1990-91 (80)
Most Ties	**21**	1974-75 (80)
Most Losses	**52**	1969-70 (76)
Most Goals	**376**	1988-89 (80)
Most Goals Against	**389**	1985-86 (80)
Fewest Points	**38**	1969-70 (76)
Fewest Wins	**14**	1969-70 (76)
Fewest Ties	**7**	1988-89 (80) 1989-90 (80)
Fewest Losses	**17**	1974-75 (80)
Fewest Goals	**168**	1969-70 (76)
Fewest Goals Against	**185**	1974-75 (80)
Longest Winning Streak		
Over-all	**8**	Oct. 21- Nov. 7/72
Home	**10**	Oct. 13- Nov. 20/90
Away	**8**	Dec. 18/74- Jan. 16/75
Longest Undefeated Streak		
Over-all	**11**	Feb. 28- Mar. 24/74 (9 wins, 2 ties)
Home	**11**	Oct. 11- Nov. 20/90 (10 wins, 1 tie)
Away	**11**	Oct. 10- Dec. 11/74 (6 wins, 5 ties)
Longest Losing Streak		
Over-all	**10**	Feb. 22- Mar. 9/84
Home	**9**	Feb. 8- Mar. 12/86
Away	**12**	Jan. 11- Feb. 15/70
Longest Winless Streak		
Over-all	**17**	Jan. 29- Mar. 5/70 (13 losses, 4 ties)
Home	**9**	Jan. 29- Mar. 5/70 (8 losses, 1 tie) Feb. 8- Mar. 12/86 (9 losses)
Away	**21**	Jan. 11- Apr. 3/70 (17 losses, 4 ties)
Most Shutouts, Season	**9**	1974-75 (80)
Most PIM, Season	**2,228**	1990-91 (80)
Most Goals, Game	**12**	Nov. 28/84 (Van. 1 at L.A. 12)

Individual

Record		
Most Seasons	**15**	Dave Taylor
Most Games	**1,030**	Dave Taylor
Most Goals, Career	**550**	Marcel Dionne
Most Assists, Career	**757**	Marcel Dionne
Most Points Career	**1,307**	Marcel Dionne
Most PIM, Career	**1,449**	Dave Taylor
Most Shutouts, Career	**32**	Rogie Vachon
Longest Consecutive Games Streak	**324**	Marcel Dionne (Jan. 7/78-Jan. 9/82)
Most Goals, Season	**70**	Bernie Nicholls (1988-89)
Most Assists, Season	**122**	Wayne Gretzky (1990-91)
Most Points, Season	**168**	Wayne Gretzky (1988-89) (54 goals, 114 assists)
Most PIM, Season	**358**	Dave Williams (1986-87)
Most Points, Defenseman Season	**76**	Larry Murphy (1980-81) (16 goals, 60 assists)
Most Points, Center, Season	**168**	Wayne Gretzky (1988-89) (54 goal, 114 assists)
Most Points, Right Wing, Season	**112**	Dave Taylor (1980-81) (47 goals, 65 assists)
Most Points, Left Wing, Season	**111**	Luc Robitaille (1987-88) (53 goals, 58 assists)
Most Points, Rookie, Season	**84**	Luc Robitaille (1986-87) (45 goals, 39 assists)
Most Shutouts, Season	**8**	Rogie Vachon (1976-77)
Most Goals, Game	**4**	Several players
Most Assists, Game	**6**	Bernie Nicholls (Dec. 1/88)
Most Points, Game	**8**	Bernie Nicholls (Dec. 1/88)

Retired Numbers

16	Marcel Dionne	1975-1987
30	Rogatien Vachon	1971-1978

All-time Record vs. Other Clubs

Regular Season

	At Home							On Road							Total						
	GP	W	L	T	GF	GA	PTS	GP	W	L	T	GF	GA	PTS	GP	W	L	T	GF	GA	PTS
Boston	51	17	29	5	175	194	39	52	10	39	3	142	247	23	103	27	68	8	317	441	62
Buffalo	44	16	20	8	150	155	40	43	14	21	8	137	179	36	87	30	41	16	287	334	76
Calgary	62	33	24	5	251	238	71	64	16	40	8	217	312	40	126	49	64	13	468	550	111
Chicago	50	22	23	5	175	174	49	50	17	26	7	151	195	41	100	39	49	12	326	369	90
Detroit	56	32	14	10	238	167	74	55	25	23	7	204	220	57	111	57	37	17	442	387	131
Edmonton	47	18	20	9	204	221	45	48	10	27	11	190	257	31	95	28	47	20	394	478	76
Hartford	20	11	6	3	87	80	25	21	6	12	3	83	88	15	41	17	18	6	170	168	40
Minnesota	55	26	15	14	210	169	66	55	14	33	8	146	221	36	110	40	48	22	356	390	102
Montreal	55	15	34	6	165	221	36	55	7	37	11	145	254	25	110	22	71	17	310	475	61
New Jersey	33	24	3	6	181	103	54	33	14	14	5	124	111	33	66	38	17	11	305	214	87
NY Islanders	35	14	14	7	118	116	35	35	12	19	4	104	130	28	70	26	33	11	222	246	63
NY Rangers	50	20	21	9	167	174	49	49	15	29	5	145	200	35	99	35	50	14	312	374	84
Philadelphia	56	17	32	7	166	190	41	54	14	33	7	140	211	35	110	31	65	14	306	401	76
Pittsburgh	60	38	14	8	232	155	84	62	19	35	8	198	235	46	122	57	49	16	430	390	130
Quebec	20	12	7	1	93	71	25	20	9	8	3	83	83	21	40	21	15	4	176	154	46
St. Louis	54	27	19	8	194	158	62	55	14	35	6	150	212	34	109	41	54	14	344	370	96
San Jose	4	3	0	1	22	15	7	3	2	1	0	9	8	4	7	5	1	1	31	23	11
Toronto	52	30	15	7	189	143	67	51	14	0	9	169	215	37	103	44	15	16	358	358	104
Vancouver	69	38	21	10	288	214	86	68	25	31	12	241	264	62	137	63	52	22	529	478	148
Washington	37	23	10	4	155	107	50	36	15	15	6	134	153	36	73	38	25	10	289	260	86
Winnipeg	44	16	20	8	181	182	40	46	17	22	7	174	203	41	90	33	42	15	355	385	81
Defunct Clubs	35	27	6	2	141	76	56	34	11	14	9	91	109	31	69	38	20	11	232	185	87
Totals	**989**	**479**	**367**	**143**	**3782**	**3323**	**1101**	**989**	**300**	**514**	**147**	**3177**	**4107**	**747**	**1978**	**779**	**881**	**290**	**6959**	**7430**	**1848**

Playoffs

	Series	W	L	GP	W	L	T	GF	GA	Last Mtg.	Round	Result
Boston	2	0	2	13	5	8	0	38	56	1977	QF	L 2-4
**Calgary	5	3	2	20	9	11	0	72	84	1990	DSF	W 4-2
Chicago	1	0	1	5	1	4	0	7	10	1974	QF	L 1-4
Edmonton	7	2	5	36	12	24	0	124	150	1992	DSF	L 2-4
Minnesota	1	0	1	7	3	4	0	21	26	1968	QF	L 3-4
NY Islanders	1	0	1	4	1	3	0	10	21	1980	PR	L 1-3
NY Rangers	2	0	2	6	1	5	0	14	32	1981	PR	L 1-3
St. Louis	1	0	1	4	0	4	0	5	16	1969	SF	L 0-4
Toronto	2	0	2	5	1	4	0	9	18	1978	PR	L 0-2
Vancouver	2	1	1	11	5	6	0	40	35	1991	DSF	W 4-2
Defunct Clubs	1	1	0	7	4	3	0	23	25			
Totals	**25**	**7**	**18**	**118**	**42**	**76**	**0**	**366**	**477**			

Playoff Results 1992-88

Year	Round	Opponent	Result	GF	GA
1992	DSF	Edmonton	L 2-4	18	23
1991	DF	Edmonton	L 2-4	20	21
	DSF	Vancouver	W 4-2	26	16
1990	DF	Edmonton	L 0-4	10	24
	DSF	Calgary	W 4-2	29	24
1989	DF	Calgary	L 0-4	11	22
	DSF	Edmonton	W 4-3	25	20
1988	DSF	Calgary	L 4-1	18	30

Abbreviations: Round: F – Final; **CF** – conference final; **DF** – division final; **DSF** – division semi-final; **SF** – semi-final; **QF** – quarter-final; **PR** – preliminary round. **GA** – goals against; **GF** – goals for.

1991-92 Results

Home				Away			
Oct.	8	Edmonton	6-3	**Oct.**	4	Winnipeg	6-3
	10	Calgary	1-7		6	Edmonton	2-2
	12	Winnipeg	3-3		22	New Jersey	2-5
	16	San Jose	8-5		23	NY Rangers	2-7
	19	Minnesota	5-2		26	NY Islanders	4-2
Nov.	7	Vancouver	3-4		28	Detroit	4-3
	9	Edmonton	4-4		30	Hartford	4-4
	14	Buffalo	2-2		31	Boston	4-2
	16	Detroit	3-5	**Nov.**	2	Toronto	5-2
	21	NY Rangers	6-1		11	Winnipeg*	2-6
	23	San Jose	6-4		12	Vancouver	2-8
	26	Toronto	4-4		19	San Jose	3-2
	30	New Jersey	1-4		28	Calgary	3-5
Dec.	12	Winnipeg	2-1	**Dec.**	3	San Jose	2-3
	14	Vancouver	4-4		5	Chicago	2-6
	17	Minnesota	1-2		7	Quebec	5-7
	21	Detroit	2-5		28	Edmonton	9-4
	26	San Jose	5-3		29	Calgary	2-6
	31	Vancouver	3-5	**Jan.**	7	Pittsburgh	5-2
Jan.	2	Edmonton	5-3		9	Philadelphia	2-5
	4	Philadelphia	7-3		10	Washington	4-7
	14	San Jose	3-3		12	New Jersey	2-5
	16	Washington	2-2		22	Minnesota	3-3
	25	Calgary	4-3		23	St Louis	6-5
	28	St Louis	3-3	**Feb.**	8	Pittsburgh*	4-3
	30	NY Rangers	1-4		9	Buffalo	5-4
Feb.	1	Chicago	2-0		11	St Louis	2-3
	4	NY Islanders	1-2		13	Chicago	2-2
	6	Hartford	5-5		19	Edmonton	3-4
	15	Washington	6-3		21	Calgary	7-9
	17	Boston*	6-3		23	Winnipeg	4-2
	27	Quebec	4-2		25	Vancouver	4-3
	29	Montreal	5-3	**Mar.**	4	San Jose	4-3
Mar.	3	Philadelphia	4-1		11	Hartford	0-4
	7	Pittsburgh	5-3		14	Montreal	2-5
	9	Toronto	4-1		15	Boston	1-5
	17	Winnipeg	5-4		26	Calgary	2-7
	19	Buffalo	2-8		27	Winnipeg	4-6
	21	Calgary*	5-2		29	Edmonton	2-2
Apr.	4	Vancouver*	2-3	**Apr.**	5	Vancouver*	6-1

*Denotes afternoon game

Entry Draft Selections 1992-78

1992
Pick
39 Justin Hocking
63 Sandy Allan
87 Kevin Brown
111 Jeff Shevalier
135 Raymond Murray
207 Magnus Wernblom
231 Ryan Pisiak
255 Jukka Tiilikainen

1991
Pick
42 Guy Leveque
79 Keith Redmond
81 Alexei Zhitnik
108 Pauli Jaks
130 Brett Seguin
152 Kelly Fairchild
196 Craig Brown
218 Mattias Olsson
240 Andre Bouliane
262 Michael Gaul

1990
Pick
7 Darryl Sydor
28 Brandy Semchuk
49 Bob Berg
91 David Goverde
112 Erik Andersson
133 Robert Lang
154 Dean Hulett
175 Denis LeBlanc
196 Patrik Ross
217 K.J. (Kevin) White
238 Troy Mohns

1989
Pick
39 Brent Thompson
81 Jim Maher
102 Eric Ricard
103 Thomas Newman
123 Daniel Rydmark
144 Ted Kramer
165 Sean Whyte
182 Jim Giacin
186 Martin Maskarinec
207 Jim Hiller
228 Steve Jaques
249 Kevin Sneddon

1988
Pick
7 Martin Gelinas
28 Paul Holden
49 John Van Kessel
70 Rob Blake
91 Jeff Robison
109 Micah Aivazoff
112 Robert Larsson
133 Jeff Kruesel
154 Timo Peltomaa
175 Jim Larkin
196 Brad Hyatt
217 Doug Laprade
238 Joe Flanagan

1987
Pick
4 Wayne McBean
27 Mark Fitzpatrick
43 Ross Wilson
90 Mike Vukonich
111 Greg Batters
132 Kyosti Karjalainen
174 Jeff Gawlicki
195 John Preston
216 Rostislav Vlach
237 Mikael Lindholm

1986
Pick
2 Jimmy Carson
44 Denis Larocque
65 Sylvain Couturier
86 Dave Guden
107 Robb Stauber
128 Sean Krakiwsky
149 Rene Chapdelaine
170 Trevor Pochipinski
191 Paul Kelly
212 Russ Mann
233 Brian Hayton

1985
Pick
9 Craig Duncanson
10 Dan Gratton
30 Par Edlund
72 Perry Florio
93 Petr Prajsler
135 Tim Flannigan
156 John Hyduke
177 Steve Horner
219 Trent Ciprick
240 Marian Horwath

1984
Pick
6 Craig Redmond
24 Brian Wilks
48 John English
69 Tom Glavine
87 Dave Grannis
108 Greg Strome
129 Tim Hanley
150 Shannon Deegan
171 Luc Robitaille
191 Jeff Crossman
212 Paul Kenny
232 Brian Martin

1983
Pick
47 Bruce Shoebottom
67 Guy Benoit
87 Bob LaForest
100 Garry Galley
107 Dave Lundmark
108 Kevin Stevens
127 Tim Burgess
147 Ken Hammond
167 Bruce Fishback
187 Thomas Ahlen
207 Miroslav Blaha
227 Chad Johnson

1982
Pick
27 Mike Heidt
48 Steve Seguin
64 Dave Gans
82 Dave Ross
90 Darcy Roy
95 Ulf Isaksson
132 Victor Nechaev
153 Peter Helander
174 Dave Chartier
195 John Franzosa
216 Ray Shero
237 Mats Ulander

1981
Pick
2 Doug Smith
39 Dean Kennedy
81 Marty Dallman
123 Brad Thompson
134 Craig Hurley
144 Peter Sawkins
165 Dan Brennan
186 Allan Tuer
207 Jeff Baikie

1980
Pick
4 Larry Murphy
10 Jim Fox
33 Greg Terrion
34 Dave Morrison
52 Steve Bozek
73 Bernie Nicholls
94 Alan Graves
115 Darren Eliot
136 Mike O'Connor
157 Bill O'Dwyer
178 Daryl Evans
199 Kim Collins

1979
Pick
16 Jay Wells
29 Dean Hopkins
30 Mark Hardy
50 John Paul Kelly
71 John Gibson
92 Jim Brown
113 Jay MacFarlane

1978
Pick
77 Paul Mancini
94 Doug Keans
111 Don Waddell
128 Rob Mierkalns
145 Ric Scully
162 Brad Thiessen
177 Jim Armstrong
193 Claude Larochelle

Luc Robitaille topped 100 points for the third time in his career in 1991-92.

Club Directory

The Great Western Forum
3900 West Manchester Blvd.
P.O. Box 17013
Inglewood, California 90308
Phone **310/419-3160**
FAX 310/673-8927
Capacity: 16,005

Executive

Chairman of the Board/Governor	Bruce McNall
President	Roy A. Mlakar
Alternate Governor	Roy A. Mlakar
Special Assistant to Chairman	Rogatien Vachon
Vice-President, Marketing/Administration	Robert Moor
Vice-President, Public Relations	Scott Carmichael
Executive Secretary to President	Susan Rowan
Secretary	Kelley Lombardozzi
Hockey Operations	
General Manager	Nick Beverley
Administrative Assistant to General Manager	John Wolf
Executive Secretary to General Manager	Marcia Galloway
Head Coach	Barry Melrose
Assistant Coach	Cap Raeder
Director of Player Personnel	Bob Owen
Scouting Staff	Jim Anderson, Ron Ansell, Serge Aubry, John Bymark, Gary Harker, Jan Lindegren, Mark Miller, Al Murray, Vaclav Nedomansky, Ted O'Connor, Don Perry, Alex Smart
Medical Staff	
Trainer	Pete Demers
Equipment Manager	Peter Millar
Assistant Equipment Manager	Mark O'Neill
Massage Therapist	Juergen Merz
Communications	
Director, Media Relations	Rick Minch
Media Relations Assistant	Adam Fell
Director, Publications	Nick Salata
Director, Community and Player Relations	Jim Fox
Communications Coordinator	Angela Ladd
Administrative Assistant	Michelle Guler
Finance/Accounting	
Executive Director, Finance	Martin Greenspun
Accounting Manager	Pete Mazur
Personnel and Payroll Manager	Barbara Mendez
Marketing/Advertising/Sales	
Executive Director, Marketing	Gregory McElroy
Director, Merchandising	Harvey Boles
Director, Sales	Dennis Metz
Traffic Manager and Event Coordinator	Tricia Webb
Advertising Account Executives	Sergio del Prado, Rory Oldham, Todd Waks, John Covarrubias
Season Seats Account Executives	Keith Jacobson, Andrew Silverman
Promotions Manager	David Resnick
Broadcasting	
Play-by-Play Announcer, Television	Bob Miller
Color Commentator, Television	Jim Fox
Play-by-Play Announcer, Radio	Nick Nickson
Color Commentator, Radio	Brian Engblom
Television	Prime Ticket Cable Network
Radio Station	XTRA (690 AM)
Home Ice	The Great Western Forum
Dimensions of Rink	200 feet by 85 feet
Colors	Black, White and Silver

General Manager

BEVERLY, NICK
General Manager, Los Angeles Kings. Born in Toronto, Ont., April 21, 1947.

Nick Beverly was appointed as the fifth general manager in Los Angeles' franchise history on June 25, 1992. Following an 11-year NHL playing career that included stops in six cities, including Los Angeles, Beverly joined the Kings' organization in 1980 after accepting the coaching position with the teams minor league affiliate in Houston. Beverly, who also coached the Kings' farm team in New Haven, was named director of player personnel and development in 1988. In 1990, he was named as assistant general manager, and continued in that capacity until being elevated to the G.M.'s office.

Coach

MELROSE, BARRY
Coach, Los Angeles Kings. Born in Kelvington, Sask., July 15, 1956.

Barry Melrose became the 17th head coach of the Los Angeles Kings on June 25, 1992, replacing Tom Webster. Melrose, who started his professional playing career at the age of 20 with the Cincinnati Stingers of the WHA, spent eight years in the NHL with Toronto, Winnipeg and Detroit. Following his successful playing career, Melrose turned his attention to coaching and led the WHL's Medicine Hat Tigers to the Memorial Cup title in 1988. For the past three seasons, he has been the coach of the AHL's Adirondack Red Wings, Detroit's top farm affiliate. In 1991-92, Melrose guided the Wings to the AHL's Calder Cup championship, the fourth title for the Adirondack franchise since 1981.

Minnesota North Stars

1991-92 Results: 32W-42L-6T 70PTS. Fourth, Norris Division

Schedule

Home		Away	
Oct.	Thur. 8 St Louis	Oct.	Tues. 6 St Louis
	Sat. 10 Tampa Bay		Thur. 15 St Louis
	Tues. 13 Calgary		Sat. 17 Montreal
	(at Saskatoon)		Sun. 18 Toronto
	Thur. 22 Quebec		Wed. 28 Edmonton
	Sat. 24 Los Angeles		Fri. 30 Vancouver
Nov.	Thur. 5 NY Islanders		Sat. 31 Calgary
	Sat. 7 Edmonton	Nov.	Sun. 15 Chicago
	Tues. 10 Pittsburgh		Wed. 18 Washington
	Thur. 12 Winnipeg		Thur. 19 Tampa Bay
	Sat. 14 Chicago*		Sat. 21 Buffalo
	Wed. 25 Vancouver		Mon. 30 NY Rangers
	Fri. 27 NY Rangers	Dec.	Tues. 1 Ottawa
	Sat. 28 San Jose		Thur. 3 Detroit
Dec.	Thur. 10 Edmonton		Sat. 5 Quebec
	Sat. 12 Chicago		Sun. 20 Chicago
	Tues. 15 Toronto		Sun. 27 Winnipeg
	Sat. 19 Detroit	Jan.	Sat. 2 NY Islanders
	Tues. 22 St Louis		Sun. 3 Hartford
	Sat. 26 Winnipeg		Wed. 6 New Jersey
	Thur. 31 Boston		Thur. 7 Pittsburgh
Jan.	Sat. 9 Tampa Bay		Thur. 14 Chicago
	Tues. 12 Chicago		Tues. 19 Tampa Bay
	Sat. 16 Calgary		Sun. 24 Tampa Bay
	Thur. 21 Ottawa		Tues. 26 Toronto
	Sat. 23 Vancouver*	Feb.	Mon. 1 Vancouver
	Thur. 28 New Jersey		Wed. 3 San Jose
	Sat. 30 Tampa Bay		Thur. 11 Tampa Bay
Feb.	Tues. 9 Washington		Sat. 13 Toronto
	Sun. 14 Toronto		Thur. 25 Boston
	Wed. 17 Los Angeles		Sat. 27 St Louis
	Sat. 20 Philadelphia*		Sun. 28 Winnipeg
	Sun. 21 Detroit*	Mar.	Wed. 3 Toronto
Mar.	Sat. 6 Montreal		Thur. 11 Vancouver
	Sun. 7 Detroit		(at Saskatoon)
	Tues. 9 San Jose		Sat. 13 St Louis
	Sun. 14 St Louis		Tues. 16 Philadelphia
	Sun. 21 Detroit*		Thur. 18 Detroit
	Thur. 25 Toronto		Wed. 31 Edmonton
	Sat. 27 Hartford	Apr.	Thur. 1 Calgary
Apr.	Tues. 6 Buffalo		Sat. 3 Los Angeles*
	Sat. 10 St Louis		Sun. 11 St Louis
	Tues. 13 Chicago		Thur. 15 Detroit

* Denotes afternoon game.

Home Starting Times:
All Games .... 7:05 p.m.
Except Matinees .... 1:05 p.m.

Franchise date: June 5, 1967

26th NHL Season

Year-by-Year Record

		Home			Road			Overall								
Season	GP	W	L	T	W	L	T	W	L	T	GF	GA	Pts.		Finished	Playoff Result
1991-92	80	20	16	4	12	26	2	32	42	6	246	278	70	4th,	Norris Div.	Lost Div. Semi-Final
1990-91	80	19	15	6	8	24	8	27	39	14	256	266	68	4th,	Norris Div.	Lost Final
1989-90	80	26	12	2	10	28	2	36	40	4	284	291	76	4th,	Norris Div.	Lost Div. Semi-Final
1988-89	80	17	15	8	10	22	8	27	37	16	258	278	70	3rd,	Norris Div.	Lost Div. Semi-Final
1987-88	80	10	24	6	9	24	7	19	48	13	242	349	51	5th,	Norris Div.	Out of Playoffs
1986-87	80	17	20	3	13	20	7	30	40	10	296	314	70	5th,	Norris Div.	Out of Playoffs
1985-86	80	21	15	4	17	18	5	38	33	9	327	305	85	2nd,	Norris Div.	Lost Div. Semi-Final
1984-85	80	14	19	7	11	24	5	25	43	12	268	321	62	4th,	Norris Div.	Lost Div. Final
1983-84	80	22	14	4	17	17	6	39	31	10	345	344	88	1st,	Norris Div.	Lost Conf. Championship
1982-83	80	23	6	11	17	18	5	40	24	16	321	290	96	2nd,	Norris Div.	Lost Div. Final
1981-82	80	21	7	12	16	16	8	37	23	20	346	288	94	1st,	Norris Div.	Lost Div. Semi-Final
1980-81	80	23	10	7	12	18	10	35	28	17	291	263	87	3rd,	Adams Div.	Lost Final
1979-80	80	25	8	7	11	20	9	36	28	16	311	253	88	3rd,	Adams Div.	Lost Semi-Final
1978-79	80	19	15	6	9	25	6	28	40	12	257	289	68	4th,	Adams Div.	Out Of Playoffs
1977-78	80	12	24	4	6	29	5	18	53	9	218	325	45	5th,	Smythe Div.	Out of Playoffs
1976-77	80	17	14	9	6	25	9	23	39	18	240	310	64	2nd,	Smythe Div.	Lost Prelim. Round
1975-76	80	15	22	3	5	31	4	20	53	7	195	303	47	4th,	Smythe Div.	Out of Playoffs
1974-75	80	17	20	3	6	30	4	23	50	7	221	341	53	4th,	Smythe Div.	Out of Playoffs
1973-74	78	18	15	6	5	23	11	23	38	17	235	275	63	7th,	West Div.	Out of Playoffs
1972-73	78	26	8	5	11	22	6	37	30	11	254	230	85	3rd,	West Div.	Lost Quarter-Final
1971-72	78	22	11	6	15	18	6	37	29	12	212	191	86	2nd,	West Div.	Lost Quarter-Final
1970-71	78	16	15	8	12	19	8	28	34	16	191	223	72	4th,	West Div.	Lost Semi-Final
1969-70	76	11	16	11	8	19	11	19	35	22	224	257	60	3rd,	West Div.	Lost Quarter-Final
1968-69	76	11	21	6	7	22	9	18	43	15	189	270	51	6th,	West Div.	Out of Playoffs
1967-68	74	17	12	8	10	20	7	27	32	15	191	226	69	4th,	West Div.	Lost Semi-Final

Dave Gagner registered his fourth consecutive season with at least 30 goals, firing 31 for the Stars in 1991-92.

Derian Hatcher had a solid 1991-92 season, compiling a plus/minus mark of +7.

1992-93 Player Personnel

FORWARDS	HT	WT	S	Place of Birth	Date	1991-92 Club
BLACK, James	6-1	195	L	Regina, Sask.	8/15/69	Hartford-Springfield
BROTEN, Neal	5-9	170	L	Roseau, MN	11/29/59	Minnesota
BUREAU, Marc	6-1	190	R	Trois-Rivières, Que.	5/19/66	Minnesota-Kalamazoo
CHURLA, Shane	6-1	200	R	Fernie, B.C.	6/24/65	Minnesota
COURTNALL, Russ	5-11	183	R	Duncan, B.C.	6/2/65	Montreal
CRAIG, Mike	6-1	180	R	St. Mary's, Ont.	6/6/71	Minnesota
DAHLEN, Ulf	6-2	195	L	Ostersund, Sweden	1/12/67	Minnesota
DUCHESNE, Gaetan	5-11	200	L	Les Saulles, Que.	7/11/62	Minnesota
ELIK, Todd	6-1	200	L	Toronto, Ont.	4/15/66	Minnesota
GAGNER, Dave	5-10	180	L	Chatham, Ont.	12/11/64	Minnesota
GAVIN, Stewart	6-0	190	L	Ottawa, Ont.	3/15/60	Minnesota
KLATT, Trent	6-1	205	R	Robbinsdale, MN	1/30/71	U. of Minn.-Minnesota
McPHEE, Mike	6-1	203	L	Sydney, N.S.	7/14/60	Montreal
MESSIER, Mitch	6-2	200	R	Regina, Sask.	8/21/65	Kalamazoo
MODANO, Mike	6-3	190	L	Livonia, MI	6/7/70	Minnesota
NESICH, Jim	5-11	185	R	Dearborn, MI	2/22/66	Kalamazoo
PROPP, Brian	5-10	195	L	Lanigan, Sask.	2/15/59	Minnesota
ROBINSON, Scott	6-2	180	L	100 Mile House, B.C.	3/29/64	Kalamazoo
RYCHEL, Warren	6-0	190	L	Tecumseh, Ont.	5/12/67	Kalamazoo-Moncton
SMITH, Bobby	6-4	210	L	N. Sydney, N.S.	2/12/58	Minnesota
SMITH, Derrick	6-2	215	L	Scarborough, Ont.	1/22/65	Minnesota-Kalamazoo
DEFENSEMEN						
BERRY, Brad	6-2	190	L	Hibbing, MN	4/1/65	Minnesota-Kalamazoo
CICCONE, Enrico	6-4	200	L	Montreal, Que.	4/10/70	Minnesota-Kalamazoo
DAHLQUIST, Chris	6-1	190	L	Fridley, MN	12/14/62	Minnesota
HATCHER, Derian	6-5	205	L	Sterling Hts., MI	6/4/72	Minnesota
JOHNSON, Jim	6-1	190	L	New Hope, MN	8/9/62	Minnesota
LUDWIG, Craig	6-3	217	L	Rhinelander, WI	3/15/61	Minnesota
MATVICHUK, Richard	6-2	190	L	Edmonton, Alta.	2/5/73	Saskatoon
SANDELIN, Scott	6-0	200	R	Hibbing, MN	8/8/64	Minnesota-Kalamazoo
SJODIN, Tommy	5-11	185	R	Sundsvall, Sweden	8/13/65	Brynas
TINORDI, Mark	6-4	205	L	Red Deer, Alta.	5/9/66	Minnesota

GOALTENDERS	HT	WT	C	Place of Birth	Date	1991-92 Club
CASEY, Jon	5-10	155	L	Grand Rapids, MN	3/29/62	Minnesota-Kalamazoo
DYCK, Larry	5-11	180	L	Winkler, Man.	12/15/65	Kalamazoo
GUENETTE, Steve	5-10	175	L	Gloucester, Ont.	11/13/65	Kalamazoo
WAKALUK, Darcy	5-11	180	L	Pincher Creek, Alta.	3/14/66	Minnesota-Kalamazoo

General Managers' History

Wren A. Blair, 1967-68 to 1973-74; Jack Gordon, 1974-75 to 1976-77; Lou Nanne, 1977-78 to 1987-88; Jack Ferreira, 1988-89 to 1989-90; Bob Clarke 1990-91 to 1991-92; Bob Gainey, 1992-93.

1991-92 Scoring

Regular Season

Pos	#	Player	Team	GP	G	A	Pts	+/-	PIM	PP	SH	GW	GT	S	%
C	9	Mike Modano	MIN	76	33	44	77	9-	46	5	0	8	2	256	12.9
L	23	Brian Bellows	MIN	80	30	45	75	20-	41	12	1	4	0	255	11.8
C	15	Dave Gagner	MIN	78	31	40	71	4-	107	17	0	3	0	229	13.5
R	22	Ulf Dahlen	MIN	79	36	30	66	5-	10	16	1	5	0	216	16.7
C	14	Todd Elik	MIN	62	14	32	46	0	125	4	3	1	0	118	11.9
C	18	Bobby Smith	MIN	68	9	37	46	24-	109	3	0	1	0	129	7.0
L	16	Brian Propp	MIN	51	12	23	35	3-	49	4	0	0	0	115	10.4
C	7	Neal Broten	MIN	76	8	26	34	15-	16	4	1	1	0	119	6.7
R	20	Mike Craig	MIN	67	15	16	31	12-	155	4	0	4	0	136	11.0
D	24	Mark Tinordi	MIN	63	4	24	28	13-	179	4	0	0	0	93	4.3
L	10	Gaetan Duchesne	MIN	73	8	15	23	6	102	0	2	1	0	106	7.5
C	25*	Kip Miller	QUE	36	5	10	15	21-	12	1	0	2	0	46	10.9
			MIN	3	1	2	3	1-	2	1	0	0	0	3	33.3
			TOTAL	39	6	12	18	22-	14	2	0	2	0	49	12.2
D	6	Jim Johnson	MIN	71	4	10	14	11	102	0	0	1	0	86	4.7
D	4	Chris Dahlquist	MIN	74	1	13	14	10-	68	0	0	0	0	63	1.6
L	17	Basil McRae	MIN	59	5	8	13	14-	245	0	0	0	0	64	7.8
D	28*	Derian Hatcher	MIN	43	8	4	12	7	88	0	0	2	0	51	15.7
D	3	Craig Ludwig	MIN	73	2	9	11	0	54	0	0	0	0	51	3.9
C	11*	Marc Bureau	MIN	46	6	4	10	5-	50	0	0	0	0	53	11.3
D	26	David Shaw	NYR	10	0	1	1	1	15	0	0	0	0	6	.0
			EDM	12	1	1	2	8-	8	0	0	0	0	15	6.7
			MIN	37	0	7	7	5-	49	0	0	0	0	49	.0
			TOTAL	59	1	9	10	12-	72	0	0	0	0	70	1.4
R	12	Stewart Gavin	MIN	35	5	4	9	0	27	0	1	1	0	49	10.2
D	5	Rob Ramage	MIN	34	4	5	9	4-	69	2	0	0	0	63	6.3
L	21	Derrick Smith	MIN	33	2	4	6	8-	33	0	0	0	0	29	6.9
R	27	Shane Churla	MIN	57	4	1	5	12-	278	0	0	0	0	42	9.5
G	30	Jon Casey	MIN	52	0	2	2	0	26	0	0	0	0	0	.0
D	41	Allen Pedersen	MIN	29	0	1	1	1-	10	0	0	0	0	17	.0
L	38	Steve Martinson	MIN	1	0	0	0	0	9	0	0	0	0	0	.0
D	32	Scott Sandelin	MIN	1	0	0	0	1-	0	0	0	0	0	1	.0
R	29*	Trent Klatt	MIN	1	0	0	0	0	0	0	0	0	0	1	.0
D	32	Brad Berry	MIN	7	0	0	0	1-	6	0	0	0	0	2	.0
C	31	Mark Janssens	NYR	4	0	0	0	1-	5	0	0	0	0	0	.0
			MIN	3	0	0	0	1-	0	0	0	0	0	1	.0
			TOTAL	7	0	0	0	2-	5	0	0	0	0	1	.0
D	39*	Enrico Ciccone	MIN	11	0	0	0	2-	48	0	0	0	0	2	.0
G	35	Darcy Wakaluk	MIN	36	0	0	0	0	20	0	0	0	0	0	.0

Goaltending

No.	Goaltender	GPI	Mins	Avg	W	L	T	EN	SO	GA	SA	S%
35	Darcy Wakaluk	36	1905	3.28	13	19	1	3	1	104	874	.881
30	Jon Casey	52	2911	3.40	19	23	5	6	2	165	1401	.882
	Totals	**80**	**4835**	**3.45**	**32**	**42**	**6**	**9**	**3**	**278**	**2284**	**.878**

Playoffs

Pos	#	Player	Team	GP	G	A	Pts	+/-	PIM	PP	SH	GW	GT	S	%
L	23	Brian Bellows	MIN	7	4	4	8	4-	14	2	0	1	0	14	28.6
C	15	Dave Gagner	MIN	7	2	4	6	3-	8	2	0	0	0	15	13.3
C	7	Neal Broten	MIN	7	1	5	6	3	2	0	0	0	0	12	8.3
C	9	Mike Modano	MIN	7	3	2	5	2-	4	1	0	0	0	19	15.8
C	18	Bobby Smith	MIN	7	1	4	5	3-	6	1	0	0	0	13	7.7
D	26	David Shaw	MIN	7	2	2	4	2-	10	1	0	0	0	13	15.4
D	6	Jim Johnson	MIN	7	1	3	4	2-	18	0	0	0	0	9	11.1
D	24	Mark Tinordi	MIN	7	1	2	3	6-	11	0	0	0	0	15	6.7
R	22	Ulf Dahlen	MIN	7	0	3	3	0	2	0	0	0	0	13	.0
C	14	Todd Elik	MIN	5	1	1	2	1-	2	0	0	1	0	3	33.3
D	28*	Derian Hatcher	MIN	5	0	2	2	1	8	0	0	0	0	10	.0
R	20	Mike Craig	MIN	4	1	0	1	0	7	0	0	0	0	1	100.0
L	10	Gaetan Duchesne	MIN	7	1	0	1	2	6	0	0	0	0	10	10.0
L	21	Derrick Smith	MIN	7	1	0	1	2-	9	0	0	1	0	12	8.3
D	3	Craig Ludwig	MIN	7	0	1	1	1	19	0	0	0	0	2	.0
L	16	Brian Propp	MIN	1	0	0	0	0	0	0	0	0	0	1	.0
D	32	Brad Berry	MIN	2	0	0	0	1	2	0	0	0	0	0	.0
C	11*	Marc Bureau	MIN	5	0	0	0	3-	14	0	0	0	0	1	.0
R	29*	Trent Klatt	MIN	6	0	0	0	4-	2	0	0	0	0	7	.0
G	30	Jon Casey	MIN	7	0	0	0	0	0	0	0	0	0	0	.0
D	4	Chris Dahlquist	MIN	7	0	0	0	5-	6	0	0	0	0	9	.0
R	12	Stewart Gavin	MIN	7	0	0	0	3-	6	0	0	0	0	11	.0

Goaltending

No.	Goaltender	GPI	Mins	Avg	W	L	EN	SO	GA	SA	S%
30	Jon Casey	7	437	3.02	3	4	1	0	22	225	.902
	Totals	**7**	**437**	**3.16**	**3**	**4**	**1**	**0**	**23**	**226**	**.898**

Coaching History

Wren Blair, 1967-68; John Muckler and Wren Blair, 1968-69; Wren Blair and Charlie Burns, 1969-70; Jackie Gordon, 1970-71 to 1972-73; Jackie Gordon and Parker MacDonald, 1973-74; Jackie Gordon and Charlie Burns, 1974-75; Ted Harris, 1975-76 to 1976-77; Ted Harris, André Beaulieu, Lou Nanne, 1977-78; Harry Howell and Glen Sonmor, 1978-79; Glen Sonmor, 1979-80 to 1981-82; Glen Sonmor and Murray Oliver, 1982-83; Bill Mahoney, 1983-84 to 1984-85; Lorne Henning, 1985-86; Lorne Henning and Glen Sonmor, 1986-87; Herb Brooks, 1987-88; Pierre Page, 1988-89 to 1989-90; Bob Gainey, 1990-91 to date.

Captains' History

Bob Woytowich, 1967-68; Elmer Vasko, 1968-69; Claude Larose, 1969-70; Ted Harris, 1970-71 to 1973-74; Bill Goldsworthy, 1974-75, 1975-76; Bill Hogaboam, 1976-77; Nick Beverly, 1977-78; J.P. Parise, 1978-79; Paul Shmyr, 1979-80, 1980-81; Tim Young, 1981-82; Craig Hartsburg, 1982-83; Brian Bellows, Craig Hartsburg, 1983-84; Craig Hartsburg, 1984-85 to 1987-88; Curt Fraser, Bob Rouse and Curt Giles, 1988-89; Curt Giles, 1989-90 to 1990-91; Mark Tinordi, 1991-92 to date.

Retired Numbers

8	Bill Goldsworthy	1967-1976
19	Bill Masterton	1967-1968

Club Records

Team

(Figures in brackets for season records are games played; records for fewest points, wins, ties, losses, goals, goals against are for 70 or more games)

Record		
Most Points	96	1982-83 (80)
Most Wins	40	1982-83 (80)
Most Ties	22	1969-70 (76)
Most Losses	53	1975-76, 1977-78 (80)
Most Goals	346	1981-82 (80)
Most Goals Against	349	1987-88 (80)
Fewest Points	45	1977-78 (80)
Fewest Wins	18	1968-69 (76) 1977-78 (80)
Fewest Ties	4	1989-90 (80)
Fewest Losses	23	1981-82 (80)
Fewest Goals	189	1968-69 (76)
Fewest Goals Against	191	1971-72 (78)
Longest Winning Streak		
Over-all	7	Mar. 16-28/80
Home	11	Nov. 4- Dec. 27/72
Away	5	Dec. 2-16/67 Feb. 5- Mar. 5/83
Longest Undefeated Streak		
Over-all	12	Feb. 18- Mar. 15/82 (9 wins, 3 ties)
Home	13	Oct. 28- Dec. 27/72 (12 wins, 1 tie) Nov. 21- Jan. 9/80 (10 wins, 3 ties) Jan. 17- Mar. 17/91 (11 wins, 2 ties)
Away	6	Nov. 30- Dec. 16/67 (5 wins, 1 tie) Nov. 7-27/71 (5 wins, 1 tie) Nov. 9-Dec. 3/83 (5 wins, 1 tie)
Longest Losing Streak		
Over-all	10	Feb. 1-20/76
Home	6	Jan. 17- Feb. 4/70
Away	8	Oct. 19- Nov. 13/75; Jan. 28- Mar. 3/88
Longest Winless Streak		
Over-all	20	Jan. 15- Feb. 28/70 (15 losses, 5 ties)
Home	12	Jan. 17- Feb. 25/70 (8 losses, 4 ties)
Away	23	Oct. 25/74- Jan. 28/75 (19 losses, 4 ties)
Most Shutouts, Season	7	1972-73 (78)
Most PIM, Season	2,313	1987-88 (80)
Most Goals, Game	15	Nov. 11/81 (Wpg. 2 at Minn. 15)

Individual

Record		
Most Seasons	12	Curt Giles
Most Games	794	Neal Broten
Most Goals, Career	342	Brian Bellows
Most Assists, Career	526	Neal Broten
Most Points Career	763	Neal Broten (237 goals, 526 assists)
Most PIM, Career	1,567	Basil McRae
Most Shutouts, Career	26	Cesare Maniago
Longest Consecutive Games Streak	442	Danny Grant (Dec. 4/68-Apr. 7/74)
Most Goals, Season	55	Dino Ciccarelli (1981-82) Brian Bellows (1989-90)
Most Assists, Season	76	Neal Broten (1985-86)
Most Points, Season	114	Bobby Smith (1981-82) (43 goals, 71 assists)
Most PIM, Season	382	Basil McRae (1987-88)
Most Points, Defenseman Season	77	Craig Hartsburg (1981-82) (17 goals, 60 assists)
Most Points, Center, Season	114	Bobby Smith (1981-82) (43 goals, 71 assists)
Most Points, Right Wing, Season	107	Dino Ciccarelli (1981-82) (55 goals, 52 assists)
Most Point, Left Wing, Season	99	Brian Bellows (1989-90) (55 goals, 44 assists)
Most Points, Rookie, Season	98	Neal Broten (1981-82) (38 goals, 60 assists)
Most Shutouts, Season	6	Cesare Maniago (1967-68)
Most Goals, Game	5	Tim Young (Jan. 15/79)
Most Assists, Game	5	Murray Oliver (Oct. 24/71) Larry Murphy (Oct. 17/89)
Most Points, Game	7	Bobby Smith (Nov. 11/81)

All-time Record vs. Other Clubs

Regular Season

	At Home							On Road							Total						
	GP	W	L	T	GF	GA	PTS	GP	W	L	T	GF	GA	PTS	GP	W	L	T	GF	GA	PTS
Boston	51	12	28	11	140	192	35	51	6	38	7	120	234	19	102	18	66	18	260	426	54
Buffalo	44	19	19	6	139	139	44	43	10	23	10	115	162	30	87	29	42	16	254	301	74
Calgary	38	18	15	5	143	125	41	38	4	24	10	101	159	18	76	22	39	15	244	284	59
Chicago	81	37	33	11	290	275	85	81	18	53	10	215	344	46	162	55	86	21	505	619	131
Detroit	77	43	21	13	303	221	99	76	28	36	12	262	300	68	153	71	57	25	565	521	167
Edmonton	21	6	11	4	78	81	16	20	1	13	6	64	104	8	41	7	24	10	142	185	24
Hartford	20	11	8	1	87	69	23	21	11	9	1	79	76	23	41	22	17	2	166	145	46
Los Angeles	55	33	14	8	221	146	74	55	15	26	14	169	210	44	110	48	40	22	390	356	118
Montreal	50	13	27	10	129	181	36	49	9	33	7	122	217	25	99	22	60	17	251	398	61
New Jersey	35	21	8	6	144	92	48	35	16	16	3	114	114	35	70	37	24	9	258	206	83
NY Islanders	37	13	19	5	109	146	31	37	9	20	8	108	146	26	74	22	39	13	217	292	57
NY Rangers	51	15	29	7	155	200	37	52	10	32	10	144	189	30	103	25	61	17	299	389	67
Philadelphia	57	22	22	13	184	194	57	57	8	39	10	129	228	26	114	30	61	23	313	422	83
Pittsburgh	55	31	19	5	214	186	67	54	15	34	5	143	210	35	109	46	53	10	357	396	102
Quebec	20	12	6	2	79	64	26	21	4	15	2	53	100	10	41	16	21	4	132	164	36
St. Louis	85	37	31	17	294	254	91	87	24	46	17	247	315	65	172	61	77	34	541	569	156
San Jose	1	1	0	0	7	4	2	2	2	0	0	11	4	4	3	3	0	0	18	8	6
Toronto	78	40	29	9	302	257	89	79	27	38	14	261	292	68	157	67	67	23	563	549	157
Vancouver	47	29	11	7	199	136	65	46	14	24	8	145	189	36	93	43	35	15	344	325	101
Washington	30	13	9	8	114	89	34	31	11	13	7	94	99	29	61	24	22	15	208	188	63
Winnipeg	23	14	7	2	108	70	30	22	11	10	1	76	76	23	45	25	17	3	184	146	53
Defunct Clubs	33	19	8	6	123	86	44	32	10	16	6	84	105	26	65	29	24	12	207	191	70
Totals	**989**	**459**	**374**	**156**	**3562**	**3207**	**1074**	**989**	**263**	**558**	**168**	**2856**	**3873**	**694**	**1978**	**722**	**932**	**324**	**6418**	**7080**	**1768**

Playoffs

	Series	W	L	GP	W	L	T	GF	GA	Last Mtg.	Round	Result
Boston	1	1	0	3	3	0	0	20	13	1981	PR	W 3-0
Buffalo	2	1	1	7	4	3	0	26	28	1981	QF	W 4-1
**Calgary	1	1	0	6	4	2	0	25	18	1981	SF	W 4-2
Chicago	6	2	4	33	14	19	0	119	119	1991	DSF	W 4-2
Detroit	1	0	1	7	3	4	0	19	23	1992	DSF	L 3-4
Edmonton	2	1	1	9	4	5	0	30	36	1991	CF	W 4-1
Los Angeles	1	1	0	7	4	3	0	26	21	1968	QF	W 4-3
Montreal	2	1	1	13	6	7	0	37	48	1980	QF	W 4-3
NY Islanders	1	0	1	5	1	4	0	16	26	1981	F	L 1-4
Philadelphia	2	0	2	11	3	8	0	26	41	1980	SF	L 1-4
Pittsburgh	1	0	1	6	2	4	0	16	28	1991	F	L 2-4
St. Louis	9	4	5	52	26	26	0	158	152	1991	DF	W 4-2
Toronto	2	2	0	7	6	1	0	35	26	1983	DSF	W 3-1
Totals	**31**	**14**	**16**	**166**	**80**	**86**	**0**	**553**	**579**			

Playoff Results 1992-88

Year	Round	Opponent	Result	GF	GA
1992	DSF	Detroit	L 3-4	19	23
1991	F	Pittsburgh	L 2-4	16	28
	CF	Edmonton	W 4-1	20	14
	DF	St. Louis	W 4-2	22	17
	DSF	Chicago	W 4-2	23	16
1990	DSF	Chicago	L 3-4	18	21
1989	DSF	St. Louis	L 1-4	15	23

Abbreviations: Round: F – Final; **CF** – conference final; **DF** – division final; **DSF** – division semi-final; **SF** – semi-final; **QF** – quarter-final; **PR** – preliminary round. **GA** – goals against; **GF** – goals for.

1991-92 Results

Home			Away		
Oct. 5	Chicago	4-2	**Oct.** 15	Calgary	3-6
10	Quebec	3-2	17	San Jose	8-2
12	Detroit	3-2	19	Los Angeles	2-5
22	Calgary	2-4	29	NY Rangers	2-3
24	Philadelphia	2-5	31	Pittsburgh	1-8
26	Boston	4-0	**Nov.** 3	Chicago	4-4
Nov. 2	Chicago	4-3	5	Detroit	3-2
9	Pittsburgh	2-3	6	Toronto	3-4
12	Toronto	7-0	16	St Louis	3-5
19	NY Islanders	4-7	22	Detroit	3-4
23	Detroit	2-2	30	Toronto	4-3
29	Toronto	2-3	**Dec.** 8	Chicago	2-7
Dec. 3	St Louis	3-3	12	Vancouver	5-7
4	St Louis	5-2	14	San Jose	3-2
7	Washington	2-4	17	Los Angeles	2-1
10	New Jersey	4-3	26	Winnipeg	3-2
21	Philadelphia	0-3	**Jan.** 2	St Louis	1-6
28	St Louis	5-2	5	Chicago	2-5
31	Chicago	6-2	7	Washington	5-3
Jan. 4	Vancouver	4-3	9	Detroit	4-9
11	San Jose	7-4	27	Boston	2-3
13	Edmonton	4-7	28	Hartford	4-3
15	Montreal	5-2	30	Philadelphia	3-5
22	Los Angeles	3-3	**Feb.** 5	Toronto	2-3
25	Chicago*	0-2	7	Buffalo	2-0
Feb. 1	NY Rangers	1-2	9	Hartford*	4-4
3	Toronto	4-2	17	Montreal	0-8
11	Edmonton	4-5	18	Quebec	0-4
13	Winnipeg	6-1	21	NY Rangers	4-5
15	Pittsburgh	5-2	22	NY Islanders	1-2
26	Montreal	1-4	24	New Jersey	3-1
29	Hartford*	4-5	**Mar.** 1	Toronto	2-6
Mar. 8	Winnipeg	4-2	3	Washington	3-1
11	Toronto	0-3	5	Detroit	4-2
14	Detroit*	4-1	10	St Louis	2-5
17	Buffalo	3-1	19	Chicago	1-4
24	Vancouver	2-4	21	Quebec	2-4
31	Buffalo	5-3	27	Edmonton	3-5
Apr. 2	St Louis	1-1	28	Calgary	3-4
4	Detroit	4-7	**Apr.** 5	St Louis	3-5

*Denotes afternoon game

Entry Draft Selections 1992-78

1992

Pick	
34	Jarkko Varvio
58	Jeff Bes
88	Jere Lehtinen
130	Michael Johnson
154	Kyle Peterson
178	Juha Lind
202	Lars Edstrom
226	Jeff Romfo
250	Jeffrey Moen

1991

Pick	
8	Richard Matvichuk
74	Mike Torchia
97	Mike Kennedy
118	Mark Lawrence
137	Geoff Finch
174	MichaelBurkett
184	Derek Herlofsky
206	Tom Nemeth
228	Shayne Green
250	Jukka Suomalainen

1990

Pick	
8	Derian Hatcher
50	Laurie Billeck
70	Cal McGowan
71	Frank Kovacs
92	Enrico Ciccone
113	Roman Turek
134	Jeff Levy
155	Doug Barrault
176	Joe Biondi
197	Troy Binnie
218	Ole-Eskild Dahlstrom
239	John McKersie

1989

Pick	
7	Doug Zmolek
28	Mike Craig
60	Murray Garbutt
75	Jean-François Quintin
87	Pat MacLeod
91	Bryan Schoen
97	Rhys Hollyman
112	Scott Cashman
154	Jonathan Pratt
175	Kenneth Blum
196	Arturs Irbe
217	Tom Pederson
238	Helmut Balderis

1988

Pick	
1	Mike Modano
40	Link Gaetz
43	Shaun Kane
64	Jeffrey Stop
148	Ken MacArthur
169	Travis Richards
190	Ari Matilainen
211	Grant Bischoff
232	Trent Andison

1987

Pick	
6	David Archibald
35	Scott McCrady
48	Kevin Kaminski
73	John Weisbrod
88	Teppo Kivela
109	Darcy Norton
130	Timo Kulonen
151	Don Schmidt
172	Jarmo Myllys
193	Larry Olimb
214	Mark Felicio
235	Dave hields

1986

Pick	
12	Warren Babe
30	Neil Wilkinson
33	Dean Kolstad
54	Eric Bennett
55	Rob Zettler
58	Brad Turner
75	Kirk Tomlinson
96	Jari Gronstrand
159	Scott Mathias
180	Lance Pitlick
201	Dan Keczmer
222	Garth Joy
243	Kurt Stahura

1985

Pick	
51	Stephane Roy
69	Mike Berger
90	Dwight Mullins
111	MikeMullowney
132	Mike Kelfer
153	Ross Johnson
174	Tim Helmer
195	Gordon Ernst
216	Ladislav Lubina
237	Tommy Sjodin

1984

Pick	
13	David Quinn
46	Ken Hodge
76	Miroslav Maly
89	Jiri Poner
97	Kari Takko
118	Gary McColgan
139	Vladimir Kyhos
160	Darin MacInnis
181	Duane Wahlin
201	Mike Orn
222	Tom Terwilliger
242	Mike Nightenale

1983

Pick	
1	Brian Lawton
36	Malcolm Parks
38	Frantisek Musil
56	Mitch Messier
76	Brian Durand
96	Rich Geist
116	Tom McComb
136	Sean Toomey
156	Don Biggs
176	Paul Pulis
196	Milos Riha
212	Oldrich Valek
236	Paul Roff

1982

Pick	
2	Brian Bellows
59	Wally Chapman
80	Rob Rouse
81	Dusan Pasek
101	Marty Wiitala
122	Todd Carlile
143	Victor Zhluktov
164	Paul Miller
185	Pat Micheletti
206	Arnold Kadlec
227	Scott Knutson

1981

Pick	
13	Ron Meighan
27	Dave Donnelly
31	Mike Sands
33	Tom Hirsch
34	Dave Preuss
41	Jali Wahlsten
69	Terry Tait
76	Jim Malwitz
97	Kelly Hubbard
118	Paul Guay
139	Jim Archibald
160	Kari Kaervo
181	Scott Bjugstad
202	Steve Kudebeh

1980

Pick	
16	Brad Palmer
37	Don Beaupre
53	Randy Velischek
79	Mark Huglen
100	Dave Jensen
121	Dan Zavarise
142	Bill Stewart
163	Jeff Walters
184	Bob Lakso
205	Dave Richter

1979

Pick	
6	Craig Hartsburg
10	Tom McCarthy
42	Neal Broten
63	Kevin Maxwell
90	Jim Dobson
111	Brian Gualazzi

1978

Pick	
1	Bobby Smith
19	Steve Payne
24	Steve Christoff
54	Curt Giles
70	Roy Kerling
87	Bob Bergloff
104	Kim Spencer
121	Mike Cotter
138	Brent Gogol
155	Mike Seide

Coach and General Manager

GAINEY, BOB

Coach and General Manager, Minnesota North Stars. Born in Peterborough, Ont., December 13, 1953.

Bob Gainey added the general manager's portfolio to his job description in June, 1992 after Bob Clarke rejoined the Philadelphia Flyers organization.

In his first season as an NHL head coach, Bob Gainey led the Minnesota North Stars through stunning playoff upsets of the League's top two teams and all the way to the Stanley Cup Finals. After surprising the League's top finishing Chicago Blackhawks in the Norris Division Semi-Finals, Gainey's Stars went on to eliminate the League's second place finishers—the St. Louis Blues—in the Norris Division Finals. The North Stars then defeated the defending Stanley Cup Champion Edmonton Oilers before bowing in six games to the Pittsburgh Penguins in the 1991 Stanley Cup Finals.

Gainey, who was appointed head coach of the North Stars on June 19, 1990 following a 16-year NHL career and a one-season coaching stint in Epinal, France, was Montreal's first choice (eighth overall) in the 1973 Amateur Draft. During his 16-year career with the Canadiens, Gainey was a member of five Stanley Cup-winning teams and was named the Conn Smythe Trophy winner in 1979. He was a four-time recipient of the Frank Selke Trophy (1978-81), awarded to the League's top defensive forward, and participated in four NHL All-Star Games (1977, 1978, 1980 and 1981). He served as team captain for eight seasons (1981-89). During his career, he played in 1,160 regular-season games, registering 239 goals and 262 assists for 501 points. In addition, he tallied 73 points (25-48-73) in 182 post-season games. He retired in July of 1989 and served as player/coach for Epinal, a second division French team.

Coaching Record

		Regular Season					Playoffs			
Season	Team	Games	W	L	T	%	Games	W	L	%
1989-90	Epinal	....	....	....	....	....	....	....	....	....
1990-91	Minnesota (NHL)	80	27	39	14	.425	23	14	9	.643
1991-92	Minnesota (NHL)	80	32	42	6	.438	7	3	4	.429
	NHL Totals	160	59	81	20	.431	30	17	13	.567

Club Directory

Met Center
7901 Cedar Avenue South
Bloomington, MN 55425
Phone **612/853-9333**
FAX 612/853-9467
GM FAX 612/853-9408
Capacity: 15,174

Owner & Governor	Norman N. Green
Alternate Governor	Pat Forciea
Hockey	
General Manager and Head Coach	Bob Gainey
Administrative Assistant	Jane Marostica
Director of Player Personnel/Hockey Operations	Les Jackson
Assistant Coaches	Doug Jarvis, Rick Wilson
Assistant to the General Manager	Doug Armstrong
Director of Amateur Scouting	Craig Button
Chief Scout	Dennis Patterson
European Scout	Matti Vaisanen
Part Time Scouts	Brad Robson, Jim Pederson, Doug Overton, Jr, Jeff Twohey, Bob Atrill, Bruce Plante, Mark Pezzin, Ray Robson, Tom Osiecki, Willard Ikola, Todd Dahl, Kevin Pottle, Smokey Cerrone
Head Athletic Trainer	Dave Surprenant
Assistant Trainer	Dave Smith
Equipment Manager	Mark Baribeau
Assistant Equipment Manager	Lance Vogt
Team Physicians	Dr. John Schaefer, Dr. Jim Schaffhausen, Dr. William Simonet, Dr. Joe Horozaniecki
Team Dentists	Dr. Paul Belvedere, Dr. Doug Lambert
Team Physical Therapists	Tom Coplin, Kent Malcomson
Team Video	Tom Zwinger
Executive	
President and Governor	Norman N. Green
Administrative Assistant	Carol Felber
Senior Vice-President and Alternate Governor	Pat Forciea
Administrative Assistant	Sue Roen
Vice-President of Administration	Pat Hoffman
Administrative Assistant	Sue Roen
Legal Counsel and Alternate Governor	Jack Donahue
Sales and Marketing	
Director of Luxury Seating	Tom Vannelli
Administrative Assistant	Sherry Rodgers
Director of Marketing	Matt Colford
Administrative Assistant	Sherry Rodgers
Group Sales Manager	Murray Cohn
Suites Manager	Tina Tano
Corporate Account Executives	Scott Erickson, Dan Richlen
Director of Ticket Sales	Murray Cohn
Administrative Assistant	Heidi Harman
Senior Account Executives	Steve Orth, Tim Wegscheid
Account Executives	Terry Bodensteiner, Tom Garrity, Bob Gazich, Bob Hanson, Kathleen Thielen, Deb Van Neste
Director of Merchandising	Peter Jocketty
Administrative Assistant	Cheryl Malmanger
Communications	
Director of Communications	Joan St. Peter
Assistant Director of Communications	Dan Stuchal
Finance	
Controller	Steve Freedman
Administrative Assistant	Kristi Cianciolo
Ticket Office Supervisors	Mark O'Hara, Micki Tschida
Ticket Office Staff	Linda DiCasmirro, Judy Goodman, Kevin Kelly
Accountants	Anne Kutzbach, John Lehman
Building Operations	
Building Manager	Mark Stoffel
Audio-Visual Coordinator	John Maher
Building Maintenance	Bob Jirik, Dave Westby
Switchboard	Marilyn Weber
West End Receptionist	Margo Quast
Arena Stadium Auditorium Productions - Game Night Services	
Parking, Ushering	Peter Kronschnabel
Facility Set-up	Scott Larson
Facility Maintenance	Doug Peterson
Star Event Management	
Directors	Paul Ridgeway, Doug McNeill
Facility Manager	Derek LaPrade
Administrative Assistant	Joey Johnson

Montreal Canadiens

1991-92 Results: 41W-28L-11T 93PTS. First, Adams Division

Patrick Roy captured his third Vezina Trophy in 1991-92, compiling a career-best GAA of 2.36

Schedule

Home			Away		
Oct.	Sat.	10 Pittsburgh	**Oct.**	Tues.	6 Hartford
	Sat.	17 Minnesota		Thur.	8 Ottawa
	Mon.	19 St Louis		Sun.	11 Buffalo
	Wed.	21 San Jose		Thur.	15 Pittsburgh
	Wed.	28 Tampa Bay		Fri.	23 NY Rangers
	Sat.	31 NY Rangers		Sat.	24 Philadelphia
Nov.	Mon.	2 Winnipeg	**Nov.**	Wed.	4 Detroit
	Sat.	7 Detroit		Wed.	11 New Jersey
	Mon.	9 Calgary		Tues.	17 Ottawa
	Sat.	14 Philadelphia		Thur.	19 Quebec
	Mon.	16 Boston		Wed.	25 Hartford
	Sat.	21 Ottawa	**Dec.**	Thur.	3 Boston
	Mon.	23 Washington		Sat.	5 Winnipeg
	Sat.	28 Vancouver		Sun.	6 Chicago
	Mon.	30 Buffalo		Tues.	8 Los Angeles
Dec.	Sat.	12 Boston		(at Phoenix)	
	Wed.	16 Quebec		Sun.	13 NY Rangers
	Sat.	19 Buffalo		Thur.	17 Quebec
	Mon.	21 Hartford		Sun.	27 Vancouver
	Wed.	23 NY Islanders		Tues.	29 Edmonton
Jan.	Mon.	4 San Jose		Thur.	31 Calgary
	(at Sacramento)		**Jan.**	Sat.	2 Los Angeles
	Sat.	9 Toronto		Tues.	5 San Jose
	Wed.	13 Hartford		Sun.	10 Hartford
	Sat.	16 NY Rangers		Thur.	14 Quebec
	Wed.	20 New Jersey		Fri.	22 New Jersey
	Mon.	25 Boston		Sat.	23 Toronto
	Wed.	27 Hartford	**Feb.**	Tues.	9 NY Islanders
	Sat.	30 Ottawa*		Thur.	11 Philadelphia
	Sun.	31 Philadelphia*		Sat.	13 Ottawa
Feb.	Wed.	3 Los Angeles		Tues.	23 St Louis
	Wed.	17 Boston		Fri.	26 Buffalo
	Sat.	20 Ottawa	**Mar.**	Mon.	1 Boston
	Sun.	21 Edmonton		Wed.	3 Tampa Bay
	Sat.	27 Buffalo		Sat.	6 Minnesota
Mar.	Wed.	10 NY Islanders		Thur.	11 Boston
	Sat.	13 Quebec		Thur.	18 Quebec
	Sat.	20 Chicago		Wed.	24 Hartford
	Mon.	22 Buffalo		Thur.	25 Boston
	Sat.	27 Ottawa	**Apr.**	Fri.	2 Washington
	Wed.	31 Quebec		Sat.	3 NY Islanders
Apr.	Sat.	10 Boston		Wed.	7 Pittsburgh
	Mon.	12 Washington		Tues.	13 Buffalo

* Denotes afternoon game.

Home Starting Times:

Weeknights	7:35 p.m.
Saturdays	8:05 p.m.
Sundays	7:05 p.m.
Matinees	1:05 p.m.

Franchise date: November 22, 1917

76th NHL Season

Year-by-Year Record

		Home			Road			Overall							
Season	GP	W	L	T	W	L	T	W	L	T	GF	GA	Pts.	Finished	Playoff Result
1991-92	80	27	8	5	14	20	6	41	28	11	267	207	93	1st, Adams Div.	Lost Div. Final
1990-91	80	23	12	5	16	18	6	39	30	11	273	249	89	2nd, Adams Div.	Lost Div. Final
1989-90	80	26	8	6	15	20	5	41	28	11	288	234	93	3rd, Adams Div.	Lost Div. Final
1988-89	80	30	6	4	23	12	5	53	18	9	315	218	115	1st, Adams Div.	Lost Final
1987-88	80	26	8	6	19	14	7	45	22	13	298	238	103	1st, Adams Div.	Lost Div. Final
1986-87	80	27	9	4	14	20	6	41	29	10	277	241	92	2nd, Adams Div.	Lost Conf. Championship
1985-86	**80**	25	11	4	15	22	3	**40**	**33**	**7**	**330**	**280**	**87**	**2nd, Adams Div.**	**Won Stanley Cup**
1984-85	80	24	10	6	17	17	6	41	27	12	309	262	94	1st, Adams Div.	Lost Div. Final
1983-84	80	19	19	2	16	21	3	35	40	5	286	295	75	4th, Adams Div.	Lost Conf. Championship
1982-83	80	25	6	9	17	18	5	42	24	14	350	286	98	2nd, Adams Div.	Lost Div. Semi-Final
1981-82	80	25	6	9	21	11	8	46	17	17	360	223	109	1st, Adams Div.	Lost Div. Semi-Final
1980-81	80	31	7	2	14	15	11	45	22	13	332	232	103	1st, Norris Div.	Lost Prelim. Round
1979-80	80	30	7	3	17	13	10	47	20	13	328	240	107	1st, Norris Div.	Lost Quarter-Final
1978-79	**80**	29	6	5	23	11	6	**52**	**17**	**11**	**337**	**204**	**115**	**1st, Norris Div.**	**Won Stanley Cup**
1977-78	**80**	32	4	4	27	6	7	**59**	**10**	**11**	**359**	**183**	**129**	**1st, Norris Div.**	**Won Stanley Cup**
1976-77	**80**	33	1	6	27	7	6	**60**	**8**	**12**	**387**	**171**	**132**	**1st, Norris Div.**	**Won Stanley Cup**
1975-76	**80**	32	3	5	26	8	6	**58**	**11**	**11**	**337**	**174**	**127**	**1st, Norris Div.**	**Won Stanley Cup**
1974-75	80	27	8	5	20	6	14	47	14	19	374	225	113	1st, Norris Div.	Lost Semi-Final
1973-74	78	24	12	3	21	12	6	45	24	9	293	240	99	2nd, East Div.	Lost Quarter-Inal
1972-73	**78**	29	4	6	23	6	10	**52**	**10**	**16**	**329**	**184**	**120**	**1st, East Div.**	**Won Stanley Cup**
1971-72	78	29	3	7	17	13	9	46	16	16	307	205	108	3rd, East Div.	Lost Quarter-Final
1970-71	**78**	29	7	3	13	16	10	**42**	**23**	**13**	**291**	**216**	**97**	**3rd, East Div.**	**Won Stanley Cup**
1969-70	76	21	9	8	17	13	8	38	22	16	244	201	92	5th, East Div.	Out of Playoffs
1968-69	**76**	26	7	5	20	12	6	**46**	**19**	**11**	**271**	**202**	**103**	**1st, East Div.**	**Won Stanley Cup**
1967-68	**74**	26	5	6	16	17	4	**42**	**22**	**10**	**236**	**167**	**94**	**1st, East Div.**	**Won Stanley Cup**
1966-67	70	19	9	7	13	16	6	32	25	13	202	188	77	2nd,	Lost Final
1965-66	**70**	23	11	1	18	10	7	**41**	**21**	**8**	**239**	**173**	**90**	**1st,**	**Won Stanley Cup**
1964-65	**70**	20	8	7	16	15	4	**36**	**23**	**11**	**211**	**185**	**83**	**2nd,**	**Won Stanley Cup**
1963-64	70	22	7	6	14	14	7	36	21	13	209	167	85	1st,	Lost Semi-Final
1962-63	70	15	10	10	13	9	13	28	19	23	225	183	79	3rd,	Lost Semi-Final
1961-62	70	26	2	7	16	12	7	42	14	14	259	166	98	1st,	Lost Semi-Final
1960-61	70	24	6	5	17	13	5	41	19	10	254	188	92	1st,	Lost Semi-Final
1959-60	**70**	23	4	8	17	14	4	**40**	**18**	**12**	**255**	**178**	**92**	**1st,**	**Won Stanley Cup**
1958-59	**70**	21	8	6	18	10	7	**39**	**18**	**13**	**58**	**158**	**91**	**1st,**	**Won Stanley Cup**
1957-58	**70**	23	8	4	20	9	6	**43**	**17**	**10**	**250**	**158**	**96**	**1st,**	**Won Stanley Cup**
1956-57	**70**	23	6	6	12	17	6	**35**	**23**	**12**	**210**	**155**	**82**	**2nd,**	**Won Stanley Cup**
1955-56	**70**	29	5	1	16	10	9	**45**	**15**	**10**	**222**	**131**	**100**	**1st,**	**Won Stanley Cup**
1954-55	70	26	5	4	15	13	7	41	18	11	228	157	93	2nd,	Lost Final
1953-54	70	7	5	3	8	19	8	35	24	11	195	141	81	2nd,	Lost Final
1952-53	**70**	18	12	5	10	11	14	**28**	**23**	**19**	**155**	**148**	**75**	**2nd,**	**Won Stanley Cup**
1951-52	70	22	8	5	12	18	5	34	26	10	195	164	78	2nd,	Lost Final
1950-51	70	17	10	8	8	20	7	25	30	15	173	184	65	3rd,	Lost Final
1949-50	70	17	8	10	12	14	9	29	22	19	172	150	77	2nd,	Lost Semi-Final
1948-49	60	19	8	3	9	15	6	28	23	9	152	126	65	3rd,	Lost Semi-Final
1947-48	60	13	13	4	7	16	7	20	29	11	147	169	51	5th,	Out of Playoffs
1946-47	60	19	6	5	15	10	5	34	16	10	189	138	78	1st,	Lost Final
1945-46	**50**	16	6	3	12	11	2	**28**	**17**	**5**	**172**	**134**	**61**	**1st,**	**Won Stanley Cup**
1944-45	50	21	2	2	17	6	2	38	8	4	228	121	80	1st,	Lost Semi-Final
1943-44	**50**	22	0	3	16	5	4	**38**	**5**	**7**	**234**	**109**	**83**	**1st,**	**Won Stanley Cup**
1942-43	50	14	4	7	5	15	5	19	19	12	181	191	50	4th,	Lost Semi-Final
1941-42	48	12	10	2	6	17	1	18	27	3	134	173	39	6th,	Lost Quarter-Final
1940-41	48	11	9	4	5	17	2	16	26	6	121	147	38	6th,	Lost Quarter-Final
1939-40	48	5	14	5	5	19	0	10	33	5	90	168	25	7th,	Out of Playoffs
1938-39	48	8	11	5	7	13	4	15	24	9	115	146	39	6th,	Lost Quarter-Final
1937-38	48	13	4	7	5	13	6	18	17	13	123	128	49	3rd, Cdn. Div.	Lost Quarter-Final
1936-37	48	16	8	0	8	10	6	24	18	6	115	111	54	1st, Cdn. Div.	Lost Semi-Final
1935-36	48	5	11	8	6	15	3	11	26	11	82	123	33	4th, Cdn. Div.	Out of Playoffs
1934-35	48	11	11	2	8	12	4	19	23	6	110	145	44	3rd, Cdn. Div.	Lost Quarter-Final
1933-34	48	16	6	2	6	14	4	22	20	6	99	101	50	2nd, Cdn. Div.	Lost Quarter-Final
1932-33	48	15	5	4	3	20	1	18	25	5	92	115	41	3rd, Cdn. Div.	Lost Quarter-Final
1931-32	48	18	3	3	7	13	4	25	16	7	128	111	57	1st, Cdn. Div.	Lost Semi-Final
1930-31	**44**	15	3	4	11	7	4	**26**	**10**	**8**	**129**	**89**	**60**	**1st, Cdn. Div.**	**Won Stanley Cup**
1929-30	**44**	13	5	4	8	9	5	**21**	**14**	**9**	**142**	**114**	**51**	**2nd, Cdn. Div.**	**Won Stanley Cup**
1928-29	44	12	4	6	10	3	9	22	7	15	71	43	59	1st, Cdn. Div.	Lost Semi-Final
1927-28	44	12	7	3	14	4	4	26	11	7	116	48	59	1st, Cdn. Div.	Lost Semi-Final
1926-27	44	15	5	2	13	9	0	28	14	2	99	67	58	2nd, Cdn. Div.	Lost Semi-Final
1925-26	36	5	12	1	6	12	0	11	24	1	79	108	23	7th,	Out of Playoffs
1924-25	30	10	5	0	7	6	2	17	11	2	93	56	36	3rd,	Lost Final
1923-24	**24**	10	2	0	3	9	0	**13**	**11**	**0**	**59**	**48**	**26**	**2nd,**	**Won Stanley Cup**
1922-23	24	10	2	0	3	7	2	13	9	2	73	61	28	2nd,	Lost NHL Final
1921-22	24	8	3	1	4	8	0	12	11	1	88	94	25	3rd,	Out of Playoffs
1920-21	24	16	8	0	8	10	6	13	11	0	112	99	26	3rd and 2nd*	Out of Playoffs
1919-20	24	8	4	0	5	7	0	13	11	0	129	113	26	2nd and 3rd*	Out of Playoffs
1918-19	18	7	2	0	3	6	0	10	8	0	88	78	20	1st and 2nd*	Cup Final but no Decision
1917-18	22	8	3	0	5	6	0	13	9	0	115	84	26	1st and 3rd*	Lost NHL Final

* Season played in two halves with no combined standing at end.
From 1917-18 through 1925-26, NHL champions played against PCHL champions for Stanley Cup.

1992-93 Player Personnel

FORWARDS	HT	WT	S	Place of Birth	Date	1991-92 Club
BELANGER, Jesse	6-0	170	R	St-Georges de Beauce, Que.	6/15/69	Montreal-Fredericton
BELLOWS, Brian	5-11	195	R	St. Catharines, Ont.	9/1/64	Minnesota
BRASHEAR, Donald	6-3	206	L	Bedford, IN	1/7/72	Verdun
BRUNET, Benoit	5-11	184	L	Ste-Anne de Bellevue, Que.	8/24/68	Montreal-Fredericton
CARBONNEAU, Guy	5-11	184	R	Sept-Iles, Que.	3/18/60	Montreal
CARNBACK, Patrik	6-0	187	L	Goteborg, Sweden	2/1/68	Frolunda
DAMPHOUSSE, Vincent	6-1	190	L	Montreal, Que.	12/17/67	Edmonton
DESJARDINS, Norman	5-10	184	R	Montréal, Que.	3/25/68	Fredericton
DIONNE, Gilbert	6-0	194	L	Drummondville, Que.	9/19/70	Montreal-Fredericton
DIPIETRO, Paul	5-9	181	R	Sault Ste-Marie, Ont.	9/8/70	Montreal-Fredericton
EWEN, Todd	6-2	220	R	Saskatoon, Sask.	3/22/66	Montreal
FERGUSON, Craig	6-0	185	L	Castro Valley, CA	4/8/70	Yale University
FERGUSON, John Jr.	6-0	192	L	Montreal, Que.	7/7/67	Fredericton
FLEETWOOD, Brent	6-1	180	L	Edmonton, Alta.	6/4/70	Fred.-W.-Salem
FLEMING, Gerry	6-5	240	L	Montréal, Que.	10/16/67	Fredericton
GUILLET, Robert	5-11	189	R	Montréal, Que.	2/22/72	Longueuil
KEANE, Mike	5-10	178	R	Winnipeg, Man.	5/29/67	Montreal
KELLEY, Robert	6-2	205	L	Cambridge, MA	2/10/69	Merrimack
KJELLBERG, Patric	6-2	196	L	Falun, Sweden	6/17/69	AIK
KUWABARA, Ryan	6-0	205	R	Hamilton, Ont.	3/23/72	Ottawa
LAROUCHE, Steve	5-11	180	R	Rouyn, Que.	4/14/71	Fredericton
LEBEAU, Patrick	5-10	172	L	St-Jérôme, Que.	3/17/70	Fred.-Cdn. Nat.-Cdn. Oly.
LEBEAU, Stephan	5-10	172	R	St-Jérôme, Que.	2/28/68	Montreal
LeCLAIR, John	6-2	205	L	St. Albans, VT	7/5/69	Montreal-Fredericton
MULLER, Kirk	6-0	205	L	Kingston, Ont.	2/8/66	Montreal
PETROV, Oleg	5-9	161	L	Moscow, USSR	4/18/71	CSKA
POULIN, Charles	6-0	172	L	St-Jean d'Iberville, Que.	7/27/72	St. Hyacinthe
ROBERGE, Mario	5-11	185	L	Québec, Que.	1/25/64	Montreal-Fredericton
RONAN, Edward	6-0	197	R	Quincy, MA	3/21/68	Montreal-Fredericton
SAGISSOR, Tom	5-11	202	R	Hastings, MN	9/12/67	Fredericton
SARAULT, Yves	6-1	170	L	Valleyfield, Que.	12/23/72	St. Jean-Trois-Rivières
SAVARD, Denis	5-10	175	R	Pointe-Gatineau, Que.	2/4/61	Montreal
SEVIGNY, Pierre	6-0	189	L	Trois-Rivières, Que.	9/8/71	Fredericton
SKRUDLAND, Brian	6-0	196	L	Peace River, Alta.	7/31/63	Montreal
STEVENSON, Turner	6-3	200	R	Prince George, B.C.	5/18/72	Seattle
TORREY, Jeff	6-0	190	R	Syracuse, NY	3/6/70	Clarkson
VALLIS, Lindsay	6-3	207	R	Winnipeg, Man.	1/12/71	Fredericton
DEFENSEMEN						
BRISEBOIS, Patrice	6-2	175	R	Montréal, Que.	1/27/71	Montreal-Fredericton
CHARRON, Eric	6-3	192	L	Verdun, Que.	1/14/70	Fredericton
COTE, Alain	6-0	200	R	Montmagny, Que.	4/14/67	Montreal-Fredericton
DAIGNEAULT, J.-J.	5-11	185	L	Montréal, Que.	10/12/65	Montreal
DESJARDINS, Eric	6-1	200	R	Rouyn, Que.	6/14/69	Montreal
DUFRESNE, Donald	6-1	206	R	Québec, Que.	4/10/67	Montreal-Fredericton
GAUTHIER, Luc	5-9	195	R	Longueuil, Que.	4/19/64	Fredericton
HALLER, Kevin	6-2	183	L	Trochu, Alta.	12/5/70	Buf.-Roch.-Mtl.
HILL, Sean	6-0	195	R	Duluth, MN	2/14/70	Fred.-U.S. Nat.-U.S. Olym.-Mtl.
MacEACHERN, Greg	6-2	205	L	Antigonish, N.S.	11/16/71	Fredericton-Laval
ODELEIN, Lyle	5-10	206	L	Quill Lake, Sask.	7/21/68	Montreal
SCHNEIDER, Mathieu	5-11	189	L	New York, NY	6/12/69	Montreal
SIMON, Darcy	6-1	200	R	North Battleford, Sask.	1/21/70	Fredericton
UNIAC, John	5-11	210	R	Stratford, Ont.	3/29/71	Winston-Salem
VEILLEUX, Steve	6-0	190	R	Lachenaie, Que.	3/9/69	Fredericton

GOALTENDERS	HT	WT	C	Place of Birth	Date	1991-92 Club
CHABOT, Frédéric	5-11	175	R	Hébertville-Stn., Que.	2/12/68	Fred.-W.-Salem
KUNTAR, Les	6-2	195	L	Elma, NY	7/28/69	Fred.-U.S. Nat.
OUELLETTE, Francis	5-10	185	R	Victoriaville, Que.	4/16/70	Peoria-Dayton
RACICOT, André	5-11	165	L	Rouyn-Noranda, Que.	6/9/69	Montreal-Fredericton
ROY, Patrick	6-0	182	L	Québec, Que.	10/5/65	Montreal

Coach

DEMERS, JACQUES

Coach, Montreal Canadiens. Born in Montreal, Que., August 25, 1944.

After spending the past two years as a radio and television analyst, Jacques Demers returns to the coaching ranks as the 21st head coach of the Montreal Canadiens. Demers, who is the only man in NHL history to win coach of the year honors in back-to-back seasons when he was with Detroit, began his coaching career in the QMJHL before making his professional coaching debut with the WHA's Chicago Cougars in 1972-73. Eventually, Demers joined the Quebec Nordiques' organization and was the teams first coach when the club joined the NHL in 1979-80. In 1981, Demers was appointed as the head of the Nordiques' AHL farm affiliate in Fredericton, where he earned Executive of the Year honors in 1983. The following season, Demers returned to the NHL with the St. Louis Blues, where he spent three seasons as head coach.

Coaching Record

		Regular Season					Playoffs			
Season	Team	Games	W	L	T	%	Games	W	L	%
1975-76	Indianapolis (WHA)	80	35	39	6	.475	7	3	4	.429
1976-77	Indianapolis (WHA)	81	36	37	8	.494	9	5	4	.556
1977-78	Cincinnati (WHA)	80	35	42	3	.456	....	....	....	....
1978-79	Quebec (WHA)	80	41	34	5	.544	4	0	4	.000
1979-80	**Quebec (NHL)**	**80**	**25**	**44**	**11**	**.381**	....	....	....	....
1981-82	Fredericton (AHL)	80	20	55	5	.281	....	....	....	....
1982-83	Fredericton (AHL)	80	45	27	8	.544	12	6	6	.500
1983-84	**St. Louis (NHL)**	**80**	**32**	**41**	**7**	**.444**	**11**	**6**	**5**	**.545**
1984-85	**St. Louis (NHL)**	**80**	**37**	**31**	**12**	**.538**	**3**	**0**	**3**	**.000**
1985-86	**St. Louis (NHL)**	**80**	**37**	**34**	**9**	**.519**	**19**	**10**	**9**	**.526**
1986-87	**Detroit (NHL)**	**80**	**36**	**34**	**10**	**.488**	**16**	**9**	**7**	**.563**
1987-88	**Detroit (NHL)**	**80**	**41**	**28**	**11**	**.581**	**16**	**9**	**7**	**.563**
1988-89	**Detroit (NHL)**	**80**	**34**	**34**	**12**	**.500**	**6**	**2**	**4**	**.333**
1989-90	**Detroit (NHL)**	**80**	**28**	**38**	**14**	**.437**	....	....	....	....
	NHL Totals	**640**	**268**	**286**	**86**	**.486**	**71**	**36**	**35**	**.507**

1991-92 Scoring

Regular Season

Pos	#.	Player	Team	GP	G	A	Pts	+/–	PIM	PP	SH	GW	GT	S	%
L	11	Kirk Muller	MTL	78	36	41	77	15	86	15	1	7	1	191	18.8
C	18	Denis Savard	MTL	77	28	42	70	6	73	12	1	5	0	174	16.1
C	47	Stephan Lebeau	MTL	77	27	31	58	18	14	13	0	5	0	178	15.2
L	27	Shayne Corson	MTL	64	17	36	53	15	118	3	0	2	0	165	10.3
C	41	Brent Gilchrist	MTL	79	23	27	50	29	57	2	0	3	2	146	15.8
R	12	Mike Keane	MTL	67	11	30	41	16	64	2	0	2	1	116	9.5
C	21	Guy Carbonneau	MTL	72	18	21	39	2	39	1	1	4	0	120	15.0
D	28	Eric Desjardins	MTL	77	6	32	38	17	50	4	0	2	0	141	4.3
L	45*	Gilbert Dionne	MTL	39	21	13	34	7	10	7	0	2	0	90	23.3
D	8	Matt Schneider	MTL	78	8	24	32	10	72	2	0	1	0	194	4.1
L	35	Mike McPhee	MTL	78	16	15	31	6	63	0	0	1	0	146	11.0
D	14*	Kevin Haller	BUF	58	6	15	21	13–	75	2	0	1	0	76	7.9
			MTL	8	2	2	4	4	17	1	0	0	0	9	22.2
			TOTAL	66	8	17	25	9–	92	3	0	1	0	85	9.4
R	6	Russ Courtnall	MTL	27	7	14	21	6	6	0	1	1	1	63	11.1
L	20	Sylvain Turgeon	MTL	56	9	11	20	4–	39	6	0	1	0	99	9.1
C	17*	John LeClair	MTL	59	8	11	19	5	14	3	0	0	0	73	11.0
D	48	J.j. Daigneault	MTL	79	4	14	18	16	36	2	0	0	1	108	3.7
D	3	Sylvain Lefebvre	MTL	69	3	14	17	9	91	0	0	0	0	85	3.5
R	30	Chris Nilan	BOS	39	5	5	10	5–	186	0	0	0	0	33	15.2
			MTL	17	1	3	4	1–	74	0	0	0	0	22	4.5
			TOTAL	56	6	8	14	6–	260	0	0	0	0	55	10.9
L	22*	Benoit Brunet	MTL	18	4	6	10	4	14	0	0	0	0	37	10.8
C	15*	Paul Di Pietro	MTL	33	4	6	10	5	25	0	0	0	0	27	14.8
D	43*	Patrice Brisebois	MTL	26	2	8	10	9	20	0	0	1	0	37	5.4
D	24	Lyle Odelein	MTL	71	1	7	8	15	212	0	0	0	0	43	2.3
C	39	Brian Skrudland	MTL	42	3	3	6	4–	36	0	0	1	0	51	5.9
G	33	Patrick Roy	MTL	67	0	5	5	0	4	0	0	0	0	0	.0
L	32	Mario Roberge	MTL	20	2	1	3	3	62	0	0	0	0	7	28.6
R	36	Todd Ewen	MTL	46	1	2	3	3	130	0	0	0	0	19	5.3
D	5	Alain Cote	MTL	13	0	3	3	7	22	0	0	0	0	6	.0
L	14*	Vladimir Vujtek	MTL	2	0	0	0	1–	0	0	0	0	0	1	.0
D	34	Donald Dufresne	MTL	3	0	0	0	2	2	0	0	0	0	2	.0
R	31*	Ed Ronan	MTL	3	0	0	0	0	0	0	0	0	0	1	.0
C	26*	Jesse Belanger	MTL	4	0	0	0	1–	0	0	0	0	0	4	.0
G	1	Roland Melanson	MTL	9	0	0	0	0	0	0	0	0	0	0	.0
G	40*	Andre Racicot	MTL	9	0	0	0	0	0	0	0	0	0	0	.0

Goaltending

No.	Goaltender	GPI	Mins	Avg	W	L	T	EN	SO	GA	SA	S%
33	Patrick Roy	67	3935	2.36	36	22	8	7	5	155	1806	.914
1	Roland Melanson	9	492	2.68	5	3	0	0	2	22	195	.887
40	* Andre Racicot	9	436	3.17	0	3	3	0	0	23	219	.895
	Totals	**80**	**4877**	**2.55**	**41**	**28**	**11**	**7**	**7**	**207**	**2227**	**.907**

Playoffs

Pos	#	Player	Team	GP	G	A	Pts	+/–	PIM	PP	SH	GW	GT	S	%
C	18	Denis Savard	MTL	11	3	9	12	1	8	1	0	0	0	33	9.1
L	11	Kirk Muller	MTL	11	4	3	7	1–	31	2	1	1	0	23	17.4
L	45*	Gilbert Dionne	MTL	11	3	4	7	2	10	1	0	1	0	33	9.1
L	27	Shayne Corson	MTL	10	2	5	7	1	15	0	0	0	0	23	8.7
D	28	Eric Desjardins	MTL	11	3	3	6	0	4	1	0	0	0	28	10.7
D	43*	Patrice Brisebois	MTL	11	2	4	6	3	6	1	0	1	0	25	8.0
C	41	Brent Gilchrist	MTL	11	2	4	6	2–	6	1	0	0	0	20	10.0
D	8	Matt Schneider	MTL	10	1	4	5	2–	6	1	0	0	0	27	3.7
C	47	Stephan Lebeau	MTL	8	1	3	4	1	4	1	0	0	0	8	12.5
D	48	J.j. Daigneault	MTL	11	0	3	3	2–	4	0	0	0	0	17	.0
R	12	Mike Keane	MTL	8	1	1	2	1	16	0	0	0	0	7	14.3
C	17*	John LeCclair	MTL	8	1	1	2	2–	4	0	0	0	0	10	10.0
L	35	Mike McPhee	MTL	8	1	1	2	1–	4	0	0	0	0	16	6.3
R	6	Russ Courtnall	MTL	10	1	1	2	2–	4	0	0	1	1	14	7.1
C	21	Guy Carbonneau	MTL	11	1	1	2	4–	6	0	0	0	0	22	4.5
C	39	Brian Skrudland	MTL	11	1	1	2	1–	20	0	0	0	0	15	6.7
D	38*	Sean Hill	MTL	4	1	0	1	1	2	0	0	0	0	4	25.0
L	20	Sylvain Turgeon	MTL	5	1	0	1	0	4	0	0	0	0	7	14.3
R	30	Chris Nilan	MTL	7	0	1	1	2–	15	0	0	0	0	4	.0
G	40*	Andre Racicot	MTL	1	0	0	0	0	0	0	0	0	0	0	.0
D	3	Sylvain Lefebvre	MTL	2	0	0	0	2	2	0	0	0	0	2	.0
R	36	Todd Ewen	MTL	3	0	0	0	0	18	0	0	0	0	1	.0
D	24	Lyle Odelein	MTL	7	0	0	0	4–	11	0	0	0	0	1	.0
D	14*	Kevin Haller	MTL	9	0	0	0	3–	6	0	0	0	0	12	.0
G	33	Patrick Roy	MTL	11	0	0	0	0	2	0	0	0	0	0	.0

Goaltending

No.	Goaltender	GPI	Mins	Avg	W	L	EN	SO	GA	SA	S%
40	* Andre Racicot	1	1	.00	0	0	0	0	0	1	1.000
33	Patrick Roy	11	686	2.62	4	7	2	1	30	312	.904
	Totals	**11**	**689**	**2.79**	**4**	**7**	**2**	**1**	**32**	**315**	**.898**

Captains' History

Newsy Lalonde, 1917-18 to 1920-21; Sprague Cleghorn, 1921-22 to 1924-25; Bill Couture, 1925-26; Sylvio Mantha, 1926-27 to 1931-32; George Hainsworth, 1932-33; Sylvio Mantha, 1933-34 to 1935-36; Babe Seibert, 1936-37 to 1938-39; Walter Buswell, 1939-40; Toe Blake, 1940-41 to 1946-47; Toe Blake, Bill Durnan (co-captains) 1947-48; Emile Bouchard, 1948-49 to 1955-56; Maurice Richard, 1956-57 to 1959-60; Doug Harvey, 1960-61; Jean Beliveau, 1961-62 to 1970-71; Henri Richard, 1971-72 to 1974-75; Yvan Cournoyer, 1975-76 to 1978-79; Serge Savard, 1979-80, 1980-81; Bob Gainey, 1981-82 to 1988-89; Guy Carbonneau and Chris Chelios (co-captains), 1989-90; Guy Carbonneau, 1990-91 to date.

Club Records

Team

(Figures in brackets for season records are games played; records for fewest points, wins, ties, losses, goals, goals against are for 70 or more games)

Record		
Most Points	*132	1976-77 (80)
Most Wins	*60	1976-77 (80)
Most Ties	23	1962-63 (70)
Most Losses	40	1983-84 (80)
Most Goals	387	1976-77 (80)
Most Goals Against	295	1983-84 (80)
Fewest Points	65	1950-51 (70)
Fewest Wins	25	1950-51 (70)
Fewest Ties	5	1983-84 (80)
Fewest Losses	*8	1976-77 (80)
Fewest Goals	155	1952-53 (70)
Fewest Goals Against	*131	1955-56 (70)
Longest WinningStreak		
Over-all	12	Jan. 6-Feb. 3/68
Home	13	Nov. 2/43-Jan. 8/44; Jan. 30-Mar. 26/77
Away	8	Dec. 18/77-Jan. 18/78; Jan. 21-Feb. 21/82
Longest Undefeated Streak		
Over-all	28	Dec. 18/77-Feb. 23/78 (23 wins, 5 ties)
Home	*34	Nov. 1/76-Apr. 2/77 (28 wins, 6 ties)
Away	*23	Nov. 27/74-Mar. 12/75 (14 wins, 9 ties)
Longest Losing Streak		
Over-all	12	Feb. 13/26-Mar. 13/26
Home	7	Dec. 16/39-Jan. 18/40
Away	10	Dec. 1/25-Feb. 2/26
Longest Winless Streak		
Over-all	12	Feb. 13-Mar. 13/26 (12 losses); Nov. 28-Dec. 29/35 (8 losses, 4 ties)
Home	*15	Dec. 16/39-Mar. 7/40 (12 losses, 3 ties)
Away	12	Oct. 20-Dec. 13/51 (8 losses, 4 ties)
Most Shutouts, Season	*22	1928-29 (44)
Most PIM, Season	1,842	1987-88 (80)
Most Goals, Game	*16	Mar. 3/20 (Mt. 16 at Que. 3)

Individual

Record		
Most Seasons	20	Henri Richard
Most Games	1,256	Henri Richard
Most Goals Career	544	Maurice Richard
Most Assists, Career	728	Guy Lafleur
Most Points Career	1,246	Guy Lafleur (518 goals, 728 assists)
Most PIM, Career	2,248	Chris Nilan
Most Shutouts, Career	75	George Hainsworth
Longest Consecutive Games Streak	560	Doug Jarvis (Oct. 8/75-Apr. 4/82)
Most Goals, Season	60	Steve Shutt (1976-77); Guy Lafleur (1977-78)
Most Assists, Season	82	Peter Mahovlich (1974-75)
Most Points, Season	136	Guy Lafleur (1976-77) (56 goals, 80 assists)
Most PIM, Season	358	Chris Nilan (1984-85)
Most Points, Defenseman Season	85	Larry Robinson (1976-77) (19 goals, 66 assists)
Most Points, Center, Season	117	Peter Mahovlich (1974-75) (35 goals, 82 assists)
Most Points, Right Wing, Season	136	Guy Lafleur (1976-77) (56 goals, 80 assists)
Most Points, Left Wing, Season	110	Mats Naslund (1985-86) (43 goals, 67 assists)
Most Points, Rookie, Season	71	Mats Naslund (1982-83) (26 goals, 45 assists); Kjell Dahlin (1985-86) (32 goals, 39 assists)
Most Shutouts, Season	*22	George Hainsworth (1928-29)
Most Goals, Game	6	Newsy Lalonde (Jan. 10/20)
Most Assists, Game	6	Elmer Lach (Feb. 6/43)
Most Points, Game	8	Maurice Richard 5G-3A (Dec. 28/44); Bert Olmstead 4G-4A (Jan. 9/54)

* NHL Record.

Retired Numbers

2	Doug Harvey	1947-1961
4	Aurèle Joliat	1922-1938
	Jean Béliveau	1950-1971
7	Howie Morenz	1923-1937
9	Maurice Richard	1942-1960
10	Guy Lafleur	1971-1984
16	Elmer Lach	1942-1954
	Henri Richard	1955-1975

All-time Record vs. Other Clubs

Regular Season

	At Home							On Road							Total						
	GP	W	L	T	GF	GA	PTS	GP	W	L	T	GF	GA	PTS	GP	W	L	T	GF	GA	PTS
Boston	301	175	82	44	1027	690	394	302	112	138	52	814	890	276	603	287	220	96	1841	1580	670
Buffalo	71	44	19	8	296	208	96	71	21	32	18	209	219	60	142	65	51	26	505	427	156
Calgary	36	20	10	6	127	88	46	35	20	10	5	127	113	45	71	40	20	11	254	201	91
Chicago	265	166	51	48	1026	624	380	265	121	90	54	742	715	296	530	287	141	102	1768	1339	676
Detroit	272	167	62	43	965	606	377	272	95	124	53	699	770	243	544	262	186	96	1664	1376	620
Edmonton	20	11	6	3	72	63	25	21	9	12	0	62	73	18	41	20	18	3	134	136	43
Hartford	48	34	8	6	221	139	74	48	23	17	8	177	151	54	96	57	25	14	398	290	128
Los Angeles	55	37	7	11	254	145	85	55	34	15	6	221	165	74	110	71	22	17	475	310	159
Minnesota	49	33	9	7	217	122	73	50	27	13	10	181	129	64	99	60	22	17	398	251	137
New Jersey	31	22	5	4	133	80	48	30	22	8	0	145	80	44	61	44	13	4	278	160	92
NY Islanders	35	21	8	6	141	106	48	37	17	16	4	115	124	38	72	38	24	10	256	230	86
NY Rangers	266	177	55	34	1052	615	388	266	109	107	50	774	761	268	532	286	162	84	1826	1376	656
Philadelphia	50	27	13	10	191	143	64	49	20	17	12	146	131	52	99	47	30	22	337	274	116
Pittsburgh	56	47	4	5	289	135	99	55	29	17	9	207	165	67	111	76	21	14	496	300	166
Quebec	48	32	8	8	214	142	72	48	21	25	2	171	169	44	96	53	33	10	385	311	116
St. Louis	50	36	8	6	222	130	78	49	25	10	14	173	126	64	99	61	18	20	395	256	142
San Jose	1	1	0	0	6	1	2	2	1	0	1	4	3	3	3	2	0	1	10	4	5
Toronto	312	190	82	40	1110	767	420	313	110	159	44	821	949	264	625	300	241	84	1931	1716	684
Vancouver	43	34	7	2	217	111	70	41	27	6	8	167	100	62	84	61	13	10	384	211	132
Washington	36	26	5	5	172	73	57	37	17	14	6	130	98	40	73	43	19	11	302	171	97
Winnipeg	20	18	2	0	113	48	36	20	8	7	5	80	66	21	40	26	9	5	193	114	57
Defunct Clubs	231	148	58	25	779	469	321	230	98	97	35	586	606	231	461	246	155	60	1365	1075	552
Totals	**2296**	**1466**	**509**	**318**	**8844**	**5505**	**3250**	**2296**	**966**	**934**	**396**	**6751**	**6603**	**2328**	**4592**	**2432**	**1443**	**717**	**15595**	**12108**	**5581**

Playoffs

	Series	W	L	GP	W	L	T	GF	GA	Last Mtg.	Round	Result
Boston	27	21	6	132	84	48	0	410	317	1992	DF	L 0-4
Buffalo	5	3	2	27	14	13	0	98	82	1991	DSF	W 4-2
Calgary	2	1	1	11	6	5	0	31	32	1989	F	L 2-4
Chicago	17	12	5	81	50	29	2	261	185	1976	QF	W 4-0
Detroit	12	5	7	62	33	29	0	161	149	1978	QF	W 4-1
Edmonton	1	0	1	3	0	3	0	6	15	1981	PR	L 0-3
Hartford	5	5	0	27	19	8	0	96	70	1992	DSF	W 4-3
Minnesota	2	1	1	13	7	6	0	48	37	1980	QF	L 3-4
NY Islanders	3	2	1	17	10	7	0	48	44	1984	CF	L 2-4
NY Rangers	13	7	6	55	32	21	2	171	139	1986	CF	W 4-1
Philadelphia	4	3	1	21	14	7	0	72	52	1989	CF	W 4-2
Quebc	4	2	2	25	13	12	0	86	69	1987	DF	W 4-3
St. Louis	3	3	0	12	12	0	0	42	14	1977	QF	W 4-0
Toronto	13	7	6	67	39	28	0	203	148	1979	QF	W 4-0
Vancouver	1	1	0	5	4	1	0	20	9	1975	QF	W 4-1
Defunct Clubs	12	7	5	32	18	10	4	82	83			
Totals	**125***	**80**	**44**	**590**	**355**	**227**	**8**	**1835**	**1445**			

* 1919 Final incomplete due to influenza epidemic.

Playoff Results 1992-88

Year	Round	Opponent	Result	GF	GA
1992	DF	Boston	L 0-4	8	14
	DSF	Hartford	W 4-3	21	18
1991	DF	Boston	L 3-4	18	18
	DSF	Buffalo	W 4-2	29	24
1990	DF	Boston	L 1-4	12	16
	DSF	Buffalo	W 4-2	17	13
1989	F	Calgary	L 2-4	16	19
	CF	Philadelphia	W 4-2	17	8
	DF	Boston	W 4-1	16	13
	DSF	Hartford	W 4-0	18	11
1988	DF	Boston	L 1-4	10	15
	DSF	Hartford	W 4-2	23	20

Abbreviations: Round: F – Final; **CF** – conference final; **DF** – division final; **DSF** – division semi-final; **SF** – semi-final; **QF** – quarter-final; **PR** – preliminary round. **GA** – goals against; **GF** – goals for.

1991-92 Results

Home				Away			
Oct.	3	Toronto	4-3	**Oct.** 8		Hartford	2-2
	5	NY Rangers	1-2		10	Detroit	4-1
	14	Hartford	3-4		12	Boston	6-0
	16	Buffalo	5-1		18	Buffalo	1-3
	23	Quebec	3-2		19	Philadelphia	1-0
	26	Pittsburgh	4-1		24	Quebec	5-0
	30	Winnipeg	6-1	**Nov.**	1	Buffalo	5-1
Nov.	2	Buffalo	5-0		6	NY Rangers	4-1
	4	New Jersey	3-2		8	New Jersey	2-3
	9	Chicago	4-2		14	Hartford	2-2
	11	Washington	2-4		21	Quebec	2-5
	16	Philadelphia	1-3		27	Washington	1-3
	18	Edmonton	1-0		29	Boston*	4-5
	23	Quebec	5-3		30	Hartford	2-3
	25	Boston	4-3	**Dec.**	5	NY Islanders	5-4
Dec.	4	Vancouver	0-3		9	Toronto	4-1
	7	Calgary	5-1		12	Boston	2-5
	14	Buffalo	4-2		19	Chicago	4-6
	16	St Louis	4-2		26	Quebec	4-1
	21	Hartford	3-2		29	Edmonton	3-1
	22	Boston	3-2		31	Calgary	2-3
Jan.	8	Boston	3-2	**Jan.**	4	San Jose	1-0
	11	Hartford	3-2		15	Minnesota	2-5
	13	Calgary	2-2		16	St Louis	6-6
	25	Buffalo*	3-4		23	Boston	3-1
	26	Hartford*	3-1		31	Buffalo	3-5
	29	New Jersey	3-4	**Feb.**	4	Vancouver	3-5
Feb.	1	Detroit	4-3		5	Edmonton	1-2
	10	Vancouver	8-3		8	Toronto	4-6
	12	San Jose	6-1		19	Hartford	2-2
	15	Quebec	4-4		26	Minnesota	4-1
	17	Minnesota	8-0		28	San Jose	3-3
	22	Pittsburgh	2-1		29	Los Angeles	3-5
	23	Quebec	3-3	**Mar.**	3	NY Islanders	4-3
Mar.	7	NY Islanders	8-2		11	Quebec	4-5
	8	Detroit	4-1		16	NY Rangers	1-4
	14	Los Angeles	5-2		25	Winnipeg	2-2
	18	Philadelphia	3-4		27	Washington	3-4
	21	St Louis	3-3		28	Pittsburgh	3-6
Apr.	4	Boston	4-4	**Apr.**	2	Buffalo	1-3

*Denotes afternoon game

Entry Draft Selections 1992-78

1992

Pick	
20	David Wilkie
33	Valeri Bure
44	Keli Corpse
68	Craig Rivet
82	Louis Bernard
92	Marc Lamothe
116	Don Chase
140	Martin Sychra
164	Christian Proulx
188	Michael Burman
212	Earl Cronan
236	Trent Cavicchi
260	Hiroyuki Miura

1991

Pick	
17	Brent Bilodeau
28	Jim Campbll
43	Craig Darby
61	Yves Sarault
73	Vladimir Vujtek
83	Sylvain Lapointe
100	Brad Layzell
105	Tony Prpic
127	Oleg Petrov
149	Brady Kramer
171	Brian Savage
193	Scott Fraser
215	Greg MacEachern
237	Paul Lepler
259	Dale Hooper

1990

Pick	
12	Turner Stevenson
39	Ryan Kuwabara
58	Charles Poulin
60	Robert Guillet
81	Gilbert Dionne
102	Paul DiPietro
123	Craig Conroy
144	Stephen Rohr
165	Brent Fleetwood
186	Derek Maguire
207	Mark Kettelhut
228	John Uniac
249	Sergei Martynyuk

1989

Pick	
13	Lindsay Vallis
30	Patrice Brisebois
41	Steve Larouche
51	Pierre Sevigny
83	Andre Racicot
104	Marc Deschamps
146	Craig Ferguson
167	Patrick Lebeu
188	Roy Mitchell
209	Ed Henrich
230	Justin Duberman
251	Steve Cadieux

1988

Pick	
20	Eric Charron
34	Martin St. Amour
46	Neil Carnes
83	Patrik Kjellberg
93	Peter Popovic
104	Jean-Claude Bergeron
125	Patrik Carnback
146	Tim Chase
167	Sean Hill
188	Harijs Vitolinsh
209	Yuri Krivokhizha
230	Kevin Dahl
251	Dave Kunda

1987

Pick	
17	Andrew Cassels
33	John LeClair
38	Eric Desjardins
44	Mathieu Schneider
58	Francois Gravel
80	Kris Miller
101	Steve McCool
122	Les Kuntar
143	Rob Kelley
164	Will Geist
185	Eric Tremblay
206	Barry McKinlay
227	Ed Ronan
248	Bryan Herring

1986

Pick	
15	Mark Pederson
27	Benoit Brunet
57	Jyrki Lumme
78	Brent Bobyck
94	Eric Aubertin
99	Mario Milani
120	Steve Bisson
141	Lyle Odelein
162	Rick Hayward
183	Antonin Routa
204	Eric Bohemier
225	Charlie Moore
246	Karel Svoboda

1985

Pick	
12	Jose Charbonneau
16	Tom Chorske
33	Todd Richards
47	Rocky Dundas
75	Martin Desjardins
79	Brent Gilchrist
96	Tom Sagissor
117	Donald Dufresne
142	Ed Cristofoli
163	Mike Claringbull
184	Roger Beedon
198	Maurice Mansi
205	Chad Arthur
226	Mike Bishop
247	John Ferguson Jr.

1984

Pick	
5	Petr Svoboda
8	Shayne Corson
29	Stephane Richer
51	Patrick Roy
54	Graeme Bonar
65	Lee Brodeur
95	Gerald Johannson
116	Jim Nesich
137	Scott MacTavish
158	Brad McCughey
179	Eric Demers
199	Ron Annear
220	Dave Tanner
240	Troy Crosby

1983

Pick	
17	Alfie Turcotte
26	Claude Lemieux
27	Sergio Momesso
35	Todd Francis
45	Daniel Letendre
78	John Kordic
98	Dan Wurst
118	Arto Javanainen
138	Vladislav Tretiak
158	Rob Bryden
178	Grant MacKay
198	Thomas Rundqvist
218	Jeff Perpich
238	Jean-Guy Bergeron

1982

Pick	
19	Alain Heroux
31	Jocelyn Gauvreau
32	Kent Carlson
33	David Maley
40	Scott Sandelin
61	Scott Harlow
69	John Devoe
103	Kevin Houle
117	Ernie Vargas
124	Michael Dark
145	Hannu Jarvenpaa
150	Steve Smith
166	Tom Kolioupoulos
187	Brian Williams
208	Bob Emery
229	Darren Acheson
250	Bill Brauer

1981

Pick	
7	Mark Hunter
18	Gilbert Delorme
19	Jan Ingman
32	Lars Eriksson
40	Chris Chelios
46	Dieter Hegen
82	Kjell Dahlin
88	Steve Rooney
124	Tom Anastos
145	Tom Kurvers
166	Paul Gess
187	Scott Ferguson
208	Danny Burrows

1980

Pick	
1	Doug Wickenheiser
27	Ric Nattress
40	John Chabot
45	John Newberry
61	Craig Ldwig
82	Jeff Teal
103	Remi Gagne
124	Mike McPhee
145	Bill Norton
166	Steve Penney
187	John Schmidt
208	Scott Robinson

1979

Pick	
27	Gaston Gingras
37	Mats Naslund
43	Craig Levie
44	Guy Carbonneau
58	Rick Wamsley
79	Dave Orleski
100	Yvan Joly
121	Greg Moffett

1978

Pick	
8	Dan Geoffrion
17	Dave Hunter
30	Dale Yakiwchuk
36	Ron Carter
42	Richard David
69	Kevin Reeves
86	Mike Boyd
103	Keith Acton
120	Jim Lawson
137	Larry Landon
154	Kevin Constantine
171	John Swan
186	Daniel Metivier
201	Viacheslav Fetisov
212	Jeff Mars
222	Greg Tignanelli
225	George Goulakos
227	Ken Moodie
229	Serge Leblanc
230	Bob Magnuson
231	Chris Nilan
232	Rick Wilson
233	Louis Sleigher
234	Doug Robb

General Managers' History

Joseph Cattarinich, 1909-1910; George Kennedy, 1910-11 to 1919-20; Leo Dandurand, 1920-21 to 1934-35; Ernest Savard, 1935-36; Cecil Hart, 1936-37 to 1938-39; Jules Dugal, 1939-40; Tom P. Gorman, 1941-42 to 1945-46; Frank J. Selke, 1946-47 to 1963-64; Sam Pollock, 1964-65 to 1977-78; Irving Grundman, 1978-79 to 1982-83; Serge Savard, 1983-84 to date.

Coaching History

George Kennedy, 1917-18 to 1919-20; Léo Dandurand, 1920-21 to 1924-25; Cecil Hart, 1925-26 to 1931-32; Newsy Lalonde, 1932-33 to 1933-34; Newsy Lalonde and Léo Dandurand, 1934-35; Sylvio Mantha, 1935-36; Cecil Hart, 1936-37 to 1937-38; Cecil Hart and Jules Dugal, 1938-39; "Babe" Siebert, 1939*; Pit Lepine, 1939-40; Dick Irvin 1940-41 to 1954-55; Toe Blake, 1955-56 to 1967-68; Claude Ruel, 1968-69 to 1969-70; Claude Ruel and Al MacNeil, 1970-71; Scott Bowman, 1971-72 to 1978-79; Bernie Geoffrion and Claude Ruel, 1979-80; Claude Ruel, 1980-81; Bob Berry, 1981-82 to 1982-83; Bob Berry and Jacques Lemaire, 1983-84; Jacques Lemaire, 1984-85; Jean Perron, 1985-86 to 1987-88; Pat Burns, 1988-89 to 1991-92; Jacques Demers, 1992-93.

* Named coach in summer but died before 1939-40 season began.

Club Directory

Montreal Forum
2313 St. Catherine Street West
Montreal, Quebec H3H 1N2
Phone **514/932-2582**
FAX (Hockey) 514/932-8736
P.R. 514/932-8285
Capacity: 16,197

Owner: The Molson Companies Limited

Chairman of the Board, President and Governor	Ronald Corey
Vice-President Hockey, Managing Director and Alternate Governor	Serge Savard
Senior Vice-President, Corporate Affairs	Jean Béliveau
Vice-President, Forum Operations	Aldo Giampaolo
Vice-President, Finance and Administration	Fred Steer
Vice-President, Marketing and Communications	Bernard Brisset
Assistant to the Managing Director & Managing Director of Fredericton Canadiens	Jacques Lemaire
Assistant to the Managing Director and Director of Scouting	André Boudrias
Head Coach	Jacques Demers
Assistant Coaches	Jacques Laperrière, Charles Thiffault
Goaltending Instructor	François Allaire
Director of Player Development and Scout	Claude Ruel
Chief Scout	Doug Robinson
Scouting Staff	Neil Armstrong, Pat Flannery, Pierre Mondou, Gerry O'Flaherty, Richard Scammell, Eric Taylor, Jean-Claude Tremblay, Del Wilson
Farm Team (AHL)Les Canadiens de Fredericton	
Head Coach	Paulin Bordeleau
Director of Operations	Wayne Gamble
Medical and Training Staff	
Club Physician	Dr. D.G. Kinnear
Athletic Trainer	Gaétan Lefebvre
Assistant to the Athletic Trainer	John Shipman
Equipment Manager	Eddy Palchak
Assistants to the Equipment Manager	Pierre Gervais, Robert Boulanger
Marketing	
EFFIX Inc.	François-Xavier Seigneur
Communications	
Director of Public Relations	Claude Mouton
Director of Press Relations	Michèle Lapointe
Director of Computer, Operations	Sylvain Roy
Finance	
Controller	Dennis McKinley
Administrative Supervisor	Dave Poulton
Accountants	Françoise Brault, Gilles Viens
Forum	
Forum Superintendent	Alain Gauthier
Director of Security	Pierre Sauvé
Director of Events	Louise Laliberté
Director of Concessions	Yvon Gosselin
Director of Purchasing	Robert Loiseau
Ticketing	
Box Office Manager	Jacques Primeau
Assistant to the Box Office Manager	Caterina D'Ascoli

Executive Secretaries
President (Lise Beaudry)/Managing Director (Donna Stuart)/Senior V.P., C.A. (Louise Richer)/V.P. Forum Operations (Vicky Mercuri)/V.P. Finance (Susan Cryans)/Public Rel. (Normande Herget)/Press Rel. (Frédérique Cardinal)

Location of Press Box	Suspended above ice — West side
Location of Radio and TV booth	Suspended above ice — East side
Dimensions of rink	200 feet by 85 feet
Ends of rink	Herculite extends above boards all around rink
Club colors	Red, White and Blue
Club trains at	Montreal Forum
Play-by-Play — Radio/TV	Dick Irvin (English) Claude Quenneville, René Pothier, Richard Garneau (French)
TV Channels	CBMT (6), CFTM (10), CBFT (2)
Radio Stations	CBF (690) (French), CJAD (800) (English)

General Manager

SAVARD, SERGE A.
Managing Director, Montreal Canadiens. Born in Montreal, Que., January 22, 1946.

When Serge Savard was named managing director of the Montreal Canadiens on April 28, 1983, he took over a club that finished in fourth place with 75 points. In 1984-85, the Canadiens were vastly improved, finishing first with 94 points. Evidence of Savard's front office efforts were visible throughout the organization where he spent 14 of his 16 NHL seasons as a standout defenseman and an important part of eight Stanley Cup winning teams. As a player, Savard captured the Conn Smythe Trophy as the most valuable player in the 1969 Stanley Cup playoffs was recipient of the Bill Masterton Trophy in 1978-79 for his dedication, perseverance and sportsmanship to the game of hockey. He was acquired by the Winnipeg Jets in the 1981 Waiver Draft and closed out his playing career with two seasons as a leader and teacher to the young Jets' team which showed remarkable improvement during Savard's term. In the 1960's, Savard twice suffered multiple leg fractures and most experts doubted he would ever play again. He was named to the NHL's Second All-Star Team in 1978-79.

New Jersey Devils

1991-92 Results: 38W-31L-11T 87PTS. Fourth, Patrick Division

Year-by-Year Record

Season	GP	Home W	Home L	Home T	Road W	Road L	Road T	Overall W	Overall L	Overall T	GF	GA	Pts.	Finished	Playoff Result
1991-92	80	24	12	4	14	19	3	38	31	11	289	259	87	4th, Patrick Div.	Lost Div. Semi-Final
1990-91	80	23	10	7	9	23	8	32	33	15	272	264	79	4th, Patrick Div.	Lost Div. Semi-Final
1989-90	80	22	15	3	15	19	6	37	34	9	295	288	83	2nd, Patrick Div.	Lost Div. Semi-Final
1988-89	80	17	18	5	10	23	7	27	41	12	281	325	66	5th, Patrick Div.	Out of Playoffs
1987-88	80	23	16	1	15	20	5	38	36	6	295	296	82	4th, Patrick Div.	Lost Conf. Championship
1986-87	80	20	17	3	9	28	3	29	45	6	293	368	64	6th, Patrick Div.	Out of Playoffs
1985-86	80	17	21	2	11	28	1	28	49	3	300	374	59	6th, Patrick Div.	Out of Playoffs
1984-85	80	13	21	6	9	27	4	22	48	10	264	346	54	5th, Patrick Div.	Out of Playoffs
1983-84	80	10	28	2	7	28	5	17	56	7	231	350	41	5th, Patrick Div.	Out of Playoffs
1982-83	80	11	20	9	6	29	5	17	49	14	230	338	48	5th, Patrick Div.	Out of Playoffs
1981-82	80	14	21	5	4	28	8	18	49	13	241	362	49	5th, Smythe Div.	Out of Playoffs
1980-81	80	15	16	9	7	29	4	22	45	13	258	344	57	5t, Smythe Div.	Out of Playoffs
1979-80	80	12	20	8	7	28	5	19	48	13	234	308	51	6th, Smythe Div.	Out of Playoffs
1978-79	80	8	24	8	7	29	4	15	53	12	210	331	42	4th, Smythe Div.	Out of Playoffs
1977-78	80	17	14	9	2	26	12	19	40	21	257	305	59	2nd, Smythe Div.	Lost Prelim. Round
1976-77	80	12	20	8	8	26	6	20	46	14	226	307	54	5th, Smythe Div.	Out of Playoffs
1975-76	80	8	24	8	4	32	4	12	56	12	190	351	36	5th, Smythe Div.	Out of Playoffs
1974-75	80	12	20	8	3	34	3	15	54	11	184	328	41	5th, Smythe Div.	Out of Playoffs

Schedule

Home	Away
Oct. Tues. 6 NY Islanders	**Oct.** Fri. 9 Philadelphia
Sat. 10 NY Rangers	Wed. 14 NY Rangers
Mon. 12 Washington	Thur. 22 Chicago
Sat. 17 Philadelphia	Wed. 28 Hartford
Tues. 20 Hartford	Sat. 31 NY Islanders
Sat. 24 Pittsburgh	**Nov.** Thur. 5 Los Angeles
Fri. 30 NY Islanders	Sat. 7 San Jose
Nov. Wed. 11 Montreal	Sat. 14 Washington
Fri. 13 Washington	Sat. 21 Pittsburgh
Wed. 18 Buffalo	Wed. 25 Ottawa
(at Hamilton)	Sat. 28 Quebec
Fri. 20 Pittsburgh	**Dec.** Thur. 3 Ottawa
Dec. Tues. 1 Toronto	Sun. 6 Buffalo
Sat. 5 Boston*	Sat. 12 Pittsburgh
Wed. 9 Washington	Tues. 15 Winnipeg
Fri. 11 Pittsburgh	Fri. 18 Tampa Bay
Mon. 21 NY Rangers	Wed. 23 NY Rangers
Sun. 27 Hartford	Tues. 29 Quebec
Jan. Sat. 2 Winnipeg	**Jan.** Fri. 1 Washington*
Wed. 6 Minnesota	Mon. 4 NY Rangers
Fri. 8 Ottawa	Sat. 9 Boston
Tues. 12 Vancouver	Wed. 20 Montreal
Thur. 14 Los Angeles	Sat. 23 Boston
Sat. 16 NY Islanders	Tues. 26 NY Islanders
Fri. 22 Montreal	Thur. 28 Minnesota
Feb. Wed. 3 Calgary	Sat. 30 St Louis
Mon. 8 NY Rangers	**Feb.** Tues. 9 Detroit
Sat. 13 Philadelphia*	Sun. 14 Philadelphia*
Wed. 17 St Louis	Tues. 23 Pittsburgh
Fri. 19 Buffalo	Thur. 25 Philadelphia
Sun. 21 Quebec	**Mar.** Wed. 3 Hartford
Sat. 27 Ottawa*	Tues. 9 Vancouver
Sun. 28 Detroit	Fri. 12 Edmonton
Mar. Fri. 5 Chicago	Sat. 13 Calgary
Sun. 7 Philadelphia	Tues. 16 Boston
Thur. 18 Edmonton	(at Providence)
Sat. 20 Quebec*	Sun. 21 Philadelphia
Tues. 23 Tampa Bay	Thur. 25 NY Islanders
Mon. 29 San Jose	Sat. 27 Washington*
Apr. Sun. 4 Pittsburgh	Wed. 31 Buffalo
Wed. 7 NY Rangers	**Apr.** Sat. 3 Toronto
Sun. 11 NY Islanders	Sat. 10 Washington
Wed. 14 Pittsburgh	Thur. 15 Pittsburgh

* Denotes afternoon game.

Home Starting Times:

All Games	7:35 p.m.
Except Matinees	2:05 p.m.
Dec. 27, Mar. 7	5:05 p.m.

Franchise date: June 30, 1982. Transferred from Denver to New Jersey, Previously transferred from Kansas City to Denver, Colorado.

19th NHL Season

Claude Lemieux, who scored a career-high 41 goals for the Devils in 1991-92, led all New Jersey scorers with 68 points.

1992-93 Player Personnel

FORWARDS	HT	WT	S	Place of Birth	Date	1991-92 Club
BARR, Dave	6-1	195	R	Toronto, Ont.	11/30/60	New Jersey
BLACK, Ryan	6-1	180	L	Guelph, Ont.	10/25/73	Peterborough
BODNARCHUK, Mike	6-1	175	R	Bramalea, Ont.	3/26/70	Utica
BROWN, Doug	5-10	185	R	Southborough, MA	6/12/64	New Jersey
CHRISTIAN, Jeff	6-1	195	L	Burlington, Ont.	7/30/70	Utica-New Jersey
CHORSKE, Tom	6-1	205	R	Minneapolis, MN	9/18/66	New Jersey
CIGER, Zdeno	6-1	190	L	Martin, Czech.	10/19/69	New Jersey
DOWD, Jim	6-1	190	R	Brick, NJ	12/25/68	Utica-New Jersey
EMMA, David	5-11	180	L	Cranston, RI	1/14/68	US National-Utica
GUERIN, Bill	6-2	200	R	Wilbraham, MA	11/9/70	US National-Utica
HANKINSON, Ben	6-2	180	R	Edina, MN	1/5/69	Utica
HEXTALL, Donevan	6-2	190	L	Wolseley, Sask.	2/24/72	Prince Albert
HOLIK, Bobby	6-3	210	R	Jihlava, Czech.	1/1/71	Hartford
LEMIEUX, Claude	6-1	215	R	Buckingham, Que.	7/16/65	New Jersey
MacLEAN, John	6-0	200	R	Oshawa, Ont.	11/20/64	New Jersey
MALLETTE, Troy	6-0	210	L	Sudbury, Ont.	2/25/70	Edmonton-New Jersey
McKAY, Randy	6-1	205	R	Montreal, Que.	1/25/67	New Jersey
MILLER, Jason	6-1	195	L	Edmonton, Alta.	3/1/71	Utica-New Jersey
OJANEN, Janne	6-2	200	L	Tampere, Finland	4/9/68	Tappara-New Jersey
PELLERIN, Scott	5-11	180	L	Shediac, N.B.	1/9/70	Maine-Utica
REGNIER, Curt	6-2	220	L	Prince Albert, Sask.	1/24/72	Prince Albert
RICHER, Stephane	6-2	215	R	Ripon, Que.	6/7/66	New Jersey
RIEHL, Kevin	5-10	180	L	Leader, Sask.	3/11/71	Medicine Hat
SEMAK, Alexander	5-10	180	R	Ufa, USSR	2/11/66	Dynamo Moscow-Utica-New Jersey
SKALDE, Jarrod	6-0	170	L	Niagara Falls, Ont.	2/26/71	Utica-New Jersey
STASTNY, Peter	6-1	200	L	Bratislava, Czech.	9/18/56	New Jersey
SULLIVAN, Brian	6-4	195	R	S. Windsor, CT	4/23/69	Utica
TODD, Kevin	5-10	185	L	Winnipeg, Man.	5/4/68	New Jersey
TOMS, Jeff	6-3	180	L	Swift Current, Sask.	6/4/74	Sault Ste. Marie
VILGRAIN, Claude	6-1	205	R	Port-au-Prince, Haiti	3/1/63	New Jersey
YELLE, Stephane	6-1	160	L	Ottawa, Ont.	5/9/74	Oshawa
ZELEPUKIN, Valeri	5-11	190	L	Voskresensk, USSR	9/17/68	Utica-New Jersey
DEFENSEMEN						
ALBELIN, Tommy	6-1	190	L	Stockholm, Sweden	5/21/64	New Jersey
COPELAND, Todd	6-2	210	L	Ridgewood, NJ	5/18/68	Utica
CRAIEVICH, David	6-1	210	R	Chatham, Ont.	5/3/71	Utica
DANEYKO, Ken	6-0	210	L	Windsor, Ont.	4/17/64	New Jersey
DEAN, Kevin	6-2	195	L	Madison, WI	4/1/69	Utica
DRIVER, Bruce	6-0	185	L	Toronto, Ont.	4/29/62	New Jersey
FETISOV, Viacheslav	6-1	215	L	Moscow, USSR	4/20/58	New Jersey
HULSE, Cale	6-3	210	R	Edmonton, Alta.	11/10/73	Portland
KASATONOV, Alexei	6-1	215	L	Leningrad, USSR	10/14/59	New Jersey
KINNEAR, Geordie	6-1	200	L	Simcoe, Ont.	7/9/73	Peterborough
KUCHYNA, Petr	6-3	180	R	Jihlava, Czech.	1/14/70	Dukla Jihlava-Utica
MALKOC, Dean	6-3	200	L	Vancouver, B.C.	1/26/70	Utica
NELSON, Chris	6-2	190	R	Philadelphia, PA	2/12/69	U. Wisconsin
NIEDERMAYER, Scott	6-0	200	L	Edmonton, Alta.	8/31/73	New Jersey-Kamloops
O'CONNOR, Myles	5-11	190	L	Calgary, Alta.	4/2/67	Utica-New Jersey
RUCHTY, Matt	6-1	210	L	Kitchener, Ont.	11/27/69	Utica
SEVERYN, Brent	6-2	210	L	Vegreville, Alta.	2/22/66	Utica
SMITH, Jason	6-3	185	R	Calgary, Alta.	11/2/73	Regina
STEVENS, Scott	6-2	210	L	Kitchener, Ont.	4/1/64	New Jersey
WEENK, Heath	6-3	210	L	Tisdale, Sask.	7/2/73	Regina

GOALTENDERS	HT	WT	C	Place of Birth	Date	1991-92 Club
BILLINGTON, Craig	5-10	165	L	London, Ont.	9/11/66	New Jersey
BRODEUR, Martin	6-1	205	L	Montreal, Que.	5/6/72	St. Hyacinthe-New Jersey
DADSWELL, Doug	5-10	180	L	Scarborough, Ont.	2/7/64	Utica
ERICKSON, Chad	5-10	180	R	Minneapolis, MN	8/21/70	Utica-New Jersey
HUGHES, Chuck	5-8	165	R	Quincy, MA	1/30/70	Harvard
SCHWAB, Corey	6-0	180	L	Battleford, Sask.	11/4/70	Utica
TERRERI, Chris	5-8	155	L	Providence, RI	11/15/64	New Jersey

1991-92 Scoring

Regular Season

Pos	#.	Player	Team	GP	G	A	Pts	+/-	PIM	PP	SH	GW	GT	S	%
R	22	Claude Lemieux	N.J.	74	41	27	68	9	109	13	1	8	3	296	13.9
R	44	Stephane Richer	N.J.	74	29	35	64	1–	25	5	1	6	1	240	12.1
C	14*	Kevin Todd	N.J.	80	21	42	63	8	69	2	0	2	1	131	16.0
C	26	Peter Stastny	N.J.	66	24	38	62	6	42	10	1	3	0	142	16.9
D	4	Scott Stevens	N.J.	68	17	42	59	24	124	7	1	2	0	156	10.9
L	19	Claude Vilgrain	N.J.	71	19	27	46	27	74	1	1	1	1	88	21.6
D	23	Bruce Driver	N.J.	78	7	35	42	5	66	3	1	1	0	205	3.4
D	7	Alexei Kasatonov	N.J.	76	12	28	40	14	70	3	2	1	0	107	11.2
L	9	Tom Chorske	N.J.	76	19	17	36	8	32	0	3	2	0	143	13.3
R	21	Randy McKay	N.J.	80	17	16	33	6	246	2	0	1	0	111	15.3
D	5	Eric Weinrich	N.J.	76	7	25	32	10	55	5	0	0	0	97	7.2
L	25*	Valeri Zelepukin	N.J.	44	13	18	31	11	28	3	0	3	0	94	13.8
R	24	Doug Brown	N.J.	71	11	17	28	17	27	1	2	1	0	140	7.9
C	16	Laurie Boschman	N.J.	75	8	20	28	9	121	0	0	2	0	89	9.0
D	2	Viacheslav Fetisov	N.J.	70	3	23	26	11	108	0	0	1	0	70	4.3
R	11	Dave Barr	N.J.	41	6	12	18	9	32	0	1	0	0	49	12.2
L	33	Zdeno Ciger	N.J.	20	6	5	11	2–	10	1	0	0	0	33	18.2
C	20*	Alexander Semak	N.J.	25	5	6	11	5	0	0	0	1	0	45	11.1
L	8	Troy Mallette	EDM	15	1	3	4	1–	36	0	0	0	0	9	11.1
			N.J.	17	3	4	7	7	43	0	0	0	0	19	15.8
			TOTAL	32	4	7	11	6	79	0	0	0	0	28	14.3
L	32	Pat Conacher	N.J.	44	7	3	10	0	16	0	1	1	0	38	18.4
D	3	Ken Daneyko	N.J.	80	1	7	8	7	170	0	0	0	0	57	1.8
C	10*	Jarrod Skalde	N.J.	15	2	4	6	1–	4	0	0	2	0	25	8.0
C	17	Patrik Sundstrom	N.J.	17	1	3	4	5–	8	1	0	0	0	16	6.3
D	6	Tommy Albelin	N.J.	19	0	4	4	7	4	0	0	0	0	18	.0
C	20	Jon Morris	N.J.	7	1	2	3	6–	6	1	0	0	0	5	20.0
L	12	Walt Poddubny	N.J.	7	1	2	3	1–	6	0	0	0	0	9	11.1
D	28*	Myles O'Connor	N.J.	9	0	2	2	2–	13	0	0	0	0	13	.0
C	10*	Neil Brady	N.J.	7	1	0	1	1	4	0	0	0	0	3	33.3
D	27*	Scott Niedermayer	N.J.	4	0	1	1	1	2	0	0	0	0	4	.0
R	12*	Bill Guerin	N.J.	5	0	1	1	1	9	0	0	0	0	8	.0
G	1	Craig Billington	N.J.	26	0	1	1	0	2	0	0	0	0	0	.0
G	31	Chris Terreri	N.J.	54	0	1	1	0	13	0	0	0	0	0	.0
C	34*	Jim Dowd	N.J.	1	0	0	0	0	0	0	0	0	0	0	.0
L	18*	Jeff Christian	N.J.	2	0	0	0	0	2	0	0	0	0	1	.0
G	30*	Chad Erickson	N.J.	2	0	0	0	0	0	0	0	0	0	0	.0
C	12*	Jason Miller	N.J.	3	0	0	0	0	0	0	0	0	0	1	.0
G	29*	Martin Brodeur	N.J.	4	0	0	0	0	0	0	0	0	0	0	.0

Goaltending

No.	Goaltender	GPI	Mins	Avg	W	L	T	EN	SO	GA	SA	S%
1	Craig Billington	26	1363	3.04	13	7	1	2	2	69	637	.892
31	Chris Terreri	54	3186	3.18	22	22	10	0	1	169	1511	.888
29	*Martin Brodeur	4	179	3.35	2	1	0	0	0	10	85	.882
30	*Chad Erickson	2	120	4.50	1	1	0	0	0	9	55	.836
	Totals	**80**	**4868**	**3.19**	**38**	**31**	**11**	**2**	**3**	**259**	**2290**	**.887**

Playoffs

Pos	#	Player	Team	GP	G	A	Pts	+/-	PIM	PP	SH	GW	GT	S	%
C	26	Peter Stastny	N.J.	7	3	7	10	1	19	0	0	0	0	12	25.0
R	22	Claude Lemieux	N.J.	7	4	3	7	1	26	1	0	0	0	33	12.1
L	33	Zdeno Ciger	N.J.	7	2	4	6	0	0	0	0	1	0	15	13.3
C	14*	Kevin Todd	N.J.	7	3	2	5	2	8	1	0	0	0	16	18.8
R	21	Randy McKay	N.J.	7	1	3	4	1	10	1	0	0	0	12	8.3
D	23	Bruce Driver	N.J.	7	0	4	4	2–	2	0	0	0	0	23	.0
R	12*	Bill Guerin	N.J.	6	3	0	3	2	4	0	0	0	0	10	30.0
D	4	Scott Stevens	N.J.	7	2	1	3	5–	29	2	0	1	0	9	22.2
R	44	Stephane Richer	N.J.	7	1	2	3	5–	0	0	0	0	0	18	5.6
D	2	Viacheslav Fetisov	N.J.	6	0	3	3	5	8	0	0	0	0	3	.0
L	9	Tom Chorske	N.J.	7	0	3	3	2–	4	0	0	0	0	16	.0
D	3	Ken Daneyko	N.J.	7	0	3	3	3	16	0	0	0	0	6	.0
D	6	Tommy Albelin	N.J.	1	1	1	2	0	0	0	0	0	0	1	100.0
L	25*	Valeri Zelepukin	N.J.	4	1	1	2	0	2	0	0	0	0	8	12.5
L	32	Pat Conacher	N.J.	7	1	1	2	3	4	0	1	0	0	5	20.0
D	7	Alexei Kasatonov	N.J.	7	1	1	2	3	12	0	0	0	0	8	12.5
L	19	Claude Vilgrain	N.J.	7	1	1	2	1	17	0	0	0	0	6	16.7
C	34	Janne Ojanen	N.J.	3	0	2	2	2–	0	0	0	0	0	0	.0
D	5	Eric Weinrich	N.J.	7	0	2	2	4–	4	0	0	0	0	4	.0
C	16	Laurie Boschman	N.J.	7	1	0	1	1	8	0	0	1	0	10	10.0
G	29*	Martin Brodeur	N.J.	1	0	0	0	0	0	0	0	0	0	0	.0
C	20*	Alexander Semak	N.J.	1	0	0	0	2–	0	0	0	0	0	3	.0
G	31	Chris Terreri	N.J.	7	0	0	0	0	0	0	0	0	0	0	.0

Goaltending

No.	Goaltender	GPI	Mins	Avg	W	L	EN	SO	GA	SA	S%
31	Chris Terreri	7	386	3.58	3	3	2	0	23	203	.887
29	*Martin Brodeur	1	32	5.63	0	1	0	0	3	15	.800
	Totals	**7**	**420**	**4.00**	**3**	**4**	**2**	**0**	**28**	**220**	**.873**

General Managers' History

(Kansas City) Sidney Abel, 1974-75 to 1975-76; (Colorado) Ray Miron, 1976-77 to 1980-81; Billy MacMillan, 1981-82 to 1982-83; Billy MacMillan and Max McNab, 1983-84; Max McNab 1984-85 to 1986-87; Lou Lamoriello, 1987-88 to date.

Coaching History

(Kansas City) Bep Guidolin, 1974-75; Bep Guidolin, Sid Abel, and Eddie Bush, 1975-76; (Colorado) John Wilson, 1976-77; Pat Kelly, 1977-78; Pat Kelly, Aldo Guidolin, 1978-79; Don Cherry, 1979-80; Bill MacMillan, 1980-81; Bert Marshall and Marshall Johnston, 1981-82; (New Jersey) Bill MacMillan, 1982-83; Bill MacMillan and Tom McVie, 1983-84; Doug Carpenter, 1984-85 to 1986-87; Doug Carpenter and Jim Schoenfeld, 1987-88; Jim Schoenfeld, 1988-89; Jim Schoenfeld and John Cunniff, 1989-90; John Cunniff and Tom McVie, 1990-91; Tom McVie, 1991-92; Herb Brooks, 1992-93.

Captains' History

Simon Nolet, 1974-75 to 1976-77; Wilf Paiement, 1977-78; Gary Croteau, 1978-79; Mike Christie, Rene Robert, Lanny McDonald, 1979-80; Lanny McDonald, 1980-81, Lanny McDonald, Rob Ramage, 1981-82; Don Lever, 1982-83; Don Lever, Mel Bridgman, 1983-84; Mel Bridgman, 1984-85, 1985-86; Kirk Muller, 1987-88 to 1990-91; Bruce Driver, 1991-92 to date.

Club Records

Team

* – Record includes Kansas City Scouts and Colorado Rockies from 1974-75 through 1981-82

Record		
Most Points	87	1991-92 (80)
Most Wins	38	1987-88 (80) 1991-92 (80)
Most Ties	21	1977-78 (80)
Most Losses	56	1983-84 (80) 1975-76 (80)
Most Goals	300	1985-86 (80)
Most Goals Against	374	1985-86
Fewest Points	*36	1975-76 (80)
	41	1983-84 (80)
Fewest Wins	*12	1975-76 (80)
	17	1982-83 (80) 1983-84 (80)
Fewest Ties	3	1985-86 (80)
Fewest Losses	31	1991-92 (80)
Fewest Goals	*184	1974-75 (80)
	230	1982-83 (80)
Fewest Goals Against	259	1991-92 (80)
Longest Winning Streak		
Over-all	6	Feb. 8- Feb. 18/92
Home	8	Oct. 9- Nov. 7/87
Away	4	Oct. 5-23/89 & Dec. 31/91-Jan 31/92
Longest Undefeated Streak		
Over-all	8	Mar. 20- Apr. 3/88 (7 wins, 1 tie) Dec. 15-30/90 (3 wins, 5 ties)
Home	9	Oct. 9- Nov. 12/87 (8 wins, 1 tie) Nov. 17- Dec. 29/90 (5 wins, 4 ties)
Away	6	Jan. 20- Feb. 9/89 (3 wins, 3 ties) Mar. 12- Apr. 3/88 (5 wins, 1 tie)
Longest Losing Streak		
Over-all	*14	Dec. 30/75- Jan. 29/76
	10	Oct. 14- Nov. 4/83
Home	9	Dec. 22/85- Feb. 6/86
Away	12	Oct. 19/83- Dec. 1/83
Longest Winless Streak		
Over-all	*27	Feb. 12- Apr. 4/76 (21 losses, 6 ties)
	18	Oct. 20- Nov. 26/82 (14 losses 4 ties)
Home	*14	Feb. 12- Mar. 30/76 (10 losses, 4 ties) Feb. 4- Mar. 31/79 (12 losses, 2 ties)
	9	Dec. 22/85- Feb. 6/86 (9 losses)
Away	*32	Nov. 12/77- Mar. 15/78 (22 losses, 10 ties)
	14	Dec. 26/82- Mar. 5/83 (13 losses, 1 tie)
Most Shutouts, Season	3	1988-89 (80)
Most PIM, Season	2,494	1988-89 (80)
Most Goals, Game	9	Apr. 1/79 (St.L. 5 at Col. 9) Feb. 12/82 (Que. 2 at Col. 9) Apr. 6/86 (NYI 7 at N.J. 9) Mar. 10/90 (Que. 3 at N.J. 9) Dec. 5/90 (Van. 4 at N.J. 9) Oct. 26/91 (S.J. 0 at N.J. 9)

Individual

Record		
Most Seasons	9	Aaron Broten
Most Games	641	Aaron Broten
Most Goals, Career	217	John MacLean
Most Assists, Career	335	Kirk Muller
Most Points, Career	520	Kirk Muller (185 goals, 335 assists)
Most PIM, Career	1,470	Ken Daneyko
Most Shutouts, Career	4	Sean Burke
Longest Consecutive Games Streak	321	Kirk Muller (Apr. 5/87-Mar. 31/91)
Most Goals, Season	46	Pat Verbeek (1987-88)
Most Assists, Season	57	Aaron Broten, Kirk Muller (1987-88)
Most Points, Season	94	Kirk Muller (1987-88) (37 goals, 57 assists)
Most PIM, Season	283	Ken Daneyko (1988-89)
Most Points, Defenseman Season	66	Tom Kurvers (1988-89) (16 goals, 50 assists)
Most Points, Center Season	94	Kirk Muller (1987-88) (37 goals, 57 assists)
Most Points, Right Wing, Season	*87	Wilf Paiement (1977-78) (31 goals, 56 assists)
	87	John MacLean (1988-89) (42 goals, 45 assists)
Most Points, Left Wing, Season	86	Kirk Muller (1989-90) (30 goals, 56 assists)
Most Points, Rookie, Season	63	Kevin Todd (1991-92) (21 goals, 42 assists)
Most Shutouts, Season	3	Sean Burke (1988-89)
Most Goals, Game	4	Bob MacMillan (Jan. 8/82) Pat Verbeek (Feb. 28/88)
Most Assists, Game	5	Kirk Muller (Mar. 25/87) Greg Adams (Oct. 10/86) Tom Kurvers (Feb. 13/89)
Most Points, Game	6	Kirk Muller (Nov. 29/86) (3 goals, 3 assists)

All-time Record vs. Other Clubs

Regular Season

	At Home							On Road							Total						
	GP	W	L	T	GF	GA	PTS	GP	W	L	T	GF	GA	PTS	GP	W	L	T	GF	GA	PTS
Boston	30	5	17	8	82	114	18	31	8	20	3	95	139	19	61	13	37	11	177	253	37
Buffalo	31	6	19	6	98	130	18	30	3	23	4	85	147	10	61	9	42	10	183	277	28
Calgary	35	10	22	3	99	136	23	34	4	26	4	88	166	12	69	14	48	7	187	302	35
Chicago	36	15	14	7	111	112	37	37	8	23	6	105	157	22	73	23	37	13	216	269	59
Detroit	31	14	9	8	109	88	36	30	11	17	2	102	128	24	61	25	26	10	211	216	60
Edmonton	23	9	12	2	78	85	20	23	7	12	4	90	115	18	46	16	24	6	168	200	38
Hartford	21	10	9	2	80	87	22	20	5	11	4	60	76	14	41	15	20	6	140	163	36
Los Angeles	33	14	14	5	111	124	33	33	3	24	6	103	181	12	66	17	38	11	214	305	45
Minnesota	35	16	16	3	114	114	35	35	8	21	6	92	144	22	70	24	37	9	206	258	57
Montreal	30	8	22	0	80	145	16	31	5	22	4	80	133	14	61	13	44	4	160	278	30
NY Islanders	53	16	28	9	171	217	41	53	4	41	8	145	254	16	106	20	69	17	316	471	57
NY Rangers	53	22	27	4	188	212	48	53	14	32	7	171	236	35	106	36	59	11	359	448	83
Philadelphia	52	23	25	4	185	210	50	53	8	38	7	122	232	23	105	31	63	11	307	442	73
Pittsburgh	50	26	16	8	198	173	60	51	18	30	3	189	224	39	101	44	46	11	387	397	99
Quebec	21	11	9	1	96	78	23	20	7	11	2	66	88	16	41	18	20	3	162	166	39
St. Louis	37	15	15	7	119	110	37	36	8	25	3	110	164	19	73	23	40	10	229	274	56
San Jose	2	2	0	0	13	3	4	1	0	1	0	2	3	0	3	2	1	0	15	6	4
Toronto	30	11	10	9	109	98	31	31	6	22	3	106	148	15	61	17	32	12	215	246	46
Vancouver	39	16	17	6	120	132	38	39	6	22	11	113	147	23	78	22	39	17	233	279	61
Washington	51	20	25	6	165	166	46	50	9	38	3	145	230	21	101	29	63	9	310	396	67
Winnipeg	19	5	9	5	57	64	15	21	3	15	3	54	88	9	40	8	24	8	111	152	24
Defunct Clubs	8	4	2	2	25	19	10	8	2	3	3	19	27	7	16	6	5	5	44	46	17
Totals	**720**	**278**	**337**	**105**	**2408**	**2617**	**661**	**720**	**147**	**477**	**96**	**2142**	**3227**	**390**	**1440**	**425**	**814**	**201**	**4550**	**5844**	**1051**

Playoffs

	Series	W	L	GP	W	L	T	GF	GA	Last Mtg.	Round	Result
Boston	1	0	1	7	3	4	0	19	30	1988	CF	L 3-4
NY Islanders	1	1	0	6	4	2	0	23	18	1988	DSF	W 4-2
NY Rangers	1	0	1	7	3	4	0	25	28	1992	DSF	L 3-4
Philadelphia	1	0	1	2	0	2	0	3	6	1978	PR	L 0-2
Pittsburgh	1	0	1	7	3	4	0	17	25	1991	DSF	L 3-4
Washington	2	1	1	13	6	7	0	43	44	1990	DSF	L 2-4
Totals	**7**	**2**	**.5**	**42**	**19**	**23**	**0**	**130**	**151**			

Playoff Results 1992-88

Year	Round	Opponent	Result	GF	GA
1992	DSF	NY Rangers	L 3-4	25	28
1991	DSF	Pittsburgh	L 3-4	17	25
1990	DSF	Washington	L 2-4	18	21
1988	CF	Boston	L 3-4	19	30
	DF	Washington	W 4-3	25	23
	DSF	NY Islanders	W 4-2	23	18

Abbreviations: Round: F – Final; **CF** – conference final; **DF** – division final; **DSF** – division semi-final; **SF** – semi-final; **QF** – quarter-final; **PR** – preliminary round. **GA** – goals against; **GF** – goals for.

1991-92 Results

Home				Away			
Oct.	5	St Louis	7-2	**Oct.**	6	Chicago	4-2
	8	Quebec	6-5		13	Philadelphia	2-4
	12	Pittsburgh*	4-1		16	NY Rangers	2-4
	19	Washington	1-5		18	Washington	5-6
	22	Los Angeles	5-2		24	Pittsburgh	4-2
	26	San Jose	9-0		29	Vancouver	3-4
Nov.	8	Montreal	3-2		30	Calgary	5-2
	12	Philadelphia	5-2	**Nov.**	1	Edmonton	3-1
	14	NY Islanders	3-4		4	Montreal	2-3
	16	Winnipeg*	0-1		9	Boston	0-4
	20	Washington	6-5		23	Philadelphia	5-5
	22	Hartford	8-2		27	Pittsburgh	4-8
Dec.	5	Calgary	6-3		30	Los Angeles	4-1
	7	Detroit	2-2	**Dec.**	8	Philadelphia	2-2
	13	Pittsburgh	3-4		10	Minnesota	3-4
	21	Chicago	1-1		14	NY Islanders	3-3
	28	Buffalo	3-0		19	Hartford	4-1
	29	Washington	3-4		23	NY Rangers	0-3
Jan.	2	Pittsburgh	4-0		26	NY Islanders	5-5
	4	NY Rangers	6-4		31	Pittsburgh	7-4
	9	St Louis	4-3	**Jan.**	24	Washington	5-2
	11	Toronto	3-4		29	Montreal	4-3
	12	Los Angeles	5-2		31	Detroit	6-3
	15	Buffalo	8-8	**Feb.**	1	Toronto	4-6
	25	Detroit	0-7		6	St Louis	1-4
Feb.	4	Philadelphia	3-1		8	Boston*	6-4
	13	Vancouver	5-3		9	Quebec*	2-1
	15	Hartford*	4-1		20	Chicago	4-4
	16	NY Rangers*	4-2		21	Winnipeg	4-6
	18	Philadelphia	4-3		25	Toronto	5-5
	24	Minnesota	1-3		29	NY Islanders	3-1
	28	NY Islanders	2-3	**Mar.**	4	NY Rangers	5-4
Mar.	2	NY Rangers	1-7		6	Buffalo	4-5
	19	Edmonton	3-5		7	Washington	2-3
	21	NY Islanders*	2-2		11	Edmonton	2-2
	24	San Jose	4-3		12	Vancouver	1-2
	26	Boston	4-2		14	San Jose	2-3
	28	Quebec*	5-2		22	NY Rangers*	3-6
Apr.	1	Washington	3-4		29	Philadelphia*	4-5
	5	Pittsburgh	5-1	**Apr.**	4	NY Islanders*	0-7

*Denotes afternoon game

Entry Draft Selections 1992-78

1992

Pick	
18	Jason Smith
42	Sergei Brylin
66	Cale Hulse
90	Vitali Tomilin
94	Scott McCabe
114	Ryan Black
138	Daniel Trebil
162	Geordie Kinnear
186	Stephane Yelle
210	Jeff Toms
234	Heath Weenk
258	Vladislav Yakovenko

1991

Pick	
3	Scott Niedermayer
11	Brian Rolston
33	Donevan Hextall
55	Fredrik Lindqvist
77	Bradley Willner
121	Curt Regnier
143	David Craievich
165	Paul Wolanski
187	Daniel Reimann
231	Kevin Riehl
253	Jason Hehr

1990

Pick	
20	Martin Brodeur
24	David Harlock
29	Chris Gotziaman
53	Michael Dunham
56	Brad Bombardir
64	Mike Bodnarchuk
95	Dean Malkoc
104	Petr Kuchyna
116	Lubomir Kolnik
137	Chris McAlpine
179	Jaroslav Modry
200	Corey Schwab
221	Valeri Zelepukin
242	Todd Reirden

1989

Pick	
5	Bill Guerin
18	Jason Miller
26	Jarrod Skalde
47	Scott Pellerin
89	Mike Heinke
110	David Emma
152	Sergei Starikov
173	Andre Faust
215	Jason Simon
236	Peter Larsson

1988

Pick	
12	Corey Foster
23	Jeff Christian
54	Zdeno Ciger
65	Matt Ruchty
75	Scott Luik
96	Chris Nelson
117	Chad Johnson
138	Chad Erickson
159	Bryan Lafort
180	Sergei Svetlov
201	Bob Woods
207	Alexander Semak
222	Charles Hughes
243	Michael Pohl

1987

Pick	
2	Brendan Shanahan
23	Rickard Persson
65	Brian Sullivan
86	Kevin Dean
107	Ben Hankinson
128	Tom Neziol
149	Jim Dowd
170	John Blessman
191	Peter Fry
212	Alain Charland

1986

Pick	
3	Neil Brady
24	Todd Copeland
45	Janne Ojanen
62	Marc Laniel
66	Anders Carlsson
108	Troy Crowder
129	Kevin Todd
150	Ryan Pardoski
171	Scott McCormack
192	Frederic Chabot
213	John Andersen
236	Doug Kirton

1985

Pick	
3	Craig Wolanin
24	Sean Burke
32	Eric Weinrich
45	Myles O'Connor
66	Gregg Polak
108	Bill McMillan
129	Kevin Schrader
150	Ed Krayer
171	Jamie Huscroft
192	Terry Shold
213	Jamie McKinley
234	David Williams

1984

Pick	
2	Kirk Muller
23	Craig Billington
44	Neil Davey
74	Paul Ysebaert
86	Jon Morris
107	Kirk McLean
128	Ian Ferguson
149	Vladimir Kames
170	Mike Roth
190	Mike Peluso
211	Jarkko Piiparinen
231	Chris Kiene

1983

Pick	
6	John MacLean
24	Shawn Evans
85	Chris Terreri
105	Gordon Mark
125	Greg Evtushevski
145	Viacheslav Fetisov
165	Jay Octeau
185	Alexander Chernykh
205	Allan Stewart
225	Alexei Kasatonov

1982

Pick	
8	Rocky Trottier
18	Ken Daneyko
43	Pat Verbeek
54	Dave Kasper
5	Scott Brydges
106	Mike Moher
127	Paul Fulcher
148	John Hutchings
169	Alan Hepple
190	Brent Shaw
207	Tony Gilliard
211	Scott Fusco
232	Dan Dorion

1981

Pick	
5	Joe Cirella
26	Rich Chernomaz
48	Uli Hiemer
66	Gus Greco
87	Doug Speck
108	Bruce Driver
129	Jeff Larmer
150	Tony Arima
171	Tim Army
192	John Johannson

1980

Pick	
19	Paul Gagne
22	Joe Ward
64	Rick LaFerriere
85	Ed Cooper
106	Aaron Broten
127	Dan Fascinato
148	Andre Hidi
169	Shawn MacKenzie
190	Bob Jansch

1979

Pick	
1	Rob Ramage
64	Steve Peters
85	Gary Dillon
106	Bob Attwell

1978

Pick	
5	Mike Gillis
27	Merlin Malinowski
41	Paul Messier
58	Dave Watson
73	Tim Thomlison
74	Rod Guimont
91	John Hynes
108	Andy Clark
125	John Oliver
142	Kevin Krook
159	Jeff Jensen
174	Bo Ericson
190	Jari Viitala
204	Ulf Zetterstrom

Coach

BROOKS, HERB
Coach, New Jersey Devils. Born in St. Paul, MN, August 5, 1937.

Herb Brooks returns to the NHL after a four-year absence to accept head coaching duties with the New Jersey Devils, the third NHL team that Brooks has directed. One of the most respected and successful coaches in U.S. college history, Brooks first captured world-wide attention when he guided the 1980 U.S. Olympic Team to a gold medal at the Lake Placid Winter Games. Brooks, who spent four seasons with the NY Rangers from 1981-82 to 1984-85 and was named coach of the year by *The Sporting News* in 1982, spent a single season behind the bench of the Minnesota North Stars in 1987-88. He first joined the Devils' family on July 11, 1991, taking over the reins of New Jersey's AHL farm affiliate, the Utica Devils, leading the youngest team in the league to a playoff berth in 1991-92.

Coaching Record

		Regular Season					Playoffs			
Season	**Team**	**Games**	**W**	**L**	**T**	**%**	**Games**	**W**	**L**	**%**
1972-73	U. Minnesota (WCHA)	34	15	16	3	.485	....	....	....	....
1973-74	U. Minnesota (WCHA)	40	22	12	6	.625	....	....	....	....
1974-75	U. Minnesota (WCHA)	53	39	11	3	.764	....	....	....	....
1975-76	U. Minnesota (WCHA)	44	28	14	2	.659	....	....	....	....
1976-77	U. Minnesota (WCHA)	42	17	22	3	.440	....	....	....	....
1977-78	U. Minnesota (WCHA)	38	22	14	2	.605	....	....	....	....
1978-79	U. Minnesota (WCHA)	44	32	11	1	.739	....	....	....	....
1979-80	U.S. National	61	42	16	3	.713	....	....	....	....
	U.S. Olympic	7	6	0	1	.929	....	....	....	....
1980-81	Davos (Switz.)					UNAVAILABLE				
1981-82	**NY Rangers (NHL)**	**80**	**39**	**27**	**14**	**.575**	**10**	**5**	**5**	**.500**
1982-83	**NY Rangers (NHL)**	**80**	**35**	**35**	**10**	**.500**	**9**	**5**	**4**	**.556**
1983-84	**NY Rangers (NHL)**	**80**	**42**	**29**	**9**	**.581**	**5**	**2**	**3**	**.400**
1984-85	**NY Rangers (NHL)**	**45**	**15**	**22**	**8**	**.422**	....	....	....	....
1986-87	St. Cloud (Div. III)	36	25	10	1	.708	....	....	....	....
1987-88	**Minnesota (NHL)**	**80**	**19**	**48**	**13**	**.319**	....	....	....	....
1991-92	Utica (AHL)	80	34	40	6	.463	4	0	4	.000
	NHL Totals	**365**	**150**	**161**	**54**	**.485**	**24**	**12**	**12**	**.500**

Club Directory

Meadowlands Arena
P.O. Box 504
East Rutherford, NJ 07073
Phone **201/935-6050**
GM FAX 201/507-0711
FAX 201/935-2127
Capacity: 19,040

Chairman	John J. McMullen
President & General Manager	Louis A. Lamoriello
Executive Vice President	Max McNab
Senior Vice President, Finance	Chris Modrzynski
Vice President, Community Development	Jerry Dailey
Vice President, Operations & Human Resources	Peter McMullen
Vice President, Administration	Mike O'Neil
Vice President, Marketing	Brian Petrovek
Hockey Club Personnel	
Director of Player Personnel	Marshall Johnston
Head Coach	Herb Brooks
Assistant Coaches	Dave Farrish, Doug Sulliman
Goaltending Coach	Warren Strelow
Head Coach, Utica Devils	Robbie Ftorek
Assistant Director of Player Personnel	David Conte
Scouting Staff	Claude Carrier, Marcel Pronovost, Milt Fisher, Frank Jay, Ed Thomlinson, Dan Labraaten, Glen Dirk, Les Widdifield, Joe Mahoney, Fernie Flaman, John Cunniff
Athletic Trainer	Ted Schuch
Equipment Managers	J.P. Mattingly, Dana Heinze
Massage Therapist	Bob Huddleston
Team Cardiologist	Dr. Joseph Niznik
Team Dentist	Dr. H. Hugh Gardy
Team Internist	Dr. Richard Commentucci
Team Orthopedists	Dr. Barry Fisher, Dr. Len Jaffe
Exercise Physiologists	Dr. Garret Caffrey, Jack Blactherwick
Physical Therapist	David Feniger
Administrative Assistants to the President/GM	Marie Carnevale, Charlotte Smaldone
Staff Assistants	Angela Gorgone, Michelle Galeano
Communications Department	
Director, Public & Media Relations	David Freed
Director, Broadcast Operations	Chris Moore
Assistant Director, Media Relations	Mike Levine
Public & Media Relations Assistant	George Moreira
Receptionist	Jelsa Belotta
Staff Assistant	David Perricone
Finance Department	
Assistant Controller	Scott Struble
Staff Accountants	Mark Spinelli, Richard Rowbotham
Secretary	Eileen Musikant
Marketing Department	
Director, Promotional Marketing	Ken Ferriter
Group Sales Managers	Neil Desormeaux, Matt Zanelli
Sales Managers	Holly Meyer, Ted Vincent, Joe Bevilacqua
Secretary	Karen Lynch
Ticket Department	
Director, Ticket Operations	Terry Farmer
Assistant Director, Ticket Operations	Scott Tanfield
Television Outlet	SportsChannel
Broadcasters	Gary Thorne, Play-by-Play; Peter McNab, Color
Radio Outlet	WABC (770 AM)
Broadcasters	Chris Moore, Play-by-Play; Sherry Ross, Color
Team Photographers	Jim Turner, Steve Crandall
Video Consultant	Mitch Kaufman
Seating Capacity	19,040
Dimensions of Rink	200 feet by 85 feet
Club Colors	Red, Black and White

General Manager

LAMORIELLO, LOU
President and General Manager, New Jersey Devils.
Born in Providence, Rhode Island, October 21, 1942.

Lou Lamoriello's life-long dedication to the game of hockey was rewarded in 1992 when he was named as a recipient of the Lester Patrick Trophy for outstanding service to hockey in the United States. Lamoriello is entering his sixth season as president and general manager of the Devils following a more than 20-year association with Providence College as a player, coach and administrator. A member of the varsity hockey Friars during his undergraduate days, he became an assistant coach with the college club after graduating in 1963. Lamoriello was later named head coach and in the ensuing 15 years, led his teams to a 248-179-13 record, a .578 winning percentage and appearances in 10 post-season tournaments, including the 1983 NCAA Final Four. Lamoriello also served a five-year term as athletic director at Providence and was a co-founder of Hockey East, one of the strongest collegiate hockey conferences in the U.S. He remained as athletic director until he was hired as president of the Devils on April 30, 1987. He assumed the dual responsibility of general manager on September 10, 1987.

New York Islanders

1991-92 Results: 34W-35L-11T 79PTS. Fifth, Patrick Division

Schedule

Home

Oct.	Sat.	17	NY Rangers
	Tues.	20	Philadelphia
	Sat.	24	Hartford
	Tues.	27	Los Angeles
	Sat.	31	New Jersey
Nov.	Sat.	7	Tampa Bay
	Sat.	14	Buffalo
	Sat.	28	Philadelphia
Dec.	Tues.	1	Pittsburgh
	Sat.	5	Washington
	Sat.	12	Winnipeg
	Sun.	13	Edmonton (at Oklahoma City)
	Thur.	17	Ottawa
	Sat.	26	NY Rangers
	Tues.	29	Toronto
Jan.	Sat.	2	Minnesota
	Tues.	5	Quebec
	Sat.	9	Vancouver
	Tues.	12	Calgary
	Thur.	14	Washington
	Tues.	19	Boston
	Sat.	23	Philadelphia
	Tues.	26	New Jersey
	Sat.	30	Boston
Feb.	Mon.	1	NY Rangers
	Tues.	9	Montreal
	Sat.	13	NY Rangers
	Tues.	16	Edmonton
	Thur.	18	St Louis
	Sat.	20	Pittsburgh*
	Tues.	23	Washington
Mar.	Tues.	2	Detroit
	Tues.	9	Philadelphia
	Sat.	13	Pittsburgh
	Sun.	14	Washington
	Thur.	25	New Jersey
	Sat.	27	San Jose
	Tues.	30	Philadelphia
Apr.	Sat.	3	Montreal
	Thur.	8	Chicago
	Sat.	10	Ottawa
	Thur.	15	Hartford

Away

Oct.	Tues.	6	New Jersey
	Thur.	8	Pittsburgh
	Sat.	10	Boston
	Thur.	15	Philadelphia
	Sun.	18	NY Rangers
	Fri.	23	Washington
	Fri.	30	New Jersey
Nov.	Tues.	3	Pittsburgh
	Thur.	5	Minnesota
	Thur.	12	Philadelphia
	Thur.	19	Boston
	Sat.	21	Calgary
	Sun.	22	Edmonton
	Tues.	24	Winnipeg
	Fri.	27	Philadelphia*
Dec.	Fri.	4	Buffalo
	Mon.	7	Tampa Bay
	Thur.	10	Chicago
	Tues.	15	St Louis (at Dallas)
	Sat.	19	Pittsburgh*
	Sun.	20	Quebec*
	Wed.	23	Montreal
	Thur.	31	St Louis
Jan.	Fri.	8	Buffalo
	Sat.	16	New Jersey
	Sun.	17	Ottawa
	Thur.	28	Pittsburgh
Feb.	Wed.	3	Toronto
	Fri.	12	NY Rangers
	Thur.	25	Quebec
	Sat.	27	Philadelphia*
	Sun.	28	Hartford
Mar.	Sun.	7	Washington*
	Wed.	10	Montreal
	Tues.	16	San Jose
	Thur.	18	Los Angeles
	Sat.	20	Vancouver
	Tues.	23	Detroit
Apr.	Fri.	2	NY Rangers
	Tues.	6	Washington
	Sun.	11	New Jersey
	Wed.	14	Hartford

* Denotes afternoon game.

Home Starting Times:

All Games	7:35 p.m.
Except Feb. 20	2:05 p.m.
Mar. 13, Mar. 14	5:05 p.m.
Apr. 3	8:05 p.m.

Franchise date: June 6, 1972

21st NHL Season

Year-by-Year Record

Season	GP	Home W	Home L	Home T	Road W	Road L	Road T	Overall W	Overall L	Overall T	GF	GA	Pts.	Finished	Playoff Result
1991-92	80	20	15	5	14	20	6	34	35	11	291	299	79	5th, Patrick Div.	Out of Playoffs
1990-91	80	15	19	6	10	26	4	25	45	10	223	290	60	6th, Patrick Div.	Out of Playoffs
1989-90	80	15	17	8	16	21	3	31	38	11	281	288	73	4th, Patrick Div.	Lost Div. Semi-Final
1988-89	80	19	18	3	9	29	2	28	47	5	265	325	61	6th, Patrick Div.	Out of Playoffs
1987-88	80	24	10	6	15	21	4	39	31	10	308	267	88	1st, Patrick Div.	Lost Div. Semi-Final
1986-87	80	20	15	5	15	18	7	35	33	12	279	281	82	3rd, Patrick Div.	Lost Div. Final
1985-86	80	22	11	7	17	18	5	39	29	12	327	284	90	3rd, Patrick Div.	Lost Div. Semi-Final
1984-85	80	26	11	3	14	23	3	40	34	6	345	312	86	3rd, Patrick Div.	Lost Div. Final
1983-84	80	28	11	1	22	15	3	50	26	4	357	269	104	1st, Patrick Div.	Lost Final
1982-83	**80**	26	11	3	16	15	9	**42**	**26**	**12**	**302**	**226**	**96**	**2nd, Patrick Div.**	**Won Stanley Cup**
1981-82	**80**	33	3	4	21	13	6	**54**	**16**	**10**	**385**	**250**	**118**	**1st, Patrick Div.**	**Won Stanley Cup**
1980-81	**80**	23	6	11	25	12	3	**48**	**18**	**14**	**355**	**260**	**110**	**1st, Patrick Div.**	**Won Stanley Cup**
1979-80	**80**	26	9	5	13	19	8	**39**	**28**	**13**	**281**	**247**	**91**	**2nd, Patrick Div.**	**Won Stanley Cup**
1978-79	80	31	3	6	20	12	8	51	15	14	358	214	116	1st, Patrick Div.	Lost Semi-Final
1977-78	80	29	3	8	19	14	7	48	17	15	334	210	111	1st, Patrick Div.	Lost Quarter-Final
1976-77	80	24	11	5	23	10	7	47	21	12	288	193	106	2nd, Patrick Div.	Lost Semi-Final
1975-76	80	24	8	8	18	13	9	42	21	17	297	190	101	2nd, Patrick Div.	Lost Semi-Final
1974-75	80	22	6	12	11	19	10	33	25	22	264	221	88	3rd, Patrick Div.	Lost Semi-Final
1973-74	78	13	17	9	6	24	9	19	41	18	182	247	56	8th, East Div.	Out of Playoffs
1972-73	78	10	25	4	2	35	2	12	60	6	170	347	30	8th, East Div.	Out of Playoffs

Ray Ferraro, who represented the Islanders at the 1992 All-Star Game, scored 40 goals in 1991-92.

1992-93 Player Personnel

FORWARDS	HT	WT	S	Place of Birth	Date	1991-92 Club
ARMSTRONG, Derek	5-11	180	R	Ottawa, Ont.	4/2/73	Sudbury
BERG, Bill	6-1	190	L	St. Catharines, Ont.	10/21/67	NYI-Capital District
CHYZOWSKI, David	6-1	190	L	Edmonton, Alta.	7/11/71	NYI-Capital District
CREIGHTON, Adam	6-5	210	L	Burlington, Ont.	6/2/65	Chicago-NY Idlanders
DALGARNO, Brad	6-3	215	R	Vancouver, B.C.	8/11/67	NYI-Capital District
DEULING, Jarrett	5-11	195	L	Vernon, B.C.	3/4/74	Kamloops
DOUCET, Wayne	6-2	203	L	Etobicoke, Ont.	6/19/70	Capital District
DUTHIE, Ryan	5-10	180	R	Red Deer, Alta.	9/2/74	Spokane
EWEN, Dean	6-2	225	L	St. Albert, Alta.	2/28/69	Capital District
FERRARO, Ray	5-10	185	L	Trail, B.C.	8/23/64	NY Islanders
FITZGERALD, Tom	6-1	197	R	Melrose, MA	8/28/68	NYI-Capital District
FLATLEY, Patrick	6-2	200	R	Toronto, Ont.	10/3/63	NY Islanders
FLEURY, Sylvain	5-11	189	L	Drummondville, Que.	4/30/70	Dayton
FRASER, Iain	5-10	184	L	Scarborough, Ont.	8/10/69	Cap. Dist.-Rich.
GREEN, Travis	6-0	196	R	Creston, B.C.	12/20/70	Capital District
GRIEVE, Brent	6-1	205	L	Oshawa, Ont.	5/9/69	Capital District
HOGUE, Benoit	5-10	190	L	Repentigny, Que.	10/28/66	Buffalo-NY Islanders
HUBER, Phil	5-11	196	L	Calgary, Alta.	1/10/69	Capital District
JABLONSKI, Jeff	6-1	185	L	Toledo, OH	6/20/67	Cap. Dist.-Nash.
JOHNSON, John	5-10	185	L	Kirkfield, Ont.	2/22/71	N. Falls-Petrboro.
JUNKER, Steve	6-0	184	L	Castlegar, B.C.	6/26/72	Spokane
KING, Derek	6-1	210	L	Hamilton, Ont.	2/11/67	NY Islanders
KROMM, Rich	6-1	192	L	Trail, B.C.	3/29/64	NYI-Capital District
LACROIX, Martin	5-11	155	R	Rosemere, Que.	1/4/70	St. Lawrence U.
LeBRUN, Sean	6-2	205	L	Prince George, B.C.	5/2/69	Cap. Dist.-Rich.
LOISELLE, Claude	5-11	195	L	Ottawa, Ont.	5/29/63	Toronto-NY Islanders
MAROIS, Daniel	6-0	190	R	Montreal, Que.	10/3/68	Toronto-NY Islanders
McINNIS, Marty	5-10	165	R	Weymouth, MA	6/2/70	NYI-US Olympic
MULLEN, Brian	5-10	180	L	New York, NY	3/16/62	San Jose
O'ROURKE, Steve	6-1	190	R	Calgary, Alta.	9/11/74	Tri-Cities
PALFFY, Zigmund	5-11	180	L	Scallca, Czech.	5/5/72	Skoda Plzen
PARADIS, Daniel	6-2	185	L	Jonquiere, Que.	11/22/72	Chicoutimi
PARKS, Greg	5-9	180	R	Edmonton, Alta.	3/25/67	NYI-Capital District
SATERDALEN, Jeff	6-1	190	R	Bloomington, MN	7/8/69	St. Cloud State
SCISSONS, Scott	6-1	200	L	Saskatoon, Sask.	10/29/71	Cdn. National
SPARKS, Todd	6-0	187	L	Edmunston, N.B.	6/9/71	Hull
TAYLOR, Chris	6-0	190	L	Stratford, Ont.	3/6/72	London
THOMAS, Steve	5-11	185	L	Stockport, U.K.	7/15/63	Chicago-NY Islanders
TOWNSHEND, Graeme	6-2	225	R	Kingston, Jamaica	10/2/65	NYI-Capital District
TURGEON, Pierre	6-1	203	L	Rouyn, Que.	8/29/69	Buffalo-NY Islanders
VANDERYDT, Rob	6-1	177	L	Blenheim, Ont.	6/8/68	Cap. Dist.-Rich.
VOLEK, David	6-0	190	L	Prague, Czech.	8/16/66	NY Islanders
VUKOTA, Mick	6-2	215	R	Saskatoon, Sask.	9/14/66	NY Islanders

DEFENSEMEN	HT	WT	S	Place of Birth	Date	1991-92 Club
CHEVELDAYOFF, Kevin	6-0	202	R	Saskatoon, Sask.	2/4/70	Capital District
CHYNOWETH, Dean	6-2	190	R	Calgary, Alta.	10/30/68	NYI-Capital District
FINLEY, Jeff	6-2	185	L	Edmonton, Alta.	4/14/67	NYI-Capital District
HAYWARD, Rick	6-0	200	L	Toledo, OH	2/25/66	Capital District
KAMPERSAL, Jeff	6-2	190	R	Beverly, MA	1/27/70	Princeton
KASPARAITIS, Darius	5-11	190	L	Elekternai, Latvia	10/16/72	Dynamo-CIS Olympic
KRUPP, Uwe	6-6	235	R	Cologne, Germany	6/24/65	Buffalo-NY Islanders
KURVERS, Tom	6-0	205	L	Minneapolis, MN	9/14/62	NY Islanders
LACHANCE, Scott	6-2	197	L	Charlottesville, VA	10/22/72	NYI-US Olympic
LEHTO, Joni	6-0	205	L	Turku, Finland	7/15/70	Cap. Dist.-Rich.
MALAKHOV, Vladimir	6-5	210	L	Sverdlovsk, USSR	8/30/68	CSKA-CIS Nat.
McBEAN, Wayne	6-2	185	L	Calgary, Alta.	2/21/69	NY Islanders
NORTON, Jeff	6-2	195	L	Acton, MA	11/25/65	NY Islanders
NYLUND, Gary	6-4	210	L	Surrey, B.C.	10/28/63	NY Islanders
PILON, Richard	6-0	211	L	Saskatoon, Sask.	4/30/68	NY Islanders
PRYOR, Chris	6-0	210	R	St. Paul, MN	1/31/61	Capital District
TURNER, Brad	6-2	190	R	Winnipeg, Man.	5/25/68	NYI-Cap. Dist.-Rich.
VASKE, Dennis	6-2	210	L	Rockford, IL	10/11/67	NYI-Capital District
WIDMER, Jason	6-0	205	L	Calgary, Alta.	8/1/73	Lethbridge

GOALTENDERS	HT	WT	C	Place of Birth	Date	1991-92 Club
FITZPATRICK, Mark	6-2	190	L	Toronto, Ont.	11/13/68	NYI-Capital District
HEALY, Glenn	5-10	185	L	Pickering, Ont.	6/23/62	NY Islanders
HNILICKA, Milan	6-0	180	L	Kladno, Czech.	6/24/73	Poldi Kladno
LORENZ, Danny	5-10	165	L	Murrayville, B.C.	12/12/69	NYI-Capital District
McLENNAN, Jamie	6-0	190	L	Edmonton, Alta.	6/30/71	Cap. Dist.-Rich.

General Managers' History

William A. Torrey, 1972-73 to 1991-92; Don Maloney, 1992-93.

Coaching History

Phil Goyette and Earl Ingarfield, 1972-73; Al Arbour, 1973-74 to 1985-86; Terry Simpson, 1986-87 to 1987-88; Terry Simpson and Al Arbour, 1988-89; Al Arbour, 1989-90 to date.

Captains' History

Ed Westfall, 1972-73 to 1975-76; Ed Westfall, Clark Gillies, 1976-77; Clark Gillies, 1977-78, 1978-79; Denis Potvin, 1979-80 to 1986-87; Brent Sutter, 1987-88 to 1990-91; Brent Sutter and Patrick Flatley, 1991-92; Patrick Flatley, 1992-93.

1991-92 Scoring

Regular Season

Pos	#.	Player	Team	GP	G	A	Pts	+/-	PIM	PP	SH	GW	GT	S	%
C	77	Pierre Turgeon	BUF	8	2	6	8	1–	4	0	0	0	0	14	14.3
			NYI	69	38	49	87	8	16	13	0	6	0	193	19.7
			TOTAL	77	40	55	95	7	20	13	0	6	0	207	19.3
C	20	Ray Ferraro	NYI	80	40	40	80	25	92	7	0	4	2	154	26.0
L	27	Derek King	NYI	80	40	38	78	10–	46	21	0	6	2	189	21.2
L	32	Steve Thomas	CHI	11	2	6	8	3–	26	0	0	1	0	35	5.7
			NYI	71	28	42	70	11	71	3	0	2	1	210	13.3
			TOTAL	82	30	48	78	8	97	3	0	3	1	245	12.2
C	33	Benoit Hogue	BUF	3	0	1	1	0	0	0	0	0	0	6	.0
			NYI	72	30	45	75	30	67	8	0	5	0	143	21.0
			TOTAL	75	30	46	76	30	67	8	0	5	0	149	20.1
L	25	Dave Volek	NYI	74	18	42	60	0	35	4	1	2	0	167	10.8
D	28	Tom Kurvers	NYI	74	9	47	56	18–	30	6	0	1	0	132	6.8
D	4	Uwe Krupp	BUF	8	2	0	2	0	6	0	0	0	0	13	15.4
			NYI	59	6	29	35	13	43	2	0	0	0	115	5.2
			TOTAL	67	8	29	37	13	49	2	0	0	0	128	6.3
C	11	Adam Creighton	CHI	11	6	6	12	1–	16	2	0	0	1	32	18.8
			NYI	66	15	9	24	4–	102	2	0	2	0	108	13.9
			TOTAL	77	21	15	36	5–	118	4	0	2	1	140	15.0
R	26	Patrick Flatley	NYI	38	8	28	36	14	31	4	1	0	0	76	10.5
R	24	Dan Marois	TOR	63	15	11	26	36–	76	4	0	0	0	140	10.7
			NYI	12	2	5	7	2	18	0	0	0	0	19	10.5
			TOTAL	75	17	16	33	34–	94	4	0	0	0	159	10.7
D	8	Jeff Norton	NYI	28	1	18	19	2	18	0	1	0	0	34	2.9
C	10	Claude Loiselle	TOR	64	6	9	15	21–	102	1	0	1	0	91	6.6
			NYI	11	1	1	2	3–	13	0	0	0	0	10	10.0
			TOTAL	75	7	10	17	24–	115	1	0	1	0	101	6.9
R	14	Tom Fitzgerald	NYI	45	6	11	17	3–	28	0	2	2	0	71	8.5
D	29	Joe Reekie	NYI	54	4	12	16	15	85	0	0	0	1	59	6.8
L	17	Bill Berg	NYI	47	5	9	14	18–	28	1	0	1	0	60	8.3
D	3	Jeff Finley	NYI	51	1	10	11	6–	26	0	0	0	0	25	4.0
C	39	Hubie McDonough	NYI	33	7	2	9	4–	15	1	1	0	0	31	22.6
C	38*	Marty Mcinnis	NYI	15	3	5	8	6	0	0	0	0	0	24	12.5
C	18	Rob Dimaio	NYI	50	5	2	7	23–	43	0	2	0	0	43	11.6
D	47	Richard Pilon	NYI	65	1	6	7	1–	183	0	0	0	0	27	3.7
D	6	Wayne McBean	NYI	25	2	4	6	11	18	0	1	1	0	51	3.9
R	12	Mick Vukota	NYI	74	0	6	6	6–	293	0	0	0	0	34	.0
D	7*	Scott Lachance	NYI	17	1	4	5	13	9	0	0	0	1	20	5.0
R	15	Brad Dalgarno	NYI	15	2	1	3	8–	12	1	0	0	0	17	11.8
L	34	Graeme Townshend	NYI	7	1	2	3	6	0	0	0	0	0	6	16.7
L	9	Dave Chyzowski	NYI	12	1	1	2	4–	17	0	0	0	0	18	5.6
G	30	Mark Fitzpatrick	NYI	30	0	2	2	0	8	0	0	0	0	0	.0
D	2	Dean Chynoweth	NYI	11	1	0	1	3–	23	0	0	0	0	6	16.7
D	36	Gary Nylund	NYI	7	0	1	1	3–	10	0	0	0	0	5	.0
G	35	Glenn Healy	NYI	37	0	1	1	0	18	0	0	0	0	0	.0
D	37*	Dennis Vaske	NYI	39	0	1	1	5	39	0	0	0	0	26	.0
L	32	Rich Kromm	NYI	1	0	0	0	0	0	0	0	0	0	0	.0
C	7*	Greg Parks	NYI	1	0	0	0	0	2	0	0	0	0	0	.0
G	1*	Danny Lorenz	NYI	2	0	0	0	0	0	0	0	0	0	0	.0
D	7*	Brad Turner	NYI	3	0	0	0	1	0	0	0	0	0	1	.0
D	23	Rick Green	NYI	4	0	0	0	1–	0	0	0	0	0	2	.0

Goaltending

No.	Goaltender	GPI	Mins	Avg	W	L	T	EN	SO	GA	SA	S%
30	Mark Fitzpatrick	30	1743	3.20	11	13	5	5	0	93	949	.902
1	Steve Weeks	23	1032	3.60	9	4	2	0	0	62	566	.890
35	Glenn Healy	37	1960	3.80	14	16	4	4	1	124	1045	.881
1	* Danny Lorenz	2	120	5.00	0	2	0	1	0	10	60	.833
	Totals	**80**	**4868**	**3.69**	**34**	**35**	**11**	**10**	**1**	**299**	**2630**	**.886**

Mark Fitzpatrick led all Islanders' goaltenders with a 3.20 GAA.

Club Records

Team

(Figures in brackets for season records are games played; records for fewest points, wins, ties, losses, goals, goals against are for 70 or more games)

Record		
Most Points	**118**	1981-82 (80)
Most Wins	**54**	1981-82 (80)
Most Ties	**22**	1974-75 (80)
Most Losses	**60**	1972-73 (78)
Most Goals	**385**	1981-82 (80)
Most Goals Against	**347**	1972-73 (78)
Fewest Points	**30**	1972-73 (78)
Fewest Wins	**12**	1972-73 (78)
Fewest Ties	**4**	1983-84 (80)
Fewest Losses	**15**	1978-79 (80)
Fewest Goals	**170**	1972-73 (78)
Fewest Goals Against	**190**	1975-76 (80)
Longest Winning Streak		
Over-all	***15**	Jan. 21/82-Feb. 20/82
Home	**14**	Jan. 2/82-Feb. 27/82
Away	**8**	Feb. 27/81-Mar. 31/81
Longest Undefeated Streak		
Over-all	**15**	Jan. 21-Feb. 21/82 (15 wins); Nov. 4-Dec. 4/80 (13 wins, 2 ties)
Home	**23**	Oct. 17/78-Jan. 27/79 (19 wins, 4 ties); Jan. 2/82-Apr. 3/82 (21 wins, 2 ties)
Away	**8**	Four times
Longest Losing Streak		
Over-all	**12**	Dec. 27/72-Jan. 18/73; Nov. 22-Dec. 17/88
Home	**5**	Jan. 2-23/33; Feb. 28-Mar. 19/74; Nov. 22-Dec. 17/88
Away	**15**	Jan. 20-Apr. 1/73
Longest Winless Streak		
Over-all	**15**	Nov. 22-Dec. 23/72 (12 losses, 3 ties)
Home	**7**	Oct. 14-Nov. 21/72 (6 losses, 1 tie); Nov. 28-Dec. 23/72 (5 losses, 2 ties); Feb. 13-Mar. 13/90 (4 losses, 3 ties)
Away	**20**	Nov. 3/72-Jan. 13/73 (19 losses, 1 tie)
Most Shutouts, Season	**10**	1975-76 (80)
Most PIM, Season	**1,857**	1986-87 (80)
Most Goals, Game	**11**	Dec. 20/83 (Pit. 3 at NYI 11); Mar. 3/84 (NYI 11 at Tor. 6)

Individual

Record		
Most Seasons	**17**	Billy Smith
Most Games	**1,123**	Bryan Trottier
Most Goals, Career	**573**	Mike Bossy
Most Assists, Career	**853**	Bryan Trottier
Most Points, Career	**1,353**	Bryan Trottier (500 goals, 853 assists)
Most PIM, Career	**1,466**	Garry Howatt
Most Shutouts, Career	**25**	Glenn Resch
Longest Consecutive Games Streak	**576**	Bill Harris (Oct. 7/72-Nov. 30/79)
Most Goals, Season	**69**	Mike Bossy (1978-79)
Most Assists, Season	**87**	Bryan Trottier (1978-79)
Most Points, Season	**147**	Mike Bossy (1981-82) (64 goals, 83 assists)
Most PIM, Season	**356**	Brian Curran (1986-87)
Most Points, Defenseman, Season	**101**	Denis Potvin (1978-79) (31 goals, 70 assists)
Most Points, Center, Season	**134**	Bryan Trottier (1978-79) (47 goals, 87 assists)
Most Points, Right Wing, Season	***147**	Mike Bossy (1981-82) (64 goals, 83 assists)
Most Points, Left Wing, Season	**100**	John Tonelli (1984-85) (42 goals, 58 assists)
Most Points, Rookie, Season	**95**	Bryan Trottier (1975-76) (32 goals, 63 assists)
Most Shutouts, Season	**7**	Glenn Resch (1975-76)
Most Goals, Game	**5**	Bryan Trottier (Dec. 23/78; Feb. 13/82); John Tonelli (Jan. 6/81)
Most Assists, Game	**6**	Mike Bossy (Jan. 6/81)
Most Points, Game	**8**	Bryan Trottier (Dec. 23/78)

* NHL Record.

Retired Numbers

5	Denis Potvin	1973-1988
22	Mike Bossy	1977-1987

All-time Record vs. Other Clubs

Regular Season

	At Home							On Road							Total						
	GP	W	L	T	GF	GA	PTS	GP	W	L	T	GF	GA	PTS	GP	W	L	T	GF	GA	PTS
Boston	36	15	18	3	116	121	33	37	9	20	8	105	145	26	73	24	38	11	221	266	59
Buffalo	38	14	17	7	113	115	35	36	12	20	4	103	126	28	74	26	37	11	216	241	63
Calgary	41	22	10	9	164	110	53	41	12	18	11	131	150	35	82	34	28	20	295	260	88
Chicago	37	16	9	12	134	106	44	39	17	17	5	139	124	39	76	33	26	17	273	230	83
Detroit	36	20	13	3	138	104	43	35	15	18	2	119	128	32	71	35	31	5	257	232	75
Edmonton	20	8	5	7	85	86	23	21	6	11	4	64	77	16	41	14	16	11	149	163	39
Hartford	21	13	6	2	88	53	28	20	10	7	3	79	63	23	41	23	13	5	167	116	51
Los Angeles	36	21	11	4	138	104	46	35	14	14	7	118	118	35	71	35	25	11	256	222	81
Minnesota	37	19	10	8	145	110	46	37	18	14	5	142	109	41	74	37	24	13	287	219	87
Montreal	36	17	15	4	120	108	38	36	9	21	6	110	139	24	72	26	36	10	230	247	62
New Jersey	52	40	5	7	245	143	87	54	27	17	10	219	180	64	106	67	22	17	464	323	151
NY Rangers	63	41	17	5	267	198	87	66	19	42	5	199	266	43	129	60	59	10	466	464	130
Philadelphia	64	33	21	10	249	188	76	64	17	37	10	194	240	44	128	50	58	20	443	428	120
Pittsburgh	59	36	15	8	257	176	80	57	21	26	10	199	220	52	116	57	41	18	456	396	132
Quebec	21	14	6	1	99	76	29	20	10	9	1	69	75	21	41	24	15	2	168	151	50
St. Louis	39	24	6	9	156	84	57	37	16	15	6	123	131	38	76	40	21	15	279	215	95
San Jose	2	2	0	0	13	3	4	1	0	1	0	2	3	0	3	2	1	0	15	6	4
Toronto	36	21	12	3	158	112	45	38	17	17	4	141	134	38	74	38	29	7	299	246	83
Vancouver	37	22	7	8	147	97	52	39	18	18	3	126	124	39	76	40	25	11	273	221	91
Washington	54	35	18	1	228	169	71	52	23	22	7	182	165	53	106	58	40	8	410	334	124
Winnipeg	20	10	5	5	76	58	25	20	12	7	1	80	68	25	40	22	12	6	156	126	50
Defunct Clubs	13	11	0	2	75	33	24	13	4	5	4	35	41	12	26	15	5	6	110	74	36
Totals	**798**	**454**	**226**	**118**	**3211**	**2354**	**1026**	**798**	**306**	**376**	**116**	**2679**	**2826**	**728**	**1596**	**760**	**602**	**234**	**5890**	**5180**	**1754**

Playoffs

	Series	W	L	GP	W	L	T	GF	GA	Last Mtg.	Round	Result
Boston	2	2	0	11	8	3	0	49	35	1983	CF	W 4-2
Buffalo	3	3	0	16	12		0	59	45	1980	SF	W 4-2
Chicago	2	2	0	6	6	0	0	21	6	1979	QF	W 4-0
Edmonton	3	2	1	15	9	6	0	58	47	1984	F	L 1-4
Los Angeles	1	1	0	4	3	1	0	21	10	1980	PR	W 3-1
Minnesota	1	1	0	5	4	1	0	26	16	1981	F	W 4-1
Montreal	3	1	2	17	7	10	0	44	48	1984	CF	W 4-2
New Jersey	1	0	1	6	2	4	0	18	23	1988	DSF	L 2-4
NY Rangers	7	5	2	35	20	15	0	126	110	1990	DSF	L 1-4
Philadelphia	4	1	3	25	11	14	0	69	83	1987	DF	L 3-4
Pittsburgh	2	2	0	12	7	5	0	43	31	1982	DSF	W 3-2
Quebec	1	1	0	4	4	0	0	18	9	1982	CF	W 4-0
Toronto	2	1	1	10	6	4	0	33	20	1981	PR	W 3-0
Vancouver	2	2	0	6	6	0	0	26	14	1982	F	W 4-0
Washington	5	4	1	24	14	10	0	76	66	1987	DSF	W 4-3
Totals	**39**	**28**	**11**	**196**	**119**	**77**	**0**	**687**	**563**			

Playoff Results 1992-88

Year	Round	Opponent	Result	GF	GA
1990	DSF	NY Rangers	L 1-4	13	22
1988	DSF	New Jersey	L 2-4	18	23

Abbreviations: Round: F – Final; **CF** – conference final; **DF** – division final; **DSF** – division semi-final; **SF** – semi-final; **QF** – quarter-final; **PR** – preliminary round. **GA** – goals against; **GF** – goals for.

1991-92 Results

Home			Away		
Oct. 12	Philadelphia	5-4	**Oct.** 5	Boston	4-3
15	Pittsburgh	6-7	9	NY Rangers	3-5
19	Edmonton	2-4	13	Quebec	1-1
22	Winnipeg	1-1	17	Pittsburgh	5-8
26	Los Angeles	2-4	31	Chicago	3-4
29	San Jose	8-4	**Nov.** 6	Edmonton	3-5
Nov. 2	Washington	4-7	9	San Jose	3-4
4	Boston	6-4	10	Vancouver	0-6
16	NY Rangers	4-2	14	New Jersey	4-3
27	Boston	2-3	19	Minnesota	7-4
30	Washington	8-1	20	Winnipeg	1-3
Dec. 5	Montreal	4-5	23	Pittsburgh	2-2
7	Chicago	2-5	29	Washington	3-2
10	St Louis	7-7	**Dec.** 11	Toronto	5-4
14	New Jersey	3-3	17	Hartford	4-2
23	Pittsburgh	3-6	19	Philadelphia	2-6
26	New Jersey	5-5	21	St Louis	2-6
28	NY Rangers	5-4	29	Hartford	4-6
Jan. 4	Quebec	5-2	**Jan.** 1	Washington*	5-8
9	Hartford	2-1	3	Buffalo	2-5
11	St Louis	3-6	7	Detroit	5-2
14	Detroit	6-2	12	Philadelphia	3-4
16	Philadelphia	4-3	30	Pittsburgh	8-5
23	Toronto	3-4	**Feb.** 4	Los Angeles	2-1
25	Pittsburgh*	3-5	6	Vancouver	5-4
Feb. 1	Philadelphia	5-5	7	Edmonton	2-4
2	Calgary	6-3	11	Calgary	3-1
15	Vancouver	3-1	14	NY Rangers	2-9
17	Winnipeg*	5-4	25	Philadelphia	1-4
20	NY Rangers	6-2	28	New Jersey	3-2
22	Minnesota	2-1	**Mar.** 5	Chicago	4-4
23	Washington	1-4	7	Montreal	2-8
29	New Jersey	1-3	8	Buffalo	6-2
Mar. 3	Montreal	3-4	12	Pittsburgh	4-6
10	Philadelphia	5-2	15	Washington*	2-5
14	Buffalo*	4-1	18	NY Rangers	1-1
26	San Jose	7-4	21	New Jersey*	2-2
28	NY Rangers	4-1	24	Quebec	2-5
29	Detroit	2-6	**Apr.** 1	Toronto	6-2
Apr. 4	New Jersey*	7-0	5	Washington*	1-1

*Denotes afternoon game

Entry Draft Selections 1992-78

1992
Pick
5 Darius Kasparaitis
56 Jarrett Deuling
104 Tomas Klimt
105 Ryan Duthie
128 Derek Armstrong
152 Vladimir Grachev
159 Steve O'Rourke
176 Jason Widmer
200 Daniel Paradis
224 David Wainwright
248 Andrei Vasiljev

1991
Pick
4 Scott Lachance
26 Zigmund Palffy
48 Jamie McLennan
70 Milan Hnilicka
92 Steve Junker
114 Robert Valicevic
136 Andreas Johansson
158 Todd Sparks
180 John Johnson
202 Robert Canavan
224 Marcus Thuresson
246 Marty Schriner

1990
Pick
6 Scott Scissons
27 Chris Taylor
48 Dan Plante
90 Chris Marinucci
111 Joni Lehto
132 Michael Guilbert
153 Sylvain Fleury
174 John Joyce
195 Richard Enga
216 Martin Lacroix
237 Andy Shirr

1989
Pick
2 Dave Chyzowski
23 Travis Green
44 Jason Zent
65 Brent Grieve
86 Jace Reed
90 Steve Young
99 Kevin O'Sullivan
128 Jon Larson
133 Brett Harkins
149 Phil Huber
170 Matthew Robbins
191 Vladimir Malakhov
212 Kelly Ens
233 Iain Fraser

1988
Pick
16 Kevin Cheveldayoff
29 Wayne Doucet
37 Sean LeBrun
58 Danny Lorenz
79 Andre Brassard
100 Paul Rutherford
111 Pavel Gross
121 Jason Rathbone
142 Yves Gaucher
163 Marty McInnis
184 Jeff Blumer
205 Jeff Kampersal
226 Phillip Neururer
247 Joe Capprini

1987
Pick
13 Dean Chynoweth
34 Jeff Hackett
55 Dean Ewen
76 George Maneluk
97 Petr Vlk
118 Rob DiMaio
139 Knut Walbye
160 Jeff Saterdalen
181 Shawn Howard
202 John Herlihy
223 Michael Erickson
244 Will Averill

1986
Pick
17 Tom Fitzgerald
38 Dennis Vaske
59 Bill Berg
80 Shawn Byram
101 Dean Sexsmith
104 Todd McLellan
122 Tony Schmalzbauer
138 Will Anderson
143 Richard Pilon
164 Peter Harris
185 Jeff Jablonski
206 Kerry Clark
227 Dan Beaudette
248 Paul Thompson

1985
Pick
6 Brad Dalgarno
13 Derek King
34 Brad Lauer
55 Jeff Finley
76 Kevin Herom
89 Tommy Hedlund
97 Jeff Sveen
118 Rod Dallman
139 Kurt Lackten
160 Hank Lammens
181 Rich Wiest
202 Real Arsenault
223 Mike Volpe
244 Tony Grenier

1984
Pick
20 Duncan MacPherson
41 Bruce Melanson
62 Jeff Norton
70 Doug Wieck
83 Ari Haanpaa
104 Mike Murray
125 Jim Wilharm
146 Kelly Murphy
167 Franco Desantis
187 Tom Warden
208 David Volek
228 Russ Becker
249 Allister Brown

1983
Pick
3 Pat LaFontaine
16 Gerald Diduck
37 Garnet McKechney
57 Mike Neill
65 Mikko Makila
84 Bob Caulfield
97 Ron Viglasi
117 Darin Illikainen
137 Jim Sprenger
157 Dale Henry
177 Kevin Vescio
197 Dave Shellington
217 John Bjorkman
237 Peter McGeough

1982
Pick
21 Patrick Flatley
42 Vern Smith
63 Garry Lacey
84 Alan Kerr
105 Rene Breton
126 Roger Kortko
147 John Tiano
168 Todd Okerlund
189 Gord Paddock
210 Eric Faust
231 Pat Goff
252 Jim Koudys

1981
Pick
21 Paul Boutilier
42 Gord Dineen
57 Ron Handy
63 Neal Coulter
84 Todd Lumbard
94 Jacques Sylvestre
126 Chuck Brimmer
147 Teppo Virta
168 Bill Dowd
189 Scott MacLellan
210 Dave Randerson

1980
Pick
17 Brent Sutter
38 Kelly Hrudey
59 Dave Simpsn
68 Monty Trottier
80 Greg Gilbert
101 Ken Leiter
122 Dan Revell
143 Mark Hamway
164 Morrison Gare
185 Peter Steblyk
206 Glen Johannesen

1979
Pick
17 Duane Sutter
25 Tomas Jonsson
38 Bill Carroll
59 Roland Melanson
80 Tim Lockridge
101 Glen Duncan
122 John Gibb

1978
Pick
15 Steve Tambellini
34 Randy Johnston
51 Dwayne Lowdermilk
84 Greg Hay
101 Kelly Davis
118 Richard Pepin
135 David Cameron
152 Paul Joswiak
169 Scott Cameron
184 Christer Lowdahl
199 Gunnar Persson

Club Directory

Nassau Veterans' Memorial Coliseum
Uniondale, NY 11553
Phone **516/794-4100**
GM FAX 516/542-9350
FAX 516/542-9348
Capacity: 16,297

Co-Chairmen	Robert Rosenthal, Stephen Walsh
President	Jerome Grossman
Executive Vice-President	Ralph Palleschi
Executive Assistant to the President	Bryan Trottier
General Manager and Vice-President/ Hockey Operations	Don Maloney
Assistant Director of Hockey Operations	Darcy Regier
Vice-President/Administration & CFO	Arthur J. McCarthy
Vice-President/Communications	Pat Calabria
Consultant	John H. Krumpe
General Counsel	William H. Skehan
Head Coach	Al Arbour
Assistant Coaches	Lorne Henning, Rick Green
Director of Scouting	Gerry Ehman
Director of Pro Scouting	Ken Morrow
Scouting Staff	Harry Boyd, Richard Green, Earl Ingarfield, Hal Laycoe, Bert Marshall, Mario Saraceno, Jack Vivian
Director of Media Relations	Greg Bouris
Assistant Director of Media Relations	Catherine Schutte
Media Relations Assistant	Eric Mirlis
Director of Publications	Chris Botta
Director of Community Affairs	Jill Knee
Director of Game Day Events	Tim Beach
Director of Amateur Hockey Development	Bob Nystrom
Director of Ticket Sales	Jim Johnson
Director of Suite Sales	Tracy Furthner
Director of Advertising Sales	Glenda Brown
Controller	Ralph Sellitti
Administrative Assistants to the General Manager	Joanne Holewa, Rosemarie Tully
Athletic Trainer	Ed Tyburski
Equipment Manager	John Doolan
Assistant Trainer	Jerry Iannarelli
Team Orthopedists	Jerry Minkoff, M.D., Barry Simonson, M.D.
Team Internists	Gerald Cordani, M.D., Larry Smith, M.D.
Physical Therapist	Steve Wirth
Team Dentists	Bruce Michnick, D.D.S., Jan Sherman, D.D.S.
Photographer	Bruce Bennett
Location of Press Box	East Side of Building
Dimensions of Rink	200 feet by 85 feet
Ends of Rink	Herculite extends above boards around rink
Club Colors	Blue, Orange and White
Television Announcers	Jiggs McDonald, Ed Westfall, Stan Fischler
Television Station	SportsChannel
Radio Announcers	Barry Landers, Bobby Nystrom
Radio Stations	WPAT (930 AM), WGBB (1240 AM), WHRD (1570 AM), WFAS (1230 AM)

Coach

ARBOUR, AL
Coach, New York Islanders. Born in Sudbury, Ont., November 1, 1932.

The 1991-92 season saw Al Arbour surpass Dick Irvin's long-standing record for career games coached. Arbour has been behind the bench for a total of 1,438 regular-season NHL games. This past season also saw Arbour become only the second coach in League history to record 700 wins. He was named head coach of the Islanders' for a second time on June 26, 1989, after serving three years as the club's vice president of player development. Arbour began his coaching career with St. Louis in 1970 before joining the Islanders at the start of the 1973-74 season. He has now won 705 regular-season games and has compiled a career winning percentage of .570.

Coaching Record

		Regular Season					Playoffs			
Season	Team	Games	W	L	T	%	Games	W	L	%
1970-71	St. Louis (NHL)	50	21	15	14	.560	....	....	....	....
1971-72	St. Louis (NHL)	44	19	19	6	.500	11	4	7	.364
1972-73	St. Louis (NHL)	13	2	6	5	.346	....	....	....	....
1973-74	NY Islanders (NHL)	78	19	41	18	.358	....	....	....	....
1974-75	NY Islanders (NHL)	80	33	25	22	.550	....	....	....	....
1975-76	NY Islanders (NHL)	80	42	21	17	.631	13	7	6	.538
1976-77	NY Islanders (NHL)	80	47	21	12	.663	12	8	4	.666
1977-78	NY Islanders (NHL)	80	48	17	15	.694	7	3	4	.429
1978-79	NY Islanders (NHL)	80	51	15	14	.725	10	6	4	.600
1979-80	NY Islanders (NHL)	80	39	28	13	.589	21	15	6	.714*
1980-81	NY Islanders (NHL)	80	48	18	14	.600	18	15	3	.833*
1981-82	NY Islanders (NHL)	80	54	16	10	.738	19	15	4	.789*
1982-83	NY Islanders (NHL)	80	42	26	12	.600	20	15	5	.750*
1983-84	NY Islanders (NHL)	80	50	26	4	.650	21	12	9	.571
1984-85	NY Islanders (NHL)	80	40	34	6	.538	10	4	6	.400
1985-86	NY Islanders (NHL)	80	39	29	12	.563	3	0	3	.000
1988-89	NY Islanders (NHL)	53	21	29	3	.425	....	....	....	.....
1989-90	NY Islanders (NHL)	80	31	38	11	.456	5	1	4	.200
1990-91	NY Islanders (NHL)	80	25	45	10	.375	....	....	....	....
1991-92	NY Islanders (NHL)	80	34	35	11	.494	....	....	....	....
	NHL Totals	1438	705	504	229	.570	187	114	73	.610

* Stanley Cup win.

General Manager

MALONEY, DON
General Manager, New York Islanders. Born in Lindsay, Ont., September 5, 1958.

Don Maloney became the second general manager in the NY Islanders' franchise history on August 17, 1992. After a 13-year playing career that included stays with the Rangers, Islanders and Whalers, Maloney joined the Islanders' organization in January, 1991 as a part-time assistant to coach Al Arbour and general manager Bill Torrey. The following season, he became assistant general manager, representing the team in contract discussions and organizing the Islanders' training camp itinerary. In his playing career, Maloney compiled 214 goals and 350 assists in 765 games.

New York Rangers

1991-92 Results: 50W-25L-5T 105PTS. First, Patrick Division

Schedule

Home	Away
Oct. Mon. 12 Hartford	**Oct.** Fri. 9 Washington
Wed. 14 New Jersey	Sat. 10 New Jersey
Sun. 18 NY Islanders	Sat. 17 NY Islanders
Wed. 21 Washington	Sat. 24 Ottawa
Fri. 23 Montreal	Sat. 31 Montreal
Mon. 26 Philadelphia	**Nov.** Sat. 7 Boston
Thur. 29 Quebec	Sat. 14 Quebec
Nov. Mon. 2 Buffalo	Thur. 19 Philadelphia
Wed. 4 Philadelphia	Sat. 21 Winnipeg
Mon. 9 Tampa Bay	Wed. 25 Pittsburgh
Wed. 11 Washington	Fri. 27 Minnesota
Mon. 23 Pittsburgh	**Dec.** Fri. 4 Washington
Mon. 30 Minnesota	Fri. 11 Tampa Bay
Dec. Wed. 2 Detroit	Thur. 17 St Louis
Sun. 6 Toronto	Sat. 19 Hartford
Wed. 9 Tampa Bay	Mon. 21 New Jersey
(at Miami)	Sat. 26 NY Islanders
Sun. 13 Montreal	Tues. 29 Washington
Tues. 15 Calgary	Thur. 31 Buffalo
Wed. 23 New Jersey	**Jan.** Sat. 2 Pittsburgh
Sun. 27 Boston	Sat. 9 Philadelphia*
Jan. Mon. 4 New Jersey	Sat. 16 Montreal
Wed. 6 Ottawa	Tues. 19 Detroit
Mon. 11 Vancouver	Sat. 23 Los Angeles
Wed. 13 Washington	Fri. 29 Buffalo
Wed. 27 Winnipeg	Sat. 30 Toronto
Feb. Wed. 3 Philadelphia	**Feb.** Mon. 1 NY Islanders
Wed. 10 Pittsburgh	Mon. 8 New Jersey
Fri. 12 NY Islanders	Sat. 13 NY Islanders
Mon. 15 St Louis*	Sat. 20 San Jose
Mar. Wed. 3 Buffalo	Mon. 22 San Jose
Fri. 5 Pittsburgh	(at Sacramento)
Tues. 9 Los Angeles	Wed. 24 Vancouver
Mon. 15 Boston	Fri. 26 Calgary
Wed. 17 Edmonton	Sat. 27 Edmonton
Fri. 19 San Jose	**Mar.** Sat. 6 Quebec
Wed. 24 Philadelphia	Thur. 11 Chicago
Fri. 26 Chicago	Sat. 13 Washington
Sun. 28 Quebec	Mon. 22 Ottawa
Apr. Fri. 2 NY Islanders	**Apr.** Sun. 4 Washington*
Mon. 5 Hartford	Wed. 7 New Jersey
Fri. 9 Pittsburgh	Sat. 10 Pittsburgh
Wed. 14 Washington	Mon. 12 Philadelphia

* Denotes afternoon game.

Home Starting Times:

All Games .... 7:35 p.m.
Except Feb. 15 .... 1:05 p.m.

Franchise date: May 15, 1926

67th NHL Season

Mark Messier captured his second Hart Trophy in 1992, leading the Rangers to a first-place finish in the NHL's overall standings.

Year-by-Year Record

		Home			Road			Overall								
Season	**GP**	**W**	**L**	**T**	**W**	**L**	**T**	**W**	**L**	**T**	**GF**	**GA**	**Pts.**		**Finished**	**Playoff Result**
1991-92	80	28	8	4	22	17	1	50	25	5	321	246	105	1st,	Patrick Div.	Lost Div. Final
1990-91	80	22	11	7	14	20	6	36	31	13	297	265	85	2nd,	Patrick Div.	Lost Div. Semi-Final
1989-90	80	20	11	9	16	20	4	36	31	13	279	267	85	1st,	Patrick Div.	Lost Div. Final
1988-89	80	21	17	2	16	18	6	37	35	8	310	307	82	3rd,	Patrick Div.	Lost Div. Semi-Final
1987-88	80	22	13	5	14	21	5	36	34	10	300	283	82	5th,	Patrick Div.	Out of Playoffs
1986-87	80	18	18	4	16	20	4	34	38	8	307	323	76	4th,	Patrick Div.	Lost Div. Semi-Final
1985-86	80	20	18	2	16	20	4	36	38	6	280	276	78	4th,	Patick Div.	Lost Conf. Championship
1984-85	80	16	18	6	10	26	4	26	44	10	295	345	62	4th,	Patrick Div.	Lost Div. Semi-Final
1983-84	80	27	12	1	15	17	8	42	29	9	314	304	93	4th,	Patrick Div.	Lost Div. Semi-Final
1982-83	80	24	13	3	11	22	7	35	35	10	306	287	80	4th,	Patrick Div.	Lost Div. Final
1981-82	80	19	15	6	20	12	8	39	27	14	316	306	92	2nd,	Patrick Div.	Lost Div. Final
1980-81	80	17	13	10	13	23	4	30	36	14	312	317	74	4th,	Patrick Div.	Lost Semi-Final
1979-80	80	22	10	8	16	22	2	38	32	10	308	284	86	3rd,	Patrick Div.	Lost Quarter-Final
1978-79	80	19	13	8	21	16	3	40	29	11	316	292	91	3rd,	Patrick Div.	Lost Final
1977-78	80	18	15	7	12	22	6	30	37	13	279	280	73	4th,	Patrick Div.	Lost Prelim. Round
1976-77	80	17	18	5	12	19	9	29	37	14	272	310	72	4th,	Patrick Div.	Out of Playoffs
1975-76	80	16	16	8	13	26	1	29	42	9	262	333	67	4th,	Patrick Div.	Out of Playoffs
1974-75	80	21	11	8	16	18	6	37	29	14	319	276	88	2nd,	Patrick Div.	Lost Prelim. Round
1973-74	78	26	7	6	14	17	8	40	24	14	300	251	94	3rd,	East Div.	Lost Semi-Final
1972-73	78	26	8	5	21	15	3	47	23	8	297	208	102	3rd,	East Div.	Lost Semi-Final
1971-72	78	26	6	7	22	11	6	48	17	13	317	192	109	2nd,	East Div.	Lost Final
1970-71	78	30	2	7	19	16	4	49	18	11	259	177	109	2nd,	East Div.	Lost Semi-Final
1969-70	76	22	8	8	16	14	8	38	22	16	246	189	92	4th,	East Div.	Lost Quarter-Final
1968-69	76	27	7	4	14	19	5	41	26	9	231	196	91	3rd,	East Div.	Lost Quarter-Final
1967-68	74	22	8	7	17	15	5	39	23	12	226	183	90	2nd,	East Div.	Lost Quarter-Final
1966-67	70	18	12	5	12	16	7	30	28	12	188	189	72	4th,		Lost Semi-Final
1965-66	70	12	16	7	6	25	4	18	41	11	195	261	47	6th,		Out of Playoffs
1964-65	70	8	19	8	12	19	4	20	38	12	179	246	52	5th,		Out of Playoffs
1963-64	70	14	13	8	8	25	2	22	38	10	186	242	54	5th,		Out of Playoffs
1962-63	70	12	17	6	10	19	6	22	36	12	211	233	56	5th,		Out of Playoffs
1961-62	70	16	11	8	10	21	4	26	32	12	195	207	64	4th,		Lost Semi-Final
1960-61	70	15	15	5	7	23	5	22	38	10	204	248	54	5th,		Out of Playoffs
1959-60	70	10	15	10	7	23	5	17	38	15	187	247	49	6th,		Out of Playoffs
1958-59	70	14	16	5	12	16	7	26	32	12	201	217	64	5th,		Out of Playoffs
1957-58	70	14	15	6	18	10	7	32	25	13	195	188	77	2nd,		Lost Semi-Final
1956-57	70	15	12		11	18	6	26	30	14	184	227	66	4th,		Lot Semi-Final
1955-56	70	20	7	8	12	21	2	32	28	10	204	203	74	3rd,		Lost Semi-Final
1954-55	70	10	12	13	7	23	5	17	35	18	150	210	52	5th,		Out of Playoffs
1953-54	70	18	12	5	11	19	5	29	31	10	161	182	68	5th,		Out of Playoffs
1952-53	70	11	14	10	6	23	6	17	37	16	152	211	50	6th,		Out of Playoffs
1951-52	70	16	13	6	7	21	7	23	34	13	192	219	59	5th,		Out of Playoffs
1950-51	70	14	11	10	6	18	11	20	29	21	169	201	61	5th,		Out of Playoffs
1949-50	70	19	12	4	9	19	7	28	31	11	170	189	67	4th,		Lost Final
1948-49	60	13	12	5	5	19	6	18	31	11	133	172	47	6th,		Out of Playoffs
1947-48	60	11	12	7	10	14	6	21	26	13	176	201	55	4th,		Lost Semi-Final
1946-47	60	11	14	5	11	18	1	22	32	6	167	186	50	5th,		Out of Playoffs
1945-46	50	8	12	5	5	16	4	13	28	9	144	191	35	6th,		Out of Playoffs
1944-45	50	7	11	7	4	18	3	11	29	10	154	247	32	6th,		Out of Playoffs
1943-44	50	4	17	4	2	22	1	6	39	5	162	310	17	6th,		Out of Playoffs
1942-43	50	7	13	5	4	18	3	11	31	8	161	253	30	6th,		Out of Playoffs
1941-42	48	15	8	1	14	9	1	29	17	2	177	143	60	1st,		Lost Semi-Final
1940-41	48	13	7	4	8	12	4	21	19	8	143	125	50	4th,		Lost Quarter-Final
1939-40	**48**	17	4	3	10	7	7	**27**	**11**	**10**	**136**	**77**	**64**	**2nd,**		**Won Stanley Cup**
1938-39	48	13	8	3	13	8	3	26	16	6	149	105	58	2nd,		Lost Semi-Final
1937-38	48	15	5	4	12	10	2	27	15	6	149	96	60	2nd,	Amn. Div.	Lost Quarter-Final
1936-37	48	9	7	8	10	13	1	19	20	9	117	106	47	3rd,	Amn. Div.	Lost Final
1935-36	48	11	6	7	8	11	5	19	17	12	91	96	50	4th,	Amn. Div.	Out of Playoffs
1934-35	48	11	8	5	11	12	1	22	20	6	137	139	50	3rd,	Amn. Div.	Lost Semi-Final
1933-34	48	11	7	6	10	12	2	21	19	8	120	113	50	3rd,	Amn. Div.	Lost Quarter-Final
1932-33	**48**	12	7	5	11	10	3	**23**	**17**	**8**	**135**	**107**	**54**	**3rd,**	**Amn. Div.**	**Won Stanley Cup**
1931-32	48	13	7	4	10	10	4	23	17	8	134	112	54	1st,	Amn. Div.	Lost Final
1930-31	44	10	9	3	9	7	6	19	16	9	106	87	47	3rd,	Amn. Div.	Lost Semi-Final
1929-30	44	11	5	6	6	12	4	17	17	10	136	143	44	3rd,	Amn. Div.	Lost Semi-Final
1928-29	44	12	6	4	9	7	6	21	13	10	72	65	52	2nd,	Amn. Div.	Lost Final
1927-28	**44**	10	8	4	9	8	5	**19**	**16**	**9**	**94**	**79**	**47**	**2nd,**	**Amn. Div.**	**Won Stanley Cup**
1926-27	44	13	5	4	12	8	2	25	13	6	95	72	56	1st,	Amn. Div.	Lost Quarter-Final

1992-93 Player Personnel

FORWARDS	HT	WT	S	Place of Birth	Date	1991-92 Club
AMONTE, Tony	6-0	180	L	Hingham, MA	8/2/70	NY Rangers
BENNETT, Ric	6-3	215	L	Springfield, MA	7/24/67	NYR-Binghamton
BIGGS, Don	5-8	180	R	Mississauga, Ont.	4/7/65	Binghamton
BROTEN, Paul	5-11	190	R	Roseau, MN	10/27/65	NY Rangers
CICHOCKI, Chris	5-11	185	R	Detroit, MI	9/17/63	Binghamton
DOMI, Tie	5-10	200	R	Windsor, Ont.	11/1/69	NY Rangers
ERIXON, Jan	6-0	196	L	Skelleftea, Sweden	7/8/62	NY Rangers
GARTNER, Mike	6-0	190	R	Ottawa, Ont.	10/29/59	NY Rangers
GILHEN, Randy	6-0	192	L	Zweibrucken, Germany	6/13/63	L.A-NY Rangers
GRAVES, Adam	6-0	185	L	Toronto, Ont.	4/12/68	NY Rangers
KING, Kris	5-11	210	L	Bracebridge, Ont.	2/18/66	NY Rangers
KING, Steven	6-0	190	R	E. Greenwich, RI	7/7/69	Binghamton
KOCUR, Joe	6-0	210	R	Calgary, Alta.	12/21/64	NY Rangers
LACROIX, Daniel	6-2	188	L	Montreal, Que.	3/11/69	Binghamton
McREYNOLDS, Brian	6-1	192	L	Penetanguishene, Ont.	1/5/85	Binghamton
MESSIER, Mark	6-1	202	L	Edmonton, Alta.	1/18/61	NY Rangers
NEMCHINOV, Sergei	6-0	200	L	Moscow, USSR	1/14/64	NY Rangers
PROSOFSKY, Jason	6-4	220	R	Medicine Hat, Alta.	5/4/71	NY Rangers
ROY, Jean-Yves	5-10	185	L	Rosemere, Que.	2/17/69	U. of Maine
STEVENS, Mike	5-11	195	L	Kitchener, Ont.	12/30/65	Moncton-Bing.
TURCOTTE, Darren	6-0	185	L	Boston, MA	3/2/68	NY Rangers
WEIGHT, Doug	5-11	185	L	Mount Clemens, MI	1/12/71	Binghamton-NYR
DEFENSEMEN						
ANDERSSON, Peter	6-0	200	L	Orebro, Sweden	8/29/65	Malmo
BEUKEBOOM, Jeff	6-4	223	R	Ajax, Ont.	3/28/65	Edm.-NYR
CIRELLA, Joe	6-3	210	R	Hamilton, Ont.	5/9/63	NY Rangers
DJOOS, Per	5-11	175	R	Mora, Sweden	5/12/68	NY Rangers
FIORENTINO, Peter	6-1	205	R	Niagara Falls, Ont.	12/22/68	Binghamton
HARDY, Mark	5-11	195	L	Semaden, Switzerland	2/1/59	NY Rangers
HURLBUT, Mike	6-2	200	L	Massena, NY	10/7/66	Binghamton
LEETCH, Brian	5-11	195	L	Corpus Christi, TX	3/3/68	NY Rangers
MOKASAK, John	5-11	200	L	Edmonton, Alta.	9/7/63	Binghamton
PATRICK, James	6-2	204	R	Winnipeg, Man.	6/14/63	NY Rangers
WELLS, Jay	6-1	210	L	Paris, Ont.	5/18/59	Buffalo-NYR

GOALTENDERS	HT	WT	C	Place of Birth	Date	1991-92 Club
HIRSCH, Corey	5-9	150	L	Medicine Hat, Alta.	7/1/72	Kamloops
RICHTER, Mike	5-10	185	L	Abington, PA	9/22/66	NY Rangers
ROUSSON, Boris	6-1	200	R	Valdor, Que.	6/14/70	Binghamton
VANBIESBROUCK, John	5-8	175	L	Detroit, MI	9/4/63	NY Rangers

Coaching History

Lester Patrick, 1926-27 to 1938-39; Frank Boucher, 1939-40 to 1947-48; Frank Boucher and Lynn Patrick, 1948-49; Lynn Patrick, 1949-50; Neil Colville, 1950-51; Neil Colville and Bill Cook, 1951-52; Bill Cook, 1952-53; Frank Boucher and Murray Patrick, 1953-54; Murray Patrick, 1954-55; Phil Watson, 1955-56 to 1958-59; Phil Watson and Alf Pike, 1959-60; Alf Pike, 1960-61; Doug Harvey, 1961-62; Murray Patrick and George Sullivan, 1962-63; George Sullivan, 1963-64 to 1964-65; George Sullivan and Emile Francis, 1965-66; Emile Francis, 1966-67 to 1967-68; Bernie Geoffrion and Emile Francis, 1968-69; Emile Francis, 1969-70 to 1972-73; Larry Popein and Emile Francis, 1973-74; Emile Francis, 1974-75; Ron Stewart and John Ferguson, 1975-76; John Ferguson, 1976-77; Jean-Guy Talbot, 1977-78; Fred Shero, 1978-79 to 1979-80; Fred Shero and Craig Patrick, 1980-81; Herb Brooks, 1981-82 to 1983-84; Herb Brooks and Craig Patrick, 1984-85; Ted Sator, 1985-86; Ted Sator, Tom Webster, Phil Esposito 1986-87; Michel Bergeron, 1987-88; Michel Bergeron and Phil Esposito, 1988-89; Roger Neilson, 1989-90 to date.

General Managers' History

Lester Patrick, 1927-28 to 1945-46; Frank Boucher, 1946-47 to 1954-55; Murray "Muzz" Patrick, 1955-56 to 1963-64; Emile Francis, 1964-65 to 1974-75; Emile Francis and John Ferguson, 1975-76; John Ferguson, 1976-77 to 1977-78; John Ferguson and Fred Shero, 1978-79; Fred Shero, 1979-80; Fred Shero and Craig Patrick, 1980-81; Craig Patrick, 1981-82 to 1985-86; Phil Esposito, 1986-87 to 1988-89; Neil Smith, 1989-90 to date.

General Manager

SMITH, NEIL
General Manager, New York Rangers. Born in Toronto, Ont., January 9, 1954.

During Neil Smith's three years as the Rangers' G.M., the team has become one of the NHL's strongest organizations, finishing in first place overall in 1991-92 with a franchise record 50 wins and 105 points. Smith's astute scouting, which has provided the Rangers with a promising group of young talent, and shrewd trading has strengthened the team into a solid Stanley Cup contender. Smith, 38-years-old, joined the Rangers on July 17, 1989 after seven seasons with the Detroit Red Wings and two with the New York Islanders. After serving as a scout for the Islanders in 1980-81 and 1981-82, Smith joined the Red Wings. While with the Red Wings, Smith held several positions including director of scouting and player development. He also served as general manager of the Adirondack Red Wings (AHL), leading that club to two Calder Cups (1985-86 and 1988-89).

A former All-American defenseman from Western Michigan University, Smith was drafted in 1974 by the New York Islanders. After receiving his degree in communications and business, Smith played two seasons in the IHL–1978-79 with the Kalamazoo Wings and Saginaw Gears and 1979-80 with the Dayton Gems, Milwaukee Admirals and Muskegon Mohawks.

1991-92 Scoring

Regular Season

Pos	#.	Player	Team	GP	G	A	Pts	+/–	PIM	PP	SH	GW	GT	S	%
C	11	Mark Messier	NYR	79	35	72	107	31	76	12	4	6	0	212	16.5
D	2	Brian Leetch	NYR	80	22	80	102	25	26	10	1	3	1	245	9.0
R	22	Mike Gartner	NYR	76	40	41	81	11	55	15	0	6	0	286	14.0
D	3	James Patrick	NYR	80	14	57	71	34	54	6	0	1	0	148	9.5
R	33*	Tony Amonte	NYR	79	35	34	69	12	55	9	0	4	0	234	15.0
C	9	Adam Graves	NYR	80	26	33	59	19	139	4	4	4	0	228	11.4
C	13	Sergei Nemchinov	NYR	73	30	28	58	19	15	2	0	5	0	124	24.2
C	8	Darren Turcotte	NYR	71	30	23	53	11	57	13	1	4	1	216	13.9
L	25	John Ogrodnick	NYR	55	17	13	30	6	22	3	0	4	0	110	15.5
C	39*	Doug Weight	NYR	53	8	22	30	3–	23	0	0	2	0	72	11.1
R	37	Paul Broten	NYR	74	13	15	28	14	102	0	3	1	0	96	13.5
C	16	Randy Gilhen	L.A.	33	3	6	9	3–	14	0	1	0	0	32	9.4
			NYR	40	7	7	14	5	14	0	0	0	0	67	10.4
			TOTAL	73	10	13	23	2	28	0	1	0	0	99	10.1
L	19	Kris King	NYR	79	10	9	19	13	224	0	0	2	0	97	10.3
D	44	Per Djoos	NYR	50	1	18	19	7	40	1	0	1	0	39	2.6
R	12	Tim Kerr	NYR	32	7	11	18	5–	12	5	0	2	0	56	12.5
L	20	Jan. Erixon	NYR	46	8	9	17	13	4	0	1	0	0	51	15.7
D	23	Jeff Beukeboom	EDM	18	0	5	5	4	78	0	0	0	0	7	.0
			NYR	56	1	10	11	19	122	0	0	0	0	41	2.4
			TOTAL	74	1	15	16	23	200	0	0	0	0	48	2.1
D	6	Joe Cirella	NYR	67	3	12	15	11	121	1	0	0	0	58	5.2
R	26	Joey Kocur	NYR	51	7	4	11	4–	121	0	0	2	0	72	9.7
D	24	Jay Wells	BUF	41	2	9	11	3–	157	0	0	0	0	26	7.7
			NYR	11	0	0	0	2	24	0	0	0	0	4	.0
			TOTAL	52	2	9	11	1–	181	0	0	0	0	30	6.7
D	14	Mark Hardy	NYR	52	1	8	9	33	65	0	0	1	0	42	2.4
R	28	Tie Domi	NYR	42	2	4	6	4–	246	0	0	1	0	20	10.0
C	31*	Rob Zamuner	NYR	9	1	2	3	0	2	0	0	0	0	11	9.1
G	34	John Vanbiesbrouck	NYR	45	0	3	3	0	23	0	0	0	0	1	.0
D	5	Normand Rochefort	NYR	26	0	2	2	10–	31	0	0	0	0	18	.0
L	17	Eric Bennett	NYR	3	0	1	1	0	2	0	0	0	0	2	.0
D	38	Jeff Bloemberg	NYR	3	0	1	1	1	0	0	0	0	0	5	.0
D	41*	Peter Fiorentino	NYR	1	0	0	0	0	0	0	0	0	0	2	.0
R	21	Jody Hull	NYR	3	0	0	0	4–	2	0	0	0	0	4	.0
G	35	Mike Richter	NYR	41	0	0	0	0	6	0	0	0	0	0	.0

Goaltending

No.	Goaltender	GPI	Mins	Avg	W	L	T	EN	SO	GA	SA	S%
34	John Vanbiesbrouck	45	2526	2.85	27	13	3	4	2	120	1331	.910
35	Mike Richter	41	2298	3.11	23	12	2	3	3	119	1205	.901
	Totals	**80**	**4836**	**3.05**	**50**	**25**	**5**	**7**	**5**	**246**	**2543**	**.903**

Playoffs

Pos	#	Player	Team	GP	G	A	Pts	+/–	PIM	PP	SH	GW	GT	S	%
R	22	Mike Gartner	NYR	13	8	8	16	3	4	3	0	1	0	66	12.1
D	2	Brian Leetch	NYR	13	4	11	15	5–	4	1	1	0	0	67	6.0
C	11	Mark Messier	NYR	11	7	7	14	4–	6	2	2	0	0	27	25.9
R	33*	Tony Amonte	NYR	13	3	6	9	7–	2	2	0	0	0	36	8.3
C	9	Adam Graves	NYR	10	5	3	8	6–	22	1	0	1	0	33	15.2
D	3	James Patrick	NYR	13	0	7	7	4–	12	0	0	0	0	21	.0
L	19	Kris King	NYR	13	4	1	5	4	14	0	0	3	1	15	26.7
D	23	Jeff Beukeboom	NYR	13	2	3	5	2–	47	0	0	0	0	10	20.0
L	20	Jan. Erixon	NYR	13	2	3	5	6–	2	0	1	1	0	11	18.2
C	13	Sergei Nemchinov	NYR	13	1	4	5	3–	8	0	0	0	0	22	4.5
C	8	Darren Turcotte	NYR	8	4	0	4	1	6	2	1	0	0	22	18.2
C	39*	Doug Weight	NYR	7	2	2	4	3	0	1	0	0	0	4	50.0
D	6	Joe Cirella	NYR	13	0	4	4	3	23	0	0	0	0	14	.0
R	37	Paul Broten	NYR	13	1	2	3	2	10	0	0	0	0	24	4.2
C	16	Randy Gilhen	NYR	13	1	2	3	0	2	0	0	0	0	17	5.9
D	14	Mark Hardy	NYR	13	0	3	3	0	31	0	0	0	0	9	.0
R	28	Tie Domi	NYR	6	1	1	2	1	32	0	0	0	0	1	100.0
R	26	Joey Kocur	NYR	12	1	1	2	3–	38	0	0	0	0	9	11.1
D	24	Jay Wells	NYR	13	0	2	2	3	10	0	0	0	0	7	.0
R	12	Tim Kerr	NYR	8	1	0	1	1–	0	1	0	0	0	7	14.3
L	25	John Ogrodnick	NYR	3	0	0	0	1–	0	0	0	0	0	4	.0
G	35	Mike Richter	NYR	7	0	0	0	0	0	0	0	0	0	0	.0
G	34	John Vanbiesbrouck	NYR	7	0	0	0	0	2	0	0	0	0	0	.0

Goaltending

No.	Goaltender	GPI	Mins	Avg	W	L	EN	SO	GA	SA	S%
35	Mike Richter	7	412	3.50	4	2	0	1	24	226	.894
34	John Vanbiesbrouck	7	368	3.75	2	5	2	0	23	179	.872
	Totals	**13**	**784**	**3.75**	**6**	**7**	**2**	**1**	**49**	**407**	**.880**

Captains' History

Bill Cook, 1926-27 to 1936-37; Art Coulter, 1937-38 to 1941-42; Ott Heller, 1942-43 to 1944-45; Neil Colville 1945-46 to 1948-49; Buddy O'Connor, 1949-50; Frank Eddolls, 1950-51; Frank Eddolls, Allan Stanley, 1951-52; Allan Stanley, 1952-53; Allan Stanley, Don Raleigh, 1953-54; Don Raleigh, 1954-55; Harry Howell, 1955-56, 1956-57; George Sullivan, 1957-58 to 1960-61; Andy Bathgate, 1961-61, 1962-63; Andy Bathgate, Camille Henry, 1963-64; Camille Henry, Bob Nevin, 1964-65; Bob Nevin 1965-66 to 1970-71; Vic Hadfield, 1971-72 to 1973-74; Brad Park, 1974-75; Brad Park, Phil Esposito, 1975-76; Phil Esposito, 1976-77, 1977-78; Dave Maloney, 1978-79, 1979-80; Dave Maloney, Walt Tkaczuk, Barry Beck, 1980-81; Barry Beck, 1981-82 to 1985-86; Ron Greschner, 1986-87; Ron Greschner and Kelly Kisio, 1987-88; Kelly Kisio, 1988-89 to 1990-91; Mark Messier, 1991-92 to date.

Retired Numbers

1	Eddie Giacomin	1965-1976
7	Rod Gilbert	1960-1978

Club Records

Team

(Figures in brackets for season records are games played; records for fewest points, wins, ties, losses, goals, goals against are for 70 or more games)

Record		
Most Points	109	1970-71 (78) 1971-72 (78)
Most Wins	50	1991-92 (80)
Most Ties	21	1950-51 (70)
Most Losses	44	1984-85 (80)
Most Goals	371	1991-92 (80)
Most Goals Against	345	1984-85 (80)
Fewest Points	47	1965-66 (70)
Fewest Wins	17	1952-53; 54-55; 59-60 (70)
Fewest Ties	5	1991-92 (80)
Fewest Losses	17	1971-72 (78)
Fewest Goals	150	1954-55 (70)
Fewest Goals Against	177	1970-71 (78)
Longest Winning Streak		
Over-all	10	Dec. 19/39-Jan. 13/40 Jan. 19-Feb. 10/73
Home	14	Dec. 19/39-Feb. 25/40
Away	7	Jan. 12-Feb. 12/35 Oct. 28-Nov. 29/78
Longest Undefeated Streak		
Over-all	19	Nov. 23/39-Jan. 13/40 (14 wins, 5 ties)
Home	26	Mar. 29/70-Feb. 2/71 (19 wins, 7 ties)
Away	11	Nov. 5/39-Jan. 13/40 (6 wins, 5 ties)
Longest Losing Streak		
Over-all	11	Oct. 30-Nov. 27/43
Home	7	Oct. 20-Nov. 14/76
Away	10	Oct. 30-Dec. 23/43
Longest Winless Streak		
Over-all	21	Jan. 23-Mar. 19/44 (17 losses, 4 ties)
Home	10	Jan. 30-Mar. 19/44 (7 losses, 3 ties)
Away	16	Oct. 9-Dec. 20/52 (12 losses, 4 ties)
Most Shutouts, Season	13	1928-29 (44)
Most PIM, Season	2,018	1989-90 (80)
Most Goals, Game	12	Nov. 21/71 (Cal. 1 at NYR 12)

Individual

Record		
Most Seasons	17	Harry Howell
Most Games	1,160	Harry Howell
Most Goals, Career	406	Rod Gilbert
Most Assists, Career	615	Rod Gilbert
Most Points, Career	1,021	Rod Gilbert (406 goals, 615 assists)
Most PIM, Career	1,226	Ron Greschner
Most Shutouts, Career	49	Ed Giacomin
Longest Consecutive Games Streak	560	Andy Hebenton (Oct. 7/55-Mar. 24/63)
Most Goals, Season	50	Vic Hadfield (1971-72)
Most Assists, Season	80	Brian Leetch (1991-92)
Most Points, Season	109	Jean Ratelle (1971-72) (46 goals, 63 assists)
Most PIM, Season	305	Troy Mallette (1989-90)
Most Points, Defenseman Season	102	Brian Leetch (1991-92) (22 goals, 80 assists)
Most Points, Center, Season	109	Jean Ratelle (1971-72) (46 goals, 63 assists)
Most Points, Right Wing, Season	97	Rod Gilbert (1971-72) (43 goals, 54 assists) Rod Gilbert (1974-75) (36 goals, 61 assists)
Most Points, Left Wing, Season	106	Vic Hadfield (1971-72) (50 goals, 56 assists)
Most Points, Rookie, Season	76	Mark Pavelich (1981-82) (33 goals, 43 assists)
Most Shutouts, Season	13	John Ross Roach (1928-29)
Most Goals, Game	5	Don Murdoch (Oct. 12/76) Mark Pavelich (Feb. 23/83)
Most Assists, Game	5	Walt Tkaczuk (Feb. 12/72) Rod Gilbert (Mar. 2/75; Mar. 30/75; Oct. 8/76) Don Maloney (Jan. 3/87)
Most Points, Game	7	Steve Vickers (Feb. 18/76)

All-time Record vs. Other Clubs

Regular Season

	At Home							On Road							Total						
	GP	W	L	T	GF	GA	PTS	GP	W	L	T	GF	GA	PTS	GP	W	L	T	GF	GA	PTS
Boston	278	121	103	54	844	774	296	275	87	150	38	767	1005	212	553	208	253	92	1611	1779	508
Buffalo	42	18	14	10	150	119	46	44	11	27	6	144	200	28	86	29	41	16	294	319	74
Calgary	42	19	18	5	155	153	43	41	10	24	7	126	188	27	83	29	42	12	281	341	70
Chicago	277	117	106	54	823	780	288	276	109	125	42	768	846	260	553	226	231	96	1591	1626	548
Detroit	274	130	86	58	844	701	318	276	75	157	44	683	970	194	550	205	243	102	1527	1671	512
Edmonton	20	6	11	3	83	85	15	20	9	10	1	71	83	19	40	15	21	4	154	168	34
Hartford	20	12	6	2	90	62	26	21	7	12	2	76	85	16	41	19	18	4	166	147	42
Los Angeles	49	29	15	5	200	145	63	50	21	20	9	174	167	51	99	50	35	14	374	312	114
Minnesota	52	32	10	10	189	144	74	51	29	15	7	200	155	65	103	61	25	17	389	299	139
Montreal	266	107	109	50	761	774	264	266	55	177	34	615	1052	144	532	162	286	84	1376	1826	408
New Jersey	53	32	14	7	236	171	71	53	27	22	4	212	188	58	106	59	36	11	448	359	129
NY Islanders	65	41	18	6	264	195	88	64	16	43	5	194	275	37	129	57	61	11	458	470	125
Philadelphia	78	35	25	18	257	229	88	78	28	37	13	230	272	69	156	63	62	31	487	501	157
Pittsburgh	72	38	27	7	302	248	83	72	35	26	11	270	257	81	144	73	53	18	572	505	164
Quebec	20	14	3	3	87	51	31	21	8	10	3	93	90	19	41	22	13	6	180	141	50
St. Louis	51	40	6	5	220	118	85	53	24	21	8	175	157	56	104	64	27	13	395	275	141
San Jose	1	1	0	0	4	3	2	1	1	0	0	4	2	2	2	2	0	0	8	5	4
Toronto	266	109	101	56	810	782	274	265	77	150	38	687	914	192	531	186	251	94	1497	1696	466
Vancouver	45	34	7	4	206	111	72	43	30	10	3	178	137	63	88	64	17	7	384	248	135
Washington	53	26	21	6	226	196	58	53	19	26	8	183	214	46	106	45	47	14	409	410	104
Winnipeg	20	10	8	2	97	86	22	21	11	8	2	81	77	24	41	21	16	4	178	163	46
Defunct Clubs	139	87	30	22	460	290	196	139	82	34	23	441	291	187	278	169	64	45	901	581	383
Totals	**2183**	**1058**	**738**	**387**	**7308**	**6217**	**2503**	**2183**	**771**	**1104**	**308**	**6372**	**7625**	**1850**	**4366**	**1829**	**1842**	**695**	**13680**	**13842**	**4353**

Playoffs

	Series	W	L	GP	W	L	T	GF	GA	Last Mtg.	Round	Result
Boston	9	3	6	42	18	22	2	104	114	1973	QF	W 4-1
Buffalo	1	0	1	3	1	2	0	6	11	1978	PR	L 1-2
**Calgary	1	1	0	4	3	1	0	14	8	1980	PR	W 3-1
Chicago	5	1	4	24	10	14	0	54	66	1973	SF	L 1-4
Detroit	5	1	4	23	10	13	0	49	57	1950	F	L 3-4
Los Angeles	2	2	0	6	5	1	0	32	14	1981	PR	W 3-1
Montreal	13	6	7	55	21	32	2	139	171	1986	CF	L 1-4
New Jersey	1	1	0	7	4	3	0	28	25	1992	DSF	W 4-3
NY Islanders	7	2	5	35	15	20	0	110	126	1990	DSF	W 4-1
Philadelphia	8	4	4	38	19	19	0	130	119	1987	DSF	L 2-4
Pittsburgh	2	0	2	10	2	8	0	30	44	1992	DF	L 2-4
St. Louis	1	1	0	6	4	2	0	29	22	1981	QF	W 4-2
Toronto	8	5	3	35	19	16	0	86	86	1971	QF	W 4-2
Washington	3	1	2	17	7	10	0	51	63	1991	DSF	L 2-4
Defunct	9	6	3	22	11	7	4	43	29			
Totals	**75**	**34**	**41**	**327**	**149**	**170**	**8**	**905**	**954**			

Playoff Results 1992-88

Year	Round	Opponent	Result	GF	GA
1992	DF	Pittsburgh	L 2-4	19	24
	DSF	New Jersey	W 4-3	28	25
1991	DSF	Washington	L 2-4	16	16
1990	DF	Washington	L 1-4	15	22
	DSF	NY Islanders	W 4-1	22	13
1989	DSF	Pittsburgh	L 0-4	11	19

Abbreviations: Round: F – Final; **CF** – conference final; **DF** – division final; **DSF** – division semi-final; **SF** – semi-final; **QF** – quarter-final; **PR** – preliminary round. **GA** – goals against; **GF** – goals for.

1991-92 Results

Home				Away			
Oct.	7	Boston	2-1	**Oct.**	3	Boston	3-5
	9	NY Islanders	5-3		5	Montreal	2-1
	14	Washington	3-5		11	Washington	1-5
	16	New Jersey	4-2		12	Hartford	2-5
	20	Edmonton	3-4		19	Pittsburgh	5-4
	23	Los Angeles	7-2		26	Quebec	5-3
	29	Minnesota	3-2	**Nov.**	2	Philadelphia*	4-2
	31	Quebec	5-4		16	NY Islanders	2-4
Nov.	4	Calgary	4-0		19	Vancouver	4-3
	6	Montreal	1-4		21	Los Angeles	1-6
	8	Toronto	3-3		23	St Louis	3-0
	11	Pittsburgh	3-1		27	Winnipeg	2-3
	13	Washington	3-5		29	Buffalo	5-4
Dec.	2	Philadelphia	4-2	**Dec.**	6	Detroit	5-6
	8	Boston	4-0		10	Pittsburgh	3-5
	16	San Jose	4-3		13	Washington	5-3
	18	Philadelphia	6-3		14	Hartford	6-2
	23	New Jersey	3-0		21	Pittsburgh	7-5
	29	Pittsburgh	3-6		26	Washington	8-6
Jan.	6	Winnipeg	4-2		28	NY Islanders	4-5
	8	St Louis	3-5		31	Winnipeg*	5-2
	14	Buffalo	6-2	**Jan.**	2	Chicago	4-3
	16	Calgary	6-4		4	New Jersey	4-6
Feb.	5	Pittsburgh	4-3		11	Quebec	7-2
	9	Detroit	5-5		12	Buffalo	3-6
	12	Vancouver	5-2		22	Calgary	4-4
	14	NY Islanders	9-2		23	Edmonton	3-1
	17	Vancouver*	3-3		28	San Jose	4-2
	21	Minnesota	5-4		30	Los Angeles	4-1
	23	Philadelphia	2-1	**Feb.**	1	Minnesota	2-1
	25	Chicago	4-1		7	Washington	2-6
Mar.	1	Hartford	9-4		16	New Jersey*	2-4
	4	New Jersey	4-5		20	NY Islanders	2-6
	9	Washington	2-5	**Mar.**	2	New Jersey	7-1
	11	Chicago	7-1		7	Philadelphia*	4-5
	16	Montreal	4-1		14	St Louis	6-0
	18	NY Islanders	1-1		20	Detroit	4-2
	22	New Jersey*	6-3		24	Philadelphia	4-3
	25	Philadelphia	4-1		28	NY Islanders	1-4
Apr.	2	Pittsburgh	7-1	**Apr.**	4	Toronto	2-4

*Denotes afternoon game

Entry Draft Selections 1992-78

1992
Pick
24 Peter Ferraro
48 Mattias Norstrom
72 Eric Cairns
85 Chris Ferraro
120 Dmitri Starostenko
144 David Dal Grande
168 Matt Oates
192 Mickey Elick
216 Dan Brierley
240 Vladimir Vorobjev

1991
Pick
15 Alexei Kovalev
37 Darcy Werenka
96 Corey Machanic
125 Fredrik Jax
128 Barry Young
147 John Rushin
169 Corey Hirsch
191 Viacheslav Uvayev
213 Jamie Ram
235 Vitali Chinakhov
257 Brian Wiseman

1990
Pick
13 Michael Stewart
34 Doug Weight
55 John Vary
69 Jeff Nielsen
76 Rick Willis
85 Sergei Zubov
99 Lubos Rob
118 Jason Weinrich
139 Bryan Lonsinger
160 Todd Hedlund
181 Andrew Silverman
202 Jon Hillebrandt
223 Brett Lievers
244 Sergei Nemchinov

1989
Pick
20 Steven Rice
40 Jason Prosofsky
45 Rob Zamuner
49 Louie DeBrusk
67 Jim Cummins
88 Aaron Miller
118 Joby Messier
139 Greg Leahy
160 Greg Spenrath
181 Mark Bavis
202 Roman Oksyuta
223 Steve Locke
244 Ken MacDermid

1988
Pick
22 Troy Mallette
26 Murray Duval
68 Tony Amonte
99 Martin Bergeron
110 Dennis Vial
131 Mike Rosati
152 Eric Couvrette
173 Shorty Forrest
194 Paul Cain
202 Eric Fenton
215 Peter Fiorentino
236 Keith Slifstien

1987
Pick
10 Jayson More
31 Daniel Lacroix
46 Simon Gagne
69 Michael Sullivan
94 Eric O'Borsky
115 Ludek Cajka
136 Clint Thomas
157 Charles Wiegand
178 Eric Burrill
199 David Porter
205 Brett Barnett
220 Lance Marciano

1986
Pick
9 Brian Leetch
51 Bret Walter
53 Shawn Clouston
72 Mark Janssens
93 Jeff Bloemberg
114 Darren Turcotte
135 Robb Graham
156 Barry Chyzowski
177 Pat Scanlon
198 Joe Ranger
219 Russell Parent
240 Soren True

1985
Pick
7 Ulf Dahlen
28 Mike Richter
49 Sam Lindstahl
70 Pat Janostin
91 Brad Stephan
112 Brian McReynolds
133 Neil Pilon
154 Larry Bernard
175 Stephane Brochu
196 Steve Nemeth
217 Robert Burakowsky
238 Rudy Poeschek

1984
Pick
14 Terry Carkner
35 Raimo Helminen
77 Paul Broten
98 Clark Donatelli
119 Kjell Samuelsson
140 Thomas Hussey
161 Brian Nelson
182 Ville Kentala
188 Heinz Ehlers
202 Kevin Miller
223 Tom Lorentz
243 Scott Brower

1983
Pick
12 Dave Gagner
33 Randy Heath
49 Vesa Salo
53 Gordie Walker
73 Peter Andersson
93 Jim Andonoff
113 Bob Alexander
133 Steve Orth
153 Peter Marcov
173 Paul Jerrard
213 Bryan Walker
233 Ulf Nilsson

1982
Pick
15 Chris Kontos
36 Tomas Sandstrom
57 Corey Millen
78 Chris Jensen
120 Tony Granato
141 Sergei Kapustin
160 Brian Glynn
162 Jan Karlsson
183 Kelly Miller
193 Simo Saarinen
204 Bob Lowes
225 Andy Otto
246 Dwayne Robinson

1981
Pick
9 James Patrick
30 Jan Erixon
50 Peter Sundstrom
51 Mark Morrison
72 John Vanbiesbrouck
114 Eric Magnuson
135 Mike Guentzel
156 Ari Lahteenmaki
177 Paul Reifenberger
198 Mario Proulx

1980
Pick
14 Jim Malone
35 Mike Allison
77 Kurt Kleinendorst
98 Scot Kleinendorst
119 Reijo Ruotsalainen
140 Bob Scurfield
161 Bart Wilson
182 Chris Wray
203 Anders Backstrom

1979
Pick
13 Doug Sulliman
34 Ed Hospodar
76 Pat Conacher
97 Dan Makuch
118 Stan Adams

1978
Pick
26 Don Maloney
43 Ray Markham
44 Dean Turner
59 Dave Silk
60 Andre Dore
76 Mike McDougal
93 Tom Laidlaw
110 Dan Clark
127 Greg Kostenko
144 Brian McDavid
161 Mark Rodrigues
176 Steve Weeks
192 Pierre Daigneault
206 Chris McLaughlin
217 Todd Johnson
223 Dan McCarthy

Club Directory

Madison Square Garden
4 Pennsylvania Plaza
New York, New York 10001
Phone **212/465-6000**
PR FAX 212/465-6494
Capacity: 18,200

Executive Management	
President & General Manager	Neil Smith
Vice-President, Legal Affairs	Kevin Billet
Vice-President, Finance	Jim Abry
Director of Communications	Barry Watkins
Director of Marketing	Kevin Kennedy
Director of Alumni Relations	Maureen Brady
Governor	Stanley R. Jaffe
Alternate Governors	Neil Smith, Kevin Billet, Bob Gutkowski
Team Management	
Assistant General Manager/Player Development	Larry Pleau
Coach	Roger Neilson
Assistant Coach	Colin Campbell, Dan Maloney
Development Coach	Ron Smith
Scouting Staff	Tony Feltrin, Bob Froese, Herb Hammond, Lou Jankowski, Martin Madden, David McNab, Christer Rockstrom
Director of Administration	TBA
Manager of Team Services	Matthew Loughran
Scouting Manager	Bill Short
Executive Administrative Assistant	Barbara Dand
Medical/Training Staff	
Team Physician/Ortho Surgeon	Barton Nisonson, M.D.
Assistant Team Physician	Anthony Maddalo
Medical Consultants	Howard Chester, James A. Nicholas, Ronald Weissman
Trainer/Medical	Dave Smith
Trainer/Equipment	Joe Murphy
Assistant Trainers	Larry Nastasi, Tim Paris
Locker-room Assistant	Benny Petrizzi
Communications Staff	
Manager of Communications	Kevin McDonald
Statistician	John Rosasco
Administrative Assistant	Ann Marie Gilmartin
Home Ice	Madison Square Garden
Press Facilities	33rd Street
Television Facilities	31st Street
Radio Facilities	33rd Street
Rink Dimensions	200 feet by 85 feet
Ends and Sides of Rink	Plexiglass (8 feet)
Club Colors	Blue, Red and White
Training Camp	Rye, New York
TV Announcers	Bruce Beck, John Davidson, Sam Rosen, Al Trautwig
Radio Announcers	Marv Albert, Sal Messina, Howie Rose
Television Outlets	Madison Square Garden Cable Network
Radio Outlet	MSG Radio – WFAN (66 AM), WEVD (1050 AM), WXPS (107.1 FM)

The New York Rangers Hockey Club is part of Madison Square Garden

Coach

NEILSON, ROGER PAUL
Coach, New York Rangers. Born in Toronto, Ont., June 16, 1934.

Roger Neilson, who started his coaching career as a 17-year old, guided the NY Rangers to their finest season in 20 years in 1991-92, compiling 105 points to finish atop the league for the first time since 1942. He began scouting Ontario prospects for the Montreal Canadiens before becoming coach of the Peterborough Petes of the OHA in 1966. He remained in Peterborough for ten seasons, winning one OHA championship while finishing lower than third in regular-season play only twice. He made his pro coaching debut with the Dallas Black Hawks of the CHL in 1976-77 and moved up to the NHL with the Toronto Maple Leafs in 1977-78. He joined the Buffalo Sabres in 1979-80 as associate coach under Scotty Bowman. He acted as the Sabres' bench coach for part of this campaign and for all of 1980-81. He became associate coach of the Vancouver Canucks under Harry Neale in 1981-82 and coached five games late in the season when Neale was serving a suspension. He also guided the Canucks in the 1982 playoffs and in 1982-83. In 1983-84, he coached the Los Angeles Kings for the last 28 games of the regular season. He served as co-coach of the Chicago Blackhawks from 1984-85 through 1986-87 before taking on special scouting assignments for the Blackhawks. He also has provided television commentary on Canadian NHL telecasts.

Coaching Record

		Regular Season					Playoffs			
Season	Team	Games	W	L	T	%	Games	W	L	%
1966-67	Peterborough (OHA)					UNAVAILABLE				
1967-68	Peterborough (OHA)	54	13	30	11	.342	....	....	....	....
1968-69	Peterborough (OHA)	54	27	18	9	.583	10	4	6	.400
1969-70	Peterborough (OHA)	54	29	13	12	.648	....	....	....	....
1970-71	Peterborough (OHA)	62	41	13	8	.726	....	....	....	....
1971-72	Peterborough (OHA)	63	34	20	9	.611	....	....	....	....
1972-73	Peterborough (OHA)	63	42	13	8	.730	....	....	....	....
1973-74	Peterborough (OHA)	70	35	21	14	.600	....	....	....	....
1974-75	Peterborough (OHA)	70	37	20	13	.621	....	....	....	....
1975-76	Peterborough (OHA)	66	18	37	11	.356	....	....	....	....
1976-77	Dallas (CHL)	76	35	25	16	.566	....	....	....	....
1977-78	**Toronto (NHL)**	**80**	**41**	**29**	**10**	**.575**	**13**	**6**	**7**	**.462**
1978-79	**Toronto (NHL)**	**80**	**34**	**33**	**13**	**.506**	**6**	**2**	**4**	**.333**
1979-80	**Buffalo (NHL)**	**26**	**14**	**6**	**6**	**.654**	....	....	....	....
1980-81	**Buffalo (NHL)**	**80**	**39**	**20**	**21**	**.619**	**8**	**4**	**4**	**.500**
1981-82	**Vancouver (NHL)**	**5**	**4**	**0**	**1**	**.900**	**17**	**11**	**6**	**.647**
1982-83	**Vancouver (NHL)**	**80**	**30**	**35**	**15**	**.469**	**4**	**1**	**3**	**.250**
1983-84	**Los Angeles (NHL)**	**28**	**8**	**17**	**3**	**.339**	....	....	....	....
1989-90	**NY Rangers (NHL)**	**80**	**36**	**31**	**13**	**.531**	**10**	**5**	**5**	**.500**
1990-91	**NY Rangers (NHL)**	**80**	**36**	**31**	**13**	**.531**	**6**	**2**	**4**	**.333**
1991-92	**NY Rangers (NHL)**	**80**	**50**	**25**	**5**	**.656**	**13**	**6**	**7**	**.462**
	NHL Totals	**667**	**309**	**253**	**105**	**.542**	**77**	**37**	**40**	**.481**

Ottawa Senators

Schedule

	Home		Away
Oct.	Thur. 8 Montreal	**Oct.**	Sat. 10 Quebec
	Thur. 22 Hartford		Mon. 12 Boston
	Sat. 24 NY Rangers		Wed. 14 Hartford
	Tues. 27 Pittsburgh		Fri. 16 Washington
	Sat. 31 Buffalo		Tues. 20 Toronto
Nov.	Mon. 9 Toronto		(at Hamilton)
	Wed. 11 Quebec		Fri. 30 Buffalo
	Tues. 17 Montreal	**Nov.**	Tues. 3 Edmonton
	Thur. 19 Hartford		Thur. 5 Calgary
	Mon. 23 Boston		Fri. 6 Vancouver
	Wed. 25 New Jersey		Fri. 13 Tampa Bay
	Sun. 29 Buffalo		Sun. 15 Philadelphia
Dec.	Tues. 1 Minnesota		Sat. 21 Montreal
	Thur. 3 New Jersey		Fri. 27 Buffalo
	Sat. 5 Philadelphia	**Dec.**	Wed. 9 Hartford
	Mon. 7 Washington		Thur. 10 Boston
	Sat. 12 Calgary		Thur. 17 NY Islanders
	Tues. 15 Detroit		Sat. 19 Toronto
	Mon. 21 Washington		Sat. 26 Quebec
	Wed. 23 Chicago		Thur. 31 Detroit
	Sun. 27 Quebec	**Jan.**	Wed. 6 NY Rangers
Jan.	Sat. 2 Buffalo		Fri. 8 New Jersey
	Sun. 10 San Jose*		Sat. 16 Pittsburgh
	Tues. 12 Los Angeles		Thur. 21 Minnesota
	Thur. 14 St Louis		Sat. 23 Washington
	Sun. 17 NY Islanders		Tues. 26 St Louis
	Tues. 19 Quebec		Sat. 30 Montreal*
	Thur. 28 Hartford	**Feb.**	Tues. 9 Philadelphia
Feb.	Mon. 1 Winnipeg		Wed. 17 Quebec
	Wed. 3 Edmonton		Sat. 20 Montreal
	Mon. 8 Buffalo		Mon. 22 Winnipeg
	Sat. 13 Montreal		Sat. 27 New Jersey*
	Tues. 23 Winnipeg	**Mar.**	Tues. 2 San Jose
	(at Saskatoon)		Thur. 4 Los Angeles
	Thur. 25 Pittsburgh		Sun. 7 Chicago*
	Sun. 28 Quebec		Sat. 13 Boston*
Mar.	Thur. 18 Boston		Sat. 20 Pittsburgh
	Mon. 22 NY Rangers		Sat. 27 Montreal
	Thur. 25 Tampa Bay		Sun. 28 Buffalo
Apr.	Thur. 1 Quebec	**Apr.**	Sat. 3 Hartford
	Sun. 4 Vancouver		Sat. 10 NY Islanders
	Wed. 7 Hartford		Sun. 11 Boston
	Wed. 14 Boston		Tues. 13 Quebec

* Denotes afternoon game.

Home Starting Times:

Weeknights	7:35 p.m.
Saturdays	8:05 p.m.
Sundays	7:05 p.m.
Matinees	1:35 p.m.
Except Nov. 29, Jan. 17, Apr. 4	8:05 p.m.

Franchise date: December 16, 1991

1st NHL Season

Mark LaForest, who was drafted by Ottawa from the roster of the NY Rangers, has played for Detroit, Toronto and Philadelphia in the NHL.

1992-93 Player Personnel

FORWARDS	HT	WT	S	Place of Birth	Date	1991-92 Club
ATCHEYNUM, Blair	6-2	190	R	Estevan, Sask.	4/20/69	Springfield
BOSCHMAN, Laurie	6-0	185	L	Major, Sask.	6/4/60	New Jersey
BRADY, Neil	6-2	200	L	Montreal, Que.	4/12/68	Utica-New Jersey
FREER, Mark	5-10	180	L	Peterborough, Ont.	7/14/63	Philadelphia-Hershey
GRIMES, Jake	6-1	196	L	Montreal, Que.	9/13/72	Belleville
GUERARD, Daniel	6-4	211	R	Lasalle, Que.	4/9/74	Victoriaville
JELINEK, Tomas	5-9	189	L	Prague, Czech.	4/29/62	HPK
LAMB, Mark	5-9	180	L	Ponteix, Sask.	8/3/64	Edmonton
LAZARO, Jeff	5-10	180	L	Waltham, MA	3/21/68	Boston-Maine
LOACH, Lonnie	5-10	180	L	New Liskeard, Ont.	4/14/68	Adirondack
LOEWEN, Darcy	5-10	192	L	Calgary, Alta.	2/26/69	Buffalo-Rochester
MURPHY, Rob	6-3	210	L	Hull, Que.	4/7/69	Vancouver-Milwaukee
OSEICKI, Mark	6-2	200	R	St. Paul, MN	7/23/68	Calgary-Salt Lake
PELUSO, Mike	6-4	225	L	Pengilly, MN	11/8/65	Chicago-Indianapolis
PENNEY, Chad	6-0	196	L	Labrador City, Nfld.	9/18/73	North Bay
SAVOIE, Claude	5-11	182	R	Montreal, Que.	3/12/73	Victoriaville
THOMSON, Jim	6-1	205	R	Edmonton, Alta.	10/30/65	Los Angeles-Phoenix
TURGEON, Sylvain	6-0	195	L	Noranda, Que.	1/17/65	Montreal
VAN KESSEL, John	6-4	193	R	Bridgewater, Ont.	12/19/69	Phoenix
YASHIN, Alexei	6-2	189	R	Sverdiovsk, USSR	11/5/73	Moscow Dynamo
DEFENSEMEN						
HAMMOND, Ken	6-1	190	L	Port Credit, Ont.	8/22/63	San Jose-Vancouver
HAMR, Radek	5-11	167	L	Usti-nad-laben, Czech.	6/15/74	Sparta Praha
KENNEY, Jay	6-2	190	L	New York, NY	9/21/73	Canterbury
LAVOIE, Dominic	6-2	205	R	Montreal, Que.	11/21/67	St. Louis-Peoria
MARSH, Brad	6-3	220	L	London, Ont.	3/31/58	Detroit
MILLER, Brad	6-4	225	L	Edmonton, Alta.	7/23/69	Buffalo-Rochester
PAYNTER, Kent	6-0	185	L	Summerside, P.E.I.	4/17/65	Winnipeg-Moncton
RUMBLE, Darren	6-1	200	L	Barrie, Ont.	1/23/69	Hershey
SHAW, Brad	6-0	190	R	Cambridge, Ont.	4/28/64	Hartford
SINCLAIR, Al	6-3	210	R	Mississauga, Ont.	4/3/73	U. of Michigan
TRAVERSE, Patrick	6-3	173	L	Montreal, Que.	3/14/74	Shawinigan

GOALTENDERS	HT	WT	C	Place of Birth	Date	1991-92 Club
LaFOREST, Mark	5-11	190	L	Welland, Ont.	7/10/62	Binghamton
MADELY, Darren	5-11	165	L	Holland Landing, Ont.	2/25/68	Lake Superior
MIKLENDA, Jaroslav	6-1	176	L	Veselina Morave, Czech.	3/7/74	Olozouc
RENNQUIST, Peter	5-10	154	L	Sweden	2/7/73	Nacka
SIDORKIEWICZ, Peter	5-9	180	L	Bialostocka, Poland	6/6/63	Hartford

Entry Draft Selections 1992

1992
Pick
2 Alexei Yashin
25 Chad Penney
50 Patrick Traverse
73 Radek Hamr
98 Daniel Guerard
121 Al Sinclair
146 Jaroslav Miklenda
169 Jay Kenney
194 Claude Savoie
217 Jake Grimes
242 Tomas Jelinek
264 Petter Ronnqvist

Club Directory

Ottawa Civic Centre

Ottawa Senators
301 Moodie Drive
Suite 200
Nepean, Ontario
K2H 9C4
Phone **613/721-0115**
FAX 613/726-1419
Capacity: 10,500

Chairman and Governor	Bruce M. Firestone
Vice-Chairman and Alternate Governor	Rod Bryden
CEO and Alternate Governor	Randy J. Sexton
General Manager and Alternate Governor	Mel Bridgman
Head Coach	Rick Bowness
Assistant Coaches	E.J. MacGuire, Alain Vigneault
Goaltending Coach	Glenn "Chico" Resch
Director, Player Personnel	John Ferguson
Director, Hockey Operations	Brian McKenna
Assistant Director, Player Personnel	TBA
Scouts	Paul Castron, André Dupont, Tim Higgins, Jim Nill, Bruce Southern
Head Equipment Trainer	Ed Georgica
Athletic Trainer	Conrad Lackten
Assistant Trainer	TBA
Executive Assistant to the General Manager	Diane Coughlan
Secretary, Hockey Department	Lisa Winslow
Vice-President, Sales	Mark Bonneau
Vice-President, Marketing	Jim Steel
Vice-President, Finance	Jim Ablett
Director, Media Relations	Laurent Benoit
Media Relations Assistant	Dominick Saillant
Public Relations Secretary	Vivianne Dumais
Director, Sales	Brian McKenna
Director, Outaouais Business Development	Enrico Valente
Sales Representatives	Mary Dellar, Brian Jokat, Steve Kulig, Darren McCartney, George Veitch
Publications Manager	Carl Lavigne
Director, Community Relations	Lisa Brazeau
Community Relations Coordinators	Marie Olney, Sylvie Guenette
Director, Guest Services	David Dakers
Director, Special Events	Randy Burgess
Special Events Coordinator	Patti Zebchuck
Merchandise Coordinator	Dave Saunders
Team Photographer	McElligot-Teckles Sports Focus Imaging

Coach

BOWNESS, RICK
Coach, Ottawa Senators. Born in Moncton, N.B., January 25, 1955.

Rick Bowness was appointed the first head coach of the Ottawa Senators on June 15, 1992. Bowness coached the Boston Bruins in 1991-92, guiding the team to a 39-32-12 record and a berth in the conference finals. The Moncton native began his coaching career with the AHL's Sherbrooke Jets as a player/coach in 1981, and returned to his hometown in 1987 as the coach and general manager of the Moncton Hawks, the Jets' AHL farm team. In February, 1989, he became the interim coach of the Winnipeg Jets, serving in that role until the conclusion of the season. Bowness then joined the Bruins' organization, coaching the AHL's Maine Mariners for two seasons before assuming head coaching duties for the Bruins for 1991-92.

Coaching Record

		Regular Season					Playoffs			
Season	**Team**	**Games**	**W**	**L**	**T**	**%**	**Games**	**W**	**L**	**%**
1987-88	Moncton (AHL)	80	27	45	8	.388	....	....	....	....
1988-89	Moncton (AHL)	53	28	20	5	.576	....	....	....	....
	Winnipeg (NHL)	**28**	**8**	**17**	**3**	**.340**	....	....	....	....
1989-90	Maine (AHL)	80	31	38	11	.457	....	....	....	....
1990-91	Maine (AHL)	80	34	34	12	.500	2	0	2	.000
1991-92	**Boston (NHL)**	**80**	**36**	**32**	**12**	**.525**	**15**	**8**	**7**	**.533**
	NHL Totals	**108**	**44**	**49**	**15**	**.477**	**15**	**8**	**7**	**.533**

General Manager

BRIDGMAN, MEL
General Manager, Ottawa Senators. Born in Trenton, Ont., April 28, 1955.

Mel Bridgman was appointed as the first general manager of the "new" Ottawa Senators on August 30, 1991. The first player selected in the 1975 Amateur Draft, Bridgman played 14 NHL seasons with Philadelphia, Calgary, New Jersey, Detroit and Vancouver. A natural team leader on and off the ice, Bridgman captained both the Flyers and the Devils during his career and was a player representative in collective bargaining issues. Bridgman, who gained valuable administrative experience when he was involved in the NHL-WHA negotiations, obtained a Master of Business Administration degree from the renowned Wharton School at the University of Pennsylvania, one of the top business schools in the United States.

Center Mark Lamb joins Ottawa after five seasons in Edmonton.

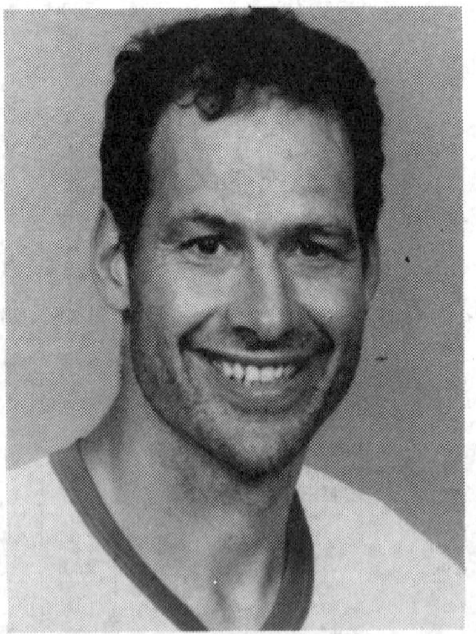

Brad Marsh, acquired from Toronto in the off-season, played his 1,000th game in 1991-92.

Sylvain Turgeon is expected to provide some offensive spark for the first-year Senators.

General Managers' History

Mel Bridgman, 1992-93.

Coaching History

Rick Bowness, 1992-93.

Philadelphia Flyers

1991-92 Results: 32W-37L-11T 75PTS. Sixth, Patrick Division

Schedule

	Home		Away
Oct.	Fri. 9 New Jersey	Oct.	Tues. 6 Pittsburgh
	Thur. 15 NY Islanders		Sat. 10 Washington
	Sun. 18 Winnipeg		Tues. 13 Quebec
	Thur. 22 Vancouver		Sat. 17 New Jersey
	Sat. 24 Montreal		Tues. 20 NY Islanders
Nov.	Sat. 7 St Louis*		Mon. 26 NY Rangers
	Thur. 12 NY Islanders		Thur. 29 Chicago
	Sun. 15 Ottawa		Sat. 31 St Louis
	Thur. 19 NY Rangers	Nov.	Wed. 4 NY Rangers
	Sun. 22 Buffalo		Sat. 14 Montreal
	Fri. 27 NY Islanders*		Sat. 21 Boston
Dec.	Thur. 3 Quebec		Sat. 28 NY Islanders
	Sun. 6 Boston	Dec.	Sat. 5 Ottawa
	Sat. 12 Washington		Fri. 11 Detroit
	Thur. 17 Pittsburgh		Tues. 15 Pittsburgh
	Sat. 19 Chicago*		Sun. 20 Tampa Bay
	Wed. 23 Pittsburgh		Sat. 26 Washington
Jan.	Thur. 7 Washington		Tues. 29 Los Angeles
	Sat. 9 NY Rangers*		Wed. 30 San Jose
	Sun. 10 Edmonton	Jan.	Sat. 2 Calgary
	Thur. 14 Calgary		Sun. 3 Edmonton
	Sun. 17 Detroit		Sat. 16 Boston
	Thur. 21 Boston		Sat. 23 NY Islanders
	Sun. 24 Hartford		Sat. 30 Pittsburgh*
	Tues. 26 Buffalo		Sun. 31 Montreal*
	Thur. 28 Quebec	Feb.	Wed. 3 NY Rangers
Feb.	Tues. 9 Ottawa		Sat. 13 New Jersey*
	Thur. 11 Montreal		Tues. 16 Calgary
	Sun. 14 New Jersey*		(at Cincinnati)
	Mon. 22 Detroit		Thur. 18 Vancouver
	(at Cleveland)		Sat. 20 Minnesota*
	Thur. 25 New Jersey		Wed. 24 Hartford
	Sat. 27 NY Islanders*	Mar.	Fri. 5 Washington
Mar.	Tues. 2 Pittsburgh		Sun. 7 New Jersey
	Thur. 11 Washington		Tues. 9 NY Islanders
	Sat. 13 Los Angeles*		Sun. 14 Hartford*
	Tues. 16 Minnesota		Thur. 18 Pittsburgh
	Sun. 21 New Jersey		Wed. 24 NY Rangers
	Thur. 25 San Jose		Sat. 27 Quebec*
Apr.	Thur. 1 Toronto		Tues. 30 NY Islanders
	Sat. 3 Tampa Bay*	Apr.	Tues. 6 Winnipeg
	Thur. 8 Washington		Sat. 10 Toronto
	Mon. 12 NY Rangers		Thur. 15 Buffalo

* Denotes afternoon game.

Home Starting Times:

Weeknights and Saturdays	7:35 p.m.
Sundays	7:05 p.m.
Matinees	1:05 p.m.
Except Oct. 24	8:05 p.m.
Dec. 5	4:35 p.m.
Feb. 27	11:05 a.m.

Franchise date: June 5, 1967

26th NHL Season

Rod Brind'Amour increased his offensive totals by 28 points in 1991-92, scoring 33 goals and adding 44 assists.

Year-by-Year Record

		Home			Road			Overall							
Season	GP	W	L	T	W	L	T	W	L	T	GF	GA	Pts.	Finished	Playoff Result
1991-92	80	22	11	7	10	26	4	32	37	11	252	273	75	6th, Patrick Div.	Out of Playoffs
1990-91	80	18	16	6	15	21	4	33	37	10	252	267	76	5th, Patrick Div.	Out of Playoffs
1989-90	80	17	19	4	13	20	7	30	39	11	290	297	71	6th, Patrick Div.	Out of Playoffs
1988-89	80	22	15	3	14	21	5	36	36	8	307	285	80	4th, Patrick Div.	Lost Conf. Championship
1987-88	80	20	14	6	18	19	3	38	33	9	292	292	85	3rd, Patrick Div.	Lost Div. Semi-Final
1986-87	80	29	9	2	17	17	6	46	26	8	310	245	100	1st, Patrick Div.	Lost Final
1985-86	80	33	6	1	20	17	3	53	23	4	335	241	110	1st, Patrick Div.	Lost Div. Semi-Final
1984-85	80	32	4	4	21	16	3	53	20	7	348	241	113	1st, Patrick Div.	Lost Final
1983-84	80	25	10	5	19	16	5	44	26	10	350	290	98	3rd, Patrick Div.	Lost Div. Semi-Final
1982-83	80	29	8	3	20	15	5	49	23	8	326	240	106	1st, Patrick Div.	Lost Div. Semi-Final
1981-82	80	25	10	5	13	21	6	38	31	11	325	313	87	3rd. Patrick Div.	Lost Div. Semi-Final
1980-81	80	23	9	8	18	15	7	41	24	15	313	249	97	2nd, Patrick Div.	Lost Quarter-Final
1979-80	80	27	5	8	21	7	12	48	12	20	327	254	116	1st, Patrick Div.	Lost Final
1978-79	80	26	10	4	14	15	11	40	25	15	281	248	95	2nd, Patrick Div.	Lost Quarter-Final
1977-78	80	29	6	5	16	14	10	45	20	15	296	200	105	2nd, Patrick Div.	Lost Semi-Final
1976-77	80	33	6	1	15	10	15	48	16	16	323	213	112	1st, Patrick Div.	Lost Semi-Final
1975-76	80	36	2	2	15	11	14	51	13	16	348	209	118	1st, Patrick Div.	Lost Final
1974-75	**80**	32	6	2	19	12	9	**51**	**18**	**11**	**293**	**181**	**113**	**1st, Patrick Div.**	**Won Stanley Cup**
1973-74	**78**	28	6	5	22	10	7	**50**	**16**	**12**	**273**	**164**	**112**	**1st, West Div.**	**Won Stanley Cup**
1972-73	78	27	8	4	10	22	7	37	30	11	296	256	85	2nd, West Div.	Lost Semi-Final
1971-72	78	19	13	7	7	25	7	26	38	14	200	236	66	5th, West Div.	Out of Playoffs
1970-71	78	20	10	9	8	23	8	28	33	17	207	225	73	3rd, West Div.	Lost Quarter-Final
1969-70	76	11	14	13	6	21	11	17	35	24	197	225	58	5th, West Div.	Out of Playoffs
1968-69	76	14	16	8	6	19	13	20	35	21	174	225	61	3rd, West Div.	Lost Quarter-Final
1967-68	74	17	13	7	14	19	4	31	32	11	173	179	73	1st, West Div.	Lost Quarter-Final

1992-93 Player Personnel

FORWARDS	HT	WT	S	Place of Birth	Date	1991-92 Club
ACTON, Keith	5-8	170	L	Stouffville, Ont.	4/15/58	Philadelphia
BARRIE, Len	6-0	200	R	Kimberly, B.C.	6/4/69	Hershey
BOIVIN, Claude	6-2	200	L	Ste. Foy, Que.	3/1/70	Hershey-Philadelphia
BRIND'AMOUR, Rod	6-1	202	L	Ottawa, Ont.	8/9/70	Philadelphia
BROWN, Dave	6-5	205	R	Saskatoon, Sask.	10/12/62	Philadelphia
CONROY, Al	5-8	170	R	Calgary, Alta.	1/17/66	Philadelphia-Hershey
COOKE, Jamie	6-2	206	R	Toronto, Ont.	11/05/68	Hershey
DANDENAULT, Eric	6-0	193	R	Sherbrooke, Que.	3/10/70	Hershey
DANIELS, Kimbi	5-10	175	R	Brandon, Man.	1/19/72	Philadelphia-Seattle
DINEEN, Kevin	5-11	190	R	Quebec City, Que.	10/28/63	Hartford-Philadelphia
DUPRE, Yanick	6-0	189	L	Montreal, Que.	11/20/72	Phi.-Drum'ville-Verdun
EKLUND, Pelle	5-10	175	L	Stockholm, Sweden	3/22/63	Philadelphia
JENSEN, Chris	5-10	170	R	Fort St. John, B.C.	10/28/63	Philadelphia-Hershey
KASPER, Steve	5-8	170	L	Montreal, Que.	9/28/61	Philadelphia
KUSHNER, Dale	6-1	195	L	Terrace, B.C.	6/13/66	Philadelphia-Hershey
LINDROS, Eric	6-5	225	R	London, Ont.	2/28/73	Oshawa-Cdn. Olympic
LOMAKIN, Andrei	5-10	176	L	Voskresensk, USSR	4/3/64	Philadelphia
MURRAY, Pat	6-3	195	L	Stratford, Ont.	8/20/69	Philadelphia-Hershey
NORRIS, Clayton	6-2	205	R	Edmonton, Alta.	3/8/72	Medicine Hat
PEDERSON, Mark	6-2	196	L	Prelate, Sask.	1/14/68	Philadelphia
RECCHI, Mark	5-10	185	L	Kamloops, B.C.	2/1/68	Pit.-Phi.
RENBERG, Mikael	6-2	183	L	Pitea, Sweden	5/5/72	Lulea
TOOKEY, Tim	5-11	190	L	Edmonton, Alta.	8/29/60	Hershey
WALZ, Wes	5-10	180	R	Calgary, Alta.	5/15/70	Philadelphia-Hershey
DEFENSEMEN						
ARMSTRONG, Bill	6-5	220	L	Richmond Hill, Ont.	5/18/70	Hershey
BENNING, Brian	6-1	195	L	Edmonton, Alta.	6/10/66	L.A.-Phi.
CARKNER, Terry	6-3	212	L	Smiths Falls, Ont.	3/7/66	Philadelphia
FENYVES, Dave	6-0	190	L	Dunnville, Ont.	4/29/60	Hershey
FOSTER, Corey	6-3	204	L	Ottawa, Ont.	10/27/69	Philadelphia-Hershey
GALLEY, Garry	6-0	190	L	Montreal, Que.	4/16/63	Boston-Philadelphia
KORDIC, Dan	6-5	220	L	Edmonton, Alta.	4/18/71	Philadelphia
MANTHA, Moe	6-2	210	R	Lakewood, OH	1/21/61	Winnipeg-Philadelphia
McGILL, Ryan	6-2	195	R	Sherwood Park, Alta.	2/28/69	Chicago-Hershey
MORROW, Steve	6-2	220	L	Evanston, IL	4/3/68	Hershey
NATTRESS, Ric	6-2	210	R	Hamilton, Ont.	5/25/62	Toronto-Calgary
PITLICK, Lance	6-0	190	R	Minneapolis, MN	11/5/67	Hershey
PORKKA, Toni	6-2	190	R	Rauma, Finland	2/4/70	Hershey
SANDWITH, Terran	6-4	220	L	Stony Plain, Alta.	4/17/72	Brandon-Saskatoon
THERIEN, Chris	6-4	230	L	Ottawa, Ont.	12/14/71	Providence
YUSHKEVICH, Dimitri	5-11	187	L	Cherepovets, USSR	11/19/71	Dynamo Moscow

GOALTENDERS	HT	WT	C	Place of Birth	Date	1991-92 Club
DEGRACE, Yanick	5-11	175	L	Lameque, N.B.	4/16/71	Hershey-Hull
HOFFORT, Bruce	5-10	185	L	Estevan, Sask.	7/30/66	San Diego
LAGRAND, Scott	6-1	170	L	Potsdam, NY	2/11/70	Boston College
ROUSSEL, Dominic	6-1	180	L	Hull, Que.	2/22/70	Hershey-Philadelphia
SODERSTROM, Tommy	5-9	163	L	Stockholm, Sweden	7/17/69	Djurgarden

1991-92 Scoring

Regular Season

Pos	#	Player	Team	GP	G	A	Pts	+/-	PIM	PP	SH	GW	GT	S	%
R	8	Mark Recchi	PIT	58	33	37	70	16–	78	16	1	4	1	156	21.2
			PHI	22	10	17	27	5–	18	4	0	1	0	54	18.5
			TOTAL	80	43	54	97	21–	96	20	1	5	1	210	20.5
C	17	Rod Brind'Amour	PHI	80	33	44	77	3–	100	8	4	5	0	202	16.3
R	20	Kevin Dineen	HFD	16	4	2	6	6–	23	1	0	1	0	28	14.3
			PHI	64	26	30	56	1	130	5	3	4	0	197	13.2
			TOTAL	80	30	32	62	5–	153	6	3	5	0	225	13.3
C	18	Mike Ricci	PHI	78	20	36	56	10–	93	11	2	0	0	149	13.4
D	28	Steve Duchesne	PHI	78	18	38	56	7–	86	7	2	3	0	229	7.9
D	19	Brian Benning	L.A.	53	2	30	32	4	99	0	0	0	0	102	2.0
			PHI	22	2	12	14	9–	35	2	0	0	0	50	4.0
			TOTAL	75	4	42	46	5–	134	2	0	0	0	152	2.6
L	14	Mark Pederson	PHI	58	15	25	40	14	22	4	0	3	0	94	16.0
C	10	Dan Quinn	PHI	67	11	26	37	13–	26	6	0	1	1	101	10.9
D	5	Kerry Huffman	PHI	60	14	18	32	1	41	4	0	2	0	123	11.4
D	3	Garry Galley	BOS	38	2	12	14	3–	83	1	0	0	0	51	3.9
			PHI	39	3	15	18	1	34	2	0	1	0	74	4.1
			TOTAL	77	5	27	32	2–	117	3	0	1	0	125	4.0
L	23	Andrei Lomakin	PHI	57	14	16	30	6–	26	2	0	0	0	82	17.1
D	2	Mark Howe	PHI	42	7	18	25	18	18	6	0	0	0	63	11.1
C	9	Per-Erik Eklund	PHI	51	7	16	23	0	4	1	2	1	0	74	9.5
L	40*	Claude Boivin	PHI	58	5	13	18	2–	187	0	0	0	0	46	10.9
L	47	Brad Jones	PHI	48	7	10	17	2–	44	0	0	1	0	67	10.4
C	25	Keith Acton	PHI	50	7	10	17	4–	98	0	0	3	0	79	8.9
D	29	Terry Carkner	PHI	73	4	12	16	14–	195	0	1	0	0	70	5.7
C	37*	Mark Freer	PHI	50	6	7	13	1–	18	0	0	2	0	41	14.6
C	46*	Allan Conroy	PHI	31	2	9	11	1	74	0	0	0	0	25	8.0
D	44*	Corey Foster	PHI	25	3	4	7	14–	20	1	0	0	0	67	4.5
R	21	Dave Brown	PHI	70	4	2	6	11–	81	0	0	0	0	50	8.0
C	15	Steve Kasper	PHI	16	3	2	5	3–	10	0	1	0	0	13	23.1
L	15	Dale Kushner	PHI	19	3	2	5	5–	18	0	0	1	0	19	15.8
C	36	Wes Walz	BOS	15	0	3	3	3–	12	0	0	0	0	17	.0
			PHI	2	1	0	1	1	0	0	0	1	0	2	50.0
			TOTAL	17	1	3	4	2–	12	0	0	1	0	19	5.3
D	6*	Dan Kordic	PHI	46	1	3	4	1	126	0	0	0	0	27	3.7
D	42	Moe Mantha	WPG	12	0	4	4	0	6	0	0	0	0	10	.0
			PHI	5	0	0	0	0	2	0	0	0	0	7	.0
			TOTAL	17	0	4	4	0	8	0	0	0	0	17	.0
D	11	Jiri Latal	PHI	10	1	2	3	1	4	0	0	1	0	22	4.5
G	27	Ron Hextall	PHI	45	0	3	3	0	35	0	0	0	0	0	.0
C	14*	Kimbi Daniels	PHI	25	1	1	2	4–	4	0	0	1	0	16	6.3
L	24*	Pat Murray	PHI	9	1	0	1	3	0	0	0	0	0	8	12.5
C	26	Martin Hostak	PHI	5	0	1	1	1–	2	0	0	0	0	8	.0
G	33*	Dominic Roussel	PHI	17	0	1	1	0	2	0	0	0	0	0	.0
L	48*	Reid Simpson	PHI	1	0	0	0	0	0	0	0	0	0	0	.0
L	66*	Yanick Dupre	PHI	1	0	0	0	0	0	0	0	0	0	0	.0
L	24*	Rod Dallman	PHI	2	0	0	0	0	5	0	0	0	0	2	.0
R	14	Chris Jensen	PHI	2	0	0	0	1–	0	0	0	0	0	2	.0

Goaltending

No.	Goaltender	GPI	Mins	Avg	W	L	T	EN	SO	GA	SA	S%
33	* Dominic Roussel	17	922	2.60	7	8	2	0	1	40	437	.908
27	Ron Hextall	45	2668	3.40	16	21	6	6	3	151	1294	.883
35	Ken Wregget	23	1259	3.57	9	8	3	1	0	75	557	.865
	Totals	**80**	**4866**	**3.37**	**32**	**37**	**11**	**7**	**4**	**273**	**2295**	**.881**

Eric Lindros will make his NHL debut in 1992-93 after a blockbuster trade brought him to Philadelphia from Quebec.

General Managers' History

Bud Poile, 1967-68 to 1968-69; Bud Poile and Keith Allen, 1969-70; Keith Allen, 1970-71 to 1982-83; Bob McCammon, 1983-84; Bobby Clarke, 1984-85 to 1989-90; Russ Farwell, 1990-91 to date.

Captains' History

Lou Angotti, 1967-68; Ed Van Impe, 1968-69 to 1971-72; Ed Van Impe, Bob Clarke, 1972-73; Bob Clarke, 1973-74 to 1978-79; Mel Bridgman, 1979-80, 1980-81; Bill Barber, 1981-82; Bill Barber, Bob Clarke, 1982-83; Bob Clarke, 1983-84; Dave Poulin, 1984-85 to 1988-89; Dave Poulin and Ron Sutter, 1989-90; Ron Sutter, 1990-91; Rick Tocchet, 1991-92.

Coaching History

Keith Allen, 1967-68 to 1968-69; Vic Stasiuk, 1969-70 to 1970-71; Fred Shero, 1971-72 to 1977-78; Bob McCammon and Pat Quinn, 1978-79; Pat Quinn, 1979-80 to 1980-81; Pat Quinn and Bob McCammon, 1981-82; Bob McCammon, 1982-83 to 1983-84; Mike Keenan, 1984-85 to 1987-88; Paul Holmgren, 1988-89 to 1990-91; Paul Holmgren and Bill Dineen, 1991-92; Bill Dineen, 1992-93.

Retired Numbers

1	Bernie Parent	1967-1971 and 1973-1979
4	Barry Ashbee	1970-1974
7	Bill Barber	1972-1985
16	Bobby Clarke	1969-1984

Club Records

Team

(Figures in brackets for season records are games played; records for fewest points, wins, ties, losses, goals, goals against are for 70 or more games)

Record		
Most Points	118	1975-76 (80)
Most Wins	53	1984-85 (80) 1985-86 (80)
Most Ties	*24	1969-70 (76)
Most Losses	38	1971-72 (78)
Most Goals	350	1983-84 (80)
Most Goals Against	313	1981-82 (80)
Fewest Points	58	1969-70 (76)
Fewest Wins	17	1969-70 (76)
Fewest Ties	4	1985-86 (80)
Fewest Losses	12	1979-80 (80)
Fewest Goals	173	1967-68 (74)
Fewest Goals Against	164	1973-74 (78)
Longest Winning Streak		
Over-all	13	Oct. 19-Nov. 17/85
Home	*20	Jan. 4- Apr. 3/76
Away	8	Dec. 22/82- Jan. 16/83
Longest Undefeated Streak		
Over-all	*35	Oct. 14/79- Jan. 6/80 (25 wins, 10 ties)
Home	26	Oct. 11/79- Feb. 3/80 (19 wins, 7 ties)
Away	16	Oct. 20/79- Jan. 6/80 (11 wins, 5 ties)
Longest Losing Streak		
Over-all	6	Mar. 25- Apr. 4/70
Home	5	Jan. 30- Feb. 15/69
Away	8	Oct. 25- Nov. 26/72
Longest Winless Streak		
Over-all	11	Nov. 21- Dec. 14/69 (9 losses, 2 ties) Dec. 10/70- Jan. 3/71 (9 losses, 2 ties)
Home	8	Dec. 19/68- Jan. 18/69 (4 losses, 4 ties)
Away	19	Oct. 23/71- Jan. 27/72 (15 losses, 4 ties)
Most Shutouts, Season	13	1974-75 (80)
Most PIM, Season	2,621	1980-81 (80)
Most Goals, Game	13	Mar. 22/84 (Pit. 4 at Phi. 13) Oct. 18/84 (Van. 2 at Phil. 13)

Individual

Record		
Most Seasons	15	Bobby Clarke
Most Games	1,144	Bobby Clarke
Most Goals, Career	420	Bill Barber
Most Assists, Career	852	Bobby Clarke
Most Points, Career	1,210	Bobby Clarke (358 goals, 852 assists)
Most PIM, Career	1,600	Paul Holmgren
Most Shutouts, Career	50	Bernie Parent
Longest Consecutive Game Streak	287	Rick MacLeish (Oct. 6/72-Feb. 5/76)
Most Goals, Season	61	Reggie Leach (1975-76)
Most Assists, Season	89	Bobby Clarke (1974-75; 1975-76)
Most Points, Season	119	Bobby Clarke (1975-76) (30 goals, 89 assists)
Most PIM, Season	*472	Dave Schultz (1974-75)
Most Points, Defenseman, Season	82	Mark Howe (1985-86) (24 goals, 58 assists)
Most Points, Center, Season	119	Bobby Clarke (1975-76) (30 goals, 89 assists)
Most Points, Right Wing, Season	98	Tim Kerr (1984-85) (54 goals, 44 assists)
Most Points, Left Wing, Season	112	Bill Barber (1975-76) (50 goals, 62 assists)
Most Points, Rookie, Season	76	Dave Poulin (1983-84) (31 goals, 45 assists)
Most Shutouts, Season	12	Bernie Parent (1973-74; 1974-75)
Most Goals, Game	4	Rick MacLeish (Feb. 13/73; Mar. 4/73) Tom Bladon (Dec. 11/77) Tim Kerr (Oct. 25/84, Jan. 17/85, Feb. 9/85, Nov. 20/86) Brian Propp (Dec. 2/86) Rick Tocchet (Feb. 27/88; Jan. 25/90)
Most Assists, Game	5	Bobby Clarke (Apr. 1/76)
Most Points, Game	8	Tom Bladon (Dec. 11/77)

* NHL Record.

All-time Record vs. Other Clubs

Regular Season

	At Home							On Road							Total						
	GP	W	L	T	GF	GA	PTS	GP	W	L	T	GF	GA	PTS	GP	W	L	T	GF	GA	PTS
Boston	49	21	22	6	164	146	48	51	11	34	6	148	213	28	100	32	56	12	312	359	76
Buffalo	43	27	9	7	161	110	61	41	14	21	6	122	148	34	84	41	30	13	283	258	95
Calgary	42	30	11	1	175	112	61	42	13	21	8	141	171	34	84	43	32	9	316	283	95
Chicago	52	27	15	10	173	142	64	51	10	24	17	136	180	37	103	37	39	27	309	322	101
Detroit	49	29	10	10	200	141	68	49	18	22	9	163	174	45	98	47	32	19	363	315	113
Edmonton	21	15	5	1	97	65	31	20	5	12	3	60	78	13	41	20	17	4	157	143	44
Hartford	21	14	6	1	87	59	29	20	7	9	0	82	85	14	41	21	15	1	169	144	43
Los Angeles	54	33	14	7	211	140	73	56	32	17	7	190	166	71	110	65	31	14	401	306	144
Minnesota	57	39	8	10	228	129	88	57	22	22	13	194	184	57	114	61	30	23	422	313	145
Montreal	49	17	20	12	131	146	46	50	13	27	10	143	191	36	99	30	47	22	274	337	82
New Jersey	53	38	8	7	232	122	83	52	25	23	4	210	185	54	105	63	31	11	442	307	137
NY Islanders	63	38	17	8	238	187	84	65	21	33	11	196	256	53	128	59	50	19	434	443	137
NY Rangers	78	37	28	13	272	230	87	78	25	35	18	229	257	68	156	62	63	31	501	487	155
Pittsburgh	78	59	12	7	347	195	125	77	31	31	15	249	249	77	155	90	43	22	596	444	202
Quebec	21	17	2	2	90	53	36	20	8	5	7	75	66	23	41	25	7	9	165	119	59
St. Louis	57	38	10	9	225	130	85	57	28	22	7	173	164	63	114	66	32	16	398	294	148
San Jose	1	1	0	0	5	2	2	2	1	1	0	2	3	2	3	2	1	0	7	5	4
Toronto	50	32	10	8	203	118	72	50	19	18	13	170	175	51	100	51	28	21	373	293	123
Vancouver	43	30	13	0	196	126	60	43	22	10	11	165	126	55	86	52	23	11	361	252	115
Washington	53	32	17	4	206	146	68	53	23	22	8	192	198	54	106	55	39	12	398	344	122
Winnipeg	21	16	5	0	96	56	32	20	10	9	1	72	68	21	41	26	14	1	168	124	53
Defunct Clubs	34	24	4	6	137	67	54	35	13	14	8	102	89	34	69	37	18	14	239	156	88
Totals	**989**	**614**	**246**	**129**	**3874**	**2622**	**1357**	**989**	**371**	**432**	**182**	**3214**	**3426**	**924**	**1978**	**985**	**678**	**311**	**7088**	**6048**	**2281**

Playoffs

	Series	W	L	GP	W	L	T	GF	GA	Last Mtg.	Round	Result
Boston	4	2	2	20	9	11	0	57	60	1978	QF	L 1-4
Buffalo	2	2	0	11	8	3	0	35	23	1978	QF	W 4-1
**Calgary	2	1	1	11	7	4	0	43	28	1981	QF	L 3-4
Chicago	1	0	1	4	0	4	0	8	20	1971	QF	L 0-4
Edmonton	3	1	2	15	7	8	0	44	49	1987	F	L 3-4
Minnesota	2	2	0	11	8	3	0	41	26	1980	SF	W 4-1
Montreal	4	1	3	21	6	15	0	52	72	1989	CF	L 2-4
*New Jersey	1	1	0	2	2	0	0	6	3	1978	PR	W 2-0
NY Islanders	4	3	1	25	14	11	0	83	69	1987	DF	W 4-3
NY Rangers	8	4	4	38	19	19	0	119	130	1987	DSF	W 4-2
Pittsburgh	1	1	0	7	4	3	0	31	24	1989	DF	W 4-3
Quebec	2	2	0	11	7	4	0	39	29	1985	CF	W 4-2
St. Louis	2	0	2	11	3	8	0	20	34	1969	QF	L 0-4
Toronto	3	3	0	17	12	5	0	67	47	1977	QF	W 4-2
Vancouver	1	1	0	3	2	1	0	15	9	1979	PR	W 2-1
Washington	3	1	2	16	7	9	0	55	65	1989	DSF	W 4-2
Totals	**43**	**25**	**18**	**223**	**116**	**107**	**0**	**715**	**688**			

Playoff Results 1992-88

Year	Round	Opponent	Result	GF	GA
1989	CF	Montreal	L 2-4	8	17
	DF	Pittsburgh	W 4-3	31	24
	DSF	Washington	W 4-2	25	19
1988	DSF	Washington	L 3-4	25	31

Abbreviations: Round: F – Final; **CF** – conference final; **DF** – division final; **DSF** – division semi-final; **SF** – semi-final; **QF** – quarter-final; **PR** – preliminary round. **GA** – goals against; **GF** – goals for.

1991-92 Results

Home				Away			
Oct.	10	Pittsburgh	3-6	**Oct.**	4	Washington	2-5
	13	New Jersey	4-2		6	Pittsburgh*	2-2
	17	Quebec	5-3		12	NY Islanders	4-5
	19	Montreal	0-1		24	Minnesota	5-2
	31	San Jose	5-2		25	Winnipeg	0-2
Nov.	2	NY Rangers*	2-4	**Nov.**	5	St Louis	4-3
	7	Buffalo	5-2		8	Buffalo	3-4
	14	Edmonton	3-1		12	New Jersey	2-5
	17	Winnipeg	1-2		16	Montreal	3-1
	23	New Jersey	5-5		20	Pittsburgh	2-5
	27	Hartford	3-7		30	Pittsburgh	1-5
	29	Pittsburgh*	3-9	**Dec.**	2	NY Rangers	2-4
Dec.	5	Washington	3-6		7	Boston	5-3
	8	New Jersey	2-2		15	Chicago	4-4
	12	Toronto	1-1		18	NY Rangers	3-6
	14	Chicago*	1-1		21	Minnesota	3-0
	19	NY Islanders	6-2		27	Vancouver	1-1
	22	Washington	4-3		28	Calgary	1-5
Jan.	7	Buffalo	5-5	**Jan.**	3	San Jose	1-3
	9	Los Angeles	5-2		4	Los Angeles	3-7
	12	NY Islanders	4-3		11	Boston	1-5
	14	Chicago	1-1		16	NY Islanders	3-4
	23	Winnipeg	0-1		21	Detroit	3-7
	28	Washington	3-2		25	Toronto	4-6
	30	Minnesota	5-3	**Feb.**	1	NY Islanders	5-5
Feb.	2	St Louis	5-1		4	New Jersey	1-3
	6	Boston	5-1		8	Quebec*	3-0
	13	Quebec	3-2		18	New Jersey	3-4
	15	Edmonton*	8-5		22	Washington	5-7
	16	Pittsburgh	3-3		23	NY Rangers	1-2
	25	NY Islanders	4-1		27	Calgary	3-0
Mar.	7	NY Rangers*	5-4		28	Edmonton	2-4
	8	Vancouver	3-7	**Mar.**	1	San Jose*	1-0
	12	Calgary	5-4		3	Los Angeles	1-4
	14	Washington*	3-1		10	NY Islanders	2-5
	22	Detroit	4-3		18	Montreal	4-3
	24	NY Rangers	3-4		20	Washington	7-6
	29	New Jersey*	5-4		25	NY Rangers	1-4
Apr.	2	Hartford	3-4		31	Pittsburgh	5-6
	5	Toronto	6-2	**Apr.**	4	Hartford*	2-4

*Denotes afternoon game

Entry Draft Selections 1992-78

1992
Pick
7 Ryan Sittler
15 Jason Bowen
31 Denis Metlyuk
103 Vladislav Buljin
127 Roman Zolotov
151 Kirk Daubenspeck
175 Claude Jutras Jr.
199 Jonas Hakansson
223 Chris Herperger
247 Patrice Paquin

1991
Pick
6 Peter Forsberg
50 Yanic Dupre
86 Aris Brimanis
94 Yanick Degrace
116 Clayton Norris
122 Dmitri Yushkevich
138 Andrei Lomakin
182 James Bode
204 Josh Bartell
226 Neil Little
248 John Porco

1990
Pick
4 Mike Ricci
25 Chris Simon
40 Mikael Renberg
42 Terran Sandwith
44 Kimbi Daniels
46 Bill Armstrong
47 Chris Therien
52 Al Kinisky
88 Dan Kordic
109 Viacheslav Butsayev
151 Patrik Englund
172 Toni Porkka
193 Greg Hanson
214 Tommy Soderstrom
235 William Lund

1989
Pick
33 Greg Johnson
34 Patrik Juhlin
72 Reid Simpson
117 Niklas Eriksson
138 John Callahan Jr.
159 Sverre Sears
180 Glen Wisser
201 Al Kummu
222 Matt Brait
243 James Pollio

1988
Pick
14 Claude Boivin
35 Pat Murray
56 Craig Fisher
63 Dominic Roussel
77 Scott Lagrand
98 Edward O'Brien
119 Gordie Frantti
140 Jamie Cooke
161 Johan Salle
182 Brian Arthur
203 Jeff Dandreta
224 Scott Billey
245 Drahomir Kadlec

1987
Pick
20 Darren Rumble
30 Jeff Harding
62 Martin Hostak
83 Tomaz Eriksson
104 Bill Gall
125 Tony Link
146 Mark Strapon
167 Darryl Ingham
188 Bruce McDonald
209 Steve Morrow
230 Darius Rusnak
251 Dale Roehl

1986
Pick
20 Kerry Huffman
23 Jukka Seppo
28 Kent Hawley
83 Mark Bar
125 Steve Scheifele
146 Sami Wahlsten
167 Murray Baron
188 Blaine Rude
209 Shawn Sabol
230 Brett Lawrence
251 Daniel Stephano

1985
Pick
21 Glen Seabrooke
42 Bruce Rendall
48 Darryl Gilmour
63 Shane Whelan
84 Paul Marshall
105 Daril Holmes
126 Ken Alexander
147 Tony Horacek
168 Mike Cusack
189 Gordon Murphy
231 Rod Williams
252 Paul Maurice

1984
Pick
22 Greg Smyth
27 Scott Mellanby
37 Jeff Chychrun
43 Dave McLay
47 John Stevens
79 Dave Hanson
100 Brian Dobbin
121 John Dzikowski
142 Tom Allen
163 Luke Vitale
184 Bill Powers
204 Daryn Fersovitch
245 Juraj Bakos

1983
Pick
41 Peter Zezel
44 Derrick Smith
81 Alan Bourbeau
101 Jerome Carrier
121 Rick Tocchet
141 Bobby Mormina
161 Per-Erik Eklund
181 Rob Nichols
201 William McCormick
221 Brian Jopling
241 Harold Duvall

1982
Pick
4 Ron Sutter
46 Miroslav Dvorak
47 Bill Campbell
77 Mikael Hjalm
98 Todd Bergen
119 Ron Hextall
140 Dave Brown
161 Alain Lavigne
182 Magnus Roupe
203 Tom Allen
224 Rick Gal
245 Mark Vichorek

1981
Pick
16 Steve Smith
37 Rich Costello
47 Barry Tabobondung
58 Ken Strong
5 David Michayluk
79 Ken Latta
100 Justin Hanley
121 Andre Villeneuve
137 Vladimir Svitek
142 Gil Hudon
163 Steve Taylor
184 Len Hachborn
205 Steve Tsujiura

1980
Pick
21 Mike Stothers
42 Jay Fraser
63 Paul Mercier
84 Taras Zytynsky
105 Daniel Held
126 Brian Tutt
147 Ross Fitzpatrick
168 Mark Botell
189 Peter Dineen
195 Bob O'Brien
210 Andy Brickley

1979
Pick
14 Brian Propp
22 Blake Wesley
35 Pelle Lindbergh
56 Lindsay Carson
77 Don Gillen
98 Thomas Eriksson
119 Gord Williams

1978
Pick
6 Behn Wilson
7 Ken Linseman
14 Dan Lucas
33 Mike Simurda
37 Gord Salt
50 Glen Cochrane
67 Russ Wilderman
83 Brad Tamblyn
100 Mark Taylor
117 Mike Ewanouski
126 Jerry Price
134 Darren Switzer
151 Greg Francis
167 Rick Berard
168 Don Lucia
182 Mark Berge
183 Ken Moore
195 Jim Olson
198 Anton Stastny

Coach

DINEEN, BILL
Coach, Philadelphia Flyers. Born in Arvida, Que., September 18, 1932.

After a long and distinguished coaching and scouting career, Bill Dineen finally realized a life-long dream of coaching in the NHL when he replaced Paul Holmgren during the 1991-92 season. Dineen, who was one of the WHA's most successful coaches with two Avco Cup titles to his credit, spent the majority of the 1980s as the coach of Detroit's AHL farm team in Adirondack, NY, leading the team to a pair of Calder Cup championships in 1986 and 1989. After Neil Smith left the Detroit organization to become general manager of the New York Rangers, Dineen was appointed as Adirondack's general manager. After the 1989 season, Dineen joined the Philadelphia Flyers' organization as a scout, assuming head coaching duties on December 4, 1991. Dineen led the team to a 24-23-9 record in the second half of the season.

Coaching Record

		Regular Season					Playoffs			
Season	**Team**	**Games**	**W**	**L**	**T**	**%**	**Games**	**W**	**L**	**%**
1970-71	Denver (WHL)					UNAVAILABLE				
1971-72	Denver (WHL)					UNAVAILABLE				
1972-73	Houston (WHA)	78	39	35	4	.526	10	4	6	.400
1973-74	Houston (WHA)	78	48	28	5	.647	14	12	2	.857
1974-75	Houston (WHA)	78	53	25	0	.679	13	12	1	.923
1975-76	Houston (WHA)	80	53	27	0	.663	17	8	9	.471
1976-77	Houston (WHA)	80	50	24	6	.663	11	6	5	.545
1977-78	Houston (WHA)	80	42	34	4	.550	6	2	4	.333
1978-79	New England (WHA)	71	34	29	8	.535	....	....	....	....
1983-84	Adirondack (AHL)	80	37	29	14	.550	7	3	4	.429
1984-85	Adirondack (AHL)	80	35	37	8	.488	....	....	....	....
1985-86	Adirondack (AHL)	80	41	31	8	.563	17	12	5	.706
1986-87	Adirondack (AHL)	80	44	31	5	.581	11	5	6	.455
1987-88	Adirondack (AHL)	80	42	27	11	.594	11	4	7	.364
1988-89	Adirondack (AHL)	80	47	27	6	.625	17	12	5	.706
1991-92	**Philadelphia (NHL)**	**56**	**24**	**23**	**9**	**.509**	....	....	....	....
	NHL Totals	**56**	**24**	**23**	**9**	**.509**	....	....	....	....

Club Directory

The Spectrum
Pattison Place
Philadelphia, PA 19148
Phone **215/465-4500**
PR FAX 215/389-9403
Pres. & GM FAX 215/389-9409
Capacity: 17,380

Board of Directors
Ed Snider, Jay Snider, Joe Scott, Keith Allen, Fred Shabel, Sylvan Tobin, Carl Hirsh, Sanford Lipstein, Ron Ryan

Majority Ownership	Ed Snider and family
Limited Partners	Sylvan and Fran Tobin
President	Jay Snider
Chairman of the Board Emeritus	Joe Scott
Chief Operating Officer	Ron Ryan
Executive Vice-President	Keith Allen
Senior Vice-President	Bob Clarke
General Manager	Russ Farwell
Head Coach	Bill Dineen
Assistant General Manager	John Blackwell
Assistant Coaches	Craig Hartsburg, Ken Hitchcock
Goaltending Instructor	Bernie Parent
Head Coach, Hershey Bears (AHL)	Mike Eaves
Physical Conditioning Coach	Pat Croce, LPT, ATC
Director of Pro Scouting	Bill Barber
Chief Scout	Jerry Melnyk
Scouts	Pete Dineen, Inge Hammarstrom, Jerry Moschella, Simon Nolet, Doug Overtow, Blair Reid, Glen Sonmor, Red Sullivan, Vaclav Slansky, Evgeny Zimin
Vice-President, Sales	Jack Betson
Vice-President, Communications	John Brogan
Vice-President, Finance	Bob Baer
Vice-President, Public Relations	Mark Piazza
Accounting Manager	Jeff Niessen
Accountant	Susann Schaffer
Accounting Clerk	Karen Pohl
Accounts Payable Clerk	Michelle Stanek
Assistant Director of Marketing/Sales	Lynn McGoldrick
Administrative Assistant	Karen Rogan
Assistant Director of Public Relations	Jill Vogel
Public Relations Assistant	Suzann Waters
Director of Community Relations	Linda Panasci
Director of Team Services	Joe Kadlec
Computer Analyst	David Gelberg
Video Coordinator	Leon Friedrich
Executive Assistants/Secretaries	Ileen Forcine, Dianna Taylor, Robin Casey, Ann Marie Nasuti
Ticket Manager	Cecilia Baker
Ticket Office Assistant	Rick Ridall
Director of Youth Hockey	Greg Scott
Archivist	Mott Linn
Office Coordinator	Joan Kadlec
Receptionist	Aggie Preston
P.A. Announcer	Lou Nolan
Team Physician	Jeff Hartzell, M.D.
Orthopedic Surgeon	Arthur Bartolozzi, M.D.
Oral Surgeon	Everett Borghesani, D.D.S.
Team Dentist	Jim Larson, D.D.S.
Athletic Therapist	Gary Smith
Trainers	Jim Evers, Harry Bricker
Manager, Practice Facility	Anthony Tomasco
Dimensions of rink	200 feet by 85 feet
Location of Press Box	Mid-ice, North side, concourse level
Club colors	Orange, Black and White
Training camp site and Practice Facility	The Coliseum, Voorhees, NJ
TV Announcers	Mike Emrick, Bill Clement
Radio Announcers	Gene Hart, Bobby Taylor
TV Stations	PRISM, SportsChannel Philadelphia, WPHL TV-17
Radio Station	610 WIP All SportsRadio

General Manager

FARWELL, RUSS
General Manager, Philadelphia Flyers. Born in Peace River, Alta., April 20, 1956.

Before being appointed to his position on June 6, 1990, Russ Farwell, 36, spent eight seasons in the Western Hockey League. He served as general manager of the Seattle Thunderbirds from 1988-90 and was named the WHL and CHL Executive of the Year in 1990. In two seasons under Farwell's leadership, the Thunderbirds were 85-52-7, including a 52-17-3 mark last year. Prior to his position with Seattle, Farwell spent six seasons as general manager of the Medicine Hat Tigers. During that time, the Tigers were 281-135-16, participated in the WHL's Eastern Division Finals five times and won consecutive Memorial Cup titles in 1986-87 and 1987-88.

Farwell is the first individual to be named an NHL general manager directly from junior hockey since Wren Blair went from Oshawa to Minnesota in 1967-68. The only other man to do so was Leighton "Hap" Emms, who went from Barrie to Boston in 1965-66.

Pittsburgh Penguins

1991-92 Results: 39W-32L-9T 87PTS. Third, Patrick Division

Year-by-Year Record

Season	Home GP	Home W	Home L	Home T	Road W	Road L	Road T	Overall W	Overall L	Overall T	GF	GA	Pts.	Finished		Playoff Result
1991-92	**80**	21	13	6	18	19	3	**39**	**32**	**9**	**343**	**308**	**87**	**3rd,**	**Patrick Div.**	**Won Stanley Cup**
1990-91	**80**	25	12	3	16	21	3	**41**	**33**	**6**	**342**	**305**	**88**	**1st,**	**Patrick Div.**	**Won Stanley Cup**
1989-90	80	22	15	3	10	25	5	32	40	8	318	359	72	5th,	Patrick Div.	Out of Playoffs
1988-89	80	24	13	3	16	20	4	40	33	7	347	349	87	2nd,	Patrick Div.	Lost Div. Final
1987-88	80	22	12	6	14	23	3	36	35	9	319	316	81	6th,	Patrick Div.	Out of Playoffs
1986-87	80	19	15	6	11	23	6	30	38	12	297	290	72	5th,	Patrick Div.	Out of Playoffs
1985-86	80	20	15	5	14	23	3	34	38	8	313	305	76	5th,	Patrick Div.	Out of Playoffs
1984-85	80	17	20	3	7	31	2	24	51	5	276	385	53	6th,	Patrick Div.	Out of Playoffs
1983-84	80	7	29	4	9	29	2	16	58	6	254	390	38	6th,	Patrick Div.	Out of Playoffs
1982-83	80	14	22	4	4	31	5	18	53	9	257	394	45	6th,	Patrick Div.	Out of Playoffs
1981-82	80	21	11	8	10	25	5	31	36	13	310	337	75	4th,	Patrick Div.	Lost Div. Semi-Final
1980-81	80	21	16	3	9	21	10	30	37	13	302	345	73	3rd,	Norris Div.	Lost Prelim. Round
1979-80	80	20	13	7	10	24	6	30	37	13	251	303	73	3rd,	Norris Div.	Lost Prelim. Round
1978-79	80	23	12	5	13	19	8	36	31	13	281	279	85	2nd,	Norris Div.	Lost Quarter-Final
1977-78	80	16	15	9	9	22	9	25	37	18	254	321	68	4th,	Norris Div.	Out of Playoffs
1976-77	80	22	12	6	12	21	7	34	33	13	240	252	81	3rd,	Norris Div.	Lost Prelim. Round
1975-76	80	23	11	6	12	22	6	35	33	12	339	303	82	3rd,	Norris Div.	Lost Prelim. Round
1974-75	80	25	5	10	12	23	5	37	28	15	326	289	89	3rd,	Norris Div.	Lost Quarter-Final
1973-74	78	15	18	6	13	23	3	28	41	9	242	273	65	5th,	West Div.	Out of Playoffs
1972-73	78	24	11	4	8	26	5	32	37	9	257	265	73	5th,	West Div.	Out of Playoffs
1971-72	78	18	15	6	8	23	8	26	38	14	220	258	66	4th,	West Div.	Lost Quarter-Final
1970-71	78	18	12	9	3	25	11	21	37	20	221	240	62	6th,	West Div.	Out of Playoffs
1969-70	76	17	13	8	9	25	4	26	38	12	182	238	64	2nd,	West Div.	Lost Semi-Final
1968-69	76	12	20	6	8	25	5	20	45	11	189	252	51	5th,	West Div.	Out of Playoffs
1967-68	74	15	12	10	12	22	3	27	34	13	195	216	67	5th,	West Div.	Out of Playoffs

Schedule

Home	Away
Oct. Tues. 6 Philadelphia	Oct. Sat. 10 Montreal
Thur. 8 NY Islanders	Sat. 17 Hartford
Tues. 13 Buffalo	Sat. 24 New Jersey
Thur. 15 Montreal	Tues. 27 Ottawa
Tues. 20 Vancouver	Thur. 29 St Louis
Thur. 22 Detroit	Nov. Sun. 1 Tampa Bay
Nov. Tues. 3 NY Islanders	Sat. 7 Toronto
Thur. 5 St Louis	Sun. 8 Chicago
Thur. 12 Quebec	Tues. 10 Minnesota
Tues. 17 Buffalo	Fri. 13 Detroit
Sat. 21 New Jersey	Fri. 20 New Jersey
Wed. 25 NY Rangers	Mon. 23 NY Rangers
Sat. 28 Washington	Fri. 27 Washington
Dec. Tues. 8 Winnipeg	Dec. Tues. 1 NY Islanders
Sat. 12 New Jersey	Thur. 3 Los Angeles
Tues. 15 Philadelphia	Sat. 5 San Jose*
Sat. 19 NY Islanders*	Fri. 11 New Jersey
Mon. 21 Quebec	Thur. 17 Philadelphia
Thur. 31 Toronto	Wed. 23 Philadelphia
Jan. Sat. 2 NY Rangers	Sun. 27 Buffalo*
Tues. 5 Boston	Jan. Sun. 10 Winnipeg
Thur. 7 Minnesota	Thur. 14 Boston
Sat. 9 Calgary*	Tues. 19 Vancouver
Sat. 16 Ottawa	Fri. 22 Edmonton
Tues. 26 Washington	Sat. 23 Calgary
Thur. 28 NY Islanders	Sun. 31 Washington*
Sat. 30 Philadelphia*	Feb. Wed. 10 NY Rangers
Feb. Mon. 8 Boston	Sun. 14 Buffalo
(at Atlanta)	Sat. 20 NY Islanders*
Sat. 13 Chicago*	Sun. 21 Hartford*
Thur. 18 Edmonton	Thur. 25 Ottawa
Tues. 23 New Jersey	Sun. 28 Washington*
Sat. 27 Tampa Bay*	Mar. Tues. 2 Philadelphia
Mar. Tues. 9 Boston	Fri. 5 NY Rangers
Thur. 11 Los Angeles	Sat. 13 NY Islanders
Thur. 18 Philadelphia	Sun. 21 Edmonton
Sat. 20 Ottawa	(at Cleveland)
Tues. 23 San Jose	Sat. 27 Boston*
Thur. 25 Washington	Sun. 28 Washington*
Apr. Thur. 1 Hartford	Apr. Sat. 3 Quebec
Wed. 7 Montreal	Sun. 4 New Jersey
Sat. 10 NY Rangers	Fri. 9 NY Rangers
Thur. 15 New Jersey	Wed. 14 New Jersey

* Denotes afternoon game.

Home Starting Times:

All Games	7:35 p.m.
Except Matinees	1:35 p.m.
Dec. 31	6:35 p.m.
Jan. 9	12:35 p.m.

Franchise date: June 5, 1967

26th NHL Season

Jaromir Jagr reached the 30-goal mark in his sophomore season, firing 32 goals for Pittsburgh in 1991-92.

1992-93 Player Personnel

FORWARDS	HT	WT	S	Place of Birth	Date	1991-92 Club
BLAESER, Jeff	6-3	190	L	Parma, OH	5/11/70	Yale
BOURQUE, Phil	6-1	196	L	Chelmeford, MA	6/8/62	Pittsburgh
CAUFIELD, Jay	6-4	235	R	Philadelphia, PA	7/17/60	Pittsburgh
DANIELS, Jeff	6-1	200	L	Oshawa, Ont.	6/24/68	Pittsburgh-Muskegon
DRAGON, Joe	5-11	180	R	Fort Smith, N.W.T.	2/20/69	Cornell
ERREY, Bob	5-10	182	L	Montreal, Que.	9/21/64	Pittsburgh
FRANCIS, Ron	6-2	200	L	Sault Ste. Marie, Ont.	3/1/63	Pittsburgh
GARDNER, Joel	6-0	175	L	Petrolia, Ont.	9/16/67	Muskegon-Knoxville
GAUTHIER, Daniel	6-2	190	L	Charlemagne, Que.	5/17/70	Muskegon
JAGR, Jaromir	6-2	208	L	Kladno, Czech.	2/15/72	Pittsburgh
LALONDE, Christian	6-1	210	L	LaSalle, Que.	5/3/66	Muskegon
LAYLIN, Cory	5-10	170	L	Minneapolis, MN	1/24/70	U. of Minnesota
LEACH, Jamie	6-1	205	R	Winnipeg, Man.	8/25/69	Pittsburgh-Muskegon
LEMIEUX, Mario	6-4	210	R	Montreal, Que.	10/5/65	Pittsburgh
LONEY, Troy	6-3	210	L	Bow Island, Alta.	9/21/63	Pittsburgh
MAJOR, Mark	6-3	223	L	Toronto, Ont.	3/20/70	Muskegon
McEACHERN, Shawn	6-0	190	L	Waltham, MA	2/28/69	US Olympic-Pittsburgh
MICK, Troy	5-11	192	L	Burnaby, B.C.	3/30/69	Knoxville
MITROVIC, Savo	5-11	185	R	Toronto, Ont.	2/4/69	New Hampshire
MULLEN, Joe	5-9	180	R	New York, NY	2/25/57	Pittsburgh
NASLUND, Markus	5-11	176	L	Ornskoldsuik, Sweden	7/30/73	MoDo
NEEDHAM, Mike	5-10	185	R	Calgary, Alta.	4/4/70	Muskegon
PATTERSON, Ed	6-2	210	R	Delta, B.C.	11/14/72	Kamloops
PRIESTLAY, Ken	5-10	190	L	Richmond, B.C.	8/24/67	Pittsburgh-Muskegon
SMART, Jason	6-4	212	L	Prince George, B.C.	1/23/70	Muskegon
SMITH, Sandy	5-11	200	R	Brainerd, MN	10/23/67	Muskegon
STEVENS, Kevin	6-3	215	L	Brockton, MA	4/15/65	Pittsburgh
STRAKA, Martin	5-10	178	L	Plzen, Czech.	9/3/72	Plzen
TOCCHET, Rick	6-0	205	R	Scarborough, Ont.	4/9/64	Philadelphia-Pittsburgh
TROTTIER, Bryan	5-11	195	L	Val Marie, Sask.	7/17/56	Pittsburgh
DEFENSEMEN						
ANDRUSAK, Greg	6-1	183	R	Cranbrook, B.C.	11/14/69	Minn.-Duluth
BRUININKS, Brian	6-0	180	R	St. Paul, MN	3/30/70	Colorado
CHYCHRUN, Jeff	6-4	215	R	LaSalle, Que.	5/3/66	Los Angeles-Pittsburgh
DYCK, Paul	6-1	192	L	Steinbach, Man.	4/15/71	Muskegon
FOGARTY, Bryan	6-2	198	L	Brantford, Ont.	6/11/69	Quebec-Halifax-New Haven-Muskegon
HEWARD, Jamie	6-2	194	R	Regina, Sask.	3/30/71	Muskegon
JENNINGS, Grant	6-3	200	L	Hudson Bay, Sask.	5/5/65	Pittsburgh
LAUS, Paul	6-1	212	R	Beamsville, Ont.	9/26/70	Muskegon
MELANSON, Robert	6-1	202	L	Antigonish, N.S.	3/5/71	Muskegon-Knoxville
MURPHY, Larry	6-1	210	R	Scarborough, Ont.	3/8/61	Pittsburgh
NELSON, Todd	6-0	201	L	Prince Albert, Sask.	5/11/69	Pittsburgh-Muskegon
PAEK, Jim	6-1	194	L	Seoul, Korea	4/7/67	Pittsburgh
PEACOCK, Shane	5-10	198	R	Winterburn, Alta.	7/7/73	Lethbridge
SAMUELSSON, Kjell	6-6	235	R	Tyngsryd, Sweden	10/18/58	Philadelphia-Pittsburgh
SAMUELSSON, Ulf	6-1	195	L	Fagersta, Sweden	3/26/64	Pittsburgh
STANTON, Paul	6-0	193	R	Boston, MA	6/22/67	Pittsburgh
THIESSEN, Travis	6-3	203	L	N. Battleford, Sask.	7/11/72	Moose Jaw

GOALTENDERS	HT	WT	C	Place of Birth	Date	1991-92 Club
BARRASSO, Tom	6-3	212	R	Boston, MA	3/31/65	Pittsburgh
DOPSON, Rob	6-0	200	L	Smith Falls, Ont.	8/21/67	Muskegon
RACINE, Bruce	6-0	178	L	Cornwall, Ont.	8/9/66	Muskegon
WREGGET, Ken	6-1	195	L	Brandon, Man.	3/25/64	Philadelphia-Pittsburgh

General Managers' History

Jack Riley, 1967-68 to 1969-70; Leonard "Red" Kelly, 1970-71 to 1971-72; Jack Riley, 1972-73 to 1973-74; Jack Button, 1974-75; Wren A. Blair, 1975-76 to 1976-77; Baz Bastien, 1977-78 to 1982-83; Ed Johnston, 1983-84 to 1987-88; Tony Esposito, 1988-89; Tony Esposito and Craig Patrick, 1989-90; Craig Patrick, 1990-91 to date.

Coaching History

George Sullivan, 1967-68 to 1968-69; Red Kelly, 1969-70 to 1971-72; Red Kelly and Ken Schinkel, 1972-73; Ken Schinkel and Marc Boileau, 1973-74; Marc Boileau, 1974-75; Marc Boileau and Ken Schinkel, 1975-76; Ken Schinkel, 1976-77; John Wilson, 1977-78 to 1979-80; Eddie Johnston, 1980-81 to 1982-83; Lou Angotti, 1983-84; Bob Berry, 1984-85 to 1986-87; Pierre Creamer, 1987-88; Gene Ubriaco, 1988-89; Gene Ubriaco and Craig Patrick, 1989-90. Bob Johnson, 1990-91 to 1991-92; Scotty Bowman, 1991-92.

1991-92 Scoring

Regular Season

Pos	#.	Player	Team	GP	G	A	Pts	+/–	PIM	PP	SH	GW	GT	S	%
C	66	Mario Lemieux	PIT	64	44	87	131	27	94	12	4	5	1	249	17.7
L	25	Kevin Stevens	PIT	80	54	69	123	8	254	19	0	4	0	325	16.6
R	7	Joe Mullen	PIT	77	42	45	87	12	30	14	0	4	1	226	18.6
D	55	Larry Murphy	PIT	77	21	56	77	33	48	7	2	3	0	206	10.2
R	68	Jaromir Jagr	PIT	70	32	37	69	12	34	4	0	4	0	194	16.5
R	92	Rick Tocchet	PHI	42	13	16	29	3	102	4	0	1	1	107	12.1
			PIT	19	14	16	30	12	49	4	1	1	0	59	23.7
			TOTAL	61	27	32	59	15	151	8	1	2	1	166	16.3
C	10	Ron Francis	PIT	70	21	33	54	7–	30	5	1	2	1	121	17.4
L	12	Bob Errey	PIT	78	19	16	35	1	119	0	3	1	0	122	15.6
C	19	Bryan Trottier	PIT	63	11	18	29	11–	54	3	1	0	2	102	10.8
L	29	Phil Bourque	PIT	58	10	16	26	6–	58	0	1	3	0	51	19.6
L	24	Troy Loney	PIT	76	10	16	26	5–	127	0	0	1	0	94	10.6
D	28	Gordie Roberts	PIT	73	2	22	24	19	87	1	0	1	0	29	6.9
D	23	Kjell Samuelsson	PHI	54	4	9	13	1	76	0	0	0	0	63	6.3
			PIT	20	1	2	3	0	34	0	0	1	0	28	3.6
			TOTAL	74	5	11	16	1	110	0	0	1	0	91	5.5
C	38	Jiri Hrdina	PIT	56	3	13	16	4	16	0	0	1	0	51	5.9
D	5	Ulf Samuelsson	PIT	62	1	14	15	2	206	1	0	1	0	75	1.3
C	18	Ken Priestlay	PIT	49	2	8	10	5	4	0	0	0	0	20	10.0
D	22	Paul Stanton	PIT	54	2	8	10	8–	62	0	0	0	0	70	2.9
R	20	Jamie Leach	PIT	38	5	4	9	2–	8	1	0	0	0	32	15.6
D	3	Grant Jennings	PIT	53	4	5	9	1–	104	0	2	2	0	35	11.4
D	2*	Jim Paek	PIT	49	1	7	8	0	36	0	0	0	0	33	3.0
D	32	Peter Taglianetti	PIT	44	1	3	4	7	57	0	0	0	0	23	4.3
C	15*	Shawn McEachern	PIT	15	0	4	4	1	0	0	0	0	0	14	.0
D	6	Jeff Chychrun	L.A.	26	0	3	3	4–	76	0	0	0	0	22	.0
			PIT	17	0	1	1	8–	35	0	0	0	0	4	.0
			TOTAL	43	0	4	4	12–	111	0	0	0	0	26	.0
G	35	Tom Barrasso	PIT	57	0	4	4	0	30	0	0	0	0	0	.0
G	31	Ken Wregget	PHI	23	0	2	2	0	0	0	0	0	0	0	.0
			PIT	9	0	0	0	0	2	0	0	0	0	0	.0
			TOTAL	32	0	2	2	0	2	0	0	0	0	0	.0
D	4	Gord Dineen	PIT	1	0	0	0	2–	0	0	0	0	0	0	.0
C	45*	Glen Mulvenna	PIT	1	0	0	0	1–	2	0	0	0	0	0	.0
D	44*	Todd Nelson	PIT	1	0	0	0	0	0	0	0	0	0	0	.0
L	43*	Jeff Daniels	PIT	2	0	0	0	0	0	0	0	0	0	0	.0
G	1	Wendell Young	PIT	18	0	0	0	0	0	0	0	0	0	0	.0
R	16	Jay Caufield	PIT	50	0	0	0	6–	175	0	0	0	0	16	.0

Goaltending

No.	Goaltender	GPI	Mins	Avg	W	L	T	EN	SO	GA	SA	S%
35	Tom Barrasso	57	3329	3.53	25	22	9	2	1	196	1702	.885
1	Wendell Young	18	838	3.79	7	6	0	4	0	53	476	.889
31	Ken Wregget	9	448	4.15	5	3	0	2	0	31	202	.847
40	Frank Pietrangelo	5	225	5.33	2	1	0	0	0	20	130	.846
	Totals	**80**	**4854**	**3.81**	**39**	**32**	**9**	**8**	**1**	**308**	**2518**	**.878**

Playoffs

Pos	#	Player	Team	GP	G	A	Pts	+/–	PIM	PP	SH	GW	GT	S	%
C	66	Mario Lemieux	PIT	15	16	18	34	6	2	8	2	5	0	69	23.2
L	25	Kevin Stevens	PIT	21	13	15	28	2	28	4	0	3	0	86	15.1
C	10	Ron Francis	PIT	21	8	19	27	8	6	2	0	2	1	58	13.8
R	68	Jaromir Jagr	PIT	21	11	13	24	4	6	2	0	4	1	59	18.6
R	92	Rick Tocchet	PIT	14	6	13	19	0	24	3	0	1	0	30	20.0
D	55	Larry Murphy	PIT	21	6	10	16	4–	19	3	0	1	0	59	10.2
L	24	Troy Loney	PIT	21	4	5	9	1	32	0	0	0	0	32	12.5
C	15*	Shawn McEachern	PIT	19	2	7	9	6	4	0	0	0	0	36	5.6
D	22	Paul Stanton	PIT	21	1	7	8	6	42	0	0	0	0	24	4.2
C	19	Bryan Trottier	PIT	21	4	3	7	0	8	0	0	0	0	30	13.3
L	29	Phil Bourque	PIT	21	3	4	7	1–	25	2	0	0	0	32	9.4
R	7	Joe Mullen	PIT	9	3	1	4	4–	4	1	0	0	0	21	14.3
R	14	Jock Callender	PIT	12	1	3	4	0	2	0	0	0	0	9	11.1
D	2*	Jim Paek	PIT	19	0	4	4	10	6	0	0	0	0	7	.0
L	12	Bob Errey	PIT	14	3	0	3	0	10	0	1	0	0	16	18.8
D	23	Kjell Samuelsson	PIT	15	0	3	3	6	12	0	0	0	0	7	.0
L	34	Dave Michayluk	PIT	7	1	1	2	1	0	0	0	0	0	1	100.0
D	28	Gordie Roberts	PIT	19	0	2	2	1–	32	0	0	0	0	8	.0
G	35	Tom Barrasso	PIT	21	0	2	2	0	4	0	0	0	0	0	.0
C	38	Jiri Hrdina	PIT	21	0	2	2	6–	16	0	0	0	0	13	.0
D	5	Ulf Samuelsson	PIT	21	0	2	2	7	39	0	0	0	0	12	.0
R	45*	Mike Needham	PIT	5	1	0	1	0	2	0	0	0	0	2	50.0
G	31	Ken Wregget	PIT	1	0	0	0	0	0	0	0	0	0	0	.0
R	16	Jay Caufield	PIT	5	0	0	0	0	2	0	0	0	0	1	.0
D	3	Grant Jennings	PIT	10	0	0	0	9–	12	0	0	0	0	12	.0

Goaltending

No.	Goaltender	GPI	Mins	Avg	W	L	EN	SO	GA	SA	S%
35	Tom Barrasso	21	1233	2.82	16	5	1	1	58	622	.907
31	Ken Wregget	1	40	6.00	0	0	0	0	4	16	.750
	Totals	**21**	**1274**	**2.97**	**16**	**5**	**1**	**1**	**63**	**639**	**.901**

Captains' History

Ab McDonald, 1967-68; no captain, 1968-69 to 1972-73; Ron Schock, 1973-74 to 1976-77; Jean Pronovost, 1977-78; Orest Kindrachuk, 1978-79 to 1980-81; Randy Carlyle, 1981-82 to 1983-84; Mike Bullard, 1984-85, 1985-86; Mike Bullard and Terry Ruskowski, 1986-87; Dan Frawley and Mario Lemieux, 1987-88; Mario Lemieux, 1988-89 to date.

Retired Numbers

21 Michel Briere 1969-1970

Club Records

Team

(Figures in brackets for season records are games played; records for fewest points, wins, ties, losses, goals, goals against are for 70 or more games)

Record		
Most Points	**89**	1974-75 (80)
Most Wins	**41**	1990-91 (80)
Most Ties	**20**	1970-71 (78)
Most Losses	**58**	1983-84 (80)
Most Goals	**347**	1988-89 (80)
Most Goals Against	**394**	1982-83 (80)
Fewest Points	**38**	1983-84 (80)
Fewest Wins	**16**	1983-84 (80)
Fewest Ties	**5**	1984-85 (80)
Fewest Losses	**28**	1974-75 (80)
Fewest Goals	**182**	1969-70 (76)
Fewest Goals Against	**216**	1967-68 (74)
Longest Winning Streak		
Over-all	**7**	Oct. 9- Oct. 22/86
Home	**11**	Jan. 5- Mar. 7/91
Away	**5**	Dec. 13- Dec. 29/91
Longest Undefeated Streak		
Over-all	**11**	Feb. 7-28/76 (7 wins, 4 ties)
Home	**20**	Nov. 30/74- Feb. 22/75 (12 wins, 8 ties)
Away	**7**	Mar. 13-27/79 (5 wins, 2 ties)
Longest Losing Streak		
Over-all	**11**	Jan. 22/83- Feb. 10/83
Home	**7**	Oct. 8-29/83
Away	**18**	Dec. 23/82- Mar. 4/83
Longest Winless Streak		
Over-all	**18**	Jan. 2- Feb. 10/83 (17 losses, 1 tie)
Home	**11**	Oct. 8- Nov. 19/83 (9 losses, 2 ties)
Away	**18**	Oct. 25/70- Jan. 14/71 (11 losses, 7 ties) Dec. 23/82- Mar. 4/83 (18 losses)
Most Shutouts, Season	**6**	1967-68 (74) 1976-77 (80)
Most PIM, Season	***2,670**	1988-89 (80)
Most Goals, Game	**12**	Mar. 15/75 (Wash. 1 at Pit. 12) Dec. 26/91 (Tor. 1 at Pit. 12)

Individual

Record		
Most Seasons	**11**	Rick Kehoe
Most Games	**753**	Jean Pronovost
Most Goals, Career	**408**	Mario Lemieux
Most Assists, Career	**606**	Mario Lemieux
Most Points, Career	**1014**	Mario Lemieux (408 goals, 606 assists)
Most PIM, Career	**959**	Rod Buskas
Most Shutouts, Career	**11**	Les Binkley
Longest Consecutive Games Streak	**320**	Ron Schock (Oct. 24/73-Apr. 3/77)
Most Goals, Season	**85**	Mario Lemieux (1988-89)
Most Assists, Season	**114**	Mario Lemieux (1988-89)
Most Points, Season	**199**	Mario Lemieux (1988-89)
Most PIM, Season	**409**	Paul Baxter (1981-82)
Most Points, Defenseman, Season	**113**	Paul Coffey (1988-89) (30 goals, 83 assists)
Most Points, Center, Season	**199**	Mario Lemieux (1988-89) (85 goals, 114 assists)
Most Points, Right Wing, Season	**115**	Rob Brown (1988-89) (49 goals, 66 assists)
Most Points, Left Wing, Season	***123**	Kevin Stevens (1991-92) (54 goals, 69 assists)
Most Points, Rookie, Season	**100**	Mario Lemieux (1984-85) (43 goals, 57 assists)
Most Shutouts, Season	**6**	Les Binkley (1967-68)
Most Goals, Game	**5**	Mario Lemieux (Dec. 31/88)
Most Assists, Game	**6**	Ron Stackhouse (Mar. 8/75) Greg Malone (Nov. 28/79) Mario Lemieux (Oct. 15/88)
Most Points, Game	**8**	Mario Lemieux (Oct. 15/88, Dec. 31/88)

* NHL Record.

All-time Record vs. Other Clubs

Regular Season

	At Home							On Road							Total						
	GP	W	L	T	GF	GA	PTS	GP	W	L	T	GF	GA	PTS	GP	W	L	T	GF	GA	PTS
Boston	51	14	26	11	160	206	39	52	7	39	6	148	244	20	103	21	65	17	308	450	59
Buffalo	44	17	15	12	169	158	46	43	7	22	14	117	196	28	87	24	37	26	286	354	74
Calgary	36	17	10	9	134	121	43	36	8	21	7	107	155	23	72	25	31	16	241	276	66
Chicago	49	22	22	5	173	166	49	50	8	33	9	141	210	25	99	30	55	14	314	376	74
Detroit	55	38	13	4	242	156	80	56	10	35	11	158	221	31	111	48	48	15	400	377	111
Edmonton	21	9	11	1	82	102	19	20	3	16	1	70	114	7	41	12	27	2	152	216	26
Hartford	21	9	9	3	92	91	21	20	7	12	1	78	92	15	41	16	21	4	170	183	36
Los Angeles	62	35	19	8	235	198	78	60	14	38	8	155	232	36	122	49	57	16	390	430	114
Minnesota	54	34	15	5	210	143	73	55	19	31	5	186	214	43	109	53	46	10	396	357	116
Montreal	55	17	29	9	165	207	43	56	4	47	5	135	289	13	111	21	76	14	300	496	56
New Jersey	51	30	18	3	224	189	63	50	16	26	8	173	198	40	101	46	44	11	397	387	103
NY Islanders	58	27	20	11	227	203	65	58	17	33	8	188	253	42	116	44	53	19	415	456	107
NY Rangers	72	26	35	11	257	270	63	72	27	38	7	248	302	61	144	53	73	18	505	572	124
Philadelphia	77	31	31	15	249	249	77	78	12	59	7	195	347	31	155	43	90	22	444	596	108
Quebec	21	12	6	3	95	85	27	20	10	10	0	80	90	20	41	22	16	3	175	175	47
St. Louis	54	24	19	11	198	165	59	55	13	37	5	147	219	31	109	37	56	16	345	384	90
San Jose	1	1	0	0	10	2	2	2	2	0	0	15	3	4	3	3	0	0	25	5	6
Toronto	52	28	19	5	218	169	61	51	17	24	10	172	212	44	103	45	43	15	390	381	105
Vancouver	41	26	8	7	184	139	59	41	18	20	3	157	156	39	82	44	28	10	341	295	98
Washington	58	28	24	6	232	202	62	60	24	32	4	231	269	52	118	52	56	10	463	471	114
Winnipeg	21	14	7	0	86	64	28	20	11	8	1	76	77	23	41	25	15	1	162	141	51
Defunct Clubs	35	22	6	7	148	93	51	34	13	10	11	108	101	37	69	35	16	18	256	194	88
Totals	**989**	**481**	**362**	**146**	**3790**	**3378**	**1108**	**989**	**267**	**591**	**131**	**3085**	**4194**	**665**	**1978**	**748**	**953**	**277**	**6875**	**7572**	**1773**

Playoffs

	Series	W	L	GP	W	L	T	GF	GA	Last Mtg.	Round	Result
Boston	4	2	2	19	10	9	0	67	62	1992	CF	W 4-0
Buffalo	1	1	0	3	2	1	0	9	9	1979	PR	W 2-1
Chicago	2	1	1	8	4	4	0	23	24	1992	F	W 4-0
Minnesota	1	1	0	6	4	2	0	28	16	1991	F	W 4-2
New Jersey	1	1	0	7	4	3	0	25	17	1991	DSF	W 4-3
NY Islanders	2	0	2	12	5	7	0	31	43	1982	DSF	L 2-3
NY Rangers	2	2	0	10	8	2	0	43	30	1992	DF	W 4-2
Philadelphia	1	0	1	7	3	4	0	24	31	1989	DF	L 3-4
St. Louis	3	1	2	13	6	7	0	40	45	1981	PR	L 2-3
Toronto	2	0	2	6	2	4	0	13	21	1977	PR	L 1-2
Washington	2	2	0	12	8	4	0	44	40	1992	DSF	W 4-3
Defunct Clubs	1	1	0	4	4	0	0	13	6			
Totals	**22**	**12**	**10**	**107**	**60**	**47**	**0**	**360**	**344**			

Playoff Results 1992-88

Year	Round	Opponent	Result	GF	GA
1992	**F**	**Chicago**	**W 4-0**	**15**	**10**
	CF	Boston	W 4-0	19	7
	DF	NY Rangers	W 4-2	24	19
	DSF	Washington	W 4-3	25	27
1991	**F**	**Minnesota**	**W 4-2**	**28**	**16**
	CF	Boston	W 4-2	27	18
	DF	Washington	W 4-1	19	13
	DSF	New Jersey	W 4-3	25	17
1989	DF	Philadelphia	L 3-4	24	31
	DSF	NY Rangers	W 4-0	19	11

Abbreviations: Round: F – Final; **CF** – conference final; **DF** – division final; **DSF** – division semi-final; **SF** – semi-final; **QF** – quarter-final; **PR** – preliminary round. **GA** – goals against; **GF** – goals for.

1991-92 Results

Home			Away		
Oct. 6	Philadelphia*	2-2	**Oct.** 4	Buffalo	5-4
17	NY Islanders	8-5	10	Philadelphia	6-3
19	NY Rangers	4-5	12	New Jersey*	1-4
22	Chicago	4-4	15	NY Islanders	7-6
24	New Jersey	2-4	26	Montreal	1-4
29	Washington	0-8	**Nov.** 8	Winnipeg	3-1
31	Minnesota	8-1	9	Minnesota	3-2
Nov. 2	Hartford	5-6	11	NY Rangers	1-3
5	Boston	5-5	15	Washington	2-6
13	Edmonton	5-4	18	Quebec	7-3
20	Philadelphia	5-2	29	Philadelphia*	9-3
23	NY Islanders	2-2	**Dec.** 3	Edmonton	3-5
27	New Jersey	8-4	5	San Jose	8-0
30	Philadelphia	5-1	7	St Louis	1-6
Dec. 10	NY Rangers	5-3	13	New Jersey	4-3
14	Washington	2-7	19	Boston	6-4
17	San Jose	10-2	23	NY Islanders	6-3
21	NY Rangers	5-7	28	Washington	6-2
26	Toronto	12-1	29	NY Rangers	6-3
31	New Jersey	4-7	**Jan.** 2	New Jersey	0-4
Jan. 4	Winnipeg*	3-2	10	Calgary	5-7
7	Los Angeles	2-5	12	Vancouver*	4-3
23	Buffalo	4-5	16	Detroit	3-3
28	Winnipeg	0-4	25	NY Islanders*	5-3
30	NY Islanders	5-8	26	Washington*	4-6
Feb. 1	St Louis	4-1	**Feb.** 5	NY Rangers	3-4
3	Detroit	4-4	9	Boston*	3-6
8	Los Angeles*	3-4	15	Minnesota	2-5
18	Toronto	7-1	16	Philadelphia	3-3
20	Quebec	4-4	22	Montreal	1-2
27	Hartford	4-8	25	Washington	3-5
29	Buffalo*	5-2	**Mar.** 3	Calgary	6-3
Mar. 10	Calgary	5-2	6	San Jose	7-3
12	NY Islanders	6-4	7	Los Angeles	3-5
17	Edmonton	6-5	14	Toronto	3-6
19	Quebec	6-3	15	Chicago	4-3
26	Vancouver	7-3	22	Hartford	2-2
28	Montreal	6-3	24	Detroit	3-4
31	Philadelphia	6-5	**Apr.** 2	NY Rangers	1-7
Apr. 4	Washington*	4-1	5	New Jersey	1-5

*Denotes afternoon game

Entry Draft Selections 1992-78

1992
Pick
19 Martin Straka
43 Marc Hussey
67 Travis Thiessen
91 Todd Klassen
115 Philipp De Rouville
139 Artem Kopot
163 Jan Alinc
187 Fran Bussey
211 Brian Bonin
235 Brian Callahan

1991
Pick
16 Markus Naslund
38 Rusty Fitzgerald
60 Shane Peacock
82 Joe Tamminen
104 Robert Melanson
126 Brian Clifford
148 Ed Patterson
170 Peter McLaughlin
192 Jeff Lembke
214 Chris Tok
236 Paul Dyck
258 Pasi Huura

1990
Pick
5 Jaromir Jagr
61 Joe Dziedzic
68 Chris Tamer
89 Brian Farrell
107 Ian Moran
110 Denis Casey
130 Mika Valila
131 Ken Plaquin
145 Pat Neaton
152 Petteri Koskimaki
173 Ladislav Karabin
194 Timothy Fingerhut
215 Michael Thompson
236 Brian Bruininks

1989
Pick
16 Jamie Heward
37 Paul Laus
58 John Brill
79 Todd Nelson
100 Tom Nevers
121 Mike Markovich
126 Mike Needham
142 Patrick Schafhauser
163 Dave Shute
184 Andrew Wolf
205 Greg Hagen
226 Scott Farrell
247 Jason Smart

1988
Pick
4 Darrin Shannon
25 Mark Major
62 Daniel Gauthier
67 Mark Recchi
88 Greg Andrusak
130 Troy Mick
151 Jeff Blaeser
172 Rob Gaudreau
193 Donald Pancoe
214 Cory Laylin
235 Darren Stolk

1987
Pick
5 Chris Joseph
26 Richard Tabaracci
47 Jamie Leach
68 Risto Kurkinen
89 Jeff Waver
110 Shawn McEachern
131 Jim Bodden
152 Jiri Kucera
173 Jack MacDougall
194 Daryn McBride
215 Mark Carlson
236 Ake Lilljebjorn

1986
Pick
4 Zarley Zalapski
25 Dave Capuano
46 Brad Aitken
67 Rob Brown
88 Sandy Smith
109 Jeff Daniels
130 Doug Hobson
151 Steve Rohlik
172 Dave McLlwain
193 Kelly Cain
214 Stan Drulia
235 Rob Wilson

1985
Pick
2 Craig Simpson
23 Lee Giffin
58 Bruce Racine
86 Steve Gotaas
107 Kevin Clemens
114 Stuart Marston
128 Steve Titus
149 Paul Stanton
170 Jim Paek
191 Steve Shaunessy
212 Doug Greschuk
233 Gregory Choules

1984
Pick
1 Mario Lemieux
9 Doug Bodger
16 Roger Belanger
64 Mark Teevens
85 Arto Javanainen
127 Tom Ryan
169 John Del Col
189 Steve Hurt
210 Jim Steen
230 Mark Ziliotto

1983
Pick
15 Bob Errey
22 Todd Charlesworth
58 Mike Rowe
63 Frank Pietrangelo
103 Patrick Emond
123 Paul Ames
163 Marty Ketola
183 Alec Haidy
203 Garth Hildebrand
223 Dave Goertz

1982
Pick
10 Rich Sutter
38 Tim Hrynewich
52 Troy Loney
94 Grant Sasser
136 Grant Couture
157 Peter Derksen
178 Greg Gravel
199 Stu Wenaas
220 Chris McCauley
241 Stan Bautch

1981
Pick
28 Steve Gatzos
49 Tom Thornbury
70 Norm Schmidt
109 Paul Edwards
112 Rod Buskas
133 Geoff Wilson
154 Mitch Lamoureux
175 Dean Defazio
196 David Hannan

1980
Pick
9 Mike Bullard
51 Randy Boyd
72 Tony Feltrin
93 Doug Shedden
114 Pat Graham
156 Robert Geale
177 Brian Lundberg
198 Steve McKenzie

1979
Pick
31 Paul Marshall
52 Bennett Wolf
73 Brian Cross
94 Nick Ricci
115 Marc Chorney

1978
Pick
25 Mike Meeker
61 Shane Pearsall
75 Rob Garner

Club Directory

Civic Arena
Pittsburgh, PA 15219
Phone **412/642-1800**
FAX 412/261-0382
Capacity: 16,164

Ownership	Howard Baldwin, Morris Belzberg, Thomas Ruta
President and Governor	Howard Baldwin
Executive Vice-President & General Manager	Craig Patrick
Executive Vice-President & Chief Financial Officer	Donn Patton
Director of Player Personnel	"Scotty" Bowman
Head Coach	TBA
Assistant Coaches	Rick Kehoe, Pierre McGuire, Rick Paterson, Barry Smith
Goaltending Coach and Scout	Gilles Meloche
Strength and Conditioning Coach	John Welday
Equipment Manager	Steve Latin
Trainer	Clark "Corky" Osburn
Assistant Equipment Manager	Kevin Greenway
Scouting Staff	Greg Malone, Les Binkley, John Gill, Charlie Hodge, Ralph Cox
Team Assistant	Howard Baldwin, Jr.
Executive Secretary	Tracey Botsford
Senior Vice-President, Marketing & Public Relations	Bill Barnes
General Counsel	J. Paul Martha
Vice-President, Public & Community Relations	TBA
Vice-President, Merchandising	Bill Cox
Vice-President, Sales & Communications	Bill Strong
Controller	Kevin Hart
Accounting Staff	Eric Brandenberg, Amy Novak, Barb Manion, Rick Patterson
Director of Public Relations	Cindy Himes
Director of Media Relations	Harry Sanders
Director of Ticket Sales	Jeff Mercer
Director of Youth Hockey Development	George Kirk
Director of Advertising Sales	Dave Peart
Director of Publications	Emily Nordstrom
Director of Merchandising	Tim Carey
Director of Promotions	Jill Thomas
General Manager, Choice Seat	Mark Watkins
Box Office Manager	Carol Coulson
Director of Promotions	Jill Thomas
Executive Secretaries	Elaine Heufelder, Paula Nichols
Director of Communications & Sales Service	Dana Young
Sales Representative	Chris Clark
Team Secretary	Christine Span
Marketing Representatives	Terri Dobos Young, Steve Swetcha, Chuck Saller
Choice Seat Staff	Julie Kapphee, Tony Miller, Tim Porco, Augie Manfredo, Edna Greeley
Merchandising Representatives	Louise Stock, Rob Redneys
Team Physician	Dr. Charles Burke
Team Dentists	Dr. Raymond Rainka, Dr. Ronald Linaburg, Dr. David Donatelli

General Manager

PATRICK, CRAIG
General Manager, Pittsburgh Penguins. Born in Detroit, MI, May 20, 1946.

Craig Patrick is the latest member of hockey's royal family to have his name inscribed on the Stanley Cup. Appointed general manager of the Penguins on December 5, 1989, Patrick laid the groundwork for Pittsburgh's two successful Stanley Cup marches through shrewd acquisitions and drafts; his trades for Ulf Samuelsson, Ron Francis, Rick Tocchet and Ken Wregget, his signing of free agent Bryan Trottier and the drafting of Jaromir Jagr are all moves considered crucial to Pittsburgh's Stanley Cup win. Patrick also hired Coach Bob Johnson, who piloted the Penguins during their first championship run in 1991.

A 1969 graduate of the University of Denver, Patrick was captain of the Pioneers' NCAA Championship hockey team that year. He returned to his alma mater in 1986 where he served as director of athletics and recreation for two years. Patrick served as administrative assistant to the president of the Amateur Hockey Association of the United States in 1980 and as an assistant coach/assistant general manager for the 1980 gold-medal winning U.S. Olympic hockey team. Before pursuing a coaching career, Patrick played professional hockey with Washington, Kansas City, St. Louis, Minnesota and California from 1971-79. In eight seasons, Patrick tallied 163 points (72-91-163) in 401 games.

NHL Coaching Record

		Regular Season					Playoffs			
Season	**Team**	**Games**	**W**	**L**	**T**	**%**	**Games**	**W**	**L**	**%**
1980-81	NY Rangers	59	26	23	10	.525	14	7	7	.500
1984-85	NY Rangers	35	11	22	2	.343	3	0	3	.000
1989-90	Pittsburgh	54	22	26	6	.463	....	....	....	....
	NHL Totals	**148**	**59**	**71**	**18**	**.459**	**17**	**7**	**10**	**.412**

Quebec Nordiques

1991-92 Results: 20W-48L-12T 52PTS. Fifth, Adams Division

Year-by-Year Record

Season	Home GP	Home W	Home L	Home T	Road W	Road L	Road T	Overall W	Overall L	Overall T	GF	GA	Pts.	Finished	Playoff Result
1991-92	80	18	19	3	2	29	9	20	48	12	255	318	52	5th, Adams Div.	Out of Playoffs
1990-91	80	9	23	8	7	27	6	16	50	14	236	354	46	5th, Adams Div.	Out of Playoffs
1989-90	80	8	26	6	4	35	1	12	61	7	240	407	31	5th, Adams Div.	Out of Playoffs
1988-89	80	16	20	4	11	26	3	27	46	7	269	342	61	5th, Adams Div.	Out of Playoffs
1987-88	80	15	23	2	17	20	3	32	43	5	271	306	69	5th, Adams Div.	Out of Playoffs
1986-87	80	20	13	7	11	26	3	31	39	10	267	276	72	4th, Adams Div.	Lost Div. Final
1985-86	80	23	13	4	20	18	2	43	31	6	330	289	92	1st, Adams Div.	Lost Div. Semi-Final
1984-85	80	24	12	4	17	18	5	41	30	9	323	275	91	2nd, Adams Div.	Lost Conf. Championship
1983-84	80	24	11	5	18	17	5	42	28	10	360	278	94	3th, Adams Div.	Lost Div. Final
1982-83	80	23	10	7	11	24	5	34	34	12	343	336	80	4th, Adams Div.	Lost Div. Semi-Final
1981-82	80	24	13	3	9	18	13	33	31	16	356	345	82	4th, Adams Div.	Lost Conf. Championship
1980-81	80	18	11	11	12	21	7	30	32	18	314	318	78	4th, Adams Div.	Lost Prelim. Round
1979-80	80	17	16	7	8	28	4	25	44	11	248	313	61	5th, Adams Div.	Out of Playoffs

Schedule

Home		Away	
Oct.	Sat. 10 Ottawa	**Oct.**	Thur. 8 Buffalo
	Tues. 13 Philadelphia		Thur. 15 Detroit
	Sat. 17 St Louis		Wed. 21 St Louis
	Tues. 27 Tampa Bay		Thur. 22 Minnesota
	Sat. 31 Winnipeg		Sat. 24 Tampa Bay
Nov.	Sat. 7 Chicago*		Thur. 29 NY Rangers
	Sun. 8 Calgary*	**Nov.**	Tues. 3 Hartford
	Sat. 14 NY Rangers		Thur. 5 Boston
	Tues. 17 Toronto		Wed. 11 Ottawa
	(at Hamilton)		Thur. 12 Pittsburgh
	Thur. 19 Montreal		Wed. 25 Buffalo
	Sat. 21 Hartford*		Thur. 26 Toronto
	Sun. 22 Washington*	**Dec.**	Thur. 3 Philadelphia
	Sat. 28 New Jersey		Thur. 10 Los Angeles
	Mon. 30 Boston		Sat. 12 San Jose
Dec.	Sat. 5 Minnesota		Sun. 13 Vancouver
	Mon. 7 Buffalo		Wed. 16 Montreal
	Thur. 17 Montreal		Mon. 21 Pittsburgh
	Sun. 20 NY Islanders*		Sun. 27 Ottawa
	Sat. 26 Ottawa		Thur. 31 Hartford
	Tues. 29 New Jersey	**Jan.**	Tues. 5 NY Islanders
Jan.	Sat. 2 Detroit		Thur. 7 Boston
	Thur. 14 Montreal		Sat. 9 Hartford
	Sat. 16 San Jose		Tues. 19 Ottawa
	Sat. 23 Buffalo		Fri. 22 Buffalo
	Tues. 26 Boston		Thur. 28 Philadelphia
Feb.	Tues. 2 Los Angeles		Fri. 29 Washington
	Wed. 3 Boston	**Feb.**	Fri. 12 Calgary
	Tues. 9 Vancouver		Sun. 14 Edmonton*
	Wed. 17 Ottawa		Sat. 20 Tampa Bay
	Tues. 23 Edmonton		(at Halifax)
	Thur. 25 NY Islanders		Sun. 21 New Jersey
	Sat. 27 Hartford		Sun. 28 Ottawa
Mar.	Sat. 6 NY Rangers	**Mar.**	Tues. 2 Winnipeg
	Mon. 8 Hartford		Thur. 4 Chicago
	Wed. 10 Buffalo		Sat. 13 Montreal
	Mon. 15 Toronto		Sat. 20 New Jersey*
	Thur. 18 Montreal		Tues. 23 Washington
	Sat. 27 Philadelphia*		Sun. 28 NY Rangers
Apr.	Sat. 3 Pittsburgh		Wed. 31 Montreal
	Tues. 6 Boston	**Apr.**	Thur. 1 Ottawa
	Sat. 10 Hartford		Thur. 8 Boston
	Tues. 13 Ottawa		Sun. 11 Buffalo

* Denotes afternoon game.

Home Starting Times:
All Games .... 7:35 p.m.
Except Matinees .... 2:05 p.m.

Franchise date: June 22, 1979

14th NHL Season

Mats Sundin finished second in team scoring in 1991-92, amassing 33 goals and 43 assists in 80 games for Quebec.

1992-93 Player Personnel

FORWARDS	HT	WT	S	Place of Birth	Date	1991-92 Club
ANDERSSON, Niclas	5-9	175	L	Kungalv, Sweden	5/20/71	Halifax
BUTTERS, Mike	6-3	220	R	St. Boniface, Man.	5/12/66	Halifax-New Haven-Adirondack-Greensboro
CAVALLINI, Gino	6-1	215	L	Toronto, Ont.	11/24/62	Québec-St. Louis
CHARBONNEAU, Stéphane	6-2	195	R	Ste-Adèle, Qué.	6/27/70	Québec-Halifax
CHASSÉ, Denis	6-2	190	R	Montréal, Qué.	2/7/70	Halifax
COOK, Brian	6-2	205	L	Waterloo, IA	1/2/67	Louisville-Greensboro
CORBET, René	6-0	176	L	Victoriaville, Qué.	6/25/73	Drummondville
DORE, Daniel	6-3	202	R	Ferme-Neuve, Qué.	4/9/70	Halifax-Greensboro
GARBUTT, Murray	6-1	205	L	Hanna, Alta.	7/29/71	Kansas City
HOUGH, Mike	6-1	192	L	Montréal, Qué.	2/6/63	Québec
HUNTER, Tim	6-2	202	R	Calgary, Alta.	9/10/60	Calgary
KAMENSKY, Valeri	6-2	198	R	Voskresensk, USSR	4/18/66	Québec
KAMINSKI, Kevin	5-9	170	L	Churchbridge, Sask.	3/13/69	Québec-Halifax
LAPOINTE, Claude	5-9	173	L	Lachine, Qué.	10/11/68	Québec
LINDSAY, Bill	5-11	185	L	Big Fork, MT	5/17/71	Québec-Tri-City
MATULIK, Ivan	6-1	205	L	Nitra, Czech.	6/17/68	Halifax
MORIN, Stéphane	6-0	175	L	Montréal, Qué.	3/27/69	Québec-Halifax
NOLAN, Owen	6-1	194	R	Belfast, N. Ireland	2/12/72	Québec
NORRIS, Dwayne	5-10	175	R	St. John, Nfld.	1/8/70	Michigan State
PEARSON, Scott	6-1	205	L	Cornwall, Ont.	12/19/69	Québec-Halifax
RAGLAN, Herb	6-0	205	R	Peterborough, Ont.	8/5/67	Québec
RICCI, Mike	6-0	190	L	Scarborough, Ont.	10/27/71	Philadelphia
RUCINSKY, Martin	5-11	178	L	Most, Czech.	3/11/71	Québec-Halifax
SAKIC, Joe	5-11	185	L	Burnaby, B.C.	7/7/69	Québec
SANIPASS, Everett	6-2	204	L	Big Cove, N.B.	2/13/68	Halifax
SIMON, Chris	6-3	230	L	Wawa, Ont.	1/30/72	Ottawa-Sault Ste. Marie
SUNDIN, Mats	6-2	190	R	Stockholm, Swe.	2/13/71	Québec
TWIST, Tony	6-1	212	L	Sherwood Park, Alta.	5/9/68	Québec
VAN DORP, Wayne	6-4	225	L	Vancouver, B.C.	5/19/61	Québec-Halifax
VERMETTE, Mark	6-1	203	R	Cochenour, Ont.	10/3/67	Québec-Halifax
WARD, Ed	6-3	190	R	Edmonton, Alta.	11/10/69	Halifax-Greensboro
YOUNG, Scott	6-0	190	R	Clinton, MA	10/1/67	Italy

DEFENSEMEN	HT	WT	S	Place of Birth	Date	1991-92 Club
BZDEL, Gerald	6-1	196	R	Wynyard, Sask.	3/13/68	Halifax
CRONIN, Shawn	6-1	215	R	Joliet, IL	8/20/63	Winnipeg
DOYON, Mario	6-0	174	R	Québec, Qué.	8/27/68	Halifax-New Haven
DUBOIS, Eric	6-0	193	R	Montréal, Qué.	5/9/70	Hfx.-N. Haven-Greensboro
DUCHESNE, Steve	5-11	195	L	Sept-Iles, Qué.	6/30/65	Philadelphia
ESAU, Len	6-3	195	R	Meadow Lake, Sask.	3/16/68	St. John
FINN, Steven	6-0	198	L	Laval, Qué.	8/20/66	Québec
FOOTE, Adam	6-1	180	R	Toronto, Ont.	7/10/71	Québec-Halifax
GUÉRARD, Stéphane	6-2	198	L	Ste. Elizabeth, Qué.	4/12/68	Did Not Play
GUSAROV, Alexei	6-2	170	L	Leningrad, USSR	7/8/64	Québec-Halifax
HUFFMAN, Kerry	6-2	200	L	Peterborough, Ont.	1/3/68	Philadelphia
KARPA, David	6-1	190	R	Regina, Sask.	5/7/71	Québec-Ferris State
KLEMM, Jon	6-3	200	R	Cranbrook, B.C.	1/8/70	Québec-Halifax
LESCHYSHYN, Curtis	6-1	205	L	Thompson, Man.	9/21/69	Québec-Halifax
RYMSHA, Andy	6-3	210	L	St. Catharines, Ont.	12/10/68	Qué.-Hfx.-New Haven
SPROTT, Jim	6-1	200	L	Oakville, Ont.	4/11/69	New Haven
TATARINOV, Mikhail	5-10	194	L	Irkutsk, USSR	7/16/66	Québec
VELISCHEK, Randy	6-0	200	L	Montréal, Qué.	2/10/62	Québec-Halifax
WOLANIN, Craig	6-3	205	L	Grosse Pointe, MI	7/27/67	Québec
ZAYONCE, Dean	6-0	200	R	Kelowna, B.C.	10/28/70	Halifax-Greensboro

GOALTENDERS	HT	WT	C	Place of Birth	Date	1991-92 Club
CLOUTIER, Jacques	5-7	168	L	Noranda, Qué.	1/3/60	Québec
FISET, Stéphane	6-0	175	L	Montréal, Qué.	6/17/70	Québec-Halifax
GORDON, Scott	5-10	175	L	Brockton, MA	2/6/63	Hfx.-N. Haven-U.S. Nat.
HEXTALL, Ron	6-3	192	L	Brandon, Man.	5/3/63	Philadelphia
KRAKE, Paul	6-0	175	L	Lloydminster, Alta.	3/25/69	Alaska-Anchorage
LABRECQUE, Patrick	6-0	187	L	Laval, Qué.	3/6/71	Halifax
TANNER, John	6-3	182	L	Cambridge, Ont.	3/17/71	Qué.-Hfx.-N. Haven

General Managers' History

Maurice Filion, 1979-80 to 1987-88; Martin Madden 1988-89; Martin Madden and Maurice Filion, 1989-90; Pierre Page, 1990-91 to date.

Coaching History

Jacques Demers, 1979-80; Maurice Filion and Michel Bergeron, 1980-81; Michel Bergeron, 1981-82 to 1986-87; André Savard and Ron Lapointe, 1987-88; Ron Lapointe, and Jean Perron, 1988-89; Michel Bergeron, 1989-90; Dave Chambers, 1990-91; Dave Chambers and Pierre Page,1991-92; Pierre Page, 1992-93.

Captains' History

Marc Tardif, 1979-80, 1980-81; Robbie Ftorek and Andre Dupont, 1981-82; Mario Marois, 1982-83 to 1984-85; Mario Marois, Peter Stastny, 1985-86; Peter Stastny, 1986-87 to 1989-90; Joe Sakic and Steven Finn, 1990-91; Mike Hough, 1991-92 to date.

Retired Numbers

3	J.C. Tremblay	1972-1979
8	Marc Tardif	1979-1983

1991-92 Scoring

Regular Season

Pos	#.	Player	Team	GP	G	A	Pts	+/-	PIM	PP	SH	GW	GT	S	%
C	19	Joe Sakic	QUE	69	29	65	94	5	20	6	3	1	1	217	13.4
R	13	Mats Sundin	QUE	80	33	43	76	19–	103	8	2	2	1	231	14.3
R	11	Owen Nolan	QUE	75	42	31	73	9–	183	17	0	0	1	190	22.1
R	23	Greg Paslawski	QUE	80	28	17	45	12–	18	5	1	4	1	134	20.9
L	18	Mike Hough	QUE	61	16	22	38	1–	77	6	2	1	0	92	17.4
D	4	Mikhail Tatarinov	QUE	66	11	27	38	8	72	5	0	1	0	191	5.8
C	47*	Claude Lapointe	QUE	78	13	20	33	8–	86	0	2	2	0	95	13.7
L	41	Doug Smail	QUE	46	10	18	28	11–	47	0	1	1	0	72	13.9
L	44	Gino Cavallini	STL	48	9	7	16	8–	40	0	0	2	1	72	12.5
			QUE	18	1	7	8	1–	4	0	0	0	0	39	2.6
			TOTAL	66	10	14	24	9–	44	0	0	2	1	111	9.0
D	5	Alexei Gusarov	QUE	68	5	18	23	9–	22	3	0	1	0	66	7.6
L	17*	Valeri Kamensky	QUE	23	7	14	21	1–	14	2	0	1	0	42	16.7
R	14	Herb Raglan	QUE	62	6	14	20	5–	120	0	0	0	2	79	7.6
C	28*	Jamie Baker	QUE	52	7	10	17	5–	32	3	0	1	0	77	9.1
D	7	Curtis Leschyshyn	QUE	42	5	12	17	28–	42	3	0	1	0	61	8.2
D	50*	Dan Lambert	QUE	28	6	9	15	5–	22	2	0	0	0	42	14.3
D	43	Bryan Fogarty	QUE	20	3	12	15	15–	16	0	0	0	0	30	10.0
C	9	Marc Fortier	QUE	39	5	9	14	7–	33	2	0	1	0	42	11.9
L	21	John Tonelli	CHI	33	1	7	8	2	37	0	0	1	0	29	3.4
			QUE	19	2	4	6	7–	14	2	0	0	0	16	12.5
			TOTAL	52	3	11	14	5–	51	2	0	1	0	45	6.7
D	6	Craig Wolanin	QUE	69	2	11	13	12–	80	0	0	0	0	71	2.8
D	29	Steven Finn	QUE	65	4	7	11	9–	194	0	0	0	0	63	6.3
C	25	Stephane Morin	QUE	30	2	8	10	2–	14	0	0	0	0	41	4.9
L	24	Wayne Van Dorp	QUE	24	3	5	8	5	109	0	0	0	0	19	15.8
D	52*	Adam Foote	QUE	46	2	5	7	4–	44	0	0	0	1	55	3.6
L	53*	Bill Lindsay	QUE	23	2	4	6	6–	14	0	0	1	0	35	5.7
D	27	Randy Velischek	QUE	38	2	3	5	3–	22	0	0	0	0	23	8.7
R	20	Mike McNeill	QUE	26	1	4	5	8–	8	1	0	0	0	15	6.7
L	50	Steve Maltais	MIN	12	2	1	3	1–	2	0	0	0	0	6	33.3
			QUE	0	0	0	0	0	0	0	0	0	0	0	.0
			TOTAL	12	2	1	3	1–	2	0	0	0	0	6	33.3
L	22	Scott Pearson	QUE	10	1	2	3	5–	14	0	0	0	0	14	7.1
L	37*	Martin Rucinsky	EDM	2	0	0	0	3–	0	0	0	0	0	1	.0
			QUE	4	1	1	2	1	2	0	0	0	0	4	25.0
			TOTAL	6	1	1	2	2–	2	0	0	0	0	5	20.0
R	44	John Kordic	QUE	18	0	2	2	3–	115	0	0	0	0	3	.0
R	45	Mark Vermette	QUE	10	1	0	1	6–	8	0	0	0	0	12	8.3
D	42*	Jon Klemm	QUE	4	0	1	1	2	0	0	0	0	0	2	.0
C	12	Ken McRae	QUE	10	0	1	1	5–	31	0	0	0	0	10	.0
D	15	Tony Twist	QUE	44	0	1	1	3–	164	0	0	0	0	9	.0
R	21*	S. Charbonneau	QUE	2	0	0	0	2–	0	0	0	0	0	4	.0
D	59*	Dave Karpa	QUE	4	0	0	0	2	14	0	0	0	0	2	.0
C	40*	Kevin Kaminski	QUE	5	0	0	0	2–	45	0	0	0	0	6	.0
D	38*	Dave Marcinyshyn	QUE	5	0	0	0	1–	26	0	0	0	0	3	.0
D	60*	Andy Rymsha	QUE	6	0	0	0	3–	23	0	0	0	0	4	.0
G	34*	John Tanner	QUE	14	0	0	0	0	4	0	0	0	0	0	.0
G	31*	Stephane Fiset	QUE	23	0	0	0	0	6	0	0	0	0	0	.0
G	32	Jacques Cloutier	QUE	26	0	0	0	0	6	0	0	0	0	0	.0

Goaltending

No.	Goaltender	GPI	Mins	Avg	W	L	T	EN	SO	GA	SA	S%
34	*John Tanner	14	796	3.47	1	7	4	1	1	46	394	.883
31	*Stephane Fiset	23	1133	3.76	7	10	2	1	1	71	646	.890
32	Jacques Cloutier	26	1345	3.93	6	14	3	0	0	88	712	.876
1	Ron Tugnutt	30	1583	4.02	6	17	3	5	1	106	782	.864
	Totals	**80**	**4876**	**3.91**	**20**	**48**	**12**	**7**	**3**	**318**	**2541**	**.875**

Owen Nolan led the Nordiques in goals (42) and powerplay goals (17) in 1991-92.

Club Records

Team

(Figures in brackets for season records are games played; records for fewest points, wins, ties, losses, goals, goals against are for 70 or more games)

Most Points	**94**	1983-84 (80)
Most Wins	**43**	1985-86 (80)
Most Ties	**18**	1980-81 (80)
Most Losses	**61**	1989-90 (80)
Most Goals	**360**	1983-84 (80)
Most Goals Against	**407**	1989-90 (80)
Fewest Points	**31**	1989-90 (80)
Fewest Wins	**12**	1989-90 (80)
Fewest Ties	**5**	1987-88 (80)
Fewest Losses	**28**	1983-84 (80)
Fewest Goals	**236**	1990-91 (80)
Fewest Goals Against	**275**	1984-85 (80)
Longest Winning Streak		
Over-all	**7**	Nov. 24-Dec. 10/83 Oct. 10-21/85 Dec. 31/85-Jan. 11/86
Home	**10**	Nov. 26/83-Jan. 10/84
Away	**5**	Feb. 28-Mar. 24, 1986
Longest Undefeated Streak		
Over-all	**11**	Mar. 10-31/81 (7 wins, 4 ties)
Home	**14**	Nov. 19/83-Jan. 21/84 (11 wins, 3 ties)
Away	**8**	Feb. 17/81-Mar. 22/81 (6 wins, 2 ties)
Longest Losing Streak		
Over-all	**14**	Oct. 21-Nov. 19/90
Home	**8**	Oct. 21-Nov. 24/90
Away	**18**	Jan. 18-Apr. 1/90
Longest Winless Streak		
Over-all	**17**	Oct. 21-Nov. 25/90 (15 losses, 2 ties)
Home	**11**	Nov. 14-Dec. 26/89 (7 losses, 4 ties)
Away	**33**	Oct. 8/91-Feb. 27/92 (25 losses, 8 ties)
Most Shutouts, Season	**6**	1985-86 (80)
Most PIM, Season	**2,104**	1989-90 (80)
Most Goals, Game	**12**	Feb. 1/83 (Hfd. 3 at Que. 12) Oct. 20/84 (Que. 12 at Tor. 3)

Individual

Most Seasons	**11**	Michel Goulet
Most Games	**813**	Michel Goulet
Most Goals, Career	**456**	Michel Goulet
Most Assists, Career	**668**	Peter Stastny
Most Points, Career	**1,048**	Peter Stastny (380 goals, 668 assists)
Most PIM, Career	**1,545**	Dale Hunter
Most Shutouts, Career	**6**	Mario Gosselin
Longest Consecutive Games Streak	**312**	Dale Hunter (Oct. 9/80-Mar. 13/84)
Most Goals, Season	**57**	Michel Goulet (1982-83)
Most Assists, Season	**93**	Peter Stastny (1981-82)
Most Points, Season	**139**	Peter Stastny (1981-82) (46 goals, 93 assists)
Most PIM, Season	**301**	Gord Donnelly (1987-88)
Most Points, Defenseman, Season	**68**	Jeff Brown (1988-89) (21 goals, 47 assists)
Most Points, Center, Season	**139**	Peter Stastny (1981-82) (46 goals, 93 assists)
Most Points, Right Wing, Season	**103**	Jacques Richard (1980-81) (52 goals, 51 assists)
Most Points, Left Wing, Season	**121**	Michel Goulet (1983-84) (56 goals, 65 assists)
Most Points, Rookie, Season	***109**	Peter Stastny (1980-81) (39 goals, 70 assists)
Most Shutouts, Season	**4**	Clint Malarchuk (1985-86)
Most Goals, Game	**5**	Mats Sundin (Mar. 5/92)
Most Assists, Game	**5**	Anton Stastny (Feb. 22/81) Michel Goulet (Jan. 3/84)
Most Points, Game	**8**	Peter Stastny (Feb. 22/81) Anton Stastny (Feb. 22/81)

* NHL Record.

All-time Record vs. Other Clubs

Regular Season

	At Home							On Road							Total						
	GP	W	L	T	GF	GA	PTS	GP	W	L	T	GF	GA	PTS	GP	W	L	T	GF	GA	PTS
Boston	48	16	28	4	184	216	36	48	15	25	8	151	195	38	96	31	53	12	335	411	74
Buffalo	48	24	16	8	185	150	56	48	13	28	7	159	200	33	96	37	44	15	344	350	89
Calagry	20	7	9	4	84	81	18	21	4	12	5	68	98	13	41	11	21	9	152	179	31
Chicago	20	8	8	4	85	81	20	21	7	13	1	69	88	15	41	15	21	5	154	169	35
Detroit	21	12	6	3	91	74	27	20	7	12	1	69	84	15	41	19	18	4	160	158	42
Edmonton	20	6	12	2	79	99	14	20	4	16	0	59	117	8	40	10	28	2	138	216	22
Hartford	48	28	13	7	210	152	63	48	17	21	10	170	172	44	96	45	34	17	380	324	107
Los Angeles	20	8	9	3	83	83	19	20	7	12	1	71	93	15	40	15	21	4	154	176	34
Minnesota	21	15	4	2	100	53	32	20	6	12	2	64	79	14	41	21	16	4	164	132	46
Montreal	48	25	21	2	169	171	52	48	8	32	8	142	214	24	96	33	53	10	311	385	76
New Jersey	20	11	7	2	88	66	24	21	9	11	1	78	96	19	41	20	18	3	166	162	43
NY Islanders	21	10	9	2	80	70	22	20	6	13	1	71	93	13	41	16	22	3	151	163	35
NY Rangers	21	10	8	3	90	93	23	20	3	14	3	51	87	9	41	13	22	6	141	180	32
Philadelphia	20	5	8	7	66	75	17	21	2	17	2	53	90	6	41	7	25	9	119	165	23
Pittsburgh	20	10	10	0	90	80	20	21	6	12	3	85	95	15	41	16	22	3	175	175	35
St. Louis	20	9	8	3	71	68	21	20	3	16	1	65	97	7	40	12	24	4	136	165	28
San Jose	1	1	0	0	6	3	2	2	0	2	0	5	11	0	3	1	2	0	11	14	2
Toronto	20	10	5	5	83	69	25	21	9	10	2	91	74	20	41	19	15	7	174	143	45
Vancouver	21	8	9	4	63	62	20	20	7	10	3	82	86	17	41	15	19	7	145	148	37
Washington	21	7	10	4	68	85	18	20	8	10	2	71	84	18	41	15	20	6	139	169	36
Winnipeg	21	9	10	2	85	88	20	20	6	9	5	78	85	17	41	15	19	7	163	173	37
Totals	**520**	**239**	**210**	**71**	**2060**	**1919**	**549**	**520**	**147**	**307**	**66**	**1752**	**2238**	**360**	**1040**	**386**	**517**	**137**	**3812**	**4157**	**909**

Playoffs

	Series	W	L	GP	W	L	T	GF	GA	Last Mtg.	Round	Result
Boston	2	1	1	11	5	6	0	36	37	1983	DSF	L 1-3
Buffalo	2	2	0	8	6	2	0	35	27	1985	DSF	W 3-2
Hartford	2	1	1	9	4	5	0	34	35	1987	DSF	W 4-2
Montreal	4	2	2	25	12	13	0	69	86	1987	DF	L 3-4
NY Islanders	1	0	1	4	0	4	0	9	18	1982	CF	L 0-4
Philadelphia	2	0	2	11	4	7	0	29	39	1985	CF	L 2-4
Totals	**13**	**6**	**7**	**68**	**31**	**37**	**0**	**212**	**242**			

Abbreviations: Round: F – Final; **CF** – conference final; **DF** – division final; **DSF** – division semi-final; **SF** – semi-final; **QF** – quarter-final; **PR** – preliminary round. **GA** – goals against; **GF** – goals for.

1991-92 Results

Home			Away		
Oct. 5	Hartford	4-2	**Oct.** 8	New Jersey	5-6
12	Buffalo	4-5	10	Minnesota	2-3
13	NY Islanders	1-1	17	Philadelphia	3-5
19	Detroit	1-6	23	Montreal	2-3
24	Montreal	0-5	31	NY Rangers	4-5
26	NY Rangers	3-5	**Nov.** 7	Chicago	2-4
29	Winnipeg	7-2	12	Hartford	4-5
Nov. 2	San Jose	6-3	14	Boston	2-5
10	Washington*	3-10	23	Montreal	3-5
16	Edmonton	2-6	27	Buffalo	4-4
18	Pittsburgh	3-7	28	St Louis	2-5
21	Montreal	5-2	**Dec.** 5	Boston	2-2
25	Hartford	5-2	12	Detroit	1-4
30	Buffalo	4-3	17	Washington	1-3
Dec. 3	Vancouver	3-0	19	Calgary	5-5
7	Los Angeles	7-5	21	San Jose	1-4
10	Boston	5-2	22	Vancouver	6-6
14	St Louis	2-4	**Jan.** 2	Hartford	1-4
26	Montreal	1-4	4	NY Islanders	2-5
28	Hartford	4-1	8	Buffalo	2-4
30	Toronto	5-2	9	Boston	4-5
Jan. 11	NY Rangers	2-7	23	Chicago	2-4
14	Calgary	3-5	29	Toronto	2-5
21	Vancouver	3-5	31	Winnipeg	4-4
25	Winnipeg*	2-1	**Feb.** 2	Edmonton*	2-8
28	Boston	2-4	5	Calgary	3-5
Feb. 8	Philadelphia*	0-3	13	Philadelphia	2-3
9	New Jersey*	1-2	15	Montreal	4-4
11	Washington	3-4	20	Pittsburgh	4-4
18	Minnesota	4-0	22	Hartford*	0-4
Mar. 3	Buffalo	4-4	23	Montreal	3-3
7	Detroit	4-4	26	San Jose	4-7
9	Hartford	2-0	27	Los Angeles	2-4
11	Montreal	5-4	**Mar.** 5	Hartford	10-4
14	Boston	4-5	15	Buffalo	4-6
21	Minnesota	4-2	17	Toronto	3-4
24	NY Islanders	5-2	19	Pittsburgh	3-6
26	Chicago	4-5	28	New Jersey*	2-5
31	Boston	4-5	**Apr.** 2	Boston	1-1
Apr. 4	Buffalo	7-3	5	Buffalo	4-3

*Denotes afternoon game

Entry Draft Selections 1992-79

1992

Pick	
4	Todd Warriner
28	Paul Brousseau
29	Tuomas Gronman
52	Emmanuel Fernandez
76	Ian McIntyre
100	Charlie Wasley
124	Paxton Schulte
148	Martin LePage
172	Mike Jickling
196	Steve Passmore
220	Anson Carter
244	Aaron Ellis

1991

Pick	
1	Eric Lindros
24	Rene Corbet
46	Richard Brennan
68	Dave Karpa
90	Patrick Labrecque
103	Bill Lindsay
134	Mikael Johansson
156	Janne Laukkanen
157	Aaron Asp
178	Adam Bartell
188	Brent Brekke
200	Paul Koch
222	Doug Friedman
244	Eric Meloche

1990

Pick	
1	Owen Nolan
22	Ryan Hughes
43	Bradley Zavisha
106	Jeff Parrott
127	Dwayne Norris
148	Andrei Kovalenko
158	Alexander Karpovtsev
169	Pat Mazzoli
190	Scott Davis
211	Mika Stromberg
232	Wade Klippenstein

1989

Pick	
1	Mats Sundin
22	Adam Foote
43	Stephane Morin
54	John Tanner
68	Niclas Andersson
76	Eric Dubois
85	Kevin Kaiser
106	Dan Lambert
127	Sergei Mylnikov
148	Paul Krake
169	Viacheslav Bykov
190	Andrei Khumutov
211	Byron Witkowski
232	Noel Rahn

1988

Pick	
3	Curtis Leschyshyn
5	Daniel Dore
24	Stephane Fiset
45	Petri Aaltonen
66	Darin Kimble
87	Stephane Venne
108	Ed Ward
129	Valeri Kamensky
150	Sakari Lindfors
171	Dan Wiebe
213	Alexei Gusarov
234	Claude Lapointe

1987

Pick	
9	Bryan Fogarty
15	Joe Sakic
51	Jim Sprott
72	Kip Miller
93	Rob Mendel
114	Garth Snow
135	Tim Hanus
156	Jake Enebak
177	Jaroslav Sevcik
183	Ladislav Tresl
198	Darren Nauss
219	Mike Williams

1986

Pick	
18	Ken McRae
39	Jean-Marc Routhier
41	Stephane Guerard
81	Ron Tugnutt
102	Gerald Bzdel
117	Scott White
123	Morgan Samuelsson
134	Mark Vermette
144	Jean-Francois Nault
165	Keith Miller
186	Pierre Millier
207	Chris Lappin
228	Martin Latreille
249	Sean Boudreault

1985

Pick	
15	David Latta
36	Jason Lafreniere
57	Max Middendorf
65	Peter Massey
78	David Espe
99	Bruce Major
120	Andy Akervik
141	Mike Oliverio
162	Mario Brunetta
183	Brit Peer
204	Tom Sasso
225	Gary Murphy
246	Jean Bois

1984

Pick	
15	Trevor Stienburg
36	Jeff Brown
57	Steve Finn
78	Terry Perkins
120	Darren Cota
141	Henrik Cedergren
162	Jyrki Maki
183	Guy Ouellette
203	Ken Quinney
244	Peter Loob

1983

Pick	
32	Yves Heroux
52	Bruce Bell
54	Iiro Jarvi
92	Luc Guenette
112	Brad Walcott
132	Craig Mack
152	Tommy Albelin
172	Wayne Groulx
192	Scott Shaunessy
232	Bo Berglund
239	Jindrich Kokrment

1982

Pick	
13	David Shaw
34	Paul Gillis
55	Mario Gosselin
76	Jiri Lala
97	Phil Stanger
131	Daniel Poudrier
181	Mike Hough
202	Vincent Lukac
223	Andre Martin
244	Jozef Lukac
248	Jan Jasko

1981

Pick	
11	Randy Moller
53	Jean-Marc Gaulin
74	Clint Malarchuk
95	Ed Lee
116	Mike Eagles
158	Andre Cote
179	Marc Brisebois
200	Kari Takko

1980

Pick	
24	Normand Rochefort
66	Jay Miller
87	Basil McRae
108	Mark Kumpel
129	Gaston Therrien
150	Michel Bolduc
171	Christian Tanguay
192	William Robinson

1979

Pick	
20	Michel Goulet
41	Dale Hunter
62	Lee Norwood
83	Anton Stastny
104	Pierre Lacroix
125	Scott McGeown

Coach and General Manager

PAGÉ, PIERRE
Coach and General Manager, Quebec Nordiques. Born in St. Hermas, Que., April 30, 1948.

Pierre Pagé added the head coaching duties of the Quebec Nordiques to his resume during 1991-92, replacing Dave Chambers 18 games into the season. Under Pagé's direction, the Nordiques compiled a 17-34-9 record. Pagé was named general manager of the Nordiques on May 4, 1990 after two seasons as head coach of the Minnesota North Stars. In his rookie season with Minnesota, the club posted a 27-37-16 record for 70 points, a 19-point improvement over the previous year and earned its first playoff berth since 1985-86. In 1989-90, the North Stars continued improving, finishing the season with 76 points (36-40-4).

Pagé, 44, joined the Calgary Flames in 1980-81 as an assistant coach to Al MacNeil. He served in that capacity through the 1981-82 season before accepting a position as coach and general manager of the Flames' top minor league affiliate in Denver (two seasons) and, later, Moncton (one season). In 1985-86, Pagé returned to Calgary as an assistant to head coach Bob Johnson and remained in that capacity through the 1987-88 season under Terry Crisp.

Before joining the Flames, Pagé was head coach of the Dalhousie University Tigers of the CIAU where in 1978-79, he guided his club to a second place finish in the national final. He also served as an assistant coach with the 1980 Canadian Olympic Team and the 1981 Team Canada entry in the Canada Cup.

Coaching Record

		Regular Season					Playoffs			
Season	**Team**	**Games**	**W**	**L**	**T**	**%**	**Games**	**W**	**L**	**%**
1978-79	Dalhousie (CIAU)	....	....	....	....	....	....	....	....	....
1982-83	Denver (CHL)	80	41	36	3	.531	6	2	4	.333
1983-84	Denver (CHL)	76	48	25	3	.651	6	2	4	.333
1984-85	Moncton (AHL)	80	32	40	8	.450	....	....	....	....
1988-89	**Minnesota (NHL)**	80	27	37	16	.438	5	1	4	.200
1989-90	**Minnesota (NHL)**	80	36	40	4	.475	7	3	4	.429
1991-92	**Quebec (NHL)**	62	17	34	11	.362	....	....	....	....
	NHL Totals	222	80	111	31	.430	12	4	8	.333

Club Directory

Colisée de Québec
2205 Ave de Colisée
Québec City, Québec
G1L 4W7
Phone **418/529-8441**
FAX 418/529-1052
Capacity: 15,399

President and Governor	Marcel Aubut
Alternate Governors	Pierre Pagé, Gilles Léger
Executive Secretaries to the President	Louise Marois, Danielle Gauthier
Coordinator – President's Agenda	Valérie Thibault
Hockey Club Personnel	
General Manager and Head Coach	Pierre Pagé
Assistant to the General Manager	Gilles Léger
Administrative Assistant to the General Manager	François Giguère
Associate Coach	Jacques Martin
Assistant Coaches	Don Jackson, André Savard, Clement Jodoin
Scouts – Professional hockey and special assignments	Dave Draper, Orval Tessier
Chief Scout	Pierre Gauthier
Assistant to the Chief Scout	Darwin Bennett
Scouts	Ross Ainsworth, Herb Boxer, Don Boyd, Yvon Gendron, Michel Georges, Mark Kelley, Bengt Lundholm, Frank Moberg, Jacques Noël, Don Paarup, Dan Summers
Physiotherapist	Jacques Lavergne
Trainers	René Lacasse, René Lavigueur, Brian Turpin
Team Physician	Dr. Pierre Beauchemin
Executive Secretary – hockey department	Martine Bélanger
Secretary – hockey department and Travel Coordinator	Nathalie Paquet
Administration and Finance	
Vice-President/Administration and Finance	Jean Laflamme
Controller	Francois Bilodeau
Assistant to the Controller	Rémi Bolduc
Executive Secretary	Ginette Parris
Sales and Marketing	
Vice-President/Corporate Development and Communications	Jean-D. Legault
Sales Director	André Lestourneau
Sales Manager – Promotional Agreements	Bernard Thiboutot
Promotional Agreements Representatives	Marc Bourassa, John Nolan
Representative – Promotional Agreements Governments and Corporations	Jean Dugré
Supervisor – Promotional Agreements Coordination	Jacquelyne Caron
Account Assistants – Promotional Agreements Coordination	Kevin Donnelly, Chantal Poirier
Head of Sector – Season tickets	Nicolas Labbé
Head of Sector – Group Sales	Michel Laporte
Head of Sector – Nordtel Service	Lise Bélanger
Sales Representatives	Reynald Roberge, Christine Côté, Bernard Nadeau
Supervisor of Novelties & Souvenirs	Tom Maguire
Executive Secretaries – Marketing & Promotions	Julienne Bois, Marie Godin
Secretaries – Marketing and Sales	Yolaine Guimont, Pauline Baron
Communications	
Director of Public Relations	Richard Thibault
Direct – Corporate and Community Affairs	Guy Lafleur
Director of Press Relations	Jean Martineau
Coordinator of Public Relations	Nicole Bouchard
Graphic Communications Coordinator	Pierre Masson
Executive Secretary – Public Relations	Marie Roy
Team Photographer	Jean-Yves Michaud
Location of Press Box	East & West side of building, upper level
Dimensions of Rink	200 feet by 85 feet
Club Colors	Blue, White and Red
Uniforms	Home – Base color white trimmed with blue and red Away – Base color blue trimmed with white and red
Training Camp Site	Québec City
Radio Station	CJRP 1060
Radio Announcers	Alain Crâte, TBA
TV Station	CFAP (2) Quatre Saisons
TV Announcers	André Côté, Claude Bédard

St. Louis Blues

1991-92 Results: 36W-33L-11T 83PTS. Third, Norris Division

Schedule

Home

Oct. Tues. 6 Minnesota
Sat. 10 Chicago
Tues. 13 Tampa Bay
Thur. 15 Minnesota
Wed. 21 Quebec
Sat. 24 Detroit
Mon. 26 San Jose
Thur. 29 Pittsburgh
Sat. 31 Philadelphia
Nov. Tues. 10 Edmonton
Sat. 14 Winnipeg
Sat. 21 Tampa Bay
Thur. 26 Vancouver
Sat. 28 Detroit
Dec. Tues. 1 Hartford
Tues. 15 NY Islanders (at Dallas)
Thur. 17 NY Rangers
Sat. 19 Winnipeg
Sun. 27 Toronto
Thur. 31 NY Islanders
Jan. Tues. 5 Edmonton
Thur. 7 Calgary
Sat. 9 Chicago
Tues. 19 Toronto
Sat. 23 Detroit
Tues. 26 Ottawa
Sat. 30 New Jersey
Feb. Mon. 1 Toronto
Tues. 9 Boston
Thur. 11 Washington
Sat. 13 Detroit
Tues. 23 Montreal
Thur. 25 Los Angeles
Sat. 27 Minnesota
Mar. Thur. 4 Calgary
Thur. 11 San Jose
Sat. 13 Minnesota
Tues. 16 Buffalo
Tues. 30 Vancouver
Apr. Sat. 3 Chicago
Sun. 11 Minnesota
Thur. 15 Tampa Bay

Away

Oct. Thur. 8 Minnesota
Sat. 17 Quebec
Mon. 19 Montreal
Nov. Tues. 3 Tampa Bay
Thur. 5 Pittsburgh
Sat. 7 Philadelphia*
Thur. 12 Chicago
Mon. 16 Toronto
Wed. 18 Hartford
Wed. 25 Detroit
Dec. Fri. 4 Calgary
Sat. 5 Edmonton
Mon. 7 Vancouver
Thur. 10 San Jose
Sat. 12 Los Angeles
Tues. 22 Minnesota
Sat. 26 Chicago
Tues. 29 Hartford (at Birmingham)
Jan. Sat. 2 Toronto
Sun. 3 Buffalo
Mon. 11 Detroit
Wed. 13 Toronto
Thur. 14 Ottawa
Sat. 16 Tampa Bay
Thur. 21 Detroit
Thur. 28 Tampa Bay
Feb. Wed. 3 Winnipeg
Mon. 15 NY Rangers*
Wed. 17 New Jersey
Thur. 18 NY Islanders
Sun. 21 Washington*
Sun. 28 Chicago
Mar. Sat. 6 Boston*
Sun. 14 Minnesota
Sat. 20 Los Angeles
Mon. 22 Vancouver
Wed. 24 Calgary
Fri. 26 Winnipeg
Apr. Sun. 4 Chicago
Tues. 6 Tampa Bay
Sat. 10 Minnesota
Tues. 13 Toronto

* Denotes afternoon game.

Home Starting Times:
Weeknights and Saturdays .... 7:35 p.m.
Sundays .... 6:05 p.m.

Franchise date: June 5, 1967

26th NHL Season

Year-by-Year Record

Season	Home GP	Home W	Home L	Home T	Road W	Road L	Road T	Overall W	Overall L	Overall T	GF	GA	Pts.	Finished	Playoff Result
1991-92	80	25	12	3	11	21	8	36	33	11	279	266	83	3rd, Norris Div.	Lost Div. Semi-Final
1990-91	80	24	9	7	23	13	4	47	22	11	310	250	105	2nd, Norris Div.	Lost Div. Final
1989-90	80	20	15	5	17	19	4	37	34	9	295	279	83	2nd, Norris Div.	Lost Div. Final
1988-89	80	22	11	7	11	24	5	33	35	12	275	285	78	2nd, Norris Div.	Lost Div. Final
1987-88	80	18	17	5	16	21	3	34	38	8	278	294	76	2nd, Norris Div.	Lost Div. Final
1986-87	80	21	12	7	11	21	8	32	33	15	281	293	79	1st, Norris Div.	Lost Div. Semi-Final
1985-86	80	23	11	6	14	23	3	37	34	9	302	291	83	3rd, Norris Div.	Lost Conf. Championship
1984-85	80	21	12	7	16	19	5	37	31	12	299	288	86	1st, Norris Div.	Lost Div. Semi-Final
1983-84	80	23	14	3	9	27	4	32	41	7	293	316	71	2nd, Norris Div.	Lost Div. Final
1982-83	80	16	16	8	9	24	7	25	40	15	285	316	65	4th, Norris Div.	Lost Div. Semi-Final
1981-82	80	22	14	4	10	26	4	32	40	8	315	349	72	3rd Norris Div.	Lost Div. Final
1980-81	80	29	7	4	16	11	13	45	18	17	352	281	107	1st, Smythe Div.	Lost Quarter-Final
1979-80	80	20	13	7	14	21	5	34	34	12	266	278	80	2nd, Smythe Div.	Lost Prelim. Round
1978-79	80	14	20	6	4	30	6	18	50	12	249	348	48	3rd, Smythe Div.	Out of Playoffs
1977-78	80	12	20	8	8	27	5	20	47	13	195	304	53	4th, Smythe Div.	Out of Playoffs
1976-77	80	22	13	5	10	26	4	32	39	9	239	276	73	1st, Smythe Div.	Lost Quarter-Final
1975-76	80	20	12	8	9	25	6	29	37	14	249	290	72	3rd, Smythe Div.	Lost Prelim. Round
1974-75	80	23	13	4	12	18	10	35	31	14	269	267	84	2nd, Smythe Div.	Lost Prelim. Round
1973-74	78	16	16	7	10	24	5	26	40	12	206	248	64	6th, West Div.	Out of Playoffs
1972-73	78	21	11	7	11	23	5	32	34	12	233	251	76	4th, West Div.	Lost Quarter-Final
1971-72	78	17	17	5	11	22	6	28	39	11	208	247	67	3rd, West Div.	Lost Semi-Final
1970-71	78	23	7	9	11	18	10	34	25	19	223	208	87	2nd, West Div.	Lost Quarter-Final
1969-70	76	24	9	5	13	18	7	37	27	12	224	179	86	1st, West Div.	Lost Final
1968-69	76	21	8	9	16	17	5	37	25	14	204	157	88	1st, West Div.	Lost Final
1967-68	74	18	12	7	9	19	9	27	31	16	177	191	70	3rd, West Div.	Lost Final

Nelson Emerson led all Blues' rookies in scoring during the 1991-92 season, registering 23 goals and 36 assists.

1992-93 Player Personnel

FORWARDS	HT	WT	S	Place of Birth	Date	1991-92 Club
BASSEN, Bob	5-11	185	L	Calgary, Alta.	5/6/65	St. Louis
BOZON, Philippe	5-10	185	L	Chamonix, France	11/30/66	St. Louis-French Oly.
CHASE, Kelly	5-11	195	R	Porcupine Pl., Sask.	10/25/67	St. Louis
CHRISTIAN, Dave	5-11	195	R	Warroad, MN	5/12/59	St. Louis
EMERSON, Nelson	5-11	180	R	Hamilton, Ont.	8/17/67	St. Louis
FELSNER, Denny	6-0	195	L	Warren, MI	4/29/70	St. Louis-Michigan
FRENETTE, Derek	6-1	210	L	Montreal, Que.	7/13/71	Peoria
HAWLEY, Joe	5-10	186	R	Peterborough, Ont.	3/13/71	Peoria
HEJNA, Tony	6-0	195	L	Buffalo, NY	1/8/68	Did not play
HOOVER, Ron	6-0	190	R	Oakville, Ont	10/28/66	St. Louis-Peoria
HULL, Brett	5-10	201	R	Belleville, Ont.	8/9/64	St. Louis
JANNEY, Craig	6-1	190	L	Hartford, CT	10/26/67	St. Louis-Boston
LOWRY, Dave	6-1	195	L	Sudbury, Ont.	2/14/65	St. Louis
MACKEY, Dave	6-4	205	L	Richmond, B.C.	7/24/66	St. Louis-Peoria
PELLERIN, Brian	5-10	185	R	Hinton, Alta.	2/20/70	Peoria
PION, Richard	5-10	180	R	Montreal, Que.	7/20/65	Peoria
PROKHOROV, Vitaly	5-9	185	L	Moscow, USSR	12/25/66	Moscow Spartak
REEVES, Kyle	5-11	190	R	Stonewall, Man.	5/12/71	Peoria
RUFF, Jason	6-3	200	L	Kelowna, B.C.	1/27/70	Peoria
SHANAHAN, Brendan	6-3	215	R	Mimico, Ont.	1/23/69	St. Louis
SUTTER, Rich	5-11	188	R	Viking, Alta.	12/2/63	St. Louis
SUTTER, Ron	6-0	180	R	Viking, Alta.	12/2/63	St. Louis
WILSON, Ron	5-9	180	L	Toronto, Ont.	5/13/56	St. Louis
DEFENSEMEN						
BARON, Murray	6-3	215	L	Prince George, B.C.	6/1/67	St. Louis
BATTERS, Jeff	6-2	215	R	Victoria, B.C.	10/23/70	Alaska-Anch.
BROWN, Jeff	6-1	204	R	Ottawa, Ont.	4/30/66	St. Louis
BUTCHER, Garth	6-0	205	R	Regina, Sask.	1/8/63	St. Louis
CAVALLINI, Paul	6-1	202	L	Toronto, Ont.	10/13/65	St. Louis
GILES, Curt	5-8	175	L	The Pas, Man.	10/30/58	St. Louis-Cdn. Nat.
HEDICAN, Bret	6-2	195	L	St. Paul, MN	8/10/70	St. L.-U.S. Nat.
HOLLINGER, Terry	6-1	200	L	Regina, Sask.	2/24/71	Peoria-Lethbridge
LaPERRIERE, Daniel	6-1	195	L	Laval, Que.	3/28/69	St. Lawrence
MARSHALL, Jason	6-2	195	R	Cranbrook, B.C.	2/22/71	St. Louis-Peoria
McKEE, Brian	5-11	185	L	Willowdale, Ont.	12/13/64	Peoria
QUINTAL, Stephane	6-3	215	R	Boucherville, Que.	10/22/68	St. Louis-Boston
ZOMBO, Rick	6-1	195	R	Des Plaines, IL	5/8/63	St. Louis-Detroit

GOALTENDERS	HT	WT	C	Place of Birth	Date	1991-92 Club
DUFFUS, Parris	6-2	193	L	Denver, CO	1/27/70	Cornell
HEBERT, Guy	5-11	180	L	Troy, NY	1/7/67	St. Louis-Peoria
JOSEPH, Curtis	5-10	182	L	Keswick, Ont.	4/29/67	St. Louis
SARJEANT, Geoff	5-9	175	L	Newmarket, Ont.	11/30/69	Michigan Tech

General Managers' History

Lynn Patrick, 1967-68 to 1968-69; Scotty Bowman, 1969-70 to 1970-71; Lynn Patrick, 1971-72; Sid Abel, 1972-73; Charles Catto, 1973-74; Gerry Ehman, 1974-75; Dennis Ball, 1975-76; Emile Francis, 1976-77 to 1982-83; Ron Caron, 1983-84 to date.

Coaching History

Lynn Patrick and Scott Bowman, 1967-68; Scott Bowman, 1968-69 to 1969-70; Al Arbour and Scott Bowman, 1970-71; Sid Abel, Bill McCreary, Al Arbour, 1971-72; Al Arbour and Jean-Guy Talbot, 1972-73; Jean-Guy Talbot and Lou Angotti, 1973-74; Lou Angotti, Lynn Patrck and Garry Young, 1974-75; Garry Young, Lynn Patrick and Leo Boivin, 1975-76; Emile Francis, 1976-77; Leo Boivin and Barclay Plager, 1977-78; Barclay Plager, 1978-79; Barclay Plager and Red Berenson, 1979-80; Red Berenson, 1980-81; Red Berenson and Emile Francis, 1981-82; Barclay Plager and Emile Francis, 1982-83; Jacques Demers, 1983-84 to 1985-86; Jacques Martin, 1986-87 to 1987-88. Brian Sutter, 1988-89 to 1991-92; Bob Plager, 1992-93.

Captains' History

Al Arbour, 1967-68 to 1969-70; Red Berenson, Barclay Plager, 1970-71; Barclay Plager, 1971-72 to 1975-76; no captain, 1976-77; Red Berenson, 1977-78; Barry Gibbs, 1978-79; Brian Sutter, 1979-80 to 1987-88; Bernie Federko, 1988-89; Rick Meagher, 1989-90; Scott Stevens, 1990-91; Garth Butcher, 1991-92.

Retired Numbers

3	Bob Gassoff	1973-1977
8	Barclay Plager	1967-1977
11	Brian Sutter	1976-1988
24	Bernie Federko	1976-1989

1991-92 Scoring

Regular Season

Pos	#.	Player	Team	GP	G	A	Pts	+/–	PIM	PP	SH	GW	GT	S	%
R	16	Brett Hull	STL	73	70	39	109	2–	48	20	5	9	1	408	17.2
C	15	Craig Janney	BOS	53	12	39	51	1	20	3	0	1	0	90	13.3
			STL	25	6	30	36	5	2	3	0	1	0	37	16.2
			TOTAL	78	18	69	87	6	22	6	0	2	0	127	14.2
R	19	Brendan Shanahan	STL	80	33	36	69	3–	171	13	0	2	2	215	15.3
C	7*	Nelson Emerson	STL	79	23	36	59	5–	66	3	0	2	0	143	16.1
D	21	Jeff Brown	STL	80	20	39	59	8	38	10	0	2	1	214	9.3
C	22	Ron Sutter	STL	68	19	27	46	9	91	5	4	1	1	106	17.9
R	27	Dave Christian	STL	78	20	24	44	2	41	1	3	3	0	142	14.1
D	14	Paul Cavallini	STL	66	10	25	35	7	95	3	1	2	1	164	6.1
C	28	Bob Bassen	STL	79	7	25	32	12	167	0	0	1	0	101	6.9
C	18	Ron Wilson	STL	64	12	17	29	10	46	5	2	2	0	100	12.0
R	23	Rich Sutter	STL	77	9	16	25	7	107	0	1	3	0	113	8.0
L	10	Dave Lowry	STL	75	7	13	20	11–	77	0	0	1	0	85	8.2
D	5	Garth Butcher	STL	68	5	15	20	5	189	0	0	0	0	50	10.0
D	33	Stephane Quintal	BOS	49	4	10	14	8–	77	0	0	0	0	52	7.7
			STL	26	0	6	6	3–	32	0	0	0	0	19	.0
			TOTAL	75	4	16	20	11–	109	0	0	0	0	71	5.6
D	4	Rick Zombo	DET	3	0	0	0	3–	15	0	0	0	0	1	.0
			STL	64	3	15	18	4	46	0	0	0	0	47	6.4
			TOTAL	67	3	15	18	1	61	0	0	0	0	48	6.3
C	41	Michel Mongeau	STL	36	3	12	15	2–	6	2	0	0	0	23	13.0
D	20	Lee Norwood	HFD	6	0	0	0	0	16	0	0	0	0	1	.0
			STL	44	3	11	14	14	94	1	0	1	0	51	5.9
			TOTAL	50	3	11	14	14	110	1	0	1	0	52	5.8
D	6	Murray Baron	STL	67	3	8	11	3–	94	0	0	0	0	55	5.5
G	31	Curtis Joseph	STL	60	0	9	9	0	12	0	0	0	0	0	.0
C	36*	Philippe Bozon	STL	9	1	3	4	5	4	0	0	0	0	19	5.3
R	29	Darin Kimble	STL	46	1	3	4	3–	166	0	0	0	0	12	8.3
R	39	Kelly Chase	STL	46	1	2	3	6–	264	0	0	0	0	29	3.4
D	2	Curt Giles	STL	13	1	1	2	3–	8	0	0	0	0	4	25.0
D	25*	Jason Marshall	STL	2	1	0	1	0	4	0	0	0	0	2	50.0
D	44*	Bret Hedican	STL	4	1	0	1	1	0	0	0	0	0	1	100.0
L	26	Dave Mackey	STL	19	1	0	1	4–	49	0	0	1	0	12	8.3
R	17*	Denny Felsner	STL	3	0	1	1	0	0	0	0	0	0	2	.0
D	38	Dominic Lavoie	STL	6	0	1	1	3–	10	0	0	0	0	11	.0
G	40*	Guy Hebert	STL	13	0	1	1	0	0	0	0	0	0	0	.0
D	4*	Rob Robinson	STL	22	0	1	1	4–	8	0	0	0	0	9	.0
L	25*	Ron Hoover	STL	1	0	0	0	0	0	0	0	0	0	1	.0
D	34*	Randy Skarda	STL	1	0	0	0	0	0	0	0	0	0	0	.0
G	1*	Pat Jablonski	STL	10	0	0	0	0	4	0	0	0	0	0	.0

Goaltending

No.	Goaltender	GPI	Mins	Avg	W	L	T	EN	SO	GA	SA	S%
40	* Guy Hebert	13	738	2.93	5	5	1	0	0	36	393	.908
31	Curtis Joseph	60	3494	3.01	27	20	10	5	2	175	1953	.910
30	Vincent Riendeau	3	157	4.20	1	2	0	0	0	11	96	.885
1	* Pat Jablonski	10	468	4.87	3	6	0	1	0	38	259	.853
	Totals	**80**	**4868**	**3.28**	**36**	**33**	**11**	**6**	**2**	**266**	**2707**	**.902**

Playoffs

Pos	#	Player	Team	GP	G	A	Pts	+/–	PIM	PP	SH	GW	GT	S	%
R	16	Brett Hull	STL	6	4	4	8	2	4	1	1	1	1	38	10.5
C	7*	Nelson Emerson	STL	6	3	3	6	0	21	2	0	0	0	11	27.3
C	15	Craig Janney	STL	6	0	6	6	4–	0	0	0	0	0	7	.0
R	19	Brendan Shanahan	STL	6	2	3	5	0	14	1	0	0	0	17	11.8
C	22	Ron Sutter	STL	6	1	3	4	1–	8	1	0	0	0	9	11.1
R	27	Dave Christian	STL	4	3	0	3	1–	0	0	0	0	0	4	75.0
D	21	Jeff Brown	STL	6	2	1	3	3–	2	0	0	1	0	19	10.5
D	33	Stephane Quintal	STL	4	1	2	3	0	6	1	0	0	0	5	20.0
D	5	Garth Butcher	STL	5	1	2	3	3	16	0	0	0	0	4	25.0
D	2	Curt Giles	STL	3	1	1	2	2–	0	1	0	0	0	2	50.0
C	28	Bob Bassen	STL	6	0	2	2	0	4	0	0	0	0	5	.0
D	4	Rick Zombo	STL	6	0	2	2	2–	12	0	0	0	0	5	.0
C	36*	Philippe Bozon	STL	6	1	0	1	2–	27	0	0	0	0	11	9.1
D	20	Lee Norwood	STL	1	0	1	1	0	0	0	0	0	0	2	.0
D	14	Paul Cavallini	STL	4	0	1	1	0	6	0	0	0	0	6	.0
G	31	Curtis Joseph	STL	6	0	1	1	0	0	0	0	0	0	0	.0
L	10	Dave Lowry	STL	6	0	1	1	0	20	0	0	0	0	6	.0
C	18	Ron Wilson	STL	6	0	1	1	3	0	0	0	0	0	6	.0
R	39	Kelly Chase	STL	1	0	0	0	0	7	0	0	0	0	0	.0
L	26	Dave Mackey	STL	1	0	0	0	0	0	0	0	0	0	3	.0
R	17*	Denny Felsner	STL	1	0	0	0	0	0	0	0	0	0	0	.0
D	6	Murray Baron	STL	2	0	0	0	1–	2	0	0	0	0	2	.0
R	29	Darin Kimble	STL	5	0	0	0	1–	7	0	0	0	0	0	.0
D	44*	Bret Hedican	STL	5	0	0	0	1	0	0	0	0	0	6	.0
R	23	Rich Sutter	STL	6	0	0	0	3–	8	0	0	0	0	8	.0

Goaltending

No.	Goaltender	GPI	Mins	Avg	W	L	EN	SO	GA	SA	S%
31	Curtis Joseph	6	379	3.64	2	4	0	0	23	217	.894
	Totals	**6**	**384**	**3.59**	**2**	**4**	**0**	**0**	**23**	**217**	**.894**

Club Records

Team

(Figures in brackets for season records are games played; records for fewest points, wins, ties, losses, goals, goals against are for 70 or more games)

Record		
Most Points	**107**	1980-81 (80)
Most Wins	**47**	1990-91 (80)
Most Ties	**19**	1970-71 (78)
Most Losses	**50**	1978-79 (80)
Most Goals	**352**	1980-81 (80)
Most Goals Against	**349**	1981-82 (80)
Fewest Points	**48**	1978-79 (80)
Fewest Wins	**18**	1978-79 (80)
Fewest Ties	**7**	1983-84 (80)
Fewest Losses	**18**	1980-81 (80)
Fewest Goals	**177**	1967-68 (74)
Fewest Goals Against	**157**	1968-69 (76)
Longest Winning Streak		
Over-all	**7**	Jan. 21-Feb. 3/88 Mar. 19-31/91
Home	**9**	Jan. 26-Feb. 26/91
Away	**4**	Four times
Longest Undefeated Streak		
Over-all	**12**	Nov. 10-Dec. 8/68 (5 wins, 7 ties)
Home	**11**	Feb. 12-Mar. 19/69 (5 wins, 6 ties) Feb. 7-Mar. 29/75 (9 wins, 2 ties)
Away	**7**	Dec. 9-26/87 (4 wins, 3 ties)
Longest Losing Streak		
Over-all	**7**	Nov. 12-26/67; Feb. 12-25/89
Home	**5**	Nov. 19-Dec. 6/77
Away	**10**	Jan. 20/82-Mar. 8/82
Longest Winless Streak		
Over-all	**12**	Jan. 17-Feb. 15/78 (10 losses, 2 ties)
Home	**7**	Dec. 28/82-Jan. 25/83 (5 losses, 2 ties)
Away	**17**	Jan. 23-Apr. 7/74 (14 losses, 3 ties)
Most Shutouts, Season	**13**	1968-69 (76)
Most PIM, Season	**2,041**	1990-91 (80)
Most Goals, Game	**10**	Feb. 2/82 (Wpg. 6 at St. L. 10) Dec. 1/84 (Det. 5 at St. L. 10) Jan. 15/86 (Tor. 1 at St. L. 10)

Individual

Record		
Most Seasons	**13**	Bernie Federko
Most Games	**927**	Bernie Federko
Most Goals, Career	**352**	Bernie Federko
Most Assists, Career	**721**	Bernie Federko
Most Points, Career	**1,073**	Bernie Federko
Most PIM, Career	**1,786**	Brian Sutter
Most Shutouts, Career	**16**	Glenn Hall
Longest Consecutive Games Streak	**662**	Garry Unger (Feb. 7/71-Apr. 8/79)
Most Goals, Season	**86**	Brett Hull (1990-91)
Most Assists, Season	**90**	Adam Oates (1990-91)
Most Points, Season	**131**	Brett Hull (1990-91) (86 goals, 45 assists)
Most PIM, Season	**306**	Bob Gassoff (1975-76)
Most Points, Defenseman Season	**66**	Rob Ramage (1985-86) (10 goals, 56 assists)
Most Points, Center, Season	**115**	Adam Oates (1990-91) (25 goals, 90 assists)
Most Points, Right Wing, Season	**131**	Brett Hull (1990-91) (86 goals, 45 assists)

Record		
Most Points, Left Wing, Season	**85**	Chuck Lefley (1975-76) (43 goals, 42 assists)
Most Points, Rookie, Season	**73**	Jorgen Pettersson (1980-81) (37 goals, 36 assists)
Most Shutouts, Season	**8**	Glenn Hall (1968-69)
Most Goals, Game	**6**	Red Berenson (Nov. 7/68)
Most Assists, Game	**5**	Brian Sutter (Nov. 22/88) Bernie Federko (Feb. 27/88) Adam Oates (Jan. 26/91)
Most Points, Game	**7**	Red Berenson (Nov. 7/68) Garry Unger (Mar. 13/71)

All-time Record vs. Other Clubs

Regular Season

	At Home							On Road							Total						
	GP	W	L	T	GF	GA	PTS	GP	W	L	T	GF	GA	PTS	GP	W	L	T	GF	GA	PTS
Boston	50	20	21	9	159	174	49	49	10	32	7	133	220	27	99	30	53	16	292	394	76
Buffalo	41	25	11	5	161	108	55	42	11	27	4	130	175	26	83	36	38	9	291	283	81
Calgary	39	15	18	6	140	129	36	38	15	20	3	109	138	33	77	30	38	9	249	267	69
Chicago	82	40	27	15	289	259	95	84	22	51	11	259	343	55	166	62	78	26	548	602	150
Detroit	76	45	21	10	287	206	100	77	34	32	11	254	280	79	153	79	53	21	541	486	179
Edmonton	20	7	10	3	77	90	17	21	5	13	3	81	101	13	41	12	23	6	158	191	30
Hartford	21	11	8	2	81	72	24	20	10	8	2	65	65	22	41	21	16	4	146	137	46
Los Angeles	55	35	14	6	212	150	76	54	19	27	8	158	194	46	109	54	41	14	370	344	122
Minnesota	87	46	24	17	315	247	109	85	31	37	17	254	294	79	172	77	61	34	569	541	188
Montreal	49	10	25	14	126	173	34	50	8	36	6	130	222	22	99	18	61	20	256	395	56
New Jersey	36	25	8	3	164	110	53	37	15	15	7	110	119	37	73	40	23	10	274	229	90
NY Islanders	37	15	16	6	133	124	36	39	7	22	10	92	155	24	76	22	38	16	225	279	60
NY Rangers	53	21	24	8	157	175	50	51	6	40	5	118	220	17	104	27	64	13	275	395	67
Philadelphia	57	22	28	7	164	173	51	57	10	38	9	130	225	29	114	32	66	16	294	398	80
Pittsburgh	55	37	13	5	219	147	79	54	19	24	11	165	198	49	109	56	37	16	384	345	128
Quebec	20	16	3	1	97	65	33	20	8	9	3	68	71	19	40	24	12	4	165	136	52
San Jose	2	2	0	0	10	3	4	1	1	0	0	4	2	2	3	3	0	0	14	5	6
Toronto	77	47	20	10	277	217	104	76	20	48	8	226	302	48	153	67	68	18	503	519	152
Vancouver	47	27	13	7	185	138	61	48	22	21	5	151	153	49	95	49	34	12	336	291	110
Washington	31	14	9	8	130	97	36	30	12	15	3	94	108	27	61	26	24	11	224	205	63
Winnipeg	22	10	4	8	93	70	28	23	5	12	6	73	85	16	45	15	16	14	166	155	44
Defunct Clubs	32	25	4	3	131	55	53	33	11	10	12	95	100	34	65	36	14	15	226	155	87
Totals	**989**	**515**	**321**	**153**	**3607**	**2982**	**1183**	**989**	**301**	**537**	**151**	**2899**	**3770**	**753**	**1978**	**816**	**858**	**304**	**6506**	**6752**	**1936**

Playoffs

	Series	W	L	GP	W	L	T	GF	GA	Last Mtg.	Round	Result
Boston	2	0	2	8	0	8	0	15	48	1972	SF	L 0-4
Buffalo	1	0	1	3	1	2	0	8	7	1976	PR	L 1-2
Calgary	1	0	1	7	3	4	0	22	28	1986	CF	L 3-4
Chicago	8	1	7	41	14	27	0	116	160	1992	DSF	L 2-4
Detroit	3	2	1	16	8	8	0	51	53	1991	DSF	W 4-3
Los Angeles	1	1	0	4	4	0	0	16	5	1969	SF	W 4-0
Minnesota	9	5	4	52	26	26	0	152	158	1991	DF	L 2-4
Montreal	3	0	3	12	0	12	0	14	42	1977	QF	L 0-4
NY Rangers	1	0	1	6	2	4	0	22	29	1981	QF	L 2-4
Philadelphia	2	2	0	11	8	3	0	34	20	1969	QF	W 4-0
Pittsburgh	3	2	1	13	7	6	0	45	40	1981	PR	W 3-2
Toronto	3	2	1	18	10	8	0	56	53	1990	DSF	W 4-1
Winnipeg	1	1	0	4	3	1	0	20	13	1982	DSF	W 3-1
Totals	**38**	**16**	**22**	**195**	**86**	**109**	**0**	**571**	**656**			

Playoff Results 1992-88

Year	Round	Opponent	Result	GF	GA
1992	DSF	Chicago	L 2-4	19	23
1991	DF	Minnesota	L 2-4	17	22
	DSF	Detroit	W 4-3	24	20
1990	DF	Chicago	L 3-4	22	28
	DSF	Toronto	W 4-1	20	16
1989	DF	Chicago	L 1-4	12	19
	DSF	Minnesota	W 4-1	23	15
1988	DF	Detroit	L 1-4	14	21
	DSF	Chicago	W 4-1	21	17

Abbreviations: Round: F – Final; **CF** – conference final; **DF** – division final; **DSF** – division semi-final; **SF** – semi-final; **QF** – quarter-final; **PR** – preliminary round. **GA** – goals against; **GF** – goals for.

1991-92 Results

Home				Away			
Oct.	10	Edmonton	3-2	**Oct.**	5	New Jersey	2-7
	12	San Jose	6-3		7	Toronto	0-3
	15	Toronto	5-1		17	Detroit	3-6
	19	Chicago	4-4		20	Chicago	4-1
	24	Boston	6-5		28	Toronto	1-1
	26	Calgary	2-2		30	Edmonton	2-2
Nov.	5	Philadelphia	3-4	**Nov.**	1	Vancouver	3-2
	9	Hartford	3-4		3	Winnipeg	3-3
	14	Winnipeg	2-1		7	Detroit	3-10
	16	Minnesota	5-3		17	Chicago	1-5
	20	Toronto	5-2		27	Detroit	4-6
	23	NY Rangers	0-3	**Dec.**	3	Minnesota	3-3
	28	Quebec	5-2		4	Minnesota	2-5
	30	Detroit	7-3		10	NY Islanders	7-7
Dec.	7	Pittsburgh	6-1		11	Buffalo	6-3
	19	San Jose	4-0		14	Quebec	4-2
	21	NY Islanders	6-2		16	Montreal	2-4
	26	Chicago	3-1		22	Chicago	2-5
Jan.	2	Minnesota	6-1		28	Minnesota	2-5
	4	Detroit	2-6		31	Buffalo	3-4
	14	Washington	1-6	**Jan.**	6	Toronto	2-3
	16	Montreal	6-6		8	NY Rangers	5-3
	21	Buffalo	5-4		9	New Jersey	3-4
	23	Los Angeles	5-6		11	NY Islanders	6-3
	25	Vancouver	0-1		28	Los Angeles	3-3
Feb.	6	New Jersey	4-1		30	San Jose	4-2
	8	Chicago	1-3	**Feb.**	1	Pittsburgh	1-4
	11	Los Angeles	3-2		2	Philadelphia	1-5
	13	Boston	4-0		17	Detroit	3-5
	15	Calgary	7-2		19	Winnipeg	4-3
	22	Toronto	4-3		23	Chicago	2-4
	27	Washington	7-3		25	Hartford	5-2
	29	Detroit	2-3	**Mar.**	2	Vancouver	5-3
Mar.	10	Minnesota	5-2		6	Edmonton	3-5
	12	Detroit	4-5		7	Calgary	1-5
	14	NY Rangers	0-6		17	Washington	4-6
	26	Hartford	7-2		19	Boston	4-1
	28	Toronto	2-3		21	Montreal	3-3
Apr.	4	Chicago	5-3		23	Toronto	2-3
	5	Minnesota	5-3	**Apr.**	2	Minnesota	1-1

*Denotes afternoon game

Entry Draft Selections 1992-78

1992
Pick
- 38 Igor Korolev
- 62 Vitali Karamnov
- 64 Vitali Prokhorov
- 86 Lee J. Leslie
- 134 Bob Lachance
- 158 Ian LaPerriere
- 160 Lance Burns
- 180 Igor Boldin
- 182 Nicholas Naumenko
- 206 Todd Harris
- 230 Yuri Gunko
- 259 Wade Salzman

1991
Pick
- 27 Steve Staios
- 64 Kyle Reeves
- 65 Nathan Lafayette
- 87 Grayden Reid
- 109 Jeff Callinan
- 131 Bruce Gardiner
- 153 Terry Hollinger
- 175 Christopher Kenady
- 197 Jed Fiebelkorn
- 219 Chris MacKenzie
- 241 Kevin Rappana
- 263 Mike Veisor

1990
Pick
- 33 Craig Johnson
- 54 Patrice Tardif
- 96 Jason Ruff
- 117 Kurtis Miller
- 138 Wayne Conlan
- 180 Parris Duffus
- 201 Steve Widmeyer
- 222 Joe Hawley
- 243 Joe Fleming

1989
Pick
- 9 Jason Marshall
- 31 Rick Corriveau
- 55 Denny Felsner
- 93 Daniel Laperriere
- 114 David Roberts
- 124 Derek Frenette
- 135 Jeff Batters
- 156 Kevin Plager
- 177 John Roderick
- 198 John Valo
- 219 Brian Lukowski

1988
Pic
- 9 Rod Brind' Amour
- 30 Adrien Plavsic
- 51 Rob Fournier
- 72 Jaan Luik
- 105 Dave Lacouture
- 114 Dan Fowler
- 135 Matt Hayes
- 156 John McCoy
- 177 Tony Twist
- 198 Bret Hedican
- 219 Heath DeBoer
- 240 Michael Francis

1987
Pick
- 12 Keith Osborne
- 54 Kevin Miehm
- 59 Robert Nordmark
- 75 Darin Smith
- 82 Andy Rymsha
- 117 Rob Robinson
- 138 Todd Crabtree
- 159 Guy Hebert
- 180 Robert Dumas
- 201 David Marvin
- 207 Andy Cesarski
- 222 Dan Rolfe
- 243 Ray Savard

1986
Pick
- 10 Jocelyn Lemieux
- 31 Mike Posma
- 52 Tony Hejna
- 73 Glen Featherstone
- 87 Michael Wolak
- 115 Mike O'Toole
- 136 Andy May
- 157 Randy Skarda
- 178 Martyn Ball
- 199 Rod Thacker
- 220 Terry MacLean
- 234 Bill Butler
- 241 David O'Brien

1985
Pick
- 37 Herb Raglan
- 44 Nelson Emerson
- 54 Ned Desmond
- 100 Dan Brooks
- 121 Rich Burchill
- 138 Pat Jablonski
- 159 Scott Brickey
- 180 Jeff Urban
- 201 Vince Guidotti
- 222 Ron Saatzer
- 243 Dave Jecha

1984
Pick
- 26 Brian Benning
- 32 Tony Hrkac
- 50 Toby Ducolon
- 53 Robert Dirk
- 56 Alan Perry
- 71 Graham Herring
- 92 Scott Paluch
- 113 Steve Tuttle
- 134 Cliff Ronning
- 148 Don Porter
- 155 Jim Vesey
- 176 Daniel Jomphe
- 196 Tom Tilley
- 217 Mark Cupolo
- 237 Mark Lanigan

1983
DID NOT DRAFT

1982
Pick
- 50 Mike Posavad
- 92 Scott Machej
- 113 Perry Ganchar
- 134 Doug Gilmour
- 155 Chris Delaney
- 176 Matt Christensen
- 197 John Shumski
- 218 Brian Ahern
- 239 Peter Smith

1981
Pick
- 20 Marty Ruff
- 36 Hakan Nordin
- 62 Gordon Donnelly
- 104 Mike Hickey
- 125 Peter Aslin
- 146 Erik Holmberg
- 167 Alain Vigneault
- 188 Dan Wood
- 209 Richard Zemlak

1980
Pick
- 12 Rik Wilson
- 54 Jim Pavese
- 75 Bob Brooke
- 96 Alain Lemieux
- 117 Perry Anderson
- 138 Roger Hagglund
- 159 Pat Rabbitt
- 180 Peter Lindgren
- 201 John Smyth

1979
Pick
- 2 Perry Turnbull
- 65 Bob Crawford
- 86 Mark Reeds
- 107 Gilles Leduc

1978
Pick
- 3 Wayne Babych
- 39 Steve Harrison
- 72 Kevin Willison
- 89 Jim Nill
- 106 Steve Stockman
- 109 Paul MacLean
- 123 Denis Houle
- 140 Tony Meagher
- 143 Rick Simpson
- 157 Jim Lockhurst
- 160 Bob Froese
- 170 Dan Lerg
- 173 Risto Siltanen
- 175 Dan Hermansson
- 181 Jean-Francois Boutin
- 185 John Sullivan
- 188 Serge Menard
- 191 Don Boyd
- 197 Paul Stasiuk
- 200 Gerhard Truntschka
- 203 Victor Shkurdyuk
- 205 Carl Bloomberg
- 207 Terry Kitching
- 209 Brian O'Connor
- 210 Brian Crombeen
- 211 Mike Pidgeon
- 214 John Cochrane
- 216 Joe Casey
- 218 Jim Farrell
- 220 Frank Johnson
- 221 Blair Wheeler

Club Directory

St. Louis Arena
5700 Oakland Avenue
St. Louis, MO 63110
Phone **314/781-5300**
FAX 314/645-1340
Capacity: 17,188

Board of Directors
Michael F. Shanahan, Jud Perkins, Andrew Craig, Edwin Trusheim, Larry Alexander, Alfred Kerth

Chairman of the Board	Michael F. Shanahan
President	Jack J. Quinn
Vice-President/General Manager	Ronald Caron
Vice-President/Director of Sales	Bruce Affleck
Vice-President/Ass't GM/Director of Player Personnel and Scouting	Ted Hampson
Vice-President/Director of Broadcast Sales	Matt Hyland
Vice-President/Director of Finance and Administration	Jerry Jasiek
Vice-President/Director of Public Relations and Marketing	Susie Mathieu
Vice-President/Head Coach	Bob Plager
Assistant General Manager	Bob Berry
Special Counsel	Thomas J. Guilfoil
Secretary/General Counsel	Timothy R. Wolf
Assistant Coach	Wayne Thomas
Assistant Coach	Harold Snepsts
Head Coach – Peoria Rivermen	Rick Meagher
Assistant Coach – Peoria Rivermen	Mark Reeds
Assistant Director of Scouting	Jack Evans
Western Canada/United States Scout	Pat Ginnell
Special Assignment/Advance Scout	Paul MacLean
New England Area Scout	Matt Keator
Director of Promotions/Community Relations	Tracy Lovasz
Assistant Director of Public Relations	Jeff Trammel
Assistant Director of Public Relations	Michael Caruso
Accounting	Marsha McBride, Rita Russell, Margaret Steinmeyer
Sales	John Casson, Wes Edwards, Tammy Iuli, Jill Mann
Merchandise Manager	George Pavlik
Head Trainer	Tom Nash
Conditioning Consultant	Mackie Shilstone
Equipment Managers	Frank Burns, Terry Roof
Executive Secretary	Lynn Diederichsen
Marketing/Public Relations Secretary	Donna Quirk
Receptionist	Pam Barrett
Orthopedic Surgeon	Dr. Jerome Gilden
Internist	Dr. Aaron Birenbaum
Dentist	Dr. Ron Sherstoff
Dentist Emeritus	Dr. Les Rich
M.D. Emeritus	Dr. J.G. Probstein
Optometrist	Dr. N. Rex Ghormley

Coach

PLAGER, BOB
Coach, St. Louis Blues. Born in Kirkland Lake, Ont., March 11, 1943.

Bob Plager became the 16th head coach of the St. Louis Blues on May 1, 1992. Plager, who was chosen by the Blues in the 1967 Expansion Draft, was one of the most popular players ever to skate for the team. He retired as a player in 1978 after 644 NHL games, 615 of those with the Blues, but remained with the organization as a scout. After serving in a number of capacities, including head coach of the Blues' Salt Lake City franchise in the CHL, Plager was appointed as the Blues' vice president in charge of player development on September 7, 1989. He became the head coach of St. Louis' IHL farm affiliate in Peoria in 1990 and led the team to the Turner Cup championship, earning IHL coach of the year honors.

Coaching Record

		Regular Season					Playoffs			
Season	Team	Games	W	L	T	%	Games	W	L	%
1990-91	Peoria (IHL)	82	58	19	5	.738	19	12	7	.632

General Manager

CARON, RON
Vice-President General Manager and Alternate Governor, St. Louis Blues. Born in Hull, Que., December 19, 1929.

Ron Caron joined the St. Louis Blues on August 13, 1983 after a 26-year association with the Montreal Canadiens' organization. He joined the Canadiens in 1957 on a part-time scouting basis after coaching in the amateur ranks. In 1966, Caron was promoted to a full-time position as chief scout of the Montreal Junior Canadiens and was instrumental in assembling two Memorial Cup championship teams. In 1968, he was named chief scout of the parent club and served as an assistant to former manager Sam Pollock. In 1969 he added the responsibilities of general manager of the Montreal Voyageurs of the AHL and maintained that role until 1978 when he was named director of scouting and player personnel for the Canadiens. Caron remained with the Montreal organization until the conclusion of the 1982-83 campaign.

San Jose Sharks

1991-92 Results: 17W-58L-5T 39PTS. Sixth, Smythe Division

Year-by-Year Record

Season	GP	Home W	Home L	Home T	Road W	Road L	Road T	Overall W	Overall L	Overall T	GF	GA	Pts.	Finished	Playoff Result
1991-92	80	14	23	3	3	35	2	17	58	5	219	359	39	6th, Smythe Div.	Out of Playoffs

Schedule

Home				Away			
Oct.	Thur.	8	Winnipeg	**Oct.**	Tues.	13	Los Angeles
	Sat.	10	Detroit		Wed.	21	Montreal
	Thur.	15	Boston		Fri.	23	Buffalo
	Sat.	17	Calgary		Sat.	24	Toronto
Nov.	Thur.	5	Buffalo		Mon.	26	St Louis
	Sat.	7	New Jersey		Wed.	28	Detroit
	Sun.	8	Los Angeles		Fri.	30	Tampa Bay
	Thur.	12	Edmonton	**Nov.**	Sun.	1	Chicago
	Sat.	14	Vancouver		Tues.	10	Vancouver
	Tues.	17	Los Angeles		Wed.	25	Calgary
	Thur.	19	Toronto		Fri.	27	Winnipeg
	Sat.	21	Chicago		Sat.	28	Minnesota
Dec.	Tues.	1	Edmonton	**Dec.**	Wed.	9	Vancouver
	Thur.	3	Hartford		Fri.	18	Vancouver
	Sat.	5	Pittsburgh*		Mon.	21	Winnipeg
	Thur.	10	St Louis		Wed.	23	Edmonton
	Sat.	12	Quebec		Tues.	29	Vancouver
	Wed.	16	Tampa Bay	**Jan.**	Mon.	4	Montreal (at Sacramento)
	Sat.	19	Vancouver		Fri.	8	Toronto
	Sat.	26	Los Angeles		Sun.	10	Ottawa*
	Wed.	30	Philadelphia		Tues.	12	Winnipeg
Jan.	Sat.	2	Vancouver		Fri.	15	Detroit
	Tues.	5	Montreal		Sat.	16	Quebec
	Fri.	29	Chicago		Mon.	18	Boston*
	Sat.	30	Calgary		Thur.	21	Hartford
Feb.	Mon.	1	Tampa Bay		Sat.	23	Tampa Bay
	Wed.	3	Minnesota		Tues.	26	Los Angeles
	Tues.	16	Washington	**Feb.**	Wed.	10	Calgary
	Thur.	18	Winnipeg		Fri.	12	Edmonton
	Sat.	20	NY Rangers		Sun.	14	Winnipeg*
	Mon.	22	NY Rangers (at Sacramento)		Sat.	27	Calgary
	Tues.	23	Calgary		Sun.	28	Edmonton
	Thur.	25	Toronto	**Mar.**	Tues.	9	Minnesota
Mar.	Tues.	2	Ottawa		Thur.	11	St Louis
	Sun.	7	Edmonton		Fri.	19	NY Rangers
	Sun.	14	Detroit*		Sun.	21	Washington*
	Tues.	16	NY Islanders		Tues.	23	Pittsburgh
Apr.	Thur.	1	Winnipeg		Thur.	25	Philadelphia
	Sat.	3	Calgary*		Sat.	27	NY Islanders
	Sun.	4	Calgary		Mon.	29	New Jersey
	Tues.	6	Edmonton	**Apr.**	Thur.	8	Los Angeles
	Sat.	10	Los Angeles		Thur.	15	Calgary

* Denotes afternoon game.

Home Starting Times:
All Games .... 7:35 p.m.
Except Matinees .... 1:35 p.m.
Dec. 5 .... 4:35 p.m.

Franchise date: May 9, 1990

2nd NHL Season

Doug Wilson solidified the Sharks' defense in the 1991-92 season, leading all San Jose rearguards in scoring with 28 points.

1992-93 Player Personnel

FORWARDS	HT	WT	S	Place of Birth	Date	1991-92 Club
BARBER, Don	6-2	205	L	Victoria, B.C.	12/2/64	S.J.-Que.-Wpg.
BEAUFAIT, Mark	5-9	165	R	Livonia, MI	5/13/70	Northern Michigan
BELLEROSE, Eric	6-1	202	L	Montreal, Que.	2/7/72	Hull-Trois-Rivières
BEREZAN, Perry	6-2	190	R	Edmonton, Alta.	12/5/64	San Jose
BRUCE, David	5-11	190	R	Thunder Bay, Ont.	10/7/64	San Jose-Kansas City
CALOUN, Jan	5-10	176	R	Usti-nad-labem, Czech.	12/20/72	Litvinov
CARTER, John	5-10	170	L	Winchester, MA	5/3/63	San Jose-Kansas City
CHERBAYEV, Alexander	6-1	187	L	Voskresensk, Russia	8/13/73	Khimik Voskresensk
COURTENAY, Ed	6-4	200	R	Verdun, Que.	2/2/68	San Jose-Kansas City
COXE, Craig	6-4	220	L	Chula Vista, CA	1/21/64	S.J.-K.C.-Milw.
CRAIGWELL, Dale	5-11	180	L	Toronto, Ont.	4/24/71	San Jose-Kansas City
DEPALMA, Larry	6-0	195	L	Trenton, MI	10/27/65	Kansas City
EVASON, Dean	5-10	180	R	Flin Flon, Man.	8/22/64	San Jose
FALLOON, Pat	5-11	192	R	Foxwarren, Man.	9/22/72	San Jose
FRANTTI, Gord	6-6	228	L	Larium, MI	6/17/70	Kansas City
FREDERICK, Troy	6-5	226	L	Virden, Man.	4/4/69	Kansas City
GARPENLOV, Johan	5-11	183	L	Stockholm, Sweden	3/21/68	San Jose-Detroit
GAUDREAU, Robert	5-11	185	R	Lincoln, RI	1/20/70	Providence C.
GRILLO, Dean	6-2	210	R	Bemidji, MN	12/8/72	Waterloo
KHOLOMEYEV, Alexandr	6-1	194	L	St. Petersburg, Russia	3/23/69	Izhorets
KISIO, Kelly	5-9	183	R	Peace River, Alta.	9/18/59	San Jose
KONOWALCHUK, Brian	5-11	180	L	Prince Albert, Sask.	10/14/71	U. of Denver
KRAVETS, Mikhail	5-10	176	L	St. Petersburg, Russia	11/12/63	San Jose-Kansas City
LAWTON, Brian	6-0	190	L	New Brunswick, N.J.	6/29/65	San Jose
McDONOUGH, Hubie	5-9	175	L	Manchester, NH	7/8/63	NYI-Capital District
McLEAN, Jeff	5-10	186	L	Port Moody, B.C.	9/6/69	U. of North Dakota
NAZAROV, Andrei	6-4	209	R	Chelyabinsk, Russia	5/22/74	Dynamo Moscow
NILSSON, Fredrick	6-1	198	L	Vasteras, Sweden	4/16/71	Vasteras
ODGERS, Jeff	6-0	195	R	Spy Hill, Sask.	5/31/69	San Jose-Kansas City
OLIMB, Larry	5-10	155	L	Warroad, MN	8/11/69	U. of Minnesota
OTEVREL, Jaroslav	6-2	185	L	Gottwaldov, Czech.	9/16/68	Zlin
QUINTIN, J.F.	6-0	187	L	St. Jean, Que.	5/28/69	San Jose-Kansas City
SKRIKO, Petri	5-10	175	L	Lapeenranta, Finland	3/12/62	Bos.-Fin. Oly.-Wpg.
SNUGGERUD, Dave	6-0	190	L	Minnetonka, MN	6/20/66	San Jose-Buffalo
SULLIVAN, Mike	6-2	185	L	Marshfield, MA	2/27/68	San Jose-Kansas City
WEISBROD, John	6-3	215	R	Syosset, NY	10/8/68	Injured
WHITNEY, Ray	5-9	160	R	Ft. Saskatchewan, Alta.	5/8/72	Cologne-S.D.-S.J.
WOOD, Dody	5-11	180	L	Chetwynd, B.C.	3/10/72	Seattle-Swift Current
DEFENSEMEN						
COLMAN, Mike	6-3	225	R	Stoneham, MA	8/4/68	San Jose-Kansas City
GAETZ, Link	6-2	210	L	Vancouver, B.C.	10/2/68	San Jose
IGNATJEV, Victor	6-3	198	L	Riga, Latvia	4/26/70	Riga
JOYCE, Duane	6-2	203	R	Pembroke, MA	5/5/65	Kansas City
KOLSTAD, Dean	6-6	210	L	Edmonton, Alta.	6/16/68	Kalamazoo
KRISS, Aaron	6-2	185	L	Parma, OH	9/17/72	Lowell U.
LESSARD, Rick	6-2	200	L	Timmins, Ont.	1/9/68	San Jose-Kansas City
MACLEOD, Pat	5-11	190	L	Melfort, Sask.	6/15/69	San Jose-Kansas City
MORE, Jayson	6-1	207	R	Souris, Man.	1/12/69	San Jose-Kansas City
OZOLNICH, Sandis	6-1	189	L	Riga, Latvia	3/8/72	Riga-Kansas City
PEDERSON, Tom	5-9	165	R	Bloomington, MN	1/1/70	US Nat.-K.C.
RAGNARSSON, Marcus	6-1	200	L	Ostervala, Sweden	8/13/71	Djurgarden
RATHJE, Mike	6-5	205	L	Mannville, Alta.	5/11/74	Medicine Hat
SCREMIN, Claudio	6-2	205	R	Burnaby, B.C.	5/28/68	San Jose-Kansas City
SMITH, Ryan	6-3	200	L	Tabor, Ont.	6/28/74	Brandon
SYKORA, Michal	6-4	198	L	Pardubice, Czech.	7/5/73	Tacoma
WILKINSON, Neil	6-3	190	R	Selkirk, Man.	8/15/67	San Jose
WILLIAMS, Dave	6-2	195	R	Plainfield, NJ	8/25/67	San Jose-Kansas City
WILSON, Doug	6-1	187	L	Ottawa, Ont.	7/5/57	San Jose
ZETTLER, Rob	6-3	190	L	Sept Iles, Que.	3/8/68	San Jose
ZMOLEK, Doug	6-2	225	L	Rochester, MN	11/3/70	U. of Minnesota

GOALTENDERS	HT	WT	C	Place of Birth	Date	1991-92 Club
BURNS, Chris	6-1	185	L	Sudbury, Ont.	5/19/73	Thunder Bay
CASHMAN, Scott	6-2	186	L	Ottawa, Ont.	9/20/69	Boston U.
FLAHERTY, Wade	6-0	170	R	Terrace, B.C.	1/11/68	San Jose-Kansas City
HACKETT, Jeff	6-1	175	L	London, Ont.	6/1/68	San Jose
HAYWARD, Brian	5-10	180	L	Toronto, Ont.	6/25/60	San Jose-Kansas City
IRBE, Arturs	5-7	180	L	Riga, Latvia	2/2/67	San Jose-Kansas City
RYDER, Dan	6-1	184	L	Kitchener, Ont.	10/24/72	Sudbury-Ottawa
SAURDIFF, Corwin	5-11	168	L	Warroad, MN	10/17/72	N. Michigan
SCHOEN, Bryan	6-2	180	L	St. Paul, MN	9/9/70	U. of Denver

1991-92 Scoring

Regular Season

Pos	#.	Player	Team	GP	G	A	Pts	+/-	PIM	PP	SH	GW	GT	S	%
R	17*	Pat Falloon	S.J.	79	25	34	59	32–	16	5	0	1	2	181	13.8
R	19	Brian Mullen	S.J.	72	18	28	46	14–	66	5	3	1	0	168	10.7
R	15	David Bruce	S.J.	60	22	16	38	20–	46	10	1	1	0	137	16.1
C	9	Brian Lawton	S.J.	59	15	22	37	25–	42	7	0	1	0	131	11.5
C	11	Kelly Kisio	S.J.	48	11	26	37	7–	54	2	3	2	0	68	16.2
D	24	Doug Wilson	S.J.	44	9	19	28	38–	26	4	0	0	1	123	7.3
D	3*	David Williams	S.J.	56	3	25	28	13–	40	2	0	1	0	91	3.3
C	8	Dean Evason	S.J.	74	11	15	26	22–	99	1	0	1	0	88	12.5
C	16	Perry Berezan	S.J.	66	12	7	19	26–	30	4	1	2	0	112	10.7
C	47*	Mike Sullivan	S.J.	64	8	11	19	18–	15	1	0	1	0	72	11.1
D	5	Neil Wilkinson	S.J.	60	4	15	19	11–	107	1	0	0	0	95	4.2
L	18	Dave Snuggerud	BUF	55	3	15	18	3–	36	0	0	0	0	75	4.0
			S.J.	11	0	1	1	12–	4	0	0	0	0	19	.0
			TOTAL	66	3	16	19	15–	40	0	0	0	0	94	3.2
D	4*	Jay More	S.J.	46	4	13	17	32–	85	1	0	1	0	60	6.7
L	14	Steve Bozek	S.J.	58	8	8	16	30–	27	2	0	0	0	105	7.6
C	33*	Dale Craigwell	S.J.	32	5	11	16	3–	8	4	0	2	0	38	13.2
D	38*	Pat Macleod	S.J.	37	5	11	16	32–	4	3	0	0	0	77	6.5
L	22	Paul Fenton	S.J.	60	11	4	15	39–	33	3	2	1	0	96	11.5
D	6	Ken Hammond	S.J.	46	5	10	15	17–	82	2	0	0	0	93	5.4
L	10	Johan Garpenlov	DET	16	1	1	2	2	4	0	0	0	0	13	7.7
			S.J.	12	5	6	11	2–	4	1	0	1	0	21	23.8
			TOTAL	28	6	7	13	0	8	1	0	1	0	34	17.6
D	23*	Link Gaetz	S.J.	48	6	6	12	27–	326	3	0	0	0	73	8.2
L	27	Perry Anderson	S.J.	48	4	8	12	17–	143	0	0	0	0	57	7.0
L	36*	Jeff Odgers	S.J.	61	7	4	11	21–	217	0	0	0	0	64	10.9
D	2	Rob Zettler	S.J.	74	1	8	9	23–	99	0	0	0	0	72	1.4
L	37	Don Barber	WPG	11	0	3	3	2	4	0	0	0	0	6	.0
			QUE	2	0	0	0	1–	0	0	0	0	0	1	.0
			S.J.	12	1	3	4	7–	2	0	0	0	0	17	5.9
			TOTAL	25	1	6	7	6–	6	0	0	0	0	24	4.2
L	28*	J-Francois Quintin	S.J.	8	3	0	3	2	0	0	0	0	0	12	25.0
C	43*	Ray Whitney	S.J.	2	0	3	3	1–	0	0	0	0	0	4	.0
L	21	Craig Coxe	S.J.	10	2	0	2	4–	19	0	0	0	0	11	18.2
D	13*	Rick Lessard	S.J.	8	0	2	2	4–	16	0	0	0	0	4	.0
G	30	Jeff Hackett	S.J.	42	0	2	2	0	8	0	0	0	0	0	.0
L	22	Mike Mchugh	S.J.	8	1	0	1	3–	14	0	0	0	0	5	20.0
C	16	Mark Pavelich	S.J.	2	0	1	1	2–	4	0	0	0	0	0	.0
L	44	Kevin Evans	S.J.	5	0	1	1	0	25	0	0	0	0	4	.0
G	32*	Arturs Irbe	S.J.	13	0	1	1	0	0	0	0	0	0	0	.0
D	34*	Michael Colman	S.J.	15	0	1	1	8–	32	0	0	0	0	7	.0
G	35	Jarmo Myllys	S.J.	27	0	1	1	0	2	0	0	0	0	0	.0
R	26*	Peter Lappin	S.J.	1	0	0	0	0	0	0	0	0	0	2	.0
L	40	Mikhail Kravets	S.J.	1	0	0	0	0	0	0	0	0	0	2	.0
G	31*	Wade Flaherty	S.J.	3	0	0	0	0	0	0	0	0	0	0	.0
L	20	John Carter	S.J.	4	0	0	0	2–	0	0	0	0	0	5	.0
R	39*	Ed Courtenay	S.J.	5	0	0	0	6–	0	0	0	0	0	7	.0
G	1	Brian Hayward	S.J.	7	0	0	0	0	14	0	0	0	0	0	.0
D	45*	Claudio Scremin	S.J.	13	0	0	0	4–	25	0	0	0	0	18	.0

Goaltending

No.	Goaltender	GPI	Mins	Avg	W	L	T	EN	SO	GA	SA	S%
30	Jeff Hackett	42	2314	3.84	11	27	1	1	0	148	1366	.892
31	* Wade Flaherty	3	178	4.38	0	3	0	2	0	13	120	.892
32	* Arturs Irbe	13	645	4.47	2	6	3	1	0	48	365	.868
1	Brian Hayward	7	305	4.92	1	4	0	0	0	25	177	.859
35	Jarmo Myllys	27	1374	5.02	3	18	1	6	0	115	862	.867
	Totals	**80**	**4829**	**4.46**	**17**	**58**	**5**	**10**	**0**	**359**	**2900**	**.876**

Office of the General Manager

LOMBARDI, DEAN
Vice President and Director of Hockey Operations, San Jose Sharks.
Born in Holyoke, Massachusetts, March 5, 1958.

Dean Lombardi enters his fifth year in the National Hockey League, his third with the Sharks organization. After two seasons as assistant general manager, he was named to his new position on June 26, 1992. Prior to joining the Sharks, he spent two seasons (1988-90) as assistant GM with the Minnesota North Stars.

Lombardi, 34, utilizes his skills in contract negotiations and knowledge of the NHL's business and legal workings to the benefit of the Sharks. In addition to spending time evaluating talent for the Entry Draft, his new position with the club also provides Lombardi with many responsibilities traditionally handled by a general manager's function.

Lombardi, raised in Ludlow, MA, sports an impressive resume along with an intense work ethic that has brought him success at all ends of his profession. He received his undergraduate degree from the University of New Haven and law degree from Tulane University, specializing in labor law. During his two years as a player agent, Lombardi represented an impressive list of clients, including five members of the 1988 United States Olympic ice hockey squad.

GRILLO, CHUCK
Vice President and Director of Player Personnel, San Jose Sharks.
Born in Hibbing, Minnesota, July 24, 1939.

Chuck Grillo fills the role of Vice President and Director of Player Personnel for the Sharks, supervising the club's scouting department and player development program. He has held that position since 1990, having the vice president's title, along with some duties of the office of general manager, added on June 26, 1992. Grillo, a native of Hibbing, MN, served as director of professional scouting from 1988-90 with the Minnesota North Stars. Prior to that he spent eight years as a scout for the New York Rangers.

Noted for his eye on talent and his innovative ideas on player development Grillo and his scouting staff were rewarded this past season as four of the Sharks 13 picks in 1991's Entry Draft saw action with the club in 1991-92. In addition, many players who contributed to the International Hockey League champion Kansas City Blades (Sharks development affiliate) were acquired and developed by Grillo and his staff while with Minnesota.

Grillo, 53, also is owner and operator of the highly-successful Minnesota Hockey Camps in Nisswa, MN, considered in the profession as the finest hockey development center in North America. Many athletes at the camp have gone on to become players, coaches and trainers in the NHL. Grillo's stimulating reason for operating the camp is his belief that "Hockey players are not born into the NHL. They are educated, nurtured and developed. The failure to do this has ultimately led to the destruction of many careers among NHL players."

Club Records

Team

(Figures in brackets for season records are games played; records for fewest points, wins, ties, losses, goals, goals against are for 70 or more games)

Most Points	**39**	1991-92 (80)
Most Wins	**17**	1991-92 (80)
Most Ties	**5**	1991-92 (80)
Most Losses	**58**	1991-92 (80)
Most Goals	**219**	1991-92 (80)
Most Goals Against	**359**	1991-92 (80)
Fewest Points	**39**	1991-92 (80)
Fewest Wins	**17**	1991-92 (80)
Fewest Ties	**5**	1991-92 (80)
Fewest Losses	**58**	1991-92 (80)
Fewest Goals	**219**	1991-92 (80)
Fewest Goals Against	**359**	1991-92 (80)
Longest Winning Streak		
Overall	**2 (3 times)**	Nov. 8/91-Nov. 9/91; Nov. 30/91-Dec. 3/91 & Feb. 4/92-Feb. 5/92.
Home	**2 (4 times)**	Nov. 8/91-Nov. 9/91; Nov. 26/91-Dec. 3/91; Feb. 4/92-Feb. 5/92 & Mar. 8/92- Mar. 14/92.
Away	**1 (3 times)**	Nov. 30/91; Jan. 12/92 & Mar. 21/92
Longest Undefeated Streak		
Overall	**4**	Nov. 26/91-Dec. 3/92 (3-0-1)
Home	**2 (6 times)**	Most recent, Mar. 8/92-Mar. 17/92 (2-0-0))
Away	**2 (2 times)**	Nov. 29/91-Nov. 30/91 (1-0-1) & Jan. 12/92-Jan. 14/92 (1-0-1)
Longest Losing Streak		
Overall	**13**	Oct. 10/91-Nov. 4/91
Home	**3 (4 times)**	Oct. 10/91-Oct. 19/91; Feb. 18/92-Feb. 23/92; Mar. 1/92- Mar. 6/92 & Mar. 17/92-Apr. 16/92
Away	**13**	Oct. 4/91-Nov. 23/92
Longest Winless Streak		
Overall	**13**	Oct. 10/91-Nov. 4/92 (0-13-0)
Home	**4 (2 times)**	Nov. 12/91-Nov. 22/91 (0-3-1) & Feb. 28/92-Mar. 6/92 (0-3-1)
Away	**13**	Oct. 4/91-Nov. 23/91 (0-13-0)
Most Shutouts, Season	**None**	
Most PIM, Season	**1894**	1991-92 (80)
Most Goals, Game	**7**	Feb. 26/92 (Quebec 4 at S.J. 7)

Individual

Most Seasons	**1**	Numerous
Most Games, Career	**79**	Pat Falloon
Most Goals, Career	**25**	Pat Falloon
Most Assists, Career	**34**	Pat Falloon
Most Points, Career	**59**	Pat Falloon (25 goals, 34 assists)
Most PIM, Career	**326**	Link Gaetz
Most Shutouts, Career	**none**	
Longest Consecutive Games Streak	**78**	Pat Falloon (Oct. 5/91-Apr. 16/92)
Most Games, Season	**79**	Pat Falloon
Most Goals, Season	**25**	Pat Falloon
Most Assists, Season	**34**	Pat Falloon
Most Points, Season	**59**	Pat Falloon (25 goals, 34 assists)
Most PIM, Season	**326**	Link Gaetz
Most Shutouts, Season	**none**	
Most Points, Defenseman Season	**28**	Doug Wilson (9 goals, 19 assists) David Williams (3 goals, 25 assists)
Most Points, Center, Season	**37**	Brian Lawton (15 goals, 22 assists)
Most Points, Right Wing, Season	**59**	Pat Falloon (25 goals, 34 assists)
Most Points, Left Wing, Season	**16**	Steve Bozek (8 goals, 8 assists)
Most Points, Rookie, Season	**59**	Pat Falloon (25 goals, 34 assists)
Most Goals, Game	**2**	17 times (Most recent Brian Lawton Mar. 23/92)
Most Assists, Game	**3**	5 times (Most recent Pat Falloon Feb. 26/92)
Most Points, Game	**4**	Pat Falloon (1G, 3A, Feb. 26/92)

1991-92 Results

Home			Away		
Oct. 5	Vancouver	2-5	**Oct.** 4	Vancouver	3-4
8	Calgary	4-3	12	St Louis	3-6
10	Winnipeg	4-5	13	Chicago	3-7
17	Minnesota	2-8	16	Los Angeles	5-8
19	Boston	1-4	23	Hartford	0-3
Nov. 8	Edmonton	6-2	25	Buffalo	1-3
9	NY Islanders	4-3	26	New Jersey	0-9
12	Buffalo	1-7	29	NY Islanders	4-8
14	Detroit	3-3	31	Philadelphia	2-5
19	Los Angeles	2-3	**Nov.** 2	Quebec	3-6
22	Toronto	1-3	4	Toronto	1-4
26	Vancouver	4-1	16	Vancouver	0-1
Dec. 3	Los Angeles	3-2	23	Los Angeles	4-6
5	Pittsburgh	0-8	29	Edmonton	4-4
10	Winnipeg	3-3	30	Calgary	2-1
12	Edmonton	6-3	**Dec.** 8	Edmonton	1-3
14	Minnesota	2-3	16	NY Rangers	3-4
21	Quebec	4-1	17	Pittsburgh	2-10
28	Vancouver	2-3	19	St Louis	0-4
Jan. 3	Philadelphia	3-1	26	Los Angeles	3-5
4	Montreal	0-1	**Jan.** 7	Vancouver	1-4
24	Calgary	2-3	8	Calgary	3-10
25	Edmonton	5-2	11	Minnesota	4-7
28	NY Rangers	2-4	12	Winnipeg	4-3
30	St Louis	2-4	14	Los Angeles	3-3
Feb. 4	Hartford	6-5	21	Edmonton	2-9
5	Chicago	5-2	**Feb.** 2	Winnipeg*	0-6
18	Washington	2-4	9	Washington*	2-6
21	Vancouver	3-5	12	Montreal	1-6
23	Calgary*	2-4	14	Buffalo	6-7
26	Quebec	7-4	15	Detroit	1-11
28	Montreal	3-3	**Mar.** 10	Chicago	1-5
Mar. 1	Philadelphia*	0-1	11	Winnipeg	0-3
4	Los Angeles	3-4	19	Calgary	1-3
6	Pittsburgh	3-7	21	Hartford	5-4
8	Toronto*	4-1	23	Boston	6-7
14	New Jersey	3-2	24	New Jersey	3-4
17	Detroit	4-5	26	NY Islanders	4-7
Apr. 1	Winnipeg	3-5	29	Winnipeg*	5-6
3	Calgary	3-4	**Apr.** 5	Edmonton*	4-6

*Denotes afternoon game

General Managers' History

Jack Ferreira, 1991-92.

Coaching History

George Kingston, 1991-92 to date.

Captains' History

Doug Wilson, 1991-92 to date.

All-time Record vs. Other Clubs

Regular Season

	At Home							On Road							Total						
	GP	W	L	T	GF	GA	PTS	GP	W	L	T	GF	GA	PTS	GP	W	L	T	GF	GA	PTS
Boston	1	0	1	0	1	4	0	1	0	1	0	6	7	0	2	0	2	0	7	11	0
Buffalo	1	0	1	0	1	7	0	2	0	2	0	7	10	0	3	0	3	0	8	17	0
Calgary	4	1	3	0	11	14	2	3	1	2	0	6	14	2	7	2	5	0	17	28	4
Chicago	1	1	0	0	5	2	2	2	0	2	0	4	12	0	3	1	2	0	9	14	2
Detroit	2	0	1	1	7	8	1	1	0	1	0	1	11	0	3	0	2	1	8	19	1
Edmonton	3	3	0	0	17	7	6	4	0	3	1	11	22	1	7	3	3	1	28	29	7
Hartford	1	1	0	0	6	5	2	2	1	1	0	5	7	2	3	2	1	0	11	12	4
Los Angeles	3	1	2	0	8	9	2	4	0	3	1	15	22	1	7	1	5	1	23	31	3
Minnesota	2	0	2	0	4	11	0	1	0	1	0	4	7	0	3	0	3	0	8	18	0
Montreal	2	0	1	1	3	4	1	1	0	1	0	1	6	0	3	0	2	1	4	10	1
New Jersey	1	1	0	0	3	2	2	2	0	2	0	3	13	0	3	1	2	0	6	15	2
NY Islanders	1	1	0	0	4	3	2	2	0	2	0	8	15	0	3	1	2	0	12	18	2
NY Rangers	1	0	1	0	2	4	0	1	0	1	0	3	4	0	2	0	2	0	5	8	0
Philadelphia	2	1	1	0	3	2	2	1	0	1	0	2	5	0	3	1	2	0	5	7	2
Pittsburgh	2	0	2	0	3	15	0	1	0	1	0	2	10	0	3	0	3	0	5	25	0
Quebec	2	2	0	0	11	5	4	1	0	1	0	3	6	0	3	2	1	0	14	11	4
St. Louis	1	0	1	0	2	4	0	2	0	2	0	3	10	0	3	0	3	0	5	14	0
Toronto	2	1	1	0	5	4	2	1	0	1	0	1	4	0	3	1	2	0	6	8	2
Vancouver	4	1	3	0	11	14	2	3	0	3	0	4	9	0	7	1	6	0	15	23	2
Washington	1	0	1	0	2	4	0	1	0	1	0	2	6	0	2	0	2	0	4	10	0
Winnipeg	3	0	2	1	10	13	1	4	1	3	0	9	18	2	7	1	5	1	19	31	3
Totals	**40**	**14**	**23**	**3**	**119**	**141**	**31**	**40**	**3**	**35**	**2**	**100**	**218**	**8**	**80**	**17**	**58**	**5**	**219**	**359**	**39**

Entry Draft Selections 1992-91

1992

Pick	
3	Mike Rathje
10	Andrei Nazarov
51	Alexander Cherbajev
75	Jan Caloun
99	Marcus Ragnarsson
123	Michal Sykora
147	Eric Bellerose
171	Ryan Smith
195	Chris Burns
219	A. Kholomeyev
243	Victor Ignatjev

1991

Pick	
2	Pat Falloon
23	Ray Whitney
30	Sandis Ozolnich
45	Dody Wood
67	Kerry Toporowski
89	Dan Ryder
111	Fredrik Nilsson
133	Jaroslav Otevrel
155	Dean Grillo
177	Corwin Saurdiff
199	Dale Craigdell
221	Aaron Kriss
243	Mikhail Kravets

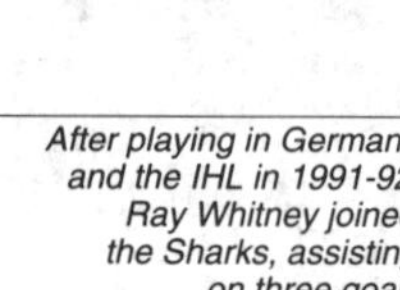

After playing in Germany and the IHL in 1991-92, Ray Whitney joined the Sharks, assisting on three goals in two games.

Coach

KINGSTON, GEORGE
Vice President and Head Coach, San Jose Sharks.
Born in Biggar, Saskatchewan, August 20, 1939.

George Kingston, 53, enters his second season as head coach of the San Jose Sharks, being named to that position on April 12, 1991. He assumed the vice president's title, along with shared responsibilities of the general manager's function, on June 26, 1992.

Under his leadership, the Sharks remained competitive and showed significant improvement throughout their inaugural season. Kingston fostered a philosophy which helped shape the Sharks into a respected, hard working team.

Kingston brings more than 30 years of hockey experience to the Sharks, most recently spending two years as sports director of the Norwegian Ice Hockey Federation and coach of Norway's national team. A native of Biggar, Saskatchewan, Kingston spent most of his coaching career in Canada, including 20 years as head coach at the University of Calgary. While there, he also worked as a part-time assistant with the NHL Calgary Flames from 1980-82. His other NHL experience came in 1988-89 as an assistant coach with the Minnesota North Stars.

Kingston has a wealth of experience on the international level including various positions with the Canadian Olympic and national programs. Among his involvement: serving as an assistant coach on the 1984 Olympic squad and head coach for the gold medal-winning Team Canada in the 1987 Spengler Cup. Kingston was chairman of the hockey tournament during the 1988 Winter Olympics in Calgary.

After starting his coaching career with six years on the high school level, Kingston guided the program at the University of Calgary from 1968-88 posting a 245-128 (.657) record over 16 seasons. During his tenure he took four, one-year leave of absences to pursue advanced degrees or work with the Canadian national program. He led Calgary to the playoffs 14 times and won five conference titles. Kingston was named Canadian college coach of the year in 1974 and 1981.

Coaching Record

		Regular Season					Playoffs			
Season	**Team**	**Games**	**W**	**L**	**T**	**%**	**Games**	**W**	**L**	**%**
1968-69	U. of Calgary (CIAU)	20	11	9	0	.550	....	....	....	....
1969-70	U. of Calgary (CIAU)	14	11	3	0	.786	....	....	....	....
1970-71	U. of Calgary (CIAU)	20	13	7	0	.650	....	....	....	....
1971-72	U. of Calgary (CIAU)	20	15	5	0	.750	....	....	....	....
1972-73	U. of Calgary (CIAU)	24	16	8	0	.667	....	....	....	....
1973-74	U. of Calgary (CIAU)	18	14	4	0	.778	....	....	....	....
1975-76	U. of Calgary (CIAU)	24	17	7	0	.708	....	....	....	....
1978-79	U. of Calgary (CIAU)	24	15	9	0	.625	....	....	....	....
1979-80	U. of Calgary (CIAU)	29	18	11	0	.629	....	....	....	....
1980-81	U. of Calgary (CIAU)	24	18	6	0	.750	....	....	....	....
1981-82	U. of Calgary (CIAU)	24	14	10	0	.583	....	....	....	....
1982-83	U. of Calgary (CIAU)	24	10	14	0	.417	....	....	....	....
1984-85	U. of Calgary (CIAU)	24	8	16	0	.333	....	....	....	....
1985-86	U. of Calgary (CIAU)	28	19	9	0	.679	....	....	....	....
1986-87	U. of Calgary (CIAU)	28	23	5	0	.821	....	....	....	....
1987-88	U. of Calgary (CIAU)	28	23	5	0	.821	....	....	....	....
1989-90	Norwegian National	....	....	....	....	....	....	....	....	....
1990-91	Norwegian National	....	....	....	....	....	....	....	....	....
1991-92	**San Jose (NHL)**	**80**	**17**	**58**	**5**	**.244**	....	....	....	....
	NHL Totals	**80**	**17**	**58**	**5**	**.244**	....	....	....	....

Club Directory

Ten Almaden Boulevard
Suite 600
P.O. Box 1240
San Jose, California 95113
Phone **408/287-7070**
FAX 408/999-5797
Capacity: 11,100

Co-Owner & Chairman	George Gund III
Co-Owner & Vice Chairman	Gordon Gund
President & CEO	Arthur L. Savage
Exec. Vice-President, Building Operations	Frank Jirik
Exec. Vice-President, Marketing & Broadcast	Matt Levine
Exec. Vice-President, C.F.O.	Grant Rollin
Vice-President, Director of Hockey Operations	Dean Lombardi
Vice-President, Director of Player Personnel	Chuck Grillo
Vice-President, Head Coach	George Kingston
Associate Coach	Bob Murdoch
Assistant Coach	Drew Remenda
Strength Coach	George Kinnear
Scouting Coordinator	Joe Will
Exec. Assistant to President	Dianna Carthew
Exec. Assistant to V.P., Director of Hockey Operations	Brenda Knight
Western Scouting Supervisor	Bob Gernander
Eastern Scouting Supervisor	Ray Payne
Professional Scouting Supervisor	Tim Burke
European Scouting Supervisor	Sakari Pietila
Regional Scout, Midwest	Rob Grillo
Regional Scout, West	Larry Ross
Area Scouts	Pat Funk (Minnesota); Tim Gorski (Alaska); Ben Hays (New England); Randy Joevenazzo (Alberta); Konstantin Krylov (Russia); Jack Morganstern (New England); Deborah Wright (Quebec)
Video Scouting Coordinator	Bob Friedlander
Head Trainer	Tom Woodcock
Equipment Manager	Bob Crocker Jr.
Assistant Equipment Manager	Arne Pappin
Team Physician	Arthur J. Ting, M.D.
Medical Staff	Warren King, M.D., James Klint, M.D., Will Straw, M.D.
Team Dentist	Robert Bonahoom, D.D.S.
Director of Media Relations	Tim Bryant
Assistant Director of Media Relations	Ken Arnold
Media Relations Assistant	Jill Freeman
Administrative Assistant	Dawn Beres
Finance	
Controller	Peggy Ferguson
Accountant	Colleen Reilly
Payroll	Bonita Tanner
Executive Assistant	Cecilia Briones
Manager, Information Systems	Alex Ignacio
Manager, Finance and Accounting	Brent M. Billinger
Business Operations	
Executive Director, Advertising Sales	David Forier
Director of Broadcasting	Mark Stulberger
Director of Executive Sales	Ted Atlee
Director of Ticket Sales	Rich Muschell
Director of Merchandise Marketing	Mary Keen Meulman
Director of Community Development	Alysse Soll
Director of Special Projects	Herb Briggin
Manager of Event Services	Kris Van Giesen
Group Account Service Manager	Mary Lewis
Account Service Managers	Wanda Mae Lombardi, Bob Fitzgerald, Andy Hawkes, Paul Solby, Gene Wiggins
Media Marketing Manager	Don Olvarado
Media Marketing Manager	Jim Josel
Merchandise Manager	Brad Porteus
Assistant Merchandise Manager	Mike Hollywood
Executive Assistant	Joyce Coppola
Media Coordinator	Valerie Bigelow
Traffic Coordinator	Martha Baumgartner
Assistant Manager Community Development/Event Services	Diane Bloom
Ticket Sales Assistant	Annie Chan-Zien
Executive Sales Assistant	Susan Leckrone
Merchandise Marketing Assistant	Kimberly Brown
Retail Manager	Jannette Scott
Store Manager	Kim Wright
Customer Service Representatives	Jill Warnock, Julie Burns
Mascot	S.J. Sharkie
Building Operations	
Vice President, Arena Construction	Jim Goddard
Arena Construction Manager	Tom Hanson
Production Director	Jack Larson
Director of Arena Marketing	Elaine Sullivan-Digre
Director of Ticket Operations	Daniel DeBoer
Assistant to Ticket Operations	Mary Enriquez
Executive Assistant	Chris Palmer
Mailroom Coordinator	Steve Perry
Administrative Assistant	Kris Lyon
P.A. Announcer	Bud Kelly
Organist	Dieter Ruehle
Receptionist	Marcia Cady
Miscellaneous	
Team Colors	Pacific Teal, Gray, Black, White
Home Ice/Capacity	Cow Palace (11,100)
Dimensions of Rink	185 feet by 85 feet
Television Stations	KICU-TV 36, SportsChannel Pacific, KGO-TV 7
Radio Network Flagship	KNEW (910 AM)
Play-By-Play (Radio)	Dan Rusanowsky
Play-By-Play (Television)	Joe Starkey
Color Commentator	TBA

Tampa Bay Lightning

Wendell Young, far right, will give the Lightning an experienced NHL goaltender for the franchise's first season. Rob Ramage, right, was selected off the roster of the Minnesota North Stars in the 1992 Expansion Draft.

Schedule

Home

Month	Day	Date	Opponent
Oct.	Wed.	7	Chicago
	Tues.	20	Edmonton
	Thur.	22	Toronto
	Sat.	24	Quebec
	Fri.	30	San Jose
Nov.	Sun.	1	Pittsburgh
	Tues.	3	St Louis
	Wed.	11	Detroit
	Fri.	13	Ottawa
	Sat.	14	Calgary
	Tues.	17	Winnipeg
	Thur.	19	Minnesota
Dec.	Sat.	5	Detroit
	Mon.	7	NY Islanders
	Fri.	11	NY Rangers
	Sat.	12	Edmonton
	Fri.	18	New Jersey
	Sun.	20	Philadelphia
Jan.	Sat.	16	St Louis
	Sun.	17	Washington
	Tues.	19	Minnesota
	Thur.	21	Toronto
	Sat.	23	San Jose
	Sun.	24	Minnesota
	Thur.	28	St Louis
Feb.	Tues.	9	Toronto
	Thur.	11	Minnesota
	Sun.	14	Boston
	Sat.	20	Quebec (at Halifax)
	Mon.	22	Los Angeles
	Thur.	25	Chicago
Mar.	Wed.	3	Montreal
	Sat.	6	Calgary
	Tues.	9	Winnipeg
	Tues.	16	Hartford
	Thur.	18	Toronto
	Sat.	20	Buffalo*
	Sat.	27	Detroit
Apr.	Thur.	1	Vancouver
	Tues.	6	St Louis
	Thur.	8	Detroit
	Sat.	10	Chicago*

Away

Month	Day	Date	Opponent
Oct.	Sat.	10	Minnesota
	Sun.	11	Chicago
	Tues.	13	St Louis
	Thur.	15	Toronto
	Fri.	16	Buffalo
	Tues.	27	Quebec
	Wed.	28	Montreal
Nov.	Fri.	6	Washington
	Sat.	7	NY Islanders
	Mon.	9	NY Rangers
	Sat.	21	St Louis
	Mon.	23	Detroit
	Tues.	24	Toronto
	Fri.	27	Calgary
	Sat.	28	Edmonton
Dec.	Wed.	9	NY Rangers (at Miami)
	Tues.	15	Los Angeles
	Wed.	16	San Jose
	Tues.	22	Boston
	Wed.	23	Hartford
	Thur.	31	Chicago
Jan.	Sat.	2	Edmonton
	Sun.	3	Vancouver
	Wed.	6	Los Angeles
	Sat.	9	Minnesota
	Mon.	11	Toronto
	Wed.	13	Detroit
	Sat.	30	Minnesota
Feb.	Mon.	1	San Jose
	Wed.	3	Vancouver
	Wed.	17	Detroit
	Fri.	19	Toronto
	Sat.	27	Pittsburgh*
Mar.	Fri.	12	Toronto
	Sun.	14	Winnipeg*
	Sun.	21	Chicago
	Tues.	23	New Jersey
	Thur.	25	Ottawa
Apr.	Sat.	3	Philadelphia*
	Sun.	11	Chicago*
	Tues.	13	Winnipeg
	Thur.	15	St Louis

* Denotes afternoon game.

Home Starting Times:

Weeknights	7:35 p.m.
Except Matinees	1:35 p.m.
Nov. 14	8:05 p.m.

Franchise date: December 16, 1991

1st NHL Season

1992-93 Player Personnel

FORWARDS	HT	WT	S	Place of Birth	Date	1991-92 Club
ANDERSSON, Mikael	5-11	185	L	Malmo, Sweden	5/10/66	Hartford
BERGLAND, Tim	6-3	194	R	Crookston, MI	1/11/65	Washington-Baltimore
BLOUIN, Jean	6-0	195	L	Montreal, Que.	2/26/71	Laval
BRADLEY, Brian	5-10	177	R	Kitchener, Ont.	1/21/65	Toronto
CALLANDER, Jock	6-1	188	R	Regina, Sask.	4/23/61	Muskegon
CAMPEAU, Christian	5-10	180	L	Verdun, Que.	6/2/71	Rouen
COLE, Danton	5-11	185	R	Pontiac, MI	1/10/67	Winnipeg
DiMAIO, Rob	5-10	190	R	Calgary, Alta.	2/19/68	NY Islanders
DUGUAY, Ron	6-2	200	R	Sudbury, Ont.	7/6/57	San Diego
ERTEL, Tyler	6-0	185	L	Kitchener, Ont.	1/15/71	Kitchener
GARDINER, Jeff	6-2	215	L	Chatham, Ont.	6/28/71	Detroit
GAVEY, Aaron	6-1	169	L	Sudbury, Ont.	2/22/74	Sault Ste. Marie
GREEN, Mark	6-4	200	R	Watertown, NY	12/26/67	Johnstown
GRETZKY, Brent	5-10	160	L	Brantford, Ont.	2/20/72	Belleville
HARDING, Jeff	6-3	220	R	Toronto, Ont.	4/6/69	Springfield
HARTMAN, Mike	6-0	192	L	Detroit, MI	2/7/67	Winnipeg
HODGE, Ken	6-1	200	L	Windsor, Ont.	4/13/66	Boston-Maine
KONTOS, Chris	6-1	195	L	Toronto, Ont.	12/10/63	Canadian National
LAFRENIERE, Jason	5-11	185	R	St. Catharines, Ont.	12/6/66	Landshut-San Diego
MacDONALD, Tom	5-11	190	L	Toronto, Ont.	4/14/74	Sault Ste. Marie
MacKAY, Kevin	5-9	164	R	S.S. Marie, Ont.	7/26/71	Windsor
MALTAIS, Steve	6-2	210	L	Arvida, Que.	1/25/69	Min.-K'zoo-Hfx.
MAXWELL, Dennis	6-0	188	L	Dauphin, Man.	6/4/74	Niagara Falls
McKEGNEY, Tony	6-1	200	L	Montreal, Que.	2/15/58	Varese
McRAE, Basil	6-2	205	L	Beaverton, Ont.	1/5/61	Minnesota
MILLER, Colin	6-0	188	R	Grimsby, Ont.	8/21/71	S.S.Marie
MONGEAU, Michel	5-9	190	L	Nun's Island, Que.	2/9/65	St. Louis-Peoria
MYHRES, Brantt	6-3	195	R	Edmonton, Alta.	3/18/74	Lethbridge
OSBORNE, Keith	6-1	180	R	Toronto, Ont.	4/2/69	St. John's
SEMENOV, Anatoli	6-2	190	L	Moscow, USSR	3/5/62	Edmonton
SIMARD, Martin	6-3	215	R	Montreal, Que.	6/25/66	Calgary-Salt Lake-Halifax
SMITH, Garin	6-0	190	L	Simcoe, Ont.	4/15/74	Gue.-Bel.-Kit.
STEVENSON, Shayne	6-1	190	R	Newmarket, Ont.	10/26/70	Boston-Maine
STILL, Allistair	6-1	197	R	Oakville, Ont.	6/10/71	Kingston
TANGUAY, Martin	5-11	185	L	Ste. Julie, Que.	1/12/73	Verdun
TARDIF, Marc	6-1	199	L	Montreal, Que.	1/6/73	Shawinigan
TUCKER, John	6-0	200	R	Windsor	9/29/64	Asiago
TUTTLE, Steve	6-1	200	R	Vancouver, B.C.	1/5/65	Peoria
VINCELETTE, Dan	6-2	200	L	Verdun, Que.	8/1/67	Chicago-Indianapolis
ZAMUNER, Rob	6-2	202	L	Oakville, Ont.	9/17/69	NY Rangers-Binghamton
DEFENSEMEN						
BANNISTER, Drew	6-1	193	R	Belleville, Ont.	4/9/74	Sault Ste. Marie
BENNING, Jim	6-0	185	L	Edmonton, Alta.	4/29/63	Varese
BERGEVIN, Marc	6-0	185	L	Montreal, Que.	8/11/65	Hartford
BOSTON, Scott	6-2	180	R	Ottawa, Ont.	7/13/71	Belleville
BLOEMBERG, Jeff	6-2	205	R	Listowel, Ont.	1/31/68	NY Rangers-Binghamton
BUCHANAN, Jeff	5-10	165	R	Swift Current, Sask.	5/23/71	Saskatoon
CHAMBERS, Shawn	6-2	200	L	Royal Oak, MI	10/11/66	Washington-Baltimore
CROSS, Cory	6-5	212	L	Lloydminster, Alta.	1/3/71	U. of Alberta
CROSSMAN, Doug	6-2	190	L	Peterborough, Ont.	6/30/60	Detroit
HAMRLIK, Roman	6-2	189	L	Gottwaldov, Czech.	4/12/74	ZPS Zlin
HERVEY, Matt	5-11	200	R	Whittier, CA	5/16/66	Boston-Maine
KEMPER, Andrew	6-2	186	R	Montreal, Que.	4/7/74	Seattle
LANZ, Rick	6-2	203	R	Kalouy Vary, Czech.	9/16/61	Phoenix
LIPUMA, Chris	6-0	183	L	Chicago, IL	3/23/71	Kitchener
McGILL, Bob	6-1	193	R	Edmonton, Alta.	4/27/62	San Jose-Detroit
MELNYK, Larry	6-0	195	L	Saskatoon, Sask.	2/21/60	
RAMAGE, Rob	6-2	195	R	Byron, Ont.	1/11/59	Minnesota
RICHER, Stephane	5-11	200	R	Hull, Que.	4/28/66	Fredericton
RIVERS, Shawn	5-10	185	L	Ottawa, Ont.	1/30/71	Sudbury
REEKIE, Joe	6-3	215	L	Victoria, B.C.	2/22/65	NYI-Capital District
ROBINSON, Rob	6-1	214	L	St. Catharines, Ont.	4/19/67	St. Louis-Peoria
TAGLIANETTI, Peter	6-2	200	L	Framingham, MA	8/15/63	Pittsburgh

GOALTENDERS	HT	WT	C	Place of Birth	Date	1991-92 Club
BERGERON, J.C.	6-2	192	L	Hauterive, Que.	10/14/68	Fredericton
GREENLAY, Mike	6-3	200	L	Vitoria, Brazil	9/15/68	C. Breton/Knoxville
JABLONSKI, Pat	6-0	170	R	Toledo, OH	6/20/67	St. Louis-Peoria
RHEAUME, Manon	5-6	136	L	Lac Beauport, Que.	2/24/72	Cdn. Nat. Women's Team
ROBINS, Trevor	5-11	175	L	Brandon, Man.	5/31/72	Saskatoon
WILKINSON, Derek	6-0	160	L	LaSalle, Que.	7/29/74	Detroit
YOUNG, Wendell	5-9	181	L	Halifax, N.S.	8/1/63	Pittsburgh

Entry Draft Selections 1992

1992
Pick
1 Roman Hamrlik
26 Drew Bannister
49 Brent Gretzky
74 Aaron Gavey
97 Brantt Myhres
122 Martin Tanguay
145 Derek Wilkinson
170 Dennis Maxwell
193 Andrew Kemper
218 Marc Tardif
241 Tom MacDonald

General Manager

ESPOSITO, PHIL
General Manager, Tampa Bay Lightning. Born in Sault Ste. Marie, Ont., February 20, 1942.

Phil Esposito, who headed up Tampa Bay's successful campaign to obtain an NHL franchise, was rewarded for his hard work when the Lightning were granted a berth in the NHL, beginning in the 1992-93 season. After an 18-year Hall-of-Fame career that included eight All-Star selections as well as winning the Hart Trophy twice, the Art Ross Trophy five times, Esposito was named vice president and general manager of the NY Rangers in 1986, remaining in that role until the start of the 1989-90 season. He also doubled as coach during the 1986-87 campaign and took over the bench duties again at the conclusion of 1988-89. Esposito, who began his career with Chicago and finished his playing days with the NY Rangers, had his most productive days with the Boston Bruins, winning a pair of Stanley Cup titles while establishing numerous team records, including most goals (76) and points (152) in a single season. In 1968-69, he became the first NHL player to record 100 points in a season.

NHL Coaching Record

		Regular Season					Playoffs			
Season	**Team**	**Games**	**W**	**L**	**T**	**%**	**Games**	**W**	**L**	**%**
1986-87	NY Rangers (NHL)	43	24	19	0	.558	6	2	4	.333
1988-89	NY Rangers (NHL)	2	0	2	0	.000	4	0	4	.000
	NHL Totals	**45**	**24**	**21**	**0**	**.533**	**10**	**2**	**8**	**.200**

Coach

CRISP, TERRY
Coach, Tampa Bay Lightning. Born in Parry Sound, Ont., May 28, 1943.

After a two-year absence, Terry Crisp returns to the NHL's coaching ranks to become the first coach of the Tampa Bay Lightning. Crisp, who won two Stanley Cups as a member of the Philadelphia Flyers, played 11 years in the NHL for the Bruins, Blues, Islanders and Flyers. After retiring in 1976, he joined the Flyers' organization as an assistant coach, serving two terms before leaving to coach the OHL's Sault Ste. Marie Greyhounds. With the Greyhounds, Crisp won three regular-season crowns and twice earned the nod as the league's coach of the year. In 1985, Crisp accepted a coaching position with the Calgary Flames' top AHL farm affiliate in Moncton and spent two seasons with the Golden Flames before being elevated to the head coaching position with their parent club. Crisp led Calgary to their best-ever finish in 1988-89, winning 54 games and capturing the franchise's first Stanley Cup championship after a six-game final series win over the Montreal Canadiens. After being released by the Flames, Crisp joined the Canadian National Team program as an assistant coach and was with the club when Team Canada won the silver medal at the 1992 Olympics.

Coaching Record

			Regular Season					Playoffs			
Season	**Team**	**Games**	**W**	**L**	**T**	**%**	**Games**	**W**	**L**	**T**	**%**
1979-80	S.S. Marie (OHL)	68	22	45	1	.331	....	....	....	....	....
1980-81	S.S. Marie (OHL)	68	47	19	2	.706	19	8	7	4	.526
1981-82	S.S. Marie (OHL)	68	40	25	3	.610	13	4	6	3	.423
1982-83	S.S. Marie (OHL)	70	48	21	1	.693	16	7	6	3	.531
1983-84	S.S. Marie (OHL)	70	38	28	4	.571	16	8	4	4	.625
1984-85	S.S. Marie (OHL)	66	54	11	1	.826	16	12	2	2	.813
1985-86	Moncton (AHL)	80	34	34	12	.500	10	5	5	0	.500
1986-87	Moncton (AHL)	80	43	31	6	.575	6	2	4	0	.333
1987-88	**Calgary (NHL)**	**80**	**48**	**23**	**9**	**.656**	**9**	**4**	**5**	**0**	**.444**
1988-89	**Calgary (NHL)**	**80**	**54**	**17**	**9**	**.731**	**22**	**16**	**6**	**0**	**.727***
1989-90	**Calgary (NHL)**	**80**	**42**	**23**	**15**	**.619**	**6**	**2**	**4**	**0**	**.333**
	NHL Totals	**240**	**144**	**63**	**33**	**.669**	**37**	**22**	**15**	**0**	**.595**

* Stanley Cup win.

General Managers' History

Phil Esposito, 1992-93.

Coaching History

Terry Crisp, 1992-93.

Club Directory

501 East Kennedy Boulevard
Suite 175
Tampa, FL 33602
Phone **813/229-2658**
FAX 813/229-3350

Expo Hall **Capacity:** 10,400

Lightning Partners, Ltd

General Partner	Lightning Partners, Inc.
Limited Partners	Lightning International, Inc. Tokyo Tower Development Co., Ltd Nippon Meat Packers, Inc. Tampa Bay Hockey Group Partners, Ltd. John Chase Equity Resources Group of Indian River County, Inc. James Murphy
Board of Directors	Yoshio Nakamura, Chairman, Phil Esposito, David LeFevre, Fukusaboro Maeda, Dr. Fujio Matsuda, Mushao Miyake, Chris Phillips, Reece Smith, Jr.
Executive Committee	Phil Esposito, David LeFevre, Chris Phillips, Reece Smith, Jr.
Executive Staff	
President	Yoshio Nakamura
Governor	David LeFevre
General Manager and Alternate Governor	Phil Esposito
Executive Vice President and Alternate Governor	Chris Phillips
Executive Vice President and Alternate Governor	Mel Lowell
Assistant to the President	Hiroyuki Nishiyama
General Counsel	
Vice President/ General Counsel	Henry Lee Paul
Hockey Operations	
President, Tampa Bay Lightning Hockey Club	Phil Esposito
Director of Hockey Operations	Tony Esposito
Head Coach	Terry Crisp
Assistant Coach	Wayne Cashman
Head Scout	John Chapman
Scouting Staff	Angelo Bumbacco, Jacques Campeau, Jake Goertzen, Doug Macauley, Don Murdoch, Richard Rose, Jonathan Sparrow, Luke Williams
Head Trainer	Skip Thayer
Equipment Manager	Jocko Cayer
Assistant Trainer	John Forristall
Strength and Conditioning Coach	Gordon Hurlburt
Director of Team Travel	Carrie Esposito
Administrative Assistant	Teresa Paedae
Administrative Assistant	Stacey Fricker
Ice Systems Supervisor	Tim Friedenberger, Michael Wall
Finance	
Chief Financial Officer	Mark Anderson
Accounting Manager	Vincent Ascanio
Accounting Assistant	Irene Canino
Administrative Assistant	Evelyn Hicks
Communications	
Vice President/Communications	Gerry Helper
Media Relations Manager	Barry Hanrahan
Communications Assistant	Lisa Katz
Communications/Marketing Assistant	Becky Cashman
Receptionist	Cheryl Pritcher
Marketing and Sales	
Vice President/Sales and Marketing	Steve Donner
Director of Corporate Sales and Sponsorship	Anne Webb
Director of Sales	Jon Swensson
Sales Representatives	Keith Brennan, Nigel Kirwan, Raymond Mihara, Missy Davis
Director of Merchandising	Kevin Murphy
Marketing Assistant	Marlene Arnold
Ticket Operations	
Director of Season Subscriptions	Jackie Staney
Ticket Office Representatives	James Ward, Andre Thompson
Medical Staff	
Team Physician	Dr. David Leffers
Team Dentist	Dr. Joseph Spoto
Television and Radio	
Television (Cable)	Sunshine Network
Over-the-air	WTOG-TV 44
Broadcaster	John Kelly, Danny Gare
Lightning Radio Network	WQYK (1010 AM)
Team Information	
Address	501 East Kennedy Boulevard Suite 175 Tampa, FL 33602
Phone	813/229-2658
FAX	813/229-3350
Home Arena	Expo Hall at Florida State Fairgrounds
Seating Capacity	10,400
Rink Dimensions	192 feet by 85 feet
Team Colors	Black, Blue, Silver and White
Training Camp Site	Lakeland Civic Center, Lakeland, Florida
Game Night Staff	
Public Address Announcer/Anthem Singer	TBA
Team Photographers	Jonathan Hayt, Dennis Osborne
Off-ice Officials	Jim Galluzzi, Ron Brace, Gerry Dollmont, Ralph Emery, Rich Galipault, Mark Losier, Tony Mancuso, Mike Rees, Dave Walkowiak, Rich Wasilewski, Dan Zabel

Toronto Maple Leafs

1991-92 Results: 30W-43L-7T 67PTS. Fifth, Norris Division

Schedule

	Home		Away
Oct.	Wed. 7 Washington	**Oct.**	Sat. 10 Calgary
	Thur. 15 Tampa Bay		Sun. 11 Edmonton
	Sat. 17 Chicago		Thur. 22 Tampa Bay
	Sun. 18 Minnesota		Fri. 30 Detroit
	Tues. 20 Ottawa	**Nov.**	Thur. 5 Chicago
	(at Hamilton)		Mon. 9 Ottawa
	Sat. 24 San Jose		Sat. 14 Boston
	Wed. 28 Buffalo		Tues. 17 Quebec
	Sat. 31 Detroit		(at Hamilton)
Nov.	Sat. 7 Pittsburgh		Thur. 19 San Jose
	Mon. 16 St Louis		Sat. 21 Los Angeles
	Tues. 24 Tampa Bay	**Dec.**	Tues. 1 New Jersey
	Thur. 26 Quebec		Thur. 3 Chicago
	Sat. 28 Los Angeles		Sun. 6 NY Rangers
Dec.	Sat. 5 Chicago		Tues. 15 Minnesota
	Wed. 9 Detroit		Sun. 20 Buffalo
	Fri. 11 Calgary		Tues. 22 Detroit
	Sat. 19 Ottawa		Sun. 27 St Louis
	Sat. 26 Detroit		Tues. 29 NY Islanders
Jan.	Sat. 2 St Louis		Thur. 31 Pittsburgh
	Wed. 6 Vancouver	**Jan.**	Mon. 4 Detroit
	Fri. 8 San Jose		Sat. 9 Montreal
	Mon. 11 Tampa Bay		Sun. 17 Chicago
	Wed. 13 St Louis		Tues. 19 St Louis
	Sat. 16 Chicago		Thur. 21 Tampa Bay
	Sat. 23 Montreal	**Feb.**	Mon. 1 St Louis
	Tues. 26 Minnesota		Tues. 9 Tampa Bay
	Sat. 30 NY Rangers		Sun. 14 Minnesota
Feb.	Wed. 3 NY Islanders		Mon. 22 Vancouver
	Thur. 11 Vancouver		Thur. 25 San Jose
	Sat. 13 Minnesota		Sat. 27 Los Angeles
	Wed. 17 Calgary	**Mar.**	Fri. 5 Detroit
	Fri. 19 Tampa Bay		Tues. 9 Washington
	Sat. 20 Boston		Mon. 15 Quebec
Mar.	Wed. 3 Minnesota		Thur. 18 Tampa Bay
	Sat. 6 Winnipeg		Tues. 23 Winnipeg
	Wed. 10 Hartford		Thur. 25 Minnesota
	Fri. 12 Tampa Bay		Sat. 27 Edmonton
	Sat. 20 Edmonton		Sun. 28 Calgary
	Wed. 31 Los Angeles	**Apr.**	Thur. 1 Philadelphia
Apr.	Sat. 3 New Jersey		Thur. 8 Winnipeg
	Sat. 10 Philadelphia		Sun. 11 Hartford
	Tues. 13 St Louis		Thur. 15 Chicago

* Denotes afternoon game.

Home Starting Times:

Weeknights	7:35 p.m.
Saturdays	8:05 p.m.
Sundays	7:05 p.m.

Franchise date: November 22, 1917

76th NHL Season

Grant Fuhr registered a pair of shutouts for the Leafs in 1991-92.

Year-by-Year Record

Season	GP	Home W	Home L	Home T	Road W	Road L	Road T	Overall W	Overall L	Overall T	GF	GA	Pts.	Finished		Playoff Result
1991-92	80	21	16	3	9	27	4	30	43	7	234	294	67	5th,	Norris Div.	Out of Playoffs
1990-91	80	15	21	4	8	25	7	23	46	11	241	318	57	5th,	Norris Div.	Out of Playoffs
1989-90	80	24	14	2	14	24	2	38	38	4	337	358	80	3rd,	Norris Div.	Lost Div. Semi-Final
1988-89	80	15	20	5	13	26	1	28	46	6	259	342	62	5th,	Norris Div.	Out of Playoffs
1987-88	80	14	20	6	7	29	4	21	49	10	273	345	52	4th,	Norris Div.	Lost Div. Semi-Final
1986-87	80	22	14	4	10	28	2	32	42	6	286	319	70	4th,	Norris Div.	Lost Div. Final
1985-86	80	16	21	3	9	27	4	25	48	7	311	386	57	4th,	Norris Div.	Lost Div. Final
1984-85	80	10	28	2	10	24	6	20	52	8	253	358	48	5th,	Norris Div.	Out of Playoffs
1983-84	80	17	16	7	9	29	2	26	45	9	303	287	61	5th,	Norris Div.	Out of Playoffs
1982-83	80	20	15	5	8	25	7	28	40	12	293	330	68	3rd,	Norris Div.	Lost Div. Semi-Final
1981-82	80	12	20	8	8	24	8	20	44	16	298	380	56	5th,	Norris Div.	Out of Playoffs
1980-81	80	14	21	5	14	16	10	28	37	15	322	367	71	5th,	Adams Div.	Lost Prelim. Round
1979-80	80	17	19	4	18	21	1	35	40	5	304	327	75	4th,	Adams Div.	Lost Prelim. Round
1978-79	80	20	12	8	14	21	5	34	33	13	267	252	81	3rd,	Adams Div.	Lost Quarter-Final
1977-78	80	21	13	6	20	16	4	41	29	10	271	237	92	3rd,	Adams Div.	Lost Semi-Final
1976-77	80	18	13	9	15	19	6	33	32	15	301	285	81	3rd,	Adams Div.	Lost Quarter-Final
1975-76	80	23	12	5	11	19	10	34	31	15	294	276	83	3rd,	Adams Div.	Lost Quarter-Final
1974-75	80	19	12	9	12	21	7	31	33	16	280	309	78	3rd,	Adams Div.	Lost Quarter-Final
1973-74	78	21	11	7	14	16	9	35	27	16	274	230	86	4th,	East Div.	Lost Quarter-Final
1972-73	78	20	12	7	7	29	3	27	41	10	247	279	64	6th,	East Div.	Out of Playoffs
1971-72	78	21	11	7	12	20	7	33	31	14	209	208	80	4th,	East Div.	Lost Quarter-Final
1970-71	78	24	9	6	13	24	2	37	33	8	248	211	82	4th,	East Div.	Lost Quarter-Final
1969-70	76	18	13	7	11	21	6	29	34	13	222	242	71	6th,	East Div.	Out of Playoffs
1968-69	76	20	8	10	15	18	5	35	26	15	234	217	85	4th,	East Div.	Lost Quarter-Final
1967-68	74	24	9	4	9	22	6	33	31	10	209	176	76	5th,	East Div.	Out of Playoffs
1966-67	**70**	21	8	6	11	19	5	**32**	**27**	**11**	**204**	**211**	**75**	**3rd,**		**Won Stanley Cup**
1965-66	70	22	9	4	12	16	7	34	25	11	208	187	79	3rd,		Lost Semi-Final
1964-65	70	17	15	3	13	11	11	30	26	14	204	173	74	4th,		Lost Semi-Final
1963-64	**70**	22	7	6	11	18	6	**33**	**25**	**12**	**192**	**172**	**78**	**3rd,**		**Won Stanley Cup**
1962-63	**70**	21	8	6	14	15	6	**35**	**23**	**12**	**221**	**180**	**82**	**1st,**		**Won Stanley Cup**
1961-62	**70**	25	5	5	12	17	6	**37**	**22**	**11**	**232**	**180**	**85**	**2nd,**		**Won Stanley Cup**
1960-61	70	21	6	8	18	13	4	39	19	12	234	176	90	2nd,		Lost Semi-Final
1959-60	70	20	9	6	15	17	3	35	26	9	199	195	79	2nd,		Lost Final
1958-59	70	17	13	5	10	19	6	27	32	11	189	201	65	4th,		Lost Final
1957-58	70	12	16	7	9	22	4	21	38	11	192	226	53	6th,		Out of Playoffs
1956-57	70	12	16	7	9	18	8	21	34	15	174	192	57	5th,		Out of Playoffs
1955-56	70	19	10	6	5	23	7	24	33	13	153	181	61	4th,		Lost Semi-Final
1954-55	70	14	10	11	10	14	11	24	24	22	147	135	70	3rd,		Lost Semi-Final
1953-54	70	22	6	7	10	18	7	32	24	14	152	131	78	3rd,		Lost Semi-Final
1952-53	70	17	12	6	10	18	7	27	30	13	156	167	67	5th,		Out of Playoffs
1951-52	70	17	10	8	12	15	8	29	25	16	168	157	74	3rd,		Lost Semi-Final
1950-51	**70**	22	8	5	19	8	8	**41**	**16**	**13**	**212**	**138**	**95**	**2nd,**		**Won Stanley Cup**
1949-50	70	18	9	8	13	18	4	31	27	12	176	173	74	3rd,		Lost Semi-Final
1948-49	**60**	12	8	10	10	17	3	**22**	**25**	**13**	**147**	**161**	**57**	**4th,**		**Won Stanley Cup**
1947-48	**60**	22	3	5	10	12	8	**32**	**15**	**13**	**182**	**143**	**77**	**1st,**		**Won Stanley Cup**
1946-47	**60**	20	8	2	11	11	8	**31**	**19**	**10**	**209**	**172**	**72**	**2nd,**		**Won Stanley Cup**
1945-46	50	10	13	2	9	11	5	19	24	7	174	185	45	5th,		Out of Playoffs
1944-45	**50**	13	9	3	11	13	1	**24**	**22**	**4**	**183**	**161**	**52**	**3rd,**		**Won Stanley Cup**
1943-44	50	13	11	1	10	12	3	23	23	4	214	174	50	3rd,		Lost Semi-Final
1942-43	50	17	6	2	5	13	7	22	19	9	198	159	53	3rd,		Lost Semi-Final
1941-42	**48**	18	6	0	9	12	3	**27**	**18**	**3**	**158**	**136**	**57**	**2nd,**		**Won Stanley Cup**
1940-41	48	16	5	3	12	9	3	28	14	6	145	99	62	2nd,		Lost Semi-Final
1939-40	48	15	3	6	10	14	0	25	17	6	134	110	56	3rd,		Lost Final
1938-39	48	13	8	3	6	12	6	19	20	9	114	107	47	3rd,		Lost Final
1937-38	48	13	6	5	11	9	4	24	15	9	151	127	57	1st,	Cdn. Div.	Lost Final
1936-37	48	14	9	1	8	12	4	22	21	5	119	115	49	3rd,	Cdn. Div.	Lost Quarter-Final
1935-36	48	15	4	5	8	15	1	23	19	6	126	106	52	2nd,	Cdn. Div.	Lost Final
1934-35	48	16	6	2	14	8	2	30	14	4	157	111	64	1st,	Cdn. Div.	Lost Final
1933-34	48	19	2	3	7	11	6	26	13	9	174	119	61	1st,	Cdn. Div.	Lost Semi-Final
1932-33	48	16	4	4	8	14	2	24	18	6	119	111	54	1st,	Cdn. Div.	Lost Final
1931-32	**48**	17	4	3	6	14	4	**23**	**18**	**7**	**155**	**127**	**53**	**2nd,**	**Cdn. Div.**	**Won Stanley Cup**
1930-31	44	15	4	3	7	9	6	22	13	9	118	99	53	2nd,	Cdn. Div.	Lost Quarter-Final
1929-30	44	10	8	4	7	13	2	17	21	6	116	124	40	4th,	Cdn. Div.	Out of Playoffs
1928-29	44	15	5	2	6	13	3	21	18	5	85	69	47	3rd,	Cdn. Div.	Lost Semi-Final
1927-28	44	9	8	5	9	10	3	18	18	8	89	88	44	4th,	Cdn. Div.	Out of Playoffs
1926-27*	44	10	10	2	5	14	3	15	24	5	79	94	35	5th,	Cdn. Div.	Out of Playoffs
1925-26	36	11	5	2	1	16	1	12	21	3	92	114	27	6th,		Out of Playoffs
1924-25	30	10	5	0	9	6	0	19	11	0	90	84	38	2nd,		Lost NHL S-Final
1923-24	24	7	5	0	3	9	0	10	14	0	59	85	20	3rd,		Out of Playoffs
1922-23	24	10	1	1	3	9	0	13	10	1	82	88	27	3rd,		Out of Playoffs
1921-22	**24**	8	4	0	5	6	1	**13**	**10**	**1**	**98**	**97**	**27**	**2nd,**		**Won Stanley Cup**
1920-21	24	9	3	0	6	6	0	15	9	0	105	100	30	2nd and 1st***		Lost NHL Final
1919-20**	24	8	4	0	4	8	0	12	12	0	119	106	24	3rd and 2nd***		Lost NHL Final
1918-19	18	5	4	0	0	9	0	5	13	0	64	92	10	3rd and 3rd***		Out of Playoffs
1917-18	**22**	10	1	0	3	8	0	**13**	**9**	**0**	**108**	**109**	**26**	**2nd and 1st*** **		**Won Stanley Cup**

* Name changed from St. Patricks to Maple Leafs. ** Name changed from Arenas to St. Patricks.
*** Season played in two halves with no combined standing at end.

1992-93 Player Personnel

FORWARDS	HT	WT	S	Place of Birth	Date	1991-92 Club
AITKEN, Brad	6-3	200	L	Scarborough, Ont.	10/30/67	St John's
ANDERSON, Glenn	6-1	190	L	Vancouver, B.C.	10/2/60	Toronto
AUGUSTA, Patrik	5-10	169	L	Jihlava, Czech.	11/13/69	Dukla Jihlava
BORSCHEVSKY, Nikolai	5-9	180	L	Tomsk, USSR	1/12/65	Spartak
CHITARONI, Terry	5-11	200	R	Haileybury, Ont.	9/12/72	Sudbury
CIMETTA, Robert	6-0	190	L	Toronto, Ont.	2/15/70	Toronto-St. John's
CLARK, Wendel	5-11	194	L	Kelvington, Sask.	10/25/66	Toronto
CLARKE, Wayne	6-2	175	R	Sterling, Ont.	8/30/72	R.P.I.
CONVERY, Brandon	6-0	180	R	Kingston, Ont.	2/4/74	Sudbury
DERUITER, Chris	6-2	190	R	Kingston, Ont.	2/27/74	Kingston
DOERS, Michael	6-0	175	R	Madison, WI	6/17/71	U. of Wisconsin
EASTWOOD, Michael	6-2	190	R	Ottawa, Ont.	7/1/67	St. John's-Toronto
ELVENAS, Roger	6-1	185	L	Lund, Sweden	5/29/68	Rogle
FOLIGNO, Mike	6-2	195	L	Sudbury, Ont.	1/29/59	Toronto
GILMOUR, Doug	5-11	165	L	Kingston, Ont.	6/25/63	Calgary-Toronto
HAKANSSON, Mikael	6-1	176	L	Stockholm, Sweden	3/31/74	Nacka
HAWKINS, Todd	6-1	195	R	Kingston, Ont.	8/2/66	St. John's-Toronto
HENDRICKSON, Darby	6-0	175	L	Richfield, MA	8/28/72	Richfield
KELLEY, Jonathan	6-1	180	R	Brighton, MA	6/25/73	Arlington
KRUSHELNYSKI, Mike	6-2	200	L	Montreal, Que.	4/27/60	Toronto
KUCHARCIK, Tomas	6-2	200	L	Mlada Boleslav, Czech.	10/5/70	Dukla Jihlava
KUDASHOV, Alexei	6-0	180	R	Elekhrostal, USSR	7/21/71	Krylja Sovetov
KUZMINSKY, Alexander	5-11	175	L	Kiev, USSR	12/7/72	Sokol Kiev
LACROIX, Eric	6-1	200	L	Montreal, Que.	7/15/71	St. Lawrence U.
LAROSE, Guy	5-9	175	L	Hull, Que.	8/31/67	Bing.-St.J.-Tor.
MALLGRAVE, Matt	6-0	180	R	Washington, DC	5/3/70	Harvard
MANDERVILLE, Kent	6-3	200	L	Edmonton, Alta.	4/12/71	Cdn. Olympic-Toronto
MARSHALL, Grant	6-1	185	R	Mississauga, Ont.	6/9/73	Ottawa
McCLELLAND, Kevin	6-2	205	R	Oshawa, Ont.	7/4/62	Toronto-St. John's
McINTYRE, Robb	6-0	180	L	Royal Oak, MI	4/27/72	Ferris St.
McLLWAIN, Dave	6-0	190	L	Seaforth, Ont.	6/9/67	Wpg.-Buf.-NYI-Tor.
McRAE, Ken	6-1	195	R	Winchester, Ont.	4/23/68	Quebec-Halifax
MERKLER, Keith	6-2	205	L	Syosset, NY	4/23/71	Princeton
OSBORNE, Mark	6-2	205	L	Toronto, Ont.	8/13/61	Winnipeg-Toronto
PEARSON, Rob	6-1	180	R	Oshawa, Ont.	3/8/71	Toronto-St. John's
PERREAULT, Yanic	5-11	182	L	Sherbrooke, Que.	4/4/71	St. John's
PERRY, Jeff	6-0	192	L	Sarnia, Ont.	12/4/71	Owen Sound-St. John's-Raleigh
PROCHAZKA, Martin	5-11	176	R	Slany, Czech.	3/3/72	Dukla Jihlava
SACCO, Joe	6-1	180	L	Medford, MA	2/4/69	Toronto-US National
St.LAURENT, Jeffrey	6-2	175	R	Sandford, ME	5/16/71	U. of New Hampshire
STIVER, Dan	6-0	185	R	Chicoutimi, Que.	9/14/71	U. of Michigan
TOMBERLIN, Justin	6-0	191	L	Grand Rapids, MN	11/15/70	U. of Maine
TOMLINSON, David	5-11	180	L	N. Vancouver, B.C.	5/8/68	Toronto-St. John's
VANDENBUSSCHE, Ryan	5-11	184	R	Simcoe, Ont.	2/28/73	Cornwall
WALTERS, Greg	6-1	195	R	Calgary, Alta.	8/12/70	St. John's-Raleigh
ZEZEL, Peter	5-9	200	L	Toronto, Ont.	4/22/65	Toronto
DEFENSEMEN						
BAUMGARTNER, Ken	6-1	200	L	Flin Flon, Man.	3/11/66	Toronto-NY Islanders
BEREHOWSKY, Drake	6-1	211	R	Toronto, Ont.	1/3/72	New Brunswick
BURKE, David	6-1	185	L	Detroit, MI	10/15/70	Cornell
CARNEY, Keith	6-1	180	L	Cumberland, RI	2/7/71	Lowell
CHEBATOR, Rob	6-0	170	L	Arlington, MA	12/1/70	U. of New Hampshire
CROWLEY, Ted	6-2	190	R	Concord, MA	5/3/70	US National-St. John's
DEMPSEY, Nathan	6-0	160	R	Spruce Grove, Alta.	7/14/74	Regina
ELLETT, Dave	6-1	200	L	Cleveland, OH	3/30/64	Toronto
GILL, Todd	6-1	185	L	Brockville, Ont.	11/9/65	Toronto
GRONVALL, Janne	6-3	187	L	Rauma, Finland	7/17/73	Lukko
HALKIDIS, Bob	6-0	200	L	Toronto, Ont.	3/5/66	Toronto
HUNT, Curtis	6-0	195	L	N. Battleford, Sask.	1/28/67	St. John's
JENSEN, Chris	6-2	190	R	Wilmette, IL	6/29/68	U. of New Hampshire
LEFEBVRE, Sylvain	6-2	204	L	Richmond, Que.	10/14/67	Montreal
LEHOUX, Guy	5-11	205	L	Disraeli, Que.	10/19/71	St. John's
MACOUN, Jamie	6-2	197	L	Newmarket, Ont.	8/17/61	Calgary-Toronto
MALONE, Scott	6-0	180	L	Boston, MA	1/16/71	U. of New Hampshire
MARTIN, Matt	6-3	190	L	Hamden, CT	4/30/71	U. of Maine
McCARTHY, Joe	6-1	200	L	Bangor, ME	11/17/70	U. of Vermont
MIRONOV, Dmitri	6-2	195	R	Moscow, USSR	12/25/65	Toronto-Krylja Sovetov
O'ROURKE, Chris	6-2	195	R	Sherwood Park, Alta.	6/1/71	Alaska-Fair.
POESCHEK, Rudy	6-2	210	R	Terrace, B.C.	9/29/66	Moncton
RAITER, Mark	6-4	220	R	Calgary, Alta.	1/27/73	Saskatoon
ROUSE, Bob	6-1	210	R	Surrey, B.C.	6/18/64	Toronto
SACCO, David	6-1	190	R	Malden, MA	7/31/70	Boston U.
SEROWIK, Jeff	6-0	190	R	Manchester, NH	10/1/67	St. John's
SHANNON, Darryl	6-2	190	L	Barrie, Ont.	6/21/68	Toronto
SIMONOV, Sergei	6-1	183	L	Saratov, USSR	5/20/74	Kristall Saratov
WEINRICH, Alex	6-0	180	R	Lewiston, ME	3/12/69	Merrimack
WOHLERS, Nick	6-2	200	L	Stillwater, MN	7/12/70	St. Thomas

GOALTENDERS	HT	WT	C	Place of Birth	Date	1991-92 Club
FUHR, Grant	5-10	186	R	Spruce Grove, Alta.	9/28/62	Toronto
GREGORIO, Mike	6-3	195	L	Reading, MA	8/17/69	Kent State
HORYNA, Robert	5-11	185	L	Hradec, Czech.	9/10/70	St. John's-Brantford
McGARRY, Pat	6-1	182	L	Ottawa, Ont.	11/3/70	U. of Dalhousie
POTVIN, Felix	6-0	185	L	Montreal, Que.	6/23/71	Toronto-St. John's
RHODES, Damian	6-0	170	L	St. Paul, MN	5/28/69	St. John's
WAMSLEY, Rick	5-11	185	L	Simcoe, Ont.	5/25/59	Toronto-Calgary

1991-92 Scoring

Regular Season

Pos	#	Player	Team	GP	G	A	Pts	+/-	PIM	PP	SH	GW	GT	S	%
C	93	Doug Gilmour	CGY	38	11	27	38	12	46	4	1	1	0	64	17.2
			TOR	40	15	34	49	13	32	6	0	3	1	104	14.4
			TOTAL	78	26	61	87	25	78	10	1	4	1	168	15.5
R	10	Glenn Anderson	TOR	72	24	33	57	13–	100	5	0	4	1	188	12.8
D	4	Dave Ellett	TOR	79	18	33	51	13–	95	9	1	4	0	225	8.0
C	25	Peter Zezel	TOR	64	16	33	49	22–	26	4	0	1	0	125	12.8
L	17	Wendel Clark	TOR	43	19	21	40	14–	123	7	0	4	0	158	12.0
C	44	Brian Bradley	TOR	59	10	21	31	3–	48	4	0	3	0	78	12.8
D	34	Jamie Macoun	CGY	37	2	12	14	10	53	1	0	0	0	58	3.4
			TOR	39	3	13	16	0	18	2	0	0	0	71	4.2
			TOTAL	76	5	25	30	10	71	3	0	0	0	129	3.9
C	22	Mike Bullard	TOR	65	14	14	28	19–	42	7	0	0	1	140	10.0
C	7	Dave McLlwain	WPG	3	1	1	2	1	2	0	0	0	0	3	33.3
			BUF	5	0	0	0	3–	2	0	0	0	0	5	.0
			NYI	54	8	15	23	8–	28	1	1	1	0	71	11.3
			TOR	11	1	2	3	1	4	0	0	1	0	12	8.3
			TOTAL	73	10	18	28	9–	36	1	1	2	0	91	11.0
R	12*	Rob Pearson	TOR	47	14	10	24	16–	58	6	0	0	1	79	17.7
C	26	Mike Krushelnyski	TOR	72	9	15	24	5–	72	0	2	1	0	100	9.0
D	3	Bob Rouse	TOR	79	3	19	22	20–	97	1	0	0	0	115	2.6
D	2	Ric Nattress	CGY	18	0	5	5	0	31	0	0	0	0	23	.0
			TOR	36	2	14	16	1–	32	0	0	1	0	43	4.7
			TOTAL	54	2	19	21	1–	63	0	0	1	0	66	3.0
L	21	Mark Osborne	WPG	43	4	12	16	8–	65	0	0	0	0	50	8.0
			TOR	11	3	1	4	2–	8	0	2	0	0	16	18.8
			TOTAL	54	7	13	20	10–	73	0	2	0	0	66	10.6
D	23	Todd Gill	TOR	74	2	15	17	22–	91	1	0	0	0	82	2.4
C	11*	Guy Larose	TOR	34	9	5	14	8–	27	0	0	0	0	60	15.0
R	71	Mike Foligno	TOR	33	6	8	14	3–	50	2	0	1	1	41	14.6
L	24*	Joe Sacco	TOR	17	7	4	11	8	4	0	0	1	0	40	17.5
D	28	Darryl Shannon	TOR	48	2	8	10	17–	23	1	0	0	0	50	4.0
L	14	Rob Cimetta	TOR	24	4	3	7	5	12	0	0	0	0	31	12.9
D	33	Bob Halkidis	TOR	46	3	3	6	9–	145	0	0	0	0	36	8.3
L	18*	Kent Manderville	TOR	15	0	4	4	1	0	0	0	0	0	14	.0
C	32*	Mike Eastwood	TOR	9	0	2	2	4–	4	0	0	0	0	6	.0
D	15	Dimitri Mironov	TOR	7	1	0	1	4–	0	0	0	1	0	7	14.3
R	18	Kevin Maguire	TOR	8	1	0	1	4–	4	0	0	0	0	8	12.5
R	16*	Greg Johnston	TOR	3	0	1	1	1–	5	0	0	0	0	2	.0
R	20	Kevin McClelland	TOR	18	0	1	1	3–	33	0	0	0	0	5	.0
L	8	Ken Baumgartner	NYI	44	0	1	1	10–	202	0	0	0	0	11	.0
			TOR	11	0	0	0	1	23	0	0	0	0	5	.0
			TOTAL	55	0	1	1	9–	225	0	0	0	0	16	.0
G	31	Grant Fuhr	TOR	66	0	1	1	0	4	0	0	0	0	0	.0
D	24*	Drake Berehowsky	TOR	1	0	0	0	0	0	0	0	0	0	0	.0
R	8*	Todd Hawkins	TOR	2	0	0	0	0	0	0	0	0	0	0	.0
C	13	Ken Linseman	TOR	2	0	0	0	2–	2	0	0	0	0	0	.0
D	36*	Leonard Esau	TOR	2	0	0	0	0	0	0	0	0	0	0	.0
C	14*	Dave Tomlinson	TOR	3	0	0	0	1–	2	0	0	0	0	6	.0
G	29*	Felix Potvin	TOR	4	0	0	0	0	0	0	0	0	0	0	.0
G	30	Rick Wamsley	CGY	9	0	0	0	0	0	0	0	0	0	0	.0
			TOR	8	0	0	0	0	0	0	0	0	0	0	.0
			TOTAL	17	0	0	0	0	0	0	0	0	0	0	.0

Goaltending

No.	Goaltender	GPI	Mins	Avg	W	L	T	EN	SO	GA	SA	S%
29	*Felix Potvin	4	210	2.29	0	2	1	1	0	8	120	.933
35	Jeff Reese	8	413	2.91	1	5	1	1	1	20	210	.905
31	Grant Fuhr	66	3774	3.66	25	33	5	7	2	230	1933	.881
30	Rick Wamsley	8	428	3.79	4	3	0	0	0	27	218	.876
	Totals	**80**	**4843**	**3.64**	**30**	**43**	**7**	**9**	**3**	**294**	**2490**	**.882**

General Managers' History

Conn Smythe, 1927-28 to 1956-57; Hap Day, 1957-58; George "Punch" Imlach, 1958-59 to 1968-69; Jim Gregory, 1969-70 to 1978-79; Punch Imlach, 1979-80 to 1980-81; Punch Imlach and Gerry McNamara, 1981-82; Gerry McNamara, 1982-83 to 1987-88; Gord Stellick, 1988-89; Floyd Smith, 1989-90 to 1990-91; Cliff Fletcher, 1991-92 to date.

Coaching History

Conn Smythe, 1927-28 to 1929-30; Conn Smythe and Art Duncan, 1930-31; Art Duncan and Dick Irvin, 1931-32; Dick Irvin, 1932-33 to 1939-40; Hap Day, 1940-41 to 1949-50; Joe Primeau, 1950-51 to 1952-53; "King" Clancy, 1953-54 to 1955-56; Howie Meeker, 1956-57; Billy Reay, 1957-58; Billy Reay and "Punch" Imlach, 1958-59; "Punch" Imlach, 1959-60 to 1968-69; John McLellan, 1969-70 to 1970-71; John McLellan and "King" Clancy, 1971-72; John McLellan, 1972-73; Red Kelly, 1973-74 to 1976-77; Roger Neilson, 1977-78 to 1978-79; Floyd Smith, Dick Duff and "Punch" Imlach, 1979-80; "Punch" Imlach, Joe Crozier and Mike Nykoluk, 1980-81; Mike Nykoluk, 1981-82 to 1983-84; Dan Maloney, 1984-85 to 1985-86; John Brophy, 1986-87 to 1987-88; John Brophy and George Armstrong, 1988-89; Doug Carpenter, 1989-90; Doug Carpenter and Tom Watt, 1990-91; Tom Watt, 1991-92; Pat Burns, 1992-93.

Club Records

Team

(Figures in brackets for season records are games played; records for fewest points, wins, ties, losses, goals, goals against are for 70 or more games)

Most Points **95** 1950-51 (70)
Most Wins **41** 1950-51 (70), 1977-78 (80)
Most Ties **22** 1954-55 (70)
Most Losses **52** 1984-85 (80)
Most Goals **337** 1989-90 (80)
Most Goals Against **387** 1983-84 (80)
Fewest Points **48** 1984-85 (80)
Fewest Wins **20** 1981-82, 1984-85 (80)
Fewest Ties **4** 1989-90 (80)
Fewest Losses **16** 1950-51 (70)
Fewest Goals **147** 1954-55 (70)
Fewest Goals Against ... ***131** 1953-54 (70)

Longest Winning Streak
Over-all .... **9** Jan. 30-Feb. 28/25
Home .... **9** Nov. 11-Dec. 26/53
Away .... **7** Nov. 14-Dec. 15/40; Dec. 4/60-Jan. 5/61

Longest Undefeated Streak
Over-all .... **11** Oct. 15-Nov. 8/50 (8 wins, 3 ties)
Home .... **18** Nov. 28/33-Mar. 10/34 (15 wins, 3 ties); Oct. 31/53-Jan. 23/54 (16 wins, 2 ties)
Away .... **9** Nov. 30/47-Jan. 11/48 (4 wins, 5 ties)

Longest Losing Streak
Over-all .... **10** Jan. 15-Feb. 8/67
Home .... **7** Nov. 10-Dec. 5/84; Jan. 26-Feb. 25/85
Away .... **11** Feb. 20/-Apr. 1/88

Longest Winless Streak
Over-all .... **15** Dec. 26/87-Jan. 25/88 (11 losses, 4 ties)
Home .... **11** Dec. 19/87-Jan. 25/88 (7 losses, 4 ties)
Away .... **18** Oct. 6/82-Jan. 5/83 (13 losses, 5 ties)

Most Shutouts, Season **13** 1953-54 (70)
Most PIM, Season **2,419** 1989-90 (80)
Most Goals, Game .... **14** Mar. 16/57 (NYR 1 at Tor. 14)

Individual

Most Seasons .... **21** George Armstrong
Most Games .... **1,187** George Armstrong
Most Goals, Career .... **389** Darryl Sittler
Most Assists, Career ...... **620** Borje Salming
Most Points, Career ...... **916** Darryl Sittler (389 goals, 527 assists)
Most PIM, Career ...... **1,670** Dave Williams
Most Shutouts, Career ..... **62** Turk Broda
Longest Consecutive Games Streak .... **486** Tim Horton (Feb. 11/61-Feb. 4/68)
Most Goals, Season .... **54** Rick Vaive (1981-82)
Most Assists, Season ...... **72** Darryl Sittler (1977-78)
Most Points, Season ...... **117** Darryl Sittler (1977-78) (45 goals, 72 assists)
Most PIM, Season .... **351** Dave Williams (1977-78)
Most Points, Defenseman Season .... **79** Ian Turnbull (1976-77) (22 goals, 57 assists)
Most Points, Center Season .... **117** Darryl Sittler (1977-78) (45 goals, 72 assists)
Most Points, Right Wing, Season .... **97** Wilf Paiement (1980-81) (40 goals, 57 assists)
Most Points, Left Wing, Season .... **94** Vince Damphousse (1989-90) (33 goals, 61 assists)
Most Points, Rookie, Season .... **66** Peter Ihnacak (1982-83) (28 goals, 38 assists)
Most Shutouts, Season .... **13** Harry Lumley (1953-54)
Most Goals, Game .... **6** Corb Denneny (Jan. 26/21); Darryl Sittler (Feb. 7/76)
Most Assists,Game .... **6** Babe Pratt (Jan. 8/44)
Most Points, Game ...... ***10** Darryl Sittler (Feb. 7/76)

* NHL Record.

Captains' History

Hap Day, 1927-28 to 1936-37; Charlie Conacher, 1937-38; Red Horner, 1938-39, 1939-40; Syl Apps, 1940-41 to 1942-43; Bob Davidson, 1943-44, 1944-45; Syl Apps, 1945-46 to 1947-48; Ted Kennedy, 1948-49 to 1954-55; Sid Smith, 1955-56; Ted Kennedy, Jim Thomson, 1956-57; George Armstrong, 1957-58 to 1968-69; Dave Keon, 1969-70 to 1974-75; Darryl Sittler, 1975-76 to 1980-81; Rick Vaive, 1981-82 to 1985-86; no captain, 1986-87 to 1988-89; Rob Ramage, 1989-90 to 1990-91; Wendel Clark, 1991-92 to date.

Retired Numbers

5	Bill Barilko	1946-1951
6	Irwin "Ace" Bailey	1927-1934

1991-92 Results

Home				Away			
Oct.	5	Detroit	8-5	**Oct.**	3	Montreal	3-4
	7	St Louis	3-0		15	St Louis	1-5
	9	Washington	4-5		17	Calgary	4-6
	12	Vancouver	1-2		19	Winnipeg	2-4
	26	Detroit	6-1		21	Vancouver	1-4
	28	St Louis	1-1		25	Detroit	0-4
Nov.	2	Los Angeles	2-5	**Nov.**	1	Washington	0-4
	4	San Jose	4-1		8	NY Rangers	3-3
	6	Minnesota	4-3		12	Minnesota	0-7
	9	Calgary	1-6		14	Chicago	0-3
	16	Chicago	2-2		20	St Louis	2-5
	17	Hartford	1-3		22	San Jose	3-1
	30	Minnesota	3-4		26	Los Angeles	4-4
Dec.	7	Vancouver	6-3		29	Minnesota	3-2
	9	Montreal	1-4	**Dec.**	4	Hartford	3-0
	11	NY Islanders	4-5		12	Philadelphia	1-1
	18	Edmonton	5-7		14	Boston	3-4
	21	Buffalo	1-4		20	Washington	3-4
	23	Winnipeg	3-1		26	Pittsburgh	1-12
	28	Detroit	4-5		30	Quebec	2-5
Jan.	4	Chicago	2-4	**Jan.**	3	Detroit	4-6
	6	St Louis	3-2		9	Chicago	0-2
	22	Boston	2-5		11	New Jersey	4-3
	25	Philadelphia	6-4		16	Chicago	0-4
	29	Quebec	5-2		23	NY Islanders	4-3
Feb.	1	New Jersey	6-4	**Feb.**	3	Minnesota	2-4
	5	Minnesota	3-2		7	Detroit	4-3
	8	Montreal	6-4		18	Pittsburgh	1-7
	11	Detroit	4-3		20	Detroit	2-3
	15	Winnipeg	1-3		22	St Louis	3-4
	16	Edmonton	7-5		27	Boston	2-4
	25	New Jersey	5-5	**Mar.**	4	Edmonton	5-2
	29	Chicago	6-5		5	Calgary	5-5
Mar.	1	Minnesota	6-2		8	San Jose*	1-4
	14	Pittsburgh	6-3		9	Los Angeles	1-4
	17	Quebec	4-3		11	Minnesota	3-0
	21	Chicago	1-3		25	Buffalo	2-5
	23	St Louis	3-2		28	St Louis	3-2
Apr.	1	NY Islanders	2-6		29	Chicago	1-5
	4	NY Rangers	4-2	**Apr.**	5	Philadelphia	2-6

*Denotes afternoon game

All-time Record vs. Other Clubs

Regular Season

	At Home							On Road							Total						
	GP	W	L	T	GF	GA	PTS	GP	W	L	T	GF	GA	PTS	GP	W	L	T	GF	GA	PTS
Boston	278	146	86	46	945	722	338	278	80	151	47	742	923	207	556	226	237	93	1687	1645	545
Buffalo	47	18	22	7	148	176	43	48	16	30	2	138	204	34	95	34	52	9	286	380	77
Calgary	36	14	15	7	144	145	35	38	11	23	4	129	178	26	74	25	38	11	273	323	61
Chicago	293	157	86	50	1012	751	364	292	106	147	39	759	903	251	585	263	233	89	1771	1654	615
Detroit	295	157	94	44	984	776	358	295	97	155	43	717	873	237	590	254	249	87	1701	1649	595
Edmonton	21	8	12	1	87	109	17	20	3	13	4	66	110	10	41	11	25	5	153	219	27
Hartford	20	6	12	2	70	85	14	20	5	12	3	67	97	13	40	11	24	5	137	182	27
Los Angeles	51	28	14	9	215	169	65	52	15	30	7	143	189	37	103	43	44	16	358	358	102
Minnesota	79	38	27	14	292	261	90	78	29	40	9	257	302	67	157	67	67	23	549	563	157
Montreal	313	159	110	44	949	821	362	312	82	190	40	767	1110	204	625	241	300	84	1716	1931	566
New Jersey	31	22	6	3	148	106	47	30	10	11	9	98	109	29	61	32	17	12	246	215	76
NY Islanders	38	16	19	3	129	143	35	36	12	21	3	112	158	27	74	28	40	6	241	301	62
NY Rangers	265	150	77	38	914	687	338	266	101	109	56	782	810	258	531	251	186	94	1696	1497	596
Philadelphia	50	18	19	13	175	170	49	50	10	32	8	118	203	28	100	28	51	21	293	373	77
Pittsburgh	51	24	17	10	212	172	58	52	19	28	5	169	218	43	103	43	45	15	381	390	101
Quebec	21	10	9	2	74	91	22	20	5	10	5	69	83	15	41	15	19	7	143	174	37
St. Louis	76	48	20	8	302	226	104	77	20	47	10	217	277	50	153	68	67	18	519	503	154
San Jose	1	1	0	0	4	1	2	2	1	1	0	4	5	2	3	2	1	0	8	6	4
Vancouver	43	18	16	9	164	151	45	42	12	23	7	132	148	31	85	30	39	16	296	299	76
Washington	32	18	10	4	152	115	40	33	11	20	2	93	128	24	65	29	30	6	245	243	64
Winnipeg	23	7	15	1	86	107	15	22	7	12	3	94	108	17	45	14	27	4	180	215	32
Defunct Clubs	232	158	53	21	860	515	337	233	84	120	29	607	745	197	465	242	173	50	1467	1260	534
Totals	**2296**	**1221**	**739**	**336**	**8066**	**6499**	**2778**	**2296**	**736**	**1225**	**335**	**6280**	**7881**	**1807**	**4592**	**1957**	**1964**	**671**	**14346**	**14380**	**4585**

Playoffs

	Series	W	L	GP	W	L	T	GF	GA	Last Mtg.	Round	Result
Boston	13	8	5	62	31	30	1	150	153	1974	QF	L 0-4
**Calgary	1	1	0	2	2	0	0	9	5	1979	PR	W 2-0
Chicago	7	5	2	25	15	9	1	76	57	1986	DSF	W 3-0
Detroit	22	11	11	110	54	56	0	287	291	1988	DSF	L 2-4
Los Angeles	2	2	0	5	4	1	0	18	9	1978	PR	W 2-0
Minnesota	2	0	2	7	1	6	0	26	35	1983	DSF	L 1-3
Montreal	13	6	7	67	28	39	0	148	203	1979	QF	L 0-4
NY Islanders	2	1	1	10	4	6	0	20	33	1981	PR	L 0-3
NY Rangers	8	3	5	35	16	19	0	86	86	1971	QF	L 2-4
Philadelphia	3	0	3	17	5	12	0	47	67	1977	QF	L 2-4
Pittsburgh	2	2	0	6	4	2	0	21	13	1977	PR	W 2-1
St. Louis	3	1	2	18	8	10	0	53	56	1990	DSF	L 1-4
Defunct	4	3	1	10	5	4	1	20	16			
Totals	**82**	**43**	**39**	**374**	**177**	**194**	**3**	**961**	**1024**			

Playoff Results 1992-88

Year	Round	Opponent	Result	GF	GA
1990	DSF	St. Louis	L 1-4	16	20
1988	DSF	Detroit	L 2-4	20	32

Abbreviations: Round: F – Final; **CF** – conference final; **DF** – division final; **DSF** – division semi-final; **SF** – semi-final; **QF** – quarter-final; **PR** – preliminary round. **GA** – goals against; **GF** – goals for.

Entry Draft Selections 1992-78

1992

Pick	
8	Brandon Convery
23	Grant Marshall
77	Nikolai Borschevsky
95	Mark Raiter
101	Janne Gronvall
106	Chris Deruiter
125	Mikael Hakansson
149	Patrik Augusta
173	Ryan Vandenbussche
197	Wayne Clarke
221	Sergei Simonov
245	Nathan Dempsey

1991

Pick	
47	Yanic Perreault
69	Terry Chitaroni
102	Alexei Kudashov
113	Jeff Perry
120	Alexander Kuzminsky
135	Martin Prochazka
160	Dmitri Mironov
164	Robb McIntyre
167	Tomas Kucharcik
179	Guy Lehoux
201	Gary Miller
223	Jonathan Kelley
245	Chris O'Rourke

1990

Pick	
10	Drake Berehowsky
31	Felix Potvin
73	Darby Hendrickson
80	Greg Walters
115	Alexander Godynyuk
136	Eric Lacroix
157	Dan Stiver
178	Robert Horyna
199	Rob Chebator
220	Scott Malone
241	Nick Vachon

1989

Pick	
3	Scott Thornton
12	Rob Pearson
21	Steve Bancroft
66	Matt Martin
96	Keith Carney
108	David Burke
125	Michael Doers
129	Keith Merkler
150	Derek Langille
171	Jeffrey St. Laurent
192	Justin Tomberlin
213	Mike Jackson
234	Steve Chartrand

1988

Pick	
6	Scott Pearson
27	Tie Domi
48	Peter Ing
69	Ted Crowley
88	Leonard Esau
132	Matt Mallgrave
153	Roger Elvenas
174	Mike Delay
195	David Sacco
216	Mike Gregorio
237	Peter DeBoer

1987

Pick	
7	Luke Richardson
28	Daniel Marois
49	John McIntyre
71	Joe Sacco
91	Mike Eastwood
112	Damian Rhodes
133	Trevor Jobe
154	Chris Jensen
175	Brian Blad
196	Ron Bernacci
217	Ken Alexander
238	Alex Weinrich

1986

Pick	
6	Vincent Damphousse
36	Darryl Shannon
48	Sean Boland
69	Kent Hulst
90	Scott Taylor
111	Stephane Giguere
132	Danny Hie
153	Stephen Brennan
174	Brian Bellefeuille
195	Sean Davidson
216	Mark Holick
237	Brian Hoard

1985

Pick	
1	Wendel Clark
22	Ken Spangler
43	Dave Thomlinson
64	Greg Vey
85	Jeff Serowik
106	Jiri Latal
127	Tim Bean
148	Andy Donahue
169	Todd Whittemore
190	Bob Reynolds
211	Tim Armstrong
232	Mitch Murphy

1984

Pick	
4	Al Iafrate
25	Todd Gill
67	Jeff Reese
88	Jack Capuano
109	Joseph Fabian
130	Joe McInnis
151	Derek Laxdal
172	Dan Turner
192	David Buckley
213	Mikael Wurst
233	Peter Slanina

1983

Pick	
7	Russ Courtnall
28	Jeff Jackson
48	Allan Bester
83	Dan Hodgson
128	Cam Plante
148	Paul Bifano
168	Cliff Albrecht
184	Greg Rolston
188	Brian Ross
208	Mike Tomlak
228	Ron Choules

1982

Pick	
3	Gary Nylund
24	Gary Leeman
25	Peter Ihnacak
45	Ken Wregget
73	Vladimir Ruzicka
87	Eduard Uvira
99	Sylvain Charland
108	Ron Dreger
115	Craig Kales
129	Dom Campedelli
139	Jeff Triano
171	Miroslav Ihnacak
192	Leigh Verstraete
213	Tim Loven
234	Jim Appleby

1981

Pick	
6	Jim Benning
24	Gary Yaremchuk
55	Ernie Godden
90	Normand LeFrancois
102	Barry Brigley
132	Andrew Wright
153	Richard Turmel
174	Greg Barber
195	Marc Magnan

1980

Pick	
25	Craig Muni
26	Bob McGill
43	Fred Boimistruck
74	Stewart Gavin
95	Hugh Larkin
116	Ron Dennis
137	Russ Adam
158	Fred Perlini
179	Darwin McCutcheon
200	Paul Higgins

1979

Pick	
9	Laurie Boschman
51	Normand Aubin
72	Vincent Tremblay
93	Frank Nigro
114	Bill McCreary

1978

Pick	
21	Joel Quenneville
48	Mark Kirton
65	Bob Parent
81	Jordy Douglas
92	Mel Hewitt
98	Normand Lefebvre
115	John Scammell
132	Kevin Reinhart
149	Mike Waghorne
166	Laurie Cuvelier

Club Directory

Maple Leaf Gardens
60 Carlton Street
Toronto, Ontario M5B 1L1
Phone **416/977-1641**
FAX 416/977-5364
Capacity: 15,642 (standing 200)

Board of Directors
Brian P. Bellmore, J. Donald Crump, Terence V. Kelly, Q.C., Ted Nikolaou, W. Ron Pringle, Steve A. Stavro, George E. Whyte, Q.C.

Chairman of the Board and CEO	Steve A. Stavro
President, Chief Operating Officer and General Manager	Cliff Fletcher
Secretary-Treasurer	J. Donald Crump
Alternate Governors	Cliff Fletcher, Brian P. Bellmore
Assistant General Manager	Bill Watters
Special Consultant to the President	Darryl Sittler
Director of Business Operations and Communications	Bob Stellick
Head Coach	Pat Burns
Assistant Coach	Mike Kitchen
Assistant Coach	Mike Murphy
Director of Scouting	Pierre Dorion
Director of Pro Scouting	Floyd Smith
Director of Professional Development	Tom Watt
Pro Scout	Dick Duff
Scouts	George Armstrong, Garth Malarchuk, Dan Marr, Jim Bzdel, Anders Hedberg, Bob Johnson, Jack Gardiner, Doug Woods, Dick Bouchard, Peter Johnson
Public Relations Coordinator	Pat Park
Public Relations Assistant	Mark Hillier
Administrative Assistants	Mary Speck
Community Relations	Ellen Salnek
Executive Secretary to the President and G.M.	Shelley Usher
Athletic Therapist	Chris Broadhurst
Trainers	Brian Papineau, Brent Smith, Jim Carey
Vice President of Building Operations	Brian Conacher
Director of Marketing	Bill Cluff
Controller	Ian Clarke
Assistant Controller	Paul Franck
Marketing Representative	Denis Cordick
Marketing Coordinator	Nancy McIlveen
Box Office Manager	Irwin "Patty" Patoff
Building Superintendent	Wayne Gillespie
Team Doctors	Dr. Michael Clarfield, Dr. Darrell Olgilvie-Harris, Dr. Leith Douglas, Dr. Michael Easterbrook, Dr. Simon McGrail
Team Dentist	Dr. Ernie Lewis
Team Psychologist	Robert Offenberger, Ph.D.

Coach

BURNS, PAT
Coach, Toronto Maple Leafs. Born in St-Henri, Que., April 4, 1952.

After four seasons behind the bench of the Montreal Canadiens, Pat Burns accepted a new challenge by assuming the head coaching duties of the Toronto Maple Leafs. A native of St-Henri, Que., Burns was the recipient of the Jack Adams Award in 1989, after taking the Canadiens to the Stanley Cup finals in his rookie seasons as an NHL coach. Burns had been coach of the QMJHL's Olympiques when he joined the Canadiens' organization as the head coach of the Sherbrooke Canadiens, the Habs' top farm team in the AHL. In addition to his other coaching responsibilities, Burns served as an assistant coach for the Canadian National Junior Team at the 1986 World Junior Championships.

Coaching Record

		Regular Season					Playoffs			
Season	Team	Games	W	L	T	%	Games	W	L	%
1983-84	Hull (QMJHL)	70	25	45	0	.357	....	....	....	....
1984-85	Hull (QMJHL)	68	33	34	1	.493	5	1	4	.200
1985-86	Hull (QMJHL)	72	54	18	0	.750	15	15	0	1.000
1986-87	Hull (QMJHL)	70	26	39	5	.407	8	4	4	.500
1987-88	Sherbrooke (AHL)	80	42	34	4	.550	6	2	4	.333
1988-89	**Montreal (NHL)**	**80**	**53**	**18**	**9**	**.719**	**21**	**14**	**7**	**.667**
1989-90	**Montreal (NHL)**	**80**	**41**	**28**	**11**	**.581**	**11**	**5**	**6**	**.455**
1990-91	**Montreal (NHL)**	**80**	**39**	**30**	**11**	**.556**	**13**	**7**	**6**	**.538**
1991-92	**Montreal (NHL)**	**80**	**41**	**28**	**11**	**.581**	**11**	**4**	**7**	**.364**
	NHL Totals	**320**	**174**	**104**	**42**	**.609**	**56**	**30**	**26**	**.536**

General Manager

FLETCHER, CLIFF
President, General Manager and Chief Operating Officer, Toronto Maple Leafs. Born in Montreal, Que., August 16, 1935.

Cliff Fletcher joined the Maple Leafs on July 1, 1991 after 19 years with the Flames franchise. Fletcher's tenure with the Flames was highlighted by the club's 1989 Stanley Cup Championship, but their success was not limited to that championship. In the Flames' eleven seasons under Fletcher after the move from Atlanta to Calgary, the club won one Stanley Cup, two Presidents' Trophies (for top overall finish), two Campbell Conference Championships and three division titles. Over the last seven seasons, the Flames have posted a 317-178-65 record for a .624 winning percentage.

A native of Montreal, Fletcher joined the Flames franchise in Atlanta in September, 1972. In the summer of 1980 he organized the successful transfer of the franchise to Calgary. He began his hockey career with the Montreal Junior Canadiens, where he served for 10 years as a scout for Sam Pollock. In 1967 he became the eastern Canada scout for the St. Louis Blues, and two seasons later was promoted to assistant general manager.

Vancouver Canucks

1991-92 Results: 42W-26L-12T 96PTS. First, Smythe Division

Schedule

Home

Oct. Sat. 10 Edmonton
Mon. 12 Winnipeg
Sun. 25 Boston*
Wed. 28 Washington
Fri. 30 Minnesota
Nov. Wed. 4 Calgary
Fri. 6 Ottawa
Sun. 8 Winnipeg*
Tues. 10 San Jose
Mon. 16 Los Angeles
Sat. 21 Edmonton
Mon. 23 Chicago
Dec. Thur. 3 Edmonton
Mon. 7 St Louis
Wed. 9 San Jose
Sun. 13 Quebec
Fri. 18 San Jose
Sun. 27 Montreal
Tues. 29 San Jose
Thur. 31 Los Angeles
Jan. Sun. 3 Tampa Bay
Fri. 15 Buffalo
Sat. 16 Hartford
Tues. 19 Pittsburgh
Wed. 27 Chicago
Sat. 30 Detroit
Feb. Mon. 1 Minnesota
Wed. 3 Tampa Bay
Thur. 18 Philadelphia
Sat. 20 Winnipeg
Mon. 22 Toronto
Wed. 24 NY Rangers
Mar. Tues. 9 New Jersey
Thur. 11 Minnesota
(at Saskatoon)
Thur. 18 Winnipeg
Sat. 20 NY Islanders
Mon. 22 St Louis
Wed. 24 Los Angeles
Fri. 26 Calgary
Apr. Wed. 7 Edmonton
Sun. 11 Calgary*
Tues. 13 Los Angeles

Away

Oct. Tues. 6 Edmonton
Fri. 16 Winnipeg
Sun. 18 Chicago
Tues. 20 Pittsburgh
Thur. 22 Philadelphia
Nov. Mon. 2 Calgary
Thur. 12 Los Angeles
Sat. 14 San Jose
Wed. 18 Edmonton
Thur. 19 Calgary
Wed. 25 Minnesota
Thur. 26 St Louis
Sat. 28 Montreal
Dec. Wed. 16 Edmonton
Sat. 19 San Jose
Tues. 22 Los Angeles
Jan. Sat. 2 San Jose
Wed. 6 Toronto
Fri. 8 Detroit
Sat. 9 NY Islanders
Mon. 11 NY Rangers
Tues. 12 New Jersey
Thur. 21 Los Angeles
Sat. 23 Minnesota*
Sun. 24 Chicago
Feb. Tues. 9 Quebec
Thur. 11 Toronto
Fri. 12 Buffalo
Mon. 15 Los Angeles*
Fri. 26 Winnipeg
Mar. Mon. 1 Buffalo
(at Hamilton)
Tues. 2 Washington
Thur. 4 Boston
Sat. 6 Hartford
Fri. 12 Winnipeg
Sun. 14 Calgary
Tues. 30 St Louis
Apr. Thur. 1 Tampa Bay
Sat. 3 Detroit*
Sun. 4 Ottawa
Fri. 9 Calgary
Thur. 15 Los Angeles

* Denotes afternoon game.

Home Starting Times:
Weeknights .... 7:35 p.m.
Saturdays .... 5:05 p.m.
Sundays .... 7:05 p.m.
Matinees .... 2:05 p.m.

Franchise date: May 22, 1970

23rd NHL Season

Year-by-Year Record

		Home			Road			Overall							
Season	GP	W	L	T	W	L	T	W	L	T	GF	GA	Pts.	Finished	Playoff Result
1991-92	80	23	10	7	19	16	5	42	26	12	285	250	96	1st, Smythe Div.	Lost Div. Final
1990-91	80	18	17	5	10	26	4	28	43	9	243	315	65	4th, Smythe Div.	Lost Div. Semi-Final
1989-90	80	13	16	11	12	25	3	25	41	14	245	306	64	5th, Smythe Div.	Out of Playoffs
1988-89	80	19	15	6	14	24	2	33	39	8	251	253	74	4th, Smythe Div.	Lost Div. Semi-Final
1987-88	80	15	20	5	10	26	4	25	46	9	272	320	59	5th, Smythe Div.	Out of Playoffs
1986-87	80	17	19	4	12	24	4	29	43	8	282	314	66	5th, Smythe Div.	Out of Playoffs
1985-86	80	17	18	5	6	26	8	23	44	13	282	333	59	4th, Smythe Div.	Lost Div. Semi-Final
1984-85	80	15	21	4	10	25	5	25	46	9	284	401	59	5th, Smythe Div.	Out of Playoffs
1983-84	80	20	16	4	12	23	5	32	39	9	306	328	73	3rd, Smythe Div.	Lost Div. Semi-Final
1982-83	80	20	12	8	10	23	7	30	35	15	303	309	75	3rd, Smythe Div.	Lost Div. Semi-Final
1981-82	80	20	8	12	10	25	5	30	33	17	290	286	77	2nd, Smythe Div.	Lost Final
1980-81	80	17	12	11	11	20	9	28	32	20	289	301	76	3rd, Smythe Div.	Lost Prelim. Round
1979-80	80	14	17	9	13	20	7	27	37	16	256	281	70	3rd, Smythe Div.	Lost Prelim. Round
1978-79	80	15	18	7	10	24	6	25	42	13	217	291	63	2nd, Smythe Div.	Lost Prelim. Round
1977-78	80	13	15	12	7	28	5	20	43	17	239	320	57	3rd, Smythe Div.	Out of Playoffs
1976-77	80	13	21	6	12	21	7	25	42	13	235	294	63	4th, Smythe Div.	Out of Playoffs
1975-76	80	22	11	7	11	21	8	33	32	15	271	272	81	2nd, Smythe Div.	Lost Prelim. Round
1974-75	80	23	12	5	15	20	5	38	32	10	271	254	86	1st, Smythe Div.	Lost Quarter-Final
1973-74	78	14	18	7	10	25	4	24	43	11	224	296	59	7th, East Div.	Out of Playoffs
1972-73	78	17	18	4	5	29	5	22	47	9	233	339	53	7th, East Div.	Out of Playoffs
1971-72	78	14	20	5	6	30	3	20	50	8	203	297	48	7th, East Div.	Out of Playoffs
1970-71	78	17	18	4	7	28	4	24	46	8	229	296	56	6th, East Div.	Out of Playoffs

Trevor Linden tied for the team lead with six game-winning goals for the Vancouver Canucks in 1991-92.

1992-93 Player Personnel

FORWARDS	HT	WT	S	Place of Birth	Date	1991-92 Club
ADAMS, Greg	6-3	198	L	Nelson, B.C.	8/1/63	Vancouver
ANTOSKI, Shawn	6-4	245	L	Brantford, Ont.	3/25/70	Milwaukee-Vancouver
BADER, Darin	6-0	202	L	Edmonton, Alta.	4/1/71	Milwaukee
BAWA, Robin	6-2	214	R	Chemainus, B.C.	3/26/66	Milwaukee-Vancouver
BURE, Pavel	5-10	180	L	Moscow, USSR	3/31/71	Vancouver
COURTNALL, Geoff	6-1	190	L	Duncan, B.C.	8/18/62	Vancouver
FERGUS, Tom	6-3	210	L	Chicago, IL	6/16/62	Vancouver-Toronto
JACKSON, Dane	6-1	200	R	Castlegar, B.C.	5/17/70	North Dakota
KESA, Dan	6-0	208	R	Vancouver, B.C.	11/23/71	Prince Albert
KRON, Robert	5-10	175	L	Brno, Czech.	2/27/67	Vancouver
LINDEN, Trevor	6-4	205	R	Medicine Hat, Alta.	4/11/70	Vancouver
MAZUR, Jay	6-2	205	R	Hamilton, Ont.	1/22/65	Vancouver-Milwaukee
MOGER, Sandy	6-3	200	R	Vernon, B.C.	3/21/69	Lake Superior State
MOMESSO, Sergio	6-3	215	L	Montreal, Que.	9/4/65	Vancouver
MURANO, Eric	6-0	200	R	LaSalle, Que.	5/4/67	Milwaukee
NEDVED, Petr	6-3	185	L	Liberec, Czech.	12/9/71	Vancouver
ODJICK, Gino	6-3	220	L	Maniwaki, Que.	9/7/70	Vancouver
PECA, Mike	5-11	180	R	Toronto, Ont.	3/26/74	Ottawa
POLISEK, Libor	6-3	198	R	Vitkovice, Czech.	4/22/74	TJ Vitkovice
RONNING, Cliff	5-8	175	L	Burnaby, B.C.	10/1/65	Vancouver
SANDLAK, Jim	6-3	220	R	Kitchener, Ont.	12/12/66	Vancouver
STOJANOV, Alek	6-4	225	L	Windsor, Ont.	4/25/73	Guelph
VALK, Garry	6-1	190	L	Edmonton, Alta.	11/27/67	Vancouver
WALTER, Ryan	6-0	200	L	Burnaby, B.C.	4/23/58	Vancouver
WARD, Dixon	6-0	200	R	Leduc, Alta.	9/23/68	North Dakota
DEFENSEMEN						
BABYCH, Dave	6-2	215	L	Edmonton, Alta.	5/23/61	Vancouver
CULLIMORE, Jassen	6-5	225	L	Simcoe, Ont.	12/4/72	Peterborough
DIDUCK, Gerald	6-2	207	R	Edmonton, Alta.	4/6/65	Vancouver
DIRK, Robert	6-4	218	L	Regina, Sask.	8/20/66	Vancouver
HERTER, Jason	6-1	190	R	Hafford, Sask.	1/15/71	Milwaukee
LIDSTER, Doug	6-1	200	R	Kamloops, B.C.	10/18/60	Vancouver
LUMME, Jyrki	6-1	207	L	Tampere, Finland	7/16/66	Vancouver
MURZYN, Dana	6-2	200	L	Calgary, Alta.	12/9/66	Vancouver
NEUMEIER, Troy	6-2	195	L	Langenburg, Sask.	9/3/70	Milwaukee
PLAVSIC, Adrien	6-1	205	L	Montreal, Que.	1/13/70	Vancouver
SLEGR, Jiri	6-1	210	L	Litvinov, Czech.	5/30/71	Litvinov
VONSTEFENELLI, Philip	6-1	183	L	Vancouver, B.C.	4/10/69	Milwaukee

GOALTENDERS	HT	WT	C	Place of Birth	Date	1991-92 Club
D'ALESSIO, Corrie	5-11	155	L	Cornwall, Ont.	9/9/69	Milwaukee
FITZSIMMONS, Jason	5-11	185	L	Regina, Sask.	6/3/71	Moose Jaw
FOUNTAIN, Mike	6-1	176	L	North York, Ont.	1/26/72	Oshawa
GAMBLE, Troy	5-11	195	L	New Glasgow, N.S.	4/7/67	Vancouver
MASON, Bob	6-1	180	R	International Falls, MN	4/22/61	Vancouver
McLEAN, Kirk	6-0	185	L	Willowdale, Ont.	6/26/66	Vancouver

General Managers' History

Normand Robert Poile, 1970-71 to 1972-73; Hal Laycoe, 1973-74; Phil Maloney, 1974-75 to 1976-77; Jake Milford, 1977-78 to 1981-82; Harry Neale, 1982-83 to 1984-85; Jack Gordon, 1985-86 to 1986-87; Pat Quinn, 1987-88 to date.

Coaching History

Hal Laycoe, 1970-71 to 1971-72; Vic Stasiuk, 1972-73; Bill McCreary and Phil Maloney, 1973-74; Phil Maloney, 1974-75 to 1975-76; Phil Maloney and Orland Kurtenbach, 1976-77; Orland Kurtenbach, 1977-78; Harry Neale, 1978-79 to 1980-81; Harry Neale and Roger Neilson, 1981-82; Roger Neilson 1982-83; Roger Neilson and Harry Neale, 1983-84; Harry Neale and Bill Laforge, 1984-85; Tom Watt, 1985-86, 1986-87; Bob McCammon, 1987-88 to 1989-90. Bob McCammon and Pat Quinn, 1990-91; Pat Quinn, 1991-92 to date.

Captains' History

Orland Kurtenbach, 1970-71 to 1973-74; no captain, 1974-75; Andre Boudrias, 1975-76; Chris Oddleifson, 1976-77; Don Lever, 1977-78; Don Lever, Kevin McCarthy, 1978-79; Kevin McCarthy, 1979-80 to 1981-82; Stan Smyl, 1982-83 to 1989-90; Dan Quinn, Doug Lidster and Trevor Linden, 1990-91; Trevor Linden, 1991-92 to date.

Retired Numbers

12	Stan Smyl	1978-1991

1991-92 Scoring

Regular Season

Pos	#.	Player	Team	GP	G	A	Pts	+/–	PIM	PP	SH	GW	GT	S	%
R	16	Trevor Linden	VAN	80	31	44	75	3	101	6	1	6	1	201	15.4
C	7	Cliff Ronning	VAN	80	24	47	71	18	42	6	0	2	1	216	11.1
C	18	Igor Larionov	VAN	72	21	44	65	7	54	10	3	4	0	97	21.6
L	10*	Pavel Bure	VAN	65	34	26	60	0	30	7	3	6	0	268	12.7
L	8	Greg Adams	VAN	76	30	27	57	8	26	13	1	5	0	184	16.3
L	14	Geoff Courtnall	VAN	70	23	34	57	6–	116	12	0	3	0	281	8.2
D	21	Jyrki Lumme	VAN	75	12	32	44	25	65	3	1	1	0	106	11.3
L	27	Sergio Momesso	VAN	58	20	23	43	16	198	2	0	3	0	153	13.1
R	25	Jim Sandlak	VAN	66	16	24	40	22	176	3	0	2	1	122	13.1
C	15	Tom Fergus	TOR	11	1	3	4	11–	4	0	0	0	0	24	4.2
			VAN	44	14	20	34	1	17	6	0	3	0	79	17.7
			TOTAL	55	15	23	38	10–	21	6	0	3	0	103	14.6
C	19	Petr Nedved	VAN	77	15	22	37	3–	36	5	0	1	1	99	15.2
D	3	Doug Lidster	VAN	66	6	23	29	9	39	3	0	2	0	89	6.7
D	44	Dave Babych	VAN	75	5	24	29	2–	63	4	0	1	0	148	3.4
D	4	Gerald Diduck	VAN	77	6	21	27	3–	229	2	0	1	0	128	4.7
L	23	Garry Valk	VAN	65	8	17	25	3	56	2	1	2	0	93	8.6
C	9	Ryan Walter	VAN	67	6	11	17	6	49	1	1	0	0	73	8.2
D	5	Dana Murzyn	VAN	70	3	11	14	15	147	0	1	0	0	99	3.0
L	29	Gino Odjick	VAN	65	4	6	10	1–	348	0	0	0	0	68	5.9
D	6	Adrien Plavsic	VAN	16	1	9	10	4	14	0	0	0	1	21	4.8
D	22	Robert Dirk	VAN	72	2	7	9	6	126	0	0	0	1	44	4.5
D	24	Randy Gregg	VAN	21	1	4	5	3–	24	0	0	0	0	19	5.3
G	1	Kirk McLean	VAN	65	0	5	5	0	0	0	0	0	0	0	.0
C	58	Robert Kron	VAN	36	2	2	4	9–	2	0	0	0	0	49	4.1
R	20	Andrew McBain	VAN	6	1	0	1	1–	0	0	0	0	0	11	9.1
C	17	Rob Murphy	VAN	6	0	1	1	2–	6	0	0	0	0	2	.0
C	41*	Robin Bawa	VAN	2	0	0	0	0	0	0	0	0	0	1	.0
L	31*	Shawn Antoski	VAN	4	0	0	0	1–	29	0	0	0	0	6	.0
R	33	Jay Mazur	VAN	5	0	0	0	2–	2	0	0	0	0	3	.0
G	35	Troy Gamble	VAN	19	0	0	0	0	8	0	0	0	0	0	.0
D	26	Jim Agnew	VAN	24	0	0	0	1–	56	0	0	0	0	9	.0

Goaltending

No.	Goaltender	GPI	Mins	Avg	W	L	T	EN	SO	GA	SA	S%
1	Kirk McLean	65	3852	2.74	38	17	9	1	5	176	1780	.901
35	Troy Gamble	19	1009	4.34	4	9	3	0	0	73	518	.859
	Totals	**80**	**4874**	**3.08**	**42**	**26**	**12**	**1**	**5**	**250**	**2299**	**.891**

Playoffs

Pos	#	Player	Team	GP	G	A	Pts	+/–	PIM	PP	SH	GW	GT	S	%
L	14	Geoff Courtnall	VAN	12	6	8	14	4	20	2	0	1	0	41	14.6
C	7	Cliff Ronning	VAN	13	8	5	13	5	6	1	0	1	0	49	16.3
R	16	Trevor Linden	VAN	13	4	8	12	5	6	2	0	1	0	37	10.8
L	10*	Pavel Bure	VAN	13	6	4	10	4	14	0	0	0	0	50	12.0
R	25	Jim Sandlak	VAN	13	4	6	10	4	22	2	0	0	0	27	14.8
C	18	Igor Larionov	VAN	13	3	7	10	1	4	1	0	0	0	12	25.0
C	15	Tom Fergus	VAN	13	5	3	8	3	6	0	0	1	0	22	22.7
D	44	Dave Babych	VAN	13	2	6	8	6	10	1	0	1	0	25	8.0
D	6	Adrien Plavsic	VAN	13	1	7	8	6	4	0	0	0	0	20	5.0
D	21	Jyrki Lumme	VAN	13	2	3	5	3	4	1	0	1	0	20	10.0
C	19	Petr Nedved	VAN	10	1	4	5	3	16	0	0	0	0	19	5.3
L	27	Sergio Momesso	VAN	13	0	5	5	1–	30	0	0	0	0	30	.0
C	58	Robert Kron	VAN	11	1	2	3	0	2	0	1	0	0	9	11.1
D	3	Doug Lidster	VAN	11	1	2	3	3	11	0	0	0	0	6	16.7
C	9	Ryan Walter	VAN	13	0	3	3	1–	8	0	0	0	0	6	.0
L	8	Greg Adams	VAN	6	0	2	2	4	4	0	0	0	0	23	.0
D	24	Randy Gregg	VAN	7	0	1	1	3	8	0	0	0	0	3	.0
G	1	Kirk McLean	VAN	13	0	1	1	0	0	0	0	0	0	0	.0
C	41*	Robin Bawa	VAN	1	0	0	0	0	0	0	0	0	0	0	.0
D	5	Dana Murzyn	VAN	1	0	0	0	0	15	0	0	0	0	0	.0
D	2	Ken Hammond	VAN	2	0	0	0	0	6	0	0	0	0	2	.0
D	26	Jim Agnew	VAN	4	0	0	0	2–	6	0	0	0	0	2	.0
L	29	Gino Odjick	VAN	4	0	0	0	0	6	0	0	0	0	1	.0
L	23	Garry Valk	VAN	4	0	0	0	2–	5	0	0	0	0	3	.0
D	4	Gerald Diduck	VAN	5	0	0	0	3–	10	0	0	0	0	7	.0
D	22	Robert Dirk	VAN	13	0	0	0	3	20	0	0	0	0	10	.0

Goaltending

No.	Goaltender	GPI	Mins	Avg	W	L	EN	SO	GA	SA	S%
1	Kirk McLean	13	785	2.52	6	7	2	2	33	364	.909
	Totals	**13**	**789**	**2.66**	**6**	**7**	**2**	**2**	**35**	**366**	**.904**

Club Records

Team

(Figures in brackets for season records are games played; records for fewest points, wins, ties, losses, goals, goals against are for 70 or more games)

Record		
Most Points	**96**	1991-92 (80)
Most Wins	**42**	1991-92 (80)
Most Ties	**20**	1980-81 (80)
Most Losses	**50**	1971-72 (78)
Most Goals	**306**	1983-84 (80)
Most Goals Against	**401**	1984-85 (80)
Fewest Points	**48**	1971-72 (78)
Fewest Wins	**20**	1971-72 (78) 1977-78 (80)
Fewest Ties	**8**	1970-71 (78) 1971-72 (78) 1986-87 (80) 1988-89 (80)
Fewest Losses	**32**	1974-75 (80) 1975-76 (80) 1980-81 (80)
Fewest Goals	**203**	1971-72 (78)
Fewest Goals Against	**250**	1991-92 (80)
Longest Winning Streak		
Over-all	**7**	Feb. 10-23/89
Home	**8**	Feb. 27/83- Mar. 21/83 Jan. 31- Mar. 10/89
Away	**5**	Jan. 14-25/92
Longest Undefeated Streak		
Over-all	**10**	Mar. 5-25/77 (5 wins, 5 ties)
Home	**12**	Oct. 29- Dec. 17/74 (11 wins, 1 tie) Jan. 29- Mar. 18/89 (10 wins, 2 ties)
Away	**5**	Four times
Longest Losing Streak		
Over-all	**9**	Four times
Home	**6**	Dec. 18/70- Jan. 20/71 Nov. 3-18/78
Away	**12**	Nov. 28/81- Feb. 6/82
Longest Winless Streak		
Over-all	**13**	Nov. 9- Dec. 7/73 (10 losses, 3 ties)
Home	**11**	Dec. 18/70- Feb. 6/71 (10 losses, 1 tie)
Away	**20**	Jan. 2/86- Apr. 2/86 (14 losses, 6 ties)
Most Shutouts, Season	**8**	1974-75 (80)
Most PIM, Season	**2,196**	1987-88 (80)
Most Goals, Game	**11**	Mar. 28/71 (Cal. 5 at Van. 11) Nov. 25/86 (L.A. 5 at Van. 11) Mar. 1/92 (Cal. 0 at Van. 11)

Individual

Record		
Most Seasons	**13**	Stan Smyl
Most Games	**896**	Stan Smyl
Most Goals, Career	**262**	Stan Smyl
Most Assists, Career	**411**	Stan Smyl
Most Points, Career	**673**	Stan Smyl (262 goals, 411 assists)
Most PIM, Career	**1,556**	Stan Smyl
Most Shutouts, Career	**11**	Gary Smith
Longest Consecutive Games Streak	**437**	Don Lever (Oct. 7/72-Jan. 14/78)
Most Goals, Season	**45**	Tony Tanti (1983-84)
Most Assists, Season	**62**	André Boudrias (1974-75)
Most Points, Season	**91**	Patrik Sundstrom (1983-84) (38 goals, 53 assists)
Most PIM, Season	**348**	Gino Odjick (1991-92)
Most Points, Defenseman, Season	**63**	Doug Lidster (1986-87) (12 goals, 51 assists)
Most Points, Center, Season	**91**	Patrik Sundstrom (1983-84) (38 goals, 53 assists)
Most Points, Right Wing, Season	**88**	Stan Smyl (1982-83) (38 goals, 50 assists)
Most Points, Left Wing, Season	**81**	Darcy Rota (1982-83) (42 goals, 39 assists)
Most Points, Rookie, Season	**60**	Ivan Hlinka (1981-82) (23 goals, 37 assists) Pavel Bure (1991-92) (34 goals, 26 assists)
Most Shutouts, Season	**6**	Gary Smith (1974-75)
Most Goals, Game	**4**	Several players
Most Assists, Game	**6**	Patrik Sundstrom (Feb. 29/84)
Most Points, Game	**7**	Patrik Sundstrom (Feb. 29/84)

All-time Record vs. Other Clubs

Regular Season

	At Home							On Road							Total						
	GP	W	L	T	GF	GA	PTS	GP	W	L	T	GF	GA	PTS	GP	W	L	T	GF	GA	PTS
Boston	42	13	21	8	141	178	34	41	3	34	4	90	188	10	83	16	55	12	231	366	44
Buffalo	42	20	12	10	161	139	50	42	12	22	8	119	156	32	84	32	34	18	280	295	82
Calgary	65	24	28	13	235	220	61	64	11	44	9	179	289	31	129	35	72	22	414	509	92
Chicago	48	22	15	11	146	137	55	47	12	30	5	112	176	29	95	34	45	16	258	313	84
Detroit	42	24	12	6	175	128	54	42	12	24	6	125	176	30	84	36	36	12	300	304	84
Edmonton	48	15	27	6	174	217	36	47	8	35	4	148	252	20	95	23	62	10	322	469	56
Hartford	21	8	7	6	72	59	22	20	8	8	4	74	67	20	41	16	15	10	146	126	42
Los Angeles	68	31	25	12	264	241	74	69	21	38	10	214	288	52	137	52	63	22	478	529	126
Minnesota	46	24	14	8	189	145	56	47	11	29	7	136	199	29	93	35	43	15	325	344	85
Montreal	41	6	27	8	100	167	20	43	7	34	2	111	217	16	84	13	61	10	211	384	36
New Jersey	39	22	6	11	147	113	55	39	17	16	6	132	120	40	78	39	22	17	279	233	95
NY Islanders	39	17	19	3	128	127	37	37	7	22	8	95	145	22	76	24	41	11	223	272	59
NY Rangers	43	10	30	3	137	178	23	45	7	34	4	111	206	18	88	17	64	7	248	384	41
Philadelphia	43	10	22	11	126	165	31	43	13	30	0	126	196	26	86	23	52	11	252	361	57
Pittsburgh	41	20	18	3	156	157	43	41	8	26	7	139	184	23	82	28	44	10	295	341	66
Quebec	20	10	7	3	86	82	23	21	9	8	4	62	63	22	41	19	15	7	148	145	45
St. Louis	48	21	22	5	153	151	47	47	13	27	7	138	185	33	95	34	49	12	291	336	80
San Jose	3	3	0	0	9	4	6	4	3	1	0	14	11	6	7	6	1	0	23	15	12
Toronto	42	23	12	7	148	132	53	43	16	18	9	151	164	41	85	39	30	16	299	296	94
Washington	30	14	12	4	103	96	32	31	11	17	3	98	105	25	61	25	29	7	201	201	57
Winnipeg	46	25	13	8	174	140	58	44	13	24	7	159	177	33	90	38	37	15	333	317	91
Defunct Clubs	19	14	3	2	82	48	30	19	10	8	1	71	68	21	38	24	11	3	153	116	51
Totals	**876**	**376**	**352**	**148**	**3106**	**3024**	**900**	**876**	**232**	**529**	**115**	**2604**	**3632**	**579**	**1752**	**608**	**881**	**263**	**5710**	**6656**	**1479**

Playoffs

	Series	W	L	GP	W	L	T	GF	GA	Last Mtg.	Round	Result
Buffalo	2	0	2	7	1	6	0	14	28	1981	PR	L 0-3
Calgary	4	1	3	18	8	10	0	57	62	1989	DSF	L 3-4
Chicago	1	1	0	5	4	1	0	18	13	1982	CF	W 4-1
Edmonton	2	0	2	9	2	7	0	20	35	1992	DF	L 2-4
Los Angeles	2	1	1	11	6	5	0	35	40	1991	DSF	L 2-4
Montreal	1	0	1	5	1	4	0	9	20	1975	QF	L 1-4
NY Islanders	2	0	2	6	0	6	0	14	26	1982	F	L 0-4
Philadelphia	1	0	1	3	1	2	0	9	15	1979	PR	L 1-2
Winnipeg	1	1	0	7	4	3	0	29	17	1992	DSF	W 4-3
Totals	**16**	**4**	**12**	**71**	**27**	**44**	**0**	**205**	**256**			

Playoff Results 1992-88

Year	Round	Opponent	Result	GF	GA
1992	DF	Edmonton	L 2-4	15	18
	DSF	Winnipeg	W 4-3	29	17
1991	DSF	Los Angeles	L 2-4	16	26
1989	DSF	Calgary	L 3-4	20	26

Abbreviations: Round: F – Final; **CF** – conference final; **DF** – division final; **DSF** – division semi-final; **SF** – semi-final; **QF** – quarter-final; **PR** – preliminary round. **GA** – goals against; **GF** – goals for.

1991-92 Results

Home				Away			
Oct.	4	San Jose	4-3	**Oct.**	5	San Jose	5-2
	17	Boston	3-3		8	Winnipeg	3-2
	19	Calgary	5-2		10	Chicago	6-7
	21	Toronto	4-1		12	Toronto	2-1
	24	Washington	3-1		13	Buffalo	3-1
	27	Edmonton	3-6		26	Edmonton	4-5
	29	New Jersey	4-3	**Nov.**	7	Los Angeles	4-3
Nov.	1	St Louis	2-3		14	Calgary	2-2
	3	Edmonton*	7-2		21	Calgary	2-3
	5	Winnipeg	2-2		26	San Jose	1-4
	10	NY Islanders	6-0	**Dec.**	1	Edmonton*	0-7
	12	Los Angeles	8-2		3	Quebec	0-3
	16	San Jose	1-0		4	Montreal	3-0
	19	NY Rangers	3-4		7	Toronto	3-6
	22	Calgary	6-5		14	Los Angeles	4-4
	29	Chicago	5-2		28	San Jose	3-2
Dec.	10	Edmonton	4-7		31	Los Angeles	5-3
	12	Minnesota	7-5	**Jan.**	3	Washington	3-3
	17	Detroit	2-1		4	Minnesota	3-4
	19	Winnipeg	3-1		14	Winnipeg	4-2
	22	Quebec	6-6		15	Edmonton	5-3
	27	Philadelphia	1-1		21	Quebec	5-3
Jan.	7	San Jose	4-1		23	Detroit	3-1
	12	Pittsburgh*	3-4		25	St Louis	1-0
	28	Edmonton	3-5	**Feb.**	10	Montreal	3-8
	30	Chicago	4-1		12	NY Rangers	2-5
Feb.	1	Hartford	4-4		13	New Jersey	3-5
	4	Montreal	5-3		15	NY Islanders	1-3
	6	NY Islanders	4-5		17	NY Rangers*	3-3
	19	Buffalo	6-5		21	San Jose	5-3
	23	Boston*	2-1	**Mar.**	5	Boston	2-2
	25	Los Angeles	3-4		7	Hartford	5-1
	28	Winnipeg	5-3		8	Philadelphia	7-3
Mar.	1	Calgary*	11-0		14	Calgary	6-4
	2	St Louis	3-5		22	Winnipeg*	1-5
	12	New Jersey	2-1		24	Minnesota	4-2
	18	Hartford	3-2		26	Pittsburgh	3-7
	20	Winnipeg	2-2		28	Detroit*	1-3
Apr.	2	Calgary	4-4		29	Washington*	4-7
	5	Los Angeles*	1-6	**Apr.**	4	Los Angeles*	3-2

*Denotes afternoon game

Entry Draft Selections 1992-78

1992

Pick	
21	Libor Polasek
40	Mike Peca
45	Michael Fountain
69	Jeff Connolly
93	Brent Tully
110	Brian Loney
117	Adrian Aucoin
141	Jason Clark
165	Scott Hollis
213	Sonny Mignacca
237	Mark Wotton
261	Aaron Boh

1991

Pick	
7	Alex Stojanov
29	Jassen Cullimore
51	Sean Pronger
95	Danny Kesa
117	Yevgeni Namestnikov
139	Brent Thurston
161	Eric Johnson
183	David Neilson
205	Brad Barton
227	Jason Fitzsimmons
249	Xavier Majic

1990

Pick	
2	Petr Nedved
18	Shawn Antoski
23	Jiri Slegr
65	Darin Bader
86	Gino Odjick
128	Daryl Filipek
149	Paul O'Hagan
170	Mark Cipriano
191	Troy Neumier
212	Tyler Ertel
233	Karri Kivi

1989

Pick	
8	Jason Herter
29	Robert Woodward
71	Brett Hauer
113	Pavel Bure
134	James Revenberg
155	Rob Sangster
176	Sandy Moger
197	Gus Morschauser
218	Hayden O'Rear
239	Darcy Cahill
248	Jan Bergman

1988

Pick	
2	Trevor Linden
33	Leif Rohlin
44	Dane Jackson
107	Corrie D'Alessio
122	Phil Von Stefenelli
128	Dixon Ward
149	Greg Geldart
170	Roger Akerstrom
191	Paul Constantin
212	Chris Wolanin
233	Stefan Nilsson

1987

Pick	
24	Rob Murphy
45	Steve Veilleux
66	Doug Torrel
87	Sean Fabian
108	Gary Valk
129	Todd Fanning
150	Viktor Tyumenev
171	Craig Daly
192	John Fletcher
213	Roger Hansson
233	Neil Eisenhut
234	Matt Evo

1986

Pick	
7	Dan Woodley
49	Don Gibson
70	Ronnie Stern
91	Eric Murano
112	Steve Herniman
133	Jon Helgeson
154	Jeff Noble
175	Matt Merton
196	Marc Lyons
217	Todd Hawkins
238	Vladimir Krutov

1985

Pick	
4	Jim Sandlak
25	Troy Gamble
46	Shane Doyle
67	Randy Siska
88	Robert Kron
109	Martin Hrstka
130	Brian McFarlane
151	Hakan Ahlund
172	Curtis Hunt
193	Carl Valimont
214	Igor Larionov
235	Darren Taylor

1984

Pick	
10	J.J. Daigneault
31	Jeff Rohlicek
52	Dave Saunders
55	Landis Chaulk
58	Mike Stevens
73	Brian Bertuzzi
94	Brett MacDonald
115	Jeff Korchinski
136	Blaine Chrest
157	Jim Agnew
178	Rex Grant
198	Ed Lowney
219	Doug Clarke
239	Ed Kister

1983

Pick	
9	Cam Neely
30	Dave Bruce
50	Scott Tottle
70	Tim Lorentz
90	Doug Quinn
110	Dave Lowry
130	Terry Maki
150	John Labatt
170	Allan Measures
190	Roger Grillo
210	Steve Kayser
230	Jay Mazur

1982

Pick	
11	Michel Petit
53	Yves Lapointe
71	Shawn Kilroy
116	Taylor Hall
137	Parie Proft
158	Newell Brown
179	Don McLaren
200	Al Raymond
221	Steve Driscoll
242	Shawn Green

1981

Pick	
10	Garth Butcher
52	Jean-Marc Lanthier
73	Wendell Young
105	Moe Lemay
115	Stu Kulak
136	Bruce Holloway
157	Petri Skriko
178	Frank Caprice
199	Rejean Vignola

1980

Pick	
7	Rick Lanz
49	Andy Schliebener
70	Marc Crawford
91	Darrell May
112	Ken Berry
133	Doug Lidster
154	John O'Connor
175	Patrik Sundstrom
196	Grant Martin

1979

Pick	
5	Rick Vaive
26	Brent Ashton
47	Ken Ellacott
68	Art Rutland
89	Dirk Graham
110	Shane Swan

1978

Pick	
4	Bill Derlago
22	Curt Fraser
40	Stan Smyl
56	Harald Luckner
57	Brad Smith
90	Gerry Minor
107	Dave Ross
124	Steve O'Neill
141	Charlie Antetomaso
158	Richard Martens

Club Directory

Pacific Coliseum
100 North Renfrew Street
Vancouver, B.C. V5K 3N7
Phone **604/254-5141**
FAX 604/251-5123
GM FAX 604/251-5514
Capacity: 16,123

Northwest Sports Enterprises Ltd.

Board of Directors
J. Lawrence Dampier, Arthur R. Griffiths, Frank A. Griffiths, C.A., F.W. Griffiths, Coleman E. Hall, Emily Griffiths-Hamilton, C.A., Douglas Holtby, Senator E.M. Lawson, W.L. McEwen, David S. Owen, Senator Ray Perrault, Peter Paul Saunders, Andrew E. Saxton, Peter W. Webster, Sydney, W. Welsh, D.A. Williams, C.A., D. Alexander Farac (Sec.)

Chairman	Frank A. Griffiths, C.A.
Vice-Chairman and Governor	Arthur R. Griffiths
President and General Manager/Head Coach	Pat Quinn
Director of Hockey Operations	George McPhee
Director of Player Personnel/Head Scout	Mike Penny
Vice-President and Director of Marketing and Communications	Glen Ringdal
Vice President of Finance/Administration	Carlos Mascarenhas
Assistant Coaches	Rick Ley, Ron Wilson, Stan Smyl
Goaltending Coach	Glen Hanlon
Trainers	Larry Ashley, Pat O'Neill, Darren Granger
Strength Coach	Wayne Wilson
Massage Therapist	Dave Schima
Director of Public and Media Relations	Steve Tambellini
Director of Pro Scouting	Murray Oliver
Scouting Staff	Scott Carter, Ron Delorme, Paul MacIntosh, Jack McCarten, Ed McColgan, Noel Price, Ken Slater, Jack Birch, Ross Mahoney
Controller	Dave Cobb
Director of Publishing	Norm Jewison
Director of Special Events	Lynn Harrison
Director of Corporate Sales	Dave Nonis
Director of Hockey Information	Steve Frost
Public Relations Assistant	Gail Nishi
Box Office Manager	Fiona Hayes
Executive Secretary, Pres. & GM	Jette Sandeford
Executive Secretary, Hockey Operations/ Player Personnel	Patti Timms
Executive Secretary, Vice-President and Director of Marketing and Communications	Carla Radiuk
Manager of Food and Beverage Operations	John Faris
Director of Retail Operations	Larry Donen
General Manager Farm Team (Hamilton Canucks)	Pat Hickey
Hamilton Head Coach	Jack McIlhargey
Hamilton Assistant Coach	TBA
Club Doctors	Dr. Ross Davidson, Dr. Doug Clemont
Club Dentist	Dr. David Lawson
Sport Psychologist	Wayne Halliwell
Club Colors	White, Black, Red and Gold
Press Box	West Side, Renfrew St. Entrance
Dimensions of rink	200 feet by 85 feet
Club Trains at	Victoria, B.C.
Play-by-Play Broadcaster	Jim Robson (radio and TV)
Radio Station	CKNW (980 AM) and Western Information Network

Cliff Ronning finished second in team scoring for the Canucks with a career-high 71 points.

Coach and General Manager

QUINN, PAT
President and General Manager/Head Coach, Vancouver Canucks.
Born in Hamilton, Ont., January 29, 1943.

Under the guidance of coach and general manager Pat Quinn, the Vancouver Canucks had the finest season in franchise history in 1991-92, compiling a record 96 points while finishing in top spot in the Smythe Division for the first time since 1975. Quinn took up management responsibilities with the Vancouver Canucks in 1987-88 after coaching in Los Angeles from 1984 to 1987 and in Philadelphia from 1978 to 1982. In Philadelphia, Quinn was awarded the Jack Adams award for leading the Flyers to the Stanley Cup finals in 1979-80. He started his coaching career with the Maine Mariners of the AHL and eventually was promoted to the head coaching job with Philadelphia. An NHL defenseman himself, Quinn played in more than 600 games over nine years.

NHL Coaching Record

		Regular Season					Playoffs			
Season	Team	Games	W	L	T	%	Games	W	L	%
1978-79	Philadelphia	30	18	8	4	.667	8	3	5	.375
1979-80	Philadelphia	80	48	12	20	.725	19	13	6	.684
1980-81	Philadelphia	80	41	24	15	.606	12	6	6	.500
1981-82	Philadelphia	72	34	29	9	.535	....	....	....	....
1984-85	Los Angeles	80	34	32	14	.513	3	0	3	.000
1985-86	Los Angeles	80	23	49	8	.338	....	....	....	....
1986-87	Los Angeles	42	18	20	4	.476	....	....	....	....
1990-91	Vancouver	26	9	13	4	.423	6	2	4	.333
1991-92	Vancouver	80	42	26	12	.600	13	6	7	.462
	NHL Totals	**570**	**267**	**213**	**90**	**.547**	**61**	**30**	**31**	**.492**

Washington Capitals

1991-92 Results: 45W-27L-8T 98PTS. Second, Patrick Division

Schedule

			Home				Away
Oct.	Fri.	9	NY Rangers	Oct.	Wed.	7	Toronto
	Sat.	10	Philadelphia		Mon.	12	New Jersey
	Fri.	16	Ottawa		Wed.	21	NY Rangers
	Sat.	17	Buffalo		Mon.	26	Winnipeg
	Fri.	23	NY Islanders		Wed.	28	Vancouver
Nov.	Tues.	3	Chicago		Fri.	30	Calgary
	(at Indianapolis)				Sat.	31	Edmonton
	Fri.	6	Tampa Bay	Nov.	Sat.	7	Hartford
	Sat.	14	New Jersey		Wed.	11	NY Rangers
	Wed.	18	Minnesota		Fri.	13	New Jersey
	Fri.	20	Detroit		Sun.	22	Quebec*
	Wed.	25	Boston		Mon.	23	Montreal
	Fri.	27	Pittsburgh		Sat.	28	Pittsburgh
Dec.	Fri.	4	NY Rangers		Mon.	30	Detroit
	Fri.	11	Winnipeg	Dec.	Sat.	5	NY Islanders
	Fri.	18	Hartford		Mon.	7	Ottawa
	Sat.	26	Philadelphia		Wed.	9	New Jersey
	Tues.	29	NY Rangers		Sat.	12	Philadelphia
Jan.	Fri.	1	New Jersey*		Wed.	16	Hartford
	Sat.	2	Chicago*		Sat.	19	Boston
	Sat.	9	Edmonton		Mon.	21	Ottawa
	Sat.	23	Ottawa		Wed.	23	Buffalo
	Fri.	29	Quebec	Jan.	Thur.	7	Philadelphia
	Sun.	31	Pittsburgh*		Wed.	13	NY Rangers
Feb.	Tues.	2	Calgary		Thur.	14	NY Islanders
	Sat.	20	Los Angeles*		Sun.	17	Tampa Bay
	Sun.	21	St Louis*		Thur.	21	Chicago
	Sun.	28	Pittsburgh*		Tues.	26	Pittsburgh
Mar.	Tues.	2	Vancouver		Wed.	27	Buffalo
	Fri.	5	Philadelphia	Feb.	Tues.	9	Minnesota
	Sun.	7	NY Islanders*		Thur.	11	St Louis
	Tues.	9	Toronto		Sat.	13	Los Angeles
	Sat.	13	NY Rangers		Tues.	16	San Jose
	Fri.	19	Hartford		Tues.	23	NY Islanders
	Sun.	21	San Jose*		Sat.	27	Boston*
	Tues.	23	Quebec	Mar.	Thur.	11	Philadelphia
	Sat.	27	New Jersey*		Sun.	14	NY Islanders
	Sun.	28	Pittsburgh*		Tues.	16	Detroit
	Tues.	30	Buffalo		(at Milwaukee)		
Apr.	Fri.	2	Montreal		Thur.	25	Pittsburgh
	Sun.	4	NY Rangers*	Apr.	Thur.	8	Philadelphia
	Tues.	6	NY Islanders		Mon.	12	Montreal
	Sat.	10	New Jersey		Wed.	14	NY Rangers

* Denotes afternoon game.

Dimitri Khristich had an outstanding season in 1991-92, leading the Capitals with 14 powerplay goals and seven game-winning goals.

Home Starting Times:

Mondays through Thursday and Saturdays	7:35 p.m.
Sundays	1:35 p.m.
Fridays	8:05 p.m.
Except Nov. 25	8:05 p.m.
Jan. 1, Jan. 2, Mar. 27	1:35 p.m.
Jan. 31	12:05 p.m.

Franchise date: June 11, 1974

19th NHL Season

Year-by-Year Record

		Home			Road			Overall							
Season	**GP**	**W**	**L**	**T**	**W**	**L**	**T**	**W**	**L**	**T**	**GF**	**GA**	**Pts.**	**Finished**	**Playoff Result**
1991-92	80	25	12	3	20	15	5	45	27	8	330	275	98	2nd, Patrick Div.	Lost Div. Semi-Final
1990-91	80	21	14	5	16	22	2	37	36	7	284	211	81	3rd, Patrick Div.	Lost Div. Final
1989-90	80	19	18	3	17	20	3	36	38	6	284	275	78	3rd, Patrick Div.	Lost Conf. Championship
1988-89	80	25	12	3	16	17	7	41	29	10	305	259	92	1st, Patrick Div.	Lost Div. Semi-Final
1987-88	80	22	14	4	16	19	5	38	33	9	281	249	85	2nd, Patrick Div.	Lost Div. Final
1986-87	80	22	15	3	16	17	7	38	32	10	285	278	86	2nd, Patrick Div.	Lost Div. Semi-Final
1985-86	80	30	8	2	20	15	5	50	23	7	315	272	107	2nd, Patrick Div.	Lost Div. Final
1984-85	80	27	11	2	19	14	7	46	25	9	322	240	101	2nd, Patrick Div.	Lost Div. Semi-Final
1983-84	80	26	11	3	22	16	2	48	27	5	308	226	101	2nd, Patrick Div.	Lost Div. Final
1982-83	80	22	12	6	17	13	10	39	25	16	306	283	94	3rd, Patrick Div.	Lost Div. Semi-Final
1981-82	80	16	16	8	10	25	5	26	41	13	319	338	65	5th, Patrick Div.	Out of Playoffs
1980-81	80	16	17	7	10	19	11	26	36	18	286	317	70	5th, Patrick Div.	Out of Playoffs
1979-80	80	20	14	6	7	26	7	27	40	13	261	293	67	5th, Patrick Div.	Out of Playoffs
1978-79	80	15	19	6	9	22	9	24	41	15	273	338	63	4th, Norris Div.	Out of Playoffs
1977-78	80	10	23	7	7	26	7	17	49	14	195	321	48	5th, Norris Div.	Out of Playoffs
1976-77	80	17	15	8	7	27	6	24	42	14	221	307	62	4th, Norris Div.	Out of Playoffs
1975-76	80	6	26	8	5	33	2	11	59	10	224	394	32	5th, Norris Div.	Out of Playoffs
1974-75	80	7	28	5	1	39	0	8	67	5	181	446	21	5th, Norris Div.	Out of Playoffs

1992-93 Player Personnel

FORWARDS	HT	WT	S	Place of Birth	Date	1991-92 Club
BOBACK, Michael	5-11	180	R	Mt. Clemens, MI	8/13/70	Providence
BONDRA, Peter	6-0	200	L	Luck, Ukraine	2/7/68	Washington
BURRIDGE, Randy	5-9	185	L	Ft. Erie, Ont.	1/7/66	Washington
BYCE, John	6-1	180	L	Madison, WI	8/9/67	Balt.-Maine-Bos.
CARPENTER, Bob	6-0	200	L	Beverley, MA	7/13/63	Boston
CORRIVEAU, Yvon	6-1	202	L	Welland, Ont.	2/8/67	Hartford-Springfield
DRUCE, John	6-2	195	R	Peterborough, Ont.	2/23/66	Washington
DUHAIME, Trevor	6-0	185	R	Toronto, Ont.	8/2/71	Trois-Rivières-St. Jean
GENDRON, Martin	5-8	182	R	Valleyfield, Que.	2/15/74	St. Hyacinthe
GREENLAW, Jeff	6-1	230	L	Toronto, Ont.	2/28/68	Washington-Baltimore
HALVERSON, Trevor	6-1	195	L	White River, Ont.	4/6/71	Baltimore
HICKS, Alexander	6-1	190	L	Calgary, Alta.	9/4/69	Wisc. Eau Claire
HUNTER, Dale	5-10	198	L	Petrolia, Ont.	7/31/60	Washington
HUNTER, Mark	6-0	200	R	Petrolia, Ont.	11/12/62	Hartford
JIRANEK, Martin	5-11	170	L	Bashaw, Alta.	10/3/69	Bowling Green-Balt.
JONES, Keith	6-2	190	R	Brantford, Ont.	11/8/68	W. Mich.-Balt.
JUBENVILLE, Jeff	6-2	195	R	Duncan, B.C.	4/2/74	Seattle-Brandon
KHRISTICH, Dimitri	6-2	195	R	Kiev, Ukraine	7/23/69	Washington
KONOWALCHUK, Steve	6-0	180	L	Salt Lake City, UT	11/11/72	Wsh.-Balt.-Pr. Alb.
KOVACS, Bill	6-4	215	L	Hamilton, Ont.	5/11/71	Balt.-Gue.-Sud.
KRYGIER, Todd	5-11	180	L	Chicago Heights, IL	10/12/65	Washington
LONGO, Chris	5-10	180	R	Belleville, Ont.	1/5/72	Peterborough
MacDERMID, Paul	6-1	205	R	Chesley, Ont.	4/14/63	Washington-Winnipeg
MacPHERSON, Billy Jo	6-1	200	L	Toronto, Ont.	9/23/73	Oshawa
MARTELL, Steve	5-10	185	R	Sydney, N.S.	3/3/70	Balt.-Ham. Rds.
MATHERS, Mike	5-10	188	L	High Prairie, Alta.	6/20/72	Kamloops
MAY, Alan	6-1	200	R	Swan Hills, Alta.	1/14/65	Washington
McAUSLAND, Darren	5-11	190	L	Grovedale, Alta.	3/3/72	Seattle
MILLER, Kelly	5-11	197	L	Lansing, MI	3/3/63	Washington
MILLER, Kevin	5-11	190	R	Lansing, MI	8/9/65	Detroit
MORRISON, Justin	5-10	180	R	Newmarket, Ont.	2/9/72	O. Sound-Kingston
NELSON, Jeff	6-0	180	L	Prince Albert, Sask.	12/18/72	Prince Albert
PEAKE, Pat	6-0	195	R	Rochester, MI	5/28/73	Detroit
PEARCE, Randy	5-11	203	L	Kitchener, Ont.	2/23/70	Balt.-Hampton Rds.
PIVONKA, Michael	6-2	198	L	Kladno, Czech.	1/28/66	Washington
RIDLEY, Mike	6-0	195	L	Winnipeg, Man.	7/8/63	Washington
SAVAGE, Reggie	5-10	187	L	Montreal, Que.	5/1/70	Baltimore
SEFTEL, Steve	6-3	200	L	Kitchener, Ont.	5/14/68	Baltimore
STAGG, Brian	6-2	177	R	North Bay, Ont.	5/23/74	Kingston
TAYLOR, Tim	6-1	180	L	Stratford, Ont.	2/6/69	Baltimore
VARGA, John	5-9	172	L	Chicago, IL	1/31/74	Tacoma
DEFENSEMEN						
BABCOCK, Bob	6-1	222	L	Toronto, Ont.	8/3/68	Baltimore
CORRIVEAU, Rick	6-0	208	L	Welland, Ont.	1/6/71	Niagara Falls-London
COTE, Sylvain	5-11	185	R	Quebec City, Que.	1/19/66	Washington
HATCHER, Kevin	6-4	225	R	Detroit, MI	9/9/66	Washington
IAFRATE, Al	6-3	220	L	Dearborn, MI	3/21/66	Washington
JOHANSSON, Calle	5-11	205	L	Goteborg, Sweden	2/14/67	Washington
LANGWAY, Rod	6-3	218	L	Maaq, Formosa	5/3/57	Washington
LAVIGNE, Eric	6-3	195	L	Victoriaville, Que.	11/4/72	Hull
LEASK, Rob	6-2	210	L	Toronto, Ont.	6/9/72	Balt.-Osh.-Gue.
MacISAAC, Al	6-0	202	L	Antigonish, N.S.	10/10/67	Hampton Roads
MATHIESON, Jim	6-1	209	L	Kindersley, Sask.	1/24/70	Baltimore
MATIER, Mark	6-1	190	L	St. Catharines, Ont.	12/14/73	Sault Ste. Marie
PUCHNIAK, Rob	6-2	205	L	Winnipeg, Man.	3/10/72	Brandon
SABOURIN, Ken	6-3	205	L	Scarborough, Ont.	4/28/66	Baltimore-Washington
SCHLEGEL, Brad	5-10	188	R	Kitchener, Ont.	7/22/68	Wsh.-Balt.-Cdn. Nat.
SLANEY, John	6-0	185	L	St. John's, Nfld.	2/7/72	Baltimore-Cornwall
VYKOUKAL, Jiri	5-11	176	R	Olomouc, Czech.	3/11/71	Baltimore-Hampton Rds.
WOOLLEY, Jason	6-0	185	L	Toronto, Ont.	7/21/69	Wsh.-Balt.-Cdn. Nat.

GOALTENDERS	HT	WT	C	Place of Birth	Date	1991-92 Club
BEAUPRE, Don	5-10	172	L	Waterloo, Ont.	9/19/61	Washington-Baltimore
DAFOE, Byron	5-11	175	L	Sussex, England	2/25/71	Balt.-N.H.-Hamp. Rds.
DERKSEN, Duane	6-1	180	L	St. Boniface, Man.	7/7/68	Wisconsin
HRIVNAK, Jim	6-2	195	L	Montreal, Que.	5/28/68	Washington-Baltimore
KOLZIG, Olaf	6-3	205	L	Johannesburg, S.A.	4/9/70	Baltimore-Hampton Rds.
SIMPSON, Shawn	6-1	190	L	Gloucester, Ont.	8/10/68	Baltimore

1991-92 Scoring

Regular Season

Pos	#.	Player	Team	GP	G	A	Pts	+/-	PIM	PP	SH	GW	GT	S	%
C	20	Michal Pivonka	WSH	80	23	57	80	10	47	7	4	2	1	177	13.0
C	32	Dale Hunter	WSH	80	28	50	78	2–	205	13	0	4	1	110	25.5
R	22	Dino Ciccarelli	WSH	78	38	38	76	10–	78	13	0	7	0	279	13.6
C	8	Dimitri Khristich	WSH	80	36	37	73	24	35	14	1	7	0	188	19.1
C	17	Mike Ridley	WSH	80	29	40	69	3	38	5	5	3	0	123	23.6
L	18	Randy Burridge	WSH	66	23	44	67	4–	50	9	0	3	0	131	17.6
R	12	Peter Bondra	WSH	71	28	28	56	16	42	4	0	3	0	158	17.7
D	6	Calle Johansson	WSH	80	14	42	56	2	49	5	2	2	0	119	11.8
D	4	Kevin Hatcher	WSH	79	17	37	54	18	105	8	1	2	1	246	6.9
L	10	Kelly Miller	WSH	78	14	38	52	20	49	0	1	3	0	144	9.7
D	34	Al Iafrate	WSH	78	17	34	51	1	180	6	0	1	1	151	11.3
D	3	Sylvain Cote	WSH	78	11	29	40	7	31	6	0	2	0	151	7.3
R	19	John Druce	WSH	67	19	18	37	14	39	1	0	3	0	129	14.7
L	21	Todd Krygier	WSH	67	13	17	30	1–	107	1	0	1	0	127	10.2
R	23	Paul MacDermid	WPG	59	10	11	21	8–	151	2	0	2	1	71	14.1
			WSH	15	2	5	7	2	43	0	0	0	0	21	9.5
			TOTAL	74	12	16	28	6–	194	2	0	2	1	92	13.0
L	16	Alan May	WSH	75	6	9	15	7–	221	0	0	1	0	43	14.0
D	5	Rod Langway	WSH	64	0	13	13	11	22	0	0	0	0	32	.0
L	14	Dave Tippett	WSH	30	2	10	12	2	16	0	0	0	0	26	7.7
L	9	Nick Kypreos	WSH	65	4	6	10	3–	206	0	0	0	0	28	14.3
R	11	Tim Bergland	WSH	22	1	4	5	3–	2	0	0	0	0	18	5.6
L	24	Jeff Greenlaw	WSH	5	0	1	1	1–	34	0	0	0	0	3	.0
D	28*	Brad Schlegel	WSH	15	0	1	1	4–	0	0	0	0	0	7	.0
G	1	Mike Liut	WSH	21	0	1	1	0	2	0	0	0	0	0	.0
D	29*	Jason Woolley	WSH	1	0	0	0	1	0	0	0	0	0	2	.0
C	40*	Steve Konowalchuk	WSH	1	0	0	0	0	0	0	0	0	0	1	.0
D	25	Shawn Chambers	WSH	2	0	0	0	3–	2	0	0	0	0	1	.0
G	39	Jim Hrivnak	WSH	12	0	0	0	0	0	0	0	0	0	0	.0
D	2	Ken Sabourin	WSH	19	0	0	0	5–	48	0	0	0	0	12	.0
G	33	Don Beaupre	WSH	54	0	0	0	0	30	0	0	0	0	0	.0

Goaltending

No.	Goaltender	GPI	Mins	Avg	W	L	T	EN	SO	GA	SA	S%
33	Don Beaupre	54	3108	3.20	29	17	6	2	1	166	1435	.884
39	Jim Hrivnak	12	605	3.47	6	3	0	1	0	35	274	.872
1	Mike Liut	21	1123	3.74	10	7	2	1	1	70	558	.875
	Totals	**80**	**4846**	**3.40**	**45**	**27**	**8**	**4**	**2**	**275**	**2271**	**.879**

Playoffs

Pos	#	Player	Team	GP	G	A	Pts	+/-	PIM	PP	SH	GW	GT	S	%
C	17	Mike Ridley	Wsh	7	0	11	11	1	0	0	0	0	0	8	.0
R	22	Dino Ciccarelli	Wsh	7	5	4	9	1–	14	1	0	0	0	12	41.7
R	12	Peter Bondra	Wsh	7	6	2	8	4	4	1	0	0	0	16	37.5
D	34	Al Iafrate	Wsh	7	4	2	6	1–	14	1	0	0	0	25	16.0
D	4	Kevin Hatcher	Wsh	7	2	4	6	4	19	0	1	0	0	18	11.1
C	20	Michal Pivonka	Wsh	7	1	5	6	4	13	1	0	1	0	19	5.3
C	8	Dimitri Khristich	Wsh	7	3	2	5	2	15	3	0	1	0	15	20.0
C	32	Dale Hunter	Wsh	7	1	4	5	1–	16	0	0	0	0	16	6.3
D	6	Calle Johansson	Wsh	7	0	5	5	4	4	0	0	0	0	10	.0
L	21	Todd Krygier	Wsh	5	2	1	3	0	4	0	0	0	0	8	25.0
D	3	Sylvain Cote	Wsh	7	1	2	3	4	4	0	0	0	0	13	7.7
L	10	Kelly Miller	Wsh	7	1	2	3	2	4	0	0	0	0	9	11.1
R	19	John Druce	Wsh	7	1	0	1	1–	2	0	0	1	0	9	11.1
L	18	Randy Burridge	Wsh	2	0	1	1	2	0	0	0	0	0	6	.0
D	5	Rod Langway	Wsh	7	0	1	1	0	2	0	0	0	0	2	.0
R	23	Paul MacDermid	Wsh	7	0	1	1	1–	22	0	0	0	0	2	.0
L	14	Dave Tippett	Wsh	7	0	1	1	2	0	0	0	0	0	8	.0
D	28*	Brad Schlegel	Wsh	7	0	1	1	1	2	0	0	0	0	1	.0
G	33	Don Beaupre	Wsh	7	0	0	0	0	0	0	0	0	0	0	.0
L	16	Alan May	Wsh	7	0	0	0	1	0	0	0	0	0	5	.0

Goaltending

No.	Goaltender	GPI	Mins	Avg	W	L	EN	SO	GA	SA	S%
33	Don Beaupre	7	419	3.15	3	4	3	0	22	212	.896
	Totals	**7**	**420**	**3.57**	**3**	**4**	**3**	**0**	**25**	**215**	**.884**

General Managers' History

Milt Schmidt, 1974-75 to 1975-76; Max McNab, 1976-77 to 1980-81; Roger Crozier, 1981-82; David Poile, 1982-83 to date.

Coaching History

Jim Anderson, George Sullivan, Milt Schmidt, 1974-75; Milt Schmidt and Tom McVie, 1975-76; Tom McVie, 1976-77 to 1977-78; Danny Belisle, 1978-79; Danny Belisle and Gary Green, 1979-80; Gary Green, 1980-81; Gary Green and Bryan Murray, 1981-82; Bryan Murray, 1982-83 to 1988-89; Bryan Murray and Terry Murray, 1989-90; Terry Murray, 1990-91 to date.

Captains' History

Doug Mohns, 1974-75; Bill Clement, Yvon Labre, 1975-76; Yvon Labre, 1976-77, 1977-78; Guy Charron, 1978-79; Ryan Walter, 1979-80 to 1981-82; Rod Langway, 1982-83 to date.

Retired Numbers

7	Yvon Labre	1973-1981

Club Records

Team

(Figures in brackets for season records are games played; records for fewest points, wins, ties, losses, goals, goals against are for 70 or more games)

Most Points 107 1985-86 (80)
Most Wins 50 1985-86 (80)
Most Ties 18 1980-81 (80)
Most Losses *67 1974-75 (80)
Most Goals 330 1991-92 (80)
Most Goals Against *446 1974-75 (80)
Fewest Points *21 1974-75 (80)
Fewest Wins *8 1974-75 (80)
Fewest Ties 5 1974-75 (80)
1983-84 (80)
Fewest Losses 23 1985-86 (80)
Fewest Goals 181 1974-75 (80)
Fewest Goals Against 226 1983-84 (80)

Longest Winning Streak
Over-all .... 10 Jan. 27-Feb. 18/84
Home .... 8 Feb. 1-Mar. 11/86
Mar. 3-April 1/89
Away .... 6 Feb. 26-Apr. 1/84

Longest Undefeated Streak
Over-all .... 14 Nov. 24-Dec. 23/82 (9 wins, 5 ties)
Home .... 12 Nov. 7/82-Dec. 14/82 (9 wins, 3 ties)
Away .... 10 Nov. 24/82-Jan. 8/83 (6 wins, 4 ties)

Longest Losing Streak
Over-all .... *17 Feb. 18-Mar. 26/75
Home .... *11 Feb. 18-Mar. 30/75
Away .... *37 Oct. 9/74-Mar. 26/75

Longest Winless Streak
Over-all .... 25 Nov. 29/75-Jan. 21/76 (22 losses, 3 ties)
Home .... 14 Dec. 3/75-Jan. 21/76 (11 losses, 3 ties)
Away .... *37 Oct. 9/74-Mar. 26/75 (37 losses)

Most Shutouts, Season 8 1983-84 (80)
Most PIM, Season ...... 2,204 [ab1989-90 (80)
Most Goals, Game .... 12 Feb. 6/90 (Que. 2 at Wash. 12)

Individual

Most Seasons .... 10 Mike Gartner
Rod Langway
Most Games .... 758 Mike Gartner
Most Goals, Career .... 397 Mike Gartner
Most Assists, Career ...... 392 Mike Gartner
Most Points, Career ...... 789 Mike Gartner (397 goals, 392 assists)
Most PIM, Career ...... 1,630 Scott Stevens
Most Shutouts, Career ...... 9 Don Beaupre
Longest Consecutive Games Streak .... 422 Bob Carpenter
Most Goals, Season .... 60 Dennis Maruk (1981-82)
Most Assists, Season ...... 76 Dennis Maruk (1981-82)
Most Points, Season ...... 136 Dennis Maruk (1981-82) (60 goals, 76 assists)
Most PIM, Season .... 339 Alan May (1989-90)
Most Points, Defenseman, Season .... 81 Larry Murphy (1986-87) (23 goals, 58 assists)
Most Points, Center, Season .... 136 Dennis Maruk (1981-82) (60 goals, 76 assists)
Most Points, Right Wing, Season .... 102 Mike Gartner (1984-85) (50 goals, 52 assists)
Most Points, Left Wing, Season .... 87 Ryan Walter (1981-82) (38 goals, 49 assists)
Most Points, Rookie, Season .... 67 Bobby Carpenter (1981-82) (32 goals, 35 assists)
Chris Valentine (1981-82) (30 goals, 37 assists)
Most Shutouts, Season ..... 5 Don Beaupre (1990-91)
Most Goals, Game .... 5 Bengt Gustafsson (Jan. 8/84)
Most Assists, Game .... 6 Mike Ridley (Jan. 7/89)
Most Points, Game .... 7 Dino Ciccarelli (Mar. 18/89)

* NHL Record.

All-time Record vs. Other Clubs

Regular Season

	At Home							On Road							Total						
	GP	W	L	T	GF	GA	PTS	GP	W	L	T	GF	GA	PTS	GP	W	L	T	GF	GA	PTS
Boston	33	8	17	8	99	129	24	32	9	19	4	91	133	22	65	17	36	12	190	262	46
Buffalo	32	5	21	6	85	135	16	33	5	24	4	89	148	14	65	10	45	10	174	283	30
Calgary	31	15	12	4	119	111	34	30	5	21	4	72	136	14	61	20	33	8	191	247	48
Chicago	30	17	10	3	117	98	37	30	6	19	5	89	125	17	60	23	29	8	206	223	54
Detroit	36	19	13	4	141	110	42	37	11	16	10	108	137	32	73	30	29	14	249	247	74
Edmonton	20	11	8	1	90	76	23	20	8	8	4	73	82	20	40	19	16	5	163	158	43
Hartford	20	11	8	1	70	61	23	21	11	7	3	83	67	25	41	22	15	4	153	128	48
Los Angeles	36	15	15	6	153	134	36	37	10	23	4	107	155	24	73	25	38	10	260	289	60
Minnesota	31	13	11	7	99	94	33	30	9	13	8	89	114	26	61	22	24	15	188	208	59
Montreal	37	14	17	6	98	130	34	36	5	26	5	73	172	15	73	19	43	11	171	302	49
New Jersey	50	38	9	3	230	145	79	51	25	20	6	166	165	56	101	63	29	9	396	310	135
NY Islanders	53	22	23	8	170	181	52	53	17	35	1	163	228	35	106	39	58	9	333	409	87
NY Rangers	53	26	19	8	214	183	60	53	21	26	6	196	226	48	106	47	45	14	410	409	108
Philadelphia	53	22	23	8	198	192	52	53	17	32	4	146	206	38	106	39	55	12	344	398	90
Pittsburgh	60	32	24	4	269	231	68	58	24	28	6	202	232	54	118	56	52	10	471	463	122
Quebec	20	10	8	2	84	71	22	21	10	7	4	85	68	24	41	20	15	6	169	139	46
St. Louis	30	15	12	3	108	94	33	31	9	14	8	97	130	26	61	24	26	11	205	224	59
San Jose	1	1	0	0	6	2	2	1	1	0	0	4	2	2	2	2	0	0	10	4	4
Toronto	33	20	11	2	128	93	42	32	10	18	4	115	152	24	65	30	29	6	243	245	66
Vancouver	31	17	11	3	105	98	37	30	12	14	4	96	103	28	61	29	25	7	201	201	65
Winnipeg	20	13	5	2	92	61	28	21	6	10	5	77	78	17	41	19	15	7	169	139	45
Defunct Clubs	10	2	8	0	28	42	4	10	4	5	1	30	39	9	20	6	13	1	58	81	13
Totals	**720**	**346**	**285**	**89**	**2703**	**2471**	**781**	**720**	**235**	**385**	**100**	**2251**	**2898**	**570**	**1440**	**581**	**670**	**189**	**4954**	**5369**	**1351**

Playoffs

	Series	W	L	GP	W	L	T	GF	GA	Last Mtg.	Round	Result
Boston	1	0	1	4	0	4	0	6	15	1990	CF	L 0-4
New Jersey	2	1	1	13	7	6	0	44	43	1990	DSF	W 4-2
NY Islanders	5	1	4	24	10	14	0	66	76	1987	DSF	L 3-4
NY Rangers	3	2	1	17	10	7	0	63	51	1991	DSF	W 4-2
Philadelphia	3	2	1	16	9	7	0	65	55	1989	DSF	L 2-4
Pittsburgh	2	0	2	12	4	8	0	40	44	1992	DSF	L 3-4
Totals	**16**	**6**	**10**	**86**	**40**	**46**	**0**	**284**	**284**			

Playoff Results 1992-88

Year	Round	Opponent	Result	GF	GA
1992	DSF	Pittsburgh	L 3-4	27	25
1991	DF	Pittsburgh	L 1-4	13	19
	DSF	NY Rangers	W 4-2	16	16
1990	CF	Boston	L 0-4	6	15
	DF	NY Rangers	W 4-1	22	15
	DSF	New Jersey	W 4-2	21	18
1989	DSF	Philadelphia	L 2-4	19	25
1988	DF	New Jersey	L 3-4	23	25
	DSF	Philadelphia	W 4-3	31	25

Abbreviations: Round: F – Final; **CF** – conference final; **DF** – division final; **DSF** – division semi-final; **SF** – semi-final; **QF** – quarter-final; **PR** – preliminary round. **GA** – goals against; **GF** – goals for.

1991-92 Results

Home			Away		
Oct. 4	Philadelphia	5-2	Oct. 9	Toronto	5-4
5	Buffalo	3-1	14	NY Rangers	5-3
11	NY Rangers	5-1	19	New Jersey	5-1
12	Chicago	2-7	23	Edmonton	6-5
18	New Jersey	6-5	24	Vancouver	1-3
Nov. 1	Toronto	4-0	27	Winnipeg	5-6
8	Detroit	4-5	29	Pittsburgh	8-0
15	Pittsburgh	6-2	Nov. 2	NY Islanders	7-4
22	Boston	6-3	10	Quebec*	10-3
27	Montreal	3-1	11	Montreal	4-2
29	NY Islanders	2-3	13	NY Rangers	5-3
Dec. 10	Calgary	4-1	20	New Jersey	5-6
13	NY Rangers	3-5	23	Hartford	3-2
17	Quebec	3-1	25	Detroit	4-5
20	Toronto	4-3	30	NY Islanders	1-8
26	NY Rangers	6-8	Dec. 5	Philadelphia	6-3
28	Pittsburgh	2-6	7	Minnesota	4-2
Jan. 1	NY Islanders*	8-5	8	Winnipeg	3-4
3	Vancouver	3-3	14	Pittsburgh	7-2
7	Minnesota	3-5	18	Buffalo	2-2
10	Los Angeles	7-4	22	Philadelphia	3-4
24	New Jersey	2-5	29	New Jersey	4-3
26	Pittsburgh*	6-4	Jan. 4	Hartford	2-2
Feb. 1	Calgary	5-2	12	Chicago	2-4
7	NY Rangers	6-2	14	St Louis	6-1
9	San Jose*	6-2	16	Los Angeles	2-2
22	Philadelphia	7-5	28	Philadelphia	2-3
25	Pittsburgh	5-3	Feb. 4	Buffalo	3-7
Mar. 1	Boston*	1-4	5	Detroit	1-4
3	Minnesota	1-3	11	Quebec	4-3
6	Winnipeg	3-3	13	Calgary	4-4
7	New Jersey	3-2	15	Los Angeles	3-6
15	NY Islanders*	5-2	18	San Jose	4-2
17	St Louis	6-4	23	NY Islanders	4-1
20	Philadelphia	6-7	27	St Louis	3-7
22	Edmonton*	6-2	29	Boston*	5-5
24	Hartford	2-8	Mar. 9	NY Rangers	5-2
27	Montreal	4-3	14	Philadelphia*	1-3
29	Vancouver*	7-4	Apr. 1	New Jersey	4-3
Apr. 5	NY Islanders*	1-1	4	Pittsburgh*	1-4

*Denotes afternoon game

Entry Draft Selections 1992-78

1992
Pick
14 Sergei Gonchar
32 Jim Carey
53 Stefan Ustorf
71 Martin Gendron
119 John Varga
167 Mark Matier
191 Mike Mathers
215 Brian Stagg
239 Gregory Callahan
263 Billy Jo MacPherson

1991
Pick
14 Pat Peake
21 Trevor Halverson
25 Eric Lavigne
36 Jeff Nelson
58 Steve Konowalchuk
80 Justin Morrison
146 Dave Morissette
168 Rick Corriveau
190 Trevor Duhaime
209 Rob Leask
212 Carl LeBlanc
234 Rob Puchniak
256 Bill Kovacs

1990
Pick
9 John Slaney
30 Rod Pasma
51 Chris Longo
72 Randy Pearce
93 Brian Sakic
94 Mark Ouimet
114 Andrei Kovalev
135 Roman Kontsek
156 Peter Bondra
159 Steve Martell
177 Ken Klee
198 Michael Boback
219 Alan Brown
240 Todd Hlushko

1989
Pick
19 Olaf Kolzig
35 Byron Dafoe
59 Jim Mathieson
61 Jason Woolley
82 Trent Klatt
145 Dave Lorentz
166 Dean Holoien
187 Victor Gervais
208 Jiri Vykoukal
229 Andrei Sidorov
250 Ken House

1988
Pick
15 Reginald Savage
36 Tim Taylor
41 Wade Bartley
57 Duane Derksen
78 Rob Krauss
120 Dmitri Khristich
141 Keith Jones
144 Brad Schlegel
162 Todd Hilditch
183 Petr Pavlas
192 Mark Sorensen
204 Claudio Scremin
225 Chris Venkus
246 Ron Pascucci

1987
Pick
36 Jeff Ballantyne
57 Steve Maltais
78 Tyler Larter
99 Pat Beauchesne
120 Rich Defreitas
141 Devon Oleniuk
162 Thomas Sjogren
204 Chris Clarke
225 Milos Vanik
240 Dan Brettschneider
246 Ryan Kummu

1986
Pick
19 Jeff Greenlaw
40 Steve Seftel
60 Shawn Simpson
61 Jimmy Hrivnak
82 Erin Ginnell
103 John Purves
124 Stefan Nilsson
145 Peter Choma
166 Lee Davidson
187 Tero Toivola
208 Bobby Bobcock
229 John Schratz
250 Scott McCrory

1985
Pick
19 Yvon Corriveau
40 John Druce
61 Rob Murray
82 Bill Houlder
83 Larry Shaw
103 Claude Dumas
124 Doug Stromback
145 Jamie Nadjiwan
166 Mark Haarmann
187 Steve Hollett
208 Dallas Eakins
229 Steve Hrynewich
250 Frank DiMuzio

1984
Pick
17 Kevin Hatcher
34 Steve Leach
59 Michal Pivonka
80 Kris King
122 Vito Cramarossa
143 Timo Iljina
164 Frank Joo
185 Jim Thomson
205 Paul Cavallini
225 Mikhail Tatarinov
246 Per Schedrin

1983
Pick
75 Tim Bergland
95 Martin Bouliane
135 Dwaine Hutton
155 Marty Abrams
175 David Cowan
195 Yves Beaudoin
215 Alain Raymond
216 Anders Huss

1982
Pick
5 Scott Stevens
58 Milan Novy
89 Dean Evason
110 Ed Kastelic
152 Wally Schreiber
173 Jamie Reeve
194 Juha Nurmi
215 Wayne Prestage
236 Jon Holden
247 Marco Kallas

1981
Pick
3 Bob Carpenter
45 Eric Calder
68 Tony Kellin
89 Mike Siltala
91 Peter Sidorkiewicz
110 Jim McGeough
131 Risto Jalo
152 Gaetan Duchesne
173 George White
194 Chris Valentine

1980
Pick
5 Darren Veitch
47 Dan Miele
55 Torrie Robertson
89 Timo Blomqvist
110 Todd Bidner
131 Frank Perkins
152 Bruce Raboin
173 Peter Andersson
194 Tony Camazzola

1979
Pick
4 Mike Gartner
24 Errol Rausse
67 Harvie Pocza
88 Tim Tookey
109 Greg Theberge

1978
Pick
2 Ryan Walter
18 Tim Coulis
20 Paul Mulvey
23 Paul MacKinnon
38 Glen Currie
45 Jay Johnston
55 Bengt-Ake Gustafsson
71 Lou Franceschetti
88 Vince Magnan
105 Mats Hallin
122 Rick Sirois
139 Denis Pomerleau
156 Barry Heard
172 Mark Toffolo
187 Paul Hogan
189 Steve Barger
202 Rod Pacholsuk
213 Wes Jarvis
215 Ray Irwin

Coach

MURRAY, TERRY RODNEY
Coach, Washington Capitals. Born in Shawville, Que., July 20, 1950.

Terry Murray, who was named head coach of the Washington Capitals on January 15, 1990, had his finest season behind the bench in 1991-92, leading the Capitals to a second-place finish in the Patrick Division with 98 points, the fourth-highest total in franchise history. Murray spent six seasons as an assistant coach with the Capitals. He was then named head coach of the Baltimore Skipjacks in June, 1988 where he led his club to a 64-point season in 1988-89 and was 26-17-1 during his 1989-90 tenure.

Murray was selected 88th overall by California in the 1970 Amateur Draft. He enjoyed a successful playing career with the Maine Mariners, leading that club to two Calder Cup championships in 1977-78 and 1978-79. He was awarded the Eddie Shore Trophy as the AHL's outstanding defenseman in 1978 and 1979. In addition he was an AHL First Team All-Star in 1975-76, 1977-78 and 1978-79. While serving as an assistant coach with the Capitals, they compiled a 259-165-66 record. His AHL coaching record stands at 56-63-5.

Coaching Record

		Regular Season					Playoffs			
Season	**Team**	**Games**	**W**	**L**	**T**	**%**	**Games**	**W**	**L**	**%**
1988-89	Baltimore (AHL)	80	30	46	4	.400	....	....	....	....
1989-90	Baltimore (AHL)	44	26	17	1	.603	....	....	....	....
1989-90	**Washington (NHL)**	**34**	**18**	**14**	**2**	**.559**	**15**	**8**	**7**	**.533**
1990-91	**Washington (NHL)**	**80**	**37**	**36**	**7**	**.506**	**11**	**5**	**6**	**.455**
1991-92	**Washington (NHL)**	**80**	**45**	**27**	**8**	**.613**	**7**	**3**	**4**	**.429**
	NHL Totals	**194**	**100**	**77**	**17**	**.559**	**33**	**16**	**17**	**.485**

Club Directory

Capital Centre
1 Harry S Truman Drive
Landover, Maryland 20785
Phone **301/386-7000**

PR FAX 301/386-7012
GM FAX 301/386-7082
Capacity: 18,130

Board of Directors
David P. Bindeman, Stuart L. Bindeman, James A. Cafritz, A. James Clark, Albert Cohen, J. Martin Irving, R. Robert Linowes, Arthur K. Mason, Dr. Jack Meshel, David M. Osnos, Richard M. Patrick

Management
Chairman and Governor .... Abe Pollin
President and Alternate Governor .... Richard M. Patrick
Legal Counsel and Alternate Governors .... David M. Osnos, Peter O'Malley
Vice-President of Finance .... Edmund Stelzer

Hockey Department
Vice-President and General Manager .... David Poile
Director of Player Personnel .... Jack Button
Head Coach .... Terry Murray
Assistant Coach .... John Perpich
Head Coach, Baltimore Skipjacks .... Barry Trotz
Assistant Coach, Baltimore Skipjacks .... Paul Gardner
Director of Team Services/Video Coordinator .... Tod Button
Administrative Assistant to the General Manager . Pat Young
Assistant to the Hockey Department .... Todd Warren
Chief Eastern Scout .... Hugh Rogers
Chief Western Scout .... Craig Channell
Chief U.S. Scout .... Jack Barzee
Chief Quebec Scout .... Gilles Cote
Scouts .... Keith Allain, Fred Devereaux, Bob Gould, Kelly Pratt, Bud Quinn, Bob Schmidt, Dan Sylvester, Darryl Young

Front Office Staff
Vice-President of Marketing .... Lew Strudler
Director of Community Relations .... Yvon Labre
Assistant Director of Marketing .... Debi Angus
Director of Promotions and Advertising .... Charles Copeland
Assistant Director of Promotions and Advertising .... Jerry Murphy
Director of Season Subscriptions .... Joanne Kowalski
Corporate Sales Manager .... Kerry Gregg
Administrative Assistant to Sales/Advertising Special Projects .... Janice Toepper
Souvenir Coordinator .... Kim Moyer
Assistant Souvenir Coordinator .... Phil Kessel
Regional Sales Managers .... Don Gore, Bryan Maust, John Oakes, Ron Potter
Sales Representatives .... David Abrutyn, Tim Bronaugh, Darren Bruening, Chris Garinger, Bill O'Brien, Brian Rupp
Administrative Assistant to the VP/Marketing .... Paula Bogley
Secretary to the Sales Department .... Shelly Finkel
Receptionist .... Nancy Woodall

Director of Public Relations .... Lou Corletto
Public Relations Assistant .... Dan Kaufman
Publications Assistant .... Rick Braunstein
Administrative Assistant to the Public Relations Department .... Julie Hensley

Controller .... Aggie Ballard
Accounting Assistants .... David Berman, Kathleen Brady, Crystal Coffren, Melanie Loveless

Medical and Training Staff
Head Trainer .... Stan Wong
Assistant Trainer/Head Equipment Manager .... Doug Shearer
Assistant Equipment Manager .... Craig Leydig
Assistant to the Equipment Manager .... Rick Harper
Strength and Conditioning Coach .... Frank Costello
Team Nutritionist .... Pat Mann
Massage Therapist .... Kurt Millar
Team Physicians .... Dr. Richard Grossman, Dr. Stephen Haas, Dr. Carl MacCartee, Dr. Frank Melograna
Team Dentist .... Dr. Howard Salob

General Manager

POILE, DAVID
Vice-President and General Manager, Washington Capitals.
Born in Toronto, Ont., February 14, 1949.

David Poile was named to the position of general manager of the Capitals on August 30, 1982 and quickly built the franchise into a solid Stanley Cup contender. During his inaugural campaign (1982-83), he led the Caps' to their first winning season (39-25-16) and a first-time berth in the Stanley Cup playoffs. He received *The Sporting News* "Executive of the Year" award in 1982-83 for his efforts and duplicated the feat in 1983-84 following the Capitals' 48-27-5 season. Poile, a graduate of Northeastern University with a degree in business administration, began his professional hockey management career in 1972 as an administrative assistant for the Atlanta Flames organization where he served until joining the Washington franchise. A former collegiate hockey star at Northeastern, he won MVP and scoring honors during his senior year.

Winnipeg Jets

1991-92 Results: 33W-32L-15T 81PTS. Fourth, Smythe Division

Year-by-Year Record

Season	GP	Home W	Home L	Home T	Road W	Road L	Road T	Overall W	Overall L	Overall T	GF	GA	Pts.	Finished	Playoff Result
1991-92	80	20	14	6	13	18	9	33	32	15	251	244	81	4th, Smythe Div.	Lost Div. Semi-Final
1990-91	80	17	18	5	9	25	6	26	43	11	260	288	63	5th, Smythe Div.	Out of Playoffs
1989-90	80	22	13	5	15	19	6	37	32	11	298	290	85	3rd, Smythe Div.	Lost Div. Semi-Final
1988-89	80	17	18	5	9	24	7	26	42	12	300	355	64	5th, Smythe Div.	Out of Playoffs
1987-88	80	20	14	6	13	22	5	33	36	11	292	310	77	3rd, Smythe Div.	Lost Div. Semi-Final
1986-87	80	25	12	3	15	20	5	40	32	8	279	271	88	3rd, Smythe Div.	Lost Div. Final
1985-86	80	18	19	3	8	28	4	26	47	7	295	372	59	3rd, Smythe Div.	Lost Div. Semi-Final
1984-85	80	21	13	6	22	14	4	43	27	10	358	332	96	2nd, Smythe Div.	Lost Div. Final
1983-84	80	17	15	8	14	23	3	31	38	11	340	374	73	4th, Smythe Div.	Lost Div. Semi-Final
1982-83	80	22	16	2	11	23	6	33	39	8	311	333	74	4th, Smythe Div.	Lost Div. Semi-Final
1981-82	80	18	13	9	15	20	5	33	33	14	319	332	80	2nd, Norris Div.	Lost Div. Semi-Final
1980-81	80	7	25	8	2	32	6	9	57	14	246	400	32	6th, Smythe Div.	Out of Playoffs
1979-80	80	13	19	8	7	30	3	20	49	11	214	314	51	5th, Smythe Div.	Out of Playoffs

Schedule

Home

Oct. Tues. 6 Detroit
Wed. 14 Edmonton
Fri. 16 Vancouver
Fri. 23 Los Angeles
Mon. 26 Washington
Wed. 28 Calgary
Nov. Fri. 6 Edmonton
Tues. 10 Los Angeles
Sat. 21 NY Rangers
Tues. 24 NY Islanders
Fri. 27 San Jose
Dec. Sat. 5 Montreal
Tues. 15 New Jersey
Mon. 21 San Jose
Wed. 23 Calgary
Sun. 27 Minnesota
Tues. 29 Boston
Thur. 31 Edmonton*
Jan. Fri. 8 Los Angeles
Sun. 10 Pittsburgh
Tues. 12 San Jose
Mon. 18 Hartford
(at Saskatoon)
Tues. 19 Chicago
Sat. 23 Edmonton
Feb. Wed. 3 St Louis
Wed. 10 Buffalo
Fri. 12 Hartford
Sun. 14 San Jose*
Mon. 22 Ottawa
Fri. 26 Vancouver
Sun. 28 Minnesota
Mar. Tues. 2 Quebec
Fri. 12 Vancouver
Sun. 14 Tampa Bay*
Sun. 21 Calgary*
Tues. 23 Toronto
Fri. 26 St Louis
Sun. 28 Los Angeles*
Apr. Tues. 6 Philadelphia
Thur. 8 Toronto
Tues. 13 Tampa Bay
Thur. 15 Edmonton

Away

Oct. Thur. 8 San Jose
Sat. 10 Los Angeles
Mon. 12 Vancouver
Sun. 18 Philadelphia
Tues. 20 Detroit
Sat. 31 Quebec
Nov. Mon. 2 Montreal
Sun. 8 Vancouver*
Thur. 12 Minnesota
Sat. 14 St Louis
Tues. 17 Tampa Bay
Thur. 19 Detroit
Dec. Wed. 2 Calgary
Tues. 8 Pittsburgh
Fri. 11 Washington
Sat. 12 NY Islanders
Thur. 17 Chicago
Sat. 19 St Louis
Sat. 26 Minnesota
Jan. Sat. 2 New Jersey
Sun. 3 Chicago
Tues. 5 Calgary
Wed. 13 Edmonton
Sat. 16 Los Angeles
Fri. 22 Calgary
Wed. 27 NY Rangers
Thur. 28 Boston
Sat. 30 Hartford
Feb. Mon. 1 Ottawa
Thur. 18 San Jose
Sat. 20 Vancouver
Tues. 23 Ottawa
(at Saskatoon)
Mar. Thur. 4 Edmonton
Sat. 6 Toronto
Sun. 7 Buffalo
Tues. 9 Tampa Bay
Tues. 16 Los Angeles
Thur. 18 Vancouver
Tues. 30 Calgary
Apr. Thur. 1 San Jose
Sat. 3 Edmonton
Sun. 11 Edmonton*

* Denotes afternoon game.

Home Starting Times:

Weeknights	7:35 p.m.
Saturdays and Sundays	7:05 p.m.
Matinees	2:05 p.m.
Except Dec 31.	4:05 p.m.
Mar. 28	1:05 p.m.

Franchise date: June 22, 1979

14th NHL Season

Winnipeg Jets' captain Troy Murray led the Jets with two shorthanded goals in 1991-92.

1992-93 Player Personnel

FORWARDS	HT	WT	S	Place of Birth	Date	1991-92 Club
BARNES, Stu	5-10	175	R	Edmonton, Alta.	12/25/70	Moncton-Winnipeg
BORSATO, Luciano	5-10	165	R	Richmond Hill, Ont.	1/7/66	Moncton-Winnipeg
CIRONE, Jason	5-9	184	L	Toronto, Ont.	2/21/71	Moncton-Winnipeg
DAVIDSON, Lee	5-11	165	L	Winnipeg, Man.	6/30/68	Moncton-Fort Wayne
DAVYDOV, Evgeny	6-0	183	R	Chelyabinsk, USSR	5/27/67	CSKA-Winnipeg
DRAPER, Kris	5-11	188	L	Toronto, Ont.	5/24/71	Moncton-Winnipeg
EAGLES, Mike	5-10	180	L	Sussex, N.B.	3/7/63	Winnipeg
ELYNUIK, Pat	6-0	185	R	Foam Lake, Sask.	10/30/67	Winnipeg
ERICKSON, Bryan	5-9	175	R	Roseau, MN	7/3/60	Winnipeg
GERNANDER, Ken	5-10	175	L	Coleraine, MN	6/30/69	Moncton
HARTJE, Tod	6-1	180	L	Anoka, MN	2/27/68	Moncton
JOYCE, Bob	6-0	195	L	Saint John, N.B.	7/11/66	Moncton
KERR, Alan	5-11	195	R	Hazelton, B.C.	3/28/64	Detroit
KOSTICHKIN, Pavel	6-1	189	L	Moscow, USSR	11/9/68	CSKA
LeBLANC, John	6-1	190	L	Campbellton, N.B.	1/21/64	Moncton-Winnipeg
LEVINS, Scott	6-3	200	R	Portland, OR	1/30/70	Moncton
MARTIN, Craig	6-2	219	R	Amherst, N.S.	1/21/71	Moncton
MURRAY, Rob	6-1	180	R	Toronto, Ont.	4/4/67	Moncton-Winnipeg
MURRAY, Troy	6-1	195	R	Calgary, Alta.	7/31/62	Winnipeg
OLCZYK, Eddie	6-1	200	L	Chicago, IL	8/16/66	Winnipeg
RAISKY, Andrei	6-2	194	L	Ust-Kamenogorsk, USSR	3/30/70	Torpedo Ust
ROMANIUK, Russ	6-0	185	L	Winnipeg, Man.	6/9/70	Moncton-Winnipeg
SELANNE, Teemu	6-0	181	R	Helsinki, Finland	7/3/70	Jokerit
SHANNON, Darrin	6-2	200	L	Barrie, Ont.	12/8/69	Winnipeg
STEEN, Thomas	5-10	195	L	Grums, Sweden	6/8/60	Winnipeg
STEVENSON, Jeremy	6-1	212	L	San Bernadino, CA	7/28/74	Cornwall
TKACHUK, Keith	6-2	200	L	Melrose, MA	3/28/72	U.S. Olym.-U.S. Jr. Nat.-Wpg.
ZHAMNOV, Alexei	6-1	187	L	Moscow, USSR	10/1/70	Dynamo Moscow
DEFENSEMEN						
BAUTIN, Sergei	6-3	185	L	Murmansk, USSR	3/11/67	Dynamo Moscow
CARLYLE, Randy	5-10	200	L	Sudbury, Ont.	4/19/56	Winnipeg
COWIE, Rob	6-0	195	L	Toronto, Ont.	11/3/67	Northeastern
EAKINS, Dallas	6-2	195	L	Dade City, FL	2/27/67	Moncton
HAYWARD, Rick	6-0	200	L	Toledo, OH	2/25/66	Capital District
HOUSLEY, Phil	5-10	179	L	St. Paul, MN	3/9/64	Winnipeg
KENNEDY, Dean	6-2	205	R	Redvers, Sask.	1/18/63	Winnipeg
LALOR, Mike	6-0	200	L	Buffalo, NY	3/8/63	Washington-Wpg.
LAMBERT, Dan	5-8	177	L	St. Boniface, Man.	1/12/70	Quebec-Halifax
NUMMINEN, Teppo	6-1	190	R	Tampere, Finland	7/3/68	Winnipeg
OLAUSSON, Fredrik	6-2	200	R	Vaxsjo, Sweden	10/5/66	Winnipeg
ULANOV, Igor	6-2	202	L	Krasnokamsk, USSR	10/1/69	Khimik-Moncton-Winnipeg
VISHEAU, Mark	6-4	197	R	Burlington, Ont.	6/27/73	London

GOALTENDERS	HT	WT	C	Place of Birth	Date	1991-92 Club
BEAUREGARD, Stephane	5-11	185	R	Cowansville, Que.	1/10/68	Winnipeg
ESSENSA, Bob	6-0	160	L	Toronto, Ont.	1/14/65	Winnipeg
GAUTHIER, Sean	5-11	202	L	Sudbury, Ont.	3/28/71	Moncton-Fort Wayne
O'NEILL, Mike	5-7	160	L	Montreal, Que.	11/3/67	Moncton-Winnipeg
RICHARDS, Mark	5-8	179	L	Jamison, PA	7/24/69	Lowell
ROY, Allain	5-10	170	L	Campbellton, N.B.	2/6/70	Harvard
TABARACCI, Richard	5-10	186	L	Toronto, Ont.	1/2/69	Moncton-Winnipeg

General Managers' History

John Ferguson, 1979-80 to 1987-88; John Ferguson and Mike Smith, 1988-89; Mike Smith, 1989-90 to date.

Coaching History

Tom McVie, 1979-80; Tom McVie and Bill Sutherland, 1980-81; Tom Watt, 1981-82 to 1982-83; Tom Watt, John Ferguson and Barry Long, 1983-84; Barry Long, 1984-85; Barry Long and John Ferguson, 1985-86. Dan Maloney, 1986-87 to 1987-88, Dan Maloney and Rick Bowness 1988-89; Bob Murdoch, 1989-90 to 1990-91; John Paddock, 1991-92 to date.

Captains' History

Lars-Erik Sjoberg, 1979-80; Morris Lukowich, 1980-81; Dave Christian, 1981-82; Dave Christian, Lucien DeBlois, 1982-83; Lucien DeBlois, 1983-84; Dale Hawerchuk, 1984-85 to 1988-89; Randy Carlyle, Dale Hawerchuk and Thomas Steen, 1989-90; Randy Carlyle and Thomas Steen, 1990-91; Troy Murray, 1991-92 to date.

Retired Numbers

9	Bobby Hull	1972-1980

1991-92 Scoring

Regular Season

Pos	#.	Player	Team	GP	G	A	Pts	+/–	PIM	PP	SH	GW	GT	S	%
D	6	Phil Housley	WPG	74	23	63	86	5–	92	11	0	4	1	234	9.8
C	16	Ed Olczyk	WPG	64	32	33	65	11	67	12	0	7	1	245	13.1
D	4	Fredrik Olausson	WPG	77	20	42	62	31–	34	13	1	2	0	227	8.8
R	15	Pat Elynuik	WPG	60	25	25	50	2–	65	9	0	1	0	127	19.7
C	19	Troy Murray	WPG	74	17	30	47	13–	69	5	2	1	1	156	10.9
L	34	Darrin Shannon	BUF	1	0	1	1	1	0	0	0	0	0	2	.0
			WPG	68	13	26	39	5	41	3	0	3	1	91	14.3
			TOTAL	69	13	27	40	6	41	3	0	3	1	93	14.0
D	27	Teppo Numminen	WPG	80	5	34	39	15	32	4	0	1	0	143	3.5
C	25	Thomas Steen	WPG	38	13	25	38	5	29	10	0	0	0	75	17.3
C	38*	Luciano Borsato	WPG	56	15	21	36	6–	45	5	0	1	0	81	18.5
C	23	Lucien DeBlois	TOR	54	8	11	19	3–	39	0	1	1	0	75	10.7
			WPG	11	1	2	3	1	2	0	0	1	0	15	6.7
			TOTAL	65	9	13	22	2–	41	0	1	2	0	90	10.0
C	14*	Stu Barnes	WPG	46	8	9	17	2–	26	4	0	0	0	75	10.7
C	36	Mike Eagles	WPG	65	7	10	17	17–	118	0	1	0	0	60	11.7
D	22	Mike Lalor	WSH	64	5	7	12	14	64	0	0	1	0	54	9.3
			WPG	15	2	3	5	11	14	0	0	0	0	20	10.0
			TOTAL	79	7	10	17	25	78	0	0	1	0	74	9.5
L	39	Doug Evans	WPG	30	7	7	14	2	68	1	0	0	0	39	17.9
R	24	Danton Cole	WPG	52	7	5	12	15–	32	1	2	0	0	65	10.8
D	32*	Igor Ulanov	WPG	27	2	9	11	5	67	0	0	0	0	23	8.7
D	8	Randy Carlyle	WPG	66	1	9	10	4	54	0	0	0	0	84	1.2
C	11	Aaron Broten	WPG	25	4	5	9	2	14	0	0	3	0	29	13.8
L	20	Mike Hartman	WPG	75	4	4	8	10–	264	0	0	1	1	89	4.5
R	7*	Keith Tkachuk	WPG	17	3	5	8	0	28	2	0	0	0	22	13.6
L	21*	Russ Romaniuk	WPG	27	3	5	8	2	18	2	0	1	0	32	9.4
R	37	John LeBlanc	WPG	16	6	1	7	6–	6	5	0	1	0	32	18.8
R	40*	Evgeny Davydov	WPG	12	4	3	7	7	8	2	0	0	0	32	12.5
L	17	Phil Sykes	WPG	52	4	2	6	12–	72	0	0	2	0	34	11.8
L	7	Petri Skriko	BOS	9	1	0	1	3–	6	1	0	0	0	20	5.0
			WPG	15	2	3	5	1–	4	0	0	0	0	27	7.4
			TOTAL	24	3	3	6	4–	10	1	0	0	0	47	6.4
C	18	Bryan Erickson	WPG	10	2	4	6	9	0	0	0	1	0	16	12.5
D	26	Dean Kennedy	WPG	18	2	4	6	2	21	0	0	1	0	20	10.0
D	33	Mario Marois	STL	17	0	1	1	3–	38	0	0	0	0	11	.0
			WPG	34	1	3	4	8–	34	0	1	0	0	32	3.1
			TOTAL	51	1	4	5	11–	72	0	1	0	0	43	2.3
D	44	Shawn Cronin	WPG	65	0	4	4	11–	271	0	0	0	0	25	.0
C	91*	Kris Draper	WPG	10	2	0	2	0	2	0	0	0	0	19	10.5
G	35	Bob Essensa	WPG	47	0	2	2	0	2	0	0	0	0	0	.0
C	50	Rob Murray	WPG	9	0	1	1	2–	18	0	0	0	0	2	.0
G	31*	Rick Tabaracci	WPG	18	0	1	1	0	4	0	0	0	0	0	.0
L	28	Bob Joyce	WPG	1	0	0	0	0	0	0	0	0	0	0	.0
G	1*	Michael O'Neill	WPG	1	0	0	0	0	0	0	0	0	0	0	.0
C	48*	Jason Cirone	WPG	3	0	0	0	0	2	0	0	0	0	1	.0
R	29	Rudy Poeschek	WPG	4	0	0	0	5–	17	0	0	0	0	1	.0
D	5	Kent Paynter	WPG	5	0	0	0	1–	4	0	0	0	0	6	.0
G	30	Steph Beauregard	WPG	26	0	0	0	0	0	0	0	0	0	0	.0

Goaltending

No.	Goaltender	GPI	Mins	Avg	W	L	T	EN	SO	GA	SA	S%
35	Bob Essensa	47	2627	2.88	21	17	6	2	5	126	1407	.910
30	Steph Beauregard	26	1267	2.89	6	8	6	1	2	61	611	.900
31	* Rick Tabaracci	18	966	3.23	6	7	3	1	0	52	470	.889
1	* Michael O'Neill	1	13	4.62	0	0	0	0	0	1	7	.857
	Totals	**80**	**4888**	**3.00**	**33**	**32**	**15**	**4**	**7**	**244**	**2499**	**.902**

Playoffs

Pos	#	Player	Team	GP	G	A	Pts	+/–	PIM	PP	SH	GW	GT	S	%
C	25	Thomas Steen	WPG	7	2	4	6	1–	2	2	0	0	0	15	13.3
D	4	Fredrik Olausson	WPG	7	1	5	6	7–	4	1	0	0	0	18	5.6
D	6	Phil Housley	WPG	7	1	4	5	6–	0	1	0	1	0	31	3.2
C	11	Aaron Broten	WPG	7	2	2	4	2–	12	0	0	0	0	10	20.0
R	15	Pat Elynuik	WPG	7	2	2	4	2–	4	2	0	0	0	9	22.2
R	40*	Evgeny Davydov	WPG	7	2	2	4	4–	2	1	0	0	0	15	13.3
R	7*	Keith Tkachuk	WPG	7	3	0	3	3–	30	0	0	0	0	14	21.4
C	16	Ed Olczyk	WPG	6	2	1	3	0	4	0	0	1	0	16	12.5
D	8	Randy Carlyle	WPG	5	1	0	1	3–	6	0	0	0	0	4	25.0
C	23	Lucien DeBlois	WPG	5	1	0	1	4–	2	0	0	1	0	8	12.5
L	34	Darrin Shannon	WPG	7	0	1	1	7–	10	0	0	0	0	11	.0
L	17	Phil Sykes	WPG	7	0	1	1	1–	9	0	0	0	0	3	.0
G	35	Bob Essensa	WPG	1	0	0	0	0	0	0	0	0	0	0	.0
L	39	Doug Evans	WPG	1	0	0	0	0	2	0	0	0	0	0	.0
C	38*	Luciano Borsato	WPG	1	0	0	0	0	0	0	0	0	0	1	.0
C	91*	Kris Draper	WPG	2	0	0	0	2–	0	0	0	0	0	1	.0
R	20	Mike Hartman	WPG	2	0	0	0	0	2	0	0	0	0	0	.0
D	26	Dean Kennedy	WPG	2	0	0	0	2–	0	0	0	0	0	1	.0
D	44	Shawn Cronin	WPG	4	0	0	0	0	6	0	0	0	0	0	.0
C	36	Mike Eagles	WPG	7	0	0	0	5–	8	0	0	0	0	5	.0
D	22	Mike Lalor	WPG	7	0	0	0	4–	19	0	0	0	0	5	.0
C	19	Troy Murray	WPG	7	0	0	0	10–	2	0	0	0	0	11	.0
D	27	Teppo Numminen	WPG	7	0	0	0	3–	0	0	0	0	0	9	.0
G	31*	Rick Tabaracci	WPG	7	0	0	0	0	0	0	0	0	0	0	.0
D	32*	Igor Ulanov	WPG	7	0	0	0	4–	39	0	0	0	0	11	.0

Goaltending

No.	Goaltender	GPI	Mins	Avg	W	L	EN	SO	GA	SA	S%
31	* Rick Tabaracci	7	387	4.03	3	4	0	0	26	212	.877
35	Bob Essensa	1	33	5.45	0	0	0	0	3	17	.824
	Totals	**7**	**420**	**4.14**	**3**	**4**	**0**	**0**	**29**	**229**	**.873**

Club Records

Team

(Figures in brackets for season records are games played; records for fewest points, wins, ties, losses, goals, goals against are for 70 or more games)

Record		
Most Points	**96**	1984-85 (80)
Most Wins	**43**	1984-85 (80)
Most Ties	**15**	1991-92 (80)
Most Losses	**57**	1980-81 (80)
Most Goals	**358**	1984-85 (80)
Most Goals Against	**400**	1980-81 (80)
Fewest Points	**32**	1980-81 (80)
Fewest Wins	**9**	1980-81 (80)
Fewest Ties	**7**	1985-86 (80)
Fewest Losses	**27**	1984-85 (80)
Fewest Goals	**214**	1979-80 (80)
Fewest Goals Against	**244**	1991-92 (80)
Longest Winning Streak		
Over-all	**9**	Mar. 8-27/85
Home	**7**	Jan. 23-Mar. 1/87
Away	**8**	Feb. 25-Apr. 6/85
Longest Undefeated Streak		
Over-all	**13**	Mar. 8-Apr. 7/85 (10 wins, 3 ties)
Home	**11**	Dec. 23/83 Feb. 5/84 (6 wins, 5 ties)
Away	**9**	Feb. 25-Apr. 7/85 (8 wins, 1 tie)
Longest Losing Streak		
Over-all	**10**	Nov. 30- Dec. 20/80
Home	**4**	Four times
Away	**9**	Dec. 26/79- Jan. 22/80
Longest Winless Streak		
Over-all	***30**	Oct. 19- Dec. 20/80 (23 losses, 7 ties)
Home	**14**	Oct. 19- Dec. 14/80 (9 losses, 5 ties)
Away	**18**	Oct. 10- Dec. 20/80 (16 losses, 2 ties)
Most Shutouts, Season	**7**	1991-92 (80)
Most PIM, Season	**2,278**	1987-88 (80)
Most Goals, Game	**12**	Feb. 25/85 (Wpg. 12 at NYR. 5)

Individual

Record		
Most Seasons	**11**	Thomas Steen
Most Games	**763**	Thomas Steen
Most Goals, Career	**379**	Dale Hawerchuk
Most Assists, Career	**550**	Dale Hawerchuk
Most Points, Career	**929**	Dale Hawerchuk (379 goals, 550 assists)
Most PIM, Career	**1,338**	Laurie Boschman
Most Shutouts, Career	**11**	Bob Essensa
Longest Consecutive Games Streak	**475**	Dale Hawerchuk (Dec. 19/82-Dec. 10/89)
Most Goals, Season	**53**	Dale Hawerchuk (1984-85)
Most Assists, Season	**77**	Dale Hawerchuk (1984-85, 1987-88)
Most Points, Season	**130**	Dale Hawerchuk (1984-85) (53 goals, 77 assists)
Most PIM, Season	**287**	Jimmy Mann (1979-80)
Most Points, Defenseman Season	**86**	Phil Housley (1991-92) (23 goals, 63 assists)
Most Points, Center, Season	**130**	Dale Hawerchuk (1984-85) (53 goals, 77 assists)
Most Points, Right Wing, Season	**101**	Paul Maclean (1984-85) (41 goals, 60 assists)
Most Points, Left Wing, Season	**92**	Morris Lukowich (1981-82) (43 goals, 49 assists)
Most Points, Rookie, Season	**103**	Dale Hawerchuk (1981-82) (45 goals, 58 assists)
Most Shutouts, Season	**5**	Bob Essensa (1991-92)
Most Goals, Game	**5**	Willy Lindstrom (Mar. 2/82)
Most Assists, Game	**5**	Dale Hawerchuk (Mar. 6/84, Mar. 18/89, Mar. 4/90)
Most Points, Game	**6**	Willy Lindstrom (Mar. 2/82) Dale Hawerchuk (Dec. 14/83, Mar. 18/89) Thomas Steen (Oct. 24/84) Eddie Olczyk (Dec. 21/91)

* NHL Record.

All-time Record vs. Other Clubs

Regular Season

	At Home							On Road							Total						
	GP	W	L	T	GF	GA	PTS	GP	W	L	T	GF	GA	PTS	GP	W	L	T	GF	GA	PTS
Boston	21	8	11	2	72	75	18	20	3	14	3	64	94	9	41	11	25	5	136	169	27
Buffalo	20	8	10	2	66	74	18	20	1	17	2	52	96	4	40	9	27	4	118	170	22
Calgary	45	21	16	8	190	163	50	45	8	32	5	140	222	21	90	29	48	13	330	385	71
Chicago	23	11	9	3	96	87	25	22	4	15	3	71	114	11	45	15	24	6	167	201	36
Detroit	22	7	7	8	74	70	22	23	9	11	3	88	91	21	45	16	18	11	162	161	43
Edmonton	44	15	25	4	179	213	34	46	12	31	3	150	218	27	90	27	56	7	329	431	61
Hartford	21	11	10	0	74	73	22	20	5	10	5	65	85	15	41	16	20	5	139	158	37
Los Angeles	46	22	17	7	203	174	51	44	20	16	8	182	181	48	90	42	33	15	385	355	99
Minnesota	22	10	11	1	76	76	21	23	7	14	2	70	108	16	45	17	25	3	146	184	37
Montreal	20	7	8	5	66	80	19	20	2	18	0	48	113	4	40	9	26	5	114	193	23
New Jersey	21	15	3	3	88	54	33	19	9	5	5	64	57	23	40	24	8	8	152	111	56
NY Islanders	20	7	12	1	65	77	15	21	4	11	6	62	82	14	41	11	23	7	127	159	29
NY Rangers	21	8	11	2	77	81	18	20	8	10	2	86	97	18	41	16	21	4	163	178	36
Philadelphia	20	9	10	1	68	72	19	21	5	16	0	56	96	10	41	14	26	1	124	168	29
Pittsburgh	20	8	11	1	77	76	17	21	7	14	0	64	86	14	41	15	25	1	141	162	31
Quebec	20	9	6	5	85	78	23	21	10	9	2	88	85	22	41	19	15	7	173	163	45
St. Louis	23	12	5	6	85	73	30	22	4	10	8	70	93	16	45	16	15	14	155	166	46
San Jose	4	3	1	0	18	9	6	3	2	0	1	13	10	5	7	5	1	1	31	19	11
Toronto	22	12	7	3	108	94	27	23	15	7	1	107	86	31	45	27	14	4	215	180	58
Vancouver	44	24	13	7	177	159	55	46	13	25	8	140	174	34	90	37	38	15	317	333	89
Washington	21	10	6	5	78	77	25	20	5	13	2	61	92	12	41	15	19	7	139	169	37
Totals	**520**	**237**	**209**	**74**	**2022**	**1935**	**548**	**520**	**153**	**298**	**69**	**1741**	**2280**	**375**	**1040**	**390**	**507**	**143**	**3763**	**4215**	**923**

Playoffs

	Series	W	L	GP	W	L	T	GF	GA	Last Mtg.	Round	Result
Calgary	3	2	1	13	7	6	0	45	43	1987	DSF	W 4-2
Edmonton	6	0	6	26	4	22	0	75	120	1990	DSF	L 3-4
St. Louis	1	0	1	4	1	3	0	13	20	1982	DSF	L 1-3
Vancouver	1	0	1	7	3	4	0	17	29	1992	DSF	L 3-4
Totals	**11**	**2**	**9**	**50**	**15**	**35**	**0**	**150**	**212**			

Playoff Results 1992-88

Year	Round	Opponent	Result	GF	GA
1992	DSF	Vancouver	L 3-4	17	29
1990	DSF	Edmonton	L 3-4	22	24
1988	DSF	Edmonton	L 1-4	17	25

Abbreviations: Round: F – Final; **CF** – conference final; **DF** – division final; **DSF** – division semi-final; **SF** – semi-final; **QF** – quarter-final; **PR** – preliminary round. **GA** – goals against; **GF** – goals for.

1991-92 Results

Home				Away			
Oct.	4	Los Angeles	3-6	**Oct.**	10	San Jose	5-4
	6	Calgary	5-3		12	Los Angeles	3-3
	8	Vancouver	2-3		22	NY Islanders	1-1
	16	Hartford	2-3		23	Detroit	3-2
	19	Toronto	4-2		29	Quebec	2-7
	25	Philadelphia	2-0		30	Montreal	1-6
	27	Washington	6-5	**Nov.**	5	Vancouver	2-2
Nov.	1	Calgary	6-7		14	St Louis	1-2
	3	St Louis	3-3		16	New Jersey*	1-0
	8	Pittsburgh	1-3		17	Philadelphia	2-1
	11	Los Angeles*	6-2		23	Edmonton	4-0
	20	NY Islanders	3-1		25	Calgary	3-3
	27	NY Rangers	3-2	**Dec.**	10	San Jose	3-3
Dec.	1	Chicago	3-2		12	Los Angeles	1-2
	4	Buffalo	5-4		14	Edmonton	5-7
	6	Edmonton	4-4		17	Calgary	4-7
	8	Washington	4-3		19	Vancouver	1-3
	21	Calgary	7-2		23	Toronto	1-3
	26	Minnesota	2-3		27	Chicago	3-3
	29	Boston	3-6	**Jan.**	2	Boston	3-1
	31	NY Rangers*	2-5		4	Pittsburgh*	2-3
Jan.	8	Edmonton	5-2		6	NY Rangers	2-4
	10	Chicago	6-2		21	Hartford	3-3
	12	San Jose	3-4		23	Philadelphia	1-0
	14	Vancouver	2-4		25	Quebec*	1-2
	31	Quebec	4-4		26	Buffalo*	2-5
Feb.	2	San Jose*	6-0		28	Pittsburgh	4-0
	4	Boston	3-3	**Feb.**	13	Minnesota	1-6
	7	Calgary	4-1		15	Toronto	3-1
	19	St Louis	3-4		17	NY Islanders*	4-5
	21	New Jersey	6-4		26	Edmonton	1-6
	23	Los Angeles	2-4		28	Vancouver	3-5
Mar.	1	Edmonton*	2-4	**Mar.**	3	Detroit	4-3
	11	San Jose	3-0		6	Washington	3-3
	13	Hartford	0-1		8	Minnesota	2-4
	15	Detroit*	1-1		17	Los Angeles	4-5
	22	Vancouver*	5-1		20	Vancouver	2-2
	25	Montreal	2-2	**Apr.**	1	San Jose	5-3
	27	Los Angeles	6-4		3	Edmonton	6-2
	29	San Jose*	6-5		5	Calgary	4-3

*Denotes afternoon game

Entry Draft Selections 1992-79

1992

Pick	
17	Sergei Bautin
27	Boris Mironov
60	Jeremy Stevenson
84	Mark Visheau
132	Alexander Alexeyev
155	Artur Oktyabrev
156	Andrei Raisky
204	Nikolai Khaibulin
228	Yevgeny Garanin
229	Teemu Numminen
252	Andrei Karpovtsev
254	Ivan Vologzhaninov

1991

Pick	
5	Aaron Ward
49	Dmitri Filimonov
91	Juha Ylonen
99	Yan Kaminsky
115	Jeff Sebastian
159	Jeff Ricciardi
181	Sean Gauthier
203	Igor Ulanov
225	Jason Jennings
247	Sergei Sorokin

1990

Pick	
19	Keith Tkachuk
35	Mike Muller
74	Roman Meluzin
75	Scott Levins
77	Alexei Zhamnov
98	Craig Martin
119	Daniel Jardemyr
140	John Lilley
161	Henrik Andersson
182	Rauli Raitanen
203	Mika Alatalo
224	Sergei Selyanin
245	Keith Morris

1989

Pick	
4	Stu Barnes
25	Dan Ratushny
46	Jason Cirone
62	Kris Draper
64	Mark Brownschidle
69	Alain Roy
109	Dan Bylsma
130	Pekka Peltola
131	Doug Evans
151	Jim Solly
172	Stephane Gauvin
193	Joe Larson
214	Bradley Podiak
235	Evgeny Davydov
240	Sergei Kharin

1988

Pick	
10	Teemu Selanne
31	Russell Romaniuk
52	Stephane Beauregard
73	Brian Hunt
94	Anthony Joseph
101	Benoit Lebeau
115	Ronald Jones
127	Markus Akerblom
136	Jukka Marttila
157	Mark Smith
178	Mike Helber
199	Pavel Kostichkin
220	Kevin Heise
241	Kyle Galloway

1987

Pick	
16	Bryan Marchment
37	Patrik Erickson
79	Don McLennan
96	Ken Gernander
100	Darrin Amundson
121	Joe Harwell
142	Tod Hartje
163	Markku Kyllonen
184	Jim Fernholz
226	Roger Rougelot
247	Hans Goran Elo

1986

Pick	
8	Pat Elynuik
29	Teppo Numminen
50	Esa Palosaari
71	Hannu Jarvenpaa
92	Craig Endean
113	Robertson Bateman
155	Frank Furlan
176	Mark Green
197	John Blue
218	Matt Cote
239	Arto Blomsten

1985

Pick	
18	Ryan Stewart
39	Roger Ohman
60	Daniel Berthiaume
81	Fredrik Olausson
102	John Borrell
123	Danton Cole
144	Brent Mowery
165	Tom Draper
186	Nevin Kardum
207	Dave Quigley
228	Chris Norton
249	Anssi Melametsa

1984

Pick	
30	Peter Douris
68	Chris Mills
72	Sean Clement
93	Scott Schneider
99	Brent Severyn
114	Gary Lorden
135	Luciano Borsato
156	Brad Jones
177	Gord Whitaker
197	Rick Forst
218	Mike Warus
238	Jim Edmonds

1983

Pick	
8	Andrew McBain
14	Bobby Dollas
29	Brad Berry
43	Peter Taglianetti
69	Bob Essensa
89	Harry Armstrong
109	Joel Baillargeon
129	Iain Duncan
149	Ron Pessetti
169	Todd Flichel
189	Cory Wright
209	Eric Cormier
229	Jamie Husgen

1982

Pick	
12	Jim Kyte
74	Tom Martin
75	Dave Ellett
96	Tim Mishler
138	Derek Ray
159	Guy Gosselin
180	Tom Ward
201	Mike Savage
222	Bob Shaw
243	Jan Urban Ericson

1981

Pick	
1	Dale Hawerchuk
22	Scott Arniel
43	Jyrki Seppa
64	Kirk McCaskill
85	Marc Behrend
106	Bob O'Connor
127	Peter Nilsson
148	Dan McFaul
169	Greg Dick
190	Vladimir Kadlec
211	Dave Kirwin

1980

Pick	
2	David Babych
23	Moe Mantha
44	Murray Eaves
65	Guy Fournier
86	Glen Ostir
107	Ron Loustel
128	Brian Mullen
135	Mike Lauen
149	Sandy Beadle
170	Ed Christian
191	Dave Chartier

1979

Pick	
19	Jimmy Mann
40	Dave Christian
61	Bill Whelton
82	Pat Daley
103	Thomas Steen
124	Tim Watters

Coach

PADDOCK, JOHN
Coach, Winnipeg Jets. Born in Brandon, Man., June 9, 1954.

John Paddock, who was named as the 10th head coach of the Winnipeg Jets on June 17, 1991, led the club to a fourth-place finish in the Smythe Division in 1991-92 with a 33-32-15 record. Paddock joined the Jets after serving one season as head coach of the Binghamton Rangers of the American Hockey League, the league where he got his coaching start in 1983. Paddock, then playing for the Maine Mariners, succeeded Tom McVie behind the Mariners bench when McVie was summoned to New Jersey; the Mariners won the AHL Calder Cup Championship that season. Paddock later joined the Hershey Bears, where he won another Calder Cup and two Coach of the Year awards. Paddock served one season as assistant general manager for the Philadelphia Flyers before joining the New York Rangers organization in 1990.

Paddock played 87 NHL games as a right wing, drafted by the Washington Capitals, and recorded eight goals and 14 assists during his career.

Coaching Record

		Regular Season					Playoffs			
Season	Team	Games	W	L	T	%	Games	W	L	%
1983-84	Maine (AHL)	80	33	36	11	.481	17	12	5	.706
1984-85	Maine (AHL)	80	38	32	10	.538	11	5	6	.454
1985-86	Hershey (AHL)	80	48	29	3	.619	18	10	8	.555
1986-87	Hershey (AHL)	80	43	36	1	.544	5	1	4	.200
1987-88	Hershey (AHL)	80	50	27	3	.644	12	12	0	1.000
1988-89	Hershey (AHL)	80	40	30	10	.563	12	7	5	.583
1990-91	Binghamton (AHL)	80	44	30	6	.588	10	4	6	.400
1991-92	**Winnipeg (NHL)**	**80**	**33**	**32**	**15**	**.506**	**7**	**3**	**4**	**.429**
	NHL Totals	**80**	**33**	**32**	**15**	**.506**	**7**	**3**	**4**	**.429**

Club Directory

Winnipeg Arena
15-1430 Maroons Road
Winnipeg, Manitoba R3G 0L5
Phone **204/982-5387**
FAX 204/788-4668
Capacity: 15,393

Board of Directors
Barry L. Shenkarow, Bill Davis, Marvin Shenkarow, Harvey Secter, Jerry Kruk, Steve Bannatyne, Dick Archer, Bob Chipman

President & Governor	Barry L. Shenkarow
Alternate Governors	Michael A. Smith, Bill Davis
Hockey Operations	
Vice-President & General Manager	Michael A. Smith
Assistant General Manager-Director of Hockey Operations	Dennis McDonald
Coach	John Paddock
Assistant Coaches	Terry Simpson, Glen Williamson, Alpo Suhonen
Moncton Director of Hockey Operations/Coach	Rob Laird
Director of Scouting	Bill Lesuk
Assistant Director of Scouting	Joe Yannetti
Scouts	Tom Savage, Connie Broden, Mike Antonovitch, Larry Hornung, Sean Coady Charlie Burroughs
Executive Ass't to Vice-President & G.M.	Pat MacDonald
Administrative Assistant-Hockey Operations	Laurie Crittenden
Communications	
Director of Communications	Mike O'Hearn
Communications Assistant	Igor Kuperman
Statistician/Communications	Bruce Barton
Director of Community Relations	Lori Summers
Administrative Assistant-Goals For Kids	Michelle McCrea
Administrative Assistant-Community Relations	Sherri Wilson
Finance and Administration	
Director of Finance & Administration	Don Binda
Director of Team Services	Murray Harding
Director of Administrative Services	Glenda Leiske
Director of Ticket Operations	Dianne Gabbs
Accounting Supervisor	Joe Leibfried
Accounting Assistants	Bryan Braun, Doug Bergman
Administrative Assistant-Team Services/ Communications	Heather Reynolds
Administrative Assistant-Novelty Operations	Lynda Sweetland
Jets' All Sports Store Managers	Charles Edwards, Jennifer Zalnasky
Marketing	
Vice-President of Marketing	Madeline Hanson
Marketing Assistant	Val Kuhn
Manager of Ticket Sales	Hartley Miller
Manager of Licensing and Retail Sales	Chris Newman
Director of Corporate Sales	Val Overwater
Senior Account Executive	Gord Dmytriw
Account Executive	Dave Baker
Sales/Licensing Assistant	Marlene Benoit
Sales/Licensing Secretary	Teresa Bastian
Dressing Room	
Athletic Therapist	Jim Ramsay
Athletic Trainer	Phil Walker
Equipment Managers	Craig Heisinger, Stan Wilson
Team Physician	Dr. Brian Lukie
Team Dentist	Dr. Gene Solmundson
Team Information	
Team Colors	Blue, Red and White
Dimensions of Rink	200 feet by 85 feet
Training Camp	Winnipeg
Press Box Location	East Side
TV Channel	CKND
Radio Station	CJOB AM 680
Play-by-Play (Radio)	Curt Keilback

General Manager

MIKE SMITH
General Manager, Winnipeg Jets. Born in Potsdam, New York, August 31, 1945.

Mike Smith was appointed general manager of the club on December 3, 1988 after ten years of service within the Jets organization. He had held the position of assistant general manager and director of scouting since 1984.

Smith began his NHL career in 1976-77 when he was an assistant coach with the New York Rangers under John Ferguson. After two seasons in New York, he assumed the same coaching duties with the Colorado Rockies. When the Jets entered the League in 1979-80, Smith was hired as general manager of their CHL franchise in Tulsa. In 1980-81, midway through the season, Smith was asked to come to Winnipeg to be head coach. In 1981-82 he became the team's director of recruiting.

1991-92 Final Statistics

Standings

Abbreviations: GA – goals against; **GF** – goals for; **GP** – games played; **L** – losses; **PTS** – points; **T** – ties; **W** – wins; **%** – percentage of games won.

CLARENCE CAMPBELL CONFERENCE

Norris Division

	GP	W	L	T	GF	GA	PTS	%
Detroit	80	43	25	12	320	256	98	.613
Chicago	80	36	29	15	257	236	87	.544
St. Louis	80	36	33	11	279	266	83	.519
Minnesota	80	32	42	6	246	278	70	.438
Toronto	80	30	43	7	234	294	67	.419

Smythe Division

	GP	W	L	T	GF	GA	PTS	%
Vancouver	80	42	26	12	285	250	96	.600
Los Angeles	80	35	31	14	287	296	84	.525
Edmonton	80	36	34	10	295	297	82	.513
Winnipeg	80	33	32	15	251	244	81	.506
Calgary	80	31	37	12	296	305	74	.463
San Jose	80	17	58	5	219	359	39	.244

PRINCE OF WALES CONFERENCE

Adams Division

	GP	W	L	T	GF	GA	PTS	%
Montreal	80	41	28	11	267	207	93	.581
Boston	80	36	32	12	270	275	84	.525
Buffalo	80	31	37	12	289	299	74	.463
Hartford	80	26	41	13	247	283	65	.406
Quebec	80	20	48	12	255	318	52	.325

Patrick Division

	GP	W	L	T	GF	GA	PTS	%
NY Rangers	80	50	25	5	321	246	105	.656
Washington	80	45	27	8	330	275	98	.613
Pittsburgh	80	39	32	9	343	308	87	.544
New Jersey	80	38	31	11	289	259	87	.544
NY Islanders	80	34	35	11	291	299	79	.494
Philadelphia	80	32	37	11	252	273	75	.469

Wayne Gretzky, who helped set up 90 goals in 1991-92, led the NHL in assists for the 13th consecutive season.

INDIVIDUAL LEADERS

Goal Scoring

Player	Team	GP	G
Brett Hull	St. L.	73	70
Kevin Stevens	Pit.	80	54
Gary Roberts	Cal.	76	53
Jeremy Roenick	Chi.	80	53
Pat LaFontaine	Buf.	57	46
Steve Yzerman	Det.	79	45
Mario Lemieux	Pit.	64	44
Luc Robitaille	L.A.	80	44
Mark Recchi	Pit.-Phi.	80	43

Assists

Player	Team	GP	A
Wayne Gretzky	L.A.	74	90
Mario Lemieux	Pit.	64	87
Brian Leetch	NYR	80	80
Adam Oates	St. L.-Bos.	80	79
Dale Hawerchuk	Buf.	77	75
Mark Messier	NYR	79	72
Craig Janney	Bos.-St. L.	78	69
Kevin Stevens	Pit.	80	69
Joe Sakic	Que.	69	65

Power-Play Goals

Player	Team	GP	PP
Dave Andreychuk	Buf.	80	28
Luc Robitaille	L.A.	80	26
Pat LaFontaine	Buf.	57	23
Jeremy Roenick	Chi.	80	22
Derek King	NYI	80	21
Brett Hull	St. L.	73	20
Mark Recchi	Pit.-Phi.	80	20
Kevin Stevens	Pit.	80	19

Short-Hand Goals

Player	Team	GP	SH
Steve Yzerman	Det.	79	8
Brett Hull	St. L.	73	5
Mike Ridley	Wsh.	80	5
Mario Lemieux	Pit.	64	4
Ron Sutter	St. L.	68	4
Murray Craven	Phi.-Hfd.	73	4
Kelly Buchberger	Edm.	79	4
Mark Messier	NYR	79	4
Paul Ysebaert	Det.	79	4
Rod Brind'Amour	Phi.	80	4
Adam Graves	NYR	80	4

Game Winning Goals

Player	Team	GP	GW
Jeremy Roenick	Chi.	80	13
Brett Hull	St. L.	73	9
Steve Yzerman	Det.	79	9
Claude Lemieux	N.J.	74	8
Mike Modano	Min.	76	8
Vincent Damphousse	Edm.	80	8
Tony Granato	L.A.	80	8

Game Tying Goals

Player	Team	GP	GT
Claude Lemieux	N.J.	74	3
Gary Roberts	Cgy.	76	3
Vladimir Ruzicka	Bos.	77	3

Shots

Player	Team	GP	S
Brett Hull	St. L.	73	408
Dave Andreychuk	Buf.	80	337
Ray Bourque	Bos.	80	334
Kevin Stevens	Pit.	80	325
Al MacInnis	Cgy.	72	304

First Goals

Player	Team	GP	FG
Brett Hull	St. L.	73	16
Stephen Leach	Bos.	78	11
Kevin Stevens	Pit.	80	10
Pat LaFontaine	Buf.	57	9
Owen Nolan	Que.	75	9

Shooting Percentage

(minimum 80 shots)

Player	Team	GP	G	S	%
Gary Roberts	Cgy.	76	53	196	27.0
Sergei Makarov	Cgy.	68	22	83	26.5
Ray Ferraro	NYI	80	40	154	26.0
Dale Hunter	Wsh.	80	28	110	25.5
Sergei Nemchinov	NYR	73	30	124	24.2

Plus/Minus

Player	Team	GP	+/–
Paul Ysebaert	Det.	79	44
Brad McCrimmon	Det.	79	39
*Nicklas Lidstrom	Det.	80	36
James Patrick	NYR	80	34
Larry Murphy	Pit.	77	33

Individual Leaders

Abbreviations: * – rookie eligible for Calder Trophy; **A** – assists; **G** – goals; **GP** – game-tying goals; **GW** – game-winning goals; **PIM** – penalties in minutes; **PP** – power play goals; **Pts** – points; **S** – shots on goal; **SH** – short-handed goals; **%** – percentage shots resulting in goals; **+/–** – difference between Goals For (**GF**) scored when a player is on the ice with his team at even strength or short-handed and Goals Against (**GA**) scored when the same player is on the ice with his team at even strength or on a power play.

Individual Scoring Leaders for Art Ross Trophy

Player	Team	GP	G	A	Pts	+/–	PIM	PP	SH	GW	GT	S	%
Mario Lemieux	Pittsburgh	64	44	87	131	27	94	12	4	5	1	249	17.7
Kevin Stevens	Pittsburgh	80	54	69	123	8	254	19	0	4	0	325	16.6
Wayne Gretzky	Los Angeles	74	31	90	121	12–	34	12	2	2	1	215	14.4
Brett Hull	St. Louis	73	70	39	109	2–	48	20	5	9	1	408	17.2
Luc Robitaille	Los Angeles	80	44	63	107	4–	95	26	0	6	1	240	18.3
Mark Messier	NY Rangers	79	35	72	107	31	76	12	4	6	0	212	16.5
Jeremy Roenick	Chicago	80	53	50	103	23	98	22	3	13	0	234	22.6
Steve Yzerman	Detroit	79	45	58	103	26	64	9	8	9	0	295	15.3
Brian Leetch	NY Rangers	80	22	80	102	25	26	10	1	3	1	245	9.0
Adam Oates	St. L.-Bos.	80	20	79	99	9–	22	6	0	4	2	191	10.5
Dale Hawerchuk	Buffalo	77	23	75	98	22–	27	13	0	4	0	242	9.5
Mark Recchi	Pit.-Phi.	80	43	54	97	21–	96	20	1	5	1	210	20.5
Pierre Turgeon	Buf.-NYI	77	40	55	95	7	20	13	0	6	0	207	19.3
Joe Sakic	Quebec	69	29	65	94	5	20	6	3	1	1	217	13.4
Pat Lafontaine	Buffalo	57	46	47	93	10	98	23	0	5	1	203	22.7
Dave Andreychuk	Buffalo	80	41	50	91	9–	71	28	0	2	2	337	12.2
Gary Roberts	Calgary	76	53	37	90	32	207	15	0	2	3	196	27.0
Vincent Damphousse	Edmonton	80	38	51	89	10	53	12	1	8	1	247	15.4
Joe Mullen	Pittsburgh	77	42	45	87	12	30	14	0	4	1	226	18.6
Doug Gilmour	Cgy.-Tor.	78	26	61	87	25	78	10	1	4	1	168	15.5
Craig Janney	Bos.-St. L.	78	18	69	87	6	22	6	0	2	0	127	14.2
Sergei Fedorov	Detroit	80	32	54	86	26	72	7	2	5	0	249	12.9
Phil Housley	Winnipeg	74	23	63	86	5–	92	11	0	4	1	234	9.8
Alexander Mogilny	Buffalo	67	39	45	84	7	73	15	0	2	0	236	16.5
Joe Murphy	Edmonton	80	35	47	82	17	52	10	2	2	2	193	18.1

Defencemen Scoring Leaders

Player	Team	GP	G	A	Pts	+/–	PIM	PP	SH	GW	GT	S	%
Brian Leetch	NY Rangers	80	22	80	102	25	26	10	1	3	1	245	9.0
Phil Housley	Winnipeg	74	23	63	86	5–	92	11	0	4	1	234	9.8
Ray Bourque	Boston	80	21	60	81	11	56	7	1	2	0	334	6.3
Larry Murphy	Pittsburgh	77	21	56	77	33	48	7	2	3	0	206	10.2
Al Macinnis	Calgary	72	20	57	77	13	83	11	0	0	1	304	6.6
James Patrick	NY Rangers	80	14	57	71	34	54	6	0	1	0	148	9.5
Paul Coffey	Pit.-L.A.	64	11	58	69	1	87	5	0	1	0	232	4.7
Fredrik Olausson	Winnipeg	77	20	42	62	31–	34	13	1	2	0	227	8.8
*Nicklas Lidstrom	Detroit	80	11	49	60	36	22	5	0	1	1	168	6.5
Jeff Brown	St. Louis	80	20	39	59	8	38	10	0	2	1	214	9.3
Scott Stevens	New Jersey	68	17	42	59	24	124	7	1	2	0	156	10.9

CONSECUTIVE SCORING STREAKS

Goals

Games	Player	Team	G
10	Brett Hull	St. Louis	14
9	Steve Yzerman	Detroit	14
6	Pat Lafontaine	Buffalo	10
6	Mario Lemieux	Pittsburgh	8
6	Mike Modano	Minnesota	7
6	Dimitri Khristich	Washington	6
6	Sergei Makarov	Calgary	6
6	Sergei Nemchinov	NY Rangers	6

Assists

Games	Player	Team	A
15	Brian Leetch	NY Rangers	23
12	Joe Sakic	Quebec	16
10	Mario Lemieux	Pittsburgh	21
10	Craig Janney	Bos.-St. L.	17
9	Tom Kurvers	NY Islanders	16
9	Mario Lemieux	Pittsburgh	16
9	Brian Leetch	NY Rangers	13
9	Larry Murphy	Pittsburgh	10

Points

Games	Player	Team	G	A	Pts
25	Brett Hull	St. Louis	31	15	46
18	Pierre Turgeon	Buf.-NYI	17	17	34
17	Dave Andreychuk	Buffalo	11	25	36
17	Brian Leetch	NY Rangers	5	24	29
16	Gary Roberts	Calgary	17	10	27
16	Derek King	NY Islanders	10	15	25

Dave Andreychuk had his finest season in 1991-92, leading the league with 28 power-play goals

Steve Yzerman victimized the opposition for a league-leading eight shorthanded goals in 1991-92.

Kevin Todd, far left, finished second among first-year scorers in 1991-92 with 63 points. Tony Amonte, left, led all rookie scorers in goals (35), points (69) and powerplay goals (9) in 1991-92.

Individual Rookie Scoring Leaders

Rookie	Team	GP	G	A	Pts	+/–	PIM	PP	SH	GW	GT	S	%
Tony Amonte	NY Rangers	79	35	34	69	12	55	9	0	4	0	234	15.0
Kevin Todd	New Jersey	80	21	42	63	8	69	2	0	2	1	131	16.0
Pavel Bure	Vancouver	65	34	26	60	0	30	7	3	6	0	268	12.7
Nicklas Lidstrom	Detroit	80	11	49	60	36	22	5	0	1	1	168	6.5
Pat Falloon	San Jose	79	25	34	59	32–	16	5	0	1	2	181	13.8
Nelson Emerson	St. Louis	79	23	36	59	5–	66	3	0	2	0	143	16.1
Donald Audette	Buffalo	63	31	17	48	1–	75	5	0	6	1	153	20.3
Luciano Borsato	Winnipeg	56	15	21	36	6–	45	5	0	1	0	81	18.5
Gilbert Dionne	Montreal	39	21	13	34	7	10	7	0	2	0	90	23.3
Vlad. Konstantinov	Detroit	79	8	26	34	25	172	1	0	2	0	108	7.4

Goal Scoring

Name	Team	GP	G
Tony Amonte	NY Rangers	79	35
Pavel Bure	Vancouver	65	34
Donald Audette	Buffalo	63	31
Pat Falloon	San Jose	79	25
Nelson Emerson	St. Louis	79	23
Gilbert Dionne	Montreal	39	21
Kevin Todd	New Jersey	80	21
Luciano Borsato	Winnipeg	56	15
Rob Pearson	Toronto	47	14
Valeri Zelepukin	New Jersey	44	13
Geoff Sanderson	Hartford	64	13
Claude Lapointe	Quebec	78	13

Assists

Name	Team	GP	A
Nicklas Lidstrom	Detroit	80	49
Kevin Todd	New Jersey	80	42
Nelson Emerson	St. Louis	79	36
Tony Amonte	NY Rangers	79	34
Pat Falloon	San Jose	79	34
Pavel Bure	Vancouver	65	26
Vlad. Konstantinov	Detroit	79	26
David Williams	San Jose	56	25
Doug Weight	NY Rangers	53	22
Luciano Borsato	Winnipeg	56	21

Power Play Goals

Name	Team	GP	PP
Tony Amonte	NY Rangers	79	9
Gilbert Dionne	Montreal	39	7
Pavel Bure	Vancouver	65	7
Rob Pearson	Toronto	47	6
Luciano Borsato	Winnipeg	56	5
Donald Audette	Buffalo	63	5
Pat Falloon	San Jose	79	5
Nicklas Lidstrom	Detroit	80	5

Short Hand Goals

Name	Team	GP	SH
Pavel Bure	Vancouver	65	3
Claude Lapointe	Quebec	78	2

Game Winning Goals

Name	Team	GP	GW
Donald Audette	Buffalo	63	6
Pavel Bure	Vancouver	65	6
Tony Amonte	NY Rangers	79	4
Valeri Zelepukin	New Jersey	44	3
Brad May	Buffalo	69	3
Peter Ahola	Los Angeles	71	1
Kevin Todd	New Jersey	80	1
Nicklas Lidstrom	Detroit	80	1

Game Tying Goals

Name	Team	GP	GT
Pat Falloon	San Jose	79	2
Scott Lachance	NY Islanders	17	1
Adam Foote	Quebec	46	1
Rob Pearson	Toronto	47	1
Donald Audette	Buffalo	63	1

Shots

Name	Team	GP	S
Pavel Bure	Vancouver	65	268
Tony Amonte	NY Rangers	79	234
Pat Falloon	San Jose	79	181
Nicklas Lidstrom	Detroit	80	168
Donald Audette	Buffalo	63	153

First Goals

Name	Team	GP	FG
Gilbert Dionne	Montreal	39	4
Rob Pearson	Toronto	47	4
Luciano Borsato	Winnipeg	56	3
Geoff Sanderson	Hartford	64	3
Pat Falloon	San Jose	79	3

Shooting Percentage

(minimum 80 shots)

Name	Team	GP	G	S	%
Gilbert Dionne	Montreal	39	21	90	23.3
Donald Audette	Buffalo	63	31	153	20.3
Luciano Borsato	Winnipeg	56	15	81	18.5
Nelson Emerson	St. Louis	79	23	143	16.1
Kevin Todd	New Jersey	80	21	131	16.0

Plus/Minus

Name	Team	GP	+/–
Nicklas Lidstrom	Detroit	80	36
Vlad. Konstantinov	Detroit	79	25
Peter Ahola	Los Angeles	71	12
Tony Amonte	NY Rangers	79	12
Kevin Todd	New Jersey	80	8

Three-or-More-Goal Games

Player	Team	Date	Final Score				G
Greg Adams	Vancouver	Dec. 4	Van	3	Mtl	0	3
Glenn Anderson	Toronto	Mar. 17	Que	3	Tor	4	3
Dave Andreychuk	Buffalo	Nov. 23	Buf	4	Bos	7	3
Dave Andreychuk	Buffalo	Mar. 19	Buf	8	L.A.	2	4
Dave Babych	Vancouver	Nov. 22	Cgy	5	Van	6	3
Brian Bellows	Minnesota	Nov. 6	Min	3	Tor	4	3
Brian Bellows	Minnesota	Dec. 31	Chi	2	Min	6	4
Paul Broten	NY Rangers	Mar. 1	Hfd	4	NYR	9	3
Mike Bullard	Toronto	Oct. 26	Det	1	Tor	6	3
Jimmy Carson	Detroit	Feb. 15	S.J.	1	Det	11	3
Wendel Clark	Toronto	Oct. 5	Det	5	Tor	8	3
Wendel Clark	Toronto	Jan. 11	Tor	4	N.J.	3	3
Murray Craven	Hartford	Dec. 7	Buf	6	Hfd	6	3
John Cullen	Hartford	Feb. 4	Hfd	5	S.J.	6	3
Vincent Damphousse	Edmonton	Dec. 14	Wpg	5	Edm	7	4
John Druce	Washington	Feb. 9	S.J.	2	Wsh	6	3
Steve Duchesne	Philadelphia	Dec. 19	NYI	2	Phi	6	3
Bob Errey	Pittsburgh	Oct. 17	NYI	5	Pit	8	3
Ray Ferraro	NY Islanders	Dec. 10	St. L.	7	NYI	7	3
Ray Ferraro	NY Islanders	Jan. 7	NYI	5	Det	2	4
Mike Gartner	NY Rangers	Mar. 11	Chi	1	NYR	7	3
Brent Gilchrist	Montreal	Feb. 17	Min	0	Mtl	8	3
Tony Granato	Los Angeles	Feb. 27	Que	2	L.A.	4	3
Adam Graves	NY Rangers	Feb. 14	NYI	2	NYR	9	3
Wayne Gretzky	Los Angeles	Nov. 23	S.J.	4	L.A.	6	3
Dale Hawerchuk	Buffalo	Feb. 14	S.J.	6	Buf	7	3
Brett Hull	St Louis	Nov. 9	Hfd	4	St. L.	3	3
Brett Hull	St Louis	Nov. 30	Det	3	St. L.	7	3
Brett Hull	St Louis	Dec. 10	St. L.	7	NYI	7	3
Brett Hull	St Louis	Dec. 21	NYI	2	St. L.	6	3
Brett Hull	St Louis	Jan. 8	St. L.	5	NYR	3	3
Brett Hull	St Louis	Jan. 16	Mtl	6	St. L.	6	3
Brett Hull	St Louis	Feb. 27	Wsh	3	St. L.	7	3
Brett Hull	St Louis	Mar. 2	St. L.	5	Van	3	3
Dale Hunter	Washington	Mar. 20	Phi	7	Wsh	6	3
Craig Janney	St Louis	Feb. 15	Cgy	2	St. L.	7	3
Derek King	NY Islanders	Oct. 15	Pit	7	NYI	6	3
Derek King	NY Islanders	Jan. 1	NYI	5	Wsh	8	3
Bob Kudelski	Los Angeles	Oct. 16	S.J.	5	L.A.	8	3
Jari Kurri	Los Angeles	Oct. 4	L.A.	6	Wpg	3	3
Pat Lafontaine	Buffalo	Nov. 12	Buf	7	S.J.	1	3
Pat Lafontaine	Buffalo	Jan. 10	Edm	2	Buf	8	3
Pat Lafontaine	Buffalo	Jan. 25	Buf	4	Mtl	3	3
Pat Lafontaine	Buffalo	Mar. 6	N.J.	4	Buf	5	3
Igor Larionov	Vancouver	Nov. 3	Edm	2	Van	7	3
Igor Larionov	Vancouver	Dec. 28	Van	3	S.J.	2	3
Steve Larmer	Chicago	Oct. 10	Van	6	Chi	7	3
Steve Larmer	Chicago	Dec. 8	Min	2	Chi	7	3
Stephan Lebeau	Montreal	Feb. 12	S.J.	1	Mtl	6	3
Mario Lemieux	Pittsburgh	Oct. 15	Pit	7	NYI	6	3
Al Macinnis	Calgary	Mar. 16	Hfd	4	Cgy	3	3
David Maley	New Jersey	Oct. 18	N.J.	5	Wsh	6	3
Mark Messier	NY Rangers	Nov. 19	NYR	4	Van	3	3
Mark Messier	NY Rangers	Dec. 13	NYR	5	Wsh	3	3
Mark Messier	NY Rangers	Mar. 22	N.J.	3	NYR	6	4
Kevin Miller	Detroit	Feb. 12	Det	9	Buf	4	3
Alexander Mogilny	Buffalo	Jan. 3	NYI	2	Buf	5	3
Kirk Muller	Montreal	Nov. 29	Mtl	4	Bos	5	3
Kirk Muller	Montreal	Jan. 16	Mtl	6	St. L.	6	3
Joe Mullen	Pittsburgh	Dec. 23	Pit	6	NYI	3	4
Joe Mullen	Pittsburgh	Dec. 26	Tor	1	Pit	12	4
Joe Mullen	Pittsburgh	Feb. 18	Tor	1	Pit	7	3
Joe Murphy	Edmonton	Jan. 13	Edm	7	Min	4	3
Brian Noonan	Chicago	Dec. 5	L.A.	2	Chi	6	3
Brian Noonan	Chicago	Dec. 27	Wpg	3	Chi	3	3
Brian Noonan	Chicago	Dec. 29	Det	6	Chi	4	4
Owen Nolan	Quebec	Oct. 12	Buf	5	Que	4	3
Owen Nolan	Quebec	Oct. 29	Wpg	2	Que	7	3
Michal Pivonka	Washington	Dec. 26	NYR	8	Wsh	6	3
Paul Ranheim	Calgary	Nov. 22	Cgy	5	Van	6	3
Mark Recchi	Pittsburgh	Nov. 18	Pit	7	Que	3	3
Stephane Richer	New Jersey	Nov. 20	Wsh	5	N.J.	6	3
Gary Roberts	Calgary	Oct. 10	Cgy	7	L.A.	1	3
Gary Roberts	Calgary	Mar. 26	L.A.	2	Cgy	7	3
Luc Robitaille	Los Angeles	Feb. 6	Hfd	5	L.A.	5	4
Jeremy Roenick	Chicago	Dec. 7	Chi	5	NYI	2	4
Vladimir Ruzicka	Boston	Nov. 5	Bos	5	Pit	5	3
Vladimir Ruzicka	Boston	Feb. 9	Pit	3	Bos	6	4
Joe Sakic	Quebec	Apr. 14	Buf	3	Que	7	4
Denis Savard	Montreal	Feb. 10	Van	3	Mtl	8	3
Ray Sheppard	Detroit	Nov. 12	Det	5	Cgy	4	3
Peter Stastny	New Jersey	Dec. 29	Wsh	4	N.J.	3	3
Ronnie Stern	Calgary	Feb. 19	Bos	4	Cgy	6	3
Kevin Stevens	Pittsburgh	Nov. 13	Edm	4	Pit	5	3
Kevin Stevens	Pittsburgh	Nov. 18	Pit	7	Que	3	3
Kevin Stevens	Pittsburgh	Nov. 29	Pit	9	Phi	3	4
Kevin Stevens	Pittsburgh	Dec. 5	Pit	8	S.J.	0	3
Mats Sundin	Quebec	Mar. 5	Que	10	Hfd	4	5
Tony Tanti	Buffalo	Dec. 20	Edm	4	Buf	4	3
Steve Thomas	NY Islanders	Apr. 15	N.J.	0	NYI	7	4
Rick Tocchet	Pittsburgh	Mar. 6	Pit	7	S.J.	3	3
Pierre Turgeon	NY Islanders	Nov. 30	Wsh	1	NYI	8	3
Pierre Turgeon	NY Islanders	Feb. 20	NYR	2	NYI	6	3
Darren Turcotte	NY Rangers	Apr. 16	Pit	1	NYR	7	3
Paul Ysebaert	Detroit	Jan. 3	Tor	4	Det	6	3
Steve Yzerman	Detroit	Dec. 3	Cgy	2	Det	5	3
Steve Yzerman	Detroit	Jan. 29	Buf	4	Det	4	3
Steve Yzerman	Detroit	Apr. 14	Det	7	Min	4	3
*Tony Amonte	NY Rangers	Mar. 14	NYR	6	St. L.	0	3
*Stu Barnes	Winnipeg	Nov. 11	L.A.	2	Wpg	6	3
*Gilbert Dionne	Montreal	Feb. 26	Mtl	4	Min	1	3

NOTE: 101 Three-or-more-goal games recorderd in 1991-92.

Wendel Clark, below, became the first Leaf in two years to record a hat-trick, notching three goals on October 5, 1991. Tim Cheveldae, right, set a Detroit Red Wings' team record by appearing in 72 games during the 1991-92 campaign.

Goaltending Leaders

Minimum 25 games

Goals Against Average

Goaltender	Team	GPI	Mins	Ga	Avg
Patrick Roy	Montreal	67	3935	155	2.36
Ed Belfour	Chicago	52	2928	132	2.70
Kirk Mclean	Vancouver	65	3852	176	2.74
John Vanbiesbrouck	NY Rangers	45	2526	120	2.85
Bob Essensa	Winnipeg	47	2627	126	2.88

Wins

Goaltender	Team	GPI	MINS	W	L	T
Kirk Mclean	Vancouver	65	3852	38	17	9
Tim Cheveldae	Detroit	72	4236	38	23	9
Patrick Roy	Montreal	67	3935	36	22	8
Don Beaupre	Washington	54	3108	29	17	6
Andy Moog	Boston	62	3640	28	22	9

Save Percentage

Goaltender	Team	GPI	MINS	GA	SA	S%	W	L	T
Patrick Roy	Montreal	67	3935	155	1806	.914	36	22	8
Curtis Joseph	St Louis	60	3494	175	1953	.910	27	20	10
Bob Essensa	Winnipeg	47	2627	126	1407	.910	21	17	6
John Vanbiesbrouck	NY Rangers	45	2526	120	1331	.910	27	13	3
Kirk McLean	Vancouver	65	3852	176	1780	.901	38	17	9
Mike Richter	NY Rangers	41	2298	119	1205	.901	23	12	2
Mark Fitzpatrick	NY Islanders	30	1743	93	949	.901	11	13	5

Shutouts

Goaltender	Team	GPI	MINS	SO	W	L	T
Bob Essensa	Winnipeg	47	2627	5	21	17	6
Ed Belfour	Chicago	52	2928	5	21	18	10
Kirk McLean	Vancouver	65	3852	5	38	17	9
Patrick Roy	Montreal	67	3935	5	36	22	8
Mike Richter	NY Rangers	41	2298	3	23	12	2
Kay Whitmore	Hartford	45	2567	3	14	21	6
Ron Hextall	Philadelphia	45	2668	3	16	21	6

Team-by-Team Point Totals

1987-88 to 1991-92

(Ranked by five-year average)

	91-92	90-91	89-90	88-89	87-88	Average
Calgary	74	100	99	117	105	**99.0**
Montreal	93	89	93	115	103	**98.6**
Boston	84	100	101	88	94	**93.4**
NY Rangers	105	85	85	82	82	**87.8**
Edmonton	82	80	90	84	99	**87.0**
Washington	98	81	78	92	85	**86.8**
St. Louis	83	105	83	78	76	**85.0**
Buffalo	74	81	98	83	85	**84.2**
Los Angeles	84	102	75	91	68	**84.0**
Detroit	98	76	70	80	93	**83.4**
Chicago	87	106	88	66	69	**83.2**
Pittsburgh	87	88	72	87	81	**83.0**
New Jersey	87	79	83	66	82	**79.4**
Philadelphia	75	76	71	80	85	**77.4**
Hartford	65	73	85	79	77	**75.8**
Winnipeg	81	63	85	64	77	**74.0**
NY Islanders	79	60	73	61	88	**72.2**
Vancouver	96	65	64	74	59	**71.6**
Minnesota	70	68	76	70	51	**67.0**
Toronto	67	57	80	62	52	**63.6**
Quebec	52	46	31	61	69	**51.8**
San Jose	39	–	–	–	–	**39.0**

Team Record When Scoring First Goal of a Game

Team	GP	FG	W	L	T
Boston	80	41	28	9	4
Buffalo	80	39	19	15	5
Calgary	80	33	19	8	6
Chicago	80	50	28	12	10
Detroit	80	46	31	7	8
Edmonton	80	42	27	11	4
Hartford	80	34	18	9	7
Los Angeles	80	37	19	11	7
Minnesota	80	38	22	13	3
Montreal	80	55	34	11	10
New Jersey	80	38	27	7	4
NY Islanders	80	34	22	7	5
NY Rangers	80	47	31	12	4
Philadelphia	80	40	21	12	7
Pittsburgh	80	48	30	14	4
Quebec	80	33	14	15	4
San Jose	80	29	11	15	3
St. Louis	80	31	21	9	1
Toronto	80	41	23	15	3
Vancouver	80	36	27	5	4
Washington	80	41	27	10	4
Winnipeg	80	47	26	11	10

Team Plus/Minus Differential

Team	GF	PPGF	Net GF	GA	PPGA	Net GA	Goal Differential
Detroit	320	72	**248**	256	78	**178**	+ 70
NY Rangers	321	81	**240**	246	60	**186**	+ 54
Montreal	267	74	**193**	207	60	**147**	+ 46
New Jersey	289	59	**230**	259	68	**191**	+ 39
Vancouver	285	85	**200**	250	76	**174**	+ 26
Washington	330	92	**238**	275	60	**215**	+ 23
Edmonton	295	68	**227**	297	93	**204**	+ 23
Pittsburgh	343	92	**251**	308	77	**231**	+ 20
Chicago	257	81	**176**	236	76	**160**	+ 16
Calgary	296	87	**209**	305	107	**198**	+ 11
St. Louis	279	69	**210**	266	64	**202**	+ 8
NY Islanders	291	75	**216**	299	90	**209**	+ 7
Boston	270	77	**193**	275	72	**203**	– 10
Los Angeles	287	79	**208**	296	76	**220**	– 12
Philadelphia	252	68	**184**	273	76	**197**	– 13
Winnipeg	251	91	**160**	244	68	**176**	– 16
Hartford	247	73	**174**	283	86	**197**	– 23
Buffalo	289	105	**184**	299	91	**208**	– 24
Minnesota	246	76	**170**	278	77	**201**	– 31
Quebec	255	66	**189**	318	87	**231**	– 42
Toronto	234	66	**168**	294	69	**225**	– 57
San Jose	219	64	**155**	359	89	**270**	–115

Team Record when Leading, Trailing, Tied

Team	Leading after 1 period			Leading after 2 periods			Trailing after 1 period			Trailing after 2 periods			Tied after 1 period			Tied after 2 periods		
	W	L	T	W	L	T	W	L	T	W	L	T	W	L	T	W	L	T
Boston	21	4	4	30	5	3	3	21	5	2	25	6	12	7	3	4	2	3
Buffalo	17	5	3	21	3	1	6	17	6	7	30	8	8	15	3	3	4	3
Calgary	16	5	3	21	1	5	5	24	4	1	30	2	10	8	5	9	6	5
Chicago	23	5	5	28	3	5	6	16	2	2	23	4	7	8	8	6	3	6
Detroit	27	7	3	35	2	0	6	13	5	2	15	5	10	5	4	6	8	7
Edmonton	23	6	3	27	4	5	6	18	4	4	26	2	7	10	3	5	4	3
Hartford	11	6	6	20	5	5	4	24	4	2	31	4	11	11	3	4	5	4
Los Angeles	21	9	8	28	2	7	7	14	3	3	24	3	7	8	3	4	5	4
Minnesota	19	3	1	27	5	2	6	25	3	1	34	1	7	14	2	4	3	3
Montreal	26	4	6	28	4	4	5	14	2	4	21	3	10	10	3	9	3	4
New Jersey	23	4	2	33	4	4	2	21	2	0	22	2	13	6	7	5	5	5
NY Islanders	21	5	3	25	3	5	3	23	3	3	23	3	10	7	5	6	9	3
NY Rangers	27	8	2	35	5	2	9	12	1	6	18	2	14	5	2	9	2	1
Philadelphia	22	4	5	24	2	3	3	16	2	4	29	2	7	17	4	4	6	6
Pittsburgh	26	6	2	27	2	3	5	20	4	8	23	3	8	6	3	4	7	3
Quebec	12	7	1	19	4	4	2	27	6	0	31	3	6	14	5	1	13	5
San Jose	7	9	2	10	4	2	3	35	2	1	44	3	7	14	1	6	10	0
St. Louis	17	5	0	31	3	1	8	18	5	2	26	6	11	10	6	3	4	4
Toronto	19	5	0	20	3	0	5	26	2	5	28	4	6	12	5	5	12	3
Vancouver	18	3	6	26	1	5	9	16	3	3	21	1	15	7	3	13	4	6
Washington	23	3	3	29	4	2	12	18	3	7	20	3	10	6	2	9	3	3
Winnipeg	17	5	6	24	2	5	3	18	3	4	24	3	13	9	6	5	6	7

Team Statistics

TEAMS' HOME-AND-ROAD RECORD

Norris Division

	Home								Road							
	GP	W	L	T	GF	GA	PTS	%	GP	W	L	T	GF	GA	PTS	%
DET	40	24	12	4	169	123	52	.650	40	19	13	8	151	133	46	.575
CHI	40	23	9	8	156	110	54	.675	40	13	20	7	101	126	33	.413
STL	40	25	12	3	160	114	53	.663	40	11	21	8	119	152	30	.375
MIN	40	20	16	4	135	116	44	.550	40	12	26	2	111	162	26	.325
TOR	40	21	16	3	146	136	45	.563	40	9	27	4	88	158	22	.275
Total	**200**	**113**	**65**	**22**	**766**	**599**	**248**	**.620**	**200**	**64**	**107**	**29**	**570**	**731**	**157**	**.393**

Smythe Division

	GP	W	L	T	GF	GA	PTS	%	GP	W	L	T	GF	GA	PTS	%
VAN	40	23	10	7	158	116	53	.663	40	19	16	5	127	134	43	.538
L.A	40	20	11	9	150	129	49	.613	40	15	20	5	137	167	35	.438
EDM	40	22	13	5	151	121	49	.613	40	14	21	5	144	176	33	.413
WPG	40	20	14	6	145	119	46	.575	40	13	18	9	106	125	35	.438
CGY	40	19	14	7	174	140	45	.563	40	12	23	5	122	165	29	.363
S.J	40	14	23	3	119	141	31	.388	40	3	35	2	100	218	8	.100
Total	**240**	**118**	**85**	**37**	**897**	**766**	**273**	**.569**	**240**	**76**	**133**	**31**	**736**	**985**	**183**	**.381**

Adams Division

	GP	W	L	T	GF	GA	PTS	%	GP	W	L	T	GF	GA	PTS	%
MTL	40	27	8	5	149	89	59	.738	40	14	20	6	118	118	34	.425
BOS	40	23	11	6	148	122	52	.650	40	13	21	6	122	153	32	.400
BUF	40	22	13	5	158	133	49	.613	40	9	24	7	131	166	25	.313
HFD	40	13	17	10	120	126	36	.450	40	13	24	3	127	157	29	.363
QUE	40	18	19	3	138	142	39	.488	40	2	29	9	117	176	13	.163
Total	**200**	**103**	**68**	**29**	**713**	**612**	**235**	**.588**	**200**	**51**	**118**	**31**	**615**	**770**	**133**	**.333**

Patrick Division

	GP	W	L	T	GF	GA	PTS	%	GP	W	L	T	GF	GA	PTS	%
NYR	40	28	8	4	170	106	60	.750	40	22	17	1	151	140	45	.563
WSH	40	25	12	3	171	137	53	.663	40	20	15	5	159	138	45	.563
PIT	40	21	13	6	192	154	48	.600	40	18	19	3	151	154	39	.488
N.J	40	24	12	4	155	115	52	.650	40	14	19	7	134	144	35	.438
NYI	40	20	15	5	164	140	45	.563	40	14	20	6	127	159	34	.425
PHI	40	22	11	7	144	122	51	.638	40	10	26	4	108	151	24	.300
Total	**240**	**140**	**71**	**29**	**996**	**774**	**309**	**.644**	**240**	**98**	**116**	**26**	**830**	**886**	**222**	**.463**
Total	**880**	**474**	**289**	**117**	**3372**	**2751**	**1065**	**.605**	**880**	**289**	**474**	**117**	**2751**	**3372**	**695**	**.395**

TEAMS' DIVISIONAL RECORD

Norris Division

	Against Own Division								Against Other Divisions							
	GP	W	L	T	GF	GA	PTS	%	GP	W	L	T	GF	GA	PTS	%
DET	32	19	10	3	130	107	41	.641	48	24	15	9	190	149	57	.594
CHI	32	15	12	5	103	84	35	.547	48	21	17	10	154	152	52	.542
STL	32	11	17	4	100	112	26	.406	48	25	16	7	179	154	57	.594
MIN	32	12	16	4	97	111	28	.438	48	20	26	2	149	167	42	.438
TOR	32	14	16	2	87	103	30	.469	48	16	27	5	147	191	37	.385
Total	**160**	**71**	**71**	**18**	**517**	**517**	**160**	**.500**	**240**	**106**	**101**	**33**	**819**	**813**	**245**	**.510**

Smythe Division

	GP	W	L	T	GF	GA	PTS	%	GP	W	L	T	GF	GA	PTS	%
VAN	35	20	10	5	133	111	45	.643	45	22	16	7	152	139	51	.567
L.A.	35	16	13	6	136	137	38	.543	45	19	18	8	151	159	46	.511
EDM	35	15	14	6	132	139	36	.514	45	21	20	4	163	158	46	.511
WPG	35	15	14	6	133	116	36	.514	45	18	18	9	118	128	45	.500
CGY	35	16	15	4	140	131	36	.514	45	15	22	8	156	174	38	.422
S.J.	35	8	24	3	102	142	19	.271	45	9	34	2	117	217	20	.222
Total	**210**	**90**	**90**	**30**	**776**	**776**	**210**	**.500**	**270**	**104**	**128**	**38**	**857**	**975**	**246**	**.456**

Adams Division

	GP	W	L	T	GF	GA	PTS	%	GP	W	L	T	GF	GA	PTS	%
MTL	32	16	10	6	106	82	38	.594	48	25	18	5	161	125	55	.573
BOS	32	16	10	6	108	112	38	.594	48	20	22	6	162	163	46	.479
BUF	32	12	14	6	110	120	30	.469	48	19	23	6	179	179	44	.458
HFD	32	10	16	6	101	108	26	.406	48	16	25	7	146	175	39	.406
QUE	32	11	15	6	110	113	28	.438	48	9	33	6	145	205	24	.250
Total	**160**	**65**	**65**	**30**	**535**	**535**	**160**	**.500**	**240**	**89**	**121**	**30**	**793**	**847**	**208**	**.433**

Patrick Division

	GP	W	L	T	GF	GA	PTS	%	GP	W	L	T	GF	GA	PTS	%
NYR	35	19	15	1	138	123	39	.557	45	31	10	4	183	123	66	.733
WSH	35	22	12	1	157	121	45	.643	45	23	15	7	173	154	53	.589
PIT	35	16	16	3	141	148	35	.500	45	23	16	6	202	160	52	.578
N.J	35	14	16	5	120	126	33	.471	45	24	15	6	169	133	54	.600
NYI	35	13	15	7	130	137	33	.471	45	21	20	4	161	162	46	.511
PHI	35	10	20	5	113	144	25	.357	45	22	17	6	139	129	50	.556
Total	**210**	**94**	**94**	**22**	**799**	**799**	**210**	**.500**	**270**	**144**	**93**	**33**	**1027**	**861**	**321**	**.594**

TEAM STREAKS

Consecutive Wins

Games	Team	From	To
9	Montreal	Oct. 19	Nov. 6
8	Los Angeles	Feb. 23	Mar. 9
7	NY Rangers	Dec. 13	Dec. 26
6	NY Rangers	Oct. 23	Nov. 4
6	Edmonton	Jan. 31	Feb. 13
6	New Jersey	Feb. 8	Feb. 18
6	Detroit	Feb. 12	Feb. 23

Consecutive Home Wins

Games	Team	From	To
9	Detroit	Nov. 7	Dec. 12
9	Buffalo	Dec. 27	Feb. 4
9	Pittsburgh	Feb. 29	Apr. 15
8	Los Angeles	Feb. 15	Mar. 17
7	Montreal	Oct. 16	Nov. 9
7	St Louis	Nov. 28	Jan. 2
7	Montreal	Dec. 7	Jan. 11

Consecutive Road Wins

Games	Team	From	To
5	Washington	Oct. 29	Nov. 13
5	Pittsburgh	Dec. 13	Dec. 29
5	Vancouver	Jan. 14	Jan. 25
4	Washington	Oct. 9	Oct. 23
4	Montreal	Oct. 19	Nov. 6
4	NY Rangers	Dec. 13	Dec. 26
4	Detroit	Dec. 21	Jan. 4
4	New Jersey	Dec. 31	Jan. 31
4	NY Rangers	Jan. 23	Feb. 1

Consecutive Undefeated

Games	Team	W	T	From	To
11	Winnipeg	8	3	Nov. 16	Dec. 10
10	Detroit	8	2	Nov. 7	Nov. 25
9	Montreal	9	0	Oct. 19	Nov. 6
9	Vancouver	5	4	Dec. 12	Jan. 3
9	Montreal	5	4	Feb. 10	Feb. 28

Consecutive Home Undefeated

Games	Team	W	T	From	To
13	Chicago	9	4	Jan. 5	Mar. 10
12	Chicago	9	3	Oct. 31	Dec. 27
11	Buffalo	9	2	Dec. 18	Feb. 4
11	NY Rangers	9	2	Jan. 14	Mar. 1
10	Montreal	8	2	Feb. 1	Mar. 14

Consecutive Road Undefeated

Games	Team	W	T	From	To
6	Vancouver	4	2	Feb. 17	Mar. 14
5	St Louis	2	3	Oct. 20	Nov. 3
5	Los Angeles	4	1	Oct. 26	Nov. 2
5	Washington	5	0	Oct. 29	Nov. 13
5	Detroit	3	2	Nov. 8	Nov. 23
5	Winnipeg	3	2	Nov. 16	Dec. 10
5	Toronto	3	2	Nov. 22	Dec. 12
5	Pittsburgh	5	0	Dec. 13	Dec. 29
5	New Jersey	4	1	Dec. 26	Jan. 31
5	Vancouver	5	0	Jan. 14	Jan. 25
5	Boston	3	2	Jan. 15	Feb. 4
5	NY Rangers	4	1	Jan. 22	Feb. 1

U.S. and Canadian Olympic 1991-92 Series Results

Each National Hockey League club played a mid-season exhibition game against either the U.S. or Canadian Olympic team in 1991-92. Team USA played 15 games, one in each U.S. NHL city. The Canadian National Team played 7 games, one in each Canadian NHL city. All games were completed before the start of the 1992 Winter Olympics. NHL clubs finished with a combined record of 11–4–7.

Date	Team	Score		NHL Team	Score
Oct. 7/91	Team USA	6	at	Minnesota	3
Oct. 23	Team USA	1	at	Buffalo	4
Oct. 24	Team USA	0	at	NY Islanders	3
Nov. 6	Team USA	4	at	New Jersey	5
Nov. 10	Team USA	1	at	Philadelphia	1
Nov. 11	Team USA	3	at	Boston	6
Nov. 17	Team USA	6	at	San Jose	2
Nov. 20	Team USA	4	at	Hartford	5(OT)
Nov. 21	Canadian National Team	2	at	Edmonton	4
Nov. 24	Canadian National Team	5	at	Vancouver	2
Nov. 25	Team USA	4	at	St. Louis	6
Dec. 1	Team USA	4	at	Detroit	4
Dec. 4	Team USA	3	at	NY Rangers	7
Dec. 8	Canadian National Team	3	at	Quebec	1
Dec. 10	Team USA	0	at	Los Angeles	5
Dec. 10	Canadian National Team	3	at	Montreal	3
Dec. 12	Team USA	3	at	Chicago	8
Dec. 12	Canadian National Team	4	at	Calgary	2
Jan. 14/92	Canadian National Team	5	at	Toronto	5
Jan. 16	Canadian National Team	4	at	Winnipeg	0
Jan. 21	Team USA	6	at	Pittsburgh	8
Jan. 22	Team USA	5	at	Washington	3

TEAM PENALTIES

Abbreviations: GP – games played; **PEN** – total penalty minutes including bench minutes; **BMI** – total bench minor minutes; **AVG** – average penalty minutes/game calculated by dividing total penalty minutes by games played

Team	GP	PEN	BMI	AVG
MTL	80	1556	12	19.5
N.J.	80	1611	8	20.1
NYI	80	1713	2	21.4
TOR	80	1734	16	21.7
BOS	80	1752	12	21.9
WSH	80	1777	32	22.2
HFD	80	1793	16	22.4
NYR	80	1805	14	22.6
PHI	80	1838	10	23.0
S.J.	80	1894	10	23.7
EDM	80	1907	24	23.8
PIT	80	1907	12	23.8
WPG	80	1907	20	23.8
STL	80	2041	12	25.5
QUE	80	2044	26	25.6
VAN	80	2075	16	25.9
DET	80	2078	28	26.0
L.A.	80	2161	10	27.0
MIN	80	2169	20	27.1
CGY	80	2643	22	33.0
CHI	80	2663	26	33.3
BUF	80	2713	14	33.9
TOTAL	**880**	**43781**	**362**	**49.8**

TEAMS' POWER PLAY RECORD

Abbreviations: ADV – total advantages; **PPGF** – power-play goals for; **%** – calculated by dividing number of power-play goals by total advantages.

	Home					Road					Overall				
	Team	**GP**	**ADV**	**PPGF**	**%**	**Team**	**GP**	**ADV**	**PPGF**	**%**	**Team**	**GP**	**ADV**	**PPGF**	**%**
1	WSH	40	210	55	26.2	PIT	40	199	46	23.1	BUF	80	466	105	22.5
2	WPG	40	236	60	25.4	BUF	40	219	47	21.5	WSH	80	412	92	22.3
3	NYI	40	172	43	25.0	BOS	40	194	39	20.1	NYI	80	339	75	22.1
4	BUF	40	247	58	23.5	HFD	40	203	40	19.7	PIT	80	423	92	21.7
5	CGY	40	194	45	23.2	NYI	40	167	32	19.2	CGY	80	414	87	21.0
6	NYR	40	212	48	22.6	CGY	40	220	42	19.1	NYR	80	387	81	20.9
7	VAN	40	233	52	22.3	L.A.	40	205	39	19.0	WPG	80	435	91	20.9
8	MTL	40	194	43	22.2	NYR	40	175	33	18.9	MTL	80	379	74	19.5
9	TOR	40	201	44	21.9	WSH	40	202	37	18.3	VAN	80	439	85	19.4
10	DET	40	191	41	21.5	N.J.	40	160	28	17.5	L.A.	80	411	79	19.2
11	ST.L.	40	192	40	20.8	ST.L.	40	167	29	17.4	ST.L.	80	359	69	19.2
12	PIT	40	224	46	20.5	QUE	40	196	34	17.3	BOS	80	406	77	19.0
13	EDM	40	187	38	20.3	EDM	40	179	30	16.8	DET	80	386	72	18.7
14	PHI	40	215	43	20.0	MTL	40	185	31	16.8	EDM	80	366	68	18.6
15	MIN	40	236	46	19.5	S.J.	40	170	28	16.5	HFD	80	414	73	17.6
16	L.A.	40	206	40	19.4	VAN	40	206	33	16.0	TOR	80	377	66	17.5
17	CHI	40	238	45	18.9	DET	40	195	31	15.9	N.J.	80	338	59	17.5
18	BOS	40	212	38	17.9	CHI	40	229	36	15.7	CHI	80	467	81	17.3
19	S.J.	40	204	36	17.6	WPG	40	199	31	15.6	S.J.	80	374	64	17.1
20	N.J.	40	178	31	17.4	MIN	40	210	30	14.3	QUE	80	385	66	17.1
21	QUE	40	189	32	16.9	PHI	40	196	25	12.8	MIN	80	446	76	17.0
22	HFD	40	211	33	15.6	TOR	40	176	22	12.5	PHI	80	411	68	16.5
TOTAL		**880**	**4582**	**957**	**20.9**		**880**	**4252**	**743**	**17.5**		**880**	**8834**	**1700**	**19.2**

TEAMS' PENALTY KILLING RECORD

Abbreviations: TSH – total times short-handed; **PPGA** – power-play goals against; **%** – calculated by dividing times short minus power-play goals against by times short.

	Home					Road					Overall				
	TEAM	**GP**	**TSH**	**PPGA**	**%**	**TEAM**	**GP**	**TSH**	**PPGA**	**%**	**TEAM**	**GP**	**TSH**	**PPGA**	**%**
1	NYR	40	202	25	87.6	WPG	40	225	32	85.8	NYR	80	395	60	84.8
2	ST.L.	40	200	26	87.0	CHI	40	261	41	84.3	CHI	80	482	76	84.2
3	WSH	40	187	26	86.1	TOR	40	180	32	82.2	WPG	80	428	68	84.1
4	MIN	40	196	30	84.7	DET	40	225	40	82.2	WSH	80	368	60	83.7
5	BOS	40	180	28	84.4	NYR	40	193	35	81.9	ST.L.	80	389	64	83.5
6	CHI	40	221	35	84.2	WSH	40	181	34	81.2	L.A.	80	417	76	81.8
7	N.J.	40	178	29	83.7	L.A.	40	211	41	80.6	N.J.	80	374	68	81.8
8	QUE	40	194	32	83.5	MTL	40	167	33	80.2	MIN	80	417	77	81.5
9	S.J.	40	211	35	83.4	N.J.	40	196	39	80.1	DET	80	419	78	81.4
10	L.A.	40	206	35	83.0	ST.L.	40	189	38	79.9	MTL	80	320	60	81.3
11	MTL	40	153	27	82.4	PHI	40	201	42	79.1	TOR	80	362	69	80.9
12	WPG	40	203	36	82.3	HFD	40	222	47	78.8	PHI	80	392	76	80.6
13	VAN	40	191	34	82.2	MIN	40	221	47	78.7	BOS	80	363	72	80.2
14	PHI	40	191	34	82.2	PIT	40	181	39	78.5	VAN	80	382	76	80.1
15	PIT	40	202	38	81.2	VAN	40	191	42	78.0	PIT	80	383	77	79.9
16	EDM	40	187	36	80.7	BUF	40	218	51	76.6	QUE	80	421	87	79.3
17	BUF	40	206	40	80.6	CGY	40	271	64	76.4	BUF	80	424	91	78.5
18	DET	40	194	38	80.4	BOS	40	183	44	76.0	HFD	80	396	86	78.3
19	CGY	40	218	43	80.3	EDM	40	236	57	75.8	CGY	80	489	107	78.1
20	TOR	40	182	37	79.7	NYI	40	207	50	75.8	S.J.	80	407	89	78.1
21	HFD	40	174	39	77.6	QUE	40	227	55	75.8	EDM	80	423	93	78.0
22	NYI	40	176	40	77.3	S.J.	40	196	54	72.4	NYI	80	383	90	76.5
TOTAL		**880**	**4252**	**743**	**82.5**		**880**	**4582**	**957**	**79.1**		**880**	**8834**	**1700**	**80.8**

SHORT HAND GOALS FOR

	Home			Road			Overall		
	Team	**GP**	**SHGF**	**Team**	**GP**	**SHGF**	**Team**	**GP**	**SHGF**
1	N.J.	40	12	DET	40	10	DET	80	18
2	PIT	40	9	ST.L.	40	10	PIT	80	16
3	CHI	40	8	HFD	40	8	ST.L.	80	16
4	WSH	40	8	QUE	40	8	PHI	80	15
5	VAN	40	8	NYR	40	7	N.J.	80	15
6	L.A.	40	8	PIT	40	7	NYR	80	14
7	DET	40	8	PHI	40	7	WSH	80	14
8	PHI	40	8	MIN	40	7	EDM	80	12
9	S.J.	40	7	EDM	40	6	VAN	80	12
10	NYR	40	7	NYI	40	6	CHI	80	11
11	BOS	40	6	WSH	40	6	L.A.	80	11
12	BUF	40	6	CGY	40	5	S.J.	80	11
13	EDM	40	6	TOR	40	4	NYI	80	11
14	ST.L.	40	6	S.J.	40	4	QUE	80	11
15	CGY	40	5	VAN	40	4	CGY	80	10
16	NYI	40	5	L.A.	40	3	HFD	80	10
17	WPG	40	4	CHI	40	3	MIN	80	9
18	QUE	40	3	N.J.	40	3	BUF	80	8
19	TOR	40	3	WPG	40	3	BOS	80	7
20	MTL	40	2	BUF	40	2	TOR	80	7
21	MIN	40	2	MTL	40	2	WPG	80	7
22	HFD	40	2	BOS	40	1	MTL	80	4
TOTAL		**880**	**133**		**880**	**116**		**880**	**249**

SHORT HAND GOALS AGAINST

	Home			Road			Overall		
	Team	**GP**	**SHGA**	**Team**	**GP**	**SHGA**	**Team**	**GP**	**SHGA**
1	MTL	40	1	DET	40	2	MTL	80	5
2	WPG	40	1	TOR	40	3	TOR	80	5
3	N.J.	40	2	CHI	40	3	WPG	80	6
4	TOR	40	2	NYI	40	4	DET	80	7
5	CGY	40	3	BUF	40	4	VAN	80	7
6	VAN	40	3	VAN	40	4	NYI	80	8
7	EDM	40	4	MTL	40	4	CHI	80	10
8	NYI	40	4	PHI	40	5	CGY	80	10
9	DET	40	5	L.A.	40	5	N.J.	80	10
10	WSH	40	6	HFD	40	5	BUF	80	11
11	QUE	40	6	ST.L.	40	5	HFD	80	11
12	S.J.	40	6	WPG	40	5	NYR	80	12
13	NYR	40	6	NYR	40	6	PHI	80	12
14	HFD	40	6	PIT	40	7	L.A.	80	12
15	BOS	40	7	CGY	40	7	ST.L.	80	12
16	CHI	40	7	BOS	40	7	BOS	80	14
17	BUF	40	7	N.J.	40	8	PIT	80	14
18	PIT	40	7	QUE	40	8	QUE	80	14
19	L.A.	40	7	WSH	40	9	WSH	80	15
20	PHI	40	7	MIN	40	10	EDM	80	15
21	ST.L.	40	7	EDM	40	11	S.J.	80	17
22	MIN	40	12	S.J.	40	11	MIN	80	22
TOTAL		**880**	**116**		**880**	**133**		**880**	**249**

Overtime Results

1984-85 to 1991-92

	1991-92				1990-91				1989-90				1988-89			
Team	GP	W	L	T	GP	W	L	T	GP	W	L	T	GP	W	L	T
Boston	9	3	0	6	17	5	0	12	14	3	2	9	19	3	2	14
Buffalo	7	1	1	5	24	3	2	19	15	4	3	8	13	2	4	7
Calgary	11	1	3	7	15	3	4	8	21	3	3	15	17	5	3	9
Chicago	8	0	0	8	12	3	1	8	10	2	2	6	17	2	3	12
Detroit	5	1	0	4	14	2	4	8	17	2	1	14	16	3	1	12
Edmonton	5	0	0	5	15	4	5	6	20	5	1	14	15	4	3	8
Hartford	11	0	1	10	18	2	5	11	9	0	0	9	10	1	4	5
Los Angeles	9	0	0	9	16	4	2	10	12	3	2	7	14	6	1	7
Minnesota	5	0	1	4	17	0	3	14	11	3	4	4	17	0	1	16
Montreal	10	4	1	5	17	3	3	11	17	4	2	11	11	2	0	9
New Jersey	8	2	2	4	17	1	1	15	16	3	4	9	17	1	4	12
NY Islanders	8	1	2	5	15	2	3	10	16	3	2	11	11	3	3	5
NY Rangers	7	0	3	4	16	1	2	13	17	2	2	13	10	1	1	8
Philadelphia	10	2	1	7	11	1	0	10	18	2	5	11	14	1	5	8
Pittsburgh	8	1	1	6	12	4	2	6	14	3	3	8	10	2	1	7
Quebec	6	0	3	3	18	1	3	14	8	0	1	7	10	2	1	7
St. Louis	6	2	1	3	18	3	4	11	15	2	4	9	16	3	1	12
San Jose	6	1	2	3												
Toronto	7	4	0	3	17	4	2	11	11	3	4	4	11	1	4	6
Vancouver	10	2	1	7	15	3	3	9	21	2	5	14	14	2	4	8
Washington	4	1	0	3	14	4	3	7	9	2	1	6	16	2	4	10
Winnipeg	9	1	2	6	14	1	2	11	19	4	4	11	20	6	2	12
Totals	**169**	**30**		**139**	**166**	**54**		**112**	**155**	**55**		**100**	**149**	**52**		**97**

	1987-88				1986-87				1985-86				1984-85			
Team	GP	W	L	T	GP	W	L	T	GP	W	L	T	GP	W	L	T
Boston	14	4	4	6	12	2	3	7	17	2	3	12	18	4	4	10
Buffalo	12	0	1	11	13	1	4	8	9	1	2	6	17	0	3	14
Calgary	15	2	4	9	4	1	0	3	12	1	2	9	14	1	1	12
Chicago	15	4	2	9	15	1	0	14	12	3	1	8	12	2	3	7
Detroit	16	2	3	11	17	2	5	10	13	2	5	6	14	0	2	12
Edmonton	16	3	2	11	14	5	3	6	14	5	2	7	12	0	1	11
Hartford	12	3	2	7	9	2	0	7	7	1	2	4	17	4	4	9
Los Angeles	12	1	3	8	12	2	2	8	14	3	3	8	19	3	2	14
Minnesota	16	1	2	13	14	2	2	10	15	4	2	9	15	1	2	12
Montreal	16	1	2	13	16	2	4	10	14	1	6	7	18	3	3	12
New Jersey	12	4	2	6	13	3	4	6	10	4	3	3	12	0	2	10
NY Islanders	13	3	0	10	20	5	3	12	17	4	1	12	15	1	8	6
NY Rangers	11	0	1	10	19	5	6	8	13	0	7	6	17	2	5	10
Philadelphia	13	1	3	9	10	1	1	8	9	4	1	4	9	1	1	7
Pittsburgh	16	5	2	9	21	5	4	12	14	3	3	8	8	3	0	5
Quebec	9	2	2	5	14	0	4	10	11	4	1	6	14	3	2	9
St. Louis	14	2	4	8	21	4	2	15	17	5	3	9	15	2	1	12
San Jose																
Toronto	13	1	2	10	13	3	4	6	17	4	6	7	15	5	2	8
Vancouver	11	0	2	9	10	2	0	8	16	1	2	13	17	7	1	9
Washington	15	2	4	9	17	5	2	10	11	4	0	7	12	3	0	9
Winnipeg	21	8	2	11	11	2	1	8	8	0	1	7	14	3	1	10
Totals	**146**	**49**		**97**	**148**	**55**		**93**	**135**	**56**		**79**	**152**	**48**		**104**

1991-92
Home Team Wins: 31
Visiting Team Wins: 23

1991-92 Penalty Shots

Scored

Kevin Miller (Detroit) scored against Patrick Roy (Montreal), October 10. Final score: Montreal 4 at Detroit 1.

Gino Odjick (Vancouver) scored against Mike Vernon (Calgary), October 19. Final score: Calgary 2 at Vancouver 5.

Bob Errey (Pittsburgh) scored against Darcy Wakaluk (Minnesota), October 31. Final score: Minnesota 1 at Pittsburgh 8.

Doug Brown (New Jersey) scored against Ken Wregget (Philadelphia), Novemeber 23. Final score: New Jersey 5 at Philadelphia 5.

Steve Yzerman (Detroit) scored against Grant Fuhr (Toronto), January 3. Final score: Toronto 4 at Detroit 6.

Dimitri Khristich (Washington) scored against Darcy Wakaluk (Minnesota), January 7. Final score: Minnesota 5 at Washington 3.

Paul Broten (NY Rangers) scored against Mike Vernon (Calgary), January 16. Final score: Calgary 4 at NY Rangers 6.

Steve Yzerman (Detroit) scored against Daren Puppa (Buffalo), January 29. Final score: Buffalo 4 at Detroit 4.

Luc Robitaille (Los Angeles) scored against Kay Whitmore (Hartford), February 6. Final score: Hartford 5 at Los Angles 5.

Pavel Bure (Vancouver) scored against Rick Tabbaracci (Winnipeg), February 28. Final score: Winnipeg 3 at Vancouver 5.

Mats Sundin (Quebec) scored against Tom Draper (Buffalo), March 3. Final score: Buffalo 4 at Quebec 4.

Murray Craven (Hartford) scored against Don Beaupre (Washington), March 24. Final score: Hartford 8 at Washington 2.

Stopped

Ron Tugnutt (Quebec) stopped Dave McLlwaine (Buffalo), October 12. Final score: Buffalo 5 at Quebec 4.

Chris Terreri (New Jersey) stopped Murray Craven (Philadelphia), October 13. Final score: New Jersey 2 at Philadelphia 4.

Tim Cheveldae (Detroit) stopped Wes Walz (Boston), November 2. Final score: Detroit 1 at Boston 4.

Mike Richter (NY Rangers) stopped Troy Murray (Winnipeg), November 27. Final score: NY Rangers 2 at Winnipeg 3.

Bill Ranford (Edmonton) stopped Greg Adams, (Vancouver), December 1. Final score: Vancouver 0 at Edmonton 7.

Wendell Young (Pittsburgh) stopped Darren Turcotte (NY Rangers), December 29. Final score: Pittsburgh 6 at NY Rangers 3.

Stephane Fiset (Quebec) stopped Craig Janney (Boston), January 9. Final score: Quebec 4 at Boston 5.

Bill Ranford (Edmonton) stopped Alexander Mogilny (Buffalo), January 10. Final score: Edmonton 2 at Buffalo 8.

Andy Moog (Boston) stopped John Cullen (Hartford), January 16. Final score: Hartford 3 at Boston 4.

Curtis Joseph (St. Louis) stopped Greg Adams (Vancouver), January 25. Final score: Vancouver 1 at St. Louis 0.

Darcy Wakaluk (Minnesota) stopped Dave Andreychuk (Buffalo), February 7. Final score: Minnesota 2 at Buffalo 0.

John Vanbiesbrouck (NY Rangers) stopped Pavel Bure (Vancouver), February 17. Final score: Vancouver 3 at NY Rangers 3.

Tom Draper (Buffalo) stopped Marty McInnis (NY Islanders), March 8. Final score: NY Islanders 6 at Buffalo 2.

Daren Puppa (Buffalo) stopped Ulf Dahlen (Minnesota), March 17. Final score: Buffalo 1 at Minnesota 3.

Stephane Fiset stopped a pair of penalty shots in 1991-92, robbing Craig Janney on January 9 and foiling Chris Dahlquist on March 21.

Bill Ranford (Edmonton) stopped Mario Lemieux (Pittsburgh), March 17. Final score: Edmonton 5 at Pittsburgh 6.

Stephane Fiset (Quebec) stopped Chris Dahlquist (Minnesota), March 21. Final score: Minnesota 2 at Quebec 4.

Curtis Joseph (St. Louis) stopped Todd Elik (Minnesota), April 16. Final score: Minnesota 3 at St. Louis 5.

Summary

29 penalty shots resulted in 12 goals.

NHL Record Book

All-Time Standings of NHL Teams

(ranked by percentage)

Team	Games	Wins	Losses	Tied	Goals For	Goals Against	Points	%
Montreal	4592	2432	1443	717	15595	12108	5581	.608
Edmonton	1040	557	349	134	4685	3911	1248	.600
Philadelphia	1978	985	678	311	7088	6048	2281	.577
Buffalo	1752	828	638	286	6373	5758	1942	.554
Boston	4432	2120	1649	663	14604	13174	4903	.553
NY Islanders	1596	760	602	234	5890	5180	1754	.549
**Calgary	1596	750	602	244	6126	5557	1744	.546
Toronto	4592	1957	1964	671	14346	14380	4585	.499
NY Rangers	4366	1829	1842	695	13680	13842	4353	.499
Detroit	4366	1802	1867	697	13250	13535	4301	.493
St. Louis	1978	816	858	304	6506	6752	1936	.489
Chicago	4366	1781	1905	680	13201	13489	4242	.486
Washington	1440	581	670	189	4954	5369	1351	.469
Los Angeles	1978	779	881	290	6959	7430	1848	.467
Pittsburgh	1978	748	953	277	6875	7572	1773	.448
Minnesota	1978	722	932	324	6418	7080	1768	.447
Hartford	1040	396	507	137	3603	4032	929	.447
Winnipeg	1040	390	507	143	3763	4215	923	.444
Quebec	1040	386	517	137	3812	4157	909	.437
Vancouver	1752	608	881	263	5710	6656	1479	.422
*New Jersey	1440	425	814	201	4550	5844	1051	.365
San Jose	80	17	58	5	219	359	39	.244

* Totals include those of Kansas City (1974-75, 1975-76) and Colorado (1976-77 through 1981-82)

**Totals include those of Atlanta (1972-73 through 1979-80)

Year-By-Year Final Standings & Leading Scorers

*Stanley Cup winner

1917-18

Team	GP	W	L	T	GF	GA	PTS
Montreal	22	13	9	0	115	84	26
*Toronto	22	13	9	0	108	109	26
Ottawa	22	9	13	0	102	114	18
**Mtl. Wanderers	6	1	5	0	17	35	2

**Montreal Arena burned down and Wanderers forced to withdraw from League. Canadiens and Toronto each counted a win for defaulted games with Wanderers.

Leading Scorers

Player	Club	GP	G	A	PTS
Malone, Joe	Montreal	20	44	—	44
Denneny, Cy	Ottawa	22	36	—	36
Noble, Reg	Toronto	20	28	—	28
Lalonde, Newsy	Montreal	14	23	—	23
Denneny, Corbett	Toronto	21	20	—	20
Pitre, Didier	Montreal	19	17	—	17
Cameron, Harry	Toronto	20	17	—	17
Darragh, Jack	Ottawa	18	14	—	14
Hyland, Harry	Mtl.W., Ott.	16	14	—	14
Skinner, Alf	Toronto	19	13	—	13
Gerard, Eddie	Ottawa	21	13	—	13

1918-19

Team	GP	W	L	T	GF	GA	PTS
Ottawa	18	12	6	0	71	53	24
Montreal	18	10	8	0	88	78	20
Toronto	18	5	13	0	64	92	10

Leading Scorers

Player	Club	GP	G	A	PTS	PIM
Lalonde, Newsy	Montreal	17	21	9	30	40
Cleghorn, Odie	Montreal	17	23	6	29	33
Denneny, Cy	Ottawa	18	18	4	22	43
Nighbor, Frank	Ottawa	18	18	4	22	27
Pitre, Didier	Montreal	17	14	4	18	9
Skinner, Alf	Toronto	17	12	3	15	26
Cameron, Harry	Tor., Ott.	14	11	3	14	35
Noble, Reg	Toronto	17	11	3	14	35
Darragh, Jack	Ottawa	14	12	1	13	27
Randall, Ken	Toronto	14	7	6	13	27

1919-20

Team	GP	W	L	T	GF	GA	PTS
*Ottawa	24	19	5	0	121	64	38
Montreal	24	13	11	0	129	113	26
Toronto	24	12	12	0	119	106	24
Quebec	24	4	20	0	91	177	8

Leading Scorers

Player	Club	GP	G	A	PTS	PIM
Malone, Joe	Quebec	24	39	9	48	12
Lalonde, Newsy	Montreal	23	36	6	42	33
Denneny, Corbett	Toronto	23	23	12	35	18
Nighbor, Frank	Ottawa	23	26	7	33	18
Noble, Reg	Toronto	24	24	7	31	51
Darragh, Jack	Ottawa	22	22	5	27	22
Arbour, Amos	Montreal	20	22	4	26	10
Wilson, Cully	Toronto	23	21	5	26	79
Broadbent, Punch	Ottawa	20	19	4	23	39
Cleghorn, Odie	Montreal	21	19	3	22	30
Pitre, Didier	Montreal	22	15	7	22	6

Alf Skinner, who fired 13 goals in 19 games during the regular season, led all playoff scorers with 8 goals for the 1918 Stanley Cup champion Toronto Arenas.

1920-21

Team	GP	W	L	T	GF	GA	PTS
Toronto	24	15	9	0	105	100	30
*Ottawa	24	14	10	0	97	75	28
Montreal	24	13	11	0	112	99	26
Hamilton	24	6	18	0	92	132	12

Leading Scorers

Player	Club	GP	G	A	PTS	PIM
Lalonde, Newsy	Montreal	24	33	8	41	36
Denneny, Cy	Ottawa	24	34	5	39	0
Dye, Babe	Ham., Tor.	24	35	2	37	32
Malone, Joe	Hamilton	20	30	4	34	2
Cameron, Harry	Toronto	24	18	9	27	35
Noble, Reg	Toronto	24	20	6	26	54
Prodgers, Goldie	Hamilton	23	18	8	26	8
Denneny, Corbett	Toronto	20	17	6	23	27
Nighbor, Frank	Ottawa	24	18	3	21	10
Berlinquette, Louis	Montreal	24	12	9	21	24

1921-22

Team	GP	W	L	T	GF	GA	PTS
Ottawa	24	14	8	2	106	84	30
*Toronto	24	13	10	1	98	97	27
Montreal	24	12	11	1	88	94	25
Hamilton	24	7	17	0	88	105	14

Leading Scorers

Player	Club	GP	G	A	PTS	PIM
Broadbent, Punch	Ottawa	24	32	14	46	24
Denneny, Cy	Ottawa	22	27	12	39	18
Dye, Babe	Toronto	24	30	7	37	18
Malone, Joe	Hamilton	24	25	7	32	4
Cameron, Harry	Toronto	24	19	8	27	18
Denneny, Corbett	Toronto	24	19	7	26	28
Noble, Reg	Toronto	24	17	8	25	10
Cleghorn, Odie	Montreal	23	21	3	24	26
Cleghorn, Sprague	Montreal	24	17	7	24	63
Reise, Leo	Hamilton	24	9	14	23	8

1922-23

Team	GP	W	L	T	GF	GA	PTS
*Ottawa	24	14	9	1	77	54	29
Montreal	24	13	9	2	73	61	28
Toronto	24	13	10	1	82	88	27
Hamilton	24	6	18	0	81	110	12

Leading Scorers

Player	Club	GP	G	A	PTS	PIM
Dye, Babe	Toronto	22	26	11	37	19
Denneny, Cy	Ottawa	24	21	10	31	20
Adams, Jack	Toronto	23	19	9	28	42
Boucher, Billy	Montreal	24	23	4	27	52
Cleghorn, Odie	Montreal	24	19	7	26	14
Roach, Mickey	Hamilton	23	17	8	25	8
Boucher, George	Ottawa	23	15	9	24	44
Joliat, Aurel	Montreal	24	13	9	22	31
Noble, Reg	Toronto	24	12	10	22	41
Wilson, Cully	Hamilton	23	16	3	19	46

1923-24

Team	GP	W	L	T	GF	GA	PTS
Ottawa	24	16	8	0	74	54	32
*Montreal	24	13	11	0	59	48	26
Toronto	24	10	14	0	59	85	20
Hamilton	24	9	15	0	63	68	18

Leading Scorers

Player	Club	GP	G	A	PTS	PIM
Denneny, Cy	Ottawa	21	22	1	23	10
Boucher, Billy	Montreal	23	16	6	22	33
Joliat, Aurel	Montreal	24	15	5	20	19
Dye, Babe	Toronto	19	17	2	19	23
Boucher, George	Ottawa	21	14	5	19	28
Burch, Billy	Hamilton	24	16	2	18	4
Clancy, King	Ottawa	24	9	8	17	18
Adams, Jack	Toronto	22	13	3	16	49
Morenz, Howie	Montreal	24	13	3	16	20
Noble, Reg	Toronto	23	12	3	15	23

1924-25

Team	GP	W	L	T	GF	GA	PTS
Hamilton	30	19	10	1	90	60	39
Toronto	30	19	11	0	90	84	38
Montreal	30	17	11	2	93	56	36
Ottawa	30	17	12	1	83	66	35
Mtl. Maroons	30	9	19	2	45	65	20
Boston	30	6	24	0	49	119	12

Leading Scorers

Player	Club	GP	G	A	PTS	PIM
Dye, Babe	Toronto	29	38	6	44	41
Denneny, Cy	Ottawa	28	27	15	42	16
Joliat, Aurel	Montreal	24	29	11	40	85
Morenz, Howie	Montreal	30	27	7	34	31
Boucher, Billy	Montreal	30	18	13	31	92
Adams, Jack	Toronto	27	21	8	29	66
Burch, Billy	Hamilton	27	20	4	24	10
Green, Red	Hamilton	30	19	4	23	63
Herberts, Jimmy	Boston	30	17	5	22	50
Day, Hap	Toronto	26	10	12	22	27

Goldie Prodgers, left, had his finest NHL season in 1920-21, compiling 26 points in 23 games for the Hamilton Tigers. Below: Reginald "Hooley" Smith's 25 points ranked him ninth on the NHL's scoring ladder in 1925-26.

1925-26

Team	GP	W	L	T	GF	GA	PTS
Ottawa	36	24	8	4	77	42	52
*Mtl. Maroons	36	20	11	5	91	73	45
Pittsburgh	36	19	16	1	82	70	39
Boston	36	17	15	4	92	85	38
NY Americans	36	12	20	4	68	89	28
Toronto	36	12	21	3	92	114	27
Montreal	36	11	24	1	79	108	23

Leading Scorers

Player	Club	GP	G	A	PTS	PIM
Stewart, Nels	Mtl. Maroons	36	34	8	42	119
Denneny, Cy	Ottawa	36	24	12	36	18
Cooper, Carson	Boston	36	28	3	31	10
Herberts, Jimmy	Boston	36	26	5	31	47
Morenz, Howie	Montreal	31	23	3	26	39
Adams, Jack	Toronto	36	21	5	26	52
Joliat, Aurel	Montreal	35	17	9	26	52
Burch, Billy	NY Americans	36	22	3	25	33
Smith, Hooley	Ottawa	28	16	9	25	53
Nighbor, Frank	Ottawa	35	12	13	25	40

1926-27

Canadian Division

Team	GP	W	L	T	GF	GA	PTS
*Ottawa	44	30	10	4	86	69	64
Montreal	44	28	14	2	99	67	58
Mtl. Maroons	44	20	20	4	71	68	44
NY Americans	44	17	25	2	82	91	36
Toronto	44	15	24	5	79	94	35

American Division

Team	GP	W	L	T	GF	GA	PTS
New York	44	25	13	6	95	72	56
Boston	44	21	20	3	97	89	45
Chicago	44	19	22	3	115	116	41
Pittsburgh	44	15	26	3	79	108	33
Detroit	44	12	28	4	76	105	28

Leading Scorers

Player	Club	GP	G	A	PTS	PIM
Cook, Bill	New York	44	33	4	37	58
Irvin, Dick	Chicago	43	18	18	36	34
Morenz, Howie	Montreal	44	25	7	32	49
Fredrickson, Frank	Det., Bos.	41	18	13	31	46
Dye, Babe	Chicago	41	25	5	30	14
Bailey, Ace	Toronto	42	15	13	28	82
Boucher, Frank	New York	44	13	15	28	17
Burch, Billy	NY Americans	43	19	8	27	40
Oliver, Harry	Boston	42	18	6	24	17
Keats, Gordon	Bos., Det.	42	16	8	24	52

1927-28

Canadian Division

Team	GP	W	L	T	GF	GA	PTS
Montreal	44	26	11	7	116	48	59
Mtl. Maroons	44	24	14	6	96	77	54
Ottawa	44	20	14	10	78	57	50
Toronto	44	18	18	8	89	88	44
NY Americans	44	11	27	6	63	128	28

American Division

Team	GP	W	L	T	GF	GA	PTS
Boston	44	20	13	11	77	70	51
*New York	44	19	16	9	94	79	47
Pittsburgh	44	19	17	8	67	76	46
Detroit	44	19	19	6	88	79	44
Chicago	44	7	34	3	68	134	17

Leading Scorers

Player	Club	GP	G	A	PTS	PIM
Morenz, Howie	Montreal	43	33	18	51	66
Joliat, Aurel	Montreal	44	28	11	39	105
Boucher, Frank	New York	44	23	12	35	15
Hay, George	Detroit	42	22	13	35	20
Stewart, Nels	Mtl. Maroons	41	27	7	34	104
Gagne, Art	Montreal	44	20	10	30	75
Cook, Fred	New York	44	14	14	28	45
Carson, Bill	Toronto	32	20	6	26	36
Finnigan, Frank	Ottawa	38	20	5	25	34
Cook, Bill	New York	43	18	6	24	42
Keats, Gordon	Chi., Det.	38	14	10	24	60

1928-29

Canadian Division

Team	GP	W	L	T	GF	GA	PTS
Montreal	44	22	7	15	71	43	59
NY Americans	44	19	13	12	53	53	50
Toronto	44	21	18	5	85	69	47
Ottawa	44	14	17	13	54	67	41
Mtl. Maroons	44	15	20	9	67	65	39

American Division

Team	GP	W	L	T	GF	GA	PTS
*Boston	44	26	13	5	89	52	57
New York	44	21	13	10	72	65	52
Detroit	44	19	16	9	72	63	47
Pittsburgh	44	9	27	8	46	80	26
Chicago	44	7	29	8	33	85	22

Leading Scorers

Player	Club	GP	G	A	PTS	PIM
Bailey, Ace	Toronto	44	22	10	32	78
Stewart, Nels	Mtl. Maroons	44	21	8	29	74
Cooper, Carson	Detroit	43	18	9	27	14
Morenz, Howie	Montreal	42	17	10	27	47
Blair, Andy	Toronto	44	12	15	27	41
Boucher, Frank	New York	44	10	16	26	8
Oliver, Harry	Boston	43	17	6	23	24
Cook, Bill	New York	43	15	8	23	41
Ward, Jimmy	Mtl. Maroons	43	14	8	22	46

Seven players tied with 19 points

1929-30

Canadian Division

Team	GP	W	L	T	GF	GA	PTS
Mtl. Maroons	44	23	16	5	141	114	51
*Montreal	44	21	14	9	142	114	51
Ottawa	44	21	15	8	138	118	50
Toronto	44	17	21	6	116	124	40
NY Americans	44	14	25	5	113	161	33

American Division

Team	GP	W	L	T	GF	GA	PTS
Boston	44	38	5	1	179	98	77
Chicago	44	21	18	5	117	111	47
New York	44	17	17	10	136	143	44
Detroit	44	14	24	6	117	133	34
Pittsburgh	44	5	36	3	102	185	13

Leading Scorers

Name	Club	GP	G	A	PTS	PIM
Weiland, Cooney	Boston	44	43	30	73	27
Boucher, Frank	New York	42	26	36	62	16
Clapper, Dit	Boston	44	41	20	61	48
Cook, Bill	New York	44	29	30	59	56
Kilrea, Hec	Ottawa	44	36	22	58	72
Stewart, Nels	Mtl. Maroons	44	39	16	55	81
Morenz, Howie	Montreal	44	40	10	50	72
Himes, Norm	NY Americans	44	28	22	50	15
Lamb, Joe	Ottawa	44	29	20	49	119
Gainor, Norm	Boston	42	18	31	49	39

1930-31

Canadian Division

Team	GP	W	L	T	GF	GA	PTS
*Montreal	44	26	10	8	129	89	60
Toronto	44	22	13	9	118	99	53
Mtl. Maroons	44	20	18	6	105	106	46
NY Americans	44	18	16	10	76	74	46
Ottawa	44	10	30	4	91	142	24

American Division

Team	GP	W	L	T	GF	GA	PTS
Boston	44	28	10	6	143	90	62
Chicago	44	24	17	3	108	78	51
New York	44	19	16	9	106	87	47
Detroit	44	16	21	7	102	105	39
Philadelphia	44	4	36	4	76	184	12

Leading Scorers

Player	Club	GP	G	A	PTS	PIM
Morenz, Howie	Montreal	39	28	23	51	49
Goodfellow, Ebbie	Detroit	44	25	23	48	32
Conacher, Charlie	Toronto	37	31	12	43	78
Cook, Bill	New York	43	30	12	42	39
Bailey, Ace	Toronto	40	23	19	42	46
Primeau, Joe	Toronto	38	9	32	41	18
Stewart, Nels	Mtl. Maroons	42	25	14	39	75
Boucher, Frank	New York	44	12	27	39	20
Weiland, Cooney	Boston	44	25	13	38	14
Cook, Fred	New York	44	18	17	35	72
Joliat, Aurel	Montreal	43	13	22	35	73

1931-32

Canadian Division

Team	GP	W	L	T	GF	GA	PTS
Montreal	48	25	16	7	128	111	57
*Toronto	48	23	18	7	155	127	53
Mtl. Maroons	48	19	22	7	142	139	45
NY Americans	48	16	24	8	95	142	40

American Division

Team	GP	W	L	T	GF	GA	PTS
New York	48	23	17	8	134	112	54
Chicago	48	18	19	11	86	101	47
Detroit	48	18	20	10	95	108	46
Boston	48	15	21	12	122	117	42

Leading Scorers

Player	Club	GP	G	A	PTS	PIM
Jackson, Harvey	Toronto	48	28	25	53	63
Primeau, Joe	Toronto	46	13	37	50	25
Morenz, Howie	Montreal	48	24	25	49	46
Conacher, Charlie	Toronto	44	34	14	48	66
Cook, Bill	New York	48	34	14	48	33
Trottier, Dave	Mtl. Maroons	48	26	18	44	94
Smith, Reg	Mtl. Maroons	43	11	33	44	49
Siebert, Albert	Mtl. Maroons	48	21	18	39	64
Clapper, Dit	Boston	48	17	22	39	21
Joliat, Aurel	Montreal	48	15	24	39	46

Hall-of-Fame defenseman Eddie Shore scored at least ten goals in each of his first five seasons in the NHL.

1932-33

Canadian Division

Team	GP	W	L	T	GF	GA	PTS
Toronto	48	24	18	6	119	111	54
Mtl. Maroons	48	22	20	6	135	119	50
Montreal	48	18	25	5	92	115	41
NY Americans	48	15	22	11	91	118	41
Ottawa	48	11	27	10	88	131	32

American Division

Team	GP	W	L	T	GF	GA	PTS
Boston	48	25	15	8	124	88	58
Detroit	48	25	15	8	111	93	58
*New York	48	23	17	8	135	107	54
Chicago	48	16	20	12	88	101	44

Leading Scorers

Player	Club	GP	G	A	PTS	PIM
Cook, Bill	New York	48	28	22	50	51
Jackson, Harvey	Toronto	48	27	17	44	43
Northcott, Lawrence	Mtl. Maroons	48	22	21	43	30
Smith, Reg	Mtl. Maroons	48	20	21	41	66
Haynes, Paul	Mtl. Maroons	48	16	25	41	18
Joliat, Aurel	Montreal	48	18	21	39	53
Barry, Marty	Boston	48	24	13	37	40
Cook, Fred	New York	48	22	15	37	35
Stewart, Nels	Boston	47	18	18	36	62
Morenz, Howie	Montreal	46	14	21	35	32
Gagnon, Johnny	Montreal	48	12	23	35	64
Shore, Eddie	Boston	48	8	27	35	102
Boucher, Frank	New York	47	7	28	35	4

1933-34

Canadian Division

Team	GP	W	L	T	GF	GA	PTS
Toronto	48	26	13	9	174	119	61
Montreal	48	22	20	6	99	101	50
Mtl. Maroons	48	19	18	11	117	122	49
NY Americans	48	15	23	10	104	132	40
Ottawa	48	13	29	6	115	143	32

American Division

Team	GP	W	L	T	GF	GA	PTS
Detroit	48	24	14	10	113	98	58
*Chicago	48	20	17	11	88	83	51
New York	48	21	19	8	120	113	50
Boston	48	18	25	5	111	130	41

Leading Scorers

Player	Club	GP	G	A	PTS	PIM
Conacher, Charlie	Toronto	42	32	20	52	38
Primeau, Joe	Toronto	45	14	32	46	8
Boucher, Frank	New York	48	14	30	44	4
Barry, Marty	Boston	48	27	12	39	12
Dillon, Cecil	New York	48	13	26	39	10
Stewart, Nels	Boston	48	21	17	38	68
Jackson, Harvey	Toronto	38	20	18	38	38
Joliat, Aurel	Montreal	48	22	15	37	27
Smith, Reg	Mtl. Maroons	47	18	19	37	58
Thompson, Paul	Chicago	48	20	16	36	17

1934-35

Canadian Division

Team	GP	W	L	T	GF	GA	PTS
Toronto	48	30	14	4	157	111	64
*Mtl. Maroons	48	24	19	5	123	92	53
Montreal	48	19	23	6	110	145	44
NY Americans	48	12	27	9	100	142	33
St. Louis	48	11	31	6	86	144	28

American Division

Team	GP	W	L	T	GF	GA	PTS
Boston	48	26	16	6	129	112	58
Chicago	48	26	17	5	118	88	57
New York	48	22	20	6	137	139	50
Detroit	48	19	22	7	127	114	45

Leading Scorers

Player	Club	GP	G	A	PTS	PIM
Conacher, Charlie	Toronto	47	36	21	57	24
Howe, Syd	St.L., Det.	50	22	25	47	34
Aurie, Larry	Detroit	48	17	29	46	24
Boucher, Frank	New York	48	13	32	45	2
Jackson, Harvey	Toronto	42	22	22	44	27
Lewis, Herb	Detroit	47	16	27	43	26
Chapman, Art	NY Americans	47	9	34	43	4
Barry, Marty	Boston	48	20	20	40	33
Schriner, Sweeney	NY Americans	48	18	22	40	6
Stewart, Nels	Boston	47	21	18	39	45
Thompson, Paul	Chicago	48	16	23	39	20

1935-36

Canadian Division

Team	GP	W	L	T	GF	GA	PTS
Mtl. Maroons	48	22	16	10	114	106	54
Toronto	48	23	19	6	126	106	52
NY Americans	48	16	25	7	109	122	39
Montreal	48	11	26	11	82	123	33

American Division

Team	GP	W	L	T	GF	GA	PTS
*Detroit	48	24	16	8	124	103	56
Boston	48	22	20	6	92	83	50
Chicago	48	21	19	8	93	92	50
New York	48	19	17	12	91	96	50

Leading Scorers

Player	Club	GP	G	A	PTS	PIM
Schriner, Sweeney	NY Americans	48	19	26	45	8
Barry, Marty	Detroit	48	21	19	40	16
Thompson, Paul	Chicago	45	17	23	40	19
Thoms, Bill	Toronto	48	23	15	38	29
Conacher, Charlie	Toronto	44	23	15	38	74
Smith, Reg	Mtl. Maroons	47	19	19	38	75
Romnes, Doc	Chicago	48	13	25	38	6
Chapman, Art	NY Americans	47	10	28	38	14
Lewis, Herb	Detroit	45	14	23	37	25
Northcott, Lawrence	Mtl. Maroons	48	15	21	36	41

Dapper Dit Clapper was the first man to play twenty seasons in the NHL, making his debut in 1927 and retiring in 1946.

1936-37

Canadian Division

Team	GP	W	L	T	GF	GA	PTS
Montreal	48	24	18	6	115	111	54
Mtl. Maroons	48	22	17	9	126	110	53
Toronto	48	22	21	5	119	115	49
NY Americans	48	15	29	4	122	161	34

American Division

Team	GP	W	L	T	GF	GA	PTS
*Detroit	48	25	14	9	128	102	59
Boston	48	23	18	7	120	110	53
New York	48	19	20	9	117	106	47
Chicago	48	14	27	7	99	131	35

Leading Scorers

Player	Club	GP	G	A	PTS	PIM
Schriner, Sweeney	NY Americans	48	21	25	46	17
Apps, Syl	Toronto	48	16	29	45	10
Barry, Marty	Detroit	48	17	27	44	6
Aurie, Larry	Detroit	45	23	20	43	20
Jackson, Harvey	Toronto	46	21	19	40	12
Gagnon, Johnny	Montreal	48	20	16	36	38
Gracie, Bob	Mtl. Maroons	47	11	25	36	18
Stewart, Nels	Bos., NYA	43	23	12	35	37
Thompson, Paul	Chicago	47	17	18	35	28
Cowley, Bill	Boston	46	13	22	35	4

1937-38

Canadian Division

Team	GP	W	L	T	GF	GA	PTS
Toronto	48	24	15	9	151	127	57
NY Americans	48	19	18	11	110	111	49
Montreal	48	18	17	13	123	128	49
Mtl. Maroons	48	12	30	6	101	149	30

American Division

Team	GP	W	L	T	GF	GA	PTS
Boston	48	30	11	7	142	89	67
New York	48	27	15	6	149	96	60
*Chicago	48	14	25	9	97	139	37
Detroit	48	12	25	11	99	133	35

Leading Scorers

Player	Club	GP	G	A	PTS	PIM
Drillon, Gord	Toronto	48	26	26	52	4
Apps, Syl	Toronto	47	21	29	50	9
Thompson, Paul	Chicago	48	22	22	44	14
Mantha, Georges	Montreal	47	23	19	42	12
Dillon, Cecil	New York	48	21	18	39	6
Cowley, Bill	Boston	48	17	22	39	8
Schriner, Sweeney	NY Americans	49	21	17	38	22
Thoms, Bill	Toronto	48	14	24	38	14
Smith, Clint	New York	48	14	23	37	0
Stewart, Nels	NY Americans	48	19	17	36	29
Colville, Neil	New York	45	17	19	36	11

1938-39

Team	GP	W	L	T	GF	GA	PTS
*Boston	48	36	10	2	156	76	74
New York	48	26	16	6	149	105	58
Toronto	48	19	20	9	114	107	47
NY Americans	48	17	21	10	119	157	44
Detroit	48	18	24	6	107	128	42
Montreal	48	15	24	9	115	146	39
Chicago	48	12	28	8	91	132	32

Leading Scorers

Player	Club	GP	G	A	PTS	PIM
Blake, Hector	Montreal	48	24	23	47	10
Schriner, Sweeney	NY Americans	48	13	31	44	20
Cowley, Bill	Boston	34	8	34	42	2
Smith, Clint	New York	48	21	20	41	2
Barry, Marty	Detroit	48	13	28	41	4
Apps, Syl	Toronto	44	15	25	40	4
Anderson, Tom	NY Americans	48	13	27	40	14
Gottselig, Johnny	Chicago	48	16	23	39	15
Haynes, Paul	Montreal	47	5	33	38	27
Conacher, Roy	Boston	47	26	11	37	12
Carr, Lorne	NY Americans	46	19	18	37	16
Colville, Neil	New York	48	18	19	37	12
Watson, Phil	New York	48	15	22	37	42

1939-40

Team	GP	W	L	T	GF	GA	PTS
Boston	48	31	12	5	170	98	67
*New York	48	27	11	10	136	77	64
Toronto	48	25	17	6	134	110	56
Chicago	48	23	19	6	112	120	52
Detroit	48	16	26	6	91	126	38
NY Americans	48	15	29	4	106	140	34
Montreal	48	10	33	5	90	168	25

Leading Scorers

Player	Club	GP	G	A	PTS	PIM
Schmidt, Milt	Boston	48	22	30	52	37
Dumart, Woody	Boston	48	22	21	43	16
Bauer, Bob	Boston	48	17	26	43	2
Drillon, Gord	Toronto	43	21	19	40	13
Cowley, Bill	Boston	48	13	27	40	24
Hextall, Bryan	New York	48	24	15	39	52
Colville, Neil	New York	48	19	19	38	22
Howe, Syd	Detroit	46	14	23	37	17
Blake, Hector	Montreal	48	17	19	36	48
Armstrong, Murray	NY Americans	48	16	20	36	12

1940-41

Team	GP	W	L	T	GF	GA	PTS
*Boston	48	27	8	13	168	102	67
Toronto	48	28	14	6	145	99	62
Detroit	48	21	16	11	112	102	53
New York	48	21	19	8	143	125	50
Chicago	48	16	25	7	112	139	39
Montreal	48	16	26	6	121	147	38
NY Americans	48	8	29	11	99	186	27

Leading Scorers

Player	Club	GP	G	A	PTS	PIM
Cowley, Bill	Boston	46	17	45	62	16
Hextall, Bryan	New York	48	26	18	44	16
Drillon, Gord	Toronto	42	23	21	44	2
Apps, Syl	Toronto	41	20	24	44	6
Patrick, Lynn	New York	48	20	24	44	12
Howe, Syd	Detroit	48	20	24	44	8
Colville, Neil	New York	48	14	28	42	28
Wiseman, Eddie	Boston	48	16	24	40	10
Bauer, Bobby	Boston	48	17	22	39	2
Schriner, Sweeney	Toronto	48	24	14	38	6
Conacher, Roy	Boston	40	24	14	38	7
Schmidt, Milt	Boston	44	13	25	38	23

1941-42

Team	GP	W	L	T	GF	GA	PTS
New York	48	29	17	2	177	143	60
*Toronto	48	27	18	3	158	136	57
Boston	48	25	17	6	160	118	56
Chicago	48	22	23	3	145	155	47
Detroit	48	19	25	4	140	147	42
Montreal	48	18	27	3	134	173	39
Brooklyn	48	16	29	3	133	175	35

Leading Scorers

Player	Club	GP	G	A	PTS	PIM
Hextall, Bryan	New York	48	24	32	56	30
Patrick, Lynn	New York	47	32	22	54	18
Grosso, Don	Detroit	48	23	30	53	13
Watson, Phil	New York	48	15	37	52	48
Abel, Sid	Detroit	48	18	31	49	45
Blake, Hector	Montreal	47	17	28	45	19
Thoms, Bill	Chicago	47	15	30	45	8
Drillon, Gord	Toronto	48	23	18	41	6
Apps, Syl	Toronto	38	18	23	41	0
Anderson, Tom	Brooklyn	48	12	29	41	54

1942-43

Team	GP	W	L	T	GF	GA	PTS
*Detroit	50	25	14	11	169	124	61
Boston	50	24	17	9	195	176	57
Toronto	50	22	19	9	198	159	53
Montreal	50	19	19	12	181	191	50
Chicago	50	17	18	15	179	180	49
New York	50	11	31	8	161	253	30

Leading Scorers

Player	Club	GP	G	A	PTS	PIM
Bentley, Doug	Chicago	50	33	40	73	18
Cowley, Bill	Boston	48	27	45	72	10
Bentley, Max	Chicago	47	26	44	70	2
Patrick, Lynn	New York	50	22	39	61	28
Carr, Lorne	Toronto	50	27	33	60	15
Taylor, Billy	Toronto	50	18	42	60	2
Hextall, Bryan	New York	50	27	32	59	28
Blake, Hector	Montreal	48	23	36	59	28
Lach, Elmer	Montreal	45	18	40	58	14
O'Connor, Herb	Montreal	50	15	43	58	2

1943-44

Team	GP	W	L	T	GF	GA	PTS
*Montreal	50	38	5	7	234	109	83
Detroit	50	26	18	6	214	177	58
Toronto	50	23	23	4	214	174	50
Chicago	50	22	23	5	178	187	49
Boston	50	19	26	5	223	268	43
New York	50	6	39	5	162	310	17

Leading Scorers

Player	Club	GP	G	A	PTS	PIM
Cain, Herb	Boston	48	36	46	82	4
Bentley, Doug	Chicago	50	38	39	77	22
Carr, Lorne	Toronto	50	36	38	74	9
Liscombe, Carl	Detroit	50	36	37	73	17
Lach, Elmer	Montreal	48	24	48	72	23
Smith, Clint	Chicago	50	23	49	72	4
Cowley, Bill	Boston	36	30	41	71	12
Mosienko, Bill	Chicago	50	32	38	70	10
Jackson, Art	Boston	49	28	41	69	8
Bodnar, Gus	Toronto	50	22	40	62	18

Conn Smythe, seen here discussing strategy with, left to right, Clancy, Horner, Hollett and Hainsworth, managed the Toronto Maple Leafs into 13 Stanley Cup finals from 1932 to 1951.

Bill Durnan was the last goaltender to captain a team, wearing the "C" during the 1947-48 season.

1944-45

Team	GP	W	L	T	GF	GA	PTS
Montreal	50	38	8	4	228	121	80
Detroit	50	31	14	5	218	161	67
*Toronto	50	24	22	4	183	161	52
Boston	50	16	30	4	179	219	36
Chicago	50	13	30	7	141	194	33
New York	50	11	29	10	154	247	32

Leading Scorers

Player	Club	GP	G	A	PTS	PIM
Lach, Elmer	Montreal	50	26	54	80	37
Richard, Maurice	Montreal	50	50	23	73	36
Blake, Hector	Montreal	49	29	38	67	15
Cowley, Bill	Boston	49	25	40	65	2
Kennedy, Ted	Toronto	49	29	25	54	14
Mosienko, Bill	Chicago	50	28	26	54	0
Carveth, Joe	Detroit	50	26	28	54	6
DeMarco, Albert	New York	50	24	30	54	10
Smith, Clint	Chicago	50	23	31	54	0
Howe, Syd	Detroit	46	17	36	53	6

1945-46

Team	GP	W	L	T	GF	GA	PTS
*Montreal	50	28	17	5	172	134	61
Boston	50	24	18	8	167	156	56
Chicago	50	23	20	7	200	178	53
Detroit	50	20	20	10	146	159	50
Toronto	50	19	24	7	174	185	45
New York	50	13	28	9	144	191	35

Leading Scorers

Player	Club	GP	G	A	PTS	PIM
Bentley, Max	Chicago	47	31	30	61	6
Stewart, Gaye	Toronto	50	37	15	52	8
Blake, Hector	Montreal	50	29	21	50	2
Smith, Clint	Chicago	50	26	24	50	2
Richard, Maurice	Montreal	50	27	21	48	50
Mosienko, Bill	Chicago	40	18	30	48	12
DeMarco, Albert	New York	50	20	27	47	20
Lach, Elmer	Montreal	50	13	34	47	34
Kaleta, Alex	Chicago	49	19	27	46	17
Taylor, Billy	Toronto	48	23	18	41	14
Horeck, Pete	Chicago	50	20	21	41	34

1946-47

Team	GP	W	L	T	GF	GA	PTS
Montreal	60	34	16	10	189	138	78
*Toronto	60	31	19	10	209	172	72
Boston	60	26	23	11	190	175	63
Detroit	60	22	27	11	190	193	55
New York	60	22	32	6	167	186	50
Chicago	60	19	37	4	193	274	42

Leading Scorers

Player	Club	GP	G	A	PTS	PIM
Bentley, Max	Chicago	60	29	43	72	12
Richard, Maurice	Montreal	60	45	26	71	69
Taylor, Billy	Detroit	60	17	46	63	35
Schmidt, Milt	Boston	59	27	35	62	40
Kennedy, Ted	Toronto	60	28	32	60	27
Bentley, Doug	Chicago	52	21	34	55	18
Bauer, Bob	Boston	58	30	24	54	4
Conacher, Roy	Detroit	60	30	24	54	6
Mosienko, Bill	Chicago	59	25	27	52	2
Dumart, Woody	Boston	60	24	28	52	12

1947-48

Team	GP	W	L	T	GF	GA	PTS
*Toronto	60	32	15	13	182	143	77
Detroit	60	30	18	12	187	148	72
Boston	60	23	24	13	167	168	59
New York	60	21	26	13	176	201	55
Montreal	60	20	29	11	147	169	51
Chicago	60	20	34	6	195	225	46

Leading Scorers

Player	Club	GP	G	A	PTS	PIM
Lach, Elmer	Montreal	60	30	31	61	72
O'Connor, Buddy	New York	60	24	36	60	8
Bentley, Doug	Chicago	60	20	37	57	16
Stewart, Gaye	Tor., Chi.	61	27	29	56	83
Bentley, Max	Chi., Tor.	59	26	28	54	14
Poile, Bud	Tor., Chi.	58	25	29	54	17
Richard, Maurice	Montreal	53	28	25	53	89
Apps, Syl	Toronto	55	26	27	53	12
Lindsay, Ted	Detroit	60	33	19	52	95
Conacher, Roy	Chicago	52	22	27	49	4

1948-49

Team	GP	W	L	T	GF	GA	PTS
Detroit	60	34	19	7	195	145	75
Boston	60	29	23	8	178	163	66
Montreal	60	28	23	9	152	126	65
*Toronto	60	22	25	13	147	161	57
Chicago	60	21	31	8	173	211	50
New York	60	18	31	11	133	172	47

Leading Scorers

Player	Club	GP	G	A	PTS	PIM
Conacher, Roy	Chicago	60	26	42	68	8
Bentley, Doug	Chicago	58	23	43	66	38
Abel, Sid	Detroit	60	28	26	54	49
Lindsay, Ted	Detroit	50	26	28	54	97
Conacher, Jim	Det., Chi.	59	26	23	49	43
Ronty, Paul	Boston	60	20	29	49	11
Watson, Harry	Toronto	60	26	19	45	0
Reay, Billy	Montreal	60	22	23	45	33
Bodnar, Gus	Chicago	59	19	26	45	14
Peirson, John	Boston	59	22	21	43	45

1949-50

Team	GP	W	L	T	GF	GA	PTS
*Detroit	70	37	19	14	229	164	88
Montreal	70	29	22	19	172	150	77
Toronto	70	31	27	12	176	173	74
New York	70	28	31	11	170	189	67
Boston	70	22	32	16	198	228	60
Chicago	70	22	38	10	203	244	54

Leading Scorers

Player	Club	GP	G	A	PTS	PIM
Lindsay, Ted	Detroit	69	23	55	78	141
Abel, Sid	Detroit	69	34	35	69	46
Howe, Gordie	Detroit	70	35	33	68	69
Richard, Maurice	Montreal	70	43	22	65	114
Ronty, Paul	Boston	70	23	36	59	8
Conacher, Roy	Chicago	70	25	31	56	16
Bentley, Doug	Chicago	64	20	33	53	28
Peirson, John	Boston	57	27	25	52	49
Prystai, Metro	Chicago	65	29	22	51	31
Guidolin, Bep	Chicago	70	17	34	51	42

Gordie Howe, who led the NHL in scoring in four straight seasons from 1951 to 1954, fires another puck past Gump Worsley, who yielded Howe's 500th, 544th and 600th career-goals.

1950-51

Team	GP	W	L	T	GF	GA	PTS
Detroit	70	44	13	13	236	139	101
*Toronto	70	41	16	13	212	138	95
Montreal	70	25	30	15	173	184	65
Boston	70	22	30	18	178	197	62
New York	70	20	29	21	169	201	62
Chicago	70	13	47	10	171	280	36

Leading Scorers

Player	Club	GP	G	A	PTS	PIM
Howe, Gordie	Detroit	70	43	43	86	74
Richard, Maurice	Montreal	65	42	24	66	97
Bentley, Max	Toronto	67	21	41	62	34
Abel, Sid	Detroit	69	23	38	61	30
Schmidt, Milt	Boston	62	22	39	61	33
Kennedy, Ted	Toronto	63	18	43	61	32
Lindsay, Ted	Detroit	67	24	35	59	110
Sloan, Tod	Toronto	70	31	25	56	105
Kelly, Red	Detroit	70	17	37	54	24
Smith, Sid	Toronto	70	30	21	51	10
Gardner, Cal	Toronto	66	23	28	51	42

1951-52

Team	GP	W	L	T	GF	GA	PTS
*Detroit	70	44	14	12	215	133	100
Montreal	70	34	26	10	195	164	78
Toronto	70	29	25	16	168	157	74
Boston	70	25	29	16	162	176	66
New York	70	23	34	13	192	219	59
Chicago	70	17	44	9	158	241	43

Leading Scorers

Player	Club	GP	G	A	PTS	PIM
Howe, Gordie	Detroit	70	47	39	86	78
Lindsay, Ted	Detroit	70	30	39	69	123
Lach, Elmer	Montreal	70	15	50	65	36
Raleigh, Don	New York	70	19	42	61	14
Smith, Sid	Toronto	70	27	30	57	6
Geoffrion, Bernie	Montreal	67	30	24	54	66
Mosienko, Bill	Chicago	70	31	22	53	10
Abel, Sid	Detroit	62	17	36	53	32
Kennedy, Ted	Toronto	70	19	33	52	33
Schmidt, Milt	Boston	69	21	29	50	57
Peirson, John	Boston	68	20	30	50	30

1952-53

Team	GP	W	L	T	GF	GA	PTS
Detroit	70	36	16	18	222	133	90
*Montreal	70	28	23	19	155	148	75
Boston	70	28	29	13	152	172	69
Chicago	70	27	28	15	169	175	69
Toronto	70	27	30	13	156	167	67
New York	70	17	37	16	152	211	50

Leading Scorers

Player	Club	GP	G	A	PTS	PIM
Howe, Gordie	Detroit	70	49	46	95	57
Lindsay, Ted	Detroit	70	32	39	71	111
Richard, Maurice	Montreal	70	28	33	61	112
Hergesheimer, Wally	New York	70	30	29	59	10
Delvecchio, Alex	Detroit	70	16	43	59	28
Ronty, Paul	New York	70	16	38	54	20
Prystai, Metro	Detroit	70	16	34	50	12
Kelly, Red	Detroit	70	19	27	46	8
Olmstead, Bert	Montreal	69	17	28	45	83
Mackell, Fleming	Boston	65	27	17	44	63
McFadden, Jim	Chicago	70	23	21	44	29

1953-54

Team	GP	W	L	T	GF	GA	PTS
*Detroit	70	37	19	14	191	132	88
Montreal	70	35	24	11	195	141	81
Toronto	70	32	24	14	152	131	78
Boston	70	32	28	10	177	181	74
New York	70	29	31	10	161	182	68
Chicago	70	12	51	7	133	242	31

Leading Scorers

Player	Club	GP	G	A	PTS	PIM
Howe, Gordie	Detroit	70	33	48	81	109
Richard, Maurice	Montreal	70	37	30	67	112
Lindsay, Ted	Detroit	70	26	36	62	110
Geoffrion, Bernie	Montreal	54	29	25	54	87
Olmstead, Bert	Montreal	70	15	37	52	85
Kelly, Red	Detroit	62	16	33	49	18
Reibel, Earl	Detroit	69	15	33	48	18
Sandford, Ed	Boston	70	16	31	47	42
Mackell, Fleming	Boston	67	15	32	47	60
Mosdell, Ken	Montreal	67	22	24	46	64
Ronty, Paul	New York	70	13	33	46	18

1954-55

Team	GP	W	L	T	GF	GA	PTS
*Detroit	70	42	17	11	204	134	95
Montreal	70	41	18	11	228	157	93
Toronto	70	24	24	22	147	135	70
Boston	70	23	26	21	169	188	67
New York	70	17	35	18	150	210	52
Chicago	70	13	40	17	161	235	43

Leading Scorers

Player	Club	GP	G	A	PTS	PIM
Geoffrion, Bernie	Montreal	70	38	37	75	57
Richard, Maurice	Montreal	67	38	36	74	125
Beliveau, Jean	Montreal	70	37	36	73	58
Reibel, Earl	Detroit	70	25	41	66	15
Howe, Gordie	Detroit	64	29	33	62	68
Sullivan, George	Chicago	69	19	42	61	51
Olmstead, Bert	Montreal	70	10	48	58	103
Smith, Sid	Toronto	70	33	21	54	14
Mosdell, Ken	Montreal	70	22	32	54	82
Lewicki, Danny	New York	70	29	24	53	8

1955-56

Team	GP	W	L	T	GF	GA	PTS
*Montreal	70	45	15	10	222	131	100
Detroit	70	30	24	16	183	148	76
New York	70	32	28	10	204	203	74
Toronto	70	24	33	13	153	181	61
Boston	70	23	34	13	147	185	59
Chicago	70	19	39	12	155	216	50

Leading Scorers

Player	Club	GP	G	A	PTS	PIM
Beliveau, Jean	Montreal	70	47	41	88	143
Howe, Gordie	Detroit	70	38	41	79	100
Richard, Maurice	Montreal	70	38	33	71	89
Olmstead, Bert	Montreal	70	14	56	70	94
Sloan, Tod	Toronto	70	37	29	66	100
Bathgate, Andy	New York	70	19	47	66	59
Geoffrion, Bernie	Montreal	59	29	33	62	66
Reibel, Earl	Detroit	68	17	39	56	10
Delvecchio, Alex	Detroit	70	25	26	51	24
Creighton, Dave	New York	70	20	31	51	43
Gadsby, Bill	New York	70	9	42	51	84

1956-57

Team	GP	W	L	T	GF	GA	PTS
Detroit	70	38	20	12	198	157	88
*Montreal	70	35	23	12	210	155	82
Boston	70	34	24	12	195	174	80
New York	70	26	30	14	184	227	66
Toronto	70	21	34	15	174	192	57
Chicago	70	16	39	15	169	225	47

Leading Scorers

Player	Club	GP	G	A	PTS	PIM
Howe, Gordie	Detroit	70	44	45	89	72
Lindsay, Ted	Detroit	70	30	55	85	103
Beliveau, Jean	Montreal	69	33	51	84	105
Bathgate, Andy	New York	70	27	50	77	60
Litzenberger, Ed	Chicago	70	32	32	64	48
Richard, Maurice	Montreal	63	33	29	62	74
McKenney, Don	Boston	69	21	39	60	31
Moore, Dickie	Montreal	70	29	29	58	56
Richard, Henri	Montreal	63	18	36	54	71
Ullman, Norm	Detroit	64	16	36	52	47

1957-58

Team	GP	W	L	T	GF	GA	PTS
*Montreal	70	43	17	10	250	158	96
New York	70	32	25	13	195	188	77
Detroit	70	29	29	12	176	207	70
Boston	70	27	28	15	199	194	69
Chicago	70	24	39	7	163	202	55
Toronto	70	21	38	11	192	226	53

Leading Scorers

Player	Club	GP	G	A	PTS	PIM
Moore, Dickie	Montreal	70	36	48	84	65
Richard, Henri	Montreal	67	28	52	80	56
Bathgate, Andy	New York	65	30	48	78	42
Howe, Gordie	Detroit	64	33	44	77	40
Horvath, Bronco	Boston	67	30	36	66	71
Litzenberger, Ed	Chicago	70	32	30	62	63
Mackell, Fleming	Boston	70	20	40	60	72
Beliveau, Jean	Montreal	55	27	32	59	93
Delvecchio, Alex	Detroit	70	21	38	59	22
McKenney, Don	Boston	70	28	30	58	22

1958-59

Team	GP	W	L	T	GF	GA	PTS
*Montreal	70	39	18	13	258	158	91
Boston	70	32	29	9	205	215	73
Chicago	70	28	29	13	197	208	69
Toronto	70	27	32	11	189	201	65
New York	70	26	32	12	201	217	64
Detroit	70	25	37	8	167	218	58

Leading Scorers

Player	Club	GP	G	A	PTS	PIM
Moore, Dickie	Montreal	70	41	55	96	61
Beliveau, Jean	Montreal	64	45	46	91	67
Bathgate, Andy	New York	70	40	48	88	48
Howe, Gordie	Detroit	70	32	46	78	57
Litzenberger, Ed	Chicago	70	33	44	77	37
Geoffrion, Bernie	Montreal	59	22	44	66	30
Sullivan, George	New York	70	21	42	63	56
Hebenton, Andy	New York	70	33	29	62	8
McKenney, Don	Boston	70	32	30	62	20
Sloan, Tod	Chicago	59	27	35	62	79

1959-60

Team	GP	W	L	T	GF	GA	PTS
*Montreal	70	40	18	12	255	178	92
Toronto	70	35	26	9	199	195	79
Chicago	70	28	29	13	191	180	69
Detroit	70	26	29	15	186	197	67
Boston	70	28	34	8	220	241	64
New York	70	17	38	15	187	247	49

Leading Scorers

Player	Club	GP	G	A	PTS	PIM
Hull, Bobby	Chicago	70	39	42	81	68
Horvath, Bronco	Boston	68	39	41	80	60
Beliveau, Jean	Montreal	60	34	40	74	57
Bathgate, Andy	New York	70	26	48	74	28
Richard, Henri	Montreal	70	30	43	73	66
Howe, Gordie	Detroit	70	28	45	73	46
Geoffrion, Bernie	Montreal	59	30	41	71	36
McKenney, Don	Boston	70	20	49	69	28
Stasiuk, Vic	Boston	69	29	39	68	121
Prentice, Dean	New York	70	32	34	66	43

1960-61

Team	GP	W	L	T	GF	GA	PTS
Montreal	70	41	19	10	254	188	92
Toronto	70	39	19	12	234	176	90
*Chicago	70	29	24	17	198	180	75
Detroit	70	25	29	16	195	215	66
New York	70	22	38	10	204	248	54
Boston	70	15	42	13	176	254	43

Leading Scorers

Player	Club	GP	G	A	PTS	PIM
Geoffrion, Bernie	Montreal	64	50	45	95	29
Béliveau, Jean	Montreal	69	32	58	90	57
Mahovlich, Frank	Toronto	70	48	36	84	131
Bathgate, Andy	New York	70	29	48	77	22
Howe, Gordie	Detroit	64	23	49	72	30
Ullman, Norm	Detroit	70	28	42	70	34
Kelly, Red	Toronto	64	20	50	70	12
Moore, Dickie	Montreal	57	35	34	69	62
Richard, Henri	Montreal	70	24	44	68	91
Delvecchio, Alex	Detroit	70	27	35	62	26

1961-62

Team	GP	W	L	T	GF	GA	PTS
Montreal	70	42	14	14	259	166	98
*Toronto	70	37	22	11	232	180	85
Chicago	70	31	26	13	217	186	75
New York	70	26	32	12	195	207	64
Detroit	70	23	33	14	184	219	60
Boston	70	15	47	8	177	306	38

Leading Scorers

Player	Club	GP	G	A	PTS	PIM
Hull, Bobby	Chicago	70	50	34	84	35
Bathgate, Andy	New York	70	28	56	84	44
Howe, Gordie	Detroit	70	33	44	77	54
Mikita, Stan	Chicago	70	25	52	77	97
Mahovlich, Frank	Toronto	70	33	38	71	87
Delvecchio, Alex	Detroit	70	26	43	69	18
Backstrom, Ralph	Montreal	66	27	38	65	29
Ullman, Norm	Detroit	70	26	38	64	54
Hay, Bill	Chicago	60	11	52	63	34
Provost, Claude	Montreal	70	33	29	62	22

Classy Ted "Teeder" Kennedy is the last member of the Leafs to win the Hart Trophy, receiving the league's MVP award in 1955.

1962-63

Team	GP	W	L	T	GF	GA	PTS
*Toronto	70	35	23	12	221	180	82
Chicago	70	32	21	17	194	178	81
Montreal	70	28	19	23	225	183	79
Detroit	70	32	25	13	200	194	77
New York	70	22	36	12	211	233	56
Boston	70	14	39	17	198	281	45

Leading Scorers

Player	Club	GP	G	A	PTS	PIM
Howe, Gordie	Detroit	70	38	48	86	100
Bathgate, Andy	New York	70	35	46	81	54
Mikita, Stan	Chicago	65	31	45	76	69
Mahovlich, Frank	Toronto	67	36	37	73	56
Richard, Henri	Montreal	67	23	50	73	57
Beliveau, Jean	Montreal	69	18	49	67	68
Bucyk, John	Boston	69	27	39	66	36
Delvecchio, Alex	Detroit	70	20	44	64	8
Hull, Bobby	Chicago	65	31	31	62	27
Oliver, Murray	Boston	65	22	40	62	38

1963-64

Team	GP	W	L	T	GF	GA	PTS
Montreal	70	36	21	13	209	167	85
Chicago	70	36	22	12	218	169	84
*Toronto	70	33	25	12	192	172	78
Detroit	70	30	29	11	191	204	71
New York	70	22	38	10	186	242	54
Boston	70	18	40	12	170	212	48

Leading Scorers

Player	Club	GP	G	A	PTS	PIM
Mikita, Stan	Chicago	70	39	50	89	146
Hull, Bobby	Chicago	70	43	44	87	50
Beliveau, Jean	Montreal	68	28	50	78	42
Bathgate, Andy	NYR, Tor.	71	19	58	77	34
Howe, Gordie	Detroit	69	26	47	73	70
Wharram, Ken	Chicago	70	39	32	71	18
Oliver, Murray	Boston	70	24	44	68	41
Goyette, Phil	New York	67	24	41	65	15
Gilbert, Rod	New York	70	24	40	64	62
Keon, Dave	Toronto	70	23	37	60	6

1964-65

Team	GP	W	L	T	GF	GA	PTS
Detroit	70	40	23	7	224	175	87
*Montreal	70	36	23	11	211	185	83
Chicago	70	34	28	8	224	176	76
Toronto	70	30	26	14	204	173	74
New York	70	20	38	12	179	246	52
Boston	70	21	43	6	166	253	48

Leading Scorers

Player	Club	GP	G	A	PTS	PIM
Mikita, Stan	Chicago	70	28	59	87	154
Ullman, Norm	Detroit	70	42	41	83	70
Howe, Gordie	Detrot	70	29	47	76	104
Hull, Bobby	Chicago	61	39	32	71	32
Delvecchio, Alex	Detroit	68	25	42	67	16
Provost, Claude	Montreal	70	27	37	64	28
Gilbert, Rod	New York	70	25	36	61	52
Pilote, Pierre	Chicago	68	14	45	59	162
Bucyk, John	Boston	68	26	29	55	24
Backstrom, Ralph	Montreal	70	25	30	55	41
Esposito, Phil	Chicago	70	23	32	55	44

1965-66

Team	GP	W	L	T	GF	GA	PTS
*Montreal	70	41	21	8	239	173	90
Chicago	70	37	25	8	240	187	82
Toronto	70	34	25	11	208	187	79
Detroit	70	31	27	12	221	194	74
Boston	70	21	43	6	174	275	48
New York	70	18	41	11	195	261	47

Leading Scorers

Player	Club	GP	G	A	PTS	PIM
Hull, Bobby	Chicago	65	54	43	97	70
Mikita, Stan	Chicago	68	30	48	78	58
Rouseau, Bobby	Montreal	70	30	48	78	20
Beliveau, Jean	Montreal	67	29	48	77	50
Howe, Gordie	Detroit	70	29	46	75	83
Ullman, Norm	Detroit	70	31	41	72	35
Delvecchio, Alex	Detroit	70	31	38	69	16
Nevin, Bob	New York	69	29	33	62	10
Richard, Henri	Montreal	62	22	39	61	47
Oliver, Murray	Boston	70	18	42	60	30

1966-67

Team	GP	W	L	T	GF	GA	PTS
Chicago	70	41	17	12	264	170	94
Montreal	70	32	25	13	202	188	77
*Toronto	70	32	27	11	204	211	75
New York	70	30	28	12	188	189	72
Detroit	70	27	39	4	212	241	58
Boston	70	17	43	10	182	253	44

Leading Scorers

Player	Club	GP	G	A	PTS	PIM
Mikita, Stan	Chicago	70	35	62	97	12
Hull, Bobby	Chicago	66	52	28	80	52
Ullman, Norm	Detroit	68	26	44	70	26
Wharram, Ken	Chicago	70	31	34	65	21
Howe, Gordie	Detroit	69	25	40	65	53
Rousseau, Bobby	Montreal	68	19	44	63	58
Esposito, Phil	Chicago	69	21	40	61	40
Goyette, Phil	New York	70	12	49	61	6
Mohns, Doug	Chicago	61	25	35	60	58
Richard, Henri	Montreal	65	21	34	55	28
Delvecchio, Alex	Detroit	70	17	38	55	10

Jean Beliveau, who scored three game-winning goals in the 1965 Finals, and Roger Crozier, who registered a 2.34 GAA in the 1966 playoffs, were the first two recipients of the Conn Smythe Trophy.

1967-68

East Division

Team	GP	W	L	T	GF	GA	PTS
*Montreal	74	42	22	10	236	167	94
New York	74	39	23	12	226	183	90
Boston	74	37	27	10	259	216	84
Chicago	74	32	26	16	212	222	80
Toronto	74	33	31	10	209	176	76
Detroit	74	27	35	12	245	257	66

West Division

Team	GP	W	L	T	GF	GA	PTS
Philadelphia	74	31	32	11	173	179	73
Los Angeles	74	31	33	10	200	224	72
St. Louis	74	27	31	16	177	191	70
Minnesota	74	27	32	15	191	226	69
Pittsburgh	74	27	34	13	195	216	67
Oakland	74	15	42	17	153	219	47

Leading Scorers

Player	Club	GP	G	A	PTS	PIM
Mikita, Stan	Chicago	72	40	47	87	14
Esposito, Phil	Boston	74	35	49	84	21
Howe, Gordie	Detroit	74	39	43	82	53
Ratelle, Jean	New York	74	32	46	78	18
Gilbert, Rod	New York	73	29	48	77	12
Hull, Bobby	Chicago	71	44	31	75	39
Ullman, Norm	Det., Tor.	71	35	37	72	28
Delvecchio, Alex	Detroit	74	22	48	70	14
Bucyk, John	Boston	72	30	39	69	8
Wharram, Ken	Chicago	74	27	42	69	18

1968-69

East Division

Team	GP	W	L	T	GF	GA	PTS
*Montreal	76	46	19	11	271	202	103
Boston	76	42	18	16	303	221	100
NewYork	76	41	26	9	231	196	91
Toronto	76	35	26	15	234	217	85
Detroit	76	33	31	12	239	221	78
Chicago	76	34	33	9	280	246	77

West Division

Team	GP	W	L	T	GF	GA	PTS
St. Louis	76	37	25	14	204	157	88
Oakland	76	29	36	11	219	251	69
Philadelphia	76	20	35	21	174	225	61
Los Angeles	76	24	42	10	185	260	58
Pittsburgh	76	20	45	11	189	252	51
Minnesota	76	18	43	5	189	270	51

Leading Scorers

Player	Club	GP	G	A	PTS	PIM
Esposito, Phil	Boston	74	49	77	126	79
Hull, Bobby	Chicago	74	58	49	107	48
Howe, Gordie	Detroit	76	44	59	103	58
Mikita, Stan	Chicago	74	30	67	97	52
Hodge, Ken	Boston	75	45	45	90	75
Cournoyer, Yvan	Montreal	76	43	44	87	31
Delvecchio, Alex	Detroit	72	25	58	83	8
Berenson, Red	St. Louis	76	35	47	82	43
Beliveau, Jean	Montreal	69	33	49	82	55
Mahovlich, Frank	Detroit	76	49	29	78	38
Ratelle, Jean	New York	75	32	46	78	26

1969-70

East Division

Team	GP	W	L	T	GF	GA	PTS
Chicago	76	45	22	9	250	170	99
*Boston	76	40	17	19	277	216	99
Detroit	76	40	21	15	246	199	95
New York	76	38	22	16	246	189	92
Montreal	76	38	22	16	244	201	92
Toronto	76	29	34	13	222	242	71

West Division

Team	GP	W	L	T	GF	GA	PTS
St. Louis	76	37	27	12	224	179	86
Pittsburgh	76	26	38	12	182	238	64
Minnesota	76	19	35	22	224	257	60
Oakland	76	22	40	14	169	243	58
Philadelphia	76	17	35	24	197	225	58
Los Angeles	76	14	52	10	168	290	38

Leading Scorers

Player	Club	GP	G	A	PTS	PIM
Orr, Bobby	Boston	76	33	87	120	125
Esposito, Phil	Boston	76	43	56	99	50
Mikita, Stan	Chicago	76	39	47	86	50
Goyette, Phil	St. Louis	72	29	49	78	16
Tkaczuk, Walt	New York	76	27	50	77	38
Ratelle, Jean	New York	75	32	42	74	28
Berenson, Red	St. Louis	67	33	39	72	38
Parise, Jean-Paul	Minnesota	74	24	48	72	72
Howe, Gordie	Detroit	76	31	40	71	58
Mahovlich, Frank	Detroit	74	38	32	70	59
Balon, Dave	New York	76	33	37	70	00
McKenzie, John	Boston	72	29	41	70	114

1970-71

East Division

Team	GP	W	L	T	GF	GA	PTS
Boston	78	57	14	7	399	207	121
New York	78	49	18	11	259	177	109
*Montreal	78	42	23	13	291	216	97
Toronto	78	37	33	8	248	211	82
Buffalo	78	24	39	15	217	291	63
Vancouver	78	24	46	8	229	296	56
Detroit	78	22	45	11	209	308	55

West Division

Team	GP	W	L	T	GF	GA	PTS
Chicago	78	49	20	9	277	184	107
St. Louis	78	34	25	19	223	208	87
Philadelphia	78	28	33	17	207	225	73
Minnesota	78	28	34	16	191	223	72
Los Angeles	78	25	40	13	239	303	63
Pittsburgh	78	21	37	20	221	240	62
California	78	20	53	5	199	320	45

Leading Scorers

Player	Club	GP	G	A	PTS	PIM
Esposito, Phil	Boston	78	76	76	152	71
Orr, Bobby	Boston	78	37	102	139	91
Bucyk, John	Boston	78	51	65	116	8
Hodge, Ken	Boston	78	43	62	105	113
Hull, Bobby	Chicago	78	44	52	96	32
Ullman, Norm	Toronto	73	34	51	85	24
Cashman, Wayne	Boston	77	21	58	79	100
McKenzie, John	Boston	65	31	46	77	120
Keon, Dave	Toronto	76	38	38	76	4
Beliveau, Jean	Montreal	70	25	51	76	40
Stanfield, Fred	Boston	75	24	52	76	12

1971-72

East Division

Team	GP	W	L	T	GF	GA	PTS
*Boston	78	54	13	11	330	204	119
New York	78	48	17	13	317	192	109
Montreal	78	46	16	16	307	205	108
Toronto	78	33	31	14	209	208	80
Detroit	78	33	35	10	261	262	76
Buffalo	78	16	43	19	203	289	51
Vancouver	78	20	50	8	203	297	48

West Division

Team	GP	W	L	T	GF	GA	PTS
Chicago	78	46	17	15	256	166	107
Minnesota	78	37	29	12	212	191	86
St. Louis	78	28	39	11	208	247	67
Pittsburgh	78	26	38	14	220	258	66
Philadelphia	78	26	38	14	200	236	66
California	78	21	39	18	216	288	60
Los Angeles	78	20	49	9	206	305	49

Leading Scorers

Player	Club	GP	G	A	PTS	PIM
Esposito, Phil	Bostn	76	66	67	133	76
Orr, Bobby	Boston	76	37	80	117	106
Ratelle, Jean	New York	63	46	63	109	4
Hadfield, Vic	New York	78	50	56	106	142
Gilbert, Rod	New York	73	43	54	97	64
Mahovlich, Frank	Montreal	76	43	53	96	36
Hull, Bobby	Chicago	78	50	43	93	24
Cournoyer, Yvan	Montreal	73	47	36	83	15
Bucyk, John	Boston	78	32	51	83	4
Clarke, Bobby	Philadelphia	78	35	46	81	87
Lemaire, Jacques	Montreal	77	32	49	81	26

1972-73

East Division

Team	GP	W	L	T	GF	GA	PTS
*Montreal	78	52	10	16	329	184	120
Boston	78	51	22	5	330	235	107
NY Rangers	78	47	23	8	297	208	102
Buffalo	78	37	27	14	257	219	88
Detroit	78	37	29	12	265	243	86
Toronto	78	27	41	10	247	279	64
Vancouver	78	22	47	9	233	339	53
NY Islaners	78	12	60	6	170	347	30

West Division

Team	GP	W	L	T	GF	GA	PTS
Chicago	78	42	27	9	284	225	93
Philadelphia	78	37	30	11	296	256	85
Minnesota	78	37	30	11	254	230	85
St. Louis	78	32	34	12	233	251	76
Pittsburgh	78	32	37	9	257	265	73
Los Angeles	78	31	36	11	232	245	73
Atlanta	78	25	38	15	191	239	65
California	78	16	46	16	213	323	48

Leading Sorers

Player	Club	GP	G	A	PTS	PIM
Esposito, Phil	Boston	78	55	75	130	87
Clarke, Bobby	Philadelphia	78	37	67	104	80
Orr, Bobby	Boston	63	29	72	101	99
MacLeish, Rick	Philadelphia	78	50	50	100	69
Lemaire, Jacques	Montreal	77	44	51	95	16
Ratelle, Jean	NY Rangers	78	41	53	94	12
Redmond, Mickey	Detroit	76	52	41	93	24
Bucyk, John	Boston	78	40	53	93	12
Mahovlich, Frank	Montreal	78	38	55	93	51
Pappin, Jim	Chicago	76	41	51	92	82

1973-74

East Division

Team	GP	W	L	T	GF	GA	PTS
Boston	78	52	17	9	349	221	113
Montreal	78	45	24	9	293	240	99
NY Rangers	78	40	24	14	300	251	94
Toronto	78	35	27	16	274	230	86
Buffalo	78	32	34	12	242	250	76
Detroit	78	29	39	10	255	319	68
Vancouver	78	24	43	11	224	296	59
NY Islanders	78	19	41	18	182	247	56

West Division

Team	GP	W	L	T	GF	GA	PTS
*Philadelphia	78	50	16	12	273	164	112
Chicago	78	41	14	23	272	164	105
Los Angeles	78	33	33	12	233	231	78
Atlanta	78	30	34	14	214	238	74
Pittsburgh	78	28	41	9	242	273	65
St. Louis	78	26	40	12	206	248	64
Minnesota	78	23	38	17	235	275	63
California	7	13	55	10	195	342	36

Leading Scorers

Player	Club	GP	G	A	PTS	PIM
Esposito, Phil	Boston	78	68	77	145	58
Orr, Bobby	Boston	74	32	90	122	82
Hodge, Ken	Boston	76	50	55	105	43
Cashman, Wayne	Boston	78	30	59	89	111
Clarke, Bobby	Philadelphia	77	35	52	87	113
Martin, Rick	Buffalo	78	52	34	86	38
Apps, Syl	Pittsburgh	75	24	61	85	37
Sittler, Darryl	Toronto	78	38	46	84	55
MacDonald, Lowell	Pitsburgh	78	43	39	82	14
Park, Brad	NY Rangers	78	25	57	82	148
Hextall, Dennis	Minnesota	78	20	62	82	138

1974-75

PRINCE OF WALES CONFERENCE

Norris Division

Team	GP	W	L	T	GF	GA	PTS
Montreal	80	47	14	19	374	225	113
Los Angeles	80	42	17	21	269	185	105
Pittsburgh	80	37	28	15	326	289	89
Detroit	80	23	45	12	259	335	58
Washington	80	8	67	5	181	446	21

Adams Division

Team	GP	W	L	T	GF	GA	PTS
Buffalo	80	49	16	15	354	240	113
Boston	80	40	26	14	345	245	94
Toronto	80	31	33	16	280	309	78
California	80	19	48	13	212	316	51

CLARENCE CAMPBELL CONFERENCE

Patrick Division

Team	GP	W	L	T	GF	GA	PTS
*Philadelphia	80	51	18	11	293	181	113
NY Rangers	80	37	29	14	319	276	88
NY Islanders	80	33	25	22	264	221	88
Atlanta	80	34	31	15	243	233	83

Smythe Division

Team	GP	W	L	T	GF	GA	PTS
Vancouver	80	38	32	10	271	254	86
St. Louis	80	35	31	14	269	267	84
Chicago	80	37	35	8	268	241	82
Minnesota	80	23	50	7	221	341	53
Kansas City	80	15	54	11	184	328	41

Leading Scorers

Player	Club	GP	G	A	PTS	PIM
Orr, Bobby	Boston	80	46	89	135	101
Esposito, Phil	Boston	79	61	66	127	62
Dionne, Marcel	Detroit	80	47	74	121	14
Lafleur, Guy	Montreal	70	53	66	119	37
Mahovlich, Pete	Montreal	80	35	82	117	64
Clarke, Bobby	Philadelphia	80	27	89	116	125
Robert, Rene	Buffalo	74	40	60	100	75
Gilbert, Rod	NY Rangers	76	36	61	97	22
Perreault, Gilbert	Buffalo	68	39	57	96	36
Martin, Rick	Buffalo	68	52	43	95	72

1975-76

PRINCE OF WALES CONFERENCE

Norris Division

Team	GP	W	L	T	GF	GA	PTS
*Montreal	80	58	11	11	337	174	127
Los Angeles	80	38	33	9	263	265	85
Pittsburgh	80	35	33	12	339	303	82
Detroit	80	26	44	10	226	300	62
Washington	80	11	59	10	224	394	32

Adams Division

Team	GP	W	L	T	GF	GA	PTS
Boston	80	48	15	17	313	237	113
Buffalo	80	46	21	13	339	240	105
Toronto	80	34	31	15	294	276	83
California	80	27	42	11	250	278	65

CLARENCE CAMPBELL CONFERENCE

Patrick Division

Team	GP	W	L	T	GF	GA	PTS
Philadelphia	80	51	13	16	348	209	118
NY Islanders	80	42	21	17	297	190	101
Atlanta	80	35	33	12	262	237	82
NY Rangers	80	29	42	9	262	333	67

Smythe Division

Team	GP	W	L	T	GF	GA	PTS
Chicago	80	32	30	18	254	261	82
Vancouver	80	33	32	15	271	272	81
St. Louis	80	29	37	14	249	290	72
Minnesota	80	20	53	7	195	303	47
Kansas City	80	12	56	12	190	351	36

Leading Scorers

Player	Club	GP	G	A	PTS	PIM
Lafleur, Guy	Montreal	80	56	69	125	36
Clarke, Bobby	Philadelphia	76	30	89	119	13
Perreault, Gilbert	Buffalo	80	44	69	113	36
Barber, Bill	Philadelphia	80	50	62	112	104
Larouche, Pierre	Pittsburgh	76	53	58	111	33
Ratelle, Jean	Bos., NYR	80	36	69	105	18
Mahovlich, Pete	Montreal	80	34	71	105	76
Pronovost, Jean	Pittsburgh	80	52	52	104	24
Sittler, Darryl	Toronto	79	41	59	100	90
Apps, Syl	Pittsburgh	80	32	67	99	24

1976-77

PRINCE OF WALES CONFERENCE

Norris Division

Team	GP	W	L	T	GF	GA	PTS
*Montreal	80	60	8	12	387	171	132
Los Angeles	80	34	31	15	271	241	83
Pittsburgh	80	34	33	13	240	252	81
Washington	80	24	42	14	221	307	62
Detroit	80	16	55	9	183	309	41

Adams Division

Team	GP	W	L	T	GF	GA	PTS
Boston	80	49	23	8	312	240	106
Buffalo	80	48	24	8	301	220	104
Toronto	80	33	32	15	301	285	81
Cleveland	80	25	42	13	240	292	63

CLARENCE CAMPBELL CONFERENCE

Patrick Division

Team	GP	W	L	T	GF	GA	PTS
Philadelphia	80	48	16	16	323	213	112
NY Islanders	80	47	21	12	288	193	106
Atlanta	80	34	34	12	264	265	80
NY Rangers	88	29	37	14	272	310	72

Smythe Division

Team	GP	W	L	T	GF	GA	PTS
St. Louis	80	32	39	9	239	276	73
Minnesota	80	23	39	18	240	310	64
Chicago	80	26	43	11	240	298	63
Vancouver	80	25	42	13	235	294	63
Colorado	80	20	46	14	226	307	54

Leading Scorers

Player	Club	GP	G	A	PTS	PIM
Lafleur, Guy	Montreal	80	56	80	136	20
Dionne, Marcel	Los Angeles	80	53	69	122	12
Shutt, Steve	Montreal	80	60	45	105	28
MacLeish, Rick	Philadelphia	79	49	48	97	42
Perreault, Gilbert	Buffalo	80	39	56	95	30
Young, Tim	Minnesota	80	29	66	95	58
Ratelle, Jean	Boston	78	33	61	94	2
McDonald, Lanny	Toronto	80	46	44	90	77
Sittler, Darryl	Toronto	73	38	52	90	89
Clarke, Bobby	Philadelphia	80	27	63	90	71

Bill Barber became the 15th player to reach the 50-goal plateau in a season when he scored against Al Smith on April 3, 1976.

1977-78

PRINCE OF WALES CONFERENCE

Norris Division

Team	GP	W	L	T	GF	GA	PTS
*Montreal	80	59	10	11	359	183	129
Detroit	80	32	34	14	252	266	78
Los Angeles	80	31	34	15	243	45	77
Pittsburgh	80	25	37	18	254	321	68
Washington	80	17	49	14	195	321	48

Adams Division

Team	GP	W	L	T	GF	GA	PTS
Boston	80	51	18	11	333	218	113
Buffalo	80	44	19	17	288	215	105
Toronto	80	41	29	10	271	237	92
Cleveland	80	22	45	13	230	325	57

CLARENCE CAMPBELL CONFERENCE

Patrick Division

Team	GP	W	L	T	GF	GA	PTS
NY Islanders	80	48	17	15	334	210	111
Philadelphia	80	45	20	15	296	200	105
Atlanta	80	34	27	19	274	252	87
NY Rangers	80	30	37	13	279	280	73

Smythe Division

Team	GP	W	L	T	GF	GA	PTS
Chicago	80	32	29	19	230	220	83
Colorado	80	19	40	21	257	305	59
Vancouver	80	20	43	17	239	320	57
St. Louis	80	20	47	13	195	304	53
Minnesota	80	18	53	9	218	325	45

Leading Scorers

Player	Club	GP	G	A	PTS	PIM
Lafleur, Guy	Montreal	79	60	72	132	26
Trottier, Bryan	NY Islanders	77	46	77	123	46
Sittler, Darryl	Toronto	80	45	72	117	100
Lemaire, Jacques	Montreal	76	36	61	97	14
Potvin, Denis	NY Islanders	80	30	64	94	81
Bossy, Mike	NY Islanders	73	53	38	91	6
O'Reilly, Terry	Boston	77	29	61	90	211
Perreault, Gilbert	Buffalo	79	41	48	89	20
Clarke, Bobby	Philadelphia	71	21	68	89	83
McDonald, Lanny	Toronto	74	47	40	87	54
Paiement, Wilf	Colorado	80	31	56	87	114

1978-79

PRINCE OF WLES CONFERENCE

Norris Division

Team	GP	W	L	T	GF	GA	PTS
*Montreal	80	52	17	11	337	204	115
Pittsburgh	80	36	31	13	281	279	85
Los Angeles	80	34	34	12	292	286	80
Washington	80	24	41	15	273	338	63
Detroit	80	23	41	16	252	295	62

Adams Division

Team	GP	W	L	T	GF	GA	PTS
Boston	80	43	23	14	316	270	100
Buffalo	80	36	28	16	280	263	88
Toronto	80	34	33	13	267	252	81
Minnesota	80	28	40	12	257	289	68

CLARENCE CAMPBELL CONFERENCE

Patrick Division

Team	GP	W	L	T	GF	GA	PTS
NY Islanders	80	51	15	14	358	214	116
Philadelphia	80	40	25	15	281	248	95
NY Rangers	80	40	29	11	316	292	91
Atlanta	80	41	31	8	327	280	90

Smythe Division

Team	GP	W	L	T	GF	GA	PTS
Chicago	80	29	36	15	244	277	73
Vancouver	80	5	42	13	217	291	63
St. Louis	80	18	50	12	249	348	48
Colorado	80	15	53	12	210	331	42

Leading Scorers

Player	Club	GP	G	A	PTS	PIM
Trottier, Bryan	NY Islanders	76	47	87	134	50
Dionne, Marcel	Los Angeles	80	59	71	130	30
Lafleur, Guy	Montreal	80	52	77	129	28
Bossy, Mike	NY Islanders	80	69	57	126	25
MacMillan, Bob	Atlanta	79	37	71	108	14
Chouinard, Guy	Atlanta	80	50	57	107	14
Potvin, Dens	NY Islanders	73	31	70	101	58
Federko, Bernie	St. Louis	74	31	64	95	14
Taylor, Dave	Los Angeles	78	43	48	91	124
Gillies, Clark	NY Islanders	75	35	56	91	68

1979-80

PRINCE OF WALES CONFERENCE

Norris Division

Team	GP	W	L	T	GF	GA	PTS
Montreal	80	47	20	13	328	240	107
Los Angeles	80	30	36	14	290	313	74
Pittsburgh	80	30	37	13	251	303	73
Hartford	80	27	34	19	303	312	73
Detroit	80	26	43	11	268	306	63

Adams Division

Team	GP	W	L	T	GF	GA	PTS
Buffalo	80	47	17	16	318	201	110
Boston	80	46	21	13	310	234	105
Minnesota	80	36	28	16	311	253	88
Toronto	80	35	40	5	304	327	75
Quebec	80	25	44	11	248	313	61

CLARENCE CAMPBELL CONFERENCE

Patrick Division

Team	GP	W	L	T	GF	GA	PTS
Philadelphia	80	48	12	20	327	254	116
*NY Islanders	80	39	28	13	281	247	91
NY Rangers	80	38	32	10	308	284	86
Atlanta	80	35	32	13	282	269	83
Washington	80	27	40	13	261	293	67

Smythe Division

Team	GP	W	L	T	GF	GA	PTS
Chicago	80	34	27	19	241	250	87
St. Louis	80	34	34	12	266	278	80
Vancouver	80	27	37	16	256	281	70
Edmonton	80	28	39	13	301	322	69
Winnipeg	80	20	49	11	214	314	51
Colorado	80	19	48	13	234	308	51

Leading Scorers

Player	Club	GP	G	A	PTS	PIM
Dionne, Marcel	Los Angeles	80	53	84	137	32
Gretzky, Wayne	Edmonton	79	51	86	137	21
Lafleur, Guy	Montreal	74	50	75	125	12
Perreault, Gilbert	Buffalo	80	40	66	106	57
Rogers, Mike	Hartford	80	44	61	105	10
Trottier, Bryan	NY Islanders	78	42	62	104	68
Simmer, Charlie	Los Angeles	64	56	45	101	65
Stoughton, Blaine	Hartford	80	56	44	100	16
Sittler, Darryl	Toronto	73	40	57	97	62
MacDonald, Blair	Edmonton	80	46	48	94	6
Federko, Bernie	St. Louis	79	38	56	94	24

Denis Savard was the first Chicago player to register back-to-back 100 point seasons, accomplishing the feat in 1984-85 and 1985-86.

1980-81

PRINCE OF WALES CONFERENCE

Norris Division

Team	GP	W	L	T	GF	GA	PTS
Montreal	80	45	22	13	332	232	103
Los Angeles	80	43	24	13	337	290	99
Pittsburgh	80	30	37	13	302	345	73
Harford	80	21	41	18	292	372	60
Detroit	80	19	43	18	252	339	56

Adams Division

Team	GP	W	L	T	GF	GA	PTS
Buffalo	80	39	20	21	327	250	99
Boston	80	37	30	13	316	272	87
Minnesota	80	35	28	17	291	263	87
Quebec	80	30	32	18	314	318	78
Toronto	80	28	37	15	322	367	71

CLARENCE CAMPBELL CONFERENCE

Patrick Division

Team	GP	W	L	T	GF	GA	PTS
*NY Islanders	80	48	18	14	355	260	110
Philadelphia	80	41	24	15	313	249	97
Calgary	80	39	27	14	329	298	92
NY Rangers	80	30	36	14	312	317	74
Washington	80	26	36	18	286	317	70

Smythe Division

Team	GP	W	L	T	GF	GA	PTS
St. Louis	80	45	18	17	352	281	107
Chicago	80	31	33	16	304	315	78
Vancouver	80	28	32	20	289	301	76
Edmonton	80	29	35	16	328	327	74
Colorado	80	22	45	13	258	344	57
Winnipeg	80	9	57	14	246	400	32

Leading Scorers

Player	Club	GP	G	A	PTS	PIM
Gretzky, Wayne	Edmonton	80	55	109	164	28
Dionne, Marcel	Los Angeles	80	58	77	135	70
Nilsson, Kent	Calgary	80	49	82	131	26
Bossy, Mike	NY Islanders	79	68	51	119	32
Taylor, Dave	Los Angeles	72	47	65	112	130
Stastny, Peter	Quebec	77	39	70	109	37
Simmer, Charlie	Los Angeles	65	56	49	105	62
Rogers, Mike	Hartford	80	40	65	105	32
Federko, Bernie	St. Louis	78	31	73	104	47
Richard, Jacques	Quebec	78	52	51	103	39
Middleton, Rick	Boston	80	44	59	103	16
Trottier, Bryan	NY Islanders	73	31	72	103	74

1981-82

CLARENCE CAMPBELL CONFERENCE

Norris Division

Team	GP	W	L	T	GF	GA	PTS
Minnesota	80	37	23	20	346	288	94
Winnipeg	80	33	33	14	319	332	80
St. Louis	80	32	40	8	315	349	72
Chicago	80	30	38	12	332	363	72
Toronto	80	20	44	16	298	380	56
Detroit	80	21	47	12	270	351	54

Smythe Division

Team	GP	W	L	T	GF	GA	PTS
Edmonton	80	48	17	15	417	295	111
Vancouver	80	30	33	17	290	286	77
Calgary	80	29	34	17	334	345	75
Los Angees	80	24	41	15	314	369	63
Colorado	80	18	49	13	241	362	49

PRINCE OF WALES CONFERENCE

Adams Division

Team	GP	W	L	T	GF	GA	PTS
Montreal	80	46	17	17	360	223	109
Boston	80	43	27	10	323	285	96
Buffalo	80	39	26	15	307	273	93
Quebec	80	33	31	16	356	345	82
Hartford	80	21	41	18	264	351	60

Patrick Division

Team	GP	W	L	T	GF	GA	PTS
*NY Islanders	80	54	16	10	385	250	118
NY Rangers	80	39	27	14	316	306	92
Philadelphia	80	38	31	11	325	313	87
Pittsburgh	80	31	36	13	310	337	75
Washington	80	26	41	13	319	338	65

Leading Scorers

Player	Club	GP	G	A	PTS	PIM
Gretzky, Wayne	Edmonton	80	92	120	212	26
Bossy, Mike	NY Islanders	80	64	83	147	22
Stastny, Peter	Quebec	80	46	93	139	91
Maruk, Dennis	Washington	80	60	76	136	128
Trottier, Bryan	NY Islanders	80	50	79	129	88
Savard, Denis	Chicago	80	32	87	119	82
Dionne, Marcel	Los Angeles	78	50	67	117	50
Smith, Bobby	Minnesota	80	43	71	114	82
Ciccarelli, Dino	Minnesota	76	55	51	106	138
Taylor, Dave	Los Angeles	78	39	67	106	130

1982-83

CLARENCE CAMPBELL CONFERENCE

Norris Division

Team	GP	W	L	T	GF	GA	PTS
Chicago	80	47	23	10	338	268	104
Minnesota	80	40	24	16	321	290	96
Toronto	80	28	40	12	293	330	68
St. Louis	80	25	40	15	285	316	65
Detroit	80	21	44	15	263	344	57

Smythe Division

Team	GP	W	L	T	GF	GA	PTS
Edmonton	80	47	21	12	424	315	106
Calgary	80	32	34	14	321	317	78
Vancouver	80	30	35	15	303	309	75
Winnipeg	80	33	39	8	311	333	74
Los Angeles	80	27	41	12	308	365	66

PRINCE OF WALES CONFERENCE

Adams Division

Team	GP	W	L	T	GF	GA	PTS
Boston	80	50	20	10	327	228	110
Montreal	80	42	24	14	350	286	98
Buffalo	80	38	29	13	318	285	89
Quebec	80	34	34	12	343	336	80
Hartford	80	19	54	7	261	403	45

Patrick Division

Team	GP	W	L	T	GF	GA	PTS
Philadelphia	80	49	23	8	32	240	106
*NY Islanders	80	42	26	12	302	226	96
Washington	80	39	25	16	306	283	94
NY Rangers	80	35	35	10	306	287	80
New Jersey	80	17	49	14	230	338	48
Pittsburgh	80	18	53	9	257	394	45

Leading Scorers

Player	Club	GP	G	A	PTS	PIM
Gretzky, Wayne	Edmonton	80	71	125	196	59
Stastny, Peter	Quebec	75	47	77	124	78
Savard, Denis	Chicago	78	35	86	121	99
Bossy, Mike	NY Islanders	79	60	58	118	20
Dionne, Marcel	Los Angeles	80	56	51	107	22
Pederson, Barry	Boston	77	46	61	107	47
Messier, Mark	Edmonton	77	48	58	106	72
Goulet, Michel	Quebec	80	57	48	105	51
Anderson, Glenn	Edmonton	72	48	56	104	70
Nilsson, Kent	Calgary	80	46	58	104	10
Kurri, Jari	Edmonton	80	45	59	104	22

Rick Vaive, a fixture in the slot for Toronto, Chicago and Buffalo, had three consecutive seasons with at least 50 goals.

1983-84

CLARENCE CAMPBELL CONFERENCE

Norris Division

Team	GP	W	L	T	GF	GA	PTS
Minnesota	80	39	31	10	345	344	88
St. Louis	80	32	41	7	293	316	71
Detroit	80	31	42	7	298	323	69
Chicago	80	30	42	8	277	311	68
Toronto	80	26	45	9	303	387	61

Smythe Division

Team	GP	W	L	T	GF	GA	PTS
*Edmonton	80	57	18	5	446	314	119
Calgary	80	34	32	14	311	314	82
Vancouver	80	2	39	9	306	328	73
Winnipeg	80	31	38	11	340	374	73
Los Angeles	80	23	44	13	309	376	59

PRINCE OF WALES CONFERENCE

Adams Division

Team	GP	W	L	T	GF	GA	PTS
Boston	80	49	25	6	336	261	104
Buffalo	80	48	25	7	315	257	103
Quebec	80	42	28	10	360	278	94
Montreal	80	35	40	5	286	295	75
Hartford	80	28	42	10	288	320	66

Patrick Division

Team	GP	W	L	T	GF	GA	PTS
NY Islanders	80	50	26	4	357	269	104
Washngton	80	48	27	5	308	226	101
Philadelphia	80	44	26	10	350	290	98
NY Rangers	80	42	29	9	314	304	93
New Jersey	80	17	56	7	231	350	41
Pittsburgh	80	16	58	6	254	390	38

Leading Scorers

Player	Club	GP	G	A	PTS	PIM
Gretzky, Wayne	Edmonton	74	87	118	205	39
Coffey, Paul	Edmonton	80	40	86	126	104
Goulet, Michel	Quebec	75	56	65	121	76
Stastny, Peter	Quebec	80	46	73	119	73
Bossy, Mike	NY Islanders	67	51	67	118	8
Pederson, Barry	Boston	80	39	77	116	64
Kurri, Jari	Edmonton	64	52	61	113	14
Trottier, Bryan	NY Islanders	68	40	71	111	59
Federko, Bernie	St. Louis	79	41	66	107	43
Middleton, Rick	Boston	80	47	58	105	14

1984-85

CLARENCE CAMPBELL CONFERENCE

Norris Division

Team	GP	W	L	T	GF	GA	PTS
St. Louis	80	37	31	12	299	288	86
Chicago	80	38	35	7	309	299	83
Detroit	80	27	41	12	313	357	66
Minnesota	80	25	43	12	268	321	62
Toronto	80	20	52	8	253	358	48

Smythe Division

Team	GP	W	L	T	GF	GA	PTS
*Edmonton	80	49	20	11	401	298	109
Winnipeg	80	43	27	10	358	332	96
Calgary	80	41	27	12	363	302	94
Los Angeles	80	34	32	14	339	326	82
Vancover	80	25	46	9	284	401	59

PRINCE OF WALES CONFERENCE

Adams Division

Team	GP	W	L	T	GF	GA	PTS
Montreal	80	41	27	12	309	262	94
Quebec	80	41	30	9	323	275	91
Buffalo	80	38	28	14	290	237	90
Boston	80	36	34	10	303	287	82
Hartford	80	30	41	9	268	318	69

Patrick Division

Team	GP	W	L	T	GF	GA	PTS
Philadelphia	80	53	20	7	348	241	113
Washington	80	46	25	9	322	240	101
NY Islanders	80	40	34	6	345	312	86
NY Rangers	80	26	44	10	295	345	62
New Jersey	80	22	48	10	264	346	54
Pittsburgh	80	24	51	5	276	385	53

Leading Scorers

Player	Club	GP	G	A	PTS	PIM
Gretzky, Wayne	Edmonton	80	73	135	208	52
Kurri, Jari	Edmonton	73	71	64	135	30
Hawerchuk, Dale	Winnipeg	80	53	77	130	74
Dionne, Marcel	Los Angeles	80	46	80	126	46
Coffey, Paul	Edmonton	80	37	84	21	97
Bossy, Mike	NY Islanders	76	58	59	117	38
Ogrodnick, John	Detroit	79	55	50	105	30
Savard, Denis	Chicago	79	38	67	105	56
Federko, Bernie	St. Louis	76	30	73	103	27
Gartner, Mike	Washington	80	50	52	102	7

1985-86

CLARENCE CAMPBELL CONFERENCE

Norris Division

Team	GP	W	L	T	GF	GA	PTS
Chicago	80	39	33	8	351	349	86
Minnesota	80	38	33	9	327	305	85
St. Louis	80	37	34	9	302	291	83
Toronto	80	25	48	7	311	386	57
Detroit	80	17	57	6	266	415	40

Smythe Division

Team	GP	W	L	T	GF	GA	PTS
Edmonton	80	56	17	7	426	310	119
Calgary	80	40	31	9	354	315	89
Winnipeg	80	26	47	7	295	372	59
Vancouver	80	23	44	13	282	333	59
Los Angeles	80	23	49	8	284	389	54

PRINCE OF WALES CONFERENE

Adams Division

Team	GP	W	L	T	GF	GA	PTS
Quebec	80	43	31	6	330	289	92
*Montreal	80	40	33	7	330	280	87
Boston	80	37	31	12	311	288	86
Hartford	80	40	36	4	332	302	84
Buffalo	80	37	37	6	296	291	80

Patrick Division

Team	GP	W	L	T	GF	GA	PTS
Philadelphia	80	53	23	4	335	241	110
Washington	80	50	23	7	315	272	107
NY Islanders	80	39	29	12	327	284	90
NY Rangers	80	36	38	6	280	276	78
Pittsburgh	80	34	38	8	313	305	76
New Jersey	80	28	49	3	300	374	59

Leading Scorers

Player	Club	GP	G	A	PTS	PIM
Gretzky, Wayne	Edmonton	80	52	163	215	52
Lemieux, Mario	Pittsburgh	79	48	93	141	43
Coffey, Paul	Edmonton	79	48	90	138	120
Kurri, Jari	Edmonton	78	68	63	131	22
Bossy, Mike	NY Islanders	80	61	62	123	14
Stastny, Peter	Quebec	76	41	81	122	60
Savard, Denis	Chicago	80	47	69	116	111
Naslund, Mats	Montreal	80	43	67	110	16
Hawerchuk, Dale	Winnipeg	80	46	59	105	44
Broten, Neal	Minnesota	80	29	76	105	47

1986-87

CLARENCE CAMPBELL CONFERENCE

Norris Division

Team	GP	W	L	T	GF	GA	PTS
St. Louis	80	32	33	15	281	293	79
Detroit	80	34	36	10	260	274	78
Chicago	80	29	37	14	290	310	72
Toronto	80	32	42	6	286	319	70
Minnesota	80	30	40	10	296	314	70

Smythe Division

Team	GP	W	L	T	GF	GA	PTS
*Edmonton	80	50	24	6	372	284	106
Calgary	80	46	31	3	318	289	95
Winnipeg	80	40	32	8	279	271	88
Los Angeles	80	31	41	8	318	341	70
Vancouver	80	29	43	8	282	314	66

PRINCE OF WALES CONFERENCE

Adams Division

Team	GP	W	L	T	GF	GA	PTS
Hartford	80	43	30	7	287	270	93
Montreal	80	41	29	10	277	241	92
Boston	80	39	34	7	301	276	85
Quebec	80	31	39	10	267	276	72
Buffalo	80	28	44	8	280	308	64

Patrick Division

Team	GP	W	L	T	GF	GA	PTS
Philadelphia	80	46	26	8	310	245	100
Washington	80	38	32	10	285	278	86
NY Islanders	80	35	33	12	279	281	82
NY Rangers	80	34	38	8	307	323	76
Pittsburg	80	30	38	12	297	290	72
New Jersey	80	29	45	6	293	368	64

Leading Scorers

Player	Club	GP	G	A	PTS	PIM
Gretzky, Wayne	Edmonton	79	62	121	183	28
Kurri, Jari	Edmonton	79	54	54	108	41
Lemieux, Mario	Pittsburgh	63	54	53	107	57
Messier, Mark	Edmonton	77	37	70	107	73
Gilmour, Doug	St. Louis	80	42	63	105	58
Ciccarelli, Dino	Minnesota	80	52	51	103	92
Hawerchuk, Dale	Winnipeg	80	47	53	100	54
Goulet, Michel	Quebec	75	49	47	96	61
Kerr, Tim	Philadelphia	75	58	37	95	57
Bourque, Ray	Boston	78	23	72	95	36

1987-88

CLARENCE CAMPBELL CONFERENCE

Norris Division

Team	GP	W	L	T	GF	GA	PTS
Detroit	80	41	28	11	322	269	93
St. Louis	80	34	38	8	278	294	76
Chicago	80	30	41	9	284	326	69
Toronto	80	21	49	10	273	345	52
Minnesota	80	19	48	13	242	349	51

Smythe Division

Team	GP	W	L	T	GF	GA	PTS
Calgary	80	48	23	9	397	305	105
*Edmonton	80	44	25	11	363	288	99
Winnipeg	80	33	36	11	292	310	77
Los Angeles	80	30	42	8	318	359	68
Vancouver	80	25	46	9	272	320	59

PRINCE OF WALES CONFERENCE

Adams Division

Team	GP	W	L	T	GF	GA	PTS
Montreal	80	45	22	13	298	238	103
Boston	80	44	30	6	300	251	94
Buffalo	80	37	32	11	283	305	85
Hartford	80	35	38	7	249	267	77
Quebec	80	32	40	5	271	306	69

Patrick Division

Team	GP	W	L	T	GF	GA	PTS
NY Islanders	80	39	31	10	308	267	88
Washington	80	38	33	9	281	249	85
Philadelphia	80	38	33	9	292	282	85
New Jersey	80	38	36	6	295	296	82
NY Rangers	80	36	34	10	300	283	82
Pittsburgh	80	36	35	9	319	316	81

Leading Scorers

Player	Club	GP	G	A	PTS	PIM
Lemieux, Mario	Pittsburgh	76	70	98	168	92
Gretzky, Wayne	Edmonton	64	40	109	149	24
Savard, Denis	Chicago	80	44	87	131	95
Hawerchuk, Dale	Winnipeg	80	44	77	121	59
Robitaille, Luc	Los Angeles	80	53	58	111	82
Stastny, Peter	Quebec	76	46	65	111	69
Messier, Mark	Edmonton	77	37	74	111	103
Carson, Jimmy	Los Angeles	80	55	52	107	45
Loob, Hakan	Calgary	80	50	56	106	47
Goulet, Michel	Quebec	80	48	58	106	56

1988-89

CLARENCE CAMBELL CONFERENCE

Norris Division

Team	GP	W	L	T	GF	GA	PTS
Detroit	80	34	34	12	313	316	80
St. Louis	80	33	35	12	275	285	78
Minnesota	80	27	37	16	258	278	70
Chicago	80	27	41	12	297	335	66
Toronto	80	28	46	6	259	342	62

Smythe Division

Team	GP	W	L	T	GF	GA	PTS
*Calgary	80	54	17	9	354	226	117
Los Angeles	80	42	31	7	376	335	91
Edmonton	80	38	34	8	325	306	84
Vancouver	80	33	39	8	251	253	74
Winnipeg	80	26	42	12	300	355	64

PRINCE OF WALES CONFERENCE

Adams Division

Team	GP	W	L	T	GF	GA	PTS
Montreal	80	53	18	9	315	218	115
Boston	80	37	29	14	289	256	88
Buffalo	80	38	35	7	291	299	83
Hartford	80	37	38	5	299	290	79
Quebec	80	27	46	7	269	342	61

Patrick Division

Team	GP	W	L	T	GF	GA	PTS
Washington	80	41	29	10	305	259	92
Pittsburgh	80	40	33	7	347	349	87
NY Rangers	80	37	35	8	310	307	82
Philadelphia	80	36	36	8	307	285	80
New Jersey	80	27	41	12	281	325	66
NY Islanders	80	28	47	5	265	325	61

Leading Scorers

Player	Club	GP	G	A	PTS	PIM
Lemieux, Mario	Pittsburgh	76	85	114	199	100
Gretzky, Wayne	Los Angeles	78	54	114	168	26
Yzerman, Steve	Detroit	80	65	90	155	61
Nicholls, Bernie	Los Angeles	79	70	80	150	96
Brown, Rob	Pittsburgh	68	49	66	115	118
Coffey, Paul	Pittsburgh	75	30	83	113	193
Mullen, Joe	Calgary	79	51	59	110	16
Kurri, Jari	Edmonton	76	44	58	102	69
Carson, Jimmy	Edmonton	80	49	51	100	36
Robitaille, Luc	Los Angeles	78	46	52	98	65

When Denis Potvin retired in 1988, he was the highest scoring defenseman in the history of the game, having registered 1,052 points in 15 NHL seasons.

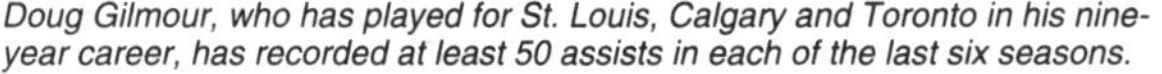

Doug Gilmour, who has played for St. Louis, Calgary and Toronto in his nine-year career, has recorded at least 50 assists in each of the last six seasons.

Mario Lemieux won his third scoring title in 1991-92, compiling 131 points on 44 goals and 87 assists in only 64 games.

1989-90

CLARENCE CAMPBELL CONFERENCE

Norris Division

Team	GP	W	L	T	GF	GA	PTS
Chicago	80	41	33	6	316	294	88
St. Louis	80	37	34	9	295	279	83
Toronto	80	38	38	4	337	358	80
Minnesota	80	36	40	4	284	291	76
Detroit	80	28	38	14	288	323	70
Smythe Division							
Calgary	80	42	23	15	348	265	99
*Edmonton	80	38	28	14	315	283	90
Winnipeg	80	37	32	11	298	290	85
Los Angeles	80	34	39	7	338	337	75
Vancouver	80	25	41	14	245	306	64

PRINCE OF WALES CONFERENCE

Adams Division

Team	GP	W	L	T	GF	GA	PTS
Boston	80	46	25	9	289	232	101
Buffalo	80	45	27	8	286	248	98
Montreal	80	41	28	11	288	234	93
Hartford	80	38	33	9	275	268	85
Quebec	80	12	61	7	240	407	31
Patrick Division							
NY Rangers	80	36	31	13	279	267	85
New Jersey	80	37	34	9	295	288	83
Washington	80	36	38	6	284	275	78
NY Islanders	80	31	38	11	281	288	73
Pittsburgh	80	32	40	8	318	359	72
Philadelphia	80	30	39	11	290	297	71

Leading Scorers

Player	Club	GP	G	A	PTS	PIM
Gretzky, Wayne	Los Angeles	73	40	102	142	42
Messier, Mark	Edmonton	79	45	84	129	79
Yzerman, Steve	Detroit	79	62	65	127	79
Lemieux, Mario	Pittsburgh	59	45	78	123	78
Hull, Brett	St. Louis	80	72	41	113	24
Nicholls, Bernie	L.A., NYR	79	39	73	112	86
Turgeon, Pierre	Buffalo	80	40	66	106	29
LaFontaine, Pat	NY Islanders	74	54	51	105	38
Coffey, Paul	Pittsburgh	80	29	74	103	95
Sakic, Joe	Quebec	80	39	63	102	27
Oates, Adam	St. Louis	80	23	79	102	30

1990-91

CLARENCE CAMPBELL CONFERENCE

Norris Division

Team	GP	W	L	T	GF	GA	PTS
Chicago	80	49	23	8	284	211	106
St. Louis	80	47	22	11	310	250	105
Detroit	80	34	38	8	273	298	76
Minnesota	80	27	39	14	256	266	68
Toronto	80	23	46	11	241	318	57
Smythe Division							
Los Angeles	80	46	24	10	340	254	102
Calgary	80	46	26	8	344	263	100
Edmonton	80	37	37	6	272	272	80
Vancouver	80	28	43	9	243	315	65
Winnipeg	80	26	43	11	260	288	63

PRINCE OF WALES CONFERENCE

Adams Division

Team	GP	W	L	T	GF	GA	PTS
Boston	80	44	24	12	299	264	100
Montreal	80	39	30	11	273	249	89
Buffalo	80	31	30	19	292	278	81
Hartford	80	31	38	11	238	276	73
Quebec	80	16	50	14	236	354	46
Patrick Division							
*Pittsburgh	80	41	33	6	342	305	88
NY Rangers	80	36	31	13	297	265	85
Washington	80	37	36	7	258	258	81
New Jersey	80	32	33	15	272	264	79
Philadelphia	80	33	37	10	252	267	76
NY Islanders	80	25	45	10	223	290	60

Leading Scorers

Player	Club	GP	G	A	PTS	PIM
Gretzky, Wayne	Los Angeles	78	41	122	163	16
Hull, Brett	St. Louis	78	86	45	131	22
Oates, Adam	St. Louis	61	25	90	115	29
Recchi, Mark	Pittsburgh	78	40	73	113	48
Cullen, John	Pit., Hfd.	78	39	71	110	101
Sakic, Joe	Quebec	80	48	61	109	24
Yzerman, Steve	Detroit	80	51	57	108	34
Fleury, Theo	Calgary	79	51	53	104	136
MacInnis, Al	Calgary	78	28	75	103	90
Larmer, Steve	Chicago	80	44	57	101	79

1991-92

CLARENCE CAMPBELL CONFERENCE

Norris Division

Team	GP	W	L	T	GF	GA	PTS
Detroit	80	43	25	12	320	256	98
Chicago	80	36	29	15	257	236	87
St. Louis	80	36	33	11	279	266	83
Minnesota	80	32	42	6	246	278	70
Toronto	80	30	43	7	234	294	67
Smythe Division							
Vancouver	80	42	26	12	285	250	96
Los Angeles	80	35	31	14	287	296	84
Edmonton	80	36	34	10	295	297	82
Winnipeg	80	33	32	15	251	244	81
Calgary	80	31	37	12	296	305	74
San Jose	80	17	58	5	219	359	39

PRINCE OF WALES CONFERENCE

Adams Division

Team	GP	W	L	T	GF	GA	PTS
Montreal	80	41	28	11	267	207	93
Boston	80	36	32	12	270	275	84
Buffalo	80	31	37	12	289	299	74
Hartford	80	26	41	13	247	283	65
Quebec	80	20	48	12	255	318	52
Patrick Division							
NY Rangers	80	50	25	5	321	246	105
Washington	80	45	27	8	330	275	98
*Pittsburgh	80	39	32	9	343	308	87
New Jersey	80	38	31	11	289	259	87
NY Islanders	80	34	35	11	291	299	79
Philadelphia	80	32	37	11	252	273	75

Leading Scorers

Player	Club	GP	G	A	PTS	PIM
Lemieux, Mario	Pittsburgh	64	44	87	131	94
Stevens, Kevin	Pittsburgh	80	54	69	123	254
Gretzky, Wayne	Los Angeles	74	31	90	121	34
Hull, Brett	St. Louis	73	70	39	109	48
Robitaille, Luc	Los Angeles	80	44	63	107	95
Messier, Mark	NY Rangers	79	35	72	107	76
Roenick, Jeremy	Chicago	80	53	50	103	23
Yzerman, Steve	Detroit	79	45	58	103	64
Leetch, Brian	NY Rangers	80	22	80	102	26
Oates, Adam	St. L., Bos.	80	20	79	99	22

Note: Detailed statistics for 1991-92 are listed in the Final Statistics, 1991-92 section of the **NHL Guide & Record Book.**

NHL History

1917 — National Hockey League organized November 22 in Montreal following suspension of operations by the National Hockey Association of Canada Limited (NHA). Montreal Canadiens, Montreal Wanderers, Ottawa Senators and Quebec Bulldogs attended founding meeting. Delegates decided to use NHA rules.

Toronto Arenas were later admitted as fifth team; Quebec decided not to operate during the first season. Quebec players allocated to remaining four teams.

Frank Calder elected president and secretary-treasurer.

First NHL games played December 19, with Toronto only arena with artificial ice. Clubs played 22-game split schedule.

1918 — Emergency meeting held January 3 due to destruction by fire of Montreal Arena which was home ice for both Canadiens and Wanderers.

Wanderers withdrew, reducing the NHL to three teams; Canadiens played remaining home games at 3,250-seat Jubilee rink.

Quebec franchise sold to P.J. Quinn of Toronto on October 18 on the condition that the team operate in Quebec City for 1918-19 season. Quinn did not attend the November League meeting and Quebec did not play in 1918-19.

1919-20 — NHL reactivated Quebec Bulldogs franchise. Former Quebec players returned to the club. New Mount Royal Arena became home of Canadiens. Toronto Arenas changed name to St. Patricks. Clubs played 24-game split schedule.

1920-21 — H.P. Thompson of Hamilton, Ontario made application for the purchase of an NHL franchise. Quebec franchise shifted to Hamilton with other NHL teams providing players to strengthen the club.

1921-22 — Split schedule abandoned. First and second place teams at the end of full schedule to play for championship.

1922-23 — Clubs agreed that players could not be sold or traded to clubs in any other league without first being offered to all other clubs in the NHL. In March, Foster Hewitt broadcast radio's first hockey game.

1923-24 — Ottawa's new 10,000-seat arena opened. First U.S. franchise granted to Boston for following season.

Dr. Cecil Hart Trophy donated to NHL to be awarded to the player judged most useful to his team.

1924-25 — Canadian Arena Company of Montreal granted a franchise to operate Montreal Maroons. NHL now six team league with two clubs in Montreal. Inaugural game in new Montreal Forum played November 29, 1924 as Canadiens defeated Toronto 7-1. Forum was home rink for the Maroons, but no ice was available in the Canadiens arena November 29, resulting in shift to Forum.

Hamilton finished first in the standings, receiving a bye into the finals. But Hamilton players, demanding $200 each for additional games in the playoffs, went on strike. The NHL suspended all players, fining them $200 each. Stanley Cup finalist to be the winner of NHL semi-final between Toronto and Canadiens.

Prince of Wales and Lady Byng trophies donated to NHL.

Clubs played 30-game schedule.

1925-26 — Hamilton club dropped from NHL. Players signed by new New York Americans franchise. Franchise granted to Pittsburgh.

Clubs played 36-game schedule.

1926-27 — New York Rangers granted franchise May 15, 1926. Chicago Black Hawks and Detroit Cougars granted franchises September 25, 1926. NHL now ten-team league with an American and a Canadian Division.

Stanley Cup came under the control of NHL. In previous seasons, winners of the now-defunct Western or Pacific Coast leagues would play NHL champion in Cup finals.

Toronto franchise sold to a new company controlled by Hugh Aird and Conn Smythe. Name changed from St. Patricks to Maple Leafs.

Clubs played 44-game schedule.

The Montreal Canadiens donated the Vezina Trophy to be awarded to the team allowing the fewest goals-against in regular season play. The winning team would, in turn, present the trophy to the goaltender playing in the greatest number of games during the season.

1929-30 — Detroit franchise changed name from Cougars to Falcons.

1930-31 — Pittsburgh transferred to Philadelphia for one season. Pirates changed name to Philadelphia Quakers. Trading deadline for teams set at February 15 of each year. NHL approved operation of farm teams by Rangers, Americans, Falcons and Bruins. Four-sided electric arena clock first demonstrated.

1931-32 — Philadelphia dropped out. Ottawa withdrew for one season. New Maple Leaf Gardens completed.

Clubs played 48-game schedule

1932-33 — Detroit franchise changed name from Falcons to Red Wings. Franchise application received from St. Louis but refused because of additional travel costs. Ottawa team resumed play.

1933-34 — First All-Star Game played as a benefit for injured player Ace Bailey. Leafs defeated All-Stars 7-3 in Toronto.

1934-35 — Ottawa franchise transferred to St. Louis. Team called St. Louis Eagles and consisted largely of Ottawa's players.

1935-36 — Ottawa-St. Louis franchise terminated. Montreal Canadiens finished season with very poor record. To strengthen the club, NHL gave Canadiens first call on the services of all French-Canadian players for three seasons.

1937-38 — Second benefit all-star game staged November 2 in Montreal in aid of the family of the late Canadiens star Howie Morenz.

Montreal Maroons withdrew from the NHL on June 22, 1938, leaving seven clubs in the League.

1938-39 — Expenses for each club regulated at $5 per man per day for meals and $2.50 per man per day for accommodation.

1939-40 — Benefit All-Star Game played October 29, 1939 in Montreal for the children of the late Albert (Babe) Siebert.

1940-41 — Ross-Tyer puck adopted as the official puck of the NHL. Early in the season it was apparent that this puck was too soft. The Spalding puck was adopted in its place.

After the playoffs, Arthur Ross, NHL governor from Boston, donated a perpetual trophy to be awarded annually to the player voted outstanding in the league.

1941-42 — New York Americans changed name to Brooklyn Americans.

1942-43 — Brooklyn Americans withdrew from NHL, leaving six teams: Boston, Chicago, Detroit, Montreal, New York and Toronto. Playoff format saw first-place team play third-place team and second play fourth.

Clubs played 50-game schedule.

Frank Calder, president of the NHL since its inception, died in Montreal. Meryn "Red" Dutton, former manager of the New York Americans, became president. The NHL commissioned the Calder Memorial Trophy to be awarded to the League's outstanding rookie each year.

1945-46 — Philadelphia, Los Angeles and San Francisco applied for NHL franchises.

The Philadelphia Arena Company of the American Hockey League applied for an injunction to prevent the possible operation of an NHL franchise in that city.

1946-47 — Mervyn Dutton retired as president of the NHL prior to the start of the season. He was succeeded by Clarence S. Campbell.

Individual trophy winners and all-star team members to receive $1,000 awards.

Playoff guarantees for players introduced.

Clubs played 60-game schedule.

1947-48 — The first annual All-Star Game for the benefit of the players' pension fund was played when the All-Stars defeated the Stanley Cup Champion Toronto Maple Leafs 4-3 in Toronto on October 13, 1947.

Ross Trophy, awarded to the NHL's outstanding player since 1941, to be awarded annually to the League's scoring leader.

Philadelphia and Los Angeles franchise applications refused.

National Hockey League Pension Society formed.

1949-50 — Clubs played 70-game schedule.

First intra-league draft held April 30, 1950. Clubs allowed to protect 30 players. Remaining players available for $25,000 each.

1951-52 — Referees included in the League's pension plan.

1952-53 — In May of 1952, City of Cleveland applied for NHL franchise. Application denied. In March of 1953, the Cleveland Barons of the AHL challenged the NHL champions for the Stanley Cup. The NHL governors did not accept this challenge.

1953-54 — The James Norris Memorial Trophy presented to the NHL for annual presentation to the League's best defenseman.

Intra-league draft rules amended to allow teams to protect 18 skaters and two goaltenders, claiming price reduced to $15,000.

1954-55 — Each arena to operate an "out-of-town" scoreboard. Referees and linesmen to wear shirts of black and white vertical stripes. Teams agree to wear white uniforms at home and colored uniforms on the road.

1956-57 — Standardized signals for referees and linesmen introduced.

1960-61 — Canadian National Exhibition, City of Toronto and NHL reach agreement for the construction of a Hockey Hall of Fame on the CNE grounds. Hall opens on August 26, 1961.

The New York Americans entered the NHL in 1925. The franchise was previously known as the Hamilton (Ontario) Tigers.

1963-64 — Player development league established with clubs operated by NHL franchises located in Minneapolis, St. Paul, Indianapolis, Omaha and, beginning in 1964-65, Tulsa. First universal amateur draft took place. All players of qualifying age (17) unaffected by sponsorship of junior teams available to be drafted.

1964-65 — Conn Smythe Trophy presented to the NHL to be awarded annually to the outstanding player in the Stanley Cup playoffs.

Minimum age of players subject to amateur draft changed to 18.

1965-66 — NHL announced expansion plans for a second six-team division to begin play in 1967-68.

1966-67 — Fourteen applications for NHL franchises received.

Lester Patrick Trophy presented to the NHL to be awarded annually for outstanding service to hockey in the United States.

NHL sponsorship of junior teams ceased, making all players of qualifying age not already on NHL-sponsored lists eligible for the amateur draft.

1967-68 — Six new teams added: California Seals, Los Angeles Kings, Minnesota North Stars, Philadelphia Flyers, Pittsburgh Penguins, St. Louis Blues. New teams to play in West Division. Remaining six teams to play in East Division.

Minimum age of players subject to amateur draft changed to 20.

Clubs played 74-game schedule.

Clarence S. Campbell Trophy awarded to team finishing the regular season in first place in West Division.

California Seals changed name to Oakland Seals on December 8, 1967.

1968-69 — Clubs played 76-game schedule.

Amateur draft expanded to cover any amateur player of qualifying age throughout the world.

1970-71 — Two new teams added: Buffalo Sabres and Vancouver Canucks. These teams joined East Division: Chicago switched to West Division.

Clubs played 78-game schedule.

1971-72 — Playoff format amended. In each division, first to play fourth; second to play third.

1972-73 — Soviet Nationals and Canadian NHL stars play eight-game pre-season series. Canadians win 4-3-1.

Two new teams added. Atlanta Flames join West Division; New York Islanders join East Division.

1974-75 — Two new teams added: Kansas City Scouts and Washington Capitals. Teams realigned into two nine-team conferences, the Prince of Wales made up of the Norris and Adams Divisions, and the Clarence Campbell made up of the Smythe and Patrick Divisions.

Clubs played 80-game schedule.

1976-77 — California franchise transferred to Cleveland. Team named Cleveland Barons. Kansas City franchise transferred to Denver. Team named Colorado Rockies.

1977-78 — Clarence S. Campbell retires as NHL president. Succeeded by John A. Ziegler, Jr.

1978-79 — Cleveland and Minnesota franchises merge, leaving NHL with 17 teams. Merged team placed in Adams Division, playing home games in Minnesota.

Minimum age of players subject to amateur draft changed to 19.

1979-80 — Four new teams added: Edmonton Oilers, Hartford Whalers, Quebec Nordiques and Winnipeg Jets.

Minimum age of players subject to entry draft changed to 18.

1980-81 — Atlanta franchise shifted to Calgary, retaining "Flames" name.

1981-82 — Unbalanced schedule adopted.

1982-83 — Colorado Rockies franchise shifted to East Rutherford, New Jersey. Team named New Jersey Devils.

1991-92 — San Jose Sharks added, making the NHL a 22-team league. NHL celebrates 75th Anniversary Season. The 1991-92 regular season suspended due to a strike by members of the NHL Players' Association on April 1, 1992. Play resumed April 12, 1992.

1992-93 — Gilbert Stein named NHL president. Ottawa Senators and Tampa Bay Lightning added, making the NHL a 24-team league. NHL celebrates Stanley Cup Centennial.

Although Reggie Bentley only saw action in 11 NHL games, brothers Max and Doug combined for 463 goals in 1,212 contests.

Major Rule Changes

1910-11 — Game changed from two 30-minute periods to three 20-minute periods.

1911-12 — National Hockey Association (forerunner of the NHL) originated six-man hockey, replacing seven-man game.

1917-18 — Goalies permitted to fall to the ice to make saves. Previously a goaltender was penalized for dropping to the ice.

1918-19 — Penalty rules amended. For minor fouls, substitutes not allowed until penalized player had served three minutes. For major fouls, no substitutes for five minutes. For match fouls, no substitutes allowed for the remainder of the game.

With the addition of two lines painted on the ice twenty feet from center, three playing zones were created, producing a forty-foot neutral center ice area in which forward passing was permitted. Kicking the puck was permitted in this neutral zone.

Tabulation of assists began.

1921-22 — Goaltenders allowed to pass the puck forward up to their own blue line.

Overtime limited to twenty minutes.

Minor penalties changed from three minutes to two minutes.

1923-24 — Match foul defined as actions deliberately injuring or disabling an opponent. For such actions, a player was fined not less than $50 and ruled off the ice for the balance of the game. A player assessed a match penalty may be replaced by a substitute at the end of 20 minutes. Match penalty recipients must meet with the League president who can assess additional punishment.

1925-26 — Delayed penalty rules introduced. Each team must have a minimum of four players on the ice at all times.

Two rules were amended to encourage offense: No more than two defensemen permitted to remain inside a team's own blue line when the puck has left the defensive zone. A faceoff to be called for ragging the puck unless short-handed.

Team captains only players allowed to talk to referees.

Goaltender's leg pads limited to 12-inch width.

Timekeeper's gong to mark end of periods rather than referee's whistle. Teams to dress a maximum of 12 players for each game from a roster of no more than 14 players.

1926-27 — Blue lines repositioned to sixty feet from each goal-line, thereby enlarging the neutral zone and standardizing distance from blueline to goal.

Uniform goal nets adopted throughout NHL with goal posts securely fastened to the ice.

1927-28 — To further encourage offense, forwar passes allowed in defending and neutral zones and goaltender's pads reduced in width from 12 to 10 inches.

Game standardized at three twenty-minute periods of stop-time separated by ten-minute intermissions.

Teams to change ends after each period.

Ten minutes of sudden-death overtime to be played if the score is tied after regulation time.

Minor penalty to be assessed to any player other than a goaltender for deliberately picking up the puck while it is in play. Minor penaly to be assessed for deliberately shooting the puck out of play.

The Art Ross goal net adopted as the official net of the NHL.

Maximum length of hockey sticks limited to 53 inches measured from heel of blade to end of handle. No minimum length stipulated.

Home teams given choice of goals to defend at start of game.

1928-29 — Forward passing permitted in defensive and neutral zones and into attacking zone if pass receiver is in neutral zone when pass is made. No forward passing allowed inside attacking zone.

Minor penalty to be assessed to any player who delays the game by passing the puck back into his defensive zone.

Ten-minute overtime without sudden-death provision to be played in games tied after regulation time. Games tied after this overtime period declared a draw.

Exclusive of goaltenders, team to dress at least 8 and no more than 12 skaters.

Major Rule Changes *— continued*

1929-30 — Forward passing permitted inside all three zones but not permitted across either blue line.

Kicking the puck allowed, but a goal cannot be scored by kicking the puck in.

No more than three players including the goaltender may remain in their defensive zone when the puck has gone up ice. Minor penalties to be assessed for the first two violations of this rule in a game; major penalties thereafter.

Goaltenders forbidden to hold the puck. Pucks caught must be cleared immediately. For infringement of this rule, a faceoff to be taken ten feet in front of the goal with no player except the goaltender standing between the faceoff spot and the goal-line.

Highsticking penalties introduced.

Maximum number of players in uniform increased from 12 to 15.

December 21, 1929 — Forward passing rules instituted at the beginning of the 1929-30 season more than doubled number of goals scored. Partway through the season, these rules were further amended to read, "No attacking player allowed to precede the play when entering the opposing defensive zone." This is similar to modern offside rule.

1930-31 — A player without a complete stick ruled out of play and forbidden from taking part in further action until a new stick is obtained. A player who has broken his stick must obtain a replacement at his bench.

A further refinement of the offside rule stated that the puck must first be propelled into the attacking zone before any player of the attacking side can enter that zone; for infringement of this rule a faceoff to take place at the spot where the inrraction took place.

1931-32 — Though there is no record of a team attempting to play with two goaltenders on the ice, a rule was instituted which stated that each team was allowed only one goaltender on the ice at one time.

Attacking players forbidden to impede the movement or obstruct the vision of opposing goaltenders.

Defending players with the exception of the goaltender forbidden from falling on the puck within 10 feet of the net.

1932-33 — Each team to have captain on the ice at all times.

If the goaltender is removed from the ice to serve a penalty, the manager of the club to appoint a substitute.

Match penalty with substitution after five minutes instituted for kicking another player.

1933-34 — Number of players permitted to stand in defensive zone restricted to three including goaltender.

Visible time clocks required in each rink.

Two referees replace one referee and one linesman.

1934-35 — Penalty shot awarded when a player is tripped and thus prevented from having a clear shot on goal, having no player to pass to other than the offending player. Shot taken from inside a 10-foot circle located 38 feet from the goal. The goaltender must not advance more than one foot from his goal-line when the shot is taken.

1937-38 — Rules introduced governing icing the puck.

Penalty shot awarded when a player other than a goaltender falls on the puck within 10 feet of the goal.

1938-39 — Penalty shot modified to allow puck carrier to skate in before shooting.

One referee and one linesman replace two referee system.

Blue line widened to 12 inches.

Maximum number of players in uniform increased from 14 to 15.

1939-40 — A substitute replacing a goaltender removed from ice to serve a penalty may use a goaltender's stick and gloves but no other goaltending equipment.

1940-41 — Flooding ice surface between periods made obligatory.

1941-42 — Penalty shots classified as minor and major. Minor shot to be taken from a line 28 feet from the goal. Major shot, awarded when a player is tripped with only the goaltender to beat, permits the player taking the penalty shot to skate right into the goalkeeper and shoot from point-blank range.

One referee and two linesmen employed to officiate games.

For playoffs, standby minor league goaltenders employed by NHL as emergency substitutes.

1942-43 — Because of wartime restrictions on train scheduling, regular-season overtime was discontinued on November 21, 1942.

Player limit reduced from 15 to 14. Minimum of 12 men in uniform abolished.

1943-44 — Red line at center ice introduced to speed up the game and reduce offside calls. This rule is considered to mark the beginning of the modern era in the NHL.

Delayed penalty rules introduced.

1945-46 — Goal indicator lights synchronized with official time clock required at all rinks.

1946-47 — System of signals by officials to indicate infractions introduced.

Linesmen from neutral cities employed for all games.

1947-48 — Goal awarded when a player with the puck has an open net to shoot at and a thrown stick prevents the shot on goal. Major penalty to any player who throws his stick in any zone other than defending zone. If a stick is thrown by a player in his defending zone but the thrown stick is not considered to have prevented a goal, a penalty shot is awarded.

All playoff games played until a winner determined, with 20-minute sudden-death overtime periods separated by 10-minute intermissions.

1949-50 — Ice surface painted white.

Clubs allowed to dress 17 players exclusive of goaltenders.

Major penalties incurred by goaltenders served by a member of the goaltender's team instead of resulting in a penalty shot.

1950-51 — Each team required to provide an emergency goaltender in attendance with full equipment at each game for use by either team in the event of illness or injury to a regular goaltender.

1951-52 — Visiting teams to wear basic white uniforms; home teams basic colored uniforms.

Goal crease enlarged from 3 × 7 feet to 4 × 8 feet.

Number of players in uniform reduced to 15 plus goaltenders.

Faceoff circles enlarged from 10-foot to 15-foot radius.

1952-53 — Teams permitted to dress 15 skaters on the road and 16 at home.

1953-54 — Number of players in uniform set at 16 plus goaltenders.

1954-55 — Number of players in uniform set at 18 plus goaltenders up to December 1 and 16 plus goaltenders thereafter.

"Bonnie Prince Charlie" Rayner led the NHL in shutouts during the 1946-47 season, blanking the opposition five times.

1956-57 — Player serving a minor penalty allowed to return to ice when a goal is scored by opposing team.

1959-60 — Players prevented from leaving their benches to enter into an altercation. Substitutions permitted providing substitutes do not enter into altercation.

1960-61 — Number of players in uniform set at 16 plus goaltenders.

1961-62 — Penalty shots to be taken by the player against whom the foul was committed. In the event of a penalty shot called in a situation where a particular player hasn't been fouled, the penalty shot to be taken by any player on the ice when the foul was committed.

1964-65 — No bodily contact on faceoffs.

In playoff games, each team to have its substitute goaltender dressed in his regular uniform except for leg pads and body protector. All previous rules governing standby goaltenders terminated.

1965-66 — Teams required to dress two goaltenders for each regular-season game.

1966-67 — Substitution allowed on coincidental major penalties.

Between-periods intermissions fixed at 15 minutes.

1967-68 — If a penalty incurred by a goaltender is a co-incident major, the penalty to be served by a player of the goaltender's team on the ice at the time the penalty was called.

1970-71 — Home teams to wear basic white uniforms; visiting teams basic colored uniforms.

Limit of curvature of hockey stick blade set at $^1/_2$ inch.

Minor penalty for deliberately shooting the puck out of the playing area.

1971-72 — Number of players in uniform set at 17 plus 2 goaltenders.

Third man to enter an altercation assessed an automatic game misconduct penalty.

1972-73 — Minimum width of stick blade reduced to 2 inches rom 2-$^1/_2$ inches.

1974-75 — Bench minor penalty imposed if a penalized player does not proceed directly and immediately to the penalty box.

1976-77 — Rule dealing with fighting amended to provide a major and game misconduct penalty for any player who is clearly the instigator of a fight.

1977-78 — Teams requesting a stick measurement to be assessed a minor penalty in the event that the measured stick does not violate the rules.

1981-82 — If both of a team's listed goaltenders are incapacitated, the team can dress and play any eligible goaltender who is available.

1982-83 — Number of players in uniform set at 18 plus 2 goaltenders.

1983-84 — Five-minute sudden-death overtime to be played in regular-season games that are tied at the end of regulation time.

1985-86 — Substitutions allowed in the event of co-incidental minor penalties.

1986-87 — Delayed off-side is no longer in effect once the players of the offending team have cleared the opponents' defensive zone.

1991-92 — Video replays employed to assist referees in goal/no goal situations. Size of goal crease increased. Crease changed to semi-circular configuration. Time clock to record tenths of a second in last minute of each period and overtime. Major and game misconduct penalty for checking from behind into boards. Penalties added for crease infringement and unnecessary contact with goaltender. Goal disallowed if puck enters net while a player of the attacking team is standing on the goal crease line, is in the goal crease or places his stick in the goal crease.

1992-93 — No substitutions allowed in the event of coincidental minor penalties called when both teams are at full strength. Wearing of helmets made optional for forwards and defensemen. Minor penalty for attempting to draw a penalty ("diving"). Major and game misconduct penalty for checking from behind into goal frame. Game misconduct penalty for instigating a fight. Highsticking redefined to include any use of the stick above waist-height. Previous rule stipulated shoulder-height.

Team Records

BEST WINNING PERCENTAGE, ONE SEASON:
.875 —Boston Bruins, 1929-30. 38W-5L-1T. 77PTS in 44GP
.830 —Montreal Canadiens, 1943-44. 38W-5L-7T. 83PTS in 50GP
.825 —Montreal Canadiens, 1976-77. 60W-8L-12T. 132PTS in 80GP
.806 —Montreal Canadiens, 1977-78. 59W-10L-11T. 129PTS in 80GP
.800 —Montreal Canadiens, 1944-45. 38W-8L-4T. 80PTS in 50GP

MOST POINTS, ONE SEASON:
132 —Montreal Canadiens, 1976-77. 60W-8L-12T. 80GP
129 —Montreal Canadien, 1977-78. 59W-10L-11T. 80GP
127 —Montreal Canadiens, 1975-76. 58W-11L-11T. 80GP

FEWEST POINTS, ONE SEASON:
8 —Quebec Bulldogs, 1919-20. 4W-20L-0T. 24GP
10 —Toronto Arenas, 1918-19. 5W-13L-0T. 18GP
12 —Hamilton Tigers, 1920-21. 6W-18L-0T. 24GP
—Hamilton Tigers, 1922-23. 6W-18L-0T. 24GP
—Boston Bruins, 1924-25. 6W-24L-0T. 30GP
—Philadelphia Quakers, 1930-31. 4W-36L-4T. 44GP

FEWEST POINTS, ONE SEASON (MINIMUM 70-GAME SCHEDULE):
21 —Washington Capitals, 1974-75. 8W-67L-5T. 80GP
30 —NY Islanders, 1972-73. 12W-60L-6T. 78GP
31 —Chicago Blackhawks, 1953-54. 12W-51L-7T. 70GP
—Quebec Nordiques, 1989-90. 12W-61L-7T. 80GP

MOST WINS, ONE SEASON:
60 —Montreal Canadiens, 1976-77. 80GP
59 —Montreal Canadien, 1977-78. 80GP
58 —Montreal Canadiens, 1975-76. 80GP

FEWEST WINS, ONE SEASON:
4 —Quebec Bulldogs, 1919-20. 24GP
—Philadelphia Quakers, 1930-31. 44GP
5 —Toronto Arenas, 1918-19. 18GP
—Pittsburgh Pirates, 1929-30. 44GP

FEWEST WINS, ONE SEASON (MINIMUM 70-GAME SCHEDULE):
8 —Washington Capitals, 1974-75. 80GP
9 —Winnipeg Jets, 1980-81 80GP
11 —Washington Capitals, 1975-76. 80GP

MOST LOSSES, ONE SEASON:
67 —Washington Capitals, 1974-75. 80GP
61 —Quebec Nordiques, 1989-90. 80GP
60 —NY Islanders, 1972-73. 78GP
59 —Washington Capitals, 1975-76. 80GP

FEWEST LOSSES, ONE SEASON:
5 —Ottawa Senators, 1919-20. 24GP
—Boston Bruins, 1929-30. 44GP
—Montreal Canadiens, 1943-44. 50GP

FEWEST LOSSES, ONE SEASON (MINIMUM 70-GAME SCHEDULE):
8 —Montreal Canadiens, 1976-77. 80GP
10 —Montreal Canadiens, 1972-73. 78GP
—Montral Canadiens, 1977-78. 80GP
11 —Montreal Canadiens, 1975-76. 80GP

MOST TIES, ONE SEASON:
24 —Philadelphia Flyers, 1969-70. 76GP
23 —Montreal Canadiens, 1962-63. 70GP
—Chicago Blackhawks, 1973-74. 78GP

FEWEST TIES, ONE SEASON (Since 1926-27):
1 —Boston Bruins, 1929-30. 44GP
2 —NY Americans, 1926-27. 44GP
—Montreal Canadiens, 1926-27. 44GP
—Boston Bruins, 1938-39. 48GP
—NY Rangers, 1941-42. 48GP

FEWEST TIES, ONE SEASON (MINIMUM 70-GAME SCHEDULE):
3 —New Jersey Devils, 1985-86. 80GP
—Calgary Flames, 1986-87. 80GP
4 —Detroit Red Wings, 1966-67. 70GP
—NY Islanders, 1983-84. 80GP
—Hartford Whalers, 1985-86. 80GP
—Philadelphia Flyers, 1985-86. 80GP
—Minnesota North Stars, 1989-90. 80GP
—Toronto Maple Leafs, 1989-90. 80GP

MOST HOME WINS, ONE SEASON:
36 —Philadelphia Flyers, 1975-76. 40GP
33 —Boston Bruins, 1970-71. 39GP
—Boston Bruins, 1973-74. 39GP
—Montreal Canadiens, 1976-77. 40GP
—Philadelphia Flyers, 1976-77. 40GP
—NY Islanders, 1981-82. 40GP
—Philadelphia Flyers,1985-86. 40GP

MOST ROAD WINS, ONE SEASON:
27 —Montreal Canadiens, 1976-77. 40GP
—Montreal Canadiens, 1977-78. 40GP
26 —Boston Bruins, 1971-72. 39GP
—Montreal Canadiens, 1975-76. 40GP
—Edmonton Oilers, 1983-84. 40GP

MOST HOME LOSSES, ONE SEASON:
29 —Pittsburgh Penguins, 1983-84. 40GP
28 —Washington Capitals, 1974-75. 40GP
—New Jersey Devils, 1983-84. 40GP
—Toronto Maple Leafs, 1984-85. 40GP
27 —Los Angeles Kings, 1985-86. 40GP

MOST ROAD LOSSES, ONE SEASON:
39 —Washington Capitals, 1974-75. 40GP
37 —California Seals, 1973-74. 39GP
35 —NY Islanders, 1972-73. 39GP
—Quebec Nordiques, 1989-90. 40GP
—San Jose Sharks, 1991-92. 40GP

MOST HOME TIES, ONE SEASON:
13 —NY Rangers, 1954-55. 35GP
—Philadelphia Flyers, 1969-70. 38GP
—California Seals, 1971-72. 39GP
—California Seals, 1972-73. 39GP
—Chicago Blackhawks, 1973-74. 39GP
12 —NY Islanders, 1974-75. 40GP
—Vancouver Canucks, 1977-78. 40GP
—Buffalo Sabres, 1980-81. 40GP
—Minnesota North Stars, 1981-82. 40GP
—Vancouver Canucks, 1981-82. 40GP
—Buffalo Sabres, 1990-91. 40GP

MOST ROAD TIES, ONE SEASON:
15 —Philadelphia Flyers, 1976-77. 40GP
14 —Montreal Canadiens, 1952-53. 35GP
—Montreal Canadiens, 1974-75. 40GP
—Philadelphia Flyers, 1975-76. 40GP

FEWEST HOME WINS, ONE SEASON:
2 —Chicago Blackhawks, 1927-28. 22GP
3 —Boston Bruins, 1924-25. 15GP
—Chicago Blackhawks, 1928-29. 22GP
—Philadelphia Quakers, 1930-31. 22GP

FEWEST HOME WINS, ONE SEASON (MINIMUM 70-GAME SCHEDULE):
6 —Chicago Blackhawks, 1954-55. 35GP
—Washington Capitals, 1975-76. 40GP
7 —Boston Bruins, 1962-63. 35GP
—Washington Capitals, 1974-75. 40GP
—Winnipeg Jets, 1980-81. 40GP
—Pittsburgh Penguins, 1983-84. 40GP

FEWEST ROAD WINS, ONE SEASON:
0 —Toronto Arenas, 1918-19. 9GP
—Quebec Bulldogs, 1919-20. 12GP
—Pittsburgh Pirates, 1929-30. 22GP
1 —Hamilton Tigers, 1921-22. 12GP
—Toronto St. Patricks, 1925-26. 18GP
—Philadelphia Quakers, 1930-31. 22GP
—NY Americans, 1940-41. 24GP
—Washington Capitals, 1974-75. 40GP

FEWEST ROAD WINS, ONE SEASON (MINIMUM 70-GAME SCHEDULE):
1 —Washington Capitals, 1974-75. 40GP
2 —Boston Bruins, 1960-61. 35GP
—Los Angeles Kings, 1969-70. 38GP
—NY Islanders, 1972-73. 39GP
—California Seals, 1973-74. 39GP
—Colorado Rockies, 1977-78. 40GP
—Winnipeg Jets, 1980-81. 40GP
—Quebec Nordiques, 1991-92. 40GP

FEWEST HOME LOSSES, ONE SEASON:
0 —Ottawa Senators, 1922-23. 12GP
—Montreal Canadiens, 1943-44. 25GP
1 —Toronto Arenas, 1917-18. 11GP
—Ottawa Senators, 19. 9GP
—Ottawa Senators, 1919-20. 12GP
—Toronto St. Patricks, 1922-23. 12GP
—Boston Bruins, 1929-30 and 1930-31. 22GP
—Montreal Canadiens, 1976-77. 40GP

FEWEST HOME LOSSES, ONE SEASON (MINIMUM 70-GAME SCHEDULE):
1 —Montreal Canadiens, 1976-77. 40GP
2 —Montreal Canadiens, 1961-62. 35GP
—NY Rangers, 1970-71. 39GP
—Philadelphia Flyers, 1975-76. 40GP

FEWEST ROAD LOSSES, ONE SEASON:
3 —Montreal Canadiens, 1928-29. 22GP
4 —Ottawa Senators, 1919-20. 12GP
—Montreal Canadiens, 1927-28. 22GP
—Boston Bruins, 1929-30. 20GP
—Boston Bruins, 1940-41. 24GP

FEWEST ROAD LOSSES, ONE SEASON (MINIMUM 70-GAME SCHEDULE):
6 —Montreal Canadiens, 1972-73. 39GP
—Montreal Canadiens, 1974-75. 40GP
—Montreal Canadiens, 1977-78. 40GP
7 —Detroit Red Wings, 1951-52. 35GP
—Montreal Canadiens, 1976-77. 40GP
—Philadelphia Flyers, 1979-80. 40GP

LONGEST WINNING STREAK:
15 Games — NY Islanders, Jan. 21, 1982 - Feb. 20, 1982.
14 Games — Boston Bruins, Dec. 3, 1929 - Jan. 9, 1930.
13 Games — Boston Bruins, Feb. 23, 1971 - March 20, 1971.
— Philadelphia Flyers, Oct. 19, 1985 - Nov. 17, 1985.

LONGEST WINNING STREAK FROM START OF SEASON:
8 Games — Toronto Maple Leafs, 1934-35.
— Buffalo Sabres, 1975-76.
7 Games — Edmonton Oilers, 1983-84.
— Quebec Nordiques, 1985-86.
— Pittsburgh Penguins, 1986-87.

LONGEST WINNING STREAK, INCLUDING PLAYOFFS:
15 Games — Detroit Red Wings, Feb. 27, 1955 -April 5, 1955. Nine regular-season games, six playoff games.

LONGEST HOME WINNING STREAK FROM START OF SEASON:
11 Games — Chicago Blackhawks, 1963-64
10 Games — Ottawa Senators, 1925-26
9 Games — Montreal Canadiens, 1953-54
— Chicago Blackhawks, 1971-72
8 Games — Boston Bruins, 1983-84
— Philadelphia Flyers, 1986-87
— New Jersey Devils, 1987-88

LONGEST HOME WINNING STREAK (ONE SEASON):
20 Games — Boston Bruins, Dec. 3, 1929 - Mar. 18, 1930.
— Philadelphia Flyers, Jan. 4, 1976 - April 3, 1976.

LONGEST HOME WINNING STREAK, INCLUDING PLAYOFFS:
24 Games — Philadelphia Flyers, Jan. 4, 1976 - April 25, 1976. 20 regular-season games, 4 playoff games.

LONGEST ROAD WINNING STREAK (ONE SEASON):
10 Games — Buffalo Sabres, Dec. 10, 1983 - Jan. 23, 1984.
8 Games — Boston Bruins, Feb. 17, 1972 - Mar. 8, 972.
— Los Angeles Kings, Dec. 18, 1974 - Jan. 16, 1975.
— Montreal Canadiens, Dec. 18, 1977 - Jan. 18. 1978.
— NY Islanders, Feb. 27, 1981 - March 29, 1981.
— Montreal Canadiens, Jan. 21, 1982 - Feb. 21, 1982.
— Philadelphia Flyers, Dec. 22, 1982 - Jan. 16, 1983.
— Winnipeg Jets, Feb. 25, 1985 - Apr. 6, 1985.
— Edmonton Oilers, Dec. 9, 1986 - Jan. 17, 1987.

LONGEST UNDEFEATED STREAK (ONE SEASON):
35 Games — Philadelphia Flyers, Oct. 14, 1979 - Jan. 6, 1980. 25W-10T.
28 Games — Montreal Canadiens, Dec. 18, 1977 - Feb. 23, 1978. 23W-5T.
23 Games — Boston Bruins, Dec. 22, 1940 - Feb. 23, 1941. 15W-8T.
— Philadelphia Flyers, Jan. 29, 1976 - Mar. 18, 1976. 17W-6T.

LONGEST UNDEFEATED STREAK FROM START OF SEASON:
15 Games — Edmonton Oilers, 1984-85. 12W-3T
14 Games — Montreal Canadiens, 1943-44. 11W-3T
13 Games — Montreal Canadiens, 1972-73. 9W-4T

LONGEST HOME UNDEFEATED STREAK (ONE SEASON):
34 Games — Montreal Canadiens, Nov. 1, 1976 - Apr. 2, 1977. 28W-6T.
27 Games — Boston Bruins, Nov. 22, 1970 - Mar. 20, 1971. 26W-1T.

LONGEST HOME UNDEFEATED STREAK, INCLUDING PLAYOFFS:
38 Games — Montreal Canadiens, Nov. 1, 1976 - April 26, 1977. 28W-6T in regular season and 4W in playoffs).

LONGEST ROAD UNDEFEATED STREAK (ONE SEASON):
23 Games — Montreal Canadiens, Nov. 27, 1974 - Mar. 12, 1975. 14W-9T.
17 Games — Montreal Canadiens, Dec. 18, 1977 - March 1, 1978. 14W-3T.
16 Games — Philadelphia Flyers, Oct. 20, 1979 - Jan. 6, 1980. 11W-5T.

LONGEST LOSING STREAK (ONE SEASON):
17 Games — Washington Capitals, Feb. 18, 1975 - Mar. 26, 1975.
15 Games — Philadelphia Quakers, Nov. 29, 1930 - Jan. 8, 1931.

LONGEST LOSING STREAK FROM START OF SEASON:
11 Games — NY Rangers, 1943-44.
7 Games — Montreal Canadiens, 1938-39.
— Chicago Blackhawks, 1947-48.
— Washington Capitals, 1983-84.

LONGEST HOME LOSING STREAK (ONE SEASON):
11 Games — Boston Bruins, Dec. 8, 1924 - Feb. 17, 1925.
— Washington Capitals, Feb. 18, 1975 - Mar. 30, 1975.

LONGEST ROAD LOSING STREAK (ONE SEASON):
37 Games — Washington Capitals, Oct. 9, 1974 - Mar. 26, 1975.

LONGEST WINLESS STREAK (ONE SEASON):
30 Games — Winnipeg Jets, Oct. 19, 1980 - Dec. 20, 1980. 23L-7T.
27 Games — Kansas City Scouts, Feb. 12, 1976 - April 4, 1976. 21L-6T.
25 Games — Washington Capitals, Nov. 29, 1975 - Jan. 21, 1976. 22L-3T.

LONGEST WINLESS STREAK FROM START OF SEASON:
15 Games — NY Rangers, 1943-44. 14L-1T
12 Games — Pittsburgh Pirates, 1927-28. 9L-3T
11 Games — Minnesota North Stars, 1973-74. 5L-6T

LONGEST HOME WINLESS STREAK (ONE SEASON):
15 Games — Chicago Blackhawks, Dec. 16, 1928 - Feb. 28, 1929. 11L-4T.
— Montreal Canadiens, Dec. 16, 1939 - Mar. 7, 1940. 12L-3T.

LONGEST ROAD WINLESS STREAK (ONE SEASON):
37 Games — Washington Capitals, Oct. 9, 1974 - Mar. 26, 1975. 37L-0T.

LONGEST NON-SHUTOUT STREAK:
264 Games — Calgary Flames, Nov. 12, 1981 - Jan. 9, 1985.
262 Games — Los Angeles Kings, Mar. 15, 1986 - Oct. 25, 1989.
230 Games — Quebec Nordiques, Feb. 10, 1980 - Jan. 13, 1983.
229 Games — Edmonton Oilers, Mar. 15, 1981 - Feb. 11, 1984.
228 Games — Chicago Blackhawks, Mar. 14, 1970 - Feb. 21, 1973.
— Washington Capitals, Oct. 31, 1989 - Apr. 13, 1992.

LONGEST NON-SHUTOUT STREAK INCLUDING PLAYOFFS:
264 Games — Los Angeles Kings, Mar. 15 1986 - Apr. 6, 1989. (5 playoff games in 1987; 5 in 1988; 2 in 1989)
262 Games — Chicago Blackhawks, Mar. 14, 1970 - Feb. 21, 1973. (8 playoff games in 1970; 18 in 1971; 8 in 1972).
251 Games — Quebec Nordiques, Feb. 10, 1980 - Jan. 13, 1983. (5 playoff games in 1981; 16 in 1982).
245 Games — Pittsburgh Penguins, Jan. 7, 1989 - Oct. 26, 1991. (11 playoff games in 1989; 23 in 1991).
235 Games — Boston Bruins, Oct. 26, 1977 - Feb. 20, 1980. (15 playoff games in 1978; 11 in 1979).

MOST CONSECUTIVE GAMES SHUT OUT:
8 — Chicago Blackhawks, 1928-29.

MOST SHUTOUTS, ONE SEASON:
22 — Montreal Canadiens, 1928-29. All by George Hainsworth. 44GP
16 — NY Americans, 1928-29. Roy Worters had 13; Flat Walsh 3. 44GP
15 — Ottawa Senators, 1925-26. All by Alex Connell. 36GP
— Ottawa Senators, 1927-28. All by Alex Connell. 44GP
— Boston Bruins, 1927-28. All by Hal Winkler. 44GP
— Chicago Blackhawks, 1969-70. All by Tony Esposito. 76GP

MOST GOALS, ONE SEASON:
446 — Edmonton Oilers, 1983-84. 80GP
426 — Edmonton Oilers, 1985-86. 80GP
424 — Edmonton Oilers, 1982-83. 80GP
417 — Edmonton Oilers, 1981-82. 80GP
401 — Edmonton Oilers, 1984-85. 80GP

HIGHEST GOALS-PER-GAME AVERAGE, ONE SEASON:
5.58 — Edmonton Oilers, 1983-84. 446G in 80GP.
5.38 — Montreal Canadiens, 1919-20. 129G in 24GP.
5.33 — Edmonton Oilers, 1985-86. 426G in 80GP.
5.30 — Edmonton Oilers, 1982-83. 424G in 80GP.
5.23 — Montreal Canadiens, 1917-18. 115G in 22GP.

FEWEST GOALS, ONE SEASON:
33 — Chicago Blackhawks, 1928-29. 44GP
45 — Montreal Maroons, 1924-25. 30GP
46 — Pittsburgh Pirates, 1928-29. 44GP

FEWEST GOALS, ONE SEASON (MINIMUM 70-GAME SCHEDULE):
133 — Chicago Blackhawks, 1953-54. 70GP
147 — Toronto Maple Leafs, 1954-55. 70GP
— Boston Bruins, 1955-56. 70GP
150 — NY Rangers, 1954-55. 70GP

LOWEST GOALS-PER-GAME AVERAGE, ONE SEASON:
.75 — Chicago Blackhawks, 1928-29, 33G in 44GP.
1.05 — Pittsburgh Pirates, 1928-29. 46G in 44GP.
1.20 — NY Americans, 1928-29. 53G in 44GP.

MOST GOALS AGAINST, ONE SEASON:
446 — Washington Capitals, 1974-75. 80GP
415 — Detroit Red Wings, 1985-86. 80GP
407 — Quebec Nordiques, 1989-90. 80GP
403 — Hartford Whalers, 1982-83. 80GP
401 — Vancouver Canucks, 1984-85. 80GP

HIGHEST GOALS-AGAINST-PER-GAME AVERAGE, ONE SEASON:
7.38 — Quebec Bulldogs, 1919-20, 177GA vs. in 24GP.
6.20 — NY Rangers, 1943-44, 310GA vs. in 50GP.
5.58 — Washington Capitals, 1974-75, 446GA vs. in 80GP.

FEWEST GOALS AGAINST, ONE SEASON:
42 — Ottawa Senators, 1925-26. 36GP
43 — Montreal Canadiens, 1928-29. 44GP
48 — Montreal Canadiens, 1923-24. 24GP
— Montreal Canadiens, 1927-28. 44GP

FEWEST GOALS AGAINST, ONE SEASON (MINIMUM 70-GAME SCHEDULE):
131 — Toronto Maple Leafs, 1953-54. 70GP
— Montreal Canadiens, 1955-56. 70GP
132 — Detroit Red Wings, 1953-54. 70GP
133 — Detroit Red Wings, 1951-52. 70GP
— Detroit Red Wings, 1952-53. 70GP

LOWEST GOALS-AGAINST-PER-GAME AVERAGE, ONE SEASON:
.98 —Montreal Canadiens, 1928-29. 43GA vs. in 44GP.
1.09 —Montreal Canadiens, 1927-28. 48GA vs. in 44GP.
1.17 —Ottawa Senators, 1925-26. 42GA vs. in 36GP.

MOST POWER-PLAY GOALS, ONE SEASON:
120 —Pittsburgh Penguins, 1988-89. 80GP
111 —NY Rangers, 1987-88. 80GP
110 —Pittsburgh Pengiins, 1987-88. 80GP
—Winnipeg Jets, 1987-88, 80GP
109 —Calgary Flames, 1987-88. 80GP

MOST POWER-PLAY GOALS AGAINST, ONE SEASON:
122 —Chicago Blackhawks, 1988-89. 80GP
120 —Pittsburgh Penguins, 1987-88. 80GP
115 —New Jersey Devils, 1988-89. 80GP
111 —Detroit Red Wings, 1985-86. 80GP
—Pittsburgh Penguins, 1988-89. 80GP
110 —Pittsburgh Penguins, 1982-83. 80GP

MOST SHORTHAND GOALS, ONE SEASON:
36 —Edmonton Oilers, 1983-84. 80GP
—Edmonton Oilers, 1986-87. 80GP
27 —Edmonton Oilers, 1985-86. 80GP
—Edmonton Oilers, 1988-89. 80GP

MOST SHORTHAND GOALS AGAINST, ONE SEASON:
22 —Pittsburgh Penguins, 1984-85. 80GP
—Minnesota North Stars, 1991-92. 80GP
21 —Calgary Flames, 1984-85. 80GP
—Pittsburgh Penguins, 1989-90. 80GP
20 —Minnesota North Stars, 1982-83. 80GP
—Quebec Nordiques, 1985-86. 80GP

MOST ASSISTS, ONE SEASON:
737 —Edmonton Oilers, 1985-86. 80GP
736 —Edmonton Oilers, 1983-84. 80GP
706 —Edmonton Oilers, 1981-82. 80GP

FEWEST ASSISTS, ONE SEASON:
45 —NY Rangers, 1926-27. 44GP

FEWEST ASSISTS, ONE SEASON (MINIMUM 70-GAME SCHEDULE):
206 —Chicago Blackhawks, 1953-54. 70GP

MOST SCORING POINTS, ONE SEASON:
1,182 —Edmonton Oilers, 1983-84. 80GP
1,163 —Edmonton Oilers, 1985-86. 80GP
1,123 —Edmonton Oilers, 1981-82. 80GP

MOST 50-OR-MORE-GOAL SCORERS, ONE SEASON:
3 —Edmonton Oilers, 1983-84. Wayne Gretzky, 87; Glenn Anderson, 54; Jari Kurri, 52 80GP.
—Edmonton Oilers, 1985-86. Jari Kurri, 68; Glenn Anderson, 54; Wayne Gretzky, 52. 80GP.
2 —Boston Bruins, 1970-71. Phil Esposito, 76; John Bucyk, 51. 78GP
—Boston Bruins, 1973-74. Phil Esposito, 68; Ken Hodge, 50. 78GP
—Philadelphia Flyers, 1975-76. Reggie Leach, 61; Bill Barber, 50. 80GP
—Pittsburgh Penguins, 1975-76. Pierre Larouche, 53; Jean Pronovost, 52. 80GP
—Montreal Canadiens, 1976-77. Steve Shutt, 60; Guy Lafleur, 56. 80GP
—Los Angeles Kings, 1979-80. Charlie Simmer, 56; Marcel Dionne, 53. 80GP
—Montreal Canadiens, 1979-80. Pierre Larouche, 50; Guy Lafleur, 50. 80GP
—Los Angeles Kings, 1980-81. Marcel Dionne, 58; Charlie Simmer, 56. 80GP
—Edmonton Oilers, 1981-82. Wayne Gretzky, 92; Mark Messier, 50. 80GP
—NY Islanders, 1981-82. Mike Bossy, 64; Bryan Trottier, 50. 80GP
—Edmonton Oilers, 1984-85. Wayne Gretzky, 73; Jari Kurri, 71. 80GP
—Washington Capitals, 1984-85. Bob Carpenter, 53; Mike Gartner, 50. 80GP
—Edmonton Oilers, 1986-87. Wayne Gretzky, 62; Jari Kurri, 54. 80GP
—Calgary Flames, 1987-88. Joe Nieuwendyk, 51; Hakan Loob, 50. 80GP
—Los Angeles Kings, 1987-88. Jimmy Carson, 55; Luc Robitaille, 53. 80GP
—Los Angeles Kings, 1988-89. Bernie Nicholls, 70; Wayne Gretzky, 54. 80GP
—Calgary Flames, 1988-89. Joe Nieuwendyk, 51; Joe Mullen, 51. 80GP

MOST 40-OR-MORE-GOAL SCORERS, ONE SEASON:
4 —Edmonton Oilers, 1982-83. Wayne Gretzky, 71; Glenn Anderson, 48; Mark Messier, 48; Jari Kurri, 45. 80GP
—Edmonton Oilers, 1983-84. Wayne Gretzky, 87; Glenn Anderson, 54; Jari Kurri, 52; Paul Coffey, 40. 80GP
—Edmonton Oilers, 1984-85. Wayne Gretzky, 73; Jari Kurri, 71; Mike Krushelnyski, 43; Glenn Anderson, 42. 80GP
—Edmonton Oilers, 1985-86. Jari Kurri, 68; Glenn Anderson, 54; Wayne Gretzky, 52; Paul Coffey, 48. 80GP
—Calgary Flames, 1987-88. Joe Nieuwendyk, 51; Hakan Loob, 50; Mike Bullard, 48; Joe Mullen, 40. 80GP
3 —Boston Bruins, 1970-71. Phil Esposito, 76; John Bucyk, 51; Ken Hodge, 43. 78GP
—NY Rangers, 1971-72. Vic Hadfield, 50; Jean Ratelle, 46; Rod Gilbert, 43. 78GP
—Buffalo Sabres, 1975-76. Danny Gare, 50; Rick Martin, 49; Gilbert Perreault, 44. 80GP
—Montreal Canadiens, 1979-80. Guy Lafleur, 50; Pierre Larouche, 50; Steve Shutt, 47. 80GP
—Buffalo Sabres, 1979-80. Danny Gare, 56; Rick Martin, 45; Gilbert Perreault, 40. 80GP
—Los Angeles Kings, 1980-81. Marcel Dionne, 58; Charlie Simmer, 56; Dave Taylor, 47. 80GP
—Los Angeles Kings, 1984-85. Marcel Dionne, 46; Bernie Nicholls, 46; Dave Taylor, 41. 80GP
—NY Islanders, 1984-85. Mike Bossy, 58; Brent Sutter, 42; John Tonelli; 42. 80GP
—Chicago Blackhawks, 1985-86. Denis Savard, 47; Troy Murray, 45; Al Secord, 40. 80GP
—Chicago Blackhawks, 1987-88. Denis Savard, 44; Rick Vaive, 43; Steve Larmer, 41. 80GP
—Edmonton Oilers, 1987-88. Craig Simpson, 43; Jari Kurri, 43; Wayne Gretzky, 40. 80GP
—Los Angeles Kings, 1988-89. Bernie Nicholls, 70; Wayne Gretzky 54; Luc Robitaille, 46. 80GP
—Los Angeles Kings, 1990-91. Luc Robitaille, 45; Tomas Sandstrom, 45; Wayne Gretzky 41. 80GP
—Pittsburgh Penguins, 1991-92. Kevin Stevens, 54; Mario Lemieux, 44; Joe Mullen, 42. 80GP

The 1946 Montreal Canadiens finished in first place in the six-team NHL and captured the Stanley Cup by winning eight post-season games against one loss.

MOST 30-OR-MORE GOAL SCORERS, ONE SEASON:
6 — **Buffalo Sabres,** 1974-75. Rick Martin, 52; Rene Robert, 40; Gilbert Perreault, 39; Don Luce, 33; Rick Dudley, Danny Gare, 31 each. 80GP
— **NY Islanders,** 1977-78, Mike Bossy, 53; Bryan Trottier, 46; Clark Gillies, 35; Denis Potvin, Bob Nystrom, Bob Bourne, 30 each. 80GP
— **Winnipeg Jets,** 1984-85. Dale Hawerchuk, 53; Paul MacLean, 41; Laurie Boschmn, 32; Brian Mullen, 32; Doug Smail, 31; Thomas Steen, 30. 80GP
5 — Chicago Blackhawks, 1968-69. 76GP
— Boston Bruins, 1970-71. 78GP
— Montreal Canadiens, 1971-72. 78GP
— Philadelphia Flyers, 1972-73. 78GP
— Boston Bruins, 1973-74. 78GP
— Montreal Canadiens, 1974-75. 80GP
— Montreal Canadiens, 1975-76. 80GP
— Pittsburgh Penguins, 1975-76. 80GP
— NY Islanders, 1978-79. 80GP
— Detroit Red Wings, 1979-80. 80GP
— Philadelphia Flyers, 1979-80. 80GP
— NY Islanders, 1980-81. 80GP
— St. Louis Blues, 1980-81. 80GP
— Chicago Blackhawks, 1981-82. 80GP
— Edmonton Oilers, 1981-82. 80GP
— Montreal Canadiens, 1981-82. 80GP
— Quebec Nordiques, 1981-82. 80GP
— Washington Capitals, 1981-82. 80GP
— Edmonton Oilers, 1982-83. 80GP
— Edmonton Oilers, 1983-84. 80GP
— Edmonton Oilers, 1984-85. 80GP
— Los Angeles Kings, 1984-85. 80GP
— Edmonton Oilers, 1985-86. 80GP
— Edmonton Oilers, 1986-87. 80GP
— Edmonton Oilers, 1987-88. 80GP
— Edmonton Oilers, 1988-89. 80GP
— Detroit Red Wings, 1991-92. 80GP
— NY Rangers, 1991-92. 80GP
— Pittsburgh Penguins, 1991-92. 80GP

MOST 20-OR-MORE GOAL SCORERS, ONE SEASON:
11 — **Boston Bruins,** 1977-78; Peter McNab, 41; Terry O'Reilly, 29; Bobby Schmautz, Stan Jonathan, 27 each; Jean Ratelle, Rick Middleton, 25 each; Wayne Cashman, 24; Gregg Sheppard, 23; Brad Park, 22; Don Marcotte, Bob Miller, 20 each. 80GP
10 — Boston Bruins, 1970-71. 78GP
— Montreal Canadiens, 1974-75. 80GP
— St. Louis Blues, 1980-81. 80GP

MOST 100 OR-MORE-POINT SCORERS, ONE SEASON:
4 — **Boston Bruins,** 1970-71, Phil Esposito, 76G-76A-152PTS; Bobby Orr, 37G-102A-139PTS; John Bucyk, 51G-65A-116PTS; Ken Hodge, 43G-62A-105PTS. 78GP
— **Edmonton Oilers,** 1982-83, Wayne Gretzky, 71G-125A-196PTS; Mark Messier, 48G-58A-106PTS; Glenn Anderson, 48G-56A-104PTS; Jari Kurri, 45G-59A-104PTS. 80GP.
— **Edmonton Oilers,** 1983-84, Wayne Gretzky, 87G-118A-205PTS; Paul Coffey, 40G-86A-126PTS; Jari Kurri, 52G-61A-113PTS; Mark Messier, 37G-64A-101PTS. 80GP.
— **Edmonton Oilers,**1985-86, Wayne Gretzky, 52G-163A-215PTS; Paul Coffey, 48G-90A-138PTS; Jari Kurri, 68G-63A-131PTS; Glenn Anderson, 54G-48A-102PTS. 80GP
3 — Boston Bruins, 1973-74, Phil Esposito, 68G-77A-145PTS; Bobby Orr, 32G-90A-122PTS; Ken Hodge, 50G-55A-105PTS. 78GP
— NY Islanders, 1978-79, Bryan Trottier, 47G-87A-134PTS; Mike Bossy, 69G-57A-126PTS; Denis Potvin, 31G-70A-101PTS. 80GP
— Los Angeles Kings, 1980-81, Marcel Dionne, 58G-77A-135PTS; Dave Taylor, 47 G-65A-112PTS; Charlie Simmer, 56G-49A-105PTS. 80GP
— Edmonton Oilers, 1984-85, Wayne Gretzky, 73G-135A-208PTS; Jari Kurri, 71G-64A-135PTS; Paul Coffey, 37G-84A-121PTS. 80GP
— NY Islanders, 1984-85. Mike Bossy, 58G-59A-117PTS; Brent Sutter, 42G-60A-102PTS; John Tonelli, 42G-58A-100PTS. 80GP
— Edmonton Oilers, 1986-87, Wayne Gretzky, 62G-121A-183PTS; Jari Kurri, 54G-54A-108PTS; Mark Messier, 37G-70A-107PTS. 80GP
— Pittsburgh Penguins, 1988-89, Mario Lemieux, 85—114A-199PTS; Rob Brown, 49G-66A-115PTS; Paul Coffey, 30G-83A-113PTS. 80GP

MOST PENALTY MINUTES, ONE SEASON:
2,713 — Buffalo Sabres, 1991-92. 80GP
2,670 — Pittsburgh Penguins, 1988-89. 80GP
2,663 — Chicago Blackhawks, 1991-92. 80GP
2,643 — Calgary Flames, 1991-92. 80GP
2,621 — Philadelphia Flyers, 1980-81. 80GP

MOST GOALS, BOTH TEAMS, ONE GAME:
21 — **Montreal Canadiens, Toronto St. Patricks,** at Montreal, Jan. 10, 1920. Montreal won 14-7.
— **Edmonton Oilers, Chicago Blackhawks,** at Chicago, Dec. 11, 1985. Edmonton won 12-9.
20 — Edmonton Oilers, Minnesota North Stars, at Edmonton, Jan. 4, 1984. Edmonton won 12-8.
— Toronto Maple Leafs, Edmonton Oilers, at Toronto, Jan. 8, 1986. Toronto won 11-9.
19 — Montreal Wanderers, Toronto Arenas, at Montreal, Dec. 19, 1917. Montreal won 10-9.
— Montreal Canadiens, Quebec Bulldogs, at Quebec, March 3, 1920, Montreal won 16-3.
— Montreal Canadiens, Hamilton Tigers, at Montreal, Feb. 26, 1921. Canadiens won 13-6.
— Boston Bruins, NY Rangers, at Boston, March 4, 1944, Boston won 10-9.
— Boston Bruins, Detroit Red Wings, at Detroit, March 16, 1944. Detroit won 10-9.
— Vancouver Canucks, Minnesota North Stars, at Vancouver, Oct. 7, 1983. Vancouver won 10-9.

MOST GOALS, ONE TEAM, ONE GAME:
16 — **Montreal Canadiens,** March 3, 1920, at Quebec. Defeated Quebec Bulldogs 16-3.

MOST CONSECUTIVE GOALS, ONE TEAM, ONE GAME:
15 — **Detroit Red Wings,** Jan. 23, 1944, at Detroit. Defeated NY Rangers 15-0.

MOST POINTS, BOTH TEAMS, ONE GAME:
62 — **Edmonton Oilers, Chicago Blackhawks,** at Chicago, Dec. 11, 1985. Edmonton won 12-9. Edmonton had 24A, Chicago, 17.
53 — Quebec Nordiques, Washington Capitals, at Washington, Feb. 22, 1981. Quebec won 11-7. Quebec had 22A, Washington, 13.
— Edmonton Oilers, Minnesota North Stars, at Edmonton, Jan. 4, 1984. Edmonton won 12-8. Edmonton had 20A, Minnesota 13.
— Minnesota North Stars, tt. Louis Blues, at St. Louis, Jan. 27, 1984. Minnesota won 10-8. Minnesota had 19A, St. Louis 16.
— Toronto Maple Leafs, Edmonton Oilers, at Toronto, Jan. 8, 1986. Toronto won 11-9. Toronto had 17A, Edmonton 16.
52 — Mtl. Maroons, NY Americans, at New York, Feb. 18, 1936. 8-8 tie. New York had 20A, Montreal 16. (3A allowed for each goal.)
— Vancouver Canucks, Minnesota North Stars, at Vancouver, Oct. 7, 1983. Vancouver won 10-9. Vancouver had 16A, Minnesota 17.

Rocket Richard was a pivotal member of the 1943-44 Montreal Canadiens, helping the club become the first team to score over 200 goals in a season.

MOST POINTS, ONE TEAM, ONE GAME:
40 — Buffalo Sabres, Dec. 21, 1975, at Buffalo. Buffalo defeated Washington 14-2, receiving 26A.
39 — Minnesota North Stars, Nov. 11, 1981, at Minnesota. Minnesota defeated Winnipeg 15-2, receiving 24A.
37 — Detroit Red Wings, Jan. 23, 1944, at Detroit. Detroit defeated NY Rangers 15-0, receiving 22A.
— Toronto Maple Leafs, March 16, 1957, at Toronto. Toronto defeated NY Rangers 14-1, receiving 23A.
— Buffalo Sabres, Feb. 25, 1978, at Cleveland. Buffalo defeated Cleveland 13-3, receiving 24A.
36 — Edmonton Oilers, Dec. 11, 1985, at Chicago. Edmonton defeated Chicago 12-9, receiving 24A.

MOST SHOTS, BOTH TEAMS, ONE GAME:
141 — NY Americans, Pittsburgh Pirates, Dec. 26, 1925, at New York. NY Americans, who won game 3-1, had 73 shots; Pit. Pirates, 68 shots.

MOST SHOTS, ONE TEAM, ONE GAME:
83 — Boston Bruins, March 4, 1941, at Boston. Boston defeated Chicago 3-2.
73 — NY Americans, Dec. 26, 1925, at New York. NY Americans defeated Pit. Pirates 3-1.
— Boston Bruins, March 21, 1991, at Boston. Boston tied Quebec 3-3.
72 — Boston Bruins, Dec. 10, 1970, at Boston. Boston defeated Buffalo 8-2.

MOST PENALTIES, BOTH TEAMS, ONE GAME:
85 Penalties — Edmonton Oilers (44), Los Angeles Kings (41) at Los Angeles, Feb. 28, 1990. Edmonton received 26 minors, 7 majors, 6 10-minute misconducts, 4 game misconducts and 1 match penalty; Los Angeles received 26 minors, 9 majors, 3 10-minute misconducts and 3 game misconducts.

MOST PENALTY MINUTES, BOTH TEAMS, ONE GAME:
406 Minutes — Minnesota North Stars, Boston Bruins at Boston, Feb. 26, 1981. Minnesota received 18 minors, 13 majors, 4 10-minute misconducts and 7 game misconducts; a total of 211PIM. Boston received 20 minors, 13 majors, 3 10-minute misconducts and six game misconducts; a total of 195PIM.

MOST PENALTIES, ONE TEAM, ONE GAME:
44 — Edmonton Oilers, Feb. 28, 1990, at Los Angeles. Edmonton received 26 minors, 7 majors, 6 10-minute misconducts, 4 game misconducts and 1 match penalty.
42 — Minnesota North Stars, Feb. 26, 1981, at Boston. Minnesota received 18 minors, 13 majors, 4 10-minute misconducts and 7 game misconducts.
— Boston Bruins, Feb. 26, 1981, at Boston vs. Minnesota. Boston received 20 minors, 13 majors, 3 10-minute misconducts and 7 game misconducts.

MOST PENALTY MINUTES, ONE TEAM, ONE GAME:
211 — Minnesota North Stars, Feb. 26, 1981, at Boston. Minnesota received 18 minors, 13 majors, 4 10-minute misconducts and 7 game misconducts.

MOST GOALS, BOTH TEAMS, ONE PERIOD:
12 — Buffalo Sabres, Toronto Maple Leafs, at Buffalo, March 19, 1981, second period. Buffalo scored 9 goals, Toronto 3. Buffalo won 14-4.
— Edmonton Oilers, Chicago Blackhawks, at Chicago, Dec. 11, 1985, second period. Edmonton scored 6 goals, Chicago 6. Edmonton won 12-9.
10 — NY Rangers, NY Americans, at NY Americans, March 16, 1939, third period. NY Rangers scored 7 goals, NY Americans 3. NY Rangers won 11-5.
— Toronto Maple Leafs, Detroit Red Wings, at Detroit, March 17, 1946, third period. Toronto scored 6 goals, Detroit 4. Toronto won 11-7.
— Vancouver Canucks, Buffalo Sabres, at Buffalo, Jan. 8, 1976, third period. Buffalo scored 6 goals, Vancouver 4. Buffalo won 8-5.
— Buffalo Sabres, Montreal Canadiens, at Montreal, Oct. 26, 1982, first period. Montreal scored 5 goals, Buffalo 5. 7-7 tie.
— Boston Bruins, Quebec Nordiques, at Quebec, Dec. 7, 1982, second period. Quebec scored 6 goals, Boston 4. Quebec won 10-5.
— Calgary Flames, Vancouver Canucks, at Vancouver, Jan. 16, 1987, first period. Vancouver scored 6 goals, Calgary 4. Vancouver won 9-5.
— Winnipeg Jets, Detroit Red Wings, at Detroit, Nov. 25, 1987, third period. Detroit scored 7 goals, Winnipeg 3. Detroit won 10-8.
— Chicago Blackhawks, St. Louis Blues, at St. Louis, Mar. 15, 1988, third period. Chicago scored 5 goals, St. Louis 5. 7-7 tie.

MOST GOALS, ONE TEAM, ONE PERIOD:
9 — Buffalo Sabres, March 19, 1981, at Buffalo, second period during 14-4 win over Toronto.
8 — Detroit Red Wings, Jan. 23, 1944, at Detroit, third period during 15-0 win over NY Rangers.
— Boston Bruins, March 16, 1969, at Boston, second period during 11-3 win over Toronto.
— NY Rangers, Nov. 21, 1971, at New York, third period during 12-1 win over California.
— Philadelphia Flyers, March 31, 1973, at Philadelphia, second period during 10-2 win over NY Islanders.
— Buffalo Sabres, Dec. 21, 1975, at Buffalo, third period during 14-2 win over Washington.
— Minnesota North Stars, Nov. 11, 1981, at Minnesota, second period during 15-2 win over Winnipeg.
— Pittsburgh Penguins, Dec. 17, 1991, at Pittsburgh, second period during 10-2 win over San Jose.

MOST POINTS, BOTH TEAMS, ONE PERIOD:
35 — Edmonton, Oilers, Chicago Blackhawks, at Chicago, Dec. 11, 1985, second period. Edmonton had 6G, 12A; Chicago, 6G, 11A. Edmonton won 12-9.
31 — Buffalo Sabres, Toronto Maple Leafs, at Buffalo, March 19, 1981, second period. Buffalo had 9G, 14A; Toronto, 3G, 5A. Buffalo won 14-4.
29 — Winnipeg Jets, Detroit Red Wings, at Detroit, Nov. 25, 1987, third period. Detroit had 7G, 13A; Winnipeg had 3G, 6A. Detroit won 10-8.
— Chicago Blackhawks, St. Louis Blues, at St. Louis, Mar. 15, 1988, third period. St. Louis had 5G, 10A; Chicago had 5G, 9A. 7-7 tie.

Gil Perreault played a major role in two of Buffalo's most lop-sided victories, 14-2 over Washington and 13-3 over Cleveland.

Thomas Steen was one of six Winnipeg Jets who scored at least 30 goals during the 1984-85 season.

MOST POINTS, ONE TEAM, ONE PERIOD:
23 — **NY Rangers,** Nov. 21, 1971, at New York, third period during 12-1 win over California. NY Rangers scored 8G and 15A.
— **Buffalo Sabres,** Dec. 21, 1975, at Buffalo, third period during 14-2 win over Washington. Buffalo scored 8G and 15A.
— **Buffalo Sabres,** March 19, 1981, at Buffalo, second period, during 14-4 win over Toronto. Buffalo scored 9G and 14A.
22 — Detroit Red Wings, Jan. 23, 1944, at Detroit, third period during 15-0 win over NY Rangers. Detroit scored 8G and 14A.
— Boston Bruins, March 16, 1969, at Boston, second period during 11-3 win over Toronto Maple Leafs. Boston scored 8G and 14A.
— Minnesota North Stars, Nov. 11, 1981, at Minnesota, second period during 15-2 win over Winnipeg. Minnesota scored 8G and 14A.
— Pittsburgh Penguins, Dec. 17, 1991, at Pittsburgh, second period during 10-2 win over San Jose. Pittsburgh scored 8G and 14A.

MOST SHOTS, ONE TEAM, ONE PERIOD:
33 — **Boston Bruins,** March 4, 1941, at Boston, second period. Boston defeated Chicago 3-2.

MOST PENALTIES, BOTH TEAMS, ONE PERIOD:
67 — **Minnesota North Stars, Boston Bruins,** at Boston, Feb. 26, 1981, first period. Minnesota received 15 minors, 8 majors, 4 10-minute misconducts and 7 game misconducts, a total of 34 penalties. Boston had 16 minors, 8 majors, 3 10-minute misconducts and 6 game misconducts, a total of 33 penalties.

MOST PENALTY MINUTES, BOTH TEAMS, ONE PERIOD:
372 — **Los Angeles Kings, Philadelphia Flyers** at Philadelphia, March 11, 1979, first period. Philadelphia received 4 minors, 8 majors, 6 10-minute misconducts and 8 game misconducts for 188 minutes. Los Angeles received 2 minors, 8 majors, 6 10-minute misconducts and 8 game misconducts for 184 minutes.

MOST PENALTIES, ONE TEAM, ONE PERIOD:
34 — **Minnesota North Stars,** Feb. 26, 1981, at Boston, first period. 15 minors, 8 majors, 4 10-minute misconducts, 7 game misconducts.

MOST PENALTY MINUTES, ONE TEAM, ONE PERIOD:
188 — **Philadelphia Flyers,** March 11, 1979, at Philadelphia vs. Los Angeles, first period. Flyers received 4 minors, 8 majors, 6 10-minute misconducts and 8 game misconducts.

FASTEST SIX GOALS, BOTH TEAMS
3 Minutes, 15 Seconds — Montreal Canadiens, Toronto Maple Leafs, at Montreal, Jan. 4, 1944, first period. Montreal scored 4G, Toronto 2. Montreal won 6-3.

FASTEST FIVE GOALS, BOTH TEAMS:
1 Minute, 24 Seconds — Chicago Blackhawks, Toronto Maple Leafs, at Toronto, Oct. 15, 1983, second period. Scorers were: Gaston Gingras, Toronto, 16:49; Denis Savard, Chicago, 17:12; Steve Larmer, Chicago, 17:27; Savard, 17:42; and John Anderson, Toronto, 18:13. Toronto won 10-8.
1 Minute, 39 Seconds — Detroit Red Wings, Toronto Maple Leafs, at Toronto, Nov. 15, 1944, third period. Scorers were: Ted Kennedy, Toronto, 10:36 and 10:55; Hal Jackson, Detroit, 11:48; Steve Wochy, Detroit, 12:02; Don Grosso, Detroit, 12:15. Detroit won 8-4.

FASTEST FIVE GOALS, ONE TEAM:
2 Minutes, 7 Seconds — Pittsburgh Penguins, at Pittsburgh, Nov. 22, 1972, third period. Scorers: Bryan Hextall, 12:00; Jean Pronovost, 12:18; Al McDonough, 13:40; Ken Schinkel, 13:49; Ron Schock, 14:07. Pittsburgh defeated St. Louis 10-4.
2 Minutes, 37 seconds — NY Islanders, at New York, Jan. 26, 1982, first period. Scorers: Duane Sutter, 1:31; John Tonelli, 2:30; Bryan Trottier, 2:46; Bryan Trottier, 3:31; Duane Sutter, 4:08. NY Islanders defeated Pittsburgh 9-2.
2 Minutes, 55 Seconds — Boston Bruins, at Boston, Dec. 19, 1974. Scorers: Bobby Schmautz, 19:13 (first period); Ken Hodge, 0:18; Phil Esposito, 0:43; Don Marcotte, 0:58; John Bucyk, 2:08 (second period). Boston defeated NY Rangers 11-3.

FASTEST FOUR GOALS, BOTH TEAMS:
53 Seconds — Chicago Blackhawks, Toronto Maple Leafs, at Toronto, Oct. 15, 1983, second period. Scorers were: Gaston Gingras, Toronto, 16:49; Denis Savard, Chicago, 17:12; Steve Larmer, Chicago, 17:27; and Savard at 17:42. Toronto won 10-8.
57 Seconds — Quebec Nordiques, Detroit Red Wings, at Quebec, Jan. 27, 1990, first period. Scorers were: Paul Gillis, Quebec, 18:01; Claude Loiselle, Quebec, 18:12; Joe Sakic, Quebec, 18:27; and Jimmy Carson, Detroit, 18:58. Detroit won 8-6.
1 Minute, 1 Second — Colorado Rockies, NY Rangers, at New York, Jan. 15, 1980, first period. Scorers were: Doug Sulliman, NY Rangers, 7:52; Ed Johnstone, NY Rangers, 7:57; Warren Miller, NY Rangers, 8:20; Rob Ramage, Colorado, 8:53. 6-6 tie.
— Chicago Blackhawks, Toronto Maple Leafs, at Toronto, Oct. 15, 1983, second period. Scorers were: Denis Savard, Chicago, 17:12; Steve Larmer, Chicago, 17:27; Savard, 17:42; John Anderson, Toronto, 18:13. Toronto won 10-8.

FASTEST FOUR GOALS, ONE TEAM:
1 Minute, 20 Seconds — Boston Bruins, at Boston, Jan. 21, 1945, second period. Scorers were: Bill Thoms at 6:34; Frank Mario at 7:08 and 7:27; and Ken Smith at 7:54. Boston defeated NY Rangers 14-3.

FASTEST THREE GOALS, BOTH TEAMS:
15 Seconds — Minnesota North Stars, NY Rangers, at Minnesota, Feb. 10, 1983, second period. Scorers were: Mark Pavelich, NY Rangers, 19:18; Ron Greschner, NY Rangers, 19:27; Willi Plett, Minnesota, 19:33. Minnesota won 7-5.
18 Seconds — Montreal Canadiens, NY Rangers, at Montreal, Dec. 12, 1963, first period. Scorers were: Dave Balon, Montreal, 0:58; Gilles Tremblay, Montreal, 1:04; Camille Henry, NY Rangers, 1:16. Montreal won 6-4.
18 Seconds — California Golden Seals, Buffalo Sabres, at California, Feb. 1, 1976, third period. Scorers were: Jim Moxey, California, 19:38; Wayne Merrick, California, 19:45; Danny Gare, Buffalo, 19:56. Buffalo won 9-5.

FASTEST THREE GOALS, ONE TEAM:
20 Seconds — Boston Bruins, at Boston, Feb. 25, 1971, third period. John Bucyk scored at 4:50, Ed Westfall at 5:02 and Ted Green at 5:10. Boston defeated Vancouver 8-3.
21 Seconds — Chicago Blackhawks, at New York, Mar. 23, 1952, third period. Bill Mosienko scored all three goals, at 6:09, 6:20 and 6:30. Chicago defeated NY Rangers 7-6.
21 Seconds — Washington Capitals, at Washington, Nov. 23, 1990, first period. Michal Pivonka scored at 16:18 and Stephen Leach scored at 16:29 and 16:39. Washington defeated Pittsburgh 7-3.

FASTEST THREE GOALS FROM START OF PERIOD, BOTH TEAMS:
1 Minute, 5 seconds — Hartford Whalers, Montreal Canadiens, at Montreal, March 11, 1989, second period. Scorers were: Kevin Dineen, Hartford, 0:11; Guy Carbonneau, Montreal, 0:36; Petr Svoboda, Montreal, 1:05. Montreal won 5-3.

FASTEST TWO GOALS, BOTH TEAMS:
2 Seconds — St. Louis Blues, Boston Bruins, at Boston, Dec. 19, 1987, third period. Scorers were: Ken Linseman, Boston, at 19:50; Doug Gilmour, St. Louis, at 19:52. St. Louis won 7-5.
3 Seconds — Chicago Blackhawks, Minnesota North Stars, at Minnesota, November 5, 1988, third period. Scorers were: Steve Thomas, Chicago, at 6:03; Dave Gagner, Minnesota, at 6:06. 5-5 tie.

FASTEST TWO GOALS, ONE TEAM:
4 Seconds — Montreal Maroons, at Montreal, Jan. 3, 1931, third period. Nels Stewart scored both goals, at 8:24 and 8:28. Mtl. Maroons defeated Boston 5-3.
— **Buffalo Sabres,** at Buffalo, Oct. 17, 1974, third period. Scorers were: Lee Fogolin at 14:55 and Don Luce at 14:59. Buffalo defeated California 6-1.
— **Toronto Maple Leafs,** at Quebec, December 29, 1988, third period. Scorers were: Ed Olczyk at 5:24 and Gary Leeman at 5:28. Toronto defeated Quebec 6-5.
— **Calgary Flames,** at Quebec, October 17, 1989, third period. Scorers were: Doug Gilmour at 19:45 and Paul Ranheim at 19:49. Calgary and Quebec tied 8-8.

FASTEST TWO GOALS FROM START OF PERIOD, BOTH TEAMS:
14 Seconds — NY Rangers, Quebec Nordiques, at Quebec, Nov. 5, 1983, third period. Scorers: Andre Savard, Quebec, 0:08; Pierre Larouche, NY Rangers, 0:14. 4-4 tie.
28 Seconds — Boston Bruins, Montreal Canadiens, at Montreal, Oct. 11, 1989, third period. Scorers: Jim Wiemer, Boston 0:10, Tom Chorske, Montreal 0:28. Montreal won 4-2.
29 Seconds — Pittsburgh Penguins, NY Islanders, at New York, Oct. 21, 1991, third period. Scorers: Randy Wood, New York 0:20, Mark Recchi, Pittsburgh 0:29. Pittsburgh won 7-6.

FASTEST TWO GOALS FROM START OF GAME, ONE TEAM:
24 Seconds — Edmonton Oilers, March 28, 1982, at Los Angeles. Mark Messier, at 0:14 and Dave Lumley, at 0:24, scored in first period. Edmonton defeated Los Angeles 6-2.
29 Seconds — Pittsburgh Penguins, Dec. 6, 1981, at Pittsburgh. George Ferguson, at 0:17, and Greg Malone, at 0:29, scored in first period. Pittsburgh defeated Chicago 6-4.
32 Seconds — Calgary Flames, Mar. 11, 1987, at Hartford. Doug Risebrough scored at 0:09 and Colin Patterson, at 0:32, in first period. Calgary defeated Hartford 6-1.

FASTEST TWO GOALS FROM START OF PERIOD, ONE TEAM:
21 Seconds — Chicago Blackhawks, Nov. 5, 1983, at Minnesota, second period. Ken Yaremchuk scored at 0:12 and Darryl Sutter at 0:21. Minnesota defeated Chicago 10-5.
30 Seconds — Washington Capitals, Jan. 27, 1980, at Washington, second period. Mike Gartner scored at 0:08 and Bengt Gustafsson at 0:30. Washington defeated NY Islanders 7-1.
31 Seconds — Buffalo Sabres, Jan. 10, 1974, at Buffalo, third period. Rene Robert scored at 0:21 and Rick Martin at 0:30. Buffalo defeated NY Rangers 7-2.
— NY Islanders, Feb. 22, 1986, at New York, third period. Roger Kortko scored at 0:10 and Bob Bourne at 0:31. NY Islanders defeated Detroit 5-2.

Individual Records

Career

MOST SEASONS:
26 — Gordie Howe, Detroit, 1946-47 – 1970-71; Hartford, 1979-80.
24 — Alex Delvecchio, Detroit, 1950-51 – 1973-74.
— Tim Horton, Toronto, NY Rangers, Pittsburgh, Buffalo, 1949-50, 1951-52 – 1973-74.
23 — John Bucyk, Detroit, Boston, 1955-56 – 1977-78.
22 — Dean Prentice, NY Rangers, Boston, Detroit, Pittsburgh, Minnesota, 1952-53 – 1973-74.
— Doug Mohns, Boston, Chicago, Minnesota, Atlanta, Washington, 1953-54 – 1974-75.
— Stan Mikita, Chicago, 1958-59 – 1979-80.

MOST GAMES:
1,767 — Gordie Howe, Detroit, 1946-47 – 1970-71; Hartford, 1979-80.
1,549 — Alex Delvecchio, Detroit, 1950-51 – 1973-74.
1,540 — John Bucyk, Detroit, Boston, 1955-56 – 1977-78.

MOST GOALS:
801 — Gordie Howe, Detroit, Hartford, in 26 seasons, 1,767GP.
749 — Wayne Gretzky, Edmonton, Los Angeles, in 13 seasons, 999GP.
731 — Marcel Dionne, Detroit, Los Angeles, NY Rangers, in 18 seasons, 1,348GP.
717 — Phil Esposito, Chicago, Boston, NY Rangers, in 18 seasons, 1,282GP.
610 — Bobby Hull, Chicago, Winnipeg, Hartford, in 16 seasons, 1,063GP.

HIGHEST GOALS-PER-GAME AVERAGE, CAREER (AMONG PLAYERS WITH 200 OR MORE GOALS):
.797 — Brett Hull, Calgary, St. Louis, 302G, 379GP, from 1986-87 – 1991-92.
.789 — Mario Lemieux, Pittsburgh, 408G, 517GP, from 1984-85 – 1991-92.
.767 — Cy Denneny, Ottawa, Boston, 250G, 326GP, from 1917-18 – 1928-29.
.762 — Mike Bossy, NY Islanders, 573G, 752GP, from 1977-78 – 1986-87.
.750 — Wayne Gretzky, Edmonton, Los Angeles, 749G, 999GP, from 1979-80 – 1991-92.

MOST ASSISTS:
1,514 — Wayne Gretzky, Edmonton, Los Angeles, in 13 seasons, 999GP.
1,049 — Gordie Howe, Detroit, Hartford in 26 seasons, 1,767GP.
1,040 — Marcel Dionne, Detroit, Los Angeles, NY Rangers in 18 seasons, 1,348GP.
926 — Stan Mikita, Chicago, in 22 seasons, 1,394GP.
890 — Bryan Trottier, NY Islanders, Pittsburgh, in 17 seasons, 1,238GP.

HIGHEST ASSIST-PER-GAME AVERAGE, CAREER (AMONG PLAYERS WITH 300 OR MORE ASSISTS):
1.516 — Wayne Gretzky, Edmonton, Los Angeles, 1,514A, 999GP from 1979-80 – 1991-92.
1.172 — Mario Lemieux, Pittsburgh, 606A, 517GP from 1984-85 – 1991-92.
.982 — Bobby Orr, Boston, Chicago, 645A, 657GP from 1966-67 – 1978-79.
.912 — Paul Coffey, Edmonton, Pittsburgh, Los Angeles, 796A, 873GP from 1980-81 – 1991-92.
.845 — Peter Stastny, Quebec, New Jersey, 754A, 892GP from 1980-81 – 1991-92.

MOST POINTS:
2,263 — Wayne Gretzky, Edmonton, Los Angeles, in 13 seasons, 999GP (749G-1,514A).
1,850 — Gordie Howe, Detroit, Hartford, in 26 seasons, 1,767GP (801G-1049A).
1,771 — Marcel Dionne, Detroit, Los Angeles, NY Rangers, in 18 seasons, 1,348GP (731G-1,040A).
1,590 — Phil Esposito, Chicago, Boston, NY Rangers in 18 seasons, 1,282GP (717G-873A).
1,467 — Stan Mikita, Chicago in 22 seasons, 1,394GP (541G-926A).

HIGHEST POINTS-PER-GAME AVERAGE, CAREER: (AMONG PLAYERS WITH 500 OR MORE POINTS):
2.265 — Wayne Gretzky, Edmonton, Los Angeles, 2,263PTS (749G-1,514A), 999GP from 1979-80 – 1991-92.
1.961 — Mario Lemieux, Pittsburgh, 1,014PTS (408G-606A), 517GP from 1984-85 – 1991-92.
1.497 — Mike Bossy, NY Islanders, 1,126PTS (573G-553A), 752GP from 1978-79 – 1986-87.
1.393 — Bobby Orr, Boston, Chicago, 915PTS (270G-645A), 657GP from 1966-67 – 1978-79.
1.342 — Steve Yzerman, Detroit, 903PTS (387G-516A), 673GP from 1983-84 – 1991-92.

MOST GOALS BY A CENTER, CAREER
749 — Wayne Gretzky, Edmonton, Los Angeles, in 13 seasons.
731 — Marcel Dionne, Detroit, Los Angeles, NY Rangers, in 18 seasons
717 — Phil Esposito, Chicago, Boston, NY Rangers, in 18 seasons.
541 — Stan Mikita, Chicago, in 22 seasons.
520 — Bryan Trottier, NY Islanders, Pittsburgh, in 17 seasons.

MOST ASSISTS BY A CENTER, CAREER;
1,514 — Wayne Gretzky, Edmonton, Los Angeles, in 13 seasons.
1,040 — Marcel Dionne, Detroit, Los Angeles, NY Rangers, in 18 seasons.
926 — Stan Mikita, Chicago, in 22 seasons.
890 — Bryan Trottier, NY Islanders, Pittsburgh, in 17 seasons.
873 — Phil Esposito, Chicago, Boston, NY Rangers, in 18 seasons.

Doug Mohns, who saw action with five NHL teams in his career, is one of only seven NHLers to play 22 seasons in the league.

MOST POINTS BY A CENTER, CAREER:
2,263 — Wayne Gretzky, Edmonton, Los Angeles, in 13 seasons.
1,771 — Marcel Dionne, Detroit, Los Angeles, NY Rangers, in 18 seasons.
1,590 — Phil Esposito, Chicago, Boston, NY Rangers, in 18 seasons.
1,467 — Stan Mikita, Chicago, in 22 seasons
1,410 — Bryan Trottier, NY Islanders, Pittsburgh, in 17 seasons.

MOST GOALS BY A LEFT WING, CAREER:
610 — Bobby Hull, Chicago, Winnipeg, Hartford, in 16 seasons.
556 — John Bucyk, Detroit, Boston, in 23 seasons.
533 — Frank Mahovlich, Toronto, Detroit, Montreal, in 18 seasons.
509 — Michel Goulet, Quebec, Chicago, in 13 seasons.
424 — Steve Shutt, Montreal, Los Angeles, in 13 seasons.

MOST ASSISTS BY A LEFT WING, CAREER:
813 — John Bucyk, Detroit, Boston, in 23 seasons.
570 — Frank Mahovlich, Toronto, Detroit, Montreal, in 18 seasons.
569 — Michel Goulet, Quebec, Chicago, in 13 seasons.
560 — Bobby Hull, Chicago, Winnipeg, Hartford, in 16 seasons.
558 — Brian Propp, Philadelphia, Boston, Minnesota, in 13 seasons.

MOST POINTS BY A LEFT WING, CAREER:
1,369 — John Bucyk, Detroit, Boston, in 23 seasons.
1,170 — Bobby Hull, Chicago, Winnipeg, Hartford, in 16 seasons.
1,103 — Frank Mahovlich, Toronto, Detroit, Montreal, in 18 seasons.
1,078 — Michel Goulet, Quebec, Chicago, in 13 seasons.
968 — Brian Propp, Philadelphia, Boston, MInnesota, in 13 seasons.

MOST GOALS BY A RIGHT WING, CAREER:
801 — Gordie Howe, Detroit, Hartford, in 26 seasons.
573 — Mike Bossy, NY Islanders, in 10 seasons.
560 — Guy Lafleur, Montreal, NY Rangers, Quebec, in 17 seasons.
544 — Maurice Richard, Montreal, in 18 seasons.
— Mike Gartner, Washington, Minnesota, NY Rangers, in 13 seasons.

MOST ASSISTS BY A RIGHT WING, CAREER:
1,049 — Gordie Howe, Detroit, Hartford, in 26 seasons.
793 — Guy Lafleur, Montreal, NY Rangers, Quebec, in 17 seasons.
626 — Dave Taylor, Los Angeles, in 15 seasons.
624 — Andy Bathgate, NY Rangers, Toronto, Detroit, Pittsburgh in 17 seasons.
615 — Rod Gilbert, NY Rangers, in 18 seasons.

MOST POINTS BY A RIGHT WING, CAREER:
1,850 — Gordie Howe, Detroit, Hartford, in 26 seasons.
1,353 — Guy Lafleur, Montreal, NY Rangers, Quebec, in 17 seasons.
1,126 — Mike Bossy, NY Islanders, in 10 seasons.
1,103 — Jari Kurri, Edmonton, Los Angeles, in 11 seasons.
1,047 — Dave Taylor, Los Angeles, in 15 seasons.

MOST GOALS BY A DEFENSEMAN, CAREER:
318 — Paul Coffey, Edmonton, Pittsburgh, Los Angeles, in 12 seasons.
310 — Denis Potvin, NY Islanders, in 15 seasons.
272 — Ray Bourque, Boston, in 13 seasons.
270 — Bobby Orr, Boston, Chicago, in 12 seasons.
248 — Doug Mohns, Boston, Chicago, Minnesota, Atlanta, Washington, in 22 seasons.

MOST ASSISTS BY A DEFENSEMAN, CAREER:
796 — Paul Coffey, Edmonton, Pittsburgh, Los Angeles, in 12 seasons.
750 — Larry Robinson, Montreal, Los Angeles, in 20 seasons.
743 — Ray Bourque, Boston, in 13 seasons.
742 — Denis Potvin, NY Islanders, in 15 seasons.
683 — Brad Park, NY Rangers, Boston, Detroit, in 17 seasons.

MOST POINTS BY A DEFENSEMAN, CAREER:
1,114 — Paul Coffey, Edmonton, Pittsburgh, Los Angeles, in 12 seasons.
1,052 — Denis Potvin, NY Islanders, in 15 seasons.
1,015 — Ray Bourque, Boston, in 13 seasons.
958 — Larry Robinson, Montreal, Los Angeles, in 20 seasons.
915 — Bobby Orr, Boston, Chicago, in 12 seasons.

MOST OVERTIME GOALS, CAREER:
7 — Mario Lemieux, Pittsburgh.
— Jari Kurri, Edmonton.
6 — Paul MacLean, Winnipeg, Detroit, St. Louis.
5 — Greg Paslawski, St. Louis, Winnipeg.
— Bernie Nicholls, Los Angeles, NY Rangers.
— Tomas Sandstrom, NY Rangers, Los Angeles.
— Bob Sweeney, Boston.
— Steve Thomas, Toronto, Chicago, NY Islanders.
— Mike Gartner, Washington, Minnesota, NY Rangers.

MOST OVERTIME ASSISTS, CAREER:
10 — Wayne Gretzky, Edmonton, Los Angeles.
9 — Bernie Federko, St. Louis.
— Dale Hawerchuk, Winnipeg, Buffalo.
8 — Mario Lemieux, Pittsburgh.
7 — Paul MacLean, Winnipeg, Detroit, St. Louis.
— Mark Messier, Edmonton, NY Rangers.
— Paul Coffey, Edmonton, Pittsburgh, Los Angeles.
— Thomas Steen, Winnipeg.

MOST OVERTIME POINTS, CAREER:
15 — Mario Lemieux, Pittsburgh, 7G-8A
13 — Paul MacLean, Winnipeg, Detroit, St. Louis. 6G-7A
— Dale Hawerchuk, Winnipeg. 4G-9A
12 — Wayne Gretzky, Edmonton, Los Angeles. 2G-10A
11 — Jari Kurri, Edmonton. 7G-4A
— Mark Messier, Edmonton, NY Rangers. 4G-7A

MOST PENALTY MINUTES:
3,966 — Dave Williams, Toronto, Vancouver, Detroit, Los Angeles, Hartford, in 14 seasons, 962GP.
3,043 — Chris Nilan, Monteal, NY Rangers, Boston, in 13 seasons, 688GP.
2,676 — Dale Hunter, Quebec, Washington, in 12 seasons, 918GP.
2,572 — Willi Plett, Atlanta, Calgary, Minnesota, Boston, in 13 seasons, 834GP.
2,405 — Tim Hunter, Calgary, in 11 seasons, 545GP.

MOST GAMES, INCLUDING PLAYOFFS:
1,924 — Gordie Howe, Detroit, Hartford, 1,767 regular-season and 157 playoff games.
1,670 — Alex Delvecchio, Detroit, 1,549 regular-season and 121 playoff games.
1,664 — John Bucyk, Detroit, Boston, 1,540 regular-season and 124 playoff games.

MOST GOALS, INCLUDING PLAYOFFS:
869 — Gordie Howe, Detroit, Hartford, 801 regular-season goals and 68 playoff goals.
844 — Wayne Gretzky, Edmonton, Los Angeles, 749 regular-season and 95 playoff goals.
778 — Phil Esposito, Chicago, Boston, NY Rangers, 717 regular-season and 61 playoff goals.
752 — Marcel Dionne, Detroit, Los Angeles, NY Rangers, 731 regular-season and 21 playoff goals.

MOST ASSISTS, INCLUDING PLAYOFFS:
1,725 — Wayne Gretzky, Edmonton, Los Angeles, 1,514 regular-season and 211 playoff assists.
1,141 — Gordie Howe, Detroit, Hartford, 1,049 regular-season and 92 playoff assists.
1,064 — Marcel Dionne, Detroit, Los Angeles, NY Rangers, 1,040 regular-season and 24 playoff assists.
1,017 — Stan Mikita, Chicago, 926 regular-season and 91 playoff assists.
1,003 — Bryan Trottier, NY Islanders, 890 regular-season and 113 playoff assists.

Goaltender Terry Sawchuk, below, appeared in an NHL record 971 NHL games from 1949 to 1970. Brad Park, right, stands fifth on the all-time leader board for assists by a defenseman, setting up 683 goals in his 17-year career.

Bobby Orr, the only defenseman in NHL history to win the Art Ross Trophy, compiled 915 points in his 12-year career, totals that rank him fifth on the NHL's all-time list among defensemen.

MOST POINTS, INCLUDING PLAYOFFS:
2,569 — Wayne Gretzky, Edmonton, Los Angeles, 2,263 regular-season and 306 playoff points.
2,010 — Gordie Howe, Detroit, Hartford, 1,850 regular-season and 160 playoff assists.
1,816 — Marcel Dionne, Detroit, Los Angeles, NY Rangers, 1,771 regular-season and 45 playoff points.
1,727 — Phil Esposito, Chicago, Boston, NY Rangers, 1,590 regular-season and 137 playoff points.
1,617 — Stan Mikita, Chicago, 1,467 regular-season and 150 playoff points.

MOST PENALTY MINUTES, INCLUDING PLAYOFFS:
4,421 — Dave Williams, Toronto, Vancouver, Los Angeles, 3,966 in regular season; 455 in playoffs.
3,584 — Chris Nilan, Montreal, NY Rangers, Boston, 3,043 in regular-season; 541 in playoffs.
3,240 — Dale Hunter, Quebec, Washington, 2,676 in regular-season; 564 in playoffs.
3,038 — Willi Plett, Atlanta, Calgary, Minnesota, Boston, 2,572 in regular-season; 466 in playoffs.
2,757 — Tim Hunter, Calgary, 2,405 regular-season; 352 in playoffs.

MOST CONSECUTIVE GAMES:
964 — Doug Jarvis, Montreal, Washington, Hartford, from Oct. 8, 1975 – Oct. 10, 1987.
914 — Garry Unger, Toronto, Detroit, St. Louis, Atlanta from Feb. 24, 1968, – Dec. 21, 1979.
800 — Steve Larmer, Chicago, from Oct. 6, 1982 to April 14, 1992.
776 — Craig Ramsay, Buffalo, from March 27, 1973, – Feb. 10, 1983.
630 — Andy Hebenton, NY Rangers, Boston, nine complete 70-game seasons from 1955-56 – 1963-64.

MOST GAMES APPEARED IN BY A GOALTENDER, CAREER:
971 — Terry Sawchuk, Detroit, Boston, Toronto, Los Angeles, NY Rangers from 1949-50 – 1969-70.
906 — Glenn Hall, Detroit, Chicago, St. Louis from 1952-53 – 1970-71.
886 — Tony Esposito, Montreal, Chicago from 1968-69 – 1983-84.
860 — Lorne "Gump" Worsley, NY Rangers, Montreal, Minnesota from 1952-53 – 1973-74.

MOST CONSECUTIVE COMPLETE GAMES BY A GOALTENDER:
502 — Glenn Hall, Detroit, Chicago. Played 502 games from beginning of 1955-56 season - first 12 games of 1962-63. In his 503rd straight game, Nov. 7, 1962, at Chicago, Hall was removed from the game against Boston with a back injury in the first period.

MOST SHUTOUTS BY A GOALTENDER, CAREER:
103 — Terry Sawchuk, Detroit, Boston, Toronto, Los Angeles, NY Rangers in 20 seasons.
94 — George Hainsworth, Montreal Canadiens, Toronto in 10 seasons.
84 — Glenn Hall, Detroit, Chicago, St. Louis in 16 seasons.

MOST GAMES SCORING THREE-OR-MORE GOALS:
49 — Wayne Gretzky, Edmonton, Los Angeles, in 13 seasons, 36 three-goal games, 9 four-goal games, 4 five-goal games.
39 — Mike Bossy, NY Islanders, in 10 seasons, 30 three-goal games, 9 four-goal games.
32 — Phil Esposito, Chicago, Boston, NY Rangers, in 18 seasons, 27 three-goal games, 5 four-goal games.
28 — Bobby Hull, Chicago, Winnipeg, Hartford, in 16 seasons, 24 three-goal games, 4 four-goal games.
— Marcel Dionne, Detroit, Los Angeles, NY Rangers, in 18 seasons, 25 three-goal games, 3 four-goal games.
27 — Mario Lemieux, Pittsburgh, in 8 seasons, 20 three-goal games, 6 four-goal games and 1 five-goal game.
26 — Cy Denneny, Ottawa in 12 seasons. 20 three-goal games, 5 four-goal games, 1 six-goal game.
— Maurice Richard, Montreal, in 18 seasons, 23 three-goal games, 2 four-goal games, 1 five-goal game.

MOST 20-OR-MORE GOAL SEASONS:
22 — Gordie Howe, Detroit, Hartford in 26 seasons.
17 — Marcel Dionne, Detroit, Los Angeles, NY Rangers, in 18 seasons.
16 — Phil Esposito, Chicago, Boston, NY Rangers, in 18 seasons.
— Norm Ullman, Detroit, Toronto, in 19 seasons.
— John Bucyk, Detroit, Boston, in 22 seasons.
15 — Frank Mahovlich, Toronto, Detroit, Montreal in 17 seasons.
— Gilbert Perreault, Buffalo, in 17 seasons.

MOST CONSECUTIVE 20-OR-MORE GOAL SEASONS:
22 — Gordie Howe, Detroit, 1949-50 – 1970-71.
17 — Marcel Dionne, Detroit, Los Angeles, NY Rangers, 1971-72 – 1987-88.
16 — Phil Esposito, Chicago, Boston, NY Rangers, 1964-65 – 1979-80.
14 — Maurice Richard, Montreal, 1943-44 – 1956-57.
— Stan Mikita, Chicago, 1961-62 — 1974-75.
13 — Bobby Hull, Chicago, 1959-60 – 1971-72.
— Guy Lafleur, Montreal, 1971-72 – 1983-84.
— Bryan Trottier, NY Islanders, 1975-76 – 1987-88.
— Wayne Gretzky, Edmonton, Los Angeles, 1979-80 – 1991-92.
— Mike Gartner, Washington, Minnesota, NY Rangers, 1979-80 – 1991-92.
— Michel Goulet, Quebec, Chicago, 1979-80 – 1991-92.

MOST 30-OR-MORE GOAL SEASONS:
14 — Gordie Howe, Detroit, Hartford in 26 seasons.
— Marcel Dionne, Detroit, Los Angeles, NY Rangers, in 18 seasons.
13 — Bobby Hull, Chicago, Winnipeg, Hartford in 16 seasons.
— Phil Esposito, Chicago, Boston, NY Rangers, in 18 seasons.
— Mike Gartner, Washington, Minnesota, NY Rangers, 1979-80 – 1991-92.
— Wayne Gretzky, Edmonton, Los Angeles, 1979-80 – 1991-92.

MOST CONSECUTIVE 30-OR-MORE GOAL SEASONS:
13 — Bobby Hull, Chicago, 1959-60 – 1971-72.
— Phil Esposito, Boston, NY Rangers, 1967-68 – 1979-80.
— Mike Gartner, Washington, Minnesota, NY Rangers, 1979-80 – 1991-92.
— Wayne Gretzky, Edmonton, Los Angeles, 1979-80 – 1991-92.
12 — Marcel Dionne, Detroit, Los Angeles,1974-75 – 1985-86.
10 — Darryl Sittler, Toronto, Philadelphia, 1973-74 – 1982-83.
— Mike Bossy, NY Islanders, 1977-78 – 1986-87.
— Jari Kurri, Edmonton, 1980-81 – 1989-90.

MOST 40-OR-MORE GOAL SEASONS:
12 — Wayne Gretzky, Edmonton, Los Angeles, in 13 seasons.
10 — Marcel Dionne, Detroit, Los Angeles, NY Rangers, in 18 seasons.
9 — Mike Bossy, NY Islanders, in 10 seasons.
8 — Bobby Hull, Chicago, Winnipeg, Hartford, in 16 seasons.
— Phil Esposito, Chicago, Boston, NY Rangers, in 18 seasons.
— Jari Kurri, Edmonton, in 10 seasons.
— Dale Hawerchuk, Winnipeg, Buffalo, in 10 seasons.
— Mike Gartner, Washington, Minnesota, NY Rangers, in 13 seasons.

MOST CONSECUTIVE 40-OR-MORE GOAL SEASONS:
12 — Wayne Gretzky, Edmonton, Los Angeles, 1979-80 – 1990-91.
9 — Mike Bossy, NY Islanders, 1977-78 – 1985-86.
7 — Phil Esposito, Boston, 1968-69 – 1974-75.
— Michel Goulet, Quebec, 1981-82 – 1987-88.
— Jari Kurri, Edmonton, 1982-83 – 1988-89.
6 — Guy Lafleur, Montreal, 1974-75 – 1979-80.
— Joe Mullen, St. Louis, Calgary, 1983-84 – 1988-89.
— Mario Lemieux, Pittsburgh, 1984-85 – 1989-90.
— Luc Robitaille, Los Angeles, 1986-87 – 1991-92.

MOST 50-OR-MORE GOAL SEASONS:
9 — Mike Bossy, NY Islanders, in 11 seasons.
— Wayne Gretzky, Edmonton, Los Angeles, in 13 seasons.
6 — Guy Lafleur, Montreal, NY Rangers, Quebec, in 17 seasons.
— Marcel Dionne, Detroit, Los Angeles, NY Rangers, in 18 seasons.
5 — Bobby Hull, Chicago, Winnipeg, Hartford, in 16 seasons.
— Phil Esposito, Chicago, Boston, NY Rangers, in 18 seasons.

MOST CONSECUTIVE 50-OR-MORE GOAL SEASONS:
9 — Mike Bossy, NY Islanders, 1977-78 – 1985-86.
8 — Wayne Gretzky, Edmonton, 1979-80 – 1986-87.
6 — Guy Lafleur, Montreal, 1974-75 – 1979-80.
5 — Phil Esposito, Boston, 1970-71 – 1974-75.
— Marcel Dionne, Los Angeles, 1978-79 – 1982-83.

MOST 60-OR-MORE GOAL SEASONS:
5 — Mike Bossy, NY Islanders, in 10 seasons.
— Wayne Gretzky, Edmonton, Los Angeles, in 13 seasons.
4 — Phil Esposito, Chicago, Boston, NY Rangers, in 18 seasons.

MOST CONSECUTIVE 60-OR-MORE GOAL SEASONS:
4 — Wayne Gretzky, Edmonton, 1981-82 – 1984-85.
3 — Mike Bossy, NY Islanders, 1980-81 – 1982-83.
— Brett Hull, St. Louis, 1989-90 – 1991-92.
2 — Phil Esposito, Boston, 1970-71 – 1971-72, 1973-74 – 1974-75.
— Jari Kurri, Edmonton, 1984-85 – 1985-86.
— Mario Lemieux, Pittsburgh, 1987-88 – 1988-89.
— Steve Yzerman, Detroit, 1988-89 – 1989-90.

MOST 100-OR-MORE POINT SEASONS:
13 — Wayne Gretzky, Edmonton, Los Angeles, 1979-80 – 1991-92.
8 — Marcel Dionne, Detroit, 1974-75; Los Angeles, 1976-77; 1978-79 – 1982-83; 1984-85.
7 — Mike Bossy, NY Islanders, 1978-79; 1980-81 – 1985-86.
— Peter Stastny, Quebec, 1980-81 – 1985-86; 1987-88.
— Mario Lemieux, Pittsburgh, 1984-85 – 1989-90; 1991-92.
6 — Phil Esposito, Boston, 1968-69; 1970-71 – 1974-75.
— Bobby Orr, Boston, 1969-70 – 1974-75.
— Guy Lafleur, Montreal, 1974-75 – 1979-80.
— Bryan Trottier, NY Islanders, 1977-78 – 1981-82; 1983-84.
— Dale Hawerchuk, Winnipeg, 1981-82; 1983-84 – 1987-88.
— Jari Kurri, Edmonton, 1982-83 – 1986-87; 1988-89.
— Mark Messier, Edmonton, 1982-83 – 1983-84; 1986-87 – 1987-88; 1989-90; NY Rangers, 1991-92.

MOST CONSECUTIVE 100-OR-MORE POINT SEASONS:
13 — Wayne Gretzky, Edmonton, Los Angeles, 1979-80 – 1991-92.
6 — Bobby Orr, Boston, 1969-70 – 1974-75.
— Guy Lafleur, Montreal, 1974-75 – 1979-80.
— Mike Bossy, NY Islanders,1980-81 – 1985-86.
— Peter Stastny, Quebec, 1980-81 – 1985-86.
— Mario Lemieux, Pittsburgh, 1984-85 – 1989-90.

Wayne Gretzky, who scored 92 goals during the 1981-82 season, holds 17 individual single-season records.

Single Season

MOST GOALS, ONE SEASON:
92 — Wayne Gretzky, Edmonton, 1981-82. 80 game schedule.
87 — Wayne Gretzky, Edmonton, 1983-84. 80 game schedule.
86 — Brett Hull, St. Louis, 1990-91. 80 game schedule.
85 — Mario Lemieux, Pittsburgh, 1988-89. 80 game schedule.
76 — Phil Esposito, Boston, 1970-71. 78 game schedule.
73 — Wayne Gretzky, Edmonton, 1984-85. 80 game schedule.
72 — Brett Hull, St. Louis, 1989-90. 80 game schedule.
71 — Jari Kurri, Edmonton, 1984-85 80 game schedule.
— Wayne Gretzky, Edmonton, 1982-83. 80 game schedule.
70 — Mario Lemieux, Pittsburgh, 1987-1988. 80 game schedule.
— Bernie Nicholls, Los Angeles, 1988-89. 80 game schedule.
— Brett Hull, St. Louis, 1991-92. 80 game schedule.
69 — Mike Bossy, NY Islanders, 1978-79. 80 game schedule.
68 — Phil Esposito, Boston, 1973-74. 78 game schedule.
— Mike Bossy, NY Islanders, 1980-81. 80 game schedule.
— Jari Kurri, Edmonton, 1985-86. 80 game schedule.

MOST ASSISTS, ONE SEASON:
163 — Wayne Gretzky, Edmonton , 1985-86. 80 game schedule.
135 — Wayne Gretzky, Edmonton, 1984-85. 80 game schedule.
125 — Wayne Gretzky, Edmonton, 1982-83. 80 game schedule.
122 — Wayne Gretzky, Los Angeles, 1990-91. 80 game schedule.
121 — Wayne Gretzky, Edmonton, 1986-87. 80 game schedule.
120 — Wayne Gretzky, Edmonton, 1981-82. 80 game schedule.
118 — Wayne Gretzky, Edmonton, 1983-84. 80 game schedule.
114 — Wayne Gretzky, Los Angeles, 1988-89. 80 game schedule.
— Mario Lemieux, Pittsburgh, 1988-89. 80 game schedule.
109 — Wayne Gretzky, Edmonton, 1980-81. 80 game schedule.
— Wayne Gretzky, Edmonton, 1987-88. 80 game schedule.
102 — Bobby Orr, Boston, 1970-71. 78 game schedule.
— Wayne Gretzky, Los Angeles, 1989-90. 80 game schedule.

MOST POINTS, ONE SEASON:
215 — Wayne Gretzky, Edmonton, 1985-86. 80 game schedule.
212 — Wayne Gretzky, Edmonton, 1981-82. 80 game schedule.
208 — Wayne Gretzky, Edmonton, 1984-85. 80 game schedule.
205 — Wayne Gretzky, Edmonton, 1983-84. 80 game schedule.
199 — Mario Lemieux, Pittsburgh, 1988-89. 80 game schedule.
196 — Wayne Gretzky, Edmonton, 1982-83. 80 game schedule.
183 — Wayne Gretzky, Edmonton, 1986-87. 80 game schedule.
168 — Mario Lemieux, Pittsburgh, 1987-88, 80 game schedule.
— Wayne Gretzky, Los Angeles, 1988-89. 80 game schedule.
164 — Wayne Gretzky, Edmonton, 1980-81. 80 game schedule.
163 — Wayne Gretzky, Los Angeles, 1990-91. 80 game schedule.
155 — Steve Yzerman, Detroit, 1988-89. 80 game schedule.
152 — Phil Esposito, Boston, 1970-71. 78 game schedule.
150 — Bernie Nicholls, Los Angeles, 1988-89. 80 game schedule.

MOST GAMES SCORING AT LEAST THREE GOALS, ONE SEASON:
10 —**Wayne Gretzky,** Edmonton, 1981-82. 6 three-goal games, 3 four-goal games, 1 five-goal game.
—**Wayne Gretzky,** Edmonton, 1983-84. 6 three-goal games, 4 four-goal games.
9 —Mike Bossy, NY Islanders, 1980-81. 6 three-goal games, 3 four-goal games.
—Mario Lemieux, Pittsburgh, 1988-89. 7 three-goal games, 1 four-goal game, 1 five-goal game.
8 —Brett Hull, St. Louis, 1991-92. 8 three-goal games.
7 —Joe Malone, Montreal, 1917-18. 2 three-goal games, 2 four-goal games, 3 five-goal games.
—Phil Esposito, Boston, 1970-71. 7 three-goal games.
—Rick Martin, Buffalo, 1975-76. 6 three-goal games, 1 four-goal game.

HIGHEST GOALS-PER-GAME AVERAGE, ONE SEASON (AMONG PLAYERS WITH 20-OR-MORE GOALS):
2.20 —Joe Malone, Montreal, 1917-18, with 44G in 20GP.
1.64 —Cy Denneny, Ottawa, 1917-18, with 36G in 22GP.
—Newsy Lalonde, Montreal, 1917-18, with 23G in 14GP.
1.63 —Joe Malone, Qebec, 1919-20, with 39G in 24GP.
1.57 —Newsy Lalonde, Montreal, 1919-20, with 36G in 23GP.
1.50 —Joe Malone, Hamilton, 1920-21, with 30G in 20GP.

HIGHEST GOALS-PER-GAME AVERAGE, ONE SEASON (AMONG PLAYERS WITH 50-OR-MORE GOALS):
1.18 —Wayne Gretzky, Edmonton, 1983-84, with 87G in 74GP.
1.15 —Wayne Gretzky, Edmonton, 1981-82, with 92G in 80GP.
1.12 —Mario Lemieux, Pittsburgh, 1988-89, with 85G in 76GP.
1.10 —Brett Hull, St. Louis, 1990-91, with 86G in 78GP.
1.00 —Maurice Richard, Montreal, 1944-45, with 50G in 50GP.
.97 —Phil Esposito, Boston, 1970-71, with 76G in 78GP.
—Jari Kurri, Edmonton, 1984-85, with 71G in 73GP.
.96 —Brett Hull, St. Louis, 1991-92, with 70G in 73GP.
.91 —Wayne Gretzky, Edmonton, 1984-85, with 73G in 80GP.
—Mario Lemieux, Pittsburgh, 1987-88, with 70G in 77GP.
.90 —Brett Hull, St. Louis, 1989-90, with 72G in 80GP.

HIGHEST ASSISTS-PER-GAME AVERAGE, ONE SEASON (AMONG PLAYERS WITH 35-OR-MORE ASSISTS):
2.04 —Wayne Gretzky, Edmonton, 1985-86, with 163A in 80GP.
1.70 —Wayne Grezky, Edmonton, 1987-88, with 109A in 64GP.
1.69 —Wayne Gretzky, Edmonton, 1984-85, with 135A in 80GP.
1.59 —Wayne Gretzky, Edmonton, 1983-84, with 118A in 74GP.
1.56 —Wayne Gretzky, Edmonton, 1982-83, with 125A in 80GP.
1.56 —Wayne Gretzky, Los Angeles, 1990-91, with 122A in 78GP.
1.53 —Wayne Gretzky, Edmonton, 1986-87, with 121A in 79GP.
1.50 —Wayne Gretzky, Edmonton, 1981-82, with 120A in 80GP.
1.50 —Mario Lemieux, Pittsburgh, 1988-89, with 114A in 76GP.
1.48 —Adam Oates, St. Louis, 1990-91, with 90A in 61GP.

HIGHEST POINTS-PER-GAME AVERAGE, ONE SEASON (AMONG PLAYERS WITH 50-OR-MORE POINTS):
2.77 —Wayne Gretzky, Edmonton, 1983-84, with 205PTS in 74GP.
2.69 —Wayne Gretzky, Edmonton, 1985-86, with 215PTS in 80GP.
2.65 —Wayne Gretzky, Edmonton, 1981-82, with 212PTS in 80GP.
2.62 —Mario Lemieux, Pittsburgh, 1988-89, with 199PTS in 78GP.
2.60 —Wayne Gretzky, Edmonton, 1984-85, with 208PTS in 80GP.
2.45 —Wayne Gretzky, Edmonton, 1982-83, with 196PTS in 80GP.
2.33 —Wayne Gretzky, Edmonton, 1987-88, with 149PTS in 64GP.
2.32 —Wayne Gretzky, Edmonton, 1986-87, with 183PTS in 79GP.
2.18 —Mario Lemieux, Pittsburgh, 1987-88 with 168PTS in 77GP.
2.15 —Wayne Gretzky, Los Angeles, 1988-89, with 168PTS in 78GP.
2.09 —Wayne Gretzky, Los Angeles, 1990-91, with 163 PTS in 78GP.
2.08 —Mario Lemieux, Pittsburgh, 1989-90, with 123 PTS in 59GP.
2.05 —Wayne Gretzky, Edmonton, 1980-81, with 164PTS in 80GP.

MOST GOALS, ONE SEASON, INCLUDING PLAYOFFS:
100 —Wayne Gretzky, Edmonton, 1983-84, 87G in 74 regular-season games and 13G in 19 playoff games.
97 —Wayne Gretzky, Edmonton, 1981-82, 92G in 80 regular-season games and 5G in 5 playoff games.
—Mario Lemieux, Pittsburgh, 1988-89, 85G in 76 regular-season games and 12G in 11 playoff games.
—Brett Hull, St. Louis, 1990-91, 86G in 78 regular-season games and 11G in 13 playoff games.
90 —Wayne Gretzky, Edmonton, 1984-85, 73G in 80 regular season games and 17G in 18 playoff games.
—Jari Kurri, Edmonton, 1984-85, 71G in 80 regular season games and 19G in 18 playoff games.
85 —Mike Bossy, NY Islanders, 1980-81, 68G in 79 regular-season games and 17G in 18 playoff games.
—Brett Hull, St. Louis, 1989-90, 72G in 80 regular season games and 13G in 12 playoff games.
83 —Wayne Gretzky, Edmonton, 1982-83, 71G in 73 regular-season games and 12G in 16 playoff games.
81 —Mike Bossy, NY Islanders, 1981-82, 64G in 80 regular-season games and 17G in 19 playoff games.
80 —Reggie Leach, Philadelphia, 1975-76, 61G in 80 regular-season games and 19G in 16 playoff games.

MOST ASSISTS, ONE SEASON, INCLUDING PLAYOFFS:
174 —Wayne Gretzky, Edmonton, 1985-86, 163A in 80 regular-season games and 11A in 10 playoff games.
165 —Wayne Gretzky, Edmonton, 1984-85, 135A in 80 regular-season games and 30A in 18 playoff games.
151 —Wayne Gretzky, Edmonton, 1982-83, 125A in 80 regular-season games and 26A in 16 playoff games.
150 —Wayne Gretzky, Edmonton, 1986-87, 121A in 79 regular-season games and 29A in 21 playoff games.
140 —Wayne Gretzky, Edmonton, 1983-84, 118A in 74 regular-season games and 22A in 19 playoff games.
—Wayne Gretzky, Edmonton, 1987-88, 109A in 64 regular-season games and 31A in 19 playoff games.
133 —Wayne Gretzky, Los Angeles, 1990-91, 122A in 78 regular-season games and 11A in 12 playoff games.
131 —Wayne Gretzky, Los Angeles, 1988-89, 114A in 78 regular-season games and 17A in 11 playoff games.
127 —Wayne Gretzky, Edmonton, 1981-82, 120A in 80 regular-season games and 7A in 5 playoff games.
123 —Wayne Gretzky, Edmonton, 1980-81, 109A in 80 regular-season games and 14A in 9 playoff games.
121 —Mario Lemieux, Pittsburgh, 1988-89, 114A in 76 regular-season games and 7A in 11 playoff games.

MOST POINTS, ONE SEASON, INCLUDING PLAYOFFS:
255 —Wayne Gretzky, Edmonton, 1984-85, 208PTS in 80 regular-season games and 47PTS in 18 playoff games.
240 —Wayne Gretzky, Edmonton, 1983-84, 205PTS in 74 regular-season games and 35PTS in 19 playoff games.
234 —Wayne Gretzky, Edmonton, 1982-83, 196PTS in 80 regular-season games and 38PTS in 16 playoff games.
—Wayne Gretzky, Edmonton, 1985-86, 215PTS in 80 regular-season games and 19PTS in 10 playoff games.
224 —Wayne Gretzky, Edmonton, 1981-82, 212PTS in 80 regular-season games and 12PTS in 5 playoff games.
218 —Mario Lemieux, Pittsburgh, 1988-89, 199PTS in 76 regular-season games and 19PTS in 11 playoff games.
217 —Wayne Gretzky, Edmonton, 1986-87, 183PTS in 79 regular-season games and 34PTS in 21 playoff games.
192 —Wayne Gretzky, Edmonton, 1987-88, 149PTS in 64 regular-season games and 43PTS in 19 playoff games.
190 —Wayne Gretzky, Los Angeles, 1988-89, 168PTS in 78 regular-season games and 22PTS in 11 playoff games.
185 —Wayne Gretzky, Edmonton, 1980-81, 164PTS in 80 regular-season games and 21PTS in 9 playoff games.

Rick Martin, who had back-to-back 50 goal seasons for the Sabres in 1974 and 1975, notched seven hat-tricks during the 1975-76 campaign.

MOST GOALS, ONE SEASON, BY A DEFENSEMAN:
48 — Paul Coffey, Edmonton, 1985-86. 80 game schedule.
46 — Bobby Orr, Boston, 1974-75. 80 game schedule.
40 — Paul Coffey, Edmonton, 1983-84. 80 game schedule.
39 — Doug Wilson, Chicago, 1981-82. 80 game schedule.
37 — Bobby Orr, Boston, 1970-71. 78 game schedule.
— Bobby Orr, Boston, 1971-72. 78 game schedule.
— Paul Coffey, Edmonton, 1984-85 80 game schedule..
33 — Bobby Orr, Boston, 1969-70. 76 game schedule.
32 — Bobby Orr, Boston, 1973-74. 78 game schedule.
31 — Denis Potvin, NY Islanders, 1975-76. 80 game schedule.
— Denis Potvin, NY Islanders, 1978-79. 80 game schedule.
— Raymond Bourque, Boston, 1983-84. 80 game schedule.
— Phil Housley, Buffalo, 1983-84. 80 game schedule.
30 — Denis Potvin, NY Islanders, 1979-80. 80 game schedule.
— Paul Coffey, Pittsburgh, 1988-89. 80 game schedule.

MOST GOALS, ONE SEASON, BY A CENTER:
92 — Wayne Gretzky, Edmonton, 1981-82. 80 game schedule.
87 — Wayne Gretzky, Edmonton, 1983-84. 80 game schedule.
85 — Mario Lemieux, Pittsburgh, 1988-89. 80 game schedule.
76 — Phil Esposito, Boston, 1970-71. 78 game schedule.
73 — Wayne Gretzky, Edmonton, 1984-85. 80 game schedule.
71 — Wayne Gretzky, Edmonton, 1982-83. 80 game schedule.
70 — Mario Lemieux, Pittsburgh, 1987-88. 80 game schedule.
— Bernie Nicholls, Los Angeles, 1988-89. 80 game schedule.

MOST GOALS, ONE SEASON, BY A RIGHT WINGER:
86 — Brett Hull, St. Louis, 1990-91. 80 game schedule.
72 — Brett Hull, St. Louis, 1989-90. 80 game schedule.
71 — Jari Kurri, Edmonton, 1984-85. 80 game schedule.
70 — Brett Hull, St. Louis, 1991-92. 80 game schedule.
69 — Mike Bossy, NY Islanders, 1978-79. 80 game schedule.
68 — Jari Kurri, Edmonton, 1985-86. 80 game schedule..
— Mike Bossy, NY Islanders, 1980-81. 80 game schedule.
66 — Lanny McDonald, Calgary, 1982-83. 80 game schedule.
64 — Mike Bossy, NY Islanders, 1981-82. 80 game schedule.
61 — Reggie Leach, Philadelphia, 1975-76. 80 game schedule.
— Mike Bossy, NY Islanders, 1985-86. 80 game schedule.
60 — Guy Lafleur, Montreal, 1977-78. 80 game schedule.
— Mike Bossy, NY Islanders, 1982-83. 80 game schedule.

MOST GOALS, ONE SEASON, BY A LEFT WINGER:
60 — Steve Shutt, Montreal, 1976-77. 80 game schedule.
58 — Bobby Hull, Chicago, 1968-69. 76 game schedule.
57 — Michel Goulet, Quebec, 1982-83. 80 game schedule.
56 — Charlie Simmer, Los Angeles, 1979-80. 80 game schedule.
— Charlie Simmer, Los Angeles, 1980-81. 80 game schedule.
— Michel Goulet, Quebec, 1983-84. 80 game schedule.
55 — Michel Goulet, Quebec, 1984-85. 80 game schedule.
— John Ogrodnick, Detroit, 1984-85. 80 game schedule.
54 — Bobby Hull, Chicago, 1965-66. 70 game schedule.
— Al Secord, Chicago, 1982-83. 80 game schedule.
— Kevin Stevens, Pittsburgh, 1991-92. 80 game schedule.

MOST GOALS, ONE SEASON, BY A ROOKIE:
53 — Mike Bossy, NY Islanders, 1977-78. 80 game schedule.
51 — Joe Nieuwendyk, Calgary, 1987-88. 80 game schedule.
45 — Dale Hawerchuk, Winnipeg, 1981-82. 80 game schedule.
— Luc Robitaille, Los Angeles, 1986-87. 80 game schedule.
44 — Richard Martin, Buffalo, 1971-72. 80 game schedule.
— Barry Pederson, Boston, 1981-82. 80 game schedule.
43 — Steve Larmer, Chicago, 1982-83. 80 game schedule.
— Mario Lemieux, Pittsburgh, 1984-85. 80 game schedule.
40 — Darryl Sutter, Chicago, 1980-81. 80 game schedule.
— Sylvain Turgeon, Hartford, 1983-84. 80 game schedule.
— Warren Young, Pittsburgh, 1984-85. 80 game schedule.

MOST GOALS, ONE SEASON, BY A ROOKIE DEFENSEMAN:
23 — Brian Leetch, NY Rangers, 1988-89. 80 game schedule.
22 — Barry Beck, Colorado, 1977-78. 80 game schedule.
19 — Reed Larson, Detroit, 1977-78. 80 game schedule.
— Phil Housley, Buffalo, 1982-83. 80 game schedule.

MOST ASSISTS, ONE SEASON, BY A DEFENSEMAN:
102 — Bobby Orr, Boston, 1970-71. 78 game schedule.
90 — Paul Coffey, Edmonton, 1985-86. 80 game schedule.
90 — Bobby Orr, Boston, 1973-74. 78 game schedule.
89 — Bobby Orr, Boston, 1974-75. 80 game schedule.

MOST ASSISTS, ONE SEASON, BY A CENTER:
163 — Wayne Gretzky, Edmonton, 1985-86. 80 game schedule.
135 — Wayne Gretzky, Edmonton, 1984-85. 80 game schedule.
125 — Wayne Gretzky, Edmonton, 1982-83. 80 game schedule.
122 — Wayne Gretzky, Los Angeles, 1990-91. 80 game schedule.
121 — Wayne Gretzky, Edmonton, 1986-87. 80 game schedule.
120 — Wayne Gretzky, Edmonton, 1981-82. 80 game schedule.
118 — Wayne Gretzky, Edmonton, 1983-84. 80 game schedule.
114 — Wayne Gretzky, Edmonton, 1988-89. 80 game schedule.
— Mario Lemieux, Pittsburgh, 1988-89. 80 game schedule.
109 — Wayne Gretzky, Edmonton, 1980-81. 80 game schedule.
— Wayne Gretzky, Edmonton, 1987-88. 80 game schedule.

MOST ASSISTS, ONE SEASON, BY A RIGHT WINGER:
83 — Mike Bossy, NY Islanders, 1981-82. 80 game schedule.
80 — Guy Lafleur, Montreal, 1976-77. 80 game schedule.
77 — Guy Lafleur, Montreal, 1978-79. 80 game schedule.

MOST ASSISTS, ONE SEASON, BY A LEFT WINGER:
69 — Kevin Stevens, Pittsburgh, 1991-92. 80 game schedule.
67 — Mats Naslund, Montreal, 1985-86. 80 game schedule.
65 — John Bucyk, Boston, 1970-71. 78 game schedule.
— Michel Goulet, Quebec, 1983-84. 80 game schedule.
64 — Mark Messier, Edmonton, 1983-84. 80 game schedule.
63 — Luc Robitaille, Los Angeles, 1991-92. 80 game schedule.

MOST ASSISTS, ONE SEASON, BY A ROOKIE:
70 — Peter Stastny, Quebec, 1980-81. 80 game schedule.
63 — Bryan Trottier, NY Islanders, 1975-76. 80 game schedule.
62 — Sergei Makarov, Calgary, 1989-90. 80 game schedule.
60 — Larry Murphy, Los Angeles, 1980-81. 80 game schedule.

MOST ASSISTS, ONE SEASON, BY A ROOKIE DEFENSEMAN:
60 — Larry Murphy, Los Angeles, 1980-81. 80 game schedule.
55 — Chris Chelios, Montreal, 1984-85. 80 game schedule.
50 — Stefan Persson, NY Islanders, 1977-78. 80 game schedule.
— Gary Suter, Calgary, 1985-86, 80 game schedule..
49 — Nicklas Lidstrom, Detroit, 1991-92. 80 game schedule.
48 — Raymond Bourque, Boston, 1979-80. 80 game schedule.
— Brian Leetch, NY Rangers, 1988-89. 80 game schedule.

Steve Shutt blasted home 60 goals during the 1976-77 season, an NHL single-season record for goals by a left winger.

MOST POINTS, ONE SEASON, BY A DEFENSEMAN:
139 — Bobby Orr, Boston, 1970-71. 78 game schedule.
138 — Paul Coffey, Edmonton,1985-86. 80 game schedule.
135 — Bobby Orr, Boston, 1974-75. 80 game schedule.
126 — Paul Coffey, Edmonton, 1983-84. 80 game schedule.
122 — Bobby Orr, Boston, 1973-74. 78 game schedule.

MOST POINTS, ONE SEASON, BY A CENTER:
215 — Wayne Gretzky, Edmonton, 1985-86. 80 game schedule.
212 — Wayne Gretzky, Edmonton, 1981-82. 80 game schedule.
208 — Wayne Gretzky, Edmonton, 1984-85. 80 game schedule.
205 — Wayne Gretzky, Edmonton, 1983-84. 80 game schedule.
199 — Mario Lemieux, Pittsburgh, 1988-89. 80 game schedule.
196 — Wayne Gretzky, Edmonton, 1982-83. 80 game schedule.
183 — Wayne Gretzky, Edmonton, 1986-87. 80 game schedule.
168 — Mario Lemieux, Pittsburgh, 1987-88. 80 game schedule.
— Wayne Gretzky, Los Angeles, 1988-89. 80 game schedule.
164 — Wayne Gretzky, Edmonton, 1980-81. 80 game schedule.
163 — Wayne Gretzky, Los Angeles, 1990-91. 80 game schedule.

MOST POINTS, ONE SEASON, BY A RIGHT WINGER:
147 — Mike Bossy, NY Islanders, 1981-82. 80 game schedule.
136 — Guy Lafleur, Montreal, 1976-77. 80 game schedule.
135 — Jari Kurri, Edmonton, 1984-85. 80 game schedule.
132 — Guy Lafleur, Montreal, 1977-78. 80 game schedule.

MOST POINTS, ONE SEASON, BY A LEFT WINGER:
123 — Kevin Stevens, Pittsburgh, 1991-92. 80 game schedule.
121 — Michel Goulet, Quebec, 1983-84. 80 game schedule.
116 — John Bucyk, Boston, 1970-71. 78 game schedule.
112 — Bill Barber, Philadelphia, 1975-76. 80 game schedule.
111 — Luc Robitaille, Los Angeles, 1987-88. 80 game schedule.

MOST POINTS, ONE SEASON, BY A ROOKIE:
109 — Peter Stastny, Quebec, 1980-81. 80 game schedule.
103 — Dale Hawerchuk, Winnipeg, 1981-82. 80 game schedule.
100 — Mario Lemieux, Pittsburgh, 1984-85. 80 game schedule.
98 — Neal Broten, Minnesota, 1981-82. 80 game schedule.

MOST POINTS, ONE SEASON, BY A ROOKIE DEFENSEMAN:
76 — Larry Murphy, Los Angeles, 1980-81. 80 game schedule.
71 — Brian Leetch, NY Rangers, 1988-89. 80 game schedule.
68 — Gary Suter, Calgary, 1985-86. 80 game schedule.
66 — Phil Housley, Buffalo, 1982-83. 80 game schedule.
65 — Raymond Bourque, Boston, 1979-80. 80 game schedule.
64 — Chris Chelios, Montreal, 1984-85. 80 game schedule.

MOST POINTS, ONE SEASON, BY A GOALTENDER:
14 — Grant Fuhr, Edmonton, 1983-84. (14A)
9 — Curtis Joseph, St. Louis, 1991-92. (9A)
8 — Mike Palmateer, Washington, 1980-81. (8A)
— Grant Fuhr, Edmonton, 1987-88. (8A)
— Ron Hextall, Philadelphia, 1988-89. (8A)
7 — Ron Hextall, Philadelphia, 1987-88. (1G-6A)
— Mike Vernon, Calgary, 1987-88. (7A)

MOST POWER-PLAY GOALS, ONE SEASON:
34 — Tim Kerr, Philadelphia, 1985-86. 80 game schedule.
31 — Joe Nieuwendyk, Calgary, 1987-88. 80 game schedule.
— Mario Lemieux, Pittsburgh, 1988-89. 80 game schedule.
29 — Michel Goulet, Quebec, 1987-88. 80 game schedule.
— Brett Hull, St. Louis, 1990-91. 80 game schedule.
28 — Phil Esposito, Boston, 1971-72. 78 game schedule.
— Mike Bossy, NY Islanders, 1980-81. 80 game schedule.
— Michel Goulet, Quebec, 1985-86. 80 game schedule.
— Dave Andreychuk, Buffalo, 1991-92. 80 game schedule.

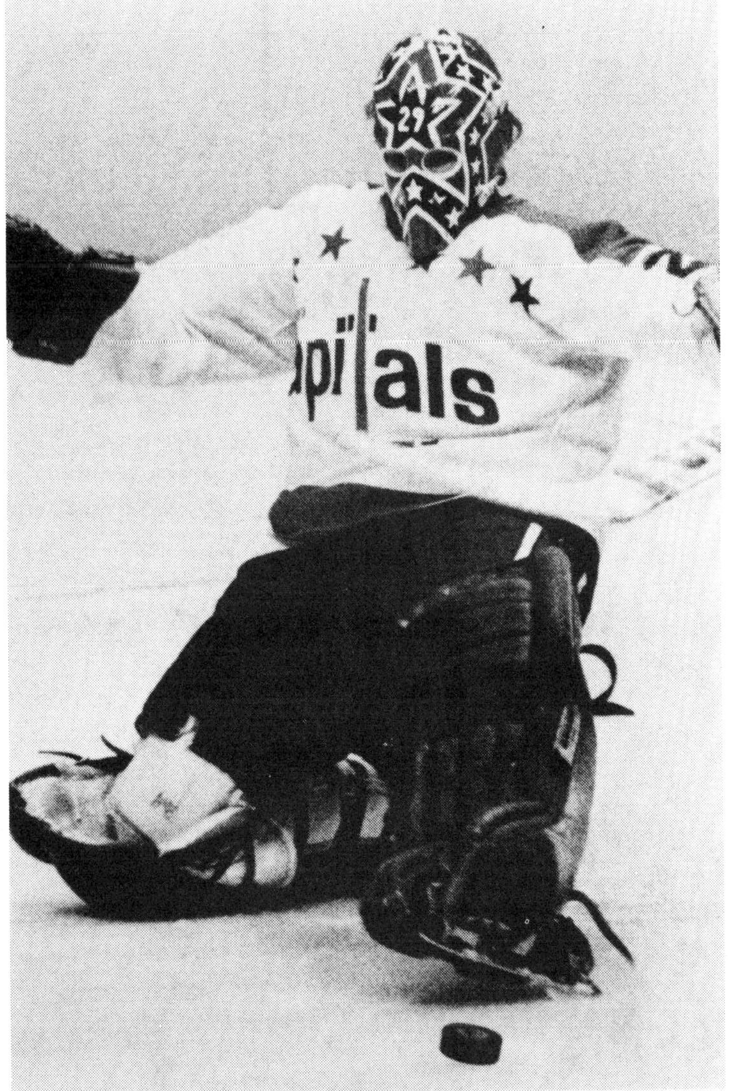

Goaltender Mike Palmateer, also known as the "Popcorn Kid," assisted on eight goals for the Washington Capitals during the 1980-81 season. Grant Fuhr holds the NHL record, gathering 14 assists for the Oilers in 1984.

MOST SHORTHAND GOALS, ONE SEASON:
13 — Mario Lemieux, Pittsburgh, 1988-89. 80 game schedule.
12 — Wayne Gretzky, Edmonton, 1983-84. 80 game schedule.
11 — Wayne Gretzky, Edmonton, 1984-85. 80 game schedule.
10 — Marcel Dionne, Detroit, 1974-75. 80 game schedule.
— Mario Lemieux, Pittsburgh, 1987-88. 80 game schedule.
— Dirk Graham, Chicago, 1988-89. 80 game schedule.

MOST SHOTS ON GOAL, ONE SEASON:
550 — Phil Esposito, Boston, 1970-71. 78 game schedule.
426 — Phil Esposito, Boston, 1971-72. 78 game schedule.
414 — Bobby Hull, Chicago, 1968-69. 76 game schedule.

MOST PENALTY MINUTES, ONE SEASON:
472 — Dave Schultz, Philadelphia, 1974-75.
409 — Paul Baxter, Pittsburgh, 1981-82.
408 — Mike Peluso, Chicago, 1991-92.
405 — Dave Schultz, Los Angeles, Pittsburgh, 1977-78.

MOST SHUTOUTS, ONE SEASON:
22 — George Hainsworth, Montreal, 1928-29. 44GP
15 — Alex Connell, Ottawa, 1925-26. 36GP
— Alex Connell, Ottawa, 1927-28. 44GP
— Hal Winkler, Boston, 1927-28. 44GP
— Tony Esposito, Chicago, 1969-70. 63GP
14 — George Hainsworth, Montreal, 1926-27. 44GP

LONGEST UNDEFEATED STREAK BY A GOALTENDER:
32 Games — Gerry Cheevers, Boston, 1971-72. 24W-8T.
31 Games — Pete Peeters, Boston, 1982-83. 26W-5T.
27 Games — Pete Peeters, Philadelphia, 1979-80. 22W-5T.
23 Games — Frank Brimsek, Boston, 1940-41. 15W-8T.
— Glenn Resch, NY Islanders, 1978-79. 15W-8T.
— Grant Fuhr, Edmonton, 1981-82. 15W-8T.

MOST GAMES, ONE SEASON, BY A GOALTENDER:
75 — Grant Fuhr, Edmonton, 1987-88.
74 — Ed Belfour, Chicago, 1990-91.
73 — Bernie Parent, Philadelphia, 1973-74.
72 — Gary Smith, Vancouver, 1974-75.
— Don Edwards, Buffalo, 1977-78.
— Tim Cheveldae, Detroit, 1991-92.
71 — Gary Smith, California, 1970-71.
— Tony Esposito, Chicago, 1974-75.

MOST WINS, ONE SEASON, BY A GOALTENDER:
47 — Bernie Parent, Philadelphia, 1973-74.
44 — Bernie Parent, Philadelphia, 1974-75.
— Terry Sawchuk, Detroit, 1950-51.
— Terry Sawchuk, Detroit, 1951-52.

LONGEST WINNING STREAK, ONE SEASON, BY A GOALTENDER:
17 — Gilles Gilbert, Boston, 1975-76.
14 — Don Beaupre, Minnesota, 1985-86.
— Ross Brooks, Boston, 1973-74.
— Tiny Thompson, Boston, 1929-30.

MOST GOALS, 50 GAMES FROM START OF SEASON:
61 — Wayne Gretzky, Edmonton, 1981-82. Oct. 7, 1981 - Jan. 22, 1982. (80-game schedule)
— **Wayne Gretzky,** Edmonton, 1983-84. Oct. 5, 1983 - Jan. 25, 1984. (80-game schedule)
54 — Mario Lemieux, Pittsburgh, 1988-89. Oct. 7, 1988 - Jan. 31, 1989. (80-game schedule)
53 — Wayne Gretzky, Edmonton, 1984-85. Oct. 11, 1984 - Jan. 28, 1985. (80-game schedule).
52 — Brett Hull, St. Louis, 1990-91. Oct. 4, 1990 - Jan. 26, 1991. (80-game schedule).
50 — Maurice Richard, Montreal, 1944-45. Oct. 28, 1944 - March 18, 1945. (50-game schedule)
— Mike Bossy, NY Islanders, 1980-81. Oct. 11, 1980 - Jan. 24, 1981. (80-game schedule)
— Brett Hull, St. Louis, 1991-92. Oct. 5, 1991 – Jan 28, 1992. (80 game schedule)

LONGEST CONSECUTIVE POINT-SCORING STREAK FROM START OF SEASON:
51 Games — Wayne Gretzky, Edmonton, 1983-84. 61G-92A-153PTS during streak which was stopped by goaltender Markus Mattsson and Los Angeles on Jan. 28, 1984.

LONGEST CONSECUTIVE POINT SCORING STREAK:
51 Games — Wayne Gretzky, Edmonton, 1983-84. 61G-92A-153PTS during streak.
46 Games — Mario Lemieux, Pittsburgh, 1989-90. 39G-64A-103PTS during streak.
39 Games — Wayne Gretzky, Edmonton, 1985-86. 33G-75A-108PTS during streak.
30 Games — Wayne Gretzky, Edmonton, 1982-83. 24G52A76PTS during streak.
28 Games — Guy Lafleur, Montreal, 1976-77. 19G-42A-61PTS during streak.
— Wayne Gretzky, Edmonton, 1984-85. 20G-43A-63PTS during streak.
— Mario Lemieux, Pittsburgh, 1985-86. 21G-38A-59PTS during streak.
— Paul Coffey, Edmonton, 1985-86. 16G-39A-55PTS during a streak.
— Steve Yzerman, Detroit, 1988-89. 29G-36A-65PTS during streak.

Known as "Suitcase" because he played for eight different teams during his 15-year career, goaltender Gary Smith played 71 games for California during the 1970-71 campaign.

LONGEST CONSECUTIVE POINT-SCORING STREAK BY A DEFENSEMAN:
28 Games — Paul Coffey, Edmonton, 1985-86. 16G-39A-55PTS during streak.
19 Games — Ray Bourque, Boston, 1987-88. 6G-21A-27PTS during streak.
17 Games — Ray Bourque, Boston, 1984-85. 4G-24A-28PTS during streak.
— Brian Leetch, NY Rangers, 1991-92. 5G-24A-29PTS during streak.
16 Games — Gary Suter, Calgary, 1987-88. 8G-17A-25PTS during streak.
15 Games — Bobby Orr, Boston, 1970-71. 10G-23A-33PTS during streak.
— Bobby Orr, Boston, 1973-74. 8G-15A-23PTS during streak.

LONGEST CONSECUTIVE GOAL-SCORING STREAK:
16 Games — Harry (Punch) Broadbent, Ottawa, 1921-22. 25 goals during streak.
14 Games — Joe Malone, Montreal, 1917-18. 35 goals during streak.
13 Games — Newsy Lalonde, Montreal, 1920-21. 24 goals during streak.
— Charlie Simmer, Los Angeles, 1979-80. 17 goals during streak.
12 Games — Cy Denneny, Ottawa, 1917-18. 23 goals during streak.
— Dave Lumley, Edmonton, 1981-82. 15 goals during streak.
11 Games — Babe Dye, Toronto, Hamilton, 1920-21. 22 goals during streak.
— Babe Dye, Toronto, 1921-22. 15 goals during streak.
— Marcel Dionne, Los Angeles, 1982-83. 14 goals during streak.
— Pat LaFontaine, NY Islanders, 1989-90. 18 goals during streak.

LONGEST CONSECUTIVE ASSIST-SCORING STREAK:
23 Games — Wayne Gretzky, Los Angeles, 1990-91. 48A during streak.
17 Games — Wayne Gretzky, Edmonton, 1983-84. 38A during streak.
— Paul Coffey, Edmonton, 1985-86. 27A during streak.
— Wayne Gretzky, Los Angeles, 1989-90. 35A during streak.
15 Games — Jari Kurri, Edmonton, 1983-84. 21A during streak.
— Brian Leetch, NY Rangers, 1991-92. 23A during streak.
14 Games — Stan Mikita, Chicago, 1967-68. 18A during streak.
— Bobby Orr, Boston, 1970-71. 23A during streak.
— Jude Drouin, Minnesota, 1971-72. 21A during streak.
— Wayne Gretzky, Edmonton, 1981-82. 26A during streak.
— Wayne Gretzky, Edmonton, 1985-86. 39A during streak.
— Mario Lemieux, Pittsburgh, 1985-86. 23A during streak.

LONGEST SHUTOUT SEQUENCE BY A GOALTENDER:
461 Minutes, 29 Seconds — Alex Connell, Ottawa, 1927-28, six consecutive shutouts. (Forward passing not permitted in attacking zones in 1927-1928.)
343 Minutes, 5 Seconds — George Hainsworth, Montreal, 1928-29, four consecutive shutouts.
324 Minutes, 40 Seconds — Roy Worters, NY Americans, 1930-31, four consecutive shutouts.
309 Minutes, 21 Seconds — Bill Durnan, Montreal, 1948-49, four consecutive shutouts.

Bengt Gustafsson scored five goals for Washington in the Capitals' 7-1 victory over the Flyers on January 8, 1984.

Paul Coffey's 28-game point-scoring streak during the 1985-86 season is the longest recorded by a defenseman and has been exceeded only by Wayne Gretzky and Mario Lemieux.

Single Game

MOST GOALS, ONE GAME:
7 — Joe Malone, Quebec Bulldogs, Jan. 31, 1920, at Quebec. Quebec 10, Toronto 6.
6 — Newsy Lalonde, Montreal, Jan. 10, 1920, at Montreal. Montreal 14, Toronto 7.
— Joe Malone, Quebec Bulldogs, March 10, 1920, at Quebec. Quebec 10, Ottawa 4.
— Corb Denneny, Toronto, Jan. 26, 1921, at Toronto. Toronto 10, Hamilton 3.
— Cy Denneny, Ottawa, March 7, 1921, at Ottawa. Ottawa 12, Hamilton 5.
— Syd Howe, Detroit, Feb. 3, 1944, at Detroit. Detroit 12, NY Rangers 2.
— Red Berenson, St. Louis, Nov. 7, 1968, at Philadelphia. St. Louis 8, Philadelphia 0
— Darryl Sittler, Toronto, Feb. 7, 1976, at Toronto. Toronto 11, Boston 4.

MOST GOALS, ONE ROAD GAME:
6 — Red Berenson, St. Louis, Nov. 7, 1968, at Philadelphia. St. Louis 8, Philadelphia 0.
5 — Joe Malone, Montreal, Dec. 19, 1917, at Ottawa. Montreal 9, Ottawa 4.
— Redvers Green, Hamilton, Dec. 5, 1924, at Toronto. Hamilton 10, Toronto 3.
— Babe Dye, Toronto, Dec. 22, 1924, at Boston. Toronto 10, Boston 2.
— Harry Broadbent, Mtl. Maroons, Jan. 7, 1925, at Hamilton. Mtl. Maroons 6, Hamilton 2.
— Don Murdoch, NY Rangers, Oct. 12, 1976, at Minnesota. NY Rangers 10, Minnesota 4.
— Tim Young, Minnesota, Jan. 15, 1979, at NY Rangers. Minnesota 8, NY Rangers 1.
— Willy Lindstrom, Winnipeg, March 2, 1982, at Philadelphia. Winnipeg 7, Philadelphia 6.
— Bengt Gustafsson, Washington, Jan. 8, 1984, at Philadelphia. Washington 7, Philadelphia 1.
— Wayne Gretzky, Edmonton, Dec. 15, 1984, at St. Louis. Edmonton 8, St. Louis 2.
— Dave Andreychuk, Buffalo, Feb. 6, 1986, at Boston. Buffalo 8, Boston 6.
— Mats Sundin, Quebec, Mar. 5, 1992, at Hartford. Quebec 10, Hartford 4.

The Quebec Nordiques' all-time leading scorer with 1,048 points, Peter Stastny scored four goals and added four assists in a 11-7 victory over Washington to set an NHL record for points in a road game.

MOST ASSISTS, ONE GAME:

7 — **Billy Taylor,** Detroit, March 16, 1947, at Chicago. Detroit 10, Chicago 6.
— **Wayne Gretzky,** Edmonton, Feb. 15, 1980, at Edmonton. Edmonton 8, Washington 2.
— **Wayne Gretzky,** Edmonton, Dec. 11, 1985, at Chicago. Edmonton 12, Chicago 9.
— **Wayne Gretzky,** Edmonton, Feb. 14, 1986, at Edmonton. Edmonton 8, Quebec 2.

6 — Elmer Lach, Montreal, Feb. 6, 1943, at Montreal. Montreal 8, Boston 3.
— Walter (Babe) Pratt, Toronto, Jan. 8, 1944, at Toronto. Toronto 12, Boston 3.
— Don Grosso, Detroit, Feb. 3, 1944, at Detroit. Detroit 12, NY Rangers 2.
— Pat Stapleton, Chicago, March 30, 1969, at Chicago. Chicago 9, Detroit 5.
— Ken Hodge, Boston, Feb. 9, 1971, at Boston. Boston 6, NY Rangers 3.
— Bobby Orr, Boston, Jan. 1, 1973, at Vancouver. Boston 8, Vancouver 2.
— Ron Stackhouse, Pittsburgh, March 8, 1975, at Pittsburgh. Pittsburgh 8, Philadelphia 2.
— Greg Malone, Pittsburgh, Nov. 28, 1979, at Pittsburgh. Pittsburgh 7, Quebec 2.
— Mike Bossy, NY Islanders, Jan. 6, 1981, at New York. NY Islanders 6, Toronto 3.
— Guy Chouinard, Calgary, Feb. 25, 1981, at Calgary. Calgary 11, NY Islanders 4.
— Mark Messier, Edmonton, Jan. 4, 1984, at Edmonton. Edmonton 12, Minnesota 8.
— Patrik Sundstrom, Vancouver, Feb 29, 1984, at Pittsburgh. Vancouver 9, Pittsburgh 5.
— Wayne Gretzky, Edmonton, Dec. 20, 1985, at Edmonton. Edmonton 9, Los Angeles 4.
— Paul Coffey, Edmonton, March 14, 1986 at Edmonton. Edmonton 12, Detroit 3.
— Gary Suter, Calgary, Apr. 4, 1986 at Calgary. Calgary 9, Edmonton 3.
— Ron Francis, Hartford, March 5, 1987 at Hartford. Hartford 10, Boston 2.
— Mario Lemieux, Pittsburgh, Oct. 15, 1988, at Pittsburgh. Pittsburgh 9, St. Louis 2.
— Bernie Nicholls, Los Angeles, Dec. 1, 1988, at Los Angeles. Los Angeles 9, Toronto 3.
— Mario Lemieux, Pittsburgh, Dec. 31, 1988 at Pittsburgh. Pittsburgh 8, New Jersey 6.

MOST ASSISTS, ONE ROAD GAME:

7 — **Billy Taylor,** Detroit, March 16, 1947, at Chicago. Detroit 10, Chicago 6.
— **Wayne Gretzky,** Edmonton, Dec. 11, 1985, at Chicago. Edmonton 12, Chicago 9.

6 — Bobby Orr, Boston, Jan. 1, 1973, at Vancouver. Boston 8, Vancouver 2.
— Patrik Sundstrom, Vancouver, Feb. 29, 1984, at Pittsburgh. Vancouver 9, Pittsburgh 5.

MOST POINTS, ONE GAME:

10 — **Darryl Sittler,** Toronto, Feb. 7, 1976, at Toronto, 6G-4A. Toronto 11, Boston 4.

8 — Maurice Richard, Montreal, Dec. 28, 1944, at Montreal, 5G-3A. Montreal 9, Detroit 1.
— Bert Olmstead, Montreal, Jan. 9, 1954, at Montreal, 4G-4A. Montreal 12, Chicago 1.
— Tom Bladon, Philadelphia, Dec. 11, 1977, at Philadelphia, 4G-4A. Philadelphia 11, Cleveland 1.
— Bryan Trottier, NY Islanders, Dec. 23, 1978, at New York, 5G-3A. NY Islanders 9, NY Rangers 4.
— Peter Stastny, Quebec, Feb. 22, 1981, at Washington, 4G-4A. Quebec 11, Washington 7.
— Anton Stastny, Quebec, Feb. 22, 1981, at Washington, 3G-5A. Quebec 11, Washington 7.
— Wayne Gretzky, Edmonton, Nov. 19, 1983, at Edmonton, 3G-5A. Edmonton 13, New Jersey 4.
— Wayne Gretzky, Edmonton, Jan. 4, 1984, at Edmonton, 4G-4A. Edmonton 12 Minnesota 8.
— Paul Coffey, Edmonton, March 14, 1986, at Edmonton, 2G-6A. Edmonton 12, Detroit 3.
— Mario Lemieux, Pittsburgh, Oct. 15, 1988, at Pittsburgh, 2G-6A. Pittsburgh 9, St. Louis 2.
— Mario Lemieux, Pittsburgh, Dec. 31, 1988, at Pittsburgh, 5G-3A. Pittsburgh 8, New Jersey 6.
— Bernie Nicholls, Los Angeles, Dec. 1, 1988, at Los Angeles, 2G-6A. Los Angeles 9, Toronto 3.

7 — Seven points have been scored by one player in one game on 35 occasions. Most recently, Mario Lemieux of Pittsburgh (Dec. 26, 1991 vs. Toronto) and Mats Sundin of Quebec (Mar. 5, 1992 vs. Hartford) had 7-point games.
Joe Malone had the first 7-point game in the NHL on Jan. 31, 1920 when his Quebec Bulldogs defeated Toronto St. Patrick's 10-6 in Quebec. All of Malone's 7 points were goals.

MOST POINTS, ONE ROAD GAME:

8 —**Peter Stastny,** Quebec, Feb. 22, 1981, at Washington, 4G-4A. Quebec 11, Washington 7.
—**Anton Stastny,** Quebec, Feb. 22, 1981, at Washington, 3G-5A. Quebec 11, Washington 7.
7 —Billy Taylor, Detroit, March 16, 1947, at Chicago, 7A. Detroit 10, Chicago. 6.
—Red Berenson, St. Louis, Nov. 7, 1968, at Philadelphia, 6G-1A. St. Louis 8, Philadelphia 0.
—Gilbert Perreault, Buffalo, Feb. 1, 1976, at California, 2G-5A. Buffalo 9, California 5.
—Peter Stastny, Quebec, April 1, 1982, at Boston, 3G-4A. Quebec 8, Boston 5.
—Wayne Gretzky, Edmonton, Nov. 6, 1983, at Winnipeg, 4G-3A. Edmonton 8, Winnipeg 5.
—Patrik Sundstrom, Vancouver, Feb. 29, 1984, at Pittsburgh, 1G-6A. Vancouver 9, Pittsburgh 5.
—Wayne Gretzky, Edmonton, Dec. 11, 1985, at Chicago. 7A, Edmonton 12, Chicago 9.
—Mario Lemieux, Pittsburgh, Jan. 21, 1989, at Edmonton, 2G, 5A. Pittsburgh 7, Edmonton 4.
—Cam Neely, Boston, Oct. 16, 1988, at Chicago, 3G, 4A. Boston 10, Chicago 3.
—Dino Ciccarelli, Washington, March 18, 1989, at Hartford, 4G, 3A. Washington 8, Hartford 2.
—Mats Sundin, Quebec, Mar. 5, 1992, at Hartford, 5G, 2A. Quebec 10, Hartford 4.

MOST GOALS, ONE GAME, BY A DEFENSEMAN:

5 —**Ian Turnbull,** Toronto, Feb. 2, 1977, at Toronto. Toronto 9, Detroit 1.
4 —Harry Cameron, Toronto, Dec. 26, 1917, at Toronto. Toronto 7, Montreal 5.
—Harry Cameron, Montreal, March 3, 1920, at Quebec City. Montreal 16, Que. Bulldogs 3.
—Sprague Cleghorn, Montreal, Jan. 14, 1922, at Montreal. Montreal 10, Hamilton 6.
—Johnny McKinnon, Pit. Pirates, Nov. 19, 1929, at Pittsburgh. Pit. Pirates 10, Toronto 5.
—Hap Day, Toronto, Nov. 19, 1929, at Pittsburgh. Pit. Pirates 10, Toronto 5.
—Tom Bladon, Philadelphia, Dec. 11, 1977, at Philadelphia. Philadelphia 11, Cleveland 1.
—Ian Turnbull, Los Angeles, Dec. 12, 1981, at Los Angeles. Los Angeles 7, Vancouver 5.
—Paul Coffey, Edmonton, Oct. 26, 1984, at Calgary. Edmonton 6, Calgary 5.

MOST GOALS BY ONE PLAYER IN HIS FIRST NHL GAME:

3 —**Alex Smart,** Montreal, Jan. 14, 1943, at Montreal. Montreal 5, Chicago 1.
—**Real Cloutier,** Quebec, Oct. 10, 1979, at Quebec. Atlanta 5, Quebec 3.

MOST GOALS, ONE GAME, BY A PLAYER IN HIS FIRST NHL SEASON:

5 —**Howie Meeker,** Toronto, Jan. 8, 1947, at Toronto. Toronto 10, Chicago 4.
—**Don Murdoch,** NY Rangers, Oct. 12, 1976, at Minnesota. NY Rangers 10, Minnesota 4.

MOST ASSISTS, ONE GAME, BY A DEFENSEMAN:

6 —**Babe Pratt,** Toronto, Jan. 8, 1944, at Toronto. Toronto 12, Boston 3.
—**Pat Stapleton,** Chicago, March 30, 1969, at Chicago. Chicago 9, Detroit 5.
—**Bobby Orr,** Boston, Jan. 1, 1973, at Vancouver, Boston 8, Vancouver 2.
—**Ron Stackhouse,** Pittsburgh, March 8, 1975, at Pittsburgh. Pittsburgh 8, Philadelphia 2.
—**Paul Coffey,** Edmonton, Mar. 14, 1986, at Edmonton. Edmonton 12, Detroit 3.
—**Gary Suter,** Calgary, Apr. 4, 1986, at Calgary. Calgary 9, Edmonton 3.

MOST ASSISTS BY ONE PLAYER IN HIS FIRST NHL GAME:

4 —**Earl (Dutch) Reibel,** Detroit, Oct. 8, 1953, at Detroit. Detroit 4, NY Rangers 1.
—**Roland Eriksson,** Minnesota, Oct. 6, 1976, at New York. NY Rangers 6, Minnesota 5.
3 —Al Hill, Philadelphia, Feb. 14, 1977, at Philadelphia. Philadelphia 6, St. Louis 4.

MOST ASSISTS, ONE GAME, BY A PLAYER IN HIS FIRST NHL SEASON:

7 —**Wayne Gretzky,** Edmonton, Feb. 15, 1980, at Edmonton. Edmonton 8, Washington 2.
6 —Gary Suter, Calgary, Apr. 4, 1986, at Calgary. Calgary 9, Edmonton 3.
5 —Jim McFadden, Detroit, Nov. 23, 1947, at Chicago. Detroit 9, Chicago 3.
—Mark Howe, Hartford, Jan. 30, 1980, at Hartford. Hartford 8, Boston 2.
—Anton Stastny, Quebec, Feb. 22, 1981, at Washington. Quebec 11, Washington 7.
—Mark Osborne, Detroit, Feb. 7, 1982, at Detroit. Detroit 8, St. Louis 5.
—Sergei Makarov, Calgary, Feb. 25, 1990, at Calgary. Calgary 10, Edmonton 4.

MOST POINTS, ONE GAME, BY A DEFENSEMAN:

8 —**Tom Bladon,** Philadelphia, Dec. 11, 1977, at Philadelphia. 4G-4A. Philadelphia 11, Cleveland 1.
—**Paul Coffey,** Edmonton, Mar. 14, 1986, at Edmonton. 2G-6A. Edmonton 12, Detroit 3.
7 —Bobby Orr, Boston, Nov. 15, 1973, at Boston, 3G-4A. Boston 10, NY Rangers 2.

MOST POINTS BY ONE PLAYER IN HIS FIRST NHL GAME:

5 —**Al Hill,** Philadelphia, Feb. 14, 1977, at Philadelphia. 2G-3A. Philadelphia 6, St. Louis 4.
4 —Alex Smart, Montreal, Jan. 14, 1943, at Montreal, 3G-1A. Montreal 5, Chicago 1.
—Earl (Dutch) Reibel, Detroit, Oct. 8, 1953, at Detroit. 4A. Detroit 4, NY Rangers 1.
—Roland Eriksson, Minnesota, Oct. 6, 1976 at New York. 4A. NY Rangers 6, Minnesota 5.

Elmer Lach, the pride of Nokomis, Saskatchewan, set up six goals in the Canadiens 8-3 win over Boston on February 6, 1943. Lach led the league in assists on three occasions, including the 1945 season when he won his first Art Ross Trophy.

MOST POINTS, ONE GAME, BY A PLAYER IN HIS FIRST NHL SEASON:
8 — **Peter Stastny,** Quebec, Feb. 22, 1981, at Washington. 4G-4A. Quebec 11, Washington 7.
— **Anton Stastny,** Quebec, Feb. 22, 1981, at Washington. 3G-5A. Quebec 11, Washington 7.
7 — Wayne Gretzky, Edmonton, Feb. 15, 1980, at Edmonton. 7A. Edmonton 8, Washington 2.
— Sergei Makarov, Calgary, Feb. 25, 1990, at Calgary, 2G-5A. Calgary 10, Edmonton 4.
6 — Wayne Gretzky, Edmonton, March 29, 1980, at Toronto. 2G-4A. Edmonton 8, Toronto 5.
— Gary Suter, Calgary, Apr. 4, 1986, at Calgary. 6A. Calgary 9, Edmonton 3.

MOST PENALTIES, ONE GAME:
10 — **Chris Nilan,** Boston, March 31, 1991, at Boston against Hartford. 6 minors, 2 majors, 1 10-minute misconduct, 1 game misconduct.
9 — Jim Dorey, Toronto, Oct. 16, 1968, at Toronto against Pittsburgh. 4 minors, 2 majors, 2 10-minute misconducts, 1 game misconduct.
— Dave Schultz, Pittsburgh, Apr. 6, 1978, at Detroit. 5 minors, 2 majors, 2 10-minute misconducts.
— Randy Holt, Los Angeles, Mar. 11, 1979, at Philadelphia. 1 minor, 3 majors, 2 10-minute misconducts, 3 game misconducts.
— Russ Anderson, Pittsburgh, Jan. 19, 1980, at Pittsburgh. 3 minors, 3 majors, 3 game misconducts.
— Kim Clackson, Quebec, March 8, 1981, at Quebec. 4 minors, 3 majors, 2 game misconducts.
— Terry O'Reilly, Boston, Dec. 19, 1984 at Hartford. 5 minors, 3 majors, 1 game misconduct.
— Larry Playfair, Los Angeles, Dec. 9, 1986, at NY Islanders. 6 minors, 2 majors, 1 10-minute misconduct.
— Marty McSorley, Los Angeles, Apr. 14, 1992, at Vancouver. 5 minors, 2 majors, 1 10-minute misconduct, 1 game misconduct.

MOST PENALTY MINUTES, ONE GAME:
67 — **Randy Holt,** Los Angeles, Mar. 11, 1979, at Philadelphia. 1 minor, 3 majors, 2 10-minute misconducts, 3 game misconducts.
55 — Frank Bathe, Philadelphia, Mar. 11, 1979, at Philadelphia. 3 majors, 2 10-minute misconducts, 2 game misconducts.
51 — Russ Anderson, Pittsburgh, Jan. 19, 1980, at Pittsburgh. 3 minors, 3 majors, 3 game misconducts.

MOST GOALS, ONE PERIOD:
4 — **Harvey (Busher) Jackson,** Toronto, Nov. 20, 1934, at St. Louis, third period. Toronto 5, St. Louis Eagles 2.
— **Max Bentley,** Chicago, Jan. 28, 1943, at Chicago, third period. Chicago 10, NY Rangers 1.
— **Clint Smith,** Chicago, March 4, 1945, at Chicago, third period. Chicago 6, Montreal 4.
— **Red Berenson,** St. Louis, Nov. 7, 1968, at Philadelphia, second period. St. Louis 8, Philadelphia 0.
— **Wayne Gretzky,** Edmonton, Feb. 18, 1981, at Edmonton, third period. Edmonton 9, St. Louis 2.
— **Grant Mulvey,** Chicago, Feb. 3, 1982, at Chicago, first period. Chicago 9, St. Louis 5.
— **Bryan Trottier,** NY Islanders, Feb. 13, 1982, at New York, second period. NY Islanders 8, Philadelphia 2.
— **Al Secord,** Chicago, Jan. 7, 1987 at Chicago, second period. Chicago 6, Toronto 4.
— **Joe Nieuwendyk,** Calgary, Jan. 11, 1989, at Calgary, second period. Calgary 8, Winnipeg 3.

MOST ASSISTS, ONE PERIOD:
5 — **Dale Hawerchuk,** Winnipeg, Mar. 6, 1984, at Los Angeles, second period. Winnipeg 7, Los Angeles 3.
4 — Four assists have been recorded in one period on 42 occasions since Buddy O'Connor of Montreal first accomplished the feat vs. NY Rangers on Nov. 8, 1942. Most recent player, Owen Nolan of Quebec (Mar. 5, 1992 vs Hartford).

MOST POINTS, ONE PERIOD:
6 — **Bryan Trottier,** NY Islanders, Dec. 23, 1978, at NY Islanders, second period. 3G, 3A. NY Islanders 9, NY Rangers 4.
5 — Les Cunningham, Chicago, Jan. 28, 1940, at Chicago, third period. 2G, 3A. Chicago 8, Montreal 1.
— Max Bentley, Chicago, Jan. 28, 1943, at Chicago, third period. 4G, 1A, Chicago 10, NY Rangers 1.
— Leo Labine, Boston, Nov. 28, 1954, at Boston, second period, 3G, 2A. Boston 6, Detroit 2.
— Darryl Sittler, Toronto, Feb. 7, 1976, at Toronto, second period. 3G, 2A. Toronto 11, Boston 4.
— Dale Hawerchuk, Winnipeg, Mar. 6, 1984, at Los Angeles, second period. 5A. Winnipeg 7, Los Angeles 3.
— Jari Kurri, Edmonton, October 26, 1984 at Edmonton, second period. Edmonton 8, Los Angeles 2.
— Pat Elynuik, Winnipeg, Jan. 20, 1989, at Winnipeg, second period. 2G, 3A. Winnipeg 7, Pittsburgh 3.
— Ray Ferraro, Hartford, Dec. 9, 1989, at Hartford, first period. 3G, 2A. Hartford 7, New Jersey 3.
— Stephane Richer, Montreal, Feb. 14, 1990, at Montreal, first period. 2G, 3A. Montreal 10, Vancouver 1.

MOST PENALTIES, ONE PERIOD:
9 — **Randy Holt,** Los Angeles, Mar. 11, 1979, at Philadelphia, first period. 1 minor, 3 majors, 2 10-minute misconducts, 3 game misconducts.

MOST PENALTY MINUTES, ONE PERIOD:
67 — **Randy Holt,** Los Angeles, Mar. 11, 1979, at Philadelphia, first period. 1 minor, 3 majors, 2 10-minute misconducts, 3 game misconducts.

FASTEST GOAL BY A ROOKIE IN HIS FIRST NHL GAME:
15 Seconds — Gus Bodnar, Toronto, Oct. 30, 1943. Toronto 5, NY Rangers 2.
18 Seconds — Danny Gare, Buffalo, Oct. 10, 1974. Buffalo 9, Boston 5.
36 Seconds — Al Hill, Philadelphia, Feb. 14, 1977. Philadelphia 6, St. Louis 4.

FASTEST GOAL FROM START OF A GAME:
5 Seconds — Doug Smail, Winnipeg, Dec. 20, 1981, at Winnipeg. Winnipeg 5, St. Louis 4.
— Bryan Trottier, NY Islanders, Mar. 22, 1984, at Boston. NY Islanders 3, Boston 3
— Alexander Mogilny, Buffalo, Dec. 21, 1991, at Toronto. Buffalo 4, Toronto 1.
6 Seconds — Henry Boucha, Detroit, Jan. 28, 1973, at Montreal. Detroit 4, Montreal 2
— Jean Pronovost, Pittsburgh, March 25, 1976, at St. Louis. St. Louis 5, Pittsburgh 2
7 Seconds — Charlie Conacher, Toronto, Feb. 6, 1932, at Toronto. Toronto 6, Boston 0
— Danny Gare, Buffalo, Dec. 17, 1978, at Buffalo. Buffalo 6, Vancouver 3
— Dave Williams, Los Angeles, Feb. 14, 1987 at Los Angeles. Los Angeles 5, Harford 2.
8 Seconds — Ron Martin, NY Americans, Dec. 4, 1932, at New York. NY Americans 4, Montreal 2
— Chuck Arnason, Colorado, Jan. 28, 1977, at Atlanta. Colorado 3, Atlanta 3
— Wayne Gretzky, Edmonton, Dec. 14, 1983, at New York. Edmonton 9, NY Rangers 4
— Gaetan Duchesne, Washington, Mar. 14, 1987, at St. Louis. Washington 3, St. Louis 3.
— Tim Kerr, Philadelphia, March 7, 1989, at Philadelphia. Philadelphia 4, Edmonton 4.
— Grant Ledyard, Buffalo, Dec. 4, 1991, at Winnipeg. Buffalo 4, Winnipeg 4.

FASTEST GOAL FROM START OF A PERIOD:
4 Seconds — Claude Provost, Montreal, Nov. 9, 1957, at Montreal, second period. Montreal 4, Boston 2.
— Denis Savard, Chicago, Jan. 12, 1986, at Chicago, third period. Chicago 4, Hartford 2.

FASTEST TWO GOALS:
4 Seconds — Nels Stewart, Mtl. Maroons, Jan. 3, 1931, at Montreal at 8:24 and 8:28, third period. Mtl. Maroons 5, Boston 3.
5 Seconds — Pete Mahovlich, Montreal, Feb. 20, 1971, at Montreal at 12:16 and 12:21, third period. Montreal 7, Chicago 1.
6 Seconds — Jim Pappin, Chicago, Feb. 16, 1972, at Chicago at 2:57 and 3:03, third period. Chicago 3, Philadelphia 3.
— Ralph Backstrom, Los Angeles, Nov. 2, 1972, at Los Angeles at 8:30 and 8:36, third period. Los Angeles 5, Boston 2.
— Lanny McDonald, Calgary, Mar. 22, 1984, at Calgary at 16:23 and 16:29, first period. Detroit 6, Calgary 4.
— Sylvain Turgeon, Hartford, Mar. 28, 1987, at Hartford at 13:59 and 14:05, second period. Hartford 5, Pittsburgh 4.

FASTEST THREE GOALS:
21 Seconds — Bill Mosienko, Chicago, March 23, 1952, at New York, against goaltender Lorne Anderson. Mosienko scored at 6:09, 6:20 and 6:30 of third period, all with both teams at full strength. Chicago 7, NY Rangers 6.
44 Seconds — Jean Béliveau, Montreal, Nov. 5, 1955, at Montreal, against goaltender Terry Sawchuk. Béliveau scored at :42, 1:08 and 1:26 of second period, all with Montreal holding a 6-4 man advantage. Montreal 4, Boston 2.

FASTEST THREE ASSISTS:
21 Seconds — Gus Bodnar, Chicago, March 23, 1952, at New York, Bodnar assisted on Bill Mosienko's three goals at 6:09, 6:20, 6:30 of third period. Chicago 7, NY Rangers 6.
44 Seconds — Bert Olmstead, Montreal, Nov. 5, 1955, at Montreal against Boston. Olmstead assisted on Jean Béliveau's three goals at :42, 1:08 and 1:26 of second period. Montreal 4, Boston 2.

Gus Bodnar helped Bill Mosienko establish a record for the fastest hat-trick by setting up all three markers.

Top 100 All-Time Goal-Scoring Leaders

* active player
(figures in parentheses indicate ranking of top 10 by goals per game)

	Player	Seasons	Games	Goals	Goals per game
1.	**Gordie Howe**, Det., Hfd.	26	1767	**801**	.453
*2.	**Wayne Gretzky**, Edm., L.A.	13	999	**749**	.750 (4)
3.	**Marcel Dionne**, Det., L.A., NYR	18	1348	**731**	.542
4.	**Phil Esposito**, Chi., Bos., NYR	18	1282	**717**	.559
5.	**Bobby Hull**, Chi., Wpg., Hfd.	16	1063	**610**	.574 (9)
6.	**Mike Bossy**, NYI	10	752	**573**	.762 (3)
7.	**Guy Lafleur**, Mtl., NYR, Que.	17	1126	**560**	.497
8.	**John Bucyk**, Det., Bos.	23	1540	**556**	.361
9.	**Maurice Richard**, Mtl.	18	978	**544**	.556
10.	**Stan Mikita**, Chi.	22	1394	**541**	.388
*11.	**Mike Gartner**, Wsh., Min., NYR	13	1005	**538**	.535
12.	**Frank Mahovlich**, Tor., Det., Mtl.	18	1181	**533**	.451
*13.	**Bryan Trottier**, NYI, Pit.	17	1238	**520**	.420
14.	**Gilbert Perreault**, Buf.	17	1191	**512**	.430
*15.	**Michel Goulet**, Que., Chi.	13	970	**509**	.525
16.	**Jean Beliveau**, Mtl.	20	1125	**507**	.451
17.	**Lanny McDonald**, Tor., Col., Cgy.	16	1111	**500**	.450
*18.	**Jari Kurri**, Edm., L.A.	11	827	**497**	.601 (6)
19.	**Jean Ratelle**, NYR, Bos.	21	1281	**491**	.383
20.	**Norm Ullman**, Det., Tor.	20	1410	**490**	.348
21.	**Darryl Sittler**, Tor., Phi., Det.	15	1096	**484**	.442
22.	**Alex Delvecchio**, Det.	24	1549	**456**	.294
23.	**Rick Middleton**, NYR, Bos.	14	1005	**448**	.446
*24.	**Dino Ciccarelli**, Min., Wsh.	12	825	**444**	.538
*25.	**Rick Vaive**, Van., Tor., Chi., Buf.	13	876	**441**	.503
*26.	**Glenn Anderson**, Edm., Tor.	12	900	**437**	.486
*27.	**Dale Hawerchuk**, Wpg., Buf.	11	870	**433**	.498
28.	**Yvan Cournoyer**, Mtl.	16	968	**428**	.442
*29.	**Peter Stastny**, Que., N.J.	12	892	**427**	.479
*30.	**Mark Messier**, Edm., NYR	13	930	**427**	.459
31.	**Steve Shutt**, Mtl., L.A.	13	930	**424**	.456
*32.	**Dave Taylor**, L.A.	15	1030	**421**	.409
33.	**Bill Barber**, Phi.	12	903	**420**	.465
34.	**Garry Unger**, Tor., Det., St.L., Atl., L.A., Edm.	16	1105	**413**	.374
*35.	**Brian Propp**, Phi., Bos., Min.	13	934	**410**	.439
*36.	**Mario Lemieux**, Pit.	8	517	**408**	.789 (2)
*37.	**Denis Savard**, Chi., Mtl.	12	883	**407**	.461
38.	**Rod Gilbert**, NYR	18	1065	**406**	.381
*39.	**Joey Mullen**, St.L., Cgy., Pit.	11	770	**400**	.519
*40.	**John Ogrodnick**, Det., Que., NYR	13	909	**396**	.436
41.	**Dave Keon**, Tor., Hfd.	18	1296	**396**	.306
42.	**Pierre Larouche**, Pit., Mtl., Hfd., NYR	14	812	**395**	.486
43.	**Bernie Geoffrion**, Mtl., NYR	16	883	**393**	.445
44.	**Jean Pronovost**, Pit., Atl., Wsh.	14	998	**391**	.392
45.	**Dean Prentice**, NYR, Bos., Det., Pit., Min.	22	1378	**391**	.284
*46.	**Steve Yzerman**, Det.	9	673	**387**	.575 (8)
47.	**Richard Martin**, Buf., L.A.	11	685	**384**	.561
*48.	**Bernie Nicholls**, L.A., NYR, Edm.	11	755	**384**	.509
49.	**Reggie Leach**, Bos., Cal., Phi., Det.	13	934	**381**	.408
50.	**Ted Lindsay**, Det., Chi.	17	1068	**379**	.355
51.	**Butch Goring**, L.A., NYI, Bos.	16	1107	**375**	.339
*52.	**Steve Larmer**, Chi.	12	807	**371**	.460
53.	**Rick Kehoe**, Tor., Pit.	14	906	**371**	.409
54.	**Tim Kerr**, Phi., NYR	12	633	**370**	.585 (7)
55.	**Bernie Federko**, St.L., Det.	14	1000	**369**	.369
*56.	**Jacques Lemaire**, Mtl.	12	853	**366**	.429
57.	**Peter McNab**, Buf., Bos., Van., N.J.	14	954	**363**	.381
58.	**Ivan Boldirev**, Bos., Cal., Chi., Atl., Van., Det.	15	1052	**361**	.343
59.	**Bobby Clarke**, Phi.	15	1144	**358**	.313
60.	**Henri Richard**, Mtl.	20	1256	**358**	.285
61.	**Dennis Maruk**, Cal., Cle., Wsh., Min.	14	888	**356**	.401
62.	**Wilf Paiment**, K.C., Col., Tor., Que., NYR, Buf., Pit.	14	946	**356**	.376
63.	**Danny Gare**, Buf., Det., Edm.	13	827	**354**	.428
*64.	**Bobby Smith**, Min., Mtl.	14	1032	**352**	.341
65.	**Rick MacLeish**, Phi., Hfd., Pit., Det.	14	846	**349**	.413
66.	**Andy Bathgate**, NYR, Tor., Det., Pit.	17	1069	**349**	.326
67.	**Charlie Simmer**, Cal., Cle., L.A., Bos., Pit.	14	712	**342**	.480
*68.	**Brian Bellows**, Min.	10	753	**342**	.454
*69.	**Mike Foligno**, Det., Buf., Tor.	13	920	**338**	.367
*70.	**Dave Christian**, Wsh., Bos., St.L.	13	940	**336**	.357
*71.	**Pat LaFontaine**, NYI, Buf.	9	587	**333**	.567(10)
72.	**Ron Ellis**, Tor.	16	1034	**332**	.321
*73.	**Mike Bullard**, Pit., Cgy., St.L., Phi., Tor.	11	727	**329**	.453
74.	**Ken Hodge**, Chi., Bos., NYR	13	881	**328**	.372
*75.	**John Tonelli**, NYI, Cgy., L.A., Chi., Que.	14	1028	**325**	.316
76.	**Nels Stewart**, Mtl. M., Bos., NYA	15	654	**324**	.495
77.	**Paul MacLean**, St.L., Wpg., Det.,	11	719	**324**	.451
78.	**Pit Martin**, Det., Bos., Chi., Van.	17	1101	**324**	.294
79.	**Vic Hadfield**, NYR, Pit.	16	1002	**323**	.322
80.	**Tony McKegney**, Buf., Que., Min., St.L., Det., Chi.	14	912	**320**	.351
*81.	**Dave Andreychuk**, Buf.	10	711	**319**	.449
82.	**Clark Gillies**, NYI, Buf.	14	958	**319**	.333
*83.	**Paul Coffey**, Edm., Pit., L.A.	12	873	**318**	.364
84.	**Don Lever**, Van., Atl., Cgy., Col., N.J., Buf.	15	1020	**313**	.307
85.	**Denis Potvin**, NYI	15	1060	**310**	.292
86.	**Bob Nevin**, Tor., NYR, Min., L.A.	18	1128	**307**	.272
*87.	**Brent Sutter**, NYI, Chi.	12	755	**305**	.404
88.	**Brian Sutter**, St.L.	12	779	**303**	.389
89.	**Dennis Hull**, Chi., Det.	14	959	**303**	.316
*90.	**Brett Hull**, Cgy., St.L.	7	379	**302**	.797 (1)
91.	**George Armstrong**, Tor.	21	1187	**296**	.249
92.	**Tom Lysiak**, Atl., Chi.	13	919	**292**	.318
93.	**Peter Mahovlich**, Det., Mtl., Pit.	16	884	**288**	.326
*94.	**Tony Tanti**, Chi., Van., Pit., Buf.	11	697	**287**	.412
*95.	**Ron Francis**, Hfd., Pit.	11	798	**287**	.360
*96.	**Luc Robitaille**, L.A.	6	473	**285**	.603 (5)
97.	**Rene Robert**, Pit., Buf., Col., Tor.	12	744	**284**	.382
98.	**Bill Goldsworthy**, Bos., Min., NYR	14	771	**283**	.367
99.	**Dick Duff**, Tor., NYR, Mtl., L.A., Buf.	18	1030	**283**	.275
*100.	**John Anderson**, Tor., Que., Hfd.	12	814	**282**	.346

The Detroit Red Wings' "Production Line" of 1969 – left to right, Gordie Howe, Alex Delvecchio and Frank Mahovlich – all rank in the NHL's top 25 all-time goal scoring leaders.

Top 100 All-Time Assist Leaders

* active player

(figures in parentheses indicate ranking of top 10 in order of assists per game)

Ted Lindsay was the fourth man to play 1,000 games in the NHL, reaching this milestone mark during the 1964-65 season.

	Player	Seasons	Games	Assists	Assists per game
*1.	**Wayne Gretzky**, Edm., L.A.	13	999	**1514**	1.516 (1)
2.	**Gordie Howe**, Det., Hfd.	26	1767	**1049**	.594
3.	**Marcel Dionne**, Det., L.A., NYR	18	1348	**1040**	.772 (9)
4.	**Stan Mikita**, Chi.	22	1394	**926**	.664
*5.	**Bryan Trottier**, NYI, Pit.	17	1238	**890**	.719
6.	**Phil Esposito**, Chi., Bos., NYR	18	1282	**873**	.681
7.	**Bobby Clarke**, Phi.	15	1144	**852**	.745
8.	**Alex Delvecchio**, Det.	24	1549	**825**	.533
9.	**Gilbert Perreault**, Buf.	17	1191	**814**	.683
10.	**John Bucyk**, Det., Bos.	23	1540	**813**	.528
*11.	**Paul Coffey**, Edm., Pit., L.A.	12	873	**796**	.912 (4)
12.	**Guy Lafleur**, Mtl., NYR, Que.	17	1126	**793**	.704
13.	**Jean Ratelle**, NYR, Bos.	21	1281	**776**	.606
14.	**Bernie Federko**, St.L., Det.	14	1000	**761**	.761
*15.	**Peter Stastny**, Que., N.J.	12	892	**754**	.845 (5)
*16.	**Larry Robinson**, Mtl., L.A.	20	1384	**750**	.542
*17.	**Ray Bourque**, Bos.	13	950	**743**	.782 (8)
18.	**Denis Potvin**, NYI	15	1060	**742**	.700
19.	**Norm Ullman**, Det., Tor.	20	1410	**739**	.524
*20.	**Denis Savard**, Chi., Mtl.	12	883	**735**	.832 (6)
*21.	**Mark Messier**, Edm., NYR	13	930	**714**	.768
22.	**Jean Beliveau**, Mtl.	20	1125	**712**	.633
23.	**Henri Richard**, Mtl.	20	1256	**688**	.548
*24.	**Dale Hawerchuk**, Wpg., Buf.	11	870	**683**	.785 (7)
25.	**Brad Park**, NYR, Bos., Det.	17	1113	**683**	.614
*26.	**Bobby Smith**, Min., Mtl.	14	1032	**672**	.651
27.	**Bobby Orr**, Bos., Chi.	12	657	**645**	.982 (3)
28.	**Darryl Sittler**, Tor., Phi., Det.	15	1096	**637**	.581
29.	**Borje Salming**, Tor., Det.	17	1148	**637**	.555
*30.	**Dave Taylor**, L.A.	15	1030	**626**	.608
31.	**Andy Bathgate**, NYR, Tor., Det., Pit.	17	1069	**624**	.584
32.	**Rod Gilbert**, NYR	18	1065	**615**	.577
*33.	**Mario Lemieux**, Pit.	8	517	**606**	1.172 (2)
*34.	**Jari Kurri**, Edm., L.A.	11	827	**606**	.733
*35.	**Ron Francis**, Hfd., Pit.	11	798	**599**	.751
36.	**Dave Keon**, Tor., Hfd.	18	1296	**590**	.455
*37.	**Doug Wilson**, Chi., S.J.	15	982	**573**	.584
38.	**Frank Mahovlich**, Tor., Det., Mtl.	18	1181	**570**	.483
*39.	**Michel Goulet**, Que., Chi.	13	970	**569**	.587
*40.	**Larry Murphy**, L.A., Wsh., Min., Pit.	12	937	**568**	.606
41.	**Bobby Hull**, Chi., Wpg., Hfd.	16	1063	**560**	.527
*42.	**Brian Propp**, Phi., Bos., Min.	13	934	**558**	.597
43.	**Mike Bossy**, NYI	10	752	**553**	.735
*44.	**Ken Linseman**, Phi., Edm., Bos., Tor.	14	860	**551**	.641
45.	**Tom Lysiak**, Atl., Chi.	13	919	**551**	.600
46.	**Red Kelly**, Det., Tor.	20	1316	**542**	.412
47.	**Rick Middleton**, NYR, Bos.	14	1005	**540**	.537
*48.	**Bernie Nicholls**, L.A., NYR, Edm.	11	755	**533**	.706
*49.	**Neal Broten**, Min.	12	794	**526**	.662
50.	**Dennis Maruk**, Cal., Cle., Wsh., Min.	14	888	**522**	.588
*51.	**Steve Yzerman**, Det.	9	673	**516**	.767
*52.	**Glenn Anderson**, Edm., Tor.	12	900	**516**	.573
53.	**Wayne Cashman**, Bos.	17	1027	**516**	.502
54.	**Butch Goring**, L.A., NYI, Bos.	16	1107	**513**	.463
*55.	**Al MacInnis**, Cgy.	11	678	**512**	.755
56.	**Dale Hunter**, Que., Wsh.	12	918	**511**	.557
*57.	**John Tonelli**, NYI, Cgy., L.A., Chi., Que.	14	1028	**511**	.497
58.	**Lanny McDonald**, Tor., Col., Cgy.	16	1111	**506**	.455
59.	**Ivan Boldirev**, Bos., Cal., Chi., Atl., Van., Det.	15	1052	**505**	.480
*60.	**Mike Gartner**, Wsh., Min., NYR	13	1005	**501**	.499
*61.	**Randy Carlyle**, Tor., Pit., Wpg.	16	1033	**498**	.482
*62.	**Phil Housley**, Buf., Wpg.	10	760	**496**	.653
*63.	**Mark Howe**, Hfd., Phi.	13	807	**489**	.606
64.	**Peter Mahovlich**, Det., Mtl., Pit.	16	884	**485**	.549
65.	**Pit Martin**, Det., Bos., Chi., Van.	17	1101	**485**	.441
*66.	**Steve Larmer**, Chi.	12	807	**482**	.597
67.	**Ken Hodge**, Chi., Bos., NYR	13	881	**472**	.536
68.	**Ted Lindsay**, Det., Chi.	17	1068	**472**	.442
69.	**Jacques Lemaire**, Mtl.	12	853	**469**	.550
70.	**Dean Prentice**, NYR, Bos., Det., Pit., Min.	22	1378	**469**	.340
*71.	**Dave Babych**, Wpg., Hfd., Van.	12	814	**468**	.575
72.	**Phil Goyette**, Mtl., NYR, St.L., Buf.	16	941	**467**	.496
73.	**Bill Barber**, Phi.	12	903	**463**	.513
74.	**Reed Larson**, Det., Bos., Edm., NYI, Min., Buf.	14	904	**463**	.512
75.	**Doug Mohns**, Bos., Chi., Min., Atl., Wsh.	22	1390	**462**	.332
*76.	**Thomas Steen**, Wpg.	11	763	**461**	.604
77.	**Bobby Rousseau**, Mtl., Min., NYR	15	942	**458**	.486
78.	**Wilf Paiment**, K.C., Col., Tor., Que., NYR, Buf., Pit.	14	946	**458**	.484
79.	**Murray Oliver**, Det., Bos., Tor., Min.	17	1127	**454**	.403
*80.	**Doug Gilmour**, St.L., Cgy., Tor.	9	690	**453**	.657
81.	**Doug Harvey**, Mtl., NYR, Det., St.L.	19	1113	**452**	.406
82.	**Guy Lapointe**, Mtl., St.L., Bos.	16	884	**451**	.510
83.	**Walt Tkachuk**, NYR	14	945	**451**	.477
84.	**Peter McNab**, Buf., Bos., Van., N.J.	14	954	**450**	.472
*85.	**Joey Mullen**, St.L., Cgy., Pit.	11	770	**449**	.583
86.	**Mel Bridgman**, Phi., Chi., N.J., Det., Van.	14	977	**449**	.460
87.	**Bill Gadsby**, Chi., NYR, Det.	20	1248	**437**	.350
88.	**Yvan Cournoyer**, Mtl.	16	968	**435**	.449
89.	**Ron Greschner**, NYR	16	982	**431**	.439
90.	**Bernie Geoffrion**, Mtl., NYR	16	883	**429**	.486
91.	**Pierre Larouche**, Pit., Mtl., Hfd., NYR	14	812	**427**	.526
92.	**Paul Reinhart**, Atl., Cgy., Van.	11	648	**426**	.657
93.	**Syl Apps Jr.**, NYR, Pit., L.A.	10	727	**423**	.582
94.	**Kent Nilsson**, Atl., Cgy., Min., Edm.	8	547	**422**	.771(10)
95.	**Bert Olmstead**, Chi., Mtl., Tor.	14	848	**421**	.496
96.	**Maurice Richard**, Mtl.	18	978	**421**	.430
97.	**Craig Ramsey**, Buf.	14	1070	**420**	.393
*98.	**John Ogrodnick**, Det., Que., NYR	13	909	**419**	.461
99.	**Bob Nevin**, Tor., NYR, Min., L.A.	18	1128	**419**	.371
100.	**Rene Robert**, Pit., Buf., Col., Tor.	12	744	**418**	.562
	Pierre Pilote, Chi., Tor.	14	890	**418**	.470
	Carol Vadnais, Mtl., Oak., Cal., Bos., NYR, N.J.	17	1087	**418**	.385

Top 100 All-Time Point Leaders

* active player

(figures in parentheses indicate ranking of top 10 by points per game)

	Player	Seasons	Games	Goals	Assists	Points	Points per game
*1.	**Wayne Gretzky**, Edm., L.A.	13	999	749	1514	**2263**	2.265 (1)
2.	**Gordie Howe**, Det., Hfd.	26	1767	801	1049	**1850**	1.047
3.	**Marcel Dionne**, Det., L.A., NYR	18	1348	731	1040	**1771**	1.314 (8)
4.	**Phil Esposito**, Chi., Bos., NYR	18	1282	717	873	**1590**	1.240
5.	**Stan Mikita**, Chi.	22	1394	541	926	**1467**	1.052
*6.	**Bryan Trottier**, NYI, Pit.	17	1238	520	890	**1410**	1.139
7.	**John Bucyk**, Det., Bos.	23	1540	556	813	**1369**	.889
8.	**Guy Lafleur**, Mtl., NYR, Que.	17	1126	560	793	**1353**	1.202
9.	**Gilbert Perreault**, Buf.	17	1191	512	814	**1326**	1.113
10.	**Alex Delvecchio**, Det.	24	1549	456	825	**1281**	.827
11.	**Jean Ratelle**, NYR, Bos.	21	1281	491	776	**1267**	.989
12.	**Norm Ullman**, Det., Tor.	20	1410	490	739	**1229**	.872
13.	**Jean Beliveau**, Mtl.	20	1125	507	712	**1219**	1.084
14.	**Bobby Clarke**, Phi.	15	1144	358	852	**1210**	1.058
*15.	**Peter Stastny**, Que., N.J.	12	892	427	754	**1181**	1.324 (7)
16.	**Bobby Hull**, Chi., Wpg., Hfd.	16	1063	610	560	**1170**	1.101
*17.	**Denis Savard**, Chi., Mtl.	12	883	407	735	**1142**	1.293 (9)
*18.	**Mark Messier**, Edm., NYR	13	930	427	714	**1141**	1.227
19.	**Bernie Federko**, St.L., Det.	14	1000	369	761	**1130**	1.130
20.	**Mike Bossy**, NYI	10	752	573	553	**1126**	1.497 (3)
21.	**Darryl Sittler**, Tor., Phi., Det.	15	1096	484	637	**1121**	1.023
*22.	**Dale Hawerchuk**, Wpg., Buf.	11	870	433	683	**1116**	1.283(10)
*23.	**Paul Coffey**, Edm., Pit., L.A.	12	873	318	796	**1114**	1.276
24.	**Frank Mahovlich**, Tor., Det., Mtl.	18	1181	533	570	**1103**	.934
*25.	**Jari Kurri**, Edm., L.A.	11	827	497	606	**1103**	1.334 (6)
*26.	**Michel Goulet**, Que., Chi.	13	970	509	569	**1078**	1.111
27.	**Denis Potvin**, NYI	15	1060	310	742	**1052**	.992
*28.	**Dave Taylor**, L.A.	15	1030	421	626	**1047**	1.017
29.	**Henri Richard**, Mtl.	20	1256	358	688	**1046**	.833
*30.	**Mike Gartner**, Wsh., Min., NYR	13	1005	538	501	**1039**	1.034
*31.	**Bobby Smith**, Min., Mtl.	14	1032	352	672	**1024**	.992
32.	**Rod Gilbert**, NYR	18	1065	406	615	**1021**	.959
*33.	**Ray Bourque**, Bos.	13	950	272	743	**1015**	1.068
*34.	**Mario Lemieux**, Pit.	8	517	408	606	**1014**	1.961 (2)
35.	**Lanny McDonald**, Tor., Col., Cgy.	16	1111	500	506	**1006**	.905
36.	**Rick Middleton**, NYR, Bos.	14	1005	448	540	**988**	.983
37.	**Dave Keon**, Tor., Hfd.	18	1296	396	590	**986**	.761
38.	**Andy Bathgate**, NYR, Tor., Det., Pit.	17	1069	349	624	**973**	.910
*39.	**Brian Propp**, Phi., Bos., Min.	13	934	410	558	**968**	1.036
40.	**Maurice Richard**, Mtl.	18	978	544	421	**965**	.987
*41.	**Larry Robinson**, Mtl., L.A.	20	1384	208	750	**958**	.692
*42.	**Glenn Anderson**, Edm., Tor.	12	900	437	516	**953**	1.059
*43.	**Bernie Nicholls**, L.A., NYR, Edm.	11	755	384	533	**917**	1.215
44.	**Bobby Orr**, Bos., Chi.	12	657	270	645	**915**	1.393 (4)
*45.	**Steve Yzerman**, Det.	9	673	387	516	**903**	1.342 (5)
46.	**Brad Park**, NYR, Bos., Det.	17	1113	213	683	**896**	.805
47.	**Butch Goring**, L.A., NYI, Bos.	16	1107	375	513	**888**	.802
*48.	**Ron Francis**, Hfd., Pit.	11	798	287	599	**886**	1.110
49.	**Bill Barber**, Phi.	12	903	420	463	**883**	.978
50.	**Dennis Maruk**, Cal., Cle., Wsh., Min.	14	888	356	522	**878**	.989
51.	**Ivan Boldirev**, Bos., Cal., Chi., Atl., Van., Det.	15	1052	361	505	**866**	.823
52.	**Yvan Cournoyer**, Mtl.	16	968	428	435	**863**	.892
*53.	**Dino Ciccarelli**, Min., Wsh.	12	825	444	416	**860**	1.042
54.	**Dean Prentice**, NYR, Bos., Det., Pit., Min.	22	1378	391	469	**860**	.624
*55.	**Steve Larmer**, Chi.	12	807	371	482	**853**	1.057
56.	**Ted Lindsay**, Det., Chi.	17	1068	379	472	**851**	.797
*57.	**Joey Mullen**, St.L., Cgy., Pit.	11	770	400	449	**849**	1.103
58.	**Tom Lysiak**, Atl., Chi.	13	919	292	551	**843**	.917
*59.	**John Tonelli**, NYI, Cgy., L.A., Chi., Que.	14	1028	325	511	**836**	.813
60.	**Jacques Lemaire**, Mtl.	12	853	366	469	**835**	.979
61.	**Red Kelly**, Det., Tor.	20	1316	281	542	**823**	.625
62.	**Pierre Larouche**, Pit., Mtl., Hfd., NYR	14	812	395	427	**822**	1.012
63.	**Bernie Geoffrion**, Mtl., NYR	16	883	393	429	**822**	.931
64.	**Steve Shutt**, Mtl., L.A.	13	930	424	393	**817**	.878
*65.	**John Ogrodnick**, Det., Que., NYR	13	909	396	419	**815**	.897
66.	**Wilf Paiment**, K.C., Col., Tor., Que., NYR, Buf., Pit.	14	946	356	458	**814**	.860
67.	**Peter McNab**, Buf., Bos., Van., N.J.	14	954	363	450	**813**	.852
68.	**Pit Martin**, Det., Bos., Chi., Van.	17	1101	324	485	**809**	.735
*69.	**Ken Linseman**, Phi., Edm., Bos., Tor.	14	860	256	551	**807**	.938
*70.	**Doug Wilson**, Chi., S.J.	15	982	234	573	**807**	.822
71.	**Garry Unger**, Tor., Det., St.L., Atl., L.A., Edm.	16	1105	413	391	**804**	.728
72.	**Ken Hodge**, Chi., Bos., NYR	13	881	328	472	**800**	.908
73.	**Wayne Cashman**, Bos.	17	1027	277	516	**793**	.772
*74.	**Rick Vaive**, Van., Tor., Chi., Buf.	13	876	441	347	**788**	.900
75.	**Borje Salming**, Tor., Det.	17	1148	150	637	**787**	.686
76.	**Jean Pronovost**, Pit., Atl., Wsh.	14	998	391	383	**774**	.776
77.	**Peter Mahovlich**, Det., Mtl., Pit.	16	884	288	485	**773**	.874
78.	**Rick Kehoe**, Tor., Pit.	14	906	371	396	**767**	.847
*79.	**Neal Broten**, Min.	12	794	237	526	**763**	.961
80.	**Dale Hunter**, Que., Wsh.	12	918	249	511	**760**	.828
81.	**Rick MacLeish**, Phi., Hfd., Pit., Det.	14	846	349	410	**759**	.897
*82.	**Dave Christian**, Wsh., Bos., St.L.	13	940	336	416	**752**	.800
*83.	**Larry Murphy**, L.A., Wsh., Min., Pit.	12	937	181	568	**749**	.799
84.	**Murray Oliver**, Det., Bos., Tor., Min.	17	1127	274	454	**728**	.646
85.	**Bob Nevin**, Tor., NYR, Min., L.A.	18	1128	307	419	**726**	.644
*86.	**Brian Bellows**, Min.	10	753	342	380	**722**	.959
*87.	**Phil Housley**, Buf., Wpg.	10	760	224	496	**720**	.947
88.	**George Armstrong**, Tor.	21	1187	296	417	**713**	.601
89.	**Vic Hadfield**, NYR, Pit.	16	1002	323	389	**712**	.711
90.	**Charlie Simmer**, Cal., Cle., L.A., Bos., Pit.	14	712	342	369	**711**	.999
*91.	**Dave Andreychuk**, Buf.	10	711	319	391	**710**	.999
92.	**Doug Mohns**, Bos., Chi., Min., Atl., Wsh.	22	1390	248	462	**710**	.511
93.	**Bobby Rousseau**, Mtl., Min., NYR	15	942	245	458	**703**	.746
94.	**Rene Robert**, Pit., Buf., Col., Tor.	12	744	284	418	**702**	.944
95.	**Richard Martin**, Buf., L.A.	11	685	384	317	**701**	1.023
96.	**Mel Bridgman**, Phi., Chi., N.J., Det., Van.	14	977	252	449	**701**	.718
*97.	**Mike Foligno**, Det., Buf., Tor.	13	920	338	362	**700**	.761
*98.	**Doug Gilmour**, St.L., Cgy., Tor.	9	690	245	453	**698**	1.012
99.	**Clark Gillies**, NYI, Buf.	14	958	319	378	**697**	.728
*100.	**Al MacInnis**, Cgy.	11	678	174	512	**686**	1.012

Dave Taylor, who reached the 1,000 career-point plateau in 1990-91, ranks 30th on the all-time assists list.

All-Time Games Played Leaders

Regular Season

* active player

	Player	Team	Seasons	GP
1.	**Gordie Howe**	Detroit	25	1,687
		Hartford	1	80
		Total	**26**	**1,767**
2.	**Alex Delvecchio**	**Detroit**	**24**	**1,549**
3.	**John Bucyk**	Detroit	2	104
		Boston	21	1,436
		Total	**23**	**1,540**
4.	**Tim Horton**	Toronto	19¾	1,185
		NY Rangers	1¼	93
		Pittsburgh	1	44
		Buffalo	2	124
		Total	**24**	**1,446**
5.	**Harry Howell**	NY Rangers	17	1,160
		California	1½	83
		Los Angeles	2½	168
		Total	**21**	**1,411**
6.	**Norm Ullman**	Detroit	12½	875
		Toronto	7½	535
		Total	**20**	**1,410**
7.	**Stan Mikita**	**Chicago**	**22**	**1,394**
8.	**Doug Mohns**	Boston	11	710
		Chicago	6½	415
		Minnesota	2½	162
		Atlanta	1	28
		Washington	1	75
		Total	**22**	**1,390**
* 9.	**Larry Robinson**	Montreal	17	1,202
		Los Angeles	3	182
		Total	**20**	**1,384**
10.	**Dean Prentice**	NY Rangers	10½	666
		Boston	3	170
		Detroit	3½	230
		Pittsburgh	2	144
		Minnesota	3	168
		Total	**22**	**1,378**
11.	**Ron Stewart**	Toronto	13	838
		Boston	2	126
		St. Louis	½	19
		NY Rangers	4	306
		Vancouver	1	42
		NY Islanders	½	22
		Total	**21**	**1,353**
12.	**Marcel Dionne**	Detroit	4	309
		Los Angeles	11¾	921
		NY Rangers	2¼	118
		Total	**18**	**1,348**
13.	**Red Kelly**	Detroit	12½	846
		Toronto	7½	470
		Total	**20**	**1,316**
14.	**Dave Keon**	Toronto	15	1,062
		Hartford	3	234
		Total	**18**	**1,296**
15.	**Phil Esposito**	Chicago	4	235
		Boston	8¼	625
		NY Rangers	5¾	422
		Total	**18**	**1,282**
16.	**Jean Ratelle**	NY Rangers	15¼	862
		Boston	5¾	419
		Total	**21**	**1,281**
17.	**Henri Richard**	**Montreal**	**20**	**1,256**
18.	**Bill Gadsby**	Chicago	8½	468
		NY Rangers	6½	457
		Detroit	5	323
		Total	**20**	**1,248**
19.	**Allan Stanley**	NY Rangers	6¼	307
		Chicago	1¾	111
		Boston	2	129
		Toronto	9	633
		Philadelphia	1	64
		Total	**21**	**1,244**
*20.	**Bryan Trottier**	NY Islanders	15	1,123
		Pittsburgh	2	115
		Total	**17**	**1,238**
21.	**Eddie Westfall**	Boston	11	734
		NY Islanders	7	493
		Total	**18**	**1,227**
22.	**Eric Nesterenko**	Toronto	5	206
		Chicago	16	1,013
		Total	**21**	**1,219**
23.	**Marcel Pronovost**	Detroit	16	983
		Toronto	5	223
		Total	**21**	**1,206**
24.	**Gilbert Perreault**	**Buffalo**	**17**	**1,191**
25.	**George Armstrong**	**Toronto**	**21**	**1,187**
26.	**Frank Mahovlich**	Toronto	11¾	720
		Detroit	2¾	198
		Montreal	3½	263
		Total	**18**	**1,181**
27.	**Don Marshall**	Montreal	10	585
		NY Rangers	7	479
		Buffalo	1	62
		Toronto	1	50
		Total	**19**	**1,176**
28.	**Bob Gainey**	**Montreal**	**16**	**1,160**
29.	**Leo Boivin**	Toronto	3¼	137
		Boston	11½	717
		Detroit	1¼	85
		Pittsburgh	1½	114
		Minnesota	1½	97
		Total	**19**	**1,150**
30.	**Borje Salming**	Toronto	16	1,099
		Detroit	1	49
		Total	**17**	**1,148**
31.	**Bobby Clarke**	**Philadelphia**	**15**	**1,144**
32.	**Bob Nevin**	Toronto	5¾	250
		NY Rangers	7¼	505
		Minnesota	2	138
		Los Angeles	3	235
		Total	**18**	**1,128**
33.	**Murray Oliver**	Detroit	2½	101
		Boston	6½	429
		Toronto	3	226
		Minnesota	5	371
		Total	**17**	**1,127**
34.	**Guy Lafleur**	Montreal	14	961
		NY Rangers	1	67
		Quebec	2	98
		Total	**17**	**1,126**
35.	**Jean Beliveau**	**Montreal**	**20**	**1,125**
36.	**Doug Harvey**	Montreal	14	890
		NY Rangers	3	151
		Detroit	1	2
		St. Louis	1	70
		Total	**19**	**1,113**
37.	**Brad Park**	NY Rangers	7½	465
		Boston	7½	501
		Detroit	2	147
		Total	**17**	**1,113**
38.	**Lanny McDonald**	Toronto	6½	477
		Colorado	1¾	142
		Calgary	7¾	441
		Total	**16**	**1,111**
39.	**Butch Goring**	Los Angeles	10¾	736
		NY Islanders	4¾	332
		Boston	½	39
		Total	**16**	**1,107**
40.	**Garry Unger**	Toronto	½	15
		Detroit	3	216
		St. Louis	8½	662
		Atlanta	1	79
		Los Angeles	¾	58
		Edmonton	2¼	75
		Total	**16**	**1,105**
41.	**Pit Martin**	Detroit	3¼	119
		Boston	1¾	111
		Chicago	10¼	740
		Vancouver	1¾	131
		Total	**17**	**1,101**
42.	**Darryl Sittler**	Toronto	11½	844
		Philadelphia	2½	191
		Detroit	1	61
		Total	**15**	**1,096**
43.	**Carol Vadnais**	Montreal	2	42
		Oakland	2	152
		California	1¾	94
		Boston	3½	263
		NY Rangers	6¾	485
		New Jersey	1	51
		Total	**17**	**1,087**
44.	**Bob Pulford**	Toronto	14	947
		Los Angeles	2	132
		Total	**16**	**1,079**
45.	**Craig Ramsay**	**Buffalo**	**14**	**1,070**
46.	**Andy Bathgate**	NY Rangers	11¾	719
		Toronto	1¼	70
		Detroit	2	130
		Pittsburgh	2	150
		Total	**17**	**1,069**
47.	**Ted Lindsay**	Detroit	14	862
		Chicago	3	206
		Total	**17**	**1,068**
48.	**Terry Harper**	Montreal	10	554
		Los Angeles	3	234
		Detroit	4	252
		St. Louis	1	11
		Colorado	1	15
		Total	**19**	**1,066**
49.	**Rod Gilbert**	**NY Rangers**	**18**	**1,065**
50.	**Bobby Hull**	Chicago	15	1,036
		Winnipeg	⅔	18
		Hartford	⅓	9
		Total	**16**	**1,063**
51.	**Denis Potvin**	**NY Islanders**	**15**	**1,060**
52.	**Jean Guy Talbot**	Montreal	13	791
		Minnesota	¼	4
		Detroit	½	32
		St. Louis	2½	172
		Buffalo	¾	57
		Total	**17**	**1,056**
53.	**Ivan Boldirev**	Boston	1¼	13
		California	2¾	191
		Chicago	4¾	384
		Atlanta	1	65
		Vancouver	2¾	216
		Detroit	2½	183
		Total	**15**	**1,052**
54.	**Eddie Shack**	NY Rangers	2¼	141
		Toronto	8¾	504
		Boston	2	120
		Los Angeles	1¼	84
		Buffalo	1½	111
		Pittsburgh	1¼	87
		Total	**17**	**1,047**
55.	**Serge Savard**	Montreal	15	917
		Winnipeg	2	123
		Total	**17**	**1,040**
56.	**Ron Ellis**	**Toronto**	**16**	**1,034**
57.	**Harold Snepsts**	Vancouver	11¾	781
		Minnesota	1	71
		Detroit	3	120
		St. Louis	1¼	61
		Total	**17**	**1,033**
*58.	**Randy Carlyle**	Toronto	2	94
		Pittsburgh	5¾	397
		Winnipeg	8¼	542
		Total	**16**	**1,033**
59.	**Ralph Backstrom**	Montreal	14½	844
		Los Angeles	2¼	172
		Chicago	¼	16
		Total	**17**	**1,032**
*60.	**Bobby Smith**	Minnesota	7¼	527
		Montreal	6¾	505
		Total	**14**	**1,032**
61.	**Dick Duff**	Toronto	9¾	582
		NY Rangers	¾	43
		Montreal	5	305
		Los Angeles	¾	39
		Buffalo	1¾	61
		Total	**18**	**1,030**
*62.	**Dave Taylor**	**Los Angeles**	**15**	**1,030**
*63.	**John Tonelli**	NY Islanders	7¾	584
		Calgary	2¼	161
		Los Angeles	3	231
		Chicago	¾	33
		Quebec	¼	19
		Total	**14**	**1,028**
64.	**Wayne Cashman**	**Boston**	**17**	**1,027**
*65.	**Brad Marsh**	Atlanta	2	160
		Calgary	1¼	97
		Philadelphia	6¾	514
		Toronto	2¾	181
		Detroit	1¼	75
		Total	**14**	**1,027**
66.	**Jim Neilson**	NY Rangers	12	810
		California	2	98
		Cleveland	2	115
		Total	**16**	**1,023**
67.	**Don Lever**	Vancouver	7⅔	593
		Atlanta	⅓	28
		Calgary	1¼	85
		Colorado	¾	59
		New Jersey	3	216
		Buffalo	2	39
		Total	**15**	**1,020**
68.	**Phil Russell**	Chicago	6¾	504
		Atlanta	1¼	93
		Calgary	3	229
		New Jersey	2¾	172
		Buffalo	1¼	18
		Total	**15**	**1,016**
69.	**Dave Lewis**	NY Islanders	6¾	514
		Los Angeles	3¼	221
		New Jersey	3	209
		Detroit	2	64
		Total	**15**	**1,008**
70.	**Bob Murray**	**Chicago**	**15**	**1,008**
71.	**Jim Roberts**	Montreal	9⅔	611
		St. Louis	5⅓	395
		Total	**15**	**1,006**
72.	**Claude Provost**	**Montreal**	**15**	**1,005**
73.	**Rick Middleton**	NY Rangers	2	124
		Boston	12	881
		Total	**14**	**1,005**
*74.	**Mike Gartner**	Washington	9¾	758
		Minnesota	1	80
		NY Rangers	2¼	167
		Total	**13**	**1,005**
75.	**Vic Hadfield**	NY Rangers	13	839
		Pittsburgh	3	163
		Total	**16**	**1,002**
76.	**Bernie Federko**	St. Louis	14	927
		Detroit	1	73
		Total	**15**	**1,000**

Goaltending Records

* active player

All-Time Shutout Leaders

Goaltender	Team	Seasons	Games	Shutouts
Terry Sawchuk	Detroit	14	734	85
(1949-1970)	Boston	2	102	11
	Toronto	3	91	4
	Los Angeles	1	36	2
	NY Rangers	1	8	1
	Total	21	971	**103**
George Hainsworth	Montreal	7½	318	75
(1926-1937)	Toronto	3½	146	19
	Total	11	464	**94**
Glenn Hall	Detroit	4	148	17
(1952-1971)	Chicago	10	618	51
	St. Louis	4	140	16
	Total	18	906	**84**
Jacques Plante	Montreal	11	556	58
(1952-1973)	NY Rangers	2	98	5
	St. Louis	2	69	10
	Toronto	2¾	106	7
	Boston	¼	8	2
	Total	18	837	**82**
Tiny Thompson	Boston	10¼	468	74
(1928-1940)	Detroit	1¾	85	7
	Total	12	553	**81**
Alex Connell	Ottawa	8	293	64
(1924-1937)	Detroit	1	48	6
	NY Americans	1	1	0
	Mtl. Maroons	2	75	11
	Total	12	417	**81**
Tony Esposito	Montreal	1	13	2
(1968-1984)	Chicago	15	873	74
	Total	16	886	**76**
Lorne Chabot	NY Rangers	2	80	21
(1926-1937)	Toronto	5	214	33
	Montreal	1	47	8
	Chicago	1	48	8
	Mtl. Maroons	1	16	2
	NY Americans	1	6	1
	Total	11	411	**73**
Harry Lumley	Detroit	6½	324	26
(1943-1960)	NY Rangers	½	1	0
	Chicago	2	134	5
	Toronto	4	267	34
	Boston	3	78	6
	Total	16	804	**71**
Roy Worters	Pittsburgh Pirates	3	123	22
(1925-1937)	NY Americans	9	360	44
	*Montreal		1	0
	Total	12	484	**66**
Turk Broda	Toronto	14	629	**62**
(1936-1952)				
John Roach	Toronto	7	223	13
(1921-1935)	NY Rangers	4	89	30
	Detroit	3	180	15
	Total	14	492	**58**
Clint Benedict	Ottawa	7	158	19
(1917-1930)	Mtl. Maroons	6	204	38
	Total	13	362	**57**
Bernie Parent	Boston	2	57	1
(1965-1979)	Philadelphia	9½	486	50
	Toronto	1½	65	4
	Total	13	608	**55**
Ed Giacomin	NY Rangers	10¼	539	49
(1965-1978)	Detroit	2¾	71	5
	Total	13	610	**54**
David Kerr	Mtl. Maroons	3	101	11
(1930-1941)	NY Americans	1	1	0
	NY Rangers	7	324	40
	Total	11	426	**51**
Rogie Vachon	Montreal	5¼	206	13
(1966-1982)	Los Angeles	6¾	389	32
	Detroit	2	109	4
	Boston	2	91	2
	Total	16	795	**51**
Ken Dryden	Montreal	8	397	**46**
(1970-1979)				
Gump Worsley	NY Rangers	10	583	24
(1952-1974)	Montreal	6½	172	16
	Minnesota	4½	107	3
	Total	**21**	**862**	**43**
Chuck Gardiner	Chicago	7	316	**42**
(1927-1934)				
Frank Brimsek	Boston	9	444	35
(1938-1950)	Chicago	1	70	5
	Total	10	514	**40**
Johnny Bower	NY Rangers	3	77	5
(1953-1970)	Toronto	12	475	32
	Total	15	552	**37**
Bill Durnan	Montreal	7	383	**34**
(1943-1950)				
Eddie Johnston	Boston	11	444	27
(1962-1978)	Toronto	1	26	1
	St. Louis	3⅔	118	4
	Chicago	⅓	4	0
	Total	16	592	**32**
Roger Crozier	Detroit	7	313	20
(1963-1977)	Buffalo	6	202	10
	Washington	1	3	0
	Total	14	518	**30**
Cesare Maniago	Toronto	1	7	0
(1960-1978)	Montreal	1	14	0
	NY Rangers	2	34	2
	Minnesota	9	420	26
	Vancouver	2	93	2
	Total	15	568	**30**

*Played 1 game for Canadiens in 1929-30.

Ten or More Shutouts, One Season

Number of Shutouts	Goaltender	Team	Season	Length of Schedule
22	George Hainsworth	Montreal	1928-29	44
15	Alex Connell	Ottawa	1925-26	36
	Alex Connell	Ottawa	1927-28	44
	Hal Winkler	Boston	1927-28	44
	Tony Esposito	Chicago	1969-70	76
14	George Hainsworth	Montreal	1926-27	44
13	Clint Benedict	Mtl. Maroons	1926-27	44
	Alex Connell	Ottawa	1926-27	44
	George Hainsworth	Montreal	1927-28	44
	John Roach	NY Rangers	1928-29	44
	Roy Worters	NY Americans	1928-29	44
	Harry Lumley	Toronto	1953-54	70
12	Tiny Thompson	Boston	1928-29	44
	Lorne Chabot	Toronto	1928-29	44
	Chuck Gardiner	Chicago	1930-31	44
	Terry Sawchuk	Detroit	1951-52	70
	Terry Sawchuk	Detroit	1953-54	70
	Terry Sawchuk	Detroit	1954-55	70
	Glenn Hall	Detroit	1955-56	70
	Bernie Parent	Philadelphia	1973-74	78
	Bernie Parent	Philadelphia	1974-75	80
11	Lorne Chabot	NY Rangers	1927-28	44
	Harry Holmes	Detroit	1927-28	44
	Clint Benedict	Mtl. Maroons	1928-29	44
	Joe Miller	Pittsburgh Pirates	1928-29	44
	Tiny Thompson	Boston	1932-33	48
	Terry Sawchuk	Detroit	1950-51	70
10	Lorne Chabot	NY Rangers	1926-27	44
	Roy Worters	Pittsburgh Pirates	1927-28	44
	Clarence Dolson	Detroit	1928-29	44
	John Roach	Detroit	1932-33	48
	Chuck Gardiner	Chicago	1933-34	48
	Tiny Thompson	Boston	1935-36	48
	Frank Brimsek	Boston	1938-39	48
	Bill Durnan	Montreal	1948-49	60
	Gerry McNeil	Montreal	1952-53	70
	Harry Lumley	Toronto	1952-53	70
	Tony Esposito	Chicago	1973-74	78
	Ken Dryden	Montreal	1976-77	80

All-Time Win Leaders

(Minimum 200 Wins)

Wins	Goaltender	GP	Decisions	Mins.	Losses	Ties	%
435	Terry Sawchuk	971	960	57,154	337	188	.551
434	Jacques Plante	837	817	49,553	246	137	.615
423	Tony Esposito	886	881	52,585	307	151	.566
407	Glenn Hall	906	899	53,484	327	165	.544
355	Rogie Vachon	795	761	46,298	291	115	.542
335	Gump Worsley	862	838	50,232	353	150	.489
332	Harry Lumley	804	799	48,097	324	143	.505
305	Billy Smith	680	643	38,431	233	105	.556
302	Turk Broda	629	627	38,173	224	101	.562
293	* Mike Liut	663	651	38,155	271	74	.507
289	Ed Giacomin	610	592	35,693	206	97	.570
286	Dan Bouchard	655	631	37,919	232	113	.543
284	Tiny Thompson	553	553	34,174	194	75	.581
270	Bernie Parent	608	588	35,136	197	121	.562
270	Gilles Meloche	788	752	45,401	351	131	.446
258	Ken Dryden	397	389	23,352	57	74	.758
252	Frank Brimsek	514	514	31,210	182	80	.568
251	* Grant Fuhr	488	466	27,684	150	59	.602
251	Johnny Bower	549	537	32,016	196	90	.551
247	George Hainsworth	464	467	29,415	146	74	.608
246	Pete Peeters	489	461	27,699	155	51	.589
242	* Andy Moog	441	410	24,763	114	54	.656
236	Eddie Johnston	592	579	34,209	256	87	.483
231	* Rejean Lemelin	497	459	27,464	148	63	.572
231	Glenn Resch	571	537	32,279	224	82	.507
230	Gerry Cheevers	418	398	24,394	94	74	.671
218	John Roach	491	491	30,423	204	69	.514
215	* Greg Millen	604	588	35,377	284	89	.441
208	Bill Durnan	383	382	22,945	112	62	.626
208	Don Edwards	459	440	26,181	155	77	.560
206	Lorne Chabot	411	411	25,309	140	65	.580
206	Roger Crozier	518	477	28,566	197	74	.509
204	* Rick Wamsley	404	378	22,963	128	46	.601
203	David Kerr	426	426	26,519	148	75	.565
203	* Don Beaupre	474	444	26,884	182	59	.524
201	* Tom Barrasso	439	418	25,246	167	50	.541

Active Shutout Leaders

Goaltender	Teams	Seasons	Games	Shutouts
Mike Liut	St. L., Hfd., Wsh.	13	663	**25**
Patrick Roy	Montreal	8	356	**18**
Greg Millen	Pit., Hfd., St. L., Que., Chi., Det.	13	604	**17**
Tom Barrasso	Buffalo, Pittsburgh	9	439	**15**
Kelly Hrudey	NY Islanders, Los Angeles	9	416	**13**
Andy Moog	Edmonton, Boston	12	441	**13**
Clint Malarchuk	Que., Wsh., Buf.	10	338	**12**
John Vanbiesbrouck	NY Rangers	10	401	**12**
Rick Wamsley	Mtl., St. L., Cgy., Tor.	12	404	**12**
Don Beaupre	Minnesota, Washington	11	474	**12**
Rejean Lemelin	Atl., Cgy., Bos.	14	497	**12**
Bob Essensa	Winnipeg	4	158	**11**
Grant Fuhr	Edmonton	11	488	**11**
Kirk McLean	New Jersey, Vancouver	7	258	**10**

Active Goaltending Leaders

(Ranked by winning percentage; minimum 250 games played)

Goaltender	Teams	Seasons	GP	Deci-sions	W	L	T	Winning %
Andy Moog	Edmonton, Boston	12	441	410	242	114	54	**.656**
Patrick Roy	Montreal	8	356	341	194	104	43	**.632**
Mike Vernon	Calgary	9	355	338	193	112	33	**.620**
Grant Fuhr	Edmonton, Toronto	11	488	460	251	150	59	**.610**
Rick Wamsley	Mtl., St. L., Cgy., Tor.	12	404	381	204	131	46	**.596**
Rejean Lemelin	Atl., Cgy., Bos.	14	497	442	231	148	63	**.594**
Kelly Hrudey	NYI, L.A.	9	416	388	190	145	53	**.558**
Rollie Melanson	NYI, L.A., N.J., Mtl.	11	291	268	129	106	33	**.543**
Tom Barrasso	Buffalo, Pittsburgh	9	439	418	201	167	50	**.541**
Ron Hextall	Philadelphia	6	281	271	130	110	31	**.537**
Bill Ranford	Boston, Edmonton	7	263	241	115	98	28	**.535**
J. Vanbiesbrouck	NY Rangers	10	401	379	180	159	40	**.528**
Don Beaupre	Minnesota, Washington	12	474	444	203	182	59	**.524**
Clint Malarchuk	Que., Wsh., Buf.	10	338	316	141	130	45	**.517**
Mike Liut	St. L., Hfd., Wsh.	13	663	638	293	271	74	**.517**
Jon Casey	Minnesota	7	265	239	102	100	37	**.504**
Brian Hayward	Wpg., Mtl., Min., S.J.	10	339	319	141	142	36	**.498**
Steve Weeks	NYR, Hfd., Van., NYI, L.A.	12	284	259	112	114	33	**.496**
Kirk McLean	New Jersey, Vancouver	7	258	245	102	115	28	**.473**
Greg Millen	Pit., Hfd., St. L., Que., Chi., Det.	14	604	588	215	284	89	**.441**
Ken Wreggett	Tor., Phi., Pit.	9	316	290	102	162	26	**.397**

Goals Against Average Leaders

(minimum 25 games played, 1926–27 to date; 15 games, 1917–18 to 1925–26)

Season	Goaltender and Club	GP	Mins.	GA	SO	AVG.
1991-92	Patrick Roy, Montreal	67	3,935	155	5	2.36
1990-91	Ed Belfour, Chicago	74	4,127	170	4	2.47
1989-90	Patrick Roy, Montreal	54	3,173	134	3	2.53
	Mike Liut, Hartford, Washington	37	2,161	91	4	2.53
1988-89	Patrick Roy, Montreal	48	2,744	113	4	2.47
1987-88	Pete Peeters, Washington	35	1,896	88	2	2.78
1986-87	Brian Hayward, Montreal	37	2,178	102	1	2.81
1985-86	Bob Froese, Philadelphia	51	2,728	116	5	2.55
1984-85	Tom Barrasso, Buffalo	54	3,248	144	5	2.66
1983-84	Pat Riggin, Washington	41	2,299	102	4	2.66
1982-83	Pete Peeters, Boston	62	3,611	142	8	2.36
1982-83	Patrick Roy, Montreal	67	3,935	155	5	2.36
1981-82	Denis Herron, Montreal	27	1,547	68	3	2.64
1980-81	Richard Sevigny, Montreal	33	1,777	71	2	2.40
1979-80	Bob Sauve, Buffalo	32	1,880	74	4	2.36
1978-79	Ken Dryden, Montreal	47	2,814	108	5	2.30
1977-78	Ken Dryden, Montreal	52	3,071	105	5	2.05
1976-77	Michel Larocque, Montreal	26	1,525	53	4	2.09
1975-76	Ken Dryden, Montreal	62	3,580	121	8	2.03
1974-75	Bernie Parent, Philadelphia	68	4,041	137	12	2.03
1973-74	Bernie Parent, Philadelphia	73	4,314	136	12	1.89
1972-73	Ken Dryden, Montreal	54	3,165	119	6	2.26
1971-72	Tony Esposito, Chicago	48	2,780	82	9	1.77
1970-71	Jacques Plante, Toronto	40	2,329	73	4	1.88
1969-70	Ernie Wakely, St. Louis	30	1,651	58	4	2.11
1968-69	Jacques Plante, St. Louis	37	2,139	70	5	1.96
1967-68	Gump Worsley, Montreal	40	2,213	73	6	1.98
1966-67	Glenn Hall, Chicago	32	1,664	66	2	2.38
1965-66	Johnny Bower, Toronto	35	1,998	75	3	2.25
1964-65	Johnny Bower, Toronto	34	2,040	81	3	2.38
1963-64	Johnny Bower, Toronto	51	3,009	106	5	2.11
1962-63	Jacques Plante, Montreal	56	3,320	138	5	2.49
1961-62	Jacques Plante, Montreal	70	4,200	166	4	2.37
1960-61	Johnny Bower, Toronto	58	3,480	145	2	2.50
1959-60	Jacques Plante, Montreal	69	4,140	175	3	2.54
1958-59	Jacques Plante, Montreal	67	4,000	144	9	2.16
1957-58	Jacques Plante, Montreal	57	3,386	119	9	2.11
1956-57	Jacques Plante, Montreal	61	3,660	123	9	2.02
1955-56	Jacques Plante, Montreal	64	3,840	119	7	1.86
1954-55	Harry Lumley, Toronto	69	4,140	134	8	1.94
	Terry Sawchuk, Detroit	68	4,080	132	12	1.94
1953-54	Harry Lumley, Toronto	69	4,140	128	13	1.86
1952-53	Terry Sawchuk, Detroit	63	3,780	120	9	1.90
1951-52	Terry Sawchuk, Detroit	70	4,200	133	12	1.90
1950-51	Al Rollins, Toronto	40	2,367	70	5	1.77
1949-50	Bill Durnan, Montreal	64	3,840	141	8	2.20
1948-49	Bill Durnan, Montreal	60	3,600	126	10	2.10
1947-48	Turk Broda, Toronto	60	3,600	143	5	2.38
1946-47	Bill Durnan, Montreal	60	3,600	138	4	2.30
1945-46	Bill Durnan, Montreal	40	2,400	104	4	2.60
1944-45	Bill Durnan, Montreal	50	3,000	121	1	2.42
1943-44	Bill Durnan, Montreal	50	3,000	109	2	2.18
1942-43	Johnny Mowers, Detroit	50	3,010	124	6	2.47
1941-42	Frank Brimsek, Boston	47	2,930	115	3	2.35
1940-41	Turk Broda, Toronto	48	2,970	99	5	2.00
1939-40	Dave Kerr, NY Rangers	48	3,000	77	8	1.54
1938-39	Frank Brimsek, Boston	43	2,610	68	10	1.56
1937-38	Tiny Thompson, Boston	48	2,970	89	7	1.80
1936-37	Normie Smith, Detroit	48	2,980	102	6	2.05
1935-36	Tiny Thompson, Boston	48	2,930	82	10	1.68
1934-35	Lorne Chabot, Chicago	48	2,940	88	8	1.80
1933-34	Wilf Cude, Detroit, Montreal	30	1,920	47	5	1.47
1932-33	Tiny Thompson, Boston	48	3,000	88	11	1.76
1931-32	Chuck Gardiner, Chicago	48	2,989	92	4	1.85
1930-31	Roy Worters, NY Americans	44	2,760	74	8	1.61
1929-30	Tiny Thompson, Boston	44	2,680	98	3	2.19
1928-29	George Hainsworth, Montreal	44	2,800	43	22	0.92
1927-28	George Hainsworth, Montreal	44	2,730	48	13	1.05
1926-27	Clint Benedict, Mtl. Maroons	43	2,748	65	13	1.42
1925-26	Alex Connell, Ottawa	36	2,251	42	15	1.12
1924-25	Georges Vezina, Montreal	30	1,860	56	5	1.81
1923-24	Georges Vezina, Montreal	24	1,459	48	3	1.97
1922-23	Clint Benedict, Ottawa	24	1,478	54	4	2.19
1921-22	Clint Benedict, Ottawa	24	1,508	84	2	3.34
1920-21	Clint Benedict, Ottawa	24	1,457	75	2	3.09
1919-20	Clint Benedict, Ottawa	24	1,444	64	5	2.66
1918-19	Clint Benedict, Ottawa	18	1,113	53	2	2.86
1917-18	Georges Vezina, Montreal	21	1,282	84	1	3.93

Coaching Records

(Minimum 600 regular-season games. Ranked by number of games coached.)

Coach	Team	Seasons	Games	Wins	Losses	Ties	%*
Al Arbour	St. Louis	1970-73	107	42	40	25	.509
	NY Islanders	1973-86; 88-92	1,331	663	464	204	.575
	Total		**1,438**	**705**	**504**	**229**	**.570**
Dick Irvin	Chicago	1930-31; 55-56	114	43	56	15	.443
	Toronto	1931-40	427	216	152	59	.575
	Montreal	1940-55	896	431	313	152	.566
	Total		**1,437**	**690**	**521**	**226**	**.559**
Scott Bowman	St. Louis	1967-71	238	110	83	45	.557
	Montreal	1971-79	634	419	110	105	.744
	Buffalo	1979-87	404	210	134	60	.594
	Pittsburgh	1991-92	80	39	32	9	.544
	Total		**1,356**	**778**	**359**	**219**	**.654**
Billy Reay	Toronto	1957-59	90	26	50	14	.367
	Chicago	1963-77	1,012	516	335	161	.589
	Total		**1,102**	**542**	**385**	**175**	**.571**
Jack Adams	Detroit	1927-44	**964**	**413**	**390**	**161**	**.512**
Sid Abel	Chicago	1952-54	140	39	79	22	.357
	Detroit	1957-68; 69-70	810	340	338	132	.501
	St. Louis	1971-72	10	3	6	1	.350
	Kansas City	1975-76	3	0	3	0	.000
	Total		**963**	**382**	**426**	**155**	**.477**
Punch Imlach	Toronto	1958-69; 79-81	840	391	311	138	.548
	Buffalo	1970-72	119	32	62	25	.374
	Total		**959**	**423**	**373**	**163**	**.526**
Toe Blake	Montreal	1955-68	**914**	**500**	**255**	**159**	**.634**
Bryan Murray	Washington	1981-90	672	343	246	83	.572
	Detroit	1990-92	160	77	63	23	.553
	Total		**832**	**420**	**309**	**106**	**.569**
Michel Bergeron	Quebec	1980-87; 89-90	634	265	283	86	.486
	NY Rangers	1987-89	158	73	67	18	.519
	Total		**792**	**338**	**350**	**104**	**.492**
Glen Sather	Edmonton	1979-89	**782**	**442**	**241**	**99**	**.629**
Emile Francis	NY Rangers	1965-75	654	347	209	98	.606
	St. Louis	1976-77, 81-83	124	46	64	14	.427
	Total		**778**	**393**	**273**	**112**	**.577**
Bob Pulford	Los Angeles	1972-77	396	178	150	68	.535
	Chicago	1977-79 1981-82; 84-87	375	158	155	62	.504
	Total		**771**	**336**	**305**	**130**	**.520**
Milt Schmidt	Boston	1954-61; 62-66	726	245	360	121	.421
	Washington	1974-76	43	5	33	5	.174
	Total		**769**	**250**	**393**	**126**	**.407**
Red Kelly	Los Angeles	1967-69	150	55	75	20	.433
	Pittsburgh	1969-73	274	90	132	52	.423
	Toronto	1973-77	318	133	123	62	.516
	Total		**742**	**278**	**330**	**134**	**465**
Fred Shero	Philadelphia	1971-78	554	308	151	95	.642
	NY Rangers	1978-81	180	82	74	24	.522
	Total		**734**	**390**	**225**	**119**	**.612**
Art Ross	Boston	1924-45	**728**	**361**	**277**	**90**	**.558**
Bob Berry	Los Angeles	1978-81	240	107	94	39	.527
	Montreal	1981-84	223	116	71	36	.601
	Pittsburgh	1984-87	240	88	127	25	.419
	Total		**703**	**311**	**292**	**100**	**.514**
Roger Neilson	Toronto	1977-79	160	75	62	23	.541
	Buffalo	1979-81	106	53	26	27	.627
	Vancouver	1982-84	133	51	61	21	.462
	Los Angeles	1984	28	8	17	3	.339
	NY Rangers	1989-92	240	122	87	31	.573
	Total		**667**	**309**	**253**	**105**	**.542**
Mike Keenan	Philadelphia	1984-88	320	190	102	28	.638
	Chicago	1988-92	320	153	126	41	.542
	Total		**640**	**343**	**228**	**69**	**.590**
Jacques Demers	Quebec	1979-80	80	25	44	11	.381
	St. Louis	1983-86	240	106	106	28	.500
	Detroit	1986-90	320	137	136	47	.502
	Total		**640**	**268**	**286**	**86**	**.486**
Jack Evans	California	1975-76	80	27	42	11	.406
	Cleveland	1976-78	160	47	87	26	.375
	Hartford	1983-88	374	163	174	37	.485
	Total		**614**	**237**	**303**	**74**	**.446**
Tommy Ivan	Detroit	1947-54	470	262	118	90	.653
	Chicago	1956-58	140	40	78	22	.364
	Total		**610**	**302**	**196**	**112**	**.587**
Lester Patrick	NY Rangers	1926-39	**604**	**281**	**216**	**107**	**.554**

* % arrived at by dividing possible points into actual points.

Dick Irvin (left) who coached three different teams to the Stanley Cup finals, confers with Toronto general manager Conn Smythe.

All-Time Penalty-Minute Leaders

* active player

(Regular season. Minimum 1,500 minutes)

Player	Teams	Seasons	Games	Penalty Minutes	Mins. per game
Dave Williams	Tor., Van., Det., L.A., Hfd.	14	962	**3,966**	4.12
***Chris Nilan**	Mtl., NYR, Bos.	13	688	**3,043**	4.42
***Dale Hunter**	Que., Wsh.	12	918	**2,676**	2.92
Willi Plett	Atl., Cgy., Minn., Bos.	13	834	**2,572**	3.08
***Tim Hunter**	Calgary	11	545	**2,405**	4.41
Dave Schultz	Phi., L.A., Pit., Buf.	9	535	**2,294**	4.29
Bryan Watson	Mtl., Det., Cal., Pit., St. L., Wsh.	16	878	**2,212**	2.52
***Laurie Boschman**	Tor., Edm., Wpg., N.J.	13	939	**2,164**	2.30
Terry O'Reilly	Boston	14	891	**2,095**	2.35
Al Secord	Bos., Chi., Tor., Phi.	12	766	**2,093**	2.73
***Rob Ramage**	Col., St. L., Cgy., Tor., Min.	13	949	**2,064**	2.17
***Basil McRae**	Que., Tor., Det., Min.	11	442	**2,061**	4.66
***Marty McSorley**	Pit., Edm., L.A.	9	520	**2,047**	3.94
Phil Russell	Chi., Atl., Cgy., N.J., Buf.	15	1,016	**2,038**	2.01
***Jay Wells**	L.A., Phi., Buf., NYR	13	826	**2,026**	2.45
Harold Snepsts	Van., Min., Det., St. L.	17	1,033	**2,009**	1.94
Andre Dupont	NYR, St. L., Phi., Que.	13	810	**1,986**	2.45
***Mike Foligno**	Det., Buf., Tor.	13	920	**1,912**	2.08
***Scott Stevens**	Wsh. St. L., N.J.	10	747	**1,902**	2.55
***Garth Butcher**	Van., St. L.	11	691	**1,889**	2.73
***Joey Kocur**	Det., NYR	8	455	**1,871**	4.11
Garry Howatt	NYI, Hfd., N.J.	12	720	**1,836**	2.55
Carol Vadnais	Mtl., Oak., Cal., Bos., NYR, N.J.	17	1,087	**1,813**	1.67
Larry Playfair	Buf., L.A.	11	688	**1,812**	2.63
Ted Lindsay	Det., Chi.	17	1,068	**1,808**	1.69
Jim Korn	Det., Tor., Buf., N.J., Cgy.	10	597	**1,801**	3.02
Brian Sutter	St. Louis	12	779	**1,786**	2.29
Wilf Paiment	K.C., Col., Tor., Que., NYR, Buf., Pit.	14	946	**1,757**	1.86
Torrie Robertson	Wsh., Hfd., Det.	10	442	**1,751**	3.96
***Mario Marois**	NYR, Van., Que., Wpg., St. L.	15	955	**1,746**	1.83
***Rick Tocchet**	Phi., Pit.	8	550	**1,734**	3.15
***Ken Linseman**	Phi., Edm., Bos., Tor.	14	860	**1,727**	2.01
***Jay Miller**	Bos., L.A.	7	446	**1,723**	3.86
***Gord Donnelly**	Que., Wpg., Buf.	9	453	**1,699**	3.75
***Bob McGill**	Tor., Chi., S.J., Det.	11	653	**1,686**	2.58
Gordie Howe	Det., Hfd.	26	1,767	**1,685**	0.95
Paul Holmgren	Phi., Min.	10	527	**1,684**	3.20
***Pat Verbeek**	N.J., Hfd.	10	699	**1,660**	2.37
***Kevin McClelland**	Pit., Edm., Det., Tor.	11	582	**1,653**	2.84
Jerry Korab	Chi., Van., Buf., L.A.	15	975	**1,629**	1.67
Mel Bridgman	Phi., Cgy., N.J., Det., Van.	14	977	**1,625**	1.66
Tim Horton	Tor., NYR, Pit., Buf.	24	1,446	**1,611**	1.11
Paul Baxter	Que., Pit., Cgy.	8	472	**1,564**	3.31
Glen Cochrane	Phi., Van., Chi., Edm.	9	411	**1,556**	3.79
Stan Smyl	Van.	13	896	**1,556**	1.74
Mike Milbury	Boston	12	754	**1,552**	2.06
Dave Hutchison	L.A., Tor., Chi., N.J.	10	584	**1,550**	2.65
Doug Risebrough	Mtl., Cal.	14	740	**1,542**	2.08
Bill Gadsby	Chi., NYR, Det.	20	1,248	**1,539**	1.23
***Bob Probert**	Detroit	7	328	**1,523**	4.64
***Dave Taylor**	Los Angeles	15	1,030	**1,512**	1.47

One Season Scoring Records

Goals-Per-Game Leaders, One Season

(Among players with 20 goals or more in one season)

Player	Team	Season	Games	Goals	Average
Joe Malone	Montreal	1917-18	20	44	2.20
Cy Denneny	Ottawa	1917-18	22	36	1.64
Newsy Lalonde	Montreal	1917-18	14	23	1.64
Joe Malone	Quebec	1919-20	24	39	1.63
Newsy Lalonde	Montreal	1919-20	23	36	1.57
Joe Malone	Hamilton	1920-21	20	30	1.50
Babe Dye	Ham., Tor.	1920-21	24	35	1.46
Cy Denneny	Ottawa	1920-21	24	34	1.42
Reg Noble	Toronto	1917-18	20	28	1.40
Newsy Lalonde	Montreal	1920-21	24	33	1.38
Odie Cleghorn	Montreal	1918-19	17	23	1.35
Harry Broadbent	Ottawa	1921-22	24	32	1.33
Babe Dye	Toronto	1924-25	29	38	1.31
Babe Dye	Toronto	1921-22	24	30	1.25
Newsy Lalonde	Montreal	1918-19	17	21	1.24
Cy Denneny	Ottawa	1921-22	22	27	1.23
Aurel Joliat	Montreal	1924-25	24	29	1.21
Wayne Gretzky	Edmonton	1983-84	74	87	1.18
Babe Dye	Toronto	1922-23	22	26	1.18
Wayne Gretzky	Edmonton	1981-82	80	92	1.15
Frank Nighbor	Ottawa	1919-20	23	26	1.13
Mario Lemieux	Pittsburgh	1988-89	76	85	1.12
Brett Hull	St. Louis	1990-91	78	86	1.10
Amos Arbour	Montreal	1919-20	20	22	1.10
Cy Denneny	Ottawa	1923-24	21	22	1.05
Joe Malone	Hamilton	1921-22	24	25	1.04
Billy Boucher	Montreal	1922-23	24	25	1.04
Maurice Richard	Montreal	1944-45	50	50	1.00
Howie Morenz	Montreal	1924-25	30	30	1.00
Reg Noble	Toronto	1919-20	24	24	1.00
Corbett Denneny	Toronto	1919-20	23	23	1.00
Jack Darragh	Ottawa	1919-20	22	22	1.00
Cooney Weiland	Boston	1929-30	44	43	.98
Phil Esposito	Boston	1970-71	78	76	.97
Jari Kurri	Edmonton	1984-85	73	71	.97

Assists-Per-Game Leaders, One Season

(Among players with 35 assists or more in one season)

Player	Team	Season	Games	Assists	Average
Wayne Gretzky	Edmonton	1985-86	80	163	2.04
Wayne Gretzky	Edmonton	1987-88	64	109	1.70
Wayne Gretzky	Edmonton	1984-85	80	135	1.69
Wayne Gretzky	Edmonton	1983-84	74	118	1.59
Wayne Gretzky	Edmonton	1982-83	80	125	1.56
Wayne Gretzky	Los Angeles	1990-91	78	122	1.56
Wayne Gretzky	Edmonton	1986-87	79	121	1.53
Wayne Gretzky	Edmonton	1981-82	80	120	1.50
Mario Lemieux	Pittsburgh	1988-89	76	114	1.50
Adam Oates	St. Louis	1990-91	61	90	1.48
Wayne Gretzky	Los Angeles	1988-89	78	114	1.46
Wayne Gretzky	Los Angeles	1989-90	73	102	1.40
Wayne Gretzky	Edmonton	1980-81	80	109	1.36
Mario Lemieux	Pittsburgh	**1991-92**	64	87	1.36
Mario Lemieux	Pittsburgh	1989-90	59	78	1.32
Bobby Orr	Boston	1970-71	78	102	1.31
Mario Lemieux	Pittsburgh	1987-88	77	98	1.27
Bobby Orr	Boston	1973-74	74	90	1.22
Wayne Gretzky	Los Angeles	**1991-92**	74	90	1.22
Mario Lemieux	Pittsburgh	1985-86	79	93	1.18
Bobby Clarke	Philadelphia	1975-76	76	89	1.17
Peter Stastny	Quebec	1981-82	80	93	1.16
Paul Coffey	Edmonton	1985-86	79	90	1.14
Bobby Orr	Boston	1969-70	76	87	1.14
Bryan Trottier	NY Islanders	1978-79	76	87	1.14
Bobby Orr	Boston	1972-73	63	72	1.14
Bill Cowley	Boston	1943-44	36	41	1.14
Steve Yzerman	Detroit	1988-89	80	90	1.13
Paul Coffey	Pittsburgh	1987-88	46	52	1.13
Bobby Orr	Boston	1974-75	80	89	1.11
Bobby Clarke	Philadelphia	1974-75	80	89	1.11
Paul Coffey	Pittsburgh	1988-89	75	83	1.11
Denis Savard	Chicago	1982-83	78	86	1.10
Denis Savard	Chicago	1981-82	80	87	1.09
Denis Savard	Chicago	1987-88	80	87	1.09
Wayne Gretzky	Edmonton	1979-80	79	86	1.09
Paul Coffey	Edmonton	1983-84	80	86	1.08
Elmer Lach	Montreal	1944-45	50	54	1.08
Peter Stastny	Quebec	1985-86	76	81	1.07
Mark Messier	Edmonton	1989-90	79	84	1.06
Paul Coffey	Edmonton	1984-85	80	84	1.05
Marcel Dionne	Los Angeles	1979-80	80	84	1.05
Bobby Orr	Boston	1971-72	76	80	1.05
Mike Bossy	NY Islanders	1981-82	80	83	1.04
Phil Esposito	Boston	1968-69	74	77	1.04
Bryan Trottier	NY Islanders	1983-84	68	71	1.04
Pete Mahovlich	Montreal	1974-75	80	82	1.03
Kent Nilsson	Calgary	1980-81	80	82	1.03
Peter Stastny	Quebec	1982-83	75	77	1.03
Bernie Nicholls	Los Angeles	1988-89	79	80	1.01
Guy Lafleur	Montreal	1979-80	74	75	1.01
Guy Lafleur	Montreal	1976-77	80	80	1.00
Marcel Dionne	Los Angeles	1984-85	80	80	1.00
Brian Leetch	NY Rangers	**1991-92**	80	80	1.00
Bryan Trottier	NY Islanders	1977-78	77	77	1.00
Mike Bossy	NY Islanders	1983-84	67	67	1.00
Jean Ratelle	NY Rangers	1971-72	63	63	1.00
Ron Francis	Hartford	1985-86	53	53	1.00
Guy Chouinard	Calgary	1980-81	52	52	1.00

Penalty Leaders

* Match Misconduct penalty not included in total penalty minutes.
** Three Match Misconduct penalties not included in total penalty minutes.
1946-47 was the first season that a Match penalty was automaticaly written into the player's total penalty minutes as 20 minutes. Now all penalties, Match, Game Misconduct, and Misconduct, are written as 10 minutes. Penalty minutes not calculated in 1917-18.

Season	Player and Club	GP	PIM
1991-92	Mike Peluso, Chicago	63	408
1990-91	Rob Ray, Buffalo	66	350
1989-90	Basil McRae, Minnesota	66	351
1988-89	Tim Hunter, Calgary	75	375
1987-88	Bob Probert, Detroit	74	398
1986-87	Tim Hunter, Calgary	73	361
1985-86	Joey Kocur, Detroit	59	377
1984-85	Chris Nilan, Montreal	77	358
1983-84	Chris Nilan, Montreal	76	338
1982-83	Randy Holt, Washington	70	275
1981-82	Paul Baxter, Pittsburgh	76	409
1980-81	Dave Williams, Vancouver	77	343
1979-80	Jimmy Mann, Winnipeg	72	287
1978-79	Dave Williams, Toronto	77	298
1977-78	Dave Schultz, L.A., Pit.	74	405
1976-77	Dave Williams, Toronto	77	338
1975-76	Steve Durbano, Pit., K.C.	69	370
1974-75	Dave Schultz, Philadelphia	76	472
1973-74	Dave Schultz, Philadelphia	73	348
1972-73	Dave Schultz, Philadelphia	76	259
1971-72	Bryan Watson, Pittsburgh	75	212
1970-71	Keith Magnuson, Chicago	76	291
1969-70	Keith Magnuson, Chicago	76	213
1968-69	Forbes Kennedy, Phi., Tor.	77	219
1967-68	Barclay Plager, St. Louis	49	153
1966-67	John Ferguson, Montreal	67	177
1965-66	Reg Fleming, Bos., NYR	69	166
1964-65	Carl Brewer, Toronto	70	177
1963-64	Vic Hadfield, NY Rangers	69	151
1962-63	Howie Young, Detroit	64	273
1961-62	Lou Fontinato, Montreal	54	167
1960-61	Pierre Pilote, Chicago	70	165
1959-60	Carl Brewer, Toronto	67	150
1958-59	Ted Lindsay, Chicago	70	184
1957-58	Lou Fontinato, NY Rangers	70	152
1956-57	Gus Mortson, Chicago	70	147
1955-56	Lou Fontinato, NY Rangers	70	202
1954-55	Fern Flaman, Boston	70	150
1953-54	Gus Mortson, Chicago	68	132
1952-53	Maurice Richard, Montreal	70	112
1951-52	Gus Kyle, Boston	69	127
1950-51	Gus Mortson, Toronto	60	142
1949-50	Bill Ezinicki, Toronto	67	144
1948-49	Bill Ezinicki, Toronto	52	145
1947-48	Bill Barilko, Toronto	57	147
1946-47	Gus Mortson, Toronto	60	133
1945-46	Jack Stewart, Detroit	47	73
1944-45	Pat Egan, Boston	48	86
1943-44	Mike McMahon, Montreal	42	98
1942-43	Jimmy Orlando, Detroit	40	89*
1941-42	Jimmy Orlando, Detroit	48	81**
1940-41	Jimmy Orlando, Detroit	48	99
1939-40	Red Horner, Toronto	30	87
1938-39	Red Horner, Toronto	48	85
1937-38	Red Horner, Toronto	47	82*
1936-37	Red Horner, Toronto	48	124
1935-36	Red Horner, Toronto	43	167
1934-35	Red Horner, Toronto	46	125
1933-34	Red Horner, Toronto	42	126*
1932-33	Red Horner, Toronto	48	144
1931-32	Red Dutton, NY Americans	47	107
1930-31	Harvey Rockburn, Detroit	42	118
1929-30	Joe Lamb, Ottawa	44	119
1928-29	Red Dutton, Mtl. Maroons	44	139
1927-28	Eddie Shore, Boston	44	165
1926-27	Nels Stewart, Mtl. Maroons	44	133
1925-26	Bert Corbeau, Toronto	36	121
1924-25	Billy Boucher, Montreal	30	92
1923-24	Bert Corbeau, Toronto	24	55
1922-23	Billy Boucher, Montreal	24	52
1921-22	Sprague Cleghorn, Montreal	24	63
1920-21	Bert Corbeau, Montreal	24	86
1919-20	Cully Wilson, Toronto	23	79
1918-19	Joe Hall, Montreal	17	85

Points-Per-Game Leaders, One Season

(Among players with 50 points or more in one season)

Player	Team	Season	Games	Points	Average
Wayne Gretzky	Edmonton	1983-84	74	205	2.77
Wayne Gretzky	Edmonton	1985-86	80	215	2.69
Wayne Gretzky	Edmonton	1981-82	80	212	2.65
Mario Lemieux	Pittsburgh	1988-89	76	199	2.62
Wayne Gretzky	Edmonton	1984-85	80	208	2.60
Wayne Gretzky	Edmonton	1982-83	80	196	2.45
Wayne Gretzky	Edmonton	1987-88	64	149	2.33
Wayne Gretzky	Edmonton	1986-87	79	183	2.32
Mario Lemieux	Pittsburgh	1987-88	77	168	2.18
Wayne Gretzky	Los Angeles	1988-89	78	168	2.15
Wayne Gretzky	Los Angeles	1990-91	78	163	2.09
Mario Lemieux	Pittsburgh	1989-90	59	123	2.08
Wayne Gretzky	Edmonton	1980-81	80	164	2.05
Mario Lemieux	Pittsburgh	**1991-92**	64	131	2.05
Bill Cowley	Boston	1943-44	36	71	1.97
Phil Esposito	Boston	1970-71	78	152	1.95
Wayne Gretzky	Los Angeles	1989-90	73	142	1.95
Steve Yzerman	Detroit	1988-89	80	155	1.94
Bernie Nicholls	Los Angeles	1988-89	79	150	1.90
Adam Oates	St. Louis	1990-91	61	115	1.89
Phil Esposito	Boston	1973-74	78	145	1.86
Jari Kurri	Edmonton	1984-85	73	135	1.85
Mike Bossy	NY Islanders	1981-82	80	147	1.84
Mario Lemieux	Pittsburgh	1985-86	79	141	1.78
Bobby Orr	Boston	1970-71	78	139	1.78
Jari Kurri	Edmonton	1983-84	64	113	1.77
Bryan Trottier	NY Islanders	1978-79	76	134	1.76
Mike Bossy	NY Islanders	1983-84	67	118	1.76
Paul Coffey	Edmonton	1985-86	79	138	1.75
Phil Esposito	Boston	1971-72	76	133	1.75
Peter Stastny	Quebec	1981-82	80	139	1.74
Wayne Gretzky	Edmonton	1979-80	79	137	1.73
Jean Ratelle	NY Rangers	1971-72	63	109	1.73
Marcel Dionne	Los Angeles	1979-80	80	137	1.71
Herb Cain	Boston	1943-44	48	82	1.71
Guy Lafleur	Montreal	1976-77	80	136	1.70
Dennis Maruk	Washington	1981-82	80	136	1.70
Phil Esposito	Boston	1968-69	74	126	1.70
Guy Lafleur	Montreal	1974-75	70	119	1.70
Mario Lemieux	Pittsburgh	1986-87	63	107	1.70
Bobby Orr	Boston	1974-75	80	135	1.69
Marcel Dionne	Los Angeles	1980-81	80	135	1.69
Guy Lafleur	Montreal	1977-78	78	132	1.69
Guy Lafleur	Montreal	1979-80	74	125	1.69
Rob Brown	Pittsburgh	1988-89	68	115	1.69
Jari Kurri	Edmonton	1985-86	78	131	1.68
Brett Hull	St. Louis	1990-91	78	131	1.68
Phil Esposito	Boston	1972-73	78	130	1.67
Cooney Weiland	Boston	1929-30	44	73	1.66
Peter Stastny	Quebec	1982-83	75	124	1.65
Bobby Orr	Boston	1973-74	74	122	1.65
Kent Nilsson	Calgary	1980-81	80	131	1.64
Wayne Gretzky	Los Angeles	**1991-92**	74	121	1.64
Denis Savard	Chicago	1987-88	80	131	1.64
Marcel Dionne	Los Angeles	1978-79	80	130	1.63
Dale Hawerchuk	Winnipeg	1984-85	80	130	1.63
Mark Messier	Edmonton	1989-90	79	129	1.63
Bryan Trottier	NY Islanders	1983-84	68	111	1.63
Pat LaFfontaine	Buffalo	**1991-92**	57	93	1.63
Charlie Simmer	Los Angeles	1980-81	65	105	1.62
Guy Lafleur	Montreal	1978-79	80	129	1.61
Bryan Trottier	NY Islanders	1981-82	80	129	1.61
Phil Esposito	Boston	1974-75	79	127	1.61
Steve Yzerman	Detroit	1989-90	79	127	1.61
Peter Stastny	Quebec	1985-86	76	122	1.61
Michel Goulet	Quebec	1983-84	75	121	1.61
Bryan Trottier	NY Islanders	1977-78	77	123	1.60
Bobby Orr	Boston	1972-73	63	101	1.60
Guy Chouinard	Calgary	1980-81	52	83	1.60
Elmer Lach	Montreal	1944-45	50	80	1.60
Steve Yzerman	Detroit	1987-88	64	102	1.59
Mike Bossy	NY Islanders	1978-79	80	126	1.58
Paul Coffey	Edmonton	1983-84	80	126	1.58
Marcel Dionne	Los Angeles	1984-85	80	126	1.58
Bobby Orr	Boston	1969-70	76	120	1.58
Charlie Simmer	Los Angeles	1979-80	64	101	1.58
Bobby Clarke	Philadelphia	1975-76	76	119	1.57
Guy Lafleur	Montreal	1975-76	80	125	1.56
Dave Taylor	Los Angeles	1980-81	72	112	1.56
Denis Savard	Chicago	1982-83	78	121	1.55
Mike Bossy	NY Islanders	1985-86	80	123	1.54
Bobby Orr	Boston	1971-72	76	117	1.54
Mike Bossy	NY Islanders	1984-85	76	117	1.54
Doug Bentley	Chicago	1943-44	50	77	1.54
Kevin Stevens	Pittsburgh	**1991-92**	80	123	1.54
Marcel Dionne	Los Angeles	1976-77	80	122	1.53
Marcel Dionne	Detroit	1974-75	80	121	1.51
Paul Coffey	Pittsburgh	1988-89	75	113	1.51

Red Dutton, left,who would later serve as president of the NHL, led the league with 139 PIM in 1928-29. Adam Oates, on the right in the photo below, averaged 1.89 points-per-game in the 1990-91 season.

Active NHL Players' Three-or-More-Goal Games

Regular Season

Teams named are the ones the players were with at the time of their multiple-scoring games. Players listed alphabetically.

Player	Team	3-Goals	4-Goals	5-Goals
Acton, Keith	Mtl., Min.	3	—	—
Adams, Greg	Vancouver	2	—	—
Amonte, Tony	NY Rangers	1	—	—
Anderson, Glenn	Edm., Tor.	18	3	—
Anderson, Perry	New Jersey	1	—	—
Andreychuk, Dave	Buffalo	6	1	1
Arniel, Scott	Winnipeg	1	—	—
Ashton, Brent	Que., Wpg.	6	—	—
Babych, Dave	Vancouver	1	—	—
Barber, Don	Minnesota	1	—	—
Barnes, Stu	Winnipeg	1	—	—
Barr, Dave	St. L., Det.	2	—	—
Bellows, Brian	Minnesota	5	2	—
Bjugstad, Scott	Minnesota	3	—	—
Bondra, Peter	Washington	1	—	—
Boschman, Laurie	Winnipeg	2	—	—
Bourque, Phil	Pittsburgh	1	—	—
Bourque, Ray	Boston	1	—	—
Bozek, Steve	Los Angeles	2	—	—
Brickley, Andy	Pit., Bos.	2	—	—
Broten, Aaron	New Jersey	1	—	—
Broten, Neal	Minnesota	6	—	—
Broten, Paul	NY Rangers	1	—	—
Brown, Rob	Pittsburgh	7	—	—
Bullard, Mike	Pit., Tor.	8	—	—
Burr, Shawn	Detroit	2	—	—
Burridge, Randy	Boston	2	—	—
Carbonneau, Guy	Montreal	—	1	—
Carpenter, Bob	Wsh, Bos.	2	1	—
Carson, Jimmy	L.A., Edm., Det.	8	1	—
Cavallini, Gino	St. Louis	1	—	—
Chabot, John	Pittsburgh	1	—	—
Christian, Dave	Wpg., Wsh.	2	—	—
Ciccarelli, Dino	Min., Wsh.	14	3	1
Clark, Wendel	Toronto	4	1	—
Coffey, Paul	Edmonton	4	1	—
Corson, Shayne	Montreal	2	—	—
Courtnall, Geoff	Bos., Wsh.	2	—	—
Courtnall, Russ	Tor., Mtl.	2	—	—
Craven, Murray	Philadelphia	3	—	—
Creighton, Adam	Buf., Chi.	2	—	—
Cullen, John	Pit., Hfd.	3	—	—
Cunneyworth, R.	Pittsburgh	1	1	—
Cyr, Paul	Buffalo	1	—	—
Dahlen, Ulf	NYR, Min.	2	—	—
Damphousse, V.	Tor., Edm.	3	1	—
DeBlois, Lucien	Winnipeg	1	—	—
Dineen, Kevin	Hartford	5	—	—
Dionne, Gilbert	Montreal	1	—	—
Druce, John	Washington	1	—	—
Duchesne, Steve	L.A., Phi.	2	—	—
Duncan, Iain	Winnipeg	1	—	—
Eklund, Pelle	Philadelphia	1	—	—
Errey, Bob	Pittsburgh	1	—	—
Evason, Dean	Hartford	1	—	—
Fergus, Tom	Toronto	4	—	—
Ferraro, Ray	Hfd., NYI	6	1	—
Flatley, Patrick	NY Islanders	1	1	—
Fleury, Theo	Calgary	5	—	—
Fogarty, Bryan	Quebec	1	—	—
Foligno, Mike	Det., Buf.	8	—	—
Francis, Ron	Hartford	8	1	—
Gagner, Dave	Minnesota	3	—	—
Gallant, Gerard	Detroit	4	—	—
Garpenlov, Johan	Detroit	—	1	—
Gartner, Mike	Wsh., Min., NYR	13	2	—
Gelinas, Martin	Edmonton	1	—	—
Gilbert, Greg	NY Islanders	2	—	—
Gilchrist, Brent	Montreal	1	—	—
Gillis, Paul	Quebec	1	—	—
Gilmour, Doug	St. Louis	2	—	—
Gould, Bobby	Calgary	1	—	—
Goulet, Michel	Que., Chi.	12	2	—
Graham, Dirk	Minnesota	1	—	—
Granato, Tony	NYR, L.A.	3	1	—
Graves, Adam	Edm., NYR	2	—	—
Gretzky, Wayne	Edm., L.A.	36	9	4
Hannan, Dave	Edmonton	1	—	—
Hawerchuk, Dale	Wpg., Buf.	13	—	—
Hodge, Ken	Boston	2	—	—
Horacek, Tony	Philadelphia	1	—	—
Housley, Phil	Buffalo	2	—	—
Howe, Mark	Hartford	1	—	—
Hrdina, Jiri	Calgary	1	1	—
Hull, Brett	Cgy., St. L.	18	—	—
Hull, Jody	Hartford	1	—	—
Hunter, Dale	Que., Wsh.	4	—	—

Gary Roberts, who hit the 50-goal mark for the first time in 1991-92, has had three hat-tricks in his six-year career with the Calgary Flames.

Player	Team	3-Goal	4-Goal	5-Goal
Hunter, Mark	St. L., Cgy.	5	1	—
Jackson, Jeff	Quebec	1	—	—
Jagr, Jaromir	Pittsburgh	1	—	—
Janney, Craig	Bos., St. L.	2	—	—
Kasper, Steve	Boston	3	—	—
Kerr, Tim	Philadelphia	13	4	—
King, Derek	NY Islanders	3	1	—
Klima, Petr	Det., Edm.	6	—	—
Krushelnyski, Mike	Edmonton	1	—	—
Kudelski, Robert	Los Angeles	2	—	—
Kurri, Jari	Edm., L.A.	19	1	1
Lacombe, Normand	Edmonton	1	—	—
LaFontaine, Pat	NYI, Buf.	11	—	—
Larionov, Igor	Vancouver	2	—	—
Larmer, Steve	Chicago	7	—	—
Lawton, Brian	Minnesota	2	—	—
Lebeau, Stephan	Montreal	1	—	—
Leeman, Gary	Toronto	4	—	—
Lemieux, Claude	Mtl., N.J.	3	—	—
Lemieux, Jocelyn	Chicago	1	—	—
Lemieux, Mario	Pittsburgh	20	6	1
Linden, Trevor	Vancouver	3	—	—
Linseman, Ken	Phi., Edm., Bos.	3	—	—
Ludzik, Steve	Chicago	1	—	—
MacInnis, Al	Calgary	1	—	—
MacLean, John	New Jersey	6	—	—
MacLellan, Brian	L.A., NYR, Min., Cgy.	2	2	—
MacTavish, Craig	Edmonton	2	—	—
Makarov, Sergei	Calgary	2	—	—
Makela, Mikko	NY Islanders	1	—	—
Maley, David	New Jersey	1	—	—
Marois, Daniel	Toronto	3	—	—
McBain, Andrew	Winnipeg	1	—	—
McKegney, Tony	Buf., Que., Min., St. L.	7	1	—
McPhee, Mike	Montreal	3	—	—
Messier, Mark	Edm., NYR	12	4	—
Miller, Kevin	Detroit	1	—	—
Modano, Mike	Minnesota	1	—	—
Mogilny, Alexander	Buffalo	2	—	—
Momesso, Sergio	Montreal	1	—	—
Mullen, Brian	Wpg., NYR	2	—	—
Mullen, Joe	St. L., Cgy., Pit.	6	4	—
Muller, Kirk	N.J., Mtl.	5	—	—
Murray, Troy	Chicago	4	—	—
Murzyn, Dana	Calgary	1	—	—
Naslund, Mats	Montreal	4	1	—
Neely, Cam	Boston	8	—	—
Nicholls, Bernie	Los Angeles	12	2	—
Nieuwendyk, Joe	Calgary	4	2	1
Noonan, Brian	Chicago	2	1	—
Nolan, Owen	Quebec	2	—	—
Ogrodnick, John	Detroit	6	—	—
Olczyk, Ed	Toronto	2	—	—
Osborne, Mark	Detroit	1	—	—
Otto, Joel	Calgary	1	—	—
Paslawski, Greg	St. Louis	2	—	—
Pivonka, Michal	Washington	1	—	—
Pederson, Barry	Boston	6	1	—
Poddubny, Walt	Tor., Que.	4	1	—
Poulin, Dave	Philadelphia	5	—	—

Player	Team	3-Goal	4-Goal	5-Goal
Presley, Wayne	Chicago	1	—	—
Probert, Bob	Detroit	1	—	—
Propp, Brian	Philadelphia	3	1	—
Quinn, Dan	Pit., Van.	4	—	—
Ranheim, Paul	Calgary	1	—	—
Recchi, Mark	Pittsburgh	1	—	—
Richer, Stephane	Mtl., N.J.	6	1	—
Ridley, Mike	NYR, Wsh.	3	1	—
Roberts, Gary	Calgary	3	—	—
Robinson, Larry	Montreal	1	—	—
Robitaille, Luc	Los Angeles	7	1	—
Roenick, Jeremy	Chicago	3	2	—
Ronning, Cliff	St. Louis	1	—	—
Ruff, Lindy	Buffalo	1	1	—
Ruzicka, Vladimir	Boston	2	—	—
Sakic, Joe	Quebec	5	—	—
Sandlak, Jim	Vancouver	1	—	—
Sandstrom, Tomas	NYR, L.A.	6	1	—
Savard, Denis	Chi., Mtl.	12	—	—
Secord, Al	Chicago	4	2	—
Shanahan, Brendan	New Jersey	1	—	—
Sheppard, Ray	Buf., Det.	3	—	—
Sinisalo, Ilkka	Philadelphia	3	—	—
Simpson, Craig	Pit., Edm.	3	—	—
Skriko, Petri	Vancouver	4	1	—
Smail, Doug	Winnipeg	2	—	—
Smith, Derrick	Philadelphia	1	—	—
Smith, Bobby	Minnesota	5	1	—
Stastny, Peter	Que., N.J.	15	2	—
Steen, Thomas	Winnipeg	3	—	—
Stern, Ronnie	Calgary	1	—	—
Stevens, Kevin	Pittsburgh	5	1	—
Sundin, Mats	Quebec	2	—	1
Sundstrom, Patrik	Vancouver	2	—	—
Sutter, Brent	NY Islanders	6	—	—
Sutter, Rich	Vancouver	1	—	—
Sweeney, Bob	Boston	1	—	—
Tanti, Tony	Van., Pit., Buf.	11	1	—
Taylor, Dave	Los Angeles	7	1	—
Thomas, Steve	Chi., NYI	3	2	—
Tikkanen, Esa	Edmonton	3	—	—
Tocchet, Rick	Phi., Pit.	7	2	—
Tonelli, John	NYI, L.A.	4	—	1
Trottier, Bryan	NY Islanders	13	1	2
Tucker, John	Buffalo	1	—	—
Turcotte, Darren	NY Rangers	4	—	—
Turgeon, Pierre	Buf., NYI	4	—	—
Turgeon, Sylvain	Hfd., N.J.	4	—	—
Vaive, Rick	Tor., Chi.	10	3	—
Verbeek, Pat	New Jersey	4	1	—
Volek, Dave	NY Islanders	1	—	—
Vukota, Mick	NY Islanders	1	—	—
Walter, Ryan	Montreal	1	—	—
Wilson, Carey	Calgary	2	—	—
Wilson, Doug	Chicago	1	—	—
Wood, Randy	NY Islanders	1	—	—
Yzerman, Steve	Detroit	14	1	—
Ysebaert, Paul	Detroit	1	—	—
Zezel, Peter	Philadelphia	1	—	—

Dale Hawerchuk, seen here being pursued by Buffalo's Craig Ramsay during his rookie season with the Winnipeg Jets in 1981-82, is one of only three freshmen to register 100 points in their first NHL campaign.

Rookie Scoring Records

All-Time Top 50 Goal-Scoring Rookies

	Rookie	Team	Position	Season	GP	G	A	PTS
1.	*Mike Bossy	NY Islanders	Right wing	1977-78	73	**53**	38	91
2.	*Joe Niewendyk	Calgary	Center	1987-88	75	**51**	41	92
3.	*Dale Hawerchuk	Winnipeg	Center	1981-82	80	**45**	58	103
	*Luc Robitaille	Los Angeles	Left wing	1986-87	79	**45**	39	84
5.	Rick Martin	Buffalo	Left wing	1971-72	73	**44**	30	74
	Barry Pederson	Boston	Center	1981-82	80	**44**	48	92
7.	*Steve Larmer	Chicago	Right wing	1982-83	80	**43**	47	90
	*Mario Lemieux	Pittsburgh	Center	1984-85	73	**43**	57	100
9.	Darryl Sutter	Chicago	Left wing	1980-81	76	**40**	22	62
	Sylvain Turgeon	Hartford	Left wing	1983-84	76	**40**	32	72
	Warren Young	Pittsburgh	Left wing	1984-85	80	**40**	32	72
12.	*Eric Vail	Atlanta	Left wing	1974-75	72	**39**	21	60
	Anton Stastny	Quebec	Left wing	1980-81	80	**39**	46	85
	*Peter Stastny	Quebec	Center	1980-81	77	**39**	70	109
	Steve Yzerman	Detroit	Center	1983-84	80	**39**	48	87
16.	*Gilbert Perreault	Buffalo	Center	1970-71	78	**38**	34	72
	Neal Broten	Minnesota	Center	1981-82	73	**38**	60	98
	Ray Sheppard	Buffalo	Right wing	1987-88	74	**38**	27	65
19.	Jorgen Pettersson	St. Louis	Left wing	1980-81	62	**37**	36	73
	Jimmy Carson	Los Angeles	Centre	1986-87	80	**37**	42	79
21.	Mike Foligno	Detroit	Right wing	1979-80	80	**36**	35	71
	Mike Bullard	Pittsburgh	Center	1981-82	75	**36**	27	63
	Paul MacLean	Winnipeg	Right wing	1981-82	74	**36**	25	61
	Tony Granato	NY Rangers	Right wing	1988-89	78	**36**	27	63
25.	Marian Stastny	Quebec	Right wing	1981-82	74	**35**	54	89
	Brian Bellows	Minnesota	Right wing	1982-83	78	**35**	30	65
	Tony Amonte	NY Rangers	Right wing	**1991-92**	79	**35**	34	69
28.	Nels Stewart	Mtl. Maroons	Center	1925-26	36	**34**	8	42
	*Danny Grant	Minnesota	Left wing	1968-69	75	**34**	31	65
	Norm Ferguson	Oakland	Right wing	1968-69	76	**34**	20	54
	Brian Propp	Philadelphia	Left wing	1979-80	80	**34**	41	75
	Wendel Clark	Toronto	Left wing	1985-86	66	**34**	11	45
	*Pavel Bure	Vancouver	Right wing	**1991-92**	65	**34**	26	60
34.	*Willi Plett	Atlanta	Right wing	1976-77	64	**33**	23	56
	Dale McCourt	Detroit	Center	1977-78	76	**33**	39	72
	Mark Pavelich	NY Rangers	Center	1981-82	79	**33**	43	76
	Ron Flockhart	Philadelphia	Center	1981-82	72	**33**	39	72
	Steve Bozek	Los Angeles	Center	1981-82	71	**33**	23	56
39.	Bill Mosienko	Chicago	Right wing	1943-44	50	**32**	38	70
	Michel Bergeron	Detroit	Right wing	1975-76	72	**32**	27	59
	*Bryan Trottier	NY Islanders	Center	1975-76	80	**32**	63	95
	Don Murdoch	NY Rangers	Right wing	1976-77	59	**32**	24	56
	Jari Kurri	Edmonton	Left wing	1980-81	75	**32**	43	75
	Bobby Carpenter	Washington	Center	1981-82	80	**32**	35	67
	Kjell Dahlin	Montreal	Right wing	1985-86	77	**32**	39	71
	Petr Klima	Detroit	Left wing	1985-86	74	**32**	24	56
	Darren Turcotte	NY Rangers	Right wing	1989-90	76	**32**	34	66
48.	Danny Gare	Buffalo	Right wing	1974-75	78	**31**	31	62
	Pierre Larouche	Pittsburgh	Center	1974-75	79	**31**	37	68
	Dave Poulin	Philadelphia	Center	1983-84	73	**31**	45	76
	Daniel Marois	Toronto	Right wing	1988-89	76	**31**	23	54
	*Sergei Fedorov	Detroit	Center	1990-91	77	**31**	48	79
	Donald Audette	Buffalo	Right wing	**1991-92**	63	**31**	17	48

* Calder Trophy Winner

All-Time Top 50 Point-Scoring Rookies

	Rookie	Team	Position	Season	GP	G	A	PTS
1.	*Peter Stastny	Quebec	Center	1980-81	77	39	70	**109**
2.	*Dale Hawerchuk	Winnipeg	Center	1981-82	80	45	58	**103**
3.	*Mario Lemieux	Pittsburgh	Center	1984-85	73	43	57	**100**
4.	Neal Broten	Minnesota	Center	1981-82	73	38	60	**98**
5.	*Bryan Trottier	NY Islanders	Center	1975-76	80	32	63	**95**
6.	Barry Pederson	Boston	Center	1981-82	80	44	48	**92**
	*Joe Nieuwendyk	Calgary	Center	1987-88	75	51	41	**92**
8.	*Mike Bossy	NY Islanders	Right wing	1977-78	73	53	38	**91**
9.	*Steve Larmer	Chicago	Right wing	1982-83	80	43	47	**90**
10.	Marian Stastny	Quebec	Right wing	1981-82	74	35	54	**89**
11.	Steve Yzerman	Detroit	Center	1983-84	80	39	48	**87**
12.	*Sergei Makarov	Calgary	Right wing	1989-90	80	24	62	**86**
13.	Anton Stastny	Quebec	Left wing	1980-81	80	39	46	**85**
14.	*Luc Robitaille	Los Angeles	Left wing	1986-87	79	45	39	**84**
15.	Jimmy Carson	Los Angeles	Center	1986-87	80	37	42	**79**
	Sergei Fedorov	Detroit	Center	1990-91	77	31	48	**79**
17.	Marcel Dionne	Detroit	Center	1971-72	78	28	49	**77**
18.	Larry Murphy	Los Angeles	Defense	1980-81	80	16	60	**76**
	Mark Pavelich	NY Rangers	Center	1981-82	79	33	43	**76**
	Dave Poulin	Philadelphia	Center	1983-84	73	31	45	**76**
21.	Brian Propp	Philadelphia	Left wing	1979-80	80	34	41	**75**
	Jari Kurri	Edmonton	Left wing	1980-81	75	32	43	**75**
	Denis Savard	Chicago	Center	1980-81	76	28	47	**75**
	Mike Modano	Minnesota	Center	1989-90	80	29	46	**75**
25.	Rick Martin	Buffalo	Left wing	1971-72	73	44	30	**74**
	*Bobby Smith	Minnesota	Center	1978-79	80	30	44	**74**
27.	Jorgen Pettersson	St. Louis	Left wing	1980-81	62	37	36	**73**
28.	*Gilbert Perreault	Buffalo	Center	1970-71	78	38	34	**72**
	Dale McCourt	Detroit	Center	1977-78	76	33	39	**72**
	Ron Flockhart	Philadelphia	Center	1981-82	72	33	39	**72**
	Sylvain Turgeon	Hartford	Left wing	1983-84	76	40	32	**72**
	Warren Young	Pittsburgh	Left wing	1984-85	80	40	32	**72**
	Carey Wilson	Calgary	Center	1984-85	74	24	48	**72**
34.	Mike Foligno	Detroit	Right wing	1979-80	80	36	35	**71**
	Dave Christian	Winnipeg	Center	1980-81	80	28	43	**71**
	Mats Naslund	Montreal	Left wing	1982-83	74	26	45	**71**
	Kjell Dahlin	Montreal	Right wing	1985-86	77	32	39	**71**
	*Brian Leetch	NY Rangers	Defense	1988-89	68	23	48	**71**
39.	Bill Mosienko	Chicago	Right wing	1943-44	50	32	38	**70**
40.	Roland Eriksson	Minnesota	Center	1976-77	80	25	44	**69**
	Tony Amonte	NY Rangers	Right wing	**1991-92**	79	35	34	**69**
42.	Jude Drouin	Minnesota	Center	1970-71	75	16	52	**68**
	Pierre Larouche	Pittsburgh	Center	1974-75	79	31	37	**68**
	Ron Francis	Hartford	Center	1981-82	59	25	43	**68**
	*Gary Suter	Calgary	Defense	1985-86	80	18	50	**68**
46.	Tom Webster	Detroit	Right wing	1970-71	78	30	37	**67**
	Bobby Carpenter	Washington	Center	1981-82	80	32	35	**67**
	Chris Valentine	Washington	Center	1981-82	60	30	37	**67**
	Mark Osborne	Detroit	Left wing	1981-82	80	26	41	**67**
	Mark Recchi	Pittsburgh	Right wing	1989-90	74	30	37	**67**

* Calder Trophy Winner

Bernie Geoffrion

Mike Bullard

Cam Neely

50-Goal Seasons

Player	Team	Date of 50th Goal	Score	Goaltender	Player's Game No.	Team Game No.	Total Goals	Total Games	Age When First 50th Scored (Yrs. & Mos.)
Maurice Richard	Mtl.	18-3-45	Mtl. 4 at Bos. 2	Harvey Bennett	50	50	50	50	23.7
Bernie Geoffrion	Mtl.	16-3-61	Tor. 2 at Mtl. 5	Cesare Maniago	62	68	50	64	30.1
Bobby Hull	Chi.	25-3-62	Chi. 1 at NYR 4	Gump Worsley	70	70	50	70	23.2
Bobby Hull	Chi.	2-3-66	Det. 4 at Chi. 5	Hank Bassen	52	57	54	65	
Bobby Hull	Chi.	18-3-67	Chi. 5 at Tor. 9	Bruce Gamble	63	66	52	66	
Bobby Hull	Chi.	5-3-69	NYR 4 at Chi. 4	Ed Giacomin	64	66	58	74	
Phil Esposito	Bos.	20-2-71	Bos. 4 at L.A. 5	Denis DeJordy	58	58	76	78	29.0
John Bucyk	Bos.	16-3-71	Bos. 11 at Det. 4	Roy Edwards	69	69	51	78	35.1
Phil Esposito	Bos.	20-2-72	Bos. 3 at Chi. 1	Tony Esposito	60	60	66	76	
Bobby Hull	Chi.	2-4-72	Det. 1 at Chi. 6	Andy Brown	78	78	50	78	
Vic Hadfield	NYR	2-4-72	Mtl. 6 at NYR 5	Denis DeJordy	78	78	50	78	31.6
Phil Esposito	Bos.	25-3-73	Buf. 1 at Bos. 6	Roger Crozier	75	75	55	78	
Mickey Redmond	Det.	27-3-73	Det. 8 at Tor. 1	Ron Low	73	75	52	76	25.3
Rick MacLeish	Phi.	1-4-73	Phi. 4 at Pit. 5	Cam Newton	78	78	50	78	23.2
Phil Esposito	Bos.	20-2-74	Bos. 5 at Min. 5	Cesare Maniago	56	56	68	78	
Mickey Redmond	Det.	23-3-74	NYR 3 at Det 5	Ed Giacomin	69	71	51	76	
Ken Hodge	Bos.	6-4-74	Bos. 2 at Mtl. 6	Michel Larocque	75	77	50	76	29.10
Rick Martin	Buf.	7-4-74	St.L. 2 at Buf. 5	Wayne Stephenson	78	78	52	78	22.9
Phil Esposito	Bos.	8-2-75	Bos. 8 at Det. 5	Jim Rutherford	54	54	61	79	
Guy Lafleur	Mtl.	29-3-75	K.C. 1 at Mtl. 4	Denis Herron	66	76	53	70	23.6
Danny Grant	Det.	2-4-75	Wsh. 3 at Det. 8	John Adams	78	78	50	80	29.2
Rick Martin	Buf.	3-4-75	Bos. 2 at Buf. 4	Ken Broderick	67	79	52	68	
Reggie Leach	Phi.	14-3-76	Atl. 1 at Phi. 6	Daniel Bouchard	69	69	61	80	25.11
Jean Pronovost	Pit.	24-3-76	Bos. 5 at Pit. 5	Gilles Gilbert	74	74	52	80	31.3
Guy Lafleur	Mtl.	27-3-76	K.C. 2 at Mtl. 8	Denis Herron	76	76	56	80	
Bill Barber	Phi.	3-4-76	Buf. 2 at Phi. 5	Al Smith	79	79	50	80	23.9
Pierre Larouche	Pit.	3-4-76	Wsh. 5 at Pit. 4	Ron Low	75	79	53	76	20.5
Danny Gare	Buf.	4-4-76	Tor. 2 at Buf. 5	Gord McRae	79	80	50	79	21.11
Steve Shutt	Mtl.	1-3-77	Mtl. 5 at NYI 4	Glenn Resch	65	65	60	80	24.8
Guy Lafleur	Mtl.	6-3-77	Mtl. 1 at Buf. 4	Don Edwards	68	68	56	80	
Marcel Dionne	L.A.	2-4-77	Min. 2 at L.A. 7	Pete LoPresti	79	79	53	80	25.8
Guy Lafleur	Mtl.	8-3-78	Wsh. 3 at Mtl. 4	Jim Bedard	63	65	60	78	
Mike Bossy	NYI	1-4-78	Wsh. 2 at NYI 3	Bernie Wolfe	69	76	53	73	21.2
Mike Bossy	NYI	24-2-79	Det. 1 at NYI 3	Rogie Vachon	58	58	69	80	
Marcel Dionne	L.A.	11-3-79	L.A. 3 at Phi. 6	Wayne Stephenson	68	68	59	80	
Guy Lafleur	Mtl.	31-3-79	Pit. 3 at Mtl. 5	Denis Herron	76	76	52	80	
Guy Chouinard	Atl.	6-4-79	NYR 2 at Atl. 9	John Davidson	79	79	50	80	22.5
Marcel Dionne	L.A.	12-3-80	L.A. 2 at Pit. 4	Nick Ricci	70	70	53	80	
Mike Bossy	NYI	16-3-80	NYI 6 at Chi. 1	Tony Esposito	68	71	51	75	
Charlie Simmer	L.A.	19-3-80	Det. 3 at L.A. 4	Jim Rutherford	57	73	56	64	26.0
Pierre Larouche	Mtl.	25-3-80	Chi. 4 at Mtl. 8	Tony Esposito	72	75	50	73	
Danny Gare	Buf.	27-3-80	Det. 1 at Buf. 10	Jim Rutherford	71	75	56	76	
Blaine Stoughton	Hfd.	28-3-80	Hfd. 4 at Van. 4	Glen Hanlon	75	75	56	80	27.0
Guy Lafleur	Mtl.	2-4-80	Mtl. 7 at Det. 2	Rogie Vachon	72	78	50	74	
Wayne Gretzky	Edm.	2-4-80	Min. 1 at Edm. 1	Gary Edwards	78	79	51	79	19.2
Reggie Leach	Phi.	3-4-80	Wsh. 2 at Phi. 4	(empty net)	75	79	50	76	
Mike Bossy	NYI	24-1-81	Que. 3 at NYI 7	Ron Grahame	50	50	68	79	
Charlie Simmer	L.A.	26-1-81	L.A. 7 at Que. 5	Michel Dion	51	51	56	65	
Marcel Dionne	L.A.	8-3-81	L.A. 4 at Wpg. 1	Markus Mattsson	68	68	58	80	
Wayne Babych	St.L.	12-3-81	St.L. 3 at Mtl. 4	Richard Sevigny	70	68	54	78	22.9
Wayne Gretzky	Edm.	15-3-81	Edm. 3 at Cgy. 3	Pat Riggin	69	69	55	80	
Rick Kehoe	Pit.	16-3-81	Pit. 7 at Edm. 6	Eddie Mio	70	70	55	80	29.7
Jacques Richard	Que.	29-3-81	Mtl. 0 at Que. 4	Richard Sevigny	76	75	52	78	28.6
Dennis Maruk	Wsh.	5-4-81	Det. 2 at Wsh. 7	Larry Lozinski	80	80	50	80	25.3
Wayne Gretzky	Edm.	30-12-81	Phi. 5 at Edm. 7	(empty net)	39	39	92	80	
Dennis Maruk	Wsh.	21-2-82	Wpg. 3 at Wsh. 6	Doug Soetaert	61	61	60	80	
Mike Bossy	NYI	4-3-82	Tor. 1 at NYI 10	Michel Larocque	66	66	64	80	
Dino Ciccarelli	Min.	8-3-82	St.L. 1 at Min. 8	Mike Liut	67	68	55	76	21.7
Rick Vaive	Tor.	24-3-82	St.L. 3 at Tor. 4	Mike Liut	72	75	54	77	22.10
Rick Middleton	Bos.	28-3-82	Bos. 5 at Buf. 9	Paul Harrison	72	77	51	75	28.11
Blaine Stoughton	Hfd.	28-3-82	Min. 5 at Hfd. 2	Gilles Meloche	76	76	52	80	28.3
Marcel Dionne	L.A.	30-3-82	Cgy. 7 at L.A. 5	Pat Riggin	75	77	50	78	
Mark Messier	Edm.	31-3-82	L.A. 3 at Edm. 7	Mario Lessard	78	79	50	78	21.3
Bryan Trottier	NYI	3-4-82	Phi. 3 at NYI 6	Pete Peeters	79	79	50	80	25.9
Lanny McDonald	Cgy.	18-2-83	Cgy. 1 at Buf. 5	Bob Sauve	60	60	66	80	30.0
Wayne Gretzky	Edm.	19-2-83	Edm. 10 at Pit. 7	Nick Ricci	60	60	1	80	
Michel Goulet	Que.	5-3-83	Que. 7 at Hfd. 3	Mike Veisor	67	67	57	80	22.11
Mike Bossy	NYI	12-3-83	Wsh. 2 at NYI 6	Al Jensen	70	71	60	79	
Marcel Dionne	L.A.	17-3-83	Que. 3 at L.A. 4	Daniel Bouchard	71	71	56	80	
Al Secord	Chi.	20-3-83	Tor. 3 at Chi. 7	Mike Palmateer	73	73	54	80	25.0
Rick Vaive	Tor.	30-3-83	Tor. 4 at Det. 2	Gilles Gilbert	76	78	51	78	
Wayne Gretzky	Edm.	7-1-84	Hfd. 3 at Edm. 5	Greg Millen	42	42	87	74	
Michel Goulet	Que.	8-3-84	Que. 8 at Pit. 6	Denis Herron	63	69	56	75	
Rick Vaive	Tor.	14-3-84	Min. 3 at Tor. 3	Gilles Meloche	69	72	52	76	
Mike Bullard	Pit.	14-3-84	Pit. 6 at L.A. 7	Markus Mattsson	71	72	51	76	23.0
Jari Kurri	Edm.	15-3-84	Edm. 2 at Mtl. 3	Rick Wamsley	57	73	52	64	23.10

Player	Team	Date of 50th Goal	Score		Goaltender	Player's Game No.	Team Game No.	Total Goals	Total Games	Age When First 50th Scored (Yrs. & Mos.)
Glenn Anderson	Edm.	21-3-84	Hfd. 3	at Edm. 5	Greg Millen	76	76	54	80	23.6
Tim Kerr	Phi.	22-3-84	Pit. 4	at Phi. 13	Denis Herron	74	75	54	79	24.3
Mike Bossy	NYI	31-3-84	NYI 3	at Wsh. 1	Pat Riggin	67	79	51	67	
Wayne Gretzky	Edm.	26-1-85	Pit. 3	at Edm. 6	Denis Herron	49	49	73	80	
Jari Kurri	Edm.	3-2-85	Hfd. 3	at Edm. 6	Greg Millen	50	53	71	73	
Mike Bossy	NYI	5-3-85	Phi. 5	at NYI 4	Bob Froese	61	65	58	76	
Tim Kerr	Phi.	7-3-85	Wsh. 6	at Phi. 9	Pat Riggin	63	65	54	74	
John Ogrodnick	Det.	13-3-85	Det. 6	at Edm. 7	Grant Fuhr	69	69	55	79	25.9
Bob Carpenter	Wsh.	21-3-85	Wsh. 2	at Mtl. 3	Steve Penney	72	72	53	80	21.9
Michel Goulet	Que.	6-3-85	Buf. 3	at Que. 4	Tom Barrasso	62	73	55	69	
Dale Hawerchuk	Wpg.	29-4-85	Chi. 5	at Wpg. 5	W. Skorodenski	77	77	53	80	21.1
Mike Gartner	Wsh.	7-4-85	Pit. 3	at Wsh. 7	Brian Ford	80	80	50	80	25.5
Jari Kurri	Edm.	4-3-86	Edm. 6	at Van. 2	Richard Brodeur	63	65	68	78	
Mike Bossy	NYI	11-3-86	Cgy. 4	at NYI 8	Rejean Lemelin	67	67	61	80	
Glenn Anderson	Edm.	14-3-86	Det. 3	at Edm. 12	Greg Stefan	63	71	54	72	
Michel Goulet	Que.	17-3-86	Que. 8	at Mtl. 6	Patrick Roy	67	72	53	75	
Wayne Gretzky	Edm.	18-3-86	Wpg. 2	at Edm. 6	Brian Hayward	72	72	52	80	
Tim Kerr	Phi.	20-3-86	Pit. 1	at Phi. 5	Roberto Romano	68	72	58	76	
Wayne Gretzky	Edm.	2-4-87	Edm. 6	at Min. 5	Don Beaupre	55	55	62	79	
Tim Kerr	Phi.	3-17-87	NYR 1	at Phi. 4	J. Vanbiesbrouck	67	71	58	75	
Jari Kurri	Edm.	3-17-87	N.J. 4	at Edm. 7	Craig Billington	69	70	54	79	
Mario Lemieux	Pit.	3-12-87	Que. 3	at Pit. 6	Mario Gosselin	53	70	54	63	21.5
Dino Ciccrelli	Min.	3-7-87	Pit. 7	at Min. 3	Gilles Meloche	66	66	52	80	
Mario Lemieux	Pit.	2-2-88	Wsh. 2	at Pit. 3	Pete Peeters	51	54	70	77	
Steve Yzerman	Det.	1-3-88	Buf. 0	at Det. 4	Tom Barrasso	64	64	50	64	22.10
Joe Nieuwendyk	Cgy.	12-3-88	Buf. 4	at Cgy. 10	Tom Barrasso	66	70	51	75	21.5
Craig Simpson	Edm.	15-3-88	Buf. 4	at Edm. 6	Jacques Cloutier	71	71	56	80	21.1
Jimmy Carson	L.A.	26-3-88	Chi. 5	at L.A. 9	Darren Pang	77	77	55	88	19.7
Luc Robitaille	L.A.	1-4-88	L.A. 6	at Cgy. 3	Mike Vernon	79	79	53	80	21.10
Hakan Loob	Cgy.	3-4-88	Min. 1	at Cgy. 4	Don Beaupre	80	80	50	80	27.9
Stephane Richer	Mtl.	3-4-88	Mtl. 4	at Buf. 4	Tom Barrasso	72	80	50	72	21.10
Mario Lemieux	Pit.	20-1-89	Pit. 3	at Wpg. 7	Eldon Reddick	44	46	85	76	
Bernie Nicholls	L.A.	28-1-89	Edm. 7	at L.A. 6	Grant Fuhr	51	51	70	79	27.7
Steve Yzerman	Det.	5-2-89	Det. 6	at Wpg. 2	Eldon Reddick	55	55	65	80	
Wayne Gretzky	L.A.	4-3-89	Phi. 2	at L.. 6	Ron Hextall	66	67	54	78	
Joe Nieuwendyk	Cgy.	21-3-89	NYI 1	at Cgy. 4	Mark Fitzpatrick	72	74	51	77	
Joe Mullen	Cgy.	31-3-89	Wpg. 1	at Cgy. 4	Bob Essensa	78	79	51	79	32.1
Brett Hull	St. L.	6-2-90	Tor. 4	at St.L. 6	Jeff Reese	54	54	72	80	25.6
Steve Yzerman	Det.	24-2-90	Det. 3	at NYI 3	Glenn Healy	63	63	62	79	
Cam Neely	Bos.	10-3-90	Bos. 3	at NYI 3	Mark Fitzpatrick	69	71	55	76	24.9
Brian Bellows	Min.	22-3-90	Min. 5	at Det. 1	Tim Cheveldae	75	75	55	80	25.
Pat LaFontaine	NYI	24-3-90	NYI 5	at Edm. 5	Bill Ranford	71	77	54	74	25.1
Luc Robitaille	L.A.	21-3-90	L.A. 3	at Van. 6	Kirk McLean	79	79	52	80	
Stephane Richer	Mtl.	24-3-90	Mtl. 4	at Hfd. 7	Peter Sidorkiewicz	75	77	51	75	
Gary Leeman	Tor.	28-3-90	NYI 6	at Tor. 3	Mark Fitzpatrick	78	78	51	80	26.1
Brett Hull	St. L.	25-1-91	St. L. 9	at Det. 4	Dave Gagnon	49	49	86	78	
Cam Neely	Bos.	26-3-91	Bos. 7	at Que. 4	empty net	67	78	51	69	
Theoren Fleury	Cgy.	26-3-91	Van. 2	at Cgy. 7	Bob Mason	77	77	51	79	22.9
Steve Yzerman	Det.	30-3-91	NYR 5	at Det. 6	Mike Richter	79	79	51	80	
Brett Hull	St. L.	28-1-92	St. L. 3	at L.A. 3	Kelly Hrudey	50	50	70	73	
Kevin Stevens	Pit.	24-3-92	Pit. 3	at Det. 4	Tim Cheveldae	74	74	54	80	26.11
Gary Roberts	Cgy.	31-3-92	Edm. 2	at Cgy. 5	Bill Ranford	73	77	53	76	25.10
Jeremy Roenick	Chi.	7-3-92	Chi. 2	at Bos. 1	Daniel Berthiaume	67	67	53	80	22.2

Brett Hull

Jeremy Roenick

Players' 500th Goals

Player	Team	Date	Game No.	Score		Opposing Goaltender	Total Goals	Total Games
Maurice Richard	Montreal	Oct. 19/57	863	Chi. 1	at Mtl. 3	Glenn Hall	544	978
Gordie Howe	Detroit	Mar. 14/62	1,045	Det. 2	at NYR 3	Gump Worsley	801	1,767
Bobby Hull	Chicago	Feb. 21/70	861	NYR. 2	at Chi. 4	Ed Giacomin	610	1,063
Jean Béliveau	Montreal	Feb. 11/71	1,101	Min. 2	at Mtl. 6	Gilles Gilbert	507	1,125
Frank Mahovlich	Montreal	Mar. 21/73	1,105	Van. 2	at Mtl. 3	Dunc Wilson	533	1,181
Phil Esposito	Boston	Dec. 22/74	803	Det. 4	at Bos. 5	Jim Rutherford	717	1,282
John Bucyk	Boston	Oct. 30/75	1,370	St. L. 2	at Bos. 3	Yves Bélanger	556	1,540
Stan Mikita	Chicago	Feb. 27/77	1,221	Van. 4	at Chi. 3	Cesare Maniago	541	1,394
Marcel Dionne	Los Angeles	Dec. 14/82	887	L.A. 2	at Wsh. 7	Al Jensen	731	1,348
Guy Lafleur	Montreal	Dec. 20/83	918	Mtl. 6	at N.J. 0	Glenn Resch	560	1,126
Mike Bossy	NYIslanders	Jan. 2/86	647	Bos. 5	at NYI 7	empty net	573	752
Gilbert Perreault	Buffalo	Mar. 9/86	1,159	NJ 3	at Buf. 4	Alain Chevrier	512	1,191
*Wayne Gretzky	Edmonton	Nov. 22/86	575	Van. 2	at Edm. 5	empty net	749	999
Lanny McDonald	Calgary	Mar. 21/89	1,107	NYI 1	at Cgy. 4	Mark Fitzpatrick	500	1,111
*Bryan Trottier	NY Islanders	Feb. 13/90	1,104	Cgy. 4	at NYI 2	Rick Wamsley	520	1,238
*Mike Gartner	NY Rangers	Oct. 14/91	936	Wsh. 5	at NYR 3	Mike Liut	538	1,005
*Michel Goulet	Chicago	Feb. 16/92	951	Cgy. 5	at Chi. 5	Jeff Reese	509	970

*Active

Bryan Trottier

100-Point Seasons

Marcel Dionne

Player	Team	Date of 100th Point	G or A	Score	Player's Game No.	Team Game No.	Points G - A PTS	Total Games	Age when first 100th point scored (Yrs. & Mos.)
Phil Esposito	Bos.	2-3-69	(G)	Pit. 0 at Bos. 4	60	62	49-77 — 126	74	27.1
Bobby Hull	Chi.	20-3-69	(G)	Chi. 5 at Bos. 5	71	71	58-49 — 107	76	30.2
Gordie Howe	Det.	30-3-69	(G)	Det. 5 at Chi. 9	76	76	44-59 — 103	76	41.0
Bobby Orr	Bos.	15-3-70	(G)	Det. 5 at Bos. 5	67	67	33-87 — 120	76	22.11
Phil Esposito	Bos.	6-2-71	(A)	Buf. 3 at Bos. 4	51	51	76-76 — 152	78	
Bobby Orr	Bos.	22-2-71	(A)	Bos. 4 at L.A. 5	58	58	37-102 — 139	78	
John Bucyk	Bos.	13-3-71	(G)	Bos. 6 at Van. 3	68	68	51-65 — 116	78	35.10
Ken Hodge	Bos.	21-3-71	(A)	Buf. 7 at Bos. 5	72	72	43-62 — 105	78	269
Jean Ratelle	NYR	18-2-72	(A)	NYR 2 at Cal. 2	58	58	46-63 — 109	63	31.4
Phil Esposito	Bos.	19-2-72	(A)	Bos. 6 at Min. 4	59	59	66-67 — 133	76	
Bobby Orr	Bos.	2-3-72	(A)	Van. 3 at Bos. 7	64	64	37-80 — 117	76	
Vic Hadfield	NYR	25-3-72	(A)	NYR 3 at Mtl. 3	74	74	50-56 — 106	78	31.5
Phil Esposito	Bos.	3-3-73	(A)	Bos. 1 at Mtl. 5	64	64	55-75 — 130	78	
Bobby Clarke	Phi	29-3-73	(G)	Atl. 2 at Phi. 4	76	76	37-67 — 104	78	23.7
Bobby Orr	Bos.	31-3-73	(G)	Bos. 3 at Tor. 7	62	77	29-72 — 101	63	
Rick MacLeish	Phi.	1-4-73	(G)	Phi. 4 at Pit. 5	78	78	50-50 — 100	78	23.3
Phil Esposito	Bos.	13-2-74	(A)	Bos. 9 at Cal. 6	53	53	68-77 — 145	78	
Bobby Orr	Bos.	12-3-74	(A)	Buf. 0 at Bos. 4	62	66	32-90 — 122	74	
Ken Hodge	Bos.	24-3-74	(A)	Mtl. 3 at Bos. 6	72	72	50-55 — 105	76	
Phil Esposito	Bos.	8-2-75	(A)	Bos. 8 at Det. 5	54	54	61-66 — 127	79	
Bobby Orr	Bos.	13-2-75	(A)	Bos. 1 at Buf. 3	57	57	46-89 — 135	80	
Guy Lafleur	Mtl.	7-3-75	(G)	Wsh. 4 at Mtl. 8	56	66	53-66 — 119	70	24.6
Pete Mahovlich	Mtl.	9-3-75	(G)	Mtl. 5 at NYR 3	67	67	35-82 — 117	80	29.5
Marcel Dionne	Det.	9-3-75	(A)	Det. 5 at Phi. 8	67	67	47-74 — 121	80	23.7
Bobby Clarke	Phi.	22-3-75	(A)	Min. 0 at Phi. 4	72	72	27-89 — 116	80	
Rene Robert	Buf.	5-4-75	(A)	Buf. 4 at Tor. 2	74	80	40-60 — 100	74	26.4
Guy Lafleur	Mtl.	10-3-76	(G)	Mtl. 5 at Chi. 1	69	69	56-69 — 125	80	
Bobby Clarke	Phi.	11-3-76	(A)	Buf. 1 at Phi. 6	64	68	30-89 — 119	76	
Bill Barber	Phi.	18-3-76	(A)	Van. 2 at Phi. 3	71	71	50-62 — 112	80	23.8
Gilbert Perreault	Buf.	21-3-76	(A)	K.C. 1 at Buf. 3	73	73	44-69 — 113	80	25.4
Pierre Larouche	Pit.	24-3-76	(G)	Bos. 5 at Pit. 5	70	74	53-58 — 111	76	20.4
Pete Mahovlich	Mtl.	28-3-76	(A)	Mtl. 2 at Bos. 2	77	77	34-71 — 105	80	
Jean Ratelle	Bos.	30-3-76	(G)	Buf. 4 at Bos. 4	77	77	36-69 — 105	80	
Jean Pronovost	Pit.	3-4-76	(A)	Wsh. 5 at Pit. 4	79	79	52-52 — 104	80	30.4
Darryl Sittler	Tor.	3-4-76	(A)	Bos. 4 at Tor. 2	78	79	41-59 — 100	79	26.7
Guy Lafleur	Mtl.	26-2-77	(A)	Clev. 3 at Mtl. 5	63	63	56-80 — 136	80	
Marcel Dionne	L.A.	5-3-77	(G)	Pit. 3 at L.A. 3	67	67	53-69 — 122	80	
Steve Shutt	Mtl.	27-3-77	(A)	Mtl. 6 at Det. 0	77	77	60-45 — 105	80	24.9
Bryan Trottier	NYI	25-2-78	(A)	Chi. 1 at NYI 7	59	60	46-77 — 123	77	21.7
Guy Lafleur	Mtl.	28-2-78	(G)	Det. 3 at Mtl. 9	69	61	60-72 — 132	78	
Darryl Sittler	Tor.	12-3-78	(A)	Tor. 7 at Pit. 1	67	67	45-72 — 117	80	
Guy Lafleur	Mtl.	27-2-79	(A)	Mtl. 3 at NYI 7	61	61	52-77 — 129	80	
Bryan Trottier	NYI	6-3-79	(A)	Buf. 3 at NYI 2	59	63	47-87 — 134	76	
Marcel Dionne	L.A.	8-3-79	(A)	L.A. 4 at Buf. 6	66	66	59-71 — 130	80	
Mike Bossy	NYI	11-3-79	(G)	NYI 4 at Bos. 4	66	66	69-57 — 126	80	22.2
Bob MacMillan	Atl.	15-3-79	(A)	Atl. 4 at Phi. 5	68	69	37-71 — 108	79	26.6
Guy Chouinard	Atl.	30-3-79	(G)	L.A. 3 at Atl. 5	75	75	50-57 — 107	80	22.5
Denis Potvin	NYI	8-4-79	(A)	NYI 5 at NYR 2	73	80	31-70 — 101	73	25.5
Marcel Dionne	L.A.	6-2-80	(A)	L.A. 3 at Hfd. 7	53	53	53-84 — 137	80	
Guy Lafleur	Mtl.	10-2-80	(A)	Mtl. 3 at Bos. 2	55	55	50-75 — 125	74	
Wayne Gretzky	Edm.	24-2-80	(A)	Bos. 4 at Edm. 2	61	62	51-86 — 137	79	19.2
Bryan Trottier	NYI	30-3-80	(A)	NYI 9 at Que. 6	75	77	42-62 — 104	78	
Gilbert Perreault	Buf.	1-4-80	(A)	Buf. 5 at Atl. 2	77	77	40-66 — 106	80	
Mike Rogers	Hfd.	4-4-80	(A)	Que. 2 at Hfd. 9	79	79	44-61 — 105	80	25.5
Charlie Simmer	L.A.	5-4-80	(G)	Van. 5 at L.A. 3	64	80	56-45 — 101	64	26.0
Blaine Stoughton	Hfd.	6-4-80	(A)	Det. 3 at Hfd. 5	80	80	56-44 — 100	80	27.0
Wayne Gretzky	Edm.	6-2-81	(G)	Wpg. 4 at Edm. 10	53	53	55-109 — 164	80	
Marcel Dionne	L.A.	12-2-81	(A)	L.A. 5 at Chi. 5	58	58	58-77 — 135	80	
Charlie Simmer	L.A.	14-2-81	(A)	Bos. 5 at L.A. 4	59	59	56-49 — 105	65	
Kent Nilsson	Cgy.	27-2-81	(G)	Hfd. 1 at Cgy. 5	64	64	49-82 — 131	80	24.6
Mike Bossy	NYI	3-3-81	(G)	Edm. 8 at NYI 8	65	66	68-51 — 119	79	
Dave Taylor	L.A.	14-3 81	(G)	Min. 4 at L.A. 10	63	70	47-65 — 112	72	25.3
Mike Rogers	Hfd.	22-3-81	(G)	Tor. 3 at Hfd. 3	74	74	40-65 — 105	80	
Bernie Federko	St.L.	28-3-81	(A)	Buf. 4 at St.L. 7	74	76	31-73 — 104	78	24.10
Rick Middleton	Bos.	28-3-81	(A)	Chi. 2 at Bos. 5	76	76	44-59 — 103	80	27.4
Jacques Richard	Que.	29-3-81	(G)	Mtl. 0 at Que. 4	75	76	52-51 — 103	78	28.6
Bryan Trottier	NYI	29-3-81	(G)	NYI 5 at Wsh. 4	69	76	31-72 — 103	73	
Peter Stastny	Que.	29-3-81	(A)	Mtl. 0 at Que. 4	73	76	39-70 — 109	77	24.6
Wayne Gretzky	Edm.	27-12-81	(G)	L.A. 3 at Edm. 10	38	38	92-120 — 212	80	
Mike Bossy	NYI	13-2-82	(A)	Phi. 2 at NYI 8	55	55	64-83 — 147	80	
Peter Stastny	Que.	16-2-82	(A)	Wpg. 3 at Que. 7	60	60	46-93 — 139	80	
Dennis Maruk	Wsh.	20-2-82	(G)	Wsh. 3 at Min. 7	60	60	60-76 — 136	80	26.3
Bryan Trottier	NYI	23-2-82	(G)	Chi. 1 at NYI 5	61	61	50-79 — 129	80	
Denis Savard	Chi.	27-2-82	(A)	Chi. 5 at L.A. 3	64	64	32-87 — 119	80	21.1
Bobby Smith	Min.	3-3-82	(A)	Det. 4 at Min. 6	66	66	43-71 — 114	80	24.1
Marcel Dionne	L.A.	6-3-82	(G)	L.A. 6 at Hfd. 7	64	66	50-67 — 117	78	
Dave Taylor	L.A.	20-3-82	(A)	Pit. 5 at L.A. 7	71	72	39-67 — 106	78	
Dale Hawerchuk	Wpg.	24-3-82	(G)	L.A. 3 at Wpg.	74	74	45-58 — 103	80	18.11
Dino Ciccarelli	Min.	27-3-82	(A)	Min. 6 at Bos. 5	72	76	55-52 — 107	76	21.8
Glenn Anderson	Edm.	28-3-82	(G)	Edm. 6 at L.A. 2	78	78	38-67 — 105	80	21.7
Mike Rogers	NYR	2-4-82	(G)	Pit. 7 at NYR 5	79	79	38-65 — 103	80	

Bobby Clarke

Kent Nilsson

Wayne Gretzky	Edm.	5-1-83	(A)	Edm. 8	at Wpg. 3	42	42	71-125 — 196	80	
Mike Bossy	NYI	3-3-83	(A)	Tor. 1	at NYI. 5	66	67	60-58 — 118	79	
Peter Stastny	Que.	5-3-83	(A)	Hfd. 3	at Que. 10	62	67	47-77 — 124	75	
Denis Savard	Chi.	6-3-83	(G)	Mtl. 4	at Chi. 5	65	67	35-86 — 121	78	
Mark Messier	Edm.	23-3-83	(G)	Edm. 4	at Wpg. 7	73	76	48-58 — 106	77	22.2
Barry Pederson	Bos.	26-3-83	(A)	Hfd. 4	at Bos. 7	73	76	46-61 — 107	77	22.0
Marcel Dionne	L.A.	26-3-83	(A)	Edm. 9	at L.A. 3	75	75	56-51 — 107	80	
Michel Goulet	Que.	27-3-83	(A)	Que. 6	at Buf. 6	77	77	57-48 — 105	80	22.11
Glenn Anderson	Edm.	29-3-83	(A)	Edm. 7	at Van. 4	70	78	48-56 — 104	72	
Jari Kurri	Edm.	29-3-83	(A)	Edm. 7	at Van. 4	78	78	45-59 — 104	80	22.10
Kent Nilsson	Cgy.	29-3-83	(G)	L.A. 3	at Cgy. 5	78	78	46-58 — 104	80	

Wayne Gretzky	Edm.	18-12-83	(G)	Edm. 7	at Wpg. 5	34	34	87-118 — 205	74	
Paul Coffey	Edm.	4-3-84	(A)	Mtl. 1	at Edm. 6	68	68	40-86 — 126	80	22.9
Michel Goulet	Que.	4-3-84	(A)	Que. 1	at Buf. 1	62	67	56-65 — 121	75	
Jari Kurri	Edm.	7-3-84	(G)	Chi. 4	at Edm. 7	53	69	52-61 — 113	64	
Peter Stastny	Que.	8-3-84	(A)	Que. 8	at Pit. 6	69	69	46-73 — 119	80	
Mike Bossy	NYI	8-3-84	(G)	Tor. 5	at NYI 9	56	68	51-67 — 118	67	
Barry Pederson	Bos.	14-3-84	(A)	Bos. 4	at Det. 2	71	71	39-77 — 116	80	
Bryan Trottier	NYI	18-3-84	(G)	NYI 4	at Hfd. 5	62	73	40-71 — 111	68	
Bernie Federko	St.L.	20-3-84	(A)	Wpg. 3	at St.L. 9	75	76	41-66 — 107	79	
Rick Middleton	Bos.	27-3-84	(G)	Bos. 6	at Que. 4	77	77	47-58 — 105	80	
Dale Hawerchuk	Wpg.	27-3-84	(G)	Wpg. 3	at L.A. 3	77	77	37-65 — 102	80	
Mark Messier	Edm.	27-3-84	(G)	Edm. 9	at Cgy. 2	72	79	37-64 — 101	73	

Wayne Gretzky	Edm.	29-12-84	(A)	Det. 3	at Edm. 6	35	35	73-135 — 208	80	
Jari Kurri	Edm.	29-1-85	(G)	Edm. 4	at Cgy. 2	48	51	71-64 — 135	73	
Mike Bossy	NYI	23-2-85	(G)	Bos. 1	at NYI 7	56	60	58-59 — 117	76	
Dale Hawerchuk	Wpg.	25-2-85	(A)	Wpg. 12	at NYR 5	64	64	53-77 — 130	80	
Marcel Dionne	L.A.	5-3-85	(A)	Pit. 0	at L.A. 6	66	66	46-80 — 126	80	
Brent Sutter	NYI	12-3-85	(A)	NYI 6	at St. L. 5	68	68	42-60 — 102	72	22.10
John Ogrodnick	Det.	22-3-85	(A)	NYR 3	at Det. 5	73	73	55-50 — 105	79	25.9
Paul Coffey	Edm.	26-3-85	(G)	Edm. 7	at NYI 5	74	74	37-84 — 121	80	
Denis Savard	Chi.	29-3-8	(A)	Chi. 5	at Wpg. 5	75	76	38-67 — 105	79	
Peter Stastny	Que.	2-4-85	(A)	Bos. 4	at Que. 6	74	77	32-68 — 100	75	
Bernie Federko	St.L.	4-4-85	(A)	NYR 5	at St.L. 4	74	78	30-73 — 103	76	
John Tonelli	NYI	6-4-85	(G)	NJ 5	at NYI 5	80	80	42-58 — 100	80	28.1
Paul MacLean	Wpg.	6-4-85	(A)	Wpg. 6	at Edm. 5	78	79	41-60 — 101	79	27.1
Mike Gartner	Wsh.	7-4-85	(G)	Pit. 3	at Wsh. 7	80	80	50-52 — 102	80	25.6
Bernie Nicholls	L.A.	6-4-85	(A)	Van. 4	at L.A. 4	80	80	46-54 — 100	80	22.9
Mario Lemieux	Pit.	7-4-85	(G)	Pit. 3	at Wsh. 7	73	80	43-57 — 100	73	19.6

Wayne Gretzky	Edm.	4-1-86	(A)	Hfd. 3	at Edm. 4	39	39	52-163 — 215	80	
Mario Lemieux	Pit.	15-2-86	(G)	Van. 4	at Pit. 9	55	56	48-93 — 141	79	
Paul Coffey	Edm.	19-2-86	(A)	Tor. 5	at Edm. 9	59	60	48-90 — 138	79	
Jari Kurri	Edm.	2-3-86	(G)	Phi. 1	at Edm. 2	62	64	68-63 — 131	78	
Peter Stastny	Que.	1-3-86	(A)	Buf. 8	at Que. 4	66	68	41-81 — 122	76	
Mike Bossy	NYI	8-3-86	(G)	Wsh. 6	at NYI 2	65	65	61-62 — 123	80	
Denis Savard	Chi.	12-3-86	(A)	Buf. 7	at Chi. 6	69	69	47-69 — 116	80	
Mats Naslund	Mtl.	13-3-86	(A)	Mtl. 2	at Bos. 3	70	70	43-67 — 110	80	26.4
Michel Goulet	Que.	24-3-86	(A)	Que. 1	at Min. 0	70	75	53-50 — 103	75	
Glenn Anderson	Edm.	25-3-86	(G)	Edm. 7	at Det. 2	66	74	54-48 — 102	72	
Neal Broten	Min.	26-3-86	(A)	Min. 6	at Tor. 1	76	76	29-76 — 105	80	26.4
Dale Hawerchuk	Wpg.	31-3-86	(A)	Wpg. 5	at L.A. 2	78	78	46-59 — 105	80	
Bernie Federko	St.L.	5-4-86	(G)	Chi. 5	at St.L. 7	79	79	34-68 — 102	80	

Wayne Gretzky	Edm.	1-11-87	(A)	Cgy. 3	at Edm. 5	42	42	62-121 — 183	79	
Jari Kurri	Edm.	3-14-87	(A)	Buf. 3	at Edm. 5	67	68	54-54 — 108	79	
Mario Lemieux	Pit.	3-18-87	(A)	St.L. 4	at Pit. 5	55	72	54-53 — 107	63	
Mark Messier	Edm.	3-19-87	(A)	Edm. 4	at Cgy. 5	71	71	37-70 — 107	77	
Doug Gilmour	St.L.	4-2-87	(A)	Buf. 3	at St.L. 5	78	78	42-63 — 105	80	23.10
Dio Ciccarelli	Min.	3-30-87	(A)	NYR 6	at Min. 5	78	78	52-51 — 103	80	
Dale Hawerchuk	Wpg.	4-5-87	(A)	Wpg. 3	at Cgy. 1	80	80	47-53 — 100	80	

Mario Lemieux	Pit.	20-1-88	(G)	Plt. 8	at Chi. 3	45	48	70-98 — 168	77	
Wayne Gretzky	Edm.	11-2-88	(A)	Edm. 7	at Van. 2	43	56	40-109 — 149	64	
Denis Savard	Chi.	12-2-88	(A)	St.L. 3	at Chi. 4	57	57	44-87 — 131	80	
Dale Hawerchuk	Wpg.	23-2-88	(G)	Wpg. 4	at Pit. 3	61	61	44-77 — 121	80	
Steve Yzerman	Det.	27-2-88	(A)	Det. 4	at Que. 5	63	63	50-52 — 102	64	22.10
Peter Stastny	Que.	8-3-88	(A)	Hfd. 4	at Que. 6	63	67	46-65 — 111	76	
Mark Messier	Edm.	15-3-88	(A)	Buf. 4	at Edm. 6	68	71	37-74 — 111	77	
Jimmy Carson	L.A.	26-3-88	(A)	Chi. 5	at L.A. 9	77	77	55-52 — 107	80	19.8
Hakan Loob	Cgy.	26-3-88	(A)	Van. 1	at Cgy. 6	76	76	50-56 — 106	80	27.9
Mike Bullard	Cgy.	26-3-88	(A)	Van. 1	at Cgy. 6	76	76	48-55 — 103	79	27.1
Michel Goulet	Que.	27-3-88	(A)	Pit. 6	at Que. 3	76	76	48-58 — 106	80	
Luc Robitaille	L.A.	30-3-88	(G)	Cgy. 7	at L.A. 9	78	78	53-58 — 111	80	22.1

Mario Lemieux	Pit.	31-12-88	(A)	N.J. 6	at Pit. 8	36	38	85-114 — 199	76	
Wayne Gretzky	L.A.	21-1-89	(A)	L.A. 4	at Hfd. 5	47	48	54-114 — 168	78	
Steve Yzerman	Det.	27-1-89	(G)	Tor. 1	at Det. 8	50	50	65-90 — 155	80	
Bernie Nicholls	L.A.	21-1-89	(A)	L.A. 4	at Hfd. 5	48	48	70-80 — 150	79	
Rob Brown	Pit.	16-3-89	(A)	Pit. 2	at N.J. 1	60	72	49-66 — 115	68	20.11
Paul Coffey	Pit.	20-3-89	(A)	Pit. 2	at Min. 7	69	74	30-83 — 113	75	
Joe Mullen	Cgy.	23-3-89	(A)	L.A. 2	at Cgy. 4	74	75	51-59 — 110	79	32.1
Jari Kurri	Edm.	29-3-89	(A)	Edm. 5	at Van. 2	75	79	44-58 — 102	76	
Jimmy Carson	Edm.	2-4-89	(A)	Edm. 2	at Cgy. 4	80	80	49-51 — 100	80	

Mario Lemieux	Pit.	28-1-90	(G)	Pit. 2	at Buf. 7	50	50	45-78 — 123	59	
Wayne Gretzky	L.A.	30-1-90	(A)	N.J. 2	at L.A. 5	51	51	40-102 — 142	73	
Steve Yzerman	Det.	19-2-90	(A)	Mtl. 5	at Det. 5	61	61	62-65 — 127	79	
Mark Messier	Edm.	20-2-90	(A)	Edm. 4	at Van. 2	62	62	45-84 — 129	79	
Brett Hull	St.L.	3-3-90	(A)	NYI 4	at St.L. 5	67	67	72-41 — 113	80	25.7
Bernie Nicholls	NYR	12-3-90	(A)	L.A. 6	at NYR 2	70	71	39-73 — 112	79	
Pierre Turgeon	Buf.	25-3-90	(G)	N.J. 4	at Buf. 3	76	76	40-66 — 106	80	20.7
Paul Coffey	Pit.	25-3-90	(A)	Pit. 2	at Hfd. 4	77	77	29-74 — 103	80	
Pat LaFontaine	NYI	27-3-90	(G)	Cgy. 4	at NYI 2	72	78	54-51 — 105	74	25.1
Adam Oates	St.L.	29-3-90	(G)	Pit 4	at St.L. 5	79	79	23-79 — 102	80	27.7
Joe Sakic	Que.	31-3-90	(G)	Hfd. 3	at Que. 2	79	79	39-63 — 102	80	20.8
Ron Francis	Hfd.	31-3-90	(G)	Hfd. 3	at Que. 2	79	79	32-69 — 101	80	27.0
Luc Robitaille	L.A.	1-4-90	(A)	L.A. 4	at Cgy. 8	80	80	52-49 — 101	80	

Bobby Smith

Michel Goulet

Brent Sutter

100-Point Seasons — *continued*

Wayne Gretzky	L.A.	30-1-91	(A) N.J. 4	at L.A. 2	50	51	41-122 — 163	78	
Brett Hull	St.L.	23-2-91	(G) Bos. 2	at St.L. 9	60	62	86-45 — 131	78	
Mark Recchi	Pit.	5-3-91	(G) Van. 1	at Pit. 4	66	67	40-73 — 113	78	23.1
Steve Yzerman	Det.	10-3-91	(G) Det. 4	at St.L. 1	72	72	51-57 — 108	80	
John Cullen	Hfd.	16-3-91	(G) N.J. 2	at Hfd. 6	71	71	39-71 — 110	78	26.7
Adam Oates	St.L.	17-3-91	(A) St.L. 4	at Chi. 6	54	73	25-90 — 115	61	
Joe Sakic	Que.	19-3-91	(G) Edm. 7	at Que. 6	74	74	48-61 — 109	80	
Steve Larmer	Chi.	24-3-91	(A) Min. 4	at Chi. 5	76	76	44-57 — 101	80	29.9
Theoren Fleury	Cgy.	26-3-91	(G) Van. 2	at Cgy. 7	77	77	51-53 — 104	79	22.9
Al MacInnis	Cgy.	28-3-91	(A) Edm. 4	at Cgy. 4	78	78	28-75 — 103	78	27.8
Mario Lemieux	Pit.	10-03-92	(A) Cgy. 2	at Pit. 5	53	67	44-87 — 131	64	
Kevin Stevens	Pit.	7-3-92	(A) Pit. 3	at L.A. 5	66	66	54-69 — 123	80	26.11
Wayne Gretzky	L.A.	3-3-92	(A) Phi. 1	at L.A. 4	60	66	31-90 — 121	74	
Brett Hull	St. L.	2-3-92	(G) St. L. 5	at Van. 3	66	66	70-39 — 109	73	
Luc Robitaille	L.A.	17-3-92	(A) Wpg. 4	at L.A. 5	73	73	44-63 — 107	80	
Mark Messier	NYR	22-3-92	(G) N.J. 3	at NYR 6	74	75	35-72 — 107	79	
Jeremy Roenick	Chi.	29-3-92	(A) Tor. 1	at Chi. 5	77	77	53-50 — 103	80	22.2
Steve Yzerman	Det.	14-4-92	(G) Det. 7	at Min. 4	79	80	45-58 — 103	79	
Brian Leetch	NYR	16-4-92	(G) Pit. 1	at NYR 7	80	80	22-80 — 102	80	24.1

Five-or-more-Goal Games

Player	Team	Date	Score		Opposing Goaltender
SEVEN GOALS					
Joe Malone	Quebec Bulldogs	Jan. 31/20	Tor. 6	at Que. 10	Ivan Mitchell
SIX GOALS					
Newsy Lalonde	Montreal	Jan. 10/20	Tor. 7	at Mtl. 14	Ivan Mitchell
Joe Malone	Quebec Bulldogs	Mar. 10/20	Ott. 4	at Que. 10	Clint Benedict
Corb Denneny	Toronto St. Pats	Jan. 26/21	Ham. 3	at Tor. 10	Howard Lockhart
Cy Denneny	Ottawa Senators	Mar. 7/21	Ham. 5	at Ott. 12	Howard Lockhart
Syd Howe	Detroit	Feb. 3/44	NYR 2	at Det. 12	Ken McAuley
Red Berenson	St. Louis	Nov. 7/68	St. L. 8	at Phil 0	Doug Favell
Darryl Sittler	Toronto	Feb. 7/76	Bos. 4	at Tor. 11	Dave Reece
FIVE GOALS					
Joe Malone	Montreal	Dec. 19/17	Mtl. 7	at Ott. 4	Clint Benedict
Harry Hyland	Mtl. Wanderers	Dec. 19/17	Tor. 9	at Mtl. W. 10	Arthur Brooks
Joe Malone	Montreal	Jan. 12/18	Ott. 4	at Mtl. 9	Clint Benedict
Joe Malone	Montreal	Feb. 2/18	Tor. 2	at Mtl. 11	Harry Holmes
Mickey Roach	Toronto St. Pats	Mar. 6/20	Que. 2	at Tor. 11	Frank Brophy
Newsy Lalonde	Montreal	Feb. 16/21	Ham. 5	at Mtl. 10	Howard Lockhart
Babe Dye	Toronto St. Pats	Dec. 16/22	Mtl. 2	at Tor. 7	Georges Vezina
Redvers Green	Hamilton Tigers	Dec. 5/24	Ham. 10	at Tor. 3	John Roach
Babe Dye	Toronto St. Pats	Dec. 22/24	Tor. 10	at Bos. 1	Charlie Stewart
Harry Broadbent	Mtl. Maroons	Jan. 7/25	Mtl. 6	at Ham. 2	Vernon Forbes
Pit Lepine	Montreal	Dec. 14/29	Ott. 4	at Mtl. 6	Alex Connell
Howie Morenz	Montreal	Mar. 18/30	NYA 3	at Mtl. 8	Roy Worters
Charlie Conacher	Toronto	Jan. 19/32	NYA 3	at Tor. 11	Roy Worters
Ray Getliffe	Montreal	Feb. 6/43	Bos. 3	at Mtl. 8	Frank Brimsek
Maurice Richard	Montreal	Dec. 28/44	Det. 1	at Mtl. 9	Harry Lumley
Howie Meeker	Toronto	Jan. 8/47	Chi. 4	at Tor. 10	Paul Bibeault
Bernie Geoffrion	Montreal	Feb. 19/55	NYR 2	at Mtl. 10	Gump Worsley
Bobby Rousseau	Montreal	Feb. 1/64	Det. 3	at Mtl. 9	Roger Crozier
Yvan Cournoyer	Montreal	Feb. 15/75	Chi. 3	at Mtl. 12	Mike Veisor
Don Murdoch	NY Rangers	Oct. 12/76	NYR 10	at Min. 4	Gary Smith
Ian Turnbull	Toronto	Feb. 2/77	Det. 1	at Tor. 9	Ed Giacomin (2) Jim Rutherford (3)
Bryan Trottier	NY Islanders	Dec. 23/78	NYR 4	at NYI 9	Wayne Thomas (4) John Davidson (1)
Tim Young	Minnesota	Jan. 15/79	Min. 8	at NYR 1	Doug Soetaert (3) Wayne Thomas (2)
John Tonelli	NY Islanders	Jan. 6/81	Tor. 3	at NYI 6	Jiri Crha
Wayne Gretzky	Edmonton	Feb. 18/81	St.L. 2	at Edm. 9	Mike Liut (3) Ed Staniowski (2)
Wayne Gretzky	Edmonton	Dec. 30/81	Phi. 5	at Edm. 7	Pete Peeters (4) Empty Net (1)
Grant Mulvey	Chicago	Feb. 3/82	St.L. 5	at Chi. 9	Mike Liut (4) Gary Edwards (1)
Bryan Trottier	NY Islanders	Feb. 13/82	Phi. 2	at NYI 8	Pete Peeters
Willy Lindstrom	Winnipeg	Mar. 2/82	Wpg. 7	at Phi. 6	Pete Peeters
Mark Pavelich	NY Rangers	Feb. 23/83	Hfd. 3	at NYR 11	Greg Millen
Jari Kurri	Edmonton	Nov. 19/83	NJ. 4	at Edm. 13	Glenn Resch (3) Ron Low (2)
Bengt Gustafsson	Washington	Jan. 8/84	Wsh. 7	at Phi. 1	Pelle Lindbergh
Pat Hughes	Edmonton	Feb. 3/84	Cgy. 5	at Edm. 10	Don Edwards (3) Rejean Lemelin (2)
Wayne Gretzky	Edmonton	Dec. 15/84	Edm. 8	at St. L. 2	Rick Wamsley (4) Mike Liut(1)
Dave Andreychuk	Buffalo	Feb. 6/86	Buf. 8	at Bos. 6	Pat Riggin (1) Doug Keans (4)
Wayne Gretzky	Edmonton	Dec. 6/87	Min. 4	at Edm. 10	Don Beaupre (4) Kari Takko (1)
Mario Lemieux	Pittsburgh	Dec. 31/88	N.J. 6	at Pit. 8	Bob Sauve (3) Chris Terreri (2)
Joe Nieuwendyk	Calgary	Jan. 11/89	Wpg. 3	at Cgy. 8	Daniel Berthiaume
Mats Sundin	Quebec	Mar. 5/92	Que. 10	at Hfd. 4	Peter Sidorkiewicz (3) Kay Whitmore (2)

Players' 1,000th Points

Player	Team	Date	Game No.	G or A		Score	Total Points G A PTS	Total Games
Gordie Howe	Detroit	Nov. 27/60	938	(A)	Tor. 0	at Det. 2	801-1,049-1,850	1,767
Jean Béliveau	Montreal	Mar. 3/68	911	(G)	Mtl. 2	at Det. 5	507-712-1,219	1,125
Alex Delvecchio	Detroit	Feb. 16/69	1,143	(A)	LA 3	at Det. 6	456-825-1,281	1,549
Norm Ullman	Toronto	Oct. 16/71	1,113	(A)	NYR 5	at Tor. 3	490-739-1,229	1,410
Bobby Hull	Chicago	Dec. 12/71	909	(A)	Minn. 3	at Chi. 5	610-560-1,170	1,063
Stan Mikita	Chicago	Oct. 15/72	924	(A)	St.L. 3	at Chi. 1	541-926-1,467	1,394
John Bucyk	Boston	Nov. 9/72	1,144	(G)	Det. 3	at Bos. 8	556-813-1,369	1,540
Frank Mahovlich	Montreal	Feb. 13/73	1,090	(A)	Phi. 7	at Mtl. 6	533-570-1,103	1,181
Henri Richard	Montreal	Dec. 20/73	1,194	(A)	Mtl. 2	at Buf. 2	358-688-1,046	1,256
Phil Esposito	Boston	Feb. 15/74	745	(A)	Bos. 4	at Van. 2	717-873-1,590	1,282
Rod Gilbert	NY Rangers	Feb. 19/77	1,027	(G)	NYR 2	at NYI 5	406-615-1,021	1,065
Jean Ratelle	Boston	Apr. 3/77	1,007	(A)	Tor. 4	at Bos. 7	491-776-1,267	1,281
Bobby Clarke	Philadelphia	Mar. 19/81	922	(G)	Bos. 3	at Phi. 5	358-852-1,210	1,144
Marcel Dionne	Los Angeles	Jan. 7/81	740	(G)	L.A. 5	at Hfd. 3	731-1,040-1,771	1,348
Guy Lafleur	Montreal	Mar. 4/81	720	(G)	Mtl. 9	at Wpg. 3	560-793-1,353	1,126
Gilbert Perreault	Buffalo	Apr. 3/82	871	(A)	Buf. 5	at Mtl.4	512-814-1,326	1,191
Darryl Sittler	Philadelphia	Jan. 20/83	927	(G)	Cgy 2	at Phi. 5	484-637-1,121	1,096
*Wayne Gretzky	Edmonton	Dec. 19/84	424	(A)	L.A. 3	at Edm. 7	749-1,514-2,263	999
*Bryan Trottier	NY Islanders	Jan. 29/85	726	(G)	Min. 4	at NYI 4	520-890-1,410	1,238
Mike Bossy	NY Islanders	Jan. 24/86	656	(A)	NYI 7	at Wsh. 5	573-553-1,126	752
Denis Potvin	NY Islanders	Apr. 4/87	987	(G)	Buf. 6	at NYI 6	310-742-1,052	1,060
Bernie Federko	St. Louis	Mar 19/88	855	(A)	Hfd. 5	at St.L. 3	369-761-1,130	1,000
Lanny McDonald	Calgary	Mar. 7/89	1,101	(G)	Wpg. 5	at Cgy. 9	500-506-1,006	1,111
*Peter Stastny	Quebec	Oct. 19/89	682	(G)	Que. 5	at Chi. 3	427-754-1,181	892
*Jari Kurri	Edmonton	Jan. 2/90	716	(A)	Edm. 6	at St.L. 4	497-606-1,103	827
*Denis Savard	Chicago	Mar. 11/90	727	(A)	St.L. 6	at Chi. 4	407-735-1,142	960
*Paul Coffey	Pittsburgh	Dec. 22/90	770	(A)	Pit. 4	at NYI 3	318-796-1,114	873
*Mark Messier	Edmonton	Jan. 13/91	822	(A)	Edm. 5	at Phi. 3	427-714-1,141	930
*Dave Taylor	Los Angeles	Feb. 5/91	930	(A)	L.A. 3	at Phi. 2	421-626-1,047	1,030
*Michel Goulet	Chicago	Feb. 23/91	878	(G)	Chi. 3	at Min. 3	509-569-1,078	970
*Dale Hawerchuk	Buffalo	Mar. 8/91	781	(G)	Chi. 5	at Buf. 3	433-683-1,116	870
*Bobby Smith	Minnesota	Nov. 30/91	986	(A)	Min. 4	at Tor. 3	352-672-1,024	1,032
*Mike Gartner	NY Rangers	Jan. 4/92	971	(G)	NYR 4	at N.J. 6	538-501-1,039	1,005
*Ray Bourque	Boston	Feb. 29/92	933	(A)	Wsh. 5	at Bos. 5	272-743-1,015	950

*Active

Jean Ratelle reached the 1,000-point plateau on April 3, 1977 in Boston's 7-4 victory over the Toronto Maple Leafs.

Individual Awards

Hart Memorial Trophy

Art Ross Trophy

Calder Memorial Trophy

James Norris Memorial Trophy

HART MEMORIAL TROPHY

An annual award "to the player adjudged to be the most valuable to his team". Winner selected in poll by Professional Hockey Writers' Association in the 24 NHL cities at the end of the regular schedule. The winner receives $10,000 and the runners-up $6,000 and $4,000.

History: The Hart Memorial Trophy was presented by the National Hockey League in 1960 after the original Hart Trophy was retired to the Hockey Hall of Fame. The original Hart Trophy was donated to the NHL in 1923 by Dr. David A. Hart, father of Cecil Hart, former manager-coach of the Montreal Canadiens.

1991-92 Winner: Mark Messier, NY Rangers
Runners-up: Patrick Roy, Montreal Canadiens
Brett Hull, St. Louis Blues

New York Rangers' center Mark Messier captured the Hart Memorial Trophy by a clear margin over runners-up Patrick Roy and Brett Hull in the voting.

Messier received 67 of 69 first-place votes and was named on all 69 ballots to earn 341 of a possible 345 points. Patrick Roy of the Montreal Canadiens placed second in the voting with 105 points, while Brett Hull, last season's Hart Trophy winner, finished third with 49 points.

Messier, obtained via trade from the Edmonton Oilers on October 4, 1991, was the Rangers' leading scorer in 1991-92 with 107 points (35–72–107) in 79 games, finishing sixth in the overall League scoring race. The Rangers' regular-season record of 50–25–5 for 105 points was the best in team history as New York finished with the NHL's top overall record for the first time since 1941-42.

He is only the second player in NHL history to win the Hart Trophy with two different clubs, having already captured the award as a member of the Edmonton Oilers in 1990. Wayne Gretzky won eight Hart Trophies with Edmonton and one with the Los Angeles Kings.

ART ROSS TROPHY

An annual award "to the player who leads the league in scoring points at the end of the regular season." The winner receives $10,000 and the runners-up $6,000 and $4,000.

History: Arthur Howie Ross, former manager-coach of Boston Bruins, presented the trophy to the National Hockey League in 1947. If two players finish the schedule with the same number of points, the trophy is awarded in the following manner: 1. Player with most goals. 2. Player with fewer games played. 3. Player scoring first goal of the season.

1991-92 Winner: Mario Lemieux, Pittsburgh Penguins
Runners-up: Kevin Stevens, Pittsburgh Penguins
Wayne Gretzky, Los Angeles Kings

Mario Lemieux of the Pittsburgh Penguins won the third Art Ross Trophy of his career in 1991-92. Lemieux had 44 goals and 87 assists for 131 points in 64 games to win the award for the first time since 1988-89. Teammate Kevin Stevens was first runner-up with 54 goals and 69 assists for 123 points. Wayne Gretzky of the Los Angeles Kings finished with 31 goals and 90 assists for 121 points.

CALDER MEMORIAL TROPHY

An annual award "to the player selected as the most proficient in his first year of competition in the National Hockey League". Winner selected in poll by Professional Hockey Writers' Association at the end of the regular schedule. The winner receives $10,000 and the runners-up $6,000 and $4,000.

History: From 1936-37 until his death in 1943, Frank Calder, NHL President, bought a trophy each year to be given permanently to the outstanding rookie. After Calder's death, the NHL presented the Calder Memorial Trophy in his memory and the trophy is to be kept in perpetuity. To be eligible for the award, a player cannot have played more than 25 games in any single preceding season nor in six or more games in each of any two preceding seasons in any major professional league. Beginning in 1990-91, to be eligible for this award a player must not have attained his twenty-sixth birthday by September 15th of the season in which he is eligible.

1991-92 Winner: Pavel Bure, Vancouver Canucks
Runners-up: Nicklas Lidstrom, Detroit Red Wings
Tony Amonte, NY Rangers

Pavel Bure of the Vancouver Canucks is the second player from the former Soviet Union, after Calgary's Sergei Makarov in 1990, to capture the Calder Memorial Trophy.

Bure received 222 points in the voting, including 26 first-place votes. He was named on 64 of the 69 ballots. Bure edged Detroit defenseman Nicklas Lidstrom and New York Rangers' right wing Tony Amonte, each finishing with 183 points, in a close three-way race.

Bure tallied 60 points (34–26–60) to finish third in rookie scoring despite missing the first 15 games of the season. He led all rookies in shorthanded goals (three), shots (268), tied for the lead in game-winning goals (six) and posted an eight-game point scoring streak. He also finished second among rookies in goals (34) and tied for second place in power-play goals (seven).

Bure is the first player in Canucks' history to capture the Calder Trophy. Current Canuck Trevor Linden finished as runner-up to Brian Leetch in Calder Trophy voting in 1989.

JAMES NORRIS MEMORIAL TROPHY

An annual award "to the defense player who demonstrates throughout the season the greatest all-round ability in the position." Winner selected in poll by Professional Hockey Writers' Association at the end of the regular schedule. The winner receives $10,000 and the runners-up $6,000 and $4,000.

History: The James Norris Memorial Trophy was presented in 1953 by the four children of the late James Norris in memory of the former owner-president of the Detroit Red Wings.

1991-92 Winner: Brian Leetch, NY Rangers
Runners-up: Ray Bourque, Boston Bruins
Phil Housley, Winnipeg Jets

New York Rangers' defenseman Brian Leetch received 335 points and appeared on all 69 ballots en route to winning his first career James Norris Trophy.

Leetch, who received 65 of 69 first-place votes, finished ahead of last season's Norris Trophy winner Ray Bourque, who received 112 points. Phil Housley of the Winnipeg Jets was third in the voting with 82 points.

Leetch led all NHL defensemen in scoring in 1991-92 with 102 points (22–80–102 in 80 games), becoming just the fifth defenseman in NHL history to record 100 points in one season. Leetch follows Bobby Orr, Denis Potvin, Paul Coffey and Al MacInnis in that exclusive category. Leetch recorded the NHL's longest consecutive game assist streak (15 games) and the third-longest point streak (17 games).

Leetch, a native of Corpus Christi, TX, became the second U.S.-born player to win the Norris Trophy since its inception in 1954. Chicago-born Chris Chelios of the Montreal Canadiens won the award in 1989. He is also the first New York Ranger to win the trophy since Harry Howell in 1967. In addition to his Norris Trophy honors, Leetch also received the Calder Trophy in 1989 as the League's top rookie.

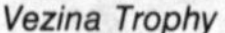
Vezina Trophy

Lady Byng Memorial Trophy

Frank J. Selke Trophy

Conn Smythe Trophy

VEZINA TROPHY

An annual award "to the goalkeeper adjudged to be the best at his position" as voted by the general managers of each of the 24 clubs. Over-all winner receives $10,000, runners-up $6,000 and $4,000.

History: Leo Dandurand, Louis Letourneau and Joe Cattarinich, former owners of the Montreal Canadiens, presented the trophy to the National Hockey League in 1926-27 in memory of Georges Vezina, outstanding goalkeeper of the Canadiens who collapsed during an NHL game November 28, 1925, and died of tuberculosis a few months later. Until the 1981-82 season, the goalkeeper(s) of the team allowing the fewest number of goals during the regular-season were awarded the Vezina Trophy.

1991-92 Winner: Patrick Roy, Montreal Canadiens
Runners-up: Kirk McLean, Vancouver Canucks
Bob Essensa, Winnipeg Jets

Patrick Roy of the Montreal Canadiens received 95 of a possible 110 points in the Vezina Trophy voting, including 17 of 22 first-place votes, to outdistance first-time Vezina Trophy finalist Kirk McLean of the Vancouver Canucks, who received 62 points. Bob Essensa of the Winnipeg Jets was third with 13 points.

Roy led the League in goals-against-average (2.36) and save percentage (.914) and tied for the lead in shutouts (five) in 1991-92 en route to posting a 36–22–8 record in 67 games. His total of 36 wins was third highest among NHL goaltenders. The Canadiens led the NHL in 1991-92 with 207 goals-against, the fewest allowed since the Buffalo Sabres' total of 201 in 1978-79.

Roy won the Vezina Trophy in 1989 and 1990 and finished as runner-up to Chicago's Ed Belfour last season. He earned his fourth career William Jennings Trophy this season as the goaltender on the team allowing the fewest goals. Roy, with three Vezina Trophies, is the only multiple winner of the award since the criteria were modified in 1981-82.

LADY BYNG MEMORIAL TROPHY

An annual award "to the player adjudged to have exhibited the best type of sportsmanship and gentlemanly conduct combined with a high standard of playing ability." Winner selected in poll by Professional Hockey Writers' Association at the end of the regular schedule. The winner receives $10,000 and the runners-up $6,000 and $4,000.

History: Lady Byng, wife of Canada's Governor-General at the time, presented the Lady Byng Trophy in 1925. After Frank Boucher of New York Rangers won the award seven times in eight seasons, he was given the trophy to keep and Lady Byng donated another trophy in 1936. After Lady Byng's death in 1949, the National Hockey League presented a new trophy, changing the name to Lady Byng Memorial Trophy.

1991-92 Winner: Wayne Gretzky, Los Angeles Kings
Runners-up: Joe Sakic, Quebec Nordiques
Brian Leetch, NY Rangers

Los Angeles Kings' center Wayne Gretzky captured the Lady Byng Trophy for the second consecutive season and the third time in his career.

Gretzky, a Lady Byng Trophy nominee for the sixth straight year and eight times in his career, received 180 points, including 29 first-place votes, to surpass Quebec Nordiques' center Joe Sakic (104 points) in the voting. Brian Leetch of the New York Rangers placed third with 74 points.

Gretzky led the Kings in scoring and finished third in the League with 121 points (31–90–121) in 74 games, while registering only 34 penalty minutes. He has never recorded more than 59 minutes in a season, 16 being the lowest. He won the Lady Byng in his first NHL season (1979-80) with the Edmonton Oilers and finished as a runner-up five times (1981 and 1987-1990) before winning the award in each of the past two seasons.

FRANK J. SELKE TROPHY

An annual award "to the forward who best excels in the defensive aspects of the game." Winner selected in poll by Professional Hockey Writers' Association at the end of the regular schedule. The winner receives $10,000 and the runners-up $6,000 and $4,000.

History: Presented to the National Hockey League in 1977 by the Board of Governors of the NHL in honour of Frank J. Selke, one of the great architects of NHL championship teams.

1991-92 Winner: Guy Carbonneau, Montreal Canadiens
Runners-up: Sergei Fedorov, Detroit Red Wings
Kelly Miller, Washington Capitals

Guy Carbonneau of the Montreal Canadiens was awarded the Frank J. Selke Trophy for the third time in the last five seasons.

Carbonneau captured 160 of a possible 345 points in the voting, to edge Sergei Fedorov of the Detroit Red Wings (120 points). Kelly Miller of the Washington Capitals placed third in the voting with 70 points.

Carbonneau, the captain of the Canadiens, tallied 39 points (18–21–39) in 72 games. He scored four game-winning goals and added a shorthanded goal. The Canadiens led the NHL in 1991-92 with 207 goals-against, the fewest allowed since the Buffalo Sabres' total of 201 in 1978-79.

Carbonneau previously won the Selke Trophy in 1988 and 1989 and finished as runner-up in 1987 and 1990. He is only one of two multiple winners of the Selke Trophy – Montreal's Bob Gainey won the award in the first four years it was presented, from 1978 through 1981.

CONN SMYTHE TROPHY

An annual award "to the most valuable player for his team in the playoffs." Winner selected by the Professional Hockey Writers' Association at the conclusion of the final game in the Stanley Cup Finals. The winner receives $10,000.

History: Presented by Maple Leaf Gardens Limited in 1964 to honor Conn Smythe, the former coach, manager, president and owner-governor of the Toronto Maple Leafs.

1991-92 Winner: Mario Lemieux, Pittsburgh Penguins

Mario Lemieux of the Pittsburgh Penguins again won the Conn Smythe Trophy as playoff MVP in 1992 as he led Pittsburgh to their second consecutive Stanley Cup triumph. The Penguins won series over Washington, (4–3), NY Rangers (4–2), Boston (4–0) and Chicago (4–0). Lemieux led all scorers in the 1992 playoffs, registering 16 goals and 18 assists for 34 points in just 15 games. Lemieux becomes just the second player (Bernie Parent won in 1974 and 1975) in NHL history to win the Conn Smythe Trophy in consecutive years.

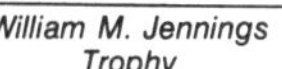
William M. Jennings Trophy

Jack Adams Award

Bill Masterton Trophy

Lester Patrick Trophy

Lester B. Pearson Award

WILLIAM M. JENNINGS TROPHY

An annual award "to the goalkeeper(s) having played a minimum of 25 games for the team with the fewest goals scored against it." Winners selected on regular-season play. Overall winner receives $10,000, runners-up $6,000 and $4,000.

History: The Jennings Trophy was presented in 1981-82 by the National Hockey League's Board of Governors to honor the late William M. Jennings, longtime governor and president of the New York Rangers and one of the great builders of hockey in the United States.

1991-92 Winner: Patrick Roy, Montreal Canadiens
Runners-up: Ed Belfour, Chicago Blackhawks
Bob Essensa, Stephane Beauregard, Winnipeg Jets

Patrick Roy of the Montreal Canadiens was instrumental in his team's League-leading goals against average of 2.55. Roy played in 67 of the Canadiens' 80 games, recording five shutouts and compiling a League-leading 2.36 goals against average.

JACK ADAMS AWARD

An annual award presented by the National Hockey League Broadcasters' Association to "the NHL coach adjudged to have contributed the most to his team's success." Winner selected by poll among members of the NHL Broadcasters' Association at the end of the regular season. The winner receives $1,000 from the NHLBA.

History: The award was presented by the NHL Broadcasters' Association in 1974 to commemorate the late Jack Adams, coach and general manager of the Detroit Red Wings, whose lifetime dedication to hockey serves as an inspiration to all who aspire to further the game.

1991-92 Winner: Pat Quinn, Vancouver Canucks
Runners-up: Roger Neilson, NY Rangers
Pat Burns, Montreal Canadiens

Vancouver Canucks' head coach Pat Quinn captured the Jack Adams Award, finishing ahead of Roger Neilson of the NY Rangers and Pat Burns of the Montreal Canadiens.

Quinn received 200 of a possible 250 points, including 34 first place votes, and was named on 48 of 50 ballots. Neilson finished in second place with 104 points, while Burns registered 48 points in the voting.

Quinn led the Canucks to a 42–26–12 record for 96 points in 1991-92, a 31-point improvement over 1990-91. It represented the best record in club history and a first-place finish in the Smythe Division for the first time since 1974-75.

Quinn is the first coach to win the Jack Adams Trophy with two different clubs, having previously won in 1980 with the Philadelphia Flyers. He becomes just the second multiple Jack Adams winner, joining Jacques Demers, who captured the honor in 1987 and 1988.

BILL MASTERTON MEMORIAL TROPHY

An annual award under the trusteeship of the Professional Hockey Writers' Association to "the National Hockey League player who best exemplifies the qualities of perseverance, sportsmanship and dedication to hockey." Winner selected by poll among the 22 chapters of the PHWA at the end of the regular season. A $2,500 grant from the PHWA is awarded annually to the Bill Masterton Scholarship Fund, based in Bloomington, MN, in the name of the Masterton Trophy winner.

History: The trophy was presented by the NHL Writers' Association in 1968 to commemorate the late William Masterton, a player of the Minnesota North Stars, who exhibited to a high degree the qualities of perseverance, sportsmanship and dedication to hockey, and who died January 15, 1968.

1991-92 Winner: Mark Fitzpatrick, NY Islanders

New York Islanders' goaltender Mark Fitzpatrick contracted eosinophilia myalgia syndrome (EMS) in the summer of 1990, an illness which has claimed 38 lives since 1989. After intense physical therapy he returned to the Islanders late in the 1990-91 season, appearing in two games. A flare-up of the disease sidelined Fitzpatrick again during training camp in September, 1991, but he returned to play in 30 games in 1991-92, posting a 11–13–5 record and 3.20 goals-against average.

Fitzpatrick regularly corresponds with other EMS patients and others with serious illnesses. He is also the Islanders' spokesman for the National Arthritis Foundation.

LESTER PATRICK TROPHY

An annual award "for outstanding service to hockey in the United States." Eligible recipients are players, officials, coaches, executives and referees. Winner selected by an award committee consisting of the President of the NHL, an NHL Governor, a representative of the New York Rangers, a member of the Hockey Hall of Fame Builder's section, a member of the Hockey Hall of Fame Player's section, a member of the U.S. Hockey Hall of Fame, a member of the NHL Broadcasters' Association and a member of the Professional Hockey Writers' Association. Each except the League President is rotated annually. The winner receives a miniature of the trophy.

History: Presented by the New York Rangers in 1966 to honor the late Lester Patrick, longtime general manager and coach of the New York Rangers, whose teams finished out of the playoffs only once in his first 16 years with the club.

1991-92 Winners: Al Arbour
Art Berglund
Lou Lamoriello

New York Islanders' coach Al Arbour, New Jersey Devils' President and General Manager Lou Lamoriello and USA Hockey Director of National Teams Art Berglund are the 1992 recipients of the Lester Patrick Trophy.

Combining his career as an NHL player and coach, Al Arbour has participated in 2,064 regular-season games in five franchise locations: Detroit, Chicago, Toronto and St. Louis as a player; St. Louis and Long Island as a coach. During that time, Arbour has been a member of eight Stanley Cup-winning teams, one each with Detroit and Chicago as a player, two with Toronto as a player, and four with the NY Islanders as a coach. This past season, Arbour became the NHL's all-time leader in games coached (1,438).

Art Berglund was an outstanding amateur player at Colorado College from 1960 to 1963. After a brief professional career in Europe, Berglund returned to the United States to manage Broadmoor World Arena in Colorado Springs for 13 years. During that time, Berglund began his career with USA Hockey in 1973 as manager of the U.S. National Team at the World Championships. Berglund also managed the U.S. National Team in 1974, 1975, 1985-87 and 1989-92 as well as the U.S. Olympic Team in 1976, 1988 and 1992.

Berglund helped pioneer USA Hockey's elite identification and development camps in the late 1970's. He was also instrumental in putting together the first U.S. National Junior Team in 1977.

Lou Lamoriello was a fixture at Providence College from 1959 through 1987 – first as a student-athlete, later as a coach and administrator. In 64 games with Providence as a player, Lamoriello scored 58 goals and had 60 assists for 118 points. After serving as an assistant coach for several years, Lamoriello became head coach of the Friars in 1968, compiling a .578 winning percentage (248–179–13) during his 15 years at the helm. During his tenure, Providence made it to 11 post-season tournaments, including a NCAA Final Four appearance in 1983.

On April 30, 1987, Lamoriello was named President of the New Jersey Devils. Prior to the start of the 1986-87 NHL season he assumed the dual role of President/General Manager. The Devils have qualified for the playoffs in four of six seasons since Lamoriello's arrival.

LESTER B. PEARSON AWARD

An annual award presented to the NHL's outstanding player as selected by the members of the National Hockey League Players' Association. The winner receives $10,000.

History: The award was presented in 1970-71 by the NHLPA in honor of the late Lester B. Pearson, former Prime Minister of Canada.

1991-92 Winner: Mark Messier, New York Rangers

King Clancy Memorial Trophy

Budweiser/NHL Man of The Year

One of the NHL's best defensive forwards, Paul Ysebaert won the Alka-Seltzer Plus Award in 1991-92, finishing with a mark of +44.

KING CLANCY MEMORIAL TROPHY

An annual award "to the player who best exemplifies leadership qualities on and off the ice and has made a noteworthy humanitarian contribution in his community". The winner receives $3,000 and the runner-up $1,000.

History: The King Clancy Memorial Trophy was presented to the National Hockey League by the Board of Governors in 1988 to honor the late Frank "King" Clancy.

1991-92 Winner: Ray Bourque, Boston Bruins
Runner-up: Keith Brown, Chicago Blackhawks

Boston Bruins' defenseman Ray Bourque has been the captain of the Bruins since 1985-86, finished second among Bruins in scoring with 81 points (20–61–81) and played in all 80 games. During the season he became just the third defenseman in NHL history to reach 1,000 career points, joining Denis Potvin and Paul Coffey. He is a four-time winner of the Norris Trophy as the NHL's outstanding defenseman and was a nominee again this season.

Off-ice, Bourque serves as honorary chairman for the main fundraiser of Boston's Floating Hospital for Infants and Children, holds an annual summer golf tournament which benefits a children's hospital in Montreal, donates all award money earned to children's charities and regularly visits sick children. In recognition of his extensive charitable work with children, Bourque was awarded with the first annual "MAC" Award at the 1991 All-Star Game in Chicago.

BUD LIGHT/NHL MAN OF THE YEAR

An annual award to the player recognized in the local community as a positive role model through his conduct on and off the ice. This includes involvement with local youth groups, charities and causes, as well as recognition among his peers and fans as a player who extols sportsmanlike qualities while maximizing his efforts toward improving his play and that of the team. The winner is selected by a special committee of distinguished NHL officials and management executives. The Bud Light/NHL Man of the Year recognizes one player from each of the local media representatives. Each nominated player receives a check for $1,000 to be given to his favorite charity. The winner receives $21,000 to be distributed to his favorite charities.

1991-92 Winner: Ryan Walter, Vancouver Canucks

Veteran forward Ryan Walter of the Vancouver Canucks was named recipient of the 1992 Bud Light/NHL Man of the Year Award.

A native of New Westminster, B.C., Walter has recorded more than 600 points and has played in over 900 NHL games. While his career on the ice has been impressive, his off-ice commitments have made him an all-star in the eyes of the community.

Walter spends numerous hours off the ice through his involvement with several charities. He is a spokesperson for World Vision, an organization that raises funds for third world countries, and Athletes for Kids, which pairs professional athletes with handicapped children.

He is also involved in the Canuck Coats for Kids program which gathers warm clothes for the less fortunate during the winter. In addition, he conducts several camps for underprivileged children through his involvement in Hockey Ministries International.

Three charities will benefit from Walter's award: the Canuck Foundation, Canuck Place and Hockey Ministries International.

ALKA-SELTZER PLUS AWARD

An annual award "to the player, having played a minimum of 60 games, who leads the League in plus/minus statistics" at the end of the regular season. Miles, Inc. will contribute $5,000 on behalf of the winner to the charity of his choice and $1000 on behalf of each individual team winner.

History: The award was presented to the NHL in 1989-90 by Miles, Inc., to recognize the League leader in plus-minus statistics. Plus-minus statistics are calculated by giving a player a "plus" when on-ice for an even-strength or shorthand goal scored by his team. He receives a "minus" when on-ice for an even-strength or shorthand goal scored by the opposing team. A plus-minus award has been presented since the 1982-83 season.

1991-92 Winner: Paul Ysebaert, Detroit Red Wings

Detroit Red Wings' leftwinger Paul Ysebaert was the NHL's leader in +/- ratings in 1991-92 with a total of +44. Ysebaert recorded an even-or-plus rating in 64 of 79 games in 1991-92. Ysebaert completed the season with a net offensive ranking of 85, having been on the ice for 114 of the Red Wings' 320 goals scored, 29 of them coming on the powerplay. His net defensive ranking was 41, having been on the ice for 56 of the 256 goals-against, 15 scored while Detroit was shorthanded. Team +/- leaders were: Ray Bourque, Boston; Mike Ramsey, Buffalo; Gary Roberts, Calgary; Chris Chelios, Chicago; Joe Murphy, Edmonton; Mikael Andersson, Hartford; Peter Ahola, Los Angeles; Jim Johnson, Minnesota; Brent Gilchrist, Montreal; Claude Vilgrain, New Jersey; Benoit Hogue, NY Islanders; James Patrick, NY Rangers; Kevin Dineen and Kerry Huffman, Philadelphia; Larry Murphy, Pittsburgh; Mikhail Tatarinov, Quebec; Bob Bassen, St. Louis; Neil Wilkinson, San Jose; Mike Krushelnyski, Toronto; Jyrki Lumme, Vancouver; Dimitri Khristich, Washington; Teppo Numminen, Winnipeg.

NHL AWARD MONEY BREAKDOWN

(Players on each club determine how team award money is divided.)

TEAM AWARDS

Stanley Cup Playoffs	Number of Clubs	Share Per Club	Total
Division Semi-Final Losers	8	$ 150,000	$1,200,000
Division Final Losers	4	300,000	1,200,000
Conference Championship Losers	2	450,000	900,000
Stanley Cup Loser	1	625,000	625,000
Stanley Cup Winners	1	1,000,000	1,000,000
TOTAL PLAYOFF AWARD MONEY			$4,925,000

Final Standings, Regular Season	Number of Clubs	Share Per Club	Total
Presidents' Trophy			
Club's Share	1	$ 100,000	$ 100,000
Players' Share	1	100,000	100,000
Division Winners	4	375,000	1,500,000
Division Second Place	4	175,000	700,000
TOTAL REGULAR SEASON AWARD MONEY			$2,400,000

INDIVIDUAL AWARDS	Winner	First Runner-up	Second Runner-up
Hart, Calder, Norris, Ross, Vezina, Byng, Selke, Jennings Trophies	$10,000	$6,000	$4,000
Conn Smythe Trophy	$10,000		
King Clancy Memorial Award	$ 3,000	$1,000	

	Number of winners	Per Player	Total
First Team All-Stars	6	$10,000	$60,000
Second Team All-Stars	6	5,000	$30,000
TOTAL INDIVIDUAL AWARD MONEY			$2,400,000
TOTAL ALL AWARDS			**$7,589,000**

Presidents' Trophy

PRESIDENTS' TROPHY

An annual award to the club finishing the regular-season with the best overall record. The winner receives $200,000, to be split evenly between the team and its players.

History: Presented to the National Hockey League in 1985-86 by the NHL Board of Governors to recognize the team compiling the top regular-season record.

1991-92 Winner: New York Rangers
Runners-up: Washington Capitals
Detroit Red Wings

The New York Rangers won the 1991-92 Presidents' Trophy with the NHL's best regular-season record of 50–25–5 for 105 points. The Washington Capitals finished second at 45–27–8 for 98 points, while the Detroit Red Wings had the third best regular-season mark of 43–25–12 for 98 points.

PRO SET/NHL PLAYER OF THE YEAR AWARD

An annual award presented by Pro Set to the National Hockey League's most valuable player in the regular-season. The winner is awarded $8,500 to benefit youth hockey.

History: In 1990, Pro Set initiated its relationship with the National Hockey League by sponsoring the Player of the Year Award. Pro Set also sponsors the Player of the Week and Player of the Month awards, donating $600 and $1,200, respectively, to youth hockey organizations chosen by the award recipient.

1991-92 Winner: Mario Lemieux, Pittsburgh Penguins

Lemieux led the League in scoring in 1991-92 with 131 points (44–87–131) despite missing 16 games due to injury. He recorded points in 56 of his 64 games, including two six-point games and one seven-point performance.

Lemieux keyed a Penguins' fourth-quarter surge by recording points in his last 17 regular-season games as Pittsburgh finished the season with the League's sixth best record (39–32–9). The Penguins went on to capture their second straight Stanley Cup Championship, with Lemieux again receiving the Conn Smythe Trophy as playoff MVP.

En route to being named Pro Set NHL Player of the Year, Lemieux garnered two Player of the Month selections (December and March/April) and three Player of the Week selections – League leading totals in both categories.

1991-92 Pro Set/NHL Award Winners

Player of the Week

Week Ending	Player	Team	Youth Hockey Organization
October 13	**Kirk McLean**	Vancouver	Semiahmoo Minor Hockey Association (B.C.)
October 20	**Pat Verbeek**	Hartford	Petrolia Minor Hockey Association (Ont.)
October 27	**Chris Terreri**	New Jersey	Warwick Junior Hockey Association (RI)
November 3	**Luc Robitaille**	Los Angeles	Los Angeles Kings Hockey Camp and Skate with the Stars (CA)
November 10	**Brett Hull**	St. Louis	Creve Coeur Youth Hockey Learn to Play (MO)
November 17	**Bob Essensa**	Winnipeg	Winnipeg Minor Hockey Association (Man.)
November 24	**Claude Lemieux**	New Jersey	New Jersey Devils Youth Hockey League (NJ)
December 1	**Mario Lemieux**	Pittsburgh	Pittsburgh Amateur Hockey Association (PA)
December 8	**Jeremy Roenick**	Chicago	Amateur Hockey Association of Illinois (IL)
December 15	**Ray Ferraro**	NY Islanders	Long Island Minor Hockey League (NY) and Trail Minor Hockey Association (B.C.)
December 22	**Patrick Roy**	Montreal	Pierrefonds Minor Hockey Association (Que.)
December 29	**Mario Lemieux**	Pittsburgh	Pittsburgh Amateur Hockey Association (PA)
January 5	**Valeri Zelepukin**	New Jersey	New Jersey Devils Youth Hockey League (NJ)
January 12	**Pat Lafontaine**	Buffalo	Hamberg Municipal Youth Hockey (NY)
January 19	**Brent Gilchrist**	Montreal	Vernon Minor Hockey Association (B.C.)
January 26	**Pat Lafontaine**	Buffalo	Grand Niagara Youth Hockey (NY)
February 2	**Bob Essensa**	Winnipeg	Winnipeg Minor Hockey Association (Man.)
February 9	**Luc Robitaille**	Los Angeles	Los Angeles Hockey Camp (CA)
February 16	**Curtis Joseph**	St. Louis	East Gwillumbury Youth Hockey (Ont.)
February 23	**Tim Cheveldae**	Detroit	Melville Minor Sports Association (Sask.)
March 1	**Bill Ranford**	Edmonton	Red Deer Minor Hockey Association (Alta.)
March 8	**Mats Sundin**	Quebec	Federation Quebecois de Hockey sur Glace (Que.)
March 15	**Kay Whitmore**	Hartford	Sudbury Minor Hockey Association (Ont.)
March 22	**Mark Messier**	NY Rangers	Hockey in Harlem (NY)
March 29	**Mario Lemieux**	Pittsburgh	Pittsburgh Amateur Hockey Association (PA)
April 16	**Sergei Makarov**	Calgary	Eston Minor Hockey Association (Sask.)

Player of the Month

Month	Player	Team	Youth Hockey Recipient
October	**Kirk McLean**	Vancouver	Semiahmoo Minor Hockey Association (B.C.)
November	**Kevin Stevens**	Pittsburgh	Pembroke Youth Hockey Association (MA)
December	**Mario Lemieux**	Pittsburgh	Pittsburgh Amateur Hockey Association (PA)
January	**Andy Moog**	Boston	Penticton Minor Hockey Association (B.C.)
	Pat Lafontaine	Buffalo	Regals/Saints/West Seneca Hockey (NY)
February	**Luc Robitaille**	Los Angeles	Los Angeles Kings Hockey Camp(CA)
March/April	**Mario Lemieux**	Pittsburgh	Pittsburgh Amateur Hockey Association (PA)

Player of the Year

Year	Player	Team	Youth Hockey Recipient
1991-92	**Mario Lemieux**	Pittsburgh	Pittsburgh Amateur Hockey Association (PA)

1991-92 Upper Deck/NHL Rookie of the Month Award

Month	Player	Team	Charitable Organization
October	**Tony Amonte**	NY Rangers	Ice Hockey in Harlem
November	**Nicklas Lidstrom**	Detroit	Goodfellow Fund of Detroit
December	**Nicklas Lidstrom**	Detroit	Leader Dogs for the Blind
January	**Valeri Zelepukin**	New Jersey	St. Jude's Childrens Hospital
February	**Gilbert Dionne**	Montreal	Drummondville Minor Hockey Assoc.
March/April	**Pavel Bure**	Vancouver	Canuck Foundation

NATIONAL HOCKEY LEAGUE INDIVIDUAL AWARD WINNERS

ART ROSS TROPHY

	Winner	Runner-up
1992	Mario Lemieux, Pit.	Kevin Stevens, Pit.
1991	Wayne Gretzky, L.A.	Brett Hull, St.L.
1990	Wayne Gretzky, L.A.	Mark Messier, Edm.
1989	Mario Lemieux, Pit.	Wayne Gretzky, L.A.
1988	Mario Lemieux, Pit.	Wayne Gretzky, Edm.
1987	Wayne Gretzky, Edm.	Jari Kurri, Edm.
1986	Wayne Gretzky, Edm.	Mario Lemieux, Pit.
1985	Wayne Gretzky, Edm.	Jari Kurri, Edm.
1984	Wayne Gretzky, Edm.	Paul Coffey, Edm.
1983	Wayne Gretzky, Edm.	Peter Stastny, Que.
1982	Wayne Gretzky, Edm.	Mike Bossy, NYI
1981	Wayne Gretzky, Edm.	Marcel Dionne, L.A.
1980	Marcel Dionne, L.A.	Wayne Gretzky, Edm.
1979	Bryan Trottier, NYI	Marcel Dionne, L.A.
1978	Guy Lafleur, Mtl.	Bryan Trottier, NYI
1977	Guy Lafleur, Mtl.	Marcel Dionne, L.A.
1976	Guy Lafleur, Mtl.	Bobby Clarke, Phi.
1975	Bobby Orr, Bos.	Phil Esposito, Bos.
1974	Phil Esposito, Bos.	Bobby Orr, Bos.
1973	Phil Esposito, Bos.	Bobby Clarke, Phi.
1972	Phil Esposito, Bos.	Bobby Orr, Bos.
1971	Phil Esposito, Bos.	Bobby Orr, Bos.
1970	Bobby Orr, Bos.	Phil Esposito, Bos.
1969	Phil Esposito, Bos.	Bobby Hull, Chi.
1968	Stan Mikita, Chi.	Phil Esposito, Bos.
1967	Stan Mikita, Chi.	Bobby Hull, Chi.
1966	Bobby Hull, Chi.	Stan Mikita, Chi.
1965	Stan Mikita, Chi.	Norm Ullman, Det.
1964	Stan Mikita, Chi.	Bobby Hull, Chi.
1963	Gordie Howe, Det.	Andy Bathgate, NYR
1962	Bobby Hull, Chi.	Andy Bathgate, NYR
1961	Bernie Geoffrion, Mtl.	Jean Beliveau, Mtl.
1960	Bobby Hull, Chi.	Bronco Horvath, Bos.
1959	Dickie Moore, Mtl.	Jean Beliveau, Mtl.
1958	Dickie Moore, Mtl.	Henri Richard, Mtl.
1957	Gordie Howe, Det.	Ted Lindsay, Det.
1956	Jean Beliveau, Mtl.	Gordie Howe, Det.
1955	Bernie Geoffrion, Mtl.	Maurice Richard, Mtl.
1954	Gordie Howe, Det.	Maurice Richard, Mtl.
1953	Gordie Howe, Det.	Ted Lindsay, Det.
1952	Gordie Howe, Det.	Ted Lindsay, Det.
1951	Gordie Howe, Det.	Maurice Richard, Mtl.
1950	Ted Lindsay, Det.	Sid Abel, Det.
1949	Roy Conacher, Chi.	Doug Bentley, Chi.
1948	Elmer Lach, Mtl.	Buddy O'Connor, NYR
1947*	Max Bentley, Chi.	Maurice Richard, Mtl.
1946	Max Bentley, Chi.	Gaye Stewart, Tor.
1945	Elmer Lach, Mtl.	Maurice Richard, Mtl.
1944	Herbie Cain, Bos.	Doug Bentley, Chi.
1943	Doug Bentley, Chi.	Bill Cowley, Bos.
1942	Bryan Hextall, NYR	Lynn Patrick, NYR
1941	Bill Cowley, Bos.	Bryan Hextall, NYR
1940	Milt Schmidt, Bos.	Woody Dumart, Bos.
1939	Toe Blake, Mtl.	Dave Schriner, NYA
1938	Gordie Drillon, Tor.	Syl Apps, Tor.
1937	Dave Schriner, NYA	Syl Apps, Tor.
1936	Dave Schriner, NYA	Marty Barry, Det.
1935	Charlie Conacher, Tor.	Syd Howe, St.L-Det.
1934	Charlie Conacher, Tor.	Joe Primeau, Tor
1933	Bill Cook, NYR	Harvey Jackson, Tor.
1932	Harvey Jackson, Tor.	Joe Primeau, Tor.
1931	Howie Morenz, Mtl.	Ebbie Goodfellow, Det.
1930	Cooney Weiland, Bos.	Frank Boucher, NYR
1929	Ace Bailey, Tor.	Nels Stewart, Mtl.M
1928	Howie Morenz, Mtl.	Aurel Joliat, Mtl.
1927	Bill Cook, NYR	Dick Irvin, Chi.
1926	Nels Stewart, Mtl.M.	Cy Denneny, Ott.
1925	Babe Dye, Tor.	Cy Denneny, Ott.
1924	Cy Denneny, Ott.	Billy Boucher, Mtl.
1923	Babe Dye, Tor.	Cy Denneny, Ott.
1922	Punch Broadbent, Ott.	Cy Denneny, Ott.
1921	Newsy Lalonde, Mtl.	Cy Denneny, Ott.
1920	Joe Malone, Que.	Newsy Lalonde, Mtl.
1919	Newsy Lalonde, Mtl.	Odie Cleghorn, Mtl.
1918	Joe Malone, Mtl.	Cy Denneny, Ott.

* Scoring leader prior to inception of Art Ross Trophy in 1947-48

FRANK J. SELKE TROPHY WINNERS

	Winner	Runner-up
1992	Guy Carbonneau, Mtl.	Sergei Fedorov, Det.
1991	Dirk Graham, Chi.	Esa Tikkanen, Edm.
1990	Rick Meagher, St.L.	Guy Carbonneau, Mtl.
1989	Guy Carbonneau, Mtl.	Esa Tikkanen, Edm.
1988	Guy Carbonneau, Mtl.	Steve Kasper, Bos.
1987	Dave Poulin, Phi.	Guy Carbonneau, Mtl.
1986	Troy Murray, Chi.	Ron Sutter, Phi.
1985	Craig Ramsay, Buf.	Doug Jarvis, Wsh.
1984	Doug Jarvis, Wsh.	Bryan Trottier, NYI
1983	Bobby Clarke, Phi.	Jari Kurri, Edm.
1982	Steve Kasper, Bos.	Bob Gainey, Mtl.
1981	Bob Gainey, Mtl.	Craig Ramsay, Buf.
1980	Bob Gainey, Mtl.	Craig Ramsay, Buf.
1979	Bob Gainey, Mtl.	Don Marcotte, Bos.
1978	Bob Gainey, Mtl.	Craig Ramsay, Buf.

HART TROPHY

	Winner	Runner-up
1992	Mark Messier, NYR	Patrick Roy, Mtl.
1991	Brett Hull, St.L.	Wayne Gretzky, L.A.
1990	Mark Messier, Edm.	Ray Bourque, Bos.
1989	Wayne Gretzky, L.A.	Mario Lemieux, Pit.
1988	Mario Lemieux, Pit.	Grant Fuhr, Edm.
1987	Wayne Gretzky, Edm.	Ray Bourque, Bos.
1986	Wayne Gretzky, Edm.	Mario Lemieux, Pit.
1985	Wayne Gretzky, Edm.	Dale Hawerchuk, Wpg.
1984	Wayne Gretzky, Edm.	Rod Langway, Wsh.
1983	Wayne Gretzky, Edm.	Pete Peeters, Bos.
1982	Wayne Gretzky, Edm.	Bryan Trottier, NYI
1981	Wayne Gretzky, Edm.	Mike Liut, St.L.
1980	Wayne Gretzky, Edm.	Marcel Dionne, L.A.
1979	Bryan Trottier, NYI	Guy Lafleur, Mtl
1978	Guy Lafleur, Mtl.	Bryan Trottier, NYI
1977	Guy Lafleur, Mtl.	Bobby Clarke, Phi.
1976	Bobby Clarke, Phi.	Denis Potvin, NYI
1975	Bobby Clarke, Phi.	Rogatien Vachon, L.A.
1974	Phil Esposito, Bos.	Bernie Parent, Phi.
1973	Bobby Clarke, Phi.	Phil Esposito, Bos.
1972	Bobby Orr, Bos.	Ken Dryden, Mtl.
1971	Bobby Orr, Bos.	Phil Esposito, Bos.
1970	Bobby Orr, Bos.	Tony Esposito, Chi.
1969	Phil Esposito, Bos.	Jean Beliveau, Mtl.
1968	Stan Mikita, Chi.	Jean Beliveau, Mtl.
1967	Stan Mikita, Chi.	Ed Giacomin, NYR
1966	Bobby Hull, Chi.	Jean Beliveau, Mtl.
1965	Bobby Hull, Chi.	Norm Ullman, Det.
1964	Jean Beliveau, Mtl.	Bobby Hull, Chi.
1963	Gordie Howe, Det.	Stan Mikita, Chi.
1962	Jacques Plante, Mtl.	Doug Harvey, NYR
1961	Bernie Geoffrion, Mtl.	Johnny Bower, Tor.
1960	Gordie Howe, Det.	Bobby Hull, Chi.
1959	Andy Bathgate, NYR	Gordie Howe, Det.
1958	Gordie Howe, Det.	Andy Bathgate, NYR
1957	Gordie Howe, Det.	Jean Beliveau, Mtl.
1956	Jean Beliveau, Mtl.	Tod Sloan, Tor.
1955	Ted Kennedy, Tor.	Harry Lumley, Tor.
1954	Al Rollins, Chi.	Red Kelly, Det.
1953	Gordie Howe, Det.	Al Rollins, Chi.
1952	Gordie Howe, Det.	Elmer Lach, Mtl.
1951	Milt Schmidt, Bos.	Maurice Richard, Mtl.
1950	Charlie Rayner, NYR	Ted Kennedy, Tor.
1949	Sid Abel, Det.	Bill Durnan, Mtl.
1948	Buddy O'Connor, NYR	Frank Brimsek, Bos.
1947	Maurice Richard, Mtl.	Milt Schmidt, Bos.
1946	Max Bentley, Chi.	Gaye Stewart, Tor.
1945	Elmer Lach, Mtl.	Maurice Richard, Mtl.
1944	Babe Pratt, Tor.	Bill Cowley, Bos.
1943	Bill Cowley, Bos.	Doug Bentley, Chi.
1942	Tom Anderson, Bro.	Syl Apps, Tor.
1941	Bill Cowley, Bos.	Dit Clapper, Bos.
1940	Ebbie Goodfellow, Det.	Syl Apps, Tor.
1939	Toe Blake, Mtl.	Syl Apps, Tor.
1938	Eddie Shore, Bos.	Paul Thompson, Chi.
1937	Babe Siebert, Mtl.	Lionel Conacher, Mtl.M
1936	Eddie Shore, Bos.	Hooley Smith, Mtl.M
1935	Eddie Shore, Bos.	Charlie Conacher, Tor.
1934	Aurel Joliat, Mtl.	Lionel Conacher, Chi.
1933	Eddie Shore, Bos.	Bill Cook, NYR
1932	Howie Morenz, Mtl.	Ching Johnson, NYR
1931	Howie Morenz, Mtl.	Eddie Shore, Bos.
1930	Nels Stewart, Mtl.M.	Lionel Hitchman, Bos.
1929	Roy Worters, NYA	Ace Bailey, Tor.
1928	Howie Morenz, Mtl.	Roy Worters, Pit.
1927	Herb Gardiner, Mtl.	Bill Cook, NYR
1926	Nels Stewart, Mtl.M.	Sprague Cleghorn, Bos.
1925	Billy Burch, Ham.	Howie Morenz, Mtl.
1924	Frank Nighbor, Ott.	Sprague Cleghorn, Mtl.

LESTER B. PEARSON AWARD WINNERS

1992	Mark Messier	NY Rangers
1991	Brett Hull	St. Louis
1990	Mark Messier	Edmonton
1989	Steve Yzerman	Detroit
1988	Mario Lemieux	Pittsburgh
1987	Wayne Gretzky	Edmonton
1986	Mario Lemieux	Pittsburgh
1985	Wayne Gretzky	Edmonton
1984	Wayne Gretzky	Edmonton
1983	Wayne Gretzky	Edmonton
1982	Wayne Gretzky	Edmonton
1981	Mike Liut	St. Louis
1980	Marcel Dionne	Los Angeles
1979	Marcel Dionne	Los Angeles
1978	Guy Lafleur	Montreal
1977	Guy Lafleur	Montreal
1976	Guy Lafleur	Montreal
1975	Bobby Orr	Boston
1974	Phil Esposito	Boston
1973	Bobby Clarke	Philadelphia
1972	Jean Ratelle	NY Rangers
1971	Phil Esposito	Boston

LADY BYNG TROPHY

	Winner	Runner-up
1992	Wayne Gretzky, L.A.	Joe Sakic, Que.
1991	Wayne Gretzky, L.A.	Brett Hull, St.L.
1990	Brett Hull, St.L.	Wayne Gretzky, L.A.
1989	Joe Mullen, Cgy.	Wayne Gretzky, L.A.
1988	Mats Naslund, Mtl.	Wayne Gretzky, Edm.
1987	Joe Mullen, Cgy.	Wayne Gretzky, Edm.
1986	Mike Bossy, NYI	Jari Kurri, Edm.
1985	Jari Kurri, Edm.	Joe Mullen, St.L.
1984	Mike Bossy, NYI	Rick Middleton, Bos.
1983	Mike Bossy, NYI	Rick Middleton, Bos.
1982	Rick Middleton, Bos.	Mike Bossy, NYI
1981	Rick Kehoe, Pit.	Wayne Gretzky, Edm.
1980	Wayne Gretzky, Edm.	Marcel Dionne, L.A.
1979	Bob MacMillan, Atl.	Marcel Dionne, L.A.
1978	Butch Goring, L.A.	Peter McNab, Bos.
1977	Marcel Dionne, L.A.	Jean Ratelle, Bos.
1976	Jean Ratelle, NYR-Bos.	Jean Pronovost, Pit.
1975	Marcel Dionne, Det.	John Bucyk, Bos.
1974	John Bucyk, Bos.	Lowell MacDonald, Pit.
1973	Gilbert Perreault, Buf.	Jean Ratelle, NYR
1972	Jean Ratelle, NYR	John Bucyk, Bos.
1971	John Bucyk, Bos.	Dave Keon, Tor.
1970	Phil Goyette, St.L.	John Bucyk, Bos.
1969	Alex Delvecchio, Det.	Ted Hampson, Oak.
1968	Stan Mikita, Chi.	John Bucyk, Bos.
1967	Stan Mikita, Chi.	Dave Keon, Tor.
1966	Alex Delvecchio, Det.	Bobby Rousseau, Mtl.
1965	Bobby Hull, Chi.	Alex Delvecchio, Det.
1964	Ken Wharram, Chi.	Dave Keon, Tor.
1963	Dave Keon, Tor.	Camille Henry, NYR
1962	Dave Keon, Tor.	Claude Provost, Mtl.
1961	Red Kelly, Tor.	Norm Ullman, Det.
1960	Don McKenney, Bos.	Andy Hebenton, NYR
1959	Alex Delvecchio, Det.	Andy Hebenton, NYR
1958	Camille Henry, NYR	Don Marshall, Mtl.
1957	Andy Hebenton, NYR	Earl Reibel, Det.
1956	Earl Reibel, Det.	Floyd Curry, Mtl.
1955	Sid Smith, Tor.	Danny Lewicki, NYR
1954	Red Kelly, Det.	Don Raleigh, NYR
1953	Red Kelly, Det.	Wally Hergesheimer, NYR
1952	Sid Smith, Tor.	Red Kelly, Det.
1951	Red Kelly, Det.	Woody Dumart, Bos.
1950	Edgar Laprade, NYR	Red Kelly, Det.
1949	Bill Quackenbush, Det.	Harry Watson, Tor.
1948	Buddy O'Connor, NYR	Syl Aps, Tor.
1947	Bobby Bauer, Bos.	Syl Apps, Tor.
1946	Toe Blake, Mtl.	Clint Smith, Chi.
1945	Bill Mosienko, Chi.	Syd Howe, Det.
1944	Clint Smith, Chi.	Herb Cain, Bos.
1943	Max Bentley, Chi.	Buddy O'Connor, Mtl.
1942	Syl Apps, Tor.	Gordie Drillon, Tor.
1941	Bobby Bauer, Bos.	Gordie Drillon, Tor.
1940	Bobby Bauer, Bos.	Clint Smith, NYR
1939	Clint Smith, NYR	Marty Barry, Det.
1938	Gordie Drillon, Tor.	Clint Smith, NYR
1937	Marty Barry, Det.	Gordie Drillon, Tor.
1936	Doc Romnes, Chi.	Dave Schriner, NYA
1935	Frank Boucher, NYR	Russ Blinco, Mtl.M
1934	Frank Boucher, NYR	Joe Primeau, Tor.
1933	Frank Boucher, NYR	Joe Primeau, Tor.
1932	Joe Primeau, Tor.	Frank Boucher, NYR
1931	Frank Boucher, NYR	Normie Himes, NYA
1930	Frank Boucher, NYR	Normie Himes, NYA
1929	Frank Boucher, NYR	Harry Darragh, Pit.

CONN SMYTHE TROPHY WINNERS

1992	Mario Lemieux	Pittsburgh
1991	Mario Lemieux	Pittsburgh
1990	Bill Ranford	Edmonton
1989	Al MacInnis	Calgary
1988	Wayne Gretzky	Edmonton
1987	Ron Hextall	Philadelphia
1986	Patrick Roy	Montreal
1985	Wayne Gretzky	Edmonton
1984	Mark Messier	Edmonton
1983	Bill Smith	NY Islanders
1982	Mike Bossy	NY Islanders
1981	Butch Goring	NY Islanders
1980	Bryan Trottier	NY Islanders
1979	Bob Gainey	Montreal
1978	Larry Robinson	Montreal
1977	Guy Lafleur	Montreal
1976	Reggie Leach	Philadelphia
1975	Bernie Parent	Philadelphia
1974	Bernie Parent	Philadelphia
1973	Yvan Cournoyer	Montreal
1972	Bobby Orr	Boston
1971	Ken Dryden	Montreal
1970	Bobby Orr	Boston
1969	Serge Savard	Montreal
1968	Glenn Hall	St. Louis
1967	Dave Keon	Toronto
1966	Roger Crozier	Detroit
1965	Jean Béliveau	Montreal

VEZINA TROPHY

	Winner	Runner-up
1992	Patrick Roy, Mtl.	Kirk McLean, Van.
1991	Ed Belfour, Chi.	Patrick Roy, Mtl.
1990	Patrick Roy, Mtl.	Daren Puppa, Buf.
1989	Patrick Roy, Mtl.	Mike Vernon, Cgy.
1988	Grant Fuhr, Edm.	Tom Barrasso, Buf.
1987	Ron Hextall, Phi.	Mike Liut, Hfd.
1986	John Vanbiesbrouck, NYR	Bob Froese, Phi.
1985	Pelle Lindbergh, Phi.	Tom Barrasso, Buf.
1984	Tom Barrasso, Buf.	Rejean Lemelin, Cgy.
1983	Pete Peeters, Bos.	Roland Melanson, NYI
1982	Bill Smith, NYI	Grant Fuhr, Edm.
1981	Richard Sevigny, Mtl.	Pete Peeters, Phi.
	Denis Herron, Mtl.	Rick St. Croix, Phi.
	Michel Larocque, Mtl.	
1980	Bob Sauve, Buf.	Gerry Cheevers, Bos.
	Don Edwards, Buf.	Gilles Gilbert, Bos.
1979	Ken Dryden, Mtl.	Glenn Resch, NYI
	Michel Larocque, Mtl.	Bill Smith, NYI
1978	Ken Dryden, Mtl.	Bernie Parent, Phi.
	Michel Larocque	Wayne Stephenson, Phi.
1977	Ken Dryden, Mtl.	Glenn Resch, NYI
	Michel Larocque, Mtl.	Bill Smith, NYI
1976	Ken Dryden, Mtl.	Glenn Resch, NYI
		Bill Smith, NYI
1975	Bernie Parent, Phi.	Rogie Vachon, L.A.
		Gary Edwards, L.A.
1974	Bernie Parent, Phi. (tie)	Gilles Gilbert, Bos.
	Tony Esposito, Chi. (tie)	
1973	Ken Dryden, Mtl.	Ed Giacomin, NYR
		Gilles Villemure, NYR
1972	Tony Esposito, Chi.	Cesare Maniago, Min.
	Gary Smith, Chi.	Lorne Worsley, Min.
1971	Ed Giacomin, NYR	Tony Esposito, Chi.
	Gilles Villemure, NYR	
1970	Tony Esposito, Chi.	Jacques Plante, St.L.
		Ernie Wakely, St.L.
1969	Jacques Plante, St.L.	Ed Giacomin, NYR
	Glenn Hall, St.L.	
1968	Lorne Worsley, Mtl.	Johnny Bower, Tor.
	Rogatien Vachon, Mtl.	Bruce Gamble, Tor.
1967	Glenn Hall, Chi.	Charlie Hodge, Mtl.
	Denis Dejordy, Chi.	
1966	Lorne Worsley, Mtl.	Glenn Hall, Chi.
	Charlie Hodge, Mtl.	
1965	Terry Sawchuk, Tor.	Roger Crozier, Det.
	Johnny Bower, Tor.	
1964	Charlie Hodge, Mtl.	Glenn Hall, Chi.
1963	Glenn Hall, Chi.	Johnny Bower, Tor.
		Don Simmons, Tor.
1962	Jacques Plante, Mtl.	Johnny Bower, Tor.
1961	Johnny Bower, Tor.	Glenn Hall, Chi.
1960	Jacques Plante, Mtl.	Glenn Hall, Chi.
1959	Jacques Plante, Mtl.	Johnny Bower, Tor.
		Ed Chadwick, Tor.
1958	Jacques Plante, Mtl.	Lorne Worsley, NYR
		Marcel Paille, NYR
1957	Jacques Plante, Mtl.	Glenn Hall, Det.
1956	Jacques Plante, Mtl.	Glenn Hall, Det.
1955	Terry Sawchuk, Det.	Harry Lumley, Tor.
1954	Harry Lumley, Tor.	Terry Sawchuk, Det.
1953	Terry Sawchuk, Det.	Gerry McNeil, Mtl.
1952	Terry Sawchuk, Det.	Al Rollins, Tor.
1951	Al Rollins, Tor.	Terry Sawchuk, Det.
1950	Bill Durnan, Mtl.	Harry Lumley, Det.
1949	Bill Durnan, Mtl.	Harry Lumley, Det.
1948	Turk Broda, Tor.	Harry Lumley, Det.
1947	Bill Durnan, Mtl.	Turk Broda, Tor.
1946	Bill Durnan, Mtl.	Frank Brimsek, Bos.
1945	Bill Durnan, Mtl.	Frank McCool, Tor. (tie)
		Harry Lumley, Det. (tie)
1944	Bill Durnan, Mtl.	Paul Bibeault, Tor.
1943	Johnny Mowers, Det.	Turk Broda, Tor.
1942	Frank Brimsek, Bos.	Turk Broda, Tor.
1941	Turk Broda, Tor.	Frank Brimsek, Bos. (tie)
		Johnny Mowers, Det. (tie)
1940	Dave Kerr, NYR	Frank Brimsek, Bos.
1939	Frank Brimsek, Bos.	Dave Kerr, NYR
1938	Tiny Thompson, Bos.	Dave Kerr, NYR
1937	Normie Smith, Det.	Dave Kerr, NYR
1936	Tiny Thompson, Bos.	Mike Karakas, Chi.
1935	Lorne Chabot, Chi.	Alex Connell, Mtl.M
1934	Charlie Gardiner, Chi.	Wilf Cude, Det.
1933	Tiny Thompson, Bos.	John Roach, Det.
1932	Charlie Gardiner, Chi.	Alex Connell, Det.
1931	Roy Worters, NYA	Charlie Gardiner, Chi.
1930	Tiny Thompson, Bos.	Charlie Gardiner, Chi.
1929	George Hainsworth, Mtl.	Tiny Thompson, Bos.
1928	George Hainsworth, Mtl.	Alex Connell, Ott.
1927	George Hainsworth, Mtl.	Clint Benedict, Mtl.M

KING CLANCY MEMORIAL TROPHY WINNERS

1992	Ray Bourque	Boston
1991	Dave Taylor	Los Angeles
1990	Kevin Lowe	Edmonton
1989	Bryan Trottier	NY Islanders
1988	Lanny McDonald	Calgary

Six members of the 1965 Detroit Red Wings, left to right, Ed Joyal, Norm Ullman, Paul Henderson, Alex Delvecchio, Coach Sid Abel and Calder Trophy winner Roger Crozier celebrate the Wings' clinching of the regular-season crown after defeating the Rangers 7-4 on March 25, 1965.

CALDER MEMORIAL TROPHY WINNERS

	Winner	Runner-up
1992	Pavel Bure, Van.	Nicklas Lidstrom, Det
1991	Ed Belfour, Chi.	Sergei Fedorov, Det.
1990	Sergei Makarov, Cgy.	Mike Modano, Min.
1989	Brian Leetch, NYR	Trevor Linden, Van.
1988	Joe Nieuwendyk, Cgy.	Ray Sheppard, Buf.
1987	Luc Robitaille, L.A.	Ron Hextall, Phi.
1986	Gary Suter, Cgy.	Wendel Clark, Tor.
1985	Mario Lemieux, Pit.	Chris Chelios, Mtl.
1984	Tom Barrasso, Buf.	Steve Yzerman, Det.
1983	Steve Larmer, Chi.	Phil Housley, Buf.
1982	Dale Hawerchuk, Wpg.	Barry Pederson, Bos.
1981	Peter Stastny, Que.	Larry Murphy, L.A.
1980	Ray Bourque, Bos.	Mike Foligno, Det.
1979	Bobby Smith, Min	Ryan Walter, Wsh.
1978	Mike Bossy, NYI	Barry Beck, Col.
1977	Willi Plett, Atl.	Don Murdoch, NYR
1976	Bryan Trottier, NYI	Glenn Resch, NYI
1975	Eric Vail, Atl.	Pierre Larouche, Pit.
1974	Denis Potvin, NYI	Tom Lysiak, Atl.
1973	Steve Vickers, NYR	Bill Barber, Phi.
1972	Ken Dryden, Mtl.	Rick Martin, Buf.
1971	Gilbert Perreault, Buf.	Jude Drouin, Min.
1970	Tony Esposito, Chi.	Bill Fairbairn, NYR
1969	Danny Grant, Min.	Norm Ferguson, Oak.
1968	Derek Sanderson, Bos.	Jacques Lemaire, Mtl.
1967	Bobby Orr, Bos.	Ed Van Impe, Chi.
1966	Brit Selby, Tor.	Bert Marshall, Det.
1965	Roger Crozier, Det.	Ron Ellis, Tor.
1964	Jacques Laperriere, Mtl.	John Ferguson, Mtl.
1963	Kent Douglas, Tor.	Doug Barkley, Det.
1962	Bobby Rousseu, Mtl.	Cliff Pennington, Bos.
1961	Dave Keon, Tor.	Bob Nevin, Tor.
1960	Bill Hay, Chi.	Murray Oliver, Det.
1959	Ralph Backstrom, Mtl.	Carl Brewer, Tor.
1958	Frank Mahovlich, Tor.	Bobby Hull, Chi.
1957	Larry Regan, Bos.	Ed Chadwick, Tor.
1956	Glenn Hall, Det.	Andy Hebenton, NYR
1955	Ed Litzenberger, Chi.	Don McKenney, Bos.
1954	Camille Henry, NYR	Earl Reibel, Det.
1953	Lorne Worsley, NYR	Gordie Hannigan, Tor.
1952	Bernie Geoffrion, Mtl.	Hy Buller, NYR
1951	Terry Sawchuk, Det.	Al Rollins, Tor.
1950	Jack Gelineau, Bos.	Phil Maloney, Bos.
1949	Pentti Lund, NYR	Allan Stanley, NYR
1948	Jim McFadden, Det.	Pete Babando, Bos.
1947	Howie Meeker, Tor.	Jimmy Conacher, Det.
1946	Edgar Laprade, NYR	George Gee, Chi.
1945	Frank McCool, Tor.	Ken Smith, Bos.
1944	Gus Bodnar, Tor.	Bill Durnan, Mtl.
1943	Gaye Stewart, Tor.	Glen Harmon, Mtl.
1942	Grant Warwick, NYR	Buddy O'Connor, Mtl.
1941	Johnny Quilty, Mtl.	Johnny Mowers, Det.
1940	Kilby MacDonald, NYR	Wally Stanowski, Tor.
1939	Frank Brimsek, Bos.	Roy Conacher, Bos.
1938	Cully Dahlstrom, Chi.	Murph Chamberlain, Tor.
1937	Syl Apps, Tor.	Gordie Drillon, Tor.
1936	Mike Karakas, Chi.	Bucko McDonald, Det.
1935	Dave Schriner, NYA	Bert Connolly, NYR
1934	Russ Blinko, Mtl.M.	
1933	Carl Voss, Det.	

JAMES NORRIS TROPHY WINNERS

	Winner	Runner-up
1992	Brian Leetch, NYR	Ray Bourque, Bos.
1991	Ray Bourque, Bos.	Al MacInnis, Cgy.
1990	Ray Bourque, Bos.	Al MacInnis, Cgy.
1989	Chris Chelios, Mtl	Paul Coffey, Pit.
1988	Ray Bourque, Bos.	Scott Stevens, Wsh.
1987	Ray Bourque, Bos.	Mark Howe, Phi.
1986	Paul Coffey, Edm.	Mark Howe, Phi.
1985	Paul Coffey, Edm.	Ray Bourque, Bos.
1984	Rod Langway, Wsh.	Paul Coffey, Edm.
1983	Rod Langway, Wsh.	Mark Howe, Phi.
1982	Doug Wilson, Chi.	Ray Bourque, Bos.
1981	Randy Carlyle, Pit.	Denis Potvin, NYI
1980	Larry Robinson, Mtl.	Borje Salming, Tor.
1979	Denis Potvin, NYI	Larry Robinson, Mtl.
1978	Denis Potvin, NYI	Brad Park, Bos.
1977	Larry Robinson, Mtl.	Borje Salming, Tor.
1976	Denis Potvin, NYI	Brad Park, NYR-Bos.
1975	Bobby Orr, Bos.	Denis Potvin, NYI
1974	Bobby Orr, Bos.	Brad Park, NYR
1973	Bobby Orr, Bos.	Guy Lapointe, Mtl.
1972	Bobby Orr, Bos.	Brad Park, NYR
1971	Bobby Orr, Bos.	Brad Park, NYR
1970	Bobby Orr, Bos.	Brad Park, NYR
1969	Bobby Orr, Bos.	Tim Horton, Tor.
1968	Bobby Orr, Bos.	J.C. Tremblay, Mtl
1967	Harry Howell, NYR	Pierre Pilote, Chi.
1966	Jacques Laperriere, Mtl.	Pierre Pilote, Chi.
1965	Pierre Pilote, Chi.	Jacques Laperriere, Mtl.
1964	Pierre Pilote, Chi.	Tim Horton, Tor.
1963	Pierre Pilote, Chi.	Carl Brewer, Tor.
1962	Doug Harvey, NYR	Pierre Pilote, Chi.
1961	Doug Harvey, Mtl.	Marcel Pronovost, Det.
1960	Doug Harvey, Mtl.	Allan Stanley, Tor.
1959	Tom Johnson, Mtl.	Bill Gadsby, NYR
1958	Doug Harvey, Mtl.	Bill Gadsby, NYR
1957	Doug Harvey, Mtl.	Red Kelly, Det.
1956	Doug Harvey, Mtl.	Bill Gadsby, NYR
1955	Doug Harvey, Mtl.	Red Kelly, Det.
1954	Red Kelly, Det.	Doug Harvey, Mtl.

JACK ADAMS AWARD WINNERS

	Winner	Runner-up
1992	Pat Quinn, Van.	Roger Neilson, NYR
1991	Brian Sutter, St.L.	Tom Webster, L.A.
1990	Bob Murdoch, Wpg.	Mike Milbury, Bos.
1989	Pat Burns, Mtl.	Bob McCammon, Van.
1988	Jacques Demers, Det.	Terry Crisp, Cgy.
1987	Jacques Demers, Det.	Jack Evans, Hfd.
1986	Glen Sather, Edm.	Jacques Demers, St.L.
1985	Mike Keenan, Phi.	Barry Long, Wpg.
1984	Bryan Murray, Wsh.	Scott Bowman, Buf.
1983	Orval Tessier, Chi.	
1982	Tom Watt, Wpg.	
1981	Red Berenson, St.L.	Bob Berry, L.A.
1980	Pat Quinn, Phi.	
1979	Al Arbour, NYI	Fred Shero, NYR
1978	Bobby Kromm, Det.	Don Cherry, Bos.
1977	Scott Bowman, Mtl.	Tom McVie, Wsh.
1976	Don Cherry, Bos.	
1975	Bob Pulford, L.A.	
1974	Fred Shero, Phi.	

LESTER PATRICK TROPHY WINNERS

1992 Al Arbour
Art Berglund
Lou Lamoriello
1991 Rod Gilbert
Mike Illitch
1990 Len Ceglarski
1989 Dan Kelly
Lou Nanne
*Lynn Patrick
Bud Poile
1988 Keith Allen
Fred Cusick
Bob Johnson
1987 *Hobey Baker
Frank Mathers
1986 John MacInnes
Jack Riley
1985 Jack Butterfield
Arthur M. Wirtz
1984 John A. Ziegler Jr.
*Arthur Howie Ross
1983 Bill Torrey
1982 Emile P. Francis
1981 Charles M. Schulz
1980 Bobby Clarke
Edward M. Snider
Frederick A. Shero
1980 U.S. Olympic Hockey Team
1979 Bobby Orr
1978 Philip A. Esposito
Tom Fitzgerald
William T. Tutt
William W. Wirtz
1977 John P. Bucyk
Murray A. Armstrong
John Mariucci
1976 Stanley Mikita
George A. Leader
Bruce A. Norris
1975 Donald M. Clark
William L. Chadwick
Thomas N. Ivan
1974 Alex Delvecchio
Murray Murdoch
*Weston W. Adams, Sr.
*Charles L. Crovat
1973 Walter L. Bush, Jr.
1972 Clarence S. Campbell
John Kelly
Ralph "Cooney" Weiland
*James D. Norris
1971 William M. Jennings
*John B. Sollenberger
*Terrance G. Sawchuk
1970 Edward W. Shore
*James C. V. Hendy
1969 Robert M. Hull
*Edward J. Jeremiah
1968 Thomas F. Lockhart
*Walter A. Brown
*Gen. John R. Kilpatrick
1967 Gordon Howe
*Charles F. Adams
*James Norris, Sr.
1966 J.J. "Jack" Adams

* awarded posthumously

BUD MAN OF THE YEAR AWARD WINNERS

1992	Ryan Walter	Vancouver
1991	Kevin Dineen	Hartford
1990	Kevin Lowe	Edmonton
1989	Lanny McDonald	Calgary
1988	Bryan Trottier	NY Islanders

PRO SET/NHL PLAYER OF THE YEAR

1992	Mario Lemieux	Pittsburgh
1991	Brett Hull	St. Louis

ALKA-SELTZER PLUS AWARD WINNERS

1992	Paul Ysebaert	Detroit
1991	Marty McSorley	Los Angeles
	Theoren Fleury	Calgary
1990	Paul Cavallini	St. Louis

BILL MASTERTON TROPHY WINNERS

1992	Mark Fitzpatrick	NY Islanders
1991	Dave Taylor	Los Angeles
1990	Gord Kluzak	Boston
1989	Tim Kerr	Philadelphia
1988	Bob Bourne	Los Angeles
1987	Doug Jarvis	Hartford
1986	Charlie Simmer	Boston
1985	Anders Hedberg	NY Rangers
1984	Brad Park	Detroit
1983	Lanny McDonald	Calgary
1982	Glenn Resch	Colorado
1981	Blake Dunlop	St. Louis
1980	Al MacAdam	Minnesota
1979	Serge Savard	Montreal
1978	Butch Goring	Los Angeles
1977	Ed Westfall	NY Islanders
1976	Rod Gilbert	NY Rangers
1975	Don Luce	Buffalo
1974	Henri Richard	Montreal
1973	Lowell MacDonald	Pittsburgh
1972	Bobby Clarke	Phiiladelphia
1971	Jean Ratelle	NY Rangers
1970	Pit Martin	Chicago
1969	Ted Hampson	Oakland
1968	Claude Provost	Montreal

WILLIAM M. JENNINGS TROPHY WINNERS

	Winner	Runner-up
1992	Patrick Roy, Mtl.	Ed Belfour, Chi.
1991	Ed Belfour, Chi.	Patrick Roy, Mtl.
1990	Andy Moog, Bos.	Patrick Roy, Mtl.
	Rejean Lemelin	Brian Hayward
1989	Patrick Roy, Mtl.	Mike Vernon, Cgy.
	Brian Hayward	Rick Wamsley
1988	Patrick Roy, Mtl.	Clint Malarchuk, Wsh.
	Brian Hayward	Pete Peeters
1987	Patrick Roy, Mtl.	Ron Hextall, Phi.
	Brian Hayward	
1986	Bob Froese, Phi.	Al Jensen, Wsh.
	Darren Jensen	Pete Peeters
1985	Tom Barrasso, Buf.	Pat Riggin, Wsh.
	Bob Sauve	
1984	Al Jensen, Wsh.	Tom Barrasso, Buf.
	Pat Riggin	Bob Sauve
1983	Roland Melanson, NYI	Pete Peeters, Bos.
	Bill Smith	
1982	Rick Wamsley, Mtl.	Billy Smith, NYI
	Denis Herron	Roland Melanson

Kevin Lowe, who replaced Mark Messier as captain of the Oilers in the 1991-92 season, was the Bud Man of the Year Award winner in 1990.

NHL Amateur and Entry Draft

History

Year	Site	Date	Total Players Drafted
1963	Queen Elizabeth Hotel	June 5	21
1964	Queen Elizabeth Hotel	June 11	24
1965	Queen Elizabeth Hotel	April 27	11
1966	Mount Royal Hotel	April 25	24
1967	Queen Elizabeth Hotel	June 7	18
1968	Queen Elizabeth Hotel	June 13	24
1969	Queen Elizabeth Hotel	June 12	84
1970	Queen Elizabeth Hotel	June 11	115
1971	Queen Elizabeth Hotel	June 10	117
1972	Queen Elizabeth Hotel	June 8	152
1973	Mount Royal Hotel	May 15	168
1974	NHL Montreal Office	May 28	247
1975	NHL Montreal Office	June 3	217
1976	NHL Montreal Office	June 1	135
1977	NHL Montreal Office	June 14	185
1978	Queen Elizabeth Hotel	June 15	234
1979	Queen Elizabeth Hotel	August 9	126
1980	Montreal Forum	June 11	210
1981	Montreal Forum	June 10	211
1982	Montreal Forum	June 9	252
1983	Montreal Forum	June 8	242
1984	Montreal Forum	June 9	250
1985	Toronto Convention Centre	June 15	252
1986	Montreal Forum	June 21	252
1987	Joe Louis Sports Arena	June 13	252
1988	Montreal Forum	June 11	252
1989	Metropolitan Sports Center	June 17	252
1990	B. C. Place	June 16	250
1991	Memorial Auditorium	June 9	264
1992	Montreal Forum	June 20	264

The NHL Amateur Draft became the NHL Entry Draft in 1979

Roman Hamrlik was chosen first overall by the Tampa Bay Lightning in the 1992 NHL Entry Draft.

First Selections

Year	Player	Pos	Drafted By	Drafted From	Age
1969	Rejean Houle	LW	Montreal	Jr. Canadiens	19.8
1970	Gilbert Perreault	C	Buffalo	Jr. Canadiens	19.7
1971	Guy Lafleur	RW	Montreal	Quebec Remparts	19.9
1972	Billy Harris	RW	NY Islanders	Toronto Marlboros	20.4
1973	Denis Potvin	D	NY Islanders	Ottawa 67's	19.7
1974	Greg Joly	D	Washington	Regina Pats	20.0
1975	Mel Bridgman	C	Philadelphia	Victoria Cougars	20.1
1976	Rick Green	D	Washington	London Knights	20.3
1977	Dale McCourt	C	Detroit	St. Catharines Fincups	20.4
1978	Bobby Smith	C	Minnesota	Ottawa 67's	20.4
1979	Bob Ramage	D	Colorado	London Knights	20.5
1980	Doug Wickenheiser	C	Montreal	Regina Pats	19.2
1981	Dale Hawerchuk	C	Winnipeg	Cornwall Royals	18.2
1982	Gord Kluzak	D	Boston	Nanaimo Islanders	18.3
1983	Brian Lawton	C	Minnesota	Mount St. Charles HS	18.11
1984	Mario Lemieux	C	Pittsburgh	Laval Voisins	18.8
1985	Wendel Clark	LW/D	Toronto	Saskatoon Blades	18.7
1986	Joe Murphy	C	Detroit	Michigan State	18.8
1987	Pierre Turgeon	C	Buffalo	Granby Bisons	17.10
1988	Mike Modano	C	Minnesota	Prince Albert Raiders	18.0
1989	Mats Sundin	RW	Quebec	Nacka (Sweden)	18.4
1990	Owen Nolan	RW	Quebec	Cornwall Royals	18.4
1991	Eric Lindros	C	Quebec	Oshawa Generals	18.3
1992	Roman Hamrlik	D	Tampa Bay	ZPS Zlin (Czech.)	18.2

Draft Summary

Following is a summary of the number of players drafted from the Ontario Hockey League (OHL), Western Hockey League (WHL), Quebec Major Junior Hockey League (QMJHL), United States Colleges, United States High Schools, European Leagues and other Leagues throughout North America since 1969:

	OHL	WHL	QMJHL	US Coll.	US HS	International	Other
1969	36	20	11	7	0	1	9
1970	51	22	13	16	0	0	13
1971	41	28	13	22	0	0	13
1972	46	44	30	21	0	0	11
1973	56	49	24	25	0	0	14
1974	69	66	40	41	0	6	25
1975	45	54	28	59	0	6	25
1976	47	33	18	26	0	8	3
1977	42	44	40	49	0	5	5
1978	59	48	22	73	0	15	17
1979	48	37	19	15	0	6	1
1980	73	41	24	42	7	13	10
1981	59	37	28	21	17	32	17
1982	60	55	17	20	47	35	18
1983	57	41	24	14	35	34	37
1984	55	37	16	22	44	40	36
1985	59	48	15	20	48	30	32
1986	66	32	22	22	40	28	42
1987	32	36	17	40	69	38	20
1988	32	30	22	48	56	39	25
1989	39	44	16	48	47	38	20
1990	39	33	14	38	57	53	16
1991	43	40	25	43	37	55	21
1992	57	45	22	9	25	82	24
Total	**1211**	**964**	**520**	**741**	**529**	**564**	**454**

Total Drafted, 1969-1992: 4,983

Ontario Hockey League

Club	'69	'70	'71	'72	'73	'74	'75	'76	'77	'78	'79	'80	'81	'82	'83	'84	'85	'86	'87	'88	'89	'90	'91	'92	Total
Peterborough	5	5	4	5	9	4	3	1	4	6	9	10	3	5	7	3	9	2	5	2	2	4	3	4	114
Oshawa	5	4	3	5	5	7	6	6	1	3	3	2	9	5	5	6	6	6	3	2	4	2	4	4	105
Kitchener	1	6	2	8	4	13	3	1	3	4	4	4	5	5	8	4	6	3	2	1	7	5	3	1	103
Ottawa	2	4	3	4	6	5	6	5	5	5	3	8	4	9	2	2	3	3	2	1	–	5	5	6	98
Toronto	3	7	6	5	6	8	4	4	7	5	4	10	2	6	4	4	3	4	1	2	2	–	–	–	97
London	4	9	1	5	6	6	3	5	4	3	6	2	5	5	3	7	1	3	2	6	3	3	1	3	96
S.S. Marie	–	–	–	–	4	5	2	5	1	5	3	3	8	1	6	4	5	7	1	2	3	1	2	7	75
Sudbury	–	–	–	–	6	6	4	5	4	4	3	7	2	4	–	2	5	3	1	–	1	2	8	2	69
Kingston	–	–	–	–	–	4	4	6	4	9	2	8	5	2	1	3	3	4	1	1	–	2	2	3	64
Hamilton	2	3	5	4	6	4	7	3	–	8	1	–	–	–	–	–	3	6	4	4	–	–	2	–	62
Niagara Falls	4	2	1	4	–	–	–	–	2	3	5	8	6	6	–	–	–	–	–	–	4	4	4	4	57
St. Catharines	5	5	8	5	4	7	3	4	6	–	–	–	–	–	–	–	–	–	–	–	–	–	–	–	47
Windsor	–	–	–	–	–	–	–	2	1	4	2	3	5	3	2	2	3	7	–	5	2	1	–	3	45
Cornwall	–	–	–	–	–	–	–	–	–	–	–	–	–	7	4	3	2	2	3	3	2	3	3	5	37
North Bay	–	–	–	–	–	–	–	–	–	–	–	–	–	–	4	4	3	3	3	3	1	4	2	5	32
Belleville	–	–	–	–	–	–	–	–	–	–	–	–	–	–	3	4	4	5	2	–	4	2	1	4	29
Brantford	–	–	–	–	–	–	–	–	–	–	3	8	5	2	7	2	–	–	–	–	–	–	–	–	27
Guelph	–	–	–	–	–	–	–	–	–	–	–	–	–	–	1	5	3	8	2	–	4	–	–	2	25
Montreal	5	6	8	1	–	–	–	–	–	–	–	–	–	–	–	–	–	–	–	–	–	–	–	–	20
Owen Sound	–	–	–	–	–	–	–	–	–	–	–	–	–	–	–	–	–	–	–	–	–	1	1	2	4
Detroit	–	–	–	–	–	–	–	–	–	–	–	–	–	–	–	–	–	–	–	–	–	–	2	2	4

Year	Total Ontario Drafted	Total Players Drafted	Ontario %
1969	36	84	42.9
1970	51	115	44.3
1971	41	117	35.0
1972	46	152	30.3
1973	56	168	33.3
1974	69	247	27.9
1975	45	217	20.7
1976	47	135	34.8
1977	42	185	22.7
1978	59	234	25.2
1979	48	126	38.1
1980	73	210	34.8
1981	59	211	28.0
1982	60	252	23.8
1983	57	242	23.6
1984	55	250	22.0
1985	59	252	23.4
1986	66	252	26.2
1987	32	252	12.7
1988	32	252	12.7
1989	39	252	15.5
1990	39	250	15.6
1991	43	264	16.3
1992	57	264	21.6
Total	**1211**	**4983**	**24.3**

Western Hockey League

Club	'69	'70	'71	'72	'73	'74	'75	'76	'77	'78	'79	'80	'81	'82	'83	'84	'85	'86	'87	'88	'89	'90	'91	'92	Total
Regina	–	–	5	5	1	8	5	3	1	4	1	3	5	6	8	4	4	3	2	–	5	1	–	4	78
Saskatoon	1	–	1	3	8	4	5	3	4	1	2	2	3	5	5	3	1	5	4	4	3	2	2	3	74
Portland	–	–	–	–	–	–	–	–	4	8	7	8	6	7	7	5	2	4	3	1	4	1	1	4	72
Calgary	3	5	2	7	4	8	4	4	4	3	–	2	5	4	3	3	3	2	–	–	–	–	–	–	66
Victoria	–	–	–	2	2	5	7	4	3	3	1	8	6	2	3	4	2	1	2	4	4	2	–	1	66
Medicine Hat	–	–	–	4	6	4	5	3	5	4	–	4	2	1	2	1	6	2	5	1	4	1	3	3	66
New Westm'r	–	–	–	6	8	7	9	5	8	6	5	1	–	–	–	2	1	1	2	1	–	–	–	–	62
Brandon	–	3	1	5	2	7	4	–	3	1	10	5	2	2	1	3	2	1	3	3	–	1	1	1	61
Kamloops	–	–	–	–	–	4	4	4	4	–	–	–	–	2	4	4	4	4	3	1	5	4	6	3	56
Lethbridge	–	–	–	–	–	–	–	2	3	5	4	1	4	7	2	1	5	1	–	3	3	4	7	3	55
Flin Flon	4	4	5	2	4	7	4	3	1	5	–	–	–	–	–	–	–	–	–	–	–	–	–	–	39
Seattle	–	–	–	–	–	–	–	–	–	4	2	3	–	6	–	1	3	1	2	4	2	6	3	2	39
Prince Albert	–	–	–	–	–	–	–	–	–	–	–	–	–	4	2	2	6	6	1	3	3	4	6	2	39
Winnipeg	3	2	4	2	5	4	4	–	4	–	–	–	1	4	1	–	–	–	–	–	–	–	–	–	34
Edmonton	4	4	5	6	6	2	3	2	–	–	2	–	–	–	–	–	–	–	–	–	–	–	–	–	34
Swift Current	1	–	1	–	3	6	–	–	–	–	–	–	–	–	–	–	–	–	5	2	2	2	1	1	24
Spokane	–	–	–	–	–	–	–	–	–	–	–	–	–	–	–	–	–	–	1	3	2	1	5	7	19
Moose Jaw	–	–	–	–	–	–	–	–	–	–	–	–	–	–	–	–	4	1	3	–	3	1	2	3	17
Tri-Cities	–	–	–	–	–	–	–	–	–	–	–	–	–	–	–	–	–	–	–	–	4	3	3	5	15
Billings	–	–	–	–	–	–	–	–	–	4	3	4	2	–	–	–	–	–	–	–	–	–	–	–	13
Estevan	4	4	4	–	–	–	–	–	–	–	–	–	–	–	–	–	–	–	–	–	–	–	–	–	12
Kelowna	–	–	–	–	–	–	–	–	–	–	–	–	–	–	2	4	5	–	–	–	–	–	–	–	11
Nanaimo	–	–	–	–	–	–	–	–	–	–	–	–	–	5	1	–	–	–	–	–	–	–	–	–	6
Tacoma	–	–	–	–	–	–	–	–	–	–	–	–	–	–	–	–	–	–	–	–	–	–	–	3	3
Vancouver	–	–	–	2	–	–	–	–	–	–	–	–	–	–	–	–	–	–	–	–	–	–	–	–	2

Year	Total Western Drafted	Total Players Drafted	Western %
1969	20	84	23.8
1970	22	115	19.1
1971	28	117	23.9
1972	44	152	28.9
1973	49	168	29.2
1974	66	247	26.7
1975	54	217	24.9
1976	33	135	24.4
1977	44	185	23.8
1978	48	234	20.5
1979	37	126	29.4
1980	41	210	19.5
1981	37	211	17.5
1982	55	252	21.8
1983	41	242	16.9
1984	37	250	14.8
1985	48	252	19.0
1986	32	252	12.7
1987	36	252	14.3
1988	30	252	11.9
1989	44	252	17.5
1990	33	250	13.2
1991	40	264	15.2
1992	45	264	17.0
Total	**964**	**4983**	**19.3**

Quebec Major Junior Hockey League

Club	'69	'70	'71	'72	'73	'74	'75	'76	'77	'78	'79	'80	'81	'82	'83	'84	'85	'86	'87	'88	'89	'90	'91	'92	Total
Shawinigan	3	2	1	6	1	5	3	–	3	–	–	2	2	5	5	2	–	2	1	–	2	–	2	3	50
Quebec	1	1	2	4	6	6	1	3	7	1	3	2	2	1	2	2	3	–	–	–	–	–	–	–	47
Trois Rivieres	–	1	2	2	2	2	3	2	6	3	2	2	2	1	3	–	3	–	1	3	3	1	2	1	47
Cornwall	2	1	2	6	4	8	1	3	1	6	1	5	5	–	–	–	–	–	–	–	–	–	–	–	45
Sherbrooke	–	–	2	2	4	3	7	5	6	3	4	1	5	2	–	–	–	–	–	–	–	–	–	–	44
Hull	–	–	–	–	–	–	3	2	2	3	–	3	1	–	3	1	–	4	3	2	2	3	3	3	38
Laval	–	–	–	1	–	2	1	1	4	2	1	–	–	2	1	2	–	5	3	1	3	3	4	1	37
Montreal	–	–	–	–	4	4	8	1	3	2	4	3	–	3	–	–	–	–	–	–	–	–	–	–	32
Chicoutimi	–	–	–	–	–	1	–	–	5	1	1	3	6	1	3	–	3	1	2	2	1	1	–	1	32
Drummondville	2	4	1	4	2	1	–	–	–	–	–	–	–	–	–	1	2	2	2	4	1	–	4	2	32
Sorel	2	3	1	3	1	8	1	1	3	–	–	–	5	–	–	–	–	–	–	–	–	–	–	–	28
Verdun	–	1	1	2	–	–	–	–	–	1	3	3	–	–	3	3	–	3	0	3	1	–	–	3	27
Granby	–	–	–	–	–	–	–	–	–	–	–	–	–	2	1	3	2	2	4	–	2	–	2	–	18
Longueuil	–	–	–	–	–	–	–	–	–	–	–	–	–	–	1	2	1	2	1	–	–	2	3	–	12
St. Jean	–	–	–	–	–	–	–	–	–	–	–	–	–	–	2	–	1	1	0	3	1	–	3	1	12
Victoriaville	–	–	–	–	–	–	–	–	–	–	–	–	–	–	–	–	–	–	–	4	–	1	–	2	7
St. Hyacinthe	–	–	–	–	–	–	–	–	–	–	–	–	–	–	–	–	–	–	–	–	–	3	1	2	6
Beauport	–	–	–	–	–	–	–	–	–	–	–	–	–	–	–	–	–	–	–	–	–	–	1	3	4
St. Jerome	1	–	1	–	–	–	–	–	–	–	–	–	–	–	–	–	–	–	–	–	–	–	–	–	2

Year	Total Quebec Drafted	Total Players Drafted	Quebec %
1969	11	84	13.1
1970	13	115	11.3
1971	13	117	11.1
1972	30	152	19.7
1973	24	168	14.3
1974	40	247	16.2
1975	28	217	12.9
1976	18	135	13.3
1977	40	185	21.6
1978	22	234	9.4
1979	19	126	15.1
1980	24	210	11.4
1981	28	211	13.3
1982	17	252	6.7
1983	24	242	9.9
1984	16	250	6.4
1985	15	252	5.9
1986	22	252	8.7
1987	17	252	6.7
1988	22	252	8.7
1989	16	252	6.3
1990	14	250	5.6
1991	25	264	9.5
1992	22	264	8.3
Total	**520**	**4983**	**10.4**

ternational

ntry	'69	'70	'71	'72	'73	'74	'75	'76	'77	'78	'79	'80	'81	'82	'83	'84	'85	'86	'87	'88	'89	'90	'91	'92	Total
eden	–	–	–	–	–	5	2	5	2	8	5	9	13	14	10	14	15	9	15	14	9	8	11	10	178
SR/CIS	–	–	–	–	–	–	1	–	–	2	–	–	–	3	5	1	2	1	2	11	18	14	25	45	130
choslovakia	–	–	–	–	–	–	–	–	–	1	1	–	4	13	9	13	8	6	11	5	8	21	9	17	126
land	1	–	–	–	–	1	3	2	3	2	–	4	13	5	9	10	4	10	6	7	3	8	6	8	115
many	–	–	–	–	–	–	–	–	–	2	–	–	2	–	1	2	1	–	1	2	–	–	1	1	13
rway	–	–	–	–	–	–	–	–	–	–	–	–	–	–	–	–	–	–	2	–	–	2	1	–	5
nmark	–	–	–	–	–	–	–	–	–	–	–	–	–	–	–	–	–	1	1	–	–	–	–	–	2
itzerland	–	–	–	–	–	–	–	1	–	–	–	–	–	–	–	–	–	–	–	–	–	–	1	–	2
otland	–	–	–	–	–	–	–	–	–	–	–	–	–	–	–	–	–	1	–	–	–	–	–	–	1
and	–	–	–	–	–	–	–	–	–	–	–	–	–	–	–	–	–	–	–	–	–	–	1	–	1
an	–	–	–	–	–	–	–	–	–	–	–	–	–	–	–	–	–	–	–	–	–	–	–	1	1

Note: Players drafted in the International category played outside North America in their draft year. European-born players drafted from the OHL, QMJHL, WHL or U.S. Colleges are not counted as International players.
See Country of Origin, bottom right, this page.

Year	Total International Drafted	Total Players Drafted	International %
1969	1	84	1.2
1970	0	115	0
1971	0	117	0
1972	0	152	0
1973	0	168	0
1974	6	247	2.4
1975	6	217	2.8
1976	8	135	5.9
1977	5	185	2.7
1978	15	234	6.4
1979	6	126	4.8
1980	13	210	6.2
1981	32	211	15.2
1982	35	252	13.9
1983	34	242	14.0
1984	40	250	17.6
1985	30	252	12.0
1986	28	252	11.1
1987	38	252	15.1
1988	39	252	15.5
1989	38	252	15.1
1990	53	250	21.2
1991	55	264	20.8
1992	82	264	31.0
Total	**567**	**4983**	**11.3**

nited States Colleges

b	'69	'70	'71	'72	'73	'74	'75	'76	'77	'78	'79	'80	'81	'82	'83	'84	'85	'86	'87	'88	'89	'90	'91	'92	Total
nnesota	1	3	2	–	–	9	4	4	5	5	2	3	1	1	1	–	–	2	1	1	1	–	–	–	46
chigan Tech	–	–	3	1	2	5	4	4	1	2	1	4	–	1	–	2	2	2	1	1	2	1	2	–	41
chigan	1	–	–	–	2	2	3	3	1	6	–	4	–	–	–	1	1	–	1	2	3	5	4	2	41
sconsin	–	1	2	4	5	4	4	2	3	–	1	–	3	2	–	1	1	–	1	–	1	–	1	–	36
nver	1	3	2	4	2	3	1	2	2	2	2	1	–	1	–	–	1	2	4	1	1	–	–	–	35
ston U.	–	4	–	–	1	1	1	1	4	5	1	–	1	–	–	1	1	2	2	3	1	2	2	1	34
rth Dakota	2	3	3	1	4	2	1	–	1	2	3	3	1	–	–	1	–	–	–	–	2	1	1	–	31
chigan State	–	–	1	–	1	1	1	1	–	–	–	2	–	2	–	2	–	1	1	4	4	5	4	1	31
ovidence	–	–	–	–	–	–	3	2	3	4	–	5	4	1	2	–	1	1	–	–	–	1	–	–	27
rkson	–	–	2	2	1	–	2	–	2	2	1	1	1	1	1	1	–	–	1	1	1	3	2	1	26
w Hampshire	–	–	–	1	1	3	6	–	4	1	1	2	1	1	1	2	–	–	–	1	–	–	–	–	25
rnell	–	–	–	2	1	1	–	1	1	1	–	1	1	1	–	1	2	–	1	2	5	2	–	–	23
wling Green	–	–	–	–	–	1	3	2	1	1	1	1	–	–	1	–	–	–	–	3	2	1	3	1	21
lorado	2	1	–	–	–	1	3	1	2	2	–	1	–	–	–	3	–	1	–	1	–	2	–	–	20
tre Dame	–	–	2	3	–	–	7	2	–	3	1	1	–	–	–	–	–	–	–	–	–	–	–	–	19
ke Superior	–	–	–	–	1	1	1	–	–	3	–	–	–	–	–	1	–	3	–	3	2	3	1	–	19
l	–	–	–	–	1	–	–	–	1	3	–	1	2	1	1	–	1	–	2	2	–	–	3	1	19
Lawrence	–	–	–	–	–	–	1	–	1	4	–	–	–	3	–	1	1	1	1	1	1	1	2	–	18
Michigan	–	–	–	–	–	–	–	–	2	–	–	2	–	–	2	2	–	2	1	1	1	1	4	–	18
ston College	–	1	–	–	–	–	1	1	–	5	–	2	1	1	–	–	–	1	2	–	2	–	–	–	17
rvard	–	–	2	–	–	–	2	–	2	2	–	–	–	1	1	–	2	–	1	1	2	–	–	–	16
rthern Mich.	–	–	–	–	–	–	–	–	–	4	–	1	2	1	–	–	–	–	4	1	2	–	1	–	16
rmont	–	–	–	–	1	–	4	–	1	1	–	1	1	–	1	1	2	–	–	1	–	–	1	–	15
nn.-Duluth	–	–	2	1	–	–	–	–	1	1	–	–	1	–	–	–	–	–	–	2	1	2	1	–	12
ami of Ohio	–	–	–	–	–	–	–	–	–	–	–	–	–	–	–	–	1	–	2	4	2	–	2	1	12
own	–	–	–	–	1	2	1	–	3	2	–	–	–	1	–	–	–	–	–	–	–	–	1	–	11
io State	–	–	–	–	–	–	–	–	2	1	–	–	–	–	–	1	–	–	2	2	–	1	1	1	11
gate	–	–	–	–	–	1	–	–	–	2	1	–	–	–	–	–	–	–	–	1	1	2	2	–	10
le	–	–	–	1	–	–	1	–	–	2	–	1	–	–	–	–	–	1	2	–	1	–	–	–	9
ine	–	–	–	–	–	–	–	–	–	–	–	–	–	1	1	–	–	1	–	3	2	1	–	–	9
rtheastern	–	–	–	–	–	1	–	–	–	1	–	1	–	–	1	–	1	1	–	–	1	1	–	–	8
nceton	–	–	–	–	–	–	1	–	–	1	–	1	1	–	1	–	–	–	1	–	1	–	–	–	7
ris State	–	–	–	–	–	–	–	–	–	–	–	–	–	–	–	–	–	–	2	1	1	1	2	–	7
Louis	–	–	–	–	–	1	2	–	1	2	–	–	–	–	–	–	–	–	–	–	–	–	–	–	6
of Ill.-Chi.	–	–	–	–	–	–	–	–	–	–	–	–	–	–	–	–	1	–	2	1	2	–	–	–	6
nnsylvania	–	–	–	–	1	2	1	–	–	–	–	1	–	–	–	–	–	–	–	–	–	–	–	–	5
rtmouth	–	–	–	1	–	–	–	–	–	1	–	1	–	–	–	–	–	–	1	–	–	–	1	–	5
ion College	–	–	–	–	–	–	–	–	4	–	–	–	–	–	–	–	–	–	–	–	–	–	–	–	4
well	–	–	–	–	–	–	–	–	1	1	–	1	–	–	–	–	1	–	–	–	–	–	–	–	4
rrimack	–	–	–	–	–	–	–	–	–	1	–	–	–	–	–	–	–	1	–	1	–	–	1	–	4
bson College	–	–	–	–	–	–	–	–	–	–	–	–	–	–	–	–	1	–	1	1	–	–	–	–	3
aska-Anchorage	–	–	–	–	–	–	–	–	–	–	–	–	–	–	–	–	–	–	–	–	2	1	–	–	3
aska-Fairbanks	–	–	–	–	–	–	–	–	–	–	–	–	–	–	–	–	–	–	–	–	–	1	1	–	2
lem State	–	–	–	–	–	–	1	–	–	–	–	–	–	–	–	–	–	–	–	–	–	–	–	–	1
midji State	–	–	1	–	–	–	–	–	–	–	–	–	–	–	–	–	–	–	–	–	–	–	–	–	1
n Diego U.	–	–	–	–	–	–	–	–	–	–	–	–	–	–	–	1	–	–	–	–	–	–	–	–	1
eenway	–	–	–	–	–	–	–	–	–	–	–	–	–	–	–	–	–	–	1	–	–	–	–	–	1
Anselen College	–	–	–	–	–	–	–	–	–	–	–	–	–	–	–	–	–	–	1	–	–	–	–	–	1
milton College	–	–	–	–	–	–	–	–	–	–	–	–	–	–	–	–	–	–	1	–	–	–	–	–	1
Thomas	–	–	–	–	–	–	–	–	–	–	–	–	–	–	–	–	–	–	–	1	–	–	–	–	1
Cloud State	–	–	–	–	–	–	–	–	–	–	–	–	–	–	–	–	–	–	–	1	–	–	–	–	1
ner. Int'l College	–	–	–	–	–	–	–	–	–	–	–	–	–	–	–	–	–	–	–	–	1	–	–	–	1

Year	Total College Drafted	Total Players Drafted	College %
1969	7	84	8.3
1970	16	115	13.9
1971	22	117	18.8
1972	21	152	13.8
1973	25	168	14.9
1974	41	247	16.6
1975	59	217	26.7
1976	26	135	19.3
1977	49	185	26.5
1978	73	234	31.2
1979	15	126	11.9
1980	42	210	20.0
1981	21	211	10.0
1982	20	252	7.9
1983	14	242	5.8
1984	22	250	8.8
1985	20	252	7.9
1986	22	252	8.7
1987	40	252	15.9
1988	48	252	19.0
1989	48	252	19.0
1990	38	250	15.2
1991	43	264	16.3
1992	9	264	3.4
Total	**741**	**4983**	**14.9**

1992 Entry Draft Analysis

Country of Origin

Country	Players Drafted
Canada	134
USSR/CIS	47
United States	38
Czechoslovakia	20
Sweden	11
Finland	10
Bahamas	1
Germany	1
Japan	1
United Kingdom	1

Position

Position	Players Drafted
Defense	86
Center	60
Right Wing	42
Left Wing	51
Goaltender	25

Birth Year

Year	Players Drafted
1974	128
1973	69
1972	44
1971	2
1970	7
1969	3
1968	2
1967	2
1966	3
1965	1
1964	2
1962	1

First Round Draft Selections, 1992

1. TAMPA BAY LIGHTNING • **ROMAN HAMRLIK** • D
A member of the Czechoslovakian National Junior Team at the 1991 and 1992 World Junior Championships, Hamrlik is an intelligent, stay-at-home defenseman with superb passing and skating skills. Best noted for his solid checking and disciplined play in his own zone, Hamrlik compiled five goals and five assists in 34 games with ZPS Zlin of the Czech National League in 1991-92.

2. OTTAWA SENATORS • **ALEXEI YASHIN** • C
One of Russia's most talented young centermen, Yashin was a key member of the CIS National Junior Team that captured the gold medal at the 1992 World Junior Championships. Blessed with speed, size and a deft touch around the net, Yashin scored seven goals in 35 games for the CIS National League champion Moscow Dynamo in 1991-92.

3. SAN JOSE SHARKS • **MIKE RATHJE** • D
Rathje is a strong, mobile defenseman with good size (6'5", 205 lbs.) and puck-carrying skills. He's nicknamed "Rat" because of his tenacious playing style. He was a member of Canada's national 17-year-old team that played in a tournament in Japan. In 67 games with the WHL's Medicine Hat Tigers, Rathje registered 11 goals and 23 assists.

4. QUEBEC NORDIQUES • **TODD WARRINER** • LW
A talented athlete who excels in a number of sports, Warriner's smooth-skating style and puck-handling skills have invited comparisons to the Canucks' Trevor Linden. Equally adept at both playmaking and scoring, this leftwinger accumulated 41 goals and an equal number of assists in only 50 games with the OHL's Windsor Spitfires.

5. NEW YORK ISLANDERS • **DARIUS KASPARAITIS** • D
Kasparitus is already renowned as a world-class defenseman, having played on three championship teams in 1991-92, including the CIS gold medal-winning team at the 1992 Olympics and the CIS National League's champion Moscow Dynamo. An intelligent rearguard who plays a calm, collected game behind the blueline, he is noted for his shot blocking and checking skills.

6. CALGARY FLAMES • **CORY STILLMAN**• C
The Flames acquired a slick, playmaking center in Stillman, who has accumulated 191 points over the past two seasons with the OHL's Windsor Spitfires. A team player whose considerable talent is coupled with outstanding determination and drive, Stillman has proven himself to be a natural on-ice leader who excels in special team situations.

7. PHILADELPHIA FLYERS • **RYAN SITTLER** • LW
The son of Hall-of-Famer Darryl Sittler, Ryan enjoyed the finest season of his young career in 1991-92, appearing with the U.S. National Junior Team at the 1992 World Junior Championships while registering 141 points in only 51 games split between Nicholls high school and the Buffalo Regals. A strong skater with a scoring touch, Sittler is a 6'2", 185 lb. power forward.

8. TORONTO MAPLE LEAFS • **BRANDON CONVERY** • C
One of the most talented offensive centermen available in the 1992 Entry Draft, Convery's speed, style, and scoring skills reminds some scouts of a young Russ Courtnall. Already a prolific scorer in the junior ranks, Convery fired 40 goals in 44 games with Sudbury during the 1991-92 campaign in just his second OHL season. A proven winner in a number of sports, he has already won awards in soccer and tennis.

9. HARTFORD WHALERS • **ROBERT PETROVICKY** • C
Petrovicky is a creative playmaking center who has proven he can escape the tight checking of man-on-man coverage. The top scorer on the Czechoslovakian National Junior Team at the 1992 World Junior Championships with nine points in seven games, Petrovicky tallied 25 goals and 36 assists in 46 games for Dukla Trencin of the Czech National League in 1991-92.

10. SAN JOSE SHARKS • **ANDREI NAZAROV** • RW
A strong skating right winger, whose size (6'4", 209 lbs.) and solid work habits are his greatest attributes, Nazarov graduated from Moscow Dynamo Juniors to the club's senior team in 1991-92, seeing action in two games. Scouting reports note that he is strong around the net, plays well without the puck and has a good wrist shot.

11. BUFFALO SABRES • **DAVID COOPER** • D
Cooper has all the qualities you look for in an NHL defenseman: quick hands, good speed and excellent playmaking abilities. He is noted for his work on the point in powerplay situations. An accurate passer who likes to rush the puck, Cooper scored 17 goals and added 47 assists in 72 games for the WHL's Medicine Hat Tigers.

12. CHICAGO BLACKHAWKS • **SERGEI KRIVOKRASOV** • RW
One of the top offensive stars of Moscow's Central Red Army team of the CIS National League, Krivokrasov was a member of the gold medal-winning USSR/CIS National Junior Team at the 1992 World Junior Championships. An exceptional skater with an excellent scoring touch from the right side, he fired 10 goals and added eight assists in 42 games during the 1991-92 season.

13. EDMONTON OILERS • **JOE HULBIG** • LW
A tall, rangy power forward whose main attributes are size (6'3", 212 lbs.) and strength, Hulbig accumulated 43 points in 17 games for St. Sebastian's high school. He also has demonstrated an ability to play a strong defensive game. Reputed to be the hardest body checker in his prep school hockey, he is also well-regarded as a playmaker and goal scorer.

14. WASHINGTON CAPITALS • **SERGEI GONCHAR** • D
The captain of the USSR/CIS National Junior Team at the 1992 World Junior Championships, Gonchar has established himself as a highly motivated on-ice team leader. Gonchar played with Traktor Chelyabinsk of the CIS National League in 1991-92. He plays a stay-at-home style and is regarded as one of the finest rearguards in the Russian game.

15. PHILADELPHIA FLYERS • **JASON BOWEN** • LW
An aggressive playmaking left winger who is not afraid of tough action in the slot, Bowen is a strong skater with good balance. Scouting reports note his hard shot and excellent passing ability and state that he is prepared to take a hit to make a play. He has played two seasons with the WHL's Tri-City Americans.

16. BOSTON BRUINS • **DMITRI KVARTALNOV** • LW
Kvartalnov was the IHL's leading scorer, MVP and rookie of the year with the San Diego Gulls in 1991-92. He is the only player drafted in the first round from another North American professional league. Kvartalnov, a left winger, tallied 60 goals and 58 assists in 77 games in 1991-92. He played with Khimik Voskresensk of the Soviet National League in 1990-91.

17. WINNIPEG JETS • **SERGEI BAUTIN** • D
Regarded as one of the toughest players in Russian Hockey, Bautin is an aggressive, hard working defenseman whose relentless forechecking earned him a first round selection by the Jets. A member of both the CIS National League champion Moscow Dynamo and the gold medal-winning Soviet National Team at the 1992 Olympics, Bautin compiled three points and 88 penalty minutes in 37 games in 1991-92.

18. NEW JERSEY DEVILS • **JASON SMITH** • D
Smith is a pro-style defenseman who likes rush the puck, plays well in his own zone and can control the point on the powerplay. He is an intelligent player with a hard, accurate, low shot. He is a good puck handler with good offensive skills. In 62 games with the WHL's Regina Pats in 1991-92, he accumulated nine goals and 29 assists.

19. PITTSBURGH PENGUINS • **MARTIN STRAKA** • C
Straka had a most impressive 1991-92 season, compiling eight points for the Czech National Junior Team at the 1992 World Junior Championships. He finished sixth in the Czech National League in scoring with 27 goals and 28 assists for Skoda Plzen. A finesse centerman who is best noted for his playmaking abilities, Straka matured into a versatile goal scorer in 1991-92, upping his total from the previous season by 20 goals.

20. MONTREAL CANADIENS • **DAVID WILKIE** • D
Wilkie has impressive speed and the ability to head-man the puck. He likes to rush and can go end to end. At 6'1" and 202 lbs., he is big, strong and mobile. He was used on special teams with Kamloops of the WHL in 1991-92 and compiled 40 points in 71 games for the Blazers.

21. VANCOUVER CANUCKS • **LIBOR POLASEK** • C
Polasek is a strong center who stands his ground in front of his opponent's net. A face-off specialist who performs best in pressure situations, he played his first season in the Czech National League in 1991-92, appearing in 17 games with TJ Vitkovice. He played a key role in Czechoslovakia's win at the 1992 European Junior Championships.

22. DETROIT RED WINGS • **CURTIS BOWEN** • LW
Bowen is a talented left winger who likes to go to the net. Hard to move out of the slot, he plays with great intensity, earning comparisons with Gary Roberts. He has breakaway skating speed and almost tripled his scoring totals with the Ottawa 67s of the OHL, finishing 1991-92 with 31 goals and 45 assists for 76 points in 65 games.

23. TORONTO MAPLE LEAFS • **GRANT MARSHALL** • RW
Marshall rebounded from serious injury in 1990 to contribute 34 goals and 100 assists to the attack of the Ottawa 67s. Although he has played much of his career on the blueline, many scouts have predicted he is best suited to right wing. He is an excellent passer with a natural scoring touch in addition to being a strong checker.

24. NEW YORK RANGERS • **PETER FERRARO** • C
Named as the top center at the 1992 World Junior Championships, Ferraro has gathered rave reviews for his outstanding performances over the past two seasons. He is a persistent forechecker with a strong, accurate shot. In addition to playing for the U.S. National junior team, Ferraro recorded 101 points in 1991-92, splitting the season between Dubuque and Waterloo of the junior USHL.

1992 Expansion Draft

OTTAWA SENATORS

Player	Pos.	Claimed From
Peter Sidorkiwicz	G	Hartford
Mark LaForest	G	NY Rangers
Brad Shaw	D	New Jersey
Darren Rumble	D	Philadelphia
Dominic Lavoie	D	St. Louis
Brad Miller	D	Buffalo
Ken Hammond	D	Vancouver
Kent Paynter	D	Winnipeg
John Van Kessell	D	Los Angeles
Sylvain Turgeon	LW	Montreal
Mike Peluso	LW/D	Chicago
Rob Murphy	LW/C	Vancouver
Mark Lamb	C	Edmonton
Laurie Boschman	C	New Jersey
Jim Thomson	RW	Los Angeles
Lonnie Loach	LW	Detroit
Mark Freer	C	Philadelphia
Chris Lindberg	LW	Calgary
Jeff Lazaro	LW	Boston
Darcy Loewen	LW	Buffalo
Blair Atcheynum	RW	Hartford

TAMPA BAY LIGHTNING

Player	Pos.	Claimed From
Wendell Young	G	Pittsburgh
Frederic Chabot	G	Montreal
Joe Reekie	D	NY Islanders
Shawn Chambers	D	Minnesota
Peter Taglianetti	D	Pittsburgh
Bob McGill	D	Detroit
Jeff Bloemberg	D	NY Rangers
Doug Crossman	D	Quebec
Rob Ramage	D	Minnesota
Michel Mongeau	C	St. Louis
Anatoli Semenov	C/LW	Edmonton
Mike Hartford	LW	Winnipeg
Basil McRae	LW	Minnesota
Rob Dimaio	C	NY Islanders
Steve Maltais	LW	Quebec
Dan Vincelette	LW	Chicago
Tim Bergland	RW	Washington
Brian Bradley	C	Toronto
Keith Osborne	RW	Toronto
Shayne Stevenson	RW	Boston
Tim Hunter	RW	Calgary

Selections two through six in the 1992 NHL Entry Draft (clockwise from right): Alexei Yashin, Mike Rathje, Todd Warriner, Darius Kasparaitis, and Cory Stillman.

1992 Entry Draft

Transferred draft choice notation:

Example: Tor.-NYI represents a draft choice transferred **from** Toronto **to** New York Islanders.

Pick	Player	Claimed By	Amateur Club	Position
ROUND # 1				
1	HAMRLIK, Roman	T.B.	ZPS Zlin	D
2	YASHIN, Alexei	Ott.	Dynamo Moscow	C
3	RATHJE, Mike	S.J.	Medicine Hat	D
4	WARRINER, Todd	Que.	Windsor	LW
5	KASPARAITIS, Darius	Tor.-NYI	Dynamo Moscow	D
6	STILLMAN, Cory	Cgy.	Windsor	C
7	SITTLER, Ryan	Phi.	Nichols	LW
8	CONVERY, Brandon	NYI-Tor.	Sudbury	C
9	PETROVICKY, Robert	Hfd.	Dukla Trencin	C
10	NAZAROV, Andrei	Min.-S.J.	Dynamo Moscow	LW
11	COOPER, David	Buf.	Medicine Hat	D
12	KRIVOKRASOV, Sergei	Wpg.-Chi.	CSKA Moscow	RW
13	HULBIG, Joe	Edm.	St. Sebastian's	LW
14	GONCHAR, Sergei	St. L.-Wsh.	Traktor Chelybinsk	D
15	BOWEN, Jason	L.A.-Pit.-Phi.	Tri-City	LW
16	KVARTALNOV, Dmitri	Bos.	San Diego	LW
17	BAUTIN, Sergei	Chi.-Wpg.	Dynamo Moscow	D
18	SMITH, Jason	N.J.	Regina	D
19	STRAKA, Martin	Pit.	Skoda Plzen	C
20	WILKIE, David	Mtl.	Kamloops	D
21	POLASEK, Libor	Van.	TJ Vitkovice	C
22	BOWEN, Curtis	Det.	Ottawa	LW
23	MARSHALL, Grant	Wsh.-Tor.	Ottawa	RW
24	FERRARO, Peter	NYR	Waterloo Jr. A	C
ROUND # 2				
25	PENNEY, Chad	Ott.	North Bay	LW
26	BANNISTER, Drew	T.B.	Sault-Ste-Marie	D
27	MIRANOV, Boris	S.J.-Chi.-Wpg.	CSKA Moscow	D
28	BROUSSEAU, Paul	Que.	Hull	RW
29	GRONMAN, Toumas	Tor.-Que.	Tacoma	D
30	O'SULLIVAN, Chris	Cgy.	Catholic Memorial	D
31	METLYUK, Denis	Phi.	Lada Togliatti	C
32	CAREY, Jim	NYI-Tor.-Wsh.	Catholic Memorial	G
33	BURE, Valeri	Hfd.-Mtl.	Spokane	LW
34	VARVIO, Jarkko	Min.	HPK	RW
35	CIERNY, Jozef	Buf.	ZTK Zvolen	LW
36	SHANTZ, Jeff	Wpg.-Chi.	Regina	C
37	REICHEL, Martin	Edm.	Freiburg	W
38	KOROLEV, Igor	St. L.	Dynamo Moscow	RW
39	HOCKING, Justin	L.A.	Spokane	D
40	PECA, Mike	Bos.-Van.	Ottawa	C
41	KLIMOVICH, Sergei	Chi.	Dynamo Moscow	C
42	BRYLIN, Sergei	N.J.	CSKA Moscow	C
43	HUSSEY, Marc	Pit.	Moose Jaw	D
44	CORPSE, Keli	Mtl.	Kingston	C
45	FOUNTAIN, Michael	Van.	Oshawa	G
46	McCARTY, Darren	Det.	Belleville	RW
47	NIKOLISHIN, Andrei	Wsh.-Hfd.	Dynamo Moscow	LW
48	NORSTROM, Mattias	NYR	AIK	D
ROUND # 3				
49	GRETZKY, Brent	T.B.	Belleville	C
50	TRAVERSE, Patrick	Ott.	Shawinigan	D
51	CHERBAJEV, Alexander	S.J.	Khimik	LW
52	FERNANDEZ, Emmanuel	Que.	Laval	G
53	USTORF, Stefan	Tor.-Wsh.	Kaufbeuren	C
54	JOHANSSON, Mathias	Cgy.	Farjestad	C
55	ZHOLTOK, Sergei	Phi.-Bos.	HC Riga	LW
56	DEULING, Jarret	NYI	Kamloops	LW
57	VOPAT, Jan	Hfd.	Litvinov	D
58	BES, Jeff	Min.	Guelph	C
59	STEINER, Ondrej	Buf.	Skoda Plzen	C
60	STEVENSON, Jeremy	Wpg.	Cornwall	LW
61	ROY, Simon	Edm.	Shawinigan	D
62	KARAMNOV, Vitali	St. L.	Dynamo Moscow	LW
63	ALLAN, Sandy	L.A.	North Bay	G
64	PROKHOROV, Vitali	Bos.-St. L.	Spartak	LW
65	MALTBY, Kirk	Chi.-Edm.	Owen Sound	RW
66	HULSE, Cale	N.J.	Portland	D
67	THIESSEN, Travis	Pit.	Moose Jaw	D
68	RIVET, Craig	Mtl.	Kingston	D
69	CONNOLLY, Jeff	Van.	St. Sebastian's	C
70	CLOUTIER, Sylvain	Det.	Guelph	C
71	GENDRON, Martin	Wsh.	St.-Hyacinthe	RW
72	CAIRNS, Eric	NYR	Detroit	D
ROUND # 4				
73	HAMR, Radek	Ott.	Sparta Praha	D
74	GAVEY, Aaron	T.B.	Sault-Ste-Marie	C
75	CALOUN, Jan	S.J.	Litvinov	RW
76	McINTYRE, Ian	Que.	Beauport	LW
77	BORSCHEVSKY, Nikolai	Tor.	Spartak	RW
78	SVEHLA, Robert	Cgy.	Dukla Trencin	D
79	SMYTH, Kevin	Phi.-Hfd.	Moose Jaw	LW
80	MELANSON, Dean	NYI-Buf.	St.-Hyacinthe	D
81	McBAIN, Jason	Hfd.	Portland	D
82	BERNARD, Louis	Min.-Mtl.	Drummondville	D
83	BARNABY, Matthew	Buf.	Beauport	LW
84	VISHEAU, Mark	Wpg.	London	D
85	FERRARO, Chris	Edm.-NYR	Waterloo Jr. A	RW
86	LESLIE, Lee J.	St. L.	Prince Albert	LW
87	BROWN, Kevin	L.A.	Belleville	RW
88	LEHTINEN, Jere	Bos.-Min.	Espoo	RW
89	MacINTYRE, Andy	Chi.	Saskatoon	LW
90	TOMILIN, Vitali	N.J.	Krylja Sovetov	C
91	KLASSEN, Todd	Pit.	Tri-City	D
92	LAMOTHE, Marc	Mtl.	Kingston	G
93	TULLY, Brent	Van.	Peterborough	D
94	McCABE, Scott	Det.-N.J.	GPD Midgets	D
95	RAITER, Mark	Wsh.-Tor.	Saskatoon	D
96	INTRANUOVO, Ralph	NYR-Edm.	Sault-Ste-Marie	C

ROUND # 5

Pick	Player	Claimed By	Amateur Club	Position
97	MYHRES, Brantt	T.B.	Lethbridge	RW
98	GUERARD, Daniel	Ott.	Victoriaville	RW
99	RAGNARSSON, Marcus	S.J.	Djurgarden	D
100	WASLEY, Charlie	Que.	St. Paul Jr. A	D
101	GRONVALL, Janne	Tor.	Lukko	D
102	HELENIUS, Sami	Cgy.	Jokerit	D
103	BULJIN, Vladislav	Phi.	Dizelist Penza	D
104	KLIMT, Tomas	NYI	Skoda Plzen	C
105	DUTHIE, Ryan	Hfd.-NYI	Spokane	C
106	DERUITER, Chris	Min.-Buf.-Tor.	Kingston Jr. A	RW
107	KETTERER, Markus	Buf.	Jokerit	G
108	KHMYLEV, Yuri	Wpg.-Buf.	Krylja Sovetov	LW
109	GAGE, Joaquin	Edm.	Portland	G
110	LONEY, Brian	St. L.-Van.	Ohio State	RW
111	SHEVALIER, Jeff	L.A.	North Bay	LW
112	BAILEY, Scott	Bos.	Spokane	G
113	HOGAN, Tim	Chi.	U. of Michigan	D
114	BLACK, Ryan	N.J.	Peterborough	LW
115	DE ROUVILLE, Philipp	Pit.	Verdun	G
116	CHASE, Don	Mtl.	Springfield Jr. B	C
117	AUCOIN, Adrian	Van.	Boston University	D
118	SULLIVAN, Mike	Det.	Reading	C
119	VARGA, John	Wsh.	Tacoma	LW
120	STAROSTENKO, Dmitri	NYR	CSKA Moscow	LW

ROUND # 6

Pick	Player	Claimed By	Amateur Club	Position
121	SINCLAIR, Al	Ott.	U. of Michigan	D
122	TANGUAY, Martin	T.B.	Verdun	C
123	SYKORA, Michal	S.J.	Tacoma	D
124	SCHULTE, Paxton	Que.	Spokane	LW
125	HAKANSSON, Mikael	Tor.	Nacka	C
126	YAKUBOV, Ravil	Cgy.	Dynamo Moscow	C
127	ZOLOTOV, Roman	Phi.	Dynamo Moscow	D
128	ARMSTRONG, Derek	NYI	Sudbury	C
129	BOUCHARD, Joel	Hfd.-Cgy.	Verdun	D
130	JOHNSON, Michael	Min.	Ottawa	D
131	RUSHFORTH, Paul	Buf.	North Bay	C
132	ALEXEYEV, Alexander	Wpg.	Sokol Kiev	D
132	DOPITA, Jiri	Edm.-Bos.	DS Olomouc	C
134	LACHANCE, Bob	St. L.	Springfield Jr. B.	RW
135	MURRAY, Raymond (Remi)	L.A.	Michigan State	LW
136	PANTELEYEV, Grigori	Bos.	HC Riga	LW
137	SKRYPEC, Gerry	Chi.	Ottawa	D
138	TREBIL, Daniel	N.J.	Bloomington-Jeffer.	D
139	KOPOT, Artem	Pit.	Traktor Chelyabinsk	D
140	SYCHRA, Martin	Mtl.	Zetor Brno	C
141	CLARK, Jason	Van.	St. Thomas Jr. B	C
142	MacDONALD, Jason	Det.	Owen Sound	RW
143	REID, Jarret	Wsh.-Hfd.	Sault-Ste-Marie	C
144	DAL GRANDE, David	NYR	Ottawa T-II Jr. A	D

ROUND # 7

Pick	Player	Claimed By	Amateur Club	Position
145	WILKINSON, Derek	T.B.	Detroit	G
146	MIKLENDA, Jaroslav	Ott.	DS Olomouc	G
147	BELLEROSE, Eric	S.J.	Trois-Rivieres	LW
148	LEPAGE, Martin	Que.	Hull	D
149	AUGUSTA, Patrik	Tor.	Dukla Jihlava	RW
150	RAJNOHA, Pavel	Cgy.	ZPS Zlin	D
151	DAUBENSPECK, Kirk	Phi.	Culver Academy	G
152	GRACHEV, Vladimir	NYI	Dynamo 2 Moscow	RW
153	BELANGER, Ken	Hfd.	Ottawa	LW
154	PETERSON, Kyle	Min.	Thunder Bay Jr. A	C
155	OKTYABREV, Artur	Buf.-Wpg.	CSKA Moscow	D
156	RAISKY, Andrei	Wpg.	Torpedo Ust	C
157	GIBSON, Steve	Edm.	Windsor	LW
158	LAPERRIERE, Ian	St. L.	Drummondville	C
159	O'ROURKE, Steve	L.A.-NYI	Tri-City	RW
160	BURNS, Lance	Bos.-St. L.	Lethbridge	C
161	PROKOPEC, Mike	Chi.	Cornwall	RW
162	KINNEAR, Geordie	N.J.	Peterborough	D
163	ALINC, Jan	Pit.	Litvinov	W
164	PROULX, Christian	Mtl.	St.-Jean	D
165	HOLLIS, Scott	Van.	Oshawa	RW
166	SCOTT, Greg	Det.	Niagara Falls	G
167	MATIER, Mark	Wsh.	Sault-Ste-Marie	D
168	OATES, Matt	NYR	Miami-Ohio	LW

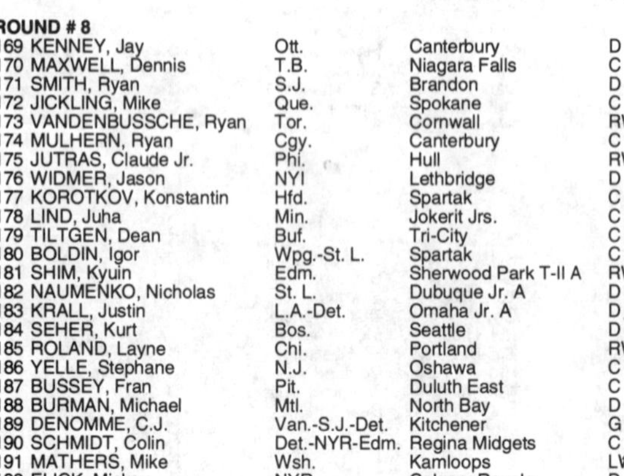

ROUND # 8

Pick	Player	Claimed By	Amateur Club	Position
169	KENNEY, Jay	Ott.	Canterbury	D
170	MAXWELL, Dennis	T.B.	Niagara Falls	C
171	SMITH, Ryan	S.J.	Brandon	D
172	JICKLING, Mike	Que.	Spokane	C
173	VANDENBUSSCHE, Ryan	Tor.	Cornwall	RW
174	MULHERN, Ryan	Cgy.	Canterbury	C
175	JUTRAS, Claude Jr.	Phi.	Hull	RW
176	WIDMER, Jason	NYI	Lethbridge	D
177	KOROTKOV, Konstantin	Hfd.	Spartak	C
178	LIND, Juha	Min.	Jokerit Jrs.	C
179	TILTGEN, Dean	Buf.	Tri-City	C
180	BOLDIN, Igor	Wpg.-St. L.	Spartak	C
181	SHIM, Kyuin	Edm.	Sherwood Park T-II A	RW
182	NAUMENKO, Nicholas	St. L.	Dubuque Jr. A	D
183	KRALL, Justin	L.A.-Det.	Omaha Jr. A	D
184	SEHER, Kurt	Bos.	Seattle	D
185	ROLAND, Layne	Chi.	Portland	RW
186	YELLE, Stephane	N.J.	Oshawa	C
187	BUSSEY, Fran	Pit.	Duluth East	C
188	BURMAN, Michael	Mtl.	North Bay	D
189	DENOMME, C.J.	Van.-S.J.-Det.	Kitchener	G
190	SCHMIDT, Colin	Det.-NYR-Edm.	Regina Midgets	C
191	MATHERS, Mike	Wsh.	Kamloops	LW
192	ELICK, Mickey	NYR	Calgary Royals	D

ROUND # 9

Pick	Player	Claimed By	Amateur Club	Position
193	KEMPER, Andrew	T.B.	Seattle	D
194	SAVOIE, Claude	Ott.	Victoriaville	RW
195	BURNS, Chris	S.J.	Thunder Bay Jr. A	G
196	PASSMORE, Steve	Que.	Victoria	G
197	CLARKE, Wayne	Tor.	R.P.I.	RW
198	CARPER, Brandon	Cgy.	Bowling Green	D
199	HAKANSSON, Jonas	Phi.	Malmo	LW
200	PARADIS, Daniel	NYI	Chicoutimi	C
201	ZWAKMAN, Greg	Hfd.	Edina	D
202	EDSTROM, Lars	Min.	Lulea	LW
203	SIMON, Todd	Buf.	Niagara Falls	C
204	KHAIBULIN, Nikolai	Wpg.	CSKA Moscow	G
205	TUOMAINEN, Marko	Edm.	Clarkson University	RW
206	HARRIS, Todd	St. L.	Tri-City	D
207	WERNBLOM, Magnus	L.A.	MoDo	RW
208	TIMANDER, Mattias	Bos.	MoDo	D
209	HYMOVITZ, David	Chi.	Thayer Academy	LW
210	TOMS, Jeff	N.J.	Sault-Ste-Marie	LW
211	BONIN, Brian	Pit.	White Bear Lake	C
212	CRONAN, Earl	Mtl.	St. Mark's	LW
213	MIGNACCA, Sonny	Van.	Medicine Hat	G
214	WALKER, Jeff	Det.	Peterborough	D
215	STAGG, Brian	Wsh.	Kingston	RW
216	BRIERLEY, Dan	NYR	Choate	D

ROUND # 10

Pick	Player	Claimed By	Amateur Club	Position
217	GRIMES, Jake	Ott.	Belleville	C
218	TARDIF, Marc	T.B.	Shawinigan	LW
219	KHOLOMEYEV, Alexander	S.J.	Izhorets	RW
220	CARTER, Anson	Que.	Wexford Jr. A	C
221	SIMONOV, Sergei	Tor.	Kristall Saratov	D
222	HOGLUND, Jonas	Cgy.	Farjestad	RW
223	HERPERGER, Chris	Phi.	Swift Current	LW
224	WAINWRIGHT, David	NYI	Thayer Academy	D
225	HALKO, Steven	Hfd.	Thornhill Jr. A	D
226	ROMFO, Jeff	Min.	Blaine	C
227	KOWALSKY, Rick	Buf.	Sault-Ste-Marie	RW
228	GARANIN, Yevgeny	Wpg.	Khimik	C
229	NUMMINEN, Teemu	Edm.-Wpg.	Stoneham	C
230	GUNKO, Yuri	St. L.	Sokol Kiev	D
231	PISIAK, Ryan	L.A.	Prince Albert	RW
232	CROMBIE, Chris	Bos.	London	LW
233	RAYMOND, Richard	Chi.	Cornwall	D
234	WEENK, Heath	N.J.	Regina	D
235	CALLAHAN, Brian	Pit.	Belmont Hill	C
236	CAVICCHI, Trent	Mtl.	Darmouth Midgets	G
237	WOTTON, Mark	Van.	Saskatoon	D
238	McGILLIS, Daniel	Det.	Hawksbury T-II Jr. A	D
239	CALLAHAN, Gregory	Wsh.	Belmont Hill	D
240	VOROBJEV, Vladimir	NYR	Metallurg	RW

ROUND # 11

Pick	Player	Claimed By	Amateur Club	Position
241	MacDONALD, Tom	T.B.	Sault-Ste-Marie	C
242	JELINEK, Tomas	Ott.	HPK	RW
243	IGNATJEV, Victor	S.J.	HC Riga	D
244	ELLIS, Aaron	Que.	Culver Mil. Academy	G
245	DEMPSEY, Nathan	Tor.	Regina	D
246	POTAICHUK, Andrei	Cgy.	Krylja Sovetov	RW
247	PAQUIN, Patrice	Phi.	Beauport	LW
248	VASILJEV, Andrei	NYI	CSKA Moscow	LW
249	ESBJORS, Joacim	Hfd.	Vastra Frolunda	D
250	MOEN, Jeffrey	Min.	Roseville	G
251	CLANCY, Chris	Buf.	Cornwall	LW
252	KARPOVTSEV, Andrei	Wpg.	Dynamo Moscow	RW
253	RASMUSSEN, Bryan	Edm.	St. Louis Park	LW
254	VOLOGZHANINOV, Ivan	St. L.-Wpg.	Sokol Kiev	F
255	TIILIKAINEN, Jukka	L.A.	Espoo	W
256	CHERVYAKOV, Denis	Bos.	HC Riga	D
257	PAVLOV, Yevgeny	Chi.-Bos.	SKA Leningrad	LW
258	YAKOVENKO, Vladislav	N.J.	Argus Moscow	LW
259	SALZMAN, Wade	Pit.-St. L.	Duluth East	G
260	MIURA, Hiroyuki	Mtl.	Japan	D
261	BOH, Aaron	Van.	Spokane	D
262	BACH, Ryan	Det.	Notre Dame T-II Jr. A	G
263	MacPHERSON, Billy Jo	Wsh.	Oshawa	LW
264	RONNQVIST, Petter	NYR-Ott.	Nacka	G

Shawn Anderson, seen here with Scotty Bowman, was the Buffalo Sabres' first selection in the 1986 Entry Draft.

Draft Choices, 1991-69

1991

FIRST ROUND

Selection	Claimed By	Amateur Club
1. LINDROS, Eric	Que.	Oshawa
2. FALLOON, Pat	S.J.	Spokane
3. NIEDERMAYER, Scott	N.J.	Kamloops
4. LACHANCE, Scott	NYI	Boston University
5. WARD, Aaron	Wpg.	U. of Michigan
6. FORSBERG, Peter	Phi.	MoDo (Sweden)
7. STOJANOV, Alex	Van.	Hamilton
8. MATVICHUK, Richard	Min.	Saskatoon
9. POULIN, Patrick	Hfd.	St.-Hyacinthe
10. LAPOINTE, Martin	Det.	Laval
11. ROLSTON, Brian	N.J.	Detroit Comp. Jr. A
12. WRIGHT, Tyler	Edm.	Swift Current
13. BOUCHER, Phillipe	Buf.	Granby
14. PEAKE, Pat	Wsh.	Detroit
15. KOVALEV, Alexei	NYR	Dynamo Moscow (USSR)
16. NASLUND, Markus	Pit.	MoDo
17. BILODEAU, Brent	Mtl.	Seattle
18. MURRAY, Glen	Bos.	Sudbury
19. SUNDBLAD, Niklas	Cgy.	AIK (Sweden)
20. RUCINSKY, Martin	Edm.	CHZ Litvinov (Czech.)
21. HALVERSON, Trevor	Wsh.	North Bay
22. McAMMOND, Dean	Chi.	Prince Albert

SECOND ROUND

Selection	Claimed By	Amateur Club
23. WHITNEY, Ray	S.J.	Spokane
24. CORBET, Rene	Que.	Drummondville
25. LAVIGNE, Eric	Wsh.	Hull
26. PALFFY, Zigmund	NYI	AC Nitra (Czech.)
27. STAIOS, Steve	St. L.	Niagara Falls
28. CAMPBELL, Jim	Mtl.	Northwood Prep
29. CULLIMORE, Jassen	Van.	Peterborough
30. OZOLINSH, Sandis	S.J.	Dynamo Riga (USSR)
31. HAMRLIK, Martin	Hfd.	TJ Zin (Czech.)
32. PUSHOR, Jamie	Det.	Lethbridge
33. HEXTALL, Donevan	N.J.	Prince Albert
34. VERNER, Andrew	Edm.	Peterborough
35. DAWE, Jason	Buf.	Peterborough
36. NELSON, Jeff	Wsh.	Prince Albert
37. WERENKA, Darcy	NYR	Lethbridge
38. FITZGERALD, Rusty	Pit.	Duluth East HS
39. POMICHTER, Michael	Chi.	Springfield Jr. B
40. STUMPEL, Jozef	Bos.	AC Nitra (Czech.)
41. GROLEAU, Francois	Cgy.	Shawinigan
42. LEVEQUE, Guy	L.A.	Cornwall
43. DARBY, Craig	Mtl.	Albany Academy
44. MATTHEWS, Jamie	Chi.	Sudbury

1990

FIRST ROUND

Selection	Claimed By	Amateur Club
1. NOLAN, Owen	Que.	Cornwall
2. NEDVED, Petr	Van.	Seattle
3. PRIMEAU, Keith	Det.	Niagara Falls
4. RICCI, Mike	Phi.	Peterborough
5. JAGR, Jaromir	Pit.	Poldi Kladno (Czech.)
6. SCISSONS, Scott	NYI	Saskatoon
7. SYDOR, Darryl	L.A.	Kamloops
8. HATCHER, Derian	Min.	North Bay
9. SLANEY, John	Wsh.	Cornwall
10. BEREHOWSKY, Drake	Tor.	Kingston
11. KIDD, Trevor	Cgy.	Brandon
12. STEVENSON, Turner	Mtl.	Seattle
13. STEWART, Michael	NYR	Michigan State
14. MAY, Brad	Buf.	Niagara Falls
15. GREIG, Mark	Hfd.	Lethbridge
16. DYKHUIS, Karl	Chi.	Hull
17. ALLISON, Scott	Edm.	Prince Albert
18. ANTOSKI, Shawn	Van.	North Bay
19. TKACHUK, Keith	Wpg.	Malden Catholic
20. BRODEUR, Martin	N.J.	St. Hyacinthe
21. SMOLINSKI, Bryan	Bos.	Michigan State

SECOND ROUND

Selection	Claimed By	Amateur Club
22. HUGHES, Ryan	Que.	Cornell
23. SLEGR, Jiri	Van.	CHZ Litvinov (Czech.)
24. HARLOCK, David	N.J.	U. of Michigan
25. SIMON, Chris	Phi.	Ottawa
26. PERREAULT, Nicolas P.	Cgy.	Hawkesbury Jr. A
27. TAYLOR, Chris	NYI	London
28. SEMCHUK, Brandy	L.A.	Canadian National
29. GOTZIAMAN, Chris	N.J.	Roseau
30. PASMA, Rod	Wsh.	Cornwall
31. POTVIN, Felix	Tor.	Chicoutimi
32. VIITAKOSKI, Vesa	Cgy.	SaiPa (Finland)
33. JOHNSON, Craig	St. L.	Hill-Murray HS
34. WEIGHT, Doug	NYR	Lake Superior
35. MULLER, Mike	Wpg.	Wayzata
36. SANDERSON, Geoff	Hfd.	Swift Current
37. DROPPA, Ivan	Chi.	Partizan (Czech.)
38. LEGAULT, Alexandre	Edm.	Boston University
39. KUWABARA, Ryan	Mtl.	Ottawa
40. RENBERG, Mikael	Phi.	Pitea (Sweden)
41. BELZILE, Etienne	Cgy.	Cornell
42. SANDWITH, Terran	Phi.	Tri-Cities

1989

FIRST ROUND

Selection	Claimed By	Amateur Club
1. SUNDIN, Mats	Que.	Nacka (Sweden)
2. CHYZOWSKI, Dave	NYI	Kamloops
3. THORNTON, Scott	Tor.	Belleville
4. BARNES, Stu	Wpg.	Tri-Cities
5. GUERIN, Bill	N.J.	Springfield Jr. B
6. BENNETT, Adam	Chi.	Sudbury
7. ZMOLEK, Doug	Min.	John Marshall
8. HERTER, Jason	Van.	U. of North Dakota
9. MARSHALL, Jason	St. L.	Vernon Jr. A
10. HOLIK, Robert	Hfd.	Dukla Jihlava (Czech.)
11. SILLINGER, Mike	Det.	Regina
12. PEARSON, Rob	Tor.	Belleville
13. VALLIS, Lindsay	Mtl.	Seattle
14. HALLER, Kevin	Buf.	Regina
15. SOULES, Jason	Edm.	Niagara Falls
16. HEWARD, Jamie	Pit.	Regina
17. STEVENSON, Shayne	Bos.	Kitchener
18. MILLER, Jason	N.J.	Medicine Hat
19. KOLZIG, Olaf	Wsh.	Tri-Cities
20. RICE, Steven	NYR	Kitchener
21. BANCROFT, Steve	Tor.	Belleville

SECOND ROUND

Selection	Claimed By	Amateur Club
22. FOOTE, Adam	Que.	Sault Ste. Marie
23. GREEN, Travis	NYI	Spokane
24. MANDERVILLE, Kent	Cgy.	Notre Dame Jr. A
25. RATUSHNY, Dan	Wpg.	Cornell
26. SKALDE, Jarrod	N.J.	Oshawa
27. SPEER, Michael	Chi.	Guelph
28. CRAIG, Mike	Min.	Oshawa
29. WOODWARD, Robert	Van.	Deerfield
30. BRISEBOIS, Patrice	Mtl.	Laval
31. CORRIVEAU, Rick	St. L.	London
32. BOUGHNER, Bob	Det.	Sault-Ste. Marie
33. JOHNSON, Greg	Phi.	Thunder Bay Jr. A
34. JUHLIN, Patrik	Phi.	Vasteras (Sweden)
35. DAFOE, Byron	Wsh.	Portland
36. BORGO, Richard	Edm.	Kitchener
37. LAUS, Paul	Pit.	Niagara Falls
38. PARSON, Mike	Bos.	Guelph
39. THOMPSON, Brent	L.A.	Medicine Hat
40. PROSOFSKY, Jason	NYR	Medicine Hat
41. LAROUCHE, Steve	Mtl.	Trois-Rivieres
42. DRURY, Ted	Cgy.	Fairfield Prep

1988

FIRST ROUND

Selection	Claimed By	Amateur Club
1. MODANO, Mike	Min.	Prince Albert
2. LINDEN, Trevor	Van.	Medicine Hat
3. LESCHYSHYN, Curtis	Que.	Saskatoon
4. SHANNON, Darrin	Pit.	Windsor
5. DORE, Daniel	Que.	Drummondville
6. PEARSON, Scott	Tor.	Kingston
7. GELINAS, Martin	L.A.	Hull
8. ROENICK, Jeremy	Chi.	Thayer Academy
9. BRIND'AMOUR, Rod	St.L.	Notre Dame Jr. A
10. SELANNE, Teemu	Wpg.	Jokerit (Finland)
11. GOVEDARIS, Chris	Hfd.	Toronto
12. FOSTER, Corey	N.J.	Peterborough
13. SAVAGE, Joel	Buf.	Victoria
14. BOIVIN, Claude	Phi.	Drummondville
15. SAVAGE, Reginald	Wsh.	Victoriaville
16. CHEVELDAYOFF, Kevin	NYI	Brandon
17. KOCUR, Kory	Det.	Saskatoon
18. CIMETTA, Robert	Bos.	Toronto
19. LEROUX, Francois	Edm.	St. Jean
20. CHARRON, Eric	Mtl.	Trois-Rivieres
21. MUZZATTI, Jason	Cgy.	Michigan State

SECOND ROUND

Selection	Claimed By	Amateur Club
22. MALLETTE, Troy	NYR	Sault Ste. Marie
23. CHRISTIAN, Jeff	N.J.	London
24. FISET, Stephane	Que.	Victoriaville
25. MAJOR, Mark	Pit.	North Bay
26. DUVAL, Murray	NYR	Spokane
27. DOMI, Tie	Tor.	Peterborough
28. HOLDEN, Paul	L.A.	London
29. DOUCET, Wayne	NYI	Hamilton
30. PLAVSIC, Adrien	St.L.	U. of New Hampshire
31. ROMANIUK, Russell	Wpg.	St. Boniface Jr. A
32. RICHTER, Barry	Hfd.	Culver Academy
33. ROHLIN, Leif	Van.	Vasteras (Sweden)
34. ST. AMOUR, Martin	Mtl.	Verdun
35. MURRAY, Pat	Phi.	Michigan State
36. TAYLOR, Tim	Wsh.	London
37. LEBRUN, Sean	NYI	New Westminster
38. ANGLEHART, Serge	Det.	Drummondville
39. KOIVUNEN, Petro	Edm.	Espoo (Finland)
40. GAETZ, Link	Min.	Spokane
41. BARTLEY, Wade	Wsh.	Dauphin Jr. A
42. HARKINS, Todd	Cgy.	Miami-Ohio

1987

FIRST ROUND

Selection	Claimed By	Amateur Club
1. TURGEON, Pierre	Buf.	Granby
2. SHANAHAN, Brendan	N.J.	London
3. WESLEY, Glen	Bos.	Portland
4. McBEAN, Wayne	L.A.	Medicine Hat
5. JOSEPH, Chris	Pit.	Seattle
6. ARCHIBALD, David	Min.	Portland
7. RICHARDSON, Luke	Tor.	Peterborough
8. WAITE, Jimmy	Chi.	Chicoutimi
9. FOGARTY, Bryan	Que.	Kingston
10. MORE, Jayson	NYR	New Westminster
11. RACINE, Yves	Det.	Longueuil
12. OSBORNE, Keith	St.L.	North Bay
13. CHYNOWETH, Dean	NYI	Medicine Hat
14. QUINTAL, Stephane	Bos.	Granby
15. SAKIC, Joe	Que.	Swift Current
16. MARCHMENT, Bryan	Wpg.	Belleville
17. CASSELS, Andrew	Mtl.	Ottawa
18. HULL, Jody	Hfd.	Peterborough
19. DEASLEY, Bryan	Cgy.	U. of Michigan
20. RUMBLE, Darren	Phi.	Kitchener
21. SOBERLAK, Peter	Edm.	Swift Current

SECOND ROUND

Selection	Claimed By	Amateur Club
22. MILLER, Brad	Buf.	Regina
23. PERSSON, Rickard	N.J.	Ostersund (Sweden)
24. MURPHY, Rob	Van.	Laval
25. MATTEAU, Stephane	Cgy.	Hull
26. TABARACCI, Richard	Pit.	Cornwall
27. FITZPATRICK, Mark	L.A.	Medicine Hat
28. MAROIS, Daniel	Tor.	Chicoutimi
29. McGILL, Ryan	Chi.	Swift Current
30. HARDING, Jeff	Phi.	St. Michael's Jr. B
31. LACROIX, Daniel	NYR	Granby
32. KRUPPKE, Gordon	Det.	Prince Albert
33. LECLAIR, John	Mtl.	Bellows Academy
34. HACKETT, Jeff	NYI	Oshawa
35. McCRADY, Scott	Min.	Medicine Hat
36. BALLANTYNE, Jeff	Wsh.	Ottawa
37. ERICKSSON, Patrik	Wpg.	Brynas (Sweden)
38. DESJARDINS, Eric	Mtl.	Granby
39. BURT, Adam	Hfd.	North Bay
40. GRANT, Kevin	Cgy.	Kitchener
41. WILKIE, Bob	Det.	Swift Current
42. WERENKA, Brad	Edm.	N. Michigan

1986

FIRST ROUND

Selection	Claimed By	Amateur Club
1. MURPHY, Joe	Det.	Michigan State
2. CARSON, Jimmy	L.A.	Verdun
3. BRADY, Neil	N.J.	Medicine Hat
4. ZALAPSKI, Zarley	Pit.	Canadian National
5. ANDERSON, Shawn	Buf.	Canadian National
6. DAMPHOUSSE, Vincent	Tor.	Laval
7. WOODLEY, Dan	Van.	Portland
8. ELYNUIK, Pat	Wpg.	Prince Albert
9. LEETCH, Brian	NYR	Avon Old Farms HS
10. LEMIEUX, Jocelyn	St.L.	Laval
11. YOUNG, Scott	Hfd.	Boston University
12. BABE, Warren	Min.	Lethbridge
13. JANNEY, Craig	Bos.	Boston College
14. SANIPASS, Everett	Chi.	Verdun
15. PEDERSON, Mark	Mtl.	Medicine Hat
16. PELAWA, George	Cgy.	Bemidji HS
17. FITZGERALD, Tom	NYI	Austin Prep
18. McRAE, Ken	Que.	Sudbury
19. GREENLAW, Jeff	Wsh.	Canadian National
20. HUFFMAN, Kerry	Phi.	Guelph
21. ISSEL, Kim	Edm.	Prince Albert

SECOND ROUND

Selection	Claimed By	Amateur Club
22. GRAVES, Adam	Det.	Windsor
23. SEPPO, Jukka	Phi.	Sport (Finland)
24. COPELAND, Todd	N.J.	Belmont Hill HS
25. CAPUANO, Dave	Pit.	Mt. St. Charles HS
26. BROWN, Greg	Buf.	St. Mark's
27. BRUNET, Benoit	Mtl.	Hull
28. HAWLEY, Kent	Phi.	Ottawa
29. NUMMINEN, Teppo	Wpg.	Tappara (Finland)
30. WILKINSON, Neil	Min.	Selkirk
31. POSMA, Mike	St.L.	Buffalo Jr. A
32. LaFORGE, Marc	Hfd.	Kingston
33. KOLSTAD, Dean	Min.	Prince Albert
34. TIRKKONEN, Pekka	Bos.	SaPKo (Finland)
35. KURZAWSKI, Mark	Chi.	Windsor
36. SHANNON, Darryl	Tor.	Windsor
37. GLYNN, Brian	Cgy.	Saskatoon
38. VASKE, Dennis	NYI	Armstrong HS
39. ROUTHIER, Jean-Marc	Que.	Hull
40. SEFTEL, Steve	Wsh.	Kingston
41. GUERARD, Stephane	Que.	Shawinigan
42. NICHOLS, Jamie	Edm.	Portland

1985

FIRST ROUND

Selection	Claimed By	Amateur Club
1. CLARK, Wendel	Tor.	Saskatoon
2. SIMPSON, Craig	Pit.	Michigan State
3. WOLANIN, Craig	N.J.	Kitchener
4. SANDLAK, Jim	Van.	London
5. MURZYN, Dana	Hfd.	Calgary
6. DALGARNO, Brad	NYI	Hamilton
7. DAHLEN, Ulf	NYR	Ostersund (Sweden)
8. FEDYK, Brent	Det.	Regina
9. DUNCANSON, Craig	L.A.	Sudbury
10. GRATTON, Dan	L.A.	Oshawa
11. MANSON, David	Chi.	Prince Albert
12. CHARBONNEAU, Jose	Mtl.	Drummondville
13. KING, Derek	NYI	Sault Ste. Marie
14. JOHANSSON, Calle	Buf.	V. Frolunda (Sweden)
15. LATTA, Dave	Que.	Kitchener
16. CHORSKE, Tom	Mtl.	Minneapolis SW HS
17. BIOTTI, Chris	Cgy.	Belmont Hill HS
18. STEWART, Ryan	Wpg.	Kamloops
19. CORRIVEAU, Yvon	Wsh.	Toronto
20. METCALFE, Scott	Edm.	Kingston
21. SEABROOKE, Glen	Phi.	Peterborough

SECOND ROUND

Selection	Claimed By	Amateur Club
22. SPANGLER, Ken	Tor.	Calgary
23. GIFFIN, Lee	Pit.	Oshawa
24. BURKE, Sean	N.J.	Toronto
25. GAMBLE, Troy	Van.	Medicine Hat
26. WHITMORE, Kay	Hfd.	Peterborough
27. NIEUWENDYK, Joe	Cgy.	Cornell
28. RICHTER, Mike	NYR	Northwood Prep.
29. SHARPLES, Jeff	Det.	Kelowna
30. EDLUND, Par	L.A.	Bjorkloven (Sweden)
31. COTE, Alain	Bos.	Quebec
32. WEINRICH, Eric	N.J.	North Yarmouth
33. RICHARD, Todd	Mtl.	Armstrong HS
34. LAUER, Brad	NYI	Regina
35. HOGUE, Benoit	Buf.	St-Jean
36. LAFRENIERE, Jason	Que.	Hamilton
37. RAGLAN, Herb	St.L.	Kingston
38. WENAAS, Jeff	Cgy.	Medicine Hat
39. OHMAN, Roger	Wpg.	Leksand (Sweden)
40. DRUCE, John	Wsh.	Peterborough
41. CARNELLEY, Todd	Edm.	Kamloops
42. RENDALL, Bruce	Phi.	Chatham

1984

FIRST ROUND

Selection	Claimed By	Amateur Club
1. LEMIEUX, Mario	Pit.	Laval
2. MULLER, Kirk	N.J.	Cdn-Nat.-Guelph
3. OLCZYK, Ed	Chi.	U.S. National
4. IAFRATE, Al	Tor.	U.S. National-Belleville
5. SVOBODA, Petr	Mtl.	CHZ (Czech.)
6. REDMOND, Craig	L.A.	Canadian National
7. BURR, Shawn	Det.	Kitchener
8. CORSON, Shayne	Mtl.	Brantford
9. BODGER, Doug	Pit.	Kamloops Jr. A
10. DAIGNEAULT, J.J.	Van.	Cdn. Nat.-Longueuil
11. COTE, Sylvain	Hfd.	Quebec
12. ROBERTS, Gary	Cgy.	Ottawa
13. QUINN, David	Min.	Kent HS
14. CARKNER, Terry	NYR	Peterborough
15. STIENBURG, Trevor	Que.	Guelph
16. BELANGER, Roger	Pit.	Kingston
17. HATCHER, Kevin	Wsh.	North Bay
18. ANDERSSON, Mikael	Buf.	V. Frolunda (Sweden)
19. PASIN, Dave	Bos.	Prince Albert
20. MacPHERSON, Duncan	NYI	Saskatoon
21. ODELEIN, Selmar	Edm.	Regina

SECOND ROUND

Selection	Claimed By	Amateur Club
22. SMYTH, Greg	Phi.	London
23. BILLINGTON, Craig	N.J.	Belleville
24. WILKS, Brian	L.A.	Kitchener
25. GILL, Todd	Tor.	Windsor
26. BENNING, Brian	St.L.	Portland
27. MELLANBY, Scott	Phi.	Henry Carr Jr. B
28. HOUDA, Doug	Det.	Calgary
29. RICHER, Stephane	Mtl.	Granby
30. DOURIS, Peter	Wpg.	U. of New Hampshire
31. ROHLICEK, Jeff	Van.	Portland
32. HRKAC, Anthony	St.L.	Orillia Jr. A
33. SABOURIN, Ken	Cgy.	Sault Ste. Marie
34. LEACH, Stephen	Wsh.	Matignon HS
35. HELMINEN, Raimo	NYR	Ilves (Finland)
36. BROWN, Jeff	Que.	Sudbury
37. CHYCHRUN, Jeff	Phi.	Kingston
38. RANHEIM, Paul	Cgy.	Edina Hornets HS
39. TRAPP, Doug	Buf.	Regina
40. PODLOSKI, Ray	Bos.	Portland
41. MELANSON, Bruce	NYI	Oshawa
42. REAUGH, Daryl	Edm.	Kamloops Jr. A

1983

FIRST ROUND

Selection	Claimed By	Amateur Club
1. LAWTON, Brian	Min.	Mount St. Charles HS
2. TURGEON, Sylvain	Hfd.	Hull
3. LaFONTAINE, Pat	NYI	Verdun
4. YZERMAN, Steve	Det.	Peterborough
5. BARRASSO, Tom	Buf.	Acton-Boxboro HS
6. MacLEAN, John	N.J.	Oshawa
7. COURTNALL, Russ	Tor.	Victoria
8. McBAIN, Andrew	Wpg.	North Bay
9. NEELY, Cam	Van.	Portland
10. LACOMBE, Normand	Buf.	U. of New Hampshire
11. CREIGHTON, Adam	Buf.	Ottawa
12. GAGNER, Dave	NYR	Brantford
13. QUINN, Dan	Cgy.	Belleville
14. DOLLAS, Bobby	Wpg.	Laval
15. ERREY, Bob	Pit.	Peterborough
16. DIDUCK, Gerald	NYI	Lethbridge
17. TURCOTTE, Alfie	Mtl.	Portland
18. CASSIDY, Bruce	Chi.	Ottawa
19. BEUKEBOOM, Jeff	Edm.	Sault Ste. Marie
20. JENSEN, David	Hfd.	Lawrence
21. MARKWART, Nevin	Bos.	Regina

SECOND ROUND

Selection	Claimed By	Amateur Club
22. CHARLESWORTH, Todd	Pit.	Oshawa
23. SIREN, Ville	Hfd.	Ilves (Finland)
24. EVANS, Shawn	N.J.	Peterborough
25. LAMBERT, Lane	Det.	Saskatoon
26. LEMIEUX, Claude	Mtl.	Trois-Rivières
27. MOMESSO, Sergio	Mtl.	Shawinigan
28. JACKSON, Jeff	Tor.	Brantford
29. BERRY, Brad	Wpg.	St. Albert
30. BRUCE, Dave	Van.	Kitchener
31. TUCKER, John	Buf.	Kitchener
32. HEROUX, Yves	Que.	Chicoutimi
33. HEATH, Randy	NYR	Portland
34. HAJDU, Richard	Buf.	Kamloops Jr. A
35. FRANCIS, Todd	Mtl.	Brantford
36. PARKS, Malcolm	Min.	St. Albert
37. McKECHNEY, Garnet	NYI	Kitchener
38. MUSIL, Frantisek	Min.	Tesla (Czech.)
39. PRESLEY, Wayne	Chi.	Kitchener
40. GOLDEN, Mike	Edm.	Reading HS
41. ZEZEL, Peter	Phi.	Toronto
42. JOHNSTON, Greg	Bos.	Toronto

1982

FIRST ROUND

Selection	Claimed By	Amateur Club
1. KLUZAK, Gord	Bos.	Nanaimo
2. BELLOWS, Brian	Min.	Kitchener
3. NYLUND, Gary	Tor.	Portland
4. SUTTER, Ron	Phi.	Lethbridge
5. STEVENS, Scott	Wsh.	Kitchener
6. HOUSLEY, Phil	Buf.	S. St. Paul HS
7. YAREMCHUK, Ken	Chi.	Portland
8. TROTTIER, Rocky	N.J.	Nanaimo
9. CYR, Paul	Buf.	Victoria
10. SUTTER, Rich	Pit.	Lethbridge
11. PETIT, Michel	Van.	Sherbrooke
12. KYTE, Jim	Wpg.	Cornwall
13. SHAW, David	Que.	Kitchener
14. LAWLESS, Paul	Hfd.	Windsor
15. KONTOS, Chris	NYR	Toronto
16. ANDREYCHUK, Dave	Buf.	Oshawa
17. CRAVEN, Murray	Det.	Medicine Hat
18. DANEYKO, Ken	N.J.	Seattle
19. HEROUX, Alain	Mtl.	Chicoutimi
20. PLAYFAIR, Jim	Edm.	Portland
21. FLATLEY, Pat	NYI	University of Wisconsin

SECOND ROUND

Selection	Claimed By	Amateur Club
22. CURRAN, Brian	Bos.	Portland
23. COURTEAU, Yves	Det.	Laval
24. LEEMAN, Gary	Tor.	Regina
25. IHNACAK, Peter	Tor.	Sparta (Czech.)
26. ANDERSON, Mike	Buf.	N. St. Paul HS
27. HEIDT, Mike	L.A.	Calgary
28. BADEAU, Rene	Chi.	Quebec
29. REIERSON, Dave	Cgy.	Prince Albert
30. JOHANSSON, Jens	Buf.	Pitea (Sweden)
31. GAUVREAU, Jocelyn	Mtl.	Granby
32. CARLSON, Kent	Mtl.	St. Lawrence University
33. MALEY, David	Mtl.	Edina HS
34. GILLIS, Paul	Que.	Niagara Falls
35. PATERSON, Mark	Hfd.	Ottawa
36. SANDSTROM, Tomas	NYR	Farjestads (Sweden)
37. KROMM, Richard	Cgy.	Portland
38. HRYNEWICH, Tim	Pit.	Sudbury
39. BYERS, yyndon	Bos.	Regina
40. SANDELIN, Scott	Mtl.	Hibbing HS
41. GRAVES, Steve	Edm.	Sault Ste. Marie
42. SMITH, Vern	NYI	Lethbridge

Brian Lawton, proudly posing with Lou Nanne and his new Minnesota North Stars' jersey, was the first selection overall in the 1983 Entry Draft.

1981

FIRST ROUND

Selection	Claimed By	Amateur Club
1. HAWERCHUK, Dale	Wpg.	Cornwall
2. SMITH, Doug	L.A.	Ottawa
3. CARPENTER, Bobby	Wsh.	St. John's HS
4. FRANCIS, Ron	Hfd.	Sault Ste. Marie
5. CIRELLA, Joe	Col.	Oshawa
6. BENNING, Jim	Tor.	Portland
7. HUNTER, Mark	Mtl.	Brantford
8. FUHR, Grant	Edm.	Victoria
9. PATRICK, James	NYR	Prince Albert
10. BUTCHER, Garth	Van.	Regina
11. MOLLER, Randy	Que.	Lethbridge
12. TANTI, Tony	Chi.	Oshawa
13. MEIGHAN, Ron	Min.	Niagara Falls
14. LEVEILLE, Normand	Bos.	Chicoutimi
15. MacINNIS, Allan	Cgy.	Kitchener
16. SMITH, Steve	Phi.	Sault Ste. Marie
17. DUDACEK, Jiri	Buf.	Poldi Kladno (Czech.)
18. DELORME, Gilbert	Mtl.	Chicoutimi
19. INGMAN, Jan	Mtl.	Farjestad (Sweden)
20. RUFF, Marty	St.L.	Lethbridge
21. BOUTILIER, Paul	NYI	Sherbrooke

SECOND ROUND

Selection	Claimed By	Amateur Club
22. ARNIEL, Scott	Wpg.	Cornwall
23. LOISELLE, Claude	Det.	Windsor
24. YAREMCHUK, Gary	Tor.	Portland
25. GRIFFIN, Kevin	Chi.	Portland
26. CHERNOMAZ, Rich	Col.	Victoria
27. DONNELLY, Dave	Min.	St. Albert
28. GATZOS, Steve	Pit.	Sault Ste. Marie
29. STRUEBY, Todd	Edm.	Regina
30. ERIXON, Jan	NYR	Skelleftea (Sweden)
31. SANDS, Mike	Min.	Sudbury
32. ERIKSSON, Lars	Mtl.	Brynas (Sweden)
33. HIRSCH, Tom	Min.	Patrick Henry HS
34. PREUSS, Dave	Min.	St. Thomas Academy
35. DUFOUR, Luc	Bos.	Chicoutimi
36. NORDIN, Hakan	St.L.	Farjestad (Sweden)
37. COSTELLO, Rich	Phi.	Natick HS
38. VIRTA, Hannu	Buf.	TPS (Finland)
39. KENNEDY, Dean	L.A.	Brandon
40. CHELIOS, Chris	Mtl.	Moose Jaw
41. WAHLSTEN, Jali	Min.	TPS (Finland)
42. DINEEN, Gord	NYI	Sault Ste. Marie

1980

FIRST ROUND

Selection	Claimed By	Amateur Club
1. WICKENHEISER, Doug	Mtl.	Regina
2. BABYCH, Dave	Wpg.	Portland
3. SAVARD, Denis	Chi.	Montreal
4. MURPHY, Larry	L.A.	Peterborough
5. VEITCH, Darren	Wsh.	Regina
6. COFFEY, Paul	Edm.	Kitchener
7. LANZ, Rick	Van.	Oshawa
8. ARTHUR, Fred	Hfd.	Cornwall
9. BULLARD, Mike	Pit.	Brantford
10. FOX, Jimmy	L.A.	Ottawa
11. BLAISDELL, Mike	Det.	Regina
12. WILSON, Rik	St.L.	Kingston
13. CYR, Denis	Cgy.	Montreal
14. MALONE, Jim	NYR	Toronto
15. DUPONT, Jerome	Chi.	Toronto
16. PALMER, Brad	Min.	Victoria
17. SUTTER, Brent	NYI	Red Deer
18. PEDERSON, Barry	Bos.	Victoria
19. GAGNE, Paul	Col.	Windsor
20. PATRICK, Steve	Buf.	Brandon
21. STOTHERS, Mike	Phi.	Kingston

SECOND ROUND

Selection	Claimed By	Amateur Club
22. WARD, Joe	Col.	Seattle
23. MANTHA, Moe	Wpg.	Toronto
24. ROCHEFORT, Normand	Que.	Quebec
25. MUNI, Craig	Tor.	Kingston
26. McGILL, Bob	Tor.	Victoria
27. NATTRESS, Ric	Mtl.	Brantford
28. LUDZIK, Steve	Chi.	Niagara Falls
29. GALARNEAU, Michel	Hfd.	Hull
30. SOLHEIM, Ken	Chi.	Medicine Hat
31. CURTALE, Tony	Cgy.	Brantford
32. LaVALLEE, Kevin	Cgy.	Brantford
33. TERRION, Greg	L.A.	Brantford
34. MORRISON, Dave	L.A.	Peterborough
35. ALLISON, Mike	NYR	Sudbury
36. DAWES, Len	Chi.	Victoria
37. BEAUPRE, Don	Min.	Sudbury
38. HRUDEY, Kelly	NYI	Medicine Hat
39. KONROYD, Steve	Cgy.	Oshawa
40. CHABOT, John	Mtl.	Hull
41. MOLLER, Mike	Buf.	Lethbridge
42. FRASER, Jay	Phi.	Ottawa

1979

FIRST ROUND

Selection	Claimed By	Amateur Club
1. RAMAGE, Rob	Col.	London
2. TURNBULL, Perry	St.L.	Portland
3. FOLIGNO, Mike	Det.	Sudbury
4. GARTNER, Mike	Wsh.	Niagara Falls
5. VAIVE, Rick	Van.	Sherbrooke
6. HARTSBURG, Craig	Min.	Sault St. Marie
7. BROWN, Keith	Chi.	Portland
8. BOURQUE, Raymond	Bos.	Verdun
9. BOSCHMAN, Laurie	Tor.	Brandon
10. McCARTHY, Tom	Min.	Oshawa
11. RAMSEY, Mike	Buf.	U. of Minnesota
12. REINHART, Paul	Atl.	Kitchener
13. SULLIMAN, Doug	NYR	Kitchener
14. PROPP, Brian	Phi.	Brandon
15. McCRIMMON, Brad	Bos.	Brandon
16. WELLS, Jay	L.A.	Kingston
17. SUTTER, Duane	NYI	Lethbridge
18. ALLISON, Ray	Hfd.	Brandon
19. MANN, Jimmy	Wpg.	Sherbrooke
20. GOULET, Michel	Que.	Quebec
21. LOWE, Kevin	Edm.	Quebec

SECOND ROUND

Selection	Claimed By	Amateur Club
22. WESLEY, Blake	Phi.	Portland
23. PEROVICH, Mike	Atl.	Brandon
24. RAUSSE, Errol	Wsh.	Seattle
25. JONSSON, Tomas	NYI	MoDo AIK (Sweden)
26. ASHTON, Brent	Van.	Saskatoon
27. GINGRAS, Gaston	Mtl.	Hamilton
28. TRIMPER, Tim	Chi.	Peterborough
29. HOPKINS, Dean	L.A.	London
30. HARDY, Mark	L.A.	Montreal
31. MARSHALL, Paul	Pit.	Brantford
32. RUFF, Lindy	Buf.	Lethbridge
33. RIGGIN, Pat	Atl.	London
34. HOSPODAR, Ed	NYR	Ottawa
35. LINDBERGH, Pelle	Phi.	AIK Solna (Sweden)
36. MORRISON, Doug	Bos.	Lethbridge
37. NASLUND, Mats	Mtl.	Brynas IFK (Sweden)
38. CARROLL, Billy	NYI	London
39. SMITH, Stuart	Hfd.	Peterborough
40. CHRISTIAN, Dave	Wpg.	U. of North Dakota
41. HUNTER, Dale	Que.	Sudbury
42. BROTEN, Neal	Min.	U. of Minnesota

1978

FIRST ROUND

Selection	Claimed By	Amateur Club
1. SMITH, Bobby	Min.	Ottawa
2. WALTER, Ryan	Wsh.	Seattle
3. BABYCH, Wayne	St.L.	Portland
4. DERLAGO, Bill	Van.	Brandon
5. GILLIS, Mike	Col.	Kingston
6. WILSON, Behn	Phi.	Kingston
7. LINSEMAN, Ken	Phi.	Kingston
8. GEOFFRION, Danny	Mtl.	Cornwall
9. HUBER, Willie	Det.	Hamilton
10. HIGGINS, Tim	Chi.	Ottawa
11. MARSH, Brad	Atl.	London
12. PETERSON, Brent	Det.	Portland
13. PLAYFAIR, Larry	Buf.	Portland
14. LUCAS, Danny	Phi.	Sault Ste. Marie
15. TAMBELLINI, Steve	NYI	Lethbridge
16. SECORD, Al	Bos.	Hamilton
17. HUNTER, Dave	Mtl.	Sudbury
18. COULIS, Tim	Wsh.	Hamilton

SECOND ROUND

Selection	Claimed By	Amateur Club
19. PAYNE, Steve	Min.	Ottawa
20. MULVEY, Paul	Wsh.	Portland
21. QUENNEVILLE, Joel	Tor.	Windsor
22. FRASER, Curt	Van.	Victoria
23. MacKINNON, Paul	Wsh.	Peterborough
24. CHRISTOFF, Steve	Min.	U. of Minnesota
25. MEEKER, Mike	Pit.	Peterborough
26. MALONEY, Don	NYR	Kitchener
27. MALINOWSKI, Merlin	Col.	Medicine Hat
28. HICKS, Glenn	Det.	Flin Flon
29. LECUYER, Doug	Chi.	Portland
30. YAKIWCHUK, Dale	Mtl.	Portland
31. JENSEN, Al	Det.	Hamilton
32. McKEGNEY, Tony	Buf.	Kingston
33. SIMURDA, Mike	Phi.	Kingston
34. JOHNSTON, Randy	NYI	Peterborough
35. NICOLSON, Graeme	Bos.	Cornwall
36. CARTER, Ron	Mtl.	Sherbrooke

1977

FIRST ROUND

Selection	Claimed By	Amateur Club
1. McCOURT, Dale	Det.	St. Catharines
2. BECK, Barry	Col.	New Westminster
3. PICARD, Robert	Wsh.	Montreal
4. GILLIS, Jere	Van.	Sherbrooke
5. CROMBEEN, Mike	Cle.	Kingston
6. WILSON, Doug	Chi.	Ottawa
7. MAXWELL, Brad	Min.	New Westminster
8. DEBLOIS, Lucien	NYR	Sorel
9. CAMPBELL, Scott	St.L.	London
10. NAPIER, Mark	Mtl.	Toronto
11. ANDERSON, John	Tor.	Toronto
12. JOHANSEN, Trevor	Tor.	Toronto
13. DUGUAY, Ron	NYR	Sudbury
14. SEILING, Ric	Buf.	St. Catharines
15. BOSSY, Mike	NYI	Laval
16. FOSTER, Dwight	Bos.	Kitchener
17. McCARTHY, Kevin	Phi.	Winnipeg
18. DUPONT, Norm	Mtl.	Montreal

SECOND ROUND

Selection	Claimed By	Amateur Club
19. SAVARD, Jean	Chi.	Quebec
20. ZAHARKO, Miles	Atl.	New Westminister
21. LOFTHOUSE, Mark	Wsh.	New Westminster
22. BANDURA, Jeff	Van.	Portland
23. CHICOINE, Daniel	Cle.	Sherbrooke
24. GLADNEY, Bob	Tor.	Oshawa
25. SEMENKO, Dave	Min.	Brandon
26. KEATING, Mike	NYR	St. Catherines
27. LABATTE, Neil	St.L.	Toronto
28. LAURENCE, Don	Atl.	Kitchener
29. SAGANIUK, Rocky	Tor.	Lethbridge
30. HAMILTON, Jim	Pit.	London
31. HILL, Brian	Atl.	Medicine Hat
32. ARESHENKOFF, Ron	Buf.	Medicine Hat
33. TONELLI, John	NYI	Toronto
34. PARRO, Dave	Bos.	Saskatoon
35. GORENCE, Tom	Phi.	U. of Minnesota
36. LANGWAY, Rod	Mtl.	U. of New Hampshire

1976

FIRST ROUND

Selection	Claimed By	Amateur Club
1. GREEN, Rick	Wsh.	London
2. CHAPMAN, Blair	Pit.	Saskatoon
3. SHARPLEY, Glen	Min.	Hull
4. WILLIAMS, Fred	Det.	Saskatoon
5. JOHANSSON, Bjorn	Cal.	Sweden
6. MURDOCH, Don	NYR	Medicine Hat
7. FEDERKO, Bernie	St.L.	Saskatoon
8. SHAND, Dave	Atl.	Peterborough
9. CLOUTIER, Real	Chi.	Quebec
10. PHILLIPOFF, Harold	Atl.	New Westminster
11. GARDNER, Paul	K.C.	Oshawa
12. LEE, Peter	Mtl.	Ottawa
13. SCHUTT, Rod	Mtl.	Sudbury
14. McKENDRY, Alex	NYI	Sudbury
15. CARROLL, Greg	Wsh.	Medicine Hat
16. PACHAL, Clayton	Bos.	New Westminster
17. SUZOR, Mark	Phi.	Kingston
18. BAKER, Bruce	Mtl.	Ottawa

SECOND ROUND

Selection	Claimed By	Amateur Club
19. MALONE, Greg	Pit.	Oshawa
20. SUTTER, Brian	St.L.	Lethbridge
21. CLIPPINGDALE, Steve	L.A.	New Westminster
22. LARSON, Reed	Det.	U. of Minnesota
23. STENLUND, Vern	Cal.	London
24. FARRISH, Dave	NYR	Sudbury
25. SMRKE, John	St.L.	Toronto
26. MANNO, Bob	Van.	St. Catharines
27. McDILL, Jeff	Chi.	Victoria
28. SIMPSON, Bobby	Atl.	Sherbrooke
29. MARSH, Peter	Pit.	Sherbrooke
30. CARLYLE, Randy	Tor.	Sudbury
31. ROBERTS, Jim	Min.	Ottawa
32. KASZYCKI, Mike	NYI	Sault Ste. Marie
33. KOWAL, Joe	Buf.	Hamilton
34. GLOECKNER, Larry	Bos.	Victoria
35. CALLANDER, Drew	Phi.	Regina
36. MELROSE, Barry	Mtl.	Kamloops

1975

FIRST ROUND

Selection	Claimed By	Amateur Club
1. BRIDGMAN, Mel	Phi.	Victoria
2. DEAN, Barry	K.C.	Medicine Hat
3. KLASSEN, Ralph	Cal.	Saskatoon
4. MAXWELL, Brian	Min.	Medicine Hat
5. LAPOINTE, Rick	Det.	Victoria
6. ASHBY, Don	Tor.	Calgary
7. VAYDIK, Greg	Chi.	Medicine Hat
8. MULHERN, Richard	Atl.	Sherbrooke
9. SADLER, Robin	Mtl.	Edmonton
10. BLIGHT, Rick	Van.	Brandon
11. PRICE, Pat	NYI	Saskatoon
12. DILLON, Wayne	NYR	Toronto
13. LAXTON, Gord	Pit.	New Westminster
14. HALWARD, Doug	Bos.	Peterborough
15. MONDOU, Pierre	Mtl.	Montreal
16. YOUNG, Tim	L.A.	Ottawa
17. SAUVE, Bob	Buf.	Laval
18. FORSYTH, Alex	Wsh.	Kingston

SECOND ROUND

Selection	Claimed By	Amateur Club
19. SCAMURRA, Peter	Wsh.	Peterborough
20. CAIRNS, Don	K.C.	Victoria
21. MARUK, Dennis	Cal.	London
22. ENGBLOM, Brian	Mtl.	U. of Wisconsin
23. ROLLINS, Jerry	Det.	Winnipeg
24. JARVIS, Doug	Tor.	Peterborough
25. ARNDT, Daniel	Chi.	Saskatoon
26. BOWNASS, Rick	Atl.	Montreal
27. STANIOWSKI, Ed	St.L.	Regina
28. GASSOFF, Brad	Van.	Kamloops
29. SALVIAN, David	NYI	St. Catharines
30. SOETAERT, Doug	NYR	Edmonton
31. ANDERSON, Russ	Pit.	U. of Minnesota
32. SMITH, Barry	Bos.	New Westminster
33. BUCYK, Terry	L.A.	Lethbridge
34. GREENBANK, Kelvin	Mtl.	Winnipeg
35. BREITENBACH, Ken	Buf.	St. Catharines
36. MASTERS, Jamie	St.L.	Ottawa

1974

FIRST ROUND

Selection	Claimed By	Amateur Club
1. JOLY, Greg	Wsh.	Regina
2. PAIEMENT, Wilfred	K.C.	St. Catharines
3. HAMPTON, Rick	Cal.	St. Catharines
4. GILLIES, Clark	NYI	Regina
5. CONNOR, Cam	Mtl.	Flin Flon
6. HICKS, Doug	Min.	Flin Flon
7. RISEBROUGH, Doug	Mtl.	Kitchener
8. LAROUCHE, Pierre	Pit.	Sorel
9. LOCHEAD, Bill	Det.	Oshawa
10. CHARTRAW, Rick	Mtl.	Kitchener
11. FOGOLIN, Lee	Buf.	Oshawa
12. TREMBLAY, Mario	Mtl.	Montreal
13. VALIQUETTE, Jack	Tor.	Sault Ste. Marie
14. MALONEY, Dave	NYR	Kitchener
15. McTAVISH, Gord	Mtl.	Sudbury
16. MULVEY, Grant	Chi.	Calgary
17. CHIPPERFIELD, Ron	Cal.	Brandon
18. LARWAY, Don	Bos.	Swift Current

SECOND ROUND

Selection	Claimed By	Amateur Club
19. MARSON, Mike	Wsh.	Sudbury
20. BURDON, Glen	K.C.	Regina
21. AFFLECK, Bruce	Cal.	U. of Denver
22. TROTTIER, Bryan	NYI	Swift Current
23. SEDLBAUER, Ron	Van.	Kitchener
24. NANTAIS, Rick	Min.	Quebec
25. HOWE, Mark	Bos.	Toronto
26. HESS, Bob	St.L.	New Westminster
27. COSSETTE, Jacques	Pit.	Sorel
28. CHOUINARD, Guy	Atl.	Quebec
29. GARE, Danny	Buf.	Calgary
30. MacGREGOR, Gary	Mtl.	Cornwall
31. WILLIAMS, Dave	Tor.	Swift Current
32. GRESCHNER, Ron	NYR	New Westminster
33. LUPIEN, Gilles	Mtl.	Montreal
34. DAIGLE, Alain	Chi.	Trois-Rivières
35. McLEAN, Don	Phi.	Sudbury
36. STURGEON, Peter	Bos.	Kitchener

1973

FIRST ROUND

Selection	Claimed By	Amateur Club
1. POTVIN, Denis	NYI	Ottawa
2. LYSIAK, Tom	Atl.	Medicine Hat
3. VERVERGAERT, Dennis	Van.	London
4. McDONALD, Lanny	Tor.	Medicine Hat
5. DAVIDSON, John	St.L.	Calgary
6. SAVARD, Andre	Bos.	Quebec
7. STOUGHTON, Blaine	Pit.	Flin Flon
8. GAINEY, Bob	Mtl.	Peterborough
9. DAILEY, Bob	Van.	Toronto
10. NEELEY, Bob	Tor.	Peterborough
11. RICHARDSON, Terry	Det.	New Westminster
12. TITANIC, Morris	Buf.	Sudbury
13. ROTA, Darcy	Chi.	Edmonton
14. MIDDLETON, Rick	NYR	Oshawa
15. TURNBULL, Ian	Tor.	Ottawa
16. MERCREDI, Vic	Atl.	New Westminster

SECOND ROUND

Selection	Claimed By	Amateur Club
17. GOLDUP, Glen	Mtl.	Toronto
18. DUNLOP, Blake	Min.	Ottawa
19. BORDELEAU, Paulin	Van.	Toronto
20. GOODENOUGH, Larry	Phi.	London
21. VAIL, Eric	Atl.	Sudbury
22. MARRIN, Peter	Mtl.	Toronto
23. BIANCHIN, Wayne	Pit.	Flin Flon
24. PESUT, George	St.L.	Saskatoon
25. ROGERS, John	Min.	Edmonton
26. LEVINS, Brent	Phi.	Swift Current
27. CAMPBELL, Colin	Pit.	Peterborough
28. LANDRY, Jean	Buf.	Quebec
29. THOMAS, Reg	Chi.	London
30. HICKEY, Pat	NYR	Hamilton
31. JONES, Jim	Bos.	Peterborough
32. ANDRUFF, Ron	Mtl.	Flin Flon

1972

FIRST ROUND

Selection	Claimed By	Amateur Club
1. HARRIS, Billy	NYI	Toronto
2. RICHARD, Jacques	Atl.	Quebec
3. LEVER, Don	Van.	Niagara Falls
4. SHUTT, Steve	Mtl.	Toronto
5. SCHOENFELD, Jim	Buf.	Niagara Falls
6. LAROCQUE, Michel	Mtl.	Ottawa
7. BARBER, Bill	Phi.	Kitchener
8. GARDNER, Dave	Mtl.	Toronto
9. MERRICK, Wayne	St.L.	Ottawa
10. BLANCHARD, Albert	NYR	Kitchener
11. FERGUSON, George	Tor.	Toronto
12. BYERS, Jerry	Min.	Kitchener
13. RUSSELL, Phil	Chi.	Edmonton
14. VAN BOXMEER, John	Mtl.	Guelph
15. MacMILLAN, Bobby	NYR	St. Catharines
16. BLOOM, Mike	Bos.	St. Catharines

SECOND ROUND

Selection	Claimed By	Amateur Club
17. HENNING Lorne	NYI	New Westminster
18. BIALOWAS, Dwight	Atl.	Regina
19. McSHEFFREY, Brian	Van.	Ottawa
20. KOZAK, Don	L.A.	Edmonton
21. SACHARUK, Larry	NYR	Saskatoon
22. CASSIDY, Tom	Cal.	Kitchener
23. BLADON, Tom	Phi.	Edmonton
24. LYNCH, Jack	Pit.	Oshawa
25. CARRIERE, Larry	Buf.	Loyola College
26. GUITE, Pierre	Det.	St. Catharines
27. OSBURN, Randy	Tor.	London
28. WEIR, Stan	Cal.	Medicine Hat
29. OGILVIE, Brian	Chi.	Edmonton
30. LUKOWICH, Bernie	Pit.	New Westminster
31. VILLEMURE, Rene	NYR	Shawinigan
32. ELDER, Wayne	Bos.	London

1971

FIRST ROUND

Selection	Claimed By	Amateur Club
1. LAFLEUR, Guy	Mtl.	Quebec
2. DIONNE, Marcel	Det.	St. Catharines
3. GUEVREMONT, Jocelyn	Van.	Montreal
4. CARR, Gene	St.L.	Flin Flon
5. MARTIN, Rick	Buf.	Montreal
6. JONES, Ron	Bos.	Edmonton
7. ARNASON, Chuck	Mtl.	Flin Flon
8. WRIGHT, Larry	Phi.	Regina
9. PLANTE, Pierre	Phi.	Drummondville
10. VICKERS, Steve	NYR	Toronto
11. WILSON, Murray	Mtl.	Ottawa
12. SPRING, Dan	Chi.	Edmonton
13. DURBANO, Steve	NYR	Toronto
14. O'REILLY, Terry	Bos.	Oshawa

SECOND ROUND

Selection	Claimed By	Amateur Club
15. BAIRD, Ken	Cal.	Flin Flon
16. BOUCHA, Henry	Det.	U.S. Nationals
17. LALONDE, Bobby	Van.	Montreal
18. McKENZIE, Brian	Pit.	St. Catharines
19. RAMSAY, Craig	Buf.	Peterborough
20. ROBINSON, Larry	Mtl.	Kitchener
21. NORRISH, Rod	Min.	Regina
22. KEHOE, Rick	Tor.	Hamilton
23. FORTIER, Dave	Tor.	St. Catharines
24. DEGUISE, Michel	Mtl.	Sorel
25. FRENCH, Terry	Mtl.	Ottawa
26. KRYSKOW, Dave	Chi.	Edmonton
27. WILLIAMS, Tom	NYR	Hamilton
28. RIDLEY, Curt	Bos.	Portage

1970

FIRST ROUND

Selection	Claimed By	Amateur Club
1. PERREAULT, Gilbert	Buf.	Montreal
2. TALLON, Dale	Van.	Toronto
3. LEACH, Reg	Bos.	Flin Flon
4. MacLEISH, Rick	Bos.	Peterborough
5. MARTINIUK, Ray	Mtl.	Flin Flon
6. LEFLEY, Chuck	Mtl.	Canadian Nationals
7. POLIS, Greg	Pit.	Estevan
8. SITTLER, Darryl	Tor.	London
9. PLUMB, Ron	Bos.	Peterborough
10. ODDLEIFSON, Chris	Oak.	Winnipeg
11. GRATTON, Norm	NYR	Montreal
12. LAJEUNESSE, Serge	Det.	Montreal
13. STEWART, Bob	Bos.	Oshawa
14. MALONEY, Dan	Chi.	London

SECOND ROUND

Selection	Claimed By	Amateur Club
15. DEADMARSH, Butch	Buf.	Brandon
16. HARGREAVES, Jim	Van.	Winnipeg
17. HARVEY, Fred	Min.	Hamilton
18. CLEMENT, Bill	Phi.	Ottawa
19. LAFRAMBOISE, Pete	Oak.	Ottawa
20. BARRETT, Fred	Min.	Toronto
21. STEWART, John	Pit.	Flin Flon
22. THOMPSON, Errol	Tor.	Charlottetown
23. KEOGAN, Murray	St.L.	U. of Minnesota
24. McDONOUGH, Al	L.A.	St. Catharines
25. MURPHY, Mike	NYR	Toronto
26. GUINDON, Bobby	Det.	Montreal
27. BOUCHARD, Dan	Bos.	London
28. ARCHAMBAULT, Mike	Chi.	Drummondville

1969

FIRST ROUND

Selection	Claimed By	Amateur Club
1. HOULE, Rejean	Mtl.	Montreal
2. TARDIF, Marc	Mtl.	Montreal
3. TANNAHILL, Don	Bos.	Niagara Falls
4. SPRING, Frank	Bos.	Edmonton
5. REDMOND, Dick	Min.	St. Catharines
6. CURRIER, Bob	Phi.	Cornwall
7. FEATHERSTONE, Tony	Oak.	Peterborough
8. DUPONT, Andr;aae	NYR	Montreal
9. MOSER, Ernie	Tor.	Estevan
10. RUTHERFORD, Jim	Det.	Hamilton
11. BOLDIREV, Ivan	Bos.	Oshawa
12. JARRY, Pierre	NYR	Ottawa
13. BORDELEAU, J.-P.	Chi.	Montreal
14. O'BRIEN, Dennis	Min.	St. Catharines

SECOND ROUND

Selection	Claimed By	Amateur Club
15. KESSELL, Rick	Pit.	Oshawa
16. HOGANSON, Dale	L.A.	Estevan
17. CLARKE, Bobby	Phi.	Flin Flon
18. STACKHOUSE, Ron	Oak.	Peterborough
19. LOWE, Mike	St.L.	Loyola College
20. BRINDLEY, Doug	Tor.	Niagara Falls
21. GARWASIUK, Ron	Det.	Regina
22. QUOQUOCHI, Art	Bos.	Montreal
23. WILSON, Bert	NYR	London
24. ROMANCHYCH, Larry	Chi.	Flin Flon
25. GILBERT, Gilles	Min.	London
26. BRIERE, Michel	Pit.	Shawinigan Falls
27. BODDY, Greg	L.A.	Edmonton
28. BROSSART, Bill	Phi.	Estevan

NHL All-Stars

Active Players' All-Star Selection Records

	First Team Selections	Second Team Selections	Total
GOALTENDERS			
Patrick Roy	(3) 1988-89; 1989-90; 1991-92.	(2) 1987-88; 1990-91.	5
Tom Barrasso	(1) 1983-84.	(1) 1984-85.	2
Grant Fuhr	(1) 1987-88.	(1) 1981-82.	2
Mike Liut	(1) 1980-81.	(1) 1986-87.	2
J.Vanbiesbrouck	(1) 1985-86.	(0)	1
Ron Hextall	(1) 1986-87.	(0)	1
Ed Belfour	(1) 1990-91.	(0)	1
R. Melanson	(0)	(1) 1982-83.	1
Mike Vernon	(0)	(1) 1988-89.	1
Darren Puppa	(0)	(1) 1989-90.	1
Kirk McLean	(0)	(1) 1991-92.	1
DEFENSEMEN			
Ray Bourque	(9) 1979-80; 1981-82; 1983-84; 1984-85; 1986-87; 1987-88; 1989-90; 1990-91; 1991-92.	(4) 1980-81; 1982-83; 1985-86; 1988-89	13
Paul Coffey	(3) 1984-85; 1985-86; 1988-89.	(4) 1981-82; 1982-83; 1983-84; 1989-90.	7
Larry Robinson	(3) 1976-77; 1978-79; 1979-80.	(3) 1977-78; 1980-81; 1985-86.	6
Al MacInnis	(2) 1989-90; 1990-91.	(2) 1986-87; 1988-89.	4
Mark Howe	(3) 1982-83; 1985-86; 1986-87.	(0)	3
Rod Langway	(2) 1982-83; 1983-84.	(1) 1984-85.	3
Doug Wilson	(1) 1981-82.	(2) 1984-85; 1989-90.	3
Chris Chelios	(1) 1988-89.	(1) 1990-91.	2
Brian Leetch	(1) 1991-92	(1) 1990-91.	2
Scott Stevens	(1) 1987-88.	(1) 1991-92	2
Randy Carlyle	(1) 1980-81.	(0)	1
Larry Murphy	(0)	(1) 1986-87.	1
Gary Suter	(0)	(1) 1987-88.	1
Brad McCrimmon	(0)	(1) 1987-88.	1
Phil Housley	(0)	(1) 1991-92	1
CENTERS			
Wayne Gretzky	(8) 1980-81; 1981-82; 1982-83; 1983-84; 1984-85; 1985-86; 1986-87; 1990-91.	(4) 1979-80; 1987-88; 1988-89; 1989-90.	12
Mario Lemieux	(2) 1987-88; 1988-89.	(3) 1985-86; 1986-87; 1991-92.	5
Bryan Trottier	(2) 1977-78; 1978-79.	(2) 1981-82; 1983-84.	4
Mark Messier	(2) 1989-90; 1991-92.	(0)	2
Denis Savard	(0)	(1) 1982-83.	1
Dale Hawerchuk	(0)	(1) 1984-85.	1
Adam Oates	(0)	(1) 1990-91.	1
RIGHT WING			
Jari Kurri	(2) 1984-85; 1986-87.	(3) 1983-84; 1985-86; 1988-89.	5
Brett Hull	(3) 1989-90; 1990-91; 1991-92.	(0)	3
Cam Neely	(0)	(3) 1987-88; 1989-90; 1990-91.	3
Joe Mullen	(1) 1988-89.	(0)	1
Dave Taylor	(0)	(1) 1980-81.	1
Tim Kerr	(0)	(1) 1986-87.	1
Mark Recchi	(0)	(1) 1991-92.	1
LEFT WING			
Luc Robitaille	(4) 1987-88; 1988-89; 1989-90; 1990-91.	(2) 1986-87; 1991-92.	6
Michel Goulet	(3) 1983-84; 1985-86; 1986-87.	(2) 1982-83; 1987-88.	5
Mark Messier	(2) 1981-82; 1982-83.	(1) 1983-84.	3
Kevin Stevens	(1) 1991-92.	(1) 1990-91.	2
John Tonelli	(0)	(2) 1981-82; 1984-85.	2
John Ogrodnick	(1) 1984-85.	(0)	1
Mats Naslund	(0)	(1) 1985-86.	1
Gerard Gallant	(0)	(1) 1988-89.	1
Brian Bellows	(0)	(1) 1989-90.	1

Leading NHL All-Stars 1930-92

Player	Pos	Team	NHL Seasons	First Team Selections	Second Team Selections	Total Selections
Howe, Gordie	RW	Detroit	26	12	9	21
Richard, Maurice	RW	Montreal	18	8	6	14
*Bourque, Ray	D	Boston	13	9	5	13
Hull, Bobby	LW	Chicago	16	10	2	12
*Gretzky, Wayne	C	Edm., L.A.	13	8	4	12
Harvey, Doug	D	Mtl., NYR	19	10	1	11
Hall, Glenn	G	Chi., St.L.	18	7	4	11
Beliveau, Jean	C	Montreal	20	6	4	10
Seibert, Earl	D	NYR., Chi	15	4	6	10
Orr, Bobby	D	Boston	12	8	1	9
Lindsay, Ted	LW	Detroit	17	8	1	9
Mahovlich, Frank	LW	Tor., Det., Mtl.	18	3	6	9
Shore, Eddie	D	Boston	14	7	1	8
Mikita, Stan	C	Chicago	22	6	2	8
Kelly, Red	D	Detroit	20	6	2	8
Esposito, Phil	C	Boston	18	6	2	8
Pilote, Pierre	D	Chicago	14	5	3	8
Brimsek, Frank	G	Boston	10	2	6	8
Bossy, Mike	RW	NY Islanders	10	5	3	8
Potvin, Denis	D	NY Islanders	15	5	2	7
Park, Brad	D	NYR, Bos.	17	5	2	7
*Coffey, Paul	D	Edm., Pit.	12	3	4	7
Plante, Jacques	G	Mtl-Tor	18	3	4	7
Gadsby, Bill	D	Chi., NYR, Det.	20	3	4	7
Sawchuk, Terry	G	Detroit	21	3	4	7
Durnan, Bill	G	Montreal	7	6	0	6
Lafleur, Guy	RW	Montreal	16	6	0	6
Dryden, Ken	G	Montreal	8	5	1	6
*Robitaille, Luc	LW	Los Angeles	6	4	2	6
*Robinson, Larry	D	Montreal	20	3	3	6
Horton, Tim	D	Toronto	24	3	3	6
Salming, Borje	D	Toronto	17	1	5	6
Cowley, Bill	C	Boston	13	4	1	5
*Messier, Mark	LW/C	Edm., NYR	13	4	1	5
Jackson, Harvey	LW	Toronto	15	4	1	5
*Goulet, Michel	LW	Quebec	13	3	2	5
Conacher, Charlie	RW	Toronto	12	3	2	5
Stewart, Jack	D	Detroit	12	3	2	5
Lach, Elmer	C	Montreal	14	3	2	5
Quackenbush, Bill	D	Det., Bos.	14	3	2	5
Blake, Toe	LW	Montreal	15	3	2	5
Esposito, Tony	G	Chicago	16	3	2	5
*Roy, Patrick	G	Montreal	8	2	3	5
Reardon, Ken	D	Montreal	7	2	3	5
*Kurri, Jari	RW	Edmonton	11	2	3	5
Apps, Syl	C	Toronto	10	2	3	5
Giacomin, Ed	G	NY Rangers	13	2	3	5
*Lemieux, Mario	C	Pittsburgh	8	2	3	5

* Active

Position Leaders in All-Star Selections

Position	Player	First Team	Second Team	Total
GOAL	Glenn Hall	7	4	11
	Frank Brimsek	2	6	8
	Jacques Plante	3	4	7
	Terry Sawchuk	3	4	7
	Bill Durnan	6	0	6
	Ken Dryden	5	1	6
DEFENSE	*Ray Bourque	9	4	13
	Doug Harvey	10	1	11
	Earl Seibert	4	6	10
	Bobby Orr	8	1	9
	Eddie Shore	7	1	8
	Red Kelly	6	2	8
	Pierre Pilote	5	3	8
LEFT WING	Bobby Hull	10	2	12
	Ted Lindsay	8	1	9
	Frank Mahovlich	3	6	9
	*Luc Robitaille	4	2	6
	Harvey Jackson	4	1	5
	*Michel Goulet	3	2	5
	Toe Blake	3	2	5
RIGHT WING	Gordie Howe	12	9	21
	Maurice Richard	8	6	14
	Mike Bossy	5	3	8
	Guy Lafleur	6	0	6
	Charlie Conacher	3	2	5
CENTER	*Wayne Gretzky	8	4	12
	Jean Beliveau	6	4	10
	Stan Mikita	6	2	8
	Phil Esposito	6	2	8
	Bill Cowley	4	1	5
	Elmer Lach	3	2	5
	Syl Apps	2	3	5
	Mario Lemieux	2	3	5

* active player

All-Star Teams

1930-92

Voting for the NHL All-Star Team is conducted among the representatives of the Professional Hockey Writers' Association at the end of the season.

Following is a list of the First and Second All-Star Teams since their inception in 1930-31.

1991-92

First Team		Second Team
Roy, Patrick, Mtl.	G	Kirk McLean, Van.
Leetch, Brian, NYR	D	Housley, Phil, Wpg.
Bourque, Ray, Bos.	D	Stevens, Scott, N.J.
Messier, Mark, NYR	C	Lemieux, Mario, Pit.
Hull, Brett, St. L.	RW	Recchi, Mark, Pit., Phi.
Stevens, Kevin, Pit.	LW	Robitaille, Luc, L.A.

1990-91

First Team		Second Team
Belfour, Ed, Chi.	G	Roy, Patrick, Mtl.
Bourque, Ray, Bos.	D	Chelios, Chris, Chi.
MacInnis, Al, Cgy.	D	Leetch, Brian, NYR
Gretzky, Wayne, L.A.	C	Oates, Adam, St. L.
Hull, Brett, St. L.	RW	Neely, Cam, Bos.
Robitaille, Luc, L.A.	LW	Stevens, Kevin, Pit.

1989-90

First Team		Second Team
Roy, Patrick, Mtl.	G	Puppa, Darren, Buf.
Bourque, Ray, Bos.	D	Coffey, Paul, Pit.
MacInnis, Al, Cgy.	D	Wilson, Doug, Chi.
Messier, Mark, Edm.	C	Gretzky, Wayne, L.A.
Hull, Brett, St. L.	RW	Neely, Cam, Bos.
Robitaille, Luc, L.A.	LW	Bellows, Brian, Min.

1988-89

First Team		Second Team
Roy, Patrick, Mtl.	G	Vernon, Mike, Cgy.
Chelios, Chris, Mtl.	D	MacInnis, Al, Cgy.
Coffey, Paul, Pit.	D	Bourque, Ray, Bos.
Lemieux, Mario, Pit.	C	Gretzky, Wayne, L.A.
Mullen, Joe, Cgy.	RW	Kurri, Jari, Edm.
Robitaille, Luc, L.A.	LW	Gallant, Gerard, Det.

1987-88

First Team		Second Team
Fuhr, Grant, Edm.	G	Roy, Patrick, Mtl.
Bourque, Ray, Bos.	D	Suter, Gary, Cgy.
Stevens, Scott, Wsh.	D	McCrimmon, Brad, Cgy.
Lemieux, Mario, Pit.	C	Gretzky, Wayne, Edm.
Loob, Hakan, Cgy.	RW	Neely, Cam, Bos.
Robitaille, Luc, L.A.	LW	Goulet, Michel, Que.

1986-87

First Team		Second Team
Hextall, Ron, Phi.	G	Liut, Mike, Hfd.
Bourque, Ray, Bos.	D	Murphy, Larry, Wsh.
Howe, Mark, Phi.	D	MacInnis, Al, Cgy.
Gretzky, Wayne, Edm.	C	Lemieux, Mario, Pit.
Kurri, Jari, Edm.	RW	Kerr, Tim, Phi.
Goulet, Michel, Que.	LW	Robitaille, Luc, L.A.

1985-86

First Team		Second Team
Vanbiesbrouck, J., NYR	G	Froese, Bob, Phi.
Coffey, Paul, Edm.	D	Robinson, Larry, Mtl.
Howe, Mark, Phi.	D	Bourque, Ray, Bos.
Gretzky, Wayne, Edm.	C	Lemieux, Mario, Pit.
Bossy, Mike, NYI	RW	Kurri, Jari, Edm.
Goulet, Michel, Que.	LW	Naslund, Mats, Mtl.

1984-85

First Team		Second Team
Lindbergh, Pelle, Phi.	G	Barrasso, Tom, Buf.
Coffey, Paul, Edm.	D	Langway, Rod, Wsh.
Bourque, Ray, Bos.	D	Wilson, Doug, Chi.
Gretzky, Wayne, Edm.	C	Hawerchuk, Dale, Wpg.
Kurri, Jari, Edm.	RW	Bossy, Mike, NYI
Ogrodnick, John, Det.	LW	Tonelli, John, NYI

1983-84

First Team		Second Team
Barrasso, Tom, Buf.	G	Riggin, Pat, Wsh.
Langway, Rod, Wsh.	D	Coffey, Paul, Edm.
Bourque, Ray, Bos.	D	Potvin, Denis, NYI
Gretzky, Wayne, Edm.	C	Trottier, Bryan, NYI
Bossy, Mike, NYI	RW	Kurri, Jari, Edm.
Goulet, Michel, Que.	LW	Messier, Mark, Edm.

1982-83

First Team		Second Team
Peeters, Pete, Bos.	G	Melanson, Roland, NYI
Howe, Mark, Phi.	D	Bourque, Ray, Bos.
Langway, Rod, Wsh.	D	Coffey, Paul, Edm.
Gretzky, Wayne, Edm.	C	Savard, Denis, Chi.
Bossy, Mike, NYI	RW	McDonald, Lanny, Cgy.
Messier, Mark, Edm.	LW	Goulet, Michel, Que.

Michel Goulet earned back-to-back First Team All-Star berths in 1986 and 1987.

1981-82

First Team		Second Team
Smith, Bill, NYI	*G*	Fuhr, Grant, Edm.
Wilson, Doug, Chi.	*D*	Coffey, Paul, Edm.
Bourque, Ray, Bos.	*D*	Engblom, Brian, Mtl.
Gretzky, Wayne, Edm.	*C*	Trottier, Bryan, NYI
Bossy, Mike, NYI	*RW*	Middleton, Rick, Bos.
Messier, Mark, Edm.	*LW*	Tonelli, John, NYI

1980-81

First Team		Second Team
Liut, Mike, St.L.	*G*	Lessard, Mario, L.A.
Potvin, Denis, NYI	*D*	Robinson, Larry, Mtl.
Carlyle, Randy, Pit.	*D*	Bourque, Ray, Bos.
Gretzky, Wayne, Edm.	*C*	Dionne, Marcel, L.A.
Bossy, Mike, NYI	*RW*	Taylor, Dave, L.A.
Simmer, Charlie, L.A.	*LW*	Barber, Bill, Phi.

1979-80

First Team		Second Team
Esposito, Tony, Chi.	*G*	Edwards, Don, Buf.
Robinson, Larry, Mtl.	*D*	Salming, Borje, Tor.
Bourque, Ray, Bos.	*D*	Schoenfeld, Jim, Buf.
Dionne, Marcel, L.A.	*C*	Gretzky, Wayne, Edm.
Lafleur, Guy, Mtl.	*RW*	Gare, Danny, Buf.
Simmer, Charlie, L.A.	*LW*	Shutt, Steve, Mtl.

1978-79

First Team		Second Team
Dryden, Ken, Mtl.	*G*	Resch, Glenn, NYI
Potvin, Denis, NYI	*D*	Salming, Borje, Tor.
Robinson, Larry, Mtl.	*D*	Savard, Serge, Mtl.
Trottier, Bryan, NYI	*C*	Dionne, Marcel, L.A.
Lafleur, Guy, Mtl.	*RW*	Bossy, Mike, NYI
Gillies, Clark, NYI	*LW*	Barber, Bill, Phi.

1977-78

First Team		Second Team
Dryden, Ken, Mtl.	*G*	Edwards, Don, Buf.
Potvin, Denis, NYI	*D*	Robinson, Larry, Mtl.
Park, Brad, Bos.	*D*	Salming, Borje, Tor.
Trottier, Bryan, NYI	*C*	Sittler, Darryl, Tor.
Lafleur, Guy, Mtl.	*RW*	Bossy, Mike, NYI
Gillies, Clark, NYI	*LW*	Shutt, Steve, Mtl.

1976-77

First Team		Second Team
Dryden, Ken, Mtl.	*G*	Vachon, Rogatien, L.A.
Robinson, Larry, Mtl.	*D*	Potvin, Denis, NYI
Salming, Borje, Tor.	*D*	Lapointe, Guy, Mtl.
Dionne, Marcel, L.A.	*C*	Perreault, Gilbert, Buf.
Lafleur, Guy, Mtl.	*RW*	McDonald, Lanny, Tor.
Shutt, Steve, Mtl.	*LW*	Martin, Richard, Buf.

1975-76

First Team		Second Team
Dryden, Ken, Mtl.	*G*	Resch, Glenn, NYI
Potvin, Denis, NYI	*D*	Salming, Borje, Tor.
Park, Brad, Bos.	*D*	Lapointe, Guy, Mtl.
Clarke, Bobby, Phi.	*C*	Perreault, Gilbert, Buf.
Lafleur, Guy, Mtl.	*RW*	Leach, Reggie, Phi.
Barber, Bill, Phi.	*LW*	Martin, Richard, Buf.

1974-75

First Team		Second Team
Parent, Bernie, Phi.	*G*	Vachon, Rogie, L.A.
Orr, Bobby, Bos.	*D*	Lapointe, Guy, Mtl.
Potvin, Denis, NYI	*D*	Salming, Borje, Tor.
Clarke, Bobby, Phi.	*C*	Esposito, Phil, Bos.
Lafleur, Guy, Mtl.	*RW*	Robert, René, Buf.
Martin, Richard, Buf.	*LW*	Vickers, Steve, NYR

1973-74

First Team		Second Team
Parent, Bernie, Phi.	*G*	Esposito, Tony, Chi.
Orr, Bobby, Bos.	*D*	White, Bill, Chi.
Park, Brad, NYR	*D*	Ashbee, Barry, Phi.
Esposito, Phil, Bos.	*C*	Clarke, Bobby, Phi.
Hodge, Ken, Bos.	*RW*	Redmond, Mickey, Det.
Martin, Richard, Buf.	*LW*	Cashman, Wayne, Bos.

1972-73

First Team		Second Team
Dryden, Ken, Mtl.	*G*	Esposito, Tony, Chi.
Orr, Bobby, Bos.	*D*	Park, Brad, NYR
Lapointe, Guy, Mtl.	*D*	White, Bill, Chi.
Esposito, Phil, Bos.	*C*	Clarke, Bobby, Phi.
Redmond, Mickey, Det.	*RW*	Cournoyer, Yvan, Mtl.
Mahovlich, Frank, Mtl.	*LW*	Hull, Dennis, Chi.

1971-72

First Team		Second Team
Esposito, Tony, Chi.	*G*	Dryden, Ken, Mtl.
Orr, Bobby, Bos.	*D*	White, Bill, Chi.
Park, Brad, NYR	*D*	Stapleton, Pat, Chi.
Esposito, Phil, Bos.	*C*	Ratelle, Jean, NYR
Gilbert, Rod, NYR	*RW*	Cournoyer, Yvan, Mtl.
Hull, Bobby, Chi.	*LW*	Hadfield, Vic, NYR

1970-71

First Team		Second Team
Giacomin, Ed, NYR	*G*	Plante, Jacques, Tor.
Orr, Bobby, Bos.	*D*	Park, Brad, NYR
Tremblay, J.C., Mtl.	*D*	Stapleton, Pat, Chi.
Esposito, Phil, Bos.	*C*	Keon, Dave, Tor.
Hodge, Ken, Bos.	*RW*	Cournoyer, Yvan, Mtl.
Bucyk, John, Bos.	*LW*	Hull, Bobby, Chi.

1969-70

First Team		Second Team
Esposito, Tony, Chi.	*G*	Giacomin, Ed, NYR
Orr, Bobby, Bos.	*D*	Brewer, Carl, Det.
Park, Brad, NYR	*D*	Laperriere, Jacques, Mtl.
Esposito, Phil, Bos.	*C*	Mikita, Stan, Chi.
Howe, Gordie, Det.	*RW*	McKenzie, John, Bos.
Hull, Bobby, Chi.	*LW*	Mahovlich, Frank, Det.

1968-69

First Team		Second Team
Hall, Glenn, St.L.	*G*	Giacomin, Ed, NYR
Orr, Bobby, Bos.	*D*	Green, Ted, Bos.
Horton, Tim, Tor.	*D*	Harris, Ted, Mtl.
Esposito, Phil, Bos.	*C*	Béliveau, Jean, Mtl.
Howe, Gordie, Det.	*RW*	Cournoyer, Yvan, Mtl.
Hull, Bobby, Chi.	*LW*	Mahovlich, Frank, Det.

1967-68

First Team		Second Team
Worsley, Lorne, Mtl.	*G*	Giacomin, Ed, NYR
Orr, Bobby, Bos.	*D*	Tremblay, J.C., Mtl.
Horton, Tim, Tor.	*D*	Neilson, Jim, NYR
Mikita, Stan, Chi.	*C*	Esposito, Phil, Bos.
Howe, Gordie, Det.	*RW*	Gilbert, Rod, NYR
Hull, Bobby, Chi.	*LW*	Bucyk, John, Bos.

1966-67

First Team		Second Team
Giacomin, Ed, NYR	*G*	Hall, Glenn, Chi.
Pilote, Pierre, Chi.	*D*	Horton, Tim, Tor.
Howell, Harry, NYR	*D*	Orr, Bobby, Bos.
Mikita, Stan, Chi.	*C*	Ullman, Norm, Det.
Wharram, Ken, Chi.	*RW*	Howe, Gordie, Det.
Hull, Bobby, Chi.	*LW*	Marshall, Don, NYR

1965-66

First Team		Second Team
Hall, Glenn, Chi.	*G*	Worsley, Lorne, Mtl.
Laperriere, Jacques, Mtl.	*D*	Stanley, Allan, Tor.
Pilote, Pierre, Chi.	*D*	Stapleton, Pat, Chi.
Mikita, Stan, Chi.	*C*	Béliveau, Jean, Mtl.
Howe, Gordie, Det.	*RW*	Rousseau, Bobby, Mtl.
Hull, Bobby, Chi.	*LW*	Mahovlich, Frank, Tor.

1964-65

First Team		Second Team
Crozier, Roger, Det.	*G*	Hodge, Charlie, Mtl.
Pilote, Pierre, Chi.	*D*	Gadsby, Bill, Det.
Laperriere, Jacques, Mtl.	*D*	Brewer, Carl, Tor.
Ullman, Norm, Det.	*C*	Mikita, Stan, Chi.
Provost, Claude, Mtl.	*RW*	Howe, Gordie, Det.
Hull, Bobby, Chi.	*LW*	Mahovlich, Frank, Tor.

1963-64

First Team		Second Team
Hall, Glenn, Chi.	*G*	Hodge, Charlie, Mtl.
Pilote, Pierre, Chi.	*D*	Vasko, Elmer, Chi.
Horton, Tim, Tor.	*D*	Laperriere, Jacques, Mtl.
Mikita, Stan, Chi.	*C*	Béliveau, Jean, Mtl.
Wharram, Ken, Chi.	*RW*	Howe, Gordie, Det.
Hull, Bobby, Chi.	*LW*	Mahovlich, Frank, Tor.

1962-63

First Team		Second Team
Hall, Glenn, Chi.	*G*	Sawchuk, Terry, Det.
Pilote, Pierre, Chi.	*D*	Horton, Tim, Tor.
Brewer, Carl, Tor.	*D*	Vasko, Elmer, Chi.
Mikita, Stan, Chi.	*C*	Richard, Henri, Mtl.
Howe, Gordie, Det.	*RW*	Bathgate, Andy, NYR
Mahovlich, Frank, Tor.	*LW*	Hull, Bobby, Chi.

1961-62

First Team		Second Team
Plante, Jacques, Mtl.	*G*	Hall, Glenn, Chi.
Harvey, Doug, NYR	*D*	Brewer, Carl, Tor.
Talbot, Jean-Guy, Mtl.	*D*	Pilote, Pierre, Chi.
Mikita, Stan, Chi.	*C*	Keon, Dave, Tor.
Bathgate, Andy, NYR	*RW*	Howe, Gordie, Det.
Hull, Bobby, Chi.	*LW*	Mahovlich, Frank, Tor.

1960-61

First Team		Second Team
Bower, Johnny, Tor.	*G*	Hall, Glenn, Chi.
Harvey, Doug, Mtl.	*D*	Stanley, Allan, Tor.
Pronovost, Marcel, Det.	*D*	Pilote, Pierre, Chi.
Béliveau, Jean, Mtl.	*C*	Richard, Henri, Mtl.
Geoffrion, Bernie, Mtl.	*RW*	Howe, Gordie, Det.
Mahovlich, Frank, Tor.	*LW*	Moore, Dickie, Mtl.

1959-60

First Team		Second Team
Hall, Glenn, Chi.	*G*	Plante, Jacques, Mtl.
Harvey, Doug, Mtl.	*D*	Stanley, Allan, Tor.
Pronovost, Marcel, Det.	*D*	Pilote, Pierre, Chi.
Béliveau, Jean, Mtl.	*C*	Horvath, Bronco, Bos.
Howe, Gordie, Det.	*RW*	Geoffrion, Bernie, Mtl.
Hull, Bobby, Chi.	*LW*	Prentice, Dean, NYR

1958-59

First Team		Second Team
Plante, Jacques, Mtl.	*G*	Sawchuk, Terry, Det.
Johnson, Tom, Mtl.	*D*	Pronovost, Marcel, Det.
Gadsby, Bill, NYR	*D*	Harvey, Doug, Mtl.
Béliveau, Jean, Mtl.	*C*	Richard, Henri, Mtl.
Bathgate, Andy, NYR	*RW*	Howe, Gordie, Det.
Moore, Dickie, Mtl.	*LW*	Delvecchio, Alex, Det.

1957-58

First Team		Second Team
Hall, Glenn, Chi.	*G*	Plante, Jacques, Mtl.
Harvey, Doug, Mtl.	*D*	Flaman, Fern, Bos.
Gadsby, Bill, NYR	*D*	Pronovost, Marcel, Det.
Richard, Henri, Mtl.	*C*	Béliveau, Jean, Mtl.
Howe, Gordie, Det.	*RW*	Bathgate, Andy, NYR
Moore, Dickie, Mtl.	*LW*	Henry, Camille, NYR

1956-57

First Team		Second Team
Hall, Glenn, Det.	*G*	Plante, Jacques, Mtl.
Harvey, Doug, Mtl.	*D*	Flaman, Fern, Bos.
Kelly, Red, Det.	*D*	Gadsby, Bill, NYR
Béliveau, Jean, Mtl.	*C*	Litzenberger, Eddie, Chi.
Howe, Gordie, Det.	*RW*	Richard, Maurice, Mtl.
Lindsay, Ted, Det.	*LW*	Chevrefils, Real, Bos.

1955-56

First Team		Second Team
Plante, Jacques, Mtl.	*G*	Hall, Glenn, Det.
Harvey, Doug, Mtl.	*D*	Kelly, Red, Det.
Gadsby, Bill, NYR	*D*	Johnson, Tom, Mtl.
Béliveau, Jean, Mtl.	*C*	Sloan, Tod, Tor.
Richard, Maurice, Mtl.	*RW*	Howe, Gordie, Det.
Lindsay, Ted, Det.	*LW*	Olmstead, Bert, Mtl.

1954-55

First Team		Second Team
Lumley, Harry, Tor.	*G*	Sawchuk, Terry, Det.
Harvey, Doug, Mtl.	*D*	Goldham, Bob, Det.
Kelly, Red, Det.	*D*	Flaman, Fern, Bos.
Béliveau, Jean, Mtl.	*C*	Mosdell, Ken, Mtl.
Richard, Maurice, Mtl.	*RW*	Geoffrion, Bernie, Mtl.
Smith, Sid, Tor.	*LW*	Lewicki, Danny, NYR

1953-54

First Team		Second Team
Lumley, Harry, Tor.	*G*	Sawchuk, Terry, Det.
Kelly, Red, Det.	*D*	Gadsby, Bill, Chi.
Harvey, Doug, Mtl.	*D*	Horton, Tim, Tor.
Mosdell, Ken, Mtl.	*C*	Kennedy, Ted, Tor.
Howe, Gordie, Det.	*RW*	Richard, Maurice, Mtl.
Lindsay, Ted, Det.	*LW*	Sandford, Ed, Bos.

1952-53

First Team		Second Team
Sawchuk, Terry, Det.	*G*	McNeil, Gerry, Mtl.
Kelly, Red, Det.	*D*	Quackenbush, Bill, Bos.
Harvey, Doug, Mtl.	*D*	Gadsby, Bill, Chi.
Mackell, Fleming, Bos.	*C*	Delvecchio, Alex, Det.
Howe, Gordie, Det.	*RW*	Richard, Maurice, Mtl.
Lindsay, Ted, Det.	*LW*	Olmstead, Bert, Mtl.

1951-52

First Team		Second Team
Sawchuk, Terry, Det.	*G*	Henry, Jim, Bos.
Kelly, Red, Det.	*D*	Buller, Hy, NYR
Harvey, Doug, Mtl.	*D*	Thomson, Jim, Tor.
Lach, Elmer, Mtl.	*C*	Schmidt, Milt, Bos.
Howe, Gordie, Det.	*RW*	Richard, Maurice, Mtl.
Lindsay, Ted, Det.	*LW*	Smith, Sid, Tor.

1950-51

First Team		Second Team
Sawchuk, Terry, Det.	*G*	Rayner, Chuck, NYR
Kelly, Red, Det.	*D*	Thomson, Jim, Tor.
Quackenbush, Bill, Bos.	*D*	Reise, Leo, Det.
Schmidt, Milt, Bos.	*C*	Abel, Sid, Det.
	(tied)	Kennedy, Ted, Tor.
Howe, Gordie, Det.	*RW*	Richard, Maurice, Mtl.
Lindsay, Ted, Det.	*LW*	Smith, Sid, Tor.

1949-50

First Team		Second Team
Durnan, Bill, Mtl.	*G*	Rayner, Chuck, NYR
Mortson, Gus, Tor.	*D*	Reise, Leo, Det.
Reardon, Kenny, Mtl.	*D*	Kelly, Red, Det.
Abel, Sid, Det.	*C*	Kennedy, Ted, Tor.
Richard, Maurice, Mtl.	*RW*	Howe, Gordie, Det.
Lindsay, Ted, Det.	*LW*	Leswick, Tony, NYR

1948-49

First Team		Second Team
Durnan, Bill, Mtl.	*G*	Rayner, Chuck, NYR
Quackenbush, Bill, Det.	*D*	Harmon, Glen, Mtl.
Stewart, Jack, Det.	*D*	Reardon, Kenny, Mtl.
Abel, Sid, Det.	*C*	Bentley, Doug, Chi.
Richard, Maurice, Mtl.	*RW*	Howe, Gordie, Det.
Conacher, Roy, Chi.	*LW*	Lindsay, Ted, Det.

1947-48

First Team		Second Team
Broda, W. "Turk", Tor.	*G*	Brimsek, Frank, Bos.
Quackenbush, Bill, Det.	*D*	Reardon, Kenny, Mtl.
Stewart, Jack, Det.	*D*	Colville, Neil, NYR
Lach, Elmer, Mtl.	*C*	O'Connor, "Buddy", NYR
Richard, Maurice, Mtl.	*RW*	Poile, "Bud", Chi.
Lindsay, Ted, Det.	*LW*	Stewart, Gaye, Chi.

1946-47

First Team		Second Team
Durnan, Bill, Mtl.	*G*	Brimsek, Frank, Bos.
Reardon, Kenny, Mtl.	*D*	Stewart, Jack, Det.
Bouchard, Emile, Mtl.	*D*	Quackenbush, Bill, Det.
Schmidt, Milt, Bos.	*C*	Bentley, Max, Chi.
Richard, Maurice, Mtl.	*RW*	Bauer, Bobby, Bos.
Bentley, Doug, Chi.	*LW*	Dumart, Woody, Bos.

1945-46

First Team		Second Team
Durnan, Bill, Mtl.	*G*	Brimsek, Frank, Bos.
Crawford, Jack, Bos.	*D*	Reardon, Kenny, Mtl.
Bouchard, Emile, Mtl.	*D*	Stewart, Jack, Det.
Bentley, Max, Chi.	*C*	Lach, Elmer, Mtl.
Richard, Maurice, Mtl.	*RW*	Mosienko, Bill, Chi.
Stewart, Gaye, Tor.	*LW*	Blake, "Toe", Mtl.
Irvin, Dick, Mtl.	*Coach*	Gottselig, John, Chi.

1944-45

First Team		Second Team
Durnan, Bill, Mtl.	*G*	Karakas, Mike, Chi.
Bouchard, Emile, Mtl.	*D*	Harmon, Glen, Mtl.
Hollett, Bill, Det.	*D*	Pratt, "Babe", Tor.
Lach, Elmer, Mtl.	*C*	Cowley, Bill, Bos.
Richard, Maurice, Mtl.	*RW*	Mosienko, Bill, Chi.
Blake, "Toe", Mtl.	*LW*	Howe, Syd, Det.
Irvin, Dick, Mtl.	*Coach*	Adams, Jack, Det.

1943-44

First Team		Second Team
Durnan, Bill, Mtl.	*G*	Bibeault, Paul, Tor.
Seibert, Earl, Chi.	*D*	Bouchard, Emile, Mtl.
Pratt, "Babe", Tor.	*D*	Clapper, "Dit", Bos.
Cowley, Bill, Bos.	*C*	Lach, Elmer, Mtl.
Carr, Lorne, Tor.	*RW*	Richard, Maurice, Mtl.
Bentley, Doug, Chi.	*LW*	Cain, Herb, Bos.
Irvin, Dick, Mtl.	*Coach*	Day, "Hap", Tor.

1942-43

First Team		Second Team
Mowers, Johnny, Det.	*G*	Brimsek, Frank, Bos.
Seibert, Earl, Chi.	*D*	Crawford, Johnny, Bos.
Stewart, Jack, Det.	*D*	Hollett, Bill, Bos.
Cowley, Bill, Bos.	*C*	Apps, Syl, Tor.
Carr, Lorne, Tor.	*RW*	Hextall, Bryan, NYR
Bentley, Doug, Chi.	*LW*	Patrick, Lynn, NYR
Adams, Jack, Det.	*Coach*	Ross, Art, Bos.

1941-42

First Team		Second Team
Brimsek, Frank, Bos.	*G*	Broda, W. "Turk", Tor.
Seibert, Earl, Chi.	*D*	Egan, Pat, NYA
Anderson, Tommy, NYA	*D*	McDonald, Bucko, Tor.
Apps, Syl, Tor.	*C*	Watson, Phil, NYR
Hextall, Bryan, NYR	*RW*	Drillon, Gord, Tor.
Patrick, Lynn, NYR	*LW*	Abel, Sid, Det.
Boucher, Frank, NYR	*Coach*	Thompson, Paul, Chi.

1940-41

First Team		Second Team
Broda, W. "Turk", Tor.	*G*	Brimsek, Frank, Bos.
Clapper, "Dit", Bos.	*D*	Seibert, Earl, Chi.
Stanowski, Wally, Tor.	*D*	Heller, Ott, NYR
Cowley, Bill, Bos.	*C*	Apps, Syl, Tor.
Hextall, Bryan, NYR	*RW*	Bauer, Bobby, Bos.
Schriner, Dave, Tor.	*LW*	Dumart, Woody, Bos.
Weiland, "Cooney", Bos.	*Coach*	Irvin, Dick, Mtl.

1939-40

First Team		Second Team
Kerr, Dave, NYR	*G*	Brimsek, Frank, Bos.
Clapper, "Dit", Bos.	*D*	Coulter, Art, NYR
Goodfellow, Ebbie, Det.	*D*	Seibert, Earl, Chi.
Schmidt, Milt, Bos.	*C*	Colville, Neil, NYR
Hextall, Bryan, NYR	*RW*	Bauer, Bobby, Bos.
Blake, "Toe", Mtl.	*LW*	Dumart, Woody, Bos.
Thompson, Paul, Chi.	*Coach*	Boucher, Frank, NYR

1938-39

First Team		Second Team
Brimsek, Frank, Bos.	*G*	Robertson, Earl, NYA
Shore, Eddie, Bos.	*D*	Seibert, Earl, Chi.
Clapper, "Dit", Bos.	*D*	Coulter, Art, NYR
Apps, Syl, Tor.	*C*	Colville, Neil, NYR
Drillon, Gord, Tor.	*RW*	Bauer, Bobby, Bos.
Blake, "Toe", Mtl.	*LW*	Gottselig, Johnny, Chi.
Ross, Art, Bos.	*Coach*	Dutton, "Red", NYA

1937-38

First Team		Second Team
Thompson, "Tiny", Bos.	*G*	Kerr, Dave, NYR
Shore, Eddie, Bos.	*D*	Coulter, Art, NYR
Seibert, "Babe", Mtl.	*D*	Seibert, Eart, Chi.
Cowley, Bill, Bos.	*C*	Apps, Syl, Tor.
Dillon, Cecil, NYR	*RW*	Dillon, Cecil, NYR
Drillon, Gord, Tor.	*(tied)*	Drillon, Gord, Tor.
Thompson, Paul, Chi.	*LW*	Blake, Toe, Mtl.
Patrick, Lester, NYR	*Coach*	Ross, Art, Bos.

1936-37

First Team		Second Team
Smith, Norm, Det.	*G*	Cude, Wilf, Mtl.
Siebert, "Babe", Mtl.	*D*	Seibert, Earl, Chi.
Goodfellow, Ebbie, Det.	*D*	Conacher, Lionel, Mtl. M.
Barry, Marty, Det.	*C*	Chapman, Art, NYA
Aurie, Larry, Det.	*RW*	Dillon, Cecil, NYR
Jackson, Harvey, Tor.	*LW*	Schriner, Dave, NYA
Adams, Jack, Det.	*Coach*	Hart, Cecil, Mtl.

1935-36

First Team		Second Team
Thompson, "Tiny", Bos.	*G*	Cude, Wilf, Mtl.
Shore, Eddie, Bos.	*D*	Seibert, Earl, Chi.
Seibert, "Babe", Bos.	*D*	Goodfellow, Ebbie, Det.
Smith, "Hooley", Mtl. M.	*C*	Thoms, Bill, Tor.
Conacher, Charlie, Tor.	*RW*	Dillon, Cecil, NYR
Schriner, Dave, NYA	*LW*	Thompson, Paul, Chi.
Patrick, Lester, NYR	*Coach*	Gorman, T.P., Mtl. M.

1934-35

First Team		Second Team
Chabot, Lorne, Chi.	*G*	Thompson, "Tiny", Bos.
Shore, Eddie, Bos.	*D*	Wentworth, Cy, Mtl. M.
Seibert, Earl, NYR	*D*	Coulter, Art, Chi.
Boucher, Frank, NYR	*C*	Weiland, "Cooney", Det.
Conacher, Charlie, Tor.	*RW*	Clapper, "Dit", Bos.
Jackson, Harvey, Tor.	*LW*	Joliat, Aurel, Mtl.
Patrick, Lester, NYR	*Coach*	Irvin, Dick, Tor.

1933-34

First Team		Second Team
Gardiner, Charlie, Chi.	*G*	Worters, Roy, NYA
Clancy, "King", Tor.	*D*	Shore, Eddie, Bos.
Conacher, Lionel, Chi.	*D*	Johnson, "Ching", NYR
Boucher, Frank, NYR	*C*	Primeau, Joe, Tor.
Conacher, Charlie, Tor.	*RW*	Cook, Bill, NYR
Jackson, Harvey, Tor.	*LW*	Joliat, Aurel, Mtl.
Patrick, Lester, NYR	*Coach*	Irvin, Dick, Tor.

1932-33

First Team		Second Team
Roach, John Ross, Det.	*G*	Gardiner, Charlie, Chi.
Shore, Eddie, Bos.	*D*	Clancy, "King", Tor.
Johnson, "Ching", NYR	*D*	Conacher, Lionel, Mtl. M.
Boucher, Frank, NYR	*C*	Morenz, Howie, Mtl.
Cook, Bill, NYR	*RW*	Conacher, Charlie, Tor.
Northcott, "Baldy", Mtl M.	*LW*	Jackson, Harvey, Tor.
Patrick, Lester, NYR	*Coach*	Irvin, Dick, Tor.

1931-32

First Team		Second Team
Gardiner, Charlie, Chi.	*G*	Worters, Roy, NYA
Shore, Eddie, Bos.	*D*	Mantha, Sylvio, Mtl.
Johnson, "Ching", NYR	*D*	Clancy, "King", Tor.
Morenz, Howie, Mtl.	*C*	Smith, "Hooley", Mtl. M.
Cook, Bill, NYR	*RW*	Conacher, Charlie, Tor.
Jackson, Harvey, Tor.	*LW*	Joliat, Aurel, Mtl.
Patrick, Lester, NYR	*Coach*	Irvin, Dick, Tor.

1930-31

First Team		Second Team
Gardiner, Charlie, Chi.	*G*	Thompson, "Tiny", Bos.
Shore, Eddie, Bos.	*D*	Mantha, Sylvio, Mtl.
Clancy, "King", Tor.	*D*	Johnson, "Ching", NYR
Morenz, Howie, Mtl.	*C*	Boucher, Frank, NYR
Cook, Bill, NYR	*RW*	Clapper, "Dit", Bos.
Joliet, Aurel, Mtl.	*LW*	Cook, "Bun", NYR
Patrick, Lester, NYR	*Coach*	Irvin, Dick, Chi.

All-Star Game Results

Year	Venue	Score	Coaches	Attendance
1992	Philadelphia	Campbell 10, Wales 6	Bob Gainey, Scotty Bowman	17,380
1991	Chicago	Campbell 11, Wales 5	John Muckler, Mike Milbury	18,472
1990	Pittsburgh	Wales 12, Campbell 7	Pat Burns, Terry Crisp	16,236
1989	Edmonton	Campbell 9, Wales 5	Glen Sather, Terry O'Reilly	17,503
1988	St. Louis	Wales 6, Campbell 5 OT	Mike Keenan, Glen Sather	17,878
1986	Hartford	Wales 4, Campbell 3 OT	Mike Keenan, Glen Sather	15,100
1985	Calgary	Wales 6, Campbell 4	Al Arbour, Glen Sather	16,825
1984	New Jersey	Wales 7, Campbell 6	Al Arbour, Glen Sather	18,939
1983	NY Islanders	Campbell 9, Wales 3	Roger Neilson, Al Arbour	15,230
1982	Washington	Wales 4, Campbell 2	Al Arbour, Glen Sonmor	18,130
1981	Los Angeles	Campbell 4, Wales 1	Pat Quinn, Scott Bowman	15,761
1980	Detroit	Wales 6, Campbell 3	Scott Bowman, Al Arbour	21,002
1978	Buffalo	Wales 3, Campbell 2 OT	Scott Bowman, Fred Shero	16,433
1977	Vancouver	Wales 4, Campbell 3	Scott Bowman, Fred Shero	15,607
1976	Philadelphia	Wales 7, Campbell 5	Floyd Smith, Fred Shero	16,436
1975	Montreal	Wales 7, Campbell 1	Bep Guidolin, Fred Shero	16,080
1974	Chicago	West 6, East 4	Billy Reay, Scott Bowman	16,426
1973	New York	East 5, West 4	Tom Johnson, Billy Reay	16,986
1972	Minnesota	East 3, West 2	Al MacNeil, Billy Reay	15,423
1971	Boston	West 2, East 1	Scott Bowman, Harry Sinden	14,790
1970	St. Louis	East 4, West 1	Claude Ruel, Scott Bowman	16,587
1969	Montreal	East 3, West 3	Toe Blake, Scott Bowman	16,260
1968	Toronto	Toronto 4, All-Stars 3	Punch Imlach, Toe Blake	15,753
1967	Montreal	Montreal 3, All-Stars 0	Toe Blake, Sid Abel	14,284
1965	Montreal	All-Stars 5, Montreal 2	Billy Reay, Toe Blake	13,529
1964	Toronto	All-Stars 3, Toronto 2	Sid Abel, Punch Imlach	14,232
1963	Toronto	All-Stars 3, Toronto 3	Sid Abel, Punch Imlach	14,034
1962	Toronto	Toronto 4, All-Stars 1	Punch Imlach, Rudy Pilous	14,236
1961	Chicago	All-Stars 3, Chicago 1	Sid Abel, Rudy Pilous	14,534
1960	Montreal	All-Stars 2, Montreal 1	Punch Imlach, Toe Blake	13,949
1959	Montreal	Montreal 6, All-Stars 1	Toe Blake, Punch Imlach	13,818
1958	Montreal	Montreal 6, All-Stars 3	Toe Blake, Milt Schmidt	13,989
1957	Montreal	All-Stars 5, Montreal 3	Milt Schmidt, Toe Blake	13,003
1956	Montreal	All-Stars 1, Montreal 1	Jim Skinner, Toe Blake	13,095
1955	Detroit	Detroit 3, All-Stars 1	Jim Skinner, Dick Irvin	10,111
1954	Detroit	All-Stars 2, Detroit 2	King Clancy, Jim Skinner	10,689
1953	Montreal	All-Stars 3, Montreal 1	Lynn Patrick, Dick Irvin	14,153
1952	Detroit	1st team 1, 2nd team 1	Tommy Ivan, Dick Irvin	10,680
1951	Toronto	1st team 2, 2nd team 2	Joe Primeau, Hap Day	11,469
1950	Detroit	Detroit 7, All-Stars 1	Tommy Ivan, Lynn Patrick	9,166
1949	Toronto	All-Stars 3, Toronto 1	Tommy Ivan, Hap Day	13,541
1948	Chicago	All-Stars 3, Toronto 1	Tommy Ivan, Hap Day	12,794
1947	Toronto	All-Stars 4, Toronto 3	Dick Irvin, Hap Day	14,169

There was no All-Star contest during the calendar year of 1966 since the game was moved from the start of season to mid-season. In 1979, the Challenge Cup series between the Soviet Union and Team NHL replaced the All-Star Game. In 1987, Rendez-Vous '87, two games between the Soviet Union and Team NHL replaced the All-Star Game. Rendez-Vous '87 scores: game one, NHL All Stars 4, Soviet Union 3; game two, Soviet Union 5, NHL All-Stars 3.

1991-92 All-Star Game Summary

January 18, 1992 at Philadelphia — Campbell 10, Wales 6

PLAYERS ON ICE: **Campbell Conference** — Belfour, Cheveldae, McLean, MacInnis, Ellett, Housley, Chelios, Roberts, Oates, Fleury, Hull, Linden, Yzerman, Robinson, Robitaille, Damphousse, Bellows, Wilson, Tinordi, Roenick, Fedorov, Gretzky

Wales Conference — Roy, Beaupre, Richter, Leetch, Stevens, Hatcher, Coffey, Muller, Messier, Nolan, Sakic, Brind'Amour, Burridge, Trottier, Cullen, Ferraro, Stevens, Desjardins, Lemieux, Jagr, Mogilny, Bourque

GOALTENDERS				
	Campbell:	Belfour	20 minutes	1 goal against
		Cheveldae	20 minutes	2 goals against
		McLean	20 minutes	3 goals against
	Wales:	Roy	20 minutes	2 goals against
		Beaupre	20 minutes	6 goals against
		Richter	20 minutes	2 goals against

SUMMARY

First Period

1. Campbell	Linden	(Roenick, Tinordi)	7:53
2. Wales	K. Stevens	(Lemieux, Jagr)	11:20
3. Campbell	Gretzky	(Hull, Robitaille)	14:56

PENALTIES: None.

Second Period

4. Campbell	Hull	(Gretzky, Robitaille)	:42
5. Wales	S. Stevens	(Mogilny, Messier)	5:37
6. Campbell	Bellows	(Fedorov, MacInnis)	7:40
7. Campbell	Roenick	(Ellett)	8:13
8. Campbell	Fleury	(Robinson)	11:06
9. Campbell	Hull	(Gretzky, Robitaille)	11:59
10. Campbell	Fleury	(Damphousse, Oates)	17:33
11. Wales	Nolan	(Sakic, Bourque)	19:29

PENALTIES: None.

Third Period

12. Wales	Trottier	(Hatcher)	4:03
13. Campbell	Bellows	(Fedorov)	4:50
14. Wales	Mogilny	(Desjardins)	5:28
15. Campbell	Roberts	(Linden)	18:42
16. Wales	Burridge	(Sakic, Nolan)	19:12

PENALTIES: None.

SHOTS ON GOAL BY:

Wales Conference	14	9	18	**41**
Campbell Conference	5	12	15	**42**

Attendance: 17,380

Referee: Don Koharski — Linesmen: Mark Vines, Mark Pare

Most Valuable Player: Brett Hull

The 1991-92 NHL/Upper Deck All-Rookie Team: Gilbert Dionne and Nicklas Lidstrom (standing), Kevin Todd, Vladimir Konstantinov and Tony Amonte (kneeling) and Dominik Hasek (on ice)

NHL/UPPER DECK ALL-ROOKIE TEAM

Voting for the NHL/Upper Deck All-Rookie Team is conducted among the representatives of the Professional Hockey Writers' Association at the end of the season. The rookie all-star team was first selected for the 1982-83 season.

1991-92		1990-91
Dominik Hasek, Chicago	*Goal*	Ed Belfour, Chicago
Nicklas Lidstrom, Detroit	*Defense*	Eric Weinrich, New Jersey
Vladimir Konstantinov, Detroit	*Defense*	Rob Blake, Los Angeles
Kevin Todd, New Jersey	*Center*	Sergei Fedorov, Detroit
Tony Amonte, NY Rangers	*Right Wing*	Ken Hodge, Boston
Gilbert Dionne, Montreal	*Left Wing*	Jaromir Jagr, Pittsburgh
1989-90		**1988-89**
Bob Essensa, Winnipeg	*Goal*	Peter Sidorkiewicz, Hartford
Brad Shaw, Hartford	*Defense*	Brian Leetch, NY Rangers
Geoff Smith, Edmonton	*Defense*	Zarley Zalapski, Pittsburgh
Mike Modano, Minnesota	*Center*	Trevor Linden, Vancouver
Sergei Makarov, Calgary	*Right Wing*	Tony Granato, NY Rangers
Rod Brind'Amour, St. Louis	*Left Wing*	David Volek, NY Islanders
1987-88		**1986-87**
Darren Pang, Chicago	*Goal*	Ron Hextall, Philadelphia
Glen Wesley, Boston	*Defense*	Steve Duchesne, Los Angeles
Calle Johansson, Buffalo	*Defense*	Brian Benning, St. Louis
Joe Nieuwendyk, Calgary	*Center*	Jimmy Carson, Los Angeles
Ray Sheppard, Buffalo	*Right Wing*	Jim Sandlak, Vancouver
Iain Duncan, Winnipeg	*Left Wing*	Luc Robitaille, Los Angeles
1985-86		**1984-85**
Patrick Roy, Montreal	*Goal*	Steve Penney, Montreal
Gary Suter, Calgary	*Defense*	Chris Chelios, Montreal
Dana Murzyn, Hartford	*Defense*	Bruce Bell, Quebec
Mike Ridley, NY Rangers	*Center*	Mario Lemieux, Pittsburgh
Kjell Dahlin, Montreal	*Right Wing*	Tomas Sandstrom, NY Rangers
Wendel Clark, Toronto	*Left Wing*	Warren Young, Pittsburgh
1983-84		**1982-83**
Tom Barrasso, Buffalo	*Goal*	Pelle Lindbergh, Philadelphia
Thomas Eriksson, Philadelphia	*Defense*	Scott Stevens, Washington
Jamie Macoun, Calgary	*Defense*	Phil Housley, Buffalo
Steve Yzerman, Detroit	*Center*	Dan Daoust, Montreal/Toronto
Hakan Loob, Calgary	*Right Wing*	Steve Larmer, Chicago
Sylvain Turgeon, Hartford	*Left Wing*	Mats Naslund, Montreal

All-Star Game Records 1947 through 1992

TEAM RECORDS

MOST GOALS, BOTH TEAMS, ONE GAME:
19 — Wales 12, Campbell 7, 1990 at Pittsburgh
16 — Campbell 11, Wales 5, 1991 at Chicago
— Campbell 10, Wales 6, 1992 at Philadelphia
14 — Campbell 9, Wales 5, 1989 at Edmonton
13 — Wales 7, Campbell 6, 1984 at New Jersey
12 — Campbell 9, Wales 3, 1983 at NY Islanders
— Wales 7, Campbell 5, 1976 at Philadelphia
11 — Wales 6, Campbell 5, 1988 at St. Louis
10 — West 6, East 4, 1974 at Chicago
— Wales 6, Campbell 4, 1985 at Calgary

FEWEST GOALS, BOTH TEAMS, ONE GAME:
2 — NHL All-Stars 1, Montreal Canadiens 1, 1956 at Montreal
— First Team All-Stars 1, Second Team All-Stars 1, 1952 at Detroit
3 — West 2, East 1, 1971 at Boston
— Montreal Canadiens 3, NHL All-Stars 0, 1967 at Montreal
— NHL All-Stars 2, Montreal Canadiens 1, 1960 at Montreal

MOST GOALS, ONE TEAM, ONE GAME:
12 — Wales 12, Campbell 7, 1990 at Pittsburgh
11 — Campbell 11, Wales 5, 1991 at Chicago
10 — Campbell 10, Wales 6, 1992 at Philadelphia
9 — Campbell 9, Wales 3, 1983 at NY Islanders
Campbell 9, Wales 5, 1989 at Edmonton
7 — Wales 7, Campbell 5, 1976 at Philadelphia
— Wales 7, Campbell 1, 1975 at Montreal
— Detroit Red Wings 7, NHL All-Stars 1, 1950 at Detroit
— Wales 7, Campbell 6, 1984 at New Jersey
— Campbell 7, Wales 12, 1990 at Pittsburgh

FEWEST GOALS, ONE TEAM, ONE GAME:
0 — NHL All-Stars 0, Montreal Canadiens 3, 1967 at Montreal
1 — 17 times (1981, 1975, 1971, 1970, 1962, 1961, 1960, 1959, both teams 1956, 1955, 1953, both teams 1952, 1950, 1949, 1948)

MOST SHOTS, BOTH TEAMS, ONE GAME (SINCE 1955):
87 — 1990 at Pittsburgh — Wales 12 (45 shots), Campbell 7 (42 shots)
83 — 1992 at Philadelphia — Campbell 10 (42 shots), Wales 6 (41 shots)
82 — 1991 at Chicago — Campbell 11 (41 shots), Wales 5 (41 shots)
81 — 1968 at Toronto — NHL All-Stars 3 (40 shots), Toronto Maple Leafs 4 (41 shots)
75 — 1955 at Detroit — NHL All-Stars 1 (31 shots), Detroit Red Wings 3 (44 shots)
— 1989 at Edmonton — Campbell 9 (37 shots), Wales 5 (38 shots)

FEWEST SHOTS, BOTH TEAMS, ONE GAME (SINCE 1955):
52 — 1978 at Buffalo — Campbell 2 (12 shots) Wales 3 (40 shots)
53 — 1960 at Montreal — NHL All-Stars 2 (27 shots) Montreal Canadiens 1 (26 shots)
55 — 1956 at Montreal — NHL All-Stars 1 (28 shots) Montreal Canadiens 1 (27 shots)
— 1971 at Boston — West 2 (28 shots) East 1 (27 shots)

MOST SHOTS, ONE TEAM, ONE GAME (SINCE 1955):
45 — 1990 at Pittsburgh — Wales (12-7 vs. Campbell)
44 — 1955 at Detroit — Detroit Red Wings (3-1 vs. NHL All-Stars)
— 1970 at St. Louis — East (4-1 vs. West)
43 — 1981 at Los Angeles — Campbell (4-1 vs. Wales)
42 — 1976 at Philadelphia — Wales (7-5 vs. Campbell)
— 1990 at Pittsburgh — Campbell (7-12 vs. Wales)
— 1992 at Philadelphia — Campbell (10-6 vs. Wales)

FEWEST SHOTS, ONE TEAM, ONE GAME (SINCE 1955):
12 — 1978 at Buffalo — Campbell (2-3 vs. Wales)
17 — 1970 at St. Louis — West (1-4 vs. East)
23 — 1961 at Chicago — Chicago Black Hawks (1-3 vs. NHL All-Stars)
24 — 1976 at Philadelphia — Campbell (5-7 vs. Wales)

MOST POWER-PLAY GOALS, BOTH TEAMS, ONE GAME (SINCE 1950):
3 — 1953 at Montreal — NHL All-Stars 3 (2 power-play goals), Montreal Canadiens 1 (1 power-play goal)
— 1954 at Detroit — NHL All-Stars 2 (1 power-play goal) Detroit Red Wings 2 (2 power-play goals)
— 1958 at Montreal — NHL All-Stars 3 (1 power-play goal) Montreal Canadiens 6 (2 power-play goals)

FEWEST POWER-PLAY GOALS, BOTH TEAMS, ONE GAME (SINCE 1950):
0 — 14 times (1952, 1959, 1960, 1967, 1968, 1969, 1972, 1973, 1976, 1980, 1981, 1984, 1985, 1992)

FASTEST TWO GOALS, BOTH TEAMS, FROM START OF GAME:
37 seconds — 1970 at St. Louis — Jacques Laperriere of East scored at 20 seconds and Dean Prentice of West scored at 37 seconds. Final score: East 4, West 1.

4:08 — 1963 at Toronto — Frank Mahovlich scored for Toronto Maple Leafs at 2:22 of first period and Henri Richard scored at 4:08 for NHL All-Stars. Final score: NHL All-Stars 3, Toronto Maple Leafs 3.

4:19 — 1980 at Detroit — Larry Robinson scored at 3:58 for Wales and Steve Payne scored at 4:19 for Wales. Final score: Wales 6, Campbell 3.

FASTEST TWO GOALS, BOTH TEAMS:
10 seconds — 1976 at Philadelphia — Dennis Ververgaert scored at 4:33 and at 4:43 of third period for Campbell. Final score: Wales 7, Campbell 5.

14 seconds — 1989 at Edmonton. Steve Yzerman and Gary Leeman scored at 17:21 and 17:35 of second period for Campbell. Final score: Campbell 9, Wales 5.

16 seconds — 1990 at Pittsburgh. Kirk Muller of Wales scored at 8:47 of second period and Al MacInnis of Campbell scored at 9:03. Final score: Wales 12, Campbell 7.

FASTEST THREE GOALS, BOTH TEAMS:
1:25 — 1992 at Philadelphia — Bryan Trottier scored at 4:03 of third period for Wales; Brian Bellows scored at 4:50 for Campbell; Alexander Mogilny scored at 5:28 for Wales. Final score: Campbell 10, Wales 6.

1:32 — 1980 at Detroit — all by Wales — Ron Stackhouse scored at 11:40 of third period, Craig Hartsburg scored at 12:40; and Reed Larson scored at 13:12. Final score: Wales 6, Campbell 3.

1:57 — 1990 at Pittsburgh — all by Wales – Rick Tocchet scored at 16:55 of first period, Mario Lemieux scored at 17:37; Pierre Turgeon scored at 18:52. Final score: Wales 12, Campbell 7.

2:01 — 1976 at Philadelphia — Curt Bennett scored at 16:59 of first period for Campbell; Pete Mahovlich scored at 18:31 for Wales; Brad Park scored at 19:00 for Wales. Final score: Wales 7, Campbell 5.

FASTEST FOUR GOALS, BOTH TEAMS:
4:21 — 1990 at Pittsbrugh — Steve Yzerman scored at 14:31 of first period for Campbell; Rick Tocchet scored at 16:55 for Wales; Mario Lemieux scored at 17:37 for Wales. Final score: Wales 12, Campbell 7.

4:26 — 1990 at Pittsbrugh — Luc Robitaille scored at 15:09 and 16:11 of third period for Campbell; Kirk Muller scored at 17:50 for Wales; Doug Smail scored at 19:35 Campbell. Final score: Wales 12, Campbell 7.

4:26 — 1980 at Detroit — all by Wales; Ron Stackhouse scored at 11:40 of third period; Craig Hartsburg scored at 12:40; Reed Larson scored at 13:12; Real Cloutier scored at 16:06. Final score: Wales 6, Campbell 3.

FASTEST TWO GOALS, ONE TEAM, FROM START OF GAME:
4:19 — 1980 at Detroit — Wales — Larry Robinson scored at 3:58 and Steve Payne scored at 4:19. Final score: Wales 6, Campbell 3.

4:38 — 1971 at Boston — West — Chico Maki scored at 36 seconds and Bobby Hull scored at 4:38. Final score: West 2, East 1.

5:13 — 1990 at Pittsburgh — Wales — Mario Lemieux scored at :21 and Dave Andreychuk scored at 5:13. Final score: Wales 12, Campbell 7.

5:25 — 1953 at Montreal — NHL All-Stars — Wally Hergesheimer scored at 4:06 and 5:25. Final score: NHL All-Stars 3, Montreal Canadiens 1.

FASTEST TWO GOALS, ONE TEAM:
10 seconds — 1976 at Philadelphia — Campbell — Dennis Ververgaert scored at 4:33 and at 4:43 of third period. Final score: Wales 7, Campbell 5.

14 seconds — 1989 at Edmonton — Campbell — Steve Yzerman and Gary Leeman scored at 17:21 and 17:35 of second period. Final score: Campbell 9, Wales 5.

21 seconds — 1980 at Detroit — Wales — Larry Robinson scored at 3:58 of first period and Steve Payne scored at 4:19. Final score: Wales 6, Campbell 3.

29 seconds — 1976 at Philadelphia — Campbell — Denis Potvin scored at 14:17 of third period and Steve Vickers scored at 14:46. Final score: Wales 7, Campbell 5.

29 seconds — 1976 at Philadelphia — Wales — Pete Mahovlich scored at 18:31 of first period and Brad Park scored at 19:00. Final score: Wales 7, Campbell 5.

FASTEST THREE GOALS, ONE TEAM:
1:32 — 1980 at Detroit — Wales — Ron Stackhouse scored at 11:40 of third period; Craig Hartsburg scored at 12:40; Reed Larson scored at 13:12. Final score: Wales 6, Campbell 3.

1:57 — 1990 at Pittsburgh — Wales — Rick Tocchett scored at 16:55 of first period; Mario Lemieux scored at 17:37; Pierre Turgeon scored at 18:52. Final score: Wales 12, Campbell 7.

2:25 — 1984 at New Jersey — Wales — Rick Middleton scored at 14:49 of first period; Mats Naslund scored at 16:40; Pierre Larouche at 17:14. Final score: Wales 7, Campbell 6.

3:26 — 1980 at Detroit — Wales — Craig Hartsburg scored at 12:40 of third period; Reed Larson scored at 13:12; Real Cloutier scored at 16:06. Final score: Wales 6, Campbell 3.

FASTEST FOUR GOALS, ONE TEAM:
4:19 — 1992 at Philadelphia — Campbell — Brian Bellows scored at 7:40 of second period, Jeremy Roenick scored at 8:13, Theoren Fleury scored at 11:06, Brett Hull scored at 11:59. Final score: Campbell 10, Wales 6.

4:26 — 1980 at Detroit — Wales — Ron Stackhouse scored at 11:40 of third period; Craig Hartsburg scored at 12:40; Reed Larson scored at 13:12; Real Cloutier scored at 16:06. Final score: Wales 6, Campbell 3.

5:52 — 1990 at Pittsburgh — Wales — Mario Lemieux scored at 13:00 of first period; Rick Tocchett scored at 16:55; Mario Lemieux scored at 17:37; Pierre Turgeon scored at 18:52. Final score: Wales 12, Campbell 7.

7:25 — 1976 at Philadelphia — Wales — Al MacAdam scored at 9:34 of second period; Guy Lafleur scored at 11:54; Marcel Dionne scored at 13:51; Dan Maloney scored at 16:59. Final score: Wales 7, Campbell 5.

MOST GOALS, BOTH TEAMS, ONE PERIOD:
9 — 1990 at Pittsburgh — First Period — Wales (7), Campbell (2). Final score: Wales 12, Campbell 7.

7 — 1983 at NY Islanders — Third period — Campbell (6), Wales (1) Final score: Campbell 9, Wales 3.

— 1991 at Chicago — Second period — Campbell (5), Wales (2). Final score: Campbell 11, Wales 5.

— 1992 at Philadelphia — Second period — Campbell (5), Wales (2). Final score: Campbell 10, Wales 6.

MOST GOALS, ONE TEAM, ONE PERIOD:
7 — 1990 at Pittsburgh — First period — Wales. Final score: Wales 12, Campbell 7.

6 — 1983 at NY Islanders — Third period — Campbell. Final score: Campbell 9, Wales 3.

5 — 1984 at New Jersey — First period — Wales. Final score: Wales 7, Campbell 6.

— 1991 at Chicago — Second period — Campbell. Final score: Campbell 11, Wales 5.

— 1992 at Philadelphia — Second period — Campbell. Final score: Campbell 10, Wales 6.

MOST SHOTS, BOTH TEAMS, ONE PERIOD:
36 — 1990 at Pittsburgh — Third period — Campbell (22), Wales (14). Final score: Wales 12, Campbell 7.

33 — 1992 at Philadelphia — Third period — Wales (18), Campbell (15). Final score: Campbell 10, Wales 6.

30 — 1959 at Montreal — Second period — NHL All-Stars (16), Montreal (14). Final score: Montreal Canadiens 6, NHL All-Stars 1.

MOST SHOTS, ONE TEAM, ONE PERIOD:
22 — 1990 at Pittsburgh — Third period — Campbell. Final score: Wales 12, Campbell 7.

— 1991 at Chicago — Third Period — Wales. Final score: Campbell 11, Wales 5.

20 — 1970 at St. Louis — Third period — East. Final score: East 4, West 1.

18 — 1955 at Detroit — Third period — Detroit Red Wings. Final score: Detroit Red Wings 3, NHL All-Stars 1.

— 1968 at Toronto — Second period — Toronto Maple Leafs. Final score: Toronto Maple Leafs 4, NHL All-Stars 3.

— 1981 at Los Angeles — First period — Campbell. Final score: Campbell 4, Wales 1.

— 1992 at Philadelphia — Third period — Wales. Final score: Campbell 10, Wales 6.

FEWEST SHOTS, BOTH TEAMS, ONE PERIOD:
9 — 1971 at Boston — Third period — East (2), West (7). Final score: West 2, East 1.

— 1980 at Detroit — Second period — Campbell (4), Wales (5). Final score: Wales 6, Campbell 3.

13 — 1982 at Washington — Third period — Campbell (6), Wales (7). Final score: Wales 4, Campbell 2.

14 — 1978 at Buffalo — First period — Campbell (7), Wales (7). Final score: Wales 3, Campbell 2.

— 1986 at Hartford — First period — Campbell (6), Wales (8). Final score: Wales 4, Campbell 3.

FEWEST SHOTS, ONE TEAM, ONE PERIOD:
2 — 1971 at Boston Third period East
Final score: West 2, East 1

— 1978 at Buffalo Second period Campbell
Final score: Wales 3, Campbell 2

3 — 1978 at Buffalo Third period Campbell
Final score: Wales 3, Campbell 2

4 — 1955 at Detroit First period NHL All-Stars
Final score: Detroit Red Wings 3, NHL All-Stars 1

4 — 1980 at Detroit Second period Campbell
Final score: Wales 6, Campbell 3

Hometown favorite Red Berenson challenges goaltender Ed Giacomin as a young Serge Savard looks on during action in the 1970 All-Star Game in St. Louis. The East downed the West 4-1.

INDIVIDUAL RECORDS

Career

MOST GAMES PLAYED:
23 — Gordie Howe from 1948 through 1980
15 — Frank Mahovlich from 1959 through 1974
13 — Jean Beliveau from 1953 through 1969
— Alex Delvecchio from 1953 through 1967
— Doug Harvey from 1951 through 1969
— Maurice Richard from 1947 through 1959

MOST GOALS:
12 — Wayne Gretzky in 12GP
10 — Gordie Howe in 23GP
9 — Mario Lemieux in 5 GP
8 — Frank Mahovlich in 15GP
7 — Maurice Richard in 13GP
5 — Bobby Hull in 12GP
— Ted Lindsay in 11GP
— Denis Potvin in 8GP
— Luc Robitaille in 4GP

MOST ASSISTS:
9 — Gordie Howe in 23GP
— Ray Bourque in 11GP
— Larry Robinson in 10GP
7 — Doug Harvey in 13GP
— Guy Lafleur in 5GP
6 — Red Kelly in 11GP
— Norm Ullman in 11GP
— Mats Naslund in 3GP
— Paul Coffey in 9GP
— Mark Messier in 9GP

MOST POINTS:
19 — Gordie Howe (10G-9A in 23GP)
17 — Wayne Gretzky (12G-5A in 12GP)
15 — Mario Lemieux (9G-6A in 6GP)
13 — Frank Mahovlich (8G-5A in 15GP)
11 — Ray Bourque (2G-9A in 11GP)
10 — Bobby Hull (5G-5A in 12GP)
— Ted Lindsay (5G-5A in 11GP)
— Luc Robitaille (5G-5A in 4GP)
— Larry Robinson (1G-9A in 10GP)

MOST PENALTY MINUTES:
27 — Gordie Howe in 23GP
21 — Gus Mortson in 9GP
16 — Harry Howell in 7GP

MOST POWER-PLAY GOALS:
6 — Gordie Howe in 23GP
3 — Bobby Hull in 12GP
2 — Maurice Richard in 13GP

Game

MOST GOALS, ONE GAME:
4 — Wayne Gretzky, Campbell, 1983
— Mario Lemieux, Wales, 1990
— Vince Damphousse, Campbell, 1991
3 — Ted Lindsay, Detroit Red Wings, 1950
— Mario Lemieux, Wales, 1988
2 — Wally Hergesheimer, NHL All-Stars, 1953
— Earl Reibel, Detroit Red Wings, 1955
— Andy Bathgate, NHL All-Stars, 1958
— Maurice Richard, Montreal Canadiens, 1958
— Frank Mahovlich, Toronto Maple Leafs, 1963
— Gordie Howe, NHL All-Stars, 1965
— John Ferguson, Montreal Canadiens, 1967
— Frank Mahovlich, East All-Stars, 1969
— Greg Polis, West All-Stars, 1973
— Syl Apps, Wales, 1975
— Dennis Ververgaert, Campbell, 1976
— Richard Martin, Wales, 1977
— Lanny McDonald, Wales, 1977
— Mike Bossy, Wales, 1982
— Pierre Larouche, Wales, 1984
— Mario Lemieux, Wales 1985
— Brian Propp, Wales, 1986
— Luc Robitaille, Campbell, 1988
— Joe Mullen, Campbell, 1989
— Pierre Turgeon, Wales, 1990
— Kirk Muller, Wales, 1990
— Luc Robitaille, Campbell, 1990
— Pat LaFontaine, Wales, 1991
— Brett Hull, Campbell, 1992
— Theoren Fleury, Campbell, 1992

Before the annual NHL All-Star Game was established in 1947, three All-Star Benefit Games were played, the first of which was staged on February 14, 1934 on behalf of injured Toronto Maple Leaf Ace Bailey. The All-Stars played the Leafs, who wore special "Ace" jerseys.

MOST ASSISTS, ONE GAME:
5 — Mats Naslund, Wales, 1988
4 — Ray Bourque, Wales, 1985
— Adam Oates, Campbell, 1991
3 — Dickie Moore, Montreal Canadiens, 1958
— Doug Harvey, Montreal Canadiens, 1959
— Guy Lafleur, Wales, 1975
— Pete Mahovlich, Wales, 1976
— Mark Messier, Campbell, 1983
— Rick Vaive, Campbell, 1984
— Mark Johnson, Wales, 1984
— Don Maloney, Wales, 1984
— Mike Krushelnyski, Campbell, 1985
— Mario Lemieux, Wales, 1988
— Brett Hull, Campbell, 1990
— Luc Robitaille, Campbell, 1992

MOST POINTS, ONE GAME:
6 — Mario Lemieux, Wales, 1988 (3G-3A)
5 — Mats Naslund, Wales, 1988 (5A)
— Adam Oates, Campbell, 1991 (1G-4A)
4 — Ted Lindsay, Detroit Red Wings, 1950 (3G-1A)
— Gordie Howe, NHL All-Stars, 1965 (2G-2A)
— Pete Mahovlich, Wales, 1976 (1G-3A)
— Wayne Gretzky, Campbell, 1983 (4G)
— Don Maloney, Wales, 1984 (1G-3A)
— Ray Bourque, Wales, 1985 (4A)
— Mario Lemieux, Wales, 1990 (4G)
— Vince Damphousse, Campbell, 1991 (4G)

MOST GOALS, ONE PERIOD:
4 — Wayne Gretzky, Campbell, Third period, 1983
3 — Mario Lemieux, Wales, First period, 1990
— Vince Damphousse, Campbell, Third period, 1991
2 — Ted Lindsay, Detroit Red Wings, First period, 1950
— Wally Hergesheimer, NHL All-Stars, First period, 1953
— Andy Bathgate, NHL All-Stars, Third period, 1958
— Frank Mahovlich, Toronto Maple Leafs, First period, 1963
— Dennis Ververgaert, Campbell, Third period, 1976
— Richard Martin, Wales, Third period, 1977
— Pierre Turgeon, Wales, First period, 1990
— Luc Robitaille, Campbell, Third period, 1990
— Theoren Fleury, Campbell, Second period, 1992
— Brett Hull, Campbell, Second period, 1992

MOST ASSISTS, ONE PERIOD:
3 — Mark Messier, Clarence Campbell, Third period, 1983
2 — By several players

MOST POINTS, ONE PERIOD:
4 — Wayne Gretzky, Campbell, Third period, 1983 (4G)
3 — Gordie Howe, NHL All-Stars, Second period, 1965 (1G-2A)
— Pete Mahovlich, Wales, First period, 1976 (1G-2A)
— Mark Messier, Campbell, Third period, 1983 (3A)
— Mario Lemieux, Wales, Second period, 1988 (1G-2A)
— Mario Lemieux, Wales, First period, 1990 (3G)
— Vince Damphousse, Campbell, Third period, 1991 (3G)

FASTEST GOAL FROM START OF GAME:
19 seconds — Ted Lindsay, Detroit Red Wings, 1950
20 seconds — Jacques Laperriere, East All-Stars, 1970
21 seconds — Mario Lemieux, Wales, 1990
36 seconds — Chico Maki, West All-Stars, 1971
37 seconds — Dean Prentice, West All-Star, 1970

FASTEST GOAL FROM START OF A PERIOD:
19 seconds — Ted Lindsay, Detroit Red Wings, 1950 (first period)
20 seconds — Jacques Laperriere, East, 1970 (first period)
21 seconds — Mario Lemieux, Wales, 1990 (first period)
26 seconds — Wayne Gretzky, Campbell, 1982 (second period)
28 seconds — Maurice Richard, NHL All-Stars, 1947 (third period)
33 seconds — Bert Olmstead, Montreal Canadiens, 1957 (second period)

FASTEST TWO GOALS FROM START OF GAME:
5:25 — Wally Hergesheimer, NHL All-Stars, 1953, at 4:06 and 5:25 of first period.

12:11 — Frank Mahovlich, Toronto, 1963, at 2:22 and 12:11 of first period.

13:00 — Mario Lemieux, Wales, 1990, at :21 and 13:00 of first period.

FASTEST TWO GOALS FROM START OF A PERIOD:
4:43 — Dennis Ververgaert, Campbell, 1976, at 4:33 and 4:43 of third period.

5:25 — Wally Hergesheimer, NHL All-Stars, 1953, at 4:06 and 5:25 of first period.

12:11 — Frank Mahovlich, Toronto, 1963. Scored at 2:22 and 12:11 of first period.

13:00 — Mario Lemieux, Wales, 1990, Scored at :21 and 13:00 of first period.

FASTEST TWO GOALS:
10 seconds — Dennis Ververgaert, Campbell, 1976. Scored at 4:33 and 4:43 of third period.

1:02 — Luc Robitaille, Campbell, 1990. Scored at 15:09 and 16:11 of third period.

1:19 — Wally Hergesheimer, NHL All-Stars, 1953. Scored at 4:06 and 5:25 of first period.

2:46 — Vince Damphousse, Campbell, 1991. Scored at 8:54 and 11:40 of third period.

Frankie Brimsek, seen here with the Calder Trophy he won in 1939, compiled a GAA of 1.02 in two All-Star Game appearances.

Goaltenders

MOST GAMES PLAYED:
13 — Glenn Hall from 1955-1969
11 — Terry Sawchuk from 1950-1968
8 — Jacques Plante from 1956-1970
6 — Tony Esposito from 1970-1980
— Ed Giacomin from 1967-1973
— Grant Fuhr from 1982 to date.

MOST GOALS AGAINST:
22 — Glenn Hall in 13GP
19 — Terry Sawchuk in 11GP
18 — Jacques Plante in 8GP
15 — Mike Vernon in 4GP
14 — Turk Broda in 4GP

BEST GOALS-AGAINST-AVERAGE AMONG THOSE WITH AT LEAST TWO GAMES PLAYED:
0.68 — Gilles Villemure in 3GP
1.02 — Frank Brimsek in 2GP
1.59 — Johnny Bower in 4GP
1.64 — Lorne "Gump" Worsley in 4GP
1.98 — Gerry McNeil in 3GP
2.03 — Don Edwards in 2GP
2.44 — Terry Sawchuk in 11GP

MOST MINUTES PLAYED:
467 — Terry Sawchuk in 11GP
421 — Glenn Hall in 13GP
370 — Jacques Plante in 8GP
209 — Turk Broda in 4GP
182 — Ed Giacomin in 6GP
177 — Grant Fuhr in 6GP
165 — Tony Esposito in 6GP

Hockey Hall of Fame

Location: Toronto's Exhibition Park, on the shore of Lake Ontario, adjacent to Ontario Place and Exhibition Stadium. The Hockey Hall of Fame building is in the middle of Exhibition Place, directly north of the stadium. The Hockey Hall of Fame is relocating to a site at the corner of Front and Yonge Streets in downtown Toronto. Opening date for the new Hall of Fame is June, 1993.

Telephone: (416) 595-1345.

Hours: Mid-May to mid-August - 10 am to 5 pm Monday through Thursday; 10 am to 7 pm Friday through Sunday. Mid-August to Labor Day - Hours vary during annual Exhibition. September after Labor Day to mid-May - 10 am to 4:30 pm. Also closed Christmas Day, New Year's Day and the day prior to the annual Exhibition.

Admission: Adults $4.50, Seniors & Students $3.25 Group rates, and reduced rate during Exhibition.

History: The Hockey Hall of Fame building was completed May 1, 1961, and officially opened August 26, 1961, by the Prime Minister of Canada, John G. Diefenbaker, and U.S. ambassador to Canada, Livingston T. Merchant. The six member clubs of the NHL operating at the time provided the funds required for construction. The City of Toronto, owner of the grounds, provided an ideal site, and the Canadian National Exhibition Association, as administrator of the park area, agreed to service and maintain the building in perpetuity for the purposes of the Hockey Hall of Fame. Hockey exhibits are provided and financed by the NHL with co-operative support of the Canadian Amateur Hockey Association. Staff and most administration costs are underwritten by the NHL.

Eligibility Requirements: Any person who is, or has been distinguished in hockey as a player, executive or referee/linesman, shall be eligible for election. Player and referee/linesman candidates will normally have completed their active participating careers three years prior to election, but in exceptional cases this period may be shortened by the Hockey Hall of Fame Board of Directors. Veteran player candidates must have concluded their careers as active players in the sport of hockey for at least 25 years. Candidates for election as executives and referees/linesmen shall be nominated only by the Board of Directors and upon election shall be known as Builders or referees/linesmen. Candidates for election as players shall be chosen on the basis of "playing ability, integrity, character and their contribution to their team and the game of hockey in general."

Honor Roll: There are 288 Honored Members of the Hockey Hall of Fame. Of the total, 199 are listed as players, 77 as Builders and 12 as Referees/Linesmen. Ian (Scotty) Morrison is Chairman of the Hall.

(Year of election to the Hall is indicated in brackets after the Members' names).

Lanny McDonald, along with Marcel Dionne, Bob Gainey and Woody Dumart, are the players who were inducted into the Hockey Hall of Fame on September 21, 1992.

PLAYERS

Abel, Sidney Gerald (1969)
*Adams, John James "Jack" (1959)
Apps, Charles Joseph Sylvanus "Syl" (1961)
Armstrong, George Edward (1975)
*Bailey, Irvine Wallace "Ace" (1975)
*Bain, Donald H. "Dan" (1945)
*Baker, Hobart "Hobey" (1945)
Barber, William Charles "Bill" (1990)
*Barry, Martin J. "Marty" (1965)
Bathgate, Andrew James "Andy" (1978)
Beliveau, Jean Arthur (1972)
*Benedict, Clinton S. (1965)
*Bentley, Douglas Wagner (1964)
*Bentley, Maxwell H. L. (1966)
Blake, Hector "Toe" (1966)
Boivin, Leo Joseph (1986)
*Boon, Richard R. "Dickie" (1952)
Bossy, Michael (1991)
Bouchard, Emile Joseph "Butch" (1966)
*Boucher, Frank (1958)
*Boucher, George "Buck" (1960)
Bower, John William (1976)
*Bowie, Russell (1945)
Brimsek, Francis Charles (1966)
*Broadbent, Harry L. "Punch" (1962)
*Broda, Walter Edward "Turk" (1967)
Bucyk, John Paul (1981)
*Burch, Billy (1974)
*Cameron, Harold Hugh "Harry" (1962)
Cheevers, Gerald Michael "Gerry" (1985)
*Clancy, Francis Michael "King" (1958)
*Clapper, Aubrey "Dit" (1947)
Clarke, Robert "Bobby" (1987)
*Cleghorn, Sprague (1958)
*Colville, Neil MacNeil (1967)
*Conacher, Charles W. (1961)
*Connell, Alex (1958)
*Cook, William Osser (1952)
Coulter, Arthur Edmund (1974)
Cournoyer, Yvan Serge (1982)
Cowley, William Mailes (1968)
*Crawford, Samuel Russell "Rusty" (1962)
*Darragh, John Proctor "Jack" (1962)
*Davidson, Allan M. "Scotty" (1950)
*Day, Clarence Henry "Hap" (1961)
Delvecchio, Alex (1977)
*Denneny, Cyril "Cy" (1959)
Dionne, Marcel (1992)
*Drillon, Gordon Arthur (1975)
*Drinkwater, Charles Graham (1950)
Dryden, Kenneth Wayne (1983)
Dumart, Woodrow "Woody" (1992)
*Dunderdale, Thomas (1974)
*Durnan, William Ronald (1964)
*Dutton, Mervyn A. "Red" (1958)
*Dye, Cecil Henry "Babe" (1970)
Esposito, Anthony James "Tony" (1988)
Esposito, Philip Anthony (1984)
*Farrell, Arthur F. (1965)
Flaman, Ferdinand Charles "Fern" (1990)
*Foyston, Frank (1958)
*Frederickson, Frank (1958)
Gadsby, William Alexander (1970)
Gainey, Bob (1992)
*Gardiner, Charles Robert "Chuck" (1945)
*Gardiner, Herbert Martin "Herb" (1958)
*Gardner, James Henry "Jimmy" (1962)
Geoffrion, Jos. A. Bernard "Boom Boom" (1972)
*Gerard, Eddie (1945)
Giacomin, Edward "Eddie" (1987)
Gilbert, Rodrigue Gabriel "Rod" (1982)
*Gilmour, Hamilton Livingstone "Billy" (1962)
*Goheen, Frank Xavier "Moose" (1952)
*Goodfellow, Ebenezer R. "Ebbie" (1963)
*Grant, Michael "Mike" (1950)
*Green, Wilfred "Shorty" (1962)
*Griffis, Silas Seth "Si" (1950)
*Hainsworth, George (1961)
Hall, Glenn Henry (1975)
*Hall, Joseph Henry (1961)
*Harvey, Douglas Norman (1973)
*Hay, George (1958)
*Hern, William Milton "Riley" (1962)
*Hextall, Bryan Aldwyn (1969)
*Holmes, Harry "Hap" (1972)
*Hooper, Charles Thomas "Tom" (1962)
Horner, George Reginald "Red" (1965)
*Horton, Miles Gilbert "Tim" (1977)
Howe, Gordon (1972)
*Howe, Sydney Harris (1965)
Howell, Henry Vernon "Harry" (1979)
Hull, Robert Marvin (1983)
*Hutton, John Bower "Bouse" (1962)
*Hyland, Harry M. (1962)
*Irvin, James Dickenson "Dick" (1958)
*Jackson, Harvey "Busher" (1971)
*Johnson, Ernest "Moose" (1952)
*Johnson, Ivan "Ching" (1958)
Johnson, Thomas Christian (1970)
*Joliat, Aurel (1947)
*Keats, Gordon "Duke" (1958)
Kelly, Leonard Patrick "Red" (1969)
Kennedy, Theodore Samuel "Teeder" (1966)
Keon, David Michael (1986)
Lach, Elmer James (1966)
Lafleur, Guy Damien (1988)
*Lalonde, Edouard Charles "Newsy" (1950)
Laperriere, Jacques (1987)
*Laviolette, Jean Baptiste "Jack" (1962)
*Lehman, Hugh (1958)
Lemaire, Jacques Gerard (1984)
*LeSueur, Percy (1961)
*Lewis, Herbert A. (1989)
Lindsay, Robert Blake Theodore "Ted" (1966)
Lumley, Harry (1980)
*MacKay, Duncan "Mickey" (1952)
Mahovlich, Frank William (1981)
*Malone, Joseph "Joe" (1950)
*Mantha, Sylvio (1960)
*Marshall, John "Jack" (1965)
*Maxwell, Fred G. "Steamer" (1962)
McDonald, Lanny (1992)
*McGee, Frank (1945)
*McGimsie, William George "Billy" (1962)
*McNamara, George (1958)
Mikita, Stanley (1983)
Moore, Richard Winston (1974)
*Moran, Patrick Joseph "Paddy" (1958)
*Morenz, Howie (1945)
Mosienko, William "Billy" (1965)
*Nighbor, Frank (1947)
*Noble, Edward Reginald "Reg" (1962)
*O'Connor, Herbert William "Buddy" (1988)
*Oliver, Harry (1967)
Olmstead, Murray Bert "Bert" (1985)
Orr, Robert Gordon (1979)
Parent, Bernard Marcel (1984)
Park, Douglas Bradford "Brad" (1988)
*Patrick, Joseph Lynn (1980)
*Patrick, Lester (1947)
Perreault, Gilbert (1990)
*Phillips, Tommy (1945)
Pilote, Joseph Albert Pierre Paul (1975)
*Pitre, Didier "Pit" (1962)
*Plante, Joseph Jacques Omer (1978)
Potvin, Denis (1991)
*Pratt, Walter "Babe" (1966)
*Primeau, A. Joseph (1963)
Pronovost, Joseph Ren;aae Marcel (1978)
Pulford, Bob (1991)
*Pulford, Harvey (1945)
Quackenbush, Hubert George "Bill" (1976)
*Rankin, Frank (1961)

Ratelle, Joseph Gilbert Yvan Jean "Jean" (1985)
Rayner, Claude Earl "Chuck" (1973)
Reardon, Kenneth Joseph (1966)
Richard, Joseph Henri (1979)
Richard, Joseph Henri Maurice "Rocket" (1961)
*Richardson, George Taylor (1950)
*Roberts, Gordon (1971)
*Ross, Arthur Howie (1945)
*Russel, Blair (1965)
*Russell, Ernest (1965)
*Ruttan, J.D. "Jack" (1962)
Savard, Serge A. (1986)
*Sawchuk, Terrance Gordon "Terry" (1971)
*Scanlan, Fred (1965)
Schmidt, Milton Conrad "Milt" (1961)
*Schriner, David "Sweeney" (1962)
*Seibert, Earl Walter (1963)
*Seibert, Oliver Levi (1961)
*Shore, Edward W. "Eddie" (1947)
*Siebert, Albert C. "Babe" (1964)
*Simpson, Harold Edward "Bullet Joe" (1962)
Sittler, Darryl Glen (1989)
*Smith, Alfred E. (1962)
Smith, Clint (1991)
*Smith, Reginald "Hooley" (1972)
*Smith, Thomas James (1973)
Stanley, Allan Herbert (1981)
*Stanley, Russell "Barney" (1962)
*Stewart, John Sherratt "Black Jack" (1964)
*Stewart, Nelson "Nels" (1962)
*Stuart, Bruce (1961)
*Stuart, Hod (1945)
*Taylor, Frederic "Cyclone" (O.B.E.) (1947)
*Thompson, Cecil R. "Tiny" (1959)
Tretiak, Vladislav (1989)
*Trihey, Col. Harry J. (1950)
Ullman, Norman Victor Alexander "Norm" (1982)
*Vezina, Georges (1945)
*Walker, John Phillip "Jack" (1960)
*Walsh, Martin "Marty" (1962)
*Watson, Harry E. (1962)
*Weiland, Ralph "Cooney" (1971)
*Westwick, Harry (1962)
*Whitcroft, Fred (1962)
*Wilson, Gordon Allan "Phat" (1962)
Worsley, Lorne John "Gump" (1980)
*Worters, Roy (1969)

BUILDERS

*Adams, Charles Francis (1960)
*Adams, Weston W. (1972)
*Aheam, Thomas Franklin "Frank" (1962)
*Ahearne, John Francis "Bunny" (1977)
*Allan, Sir Montagu (C.V.O.) (1945)
Allen, Keith (1992)
*Ballard, Harold Edwin (1977)
*Bauer, Father David (1989)
*Bickell, John Paris (1978)
Bowman, Scott (1991)
*Brown, George V. (1961)
*Brown, Walter A. (1962)
*Buckland, Frank (1975)
Butterfield, Jack Arlington (1980)
*Calder, Frank (1947)
*Campbell, Angus D. (1964)
*Campbell, Clarence Sutherland (1966)
*Cattarinich, Joseph (1977)
*Dandurand, Joseph Viateur "Leo" (1963)
Dilio, Francis Paul (1964)
*Dudley, George S. (1958)
*Dunn, James A. (1968)
Eagleson, Robert Alan (1989)
Francis, Emile (1982)
*Gibson, Dr. John L. "Jack" (1976)
*Gorman, Thomas Patrick "Tommy" (1963)
*Hanley, William (1986)
*Hay, Charles (1974)
*Hendy, James C. (1968)
*Hewitt, Foster (1965)
*Hewitt, William Abraham (1947)
*Hume, Fred J. (1962)
*Imlach, George "Punch" (1984)
Ivan, Thomas N. (1974)
*Jennings, William M. (1975)
*Johnson, Bob (1992)
Juckes, Gordon W. (1979)
*Kilpatrick, Gen. John Reed (1960)
*Leader, George Alfred (1969)
LeBel, Robert (1970)
*Lockhart, Thomas F. (1965)
*Loicq, Paul (1961)
*Mariucci, John (1985)
Mathers, Frank (1992)
*McLaughlin, Major Frederic (1963)
*Milford, John "Jake" (1984)
Molson, Hon. Hartland de Montarville (1973)
*Nelson, Francis (1947)
*Norris, Bruce A. (1969)
*Norris, Sr., James (1958)
*Norris, James Dougan (1962)
*Northey, William M. (1947)
*O'Brien, John Ambrose (1962)
*Patrick, Frank (1958)
*Pickard, Allan W. (1958)
Pilous, Rudy (1985)
Poile, Norman "Bud" (1990)
Pollock, Samuel Patterson Smyth (1978)
*Raymond, Sen. Donat (1958)
*Robertson, John Ross (1947)
*Robinson, Claude C. (1947)
*Ross, Philip D. (1976)
*Selke, Frank J. (1960)
Sinden, Harry James (1983)
*Smith, Frank D. (1962)
*Smythe, Conn (1958)
Snider, Edward M. (1988)
*Stanley of Preston, Lord (G.C.B.) (1945)
*Sutherland, Cap. James T. (1947)
Tarasov, Anatoli V. (1974)
*Turner, Lloyd (1958)
*Tutt, William Thayer (1978)
Voss, Carl Potter (1974)
*Waghorn, Fred C. (1961)
*Wirtz, Arthur Michael (1971)
Wirtz, William W. "Bill" (1976)
Ziegler, John A. Jr. (1987)

REFEREES/LINESMEN

Armstrong, Neil (1991)
Ashley, John George (1981)
Chadwick, William L. (1964)
*Elliott, Chaucer (1961)
*Hayes, George William (1988)
*Hewitson, Robert W. (1963)
*Ion, Fred J. "Mickey" (1961)
Pavelich, Matt (1987)
*Rodden, Michael J. "Mike" (1962)
*Smeaton, J. Cooper (1961)
Storey, Roy Alvin "Red" (1967)
Udvari, Frank Joseph (1973)

*Deceased

Elmer Ferguson Memorial Award Winners

In recognition of distinguished members of the newspaper profession whose words have brought honor to journalism and to hockey. Selected by the Professional Hockey Writers' Association.

*Barton, Charlie, Buffalo-Courier Express
*Beauchamp, Jacques, Montreal Matin/Journal de Montreal
Brennan, Bill, Detroit News
*Burchard, Jim, New York World Telegram
*Burnett, Red, Toronto Star
*Carroll, Dink, Montreal Gazette
Coleman, Jim, Southam Newspapers
*Damata, Ted, Chicago Daily News
Delano, Hugh, New York Post
Desjardins, Marcel, Montreal La Presse
Dulmage, Jack, Windsor Star
Dunnell, Milt, Toronto Star
*Ferguson, Elmer, Montreal Newspapers
Fisher, Red, Montreal Star/Gazette
*Fitzgerald, Tom, Boston Globe
Frayne, Trent, Toronto Telegram/Globe and Mail/Sun
Gross, George, Toronto Telegram
Johnston, Dick, Buffalo News
*Laney, Al, New York Herald-Tribune
Larochelle, Claude, Le Soleil
L'Esperance, Zotique, le Journal de Montréal
*Mayer, Charles, le Journal de Montréal
MacLeod, Rex, Toronto Globe and Mail
Monahan, Leo, Boston Herald
Moriarty, Tim, UPI/Newsday
*Nichols, Joe, New York Times
*O'Brien, Andy, Weekend Magazine
Orr, Frank, Toronto Star
Olan, Ben, New York Associated Press
*O'Meara, Basil, Montreal Star
Proudfoot, Jim, Toronto Star
Raymond, Bertrand, le Journal de Montréal
Rosa, Fran, Boston Globe
*Vipond, Jim, Toronto Globe and Mail
Walter, Lewis, Detroit Times
Young, Scott, Toronto Globe and Mail/Telegram

Foster Hewitt Memorial Award Winners

In recognition of members of the radio and television industry who made outstanding contributions to their profession and the game during their career in hockey broadcasting. Selected by the NHL Broadcasters' Association.

Cusick, Fred, Boston
Gallivan, Danny, Montreal
*Hewitt, Foster, Toronto
Irvin, Dick, Montreal
*Kelly, Dan, St. Louis
Lecavelier, Rene, Montreal
Lynch, Budd, Detroit
Martyn, Bruce, Detroit
McDonald, Jiggs, NY Islanders
*McKnight, Wes, Toronto
Petit, Lloyd, Chicago
Robson, Jim, Vancouver
*Smith, Doug, Montreal
Wilson, Bob, Boston
*Deceased

United States Hockey Hall of Fame

The United States Hockey Hall of Fame is located in Eveleth, Minnesota, 60 miles north of Duluth, on Highway 53. The facility is open Monday to Saturday 9 a.m. to 5 p.m. and Sundays 11 a.m to 5 p.m.; Adult $2.50; Seniors $2.25; Juniors $1.50; and Children 7-12 $1.25; Children under 6 free. Group rates available.

The Hall was dedicated and opened on June 21, 1973, largely as the result of the work of D. Kelly Campbell, Chairman of the Eveleth Civic Association's Project H Committee. The National Hockey League contributed $100,000 towards the construction of the building. There are now 75 enshrinees consisting of 47 players, 13 coaches, 14 administrators, and one referee. New members are inducted annually in October and must have made a significant contribution toward hockey in the United States through the vehicle of their careers.

PLAYERS

*Abel, Clarence "Taffy"
*Baker, Hobart "Hobey"
Bartholome, Earl
Bessone, Peter
Blake, Robert
Brimsek, Frank
*Chaisson, Ray
Chase, John P.
Christian, Roger
Christian, William "Bill"
Cleary, Robert
Cleary, William
*Conroy, Anthony
Dahlstrom, Carl "Cully"
DesJardins, Victor
Desmond, Richard
*Dill, Robert
Everett, Doug
Ftorek, Robbie
*Garrison, John B.
Garrity, Jack
*Goheen, Frank "Moose"
Harding, Austin "Austie"
Iglehart, Stewart
Johnson, Virgil
Karakas, Mike
Kirrane, Jack
*Lane, Myles J.
*Linder, Joseph
*LoPresti, Sam L.
*Mariucci, John
Matchefts, John
Mayasich, John
McCartan, Jack
Moe, William
*Moseley, Fred
*Murray, Hugh "Muzz" Sr.
*Nelson, Hubert "Hub"
Olson , Eddie
*Owen, Jr., George
*Palmer, Winthrop
Paradise, Robert
Purpur, Clifford "Fido"
Riley, William
*Romnes, Elwin "Doc"
Rondeau, Richard
*Williams, Thomas
*Winters, Frank "Coddy"
*Yackel, Ken

COACHES

*Almquist, Oscar
Bessone, Amo
Brooks, Herbert
Ceglarski, Len
*Fullerton, James
*Gordon, Malcolm K.
Heyliger, Victor
Ikola, Willard
*Jeremiah, Edward J.
*Johnson, Bob
*Kelley, John "Snooks"
Pleban, John "Connie"
Riley, Jack
Ross, Larry
*Thompson, Clifford, R.
*Stewart, William
*Winsor, Alfred "Ralph"

ADMINISTRATORS

*Brown, George V.
*Brown, Walter A.
Bush, Walter
Clark, Donald
*Gibson, J.C. "Doc"
*Jennings, William M.
*Kahler, Nick
*Lockhart, Thomas F.
Marvin, Cal
Ridder, Robert
Trumble, Harold
*Tutt, William Thayer
Wirtz, William W. "Bill"
*Wright, Lyle Z.

REFEREE

Chadwick, William

*Deceased

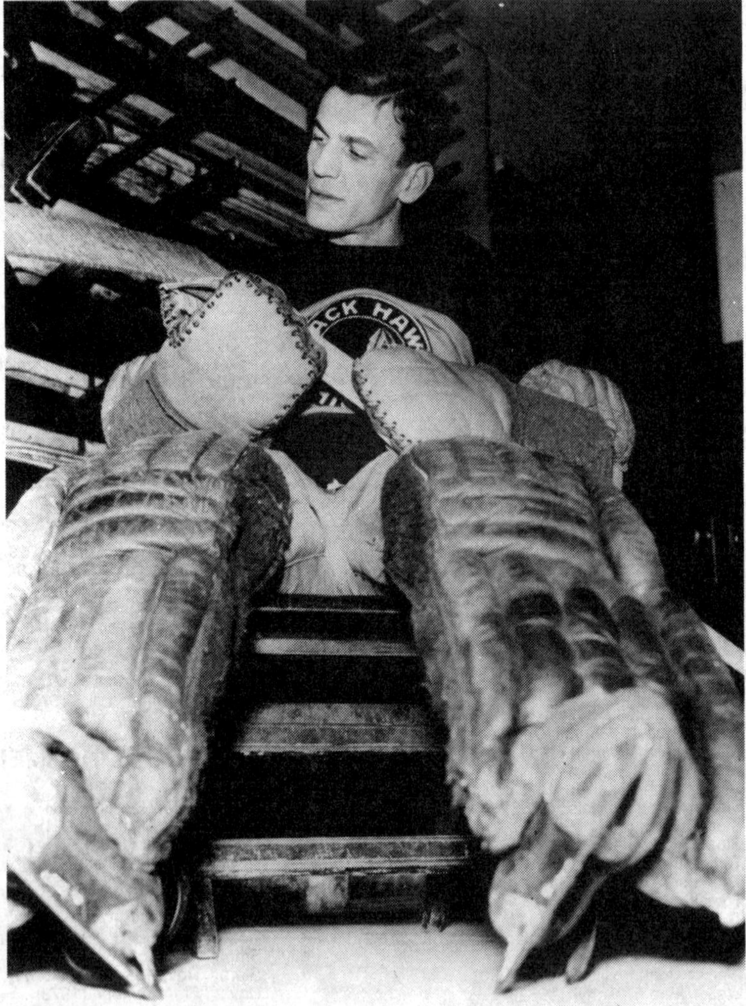

Mike Karakas, the Calder Trophy winner in 1936 and member of the U.S. Hockey Hall of Fame, led the league with four shutouts in 1945.

1992 Stanley Cup Playoffs

Larry Murphy topped all Pittsburgh defensemen in scoring during the 1992 playoffs with 16 points.

Team Playoff Records

	Gp	W	L	Gf	Ga	Pctg
Pittsburgh	21	16	5	83	63	.762
Chicago	18	12	6	65	48	.667
Boston	15	8	7	40	51	.533
Edmonton	16	8	8	49	54	.500
NY Rangers	13	6	7	47	49	.462
Vancouver	13	6	7	44	35	.462
Montreal	11	4	7	29	32	.364
Detroit	11	4	7	29	30	.364
Washington	7	3	4	27	25	.429
New Jersey	7	3	4	25	28	.429
Buffalo	7	3	4	24	19	.429
Minnesota	7	3	4	19	23	.429
Hartford	7	3	4	18	21	.429
Winnipeg	7	3	4	17	29	.429
St Louis	6	2	4	19	23	.333
Los Angeles	6	2	4	18	23	.333

Results

DIVISION SEMI-FINALS

(Best-of-seven series)

Prince of Wales Conference

Series 'A'

Sun. Apr. 19	Hartford 0	at	Montreal 2
Tue. Apr. 21	Hartford 2	at	Montreal 5
Thu. Apr. 23	Montreal 2	at	Hartford 5
Sat. Apr. 25	Montreal 1	at	Hartford 3
Mon. Apr. 27	Hartford 4	at	Montreal 7
Wed. Apr. 29	Montreal 1	at	Hartford 2*
Fri. May 1	Hartford 2	at	Montreal 3**

* Yvon Corriveau scored at 0:24 of overtime
** Russ Courtnall scored at 25:26 of overtime

Montreal won series 4-3

Series 'B'

Sun. Apr. 19	Buffalo 3	at	Boston 2
Tue. Apr. 21	Buffalo 2	at	Boston 3*
Thu. Apr. 23	Boston 3	at	Buffalo 2
Sat. Apr. 25	Boston 5	at	Buffalo 4**
Mon. Apr. 27	Buffalo 2	at	Boston 0
Wed. Apr. 29	Boston 3	at	Buffalo 9
Fri. May 1	Buffalo 2	at	Boston 3

* Adam Oates scored at 11:14 of overtime
** Ted Donato scored at 2:08 of overtime

Boston won series 4-3

Series 'C'

Sun. Apr. 19	New Jersey 1	at	NY Rangers 2
Tue. Apr. 21	New Jersey 7	at	NY Rangers 3
Thu. Apr. 23	NY Rangers 1	at	New Jersey 3
Sat. Apr. 25	NY Rangers 3	at	New Jersey 0
Mon. Apr. 27	New Jersey 5	at	NY Rangers 8
Wed. Apr. 29	NY Rangers 3	at	New Jersey 5
Fri. May 1	New Jersey 4	at	NY Rangers 8

NY Rangers won series 4-3

Series 'D'

Sun. Apr. 19	Pittsburgh 1	at	Washington 3
Tue. Apr. 21	Pittsburgh 2	at	Washington 6
Thu. Apr. 23	Washington 4	at	Pittsburgh 6
Sat. Apr. 25	Washington 7	at	Pittsburgh 2
Mon. Apr. 27	Pittsburgh 5	at	Washington 2
Wed. Apr. 29	Washington 4	at	Pittsburgh 6
Fri. May 1	Pittsburgh 3	at	Washington 1

Pittsburgh won series 4-3

Clarence Campbell Conference

Series 'E'

Sat. Apr. 18	Minnesota 4	at	Detroit 3
Mon. Apr. 20	Minnesota 4	at	Detroit 2
Wed. Apr. 22	Detroit 5	at	Minnesota 4*
Fri. Apr. 24	Detroit 4	at	Minnesota 5
Sun. Apr. 26	Minnesota 0	at	Detroit 3
Tue. Apr. 28	Detroit 1	at	Minnesota 0**
Thu. Apr. 30	Minnesota 2	at	Detroit 5

* Yves Racine scored at 1:15 of overtime
** Sergei Fedorov scored at 16:13 of overtime

Detroit won series 4-3

Series 'F'

Sat. Apr. 18	St Louis 1	at	Chicago 3
Mon. Apr. 20	St Louis 5	at	Chicago 3
Wed. Apr. 22	Chicago 4	at	St Louis 5*
Fri. Apr. 24	Chicago 5	at	St Louis 3
Sun. Apr. 26	St Louis 4	at	Chicago 6
Tue. Apr. 28	Chicago 2	at	St Louis 1

* Brett Hull scored at 23:33 of overtime

Chicago won series 4-2

Series 'G'

Sat. Apr. 18	Winnipeg 3	at	Vancouver 2
Mon. Apr. 20	Winnipeg 2	at	Vancouver 3
Wed. Apr. 22	Vancouver 2	at	Winnipeg 4
Fri. Apr. 24	Vancouver 1	at	Winnipeg 3
Sun. Apr. 26	Winnipeg 2	at	Vancouver 8
Tue. Apr. 28	Vancouver 8	at	Winnipeg 3
Thu. Apr. 30	Winnipeg 0	at	Vancouver 5

Vancouver won series 4-3

Series 'H'

Sat. Apr. 18	Edmonton 3	at	Los Angeles 1
Mon. Apr. 20	Edmonton 5	at	Los Angeles 8
Wed. Apr. 22	Los Angeles 3	at	Edmonton 4
Fri. Apr. 24	Los Angeles 4	at	Edmonton 3
Sun. Apr. 26	Edmonton 5	at	Los Angeles 2
Tue. Apr. 28	Los Angeles 0	at	Edmonton 3

Edmonton won series 4-2

DIVISION FINALS

(Best-of-seven series)

Prince of Wales Conference

Series 'I'

Sun. May 3	Boston 6	at	Montreal 4
Tue. May 5	Boston 3	at	Montreal 2*
Thu. May 7	Montreal 2	at	Boston 3
Sat. May 9	Montreal 0	at	Boston 2

* Peter Douris scored at 3:12 of overtime

Boston won series 4-0

Series 'J'

Sun. May 3	Pittsburgh 4	at	NY Rangers 2
Tue. May 5	Pittsburgh 2	at	NY Rangers 4
Thu. May 7	NY Rangers 6	at	Pittsburgh 5*
Sat. May 9	NY Rangers 4	at	Pittsburgh 5**
Mon. May 11	Pittsburgh 3	at	NY Rangers 2
Wed. May 13	NY Rangers 1	at	Pittsburgh 5

* Kris King scored at 1:29 of overtime
** Ron Francis scored at 2:47 of overtime

Pittsburgh won series 4-2

Clarence Campbell Conference

Series 'K'

Sat. May 2	Chicago 2	at	Detroit 1
Mon. May 4	Chicago 3	at	Detroit 1
Wed. May 6	Detroit 4	at	Chicago 5
Fri. May 8	Detroit 0	at	Chicago 1

Chicago won series 4-0

Series 'L'

Sun. May 3	Edmonton 4	at	Vancouver 3*
Mon. May 4	Edmonton 0	at	Vancouver 4
Wed. May 6	Vancouver 2	at	Edmonton 5
Fri. May 8	Vancouver 2	at	Edmonton 3
Sun. May 10	Edmonton 3	at	Vancouver 4
Tue. May 12	Vancouver 0	at	Edmonton 3

* Joe Murphy scored at 8:36 of overtime

Edmonton won series 4-2

CONFERENCE CHAMPIONSHIPS

(Best-of-seven series)

Prince of Wales Conference

Series 'M'

Sun. May 17	Boston 3	at	Pittsburgh 4*
Tue. May 19	Boston 2	at	Pittsburgh 5
Thu. May 21	Pittsburgh 5	at	Boston 1
Sat. May 23	Pittsburgh 5	at	Boston 1

* Jaromir Jagr scored at 9:44 of overtime

Pittsburgh won series 4-0

Clarence Campbell Conference

Series 'N'

Sat. May 16	Edmonton 2	at	Chicago 8
Mon. May 18	Edmonton 2	at	Chicago 4
Wed. May 20	Chicago 4	at	Edmonton 3*
Fri. May 22	Chicago 5	at	Edmonton 1

* Jeremy Roenick scored at 2:45 of overtime

Chicago won series 4-0

STANLEY CUP CHAMPIONSHIP

(Best-of-seven series)

Series 'O'

Tue. May 26	Chicago 4	at	Pittsburgh 5
Thu. May 28	Chicago 1	at	Pittsburgh 3
Sat. May 30	Pittsburgh 1	at	Chicago 0
Mon. June 1	Pittsburgh 6	at	Chicago 5

Pittsburgh won series 4-0

Individual Leaders

Abbreviations: * – rookie eligible for Calder Trophy; **A** – assists; **G** – goals; **GP** – Games Played; **GT** – game-tying goals; **GW** – game-winning goals; **PIM** – penalties in minutes; **PP** – power play goals; **Pts** – points; **S** – shots on goal; **SH** – short-handed goals; **%** – percentage shots resulting in goals; **+/–** – difference between Goals For (**GF**) scored when a player is on the ice with his team at even strength or short-handed and Goals Against (**GA**) scored when the same player is on the ice with his team at even strength or on a power play.

Playoff Scoring Leaders

Player	Team	GP	G	A	Pts	+/–	PIM	PP	SH	GW	GT	S	%
Mario Lemieux	Pittsburgh	15	16	18	34	6	2	8	2	5	0	69	23.2
Kevin Stevens	Pittsburgh	21	13	15	28	2	28	4	0	3	0	86	15.1
Ron Francis	Pittsburgh	21	8	19	27	8	6	2	0	2	1	58	13.8
Jaromir Jagr	Pittsburgh	21	11	13	24	4	6	2	0	4	1	59	18.6
Joe Murphy	Edmonton	16	8	16	24	2	12	4	0	2	1	32	25.0
Jeremy Roenick	Chicago	18	12	10	22	11	12	4	0	3	1	56	21.4
Chris Chelios	Chicago	18	6	15	21	19	37	3	0	1	0	54	11.1
Bernie Nicholls	Edmonton	16	8	11	19	2	25	4	0	1	0	32	25.0
Rick Tocchet	Pittsburgh	14	6	13	19	0	24	3	0	1	0	30	20.0
Adam Oates	Boston	15	5	14	19	6-	4	3	0	2	1	35	14.3
Mike Gartner	NY Rangers	13	8	8	16	3	4	3	0	1	0	66	12.1
Larry Murphy	Pittsburgh	21	6	10	16	4-	19	3	0	1	0	59	10.2
Steve Larmer	Chicago	18	8	7	15	9	6	3	0	0	0	69	11.6
Brian Noonan	Chicago	18	6	9	15	3-	30	3	0	1	0	37	16.2
Brian Leetch	NY Rangers	13	4	11	15	5-	4	1	1	0	0	67	6.0
Mark Messier	NY Rangers	11	7	7	14	4-	6	2	2	0	0	27	25.9
Geoff Courtnall	Vancouver	12	6	8	14	4	20	2	0	1	0	41	14.6
Vincent Damphousse	Edmonton	16	6	8	14	5	8	1	0	0	0	45	13.3
Cliff Ronning	Vancouver	13	8	5	13	5	6	1	0	1	0	49	16.3
Dirk Graham	Chicago	18	7	5	12	9	8	0	0	1	0	45	15.6
Trevor Linden	Vancouver	13	4	8	12	5	6	2	0	1	0	37	10.8
*Joe Juneau	Boston	15	4	8	12	3-	21	2	0	0	0	29	13.8
Denis Savard	Montreal	11	3	9	12	1	8	1	0	0	0	33	9.1
Dave Manson	Edmonton	16	3	9	12	2-	44	1	0	0	0	47	6.4
Steve Smith	Chicago	18	1	11	12	12	16	1	0	0	0	37	2.7

Playoff Defensemen Scoring Leaders

Player	Team	GP	G	A	Pts	+/–	PIM	PP	SH	GW	GT	S	%
Chris Chelios	Chicago	18	6	15	21	19	37	3	0	1	0	54	11.1
Larry Murphy	Pittsburgh	21	6	10	16	4-	19	3	0	1	0	59	10.2
Brian Leetch	NY Rangers	13	4	11	15	5-	4	1	1	0	0	67	6.0
Dave Manson	Edmonton	16	3	9	12	2-	44	1	0	0	0	47	6.4
Steve Smith	Chicago	18	1	11	12	12	16	1	0	0	0	37	2.7
Ray Bourque	Boston	12	3	6	9	10-	12	2	0	0	0	51	5.9
Dave Babych	Vancouver	13	2	6	8	6	10	1	0	1	0	25	8.0
*Igor Kravchuk	Chicago	18	2	6	8	2-	8	1	0	0	0	48	4.2
Adrien Plavsic	Vancouver	13	1	7	8	6	4	0	0	0	0	20	5.0
Paul Stanton	Pittsburgh	21	1	7	8	6	42	0	0	0	0	24	4.2

GOALTENDING LEADERS

Goals Against Average

Goaltender	Team	GPI	Mins.	GA	Avg.
Ed Belfour	Chicago	18	949	39	2.47
Tim Cheveldae	Detroit	11	597	25	2.51
Kirk McLean	Vancouver	13	785	33	2.52
Patrick Roy	Montreal	11	686	30	2.62
Tom Barrasso	Pittsburgh	21	1233	58	2.82

Wins

Goaltender	Team	GPI	Mins.	W	L
Tom Barrasso	Pittsburgh	21	1233	16	5
Ed Belfour	Chicago	18	949	12	4
Andy Moog	Boston	15	866	8	7
Bill Ranford	Edmonton	16	909	8	8
Kirk McLean	Vancouver	13	785	6	7

Save Percentage

Goaltender	Team	GPI	Mins.	GA	SA	S%	W	L
Kirk McLean	Vancouver	13	785	33	364	.909	6	7
Tim Cheveldae	Detroit	11	597	25	277	.909	3	7
Tom Barrasso	Pittsburgh	21	1233	58	622	.907	16	5
Patrick Roy	Montreal	11	686	30	312	.903	4	7
Ed Belfour	Chicago	18	949	39	398	.902	12	4

Shutouts

Goaltender	Team	GPI	Mins.	SO
Tim Cheveldae	Detroit	11	597	2
Kirk McLean	Vancouver	13	785	2
Bill Ranford	Edmonton	16	909	2

Plus/Minus

Name	Team	GP	+/–
Chris Chelios	Chicago	18	19
Steve Smith	Chicago	18	12
Jeremy Roenick	Chicago	18	11
*Jim Paek	Pittsburgh	19	10
Dirk Graham	Chicago	18	9
Steve Larmer	Chicago	18	9

First Goals

Name	Team	GP	FG
Kevin Stevens	Pittsburgh	21	4
Sergei Fedorov	Detroit	11	3
Jeremy Roenick	Chicago	18	3

Goal Scoring

Name	Team	GP	G
Mario Lemieux	Pittsburgh	15	16
Kevin Stevens	Pittsburgh	21	13
Jeremy Roenick	Chicago	18	12
Jaromir Jagr	Pittsburgh	21	11
Pat Lafontaine	Buffalo	7	8
Mike Gartner	NY Rangers	13	8
Cliff Ronning	Vancouver	13	8
Joe Murphy	Edmonton	16	8
Bernie Nicholls	Edmonton	16	8
Steve Larmer	Chicago	18	8
Ron Francis	Pittsburgh	21	8
Mark Messier	Ny Rangers	11	7
Dirk Graham	Chicago	18	7

Assists

Name	Team	GP	A
Ron Francis	Pittsburgh	21	19
Mario Lemieux	Pittsburgh	15	18
Joe Murphy	Edmonton	16	16
Chris Chelios	Chicago	18	15
Kevin Stevens	Pittsburgh	21	15
Adam Oates	Boston	15	14
Rick Tocchet	Pittsburgh	14	13
Jaromir Jagr	Pittsburgh	21	13
Mike Ridley	Washington	7	11
Brian Leetch	NY Rangers	13	11
Bernie Nicholls	Edmonton	16	11
Steve Smith	Chicago	18	11

Power Play Goals

Name	Team	GP	PP
Mario Lemieux	Pittsburgh	15	8
Pat Lafontaine	Buffalo	7	5
Joe Murphy	Edmonton	16	4
Bernie Nicholls	Edmonton	16	4
Jeremy Roenick	Chicago	18	4
Kevin Stevens	Pittsburgh	21	4

Short Hand Goals

Name	Team	GP	SH
Sergei Fedorov	Detroit	11	2
Mark Messier	NY Rangers	11	2
Mario Lemieux	Pittsburgh	15	2

Game Winning Goals

Name	Team	GP	GW
Mario Lemieux	Pittsburgh	15	5
Jaromir Jagr	Pittsburgh	21	4
Kris King	NY Rangers	13	3
Jeremy Roenick	Chicago	18	3
Kevin Stevens	Pittsburgh	21	3
Adam Oates	Boston	15	2
Joe Murphy	Edmonton	16	2
Jocelyn Lemieux	Chicago	18	2
Ron Francis	Pittsburgh	21	2

Overtime Goals

Name	Team	GP	OT
Brett Hull	St Louis	6	1
Yvon Corriveau	Hartford	7	1
Peter Douris	Boston	7	1
Russ Courtnall	Montreal	10	1
Sergei Fedorov	Detroit	11	1
Yves Racine	Detroit	11	1
Kris King	NY Rangers	13	1
Adam Oates	Boston	15	1
*Ted Donato	Boston	15	1
Joe Murphy	Edmonton	16	1
Jeremy Roenick	Chicago	18	1
Ron Francis	Pittsburgh	21	1
Jaromir Jagr	Pittsburgh	21	1

Shots

Name	Team	GP	S
Kevin Stevens	Pittsburgh	21	86
Mario Lemieux	Pittsburgh	15	69
Steve Larmer	Chicago	18	69
Brian Leetch	NY Rangers	13	67
Mike Gartner	NY Rangers	13	66

Team Statistics

TEAMS' HOME-AND-ROAD RECORD

	Home						Road					
	GP	W	L	GF	GA	%	GP	W	L	GF	GA	%
PIT	10	8	2	46	36	.800	11	8	3	37	27	.727
CHI	9	6	3	35	25	.667	9	6	3	30	23	.667
BOS	8	4	4	15	21	.500	7	4	3	25	30	.571
EDM	8	5	3	25	20	.625	8	3	5	24	34	.375
NYR	7	4	3	29	26	.571	6	2	4	18	23	.333
VAN	7	5	2	29	14	.714	6	1	5	15	21	.167
MTL	6	4	2	23	17	.667	5	0	5	6	15	.000
DET	6	2	4	15	15	.333	5	2	3	14	15	.400
WSH	4	2	2	12	11	.500	3	1	2	15	14	.333
N.J.	3	2	1	8	7	.667	4	1	3	17	21	.250
BUF	3	1	2	15	11	.333	4	2	2	9	8	.500
MIN	3	1	2	9	10	.333	4	2	2	10	13	.500
HFD	3	3	0	10	4	1.000	4	0	4	8	17	.000
WPG	3	2	1	10	11	.667	4	1	3	7	18	.250
STL	3	1	2	9	11	.333	3	1	2	10	12	.333
L.A.	3	1	2	11	13	.333	3	1	2	7	10	.333
TOTAL	86	51	35	301	252	.593	86	35	51	252	301	.407

TEAM PENALTIES

Abbreviations: GP – games played; **PEN** – total penalty minutes, including bench penalties; **BMI** – total bench penalty minutes; **AVG** – average penalty minutes per game.

Team	GP	PEN	BMI	AVG
BUF	7	80	0	11.4
PIT	21	339	2	16.1
BOS	15	254	2	16.9
DET	11	206	0	18.7
VAN	13	243	0	18.7
CHI	18	340	4	18.9
MTL	11	208	0	18.9
WSH	7	139	0	19.9
HFD	7	147	0	21.0
EDM	16	340	0	21.3
NYR	13	277	2	21.3
MIN	7	156	0	22.3
WPG	7	167	4	23.9
N.J.	7	177	4	25.3
L.A.	6	153	2	25.5
STL	6	166	2	27.7
TOTAL	**86**	**3392**	**22**	**39.4**

TEAMS' POWER PLAY RECORD

Abbreviations: Adv-total advantages; **PPGF**-power play goals for; **%** arrived by dividing number of power-play goals by total advantages.

Home					Road					Overall				
Team	GP	ADV	PPGF	%	Team	GP	ADV	PPGF	%	Team	GP	ADV	PPGF	%
1 NYR	7	27	8	29.6	BOS	7	29	7	24.1	BUF	7	40	10	25.0
2 WPG	3	18	5	27.8	MIN	4	21	5	23.8	PIT	21	102	25	24.5
3 PIT	10	65	17	26.2	BUF	4	17	4	23.5	NYR	13	58	13	22.4
4 BUF	3	23	6	26.1	DET	5	23	5	21.7	MIN	7	35	7	20.0
5 STL	3	22	5	22.7	PIT	11	37	8	21.6	STL	6	36	7	19.4
6 VAN	7	42	8	19.0	WSH	3	20	4	20.0	WSH	7	37	7	18.9
7 MTL	6	33	6	18.2	EDM	8	40	8	20.0	WPG	7	38	7	18.4
8 HFD	3	17	3	17.6	CHI	9	55	11	20.0	BOS	15	61	11	18.0
9 WSH	4	17	3	17.6	N.J	4	17	3	17.6	EDM	16	78	14	17.9
10 L.A	3	23	4	17.4	L.A	3	12	2	16.7	N.J	7	29	5	17.2
11 N.J	3	12	2	16.7	NYR	6	31	5	16.1	L.A	6	35	6	17.1
12 EDM	8	38	6	15.8	STL	3	14	2	14.3	CHI	18	108	18	16.7
13 MIN	3	14	2	14.3	HFD	4	23	3	13.0	MTL	11	59	9	15.3
14 CHI	9	53	7	13.2	MTL	5	26	3	11.5	HFD	7	40	6	15.0
15 BOS	8	32	4	12.5	WPG	4	20	2	10.0	VAN	13	70	10	14.3
16 DET	6	28	2	7.1	VAN	6	28	2	7.1	DET	11	51	7	13.7
TOTAL	**86**	**464**	**88**	**19.0**		**86**	**413**	**74**	**17.9**		**86**	**877**	**162**	**18.5**

TEAMS' PENALTY KILLING RECORD

Abbreviations: TSH – Total times short-handed; **PPGA** – power-play goals against; **%** arrived by dividing times short minus power-play goals against by times short.

Home					Road					Overall				
Team	GP	TSH	PPGA	%	Team	GP	TSH	PPGA	%	Team	GP	TSH	PPGA	%
1 WPG	3	15	1	93.3	MIN	4	18	1	94.4	WPG	7	39	5	87.2
2 CHI	9	38	4	89.5	DET	5	25	3	88.0	PIT	21	92	13	85.9
3 VAN	7	33	4	87.9	PIT	11	41	5	87.8	CHI	18	90	13	85.6
4 HFD	3	16	2	87.5	BUF	4	16	2	87.5	DET	11	61	9	85.2
5 NYR	7	32	5	84.4	WPG	4	24	4	83.3	MIN	7	32	5	84.4
6 PIT	10	51	8	84.3	MTL	5	29	5	82.8	MTL	11	57	10	82.5
7 N.J.	3	19	3	84.2	CHI	9	52	9	82.7	VAN	13	63	11	82.5
8 DET	6	36	6	83.3	EDM	8	54	10	81.5	NYR	13	62	11	82.3
9 MTL	6	28	5	82.1	STL	3	20	4	80.0	EDM	16	90	17	81.1
10 BOS	8	32	6	81.3	NYR	6	30	6	80.0	HFD	7	41	8	80.5
11 EDM	8	36	7	80.6	BOS	7	45	9	80.0	BOS	15	77	15	80.5
12 STL	3	22	5	77.3	VAN	6	30	7	76.7	STL	6	42	9	78.6
13 MIN	3	14	4	71.4	L.A.	3	17	4	76.5	BUF	7	28	6	78.6
14 BUF	3	12	4	66.7	HFD	4	25	6	76.0	N.J.	7	35	9	74.3
15 WSH	4	12	4	66.7	WSH	3	22	7	68.2	L.A.	6	34	10	70.6
16 L.A.	3	17	6	64.7	N.J.	4	16	6	62.5	WSH	7	34	11	67.6
TOTAL	**86**	**413**	**74**	**82.1**		**86**	**464**	**88**	**81.0**		**86**	**877**	**162**	**81.5**

SHORT-HANDED GOALS

For			Against		
Team	Games	Goals	Team	Games	Goals
NYR	13	5	EDM	16	0
DET	11	3	DET	11	0
PIT	21	3	BUF	7	0
HFD	7	2	L.A.	6	0
BUF	7	2	NYR	13	1
STL	6	1	VAN	13	1
N.J.	7	1	HFD	7	1
WSH	7	1	WSH	7	1
MTL	11	1	WPG	7	1
VAN	13	1	STL	6	1
BOS	15	1	CHI	18	2
EDM	16	1	MTL	11	2
CHI	18	1	PIT	21	3
L.A.	6	0	BOS	15	3
MIN	7	0	MIN	7	3
WPG	7	0	N.J.	7	4
TOTAL	86	23	**TOTAL**	86	23

Chicago's Chris Chelios led all defensemen with six goals and 15 assists during the 1992 playoffs.

Stanley Cup Record Book

History: The Stanley Cup, the oldest trophy competed for by professional athletes in North America, was donated by Frederick Arthur, Lord Stanley of Preston and son of the Earl of Derby, in 1893. Lord Stanley purchased the trophy for 10 guineas ($50 at that time) for presentation to the amateur hockey champions of Canada. Since 1910, when the National Hockey Association took possession of the Stanley Cup, the trophy has been the symbol of professional hockey supremacy. It has been competed for only by NHL teams since 1926 and has been under the exclusive control of the NHL since 1946.

Stanley Cup Standings

1918-92

(ranked by Cup wins)

Teams	Cup Wins	Yrs.	Series	Wins	Losses	Games	Wins	Losses	Ties	Goals For	Goals Against	Winning %
Montreal	22*	67	125*	80	44	590	355	227	8	1835	1445	.608
Toronto	13	54	82	43	39	374	177	194	3	961	1024	.477
Detroit	7	41	70	36	34	337	162	174	1	903	918	.482
Boston	5	53	93	45	48	449	220	223	6	1333	1325	.497
Edmonton	5	13	37	29	8	180	120	60	0	770	579	.667
NY Islanders	4	15	39	28	11	196	119	77	0	687	563	.607
Chicago	3	47	81	37	44	364	168	191	5	1066	1175	.468
NY Rangers	3	44	75	34	41	327	149	170	8	905	954	.468
Philadelphia	2	20	43	25	18	223	116	107	0	715	688	.520
Pittsburgh	2	12	22	12	10	107	60	47	0	356	348	.561
Calgary* **	1	18	28	12	16	132	61	71	0	439	475	.462
St. Louis	0	22	38	16	22	195	86	109	0	571	656	.441
Los Angeles	0	18	25	7	18	118	42	76	0	366	477	.356
Minnesota	0	17	31	14	17	166	80	86	0	554	579	.482
Buffalo	0	17	26	9	17	123	54	69	0	390	420	.439
Vancouver	0	12	16	4	12	71	27	44	0	205	256	.380
Washington	0	10	16	6	10	86	40	46	0	284	284	.465
Winnipeg	0	9	11	2	9	50	15	35	0	150	212	.300
Hartford	0	8	9	1	8	49	18	31	0	143	177	.367
Quebec	0	7	13	6	7	68	31	37	0	212	242	.456
New Jersey****	0	5	7	2	5	42	19	23	0	134	147	.452
San Jose	0	0	0	0	0	0	0	0	0	0	0	.000

* 1919 final incomplete due to influenza epidemic.
** Montreal Canadiens also won Stanley Cup in 1916.
*** Includes totals of Atlanta 1972-80.
**** Includes totals of Colorado 1976-82.

Stanley Cup Winners Prior to Formation of NHL in 1917

Season	Champions	Manager	Coach
1916-17	Seattle Metropolitans	Pete Muldoon	Pete Muldoon
1915-16	Montreal Candiens	George Kennedy	George Kennedy
1914-15	Vancouver Millionaires	Frank Patrick	Frank Patrick
1913-14	Toronto Blueshirts	Jack Marshall	Scotty Davidson*
1912-13**	Quebec Bulldogs	M.J. Quinn	Joe Malone*
1911-12	Quebec Bulldogs	M.J. Quinn	C. Nolan
1910-11	Ottawa Senators		Bruce Stuart*
1909-10	Montreal Wanderers	R. R. Boon	Pud Glass*
1908-09	Ottawa Senators		Bruce Stuart*
1907-08	Montreal Wanderers	R. R. Boon	Cecil Blachford
1906-07	Montreal Wanderers (March)	R. R. Boon	Cecil Blachford
1906-07	Kenora Thistles (January)	F.A. Hudson	Tommy Phillips*
1905-06	Montreal Wanderers		Cecil Blachford*
1904-05	Ottawa Silver Seven		A. T. Smith
1903-04	Ottawa Silver Seven		A. T. Smith
1902-03	Ottawa Silver Seven		A. T. Smith
1901-02	Montreal A.A.A.		C. McKerrow
1900-01	Winnipeg Victoria		D. H. Bain
1899-1900	Montreal Shamrocks		H.J. Trihey*
1898-99	Montrel Shamrocks		H.J. Trihey*
1897-98	Montreal Victorias		F. Richardson
1896-97	Montreal Victorias		Mike Grant*
1895-96	Montreal Victorias (December, 1896)		Mike Grant*
1895-96	Winnipeg Victorias (February)		J.C. G. Armytage
1894-95	Montreal Victorias		Mike Grant*
1893-94	Montreal A.A.A.		
1892-93	Montreal A.A.A.		

** Victoria defeated Quebec in challenge series. No official recognition.
* In the early years the teams were frequently run by the Captain. *Indicates Captain

Stanley Cup Winners

Season	Champions	Manager	Coach
1991-92	Pittsburgh Penguins	Craig Patrick	Scotty Bowman
1990-91	Pittsburgh Penguins	Craig Patrick	Bob Johnson
1989-90	Edmonton Oilers	Glen Sather	John Muckler
1988-89	Calgary Flames	Cliff Fletcher	Terry Crisp
1987-88	Edmonton Oilers	Glen Sather	Glen Sather
1986-87	Edmonton Oilers	Glen Sather	Glen Sather
1985-86	Montreal Canadiens	Serge Savard	Jean Perron
1984-85	Edmonton Oilers	Glen Sather	Glen Sather
1983-84	Edmonton Oilers	Glen Sather	Gle Sather
1982-83	New York Islanders	Bill Torrey	Al Arbour
1981-82	New York Islanders	Bill Torrey	Al Arbour
1980-81	New York Islanders	Bill Torrey	Al Arbour
1979-80	New York Islanders	Bill Torrey	Al Arbour
1978-79	Montreal Canadiens	Irving Grundman	Scotty Bowman
1977-78	Montreal Canadiens	Sam Pollock	Scotty Bowman
1976-77	Montreal Canadiens	Sam Pollock	Scotty Bowman
1975-76	Montreal Canadiens	Sam Pollock	Scotty Bowman
1974-75	Philadelphia Flyers	Keith Allen	Fred Shero
1973-74	Philadelphia Flyers	Keith Allen	Fred Shero
1972-73	Montreal Canadiens	Sam Pollock	Scotty Bowman
1971-72	Boston Bruins	Milt Schmidt	Tom Johnson
1970-71	Montreal Canadiens	Sam Pollock	Al MacNeil
1969-70	Boston Bruins	Milt Schmidt	Harry Sinden
1968-69	Montreal Canadiens	Sam Pollock	Claude Ruel
1967-68	Montreal Canadiens	Sam Pollock	Toe Blake
1966-67	Toronto Maple Leafs	Punch Imach	Punch Imlach
1965-66	Montreal Canadiens	Sam Pollock	Toe Blake
1964-65	Montreal Canadiens	Sam Pollock	Toe Blake
1963-64	Toronto Maple Leafs	Punch Imlach	Punch Imlach
1962-63	Toronto Maple Leafs	Punch Imlach	Punch Imlach
1961-62	Toronto Maple Leafs	Punch Imlach	Punch Imlach
1960-61	Chicago Black Hawks	Tommy Ivan	Rudy Pilous
1959-60	Montreal Canadiens	Frank Selke	Toe Blake
1958-59	Montreal Canadiens	Frank Selke	Toe Blake
1957-58	Montreal Canadiens	Frank Selke	Toe Blake
1956-57	Montreal Canadiens	Frank Selke	Toe Blake
1955-56	Montreal Canadiens	Frank Selke	Toe Blake
1954-55	Detroit Red Wings	Jack Adams	Jimmy Skinner
1953-54	Detroit Red Wings	Jack Adams	Tommy Ivan
1952-53	Montreal Canadiens	Frank Selke	Dick Irvin
1951-52	Detroit Red Wings	Jack Adams	Tommy Ivan
1950-51	Toronto Maple Leafs	Conn Smythe	Joe Primeau
1949-50	Detroit Red Wings	Jack dams	Tommy Ivan
1948-49	Toronto Maple Leafs	Conn Smythe	Hap Day
1947-48	Toronto Maple Leafs	Conn Smythe	Hap Day
1946-47	Toronto Maple Leafs	Conn Smythe	Hap Day
1945-46	Montreal Canadiens	Tommy Gorman	Dick Irvin
1944-45	Toronto Maple Leafs	Conn Smythe	Hap Day
1943-44	Montreal Canadiens	Tommy Gorman	Dick Irvin
1942-43	Detroit Red Wings	Jack Adams	Jack Adams
1941-42	Toronto Maple Leafs	Conn Smythe	Hap Day
1940-41	Boston Bruins	Art Ross	Cooney Weiland
1939-40	New York Rangers	Lester Patrick	Frank Boucher
1938-39	Boston Bruins	Art Ross	Art Ross
1937-38	Chicago Black Hawks	Bill Stewart	Bill Stewart
1936-37	Detroit Red Wings	Jack Adams	Jack Adams
1935-36	Detroit Red Wings	Jack Adams	Jack Adams
1934-35	Montreal Maroons	Tommy Gorman	Tommy Gorman
1933-34	Chicago Black Hawks	Tommy Gorman	Tommy Gorman
1932-33	New York Rangers	Lester Patrick	Lester Patrick
1931-32	Toronto Maple Leafs	Conn Smythe	Dick Irvin
1930-31	Montreal Canadiens	Cecil Hart	Cecil Hart
1929-30	Montreal Canadiens	Cecil Hart	Cecil Hart
1928-29	Boston Bruins	Art Ross	Cy Denneny
1927-28	New York Rangers	Lester Patrick	Lester Patrick
1926-27	Ottawa Senators	Dave Gill	Dave Gill
1925-26	Montreal Maroons	Eddie Gerard	Eddie Gerard
1924-25	Victoria Cougars	Lester Patrick	Lester Patrick
1923-24	Montreal Canadiens	Leo Dandurand	Leo Dandurand
1922-23	Ottawa Senators	Tommy Gorman	Pete Green
1921-22	Toronto St. Pats	Charlie Querrie	Eddie Powers
1920-21	Ottawa Senators	Tommy Gorman	Pete Green
1919-20	Ottawa Senators	Tommy Gorman	Pete Green
1918-19	No decision*		
1917-18	Toronto Arenas	Charlie Querrie	Dick Carroll

* In the spring of 1919 the Montreal Canadiens travelled to Seattle to meet Seattle, PCHL champions. After five games had been payed — teams were tied at 2 wins and 1 tie — the series was called off by the local Department of Health because of the influenza epidemic and the death from influenza of Joe Hall.

Championship Trophies

PRINCE OF WALES TROPHY

Beginning with the 1981-82 season, the club which advances to the Stanley Cup Finals as the winner of the Wales Conference Championship is presented with the Prince of Wales Trophy.

History: His Royal Highnesss, the Prince of Wales, donated the trophy to the National Hockey League in 1924. From 1927-28 through 1937-38, the award was presented to the team finishing first in the American Division of the NHL. From 1938-39, when the NHL reverted to one section, to 1966-67, it was presented to the team wining the NHL championship. With expansion in 1967-68, it again became a divisional trophy, awarded to the champions of the East Division through to the end of the 1973-74 season. Beginning in 1974-75, it was awarded to the regular-season winner of the conference bearing the name of the trophy. Starting with the 1981-82 season, the trophy has been presented to the playoff champion in the Wales Conference.

1991-92 Winner: Pittsburgh Penguins

The Pittsburgh Penguins won their second consecutive Prince of Wales Trophy on May 23, 1992, after defeating the Boston Bruins in game four of the Prince of Wales Conference Championship series. Before defeating the Bruins, the Penguins had series wins over Washington and the New York Rangers.

PRINCE OF WALES TROPHY WINNERS

1991-92	**Pittsburgh Penguins**	1957-58	Montreal Canadiens
1990-91	Pittsburgh Penguins	1956-57	Detroit Red Wings
1989-90	Boston Bruins	1955-56	Montreal Canadiens
1988-89	Montreal Canadiens	1954-55	Detroit Red Wings
1987-88	Boston Bruins	1953-54	Detroit Red Wings
1986-87	Philadelphia Flyers	1952-53	Detroit Red Wings
1985-86	Montreal Canadiens	1951-52	Detroit Red Wings
1984-85	Philadelphia Flyers	1950-51	Detroit Red Wings
1983-84	New York Islanders	1949-50	Detroit Red Wings
1982-83	New York Islanders	1948-49	Detroit Red Wings
1981-82	New York Islanders	1947-48	Toronto Maple Leafs
1980-81	Montreal Canadiens	1946-47	Montreal Canadiens
1979-80	Buffalo Sabres	1945-46	Montreal Canadiens
1978-79	Montreal Canadiens	1944-45	Montreal Canadiens
1977-78	Montreal Canadiens	1943-44	Montreal Canadiens
1976-77	Montreal Canadiens	1942-43	Detroit Red Wings
1975-76	Montreal Canadiens	1941-42	New York Rangers
1974-75	Buffalo Sabres	1940-41	Boston Bruins
1973-74	Boston Bruins	1939-40	Boston Bruins
1972-73	Montreal Canadiens	1938-39	Boston Bruins
1971-72	Boston Bruins	1937-38	Boston Bruins
1970-71	Boston Bruins	1936-37	Detroit Red Wings
1969-70	Chicago Blackhawks	1935-36	Detroit Red Wings
1968-69	Montreal Canadiens	1934-35	Boston Bruins
1967-68	Montreal Canadiens	1933-34	Detroit Red Wings
1966-67	Chicago Blackhawks	1932-33	Boston Bruins
1965-66	Montreal Canadiens	1931-32	New York Rangers
1964-65	Detroit Red Wings	1930-31	Boston Bruins
1963-64	Montreal Canadiens	1929-30	Boston Bruins
1962-63	Toronto Maple Leafs	1928-29	Boston Bruins
1961-62	Montreal Canadiens	1927-28	Boston Bruins
1960-61	Montreal Canadiens	1926-27	Ottawa Senators
1959-60	Montreal Canadiens	1925-26	Montreal Maroons
1958-59	Montreal Canadiens	1924-25	Montreal Canadiens

Prince of Wales Trophy

Stanley Cup

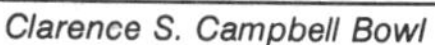

Clarence S. Campbell Bowl

CLARENCE S. CAMPBELL BOWL

Beginning with the 1981-82 season, the club which advances to the Stanley Cup Finals as the winner of the Campbell Conference championship is presented with the Clarence S. Campbell Bowl.

History: Presented by the member clubs in 1968 for perpetual competition by the National Hockey League in recognition of the services of Clarence S. Campbell, President of the NHL from 1946 to 1977. From 1967-68 through 1973-74, the trophy was awarded to the champions of the West Division. Beginning in 1974-75, it was awarded to the regular-season winner of the conference bearing the name of the trophy. Starting with the 1981-82 season, the trophy has been presented to the playoff champion in the Campbell Conference. The trophy itself is a hallmark piece made of sterling silver and was crafted by a British silversmith in 1878.

1991-92 Winner: Chicago Blackhawks

The Chicago Blackhawks won their first Clarence S. Campbell Bowl in 19 seasons after a four-game sweep of the Edmonton Oilers. Prior to facing the Oilers, Chicago had series wins over St. Louis and Detroit.

CLARENCE S. CAMPBELL BOWL WINNERS

1991-92	**Chicago Blackhawks**	1978-79	New York Islanders
1990-91	Minnesota North Stars	1977-78	New York Islanders
1989-90	Edmonton Oilers	1976-77	Philadelphia Flyers
1988-89	Calgary Flames	1975-76	Philadelphia Flyers
1987-88	Edmonton Oilers	1974-75	Philadelphia Flyers
1986-87	Edmonton Oilers	1973-74	Philadelphia Flyers
1985-86	Calgary Flames	1972-73	Chicago Blackhawks
1984-85	Edmonton Oilers	1971-72	Chicago Blackhawks
1983-84	Edmonton Oilers	1970-71	Chicago Blackhawks
1982-83	Edmonton Oilers	1969-70	St. Louis Blues
1981-82	Vancouver Canucks	1968-69	St. Louis Blues
1980-81	New York Islanders	1967-68	Philadelphia Flyers
1979-80	Philadelphia Flyers		

Stanley Cup Winners:

Rosters and Final Series Scores

1991-92 — Pittsburgh Penguins — Mario Lemieux (Captain), Ron Francis, Bryan Trottier, Kevin Stevens, Bob Errey, Phil Bourque, Troy Loney, Rick Tocchet, Joe Mullen, Jaromir Jagr, Jiri Hrdina, Shawn McEachern, Ulf Samuelsson, Kjell Samuelsson, Larry Murphy, Gord Roberts, Jim Paek, Paul Stanton, Tom Barrasso, Ken Wregget, Jay Caufield, Jamie Leach, Wendell Young, Grant Jennings, Peter Taglianetti, Jock Callander, Dave Michayluk, Mike Needham, Jeff Chychrun, Ken Priestlay, Jeff Daniels, Howard Baldwin (Owner and President), Morris Belzberg (Owner), Thomas Ruta (Owner), Donn Patton (Executive Vice President and Chief Financial Officer), Paul Martha (Executive Vice President and General Counsel), Craig Patrick (Executive Vice President and General Manager), Bob Johnson (Coach), Scott Bowman (Director of Player Development and Coach), Barry Smith, Rick Kehoe, Pierre McGuire, Gilles Meloche, Rick Paterson (Assistant Coaches), Steve Latin (Equipment Manager), Skip Thayer (Trainer), John Welday (Strength and Conditioning Coach), Greg Malone, Les Binkley, Charlie Hodge, John Gill, Ralph Cox (Scouts).

Scores: May 26 at Pittsburgh — Pittsburgh 5, Chicago 4; May 28 at Pittsburgh — Pittsburgh 3, Chicago 1; May 30 at Chicago — Pittsburgh 1, Chicago 0; June 1 at Chicago — Pittsburgh 6, Chicago 5.

1990-91 — Pittsburgh Penguins — Mario Lemieux (Captain), Paul Coffey, Randy Hillier, Bob Errey, Tom Barrasso, Phil Bourque, Jay Caufield, Ron Francis, Randy Gilhen, Jiri Hrdina, Jaromir Jagr, Grant Jennings, Troy Loney, Joe Mullen, Larry Murphy, Jim Paek, Frank Pietrangelo, Barry Pederson, Mark Recchi, ordie Roberts, Ulf Samuelsson, Paul Stanton, Kevin Stevens, Peter Taglianetti, Bryan Trottier, Scott Young, Wendell Young, Edward J. DeBartolo, Sr. (Owner), Marie D. DeBartolo York (President), Paul Martha (Vice-President & General Counsel), Craig Patrick (General Manager), Scotty Bowman (Director of Player Development & Recruitment), Bob Johnson (Coach), Rick Kehoe (Assistant Coach), Gilles Meloche (Goaltending Coach & Scout), Rick Paterson (Assistant Coach), Barry Smith (Assistant Coach), Steve Latin (Eqipment Manager), Skip Thayer (Trainer), John Welday (Strength & Conditioning Coach), Greg Malone (Scout).

Scores: May 15 at Pittsburgh — Minnesota 5, Pittsburgh 4; May 17 at Pittsburgh — Pittsburgh 4, Minnesota 1; May 19 at Minnesota — Minnesota 3, Pittsburgh 1; May 21 at Minnesota — Pittsburgh 5, Minnesota 3; May 23 at Pittsburgh — Pittsburgh 6, Minnesota 4; May 25 at Minnesota — Pittsburgh 8, Minnesota 0.

1989-90 — Edmonton Oilers — Kevin Lowe, Steve Smith, Jeff Beukeboom, Mark Lamb, Joe Murphy, Glenn Anderson, Mark Messier, Adam Graves, Craig MacTavish, Kelly Buchberger, Jari Kurri, Caig Simpson, Martin Gelinas, Randy Gregg, Charlie Huddy, Geoff Smith, Reijo Ruotsalainen, Craig Muni, Bill Ranford, Dave Brown, Eldon Reddick, Petr Klima, Esa Tikkanen, Grant Fuhr, Peter Pocklington (Owner), Glen Sather (President/General Manager), John Muckler (Coach), Ted Green (Co-Coach), Ron Low (Ass't Coach), Bruce MacGregor (Ass't General Manager), Barry Fraser (Director of Player Personnel), John Blackwell (Director of Operations, AHL), Ace Bailey, Ed Chadwick, Lorne Davis, Harry Howell, Matti Vaisanen and Albert Reeves (Scouts), Bill Tuele (Director of Public Relations), Werner Baum (Controller), Dr. Gordon Cameron (Medical Chief of Staff), Dr. David Reid (Team Physician), Barrie Stafford (Athletic Trainer), Ken Lowe (Athletic Therapist), Stuart Poirier (Massage Therapist), Lyle Kulchisky (Ass't Trainer).
Scores: May 15 at Boston — Edmonton 3, Boston 2; May 18 at Boston — Edmonton 7, Boston 2; May 20 at Edmonton — Boston 2, Edmonton 1; May 22 at Edmonton — Edmonton 5, Boston 1; May 24 at Boston — Edmonton 4, Boston 1.

1988-89 — Calgary Flames — Mike Vernon, Rick Wamsley, Al MacInnis, Brad McCrimmon, Dana Murzyn, Ric Nattress, Joe Mullen, Lanny McDonald (Co-captain), Gary Roberts, Colin Patterson, Hakan Loob, Theoren Fleury, Jiri Hrdina, Tim Hunter (Ass't. captain), Gary Suter, Mark Hunter, Jim Peplinski (Co-captain), Joe Nieuwendyk, Brian MacLellan, Joel Otto, Jamie Macon, Doug Gilmour, Rob Ramage. Norman Green, Harley Hotchkiss, Norman Kwong, Sonia Scurfield, B.J. Seaman, D.K. Seaman (Owners), Cliff Fletcher (President and General Manager), Al MacNeil (Ass't General Manager), Al Coates (Ass't to the President), Terry Crisp (Head Coach), Doug Risebrough, Tom Watt (Ass't Coaches), Glenn Hall (Goaltending Consultant), Jim Murray (Trainer), Bob Stewart (Equipment Manager), Al Murray (Ass't Trainer).
Scores: May 14 at Calgary — Calgary 3, Montreal 2; May 17 at Calgary— Montreal 4, Calgary 2; May 19 at Montreal — Montreal 4, Calgary 3; May 21 at Montreal — Calgary 4, Montreal 2; May 23 at Calgary — Calgary 3, Montreal 2; May 25 at Montreal — Calgary 4, Montreal 2.

1987-88 — Edmonton Oilers — Keith Acton, Glenn Anderson, Jeff Beukeboom, Geoff Courtnall, Grant Fuhr, Randy Gregg, Wayne Gretzky, Dave Hannan, Charlie Huddy, Mike Krushelnyski, Jari Kurri, Normand Lacombe, Kevin Lowe, Craig MacTavish, Kevin McClelland, Marty McSorley, Mark Messier, Craig Muni,Bill Ranford, Craig Simpson, Steve Smith, Esa Tikkanen, Peter Pocklington (Owner), Glen Sather (General Manager/Coach), John Muckler (Co-Coach), Ted Green (Ass't Coach), Barry Fraser (Director of Player Personnel), Bill Tuele (Director of Public Relations), Dr. Gordon Cameron (Team Physician), Peter Millar (Athletic Therapist), Barrie Stafford (Trainer), Juergen Mers (Massage Therapist), Lyle Kulchisky (Ass't Trainer).
Scores: May 18 at Edmonton — Edmonton 2, Boston 1; May 20 at Edmonton — Edmonto 4, Boston 2; May 22 at Boston — Edmonton 6, Boston 3; May 24 at Boston — Boston 3, Edmonton 3 (suspended due to power failure); May 26 at Edmonton — Edmonton 6, Boston 3.

1986-87 — Edmonton Oilers — Glenn Anderson, Jeff Beukeboom, Kelly Buchberger, Paul Coffey, Grant Fuhr, Randy Gregg, Wayne Gretzky, Charlie Huddy, Dave Hunter, Mike Krushelnyski, Jari Kurri, Moe Lemay, Kevin Lowe, Craig MacTavish, Kevin McClelland, Marty McSorley, Mark Messier, Andy Moog, Craig Muni, Kent Nilsson, Jaroslav Pouzar, Reijo Ruotsalainen, Steve Smith, Esa Tikkanen, Peter Pocklington (Owner), Glen Sather (General Manager/Coach), John Muckler (Co-Coach), Ted Green (Ass't. Coach), Ron Low (Ass't. Coach), Bruce MacGregor (Ass't. General Manager), Barry Fraser (Director of Player Personnel), Peter Millar (Athletic Therapist), Barrie Stafford (Trainer), Lyle Kulchisky (Ass't Trainer).
Scores: May 17 at Edmonton — Edmonton 4, Philadelphia 3; May 20 at Edmonton — Edmonton 3, Philadelphia 2; May 22 at Philadelpia — Philadelphia 5, Edmonton 3; May 24 at Philadelphia — Edmonton 4, Philadelphia 1; May 26 at Edmonton — Philadelphia 4, Edmonton 3; May 28 at Philadelphia — Philadelphia 3, Edmonton 2; May 31 at Edmonton —
Edmonton 3, Philadelphia 1.

1985-86 — Montreal Canadiens — Bob Gainey, Doug Soetaert, Patrick Roy, Rick Green, David Maley, Ryan Walter, Serge Boisvert, Mario Tremblay, Bobby Smith, Craig Ludwig, Tom Kurvers, Kjell Dahlin, Larry Robinson, Guy Carbonneau, Chris Chelios, Petr Svoboda, Mats aslund, Lucien DeBlois, Steve Rooney, Gaston Gingras, Mike Lalor, Chris Nilan, John Kordic, Claude Lemieux, Mike McPhee, Brian Skrudland, Stephane Richer, Ronald Corey (President), Serge Savard (General Manager), Jean Perron (Coach), Jacques Laperriere (Ass't. Coach), Jean Beliveau (Vice President), Francois-Xavier Seigneur (Vice President), Fred Steer (Vice President), Jacques Lemaire (Ass't. General Manager), Andre Boudrias (Ass't. General Manager), Claude Ruel, Yves Belanger (Athletic Therapist), Gaetan Lfebvre (Ass't. Athletic Therapist), Eddy Palchek (Trainer), Sylvain Toupin (Ass't. Trainer).
Scores: May 16 at Calgary — Calgary 5, Montreal 3; May 18 at Calgary — Montreal 3, Calgary 2; May 20 at Montreal — Montreal 5, Calgary 3; May 22 at Montreal — Montreal 1, Calgary 0; May 24 at Calgary — Montreal 4, Calgary 3.

1984-85 — Edmonton Oilers — Glenn Anderson, Bill Carroll, Paul Coffey, Lee Fogolin, Grant Fuhr, Randy Gregg, Wayne Gretzky, Charlie Huddy, Pat Hughes, Dave Hunter, Don Jackson, Mike Krushelnyski, Jari Kurri, Willy Lindstrom, Kevin Lowe, Dave Lumley, Kevin McClelland, Larry Melnyk, Mark Messier, Andy Moog, Mark Napier, Jaroslav Pouzar, Dave Semenko, Esa Tikkanen, Peter Pocklington (Owner), Glen Sather (General Manager/Coach), John Muckler (Ass't. Coach), Ted Green (Ass't. Coach), Bruce MacGregor (Ass't. General Manager), Barry Fraser (Director of Player Personnel/Chief Scout), Peter Millar (Athletic Therapist), Barrie Stafford, Lyle Kulchisky (Trainers)
Scores: May21 at Philadelphia — Philadelphia 4, Edmonton 1; May 23 at Philadelphia — Edmonton 3, Philadelphia 1; May 25 at Edmonton — Edmonton 4, Philadelphia 3; May 28 at Edmonton — Edmonton 5, Philadelphia 3; May 30 at Edmonton — Edmonton 8, Philadelphia 3.

1983-84 — Edmonton Oilers — Glenn Anderson, Paul Coffey, Pat Conacher, Lee Fogolin, Grant Fuhr, Randy Gregg, Wayne Gretzky, Charlie Huddy, Pat Hughes, Dave Hunter, Don Jackson, Jari Kurri, Willy Lindstrom, Ken Linseman, Kevin Lowe, Dave Lmley, Kevin McClelland, Mark Messier, Andy Moog, Jaroslav Pouzar, Dave Semenko, Peter Pocklington (Owner), Glen Sather (General Manager/Coach), John Muckler (Ass't. Coach), Ted Green (Ass't. Coach), Bruce MacGregor (Ass't. General Manager), Barry Fraser (Director of Player Personnel/Chief Scout), Peter Millar (Athletic Therapist), Barrie Stafford (Trainer)
Scores: May 10 at New York — Edmonton 1, NY Islanders 0; May 12 at New York — NY Islanders 6, Edmonton 1; May 15 at Edmonton — Edmonton 7, NY Islanders 2; May 17 at Edmonton — Edmonton 7, NY Islanders 2; May 19 at Edmonton — Edmonton 5, NY Islanders 2.

1982-83 — New York Islanders — Mike Bossy, Bob Bourne, Paul Boutilier, Bill Carroll, Greg Gilbert, Clark Gillies, Butch Goring, Mats Hallin, Tomas Jonsson, Anders Kallur, Gord Lane, Dave Langevin, Mike McEwen, Roland Melanson, Wayne Merrick, Ken Morrow, Bob Nystrom, Stefan Persson, Denis Potvin, Bill Smith, Brent Sutter, Duane Sutter, John Tonelli, Bryan Trottier, Al Arbour (coch), Lorne Henning (ass't coach), Bill Torrey (general manager), Ron Waske, Jim Pickard (trainers)
Scores: May 10 at Edmonton — NY Islanders 2, Edmonton 0; May 12 at Edmonton — NY Islanders 6, Edmonton 3; May 14 at New York — NY Islanders 5, Edmonton 1; May 17 at New York — NY Islanders 4, Edmonton 2

1981-82 — New York Islanders — Mike Bossy, Bob Bourne, Bill Carroll, Butch Goring, Greg Gilbert, Clark Gillies, Tomas Jonsson, Anders Kallur, Gord Lane, Dave Langevin, Hector Marin, Mike McEwen, Roland Melanson, Wayne Merrick, Ken Morrow, Bob Nystrom, Stefan Persson, Denis Potvin, Bill Smith, Brent Sutter, Duane Sutter, John Tonelli, Bryan Trottier, Al Arbour (coach), Lorne Henning (ass't coach), Bill Torrey (general manager), Ron Waske, Jim Pickard (trainers)
Scores: May 8 at New York — NY Islanders 6, Vancouver 5; May 11 at New York — NY Islanders 6, Vancouver 4; May 13 at Vancouver — NY Islanders 3, Vancouver 0; May 16 at Vancouver — NY Islanders 3, Vancouver 1

1980-81 — New York Islanders — Denis Potvin, Mike McEwen, Ken Morrow, Gord Lane, Bob Lorimer, Stefan Persson, Dave Langevin, Mike Bossy, Bryan Trottier, Butch Goring, Wayne Merrick, Clark Gillies, John Tonelli, Bob Nystrom, Bill Carroll, Bob Bourne, Hector Marini, Anders Kallur, Duane Sutter, Garry Howatt, Lorne Henning, Bill Smith, Roland Melanson, Al Arbour (coach), Bill Torrey (general manager), Ron Waske, Jim Pickard (trainers).
Scores: May 12 at New York — NY Islaners 6, Minnesota 3; May 14 at New York — NY Islanders 6, Minnesota 3; May 17 at Minnesota — NY Islanders 7, Minnesota 5; May 19 at Minnesota— Minnesota 4, NY Islanders 2; May 21 at New York — NY Islanders 5, Minnesota 1.

1979-80 — New York Islanders — Gord Lane, Jean Potvin, Bob Lorimer, Denis Potvin, Stefan Persson, Ken Morrow, Dave Langevin, Duane Sutter, Garry Howatt, Clark Gillies, Lorne Henning, Wayne Merrick, Bob Bourne, Steve Tambellini, Bryan Trottier, Mike Bossy, Bob Nystrom, John Tonelli, Anders Kallur, Butch Goring, Alex McKendry, Glenn Resch, Billy Smith, Al Arbour (coach), Bill Torrey (general manager), Ron Waske, Jim Pickard (trainers).
Scores: May 13 at Philadelphia — NY Islanders 4, Philadelphia 3; May 15 at Philadelphia — Philadelphia 8, NY Islanders 3; May 17 at Long Island — NY Islanders 6, Philadelphia 2; May 19 at Long Island — NY Islanders 5, Philadelphia 2; May 22 at Philadelphia — Philadelphia 6, NY Islanders 3; May 24 at Long Island — NY Islandes 5, Philadelphia 4.

1978-79 — Montreal Canadiens — Ken Dryden, Larry Robinson, Serge Savard, Guy Lapointe, Brian Engblom, Gilles Lupien, Rick Chartraw, Guy Lafleur, Steve Shutt, Jacques Lemaire, Yvan Cournoyer, Rejean Houle, Pierre Mondou, Bob Gainey, Doug Jarvis, Yvon Lambert, Doug Risebrough, Pierre Larouche, Mario Tremblay, Cam Connor, Pat Hughes, Rod Langway, Mark Napier, Michel Larocque, Richard Sevigny, Scotty Bowman (coach), Irving Grundman (managing director), Eddy Palchak, Piere Meilleur (trainers).
Scores: May 13 at Montreal — NY Rangers 4, Montreal 1; May 15 at Montreal — Montreal 6, NY Rangers 2; May 17 at New York — Montreal 4, NY Rangers 1; May 19 at New York — Montreal 4, NY Rangers 3; May 21 at Montreal — Montreal 4, NY Rangers 1.

1977-78 — Montreal Canadiens — Ken Dryden, Larry Robinson, Serge Savard, Guy Lapointe, Bill Nyrop, Pierre Bouchard, Brian Engblom, Gilles Lupien, Rick Chartraw, Guy Lafleur, Steve Shutt, Jacques Lemaire, Yvan Cournoyer, Rejean Houle, Pierre Mondou, Bob Gainey, Doug Jarvis, Yvon Lambert, Doug Risebrough, Pierre Larouche, Mario Tremblay, Michel Larocque, Scotty Bowman (coach), Sam Pollock (general manager), Eddy Palchak, Pierre Meilleur (trainers).
Scores: May 13 at Montreal — Montreal 4, Boston 1; May 16 at Montreal — Montreal 3, Boston 2; May 18 at Boston — Boston 4, Montreal 0; May 21 at Boston — Boston 4, Montreal 3; May 23 at Montreal — Montreal 4, Boston 1; May 25 at Boston — Montreal 4, Boston 1.

1976-77 — Montreal Canadiens — Ken Dryden, Guy Lapointe, Larry Robinson, Serge Savard, Jimmy Roberts, Rick Chartraw, Bill Nyrop, Pierre Bouchard, Brian Engblom, Yvan Cournoyer, Guy Lafleur, Jacques Lemaire, Steve Shutt, Pete Mahovlich, Murray Wilson, Doug Jarvis, Yvon Lambert, Bob Gainey, Doug Risebrough, Mario Tremblay, Rejean Houle, Pierre Mondou, Mike Polich, Michel Larocque, Scotty Bowman (coach), Sam Pollock (general manager), Eddy Palchak, Pierre Meilleur (trainers).
Scores: May 7 at Montreal — Montreal 7, Boston 3; May 10 at Montreal — Montreal 3, Boston 0; May 12 at Boston — Montreal 4, Boston 2; May 14 at Boston — Montreal 2, Boston 1.

1975-76 — Montreal Canadiens — Ken Dryden, Serge Savard, Guy Lapointe, Larry Robinson, Bill Nyrop, Pierre Bouchard, Jim Roberts, Guy Lafleur, Steve Shutt, Pete Mahovlich, Yvan Cournoyer, Jacques Lemaire, Yvon Lambert, Bob Gainey, Doug Jarvis, Doug Risebrough, Murray Wilson, Mario Tremblay, Rick Chartraw,Michel Larocque, Scotty Bowman (coach), Sam Pollock (general manager), Eddy Palchak, Pierre Meilleur (trainers).
Scores: May 9 at Montreal — Montreal 4, Philadelphia 3; May 11 at Montreal — Montreal 2, Philadelphia 1; May 13 at Philadelphia — Montreal 3, Philadelphia 2; May 16 at Philadelphia — Montreal 5, Philadelphia 3.

1974-75 — Philadelphia Flyers — Bernie Parent, Wayne Stephenson, Ed Van Impe, Tom Bladon, André Dupont, Joe Watson, Jim Watson, Ted Harris, Larry Goodenoug, Rick MacLeish, Bobby Clarke, Bill Barber, Reggie Leach, Gary Dornhoefer, Ross Lonsberry, Bob Kelly, Terry Crisp, Don Saleski, Dave Schultz, Orest Kindrachuk, Bill Clement, Fred Shero (coach), Keith Allen (general manager), Frank Lewis, Jim McKenzie (trainers).
Scores: May 15 at Philadelphia — Philadelphia 4, Buffalo 1; May 18 at Philadelphia — Philadelphia 2, Buffalo 1; May 20 at Buffalo — Buffalo 5, Philadelphia 4; May 22 at Buffalo — Buffalo 4, Philadelphia 2; May 25 at Philadelphia — Piladelphia 5, Buffalo 1; May 27 at Buffalo — Philadelphia 2, Buffalo 0.

1973-74 — Philadelphia Flyers — Bernie Parent, Ed Van Impe, Tom Bladon, André Dupont, Joe Watson, Jim Watson, Barry Ashbee, Bill Barber, Dave Schultz, Don Saleski, Gary Dornhoefer, Terry Crisp, Bobby Clarke, Simon Nolet, Ross Lonsberry, Rick MacLeish, Bill Flett, Orest Kindrachuk, Bill Clement, Bob Kelly, Bruce Cowick, Al MacAdam, Bobby Taylor, Fred Shero (coach), Keith Allen (general manager), Frank Lewis, Jim McKenzie (trainers).
Scores: May 7 at Boston — Boston 3, Philadelphia 2; May 9 at Boston — Philadelphia 3, Boston 2; May 12 at Philadelphia — Philadelphia 4, Boston 1; May 14 at Philadelphia — Philadelphia 4, Boston 2; May 16 at Boston — Boston 5, Philadelphia 1; May 19 at Philadelphia — Philadelphia 1, Boston 0.

Kenny Wharram (11) steers a rebound away from the Canadiens' Phil Goyette (20) as Jack Evans (5), goaltender Glenn Hall and Al Arbour (2) watch the proceedings.

1972-73 — Montreal Canadiens — Ken Dryden, Guy Lapointe, Serge Savard, Larry Robinson, Jacques Laperriere, Bob Murdoch, Pierre Bouchard, Jim Roberts, Yvan Cournoyer, Frak Mahovlich, Jacques Lemaire, Pete Mahovlich, Marc Tardif, Henri Richard, Rejean Houle, Guy Lafleur, Chuck Lefley, Claude Larose, Murray Wilson, Steve Shutt, Michel Plasse, Scotty Bowman (coach), Sam Pollock (general manager), Ed Palchak, Bob Williams (trainers).
Scores: April 29 at Montreal — Montreal 8, Chicago 3; May 1 at Montreal — Montreal 4, Chicago 1; May 3 at Chicago — Chicago 7, Montreal 4; May 6 at Chicago — Montreal 4, Chicago 0; May 8 at Montreal — Chicago 8, Montreal 7; May 10at Chicago — Montreal 6, Chicago 4.

1971-72 — Boston Bruins — Gerry Cheevers, Ed Johnston, Bobby Orr, Ted Green, Carol Vadnais, Dallas Smith, Don Awrey, Phil Esposito, Ken Hodge, John Bucyk, Mike Walton, Wayne Cashman, Garnet Bailey, Derek Sanderson, Fred Stanfield, Ed Westfall, John McKenzie, Don Marcotte, Garry Peters, Chris Hayes, Tom Johnson (coach), Milt Schmidt (general manager), Dan Canney, John Forristall (trainers).
Scores: April 30 at Boston — Boson 6, NY Rangers 5; May 2 at Boston — Boston 2, NY Rangers 1; May 4 at New York — NY Rangers 5, Boston 2; May 7 at New York — Boston 3, NY Rangers 2; May 9 at Boston — NY Rangers 3, Boston 2; May 11 at New York — Boston 3, NY Rangers 0.

1970-71 — Montreal Canadiens — Ken Dryden, Rogatien Vachon, Jacques Laperriere, Jean-Claude Tremblay, Guy Lapointe, Terry Harper, Pierre Bouchard, Jean Beliveau, Marc Tardif, Yvan Cournoyer, Rejean Houle, Claude Larose, Henri Richard, Phil Roberto Pete Mahovlich, Leon Rochefort, John Ferguson, Bobby Sheehan, Jacques Lemaire, Frank Mahovlich, Bob Murdoch, Chuck Lefley, Al MacNeil (coach), Sam Pollock (general manager), Yvon Belanger, Ed Palchak (trainers).
Scores: May 4 at Chicago — Chicago 2, Montreal 1; May 6 at Chicago — Chicago 5, Montreal 3; May 9 at Montreal — Montreal 4, Chicago 2; May 11 at Montreal — Montreal 5, Chicago 2; May 13 at Chicago — Chicago 2, Montreal 0; May 16 at Montreal — Montreal 4, Chicago 3; May 18 at Chicago — Montreal 3, Chicago 2.

1969-70 — Boston Bruins — Gerry Cheevers, Ed Johnston, Bobby Orr, Rick Smith, Dallas Smith, Bill Speer, Gary Doak, Don Awrey, Phil Esposito, Ken Hodge, John Bucyk, Wayne Carleton, Wayne Cashman, Derek Sanderson, Fred Stanfield, Ed Westfall, John McKenzie, Jim Lorentz, Don Marcotte, Bill Lesuk, Dan Schock, Harry Sinden (coach), Milt Schmidt (general manager), Dan Canney, John Forristall (trainers).
Scores: May 3 at St. Louis — Boston 6, St. Louis 1; May 5 at St. Louis — Boston 6, St. Louis 2; May 7 at Boston — Boston 4, St. Louis 1; May 10 at Boston — Boston 4, St. Louis 3.

1968-69 — Montreal Canadiens — Lorne Worsley, Rogatien Vachon, Jacques Laperriere, Jean-Claude Tremblay, Ted Harris, Serge Savard, Terry Harper, Larry Hillman, Jean Beliveau, Ralph Backstrom, Dick Duff, Yvan Cournoyer, Claude Provost, Bobby Rousseau, Henri Richard, John Ferguson, Christian Bordeleau, Mickey Redmond, Jacques Lemaire, Lucien Grenier, Tony Esposito, ClaudeRuel (coach), Sam Pollock (general manager), Larry Aubut, Eddy Palchak (trainers).
Scores: April 27 at Montreal — Montreal 3, St. Louis 1; April 29 at Montreal — Montreal 3, St. Louis 1; May 1 at St. Louis — Montreal 4, St. Louis 0; May 4 at St. Louis — Montreal 2, St. Louis 1.

1967-68 — Montreal Canadiens — Lorne Worsley, Rogatien Vachon, Jacques Laperriere, Jean-Claude Tremblay, Ted Harris, Serge Savard, Terry Harper, Carol Vadnais, Jean Beliveau, Gilles Tremblay, Ralph Backtrom, Dick Duff, Claude Larose, Yvan Cournoyer, Claude Provost, Bobby Rousseau, Henri Richard, John Ferguson, Danny Grant, Jacques Lemaire, Mickey Redmond, Toe Blake (coach), Sam Pollock (general manager), Larry Aubut, Eddy Palchak (trainers).
Scores: May 5 at St. Louis — Montreal 3, St. Louis 2; May 7 at St. Louis — Montreal 1, St. Louis 0; May 9 at Montreal — Montreal 4, St. Louis 3; May 11 at Montreal — Montreal 3, St. Louis 2.

1966-67 — Toronto Maple Leafs — Johnny Bower, Terry Sachuk, Larry Hillman, Marcel Pronovost, Tim Horton, Bob Baun, Aut Erickson, Allan Stanley, Red Kelly, Ron Ellis, George Armstrong, Pete Stemkowski, Dave Keon, Mike Walton, Jim Pappin, Bob Pulford, Brian Conacher, Eddie Shack, Frank Mahovlich, Milan Marcetta, Larry Jeffrey, Bruce Gamble, Punch Imlach (manager-coach), Bob Haggart (trainer).
Scores: April 20 at Montreal — Toronto 2, Montreal 6; April 22 at Montreal — Toronto 3, Montreal 0; April 25 at Toronto — Toronto 3, Montreal 2; April 27 at Toronto — Toronto 2, Montreal 6; April 29 at Montreal — Toronto 4, Montreal 1; May 2 at Toronto — Toronto 3, Montreal 1.

1965-66 — Montreal Canadiens — Lorne Worsley, Charlie Hodge, Jean-Claude Tremblay, Ted Harris, Jean-Guy Talbot, Terry Harper, Jacques Laperriere, Noel Price, Jean Beliveau, Ralph Backstrom, Dick Duff, Gilles Tremblay, Claude Larose, Yvan Cournoyer, Claude Provost, Bobby Rousseau, Henri Richard, Dave Balon, John Ferguson, Leon Rochefort, Jim Roberts, Toe Blake (coch), Sam Pollock (general manager), Larry Aubut, Andy Galley (trainers).
Scores: April 24 at Montreal — Detroit 3, Montreal 2; April 26 at Montreal — Detroit 5, Montreal 2; April 28 at Detroit — Montreal 4, Detroit 2; May 1 at Detroit — Montreal 2, Detroit 1; May 3 at Montreal — Montreal 5, Detroit 1; May 5 at Detroit — Montreal 3, Detroit 2.

1964-65 — Montreal Canadiens — Lorne Worsley, Charlie Hodge, Jean-Claude Tremblay, Ted Harris, Jean-Guy Talbot, Terry Harper, Jacques Laperriere, Jean Gauthier, Noel Picard, Jean Beliveau, Ralph Backstrom, Dick Duff, Claude Larose, Yvan Cournoyer, Claude Provost, Bobby Rousseau, Henri Richard, Dave Balon, John Ferguson, Red Berenson, Jim Roberts, Toe Blake (coach), Sam Pollock (general manager), Larry Aubut, Andy Galley (trainers).
Scores: April 17 at Montreal — Montreal 3, Chicago 2; April 20 at Montreal — Montreal 2, Chicago 0; April 22 at Chicago — Montreal 1, Chicago 3; April 25 at Chicago — Montreal 1, Chicago 5; April 7 at Montreal — Montreal 6, Chicago 0; April 29 at Chicago — Montreal 1, Chicago 2; May 1 at Montreal — Montreal 4, Chicago 0.

1963-64 — Toronto Maple Leafs — Johnny Bower, Carl Brewer, Tim Horton, Bob Baun, Allan Stanley, Larry Hillman, Al Arbour, Red Kelly, Gerry Ehman, Andy Bathgate, George Armstrong, Ron Stewart, Dave Keon, Billy Harris, Don McKenney, Jim Pappin, Bob Pulford, Eddie Shack, Frank Mahovlich, Eddie Litzenberger, Punch Imlach (manager-coach), Bob Haggert (trainer).
Scores April 11 at Toronto — Toronto 3, Detroit 2; April 14 at Toronto — Toronto 3, Detroit 4; April 16 at Detroit — Toronto 3, Detroit 4; April 18 at Detroit — Toronto 4, Detroit 2; April 21 at Toronto — Toronto 1, Detroit 2; April 23 at Detroit — Toronto 4, Detroit 3; April 25 at Toronto — Toronto 4, Detroit 0.

1962-63 — Toronto Maple Leafs — Johnny Bower, Don Simmons, Carl Brewer, Tim Horton, Kent Douglas, Allan Stanley, Bob Baun, Larry Hillman, Red Kelly, Dick Duff, George Armstrong,Bob Nevin, Ron Stewart, Dave Keon, Billy Harris, Bob Pulford, Eddie Shack, Ed Litzenberger, Frank Mahovlich, John MacMillan, Punch Imlach (manager-coach), Bob Haggert (trainer).
Scores: April 9 at Toronto — Toronto 4, Detroit 2; April 11 at Toronto — Toronto 4, Detroit 2; April 14 at Detroit — Toronto 2, Detroit 3; April 16 at Detroit — Toronto 4, Detroit 2; April 18 at Toronto — Toronto 3, Detroit 1.

1961-62 — Toronto Maple Leafs — Johnny Bower, Don Simmons, Carl Brewer, Tim Hrton, Bob Baun, Allan Stanley, Al Arbour, Larry Hillman, Red Kelly, Dick Duff, George Armstrong, Frank Mahovlich, Bob Nevin, Ron Stewart, Bill Harris, Bert Olmstead, Bob Pulford, Eddie Shack, Dave Keon, Ed Litzenberger, John MacMillan, Punch Imlach (manager-coach), Bob Haggert (trainer).
Scores: April 10 at Toronto — Toronto 4, Chicago 1; April 12 at Toronto — Toronto 3, Chicago 2; April 15 at Chicago — Toronto 0, Chicago 3; April 17 at Chicago — Toronto 1, Chicago 4; April 19 at Toronto —Toronto 8, Chicago 4; April 22 at Chicago — Toronto 2, Chicago 1.

1960-61 — Chicago Blackhawks — Glenn Hall, Al Arbour, Pierre Pilote, Elmer Vasko, Jack Evans, Dollard St. Laurent, Reg Fleming, Tod Sloan, Ron Murphy, Eddie Litzenberger, Bill Hay, Bobby Hull, Ab McDonald, Eric Nesterenko, Ken Wharram, Earl Balfour, Stan Mikita, Murray Balfour, Chico Maki, Wayne Hicks, Tommy Ivan (manager), Rudy Pilous (coach), Nick Garen (trainer).
Scores: April 6 at Chicago — Chicago 3, Detroit 2; Aprl 8 at Detroit — Detroit 3, Chicago 1; April 10 at Chicago — Chicago 3, Detroit 1; April 12 at Detroit — Detroit 2, Chicago 1; April 14 at Chicago — Chicago 6, Detroit 3; April 16 at Detroit — Chicago 5, Detroit 1.

1959-60 — Montreal Canadiens — Jacques Plante, Charlie Hodge, Doug Harvey, Tom Johnson, Bob Turner, Jean-Guy Talbot, Albert Langlois, Ralph Backstrom, Jean Beliveau, Marcel Bonin, Bernie Geoffrion, Phil Goyette, Bill Hicke, Don Marshall, Ab McDonald, Dickie Moore, Andr;aae Pronvost, Claude Provost, Henri Richard, Maurice Richard, Frank Selke (manager), Toe Blake (coach), Hector Dubois, Larry Aubut (trainers).
Scores: April 7 at Montreal — Montreal 4, Toronto 2; April 9 at Montreal — Montreal 2, Toronto 1; April 12 at Toronto — Montreal 5, Toronto 2; April 14 at Toronto — Montreal 4, Toronto 0.

1958-59 — Montreal Canadiens — Jacques Plante, Charlie Hodge, Doug Harvey, Tom Johnson, Bob Turner, Jean-Guy Talbot, Albert Langlois, Bernie Geoffrion, Ralp Backstrom, Bill Hicke, Maurice Richard, Dickie Moore, Claude Provost, Ab McDonald, Henri Richard, Marcel Bonin, Phil Goyette, Don Marshall, Andr;aae Pronovost, Jean B;aaeliveau, Frank Selke (manager), Toe Blake (coach), Hector Dubois, Larry Aubut (trainers).
Scores: April 9 at Montreal — Montreal 5, Toronto 3; April 11 at Montreal — Montreal 3, Toronto 1; April 14 at Toronto — Toronto 3, Montreal 2; April 16 at Toronto — Montreal 3, Toronto 2; April 18 at Montreal — Montreal 5, Toronto 3.

1957-58 — Montreal Canadiens — Jacques Plante, Gerry McNeil, Doug Harvey, Tom Johnson, Bob Turner, Dollard St-Laurent, Jean-Guy Talbot, Albert Langlois, Jean B;aaeliveau, Bernie Geoffrion, Maurice Richard, Dickie Moore, Claude Provost, Floyd Curry, Bert Olmstead, Henri Richard, Marcel Bonin, Phil Goyette, Don Marshall, Andr;aae Pronovost, Connie Broden, Frank Selke (manager), Toe Blake (coach), Hector Dubois, Larry Aubut (trainers).
Scores: April 8 at Montreal —Montreal 2, Boston 1; April 10 at Montreal — Boston 5, Montreal 2; April 13 at Boston — Montreal 3, Boston 0; April 15 at Boston — Boston 3, Montreal 1; April 17 at Montreal — Montreal 3, Boston 2; April 20 at Boston — Montreal 5, Boston 3.

1956-57 — Montreal Canadiens — Jacques Plante, Gerry McNeil, Doug Harvey, Tom Johnson, Bob Turner, Dollard St. Laurent, Jean-Guy Talbot, Jean B;aaeliveau, Bernie Geoffrion, Floyd Curry, Dickie Moore, Maurice Richard, Claude Provost, Bert Olmstead, Henri Richard, Phil Goyette, Don Marshall, Andr;aae Pronovost, Connie Broden, Frank Selke (manager), Toe Blake (coach), Hector Dubois, Larry Aubut (trainers).
Scores: April 6, at Montreal — Montreal 5, Boston 1; April 9, at Montreal — Montreal 1, Boston 0; April 11, at Boston — Montreal 4, Boston 2; April 14, at Boston — Boston 2, Montreal 0; April 16, at Montreal — Montreal 5, Boston 1.

1955-56 — Montreal Canadiens — Jacques Plante, Doug Harvey, Emile Bouchard, Bob Turner, Tom Johnson, Jean-Guy Talbot, Dollard St. Laurent, Jean B;aaeliveau, Bernie Geoffrion, Bert Olmstead, Floyd Curry, Jackie Leclair, Maurice Richard, Dickie Moore, Henri Richard, Ken Mosdell, Don Marshall, Claude Provost, Frank Selke (manager), Toe Blake (coach), Hector Dubois (trainer).
Scores: March 31, at Montreal — Montreal 6, Detroit 4; April 3, at Montreal — Montreal 5, Detroit 1; April 5, at Detroit — Detroit 3, Montreal 1; April 8, at Detroit — Montreal 3, Detroit 0; April 10, at Montreal — Montreal 3, Detroit 1.

1954-55 — Detroit Red Wings — Terry Sawchuk, Red Kelly, Bob Goldham, Marcel Pronovost, Ben Woit, Jim Hay, Larry Hillman, Ted Lindsay, Tony Leswick, Gordie Howe, Alex Delvecchio, Marty Pavelich, Glen Skov, Earl Reibel, John Wilson, Bill Dineen, Vic Stasiuk, Marcel Bonin, Jack Adams (manager), Jimmy Skinner (coach), Carl Mattson (trainer).
Scores: April 3, at Detroit — Detroit 4, Montreal 2; April 5, at Detroit — Detroit 7, Montreal 1, April 7 at Monreal — Montreal 4, Detroit 2; April 9, at Montreal — Montreal 5, Detroit 3; April 10, at Detroit — Detroit 5, Montreal 1; April 12, at Montreal — Montreal 6, Detroit 3; April 14, at Detroit — Detroit 3, Montreal 1

1953-54 — Detroit Red Wings — Terry Sawchuk, Red Kelly, Bob Goldham, Ben Woit, Marcel Pronovost, Al Arbour, Keith Allen, Ted Lindsay, Tony Leswick, Gordie Howe, Marty Pavelich, Alex Delvecchio, Metro Prystai, Glen Skov, John Wilson, Bill Dineen, Jim Peters, Earl Reibel, Vic Stasiu, Jack Adams (manager), Tommy Ivan (coach), Carl Mattson (trainer).
Scores: April 4, at Detroit — Detroit 3, Montreal 1; April 6, at Detroit — Montreal 3, Detroit 1; April 8, at Montreal — Detroit 5, Montreal 2; April 10, at Montreal — Detroit 2, Montreal 0; April 11, at Detroit — Montreal 1, Detroit 0; April 13, at Montreal — Montreal 4, Detroit 1; April 16, at Detroit — Detroit 2, Montreal 1.

1952-53 — Montreal Canadiens — Gerry McNeil, Jacques Plante, Doug Harvey, Emile Bouchard, Tom Johnson, Dollard St. Laurent, Bud MacPherson, Maurice Richard, Elmer Lach, Bert Olmstead, Bernie Geoffrion, Floyd Curry, Paul Masnick, Billy Reay, Dickie Moore, Ken Mosdell, Dick Gamble, Johnny McCormack, Lorne Davis, Calum McKay, Eddie Mazur, Frank Selke (manager), Dick Irvin (coach), Hector Dubois (trainer).
Scores: April 9, at Montreal — Montreal 4, Boston 2; April 11, at Montreal — Boston 4, Montreal 1; April 12, at Boston — Montreal 3, Boston 0; April 14, at Boston — Montreal 7, Boston 3; April 16, at Montreal — Montreal 1, Boston 0.

1951-52 — Detroit Red Wings — Terry Sawchuk, Bob Goldham, Ben Woit, Red Kelly, Leo Reise, Marcel Pronovost, Ted Lindsay, Tony Leswick, Gordie Howe, Metro Prystai, Marty Pavelich, Sid Abel, Glen Skov, Alex Delvecchio, John Wilson, Vic Stasiuk, Larry Zeidel, Jack Adams (manager) Tommy Ivan (coach), Carl Mattson (trainer).
Scores: April 10, at Montreal — Detroit 3, Montreal 1; April 12 at Montreal — Detroit 2, Montreal 1; April 13, at Detroit — Detroit 3, Montreal 0; April 15, at Detroit — Detroit 3, Montreal 0.

1950-51 — Toronto Maple Leafs — Turk Broda, Al Rollins, Jim Thomson, Gus Mortson, Bill Barilko, Bill Juzda, Fern Flaman, Hugh Bolton, Ted Kennedy, Sid Smith, Tod Sloan, Cal Gardner, Howie Meeker, Harry Watson, Max Bentley, Joe Klukay, Danny Lewicki, Ray Timgren, Fleming Mackell, Johnny McCormack, Bob Hassard, Conn Smythe (manager), Joe Primeau (coach), Tim Daly (trainer).
Scores: April 11, at Toronto — Toronto 3, Montreal 2; April 14, at Toronto — Montreal 3, Toronto 2; April 17, at Montreal — Toronto 2, Montreal 1; April 19, at Montreal — Toronto 3, Montreal 2; April 21, at Toronto — Toronto 3, Montreal 2.

1949-50 — Detroit Red Wings — Harry Lumley, Jack Stewart, Leo Reise, Clare Martin, Al Dewsbury, Lee Fogolin, Marcel Pronovost, Red Kelly, Ted Lindsay, Sid Abel, Gordie Howe, George Gee, Jimmy Peters, Marty Pavelich, Jim McFadden, Pete Babando, Max McNab, Gerry Coutur, Joe Carveth, Steve Black, John Wilson, Larry Wilson, Jack Adams (manager), Tommy Ivan (coach), Carl Mattson (trainer).
Scores: April 11, at Detroit — Detroit 4, NY Rangers 1; April 13, at Toronto* — NY Rangers 3, Detroit 1; April 15, at Toronto — Detroit 4, NY Rangers 0; April 18, at Detroit — NY Rangers 4, Detroit 3; April 20, at Detroit — NY Rangers 2, Detroit 1; April 22, at Detroit — Detroit 5, NY Rangers 4; April 23, at Detroit — Detroit 4, NY Rangers 3.
* Ice was unavailable in Madison Square Garden and Rangers elected to play second and third games on Toronto ice.

1948-49 — Toronto Maple Leafs — Turk Broda, Jim Thomson, Gus Mortson, Bill Barilko, Garth Boesch, Bill Juzda, Ted Kennedy, Howie Meeker, Vic Lynn, Harry Watson, Bill Ezinicki, Cal Gardner, Max Bentley, Joe Klukay, Sid Smith, Don Metz, Ray Timgren, Fleming Mackell, Harry Taylor, Bob Dawes, Tod Sloan, Conn Smythe (manager), Hap Day (coach), Tim Daly (trainer).
Scores: April 8, t Detroit — Toronto 3, Detroit 2; April 10, at Detroit — Toronto 3, Detroit 1; April 13, at Toronto — Toronto 3, Detroit 1; April 16, at Toronto — Toronto 3, Detroit 1.

1947-48 — Toronto Maple Leafs — Turk Broda, Jim Thomson, Wally Stanowski, Garth Boesch, Bill Barilko. Gus Mortson, Phil Samis, Syl Apps, Bill Ezinicki, Harry Watson, Ted Kennedy, Howie Meeker, Vic Lynn, Nick Metz, Max Bentley, Joe Klukay, Les Costello, Don Metz, Sid Smith, Conn Smythe (manager), Hap Day (coach), Tim Daly (trainer).
Scores: April 7, at Toronto — Toronto 5, Detroit 3; April 10, at Toronto — Toronto 4, Detroit 2; April 11, at Detroit — Toronto 2, Detroit 0; April 14, at Detroit — Toronto 7, Detroit 2.

1946-47 — Toronto Maple Leafs — Turk Broda, Garth Boesch, Gus Mortson, Jim Thomson, Wally Stanowski, Bill Barilko, Harry Watson, Bud Poile, Ted Kennedy, Syl Apps, Don Metz, Nick Metz, Bill Ezinicki, Vic Lynn, Howie Meeker, Gaye Stewart, Joe Klukay, Gus Bodnar, Bob Goldham, Conn Smythe (manager), Hap Day (coach), Tim Daly (trainer).
Scores: April 8, at Montreal — Montreal 6, Toronto 0; April 10, at Montreal — Toronto 4, Montreal 0; April 12, at Toronto — Toronto 4, Montreal 2; April 15, at Toronto — Toronto 2, Montreal 1; April 17, at Montreal — Montreal 3, Toronto 1; April 19, at Toronto — Toronto 2, Montreal 1.

1945-46 — Montreal Canadiens — Elmer Lach, Toe Blake, Maurice Richard, Bob Fillion, Dutch Hiller, Murph Chamberlain, Ken Mosdell, Buddy O'Connor, Glen Harmon, Jim Peters, Emile Bouchard, Bill Reay, Ken Reardon, Leo Lamoureux, Frank Eddolls, Gerry Plamondon, Bill Durnan, Tommy Gorman (manager), Dick Irvin (coach), Ernie Cook (trainer).
Scores: March 30, at Montreal — Montreal 4, Boston 3; April 2, at Montreal — Montreal 3, Boston 2; April 4, at Boston — Montreal 4, Boston 2; April 7, at Boston — Boston 3, Montreal 2; April 9, at Montreal — Montreal 6, Boston 3.

1944-45 — Toronto Maple Leafs — Don Metz, Frank McCool, Wally Stanowski, Reg Hamilton, Elwyn Morris, Johnny McCreedy, Tommy O'Neill, Ted Kennedy, Babe Pratt, Gus Bodnar, Art Jackson, Jack McLean, Mel Hill, Nick Metz, Bob Davidson, Dave Schriner, Lorne Carr, Conn Smythe (manager), Frank Selke (business manager), Hap Day (coach), Tim Daly (trainer).
Scores: April 6, at Detroit — Toronto 1, Detroit 0; April 8, at Detroit — Toronto 2, Detroit 0; April 12, at Toronto — Toronto 1, Detroit 0; April 14, at Toronto — Detroit 5, Toronto 3; April 19, at Detroit — Detroit 2, Toronto 0; April 21, at Toronto — Detroit 1, Toronto 0; April 22, at Detroit — Toronto 2, Detroit 1.

1943-44 — Montreal Canadiens — Toe Blake, Maurice Richard, Elmer Lach, Ray Getliffe, Murph Chamberlain, Phil Watson, Emile Bouchard, Glen Harmon, Buddy O'Connor, Jerry Heffernan, Mike McMahon, Leo Lamoureux, Fernand Majeau, Bob Fillion, Bill Durnan, Tommy Gorman (manager), Dick Irvin (coach), Ernie Cook (trainer).
Scores: April 4, at Montreal — Montreal 5, Chicago 1; April 6, at Chicago — Montreal 3, Chicago 1; April 9, at Chicago — Montreal 3, Chicago 2; April 13, at Montreal — Montreal 5, Chicago 4.

1942-43 — Detroit Red Wings — Jack Stewart, Jimmy Orlando, Sid Abel, Alex Motter, Harry Watson, Joe Carveth, Mud Bruneteau, Eddie Wares, Johnny Mowers, Cully Simon, Don Grosso, Carl Liscombe, Connie Brown, Syd Howe, Les Douglas, Hal Jackson, Joe Fisher, Jack Adams (manager), Ebbie Goodfellow (playing-coach), Honey Walker (trainer).
Scores: April 1, at Detroit — Detroit 6, Boston 2; April 4, at Detroit — Detroit 4, Boston 3; April 7, at Boston — Detroit 4, Boston 0; April 8, at Boston — Detroit 2, Boston 0.

1941-42 — Toronto Maple Leafs — Wally Stanowski, Syl Apps, Bob Goldham, Gord Drillon, Hank Goldup, Ernie Dickens, Dave Schriner, Bucko McDonald, Bob Davidson, Nick Metz, Bingo Kampman, Don Metz, Gaye Stewart, Turk Broda, Johnny McCreedy, Lorne Carr, Pete Langelle, Billy Taylor, Conn Smyte (manager), Hap Day (coach), Frank Selke (business manager), Tim Daly (trainer).
Scores: April 4, at Toronto — Detroit 3, Toronto 2; April 7, at Toronto — Detroit 4, Toronto 2; April 9, at Detroit — Detroit 5, Toronto 2; April 12, at Detroit — Toronto 4, Detroit 3; April 14, at Toronto — Toronto 9, Detroit 3; April 16, at Detroit — Toronto 3, Detroit 0; April 18, at Toronto — Toronto 3, Detroit 1.

1940-41 — Boston Bruins — Bill Cowley, Des Smith, Dit Clapper, Frank Brimsek, Flash Hollett, John Crawford, Bobby Bauer, Pat McCreavy, Herb Cain, Mel Hill, Milt Schmidt, Woody Dumart, Roy Conacher, Terry Reardon, Art Jackson, Eddie Wiseman, Art Ross (manager), Cooney Weiland (coach), Win Green (trainer).
Scores: April 6, at Boston — Detroit 2, Boston 3; April 8, at Boston — Detroit 1, Boston 2; April 10, at Detroit — Boston 4, Detroit 2; April 12, at Detroit — Boston 3, Detroit 1.

1939-40 — New York Rangers — Dave Kerr, Art Coulter, Ott Heller, Alex Shibicky, Mac Colville, Neil Colville, Phil Watson, Lynn Patrick, Clint Smith, Muzz Patrick, Babe Pratt, Bryan Hextall, Kilby Macdonald, Dutch Hiller, Alf Pike, Sanford Smith, Lester Patrick (manager), Frank Boucher (coach), Harry Westerby (trainer).
Scores: April 2, at New York — NY Rangers 2, Toronto 1; April 3, at New York — NY Rangers 6, Toronto 2; April 6, at Toronto — NY Rangers 1, Toronto 2; April 9, at Toronto — NY Rangers 0, Toronto 3; April 11, at Toronto — NY Rangers 2, Toronto 1; April 13, at Toronto — NY Rangers 3, Toronto 2.

1938-39 — Boston Bruins — Bobby Bauer, Mel Hill, Flash Hollett, Roy Conacher, Gord Pettinger, Milt Schmidt, Woody Dumart, Jack Crawford, Ray Getliffe, Frank Brimsek, Eddie Shore, Dit Clapper, Bill Cowley, Jack Portland, Red Hamill, Cooney Weiland, Art Ross (manager-coach), Win Green (trainer).
Scores: April 6, at Boston — Toronto 1, Boston 2; April 9, at Boston — Toronto 3, Boston 2; April 11, at Toronto — Toronto 1, Boston 3; April 13 at Toronto — Toronto 0, Boston 2; April 16, at Boston — Toronto 1, Boston 3.

1937-38 — Chicago Blackhawks — Art Wiebe, Carl Voss, Hal Jackson, Mike Karakas, Mush March, Jack Shill, Earl Seibert, Cully Dahlstrom, Alex Levinsky, Johnny Gottselig, Lou Trudel, Pete Palangio, Bill MacKenzie, Doc Romnes, Paul Thompson, Roger Jenkins, Alf Moore, Bert Connolly, Virgil Johnson, Paul Goodman, Bill Stewart (manager-coach), Eddie Froelich (trainer).
Scores: April 5, at Toronto — Chicago 3, Toronto 1; Aril 7, at Toronto — Chicago 1, Toronto 5; April 10 at Chicago — Chicago 2, Toronto 1; April 12, at Chicago — Chicago 4, Toronto 1.

1936-37 — Detroit Red Wings — Normie Smith, Pete Kelly, Larry Aurie, Herbie Lewis, Hec Kilrea, Mud Bruneteau, Syd Howe, Wally Kilrea, Jimmy Franks, Bucko McDonald, Gordon Pettinger, Ebbie Goodfellow, Johnny Gallagher, Scotty Bowman, Johnny Sorrell, Marty Barry, Earl Robertson, Johnny Sherf, Howard Mackie, Jack Adams (manager-coach), Honey Walker (trainer).
Scores: April 6, at New York — Detroit 1, NY Rangers 5; April 8, at Detroit — Detroit 4, NY Rangers 2; April 11, at Detroit — Detroit 0, NY Rangers 1; April 13, at Detroit — Detroit 1, NY Rangers 0; April 15, at Detroit — Detroit 3, NY Rangers 0.

1935-36 — Detroit Red Wings — Johnny Sorrell, Syd Howe, Marty Barry, Herbie Lewis, Mud Bruneteau, Wally Kilrea, Hec Kilrea, Gordon Pettinger, Bucko McDonald, Scotty Bowman, Pete Kelly, Doug Young, Ebbie Goodfellow, Normie Smith, Jack Adams (manager-coach), Honey Walker (trainer).
Scores: April 5, at Detroit — Detroit 3, Toronto 1; April 7, at Detroit — Detroit 9, Toronto 4; April 9, at Toronto — Detroit 3, Toronto 4; April 11, at Toronto — Detroit 3, Toronto 2.

1934-35 — Montreal Maroons — Marvin (Cy) Wentworth, Alex Connell, Toe Blake, Stew Evans, Earl Robinson, Bill Miller, Dave Trottier, Jimmy Ward, Larry Northcott, Hooley Smith, Russ Blinco, Allan Shields, Sammy McManus, Gus Marker, Bob Gracie, Herb Cain, Tommy Gorman (manager), Lionel Conacher (coach), Bill O'Brien (trainer).
Scores: April 4, at Toronto — Mtl. Maroons 3, Toronto 2; April 6, at Toronto — Mtl. Maroons 3, Toronto 1; April 9, at Montreal — Mtl. Maroons 4, Toronto 1.

1933-34 — Chicago Blackhawks — Taffy Abel, Lolo Couture, Lou Trudel, Lionel Conacher, Paul Thompson, Leroy Goldsworthy, Art Coulter, Roger Jenkins, Don McFayden, Tommy Cook, Doc Romnes, Johnny Gottselig, Mush March, Johny Sheppard, Chuck Gardiner (captain), Bill Kendall, Tommy Gorman (manager-coach), Eddie Froelich (trainer).
Scores: April 3, at Detroit — Chicago 2, Detroit 1; April 5, at Detroit — Chicago 4, Detroit 1; April 8, at Chicago — Detroit 5, Chicago 2; April 10, at Chicago — Chicago 1, Detroit 0.

1932-33 — New York Rangers — Ching Johnson, Butch Keeling, Frank Boucher, Art Somers, Babe Siebert, Bun Cook, Andy Aitkinhead, Ott Heller, Ozzie Asmundson, Gord Pettinger, Doug Brennan, Cecil Dillon, Bill Cook (captain), Murray Murdock, Earl Seibert, Lester Patrick (manager-coach), Harry Westerby (trainer).
Scores: April 4, at New York — NY Rangers 5, Toronto 1; April 8, at Toronto — NY Rangers 3, Toronto 1; April 11, at Toronto — Toronto 3, NY Rangers 2, April 13, at Toronto — NY Rangers 1, Toronto 0.

1931-32 — Toronto Maple Leafs — Charlie Conacher, Harvey Jackson, King Clancy, Andy Blair, Red Horner, Lorne Chabot, Alex Levinsky, Joe Primeau, Hal Darragh, Hal Cotton, Frank Finnigan, Hap Day, Ace Bailey, Bob Gracie, Fred Robertson, Earl Miller, Conn Smythe (manager), Dick Irvin (coach), Tim Daly (trainer).
Scores: April 5 at New York — Toronto 6, NY Rangers 4; April 7, at Boston* — Toronto 6, NY Rangers 2; April 9, at Toronto — Toronto 6, NY Rangers 4.
* Ice was unavailable in Madison Square Garden and Rangers elected to play the second game on neutral ice.

1930-31 — Montreal Canadiens — George Hainsworth, Wildor Larochelle, Marty Burke, Sylvio Mantha, Howie Morenz, Johnny Gagnon, Aurel Joliat, Armand Mondou, Pit Lepine, Albert Leduc, Georges Mantha, Art Lesieur, Nick Wasnie, Bert McCaffrey, Gus Rivers, Jean Pusie, Leo Dandurand (manager), Cecil Hart (coach), Ed Dufour (trainer).
Scores: April 3, at Chicago — Montreal 2, Chicago 1; April 5, at Chicago — Chicago 2, Montreal 1; April 9, at Montreal — Chicago 3, Montreal 2; April 11, at Montreal — Montreal 4, Chicago 2; April 14, at Montreal — Montreal 2, Chicago 0.

1929-30 — Montreal Canadiens — George Hainsworth, Marty Burke, Sylvio Mantha, Howie Morenz, Bert McCaffrey, Aurel Joliat, Albert Leduc, Pit Lepine, Wildor Larochelle, Nick Wasnie, Gerald Carson, Armand Mondou, Georges Mantha, Gus Rivers, Leo Dandurand (manager), Cecil Hart (coach), Ed Dufour (trainer).
Scores: April 1 at Boston — Montreal 3, Boston 0; April 3 at Montreal — Montreal 4, Boston 3.

1928-29 — Boston Bruins — Cecil (Tiny) Thompson, Eddie Shore, Lionel Hitchman, Perk Galbraith, Eric Pettinger, Frank Fredrickson, Mickey Mackay, Red Green, Dutch Gainor, Harry Oliver, Eddie Rodden, Dit Clapper, Cooney Weiland, Lloyd Klein, Cy Denneny, Bill Carson, George Owen, Myles Lane, Art Ross (manager-coach), Win Green (trainer).
Scores: March 28 at Boston — Boston 2, NY Rangers 0; March 29 at New York — Boston 2, NY Rangers 1.

1927-28 — New York Rangers — Lorne Chabot, Taffy Abel, Leon Bourgault, Ching Johnson, Bill Cook, Bun Cook, Frank Boucher, Billy Boyd, Murray Murdoch, Paul Thompson, Alex Gray, Joe Miller, Patsy Callighen, Lester Patrick (manager-coach), Harry Westerby (trainer).
Scores: April 5 at Montreal — Mtl. Maroons 2, NY Rangers 0; April 7 at Montreal — NY Rangers 2, Mtl. Maroons 1; April 10 at Montreal — Mtl. Maroons 2, NY Rangers 1; April 12 at Montreal — NY Rangers 1, Mtl. Maroons 0; April 14 at Montreal — NY Rangers 2, Mtl. Maroons 1.

1926-27 — Ottawa Senators — Alex Connell, King Clancy, George (Buck) Boucher, Ed Gorman, Frank Finnigan, Alex Smith, Hec Kilrea, Hooley Smith, Cy Denneny, Frank Nighbor, Jack Adams, Milt Halliday, Dave Gil (manager-coach).
Scores: April 7 at Boston — Ottawa 0, Boston 0; April 9 at Boston — Ottawa 3, Boston 1; April 11 at Ottawa — Boston 1, Ottawa 1; April 13 at Ottawa — Ottawa 3, Boston 1.

1925-26 — Montreal Maroons — Clint Benedict, Reg Noble, Frank Carson, Dunc Munro, Nels Stewart, Harry Broadbent, Babe Siebert, Dinny Dinsmore, Bill Phillips, Hobart (Hobie) Kitchen, Sammy Rothschiel, Albert (Toots) Holway, Shorty Horne, Bern Brophy, Eddie Gerard (manager-coach), Bill O'Brien (trainer).
Scores: March 30 at Montreal — Mtl. Maroons 3, Victoria 0; April 1 at Montreal — Mtl. Maroons 3, Victoria 0; April 3 at Montreal — Victoria 3, Mtl. Maroons 2; April 6 at Montreal — Mtl. Maroons 2, Victoria 0.

The series in the spring of 1926 ended the annual playoffs between the champions of the east and the champions of the west. The west coast league disbanded, selling its players to Chicago, Detroit and New York Rangers. Since 1926-27 the annual playoffs in the National Hockey League have decided the Stanley Cup champions.

1924-25 — Victoria Cougars — Harry (Happy) Holmes, Clem Loughlin, Gordie Fraser, Frank Fredrickson, Jack Walker, Harold (Gizzy) Hart, Harold (Slim) Halderson, Frank Foyston, Wally Elmer, Harry Meeking, Jocko Anderson, Lester Patrick (manager-coach).
Scores: March 21 at Victoria — Victoria 5, Montreal 2; March 23 at Vancouver — Victoria 3, Montreal 1; March 27 at Victoria — Montreal 4, Victoria 2; March 30 at Victoria — Victoria 6, Montreal 1.

1923-24 — Montreal Canadiens — Georges Vezina, Sprague Cleghorn, Billy Couture, Howie Morenz, Aurel Joliat, Billy Boucher, Odie Cleghorn, Sylvio Mantha, Bobby Boucher, Billy Bell, Billy Cameron, Joe Malone, Fortier, Leo Dandurand (manager-coach).
Scores: March 18 at Montreal — Montreal 3, Van. Maroons 2; March 20 at Montreal — Montreal 2, Van. Maroons 1. March 22 at Montreal — Montreal 6, Cgy. Tigers 1; March 25 at Ottawa* — Montreal 3, Cgy. Tigers 0. (Because of an agreement between the NHL and the two western leagues WCHL and PCHA, Montreal had to play the champions of each league during the Stanley Cup series of 1924.)
*Game transferred to Ottawa to benefit from an artificial ice surface.

1922-23 — Ottawa Senators — George (Buck) Boucher, Lionel Hitchman, Frank Nighbor, King Clancy, Harry Helman, Clint Benedict, Jack Darragh, Eddie Gerard, Cy Denneny, Harry Broadbent, Tommy Gorman (manager), Pete Green (coach), F. Dolan (trainer).
Scores: March 16 at Vancouver — Ottawa 1, Van. Maroons 0; March 19 at Vancouver — Van. Maroons 4, Ottawa 1; March 23 at Vancouver — Ottawa 3, Van. Maroons 2; March 26 at Vancouver — Ottawa 5, Van. Maroons 1; March 29 at Vancouver — Ottawa 2, Edm. Eskimos 1; March 31 at Vancouver — Ottawa 1, Edm. Eskimos 0. (Because of an agreement between the NHL and the two western leagues, WCHL and PCHA, Ottawa had to play the champions of each league during the Stanley Cup series of 1923.)

1921-22 — Toronto St. Pats — Ted Stackhouse, Corb Denneny, Rod Smylie, Lloyd Andrews, John Ross Roach, Harry Cameron, Bill (Red) Stuart, Cecil (Babe) Dye, Ken Randall, Reg Noble, Eddie Gerard (borrowed for one game from Ottawa), Stan Jackson, Nolan Mitchell, Charlie Querrie (manager), Eddie Powers (coach).
Scores: March 17 at Toronto — Van. Millionaires 4, Toronto 3; March 20 at Toronto — Toronto 2, Van. Millionaires 1; March 23 at Toronto — Van. Millionaires 3, Toronto 0; March 25 at Toronto — Toronto 6, Van. Millionaires 0; March 28 at Toronto — Toronto 5, Van. Millionaires 1.

1920-21 — Ottawa Senators — Jack McKell, Jack Darragh, Morley Bruce, George (Buck) Boucher, Eddie Gerard, Clint Benedict, Sprague Cleghorn, Frank Nighbor, Harry Broadbent, Cy Denneny, Leth Graham, Tommy Gorman (manager),Pete Green (coach), F. Dolan (trainer).
Scores: March 21 at Vancouver — Van. Millionaires 2, Ottawa 1; March 24 at Vancouver — Ottawa 4, Van. Millionaires 3; March 28 at Vancouver — Ottawa 3, Van. Millionaires 2; March 31 at Vancouver — Van. Millionaires 3, Ottawa 2; April 4 at Vancouver — Ottawa 2, Van. Millionaires 1

1919-20 — Ottawa Senators — Jack McKell, Jack Darragh, Morley Bruce, Horrace Merrill, George (Buck) Boucher, Eddie Gerard, Clint Benedict, Sprague Cleghorn, Frank Nighbor, Harry Broadbent, Cy Denneny, Price, Tommy Gorman (manager), Pete Green (coach).
Scores: March 22 at Ottawa — Ottawa 3, Seattle 2; March 24 at Ottawa — Ottawa 3, Seattle 0; March 27 at Ottawa — Seattle 3, Ottawa 1; March 30 at Toronto* — Seattle 5, Ottawa 2; April 1 at Toronto* — Ottawa 6, Seattle 1.
*Games transferred to Toronto to benefit from artificial ice surface.

1918-19 — No decision, Series halted by Spanish influenza epidemic, illness of several players and dath of Joe Hall of Montreal Canadiens from flu. Five games had been played when the series was halted, each team having won two and tied one. The results are shown:
Scores: March 19 at Seattle — Seattle 7, Montreal 0; March 22 at Seattle — Montreal 4, Seattle 2; March 24 at Seattle — Seattle 7, Montreal 2; March 26 at Seattle — Montreal 0, Seattle 0; March 30 at Seattle — Montreal 4, Seattle 3.

1917-18 — Toronto Arenas — Rusty Crawford, Harry Meeking, Ken Randall, Corb Denneny, Harry Cameron, Jack Adams, Alf Skinner, Harry Mummery, Harry (Happy) Holmes, Reg Noble, Sammy Hebert, Jack Marks, Jack Coughlin, Neville, Charlie Querrie (manager), Dick Carroll (coach), Frank Carroll (trainer).
Scores: March 20 at Toronto — Toronto 5, Van. Millionaires 3; March 23 at Toronto — Van. Millionaires 6, Toronto 4; March 26 at Toronto — Toronto 6, Van. Millionaires 3; March 28 at Toronto — Van. Millionaires 8, Toronto 1; March 30 at Toronto — Toronto 2, Van. Millionaires 1.

1916-17 — Seattle Metropolitans — Harry (Happy) Holmes, Ed Carpenter, Cully Wilson, Jack Walker, Bernie Morris, Frank Foyston, Roy Rickey, Jim Riley, Bobby Rowe (captain), Peter Muldoon (manager).
Scores: March 17 at Seattle — Montreal 8, Seattle 4; March 20 at Seattle — Seattle 6, Montreal 1; March 23 at Seattle — Seattle 4, Montreal 1; March 25 at Seattle — Seattle 9, Montreal 1.

1915-16 — Montreal Canadiens — Georges Vezina, Bert Corbeau, Jack Laviolette, Newsy Lalonde, Louis Berlinguette, Goldie Prodgers, Howard McNamara, Didier Pitre, Skene Ronan, Amos Arbour, Skinner Poulin, Jack Fournier, George Kennedy (manager).
Scores: March 20 at Montreal — Portland 2, Montreal 0; March 22 at Montreal — Montreal 2, Portland 1; March 25 at Montreal — Montreal 6, Portland 3; March 28 at Montreal — Portland 6, Montreal 5; March 30 at Montreal — Montreal 2, Portland 1.

1914-15 — Vancouver Millionaires — Kenny Mallen, Frank Nighbor, Fred (Cyclone) Taylor, Hughie Lehman, Lloyd Cook, Mickey MacKay, Barney Stanley, Jim Seaborn, Si Griffis (captain), Jean Matz, Frank Patrick (playing manager).
Scores: March 22 at Vancouver — Van. Millionaires 6, Ottawa 2; March 24 at Vancouver — Van. Millionaires 8, Ottawa 3; March 26 at Vancouver — Van. Millionaires 12, Ottawa 3.

1913-14 — Toronto Blueshirts — Con Corbeau, F. Roy McGiffen, Jack Walker, George McNamara, Cully Wilson, Frank Foyston, Harry Cameron, Harry (Happy) Holmes, Alan M. Davidson (captain), Harriston, Jack Marshall (playing-manager), Frank and Dick Carroll (trainers).
Scores: March 7 at Montreal — Montreal 2, Toronto 0; March 11 at Toronto — Toronto 6, Montreal 0; Total goals: Toronto 6, Montreal 2. March 14 at Toronto — Toronto 5, Victoria 2; March 17 at Toronto — Toronto 6, Victoria 5; March 19 at Toronto — Toronto 2, Victoria 1.

1912-13 — Quebec Bulldogs — Joe Malone, Joe Hall, Paddy Moran, Harry Mummery, Tommy Smith, Jack Marks, Russell Crawford, Billy Creighton, Jeff Malone, Rocket Power, M.J. Quinn (manager), D. Beland (trainer).
Scores: March 8 at Quebec — Que. Bulldogs 14, Sydney 3; March 10 at Quebec — Que. Bulldogs 6, Sydney 2.

Victoria challenged Quebec but the Bulldogs refused to put the Stanley Cup in competition so the two teams played an exhibition series with Victoria winning two games to one by scores of 7-5, 3-6, 6-1. It was the first meeting between the Eastern champions and the Western champions. The following year, and until the Western Hockey League disbanded after the 1926 playoffs, the Cup went to the winner of the series between East and West.

1911-12 — Quebec Bulldogs — Goldie Prodgers, Joe Hall, Walter Rooney, Paddy Moran, Jack Marks, Jack McDonald, Eddie Oatman, Leonard, Joe Malone (captain), C. Nolan (coach), M.J. Quinn (manager), D. Beland (trainer).
Scores: March 11 at Quebec — Que. Bulldogs 9, Moncton 3; March 13 at Quebec — Que. Bulldogs 8,Moncton 0.

Prior to 1912, teams could challenge the Stanley Cup champions for the title, thus there was more than one Championship Series played in most of the seasons between 1894 and 1911.

1910-11 — Ottawa Senators — Hamby Shore, Percy LeSueur, Jack Darragh, Bruce Stuart, Marty Walsh, Bruce Ridpath, Fred Lake, Albert (Dubby) Kerr, Alex Currie, Horace Gaul.
Scores: March 13 at Ottawa — Ottawa 7, Galt 4; March 16 at Ottawa — Ottawa 13, Port Arthur 4.

1909-10 — Monteal Wanderers — Cecil W. Blackford, Ernie (Moose) Johnson, Ernie Russell, Riley Hern, Harry Hyland, Jack Marshall, Frank (Pud) Glass (captain), Jimmy Gardner, R. R. Boon (manager).
Scores: March 12 at Montreal — Mtl. Wanderers 7, Berlin (Kitchener) 3.

1908-09 — Ottawa Senators — Fred Lake, Percy LeSueur, Fred (Cyclone) Taylor, H.L. (Billy) Gilmour, Albert Kerr, Edgar Dey, Marty Walsh, Bruce Stuart (captain).
Scores: Ottawa, as champions of the Eastern Canada Hockey Association took over the Stanley Cup in 1909 and, although a challenge was accepted by the Cup trustees from Winnipeg Shamrocks but could not be arranged because of the lateness of the season, no other challenges were made in 1909. The following season — 1909-10 — however, the Senators accepted two challenges as defending Cup Champions. The first was against Galt in a two-game, total-point series, and the second against Edmonton, also a two-game, total-point series. Results: January 5 at Ottawa —Ottawa 12, Galt 3; January 7 at Ottawa — Ottawa 3, Galt 1. January 18 at Ottawa — Ottawa 8, Edm. Eskimos 4; January 20 at Ottawa — Ottawa 13, Edm. Eskimos 7.

1907-08 — Montreal Wanderers — Riley Hern, Art Ross, Walter Small, Frank (Pud) Glass, Bruce Stuart, Ernie Russell, Ernie (Moose) Johnson, Cecil Blachford (captain), Tom Hooper, Larry Gilmour, Ernie Liffiton, R.R. Boon (manager).
Scores: Wanderers accepted four challenges for the Cup: January 9 at Montreal — Mtl. Wanderers 9, Ott. Victorias 3; January 13 at Montreal — Mtl. Wanderers 13, Ott. Victorias 1; March 10 at Montreal — Mtl. Wanderers 11, Wpg. Maple Leafs 5; March 12 at Montreal — Mtl. Wanderers 9, Wpg. Maple Leafs 3; March 14 at Montreal — Mtl. Wanderers 6, Tor. Maple Leafs 4. Note: Toronto played in the Ontario Professional Hockey League (1908, 1909). This club was not associated with the current NHL franchise. At start of following season, 1908-09, Wanderers were challenged by Edmonton. Results: December 28 at Montreal — Mtl. Wanderers 7, Edm. Eskimos 3; December 30 at Montreal — Edm. Eskimos 7, Mtl. Wanderers 6. Total goals:
Mtl. Wanderers 13, Edm. Eskimos 10.

1906-07 — (March) — **Montreal Wanderers** — W. S. (Billy) Strachan, Riley Hern, Lester Patrick, Hod Stuart, Frank (Pud) Glass, Ernie Russell, Cecil Blachford (captain), Ernie (Moose) Johnson, Rod Kennedy, Jack Marshall, R. R. Boon (manager).
Scores: March 23 at Winnipeg — Mtl. Wanderers 7, Kenora 2; March 25 at Winnipeg — Kenora 6, Mtl. Wanderers 5. Total goals: Mtl. Wanderers 12, Kenora 8.

1906-07 — (January) — **Kenora Thistles** — Eddie Geroux, Art Ross, Si Griffis, Tom Hooper, Billy McGimsie, Roxy Beaudro, Tom Phillips.
Scores: January 17 at Montreal — Kenora 4, Mtl. Wanderers 2; Jan. 21 at Montreal — Kenora 8, Mtl. Wanderers 6.

1905-06 — (March) — **Montreal Wanderers** — H. Menard, Billy Strachan, Rod Kennedy, Lester Patrick, Frank (Pud) Glass, Ernie Russell Ernie (Moose) Johnson, Cecil Blachford (captain), Josh Arnold, R. R. Boon (manager).
Scores: March 14 at Montreal — Mtl. Wanderers 9, Ottawa 1; March 17 at Ottawa — Ottawa 9, Mtl. Wanderers 3. Total goals: Mtl. Wanderers 12, Ottawa 10. Wanderers accepted a challenge from New Glasgow, N.S., prior to the start of the 1906-07 season. Results: December 27 at Montreal — Mtl. Wanderers 10, New Glasgow 3; December 29 at Montreal — Mtl. Wanderers 7, New Glasgow 2.

1905-06 — (February) — **Ottawa Silver Seven** — Harvey Pulford (captain), Arthur Moore, Harry Westwick, Frank McGee, Alf Smith (playing coach), Billy Gilmour, Billy Hague, Percy LeSueur, Harry Smith, Tommy Smith, Dion, Ebbs.
Scores: February 27 at Ottawa — Ottawa 16, Queen's University 7; February 28 at Ottawa — Ottawa 12, Queen's University 7; March 6 at Ottawa — Ottawa 6, Smith's Falls 5; March 8 at Ottawa — Ottawa 8, Smith's Falls 2.

1904-05 — Ottawa Silver Seven — Dave Finnie, Harvey Pulford (captain), Arthur Moore, Harry Westwick, Frank McGee, Alf Smith (playing coach), Billy Gilmour, Frank White, Horace Gaul, Hamby Shore, Allen.
Scores: January 13 at Ottawa — Ottawa 9, Dawson City 2; January 16 at Ottawa — Ottawa 23, Dawson City 2; March 7 at Ottawa — Rat Portage 9, Ottawa 3; March 9 at Ottawa — Ottawa 4, Rat Portage 2; March 11 at Ottawa — Ottawa 5, Rat Portage 4.

1903-04 — Ottawa Silver Seven — S. C. (Suddy) Gilmour, Arthur Moore, Frank McGee, J.B. (Bouse) Hutton, H.L. (Billy) Gilmour, Jim McGee, Harry Westwick, E. H. (Harvey) Pulford (captain), Scott, A. T. (Alf) Smith (playing coach).
Scores: December 30 at Ottawa — Ottawa 9, Wpg. Rowing Club 1; January 1 at Ottawa — Wpg. Rowing Club 6, Ottawa 2; January 4 at Ottawa — Ottawa 2, Wpg. Rowing Club 0. February 23 at Ottawa — Ottawa 6, Tor. Malboros 3; February 25 at Ottawa — Ottawa 11, Tor. Marlboros 2; March 2 at Montreal — Ottawa 5, Mtl. Wanderers 5. Following the tie game, a new two-game series was ordered to be played in Ottawa but Wanderers refused unless the tie-game was replayed in Montreal. When no settlement could be reached, the series was abandoned and Ottawa retained the Cup and accepted a two-game challenge from Brandon. Results: (both games at Ottawa), March 9, Ottawa 6, Brandon 3; March 11, Ottawa 9, Brandon 3.

1902-03 — (March) — **Ottawa Silver Seven** — S. C. (Suddy) Gilmour, P.T. (Percy) Sims, J. B. (Bouse) Hutton, D. J. (Dave) Gilmour, H. L. (Billy) ilmour, Harry Westwick, Frank McGee, F. H. Wood, A. A. Fraser, Charles D. Spittal, E. H. (Harvey) Pulford (captain), Arthur Moore, A. T. (Alf) Smith (coach.)
Scores: March 7 at Montreal — Ottawa 1, Mtl. Victorias 1; March 10 at Ottawa — Ottawa 8, Mtl. Victorias 0. Total goals: Ottawa 9, Mtl. Victorias 1; March 12 at Ottawa — Ottawa 6, Rat Portage 2; March 14 at Ottawa — Ottawa 4, Rat Portage 2,

1902-03 — (February) — **Montreal AAA** — Tom Hodge, R.R. (Dickie) Boon, W.C. (Billy) Nicholson, Art Hooper, W.J. (Billy) Bellingham, Charles A. Liffiton, Jack Marshall, Jim Gardner, Cecil Blachford, George Smith.
Scores: January 29 at Montreal — Mtl. AAA 8, Wpg. Victorias 1; January 31 at Montreal — Wpg. Victorias 2, Mtl. AAA 2; February 2 at Montreal — Wpg. Victorias 4, Mtl. AAA 2; February 4 at Montreal — Mtl. AAA 5, Wpg. Victorias 1.

1901-02 — (March) — **Montreal AAA** — Tom Hodge, R. R. (Dickie) Boon, W.C. (Billy) Nicholson, Art Hooper, W. J. (Billy) Bellingham, Charles A. Liffiton, Jack Marshall, Roland Elliott, Jim Gardner.
Scores: March 13 at Winnipeg — Wpg. Victorias 1, Mtl. AAA 0; March 15 at Winnipeg — Mtl. AAA 5, Wpg. Victorias 0; March 17 at Winnipeg — Mtl. AAA 2, Wpg. Victorias 1.

1901-02 — (January) — **Winnipeg Victorias** — Burke Wood, A.B. (Tony) Gingras, Charles W. Johnstone, R.M. (Rod) Flett, Magnus L. Flett, Dan Bain (captain), Fred Scanlon, F. Cadham, G. Brown.
Scores: January 21 at Winnipeg — Wpg. Victorias 5, Tor Wellingtons 3; January 23 at Winnipeg — Wpg. Victorias 5, Tor. Wellingtons 3.

1900-01 — Winnipeg Victorias — Burke Wood, Jack Marshall, A.B. (Tony) Gingras, Charles W. Johnstone, R. M. (Rod) Flett, Magnus L. Flett, Dan Bain (captain), G. Brown.
Scores: January 29 at Montreal — Wpg. Victorias 4, Mtl. Shamrocks 3; January 31 at Montreal — Wpg. Victorias 2, Mtl. Shamrocks 1.

1899-1900 — Montreal Shamrocks — Joe McKenna, Frank Tansey, Frank Wall, Art Farrell, Fred Scanlon, Harry Trihey (captain), Jack Brannen.
Scores: February 12 at Montreal — Mtl. Shamrocks 4, Wpg. Victorias 3; February at Montreal — Wpg. Victorias 3, Mtl. Shamrocks 2; February 16 at Montreal — Mtl. Shamrocks 5, Wpg. Victorias 4; March 5 at Montreal — Mtl. Shamrocks 10, Halifax 2; March 7 at Montreal — Mtl. Shamrocks 11, Halifax 0.

1898-99 — (March) — **Montreal Shamrocks** — Joe McKenna, Frank Tansey, Frank Wall, Harry Trihey (captain), Art Farrell, Fred Scanlon, Jack Brannen, Dalby, Hoerner.
Scores: March 14 at Montreal — Mtl. Shamrocks 6, Queen's University 2.

1898-99 — (February) — **Montreal Victorias** — Gordon Lewis, Mike Grant, Graham Drinkwater, Cam Davidson, Bob McDougall, Ernie McLea, Frank Richardson, Jack Ewing, Russell Bowie, Douglas Acer, Fred McRobie.
Scores: February 15 at Montreal — Mtl. Victorias 2, Wpg. Victorias 1; February 18 at Montreal — Mtl. Victorias 3, Wpg. Victorias 2.

1897-98 — Montreal Victorias — Gordon Lewis, Hartland McDougall, Mike Grant, Graham Drinkwater, Cam Davidson, Bob McDougall, Ernie McLea, Frank Richardson (captain), Jack Ewing. The Victorias as champions of the Amateur Hockey Association, retained the Cup and were not called upon to defend it.

1896-97 — Montreal Victorias — Gordon Lewis, Harold Henderson, Mike Grant (captain), Cam Davidson, Graham Drinkwater, Robert McDougall, Ernie McLea, Shirley Davidson, Hartland McDougall, Jack Ewing, Percy Molson, David Gillilan, McLellan.
Scores: December 27 at Montreal — Mtl. Victorias 15, Ott. Capitals 2.

1895-96 — (December) — **Montreal Victorias** — Gordon Lewis, Harold Henderson, Mike Grant (captain), Robert McDougall, Graham Drinkwater, Shirley Davidson, Ernie McLea, Robert Jones, Cam Davidson, Hartland McDougall, David Gillilan, Reg Wallace, Stanley Willett.
Scores: December 30 at Winnipeg — Mtl. Victorias 6, Wpg. Victorias 5.

1895-96 — (February) — **Winnipeg Victorias** — G.H. Merritt, Rod Flett, Fred Higginbotham, Jack Armitage (captain), C.J. (Tote) Campbell, Dan Bain, Charles Johnstone, H. Howard.
Scores: February 14 at Montreal — Wpg. Victorias 2, Mtl. Victorias 0.

1894-95 — Montreal Victorias — Robert Jones, Harold Henderson, Mike Grant (captain), Shirley Davidson, Bob McDougall, Norman Rankin, Graham Drinkwater, Roland Elliot, William Pullan, Hartland McDougall, Arthur Fenwick, A. McDougall. Montreal Victorias as champions of the Amateur Hockey Association were prepared to defend the Stanley Cup. However, the Stanley Cup trustees had already accepted a challenge match between the 1894 champion Montreal AAA and Queen's University. It was declared that if Montreal AAA defeated Queen's University, Montreal Victorias would be declared Stanley Cup champions. If Queen's University won, the Cup would go to the university club. In a game played March 9, 1895, Montreal AAA defeated Queen's University 5-1. As a result, Montreal Victorias were awarded the Stanley Cup.

1893-94 — Montreal AAA — Herbert Collins, Allan Cameron, George James, Billy Barlow, Clare Mussen, Archie Hodgson, Haviland Routh, Alex Irving, James Stewart, A.C. (Toad) Waud, A. Kingan, E. O'Brien.
Scores: March 17 at Mtl. Victorias — Mtl. AAA 3, Mtl. Victorias 2; March 22 at Montreal — Mtl. AAA 3, Ott. Generals 1.

1892-93 — Montreal AAA — Tom Paton, James Stewart, Allan Cameron, Alex Irving, Haviland Routh, Archie Hodgson, Billy Barlow, A.B. Kingan, J. Lowe.
In accordance with the terms governing the presentation of the Stanley Cup, it was awarded for the first time to the Montreal AAA as champions of the Amateur Hockey Association in 1893. Once Montreal AAA had been declared holders of the Stanley Cup, any Canadian hockey team could challenge for the trophy.

All-Time NHL Playoff Formats

1917-18 — The regular-season was split into two halves. The winners of both halves faced each other in a two-game, total-goals series for the NHL championship and the right to meet the PCHA champion in the best-of-five Stanley Cup Finals.

1918-19 — Same as 1917-18, except that the Stanley Cup Finals was extended to a best-of-seven series.

1919-20 — Same as 1917-1918, except that Ottawa won both halves of the split regular-season schedule to earn an automatic berth into the best-of-five Stanley Cup Finals against the PCHA champions.

1921-22 — The top two teams at the conclusion of the regular-season faced each other in a two-game, total-goals series for the NHL championship. The NHL champion then moved on to play the winner of the PCHA-WCHL playoff series in the best-of-five Stanley Cup Finals.

1922-23 — The top two teams at the conclusion of the regular-season faced each other in a two-game, total-goals series for the NHL championship. The NHL champion then moved on to play the PCHA champion in the best-of-three Stanley Cup Semi-Finals, and the winner of the Semi-Finals played the WCHL champion, which had been given a bye, in the best-of-three Stanley Cup Finals.

1923-24 — The top two teams at the conclusion of the regular-season faced each other in a two-game, total-goals series for the NHL championship. The NHL champion then moved to play the loser of the PCHA-WCHL playoff (the winner of the PCHA-WCHL playoff earned a bye into the Stanley Cup Finals) in the best-of-three Stanley Cup Semi-Finals. The winner of this series met the PCHA-WCHL playoff winner in the best-of-three Stanley Cup Finals.

1924-25 — The first place team (Hamilton)at the conclusion of the regular-season was supposed to play the winner of a two-game, total goals series between the second (Toronto) and third (Montreal) place clubs. However, Hamilton refused to abide by this new format, demanding greater compensation than offered by the League. Thus, Toronto and Montreal played their two-game, total-goals series, and the winner (Montreal) earned the NHL title and then played the WCHL champion (Victoria) in the best-of-five Stanley Cup Finals.

1925-26 — The format which was intended for 1924-25 went into effect. The winner of the two-game, total-goals series between the second and third place teams squared off against the first place team in the two-game, total-goals NHL championship series. The NHL champion then moved on to play the WHL champion in the best-of-five Stanley Cup Finals.

After the 1925 season, the NHL was the only major professional hockey league still in existence and consequently took over sole control of the Stanley Cup competition.

1926-27 — The 10-team league was divided into two divisions — Candian and American — of five teams apiece. In each division, the winner of the two-game, total-goals series between the second and third place teams faced the first place team in a two-game, total-goals series for the division title. The two division title winners then met in the best-of-five Stanley Cup Finals.

1928-29 — Both first place teams in the two divisions played each other in a best-of-five series. Both second place teams in the two divisions played each other in a two-game, total-goals series as did the two third place teams. The winners of these latter two series then played each other in a best-of-three series for the right to meet the winner of the series between the two first place clubs. This Stanley Cup Finals was a best-of-three.

Series A: First in Canadian Division versus first in American (best-of-five)
Series B: Second in Canadian Division versus second in American (two-game, total-goals)
Series C: Third in Canadian Division versus third in American (two-game, total-goals)
Series D: Winner of Series B versus winner of Series C (best-of-three)
Series E: Winner of Series A versus winner of Series D (best of three) for Stanley Cup

1931-32 — Same as 1928-29, except that Series D was changed to a two-game, total-goals format and Series E was changed to best of five.

1936-37 — Same as 1931-32, except that Series B, C, and D were each best-of-three.

1938-39 — With the NHL reduced to seven teams, the two-division system was replaced by one seven-team league. Based on final regular-season standings, the following playoff format was adopted:

Series A: First versus Second (best-of-seven)
Series B: Third versus Fourth (best-of-three)
Series C: Fifth versus Sixth (best-of-three)
Series D: Winner of Series B versus winner of Series C (best-of-three)
Series E: Winner of Series A versus winner of Series D (best-of-seven)

1942-43 — With the NHL reduced to six teams (the "original six"), only the top four finishers qualified for playoff action. The best-of-seven Semi-Finals pitted Team #1 vs Team #3 and Team #2 vs Team #4. The winners of each Semi-Final series met in the best-of-seven Stanley Cup Finals.

1967-68 — When it doubled in size from 6 to 12 teams, the NHL once again was divided into two divisions — East and West — of six teams apiece. The top four clubs in each division qualified for the playoffs (all series were best-of-seven):

Series A; Team #1 (East) vs Team #3 (East)
Series B: Team #2 (East) vs Team #4 (East)
Series C: Team #1 (West) vs Team #3 (West)
Series D: Team #2 (West) vs Team #4 (West)
Series E: Winner of Series A vs winner of Series B
Series F: Winner of Series C vs winner of Series D
Series G: Winner of Series E vs Winner of Series F

1970-71 — Same as 1967-68 except that Series E mtched the winners of Series A and D, and Series F matched the winners of Series B and C.

1971-72 — Same as 1970-71, except that Series A and C matched Team #1 vs Team #4, and Series B and D matched Team #2 vs Team #3.

1974-75 — With the League now expanded to 18 teams in four divisions, a completely new playoff format was introduced. First, the #2 and #3 teams in each of the four divisions were pooled together in the Preliminary round. These eight (#2 and #3) clubs were ranked #1 to #8 based on regular-season record:

Series A: Team #1 vs Team #8 (best-of-three)
Series B: Team #2 vs Team #7 (best-of-three)
Series C: Team #3 vs Team #6 (best-of-three)
Series D: Team #4 vs Team #5 (best-of-three)
The winners of this Preliminary round then pooled together with the four division winners, which had received byes into this Quarter-Final round. These eight teams were again ranked #1 to #8 based on regular-season record:
Series E: Team #1 vs Team #8 (best-of-seven)
Series F: Team #2 vs Team #7 (best-of-seven)
Series G: Team #3 vs Team #6 (best-of-seven)
Series H: Team #4 vs Team #5 (best-of-seven)
The four Quarter-Finals winners, which moved on to the Semi-Finals, were then ranked #1 to #4 based on regular season record:
Series I: Team #1 vs Team #4 (best-of-seven)
Series J: Team #2 vs Team #3 (best-of-seven)
Series K: Winner of Series I vs winner of Series J (best-of-seven)

1977-78 — Same as 1974-75, except that the Preliminary round consisted of the #2 teams in the four divisions and the next four teams based on regular-season record (not their standings within their divisions).

1979-80 — With the addition of four WHA franchises, the League expanded its playoff structure to include 16 of its 21 teams. The four first place teams in the four divisions automatically earned playoff berths. Among the 17 other clubs, the top 12, according to regular-season record, also earned berths. All 16 teams were then pooled together and ranked #1 to #16 based on regular-season record:

Series A: Team #1 vs Team #16 (best-of-five)
Series B: Team #2 vs Team #15 (best-of-five)
Series C: Team #3 vs Team #14 (best-of-five)
Series D: Team #4 vs Team #13 (best-of-five)
Series E: Team #5 vs Team #12 (best-of-five)
Series F: Team #6 vs Team #11 (best-of-five)
Series G: Team #7 vs Team #10 (best-of-five)
Series H: Team #8 vs Team # 9 (best-of-five)
The eight Preliminary round winners, ranked #1 to #8 based on regular-season record, moved on to the Quarter-Finals:
Series I: Team #1 vs Team #8 (best-of-seven)
Series J: Team #2 vs Team #7 (best-of-seven)
Series K: Team #3 vs Team #6 (best-of-seven)
Series L: Team #4 vs Team #5 (best-of-seven)
The eight Quarter-Finals winners, ranked #1 to #4 based on regular-season record, moved on to the semi-finals:
Series M: Team #1 vs Team #4 (best-of-seven)
Series N: Team #2 vs Team #3 (best-of-seven)
Series O: Winner of Series M vs winner of Series N (best-of-seven)

1981-82 — The first four teams in each division earn playoff berths. In each division, the first-place team opposes the fourth-place team and the second-place team opposes the third-place team in a best-of-five Division Semi-Final series (DSF). In each division, the two winners of the DSF meet in a best-of-seven Division Final series (DF). The two winners in each conference meet in a best-of-seven Conference Final series (CF). In the Prince of Wales Conference, the Adams Division winner opposes the Patrick Division winner; in the Clarence Campbell Conference, the Smythe Division winner opposes the Norris Division winner. The two CF winners meet in a best-of-seven Stanley Cup Final (F) series.

1986-87 to date — Division Semi-Final series changed from best-of-five to best-of-seven.

Team Records

1918-1992

MOST STANLEY CUP CHAMPIONSHIPS:
22 — Montreal Canadiens 1924-30-31-44-46-53-56-57-58-59-60-65-66-68-69-71-73-76-77-78-79-86
13 — Toronto Maple Leafs 1918-22-32-42-45-47-48-49-51-62-63-64-67
7 — Detroit Red Wings 1936-37-43-50-52-54-55

MOST FINAL SERIES APPEARANCES:
32 — Montreal Canadiens in 75-year history.
21 — Toronto Maple Leafs in 75-year history.
18 — Detroit Red Wings in 66-year history.

MOST YEARS IN PLAYOFFS:
67 — Montreal Canadiens in 75-year history.
54 — Toronto Maple Leafs in 75-year history.
53 — Boston Bruins in 68-year history.

MOST CONSECUTIVE STANLEY CUP CHAMPIONSHIPS:
5 — Montreal Canadiens (1956-57-58-59-60)
4 — Montreal Canadiens (1976-77-78-79)
— NY Islanders (1980-81-82-83)

MOST CONSECUTIVE FINAL SERIES APPEARANCES:
10 — Montreal Canadiens (1951-60, inclusive)

MOST CONSECUTIVE PLAYOFF APPEARANCES:
25 — Boston Bruins (1968-92, inclusive)
23 — Chicago Blackhawks (1970-92, inclusive)
22 — Montreal Canadiens (1971-92, inclusive)
21 — Montreal Canadiens (1949-69, inclusive)
20 — Detroit Red Wings (1939-58, inclusive)

MOST GOALS BOTH TEAMS, ONE PLAYOFF SERIES:
69 — Edmonton Oilers, Chicago Blackhawks in 1985 CF. Edmonton won best-of-seven series 4-2, outscoring Chicago 44-25.
62 — Chicago Blackhawks, Minnesota North Stars in 1985 DF. Chicago won best-of-seven series 4-2, outscoring Minnesota 33-29.
60 — Edmonton Oilers, Calgary Flames in 1984 DF. Edmonton won best-of-seven series 4-3, outscoring Calgary 33-27.

MOST GOALS ONE TEAM, ONE PLAYOFF SERIES:
44 — Edmonton Oilers in 1985 CF. Edmonton won best-of-seven series 4-2, outscoring Chicago 44-25.
35 — Edmonton Oilers in 1983 DF. Edmonton won best-of-seven series 4-1, outscoring Calgary 35-13.

MOST GOALS, BOTH TEAMS, TWO-GAME SERIES:
17 — Toronto St. Patricks, Montreal Canadiens in 1918 NHL F. Toronto won two-game tota goal series 10-7.
15 — Boston Bruins, Chicago Blackhawks in 1927 QF. Boston won two-game total goal series 10-5.
— Pittsburgh Penguins, St. Louis Blues in 1975 PR. Pittsburgh won best-of-three series 2-0, outscoring St. Louis 9-6.

MOST GOALS, ONE TEAM, TWO-GAME SERIES:
11 — Buffalo Sabres in 1977 PR. Buffalo won best-of-three series 2-0, outscoring Minnesota 11-3.
— Toronto Maple Leafs in 1978 PR. Toronto won best-of-three series 2-0, outscoring Los Angeles 11-3.
10 — Boston Bruins in 1927 QF. Boston won two-game total goal series 10-5.

MOST GOALS, BOTH TEAMS, THREE-GAME SERIES:
33 — Minnesota North Stars, Boston Bruins in 1981 PR. Minnesota won best-of-five series 3-0, outscoring Boston 20-13.
31 — Chicago Blackhawks, Detroit Red Wings in 1985 DSF. Chicago won best-of-five series 3-0, outscoring Detroit 23-8.
28 — Toronto Maple Leafs, NY Rangers in 1932 F. Toronto won best-of-five series 3-0, outscoring New York 18-10.

MOST GOALS, ONE TEAM, THREE-GAME SERIES:
23 — Chicago Blackhawks in 1985 DSF. Chicago won best-of-five series 3-0, outscoring Detroit 23-8.
20 — Minnesota North Stars in 1981 PR. Minnesota won best-of-five series 3-0, outscoring Boston 20-13.
— NY Islanders in 1981 PR. New York won best-of-five series 3-0, outscorig Toronto 20-4.

MOST GOALS, BOTH TEAMS, FOUR-GAME SERIES:
36 — Boston Bruins, St. Louis Blues in 1972 SF. Boston won best-of-seven series 4-0, outscoring St. Louis 28-8.
— Edmonton Oilers, Chicago Blackhawks in 1983 CF. Edmonton won best-of-seven series 4-0, outscoring Chicago 25-11.
— Minnesota North Stars, Toronto Maple Leafs in 1983 DSF. Minnesota won best-of-five series 3-1; teams tied i scoring 18-18.
35 — NY Rangers, Los Angeles Kings in 1981 PR. NY Rangers won best-of-five series 3-1, outscoring Los Angeles 23-12.

MOST GOALS, ONE TEAM, FOUR-GAME SERIES:
28 — Boston Bruins in 1972 SF. Boston won best-of-seven series 4-0, outscoring St. Louis 28-8.

MOST GOALS, BOTH TEAMS, FIVE-GAME SERIES:
52 — Edmonton Oilers, Los Angeles Kings in 1987 DSF. Edmonton won best-of-seven series 4-1, outscoring Los Angeles 32-20.
50 — Los Angeles Kings, Edmonton Oilers in 1982 DSF. Los Angeles won best-of-five series 3-2, outscoring Edmonton 27-23.
48 — Edmonton Oilers, Calgary Flames in 1983 DF. Edmonton won best-of-seven series 4-1, outscoring Calgary 35-13.
— Calgary Flames, Los Angeles Kings in 1988 DSF. Calgary won best-of-seven series 4-1, outscoring Los Angeles 30-18.

MOST GOALS, ONE TEAM, FIVE-GAME SERIES:
35 — Edmonton Oilers in 1983 DF. Edmonton won best-of-seven series 4-1, outscoring Calgary 35-13.
32 — Edmonton Oilers in 1987 DSF. Edmonton won best-of-seven series 4-1, outscoring Los Angeles 32-20.
28 — NY Rangers in 1979 QF. NY Rangers won best-of-seven series 4-1, outscoring Philadelphia 28-8.
27 — Philadelphia Flyers in 1980 SF. Philadelphia won best-of-seven series 4-1, outscoring Minnesota 27-14.
— Los Angeles Kings, in 1982 DSF. Los Angeles won best-of-five series 3-2, outscoring Edmonton 27-23.

MOST GOALS, BOTH TEAMS, SIX-GAME SERIES:
69 — Edmonton Oilers, Chicago Blackhawks in 1985 CF. Edmonton won best-of-seven series 4-2, outscoring Chicago 44-25.
62 — Chicago Blackhawks, Minnesota North Stars in 1985 DF. Chicago won best-of-seven series 4-2, outscoring Minnesota 33-29.
56 — Montreal Canadiens, Chicago Blackhawks in 1973 F. Montreal won best-of-seven series 4-2, outscoring Chicago 33-23.

MOST GOALS, ONE TEAM, SIX-GAME SERIES:
44 — Edmonton Oilers in 1985 CF. Edmonton won best-of-seven series 4-2, outscoring Chicago 44-25.
33 — Chicago Blackhawks in 1985 DF. Chicago won best-of-seven series 4-2, outscoring Minnesota 33-29.
— Montreal Canadiens in 1973 F. Montreal won best-of-seven series 4-2, outscoring Chicago 33-23.

MOST GOALS, BOTH TEAMS, SEVEN-GAME SERIES:
60 — Edmonton Oilers, Calgary Flames in 1984 DF. Edmonton won best-of-seven series 4-3, outscoring Calgary 33-27.

MOST GOALS, ONE TEAM, SEVEN-GAME SERIES:
33 — Philadelphia Flyers in 1976 QF. Philadelphia won best-of-seven series 4-3, outscoring Toronto 33-23.
— Boston Bruins in 1983 DF. Boston won best-of-seven series 4-3, outscoring Buffalo 33-23.
— Edmonton Oilers in 1984 DF. Edmonton won best-of-seven series 4-3, outscoring Calgary 33-27.

FEWEST GOALS, BOTH TEAMS, TWO-GAME SERIES:
1 — NY Rangers, NY Americans, in 1929 SF. NY Rangers defeated NY Americans 1-0 in two-game, total-goal series.
— Mtl. Maroons, Chicago Blackhawks in 1935 SF. Mtl. Maroons defeated Chicago 1-0 in two-game, total-goal series.

FEWEST GOALS, ONE TEAM, TWO-GAME SERIES:
0 — NY Americans in 1929 SF. Lost two-game total-goal series 1-0 against NY Rangers.
— Chicago Blackhawks in 1935 SF. Lost two-game total-goal series 1-0 against Mtl. Maroons.
— Mtl. Maroons in 1937 SF. Lost best-of-three series 2-0 to NY Rangers while being outscored 5-0.
— NY Americans in 1939 QF. Lost best-of-three series 2-0 to Toronto while being outscored 6-0.

FEWEST GOALS, BOTH TEAMS, THREE-GAME SERIES:
7 — Boston Bruins, Montreal Canadiens in 1929 SF. Boston won best-of-five series 3-0, outscoring Montreal 5-2.
— Detroit Red Wings, Mtl. Maroons in 1936 SF. Detroit won best-of-five series 3-0, outscoring Mtl. Maroons 6-1.

FEWEST GOALS, ONE TEAM, THREE-GAME SERIES:
1 — Mtl. Maroons in 1936 SF. Lost best-of-five series 3-0 to Detroit and were outscored 6-1.

FEWEST GOALS, BOTH TEAMS, FOUR-GAME SERIES:
9 — Toronto Maple Leafs, Boston Bruins in 1935 SF. Toronto won best-of-five series 3-1, outscoring Boston 7-2.

FEWEST GOALS, ONE TEAM, FOUR-GAME SERIES:
2 — Boston Bruins in 1935 SF. Toronto won best-of-five series 3-1, outscoring Boston 7-2.
— Montreal Canadiens in 1952 F. Detroit won best-of-seven series 4-0, outscoring Montreal 11-2.

FEWEST GOALS, BOTH TEAMS, FIVE-GAME SERIES:
11 — NY Rangers, Mtl. Maroons in 1928 F. NY Rangers won best-of-five series 3-2 , while outscored by Mtl. Maroons 6-5.

FEWEST GOALS, ONE TEAM, FIVE-GAME SERIES:
5 — NY Rangers in 1928 F. NY Rangers won best-of-five series 3-2, while outscored by Mtl. Maroons 6-5.

FEWEST GOALS, BOTH TEAMS, SIX-GAME SERIES:
22 — Toronto Maple Leafs, Boston Bruins in 1951 SF. Toronto won best-of-seven series 4-1 with 1 tie, outscoring Boston 17-5.

FEWEST GOALS, ONE TEAM, SIX-GAME SERIES:
5 — Boston Bruins in 1951 SF. Toronto won best-of-seven series 4-1 with 1 tie, outscoring Boston 17-5.

FEWEST GOALS, BOTH TEAMS, SEVEN-GAME SERIES:
18 — Toronto Maple Leafs, Detroit Red Wings in 1945 F. Toronto won best-of-seven series 4-3; teams tied in scoring 9-9.

FEWEST GOALS, ONE TEAM, SEVEN-GAME SERIES:

9 — Toronto Maple Leafs, in 1945 F. Toronto won best-of- seven series 4-3; teams tied in scoring 9-9.

— Detroit Red Wings, in 1945 F. Toronto won best-of-seven series 4-3; teams tied in scoring 9-9.

MOST GOALS, BOTH TEAMS, ONE GAME:

18 — Los Angeles Kings, Edmonton Oilers at Edmonton, April 7, 1982. Los Angeles 10, Edmonton 8. Los Angeles won best-of-five DSF 3-2.

17 — Pittsburgh Penguins, Philadelphia Flyers at Pittsburgh, April 25, 1989. Pittsburgh 10, Philadelphia 7. Philadelphia won best-of-seven DF 4-3.

16 — Edmonton Oilers, Los Angeles Kings at Edmonton, April 9, 1987. Edmonton 13, Los Angeles 3. Edmonton won best-of-seven DSF 4-1.

— Los Angeles Kings, Calgary Flames at Los Angeles, April 10, 1990. Los Angeles 12, Calgary 4. Los Angeles won best-of-seven DF 4-2.

MOST GOALS, ONE TEA, ONE GAME:

13 — Edmonton Oilers at Edmonton, April 9, 1987. Edmonton 13, Los Angeles 3. Edmonton won best-of-seven DSF 4-1.

12 — Los Angeles Kings at Los Angeles, April 10, 1990. Los Angeles 12, Calgary 4. Los Angeles won best-of-seven DSF 4-2.

11 — Montreal Canadiens at Montreal, March 30, 1944. Montreal 11, Toronto 0. Canadiens won best-of-seven SF 4-1.

— Edmonton Oilers at Edmonton May 4, 1985. Edmonton 11, Chicago 2. Edmonton won best-of-seven CF 4-2.

MOST GOALS, BOTH TEAMS, ONE PERIOD:

9 — NY Rangers, Philadelphia Flyers, April 24, 1979, at Philadelphia, third period. NY Rangers won 8-3 scoring six of nine third-period goals.

— **Los Angeles Kings, Calgary Flames** at Los Angeles, April 10, 1990, second period. Los Angeles won game 12-4, scoring five of nine second-period goals.

8 — Chicago Blackhawks, Montreal Canadiens at Montreal, May 8, 1973, in the second period. Chicago won 8-7 scoring five of eight second-period goals.

— Chicago Blackhawks, Edmonton Oilers at Chicago, May 12, 1985 in the first period. Chicago won 8-6, scoring five of eight first-period goals.

— Edmonton Oilers, Winnipeg Jets at Edmonton, April 6, 1988 in the third period. Edmonton won 7-4, scoring six of eight third period goals.

— Hartford Whalers, Montreal Canadiens at Hartford, April 10, 1988 in the third period. Hartford won 7-5, scoring five of eight third period goals.

MOST GOALS, ONE TEAM, ONE PERIOD:

7 — Montreal Canadiens, March 30, 1944, at Montreal in third period, during 11-0 win against Toronto.

LONGEST OVERTIME:

116 Minutes, 30 Seconds — Detroit Red Wings, Mtl. Maroons at Montreal, March 24, 25, 1936. Detroit 1, Mtl. Maroons 0. Mud Bruneteau scored, assisted by Hec Kilrea, at 16:30 of sixth overtime period, or after 176 minutes, 30 seconds from start of game, which ended at 2:25 a.m. Detroit won best-of-five SF 3-0.

Brian Skrudland holds the record for the fastest overtime goal in playoff competition, scoring on Calgary's Mike Vernon nine seconds into extra time on May 18, 1986.

SHORTEST OVERTIME:

9 Seconds — Montreal Canadiens, Calgary Flames, at Calgary, May 18, 1986. Montreal won 3-2 on Brian Skrudland's goal and captured the best-of-seven F 4-1.

11 Seconds — NY Islanders, NY Rangers, at NY Rangers, April 11, 1975. NY Islanders won 4-3 on Jean-Paul Parise's goal and captured the best-of-three PR 2-1.

MOST OVERTIME GAMES, ONE PLAYOFF YEAR:

16 — 1982. Of 71 games played, 16 went into overtime.

FEWEST OVERTIME GAMES, ONE PLAYOFF YEAR:

0 — 1963. None of the 16 games went into overtime, the only year since 1926 that no overtime was required in any playoff series.

MOST OVERTIME-GAME VICTORIES, ONE TEAM, ONE PLAYOFF YEAR:

6 — NY Islanders, 1980. One against Los Angeles in the PR; two against Boston in the QF; one against Buffalo in the SF; and two against Philadelphia in the F. Islanders played 21 games.

MOST OVERTIME GAMES, FINAL SERIES:

5 — Toronto Maple Leafs,, Montreal Canadiens in 1951. Toronto defeated Montreal 4-1 in best-of-seven series.

MOST OVERTIME GAMES, SEMI-FINAL SERIES:

4 — Toronto Maple Leafs, Boston Bruins in 1933. Toronto won best-of-five series 3-2.

— Boston Bruins, NY Rangers in 1939.BBoston won best-of-seven series 4-3.

— St. Louis Blues, Minnesota North Stars in 1968. St. Louis won best-of-seven series 4-3.

MOST GAMES PLAYED BY ALL TEAMS, ONE PLAYOFF YEAR:

92 — 1991. There were 51 DSF, 24 DF, 11 CF and 6 F games.

87 — 1987. There were 44 DSF, 25 DF, 11 CF and 7 F games.

86 — 1992. There were 54 DSF, 20 DF, 8 CF and 4 F games.

85 — 1990. There were 49 DSF, 21 DF, 10 CF and 5 F games.

83 — 1988. There were 46 DSF, 27 DF, 12 CF and 4 F games.

MOST GAMES PLAYED, ONE TEAM, ONE PLAYOFF YEAR:

26 — Philadelphia Flyers, 1987. Won DSF 4-2 against NY Rangers, DF 4-3 against NY Islanders, CF 4-2 against Montreal, and lost F 4-3 against Edmonton.

24 — Pittsburgh Penguins,1991. Won DSF 4-3 against New Jersey, DF 4-1 against Washington, CF 4-2 against Boston, and F 4-2 against Minnesota.

23 — Minnesota North Stars, 1991. Won DSF 4-2 against Chicago, DF 4-2 against St. Louis, CF 4-1 against Edmonton, and lost F 4-2 against Pittsburgh.

MOST ROAD VICTORIES, ONE TEAM, ONE PLAYOFF YEAR:

8 — NY Islanders, 1980. Won two at Los Angeles in PR; three at Boston in QF; two at Buffalo in SF; and one at Philadelphia in F series.

— Philadelphia Flyers, 1987. Won two at NY Rangers in DSF; two at NY Islanders in DF; three at Montreal in CF; and one at Edmonton in F series.

— Edmonton Oilers, 1990. Won one at Winnipeg in DSF; two at Los Angeles in DF; two at Chicago in CF and three at Boston in F series.

— Pittsburgh Penguins, 1992. Won two at Washington in DSF; two at NY Rangers in DF; two at Boston in CF; and two at Chicago in F series.

MOST HOME VICTORIES, ONE TEAM, ONE PLAYOFF YEAR:

11 — Edmonton Oilers, 1988

10 — Edmonton Oilers, 1985 in 10 home-ice games.

— Montreal Canadiens, 1986

9 — Philadelphia Flyers, 1974

— Philadelphia Flyers, 1980

— NY Islanders, 1981

— NY Islanders, 1983

— Edmonton Oilers, 1984

— Edmonton Oilers, 1987

— Calgary Flames, 1989

— Pittsburgh Penguins, 1991

MOST ROAD VICTORIES, ALL TEAMS, ONE PLAYOFF YEAR:

46 — 1987. Of 87 games played, road teams won 46 (22 DSF, 14 DF, 8 CF and 2 Stanley Cup).

MOST CONSECUTIVE PLAYOFF GAME VICTORIES:

12 — Edmonton Oilers. Streak began May 15, 1984 at Edmonton with a 7-2 win over NY Islanders in third game of F series, and ended May 9, 1985 when Chicago defeated Edmonton 5-2 at Chicago. Included in the streak were three wins over the NY Islanders, in 1984, three over Los Angeles, four over Winnipeg and two over Chicago, all in 1985.

11 — Montreal Canadiens. Streak began April 16, 1959, at Toronto with 3-2 win in fourth game of F series, won by Montreal 4-1, and ended March 23, 1961, when Chicago defeated Montreal 4-3 in second game of SF series. Included in streak were eight straight victories in 1960.

— Montreal Canadiens. Streak began April 28, 1968, at Montreal with 4-3 win in fifth game of SF series, won by Montreal 4-1, and ended April 17, 1969, at Boston when Boston defeated them 5-0 in third game of SF series. Included in the streak were four straight wins over St. Louis in the 1968 F and four straight wins over NY Rangers in a 1969 QF series.

— Boston Bruins. Streak began April 14, 1970, at Boston with 3-2 victory over NY Rangers in fifth game of a QF series, won by Boston 4-2. It continued with a four-game victory over Chicago in the 1970 SF and a four-game win over St. Louis in the 1970 F. Boston then won the first game of a 1971 QF series against Montreal. Montreal ended the streak April 8, 1971, at Boston with a 7-5 victory.

— Montreal Canadiens. Streak started May 6, 1976, at Montreal with 5-2 win in fifth game of a SF series against NY Islanders, won by Montreal 4-1. Continued with a four-game sweep over Philadelphia in the 1976 F and a four-game win against St. Louis in the 1977 QF. Montreal won the first two games of a 1977 SF series against the NY Islanders before NY Islanders ended the streak, April 2, 1977 at New York with a 5-3 victory.

— Chicago Blackhawks. Streak started April 24, 1992, at St. Louis with a 5-3 win in fourth game of a DSF series against St. Louis, won by Chicago 4-2. Continued with a four-game sweep over Detroit in the 1992 DF and a four-game win over Edmonton in the 1992 CF. Pittsburgh ended the streak May 26, 1992, at Pittsburgh with a 5-4 victory.

— Pittsburgh Penguins. Streak started May 9, 1992, at Pittsburgh with a 5-4 in fourth game of a DF series against NY Rangers, won by Pittsburgh 4-2. Continued with a four-game sweep over Boston in the 1992 CF and a four-game win over Chicago in the 1992 F.

MOST CONSECUTIVE VICTORIES, ONE PLAYOFF YEAR:
11 — Chicago Blackhawks in 1992. Chicago won last three games of best-of-seven DSF against St. Louis to win series 4-2 and then defeated Detroit 4-0 in best-of-seven DF and Edmonton 4-0 in best-of-seven CF.
— Pittsburgh Penguins in 1992. Pittsburgh won last three games of best-of-seven DF against NY Rangers to win series 4-2 and then defeated Boston 4-0 in best-of-seven CF and Chicago 4-0 in best-of-seven F.

LONGEST PLAYOFF LOSING STREAK:
16 Games — Chicago Blackhawks. Streak started in 1975 QF against Buffalo when Chicago lost last two games. Then Chicago lost four games to Montreal in 1976 QF; two games to NY Islanders in 1977 PR; four games to Boston in 1978 QF and four games to NY Islanders in 1979 QF. Streak ended on April 8, 1980 when Chicago defeated St. Louis 3-2 in the opening game of their 1980 PR series.
12 Games — Toronto Maple Leafs. Streak started on April 16, 1979 as Toronto lost four straight games in a QF series against Montreal. Continued with three-game PR defeats versus Philadelphia and NY Islanders in 1980 and 1981 respectively. Toronto failed to qualify for the 1982 playoffs and lost the first two games of a 1983 DSF against Minnesota. Toronto ended the streak with a 6-3 win against the North Stars on April 9, 1983.
10 Games — NY Rangers. Streak started in 1968 QF against Chicago when NY Rangers lost last four games and continued through 1969 (four straight losses to Montreal in QF) and 1970 (two straight losses to Boston in QF) before ending with a 4-3 win against Boston, at New York, April 11, 1970.
— Philadelphia Flyers. Streak started on April 18, 1968, the last game in the 1968 QF series against St. Louis, and continued through 1969 (four straight losses to St. Louis in QF), 1971 (four straight losses to Chicago in QF) and 1973 (opening game loss to Minnesota in QF) before ending with a 4-1 win against Minnesota, at Philadelphia, April 5, 1973.

MOST SHUTOUTS, ONE PLAYOFF YEAR, ALL TEAMS:
12 — 1992. Of 86 games played, Detroit, Edmonton and Vancouver had 2 each, while Boston, Buffalo, Chicago, Montreal, NY Rangers and Pittsburgh had 1 each.
8 — 1937. Of 17 games played, NY Rangers had 4. Detroit 3, Boston 1.
— 1975. Of 51 games played, Philadelphia had 5, Montreal 2, NY Islanders 1.
— 1980. Of 67 games played, Buffalo had 3, Philadelphia 2, Montreal, NY Islanders and Minnesota 1 each.
— 1984. Of 70 games played, Montreal had 3, Edmonton, Minnesota, NY Rangers, St. Louis and Vancouver 1 each.

FEWEST SHUTOUTS, ONE PLAYOFF YEAR, ALL TEAMS:
0 — 1959. 18 games played.

MOST SHUTOUTS, BOTH TEAMS, ONE SERIES:
5 — 1945 F, Toronto Maple Leafs, Detroit Red Wings. Toronto had 3 shutouts, Detroit 2. Toronto won best-of-seven series 4-3.
— 1950 SF, Toronto Maple Leafs, Detroit Red Wings. Toronto had 3 shutouts, Detroit 2. Detroit won best-of-seven series 4-3.

MOST PENALTIES, BOTH TEAMS, ONE SERIES:
219 — New Jersey Devils, Washington Capitals in 1988 DF won by New Jersey 4-3. New Jersey received 98 minors, 11 majors, 9 misconducts and 1 match penalty. Washington received 80 minors, 11 majors, 8 misconducts and 1 match penalty.

MOST PENALTY MINUTES, BOTH TEAMS, ONE SERIES:
656 — New Jersey Devils, Washington Capitals in 1988 DF won by New Jersey 4-3. New Jersey had 351 minutes; Washington 305.

MOST PENALTIES, ONE TEAM, ONE SERIES:
119 — New Jersey Devils in 1988 DF versus Washington. New Jersey received 98 minors, 11 majors, 9 misconducts and 1 match penalty.

MOST PENALTY MINUTES, ON TEAM, ONE SERIES:
351 — New Jersey Devils in 1988 DF versus Washington. Series won by New Jersey 4-3.

MOST PENALTY MINUTES, BOTH TEAMS, ONE GAME:
298 Minutes — Detroit Red Wings, St. Louis Blues, at St. Louis, April 12, 1991. Detroit received 33 penalties for 152 minutes; St. Louis 33 penalties for 146 minutes. St. Louis won 6-1.
267 Minutes — NY Rangers, Los Angeles Kings, at Los Angeles, April 9, 1981. NY Rangers received 31 penalties for 142 minutes; Los Angeles 28 penalties for 125 minutes. Los Angeles won 5-4.

MOST PENALTIES, BOTH TEAMS, ONE GAME:
66 — Detroit Red Wings, St. Louis Blues, at St. Louis, April 12, 1991. Detroit received 33 penalties; St. Louis 33. St. Louis won 6-1.
62 — New Jersey Devils, Washington Capitals, at New Jersey, April 22, 1988. New Jersey received 32 penalties; Washington 30. New Jersey won 10-4.

MOST PENALTIES, ONE TEAM, ONE GAME:
33 — Detroit Red Wings, at St. Louis, April 12,1991. St. Louis won 6-1.
— St. Louis Blues, at St. Louis, April 12, 1991. St. Louis won 6-1.
32 — New Jersey Devils, at Washington, April 22,1988. New Jersey won 10-4.
31 — NY Rangers, at Los Angeles, April 9, 1981. Los Angeles won 5-4.
30 — Philadelphia Flyers, at Toronto, April 15, 1976. Toronto won 5-4.

MOST PENALTY MINUTES, ONE TEAM, ONE GAME:
152 — Detroit Red Wings, at St. Louis, April 12, 1991. St. Louis won 6-1.
146 — St. Louis Blues, at St. Louis, April 12, 1991. St. Louis won 6-1.
142 — NY Rangers, at Los Angeles, April 9, 1981. Los Angeles won 5-4.

MOST PENALTIES, BOTH TEAMS, ONE PERIOD:
43 — NY Rangers, Los Angeles Kings, April 9, 1981, at Los Angeles, first period. NY Rangers had 24 penalties; Los Angeles 19. Los Angeles won 5-4.

MOST PENALTY MINUTES, BOTH TEAMS, ONE PERIOD:
248 — NY Islanders, Boston Bruins, April 17, 1980, first period, at Boston. Each team received 124 minutes. Islanders won 5-4.

MOST PENALTIES, ONE TEAM, ONE PERIOD: (AND) MOST PENALTY MINUTES, ONE TEAM, ONE PERIOD:
24 Penalties; 125 Minutes — NY Rangers, April 9, 1981, at Los Angeles, first period. Los Angeles won 5-4.

FEWEST PENALTIES, BOTH TEAMS, BEST-OF-SEVEN SERIES:
19 — Detroit Red Wings, Toronto Maple Leafs in 1945 F, won by Toronto 4-3. Detroit received 10 minors. Toronto 9 minors.

FEWEST PENALTIES, ONE TEAM, BEST-OF-SEVEN SERIES:
9 — Toronto Maple Leafs in 1945 F, won by Toronto 4-3 against Detroit.

MOST POWER-PLAY GOALS BY ALL TEAMS, ONE PLAYOFF YEAR:
~~199~~1988 in 83 games.

MOST POWER-PLAY GOALS, ONE TEAM, ONE PLAYOFF YEAR:
35 — Minnesota North Stars, 1991 in 23 games.
32 — Edmonton Oilers, 1988 in 18 games.
31 — NY Islanders, 1981, in 18 games.

MOST POWER-PLAY GOALS, BOTH TEAMS, ONE SERIES:
21 — NY Islanders, Philadelphia Flyers in 1980 F, won by NY Islanders 4-2. NY Islanders had 15 and Flyers 6.
— NY Islanders, Edmonton Oilers in 1981 QF, won by NY Islanders 4-2. NY Islanders had 13 and Edmonton 8.
— Philadelphia Flyers, Pittsburgh Penguins in 1989 DF, won by Philadelphia 4-3. Philadelphia had 11 and Pittsburgh 10.
— Minnesota North Stars, Chicago Blackhawks in 1991 DSF, won by Minnesota 4-2. Minnesota had 15 and Chicago 6.
20 — Toronto Maple Leafs, Philadelphia Flyers in 1976 QF series won by Philadelphia 4-3. Toronto had 12 power-pay goals; Philadelphia 8.

MOST POWER-PLAY GOALS, ONE TEAM, ONE SERIES:
15 — NY Islanders in 1980 F against Philadelphia. NY Islanders won series 4-2.
— Minnesota North Stars in 1991 DSF against Chicago. Minnesota won series 4-2.
13 — NY Islanders in 1981 QF against Edmonton. NY Islanders won series 4-2.
— Calgary Flames in 1986 CF against St. Louis. Calgary won series 4-3.
12 — Toronto Maple Leafs in 1976 QF series won by Philadelphia 4-3.

MOST POWER-PLAY GOALS, BOTH TEAMS, ONE GAME:
8 — Minnesota North Stars, St. Louis Blues, April 24, 1991 at Minnesota. Minnesota had 4, St. Louis 4. Minnesota won 8-4.
7 — Minnesota North Stars, Edmonton Oilers, April 28, 1984 at Minnesota. Minnesota had 4, Edmonton 3. Edmonton won 8-5.
— Philadelphia Flyers, NY Rangers, April 13, 1985 at New York. Philadelphia had 4, NY Rangers 3. Philadelphia won 6-5.
— Edmonton Oilers, Chicago Blackhawks, May 14, 1985 at Edmonton. Chicago had 5, Edmonton 2. Edmonton won 10-5.
— Edmonton Oilers, Los Angeles Kings, April 9, 1987 at Edmonton. Edmonton had 5, Los Angeles 2. Edmonton won 13-3.
— Vancouver Canucks, Calgary Flames, April 9, 1989 at Vancouver. Vancouver had 4, Calgary 3. Vancouver won 5-3.

MOST POWER-PLAY GOALS, ONE TEAM, ONE GAME:
6 — Boston Bruins, April 2, 1969, at Boston against Toronto. Boston won 10-0.

MOST POWER-PLAY GOALS, BOTH TEAMS, ONE PERIOD:
5 — Minnesota North Stars, Edmonton Oilers, April 28, 1984, second period, at Minnesota. Minnesota had 4 and Edmonton 1. Edmonton won 8-5.
— Vancouver Canucks, Calgary Flames, April 9, 1989, third period at Vancouver. Vancouver had 3 and Calgary 2. Vancouver won 5-3.
— Minnesota North Stars, St. Louis Blues, April 24, 1991, second period, at Minnesota. Minnesota had 4 and St. Louis 1. Minnesota won 8-4.

MOST POWER-PLAY GOALS, ONE TEAM, ONE PERIOD:
4 — Toronto Maple Leafs, March 26, 1936, second period against Boston at Toronto. Toronto won 8-3.
— Minnesota North Stars, April 28, 1984, second period against Edmonton at Minnesota. Edmonton won 8-5.
— Boston Bruins, April 11, 1991, third period against Hartford at Boston. Boston won 6-1.
— Minnesota North Stars, April 24, 1991, second period against St. Louis at Minnesota. Minnesota won 8-4.

MOST SHORTHAND GOALS BY ALL TEAMS, ONE PLAYOFF YEAR:
33 — 1988, in 83 games.

MOST SHORTHAND GOALS, ONE TEAM, ONE PLAYOFF YEAR:
10 — Edmonton Oilers 1983, in 16 games.
9 — NY Islanders, 1981, in 19 games.
8 — Philadelphia Flyers, 1989, in 19 games.
7 — NY Islanders, 1980, in 21 games.
7 — Chicago Blackhawks, 1989, in 16 games.

MOST SHORTHAND GOALS, BOTH TEAMS, ONE SERIES:
7 — Boston Bruins (4), NY Rangers (3), in 1958 SF, won by Boston 4-2.
— Edmonton Oilers (5), Calgary Flames (2), in 1983 DF won by Edmonton 4-1.

MOST SHORTHAND GOALS, ONE TEAM, ONE SERIES:
5 — Edmonton Oilers in 1983 against Calgary in best-of-seven DF won by Edmonton 4-1.
— NY Rangers in 1979 against Philadelphia in best-of-seven QF, won by NY Rangers 4-1.
4 — Boston Bruins in 1958 against NY Rangers in best-of-seven SF series, won by Boston 4-2.
— Minnesota North Stars in 1981 against Calgary in best-of-seven SF, won by Minnesota 4-2.
— Chicago Blackhawks in 1989 against Detroit in best-of-seven DSF won by Chicago 4-2.
— Philadelphia Flyers in 1989 against Pittsburgh in best-of-seven DF won by Philadelphia 4-3.
— NY Rangers in 1992 against New Jersey in best-of-seven DSF won by NY Rangers 4-3.

MOST SHORTHAND GOALS, BOTH TEAMS, ONE GAME:
4 — NY Islanders, NY Rangers, April 17, 1983 at NY Rangers. NY Islanders had 3 shorthand goals, NY Rangers 1. NY Rangers won 7-6.
— Boston Bruins, Minnesota North Stars, April 11, 1981, at Minnesota. Boston had 3 shorthand goals, Minnesota 1. Minnesota won 6-3.
3 — Toronto Maple Leafs, Detroit Red Wings, April 5, 1947, at Toronto. Toronto had 2 shorthand goals, Detroit 1. Toronto won 6-1.
— NY Rangers, Boston Bruins, April 1, 1958, at Boston. NY Rangers had 2 shorthand goals, Boston 1. NY Rangers won 5-2.
— Minnesota North Stars, Philadelphia Flyers, May 4, 1980, at Minnesota. Minnesota had 2 shorthand goals, Philadelphia 1. Philadelphia won 5-3.
— Edmonton Oilers, Winnipeg Jets, April 9, 1988 at Winnipeg. Winnipeg had 2 shorthand goals, Edmonton 1. Winnipeg won 6-4.
— New Jersey Devils, NY Islanders, April 14, 1988 at New Jersey. NY Islanders had 2 shorthand goals, New Jersey 1. New Jersey won 6-5.

MOST SHORTHAND GOALS, ONE TEAM, ONE GAME:
3 — Boston Bruins, April 11, 1981, at Minnesota. Minnesota won 6-3.
— NY Islanders, April 17, 1983, at NY Rangers. NY Rangers won 7-6.

MOST SHORTHAND GOALS, BOTH TEAMS, ONE PERIOD:
3 — Toronto Maple Leafs, Detroit Red Wings, April 5, 1947, at Toronto, first period. Toronto had 2 shorthand goals, Detroit 1. Toronto won 6-1.

MOST SHORTHAND GOALS ONE TEAM, ONE PERIOD:
2 — Toronto Maple Leafs, April 5, 1947, at Toronto against Detroit, first period. Toronto won 6-1.
— Toronto Maple Leafs, April 13, 1965, at Toronto against Montreal, first period. Montreal won 4-3.
— Boston Bruins, April 20, 1969, at Boston against Montreal, first period. Boston won 3-2.
— Boston Bruins, April 8, 1970, at Boston against NY Rangers, second period. Boston won 8-2.
— Boston Bruins, April 30, 1972, at Boston against NY Rangers, first period. Boston won 6-5.
— Chicago Blackhawks, May 3, 1973, at Chicago against Montreal, first period. Chicago won 7-4.
— Montreal Canadiens, April 23, 1978, at Detroit, first period. Montreal won 8-0.
— NY Islanders, April 8, 1980, at New York against Los Angeles, second period. NY Islanders won 8-1.
— Los Angeles Kings, April 9, 1980, at NY Islanders, first period. Los Angeles won 6-3.
— Boston Bruins, April 13, 1980, at Pittsburgh, second period. Boston won 8-3.
— Minnesota North Stars, May 4, 1980, at Minnesota against Philadelphia, second period. Philadelphia won 5-3.
— Boston Bruins, April 11, 1981, at Minnesota, third period. Minnesota won 6-3.
— NY Islanders, May 12, 1981, at New York against Minnesota, first period. NY Islanders won 6-3.
— Montreal Canadiens, April 7, 1982, at Montreal against Quebec, third period. Montreal won 5-1.
— Edmonton Oilers, April 24, 1983, at Edmonton against Chicago, third period. Edmonton won 8-4.
— Winnipeg Jets, April 14, 1985, at Calgary, second period. Winnipeg won 5-3.
— Boston Bruins, April 6, 1988 at Boston against Buffalo, first period. Boston won 7-3.
— NY Islanders, April 14, 1988 at New Jersey, third period. New Jersey won 6-5.

FASTEST TWO GOALS, BOTH TEAMS:
5 Seconds — Pittsburgh Penguins, Buffalo Sabres at Buffalo, April 14, 1979. Gilbert Perreault scored for Buffalo at 12:59 and Jim Hamilton for Pittsburgh at 13:04 of first period. Pittsburgh won 4-3 and best-of-three PR 2-1.
8 Seconds — Minnesota North Stars, St. Louis Blues at Minnesota, April 9, 1989. Bernie Federko scored for St. Louis at 2:28 of third period and Perry Berezan at 2:36 for Minnesota. Minnesota won 5-4. St. Louis won best-of-seven DSF 4-1.
9 Seconds — NY Islanders, Washington Capitals at Washington, April 10, 1986. Bryan Trottier scored for New York at 18:26 of second period and Scott Stevens at 18:35 for Washington. Washington won 5-2, and won best-of-five DSF 3-0.
10 Seconds — Washington Capitals, New Jersey Devils at New Jersey, April 5, 1990. Pat Conacher scored for New Jersey at 8:02 of second period and Dale Hunter at 8:12 for Washington. Washington won 5-4, and won best-of-seven DSF 4-2.
— Calgary Flames, Edmonton Oilers at Edmonton, April 8, 1991. Joe Nieuwendyk scored for Calgary at 2:03 of first period and Esa Tikkanen at 2:13 for Edmonton. Edmonton won 4-3, and won best-of-seven DSF 4-3.

FASTEST TWO GOALS, ONE TEAM:
5 Seconds — Detroit Red Wings at Detroit, April 11, 1965, against Chicago. Norm Ullman scored at 17:35 and 17:40, second period. Detroit won 4-2. Chicago won best-of-seven SF 4-3.

FASTEST THREE GOALS, BOTH TEAMS:
21 Seconds — Edmonton Oilers, Chicago Blackhawks at Edmonton, May 7, 1985. Behn Wilson scored for Chicago at 19:22 of third period, Jari Kurri at 19:36 and Glenn Anderson at 19:43 for Edmonton. Edmonton won 7-3 and best-of-seven CF 4-2.
30 Seconds — Chicago Blackhawks, Pittsburgh Penguins at Chicago, June 1, 1992. Dirk Graham scored for Chicago at 6:21 of first period, Kevin Stevens for Pittsburgh at 6:33 and Graham for Chicago at 6:51. Pittsburgh won 6-5 and best-of-seven F 4-0.
31 Seconds — Edmonton Oilers, Philadelphia Flyers at Edmonton, May 25, 1985. Wayne Gretzky scored for Edmonton at 1:10 and 1:25 of first period, Derrick Smith scored for Philadelphia at 1:41. Edmonton won 4-3 and best-of-seven F 4-1.

FASTEST THREE GOALS, ONE TEAM:
23 Seconds — Toronto Maple Leafs at Toronto, April 12, 1979, against Atlanta Flames. Darryl Sittler scored at 4:04 of first period and again at 4:16 and Ron Ellis at 4:27. Leafs won 7-4 and best-of-three PR 2-0.
38 Seconds — NY Rangers at New York, April 12, 1986. Jim Wiemer scored at 12:29 of third period, Bob Brooke at 12:43 and Ron Grescher at 13:07. NY Rangers won 5-2 and best-of-five DSF 3-2.
56 Seconds — Montreal Canadiens at Detroit, April 6, 1954. Dickie Moore scored at 15:03 of first period, Maurice Richard at 15:28 and again at 15:59. Montreal won 3-1. Detroit won best-of-seven F 4-3.

FASTEST FOUR GOALS, BOTH TEAMS:
1 Minute, 33 Seconds — Philadelphia Flyers, Toronto Maple Leafs at Philadelphia, April 20, 1976. Don Saleski of Philadelphia scored at 10:04 of second period; Bob Neely, Toronto, 10:42; Gary Dornhoefer, Philadelphia, 11:24; and Don Saleski, 11:37. Philadelphia won 7-1 and best-of-seven QF series 4-3.
1 minute, 34 seconds — Montreal Canadiens, Calgary Flames at Montreal, May 20, 1986. Joel Otto of Calgary scored at 17:59 of first period; Bobby Smith, Montreal, 18:25; Mats Naslund, Montreal, 19:17; and Bob Gainey, Montreal, 19:33. Montreal won 5-3 and best-of-seven F series 4-1.
1 Minute, 38 Seconds — Boston Bruins, Philadelphia Flyers at Philadelphia, April 26, 1977. Gregg Sheppard of Boston scored at 14:01 of second period; Mike Milbury, Boston, 15:01; Gary Dornhoefer, Philadelphia, 15:16; and Jean Ratelle, Boston, 15:39. Boston won 5-4 and best-of-seven SF series 4-0.

FASTEST FOUR GOALS, ONE TEAM:
2 Minutes, 35 Seconds — Montreal Canadiens at Montreal, March 30, 1944, against Toronto. Toe Blake scored at 7:58 of third period and again at 8:37; Maurice Richard, 9:17; Ray Getliffe, 10:33. Montreal won 11-0 and best-of-seven SF 4-1.

FASTEST FIVE GOALS, BOTH TEAMS:
3 Minutes, 6 Seconds — Chicago Blackhawks, Minnesota North Stars, at Chicago April 21, 1985. Keith Brown scored for Chicago at 1:12, second period; Ken Yaremchuk, Chicago, 1:27; Dino Ciccarelli, Minnesota, 2:48; Tony McKegney, Minnesota, 4:07; and Curt Fraser, Chicago, 4:18. Chicago won 6-2 and best-of-seven DF 4-2.
3 Minutes, 20 Seconds — Minnesota North Stars, Philadelphia Flyers, at Philadelphia, April 29, 1980. Paul Shmyr scored for Minnesota at 13:20, first period; Steve Christoff, Minnesota, 13:59; Ken Linseman, Philadelphia, 14:54; Tom Gorence, Philadelphia, 15:36; and Linseman, 16:40. Minnesota won 6-5. Philadelphia won best-of-seven SF 4-1.
4 Minutes, 19 Seconds — Toronto Maple Leafs, NY Rangers at Toronto, April 9, 1932. Ace Bailey scored for Toronto at 15:07, third period; Fred Cook, NY Rangers, 16:32; Bob Gracie, Toronto, 17:36; Frank Boucher, NY Rangers, 18:26 and again at 19:26. Toronto won 6-4 and best-of-five F 3-0.

FASTEST FIVE GOALS, ONE TEAM:
3 Minutes, 36 Seconds — Montreal Canadiens at Montreal, March 30, 1944, against Toronto. Toe Blake scored at 7:58 of third period and again at 8:37; Maurice Richard, 9:17; Ray Getliffe, 10:33; and Buddy O'Connor, 11:34. Canadiens won 11-0 and best-of-seven SF 4-1.

MOST THREE-OR-MORE GOAL GAMES BY ALL TEAMS, ONE PLAYOFF YEAR:
12 — 1983 in 66 games.
— 1988 in 83 games.
11 — 1985 in 70 games.
— 1992 in 86 games.

MOST THREE-OR-MORE GOAL GAMES, ONE TEAM, ONE PLAYOFF YEAR:
6 — Edmonton Oilers in 16 games, 1983.
— Edmonton Oilers in 18 games, 1985.

Henri Richard, who won eleven Stanley Cup championships as a member of the Montreal Canadiens, scored the Cup-winning goal in 1966 and 1971.

Individual Records

Career

MOST YEARS IN PLAYOFFS:
20 — Gordie Howe, Detroit, Hartford (1947-58 incl.; 60-61; 63-66 incl.; 70 & 80)
— Larry Robinson, Montreal, Los Angeles (1973-92 incl.)
19 — Red Kelly, Detroit, Toronto
18 — Stan Mikita, Chicago
— Henri Richard, Montreal

MOST CONSECUTIVE YEARS IN PLAYOFFS:
20 — Larry Robinson, Montreal, Los Angeles (1973-1992, inclusive).
17 — Brad Park, NY Rangers, Boston, Detroit (1969-1985, inclusive).
16 — Jean Beliveau, Montreal (1954-69, inclusive).

MOST PLAYOFF GAMES:
227 — Larry Robinson, Montreal, Los Angeles
219 — Bryan Trottier, NY Islanders, Pittsburgh
185 — Denis Potvin, NY Islanders
184 — Bobby Smith, Minnesota, Montreal
182 — Bob Gainey, Montreal

MOST POINTS IN PLAYOFFS (CAREER):
306 — Wayne Gretzky, Edmonton, Los Angeles, 95G, 211A
229 — Mark Messier, Edmonton, NY Rangers, 87G, 142A
205 — Jari Kurri, Edmonton, Los Angeles, 93G, 112A
184 — Bryan Trottier, NY Islanders, Pittsburgh 71G, 113A
183 — Glenn Anderson, Edmonton, 81G, 102A
176 — Jean Beliveau, Montreal, 79G, 97A

MOST GOALS IN PLAYOFFS (CAREER):
95 — Wayne Gretzky, Edmonton, Los Angeles
93 — Jari Kurri, Edmonton, Los Angeles
87 — Mark Messier, Edmonton, NY Rangers
85 — Mike Bossy, NY Islanders
82 — Maurice Richard, Montreal
81 — Glenn Anderson, Edmonton

MOST GAME-WINNING GOALS IN PLAYOFFS (CAREER):
18 — Maurice Richard, Montreal
— Wayne Gretzky, Edmonton, Los Angeles
17 — Mike Bossy, NY Islanders
15 — Jean Beliveau, Montreal
— Yvan Cournoyer, Montreal

MOST OVERTIME GOALS IN PLAYOFFS (CAREER):
6 — Maurice Richard, Montreal (1 in 1946; 3 in 1951; 1 in 1957; 1 in 1958.)
4 — Bob Nystrom, NY Islanders
— Dale Hunter, Quebec, Washington
3 — Mel Hill, Boston
— Rene Robert, Buffalo
— Danny Gare, Buffalo
— Jacques Lemaire, Montreal
— Bobby Clarke, Philadelphia
— Terry O'Reilly, Boston
— Mike Bossy, NY Islanders
— Steve Payne, Minnesota
— Ken Morrow, NY Islanders
— Lanny McDonald, Toronto, Calgary
— Glenn Anderson, Edmonton
— Peter Stastny, Quebec
— Dino Ciccarelli, Minnesota, Washington
— Wayne Gretzky, Edmonton, Los Angeles
— Russ Courtnall, Montreal

MOST POWER-PLAY GOALS IN PLAYOFFS (CAREER):
35 — Mike Bossy, NY Islanders
27 — Denis Potvin, NY Islanders
26 — Jean Beliveau, Montreal
— Wayne Gretzky, Edmonton, Los Angeles
24 — Bobby Smith, Minnesota, Montreal
23 — Glenn Anderson, Edmonton
— Brian Propp, Philadelphia, Boston, Minnesota
— Cam Neely, Vancouver, Boston
— Jari Kurri, Edmonton, Los Angeles

MOST SHORTHAND GOALS IN PLAYOFFS (CAREER):
13 — Mark Messier, Edmonton, NY Rangers
10 — Wayne Gretzky, Edmonton, Los Angeles
8 — Ed Westfall, Boston, NY Islanders
— Hakan Loob, Calgary
7 — Jari Kurri, Edmonton

MOST THREE-OR-MORE-GOAL GAMES IN PLAYOFFS (CAREER):
7 — Maurice Richard, Montreal. Four three-goal games; two four-goal games; one five-goal game.
— Wayne Gretzky, Edmonton. Five three-goal games; two four-goal games.
— Jari Kurri, Edmonton. One four-goal game; six three-goal games.
5 — Mike Bossy, NY Islanders. Four three-goal games; one four-goal game.

MOST ASSISTS IN PLAYOFFS (CAREER):
211 — Wayne Gretzky, Edmonton, Los Angeles
142 — Mark Messier, Edmonton, NY Rangers
116 — Larry Robinson, Montreal, Los Angeles
113 — Bryan Trottier, NY Islanders, Pittsburgh
112 — Jari Kurri, Edmonton, Los Angeles
108 — Denis Potvin, NY Islanders

MOST PENALTY MINUTES IN PLAYOFFS (CAREER):
564 — Dale Hunter, Quebec, Washington
541 — Chris Nilan, Montreal, NY Rangers, Boston
466 — Willi Plett, Atlanta, Calgary, Minnesota, Boston
455 — Dave Williams, Toronto, Vancouver, Los Angeles
412 — Dave Schultz, Philadelphia, Los Angeles, Buffalo

MOST SHUTOUTS IN PLAYOFFS (CAREER):
15 — Clint Benedict, Ottawa, Mtl. Maroons
14 — Jacques Plante, Montreal, St. Louis
13 — Turk Broda, Toronto
12 — Terry Sawchuk, Detroit, Toronto, Los Angeles

MOST PLAYOFF GAMES APPEARED IN BY A GOALTENDER (CAREER):
132 — Bill Smith, NY Islanders
115 — Glenn Hall, Detroit, Chicago, St. Louis
112 — Jacques Plante, Montreal, St. Louis, Toronto, Boston
— Ken Dryden, Montreal
111 — Grant Fuhr, Edmonton
106 — Terry Sawchuk, Detroit, Toronto, Los Angeles, NY Rangers

MOST MINUTES PLAYED BY A GOALTENDER (CAREER):
7,645 — Billy Smith, NY Islanders
6,899 — Glenn Hall, Detroit, Chicago, St. Louis
6,846 — Ken Dryden, Montreal
6,651 — Jacques Plante, Montreal, St. Louis, Toronto, Boston

Single Playoff Year

MOST POINTS, ONE PLAYOFF YEAR:
47 — Wayne Gretzky, Edmonton, in 1985. 17 goals, 30 assists in 18 games.
44 — Mario Lemieux, Pittsburgh, in 1991. 16 goals, 28 assists in 23 games.
43 — Wayne Gretzky, Edmonton, in 1988. 12 goals, 31 assists in 19 games.
38 — Wayne Gretzky, Edmonton, in 1983. 12 goals, 26 assists in 16 games.
37 — Paul Coffey, Edmonton, in 1985. 12 goals, 25 assists in 18 games.
35 — Mike Bossy, NY Islanders, in 1981. 17 goals, 18 assists in 18 games.
— Wayne Gretzky, Edmonton, in 1984. 13 goals, 22 assists in 19 games.
— Mark Messier, Edmonton, in 1988. 11 goals, 23 assists in 19 games.
34 — Wayne Gretzky, Edmonton, in 1987. 5 goals, 29 assists in 21 games.
— Mark Recchi, Pittsburgh, in 1991. 10 goals, 24 assists in 24 games.
— Mario Lemieux, Pittsburgh, in 1992. 16 goals, 18 assists in 15 games.
33 — Rick Middleton Boston, in 1983. 11 goals, 22 assists in 17 games.
— Kevin Stevens, Pittsburgh, in 1991. 17 goals, 16 assists in 24 games.
32 — Barry Pederson, Boston, in 1983. 14 goals, 18 assists in 17 games.

MOST POINTS BY A DEFENSEMAN, ONE PLAYOFF YEAR:
37 — Paul Coffey, Edmonton, in 1985. 12 goals, 25 assists in 18 games.
31 — Al MacInnis, Calgary, in 1989. 7 goals, 24 assists in 18 games.
25 — Denis Potvin, NY Islanders, in 1981. 8 goals, 17 assists in 18 games.
— Ray Bourque, Boston, in 1991. 7 goals, 18 assists in 19 games.
24 — Bobby Orr, Boston, in 1972. 5 goals, 19 assists in 15 games.

MOST POINTS BY A ROOKIE, ONE PLAYOFF YEAR:
21 — Dino Ciccarelli, Minnesota, in 1981. 14 goals, 7 assists in 19 games.
20 — Don Maloney, NY Rangers, in 1979. 7 goals, 13 assists in 18 games.

LONGEST CONSECUTIVE POINT-SCORING STREAK, ONE PLAYOFF YEAR:
18 games — Bryan Trottier, NY Islanders, 1981. 11 goals, 18 assists, 29 points.
17 games — Wayne Gretzky, Edmonton, 1988. 12 goals, 29 assists, 41 points.
— Al MacInnis, Calgary, 1989. 7 goals, 19 assists, 24 points.

LONGEST CONSECUTIVE POINT-SCORING STREAK, MORE THAN ONE PLAYOFF YEAR:
27 games — Bryan Trottier, NY Islanders, 1980, 1981 and 1982. 7 games in 1980 (3 G, 5 A, 8 PTS), 18 games in 1981 (11 G, 18 A, 29 PTS), and two games in 1982 (2 G, 3 A, 5 PTS). Total points, 42.
19 games — Wayne Gretzky, Edmonton, Los Angeles 1988 and 1989. 17 games in 1988 (12 G, 29 A, 41 PTS with Edmonton), 2 games in 1989 (1 G, 2 A, 3 PTS with Los Angeles). Total points, 44.
18 games — Phil Esposito, Boston, 1970 and 1971. 13 G, 20 A, 33 PTS.

MOST GOALS, ONE PLAYOFF YEAR:
19 — Reggie Leach, Philadelphia, 1976. 16 games.
— Jari Kurri, Edmonton, 1985. 18 games.
17 — Newsy Lalonde, Montreal, 1919. 10 games.
— Mike Bossy, NY Islanders, 1981. 18 games.
— Steve Payne, Minnesota, 1981. 19 games.
— Mike Bossy, NY Islanders, 1982. 19 games.
— Mike Bossy, NY Islanders, 1983. 19 games
— Wayne Gretzky, Edmonton, 1985. 18 games.
— Kevin Stevens, Pittsburgh, 1991. 24 games.

MOST GOALS BY A DEFENSEMAN, ONE PLAYOFF YEAR:
12 — Paul Coffey, Edmonton, 1985. 18 games.
9 — Bobby Orr, Boston, 1970. 14 games.
— Brad Park, Boston, 1978. 15 games.
8 — Denis Potvin, NY Islanders, 1981. 18 games.
— Raymond Bourque, Boston, 1983. 17 games.
— Denis Potvin, NY Islanders, 1983. 20 games.
— Paul Coffey, Edmonton, 1984. 19 games

MOST GOALS BY A ROOKIE, ONE PLAYOFF YEAR:
14 — Dino Ciccarelli, Minnesota, 1981. 19 games.
11 — Jeremy Roenick, Chicago, 1990. 20 games.
10 — Claude Lemieux, Montreal, 1986. 20 games.
9 — Pat Flatley, NY Islanders, 1984. 21 games
8 — Steve Christoff, Minnesota, 1980. 14 games.
— Brad Palmer, Minnesota, 1981. 19 games.
— Mike Krushelnyski, Boston, 1983. 17 games.
— Bob Joyce, Boston, 1988. 23 games.

MOST GAME-WINNING GOALS, ONE PLAYOFF YEAR:
5 — Mike Bossy, NY Islanders, 1983. 19 games.
— Jari Kurri, Edmonton, 1987. 21 games.
— Bobby Smith, Minnesota, 1991. 23 games.
— Mario Lemieux, Pittsburgh, 1992. 15 games.

MOST OVERTIME GOALS, ONE PLAYOFF YEAR:
3 — Mel Hill, Boston, 1939. All against NY Rangers in best-of-seven SF, won by Boston 4-3.
— Maurice Richard, Montreal, 1951. 2 against Detroit in best-of-seven SF, won by Montreal 4-2; 1 against Toronto best-of-seven F, won by Toronto 4-1.

MOST POWER-PLAY GOALS, ONE PLAYOFF YEAR:
9 — Mike Bossy, NY Islanders, 1981. 18 games against Toronto, Edmonton, NY Rangers and Minnesota.
— Cam Neely, Boston, 1991. 19 games against Hartford, Montreal, Pittsburgh.
8 — Tim Kerr, Philadelphia, 1989. 19 games.
— John Druce, Washington, 1990. 15 games
— Brian Propp, Minnesota, 1991. 23 games.
— Mario Lemieux, Pittsburgh, 1992. 15 games.
7 — Michel Goulet, Quebec, 1985. 17 games.
— Mark Messier, Edmonton, 1988. 19 games.
— Mario Lemieux, Pittsburgh, 1989. 11 games.
— Brett Hull, St. Louis, 1990. 12 games.
— Kevin Stevens, Pittsburgh, 1991. 24 games.

MOST SHORTHAND GOALS, ONE PLAYOFF YEAR:
3 — Derek Sanderson, Boston, 1969. 1 against Toronto in QF, won by Boston 4-0; 2 against Montreal in SF, won by Montreal, 4-2.
— Bill Barber, Philadelphia, 1980. All against Minnesota in SF, won by Philadelphia 4-1.
— Lorne Henning, NY Islanders, 1980. 1 against Boston in QF won by NY Islanders 4-1; 1 against Buffalo in SF, won by NY Islanders 4-2, 1 against Philadelphia in F, won by NY Islanders 4-2.
— Wayne Gretzky, Edmonton, 1983. 2 against Winnipeg in DSF won by Edmonton 3-0; 1 against Calgary in DF, won by Edmonton 4-1.
— Wayne Presley, Chicago, 1989. All against Detroit in DSF won by Chicago 4-2.

MOST THREE-OR-MORE GOAL GAMES, ONE PLAYOFF YEAR:
4 — Jari Kurri, Edmonton, 1985. 1 four-goal game, 3 three-goal games.
3 — Mark Messier, Edmonton, 1983. 3 three-goal games.
— Mike Bossy, NY Islanders, 1983. 1 four-goal game, 2 three-goal games
2 — Newsy Lalonde, Montreal, 1919. 1 five-goal game, 1 four-goal game.
— Maurice Richard, Montreal, 1944. 1 five-goal game; 1 three-goal game.
— Doug Bentley, Chicago, 1944. 2 three-goal games.
— Norm Ullman, Detroit, 1964. 2 three-goal games.
— Phil Esposito, Boston, 1970. 2 three-goal games.
— Pit Martin, Chicago, 1973. 2 three-goal games.
— Rick MacLeish, Philadelphia, 1975. 2 three-goal games.
— Lanny McDonald, Toronto, 1977. 1 three-goal game; 1 four-goal game.
— Wayne Gretzky, Edmonton, 1981. 2 three-goal games.
— Wayne Gretzky, Edmonton, 1983. 2 four-goal games.
— Wayne Gretzky, Edmonton, 1985. 2 three-goal games.
— Petr Klima, Detroit, 1988. 2 three-goal games.
— Cam Neely, Boston, 1991. 2 three-goal games.

LONGEST CONSECUTIVE GOAL-SCORING STREAK, ONE PLAYOFF YEAR:
9 Games — Reggie Leach, Philadelphia, 1976. Streak started April 17 at Toronto and ended May 9 at Montreal. He scored one goal in each of seven games; two in one game; and five in another; a total of 14 goals.

MOST ASSISTS, ONE PLAYOFF YEAR:
31 — Wayne Gretzky, Edmonton, 1988. 19 games.
30 — Wayne Gretzky, Edmonton, 1985. 18 games.
29 — Wayne Gretzky, Edmonton, 1987. 21 games.
28 — Mario Lemieux, Pittsburgh, 1991. 23 games.
26 — Wayne Gretzky, Edmonton, 1983. 16 games.
25 — Paul Coffey, Edmonton, 1985. 18 games.
24 — Al MacInnis, Calgary, 1989. 22 games.
— Mark Recchi, Pittsburgh, 1991. 24 games.

MOST ASSISTS BY A DEFENSEMAN, ONE PLAYOFF YEAR:
25 — Paul Coffey, Edmonton, 1985. 18 games.
24 — Al MacInnis, Calgary, 1989. 22 games.
19 — Bobby Orr, Boston, 1972. 15 games.
18 — Ray Bourque, Boston, 1988. 23 games.
— Ray Bourque, Boston, 1991. 19 games.
— Larry Murphy, Pittsburgh, 1991. 23 games.
17 — Larry Robinson, Montreal, 1978. 15 games.
— Denis Potvin, NY Islanders, 1981. 18 games.
— Charlie Huddy, Edmonton, 1985. 18 games.
— Larry Robinson, Montreal, 1987. 17 games.

Ron Hextall appeared in a record 26 games during the 1987 playoffs.

MOST MINUTES PLAYED BY A GOALTENDER, ONE PLAYOFF YEAR:
1,540 — Ron Hextall, Philadelphia, 1987. 26 games.
1,401 — Bill Ranford, Edmonton, 1990. 22 games.
1,381 — Mike Vernon, Calgary, 1989. 22 games.
1,233 — Tom Barrasso, Pittsburgh, 1992. 21 games.
1,229 — Mike Vernon, Calgary, 1986. 21 games.
1,221 — Ken Dryden, Montreal, 1971. 20 games.
1,218 — Patrick Roy, Montreal, 1986. 20 games.
1,206 — Patrick Roy, Montreal, 1989. 19 games.

MOST WINS BY A GOALTENDER, ONE PLAYOFF YEAR:
16 — Grant Fuhr, Edmonton, 1988. 19 games.
— Mike Vernon, Calgary, 1989. 22 games.
— Bill Ranford, Edmonton, 1990. 22 games
— Tom Barrasso, Pittsburgh, 1992. 21 games.
15 — Bill Smith, NY Islanders, 1980. 20 games.
— Bill Smith, NY Islanders, 1982. 18 games.
— Grant Fuhr, Edmonton, 1985. 18 games.
— Patrick Roy, Montreal, 1986. 20 games.
— Ron Hextall, Philadelphia, 1987. 26 games.
14 — Bill Smith, NY Islanders, 1981. 17 games.
— Grant Fuhr, Edmonton, 1987. 19 games.
— Jon Casey, Minnesota, 1991. 23 games.

MOST CONSECUTIVE WINS BY A GOALTENDER, ONE PLAYOFF YEAR:
11 — Ed Belfour, Chicago, 1992. 3 wins against St. Louis in DSF, won by Chicago 4-2; 4 wins against Detroit in DF, won by Chicago 4-0; and 4 wins against Edmonton in CF, won by Chicago 4-0.
— Tom Barrasso, Pittsburgh, 1992. 3 wins against NY Rangers in DF, won by Pittsburgh 4-2; 4 wins against Boston in CF, won by Pittsburgh 4-0; and 4 wins against Chicago in F, won by Pittsburgh 4-0.

MOST SHUTOUTS, ONE PLAYOFF YEAR:
4 — Clint Benedict, Mtl. Maroons, 1926. 8 games.
— Clint Benedict, Mtl. Maroons, 1928. 9 games.
— Dave Kerr, NY Rangers, 1937. 9 games.
— Frank McCool, Toronto, 1945. 13 games.
— Terry Sawchuk, Detroit, 1952. 8 games.
— Bernie Parent, Philadelphia, 1975. 17 games.
— Ken Dryden, Montreal, 1977. 14 games.

MOST CONSECUTIVE SHUTOUTS:
3 — Clint Benedict, Mtl. Maroons, 1926. Benedict shut out Ottawa 1-0, Mar. 27; he then shut out Victoria twice, 3-0, Mar. 30; 3-0, Apr. 1. Mtl. Maroons won NHL F vs. Ottawa 2 goals to 1 and won the best-of-five F vs. Victoria 3-1.
— Frank McCool, Toronto, 1945. McCool shut out Detroit 1-0, April 6; 2-0, April 8; 1-0, April 12. Toronto won the best-of-seven F 4-3.

LONGEST SHUTOUT SEQUENCE:
248 Minutes, 32 Seconds — Norm Smith, Detroit, 1936. In best-of-five SF, Smith shut out Mtl. Maroons 1-0, March 24, in 116:30 overtime; shut out Maroons 3-0 in second game, March 26; and was scored against at 12:02 of first period, March 29, by Gus Marker. Detroit won SF 3-0.

One-Series Records

MOST POINTS IN FINAL SERIES:
13 — Wayne Gretzky, Edmonton, in 1988, 4 games plus suspended game vs. Boston. 3 goals, 10 assists.
12 — Gordie Howe, Detroit, in 1955, 7 games vs. Montreal. 5 goals, 7 assists.
— Yvan Cournoyer, Montreal, in 1973, 6 games vs. Chicago. 6 goals, 6 assists.
— Jacques Lemaire, Montreal, in 1973, 6 games vs. Chicago. 3 goals, 9 assists.
— Mario Lemieux, Pittsburgh, in 1991, 5 games vs. Minnesota. 5 goals, 7 assists.

MOST GOALS IN FINAL SERIES:
9 — Babe Dye, Toronto, in 1922, 5 games vs. Van. Millionaires.
8 — Alf Skinner, Toronto, in 1918, 5 games vs. Van. Millionaires.
7 — Jean Beliveau, Montreal, in 1956, during 5 games vs. Detroit.
— Mike Bossy, NY Islanders, in 1982, during 4 games vs. Vancouver.
— Wayne Gretzky, Edmonton, in 1985, during 5 games vs. Philadelphia.

MOST ASSISTS IN FINLL SERIES:
10 — Wayne Gretzky, Edmonton, in 1988, 4 games plus suspended game vs. Boston.
9 — Jacques Lemaire, Montreal, in 1973, 6 games vs. Chicago.
— Wayne Gretzky, Edmonton, in 1987, 7 games vs. Philadelphia
— Larry Murphy, Pittsburgh, in 1991, 6 games vs. Minnesota.

MOST POINTS IN ONE SERIES (OTHER THAN FINAL):
19 — Rick Middleton, Boston, in 1983 DF, 7 games vs. Buffalo. 5 goals, 14 assists.
18 — Wayne Gretzky, Edmonton, in 1985 CF, 6 games vs. Chicago. 4 goals, 14 assists.
17 — Mario Lemieux, Pittsburgh, in 1992 DSF, 6 games vs. Washington. 7 goals, 10 assists.
16 — Barry Pederson, Boston, in 1983 DF, 7 games vs. Buffalo. 7 goals, 9 assists.
15 — Jari Kurri, Edmonton, in 1985 CF, 6 games vs. Chicago. 12 goals, 3 assists.
— Wayne Gretzky, Edmonton, in 1987 DSF, 5 games vs. Los Angeles. 2 goals, 13 assists.
— Tim Kerr, Philadelphia, in 1989 DF, 7 games vs. Pittsburgh. 10 goals, 5 assists.
— Mario Lemieux, Pittsburgh, in 1991 CF, 6 games vs. Boston. 6 goals, 9 assists.

MOST GOALS IN ONE SERIES (OTHER THAN FINAL):
12 — Jari Kurri, Edmonton, in 1985 CF, 6 games vs. Chicago.
11 — Newsy Lalonde, Montreal, in 1919 NHL F, 5 games vs. Ottawa.
10 — Tim Kerr, Philadelphia, in 1989 DF, 7 games vs. Pittsburgh.
9 — Reggie Leach, Philadelphia, in 1976 SF, 5 games vs. Boston.
— Bill Barber, Philadelphia, in 1980 SF, 5 games vs. Minnesota.
— Mike Bossy, NY Islanders, in 1983 CF, 6 games vs. Boston.
— Mario Lemieux, Pittsburgh, in 1989 DF, 7 games vs. Philadelphia.

MOST ASSISTS IN ONE SERIES (OTHER THAN FINAL):
14 — Rick Middleton, Boston, in 1983 DF, 7 games vs. Buffalo.
— Wayne Gretzky, Edmonton, in 1985 CF, 6 games vs. Chicago.
13 — Wayne Gretzky, Edmonton, in 1987 DSF, 5 games vs. Los Angeles.
11 — Mark Messier, Edmonton, in 1989 DSF, 7 games vs. Los Angeles.
— Al MacInnis, Calgary, in 1984 DF, 7 games vs. Edmonton.
— Mike Ridley, Washington, in 1992 DSF, 7 games vs. Pittsburgh.
10 — Fleming Mackell, Boston, in 1958 SF, 6 games vs. NY Rangers.
— Stan Mikita, Chicago, in 1962 SF, 6 games vs. Montreal.
— Bob Bourne, NY Islanders, in 1983 DF, 6 games vs. NY Rangers.
— Wayne Gretzky, Edmonton, in 1988 DSF, 5 games vs. Winnipeg.
— Mario Lemieux, Pittsburgh, in 1992 DSF, 6 games vs. Washington.

MOST GAME-WINNING GOALS, ONE PLAYOFF SERIES:
4 — Mike Bossy, NY Islanders, 1983, CF vs. Boston, won by NY Islanders 4-2.

MOST OVERTIME GOALS, ONE PLAYOFF SERIES:
3 — Mel Hill, Boston, 1939, SF vs. NY Rangers, won by Boston 4-3. Hill scored at 59:25 overtime March 21 for a 2-1 win; at 8:24, March 23 for a 3-2 win; and at 48:00, April 2 for a 2-1 win.

MOST POWER-PLAY GOALS, ONE PLAYOFF SERIES:
6 — Chris Kontos, Los Angeles, 1989, DSF vs. Edmonton, won by Los Angeles 4-3.
5 — Andy Bathgate, Detroit, 1966, SF vs. Chicago, won by Detroit 4-2.
— Denis Potvin, NY Islanders, 1981, QF vs. Edmonton, won by NY Islanders 4-2.
— Ken Houston, Calgary, 1981, QF vs. Philadelphia, won by Calgary 4-3.
— Rick Vaive, Chicago, 1988, DSF vs. St. Louis, won by St. Louis 4-1.
— Tim Kerr, Philadelphia, 1989, DF vs. Pittsburgh, won by Philadelphia 4-3.
— Mario Lemieux, Pittsburgh, 1989, DF vs. Philadelphia won by Philadelphia 4-3.
— John Druce, Washington, 1990, DF vs. NY Rangers won by Washington 4-1.
— Pat LaFontaine, Buffalo, 1992, DSF vs. Boston won by Boston 4-3.

MOST SHORTHAND GOALS, ONE PLAYOFF SERIES:
3 — **Bill Barber, Philadelphia,** 1980, SF vs. Minnesota, won by Philadelphia 4-1.
— **Wayne Presley, Chicago,** 1989, DSF vs. Detroit, won by Chicago 4-2.
2 — Mac Colville, NY Rangers, 1940, SF vs. Boston, won by NY Rangers 4-2.
— Jerry Toppazzini, Boston, 1958, SF vs. NY Rangers, won by Boston 4-2.
— Dave Keon, Toronto, 1963, F vs. Detroit, won by Toronto 4-1.
— Bob Pulford, Toronto, 1964, F vs. Detroit, won by Toronto 4-3.
— Serge Savard, Montreal, 1968, F vs. St. Louis, won by Montreal 4-0.
— Derek Sanderson, Boston, 1969, SF vs. Montreal, won by Montreal 4-2.
— Bryan Trottier, NY Islanders, 1980, PR vs. Los Angeles, won by NY Islanders 3-1.
— Bobby Lalonde, Boston, 1981, PR vs. Minnesota, won by Minnesota 3-0.
— Butch Goring, NY Islanders, 1981, SF vs. NY Rangers, won by NY Islanders 4-0.
— Wayne Gretzky, Edmonton, 1983, DSF vs. Winnipeg, won by Edmonton 3-0.
— Mark Messier, Edmonton, 1983, DF vs. Calgary, won by Edmonton 4-1.
— Jari Kurri, Edmonton, 1983, CF vs. Chicago, won by Edmonton 4-0.
— Wayne Gretzky, Edmonton, 1985, DF vs. Winnipeg, won by Edmonton 4-0.
— Kevin Lowe, Edmonton, 1987, F vs. Philadelphia, won by Edmonton 4-3.
— Bob Gould, Washington, 1988, DSF vs. Philadelphia, won by Washington 4-3.
— Dave Poulin, Philadelphia, 1989, DF vs. Pittsburgh, won by Philadelphia 4-3.
— Russ Courtnall, Montreal, 1991, DF vs. Boston, won by Boston 4-3.
— Sergei Fedorov, Detroit, 1992 DSF vs. Minnesota, won by Detroit 4-3.
— Mark Messier, NY Rangers, 1992, DSF vs. New Jersey, won by NY Rangers 4-3.

MOST THREE-OR-MORE-GOAL GAMES, ONE PLAYOFF SERIES:
3 — **Jari Kurri, Edmonton** 1985, CF vs. Chicago won by Edmonton 4-2. Kurri scored 3 G May 7 at Edmonton in 7-3 win, 3 G May 14 in 10-5 win and 4 G May 16 at Chicago in 8-2 win.
2 — Doug Bentley, Chicago, 1944, SF vs. Detroit, won by Chicago 4-1. Bentley scored 3 G Mar. 28 at Chicago in 7-1 win and 3 G Mar. 30 at Detroit in 5-2 win.
— Norm Ullman, Detroit, 1964, SF vs. Chicago, won by Detroit 4-3. Ullman scored 3 G Mar. 29 at Chicago in 7-1 win and 3 G April 7 at Detroit in 7-2 win.
— Mark Messier, Edmonton, 1983, DF vs. Calgary won by Edmonton 4-1. Messier scored 4 G April 14 at Edmonton in 6-3 win and 3 G April 17 at Calgary in 10-2 win.
— Mike Bossy, NY Islanders, 1983, CF vs. Boston won by NY Islanders 4-2. Bossy scored 3 G May 3 at New York in 8-3 win and 4 G on May 7 at New York in 8-4 win.

Single Playoff Game Records

MOST POINTS, ONE GAME:
8 — **Patrik Sundstrom, New Jersey,** April 22, 1988 at New Jersey during 10-4 win over Washington. Sundstrom had 3 goals, 5 assists.
— **Mario Lemieux, Pittsburgh,** April 25, 1989 at Pittsburgh during 10-7 win over Philadelphia. Lemieux had 5 goals, 3 assists.
7 — Wayne Gretzky, Edmonton, April 17, 1983 at Calgary during 10-2 win. Gretzky had 4 goals, 3 assists.
— Wayne Gretzky, Edmonton, April 25,1985 at Winnipeg during 8-3 win. Gretzky had 3 goals, 4 assists.
— Wayne Gretzky, Edmonton, April 9, 1987, at Edmonton during 13-3 win over Los Angeles. Gretzky had 1 goal, 6 assists.
6 — Dickie Moore, Montreal, March 25, 1954, at Montreal during 8-1 win over Boston. Moore had 2 goals, 4 assists.
— Phil Esposito, Boston, April 2, 1969, at Boston during 10-0 win over Toronto. Esposito had 4 goals, 2 assists.
— Darryl Sittler, Toronto, April 22, 1976, at Toronto during 8-5 win over Philadelphia. Sittler had 5 goals, 1 assist.
— Guy Lafleur, Montreal, April 11, 1977, at Montreal during 7-2 victory vs. St. Louis. Lafleur had 3 goals, 3 assists.
— Mikko Leinonen, NY Rangers, April 8, 1982, at New York during 7-3 win over Philadelphia. Leinonen had 6 assists.
— Paul Coffey, Edmonton, May 14, 1985 at Edmonton during 10-5 win over Chicago. Coffey had 1 goal, 5 assists.
— John Anderson, Hartford, April 12, 1986 at Hartford during 9-4 win over Quebec. Anderson had 2 goals, 4 assists.
— Mario Lemieux, Pittsburgh, April 23, 1992 at Pittsburgh during 6-4 win over Washington. Lemieux had 3 goals, 3 assists.

MOST POINTS BY A DEFENSEMAN, ONE GAME:
6 — **Paul Coffey, Edmonton,** May 14, 1985 at Edmonton vs. Chicago. 1 goal, 5 assists. Edmonton won 10-5.
5 — Eddie Bush, Detroit, April 9, 1942, at Detroit vs. Toronto. 1 goal, 4 assists. Detroit won 5-2.
— Bob Dailey, Philadelphia, May 1, 1980, at Philadelphia vs. Minnesota. 1 goal, 4 assists. Philadelphia won 7-0.
— Denis Potvin, NY Islanders, April 17, 1981, at New York vs. Edmonton. 3 goals, 2 assists. NY Islanders won 6-3.
— Risto Siltanen, Quebec, April 14, 1987 at Hartford. 5 assists. Quebec won 7-5.

MOST GOALS, ONE GAME:
5 — **Newsy Lalonde, Montreal,** March 1, 1919, at Montreal. Final score: Montreal 6, Ottawa 3.
— **Maurice Richard, Montreal,** March 23, 1944, at Montreal. Final score: Montreal 5, Toronto 1.
— **Darryl Sittler, Toronto,** April 22, 1976, at Toronto. Final score: Toronto 8, Philadelphia 5.
— **Reggie Leach, Philadelphia,** May 6, 1976, at Philadelphia. Final score: Philadelphia 6, Boston 3.
— **Mario Lemieux, Pittsburgh,** April 25, 1989 at Pittsburgh. Final score: Pittsburgh 10, Philadelphia 7.

MOST GOALS BY A DEFENSEMAN, ONE GAME:
3 — **Bobby Orr, Boston,** April 11, 1971 at Montreal. Final score: Boston 5, Montreal 2.
— **Dick Redmond, Chicago,** April 4, 1973 at Chicago. Final score: Chicago 7, St. Louis 1.
— **Denis Potvin, NY Islanders,** April 17, 1981 at New York. Final score: NY Islanders 6, Edmonton 3.
— **Paul Reinhart, Calgary,** April 14, 1983 at Edmonton. Final score: Edmonton 6, Calgary 3.
— **Paul Reinhart, Calgary,** April 8, 1984 at Vancouver. Final score: Calgary 5, Vancouver 1.
— **Doug Halward, Vancouver,** April 7, 1984 at Vancouver. Final score: Vancouver 7, Calgary 0.

MOST POWER-PLAY GOALS, ONE GAME:
3 — **Syd Howe, Detroit,** March 23, 1939, at Detroit vs. Montreal, Detroit won 7-3.
— **Sid Smith, Toronto,** April 10, 1949, at Detroit. Toronto won 3-1.
— **Phil Esposito, Boston,** April 2, 1969, at Boston vs. Toronto. Boston won 10-0.
— **John Bucyk, Boston,** April 21, 1974, at Boston vs. Chicago. Boston won 8-6.
— **Denis Potvin, NY Islanders,** April 17, 1981, at New York vs. Edmonton. NY Islanders won 6-3.
— **Tim Kerr, Philadelphia,** April 13, 1985, at NY Rangers. Philadelphia won 6-5.
— **Jari Kurri, Edmonton,** April 9, 1987, at Edmonton vs. Los Angeles. Edmonton won 13-3.
— **Mark Johnson, New Jersey,** April 22, 1988, at New Jersey vs. Washington. New Jersey won 10-4.

MOST SHORTHAND GOALS, ONE GAME:
2 — **Dave Keon, Toronto,** April 18, 1963, at Toronto, in 3-1 win vs. Detroit.
— **Bryan Trottier, NY Islanders,** April 8, 1980 at New York, in 8-1 win vs. Los Angeles.
— **Bobby Lalonde, Boston,** April 11, 1981 at Minnesota, in 6-3 win by Minnesota.
— **Wayne Gretzky, Edmonton,** April 6, 1983 at Edmonton, in 6-3 win vs. Winnipeg.
— **Jari Kurri, Edmonton,** April 24, 1983, at Edmonton, in 8-3 win vs. Chicago.
— **Mark Messier, NY Rangers,** April 21, 1992, at New York, in 7-3 loss vs. New Jersey.

MOST ASSISTS, ONE GAME:
6 — **Mikko Leinonen, NY Rangers,** April 8, 1982, at New York. Final score: NY Rangers 7, Philadelphia 3.
— **Wayne Gretzky, Edmonton,** April 9, 1987, at Edmonton. Final score: Edmonton 13, Los Angeles 3.
5 — Toe Blake, Montreal, March 23, 1944, at Montreal. Final score: Montreal 5, Toronto 1.
— Maurice Richard, Montreal, March 27, 1956, at Montreal. Final score: Montreal 7, NY Rangers 0.
— Bert Olmstead, Montreal, March 30, 1957, at Montreal. Final score: Montreal 8, NY Rangers 3.
— Don McKenney, Boston, April 5, 1958, at Boston. Final score: Boston 8, NY Rangers 2.
— Stan Mikita, Chicago, April 4, 1973, at Chicago. Final score: Chicago 7, St. Louis 1.
— Wayne Gretzky, Edmonton, April 8, 1981, at Montreal. Final score: Edmonton 6, Montreal 3.
— Paul Coffey, Edmonton, May 14, 1985, at Edmonton. Final score: Edmonton 10, Chicago 5.
— Doug Gilmour, St. Louis, April 15, 1986, at Minnesota. Final score: St. Louis 6, Minnesota 3.
— Risto Siltanen, Quebec, April 14, 1987 at Hartford. Final score: Quebec 7, Hartford 5.
— Patrik Sundstrom, New Jersey, April 22, 1988, at New Jersey. Final score: New Jersey 10, Washington 4.

MOST PENALTY MINUTES, ONE GAME:
42 — **Dave Schultz, Philadelphia,** April 22, 1976, at Toronto. One minor, 2 majors, 1 10-minute misconduct and 2 game-misconducts. Final score: Toronto 8, Philadelphia 5.

MOST PENALTIES, ONE GAME:
8 — **Forbes Kennedy, Toronto,** April 2, 1969, at Boston. Four minors, 2 majors, 1 10-minute misconduct, 1 game misconduct. Final score: Boston 10, Toronto 0.
— **Kim Clackson, Pittsburgh,** April 14, 1980, at Boston. Five minors, 2 majors, 1 10-minute misconduct. Final score: Boston 6, Pittsburgh 2

MOST POINTS, ONE PERIOD:
4 — **Maurice Richard, Montreal,** March 29, 1945, at Montreal vs. Toronto. Third period, 3 goals, 1 assist. Final score: Montreal 10, Toronto 3.
— **Dickie Moore, Montreal,** March 25, 1954, at Montreal vs. Boston. First period, 2 goals, 2 assists. Final score: Montreal 8, Boston 1.
— **Barry Pederson, Boston,** April 8, 1982, at Boston vs. Buffalo. Second period, 3 goals, 1 assist. Final score: Boston 7, Buffalo 3.
— **Peter McNab, Boston,** April 11, 1982, at Buffalo. Second period, 1 goal, 3 assists. Final score: Boston 5, Buffalo 2.
— **Tim Kerr, Philadelphia,** April 13, 1985 at New York. Second period, 4 goals. Final score: Philadelphia 6, Rangers 5.
— **Ken Linseman, Boston,** April 14, 1985 at Boston vs. Montreal. Second period, 2 goals, 2 assists. Final score: Boston 7, Montreal 6.
— **Wayne Gretzky, Edmonton,** April 12, 1987, at Los Angeles. Third period, 1 goal, 3 assists. Final score: Edmonton 6, Los Angeles 3.
— **Glenn Anderson, Edmonton,** April 6, 1988, at Edmonton vs. Winnipeg. Third period, 3 goals, 1 assist. Final score: Edmonton 7, Winnipeg 4.
— **Mario Lemieux, Pittsburgh,** April 25, 1989, at Pittsburgh vs. Philadelphia. First period, 4 goals. Final score: Pittsburgh 10, Philadelphia 7.
— **Dave Gagner, Minnesota,** April 8, 1991, at Minnesota vs. Chicago. First period, 2 goals, 2 assists. Final score: Chicago 6, Minnesota 5.
— **Mario Lemieux, Pittsburgh,** April 23, 1992, at Pittsburgh vs. Washington. Second period, 2 goals, 2 assists. Final score: Pittsburgh 6, Washington 4.

MOST GOALS, ONE PERIOD:
4 — Tim Kerr, Philadelphia, April 13, 1985, at New York vs. NY Rangers, second period. Final score: Philadelphia 6, NY Rangers 5.
— Mario Lemieux, Pittsburgh, April 25, 1989, at Pittsburgh vs. Philadelphia, first period. Final score: Pittsburgh 10, Philadelphia 7.
3 — Harvey (Busher) Jackson, Toronto, April 5, 1932, at New York vs. NY Rangers, second period. Final score: Toronto 6, NY Rangers 4.
— Maurice Richard, Montreal, March 23, 1944, at Montreal vs. Toronto, second period. Final score: Montreal 5, Toronto 1.
— Maurice Richard, Montreal, March 29, 1945, at Montreal vs. Toronto, third period. Final score: Montreal 10, Toronto 3.
— Maurice Richard, Montreal, April 6, 1957 at Montreal vs. Boston, second period. Final score: Montreal 5, Boston 1.
— Ted Lindsay, Detroit, April 5, 1955, at Detroit vs. Montreal, second period. Final score: Detroit 7, Montreal 1.
— Red Berenson, St. Louis, April 15, 1969, at St. Louis vs. Los Angeles, second period. Final score: St. Louis 4, Los Angeles 0.
— Jacques Lemaire, Montreal, April 20, 1971, at Montreal vs. Minnesota, second period. Final score: Montreal 7, Minnesota 2.
— Rick MacLeish, Philadelphia, April 11, 1974, at Philadelphia vs. Atlanta, second period. Final score: Philadelphia 5, Atlanta 1.
— Tom Williams, Los Angeles, April 14, 1974, at Los Angeles vs. Chicago, third period. Final score: Los Angeles 5, Chicago 1.
— Darryl Sittler, Toronto, April 22, 1976, at Toronto vs. Philadelphia, second period. Final score: Toronto 8, Philadelphia 5.
— Reggie Leach, Philadelphia, May 6, 1976, at Philadelphia vs. Boston, second period. Final score: Philadelphia 6, Boston 3.
— Bobby Schmautz, Boston, April 11, 1977, at Boston vs. Los Angeles, first period. Final score: Boston 8, Los Angeles 3.
— George Ferguson, Toronto, April 11, 1978, at Toronto vs. Los Angeles, third period. Final score: Toronto 7, Los Angeles 3.
— Barry Pederson, Boston, April 8, 1982, at Boston vs. Buffalo, second period. Final score: Boston 7, Buffalo 3.
— Peter Stastny, Quebec, April 5, 1983, at Boston, first period. Final score: Boston 4, Quebec 3.
— Wayne Gretzky, Edmonton, April 6, 1983 at Edmonton, second period. Final score: Edmonton 6, Winnipeg 3.
— Mike Bossy, NY Islanders, May 7, 1983 at New York, second period. Final score: NY Islanders 8, Boston 4.
— Dave Andreychuk, Buffalo, April 14, 1985, at Buffalo vs. Quebec, third period. Final score: Buffalo 7, Quebec 4.
— Wayne Gretzky, Edmonton, May 25, 1985, at Edmonton vs. Philadelphia, first period. Final score: Edmonton 4, Philadelphia 3.
— Glenn Anderson, Edmonton, April 6, 1988, at Edmonton vs. Winnipeg, third period. Final score: Edmonton 7, Winnipeg 4.
— Tim Kerr, Philadelphia, April 19, 1989, at Pittsburgh vs. Penguins, first period. Final score: Philadelphia 4, Pittsburgh 2.
— Petr Klima, Edmonton, May 4, 1991, at Edmonton vs. Minnesota, first period. Final score: Edmonton 7, Minnesota 2.
— Dino Ciccarelli, Washington, April 25, 1992, at Pittsburgh, third period. Final score: Washington 7, Pittsburgh 2.
— Kevin Stevens, Pittsburgh, May 17, 1992, at Boston, first period. Final score: Pittsburgh 5, Boston 1.
— Dirk Graham, Chicago, June 1, 1992, at Chicago vs. Pittsburgh, first period. Final score: Pittsburgh 6, Chicago 5.

MOST POWER-PLAY GOALS, ONE PERIOD:
3 — Tim Kerr, Philadelphia, April 13, 1985 at New York, second period in 6-5 win vs. NY Rangers.
2 — Two power-play goals have been scored by one player in one period on 40 occasions. Charlie Conacher of Toronto was the first to score two power-play goals in one period, setting the mark on Mar. 26, 1936. Nelson Emerson of St. Louis is the most recent to equal this mark with two power-play goals in the first period at St. Louis, April 22, 1992. Final score: St. Louis 5, Chicago 4.

MOST SHORTHAND GOALS, ONE PERIOD:
2 — Bryan Trottier, NY Islanders, April 8, 1980, second period at New York in 8-1 win vs. Los Angeles.
— Bobby Lalonde, Boston, April 11, 1981, third period at Minnesota in 6-3 win by Minnesota.
— Jari Kurri, Edmonton, April 24, 1983, third period at Edmonton in 8-4 win vs. Chicago.

MOST ASSISTS, ONE PERIOD:
3 — Three assists by one player in one period of a playoff game have been recorded on **56** occasions. Chris Chelios of Chicago is the most recent to equal this mark with 3 assists in the third period at Chicago vs. Edmonton, May 18, 1992. Final score: Chicago 4, Edmonton 2.
Wayne Gretzky has had 3 assists in one period 5 times; Ray Bourque, 3 times; Toe Blake, Jean Beliveau, Doug Harvey and Bobby Orr, twice. Nick Metz of Toronto was the first player to be credited with 3 assists in one period of a playoff game Mar. 21, 1941 at Toronto vs. Boston.

MOST PENALTIES, ONE PERIOD AND MOST PENALTY MINUTES, ONE PERIOD:
6 Penalties; 39 Minutes — Ed Hospodar, NY Rangers, April 9, 1981, at Los Angeles, first period. Two minors, 1 major, 1 10-minute misconduct, 2 game misconducts. Final score: Los Angeles 5, NY Rangers 4.

FASTEST TWO GOALS:
5 Seconds — Norm Ullman, Detroit, at Detroit, April 11, 1965, vs. Chicago and goaltender Glenn Hall. Ullman scored at 17:35 and 17:40 of second period. Detroit won 4-2.

FASTEST GOAL FROM START OF GAME:
6 Seconds — Don Kozak, Los Angeles, April 17, 1977, at Los Angeles vs. Boston and goaltender Gerry Cheevers. Los Angeles won 7-4.
7 Seconds — Bob Gainey, Montreal, May 5, 1977, at New York vs. NY Islanders and goaltender Glenn Resch. Montreal won 2-1.
— Terry Murray, Philadelphia, April 12, 1981, at Quebec vs. goaltender Dan Bouchard. Quebec won 4-3 in overtime.
8 Seconds — Stan Smyl, Vancouver, April 7, 1982, at Vancouver vs. Calgary and goaltender Pat Riggin. Vancouver won 5-3.

FASTEST GOAL FROM START OF PERIOD (OTHER THAN FIRST):
6 Seconds — Pelle Eklund, Philadelphia, April 25, 1989, at Pittsburgh vs. goaltender Tom Barrasso, second period. Pittsburgh won 10-7.
9 Seconds — Bill Collins, Minnesota, April 9, 1968, at Minnesota vs. Los Angeles and goaltender Wayne Rutledge, third period. Minnesota won 7-5.
— Dave Balon, Minnesota, April 25, 1968, at St. Louis vs. goaltender Glenn Hall, third period. Minnesota won 5-1.
— Murray Oliver, Minnesota, April 8, 1971, at St. Louis vs. goaltender Ernie Wakely, third period. St. Louis won 4-2.
— Clark Gillies, NY Islanders, April 15, 1977, at Buffalo vs. goaltender Don Edwards, third period. NY Islanders won 4-3.
— Eric Vail, Atlanta, April 11, 1978, at Atlanta vs. Detroit and goaltender Ron Low, third period. Detroit won 5-3.
— Stan Smyl, Vancouver, April 10, 1979, at Philadelphia vs. goaltender Wayne Stephenson, third period. Vancouver won 3-2.
— Wayne Gretzky, Edmonton, April 6, 1983, at Edmonton vs. Winnipeg and goaltender Brian Hayward, second period. Edmonton won 6-3.
— Mark Messier, Edmonton, April 16, 1984, at Calgary vs. goaltender Don Edwards, third period. Edmonton won 5-3.
— Brian Skrudland, Montreal, May 18, 1986 at Calgary vs. Calgary and goaltender Mike Vernon, overtime. Montreal won 3-2.

FASTEST TWO GOALS FROM START OF GAME:
1 Minute, 8 Seconds — Dick Duff, Toronto, April 9, 1963 at Toronto vs. Detroit and goaltender Terry Sawchuk. Duff scored at 49 seconds and 1:08. Final score: Toronto 4, Detroit 2.

FASTEST TWO GOALS FROM START OF PERIOD:
35 Seconds — Pat LaFontaine, NY Islanders, May 19, 1984 at Edmonton vs. goaltender Andy Moog. LaFontaine scored at 13 and 35 seconds of third period. Final score: Edmonton 5, NY Islanders 2.

Early Playoff Records

1893-1918

Team Records

MOST GOALS, BOTH TEAMS, ONE GAME:
25 — Ottawa Silver Seven, Dawson City at Ottawa, Jan. 16, 1905. Ottawa 23, Dawson City 2. Ottawa won best-of-three series 2-0.

MOST GOALS, ONE TEAM, ONE GAME:
23 — Ottawa Silver Seven at Ottawa, Jan. 16, 1905. Ottawa defeated Dawson City 23-2.

MOST GOALS, BOTH TEAMS, BEST-OF-THREE SERIES:
42 — Ottawa Silver Seven, Queen's University at Ottawa, 1906. Ottawa defeated Queen's 16-7, Feb. 27, and 12-7, Feb. 28.

MOST GOALS, ONE TEAM, BEST-OF-THREE SERIES:
32 — Ottawa Silver Seven in 1905 at Ottawa. Defeated Dawson City 9-2, Jan. 13, and 23-2, Jan. 16.

MOST GOALS, BOTH TEAMS, BEST-OF-FIVE SERIES:
39 — Toronto Arenas, Vancouver Millionaires at Toronto, 1918. Toronto won 5-3, Mar. 20; 6-3, Mar. 26; 2-1, Mar. 30. Vancouver won 6-4, Mar. 23, and 8-1, Mar. 28. Toronto scored 18 goals; Vancouver 21.

MOST GOALS, ONE TEAM, BEST-OF-FIVE SERIES:
26 — Vancouver Millionaires in 1915 at Vancouver. Defeated Ottawa Senators 6-2, Mar. 22; 8-3, Mar. 24; and 12-3 Mar. 26.

Individual Records

MOST GOALS IN PLAYOFFS:
63 — Frank McGee, Ottawa Silver Seven, in 22 playoff games. Seven goals in four games, 1903; 21 goals in eight games, 1904; 18 goals in four games, 1905; 17 goals in six games, 1906.

MOST GOALS, ONE PLAYOFF SERIES:
15 — Frank McGee, Ottawa Silver Seven, in two games in 1905 at Ottawa. Scored one goal, Jan. 13, in 9-2 victory over Dawson City and 14 goals, Jan. 16, in 23-2 victory.

MOST GOALS, ONE PLAYOFF GAME:
14 — Frank McGee, Ottawa Silver Seven, Jan. 16, 1905 at Ottawa in 23-2 victory over Dawson City.

FASTEST THREE GOALS:
40 Seconds — Marty Walsh, Ottawa Senators, at Ottawa, March 16, 1911, at 3:00, 3:10, and 3:40 of third period. Ottawa defeated Port Arthur 13-4.

Reg Leach (far left) scored 47 goals in 94 playoff games, including a record 19 in the 1976 post-season. Brian Propp (left) ranks tenth among all-time playoff goal scorers with 64 goals in 147 post-season games.

All-Time Playoff Goal Leaders since 1918

(40 or more goals)

Player	Teams	Yrs.	GP	G
*Wayne Gretzky	Edm., L.A.	13	156	95
*Jari Kurri	Edm., L.A.	11	150	93
*Mark Messier	Edm., NYR	13	177	87
Mike Bossy	NY Islanders	10	129	85
Maurice Richard	Montreal	15	133	82
*Glenn Anderson	Edmonton	11	164	81
Jean Beliveau	Montreal	17	162	79
Bryan Trottier	NYI, Pit.	16	219	71
Gordie Howe	Det., Hfd.	20	157	68
*Brian Propp	Phi., Bos., Min.	14	160	64
Yvan Cournoyer	Montreal	12	147	64
*Bobby Smith	Min., Mtl.	13	184	64
Bobby Hull	Chi., Hfd.	14	119	62
Phil Esposito	Chi., Bos., NYR	15	130	61
Jacques Lemaire	Montreal	11	145	61
Stan Mikita	Chicago	18	155	59
Guy Lafleur	Mtl., NYR	14	128	58
Bernie Geoffrion	Mtl., NYR	16	132	58
*Denis Savard	Chicago, Mtl.	12	123	58
Denis Potvin	NY Islanders	14	185	56
*Joe Mullen	St.L., Cgy., Pit.	10	112	55
Rick MacLeish	Phi., Pit., Det.	11	114	54
Bill Barber	Philadelphia	11	129	53
*Cam Neely	Bos.	6	84	51
*Esa Tikkanen	Edm.	8	114	51
Frank Mahovlich	Tor., Det., Mtl.	14	137	51
Steve Shutt	Mtl., LA.	12	99	50
*Dino Ciccarelli	Min., Wsh	10	94	49
Henri Richard	Montreal	18	180	49
Reggie Leach	Bos., Phi.	8	94	47
Ted Lindsay	Det., Chi.	16	133	47
Clark Gillies	NYI, Buf.	13	164	47
Dickie Moore	Mtl., Tor., St. L.	14	135	46
Rick Middleton	NYR, Bos.	12	114	45
*Steve Larmer	Chicago	10	103	45
*Mario Lemieux	Pittsburgh	3	49	44
*Paul Coffey	Edm., Pit., L.A.	10	123	44
Lanny McDonald	Tor., Cgy.	13	117	44
*Ken Linseman	Phi., Edm., Bos.	11	113	43
*Brett Hull	Cgy., St. L.	7	57	42
Bobby Clarke	Philadelphia	13	136	42
John Bucyk	Det., Bos.	14	124	41
*Tim Kerr	Phi., NYR	10	81	40
Peter McNab	Bos., Van.	10	107	40
Bob Bourne	NYI, L.A.	13	139	40
*John Tonelli	NYI, Cgy., L.A.	13	172	40

* — Active player.

All-Time Playoff Assist Leaders since 1918

(60 or more assists)

Player	Teams	Yrs.	GP	A
*Wayne Gretzky	Edm., L.A.	13	156	211
*Mark Messier	Edm., NYR	13	177	142
Larry Robinson	Mtl., L.A.	20	227	116
Bryan Trottier	NY, Pit.	16	219	113
*Jari Kurri	Edm., L.A.	11	150	112
Denis Potvin	NY Islanders	14	185	108
*Glenn Anderson	Edmonton	11	164	102
Jean Beliveau	Montreal	17	162	97
*Bobby Smith	Min., Mtl.	13	184	96
*Ray Bourque	Boston	13	135	95
Gordie Howe	Det., Hfd.	20	157	92
*Paul Coffey	Edm., Pit., L.A.	10	123	92
Stan Mikita	Chicago	18	155	91
Brad Park	NYR, Bos., Det.	17	161	90
*Denis Savard	Chi., Mtl.	12	123	89
*Brian Propp	Phi., Bos., Min.	14	160	84
Henri Richard	Montreal	18	180	80
Jacques Lemaire	Montreal	11	145	78
*Ken Linseman	Phi., Edm., Bos.	11	113	77
Bobby Clarke	Philadelphia	13	136	77
Guy Lafleur	Mtl., NYR	14	128	76
Phil Esposito	Chi., Bos., NYR	15	130	76
Mike Bossy	NY Islanders	10	129	75
*John Tonelli	NYI, Cgy., L.A.	13	172	75
*Chris Chelios	Mtl., Chi.	9	122	74
*Peter Stastny	Que., N.J.	10	84	70
Gilbert Perreault	Buffalo	11	90	70
Alex Delvecchio	Detroit	14	121	69
Bobby Hull	Chi., Hfd.	14	119	67
Frank Mahovlich	Tor., Det., Mtl.	14	137	67
Bobby Orr	Boston	8	74	66
*Adam Oates	Det., St. L., Bos.	6	78	66
Bernie Federko	St. Louis	11	91	66
Jean Ratelle	NYR, Bos.	15	123	66
*Al MacInnis	Calgary	8	82	65
Dickie Moore	Mtl., Tor., St. L.	14	135	64
Doug Harvey	Mtl., NYR, St. L.	15	137	64
*Steve Larmer	Chicago	10	103	63
Yvan Cournoyer	Montreal	12	147	63
*Craig Janney	Bos., St. L.	5	75	62
*Charlie Huddy	Edm., L.A.	11	144	62
John Bucyk	Det., Bos.	14	124	62
*Doug Wilson	Chicago	12	95	61

All-Time Playoff Point Leaders since 1918

(100 or more points)

Player	Teams	Yrs.	GP	G	A	Pts.
*Wayne Gretzky	Edm., L.A.	13	156	95	211	306
*Mark Messier	Edm., NYR	13	177	87	142	229
*Jari Kurri	Edm., L.A.	11	150	93	112	205
Bryan Trottier	NYI, Pit.	16	219	71	113	184
*Glenn Anderson	Edmonton	11	164	81	102	183
Jean Beliveau	Montreal	17	162	79	97	176
Denis Potvin	NY Islanders	14	185	56	108	164
Mike Bossy	NY Islanders	10	129	85	75	160
Gordie Howe	Det., Hfd.	20	157	68	92	160
*Bobby Smith	Min., Mtl.	13	184	64	96	160
Stan Mikita	Chicago	18	155	59	91	150
*Brian Propp	Phi., Bos., Min.	13	160	64	84	148
*Denis Savard	Chi., Mtl.	12	123	58	89	147
Larry Robinson	Mtl., L.A.	20	227	28	116	144
Jacques Lemaire	Montreal	11	145	61	78	139
Phil Esposito	Chi., Bos., NYR	15	130	61	76	137
*Paul Coffey	Edm., Pit., L.A.	10	123	44	92	136
Guy Lafleur	Mtl, NYR	14	128	58	76	134
Bobby Hull	Chi., Hfd.	14	119	62	67	129
Henri Richard	Montreal	18	180	49	80	129
Yvan Cornoyer	Montreal	12	147	64	63	127
Maurice Richard	Montreal	15	133	82	44	126
*Ray Bourque	Boston	13	135	30	95	125
Brad Park	NYR, Bos., Det.	17	161	35	90	125
*Ken Linseman	Phi., Edm., Bos.	11	113	43	77	120
Bobby Clarke	Philadelphia	13	136	42	77	119
Bernie Geoffrion	Mtl., NYR	16	132	58	60	118
Frank Mahovlich	Tor., Det., Mtl.	14	137	51	67	118
*John Tonelli	NYI, Cgy., L.A.	13	172	40	75	115
Dickie Moore	Mtl., Tor., St. L.	14	135	46	64	110
Bill Barber	Philadelphia	11	129	53	55	108
*Steve Larmer	Chicago	10	103	45	63	108
Rick MacLeish	Phi., Pit., Det.	11	114	54	53	107
Alex Delveccio	Detroit	14	121	35	69	104
John Bucyk	Det., Bos.	14	124	41	62	103
*Peter Stastny	Que., N.J.	10	84	33	70	103
Gilbert Perreault	Buffalo	11	90	33	70	103
Bernie Federko	St. Louis	11	91	35	66	101
Rick Middleton	NYR, Bos.	12	114	45	55	100

Three-or-more-Goal Games, Playoffs 1918–1992

Player	Team	Date	City	Total Goals	Opposing Goaltender	Score	
Maurice Richard (7)	Mtl.	Mar.23/44	Mtl.	5	Paul Bibeault	Mtl. 5	Tor. 1
		Apr. 7/44	Chi.	3	Mike Karakas	Mtl. 3	Chi. 1
		Mar.29/45	Mtl.	4	Frank McCool	Mtl. 10	Tor. 3
		Apr.14/53	Bos.	3	Gord Henry	Mtl. 7	Bos. 3
		Mar.20/56	Mtl.	3	Lorne Worsley	Mtl. 7	NYR 1
		Apr. 6/57	Mtl.	4	Don Simmons	Mtl. 5	Bos. 1
		Apr. 1/58	Det.	3	Terry Sawchuk	Mtl. 4	Det. 3
Wayne Gretzky (7)	Edm.	Apr.11/81	Edm.	3	Richard Sevigny	Edm. 6	Mtl. 2
		Apr.19/81	Edm.	3	Billy Smith	Edm. 5	NYI 2
		Apr. 6/83	Edm.	4	Brian Hayward	Edm. 6	Wpg. 3
		Apr.17/83	Cgy.	4	Rejean Lemelin	Edm. 10	Cgy. 2
		Apr.25/85	Wpg.	3	Bryan Hayward (2)		
					Marc Behrend (1)	Edm. 8	Wpg. 3
		May25/85	Edm.	3	Pelle Lindbergh	Edm. 4	Phi. 3
		Apr.24/86	Cgy.	3	Mike Vernon	Edm. 7	Cgy. 4
		Apr. 4/84	Edm.	3	Doug Soetaert (1)		
					Mike Veisor (2)	Edm. 9	Wpg. 2
Jari Kurri (7)	Edm.	Apr.25/85	Wpg.	3	Bryan Hayward (2)		
					Marc Behrend (1)	Edm. 8	Wpg. 3
		May 7/85	Edm.	3	Murray Bannerman	Edm. 7	Chi. 3
		May14/85	Edm.	3	Murray Bannerman	Edm. 10	Chi. 5
		May16/85	Chi.	4	Murray Bannerman	Edm. 8	Chi. 2
		Apr. 9/87	Edm.	4	Roland Melanson (2)		
					Daren Eliot (2)	Edm. 13	L.A. 3
		May18/90	Bos.	3	Andy Moog (2)		
					Rejean Lemelin (1)	Edm. 7	Bos. 2
Mike Bossy (5)	NYI	Apr.16/79	NYI	3	Tony Esposito	NYI 6	Chi. 2
		May 8/82	NYI	3	Richard Brodeur	NYI 6	Van. 5
		Apr.10/83	Wsh.	3	Al Jensen	NYI 6	Wsh. 3
		May 3/83	NYI	3	Pete Peeters	NYI 8	Bos. 3
		May 7/83	NYI	4	Pete Peeters	NYI 8	Bos. 4
Phil Esposito (4)	Bos.	Apr. 2/69	Bos.	4	Bruce Gamble	Bos. 10	Tor. 0
		Apr. 8/70	Bos.	3	Ed Giacomin	Bos. 8	NYR 2
		Apr.19/70	Chi.	3	Tony Esposito	Bos. 6	Chi. 3
		Apr. 8/75	Bos.	3	Tony Esposito (2)		
					Michel Dumas (1)	Bos. 8	Chi. 2
Dino Ciccarelli (4)	Min.	May 5/81	Min.	3	Pat Riggin	Min. 7	Cgy. 4
		Apr.10/82	Min.	3	Murray Bannerman	Min. 7	Chi. 1
	Wsh.	Apr. 5/90	N.J.	3	Sean Burke	Wsh. 5	N.J. 4
	Wsh.	Apr.25/92	Pit.	4	Tom Barrasso (1)		
					Ken Wregget (3)	Wsh. 7	Pit. 2
Bernie Geoffrion (3)	Mtl.	Mar.27/52	Mtl.	3	Jim Henry	Mtl. 4	Bos. 0
		Apr. 7/55	Mtl.	3	Terry Sawchuk	Mtl. 4	Det. 2
		Mar.30/57	Mtl.	3	Lorne Worsley	Mtl. 8	NYR 3
Norm Ullman (3)	Det.	Mar.29/64	Chi.	3	Glenn Hall	Det. 5	Chi. 4
		Apr. 7/64	Det.	3	Glenn Hall (2)		
					Denis DeJordy (1)	Det. 7	Chi. 2
		Apr.11/65	Det.	3	Glenn Hall	Det. 4	Chi. 2
John Bucyk (3)	Bos.	May 3/70	St. L.	3	Jacques Plante (1)		
					Ernie Wakely (2)	Bos. 6	St.L. 1
		Apr.20/72	Bos.	3	Jacques Caron (1)		
					Ernie Wakely (2)	Bos. 10	St.L. 2
		Apr.21/74	Bos.	3	Tony Esposito	Bos. 8	Chi. 6
Rick MacLeish (3)	Phil	Apr.11/74	Phil	3	Phil Myre	Phi. 5	Atl. 1
		Apr.13/75	Phil	3	Gord McRae	Phi. 6	Tor. 3
		May13/75	Phil	3	Glenn Resch	Phi. 4	NYI 1
Denis Savard (3)	Chi.	Apr.19/82	Chi.	3	Mike Liut	Chi. 7	StL. 4
		Apr.10/86	Chi.	4	Ken Wregget	Tor. 6	Chi. 4
		Apr. 9/88	St.L.	3	Greg Millen	Chi. 6	St.L. 3
Mark Messier (3)	Edm.	Apr.14/83	Edm.	4	Rejean Lemelin	Edm. 6	Cgy. 3
		Apr.17/83	Cgy.	3	Rejean Lemelin (1)	Edm. 10	Cgy. 2
					Don Edwards (2)		
		Apr.26/83	Edm.	3	Murray Bannerman	Edm. 8	Chi. 2
Tim Kerr (3)	Phi.	Apr.13/85	NYR	4	Glen Hanlon	Phi. 6	NYR 5
		Apr.20/87	Phi.	3	Kelly Hrudey	Phi. 4	NYI 2
		Apr.19/89	Pit.	3	Tom Barrasso	Phi. 4	Pit. 2
Cam Neely (3)	Bos.	Apr. 9/87	Mtl.	3	Patrick Roy	Mtl. 4	Bos. 3
	Bos.	Apr. 5/91	Bos.	3	Peter Sidorkiewicz	Bos. 4	Hfd. 3
	Bos.	Apr.25/91	Bos.	3	Patrick Roy	Bos. 4	Mtl. 1
Petr Klima (3)	Det.	Apr. 7/88	Tor.	3	Alan Bester (2)		
					Ken Wregett (1)	Det. 6	Tor. 2
		Apr.21/88	St.L.	3	Greg Millen	Det. 6	St.L. 0
	Edm.	May 4/91	Edm.	3	Jon Casey	Edm. 7	Min. 2
Esa Tikkanen (3)	Edm.	May22/88	Edm.	3	Rejean Lemelin	Edm. 6	Bos. 3
	Edm.	Apr.16/91	Cgy.	3	Mike Vernon	Edm. 5	Cgy. 4
	Edm.	Apr.26/92	L.A.	3	Kelly Hrudey	Edm. 5	L.A. 2
Newsy Lalonde (2)	Mtl.	Mar. 1/19	Mtl.	5	Clint Benedict	Mtl. 6	Ott. 3
	Mtl.	Mar.22/19	Sea.	4	Harry Holmes	Mtl. 4	Sea. 2
Howie Morenz (2)	Mtl.	Mar.22/24	Mtl.	3	Charles Reid	Mtl. 6	Cgy.T. 1
	Mtl.	Mar.27/25	Mtl.	3	Harry Holmes	Mtl. 4	Vic. 2
Toe Blake (2)	Mtl.	Mar.22/38	Mtl.	3	Mike Karakas	Mtl. 6	Chi. 4
		Mar.26/46	Chi.	3	Mike Karakas	Mtl. 7	Chi. 2
Doug Bentley (2)	Chi.	Mar.28/44	Chi.	3	Connie Dion	Chi. 7	Det. 1
		Mar.30/44	Det.	3	Connie Dion	Chi. 5	Det. 2
Ted Kennedy (2)	Tor.	Apr.14/45	Tor.	3	Harry Lumley	Det. 5	Tor. 3
		Mar.27/48	Tor.	4	Frank Brimsek	Tor. 5	Bos. 3
Bobby Hull (2)	Chi.	Apr. 7/63	Det.	3	Terry Sawchuk	Det. 7	Chi. 4
		Apr. 9/72	Pitt	3	Jim Rutherford	Chi. 6	Pit. 5
F. St. Marseille (2)	St. L.	Apr.28/70	St.L	3	Al Smith	St.L. 5	Pit. 0
		Apr. 6/72	Min.	3	Cesare Maniago	Min. 6	St.L. 5
Pit Martin (2)	Chi.	Apr. 4/73	Chi.	3	W. Stephenson	Chi. 7	St.L. 1
		May10/73	Chi.	3	Ken Dryden	Mtl. 6	Chi. 4
Yvan Cournoyer (2)	Mtl.	Apr. 5/73	Mtl.	3	Dave Dryden	Mtl. 7	Buf. 3
		Apr.11/74	Mtl.	3	Ed Giacomin	Mtl. 4	NYR 1
Guy Lafleur (2)	Mtl.	May 1/75	Mtl.	3	Roger Crozier (1)		
					Gerry Desjardins (2)	Mtl. 7	Buf. 0
		Apr.11/77	Mtl.	3	Ed Staniowski	Mtl. 7	St.L. 2
Lanny McDonald (2)	Tor.	Apr. 9/77	Pitt	3	Denis Herron	Tor. 5	Pit. 2
		Apr.17/77	Tor.	4	W. Stephenson	Phi. 6	Tor. 5
Butch Goring (2)	L.A.	Apr. 9/77	L.A.	3	Phil Myre	L.A. 4	Atl. 2
	NYI	May17/81	Min.	3	Gilles Meloche	NYI 7	Min. 5
Bryan Trottier (2)	NYI	Apr. 8/80	NYI	3	Doug Keans	NYI 8	L.A. 1
		Apr. 9/81	NYI	3	Michel Larocque	NYI 5	Tor. 1
Bill Barber (2)	Phil	May 4/80	Min.	4	Gilles Meloche	Phi. 5	Min. 3
		Apr. 9/81	Phil	3	Dan Bouchard	Phi. 8	Que. 5
Brian Propp (2)	Phi.	Apr.22/81	Phi.	3	Pat Riggin	Phi. 9	Cgy. 4
		Apr.21/85	Phi.	3	Billy Smith	Phi. 5	NYI 2
Paul Reinhart (2)	Cgy	Apr.14/83	Edm.	3	Andy Moog	Edm. 6	Cgy. 3
		Apr. 8/84	Van	3	Richard Brodeur	Cgy. 5	Van. 1
Peter Stastny (2)	Que.	Apr. 5/83	Bos.	3	Pete Peeters	Bos. 4	Que. 3
		Apr.11/87	Que.	3	Mike Liut (2)		
					Steve Weeks (1)	Que. 5	Hfd. 1
Glenn Anderson (2)	Edm.	Apr.26/83	Edm.	4	Murray Bannerman	Edm. 8	Chi. 2
		Apr. 6/88	Wpg.	3	Daniel Berthiaume	Edm. 7	Wpg. 4
Michel Goulet (2)	Que.	Apr.23/85	Que.	3	Steve Penney	Que. 7	Mtl. 6
		Apr.12/87	Que.	3	Mike Liut	Que. 4	Hfd. 1
Peter Zezel (2)	Phi.	Apr.13/86	NYR	3	J. Vanbiesbrouck	Phi. 7	NYR 1
	St. L.	Apr.11/89	St. L.	3	Jon Casey (2)		
					Kari Takko (1)	St. L. 6	Min. 1
Steve Yzerman (2)	Det.	Apr. 6/89	Det.	3	Alain Chevrier	Chi. 5	Det. 4
	Det.	Apr. 4/91	St.L.	3	Vincent Riendeau (2)	Det. 6	St. L. 3
					Pat Jablonski (1)		
Mario Lemieux (2)	Pit.	Apr.25/89	Pit.	5	Ron Hextall	Pit. 10	Phi. 7
	Pit.	Apr.23/92	Pit.	3	Don Beaupre	Pit. 6	Wsh. 4
Mike Gartner (2)	NYR	Apr.13/90	NYR	3	Mark Fitzpatrick (2)		
					Glenn Healy (1)	NYR 6	NYI 5
	NYR	Apr.27/92	NYR	3	Chris Terreri	NYR 8	N.J. 5
Geoff Courtnall (2)	Van.	Apr. 4/91	L.A.	3	Kelly Hrudey	Van. 6	L.A. 5
	Van.	Apr.30/92	Van.	3	Rick Tabaracci	Van. 5	Win. 5
Harry Meeking	Tor.	Mar.11/18	Tor.	3	Georges Vezina	Tor. 7	Mtl. 3
Alf Skinner	Tor.	Mar.23/18	Tor.	3	Hugh Lehman	Van.M. 6	Tor. 4
Joe Malone	Mtl.	Feb.23/19	Mtl.	3	Clint Benedict	Mtl. 8	Ott. 4
Odie Cleghorn	Mtl.	Feb.27/19	Ott.	3	Clint Benedict	Mtl. 5	Ott. 3
Jack Darragh	Ott.	Apr. 1/20	Tor.	3	Harry Holmes	Ott. 6	Sea. 1
George Boucher	Ott.	Mar.10/21	Ott.	3	Jake Forbes	Ott. 5	Tor. 0
Babe Dye	Tor.	Mar.28/22	Tor.	4	Hugh Lehman	Tor. 5	Van.M. 1
Perk Galbraith	Bos.	Mar.31/27	Bos.	3	Hugh Lehman	Bos. 4	Chi. 4
Busher Jackson	Tor.	Apr. 5/32	NYR	3	John Ross Roach	Tor. 6	NYR 4
Frank Boucher	NYR	Apr. 9/32	Tor.	3	Lorne Chabot	Tor. 6	NYR 4
Charlie Conacher	Tor.	Mar.26/36	Tor.	3	Tiny Thompson	Tor. 8	Bos. 3
Syd Howe	Det.	Mar.23/39	Det.	3	Claude Bourque	Det. 7	Mtl. 3
Bryan Hextall	NYR	Apr. 3/40	NYR	3	Turk Broda	NYR 6	Tor. 2
Joe Benoit	Mtl.	Mar.22/41	Mtl.	3	Sam LoPresti	Mtl. 4	Chi. 3
Syl Apps	Tor.	Mar.25/41	Tor.	3	Frank Brimsek	Tor. 7	Bos. 2
Jack McGill	Bos.	Mar.29/42	Bos.	3	Johnny Mowers	Det. 6	Bos. 4
Don Metz	Tor.	Apr.14/42	Tor.	3	Johnny Mowers	Tor. 9	Det. 3
Mud Bruneteau	Det.	Apr. 1/43	Det.	3	Frank Brimsek	Det. 6	Bos. 2
Don Grosso	Det.	Apr. 7/43	Bos.	3	Frank Brimsek	Det. 4	Bos. 0
Carl Liscombe	Det.	Apr. 3/45	Bos.	4	Paul Bibeault	Det. 5	Bos. 3
Billy Reay	Mtl.	Apr. 1/47	Bos.	4	Frank Brimsek	Mtl. 5	Bos. 1
Gerry Plamondon	Mtl.	Mar.24/49	Det.	3	Harry Lumley	Mtl. 4	Det. 3
Sid Smith	Tor.	Apr.10/49	Det.	3	Harry Lumley	Tor. 3	Det. 1
Pentti Lund	NYR	Apr. 2/50	NYR	3	Bill Durnan	NYR 4	Mtl. 1
Ted Lindsay	Det.	Apr. 5/55	Det.	4	Charlie Hodge (1)		
					Jacques Plante (3)	Det. 7	Mtl. 1
Gordie Howe	Det.	Apr.10/55	Det.	3	Jacques Plante	Det. 5	Mtl. 1
Phil Goyette	Mtl.	Mar.25/58	Mtl.	3	Terry Sawchuk	Mtl. 8	Det. 1
Jerry Toppazzini	Bos.	Apr. 5/58	Bos.	3	Lorne Worsley	Bos. 8	NYR 2
Bob Pulford	Tor.	Apr.19/62	Tor.	3	Glenn Hall	Tor. 8	Chi. 4
Dave Keon	Tor.	Apr. 9/64	Mtl.	3	Charlie Hodge	Tor. 3	Mtl. 1
Henri Richard	Mtl.	Apr.20/67	Mtl.	3	Terry Sawchuk (2)		
					Johnny Bower (1)	Mtl. 6	Tor. 2
Rosaire Paiement	Phi.	Apr.13/68	Phi.	3	Glenn Hall (1)		
					Seth Martin (2)	Phi. 6	St. L. 1
Jean Beliveau	Mtl.	Apr.20/68	Mtl.	3	Denis DeJordy	Mtl. 4	Chi. 1
Red Berenson	St. L.	Apr.15/69	St. L.	3	Gerry Desjardins	St. L. 4	L.A. 0
Ken Schinkel	Pit.	Apr.11/70	Oak.	3	Gary Smith	Pit. 5	Oak. 2
Jim Pappin	Chi.	Apr.11/71	Phi.	3	Bruce Gamble	Chi. 6	Phi. 2
Bobby Orr	Bos.	Apr.11/71	Mtl.	3	Ken Dryden	Bos. 5	Mtl. 2
Jacques Lemaire	Mtl.	Apr.20/71	Mtl.	3	Lorne Worsley	Mtl. 7	Min. 2
Vic Hadfield	NYR	Apr.22/71	NYR	3	Tony Esposito	NYR 4	Chi. 1
Fred Stanfield	Bos.	Apr.18/72	Bos.	3	Jacques Caron	Bos. 6	St. L. 1
Ken Hodge	Bos.	Apr.30/72	Bos.	3	Ed Giacomin	Bos. 6	NYR 5
Steve Vickers	NYR	Apr.10/73	Bos.	3	Ross Brooks (2)		
					Ed Johnston (1)	NYR 6	Bos. 3
Dick Redmond	Chi.	Apr. 4/73	Chi.	3	Wayne Stephenson	Chi. 7	St. L. 1
Tom Williams	L.A.	Apr.14/74	L.A.	3	Mike Veisor	L.A. 5	Chi. 1
Marcel Dionne	L.A.	Apr.15/76	L.A.	3	Gilles Gilbert	L.A. 6	Bos. 4
Don Saleski	Phi.	Apr.20/76	Phil	3	Wayne Thomas	Phi. 7	Tor. 1
Darryl Sittler	Tor.	Apr.22/76	Tor.	5	Bernie Parent	Tor. 8	Phi. 5
Reggie Leach	Phi.	May 6/76	Phi.	5	Gilles Gilbert	Phi. 6	Bos. 3
Jim Lorentz	Buf.	Apr. 7/77	Min.	3	Pete LoPresti (2)		
					Gary Smith (1)	Buf. 7	Min. 1
Bobby Schmautz	Bos.	Apr.11/77	Bos.	3	Rogatien Vachon	Bos. 8	L.A. 3
Billy Harris	NYI	Apr.23/77	Mtl.	3	Ken Dryden	Mtl. 4	NYI 3

Butch Goring, who tallied two playoff hat-tricks in his career, won the Conn Smythe Trophy in 1982.

Player	Team	Date	City	Total Goals	Opposing Goaltender	Score	
George Ferguson	Tor.	Apr.11/78	Tor.	3	Rogatien Vachon	Tor. 7	L.A. 3
Jean Ratelle	Bos.	May 3/79	Bos.	3	Ken Dryden	Bos. 4	Mtl. 3
Stan Jonathan	Bos.	May 8/79	Bos.	3	Ken Dryden	Bos. 5	Mtl. 2
Ron Duguay	NYR	Apr.20/80	NYR	3	Pete Peeters	NYR 4	Phi. 2
Steve Shutt	Mtl.	Apr.22/80	Mtl.	3	Gilles Meloche	Mtl. 6	Min. 2
Gilbert Perreault	Buf.	May 6/80	NYI	3	Billy Smith (2) ENG (1)	Buf. 7	NYI 4
Paul Holmgren	Phi.	May15/80	Phil	3	Billy Smith	Phi. 8	NYI 3
Steve Payne	Min.	Apr. 8/81	Bos.	3	Rogatien Vachon	Min. 5	Bos. 4
Denis Potvin	NYI	Apr.17/81	NYI	3	Andy Moog	NYI 6	Edm. 3
Barry Pederson	Bos.	Apr. 8/82	Bos.	3	Don Edwards	Bos. 7	Buf. 3
Duane Sutter	NYI	Apr.15/83	NYI	3	Glen Hanlon	NYI 5	NYR 0
Doug Halward	Van.	Apr. 7/84	Van.	3	Rejean Lemelin (2) Don Edwards (1)	Van. 7	Cgy. 0
Jorgen Pettersson	St. L.	Apr. 8/84	Det.	3	Ed Mio	St. L. 3	Det. 2
Clark Gillies	NYI	May12/84	NYI	3	Grant Fuhr	NYI 6	Edm. 1
Ken Linseman	Bos.	Apr.14/85	Bos.	3	Steve Penney	Bos. 7	Mtl. 6
Dave Andreychuk	Buf.	Apr.14/85	Buf.	3	Dan Bouchard	Que. 4	Buf. 7
Greg Paslawski	StL.	Apr.15/86	Min.	3	Don Beaupre	St. L. 6	Min. 3
Doug Risebrough	Cgy.	May 4/86	Cgy.	3	Rick Wamsley	Cgy. 8	St.L. 2
Mike McPhee	Mtl.	Apr.11/87	Bos.	3	Doug Keans	Mtl. 5	Bos. 4
John Ogrodnick	Que.	Apr.14/87	Hfd.	3	Mike Liut	Que. 7	Hfd. 5
Pelle Eklund	Phi.	May10/87	Mtl.	3	Patrick Roy (1) Bryan Hayward (2)	Phi. 6	Mtl. 3
John Tucker	Buf.	Apr. 9/88	Bos.	4	Andy Moog	Buf. 6	Bos. 2
Tony Hrkac	St.L.	Apr.10/88	St.L.	4	Darren Pang	St.L. 6	Chi. 5
Hakan Loob	Cgy.	Apr.10/88	Cgy.	3	Glenn Healy	Cgy. 7	L.A. 3
Ed Olczyk	Tor.	Apr.12/88	Tor.	3	Greg Stefan (2) Glen Hanlon (1)	Tor. 6	Det. 5
Aaron Broten	N.J.	Apr.20/88	N.J.	3	Pete Peeters	N.J. 5	Wsh. 2
Mark Johnson	N.J.	Apr.22/88	Wsh.	4	Pete Peeters	N.J. 10	Wsh. 4
Patrik Sundstrom	N.J.	Apr.22/88	Wsh.	3	Pete Peeters (2) Clint Malarchuk (1)	N.J. 10	Wsh. 4
Bob Brooke	Min.	Apr. 5/89	St. L.	3	Greg Millen	St. L. 4	Min. 3
Chris Kontos	L.A.	Apr. 6/89	L.A.	3	Grant Fuhr	L.A. 5	Edm. 2
Wayne Presley	Chi.	Apr.13/89	Chi.	3	Greg Stefan (1) Glen Hanlon (2)	Chi. 7	Det. 1
Tony Granato	L.A.	Apr.10/90	L.A.	3	Mike Vernon (1) Rick Wamsley (2)	L.A. 12	Cgy. 4
Tomas Sandstrom	L.A.	Apr.10/90	L.A.	3	Mike Vernon (1) Rick Wamsley (2)	L.A. 12	Cgy. 4
Dave Taylor	L.A.	Apr.10/90	L.A.	3	Mike Vernon (1) Rick Wamsley (2)	L.A. 12	Cgy. 4
Bernie Nicholls	NYR	Apr.19/90	NYR	3	Mike Liut	NYR 7	Wsh. 3
John Druce	Wsh.	Apr.21/90	NYR	3	John Vanbiesbrouck	Wsh. 6	NYR 3
Adam Oates	St. L.	Apr.12/91	St. L.	3	Tim Chevaldae	St. L. 6	Det. 1
Luc Robitaille	L.A.	Apr.26/91	L.A.	3	Grant Fuhr	L.A. 5	Edm. 2
Ron Francis	Pit.	May. 9/92	Pit.	3	Mike Richter (2) John V'brouck (1)	Pit. 5	NYR. 4
Dirk Graham	Chi.	June 1/92	Chi.	3	Tom Barrasso	Pit. 5	Chi. 2
Joe Murphy	Edm.	May 6/92	Edm.	3	Kirk McLean	Edm. 5	Van. 2
Ray Sheppard	Det.	Apr.24/92	Min.	3	Jon Casey	Min. 5	Det. 2
Kevin Stevens	Pit.	May21/92	Bos.	4	Andy Moog	Pit. 5	Bos. 2
Pavel Bure	Van.	Apr.28/92	Wpg.	3	Rick Tabaracci	Van. 8	Wpg. 3

Leading Playoff Scorers, 1918–1992

Season	Player and Club	Games Played	Goals	Assists	Points
1991-92	Mario Lemieux, Pittsburgh	15	16	18	34
1990-91	Mario Lemieux, Pittsburgh	23	16	28	44
1989-90	Craig Simpson, Edmonton	22	16	15	31
	Mark Messier, Edmonton	22	9	22	31
1988-89	Al MacInnis, Calgary	22	7	24	31
1987-88	Wayne Gretzky, Edmonton	19	12	31	43
1986-87	Wayne Gretzky, Edmonton	21	5	29	34
1985-86	Doug Gilmour, St. Louis	19	9	12	21
	Bernie Federko, St. Louis	19	7	14	21
1984-85	Wayne Gretzky, Edmonton	18	17	30	47
1983-84	Wayne Gretzky, Edmonton	19	13	22	35
1982-83	Wayne Gretzky, Edmonton	16	12	26	38
1981-82	Bryan Trottier, NY Islanders	19	6	23	29
1980-81	Mike Bossy, NY Islanders	18	17	18	35
1979-80	Bryan Trottier, NY Islanders	21	12	17	29
1978-79	Jacques Lemaire, Montreal	16	11	12	23
	Guy Lafleur, Montreal	16	10	13	23
1977-78	Guy Lafleur, Montreal	15	10	11	21
	Larry Robinson, Montreal	15	4	17	21
1976-77	Guy Lafleur, Montreal	14	9	17	26
1975-76	Reggie Leach, Philadelphia	16	19	5	24
1974-75	Rick MacLeish, Philadelphia	17	11	9	20
1973-74	Rick MacLeish, Philadelphia	17	13	9	22
1972-73	Yvan Cournoyer, Montreal	17	15	10	25
1971-72	Phil Esposito, Boston	15	9	15	24
	Bobby Orr, Boston	15	5	19	24
1970-71	Frank Mahovlich, Montreal	20	14	13	27
1969-70	Phil Esposito, Boston	14	13	14	27
1968-69	Phil Esposito, Boston	10	8	10	18
1967-68	Bill Goldsworthy, Minnesota	14	8	7	15
1966-67	Jim Pappin, Toronto	12	7	8	15
1965-66	Norm Ullman, Detroit	12	6	9	15
1964-65	Bobby Hull, Chicago	14	10	7	17
1963-64	Gordie Howe, Detroit	14	9	10	19
1962-63	Gordie Howe, Detroit	11	7	9	16
	Norm Ullman, Detroit	11	4	12	16
1961-62	Stan Mikita, Chicago	12	6	15	21
1960-61	Gordie Howe, Detroit	11	4	11	15
	Pierre Pilote, Chicago	12	3	12	15
1959-60	Henri Richard, Montreal	8	3	9	12
	Bernie Geoffrion, Montreal	8	2	10	12
1958-59	Dickie Moore, Montreal	11	5	12	17
1957-58	Fleming Mackell, Boston	12	5	14	19
1956-57	Bernie Geoffrion, Montreal	11	11	7	18
1955-56	Jean Béliveau, Montreal	10	12	7	19
1954-55	Gordie Howe, Detroit	11	9	11	20
1953-54	Dickie Moore, Montreal	11	5	8	13
1952-53	Ed Sanford, Boston	11	8	3	11
1951-52	Ted Lindsay, Detroit	8	5	2	7
	Floyd Curry, Montreal	11	4	3	7
	Metro Prystai, Detroit	8	2	5	7
	Gordie Howe, Detroit	8	2	5	7
1950-51	Maurice Richard, Montreal	11	9	4	13
	Max Bentley, Toronto	11	2	11	13
1949-50	Pentti Lund, NY Rangers	12	6	5	11
1948-49	Gordie Howe, Detroit	11	8	3	11
1947-48	Ted Kennedy, Toronto	9	8	6	14
1946-47	Maurice Richard, Montreal	10	6	5	11
1945-46	Elmer Lach, Montreal	9	5	12	17
1944-45	Joe Carveth, Detroit	14	5	6	11
1943-44	Toe Blake, Montreal	9	7	11	18
1942-43	Carl Liscombe, Detroit	10	6	8	14
1941-42	Don Grosso, Detroit	12	8	6	14
1940-41	Milt Schmidt, Boston	11	5	6	11
1939-40	Phil Watson, NY Rangers	12	3	6	9
	Neil Colville, NY Rangers	12	2	7	9
1938-39	Bill Cowley, Boston	12	3	11	14
1937-38	Johnny Gottselig, Chicago	10	5	3	8
1936-37	Marty Barry, Detroit	10	4	7	11
1935-36	Buzz Boll, Toronto	9	7	3	10
1934-35	Baldy Northcott, Mtl. Maroons	7	4	1	5
	Harvey Jackson, Toronto	7	3	2	5
	Marvin Wentworth, Mtl. Maroons	7	3	2	5
1933-34	Larry Aurie, Detroit	9	3	7	10
1932-33	Cecil Dillon, NY Rangers	8	8	2	10
1931-32	Frank Boucher, NY Rangers	7	3	6	9
1930-31	Cooney Weiland, Boston	5	6	3	9
1929-30	Marty Barry, Boston	6	3	3	6
	Cooney Weiland, Boston	6	1	5	6
1928-29	Andy Blair, Toronto	4	3	0	3
	Butch Keeling, NY Rangers	6	3	0	3
	Ace Bailey, Toronto	4	1	2	3
1927-28	Frank Boucher, NY Rangers	9	7	3	10
1926-27	Harry Oliver, Boston	8	4	2	6
	Perk Galbraith, Boston	8	3	3	6
	Frank Fredrickson, Boston	8	2	4	6
1925-26	Nels Stewart, Mtl. Maroons	8	6	3	9
1924-25	Howie Morenz, Montreal	6	7	1	8
1923-24	Howie Morenz, Montreal	6	7	2	9
1922-23	Punch Broadbent, Ottawa	8	6	1	7
1921-22	Babe Dye, Toronto	7	11	2	13
1920-21	Cy Denneny, Ottawa	7	4	2	6
1919-20	Frank Nighbor, Ottawa	5	6	1	7
	Jack Darragh, Ottawa	5	5	2	7
1918-19	Newsy Lalonde, Montreal	10	17	1	18
1917-18	Alf Skinner, Toronto	7	8	1	9

Overtime Games since 1918

Abbreviations: Teams/Cities: — **Atl.** - Atlanta; **Bos.** - Boston; **Buf.** - Buffalo; **Cgy.** - Calgary; **Cgy. T.** - Calgary Tigers (Western Canada Hockey League); **Chi.** - Chicago; **Col.** - Colorado; **Det.** - Detroit; **Edm.** - Edmonton; **Edm. E.** - Edmonton Eskimos (WCHL); **Hfd.** - Hartford; **K.C.** - Kansas City; **L.A.** - Los Angeles; **Min.** - Minnesota; **Mtl.** - Montreal; **Mtl.M.** - Montreal Maroons; **N.J.** - New Jersey; **NY** - New York; **NYA** - NY Americans; **NYI** - New York Islanders; **NYR** - New York Rangers; **Oak.** - Oakland; **Ott.** - Ottawa; **Phi.** - Philadelphia; **Pit.** - Pittsburgh; **Que.** - Quebec; **St.L.** - St. Louis; **Sea.** - Seattle Metropolitans (Pacific Coast Hockey Association); **Tor.** - Toronto; **Van.** - Vancouver; **Van. M** - Vancouver Millionaires (PCHA); **Vic.** - Victoria Cougars (WCHL); **Wpg.** - Winnipeg; **Wsh.** - Washington.
SERIES — **CF** - conference final; **DF** - division final; **DSF** - division semi-final; **F** - final; **PR** - preliminary round; **QF** - quarter final; **SF** - semi-final.

Date	City	Series	Score		Scorer	Overtime	Series Winner
Mar.26/19	Sea.	F	Mtl. 0	Sea. 0	no scorer	20:00	
Mar.29/19	Sea.	F	Mtl. 4	Sea. 3	Odie Cleghorn	15:57	
Mar.21/22	Tor.	F	Tor 2	Van.M. 1	Babe Dye	4:50	Tor.
Mar.29/23	Van.	F	Ott. 2	Edm.E. 1	Cy Denneny	2:08	Ott.
Mar.31/27	Mtl.	QF	Mtl. 1	Mtl. M. 0	Howie Morenz	12:05	Mtl.
Apr. 7/27	Bos.	F	Ott. 0	Bos. 0	no scorer	20:00	Ott.
Apr. 11/27	Ott.	F	Bos. 1	Ott. 1	no scorer	20:00	Ott.
Apr. 3/28	Mtl.	QF	Mtl. M. 1	Mtl. 0	Russ Oatman	8:20	Mtl. M.
Apr. 7/28	Mtl.	F	NYR 2	Mtl. M. 1	Frank Boucher	7:05	NYR
Mar.21/29	NY	QF	NYR 1	NYA 0	Butch Keeling	29:50	NYR
Mar.26/29	Tor.	SF	NYR 2	Tor. 1	Frank Boucher	2:03	NYR
Mar.20/30	Mtl.	SF	Bos. 2	Mtl. M. 1	Harry Oliver	45:35	Bos.
Mar.25/30	Bos.	SF	Mtl. M. 1	Bos. 0	Archie Wilcox	26:27	Bos.
Mar.26/30	Mtl.	QF	Chi. 2	Mtl. 2	Howie Morenz (Mtl.)	51:43	Mtl.
Mar.28/30	Mtl.	SF	Mtl. 2	NYR 1	Gus Rivers	68:52	Mtl.
Mar.24/31	Bos.	SF	Bos. 5	Mtl. 4	Cooney Weiland	18:56	Mtl.
Mar.26/31	Chi.	QF	Chi. 2	Tor. 1	Steward Adams	19:20	Chi.
Mar.28/31	Mtl.	SF	Mtl. 4	Bos. 3	Georges Mantha	5:10	Mtl.
Apr. 1/31	Mtl.	SF	Mtl. 3	Bos. 2	Wildor Larochelle	19:00	Mtl.
Apr. 5/31	Chi.	F	Chi. 2	Mtl. 1	Johnny Gottselig	24:50	Mtl.
Apr. 9/31	Mtl.	F	Chi. 3	Mtl. 2	Cy Wentworth	53:50	Mtl.
Mar.26/32	Mtl.	SF	NYR 4	Mtl. 3	Fred Cook	59:32	NYR
Apr. 2/32	Tor.	SF	Tor. 3	Mtl. M. 2	Bob Gracie	17:59	Tor.
Mar.25/33	Bos.	SF	Bos. 2	Tor. 1	Marty Barry	14:14	Tor.
Mar.28/33	Bos.	SF	Tor. 1	Bos. 0	Busher Jackson	15:03	Tor.
Mar.30/33	Tor.	SF	Bos. 2	Tor. 1	Eddie Shore	4:23	Tor.
Apr. 3/33	Tor.	SF	Tor. 1	Bos. 0	Ken Doraty	104:46	Tor.
Apr. 13/33	Tor.	F	NYR 1	Tor. 0	Bill Cook	7:33	NYR
Mar.22/34	Tor.	SF	Det. 2	Tor. 1	Herbie Lewis	1:33	Det.
Mar.25/34	Chi.	QF	Chi. 1	Mtl. 1	Mush March (Chi)	11:05	Chi.
Apr. 3/34	Det.	F	Chi. 2	Det. 1	Paul Thompson	21:05	Chi.
Apr. 10/34	Chi.	F	Chi. 1	Det. 0	Mush March	30:05	Chi.
Mar.23/35	Bos.	SF	Bos. 1	Tor. 0	Dit Clapper	33:26	Tor.
Mar.26/35	Chi.	QF	Mtl. M. 1	Chi. 0	Baldy Northcott	4:02	Mtl. M.
Mar.30/35	Tor.	SF	Tor. 2	Bos. 1	Pep Kelly	1:36	Tor.
Apr. 4/35	Tor.	F	Mtl. M. 3	Tor. 2	Dave Trottier	5:20	Mtl. M.
Mar.24/36	Mtl.	SF	Det. 1	Mtl. M. 0	Mud Bruneteau	116:30	Det.
Apr. 9/36	Tor.	F	Tor. 4	Det. 3	Buzz Boll	0:31	Det.
Mar.25/37	NY	QF	NYR 2	Tor. 1	Babe Pratt	13:05	NYR
Apr. 1/37	Mtl.	SF	Det. 2	Mtl. 1	Hec Kilrea	51:49	Det.
Mar.22/38	NY	QF	NYA 2	NYR 1	Johnny Sorrell	21:25	NYA
Mar.25/38	Tor.	SF	Tor. 1	Bos. 0	George Parsons	21:31	Tor.
Mar.26/38	Mtl.	QF	Chi. 3	Mtl. 2	Paul Thompson	11:49	Chi.
Mar.27/38	NY	QF	NYA 3	NYR 2	Lorne Carr	60:40	NYA
Mar.29/38	Bos.	SF	Tor. 3	Bos. 2	Gord Drillon	10:04	Tor.
Mar.31/38	Chi.	SF	Chi. 1	NYA 0	Cully Dahlstrom	33:01	Chi.
Mar.21/39	NY	SF	Bos. 2	NYR 1	Mel Hill	59:25	Bos.
Mar.23/39	Bos.	SF	Bos. 3	NYR 2	Mel Hill	8:24	Bos.
Mar.26/39	Det.	QF	Det. 1	Mtl. 0	Marty Barry	7:47	Det.
Mar.30/39	Bos.	SF	NYR 2	Bos. 1	Clint Smith	17:19	Bos.
Apr. 1/39	Tor.	SF	Tor. 5	Det. 4	Gord Drillon	5:42	Tor.
Apr. 2/39	Bos.	SF	Bos. 2	NYR 1	Mel Hill	48:00	Bos.
Apr. 9/39	Bos.	F	Tor. 3	Bos. 2	Doc Romnes	10:38	Bos.
Mar.19/40	Det.	QF	Det. 2	NYA 1	Syd Howe	0:25	Det.
Mar.19/40	Tor.	QF	Tor. 3	Chi. 2	Syl Apps	6:35	Tor.
Apr. 2/40	NY	F	NYR 2	Tor. 1	Alf Pike	15:30	NYR
Apr. 11/40	Tor.	F	NYR 2	Tor. 1	Muzz Patrick	31:43	NYR
Apr. 13/40	Tor.	F	NYR 3	Tor. 2	Bryan Hextall	2:07	NYR
Mar.20/41	Det.	QF	Det. 2	NYR 1	Gus Giesebrecht	12:01	Det.
Mar.22/41	Mtl.	QF	Mtl. 4	Chi. 3	Charlie Sands	34:04	Chi.
Mar.29/41	Bos.	SF	Tor. 2	Bos. 1	Pete Langelle	17:31	Bos.
Mar.30/41	Chi.	SF	Det. 2	Chi. 1	Gus Giesebrecht	9:15	Det.
Mar.22/42	Chi.	QF	Bos. 2	Chi. 1	Des Smith	9:51	Bos.
Mar.21/43	Bos.	SF	Bos. 5	Mtl. 4	Don Gallinger	12:30	Bos.
Mar.23/43	Det.	SF	Tor. 3	Det. 2	Jack McLean	70:18	Det.
Mar.25/43	Mtl.	SF	Bos. 3	Mtl. 2	Harvey Jackson	3:20	Bos.
Mar.30/43	Tor.	SF	Det. 3	Tor. 2	Adam Brown	9:21	Det.
Mar.30/43	Bos.	SF	Bos. 5	Mtl. 4	Ab DeMarco	3:41	Bos.
Apr. 13/44	Mtl.	F	Mtl. 5	Chi. 4	Toe Blake	9:12	Mtl.
Mar.27/45	Tor.	SF	Tor. 4	Mtl. 3	Gus Bodnar	12:36	Tor.
Mar.29/45	Det.	SF	Det. 3	Bos. 2	Mud Bruneteau	17:12	Det.
Apr. 21/45	Tor.	F	Det. 1	Tor. 0	Ed Bruneteau	14:16	Tor.
Mar.28/46	Bos.	SF	Bos. 4	Det. 3	Don Gallinger	9:51	Bos.
Mar.30/46	Mtl.	F	Mtl. 4	Bos. 3	Maurice Richard	9:08	Mtl.
Apr. 2/46	Mtl.	F	Mtl. 3	Bos. 2	Jim Peters	16:55	Mtl.
Apr. 7/46	Bos.	F	Bos. 3	Mtl. 2	Terry Reardon	15:13	Mtl.
Mar.26/47	Tor.	SF	Tor. 3	Det. 2	Howie Meeker	3:05	Tor.
Mar.27/47	Mtl.	SF	Mtl. 2	Bos. 1	Ken Mosdell	5:38	Mtl.
Apr. 3/47	Mtl.	SF	Mtl. 4	Bos. 3	John Quilty	36:40	Mtl.
Apr. 15/47	Tor.	F	Tor. 2	Mtl. 1	Syl Apps	16:36	Tor.
Mar.24/48	Tor.	SF	Tor. 5	Bos. 4	Nick Metz	17:03	Tor.
Mar.22/49	Det.	SF	Det. 2	Mtl. 1	Max McNab	44:52	Det.
Mar.24/49	Det.	SF	Mtl. 4	Det. 3	Gerry Plamondon	2:59	Det.
Mar.26/49	Tor.	SF	Bos. 5	Tor. 4	Woody Dumart	16:14	Tor.
Apr. 8/49	Det.	F	Tor. 3	Det. 2	Joe Klukay	17:31	Tor.
Apr. 4/50	Tor.	SF	Det. 2	Tor. 1	Leo Reise	20:38	Det.
Apr. 4/50	Mtl.	SF	Mtl. 3	NYR 2	Elmer Lach	15:19	Mtl.
Apr. 9/50	Det.	SF	Det. 1	Tor. 0	Leo Reise	8:39	Det.
Apr. 18/50	Det.	F	NYR 4	Det. 3	Don Raleigh	8:34	Det.
Apr. 20/50	Det.	F	NYR 2	Det. 1	Don Raleigh	1:38	Det.
Apr. 23/50	Det.	F	Det. 4	NYR 3	Pete Babando	28:31	Det.
Mar.27/51	Det.	SF	Mtl. 3	Det. 2	Maurice Richard	61:09	Mtl.
Mar.29/51	Det.	SF	Mtl. 1	Det. 0	Maurice Richard	42:20	Mtl.
Mar.31/51	Tor.	SF	Bos. 1	Tor. 1	no scorer	20:00	Tor.
Apr. 11/51	Tor.	F	Tor. 3	Mtl. 2	Sid Smith	5:51	Tor.
Apr. 14/51	Tor.	F	Mtl. 3	Tor. 2	Maurice Richard	2:55	Tor.
Apr. 17/51	Mtl.	F	Tor. 2	Mtl. 1	Ted Kennedy	4:47	Tor.
Apr. 19/51	Mtl.	F	Tor. 3	Mtl. 2	Harry Watson	5:15	Tor.
Apr. 21/51	Tor.	F	Tor. 3	Mtl. 2	Bill Barilko	2:53	Tor.
Apr. 6/52	Bos.	SF	Mtl. 3	Bos. 2	Paul Masnick	27:49	Mtl.
Mar.29/53	Bos.	SF	Bos. 2	Det. 1	Jack McIntyre	12:29	Bos.
Mar.29/53	Chi.	SF	Chi. 2	Mtl. 1	Al Dewsbury	5:18	Mtl.
Apr. 16/53	Mtl.	F	Mtl. 1	Bos. 0	Elmer Lach	1:22	Mtl.
Apr. 1/54	Det.	SF	Det. 4	Tor. 3	Ted Lindsay	21:01	Det.
Apr. 11/54	Det.	F	Mtl. 1	Det. 0	Ken Mosdell	5:45	Det.
Apr. 16/54	Det.	F	Det. 2	Mtl. 1	Tony Leswick	4:29	Det.
Mar.29/55	Bos.	SF	Mtl. 4	Bos. 3	Don Marshall	3:05	Mtl.
Mar.24/56	Tor.	SF	Det. 5	Tor. 4	Ted Lindsay	4:22	Det.
Mar.28/57	NY	SF	NYR 4	Mtl. 3	Andy Hebenton	13:38	Mtl.
Apr. 4/57	Mtl.	SF	Mtl. 4	NYR 3	Maurice Richard	1:11	Mtl.
Mar.27/58	NY	SF	Bos. 4	NYR 3	Jerry Toppazzini	4:46	Bos.
Mar.30/58	Det.	SF	Mtl. 2	Det. 1	André Pronovost	11:52	Mtl.
Apr. 17/58	Mtl.	F	Mtl. 3	Bos. 2	Maurice Richard	5:45	Mtl.
Mar.28/59	Tor.	SF	Tor. 3	Bos. 2	Gerry Ehman	5:02	Tor.
Mar.31/59	Tor.	SF	Tor. 3	Bos. 2	Frank Mahovlich	11:21	Tor.
Apr. 14/59	Tor.	F	Tor. 3	Mtl. 2	Dick Duff	10:06	Mtl.
Mar.26/60	Mtl.	SF	Mtl. 4	Chi. 3	Doug Harvey	8:38	Mtl.
Mar.27/60	Det.	SF	Tor. 5	Det. 4	Frank Mahovlich	43:00	Tor.
Mar.29/60	Det.	SF	Det. 2	Tor. 1	Gerry Melnyk	1:54	Tor.
Mar.22/61	Tor.	SF	Tor. 3	Det. 2	George Armstrong	24:51	Det.
Mar.26/61	Chi.	SF	Chi. 2	Mtl. 1	Murray Balfour	52:12	Chi.
Apr. 5/62	Tor.	SF	Tor. 3	NYR 2	Red Kelly	24:23	Tor.
Apr. 2/64	Det.	SF	Chi. 3	Det. 2	Murray Balfour	8:21	Det.
Apr. 14/64	Tor.	F	Det. 3	Tor. 2	Larry Jeffrey	7:52	Tor.
Apr. 23/64	Det.	F	Tor. 4	Det. 3	Bobby Baun	1:43	Tor.
Apr. 6/65	Tor.	SF	Tor. 3	Mtl. 2	Dave Keon	4:17	Mtl.
Apr. 13/65	Tor.	SF	Mtl. 4	Tor. 3	Claude Provost	16:33	Mtl.
May 5/66	Det.	F	Mtl. 3	Det. 2	Henri Richard	2:20	Mtl.
Apr. 13/67	NY	SF	Mtl. 2	NYR 1	John Ferguson	6:28	Mtl.
Apr. 25/67	Tor.	F	Tor. 3	Mtl. 2	Bob Pulford	28:26	Tor.
Apr. 10/68	St. L.	QF	St. L. 3	Phi. 2	Larry Keenan	24:10	St. L.
Apr. 16/68	St. L.	QF	Phi. 2	St. L. 1	Don Blackburn	31:38	St. L.
Apr. 16/68	Min.	QF	Min. 4	L.A. 3	Milan Marcetta	9:11	Min.
Apr. 22/68	Min.	SF	Min. 3	St. L. 2	Parker MacDonald	3:41	St. L.
Apr. 27/68	St. L.	SF	St. L. 4	Min. 3	Gary Sabourin	1:32	St. L.
Apr. 28/68	Mtl.	SF	Mtl. 4	Chi. 3	Jacques Lemaire	2:14	Mtl.
Apr. 29/68	St. L.	SF	St. L. 3	Min. 2	Bill McCreary	17:27	St. L.
May 3/68	St. L.	SF	St. L. 2	Min. 1	Ron Schock	22:50	St. L.
May 5/68	St. L.	F	Mtl. 3	St. L. 2	Jacques Lemaire	1:41	Mtl.
May 9/68	Mtl.	F	Mtl. 4	St. L. 3	Bobby Rousseau	1:13	Mtl.
Apr. 2/69	Oak.	QF	L.A. 5	Oak. 4	Ted Irvine	0:19	L.A.
Apr. 10/69	Mtl.	SF	Mtl. 3	Bos. 2	Ralph Backstrom	0:42	Mtl.
Apr. 13/69	Mtl.	SF	Mtl. 4	Bos. 3	Mickey Redmond	4:55	Mtl.
Apr. 24/69	Bos.	SF	Mtl. 2	Bos. 1	Jean Béliveau	31:28	Mtl.
Apr. 12/70	Oak.	QF	Pit. 3	Oak. 2	Michel Briere	8:28	Pit.
May 10/70	Bos.	F	Bos. 4	St. L. 3	Bobby Orr	0:40	Bos.
Apr. 15/71	Tor.	QF	NYR 2	Tor. 1	Bob Nevin	9:07	NYR
Apr. 18/71	Chi.	SF	NYR 2	Chi. 1	Pete Stemkowski	1:37	Chi.
Apr. 27/71	Chi.	SF	Chi. 3	NYR 2	Bobby Hull	6:35	Chi.
Apr. 29/71	NY	SF	NYR 3	Chi. 2	Pete Stemkowski	41:29	Chi.
May 4/71	Chi.	F	Chi. 2	Mtl. 1	Jim Pappin	21:11	Mtl.
Apr. 6/72	Bos.	OF	Tor. 4	Bos. 3	Jim Harrison	2:58	Bos.
Apr. 6/72	Min.	QF	Min. 6	St. L. 5	Bill Goldsworthy	1:36	St. L.
Apr. 9/72	Pit.	QF	Chi. 6	Pit. 5	Pit Martin	0:12	Chi.
Apr. 16/72	Min.	QF	St. L. 2	Min. 1	Kevin O'Shea	10:07	St. L.
Apr. 01/73	Mtl.	QF	Buf. 3	Mtl. 2	René Robert	9:18	Mtl.
Apr. 10/73	Phi.	QF	Phi. 3	Min. 2	Gary Dornhoefer	8:35	Phi.
Apr. 14/73	Mtl.	SF	Phi. 5	Mtl. 4	Rick MacLeish	2:56	Mtl.
Apr. 17/73	Mtl.	SF	Mtl. 4	Phi. 3	Larry Robinson	6:45	Mtl.
Apr. 14/74	Tor.	QF	Bos. 4	Tor. 3	Ken Hodge	1:27	Bos.
Apr. 14/74	Atl.	QF	Phi. 4	Atl. 3	Dave Schultz	5:40	Phi.
Apr. 16/74	Mtl.	QF	NYR 3	Mtl. 2	Ron Harris	4:07	NYR
Apr. 23/74	Chi.	SF	Chi. 4	Bos. 3	Jim Pappin	3:48	Bos.
Apr. 28/74	NY	SF	NYR 2	Phi. 1	Rod Gilbert	4:20	Phi.
May 9/74	Bos.	F	Phi. 3	Bos. 2	Bobby Clarke	12:01	Phi.
Apr. 8/75	L.A.	PR	L.A. 3	Tor. 2	Mike Murphy	8:53	Tor.
Apr. 10/75	Tor.	PR	Tor. 3	L.A. 2	Blaine Stoughton	10:19	Tor.
Apr. 10/75	Chi.	PR	Chi. 4	Bos. 3	Ivan Boldirev	7:33	Chi.
Apr. 11/75	NY	PR	NYI 4	NYR 3	Jean-Paul Parise	0:11	NYI
Apr. 19/75	Tor.	QF	Phi. 4	Tor. 3	André Dupont	1:45	Phi.
Apr. 17/75	Chi.	QF	Chi. 5	Buf. 4	Stan Mikita	2:31	Buf.
Apr. 22/75	Mtl.	QF	Mtl. 5	Van. 4	Guy Lafleur	17:06	Mtl.
May 1/75	Phi.	SF	Phi. 5	NYI 4	Bobby Clarke	2:56	Phi.
May 7/75	NYI	SF	NYI 4	Phi. 3	Jude Drouin	1:53	Phi.
Apr. 27/75	Buf.	SF	Buf. 6	Mtl. 5	Danny Gare	4:42	Buf.
May 6/75	Buf.	SF	Buf. 5	Mtl. 4	René Robert	5:56	Buf.
May 20/75	Buf.	F	Buf. 5	Phi. 4	René Robert	18:29	Phi.
Apr. 8/76	Buf.	PR	Buf. 3	St. L. 2	Danny Gare	11:43	Buf.
Apr. 9/76	Buf.	PR	Buf. 2	St. L. 1	Don Luce	14:27	Buf.
Apr. 13/76	Bos.	QF	L.A. 3	Bos. 2	Butch Goring	0:27	Bos.
Apr. 13/76	Buf.	QF	Buf. 3	NYI 2	Danny Gare	14:04	NYI
Apr. 22/76	L.A.	QF	L.A. 4	Bos. 3	Butch Goring	18:28	Bos.
Apr. 29/76	Phi.	SF	Phi. 2	Bos. 1	Reggie Leach	13:38	Phi.

Date	City	Series	Score		Scorer	Overtime	Series Winner
Apr.15/77	Tor.	QF	Phi. 4	Tor. 3	Rick MacLeish	2:55	Phi.
Apr.17/77	Tor.	QF	Phi. 6	Tor. 5	Reggie Leach	19:10	Phi.
Apr.24/77	Phi.	SF	Bos. 4	Phi. 3	Rick Middleton	2:57	Bos.
Apr.26/77	Phi.	SF	Bos. 5	Phi. 4	Terry O'Reilly	30:07	Bos.
May 3/77	Mtl.	SF	NYI 4	Mtl. 3	Billy Harris	3:58	Mtl.
May14/77	Bos.	F	Mtl. 2	Bos. 1	Jacques Lemaire	4:32	Mtl.
Apr.11/78	Phi.	PR	Phi. 3	Col. 2	Mel Bridgman	0:23	Phi.
Apr.13/78	NY	PR	NYR 4	Buf. 3	Don Murdoch	1:37	Buf.
Apr.19/78	Bos.	QF	Bos. 4	Chi. 3	Terry O'Reilly	1:50	Bos.
Apr.19/78	NYI	QF	NYI 3	Tor. 2	Mike Bossy	2:50	Tor.
Apr.21/78	Chi.	QF	Bos. 4	Chi. 3	Peter McNab	10:17	Bos.
Apr.25/78	NYI	QF	NYI 2	Tor. 1	Bob Nystrom	8:02	Tor.
Apr.29/78	NYI	QF	Tor. 2	NYI 1	Lanny McDonald	4:13	Tor.
May 2/78	Bos.	SF	Bos. 3	Phi. 2	Rick Middleton	1:43	Bos.
May16/78	Mtl.	F	Mtl. 3	Bos. 2	Guy Lafleur	13:09	Mtl.
May21/78	Bos.	F	Bos. 4	Mtl. 3	Bobby Schmautz	6:22	Mtl.
Apr.12/79	L.A.	PR	NYR 2	L.A. 1	Phil Esposito	6:11	NYR
Apr.14/79	Buf.	PR	Pit. 4	Buf. 3	George Ferguson	0:47	Pit.
Apr.16/79	Phi.	QF	Phi. 3	NYR 2	Ken Linseman	0:44	NYR
Apr.18/79	NYI	QF	NYI 1	Chi. 0	Mike Bossy	2:31	NYI
Apr.21/79	Tor.	QF	Mtl. 4	Tor. 3	Cam Connor	25:25	Mtl.
Apr.22/79	Tor.	QF	Mtl. 5	Tor. 4	Larry Robinson	4:14	Mtl.
Apr.28/79	NYI	SF	NYI 4	NYR 3	Denis Potvin	8:02	NYR
May 3/79	NY	SF	NYI 3	NYR 2	Bob Nystrom	3:40	NYR
May 3/79	Bos.	SF	Bos. 4	Mtl. 3	Jean Ratelle	3:46	Mtl.
May10/79	Mtl.	SF	Mtl. 5	Bos. 4	Yvon Lambert	9:33	Mtl.
May19/79	NY	F	Mtl. 4	NYR 3	Serge Savard	7:25	Mtl.
Apr. 8/80	NY	PR	NYR 2	Atl. 1	Steve Vickers	0:33	NYR
Apr. 8/80	Phi.	PR	Phi. 4	Edm. 3	Bobby Clarke	8:06	Phi.
Apr. 8/80	Chi.	PR	Chi. 3	St. L. 2	Doug Lecuyer	12:34	Chi.
Apr.11/80	Hfd.	PR	Mtl. 4	Hfd. 3	Yvon Lambert	0:29	Mtl.
Apr.11/80	Tor.	PR	Min. 4	Tor. 3	Al MacAdam	0:32	Min.
Apr.11/80	L.A.	PR	NYI 4	L.A. 3	Ken Morrow	6:55	NYI
Apr.11/80	Edm.	PR	Phi. 3	Edm. 2	Ken Linseman	23:56	Phi.
Apr.16/80	Bos.	QF	NYI 2	Bos. 1	Clark Gillies	1:02	NYI
Apr.17/80	Bos.	QF	NYI 5	Bos. 4	Bob Bourne	1:24	NYI
Apr.21/80	NYI	QF	Bos. 4	NYI 3	Terry O'Reilly	17:13	NYI
May 1/80	Buf.	SF	NYI 2	Buf. 1	Bob Nystrom	21:20	NYI
May13/80	Phi.	F	NYI 4	Phi. 3	Denis Potvin	4:07	NYI
May24/80	NYI	F	NYI 5	Phi. 4	Bob Nystrom	7:11	NYI
Apr. 8/81	Buf.	PR	Buf. 3	Van. 2	Alan Haworth	5:00	Buf.
Apr. 8/81	Bos.	PR	Min. 5	Bos. 4	Steve Payne	3:34	Min.
Apr.11/81	Chi.	PR	Cgy. 5	Chi. 4	Willi Plett	35:17	Cgy.
Apr.12/81	Que.	PR	Que. 4	Phi. 3	Dale Hunter	:37	Phi.
Apr.14/81	St. L.	PR	St. L. 4	Pit. 3	Mike Crombeen	25:16	St. L.
Apr.16/81	Buf.	QF	Min. 4	Buf. 3	Steve Payne	0:22	Min.
Apr.20/81	Min.	QF	Buf. 5	Min. 4	Craig Ramsay	16:32	Min.
Apr.20/81	Edm.	QF	NYI 5	Edm. 4	Ken Morrow	5:41	NYI
Apr. 7/82	Min.	DSF	Chi. 3	Min. 2	Greg Fox	3:34	Chi.
Apr. 8/82	Edm.	DSF	Edm. 3	L.A. 2	Wayne Gretzky	6:20	L.A.
Apr. 8/82	Van.	DSF	Van. 2	Cgy. 1	Dave Williams	14:20	Van.
Apr.10/82	Pit.	DSF	Pit. 2	NYI 1	Rick Kehoe	4:14	NYI
Apr.10/82	L.A.	DSF	L.A. 6	Edm. 5	Daryl Evans	2:35	L.A.
Apr.13/82	Mtl.	DSF	Que. 3	Mtl. 2	Dale Hunter	0:22	Que.
Apr.13/82	NY	DSF	NYI 4	Pit. 3	John Tonelli	6:19	NYI
Apr.16/82	Van.	DF	L.A. 3	Van. 2	Steve Bozek	4:33	Van.
Apr.18/82	Que.	DF	Que. 3	Bos. 2	Wilf Paiement	11:44	Que.
Apr.18/82	NY	DF	NYI 4	NYR 3	Bryan Trottier	3:00	NYI
Apr.18/82	L.A.	DF	Van. 4	L.A. 3	Colin Campbell	1:23	Van.
Apr.21/82	St. L.	DF	St. L. 3	Chi. 2	Bernie Federko	3:28	Chi.
Apr.23/82	Que.	DF	Bos. 6	Que. 5	Peter McNab	10:54	Que.
Apr.27/82	Chi.	CF	Van. 2	Chi. 1	Jim Nill	28:58	Van.
May 1/82	Que.	CF	NYI 5	Que. 4	Wayne Merrick	16:52	NYI
May 8/82	NYI	F	NYI 6	Van. 5	Mike Bossy	19:58	NYI
Apr. 5/83	Bos.	DSF	Bos. 4	Que. 3	Barry Pederson	1:46	Bos.
Apr. 6/83	Cgy.	DSF	Cgy. 4	Van. 3	Eddy Beers	12:27	Cgy.
Apr. 7/83	Min.	DSF	Min. 5	Tor. 4	Bobby Smith	5:03	Min.
Apr.10/83	Tor.	DSF	Min. 5	Tor. 4	Dino Ciccarelli	8:05	Min.
Apr.10/83	Van.	DSF	Cgy. 4	Van. 3	Greg Meredith	1:06	Cgy.
Apr.18/83	Min.	DF	Chi. 4	Min. 3	Rich Preston	10:34	Chi.
Apr.24/83	Bos.	DF	Bos. 3	Buf. 2	Brad Park	1:52	Bos.
Apr. 5/84	Edm.	DSF	Edm. 5	Wpg. 4	Randy Gregg	0:21	Edm.
Apr. 7/84	Det.	DSF	St. L. 4	Det. 3	Mark Reeds	37:07	St. L.
Apr. 8/84	Det.	DSF	St. L. 3	Det. 2	Jorgen Pettersson	2:42	St. L.
Apr.10/84	NYI	DSF	NYI 3	NYR 2	Ken Morrow	8:56	NYI
Apr.13/84	Min.	DF	St. L. 4	Min. 3	Doug Gilmour	16:16	Min.
Apr.13/84	Edm.	DF	Cgy. 6	Edm. 5	Carey Wilson	3:42	Edm.
Apr.13/84	NYI	DF	NYI 5	Wsh. 4	Anders Kallur	7:35	NYI
Apr.16/84	Mtl.	DF	Que. 4	Mtl. 3	Bo Berglund	3:00	Mtl.
Apr.20/84	Cgy.	DF	Cgy. 5	Edm. 4	Lanny McDonald	1:04	Edm.
Apr.22/84	Min.	DF	Min. 4	St. L. 3	Steve Payne	6:00	Min.
Apr.10/85	Phi.	DSF	Phi. 5	NYR 4	Mark Howe	8:01	Phi.
Apr.10/85	Wsh.	DSF	Wsh. 4	NYI 3	Alan Haworth	2:28	NYI
Apr.10/85	Edm.	DSF	Edm. 3	L.A. 2	Lee Fogolin	3:01	Edm.
Apr.10/85	Wpg.	DSF	Wpg. 5	Cgy. 4	Brian Mullen	7:56	Wpg.
Apr.11/85	Wsh.	DSF	Wsh. 2	NYI 1	Mike Gartner	21:23	NYI
Apr.13/85	L.A.	DSF	Edm. 4	L.A. 3	Glenn Anderson	0:46	Edm.
Apr.18/85	Mtl.	DF	Que. 2	Mtl. 1	Mark Kumpel	12:23	Que.
Apr.23/85	Que.	DF	Que. 7	Mtl. 6	Dale Hunter	18:36	Que.
May 2/85	Mtl.	DF	Que. 3	Mtl. 2	Peter Stastny	2:22	Que.
Apr.25/85	Min.	DF	Chi. 7	Min. 6	Darryl Sutter	21:57	Chi.
Apr.28/85	Chi.	DF	Min. 5	Chi. 4	Dennis Maruk	1:14	Chi.
Apr.30/85	Min.	DF	Chi. 6	Min. 5	Darryl Sutter	15:41	Chi.
May 5/85	Que.	CF	Que. 2	Phi. 1	Peter Stastny	6:20	Phi.
Apr. 9/86	Que.	DSF	Hfd. 3	Que. 2	Sylvain Turgeon	2:36	Hfd.
Apr.12/86	Wpg.	DSF	Cgy. 4	Wpg. 3	Lanny McDonald	8:25	Cgy.
Apr.17/86	Wsh.	DF	NYR 4	Wsh. 3	Brian MacLellan	1:16	NYR
Apr.20/86	Edm.	DF	Edm. 6	Cgy. 5	Glenn Anderson	1:04	Cgy.
Apr.23/86	Hfd.	DF	Hfd. 2	Mtl. 1	Kevin Dineen	1:07	Mtl.
Apr.23/86	NYR	DF	NYR 6	Wsh. 5	Bob Brooke	2:40	NYR
Apr.26/86	St L.	DF	St L. 4	Tor. 3	Mark Reeds	7:11	St L.
Apr.29/86	Mtl.	DF	Mtl. 2	Hfd. 1	Claude Lemieux	5:55	Mtl.
May 5/86	NYR	CF	Mtl. 4	NYR 3	Claude Lemieux	9:41	Mtl.
May12/86	St L.	CF	St L. 6	Cgy. 5	Doug Wickenheiser	7:30	Cgy.
May18/86	Cgy.	F	Mtl. 3	Cgy. 2	Brian Skrudland	0:09	Mtl.
Apr. 8/87	Hfd.	DSF	Hfd. 3	Que. 2	Paul MacDermid	2:20	Que.
Apr. 9/87	Mtl.	DSF	Mtl. 4	Bos. 3	Mats Naslund	2:38	Mtl.
Apr. 9/87	St. L.	DSF	Tor. 3	St. L. 2	Rick Lanz	10:17	Tor.
Apr.11/87	Wpg.	DSF	Cgy. 3	Wpg. 2	Mike Bullard	3:53	Wpg.
Apr.11/87	Chi.	DSF	Det. 4	Chi. 3	Shawn Burr	4:51	Det.
Apr.16/87	Que.	DSF	Que. 5	Hfd. 4	Peter Stastny	6:05	Que.
Apr.18/87	Wsh.	DSF	NYI 3	Wsh. 2	Pat LaFontaine	68:47	NYI
Apr.21/87	Edm.	DF	Edm. 3	Wpg. 2	Glenn Anderson	0:36	Edm.
Apr.26/87	Que.	DF	Mtl. 3	Que. 2	Mats Naslund	5:30	Mtl.
Apr.27/87	Tor.	DF	Tor. 3	Det. 2	Mike Allison	9:31	Det.
May 4/87	Phi.	CF	Phi. 4	Mtl. 3	Ilkka Sinislao	9:11	Phi.
May20/87	Edm.	F	Edm. 3	Phi. 2	Jari Kurri	6:50	Edm.
Apr. 6/88	NYI	DSF	NYI 4	N.J. 3	Pat LaFontaine	6:11	N.J.
Apr.10/88	Phi.	DSF	Phi. 5	Wsh. 4	Murray Craven	1:18	Wsh.
Apr.10/88	N.J.	DSF	NYI 5	N.J. 4	Brent Sutter	15:07	N.J.
Apr.10/88	Buf.	DSF	Buf. 6	Bos. 5	John Tucker	5:32	Bos.
Apr.12/88	Det.	DSF	Tor. 6	Det. 5	Ed Olczyk	0:34	Det.
Apr.16/88	Wsh.	DSF	Wsh. 5	Phi. 4	Dale Hunter	5:57	Wsh.
Apr.21/88	Cgy.	DF	Edm. 5	Cgy. 4	Wayne Gretzky	7:54	Edm.
May 4/88	Bos.	CF	N.J. 3	Bos. 2	Doug Brown	17:46	Bos.
May 9/88	Det.	CF	Edm. 4	Det. 3	Jari Kurri	11:02	Edm.
Apr. 5/89	St. L.	DSF	St. L. 4	Min. 3	Brett Hull	11:55	St. L.
Apr. 5/89	Cgy.	DSF	Van. 4	Cgy. 3	Paul Reinhart	2:47	Cgy.
Apr. 6/89	St. L.	DSF	St. L. 4	Min. 3	Rick Meagher	5:30	St. L.
Apr. 6/89	Det.	DSF	Chi. 5	Det. 4	Duane Sutter	14:36	Chi.
Apr. 8/89	Hfd.	DSF	Mtl. 5	Hfd. 4	Stephane Richer	5:01	Mtl.
Apr. 8/89	Phi.	DSF	Wsh. 4	Phi. 3	Kelly Miller	0:51	Phi.
Apr. 9/89	Hfd.	DSF	Mtl. 4	Hfd. 3	Russ Courtnall	15:12	Mtl.
Apr.15/89	Cgy.	DSF	Cgy. 4	Van. 3	Joel Otto	19:21	Cgy.
Apr.18/89	Cgy.	DF	Cgy. 4	L.A. 3	Doug Gilmour	7:47	Cgy.
Apr.19/89	Mtl.	DF	Mtl. 3	Bos. 2	Bobby Smith	12:24	Mtl.
Apr.20/89	St. L.	DF	St. L. 5	Chi. 4	Tony Hrkac	33:49	Chi.
Apr.21/89	Phi.	DF	Pit. 4	Phi. 3	Phil Bourque	12:08	Phi.
May 8/89	Chi.	CF	Cgy. 2	Chi. 1	Al MacInnis	15:05	Cgy.
May 9/89	Mtl.	CF	Phi. 2	Mtl. 1	Dave Poulin	5:02	Mtl.
May19/89	Mtl.	F	Mtl. 4	Cgy. 3	Ryan Walter	38:08	Cgy.
Apr. 5/90	N.J.	DSF	Wsh. 5	N.J. 4	Dino Ciccarelli	5:34	Wsh.
Apr. 6/90	Edm.	DSF	Edm. 3	Wpg. 2	Mark Lamb	4:21	Edm.
Apr. 8/90	Tor.	DSF	St. L. 6	Tor. 5	Sergio Momesso	6:04	St. L.
Apr. 8/90	L.A.	DSF	L.A. 2	Cgy. 1	Tony Granato	8:37	L.A.
Apr. 9/90	Mtl.	DSF	Mtl. 2	Buf. 1	Brian Skrudland	12:35	Mtl.
Apr. 9/90	NYI	DSF	NYI 4	NYR 3	Brent Sutter	20:59	NYR
Apr.10/90	Wpg.	DSF	Wpg. 4	Edm. 3	Dave Ellett	21:08	Edm.
Apr.14/90	L.A.	DSF	L.A. 4	Cgy. 3	Mike Krushelnyski	23:14	L.A.
Apr.15/90	Hfd.	DSF	Hfd. 3	Bos. 2	Kevin Dineen	12:30	Bos.
Apr.21/90	Bos.	DF	Bos. 5	Mtl. 4	Garry Galley	3:42	Bos.
Apr.24/90	L.A.	DF	Edm. 6	L.A. 5	Joe Murphy	4:42	Edm.
Apr.25/90	Wsh.	DF	Wsh. 4	NYR 3	Rod Langway	0:34	Wsh.
Apr.27/90	NYR	DF	Wsh. 2	NYR 1	John Druce	6:48	Wsh.
May15/90	Bos.	F	Edm. 3	Bos. 2	Petr Klima	55:13	Edm.
Apr. 4/91	Chi.	DSF	Min. 4	Chi. 3	Brian Propp	4:14	Min.
Apr. 5/91	Pit.	DSF	Pit. 5	N.J. 4	Jaromir Jagr	8:52	Pit.
Apr. 6/91	L.A.	DSF	L.A. 3	Van. 2	Wayne Gretzky	11:08	L.A.
Apr. 8/91	Van.	DSF	Van. 2	L.A. 1	Cliff Ronning	3:12	L.A.
Apr.11/91	NYR	DSF	Wsh. 5	NYR 4	Dino Ciccarelli	6:44	Wsh.
Apr.11/91	Mtl.	DSF	Mtl. 4	Buf. 3	Russ Courtnall	5:56	Mtl.
Apr.14/91	Edm.	DSF	Cgy. 2	Edm. 1	Theo Fleury	4:40	Edm.
Apr.16/91	Cgy.	DSF	Edm. 5	Cgy. 4	Esa Tikkanen	6:58	Edm.
Apr.18/91	L.A.	DF	L.A. 4	Edm. 3	Luc Robitaille	2:13	Edm.
Apr.19/91	Bos.	DF	Mtl. 4	Bos. 3	Stephane Richer	0:27	Bos.
Apr.19/91	Pit.	DF	Pit. 7	Wsh. 6	Kevin Stevens	8:10	Pit.
Apr.20/91	L.A.	DF	Edm. 4	L.A. 3	Petr Klima	24:48	Edm.
Apr.22/91	Edm.	DF	Edm. 4	L.A. 3	Esa Tikkanen	20:48	Edm.
Apr.27/91	Mtl.	DF	Mtl. 3	Bos. 2	Shayne Corson	17:47	Bos.
Apr.28/91	Edm.	DF	Edm. 4	L.A. 3	Craig MacTavish	16:57	Edm.
May 3/91	Bos.	CF	Bos. 5	Pit. 4	Vladimir Ruzicka	8:14	Pit.
Apr.21/92	Bos.	DSF	Bos. 3	Buf. 2	Adam Oates	11:24	Bos.
Apr.22/92	Min.	DSF	Det. 5	Min. 4	Yves Racine	1:15	Det.
Apr.22/92	St. L.	DSF	St. L. 5	Chi. 4	Brett Hull	23:33	Chi.
Apr.25/92	Buf.	DSF	Bos. 5	Buf. 4	Ted Donato	2:08	Bos.
Apr.28/92	Min.	DSF	Det. 1	Min. 0	Sergei Fedorov	16:13	Det.
Apr.29/92	Hfd.	DSF	Hfd. 2	Mon. 1	Yvon Corriveau	0:24	Mtl.
May 1/92	Mtl.	DSF	Mtl. 3	Hfd. 2	Russ Courtnall	25:26	Mtl.
May 3/92	Van.	DF	Edm. 4	Van. 3	Joe Murphy	8:36	Edm.
May 5/92	Mtl.	DF	Bos. 3	Mtl. 2	Peter Douris	3:12	Bos.
May 7/92	Pit.	DF	NYR 6	Pit. 5	Kris King	1:29	Pit.
May 9/92	Pit.	DF	Pit. 5	NYR 4	Ron Francis	2:47	Pit.
May17/92	Pit.	CF	Pit. 4	Bos. 3	Jaromir Jagr	9:44	Pit.

Ten Longest Overtime Games

Date	City	Series	Score		Scorer	Overtime	Series Winner
Mar.24/36	Mtl.	SF	Det. 1	Mtl. M. 0	Mud Bruneteau	116:30	Det.
Apr. 3/33	Tor.	SF	Tor. 1	Bos. 0	Ken Doraty	104:46	Tor.
Mar.23/43	Det.	SF	Tor. 3	Det. 2	Jack McLean	70:18	Det.
Mar.28/30	Mtl.	SF	Mtl. 2	NYR 1	Gus Rivers	68:52	Mtl.
Apr.18/87	Wsh.	DSF	NYI 3	Wsh. 2	Pat LaFontaine	68:47	NYI
Mar.27/51	Det.	SF	Mtl. 3	Det. 2	Maurice Richard	61:09	Mtl.
Mar.27/38	NY	QF	NYA 3	NYR 2	Lorne Carr	60:40	NYA
Mar.26/32	Mtl.	SF	NYR 4	Mtl. 3	Fred Cook	59:32	NYR
Mar.21/39	NY	SF	Bos. 2	NYR 1	Mel Hill	59:25	Bos.
May15/90	Bos.	F	Edm. 3	Bos. 2	Petr Klima	55:13	Edm.

Stanley Cup Coaching Records

Coaches listed in order of total games coached in playoffs. Minimum: 65 games.

Coach	Team	Years	Series	Series W	Series L	Games G	Games W	Games L	T	Cups	%
Bowman, Scott	St. Louis	4	10	6	4	52	26	26	0	0	.500
	Montreal	8	19	16	3	98	70	28	0	5	.714
	Buffalo	5	8	3	5	36	18	18	0	0	.500
	Pittsburgh	1	4	4	0	21	16	5	0	1	.762
	TOTALS	**18**	**41**	**29**	**12**	**207**	**130**	**77**	**0**	**6**	**.628**
Irvin, Dick	Chicago	1	3	2	1	9	5	3	1	0	.611
	Toronto	9	20	12	8	66	33	32	1	1	.508
	Montreal	14	22	11	11	115	62	53	0	3	.539
	TOTALS	**24**	**45**	**25**	**20**	**190**	**100**	**88**	**2**	**4**	**.532**
Arbour, Al	St. Louis	1	2	1	1	11	4	7	0	0	.364
	NY Islanders	13	36	27	9	176	110	66	0	4	.625
	TOTALS	**14**	**38**	**28**	**10**	**187**	**114**	**73**	**0**	**4**	**.610**
Sather, Glen	Edmonton	**10**	**27**	**21**	**6**	***126**	**89**	**37**	**0**	**4**	**.706**
Blake, Toe	Montreal	**13**	**23**	**18**	**5**	**119**	**82**	**37**	**0**	**8**	**.689**
Keenan, Mike	Philadelphia	4	10	6	4	57	32	25	0	0	.561
	Chicago	4	11	7	4	60	33	27	0	0	.550
	TOTALS	**8**	**21**	**13**	**8**	**117**	**65**	**52**	**0**	**0**	**.556**
Reay, Billy	Chicago	**12**	**22**	**10**	**12**	**117**	**57**	**60**	**0**	**0**	**.487**
Shero, Fred	Philadelphia	6	16	12	4	83	48	35	0	2	.578
	NY Rangers	2	5	3	2	25	13	12	0	0	.520
	TOTALS	**8**	**21**	**15**	**6**	**108**	**61**	**47**	**0**	**2**	**.565**
Adams, Jack	Detroit	**15**	**27**	**15**	**12**	**105**	**52**	**52**	**1**	**3**	**.500**
Francis, Emile	NY Rangers	9	14	5	9	75	34	41	0	0	.453
	St. Louis	3	4	1	3	18	6	12	0	0	.333
	TOTALS	**12**	**18**	**6**	**12**	**93**	**40**	**53**	**0**	**0**	**.430**
Imlach, Punch	Toronto	**11**	**17**	**10**	**7**	**92**	**44**	**48**	**0**	**4**	**.478**
Day, Hap	Toronto	**9**	**14**	**10**	**4**	**80**	**49**	**31**	**0**	**5**	**.613**
Johnson, Bob	Calgary	5	10	5	5	52	25	27	0	0	.481
	Pittsburgh	1	4	4	0	24	16	8	0	1	.666
	TOTALS	**6**	**14**	**9**	**5**	**76**	**41**	**35**	**0**	**1**	**.539**
Abel, Sid	Chicago	1	1	0	1	7	3	4	0	0	.429
	Detroit	8	12	4	8	69	29	40	0	0	.420
	TOTALS	**9**	**13**	**4**	**9**	**76**	**32**	**44**	**0**	**0**	**.421**
Demers, Jacques	St. Louis	3	6	3	3	33	16	17	0	0	.485
	Detroit	3	7	4	3	38	20	18	0	0	.526
	TOTALS	**6**	**13**	**7**	**6**	**71**	**36**	**35**	**0**	**0**	**.507**
Murray, Bryan	Washington	7	10	3	7	53	24	29	0	0	.452
	Detroit	2	3	1	2	18	7	11	0	0	.388
	TOTALS	**9**	**13**	**4**	**9**	**71**	**31**	**40**	**0**	**0**	**.436**
Ross, Art	Boston	**12**	**19**	**9**	**10**	**70**	**32**	**33**	**5**	**2**	**.493**
Bergeron, Michel	Quebec	**7**	**13**	**6**	**7**	**68**	**31**	**37**	**0**	**0**	**.456**
Ivan, Tommy	Detroit	**7**	**12**	**8**	**4**	**67**	**36**	**31**	**0**	**3**	**.537**
Nelson, Roger	Toronto	2	5	3	2	19	8	11	0	0	.421
	Buffalo	1	2	1	1	8	4	4	0	0	.500
	Vancouver	2	5	3	2	21	12	9	0	0	.571
	NY Rangers	2	3	1	2	19	8	11	0	0	.421
	TOTALS	**7**	**15**	**8**	**7**	**67**	**32**	**35**	**0**	**0**	**.473**
Pulford, Bob	Los Angeles	4	6	2	4	26	11	15	0	0	.423
	Chicago	5	9	4	5	41	17	24	0	0	.415
	TOTALS	**9**	**15**	**6**	**9**	**67**	**28**	**39**	**0**	**0**	**.418**
Patrick, Lester	NY Rangers	**12**	**24**	**14**	**10**	**65**	**31**	**26**	**8**	**2**	**.538**

* Does not include suspended game, May 24, 1988.

Overtime Record of Current Teams

(Listed by number of OT games played)

Team	Overall GP	W	L	T	Home GP	W	L	T	Last OT Game	Road GP	W	L	T	Last OT Game
Montreal	103	55	46	2	49	31	17	1	May 5/92	54	24	29	1	Apr. 29/92
Boston	86	35	48	3	40	20	19	1	Apr. 21/92	46	15	29	2	May 5/92
Toronto	75	36	38	1	48	22	25	1	Apr. 8/90	27	14	13	0	Apr. 12/88
NY Rangers	52	24	28	0	21	9	12	0	Apr. 11/91	31	15	16	0	May 9/92
Detroit	49	22	27	0	29	10	19	0	Apr. 6/89	20	12	8	0	Apr. 28/92
Chicago	46	22	22	2	23	12	10	1	Apr. 4/91	23	10	12	1	May 20/92
Philadelphia	34	18	16	0	13	8	5	0	Apr. 21/89	21	10	11	0	May 9/89
NY Islanders	32	25	7	0	14	12	2	0	Apr. 9/90	18	13	5	0	Apr. 10/88
St. Louis	28	17	11	0	14	12	2	0	Apr. 22/92	14	5	9	0	Apr. 8/90
Edmonton	27	17	10	0	14	9	5	0	May 20/92	13	8	5	0	May 3/92
Minnesota	26	11	15	0	14	5	9	0	Apr. 28/92	12	6	6	0	Apr. 4/91
* Calgary	24	11	13	0	9	4	5	0	Apr. 16/91	15	7	8	0	Apr. 14/91
Los Angeles	24	10	14	0	13	7	6	0	Apr. 20/91	11	3	8	0	Apr. 28/91
Buffalo	20	10	10	0	12	8	4	0	Apr. 25/92	8	2	6	0	Apr. 21/92
Quebec	15	9	6	0	9	5	4	0	Apr. 26/87	6	4	2	0	Apr. 8/87
Washington	14	8	6	0	6	4	2	0	Apr. 25/90	8	4	4	0	Apr. 19/91
Vancouver	14	5	9	0	5	2	3	0	May 3/92	9	3	6	0	Apr. 6/91
Pittsburgh	13	8	5	0	7	5	2	0	May 17/92	6	3	3	0	May 3/91
Hartford	11	5	6	0	7	4	3	0	Apr. 29/92	4	1	3	0	May 1/92
Winnipeg	7	3	4	0	4	2	2	0	Apr. 10/90	3	1	2	0	Apr. 6/90
** New Jersey	6	1	5	0	2	0	2	0	Apr. 5/90	4	1	3	0	Apr. 5/91

*Totals include those of Atlanta 1974-80.
**Totals include those of Kansas City and Colorado 1975-82.

Penalty Shots in Stanley Cup Playoff Games

Date	Player	Goaltender	Scored		Final Score	Series	
Mar. 25/37	Lionel Conacher, Mtl. Maroons	Tiny Thompson, Boston	No	Mtl.	0 at Bos.	4	QF
Apr. 15/37	Alex Shibicky, NY Rangers	Earl Robertson, Detroit	No	NYR	0 at Det.	3	F
Apr. 13/44	Virgil Johnson, Chicago	Bill Durnan, Montreal	No	Chi.	4 at Mtl.	5*	F
Apr. 9/68	Wayne Connelly, Minnesota	Terry Sawchuk, Los Angeles	Yes	L.A.	5 at Min.	7	QF
Apr. 27/68	Jim Roberts, St. Louis	Cesare Maniago, Minnesota	No	St. L.	4 at Min.	3	SF
May 16/71	Frank Mahovlich, Montreal	Tony Esposito, Chicago	No	Chi.	3 at Mtl.	4	F
May 7/75	Bill Barber, Philadelphia	Glenn Resch, NY Islanders	No	Phi.	3 at NYI	4*	SF
Apr. 20/79	Mike Walton, Chicago	Glenn Resch, NY Islanders	No	NYI	4 at Chi.	0	QF
Apr. 9/81	Peter McNab, Boston	Don Beaupre, Minnesota	No	Min.	5 at Bos.	4*	PR
Apr. 17/81	Anders Hedberg, NY Rangers	Mike Liut, St. Louis	Yes	NYR	6 at St. L.	4	QF
Apr. 9/83	Denis Potvin, NY Islanders	Pat Riggin, Washington	No	NYI	6 at Wsh.	2	DSF
Apr. 28/84	Wayne Gretzky, Edmonton	Don Beaupre, Minnesota	Yes	Edm.	8 at Min.	5	CF
May 1/84	Mats Naslund, Montreal	Bill Smith, NY Islanders	No	Mtl.	1 at NYI	3	CF
Apr. 14/85	Bob Carpenter, Washington	Bill Smith, NY Islanders	No	Wsh.	4 at NYI.	6	DF
May 28/85	Ron Sutter, Philadelphia	Grant Fuhr, Edmonton	No	Phi	3 at Edm.	5	F
May 30/85	Dave Poulin, Philadelphia	Grant Fuhr, Edmonton	No	Phi.	3 at Edm.	8	F
Apr. 9/88	John Tucker, Buffalo	Andy Moog, Boston	Yes	Bos.	2 at Buf	6	DSF
Apr. 9/88	Petr Klima, Detroit	Allan Bester, Toronto	Yes	Det.	6 at Tor.	3	DSF
Apr. 8/89	Neal Broten, Minnesota	Greg Millen, St. Louis	Yes	St.L.	5 at Min.	3	DSF
Apr. 4/90	Al MacInnis, Calgary	Kelly Hrudey, Los Angeles	Yes	L.A.	5 at Cgy.	3	DSF
Apr. 5/90	Randy Wood, NY Islanders	Mike Richter, NY Rangers	No	NYI	1 at NYR	2	DSF
May 3/90	Kelly Miller, Washington	Andy Moog, Boston	No	Wsh.	3 at Bos.	5	CF
May 18/90	Petr Klima, Edmonton	Rejean Lemelin, Boston	No	Edm.	7 at Bos.	2	F
Apr. 6/91	Basil McRae, Minnesota	Ed Belfour, Chicago	Yes	Min.	2 at Chi.	5	DSF
Apr. 10/91	Steve Duchesne, Los Angeles	Kirk McLean, Vancouver	Yes	L.A.	6 at Van.	1	DSF
May 11/92	Jaromir Jagr, Pittsburgh	John Vanbiesbrouck, NYR	Yes	Pit.	3 at NYR	2	DF
May 13/92	Shawn McEachern, Pittsburgh	John Vanbiesbrouck, NYR	No	NYR	1 at Pit.	5	DF

* Game was decided in overtime, but shot taken during regulation time.

The Islanders' Bill Smith stopped two penalty shots in the playoffs, blanking Mats Naslund in 1984 and Bobby Carpenter in 1985.

1992-93 Player Register

Note: The 1992-93 Player Register lists forwards and defensemen only. Goaltenders are listed separately. The Player Register lists every skater who appeared in an NHL game in the 1991-92 season, every skater drafted in the first six rounds of the 1992 Entry Draft and the first three rounds of the 1991 Entry Draft and other players on NHL Reserve Lists. Trades and roster changes are current as of August 24, 1992.

Abbreviations: A – assists; **G** – goals; **GP** – games played; **Lea** – league; **PIM** – penalties in minutes; **TP** – total points; * – league-leading total.

Pronunciations courtesy of the NHL Broadcasters' Association and Igor Kuperman, Winnipeg Jets

Goaltender Register begins on page 397.

LEAGUES:

ACHL	Atlantic Coast Hockey League
AHL	American Hockey League
AJHL	Alberta Junior Hockey League
AUAA	Atlantic Universities Athletic Association
BCJHL	British Columbia Junior Hockey League
CCHA	Central Collegiate Hockey Association
CHL	Central Hockey League
CIAU	Canadian Interuniversity Athletic Union
COJHL	Central Ontario Junior Hockey League
CWUAA	Canada West Universities Athletic Association
ECAC	Eastern Collegiate Athletic Association
ECHL	East Coast Hockey League
G.N.	Great Northern
GPAC	Great Plains Athletic Conference
H.E.	Hockey East
HS	High School
IHL	International Hockey League
Jr.	Junior
MJHA	(New York) Metropolitan Junior Hockey Association
MJHL	Manitoba Junior Hockey League
NAHL	North American Hockey League
NCAA	National Collegiate Athletic Association
NHL	**National Hockey League**
OHA	Ontario Hockey Association
OHL	Ontario Hockey League
OMJHL	Ontario Major Junior Hockey League
OPJHL	Ontario Provincial Junior Hockey League
OUAA	Ontario Universities Athletic Association
QJHL	Quebec Junior Hockey League
QMJHL	Quebec Major Junior Hockey League
SJHL	Saskatchewan Junior Hockey League
SOHL	Southern Ontario Hockey League
USHL	United States Hockey League (Junior)
WCHA	Western Collegiate Hockey Association
WHA	World Hockey Association
WHL	Western Hockey League

AALTONEN, PETRI (AL-tuh-nehn)

Center. Shoots left. 5'10", 185 lbs. Born, Tampere, Finland, May 31, 1970.
(Quebec's 4th choice, 45th overall, in 1988 Entry Draft).

			Regular Season					Playoffs				
Season	Club	Lea	GP	G	A	TP	PIM	GP	G	A	TP	PIM
1986-87	HIFK	Fin. Jr.	30	8	5	13	24	4	0	0	0	0
1987-88	HIFK	Fin. Jr.	34	37	20	57	25	....	....	....	....	....
1988-89	HIFK	Fin.	2	0	0	0	0	....	....	....	....	....
1989-90	HIFK	Fin.	3	0	0	0	0	....	....	....	....	....
1990-91	HIFK	Fin.	43	6	9	15	12	3	1	1	2	0
1991-92	Tappara	Fin.	36	3	4	7	18	....	....	....	....	....

ACTON, KEITH EDWARD

Center. Shoots left. 5'8", 170 lbs. Born, Stouffville, Ont., April 15, 1958.
(Montreal's 8th choice, 103rd overall, in 1978 Amateur Draft).

			Regular Season					Playoffs				
Season	Club	Lea	GP	G	A	TP	PIM	GP	G	A	TP	PIM
1976-77	Peterborough	OHA	65	52	69	121	93	4	1	4	5	6
1977-78	Peterborough	OHA	68	42	86	128	52	21	10	8	18	16
1978-79	Nova Scotia	AHL	79	15	26	41	22	10	4	2	6	4
1979-80	**Montreal**	**NHL**	**2**	**0**	**1**	**1**	**0**	....	....	....	....	....
a	Nova Scotia	AHL	75	45	53	98	38	6	1	2	3	8
1980-81	**Montreal**	**NHL**	**61**	**15**	**24**	**39**	**74**	**2**	**0**	**0**	**0**	**6**
1981-82	**Montreal**	**NHL**	**78**	**36**	**52**	**88**	**88**	**5**	**0**	**4**	**4**	**16**
1982-83	**Montreal**	**NHL**	**78**	**24**	**26**	**50**	**63**	**3**	**0**	**0**	**0**	**0**
1983-84	**Montreal**	**NHL**	**9**	**3**	**7**	**10**	**4**	....	....	....	....	....
	Minnesota	**NHL**	**62**	**17**	**38**	**55**	**60**	**15**	**4**	**7**	**11**	**12**
1984-85	**Minnesota**	**NHL**	**78**	**20**	**38**	**58**	**90**	**9**	**4**	**4**	**8**	**6**
1985-86	**Minnesota**	**NHL**	**79**	**26**	**32**	**58**	**100**	**5**	**0**	**3**	**3**	**6**
1986-87	**Minnesota**	**NHL**	**78**	**16**	**29**	**45**	**56**	....	....	....	....	....
1987-88	**Minnesota**	**NHL**	**46**	**8**	**11**	**19**	**74**	....	....	....	....	....
	Edmonton	**NHL**	**26**	**3**	**6**	**9**	**21**	**7**	**2**	**0**	**2**	**16**
1988-89	**Edmonton**	**NHL**	**46**	**11**	**15**	**26**	**47**	....	....	....	....	....
	Philadelphia	**NHL**	**25**	**3**	**10**	**13**	**64**	**16**	**2**	**3**	**5**	**18**
1989-90	**Philadelphia**	**NHL**	**69**	**13**	**14**	**27**	**80**	....	....	....	....	....
1990-91	**Philadelphia**	**NHL**	**76**	**14**	**23**	**37**	**131**	....	....	....	....	....
1991-92	**Philadelphia**	**NHL**	**50**	**7**	**10**	**17**	**98**	....	....	....	....	....
	NHL Totals		**863**	**216**	**336**	**552**	**1050**	**62**	**12**	**21**	**33**	**80**

a AHL Second All-Star Team (1980)

Played in NHL All-Star Game (1982)

Traded to **Minnesota** by **Montreal** with Mark Napier and Toronto's third round choice (Ken Hodge) in 1984 Entry Draft — Montreal's property via earlier transaction — for Bobby Smith, October 28, 1983. Traded to **Edmonton** by **Minnesota** for Moe Mantha, January 22, 1988. Traded to **Philadelphia** by **Edmonton** with Edmonton's fifth round choice (Dimitri Yushkevich) in 1991 Entry Draft for Dave Brown, February 7, 1989. Traded to **Winnipeg** by **Philadelphia** with Pete Peeters for future considerations, September 28, 1989. Traded to **Philadelphia** by **Winnipeg** with Pete Peeters for Toronto's fifth round choice in 1991 Entry Draft (Juha Ylonen) — previously acquired by Philadelphia — and the cancellation of future considerations owed Philadelphia from the trade of Shawn Cronin, October 3, 1989.

ADAMS, GREG

Left wing. Shoots left. 6'3", 198 lbs. Born, Nelson, B.C., August 1, 1963.

			Regular Season					Playoffs				
Season	Club	Lea	GP	G	A	TP	PIM	GP	G	A	TP	PIM
1982-83	N. Arizona	NCAA	29	14	21	35	19	....	....	....	....	....
1983-84	N. Arizona	NCAA	26	44	29	73	24	....	....	....	....	....
1984-85	**New Jersey**	**NHL**	**36**	**12**	**9**	**21**	**14**	....	....	....	....	....
	Maine	AHL	41	15	20	35	12	11	3	4	7	0
1985-86	**New Jersey**	**NHL**	**78**	**35**	**42**	**77**	**30**	....	....	....	....	....
1986-87	**New Jersey**	**NHL**	**72**	**20**	**27**	**47**	**19**	....	....	....	....	....
1987-88	**Vancouver**	**NHL**	**80**	**36**	**40**	**76**	**30**	....	....	....	....	....
1988-89	**Vancouver**	**NHL**	**61**	**19**	**14**	**33**	**24**	**7**	**2**	**3**	**5**	**2**
1989-90	**Vancouver**	**NHL**	**65**	**30**	**20**	**50**	**18**	....	....	....	....	....
1990-91	**Vancouver**	**NHL**	**55**	**21**	**24**	**45**	**10**	**5**	**0**	**0**	**0**	**2**
1991-92	**Vancouver**	**NHL**	**76**	**30**	**27**	**57**	**26**	**6**	**0**	**2**	**2**	**4**
	NHL Totals		**523**	**203**	**203**	**406**	**171**	**18**	**2**	**5**	**7**	**8**

Played in NHL All-Star Game (1988)

Signed as a free agent by **New Jersey**, June 25, 1984. Traded to **Vancouver** by **New Jersey** with Kirk McLean for Patrik Sundstrom and Vancouver's fourth round choice (Matt Ruchty) in 1988 Entry Draft, September 10, 1987.

AGNEW, JIM

Defense. Shoots left. 6'1", 190 lbs. Born, Hartney, Man., March 21, 1966.
(Vancouver's 10th choice, 157th overall, in 1984 Entry Draft).

			Regular Season					Playoffs				
Season	Club	Lea	GP	G	A	TP	PIM	GP	G	A	TP	PIM
1982-83	Brandon	WHL	14	1	1	2	9	....	....	....	....	....
1983-84	Brandon	WHL	71	6	17	23	107	12	0	1	1	39
1984-85	Brandon	WHL	19	3	15	18	82	....	....	....	....	....
	Portland	WHL	44	5	24	29	223	6	0	2	2	44
1985-86a	Portland	WHL	70	6	30	36	286	9	0	1	1	48
1986-87	**Vancouver**	**NHL**	**4**	**0**	**0**	**0**	**0**	....	....	....	....	....
	Fredericton	AHL	67	0	5	5	261	....	....	....	....	....
1987-88	**Vancouver**	**NHL**	**10**	**0**	**1**	**1**	**16**	....	....	....	....	....
	Fredericton	AHL	63	2	8	10	188	14	0	2	2	43
1988-89	Milwaukee	IHL	47	2	10	12	181	11	0	2	2	34
1989-90	**Vancouver**	**NHL**	**7**	**0**	**0**	**0**	**36**	....	....	....	....	....
b	Milwaukee	IHL	51	4	10	14	238	....	....	....	....	....
1990-91	**Vancouver**	**NHL**	**20**	**0**	**0**	**0**	**81**	....	....	....	....	....
	Milwaukee	IHL	3	0	0	0	33	....	....	....	....	....
1991-92	**Vancouver**	**NHL**	**24**	**0**	**0**	**0**	**56**	**4**	**0**	**0**	**0**	**6**
	NHL Totals		**65**	**0**	**1**	**1**	**189**	**4**	**0**	**0**	**0**	**6**

a WHL First All-Star Team, West Division (1986)
b IHL Second All-Star Team (1990)

AHLUND, HAKAN

Right wing. Shoots left. 5'10", 190 lbs. Born, Orebro, Sweden, August 16, 1967.
(Vancouver's 8th choice, 151st overall, in 1985 Entry Draft).

			Regular Season					Playoffs				
Season	Club	Lea	GP	G	A	TP	PIM	GP	G	A	TP	PIM
1988-89	Malmo	Swe.	35	20	27	47	....	....	....	....	....	....
1989-90	Malmo	Swe.	35	12	38	50	30	....	....	....	....	....
1990-91	Malmo	Swe.	39	9	18	27	46	....	....	....	....	....
1991-92	Malmo	Swe.	38	5	11	16	48	10	2	2	4	8

AHOLA, PETER

Defense. Shoots left. 6'3", 205 lbs. Born, Espoo, Finland, May 14, 1968.

			Regular Season					Playoffs				
Season	Club	Lea	GP	G	A	TP	PIM	GP	G	A	TP	PIM
1989-90	Boston U.	H.E.	43	3	20	23	65	....	....	....	....	....
1990-91a	Boston U.	H.E.	39	12	24	36	88	....	....	....	....	....
1991-92	**Los Angeles**	**NHL**	**71**	**7**	**12**	**19**	**101**	**6**	**0**	**0**	**0**	**2**
	Phoenix	IHL	7	3	3	6	34	....	....	....	....	....
	NHL Totals		**71**	**7**	**12**	**19**	**101**	**6**	**0**	**0**	**0**	**2**

a NCAA East Second All-American Team (1991)

Signed as a free agent by **Los Angeles**, April 5, 1991.

AIKEN, DAVID (AY-kin)

Left wing. Shoots left. 6', 200 lbs. Born, St. Stephen, N.B., September 27, 1967.
(Edmonton's 1st choice, 20th overall, in 1989 Supplemental Draft).

			Regular Season					Playoffs				
Season	Club	Lea	GP	G	A	TP	PIM	GP	G	A	TP	PIM
1986-87	N. Hampshire	H.E.	37	19	9	28	10	....	....	....	....	....
1987-88	N. Hampshire	H.E.	29	7	15	22	24	....	....	....	....	....
1988-89	N. Hampshire	H.E.	34	14	17	31	30	....	....	....	....	....
1989-90	N. Hampshire	H.E.	39	12	19	31	37	....	....	....	....	....
1990-91	Richmond	ECHL	64	28	52	80	29	4	1	3	4	0
1991-92	Richmond	ECHL	63	31	36	67	25	7	5	2	7	0

AITKEN, BRAD (ATE-kin)

Left wing. Shoots left. 6'2", 200 lbs. Born, Scarborough, Ont., October 30, 1967.
(Pittsburgh's 3rd choice, 46th overall, in 1986 Entry Draft).

			Regular Season					Playoffs				
Season	Club	Lea	GP	G	A	TP	PIM	GP	G	A	TP	PIM
1985-86	Peterborough	OHL	48	9	28	37	77	....	....	....	....	....
	S.S. Marie	OHL	20	8	19	27	11	....	....	....	....	....
1986-87	S.S. Marie	OHL	52	27	38	65	86	4	1	2	3	5
1987-88	**Pittsburgh**	**NHL**	**5**	**1**	**1**	**2**	**0**	....	....	....	....	....
	Muskegon	IHL	74	32	31	63	128	1	0	0	0	0
1988-89	Muskegon	IHL	74	35	30	65	139	13	5	5	10	75
1989-90	Muskegon	IHL	46	10	23	33	172	....	....	....	....	....
	Phoenix	IHL	8	2	1	3	18	....	....	....	....	....
	Fort Wayne	IHL	13	5	2	7	0	5	2	1	3	12
1990-91	**Pittsburgh**	**NHL**	**6**	**0**	**1**	**1**	**25**	....	....	....	....	....
	Muskegon	IHL	44	14	17	31	143	....	....	....	....	....
	Kansas City	IHL	6	4	6	10	2	....	....	....	....	....
	Edmonton	**NHL**	**3**	**0**	**1**	**1**	**0**	....	....	....	....	....
	Cape Breton	AHL	6	2	3	5	17	3	0	2	2	6
1991-92	St. John's	AHL	59	12	27	39	169	....	....	....	....	....
	NHL Totals		**14**	**1**	**3**	**4**	**25**	....	....	....	....	....

Traded to **Edmonton** by **Pittsburgh** for Kim Issel, March 5, 1991. Signed as a free agent by **Toronto**, July 30, 1991.

AIVAZOFF, MICAH (AY-va-zoff)

Center. Shoots left. 6', 192 lbs. Born, Powell River, B.C., May 4, 1969.
(Los Angeles' 6th choice, 109th overall, in 1988 Entry Draft).

			Regular Season					Playoffs				
Season	Club	Lea	GP	G	A	TP	PIM	GP	G	A	TP	PIM
1986-87	Victoria	WHL	72	18	39	57	112	5	1	0	1	2
1987-88	Victoria	WHL	69	26	57	83	79	8	3	4	7	14
1988-89	Victoria	WHL	70	35	65	100	136	8	5	7	12	2
1989-90	New Haven	AHL	77	20	39	59	71	....	....	....	....	....
1990-91	New Haven	AHL	79	11	29	40	84	....	....	....	....	....
1991-92	Adirondack	AHL	61	9	20	29	50	19	2	8	10	25

AKERBLOM, MARKUS (OHK-uhr-blum)

Left wing. Shoots left. 6', 189 lbs. Born, Ostersund, Sweden, November 22, 1969.
(Winnipeg's 8th choice, 127th overall, in 1988 Entry Draft).

			Regular Season					Playoffs				
Season	Club	Lea	GP	G	A	TP	PIM	GP	G	A	TP	PIM
1986-87	Ostersund	Swe.2	32	14	18	32	....	....	....	....	....	....
1987-88	Bjorkloven	Swe.	32	6	8	14	....	....	....	....	....	....
1988-89	Bjorkloven	Swe.	21	6	10	16	....	....	....	....	....	....
1989-90	Bjorkloven	Swe.2	15	10	10	20	....	....	....	....	....	....
1990-91	Bjorkloven	Swe.2	22	7	4	11	16	....	....	....	....	....
1991-92	Leksand	Swe.	21	3	5	8	6	....	....	....	....	....

AKERSTROM, ROGER (OHK-uhr-struhm)

Defense. Shoots left. 5'11", 189 lbs. Born, Lulea, Sweden, April 5, 1967.
(Vancouver's 8th choice, 170th overall, in 1988 Entry Draft).

			Regular Season					Playoffs				
Season	Club	Lea	GP	G	A	TP	PIM	GP	G	A	TP	PIM
1987-88	Lulea	Swe.	34	4	3	7	28	....	....	....	....	....
1988-89	Lulea	Swe.	38	6	12	18	32	....	....	....	....	....
1989-90	Lulea	Swe.	36	5	10	15	44	5	3	2	5	2
1990-91	Lulea	Swe.	38	2	10	12	38	....	....	....	....	....
1991-92	Vasteras	Swe.	39	3	9	12	20	....	....	....	....	....

AKERVIK, ANDY

Right wing. Shoots right. 6'4", 204 lbs. Born, Duluth, MN, August 11, 1967.
(Quebec's 7th choice, 120th overall, in 1985 Entry Draft).

			Regular Season					Playoffs				
Season	Club	Lea	GP	G	A	TP	PIM	GP	G	A	TP	PIM
1989-90	Skovde	Swe.2	33	22	24	46	....	....	....	....	....	....
1990-91	Kansas City	IHL	56	8	11	19	36	....	....	....	....	....
1991-92	Kansas City	IHL	22	1	5	6	12	....	....	....	....	....

Signed as a free agent by **San Jose**, September 3, 1991.

ALATALO, MIKA

Left wing. Shoots left. 5'11", 185 lbs. Born, Oulu, Finland, August 11, 1971.
(Winnipeg's 11th choice, 203rd overall, in 1990 Entry Draft).

			Regular Season					Playoffs				
Season	Club	Lea	GP	G	A	TP	PIM	GP	G	A	TP	PIM
1989-90	KooKoo	Fin.	41	3	5	8	22	....	....	....	....	....
1990-91	Lukko	Fin.	39	10	1	11	10	....	....	....	....	....
1991-92	Lukko	Fin.	43	20	17	37	32	2	0	0	0	0

ALBELIN, TOMMY (AL-buh-LEEN)

Defense. Shoots left. 6'1", 190 lbs. Born, Stockholm, Sweden, May 21, 1964.
(Quebec's 7th choice, 152nd overall, in 1983 Entry Draft).

			Regular Season					Playoffs				
Season	Club	Lea	GP	G	A	TP	PIM	GP	G	A	TP	PIM
1982-83	Djurgarden	Swe.	19	2	5	7	4	6	1	0	1	2
1983-84	Djurgarden	Swe.	30	9	5	14	26	4	0	1	1	2
1984-85	Djurgarden	Swe.	32	9	8	17	22	8	2	1	3	4
1985-86	Djurgarden	Swe.	35	4	8	12	26	....	....	....	....	....
1986-87	Djurgarden	Swe.	33	7	5	12	49	2	0	0	0	0
1987-88	**Quebec**	**NHL**	**60**	**3**	**23**	**26**	**47**	....	....	....	....	....
1988-89	**Quebec**	**NHL**	**14**	**2**	**4**	**6**	**27**	....	....	....	....	....
	Halifax	AHL	8	2	5	7	4	....	....	....	....	....
	New Jersey	**NHL**	**46**	**7**	**24**	**31**	**40**	....	....	....	....	....
1989-90	**New Jersey**	**NHL**	**68**	**6**	**23**	**29**	**63**	....	....	....	....	....
1990-91	**New Jersey**	**NHL**	**47**	**2**	**12**	**14**	**44**	**3**	**0**	**1**	**1**	**2**
	Utica	AHL	14	4	2	6	10	....	....	....	....	....
1991-92	**New Jersey**	**NHL**	**19**	**0**	**4**	**4**	**4**	**1**	**1**	**1**	**2**	**0**
	Utica	AHL	11	4	6	10	4	....	....	....	....	....
	NHL Totals		**254**	**20**	**90**	**110**	**225**	**4**	**1**	**2**	**3**	**2**

Traded to **New Jersey** by **Quebec** for New Jersey's fourth round choice (Niclas Andersson) in 1989 Entry Draft, December 12, 1988.

ALEXEYEV, ALEXANDER

Defense. Shoots left. 6', 185 lbs. Born, Kiev, Soviet Union, March 21, 1974.
(Winnipeg's 5th choice, 132nd overall, in 1992 Entry Draft).

			Regular Season					Playoffs				
Season	Club	Lea	GP	G	A	TP	PIM	GP	G	A	TP	PIM
1990-91	Sokol Kiev	USSR	5	0	0	0	2	....	....	....	....	....
1991-92	Sokol Kiev	CIS	25	1	5	6	22	....	....	....	....	....

ALLAIN, RICK

Defense. Shoots left. 6', 190 lbs. Born, Guelph, Ont., May 20, 1969.
(Boston's 8th choice, 164th overall, in 1989 Entry Draft).

			Regular Season					Playoffs				
Season	Club	Lea	GP	G	A	TP	PIM	GP	G	A	TP	PIM
1986-87	Kitchener	OHL	18	0	0	0	32	....	....	....	....	....
1987-88	Kitchener	OHL	45	4	9	13	267	....	....	....	....	....
1988-89	Kitchener	OHL	62	2	16	18	245	5	0	0	0	10
1989-90	Kitchener	OHL	55	5	16	21	156	17	0	4	4	46
1990-91	Maine	AHL	13	0	1	1	33	....	....	....	....	....
	Johnstown	ECHL	36	2	12	14	100	10	0	0	0	50
1991-92	Maine	AHL	66	1	11	12	249	....	....	....	....	....

ALLEN, PETER

Defense. Shoots right. 6'2", 185 lbs. Born, Calgary, Alta., March 6, 1970.
(Boston's 1st choice, 24th overall, in 1991 Supplemental Draft).

			Regular Season					Playoffs				
Season	Club	Lea	GP	G	A	TP	PIM	GP	G	A	TP	PIM
1989-90	Yale	ECAC	26	2	4	6	16	....	....	....	....	....
1990-91	Yale	ECAC	17	0	6	6	14	....	....	....	....	....
1991-92	Yale	ECAC	26	5	13	18	26	....	....	....	....	....

ALLISON, SCOTT

Center. Shoots left. 6'4", 194 lbs. Born, St. Boniface, Man., April 22, 1972.
(Edmonton's 1st choice, 17th overall, in 1990 Entry Draft).

			Regular Season					Playoffs				
Season	Club	Lea	GP	G	A	TP	PIM	GP	G	A	TP	PIM
1988-89	Prince Albert	WHL	51	6	9	15	37	3	0	0	0	0
1989-90	Prince Albert	WHL	66	22	16	38	73	11	1	4	5	8
1990-91	Prince Albert	WHL	30	5	5	10	57	....	....	....	....	....
	Portland	WHL	44	5	17	22	105	....	....	....	....	....
1991-92	Moose Jaw	WHL	72	37	45	82	238	3	1	1	2	25

AMBROZIAK, PETER

Left wing. Shoots left. 6', 191 lbs. Born, Toronto, Ont., September 15, 1971.
(Buffalo's 4th choice, 72nd overall, in 1991 Entry Draft).

			Regular Season					Playoffs				
Season	Club	Lea	GP	G	A	TP	PIM	GP	G	A	TP	PIM
1990-91	Ottawa	OHL	62	30	32	62	56	17	15	9	24	24
1991-92	Ottawa	OHL	49	32	49	81	50	11	3	7	10	33

AMONTE, ANTHONY (TONY)

Right wing. Shoots left. 6', 180 lbs. Born, Hingham, MA, August 2, 1970.
(NY Rangers' 3rd choice, 68th overall, in 1988 Entry Draft).

			Regular Season					Playoffs				
Season	Club	Lea	GP	G	A	TP	PIM	GP	G	A	TP	PIM
1989-90	Boston U.	H.E.	41	25	33	58	52	....	....	....	....	....
1990-91ab	Boston U.	H.E.	38	31	37	68	82	....	....	....	....	....
	NY Rangers	**NHL**	....	....	....	....	....	**2**	**0**	**2**	**2**	**2**
1991-92c	**NY Rangers**	**NHL**	**79**	**35**	**34**	**69**	**55**	**13**	**3**	**6**	**9**	**2**
	NHL Totals		**79**	**35**	**34**	**69**	**55**	**15**	**3**	**8**	**11**	**4**

a Hockey East Second All-Star Team (1991)
b NCAA Final Four All-Tournament Team (1991)
c NHL/Upper Deck All-Rookie Team (1992)

ANDERSON, GLENN CHRIS

Right wing. Shoots left. 6'1", 190 lbs. Born, Vancouver, B.C., October 2, 1960.
(Edmonton's 3rd choice, 69th overall, in 1979 Entry Draft).

			Regular Season					Playoffs				
Season	Club	Lea	GP	G	A	TP	PIM	GP	G	A	TP	PIM
1978-79	U. of Denver	WCHA	40	26	29	55	58	....	....	....	....	....
1979-80	Seattle	WHL	7	5	5	10	4	....	....	....	....	....
	Cdn. Olympic	....	49	21	21	42	46	....	....	....	....	....
1980-81	**Edmonton**	**NHL**	**58**	**30**	**23**	**53**	**24**	**9**	**5**	**7**	**12**	**12**
1981-82	**Edmonton**	**NHL**	**80**	**38**	**67**	**105**	**71**	**5**	**2**	**5**	**7**	**8**
1982-83	**Edmonton**	**NHL**	**72**	**48**	**56**	**104**	**70**	**16**	**10**	**10**	**20**	**32**
1983-84	**Edmonton**	**NHL**	**80**	**54**	**45**	**99**	**65**	**19**	**6**	**11**	**17**	**33**
1984-85	**Edmonton**	**NHL**	**80**	**42**	**39**	**81**	**69**	**18**	**10**	**16**	**26**	**38**
1985-86	**Edmonton**	**NHL**	**72**	**54**	**48**	**102**	**90**	**10**	**8**	**3**	**11**	**14**
1986-87	**Edmonton**	**NHL**	**80**	**35**	**38**	**73**	**65**	**21**	**14**	**13**	**27**	**59**
1987-88	**Edmonton**	**NHL**	**80**	**38**	**50**	**88**	**58**	**19**	**9**	**16**	**25**	**49**
1988-89	**Edmonton**	**NHL**	**79**	**16**	**48**	**64**	**93**	**7**	**1**	**2**	**3**	**8**
1989-90	**Edmonton**	**NHL**	**73**	**34**	**38**	**72**	**107**	**22**	**10**	**12**	**22**	**20**
1990-91	**Edmonton**	**NHL**	**74**	**24**	**31**	**55**	**59**	**18**	**6**	**7**	**13**	**41**
1991-92	**Toronto**	**NHL**	**72**	**24**	**33**	**57**	**100**	....	....	....	....	....
	NHL Totals		**900**	**437**	**516**	**953**	**871**	**164**	**81**	**102**	**183**	**314**

Played in NHL All-Star Game (1984-86, 1988)

Traded to **Toronto** by **Edmonton** with Grant Fuhr and Craig Berube for Vincent Damphousse, Peter Ing, Scott Thornton, Luke Richardson, future considerations and cash, September 19, 1991.

ANDERSON, JOHN MURRAY

Right wing. Shoots left. 5'11", 200 lbs. Born, Toronto, Ont., March 28, 1957.
(Toronto's 1st choice, 11th overall, in 1977 Amateur Draft).

			Regular Season					Playoffs				
Season	Club	Lea	GP	G	A	TP	PIM	GP	G	A	TP	PIM
1973-74	Toronto	OMJHL	38	22	22	44	6	....	....	....	....	....
1974-75	Toronto	OMJHL	70	49	64	113	31	22	16	14	30	14
1975-76	Toronto	OHA	39	26	25	51	19	10	7	4	11	7
1976-77a	Toronto	OHA	64	57	62	119	42	6	3	5	8	0
1977-78	**Toronto**	**NHL**	**17**	**1**	**2**	**3**	**2**	**2**	**0**	**0**	**0**	**0**
	Dallas	CHL	55	22	23	45	6	13	*11	8	*19	2
1978-79	**Toronto**	**NHL**	**71**	**15**	**11**	**26**	**10**	**6**	**0**	**2**	**2**	**0**
1979-80	**Toronto**	**NHL**	**74**	**25**	**28**	**53**	**22**	**3**	**1**	**1**	**2**	**0**
1980-81	**Toronto**	**NHL**	**75**	**17**	**26**	**43**	**31**	**2**	**0**	**0**	**0**	**0**
1981-82	**Toronto**	**NHL**	**69**	**31**	**26**	**57**	**30**	....	....	....	....	....
1982-83	**Toronto**	**NHL**	**80**	**31**	**49**	**80**	**24**	**4**	**2**	**4**	**6**	**0**
1983-84	**Toronto**	**NHL**	**73**	**37**	**31**	**68**	**22**	....	....	....	....	....
1984-85	**Toronto**	**NHL**	**75**	**32**	**31**	**63**	**27**	....	....	....	....	....
1985-86	**Quebec**	**NHL**	**65**	**21**	**28**	**49**	**26**	....	....	....	....	....
	Hartford	**NHL**	**14**	**8**	**17**	**25**	**2**	**10**	**5**	**8**	**13**	**0**
1986-87	**Hartford**	**NHL**	**76**	**31**	**44**	**75**	**19**	**6**	**1**	**2**	**3**	**0**
1987-88	**Hartford**	**NHL**	**63**	**17**	**32**	**49**	**20**	....	....	....	....	....
1988-89	**Hartford**	**NHL**	**62**	**16**	**24**	**40**	**28**	**4**	**0**	**1**	**1**	**2**
1989-90	Binghamton	AHL	3	1	1	2	0	....	....	....	....	....
	Milano	Italy	9	7	9	16	18	....	....	....	....	....
1990-91	Fort Wayne	IHL	63	40	43	83	24	1	3	0	3	0
1991-92bcd	New Haven	AHL	68	41	54	95	24	4	0	4	4	0
	NHL Totals		**814**	**282**	**349**	**631**	**263**	**37**	**9**	**18**	**27**	**2**

a OHA First All-Star Team (1977)
b Won Fred Hunt Award (Sportsmanship-AHL) (1992)
c AHL First All-Star Team (1992)
d Won Les Cunningham Trophy (MVP-AHL) (1992)

Traded to **Quebec** by **Toronto** for Brad Maxwell, August 21, 1985. Traded to **Hartford** by **Quebec** for Risto Siltanen, March 8, 1986.

ANDERSON, PERRY LYNN

Left wing. Shoots left. 6'1", 225 lbs. Born, Barrie, Ont., October 14, 1961.
(St. Louis' 5th choice, 117th overall, in 1980 Entry Draft).

			Regular Season					Playoffs				
Season	Club	Lea	GP	G	A	TP	PIM	GP	G	A	TP	PIM
1978-79	Kingston	OHA	61	6	13	19	85	5	2	1	3	6
1979-80	Kingston	OHA	63	17	16	33	52	3	0	0	0	6
1980-81	Kingston	OHA	38	9	13	22	118	....	....	....	....	....
	Brantford	OHA	31	8	27	35	43	6	4	2	6	15
1981-82	**St. Louis**	**NHL**	**5**	**1**	**2**	**3**	**0**	**10**	**2**	**0**	**2**	**4**
	Salt Lake	CHL	71	32	32	64	117	2	1	0	1	2
1982-83	**St. Louis**	**NHL**	**18**	**5**	**2**	**7**	**14**	....	....	....	....	....
	Salt Lake	CHL	57	23	19	42	140	....	....	....	....	....
1983-84	**St. Louis**	**NHL**	**50**	**7**	**5**	**12**	**195**	**9**	**0**	**0**	**0**	**27**
	Montana	CHL	8	7	3	10	34	....	....	....	....	....
1984-85	**St. Louis**	**NHL**	**71**	**9**	**9**	**18**	**146**	**3**	**0**	**0**	**0**	**7**
1985-86	**New Jersey**	**NHL**	**51**	**7**	**12**	**19**	**91**	....	....	....	....	....
1986-87	**New Jersey**	**NHL**	**57**	**10**	**9**	**19**	**107**	....	....	....	....	....
	Maine	AHL	9	5	4	9	42	....	....	....	....	....
1987-88	**New Jersey**	**NHL**	**60**	**4**	**6**	**10**	**222**	**10**	**0**	**0**	**0**	**113**
1988-89	**New Jersey**	**NHL**	**39**	**3**	**6**	**9**	**128**	....	....	....	....	....
1989-90	Utica	AHL	71	13	17	30	128	5	0	0	0	24
1990-91	**New Jersey**	**NHL**	**1**	**0**	**0**	**0**	**5**	**4**	**0**	**1**	**1**	**10**
	Utica	AHL	68	19	14	33	245	....	....	....	....	....
1991-92	**San Jose**	**NHL**	**48**	**4**	**8**	**12**	**143**	....	....	....	....	....
	NHL Totals		**400**	**50**	**59**	**109**	**1051**	**36**	**2**	**1**	**3**	**161**

Traded to **New Jersey** by **St. Louis** for Rick Meagher and New Jersey's 12th round choice (Bill Butler) in 1986 Entry Draft, August 29, 1985. Signed as a free agent by **San Jose**, July 8, 1991.

ANDERSON, SHAWN

Defense. Shoots left. 6'1", 200 lbs. Born, Montreal, Que., February 7, 1968.
(Buffalo's 1st choice, 5th overall, in 1986 Entry Draft).

			Regular Season					Playoffs				
Season	Club	Lea	GP	G	A	TP	PIM	GP	G	A	TP	PIM
1985-86	Maine	H.E.	16	5	8	13	22	....	....	....	....	....
	Cdn. Olympic	....	49	4	14	18	38	....	....	....	....	....
1986-87	**Buffalo**	**NHL**	**41**	**2**	**11**	**13**	**23**	....	....	....	....	....
	Rochester	AHL	15	2	5	7	11	....	....	....	....	....
1987-88	**Buffalo**	**NHL**	**23**	**1**	**2**	**3**	**17**	....	....	....	....	....
	Rochester	AHL	22	5	16	21	19	6	0	0	0	0
1988-89	**Buffalo**	**NHL**	**33**	**2**	**10**	**12**	**18**	**5**	**0**	**1**	**1**	**4**
	Rochester	AHL	31	5	14	19	24	....	....	....	....	....
1989-90	**Buffalo**	**NHL**	**16**	**1**	**3**	**4**	**8**	....	....	....	....	....
	Rochester	AHL	39	2	16	18	41	9	1	0	1	4
1990-91	**Quebec**	**NHL**	**31**	**3**	**10**	**13**	**21**	....	....	....	....	....
	Halifax	AHL	4	0	1	1	2	....	....	....	....	....
1991-92	Weiswasser	Ger.	38	7	15	22	83	....	....	....	....	....
	NHL Totals		**144**	**9**	**36**	**45**	**87**	**5**	**0**	**1**	**1**	**4**

Traded to **Washington** by **Buffalo** for Bill Houlder, September 30, 1990. Claimed by **Quebec** in NHL Waiver Draft, October 1, 1990. Traded to **Winnipeg** by **Quebec** for Sergei Kharin, October 22, 1991. Traded to **Washington** by **Winnipeg** for future considerations, October 23, 1991.

ANDERSSON, BO MIKAEL (AN-duhr-suhn)

Left wing. Shoots left. 5'11", 185 lbs. Born, Malmo, Sweden, May 10, 1966.
(Buffalo's 1st choice, 18th overall, in 1984 Entry Draft).

			Regular Season					Playoffs				
Season	Club	Lea	GP	G	A	TP	PIM	GP	G	A	TP	PIM
1982-83	V. Frolunda	Swe.	1	1	0	1	0	....	....	....	....	....
1983-84	V. Frolunda	Swe.	18	0	3	6	....	....	....	....	....	....
1984-85	V. Frolunda	Swe.	30	16	11	27	18	6	3	2	5	2
1985-86	**Buffalo**	**NHL**	**32**	**1**	**9**	**10**	**4**	....	....	....	....	....
	Rochester	AHL	20	10	4	14	6	....	....	....	....	....
1986-87	**Buffalo**	**NHL**	**16**	**0**	**3**	**3**	**0**	....	....	....	....	....
	Rochester	AHL	42	6	20	26	14	9	1	2	3	2
1987-88	**Buffalo**	**NHL**	**37**	**3**	**20**	**23**	**10**	**1**	**1**	**0**	**1**	**0**
	Rochester	AHL	35	12	24	36	16	....	....	....	....	....
1988-89	**Buffalo**	**NHL**	**14**	**0**	**1**	**1**	**4**	....	....	....	....	....
	Rochester	AHL	56	18	33	51	12	....	....	....	....	....
1989-90	**Hartford**	**NHL**	**50**	**13**	**24**	**37**	**6**	**5**	**0**	**3**	**3**	**2**
1990-91	**Hartford**	**NHL**	**41**	**4**	**7**	**11**	**8**	....	....	....	....	....
	Springfield	AHL	26	7	22	29	10	18	*10	8	18	12
1991-92	**Hartford**	**NHL**	**74**	**18**	**29**	**47**	**14**	**7**	**0**	**2**	**2**	**6**
	NHL Totals		**264**	**39**	**93**	**132**	**46**	**13**	**1**	**5**	**6**	**8**

Claimed by **Hartford** in NHL Waiver Draft, October 2, 1989. Signed as a free agent by **Tampa Bay**, June 29, 1992.

ANDERSSON, ERIK

Right wing. Shoots left. 6'2", 187 lbs. Born, Stockholm, Sweden, August 19, 1971.
(Los Angeles' 5th choice, 112th overall, in 1990 Entry Draft).

			Regular Season					Playoffs				
Season	Club	Lea	GP	G	A	TP	PIM	GP	G	A	TP	PIM
1989-90	Danderyd	Swe.	30	14	5	19	16	....	....	....	....	....
1990-91	AIK	Swe.	32	1	1	2	10	....	....	....	....	....
1991-92	AIK	Swe.	3	0	0	0	0	....	....	....	....	....

ANDERSSON, HENRIK

Defense. Shoots left. 6'4", 187 lbs. Born, Vasteras, Sweden, January 19, 1970.
(Winnipeg's 9th choice, 161st overall, in 1990 Entry Draft).

			Regular Season					Playoffs				
Season	Club	Lea	GP	G	A	TP	PIM	GP	G	A	TP	PIM
1989-90	Vasteras	Swe.	36	2	2	4	10	....	....	....	....	....
1990-91	Vasteras	Swe.	34	2	5	7	10	....	....	....	....	....
1991-92	Vasteras	Swe.	2	0	0	0	0	....	....	....	....	....

ANDERSSON, NICLAS (AN-duhr-suhn)

Left wing. Shoots left. 5'9", 175 lbs. Born, Kungalv, Sweden, May 20, 1971.
(Quebec's 5th choice, 68th overall, in 1989 Entry Draft).

			Regular Season					Playoffs				
Season	Club	Lea	GP	G	A	TP	PIM	GP	G	A	TP	PIM
1987-88	V. Frolunda	Swe.	15	5	5	10	....	....	....	....	....	....
1988-89	V. Frolunda	Swe.	30	13	24	37	....	....	....	....	....	....
1989-90	V. Frolunda	Swe.	38	10	21	31	14	....	....	....	....	....
1990-91	V. Frolunda	Swe.	22	6	10	16	16	....	....	....	....	....
1991-92	Halifax	AHL	57	8	26	34	41	....	....	....	....	....

ANDREYCHUK, DAVID (DAVE)

Left wing. Shoots right. 6'3", 225 lbs. Born, Hamilton, Ont., September 29, 1963.
(Buffalo's 3rd choice, 16th overall, in 1982 Entry Draft).

			Regular Season					Playoffs				
Season	Club	Lea	GP	G	A	TP	PIM	GP	G	A	TP	PIM
1980-81	Oshawa	OHA	67	22	22	44	80	10	3	2	5	20
1981-82	Oshawa	OHL	67	57	43	100	71	3	1	4	5	16
1982-83	**Buffalo**	**NHL**	**43**	**14**	**23**	**37**	**16**	**4**	**1**	**0**	**1**	**4**
	Oshawa	OHL	14	8	24	32	6	....	....	....	....	....
1983-84	**Buffalo**	**NHL**	**78**	**38**	**42**	**80**	**42**	**2**	**0**	**1**	**1**	**2**
1984-85	**Buffalo**	**NHL**	**64**	**31**	**30**	**61**	**54**	**5**	**4**	**2**	**6**	**4**
1985-86	**Buffalo**	**NHL**	**80**	**36**	**51**	**87**	**61**	....	....	....	....	....
1986-87	**Buffalo**	**NHL**	**77**	**25**	**48**	**73**	**46**	....	....	....	....	....
1987-88	**Buffalo**	**NHL**	**80**	**30**	**48**	**78**	**112**	**6**	**2**	**4**	**6**	**0**
1988-89	**Buffalo**	**NHL**	**56**	**28**	**24**	**52**	**40**	**5**	**0**	**3**	**3**	**0**
1989-90	**Buffalo**	**NHL**	**73**	**40**	**42**	**82**	**42**	**6**	**2**	**5**	**7**	**2**
1990-91	**Buffalo**	**NHL**	**80**	**36**	**33**	**69**	**32**	**6**	**2**	**2**	**4**	**8**
1991-92	**Buffalo**	**NHL**	**80**	**41**	**50**	**91**	**71**	**7**	**1**	**3**	**4**	**12**
	NHL Totals		**711**	**319**	**391**	**710**	**516**	**41**	**12**	**20**	**32**	**32**

Played in NHL All-Star Game (1990)

ANDRUSAK, GREG

Defense. Shoots right. 6'1", 183 lbs. Born, Cranbrook, B.C., November 14, 1969.
(Pittsburgh's 5th choice, 88th overall, in 1988 Entry Draft).

			Regular Season									
Season	Club	Lea	GP	G	A	TP	PIM	GP	G	A	TP	PIM
1987-88	Minn.-Duluth	WCHA	37	4	5	9	42	....	....	....	....	....
1988-89	Minn.-Duluth	WCHA	35	4	8	12	74	....	....	....	....	....
	Cdn. Olympic	....	2	0	0	0	0	....	....	....	....	....
1989-90	Minn.-Duluth	WCHA	35	5	29	34	74	....	....	....	....	....
1990-91	Cdn. National	....	53	4	11	15	34	....	....	....	....	....
1991-92a	Minn.-Duluth	WCHA	36	7	27	34	125	....	....	....	....	....

a WCHA First All-Star Team (1992)

ANGLEHART, SERGE

Defense. Shoots right. 6'2", 190 lbs. Born, Hull, Que., April 18, 1970.
(Detroit's 2nd choice, 38th overall, in 1988 Entry Draft).

			Regular Season					Playoffs				
Season	Club	Lea	GP	G	A	TP	PIM	GP	G	A	TP	PIM
1987-88	Drummondville	QMJHL	44	1	8	9	122	17	0	3	3	19
1988-89	Drummondville	QMJHL	39	6	15	21	89	3	0	0	0	37
	Adirondack	AHL	....	....	....	....	....	2	0	0	0	0
1989-90	Laval	QMJHL	48	2	19	21	131	10	1	6	7	69
1990-91	Adirondack	AHL	52	3	8	11	113	....	....	....	....	....
1991-92	Adirondack	AHL	16	0	1	1	43	....	....	....	....	....

ANTOS, DEAN

Center. Shoots left. 5'11", 175 lbs. Born, Killam, Alta., May 20, 1967.

			Regular Season					Playoffs				
Season	Club	Lea	GP	G	A	TP	PIM	GP	G	A	TP	PIM
1987-88	N. Michigan	WCHA	35	14	23	37	32	....	....	....	....	....
1988-89	N. Michigan	WCHA	45	25	24	49	28	....	....	....	....	....
1989-90	N. Michigan	WCHA	42	19	22	41	50	....	....	....	....	....
1990-91	N. Michigan	WCHA	40	17	26	43	63	....	....	....	....	....
1991-92	Cape Breton	AHL	15	1	4	5	2	....	....	....	....	....

Signed as a free agent by **Edmonton**, July 17, 1991.

ANTOSKI, SHAWN

Left wing. Shoots left. 6'4", 235 lbs. Born, Brantford, Ont., March 25, 1970.
(Vancouver's 2nd choice, 18th overall, in 1990 Entry Draft).

			Regular Season					Playoffs				
Season	Club	Lea	GP	G	A	TP	PIM	GP	G	A	TP	PIM
1987-88	North Bay	OHL	52	3	4	7	163	....	....	....	....	....
1988-89	North Bay	OHL	57	6	21	27	201	9	5	3	8	24
1989-90	North Bay	OHL	59	25	31	56	201	5	1	2	3	17
1990-91	**Vancouver**	**NHL**	**2**	**0**	**0**	**0**	**0**	....	....	....	....	....
	Milwaukee	IHL	62	17	7	24	330	5	1	2	3	10
1991-92	**Vancouver**	**NHL**	**4**	**0**	**0**	**0**	**29**	....	....	....	....	....
	Milwaukee	IHL	52	17	16	33	346	5	2	0	2	20
	NHL Totals		**6**	**0**	**0**	**0**	**29**	....	....	....	....	....

ARCHIBALD, DAVE

Center/Left wing. Shoots left. 6'1", 190 lbs. Born, Chilliwack, B.C., April 14, 1969.
(Minnesota's 1st choice, 6th overall, in 1987 Entry Draft).

			Regular Season					Playoffs				
Season	Club	Lea	GP	G	A	TP	PIM	GP	G	A	TP	PIM
1984-85	Portland	WHL	47	7	11	18	10	3	0	2	2	0
1985-86	Portland	WHL	70	29	35	64	56	15	6	7	13	11
1986-87	Portland	WHL	65	50	57	107	40	20	10	18	28	11
1987-88	**Minnesota**	**NHL**	**78**	**13**	**20**	**33**	**26**	....	....	....	....	....
1988-89	**Minnesota**	**NHL**	**72**	**14**	**19**	**33**	**14**	**5**	**0**	**1**	**1**	**0**
1989-90	**Minnesota**	**NHL**	**12**	**1**	**5**	**6**	**6**	....	....	....	....	....
	NY Rangers	**NHL**	**19**	**2**	**3**	**5**	**6**	....	....	....	....	....
	Flint	IHL	41	14	38	52	16	4	3	2	5	0
1990-91	Cdn. National	....	29	19	12	31	20	....	....	....	....	....
1991-92	Cdn. National	....	58	20	43	63	62	....	....	....	....	....
	Cdn. Olympic	....	8	7	1	8	18	....	....	....	....	....
	Bolzano	Italy	5	4	3	7	16	7	8	5	13	7
	NHL Totals		**181**	**30**	**47**	**77**	**52**	**5**	**0**	**1**	**1**	**0**

Traded to **NY Rangers** by **Minnesota** for Jayson More, November 1, 1989.

ARMSTRONG, BILL

Defense. Shoots left. 6'4", 215 lbs. Born, Richmond Hill, Ont., May 18, 1970.
(Philadelphia's 6th choice, 46th overall, in 1990 Entry Draft).

			Regular Season					Playoffs				
Season	Club	Lea	GP	G	A	TP	PIM	GP	G	A	TP	PIM
1987-88	Toronto	OHL	64	1	10	11	99	....	....	....	....	....
1988-89	Toronto	OHL	64	1	16	17	82	....	....	....	....	....
1989-90	Hamilton	OHL	18	0	2	2	38	....	....	....	....	....
	Niagara Falls	OHL	4	0	1	1	13	....	....	....	....	....
	Oshawa	OHL	41	2	8	10	115	17	0	7	7	39
1990-91	Hershey	AHL	56	1	9	10	117	....	....	....	....	....
1991-92	Hershey	AHL	64	26	22	48	186	6	2	2	4	6

ARMSTRONG, DEREK

Center. Shoots right. 5'11", 180 lbs. Born, Ottawa, Ont., April 23, 1973.
(NY Islanders' 5th choice, 128 overall, in 1992 Entry Draft).

			Regular Season					Playoffs				
Season	Club	Lea	GP	G	A	TP	PIM	GP	G	A	TP	PIM
1990-91	Hawkesbury	COJHL	54	27	45	72	49	....	....	....	....	....
1991-92	Sudbury	OHL	66	31	54	85	22	....	....	....	....	....

ARMSTRONG, WILLIAM (BILL)

Left wing. Shoots left. 6'2", 195 lbs. Born, London, Ont., June 25, 1966.

			Regular Season					Playoffs				
Season	Club	Lea	GP	G	A	TP	PIM	GP	G	A	TP	PIM
1986-87	W. Michigan	CCHA	43	13	20	33	86	....	....	....	....	....
1987-88	W. Michigan	CCHA	41	22	17	39	88	....	....	....	....	....
1988-89	W. Michigan	CCHA	40	23	19	42	97	....	....	....	....	....
1989-90	Hershey	AHL	58	10	6	16	99	....	....	....	....	....
1990-91	**Philadelphia**	**NHL**	**1**	**0**	**1**	**1**	**0**	....	....	....	....	....
	Hershey	AHL	70	36	27	63	150	6	2	8	10	19
1991-92	Hershey	AHL	80	2	14	16	159	3	0	0	0	2
	NHL Totals		**1**	**0**	**1**	**1**	**0**	....	....	....	....	....

Signed as a free agent by **Philadelphia**, May 16, 1989.

ARNIEL, SCOTT (ar-NEEL)

Left wing. Shoots left. 6'1", 188 lbs. Born, Kingston, Ont., September 17, 1962.
(Winnipeg's 2nd choice, 22nd overall, in 1981 Entry Draft).

			Regular Season					Playoffs				
Season	Club	Lea	GP	G	A	TP	PIM	GP	G	A	TP	PIM
1980-81	Cornwall	QJHL	68	52	71	123	102	19	14	19	33	24
1981-82	**Winnipeg**	**NHL**	**17**	**1**	**8**	**9**	**14**	**3**	**0**	**0**	**0**	**0**
	Cornwall	OHL	24	18	26	44	43	....	....	....	....	....
1982-83	**Winnipeg**	**NHL**	**75**	**13**	**5**	**18**	**46**	**2**	**0**	**0**	**0**	**0**
1983-84	**Winnipeg**	**NHL**	**80**	**21**	**35**	**56**	**68**	**2**	**0**	**0**	**0**	**5**
1984-85	**Winnipeg**	**NHL**	**79**	**22**	**22**	**44**	**81**	**8**	**1**	**2**	**3**	**9**
1985-86	**Winnipeg**	**NHL**	**80**	**18**	**25**	**43**	**40**	**3**	**0**	**0**	**0**	**12**
1986-87	**Buffalo**	**NHL**	**63**	**11**	**14**	**25**	**59**	....	....	....	....	....
1987-88	**Buffalo**	**NHL**	**73**	**17**	**23**	**40**	**61**	**6**	**0**	**1**	**1**	**5**
1988-89	**Buffalo**	**NHL**	**80**	**18**	**23**	**41**	**46**	**5**	**1**	**0**	**1**	**4**
1989-90	**Buffalo**	**NHL**	**79**	**18**	**14**	**32**	**77**	**5**	**1**	**0**	**1**	**4**
1990-91	**Winnipeg**	**NHL**	**75**	**5**	**17**	**22**	**87**	....	....	....	....	....
1991-92	**Boston**	**NHL**	**29**	**5**	**3**	**8**	**20**	....	....	....	....	....
	Maine	AHL	14	4	4	8	8	....	....	....	....	....
	New Haven	AHL	11	3	3	6	10	....	....	....	....	....
	NHL Totals		**730**	**149**	**189**	**338**	**599**	**34**	**3**	**3**	**6**	**39**

Traded to **Buffalo** by **Winnipeg** for Gilles Hamel, June 21, 1986. Traded to **Winnipeg** by **Buffalo** with Phil Housley, Jeff Parker and Buffalo's first round choice (Keith Tkachuk) in 1990 Entry Draft for Dale Hawerchuk, Winnipeg's first round choice (Brad May) in 1990 Entry Draft and future considerations, June 16, 1990. Traded to **Boston** by **Winnipeg** for future considerations, November 22, 1991.

ASHTON, BRENT KENNETH

Left wing. Shoots left. 6'1", 210 lbs. Born, Saskatoon, Sask., May 18, 1960.
(Vancouver's 2nd choice, 26th overall, in 1979 Entry Draft).

			Regular Season					Playoffs				
Season	Club	Lea	GP	G	A	TP	PIM	GP	G	A	TP	PIM
1977-78	Saskatoon	WHL	46	38	26	64	47	....	....	....	....	....
1978-79	Saskatoon	WHL	62	64	55	119	80	11	14	4	18	5
1979-80	**Vancouver**	**NHL**	**47**	**5**	**14**	**19**	**11**	**4**	**1**	**0**	**1**	**6**
1980-81	**Vancouver**	**NHL**	**77**	**18**	**11**	**29**	**57**	**3**	**0**	**0**	**0**	**0**
1981-82	**Colorado**	**NHL**	**80**	**24**	**36**	**60**	**26**	....	....	....	....	....
1982-83	**New Jersey**	**NHL**	**76**	**14**	**19**	**33**	**47**	....	....	....	....	....
1983-84	**Minnesota**	**NHL**	**68**	**7**	**10**	**17**	**54**	**12**	**1**	**2**	**3**	**22**
1984-85	**Minnesota**	**NHL**	**29**	**4**	**7**	**11**	**15**	....	....	....	....	....
	Quebec	**NHL**	**49**	**27**	**24**	**51**	**38**	**18**	**6**	**4**	**10**	**13**
1985-86	**Quebec**	**NHL**	**77**	**26**	**32**	**58**	**64**	**3**	**2**	**1**	**3**	**9**
1986-87	**Quebec**	**NHL**	**46**	**25**	**19**	**44**	**17**	....	....	....	....	....
	Detroit	**NHL**	**35**	**15**	**16**	**31**	**22**	**16**	**4**	**9**	**13**	**6**
1987-88	**Detroit**	**NHL**	**73**	**26**	**27**	**53**	**50**	**16**	**7**	**5**	**12**	**10**
1988-89	**Winnipeg**	**NHL**	**75**	**31**	**37**	**68**	**36**	....	....	....	....	....
1989-90	**Winnipeg**	**NHL**	**79**	**22**	**34**	**56**	**37**	**7**	**3**	**1**	**4**	**2**
1990-91	**Winnipeg**	**NHL**	**61**	**12**	**24**	**36**	**58**	....	....	....	....	....
1991-92	**Winnipeg**	**NHL**	**7**	**1**	**0**	**1**	**4**	....	....	....	....	....
	Boston	**NHL**	**61**	**17**	**22**	**39**	**47**	....	....	....	....	....
	NHL Totals		**940**	**274**	**332**	**606**	**583**	**79**	**24**	**22**	**46**	**68**

Traded to **Winnipeg** by **Vancouver** with Vancouver's fourth round choice (Tom Martin) in the 1982 Entry Draft as compensation for Vancouver's signing of Ivan Hlinka, July 15, 1981. Traded to **Colorado** by **Winnipeg** with Winnipeg's third round choice (Dave Kasper) in 1982 Entry Draft for Lucien DeBlois, July 15, 1981. Traded to **Minnesota** by **New Jersey** for Dave Lewis, October 3, 1983. Traded to **Quebec** by **Minnesota** with Brad Maxwell for Tony McKegney and Bo Berglund, December 14, 1984. Traded to **Detroit** by **Quebec** with Gilbert Delorme and Mark Kumpel for Basil McRae, John Ogrodnick and Doug Shedden, January 17, 1987. Traded to **Winnipeg** by **Detroit** for Paul MacLean, June 13, 1988. Traded to **Boston** by **Winnipeg** for Petri Skriko, October 29, 1991.

ASP, AARON

Center. Shoots right. 6'2", 180 lbs. Born, Cobble Hill, B.C., February 16, 1971.
(Quebec's 8th choice, 157th overall, in 1991 Entry Draft).

			Regular Season					Playoffs				
Season	Club	Lea	GP	G	A	TP	PIM	GP	G	A	TP	PIM
1990-91	Ferris State	CCHA	37	11	23	34	12	....	....	....	....	....
1991-92	Ferris State	CCHA	33	9	10	19	14	....	....	....	....	....

ASTLEY, MARK

Defense. Shoots left. 5'11", 185 lbs. Born, Calgary, Alta., March 30, 1969.
(Buffalo's 9th choice, 194th overall, in 1989 Entry Draft).

			Regular Season					Playoffs				
Season	Club	Lea	GP	G	A	TP	PIM	GP	G	A	TP	PIM
1988-89	Lake Superior	CCHA	42	3	12	15	26	....	....	....	....	....
1989-90	Lake Superior	CCHA	43	7	25	32	29	....	....	....	....	....
1990-91a	Lake Superior	CCHA	45	19	27	46	50	....	....	....	....	....
1991-92bcd	Lake Superior	CCHA	39	11	36	47	65	....	....	....	....	....

a CCHA Second All-Star Team (1991)
b CCHA First All-Star Team (1992)
c NCAA West First All-Star Team (1992)
d NCAA All-Tournament Team (1992)

ATCHEYNUM, BLAIR (ATCH-uh-num)

Right wing. Shoots right. 6'2", 190 lbs. Born, Estevan, Sask., April 20, 1969.
(Hartford's 2nd choice, 52nd overall, in 1989 Entry Draft).

			Regular Season					Playoffs				
Season	Club	Lea	GP	G	A	TP	PIM	GP	G	A	TP	PIM
1985-86	Saskatoon	WHL	19	1	4	5	22	....	....	....	....	....
1986-87	Saskatoon	WHL	21	0	4	4	4	....	....	....	....	....
	Swift Current	WHL	5	2	1	3	0	....	....	....	....	....
	Moose Jaw	WHL	12	3	0	3	2	....	....	....	....	....
1987-88	Moose Jaw	WHL	60	32	16	48	52	....	....	....	....	....
1988-89a	Moose Jaw	WHL	71	70	68	138	70	7	2	5	7	13
1989-90	Binghamton	AHL	78	20	21	41	45	....	....	....	....	....
1990-91	Springfield	AHL	72	25	27	52	42	13	0	6	6	6
1991-92	Springfield	AHL	62	16	21	37	64	6	1	1	2	2

a WHL First All-Star Team (1989)

Claimed by **Ottawa** from **Hartford** in Expansion Draft, June 18, 1992.

AUCOIN, ADRIAN

Defense. Shoots right. 6'1", 194 lbs. Born, Ottawa, Ont., July 3, 1973.
(Vancouver's 7th choice, 117th overall, in 1992 Entry Draft).

			Regular Season					Playoffs				
Season	Club	Lea	GP	G	A	TP	PIM	GP	G	A	TP	PIM
1991-92	Boston U.	H.E.	32	2	10	12	60	....	....	....	....	....

AUDETTE, DONALD

Right wing. Shoots right. 5'8", 175 lbs. Born, Laval, Que., September 23, 1969.
(Buffalo's 8th choice, 183rd overall, in 1989 Entry Draft).

			Regular Season					Playoffs				
Season	Club	Lea	GP	G	A	TP	PIM	GP	G	A	TP	PIM
1986-87	Laval	QMJHL	66	17	22	39	36	14	2	6	8	10
1987-88	Laval	QMJHL	63	48	61	109	56	14	7	12	19	20
1988-89a	Laval	QMJHL	70	76	85	161	123	17	17	12	29	43
1989-90bc	Rochester	AHL	70	42	46	88	78	15	9	8	17	29
	Buffalo	**NHL**	....	....	....	....	....	**2**	**0**	**0**	**0**	**0**
1990-91	**Buffalo**	**NHL**	**8**	**4**	**3**	**7**	**4**	....	....	....	....	....
	Rochester	AHL	5	4	0	4	2	....	....	....	....	....
1991-92	**Buffalo**	**NHL**	**63**	**31**	**17**	**48**	**75**	....	....	....	....	....
	NHL Totals		**71**	**35**	**20**	**55**	**79**	**2**	**0**	**0**	**0**	**0**

a QMJHL First All-Star Team (1989)
b AHL First All-Star Team (1990)
c Won Dudley "Red" Garret Memorial Trophy (Top Rookie-AHL) (1990)

AUGER, JACQUES

Defense. Shoots right. 6'1", 215 lbs. Born, Levis, Que., April 20, 1972.
(Chicago's 6th choice, 132nd overall, in 1991 Entry Draft).

			Regular Season					Playoffs				
Season	Club	Lea	GP	G	A	TP	PIM	GP	G	A	TP	PIM
1990-91	U. Wisconsin	WCHA	31	1	3	4	49	....	....	....	....	....
1991-92	Beauport	QMJHL	6	1	2	3	14	....	....	....	....	....
	Hull	QMJHL	41	1	8	9	114	6	0	1	1	10

AUGUSTA, PATRICK

Right wing. Shoots left. 5'10", 169 lbs. Born, Jihlava, Czechoslovakia, November 13, 1969.
(Toronto's 8th choice, 149th overall, in 1992 Entry Draft).

			Regular Season					Playoffs				
Season	Club	Lea	GP	G	A	TP	PIM	GP	G	A	TP	PIM
1989-90	Dukla Jihlava	Czech.	46	12	12	24	....	....	....	....	....	....
1990-91	Dukla Jihlava	Czech.	49	20	22	42	18	....	....	....	....	....
1991-92	Dukla Jihlava	Czech.	42	16	16	32	....	....	....	....	....	....

AVERILL, WILLIAM

Defense. Shoots right. 5'11", 175 lbs. Born, Wayland, MA, December 20, 1968.
(NY Islanders' 12th choice, 244th overall, in 1987 Entry Draft).

			Regular Season					Playoffs				
Season	Club	Lea	GP	G	A	TP	PIM	GP	G	A	TP	PIM
1987-88	Northeastern	H.E.	36	2	23	25	36	....	....	....	....	....
1988-89	Northeastern	H.E.	36	4	16	20	40	....	....	....	....	....
1989-90	Northeastern	H.E.	35	6	13	19	41	....	....	....	....	....
1990-91	Northeastern	H.E.	35	6	16	22	40	....	....	....	....	....
1991-92	Capital Dist.	AHL	12	0	0	0	0	....	....	....	....	....
	Richmond	ECHL	33	3	23	26	18	....	....	....	....	....

BABCOCK, BOBBY

Defense. Shoots left. 6'1", 222 lbs. Born, Agincourt, Ont., August 3, 1968.
(Washington's 11th choice, 208th overall, in 1986 Entry Draft).

			Regular Season					Playoffs				
Season	Club	Lea	GP	G	A	TP	PIM	GP	G	A	TP	PIM
1985-86	S.S. Marie	OHL	50	1	7	8	188	....	....	....	....	....
1986-87	S.S. Marie	OHL	62	7	8	15	243	4	0	0	0	11
1987-88	S.S. Marie	OHL	8	0	2	2	30	....	....	....	....	....
	Cornwall	OHL	42	0	16	16	120	....	....	....	....	....
1988-89	Cornwall	OHL	42	0	9	9	163	18	1	3	4	29
1989-90	Baltimore	AHL	67	0	4	4	249	7	0	0	0	23
1990-91	**Washington**	**NHL**	**1**	**0**	**0**	**0**	**0**	....	....	....	....	....
	Baltimore	AHL	38	0	3	3	112	....	....	....	....	....
1991-92	Baltimore	AHL	26	0	2	2	55	....	....	....	....	....
	NHL Totals		**1**	**0**	**0**	**0**	**0**	....	....	....	....	....

BABYCH, DAVID MICHAEL (DAVE) (BAB-itch)

Defense. Shoots left. 6'2", 215 lbs. Born, Edmonton, Alta., May 23, 1961.
(Winnipeg's 1st choice, 2nd overall, in 1980 Entry Draft).

			Regular Season					Playoffs				
Season	Club	Lea	GP	G	A	TP	PIM	GP	G	A	TP	PIM
1978-79	Portland	WHL	67	20	59	79	63	25	7	22	29	22
1979-80ab	Portland	WHL	50	22	60	82	71	8	1	10	11	2
1980-81	**Winnipeg**	**NHL**	**69**	**6**	**38**	**44**	**90**	....	....	....	....	....
1981-82	**Winnipeg**	**NHL**	**79**	**19**	**49**	**68**	**92**	**4**	**1**	**2**	**3**	**29**
1982-83	**Winnipeg**	**NHL**	**79**	**13**	**61**	**74**	**56**	**3**	**0**	**0**	**0**	**0**
1983-84	**Winnipeg**	**NHL**	**66**	**18**	**39**	**57**	**62**	**3**	**1**	**1**	**2**	**0**
1984-85	**Winnipeg**	**NHL**	**78**	**13**	**49**	**62**	**78**	**8**	**2**	**7**	**9**	**6**
1985-86	**Winnipeg**	**NHL**	**19**	**4**	**12**	**16**	**14**	....	....	....	....	....
	Hartford	**NHL**	**62**	**10**	**43**	**53**	**36**	**8**	**1**	**3**	**4**	**14**
1986-87	**Hartford**	**NHL**	**66**	**8**	**33**	**41**	**44**	**6**	**1**	**1**	**2**	**14**
1987-88	**Hartford**	**NHL**	**71**	**14**	**36**	**50**	**54**	**6**	**3**	**2**	**5**	**2**
1988-89	**Hartford**	**NHL**	**70**	**6**	**41**	**47**	**54**	**4**	**1**	**5**	**6**	**2**
1989-90	**Hartford**	**NHL**	**72**	**6**	**37**	**43**	**62**	**7**	**1**	**2**	**3**	**0**
1990-91	**Hartford**	**NHL**	**8**	**0**	**6**	**6**	**4**	....	....	....	....	....
1991-92	**Vancouver**	**NHL**	**75**	**5**	**24**	**29**	**63**	**13**	**2**	**6**	**8**	**10**
	NHL Totals		**814**	**122**	**468**	**590**	**709**	**62**	**13**	**29**	**42**	**77**

a WHL First All-Star Team (1980)
b Named WHL's Top Defenseman (1980)

Played in NHL All-Star Game (1983, 1984)

Traded to **Hartford** by **Winnipeg** for Ray Neufeld, November 21, 1985. Claimed by **Minnesota** from **Hartford** in Expansion Draft, May 30, 1991. Traded to **Vancouver** by **Minnesota** for Tom Kurvers, June 22, 1991.

BACA, JERGUS

Defense. Shoots left. 6'2", 211 lbs. Born, Liptovsky Mikulas, Czech., January 4, 1965.
(Hartford's 6th choice, 141st overall, in 1990 Entry Draft).

			Regular Season					Playoffs				
Season	Club	Lea	GP	G	A	TP	PIM	GP	G	A	TP	PIM
1987-88	VSZ Kosice	Czech.	40	5	5	10	32	....	....	....	....	....
1988-89a	VSZ Kosice	Czech.	42	3	10	13	46	....	....	....	....	....
	Czech. National	....	32	2	5	7	42	....	....	....	....	....
1989-90a	VSZ Kosice	Czech.	47	9	16	25	....	....	....	....	....	....
	Czech. National	....	25	0	1	1	44	....	....	....	....	....
1990-91	**Hartford**	**NHL**	**9**	**0**	**2**	**2**	**14**	....	....	....	....	....
	Springfield	AHL	57	6	23	29	89	18	3	13	16	18
1991-92	**Hartford**	**NHL**	**1**	**0**	**0**	**0**	**0**	....	....	....	....	....
	Springfield	AHL	64	6	20	26	88	11	0	6	6	20
	NHL Totals		**10**	**0**	**2**	**2**	**14**	....	....	....	....	....

a Czechoslovakian National League First Team All-Star (1989, 1990)

BADER, DARIN

Left wing. Shoots left. 6', 202 lbs. Born, Edmonton, Alta., April 1, 1971.
(Vancouver's 4th choice, 65th overall, in 1990 Entry Draft).

			Regular Season					Playoffs				
Season	Club	Lea	GP	G	A	TP	PIM	GP	G	A	TP	PIM
1987-88	Saskatoon	WHL	53	5	9	14	73	10	2	0	2	11
1988-89	Saskatoon	WHL	66	19	14	33	214	8	7	3	10	25
1989-90	Saskatoon	WHL	54	26	31	57	107	10	6	4	10	30
1990-91	Saskatoon	WHL	40	35	32	67	106	....	....	....	....	....
1991-92	Milwaukee	IHL	4	0	0	0	5	....	....	....	....	....

BAKER, JAMIE

Center. Shoots left. 6', 190 lbs. Born, Ottawa, Ont., August 31, 1966.
(Quebec's 2nd choice, 8th overall, in 1988 Supplemental Draft).

			Regular Season					Playoffs				
Season	Club	Lea	GP	G	A	TP	PIM	GP	G	A	TP	PIM
1985-86	St. Lawrence	ECAC	31	9	16	25	52	....	....	....	....	....
1986-87	St. Lawrence	ECAC	32	8	24	32	59	....	....	....	....	....
1987-88	St. Lawrence	ECAC	34	26	24	50	38	....	....	....	....	....
1988-89	St. Lawrence	ECAC	13	11	16	27	16	....	....	....	....	....
1989-90	**Quebec**	**NHL**	**1**	**0**	**0**	**0**	**0**	....	....	....	....	....
	Halifax	AHL	74	17	43	60	47	6	0	0	0	7
1990-91	**Quebec**	**NHL**	**18**	**2**	**0**	**2**	**8**	....	....	....	....	....
	Halifax	AHL	50	14	22	36	85	....	....	....	....	....
1991-92	**Quebec**	**NHL**	**52**	**7**	**10**	**17**	**32**	....	....	....	....	....
	Halifax	AHL	9	5	0	5	12	....	....	....	....	....
	NHL Totals		**71**	**9**	**10**	**19**	**40**	....	....	....	....	....

BALKOVEC, MACO

Defense. Shoots left. 6'2", 190 lbs. Born, New Westminster, B.C., January 17, 1971.
(Chicago's 5th choice, 110th overall, in 1991 Entry Draft).

			Regular Season					Playoffs				
Season	Club	Lea	GP	G	A	TP	PIM	GP	G	A	TP	PIM
1990-91	Merrit	BCJHL	57	14	64	78	145	....	....	....	....	....
1991-92	U. Wisconsin	WCHA	35	7	11	18	95	....	....	....	....	....

BANCROFT, STEVE

Defense. Shoots left. 6'1", 214 lbs. Born, Toronto, Ont., October 6, 1970.
(Toronto's 3rd choice, 21st overall, in 1989 Entry Draft).

			Regular Season					Playoffs				
Season	Club	Lea	GP	G	A	TP	PIM	GP	G	A	TP	PIM
1987-88	Belleville	OHL	56	1	8	9	42	....	....	....	....	....
1988-89	Belleville	OHL	66	7	30	37	99	5	0	2	2	10
1989-90	Belleville	OHL	53	10	33	43	135	11	3	9	12	38
1990-91	Newmarket	AHL	9	0	3	3	22	....	....	....	....	....
	Maine	AHL	53	2	12	14	46	2	0	0	0	2
1991-92	Maine	AHL	26	1	3	4	45	....	....	....	....	....
	Indianapolis	IHL	36	8	23	31	49	....	....	....	....	....

Traded to **Boston** by **Toronto** for Rob Cimetta, November 9, 1990. Traded to **Chicago** by **Boston** with Boston's eleventh round choice in 1993 Entry Draft for Chicago's eleventh round choice (Eugene Pavlov) in 1992 Entry Draft and Chicago's third round choice in 1993 Entry Draft, January 9, 1992.

BANKS, DARREN ALEXANDER

Left wing. Shoots left. 6'2", 215 lbs. Born, Toronto, Ont., March 18, 1966.

			Regular Season					Playoffs				
Season	Club	Lea	GP	G	A	TP	PIM	GP	G	A	TP	PIM
1986-87	Brock	OUAA	24	5	3	8	82	....	....	....	....	....
1987-88	Brock	OUAA	26	10	11	21	110	....	....	....	....	....
1988-89	Brock	OUAA	26	19	14	33	88	....	....	....	....	....
1989-90	Salt Lake	IHL	6	0	0	0	11	1	0	0	0	10
	Fort Wayne	IHL	2	0	1	1	0	....	....	....	....	....
	Knoxville	ECHL	52	25	22	47	258	....	....	....	....	....
1990-91	Salt Lake	IHL	56	9	7	16	286	3	0	1	1	6
1991-92	Salt Lake	IHL	55	5	5	10	303	....	....	....	....	....

Signed as a free agent by **Calgary**, December 12, 1990. Signed as a free agent by **Boston**, July 23, 1992.

BANNISTER, DARIN

Defense. Shoots right. 6', 185 lbs. Born, Calgary, Alta., January 16, 1967.
(Detroit's 11th choice, 200th overall, in 1987 Entry Draft).

			Regular Season					Playoffs				
Season	Club	Lea	GP	G	A	TP	PIM	GP	G	A	TP	PIM
1986-87	Ill.-Chicago	CCHA	38	4	16	20	38	....	....	....	....	....
1987-88	Ill.-Chicago	CCHA	39	2	26	28	96	....	....	....	....	....
1988-89	Ill.-Chicago	CCHA	41	7	26	33	88	....	....	....	....	....
1989-90	Ill.-Chicago	CCHA	37	5	22	27	72	....	....	....	....	....
	Hampton Rds.	ECHL	5	0	2	2	22	4	0	2	2	9
1990-91	San Diego	IHL	81	4	11	15	108	....	....	....	....	....
1991-92	Adirondack	AHL	26	0	3	3	32	....	....	....	....	....
	Toledo	ECHL	27	3	29	32	68	5	1	3	4	14

BANNISTER, DREW

Defense. Shoots right. 6'1", 193 lbs. Born, Bellevile, Ont., April 9, 1974.
(Tampa Bay's 2nd choice, 26th overall, in 1992 Entry Draft).

			Regular Season					Playoffs				
Season	Club	Lea	GP	G	A	TP	PIM	GP	G	A	TP	PIM
1990-91	S.S. Marie	OHL	41	2	8	10	51	4	0	0	0	0
1991-92	S.S. Marie	OHL	64	4	21	25	122	16	3	10	13	36

BARAHONA, RALPH J.

Center. Shoots left. 5'10", 180 lbs. Born, Long Beach, CA, November 16, 1965.

			Regular Season					Playoffs				
Season	Club	Lea	GP	G	A	TP	PIM	GP	G	A	TP	PIM
1988-89	U.Wisc.-S.Pt.	NCAA	41	33	47	80	....	....	....	....	....	....
1989-90	U.Wisc.-S.Pt.	NCAA	35	22	30	52	18	....	....	....	....	....
1990-91	**Boston**	**NHL**	**3**	**2**	**1**	**3**	**0**	....	....	....	....	....
	Maine	AHL	72	24	33	57	14	2	1	1	2	0
1991-92	**Boston**	**NHL**	**3**	**0**	**1**	**1**	**0**	....	....	....	....	....
	Maine	AHL	74	27	32	59	39	....	....	....	....	....
	NHL Totals		**6**	**2**	**2**	**4**	**0**	....	....	....	....	....

Signed as a free agent by **Boston**, September 26, 1990.

BARBER, DON

Right/Left wing. Shoots left. 6'2", 205 lbs. Born, Victoria, B.C., December 2, 1964.
(Edmonton's 5th choice, 120th overall, in 1983 Entry Draft).

			Regular Season					Playoffs				
Season	Club	Lea	GP	G	A	TP	PIM	GP	G	A	TP	PIM
1984-85	Bowling Green	CCHA	39	15	22	37	44	....	....	....	....	....
1985-86	Bowling Green	CCHA	35	21	22	43	64	....	....	....	....	....
1986-87	Bowling Green	CCHA	43	29	34	63	107	....	....	....	....	....
1987-88	Bowling Green	CCHA	38	18	47	65	62	....	....	....	....	....
1988-89	**Minnesota**	**NHL**	**23**	**8**	**5**	**13**	**8**	**4**	**1**	**1**	**2**	**2**
	Kalamazoo	IHL	39	14	17	31	23	....	....	....	....	....
1989-90	**Minnesota**	**NHL**	**44**	**15**	**19**	**34**	**32**	**7**	**3**	**3**	**6**	**8**
	Kalamazoo	IHL	10	4	4	8	38	....	....	....	....	....
1990-91	**Minnesota**	**NHL**	**7**	**0**	**0**	**0**	**4**	....	....	....	....	....
	Winnipeg	**NHL**	**16**	**1**	**2**	**3**	**14**	....	....	....	....	....
	Moncton	AHL	38	17	21	38	32	9	4	6	10	8
1991-92	**Winnipeg**	**NHL**	**11**	**0**	**3**	**3**	**4**	....	....	....	....	....
	Halifax	AHL	25	12	10	22	8	....	....	....	....	....
	Quebec	**NHL**	**2**	**0**	**0**	**0**	**0**	....	....	....	....	....
	San Jose	**NHL**	**12**	**1**	**3**	**4**	**2**	....	....	....	....	....
	NHL Totals		**115**	**25**	**32**	**57**	**64**	**11**	**4**	**4**	**8**	**10**

Traded to **Minnesota** by **Edmonton** with Marc Habscheid and Emanuel Viveiros for Gord Sherven and Don Biggs, December 20, 1985. Traded to **Winnipeg** by **Minnesota** for Doug Smail, November 7, 1990. Claimed on waivers by **Quebec** from **Winnipeg**, November 12, 1991. Traded to **San Jose** by **Quebec** for Murray Garbutt, March 7, 1992.

BARKLEY, MICHAEL

Right wing. Shoots right. 6', 185 lbs. Born, Port Alberni, B.C., April 7, 1970.
(Buffalo's 6th choice, 119th overall, in 1989 Entry Draft).

			Regular Season					Playoffs				
Season	Club	Lea	GP	G	A	TP	PIM	GP	G	A	TP	PIM
1988-89	U. of Maine	H.E.	41	12	13	25	16	....	....	....	....	....
1989-90	U. of Maine	H.E.	43	11	19	30	20	....	....	....	....	....
1990-91	U. of Maine	H.E.	23	6	8	14	6	....	....	....	....	....
1991-92	U. of Maine	H.E.	15	1	4	5	14	....	....	....	....	....

BARNABY, MATTHEW

Left wing. Shoots left. 6', 170 lbs. Born, Ottawa, Ont., May 4, 1973.
(Buffalo's 5th choice, 83rd overall, in 1992 Entry Draft).

			Regular Season					Playoffs				
Season	Club	Lea	GP	G	A	TP	PIM	GP	G	A	TP	PIM
1990-91	Beauport	QMJHL	52	9	5	14	262	....	....	....	....	....
1991-92	Beauport	QMJHL	63	29	37	66	*476	....	....	....	....	....

BARNES, STU

Center. Shoots right. 5'10", 175 lbs. Born, Edmonton, Alta., December 25, 1970.
(Winnipeg's 1st choice, 4th overall, in 1989 Entry Draft).

			Regular Season					Playoffs				
Season	Club	Lea	GP	G	A	TP	PIM	GP	G	A	TP	PIM
1987-88	N. Westminster	WHL	71	37	64	101	88	5	2	3	5	6
1988-89ab	Tri-Cities	WHL	70	59	82	141	117	7	6	5	11	10
1989-90	Tri-Cities	WHL	63	52	92	144	165	7	1	5	6	26
1990-91	Cdn. National	....	53	22	27	49	68	....	....	....	....	....
1991-92	**Winnipeg**	**NHL**	**46**	**8**	**9**	**17**	**26**	....	....	....	....	....
	Moncton	AHL	30	13	19	32	10	11	3	9	12	6
	NHL Totals		**46**	**8**	**9**	**17**	**26**	....	....	....	....	....

a WHL West Second All-Star Team (1989)
b WHL Player of the Year (1989)

BARON, MURRAY

Defense. Shoots left. 6'3", 210 lbs. Born, Prince George, B.C., June 1, 1967.
(Philadelphia's 7th choice, 167th overall, in 1986 Entry Draft).

			Regular Season					Playoffs				
Season	Club	Lea	GP	G	A	TP	PIM	GP	G	A	TP	PIM
1986-87	North Dakota	WCHA	41	4	10	14	62	....	....	....	....	....
1987-88	North Dakota	WCHA	41	1	10	11	95	....	....	....	....	....
1988-89	North Dakota	WCHA	40	2	6	8	92	....	....	....	....	....
	Hershey	AHL	9	0	3	3	8	....	....	....	....	....
1989-90	**Philadelphia**	**NHL**	**16**	**2**	**2**	**4**	**12**	....	....	....	....	....
	Hershey	AHL	50	0	10	10	101	....	....	....	....	....
1990-91	**Philadelphia**	**NHL**	**67**	**8**	**8**	**16**	**74**	....	....	....	....	....
	Hershey	AHL	6	2	3	5	0	....	....	....	....	....
1991-92	**St. Louis**	**NHL**	**67**	**3**	**8**	**11**	**94**	**2**	**0**	**0**	**0**	**2**
	NHL Totals		**150**	**13**	**18**	**31**	**180**	**2**	**0**	**0**	**0**	**2**

Traded to **St. Louis** by **Philadelphia** with Ron Sutter for Dan Quinn and Rod Brind'Amour, September 22, 1991.

BARR, DAVID (DAVE)

Right wing. Shoots right. 6'1", 195 lbs. Born, Toronto, Ont., November 30, 1960.

			Regular Season					Playoffs				
Season	Club	Lea	GP	G	A	TP	PIM	GP	G	A	TP	PIM
1979-80	Lethbridge	WHL	60	16	38	54	47	....	....	....	....	....
1980-81	Lethbridge	WHL	72	26	62	88	106	....	....	....	....	....
1981-82	**Boston**	**NHL**	**2**	**0**	**0**	**0**	**0**	**5**	**1**	**0**	**1**	**0**
	Erie	AHL	76	18	48	66	29	....	....	....	....	....
1982-83	**Boston**	**NHL**	**10**	**1**	**1**	**2**	**7**	**10**	**0**	**0**	**0**	**2**
	Baltimore	AHL	72	27	51	78	67	....	....	....	....	....
1983-84	**NY Rangers**	**NHL**	**6**	**0**	**0**	**0**	**2**	....	....	....	....	....
	Tulsa	CHL	50	28	37	65	24	....	....	....	....	....
	St. Louis	**NHL**	**1**	**0**	**0**	**0**	**0**	....	....	....	....	....
1984-85	**St. Louis**	**NHL**	**75**	**16**	**18**	**34**	**32**	**2**	**0**	**0**	**0**	**2**
1985-86	**St. Louis**	**NHL**	**72**	**13**	**38**	**51**	**70**	**11**	**1**	**1**	**2**	**14**
1986-87	**St. Louis**	**NHL**	**2**	**0**	**0**	**0**	**0**	....	....	....	....	....
	Hartford	**NHL**	**30**	**2**	**4**	**6**	**19**	....	....	....	....	....
	Detroit	**NHL**	**37**	**13**	**13**	**26**	**49**	**13**	**1**	**0**	**1**	**14**
1987-88	**Detroit**	**NHL**	**51**	**14**	**26**	**40**	**58**	**16**	**5**	**7**	**12**	**22**
1988-89	**Detroit**	**NHL**	**73**	**27**	**32**	**59**	**69**	**6**	**3**	**1**	**4**	**6**
1989-90	**Detroit**	**NHL**	**62**	**10**	**25**	**35**	**45**	....	....	....	....	....
	Adirondack	AHL	9	1	14	15	17	....	....	....	....	....
1990-91	**Detroit**	**NHL**	**70**	**18**	**22**	**40**	**55**	....	....	....	....	....
1991-92	**New Jersey**	**NHL**	**41**	**6**	**12**	**18**	**32**	....	....	....	....	....
	Utica	AHL	1	0	0	0	7	....	....	....	....	....
	NHL Totals		**532**	**120**	**191**	**311**	**438**	**63**	**11**	**9**	**20**	**60**

Signed as a free agent by **Boston**, September 28, 1981. Traded to **NY Rangers** by **Boston** for Dave Silk, October 5, 1983. Traded to **St. Louis** by **NY Rangers** with NY Rangers' third round choice (Alan Perry) in the 1984 Entry Draft for Larry Patey and Bob Brooke, March 5, 1984. Traded to **Hartford** by **St. Louis** for Tim Bothwell, October 21, 1986. Traded to **Detroit** by **Hartford** for Randy Ladouceur, January 12, 1987. Acquired by **New Jersey** from **Detroit** with Randy McKay as compensation for Detroit's signing of free agent Troy Crowder, September 9, 1991.

BARRAULT, DOUGLAS

Right wing. Shoots right. 6'2", 205 lbs. Born, Golden, B.C., April 21, 1970.
(Minnesota's 8th choice, 155th overall, in 1990 Entry Draft).

			Regular Season					Playoffs				
Season	Club	Lea	GP	G	A	TP	PIM	GP	G	A	TP	PIM
1988-89	Lethbridge	WHL	57	14	13	27	34	....	....	....	....	....
1989-90	Lethbridge	WHL	54	14	16	30	36	19	7	3	10	0
1990-91a	Lethbridge	WHL	4	2	2	4	16	....	....	....	....	....
	Seattle	WHL	61	42	42	84	69	6	5	3	8	4
1991-92	Kalamazoo	IHL	60	5	14	19	26	....	....	....	....	....

a WHL West Second All-Star Team (1991)

BARRIE, LEN

Center. Shoots left. 6', 200 lbs. Born, Kimberley, B.C., June 4, 1969.
(Edmonton's 7th choice, 124th overall, in 1988 Entry Draft).

			Regular Season					Playoffs				
Season	Club	Lea	GP	G	A	TP	PIM	GP	G	A	TP	PIM
1985-86	Calgary	WHL	32	3	0	3	18	....	....	....	....	....
1986-87	Calgary	WHL	34	13	13	26	81	....	....	....	....	....
	Victoria	WHL	34	7	6	13	92	5	0	1	1	15
1987-88	Victoria	WHL	70	37	49	86	192	8	2	0	2	29
1988-89	Victoria	WHL	67	39	48	87	157	7	5	2	7	23
1989-90	**Philadelphia**	**NHL**	**1**	**0**	**0**	**0**	**0**	....	....	....	....	....
a	Kamloops	WHL	70	*85	*100	*185	108	17	*14	23	*37	24
1990-91	Hershey	AHL	63	26	32	58	60	7	4	0	4	12
1991-92	Hershey	AHL	75	42	43	85	78	3	0	2	2	32
	NHL Totals		**1**	**0**	**0**	**0**	**0**	....	....	....	....	....

a WHL West First All-Star Team (1990)

Signed as a free agent by **Philadelphia**, February 28, 1990.

BARTELL, ADAM

Defense. Shoots right. 6'1", 182 lbs. Born, Buffalo, NY, April 27, 1973.
(Quebec's 9th choice, 178th overall, in 1991 Entry Draft).

			Regular Season					Playoffs				
Season	Club	Lea	GP	G	A	TP	PIM	GP	G	A	TP	PIM
1990-91	Niagara	USHL	31	0	17	17	20	....	....	....	....	....
1991-92	RPI	ECAC	31	5	13	18	18	....	....	....	....	....

BARTHE, CLAUDE

Defense. Shoots right. 6'2", 197 lbs. Born, St. Pierre De Sorel, Que., June 15, 1970.
(Detroit's 5th choice, 108th overall, in 1990 Entry Draft).

			Regular Season					Playoffs				
Season	Club	Lea	GP	G	A	TP	PIM	GP	G	A	TP	PIM
1989-90a	Victoriaville	QMJHL	68	20	55	75	148	16	0	9	9	44
1990-91	Trois-Rivières	QMJHL	28	4	17	21	43	6	1	3	4	35
1991-92	Winston-Salem	ECHL	54	3	13	16	136	....	....	....	....	....

a QMJHL First All-Star Team (1990)

BARTLEY, WADE

Defense. Shoots right. 6', 190 lbs. Born, Killarney, Man., May 16, 1970.
(Washington's 3rd choice, 41st overall, in 1988 Entry Draft).

			Regular Season					Playoffs				
Season	Club	Lea	GP	G	A	TP	PIM	GP	G	A	TP	PIM
1988-89	North Dakota	WCHA	32	1	1	2	8	....	....	....	....	....
1989-90	Sudbury	OHL	60	23	36	59	53	7	1	4	5	10
1990-91	Sudbury	OHL	47	11	37	48	57	5	1	3	4	4
	Baltimore	AHL	2	0	0	0	0	....	....	....	....	....
1991-92	Baltimore	AHL	20	0	7	7	25	....	....	....	....	....
	Hampton Rds.	ECHL	43	8	26	34	75	14	4	8	12	38

BARTON, BRAD

Defense. Shoots right. 6'2", 192 lbs. Born, Uxbridge, Ont., May 15, 1972.
(Vancouver's 10th choice, 205th overall, in 1991 Entry Draft).

			Regular Season					Playoffs				
Season	Club	Lea	GP	G	A	TP	PIM	GP	G	A	TP	PIM
1990-91	Kitchener	OHL	55	2	18	20	125	6	1	4	5	23
1991-92	Kitchener	OHL	64	9	26	35	160	14	1	2	3	14

BASSEN, BOB

Center/Left wing. Shoots left. 5'11", 180 lbs. Born, Calgary, Alta., May 6, 1965.

			Regular Season					Playoffs				
Season	Club	Lea	GP	G	A	TP	PIM	GP	G	A	TP	PIM
1982-83	Medicine Hat	WHL	4	3	2	5	0	3	0	0	0	4
1983-84	Medicine Hat	WHL	72	29	29	58	93	14	5	11	16	12
1984-85a	Medicine Hat	WHL	65	32	50	82	143	10	2	8	10	39
1985-86	**NY Islanders**	**NHL**	**11**	**2**	**1**	**3**	**6**	**3**	**0**	**1**	**1**	**0**
	Springfield	AHL	54	13	21	34	111	....	....	....	....	....
1986-87	**NY Islanders**	**NHL**	**77**	**7**	**10**	**17**	**89**	**14**	**1**	**2**	**3**	**21**
1987-88	**NY Islanders**	**NHL**	**77**	**6**	**16**	**22**	**99**	**6**	**0**	**1**	**1**	**23**
1988-89	**NY Islanders**	**NHL**	**19**	**1**	**4**	**5**	**21**	....	....	....	....	....
	Chicago	**NHL**	**49**	**4**	**12**	**16**	**62**	**10**	**1**	**1**	**2**	**34**
1989-90	**Chicago**	**NHL**	**6**	**1**	**1**	**2**	**8**	**1**	**0**	**0**	**0**	**2**
b	Indianapolis	IHL	73	22	32	54	179	12	3	8	11	33
1990-91	**St. Louis**	**NHL**	**79**	**16**	**18**	**34**	**183**	**13**	**1**	**3**	**4**	**24**
1991-92	**St. Louis**	**NHL**	**79**	**7**	**25**	**32**	**167**	**6**	**0**	**2**	**2**	**4**
	NHL Totals		**397**	**44**	**87**	**131**	**635**	**52**	**3**	**10**	**13**	**106**

a WHL First All-Star Team (1985)
b IHL First All-Star Team (1990)

Signed as a free agent by **NY Islanders**, October 19, 1984.Traded to **Chicago** by **NY Islanders** with Steve Konroyd for Marc Bergevin and Gary Nylund, November 25, 1988. Claimed by **St. Louis** in NHL Waiver Draft, October 1, 1990.

BASSEN, MARK

Center. Shoots right. 5'10", 170 lbs. Born, Calgary, Alta., May 9, 1969.

			Regular Season					Playoffs				
Season	Club	Lea	GP	G	A	TP	PIM	GP	G	A	TP	PIM
1986-87	Calgary	WHL	4	1	1	2	4	....	....	....	....	....
1987-88	Lethbridge	WHL	70	19	28	47	48	....	....	....	....	....
1988-89	Lethbridge	WHL	7	1	4	5	12	....	....	....	....	....
	Brandon	WHL	65	31	65	96	74	....	....	....	....	....
1989-90	Hershey	AHL	57	5	9	14	128	....	....	....	....	....
1990-91	Hershey	AHL	42	3	1	4	86	....	....	....	....	....
1991-92	Peoria	IHL	82	18	23	41	228	10	0	4	4	15

Signed as a free agent by **Philadelphia**, October 5, 1989.

BATTERS, JEFF

Defense. Shoots right. 6'2", 215 lbs. Born, Victoria, B.C., October 23, 1970.
(St. Louis' 7th choice, 135th overall, in 1989 Entry Draft).

			Regular Season					Playoffs				
Season	Club	Lea	GP	G	A	TP	PIM	GP	G	A	TP	PIM
1988-89	Alaska-Anch.	G.N.	33	8	14	22	123	....	....	....	....	....
1989-90	Alaska-Anch.	G.N.	34	6	9	15	102	....	....	....	....	....
1990-91	Alaska-Anch.	G.N.	39	16	14	30	90	....	....	....	....	....
1991-92	Alaska-Anch.	G.N.	33	6	16	22	84	....	....	....	....	....

BAUER, COLLIN

Defense. Shoots left. 6'1", 180 lbs. Born, Edmonton, Alta., September 6, 1970.
(Edmonton's 4th choice, 61st overall, in 1988 Entry Draft).

			Regular Season					Playoffs				
Season	Club	Lea	GP	G	A	TP	PIM	GP	G	A	TP	PIM
1986-87	Saskatoon	WHL	61	1	25	26	37	11	0	6	6	10
1987-88	Saskatoon	WHL	70	9	53	62	66	10	2	5	7	16
1988-89a	Saskatoon	WHL	61	17	62	79	71	8	1	8	9	8
1989-90	Saskatoon	WHL	29	4	25	29	49	10	1	8	9	14
1990-91	Cape Breton	AHL	40	4	14	18	18	4	1	1	2	4
1991-92	Cape Breton	AHL	55	7	15	22	36	3	0	0	0	7

a WHL East All-Star Team (1989)

Traded to **Minnesota** by **Edmonton** for future considerations, August 4, 1992.

BAUMGARTNER, KEN

Defense/Center. Shoots left. 6'1", 200 lbs. Born, Flin Flon, Man., March 11, 1966.
(Buffalo's 12th choice, 245th overall, in 1985 Entry Draft).

			Regular Season					Playoffs				
Season	Club	Lea	GP	G	A	TP	PIM	GP	G	A	TP	PIM
1984-85	Prince Albert	WHL	60	3	9	12	252	13	1	3	4	89
1985-86	Prince Albert	WHL	70	4	23	27	277	20	3	9	12	112
1986-87	New Haven	AHL	13	0	3	3	99	6	0	0	0	60
1987-88	**Los Angeles**	**NHL**	**30**	**2**	**3**	**5**	**189**	**5**	**0**	**1**	**1**	**28**
	New Haven	AHL	48	1	5	6	181	....	....	....	....	....
1988-89	**Los Angeles**	**NHL**	**49**	**1**	**3**	**4**	**288**	**5**	**0**	**0**	**0**	**8**
	New Haven	AHL	10	1	3	4	26	....	....	....	....	....
1989-90	**Los Angeles**	**NHL**	**12**	**1**	**0**	**1**	**28**	....	....	....	....	....
	NY Islanders	**NHL**	**53**	**0**	**5**	**5**	**194**	**4**	**0**	**0**	**0**	**27**
1990-91	**NY Islanders**	**NHL**	**78**	**1**	**6**	**7**	**282**	....	....	....	....	....
1991-92	**NY Islanders**	**NHL**	**44**	**0**	**1**	**1**	**202**	....	....	....	....	....
	Toronto	**NHL**	**11**	**0**	**0**	**0**	**23**	....	....	....	....	....
	NHL Totals		**277**	**5**	**18**	**23**	**1206**	**14**	**0**	**1**	**1**	**63**

Traded to **Los Angeles** by **Buffalo** with Sean McKenna and Larry Playfair for Brian Engblom and Doug Smith, January 29, 1986. Traded to **NY Islanders** by **Los Angeles** with Hubie McDonough for Mikko Makela, November 29, 1989. Traded to **Toronto** by **NY Islanders** with Dave McLlwain for Daniel Marois and Claude Loiselle, March 10, 1992.

BAUTIN, SERGEI (bow-OO-tin)

Defense. Shoots left. 6'3", 185 lbs. Born, Murmansk, Soviet Union, March 11, 1967.
(Winnipeg's 1st choice, 17th overall, in 1992 Entry Draft).

			Regular Season					Playoffs				
Season	Club	Lea	GP	G	A	TP	PIM	GP	G	A	TP	PIM
1990-91	Moscow D'amo	USSR	33	2	0	2	28	....	....	....	....	....
1991-92	Moscow D'amo	CIS	37	1	3	4	88	....	....	....	....	....

BAVIS, MARK

Center. Shoots left. 6', 175 lbs. Born, Roslindale, MA, March 13, 1970.
(NY Rangers' 10th choice, 181st overall, in 1989 Entry Draft).

			Regular Season					Playoffs				
Season	Club	Lea	GP	G	A	TP	PIM	GP	G	A	TP	PIM
1989-90	Boston U.	H.E.	44	6	5	11	50	....	....	....	....	....
1990-91	Boston U.	H.E.	33	7	9	16	30	....	....	....	....	....
1991-92	Boston U.	H.E.	34	9	17	26	30	....	....	....	....	....

BAVIS, MICHAEL

Right wing. Shoots right. 6', 180 lbs. Born, Roslindale, MA, March 13, 1970.
(Buffalo's 12th choice, 245th overall, in 1989 Entry Draft).

			Regular Season					Playoffs				
Season	Club	Lea	GP	G	A	TP	PIM	GP	G	A	TP	PIM
1989-90	Boston U.	H.E.	44	2	11	13	28	....	....	....	....	....
1990-91	Boston U.	H.E.	40	5	18	23	47	....	....	....	....	....
1991-92	Boston U.	H.E.	34	11	13	24	32	....	....	....	....	....

BAWA, ROBIN (BAH-wuh)

Right wing. Shoots right. 6'2", 214 lbs. Born, Chemainus, B.C., March 26, 1966.

			Regular Season					Playoffs				
Season	Club	Lea	GP	G	A	TP	PIM	GP	G	A	TP	PIM
1982-83	Kamloops	WHL	66	10	24	34	17	7	1	2	3	0
1983-84	Kamloops	WHL	64	16	28	44	40	13	4	2	6	4
1984-85	Kamloops	WHL	52	6	19	25	45	15	4	9	13	14
1985-86	Kamloops	WHL	63	29	43	72	78	16	5	13	18	4
1986-87a	Kamloops	WHL	62	57	56	113	91	13	6	7	13	22
1987-88	Fort Wayne	IHL	55	12	27	39	239	6	1	3	4	24
1988-89	Baltimore	AHL	75	23	24	47	205	....	....	....	....	....
1989-90	**Washington**	**NHL**	**5**	**1**	**0**	**1**	**6**	....	....	....	....	....
	Baltimore	AHL	61	7	18	25	189	11	1	2	3	49
1990-91	Fort Wayne	IHL	72	21	26	47	381	18	4	4	8	87
1991-92	**Vancouver**	**NHL**	**2**	**0**	**0**	**0**	**0**	**1**	**0**	**0**	**0**	**0**
	Milwaukee	IHL	70	27	14	41	238	5	2	2	4	8
	NHL Totals		**7**	**1**	**0**	**1**	**6**	**1**	**0**	**0**	**0**	**0**

a WHL West All-Star Team (1987)

Signed as a free agent by **Washington**, May 22, 1987. Traded to **Vancouver** by **Washington** for cash, July 31, 1991.

BEAUFAIT, MARK

Center. Shoots right. 5'9", 165 lbs. Born, Royal Oak, MI, May 13, 1970.
(San Jose's 2nd choice, 7th overall, in 1991 Supplemental Draft).

			Regular Season					Playoffs				
Season	Club	Lea	GP	G	A	TP	PIM	GP	G	A	TP	PIM
1988-89	N. Michigan	WCHA	11	2	1	3	2	....	....	....	....	....
1989-90	N. Michigan	WCHA	34	10	14	24	12	....	....	....	....	....
1990-91	N. Michigan	WCHA	47	19	30	49	18	....	....	....	....	....
1991-92	N. Michigan	WCHA	39	31	44	75	43	....	....	....	....	....

BEAULIEU, COREY

Defense. Shoots left. 6'1", 210 lbs. Born, Winnipeg, Man., September 10, 1969.
(Hartford's 5th choice, 116th overall, in 1988 Entry Draft).

			Regular Season					Playoffs				
Season	Club	Lea	GP	G	A	TP	PIM	GP	G	A	TP	PIM
1985-86	Moose Jaw	WHL	68	3	1	4	111	13	1	1	2	13
1986-87	Moose Jaw	WHL	63	2	7	9	188	9	0	0	0	17
1987-88	Seattle	WHL	67	2	9	11	225	....	....	....	....	....
1988-89	Seattle	WHL	32	0	3	3	134	....	....	....	....	....
	Moose Jaw	WHL	29	3	17	20	91	7	1	2	3	16
1989-90	Binghamton	AHL	56	0	2	2	191	....	....	....	....	....
1990-91			DID NOT PLAY									
1991-92	Louisville	ECHL	8	1	5	6	60	....	....	....	....	....
	Springfield	AHL	52	0	0	0	157	2	0	0	0	2

BEERS, BOB

Defense. Shoots right. 6'2", 200 lbs. Born, Pittsburgh, PA, May 20, 1967.
(Boston's 10th choice, 210th overall, in 1985 Entry Draft).

			Regular Season					Playoffs				
Season	Club	Lea	GP	G	A	TP	PIM	GP	G	A	TP	PIM
1985-86	N. Arizona	NCAA	28	11	39	50	96	....	....	....	....	....
1986-87	U. of Maine	H.E.	38	0	13	13	45	....	....	....	....	....
1987-88	U. of Maine	H.E.	41	3	11	14	72	....	....	....	....	....
1988-89ab	U. of Maine	H.E.	44	10	27	37	53	....	....	....	....	....
1989-90	**Boston**	**NHL**	**3**	**0**	**1**	**1**	**6**	**14**	**1**	**1**	**2**	**18**
	Maine	AHL	74	7	36	43	63	....	....	....	....	....
1990-91	**Boston**	**NHL**	**16**	**0**	**1**	**1**	**10**	**6**	**0**	**0**	**0**	**4**
	Maine	AHL	36	2	16	18	21	....	....	....	....	....
1991-92	**Boston**	**NHL**	**31**	**0**	**5**	**5**	**29**	**1**	**0**	**0**	**0**	**0**
	Maine	AHL	33	6	23	29	24	....	....	....	....	....
	NHL Totals		**50**	**0**	**7**	**7**	**45**	**21**	**1**	**1**	**2**	**22**

a Hockey East Second All-Star Team (1989)
b NCAA East Second All-American Team (1989)

BELANGER, CHRIS

Defense. Shoots right. 6'2", 185 lbs. Born, Welland, Ont., April 4, 1972.
(Hartford's 9th choice, 185th overall, in 1991 Entry Draft).

			Regular Season					Playoffs				
Season	Club	Lea	GP	G	A	TP	PIM	GP	G	A	TP	PIM
1990-91	W. Michigan	CCHA	2	0	0	0	2	....	....	....	....	....
1991-92	W. Michigan	CCHA	36	7	24	31	28	....	....	....	....	....

BELANGER, HUGO

Left wing. Shoots left. 6'1", 190 lbs. Born, St. Hubert, Que., May 28, 1970.
(Chicago's 6th choice, 163rd overall, in 1990 Entry Draft).

			Regular Season					Playoffs				
Season	Club	Lea	GP	G	A	TP	PIM	GP	G	A	TP	PIM
1989-90	Clarkson	ECAC	36	14	25	39	12	....	....	....	....	....
1990-91	Clarkson	ECAC	40	32	43	75	18	....	....	....	....	....
1991-92a	Clarkson	ECAC	32	18	31	49	26	....	....	....	....	....

a ECAC Second All-Star Team (1992)

BÉLANGER, JESSE

Center. Shoots right. 6', 170 lbs. Born, St. Georges de Beauce, Que., June 15, 1969.

			Regular Season					Playoffs				
Season	Club	Lea	GP	G	A	TP	PIM	GP	G	A	TP	PIM
1987-88	Granby	QMJHL	69	33	43	76	10	5	3	3	6	0
1988-89	Granby	QMJHL	67	40	63	103	26	4	0	5	5	0
1989-90	Granby	QMJHL	67	53	54	107	53	....	....	....	....	....
1990-91	Fredericton	AHL	75	40	58	98	30	6	2	4	6	0
1991-92	**Montreal**	**NHL**	**4**	**0**	**0**	**0**	**0**	....	....	....	....	....
	Fredericton	AHL	65	30	41	71	26	7	3	3	6	2
	NHL Totals		**4**	**0**	**0**	**0**	**0**	....	....	....	....	....

Signed as a free agent by **Montreal**, October 3, 1990.

BELL, BRUCE

Defense. Shoots left. 6'1", 190 lbs. Born, Toronto, Ont., February 15, 1965.
(Quebec's 2nd choice, 52nd overall, in 1983 Entry Draft).

			Regular Season					Playoffs				
Season	Club	Lea	GP	G	A	TP	PIM	GP	G	A	TP	PIM
1981-82	S.S. Marie	OHL	67	11	18	29	63	12	0	2	2	24
1982-83	S.S. Marie	OHL	5	0	2	2	2	....	....	....	....	....
	Windsor	OHL	61	10	35	45	39	3	0	4	4	0
1983-84a	Brantford	OHL	63	7	41	48	55	6	0	3	3	16
1984-85b	**Quebec**	**NHL**	**75**	**6**	**31**	**37**	**44**	**16**	**2**	**2**	**4**	**21**
1985-86	**St. Louis**	**NHL**	**75**	**2**	**18**	**20**	**43**	**14**	**0**	**2**	**2**	**13**
1986-87	**St. Louis**	**NHL**	**45**	**3**	**13**	**16**	**18**	**4**	**1**	**1**	**2**	**7**
1987-88	**NY Rangers**	**NHL**	**13**	**1**	**2**	**3**	**8**	....	....	....	....	....
	Colorado	IHL	65	11	34	45	107	4	2	3	5	0
1988-89	Halifax	AHL	12	0	6	6	0	2	0	1	1	2
	Adirondack	AHL	9	1	4	5	4	....	....	....	....	....
1989-90	**Edmonton**	**NHL**	**1**	**0**	**0**	**0**	**0**	....	....	....	....	....
	Cape Breton	AHL	52	8	26	34	64	6	3	4	7	2
1990-91	Cape Breton	AHL	14	2	5	7	7	....	....	....	....	....
	Kalamazoo	IHL	48	5	21	26	32	3	0	0	0	8
1991-92	St. John's	AHL	45	5	16	21	70	10	4	7	11	8
	NHL Totals		**209**	**12**	**64**	**76**	**113**	**34**	**3**	**5**	**8**	**41**

a OHL First All-Star Team (1984)
b NHL All-Rookie Team (1985)

Traded to **St. Louis** by **Quebec** for Gilbert Delorme, October 2, 1985. Traded to **NY Rangers** by **St. Louis** with future considerations for Tony McKegney and Rob Whistle, May 28, 1987. Traded to **Quebec** by **NY Rangers** with Jari Gronstrand, Walt Poddubny and NY Rangers' fourth round choice (Eric Dubois) in 1989 Entry Draft for Jason Lafreniere and Normand Rochefort, August 1, 1988. Claimed by **Detroit** on waivers, December 19, 1988. Signed as a free agent by **Edmonton**, February 1, 1990. Traded to **Minnesota** by **Edmonton** for Kari Takko, November 22, 1990.

BELLEROSE, ERIC

Left wing. Shoots left. 6'1", 202 lbs. Born, Montreal, Que., February 7, 1972.
(San Jose's 7th choice, 147th overall, in 1992 Entry Draft).

			Regular Season					Playoffs				
Season	Club	Lea	GP	G	A	TP	PIM	GP	G	A	TP	PIM
1988-89	Trois-Rivières	QMJHL	10	0	0	0	4	....	....	....	....	....
1989-90	St-Hyacinthe	QMJHL	69	20	57	77	63	12	4	8	12	21
1990-91	St-Hyacinthe	QMJHL	22	5	16	21	12	....	....	....	....	....
	Hull	QMJHL	46	23	35	58	75	6	2	3	5	4
1991-92	Hull	QMJHL	8	7	6	13	35	....	....	....	....	....
	Trois-Rivières	QMJHL	62	36	59	95	98	15	7	16	23	26

BELLOWS, BRIAN

Left wing. Shoots right. 5'11", 195 lbs. Born, St. Catharines, Ont., September 1, 1964.
(Minnesota's 1st choice, 2nd overall, in 1982 Entry Draft).

			Regular Season					Playoffs				
Season	Club	Lea	GP	G	A	TP	PIM	GP	G	A	TP	PIM
1980-81a	Kitchener	OHA	66	49	67	116	23	16	14	13	27	13
1981-82bc	Kitchener	OHL	47	45	52	97	23	15	16	13	29	11
1982-83	**Minnesota**	**NHL**	**78**	**35**	**30**	**65**	**27**	**9**	**5**	**4**	**9**	**18**
1983-84	**Minnesota**	**NHL**	**78**	**41**	**42**	**83**	**66**	**16**	**2**	**12**	**14**	**6**
1984-85	**Minnesota**	**NHL**	**78**	**26**	**36**	**62**	**72**	**9**	**2**	**4**	**6**	**9**
1985-86	**Minnesota**	**NHL**	**77**	**31**	**48**	**79**	**46**	**5**	**5**	**0**	**5**	**16**
1986-87	**Minnesota**	**NHL**	**65**	**26**	**27**	**53**	**34**	....	....	....	....	....
1987-88	**Minnesota**	**NHL**	**77**	**40**	**41**	**81**	**81**	....	....	....	....	....
1988-89	**Minnesota**	**NHL**	**60**	**23**	**27**	**50**	**55**	**5**	**2**	**3**	**5**	**8**
1989-90d	**Minnesota**	**NHL**	**80**	**55**	**44**	**99**	**72**	**7**	**4**	**3**	**7**	**10**
1990-91	**Minnesota**	**NHL**	**80**	**35**	**40**	**75**	**43**	**23**	**10**	**19**	**29**	**30**
1991-92	**Minnesota**	**NHL**	**80**	**30**	**45**	**75**	**41**	**7**	**4**	**4**	**8**	**14**
	NHL Totals		**753**	**342**	**380**	**722**	**537**	**81**	**34**	**49**	**83**	**111**

a OHA Third All-Star Team (1981)
b OHL First All-Star Team (1982)
c Most Sportsmanlike Player, Memorial Cup Tournament (1982)
d NHL Second All-Star Team (1990)

Played in NHL All-Star Game (1984, 1988, 1992)

BELZILE, ETIENNE

Defense. Shoots left. 6'1", 179 lbs. Born, Quebec City, Que., May 2, 1972.
(Calgary's 4th choice, 41st overall, in 1990 Entry Draft).

			Regular Season					Playoffs				
Season	Club	Lea	GP	G	A	TP	PIM	GP	G	A	TP	PIM
1989-90	Cornell	ECAC	27	1	5	6	22	....	....	....	....	....
1990-91	Cornell	ECAC	32	2	3	5	40	....	....	....	....	....
1991-92	Cornell	ECAC	29	1	1	2	20	....	....	....	....	....

BENNETT, ADAM

Defense. Shoots right. 6'4", 206 lbs. Born, Georgetown, Ont., March 30, 1971.
(Chicago's 1st choice, 6th overall, in 1989 Entry Draft).

			Regular Season					Playoffs				
Season	Club	Lea	GP	G	A	TP	PIM	GP	G	A	TP	PIM
1988-89	Sudbury	OHL	66	7	22	29	133	....	....	....	....	....
1989-90a	Sudbury	OHL	65	18	43	61	116	7	1	2	3	23
1990-91b	Sudbury	OHL	54	21	29	50	123	5	1	2	3	11
	Indianapolis	IHL	3	0	1	1	12	2	0	0	0	0
1991-92	**Chicago**	**NHL**	**5**	**0**	**0**	**0**	**12**	....	....	....	....	....
	Indianapolis	IHL	59	4	10	14	89	....	....	....	....	....
	NHL Totals		**5**	**0**	**0**	**0**	**12**	....	....	....	....	....

a OHL Third All-Star Team (1990)
b OHL Second All-Star Team (1991)

BENNETT, ERIC (RICK)

Left wing. Shoots left. 6'4", 215 lbs. Born, Springfield, MA, July 24, 1967.
(Minnesota's 4th choice, 54th overall, in 1986 Entry Draft).

			Regular Season					Playoffs				
Season	Club	Lea	GP	G	A	TP	PIM	GP	G	A	TP	PIM
1986-87	Providence	H.E.	32	15	12	27	34	....	....	....	....	....
1987-88	Providence	H.E.	33	9	16	25	70	....	....	....	....	....
1988-89a	Providence	H.E.	32	14	32	46	74	....	....	....	....	....
1989-90b	Providence	H.E.	31	12	24	36	74	....	....	....	....	....
	NY Rangers	**NHL**	**6**	**1**	**0**	**1**	**5**	....	....	....	....	....
1990-91	**NY Rangers**	**NHL**	**6**	**0**	**0**	**0**	**6**	....	....	....	....	....
	Binghamton	AHL	71	27	32	59	206	10	2	1	3	27
1991-92	**NY Rangers**	**NHL**	**3**	**0**	**1**	**1**	**2**	....	....	....	....	....
	Binghamton	AHL	69	19	23	42	112	11	0	1	1	23
	NHL Totals		**15**	**1**	**1**	**2**	**13**	....	....	....	....	....

a NCAA East Second All-American Team (1989)
b Hockey East All-Star Team (1990)

Rights traded to **NY Rangers** by **Minnesota** with Brian Lawton and Igor Liba for Paul Jerrard and Mark Tinordi, the rights to Bret Barnett and Mike Sullivan, and Los Angeles' third round choice (Murray Garbutt) in 1989 Entry Draft - acquired March 10, 1987 by Minnesota - October 11, 1988.

BENNING, BRIAN

Defense. Shoots left. 6', 195 lbs. Born, Edmonton, Alta., June 10, 1966.
(St. Louis' 1st choice, 26th overall, in 1984 Entry Draft).

			Regular Season					Playoffs				
Season	Club	Lea	GP	G	A	TP	PIM	GP	G	A	TP	PIM
1983-84	Portland	WHL	38	6	41	47	108	....	....	....	....	....
1984-85	**St. Louis**	**NHL**	**4**	**0**	**2**	**2**	**0**	....	....	....	....	....
	Kamloops	WHL	17	3	18	21	26	....	....	....	....	....
1985-86	Cdn. Olympic	....	60	6	13	19	43	....	....	....	....	....
	St. Louis	**NHL**	....	....	....	....	....	**6**	**1**	**2**	**3**	**13**
1986-87a	**St. Louis**	**NHL**	**78**	**13**	**36**	**49**	**110**	**6**	**0**	**4**	**4**	**9**
1987-88	**St. Louis**	**NHL**	**77**	**8**	**29**	**37**	**107**	**10**	**1**	**6**	**7**	**25**
1988-89	**St. Louis**	**NHL**	**66**	**8**	**26**	**34**	**102**	**7**	**1**	**1**	**2**	**11**
1989-90	**St. Louis**	**NHL**	**7**	**1**	**1**	**2**	**2**	....	....	....	....	....
	Los Angeles	**NHL**	**48**	**5**	**18**	**23**	**104**	**7**	**0**	**2**	**2**	**10**
1990-91	**Los Angeles**	**NHL**	**61**	**7**	**24**	**31**	**127**	**12**	**0**	**5**	**5**	**6**
1991-92	**Los Angeles**	**NHL**	**53**	**2**	**30**	**32**	**99**	....	....	....	....	....
	Philadelphia	**NHL**	**22**	**2**	**12**	**14**	**35**	....	....	....	....	....
	NHL Totals		**416**	**46**	**178**	**224**	**686**	....	....	....	....	....

a NHL All-Rookie Team (1987)

Traded to **Los Angeles** by **St Louis** for Los Angeles' third round choice (Kyle Reeves) in 1991 Entry Draft, November 10, 1989. Traded to **Pittsburgh** by **Los Angeles** with Jeff Chychrun and Los Angeles' first round choice in 1992 Entry Draft (later traded to Philadelphia - Jason Bowen) for Paul Coffey, February 19, 1992. Traded to **Philadelphia** by **Pittsburgh** with Mark Recchi and Los Angeles' first choice in 1992 Entry Draft (Jason Bowen) previously acquired in the Paul Coffey trade, February 19, 1992.

BENNING, JAMES (JIM)

Defense. Shoots left. 6', 180 lbs. Born, Edmonton, Alta., April 29, 1963.
(Toronto's 1st choice, 6th overall, in 1981 Entry Draft).

			Regular Season					Playoffs				
Season	Club	Lea	GP	G	A	TP	PIM	GP	G	A	TP	PIM
1979-80	Portland	WHL	71	11	60	71	42	8	3	9	12	6
1980-81ab	Portland	WHL	72	28	*111	139	61	9	1	5	6	16
1981-82	**Toronto**	**NHL**	**74**	**7**	**24**	**31**	**46**	....	....	....	....	....
1982-83	**Toronto**	**NHL**	**74**	**5**	**17**	**22**	**47**	**4**	**1**	**1**	**2**	**2**
1983-84	**Toronto**	**NHL**	**79**	**12**	**39**	**51**	**66**	....	....	....	....	....
1984-85	**Toronto**	**NHL**	**80**	**9**	**35**	**44**	**55**	....	....	....	....	....
1985-86	**Toronto**	**NHL**	**52**	**4**	**21**	**25**	**71**	....	....	....	....	....
1986-87	**Toronto**	**NHL**	**5**	**0**	**0**	**0**	**4**	....	....	....	....	....
	Newmarket	AHL	10	1	5	6	0	....	....	....	....	....
	Vancouver	**NHL**	**54**	**2**	**11**	**13**	**40**	....	....	....	....	....
1987-88	**Vancouver**	**NHL**	**77**	**7**	**26**	**33**	**58**	....	....	....	....	....
1988-89	**Vancouver**	**NHL**	**65**	**3**	**9**	**12**	**48**	**3**	**0**	**0**	**0**	**0**
1989-90	**Vancouver**	**NHL**	**45**	**3**	**9**	**12**	**26**	....	....	....	....	....
1990-91	Milwaukee	IHL	66	1	31	32	75	6	0	0	0	0
1991-92	Varese	Italy	18	0	12	12	14	7	0	2	2	50
	NHL Totals		**605**	**52**	**191**	**243**	**461**	**7**	**1**	**1**	**2**	**2**

a WHL First All-Star Team (1981)
b Named WHL's Top Defenseman (1981)

Traded to **Vancouver** by **Toronto** with Dan Hodgson for Rick Lanz, December 12, 1986.

BERALDO, PAUL

Right wing. Shoots right. 5'11", 175 lbs. Born, Hamilton, Ont., October 5, 1967.
(Boston's 6th choice, 139th overall, in 1986 Entry Draft).

			Regular Season					Playoffs				
Season	Club	Lea	GP	G	A	TP	PIM	GP	G	A	TP	PIM
1985-86	S.S. Marie	OHL	61	15	13	28	48	....	....	....	....	....
1986-87	S.S. Marie	OHL	63	39	51	90	117	4	3	2	5	6
1987-88	**Boston**	**NHL**	**3**	**0**	**0**	**0**	**0**	....	....	....	....	....
	Maine	AHL	62	22	15	37	112	2	0	0	0	19
1988-89	**Boston**	**NHL**	**7**	**0**	**0**	**0**	**4**	....	....	....	....	....
	Maine	AHL	73	25	28	53	134	....	....	....	....	....
1989-90	Cdn. National	....	9	2	8	10	20	....	....	....	....	....
	Maine	AHL	51	14	27	41	31	....	....	....	....	....
1990-91	Milano	Italy	34	34	27	61	77	10	12	12	24	13
1991-92	Milano	Italy	16	23	13	36	24	12	10	5	15	11
	NHL Totals		**10**	**0**	**0**	**0**	**4**	....	....	....	....	....

BERANEK, JOSEF (beh-RAH-nehk)

Right wing. Shoots left. 6'2", 185 lbs. Born, Litvinov, Czechoslovakia, October 25, 1969.
(Edmonton's 3rd choice, 78th overall, in 1989 Entry Draft).

			Regular Season					Playoffs				
Season	Club	Lea	GP	G	A	TP	PIM	GP	G	A	TP	PIM
1988-89	CHZ Litvinov	Czech.	23	14	8	22	....	....	....	....	....	....
1989-90	Dukla Trencin	Czech.	49	19	23	42	....	....	....	....	....	....
1990-91	CHZ Litvinov	Czech.	50	27	27	54	98	....	....	....	....	....
1991-92	**Edmonton**	**NHL**	**58**	**12**	**16**	**28**	**18**	**12**	**2**	**1**	**3**	**0**
	NHL Totals		**58**	**12**	**16**	**28**	**18**	**12**	**2**	**1**	**3**	**0**

BEREHOWSKY, DRAKE

Defense. Shoots right. 6'1", 211 lbs. Born, Toronto, Ont., January 3, 1972.
(Toronto's 1st choice, 10th overall, in 1990 Entry Draft).

			Regular Season					Playoffs				
Season	Club	Lea	GP	G	A	TP	PIM	GP	G	A	TP	PIM
1988-89	Kingston	OHL	63	7	39	46	85	....	....	....	....	....
1989-90	Kingston	OHL	9	3	11	14	28	....	....	....	....	....
1990-91	**Toronto**	**NHL**	**8**	**0**	**1**	**1**	**25**	....	....	....	....	....
	Kingston	OHL	13	5	13	18	38	....	....	....	....	....
	North Bay	OHL	26	7	23	30	51	10	2	7	9	21
1991-92	**Toronto**	**NHL**	**1**	**0**	**0**	**0**	**0**	....	....	....	....	....
ab	North Bay	OHL	62	19	63	82	147	21	7	24	31	22
	St. John's	AHL	....	....	....	....	....	6	0	5	5	21
	NHL Totals		**9**	**0**	**1**	**1**	**25**	....	....	....	....	....

a Canadian Major Junior Defenseman of the Year (1992)
b OHL First All-Star Team (1992)

BEREZAN, PERRY EDMUND (BAIR-ih-ZAN)

Center. Shoots right. 6'2", 190 lbs. Born, Edmonton, Alta., December 5, 1964.
(Calgary's 3rd choice, 56th overall, in 1983 Entry Draft).

			Regular Season					Playoffs				
Season	Club	Lea	GP	G	A	TP	PIM	GP	G	A	TP	PIM
1983-84	North Dakota	WCHA	44	28	24	52	29	....	....	....	....	....
1984-85a	North Dakota	WCHA	42	23	35	58	32	....	....	....	....	....
	Calgary	**NHL**	**9**	**3**	**2**	**5**	**4**	**2**	**1**	**0**	**1**	**4**
1985-86	**Calgary**	**NHL**	**55**	**12**	**21**	**33**	**39**	**8**	**1**	**1**	**2**	**6**
1986-87	**Calgary**	**NHL**	**24**	**5**	**3**	**8**	**24**	**2**	**0**	**2**	**2**	**7**
1987-88	**Calgary**	**NHL**	**29**	**7**	**12**	**19**	**66**	**8**	**0**	**2**	**2**	**13**
1988-89	**Calgary**	**NHL**	**35**	**4**	**4**	**8**	**23**	....	....	....	....	....
	Minnesota	**NHL**	**16**	**1**	**4**	**5**	**4**	**5**	**1**	**2**	**3**	**4**
1989-90	**Minnesota**	**NHL**	**64**	**3**	**12**	**15**	**31**	**5**	**1**	**0**	**1**	**0**
1990-91	**Minnesota**	**NHL**	**52**	**11**	**6**	**17**	**30**	**1**	**0**	**0**	**0**	**0**
	Kalamazoo	IHL	2	0	0	0	2	....	....	....	....	....
1991-92	**San Jose**	**NHL**	**66**	**12**	**7**	**19**	**30**	....	....	....	....	....
	NHL Totals		**350**	**58**	**71**	**129**	**251**	**31**	**4**	**7**	**11**	**34**

a WCHA Second All-Star Team (1985)

Traded to **Minnesota** by **Calgary** with Shane Churla for Brian MacLellan and Minnesota's fourth round choice (Robert Reichel) in 1989 Entry Draft, March 4, 1989. Signed as a free agent by **San Jose**, October 10, 1991.

BERG, BILL

Left wing. Shoots left. 6'1", 190 lbs. Born, St. Catharines, Ont., October 21, 1967.
(NY Islanders' 3rd choice, 59th overall, in 1986 Entry Draft).

			Regular Season					Playoffs				
Season	Club	Lea	GP	G	A	TP	PIM	GP	G	A	TP	PIM
1985-86	Toronto	OHL	64	3	35	38	143	4	0	0	0	19
	Springfield	AHL	4	1	1	2	4	....	....	....	....	....
1986-87	Toronto	OHL	57	3	15	18	138	....	....	....	....	....
1987-88	Springfield	AHL	76	6	26	32	148	....	....	....	....	....
	Peoria	IHL	5	0	1	1	8	7	0	3	3	31
1988-89	**NY Islanders**	**NHL**	**7**	**1**	**2**	**3**	**10**	....	....	....	....	....
	Springfield	AHL	69	17	32	49	122	....	....	....	....	....
1989-90	Springfield	AHL	74	12	42	54	74	15	5	12	17	35
1990-91	**NY Islanders**	**NHL**	**78**	**9**	**14**	**23**	**67**	....	....	....	....	....
1991-92	**NY Islanders**	**NHL**	**47**	**5**	**9**	**14**	**28**	....	....	....	....	....
	Capital Dist.	AHL	3	0	2	2	16	....	....	....	....	....
	NHL Totals		**132**	**15**	**25**	**40**	**105**	....	....	....	....	....

BERG, BOB

Left wing. Shoots left. 6'2", 190 lbs. Born, Beamsville, Ont., July 2, 1970.
(Los Angeles' 3rd choice, 49th overall, in 1990 Entry Draft).

			Regular Season					Playoffs				
Season	Club	Lea	GP	G	A	TP	PIM	GP	G	A	TP	PIM
1987-88	Belleville	OHL	61	15	27	42	59	....	....	....	....	....
1988-89	Belleville	OHL	66	33	51	84	88	5	1	3	4	8
1989-90a	Belleville	OHL	66	48	49	97	124	8	2	2	4	14
1990-91	New Haven	AHL	19	0	1	1	8	....	....	....	....	....
	Niagara Falls	OHL	12	8	4	12	11	....	....	....	....	....
	Sudbury	OHL	23	12	15	27	34	5	2	1	3	6
1991-92	Phoenix	IHL	24	2	8	10	18	....	....	....	....	....
	Richmond	ECHL	37	19	14	33	65	6	2	1	3	0

a OHL First All-Star Team (1990)

BERGER, PHILIP (PHIL)

Left wing. Shoots left. 6', 190 lbs. Born, Dearborn, MI, December 3, 1966.
(Quebec's 1st choice, 3rd overall, in 1988 Supplemental Draft).

			Regular Season					Playoffs				
Season	Club	Lea	GP	G	A	TP	PIM	GP	G	A	TP	PIM
1985-86	N. Michigan	WCHA	21	5	2	7	20	....	....	....	....	....
1986-87	N. Michigan	WCHA	24	11	10	21	6	....	....	....	....	....
1987-88a	N. Michigan	WCHA	38	40	32	72	22	....	....	....	....	....
1988-89b	N. Michigan	WCHA	44	30	33	63	24	....	....	....	....	....
1989-90	Fort Wayne	IHL	3	2	2	4	2	....	....	....	....	....
	Greensboro	ECHL	46	38	44	82	119	10	11	3	14	32
1990-91	Halifax	AHL	4	1	0	1	0	....	....	....	....	....
	Greensboro	ECHL	44	22	34	56	112	13	11	11	22	17
1991-92cde	Greensboro	ECHL	60	60	70	*130	158	11	8	13	21	56
	Fort Wayne	IHL	....	....	....	....	....	4	3	3	6	0

a WCHA First All-Star Team (1988)
b WCHA Second All-Star Team (1989)
c ECHL Second All-Star Team (1992)
d ECHL MVP
e ECHL Scoring Leader

BERGEVIN, MARC

Defense. Shoots left. 6', 185 lbs. Born, Montreal, Que., August 11, 1965.
(Chicago's 3rd choice, 59th overall, in 1983 Entry Draft).

			Regular Season					Playoffs				
Season	Club	Lea	GP	G	A	TP	PIM	GP	G	A	TP	PIM
1982-83	Chicoutimi	QMJHL	64	3	27	30	113	....	....	....	....	....
1983-84	Chicoutimi	QMJHL	70	10	35	45	125	....	....	....	....	....
	Springfield	AHL	7	0	1	1	2	....	....	....	....	....
1984-85	**Chicago**	**NHL**	**60**	**0**	**6**	**6**	**54**	**6**	**0**	**3**	**3**	**2**
	Springfield	AHL	....	....	....	....	....	4	0	0	0	0
1985-86	**Chicago**	**NHL**	**71**	**7**	**7**	**14**	**60**	**3**	**0**	**0**	**0**	**0**
1986-87	**Chicago**	**NHL**	**66**	**4**	**10**	**14**	**66**	**3**	**1**	**0**	**1**	**2**
1987-88	**Chicago**	**NHL**	**58**	**1**	**6**	**7**	**85**	....	....	....	....	....
	Saginaw	IHL	10	2	7	9	20	....	....	....	....	....
1988-89	**Chicago**	**NHL**	**11**	**0**	**0**	**0**	**18**	....	....	....	....	....
	NY Islanders	**NHL**	**58**	**2**	**13**	**15**	**62**	....	....	....	....	....
1989-90	**NY Islanders**	**NHL**	**18**	**0**	**4**	**4**	**30**	....	....	....	....	....
	Springfield	AHL	47	7	16	23	66	17	2	11	13	16
1990-91	Capital Dist.	AHL	7	0	5	5	6	....	....	....	....	....
	Hartford	**NHL**	**4**	**0**	**0**	**0**	**4**	....	....	....	....	....
	Springfield	AHL	58	4	23	27	85	18	0	7	7	26
1991-92	**Hartford**	**NHL**	**75**	**7**	**17**	**24**	**64**	**5**	**0**	**0**	**0**	**2**
	NHL Totals		**421**	**21**	**63**	**84**	**443**	**17**	**1**	**3**	**4**	**6**

Traded to **NY Islanders** by **Chicago** with Gary Nylund for Steve Konroyd and Bob Bassen, November 25, 1988. Traded to **Hartford** by **NY Islanders** for future considerations, October 30, 1990.

BERGLAND, TIM

Right wing. Shoots right. 6'3", 194 lbs. Born, Crookston, MN, January 11, 1965.
(Washington's 1st choice, 75th overall, in 1983 Entry Draft).

			Regular Season					Playoffs				
Season	Club	Lea	GP	G	A	TP	PIM	GP	G	A	TP	PIM
1983-84	U. Minnesota	WCHA	24	4	11	15	4	....	....	....	....	....
1984-85	U. Minnesota	WCHA	34	5	9	14	8	....	....	....	....	....
1985-86	U. Minnesota	WCHA	48	11	16	27	26	....	....	....	....	....
1986-87	U. Minnesota	WCHA	49	18	17	35	48	....	....	....	....	....
1987-88	Fort Wayne	IHL	13	2	1	3	9	....	....	....	....	....
	Binghamton	AHL	63	21	26	47	31	4	0	0	0	0
1988-89	Baltimore	AHL	78	24	29	53	39	....	....	....	....	....
1989-90	**Washington**	**NHL**	**32**	**2**	**5**	**7**	**31**	**15**	**1**	**1**	**2**	**10**
	Baltimore	AHL	47	12	19	31	55	....	....	....	....	....
1990-91	**Washington**	**NHL**	**47**	**5**	**9**	**14**	**21**	**11**	**1**	**1**	**2**	**12**
	Baltmore	AHL	15	8	9	17	16	....	....	....	....	....
1991-92	**Washington**	**NHL**	**22**	**1**	**4**	**5**	**2**	....	....	....	....	....
	Baltimore	AHL	11	6	10	16	5	....	....	....	....	....
	NHL Totals		**101**	**8**	**18**	**26**	**54**	**26**	**2**	**2**	**4**	**22**

Claimed by **Tampa Bay** from **Washington** in Expansion Draft, June 18, 1992.

BERGMAN, JAN (BURG-muhn)

Defense. Shoots left. 5'11", 194 lbs. Born, Sodertalje, Sweden, August 7, 1969.
(Vancouver's 11th choice, 248th overall, in 1989 Entry Draft).

			Regular Season					Playoffs				
Season	Club	Lea	GP	G	A	TP	PIM	GP	G	A	TP	PIM
1988-89	Sodertalje	Swe.	34	2	4	6	14	....	....	....	....	....
1989-90	Sodertalje	Swe.	31	0	4	4	10	2	1	0	1	0
1990-91	Sodertalje	Swe.	40	4	4	8	16	....	....	....	....	....
1991-92	Sodertalje	Swe.	21	1	1	2	8	....	....	....	....	....

BERMINGHAM, JIM

Center. Shoots left. 6'3", 201 lbs. Born, Montreal, Que., November 12, 1971.
(Detroit's 7th choice, 186th overall, in 1991 Entry Draft).

			Regular Season					Playoffs				
Season	Club	Lea	GP	G	A	TP	PIM	GP	G	A	TP	PIM
1990-91	Laval	QMJHL	67	21	39	60	109	13	4	8	12	17
1991-92	Laval	QMJHL	65	37	66	103	88	10	3	6	9	28

BERNARD, LOUIS

Defense. Shoots right. 6'1", 198 lbs. Born, Victoriaville, Que., July 10, 1974.
(Montreal's 5th choice, 82nd overall, in 1992 Entry Draft).

			Regular Season					Playoffs				
Season	Club	Lea	GP	G	A	TP	PIM	GP	G	A	TP	PIM
1990-91	Cant. de'l'Est.	Midget	40	7	14	21	88	....	....	....	....	....
1991-92	Drummondville	QMJHL	70	8	24	32	59	4	0	1	1	4

BERRY, BRAD

Defense. Shoots left. 6'2", 190 lbs. Born, Bashaw, Alta., April 1, 1965.
(Winnipeg's 3rd choice, 29th overall, in 1983 Entry Draft).

			Regular Season					Playoffs				
Season	Club	Lea	GP	G	A	TP	PIM	GP	G	A	TP	PIM
1983-84	North Dakota	WCHA	32	2	7	9	8	....	....	....	....	....
1984-85	North Dakota	WCHA	40	4	26	30	26	....	....	....	....	....
1985-86	North Dakota	WCHA	40	6	29	35	26	....	....	....	....	....
	Winnipeg	**NHL**	**13**	**1**	**0**	**1**	**10**	**3**	**0**	**0**	**0**	**0**
1986-87	**Winnipeg**	**NHL**	**52**	**2**	**8**	**10**	**60**	**7**	**0**	**1**	**1**	**14**
1987-88	**Winnipeg**	**NHL**	**48**	**0**	**6**	**6**	**75**	....	....	....	....	....
	Moncton	AHL	10	1	3	4	14	....	....	....	....	....
1988-89	**Winnipeg**	**NHL**	**38**	**0**	**9**	**9**	**45**	....	....	....	....	....
	Moncton	AHL	38	3	16	19	39	....	....	....	....	....
1989-90	**Winnipeg**	**NHL**	**12**	**1**	**2**	**3**	**6**	**1**	**0**	**0**	**0**	**0**
	Moncton	AHL	38	1	9	10	58	....	....	....	....	....
1990-91	Brynas	Swe.	38	3	1	4	38	....	....	....	....	....
1991-92	**Minnesota**	**NHL**	**7**	**0**	**0**	**0**	**6**	**2**	**0**	**0**	**0**	**2**
	Kalamazoo	IHL	65	5	18	23	90	5	2	0	2	6
	NHL Totals		**170**	**4**	**25**	**29**	**202**	**13**	**0**	**1**	**1**	**16**

Signed as a free agent by **Minnesota**, October 4, 1991.

BERUBE, CRAIG (buh-ROO-bee)

Left wing. Shoots left. 6'1", 205 lbs. Born, Calahoo, Alta., December 17, 1965.

			Regular Season					Playoffs				
Season	Club	Lea	GP	G	A	TP	PIM	GP	G	A	TP	PIM
1982-83	Kamloops	WHL	4	0	0	0	0	....	....	....	....	....
1983-84	N. Westminster	WHL	70	11	20	31	104	8	1	2	3	5
1984-85	N. Westminster	WHL	70	25	44	69	191	10	3	2	5	4
1985-86	Kamloops	WHL	32	17	14	31	119	....	....	....	....	....
	Medicine Hat	WHL	34	14	16	30	95	25	7	8	15	102
1986-87	**Philadelphia**	**NHL**	**7**	**0**	**0**	**0**	**57**	**5**	**0**	**0**	**0**	**17**
	Hershey	AHL	63	7	17	24	325	....	....	....	....	....
1987-88	**Philadelphia**	**NHL**	**27**	**3**	**2**	**5**	**108**	....	....	....	....	....
	Hershey	AHL	31	5	9	14	119	....	....	....	....	....
1988-89	**Philadelphia**	**NHL**	**53**	**1**	**1**	**2**	**199**	**16**	**0**	**0**	**0**	**56**
	Hershey	AHL	7	0	2	2	19	....	....	....	....	....
1989-90	**Philadelphia**	**NHL**	**74**	**4**	**14**	**18**	**291**	....	....	....	....	....
1990-91	**Philadelphia**	**NHL**	**74**	**8**	**9**	**17**	**293**	....	....	....	....	....
1991-92	**Toronto**	**NHL**	**40**	**5**	**7**	**12**	**109**	....	....	....	....	....
	Calgary	**NHL**	**36**	**1**	**4**	**5**	**155**	....	....	....	....	....
	NHL Totals		**311**	**22**	**37**	**59**	**1212**	**21**	**0**	**0**	**0**	**73**

Signed as a free agent by **Philadelphia**, March 19, 1986. Traded to **Edmonton** by **Philadelphia** with Craig Fisher and Scott Mellanby for Dave Brown, Corey Foster and Jari Kurri, May 30, 1991. Traded to **Toronto** by **Edmonton** with Grant Fuhr and Glenn Anderson for Vincent Damphousse, Peter Ing, Scott Thornton, Luke Richardson, future considerations and cash, September 19, 1991. Traded to **Calgary** by **Toronto** with Alexander Godynyuk, Gary Leeman, Michel Petit and Jeff Reese for Doug Gilmour, Jamie Macoun, Ric Nattress, Rick Wamsley and Kent Manderville, January 2, 1992.

BES, JEFF

Center. Shoots left. 6', 186 lbs. Born, Tillsonburg, Ont., July 31, 1973.
(Minnesota's 2nd choice, 58th overall, in 1992 Entry Draft).

			Regular Season					Playoffs				
Season	Club	Lea	GP	G	A	TP	PIM	GP	G	A	TP	PIM
1990-91	Hamilton	OHL	66	23	47	70	53	4	1	4	5	4
1991-92	Guelph	OHL	62	40	62	102	123	....	....	....	....	....

BEUKEBOOM, JEFF (BOO-kuh-BOOM)

Defense. Shoots right. 6'4", 215 lbs. Born, Ajax, Ont., March 28, 1965.
(Edmonton's 1st choice, 19th overall, in 1983 Entry Draft).

			Regular Season					Playoffs				
Season	Club	Lea	GP	G	A	TP	PIM	GP	G	A	TP	PIM
1982-83	S.S. Marie	OHL	70	0	25	25	143	16	1	4	5	46
1983-84	S.S. Marie	OHL	61	6	30	36	178	16	1	7	8	43
1984-85a	S.S. Marie	OHL	37	4	20	24	85	16	4	6	10	47
1985-86	Nova Scotia	AHL	77	9	20	29	175	....	....	....	....	....
	Edmonton	**NHL**	....	....	....	....	....	**1**	**0**	**0**	**0**	**4**
1986-87	**Edmonton**	**NHL**	**44**	**3**	**8**	**11**	**124**	....	....	....	....	....
	Nova Scotia	AHL	14	1	7	8	35	....	....	....	....	....
1987-88	**Edmonton**	**NHL**	**73**	**5**	**20**	**25**	**201**	**7**	**0**	**0**	**0**	**16**
1988-89	**Edmonton**	**NHL**	**36**	**0**	**5**	**5**	**94**	**1**	**0**	**0**	**0**	**2**
	Cape Breton	AHL	8	0	4	4	36	....	....	....	....	....
1989-90	**Edmonton**	**NHL**	**46**	**1**	**12**	**13**	**86**	**2**	**0**	**0**	**0**	**0**
1990-91	**Edmonton**	**NHL**	**67**	**3**	**7**	**10**	**150**	**18**	**1**	**3**	**4**	**28**
1991-92	**Edmonton**	**NHL**	**18**	**0**	**5**	**5**	**78**	....	....	....	....	....
	NY Rangers	**NHL**	**56**	**1**	**10**	**11**	**122**	**13**	**2**	**3**	**5**	**47**
	NHL Totals		**340**	**13**	**67**	**80**	**855**	**42**	**3**	**6**	**9**	**97**

a OHL First All-Star Team (1985)

Traded to **NY Rangers** by **Edmonton** for David Shaw, November 12, 1991.

BIGGS, DON

Center. Shoots right. 5'8", 185 lbs. Born, Mississauga, Ont., April 7, 1965.
(Minnesota's 9th choice, 156th overall, in 1983 Entry Draft).

			Regular Season					Playoffs				
Season	Club	Lea	GP	G	A	TP	PIM	GP	G	A	TP	PIM
1982-83	Oshawa	OHL	70	22	53	75	145	16	3	6	9	17
1983-84	Oshawa	OHL	58	31	60	91	149	7	4	4	8	18
1984-85	**Minnesota**	**NHL**	**1**	**0**	**0**	**0**	**0**	....	....	....	....	....
	Springfield	AHL	6	0	3	3	0	2	1	0	1	0
	Oshawa	OHL	60	48	69	117	105	5	3	4	7	6
1985-86	Springfield	AHL	28	15	16	31	46	....	....	....	....	....
	Nova Scotia	AHL	47	6	23	29	36	....	....	....	....	....
1986-87	Nova Scotia	AHL	80	22	25	47	165	5	1	2	3	4
1987-88	Hershey	AHL	77	38	41	79	151	12	5	*11	*16	22
1988-89	Hershey	AHL	76	36	67	103	158	11	5	9	14	30
1989-90	**Philadelphia**	**NHL**	**11**	**2**	**0**	**2**	**8**	....	....	....	....	....
	Hershey	AHL	66	39	53	92	125	....	....	....	....	....
1990-91	Rochester	AHL	65	31	57	88	115	15	9	*14	*23	14
1991-92	Binghamton	AHL	74	32	50	82	122	11	3	7	10	8
	NHL Totals		**12**	**2**	**0**	**2**	**8**	....	....	....	....	....

Traded to **Edmonton** by **Minnesota** with Gord Sherven for Marc Habscheid, Don Barber and Emanuel Viveiros, December 20, 1985. Signed as a free agent by **Philadelphia**, July 17, 1987. Traded to **NY Rangers** by **Philadelphia** for future considerations, August 8, 1991.

BIGNELL, GREG

Defense. Shoots left. 6', 188 lbs. Born, Kitchener, Ont., May 9, 1969.
(Detroit's 10th choice, 200th overall, in 1989 Entry Draft).

			Regular Season					Playoffs				
Season	Club	Lea	GP	G	A	TP	PIM	GP	G	A	TP	PIM
1988-89	Belleville	OHL	54	6	27	33	180	5	0	1	1	16
1989-90	Belleville	OHL	58	6	26	32	141	11	0	6	6	31
1990-91	Hampton Rds.	ECHL	55	7	21	28	265	....	....	....	....	....
1991-92	Toledo	ECHL	22	0	5	5	167	....	....	....	....	....
	Richmond	ECHL	12	1	2	3	42	6	0	1	1	40

BILLECK, LAURIE

Defense. Shoots right. 6'3", 210 lbs. Born, Dauphin, Man., February 2, 1971.
(Minnesota's 2nd choice, 50th overall, in 1990 Entry Draft).

			Regular Season					Playoffs				
Season	Club	Lea	GP	G	A	TP	PIM	GP	G	A	TP	PIM
1988-89	Prince Albert	WHL	60	2	4	6	65	4	1	0	1	14
1989-90	Prince Albert	WHL	67	7	28	35	135	14	2	3	5	24
1990-91	Prince Albert	WHL	35	1	10	11	60	3	0	0	0	5
1991-92	Tacoma	WHL	65	14	29	43	168	4	0	1	1	18

BILODEAU, BRENT

Defense. Shoots left. 6'3", 220 lbs. Born, Dallas, TX, March 27, 1973.
(Montreal's 1st choice, 17th overall, in 1991 Entry Draft).

			Regular Season					Playoffs				
Season	Club	Lea	GP	G	A	TP	PIM	GP	G	A	TP	PIM
1989-90	Seattle	WHL	68	14	29	43	170	13	3	5	8	31
1990-91	Seattle	WHL	55	7	18	25	145	6	1	0	1	12
1991-92a	Seattle	WHL	7	1	2	3	43	....	....	....	....	....
	Swift Current	WHL	56	10	47	57	118	8	2	3	5	11

a WHL East Second All-Star Team (1992)

BIONDI, JOSEPH

Center. Shoots left. 6'1", 175 lbs. Born, Warroad, MN, June 25, 1970.
(Minnesota's 9th choice, 176th overall, in 1990 Entry Draft).

			Regular Season					Playoffs				
Season	Club	Lea	GP	G	A	TP	PIM	GP	G	A	TP	PIM
1989-90	Minn.-Duluth	WCHA	37	10	17	27	8	....	....	....	....	....
1990-91	Minn.-Duluth	WCHA	30	6	8	14	4	....	....	....	....	....
1991-92	Minn.-Duluth	WCHA	34	8	6	14	10	....	....	....	....	....

BISSETT, TOM (BIH-siht)

Center. Shoots left. 6', 180 lbs. Born, Seattle, WA, March 13, 1966.
(Detroit's 11th choice, 211th overall, in 1986 Entry Draft).

			Regular Season					Playoffs				
Season	Club	Lea	GP	G	A	TP	PIM	GP	G	A	TP	PIM
1985-86	Michigan Tech	WCHA	40	12	21	33	18	....	....	....	....	....
1986-87	Michigan Tech	WCHA	40	16	19	35	12	....	....	....	....	....
1987-88	Michigan Tech	WCHA	41	18	26	44	20	....	....	....	....	....
1988-89	Adirondack	AHL	5	0	1	1	0	....	....	....	....	....
	Michigan Tech	WCHA	42	19	28	47	16	....	....	....	....	....
1989-90	Adirondack	AHL	16	11	4	15	4	....	....	....	....	....
	Hampton Rds.	ECHL	5	7	7	14	2	....	....	....	....	....
1990-91	**Detroit**	**NHL**	**5**	**0**	**0**	**0**	**0**	....	....	....	....	....
	Adirondack	AHL	73	44	38	82	12	2	0	0	0	0
1991-92	Brynas	Swe.	40	25	15	40	32	....	....	....	....	....
	NHL Totals		**5**	**0**	**0**	**0**	**0**	....	....	....	....	....

BJUGSTAD, SCOTT (BYOOG-stad)

Right wing. Shoots left. 6'1", 185 lbs. Born, St. Paul, MN, June 2, 1961.
(Minnesota's 13th choice, 181st overall, in 1981 Entry Draft).

			Regular Season					Playoffs				
Season	Club	Lea	GP	G	A	TP	PIM	GP	G	A	TP	PIM
1979-80	U. Minnesota	WCHA	18	2	2	4	2	....	....	....	....	....
1980-81	U. Minnesota	WCHA	35	12	23	25	34	....	....	....	....	....
1981-82	U. Minnesota	WCHA	36	29	14	43	24	....	....	....	....	....
1982-83a	U. Minnesota	WCHA	26	21	35	56	12	....	....	....	....	....
1983-84	U.S. National	....	54	31	20	51	28	....	....	....	....	....
	U.S. Olympic	....	6	3	2	5	6	....	....	....	....	....
	Minnesota	**NHL**	**5**	**0**	**0**	**0**	**2**	....	....	....	....	....
	Salt Lake	CHL	15	10	8	18	6	5	3	4	7	0
1984-85	**Minnesota**	**NHL**	**72**	**11**	**4**	**15**	**32**	....	....	....	....	....
	Springfield	AHL	5	2	3	5	2	....	....	....	....	....
1985-86	**Minnesota**	**NHL**	**80**	**43**	**33**	**76**	**24**	**5**	**0**	**1**	**1**	**0**
1986-87	**Minnesota**	**NHL**	**39**	**4**	**9**	**13**	**43**	....	....	....	....	....
	Springfield	AHL	11	4	6	10	7	....	....	....	....	....
1987-88	**Minnesota**	**NHL**	**33**	**10**	**12**	**22**	**15**	....	....	....	....	....
1988-89	**Pittsburgh**	**NHL**	**24**	**3**	**0**	**3**	**4**	....	....	....	....	....
	Kalamazoo	IHL	4	5	0	5	4	....	....	....	....	....
1989-90	**Los Angeles**	**NHL**	**11**	**1**	**2**	**3**	**2**	**2**	**0**	**0**	**0**	**2**
	New Haven	AHL	47	45	21	66	40	....	....	....	....	....
1990-91	**Los Angeles**	**NHL**	**31**	**2**	**4**	**6**	**12**	**2**	**0**	**0**	**0**	**0**
	Phoenix	IHL	3	7	2	9	2	....	....	....	....	....
1991-92	**Los Angeles**	**NHL**	**22**	**2**	**4**	**6**	**10**	....	....	....	....	....
	Phoenix	IHL	28	14	14	28	12	....	....	....	....	....
	NHL Totals		**317**	**76**	**68**	**144**	**144**	**9**	**0**	**1**	**1**	**2**

a WCHA First All-Star Team (1983)

Traded to **Pittsburgh** by **Minnesota** with Gord Dineen for Ville Siren and Steve Gotaas, December 17, 1988. Signed as a free agent by **Los Angeles**, August 21, 1989.

BJUHR, THOMAS (BYOOR)

Right wing. Shoots left. 6'1", 216 lbs. Born, Stockholm, Sweden, August 28, 1966.
(Detroit's 7th choice, 134th overall, in 1985 Entry Draft).

			Regular Season					Playoffs				
Season	Club	Lea	GP	G	A	TP	PIM	GP	G	A	TP	PIM
1984-85	AIK	Swe. Jr.	33	38	18	56	28	....	....	....	....	....
	AIK	Swe.	3	1	0	1	0	....	....	....	....	....
1985-86	AIK	Swe.	14	0	1	1	8	....	....	....	....	....
1986-87	Portland	WHL	39	28	26	54	23	....	....	....	....	....
1987-88	Adirondack	AHL	58	4	2	6	21	....	....	....	....	....
1988-89	AIK	Swe.	34	8	9	17	40	....	....	....	....	....
1989-90	AIK	Swe.	40	19	12	31	22	3	0	1	1	4
1990-91	AIK	Swe.	39	11	7	18	51	....	....	....	....	....
1991-92	AIK	Swe.	39	3	1	4	10	3	0	0	0	0

BLACK, JAMES

Center. Shoots left. 5'11", 185 lbs. Born, Regina, Sask., August 15, 1969.
(Hartford's 4th choice, 94th overall, in 1989 Entry Draft).

			Regular Season					Playoffs				
Season	Club	Lea	GP	G	A	TP	PIM	GP	G	A	TP	PIM
1987-88	Portland	WHL	72	30	50	80	50	....	....	....	....	....
1988-89	Portland	WHL	71	45	51	96	57	19	13	6	19	28
1989-90	**Hartford**	**NHL**	**1**	**0**	**0**	**0**	**0**	....	....	....	....	....
	Binghamton	AHL	80	37	35	72	34	....	....	....	....	....
1990-91	**Hartford**	**NHL**	**1**	**0**	**0**	**0**	**0**	....	....	....	....	....
	Springfield	AHL	79	35	61	96	34	18	9	9	18	6
1991-92	**Hartford**	**NHL**	**30**	**4**	**6**	**10**	**10**	....	....	....	....	....
	Springfield	AHL	47	15	25	40	33	10	3	2	5	18
	NHL Totals		**32**	**4**	**6**	**10**	**10**	....	....	....	....	....

BLACK, RYAN

Left wing. Shoots left. 6', 180 lbs. Born, Guelph, Ont., October 25, 1973.
(New Jersey's 6th choice, 114th overall, in 1992 Entry Draft).

			Regular Season					Playoffs				
Season	Club	Lea	GP	G	A	TP	PIM	GP	G	A	TP	PIM
1990-91	Peterborough	OHL	59	7	16	23	41	4	0	1	1	0
1991-92	Peterborough	OHL	66	18	33	51	57	7	1	1	2	11

BLAD, BRIAN

Defense. Shoots left. 6'2", 200 lbs. Born, Brockville, Ont., July 22, 1967.
(Toronto's 9th choice, 175th overall, in 1987 Entry Draft).

			Regular Season					Playoffs				
Season	Club	Lea	GP	G	A	TP	PIM	GP	G	A	TP	PIM
1984-85	Windsor	OHL	56	1	7	8	126	....	....	....	....	....
1985-86	Windsor	OHL	56	2	9	11	195	....	....	....	....	....
1986-87	Windsor	OHL	15	1	1	2	30	....	....	....	....	....
	Belleville	OHL	20	1	5	6	43	....	....	....	....	....
1987-88	Milwaukee	IHL	28	1	6	7	45	....	....	....	....	....
	Newmarket	AHL	39	0	4	4	74	....	....	....	....	....
1988-89	Newmarket	AHL	59	2	4	6	149	5	0	1	1	5
1989-90	Newmarket	AHL	58	2	4	6	216	....	....	....	....	....
1990-91	Newmarket	AHL	28	0	0	0	100	....	....	....	....	....
	Milwaukee	IHL	37	1	2	3	98	6	0	2	2	8
1991-92	Milwaukee	IHL	58	1	3	4	162	5	0	0	0	0

Traded to **Vancouver** by **Toronto** for Todd Hawkins, January 22, 1991.

BLAESER, JEFFREY

Left wing. Shoots left. 6'3", 190 lbs. Born, Parma, OH, May 11, 1970.
(Pittsburgh's 7th choice, 151st overall, in 1988 Entry Draft).

			Regular Season					Playoffs				
Season	Club	Lea	GP	G	A	TP	PIM	GP	G	A	TP	PIM
1988-89	Yale	ECAC	31	8	19	27	12	....	....	....	....	....
1989-90	Yale	ECAC	29	17	14	31	16	....	....	....	....	....
1990-91	Yale	ECAC	29	12	14	26	22	....	....	....	....	....
1991-92	Yale	ECAC	24	8	15	23	4	....	....	....	....	....

BLAIN, JOEL

Left wing. Shoots left. 6', 195 lbs. Born, Malartic, Que., October 12, 1971.
(Edmonton's 4th choice, 67th overall, in 1990 Entry Draft).

			Regular Season					Playoffs				
Season	Club	Lea	GP	G	A	TP	PIM	GP	G	A	TP	PIM
1989-90	Hull	QMJHL	65	31	47	78	137	11	6	6	12	16
1990-91	Hull	QMJHL	61	19	31	50	95	6	4	3	7	17
1991-92	Hull	QMJHL	60	24	35	59	146	6	4	2	6	27

BLAKE, ROBERT (ROB)

Defense. Shoots right. 6'3", 215 lbs. Born, Simcoe, Ont., December 10, 1969.
(Los Angeles' 4th choice, 70th overall, in 1988 Entry Draft).

			Regular Season					Playoffs				
Season	Club	Lea	GP	G	A	TP	PIM	GP	G	A	TP	PIM
1987-88	Bowling Green	CCHA	43	5	8	13	88	....	....	....	....	....
1988-89a	Bowling Green	CCHA	46	11	21	32	140	....	....	....	....	....
1989-90bc	Bowling Green	CCHA	42	23	36	59	140	....	....	....	....	....
	Los Angeles	**NHL**	**4**	**0**	**0**	**0**	**4**	**8**	**1**	**3**	**4**	**4**
1990-91d	**Los Angeles**	**NHL**	**75**	**12**	**34**	**46**	**125**	**12**	**1**	**4**	**5**	**26**
1991-92	**Los Angeles**	**NHL**	**57**	**7**	**13**	**20**	**102**	**6**	**2**	**1**	**3**	**12**
	NHL Totals		**136**	**19**	**47**	**66**	**231**	**26**	**4**	**8**	**12**	**42**

a CCHA Second All-Star Team (1989)
b CCHA First All-Star Team (1990)
c NCAA West First All-American Team (1990)
d NHL/Upper Deck All-Rookie Team (1991)

BLESSMAN, JOHN

Defense. Shoots left. 6'3", 211 lbs. Born, Toronto, Ont., April 27, 1967.
(New Jersey's 8th choice, 170th overall, in 1987 Entry Draft).

			Regular Season					Playoffs				
Season	Club	Lea	GP	G	A	TP	PIM	GP	G	A	TP	PIM
1984-85	Toronto	OHL	25	1	3	4	42	5	0	0	0	0
1985-86	Toronto	OHL	64	2	13	15	116	4	0	0	0	11
1986-87	Toronto	OHL	61	6	24	30	130	....	....	....	....	....
1987-88	Utica	AHL	24	0	2	2	50	....	....	....	....	....
	Toronto	OHL	23	8	11	19	64	4	0	4	4	0
1988-89	Utica	AHL	26	2	3	5	46	....	....	....	....	....
	Indianapolis	IHL	31	2	5	7	60	....	....	....	....	....
1989-90	Hershey	AHL	1	0	0	0	0	....	....	....	....	....
	Winston-Salem	ECHL	17	1	6	7	108	....	....	....	....	....
	Greensboro	ECHL	19	0	7	7	81	11	3	6	9	50
1990-91	Greensboro	ECHL	29	7	14	21	131	13	1	9	10	36
1991-92	Greensboro	ECHL	2	0	0	0	14	....	....	....	....	....
	Kansas City	IHL	25	0	2	2	24	....	....	....	....	....
	Cape Breton	AHL	27	2	8	10	16	5	0	1	1	2

BLOEMBERG, JEFF (BLOOM-buhrg)

Defense. Shoots right. 6'2", 205 lbs. Born, Listowel, Ont., January 31, 1968.
(NY Rangers' 5th choice, 93rd overall, in 1986 Entry Draft).

			Regular Season					Playoffs				
Season	Club	Lea	GP	G	A	TP	PIM	GP	G	A	TP	PIM
1985-86	North Bay	OHL	60	2	11	13	76	8	1	2	3	9
1986-87	North Bay	OHL	60	5	13	18	91	21	1	6	7	13
1987-88	Colorado	IHL	5	0	0	0	0	11	1	0	1	8
	North Bay	OHL	46	9	26	35	60	4	1	4	5	2
1988-89	**NY Rangers**	**NHL**	**9**	**0**	**0**	**0**	**0**	....	....	....	....	....
	Denver	IHL	64	7	22	29	55	1	0	0	0	0
1989-90	**NY Rangers**	**NHL**	**28**	**3**	**3**	**6**	**25**	**7**	**0**	**3**	**3**	**5**
	Flint	IHL	41	7	14	21	24	....	....	....	....	....
1990-91	**NY Rangers**	**NHL**	**3**	**0**	**2**	**2**	**0**	....	....	....	....	....
a	Binghamton	AHL	77	16	46	62	28	10	0	6	6	10
1991-92	**NY Rangers**	**NHL**	**3**	**0**	**1**	**1**	**0**	....	....	....	....	....
	Binghamton	AHL	66	6	41	47	22	11	1	10	11	10
	NHL Totals		**43**	**3**	**6**	**9**	**25**	**7**	**0**	**3**	**3**	**5**

a AHL Second All-Star Team (1991)

Claimed by **Tampa Bay** from **NY Rangers** in Expansion Draft, June 18, 1992.

BLOMSTEN, ARTO (BLOOM-stehn)

Defense. Shoots left. 6'3", 191 lbs. Born, Vaasa, Finland, March 16, 1965.
(Winnipeg's 11th choice, 239th overall, in 1986 Entry Draft).

			Regular Season					Playoffs				
Season	Club	Lea	GP	G	A	TP	PIM	GP	G	A	TP	PIM
1986-87	Djurgarden	Swe.	29	2	4	6	28	....	....	....	....	....
1987-88	Djurgarden	Swe.	39	12	6	18	36	2	1	0	1	0
1988-89	Djurgarden	Swe.	40	10	9	19	38	....	....	....	....	....
1989-90	Djurgarden	Swe.	36	5	21	26	28	8	4	1	5	6
1990-91	Djurgarden	Swe.	38	2	9	11	42	....	....	....	....	....
1991-92	Djurgarden	Swe.	39	6	8	14	34	10	2	0	2	8

BLUM, JOHN JOSEPH

Defense. Shoots right. 6'3", 205 lbs. Born, Detroit, MI, October 8, 1959.

			Regular Season					Playoffs				
Season	Club	Lea	GP	G	A	TP	PIM	GP	G	A	TP	PIM
1980-81	Michigan	WCHA	38	9	43	52	93	....	....	....	....	....
1981-82	Wichita	CHL	78	8	33	41	247	7	0	3	3	24
1982-83	**Edmonton**	**NHL**	**5**	**0**	**3**	**3**	**24**	....	....	....	....	....
	Moncton	AHL	76	10	30	40	219	....	....	....	....	....
1983-84	**Edmonton**	**NHL**	**4**	**0**	**1**	**1**	**2**	....	....	....	....	....
	Moncton	AHL	57	3	22	25	202	....	....	....	....	....
	Boston	**NHL**	**12**	**1**	**1**	**2**	**30**	**3**	**0**	**0**	**0**	**4**
1984-85	**Boston**	**NHL**	**75**	**3**	**13**	**16**	**263**	**5**	**0**	**0**	**0**	**13**
1985-86	**Boston**	**NHL**	**61**	**1**	**7**	**8**	**80**	**3**	**0**	**0**	**0**	**6**
	Moncton	AHL	12	1	5	6	37	....	....	....	....	....
1986-87	**Washington**	**NHL**	**66**	**2**	**8**	**10**	**133**	**6**	**0**	**1**	**1**	**4**
1987-88	**Boston**	**NHL**	**19**	**0**	**1**	**1**	**70**	**3**	**0**	**1**	**1**	**0**
	Maine	AHL	43	5	18	23	136	8	0	6	6	35
1988-89	**Detroit**	**NHL**	**6**	**0**	**0**	**0**	**8**	....	....	....	....	....
	Adirondack	AHL	56	1	19	20	168	12	0	1	1	18
1989-90	**Boston**	**NHL**	**2**	**0**	**0**	**0**	**0**	....	....	....	....	....
	Maine	AHL	77	1	20	21	134	....	....	....	....	....
1990-91	Maine	AHL	57	4	8	12	75	1	0	0	0	2
1991-92	Capital Dist.	AHL	51	0	6	6	76	1	0	0	0	2
	NHL Totals		**250**	**7**	**34**	**41**	**610**	**20**	**0**	**2**	**2**	**27**

Signed as a free agent by **Edmonton**, May 5, 1981. Traded to **Boston** by **Edmonton** for Larry Melnyk, March 6, 1984. Claimed by **Washington** from **Boston** in NHL Waiver Draft, October 6, 1986. Traded to **Boston** by **Washington** for Boston's seventh round choice (Brad Schlegal) in 1988 Entry Draft, June 1, 1987. Signed as a free agent by **Detroit**, August 12, 1988. Signed as a free agent by **Boston**, July 6, 1989.

BOBACK, MICHAEL

Center. Shoots right. 5'11", 180 lbs. Born, Mt. Clemens, MI, August 13, 1970.
(Washington's 12th choice, 198th overall, in 1990 Entry Draft).

			Regular Season					Playoffs				
Season	Club	Lea	GP	G	A	TP	PIM	GP	G	A	TP	PIM
1988-89	Providence	H.E.	29	19	19	38	24	....	....	....	....	....
1989-90a	Providence	H.E.	31	13	29	42	28	....	....	....	....	....
1990-91	Providence	H.E.	26	15	24	39	6	....	....	....	....	....
1991-92b	Providence	H.E.	36	24	*48	*72	34	....	....	....	....	....

a Hockey East All-Star Team (1990)
b Hockey East First All-Star Team (1992)

BODE, JAMES

Right wing. Shoots right. 5'11", 183 lbs. Born, Robbinsdale, MN, July 26, 1973.
(Philadelphia's 9th choice, 182nd overall, in 1991 Entry Draft).

			Regular Season					Playoffs				
Season	Club	Lea	GP	G	A	TP	PIM	GP	G	A	TP	PIM
1990-91	Armstrong	HS	....	19	19	38	....	....	....	....	....	....
1991-92	Armstrong	HS	24	19	21	40	....	....	....	....	....	....

BODGER, DOUG

Defense. Shoots left. 6'2", 213 lbs. Born, Chemainus, B.C., June 18, 1966.
(Pittsburgh's 2nd choice, 9th overall, in 1984 Entry Draft).

			Regular Season					Playoffs				
Season	Club	Lea	GP	G	A	TP	PIM	GP	G	A	TP	PIM
1982-83a	Kamloops	WHL	72	26	66	92	98	7	0	5	5	2
1983-84	Kamloops	WHL	70	21	77	98	90	17	2	15	17	12
1984-85	**Pittsburgh**	**NHL**	**65**	**5**	**26**	**31**	**67**	....	....	....	....	....
1985-86	**Pittsburgh**	**NHL**	**79**	**4**	**33**	**37**	**63**	....	....	....	....	....
1986-87	**Pittsburgh**	**NHL**	**76**	**11**	**38**	**49**	**52**	....	....	....	....	....
1987-88	**Pittsburgh**	**NHL**	**69**	**14**	**31**	**45**	**103**	....	....	....	....	....
1988-89	**Pittsburgh**	**NHL**	**10**	**1**	**4**	**5**	**7**	....	....	....	....	....
	Buffalo	**NHL**	**61**	**7**	**40**	**47**	**52**	**5**	**1**	**1**	**2**	**11**
1989-90	**Buffalo**	**NHL**	**71**	**12**	**36**	**48**	**64**	**6**	**1**	**5**	**6**	**6**
1990-91	**Buffalo**	**NHL**	**58**	**5**	**23**	**28**	**54**	**4**	**0**	**1**	**1**	**0**
1991-92	**Buffalo**	**NHL**	**73**	**11**	**35**	**46**	**108**	**7**	**2**	**1**	**3**	**2**
	NHL Totals		**562**	**70**	**266**	**336**	**570**	**22**	**4**	**8**	**12**	**19**

a WHL Second All-Star Team (1983)

Traded to **Buffalo** by **Pittsburgh** wih Darrin Shannon for Tom Barrasso and Buffalo's third round choice (Joe Dziedzic) in 1990 Entry Draft, November 12, 1988.

BODNARCHUK, MICHAEL

Right wing. Shoots right. 6'1", 175 lbs. Born, Bramalea, Ont., March 26, 1970.
(New Jersey's 6th choice, 64th overall, in 1990 Entry Draft).

			Regular Season					Playoffs				
Season	Club	Lea	GP	G	A	TP	PIM	GP	G	A	TP	PIM
1988-89	Kingston	OHL	63	22	38	60	30	....	....	....	....	....
1989-90	Kingston	OHL	66	41	59	100	31	....	....	....	....	....
1990-91	Utica	AHL	69	23	32	55	28	....	....	....	....	....
1991-92	Utica	AHL	76	21	19	40	36	4	0	2	2	0

BOIVIN, CLAUDE

Left wing. Shoots left. 6'2", 200 lbs. Born, Ste. Foy, Que., March 1, 1970.
(Philadelphia's 1st choice, 14th overall, in 1988 Entry Draft).

			Regular Season					Playoffs				
Season	Club	Lea	GP	G	A	TP	PIM	GP	G	A	TP	PIM
1987-88	Drummondville	QMJHL	63	23	26	49	233	17	5	3	8	74
1988-89	Drummondville	QMJHL	63	20	36	56	218	4	0	2	2	27
1989-90	Laval	QMJHL	59	24	51	75	309	13	7	13	20	59
1990-91	Hershey	AHL	65	13	32	45	159	7	1	5	6	28
1991-92	**Philadelphia**	**NHL**	**58**	**5**	**13**	**18**	**187**	....	....	....	....	....
	Hershey	AHL	20	4	5	9	96	....	....	....	....	....
	NHL Totals		**58**	**5**	**13**	**18**	**187**	....	....	....	....	....

BOLDIN, IGOR

Center. Shoots left. 5'11", 174 lbs. Born, Moscow, Soviet Union, February 2, 1964.
(St. Louis' 8th choice, 180th overall, in 1992 Entry Draft).

			Regular Season					Playoffs				
Season	Club	Lea	GP	G	A	TP	PIM	GP	G	A	TP	PIM
1989-90	Spartak	USSR	45	13	18	31	8	....	....	....	....	....
1990-91	Spartak	USSR	43	8	15	23	8	....	....	....	....	....
1991-92	Spartak	CIS	41	8	*25	33	4	....	....	....	....	....

BOMBARDIR, BRAD

Defense. Shoots left. 6'2", 190 lbs. Born, Powell River, B.C., May 5, 1972.
(New Jersey's 5th choice, 56th overall, in 1990 Entry Draft).

			Regular Season					Playoffs				
Season	Club	Lea	GP	G	A	TP	PIM	GP	G	A	TP	PIM
1990-91	North Dakota	WCHA	33	3	6	9	18	....	....	....	....	....
1991-92	North Dakota	WCHA	35	3	14	17	54	....	....	....	....	....

BONDRA, PETER

Right wing. Shoots left. 6', 200 lbs. Born, Luck, Soviet Union, February 7, 1968.
(Washington's 9th choice, 156th overall, in 1990 Entry Draft).

			Regular Season					Playoffs				
Season	Club	Lea	GP	G	A	TP	PIM	GP	G	A	TP	PIM
1988-89	VSZ Kosice	Czech.	40	30	10	40	20	....	....	....	....	....
1989-90	VSZ Kosice	Czech.	42	29	17	46	....	....	....	....	....	....
1990-91	**Washington**	**NHL**	**54**	**12**	**16**	**28**	**47**	**4**	**0**	**1**	**1**	**2**
1991-92	**Washington**	**NHL**	**71**	**28**	**28**	**56**	**42**	**7**	**6**	**2**	**8**	**4**
	NHL Totals		**125**	**40**	**44**	**84**	**89**	**11**	**6**	**3**	**9**	**6**

BONNER, JAMES

Defense. Shoots left. 6', 195 lbs. Born, Grand Rapids, MN, November 17, 1970.
(NY Islanders' 1st choice, 4th overall, in 1991 Supplemental Draft).

			Regular Season					Playoffs				
Season	Club	Lea	GP	G	A	TP	PIM	GP	G	A	TP	PIM
1989-90	Michigan Tech	WCHA	36	3	3	6	32	....	....	....	....	....
1990-91	Michigan Tech	WCHA	37	1	1	2	30	....	....	....	....	....
1991-92	Michigan Tech	WCHA	10	0	0	0	14	....	....	....	....	....

BORGO, RICHARD

Right wing. Shoots right. 5'11", 190 lbs. Born, Thunder Bay, Ont., September 25, 1970.
(Edmonton's 2nd choice, 36th overall, in 1989 Entry Draft).

			Regular Season					Playoffs				
Season	Club	Lea	GP	G	A	TP	PIM	GP	G	A	TP	PIM
1986-87	Kitchener	OHL	62	5	10	15	29	....	....	....	....	....
1987-88	Kitchener	OHL	64	24	22	46	81	4	0	4	4	0
1988-89	Kitchener	OHL	66	23	23	46	75	5	0	1	1	4
1989-90	Kitchener	OHL	32	13	22	35	43	17	5	5	10	10
1990-91	Kitchener	OHL	60	43	56	99	50	6	1	0	1	12
1991-92	Cape Breton	AHL	52	10	14	24	90	3	0	0	0	6

BORSATO, LUCIANO

Center. Shoots right. 5'10", 165 lbs. Born, Richmond Hill, Ont., January 7, 1966.
(Winnipeg's 7th choice, 135th overall, in 1984 Entry Draft).

			Regular Season					Playoffs				
Season	Club	Lea	GP	G	A	TP	PIM	GP	G	A	TP	PIM
1984-85	Clarkson	ECAC	33	15	17	32	37	....	....	....	....	....
1985-86	Clarkson	ECAC	28	14	17	31	44	....	....	....	....	....
1986-87	Clarkson	ECAC	31	16	41	57	55	....	....	....	....	....
1987-88ab	Clarkson	ECAC	33	15	29	44	38	....	....	....	....	....
	Moncton	AHL	3	1	1	2	0	....	....	....	....	....
1988-89	Moncton	AHL	6	2	5	7	4	....	....	....	....	....
	Tappara	Fin.	44	31	36	67	69	7	0	3	3	4
1989-90	Moncton	AHL	1	1	0	1	0	....	....	....	....	....
1990-91	**Winnipeg**	**NHL**	**1**	**0**	**1**	**1**	**2**	....	....	....	....	....
	Moncton	AHL	41	14	24	38	40	9	3	7	10	22
1991-92	**Winnipeg**	**NHL**	**56**	**15**	**21**	**36**	**45**	**1**	**0**	**0**	**0**	**0**
	Moncton	AHL	14	2	7	9	39	....	....	....	....	....
	NHL Totals		**57**	**15**	**22**	**37**	**47**	**1**	**0**	**0**	**0**	**0**

a ECAC Second All-Star Team (1988)
b NCAA East Second All-American Team (1988)

BORSCHEVSKY, NIKOLAI

Right wing. Shoots left. 5'9", 180 lbs. Born, Tomsk, Soviet Union, January 12, 1965.
(Toronto's 3rd choice, 77th overall, in 1992 Entry Draft).

			Regular Season					Playoffs				
Season	Club	Lea	GP	G	A	TP	PIM	GP	G	A	TP	PIM
1990-91	Spartak	USSR	45	19	16	35	16	....	....	....	....	....
1991-92	Spartak	CIS	40	25	14	39	16	....	....	....	....	....

BOSCHMAN, LAURIE JOSEPH (BOSH-man)

Center. Shoots left. 6', 185 lbs. Born, Major, Sask., June 4, 1960.
(Toronto's 1st choice, 9th overall, in 1979 Entry Draft).

			Regular Season					Playoffs				
Season	Club	Lea	GP	G	A	TP	PIM	GP	G	A	TP	PIM
1976-77	Brandon	WHL	3	0	1	1	0	12	1	1	2	17
1977-78	Brandon	WHL	72	42	57	99	227	8	2	5	7	45
1978-79a	Brandon	WHL	65	66	83	149	215	22	11	23	34	56
1979-80	**Toronto**	**NHL**	**80**	**16**	**32**	**48**	**78**	**3**	**1**	**1**	**2**	**18**
1980-81	**Toronto**	**NHL**	**53**	**14**	**19**	**33**	**178**	**3**	**0**	**0**	**0**	**7**
	New Brunswick	AHL	4	4	1	5	47	....	....	....	....	....
1981-82	**Toronto**	**NHL**	**54**	**9**	**19**	**28**	**150**	....	....	....	....	....
	Edmonton	**NHL**	**11**	**2**	**3**	**5**	**37**	**3**	**0**	**1**	**1**	**4**
1982-83	**Edmonton**	**NHL**	**62**	**8**	**12**	**20**	**183**	....	....	....	....	....
	Winnipeg	**NHL**	**12**	**3**	**5**	**8**	**36**	**3**	**0**	**1**	**1**	**12**
1983-84	**Winnipeg**	**NHL**	**61**	**28**	**46**	**74**	**234**	**3**	**0**	**1**	**1**	**5**
1984-85	**Winnipeg**	**NHL**	**80**	**32**	**44**	**76**	**180**	**8**	**2**	**1**	**3**	**21**
1985-86	**Winnipeg**	**NHL**	**77**	**27**	**42**	**69**	**241**	**3**	**0**	**1**	**1**	**6**
1986-87	**Winnipeg**	**NHL**	**80**	**17**	**24**	**41**	**152**	**10**	**2**	**3**	**5**	**32**
1987-88	**Winnipeg**	**NHL**	**80**	**25**	**23**	**48**	**229**	**5**	**1**	**3**	**4**	**9**
1988-89	**Winnipeg**	**NHL**	**70**	**10**	**26**	**36**	**163**	....	....	....	....	....
1989-90	**Winnipeg**	**NHL**	**66**	**10**	**17**	**27**	**103**	**2**	**0**	**0**	**0**	**2**
1990-91	**New Jersey**	**NHL**	**78**	**11**	**9**	**20**	**79**	**7**	**1**	**1**	**2**	**16**
1991-92	**New Jersey**	**NHL**	**75**	**8**	**20**	**28**	**121**	**7**	**1**	**0**	**1**	**8**
	NHL Totals		**939**	**220**	**341**	**561**	**2164**	**57**	**8**	**13**	**21**	**140**

a WHL First All-Star Team (1979)

Traded to **Edmonton** by **Toronto** for Walt Poddubny and Phil Drouilliard, March 8, 1982. Traded to **Winnipeg** by **Edmonton** for Willy Lindstrom, March 7, 1983. Traded to **New Jersey** by **Winnipeg** for Bob Brooke, September 6, 1990. Claimed by **Ottawa** from **New Jersey** in Expansion Draft, June 18, 1992.

BOUCHARD, JOEL

Defense. Shoots left. 6', 180 lbs. Born, Montreal, Que., January 23, 1974.
(Calgary's 7th choice, 129th overall, in 1992 Entry Draft).

			Regular Season					Playoffs				
Season	Club	Lea	GP	G	A	TP	PIM	GP	G	A	TP	PIM
1990-91	Longueuil	QMJHL	53	3	19	22	34	8	1	0	1	11
1991-92	Verdun	QMJHL	70	9	20	29	55	19	1	7	8	20

BOUCHER, PHILIPPE

Defense. Shoots right. 6'2", 189 lbs. Born, St. Apollinaire, Que., March 24, 1973.
(Buffalo's 1st choice, 13th overall, in 1991 Entry Draft).

			Regular Season					Playoffs				
Season	Club	Lea	GP	G	A	TP	PIM	GP	G	A	TP	PIM
1990-91ab	Granby	QMJHL	69	21	46	67	92	....	....	....	....	....
1991-92	Granby	QMJHL	49	22	37	59	47	....	....	....	....	....
b	Laval	QMJHL	16	7	11	18	36	10	5	6	11	8

a Canadian Major Junior Rookie of the Year (1991)
b QMJHL Second All-Star Team (1991, 1992)

BOUDREAU, BRUCE ALLAN (BOO-droh)

Center. Shoots left. 5'9", 170 lbs. Born, Toronto, Ont., January 9, 1955.
(Toronto's 3rd choice, 42nd overall, in 1975 Amateur Draft).

			Regular Season					Playoffs				
Season	Club	Lea	GP	G	A	TP	PIM	GP	G	A	TP	PIM
1973-74	Toronto	OMJHL	53	46	67	113	51	....	....	....	....	....
1974-75	Toronto	OMJHL	69	*68	97	*165	52	22	12	*28	40	26
1975-76	Minnesota	WHA	30	3	6	9	4	....	....	....	....	....
	Johnstown	NAHL	34	25	35	60	14	....	....	....	....	....
1976-77	**Toronto**	**NHL**	**15**	**2**	**5**	**7**	**4**	**3**	**0**	**0**	**0**	**0**
	Dallas	CHL	58	*37	34	71	40	1	1	1	2	0
1977-78	**Toronto**	**NHL**	**40**	**11**	**18**	**29**	**12**	....	....	....	....	....
	Dallas	CHL	22	13	9	22	11	....	....	....	....	....
1978-79	**Toronto**	**NHL**	**26**	**4**	**3**	**7**	**2**	....	....	....	....	....
	New Brunswick	AHL	49	20	38	58	20	5	1	1	2	8
1979-80	**Toronto**	**NHL**	**2**	**0**	**0**	**0**	**2**	....	....	....	....	....
	New Brunswick	AHL	75	36	54	90	47	17	6	7	13	23
1980-81	**Toronto**	**NHL**	**39**	**10**	**14**	**24**	**18**	**2**	**1**	**0**	**1**	**0**
	New Brunswick	AHL	40	17	41	58	22	8	6	5	11	14
1981-82	**Toronto**	**NHL**	**12**	**0**	**2**	**2**	**6**	....	....	....	....	....
	Cincinnati	CHL	65	42	61	103	42	4	3	1	4	8
1982-83	St. Catharines	AHL	80	50	72	122	65	....	....	....	....	....
	Toronto	**NHL**	....	....	....	....	....	**4**	**1**	**0**	**1**	**0**
1983-84	St. Catharines	AHL	80	47	62	109	44	7	0	5	5	11
1984-85	Baltimore	AHL	17	4	7	11	4	15	3	9	12	4
1985-86	**Chicago**	**NHL**	**7**	**1**	**0**	**1**	**2**	....	....	....	....	....
	Nova Scotia	AHL	65	30	36	66	36	....	....	....	....	....
1986-87	Nova Scotia	AHL	78	35	47	82	40	5	3	3	6	4
1987-88abc	Springfield	AHL	80	42	*74	*116	84	....	....	....	....	....
1988-89	Springfield	AHL	50	28	36	64	42	....	....	....	....	....
	Newmarket	AHL	20	7	16	23	12	4	0	1	1	6
1989-90	Phoenix	IHL	82	41	68	109	89	....	....	....	....	....
1990-91	Fort Wayne	IHL	81	40	*80	120	111	19	11	7	18	30
1991-92	Fort Wayne	IHL	77	34	50	84	100	7	3	4	7	10
	Adirondack	AHL	....	....	....	....	....	4	1	1	2	2
	NHL Totals		**141**	**28**	**42**	**70**	**46**	**9**	**2**	**0**	**2**	**0**

a AHL First All-Star Team (1988)
b Won Fred Hunt Award (Sportsmanship-AHL) (1988)
c Won John Sollenberger Trophy (Top Scorer-AHL) (1988)

Claimed by **Toronto** as fill in Expansion Draft, June 13, 1979. Signed as a free agent by **Chicago**, October 10, 1985.

BOUGHNER, BOB (BOOG-nuhr)

Defense. Shoots right. 5'11", 201 lbs. Born, Windsor, Ont., March 8, 1971.
(Detroit's 2nd choice, 32nd overall, in 1989 Entry Draft).

			Regular Season					Playoffs				
Season	Club	Lea	GP	G	A	TP	PIM	GP	G	A	TP	PIM
1988-89	S.S. Marie	OHL	64	6	15	21	182	....	....	....	....	....
1989-90	S.S. Marie	OHL	49	7	23	30	122	....	....	....	....	....
1990-91	S.S. Marie	OHL	64	13	33	46	156	14	2	9	11	35
1991-92	Toledo	ECHL	28	3	10	13	79	5	2	0	2	15
	Adirondack	AHL	1	0	0	0	7	....	....	....	....	....

BOURQUE, PHILLIPPE RICHARD (PHIL) (BOHRK)

Left wing. Shoots left. 6'1", 196 lbs. Born, Chelmsford, MA, June 8, 1962.

			Regular Season					Playoffs				
Season	Club	Lea	GP	G	A	TP	PIM	GP	G	A	TP	PIM
1980-81	Kingston	OHL	47	4	4	8	46	6	0	0	0	10
1981-82	Kingston	OHL	67	11	40	51	111	4	0	0	0	0
1982-83	Baltimore	AHL	65	1	15	16	93	....	....	....	....	....
1983-84	**Pittsburgh**	**NHL**	**5**	**0**	**1**	**1**	**12**	....	....	....	....	....
	Baltimore	AHL	58	5	17	22	96	....	....	....	....	....
1984-85	Baltimore	AHL	79	6	15	21	164	13	2	5	7	23
1985-86	**Pittsburgh**	**NHL**	**4**	**0**	**0**	**0**	**2**	....	....	....	....	....
	Baltimore	AHL	74	8	18	26	226	....	....	....	....	....
1986-87	**Pittsburgh**	**NHL**	**22**	**2**	**3**	**5**	**32**	....	....	....	....	....
	Baltimore	AHL	49	15	16	31	183	....	....	....	....	....
1987-88	**Pittsburgh**	**NHL**	**21**	**4**	**12**	**16**	**20**	....	....	....	....	....
ab	Muskegon	IHL	52	16	36	52	66	6	1	2	3	16
1988-89	**Pittsburgh**	**NHL**	**80**	**17**	**26**	**43**	**97**	**11**	**4**	**1**	**5**	**66**
1989-90	**Pittsburgh**	**NHL**	**76**	**22**	**17**	**39**	**108**	....	....	....	....	....
1990-91	**Pittsburgh**	**NHL**	**78**	**20**	**14**	**34**	**106**	**24**	**6**	**7**	**13**	**16**
1991-92	**Pittsburgh**	**NHL**	**58**	**10**	**16**	**26**	**58**	**21**	**3**	**4**	**7**	**25**
	NHL Totals		**344**	**75**	**89**	**164**	**435**	**56**	**13**	**12**	**25**	**107**

a IHL First All-Star Team (1988)
b Won Governor's Trophy (Outstanding Defenseman-IHL) (1988)

Signed as a free agent by **Pittsburgh**, October 4, 1982.

BOURQUE, RAYMOND JEAN (BOHRK)

Defense. Shoots left. 5'11", 210 lbs. Born, Montreal, Que., December 28, 1960.
(Boston's 1st choice, 8th overall, in 1979 Entry Draft).

			Regular Season					Playoffs				
Season	Club	Lea	GP	G	A	TP	PIM	GP	G	A	TP	PIM
1976-77	Sorel	QJHL	69	12	36	48	61	....	....	....	....	....
1977-78	Verdun	QJHL	72	22	57	79	90	4	2	1	3	0
1978-79	Verdun	QJHL	63	22	71	93	44	11	3	16	19	18
1979-80ab	**Boston**	**NHL**	**80**	**17**	**48**	**65**	**73**	**10**	**2**	**9**	**11**	**27**
1980-81c	**Boston**	**NHL**	**67**	**27**	**29**	**56**	**96**	**3**	**0**	**1**	**1**	**2**
1981-82b	**Boston**	**NHL**	**65**	**17**	**49**	**66**	**51**	**9**	**1**	**5**	**6**	**16**
1982-83c	**Boston**	**NHL**	**65**	**22**	**51**	**73**	**20**	**17**	**8**	**15**	**23**	**10**
1983-84b	**Boston**	**NHL**	**78**	**31**	**65**	**96**	**57**	**3**	**0**	**2**	**2**	**0**
1984-85b	**Boston**	**NHL**	**73**	**20**	**66**	**86**	**53**	**5**	**0**	**3**	**3**	**4**
1985-86c	**Boston**	**NHL**	**74**	**19**	**58**	**77**	**68**	**3**	**0**	**0**	**0**	**0**
1986-87bd	**Boston**	**NHL**	**78**	**23**	**72**	**95**	**36**	**4**	**1**	**2**	**3**	**0**
1987-88bd	**Boston**	**NHL**	**78**	**17**	**64**	**81**	**72**	**23**	**3**	**18**	**21**	**26**
1988-89c	**Boston**	**NHL**	**60**	**18**	**43**	**61**	**52**	**10**	**0**	**4**	**4**	**6**
1989-90bd	**Boston**	**NHL**	**76**	**19**	**65**	**84**	**50**	**17**	**5**	**12**	**17**	**16**
1990-91bd	**Boston**	**NHL**	**76**	**21**	**73**	**94**	**75**	**19**	**7**	**18**	**25**	**12**
1991-92be	**Boston**	**NHL**	**80**	**21**	**60**	**81**	**56**	**12**	**3**	**6**	**9**	**12**
	NHL Totals		**950**	**272**	**743**	**1015**	**759**	**135**	**30**	**95**	**125**	**131**

a Won Calder Memorial Trophy (1980)
b NHL First All-Star Team (1980, 1982, 1984, 1985, 1987, 1988, 1990, 1991, 1992)
c NHL Second All-Star Team (1981, 1983, 1986, 1989)
d Won James Norris Memorial Trophy (1987, 1988, 1990, 1991)
e Won King Clancy Memorial Trophy (1992)

Played in NHL All-Star Game (1981-86, 1988-92)

BOWEN, CURTIS

Left wing. Shoots left. 6'1", 189 lbs. Born, Kenora, Ont., March 24, 1974.
(Detroit's 1st choice, 22nd overall, in 1992 Entry Draft).

			Regular Season					Playoffs				
Season	Club	Lea	GP	G	A	TP	PIM	GP	G	A	TP	PIM
1990-91	Ottawa	OHL	42	12	14	26	31	....	....	....	....	....
1991-92	Ottawa	OHL	65	31	45	76	94	11	3	7	10	11

BOWEN, JASON

Left wing. Shoots left. 6'4", 210 lbs. Born, Port Alice, B.C., November 11, 1973.
(Philadelphia's 2nd choice, 15th overall, in 1992 Entry Draft).

			Regular Season					Playoffs				
Season	Club	Lea	GP	G	A	TP	PIM	GP	G	A	TP	PIM
1990-91	Tri-Cities	WHL	60	7	13	20	252	6	2	2	4	18
1991-92	Tri-Cities	WHL	19	5	3	8	135	5	0	1	1	42

BOYER, ZAC

Right wing. Shoots right. 6'1", 185 lbs. Born, Inuvik, N.W.T., October 25, 1971.
(Chicago's 4th choice, 88th overall, in 1991 Entry Draft).

			Regular Season					Playoffs				
Season	Club	Lea	GP	G	A	TP	PIM	GP	G	A	TP	PIM
1990-91	Kamloops	WHL	64	45	60	105	58	12	6	10	16	8
1991-92	Kamloops	WHL	70	40	69	109	90	17	9	*20	*29	16

BOZON, PHILIPPE

Left wing. Shoots left. 5'10", 175 lbs. Born, Chamonix, France, November 30, 1966.

Season	Club	Lea	Regular Season GP	G	A	TP	PIM	Playoffs GP	G	A	TP	PIM
1984-85	St-Jean	QMJHL	67	32	50	82	82	5	0	5	5	4
1985-86a	St-Jean	QMJHL	65	59	52	111	72	10	10	6	16	16
	Peoria	IHL	....	....	....	....	....	5	1	0	1	0
1986-87	Peoria	IHL	28	4	11	15	17	....	....	....	....	....
	St-Jean	QMJHL	25	20	21	41	75	8	5	5	10	30
1987-88	Mont-Blanc	France	18	11	15	26	34	10	15	6	21	6
1988-89			DID NOT PLAY									
1989-90	Grenoble	France	36	45	38	83	34	....	....	....	....	....
1990-91	Grenoble	France	UNAVAILABLE									
1991-92	Chamonix	France	10	12	8	20	20	....	....	....	....	....
	French Oly.	....	7	3	2	5	4	....	....	....	....	....
	St. Louis	**NHL**	**9**	**1**	**3**	**4**	**4**	**6**	**1**	**0**	**1**	**27**
	NHL Totals		**9**	**1**	**3**	**4**	**4**	**6**	**1**	**0**	**1**	**27**

a QMJHL Second All-Star Team (1986)

Signed as a free agent by **St. Louis**, September 29, 1985.

BRADLEY, BRIAN WALTER RICHARD

Center. Shoots right. 5'10", 177 lbs. Born, Kitchener, Ont., January 21, 1965.
(Calgary's 2nd choice, 51st overall, in 1983 Entry Draft).

Season	Club	Lea	Regular Season GP	G	A	TP	PIM	Playoffs GP	G	A	TP	PIM
1982-83	London	OHL	67	37	82	119	37	3	1	0	1	0
1983-84	London	OHL	49	40	60	100	24	4	2	4	6	0
1984-85	London	OHL	32	27	49	76	22	8	5	10	15	4
1985-86	**Calgary**	**NHL**	**5**	**0**	**1**	**1**	**0**	**1**	**0**	**0**	**0**	**0**
	Moncton	AHL	59	23	42	65	40	10	6	9	15	4
1986-87	**Calgary**	**NHL**	**40**	**10**	**18**	**28**	**16**	....	....	....	....	....
	Moncton	AHL	20	12	16	28	8	....	....	....	....	....
1987-88	Cdn. National	....	47	8	19	37	42	....	....	....	....	....
	Cdn. Olympic	....	7	0	4	4	0	....	....	....	....	....
	Vancouver	**NHL**	**11**	**3**	**5**	**8**	**6**	....	....	....	....	....
1988-89	**Vancouver**	**NHL**	**71**	**18**	**27**	**45**	**42**	**7**	**3**	**4**	**7**	**10**
1989-90	**Vancouver**	**NHL**	**67**	**19**	**29**	**48**	**65**	....	....	....	....	....
1990-91	**Vancouver**	**NHL**	**44**	**11**	**20**	**31**	**42**	....	....	....	....	....
	Toronto	**NHL**	**26**	**0**	**11**	**11**	**20**	....	....	....	....	....
1991-92	**Toronto**	**NHL**	**59**	**10**	**21**	**31**	**48**	....	....	....	....	....
	NHL Totals		**323**	**71**	**132**	**203**	**239**	**8**	**3**	**4**	**7**	**10**

Traded to **Vancouver** by **Calgary** with Peter Bakovic and Kevin Guy for Craig Coxe, March 6, 1988. Traded to **Toronto** by **Vancouver** for Tom Kurvers, January 12, 1991. Claimed by **Tampa Bay** from **Toronto** in Expansion Draft, June 18, 1992.

BRADY, NEIL

Center. Shoots left. 6'2", 200 lbs. Born, Montreal, Que., April 12, 1968.
(New Jersey's 1st choice, 3rd overall, in 1986 Entry Draft).

Season	Club	Lea	Regular Season GP	G	A	TP	PIM	Playoffs GP	G	A	TP	PIM
1984-85	Calgary	Midget	37	25	50	75	75	....	....	....	....	....
	Medicine Hat	WHL	....	....	....	....	....	3	0	0	0	2
1985-86a	Medicine Hat	WHL	72	21	60	81	104	21	9	11	20	23
1986-87	Medicine Hat	WHL	57	19	64	83	126	18	1	4	5	25
1987-88	Medicine Hat	WHL	61	16	35	51	110	15	0	3	3	19
1988-89	Utica	AHL	75	16	21	37	56	4	0	3	3	0
1989-90	**New Jersey**	**NHL**	**19**	**1**	**4**	**5**	**13**	....	....	....	....	....
	Utica	AHL	38	10	13	23	21	5	0	1	1	10
1990-91	**New Jersey**	**NHL**	**3**	**0**	**0**	**0**	**0**	....	....	....	....	....
	Utica	AHL	77	33	63	96	91	....	....	....	....	....
1991-92	**New Jersey**	**NHL**	**7**	**1**	**0**	**1**	**4**	....	....	....	....	....
	Utica	AHL	33	12	30	42	28	....	....	....	....	....
	NHL Totals		**29**	**2**	**4**	**6**	**17**	....	....	....	....	....

a WHL Rookie of the Year (1986)

BRAIT, MATTHEW

Defense. Shoots left. 6'2", 210 lbs. Born, Toronto, Ont., June 29, 1969.
(Philadelphia's 9th choice, 222nd overall, in 1989 Entry Draft).

Season	Club	Lea	Regular Season GP	G	A	TP	PIM	Playoffs GP	G	A	TP	PIM
1989-90	Kent State	NCAA	30	4	8	12	81	....	....	....	....	....
1990-91	Kent State	NCAA	24	2	3	5	92	....	....	....	....	....
1991-92	Kent State	NCAA	30	0	5	5	68	....	....	....	....	....

BRAUER, CAM

Defense. Shoots left. 6'3", 210 lbs. Born, Calgary, Alta., January 4, 1970.
(Edmonton's 5th choice, 82nd overall, in 1988 Entry Draft).

Season	Club	Lea	Regular Season GP	G	A	TP	PIM	Playoffs GP	G	A	TP	PIM
1987-88	RPI	ECAC	18	0	1	1	4	....	....	....	....	....
1988-89	Regina	WHL	49	0	9	9	59	....	....	....	....	....
1989-90	Regina	WHL	4	0	0	0	20	....	....	....	....	....
a	Seattle	WHL	64	1	9	10	229	10	0	0	0	27
1990-91	Springfield	AHL	45	0	1	1	65	....	....	....	....	....
	Louisville	ECHL	5	0	1	1	9	....	....	....	....	....
1991-92	Louisville	ECHL	44	2	10	12	182	13	0	1	1	28
	Springfield	AHL	5	0	0	0	6	....	....	....	....	....

a WHL West Second All-Star Team (1990)

Rights traded to **Hartford** by **Edmonton** for Mark Laforge, March 6, 1990.

BRAZDA, RADOMIR (BRAHZ-duh)

Defense. Shoots right. 6'2", 175 lbs. Born, Pardubice, Czechoslovakia, October 11, 1967.
(Detroit's 6th choice, 95th overall, in 1987 Entry Draft).

Season	Club	Lea	Regular Season GP	G	A	TP	PIM	Playoffs GP	G	A	TP	PIM
1986-87	Pardubice	Czech.	31	1	1	2	....	....	....	....	....	....
1987-88	Pardubice	Czech.	11	1	2	3	....	....	....	....	....	....
1988-89	Dukla Trencin	Czech.	35	1	1	2	....	....	....	....	....	....
1989-90	Pardubice	Czech.	26	2	1	3	....	....	....	....	....	....
1990-91	Pardubice	Czech.	40	5	11	16	24	....	....	....	....	....
1991-92	Pardubice	Czech.	42	4	9	13	....	....	....	....	....	....

BREAULT, FRANCOIS

Right wing. Shoots left. 5'11", 185 lbs. Born, Acton Vale, Que., May 11, 1967.

Season	Club	Lea	Regular Season GP	G	A	TP	PIM	Playoffs GP	G	A	TP	PIM
1986-87	Granby	QMJHL	60	24	33	57	134	....	....	....	....	....
1987-88	Trois-Rivières	QMJHL	28	16	19	35	108	....	....	....	....	....
	Maine	AHL	11	0	1	1	37	....	....	....	....	....
1988-89	New Haven	AHL	68	21	24	45	51	....	....	....	....	....
1989-90	New Haven	AHL	37	17	21	38	33	....	....	....	....	....
1990-91	**Los Angeles**	**NHL**	**17**	**1**	**4**	**5**	**6**	....	....	....	....	....
1991-92	**Los Angeles**	**NHL**	**6**	**1**	**0**	**1**	**30**	....	....	....	....	....
	Phoenix	IHL	54	14	19	33	40	....	....	....	....	....
	NHL Totals		**23**	**2**	**4**	**6**	**36**	....	....	....	....	....

Signed as a free agent by **Los Angeles**, July, 1988.

BREEN, GEORGE

Right wing. Shoots right. 6'2", 200 lbs. Born, Webster, MA, August 3, 1973.
(Edmonton's 4th choice, 56th overall, in 1991 Entry Draft).

Season	Club	Lea	Regular Season GP	G	A	TP	PIM	Playoffs GP	G	A	TP	PIM
1989-90	Cushing Aca.	HS	20	9	8	17	....	....	....	....	....	....
1991-92	Providence	H.E.	36	8	4	12	24	....	....	....	....	....

BREKKE, BRENT

Defense. Shoots left. 6'1", 175 lbs. Born, Minot, ND, August 16, 1971.
(Quebec's 9th choice, 188th overall, in 1991 Entry Draft).

Season	Club	Lea	Regular Season GP	G	A	TP	PIM	Playoffs GP	G	A	TP	PIM
1990-91	W. Michigan	CCHA	38	1	8	9	57	....	....	....	....	....
1991-92	W. Michigan	CCHA	36	1	10	11	68	....	....	....	....	....

BRENNAN, RICHARD

Defense. Shoots right. 6'2", 200 lbs. Born, Schnectady, NY, November 26, 1972.
(Quebec's 3rd choice, 46th overall, in 1991 Entry Draft).

Season	Club	Lea	Regular Season GP	G	A	TP	PIM	Playoffs GP	G	A	TP	PIM
1990-91	Tabor Aca.	HS	34	13	37	50	91	....	....	....	....	....
1991-92	Boston U.	H.E.	30	4	13	17	50	....	....	....	....	....

BRESLIN, TIM

Left wing. Shoots left. 6', 180 lbs. Born, Downers Grove, IL, December 8, 1967.

Season	Club	Lea	Regular Season GP	G	A	TP	PIM	Playoffs GP	G	A	TP	PIM
1990-91	Lake Superior	CCHA	45	25	37	62	26	....	....	....	....	....
1991-92	Phoenix	IHL	45	8	21	29	12	....	....	....	....	....

Signed as a free agent by **Los Angeles**, July 16, 1992.

BREWER, MIKE

Center. Shoots left. 5'10", 175 lbs. Born, Chestwick, Ont., April 13, 1969.
(Washington's 1st choice, 20th overall, in 1991 Supplemental Draft).

Season	Club	Lea	Regular Season GP	G	A	TP	PIM	Playoffs GP	G	A	TP	PIM
1988-89	Brown	ECAC	23	5	8	13	10	....	....	....	....	....
1989-90a	Brown	ECAC	29	7	24	31	64	....	....	....	....	....
1990-91b	Brown	ECAC	21	4	18	22	44	....	....	....	....	....
1991-92ac	Brown	ECAC	28	13	34	47	62	....	....	....	....	....

a ECAC First All-Star Team (1990, 1992)
b ECAC Second All-Star Team (1991)
c NCAA East First All-Star Team (1992)

BRICKLEY, ANDY

Left wing/Center. Shoots left. 5'11", 200 lbs. Born, Melrose, MA, August 9, 1961.
(Philadelphia's 10th choice, 210th overall, in 1980 Entry Draft).

Season	Club	Lea	Regular Season GP	G	A	TP	PIM	Playoffs GP	G	A	TP	PIM
1979-80	N. Hampshire	ECAC	27	15	17	32	8	....	....	....	....	....
1980-81	N. Hampshire	ECAC	31	27	25	52	16	....	....	....	....	....
1981-82ab	N. Hampshire	ECAC	35	26	27	53	6	....	....	....	....	....
1982-83	**Philadelphia**	**NHL**	**3**	**1**	**1**	**2**	**0**	....	....	....	....	....
c	Maine	AHL	76	29	54	83	10	17	9	5	14	0
1983-84	Springfield	AHL	7	1	5	6	2	....	....	....	....	....
	Pittsburgh	**NHL**	**50**	**18**	**20**	**38**	**9**	....	....	....	....	....
	Baltimore	AHL	4	0	5	5	2	....	....	....	....	....
1984-85	**Pittsburgh**	**NHL**	**45**	**7**	**15**	**22**	**10**	....	....	....	....	....
	Baltimore	AHL	31	13	14	27	8	15	*10	8	18	0
1985-86	Maine	AHL	60	26	34	60	20	5	0	4	4	0
1986-87	**New Jersey**	**NHL**	**51**	**11**	**12**	**23**	**8**	....	....	....	....	....
1987-88	**New Jersey**	**NHL**	**45**	**8**	**14**	**22**	**14**	**4**	**0**	**1**	**1**	**4**
	Utica	AHL	9	5	8	13	4	....	....	....	....	....
1988-89	**Boston**	**NHL**	**71**	**13**	**22**	**35**	**20**	**10**	**0**	**2**	**2**	**0**
1989-90	**Boston**	**NHL**	**43**	**12**	**28**	**40**	**8**	**2**	**0**	**0**	**0**	**0**
1990-91	**Boston**	**NHL**	**40**	**2**	**9**	**11**	**8**	....	....	....	....	....
	Maine	AHL	17	8	17	25	2	1	0	0	0	0
1991-92	**Boston**	**NHL**	**23**	**10**	**17**	**27**	**2**	....	....	....	....	....
	Maine	AHL	14	5	15	20	2	....	....	....	....	....
	NHL Totals		**371**	**82**	**138**	**220**	**79**	**16**	**0**	**3**	**3**	**4**

a ECAC First All-Star Team (1982)
b NCAA All-American Team (1982)
c AHL Second All-Star Team (1983)

Traded to **Pittsburgh** by **Philadelphia** with Mark Taylor, Ron Flockhart, Philadephia's first round (Roger Belanger) and third round (Mike Stevens — later transferred to Vancouver) choices in 1984 Entry Draft for Rich Sutter and Pittsburgh's second round (Greg Smyth) and third round (David McLay) choices in 1984 Entry Draft, October 23, 1983. Signed as a free agent by **New Jersey**, July 8, 1986. Claimed by **Boston** in NHL Waiver Draft, October 3, 1988,

BRIGHT, CHRIS

Center. Shoots left. 6', 185 lbs. Born, Guelph, Ont., October 14, 1970.
(Hartford's 4th choice, 78th overall, in 1990 Entry Draft).

			Regular Season					Playoffs				
Season	Club	Lea	GP	G	A	TP	PIM	GP	G	A	TP	PIM
1987-88	Moose Jaw	WHL	20	2	2	4	10	....	....	....	....	....
1988-89	Moose Jaw	WHL	71	18	27	45	61	7	2	0	0	6
1989-90	Moose Jaw	WHL	72	36	38	74	107	....	....	....	....	....
1990-91	Springfield	AHL	37	3	4	7	32	....	....	....	....	....
1991-92	Louisville	ECHL	46	17	39	56	61	13	9	8	17	18
	Springfield	AHL	8	1	0	1	6	....	....	....	....	....

BRILL, JOHN

Right wing. Shoots left. 6'3", 180 lbs. Born, St. Paul, MN, December 3, 1970.
(Pittsburgh's 3rd choice, 58th overall, in 1989 Entry Draft).

			Regular Season					Playoffs				
Season	Club	Lea	GP	G	A	TP	PIM	GP	G	A	TP	PIM
1989-90	U. Minnesota	WCHA	34	2	8	10	22	....	....	....	....	....
1990-91	U. Minnesota	WCHA	44	6	13	19	36	....	....	....	....	....
1991-92	U. Minnesota	WCHA	35	7	9	16	46	....	....	....	....	....

BRIMANIS, ARIS

Defense. Shoots right. 6'3", 195 lbs. Born, Cleveland, OH, March 14, 1972.
(Philadelphia's 4th choice, 86th overall, in 1991 Entry Draft).

			Regular Season					Playoffs				
Season	Club	Lea	GP	G	A	TP	PIM	GP	G	A	TP	PIM
1990-91	Bowling Green	CCHA	38	3	6	9	42	....	....	....	....	....
1991-92	Bowling Green	CCHA	32	2	9	11	38	....	....	....	....	....

BRIND'AMOUR, ROD

Center. Shoots left. 6'1", 202 lbs. Born, Ottawa, Ont., August 9, 1970.
(St. Louis' 1st choice, 9th overall, in 1988 Entry Draft).

			Regular Season					Playoffs				
Season	Club	Lea	GP	G	A	TP	PIM	GP	G	A	TP	PIM
1988-89a	Michigan State	CCHA	42	27	32	59	63	....	....	....	....	....
	St. Louis	NHL	....	....	....	....	....	5	2	0	2	4
1989-90b	St. Louis	NHL	79	26	35	61	46	12	5	8	13	6
1990-91	St. Louis	NHL	78	17	32	49	93	13	2	5	7	10
1991-92	Philadelphia	NHL	80	33	44	77	100	....	....	....	....	....
	NHL Totals		237	76	111	187	239	30	9	13	22	20

a CCHA Freshman of the Year (1989)
b NHL All-Rookie Team (1990)

Played in NHL All-Star Game (1992)

Traded to **Philadelphia** by **St. Louis** with Dan Quinn for Ron Sutter and Murray Baron, September 22, 1991.

BRISEBOIS, PATRICE

Defense. Shoots right. 6'2", 175 lbs. Born, Montreal, Que., January 27, 1971.
(Montreal's 2nd choice, 30th overall, in 1989 Entry Draft).

			Regular Season					Playoffs				
Season	Club	Lea	GP	G	A	TP	PIM	GP	G	A	TP	PIM
1987-88	Laval	QMJHL	48	10	34	44	95	6	0	2	2	2
1988-89	Laval	QMJHL	50	20	45	65	95	17	8	14	22	45
1989-90a	Laval	QMJHL	56	18	70	88	108	13	7	9	16	26
1990-91	Montreal	NHL	10	0	2	2	4	....	....	....	....	....
bcd	Drummondville	QMJHL	54	17	44	61	72	14	6	18	24	49
1991-92	Montreal	NHL	26	2	8	10	20	11	2	4	6	6
	Fredericton	AHL	53	12	27	39	51	....	....	....	....	....
	NHL Totals		36	2	10	12	24	11	2	4	6	6

a QMJHL Second All-Star Team (1990)
b QMJHL and Canadian Major Junior Defenseman of the Year (1991)
c QMJHL First All-Star Team (1991)
d Memorial Cup All-Star Team (1991)

BROTEN, AARON (BRAH-tuhn)

Left wing/Center. Shoots left. 5'10", 180 lbs. Born, Roseau, MN, November 14, 1960.
(Colorado's 5th choice, 106th overall, in 1980 Entry Draft).

			Regular Season					Playoffs				
Season	Club	Lea	GP	G	A	TP	PIM	GP	G	A	TP	PIM
1979-80	U. Minnesota	WCHA	41	25	47	72	8	....	....	....	....	....
1980-81	U. Minnesota	WCHA	45	*47	*59	*106	24	....	....	....	....	....
	Colorado	NHL	2	0	0	0	0	....	....	....	....	....
1981-82	Colorado	NHL	58	15	24	39	6	....	....	....	....	....
	Fort Worth	CHL	19	15	21	36	11	....	....	....	....	....
1982-83	New Jersey	NHL	73	16	39	55	28	....	....	....	....	....
	Wichita	CHL	4	0	4	4	0	....	....	....	....	....
1983-84	New Jersey	NHL	80	13	23	36	36	....	....	....	....	....
1984-85	New Jersey	NHL	80	22	35	57	38	....	....	....	....	....
1985-86	New Jersey	NHL	66	18	25	43	26	....	....	....	....	....
1986-87	New Jersey	NHL	80	26	53	79	36	....	....	....	....	....
1987-88	New Jersey	NHL	80	26	57	83	80	20	5	11	16	20
1988-89	New Jersey	NHL	80	16	43	59	81	....	....	....	....	....
1989-90	New Jersey	NHL	42	10	8	18	36	....	....	....	....	....
	Minnesota	NHL	35	9	9	18	22	7	0	5	5	8
1990-91	Quebec	NHL	20	5	4	9	6	....	....	....	....	....
	Toronto	NHL	27	6	4	10	32	....	....	....	....	....
1991-92	Winnipeg	NHL	25	4	5	9	14	7	2	2	4	12
	Moncton	AHL	4	0	2	2	0	....	....	....	....	....
	NHL Totals		748	186	329	515	441	34	7	18	25	40

Traded to **Minnesota** by **New Jersey** for Bob Brooke, January 5, 1990. Claimed by **Quebec** in NHL Waiver Draft, October 1, 1990. Traded to **Toronto** by **Quebec** with Lucien Deblois and Michel Petit for Scott Pearson and Toronto's second round choices in 1991 (later traded to Washington — Eric Lavigne) and 1992 Entry Drafts, November 17, 1990. Signed as a free agent by **Winnipeg**, January 21, 1992.

BROTEN, NEAL (BRAH-tuhn)

Center. Shoots left. 5'9", 170 lbs. Born, Roseau, MN, November 29, 1959.
(Minnesota's 3rd choice, 42nd overall, in 1979 Entry Draft).

			Regular Season					Playoffs				
Season	Club	Lea	GP	G	A	TP	PIM	GP	G	A	TP	PIM
1978-79	U. Minnesota	WCHA	40	21	50	71	18	....	....	....	....	....
1979-80	U.S. National	....	55	25	30	55	20	....	....	....	....	....
	U.S. Olympic	....	7	2	1	3	2	....	....	....	....	....
1980-81ab	U. Minnesota	WCHA	36	17	54	71	56	....	....	....	....	....
	Minnesota	NHL	3	2	0	2	12	19	1	7	8	9
1981-82	Minnesota	NHL	73	38	60	98	42	4	0	2	2	0
1982-83	Minnesota	NHL	79	32	45	77	43	9	1	6	7	10
1983-84	Minnesota	NHL	76	28	61	89	43	16	5	5	10	4
1984-85	Minnesota	NHL	80	19	37	56	39	9	2	5	7	10
1985-86	Minnesota	NHL	80	29	76	105	47	5	3	2	5	2
1986-87	Minnesota	NHL	46	18	35	53	33	....	....	....	....	....
1987-88	Minnesota	NHL	54	9	30	39	32	....	....	....	....	....
1988-89	Minnesota	NHL	68	18	38	56	57	5	2	2	4	4
1989-90	Minnesota	NHL	80	23	62	85	45	7	2	2	4	18
1990-91	Minnesota	NHL	79	13	56	69	26	23	9	13	22	6
1991-92	Preussen	Ger.	8	3	5	8	2	....	....	....	....	....
	Minnesota	NHL	76	8	26	34	16	7	1	5	6	2
	NHL Totals		794	237	526	763	435	104	26	49	75	65

a WCHA First All-Star Team (1981)
b Won Hobey Baker Memorial Trophy (Top U.S. College Player) (1981)

Played in NHL All-Star Game (1983-86)

BROTEN, PAUL (BRAH-tuhn)

Right wing. Shoots right. 5'11", 190 lbs. Born, Roseau, MN, October 27, 1965.
(NY Rangers' 3rd choice, 77th overall, in 1984 Entry Draft).

			Regular Season					Playoffs				
Season	Club	Lea	GP	G	A	TP	PIM	GP	G	A	TP	PIM
1984-85	U. Minnesota	WCHA	44	8	8	16	26	....	....	....	....	....
1985-86	U. Minnesota	WCHA	38	6	16	22	24	....	....	....	....	....
1986-87	U. Minnesota	WCHA	48	17	22	39	52	....	....	....	....	....
1987-88	U. Minnesota	WCHA	38	18	21	39	42	....	....	....	....	....
1988-89	Denver	IHL	77	28	31	59	133	4	0	2	2	6
1989-90	NY Rangers	NHL	32	5	3	8	26	6	1	1	2	2
	Flint	IHL	28	17	9	26	55	....	....	....	....	....
1990-91	NY Rangers	NHL	28	4	6	10	18	5	0	0	0	2
	Binghamton	AHL	8	2	2	4	4	....	....	....	....	....
1991-92	NY Rangers	NHL	74	13	15	28	102	13	1	2	3	10
	NHL Totals		134	22	24	46	146	24	2	3	5	14

BROUSSEAU, PAUL

Right wing. Shoots right. 6'2", 212 lbs. Born, Pierrefonds, Que., September 18, 1973.
(Quebec's 2nd choice, 28th overall, in 1992 Entry Draft).

			Regular Season					Playoffs				
Season	Club	Lea	GP	G	A	TP	PIM	GP	G	A	TP	PIM
1989-90	Chicoutimi	QMJHL	57	17	24	41	32	....	....	....	....	....
1990-91	Trois-Rivières	QMJHL	67	30	66	96	48	6	3	2	5	2
1991-92	Hull	QMJHL	57	35	61	96	54	6	3	5	8	10

BROWN, ALAN

Defense. Shoots left. 6', 180 lbs. Born, Nepean, Ont., January 26, 1971.
(Washington's 13th choice, 219th overall, in 1990 Entry Draft).

			Regular Season					Playoffs				
Season	Club	Lea	GP	G	A	TP	PIM	GP	G	A	TP	PIM
1989-90	Colgate	ECAC	33	2	3	5	22	....	....	....	....	....
1990-91	Colgate	ECAC	32	0	5	5	26	....	....	....	....	....
1991-92	Colgate	ECAC	29	1	10	11	28	....	....	....	....	....

BROWN, DAVID

Right wing. Shoots right. 6'5", 205 lbs. Born, Saskatoon, Sask., October 12, 1962.
(Philadelphia's 7th choice, 140th overall, in 1982 Entry Draft).

			Regular Season					Playoffs				
Season	Club	Lea	GP	G	A	TP	PIM	GP	G	A	TP	PIM
1980-81	Spokane	WHL	9	2	2	4	21	....	....	....	....	....
1981-82	Saskatoon	WHL	62	11	33	44	344	5	1	0	1	4
1982-83	Philadelphia	NHL	2	0	0	0	5	....	....	....	....	....
	Maine	AHL	71	8	6	14	*418	16	0	0	0	*107
1983-84	Philadelphia	NHL	19	1	5	6	98	2	0	0	0	12
	Springfield	AHL	59	17	14	31	150	....	....	....	....	....
1984-85	Philadelphia	NHL	57	3	6	9	165	11	0	0	0	59
1985-86	Philadelphia	NHL	76	10	7	17	277	5	0	0	0	16
1986-87	Philadelphia	NHL	62	7	3	10	274	26	1	2	3	59
1987-88	Philadelphia	NHL	47	12	5	17	114	7	1	0	1	27
1988-89	Philadelphia	NHL	50	0	3	3	100	....	....	....	....	....
	Edmonton	NHL	22	0	2	2	56	7	0	0	0	6
1989-90	Edmonton	NHL	60	0	6	6	145	3	0	0	0	0
1990-91	Edmonton	NHL	58	3	4	7	160	16	0	1	1	30
1991-92	Philadelphia	NHL	70	4	2	6	81	....	....	....	....	....
	NHL Totals		453	36	41	77	1394	77	2	3	5	209

Traded to **Edmonton** by **Philadelphia** for Keith Acton and Edmonton's fifth round choice (Dimitri Yushkevich) in 1991 Entry Draft, February 7, 1989. Traded to **Philadelphia** by **Edmonton** with Corey Foster and Jari Kurri for Craig Fisher, Scott Mellanby and Craig Berube, May 30, 1991.

BROWN, DOUG

Right wing. Shoots right. 5'10", 180 lbs. Born, Southborough, MA, June 12, 1964.

			Regular Season					Playoffs				
Season	Club	Lea	GP	G	A	TP	PIM	GP	G	A	TP	PIM
1982-83	Boston College	ECAC	22	9	8	17	0	....	....	....	....	....
1983-84	Boston College	ECAC	38	11	10	21	6	....	....	....	....	....
1984-85	Boston College	H.E.	45	37	31	68	10	....	....	....	....	....
1985-86	Boston College	H.E.	38	16	40	56	16	....	....	....	....	....
1986-87	**New Jersey**	**NHL**	**4**	**0**	**1**	**1**	**0**	....	....	....	....	....
	Maine	AHL	73	24	34	58	15	....	....	....	....	....
1987-88	**New Jersey**	**NHL**	**70**	**14**	**11**	**25**	**20**	**19**	**5**	**1**	**6**	**6**
	Utica	AHL	2	0	2	2	2	....	....	....	....	....
1988-89	**New Jersey**	**NHL**	**63**	**15**	**10**	**25**	**15**	....	....	....	....	....
	Utica	AHL	4	1	4	5	0	....	....	....	....	....
1989-90	**New Jersey**	**NHL**	**69**	**14**	**20**	**34**	**16**	**6**	**0**	**1**	**1**	**2**
1990-91	**New Jersey**	**NHL**	**58**	**14**	**16**	**30**	**4**	**7**	**2**	**2**	**4**	**2**
1991-92	**New Jersey**	**NHL**	**71**	**11**	**17**	**28**	**27**	....	....	....	....	....
	NHL Totals		**335**	**68**	**75**	**143**	**82**	**32**	**7**	**4**	**11**	**10**

Signed as a free agent by **New Jersey**, August 6, 1986.

BROWN, GREG

Defense. Shoots right. 6', 185 lbs. Born, Hartford, CT, March 7, 1968.
(Buffalo's 2nd choice, 26th overall, in 1986 Entry Draft).

			Regular Season					Playoffs				
Season	Club	Lea	GP	G	A	TP	PIM	GP	G	A	TP	PIM
1986-87	Boston College	H.E.	37	10	27	37	22	....	....	....	....	....
1987-88	U.S. National	....	55	6	29	35	22	....	....	....	....	....
	U.S. Olympic	....	6	0	4	4	2	....	....	....	....	....
1988-89abc	Boston College	H.E.	40	9	34	43	24	....	....	....	....	....
1989-90abc	Boston College	H.E.	42	5	35	40	42	....	....	....	....	....
1990-91	**Buffalo**	**NHL**	**39**	**1**	**2**	**3**	**35**	....	....	....	....	....
	Rochester	AHL	31	6	17	23	16	14	1	4	5	8
1991-92	Rochester	AHL	56	8	30	38	25	16	1	5	6	4
	U.S. National	....	8	0	0	0	5	....	....	....	....	....
	U.S. Olympic	....	7	0	0	0	2	....	....	....	....	....
	NHL Totals		**39**	**1**	**2**	**3**	**35**	....	....	....	....	....

a Hockey East First All-Star Team (1989, 1990)
b Hockey East Player of the Year (1989, 1990)
c NCAA East First All-American Team (1989, 1990)

BROWN, JEFF

Defense. Shoots right. 6'1", 204 lbs. Born, Ottawa, Ont., April 30, 1966.
(Quebec's 2nd choice, 36th overall, in 1984 Entry Draft).

			Regular Season					Playoffs				
Season	Club	Lea	GP	G	A	TP	PIM	GP	G	A	TP	PIM
1982-83	Sudbury	OHL	65	9	37	46	39	....	....	....	....	....
1983-84	Sudbury	OHL	68	17	60	77	39	....	....	....	....	....
1984-85	Sudbury	OHL	56	16	48	64	26	....	....	....	....	....
1985-86	**Quebec**	**NHL**	**8**	**3**	**2**	**5**	**6**	**1**	**0**	**0**	**0**	**0**
a	Sudbury	OHL	45	22	28	50	24	4	0	2	2	11
	Fredericton	AHL	....	....	....	....	....	1	0	1	1	0
1986-87	**Quebec**	**NHL**	**44**	**7**	**22**	**29**	**16**	**13**	**3**	**3**	**6**	**2**
	Fredericton	AHL	26	2	14	16	16	....	....	....	....	....
1987-88	**Quebec**	**NHL**	**78**	**16**	**36**	**52**	**64**	....	....	....	....	....
1988-89	**Quebec**	**NHL**	**78**	**21**	**47**	**68**	**62**	....	....	....	....	....
1989-90	**Quebec**	**NHL**	**29**	**6**	**10**	**16**	**18**	....	....	....	....	....
	St. Louis	**NHL**	**48**	**10**	**28**	**38**	**37**	**12**	**2**	**10**	**12**	**4**
1990-91	**St. Louis**	**NHL**	**67**	**12**	**47**	**59**	**39**	**13**	**3**	**9**	**12**	**6**
1991-92	**St. Louis**	**NHL**	**80**	**20**	**39**	**59**	**38**	**6**	**2**	**1**	**3**	**2**
	NHL Totals		**432**	**95**	**231**	**326**	**280**	**45**	**10**	**23**	**33**	**14**

a OHL First All-Star Team (1986)

Traded to **St Louis** by **Quebec** for Tony Hrkac and Greg Millen, December 13, 1989.

BROWN, KEITH JEFFREY

Defense. Shoots right. 6'1", 192 lbs. Born, Corner Brook, Nfld., May 6, 1960.
(Chicago's 1st choice, 7th overall, in 1979 Entry Draft).

			Regular Season					Playoffs				
Season	Club	Lea	GP	G	A	TP	PIM	GP	G	A	TP	PIM
1977-78a	Portland	WHL	72	11	53	64	51	8	0	3	3	2
1978-79bc	Portland	WHL	70	11	85	96	75	25	3	*30	33	21
1979-80	**Chicago**	**NHL**	**76**	**2**	**18**	**20**	**27**	**6**	**0**	**0**	**0**	**4**
1980-81	**Chicago**	**NHL**	**80**	**9**	**34**	**43**	**80**	**3**	**0**	**2**	**2**	**2**
1981-82	**Chicago**	**NHL**	**33**	**4**	**20**	**24**	**26**	**4**	**0**	**2**	**2**	**5**
1982-83	**Chicago**	**NHL**	**50**	**4**	**27**	**31**	**20**	**7**	**0**	**0**	**0**	**11**
1983-84	**Chicago**	**NHL**	**74**	**10**	**25**	**35**	**94**	**5**	**0**	**1**	**1**	**10**
1984-85	**Chicago**	**NHL**	**56**	**1**	**22**	**23**	**55**	**11**	**2**	**7**	**9**	**31**
1985-86	**Chicago**	**NHL**	**70**	**11**	**29**	**40**	**87**	**3**	**0**	**1**	**1**	**9**
1986-87	**Chicago**	**NHL**	**73**	**4**	**23**	**27**	**86**	**4**	**0**	**1**	**1**	**6**
1987-88	**Chicago**	**NHL**	**24**	**3**	**6**	**9**	**45**	**5**	**0**	**2**	**2**	**10**
1988-89	**Chicago**	**NHL**	**74**	**2**	**16**	**18**	**84**	**13**	**1**	**3**	**4**	**25**
1989-90	**Chicago**	**NHL**	**67**	**5**	**20**	**25**	**87**	**18**	**0**	**4**	**4**	**43**
1990-91	**Chicago**	**NHL**	**45**	**1**	**10**	**11**	**55**	**6**	**1**	**0**	**1**	**8**
1991-92	**Chicago**	**NHL**	**57**	**6**	**10**	**16**	**69**	**14**	**0**	**8**	**8**	**18**
	NHL Totals		**779**	**62**	**260**	**322**	**815**	**99**	**4**	**31**	**35**	**182**

a Shared WHL's Rookie of the Year with John Ogrodnick (New Westminster) (1978)
b Named WHL's Top Defenseman (1979)
c WHL First All-Star Team (1979)

BROWN, KEVIN

Right wing. Shoots right. 6'1", 212 lbs. Born, Birmingham, England, May 11, 1974.
(Los Angeles' 3rd choice, 87th overall, in 1992 Entry Draft).

			Regular Season					Playoffs				
Season	Club	Lea	GP	G	A	TP	PIM	GP	G	A	TP	PIM
1990-91	Waterloo	Jr. B	46	25	33	58	111	....	....	....	....	....
1991-92	Belleville	OHL	66	24	24	48	52	5	1	4	5	8

BROWN, RICHARD (CAM)

Left wing. Shoots left. 6'1", 210 lbs. Born, Saskatoon, Sask., May 15, 1969.

			Regular Season					Playoffs				
Season	Club	Lea	GP	G	A	TP	PIM	GP	G	A	TP	PIM
1989-90	Brandon	WHL	68	34	41	75	182	....	....	....	....	....
1990-91	**Vancouver**	**NHL**	**1**	**0**	**0**	**0**	**7**	....	....	....	....	....
	Milwaukee	IHL	74	11	13	24	218	3	0	0	0	0
1991-92	Milwaukee	IHL	51	6	8	14	179	1	0	0	0	0
	NHL Totals		**1**	**0**	**0**	**0**	**7**	....	....	....	....	....

Signed as a free agent by **Vancouver**, April 6, 1990.

BROWN, ROB

Right wing. Shoots left. 5'11", 185 lbs. Born, Kingston, Ont., April 10, 1968.
(Pittsburgh's 4th choice, 67th overall, in 1986 Entry Draft).

			Regular Season					Playoffs				
Season	Club	Lea	GP	G	A	TP	PIM	GP	G	A	TP	PIM
1984-85	Kamloops	WHL	60	29	50	79	95	15	8	8	26	28
1985-86ab	Kamloops	WHL	69	58	*115	*173	171	16	*18	*28	*46	14
1986-87abc	Kamloops	WHL	63	*76	*136	*212	101	5	6	5	11	6
1987-88	**Pittsburgh**	**NHL**	**51**	**24**	**20**	**44**	**56**	....	....	....	....	....
1988-89	**Pittsburgh**	**NHL**	**68**	**49**	**66**	**115**	**118**	**11**	**5**	**3**	**8**	**22**
1989-90	**Pittsburgh**	**NHL**	**80**	**33**	**47**	**80**	**102**	....	....	....	....	....
1990-91	**Pittsburgh**	**NHL**	**25**	**6**	**10**	**16**	**31**	....	....	....	....	....
	Hartford	**NHL**	**44**	**18**	**24**	**42**	**101**	**5**	**1**	**0**	**1**	**7**
1991-92	**Hartford**	**NHL**	**42**	**16**	**15**	**31**	**39**	....	....	....	....	....
	Chicago	**NHL**	**25**	**5**	**11**	**16**	**34**	**8**	**2**	**4**	**6**	**4**
	NHL Totals		**335**	**151**	**193**	**344**	**481**	**24**	**8**	**7**	**15**	**33**

a WHL Player of the Year (1986, 1987)
b WHL First All-Star Team (1986, 1987)
c Canadian Major Junior Player of the Year (1987)

Played in NHL All-Star Game (1989)

Traded to **Hartford** by **Pittsburgh** for Scott Young, December 21, 1990. Traded to **Chicago** by **Hartford** for Steve Konroyd, January 24, 1992.

BROWNSCHIDLE, MARK

Defense. Shoots right. 6'2", 185 lbs. Born, East Amherst, NY, October 26, 1970.
(Winnipeg's 5th choice, 64th overall, in 1989 Entry Draft).

			Regular Season					Playoffs				
Season	Club	Lea	GP	G	A	TP	PIM	GP	G	A	TP	PIM
1988-89	Boston U.	H.E.	35	0	7	7	12	....	....	....	....	....
1989-90	Boston U.	H.E.	38	1	4	5	12	....	....	....	....	....
1990-91	Boston U.	H.E.	13	0	1	1	10	....	....	....	....	....
1991-92	Boston U.	H.E.	26	2	6	8	6	....	....	....	....	....

BRUCE, DAVID

Right wing/Center. Shoots right. 5'11", 190 lbs. Born, Thunder Bay, Ont., October 7, 1964.
(Vancouver's 2nd choice, 30th overall, in 1983 Entry Draft).

			Regular Season					Playoffs				
Season	Club	Lea	GP	G	A	TP	PIM	GP	G	A	TP	PIM
1982-83	Kitchener	OHL	67	36	35	71	199	12	7	9	16	27
1983-84	Kitchener	OHL	62	52	40	92	203	10	5	8	13	20
1984-85	Fredericton	AHL	56	14	11	25	104	5	0	0	0	37
1985-86	**Vancouver**	**NHL**	**12**	**0**	**1**	**1**	**14**	**1**	**0**	**0**	**0**	**0**
	Fredericton	AHL	66	25	16	41	151	2	0	1	1	12
1986-87	**Vancouver**	**NHL**	**50**	**9**	**7**	**16**	**109**	....	....	....	....	....
	Fredericton	AHL	17	7	6	13	73	....	....	....	....	....
1987-88	**Vancouver**	**NHL**	**28**	**7**	**3**	**10**	**57**	....	....	....	....	....
	Fredericton	AHL	30	27	18	45	115	....	....	....	....	....
1988-89	**Vancouver**	**NHL**	**53**	**7**	**7**	**14**	**65**	....	....	....	....	....
1989-90a	Milwaukee	IHL	68	40	35	75	148	6	5	3	8	0
1990-91	**St. Louis**	**NHL**	**12**	**1**	**2**	**3**	**14**	**2**	**0**	**0**	**0**	**2**
ab	Peoria	IHL	60	*64	52	116	78	18	*18	11	*29	40
1991-92	**San Jose**	**NHL**	**60**	**22**	**16**	**38**	**46**	....	....	....	....	....
	Kansas City	IHL	7	5	5	10	6	....	....	....	....	....
	NHL Totals		**215**	**46**	**36**	**82**	**305**	**3**	**0**	**0**	**0**	**2**

a IHL First All-Star Team (1990, 1991)
b Won James Gatschene Memorial Trophy (MVP—IHL) (1991)

Signed as a free agent by **St. Louis**, July 6, 1990. Claimed by **San Jose** from **St. Louis** in Expansion Draft, May 30, 1991.

BRUININKS, BRIAN

Defense. Shoots right. 6', 180 lbs. Born, St. Paul, MN, March 30, 1970.
(Pittsburgh's 14th choice, 236th overall, in 1990 Entry Draft).

			Regular Season					Playoffs				
Season	Club	Lea	GP	G	A	TP	PIM	GP	G	A	TP	PIM
1988-89	Colorado	WCHA	31	1	2	3	35	....	....	....	....	....
1989-90	Colorado	WCHA	30	3	7	10	8	....	....	....	....	....
1990-91	Colorado	WCHA	38	3	8	11	35	....	....	....	....	....
1991-92	Colorado	WCHA	40	3	8	11	29	....	....	....	....	....

BRUNET, BENOIT (broo-NAY)

Left wing. Shoots left. 5'11", 184 lbs. Born, Ste-Anne de Bellevue, Que., August 24, 1968.
(Montreal's 2nd choice, 27th overall, in 1986 Entry Draft).

			Regular Season					Playoffs				
Season	Club	Lea	GP	G	A	TP	PIM	GP	G	A	TP	PIM
1985-86	Hull	QMJHL	71	33	37	70	81	....	....	....	....	....
1986-87a	Hull	QMJHL	60	43	67	110	105	6	7	5	12	8
1987-88	Hull	QMJHL	62	54	89	143	131	10	3	10	13	11
1988-89	**Montreal**	**NHL**	**2**	**0**	**1**	**1**	**0**	....	....	....	....	....
b	Sherbrooke	AHL	73	41	76	117	95	6	2	0	2	4
1989-90	Sherbrooke	AHL	72	32	35	67	82	12	8	7	15	20
1990-91	**Montreal**	**NHL**	**17**	**1**	**3**	**4**	**0**	....	....	....	....	....
	Fredericton	AHL	24	13	18	31	16	6	5	6	11	2
1991-92	**Montreal**	**NHL**	**18**	**4**	**6**	**10**	**14**	....	....	....	....	....
	Fredericton	AHL	6	7	9	16	27	....	....	....	....	....
	NHL Totals		**37**	**5**	**10**	**15**	**14**	....	....	....	....	....

a QMJHL Second All-Star Team (1987)
b AHL First All-Star Team (1989)

BRYLIN, SERGEI (BRIH-lin)

Center. Shoots left. 5'9", 176 lbs. Born, Moscow, Soviet Union, January 13, 1974.
(New Jersey's 2nd choice, 42nd overall, in 1992 Entry Draft).

			Regular Season					Playoffs				
Season	Club	Lea	GP	G	A	TP	PIM	GP	G	A	TP	PIM
1991-92	CSKA	CIS	44	1	6	7	4	....	....	....	....	....

BUCHBERGER, KELLY (BUHK-BUHR-GUHR)

Left wing. Shoots left. 6'2", 210 lbs. Born, Langenburg, Sask., December 2, 1966.
(Edmonton's 8th choice, 188th overall, in 1985 Entry Draft).

			Regular Season					Playoffs				
Season	Club	Lea	GP	G	A	TP	PIM	GP	G	A	TP	PIM
1984-85	Moose Jaw	WHL	51	12	17	29	114	....	....	....	....	....
1985-86	Moose Jaw	WHL	72	14	22	36	206	13	11	4	15	37
1986-87	Nova Scotia	AHL	70	12	20	32	257	5	0	1	1	23
	Edmonton	**NHL**	....	....	....	....	....	**3**	**0**	**1**	**1**	**5**
1987-88	**Edmonton**	**NHL**	**19**	**1**	**0**	**1**	**81**	....	....	....	....	....
	Nova Scotia	AHL	49	21	23	44	206	2	0	0	0	11
1988-89	**Edmonton**	**NHL**	**66**	**5**	**9**	**14**	**234**	....	....	....	....	....
1989-90	**Edmonton**	**NHL**	**55**	**2**	**6**	**8**	**168**	**19**	**0**	**5**	**5**	**13**
1990-91	**Edmonton**	**NHL**	**64**	**3**	**1**	**4**	**160**	**12**	**2**	**1**	**3**	**25**
1991-92	**Edmonton**	**NHL**	**79**	**20**	**24**	**44**	**157**	**16**	**1**	**4**	**5**	**32**
	NHL Totals		**283**	**31**	**40**	**71**	**800**	**50**	**3**	**11**	**14**	**75**

BUCKLEY, JEROME

Right wing. Shoots right. 6'2", 200 lbs. Born, Needham, MA, June 27, 1971.
(Boston's 3rd choice, 84th overall, in 1990 Entry Draft).

			Regular Season					Playoffs				
Season	Club	Lea	GP	G	A	TP	PIM	GP	G	A	TP	PIM
1990-91	Northwood	HS	26	31	26	57	65	....	....	....	....	....
1991-92	Boston College	H.E.	30	2	0	2	46	....	....	....	....	....

BULLARD, MICHAEL BRIAN (MIKE) (BULL-ard)

Center. Shoots left. 6', 195 lbs. Born, Ottawa, Ont., March 10, 1961.
(Pittsburgh's 1st choice, 9th overall, in 1980 Entry Draft).

			Regular Season					Playoffs				
Season	Club	Lea	GP	G	A	TP	PIM	GP	G	A	TP	PIM
1978-79	Brantford	OHA	66	43	56	99	66	....	....	....	....	....
1979-80a	Brantford	OHA	66	66	84	150	86	11	10	6	16	29
1980-81	**Pittsburgh**	**NHL**	**15**	**1**	**2**	**3**	**19**	**4**	**3**	**3**	**6**	**0**
b	Brantford	OHA	42	47	60	107	55	6	4	5	9	10
1981-82	**Pittsburgh**	**NHL**	**75**	**36**	**27**	**63**	**91**	**5**	**1**	**1**	**2**	**4**
1982-83	**Pittsburgh**	**NHL**	**57**	**22**	**22**	**44**	**60**	....	....	....	....	....
1983-84	**Pittsburgh**	**NHL**	**76**	**51**	**41**	**92**	**57**	....	....	....	....	....
1984-85	**Pittsburgh**	**NHL**	**68**	**32**	**31**	**63**	**75**	....	....	....	....	....
1985-86	**Pittsburgh**	**NHL**	**77**	**41**	**42**	**83**	**69**	....	....	....	....	....
1986-87	**Pittsburgh**	**NHL**	**14**	**2**	**10**	**12**	**17**	....	....	....	....	....
	Calgary	**NHL**	**57**	**28**	**26**	**54**	**34**	**6**	**4**	**3**	**7**	**2**
1987-88	**Calgary**	**NHL**	**79**	**48**	**55**	**103**	**68**	**6**	**0**	**2**	**2**	**6**
1988-89	**St. Louis**	**NHL**	**20**	**4**	**12**	**16**	**46**	....	....	....	....	....
	Philadelphia	**NHL**	**54**	**23**	**26**	**49**	**60**	**19**	**3**	**9**	**12**	**32**
1989-90	**Philadelphia**	**NHL**	**70**	**27**	**37**	**64**	**67**	....	....	....	....	....
1990-91	Ambri Piotta	Switz.	36	36	33	69	....	5	6	4	10	....
1991-92	**Toronto**	**NHL**	**65**	**14**	**14**	**28**	**40**	....	....	....	....	....
	NHL Totals		**727**	**329**	**345**	**674**	**703**	**40**	**11**	**18**	**29**	**44**

a OHA Third All-Star Team (1979)
b OHA Second All-Star Team (1980)

Traded to **Calgary** by **Pittsburgh** for Dan Quinn, November 12, 1986. Traded to **St. Louis** by **Calgary** with Craig Coxe and Tim Corkery for Mark Hunter, Doug Gilmour, Steve Bozek and Michael Dark, September 6, 1988. Traded to **Philadelphia** by **St. Louis** for Peter Zezel, November 29, 1988. Rights traded to **Toronto** by **Philadelphia** for Toronto's fourth round choice in 1992 Entry Draft or Toronto's third round choice in 1993 Entry Draft, July 29, 1991.

BURAKOWSKY, ROBERT (boo-ruh-KAHV-skee)

Right wing. Shoots right. 5'10", 178 lbs. Born, Malmo, Sweden, November 24, 1966.
(NY Rangers' 11th choice, 217th overall, in 1985 Entry Draft).

			Regular Season					Playoffs				
Season	Club	Lea	GP	G	A	TP	PIM	GP	G	A	TP	PIM
1985-86	Leksand	Swe.	19	4	3	7	4	....	....	....	....	....
1986-87	Leksand	Swe.	36	21	15	36	26	....	....	....	....	....
1987-88	Leksand	Swe.	36	10	11	21	10	....	....	....	....	....
1988-89	Leksand	Swe.	40	23	20	43	44	10	6	7	13	4
1989-90	AIK	Swe.	37	27	29	56	32	3	0	2	2	12
1990-91	AIK	Swe.	30	8	15	23	26	....	....	....	....	....
1991-92	Malmo	Swe.	40	19	22	41	42	9	5	0	5	4

BURE, PAVEL (boo-RAI)

Right wing. Shoots left. 5'9", 180 lbs. Born, Moscow, Soviet Union, March 31, 1971.
(Vancouver's 4th choice, 113th overall, in 1989 Entry Draft).

			Regular Season					Playoffs				
Season	Club	Lea	GP	G	A	TP	PIM	GP	G	A	TP	PIM
1987-88	CSKA	USSR	5	1	1	2	0	....	....	....	....	....
1988-89a	CSKA	USSR	32	17	9	26	8	....	....	....	....	....
1989-90	CSKA	USSR	46	14	10	24	20	....	....	....	....	....
1990-91	CSKA	USSR	44	35	11	46	24	....	....	....	....	....
1991-92b	**Vancouver**	**NHL**	**65**	**34**	**26**	**60**	**30**	**13**	**6**	**4**	**10**	**14**
	NHL Totals		**65**	**34**	**26**	**60**	**30**	**13**	**6**	**4**	**10**	**14**

a Named Soviet National League Rookie-of-the-Year (1989)
b Won Calder Memorial Trophy (1992)

BURE, VALERI

Right wing. Shoots right. 5'9", 155 lbs. Born, Moscow, Soviet Union, June 13, 1974.
(Montreal's 2nd choice, 33rd overall, in 1992 Entry Draft).

			Regular Season					Playoffs				
Season	Club	Lea	GP	G	A	TP	PIM	GP	G	A	TP	PIM
1990-91	CSKA	USSR	3	0	0	0	0	....	....	....	....	....
1991-92	Spokane	WHL	53	27	22	49	78	10	11	6	17	10

BUREAU, MARC (BEWR-oh)

Center. Shoots right. 6'1", 198 lbs. Born, Trois-Rivières, Que., May 19, 1966.

			Regular Season					Playoffs				
Season	Club	Lea	GP	G	A	TP	PIM	GP	G	A	TP	PIM
1983-84	Chicoutimi	QMJHL	56	6	16	22	14	....	....	....	....	....
1984-85	Chicoutimi	QMJHL	41	30	25	55	15	....	....	....	....	....
	Granby	QMJHL	27	20	45	65	14	....	....	....	....	....
1985-86	Granby	QMJHL	19	6	17	23	36	....	....	....	....	....
	Chicoutimi	QMJHL	44	30	45	75	33	9	3	7	10	10
1986-87	Longueuil	QMJHL	66	54	58	112	68	20	17	20	37	12
1987-88	Salt Lake	IHL	69	7	20	27	86	7	0	3	3	8
1988-89	Salt Lake	IHL	76	28	36	64	119	14	7	5	12	31
1989-90	**Calgary**	**NHL**	**5**	**0**	**0**	**0**	**4**	....	....	....	....	....
a	Salt Lake	IHL	67	43	48	91	173	11	4	8	12	0
1990-91	**Calgary**	**NHL**	**5**	**0**	**0**	**0**	**2**	....	....	....	....	....
a	Salt Lake	IHL	54	40	48	88	101	....	....	....	....	....
	Minnesota	**NHL**	**9**	**0**	**6**	**6**	**4**	**23**	**3**	**2**	**5**	**20**
1991-92	**Minnesota**	**NHL**	**46**	**6**	**4**	**10**	**50**	**5**	**0**	**0**	**0**	**14**
	Kalamazoo	IHL	7	2	8	10	2	....	....	....	....	....
	NHL Totals		**65**	**6**	**10**	**16**	**60**	**28**	**3**	**2**	**5**	**34**

a IHL Second All-Star Team (1990, 1991)

Signed as a free agent by **Calgary**, May 19, 1987. Traded to **Minnesota** by **Calgary** for Minnesota's third round choice (Sandy McCarthy) in 1991 Entry Draft, March 5, 1991.

BURKE, DAVID

Defense. Shoots left. 6'1", 182 lbs. Born, Detroit, MI, October 15, 1970.
(Toronto's 6th choice, 108th overall, in 1989 Entry Draft).

			Regular Season					Playoffs				
Season	Club	Lea	GP	G	A	TP	PIM	GP	G	A	TP	PIM
1988-89	Cornell	ECAC	26	0	3	3	22	....	....	....	....	....
1989-90	Cornell	ECAC	29	0	12	12	28	....	....	....	....	....
1990-91	Cornell	ECAC	32	2	8	10	43	....	....	....	....	....
1991-92	Cornell	ECAC	29	5	9	14	30	....	....	....	....	....

BURKETT, MICHAEL

Left wing. Shoots left. 6'3", 180 lbs. Born, Toronto, Ont., March 15, 1972.
(Minnesota's 8th choice, 174th overall, in 1991 Entry Draft).

			Regular Season					Playoffs				
Season	Club	Lea	GP	G	A	TP	PIM	GP	G	A	TP	PIM
1990-91	Michigan State	CCHA	35	3	6	9	14	....	....	....	....	....
1991-92	Michigan State	CCHA	33	7	5	12	42	....	....	....	....	....

BURNS, TONY

Defense. Shoots left. 6'1", 195 lbs. Born, Duluth, MN, September 18, 1971.
(Detroit's 4th choice, 87th overall, in 1990 Entry Draft).

			Regular Season					Playoffs				
Season	Club	Lea	GP	G	A	TP	PIM	GP	G	A	TP	PIM
1989-90	Duluth-Denfield	HS	25	21	23	44	....	....	....	....	....	....
1990-91	St. Cloud	WCHA	35	2	6	8	35	....	....	....	....	....
1991-92	St. Cloud	WCHA	5	0	1	1	6	....	....	....	....	....
	Toledo	ECHL	34	8	9	17	36	....	....	....	....	....

BURR, SHAWN

Left wing/Center. Shoots left. 6'1", 200 lbs. Born, Sarnia, Ont., July 1, 1966.
(Detroit's 1st choice, 7th overall, in 1984 Entry Draft).

			Regular Season					Playoffs				
Season	Club	Lea	GP	G	A	TP	PIM	GP	G	A	TP	PIM
1983-84	Kitchener	OHL	68	41	44	85	50	16	5	12	17	22
1984-85	**Detroit**	**NHL**	**9**	**0**	**0**	**0**	**2**	....	....	....	....	....
	Adirondack	AHL	4	0	0	0	2	....	....	....	....	....
	Kitchener	OHL	48	24	42	66	50	4	3	3	6	2
1985-86	**Detroit**	**NHL**	**5**	**1**	**0**	**1**	**4**	....	....	....	....	....
	Adirondack	AHL	3	2	2	4	2	17	5	7	12	32
a	Kitchener	OHL	59	60	67	127	104	5	2	3	5	8
1986-87	**Detroit**	**NHL**	**80**	**22**	**25**	**47**	**107**	**16**	**7**	**2**	**9**	**20**
1987-88	**Detroit**	**NHL**	**78**	**17**	**23**	**40**	**97**	**9**	**3**	**1**	**4**	**14**
1988-89	**Detroit**	**NHL**	**79**	**19**	**27**	**46**	**78**	**6**	**1**	**2**	**3**	**6**
1989-90	**Detroit**	**NHL**	**76**	**24**	**32**	**56**	**82**	....	....	....	....	....
	Adirondack	AHL	3	4	2	6	2	....	....	....	....	....
1990-91	**Detroit**	**NHL**	**80**	**20**	**30**	**50**	**112**	**7**	**0**	**4**	**4**	**15**
1991-92	**Detroit**	**NHL**	**79**	**19**	**32**	**51**	**118**	**11**	**1**	**5**	**6**	**10**
	NHL Totals		**486**	**122**	**169**	**291**	**600**	**49**	**12**	**14**	**26**	**65**

a OHL Second All-Star Team (1986)

BURRIDGE, RANDY

Left wing. Shoots left. 5'9", 185 lbs. Born, Fort Erie, Ont., January 7, 1966.
(Boston's 7th choice, 157th overall, in 1985 Entry Draft).

			Regular Season					Playoffs				
Season	Club	Lea	GP	G	A	TP	PIM	GP	G	A	TP	PIM
1983-84	Peterborough	OHL	55	6	7	13	44	8	3	2	5	7
1984-85	Peterborough	OHL	66	49	57	106	88	17	9	16	25	18
1985-86	**Boston**	**NHL**	**52**	**17**	**25**	**42**	**28**	**3**	**0**	**4**	**4**	**12**
	Peterborough	OHL	17	15	11	26	23	3	1	3	4	2
	Moncton	AHL	....	....	....	....	....	3	0	2	2	2
1986-87	**Boston**	**NHL**	**23**	**1**	**4**	**5**	**16**	**2**	**1**	**0**	**1**	**2**
	Moncton	AHL	47	26	41	67	139	3	1	2	3	30
1987-88	**Boston**	**NHL**	**79**	**27**	**28**	**55**	**105**	**23**	**2**	**10**	**12**	**16**
1988-89	**Boston**	**NHL**	**80**	**31**	**30**	**61**	**39**	**10**	**5**	**2**	**7**	**6**
1989-90	**Boston**	**NHL**	**63**	**17**	**15**	**32**	**47**	**21**	**4**	**11**	**15**	**14**
1990-91	**Boston**	**NHL**	**62**	**15**	**13**	**28**	**40**	**19**	**0**	**3**	**3**	**39**
1991-92	**Washington**	**NHL**	**66**	**23**	**44**	**67**	**50**	**2**	**0**	**1**	**1**	**0**
	NHL Totals		**425**	**131**	**159**	**290**	**325**	**80**	**12**	**31**	**43**	**89**

Played in NHL All-Star Game (1992)

Traded to **Washington** by **Boston** for Stephen Leach, June 21, 1991.

BURT, ADAM

Defense. Shoots left. 6', 190 lbs. Born, Detroit, MI, January 15, 1969.
(Hartford's 2nd choice, 39th overall, in 1987 Entry Draft).

			Regular Season					Playoffs				
Season	Club	Lea	GP	G	A	TP	PIM	GP	G	A	TP	PIM
1985-86	North Bay	OHL	49	0	11	11	81	10	0	0	0	24
1986-87	North Bay	OHL	57	4	27	31	138	24	1	6	7	68
1987-88	Binghamton	AHL	....	....	....	....	....	2	1	1	2	0
a	North Bay	OHL	66	17	53	70	176	2	0	3	3	6
1988-89	**Hartford**	**NHL**	**5**	**0**	**0**	**0**	**6**	....	....	....	....	....
	Binghamton	AHL	5	0	2	2	13	....	....	....	....	....
	North Bay	OHL	23	4	11	15	45	12	2	12	14	12
1989-90	**Hartford**	**NHL**	**63**	**4**	**8**	**12**	**105**	**2**	**0**	**0**	**0**	**0**
1990-91	**Hartford**	**NHL**	**42**	**2**	**7**	**9**	**63**	....	....	....	....	....
	Springfield	AHL	9	1	3	4	22	....	....	....	....	....
1991-92	**Hartford**	**NHL**	**66**	**9**	**15**	**24**	**93**	**2**	**0**	**0**	**0**	**0**
	NHL Totals		**176**	**15**	**30**	**45**	**267**	**4**	**0**	**0**	**0**	**0**

a OHL Second All-Star Team (1988)

BUSKAS, ROD

Defense. Shoots right. 6'1", 206 lbs. Born, Wetaskiwin, Alta., January 7, 1961.
(Pittsburgh's 5th choice, 112th overall, in 1981 Entry Draft).

			Regular Season					Playoffs				
Season	Club	Lea	GP	G	A	TP	PIM	GP	G	A	TP	PIM
1978-79	Billings	WHL	1	0	0	0	0	....	....	....	....	....
	Medicine Hat	WHL	34	1	12	13	60	....	....	....	....	....
1979-80	Medicine Hat	WHL	72	7	40	47	284	....	....	....	....	....
1980-81	Medicine Hat	WHL	72	14	46	60	164	5	1	1	2	8
1981-82	Erie	AHL	69	1	18	19	78	....	....	....	....	....
1982-83	**Pittsburgh**	**NHL**	**41**	**2**	**2**	**4**	**102**	....	....	....	....	....
	Baltimore	AHL	31	2	8	10	45	....	....	....	....	....
1983-84	**Pittsburgh**	**NHL**	**47**	**2**	**4**	**6**	**60**	....	....	....	....	....
	Baltimore	AHL	33	2	12	14	100	10	1	3	4	22
1984-85	**Pittsburgh**	**NHL**	**69**	**2**	**7**	**9**	**191**	....	....	....	....	....
1985-86	**Pittsburgh**	**NHL**	**72**	**2**	**7**	**9**	**159**	....	....	....	....	....
1986-87	**Pittsburgh**	**NHL**	**68**	**3**	**15**	**18**	**123**	....	....	....	....	....
1987-88	**Pittsburgh**	**NHL**	**76**	**4**	**8**	**12**	**206**	....	....	....	....	....
1988-89	**Pittsburgh**	**NHL**	**52**	**1**	**5**	**6**	**105**	**10**	**0**	**0**	**0**	**23**
1989-90	**Vancouver**	**NHL**	**17**	**0**	**3**	**3**	**36**	....	....	....	....	....
	Pittsburgh	**NHL**	**6**	**0**	**0**	**0**	**13**	....	....	....	....	....
1990-91	**Los Angeles**	**NHL**	**57**	**3**	**8**	**11**	**182**	**2**	**0**	**2**	**2**	**22**
1991-92	**Los Angeles**	**NHL**	**5**	**0**	**0**	**0**	**11**	....	....	....	....	....
	Chicago	**NHL**	**42**	**0**	**4**	**4**	**80**	**6**	**0**	**1**	**1**	**0**
	NHL Totals		**552**	**19**	**63**	**82**	**1268**	**18**	**0**	**3**	**3**	**45**

Traded to **Vancouver** by **Pittsburgh** for Vancouver's sixth round choice (Ian Moran) in 1990 Entry Draft, October 24, 1989. Traded to **Pittsburgh** by **Vancouver** with Barry Pederson and Tony Tanti for Dave Capuano, Andrew McBain and Dan Quinn, January 8, 1990. Claimed by **Los Angeles** in NHL Waiver Draft, October 1, 1990. Traded to **Chicago** by **Los Angeles** for Chris Norton and future considerations, October 28, 1991.

BUTCHER, GARTH

Defense. Shoots right. 6', 200 lbs. Born, Regina, Sask., January 8, 1963.
(Vancouver's 1st choice, 10th overall, in 1981 Entry Draft).

			Regular Season					Playoffs				
Season	Club	Lea	GP	G	A	TP	PIM	GP	G	A	TP	PIM
1979-80	Regina	WHL	13	0	4	4	20	....	....	....	....	....
1980-81a	Regina	WHL	69	9	77	86	230	11	5	17	22	60
1981-82	**Vancouver**	**NHL**	**5**	**0**	**0**	**0**	**9**	**1**	**0**	**0**	**0**	**0**
a	Regina	WHL	65	24	68	92	318	19	3	17	20	95
1982-83	**Vancouver**	**NHL**	**55**	**1**	**13**	**14**	**104**	**3**	**1**	**0**	**1**	**2**
1983-84	**Vancouver**	**NHL**	**28**	**2**	**0**	**2**	**34**	....	....	....	....	....
	Fredericton	AHL	25	4	13	17	43	6	0	2	2	19
1984-85	**Vancouver**	**NHL**	**75**	**3**	**9**	**12**	**152**	....	....	....	....	....
	Fredericton	AHL	3	1	0	1	11	....	....	....	....	....
1985-86	**Vancouver**	**NHL**	**70**	**4**	**7**	**11**	**188**	**3**	**0**	**0**	**0**	**0**
1986-87	**Vancouver**	**NHL**	**70**	**5**	**15**	**20**	**207**	....	....	....	....	....
1987-88	**Vancouver**	**NHL**	**80**	**6**	**17**	**23**	**285**	....	....	....	....	....
1988-89	**Vancouver**	**NHL**	**78**	**0**	**20**	**20**	**227**	**7**	**1**	**1**	**2**	**22**
1989-90	**Vancouver**	**NHL**	**80**	**6**	**14**	**20**	**205**	....	....	....	....	....
1990-91	**Vancouver**	**NHL**	**69**	**6**	**12**	**18**	**257**	....	....	....	....	....
	St. Louis	**NHL**	**13**	**0**	**4**	**4**	**32**	**13**	**2**	**1**	**3**	**54**
1991-92	**St. Louis**	**NHL**	**68**	**5**	**15**	**20**	**189**	**5**	**1**	**2**	**3**	**16**
	NHL Totals		**691**	**38**	**126**	**164**	**1889**	**32**	**5**	**4**	**9**	**92**

a WHL First All-Star Team (1981, 1982)

Traded to **St. Louis** by **Vancouver** with Dan Quinn for Geoff Courtnall, Robert Dirk, Sergio Momesso, Cliff Ronning and future considerations, March 5, 1991.

BUTSAYEV, VYACHESLAV

Center. Shoots left. 6'2", 200 lbs. Born, Togliatti, Soviet Union, June 13, 1970.
(Philadelphia's 10th choice, 109th overall, in 1990 Entry Draft).

			Regular Season					Playoffs				
Season	Club	Lea	GP	G	A	TP	PIM	GP	G	A	TP	PIM
1989-90	CSKA	USSR	48	13	4	17	30	....	....	....	....	....
1990-91	CSKA	USSR	46	14	9	23	32	....	....	....	....	....
1991-92	CSKA	CIS	36	12	13	25	26	....	....	....	....	....

BYCE, JOHN

Center. Shoots left. 6'1", 180 lbs. Born, Madison, WI, August 9, 1967.
(Boston's 11th choice, 220th overall, in 1985 Entry Draft).

			Regular Season					Playoffs				
Season	Club	Lea	GP	G	A	TP	PIM	GP	G	A	TP	PIM
1986-87	U. Wisconsin	WCHA	40	1	4	5	12	....	....	....	....	....
1987-88	U. Wisconsin	WCHA	41	22	12	34	18	....	....	....	....	....
1988-89a	U. Wisconsin	WCHA	42	27	28	55	16	....	....	....	....	....
1989-90ab	U. Wisconsin	WCHA	46	27	44	71	20	....	....	....	....	....
	Boston	**NHL**	....	....	....	....	....	**8**	**2**	**0**	**2**	**2**
1990-91	**Boston**	**NHL**	**18**	**1**	**3**	**4**	**6**	....	....	....	....	....
	Maine	AHL	53	19	29	48	20	....	....	....	....	....
1991-92	**Boston**	**NHL**	**3**	**1**	**0**	**1**	**0**	....	....	....	....	....
	Maine	AHL	55	29	21	50	41	....	....	....	....	....
	Baltimore	AHL	20	9	5	14	4	....	....	....	....	....
	NHL Totals		**21**	**2**	**3**	**5**	**6**	**8**	**2**	**0**	**2**	**2**

a WCHA Second All-Star Team (1989, 1990)
b NCAA All-Tournament Team (1990)

Traded to **Washington** by **Boston** with Dennis Smith for Brent Hughes and future considerations, February 24, 1992.

BYERS, LYNDON

Right wing. Shoots right. 6'1", 200 lbs. Born, Nipawin, Sask., February 29, 1964.
(Boston's 3rd choice, 39th overall, in 1982 Entry Draft).

			Regular Season					Playoffs				
Season	Club	Lea	GP	G	A	TP	PIM	GP	G	A	TP	PIM
1981-82	Regina	WHL	57	18	25	43	169	20	5	6	11	48
1982-83	Regina	WHL	70	32	38	70	153	5	1	1	2	16
1983-84	**Boston**	**NHL**	**10**	**2**	**4**	**6**	**32**	....	....	....	....	....
	Regina	WHL	58	32	57	89	154	23	17	18	35	78
1984-85	**Boston**	**NHL**	**33**	**3**	**8**	**11**	**41**	....	....	....	....	....
	Hershey	AHL	27	4	6	10	55	....	....	....	....	....
1985-86	**Boston**	**NHL**	**5**	**0**	**2**	**2**	**9**	....	....	....	....	....
	Moncton	AHL	14	2	4	6	26	....	....	....	....	....
	Milwaukee	IHL	8	0	2	2	22	....	....	....	....	....
1986-87	**Boston**	**NHL**	**18**	**2**	**3**	**5**	**53**	**1**	**0**	**0**	**0**	**0**
	Moncton	AHL	27	5	5	10	63	....	....	....	....	....
1987-88	**Boston**	**NHL**	**53**	**10**	**14**	**24**	**236**	**11**	**1**	**2**	**3**	**62**
	Maine	AHL	2	0	1	1	18	....	....	....	....	....
1988-89	**Boston**	**NHL**	**49**	**0**	**4**	**4**	**218**	**2**	**0**	**0**	**0**	**0**
	Maine	AHL	4	1	3	4	2	....	....	....	....	....
1989-90	**Boston**	**NHL**	**43**	**4**	**4**	**8**	**159**	**17**	**1**	**0**	**1**	**12**
1990-91	**Boston**	**NHL**	**19**	**2**	**2**	**4**	**82**	**1**	**0**	**0**	**0**	**10**
1991-92	**Boston**	**NHL**	**31**	**1**	**1**	**2**	**129**	**5**	**0**	**0**	**0**	**12**
	Maine	AHL	11	5	4	9	47	....	....	....	....	....
	NHL Totals		**261**	**24**	**42**	**66**	**959**	**37**	**2**	**2**	**4**	**96**

BYKOV, VIACHESLAV (BIH-kahf)

Center. 5'8", 175 lbs. Born, Chelyabinsk, Soviet Union, July 24, 1960.
(Quebec's 11th choice, 169th overall, in 1989 Entry Draft).

			Regular Season					Playoffs				
Season	Club	Lea	GP	G	A	TP	PIM	GP	G	A	TP	PIM
1979-80	Chelyabinsk	USSR	3	2	0	2	0	....	....	....	....	....
1980-81	Chelyabinsk	USSR	48	26	16	42	4	....	....	....	....	....
1981-82	Chelyabinsk	USSR	44	20	16	36	14	....	....	....	....	....
1982-83	CSKA	USSR	44	22	22	44	10	....	....	....	....	....
1983-84	CSKA	USSR	44	22	11	33	12	....	....	....	....	....
1984-85	CSKA	USSR	36	21	14	35	4	....	....	....	....	....
1985-86	CSKA	USSR	36	10	10	20	6	....	....	....	....	....
1986-87	CSKA	USSR	40	18	15	33	10	....	....	....	....	....
1987-88	CSKA	USSR	47	17	30	47	26	....	....	....	....	....
1988-89	CSKA	USSR	40	16	20	36	10	....	....	....	....	....
1989-90	CSKA	USSR	48	21	16	37	16	....	....	....	....	....
1990-91	Fribourg	Switz.	36	35	49	84	....	8	8	16	24	....
1991-92	Fribourg	Switz.	34	40	49	89	24	....	....	....	....	....

BYLSMA, DAN

Left wing. Shoots left. 6'2", 205 lbs. Born, Grand Rapids, MI, September 19, 1970.
(Winnipeg's 7th choice, 109th overall, in 1989 Entry Draft).

			Regular Season					Playoffs				
Season	Club	Lea	GP	G	A	TP	PIM	GP	G	A	TP	PIM
1988-89	Bowling Green	CCHA	32	3	7	10	10	....	....	....	....	....
1989-90	Bowling Green	CCHA	44	13	17	30	30	....	....	....	....	....
1990-91	Bowling Green	CCHA	40	9	12	21	48	....	....	....	....	....
1991-92	Bowling Green	CCHA	34	11	14	25	24	....	....	....	....	....

BYRAM, SHAWN

Left wing. Shoots left. 6'2", 204 lbs. Born, Neepawa, Man., September 12, 1968.
(NY Islanders' 4th choice, 80th overall, in 1986 Entry Draft).

			Regular Season					Playoffs				
Season	Club	Lea	GP	G	A	TP	PIM	GP	G	A	TP	PIM
1985-86	Regina	WHL	46	7	6	13	45	9	0	1	1	11
1986-87	Prince Albert	WHL	67	19	21	40	147	7	1	1	2	10
1987-88	Prince Albert	WHL	61	23	28	51	178	10	5	2	7	27
1988-89	Springfield	AHL	45	5	11	16	195	....	....	....	....	....
	Indianapolis	IHL	1	0	0	0	2	....	....	....	....	....
1989-90	Springfield	AHL	31	4	4	8	30	....	....	....	....	....
	Johnstown	ECHL	8	5	5	10	35	....	....	....	....	....
1990-91	**NY Islanders**	**NHL**	**4**	**0**	**0**	**0**	**14**	....	....	....	....	....
	Capital Dist.	AHL	62	28	35	63	162	....	....	....	....	....
1991-92	**Chicago**	**NHL**	**1**	**0**	**0**	**0**	**0**	....	....	....	....	....
	Indianapolis	IHL	69	18	21	39	154	....	....	....	....	....
	NHL Totals		**5**	**0**	**0**	**0**	**14**	....	....	....	....	....

Signed as a free agent by **Chicago**, August 15, 1991.

BZDEL, GERALD (bayz-DEHL)

Defense. Shoots right. 6'1", 196 lbs. Born, Wynyard, Sask., March 13, 1968.
(Quebec's 5th choice, 102nd overall, in 1986 Entry Draft).

			Regular Season					Playoffs				
Season	Club	Lea	GP	G	A	TP	PIM	GP	G	A	TP	PIM
1985-86	Regina	WHL	72	2	15	17	107	10	0	3	3	14
1986-87	Regina	WHL	13	0	3	3	38	....	....	....	....	....
	Seattle	WHL	48	4	12	16	137	....	....	....	....	....
1987-88	Moose Jaw	WHL	72	4	17	21	217	....	....	....	....	....
1988-89	Halifax	AHL	36	1	3	4	46	....	....	....	....	....
1989-90	Halifax	AHL	59	2	20	22	84	6	0	1	1	24
1990-91	Halifax	AHL	74	3	11	14	99	....	....	....	....	....
1991-92	Halifax	AHL	35	0	6	6	42	....	....	....	....	....

CAIRNS, ERIC

Defense. Shoots left. 6'5", 217 lbs. Born, Oakville, Ont., June 27, 1974.
(NY Rangers' 3rd choice, 72nd overall, in 1992 Entry Draft).

			Regular Season					Playoffs				
Season	Club	Lea	GP	G	A	TP	PIM	GP	G	A	TP	PIM
1990-91	Burlington	Jr. B	37	5	16	21	120	....	....	....	....	....
1991-92	Detroit	OHL	64	1	11	12	232	7	0	0	0	31

CALLAHAN, JOHN JR. (JACK)

Center. Shoots right. 6'3", 208 lbs. Born, Melrose, MA, April 21, 1971.
(Philadelphia's 5th choice, 138th overall, in 1989 Entry Draft).

			Regular Season					Playoffs				
Season	Club	Lea	GP	G	A	TP	PIM	GP	G	A	TP	PIM
1990-91	Boston College	H.E.	30	11	5	16	16	....	....	....	....	....
1991-92	Boston College	H.E.	35	15	11	26	52	....	....	....	....	....

CALLANDER, JOHN (JOCK)

Right wing. Shoots right. 6'1", 188 lbs. Born, Regina, Sask., April 23, 1961.

			Regular Season					Playoffs				
Season	Club	Lea	GP	G	A	TP	PIM	GP	G	A	TP	PIM
1979-80	Regina	WHL	39	9	11	20	25	18	8	5	13	0
1980-81	Regina	WHL	72	67	86	153	37	11	6	7	13	14
1981-82	Regina	WHL	71	79	111	*190	59	20	13	*26	39	37
1982-83	Salt Lake	CHL	68	20	27	47	26	6	0	1	1	9
1983-84	Montana	CHL	72	27	32	59	69	....	....	....	....	....
	Toledo	IHL	2	0	0	0	0	....	....	....	....	....
1984-85	Muskegon	IHL	82	39	68	107	86	17	13	*21	*34	33
1985-86a	Muskegon	IHL	82	39	72	111	121	14	*12	11	*23	12
1986-87bcd	Muskegon	IHL	82	54	82	*136	110	15	13	7	20	23
1987-88	**Pittsburgh**	**NHL**	**41**	**11**	**16**	**27**	**45**	....	....	....	....	....
	Muskegon	IHL	31	20	36	56	49	6	2	3	5	25
1988-89	**Pittsburgh**	**NHL**	**30**	**6**	**5**	**11**	**20**	**10**	**2**	**5**	**7**	**10**
	Muskegon	IHL	48	25	39	64	40	7	5	5	10	30
1989-90	**Pittsburgh**	**NHL**	**30**	**4**	**7**	**11**	**49**	....	....	....	....	....
	Muskegon	IHL	46	29	49	78	118	15	6	*14	20	54
1990-91	Muskegon	IHL	30	14	20	34	102	....	....	....	....	....
1991-92b	Muskegon	IHL	81	42	70	112	160	10	4	10	14	13
	Pittsburgh	**NHL**	....	....	....	....	....	**12**	**1**	**3**	**4**	**2**
	NHL Totals		**101**	**21**	**28**	**49**	**114**	**22**	**3**	**8**	**11**	**12**

a IHL Playoff MVP (1986)
b IHL First All-Star Team (1987, 1992)
c Shared James Gatschene Memorial Trophy (MVP-IHL) with Jeff Pyle (1987)
d Shared Leo P. Lamoureux Memorial Trophy (Top Scorer-IHL) with Jeff Pyle (1987)

Signed as a free agent by **St. Louis**, September 28, 1981. Signed as a free agent by **Pittsburgh**, July 31, 1987. Signed as a free agent by **Tampa Bay**, July 29, 1992.

CALOUN, JAN

Right wing. Shoots right. 5'10", 176 lbs. Born, Usti-Nad-Labem, Czech., December 20, 1972.
(San Jose's 4th choice, 75th overall, in 1992 Entry Draft).

			Regular Season					Playoffs				
Season	Club	Lea	GP	G	A	TP	PIM	GP	G	A	TP	PIM
1990-91	Litvinov	Czech.	58	29	31	60	12	....	....	....	....	....
1991-92	Litvinov	Czech.	46	39	18	57	0	....	....	....	....	....

CAMPBELL, JIM

Center. Shoots right. 6'1", 175 lbs. Born, Worcester, MA, April 3, 1973.
(Montreal's 2nd choice, 28th overall, in 1991 Entry Draft).

			Regular Season					Playoffs				
Season	Club	Lea	GP	G	A	TP	PIM	GP	G	A	TP	PIM
1990-91	Northwood	HS	26	36	47	83	36	....	....	....	....	....
1991-92	Hull	QMJHL	64	41	44	85	51	6	7	3	10	8

CANAVAN, ROBERT

Left wing. Shoots left. 5'11", 180 lbs. Born, Boston, MA, February 4, 1973.
(NY Islanders' 10th choice, 202nd overall, in 1991 Entry Draft).

			Regular Season					Playoffs				
Season	Club	Lea	GP	G	A	TP	PIM	GP	G	A	TP	PIM
1990-91	Hingham	HS	17	28	22	50	18	....	....	....	....	....
1991-92	Boston College	H.E.	30	7	4	11	28	....	....	....	....	....

CAPUANO, DAVE (KAP-yew-AN-oh)

Left wing. Shoots left. 6'2", 190 lbs. Born, Warwick, RI, July 27, 1968.
(Pittsburgh's 2nd choice, 25th overall, in 1986 Entry Draft).

			Regular Season					Playoffs				
Season	Club	Lea	GP	G	A	TP	PIM	GP	G	A	TP	PIM
1986-87	U. of Maine	H.E.	38	18	41	59	14	....	....	....	....	....
1987-88abc	U. of Maine	H.E.	42	*34	*51	*85	51	....	....	....	....	....
1988-89ac	U. of Maine	H.E.	41	37	30	67	38	....	....	....	....	....
1989-90	**Pittsburgh**	**NHL**	**6**	**0**	**0**	**0**	**2**	....	....	....	....	....
	Muskegon	IHL	27	15	15	30	22	....	....	....	....	....
	Vancouver	**NHL**	**27**	**3**	**5**	**8**	**10**	....	....	....	....	....
	Milwaukee	IHL	2	0	4	4	0	6	1	5	6	0
1990-91	**Vancouver**	**NHL**	**61**	**13**	**31**	**44**	**42**	**6**	**1**	**1**	**2**	**5**
1991-92	Milwaukee	IHL	9	2	6	8	8	....	....	....	....	....
	NHL Totals		**94**	**16**	**36**	**52**	**54**	**6**	**1**	**1**	**2**	**5**

a NCAA East First All-American Team (1988, 1989)
b NCAA All-Tournament Team (1988)
c Hockey East First All-Star Team (1988, 1989)

Traded to **Vancouver** by **Pittsburgh** with Andrew McBain and Dan Quinn for Rod Buskas, Barry Pederson and Tony Tanti, January 8, 1990.

CAPUANO, DEAN

Defense. Shoots left. 6'1", 175 lbs. Born, Providence, RI, November 3, 1971.
(Boston's 9th choice, 210th overall, in 1990 Entry Draft).

			Regular Season					Playoffs				
Season	Club	Lea	GP	G	A	TP	PIM	GP	G	A	TP	PIM
1989-90	Mt. St. Charles	HS	....	5	20	25	....	....	....	....	....	....
1990-91	Providence	H.E.	19	3	5	8	6	....	....	....	....	....
1991-92	Providence	H.E.	3	0	0	0	0	....	....	....	....	....

CAPUANO, JACK (KAP-yew-AN-oh)

Defense. Shoots left. 6'2", 210 lbs. Born, Cranston, RI, July 7, 1966.
(Toronto's 4th choice, 67th overall, in 1984 Entry Draft).

			Regular Season					Playoffs				
Season	Club	Lea	GP	G	A	TP	PIM	GP	G	A	TP	PIM
1985-86	U. of Maine	H.E.	39	9	18	27	51	....	....	....	....	....
1986-87a	U. of Maine	H.E.	42	10	34	44	20	....	....	....	....	....
1987-88bc	U. of Maine	H.E.	43	13	37	50	87	....	....	....	....	....
1988-89	Newmarket	AHL	74	5	16	21	52	1	0	0	0	0
1989-90	**Toronto**	**NHL**	**1**	**0**	**0**	**0**	**0**	....	....	....	....	....
	Newmarket	AHL	8	0	2	2	7	....	....	....	....	....
	Springfield	AHL	14	0	4	4	8	....	....	....	....	....
	Milwaukee	IHL	17	3	10	13	60	6	0	1	1	12
1990-91	**Vancouver**	**NHL**	**3**	**0**	**0**	**0**	**0**	....	....	....	....	....
	Milwaukee	IHL	80	20	30	50	76	6	0	1	1	2
1991-92	**Boston**	**NHL**	**2**	**0**	**0**	**0**	**0**	....	....	....	....	....
	Maine	AHL	74	14	26	40	35	....	....	....	....	....
	NHL Totals		**6**	**0**	**0**	**0**	**0**	....	....	....	....	....

a Hockey East Second All-Star Team (1987)
b NCAA East First All-American Team (1988)
c Hockey East First All-Star Team (1988)

Traded to **NY Islanders** by **Toronto** with Paul Gagne and Derek Laxdal for Mike Stevens and Gilles Thibaudeau, December 20, 1989. Traded to **Vancouver** by **NY Islanders** for Jeff Rohlicek, March 6, 1990. Signed as a free agent by **Boston**, August 1, 1991.

CARBONNEAU, GUY (KAR-buhn-oh, GEE)

Center. Shoots right. 5'11", 184 lbs. Born, Sept-Iles, Que., March 18, 1960.
(Montreal's 4th choice, 44th overall, in 1979 Entry Draft).

			Regular Season					Playoffs				
Season	Club	Lea	GP	G	A	TP	PIM	GP	G	A	TP	PIM
1976-77	Chicoutimi	QJHL	59	9	20	29	8	4	1	0	1	0
1977-78	Chicoutimi	QJHL	70	28	55	83	60	....	....	....	....	....
1978-79	Chicoutimi	QJHL	72	62	79	141	47	4	2	1	3	4
1979-80	Chicoutimi	QJHL	72	72	110	182	66	12	9	15	24	28
	Nova Scotia	AHL	....	....	....	....	....	2	1	1	2	2
1980-81	**Montreal**	**NHL**	**2**	**0**	**1**	**1**	**0**	....	....	....	....	....
	Nova Scotia	AHL	78	35	53	88	87	6	1	3	4	9
1981-82	Nova Scotia	AHL	77	27	67	94	124	9	2	7	9	8
1982-83	**Montreal**	**NHL**	**77**	**18**	**29**	**47**	**68**	**3**	**0**	**0**	**0**	**2**
1983-84	**Montreal**	**NHL**	**78**	**24**	**30**	**54**	**75**	**15**	**4**	**3**	**7**	**12**
1984-85	**Montreal**	**NHL**	**79**	**23**	**34**	**57**	**43**	**12**	**4**	**3**	**7**	**8**
1985-86	**Montreal**	**NHL**	**80**	**20**	**36**	**56**	**57**	**20**	**7**	**5**	**12**	**35**
1986-87	**Montreal**	**NHL**	**79**	**18**	**27**	**45**	**68**	**17**	**3**	**8**	**11**	**20**
1987-88a	**Montreal**	**NHL**	**80**	**17**	**21**	**38**	**61**	**11**	**0**	**4**	**4**	**2**
1988-89a	**Montreal**	**NHL**	**79**	**26**	**30**	**56**	**44**	**21**	**4**	**5**	**9**	**10**
1989-90	**Montreal**	**NHL**	**68**	**19**	**36**	**55**	**37**	**11**	**2**	**3**	**5**	**6**
1990-91	**Montreal**	**NHL**	**78**	**20**	**24**	**44**	**63**	**13**	**1**	**5**	**6**	**10**
1991-92a	**Montreal**	**NHL**	**72**	**18**	**21**	**39**	**39**	**11**	**1**	**1**	**2**	**6**
	NHL Totals		**772**	**203**	**289**	**492**	**555**	**134**	**26**	**37**	**63**	**111**

a Won Frank J. Selke Trophy (1988, 1989, 1992)

CARKNER, TERRY

Defense. Shoots left. 6'3", 212 lbs. Born, Smiths Falls, Ont., March 7, 1966.
(NY Rangers' 1st choice, 14th overall, in 1984 Entry Draft).

			Regular Season					Playoffs				
Season	Club	Lea	GP	G	A	TP	PIM	GP	G	A	TP	PIM
1983-84	Peterborough	OHL	58	4	19	23	77	8	0	6	6	13
1984-85a	Peterborough	OHL	64	14	47	61	125	17	2	10	12	11
1985-86b	Peterborough	OHL	54	12	32	44	106	16	1	7	8	17
1986-87	**NY Rangers**	**NHL**	**52**	**2**	**13**	**15**	**118**	**1**	**0**	**0**	**0**	**0**
	New Haven	AHL	12	2	6	8	56	3	1	0	1	0
1987-88	**Quebec**	**NHL**	**63**	**3**	**24**	**27**	**159**	....	....	....	....	....
1988-89	**Philadelphia**	**NHL**	**78**	**11**	**32**	**43**	**149**	**19**	**1**	**5**	**6**	**28**
1989-90	**Philadelphia**	**NHL**	**63**	**4**	**18**	**22**	**169**	....	....	....	....	....
1990-91	**Philadelphia**	**NHL**	**79**	**7**	**25**	**32**	**204**	....	....	....	....	....
1991-92	**Philadelphia**	**NHL**	**73**	**4**	**12**	**16**	**195**	....	....	....	....	....
	NHL Totals		**408**	**31**	**124**	**155**	**994**	**20**	**1**	**5**	**6**	**28**

a OHL Second All-Star Team (1985)
b OHL First All-Star Team (1986)

Traded to **Quebec** by **NY Rangers** with Jeff Jackson for John Ogrodnick and David Shaw, September 30, 1987. Traded to **Philadelphia** by **Quebec** for Greg Smyth and Philadelphia's third round choice (John Tanner) in the 1989 Entry Draft, July 25, 1988.

CARLSON, MARK

Left wing. Shoots left. 6', 193 lbs. Born, Danbury, CT, February 5, 1969.
(Pittsburgh's 11th choice, 215th overall, in 1987 Entry Draft).

			Regular Season					Playoffs				
Season	Club	Lea	GP	G	A	TP	PIM	GP	G	A	TP	PIM
1990-91	Lowell	H.E.	11	0	1	1	20	....	....	....	....	....
1991-92	Lowell	H.E.	23	3	1	4	20	....	....	....	....	....

CARLYLE, RANDY ROBERT

Defense. Shoots left. 5'10", 200 lbs. Born, Sudbury, Ont., April 19, 1956.
(Toronto's 1st choice, 30th overall, in 1976 Amateur Draft).

			Regular Season					Playoffs				
Season	Club	Lea	GP	G	A	TP	PIM	GP	G	A	TP	PIM
1974-75	Sudbury	OMJHL	67	17	47	64	118	15	3	6	9	21
1975-76a	Sudbury	OHA	60	15	64	79	126	17	6	13	19	50
1976-77	**Toronto**	**NHL**	**45**	**0**	**5**	**5**	**51**	**9**	**0**	**1**	**1**	**20**
	Dallas	CHL	26	2	7	9	63	....	....	....	....	....
1977-78	**Toronto**	**NHL**	**49**	**2**	**11**	**13**	**31**	**7**	**0**	**1**	**1**	**8**
	Dallas	CHL	21	3	14	17	31	....	....	....	....	....
1978-79	**Pittsburgh**	**NHL**	**70**	**13**	**34**	**47**	**78**	**7**	**0**	**0**	**0**	**12**
1979-80	**Pittsburgh**	**NHL**	**67**	**8**	**28**	**36**	**45**	**5**	**1**	**0**	**1**	**4**
1980-81bc	**Pittsburgh**	**NHL**	**76**	**16**	**67**	**83**	**136**	**5**	**4**	**5**	**9**	**9**
1981-82	**Pittsburgh**	**NHL**	**73**	**11**	**64**	**75**	**131**	**5**	**1**	**3**	**4**	**16**
1982-83	**Pittsburgh**	**NHL**	**61**	**15**	**41**	**56**	**110**	....	....	....	....	....
1983-84	**Pittsburgh**	**NHL**	**50**	**3**	**23**	**26**	**82**	....	....	....	....	....
	Winnipeg	**NHL**	**5**	**0**	**3**	**3**	**2**	**3**	**0**	**2**	**2**	**4**
1984-85	**Winnipeg**	**NHL**	**71**	**13**	**38**	**51**	**98**	**8**	**1**	**5**	**6**	**13**
1985-86	**Winnipeg**	**NHL**	**68**	**16**	**33**	**49**	**93**	....	....	....	....	....
1986-87	**Winnipeg**	**NHL**	**71**	**16**	**26**	**42**	**93**	**10**	**1**	**5**	**6**	**18**
1987-88	**Winnipeg**	**NHL**	**78**	**15**	**44**	**59**	**210**	**5**	**0**	**2**	**2**	**10**
1988-89	**Winnipeg**	**NHL**	**78**	**6**	**38**	**44**	**78**	....	....	....	....	....
1989-90	**Winnipeg**	**NHL**	**53**	**3**	**15**	**18**	**50**	....	....	....	....	....
1990-91	**Winnipeg**	**NHL**	**52**	**9**	**19**	**28**	**44**	....	....	....	....	....
1991-92	**Winnipeg**	**NHL**	**66**	**1**	**9**	**10**	**54**	**5**	**1**	**0**	**1**	**6**
	NHL Totals		**1033**	**147**	**498**	**645**	**1386**	**69**	**9**	**24**	**33**	**120**

a OHA Second All-Star Team (1976)
b Won James Norris Memorial Trophy (1981)
c NHL First All-Star Team (1981)

Played in NHL All-Star Game (1981-83, 1985)

Traded to **Pittsburgh** by **Toronto** with George Ferguson for Dave Burrows, June 14, 1978. Traded to **Winnipeg** by **Pittsburgh** for Winnipeg's first round choice (Doug Bodger) in 1984 Entry Draft and future considerations (Moe Mantha), March 5, 1984.

CARNBACK, PATRIK (KAHRN-buhk)

Left wing. Shoots left. 6', 189 lbs. Born, Goteborg, Sweden, February 1, 1968.
(Montreal's 7th choice, 125th overall, in 1988 Entry Draft).

			Regular Season					Playoffs				
Season	Club	Lea	GP	G	A	TP	PIM	GP	G	A	TP	PIM
1986-87	V. Frolunda	Swe.2	28	3	1	4	4	....	....	....	....	....
1987-88	V. Frolunda	Swe.2	33	16	19	35	10	....	....	....	....	....
1988-89	V. Frolunda	Swe.2	53	39	36	75	52	....	....	....	....	....
1989-90	V. Frolunda	Swe.	40	26	27	53	34	....	....	....	....	....
1990-91	V. Frolunda	Swe.2	22	10	9	19	46	....	....	....	....	....
1991-92	V. Frolunda	Swe.	33	17	24	41	32	....	....	....	....	....

CARNEY, KEITH

Defense. Shoots left. 6'1", 180 lbs. Born, Cumberland, RI, February 7, 1971.
(Toronto's 5th choice, 96th overall, in 1989 Entry Draft).

			Regular Season					Playoffs				
Season	Club	Lea	GP	G	A	TP	PIM	GP	G	A	TP	PIM
1989-90	Lowell	H.E.	8	0	2	2	2	....	....	....	....	....
1990-91	Lowell	H.E.	11	0	2	2	8	....	....	....	....	....
1991-92	Lowell	H.E.	22	1	6	7	24	....	....	....	....	....

CARNEY, KEITH E.

Defense. Shoots left. 6'2", 205 lbs. Born, Providence, RI, February 3, 1970.
(Buffalo's 3rd choice, 76th overall, in 1988 Entry Draft).

			Regular Season					Playoffs				
Season	Club	Lea	GP	G	A	TP	PIM	GP	G	A	TP	PIM
1988-89	U. of Maine	H.E.	40	4	22	26	24	....	....	....	....	....
1989-90ab	U. of Maine	H.E.	41	3	41	44	43	....	....	....	....	....
1990-91cd	U. of Maine	H.E.	40	7	49	56	38	....	....	....	....	....
1991-92	**Buffalo**	**NHL**	**14**	**1**	**2**	**3**	**18**	**7**	**0**	**3**	**3**	**0**
	Rochester	AHL	24	1	10	11	2	2	0	2	2	0
	NHL Totals		**14**	**1**	**2**	**3**	**18**	....	....	....	....	....

a Hockey East Second All-Star Team (1990)
b NCAA East Second All-American Team (1990)
c Hockey East First All-Star Team (1991)
d NCAA East First All-American Team (1991)

CARPENTER, ROBERT (BOB)

Center/Left wing. Shoots left. 6', 190 lbs. Born, Beverly, MA, July 13, 1963.
(Washington's 1st choice, 3rd overall, in 1981 Entry Draft).

			Regular Season					Playoffs				
Season	Club	Lea	GP	G	A	TP	PIM	GP	G	A	TP	PIM
1980-81	St. John's	HS	18	14	24	38	....	....	....	....	....	....
1981-82	**Washington**	**NHL**	**80**	**32**	**35**	**67**	**69**	....	....	....	....	....
1982-83	**Washington**	**NHL**	**80**	**32**	**37**	**69**	**64**	**4**	**1**	**0**	**1**	**2**
1983-84	**Washington**	**NHL**	**80**	**28**	**40**	**68**	**51**	**8**	**2**	**1**	**3**	**25**
1984-85	**Washington**	**NHL**	**80**	**53**	**42**	**95**	**87**	**5**	**1**	**4**	**5**	**8**
1985-86	**Washington**	**NHL**	**80**	**27**	**29**	**56**	**105**	**9**	**5**	**4**	**9**	**12**
1986-87	**Washington**	**NHL**	**22**	**5**	**7**	**12**	**21**	....	....	....	....	....
	NY Rangers	**NHL**	**28**	**2**	**8**	**10**	**20**	....	....	....	....	....
	Los Angeles	**NHL**	**10**	**2**	**3**	**5**	**6**	**5**	**1**	**2**	**3**	**2**
1987-88	**Los Angeles**	**NHL**	**71**	**19**	**33**	**52**	**84**	**5**	**1**	**1**	**2**	**0**
1988-89	**Los Angeles**	**NHL**	**39**	**11**	**15**	**26**	**16**	....	....	....	....	....
	Boston	**NHL**	**18**	**5**	**9**	**14**	**10**	**8**	**1**	**1**	**2**	**4**
1989-90	**Boston**	**NHL**	**80**	**25**	**31**	**56**	**97**	**21**	**4**	**6**	**10**	**39**
1990-91	**Boston**	**NHL**	**29**	**8**	**8**	**16**	**22**	**1**	**0**	**1**	**1**	**2**
1991-92	**Boston**	**NHL**	**60**	**25**	**23**	**48**	**46**	**8**	**0**	**1**	**1**	**6**
	NHL Totals		**757**	**274**	**320**	**594**	**698**	**74**	**16**	**21**	**37**	**100**

Played in NHL All-Star Game (1985)

Traded to **NY Rangers** by **Washington** with Washington's second round choice (Jason Prosofsky) in 1989 Entry Draft for Bob Crawford, Kelly Miller and Mike Ridley, January 1, 1987. Traded to **Los Angeles** by **NY Rangers** with Tom Laidlaw for Jeff Crossman, Marcel Dionne and Los Angeles' third round choice in 1989 Entry Draft (Draft choice acquired by **Minnesota,** October 12, 1988. **Minnesota** selected Murray Garbutt.) Traded to **Boston** by **Los Angeles** for Steve Kasper, January 23, 1989.

CARSON, JIMMY

Center. Shoots right. 6', 200 lbs. Born, Southfield, MI, July 20, 1968.
(Los Angeles' 1st choice, 2nd overall, in 1986 Entry Draft).

			Regular Season					Playoffs				
Season	Club	Lea	GP	G	A	TP	PIM	GP	G	A	TP	PIM
1984-85	Verdun	QMJHL	68	44	72	116	12	14	9	17	26	12
1985-86a	Verdun	QMJHL	69	70	83	153	46	5	2	6	8	0
1986-87b	**Los Angeles**	**NHL**	**80**	**37**	**42**	**79**	**22**	**5**	**1**	**2**	**3**	**6**
1987-88	**Los Angeles**	**NHL**	**80**	**55**	**52**	**107**	**45**	**5**	**5**	**3**	**8**	**4**
1988-89	**Edmonton**	**NHL**	**80**	**49**	**51**	**100**	**36**	**7**	**2**	**1**	**3**	**6**
1989-90	**Edmonton**	**NHL**	**4**	**1**	**2**	**3**	**0**	....	....	....	....	....
	Detroit	**NHL**	**44**	**20**	**16**	**36**	**8**	....	....	....	....	....
1990-91	**Detroit**	**NHL**	**64**	**21**	**25**	**46**	**28**	**7**	**2**	**1**	**3**	**4**
1991-92	**Detroit**	**NHL**	**80**	**34**	**35**	**69**	**30**	**11**	**2**	**3**	**5**	**0**
	NHL Totals		**432**	**217**	**223**	**440**	**169**	**35**	**12**	**10**	**22**	**20**

a QMJHL Second All-Star Team (1986)
b Named to NHL All-Rookie Team (1987)

Played in NHL All-Star Game (1989)

Traded to **Edmonton** by **Los Angeles** with Martin Gelinas, Los Angeles' first round choices in 1989 (acquired by New Jersey, June 17, 1989. New Jersey selected Jason Miller), 1991 (Martin Rucinsky) and 1993 Entry Drafts and cash for Wayne Gretzky, Mike Krushelnyski and Marty McSorley, August 9, 1988. Traded to **Detroit** by **Edmonton** with Kevin McClelland and Edmonton's fifth round choice (later traded to Montreal for Rick Green. Montreal selected Brad Layzell) in 1991 Entry Draft for Petr Klima, Joe Murphy, Adam Graves and Jeff Sharples, November 2, 1989.

CARTER, JOHN

Left wing. Shoots left. 5'10", 181 lbs. Born, Winchester, MA, May 3, 1963.

			Regular Season					Playoffs				
Season	Club	Lea	GP	G	A	TP	PIM	GP	G	A	TP	PIM
1982-83	RPI	ECAC	29	16	22	38	33	....	....	....	....	....
1983-84	RPI	ECAC	38	35	39	74	52	....	....	....	....	....
1984-85	RPI	ECAC	37	43	29	72	52	....	....	....	....	....
1985-86	RPI	ECAC	27	23	18	41	68	....	....	....	....	....
	Boston	**NHL**	**3**	**0**	**0**	**0**	**0**	....	....	....	....	....
1986-87	**Boston**	**NHL**	**8**	**0**	**1**	**1**	**0**	....	....	....	....	....
	Moncton	AHL	58	25	30	55	60	6	2	3	5	5
1987-88	**Boston**	**NHL**	**4**	**0**	**1**	**1**	**2**	....	....	....	....	....
	Maine	AHL	76	38	38	76	145	10	4	4	8	44
1988-89	**Boston**	**NHL**	**44**	**12**	**10**	**22**	**24**	**10**	**1**	**2**	**3**	**6**
	Maine	AHL	24	13	6	19	12	....	....	....	....	....
1989-90	**Boston**	**NHL**	**76**	**17**	**22**	**39**	**26**	**21**	**6**	**3**	**9**	**45**
	Maine	AHL	2	2	2	4	2	....	....	....	....	....
1990-91	**Boston**	**NHL**	**50**	**4**	**7**	**11**	**68**	....	....	....	....	....
	Maine	AHL	16	5	9	14	16	1	0	0	0	10
1991-92	**San Jose**	**NHL**	**4**	**0**	**0**	**0**	**0**	....	....	....	....	....
	Kansas City	IHL	42	11	15	26	116	15	6	9	15	18
	NHL Totals		**189**	**33**	**41**	**74**	**120**	**31**	**7**	**5**	**12**	**51**

Signed as a free agent by **Boston**, May 3, 1986. Signed as a free agent by **San Jose**, August 22, 1991.

CARUSO, BRIAN

Left wing. Shoots left. 6'2", 225 lbs. Born, Thunder Bay, Ont., September 20, 1972.
(Calgary's 4th choice, 63rd overall, in 1991 Entry Draft).

			Regular Season					Playoffs				
Season	Club	Lea	GP	G	A	TP	PIM	GP	G	A	TP	PIM
1990-91	Minn.-Duluth	WCHA	31	5	6	11	24	....	....	....	....	....
1991-92	Minn.-Duluth	WCHA	29	2	3	5	34	....	....	....	....	....

CARVEL, GREG

Center. Shoots left. 5'11", 185 lbs. Born, Canton, NY, August 17, 1970.
(Pittsburgh's 1st choice, 22nd overall, in 1991 Supplemental Draft).

			Regular Season					Playoffs				
Season	Club	Lea	GP	G	A	TP	PIM	GP	G	A	TP	PIM
1989-90	St. Lawrence	ECAC	30	5	16	21	18	....	....	....	....	....
1990-91	St. Lawrence	ECAC	34	7	15	22	18	....	....	....	....	....
1991-92	St. Lawrence	ECAC	34	12	20	32	23	....	....	....	....	....

CASSELMAN, MIKE

Center. Shoots left. 5'11", 180 lbs. Born, Morrisburg, Ont., August 23, 1968.
(Detroit's 1st choice, 3rd overall, in 1990 Supplemental Draft).

			Regular Season					Playoffs				
Season	Club	Lea	GP	G	A	TP	PIM	GP	G	A	TP	PIM
1987-88	Clarkson	ECAC	24	4	1	5	....	....	....	....	....	....
1988-89	Clarkson	ECAC	31	3	14	17	....	....	....	....	....	....
1989-90	Clarkson	ECAC	34	22	21	43	69	....	....	....	....	....
1990-91	Clarkson	ECAC	40	19	35	54	44	....	....	....	....	....
1991-92a	Toledo	ECHL	61	39	60	99	83	5	0	1	1	6
	Adirondack	AHL	1	0	0	0	0	....	....	....	....	....

a ECHL Second All-Star Team (1992)

CASSELS, ANDREW (CASTLES)

Center. Shoots left. 6', 192 lbs. Born, Bramalea, Ont., July 23, 1969.
(Montreal's 1st choice, 17th overall, in 1987 Entry Draft).

			Regular Season					Playoffs				
Season	Club	Lea	GP	G	A	TP	PIM	GP	G	A	TP	PIM
1986-87a	Ottawa	OHL	66	26	66	92	28	11	5	9	14	7
1987-88bc	Ottawa	OHL	61	48	*103	*151	39	16	8	*24	*32	13
1988-89c	Ottawa	OHL	56	37	97	134	66	12	5	10	15	10
1989-90	**Montreal**	**NHL**	**6**	**2**	**0**	**2**	**2**	....	....	....	....	....
	Sherbrooke	AHL	55	22	45	67	25	12	2	11	13	6
1990-91	**Montreal**	**NHL**	**54**	**6**	**19**	**25**	**20**	**8**	**0**	**2**	**2**	**2**
1991-92	**Hartford**	**NHL**	**67**	**11**	**30**	**41**	**18**	**7**	**2**	**4**	**6**	**6**
	NHL Totals		**127**	**19**	**49**	**68**	**40**	**15**	**2**	**6**	**8**	**8**

a OHL Rookie of the Year (1987)
b OHL Player of the Year (1988)
c OHL First All-Star Team (1988,1989)

Traded to **Hartford** by **Montreal** for Hartford's second round choice (Valeri Bure) in 1992 Entry Draft, September 17, 1991.

CAUFIELD, JAY

Right wing. Shoots right. 6'4", 237 lbs. Born, Philadelphia, PA, July 17, 1960.

			Regular Season					Playoffs				
Season	Club	Lea	GP	G	A	TP	PIM	GP	G	A	TP	PIM
1984-85	North Dakota	WCHA	1	0	0	0	0	....	....	....	....	....
1985-86	Toledo	IHL	30	5	4	9	54	....	....	....	....	....
	New Haven	AHL	40	2	3	5	40	1	0	0	0	0
1986-87	**NY Rangers**	**NHL**	**13**	**2**	**1**	**3**	**45**	**3**	**0**	**0**	**0**	**12**
	Flint	IHL	12	4	3	7	59	....	....	....	....	....
	New Haven	AHL	13	0	0	0	43	....	....	....	....	....
1987-88	**Minnesota**	**NHL**	**1**	**0**	**0**	**0**	**0**	....	....	....	....	....
	Kalamazoo	IHL	65	5	10	15	273	6	0	1	1	47
1988-89	**Pittsburgh**	**NHL**	**58**	**1**	**4**	**5**	**285**	**9**	**0**	**0**	**0**	**28**
1989-90	**Pittsburgh**	**NHL**	**37**	**1**	**2**	**3**	**123**	....	....	....	....	....
1990-91	**Pittsburgh**	**NHL**	**23**	**1**	**1**	**2**	**71**	....	....	....	....	....
	Muskegon	IHL	3	1	0	1	18	....	....	....	....	....
1991-92	**Pittsburgh**	**NHL**	**50**	**0**	**0**	**0**	**175**	**5**	**0**	**0**	**0**	**2**
	NHL Totals		**182**	**5**	**8**	**13**	**699**	**17**	**0**	**0**	**0**	**42**

Signed as a free agent by **NY Rangers**, October 8, 1985. Traded to **Minnesota** by **NY Rangers** with Dave Gagne for Jari Gronstrand and Paul Boutilier, October 8, 1987. Claimed by **Pittsburgh** in NHL Waiver Draft, October 3, 1988.

CAVALLINI, GINO JOHN

Left wing. Shoots left. 6'1", 215 lbs. Born, Toronto, Ont., November 24, 1962.

			Regular Season					Playoffs				
Season	Club	Lea	GP	G	A	TP	PIM	GP	G	A	TP	PIM
1982-83	Bowling Green	CCHA	40	8	16	24	52	....	....	....	....	....
1983-84	Bowling Green	CCHA	43	25	23	48	16	....	....	....	....	....
1984-85	**Calgary**	**NHL**	**27**	**6**	**10**	**16**	**14**	**3**	**0**	**0**	**0**	**4**
	Moncton	AHL	51	29	19	48	28	....	....	....	....	....
1985-86	**Calgary**	**NHL**	**27**	**7**	**7**	**14**	**26**	....	....	....	....	....
	Moncton	AHL	4	3	2	5	7	....	....	....	....	....
	St. Louis	**NHL**	**30**	**6**	**5**	**11**	**36**	**17**	**4**	**5**	**9**	**10**
1986-87	**St. Louis**	**NHL**	**80**	**18**	**26**	**44**	**54**	**6**	**3**	**1**	**4**	**2**
1987-88	**St. Louis**	**NHL**	**64**	**15**	**17**	**32**	**62**	**10**	**5**	**5**	**10**	**19**
1988-89	**St. Louis**	**NHL**	**74**	**20**	**23**	**43**	**79**	**9**	**0**	**2**	**2**	**17**
1989-90	**St. Louis**	**NHL**	**80**	**15**	**15**	**30**	**77**	**12**	**1**	**3**	**4**	**12**
1990-91	**St. Louis**	**NHL**	**78**	**8**	**27**	**35**	**81**	**13**	**1**	**3**	**4**	**2**
1991-92	**St. Louis**	**NHL**	**48**	**9**	**7**	**16**	**40**	....	....	....	....	....
	Quebec	**NHL**	**18**	**1**	**7**	**8**	**4**	....	....	....	....	....
	NHL Totals		**526**	**105**	**144**	**249**	**473**	**70**	**14**	**19**	**33**	**66**

Signed as a free agent by **Calgary**, May 16, 1984. Traded to **St. Louis** by **Calgary** with Eddy Beers and Charles Bourgeois for Joe Mullen, Terry Johnson and Rik Wilson, February 1, 1986. Claimed on waivers by **Quebec**, February 27, 1992.

CAVALLINI, PAUL

Defense. Shoots left. 6'1", 210 lbs. Born, Toronto, Ont., October 13, 1965.
(Washington's 9th choice, 205th overall, in 1984 Entry Draft).

			Regular Season					Playoffs				
Season	Club	Lea	GP	G	A	TP	PIM	GP	G	A	TP	PIM
1984-85	Providence	H.E.	37	4	10	14	52	....	....	....	....	....
1985-86	Cdn. Olympic	....	52	1	11	12	95	....	....	....	....	....
	Binghamton	AHL	15	3	4	7	20	6	0	2	2	56
1986-87	**Washington**	**NHL**	**6**	**0**	**2**	**2**	**8**	....	....	....	....	....
	Binghamton	AHL	66	12	24	36	188	13	2	7	9	35
1987-88	**Washington**	**NHL**	**24**	**2**	**3**	**5**	**66**	....	....	....	....	....
	St. Louis	**NHL**	**48**	**4**	**7**	**11**	**86**	**10**	**1**	**6**	**7**	**26**
1988-89	**St. Louis**	**NHL**	**65**	**4**	**20**	**24**	**128**	**10**	**2**	**2**	**4**	**14**
1989-90a	**St. Louis**	**NHL**	**80**	**8**	**39**	**47**	**106**	**12**	**2**	**3**	**5**	**20**
1990-91	**St. Louis**	**NHL**	**67**	**10**	**25**	**35**	**89**	**13**	**2**	**3**	**5**	**20**
1991-92	**St. Louis**	**NHL**	**66**	**10**	**25**	**35**	**95**	**4**	**0**	**1**	**1**	**6**
	NHL Totals		**356**	**38**	**121**	**159**	**578**	**49**	**7**	**15**	**22**	**86**

a Won Alka-Seltzer Plus Award (NHL plus/minus leader) (1990)

Played in NHL All-Star Game (1990)

Traded to **St. Louis** by **Washington** for Montreal's second round choice (Wade Bartley) in 1988 Entry Draft — St. Louis' property via earlier deal — December 11, 1987.

CERNICH, KORD

Defense, Shoots left. 5'11", 195 lbs. Born, Ketchikan, AK, October 20, 1966.

			Regular Season					Playoffs				
Season	Club	Lea	GP	G	A	TP	PIM	GP	G	A	TP	PIM
1986-87	Lake Superior	CCHA	39	4	18	22	32	....	....	....	....	....
1987-88a	Lake Superior	CCHA	46	17	22	39	78	....	....	....	....	....
1988-89b	Lake Superior	CCHA	46	7	31	38	74	....	....	....	....	....
1989-90bc	Lake Superior	CCHA	46	11	25	36	59	....	....	....	....	....
1990-91	Binghamton	AHL	52	5	10	15	36	....	....	....	....	....
1991-92	Binghamton	AHL	5	1	3	4	6	....	....	....	....	....
	San Diego	IHL	64	5	18	23	53	3	1	0	1	0

a CCHA Second All-Star Team (1988)
b CCHA First All-Star Team (1989, 1990)
c NCAA West Second All-American Team (1990)

Signed as a free agent by **NY Rangers**, July 19, 1990.

CHABOT, JOHN DAVID (shah-BAHT)

Center. Shoots left. 6'2", 200 lbs. Born, Summerside, P.E.I., May 18, 1962.
(Montreal's 3rd choice, 40th overall, in 1980 Entry Draft).

			Regular Season					Playoffs				
Season	Club	Lea	GP	G	A	TP	PIM	GP	G	A	TP	PIM
1979-80	Hull	QMJHL	68	26	57	83	28	4	1	2	3	0
1980-81	Hull	QMJHL	70	27	62	89	24	....	....	....	....	....
	Nova Scotia	AHL	1	0	0	0	0	2	0	0	0	0
1981-82ab	Sherbrooke	QMJHL	62	34	*109	143	42	19	6	26	32	6
1982-83	Nova Scotia	AHL	76	16	73	89	19	7	1	3	4	0
1983-84	**Montreal**	**NHL**	**56**	**18**	**25**	**43**	**13**	**11**	**1**	**4**	**5**	**0**
1984-85	**Montreal**	**NHL**	**10**	**1**	**6**	**7**	**2**	....	....	....	....	....
	Pittsburgh	**NHL**	**67**	**8**	**45**	**53**	**12**	....	....	....	....	....
1985-86	**Pittsburgh**	**NHL**	**77**	**14**	**31**	**45**	**6**	....	....	....	....	....
1986-87	**Pittsburgh**	**NHL**	**72**	**14**	**22**	**36**	**8**	....	....	....	....	....
1987-88	**Detroit**	**NHL**	**78**	**13**	**44**	**57**	**10**	**16**	**4**	**15**	**19**	**2**
1988-89	**Detroit**	**NHL**	**52**	**2**	**10**	**12**	**6**	**6**	**1**	**1**	**2**	**0**
	Adirondack	AHL	8	3	12	15	0	....	....	....	....	....
1989-90	**Detroit**	**NHL**	**69**	**9**	**40**	**49**	**24**	....	....	....	....	....
1990-91	**Detroit**	**NHL**	**27**	**5**	**5**	**10**	**4**	....	....	....	....	....
	Adirondack	AHL	27	11	30	41	4	2	0	1	1	0
1991-92	Milano	Italy	18	10	36	46	4	12	3	13	16	2
	NHL Totals		**508**	**84**	**228**	**312**	**85**	**33**	**6**	**20**	**26**	**2**

a QMJHL First All-Star Team (1982)
b QMJHL Most Valuable Player (1982)

Traded to **Pittsburgh** by **Montreal** for Ron Flockhart, November 9, 1984. Signed as a free agent by **Detroit**, June 25, 1987.

CHALIFOUX, DENIS

Center. Shoots right. 5'8", 165 lbs. Born, Laval, Que., February 28, 1971.
(Hartford's 11th choice, 246th overall, in 1990 Entry Draft).

			Regular Season					Playoffs				
Season	Club	Lea	GP	G	A	TP	PIM	GP	G	A	TP	PIM
1989-90	Laval	QMJHL	70	41	68	109	32	14	*14	14	*28	14
1990-91a	Laval	QMJHL	67	38	79	117	77	4	1	1	2	4
1991-92	Springfield	AHL	66	17	20	37	26	4	1	0	1	4

a QMJHL Second All-Star Team (1991)

CHAMBERS, SHAWN

Defense. Shoots left. 6'2", 200 lbs. Born, Royal Oaks, MI, October 11, 1966.
(Minnesota's 1st choice, 4th overall, in 1987 Supplemental Draft).

			Regular Season					Playoffs				
Season	Club	Lea	GP	G	A	TP	PIM	GP	G	A	TP	PIM
1985-86	Alaska-Fair.	G.N.	25	15	21	36	34	....	....	....	....	....
1986-87	Alaska-Fair.	G.N.	28	8	29	37	84	....	....	....	....	....
	Seattle	WHL	28	8	25	33	58	....	....	....	....	....
	Fort Wayne	IHL	12	2	6	8	0	10	1	4	5	5
1987-88	**Minnesota**	**NHL**	**19**	**1**	**7**	**8**	**21**	....	....	....	....	....
	Kalamazoo	IHL	19	1	6	7	22	....	....	....	....	....
1988-89	**Minnesota**	**NHL**	**72**	**5**	**19**	**24**	**80**	**3**	**0**	**2**	**2**	**0**
1989-90	**Minnesota**	**NHL**	**78**	**8**	**18**	**26**	**81**	**7**	**2**	**1**	**3**	**10**
1990-91	**Minnesota**	**NHL**	**29**	**1**	**3**	**4**	**24**	**23**	**0**	**7**	**7**	**16**
	Kalamazoo	IHL	3	1	1	2	0	....	....	....	....	....
1991-92	**Washington**	**NHL**	**2**	**0**	**0**	**0**	**2**	....	....	....	....	....
	Baltimore	AHL	5	2	3	5	9	....	....	....	....	....
	NHL Totals		**200**	**15**	**47**	**62**	**208**	**33**	**2**	**10**	**12**	**26**

Traded to **Washington** by **Minnesota** for Steve Maltais and Trent Klatt, June 21, 1991. Claimed by **Tampa Bay** from **Minnesota** in Expansion Draft, June 18, 1992.

CHAPDELAINE, RENE (SHAP-duh-LAYN)

Defense. Shoots right. 6'1", 195 lbs. Born, Weyburn, Sask., September 27, 1966.
(Los Angeles' 7th choice, 149th overall, in 1986 Entry Draft).

			Regular Season					Playoffs				
Season	Club	Lea	GP	G	A	TP	PIM	GP	G	A	TP	PIM
1985-86	Lake Superior	CCHA	32	1	4	5	47	....	....	....	....	....
1986-87	Lake Superior	CCHA	28	1	5	6	51	....	....	....	....	....
1987-88	Lake Superior	CCHA	35	1	9	10	44	....	....	....	....	....
1988-89	Lake Superior	CCHA	46	4	9	13	62	....	....	....	....	....
1989-90	New Haven	AHL	41	0	1	1	35	....	....	....	....	....
1990-91	**Los Angeles**	**NHL**	**3**	**0**	**1**	**1**	**10**	....	....	....	....	....
	New Haven	AHL	65	3	11	14	49	....	....	....	....	....
	Phoenix	IHL	17	0	2	2	10	11	0	0	0	8
1991-92	**Los Angeles**	**NHL**	**16**	**0**	**1**	**1**	**10**	....	....	....	....	....
	Phoenix	IHL	62	4	22	26	87	....	....	....	....	....
	New Haven	AHL	....	....	....	....	....	4	0	2	2	0
	NHL Totals		**19**	**0**	**2**	**2**	**20**	....	....	....	....	....

CHAPMAN, BRIAN

Defense. Shoots left. 6', 195 lbs. Born, Brockville, Ont., February 10, 1968.
(Hartford's 3rd choice, 74th overall, in 1986 Entry Draft).

			Regular Season					Playoffs				
Season	Club	Lea	GP	G	A	TP	PIM	GP	G	A	TP	PIM
1985-86	Belleville	OHL	66	6	31	37	168	24	2	6	8	54
1986-87	Belleville	OHL	54	4	32	36	142	6	1	1	2	10
1987-88	Belleville	OHL	63	11	57	68	180	6	1	4	5	13
1988-89	Binghamton	AHL	71	5	25	30	216	....	....	....	....	....
1989-90	Binghamton	AHL	68	2	15	17	180	....	....	....	....	....
1990-91	**Hartford**	**NHL**	**3**	**0**	**0**	**0**	**29**	....	....	....	....	....
	Springfield	AHL	60	4	23	27	200	18	1	4	5	62
1991-92	Springfield	AHL	73	3	26	29	245	10	2	2	4	25
	NHL Totals		**3**	**0**	**0**	**0**	**29**	....	....	....	....	....

CHARBONNEAU, JOSE (JOE) (SHAHR-buh-NOH)

Right wing. Shoots right. 6', 195 lbs. Born, Ferme-Neuve, Que., November 21, 1966.
(Montreal's 1st choice, 12th overall, in 1985 Entry Draft).

			Regular Season					Playoffs				
Season	Club	Lea	GP	G	A	TP	PIM	GP	G	A	TP	PIM
1983-84	Drummondville	QMJHL	65	31	59	90	110	....	....	....	....	....
1984-85	Drummondville	QMJHL	46	34	40	74	91	12	5	10	15	20
1985-86	Drummondville	QMJHL	57	44	45	89	158	23	16	20	36	40
1986-87	Sherbrooke	AHL	72	14	27	41	94	16	5	12	17	17
1987-88	**Montreal**	**NHL**	**16**	**0**	**2**	**2**	**6**	**8**	**0**	**0**	**0**	**4**
	Sherbrooke	AHL	55	30	35	65	108	....	....	....	....	....
1988-89	**Montreal**	**NHL**	**9**	**1**	**3**	**4**	**6**	....	....	....	....	....
	Sherbrooke	AHL	33	13	15	28	95	....	....	....	....	....
	Vancouver	**NHL**	**13**	**0**	**1**	**1**	**6**	....	....	....	....	....
	Milwaukee	IHL	13	8	5	13	46	10	3	2	5	23
1989-90	Milwaukee	IHL	65	23	38	61	137	5	0	1	1	8
1990-91	Cdn. National	....	56	22	29	51	54					
1991-92	Cdn. National	....			UNAVAILABLE							
	NHL Totals		**38**	**1**	**6**	**7**	**18**	**8**	**0**	**0**	**0**	**4**

Traded to **Vancouver** by **Montreal** for Dan Woodley, January 25, 1989.

CHARBONNEAU, STEPHANE (SHAHR-buh-NOH)

Right wing. Shoots right. 6'2", 195 lbs. Born, Ste-Adele, Que., June 27, 1970.

			Regular Season					Playoffs				
Season	Club	Lea	GP	G	A	TP	PIM	GP	G	A	TP	PIM
1989-90	Shawinigan	QMJHL	62	37	58	95	154	....	....	....	....	....
1990-91	Shawinigan	QMJHL	6	4	3	7	2	....	....	....	....	....
	Chicoutimi	QMJHL	55	37	30	67	109	17	13	9	22	43
1991-92	**Quebec**	**NHL**	**2**	**0**	**0**	**0**	**0**	....	....	....	....	....
	Halifax	AHL	64	22	25	47	183	....	....	....	....	....
	NHL Totals		**2**	**0**	**0**	**0**	**0**	....	....	....	....	....

Signed as a free agent by **Quebec**, April 25, 1991.

CHARRON, ERIC

Defense. Shoots left. 6'3", 192 lbs. Born, Verdun, Que., January 14, 1970.
(Montreal's 1st choice, 20th overall, in 1988 Entry Draft).

			Regular Season					Playoffs				
Season	Club	Lea	GP	G	A	TP	PIM	GP	G	A	TP	PIM
1987-88	Trois-Rivières	QMJHL	67	3	13	16	135	....	....	....	....	....
1988-89	Trois-Rivières	QMJHL	38	2	16	18	111	....	....	....	....	....
	Verdun	QMJHL	28	2	15	17	66	....	....	....	....	....
	Sherbrooke	AHL	1	0	0	0	0	....	....	....	....	....
1989-90	St-Hyacinthe	QMJHL	68	13	38	51	152	11	3	4	7	67
	Sherbrooke	AHL	....	....	....	....	....	2	0	0	0	0
1990-91	Fredericton	AHL	71	1	11	12	108	2	1	0	1	29
1991-92	Fredericton	AHL	59	2	11	13	98	6	1	0	1	4

CHASE, DON

Center. Shoots right. 5'11", 190 lbs. Born, Springfield, MA, March 17, 1974.
(Montreal's 7th choice, 116th overall, in 1992 Entry Draft).

			Regular Season					Playoffs				
Season	Club	Lea	GP	G	A	TP	PIM	GP	G	A	TP	PIM
1991-92	Springfield	US Jr.	49	69	75	144	80					

CHASE, KELLY WAYNE

Right wing. Shoots right. 5'11", 195 lbs. Born, Porcupine Plain, Sask., October 25, 1967.

			Regular Season					Playoffs				
Season	Club	Lea	GP	G	A	TP	PIM	GP	G	A	TP	PIM
1985-86	Saskatoon	WHL	57	7	18	25	172	10	3	4	7	37
1986-87	Saskatoon	WHL	68	17	29	46	285	11	2	8	10	37
1987-88	Saskatoon	WHL	70	21	34	55	*343	9	3	5	8	32
1988-89	Peoria	IHL	38	14	7	21	278	....	....	....	....	....
1989-90	**St. Louis**	**NHL**	**43**	**1**	**3**	**4**	**244**	**9**	**1**	**0**	**1**	**8**
	Peoria	IHL	10	1	2	3	76	....	....	....	....	....
1990-91	**St. Louis**	**NHL**	**2**	**1**	**0**	**1**	**15**	**6**	**0**	**0**	**0**	**18**
	Peoria	IHL	61	20	34	54	406	10	4	3	7	61
1991-92	**St. Louis**	**NHL**	**46**	**1**	**2**	**3**	**264**	**1**	**0**	**0**	**0**	**7**
	NHL Totals		**91**	**3**	**5**	**8**	**523**	**16**	**1**	**0**	**1**	**33**

Signed as a free agent by **St. Louis**, February 23, 1988.

CHASE, TIMOTHY

Center. Shoots left. 6'2", 180 lbs. Born, Gaithersburg, MD, March 23, 1970.
(Montreal's 8th choice, 146th overall, in 1988 Entry Draft).

			Regular Season					Playoffs				
Season	Club	Lea	GP	G	A	TP	PIM	GP	G	A	TP	PIM
1989-90	Brown	ECAC	8	0	0	0	0	....	....	....	....	....
1990-91	Brown	ECAC	19	5	8	13	18	....	....	....	....	....
1991-92	Brown	ECAC	29	19	10	29	25	....	....	....	....	....

CHEBATOR, ROB

Defense. Shoots left. 6', 170 lbs. Born, Arlington, MA, December 1, 1970.
(Toronto's 9th choice, 199th overall, in 1990 Entry Draft).

			Regular Season					Playoffs				
Season	Club	Lea	GP	G	A	TP	PIM	GP	G	A	TP	PIM
1990-91	N. Hampshire	H.E.	33	4	2	6	14	....	....	....	....	....
1991-92	N. Hampshire	H.E.	36	5	6	11	24	....	....	....	....	....

CHELIOS, CHRIS (CHELL-EE-ohs)

Defense. Shoots right. 6'1", 186 lbs. Born, Chicago, IL, January 25, 1962.
(Montreal's 5th choice, 40th overall, in 1981 Entry Draft).

			Regular Season					Playoffs				
Season	Club	Lea	GP	G	A	TP	PIM	GP	G	A	TP	PIM
1981-82	U. Wisconsin	WCHA	43	6	43	49	50	....	....	....	....	....
1982-83ab	U. Wisconsin	WCHA	26	9	17	26	50	....	....	....	....	....
1983-84	U.S. National	....	60	14	35	49	58	....	....	....	....	....
	U.S. Olympic	....	6	0	4	4	8	....	....	....	....	....
	Montreal	**NHL**	**12**	**0**	**2**	**2**	**12**	**15**	**1**	**9**	**10**	**17**
1984-85c	**Montreal**	**NHL**	**74**	**9**	**55**	**64**	**87**	**9**	**2**	**8**	**10**	**17**
1985-86	**Montreal**	**NHL**	**41**	**8**	**26**	**34**	**67**	**20**	**2**	**9**	**11**	**49**
1986-87	**Montreal**	**NHL**	**71**	**11**	**33**	**44**	**124**	**17**	**4**	**9**	**13**	**38**
1987-88	**Montreal**	**NHL**	**71**	**20**	**41**	**61**	**172**	**11**	**3**	**1**	**4**	**29**
1988-89de	**Montreal**	**NHL**	**80**	**15**	**58**	**73**	**185**	**21**	**4**	**15**	**19**	**28**
1989-90	**Montreal**	**NHL**	**53**	**9**	**22**	**31**	**136**	**5**	**0**	**1**	**1**	**8**
1990-91f	**Chicago**	**NHL**	**77**	**12**	**52**	**64**	**192**	**6**	**1**	**7**	**8**	**46**
1991-92	**Chicago**	**NHL**	**80**	**9**	**47**	**56**	**245**	**18**	**6**	**15**	**21**	**37**
	NHL Totals		**559**	**93**	**336**	**429**	**1220**	**122**	**23**	**74**	**97**	**269**

a WCHA Second All-Star Team (1983)
b NCAA All-Tournament Team (1983)
c NHL All-Rookie Team (1985)
d NHL First All-Star Team (1989)
e Won Norris Trophy (1989)
f NHL Second All-Star Team (1991)

Played in NHL All-Star Game (1985, 1990, 1991, 1992)

Traded to **Chicago** by **Montreal** with Montreal's second round choice (Michael Pomichter) in 1991 Entry Draft for Denis Savard, June 29, 1990.

CHERBAYEV, ALEXANDER (cher-BIGH-ev)

Left wing. Shoots left. 6'1", 187 lbs. Born, Voskresensk, Soviet Union, August 13, 1973.
(San Jose's 3rd choice, 51st overall, in 1992 Entry Draft).

			Regular Season					Playoffs				
Season	Club	Lea	GP	G	A	TP	PIM	GP	G	A	TP	PIM
1990-91	Khimik	USSR	16	2	2	4	0	....	....	....	....	....
1991-92	Khimik	CIS	38	3	3	6	14	....	....	....	....	....

CHERNOMAZ, RICHARD (RICH) (CHUR-noh-maz)

Right wing. Shoots right. 5'8", 185 lbs. Born, Selkirk, Man., September 1, 1963.
(Colorado's 2nd choice, 26th overall, in 1981 Entry Draft).

			Regular Season					Playoffs				
Season	Club	Lea	GP	G	A	TP	PIM	GP	G	A	TP	PIM
1980-81	Victoria	WHL	72	49	64	113	92	15	11	15	26	38
1981-82	**Colorado**	**NHL**	**2**	**0**	**0**	**0**	**0**	....	....	....	....	....
	Victoria	WHL	49	36	62	98	69	4	1	2	3	13
1982-83a	Victoria	WHL	64	71	53	124	113	12	10	5	15	18
1983-84	**New Jersey**	**NHL**	**7**	**2**	**1**	**3**	**2**	....	....	....	....	....
	Maine	AHL	69	17	29	46	39	2	0	1	1	0
1984-85	**New Jersey**	**NHL**	**3**	**0**	**2**	**2**	**2**	....	....	....	....	....
	Maine	AHL	64	17	34	51	64	10	2	2	4	4
1985-86	Maine	AHL	78	21	28	49	82	5	0	0	0	2
1986-87	**New Jersey**	**NHL**	**25**	**6**	**4**	**10**	**8**	....	....	....	....	....
	Maine	AHL	58	35	27	62	65	....	....	....	....	....
1987-88	**Calgary**	**NHL**	**2**	**1**	**0**	**1**	**0**	....	....	....	....	....
b	Salt Lake	IHL	73	48	47	95	122	18	4	14	18	30
1988-89	**Calgary**	**NHL**	**1**	**0**	**0**	**0**	**0**	....	....	....	....	....
	Salt Lake	IHL	81	33	68	101	122	14	7	5	12	47
1989-90	Salt Lake	IHL	65	39	35	74	170	11	6	6	12	32
1990-91b	Salt Lake	IHL	81	39	58	97	213	4	3	1	4	8
1991-92	**Calgary**	**NHL**	**11**	**0**	**0**	**0**	**6**	....	....	....	....	....
	Salt Lake	IHL	66	20	40	60	201	5	1	2	3	10
	NHL Totals		**51**	**9**	**7**	**16**	**18**	....	....	....	....	....

a WHL First All-Star Team (1983)
b IHL Second All-Star Team (1988, 1991)

Signed as a free agent by **Calgary**, August 4, 1987.

CHEVELDAYOFF, KEVIN (sheh-vehl-DAY-ahf)

Defense. Shoots right. 6', 202 lbs. Born, Saskatoon, Sask., February 4, 1970.
(NY Islanders' 1st choice, 16th overall, in 1988 Entry Draft).

			Regular Season					Playoffs				
Season	Club	Lea	GP	G	A	TP	PIM	GP	G	A	TP	PIM
1986-87	Brandon	WHL	70	0	16	16	259	....	....	....	....	....
1987-88	Brandon	WHL	71	3	29	32	265	4	0	2	2	20
1988-89	Brandon	WHL	40	4	12	16	135	....	....	....	....	....
1989-90	Brandon	WHL	33	5	12	17	56	....	....	....	....	....
	Springfield	AHL	4	0	0	0	0	....	....	....	....	....
1990-91	Capital Dist.	AHL	76	0	14	14	203	....	....	....	....	....
1991-92	Capital Dist.	AHL	44	0	4	4	110	7	0	0	0	22

CHIASSON, STEVE (CHAY-sahn)

Defense. Shoots left. 6'1", 205 lbs. Born, Barrie, Ont., April 14, 1967.
(Detroit's 3rd choice, 50th overall, in 1985 Entry Draft).

			Regular Season					Playoffs				
Season	Club	Lea	GP	G	A	TP	PIM	GP	G	A	TP	PIM
1984-85	Guelph	OHL	61	8	22	30	139	....	....	....	....	....
1985-86	Guelph	OHL	54	12	30	42	126	18	10	10	20	37
1986-87	**Detroit**	**NHL**	**45**	**1**	**4**	**5**	**73**	**2**	**0**	**0**	**0**	**19**
1987-88	**Detroit**	**NHL**	**29**	**2**	**9**	**11**	**57**	**9**	**2**	**2**	**4**	**31**
	Adirondack	AHL	23	6	11	17	58	....	....	....	....	....
1988-89	**Detroit**	**NHL**	**65**	**12**	**35**	**47**	**149**	**5**	**2**	**1**	**3**	**6**
1989-90	**Detroit**	**NHL**	**67**	**14**	**28**	**42**	**114**	....	....	....	....	....
1990-91	**Detroit**	**NHL**	**42**	**3**	**17**	**20**	**80**	**5**	**3**	**1**	**4**	**19**
1991-92	**Detroit**	**NHL**	**62**	**10**	**24**	**34**	**136**	**11**	**1**	**5**	**6**	**12**
	NHL Totals		**310**	**42**	**117**	**159**	**609**	**32**	**8**	**9**	**17**	**87**

CHINAKHOV, VITALI (chih-NAH-khov)

Center. Shoots left. 5'11", 183 lbs. Born, Yaroslavl, Soviet Union, January 15, 1972.
(NY Rangers' 11th choice, 235th overall, in 1991 Entry Draft).

			Regular Season					Playoffs				
Season	Club	Lea	GP	G	A	TP	PIM	GP	G	A	TP	PIM
1990-91	Torpedo Yaro.	USSR	20	1	1	2	10	....	....	....	....	....
1991-92	Torpedo Yaro.	CIS	18	4	1	5	4	....	....	....	....	....

CHORSKE, TOM

Right/Left wing. Shoots right. 6'1", 204 lbs. Born, Minneapolis, MN, September 18, 1966.
(Montreal's 2nd choice, 16th overall, in 1985 Entry Draft).

			Regular Season					Playoffs				
Season	Club	Lea	GP	G	A	TP	PIM	GP	G	A	TP	PIM
1985-86	U. Minnesota	WCHA	39	6	4	10	16	....	....	....	....	....
1986-87	U. Minnesota	WCHA	47	20	22	42	20	....	....	....	....	....
1987-88	U.S. National	....	36	9	16	25	24	....	....	....	....	....
1988-89a	U. Minnesota	WCHA	37	25	24	49	28	....	....	....	....	....
1989-90	**Montreal**	**NHL**	**14**	**3**	**1**	**4**	**2**	....	....	....	....	....
	Sherbrooke	AHL	59	22	24	46	54	12	4	4	8	8
1990-91	**Montreal**	**NHL**	**57**	**9**	**11**	**20**	**32**	....	....	....	....	....
1991-92	**New Jersey**	**NHL**	**76**	**19**	**17**	**36**	**32**	**7**	**0**	**3**	**3**	**4**
	NHL Totals		**147**	**31**	**29**	**60**	**66**	**7**	**0**	**3**	**3**	**4**

a WCHA First All-Star Team (1989)

Traded to **New Jersey** by **Montreal** with Stephane Richer for Kirk Muller and Roland Melanson, September 20, 1991.

CHRISTIAN, DAVID (DAVE)

Right wing. Shoots right. 5'11", 175 lbs. Born, Warroad, MN, May 12, 1959.
(Winnipeg's 2nd choice, 40th overall, in 1979 Entry Draft).

			Regular Season					Playoffs				
Season	Club	Lea	GP	G	A	TP	PIM	GP	G	A	TP	PIM
1977-78	North Dakota	WCHA	38	8	16	24	14	....	....	....	....	....
1978-79	North Dakota	WCHA	40	22	24	46	22	....	....	....	....	....
1979-80	U.S. National	....	59	10	20	30	26	....	....	....	....	....
	U.S. Olympic	....	7	0	8	8	6	....	....	....	....	....
	Winnipeg	**NHL**	**15**	**8**	**10**	**18**	**2**	....	....	....	....	....
1980-81	**Winnipeg**	**NHL**	**80**	**28**	**43**	**71**	**22**	....	....	....	....	....
1981-82	**Winnipeg**	**NHL**	**80**	**25**	**51**	**76**	**28**	**4**	**0**	**1**	**1**	**2**
1982-83	**Winnipeg**	**NHL**	**55**	**18**	**26**	**44**	**23**	**3**	**0**	**0**	**0**	**0**
1983-84	**Washington**	**NHL**	**80**	**29**	**52**	**81**	**28**	**8**	**5**	**4**	**9**	**5**
1984-85	**Washington**	**NHL**	**80**	**26**	**43**	**69**	**14**	**5**	**1**	**1**	**2**	**0**
1985-86	**Washington**	**NHL**	**80**	**41**	**42**	**83**	**15**	**9**	**4**	**4**	**8**	**0**
1986-87	**Washington**	**NHL**	**76**	**23**	**27**	**50**	**8**	**7**	**1**	**3**	**4**	**6**
1987-88	**Washington**	**NHL**	**80**	**37**	**21**	**58**	**26**	**14**	**5**	**6**	**11**	**6**
1988-89	**Washington**	**NHL**	**80**	**34**	**31**	**65**	**12**	**6**	**1**	**1**	**2**	**0**
1989-90	**Washington**	**NHL**	**28**	**3**	**8**	**11**	**4**	....	....	....	....	....
	Boston	**NHL**	**50**	**12**	**17**	**29**	**8**	**21**	**4**	**1**	**5**	**4**
1990-91	**Boston**	**NHL**	**78**	**32**	**21**	**53**	**41**	**19**	**8**	**4**	**12**	**4**
1991-92	**St. Louis**	**NHL**	**78**	**20**	**24**	**44**	**41**	**4**	**3**	**0**	**3**	**0**
	NHL Totals		**940**	**336**	**416**	**752**	**272**	**100**	**32**	**25**	**57**	**27**

Played in NHL All-Star Game (1991)

Traded to **Washington** by **Winnipeg** for Washington's first round choice (Bob Dollas) in the 1983 Entry Draft, June 8, 1983. Traded to **Boston** by **Washington** for Bob Joyce, December 13, 1989. Acquired by **St. Louis** from **Boston** with Boston's third round choice in 1992 Entry Draft and either Boston's seventh round choice in 1992 Entry Draft or sixth round choice in 1993 Entry Draft as compensation for Boston's free agent signings of Glen Featherstone and Dave Thomlinson, July 30, 1991.

CHRISTIAN, JEFF

Left wing. Shoots left. 6'1", 195 lbs. Born, Burlington, Ont., July 30, 1970.
(New Jersey's 2nd choice, 23rd overall, in 1988 Entry Draft).

			Regular Season					Playoffs				
Season	Club	Lea	GP	G	A	TP	PIM	GP	G	A	TP	PIM
1987-88	London	OHL	64	15	29	44	154	9	1	5	6	27
1988-89	London	OHL	64	27	30	57	221	20	3	4	7	56
1989-90	London	OHL	18	14	7	21	64	....	....	....	....	....
	Owen Sound	OHL	37	19	26	45	145	10	6	7	13	43
1990-91	Utica	AHL	80	24	42	66	165	....	....	....	....	....
1991-92	**New Jersey**	**NHL**	**2**	**0**	**0**	**0**	**2**	....	....	....	....	....
	Utica	AHL	76	27	24	51	198	4	0	0	0	16
	NHL Totals		**2**	**0**	**0**	**0**	**2**	....	....	....	....	....

CHURLA, SHANE

Right wing. Shoots right. 6'1", 200 lbs. Born, Fernie, B.C., June 24, 1965.
(Hartford's 4th choice, 110th overall, in 1985 Entry Draft).

			Regular Season					Playoffs				
Season	Club	Lea	GP	G	A	TP	PIM	GP	G	A	TP	PIM
1983-84	Medicine Hat	WHL	48	3	7	10	115	14	1	5	6	41
1984-85	Medicine Hat	WHL	70	14	20	34	370	9	1	0	1	55
1985-86	Binghamton	AHL	52	4	10	14	306	3	0	0	0	22
1986-87	**Hartford**	**NHL**	**20**	**0**	**1**	**1**	**78**	**2**	**0**	**0**	**0**	**42**
	Binghamton	AHL	24	1	5	6	249	....	....	....	....	....
1987-88	**Hartford**	**NHL**	**2**	**0**	**0**	**0**	**14**	....	....	....	....	....
	Binghamton	AHL	25	5	8	13	168	....	....	....	....	....
	Calgary	**NHL**	**29**	**1**	**5**	**6**	**132**	**7**	**0**	**1**	**1**	**17**
1988-89	**Calgary**	**NHL**	**5**	**0**	**0**	**0**	**25**	....	....	....	....	....
	Salt Lake	IHL	32	3	13	16	278	....	....	....	....	....
	Minnesota	**NHL**	**13**	**1**	**0**	**1**	**54**	....	....	....	....	....
1989-90	**Minnesota**	**NHL**	**53**	**2**	**3**	**5**	**292**	**7**	**0**	**0**	**0**	**44**
1990-91	**Minnesota**	**NHL**	**40**	**2**	**2**	**4**	**286**	**22**	**2**	**1**	**3**	**90**
1991-92	**Minnesota**	**NHL**	**57**	**4**	**1**	**5**	**278**	....	....	....	....	....
	NHL Totals		**219**	**10**	**12**	**22**	**1159**	**38**	**2**	**2**	**4**	**193**

Traded to **Calgary** by **Hartford** with Dana Murzyn for Neil Sheehy, Carey Wilson, and the rights to Lane MacDonald, January 3, 1988. Traded to **Minnesota** by **Calgary** with Perry Berezan for Brian MacLellan and Minnesota's fourth round choice (Robert Reichel) in 1989 Entry Draft, March 4, 1989. Claimed by **San Jose** from **Minnesota** in Dispersal Draft, May 30, 1991. Traded to **Minnesota** by **San Jose** for Kelly Kisio, June 3, 1991.

CHYCHRUN, JEFF (CHIHK-rihn)

Defense. Shoots right. 6'4", 215 lbs. Born, LaSalle, Que., May 3, 1966.
(Philadelphia's 3rd choice, 37th overall, in 1984 Entry Draft).

			Regular Season					Playoffs				
Season	Club	Lea	GP	G	A	TP	PIM	GP	G	A	TP	PIM
1983-84	Kingston	OHL	63	1	13	14	137	....	....	....	....	....
1984-85	Kingston	OHL	58	4	10	14	206	....	....	....	....	....
1985-86	Kingston	OHL	61	4	21	25	127	10	2	1	3	17
	Hershey	AHL	....	....	....	....	....	4	0	1	1	9
	Kalamazoo	IHL	....	....	....	....	....	3	1	0	1	0
1986-87	**Philadelphia**	**NHL**	**1**	**0**	**0**	**0**	**4**	....	....	....	....	....
	Hershey	AHL	74	1	17	18	239	4	0	0	0	10
1987-88	**Philadelphia**	**NHL**	**3**	**0**	**0**	**0**	**4**	....	....	....	....	....
	Hershey	AHL	55	0	5	5	210	12	0	2	2	44
1988-89	**Philadelphia**	**NHL**	**80**	**1**	**4**	**5**	**245**	**19**	**0**	**2**	**2**	**65**
1989-90	**Philadelphia**	**NHL**	**79**	**2**	**7**	**9**	**250**	....	....	....	....	....
1990-91	**Philadelphia**	**NHL**	**36**	**0**	**6**	**6**	**105**	....	....	....	....	....
1991-92	**Los Angeles**	**NHL**	**26**	**0**	**3**	**3**	**76**	....	....	....	....	....
	Phoenix	IHL	3	0	0	0	6	....	....	....	....	....
	Pittsburgh	**NHL**	**17**	**0**	**1**	**1**	**35**	....	....	....	....	....
	NHL Totals		**242**	**3**	**21**	**24**	**719**	**19**	**0**	**2**	**2**	**65**

Traded to **Los Angeles** by **Philadelphia** with Jari Kurri for Steve Duchesne, Steve Kasper and Los Angeles' fourth round choice (Aris Brimanis) in 1991 Entry Draft, May 30, 1991. Traded to **Pittsburgh** by **Los Angeles** with Brian Benning and Los Angeles' first round choice in 1992 Entry Draft (later traded to Philadelphia - Jason Bowen), for Paul Coffey, February 19, 1992.

CHYNOWETH, DEAN (shih-NOWTH)

Defense. Shoots right. 6'2", 190 lbs. Born, Calgary, Alta., October 30, 1968.
(NY Islanders' 1st choice, 13th overall, in 1987 Entry Draft).

			Regular Season					Playoffs				
Season	Club	Lea	GP	G	A	TP	PIM	GP	G	A	TP	PIM
1985-86	Medicine Hat	WHL	69	3	12	15	208	17	3	2	5	52
1986-87	Medicine Hat	WHL	67	3	18	21	285	13	4	2	6	28
1987-88	Medicine Hat	WHL	64	1	21	22	274	16	0	6	6	*87
1988-89	**NY Islanders**	**NHL**	**6**	**0**	**0**	**0**	**48**	....	....	....	....	....
1989-90	**NY Islanders**	**NHL**	**20**	**0**	**2**	**2**	**39**	....	....	....	....	....
	Springfield	AHL	40	0	7	7	98	17	0	4	4	36
1990-91	**NY Islanders**	**NHL**	**25**	**1**	**1**	**2**	**59**	....	....	....	....	....
	Capital Dist.	AHL	44	1	5	6	176	....	....	....	....	....
1991-92	**NY Islanders**	**NHL**	**11**	**1**	**0**	**1**	**23**	....	....	....	....	....
	Capital Dist.	AHL	43	4	6	10	164	6	1	1	2	39
	NHL Totals		**62**	**2**	**3**	**5**	**169**	....	....	....	....	....

CHYZOWSKI, DAVID (chih-ZOW-skee)

Left wing. Shoots left. 6'1", 190 lbs. Born, Edmonton, Alta., July 11, 1971.
(NY Islanders' 1st choice, 2nd overall, in 1989 Entry Draft).

			Regular Season					Playoffs				
Season	Club	Lea	GP	G	A	TP	PIM	GP	G	A	TP	PIM
1987-88	Kamloops	WHL	66	16	17	33	117	18	2	4	6	26
1988-89a	Kamloops	WHL	68	56	48	104	139	16	15	13	28	32
1989-90	**NY Islanders**	**NHL**	**34**	**8**	**6**	**14**	**45**	....	....	....	....	....
	Springfield	AHL	4	0	0	0	7	....	....	....	....	....
	Kamloops	WHL	4	5	2	7	17	17	11	6	17	46
1990-91	**NY Islanders**	**NHL**	**56**	**5**	**9**	**14**	**61**	....	....	....	....	....
	Capital Dist.	AHL	7	3	6	9	22	....	....	....	....	....
1991-92	**NY Islanders**	**NHL**	**12**	**1**	**1**	**2**	**17**	....	....	....	....	....
	Capital Dist.	AHL	55	15	18	33	121	6	1	1	2	23
	NHL Totals		**102**	**14**	**16**	**30**	**123**	....	....	....	....	....

a WHL West All-Star Team (1989)

CIAVAGLIA, PETER

Center. Shoots left. 5'10", 173 lbs. Born, Albany, NY, July 15, 1969.
(Calgary's 8th choice, 145th overall, in 1987 Entry Draft).

			Regular Season					Playoffs				
Season	Club	Lea	GP	G	A	TP	PIM	GP	G	A	TP	PIM
1987-88	Harvard	ECAC	30	10	23	33	16	....	....	....	....	....
1988-89a	Harvard	ECAC	34	15	48	63	36	....	....	....	....	....
1989-90	Harvard	ECAC	28	17	18	35	22	....	....	....	....	....
1990-91abc	Harvard	ECAC	27	24	*38	*62	2	....	....	....	....	....
1991-92	**Buffalo**	**NHL**	**2**	**0**	**0**	**0**	**0**	....	....	....	....	....
	Rochester	AHL	77	37	61	98	16	6	2	5	7	6
	NHL Totals		**2**	**0**	**0**	**0**	**0**	....	....	....	....	....

a ECAC Second All-Star Team (1989, 1991)
b ECAC Player of the Year (1991)
c NCAA East Second All-American Team (1991)

Signed as a free agent by **Buffalo**, August 30, 1991.

CICCARELLI, DINO (sih-sih-REHL-ee)

Right wing. Shoots right. 5'10", 175 lbs. Born, Sarnia, Ont., February 8, 1960.

			Regular Season					Playoffs				
Season	Club	Lea	GP	G	A	TP	PIM	GP	G	A	TP	PIM
1977-78a	London	OHA	68	72	70	142	49	9	6	10	16	6
1978-79	London	OHA	30	8	11	19	35	7	3	5	8	0
1979-80	London	OHA	62	50	53	103	72	5	2	6	8	15
1980-81	**Minnesota**	**NHL**	**32**	**18**	**12**	**30**	**29**	**19**	**14**	**7**	**21**	**25**
	Oklahoma City	CHL	48	32	25	57	45	....	....	....	....	....
1981-82	**Minnesota**	**NHL**	**76**	**55**	**51**	**106**	**138**	**4**	**3**	**1**	**4**	**2**
1982-83	**Minnesota**	**NHL**	**77**	**37**	**38**	**75**	**94**	**9**	**4**	**6**	**10**	**11**
1983-84	**Minnesota**	**NHL**	**79**	**38**	**33**	**71**	**58**	**16**	**4**	**5**	**9**	**27**
1984-85	**Minnesota**	**NHL**	**51**	**15**	**17**	**32**	**41**	**9**	**3**	**3**	**6**	**8**
1985-86	**Minnesota**	**NHL**	**75**	**44**	**45**	**89**	**51**	**5**	**0**	**1**	**1**	**6**
1986-87	**Minnesota**	**NHL**	**80**	**52**	**51**	**103**	**88**	....	....	....	....	....
1987-88	**Minnesota**	**NHL**	**67**	**41**	**45**	**86**	**79**	....	....	....	....	....
1988-89	**Minnesota**	**NHL**	**65**	**32**	**27**	**59**	**64**	....	....	....	....	....
	Washington	**NHL**	**11**	**12**	**3**	**15**	**12**	**6**	**3**	**3**	**6**	**12**
1989-90	**Washington**	**NHL**	**80**	**41**	**38**	**79**	**122**	**8**	**8**	**3**	**11**	**6**
1990-91	**Washington**	**NHL**	**54**	**21**	**18**	**39**	**66**	**11**	**5**	**4**	**9**	**22**
1991-92	**Washington**	**NHL**	**78**	**38**	**38**	**76**	**78**	**7**	**5**	**4**	**9**	**14**
	NHL Totals		**825**	**444**	**416**	**860**	**920**	**94**	**49**	**37**	**86**	**133**

a OHA Second All-Star Team (1978)

Played in NHL All-Star Game (1982, 1983,1989)

Signed as a free agent by **Minnesota**, September 28, 1979. Traded to **Washington** by **Minnesota** with Bob Rouse for Mike Gartner and Larry Murphy, March 7, 1989. Traded to **Detroit** by **Washington** for Kevin Miller, June 20, 1992.

CICCONE, ENRICO

Defense. Shoots left. 6'4", 200 lbs. Born, Montreal, Que., April 10, 1970.
(Minnesota's 5th choice, 92nd overall, in 1990 Entry Draft).

			Regular Season					Playoffs				
Season	Club	Lea	GP	G	A	TP	PIM	GP	G	A	TP	PIM
1987-88	Shawinigan	QMJHL	61	2	12	14	324	....	....	....	....	....
1988-89	Shawinigan	QMJHL	34	7	11	18	132	....	....	....	....	....
	Trois-Rivières	QMJHL	24	0	7	7	153	....	....	....	....	....
1989-90	Trois-Rivières	QMJHL	40	4	24	28	227	3	0	0	0	15
1990-91	Kalamazoo	IHL	57	4	9	13	384	4	0	1	1	32
1991-92	**Minnesota**	**NHL**	**11**	**0**	**0**	**0**	**48**	....	....	....	....	....
	Kalamazoo	IHL	53	4	16	20	406	10	0	1	1	58
	NHL Totals		**11**	**0**	**0**	**0**	**48**	....	....	....	....	....

CICHOCKI, CHRIS (chih-HAH-kee)

Right wing. Shoots right. 5'11", 185 lbs. Born, Detroit, MI, September 17, 1963.

			Regular Season					Playoffs				
Season	Club	Lea	GP	G	A	TP	PIM	GP	G	A	TP	PIM
1982-83	Michigan Tech	CCHA	36	12	10	22	10	....	....	....	....	....
1983-84	Michigan Tech	CCHA	40	25	20	45	36	....	....	....	....	....
1984-85	Michigan Tech	CCHA	40	30	24	54	14	....	....	....	....	....
1985-86	**Detroit**	**NHL**	**59**	**10**	**11**	**21**	**21**	....	....	....	....	....
	Adirondack	AHL	9	4	4	8	6	....	....	....	....	....
1986-87	**Detroit**	**NHL**	**2**	**0**	**0**	**0**	**2**	....	....	....	....	....
	Adirondack	AHL	55	31	34	65	27	....	....	....	....	....
	Maine	AHL	7	2	2	4	0	....	....	....	....	....
1987-88	**New Jersey**	**NHL**	**5**	**1**	**0**	**1**	**2**	....	....	....	....	....
	Utica	AHL	69	36	30	66	66	....	....	....	....	....
1988-89	**New Jersey**	**NHL**	**2**	**0**	**1**	**1**	**2**	....	....	....	....	....
	Utica	AHL	59	32	31	63	50	5	0	1	1	2
1989-90	Utica	AHL	11	3	1	4	10	....	....	....	....	....
	Binghamton	AHL	60	21	26	47	22	....	....	....	....	....
1990-91	Binghamton	AHL	80	35	30	65	70	9	0	4	4	2
1991-92	Binghamton	AHL	75	28	29	57	132	6	5	4	9	4
	NHL Totals		**68**	**11**	**12**	**23**	**27**	....	....	....	....	....

Signed as a free agent by **Detroit**, June 28, 1985. Traded to **New Jersey** by **Detroit** with Detroit's third round choice (later transferred to Buffalo - Andrew MacVicar) in 1987 Entry Draft for Mel Bridgman, March 9, 1987. Traded to **Hartford** by **New Jersey** for Jim Thomson, October 31, 1989. Signed as a free agent by **NY Rangers**, September 6, 1990.

CIERNY, JOZEF (chee-ER-nee)

Left wing. Shoots left. 6'2", 176 lbs. Born, Zvolen, Czech., May 13, 1974.
(Buffalo's 2nd choice, 35th overall, in 1992 Entry Draft).

			Regular Season					Playoffs				
Season	Club	Lea	GP	G	A	TP	PIM	GP	G	A	TP	PIM
1991-92	ZK Zvolen	Czech.2	26	10	3	13	8	....	....	....	....	....

CIGER, ZDENO (SEE-gur)

Left wing. Shoots left. 6'1", 190 lbs. Born, Martin, Czech., October 19, 1969.
(New Jersey's 3rd choice, 54th overall, in 1988 Entry Draft).

			Regular Season					Playoffs				
Season	Club	Lea	GP	G	A	TP	PIM	GP	G	A	TP	PIM
1988-89	Dukla Trencin	Czech.	32	15	21	36	18	....	....	....	....	....
1989-90	Dukla Trencin	Czech.	53	18	28	46	....	....	....	....	....	....
1990-91	**New Jersey**	**NHL**	**45**	**8**	**17**	**25**	**8**	**6**	**0**	**2**	**2**	**4**
	Utica	AHL	8	5	4	9	2	....	....	....	....	....
1991-92	**New Jersey**	**NHL**	**20**	**6**	**5**	**11**	**10**	**7**	**2**	**4**	**6**	**0**
	NHL Totals		**65**	**14**	**22**	**36**	**18**	**13**	**2**	**6**	**8**	**4**

CIMETTA, ROBERT

Left/Right wing. Shoots left. 6', 190 lbs. Born, Toronto, Ont., February 15, 1970.
(Boston's 1st choice, 18th overall, in 1988 Entry Draft).

			Regular Season					Playoffs				
Season	Club	Lea	GP	G	A	TP	PIM	GP	G	A	TP	PIM
1986-87	Toronto	OHL	66	21	35	56	65	....	....	....	....	....
1987-88	Toronto	OHL	64	34	42	76	90	4	2	2	4	7
1988-89	**Boston**	**NHL**	**7**	**2**	**0**	**2**	**0**	**1**	**0**	**0**	**0**	**15**
a	Toronto	OHL	58	*55	47	102	89	6	3	3	6	0
1989-90	**Boston**	**NHL**	**47**	**8**	**9**	**17**	**33**	....	....	....	....	....
	Maine	AHL	9	3	2	5	13	....	....	....	....	....
1990-91	**Toronto**	**NHL**	**25**	**2**	**4**	**6**	**21**	....	....	....	....	....
	Newmarket	AHL	29	16	18	34	24	....	....	....	....	....
1991-92	**Toronto**	**NHL**	**24**	**4**	**3**	**7**	**12**	....	....	....	....	....
	St. John's	AHL	19	4	13	17	23	10	3	7	10	24
	NHL Totals		**103**	**16**	**16**	**32**	**66**	**1**	**0**	**0**	**0**	**15**

a OHL First All-Star Team (1989)

Traded to **Toronto** by **Boston** for Steve Bancroft, November 9, 1990.

CIPRIANO, MARK

Right wing. Shoots right. 5'10", 195 lbs. Born, Delta, B.C., June 1, 1971.
(Vancouver's 8th choice, 170th overall, in 1990 Entry Draft).

			Regular Season					Playoffs				
Season	Club	Lea	GP	G	A	TP	PIM	GP	G	A	TP	PIM
1988-89	Victoria	WHL	19	0	1	1	20	....	....	....	....	....
1989-90	Victoria	WHL	66	15	27	42	264	....	....	....	....	....
1990-91	Victoria	WHL	51	15	22	37	235	....	....	....	....	....
1991-92	Columbus	ECHL	48	17	14	31	333	....	....	....	....	....

CIRELLA, JOE (suh-REHL-uh)

Defense. Shoots right. 6'3", 210 lbs. Born, Hamilton, Ont., May 9, 1963.
(Colorado's 1st choice, 5th overall, in 1981 Entry Draft).

			Regular Season					Playoffs				
Season	Club	Lea	GP	G	A	TP	PIM	GP	G	A	TP	PIM
1980-81	Oshawa	OHA	56	5	31	36	220	11	0	2	2	41
1981-82	**Colorado**	**NHL**	**65**	**7**	**12**	**19**	**52**	....	....	....	....	....
	Oshawa	OHL	3	0	1	1	0	11	7	10	17	32
1982-83	**New Jersey**	**NHL**	**2**	**0**	**1**	**1**	**4**	....	....	....	....	....
a	Oshawa	OHL	56	13	55	68	110	17	4	16	20	37
1983-84	**New Jersey**	**NHL**	**79**	**11**	**33**	**44**	**137**	....	....	....	....	....
1984-85	**New Jersey**	**NHL**	**66**	**6**	**18**	**24**	**141**	....	....	....	....	....
1985-86	**New Jersey**	**NHL**	**66**	**6**	**23**	**29**	**147**	....	....	....	....	....
1986-87	**New Jersey**	**NHL**	**65**	**9**	**22**	**31**	**111**	....	....	....	....	....
1987-88	**New Jersey**	**NHL**	**80**	**8**	**31**	**39**	**191**	**19**	**0**	**7**	**7**	**49**
1988-89	**New Jersey**	**NHL**	**80**	**3**	**19**	**22**	**155**	....	....	....	....	....
1989-90	**Quebec**	**NHL**	**56**	**4**	**14**	**18**	**67**	....	....	....	....	....
1990-91	**Quebec**	**NHL**	**39**	**2**	**10**	**12**	**59**	....	....	....	....	....
	NY Rangers	**NHL**	**19**	**1**	**0**	**1**	**52**	**6**	**0**	**2**	**2**	**26**
1991-92	**NY Rangers**	**NHL**	**67**	**3**	**12**	**15**	**121**	**13**	**0**	**4**	**4**	**23**
	NHL Totals		**684**	**60**	**195**	**255**	**1237**	**38**	**0**	**13**	**13**	**98**

a OHL First All-Star Team (1983)

Played in NHL All-Star Game (1984)

Traded to **Quebec** by **New Jersey** with Claude Loiselle and New Jersey's eighth round choice (Alexander Karpovtsev) in 1990 Entry Draft for Walt Poddubny and Quebec's fourth round choice (Mike Bodnarchuk) in 1990 Entry Draft, June 17, 1989. Traded to **NY Rangers** by **Quebec** for Aaron Miller and NY Rangers' fifth round choice (Bill Lindsay) in 1991 Entry Draft, January 17, 1991.

CIRONE, JASON (sih-ROHN)

Center. Shoots left. 5'9", 185 lbs. Born, Toronto, Ont., February 21, 1971.
(Winnipeg's 3rd choice, 46th overall, in 1989 Entry Draft).

			Regular Season					Playoffs				
Season	Club	Lea	GP	G	A	TP	PIM	GP	G	A	TP	PIM
1987-88	Cornwall	OHL	53	12	11	23	41	11	1	2	3	4
1988-89	Cornwall	OHL	64	39	44	83	67	17	19	8	27	14
1989-90	Cornwall	OHL	32	22	41	63	56	6	4	2	6	14
1990-91	Cornwall	OHL	40	31	29	60	66	....	....	....	....	....
a	Windsor	OHL	23	27	23	50	31	11	9	8	17	14
1991-92	**Winnipeg**	**NHL**	**3**	**0**	**0**	**0**	**2**	....	....	....	....	....
	Moncton	AHL	64	32	27	59	124	10	1	1	2	8
	NHL Totals		**3**	**0**	**0**	**0**	**2**	....	....	....	....	....

a OHL Third All-Star Team (1991)

CLARK, JASON

Center. Shoots left. 6', 180 lbs. Born, London, Ont., May 6, 1972.
(Vancouver's 8th choice, 141st overall, in 1992 Entry Draft).

			Regular Season					Playoffs				
Season	Club	Lea	GP	G	A	TP	PIM	GP	G	A	TP	PIM
1991-92	St. Thomas	Jr. B	47	25	52	77	66	....	....	....	....	....

CLARK, KERRY

Right wing. Shoots right. 6'1", 190 lbs. Born, Kelvington, Sask., August 21, 1968.
(NY Islanders' 12th choice, 206th overall, in 1986 Entry Draft).

			Regular Season					Playoffs				
Season	Club	Lea	GP	G	A	TP	PIM	GP	G	A	TP	PIM
1985-86	Regina	WHL	23	4	4	8	58	....	....	....	....	....
	Saskatoon	WHL	39	5	8	13	104	13	2	2	4	33
1986-87	Saskatoon	WHL	54	12	10	22	229	8	0	1	1	23
1987-88	Saskatoon	WHL	67	15	11	26	241	10	2	2	4	16
1988-89	Springfield	AHL	63	7	7	14	264	....	....	....	....	....
	Indianapolis	IHL	3	0	1	1	12	....	....	....	....	....
1989-90	Springfield	AHL	21	0	1	1	73	....	....	....	....	....
	Phoenix	IHL	38	4	8	12	262	....	....	....	....	....
1990-91	Salt Lake	IHL	62	14	14	28	372	4	1	1	2	12
1991-92	Salt Lake	IHL	74	12	14	26	266	5	1	0	1	34

Signed as a free agent by **Calgary**, July 23, 1990.

CLARK, WENDEL

Left wing. Shoots left. 5'11", 194 lbs. Born, Kelvington, Sask., October 25, 1966.
(Toronto's 1st choice, 1st overall, in 1985 Entry Draft).

			Regular Season					Playoffs				
Season	Club	Lea	GP	G	A	TP	PIM	GP	G	A	TP	PIM
1983-84	Saskatoon	WHL	72	23	45	68	225	....	....	....	....	....
1984-85a	Saskatoon	WHL	64	32	55	87	253	3	3	3	6	7
1985-86b	**Toronto**	**NHL**	**66**	**34**	**11**	**45**	**227**	**10**	**5**	**1**	**6**	**47**
1986-87	**Toronto**	**NHL**	**80**	**37**	**23**	**60**	**271**	**13**	**6**	**5**	**11**	**38**
1987-88	**Toronto**	**NHL**	**28**	**12**	**11**	**23**	**80**	....	....	....	....	....
1988-89	**Toronto**	**NHL**	**15**	**7**	**4**	**11**	**66**	....	....	....	....	....
1989-90	**Toronto**	**NHL**	**38**	**18**	**8**	**26**	**116**	**5**	**1**	**1**	**2**	**19**
1990-91	**Toronto**	**NHL**	**63**	**18**	**16**	**34**	**152**	....	....	....	....	....
1991-92	**Toronto**	**NHL**	**43**	**19**	**21**	**40**	**123**	....	....	....	....	....
	NHL Totals		**333**	**145**	**94**	**239**	**1035**	**28**	**12**	**7**	**19**	**104**

a WHL First All-Star Team, East Division (1985)
b NHL All-Rookie Team (1986)

Played in NHL All-Star Game (1986)

CLEARY, JOSEPH

Defense. Shoots right. 5'11", 186 lbs. Born, Buffalo, NY, January 17, 1970.
(Chicago's 4th choice, 92nd overall, in 1988 Entry Draft).

			Regular Season					Playoffs				
Season	Club	Lea	GP	G	A	TP	PIM	GP	G	A	TP	PIM
1988-89	Boston College	H.E.	38	5	7	12	36	....	....	....	....	....
1989-90	Boston College	H.E.	42	5	21	26	56	....	....	....	....	....
1990-91	Boston College	H.E.	36	4	19	23	34	....	....	....	....	....
1991-92	Boston College	H.E.	29	5	20	25	66	....	....	....	....	....

CLIFFORD, BRIAN

Center. Shoots right. 5'11", 170 lbs. Born, Buffalo, NY, July 7, 1973.
(Pittsburgh's 6th choice, 126th overall, in 1991 Entry Draft).

			Regular Season					Playoffs				
Season	Club	Lea	GP	G	A	TP	PIM	GP	G	A	TP	PIM
1990-91	Nichols	HS	29	29	33	62	74	....	....	....	....	....
1991-92	Nichols	HS	29	27	31	58	46	....	....	....	....	....

CLOUSTON, SHAUN

Left wing. Shoots left. 6'1", 205 lbs. Born, Viking, Alta., February 21, 1968.
(NY Rangers' 3rd choice, 53rd overall, in 1986 Entry Draft).

			Regular Season					Playoffs				
Season	Club	Lea	GP	G	A	TP	PIM	GP	G	A	TP	PIM
1985-86	U. of Alberta	CWUAA	53	18	21	39	75	....	....	....	....	....
1986-87	Portland	WHL	70	6	25	31	93	19	0	5	5	45
1987-88	Portland	WHL	68	29	50	79	144	....	....	....	....	....
1988-89	Portland	WHL	72	45	47	92	150	19	7	10	17	28
1989-90	Milwaukee	IHL	54	6	16	22	61	....	....	....	....	....
	Virginia	ECHL	5	3	2	5	14	2	0	0	0	2
1990-91	Milwaukee	IHL	78	13	27	40	93	6	2	0	2	8
1991-92	Cincinnati	ECHL	33	16	27	43	42	9	6	5	11	8

Signed as a free agent by **Vancouver**, May 27, 1989.

CLOUTIER, SYLVAIN (kloo-CHAY)

Center. Shoots left. 6', 195 lbs. Born, Mont-Laurier, Que., February 13, 1974.
(Detroit's 3rd choice, 70th overall, in 1992 Entry Draft).

			Regular Season					Playoffs				
Season	Club	Lea	GP	G	A	TP	PIM	GP	G	A	TP	PIM
1990-91	S.S. Marie	Midget	34	51	40	91	92	....	....	....	....	....
1991-92	Guelph	OHL	62	35	31	66	74	....	....	....	....	....

COFFEY, PAUL DOUGLAS

Defense. Shoots left. 6', 200 lbs. Born, Weston, Ont., June 1, 1961.
(Edmonton's 1st choice, 6th overall, in the 1980 Entry Draft).

			Regular Season					Playoffs				
Season	Club	Lea	GP	G	A	TP	PIM	GP	G	A	TP	PIM
1978-79a	S.S. Marie	OHA	68	17	72	89	103	....	....	....	....	....
1979-80b	S.S. Marie	OHA	23	10	21	31	63	....	....	....	....	....
	Kitchener	OHA	52	19	52	71	130	....	....	....	....	....
1980-81	**Edmonton**	**NHL**	**74**	**9**	**23**	**32**	**130**	**9**	**4**	**3**	**7**	**22**
1981-82c	**Edmonton**	**NHL**	**80**	**29**	**60**	**89**	**106**	**5**	**1**	**1**	**2**	**6**
1982-83c	**Edmonton**	**NHL**	**80**	**29**	**67**	**96**	**87**	**16**	**7**	**7**	**14**	**14**
1983-84c	**Edmonton**	**NHL**	**80**	**40**	**86**	**126**	**104**	**19**	**8**	**14**	**22**	**21**
1984-85de	**Edmonton**	**NHL**	**80**	**37**	**84**	**121**	**97**	**18**	**12**	**25**	**37**	**44**
1985-86de	**Edmonton**	**NHL**	**79**	**48**	**90**	**138**	**120**	**10**	**1**	**9**	**10**	**30**
1986-87	**Edmonton**	**NHL**	**59**	**17**	**50**	**67**	**49**	**17**	**3**	**8**	**11**	**30**
1987-88	**Pittsburgh**	**NHL**	**46**	**15**	**52**	**67**	**93**	....	....	....	....	....
1988-89e	**Pittsburgh**	**NHL**	**75**	**30**	**83**	**113**	**195**	**11**	**2**	**13**	**15**	**31**
1989-90c	**Pittsburgh**	**NHL**	**80**	**29**	**74**	**103**	**95**	....	....	....	....	....
1990-91	**Pittsburgh**	**NHL**	**76**	**24**	**69**	**93**	**128**	**12**	**2**	**9**	**11**	**6**
1991-92	**Pittsburgh**	**NHL**	**54**	**10**	**54**	**64**	**62**	....	....	....	....	....
	Los Angeles	**NHL**	**10**	**1**	**4**	**5**	**25**	**6**	**4**	**3**	**7**	**2**
	NHL Totals		**873**	**318**	**796**	**1114**	**1291**	**123**	**44**	**92**	**136**	**206**

a OHA Third All-Star Team (1979)
b OHA Second All-Star Team (1980)
c NHL Second All-Star Team (1982, 1983, 1984, 1990)
d Won James Norris Memorial Trophy (1985, 1986)
e NHL First All-Star Team (1985, 1986, 1989)

Played in NHL All-Star Game (1982-86, 1988-92)

Traded to **Pittsburgh** by **Edmonton** with Dave Hunter and Wayne Van Dorp for Craig Simpson, Dave Hannan, Moe Mantha and Chris Joseph, November 24, 1987. Traded to **Los Angeles** by **Pittsburgh** for Brian Benning, Jeff Chychrun and Los Angeles' first round choice (later traded to Philadelphia - Jason Bowen) in 1992 Entry Draft, February 19, 1992.

COLE, DANTON

Center/Right wing. Shoots right. 5'11", 189 lbs. Born, Pontiac, MI, January 10, 1967.
(Winnipeg's 6th choice, 123rd overall, in 1985 Entry Draft).

			Regular Season					Playoffs				
Season	Club	Lea	GP	G	A	TP	PIM	GP	G	A	TP	PIM
1985-86	Michigan State	CCHA	43	11	10	21	22	....	....	....	....	....
1986-87	Michigan State	CCHA	44	9	15	24	16	....	....	....	....	....
1987-88	Michigan State	CCHA	46	20	36	56	38	....	....	....	....	....
1988-89	Michigan State	CCHA	47	29	33	62	46	....	....	....	....	....
1989-90	**Winnipeg**	**NHL**	**2**	**1**	**1**	**2**	**0**	....	....	....	....	....
	Moncton	AHL	80	31	42	73	18	....	....	....	....	....
1990-91	**Winnipeg**	**NHL**	**66**	**13**	**11**	**24**	**24**	....	....	....	....	....
	Moncton	AHL	3	1	1	2	0	....	....	....	....	....
1991-92	**Winnipeg**	**NHL**	**52**	**7**	**5**	**12**	**32**	....	....	....	....	....
	NHL Totals		**120**	**21**	**17**	**38**	**56**	....	....	....	....	....

Traded to **Tampa Bay** by **Winnipeg** for future considerations, June 19, 1992.

COLMAN, MICHAEL

Defense. Shoots right. 6'3", 218 lbs. Born, Stoneham, MA, August 4, 1968.

			Regular Season					Playoffs				
Season	Club	Lea	GP	G	A	TP	PIM	GP	G	A	TP	PIM
1989-90	Ferris State	CCHA	23	0	4	4	62	....	....	....	....	....
1990-91	Kansas City	IHL	66	1	6	7	115	....	....	....	....	....
1991-92	**San Jose**	**NHL**	**15**	**0**	**1**	**1**	**32**	....	....	....	....	....
	Kansas City	IHL	59	0	4	4	130	3	0	0	0	4
	NHL Totals		**15**	**0**	**1**	**1**	**32**	....	....	....	....	....

Signed as a free agent by **San Jose**, September 3, 1991.

CONACHER, PATRICK JOHN (PAT) (KAH-nuh-kuhr)

Left wing. Shoots left. 5'8", 190 lbs. Born, Edmonton, Alta., May 1, 1959.
(NY Rangers' 3rd choice, 76th overall, in 1979 Entry Draft).

			Regular Season					Playoffs				
Season	Club	Lea	GP	G	A	TP	PIM	GP	G	A	TP	PIM
1977-78	Billings	WHL	72	31	44	75	105	20	15	14	29	22
1978-79	Billings	WHL	39	25	37	62	50	....	....	....	....	....
	Saskatoon	WHL	33	15	32	47	37	....	....	....	....	....
1979-80	**NY Rangers**	**NHL**	**17**	**0**	**5**	**5**	**4**	**3**	**0**	**1**	**1**	**2**
	New Haven	AHL	53	11	14	25	43	7	1	1	2	4
1980-81						DID NOT PLAY						
1981-82	Springfield	AHL	77	23	22	45	38	....	....	....	....	....
1982-83	**NY Rangers**	**NHL**	**5**	**0**	**1**	**1**	**4**	....	....	....	....	....
	Tulsa	CHL	63	29	28	57	44	....	....	....	....	....
1983-84	**Edmonton**	**NHL**	**45**	**2**	**8**	**10**	**31**	**3**	**1**	**0**	**1**	**2**
	Moncton	AHL	28	7	16	23	30	....	....	....	....	....
1984-85	Nova Scotia	AHL	68	20	45	65	44	6	3	2	5	0
1985-86	**New Jersey**	**NHL**	**2**	**0**	**2**	**2**	**2**	....	....	....	....	....
	Maine	AHL	69	15	30	45	83	5	1	1	2	11
1986-87	Maine	AHL	56	12	14	26	47	....	....	....	....	....
1987-88	**New Jersey**	**NHL**	**24**	**2**	**5**	**7**	**12**	**17**	**2**	**2**	**4**	**14**
	Utica	AHL	47	14	33	47	32	....	....	....	....	....
1988-89	**New Jersey**	**NHL**	**55**	**7**	**5**	**12**	**14**	....	....	....	....	....
1989-90	**New Jersey**	**NHL**	**19**	**3**	**3**	**6**	**4**	**5**	**1**	**0**	**1**	**10**
	Utica	AHL	57	13	36	49	53	....	....	....	....	....
1990-91	**New Jersey**	**NHL**	**49**	**5**	**11**	**16**	**27**	**7**	**0**	**2**	**2**	**2**
	Utica	AHL	4	0	1	1	6	....	....	....	....	....
1991-92	**New Jersey**	**NHL**	**44**	**7**	**3**	**10**	**16**	**7**	**1**	**1**	**2**	**4**
	NHL Totals		**260**	**26**	**43**	**69**	**114**	**42**	**5**	**6**	**11**	**34**

Signed as a free agent by **Edmonton**, October 4, 1983. Signed as a free agent by **New Jersey**, August 14, 1985.

CONLAN, WAYNE

Center. Shoots right. 5'10", 170 lbs. Born, Minneapolis, MN, January 9, 1972.
(St. Louis' 5th choice, 138th overall, in 1990 Entry Draft).

			Regular Season					Playoffs				
Season	Club	Lea	GP	G	A	TP	PIM	GP	G	A	TP	PIM
1990-91	Trinity-Pawling	HS	23	31	33	64	....	....	....	....	....	....
1991-92	U. of Maine	H.E.	22	8	1	9	10	....	....	....	....	....

CONN, ROB

Left/Right wing. Shoots right. 6'2", 200 lbs. Born, Calgary, Alta., September 3, 1968.

			Regular Season					Playoffs				
Season	Club	Lea	GP	G	A	TP	PIM	GP	G	A	TP	PIM
1988-89	Alaska-Anch.	G.N.	33	21	17	38	46	....	....	....	....	....
1989-90	Alaska-Anch.	G.N.	34	27	21	48	46	....	....	....	....	....
1990-91	Alaska-Anch.	G.N.	43	28	32	60	53	....	....	....	....	....
1991-92	**Chicago**	**NHL**	**2**	**0**	**0**	**0**	**2**	....	....	....	....	....
	Indianapolis	IHL	72	19	16	35	100	....	....	....	....	....
	NHL Totals		**2**	**0**	**0**	**0**	**2**	....	....	....	....	....

Signed as a free agent by **Chicago**, July 31, 1991.

CONNOLLY, JEFF

Center. Shoots right. 6', 185 lbs. Born, Worcester, MA, February 1, 1974.
(Vancouver's 4th choice, 69th overall, in 1992 Entry Draft).

			Regular Season					Playoffs				
Season	Club	Lea	GP	G	A	TP	PIM	GP	G	A	TP	PIM
1990-91	Milton Academy	HS	23	28	19	47	....	....	....	....	....	....
1991-92	St. Sebastiens'	HS	28	31	35	66	....	....	....	....	....	....

CONROY, CRAIG

Center. Shoots right. 6'2", 190 lbs. Born, Potsdam, NY, September 4, 1971.
(Montreal's 7th choice, 123rd overall, in 1990 Entry Draft).

			Regular Season					Playoffs				
Season	Club	Lea	GP	G	A	TP	PIM	GP	G	A	TP	PIM
1990-91	Clarkson	ECAC	40	8	21	29	24	....	....	....	....	....
1991-92	Clarkson	ECAC	31	19	17	36	36	....	....	....	....	....

CONROY, JOHN (AL)

Center. Shoots right. 5'8", 170 lbs. Born, Calgary, Alta., January 17, 1966.

			Regular Season					Playoffs				
Season	Club	Lea	GP	G	A	TP	PIM	GP	G	A	TP	PIM
1989-90	Adirondack	AHL	77	23	33	56	147	....	....	....	....	....
1990-91	Adirondack	AHL	80	26	39	65	172	....	....	....	....	....
1991-92	**Philadelphia**	**NHL**	**31**	**2**	**9**	**11**	**74**	....	....	....	....	....
	Hershey	AHL	47	17	28	45	90	6	4	2	6	12
	NHL Totals		**31**	**2**	**9**	**11**	**74**	....	....	....	....	....

Signed as a free agent by **Detroit**, August, 1989. Signed as a free agent by **Philadelphia**, August 21, 1991.

CONSTANTIN, PAUL

Center. Shoots left. 6', 180 lbs. Born, Burlington, Ont., May 16, 1968.
(Vancouver's 9th choice, 191st overall, in 1988 Entry Draft).

			Regular Season					Playoffs				
Season	Club	Lea	GP	G	A	TP	PIM	GP	G	A	TP	PIM
1988-89	Lake Superior	CCHA	28	5	5	10	0	....	....	....	....	....
1989-90	Lake Superior	CCHA	29	6	2	8	10	....	....	....	....	....
1990-91	Lake Superior	CCHA	32	9	9	18	4	....	....	....	....	....
1991-92a	Lake Superior	CCHA	39	15	30	45	34	....	....	....	....	....

a NCAA All-Tournament Team (1992)

CONVERY, BRANDON

Center. Shoots right. 6', 180 lbs. Born, Kingston, Ont., February 4, 1974.
(Toronto's 1st choice, 8th overall, in 1992 Entry Draft).

			Regular Season					Playoffs				
Season	Club	Lea	GP	G	A	TP	PIM	GP	G	A	TP	PIM
1990-91	Sudbury	OHL	56	26	22	48	18	5	1	1	2	2
1991-92	Sudbury	OHL	44	40	26	66	44	5	3	2	5	4

COOKE, JAMES (JAMIE)

Right wing. Shoots right. 6'1", 195 lbs. Born, Bramalea, Ont., November 5, 1968.
(Philadelphia's 8th choice, 140th overall, in 1988 Entry Draft).

			Regular Season					Playoffs				
Season	Club	Lea	GP	G	A	TP	PIM	GP	G	A	TP	PIM
1988-89	Colgate	ECAC	28	13	11	24	26	....	....	....	....	....
1989-90	Colgate	ECAC	38	16	20	36	24	....	....	....	....	....
1990-91	Colgate	ECAC	32	29	26	55	22	....	....	....	....	....
1991-92	Hershey	AHL	66	15	26	41	49	....	....	....	....	....

COOPER, DAVID

Defense. Shoots left. 6'2", 204 lbs. Born, Ottawa, Ont., November 2, 1973.
(Buffalo's 1st choice, 11th overall, in 1992 Entry Draft).

			Regular Season					Playoffs				
Season	Club	Lea	GP	G	A	TP	PIM	GP	G	A	TP	PIM
1989-90	Medicine Hat	WHL	61	4	11	15	65	....	....	....	....	....
1990-91	Medicine Hat	WHL	64	12	31	43	66	11	1	3	4	23
1991-92	Medicine Hat	WHL	72	17	47	64	176	4	1	4	5	8

COPELAND, TODD

Defense. Shoots left. 6'2", 210 lbs. Born, Ridgewood, NJ, May 18, 1967.
(New Jersey's 2nd choice, 24th overall, in 1986 Entry Draft).

			Regular Season					Playoffs				
Season	Club	Lea	GP	G	A	TP	PIM	GP	G	A	TP	PIM
1986-87	U. of Michigan	CCHA	34	2	11	13	59	....	....	....	....	....
1987-88	U. of Michigan	CCHA	41	3	10	13	58	....	....	....	....	....
1988-89	U. of Michigan	CCHA	39	5	14	19	102	....	....	....	....	....
1989-90	U. of Michigan	CCHA	34	6	16	22	62	....	....	....	....	....
1990-91	Utica	AHL	79	6	24	30	53	....	....	....	....	....
1991-92	Utica	AHL	80	4	23	27	98	4	2	2	4	2

CORBET, RENE

Left wing. Shoots left. 6', 176 lbs. Born, Victoriaville, Que., June 25, 1973.
(Quebec's 2nd choice, 24th overall, in 1991 Entry Draft).

			Regular Season					Playoffs				
Season	Club	Lea	GP	G	A	TP	PIM	GP	G	A	TP	PIM
1990-91	Drummondville	QMJHL	45	25	40	65	34	14	11	6	17	15
1991-92	Drummondville	QMJHL	56	46	50	96	90	4	1	2	3	17

CORKUM, BOB

Center. Shoots right. 6'2", 212 lbs. Born, Salisbury, MA, December 18, 1967.
(Buffalo's 3rd choice, 47th overall, in 1986 Entry Draft).

			Regular Season					Playoffs				
Season	Club	Lea	GP	G	A	TP	PIM	GP	G	A	TP	PIM
1985-86	U. of Maine	H.E.	39	7	26	33	53	....	....	....	....	....
1986-87	U. of Maine	H.E.	35	18	11	29	24	....	....	....	....	....
1987-88	U. of Maine	H.E.	40	14	18	32	64	....	....	....	....	....
1988-89	U. of Maine	H.E.	45	17	31	48	64	....	....	....	....	....
1989-90	**Buffalo**	**NHL**	**8**	**2**	**0**	**2**	**2**	**5**	**1**	**0**	**1**	**4**
	Rochester	AHL	43	8	11	19	45	12	2	5	7	16
1990-91	Rochester	AHL	69	13	21	34	77	15	4	4	8	4
1991-92	**Buffalo**	**NHL**	**20**	**2**	**4**	**6**	**21**	**4**	**1**	**0**	**1**	**0**
	Rochester	AHL	52	16	12	28	47	8	0	6	6	8
	NHL Totals		**28**	**4**	**4**	**8**	**23**	**9**	**2**	**0**	**2**	**4**

CORPSE, KELI

Center. Shoots left. 5'11", 176 lbs. Born, London, Ont., May 14, 1974.
(Montreal's 3rd choice, 44th overall, in 1992 Entry Draft).

			Regular Season					Playoffs				
Season	Club	Lea	GP	G	A	TP	PIM	GP	G	A	TP	PIM
1990-91	Kingston	OHL	58	18	33	51	34	....	....	....	....	....
1991-92	Kingston	OHL	65	31	52	83	20	....	....	....	....	....

CORRIVEAU, RICK

Defense. Shoots left. 6', 208 lbs. Born, Welland, Ont., January 6, 1971.
(Washington's 8th choice, 168th overall, in 1991 Entry Draft).

			Regular Season					Playoffs				
Season	Club	Lea	GP	G	A	TP	PIM	GP	G	A	TP	PIM
1987-88a	London	OHL	62	19	47	66	51	12	4	10	14	18
1988-89	London	OHL	12	4	10	14	21	1	0	0	0	0
1989-90b	London	OHL	63	22	55	77	63	6	4	3	7	12
1990-91	London	OHL	64	27	60	87	83	7	3	7	10	16
1991-92	London	OHL	4	0	7	7	6	....	....	....	....	....
	Niagara Falls	OHL	54	21	57	78	72	17	5	16	21	36

a OHL Rookie of the Year (1988)
b OHL Third All-Star Team (1990)

Previously drafted 31st overall by **St. Louis** in 1989 Entry Draft.

CORRIVEAU, YVON (koh-RIV-oh)

Left wing. Shoots left. 6'1", 195 lbs. Born, Welland, Ont., February 8, 1967.
(Washington's 1st choice, 19th overall, in 1985 Entry Draft).

			Regular Season					Playoffs				
Season	Club	Lea	GP	G	A	TP	PIM	GP	G	A	TP	PIM
1984-85	Toronto	OHL	59	23	28	51	65	3	0	0	0	5
1985-86	**Washington**	**NHL**	**2**	**0**	**0**	**0**	**0**	**4**	**0**	**3**	**3**	**2**
	Toronto	OHL	59	54	36	90	75	4	1	1	2	0
1986-87	**Washington**	**NHL**	**17**	**1**	**1**	**2**	**24**	....	....	....	....	....
	Toronto	OHL	23	14	19	33	23	....	....	....	....	....
	Binghamton	AHL	7	0	0	0	2	8	0	1	1	0
1987-88	**Washington**	**NHL**	**44**	**10**	**9**	**19**	**84**	**13**	**1**	**2**	**3**	**30**
	Binghamton	AHL	35	15	14	29	64	....	....	....	....	....
1988-89	**Washington**	**NHL**	**33**	**3**	**2**	**5**	**62**	**1**	**0**	**0**	**0**	**0**
	Baltimore	AHL	33	16	23	39	65	....	....	....	....	....
1989-90	**Washington**	**NHL**	**50**	**9**	**6**	**15**	**50**	....	....	....	....	....
	Hartford	**NHL**	**13**	**4**	**1**	**5**	**22**	**4**	**1**	**0**	**1**	**0**
1990-91	**Hartford**	**NHL**	**23**	**1**	**1**	**2**	**18**	....	....	....	....	....
	Springfield	AHL	44	17	25	42	10	18	*10	6	16	31
1991-92	**Hartford**	**NHL**	**38**	**12**	**8**	**20**	**36**	**7**	**3**	**2**	**5**	**18**
	Springfield	AHL	39	26	15	41	40	....	....	....	....	....
	NHL Totals		**220**	**40**	**28**	**68**	**296**	**29**	**5**	**7**	**12**	**50**

Traded to **Hartford** by **Washington** for Mike Liut, March 6, 1990. Traded to **Washington** by **Hartford** to complete June 15 deal in which Mark Hunter and future considerations were traded for Nick Kypreos, August 20, 1992.

CORSON, SHAYNE

Left wing. Shoots left. 6', 201 lbs. Born, Barrie, Ont., August 13, 1966.
(Montreal's 2nd choice, 8th overall, in 1984 Entry Draft).

			Regular Season					Playoffs				
Season	Club	Lea	GP	G	A	TP	PIM	GP	G	A	TP	PIM
1983-84	Brantford	OHL	66	25	46	71	165	6	4	1	5	26
1984-85	Hamilton	OHL	54	27	63	90	154	11	3	7	10	19
1985-86	**Montreal**	**NHL**	**3**	**0**	**0**	**0**	**2**	....	....	....	....	....
	Hamilton	OHL	47	41	57	98	153	....	....	....	....	....
1986-87	**Montreal**	**NHL**	**55**	**12**	**11**	**23**	**144**	**17**	**6**	**5**	**11**	**30**
1987-88	**Montreal**	**NHL**	**71**	**12**	**27**	**39**	**152**	**3**	**1**	**0**	**1**	**12**
1988-89	**Montreal**	**NHL**	**80**	**26**	**24**	**50**	**193**	**21**	**4**	**5**	**9**	**65**
1989-90	**Montreal**	**NHL**	**76**	**31**	**44**	**75**	**144**	**11**	**2**	**8**	**10**	**20**
1990-91	**Montreal**	**NHL**	**71**	**23**	**24**	**47**	**138**	**13**	**9**	**6**	**15**	**36**
1991-92	**Montreal**	**NHL**	**64**	**17**	**36**	**53**	**118**	**10**	**2**	**5**	**7**	**15**
	NHL Totals		**420**	**121**	**166**	**287**	**891**	**75**	**24**	**29**	**53**	**178**

Played in NHL All-Star Game (1990)

COTE, ALAIN GABRIEL (koh-TAY)

Defense. Shoots right. 6', 200 lbs. Born, Montmagny, Que., April 14, 1967.
(Boston's 1st choice, 31st overall, in 1985 Entry Draft).

			Regular Season					Playoffs				
Season	Club	Lea	GP	G	A	TP	PIM	GP	G	A	TP	PIM
1983-84	Quebec	QMJHL	60	3	17	20	40	5	1	3	4	8
1984-85	Quebec	QMJHL	68	9	25	34	173	4	0	1	1	12
1985-86	**Boston**	**NHL**	**32**	**0**	**6**	**6**	**14**	....	....	....	....	....
	Granby	QMJHL	22	4	12	16	48	....	....	....	....	....
1986-87	**Boston**	**NHL**	**3**	**0**	**0**	**0**	**0**	....	....	....	....	....
	Granby	QMJHL	43	7	24	31	185	4	0	3	3	2
1987-88	**Boston**	**NHL**	**2**	**0**	**0**	**0**	**0**	....	....	....	....	....
	Maine	AHL	69	9	34	43	108	9	2	4	6	19
1988-89	**Boston**	**NHL**	**31**	**2**	**3**	**5**	**51**	....	....	....	....	....
	Maine	AHL	37	5	16	21	111	....	....	....	....	....
1989-90	**Washington**	**NHL**	**2**	**0**	**0**	**0**	**2**	....	....	....	....	....
	Baltimore	AHL	57	5	19	24	161	3	0	0	0	9
1990-91	**Montreal**	**NHL**	**28**	**0**	**6**	**6**	**26**	**11**	**0**	**2**	**2**	**26**
	Fredericton	AHL	49	8	19	27	110	....	....	....	....	....
1991-92	**Montreal**	**NHL**	**13**	**0**	**3**	**3**	**22**	....	....	....	....	....
	Fredericton	AHL	20	1	10	11	24	7	0	1	1	4
	NHL Totals		**111**	**2**	**18**	**20**	**115**	**11**	**0**	**2**	**2**	**26**

Traded to **Washington** by **Boston** for Bob Gould, September 28, 1989. Traded to **Montreal** by **Washington** for Marc Deschamps, June 22, 1990.

COTE, SYLVAIN (COH-tay)

Defense. Shoots right. 5'11", 185 lbs. Born, Quebec City, Que., January 19, 1966.
(Hartford's 1st choice, 11th overall, in 1984 Entry Draft).

			Regular Season					Playoffs				
Season	Club	Lea	GP	G	A	TP	PIM	GP	G	A	TP	PIM
1982-83	Quebec	QMJHL	66	10	24	34	50	....	....	....	....	....
1983-84	Quebec	QMJHL	66	15	50	65	89	5	1	1	2	0
1984-85	**Hartford**	**NHL**	**67**	**3**	**9**	**12**	**17**	....	....	....	....	....
1985-86	**Hartford**	**NHL**	**2**	**0**	**0**	**0**	**0**	....	....	....	....	....
a	Hull	QMJHL	26	10	33	43	14	13	6	*28	34	22
	Binghamton	AHL	12	2	4	6	0	....	....	....	....	....
1986-87	**Hartford**	**NHL**	**67**	**2**	**8**	**10**	**20**	**2**	**0**	**2**	**2**	**2**
1987-88	**Hartford**	**NHL**	**67**	**7**	**21**	**28**	**30**	**6**	**1**	**1**	**2**	**4**
1988-89	**Hartford**	**NHL**	**78**	**8**	**9**	**17**	**49**	**3**	**0**	**1**	**1**	**4**
1989-90	**Hartford**	**NHL**	**28**	**4**	**2**	**6**	**14**	....	....	....	....	....
1990-91	**Hartford**	**NHL**	**73**	**7**	**12**	**19**	**17**	**6**	**0**	**2**	**2**	**2**
1991-92	**Washington**	**NHL**	**78**	**11**	**29**	**40**	**31**	**7**	**1**	**2**	**3**	**4**
	NHL Totals		**460**	**42**	**90**	**132**	**178**	**24**	**2**	**8**	**10**	**16**

a QMJHL First All-Star Team (1986).

Traded to **Washington** by **Hartford** for Washington's second round choice (Andrei Nikolishin) in 1992 Entry Draft, September 8, 1991.

COURTENAY, EDWARD

Right wing. Shoots right. 6'4", 216 lbs. Born, Verdun, Que., February 2, 1968.

			Regular Season					Playoffs				
Season	Club	Lea	GP	G	A	TP	PIM	GP	G	A	TP	PIM
1987-88	Granby	QMJHL	54	37	34	71	19	5	1	1	2	2
1988-89	Granby	QMJHL	68	59	55	114	68	4	1	1	2	22
	Kalamazoo	IHL	1	0	0	0	0	1	0	0	0	2
1989-90	Kalamazoo	IHL	57	25	28	53	16	....	....	....	....	....
1990-91	Kalamazoo	IHL	76	35	36	71	37	....	....	....	....	....
1991-92	**San Jose**	**NHL**	**5**	**0**	**0**	**0**	**0**	....	....	....	....	....
	Kansas City	IHL	36	14	12	26	46	15	8	9	17	15
	NHL Totals		**5**	**0**	**0**	**0**	**0**	....	....	....	....	....

Signed as a free agent by **Minnesota**, October 1, 1989. Claimed by **San Jose** from **Minnesota** in Dispersal Draft, May 30, 1991.

COURTNALL, GEOFF

Left wing. Shoots left. 6'1", 190 lbs. Born, Victoria, B.C., August 18, 1962.

			Regular Season					Playoffs				
Season	Club	Lea	GP	G	A	TP	PIM	GP	G	A	TP	PIM
1980-81	Victoria	WHL	11	3	4	7	6	15	2	1	3	7
1981-82	Victoria	WHL	72	35	57	90	100	4	1	0	1	2
1982-83	Victoria	WHL	71	41	73	114	186	12	6	7	13	42
1983-84	**Boston**	**NHL**	**4**	**0**	**0**	**0**	**0**	....	....	....	....	....
	Hershey	AHL	74	14	12	26	51	....	....	....	....	....
1984-85	**Boston**	**NHL**	**64**	**12**	**16**	**28**	**82**	**5**	**0**	**2**	**2**	**7**
	Hershey	AHL	9	8	4	12	4	....	....	....	....	....
1985-86	**Boston**	**NHL**	**64**	**21**	**16**	**37**	**61**	**3**	**0**	**0**	**0**	**2**
	Moncton	AHL	12	8	8	16	6	....	....	....	....	....
1986-87	**Boston**	**NHL**	**65**	**13**	**23**	**36**	**117**	**1**	**0**	**0**	**0**	**0**
1987-88	**Boston**	**NHL**	**62**	**32**	**26**	**58**	**108**	....	....	....	....	....
	Edmonton	**NHL**	**12**	**4**	**4**	**8**	**15**	**19**	**0**	**3**	**3**	**23**
1988-89	**Washington**	**NHL**	**79**	**42**	**38**	**80**	**112**	**6**	**2**	**5**	**7**	**12**
1989-90	**Washington**	**NHL**	**80**	**35**	**39**	**74**	**104**	**15**	**4**	**9**	**13**	**32**
1990-91	**St. Louis**	**NHL**	**66**	**27**	**30**	**57**	**56**	....	....	....	....	....
	Vancouver	**NHL**	**11**	**6**	**2**	**8**	**8**	**6**	**3**	**5**	**8**	**4**
1991-92	**Vancouver**	**NHL**	**70**	**23**	**34**	**57**	**116**	**12**	**6**	**8**	**14**	**20**
	NHL Totals		**577**	**215**	**228**	**443**	**779**	**67**	**15**	**32**	**47**	**100**

Signed as a free agent by **Boston**, July 6, 1983. Traded to **Edmonton** by **Boston** with Bill Ranford and future considerations for Andy Moog, March 8, 1988. Rights traded to **Washington** by **Edmonton** for Greg C. Adams, July 22, 1988. Traded to **St. Louis** by **Washington** for Peter Zezel and Mike Lalor, July 13, 1990. Traded to **Vancouver** by **St. Louis** with Robert Dirk, Sergio Momesso, Cliff Ronning and future considerations for Dan Quinn and Garth Butcher, March 5, 1991.

COURTNALL, RUSSELL (RUSS)

Center/Right wing. Shoots right. 5'11", 183 lbs. Born, Duncan, B.C., June 2, 1965.
(Toronto's 1st choice, 7th overall, in 1983 Entry Draft).

			Regular Season					Playoffs				
Season	Club	Lea	GP	G	A	TP	PIM	GP	G	A	TP	PIM
1982-83	Victoria	WHL	60	36	61	97	33	12	11	7	18	6
1983-84	Victoria	WHL	32	29	37	66	63	....	....	....	....	....
	Cdn. Olympic	....	16	4	7	11	10	....	....	....	....	....
	Toronto	**NHL**	**14**	**3**	**9**	**12**	**6**	....	....	....	....	....
1984-85	**Toronto**	**NHL**	**69**	**12**	**10**	**22**	**44**	....	....	....	....	....
1985-86	**Toronto**	**NHL**	**73**	**22**	**38**	**60**	**52**	**10**	**3**	**6**	**9**	**8**
1986-87	**Toronto**	**NHL**	**79**	**29**	**44**	**73**	**90**	**13**	**3**	**4**	**7**	**11**
1987-88	**Toronto**	**NHL**	**65**	**23**	**26**	**49**	**47**	**6**	**2**	**1**	**3**	**0**
1988-89	**Toronto**	**NHL**	**9**	**1**	**1**	**2**	**4**	....	....	....	....	....
	Montreal	**NHL**	**64**	**22**	**17**	**39**	**15**	**21**	**8**	**5**	**13**	**18**
1989-90	**Montreal**	**NHL**	**80**	**27**	**32**	**59**	**27**	**11**	**5**	**1**	**6**	**10**
1990-91	**Montreal**	**NHL**	**79**	**26**	**50**	**76**	**29**	**13**	**8**	**3**	**11**	**7**
1991-92	**Montreal**	**NHL**	**27**	**7**	**14**	**21**	**6**	**10**	**1**	**1**	**2**	**4**
	NHL Totals		**559**	**172**	**241**	**413**	**320**	**84**	**30**	**21**	**51**	**58**

Traded to **Montreal** by **Toronto** for John Kordic and Montreal's sixth round choice (Michael Doers) in 1989 Entry Draft, November 7, 1988.

COUTURIER, SYLVAIN (koo-TOOR-ee-yah, SIHL-vay)

Center. Shoots left. 6'2", 205 lbs. Born, Greenfield Park, Que., April 23, 1968.
(Los Angeles' 3rd choice, 65th overall, in 1986 Entry Draft).

			Regular Season					Playoffs				
Season	Club	Lea	GP	G	A	TP	PIM	GP	G	A	TP	PIM
1985-86	Laval	QMJHL	68	21	37	58	64	14	1	7	8	28
1986-87	Laval	QMJHL	67	39	51	90	77	13	12	14	26	19
1987-88a	Laval	QMJHL	67	70	67	137	115	....	....	....	....	....
1988-89	**Los Angeles**	**NHL**	**16**	**1**	**3**	**4**	**2**	....	....	....	....	....
	New Haven	AHL	44	18	20	38	33	10	2	2	4	11
1989-90	New Haven	AHL	50	9	8	17	47	....	....	....	....	....
1990-91	**Los Angeles**	**NHL**	**3**	**0**	**1**	**1**	**0**	....	....	....	....	....
	Phoenix	IHL	66	50	37	87	49	10	8	2	10	10
1991-92	**Los Angeles**	**NHL**	**14**	**3**	**1**	**4**	**2**	....	....	....	....	....
	Phoenix	IHL	39	19	20	39	68	....	....	....	....	....
	NHL Totals		**33**	**4**	**5**	**9**	**4**	....	....	....	....	....

a QMJHL Third All-Star Team (1988)

COWIE, ROB

Defense. Shoots left. 6', 195 lbs. Born, Toronto, Ont., November 3, 1967.

			Regular Season					Playoffs				
Season	Club	Lea	GP	G	A	TP	PIM	GP	G	A	TP	PIM
1987-88	Northeastern	H.E.	36	7	8	15	38	....	....	....	....	....
1988-89	Northeastern	H.E.	36	7	34	41	60	....	....	....	....	....
1989-90	Northeastern	H.E.	34	14	31	45	54	....	....	....	....	....
1990-91	Northeastern	H.E.	33	18	23	41	56	....	....	....	....	....
1991-92	Moncton	AHL	64	11	30	41	89	5	1	1	2	0

Signed as a free agent by **Winnipeg**, July 4, 1991.

COXE, CRAIG

Left wing. Shoots left. 6'4", 210 lbs. Born, Chula Vista, CA, January 21, 1964.
(Detroit's 4th choice, 66th overall, in 1982 Entry Draft).

			Regular Season					Playoffs				
Season	Club	Lea	GP	G	A	TP	PIM	GP	G	A	TP	PIM
1982-83	Belleville	OHL	64	14	27	41	102	4	1	2	3	2
1983-84	Belleville	OHL	45	17	28	45	90	3	2	0	2	4
1984-85	**Vancouver**	**NHL**	**9**	**0**	**0**	**0**	**49**	....	....	....	....	....
	Fredericton	AHL	62	8	7	15	242	4	2	1	3	16
1985-86	**Vancouver**	**NHL**	**57**	**3**	**5**	**8**	**176**	**3**	**0**	**0**	**0**	**2**
1986-87	**Vancouver**	**NHL**	**15**	**1**	**0**	**1**	**31**	....	....	....	....	....
	Fredericton	AHL	46	1	12	13	168	....	....	....	....	....
1987-88	**Vancouver**	**NHL**	**64**	**5**	**12**	**17**	**186**	....	....	....	....	....
	Calgary	**NHL**	**7**	**2**	**3**	**5**	**32**	**2**	**1**	**0**	**1**	**16**
1988-89	**St. Louis**	**NHL**	**41**	**0**	**7**	**7**	**127**	....	....	....	....	....
	Peoria	IHL	8	2	7	9	38	....	....	....	....	....
1989-90	**Vancouver**	**NHL**	**25**	**1**	**4**	**5**	**66**	....	....	....	....	....
	Milwaukee	IHL	5	0	5	5	4	....	....	....	....	....
1990-91	**Vancouver**	**NHL**	**7**	**0**	**0**	**0**	**27**	....	....	....	....	....
	Milwaukee	IHL	36	9	21	30	116	6	3	2	5	22
1991-92	**San Jose**	**NHL**	**10**	**2**	**0**	**2**	**19**	....	....	....	....	....
	Kansas City	IHL	51	17	21	38	106	....	....	....	....	....
	Kalamazoo	IHL	6	4	5	9	13	10	2	4	6	37
	NHL Totals		**235**	**14**	**31**	**45**	**713**	**5**	**1**	**0**	**1**	**18**

Signed as a free agent by **Vancouver**, June 26, 1984. Traded to **Calgary** by **Vancouver** for Brian Bradley and Peter Bakovic, March 6, 1988. Traded to **St. Louis** by **Calgary** with Mike Bullard and Tim Corkery for Mark Hunter, Doug Gilmour, Steve Bozek and Michael Dark, September 6, 1988. Traded to **Chicago** by **St. Louis** for Rik Wilson, September 27, 1989. Claimed by **Vancouver** in NHL Waiver Draft, October 2, 1989. Claimed by **San Jose** from **Vancouver** in Expansion Draft, May 30, 1991.

CRAIEVICH, DAVID

Defense. Shoots right. 6'1", 209 lbs. Born, Chatham, Ont., May 3, 1971.
(New Jersey's 7th choice, 143rd overall, in 1991 Entry Draft).

			Regular Season					Playoffs				
Season	Club	Lea	GP	G	A	TP	PIM	GP	G	A	TP	PIM
1990-91	Oshawa	OHL	66	12	30	42	118	16	4	5	9	21
1991-92	Utica	AHL	9	0	0	0	4	1	0	0	0	4

CRAIG, MIKE

Right wing. Shoots right. 6'1", 185 lbs. Born, St. Mary's, Ont., June 6, 1971.
(Minnesota's 2nd choice, 28th overall, in 1989 Entry Draft).

			Regular Season					Playoffs				
Season	Club	Lea	GP	G	A	TP	PIM	GP	G	A	TP	PIM
1987-88	Oshawa	OHL	61	6	10	16	39	7	7	0	1	11
1988-89	Oshawa	OHL	63	36	36	72	34	6	3	1	4	6
1989-90	Oshawa	OHL	43	36	40	76	85	17	10	16	26	46
1990-91	**Minnesota**	**NHL**	**39**	**8**	**4**	**12**	**32**	**10**	**1**	**1**	**2**	**20**
1991-92	**Minnesota**	**NHL**	**67**	**15**	**16**	**31**	**155**	**4**	**1**	**0**	**1**	**7**
	NHL Totals		**106**	**23**	**20**	**43**	**187**	**14**	**2**	**1**	**3**	**27**

CRAIGWELL, DALE

Center. Shoots left. 5'11", 180 lbs. Born, Toronto, Ont., April 24, 1971.
(San Jose's 11th choice, 199th overall, in 1991 Entry Draft).

			Regular Season					Playoffs				
Season	Club	Lea	GP	G	A	TP	PIM	GP	G	A	TP	PIM
1988-89	Oshawa	OHL	55	9	14	23	15	....	....	....	....	....
1989-90	Oshawa	OHL	64	22	41	63	39	17	7	7	14	11
1990-91	Oshawa	OHL	56	27	68	95	34	16	7	16	23	9
1991-92	**San Jose**	**NHL**	**32**	**5**	**11**	**16**	**8**	....	....	....	....	....
	Kansas City	IHL	48	6	19	25	29	12	4	7	11	4
	NHL Totals		**32**	**5**	**11**	**16**	**8**	....	....	....	....	....

CRAVEN, MURRAY

Left wing. Shoots left. 6'2", 185 lbs. Born, Medicine Hat, Alta., July 20, 1964.
(Detroit's 1st choice, 17th overall, in 1982 Entry Draft).

			Regular Season					Playoffs				
Season	Club	Lea	GP	G	A	TP	PIM	GP	G	A	TP	PIM
1980-81	Medicine Hat	WHL	69	5	10	15	18	5	0	0	0	2
1981-82	Medicine Hat	WHL	72	35	46	81	49	....	....	....	....	....
1982-83	**Detroit**	**NHL**	**31**	**4**	**7**	**11**	**6**	....	....	....	....	....
	Medicine Hat	WHL	28	17	29	46	35	....	....	....	....	....
1983-84	**Detroit**	**NHL**	**15**	**0**	**4**	**4**	**6**	....	....	....	....	....
	Medicine Hat	WHL	48	38	56	94	53	4	5	3	8	4
1984-85	**Philadelphia**	**NHL**	**80**	**26**	**35**	**61**	**30**	**19**	**4**	**6**	**10**	**11**
1985-86	**Philadelphia**	**NHL**	**78**	**21**	**33**	**54**	**34**	**5**	**0**	**3**	**3**	**4**
1986-87	**Philadelphia**	**NHL**	**77**	**19**	**30**	**49**	**38**	**12**	**3**	**1**	**4**	**9**
1987-88	**Philadelphia**	**NHL**	**72**	**30**	**46**	**76**	**58**	**7**	**2**	**5**	**7**	**4**
1988-89	**Philadelphia**	**NHL**	**51**	**9**	**28**	**37**	**52**	**1**	**0**	**0**	**0**	**0**
1989-90	**Philadelphia**	**NHL**	**76**	**25**	**50**	**75**	**42**	....	....	....	....	....
1990-91	**Philadelphia**	**NHL**	**77**	**19**	**47**	**66**	**53**	....	....	....	....	....
1991-92	**Philadelphia**	**NHL**	**12**	**3**	**3**	**6**	**8**	....	....	....	....	....
	Hartford	**NHL**	**61**	**24**	**30**	**54**	**38**	**7**	**3**	**3**	**6**	**6**
	NHL Totals		**630**	**180**	**313**	**493**	**365**	**51**	**12**	**18**	**30**	**34**

Traded to **Philadelphia** by **Detroit** with Joe Paterson for Darryl Sittler, October 10, 1984. Traded to **Hartford** by **Philadelphia** with future considerations for Kevin Dineen, November 13, 1991.

CRAWFORD, LOUIS (LOU)

Left wing. Shoots left. 6', 185 lbs. Born, Belleville, Ont., November 5, 1962.

			Regular Season					Playoffs				
Season	Club	Lea	GP	G	A	TP	PIM	GP	G	A	TP	PIM
1980-81	Kitchener	OHA	53	2	7	9	134	....	....	....	....	....
1981-82	Kitchener	OHL	64	11	17	28	243	15	3	4	7	71
1982-83	Rochester	AHL	64	5	11	16	142	13	1	1	2	7
1983-84	Rochester	AHL	76	7	6	13	234	17	2	4	6	87
1984-85	Rochester	AHL	70	8	7	15	213	1	0	0	0	10
1985-86	Nova Scotia	AHL	78	8	11	19	214	....	....	....	....	....
1986-87	Nova Scotia	AHL	35	3	4	7	48	....	....	....	....	....
1987-88	Nova Scotia	AHL	65	15	15	30	170	4	1	2	3	9
1988-89	Adirondack	AHL	74	23	23	46	179	9	0	6	6	32
1989-90	**Boston**	**NHL**	**7**	**0**	**0**	**0**	**20**	....	....	....	....	....
	Maine	AHL	62	15	13	28	162	....	....	....	....	....
1990-91	Maine	AHL	80	18	17	35	215	2	0	0	0	5
1991-92	**Boston**	**NHL**	**19**	**2**	**1**	**3**	**9**	....	....	....	....	....
	Maine	AHL	54	17	15	32	171	....	....	....	....	....
	NHL Totals		**26**	**2**	**1**	**3**	**29**	....	....	....	....	....

Signed as a free agent by **Buffalo**, August 23, 1984. Signed as a free agent by **Detroit**, August 11, 1988. Signed as a free agent by **Boston**, July 6, 1989.

CREAGH, BRENDAN

Defense. Shoots left. 6', 195 lbs. Born, Hartford, CT, February 1, 1970.
(Los Angeles' 1st choice, 26th overall, in 1991 Supplemental Draft).

			Regular Season					Playoffs				
Season	Club	Lea	GP	G	A	TP	PIM	GP	G	A	TP	PIM
1989-90	U. of Vermont	ECAC	30	4	7	11	12	....	....	....	....	....
1990-91	U. of Vermont	ECAC	31	3	7	10	26	....	....	....	....	....
1991-92	U. of Vermont	ECAC	21	6	7	13	10	....	....	....	....	....

CREIGHTON, ADAM (KRAY-ton)

Center. Shoots left. 6'5", 210 lbs. Born, Burlington, Ont., June 2, 1965.
(Buffalo's 3rd choice, 11th overall, in 1983 Entry Draft).

			Regular Season					Playoffs				
Season	Club	Lea	GP	G	A	TP	PIM	GP	G	A	TP	PIM
1981-82	Ottawa	OHL	60	15	27	42	73	17	7	1	8	40
1982-83	Ottawa	OHL	68	44	46	90	88	9	0	2	2	12
1983-84	**Buffalo**	**NHL**	**7**	**2**	**2**	**4**	**4**	....	....	....	....	....
	Ottawa	OHL	56	42	49	91	79	13	16	11	27	28
1984-85	**Buffalo**	**NHL**	**30**	**2**	**8**	**10**	**33**	....	....	....	....	....
	Rochester	AHL	6	5	3	8	2	5	2	1	3	20
	Ottawa	OHL	10	4	14	18	23	5	6	2	8	11
1985-86	**Buffalo**	**NHL**	**19**	**1**	**1**	**2**	**2**	....	....	....	....	....
	Rochester	AHL	32	17	21	38	27	....	....	....	....	....
1986-87	**Buffalo**	**NHL**	**56**	**18**	**22**	**40**	**26**	....	....	....	....	....
1987-88	**Buffalo**	**NHL**	**36**	**10**	**17**	**27**	**87**	....	....	....	....	....
1988-89	**Buffalo**	**NHL**	**24**	**7**	**10**	**17**	**44**	....	....	....	....	....
	Chicago	**NHL**	**43**	**15**	**14**	**29**	**92**	**15**	**5**	**6**	**11**	**44**
1989-90	**Chicago**	**NHL**	**80**	**34**	**36**	**70**	**224**	**20**	**3**	**6**	**9**	**59**
1990-91	**Chicago**	**NHL**	**72**	**22**	**29**	**51**	**135**	**6**	**0**	**1**	**1**	**10**
1991-92	**Chicago**	**NHL**	**11**	**6**	**6**	**12**	**16**	....	....	....	....	....
	NY Islanders	**NHL**	**66**	**15**	**9**	**24**	**102**	....	....	....	....	....
	NHL Totals		**444**	**132**	**154**	**286**	**765**	**41**	**8**	**13**	**21**	**113**

Traded to **Chicago** by **Buffalo** for Rick Vaive, December 26, 1988. Traded to **NY Islanders** by **Chicago** with Steve Thomas for Brent Sutter and Brad Lauer, October 25, 1991.

CRONIN, SHAWN

Defense. Shoots left. 6'2", 210 lbs. Born, Joliet, IL, August 20, 1963.

			Regular Season					Playoffs				
Season	Club	Lea	GP	G	A	TP	PIM	GP	G	A	TP	PIM
1983-84	Ill.-Chicago	CCHA	32	0	4	4	41	....	....	....	....	....
1984-85	Ill.-Chicago	CCHA	31	2	6	8	52	....	....	....	....	....
1985-86	Ill.-Chicago	CCHA	35	3	8	11	70	....	....	....	....	....
1986-87	Salt Lake	IHL	53	8	16	24	118	....	....	....	....	....
	Binghamton	AHL	12	0	1	1	60	10	0	0	0	41
1987-88	Binghamton	AHL	65	3	8	11	212	4	0	0	0	15
1988-89	**Washington**	**NHL**	**1**	**0**	**0**	**0**	**0**	....	....	....	....	....
	Baltimore	AHL	75	3	9	12	267	....	....	....	....	....
1989-90	**Winnipeg**	**NHL**	**61**	**0**	**4**	**4**	**243**	**5**	**0**	**0**	**0**	**7**
1990-91	**Winnipeg**	**NHL**	**67**	**1**	**5**	**6**	**189**	....	....	....	....	....
1991-92	**Winnipeg**	**NHL**	**65**	**0**	**4**	**4**	**271**	**4**	**0**	**0**	**0**	**6**
	NHL Totals		**194**	**1**	**13**	**14**	**703**	**9**	**0**	**0**	**0**	**13**

Signed as a free agent by **Hartford**, March, 1986. Signed as a free agent by **Washington**, June 6, 1988. Signed as a free agent by **Philadelphia**, June 12, 1989. Traded to **Winnipeg** by **Philadelphia** for future considerations, July 21, 1989.

CROSSMAN, DOUGLAS (DOUG)

Defense. Shoots left. 6'2", 190 lbs. Born, Peterborough, Ont., June 30, 1960.
(Chicago's 6th choice, 112th overall, in 1979 Entry Draft).

			Regular Season					Playoffs				
Season	Club	Lea	GP	G	A	TP	PIM	GP	G	A	TP	PIM
1977-78	Ottawa	OHA	65	4	17	21	17	....	....	....	....	....
1978-79	Ottawa	OHA	67	12	51	63	65	4	1	3	4	0
1979-80	Ottawa	OHA	66	20	96	116	48	11	7	6	13	19
1980-81	**Chicago**	**NHL**	**9**	**0**	**2**	**2**	**2**	....	....	....	....	....
	New Brunswick	AHL	70	13	43	56	90	13	5	6	11	36
1981-82	**Chicago**	**NHL**	**70**	**12**	**28**	**40**	**24**	**11**	**0**	**3**	**3**	**4**
1982-83	**Chicago**	**NHL**	**80**	**13**	**40**	**53**	**46**	**13**	**3**	**7**	**10**	**6**
1983-84	**Philadelphia**	**NHL**	**78**	**7**	**28**	**35**	**63**	**3**	**0**	**0**	**0**	**0**
1984-85	**Philadelphia**	**NHL**	**80**	**4**	**33**	**37**	**65**	**19**	**4**	**6**	**10**	**38**
1985-86	**Philadelphia**	**NHL**	**80**	**6**	**37**	**43**	**55**	**5**	**0**	**1**	**1**	**4**
1986-87	**Philadelphia**	**NHL**	**78**	**9**	**31**	**40**	**29**	**26**	**4**	**14**	**18**	**31**
1987-88	**Philadelphia**	**NHL**	**76**	**9**	**29**	**38**	**43**	**7**	**1**	**1**	**2**	**8**
1988-89	**Los Angeles**	**NHL**	**74**	**10**	**15**	**25**	**53**	**2**	**0**	**1**	**1**	**2**
	New Haven	AHL	3	0	0	0	0	....	....	....	....	....
1989-90	**NY Islanders**	**NHL**	**80**	**15**	**44**	**59**	**54**	**5**	**0**	**1**	**1**	**6**
1990-91	**NY Islanders**	**NHL**	**16**	**1**	**6**	**7**	**12**	....	....	....	....	....
	Hartford	**NHL**	**41**	**4**	**19**	**23**	**19**	....	....	....	....	....
	Detroit	**NHL**	**17**	**3**	**4**	**7**	**17**	**6**	**0**	**5**	**5**	**6**
1991-92	**Detroit**	**NHL**	**26**	**0**	**8**	**8**	**14**	....	....	....	....	....
	NHL Totals		**805**	**93**	**324**	**417**	**496**	**97**	**12**	**39**	**51**	**105**

Traded to **Philadelphia** by **Chicago** with Chicago's second round choice (Scott Mellanby) in the 1984 Entry Draft for Behn Wilson, June 8, 1983. Traded to **Los Angeles** by **Philadelphia** for Jay Wells, September 29, 1988. Traded to **NY Islanders** by **Los Angeles** to complete February 22, 1989, transaction in which Mark Fitzpatrick and Wayne McBean were traded to **NY Islanders** by **Los Angeles** for Kelly Hrudey, May 23, 1989. Traded to **Hartford** by **NY Islanders** for Ray Ferraro, November 13, 1990. Traded to **Detroit** by **Hartford** for Doug Houda, February 20, 1991. Traded to **Quebec** by **Detroit** with Dennis Vial for cash, June 15, 1992. Claimed by **Tampa Bay** from **Quebec** in Expansion Draft, June 18, 1992.

CROWDER, TROY

Right wing. Shoots right. 6'4", 220 lbs. Born, Sudbury, Ont., May 3, 1968.
(New Jersey's 6th choice, 108th overall, in 1986 Entry Draft).

			Regular Season					Playoffs				
Season	Club	Lea	GP	G	A	TP	PIM	GP	G	A	TP	PIM
1985-86	Hamilton	OHL	56	4	4	8	178	....	....	....	....	....
1986-87	Belleville	OHL	21	5	5	10	52	....	....	....	....	....
	North Bay	OHL	35	6	11	17	90	23	3	9	12	99
1987-88	North Bay	OHL	9	1	2	3	44	....	....	....	....	....
	Belleville	OHL	46	12	27	39	103	6	2	3	5	24
	Utica	AHL	3	0	0	0	36	....	....	....	....	....
	New Jersey	**NHL**	....	....	....	....	....	**1**	**0**	**0**	**0**	**12**
1988-89	Utica	AHL	62	6	4	10	152	2	0	0	0	25
1989-90	**New Jersey**	**NHL**	**10**	**0**	**0**	**0**	**23**	**2**	**0**	**0**	**0**	**10**
	Nashville	ECHL	3	0	0	0	15	....	....	....	....	....
1990-91	**New Jersey**	**NHL**	**59**	**6**	**3**	**9**	**182**	....	....	....	....	....
1991-92	**Detroit**	**NHL**	**7**	**0**	**0**	**0**	**35**	**1**	**0**	**0**	**0**	**0**
	NHL Totals		**76**	**6**	**3**	**9**	**240**	**4**	**0**	**0**	**0**	**22**

Signed as a free agent by **Detroit**, August 27, 1991.

CROWLEY, EDWARD (TED)

Defense. Shoots right. 6'2", 188 lbs. Born, Concord, MA, May 3, 1970.
(Toronto's 4th choice, 69th overall, in 1988 Entry Draft).

			Regular Season					Playoffs				
Season	Club	Lea	GP	G	A	TP	PIM	GP	G	A	TP	PIM
1989-90	Boston College	H.E.	39	7	24	31	34	....	....	....	....	....
1990-91ab	Boston College	H.E.	39	12	24	36	61	....	....	....	....	....
1991-92	St. John's	AHL	29	5	4	9	33	10	3	1	4	11

a Hockey East First All-Star Team (1991)
b NCAA East Second All-American Team (1991)

CROWLEY, JOE

Left wing. Shoots left. 6'2", 195 lbs. Born, Concord, MA, February 29, 1972.
(Edmonton's 3rd choice, 59th overall, in 1990 Entry Draft).

			Regular Season					Playoffs				
Season	Club	Lea	GP	G	A	TP	PIM	GP	G	A	TP	PIM
1989-90	Lawrence Aca.	HS	10	8	5	13	....	....	....	....	....	....
1990-91	Boston College	H.E.	17	3	0	3	14	....	....	....	....	....
1991-92	Hull	QMJHL	37	10	9	19	120	....	....	....	....	....
	Trois-Rivières	QMJHL	4	1	3	4	4	....	....	....	....	....
	Winston-Salem	ECHL	6	0	0	0	0	....	....	....	....	....

CULLEN, JOHN

Center. Shoots right. 5'10", 187 lbs. Born, Puslinch, Ont., August 2, 1964.
(Buffalo's 2nd choice, 10th overall, in 1986 Supplemental Draft).

			Regular Season					Playoffs				
Season	Club	Lea	GP	G	A	TP	PIM	GP	G	A	TP	PIM
1983-84a	Boston U.	ECAC	40	23	33	56	28	....	....	....	....	....
1984-85b	Boston U.	H.E.	41	27	32	59	46	....	....	....	....	....
1985-86bc	Boston U.	H.E.	43	25	49	74	54	....	....	....	....	....
1986-87d	Boston U.	H.E.	36	23	29	52	35	....	....	....	....	....
1987-88efgh	Flint	IHL	81	48	*109	*157	113	16	11	*15	26	16
1988-89	**Pittsburgh**	**NHL**	**79**	**12**	**37**	**49**	**112**	**11**	**3**	**6**	**9**	**28**
1989-90	**Pittsburgh**	**NHL**	**72**	**32**	**60**	**92**	**138**	....	....	....	....	....
1990-91	**Pittsburgh**	**NHL**	**65**	**31**	**63**	**94**	**83**	....	....	....	....	....
	Hartford	**NHL**	**13**	**8**	**8**	**16**	**18**	**6**	**2**	**7**	**9**	**10**
1991-92	**Hartford**	**NHL**	**77**	**26**	**51**	**77**	**141**	**7**	**2**	**1**	**3**	**12**
	NHL Totals		**306**	**109**	**219**	**328**	**492**	**24**	**7**	**14**	**21**	**50**

a ECAC Rookie of the Year (1984)
b Hockey East First All-Star Team (1985, 1986)
c NCAA East Second All-American Team (1986)
d Hockey East Second All-Star Team (1987)
e IHL First All-Star Team (1988)
f Won James Gatschene Memorial Trophy (MVP-IHL) (1988)
g Shared Garry F. Longman Memorial Trophy (Top Rookie-IHL) with Ed Belfour (1988)
h Won Leo P. Lamoureux Memorial Trophy (Top Scorer-IHL) (1988)

Played in NHL All-Star Game (1991, 1992)

Signed as a free agent by **Pittsburgh**, June 21, 1988. Traded to **Hartford** by **Pittsburgh** with Jeff Parker and Zarley Zalapski for Ron Francis, Grant Jennings and Ulf Samuelsson, March 4, 1991.

CULLIMORE, JASSEN

Defense. Shoots left. 6'5", 225 lbs. Born, Simcoe, Ont., December 4, 1972.
(Vancouver's 2nd choice, 29th overall, in 1991 Entry Draft).

			Regular Season					Playoffs				
Season	Club	Lea	GP	G	A	TP	PIM	GP	G	A	TP	PIM
1989-90	Peterborough	OHL	59	2	6	8	61	11	0	2	2	8
1990-91	Peterborough	OHL	62	8	16	24	74	4	1	0	1	7
1991-92a	Peterborough	OHL	54	9	37	46	65	10	3	6	9	8

a OHL Second All-Star Team (1992)

CUMMINS, JIM

Right wing. Shoots right. 6'2", 203 lbs. Born, Dearborn, MI, May 17, 1970.
(NY Rangers' 5th choice, 67th overall, in 1989 Entry Draft).

			Regular Season					Playoffs				
Season	Club	Lea	GP	G	A	TP	PIM	GP	G	A	TP	PIM
1988-89	Michigan State	CCHA	30	3	8	11	98	....	....	....	....	....
1989-90	Michigan State	CCHA	41	8	7	15	94	....	....	....	....	....
1990-91	Michigan State	CCHA	34	9	6	15	110	....	....	....	....	....
1991-92	**Detroit**	**NHL**	**1**	**0**	**0**	**0**	**7**	....	....	....	....	....
	Adirondack	AHL	65	7	13	20	338	5	0	0	0	19
	NHL Totals		**1**	**0**	**0**	**0**	**7**	....	....	....	....	....

Traded to **Detroit** by **NY Rangers** with Kevin Miller and Dennis Vial for Joey Kocur and Per Djoos, March 5, 1991.

CUNNEYWORTH, RANDY WILLIAM

Left wing. Shoots left. 6', 180 lbs. Born, Etobicoke, Ont., May 10, 1961.
(Buffalo's 9th choice, 167th overall, in 1980 Entry Draft).

			Regular Season					Playoffs				
Season	Club	Lea	GP	G	A	TP	PIM	GP	G	A	TP	PIM
1979-80	Ottawa	OHA	63	16	25	41	145	11	0	1	1	13
1980-81	**Buffalo**	**NHL**	**1**	**0**	**0**	**0**	**2**	....	....	....	....	....
	Rochester	AHL	1	0	1	1	2	....	....	....	....	....
	Ottawa	OHA	67	54	74	128	240	15	5	8	13	35
1981-82	**Buffalo**	**NHL**	**20**	**2**	**4**	**6**	**47**	....	....	....	....	....
	Rochester	AHL	57	12	15	27	86	9	4	0	4	30
1982-83	Rochester	AHL	78	23	33	56	111	16	4	4	8	35
1983-84	Rochester	AHL	54	18	17	35	85	17	5	5	10	55
1984-85	Rochester	AHL	72	30	38	68	148	5	2	1	3	16
1985-86	**Pittsburgh**	**NHL**	**75**	**15**	**30**	**45**	**74**	....	....	....	....	....
1986-87	**Pittsburgh**	**NHL**	**79**	**26**	**27**	**53**	**142**	....	....	....	....	....
1987-88	**Pittsburgh**	**NHL**	**71**	**35**	**39**	**74**	**141**	....	....	....	....	....
1988-89	**Pittsburgh**	**NHL**	**70**	**25**	**19**	**44**	**156**	**11**	**3**	**5**	**8**	**26**
1989-90	**Winnipeg**	**NHL**	**28**	**5**	**6**	**11**	**34**	....	....	....	....	....
	Hartford	**NHL**	**43**	**9**	**9**	**18**	**41**	**4**	**0**	**0**	**0**	**2**
1990-91	**Hartford**	**NHL**	**32**	**9**	**5**	**14**	**49**	**1**	**0**	**0**	**0**	**0**
	Springfield	AHL	2	0	0	0	5	....	....	....	....	....
1991-92	**Hartford**	**NHL**	**39**	**7**	**10**	**17**	**71**	**7**	**3**	**0**	**3**	**9**
	NHL Totals		**458**	**133**	**149**	**282**	**757**	**23**	**6**	**5**	**11**	**37**

Traded to **Pittsburgh** by **Buffalo** with Mike Moller for Pat Hughes, October 4, 1985. Traded to **Winnipeg** by **Pittsburgh** with Rick Tabaracci and Dave McLlwain for Jim Kyte, Andrew McBain and Randy Gilhen, June 17, 1989. Traded to **Hartford** by **Winnipeg** for Paul MacDermid, December 13, 1989.

CURRAN, BRIAN

Defense. Shoots left. 6'5", 220 lbs. Born, Toronto, Ont., November 5, 1963.
(Boston's 2nd choice, 22nd overall, in 1982 Entry Draft).

			Regular Season					Playoffs				
Season	Club	Lea	GP	G	A	TP	PIM	GP	G	A	TP	PIM
1980-81	Portland	WHL	59	2	28	30	275	7	0	1	1	13
1981-82	Portland	WHL	51	2	16	18	132	14	1	7	8	63
1982-83	Portland	WHL	56	1	30	31	187	14	1	3	4	57
1983-84	**Boston**	**NHL**	**16**	**1**	**1**	**2**	**57**	**3**	**0**	**0**	**0**	**7**
	Hershey	AHL	23	0	2	2	94	....	....	....	....	....
1984-85	**Boston**	**NHL**	**56**	**0**	**1**	**1**	**158**	....	....	....	....	....
	Hershey	AHL	4	0	0	0	19	....	....	....	....	....
1985-86	**Boston**	**NHL**	**43**	**2**	**5**	**7**	**192**	**2**	**0**	**0**	**0**	**4**
1986-87	**NY Islanders**	**NHL**	**68**	**0**	**10**	**10**	**356**	**8**	**0**	**0**	**0**	**51**
1987-88	**NY Islanders**	**NHL**	**22**	**0**	**1**	**1**	**68**	....	....	....	....	....
	Springfield	AHL	8	1	0	1	43	....	....	....	....	....
	Toronto	**NHL**	**7**	**0**	**1**	**1**	**19**	**6**	**0**	**0**	**0**	**41**
1988-89	**Toronto**	**NHL**	**47**	**1**	**4**	**5**	**185**	....	....	....	....	....
1989-90	**Toronto**	**NHL**	**72**	**2**	**9**	**11**	**301**	**5**	**0**	**1**	**1**	**19**
1990-91	**Toronto**	**NHL**	**4**	**0**	**0**	**0**	**7**	....	....	....	....	....
	Newmarket	AHL	6	0	1	1	32	....	....	....	....	....
	Buffalo	**NHL**	**17**	**0**	**1**	**1**	**43**	....	....	....	....	....
	Rochester	AHL	10	0	0	0	36	....	....	....	....	....
1991-92	**Buffalo**	**NHL**	**3**	**0**	**0**	**0**	**14**	....	....	....	....	....
	Rochester	AHL	36	0	3	3	122	....	....	....	....	....
	NHL Totals		**355**	**6**	**33**	**39**	**1400**	**24**	**0**	**1**	**1**	**122**

Signed as a free agent by **NY Islanders**, August 29, 1987. Traded to **Toronto** by **NY Islanders** for Toronto's sixth round choice (Pavel Gross) in 1988 Entry Draft, March 8, 1988. Traded to **Buffalo** by **Toronto** with Lou Franceschetti for Mike Foligno and Buffalo's eighth round choice (Thomas Kucharcik) in 1991 Entry Draft, December 17, 1990.

CURRIE, DAN

Left wing. Shoots left. 6'2", 195 lbs. Born, Burlington, Ont., March 15, 1968.
(Edmonton's 4th choice, 84th overall, in 1986 Entry Draft).

			Regular Season					Playoffs				
Season	Club	Lea	GP	G	A	TP	PIM	GP	G	A	TP	PIM
1985-86	S.S. Marie	OHL	66	21	24	45	37	....	....	....	....	....
1986-87	S.S. Marie	OHL	66	31	52	83	53	4	2	1	3	2
1987-88	Nova Scotia	AHL	3	4	2	6	0	5	4	3	7	0
	S.S. Marie	OHL	57	50	59	109	53	6	3	9	12	4
1988-89	Cape Breton	AHL	77	29	36	65	29	....	....	....	....	....
1989-90	Cape Breton	AHL	77	36	40	76	28	6	4	4	8	0
1990-91	**Edmonton**	**NHL**	**5**	**0**	**0**	**0**	**0**	....	....	....	....	....
	Cape Breton	AHL	71	47	45	92	51	4	3	1	4	8
1991-92	**Edmonton**	**NHL**	**7**	**1**	**0**	**1**	**0**	....	....	....	....	....
a	Cape Breton	AHL	66	*50	42	92	39	5	4	5	9	4
	NHL Totals		**12**	**1**	**0**	**1**	**0**	....	....	....	....	....

a AHL Second All-Star Team (1992)

CYR, PAUL

Left wing. Shoots left. 5'10", 180 lbs. Born, Port Alberni, B.C., October 31, 1963.
(Buffalo's 2nd choice, 9th overall, in 1982 Entry Draft).

			Regular Season					Playoffs				
Season	Club	Lea	GP	G	A	TP	PIM	GP	G	A	TP	PIM
1980-81	Victoria	WHL	64	36	22	58	85	14	6	5	11	46
1981-82a	Victoria	WHL	58	52	56	108	167	4	3	2	5	12
1982-83	Victoria	WHL	20	21	22	43	61	....	....	....	....	....
	Buffalo	**NHL**	**36**	**15**	**12**	**27**	**59**	**10**	**1**	**3**	**4**	**6**
1983-84	**Buffalo**	**NHL**	**71**	**16**	**27**	**43**	**52**	**3**	**0**	**1**	**1**	**0**
1984-85	**Buffalo**	**NHL**	**71**	**22**	**24**	**46**	**63**	**5**	**2**	**2**	**4**	**15**
1985-86	**Buffalo**	**NHL**	**71**	**20**	**31**	**51**	**120**	....	....	....	....	....
1986-87	**Buffalo**	**NHL**	**73**	**11**	**16**	**27**	**122**	....	....	....	....	....
1987-88	**Buffalo**	**NHL**	**20**	**1**	**1**	**2**	**38**	....	....	....	....	....
	NY Rangers	**NHL**	**40**	**4**	**13**	**17**	**41**	....	....	....	....	....
1988-89	**NY Rangers**	**NHL**	**1**	**0**	**0**	**0**	**2**	....	....	....	....	....
1989-90	**NY Rangers**	**NHL**	DID NOT PLAY - INJURED									
1990-91	**Hartford**	**NHL**	**70**	**12**	**13**	**25**	**107**	**6**	**1**	**0**	**1**	**10**
1991-92	**Hartford**	**NHL**	**17**	**0**	**3**	**3**	**19**	....	....	....	....	....
	Springfield	AHL	43	11	18	29	30	11	0	3	3	12
	NHL Totals		**470**	**101**	**140**	**241**	**623**	**24**	**4**	**6**	**10**	**31**

a WHL Second All-Star Team (1982)

Traded to **NY Rangers** by **Buffalo** with Buffalo's 10th round choice (Eric Fenton) in 1988 Entry Draft for Mike Donnelly and NY Rangers' fifth round choice (Alexander Mogilny) in 1988 Entry Draft, December 31, 1987. Signed as a free agent by **Hartford**, September 30, 1990.

CZERKAWSKI, MARIUSZ

Right wing. Shoots right. 5'11", 185 lbs. Born, Radomsko, Poland, April 13, 1972.
(Boston's 5th choice, 106th overall, in 1991 Entry Draft).

			Regular Season					Playoffs				
Season	Club	Lea	GP	G	A	TP	PIM	GP	G	A	TP	PIM
1991-92	Djurgarden	Swe.	39	8	5	13	4	9	0	0	0	2

DAGENAIS, MIKE

Defense. Shoots left. 6'3", 200 lbs. Born, Gloucester, Ont., July 22, 1969.
(Chicago's 4th choice, 60th overall, in 1987 Entry Draft).

			Regular Season					Playoffs				
Season	Club	Lea	GP	G	A	TP	PIM	GP	G	A	TP	PIM
1985-86	Peterborough	OHL	45	1	3	4	40	....	....	....	....	....
1986-87	Peterborough	OHL	56	1	17	18	66	12	4	1	5	20
1987-88	Peterborough	OHL	66	11	23	34	125	12	1	1	2	31
1988-89	Peterborough	OHL	62	14	23	37	122	13	3	3	6	12
1989-90	Peterborough	OHL	44	14	26	40	74	12	4	1	5	18
1990-91	Indianapolis	IHL	76	13	14	27	115	4	0	0	0	4
1991-92	Halifax	AHL	69	11	21	32	143	....	....	....	....	....

Traded to **Quebec** by **Chicago** for Ryan McGill, September 25, 1991.

DAHL, KEVIN

Defense. Shoots right. 5'11", 190 lbs. Born, Regina, Sask., December 30, 1968.
(Montreal's 12th choice, 230th overall, in 1988 Entry Draft).

			Regular Season					Playoffs				
Season	Club	Lea	GP	G	A	TP	PIM	GP	G	A	TP	PIM
1987-88	Bowling Green	CCHA	44	2	23	25	78	....	....	....	....	....
1988-89	Bowling Green	CCHA	46	9	26	35	51	....	....	....	....	....
1989-90	Bowling Green	CCHA	43	8	22	30	74	....	....	....	....	....
1990-91	Fredericton	AHL	32	1	15	16	45	9	0	1	1	11
	Winston-Salem	ECHL	36	7	17	24	58	....	....	....	....	....
1991-92	Cdn. National	....	45	2	15	17	44	....	....	....	....	....
	Cdn. Olympic	....	8	2	0	2	6	....	....	....	....	....
	Salt Lake	IHL	13	0	2	2	12	5	0	0	0	13

DAHLEN, ULF (DAH-lehn)

Right wing. Shoots left. 6'2", 195 lbs. Born, Ostersund, Sweden, January 12, 1967.
(NY Rangers' 1st choice, 7th overall, in 1985 Entry Draft).

			Regular Season					Playoffs				
Season	Club	Lea	GP	G	A	TP	PIM	GP	G	A	TP	PIM
1983-84	Ostersund	Swe.2	36	15	11	26	10	....	....	....	....	....
1984-85	Ostersund	Swe.2	36	33	26	59	20	....	....	....	....	....
1985-86	Bjorkloven	Swe.	21	4	3	7	8	....	....	....	....	....
1986-87	Bjorkloven	Swe.	31	9	12	21	20	6	6	2	8	4
1987-88	**NY Rangers**	**NHL**	**70**	**29**	**23**	**52**	**26**	....	....	....	....	....
	Colorado	IHL	2	2	2	4	0	....	....	....	....	....
1988-89	**NY Rangers**	**NHL**	**56**	**24**	**19**	**43**	**50**	**4**	**0**	**0**	**0**	**0**
1989-90	**NY Rangers**	**NHL**	**63**	**18**	**18**	**36**	**30**	....	....	....	....	....
	Minnesota	**NHL**	**13**	**2**	**4**	**6**	**0**	**7**	**1**	**4**	**5**	**2**
1990-91	**Minnesota**	**NHL**	**66**	**21**	**18**	**39**	**6**	**15**	**2**	**6**	**8**	**4**
1991-92	**Minnesota**	**NHL**	**79**	**36**	**30**	**66**	**10**	**7**	**0**	**3**	**3**	**2**
	NHL Totals		**347**	**130**	**112**	**242**	**122**	**33**	**3**	**13**	**16**	**8**

Traded to **Minnesota** by **NY Rangers** with Los Angeles' fourth round choice (Cal McGowan) – previously acquired by NY Rangers – in 1990 Entry Draft and future considerations, March 6, 1990.

DAHLQUIST, CHRIS (DAHL-kwist)

Defense. Shoots left. 6'1", 195 lbs. Born, Fridley, MN, December 14, 1962.

			Regular Season					Playoffs				
Season	Club	Lea	GP	G	A	TP	PIM	GP	G	A	TP	PIM
1981-82	Lake Superior	CCHA	39	4	10	14	62	....	....	....	....	....
1982-83	Lake Superior	CCHA	35	0	12	12	63	....	....	....	....	....
1983-84	Lake Superior	CCHA	40	4	19	23	76	....	....	....	....	....
1984-85	Lake Superior	CCHA	32	4	10	14	18	....	....	....	....	....
1985-86	**Pittsburgh**	**NHL**	**5**	**1**	**2**	**3**	**2**	....	....	....	....	....
	Baltimore	AHL	65	4	21	25	64	....	....	....	....	....
1986-87	**Pittsburgh**	**NHL**	**19**	**0**	**1**	**1**	**20**	....	....	....	....	....
	Baltimore	AHL	51	1	16	17	50	....	....	....	....	....
1987-88	**Pittsburgh**	**NHL**	**44**	**3**	**6**	**9**	**69**	....	....	....	....	....
1988-89	**Pittsburgh**	**NHL**	**43**	**1**	**5**	**6**	**42**	**2**	**0**	**0**	**0**	**0**
	Muskegon	IHL	10	3	6	9	14	....	....	....	....	....
1989-90	**Pittsburgh**	**NHL**	**62**	**4**	**10**	**14**	**56**	....	....	....	....	....
	Muskegon	IHL	6	1	1	2	8	....	....	....	....	....
1990-91	**Pittsburgh**	**NHL**	**22**	**1**	**2**	**3**	**30**	....	....	....	....	....
	Minnesota	**NHL**	**42**	**2**	**6**	**8**	**33**	**23**	**1**	**6**	**7**	**20**
1991-92	**Minnesota**	**NHL**	**74**	**1**	**13**	**14**	**68**	**7**	**0**	**0**	**0**	**6**
	NHL Totals		**311**	**13**	**45**	**58**	**320**	**32**	**1**	**6**	**7**	**26**

Signed as a free agent by **Pittsburgh**, May 7, 1985. Traded to **Minnesota** by **Pittsburgh** with Jim Johnson for Larry Murphy and Peter Taglianetti, December 11, 1990.

DAIGNEAULT, JEAN-JACQUES (DAYN-yoh)

Defense. Shoots left. 5'11", 185 lbs. Born, Montreal, Que., October 12, 1965.
(Vancouver's 1st choice, 10th overall, in 1984 Entry Draft).

			Regular Season					Playoffs				
Season	Club	Lea	GP	G	A	TP	PIM	GP	G	A	TP	PIM
1981-82	Laval	QMJHL	64	4	25	29	41	18	1	3	4	2
1982-83ab	Longueuil	QMJHL	70	26	58	84	58	15	4	11	15	35
1983-84	Cdn. Olympic	....	62	6	15	21	40	....	....	....	....	....
	Longueuil	QMJHL	10	2	11	13	6	14	3	13	16	30
1984-85	**Vancouver**	**NHL**	**67**	**4**	**23**	**27**	**69**	....	....	....	....	....
1985-86	**Vancouver**	**NHL**	**64**	**5**	**23**	**28**	**45**	**3**	**0**	**2**	**2**	**0**
1986-87	**Philadelphia**	**NHL**	**77**	**6**	**16**	**22**	**56**	**9**	**1**	**0**	**1**	**0**
1987-88	**Philadelphia**	**NHL**	**28**	**2**	**2**	**4**	**12**	....	....	....	....	....
	Hershey	AHL	10	1	5	6	8	....	....	....	....	....
1988-89	Hershey	AHL	12	0	10	10	13	....	....	....	....	....
	Sherbrooke	AHL	63	10	33	43	48	6	1	3	4	2
1989-90	**Montreal**	**NHL**	**36**	**2**	**10**	**12**	**14**	**9**	**0**	**0**	**0**	**2**
	Sherbrooke	AHL	28	8	19	27	18	....	....	....	....	....
1990-91	**Montreal**	**NHL**	**51**	**3**	**16**	**19**	**31**	**5**	**0**	**1**	**1**	**0**
1991-92	**Montreal**	**NHL**	**79**	**4**	**14**	**18**	**36**	**11**	**0**	**3**	**3**	**4**
	NHL Totals		**402**	**26**	**104**	**130**	**263**	**37**	**1**	**6**	**7**	**6**

a QMJHL First All-Star Team (1983)
b Named QMJHL's Top Defenseman (1983)

Traded to **Philadelphia** by **Vancouver** with Vancouver's second round choice (Kent Hawley) in 1986 Entry Draft for Dave Richter, Rich Sutter and Vancouver's third round choice (Don Gibson) — acquired earlier — in 1986 Entry Draft, June 6, 1986. Traded to **Montreal** by **Philadelphia** for Scott Sandelin, November 7, 1988.

DALGARNO, BRAD

Right wing. Shoots right. 6'3", 215 lbs. Born, Vancouver, B.C., August 11, 1967.
(NY Islanders' 1st choice, 6th overall, in 1985 Entry Draft).

			Regular Season					Playoffs				
Season	Club	Lea	GP	G	A	TP	PIM	GP	G	A	TP	PIM
1984-85	Hamilton	OHA	66	23	30	53	86	....	....	....	....	....
1985-86	**NY Islanders**	**NHL**	**2**	**1**	**0**	**1**	**0**	....	....	....	....	....
	Hamilton	OHL	54	22	43	65	79	....	....	....	....	....
1986-87	Hamilton	OHL	60	27	32	59	100	....	....	....	....	....
1987-88	**NY Islanders**	**NHL**	**38**	**2**	**8**	**10**	**58**	....	....	....	....	....
	Springfield	AHL	39	13	11	24	76	....	....	....	....	....
1988-89	**NY Islanders**	**NHL**	**55**	**11**	**10**	**21**	**86**	....	....	....	....	....
1989-90						DID NOT PLAY						
1990-91	**NY Islanders**	**NHL**	**41**	**3**	**12**	**15**	**24**	....	....	....	....	....
	Capital Dist.	AHL	27	6	14	20	26	....	....	....	....	....
1991-92	**NY Islanders**	**NHL**	**15**	**2**	**1**	**3**	**12**	....	....	....	....	....
	Capital Dist.	AHL	14	7	8	15	34	....	....	....	....	....
	NHL Totals		**151**	**19**	**31**	**50**	**180**	**5**	**0**	**1**	**1**	**19**

DAL GRANDE, DAVID

Defense. Shoots left. 6'5", 195 lbs. Born, Ottawa, Ont., July 8, 1974.
(NY Rangers' 6th choice, 144th overall, in 1992 Entry Draft).

			Regular Season					Playoffs				
Season	Club	Lea	GP	G	A	TP	PIM	GP	G	A	TP	PIM
1990-91	Nepean	Midget	36	6	35	41	12	....	....	....	....	....
1991-92	Ottawa	COJHL	53	7	28	35	54	....	....	....	....	....

DALLMAN, ROD

Left wing. Shoots left. 5'11", 185 lbs. Born, Prince Albert, Sask., January 26, 1967.
(NY Islanders' 8th choice, 118th overall, in 1985 Entry Draft).

			Regular Season					Playoffs				
Season	Club	Lea	GP	G	A	TP	PIM	GP	G	A	TP	PIM
1984-85	Prince Albert	WHL	40	8	11	19	133	12	3	4	7	51
1985-86	Prince Albert	WHL	59	20	21	41	198	....	....	....	....	....
1986-87	Prince Albert	WHL	47	13	21	34	240	5	0	1	1	32
1987-88	**NY Islanders**	**NHL**	**3**	**1**	**0**	**1**	**6**	....	....	....	....	....
	Springfield	AHL	59	9	17	26	355	....	....	....	....	....
	Peoria	IHL	8	3	4	7	18	7	0	2	2	65
1988-89	**NY Islanders**	**NHL**	**1**	**0**	**0**	**0**	**15**	....	....	....	....	....
	Springfield	AHL	67	12	12	24	360	....	....	....	....	....
1989-90	**NY Islanders**	**NHL**	....	....	....	....	....	**1**	**0**	**1**	**1**	**0**
	Springfield	AHL	43	10	20	30	129	15	5	5	10	59
1990-91	Hershey	AHL	2	0	0	0	0	....	....	....	....	....
	San Diego	IHL	15	3	5	8	85	....	....	....	....	....
1991-92	**Philadelphia**	**NHL**	**2**	**0**	**0**	**0**	**5**	....	....	....	....	....
	Hershey	AHL	31	4	13	17	114	....	....	....	....	....
	NHL Totals		**6**	**1**	**0**	**1**	**26**	**1**	**0**	**1**	**1**	**0**

Signed as a free agent by **Philadelphia**, July 31, 1990.

DAM, TREVOR

Right wing. Shoots right. 5'10", 208 lbs. Born, Scarborough, Ont., April 20, 1970.
(Chicago's 2nd choice, 50th overall, in 1988 Entry Draft).

			Regular Season					Playoffs				
Season	Club	Lea	GP	G	A	TP	PIM	GP	G	A	TP	PIM
1986-87	London	OHL	64	6	17	23	88	....	....	....	....	....
1987-88	London	OHL	66	25	38	63	169	12	0	3	3	19
1988-89	London	OHL	66	33	59	92	111	21	9	11	20	39
1989-90	London	OHL	56	20	54	74	91	6	2	5	7	15
1990-91	Indianapolis	IHL	50	9	10	19	28	1	0	0	0	2
1991-92	Indianapolis	IHL	79	19	23	42	132	....	....	....	....	....

DAMPHOUSSE, VINCENT (DAM-fooz)

Left wing. Shoots left. 6'1", 190 lbs. Born, Montreal, Que., December 17, 1967.
(Toronto's 1st choice, 6th overall, in 1986 Entry Draft).

			Regular Season					Playoffs				
Season	Club	Lea	GP	G	A	TP	PIM	GP	G	A	TP	PIM
1983-84	Laval	QMJHL	66	29	36	65	25	....	....	....	....	....
1984-85	Laval	QMJHL	68	35	68	103	62	....	....	....	....	....
1985-86a	Laval	QMJHL	69	45	110	155	70	14	9	27	36	12
1986-87	**Toronto**	**NHL**	**80**	**21**	**25**	**46**	**26**	**12**	**1**	**5**	**6**	**8**
1987-88	**Toronto**	**NHL**	**75**	**12**	**36**	**48**	**40**	**6**	**0**	**1**	**1**	**10**
1988-89	**Toronto**	**NHL**	**80**	**26**	**42**	**68**	**75**	....	....	....	....	....
1989-90	**Toronto**	**NHL**	**80**	**33**	**61**	**94**	**56**	**5**	**0**	**2**	**2**	**2**
1990-91	**Toronto**	**NHL**	**79**	**26**	**47**	**73**	**65**	....	....	....	....	....
1991-92	**Edmonton**	**NHL**	**80**	**38**	**51**	**89**	**53**	**16**	**6**	**8**	**14**	**8**
	NHL Totals		**474**	**156**	**262**	**418**	**315**	**39**	**7**	**16**	**23**	**28**

a QMJHL Second All-Star Team (1986)

Played in NHL All-Star Game (1991, 1992)

Traded to **Edmonton** by **Toronto** with Peter Ing, Scott Thornton, Luke Richardson, future considerations and cash for Grant Fuhr, Glenn Anderson and Craig Berube, September 19, 1991.

DANDENAULT, ERIC

Defense. Shoots right. 6', 193 lbs. Born, Sherbrooke, Que., March 10, 1970.

			Regular Season					Playoffs				
Season	Club	Lea	GP	G	A	TP	PIM	GP	G	A	TP	PIM
1990-91	Drummondville	QMJHL	67	14	33	47	215	14	5	6	11	84
1991-92	Hershey	AHL	69	6	13	19	149	3	0	0	0	4

Signed as a free agent by **Philadelphia**, December 4, 1991.

DANEYKO, KENNETH (KEN) (DAN-ee-koh)

Defense. Shoots left. 6', 210 lbs. Born, Windsor, Ont., April 17, 1964.
(New Jersey's 2nd choice, 18th overall, in 1982 Entry Draft).

			Regular Season					Playoffs				
Season	Club	Lea	GP	G	A	TP	PIM	GP	G	A	TP	PIM
1980-81	Spokane	WHL	62	6	13	19	40	4	0	0	0	6
1981-82	Spokane	WHL	26	1	11	12	147	....	....	....	....	....
	Seattle	WHL	38	1	22	23	151	14	1	9	10	49
1982-83	Seattle	WHL	69	17	43	60	150	4	1	3	4	14
1983-84	**New Jersey**	**NHL**	**11**	**1**	**4**	**5**	**17**	....	....	....	....	....
	Kamloops	WH	19	6	28	34	52	17	4	9	13	28
1984-85	**New Jersey**	**NHL**	**1**	**0**	**0**	**0**	**10**	....	....	....	....	....
	Maine	AHL	80	4	9	13	206	11	1	3	4	36
1985-86	**New Jersey**	**NHL**	**44**	**0**	**10**	**10**	**100**	....	....	....	....	....
	Maine	AHL	21	3	2	5	75	....	....	....	....	....
1986-87	**New Jersey**	**NHL**	**79**	**2**	**12**	**14**	**183**	....	....	....	....	....
1987-88	**New Jersey**	**NHL**	**80**	**5**	**7**	**12**	**239**	**20**	**1**	**6**	**7**	**83**
1988-89	**New Jersey**	**NHL**	**80**	**5**	**5**	**10**	**283**	....	....	....	....	....
1989-90	**New Jersey**	**NHL**	**74**	**6**	**15**	**21**	**216**	**6**	**2**	**0**	**2**	**21**
1990-91	**New Jersey**	**NHL**	**80**	**4**	**16**	**20**	**249**	**7**	**0**	**1**	**1**	**10**
1991-92	**New Jersey**	**NHL**	**80**	**1**	**7**	**8**	**170**	**7**	**0**	**3**	**3**	**16**
	NHL Totals		**529**	**24**	**76**	**100**	**1467**	**40**	**3**	**10**	**13**	**130**

DANIELS, JEFF

Left wing. Shoots left. 6'1", 200 lbs. Born, Oshawa, Ont., June 24, 1968.
(Pittsburgh's 6th choice, 109th overall, in 1986 Entry Draft).

			Regular Season					Playoffs				
Season	Club	Lea	GP	G	A	TP	PIM	GP	G	A	TP	PIM
1984-85	Oshawa	OHL	59	7	11	18	16	....	....	....	....	....
1985-86	Oshawa	OHL	62	13	19	32	23	6	0	1	1	0
1986-87	Oshawa	OHL	54	14	9	23	22	15	3	2	5	5
1987-88	Oshawa	OHL	64	29	39	68	59	4	2	3	5	0
1988-89	Muskegon	IHL	58	21	21	42	58	11	3	5	8	11
1989-90	Muskegon	IHL	80	30	47	77	39	6	1	1	2	7
1990-91	**Pittsburgh**	**NHL**	**11**	**0**	**2**	**2**	**2**	....	....	....	....	....
	Muskegon	IHL	62	23	29	52	18	5	1	3	4	2
1991-92	**Pittsburgh**	**NHL**	**2**	**0**	**0**	**0**	**0**	....	....	....	....	....
	Muskegon	IHL	44	19	16	35	38	10	5	4	9	9
	NHL Totals		**13**	**0**	**2**	**2**	**2**	....	....	....	....	....

DANIELS, KIMBI

Center. Shoots right. 5'10", 175 lbs. Born, Brandon, Man., January 19, 1972.
(Philadelphia's 5th choice, 44th overall, in 1990 Entry Draft).

			Regular Season					Playoffs				
Season	Club	Lea	GP	G	A	TP	PIM	GP	G	A	TP	PIM
1988-89	Swift Current	WHL	68	30	31	61	48	12	6	6	12	12
1989-90	Swift Current	WHL	69	43	51	94	84	4	1	3	4	10
1990-91	**Philadelphia**	**NHL**	**2**	**0**	**1**	**1**	**0**	....	....	....	....	....
	Swift Current	WHL	69	54	64	118	68	3	4	2	6	6
1991-92	**Philadelphia**	**NHL**	**25**	**1**	**1**	**2**	**4**	....	....	....	....	....
	Seattle	WHL	19	7	14	21	133	15	5	10	15	27
	NHL Totals		**27**	**1**	**2**	**3**	**4**	....	....	....	....	....

DANIELS, SCOTT

Left wing. Shoots left. 6'3", 200 lbs. Born, Prince Albert, Sask., September 19, 1969.
(Hartford's 6th choice, 136th overall, in 1989 Entry Draft).

			Regular Season					Playoffs				
Season	**Club**	**Lea**	**GP**	**G**	**A**	**TP**	**PIM**	**GP**	**G**	**A**	**TP**	**PIM**
1986-87	Kamloops	WHL	43	6	4	10	68	....	....	....	....	....
	N. Westminster	WHL	19	4	7	11	30	....	....	....	....	....
1987-88	N. Westminster	WHL	37	6	11	17	157	....	....	....	....	....
	Regina	WHL	19	2	3	5	83	....	....	....	....	....
1988-89	Regina	WHL	64	21	26	47	241	....	....	....	....	....
1989-90	Regina	WHL	52	28	31	59	171	....	....	....	....	....
1990-91	Springfield	AHL	40	2	6	8	121	....	....	....	....	....
	Louisville	ECHL	9	5	3	8	34	1	0	2	2	0
1991-92	Springfield	AHL	54	7	15	22	213	10	0	0	0	32

DARBY, CRAIG

Center. Shoots right. 6'3", 180 lbs. Born, Oneida, NY, September 26, 1972.
(Montreal's 3rd choice, 43rd overall, in 1991 Entry Draft).

			Regular Season					Playoffs				
Season	**Club**	**Lea**	**GP**	**G**	**A**	**TP**	**PIM**	**GP**	**G**	**A**	**TP**	**PIM**
1990-91	Albany Aca.	HS	....	33	61	94	....	....	....	....	....	....
1991-92	Providence	H.E.	35	17	24	41	47	....	....	....	....	....

DAVIDSON, LEE

Center/Left wing. Shoots left. 5'10", 165 lbs. Born, Winnipeg, Man., June 30, 1968.
(Washington's 9th choice, 166th overall, in 1986 Entry Draft).

			Regular Season					Playoffs				
Season	**Club**	**Lea**	**GP**	**G**	**A**	**TP**	**PIM**	**GP**	**G**	**A**	**TP**	**PIM**
1986-87	North Dakota	WCHA	41	16	12	28	65	....	....	....	....	....
1987-88	North Dakota	WCHA	40	22	24	46	74	....	....	....	....	....
1988-89	North Dakota	WCHA	41	16	37	53	60	....	....	....	....	....
1989-90ab	North Dakota	WCHA	45	26	*49	75	0	....	....	....	....	....
1990-91	Moncton	AHL	69	15	17	32	24	....	....	....	....	....
1991-92	Moncton	AHL	43	3	12	15	32	....	....	....	....	....
	Fort Wayne	IHL	22	4	10	14	30	7	2	5	7	8

a WCHA Second All-Star Team (1990)
b NCAA West Second All-American Team (1990)

Signed as a free agent by **Winnipeg**, 1990.

DAVYDOV, EVGENY (dah-VEE-dohv, yev-GAIN-ee)

Left wing. Shoots right. 6', 183 lbs. Born, Chelyabinsk,Soviet Union, May 27, 1967.
(Winnipeg's 14th choice, 235th overall, in 1989 Entry Draft).

			Regular Season					Playoffs				
Season	**Club**	**Lea**	**GP**	**G**	**A**	**TP**	**PIM**	**GP**	**G**	**A**	**TP**	**PIM**
1984-85	Chelyabinsk	USSR	5	1	0	1	2	....	....	....	....	....
1985-86	Chelyabinsk	USSR	39	11	5	16	22	....	....	....	....	....
1986-87	CSKA	USSR	32	11	2	13	8	....	....	....	....	....
1987-88	CSKA	USSR	44	16	7	23	18	....	....	....	....	....
1988-89	CSKA	USSR	35	9	7	16	4	....	....	....	....	....
1989-90	CSKA	USSR	44	17	6	23	16	....	....	....	....	....
1990-91	CSKA	USSR	44	10	10	20	26	....	....	....	....	....
1991-92	CSKA	CIS	27	13	12	25	14	....	....	....	....	....
	CIS Olympic	....	8	3	3	6	2	....	....	....	....	....
	Winnipeg	**NHL**	**12**	**4**	**3**	**7**	**8**	**7**	**2**	**2**	**4**	**2**
	NHL Totals		**12**	**4**	**3**	**7**	**8**	**7**	**2**	**2**	**4**	**2**

DAWE, JASON

Left wing. Shoots left. 5'10", 195 lbs. Born, Scarborough, Ont., May 29, 1973.
(Buffalo's 2nd choice, 35th overall, in 1991 Entry Draft).

			Regular Season					Playoffs				
Season	**Club**	**Lea**	**GP**	**G**	**A**	**TP**	**PIM**	**GP**	**G**	**A**	**TP**	**PIM**
1989-90	Peterborough	OHL	50	15	18	33	19	12	4	7	11	4
1990-91	Peterborough	OHL	66	43	27	70	43	4	3	1	4	0
1991-92a	Peterborough	OHL	66	53	55	108	55	4	5	0	5	0

a OHL Third All-Star Team (1992)

DAY, JOSEPH (JOE)

Left wing. Shoots left. 5'11", 180 lbs. Born, Chicago, IL, May 11, 1968.
(Hartford's 8th choice, 186th overall, in 1987 Entry Draft).

			Regular Season					Playoffs				
Season	**Club**	**Lea**	**GP**	**G**	**A**	**TP**	**PIM**	**GP**	**G**	**A**	**TP**	**PIM**
1986-87	St. Lawrence	ECAC	33	9	11	20	25	....	....	....	....	....
1987-88	St. Lawrence	ECAC	30	21	16	37	36	....	....	....	....	....
1988-89	St. Lawrence	ECAC	36	21	27	48	44	....	....	....	....	....
1989-90a	St. Lawrence	ECAC	32	19	26	45	30	....	....	....	....	....
1990-91	Springfield	AHL	75	24	29	53	82	18	5	5	10	27
1991-92	**Hartford**	**NHL**	**24**	**0**	**3**	**3**	**10**	....	....	....	....	....
	Springfield	AHL	50	33	25	58	92	....	....	....	....	....
	NHL Totals		**24**	**0**	**3**	**3**	**10**	....	....	....	....	....

a ECAC Second All-Star Team (1990)

DEAN, KEVIN

Defense. Shoots left. 6'2", 195 lbs. Born, Madison, WI, April 1, 1969.
(New Jersey's 4th choice, 86th overall, in 1987 Entry Draft).

			Regular Season					Playoffs				
Season	**Club**	**Lea**	**GP**	**G**	**A**	**TP**	**PIM**	**GP**	**G**	**A**	**TP**	**PIM**
1987-88	N. Hampshire	H.E.	27	1	6	7	34	....	....	....	....	....
1988-89	N. Hampshire	H.E.	34	1	12	13	28	....	....	....	....	....
1989-90	N. Hampshire	H.E.	39	2	6	8	42	....	....	....	....	....
1990-91	N. Hampshire	H.E.	31	10	12	22	22	....	....	....	....	....
	Utica	AHL	7	0	1	1	2	....	....	....	....	....
1991-92	Utica	AHL	23	0	3	3	6	....	....	....	....	....
	Cincinnati	ECHL	30	3	22	25	43	9	1	6	7	8

DEAN, SCOTT

Defense. Shoots left. 5'11", 200 lbs. Born, Lake Forrest, IL, June 12, 1972.
(Chicago's 12th choice, 264th overall, in 1991 Entry Draft).

			Regular Season					Playoffs				
Season	**Club**	**Lea**	**GP**	**G**	**A**	**TP**	**PIM**	**GP**	**G**	**A**	**TP**	**PIM**
1990-91	Lake Forrest	HS	25	27	24	51	83	....	....	....	....	....
1991-92	Michigan State	CCHA	18	1	2	3	26	....	....	....	....	....

DEASLEY, BRYAN

Left wing. Shoots left. 6'3", 205 lbs. Born, Toronto, Ont., November 26, 1968.
(Calgary's 1st choice, 19th overall, in 1987 Entry Draft).

			Regular Season					Playoffs				
Season	**Club**	**Lea**	**GP**	**G**	**A**	**TP**	**PIM**	**GP**	**G**	**A**	**TP**	**PIM**
1986-87	U. of Michigan	CCHA	38	13	11	24	74	....	....	....	....	....
1987-88	U. of Michigan	CCHA	27	18	4	22	38	....	....	....	....	....
1988-89	Cdn. National	....	54	19	19	38	32	....	....	....	....	....
	Salt Lake	IHL	....	....	....	....	....	7	3	3	6	25
1989-90	Salt Lake	IHL	71	16	11	27	46	11	4	0	4	8
1990-91	Salt Lake	IHL	75	24	21	45	63	....	....	....	....	....
1991-92	Salt Lake	IHL	65	12	23	35	67	2	0	0	0	4

DeBLOIS, LUCIEN (DEHB-loh-wah)

Center. Shoots right. 5'11", 200 lbs. Born, Joliette, Que., June 21, 1957.
(NY Rangers' 1st choice, 8th overall, in 1977 Amateur Draft).

			Regular Season					Playoffs				
Season	**Club**	**Lea**	**GP**	**G**	**A**	**TP**	**PIM**	**GP**	**G**	**A**	**TP**	**PIM**
1975-76	Sorel	QJHL	70	56	55	111	112	5	1	1	2	32
1976-77	Sorel	QJHL	72	56	78	134	131	....	....	....	....	....
1977-78	**NY Rangers**	**NHL**	**71**	**22**	**8**	**30**	**27**	**3**	**0**	**0**	**0**	**2**
1978-79	**NY Rangers**	**NHL**	**62**	**11**	**17**	**28**	**26**	**9**	**2**	**0**	**2**	**4**
	New Haven	AHL	7	4	6	10	6	....	....	....	....	....
1979-80	**NY Rangers**	**NHL**	**6**	**3**	**1**	**4**	**7**	....	....	....	....	....
	Colorado	**NHL**	**70**	**24**	**19**	**43**	**36**	....	....	....	....	....
1980-81	**Colorado**	**NHL**	**74**	**26**	**16**	**42**	**78**	....	....	....	....	....
1981-82	**Winnipeg**	**NHL**	**65**	**25**	**27**	**52**	**87**	**4**	**2**	**1**	**3**	**4**
1982-83	**Winnipeg**	**NHL**	**79**	**27**	**27**	**54**	**69**	**3**	**0**	**0**	**0**	**5**
1983-84	**Winnipeg**	**NHL**	**80**	**34**	**45**	**79**	**50**	**3**	**0**	**1**	**1**	**4**
1984-85	**Montreal**	**NHL**	**51**	**12**	**11**	**23**	**20**	**8**	**2**	**4**	**6**	**4**
1985-86	**Montreal**	**NHL**	**61**	**14**	**17**	**31**	**48**	**11**	**0**	**0**	**0**	**7**
1986-87	**NY Rangers**	**NHL**	**40**	**3**	**8**	**11**	**27**	**2**	**0**	**0**	**0**	**2**
1987-88	**NY Rangers**	**NHL**	**74**	**9**	**21**	**30**	**103**	....	....	....	....	....
1988-89	**NY Rangers**	**NHL**	**73**	**9**	**24**	**33**	**107**	**4**	**0**	**0**	**0**	**4**
1989-90	**Quebec**	**NHL**	**70**	**9**	**8**	**17**	**45**	....	....	....	....	....
1990-91	**Quebec**	**NHL**	**14**	**2**	**2**	**4**	**13**	....	....	....	....	....
	Toronto	**NHL**	**38**	**10**	**12**	**22**	**30**	....	....	....	....	....
1991-92	**Toronto**	**NHL**	**54**	**8**	**11**	**19**	**39**	....	....	....	....	....
	Winnipeg	**NHL**	**11**	**1**	**2**	**3**	**2**	**5**	**1**	**0**	**1**	**2**
	NHL Totals		**993**	**249**	**276**	**525**	**814**	**52**	**7**	**6**	**13**	**38**

Traded to **Colorado** by **NY Rangers** with Pat Hickey, Mike McEwen, Dean Turner and future consideration (Bobby Crawford) for Barry Beck, November 2, 1979. Traded to **Winnipeg** by **Colorado** for Brent Ashton and Winnipeg's third round choice (Dave Kasper) in the 1982 Entry Draft, July 15, 1981. Traded to **Montreal** by **Winnipeg** for Perry Turnbull, June 13, 1984. Signed as a free agent by **NY Rangers**, September 8, 1986. Signed as a free agent by **Quebec**, August 2, 1989. Traded to **Toronto** by **Quebec** with Aaron Broten and Michel Petit for Scott Pearson and Toronto's second round choices in 1991 (later traded to Washington — Eric Lavigne) and 1992 Entry Drafts, November 17, 1990. Traded to **Winnipeg** by **Toronto** for Mark Osborne, March 10, 1992.

DeBRUSK, LOUIE (dah-BRUHSK)

Left wing. Shoots left. 6'1", 225 lbs. Born, Cambridge, Ont., March 19, 1971.
(NY Rangers' 4th choice, 49th overall, in 1989 Entry Draft).

			Regular Season					Playoffs				
Season	**Club**	**Lea**	**GP**	**G**	**A**	**TP**	**PIM**	**GP**	**G**	**A**	**TP**	**PIM**
1988-89	London	OHL	59	11	11	22	149	19	1	1	2	43
1989-90	London	OHL	61	21	19	40	198	6	2	2	4	24
1990-91	London	OHL	61	31	33	64	*223	7	2	2	4	14
	Binghamton	AHL	2	0	0	0	7	2	0	0	0	9
1991-92	**Edmonton**	**NHL**	**25**	**2**	**1**	**3**	**124**	....	....	....	....	....
	Cape Breton	AHL	28	2	2	4	73	....	....	....	....	....
	NHL Totals		**25**	**2**	**1**	**3**	**124**	....	....	....	....	....

Traded to **Edmonton** by **NY Rangers** with Bernie Nicholls and Steven Rice for Mark Messier and future considerations, October 4, 1991.

de CARLE, MIKE

Left wing. Shoots left. 6', 200 lbs. Born, Covina, CA, August 20, 1966.
(Buffalo's 2nd choice, 6th overall, in 1987 Supplemental Draft).

			Regular Season					Playoffs				
Season	**Club**	**Lea**	**GP**	**G**	**A**	**TP**	**PIM**	**GP**	**G**	**A**	**TP**	**PIM**
1985-86	Lake Superior	CCHA	36	12	21	33	40	....	....	....	....	....
1986-87	Lake Superior	CCHA	38	34	18	52	122	....	....	....	....	....
1987-88ab	Lake Superior	CCHA	43	27	39	66	83	....	....	....	....	....
1988-89	Lake Superior	CCHA	38	20	24	44	76	....	....	....	....	....
1989-90	Phoenix	IHL	24	5	4	9	44	....	....	....	....	....
	Fort Wayne	IHL	12	4	5	9	7	5	2	6	8	15
1990-91	Erie	ECHL	51	15	31	46	180	5	1	1	2	6
1991-92	Nashville	ECHL	62	28	27	55	205	....	....	....	....	....

a NCAA All-Tournament Team (1988)
b CCHA Second All-Star Team (1988)

DELAY, MICHAEL

Defense. Shoots left. 6', 190 lbs. Born, Boston, MA, August 31, 1969.
(Toronto's 8th choice, 174th overall, in 1988 Entry Draft).

			Regular Season					Playoffs				
Season	**Club**	**Lea**	**GP**	**G**	**A**	**TP**	**PIM**	**GP**	**G**	**A**	**TP**	**PIM**
1988-89	Boston College	H.E.	1	1	0	1	0	....	....	....	....	....
1989-90	Boston College	H.E.	7	0	0	0	0	....	....	....	....	....
1990-91	Boston College	H.E.	6	0	0	0	2	....	....	....	....	....
1991-92	Boston College	H.E.	34	1	2	3	28	....	....	....	....	....

DELORME, GILBERT (duh-LOHRM)

Defense. Shoots right. 6'1", 199 lbs. Born, Boucherville, Que., November 25, 1962.
(Montreal's 2nd choice, 18th overall, in 1981 Entry Draft).

			Regular Season					Playoffs				
Season	Club	Lea	GP	G	A	TP	PIM	GP	G	A	TP	PIM
1979-80	Chicoutimi	QJHL	71	25	86	111	68	12	2	10	12	26
1980-81	Chicoutimi	QJHL	70	27	79	106	77	12	10	12	22	16
1981-82	Montreal	NHL	60	3	8	11	55	....	....	....	....	....
1982-83	Montreal	NHL	78	12	21	33	89	3	0	0	0	2
1983-84	Montreal	NHL	27	2	7	9	8	....	....	....	....	....
	St. Louis	NHL	44	0	5	5	41	11	1	3	4	11
1984-85	St. Louis	NHL	74	2	12	14	53	3	0	0	0	0
1985-86	Quebec	NHL	64	2	18	20	51	2	0	0	0	5
1986-87	Quebec	NHL	19	2	0	2	14	....	....	....	....	....
	Detroit	NHL	24	2	3	5	33	16	0	2	2	14
1987-88	Detroit	NHL	55	2	8	10	81	15	0	3	3	22
1988-89	Detroit	NHL	42	1	3	4	51	6	0	1	1	2
1989-90	Pittsburgh	NHL	54	3	7	10	44	....	....	....	....	....
1990-91	Pittsburgh	NHL	DID NOT PLAY									
1991-92	Muskegon	IHL	60	6	6	12	89	7	2	2	4	12
	NHL Totals		**541**	**31**	**92**	**123**	**520**	**56**	**1**	**9**	**10**	**56**

Traded to **St. Louis** by **Montreal** with Greg Paslawski and Doug Wickenheiser for Perry Turnbull, December 21, 1983. Traded to **Quebec** by **St. Louis** for Bruce Bell, October 2, 1985. Traded to **Detroit** by **Quebec** with Brent Ashton and Mark Kumpel for Basil McRae, John Ogrodnick and Doug Shedden, January 17, 1987. Signed as a free agent by **Pittsburgh**, June 28, 1989.

DePALMA, LARRY

Left wing. Shoots left. 6', 195 lbs. Born, Trenton, MI, October 27, 1965.

			Regular Season					Playoffs				
Season	Club	Lea	GP	G	A	TP	PIM	GP	G	A	TP	PIM
1984-85	N. Westminster	WHL	65	14	16	30	87	10	1	1	2	25
1985-86	Saskatoon	WHL	65	61	51	112	232	13	7	9	16	58
	Minnesota	NHL	1	0	0	0	0	....	....	....	....	....
1986-87	Minnesota	NHL	56	9	6	15	219	....	....	....	....	....
	Springfield	AHL	9	2	2	4	82	....	....	....	....	....
1987-88	Minnesota	NHL	7	1	1	2	15	....	....	....	....	....
	Baltimore	AHL	16	8	10	18	121	....	....	....	....	....
	Kalamazoo	IHL	22	6	11	17	215	....	....	....	....	....
1988-89	Minnesota	NHL	43	5	7	12	102	2	0	0	0	6
1989-90	Kalamazoo	IHL	36	7	14	21	218	4	1	1	2	32
1990-91	Minnesota	NHL	14	3	0	3	26	....	....	....	....	....
	Kalamazoo	IHL	55	27	32	59	160	11	5	4	9	25
1991-92	Kansas City	IHL	62	28	29	57	188	15	7	*13	20	34
	NHL Totals		**121**	**18**	**14**	**32**	**362**	**2**	**0**	**0**	**0**	**6**

Signed as a free agent by **San Jose**, August 30, 1991.

DE RUITER, CHRIS

Right wing. Shoots right. 6'2", 190 lbs. Born, Kingston, Ont., February 27, 1974.
(Toronto's 6th choice, 106th overall, in 1992 Entry Draft).

			Regular Season					Playoffs				
Season	Club	Lea	GP	G	A	TP	PIM	GP	G	A	TP	PIM
1990-91	Kingston	Jr. B	43	8	33	41	78	....	....	....	....	....
1991-92	Kingston	Tier II	29	27	24	51	52	....	....	....	....	....

DESCHAMPS, MARC

Defense. Shoots right. 6'3", 210 lbs. Born, Kapuskasing, Ont., September 29, 1970.
(Montreal's 6th choice, 104th overall, in 1989 Entry Draft).

			Regular Season					Playoffs				
Season	Club	Lea	GP	G	A	TP	PIM	GP	G	A	TP	PIM
1988-89	Cornell	ECAC	26	0	7	7	26	....	....	....	....	....
1989-90	Cornell	ECAC	13	0	2	2	10	....	....	....	....	....
1990-91	Cornell	ECAC	7	0	1	1	0	....	....	....	....	....
1991-92	Cornell	ECAC	25	0	8	8	60	....	....	....	....	....

Traded to **Washington** by **Montreal** for Alain Cote, June 22, 1990.

DESJARDINS, ERIC (day-jar-DAN)

Defense. Shoots right. 6'1", 200 lbs. Born, Rouyn, Que., June 14, 1969.
(Montreal's 3rd choice, 38th overall, in 1987 Entry Draft).

			Regular Season					Playoffs				
Season	Club	Lea	GP	G	A	TP	PIM	GP	G	A	TP	PIM
1986-87a	Granby	QMJHL	66	14	24	38	178	8	3	2	5	10
1987-88	Sherbrooke	AHL	3	0	0	0	6	4	0	2	2	2
bc	Granby	QMJHL	62	18	49	67	138	5	0	3	3	10
1988-89	Montreal	NHL	36	2	12	14	26	14	1	1	2	6
1989-90	Montreal	NHL	55	3	13	16	51	6	0	0	0	10
1990-91	Montreal	NHL	62	7	18	25	27	13	1	4	5	8
1991-92	Montreal	NHL	77	6	32	38	50	11	3	3	6	4
	NHL Totals		**230**	**18**	**75**	**93**	**154**	**44**	**5**	**8**	**13**	**28**

a QMJHL Second All-Star Team (1987)
b QMJHL First All-Star Team (1988)
c QMJHL Top Defenseman (1988)

Played in NHL All-Star Game (1992)

DESJARDINS, MARTIN (day-jar-DAN)

Center. Shoots left. 6', 180 lbs. Born, Ste-Rose, Que., January 28, 1967.
(Montreal's 5th choice, 75th overall, in 1985 Entry Draft).

			Regular Season					Playoffs				
Season	Club	Lea	GP	G	A	TP	PIM	GP	G	A	TP	PIM
1984-85	Trois-Rivières	QMJHL	66	29	34	63	76	7	4	6	10	6
1985-86	Trois-Rivières	QMJHL	71	49	69	118	103	4	2	4	6	4
1986-87	Trois-Rivières	QMJHL	52	32	52	84	77	....	....	....	....	....
	Longueuil	QMJHL	17	7	10	17	12	19	8	10	18	18
1987-88	Sherbrooke	AHL	75	34	36	70	117	5	1	1	2	8
1988-89	Sherbrooke	AHL	70	17	27	44	104	6	2	7	9	21
1989-90	Montreal	NHL	8	0	2	2	2	....	....	....	....	....
	Sherbrooke	AHL	65	21	26	47	72	12	4	*13	17	28
1990-91	Fredericton	AHL	2	0	1	1	6	....	....	....	....	....
	Indianapolis	IHL	71	15	42	57	110	7	2	1	3	8
1991-92	Indianapolis	IHL	36	4	7	11	52	....	....	....	....	....
	NHL Totals		**8**	**0**	**2**	**2**	**2**	....	....	....	....	....

Traded to **Chicago** by **Montreal** for future considerations, October 10, 1990.

DESJARDINS, NORMAN

Right wing. Shoots right. 5'10", 184 lbs. Born, Montreal, Que., March 25, 1968.

			Regular Season					Playoffs				
Season	Club	Lea	GP	G	A	TP	PIM	GP	G	A	TP	PIM
1986-87	Granby	QMJHL	52	19	22	41	61	....	....	....	....	....
	Verdun	QMJHL	14	3	5	8	45	....	....	....	....	....
1987-88	Verdun	QMJHL	69	31	44	75	95	....	....	....	....	....
1988-89	Longueuil	QMJHL	63	26	61	87	72	....	....	....	....	....
1989-90	Sherbrooke	AHL	58	13	19	32	91	12	4	3	7	15
1990-91	Fredericton	AHL	74	11	13	24	110	9	2	2	4	6
1991-92	Fredericton	AHL	50	9	9	18	62	....	....	....	....	....

Signed as a free agent by **Montreal**, November 27, 1989.

DEULING, JARRETT

Left wing. Shoots left. 5'11", 194 lbs. Born, Vernon, B.C., March 4, 1974.
(NY Islanders' 2nd choice, 56th overall, in 1992 Entry Draft).

			Regular Season					Playoffs				
Season	Club	Lea	GP	G	A	TP	PIM	GP	G	A	TP	PIM
1990-91	Kamloops	WHL	48	4	12	16	43	12	5	2	7	7
1991-92	Kamloops	WHL	68	28	26	54	79	17	10	6	16	18

DIDUCK, GERALD (DID-uck)

Defense. Shoots right. 6'2", 207 lbs. Born, Edmonton, Alta., April 6, 1965.
(NY Islanders' 2nd choice, 16th overall, in 1983 Entry Draft).

			Regular Season					Playoffs				
Season	Club	Lea	GP	G	A	TP	PIM	GP	G	A	TP	PIM
1981-82	Lethbridge	WHL	71	1	15	16	81	12	0	3	3	27
1982-83	Lethbridge	WHL	67	8	16	24	151	20	3	12	15	49
1983-84	Lethbridge	WHL	65	10	24	34	133	5	1	4	5	27
	Indianapolis	IHL	....	....	....	....	....	10	1	6	7	19
1984-85	NY Islanders	NHL	65	2	8	10	80	....	....	....	....	....
1985-86	NY Islanders	NHL	10	1	2	3	2	....	....	....	....	....
	Springfield	AHL	61	6	14	20	173	....	....	....	....	....
1986-87	NY Islanders	NHL	30	2	3	5	67	14	0	1	1	35
	Springfield	AHL	45	6	8	14	120	....	....	....	....	....
1987-88	NY Islanders	NHL	68	7	12	19	113	6	1	0	1	42
1988-89	NY Islanders	NHL	65	11	21	32	155	....	....	....	....	....
1989-90	NY Islanders	NHL	76	3	17	20	163	5	0	0	0	12
1990-91	Montreal	NHL	32	1	2	3	39	....	....	....	....	....
	Vancouver	NHL	31	3	7	10	66	6	1	0	1	11
1991-92	Vancouver	NHL	77	6	21	27	229	5	0	0	0	10
	NHL Totals		**454**	**36**	**93**	**129**	**914**	**36**	**2**	**1**	**3**	**110**

Traded to **Montreal** by **NY Islanders** for Craig Ludwig, September 4, 1990. Traded to **Vancouver** by **Montreal** for Vancouver's fourth round choice (Vladimir Vujtek) in 1991 Entry Draft, January 12, 1991.

DiMAIO, ROBERT (ROB) (duh-MIGH-oh)

Center. Shoots right. 5'8", 175 lbs. Born, Calgary, Alta., February 19, 1968.
(NY Islanders' 6th choice, 118th overall, in 1987 Entry Draft).

			Regular Season					Playoffs				
Season	Club	Lea	GP	G	A	TP	PIM	GP	G	A	TP	PIM
1986-87	Medicine Hat	WHL	70	27	43	70	130	20	7	11	18	46
1987-88	Medicine Hat	WHL	54	47	43	90	120	14	12	19	*31	59
1988-89	NY Islanders	NHL	16	1	0	1	30	....	....	....	....	....
	Springfield	AHL	40	13	18	31	67	....	....	....	....	....
1989-90	NY Islanders	NHL	7	0	0	0	2	1	1	0	1	4
	Springfield	AHL	54	25	27	52	69	16	4	7	11	45
1990-91	NY Islanders	NHL	1	0	0	0	0	....	....	....	....	....
	Capital Dist.	AHL	12	3	4	7	22	....	....	....	....	....
1991-92	NY Islanders	NHL	50	5	2	7	43	....	....	....	....	....
	NHL Totals		**74**	**6**	**2**	**8**	**75**	**1**	**1**	**0**	**1**	**4**

Claimed by **Tampa Bay** from **NY Islanders** in Expansion Draft, June 18, 1992.

DINEEN, GORDON (GORD)

Defense. Shoots right. 6', 195 lbs. Born, Quebec City, Que., September 21, 1962.
(NY Islanders' 2nd choice, 42nd overall, in 1981 Entry Draft).

			Regular Season					Playoffs				
Season	Club	Lea	GP	G	A	TP	PIM	GP	G	A	TP	PIM
1980-81	S.S. Marie	OHA	68	4	26	30	158	19	1	7	8	58
1981-82	S.S. Marie	OHL	68	9	45	54	185	13	1	2	3	52
1982-83	NY Islanders	NHL	2	0	0	0	4	....	....	....	....	....
abc	Indianapolis	CHL	73	10	47	57	78	13	2	10	12	29
1983-84	NY Islanders	NHL	43	1	11	12	32	9	1	1	2	28
	Indianapolis	CHL	26	4	13	17	63	....	....	....	....	....
1984-85	NY Islanders	NHL	48	1	12	13	89	10	0	0	0	26
	Springfield	AHL	25	1	8	9	46	....	....	....	....	....
1985-86	NY Islanders	NHL	57	1	8	9	81	3	0	0	0	2
	Springfield	AHL	11	2	3	5	20	....	....	....	....	....
1986-87	NY Islanders	NHL	71	4	10	14	110	7	0	4	4	4
1987-88	NY Islanders	NHL	57	4	12	16	62	....	....	....	....	....
	Minnesota	NHL	13	1	1	2	21	....	....	....	....	....
1988-89	Minnesota	NHL	2	0	1	1	2	....	....	....	....	....
	Kalamazoo	IHL	25	2	6	8	49	....	....	....	....	....
	Pittsburgh	NHL	38	1	2	3	42	11	0	2	2	8
1989-90	Pittsburgh	NHL	69	1	8	9	125	....	....	....	....	....
1990-91	Pittsburgh	NHL	9	0	0	0	4	....	....	....	....	....
	Muskegon	IHL	40	1	14	15	57	5	0	2	2	0
1991-92	Pittsburgh	NHL	1	0	0	0	0	....	....	....	....	....
d	Muskegon	IHL	79	8	37	45	83	14	2	4	6	33
	NHL Totals		**410**	**14**	**65**	**79**	**572**	**40**	**1**	**7**	**8**	**68**

a CHL First All-Star Team (1983)
b Won Bob Gassoff Trophy (CHL's Most Improved Defenseman) (1983)
c Won Bobby Orr Trophy (CHL's Top Defenseman) (1983)
d IHL First All-Star Team (1992)

Traded to **Minnesota** by **NY Islanders** for Chris Pryor and future considerations, March 8, 1988. Traded to **Pittsburgh** by **Minnesota** with Scott Bjugstad for Ville Siren and Steve Gotaas, December 17, 1988.

DINEEN, KEVIN

Right wing. Shoots right. 5'11", 190 lbs. Born, Quebec City, Que., October 28, 1963.
(Hartford's 3rd choice, 56th overall, in 1982 Entry Draft).

			Regular Season					Playoffs				
Season	Club	Lea	GP	G	A	TP	PIM	GP	G	A	TP	PIM
1981-82	U. of Denver	WCHA	26	10	10	20	70	....	....	....	....	....
1982-83	U. of Denver	WCHA	36	16	13	29	108	....	....	....	....	....
1983-84	Cdn. Olympic	....	52	5	11	16	2	....	....	....	....	....
1984-85	**Hartford**	**NHL**	**57**	**25**	**16**	**41**	**120**	....	....	....	....	....
	Binghamton	AHL	25	15	8	23	41	....	....	....	....	....
1985-86	**Hartford**	**NHL**	**57**	**33**	**35**	**68**	**124**	**10**	**6**	**7**	**13**	**18**
1986-87	**Hartford**	**NHL**	**78**	**40**	**39**	**79**	**110**	**6**	**2**	**1**	**3**	**31**
1987-88	**Hartford**	**NHL**	**74**	**25**	**25**	**50**	**217**	**6**	**4**	**4**	**8**	**8**
1988-89	**Hartford**	**NHL**	**79**	**45**	**44**	**89**	**167**	**4**	**1**	**0**	**1**	**10**
1989-90	**Hartford**	**NHL**	**67**	**25**	**41**	**66**	**164**	**6**	**3**	**2**	**5**	**18**
1990-91a	**Hartford**	**NHL**	**61**	**17**	**30**	**47**	**104**	**6**	**1**	**0**	**1**	**16**
1991-92	**Hartford**	**NHL**	**16**	**4**	**2**	**6**	**23**	....	....	....	....	....
	Philadelphia	**NHL**	**64**	**26**	**30**	**56**	**130**	....	....	....	....	....
	NHL Totals		**553**	**240**	**262**	**502**	**1159**	**38**	**17**	**14**	**31**	**101**

a Won Bud Light/NHL Man of the Year Award (1991)

Played in NHL All-Star Game (1988, 1989)

Traded to **Philadelphia** by **Hartford** for Murray Craven and future considerations, November 13, 1991.

DIONNE, GILBERT

Left wing. Shoots left. 6', 194 lbs. Born, Drummondville, Que., September 19, 1970.
(Montreal's 5th choice, 81st overall, in 1990 Entry Draft).

			Regular Season					Playoffs				
Season	Club	Lea	GP	G	A	TP	PIM	GP	G	A	TP	PIM
1988-89	Kitchener	OHL	66	11	33	44	13	5	1	1	2	4
1989-90a	Kitchener	OHL	64	48	57	105	85	17	13	10	23	22
1990-91	**Montreal**	**NHL**	**2**	**0**	**0**	**0**	**0**	....	....	....	....	....
	Fredericton	AHL	77	40	47	87	62	9	6	5	11	8
1991-92b	**Montreal**	**NHL**	**39**	**21**	**13**	**34**	**10**	**11**	**3**	**4**	**7**	**10**
	Fredericton	AHL	29	19	27	46	20	....	....	....	....	....
	NHL Totals		**41**	**21**	**13**	**34**	**10**	**11**	**3**	**4**	**7**	**10**

a OHL Third All-Star Team (1990)
b NHL/Upper Deck All-Rookie Team (1992)

DIPIETRO, PAUL

Center. Shoots right. 5'9", 181 lbs. Born, Sault Ste. Marie, Ont., September 8, 1970.
(Montreal's 6th choice, 102nd overall, in 1990 Entry Draft).

			Regular Season					Playoffs				
Season	Club	Lea	GP	G	A	TP	PIM	GP	G	A	TP	PIM
1986-87	Sudbury	OHL	49	5	11	16	13	....	....	....	....	....
1987-88	Sudbury	OHL	63	25	42	67	27	....	....	....	....	....
1988-89	Sudbury	OHL	57	31	48	79	27	....	....	....	....	....
1989-90a	Sudbury	OHL	66	56	63	119	57	7	3	6	9	7
1990-91	Fredericton	AHL	78	39	31	70	38	9	5	6	11	2
1991-92	**Montreal**	**NHL**	**33**	**4**	**6**	**10**	**25**	....	....	....	....	....
	Fredericton	AHL	43	26	31	57	52	7	3	4	7	8
	NHL Totals		**33**	**4**	**6**	**10**	**25**	....	....	....	....	....

a OHL Third All-Star Team (1990)

DIRK, ROBERT

Defense. Shoots left. 6'4", 218 lbs. Born, Regina, Sask., August 20, 1966.
(St. Louis' 4th choice, 53rd overall, in 1984 Entry Draft).

			Regular Season					Playoffs				
Season	Club	Lea	GP	G	A	TP	PIM	GP	G	A	TP	PIM
1982-83	Regina	WHL	1	0	0	0	0	....	....	....	....	....
1983-84	Regina	WHL	62	2	10	12	64	23	1	12	13	24
1984-85	Regina	WHL	69	10	34	44	97	8	0	0	0	4
1985-86	Regina	WHL	72	19	60	79	140	10	3	5	8	8
1986-87	Peoria	IHL	76	5	17	22	155	....	....	....	....	....
1987-88	**St. Louis**	**NHL**	**7**	**0**	**1**	**1**	**16**	**6**	**0**	**1**	**1**	**2**
	Peoria	IHL	54	4	21	25	126	....	....	....	....	....
1988-89	**St. Louis**	**NHL**	**9**	**0**	**1**	**1**	**11**	....	....	....	....	....
	Peoria	IHL	22	0	2	2	54	....	....	....	....	....
1989-90	**St. Louis**	**NHL**	**37**	**1**	**1**	**2**	**128**	**3**	**0**	**0**	**0**	**0**
	Peoria	IHL	24	1	2	3	79	....	....	....	....	....
1990-91	**St. Louis**	**NHL**	**41**	**1**	**3**	**4**	**100**	....	....	....	....	....
	Peoria	IHL	3	0	0	0	2	....	....	....	....	....
	Vancouver	**NHL**	**11**	**1**	**0**	**1**	**20**	**6**	**0**	**0**	**0**	**13**
1991-92	**Vancouver**	**NHL**	**72**	**2**	**7**	**9**	**126**	**13**	**0**	**0**	**0**	**20**
	NHL Totals		**177**	**5**	**13**	**18**	**501**	**28**	**0**	**1**	**1**	**35**

Traded to **Vancouver** by **St. Louis** with Geoff Courtnall, Sergio Momesso, Cliff Ronning and future considerations for Dan Quinn and Garth Butcher, March 5, 1991.

DI VITA, DAVID

Defense. Shoots left. 6'2", 195 lbs. Born, St. Clair Shores, MI, February 3, 1969.
(Buffalo's 6th choice, 106th overall, in 1988 Entry Draft).

			Regular Season					Playoffs				
Season	Club	Lea	GP	G	A	TP	PIM	GP	G	A	TP	PIM
1987-88	Lake Superior	CCHA	26	1	0	1	20	....	....	....	....	....
1988-89	Lake Superior	CCHA	25	1	4	5	28	....	....	....	....	....
1989-90	Lake Superior	CCHA	46	4	12	16	58	....	....	....	....	....
1990-91	Lake Superior	CCHA	43	3	5	8	63	....	....	....	....	....
1991-92	Rochester	AHL	25	1	2	3	59	....	....	....	....	....
	Erie	ECHL	21	2	10	12	46	4	0	0	0	7

DJOOS, PER (JUICE)

Defense. Shoots right. 5'11", 176 lbs. Born, Mora, Sweden, May 11, 1968.
(Detroit's 7th choice, 127th overall, in 1986 Entry Draft).

			Regular Season					Playoffs				
Season	Club	Lea	GP	G	A	TP	PIM	GP	G	A	TP	PIM
1986-87	Brynas	Swe.	23	1	2	3	16	....	....	....	....	....
1987-88	Brynas	Swe.	34	4	11	15	18	....	....	....	....	....
1988-89	Brynas	Swe.	40	1	17	18	44	....	....	....	....	....
1989-90	Brynas	Swe.	37	5	13	18	34	5	1	3	4	6
1990-91	**Detroit**	**NHL**	**26**	**0**	**12**	**12**	**16**	....	....	....	....	....
	Adirondack	AHL	20	2	9	11	6	....	....	....	....	....
	Binghamton	AHL	14	1	8	9	10	9	2	2	4	4
1991-92	**NY Rangers**	**NHL**	**50**	**1**	**18**	**19**	**40**	....	....	....	....	....
	NHL Totals		**76**	**1**	**30**	**31**	**56**	....	....	....	....	....

Traded to **NY Rangers** by **Detroit** with Joey Kocur for Kevin Miller, Jim Cummins and Dennis Vial, March 5, 1991.

DOBBIN, BRIAN

Right wing. Shoots right. 5'11", 205 lbs. Born, Petrolia, Ont., August 18, 1966.
(Philadelphia's 7th choice, 100th overall, in 1984 Entry Draft).

			Regular Season					Playoffs				
Season	Club	Lea	GP	G	A	TP	PIM	GP	G	A	TP	PIM
1982-83	Kingston	OHL	69	16	39	55	35	....	....	....	....	....
1983-84	London	OHL	70	30	40	70	70	....	....	....	....	....
1984-85	London	OHL	53	42	57	99	63	8	7	4	11	2
1985-86	London	OHL	59	38	55	93	113	5	2	1	3	9
	Hershey	AHL	2	1	0	1	0	18	5	5	10	21
1986-87	**Philadelphia**	**NHL**	**12**	**2**	**1**	**3**	**14**	....	....	....	....	....
	Hershey	AHL	52	26	35	61	66	5	4	2	6	15
1987-88	**Philadelphia**	**NHL**	**21**	**3**	**5**	**8**	**6**	....	....	....	....	....
	Hershey	AHL	54	36	47	83	58	12	7	8	15	15
1988-89	**Philadelphia**	**NHL**	**14**	**0**	**1**	**1**	**8**	**2**	**0**	**0**	**0**	**17**
a	Hershey	AHL	59	43	48	91	61	11	7	6	13	12
1989-90	**Philadelphia**	**NHL**	**9**	**1**	**1**	**2**	**11**	....	....	....	....	....
b	Hershey	AHL	68	38	47	85	58	....	....	....	....	....
1990-91	Hershey	AHL	80	35	43	78	82	7	1	2	3	7
1991-92	New Haven	AHL	33	16	21	37	20	....	....	....	....	....
	Boston	**NHL**	**7**	**1**	**0**	**1**	**22**	....	....	....	....	....
	Maine	AHL	33	21	15	36	14	....	....	....	....	....
	NHL Totals		**63**	**7**	**8**	**15**	**61**	**2**	**0**	**0**	**0**	**17**

a AHL First All-Star Team (1989)
b AHL Second All-Star Team (1990)

Traded to **Boston** by **Philadelphia** with Gord Murphy and Philadelphia's third round choice (Sergei Zholtok) in 1992 Entry Draft for Garry Galley, Wes Walz and future considerations, January 2, 1992.

DOERS, MICHAEL

Right wing. Shoots right. 6', 175 lbs. Born, Madison, WI, June 17, 1971.
(Toronto's 7th choice, 125th overall, in 1989 Entry Draft).

			Regular Season					Playoffs				
Season	Club	Lea	GP	G	A	TP	PIM	GP	G	A	TP	PIM
1990-91	Madison	USHL	20	3	8	11	4	....	....	....	....	....
1991-92	U. of Wisconsin	WCHA	37	3	3	6	18	....	....	....	....	....

DOLLAS, BOBBY

Defense. Shoots left. 6'2", 212 lbs. Born, Montreal, Que., January 31, 1965.
(Winnipeg's 2nd choice, 14th overall, in 1983 Entry Draft).

			Regular Season					Playoffs				
Season	Club	Lea	GP	G	A	TP	PIM	GP	G	A	TP	PIM
1982-83a	Laval	QMJHL	63	16	45	61	144	11	5	5	10	23
1983-84	**Winnipeg**	**NHL**	**1**	**0**	**0**	**0**	**0**	....	....	....	....	....
	Laval	QMJHL	54	12	33	45	80	14	1	8	9	23
1984-85	**Winnipeg**	**NHL**	**9**	**0**	**0**	**0**	**0**	....	....	....	....	....
	Sherbrooke	AHL	8	1	3	4	4	17	3	6	9	17
1985-86	**Winnipeg**	**NHL**	**46**	**0**	**5**	**5**	**66**	**3**	**0**	**0**	**0**	**2**
	Sherbrooke	AHL	25	4	7	11	29	....	....	....	....	....
1986-87	Sherbrooke	AHL	75	6	18	24	87	16	2	4	6	13
1987-88	**Quebec**	**NHL**	**9**	**0**	**0**	**0**	**2**	....	....	....	....	....
	Moncton	AHL	26	4	10	14	20	....	....	....	....	....
	Fredericton	AHL	33	4	8	12	27	15	2	2	4	24
1988-89	**Quebec**	**NHL**	**16**	**0**	**3**	**3**	**16**	....	....	....	....	....
	Halifax	AHL	57	5	19	24	65	4	1	0	1	14
1989-90	Cdn. National	....	68	8	29	37	60	....	....	....	....	....
1990-91	**Detroit**	**NHL**	**56**	**3**	**5**	**8**	**20**	**7**	**1**	**0**	**1**	**13**
1991-92	**Detroit**	**NHL**	**27**	**3**	**1**	**4**	**20**	**2**	**0**	**1**	**1**	**0**
	Adirondack	AHL	19	1	6	7	33	18	7	4	11	22
	NHL Totals		**164**	**6**	**14**	**20**	**124**	**12**	**1**	**1**	**2**	**15**

a QMJHL Second All-Star Team (1983)

Traded to **Quebec** by **Winnipeg** for Stu Kulak, December 17, 1987. Signed as a free agent by **Detroit**, October 18, 1990.

DOMI, TAHIR (TIE) (DOH-mee)

Right wing. Shoots right. 5'10", 200 lbs. Born, Windsor, Ont., November 1, 1969.
(Toronto's 2nd choice, 27th overall, in 1988 Entry Draft).

			Regular Season					Playoffs				
Season	Club	Lea	GP	G	A	TP	PIM	GP	G	A	TP	PIM
1986-87	Peterborough	OHL	18	1	1	2	79	....	....	....	....	....
1987-88	Peterborough	OHL	60	22	21	43	292	12	3	9	12	24
1988-89	Peterborough	OHL	43	14	16	30	175	17	10	9	19	70
1989-90	**Toronto**	**NHL**	**2**	**0**	**0**	**0**	**42**	....	....	....	....	....
	Newmarket	AHL	57	14	11	25	285	....	....	....	....	....
1990-91	**NY Rangers**	**NHL**	**28**	**1**	**0**	**1**	**185**	....	....	....	....	....
	Binghamton	AHL	25	11	6	17	219	7	3	2	5	16
1991-92	**NY Rangers**	**NHL**	**42**	**2**	**4**	**6**	**246**	**6**	**1**	**1**	**2**	**32**
	NHL Totals		**72**	**3**	**4**	**7**	**473**	**6**	**1**	**1**	**2**	**32**

Traded to **NY Rangers** by **Toronto** with Mark LaForest for Greg Johnston, June 28, 1990.

DONATELLI, CLARK

Left wing. Shoots left. 5'10", 180 lbs. Born, Providence, RI, November 22, 1967.
(NY Rangers' 4th choice, 98th overall, in 1984 Entry Draft).

			Regular Season					Playoffs				
Season	Club	Lea	GP	G	A	TP	PIM	GP	G	A	TP	PIM
1984-85	Boston U.	H.E.	40	17	18	35	46	....	....	....	....	....
1985-86ab	Boston U.	H.E.	43	28	34	62	30	....	....	....	....	....
1986-87	Boston U.	H.E.	37	15	23	38	46	....	....	....	....	....
1987-88	U.S. National	....	50	11	27	38	26	....	....	....	....	....
	U.S. Olympic	....	6	2	1	3	5	....	....	....	....	....
1988-89					DID NOT PLAY							
1989-90	**Minnesota**	**NHL**	**25**	**3**	**3**	**6**	**17**	....	....	....	....	....
	Kalamazoo	IHL	27	8	9	17	47	4	0	2	2	12
1990-91	San Diego	IHL	46	17	10	27	45	....	....	....	....	....
1991-92	U.S. National	....	42	13	25	38	50	....	....	....	....	....
	U.S. Olympic	....	8	2	1	3	6	....	....	....	....	....
	Boston	**NHL**	**10**	**0**	**1**	**1**	**22**	**2**	**0**	**0**	**0**	**0**
	NHL Totals		**35**	**3**	**4**	**7**	**39**	**2**	**0**	**0**	**0**	**0**

a NCAA East Second All-American Team (1986)
b Hockey East Second All-Star Team (1986)

Traded to **Edmonton** by **NY Rangers** with Ville Kentala, Reijo Ruotsalainen and Jim Wiemer for Mike Golden, Don Jackson and Miloslav Horava, October 2, 1986. Signed as a free agent by **Minnesota**, June 20, 1989. Signed as a free agent by **Boston**, March 10, 1992.

DONATO, EDWARD (TED)

Center. Shoots left. 5'10", 170 lbs. Born, Dedham, MA, April 28, 1969.
(Boston's 6th choice, 98th overall, in 1987 Entry Draft).

			Regular Season					Playoffs				
Season	Club	Lea	GP	G	A	TP	PIM	GP	G	A	TP	PIM
1987-88	Harvard	ECAC	28	12	14	26	24	....	....	....	....	....
1988-89	Harvard	ECAC	34	14	37	51	30	....	....	....	....	....
1989-90	Harvard	ECAC	16	5	6	11	34	....	....	....	....	....
1990-91a	Harvard	ECAC	27	19	*37	56	26	....	....	....	....	....
1991-92	U.S. National	....	52	11	22	33	24	....	....	....	....	....
	U.S. Olympic	....	8	4	3	7	8	....	....	....	....	....
	Boston	**NHL**	**10**	**1**	**2**	**3**	**8**	**15**	**3**	**4**	**7**	**4**
	NHL Totals		**10**	**1**	**2**	**3**	**8**	**15**	**3**	**4**	**7**	**4**

a ECAC First All-Star Team (1991)

DONNELLY, GORDON (GORD)

Right wing. Shoots right. 6'1", 202 lbs. Born, Montreal, Que., April 5, 1962.
(St. Louis' 3rd choice, 62nd overall, in 1981 Entry Draft).

			Regular Season					Playoffs				
Season	Club	Lea	GP	G	A	TP	PIM	GP	G	A	TP	PIM
1980-81	Sherbrooke	QMJHL	67	15	23	38	252	14	1	2	3	35
1981-82	Sherbrooke	QMJHL	60	8	41	49	250	22	2	7	9	106
1982-83	Salt Lake	CHL	67	3	12	15	222	6	1	1	2	8
1983-84	**Quebec**	**NHL**	**38**	**0**	**5**	**5**	**60**	....	....	....	....	....
	Fredericton	AHL	30	2	3	5	146	7	1	1	2	43
1984-85	**Quebec**	**NHL**	**22**	**0**	**0**	**0**	**33**	....	....	....	....	....
	Fredericton	AHL	42	1	5	6	134	6	0	1	1	25
1985-86	**Quebec**	**NHL**	**36**	**2**	**2**	**4**	**85**	**1**	**0**	**0**	**0**	**0**
	Fredericton	AHL	38	3	5	8	103	5	0	0	0	33
1986-87	**Quebec**	**NHL**	**38**	**0**	**2**	**2**	**143**	**13**	**0**	**0**	**0**	**53**
1987-88	**Quebec**	**NHL**	**63**	**4**	**3**	**7**	**301**	....	....	....	....	....
1988-89	**Quebec**	**NHL**	**16**	**4**	**0**	**4**	**46**	....	....	....	....	....
	Winnipeg	**NHL**	**57**	**6**	**10**	**16**	**228**	....	....	....	....	....
1989-90	**Winnipeg**	**NHL**	**55**	**3**	**3**	**6**	**222**	**6**	**0**	**1**	**1**	**8**
1990-91	**Winnipeg**	**NHL**	**57**	**3**	**4**	**7**	**265**	....	....	....	....	....
1991-92	**Winnipeg**	**NHL**	**4**	**0**	**0**	**0**	**11**	....	....	....	....	....
	Buffalo	**NHL**	**67**	**2**	**3**	**5**	**305**	**6**	**0**	**1**	**1**	**0**
	NHL Totals		**453**	**24**	**32**	**56**	**1699**	**26**	**0**	**2**	**2**	**61**

Rights transferred to **Quebec** by **St. Louis** with rights to Claude Julien when St. Louis signed Jacques Demers as coach, August 19, 1983. Traded to **Winnipeg** by **Quebec** for Mario Marois, December 6, 1988. Traded to **Buffalo** by **Winnipeg** with Dave McLlwain, Winnipeg's fifth round choice (Yuri Khmylev) in 1992 Entry Draft and future considerations for Darrin Shannon, Mike Hartman and Dean Kennedy, October 11, 1991.

DONNELLY, MIKE

Left wing. Shoots left. 5'11", 185 lbs. Born, Detroit, MI, October 10, 1963.

			Regular Season					Playoffs				
Season	Club	Lea	GP	G	A	TP	PIM	GP	G	A	TP	PIM
1982-83	Michigan State	CCHA	24	7	13	20	8	....	....	....	....	....
1983-84	Michigan State	CCHA	44	18	14	32	40	....	....	....	....	....
1984-85	Michigan State	CCHA	44	26	21	47	48	....	....	....	....	....
1985-86ab	Michigan State	CCHA	44	*59	38	97	65	....	....	....	....	....
1986-87	**NY Rangers**	**NHL**	**5**	**1**	**1**	**2**	**0**	....	....	....	....	....
	New Haven	AHL	58	27	34	61	52	7	2	0	2	9
1987-88	**NY Rangers**	**NHL**	**17**	**2**	**2**	**4**	**8**	....	....	....	....	....
	Colorado	IHL	8	7	11	18	15	....	....	....	....	....
	Buffalo	**NHL**	**40**	**6**	**8**	**14**	**44**	....	....	....	....	....
1988-89	**Buffalo**	**NHL**	**22**	**4**	**6**	**10**	**10**	....	....	....	....	....
	Rochester	AHL	53	32	37	69	53	....	....	....	....	....
1989-90	**Buffalo**	**NHL**	**12**	**1**	**2**	**3**	**8**	....	....	....	....	....
	Rochester	AHL	68	43	55	98	71	16	*12	7	19	9
1990-91	**Los Angeles**	**NHL**	**53**	**7**	**5**	**12**	**41**	**12**	**5**	**4**	**9**	**6**
	New Haven	AHL	18	10	6	16	2	....	....	....	....	....
1991-92	**Los Angeles**	**NHL**	**80**	**29**	**16**	**45**	**20**	**6**	**1**	**0**	**1**	**4**
	NHL Totals		**229**	**50**	**40**	**90**	**131**	**18**	**6**	**4**	**10**	**10**

a CCHA First All-Star Team (1986)
b NCAA West First All-American Team (1986)

Signed as a free agent by **NY Rangers**, August 15, 1986. Traded to **Buffalo** by **NY Rangers** with Rangers' fifth round choice (Alexander Mogilny) in 1988 Entry Draft for Paul Cyr and Buffalo's tenth round choice (Eric Fenton) in 1988 Entry Draft, December 31, 1987. Traded to **Los Angeles** by **Buffalo** for Mikko Makela, September 30, 1990.

DOOLEY, SEAN

Defense. Shoots left. 6'3", 215 lbs. Born, Ipswich, MA, March 22, 1969.
(Buffalo's 8th choice, 148th overall, in 1987 Entry Draft).

			Regular Season					Playoffs				
Season	Club	Lea	GP	G	A	TP	PIM	GP	G	A	TP	PIM
1987-88	Merrimack	NCAA	3	0	0	0	0	....	....	....	....	....
1988-89	Merrimack	NCAA	19	2	8	10	10	....	....	....	....	....
1989-90	Merrimack	H.E.	22	1	2	3	31	....	....	....	....	....
1990-91	Merrimack	H.E.	7	0	3	3	12	....	....	....	....	....
1991-92	Nashville	ECHL	19	2	7	9	13	....	....	....	....	....

DOPITA, JIRI

Center. Shoots left. 6'4", 202 lbs. Born, Sumperk, Czech., December 2, 1968.
(Boston's 4th choice, 133rd overall, in 1992 Entry Draft).

			Regular Season					Playoffs				
Season	Club	Lea	GP	G	A	TP	PIM	GP	G	A	TP	PIM
1990-91	D.S. Olomouc	Czech.	42	11	13	24	26	....	....	....	....	....
1991-92	D.S. Olomouc	Czech.	41	25	24	49	....	....	....	....	....	....

DORE, DANIEL

Right wing. Shoots right. 6'3", 202 lbs. Born, Ferme-Neuve, Que., April 9, 1970.
(Quebec's 2nd choice, 5th overall, in 1988 Entry Draft).

			Regular Season					Playoffs				
Season	Club	Lea	GP	G	A	TP	PIM	GP	G	A	TP	PIM
1986-87	Drummondville	QMJHL	68	23	41	64	229	8	0	1	1	18
1987-88	Drummondville	QMJHL	64	24	39	63	218	17	7	11	18	42
1988-89	Drummondville	QMJHL	62	33	58	91	236	4	2	3	5	14
1989-90	**Quebec**	**NHL**	**16**	**2**	**3**	**5**	**59**	....	....	....	....	....
	Chicoutimi	QMJHL	24	6	23	29	112	6	0	3	3	27
1990-91	**Quebec**	**NHL**	**1**	**0**	**0**	**0**	**0**	....	....	....	....	....
	Halifax	AHL	50	7	10	17	139	....	....	....	....	....
1991-92	Halifax	AHL	29	4	1	5	45	....	....	....	....	....
	Greensboro	ECHL	6	1	0	1	34	....	....	....	....	....
	NHL Totals		**17**	**2**	**3**	**5**	**59**	....	....	....	....	....

D'ORSONNENS, MARTIN

Defense. Shoots left. 5'11", 185 lbs. Born, Repentigny, Que., February 11, 1972.
(Hartford's 7th choice, 162nd overall, in 1990 Entry Draft).

			Regular Season					Playoffs				
Season	Club	Lea	GP	G	A	TP	PIM	GP	G	A	TP	PIM
1989-90	Clarkson	ECAC	35	5	8	13	81	....	....	....	....	....
1990-91	Clarkson	ECAC	39	2	8	10	84	....	....	....	....	....
1991-92	Clarkson	ECAC	31	2	10	12	49	....	....	....	....	....

DOUCET, WAYNE

Left wing. Shoots left. 6'2", 203 lbs. Born, Etobicoke, Ont., June 19, 1970.
(NY Islanders' 2nd choice, 29th overall, in 1988 Entry Draft).

			Regular Season					Playoffs				
Season	Club	Lea	GP	G	A	TP	PIM	GP	G	A	TP	PIM
1986-87	Sudbury	OHL	64	20	28	48	85	....	....	....	....	....
1987-88	Sudbury	OHL	23	9	4	13	53	....	....	....	....	....
	Hamilton	OHL	37	11	14	25	7	1	0	0	0	8
1988-89	Springfield	AHL	6	2	2	4	4	....	....	....	....	....
	Niagara Falls	OHL	11	3	2	5	58	....	....	....	....	....
	Kingston	OHL	53	22	29	51	193	....	....	....	....	....
1989-90	Kingston	OHL	66	32	47	79	127	7	2	5	7	18
1990-91	Capital Dist.	AHL	21	11	6	17	93	....	....	....	....	....
1991-92	Capital Dist.	AHL	60	11	7	18	116	7	1	1	2	6

DOURIS, PETER

Right wing. Shoots right. 6'1", 195 lbs. Born, Toronto, Ont., February 19, 1966.
(Winnipeg's 1st choice, 30th overall, in 1984 Entry Draft).

			Regular Season					Playoffs				
Season	Club	Lea	GP	G	A	TP	PIM	GP	G	A	TP	PIM
1983-84	N. Hampshire	ECAC	37	19	15	34	14	....	....	....	....	....
1984-85	N. Hampshire	H.E.	42	27	24	51	34	....	....	....	....	....
1985-86	**Winnipeg**	**NHL**	**11**	**0**	**0**	**0**	**0**	....	....	....	....	....
	Cdn. Olympic	....	33	16	7	23	18	....	....	....	....	....
1986-87	**Winnipeg**	**NHL**	**6**	**0**	**0**	**0**	**0**	....	....	....	....	....
	Sherbrooke	AHL	62	14	28	42	24	17	7	*15	*22	16
1987-88	**Winnipeg**	**NHL**	**4**	**0**	**2**	**2**	**0**	**1**	**0**	**0**	**0**	**0**
	Moncton	AHL	73	42	37	79	53	....	....	....	....	....
1988-89	Peoria	IHL	81	28	41	69	32	4	1	2	3	0
1989-90	**Boston**	**NHL**	**36**	**5**	**6**	**11**	**15**	**8**	**0**	**1**	**1**	**8**
	Maine	AHL	38	17	20	37	14	....	....	....	....	....
1990-91	**Boston**	**NHL**	**39**	**5**	**2**	**7**	**9**	**7**	**0**	**1**	**1**	**6**
	Maine	AHL	35	16	15	31	9	2	3	0	3	2
1991-92	**Boston**	**NHL**	**54**	**10**	**13**	**23**	**10**	**7**	**2**	**3**	**5**	**0**
	Maine	AHL	12	4	3	7	2	....	....	....	....	....
	NHL Totals		**150**	**20**	**23**	**43**	**34**	**23**	**2**	**5**	**7**	**14**

Traded to **St. Louis** by **Winnipeg** for Kent Carlson and St. Louis' twelfth round choice (Sergei Kharin) in 1989 Entry Draft and St. Louis' fourth round choice (Scott Levins) in 1990 Entry Draft, September 29, 1988. Signed as a free agent by **Boston**, June 27, 1989.

DOWD, JAMES (JIM)

Right wing. Shoots right. 6'1", 185 lbs. Born, Brick, NJ, December 25, 1968.
(New Jersey's 7th choice, 149th overall, in 1987 Entry Draft).

			Regular Season					Playoffs				
Season	Club	Lea	GP	G	A	TP	PIM	GP	G	A	TP	PIM
1987-88	Lake Superior	CCHA	45	18	27	45	16	....	....	....	....	....
1988-89	Lake Superior	CCHA	46	24	35	59	40	....	....	....	....	....
1989-90ab	Lake Superior	CCHA	46	25	*67	92	30	....	....	....	....	....
1990-91cde	Lake Superior	CCHA	44	24	*54	*78	53	....	....	....	....	....
1991-92	**New Jersey**	**NHL**	**1**	**0**	**0**	**0**	**0**	....	....	....	....	....
	Utica	AHL	78	17	42	59	47	4	2	2	4	4
	NHL Totals		**1**	**0**	**0**	**0**	**0**	....	....	....	....	....

a CCHA Second All-Star Team (1990)
b NCAA West Second All-American Team (1990)
c CCHA Player of the Year (1991)
d CCHA First All-Star Team (1991)
e NCAA West First All-American Team (1991)

DOYON, MARIO (doh-YAWN)

Defense. Shoots right. 6', 174 lbs. Born, Quebec City, Que., August 27, 1968.
(Chicago's 5th choice, 119th overall, in 1986 Entry Draft).

			Regular Season					Playoffs				
Season	Club	Lea	GP	G	A	TP	PIM	GP	G	A	TP	PIM
1985-86	Drummondville	QMJHL	71	5	14	19	129	23	5	4	9	32
1986-87	Drummondville	QMJHL	65	18	47	65	150	8	1	3	4	30
1987-88	Drummondville	QMJHL	68	23	54	77	233	17	3	14	17	46
1988-89	**Chicago**	**NHL**	**7**	**1**	**1**	**2**	**6**	....	....	....	....	....
	Saginaw	IHL	71	16	32	48	69	6	0	0	0	8
1989-90	Indianapolis	IHL	66	9	25	34	50	....	....	....	....	....
	Quebec	**NHL**	**9**	**2**	**3**	**5**	**6**	....	....	....	....	....
	Halifax	AHL	5	1	2	3	0	6	1	3	4	2
1990-91	**Quebec**	**NHL**	**12**	**0**	**0**	**0**	**4**	....	....	....	....	....
	Halifax	AHL	59	14	23	37	58	....	....	....	....	....
1991-92	Halifax	AHL	9	0	0	0	22	....	....	....	....	....
	New Haven	AHL	64	11	29	40	44	5	1	1	2	2
	NHL Totals		**28**	**3**	**4**	**7**	**16**					

Traded to **Quebec** by **Chicago** with Everett Sanipass and Dan Vincelette for Greg Millen, Michel Goulet and Quebec's sixth round choice (Kevin St. Jacques) in 1991 Entry Draft, March 5, 1990.

DRAGON, JOE

Right wing. Shoots right. 5'11", 180 lbs. Born, Fort Smith, N.W.T., February 20, 1969.
(Pittsburgh's 1st choice, 5th overall, in 1990 Supplemental Draft).

			Regular Season					Playoffs				
Season	Club	Lea	GP	G	A	TP	PIM	GP	G	A	TP	PIM
1988-89	Cornell	ECAC	3	1	1	2	2	....	....	....	....	....
1989-90	Cornell	ECAC	29	15	24	39	26	....	....	....	....	....
1990-91	Cornell	ECAC	32	8	18	26	46	....	....	....	....	....
1991-92	Cornell	ECAC	29	10	16	26	37	....	....	....	....	....

DRAKE, DALLAS

Center. Shoots left. 6', 170 lbs. Born, Trail, B.C., February 4, 1969.
(Detroit's 6th choice, 116th overall, in 1989 Entry Draft).

			Regular Season					Playoffs				
Season	Club	Lea	GP	G	A	TP	PIM	GP	G	A	TP	PIM
1988-89	N. Michigan	WCHA	38	17	22	39	22	....	....	....	....	....
1989-90	N. Michigan	WCHA	46	13	24	37	42	....	....	....	....	....
1990-91	N. Michigan	WCHA	44	22	36	58	89	....	....	....	....	....
1991-92ab	N. Michigan	WCHA	38	39	41	80	46	....	....	....	....	....

a WCHA First All-Star Team (1992)
b NCAA West First All-Star Team (1992)

DRAPER, KRIS

Center. Shoots left. 5'11", 190 lbs. Born, Toronto, Ont., May 24, 1971.
(Winnipeg's 4th choice, 62nd overall, in 1989 Entry Draft).

			Regular Season					Playoffs				
Season	Club	Lea	GP	G	A	TP	PIM	GP	G	A	TP	PIM
1988-89	Cdn. National	....	60	11	15	26	16	....	....	....	....	....
1989-90	Cdn. National	....	61	12	22	34	44	....	....	....	....	....
1990-91	**Winnipeg**	**NHL**	**3**	**1**	**0**	**1**	**5**	....	....	....	....	....
	Ottawa	OHL	39	19	42	61	35	17	8	11	19	20
	Moncton	AHL	7	2	1	3	2	....	....	....	....	....
1991-92	**Winnipeg**	**NHL**	**10**	**2**	**0**	**2**	**2**	**2**	**0**	**0**	**0**	**0**
	Moncton	AHL	61	11	18	29	113	4	0	1	1	6
	NHL Totals		**13**	**3**	**0**	**3**	**7**	**2**	**0**	**0**	**0**	**0**

DRIVER, BRUCE

Defense. Shoots left. 6', 185 lbs. Born, Toronto, Ont., April 29, 1962.
(Colorado's 6th choice, 108th overall, in 1981 Entry Draft).

			Regular Season					Playoffs				
Season	Club	Lea	GP	G	A	TP	PIM	GP	G	A	TP	PIM
1980-81	U. Wisconsin	WCHA	42	5	15	20	42	....	....	....	....	....
1981-82ab	U. Wisconsin	WCHA	46	7	37	44	84	....	....	....	....	....
1982-83	U. Wisconsin	WCHA	49	19	42	61	100	....	....	....	....	....
1983-84	Cdn. Olympic	....	61	11	17	28	44	....	....	....	....	....
	New Jersey	**NHL**	**4**	**0**	**2**	**2**	**0**	....	....	....	....	....
	Maine	AHL	12	2	6	8	15	16	0	10	10	8
1984-85	**New Jersey**	**NHL**	**67**	**9**	**23**	**32**	**36**	....	....	....	....	....
1985-86	**New Jersey**	**NHL**	**40**	**3**	**15**	**18**	**32**	....	....	....	....	....
	Maine	AHL	15	4	7	11	16	....	....	....	....	....
1986-87	**New Jersey**	**NHL**	**74**	**6**	**28**	**34**	**36**	....	....	....	....	....
1987-88	**New Jersey**	**NHL**	**74**	**15**	**40**	**55**	**68**	**20**	**3**	**7**	**10**	**14**
1988-89	**New Jersey**	**NHL**	**27**	**1**	**15**	**16**	**24**	....	....	....	....	....
1989-90	**New Jersey**	**NHL**	**75**	**7**	**46**	**53**	**63**	**6**	**1**	**5**	**6**	**6**
1990-91	**New Jersey**	**NHL**	**73**	**9**	**36**	**45**	**62**	**7**	**1**	**2**	**3**	**12**
1991-92	**New Jersey**	**NHL**	**78**	**7**	**35**	**42**	**66**	**7**	**0**	**4**	**4**	**2**
	NHL Totals		**512**	**57**	**240**	**297**	**387**	**40**	**5**	**18**	**23**	**34**

a WCHA First All-Star Team (1982)
b NCAA All-Tournament Team (1982)

DROPPA, IVAN

Defense. Shoots left. 6'2", 209 lbs. Born, Liptovsky Mikulas, Czech., February 1, 1972.
(Chicago's 2nd choice, 37th overall, in 1990 Entry Draft).

			Regular Season					Playoffs				
Season	Club	Lea	GP	G	A	TP	PIM	GP	G	A	TP	PIM
1990-91	VSZ Kosice	Czech.	49	1	7	8	12	....	....	....	....	....
1991-92	VSZ Kosice	Czech.	43	4	9	13	....	....	....	....	....	....

DRUCE, JOHN

Right wing. Shoots right. 6'2", 195 lbs. Born, Peterborough, Ont., February 23, 1966.
(Washington's 2nd choice, 40th overall, in 1985 Entry Draft).

			Regular Season					Playoffs				
Season	Club	Lea	GP	G	A	TP	PIM	GP	G	A	TP	PIM
1984-85	Peterborough	OHL	54	12	14	26	90	17	6	2	8	21
1985-86	Peterborough	OHL	49	22	24	46	84	16	0	5	5	34
1986-87	Binghamton	AHL	77	13	9	22	131	12	0	3	3	28
1987-88	Binghamton	AHL	68	32	29	61	82	1	0	0	0	0
1988-89	**Washington**	**NHL**	**48**	**8**	**7**	**15**	**62**	**1**	**0**	**0**	**0**	**0**
	Baltimore	AHL	16	2	11	13	10	....	....	....	....	....
1989-90	**Washington**	**NHL**	**45**	**8**	**3**	**11**	**52**	**15**	**14**	**3**	**17**	**23**
	Baltimore	AHL	26	15	16	31	38	....	....	....	....	....
1990-91	**Washington**	**NHL**	**80**	**22**	**36**	**58**	**46**	**11**	**1**	**1**	**2**	**7**
1991-92	**Washington**	**NHL**	**67**	**19**	**18**	**37**	**39**	**7**	**1**	**0**	**1**	**2**
	NHL Totals		**240**	**57**	**64**	**121**	**199**	**34**	**16**	**4**	**20**	**32**

DRULIA, STAN

Right wing. Shoots right. 5'11", 190 lbs. Born, Elmira, NY, January 5, 1968.
(Pittsburgh's 11th choice, 214th overall, in 1986 Entry Draft).

			Regular Season					Playoffs				
Season	Club	Lea	GP	G	A	TP	PIM	GP	G	A	TP	PIM
1985-86	Belleville	OHL	66	43	36	79	73	....	....	....	....	....
1986-87	Hamilton	OHL	55	27	51	78	26	....	....	....	....	....
1987-88a	Hamilton	OHL	65	52	69	121	44	14	8	16	24	12
1988-89	Maine	AHL	3	1	1	2	0	....	....	....	....	....
b	Niagara Falls	OHL	47	52	93	145	59	17	11	*26	37	18
1989-90	Phoenix	IHL	16	6	3	9	2	....	....	....	....	....
	Cape Breton	AHL	31	5	7	12	2	....	....	....	....	....
1990-91cd	Knoxville	ECHL	64	*63	77	*140	39	3	3	2	5	4
1991-92e	New Haven	AHL	77	49	53	102	46	5	2	4	6	4

a OHL Third All-Star Team (1988)
b OHL First All-Star Team (1989)
c MVP — ECHL (1991)
d ECHL First All-Star Team (1991)
e AHL Second All-Star Team (1992)

Signed as a free agent by **Edmonton**, February 24, 1989.

DRURY, TED

Center. Shoots left. 6', 185 lbs. Born, Boston, MA, September 13, 1971.
(Calgary's 2nd choice, 42nd overall, in 1989 Entry Draft).

			Regular Season					Playoffs				
Season	Club	Lea	GP	G	A	TP	PIM	GP	G	A	TP	PIM
1989-90	Harvard	ECAC	17	9	13	22	10	....	....	....	....	....
1990-91	Harvard	ECAC	25	18	18	36	22	....	....	....	....	....
1991-92	U.S. National	....	53	11	23	34	30	....	....	....	....	....
	U.S. Olympic	....	7	1	1	2	0	....	....	....	....	....

DUBERMAN, JUSTIN

Right wing. Shoots right. 6'1", 185 lbs. Born, New Haven, CT, March 23, 1970.
(Montreal's 11th choice, 230th overall, in 1989 Entry Draft).

			Regular Season					Playoffs				
Season	Club	Lea	GP	G	A	TP	PIM	GP	G	A	TP	PIM
1988-89	North Dakota	WCHA	33	3	1	4	30	....	....	....	....	....
1989-90	North Dakota	WCHA	42	10	9	19	50	....	....	....	....	....
1990-91	North Dakota	WCHA	42	19	18	37	68	....	....	....	....	....
1991-92	North Dakota	WCHA	39	17	27	44	90	....	....	....	....	....

DUBINSKY, STEVE

Center. Shoots left. 6', 190 lbs. Born, Montreal, Que., July 9, 1970.
(Chicago's 9th choice, 226th overall, in 1990 Entry Draft).

			Regular Season					Playoffs				
Season	Club	Lea	GP	G	A	TP	PIM	GP	G	A	TP	PIM
1989-90	Clarkson	ECAC	35	7	10	17	24	....	....	....	....	....
1990-91	Clarkson	ECAC	39	13	23	36	26	....	....	....	....	....
1991-92	Clarkson	ECAC	32	20	31	51	40	....	....	....	....	....

DUBOIS, ERIC

Defense. Shoots right. 6', 195 lbs. Born, Montreal, Que., May 9, 1970.
(Quebec's 6th choice, 76th overall, in 1989 Entry Draft).

			Regular Season					Playoffs				
Season	Club	Lea	GP	G	A	TP	PIM	GP	G	A	TP	PIM
1986-87	Laval	QMJHL	61	1	17	18	29	....	....	....	....	....
1987-88	Laval	QMJHL	69	8	32	40	132	14	1	7	8	12
1988-89	Laval	QMJHL	68	15	44	59	126	17	1	11	12	55
1989-90	Laval	QMJHL	66	9	36	45	153	13	3	8	11	29
1990-91	Laval	QMJHL	57	15	45	60	122	13	3	5	8	29
1991-92	Halifax	AHL	14	0	0	0	8	....	....	....	....	....
	New Haven	AHL	1	0	0	0	2	....	....	....	....	....
	Greensboro	ECHL	36	7	17	24	62	11	4	4	8	40

DUCHESNE, GAETAN (doo-SHAYN)

Left wing. Shoots left. 5'11", 200 lbs. Born, Les Saulles, Que., July 11, 1962.
(Washington's 8th choice, 152nd overall, in 1981 Entry Draft).

			Regular Season					Playoffs				
Season	Club	Lea	GP	G	A	TP	PIM	GP	G	A	TP	PIM
1979-80	Quebec	QJHL	46	9	28	37	22	5	0	2	2	9
1980-81	Quebec	QJHL	72	27	45	72	63	7	1	4	5	6
1981-82	**Washington**	**NHL**	**74**	**9**	**14**	**23**	**46**	....	....	....	....	....
1982-83	**Washington**	**NHL**	**77**	**18**	**19**	**37**	**52**	**4**	**1**	**1**	**2**	**4**
	Hershey	AHL	1	1	0	1	0	....	....	....	....	....
1983-84	**Washington**	**NHL**	**79**	**17**	**19**	**36**	**29**	**8**	**2**	**1**	**3**	**2**
1984-85	**Washington**	**NHL**	**67**	**15**	**23**	**38**	**32**	**5**	**0**	**1**	**1**	**7**
1985-86	**Washington**	**NHL**	**80**	**11**	**28**	**39**	**39**	**9**	**4**	**3**	**7**	**12**
1986-87	**Washington**	**NHL**	**74**	**17**	**35**	**52**	**53**	**7**	**3**	**0**	**3**	**14**
1987-88	**Quebec**	**NHL**	**80**	**24**	**23**	**47**	**83**	....	....	....	....	....
1988-89	**Quebec**	**NHL**	**70**	**8**	**21**	**29**	**56**	....	....	....	....	....
1989-90	**Minnesota**	**NHL**	**72**	**12**	**8**	**20**	**33**	**7**	**0**	**0**	**0**	**6**
1990-91	**Minnesota**	**NHL**	**68**	**9**	**9**	**18**	**18**	**23**	**2**	**3**	**5**	**34**
1991-92	**Minnesota**	**NHL**	**73**	**8**	**15**	**23**	**102**	**7**	**1**	**0**	**1**	**6**
	NHL Totals		**814**	**148**	**214**	**362**	**543**	**70**	**13**	**9**	**22**	**85**

Traded to **Quebec** by **Washington** with Alan Haworth and Washington's first round choice (Joe Sakic) in 1987 Entry Draft for Clint Malarchuk and Dale Hunter, June 13, 1987. Traded to **Minnesota** by **Quebec** for Kevin Kaminski, June 19, 1989.

DUCHESNE, STEVE (doo-SHAYN)

Defense. Shoots left. 5'11", 195 lbs. Born, Sept-Iles, Que., June 30, 1965.

			Regular Season					Playoffs				
Season	Club	Lea	GP	G	A	TP	PIM	GP	G	A	TP	PIM
1983-84	Drummondville	QMJHL	67	1	34	35	79	....	....	....	....	....
1984-85a	Drummondville	QMJHL	65	22	54	76	94	5	4	7	11	8
1985-86	New Haven	AHL	75	14	35	49	76	5	0	2	2	9
1986-87b	**Los Angeles**	**NHL**	**75**	**13**	**25**	**38**	**74**	**5**	**2**	**2**	**4**	**4**
1987-88	**Los Angeles**	**NHL**	**71**	**16**	**39**	**55**	**109**	**5**	**1**	**3**	**4**	**14**
1988-89	**Los Angeles**	**NHL**	**79**	**25**	**50**	**75**	**92**	**11**	**4**	**4**	**8**	**12**
1989-90	**Los Angeles**	**NHL**	**79**	**20**	**42**	**62**	**36**	**10**	**2**	**9**	**11**	**6**
1990-91	**Los Angeles**	**NHL**	**78**	**21**	**41**	**62**	**66**	**12**	**4**	**8**	**12**	**8**
1991-92	**Philadelphia**	**NHL**	**78**	**18**	**38**	**56**	**86**	....	....	....	....	....
	NHL Totals		**460**	**113**	**235**	**348**	**463**	**43**	**13**	**26**	**39**	**44**

a QMJHL First All-Star Team (1985)
b NHL All-Rookie Team (1987)

Played in NHL All-Star Game (1989, 1990)

Signed as a free agent by **Los Angeles,** October 1, 1984. Traded to **Philadelphia** by **Los Angeles** with Steve Kasper and Los Angeles' fourth round choice (Aris Brimanis) in 1991 Entry Draft for Jari Kurri and Jeff Chychrun, May 30, 1991. Traded to **Quebec** by **Philadelphia** with Peter Forsberg, Kerry Huffman, Mike Ricci, Ron Hextall, Chris Simon, Philadelphia's first choice in the 1993 and 1994 Entry Drafts and cash for Eric Lindros, June 30, 1992.

DUFFY, JACK

Defense. Shoots right. 6'1", 195 lbs. Born, Northford, CT, September 25, 1970.
(NY Islanders' 2nd choice, 10th overall, in 1991 Supplemental Draft).

			Regular Season					Playoffs				
Season	Club	Lea	GP	G	A	TP	PIM	GP	G	A	TP	PIM
1989-90	Yale	ECAC	26	1	6	7	48	....	....	....	....	....
1990-91	Yale	ECAC	29	4	8	12	48	....	....	....	....	....
1991-92a	Yale	ECAC	27	3	24	27	78	....	....	....	....	....

a ECAC Second All-Star Team (1992)

DUFRESNE, DONALD (DOO-FRAYN)

Defense. Shoots right. 6'1", 206 lbs. Born, Quebec City, Que., April 10, 1967.
(Montreal's 8th choice, 117th overall, in 1985 Entry Draft).

			Regular Season					Playoffs				
Season	Club	Lea	GP	G	A	TP	PIM	GP	G	A	TP	PIM
1983-84	Trois-Rivières	QMJHL	67	7	12	19	97	....	....	....	....	....
1984-85	Trois-Rivières	QMJHL	65	5	30	35	112	7	1	3	4	12
1985-86a	Trois-Rivières	QMJHL	63	8	32	40	160	1	0	0	0	0
1986-87a	Trois-Rivières	QMJHL	51	5	21	26	79	....	....	....	....	....
	Longueuil	QMJHL	16	0	8	8	18	20	1	8	9	38
1987-88	Sherbrooke	AHL	47	1	8	9	107	6	1	0	1	34
1988-89	**Montreal**	**NHL**	**13**	**0**	**1**	**1**	**43**	**6**	**1**	**1**	**2**	**4**
	Sherbrooke	AHL	47	0	12	12	170	....	....	....	....	....
1989-90	**Montreal**	**NHL**	**18**	**0**	**4**	**4**	**23**	**10**	**0**	**1**	**1**	**18**
	Sherbrooke	AHL	38	2	11	13	104	....	....	....	....	....
1990-91	**Montreal**	**NHL**	**53**	**2**	**13**	**15**	**55**	**10**	**0**	**1**	**1**	**21**
	Fredericton	AHL	10	1	4	5	35	1	0	0	0	0
1991-92	**Montreal**	**NHL**	**3**	**0**	**0**	**0**	**2**	....	....	....	....	....
	Fredericton	AHL	31	8	12	20	60	7	0	0	0	10
	NHL Totals		**87**	**2**	**18**	**20**	**123**	**26**	**1**	**3**	**4**	**43**

a QMJHL Second All-Star Team (1986, 1987)

DUGUAY, RONALD (RON) (doo-GAY)

Center/Right wing. Shoots right. 6'2", 200 lbs. Born, Sudbury, Ont., July 6, 1957.
(NY Rangers' 2nd choice, 13th overall, in 1977 Amateur Draft).

			Regular Season					Playoffs				
Season	Club	Lea	GP	G	A	TP	PIM	GP	G	A	TP	PIM
1975-76a	Sudbury	OHA	61	42	92	134	101	17	11	9	20	37
1976-77	Sudbury	OHA	61	43	66	109	109	6	4	3	7	5
1977-78	**NY Rangers**	**NHL**	**71**	**20**	**20**	**40**	**43**	**3**	**1**	**1**	**2**	**2**
1978-79	**NY Rangers**	**NHL**	**79**	**27**	**36**	**63**	**35**	**18**	**5**	**4**	**9**	**11**
1979-80	**NY Rangers**	**NHL**	**73**	**28**	**22**	**50**	**37**	**9**	**5**	**2**	**7**	**11**
1980-81	**NY Rangers**	**NHL**	**50**	**17**	**21**	**38**	**83**	**14**	**8**	**9**	**17**	**16**
1981-82	**NY Rangers**	**NHL**	**72**	**40**	**36**	**76**	**82**	**10**	**5**	**1**	**6**	**31**
1982-83	**NY Rangers**	**NHL**	**72**	**19**	**25**	**44**	**58**	**9**	**2**	**2**	**4**	**28**
1983-84	**Detroit**	**NHL**	**80**	**33**	**47**	**80**	**34**	**4**	**2**	**3**	**5**	**2**
1984-85	**Detroit**	**NHL**	**80**	**38**	**51**	**89**	**51**	**3**	**1**	**0**	**1**	**7**
1985-86	**Detroit**	**NHL**	**67**	**19**	**29**	**48**	**26**	....	....	....	....	....
	Pittsburgh	**NHL**	**13**	**6**	**7**	**13**	**6**	....	....	....	....	....
1986-87	**Pittsburgh**	**NHL**	**40**	**5**	**13**	**18**	**30**	....	....	....	....	....
	NY Rangers	**NHL**	**34**	**9**	**12**	**21**	**9**	**6**	**2**	**0**	**2**	**4**
1987-88	**NY Rangers**	**NHL**	**48**	**4**	**4**	**8**	**23**	....	....	....	....	....
	Colorado	IHL	2	0	0	0	0	....	....	....	....	....
	Los Angeles	**NHL**	**15**	**2**	**6**	**8**	**17**	**2**	**0**	**0**	**0**	**0**
1988-89	**Los Angeles**	**NHL**	**70**	**7**	**17**	**24**	**48**	**11**	**0**	**0**	**0**	**6**
1989-90	Mannheimer	W.Ger.	22	11	7	18	38	....	....	....	....	....
1990-91	San Diego	IHL	51	15	24	39	87	....	....	....	....	....
1991-92	San Diego	IHL	60	18	18	36	32	4	0	1	1	0
	NHL Totals		**864**	**274**	**346**	**620**	**582**	**89**	**31**	**22**	**53**	**118**

a OHA Third All-Star Team (1976)

Played in NHL All-Star Game (1982)

Traded to **Detroit** by **NY Rangers** with Eddie Mio and Eddie Johnstone for Willie Huber, Mark Osborne and Mike Blaisdell, June 13, 1983. Traded to **Pittsburgh** by **Detroit** for Doug Shedden, March 11, 1986. Traded to **NY Rangers** by **Pittsburgh** for Chris Kontos, January 21, 1987. Traded to **Los Angeles** by **NY Rangers** for Mark Hardy, February 23, 1988.

DUHAIME, TREVOR

Right wing. Shoots right. 6', 188 lbs. Born, Toronto, Ont., August 2, 1971.
(Washington's 9th choice, 190th overall, in 1991 Entry Draft).

			Regular Season					Playoffs				
Season	Club	Lea	GP	G	A	TP	PIM	GP	G	A	TP	PIM
1989-90	St-Jean	QMJHL	66	12	17	29	132	....	....	....	....	....
1990-91	St-Jean	QMJHL	70	29	31	60	240	....	....	....	....	....
1991-92	St-Jean	QMJHL	21	4	14	18	49	....	....	....	....	....
	Trois-Rivières	QMJHL	45	20	14	34	135	14	0	11	11	36

DUKOVAC, PAUL C.

Defense. Shoots right. 6'1", 190 lbs. Born, New Liskeard, Ont., January 18, 1969.
(Vancouver's 1st choice, 2nd overall, in 1990 Supplemental Draft).

			Regular Season					Playoffs				
Season	Club	Lea	GP	G	A	TP	PIM	GP	G	A	TP	PIM
1988-89	Cornell	ECAC	14	1	4	5	8	....	....	....	....	....
1989-90	Cornell	ECAC	29	1	8	9	34	....	....	....	....	....
1990-91	Cornell	ECAC	32	0	7	7	36	....	....	....	....	....
1991-92	Cornell	ECAC	8	2	2	4	6	....	....	....	....	....

DUNCAN, IAIN

Left wing. Shoots left. 6'1", 200 lbs. Born, Weston, Ont., August 4, 1963.
(Winnipeg's 8th choice, 129th overall, in 1983 Entry Draft).

			Regular Season					Playoffs				
Season	Club	Lea	GP	G	A	TP	PIM	GP	G	A	TP	PIM
1983-84	Bowling Green	CCHA	44	11	20	31	65	....	....	....	....	....
1984-85	Bowling Green	CCHA	37	9	21	30	105	....	....	....	....	....
1985-86	Bowling Green	CCHA	41	26	26	52	124	....	....	....	....	....
1986-87a	Bowling Green	CCHA	39	28	40	68	141	....	....	....	....	....
	Winnipeg	**NHL**	**6**	**1**	**2**	**3**	**0**	**7**	**0**	**2**	**2**	**6**
1987-88b	**Winnipeg**	**NHL**	**62**	**19**	**23**	**42**	**73**	**4**	**0**	**1**	**1**	**0**
	Moncton	AHL	8	1	3	4	26	....	....	....	....	....
1988-89	**Winnipeg**	**NHL**	**57**	**14**	**30**	**44**	**74**	....	....	....	....	....
1989-90	Moncton	AHL	49	16	25	41	81	....	....	....	....	....
1990-91	**Winnipeg**	**NHL**	**2**	**0**	**0**	**0**	**2**	....	....	....	....	....
	Moncton	AHL	66	19	45	64	105	8	3	4	7	40
1991-92	Phoenix	IHL	46	12	24	36	103	....	....	....	....	....
	NHL Totals		**127**	**34**	**55**	**89**	**149**	**11**	**0**	**3**	**3**	**6**

a CCHA First All-Star Team (1987)
b NHL All-Rookie Team (1988)

DUNCANSON, CRAIG

Left wing. Shoots left. 6', 190 lbs. Born, Sudbury, Ont., March 17, 1967.
(Los Angeles' 1st choice, 9th overall, in 1985 Entry Draft).

			Regular Season					Playoffs				
Season	Club	Lea	GP	G	A	TP	PIM	GP	G	A	TP	PIM
1983-84	Sudbury	OHL	62	38	38	76	176	....	....	....	....	....
1984-85a	Sudbury	OHL	53	35	28	63	129	....	....	....	....	....
1985-86	**Los Angeles**	**NHL**	**2**	**0**	**1**	**1**	**0**	....	....	....	....	....
	Sudbury	OHL	21	12	17	29	55	....	....	....	....	....
	Cornwall	OHL	40	31	50	81	135	6	4	7	11	2
	New Haven	AHL	....	....	....	....	....	2	0	0	0	5
1986-87	**Los Angeles**	**NHL**	**2**	**0**	**0**	**0**	**24**	....	....	....	....	....
	Cornwall	OHL	52	22	45	67	88	5	4	3	7	20
1987-88	**Los Angeles**	**NHL**	**9**	**0**	**0**	**0**	**12**	....	....	....	....	....
	New Haven	AHL	57	15	25	40	170	....	....	....	....	....
1988-89	**Los Angeles**	**NHL**	**5**	**0**	**0**	**0**	**0**	....	....	....	....	....
	New Haven	AHL	69	25	39	64	200	17	4	8	12	60
1989-90	**Los Angeles**	**NHL**	**10**	**3**	**2**	**5**	**9**	....	....	....	....	....
	New Haven	AHL	51	17	30	47	152	....	....	....	....	....
1990-91	**Winnipeg**	**NHL**	**7**	**2**	**0**	**2**	**16**	....	....	....	....	....
	Moncton	AHL	58	16	34	50	107	9	3	11	14	31
1991-92	Baltimore	AHL	46	20	26	46	98	....	....	....	....	....
	Moncton	AHL	19	12	9	21	6	11	6	4	10	10
	NHL Totals		**35**	**5**	**3**	**8**	**61**	....	....	....	....	....

a OHL Third All-Star Team (1985)

Traded to **Minnesota** by **Los Angeles** for Daniel Berthiaume, September 6, 1990. Traded to **Washington** by **Winnipeg** with Brent Hughes and Simon Wheeldon for Bob Joyce, Tyler Larter and Kent Paynter, May 21, 1991. Traded to **Winnipeg** by **Minnesota** for Brian Hunt, September 6, 1990.

DUPRE, YANICK (dew-PRAY)

Left wing. Shoots left. 6', 189 lbs. Born, Montreal, Que., November 20, 1972.
(Philadelphia's 2nd choice, 50th overall, in 1991 Entry Draft).

			Regular Season					Playoffs				
Season	Club	Lea	GP	G	A	TP	PIM	GP	G	A	TP	PIM
1989-90	Drummondville	QMJHL	53	15	19	34	69	....	....	....	....	....
1990-91	Drummondville	QMJHL	58	29	38	67	87	11	8	5	13	33
1991-92	**Philadelphia**	**NHL**	**1**	**0**	**0**	**0**	**0**	....	....	....	....	....
	Drummondville	QMJHL	28	19	17	36	48	....	....	....	....	....
	Verdun	QMJHL	12	7	14	21	21	19	9	9	18	20
	NHL Totals		**1**	**0**	**0**	**0**	**0**	....	....	....	....	....

DUPUIS, GUY (dew-PWEE)

Defense. Shoots right. 6'2", 200 lbs. Born, Moncton, N.B., May 10, 1970.
(Detroit's 3rd choice, 47th overall, in 1988 Entry Draft).

			Regular Season					Playoffs				
Season	Club	Lea	GP	G	A	TP	PIM	GP	G	A	TP	PIM
1986-87	Hull	QMJHL	69	5	10	15	35	8	1	2	3	2
1987-88	Hull	QMJHL	69	14	34	48	72	19	3	8	11	29
1988-89a	Hull	QMJHL	70	15	56	71	89	9	3	3	6	8
1989-90	Hull	QMJHL	70	8	41	49	96	11	1	3	4	8
1990-91	Adirondack	AHL	57	4	10	14	73	....	....	....	....	....
1991-92	Adirondack	AHL	49	3	6	9	59	3	0	0	0	4
	Fort Wayne	IHL	10	2	7	9	0	....	....	....	....	....

a QMJHL Second All-Star Team (1989)

DUTHIE, RYAN

Center. Shoots right. 5'10", 180 lbs. Born, Red Deer, Alta., September 2, 1974.
(NY Islanders' 4th choice, 105th overall, in 1992 Entry Draft).

			Regular Season					Playoffs				
Season	Club	Lea	GP	G	A	TP	PIM	GP	G	A	TP	PIM
1990-91	Calgary	AJHL	60	45	64	109	81	....	....	....	....	....
1991-92	Spokane	WHL	67	23	37	60	119	10	5	10	15	18

DUUS, JESPER (DOO-uhs)

Defense. Shoots right. 5'11", 176 lbs. Born, Rodovre, Denmark, November 24, 1967.
(Edmonton's 12th choice, 241st overall, in 1987 Entry Draft).

			Regular Season					Playoffs				
Season	Club	Lea	GP	G	A	TP	PIM	GP	G	A	TP	PIM
1985-86	Rodovre	Den.	24	3	5	8	28	6	1	2	3	4
1986-87	Rodovre	Den.	24	6	14	20	14	6	1	3	4	6
1987-88	Farjestad	Swe.	26	2	5	7	8	....	....	....	....	....
1988-89	Farjestad	Swe.	36	4	4	8	10	....	....	....	....	....
1989-90	Farjestad	Swe.	41	4	9	13	28	10	1	0	1	4
1990-91	Farjestad	Swe.	40	1	7	8	20	....	....	....	....	....
1991-92	Farjestad	Swe.	40	6	14	20	14	6	0	2	2	0

DUVAL, MURRAY

Defense. Shoots left. 6'1", 203 lbs. Born, Thompson, Man., January 22, 1970.
(NY Rangers' 2nd choice, 26th overall, in 1988 Entry Draft).

			Regular Season					Playoffs				
Season	Club	Lea	GP	G	A	TP	PIM	GP	G	A	TP	PIM
1986-87	Spokane	WHL	27	2	6	8	21	....	....	....	....	....
1987-88	Spokane	WHL	70	26	37	63	104	15	5	2	7	22
1988-89	Spokane	WHL	4	0	3	3	22	....	....	....	....	....
	Tri-Cities	WHL	67	14	25	39	122	....	....	....	....	....
1989-90	Tri-Cities	WHL	7	4	4	8	10	....	....	....	....	....
	Swift Current	WHL	7	3	5	8	31	....	....	....	....	....
	Kamloops	WHL	56	14	36	50	94	17	8	7	15	29
1990-91a	Kamloops	WHL	67	47	66	113	187	12	8	5	13	30
1991-92	San Diego	IHL	10	1	2	3	6	....	....	....	....	....
	Binghamton	AHL	15	1	6	7	8	....	....	....	....	....
	Erie	ECHL	19	5	8	13	26	4	1	0	1	4

a WHL West Second All-Star Team (1991)

DYCK, PAUL

Defense. Shoots left. 6'1", 192 lbs. Born, Steinbach, Man., April 15, 1971.
(Pittsburgh's 11th choice, 236th overall, in 1991 Entry Draft).

			Regular Season					Playoffs				
Season	Club	Lea	GP	G	A	TP	PIM	GP	G	A	TP	PIM
1990-91	Moose Jaw	WHL	72	12	41	53	63	8	0	7	7	17
1991-92	Muskegon	IHL	73	6	21	27	40	14	1	3	4	4

DYKHUIS, KARL

Defense. Shoots left. 6'3", 195 lbs. Born, Sept-Iles, Que., July 8, 1972.
(Chicago's 1st choice, 16th overall, in 1990 Entry Draft).

			Regular Season					Playoffs				
Season	Club	Lea	GP	G	A	TP	PIM	GP	G	A	TP	PIM
1988-89	Hull	QMJHL	63	2	29	31	59	9	1	9	10	6
1989-90a	Hull	QMJHL	69	10	46	56	119	11	2	5	7	2
1990-91	Cdn. National	....	37	2	9	11	16	....	....	....	....	....
	Longueuil	QMJHL	3	1	4	4	6	8	2	5	7	6
1991-92	**Chicago**	**NHL**	**6**	**1**	**3**	**4**	**4**	....	....	....	....	....
	Verdun	QMJHL	29	5	19	24	55	17	0	12	12	14
	NHL Totals		**6**	**1**	**3**	**4**	**4**	....	....	....	....	....

a QMJHL First All-Star Team (1990)

DZIEDZIC, JOE

Left wing. Shoots left. 6'3", 200 lbs. Born, Minneapolis, MN, December 18, 1971.
(Pittsburgh's 2nd choice, 61st overall, in 1990 Entry Draft).

			Regular Season					Playoffs				
Season	Club	Lea	GP	G	A	TP	PIM	GP	G	A	TP	PIM
1990-91	U. Minnesota	WCHA	20	6	4	10	26	....	....	....	....	....
1991-92	U. Minnesota	WCHA	34	8	9	17	68	....	....	....	....	....

EAGLES, MICHAEL (MIKE)

Center/Left wing. Shoots left. 5'10", 180 lbs. Born, Sussex, N.B., March 7, 1963.
(Quebec's 5th choice, 116th overall, in 1981 Entry Draft).

			Regular Season					Playoffs				
Season	Club	Lea	GP	G	A	TP	PIM	GP	G	A	TP	PIM
1980-81	Kitchener	OHA	56	11	27	38	64	18	4	2	6	36
1981-82	Kitchener	OHL	62	26	40	66	148	15	3	11	14	27
1982-83	**Quebec**	**NHL**	**2**	**0**	**0**	**0**	**2**	....	....	....	....	....
	Kitchener	OHL	58	26	36	62	133	12	5	7	12	27
1983-84	Fredericton	AHL	68	13	29	42	85	4	0	0	0	5
1984-85	Fredericton	AHL	36	4	20	24	80	3	0	0	0	2
1985-86	**Quebec**	**NHL**	**73**	**11**	**12**	**23**	**49**	**3**	**0**	**0**	**0**	**2**
1986-87	**Quebec**	**NHL**	**73**	**13**	**19**	**32**	**55**	**4**	**1**	**0**	**1**	**10**
1987-88	**Quebec**	**NHL**	**76**	**10**	**10**	**20**	**74**	....	....	....	....	....
1988-89	**Chicago**	**NHL**	**47**	**5**	**11**	**16**	**44**	....	....	....	....	....
1989-90	**Chicago**	**NHL**	**23**	**1**	**2**	**3**	**34**	....	....	....	....	....
	Indianapolis	IHL	24	11	13	24	47	13	*10	10	20	34
1990-91	**Winnipeg**	**NHL**	**44**	**0**	**9**	**9**	**79**	....	....	....	....	....
	Indianapolis	IHL	25	15	14	29	47	....	....	....	....	....
1991-92	**Winnipeg**	**NHL**	**65**	**7**	**10**	**17**	**118**	**7**	**0**	**0**	**0**	**8**
	NHL Totals		**403**	**47**	**73**	**120**	**455**	**14**	**1**	**0**	**1**	**20**

Traded to **Chicago** by **Quebec** for Bob Mason, July 5, 1988. Traded to **Winnipeg** by **Chicago** for Winnipeg's fourth round choice (Igor Kravchuk) in 1991 Entry Draft, December 14, 1990.

EAKINS, DALLAS

Defense. Shoots left. 6'2", 195 lbs. Born, Dade City, FL, February 27, 1967.
(Washington's 11th choice, 208th overall, in 1985 Entry Draft).

			Regular Season					Playoffs				
Season	Club	Lea	GP	G	A	TP	PIM	GP	G	A	TP	PIM
1984-85	Peterborough	OHL	48	0	8	8	96	7	0	0	0	18
1985-86	Peterborough	OHL	60	6	16	22	134	16	0	1	1	30
1986-87	Peterborough	OHL	54	3	11	14	145	12	1	4	5	37
1987-88	Peterborough	OHL	64	11	27	38	129	12	3	12	15	16
1988-89	Baltimore	AHL	62	0	10	10	139	....	....	....	....	....
1989-90	Moncton	AHL	75	2	11	13	189	....	....	....	....	....
1990-91	Moncton	AHL	75	1	12	13	132	9	0	1	1	44
1991-92	Moncton	AHL	67	3	13	16	136	11	2	1	3	16

Signed as a free agent by **Winnipeg**, October 17, 1989.

EASTWOOD, MICHAEL

Center. Shoots right. 6'2", 190 lbs. Born, Ottawa, Ont., July 1, 1967.
(Toronto's 5th choice, 91st overall, in 1987 Entry Draft).

			Regular Season					Playoffs				
Season	Club	Lea	GP	G	A	TP	PIM	GP	G	A	TP	PIM
1987-88	W. Michigan	CCHA	42	5	8	13	14	....	....	....	....	....
1988-89	W. Michigan	CCHA	40	10	13	23	87	....	....	....	....	....
1989-90	W. Michigan	CCHA	40	25	27	52	36	....	....	....	....	....
1990-91a	W. Michigan	CCHA	42	29	32	61	84	....	....	....	....	....
1991-92	**Toronto**	**NHL**	**9**	**0**	**2**	**2**	**4**	....	....	....	....	....
	St. John's	AHL	61	18	25	43	28	16	9	10	19	16
	NHL Totals		**9**	**0**	**2**	**2**	**4**	....	....	....	....	....

a CCHA Second All-Star Team (1991)

EDGERLY, DEREK

Center. Shoots left. 6'1", 190 lbs. Born, Malden, MA, April 3, 1971.
(Chicago's 5th choice, 124th overall, in 1990 Entry Draft).

			Regular Season					Playoffs				
Season	Club	Lea	GP	G	A	TP	PIM	GP	G	A	TP	PIM
1990-91	Northeastern	H.E.	34	3	11	14	12	....	....	....	....	....
1991-92	Northeastern	H.E.	15	2	1	3	14	....	....	....	....	....

EDLUND, PAR (EHD-luhnd, PEHR)

Left wing. Shoots right. 5'11", 196 lbs. Born, Sodertalje, Sweden, April 9, 1967.
(Los Angeles' 3rd choice, 30th overall, in 1985 Entry Draft).

			Regular Season					Playoffs				
Season	Club	Lea	GP	G	A	TP	PIM	GP	G	A	TP	PIM
1986-87	Bjorkloven	Swe.	4	0	0	0	0	....	....	....	....	....
1987-88	Bjorkloven	Swe.	37	6	4	10	14	7	1	0	1	2
1988-89	Bjorkloven	Swe.	18	9	10	19	....	....	....	....	....	....
1989-90	Bjorkloven	Swe.2	18	13	9	22	0	....	....	....	....	....
1990-91	V. Frolunda	Swe.2	15	5	4	9	10	....	....	....	....	....
1991-92	V. Frolunda	Swe.	35	13	9	22	46	2	0	0	0	4

EDSTROM, LARS (EHD-struhm)

Left wing. Shoots left. 5'11", 185 lbs. Born, Lulea, Sweden, July 16, 1966.
(Minnesota's 7th choice, 202nd overall, in 1992 Entry Draft).

			Regular Season					Playoffs				
Season	Club	Lea	GP	G	A	TP	PIM	GP	G	A	TP	PIM
1989-90	Lulea	Swe.	32	11	15	26	16	....	....	....	....	....
1990-91	Lulea	Swe.	37	8	19	27	43	....	....	....	....	....
1991-92	Lulea	Swe.	35	17	19	36	20	1	0	0	0	0

EGELAND, TRACY

Left wing. Shoots right. 6'1", 180 lbs. Born, Lethbridge, Alta., August 20, 1970.
(Chicago's 5th choice, 132nd overall, in 1989 Entry Draft).

			Regular Season					Playoffs				
Season	Club	Lea	GP	G	A	TP	PIM	GP	G	A	TP	PIM
1986-87	Swift Current	WHL	48	3	2	5	20	....	....	....	....	....
1987-88	Swift Current	WHL	63	10	22	32	34	....	....	....	....	....
1988-89	Medicine Hat	WHL	42	11	12	23	64	....	....	....	....	....
	Prince Albert	WHL	24	17	10	27	24	4	0	1	1	13
1989-90	Prince Albert	WHL	61	39	26	65	160	13	7	10	17	26
1990-91	Indianapolis	IHL	79	17	22	39	205	7	2	1	3	21
1991-92	Indianapolis	IHL	66	20	11	31	214	....	....	....	....	....

EISENHUT, NEIL

Center. Shoots left. 5'11", 190 lbs. Born, Oliver, B.C., January 9, 1967.
(Vancouver's 11th choice, 238th overall, in 1987 Entry Draft).

			Regular Season					Playoffs				
Season	Club	Lea	GP	G	A	TP	PIM	GP	G	A	TP	PIM
1987-88	North Dakota	WCHA	42	12	20	32	14	....	....	....	....	....
1988-89	North Dakota	WCHA	41	22	16	38	20	....	....	....	....	....
1989-90	North Dakota	WCHA	45	22	32	54	46	....	....	....	....	....
1990-91	North Dakota	WCHA	20	9	15	24	10	....	....	....	....	....
1991-92	Milwaukee	IHL	76	13	23	36	26	2	1	2	3	0

EKLUND, PER-ERIK (PELLE) (EHK-luhnd)

Center. Shoots left. 5'10", 175 lbs. Born, Stockholm, Sweden, March 22, 1963.
(Philadelphia's 7th choice, 161st overall, in 1983 Entry Draft).

			Regular Season					Playoffs				
Season	Club	Lea	GP	G	A	TP	PIM	GP	G	A	TP	PIM
1981-82	AIK	Swe.	23	2	3	5	2	....	....	....	....	....
1982-83	AIK	Swe.	34	13	17	30	14	3	1	4	5	2
1983-84	AIK	Swe.	35	9	18	27	24	6	6	7	13	2
1984-85	AIK	Swe.	35	16	33	49	10	....	....	....	....	....
1985-86	**Philadelphia**	**NHL**	**70**	**15**	**51**	**66**	**12**	**5**	**0**	**2**	**2**	**0**
1986-87	**Philadelphia**	**NHL**	**72**	**14**	**41**	**55**	**2**	**26**	**7**	**20**	**27**	**2**
1987-88	**Philadelphia**	**NHL**	**71**	**10**	**32**	**42**	**12**	**7**	**0**	**3**	**3**	**0**
1988-89	**Philadelphia**	**NHL**	**79**	**18**	**51**	**69**	**23**	**19**	**3**	**8**	**11**	**2**
1989-90	**Philadelphia**	**NHL**	**70**	**23**	**39**	**62**	**16**	....	....	....	....	....
1990-91	**Philadelphia**	**NHL**	**73**	**19**	**50**	**69**	**14**	....	....	....	....	....
1991-92	**Philadelphia**	**NHL**	**51**	**7**	**16**	**23**	**4**	....	....	....	....	....
	NHL Totals		**486**	**106**	**280**	**386**	**83**	**57**	**10**	**33**	**43**	**4**

ELIK, TODD (EL-ik)

Center. Shoots left. 6'2", 190 lbs. Born, Brampton, Ont., April 15, 1966.

			Regular Season					Playoffs				
Season	Club	Lea	GP	G	A	TP	PIM	GP	G	A	TP	PIM
1984-85	Kingston	OHL	34	14	11	25	6	....	....	....	....	....
	North Bay	OHL	23	4	6	10	2	4	2	0	2	0
1985-86	North Bay	OHL	40	12	34	46	20	10	7	6	13	0
1986-87	U. of Regina	CWUAA	27	26	34	60	137	....	....	....	....	....
1987-88	Colorado	IHL	81	44	56	100	83	12	8	12	20	9
1988-89	Denver	IHL	28	20	15	35	22	....	....	....	....	....
	New Haven	AHL	43	11	25	36	31	17	10	12	22	44
1989-90	**Los Angeles**	**NHL**	**48**	**10**	**23**	**33**	**4**	**10**	**3**	**9**	**12**	**10**
	New Haven	AHL	32	20	23	43	42	....	....	....	....	....
1990-91	**Los Angeles**	**NHL**	**74**	**21**	**37**	**58**	**58**	**12**	**2**	**7**	**9**	**6**
1991-92	**Minnesota**	**NHL**	**62**	**14**	**32**	**46**	**125**	**5**	**1**	**1**	**2**	**2**
	NHL Totals		**184**	**45**	**92**	**137**	**187**	**27**	**6**	**17**	**23**	**18**

Signed as a free agent by **NY Rangers**, February 26, 1988. Traded to **Los Angeles** by **NY Rangers** with Igor Liba, Michael Boyce and future considerations for Dean Kennedy and Denis Larocque, December 12, 1988. Traded to **Minnesota** by **Los Angeles** for Randy Gilhen, Charlie Huddy, Jim Thomson and NY Rangers' fourth round choice (previously acquired by Minnesota — Alexei Zhitnik) in 1991 Entry Draft, June 22, 1991.

ELLETT, DAVID

Defense. Shoots left. 6'1", 200 lbs. Born, Cleveland, OH, March 30, 1964.
(Winnipeg's 3rd choice, 75th overall, in 1982 Entry Draft).

			Regular Season					Playoffs				
Season	Club	Lea	GP	G	A	TP	PIM	GP	G	A	TP	PIM
1982-83	Bowling Green	CCHA	40	4	13	17	34	....	....	....	....	....
1983-84ab	Bowling Green	CCHA	43	15	39	54	96	....	....	....	....	....
1984-85	**Winnipeg**	**NHL**	**80**	**11**	**27**	**38**	**85**	**8**	**1**	**5**	**6**	**4**
1985-86	**Winnipeg**	**NHL**	**80**	**15**	**31**	**46**	**96**	**3**	**0**	**1**	**1**	**0**
1986-87	**Winnipeg**	**NHL**	**78**	**13**	**31**	**44**	**53**	**10**	**0**	**8**	**8**	**2**
1987-88	**Winnipeg**	**NHL**	**68**	**13**	**45**	**58**	**106**	**5**	**1**	**2**	**3**	**10**
1988-89	**Winnipeg**	**NHL**	**75**	**22**	**34**	**56**	**62**	....	....	....	....	....
1989-90	**Winnipeg**	**NHL**	**77**	**17**	**29**	**46**	**96**	**7**	**2**	**0**	**2**	**6**
1990-91	**Winnipeg**	**NHL**	**17**	**4**	**7**	**11**	**6**	....	....	....	....	....
	Toronto	**NHL**	**60**	**8**	**30**	**38**	**69**	....	....	....	....	....
1991-92	**Toronto**	**NHL**	**79**	**18**	**33**	**51**	**95**	....	....	....	....	....
	NHL Totals		**614**	**121**	**267**	**388**	**668**	**33**	**4**	**16**	**20**	**22**

a CCHA Second All-Star Team (1984)
b Named to NCAA All-Tournament Team (1984)

Played in NHL All-Star Game (1989, 1992)

Traded to **Toronto** by **Winnipeg** with Paul Fenton for Ed Olczyk and Mark Osborne, November 10, 1990.

ELVENAS, ROGER

Center. Shoots left. 6'1", 183 lbs. Born, Lund, Sweden, May 29, 1968.
(Toronto's 7th choice, 153rd overall, in 1988 Entry Draft).

			Regular Season					Playoffs				
Season	Club	Lea	GP	G	A	TP	PIM	GP	G	A	TP	PIM
1987-88	Rogle	Swe.	35	21	18	39	....	....	....	....	....	....
1988-89	Rogle	Swe.	36	24	40	64	....	....	....	....	....	....
1989-90	Rogle	Swe.	35	16	25	41	24	....	....	....	....	....
1990-91	Rogle	Swe.	32	17	26	43	12	....	....	....	....	....
1991-92	Rogle	Swe.2			UNAVAILABLE							

ELVENAS, STEFAN

Right wing. Shoots left. 6'1", 183 lbs. Born, Lund, Sweden, March 30, 1970.
(Chicago's 3rd choice, 71st overall, in 1988 Entry Draft).

			Regular Season					Playoffs				
Season	Club	Lea	GP	G	A	TP	PIM	GP	G	A	TP	PIM
1989-90	Rogle	Swe.	35	18	25	43	56	....	....	....	....	....
1990-91	Rogle	Swe.	18	14	6	20	10	....	....	....	....	....
1991-92	Rogle	Swe.2			UNAVAILABLE							

ELYNUIK, PAT (EL-ih-NYUK)

Right wing. Shoots right. 6', 185 lbs. Born, Foam Lake, Sask., October 30, 1967.
(Winnipeg's 1st choice, 8th overall, in 1986 Entry Draft).

			Regular Season					Playoffs				
Season	Club	Lea	GP	G	A	TP	PIM	GP	G	A	TP	PIM
1984-85	Prince Albert	WHL	70	23	20	43	54	13	9	3	12	7
1985-86a	Prince Albert	WHL	68	53	53	106	62	20	7	9	16	17
1986-87a	Prince Albert	WHL	64	51	62	113	40	8	5	5	10	12
1987-88	**Winnipeg**	**NHL**	**13**	**1**	**3**	**4**	**12**	....	....	....	....	....
	Moncton	AHL	30	11	18	29	35	....	....	....	....	....
1988-89	**Winnipeg**	**NHL**	**56**	**26**	**25**	**51**	**29**	....	....	....	....	....
	Moncton	AHL	7	8	2	10	2	....	....	....	....	....
1989-90	**Winnipeg**	**NHL**	**80**	**32**	**42**	**74**	**83**	**7**	**2**	**4**	**6**	**2**
1990-91	**Winnipeg**	**NHL**	**80**	**31**	**34**	**65**	**73**	....	....	....	....	....
1991-92	**Winnipeg**	**NHL**	**60**	**25**	**25**	**50**	**65**	**7**	**2**	**2**	**4**	**4**
	NHL Totals		**289**	**115**	**129**	**244**	**262**	**14**	**4**	**6**	**10**	**6**

a WHL East All-Star Team (1986, 1987)

EMERSON, NELSON

Center. Shoots right. 5'11", 175 lbs. Born, Hamilton, Ont., August 17, 1967.
(St. Louis' 2nd choice, 44th overall, in 1985 Entry Draft).

			Regular Season					Playoffs				
Season	Club	Lea	GP	G	A	TP	PIM	GP	G	A	TP	PIM
1986-87a	Bowling Green	CCHA	45	26	35	61	28	....	....	....	....	....
1987-88bc	Bowling Green	CCHA	45	34	49	83	54	....	....	....	....	....
1988-89d	Bowling Green	CCHA	44	22	46	68	46	....	....	....	....	....
1989-90ce	Bowling Green	CCHA	44	30	52	82	42	....	....	....	....	....
	Peoria	IHL	3	1	1	2	0	....	....	....	....	....
1990-91	**St. Louis**	**NHL**	**4**	**0**	**3**	**3**	**2**	....	....	....	....	....
fg	Peoria	IHL	73	36	79	115	91	17	9	12	21	16
1991-92	**St. Louis**	**NHL**	**79**	**23**	**36**	**59**	**66**	**6**	**3**	**3**	**6**	**21**
	NHL Totals		**83**	**23**	**39**	**62**	**68**	**6**	**3**	**3**	**6**	**21**

a CCHA Freshman of the Year (1987)
b NCAA West Second All-American Team (1988)
c CCHA First All-Star Team (1988, 1990)
d CCHA Second All-Star Team (1989)
e NCAA West First All-American Team (1990)
f IHL First All-Star Team (1991)
g Won Garry F. Longman Memorial Trophy (Top Rookie — IHL) (1991)

EMMA, DAVID

Center. Shoots left. 5'11", 180 lbs. Born, Cranston, RI, January 14, 1969.
(New Jersey's 6th choice, 110th overall, in 1989 Entry Draft).

			Regular Season					Playoffs				
Season	Club	Lea	GP	G	A	TP	PIM	GP	G	A	TP	PIM
1987-88	Boston College	H.E.	30	19	16	35	30	....	....	....	....	....
1988-89	Boston College	H.E.	36	20	31	51	36	....	....	....	....	....
1989-90ab	Boston College	H.E.	42	38	34	*72	46	....	....	....	....	....
1990-91abcd	Boston College	H.E.	39	*35	46	*81	44	....	....	....	....	....
1991-92	U.S. National	....	55	15	16	31	32	....	....	....	....	....
	U.S. Olympic	....	6	0	1	1	6	....	....	....	....	....
	Utica	AHL	15	4	7	11	12	4	1	1	2	2

a Hockey East First All-Star Team (1990, 1991)
b NCAA East First All-American Team (1990, 1991)
c Hockey East Player of the Year (1991)
d Won Hobey Baker Award (Top U.S. Collegiate Player) (1991)

ENGA, RICHARD

Center. Shoots right. 5'10", 156 lbs. Born, Bitburg, Germany, February 15, 1972.
(NY Islanders' 9th choice, 195th overall, in 1990 Entry Draft).

			Regular Season					Playoffs				
Season	Club	Lea	GP	G	A	TP	PIM	GP	G	A	TP	PIM
1990-91	Culver Aca.	HS	37	41	48	89	13	....	....	....	....	....
1991-92	Colorado	WCHA	40	11	16	27	18	....	....	....	....	....

ENGLUND, PATRIK

Left wing. Shoots right. 6', 172 lbs. Born, Stockholm, Sweden, June 3, 1970.
(Philadelphia's 11th choice, 151st overall, in 1990 Entry Draft).

			Regular Season					Playoffs				
Season	Club	Lea	GP	G	A	TP	PIM	GP	G	A	TP	PIM
1989-90	AIK	Swe.	31	11	7	18	....	....	....	....	....	....
1990-91	AIK	Swe.	40	9	7	16	4	....	....	....	....	....
1991-92	AIK	Swe.	39	8	5	13	8	3	0	0	0	0

ENS, KELLY

Center. Shoots left. 6'2", 195 lbs. Born, Saskatoon, Sask., June 15, 1969.
(NY Islanders' 13th choice, 212th overall, in 1989 Entry Draft).

			Regular Season					Playoffs				
Season	Club	Lea	GP	G	A	TP	PIM	GP	G	A	TP	PIM
1988-89	Lethbridge	WHL	72	46	36	82	146	19	14	14	28	36
1989-90a	Lethbridge	WHL	72	62	58	120	139	19	14	14	28	36
1990-91	Springfield	AHL	21	4	2	6	13	....	....	....	....	....
	Louisville	ECHL	8	2	2	4	21	....	....	....	....	....
1991-92	Springfield	AHL	10	0	2	2	10	....	....	....	....	....
	Louisville	ECHL	34	20	24	44	45	13	6	4	10	50

a WHL East Second All-Star Team (1990)

Signed as a free agent by **Hartford**, July 5, 1990.

ERICKSON, BRYAN

Right wing. Shoots right. 5'9", 170 lbs. Born, Roseau, MN, March 7, 1960.

			Regular Season					Playoffs				
Season	Club	Lea	GP	G	A	TP	PIM	GP	G	A	TP	PIM
1981-82	U. Minnesota	WCHA	35	25	20	45	20	....	....	....	....	....
1982-83	U. Minnesota	WCHA	42	35	47	82	34	....	....	....	....	....
	Hershey	AHL	1	0	1	1	0	3	3	0	3	0
1983-84	**Washington**	**NHL**	**45**	**12**	**17**	**29**	**16**	**8**	**2**	**3**	**5**	**7**
	Hershey	AHL	31	16	12	28	11	....	....	....	....	....
1984-85	**Washington**	**NHL**	**57**	**15**	**13**	**28**	**23**	....	....	....	....	....
	Binghamton	AHL	13	6	11	17	8	....	....	....	....	....
1985-86	**Los Angeles**	**NHL**	**55**	**20**	**23**	**43**	**36**	....	....	....	....	....
	Binghamton	AHL	7	5	3	8	2	....	....	....	....	....
	New Haven	AHL	14	8	3	11	11	....	....	....	....	....
1986-87	**Los Angeles**	**NHL**	**68**	**20**	**30**	**50**	**26**	**3**	**1**	**1**	**2**	**0**
1987-88	**Los Angeles**	**NHL**	**42**	**6**	**15**	**21**	**20**	....	....	....	....	....
	New Haven	AHL	3	0	0	0	0	....	....	....	....	....
	Pittsburgh	**NHL**	**11**	**1**	**4**	**5**	**0**	....	....	....	....	....
1988-89						DID NOT PLAY						
1989-90	Moncton	AHL	13	4	7	11	4	....	....	....	....	....
1990-91	**Winnipeg**	**NHL**	**6**	**0**	**7**	**7**	**0**	....	....	....	....	....
	Moncton	AHL	36	18	14	32	16	9	9	2	11	6
1991-92	**Winnipeg**	**NHL**	**10**	**2**	**4**	**6**	**0**	....	....	....	....	....
	NHL Totals		**294**	**76**	**113**	**189**	**121**	**11**	**3**	**4**	**7**	**7**

Signed as a free agent by **Washington**, April 5, 1983. Traded to **Los Angeles** by **Washington** for Bruce Shoebottom, October 31, 1985. Traded to **Pittsburgh** by **Los Angeles** for Chris Kontos and Pittsburgh's sixth round draft choice in 1988 Entry Draft (Micah Aivazoff), February 5, 1988. Signed as a free agent by **Winnipeg**, March 2, 1990.

ERICKSON, PATRIK (AIR-ihk-suhn)

Right wing. Shoots left. 5'11", 183 lbs. Born, Gavle, Sweden, March 13, 1969.
(Winnipeg's 2nd choice, 37th overall, in 1987 Entry Draft).

			Regular Season					Playoffs				
Season	Club	Lea	GP	G	A	TP	PIM	GP	G	A	TP	PIM
1986-87	Brynas	Swe.	25	10	5	15	8	....	....	....	....	....
1987-88	Brynas	Swe.	35	14	9	23	6	....	....	....	....	....
1988-89	Brynas	Swe.	33	6	10	16	14	....	....	....	....	....
1989-90	Brynas	Swe.	40	16	17	33	18	5	3	2	3	4
1990-91	Brynas	Swe.	33	9	14	23	36	....	....	....	....	....
1991-92	AIK	Swe.	37	7	19	26	34	3	1	0	1	0

ERICKSSON, TOMMY

Left wing. Shoots right. 5'11", 183 lbs. Born, Umea, Sweden, May 3, 1966.
(Chicago's 3rd choice, 66th overall, in 1984 Entry Draft).

			Regular Season					Playoffs				
Season	Club	Lea	GP	G	A	TP	PIM	GP	G	A	TP	PIM
1987-88	Djurgarden	Swe.	39	13	17	30	36	....	....	....	....	....
1988-89	Djurgarden	Swe.	4	0	0	0	0	....	....	....	....	....
1989-90	Djurgarden	Swe.	39	11	12	23	106	....	....	....	....	....
1990-91	Djurgarden	Swe.	39	16	11	27	64	10	1	0	1	2

ERIKSSON, NIKLAS (AIR-ihk-suhn)

Center. Shoots left. 5'11", 180 lbs. Born, Vastervik, Sweden, February 17, 1969.
(Philadelphia's 4th choice, 117th overall, in 1989 Entry Draft).

			Regular Season					Playoffs				
Season	Club	Lea	GP	G	A	TP	PIM	GP	G	A	TP	PIM
1988-89	Leksand	Swe.	33	18	12	30	22	....	....	....	....	....
1989-90	Leksand	Swe.	40	18	16	34	16	3	0	2	2	2
1990-91	Leksand	Swe.2	8	2	2	4	2	....	....	....	....	....
1991-92	Leksand	Swe.	22	10	6	16	16	....	....	....	....	....

ERIKSSON, TOMAZ (AIR-ihk-suhn)

Left wing. Shoots left. 6', 194 lbs. Born, Stockholm, Sweden, March 23, 1967.
(Philadelphia's 4th choice, 83rd overall, in 1987 Entry Draft).

			Regular Season					Playoffs				
Season	Club	Lea	GP	G	A	TP	PIM	GP	G	A	TP	PIM
1986-87	Djurgarden	Swe.	20	7	4	11	14	2	2	0	2	0
1987-88	Djurgarden	Swe.	26	4	5	9	16	....	....	....	....	....
1988-89	Sodertalje	Swe.	38	6	13	19	50	....	....	....	....	....
1989-90	Sodertalje	Swe.	39	14	10	24	26	....	....	....	....	....
1990-91	Sodertalje	Swe.	26	12	14	26	26	....	....	....	....	....
1991-92	Sodertalje	Swe.	22	3	6	9	14	....	....	....	....	....

ERIXON, JAN (AIR-ihk-suhn)

Left wing. Shoots left. 6', 196 lbs. Born, Skelleftea, Sweden, July 8, 1962.
(NY Rangers' 2nd choice, 30th overall, in 1981 Entry Draft).

			Regular Season					Playoffs				
Season	Club	Lea	GP	G	A	TP	PIM	GP	G	A	TP	PIM
1979-80	Skelleftea	Swe.	15	1	0	1	2	....	....	....	....	....
1980-81	Skelleftea	Swe.	32	6	6	12	4	3	1	0	1	0
1981-82	Skelleftea	Swe.	30	7	7	14	26	....	....	....	....	....
1982-83	Skelleftea	Swe.	36	10	19	29	32	....	....	....	....	....
1983-84	**NY Rangers**	**NHL**	**75**	**5**	**25**	**30**	**16**	**5**	**2**	**0**	**2**	**4**
1984-85	**NY Rangers**	**NHL**	**66**	**7**	**22**	**29**	**33**	**2**	**0**	**0**	**0**	**2**
1985-86	**NY Rangers**	**NHL**	**31**	**2**	**17**	**19**	**4**	**12**	**0**	**1**	**1**	**4**
1986-87	**NY Rangers**	**NHL**	**68**	**8**	**18**	**26**	**24**	**6**	**1**	**0**	**1**	**0**
1987-88	**NY Rangers**	**NHL**	**70**	**7**	**19**	**26**	**33**	....	....	....	....	....
1988-89	**NY Rangers**	**NHL**	**44**	**4**	**11**	**15**	**27**	**4**	**0**	**1**	**1**	**2**
1989-90	**NY Rangers**	**NHL**	**58**	**4**	**9**	**13**	**8**	**10**	**1**	**0**	**1**	**2**
1990-91	**NY Rangers**	**NHL**	**53**	**7**	**18**	**25**	**8**	**6**	**1**	**2**	**3**	**0**
1991-92	**NY Rangers**	**NHL**	**46**	**8**	**9**	**17**	**4**	**13**	**2**	**3**	**5**	**2**
	NHL Totals		**511**	**52**	**148**	**200**	**157**	**58**	**7**	**7**	**14**	**16**

ERREY, BOB (AIRY)

Left wing. Shoots left. 5'10", 183 lbs. Born, Montreal, Que., September 21, 1964.
(Pittsburgh's 1st choice, 15th overall, in 1983 Entry Draft).

			Regular Season					Playoffs				
Season	Club	Lea	GP	G	A	TP	PIM	GP	G	A	TP	PIM
1981-82	Peterborough	OHL	68	29	31	60	39	9	3	1	4	9
1982-83a	Peterborough	OHL	67	53	47	100	74	4	1	3	4	7
1983-84	**Pittsburgh**	**NHL**	**65**	**9**	**13**	**22**	**29**	....	....	....	....	....
1984-85	**Pittsburgh**	**NHL**	**16**	**0**	**2**	**2**	**7**	....	....	....	....	....
	Baltimore	AHL	59	17	24	41	14	8	3	4	7	11
1985-86	**Pittsburgh**	**NHL**	**37**	**11**	**6**	**17**	**8**	....	....	....	....	....
	Baltimore	AHL	18	8	7	15	28	....	....	....	....	....
1986-87	**Pittsburgh**	**NHL**	**72**	**16**	**18**	**34**	**46**	....	....	....	....	....
1987-88	**Pittsburgh**	**NHL**	**17**	**3**	**6**	**9**	**18**	....	....	....	....	....
1988-89	**Pittsburgh**	**NHL**	**76**	**26**	**32**	**58**	**124**	**11**	**1**	**2**	**3**	**12**
1989-90	**Pittsburgh**	**NHL**	**78**	**20**	**19**	**39**	**109**	....	....	....	....	....
1990-91	**Pittsburgh**	**NHL**	**79**	**20**	**22**	**42**	**115**	**24**	**5**	**2**	**7**	**29**
1991-92	**Pittsburgh**	**NHL**	**78**	**19**	**16**	**35**	**119**	**14**	**3**	**0**	**3**	**10**
	NHL Totals		**518**	**124**	**134**	**258**	**575**	**49**	**9**	**4**	**13**	**51**

a OHL First All-Star Team (1983)

ESAU, LEONARD

Defense. Shoots right. 6'3", 190 lbs. Born, Meadow Lake, Sask., June 3, 1968.
(Toronto's 5th choice, 86th overall, in 1988 Entry Draft).

			Regular Season					Playoffs				
Season	Club	Lea	GP	G	A	TP	PIM	GP	G	A	TP	PIM
1988-89	St. Cloud	NCAA	35	12	27	39	69	....	....	....	....	....
1989-90	St. Cloud	NCAA	29	8	11	19	83	....	....	....	....	....
1990-91	Newmarket	AHL	76	4	14	18	28	....	....	....	....	....
1991-92	**Toronto**	**NHL**	**2**	**0**	**0**	**0**	**0**	....	....	....	....	....
	St. John's	AHL	78	9	29	38	68	13	0	2	2	14
	NHL Totals		**2**	**0**	**0**	**0**	**0**	....	....	....	....	....

Traded to **Quebec** by **Toronto** for Ken McRae, July 21, 1992.

ESPE, DAVID (ES-pee)

Defense. Shoots left. 6', 185 lbs. Born, St. Paul, MN, November 3, 1966.
(Quebec's 5th choice, 78th overall, in 1985 Entry Draft).

			Regular Season					Playoffs				
Season	Club	Lea	GP	G	A	TP	PIM	GP	G	A	TP	PIM
1985-86	U. Minnesota	WCHA	27	0	6	6	18	....	....	....	....	....
1986-87	U. Minnesota	WCHA	45	4	8	12	28	....	....	....	....	....
1987-88	U. Minnesota	WCHA	43	4	10	14	68	....	....	....	....	....
1988-89	U. Minnesota	WCHA	47	0	11	11	61	....	....	....	....	....
1989-90	Halifax	AHL	48	2	16	18	26	1	0	0	0	4
1990-91	Halifax	AHL	49	5	16	21	51	....	....	....	....	....
1991-92	Halifax	AHL	43	4	7	11	22	....	....	....	....	....

EVANS, DOUG

Left wing. Shoots left. 5'9", 185 lbs. Born, Peterborough, Ont., June 2, 1963.

			Regular Season					Playoffs				
Season	Club	Lea	GP	G	A	TP	PIM	GP	G	A	TP	PIM
1981-82	Peterborough	OHL	56	17	49	66	176	9	0	2	2	41
1982-83	Peterborough	OHL	65	31	55	86	165	4	0	3	3	23
1983-84	Peterborough	OHL	61	45	79	124	98	8	4	12	16	26
1984-85	Peoria	IHL	81	36	61	97	189	20	18	14	32	*88
1985-86	**St. Louis**	**NHL**	**13**	**1**	**0**	**1**	**2**	....	....	....	....	....
a	Peoria	IHL	60	46	51	97	179	10	4	6	10	32
1986-87	**St. Louis**	**NHL**	**53**	**3**	**13**	**16**	**91**	**5**	**0**	**0**	**0**	**10**
	Peoria	IHL	18	10	15	25	39	....	....	....	....	....
1987-88	**St. Louis**	**NHL**	**41**	**5**	**7**	**12**	**49**	**2**	**0**	**0**	**0**	**0**
	Peoria	IHL	11	4	16	20	64	....	....	....	....	....
1988-89	**St. Louis**	**NHL**	**53**	**7**	**12**	**19**	**81**	**7**	**1**	**2**	**3**	**16**
1989-90	**St. Louis**	**NHL**	**3**	**0**	**0**	**0**	**0**	....	....	....	....	....
	Peoria	IHL	42	19	28	47	128	....	....	....	....	....
	Winnipeg	**NHL**	**27**	**10**	**8**	**18**	**33**	**7**	**2**	**2**	**4**	**10**
1990-91	**Winnipeg**	**NHL**	**70**	**7**	**27**	**34**	**108**	....	....	....	....	....
1991-92	Peoria	IHL	16	5	14	19	38	....	....	....	....	....
	Winnipeg	**NHL**	**30**	**7**	**7**	**14**	**68**	**1**	**0**	**0**	**0**	**2**
	Moncton	AHL	10	7	8	15	10	....	....	....	....	....
	NHL Totals		**290**	**40**	**74**	**114**	**432**	**22**	**3**	**4**	**7**	**38**

a IHL First All-Star Team (1986)

Signed as a free agent by **St. Louis**, June 10, 1985. Traded to **Winnipeg** by **St. Louis** for Ron Wilson, January 22, 1990. Traded to **Boston** by **Winnipeg** for Daniel Berthiaume, June 10, 1992.

EVANS, DOUGLAS B.

Defense. Shoots right. 6', 200 lbs. Born, San Jose, CA, July 12, 1971.
(Winnipeg's 9th choice, 131st overall, in 1989 Entry Draft).

			Regular Season					Playoffs				
Season	Club	Lea	GP	G	A	TP	PIM	GP	G	A	TP	PIM
1988-89	U. of Michigan	CCHA	38	0	8	8	41	....	....	....	....	....
1989-90	U. of Michigan	CCHA	31	2	3	5	24	....	....	....	....	....
1990-91	U. of Michigan	CCHA	42	0	9	9	47	....	....	....	....	....
1991-92	U. of Michigan	CCHA	39	2	3	5	32	....	....	....	....	....

EVANS, KEVIN ROBERT

Left wing. Shoots left. 5'9", 185 lbs. Born, Peterborough, Ont., July 10, 1965.

			Regular Season					Playoffs				
Season	Club	Lea	GP	G	A	TP	PIM	GP	G	A	TP	PIM
1984-85	London	OHL	52	3	7	10	148	....	....	....	....	....
1985-86	Victoria	WHL	66	16	39	55	441	....	....	....	....	....
	Kalamazoo	IHL	11	3	5	8	97	6	3	0	3	56
1986-87	Kalamazoo	IHL	73	19	31	50	*648	3	1	0	1	24
1987-88	Kalamazoo	IHL	54	9	28	37	404	5	1	1	2	46
1988-89	Kalamazoo	IHL	50	22	34	56	326	....	....	....	....	....
1989-90	Kalamazoo	IHL	76	30	54	84	346	10	8	4	12	86
1990-91	**Minnesota**	**NHL**	**4**	**0**	**0**	**0**	**19**	....	....	....	....	....
	Kalamazoo	IHL	16	10	12	22	70	....	....	....	....	....
1991-92	**San Jose**	**NHL**	**5**	**0**	**1**	**1**	**25**	....	....	....	....	....
	Kansas City	IHL	66	10	39	49	342	14	2	13	15	70
	NHL Totals		**9**	**0**	**1**	**1**	**44**	....	....	....	....	....

Signed as a free agent by **Minnesota**, August 8, 1988. Claimed by **San Jose** from **Minnesota** in Dispersal Draft, May 30, 1991.

EVANS, SHAWN

Defense. Shoots left. 6'3", 195 lbs. Born, Kingston, Ont., September 7, 1965.
(New Jersey's 2nd choice, 24th overall, in 1983 Entry Draft).

			Regular Season					Playoffs				
Season	Club	Lea	GP	G	A	TP	PIM	GP	G	A	TP	PIM
1982-83	Peterborough	OHL	58	7	41	48	116	4	2	0	2	12
1983-84a	Peterborough	OHL	67	21	88	109	116	8	1	16	17	8
1984-85b	Peterborough	OHL	66	16	83	99	78	16	6	18	24	6
1985-86	**St. Louis**	**NHL**	**7**	**0**	**0**	**0**	**2**	....	....	....	....	....
	Peoria	IHL	55	8	26	34	36	....	....	....	....	....
1986-87	Nova Scotia	AHL	55	7	28	35	29	5	0	4	4	6
1987-88	Nova Scotia	AHL	79	8	62	70	109	5	1	1	2	40
1988-89	Springfield	AHL	68	9	50	59	125	....	....	....	....	....
1989-90	**NY Islanders**	**NHL**	**2**	**1**	**0**	**1**	**0**	....	....	....	....	....
	Springfield	AHL	63	6	35	41	102	18	6	11	17	35
1990-91	Maine	AHL	51	9	37	46	44	2	0	1	1	0
1991-92c	Springfield	AHL	80	11	67	78	81	11	0	8	8	16
	NHL Totals		**9**	**1**	**0**	**1**	**2**	....	....	....	....	....

a OHL Second All-Star Team (1984)
b OHL Third All-Star Team (1985)
c AHL First All-Star Team (1992)

Traded to **St. Louis** by **New Jersey** with New Jersey's fifth round choice (Michael Wolak) in 1986 Entry Draft for Mark Johnson, September 19, 1985. Traded to **Edmonton** by **St. Louis** for Todd Ewen, October 15, 1986. Signed as a free agent by **NY Islanders**, June 20, 1988. Signed as a free agent by **Boston**, December 19, 1990. Signed as a free agent by **Hartford**, August 14, 1991.

EVASON, DEAN (EH-vuh-suhn)

Center. Shoots right. 5'10", 180 lbs. Born, Flin Flon, Man., August 22, 1964.
(Washington's 3rd choice, 89th overall, in 1982 Entry Draft).

			Regular Season					Playoffs				
Season	Club	Lea	GP	G	A	TP	PIM	GP	G	A	TP	PIM
1980-81	Spokane	WHL	3	1	1	2	0	....	....	....	....	....
1981-82	Spokane	WHL	26	8	14	22	65	....	....	....	....	....
	Kamloops	WHL	44	21	55	76	47	4	2	1	3	0
1982-83	Kamloops	WHL	70	71	93	164	102	7	5	7	12	18
1983-84	**Washington**	**NHL**	**2**	**0**	**0**	**0**	**2**	....	....	....	....	....
a	Kamloops	WHL	57	49	88	137	89	17	*21	20	41	33
1984-85	**Washington**	**NHL**	**15**	**3**	**4**	**7**	**2**	....	....	....	....	....
	Hartford	**NHL**	**2**	**0**	**0**	**0**	**0**	....	....	....	....	....
	Binghamton	AHL	65	27	49	76	38	8	3	5	8	9
1985-86	**Hartford**	**NHL**	**55**	**20**	**28**	**48**	**65**	**10**	**1**	**4**	**5**	**10**
	Binghamton	AHL	26	9	17	26	29	....	....	....	....	....
1986-87	**Hartford**	**NHL**	**80**	**22**	**37**	**59**	**67**	**5**	**3**	**2**	**5**	**35**
1987-88	**Hartford**	**NHL**	**77**	**10**	**18**	**28**	**115**	**6**	**1**	**1**	**2**	**2**
1988-89	**Hartford**	**NHL**	**67**	**11**	**17**	**28**	**60**	**4**	**1**	**2**	**3**	**10**
1989-90	**Hartford**	**NHL**	**78**	**18**	**25**	**43**	**138**	**7**	**2**	**2**	**4**	**22**
1990-91	**Hartford**	**NHL**	**75**	**6**	**23**	**29**	**170**	**6**	**0**	**4**	**4**	**29**
1991-92	**San Jose**	**NHL**	**74**	**11**	**15**	**26**	**99**	....	....	....	....	....
	NHL Totals		**525**	**101**	**167**	**268**	**718**	**38**	**8**	**15**	**23**	**108**

a WHL First All-Star Team, West Division (1984)

Traded to **Hartford** by **Washington** with Peter Sidorkiewicz for David Jensen, March 12, 1985. Traded to **San Jose** by **Hartford** for Dan Keczmer, October 2, 1991.

EWEN, DEAN

Left wing. Shoots left. 6'2", 225 lbs. Born, St. Albert, Alta., February 28, 1969.
(NY Islanders' 3rd choice, 55th overall, in 1987 Entry Draft).

			Regular Season					Playoffs				
Season	Club	Lea	GP	G	A	TP	PIM	GP	G	A	TP	PIM
1988-89	Spokane	WHL	5	0	0	0	5	....	....	....	....	....
	Seattle	WHL	56	22	30	52	254	....	....	....	....	....
1989-90	Springfield	AHL	34	0	7	7	....	....	....	....	....	....
1990-91	Capital Dist.	AHL				DID NOT PLAY						
1991-92	Capital Dist.	AHL	41	5	8	13	106	....	....	....	....	....

EWEN, TODD

Right wing. Shoots right. 6'2", 220 lbs. Born, Saskatoon, Sask., March 22, 1966.
(Edmonton's 9th choice, 168th overall, in 1984 Entry Draft).

			Regular Season					Playoffs				
Season	Club	Lea	GP	G	A	TP	PIM	GP	G	A	TP	PIM
1982-83	Kamloops	WHL	3	0	0	0	2	2	0	0	0	0
1983-84	N. Westminster	WHL	68	11	13	24	176	7	2	1	3	15
1984-85	N. Westminster	WHL	56	11	20	31	304	10	1	8	9	60
1985-86	N. Westminster	WHL	60	28	24	52	289	....	....	....	....	....
	Maine	AHL	....	....	....	....	....	3	0	0	0	7
1986-87	**St. Louis**	**NHL**	**23**	**2**	**0**	**2**	**84**	**4**	**0**	**0**	**0**	**23**
	Peoria	IHL	16	3	3	6	110	....	....	....	....	....
1987-88	**St. Louis**	**NHL**	**64**	**4**	**2**	**6**	**227**	**6**	**0**	**0**	**0**	**21**
1988-89	**St. Louis**	**NHL**	**34**	**4**	**5**	**9**	**171**	**2**	**0**	**0**	**0**	**21**
1989-90	**St. Louis**	**NHL**	**3**	**0**	**0**	**0**	**11**	....	....	....	....	....
	Peoria	IHL	2	0	0	0	12	....	....	....	....	....
	Montreal	**NHL**	**41**	**4**	**6**	**10**	**158**	**10**	**0**	**0**	**0**	**4**
1990-91	**Montreal**	**NHL**	**28**	**3**	**2**	**5**	**128**	....	....	....	....	....
1991-92	**Montreal**	**NHL**	**46**	**1**	**2**	**3**	**130**	**3**	**0**	**0**	**0**	**18**
	NHL Totals		**239**	**18**	**17**	**35**	**909**	**25**	**0**	**0**	**0**	**87**

Traded to **St. Louis** by **Edmonton** for Shawn Evans, October 15, 1986. Traded to **Montreal** by **St. Louis** for future considerations, December 12, 1989.

FABIAN, SEAN

Defense. Shoots right. 6'1", 200 lbs. Born, Minneapolis, MN, May 11, 1969.
(Vancouver's 4th choice, 87th overall, in 1987 Entry Draft).

			Regular Season					Playoffs				
Season	Club	Lea	GP	G	A	TP	PIM	GP	G	A	TP	PIM
1987-88	U. Minnesota	WCHA	10	0	1	1	11	....	....	....	....	....
1988-89	U. Minnesota	WCHA				DID NOT PLAY						
1989-90	U. Minnesota	WCHA	40	0	10	10	74	....	....	....	....	....
1990-91	U. Minnesota	WCHA	41	0	7	7	23	....	....	....	....	....
1991-92	U. Minnesota	WCHA	32	1	3	4	45	....	....	....	....	....

FAIRCHILD, KELLY

Defense. Shoots left. 5'11", 180 lbs. Born, Hibbing, MN, April 9, 1973.
(Los Angeles' 7th choice, 152nd overall, in 1991 Entry Draft).

			Regular Season					Playoffs				
Season	Club	Lea	GP	G	A	TP	PIM	GP	G	A	TP	PIM
1990-91	Grand Rapids	HS	28	12	17	29	25	....	....	....	....	....
1991-92	U. of Wisconsin	WCHA	37	11	10	21	45	....	....	....	....	....

FALLOON, PAT

Right wing. Shoots right. 5'11", 192 lbs. Born, Foxwarren, Man., September 22, 1972.
(San Jose's 1st choice, 2nd overall, in 1991 Entry Draft).

			Regular Season					Playoffs				
Season	Club	Lea	GP	G	A	TP	PIM	GP	G	A	TP	PIM
1988-89	Spokane	WHL	72	22	56	78	41	....	....	....	....	....
1989-90	Spokane	WHL	71	60	64	124	48	6	5	8	13	4
1990-91abcd	Spokane	WHL	61	64	74	138	33	15	10	14	24	10
1991-92	**San Jose**	**NHL**	**79**	**25**	**34**	**59**	**16**	....	....	....	....	....
	NHL Totals		**79**	**25**	**34**	**59**	**16**	....	....	....	....	....

a WHL West First All-Star Team (1991)
b Canadian Major Junior Most Sportsmanlike Player of the Year (1991)
c Memorial Cup All-Star Team (1991)
d Won Stafford Smythe Memorial Trophy (Memorial Cup MVP) (1991)

FARRELL, BRIAN

Center. Shoots left. 5'11", 182 lbs. Born, West Hartford, CT, April 16, 1972.
(Pittsburgh's 4th choice, 89th overall, in 1990 Entry Draft).

			Regular Season					Playoffs				
Season	Club	Lea	GP	G	A	TP	PIM	GP	G	A	TP	PIM
1990-91	Harvard	ECAC	28	3	8	11	16	....	....	....	....	....
1991-92	Harvard	ECAC	9	5	3	8	6	....	....	....	....	....

FAUST, ANDRE

Center. Shoots left. 6'1", 180 lbs. Born, Joliette, Que., October 7, 1969.
(New Jersey's 8th choice, 173rd overall, in 1989 Entry Draft).

			Regular Season					Playoffs				
Season	Club	Lea	GP	G	A	TP	PIM	GP	G	A	TP	PIM
1988-89	Princeton	ECAC	27	15	24	39	28	....	....	....	....	....
1989-90a	Princeton	ECAC	22	9	28	37	20	....	....	....	....	....
1990-91	Princeton	ECAC	26	15	22	37	51	....	....	....	....	....
1991-92a	Princeton	ECAC	27	14	21	35	38	....	....	....	....	....

a ECAC Second All-Star Team (1990, 1992)

FEATHERSTONE, GLEN

Defense. Shoots left. 6'4", 216 lbs. Born, Toronto, Ont., July 8, 1968.
(St. Louis' 4th choice, 73rd overall, in 1986 Entry Draft).

			Regular Season					Playoffs				
Season	Club	Lea	GP	G	A	TP	PIM	GP	G	A	TP	PIM
1985-86	Windsor	OHL	49	0	6	6	135	14	1	1	2	23
1986-87	Windsor	OHL	47	6	11	17	154	14	2	6	8	19
1987-88	Windsor	OHL	53	7	27	34	201	12	6	9	15	47
1988-89	**St. Louis**	**NHL**	**18**	**0**	**2**	**2**	**22**	**6**	**0**	**0**	**0**	**0**
	Peoria	IHL	37	5	19	24	97	....	....	....	....	....
1989-90	**St. Louis**	**NHL**	**58**	**0**	**12**	**12**	**145**	**12**	**0**	**2**	**2**	**47**
	Peoria	IHL	15	1	4	5	43	....	....	....	....	....
1990-91	**St. Louis**	**NHL**	**68**	**5**	**15**	**20**	**204**	**9**	**0**	**0**	**0**	**31**
1991-92	**Boston**	**NHL**	**7**	**1**	**0**	**1**	**20**	....	....	....	....	....
	NHL Totals		**151**	**6**	**29**	**35**	**391**	**27**	**0**	**2**	**2**	**78**

Signed as a free agent by **Boston**, July 25, 1991.

FEDOROV, SERGEI (FE-duh-rahf)

Center. Shoots left. 6'1", 191 lbs. Born, Pskov, Soviet Union, December 13, 1969.
(Detroit's 4th choice, 74th overall, in 1989 Entry Draft).

			Regular Season					Playoffs				
Season	Club	Lea	GP	G	A	TP	PIM	GP	G	A	TP	PIM
1985-86	CSKA	USSR	15	6	1	7	10	....	....	....	....	....
1986-87	CSKA	USSR	29	6	6	12	12	....	....	....	....	....
1987-88	CSKA	USSR	48	7	9	16	20	....	....	....	....	....
1988-89	CSKA	USSR	44	9	8	17	35	....	....	....	....	....
1989-90	CSKA	USSR	48	19	10	29	22	....	....	....	....	....
1990-91a	**Detroit**	**NHL**	**77**	**31**	**48**	**79**	**66**	**7**	**1**	**5**	**6**	**4**
1991-92	**Detroit**	**NHL**	**80**	**32**	**54**	**86**	**72**	**11**	**5**	**5**	**10**	**8**
	NHL Totals		**157**	**63**	**102**	**165**	**138**	**18**	**6**	**10**	**16**	**12**

a NHL/Upper Deck All-Rookie Team (1991)

Played in NHL All-Star Game (1992)

FEDYK, BRENT (FEH-dihk)

Right wing. Shoots right. 6', 195 lbs. Born, Yorkton, Sask., March 8, 1967.
(Detroit's 1st choice, 8th overall, in 1985 Entry Draft).

			Regular Season					Playoffs				
Season	Club	Lea	GP	G	A	TP	PIM	GP	G	A	TP	PIM
1983-84	Regina	WHL	63	15	28	43	30	23	8	7	15	6
1984-85	Regina	WHL	66	35	35	70	48	8	5	4	9	0
1985-86	Regina	WHL	50	43	34	77	47	5	0	1	1	0
1986-87	Regina	WHL	12	9	6	15	9	....	....	....	....	....
	Seattle	WHL	13	5	11	16	9	....	....	....	....	....
	Portland	WHL	11	5	4	9	6	14	5	6	11	0
1987-88	**Detroit**	**NHL**	**2**	**0**	**1**	**1**	**2**	....	....	....	....	....
	Adirondack	AHL	34	9	11	20	22	5	0	2	2	6
1988-89	**Detroit**	**NHL**	**5**	**2**	**0**	**2**	**0**	....	....	....	....	....
	Adirondack	AHL	66	40	28	68	33	15	7	8	15	23
1989-90	**Detroit**	**NHL**	**27**	**1**	**4**	**5**	**6**	....	....	....	....	....
	Adirondack	AHL	33	14	15	29	24	6	2	1	3	4
1990-91	**Detroit**	**NHL**	**67**	**16**	**19**	**35**	**38**	**6**	**1**	**0**	**1**	**2**
1991-92	**Detroit**	**NHL**	**61**	**5**	**8**	**13**	**42**	**1**	**0**	**0**	**0**	**2**
	Adirondack	AHL	1	0	2	2	0	....	....	....	....	....
	NHL Totals		**162**	**24**	**32**	**56**	**88**	**7**	**1**	**0**	**1**	**4**

FELSNER, DENNY

Left wing. Shoots left. 6', 185 lbs. Born, Warren, MI, April 29, 1970.
(St. Louis' 3rd choice, 55th overall, in 1989 Entry Draft).

			Regular Season					Playoffs				
Season	Club	Lea	GP	G	A	TP	PIM	GP	G	A	TP	PIM
1988-89	U. of Michigan	CCHA	39	30	19	49	22	....	....	....	....	....
1989-90	U. of Michigan	CCHA	33	27	16	43	24	....	....	....	....	....
1990-91ab	U. of Michigan	CCHA	46	*40	35	75	58	....	....	....	....	....
1991-92ac	U. of Michigan	CCHA	44	42	52	94	46	....	....	....	....	....
	St. Louis	**NHL**	**3**	**0**	**1**	**1**	**0**	**1**	**0**	**0**	**0**	**0**
	NHL Totals		**3**	**0**	**1**	**1**	**0**	**1**	**0**	**0**	**0**	**0**

a CCHA First All-Star Team (1991, 1992)
b NCAA West Second All-American Team (1991)
c NCAA West First All-Star Team (1992)

FENTON, ERIC

Center. Shoots right. 6'2", 190 lbs. Born, Troy, NY, July 17, 1969.
(NY Rangers' 10th choice, 202nd overall, in 1988 Entry Draft).

			Regular Season					Playoffs				
Season	Club	Lea	GP	G	A	TP	PIM	GP	G	A	TP	PIM
1989-90	U. of Maine	H.E.	7	2	2	4	2	....	....	....	....	....
1990-91	U. of Maine	H.E.	10	0	1	1	16	....	....	....	....	....

FENTON, PAUL JOHN

Left wing. Shoots left. 5'11", 180 lbs. Born, Springfield, MA, December 22, 1959.

			Regular Season					Playoffs				
Season	Club	Lea	GP	G	A	TP	PIM	GP	G	A	TP	PIM
1979-80	Boston U.	ECAC	24	8	17	25	14	....	....	....	....	....
1980-81	Boston U.	ECAC	5	3	2	5	0	....	....	....	....	....
1981-82	Boston U.	ECAC	28	20	13	33	20	....	....	....	....	....
1982-83a	Peoria	IHL	82	60	51	111	53	....	....	....	....	....
	Colorado	CHL	1	0	1	1	0	3	2	0	2	2
1983-84	Binghamton	AHL	78	41	24	65	67	....	....	....	....	....
1984-85	**Hartford**	**NHL**	**33**	**7**	**5**	**12**	**10**	....	....	....	....	....
	Binghamton	AHL	45	26	21	47	18	....	....	....	....	....
1985-86	**Hartford**	**NHL**	**1**	**0**	**0**	**0**	**0**	....	....	....	....	....
b	Binghamton	AHL	75	53	35	88	87	6	2	0	2	2
1986-87	**NY Rangers**	**NHL**	**8**	**0**	**0**	**0**	**2**	....	....	....	....	....
c	New Haven	AHL	70	37	38	75	45	7	6	4	10	6
1987-88	**Los Angeles**	**NHL**	**71**	**20**	**23**	**43**	**46**	**5**	**2**	**1**	**3**	**2**
	New Haven	AHL	5	11	5	16	9	....	....	....	....	....
1988-89	**Los Angeles**	**NHL**	**21**	**2**	**3**	**5**	**6**	....	....	....	....	....
	Winnipeg	**NHL**	**59**	**14**	**9**	**23**	**33**	....	....	....	....	....
1989-90	**Winnipeg**	**NHL**	**80**	**32**	**18**	**50**	**40**	**7**	**2**	**0**	**2**	**23**
1990-91	**Winnipeg**	**NHL**	**17**	**4**	**4**	**8**	**18**	....	....	....	....	....
	Toronto	**NHL**	**30**	**5**	**10**	**15**	**0**	....	....	....	....	....
	Calgary	**NHL**	**31**	**5**	**7**	**12**	**10**	**5**	**0**	**0**	**0**	**2**
1991-92	**San Jose**	**NHL**	**60**	**11**	**4**	**15**	**33**	....	....	....	....	....
	NHL Totals		**411**	**100**	**83**	**183**	**198**	**17**	**4**	**1**	**5**	**27**

a IHL First All-Star Team (1983)
b AHL First All-Star Team (1986)
c AHL Second All-Star Team (1987)

Signed as a free agent by **Hartford**, October 6, 1983. Claimed by **Los Angeles** in NHL Waiver Draft, October 5, 1987. Traded to **Winnipeg** by **Los Angeles** for Gilles Hamel, November 25, 1988. Traded to **Toronto** by **Winnipeg** with Dave Ellett for Ed Olczyk and Mark Osborne, November 10, 1990. Traded to **Washington** by **Toronto** with John Kordic for Washington's fifth round choice (Alexei Kudashov) in 1991 Entry Draft, January 24, 1991. Traded to **Calgary** by **Washington** for Ken Sabourin, January 24, 1991. Traded to **Hartford** by **Calgary** for future considerations, August 26, 1991. Traded to **San Jose** by **Hartford** for Mike McHugh, October 18, 1991.

FENYVES, DAVID (FEHN-vehs)

Defense. Shoots left. 5'11", 192 lbs. Born, Dunnville, Ont., April 29, 1960.

			Regular Season					Playoffs				
Season	Club	Lea	GP	G	A	TP	PIM	GP	G	A	TP	PIM
1978-79	Peterborough	OHA	66	2	23	25	122	19	0	5	5	18
1979-80a	Peterborough	OHA	66	9	36	45	92	14	0	3	3	14
1980-81	Rochester	AHL	77	6	16	22	146	....	....	....	....	....
1981-82	Rochester	AHL	73	3	14	17	68	5	0	1	1	4
1982-83	**Buffalo**	**NHL**	**24**	**0**	**8**	**8**	**14**	**4**	**0**	**0**	**0**	**0**
	Rochester	AHL	51	2	19	21	45	....	....	....	....	....
1983-84	**Buffalo**	**NHL**	**10**	**0**	**4**	**4**	**9**	**2**	**0**	**0**	**0**	**7**
	Rochester	AHL	70	3	16	19	55	16	1	4	5	22
1984-85	**Buffalo**	**NHL**	**60**	**1**	**8**	**9**	**27**	**5**	**0**	**0**	**0**	**2**
	Rochester	AHL	9	0	3	3	8	....	....	....	....	....
1985-86	**Buffalo**	**NHL**	**47**	**0**	**7**	**7**	**37**	....	....	....	....	....
1986-87	**Buffalo**	**NHL**	**7**	**1**	**0**	**1**	**0**	....	....	....	....	....
bc	Rochester	AHL	71	6	16	22	57	18	3	12	15	10
1987-88	**Philadelphia**	**NHL**	**5**	**0**	**0**	**0**	**0**	....	....	....	....	....
de	Hershey	AHL	75	11	40	51	47	12	1	8	9	10
1988-89	**Philadelphia**	**NHL**	**1**	**0**	**1**	**1**	**0**	....	....	....	....	....
de	Hershey	AHL	79	15	51	66	41	12	2	6	8	6
1989-90	**Philadelphia**	**NHL**	**12**	**0**	**0**	**0**	**4**	....	....	....	....	....
	Hershey	AHL	66	6	37	43	57	....	....	....	....	....
1990-91	**Philadelphia**	**NHL**	**40**	**1**	**4**	**5**	**28**	....	....	....	....	....
	Hershey	AHL	29	4	11	15	13	7	0	3	3	6
1991-92	Hershey	AHL	68	4	24	28	29	6	1	1	2	10
	NHL Totals		**206**	**3**	**32**	**35**	**119**	**11**	**0**	**0**	**0**	**9**

a OHA Second All-Star Team (1980)
b AHL Second All-Star Team (1987)
c Named AHL Playoff MVP (1987)
d AHL First All-Star Team (1988, 1989)
e Won Eddie Shore Plaque (Outstanding Defenseman-AHL) (1988, 1989)

Signed as a free agent by **Buffalo**, October 31, 1979. Claimed by **Philadelphia** in NHL Waiver Draft, October 5, 1987.

FERGUS, THOMAS JOSEPH (TOM)

Center. Shoots left. 6'3", 210 lbs. Born, Chicago, IL, June 16, 1962.
(Boston's 2nd choice, 60th overall, in 1980 Entry Draft).

			Regular Season					Playoffs				
Season	Club	Lea	GP	G	A	TP	PIM	GP	G	A	TP	PIM
1979-80	Peterborough	OHA	63	8	6	14	14	14	1	5	6	6
1980-81	Peterborough	OHA	63	43	45	88	33	5	1	4	5	2
1981-82	**Boston**	**NHL**	**61**	**15**	**24**	**39**	**12**	**6**	**3**	**0**	**3**	**0**
1982-83	**Boston**	**NHL**	**80**	**28**	**35**	**63**	**39**	**15**	**2**	**2**	**4**	**15**
1983-84	**Boston**	**NHL**	**69**	**25**	**36**	**61**	**12**	**3**	**2**	**0**	**2**	**9**
1984-85	**Boston**	**NHL**	**79**	**30**	**43**	**73**	**75**	**5**	**0**	**0**	**0**	**4**
1985-86	**Toronto**	**NHL**	**78**	**31**	**42**	**73**	**64**	**10**	**5**	**7**	**12**	**6**
1986-87	**Toronto**	**NHL**	**57**	**21**	**28**	**49**	**57**	**2**	**0**	**1**	**1**	**2**
	Newmarket	AHL	1	0	1	1	0	....	....	....	....	....
1987-88	**Toronto**	**NHL**	**63**	**19**	**31**	**50**	**81**	**6**	**2**	**3**	**5**	**2**
1988-89	**Toronto**	**NHL**	**80**	**22**	**45**	**67**	**48**	....	....	....	....	....
1989-90	**Toronto**	**NHL**	**54**	**19**	**26**	**45**	**62**	**5**	**2**	**1**	**3**	**4**
1990-91	**Toronto**	**NHL**	**14**	**5**	**4**	**9**	**8**	....	....	....	....	....
1991-92	**Toronto**	**NHL**	**11**	**1**	**3**	**4**	**4**	....	....	....	....	....
	Vancouver	**NHL**	**44**	**14**	**20**	**34**	**17**	**13**	**5**	**3**	**8**	**6**
	NHL Totals		**690**	**230**	**337**	**567**	**479**	**65**	**21**	**17**	**38**	**48**

Traded to **Toronto** by **Boston** for Bill Derlago, October 11, 1985. Traded to **Vancouver** by **Toronto** for cash, December 18, 1991.

FERGUSON, CRAIG

Right wing. Shoots left. 6', 185 lbs. Born, Castro Valley, CA, April 8, 1970.
(Montreal's 7th choice, 146th overall, in 1989 Entry Draft).

			Regular Season					Playoffs				
Season	Club	Lea	GP	G	A	TP	PIM	GP	G	A	TP	PIM
1988-89	Yale	ECAC	24	11	6	17	20	....	....	....	....	....
1989-90	Yale	ECAC	28	6	13	19	36	....	....	....	....	....
1990-91	Yale	ECAC	29	11	10	21	34	....	....	....	....	....
1991-92	Yale	ECAC	27	9	16	25	26	....	....	....	....	....

FERGUSON, JOHN Jr.

Left wing. Shoots left. 6', 192 lbs. Born, Montreal, Que., July 7, 1967.
(Montreal's 15th choice, 247th overall, in 1985 Entry Draft).

			Regular Season					Playoffs				
Season	Club	Lea	GP	G	A	TP	PIM	GP	G	A	TP	PIM
1985-86	Providence	H.E.	18	1	2	3	2	....	....	....	....	....
1986-87	Providence	H.E.	23	0	0	0	6	....	....	....	....	....
1987-88	Providence	H.E.	34	0	5	5	31	....	....	....	....	....
1988-89	Providence	H.E.	40	14	15	29	61	....	....	....	....	....
1989-90	Sherbrooke	AHL	17	4	3	7	8	1	0	0	0	0
	Peoria	IHL	18	1	8	9	14	3	0	0	0	2
1990-91	Fredericton	AHL	73	14	8	22	96	9	3	3	6	21
1991-92	Fredericton	AHL	62	18	21	39	74	5	1	1	2	4

FERNER, MARK

Defense. Shoots left. 6', 193 lbs. Born, Regina, Sask., September 5, 1965.
(Buffalo's 12th choice, 194th overall, in 1983 Entry Draft).

			Regular Season					Playoffs				
Season	Club	Lea	GP	G	A	TP	PIM	GP	G	A	TP	PIM
1982-83	Kamloops	WHL	69	6	15	21	81	7	0	0	0	7
1983-84	Kamloops	WHL	72	9	30	39	169	14	1	8	9	20
1984-85a	Kamloops	WHL	69	15	39	54	91	15	4	9	13	21
1985-86	Rochester	AHL	63	3	14	17	87	....	....	....	....	....
1986-87	**Buffalo**	**NHL**	**13**	**0**	**3**	**3**	**9**	....	....	....	....	....
	Rochester	AHL	54	0	12	12	157	....	....	....	....	....
1987-88	Rochester	AHL	69	1	25	26	165	7	1	4	5	31
1988-89	**Buffalo**	**NHL**	**2**	**0**	**0**	**0**	**2**	....	....	....	....	....
	Rochester	AHL	55	0	18	18	97	....	....	....	....	....
1989-90	**Washington**	**NHL**	**2**	**0**	**0**	**0**	**0**	....	....	....	....	....
	Baltimore	AHL	74	7	28	35	76	11	1	2	3	21
1990-91	**Washington**	**NHL**	**7**	**0**	**1**	**1**	**4**	....	....	....	....	....
b	Baltimore	AHL	61	14	40	54	38	6	1	4	5	24
1991-92	Baltimore	AHL	57	7	38	45	67	....	....	....	....	....
	St. John's	AHL	15	1	8	9	6	14	2	14	16	38
	NHL Totals		**24**	**0**	**4**	**4**	**15**	....	....	....	....	....

a WHL First All-Star Team, West Division (1985)
b AHL Second All-Star Team (1991)

Traded to **Washington** by **Buffalo** for Scott McCrory, June 1, 1989. Traded to **Toronto** by **Washington** for future considerations, February 27, 1992.

FERRARO, CHRIS

Right wing. Shoots right. 5'10", 175 lbs. Born, Port Jefferson, NY, January 24, 1973.
(NY Rangers' 4th choice, 85th overall, in 1992 Entry Draft).

			Regular Season					Playoffs				
Season	Club	Lea	GP	G	A	TP	PIM	GP	G	A	TP	PIM
1990-91	Dubuque	USHL	45	53	44	97	....	....	....	....	....	....
1991-92	Dubuque	USHL	20	30	19	49	52	....	....	....	....	....
	Waterloo	USHL	18	19	31	50	54	....	....	....	....	....

FERRARO, PETER

Center. Shoots right. 5'10", 175 lbs. Born, Port Jefferson, NY, January 24, 1973.
(NY Rangers' 1st choice, 24th overall, in 1992 Entry Draft).

			Regular Season					Playoffs				
Season	Club	Lea	GP	G	A	TP	PIM	GP	G	A	TP	PIM
1990-91	Dubuque	USHL	29	21	31	52	83	....	....	....	....	....
1991-92	Dubuque	USHL	21	25	25	50	92	....	....	....	....	....
	Waterloo	USHL	21	23	28	51	76	....	....	....	....	....

FERRARO, RAY

Center. Shoots left. 5'10", 185 lbs. Born, Trail, B.C., August 23, 1964.
(Hartford's 5th choice, 88th overall, in 1982 Entry Draft).

			Regular Season					Playoffs				
Season	Club	Lea	GP	G	A	TP	PIM	GP	G	A	TP	PIM
1982-83	Portland	WHL	50	41	49	90	39	14	14	10	24	13
1983-84a	Brandon	WHL	72	*108	84	*192	84	11	13	15	28	20
1984-85	**Hartford**	**NHL**	**44**	**11**	**17**	**28**	**40**	....	....	....	....	....
	Binghamton	AHL	37	20	13	33	29	....	....	....	....	....
1985-86	**Hartford**	**NHL**	**76**	**30**	**47**	**77**	**57**	**10**	**3**	**6**	**9**	**4**
1986-87	**Hartford**	**NHL**	**80**	**27**	**32**	**59**	**42**	**6**	**1**	**1**	**2**	**8**
1987-88	**Hartford**	**NHL**	**68**	**21**	**29**	**50**	**81**	**6**	**1**	**1**	**2**	**6**
1988-89	**Hartford**	**NHL**	**80**	**41**	**35**	**76**	**86**	**4**	**2**	**0**	**2**	**4**
1989-90	**Hartford**	**NHL**	**79**	**25**	**29**	**54**	**109**	**7**	**0**	**3**	**3**	**2**
1990-91	**Hartford**	**NHL**	**15**	**2**	**5**	**7**	**18**	....	....	....	....	....
	NY Islanders	**NHL**	**61**	**19**	**16**	**35**	**52**	....	....	....	....	....
1991-92	**NY Islanders**	**NHL**	**80**	**40**	**40**	**80**	**92**	....	....	....	....	....
	NHL Totals		**583**	**216**	**250**	**466**	**577**	**33**	**7**	**11**	**18**	**24**

a WHL First All-Star Team (1984)

Played in NHL All-Star Game (1992)

Traded to **NY Islanders** by **Hartford** for Doug Crossman, November 13, 1990.

FETISOV, VIACHESLAV (SLAVA) (feh-TEE-sahf)

Defense. Shoots left. 6'1", 220 lbs. Born, Moscow, Soviet Union, April 20, 1958.
(New Jersey's 6th choice, 145th overall, in 1983 Entry Draft).

			Regular Season					Playoffs				
Season	Club	Lea	GP	G	A	TP	PIM	GP	G	A	TP	PIM
1974-75	CSKA	USSR	1	0	0	0	0	....	....	....	....	....
1976-77	CSKA	USSR	27	3	4	7	14	....	....	....	....	....
1977-78a	CSKA	USSR	35	9	18	27	46	....	....	....	....	....
1978-79	CSKA	USSR	29	10	19	29	40	....	....	....	....	....
1979-80	CSKA	USSR	37	10	14	24	46	....	....	....	....	....
1980-81	CSKA	USSR	48	13	16	29	44	....	....	....	....	....
1981-82ac	CSKA	USSR	46	15	26	41	20	....	....	....	....	....
1982-83a	CSKA	USSR	43	6	17	23	46	....	....	....	....	....
1983-84ab	CSKA	USSR	44	19	30	49	38	....	....	....	....	....
1984-85a	CSKA	USSR	20	13	12	25	6	....	....	....	....	....
1985-86abc	CSKA	USSR	40	15	19	34	12	....	....	....	....	....
1986-87ab	CSKA	USSR	39	13	20	33	18	....	....	....	....	....
1987-88ab	CSKA	USSR	46	18	17	35	26	....	....	....	....	....
1988-89	CSKA	USSR	23	9	9	18	18	....	....	....	....	....
1989-90	**New Jersey**	**NHL**	**72**	**8**	**34**	**42**	**52**	**6**	**0**	**2**	**2**	**10**
1990-91	**New Jersey**	**NHL**	**67**	**3**	**16**	**19**	**62**	**7**	**0**	**0**	**0**	**15**
	Utica	AHL	1	1	1	2	0	....	....	....	....	....
1991-92	**New Jersey**	**NHL**	**70**	**3**	**23**	**26**	**108**	**6**	**0**	**3**	**3**	**8**
	NHL Totals		**209**	**14**	**73**	**87**	**222**	**19**	**0**	**5**	**5**	**33**

a Soviet National League All-Star Team (1979, 1980, 1982-88)
b Leningradskaya-Pravda Trophy-Top Scoring Defenseman (1984, 1986-88)
c Soviet Player of the Year (1982, 1986, 1988)

FIEDELKORN, JED

Right wing. Shoots right. 6'3", 211 lbs. Born, Minneapolis, MN, September 1, 1972.
(St. Louis' 9th choice, 197th overall, in 1991 Entry Draft).

			Regular Season					Playoffs				
Season	Club	Lea	GP	G	A	TP	PIM	GP	G	A	TP	PIM
1990-91	Osseo	HS	22	21	21	42	32	....	....	....	....	....
1991-92	U. Minnesota	WCHA	7	0	0	0	10	....	....	....	....	....

FILIMONOV, DIMITRI

Defense. Shoots right. 6'4", 207 lbs. Born, Perm, Soviet Union, October 14, 1971.
(Winnipeg's 2nd choice, 49th overall, in 1991 Entry Draft).

			Regular Season					Playoffs				
Season	Club	Lea	GP	G	A	TP	PIM	GP	G	A	TP	PIM
1990-91	Moscow D'amo	USSR	45	4	6	10	12	....	....	....	....	....
1991-92	Moscow D'amo	CIS	38	3	2	5	12	....	....	....	....	....

FILIPEK, DARYL

Defense. Shoots left. 6'1", 185 lbs. Born, Hay River, NWT, November 30, 1970.
(Vancouver's 6th choice, 128th overall, in 1990 Entry Draft).

			Regular Season					Playoffs				
Season	Club	Lea	GP	G	A	TP	PIM	GP	G	A	TP	PIM
1989-90	Ferris State	CCHA	38	4	20	24	44	....	....	....	....	....
1990-91	Ferris State	CCHA	39	6	11	17	68	....	....	....	....	....
1991-92	Ferris State	CCHA	30	4	6	10	28	....	....	....	....	....

FINGERHUT, TIMOTHY

Left wing. Shoots left. 6', 175 lbs. Born, Camden, NJ, May 20, 1971.
(Pittsburgh's 12th choice, 194th overall, in 1990 Entry Draft).

			Regular Season					Playoffs				
Season	Club	Lea	GP	G	A	TP	PIM	GP	G	A	TP	PIM
1990-91	U. of Vermont	ECAC	23	6	7	13	19	....	....	....	....	....
1991-92	U. of Vermont	ECAC	30	9	10	19	14	....	....	....	....	....

FINLEY, JEFF

Defense. Shoots left. 6'2", 204 lbs. Born, Edmonton, Alta., April 14, 1967.
(NY Islanders' 4th choice, 55th overall, in 1985 Entry Draft).

			Regular Season					Playoffs				
Season	Club	Lea	GP	G	A	TP	PIM	GP	G	A	TP	PIM
1983-84	Portland	WHL	5	0	0	0	5	5	0	1	1	4
1984-85	Portland	WHL	69	6	44	50	57	6	1	2	3	2
1985-86	Portland	WHL	70	11	59	70	83	15	1	7	8	16
1986-87	Portland	WHL	72	13	53	66	113	20	1	*21	22	27
1987-88	**NY Islanders**	**NHL**	**10**	**0**	**5**	**5**	**15**	**1**	**0**	**0**	**0**	**2**
	Springfield	AHL	52	5	18	23	50	....	....	....	....	....
1988-89	**NY Islanders**	**NHL**	**4**	**0**	**0**	**0**	**6**	....	....	....	....	....
	Springfield	AHL	65	3	16	19	55	....	....	....	....	....
1989-90	**NY Islanders**	**NHL**	**11**	**0**	**1**	**1**	**0**	**5**	**0**	**2**	**2**	**2**
	Springfield	AHL	57	1	15	16	41	13	1	4	5	23
1990-91	**NY Islanders**	**NHL**	**11**	**0**	**0**	**0**	**4**	....	....	....	....	....
	Capital Dist.	AHL	67	10	34	44	34	....	....	....	....	....
1991-92	**NY Islanders**	**NHL**	**51**	**1**	**10**	**11**	**26**	....	....	....	....	....
	Capital Dist.	AHL	20	1	9	10	6	....	....	....	....	....
	NHL Totals		**87**	**1**	**16**	**17**	**51**	**6**	**0**	**2**	**2**	**4**

FINN, STEVEN

Defense. Shoots left. 6', 198 lbs. Born, Laval, Que., August 20, 1966.
(Quebec's 3rd choice, 57th overall, in 1984 Entry Draft).

			Regular Season					Playoffs				
Season	Club	Lea	GP	G	A	TP	PIM	GP	G	A	TP	PIM
1982-83	Laval	QMJHL	69	7	30	37	108	6	0	2	2	6
1983-84	Laval	QMJHL	68	7	39	46	159	14	1	6	7	27
1984-85a	Laval	QMJHL	61	20	33	53	169	....	....	....	....	....
	Fredericton	AHL	4	0	0	0	14	6	1	1	2	4
1985-86	**Quebec**	**NHL**	**17**	**0**	**1**	**1**	**28**	....	....	....	....	....
	Laval	QMJHL	29	4	15	19	111	14	6	16	22	57
1986-87	**Quebec**	**NHL**	**36**	**2**	**5**	**7**	**40**	**13**	**0**	**2**	**2**	**29**
	Fredericton	AHL	38	7	19	26	73	....	....	....	....	....
1987-88	**Quebec**	**NHL**	**75**	**3**	**7**	**10**	**198**	....	....	....	....	....
1988-89	**Quebec**	**NHL**	**77**	**2**	**6**	**8**	**235**	....	....	....	....	....
1989-90	**Quebec**	**NHL**	**64**	**3**	**9**	**12**	**208**	....	....	....	....	....
1990-91	**Quebec**	**NHL**	**71**	**6**	**13**	**19**	**228**	....	....	....	....	....
1991-92	**Quebec**	**NHL**	**65**	**4**	**7**	**11**	**194**	....	....	....	....	....
	NHL Totals		**405**	**20**	**48**	**68**	**1131**	**13**	**0**	**2**	**2**	**29**

a QMJHL Second All-Star Team (1985)

FIORENTINO, PETER

Defense. Shoots right. 6'1", 200 lbs. Born, Niagara Falls, Ont., December 22, 1968.
(NY Rangers' 11th choice, 215th overall, in 1988 Entry Draft).

			Regular Season					Playoffs				
Season	Club	Lea	GP	G	A	TP	PIM	GP	G	A	TP	PIM
1985-86	S.S. Marie	OHL	58	1	6	7	87	....	....	....	....	....
1986-87	S.S. Marie	OHL	64	1	12	13	187	....	....	....	....	....
1987-88	S.S. Marie	OHL	65	5	27	32	252	6	2	2	4	21
1988-89	S.S. Marie	OHL	55	5	24	29	220	....	....	....	....	....
	Denver	IHL	10	0	0	0	39	4	0	0	0	24
1989-90	Flint	IHL	64	2	7	9	302	....	....	....	....	....
1990-91	Binghamton	AHL	55	2	11	13	361	1	0	0	0	0
1991-92	**NY Rangers**	**NHL**	**1**	**0**	**0**	**0**	**0**	....	....	....	....	....
	Binghamton	AHL	70	2	11	13	340	5	0	1	1	24
	NHL Totals		**1**	**0**	**0**	**0**	**0**	....	....	....	....	....

FIRTH, JASON

Center. Shoots left. 5'11", 175 lbs. Born, Dartmouth, N.S., March 29, 1971.
(Detroit's 8th choice, 208th overall, in 1991 Entry Draft).

			Regular Season					Playoffs				
Season	Club	Lea	GP	G	A	TP	PIM	GP	G	A	TP	PIM
1990-91	Kitchener	OHL	62	41	70	111	27	6	5	7	12	2
1991-92	North Bay	OHL	53	25	72	97	22	21	10	15	25	29

FISHER, CRAIG

Center. Shoots left. 6'3", 180 lbs. Born, Oshawa, Ont., June 30, 1970.
(Philadelphia's 3rd choice, 56th overall, in 1988 Entry Draft).

			Regular Season					Playoffs				
Season	Club	Lea	GP	G	A	TP	PIM	GP	G	A	TP	PIM
1988-89	Miami-Ohio	CCHA	37	22	20	42	37	....	....	....	....	....
1989-90a	Miami-Ohio	CCHA	39	37	29	66	38	....	....	....	....	....
	Philadelphia	**NHL**	**2**	**0**	**0**	**0**	**0**	....	....	....	....	....
1990-91	**Philadelphia**	**NHL**	**2**	**0**	**0**	**0**	**0**	....	....	....	....	....
	Hershey	AHL	77	43	36	79	46	7	5	3	8	2
1991-92	Cape Breton	AHL	60	20	25	45	28	1	0	0	0	0
	NHL Totals		**4**	**0**	**0**	**0**	**0**	....	....	....	....	....

a CCHA First All-Star Team (1990)

Traded to **Edmonton** by **Philadelphia** with Scott Mellanby and Craig Berube for Dave Brown, Corey Foster and Jari Kurri, May 30, 1991.

FITZGERALD, RUSTY

Center. Shoots left. 6'1", 186 lbs. Born, Minneapolis, MN, October 4, 1972.
(Pittsburgh's 2nd choice, 38th overall, in 1991 Entry Draft).

			Regular Season					Playoffs				
Season	Club	Lea	GP	G	A	TP	PIM	GP	G	A	TP	PIM
1990-91	Silverbay	HS	21	25	27	52	24	....	....	....	....	....
1991-92	Minn.-Duluth	WCHA	37	9	11	20	40	....	....	....	....	....

FITZGERALD, TOM

Right wing/Center. Shoots right. 6'1", 195 lbs. Born, Melrose, MA, August 28, 1968.
(NY Islanders' 1st choice, 17th overall, in 1986 Entry Draft).

			Regular Season					Playoffs				
Season	Club	Lea	GP	G	A	TP	PIM	GP	G	A	TP	PIM
1986-87	Providence	H.E.	27	8	14	22	22	....	....	....	....	....
1987-88	Providence	H.E.	36	19	15	34	50	....	....	....	....	....
1988-89	**NY Islanders**	**NHL**	**23**	**3**	**5**	**8**	**10**	....	....	....	....	....
	Springfield	AHL	61	24	18	42	43	....	....	....	....	....
1989-90	**NY Islanders**	**NHL**	**19**	**2**	**5**	**7**	**4**	**4**	**1**	**0**	**1**	**4**
	Springfield	AHL	53	30	23	53	32	14	2	9	11	13
1990-91	**NY Islanders**	**NHL**	**41**	**5**	**5**	**10**	**24**	....	....	....	....	....
	Capital Dist.	AHL	27	7	7	14	50	....	....	....	....	....
1991-92	**NY Islanders**	**NHL**	**45**	**6**	**11**	**17**	**28**	....	....	....	....	....
	Capital Dist.	AHL	4	1	1	2	4	....	....	....	....	....
	NHL Totals		**128**	**16**	**26**	**42**	**66**	**4**	**1**	**0**	**1**	**4**

FLANAGAN, JOSEPH

Center. Shoots right. 6', 180 lbs. Born, Arlington, MA, March 5, 1969.
(Los Angeles' 13th choice, 238th overall, in 1988 Entry Draft).

			Regular Season					Playoffs				
Season	Club	Lea	GP	G	A	TP	PIM	GP	G	A	TP	PIM
1988-89	N. Hampshire	H.E.	23	11	34	45	4	....	....	....	....	....
1989-90	N. Hampshire	H.E.	34	12	24	36	6	....	....	....	....	....
1990-91	N. Hampshire	H.E.	35	24	20	44	18	....	....	....	....	....
1991-92	N. Hampshire	H.E.	37	26	34	60	12	....	....	....	....	....

FLANAGAN, PAUL

Defense. Shoots left. 6', 190 lbs. Born, Acton, MA, May 17, 1969.
(Buffalo's 7th choice, 127th overall, in 1987 Entry Draft).

			Regular Season					Playoffs				
Season	Club	Lea	GP	G	A	TP	PIM	GP	G	A	TP	PIM
1990-91	Northeastern	H.E.	34	1	7	8	58	....	....	....	....	....
1991-92	Northeastern	H.E.	30	4	5	9	48	....	....	....	....	....

FLATLEY, PATRICK (FLAT-lee)

Right wing. Shoots right. 6'2", 197 lbs. Born, Toronto, Ont., October 3, 1963.
(NY Islanders' 1st choice, 21st overall, in 1982 Entry Draft).

			Regular Season					Playoffs				
Season	Club	Lea	GP	G	A	TP	PIM	GP	G	A	TP	PIM
1981-82	U. Wisconsin	WCHA	17	10	9	19	40	....	....	....	....	....
1982-83ab	U. Wisconsin	WCHA	26	17	24	41	48	....	....	....	....	....
1983-84	Cdn. Olympic	....	57	33	17	50	136	....	....	....	....	....
	NY Islanders	**NHL**	**16**	**2**	**7**	**9**	**6**	**21**	**9**	**6**	**15**	**14**
1984-85	**NY Islanders**	**NHL**	**78**	**20**	**31**	**51**	**106**	**4**	**1**	**0**	**1**	**6**
1985-86	**NY Islanders**	**NHL**	**73**	**18**	**34**	**52**	**66**	**3**	**0**	**0**	**0**	**21**
1986-87	**NY Islanders**	**NHL**	**63**	**16**	**35**	**51**	**81**	**11**	**3**	**2**	**5**	**6**
1987-88	**NY Islanders**	**NHL**	**40**	**9**	**15**	**24**	**28**	....	....	....	....	....
1988-89	**NY Islanders**	**NHL**	**41**	**10**	**15**	**25**	**31**	....	....	....	....	....
	Springfield	AHL	2	1	1	2	2	....	....	....	....	....
1989-90	**NY Islanders**	**NHL**	**62**	**17**	**32**	**49**	**101**	**5**	**3**	**0**	**3**	**2**
1990-91	**NY Islanders**	**NHL**	**56**	**20**	**25**	**45**	**74**	....	....	....	....	....
1991-92	**NY Islanders**	**NHL**	**38**	**8**	**28**	**36**	**31**	....	....	....	....	....
	NHL Totals		**467**	**120**	**222**	**342**	**524**	**44**	**16**	**8**	**24**	**49**

a WCHA First All-Star Team (1983)
b Named to NCAA All-Tournament Team (1983)

FLEETWOOD, BRENT

Left wing. Shoots left. 6'1", 180 lbs. Born, Edmonton, Alta., June 4, 1970.
(Montreal's 9th choice, 165th overall, in 1990 Entry Draft).

			Regular Season					Playoffs				
Season	Club	Lea	GP	G	A	TP	PIM	GP	G	A	TP	PIM
1987-88	Portland	WHL	28	7	6	13	20	....	....	....	....	....
1988-89	Portland	WHL	70	20	31	51	87	19	5	2	7	22
1989-90	Portland	WHL	72	41	43	84	114	....	....	....	....	....
1990-91	Fredericton	AHL	5	0	1	1	2	....	....	....	....	....
	Winston-Salem	ECHL	61	28	32	60	75	....	....	....	....	....
1991-92	Winston-Salem	ECHL	56	27	32	59	73	4	0	0	0	7
	Fredericton	AHL	3	0	0	0	0	....	....	....	....	....

FLEURY, SYLVAIN

Left wing. Shoots left. 5'11", 189 lbs. Born, Drummondville, Que., April 30, 1970.
(NY Islanders' 7th choice, 153rd overall, in 1990 Entry Draft).

			Regular Season					Playoffs				
Season	Club	Lea	GP	G	A	TP	PIM	GP	G	A	TP	PIM
1989-90	Longueuil	QMJHL	70	50	74	124	26	....	....	....	....	....
1990-91	Longueuil	QMJHL	68	36	61	97	29	8	7	6	13	2
1991-92	Dayton	ECHL	59	27	30	57	13	3	3	0	3	2

FLEURY, THEOREN

Center/Right wing. Shoots right. 5'6", 160 lbs. Born, Oxbow, Sask., June 29, 1968.
(Calgary's 9th choice, 166th overall, in 1987 Entry Draft).

			Regular Season					Playoffs				
Season	Club	Lea	GP	G	A	TP	PIM	GP	G	A	TP	PIM
1984-85	Moose Jaw	WHL	71	29	46	75	82	....	....	....	....	....
1985-86	Moose Jaw	WHL	72	43	65	108	124	....	....	....	....	....
1986-87	Moose Jaw	WHL	66	61	68	129	110	9	7	9	16	34
1987-88	Moose Jaw	WHL	65	68	92	*160	235	....	....	....	....	....
	Salt Lake	IHL	2	3	4	7	7	8	11	5	16	16
1988-89	**Calgary**	**NHL**	**36**	**14**	**20**	**34**	**46**	**22**	**5**	**6**	**11**	**24**
	Salt Lake	IHL	40	37	37	74	81	....	....	....	....	....
1989-90	**Calgary**	**NHL**	**80**	**31**	**35**	**66**	**157**	**6**	**2**	**3**	**5**	**10**
1990-91a	**Calgary**	**NHL**	**79**	**51**	**53**	**104**	**136**	**7**	**2**	**5**	**7**	**14**
1991-92	**Calgary**	**NHL**	**80**	**33**	**40**	**73**	**133**	....	....	....	....	....
	NHL Totals		**275**	**129**	**148**	**277**	**472**	**35**	**9**	**14**	**23**	**48**

a Co-winner of Alka-Seltzer Plus Award with Marty McSorley (1991)
Played in NHL All-Star Game (1991, 1992)

FLOMENHOFT, STEVE

Center. Shoots right. 6', 215 lbs. Born, Riverwoods, IL, May 4, 1971.
(Ottawa's 1st choice, 2nd overall, in 1992 Supplemental Draft).

			Regular Season					Playoffs				
Season	Club	Lea	GP	G	A	TP	PIM	GP	G	A	TP	PIM
1989-90	Harvard	ECAC	28	5	5	10	22	....	....	....	....	....
1990-91	Harvard	ECAC	29	12	14	26	48	....	....	....	....	....
1991-92	Harvard	ECAC	27	14	17	31	30	....	....	....	....	....

FOGARTY, BRYAN

Defense. Shoots left. 6'2", 198 lbs. Born, Brantford, Ont., June 11, 1969.
(Quebec's 1st choice, 9th overall, in 1987 Entry Draft).

			Regular Season					Playoffs				
Season	Club	Lea	GP	G	A	TP	PIM	GP	G	A	TP	PIM
1985-86	Kingston	OHL	47	2	19	21	14	10	1	3	4	4
1986-87a	Kingston	OHL	56	20	50	70	46	12	2	3	5	5
1987-88	Kingston	OHL	48	11	36	47	50	....	....	....	....	....
1988-89abc	Niagara Falls	OHL	60	47	*108	*155	88	17	10	22	32	36
1989-90	**Quebec**	**NHL**	**45**	**4**	**10**	**14**	**31**	....	....	....	....	....
	Halifax	AHL	22	5	14	19	6	6	2	4	6	0
1990-91	**Quebec**	**NHL**	**45**	**9**	**22**	**31**	**24**	....	....	....	....	....
	Halifax	AHL	5	0	2	2	0	....	....	....	....	....
1991-92	**Quebec**	**NHL**	**20**	**3**	**12**	**15**	**16**	....	....	....	....	....
	Halifax	AHL	2	0	0	0	2	....	....	....	....	....
	New Haven	AHL	4	0	1	1	6	....	....	....	....	....
	Muskegon	IHL	8	2	4	6	30	....	....	....	....	....
	NHL Totals		**110**	**16**	**44**	**60**	**71**	....	....	....	....	....

a OHL First All-Star Team (1987, 1989)
b OHL Player of the Year (1989)
c Canadian Major Junior Player of the Year (1989)
Traded to **Pittsburgh** by **Quebec** for Scott Young, March 10, 1992.

FOLIGNO, MIKE ANTHONY (foh-LEE-noh)

Right wing. Shoots right. 6'2", 195 lbs. Born, Sudbury, Ont., January 29, 1959.
(Detroit's 1st choice, 3rd overall, in 1979 Entry Draft).

			Regular Season					Playoffs				
Season	Club	Lea	GP	G	A	TP	PIM	GP	G	A	TP	PIM
1975-76	Sudbury	OHA	57	22	14	36	45	....	....	....	....	....
1976-77	Sudbury	OHA	66	31	44	75	62	....	....	....	....	....
1977-78	Sudbury	OHA	67	47	39	86	112	....	....	....	....	....
1978-79a	Sudbury	OHA	68	65	85	*150	98	10	5	5	10	14
1979-80	**Detroit**	**NHL**	**80**	**36**	**35**	**71**	**109**	....	....	....	....	....
1980-81	**Detroit**	**NHL**	**80**	**28**	**35**	**63**	**210**	....	....	....	....	....
1981-82	**Detroit**	**NHL**	**26**	**13**	**13**	**26**	**28**	....	....	....	....	....
	Buffalo	**NHL**	**56**	**20**	**31**	**51**	**149**	**4**	**2**	**0**	**2**	**9**
1982-83	**Buffalo**	**NHL**	**66**	**22**	**25**	**47**	**135**	**10**	**2**	**3**	**5**	**39**
1983-84	**Buffalo**	**NHL**	**70**	**32**	**31**	**63**	**151**	**3**	**2**	**1**	**3**	**19**
1984-85	**Buffalo**	**NHL**	**77**	**27**	**29**	**56**	**154**	**5**	**1**	**3**	**4**	**12**
1985-86	**Buffalo**	**NHL**	**79**	**41**	**39**	**80**	**168**	....	....	....	....	....
1986-87	**Buffalo**	**NHL**	**75**	**30**	**29**	**59**	**176**	....	....	....	....	....
1987-88	**Buffalo**	**NHL**	**74**	**29**	**28**	**57**	**220**	**6**	**3**	**2**	**5**	**31**
1988-89	**Buffalo**	**NHL**	**75**	**27**	**22**	**49**	**156**	**5**	**3**	**1**	**4**	**21**
1989-90	**Buffalo**	**NHL**	**61**	**15**	**25**	**40**	**99**	**6**	**0**	**1**	**1**	**12**
1990-91	**Buffalo**	**NHL**	**31**	**4**	**5**	**9**	**42**	....	....	....	....	....
	Toronto	**NHL**	**37**	**8**	**7**	**15**	**65**	....	....	....	....	....
1991-92	**Toronto**	**NHL**	**33**	**6**	**8**	**14**	**50**	....	....	....	....	....
	NHL Totals		**920**	**338**	**362**	**700**	**1912**	**39**	**13**	**11**	**24**	**143**

a OHL First All-Star Team (1979)
Traded to **Buffalo** by **Detroit** with Dale McCourt and Brent Peterson for Danny Gare, Jim Schoenfeld and Derek Smith, December 2, 1981. Traded to **Toronto** by **Buffalo** with Buffalo's eighth round choice (Thomas Kucharcik) in 1991 Entry Draft for Brian Curran and Lou Franceschetti, December 17, 1990.

FOOTE, ADAM

Defense. Shoots right. 6'1", 180 lbs. Born, Toronto, Ont., July 10, 1971.
(Quebec's 2nd choice, 22nd overall, in 1989 Entry Draft).

			Regular Season					Playoffs				
Season	Club	Lea	GP	G	A	TP	PIM	GP	G	A	TP	PIM
1988-89	S.S. Marie	OHL	66	7	32	39	120	....	....	....	....	....
1989-90	S.S. Marie	OHL	61	12	43	55	199	....	....	....	....	....
1990-91a	S.S. Marie	OHL	59	18	51	69	93	14	5	12	17	28
1991-92	**Quebec**	**NHL**	**46**	**2**	**5**	**7**	**44**	....	....	....	....	....
	Halifax	AHL	6	0	1	1	2	....	....	....	....	....
	NHL Totals		**46**	**2**	**5**	**7**	**44**	....	....	....	....	....

a OHL First All-Star Team (1991)

FORSBERG, PETER

Center. Shoots left. 5'11", 190 lbs. Born, Ornskoldsvik, Sweden, July 20, 1973.
(Philadelphia's 1st choice, 6th overall, in 1991 Entry Draft).

			Regular Season					Playoffs				
Season	Club	Lea	GP	G	A	TP	PIM	GP	G	A	TP	PIM
1989-90	MoDo	Swe. Jr.	30	15	12	27	42	....	....	....	....	....
1990-91	MoDo	Swe.	23	7	10	14	22	....	....	....	....	....
1991-92	MoDo	Swe.	39	9	19	28	78	....	....	....	....	....

Traded to **Quebec** by **Philadelphia** with Steve Duchesne, Kerry Huffman, Mike Ricci, Ron Hextall, Chris Simon, Philadelphia's first choice in the 1993 and 1994 Entry Drafts and cash for Eric Lindros, June 30, 1992.

FORSLUND, TOMAS (FOHRS-luhnd)

Right wing. Shoots left. 5'11", 200 lbs. Born, Falun, Sweden, November 24, 1968.
(Calgary's 4th choice, 85th overall, in 1988 Entry Draft).

			Regular Season					Playoffs				
Season	Club	Lea	GP	G	A	TP	PIM	GP	G	A	TP	PIM
1986-87	Leksand	Swe.	23	3	5	8	....	....	....	....	....	....
1987-88	Leksand	Swe.	37	9	10	19	....	....	....	....	....	....
1988-89	Leksand	Swe.	39	14	16	30	56	....	....	....	....	....
1989-90	Leksand	Swe.	38	14	21	35	48	3	0	1	1	2
1990-91	Leksand	Swe.2	23	5	10	15	10	....	....	....	....	....
1991-92	**Calgary**	**NHL**	**38**	**5**	**9**	**14**	**12**	....	....	....	....	....
	Salt Lake	IHL	22	10	6	16	25	5	2	2	4	2
	NHL Totals		**38**	**5**	**9**	**14**	**12**	....	....	....	....	....

FORTIER, MARC

Center. Shoots right. 6', 192 lbs. Born, Windsor, Que., February 26, 1966.

			Regular Season					Playoffs				
Season	Club	Lea	GP	G	A	TP	PIM	GP	G	A	TP	PIM
1983-84	Chicoutimi	QMJHL	67	16	30	46	51	....	....	....	....	....
1984-85	Chicoutimi	QMJHL	68	35	63	98	114	14	8	4	12	16
1985-86	Chicoutimi	QMJHL	71	47	86	133	49	9	2	14	16	12
1986-87	Chicoutimi	QMJHL	65	66	135	201	39	19	11	40	51	20
1987-88	**Quebec**	**NHL**	**27**	**4**	**10**	**14**	**12**	....	....	....	....	....
	Fredericton	AHL	50	26	36	62	48	....	....	....	....	....
1988-89	**Quebec**	**NHL**	**57**	**20**	**19**	**39**	**45**	....	....	....	....	....
	Halifax	AHL	16	11	11	22	14	....	....	....	....	....
1989-90	**Quebec**	**NHL**	**59**	**13**	**17**	**30**	**28**	....	....	....	....	....
	Halifax	AHL	15	5	6	11	6	....	....	....	....	....
1990-91	**Quebec**	**NHL**	**14**	**0**	**4**	**4**	**6**	....	....	....	....	....
	Halifax	AHL	58	24	32	56	85	....	....	....	....	....
1991-92	**Quebec**	**NHL**	**39**	**5**	**9**	**14**	**33**	....	....	....	....	....
	Halifax	AHL	16	9	16	25	44	....	....	....	....	....
	NHL Totals		**196**	**42**	**59**	**101**	**124**	....	....	....	....	....

Signed as a free agent by **Quebec**, February 3, 1987.

FOSTER, COREY

Defense. Shoots left. 6'3", 204 lbs. Born, Ottawa, Ont., October 27, 1969.
(New Jersey's 1st choice, 12th overall, in 1988 Entry Draft).

			Regular Season					Playoffs				
Season	Club	Lea	GP	G	A	TP	PIM	GP	G	A	TP	PIM
1986-87	Peterborough	OHL	30	3	4	7	4	1	0	0	0	0
1987-88	Peterborough	OHL	66	13	31	44	58	11	5	9	14	13
1988-89	**New Jersey**	**NHL**	**2**	**0**	**0**	**0**	**0**	....	....	....	....	....
a	Peterborough	OHL	55	14	42	56	42	17	1	17	18	12
1989-90	Cape Breton	AHL	54	7	17	24	32	1	0	0	0	0
1990-91	Cape Breton	AHL	67	14	11	25	51	4	2	4	6	4
1991-92	**Philadelphia**	**NHL**	**25**	**3**	**4**	**7**	**20**	....	....	....	....	....
	Hershey	AHL	19	5	9	14	26	6	1	1	2	5
	NHL Totals		**27**	**3**	**4**	**7**	**20**	....	....	....	....	....

a OHL Third All-Star Team (1989)

Traded to **Edmonton** by **New Jersey** for Edmonton's first round choice (Jason Miller) in 1989 Entry Draft, June 17, 1989. Traded to **Philadelphia** by **Edmonton** with Dave Brown and Jari Kurri for Craig Fisher, Scott Mellanby and Craig Berube, May 30, 1991.

FOSTER, STEPHEN

Defense. Shoots right. 6'3", 210 lbs. Born, Brockton, MA, March 21, 1971.
(Boston's 6th choice, 122nd overall, in 1989 Entry Draft).

			Regular Season					Playoffs				
Season	Club	Lea	GP	G	A	TP	PIM	GP	G	A	TP	PIM
1989-90	Boston U.	H.E.	28	0	8	8	26	....	....	....	....	....
1990-91	Boston U.	H.E.			DID NOT PLAY							
1991-92	Boston U.	H.E.	12	0	4	4	12	....	....	....	....	....

FOY, CHRIS

Defense. Shoots left. 6', 190 lbs. Born, Toronto, Ont., September 16, 1970.
(NY Islanders' 1st choice, 8th overall, in 1992 Supplemental Draft).

			Regular Season					Playoffs				
Season	Club	Lea	GP	G	A	TP	PIM	GP	G	A	TP	PIM
1990-91	Northeastern	H.E.	33	0	3	3	20	....	....	....	....	....
1991-92	Northeastern	H.E.	33	8	11	19	45	....	....	....	....	....

FRANCESCHETTI, LOU (FRAN-sihs-KEH-tee)

Right wing. Shoots left. 6', 200 lbs. Born, Toronto, Ont., March 28, 1958.
(Washington's 8th choice, 71st overall, in 1978 Amateur Draft).

			Regular Season					Playoffs				
Season	Club	Lea	GP	G	A	TP	PIM	GP	G	A	TP	PIM
1976-77	Niagara Falls	OHA	61	23	30	53	80	....	....	....	....	....
1977-78	Niagara Falls	OHA	62	40	50	90	46	....	....	....	....	....
1978-79	Saginaw	IHL	2	1	1	2	0	....	....	....	....	....
	Port Huron	IHL	76	45	58	103	131	....	....	....	....	....
1979-80	Port Huron	IHL	15	3	8	11	31	....	....	....	....	....
	Hershey	AHL	65	27	29	56	58	14	6	9	15	32
1980-81	Hershey	AHL	79	32	36	68	173	10	3	7	10	30
1981-82	Hershey	AHL	50	22	33	55	89	....	....	....	....	....
	Washington	**NHL**	**30**	**2**	**10**	**12**	**23**	....	....	....	....	....
1982-83	Hershey	AHL	80	31	44	75	176	5	1	2	3	16
1983-84	**Washington**	**NHL**	**2**	**0**	**0**	**0**	**0**	**3**	**0**	**0**	**0**	**8**
	Hershey	AHL	73	26	34	60	130	....	....	....	....	....
1984-85	**Washington**	**NHL**	**22**	**4**	**7**	**11**	**45**	**5**	**1**	**1**	**2**	**15**
	Binghamton	AHL	52	29	43	72	75	....	....	....	....	....
1985-86	**Washington**	**NHL**	**76**	**7**	**14**	**21**	**131**	**8**	**0**	**0**	**0**	**15**
1986-87	**Washington**	**NHL**	**75**	**12**	**9**	**21**	**127**	**7**	**0**	**0**	**0**	**23**
1987-88	**Washington**	**NHL**	**59**	**4**	**8**	**12**	**113**	**4**	**0**	**0**	**0**	**14**
	Binghamton	AHL	6	2	4	6	4	....	....	....	....	....
1988-89	**Washington**	**NHL**	**63**	**7**	**10**	**17**	**123**	**6**	**1**	**0**	**1**	**8**
	Baltimore	AHL	10	8	7	15	30	....	....	....	....	....
1989-90	**Toronto**	**NHL**	**80**	**21**	**15**	**36**	**127**	**5**	**0**	**1**	**1**	**26**
1990-91	**Toronto**	**NHL**	**16**	**1**	**1**	**2**	**30**	....	....	....	....	....
	Buffalo	**NHL**	**35**	**1**	**7**	**8**	**28**	**6**	**1**	**0**	**1**	**2**
1991-92	**Buffalo**	**NHL**	**1**	**0**	**0**	**0**	**0**	....	....	....	....	....
	New Haven	AHL	25	6	7	13	59	....	....	....	....	....
	Rochester	AHL	49	15	25	40	64	15	3	5	8	31
	NHL Totals		**459**	**59**	**81**	**140**	**747**	**44**	**3**	**2**	**5**	**111**

Traded to **Toronto** by **Washington** for Toronto's fifth round choice (Mark Ouimet) in 1990 Entry Draft, June 29, 1989. Traded to **Buffalo** by **Toronto** with Brian Curran for Mike Foligno and Buffalo's eighth round choice (Thomas Kucharcik) in 1991 Entry Draft, December 17, 1990.

FRANCIS, RONALD (RON)

Center. Shoots left. 6'2", 200 lbs. Born, Sault Ste. Marie, Ont., March 1, 1963.
(Hartford's 1st choice, 4th overall, in 1981 Entry Draft).

			Regular Season					Playoffs				
Season	Club	Lea	GP	G	A	TP	PIM	GP	G	A	TP	PIM
1980-81	S.S. Marie	OHA	64	26	43	69	33	19	7	8	15	34
1981-82	**Hartford**	**NHL**	**59**	**25**	**43**	**68**	**51**	....	....	....	....	....
	S.S. Marie	OHL	25	18	30	48	46	....	....	....	....	....
1982-83	**Hartford**	**NHL**	**79**	**31**	**59**	**90**	**60**	....	....	....	....	....
1983-84	**Hartford**	**NHL**	**72**	**23**	**60**	**83**	**45**	....	....	....	....	....
1984-85	**Hartford**	**NHL**	**80**	**24**	**57**	**81**	**66**	....	....	....	....	....
1985-86	**Hartford**	**NHL**	**53**	**24**	**53**	**77**	**24**	**10**	**1**	**2**	**3**	**4**
1986-87	**Hartford**	**NHL**	**75**	**30**	**63**	**93**	**45**	**6**	**2**	**2**	**4**	**6**
1987-88	**Hartford**	**NHL**	**80**	**25**	**50**	**75**	**87**	**6**	**2**	**5**	**7**	**2**
1988-89	**Hartford**	**NHL**	**69**	**29**	**48**	**77**	**36**	**4**	**0**	**2**	**2**	**0**
1989-90	**Hartford**	**NHL**	**80**	**32**	**69**	**101**	**73**	**7**	**3**	**3**	**6**	**8**
1990-91	**Hartford**	**NHL**	**67**	**21**	**55**	**76**	**51**	....	....	....	....	....
	Pittsburgh	**NHL**	**14**	**2**	**9**	**11**	**21**	**24**	**7**	**10**	**17**	**24**
1991-92	**Pittsburgh**	**NHL**	**70**	**21**	**33**	**54**	**30**	**21**	**8**	***19**	**27**	**6**
	NHL Totals		**798**	**287**	**599**	**886**	**589**	**78**	**23**	**43**	**66**	**50**

Played in NHL All-Star Game (1983, 1985, 1990)

Traded to **Pittsburgh** by **Hartford** with Grant Jennings and Ulf Samuelsson for John Cullen, Jeff Parker and Zarley Zalapski, March 4, 1991.

FRANTTI, GORDON

Center. Shoots left. 6'6", 228 lbs. Born, Laurium, MI, July 17, 1970.
(Philadelphia's 7th choice, 119th overall, in 1988 Entry Draft).

			Regular Season					Playoffs				
Season	Club	Lea	GP	G	A	TP	PIM	GP	G	A	TP	PIM
1989-90	W. Michigan	CCHA	30	7	4	11	16	....	....	....	....	....
1990-91	W. Michigan	CCHA	3	0	1	1	7	....	....	....	....	....
	Tri-Cities	WHL	48	20	21	41	86	7	3	2	5	8
1991-92	Kansas City	IHL	55	17	15	32	40	2	0	0	0	0

FRANZOSA, DAVID

Left wing. Shoots left. 5'11", 175 lbs. Born, Reading, MA, November 20, 1970.
(Boston's 11th choice, 227th overall, in 1989 Entry Draft).

			Regular Season					Playoffs				
Season	Club	Lea	GP	G	A	TP	PIM	GP	G	A	TP	PIM
1988-89	Boston College	H.E.	16	2	1	3	0	....	....	....	....	....
1989-90	Boston College	H.E.	42	8	20	28	20	....	....	....	....	....
1990-91	Boston College	H.E.	39	14	19	33	14	....	....	....	....	....
1991-92	Boston College	H.E.	35	18	35	53	38	....	....	....	....	....

FRASER, IAIN

Center. Shoots left. 5'10", 175 lbs. Born, Scarborough, Ont., August 10, 1969.
(NY Islanders' 12th choice, 233rd overall, in 1989 Entry Draft).

			Regular Season					Playoffs				
Season	Club	Lea	GP	G	A	TP	PIM	GP	G	A	TP	PIM
1986-87	Oshawa	OHL	5	1	2	3	0	....	....	....	....	....
1987-88	Oshawa	OHL	16	4	4	8	22	6	2	3	5	2
1988-89	Oshawa	OHL	62	33	57	90	87	6	2	8	10	12
1989-90a	Oshawa	OHL	56	40	65	105	75	17	10	*22	32	8
1990-91	Capital Dist.	AHL	32	5	13	18	16	....	....	....	....	....
	Richmond	ECHL	3	1	1	2	0	....	....	....	....	....
1991-92	Capital Dist.	AHL	45	9	11	20	24	....	....	....	....	....

a Memorial Cup All-Star Team, Tournament MVP (1990)

FRASER, SCOTT

Center. Shoots right. 6'1", 178 lbs. Born, Moncton, N.B., May 3, 1972.
(Montreal's 9th choice, 193rd overall, in 1991 Entry Draft).

			Regular Season					Playoffs				
Season	Club	Lea	GP	G	A	TP	PIM	GP	G	A	TP	PIM
1990-91	Dartmouth	ECAC	24	10	10	20	30	....	....	....	....	....
1991-92	Dartmouth	ECAC	24	11	7	18	60	....	....	....	....	....

FREDERICK, JOSEPH

Right wing. Shoots right. 6'1", 190 lbs. Born, St. Hubert, Que., August 6, 1969.
(Detroit's 13th choice, 242nd overall, in 1989 Entry Draft).

			Regular Season					Playoffs				
Season	Club	Lea	GP	G	A	TP	PIM	GP	G	A	TP	PIM
1990-91	N. Michigan	WCHA	40	9	11	20	77	....	....	....	....	....
1991-92	N. Michigan	WCHA	36	23	8	31	100	....	....	....	....	....

FREDERICK, TROY

Center. Shoots left. 6'5", 226 lbs. Born, Virden, Man., April 4, 1969.

			Regular Season					Playoffs				
Season	Club	League	GP	G	A	TP	PIM	GP	G	A	TP	PIM
1987-88	Brandon	WHL	66	15	13	28	17	4	3	1	4	6
1988-89	Brandon	WHL	72	26	30	56	72	....	....	....	....	....
1989-90	Brandon	WHL	70	27	29	56	133	....	....	....	....	....
1990-91	Kansas City	IHL	39	2	3	5	79	....	....	....	....	....
	Knoxville	ECHL	4	0	3	3	71	....	....	....	....	....
1991-92	Kansas City	IHL	13	0	3	3	29	....	....	....	....	....

Signed as a free agent by **San Jose,** September 3, 1991.

FREER, MARK (FRIHR)

Center. Shoots left. 5'10", 180 lbs. Born, Peterborough, Ont., July 14, 1968.

			Regular Season					Playoffs				
Season	Club	Lea	GP	G	A	TP	PIM	GP	G	A	TP	PIM
1985-86	Peterborough	OHL	65	16	28	44	24	14	3	4	7	13
1986-87	**Philadelphia**	**NHL**	**1**	**0**	**1**	**1**	**0**	....	....	....	....	....
	Peterborough	OHL	65	39	43	82	44	12	2	6	8	5
1987-88	**Philadelphia**	**NHL**	**1**	**0**	**0**	**0**	**0**	....	....	....	....	....
	Peterborough	OHL	63	38	70	108	63	12	5	12	17	4
1988-89	**Philadelphia**	**NHL**	**5**	**0**	**1**	**1**	**0**	....	....	....	....	....
	Hershey	AHL	75	30	49	79	77	12	4	6	10	2
1989-90	**Philadelphia**	**NHL**	**2**	**0**	**0**	**0**	**0**	....	....	....	....	....
	Hershey	AHL	65	28	36	64	31	....	....	....	....	....
1990-91	Hershey	AHL	77	18	44	62	45	7	1	3	4	17
1991-92	**Philadelphia**	**NHL**	**50**	**6**	**7**	**13**	**18**	....	....	....	....	....
	Hershey	AHL	31	13	11	24	38	6	0	3	3	2
	NHL Totals		**59**	**6**	**9**	**15**	**18**	....	....	....	....	....

Signed as a free agent by **Philadelphia**, October 7, 1986. Claimed by **Ottawa** from **Philadelphia** in Expansion Draft, June 18, 1992.

FRENETTE, DEREK

Left wing/Defense. Shoots left. 6'1", 175 lbs. Born, Montreal, Que., July 13, 1971.
(St. Louis' 6th choice, 124th overall, in 1989 Entry Draft).

			Regular Season					Playoffs				
Season	Club	Lea	GP	G	A	TP	PIM	GP	G	A	TP	PIM
1988-89	Ferris State	CCHA	25	3	4	7	17	....	....	....	....	....
1989-90	Ferris State	CCHA	28	1	4	5	48	....	....	....	....	....
1990-91	Hull	QMJHL	66	27	42	69	72	6	4	3	7	12
	Peoria	IHL	....	....	....	....	....	6	0	0	0	0
1991-92	Peoria	IHL	46	2	11	13	51	10	0	3	3	4

FRIEDMAN, DOUG

Left wing. Shoots left. 6'1", 189 lbs. Born, Cape Elizabeth, ME, September 1, 1971.
(Quebec's 11th choice, 222nd overall, in 1991 Entry Draft).

			Regular Season					Playoffs				
Season	Club	Lea	GP	G	A	TP	PIM	GP	G	A	TP	PIM
1990-91	Boston U.	H.E.	36	6	6	12	37	....	....	....	....	....
1991-92	Boston U.	H.E.	34	11	8	19	42	....	....	....	....	....

FROLOV, DIMITRI

Defense. Shoots left. 6'3", 213 lbs. Born, Moscow, Soviet Union, August 22, 1966.
(Calgary's 8th choice, 146th overall, in 1990 Entry Draft).

			Regular Season					Playoffs				
Season	Club	Lea	GP	G	A	TP	PIM	GP	G	A	TP	PIM
1989-90	Moscow D'amo	USSR	45	2	9	11	18	....	....	....	....	....
1990-91	Moscow D'amo	USSR	46	5	7	12	26	....	....	....	....	....
1991-92	Moscow D'amo	CIS	27	0	4	4	12	....	....	....	....	....

GAETZ, LINK (GAYTZ)

Defense. Shoots left. 6'2", 223 lbs. Born, Vancouver, B.C., October 2, 1968.
(Minnesota's 2nd choice, 40th overall, in 1988 Entry Draft).

			Regular Season					Playoffs				
Season	Club	Lea	GP	G	A	TP	PIM	GP	G	A	TP	PIM
1986-87	N. Westminster	WHL	44	2	7	9	52	....	....	....	....	....
1987-88	Spokane	WHL	59	9	20	29	313	10	2	2	4	70
1988-89	**Minnesota**	**NHL**	**12**	**0**	**2**	**2**	**53**	....	....	....	....	....
	Kalamazoo	IHL	37	3	4	7	192	5	0	0	0	56
1989-90	**Minnesota**	**NHL**	**5**	**0**	**0**	**0**	**33**	....	....	....	....	....
	Kalamazoo	IHL	61	5	16	21	318	9	2	2	4	59
1990-91	Kalamazoo	IHL	9	0	1	1	44	....	....	....	....	....
	Kansas City	IHL	18	1	10	11	178	....	....	....	....	....
1991-92	**San Jose**	**NHL**	**48**	**6**	**6**	**12**	**326**	....	....	....	....	....
	NHL Totals		**65**	**6**	**8**	**14**	**412**	....	....	....	....	....

Claimed by **San Jose** from **Minnesota** in Dispersal Draft, May 30, 1991.

GAGE, JOSEPH WILLIAM (JODY)

Right wing. Shoots right. 6', 190 lbs. Born, Toronto, Ont., November 29, 1959.
(Detroit's 2nd choice, 45th overall, in 1979 Entry Draft).

			Regular Season					Playoffs				
Season	Club	Lea	GP	G	A	TP	PIM	GP	G	A	TP	PIM
1977-78	Hamilton	OHA	32	15	18	33	19	....	....	....	....	....
	Kitchener	OHA	36	17	27	44	21	9	4	3	7	4
1978-79	Kitchener	OHA	58	46	43	89	40	10	1	2	3	6
1979-80	Adirondack	AHL	63	25	21	46	15	5	2	1	3	0
1980-81	**Detroit**	**NHL**	**16**	**2**	**2**	**4**	**22**	....	....	....	....	....
	Adirondack	AHL	59	17	31	48	44	17	9	6	15	12
1981-82	**Detroit**	**NHL**	**31**	**9**	**10**	**19**	**2**	....	....	....	....	....
	Adirondack	AHL	47	21	20	41	21	....	....	....	....	....
1982-83	Adirondack	AHL	65	23	30	53	33	6	1	5	6	8
1983-84	**Detroit**	**NHL**	**3**	**0**	**0**	**0**	**0**	....	....	....	....	....
	Adirondack	AHL	73	40	32	72	32	6	3	4	7	2
1984-85	Adirondack	AHL	78	27	33	60	55	....	....	....	....	....
1985-86	**Buffalo**	**NHL**	**7**	**3**	**2**	**5**	**0**	....	....	....	....	....
a	Rochester	AHL	73	42	57	99	56	....	....	....	....	....
1986-87	Rochester	AHL	70	26	39	65	60	17	*14	5	19	24
1987-88	**Buffalo**	**NHL**	**2**	**0**	**0**	**0**	**0**	....	....	....	....	....
ab	Rochester	AHL	76	*60	44	104	46	5	2	5	7	10
1988-89	Rochester	AHL	65	31	38	69	60	....	....	....	....	....
1989-90	Rochester	AHL	75	45	38	83	42	17	4	6	10	12
1990-91a	Rochester	AHL	73	42	43	85	34	15	6	10	16	14
1991-92	**Buffalo**	**NHL**	**9**	**0**	**1**	**1**	**2**	....	....	....	....	....
	Rochester	AHL	67	40	40	80	54	16	5	9	14	10
	NHL Totals		**68**	**14**	**15**	**29**	**26**	....	....	....	....	....

a AHL First All-Star Team (1986, 1988, 1991)
b Won Les Cunningham Trophy (MVP-AHL) (1988)

Signed as a free agent by **Buffalo**, July 31, 1985.

GAGNER, DAVE (GAH-nyay)

Center. Shoots left. 5'10", 180 lbs. Born, Chatham, Ont., December 11, 1964.
(NY Rangers' 1st choice, 12th overall, in 1983 Entry Draft).

			Regular Season					Playoffs				
Season	Club	Lea	GP	G	A	TP	PIM	GP	G	A	TP	PIM
1981-82	Brantford	OHL	68	30	46	76	31	11	3	6	9	6
1982-83a	Brantford	OHL	70	55	66	121	57	8	5	5	10	4
1983-84	Cdn. Olympic	....	50	19	18	37	26	....	....	....	....	....
	Brantford	OHL	12	7	13	20	4	6	0	4	4	6
1984-85	**NY Rangers**	**NHL**	**38**	**6**	**6**	**12**	**16**	....	....	....	....	....
	New Haven	AHL	38	13	20	33	23	....	....	....	....	....
1985-86	**NY Rangers**	**NHL**	**32**	**4**	**6**	**10**	**19**	....	....	....	....	....
	New Haven	AHL	16	10	11	21	11	4	1	2	3	2
1986-87	**NY Rangers**	**NHL**	**10**	**1**	**4**	**5**	**12**	....	....	....	....	....
	New Haven	AHL	56	22	41	63	50	7	1	5	6	18
1987-88	**Minnesota**	**NHL**	**51**	**8**	**11**	**19**	**55**	....	....	....	....	....
	Kalamazoo	IHL	14	16	10	26	26	....	....	....	....	....
1988-89	**Minnesota**	**NHL**	**75**	**35**	**43**	**78**	**104**	....	....	....	....	....
	Kalamazoo	IHL	1	0	1	1	4	....	....	....	....	....
1989-90	**Minnesota**	**NHL**	**79**	**40**	**38**	**78**	**54**	**7**	**2**	**3**	**5**	**16**
1990-91	**Minnesota**	**NHL**	**73**	**40**	**42**	**82**	**114**	**23**	**12**	**15**	**27**	**28**
1991-92	**Minnesota**	**NHL**	**78**	**31**	**40**	**71**	**107**	**7**	**2**	**4**	**6**	**8**
	NHL Totals		**436**	**165**	**190**	**355**	**481**	**37**	**16**	**22**	**38**	**52**

a OHL Second All-Star Team (1983)

Played in NHL All-Star Game (1991)

Traded to **Minnesota** by **NY Rangers** with Jay Caulfield for Jari Gronstrand and Paul Boutilier, October 8, 1987.

GALLANT, GERARD (guh-LAHNT)

Left wing. Shoots left. 5'10", 190 lbs. Born, Summerside, P.E.I., September 2, 1963.
(Detroit's 4th choice, 107th overall, in 1981 Entry Draft).

			Regular Season					Playoffs				
Season	Club	Lea	GP	G	A	TP	PIM	GP	G	A	TP	PIM
1980-81	Sherbrooke	QMJHL	68	41	59	100	265	14	6	13	19	46
1981-82	Sherbrooke	QMJHL	58	34	58	92	260	22	14	24	38	84
1982-83	St-Jean	QMJHL	33	28	25	53	139	....	....	....	....	....
	Verdun	QMJHL	29	26	49	75	105	15	14	19	33	84
1983-84	Adirondack	AHL	77	31	33	64	195	7	1	3	4	34
1984-85	**Detroit**	**NHL**	**32**	**6**	**12**	**18**	**66**	**3**	**0**	**0**	**0**	**11**
	Adirondack	AHL	46	18	29	47	131	....	....	....	....	....
1985-86	**Detroit**	**NHL**	**52**	**20**	**19**	**39**	**106**	....	....	....	....	....
1986-87	**Detroit**	**NHL**	**80**	**38**	**34**	**72**	**216**	**16**	**8**	**6**	**14**	**43**
1987-88	**Detroit**	**NHL**	**73**	**34**	**39**	**73**	**242**	**16**	**6**	**9**	**15**	**55**
1988-89a	**Detroit**	**NHL**	**76**	**39**	**54**	**93**	**230**	**6**	**1**	**2**	**3**	**40**
1989-90	**Detroit**	**NHL**	**69**	**36**	**44**	**80**	**254**	....	....	....	....	....
1990-91	**Detroit**	**NHL**	**45**	**10**	**16**	**26**	**111**	....	....	....	....	....
1991-92	**Detroit**	**NHL**	**69**	**14**	**22**	**36**	**187**	**11**	**2**	**2**	**4**	**25**
	NHL Totals		**496**	**197**	**240**	**437**	**1412**	**52**	**17**	**19**	**36**	**174**

a NHL Second All-Star Team (1989)

GALLEY, GARRY

Defense. Shoots left. 6', 190 lbs. Born, Montreal, Que., April 16, 1963.
(Los Angeles' 4th choice, 100th overall, in 1983 Entry Draft).

			Regular Season					Playoffs				
Season	Club	Lea	GP	G	A	TP	PIM	GP	G	A	TP	PIM
1981-82	Bowling Green	CCHA	42	3	36	39	48	....	....	....	....	....
1982-83	Bowling Green	CCHA	40	17	29	46	40	....	....	....	....	....
1983-84ab	Bowling Green	CCHA	44	15	52	67	61	....	....	....	....	....
1984-85	**Los Angeles**	**NHL**	**78**	**8**	**30**	**38**	**82**	**3**	**1**	**0**	**1**	**2**
1985-86	**Los Angeles**	**NHL**	**49**	**9**	**13**	**22**	**46**	....	....	....	....	....
	New Haven	AHL	4	2	6	8	6	....	....	....	....	....
1986-87	**Los Angeles**	**NHL**	**30**	**5**	**11**	**16**	**57**	....	....	....	....	....
	Washington	**NHL**	**18**	**1**	**10**	**11**	**10**	**2**	**0**	**0**	**0**	**0**
1987-88	**Washington**	**NHL**	**58**	**7**	**23**	**30**	**44**	**13**	**2**	**4**	**6**	**13**
1988-89	**Boston**	**NHL**	**78**	**8**	**21**	**29**	**80**	**9**	**0**	**1**	**1**	**33**
1989-90	**Boston**	**NHL**	**71**	**8**	**27**	**35**	**75**	**21**	**3**	**3**	**6**	**34**
1990-91	**Boston**	**NHL**	**70**	**6**	**21**	**27**	**84**	**16**	**1**	**5**	**6**	**17**
1991-92	**Boston**	**NHL**	**38**	**2**	**12**	**14**	**83**	....	....	....	....	....
	Philadelphia	**NHL**	**39**	**3**	**15**	**18**	**34**	....	....	....	....	....
	NHL Totals		**529**	**57**	**183**	**240**	**595**	**64**	**7**	**13**	**20**	**109**

a CCHA First All-Star Team (1984)
b NCAA All-American (1984)

Played in NHL All-Star Game (1991)

Traded to **Washington** by **Los Angeles** for Al Jensen, February 14, 1987. Signed as a free agent by **Boston**, July 8, 1988. Traded to **Philadelphia** by **Boston** with Wes Walz and future considerations for Gord Murphy, Brian Dobbin and Philadelphia's third round choice (Sergei Zholtok) in 1992 Entry Draft, January 2, 1992.

GANCHAR, PERRY

Right wing. Shoots right. 5'9", 180 lbs. Born, Saskatoon, Sask., October 28, 1963.
(St. Louis' 3rd choice, 113th overall, in 1982 Entry Draft).

			Regular Season					Playoffs				
Season	Club	Lea	GP	G	A	TP	PIM	GP	G	A	TP	PIM
1979-80	Saskatoon	WHL	27	9	14	23	60	....	....	....	....	....
1980-81	Saskatoon	WHL	72	26	53	79	117	....	....	....	....	....
1981-82	Saskatoon	WHL	53	38	52	90	82	5	3	3	6	17
1982-83	Saskatoon	WHL	68	68	48	116	105	6	1	4	5	24
	Salt Lake	CHL	....	....	....	....	....	1	0	1	1	0
1983-84	**St. Louis**	**NHL**	**1**	**0**	**0**	**0**	**0**	**7**	**3**	**1**	**4**	**0**
	Montana	CHL	59	23	22	45	77	....	....	....	....	....
1984-85	**St. Louis**	**NHL**	**7**	**0**	**2**	**2**	**0**	....	....	....	....	....
a	Peoria	IHL	63	41	29	70	114	20	4	11	15	49
1985-86	Sherbrooke	AHL	75	25	29	54	42	....	....	....	....	....
1986-87	Sherbrooke	AHL	68	22	29	51	64	17	9	8	17	37
1987-88	**Montreal**	**NHL**	**1**	**1**	**0**	**1**	**0**	....	....	....	....	....
	Sherbrooke	AHL	28	12	18	30	61	....	....	....	....	....
	Pittsburgh	**NHL**	**30**	**2**	**5**	**7**	**36**	....	....	....	....	....
1988-89	**Pittsburgh**	**NHL**	**3**	**0**	**0**	**0**	**0**	....	....	....	....	....
	Muskegon	IHL	70	39	34	73	114	14	7	8	15	6
1989-90	Muskegon	IHL	79	40	45	85	111	14	3	5	8	27
1990-91	Muskegon	IHL	80	37	38	75	87	5	2	1	3	0
1991-92	Muskegon	IHL	65	29	20	49	65	14	9	9	18	18
	NHL Totals		**42**	**3**	**7**	**10**	**36**	**7**	**3**	**1**	**4**	**0**

a IHL Second All-Star Team (1985)

Traded to **Montreal** by **St. Louis** for Ron Flockhart, August 26, 1985. Traded to **Pittsburgh** by **Montreal** for future considerations, December 17, 1987.

GARBUTT, MURRAY

Center. Shoots left. 6'1", 205 lbs. Born, Hanna, Alta., July 29, 1971.
(Minnesota's 3rd choice, 60th overall, in 1989 Entry Draft).

			Regular Season					Playoffs				
Season	Club	Lea	GP	G	A	TP	PIM	GP	G	A	TP	PIM
1987-88	Medicine Hat	WHL	9	2	1	3	15	16	0	1	1	15
1988-89	Medicine Hat	WHL	64	14	24	38	145	3	1	0	1	6
1989-90	Medicine Hat	WHL	72	38	27	65	221	3	1	0	1	21
1990-91	Medicine Hat	WHL	30	15	26	41	97	....	....	....	....	....
	Spokane	WHL	31	17	19	36	90	15	4	8	12	44
1991-92	Kansas City	IHL	25	2	6	8	19	....	....	....	....	....

Claimed by **San Jose** from **Minnesota** in Dispersal Draft, May 30, 1991. Traded to **Quebec** by **San Jose** for Don Barber, March 7, 1992.

GARDINER, BRUCE

Center. Shoots right. 6'1", 170 lbs. Born, Barrie, Ont., February 11, 1971.
(St. Louis' 6th choice, 131st overall, in 1991 Entry Draft).

			Regular Season					Playoffs				
Season	Club	Lea	GP	G	A	TP	PIM	GP	G	A	TP	PIM
1990-91	Colgate	ECAC	27	4	9	13	72	....	....	....	....	....
1991-92	Colgate	ECAC	23	7	8	15	77	....	....	....	....	....

GARDNER, JOEL

Center. Shoots left. 6', 175 lbs. Born, Petrolia, Ont., September 16, 1967.
(Boston's 11th choice, 244th overall, in 1986 Entry Draft).

			Regular Season					Playoffs				
Season	Club	Lea	GP	G	A	TP	PIM	GP	G	A	TP	PIM
1986-87	Colgate	ECAC	31	10	20	30	20	....	....	....	....	....
1987-88	Colgate	ECAC	31	14	32	46	24	....	....	....	....	....
1988-89	Colgate	ECAC	30	21	25	46	38	....	....	....	....	....
1989-90abc	Colgate	ECAC	38	26	36	62	62	....	....	....	....	....
1990-91	Muskegon	IHL	49	9	13	22	30	2	0	1	1	0
1991-92	Muskegon	IHL	5	1	2	3	2	....	....	....	....	....
	Knoxville	ECHL	36	20	34	54	30	....	....	....	....	....

a ECAC First All-Star Team (1990)
b NCAA East Second All-American Team (1990)
c NCAA All-Tournament Team (1990)

Signed as a free agent by **Pittsburgh**, September 11, 1990.

GARPENLOV, JOHAN (GAHR-puhn-luhv)

Left wing. Shoots left. 5′11″, 183 lbs. Born, Stockholm, Sweden, March 21, 1968.
(Detroit's 5th choice, 85th overall, in 1986 Entry Draft).

			Regular Season					Playoffs				
Season	Club	Lea	GP	G	A	TP	PIM	GP	G	A	TP	PIM
1986-87	Djurgarden	Swe.	29	5	8	13	20	....	....	....	....	....
1987-88	Djurgarden	Swe.	30	7	10	17	12	....	....	....	....	....
1988-89	Djurgarden	Swe.	36	12	19	31	20	....	....	....	....	....
1989-90	Djurgarden	Swe.	39	20	13	33	35	8	2	4	6	4
1990-91	**Detroit**	**NHL**	**71**	**18**	**22**	**40**	**18**	**6**	**0**	**1**	**1**	**4**
1991-92	**Detroit**	**NHL**	**16**	**1**	**1**	**2**	**4**	....	....	....	....	....
	San Jose	**NHL**	**12**	**5**	**6**	**11**	**4**	....	....	....	....	....
	NHL Totals		**99**	**24**	**29**	**53**	**26**	**6**	**0**	**1**	**1**	**4**

Traded to **San Jose** by **Detroit** for Bob McGill and Vancouver's eighth round choice in 1992 Entry Draft (C.J. Denomme) previously acquired by Detroit, March 9, 1992.

GARTNER, MICHAEL ALFRED (MIKE)

Right wing. Shoots right. 6′, 190 lbs. Born, Ottawa, Ont., October 29, 1959.
(Washington's 1st choice, 4th overall, in 1979 Entry Draft).

			Regular Season					Playoffs				
Season	Club	Lea	GP	G	A	TP	PIM	GP	G	A	TP	PIM
1976-77	Niagara Falls	OHA	62	33	42	75	125	....	....	....	....	....
1977-78a	Niagara Falls	OHA	64	41	49	90	56	....	....	....	....	....
1978-79	Cincinnati	WHA	78	27	25	52	123	3	0	2	2	2
1979-80	**Washington**	**NHL**	**77**	**36**	**32**	**68**	**66**	....	....	....	....	....
1980-81	**Washington**	**NHL**	**80**	**48**	**46**	**94**	**100**	....	....	....	....	....
1981-82	**Washington**	**NHL**	**80**	**35**	**45**	**80**	**121**	....	....	....	....	....
1982-83	**Washington**	**NHL**	**73**	**38**	**38**	**76**	**54**	**4**	**0**	**0**	**0**	**4**
1983-84	**Washington**	**NHL**	**80**	**40**	**45**	**85**	**90**	**8**	**3**	**7**	**10**	**16**
1984-85	**Washington**	**NHL**	**80**	**50**	**52**	**102**	**71**	**5**	**4**	**3**	**7**	**9**
1985-86	**Washington**	**NHL**	**74**	**35**	**40**	**75**	**63**	**9**	**2**	**10**	**12**	**4**
1986-87	**Washington**	**NHL**	**78**	**41**	**32**	**73**	**61**	**7**	**4**	**3**	**7**	**14**
1987-88	**Washington**	**NHL**	**80**	**48**	**33**	**81**	**73**	**14**	**3**	**4**	**7**	**14**
1988-89	**Washington**	**NHL**	**56**	**26**	**29**	**55**	**71**	....	....	....	....	....
	Minnesota	**NHL**	**13**	**7**	**7**	**14**	**2**	**5**	**0**	**0**	**0**	**6**
1989-90	**Minnesota**	**NHL**	**67**	**34**	**36**	**70**	**32**	....	....	....	....	....
	NY Rangers	**NHL**	**12**	**11**	**5**	**16**	**6**	**10**	**5**	**3**	**8**	**12**
1990-91	**NY Rangers**	**NHL**	**79**	**49**	**20**	**69**	**53**	**6**	**1**	**1**	**2**	**0**
1991-92	**NY Rangers**	**NHL**	**76**	**40**	**41**	**81**	**55**	**13**	**8**	**8**	**16**	**4**
	NHL Totals		**1005**	**538**	**501**	**1039**	**918**	**81**	**30**	**39**	**69**	**83**

a OHA First All-Star Team (1978)

Played in NHL All-Star Game (1980, 1985, 1986, 1988, 1990)

Traded to **Minnesota** by **Washington** with Larry Murphy for Dino Ciccarelli and Bob Rouse, March 7, 1989. Traded to **NY Rangers** by **Minnesota** for Ulf Dahlen, Los Angeles' fourth round choice (Cal McGowan) – previously acquired by NY Rangers – in 1990 Entry Draft and future considerations, March 6, 1990.

GAUDREAU, ROBERT (ROB)

Right wing. Shoots right. 5′11″, 185 lbs. Born, Lincoln, RI, January 20, 1970.
(Pittsburgh's 8th choice, 172nd overall, in 1988 Entry Draft).

			Regular Season					Playoffs				
Season	Club	Lea	GP	G	A	TP	PIM	GP	G	A	TP	PIM
1988-89a	Providence	H.E.	42	28	29	57	32	....	....	....	....	....
1989-90	Providence	H.E.	32	20	18	38	12	....	....	....	....	....
1990-91b	Providence	H.E.	36	34	27	61	20	....	....	....	....	....
1991-92cd	Providence	H.E.	36	21	34	55	22	....	....	....	....	....

a Co-winner Hockey East Rookie of the Year (1989)
b Hockey East Second All-Star Team (1991)
c NCAA East Second All-Star Team (1992)
d Hockey East First All-Star Team (1992)

Rights traded to **Minnesota** by **Pittsburgh** for Richard Zemlak, November 1, 1988. Claimed by **San Jose** from **Minnesota** in Dispersal Draft, May 30, 1991.

GAUL, MICHAEL

Defense. Shoots right. 6′1″, 197 lbs. Born, Dorval, Que., April 22, 1973.
(Los Angeles' 12th choice, 262nd overall, in 1991 Entry Draft).

			Regular Season					Playoffs				
Season	Club	Lea	GP	G	A	TP	PIM	GP	G	A	TP	PIM
1990-91	St. Lawrence	ECAC	31	1	3	4	46	....	....	....	....	....
1991-92	Laval	QMJHL	50	6	38	44	44	10	0	2	2	20

GAUTHIER, DANIEL

Left wing. Shoots left. 6′1″, 190 lbs. Born, Charlemagne, Que., May 17, 1970.
(Pittsburgh's 3rd choice, 62nd overall, in 1988 Entry Draft).

			Regular Season					Playoffs				
Season	Club	Lea	GP	G	A	TP	PIM	GP	G	A	TP	PIM
1986-87	Longueuil	QMJHL	64	23	22	45	23	18	4	5	9	15
1987-88	Victoriaville	QMJHL	66	43	47	90	53	5	2	1	3	0
1988-89	Victoriaville	QMJHL	64	41	75	116	84	16	12	17	29	30
1989-90	Victoriaville	QMJHL	62	45	69	114	32	16	8	*19	27	16
1990-91	Albany	IHL	1	1	0	1	0	....	....	....	....	....
ab	Knoxville	ECHL	61	41	*93	134	40	2	0	4	4	4
1991-92	Muskegon	IHL	68	19	18	37	28	9	3	6	9	8

a ECHL First All-Star Team (1991)
b Top Rookie — ECHL (1991)

GAUTHIER, LUC (GOH-chay)

Defense. Shoots right. 5′9″, 195 lbs. Born, Longueuil, Que., April 19, 1964.

			Regular Season					Playoffs				
Season	Club	Lea	GP	G	A	TP	PIM	GP	G	A	TP	PIM
1983-84	Longueuil	QMJHL	70	8	54	62	207	....	....	....	....	....
1984-85	Longueuil	QMJHL	60	13	47	60	111	....	....	....	....	....
1985-86	Saginaw	IHL	66	9	29	38	160	....	....	....	....	....
1986-87	Sherbrooke	AHL	78	5	17	22	8	17	2	4	6	31
1987-88	Sherbrooke	AHL	61	4	10	14	105	6	0	0	0	18
1988-89	Sherbrooke	AHL	77	8	20	28	178	6	0	0	0	10
1989-90	Sherbrooke	AHL	79	3	23	26	139	12	0	4	4	35
1990-91	**Montreal**	**NHL**	**3**	**0**	**0**	**0**	**2**	....	....	....	....	....
	Fredericton	AHL	69	7	20	27	238	9	1	1	2	10
1991-92	Fredericton	AHL	80	4	14	18	252	7	1	1	2	26
	NHL Totals		**3**	**0**	**0**	**0**	**2**	....	....	....	....	....

Signed as a free agent by **Montreal**, October 7, 1986.

GAUVIN, STEPHANE

Left wing. Shoots left. 6′, 175 lbs. Born, Vancouver, B.C., April 16, 1970.
(Winnipeg's 11th choice, 172nd overall, in 1989 Entry Draft).

			Regular Season					Playoffs				
Season	Club	Lea	GP	G	A	TP	PIM	GP	G	A	TP	PIM
1988-89	Cornell	ECAC	30	2	5	7	24	....	....	....	....	....
1989-90	Cornell	ECAC	29	2	2	4	34	....	....	....	....	....
1990-91	Cornell	ECAC	32	3	5	8	24	....	....	....	....	....
1991-92	Cornell	ECAC	29	6	10	16	28	....	....	....	....	....

GAVEY, AARON

Center. Shoots left. 6′1″, 169 lbs. Born, Sudbury, Ont., February 22, 1974.
(Tampa Bay's 4th choice, 74th overall, in 1992 Entry Draft).

			Regular Season					Playoffs				
Season	Club	Lea	GP	G	A	TP	PIM	GP	G	A	TP	PIM
1990-91	Peterborough	Jr. B	42	26	30	56	68	....	....	....	....	....
1991-92	S.S. Marie	OHL	48	7	11	18	27	19	5	1	6	10

GAVIN, ROBERT (STEWART)

Left/Right wing. Shoots left. 6′, 190 lbs. Born, Ottawa, Ont., March 15, 1960.
(Toronto's 4th choice, 74th overall, in 1980 Entry Draft).

			Regular Season					Playoffs				
Season	Club	Lea	GP	G	A	TP	PIM	GP	G	A	TP	PIM
1978-79	Toronto	OHA	61	24	25	49	83	3	1	0	1	0
1979-80	Toronto	OHA	68	27	30	57	52	4	1	1	2	2
1980-81	**Toronto**	**NHL**	**14**	**1**	**2**	**3**	**13**	....	....	....	....	....
	New Brunswick	AHL	46	7	12	19	42	13	1	0	1	2
1981-82	**Toronto**	**NHL**	**38**	**5**	**6**	**11**	**29**	....	....	....	....	....
1982-83	**Toronto**	**NHL**	**63**	**6**	**5**	**11**	**44**	**4**	**0**	**0**	**0**	**0**
	St. Catharines	AHL	6	2	4	6	17	....	....	....	....	....
1983-84	**Toronto**	**NHL**	**80**	**10**	**22**	**32**	**90**	....	....	....	....	....
1984-85	**Toronto**	**NHL**	**73**	**12**	**13**	**25**	**38**	....	....	....	....	....
1985-86	**Hartford**	**NHL**	**76**	**26**	**29**	**55**	**51**	**10**	**4**	**1**	**5**	**13**
1986-87	**Hartford**	**NHL**	**79**	**20**	**21**	**41**	**28**	**6**	**2**	**4**	**6**	**10**
1987-88	**Hartford**	**NHL**	**56**	**11**	**10**	**21**	**59**	**6**	**2**	**2**	**4**	**4**
1988-89	**Minnesota**	**NHL**	**73**	**8**	**18**	**26**	**34**	**5**	**3**	**1**	**4**	**10**
1989-90	**Minnesota**	**NHL**	**80**	**12**	**13**	**25**	**76**	**7**	**0**	**2**	**2**	**12**
1990-91	**Minnesota**	**NHL**	**38**	**4**	**4**	**8**	**36**	**21**	**3**	**10**	**13**	**20**
1991-92	**Minnesota**	**NHL**	**35**	**5**	**4**	**9**	**27**	**7**	**0**	**0**	**0**	**6**
	NHL Totals		**705**	**120**	**147**	**267**	**525**	**66**	**14**	**20**	**34**	**75**

Traded to **Hartford** by **Toronto** for Chris Kotsopoulos, October 7, 1985. Claimed by **Minnesota** in NHL Waiver Draft, October 3, 1988.

GEARY, DEREK

Right wing. Shoots right. 6′3″, 180 lbs. Born, Gloucester, MA, February 18, 1970.
(Boston's 5th choice, 123rd overall, in 1988 Entry Draft).

			Regular Season					Playoffs				
Season	Club	Lea	GP	G	A	TP	PIM	GP	G	A	TP	PIM
1990-91	Boston U.	H.E.				DID NOT PLAY						
1991-92	Dartmouth	ECAC	26	7	6	13	30	....	....	....	....	....

GELINAS, MARTIN (JEL-in-uh)

Left wing. Shoots left. 5′11″, 195 lbs. Born, Shawinigan, Que., June 5, 1970.
(Los Angeles' 1st choice, 7th overall, in 1988 Entry Draft).

			Regular Season					Playoffs				
Season	Club	Lea	GP	G	A	TP	PIM	GP	G	A	TP	PIM
1987-88	Hull	QMJHL	65	63	68	131	74	17	15	18	33	32
1988-89	**Edmonton**	**NHL**	**6**	**1**	**2**	**3**	**0**	....	....	....	....	....
	Hull	QMJHL	41	38	39	77	31	9	5	4	9	14
1989-90	**Edmonton**	**NHL**	**46**	**17**	**8**	**25**	**30**	**20**	**2**	**3**	**5**	**6**
1990-91	**Edmonton**	**NHL**	**73**	**20**	**20**	**40**	**34**	**18**	**3**	**6**	**9**	**25**
1991-92	**Edmonton**	**NHL**	**68**	**11**	**18**	**29**	**62**	**15**	**1**	**3**	**4**	**10**
	NHL Totals		**193**	**49**	**48**	**97**	**126**	**53**	**6**	**12**	**18**	**41**

Traded to **Edmonton** by **Los Angeles** with Jimmy Carson and Los Angeles' first round choices in 1989, (acquired by New Jersey, June 17, 1989. New Jersey selected Jason Miller), 1991 (Martin Rucinsky) and 1993 Entry Drafts and cash for Wayne Gretzky, Mike Krushelnyski and Marty McSorley, August 9, 1988.

GENDRON, MARTIN

Right wing. Shoots right. 5′8″, 182 lbs. Born, Valleyfield, Que., February 15, 1974.
(Washington's 4th choice, 71st overall, in 1992 Entry Draft).

			Regular Season					Playoffs				
Season	Club	Lea	GP	G	A	TP	PIM	GP	G	A	TP	PIM
1990-91	St-Hyacinthe	QMJHL	55	34	23	57	33	4	1	2	3	0
1991-92	St-Hyacinthe	QMJHL	69	*71	66	137	45	6	7	4	11	14

GERMAIN, ERIC

Defense. Shoots left. 6′1″, 195 lbs. Born, Quebec City, Que., June 26, 1966.

			Regular Season					Playoffs				
Season	Club	Lea	GP	G	A	TP	PIM	GP	G	A	TP	PIM
1983-84	St-Jean	QMJHL	57	2	15	17	60	4	1	0	1	6
1984-85	St-Jean	QMJHL	66	10	31	41	243	5	4	0	4	14
1985-86	St-Jean	QMJHL	66	5	38	43	183	10	0	6	6	56
1986-87	Flint	IHL	21	0	2	2	23	....	....	....	....	....
	Fredericton	AHL	44	2	8	10	28	....	....	....	....	....
1987-88	**Los Angeles**	**NHL**	**4**	**0**	**1**	**1**	**13**	**1**	**0**	**0**	**0**	**4**
	New Haven	AHL	69	0	10	10	0	....	....	....	....	....
1988-89	New Haven	AHL	55	0	9	9	93	17	0	3	3	23
1989-90	New Haven	AHL	59	3	12	15	112	....	....	....	....	....
1990-91	Binghamton	AHL	60	4	10	14	144	10	0	1	1	14
1991-92	Moncton	AHL	3	0	2	2	4	....	....	....	....	....
	Binghamton	AHL	47	3	6	9	86	3	0	0	0	0
	NHL Totals		**4**	**0**	**1**	**1**	**13**	**1**	**0**	**0**	**0**	**4**

Signed as a free agent by **Los Angeles**, July 1, 1986. Signed as a free agent by **NY Rangers**, July 11, 1990.

GERNANDER, KEN

Center. Shoots left. 5'10", 175 lbs. Born, Coleraine, MN, June 30, 1969.
(Winnipeg's 4th choice, 96th overall, in 1987 Entry Draft).

			Regular Season					Playoffs				
Season	Club	Lea	GP	G	A	TP	PIM	GP	G	A	TP	PIM
1987-88	U. Minnesota	WCHA	44	14	14	28	14	....	....	....	....	....
1988-89	U. Minnesota	WCHA	44	9	11	20	2	....	....	....	....	....
1989-90	U. Minnesota	WCHA	44	32	17	49	24	....	....	....	....	....
1990-91	U. Minnesota	WCHA	44	23	20	43	24	....	....	....	....	....
1991-92	Fort Wayne	IHL	13	7	6	13	2	....	....	....	....	....
	Moncton	AHL	43	8	18	26	9	8	1	1	2	2

GIACIN, JIM

Left wing. Shoots left. 6'1", 200 lbs. Born, St. Louis, MO, January 6, 1971.
(Los Angeles' 8th choice, 182nd overall, in 1989 Entry Draft).

			Regular Season					Playoffs				
Season	Club	Lea	GP	G	A	TP	PIM	GP	G	A	TP	PIM
1989-90	St. Lawrence	ECAC	28	4	2	6	32	....	....	....	....	....
1990-91	St. Lawrence	ECAC	35	3	5	8	22	....	....	....	....	....

GIBSON, DON

Defense. Shoots right. 6'1", 210 lbs. Born, Deloraine, Man., December 29, 1967.
(Vancouver's 2nd choice, 49th overall, in 1986 Entry Draft).

			Regular Season					Playoffs				
Season	Club	Lea	GP	G	A	TP	PIM	GP	G	A	TP	PIM
1986-87	Michigan State	CCHA	43	3	3	6	74	....	....	....	....	....
1987-88	Michigan State	CCHA	43	7	12	19	118	....	....	....	....	....
1988-89	Michigan State	CCHA	39	7	10	17	107	....	....	....	....	....
1989-90a	Michigan State	CCHA	44	5	22	27	167	....	....	....	....	....
	Milwaukee	IHL	1	0	0	0	4	5	0	1	1	41
1990-91	**Vancouver**	**NHL**	**14**	**0**	**3**	**3**	**20**	....	....	....	....	....
	Milwaukee	IHL	21	4	3	7	76	....	....	....	....	....
1991-92	Milwaukee	IHL	35	6	9	15	105	4	1	0	1	7
	NHL Totals		**14**	**0**	**3**	**3**	**20**	....	....	....	....	....

a CCHA Second All-Star Team (1990)

GILBERT, GREGORY SCOTT (GREG)

Left wing. Shoots left. 6'1", 191 lbs. Born, Mississauga, Ont., January 22, 1962.
(NY Islanders' 5th choice, 80th overall, in 1980 Entry Draft).

			Regular Season					Playoffs				
Season	Club	Lea	GP	G	A	TP	PIM	GP	G	A	TP	PIM
1979-80	Toronto	OHA	68	10	11	21	35	....	....	....	....	....
1980-81	Toronto	OHA	64	30	37	67	73	5	2	6	8	16
1981-82	**NY Islanders**	**NHL**	**1**	**1**	**0**	**1**	**0**	**4**	**1**	**1**	**2**	**2**
a	Toronto	OHL	65	41	67	108	119	10	4	12	16	23
1982-83	**NY Islanders**	**NHL**	**45**	**8**	**11**	**19**	**30**	**10**	**1**	**0**	**1**	**14**
	Indianapolis	CHL	24	11	16	27	23	....	....	....	....	....
1983-84	**NY Islanders**	**NHL**	**79**	**31**	**35**	**66**	**59**	**21**	**5**	**7**	**12**	**39**
1984-85	**NY Islanders**	**NHL**	**58**	**13**	**25**	**38**	**36**	....	....	....	....	....
1985-86	**NY Islanders**	**NHL**	**60**	**9**	**19**	**28**	**82**	**2**	**0**	**0**	**0**	**9**
	Springfield	AHL	2	0	0	0	2	....	....	....	....	....
1986-87	**NY Islanders**	**NHL**	**51**	**6**	**7**	**13**	**26**	**10**	**2**	**2**	**4**	**6**
1987-88	**NY Islanders**	**NHL**	**76**	**17**	**28**	**45**	**46**	**4**	**0**	**0**	**0**	**6**
1988-89	**NY Islanders**	**NHL**	**55**	**8**	**13**	**21**	**45**	....	....	....	....	....
	Chicago	**NHL**	**4**	**0**	**0**	**0**	**0**	**15**	**1**	**5**	**6**	**20**
1989-90	**Chicago**	**NHL**	**70**	**12**	**25**	**37**	**54**	**19**	**5**	**8**	**13**	**34**
1990-91	**Chicago**	**NHL**	**72**	**10**	**15**	**25**	**58**	**5**	**0**	**1**	**1**	**2**
1991-92	**Chicago**	**NHL**	**50**	**7**	**5**	**12**	**35**	**10**	**1**	**3**	**4**	**16**
	NHL Totals		**621**	**122**	**183**	**305**	**471**	**100**	**16**	**27**	**43**	**148**

a OHL Third All-Star Team (1982)

Traded to **Chicago** by **NY Islanders** for Chicago's fifth round choice (Steve Young) in 1989 Entry Draft, March 7, 1989.

GILCHRIST, BRENT

Left wing. Shoots left. 5'11", 181 lbs. Born, Moose Jaw, Sask., April 3, 1967.
(Montreal's 6th choice, 79th overall, in 1985 Entry Draft).

			Regular Season					Playoffs				
Season	Club	Lea	GP	G	A	TP	PIM	GP	G	A	TP	PIM
1983-84	Kelowna	WHL	69	16	11	27	16	....	....	....	....	....
1984-85	Kelowna	WHL	51	35	38	73	58	6	5	2	7	8
1985-86	Spokane	WHL	52	45	45	90	57	9	6	7	13	19
1986-87	Spokane	WHL	46	45	55	100	71	5	2	7	9	6
	Sherbrooke	AHL	....	....	....	....	....	10	2	7	9	2
1987-88	Sherbrooke	AHL	77	26	48	74	83	6	1	3	4	6
1988-89	**Montreal**	**NHL**	**49**	**8**	**16**	**24**	**16**	**9**	**1**	**1**	**2**	**10**
	Sherbrooke	AHL	7	6	5	11	7	....	....	....	....	....
1989-90	**Montreal**	**NHL**	**57**	**9**	**15**	**24**	**28**	**8**	**2**	**0**	**2**	**2**
1990-91	**Montreal**	**NHL**	**51**	**6**	**9**	**15**	**10**	**13**	**5**	**3**	**8**	**6**
1991-92	**Montreal**	**NHL**	**79**	**23**	**27**	**50**	**57**	**11**	**2**	**4**	**6**	**6**
	NHL Totals		**236**	**46**	**67**	**113**	**111**	**41**	**10**	**8**	**18**	**24**

GILES, CURT (JIGHLS)

Defense. Shoots left. 5'8", 175 lbs. Born, The Pas, Man., November 30, 1958.
(Minnesota's 4th choice, 54th overall, in 1978 Amateur Draft).

			Regular Season					Playoffs				
Season	Club	Lea	GP	G	A	TP	PIM	GP	G	A	TP	PIM
1977-78	Minn.-Duluth	WCHA	34	11	36	47	62	....	....	....	....	....
1978-79	Minn.-Duluth	WCHA	30	3	38	41	38	....	....	....	....	....
1979-80	**Minnesota**	**NHL**	**37**	**2**	**7**	**9**	**31**	**12**	**2**	**4**	**6**	**10**
	Oklahoma City	CHL	42	4	24	28	35	....	....	....	....	....
1980-81	**Minnesota**	**NHL**	**67**	**5**	**22**	**27**	**56**	**19**	**1**	**4**	**5**	**14**
1981-82	**Minnesota**	**NHL**	**74**	**3**	**12**	**15**	**87**	**4**	**0**	**0**	**0**	**2**
1982-83	**Minnesota**	**NHL**	**76**	**2**	**21**	**23**	**70**	**5**	**0**	**2**	**2**	**6**
1983-84	**Minnesota**	**NHL**	**70**	**6**	**22**	**28**	**59**	**16**	**1**	**3**	**4**	**25**
1984-85	**Minnesota**	**NHL**	**77**	**5**	**25**	**30**	**49**	**9**	**0**	**0**	**0**	**17**
1985-86	**Minnesota**	**NHL**	**69**	**6**	**21**	**27**	**30**	**5**	**0**	**1**	**1**	**10**
1986-87	**Minnesota**	**NHL**	**11**	**0**	**3**	**3**	**4**	....	....	....	....	....
	NY Rangers	**NHL**	**61**	**2**	**17**	**19**	**50**	**5**	**0**	**0**	**0**	**6**
1987-88	**NY Rangers**	**NHL**	**13**	**0**	**0**	**0**	**10**	....	....	....	....	....
	Minnesota	**NHL**	**59**	**1**	**12**	**13**	**66**	....	....	....	....	....
1988-89	**Minnesota**	**NHL**	**76**	**5**	**10**	**15**	**77**	**5**	**0**	**0**	**0**	**4**
1989-90	**Minnesota**	**NHL**	**74**	**1**	**12**	**13**	**48**	**7**	**0**	**1**	**1**	**6**
1990-91	**Minnesota**	**NHL**	**70**	**4**	**10**	**14**	**48**	**10**	**1**	**0**	**1**	**16**
1991-92	Cdn. National	....	31	3	6	9	37	....	....	....	....	....
	Cdn. Olympic	....	8	1	0	1	6	....	....	....	....	....
	St. Louis	**NHL**	**13**	**1**	**1**	**2**	**8**	**3**	**1**	**1**	**2**	**0**
	NHL Totals		**847**	**43**	**195**	**238**	**693**	**100**	**6**	**16**	**22**	**116**

Traded to **NY Rangers** by **Minnesota** with Tony McKegney and Minnesota's second round choice (Troy Mallette) in 1988 Entry Draft for Bob Brooke and NY Rangers' rights to Minnesota's fourth round choice (Jeffery Stolp) in 1988 Entry Draft previously acquired by NY Rangers in Mark Pavelich deal, November 13, 1986. Traded to **Minnesota** by **NY Rangers** for Byron Lomow and future considerations, November 20, 1987. Signed as a free agent by **St. Louis**, February 29, 1992.

GILHEN, RANDY (GIHL-uhn)

Center. Shoots left. 6', 190 lbs. Born, Zweibrucken, West Germany, June 13, 1963.
(Hartford's 6th choice, 109th overall, in 1982 Entry Draft).

			Regular Season					Playoffs				
Season	Club	Lea	GP	G	A	TP	PIM	GP	G	A	TP	PIM
1980-81	Saskatoon	WHL	68	10	5	15	154	....	....	....	....	....
1981-82	Saskatoon	WHL	25	15	9	24	45	....	....	....	....	....
	Winnipeg	WHL	36	26	28	54	42	....	....	....	....	....
1982-83	**Hartford**	**NHL**	**2**	**0**	**1**	**1**	**0**	....	....	....	....	....
	Winnipeg	WHL	71	57	44	101	84	3	2	2	4	0
1983-84	Binghamton	AHL	73	8	12	20	72	....	....	....	....	....
1984-85	Salt Lake	IHL	57	20	20	40	28	....	....	....	....	....
	Binghamton	AHL	18	3	3	6	9	8	4	1	5	16
1985-86	Fort Wayne	IHL	82	44	40	84	48	15	10	8	18	6
1986-87	**Winnipeg**	**NHL**	**2**	**0**	**0**	**0**	**0**	....	....	....	....	....
	Sherbrooke	AHL	75	36	29	65	44	17	7	13	20	10
1987-88	**Winnipeg**	**NHL**	**13**	**3**	**2**	**5**	**15**	**4**	**1**	**0**	**1**	**10**
	Moncton	AHL	68	40	47	87	51	....	....	....	....	....
1988-89	**Winnipeg**	**NHL**	**64**	**5**	**3**	**8**	**38**	....	....	....	....	....
1989-90	**Pittsburgh**	**NHL**	**61**	**5**	**11**	**16**	**54**	....	....	....	....	....
1990-91	**Pittsburgh**	**NHL**	**72**	**15**	**10**	**25**	**51**	**16**	**1**	**0**	**1**	**14**
1991-92	**Los Angeles**	**NHL**	**33**	**3**	**6**	**9**	**14**	....	....	....	....	....
	NY Rangers	**NHL**	**40**	**7**	**7**	**14**	**14**	**13**	**1**	**2**	**3**	**2**
	NHL Totals		**287**	**38**	**40**	**78**	**186**	**33**	**3**	**2**	**5**	**26**

Signed as a free agent by **Winnipeg**, August, 1985. Traded to **Pittsburgh** by **Winnipeg** with Jim Kyte and Andrew McBain for Randy Cunnyworth, Rick Tabaracci and Dave McLlwain, June 17, 1989. Claimed by **Minnesota** from **Pittsburgh** in Expansion Draft, May 30, 1991. Traded to **Los Angeles** by **Minnesota** with Charlie Huddy, Jim Thomson and NY Rangers' fourth round choice (previously acquired by Minnesota — Alexei Zhitnik) in 1991 Entry Draft for Todd Elik, June 22, 1991. Traded to **NY Rangers** by **Los Angeles** for Corey Millen, December 23, 1991.

GILL, TODD

Defense. Shoots left. 6', 185 lbs. Born, Brockville, Ont., November 9, 1965.
(Toronto's 2nd choice, 25th overall, in 1984 Entry Draft).

			Regular Season					Playoffs				
Season	Club	Lea	GP	G	A	TP	PIM	GP	G	A	TP	PIM
1982-83	Windsor	OHL	70	12	24	36	108	3	0	0	0	11
1983-84	Windsor	OHL	68	9	48	57	184	3	1	1	2	10
1984-85	**Toronto**	**NHL**	**10**	**1**	**0**	**1**	**13**	....	....	....	....	....
a	Windsor	OHL	53	17	40	57	148	4	0	1	1	14
1985-86	**Toronto**	**NHL**	**15**	**1**	**2**	**3**	**28**	**1**	**0**	**0**	**0**	**0**
	St. Catharines	AHL	58	8	25	33	90	10	1	6	7	17
1986-87	**Toronto**	**NHL**	**61**	**4**	**27**	**31**	**92**	**13**	**2**	**2**	**4**	**42**
	Newmarket	AHL	11	1	8	9	33	....	....	....	....	....
1987-88	**Toronto**	**NHL**	**65**	**8**	**17**	**25**	**131**	**6**	**1**	**3**	**4**	**20**
	Newmarket	AHL	2	0	1	1	2	....	....	....	....	....
1988-89	**Toronto**	**NHL**	**59**	**11**	**14**	**25**	**72**	....	....	....	....	....
1989-90	**Toronto**	**NHL**	**48**	**1**	**14**	**15**	**92**	**5**	**0**	**3**	**3**	**16**
1990-91	**Toronto**	**NHL**	**72**	**2**	**22**	**24**	**113**	....	....	....	....	....
1991-92	**Toronto**	**NHL**	**74**	**2**	**15**	**17**	**91**	....	....	....	....	....
	NHL Totals		**404**	**30**	**111**	**141**	**632**	**25**	**3**	**8**	**11**	**78**

a OHL Third All-Star Team (1985)

GILLINGHAM, TODD

Left wing. Shoots left. 6'2", 200 lbs. Born, Labrador City, Nfld., January 31, 1970.

			Regular Season					Playoffs				
Season	Club	Lea	GP	G	A	TP	PIM	GP	G	A	TP	PIM
1988-89	Verdun	QMJHL	67	16	25	41	253	....	....	....	....	....
1989-90	Trois-Rivières	QMJHL	62	22	36	58	349	....	....	....	....	....
1990-91	Trois-Rivières	QMJHL	66	46	102	148	353	6	2	4	6	40
1991-92	St. John's	AHL	66	12	35	47	306	16	4	7	11	80

Signed as a free agent by **Calgary**, May 1, 1991. Traded to **Toronto** by **Calgary** for cash, January 15, 1992. Traded to **Calgary** by **Toronto** for cash, June 2, 1992.

GILLIS, PAUL

Center. Shoots left. 5'11", 198 lbs. Born, Toronto, Ont., December 31, 1963.
(Quebec's 2nd choice, 34th overall, in 1982 Entry Draft).

			Regular Season					Playoffs				
Season	Club	Lea	GP	G	A	TP	PIM	GP	G	A	TP	PIM
1980-81	Niagara Falls	OHA	59	14	19	33	165	....	....	....	....	....
1981-82	Niagara Falls	OHL	65	27	62	89	247	5	1	5	6	26
1982-83	Quebec	NHL	7	0	2	2	2	....	....	....	....	....
	North Bay	OHL	61	34	52	86	151	6	1	3	4	26
1983-84	Quebec	NHL	57	8	9	17	59	1	0	0	0	2
	Fredericton	AHL	18	7	8	15	47	....	....	....	....	....
1984-85	Quebec	NHL	77	14	28	42	168	18	1	7	8	73
1985-86	Quebec	NHL	80	19	24	43	203	3	0	2	2	14
1986-87	Quebec	NHL	76	13	26	39	267	13	2	4	6	65
1987-88	Quebec	NHL	80	7	10	17	164	....	....	....	....	....
1988-89	Quebec	NHL	79	15	25	40	163	....	....	....	....	....
1989-90	Quebec	NHL	71	8	14	22	234	....	....	....	....	....
1990-91	Quebec	NHL	49	3	8	11	91	....	....	....	....	....
	Chicago	NHL	13	0	5	5	53	2	0	0	0	2
1991-92	Chicago	NHL	2	0	0	0	6	....	....	....	....	....
	Indianapolis	IHL	42	10	15	25	170	....	....	....	....	....
	Hartford	NHL	12	0	2	2	48	5	0	1	1	0
	NHL Totals		603	87	153	240	1458	42	3	14	17	156

Traded to **Chicago** by **Quebec** with Dan Vincelette for Ryan McGill and Mike McNeil, March 5, 1991. Traded to **Hartford** by **Chicago** for future considerations, January 27, 1992.

GILMOUR, DOUGLAS (DOUG)

Center. Shoots left. 5'11", 165 lbs. Born, Kingston, Ont., June 25, 1963.
(St. Louis' 4th choice, 134th overall, in 1982 Entry Draft).

			Regular Season					Playoffs				
Season	Club	Lea	GP	G	A	TP	PIM	GP	G	A	TP	PIM
1981-82	Cornwall	OHL	67	46	73	119	42	5	6	9	15	2
1982-83ab	Cornwall	OHL	68	70	*107	*177	62	8	8	10	18	16
1983-84	St. Louis	NHL	80	25	28	53	57	11	2	9	11	10
1984-85	St. Louis	NHL	78	21	36	57	49	3	1	1	2	2
1985-86	St. Louis	NHL	74	25	28	53	41	19	9	12	*21	25
1986-87	St. Louis	NHL	80	42	63	105	58	6	2	2	4	16
1987-88	St. Louis	NHL	72	36	50	86	59	10	3	14	17	18
1988-89	Calgary	NHL	72	26	59	85	44	22	11	11	22	20
1989-90	Calgary	NHL	78	24	67	91	54	6	3	1	4	8
1990-91	Calgary	NHL	78	20	61	81	144	7	1	1	2	0
1991-92	Calgary	NHL	38	11	27	38	46	....	....	....	....	....
	Toronto	NHL	40	15	34	49	32	....	....	....	....	....
	NHL Totals		690	245	453	698	584	86	32	51	83	99

a OHL First All-Star Team (1983)
b Named OHL's Most Outstanding Player (1983)

Traded to **Calgary** by **St. Louis** with Mark Hunter, Steve Bozek and Michael Dark for Mike Bullard, Craig Coxe and Tim Corkery, September 6, 1988. Traded to **Toronto** by **Calgary** with Jamie Macoun, Ric Natress, Kent Manderville and Rick Wamsley for Gary Leeman, Alexander Godynyuk, Jeff Reese, Michel Petit and Craig Berube, January 2, 1992.

GLENNON, MATTHEW (MATT)

Left wing. Shoots left. 6', 185 lbs. Born, Hull, MA, September 20, 1968.
(Boston's 7th choice, 119th overall, in 1987 Entry Draft).

			Regular Season					Playoffs				
Season	Club	Lea	GP	G	A	TP	PIM	GP	G	A	TP	PIM
1987-88	Boston College	H.E.	16	3	3	6	16	....	....	....	....	....
1988-89	Boston College	H.E.	16	1	6	7	4	....	....	....	....	....
1989-90	Boston College	H.E.	31	7	11	18	16	....	....	....	....	....
1990-91	Boston College	H.E.	33	6	9	15	36	....	....	....	....	....
1991-92	Boston	NHL	3	0	0	0	2	....	....	....	....	....
	Maine	AHL	32	6	12	18	13	....	....	....	....	....
	Johnstown	ECHL	30	9	46	55	77	6	2	4	6	25
	NHL Totals		3	0	0	0	2	....	....	....	....	....

GLYNN, BRIAN

Defense. Shoots left. 6'4", 215 lbs. Born, Iserlohn, West Germany, November 23, 1967.
(Calgary's 2nd choice, 37th overall, in 1986 Entry Draft).

			Regular Season					Playoffs				
Season	Club	Lea	GP	G	A	TP	PIM	GP	G	A	TP	PIM
1984-85	Saskatoon	WHL	12	1	0	1	2	3	0	0	0	0
1985-86	Saskatoon	WHL	66	7	25	32	131	13	0	3	3	30
1986-87	Saskatoon	WHL	44	2	26	28	163	11	1	3	4	19
1987-88	Calgary	NHL	67	5	14	19	87	1	0	0	0	0
1988-89	Calgary	NHL	9	0	1	1	19	....	....	....	....	....
	Salt Lake	IHL	31	3	10	13	105	14	3	7	10	31
1989-90	Calgary	NHL	1	0	0	0	0	....	....	....	....	....
ab	Salt Lake	IHL	80	17	44	61	164	....	....	....	....	....
1990-91	Salt Lake	IHL	8	1	3	4	18	....	....	....	....	....
	Minnesota	NHL	66	8	11	19	83	23	2	6	8	18
1991-92	Minnesota	NHL	37	2	12	14	24	....	....	....	....	....
	Edmonton	NHL	25	2	6	8	6	16	4	1	5	12
	NHL Totals		205	17	44	61	219	40	6	7	13	30

a IHL First All-Star Team (1990)
b Won Governors' Trophy (Outstanding Defenseman-IHL) (1990)

Traded to **Minnesota** by **Calgary** for Frantisek Musil, October 26, 1990. Traded to **Edmonton** by **Minnesota** for David Shaw, January 21, 1992.

GODYNYUK, ALEXANDER (goh-dih-NYOOK)

Defense. Shoots left. 6', 207 lbs. Born, Kiev, Soviet Union, January 27, 1970.
(Toronto's 5th choice, 115th overall, in 1990 Entry Draft).

			Regular Season					Playoffs				
Season	Club	Lea	GP	G	A	TP	PIM	GP	G	A	TP	PIM
1989-90	Sokol Kiev	USSR	38	3	2	5	31	....	....	....	....	....
1990-91	Sokol Kiev	USSR	19	3	1	4	20	....	....	....	....	....
	Toronto	NHL	18	0	3	3	16	....	....	....	....	....
	Newmarket	AHL	11	0	1	1	29	....	....	....	....	....
1991-92	Toronto	NHL	31	3	6	9	59	....	....	....	....	....
	Calgary	NHL	6	0	1	1	4	....	....	....	....	....
	Salt Lake	IHL	17	2	1	3	24	....	....	....	....	....
	NHL Totals		55	3	10	13	79	....	....	....	....	....

Traded to **Calgary** by **Toronto** with Craig Berube, Gary Leeman, Michel Petit and Jeff Reese for Doug Gilmour, Jamie Macoun, Ric Nattress, Rick Wamsley and Kent Manderville, January 2, 1992.

GOLCZEWSKI, GARY

Left wing. Shoots left. 6', 190 lbs. Born, Morristown, NJ, February 16, 1973.
(Boston's 6th choice, 150th overall, in 1991 Entry Draft).

			Regular Season					Playoffs				
Season	Club	Lea	GP	G	A	TP	PIM	GP	G	A	TP	PIM
1990-91	Trinity Pawling	HS	19	19	22	41	38	....	....	....	....	....
1991-92	Trinity Pawling	HS	15	16	17	33	....	....	....	....	....	....

GONCHAR, SERGEI (gohn-CHAR)

Defense. Shoots left. 6', 178 lbs. Born, Chelyabinsk, Soviet Union, April 13, 1974.
(Washington's 1st choice, 14th overall, in 1992 Entry Draft).

			Regular Season					Playoffs				
Season	Club	Lea	GP	G	A	TP	PIM	GP	G	A	TP	PIM
1991-92	Chelyabinsk	CIS	31	1	0	1	6	....	....	....	....	....

GOODALL, GLEN

Center. Shoots right. 5'8", 170 lbs. Born, Fort Nelson, B.C., January 22, 1970.
(Detroit's 9th choice, 206th overall, in 1988 Entry Draft).

			Regular Season					Playoffs				
Season	Club	Lea	GP	G	A	TP	PIM	GP	G	A	TP	PIM
1984-85	Seattle	WHL	59	5	21	26	6	....	....	....	....	....
1985-86	Seattle	WHL	65	13	28	41	53	4	1	1	2	0
1986-87	Seattle	WHL	68	63	49	112	64	....	....	....	....	....
1987-88	Seattle	WHL	70	53	64	117	88	....	....	....	....	....
1988-89	Seattle	WHL	70	52	62	114	58	....	....	....	....	....
	Flint	IHL	9	5	4	9	4	....	....	....	....	....
1989-90ab	Seattle	WHL	67	76	87	163	83	10	7	7	14	2
1990-91	Adirondack	AHL	69	18	23	41	49	2	0	0	0	2
1991-92	San Diego	IHL	19	1	11	12	10	....	....	....	....	....
	Binghamton	AHL	6	0	2	2	0	....	....	....	....	....
	Erie	ECHL	14	6	20	26	12	4	1	1	2	2

a WHL West Second All-Star Team (1990)
b WHL Player of the Year (1990)

Signed as a free agent by **NY Rangers**, August 28, 1991.

GORDIJUK, VIKTOR (gohr-dee-YOOK)

Right wing. Shoots right. 5'10", 176 lbs. Born, Moscow, Soviet Union, April 11, 1970.
(Buffalo's 6th choice, 142nd overall, in 1990 Entry Draft).

			Regular Season					Playoffs				
Season	Club	Lea	GP	G	A	TP	PIM	GP	G	A	TP	PIM
1989-90	Soviet Wings	USSR	48	11	4	15	24	....	....	....	....	....
1990-91	Soviet Wings	USSR	46	12	10	22	22	....	....	....	....	....
1991-92	Soviet Wings	CIS	42	16	7	23	24	....	....	....	....	....

GOSSELIN, GUY (GOHS-lin, GEE)

Defense. Shoots right. 5'10", 185 lbs. Born, Rochester, MN, January 6, 1964.
(Winnipeg's 6th choice, 159th overall, in 1982 Entry Draft).

			Regular Season					Playoffs				
Season	Club	Lea	GP	G	A	TP	PIM	GP	G	A	TP	PIM
1982-83	Minn.-Duluth	WCHA	4	0	0	0	0	....	....	....	....	....
1983-84	Minn.-Duluth	WCHA	37	3	3	6	26	....	....	....	....	....
1984-85	Minn.-Duluth	WCHA	47	3	7	10	25	....	....	....	....	....
1985-86	Minn.-Duluth	WCHA	39	2	16	18	53	....	....	....	....	....
1986-87a	Minn.-Duluth	WCHA	33	7	8	15	66	....	....	....	....	....
1987-88	U.S. National	....	50	3	19	22	82	....	....	....	....	....
	U.S. Olympic	....	6	0	3	3	2	....	....	....	....	....
	Winnipeg	NHL	5	0	0	0	6	....	....	....	....	....
1988-89	Moncton	AHL	58	2	8	10	56	10	1	1	2	2
1989-90	Moncton	AHL	70	2	10	12	37	....	....	....	....	....
1990-91	Skelleftea	Swe.2	16	0	1	1	8	....	....	....	....	....
1991-92	U.S. National	....	18	1	3	4	20	....	....	....	....	....
	U.S. Olympic	....	8	0	0	0	6	....	....	....	....	....
	NHL Totals		5	0	0	0	6	....	....	....	....	....

a WCHA Second All-Star Team (1987)

GOTAAS, STEVE (GAH-tihs)

Center. Shoots right. 5'10", 180 lbs. Born, Camrose, Alta., May 10, 1967.
(Pittsburgh's 4th choice, 86th overall, in 1985 Entry Draft).

			Regular Season					Playoffs				
Season	Club	Lea	GP	G	A	TP	PIM	GP	G	A	TP	PIM
1983-84	Prince Albert	WHL	65	10	22	32	47	5	0	1	1	0
1984-85	Prince Albert	WHL	72	32	41	73	66	13	3	6	9	17
1985-86	Prince Albert	WHL	61	40	61	101	31	....	....	....	....	....
1986-87	Prince Albert	WHL	68	53	55	108	94	8	5	6	11	16
1987-88	Pittsburgh	NHL	36	5	6	11	45	....	....	....	....	....
	Muskegon	IHL	34	16	22	38	4	....	....	....	....	....
1988-89	Minnesota	NHL	12	1	3	4	6	3	0	1	1	5
	Muskegon	IHL	19	9	16	25	34	....	....	....	....	....
	Kalamazoo	IHL	30	24	22	46	12	5	2	3	5	2
1989-90	Kalamazoo	IHL	1	1	0	1	0	2	0	0	0	2
1990-91	Minnesota	NHL	1	0	0	0	2	....	....	....	....	....
	Kalamazoo	IHL	78	30	49	79	88	7	3	5	8	4
1991-92	Kalamazoo	IHL	72	34	29	63	115	12	4	10	14	20
	NHL Totals		49	6	9	15	53	3	0	1	1	5

Traded to **Minnesota** by **Pittsburgh** with Ville Siren for Gord Dineen and Scott Bjugstad, December 17, 1988.

GOTZIAMAN, CHRIS

Right wing. Shoots right. 6'3", 200 lbs. Born, Roseau, MN, November 29, 1971.
(New Jersey's 3rd choice, 29th overall, in 1990 Entry Draft).

			Regular Season					Playoffs				
Season	Club	Lea	GP	G	A	TP	PIM	GP	G	A	TP	PIM
1990-91	North Dakota	WCHA	40	11	8	19	26	....	....	....	....	....
1991-92	North Dakota	WCHA	38	9	6	15	47	....	....	....	....	....

GOULET, MICHEL (goo-LAY)

Left wing. Shoots left. 6'1", 195 lbs. Born, Peribonka, Que., April 21, 1960.
(Quebec's 1st choice, 20th overall, in 1979 Entry Draft).

			Regular Season					Playoffs				
Season	Club	Lea	GP	G	A	TP	PIM	GP	G	A	TP	PIM
1976-77	Quebec	QJHL	37	17	18	35	9	14	3	8	11	19
1977-78	Quebec	QJHL	72	73	62	135	109	1	0	1	1	0
1978-79	Birmingham	WHA	78	28	30	58	65	....	....	....	....	....
1979-80	**Quebec**	**NHL**	**77**	**22**	**32**	**54**	**48**	....	....	....	....	....
1980-81	**Quebec**	**NHL**	**76**	**32**	**39**	**71**	**45**	**4**	**3**	**4**	**7**	**7**
1981-82	**Quebec**	**NHL**	**80**	**42**	**42**	**84**	**48**	**16**	**8**	**5**	**13**	**6**
1982-83a	**Quebec**	**NHL**	**80**	**57**	**48**	**105**	**51**	**4**	**0**	**0**	**0**	**6**
1983-84b	**Quebec**	**NHL**	**75**	**56**	**65**	**121**	**76**	**9**	**2**	**4**	**6**	**17**
1984-85	**Quebec**	**NHL**	**69**	**55**	**40**	**95**	**55**	**17**	**11**	**10**	**21**	**17**
1985-86b	**Quebec**	**NHL**	**75**	**53**	**51**	**104**	**64**	**3**	**1**	**2**	**3**	**10**
1986-87b	**Quebec**	**NHL**	**75**	**49**	**47**	**96**	**61**	**13**	**9**	**5**	**14**	**35**
1987-88a	**Quebec**	**NHL**	**80**	**48**	**58**	**106**	**56**	....	....	....	....	....
1988-89	**Quebec**	**NHL**	**69**	**26**	**38**	**64**	**67**	....	....	....	....	....
1989-90	**Quebec**	**NHL**	**57**	**16**	**29**	**45**	**42**	....	....	....	....	....
	Chicago	**NHL**	**8**	**4**	**1**	**5**	**9**	**14**	**2**	**4**	**6**	**6**
1990-91	**Chicago**	**NHL**	**74**	**27**	**38**	**65**	**65**	....	....	....	....	....
1991-92	**Chicago**	**NHL**	**75**	**22**	**41**	**63**	**69**	**9**	**3**	**4**	**7**	**6**
	NHL Totals		**970**	**509**	**569**	**1078**	**756**	**89**	**39**	**38**	**77**	**110**

a NHL Second All-Star Team (1983, 1988)
b NHL First All-Star Team (1984, 1986, 1987)

Played in NHL All-Star Game (1983-86, 1988)

Traded to **Chicago** by **Quebec** with Greg Millen and Quebec's sixth round choice (Kevin St. Jacques) in 1991 Entry Draft for Mario Doyon, Everett Sanipass and Dan Vincelette, March 5, 1990.

GOVEDARIS, CHRIS (goh-va-DAIR-us)

Left wing. Shoots left. 6', 200 lbs. Born, Toronto, Ont., February 2, 1970.
(Hartford's 1st choice, 11th overall, in 1988 Entry Draft).

			Regular Season					Playoffs				
Season	Club	Lea	GP	G	A	TP	PIM	GP	G	A	TP	PIM
1986-87	Toronto	OHL	64	36	28	64	148	....	....	....	....	....
1987-88	Toronto	OHL	62	42	38	80	118	4	2	1	3	10
1988-89	Toronto	OHL	49	41	38	79	117	6	2	3	5	0
1989-90	**Hartford**	**NHL**	**12**	**0**	**1**	**1**	**6**	**2**	**0**	**0**	**0**	**2**
	Binghamton	AHL	14	3	3	6	4	....	....	....	....	....
	Hamilton	OHL	23	11	21	32	53	....	....	....	....	....
1990-91	**Hartford**	**NHL**	**14**	**1**	**3**	**4**	**4**	....	....	....	....	....
	Springfield	AHL	56	26	36	62	133	9	2	5	7	36
1991-92	Springfield	AHL	43	14	25	39	55	11	3	2	5	25
	NHL Totals		**26**	**1**	**4**	**5**	**10**	**2**	**0**	**0**	**0**	**2**

GRAHAM, DIRK MILTON

Left/Right wing. Shoots right. 5'11", 198 lbs. Born, Regina, Sask., July 29, 1959.
(Vancouver's 5th choice, 89th overall, in 1979 Entry Draft).

			Regular Season					Playoffs				
Season	Club	Lea	GP	G	A	TP	PIM	GP	G	A	TP	PIM
1975-76	Regina	WCHL	2	0	0	0	0	6	1	1	2	5
1976-77	Regina	WCHL	65	37	28	65	66	....	....	....	....	....
1977-78	Regina	WCHL	72	49	61	110	87	13	15	19	34	37
1978-79	Regina	WHL	71	48	60	108	252	....	....	....	....	....
1979-80	Dallas	CHL	62	17	15	32	96	....	....	....	....	....
1980-81	Fort Wayne	IHL	6	1	2	3	12	....	....	....	....	....
a	Toledo	IHL	61	40	45	85	88	....	....	....	....	....
1981-82	Toledo	IHL	72	49	56	105	68	13	10	11	*21	8
1982-83b	Toledo	IHL	78	70	55	125	88	11	13	7	*20	30
1983-84	**Minnesota**	**NHL**	**6**	**1**	**1**	**2**	**0**	**1**	**0**	**0**	**0**	**2**
c	Salt Lake	CHL	57	37	57	94	72	5	3	8	11	2
1984-85	**Minnesota**	**NHL**	**36**	**12**	**11**	**23**	**23**	**9**	**0**	**4**	**4**	**7**
	Springfield	AHL	37	20	28	48	41	....	....	....	....	....
1985-86	**Minnesota**	**NHL**	**80**	**22**	**33**	**55**	**87**	**5**	**3**	**1**	**4**	**2**
1986-87	**Minnesota**	**NHL**	**76**	**25**	**29**	**54**	**142**	....	....	....	....	....
1987-88	**Minnesota**	**NHL**	**28**	**7**	**5**	**12**	**39**	....	....	....	....	....
	Chicago	**NHL**	**42**	**17**	**19**	**36**	**32**	**4**	**1**	**2**	**3**	**4**
1988-89	**Chicago**	**NHL**	**80**	**33**	**45**	**78**	**89**	**16**	**2**	**4**	**6**	**38**
1989-90	**Chicago**	**NHL**	**73**	**22**	**32**	**54**	**102**	**5**	**1**	**5**	**6**	**2**
1990-91d	**Chicago**	**NHL**	**80**	**24**	**21**	**45**	**88**	**6**	**1**	**2**	**3**	**17**
1991-92	**Chicago**	**NHL**	**80**	**17**	**30**	**47**	**89**	**18**	**7**	**5**	**12**	**8**
	NHL Totals		**581**	**180**	**226**	**406**	**691**	**64**	**15**	**23**	**38**	**80**

a IHL Second All-Star Team (1981)
b IHL First All-Star Team (1983)
c CHL First All-Star Team (1984)
d Won Frank J. Selke Trophy (1991)

Signed as a free agent by **Minnesota**, August 17, 1983. Traded to **Chicago** by **Minnesota** for Curt Fraser, January 4, 1988.

GRANATO, TONY

Left wing. Shoots right. 5'10", 185 lbs. Born, Downers Grove, IL, July 25, 1964.
(NY Rangers' 5th choice, 120th overall, in 1982 Entry Draft).

			Regular Season					Playoffs				
Season	Club	Lea	GP	G	A	TP	PIM	GP	G	A	TP	PIM
1983-84	U. Wisconsin	WCHA	35	14	17	31	48	....	....	....	....	....
1984-85	U. Wisconsin	WCHA	42	33	34	67	94	....	....	....	....	....
1985-86	U. Wisconsin	WCHA	33	25	24	49	36	....	....	....	....	....
1986-87ab	U. Wisconsin	WCHA	42	28	45	73	64	....	....	....	....	....
1987-88	U.S. National	....	49	40	31	71	55	....	....	....	....	....
	U.S. Olympic	....	6	1	7	8	4	....	....	....	....	....
	Colorado	IHL	22	13	14	27	36	8	9	4	13	16
1988-89c	**NY Rangers**	**NHL**	**78**	**36**	**27**	**63**	**140**	**4**	**1**	**1**	**2**	**21**
1989-90	**NY Rangers**	**NHL**	**37**	**7**	**18**	**25**	**77**	....	....	....	....	....
	Los Angeles	**NHL**	**19**	**5**	**6**	**11**	**45**	**10**	**5**	**4**	**9**	**12**
1990-91	**Los Angeles**	**NHL**	**68**	**30**	**34**	**64**	**154**	**12**	**1**	**4**	**5**	**28**
1991-92	**Los Angeles**	**NHL**	**80**	**39**	**29**	**68**	**187**	**6**	**1**	**5**	**6**	**10**
	NHL Totals		**282**	**117**	**114**	**231**	**603**	**32**	**8**	**14**	**22**	**71**

a WCHA Second All-Star Team (1987)
b NCAA West Second All-American Team (1987)
c NHL All-Rookie Team (1989)

Traded to **Los Angeles** by **NY Rangers** with Tomas Sandstrom for Bernie Nicholls, January 20, 1990.

GRANT, KEVIN

Defense. Shoots right. 6'3", 210 lbs. Born, Toronto, Ont., January 9, 1969.
(Calgary's 3rd choice, 40th overall, in 1987 Entry Draft).

			Regular Season					Playoffs				
Season	Club	Lea	GP	G	A	TP	PIM	GP	G	A	TP	PIM
1985-86	Kitchener	OHL	63	2	15	17	204	5	0	1	1	11
1986-87	Kitchener	OHL	52	5	18	23	125	4	0	1	1	16
1987-88	Kitchener	OHL	48	3	20	23	138	4	0	1	1	4
1988-89	Salt Lake	IHL	3	0	1	1	5	3	0	0	0	12
	Sudbury	OHL	60	9	41	50	186	....	....	....	....	....
1989-90	Salt Lake	IHL	78	7	17	24	117	11	0	2	2	22
1990-91	Salt Lake	IHL	63	6	19	25	200	3	0	0	0	8
1991-92	Salt Lake	IHL	73	7	16	23	181	....	....	....	....	....

GRAVELLE, DAN

Center. Shoots left. 5'11", 190 lbs. Born, Montreal, Que., March 10, 1970.
(Chicago's 1st choice, 28th overall, in 1991 Supplemental Draft).

			Regular Season					Playoffs				
Season	Club	Lea	GP	G	A	TP	PIM	GP	G	A	TP	PIM
1989-90	Merrimack	H.E.	10	2	1	3	13	....	....	....	....	....
1990-91	Merrimack	H.E.	32	18	21	39	22	....	....	....	....	....
1991-92	Merrimack	H.E.	34	23	28	51	40	....	....	....	....	....

GRAVES, ADAM

Center. Shoots left. 5'11", 185 lbs. Born, Toronto, Ont., April 12, 1968.
(Detroit's 2nd choice, 22nd overall, in 1986 Entry Draft).

			Regular Season					Playoffs				
Season	Club	Lea	GP	G	A	TP	PIM	GP	G	A	TP	PIM
1985-86	Windsor	OHL	62	27	37	64	35	16	5	11	16	10
1986-87	Windsor	OHL	66	45	55	100	70	14	9	8	17	32
	Adirondack	AHL	....	....	....	....	....	5	0	1	1	0
1987-88	**Detroit**	**NHL**	**9**	**0**	**1**	**1**	**8**	....	....	....	....	....
	Windsor	OHL	37	28	32	60	107	12	14	18	*32	16
1988-89	**Detroit**	**NHL**	**56**	**7**	**5**	**12**	**60**	**5**	**0**	**0**	**0**	**4**
	Adirondack	AHL	14	10	11	21	28	14	11	7	18	17
1989-90	**Detroit**	**NHL**	**13**	**0**	**1**	**1**	**13**	....	....	....	....	....
	Edmonton	**NHL**	**63**	**9**	**12**	**21**	**123**	**22**	**5**	**6**	**11**	**17**
1990-91	**Edmonton**	**NHL**	**76**	**7**	**18**	**25**	**127**	**18**	**2**	**4**	**6**	**22**
1991-92	**NY Rangers**	**NHL**	**80**	**26**	**33**	**59**	**139**	**10**	**5**	**3**	**8**	**22**
	NHL Totals		**297**	**49**	**70**	**119**	**470**	**55**	**12**	**13**	**25**	**65**

Traded to **Edmonton** by **Detroit** with Petr Klima, Joe Murphy and Jeff Sharples for Jimmy Carson, Kevin McClelland and Edmonton's fifth round choice (later traded to Montreal for Rick Green. Montreal selected Brad Layzell) in 1991 Entry Draft, November 2, 1989. Signed as a free agent by **NY Rangers**, September 3, 1991.

GRAVES, STEVE

Left wing. Shoots left. 5'10", 175 lbs. Born, Trenton, Ont., April 7, 1964.
(Edmonton's 2nd choice, 41st overall, in 1982 Entry Draft).

			Regular Season					Playoffs				
Season	Club	Lea	GP	G	A	TP	PIM	GP	G	A	TP	PIM
1981-82	S.S. Marie	OHL	66	12	15	27	49	13	8	5	13	14
1982-83	S.S. Marie	OHL	60	21	20	41	48	5	0	0	0	4
1983-84	**Edmonton**	**NHL**	**2**	**0**	**0**	**0**	**0**	....	....	....	....	....
a	S.S. Marie	OHL	67	41	48	89	47	16	6	8	14	8
1984-85	Nova Scotia	AHL	80	17	15	32	20	6	0	1	1	4
1985-86	Nova Scotia	AHL	78	19	18	37	22	....	....	....	....	....
1986-87	**Edmonton**	**NHL**	**12**	**2**	**0**	**2**	**0**	....	....	....	....	....
	Nova Scotia	AHL	59	18	10	28	22	5	1	1	2	2
1987-88	**Edmonton**	**NHL**	**21**	**3**	**4**	**7**	**10**	....	....	....	....	....
	Nova Scotia	AHL	11	6	2	8	4	....	....	....	....	....
1988-89	Cdn. National	....	3	5	1	6	2	....	....	....	....	....
	TPS	Fin.	43	16	12	28	48	10	2	8	10	12
1989-90	Cdn. National	....	53	24	19	43	50	....	....	....	....	....
1990-91	New Haven	AHL	3	0	1	1	2	....	....	....	....	....
	Phoenix	IHL	56	11	20	31	64	5	1	3	4	2
1991-92	Asiago	Italy	12	4	6	10	4	....	....	....	....	....
	NHL Totals		**35**	**5**	**4**	**9**	**10**	....	....	....	....	....

a OHL Third All-Star Team (1984)

Signed as a free agent by **Los Angeles**, July 16, 1990.

GREEN, MARK

Center. Shoots right. 6'4", 200 lbs. Born, Watertown, NY, December 26, 1967.
(Winnipeg's 8th choice, 176th overall, in 1986 Entry Draft).

			Regular Season					Playoffs				
Season	Club	Lea	GP	G	A	TP	PIM	GP	G	A	TP	PIM
1987-88	Clarkson	ECAC	18	3	6	9	18	....	....	....	....	....
1988-89	Clarkson	ECAC	30	16	11	27	42	....	....	....	....	....
1989-90	Clarkson	ECAC	32	18	17	35	42	....	....	....	....	....
1990-91	Clarkson	ECAC	38	21	24	45	32	....	....	....	....	....
1991-92a	Johnstown	ECHL	64	68	49	117	44	6	2	3	5	4

a ECHL First All-Star Team (1992)

Signed as a free agent by **Tampa Bay**, August 18, 1992.

GREEN, RICHARD DOUGLAS (RICK)

Defense. Shoots left. 6'3", 220 lbs. Born, Belleville, Ont., February 20, 1956.
(Washington's 1st choice, 1st overall, in 1976 Amateur Draft).

			Regular Season					Playoffs				
Season	Club	Lea	GP	G	A	TP	PIM	GP	G	A	TP	PIM
1974-75	London	OMJHL	65	8	45	53	68	....	....	....	....	....
1975-76ab	London	OHA	61	13	47	60	69	5	1	0	1	4
1976-77	**Washington**	**NHL**	**45**	**3**	**12**	**15**	**16**	....	....	....	....	....
1977-78	**Washington**	**NHL**	**60**	**5**	**14**	**19**	**67**	....	....	....	....	....
1978-79	**Washington**	**NHL**	**71**	**8**	**33**	**41**	**62**	....	....	....	....	....
1979-80	**Washington**	**NHL**	**71**	**4**	**20**	**24**	**52**	....	....	....	....	....
1980-81	**Washington**	**NHL**	**65**	**8**	**23**	**31**	**91**	....	....	....	....	....
1981-82	**Washington**	**NHL**	**65**	**3**	**25**	**28**	**93**	....	....	....	....	....
1982-83	**Montreal**	**NHL**	**66**	**2**	**24**	**26**	**58**	**3**	**0**	**0**	**0**	**2**
1983-84	**Montreal**	**NHL**	**7**	**0**	**1**	**1**	**7**	**15**	**1**	**2**	**3**	**33**
1984-85	**Montreal**	**NHL**	**77**	**1**	**18**	**19**	**30**	**12**	**0**	**3**	**3**	**14**
1985-86	**Montreal**	**NHL**	**46**	**3**	**2**	**5**	**20**	**18**	**1**	**4**	**5**	**8**
1986-87	**Montreal**	**NHL**	**72**	**1**	**9**	**10**	**10**	**17**	**0**	**4**	**4**	**8**
1987-88	**Montreal**	**NHL**	**59**	**2**	**11**	**13**	**33**	**11**	**0**	**2**	**2**	**2**
1988-89	**Montreal**	**NHL**	**72**	**1**	**14**	**15**	**25**	**21**	**1**	**1**	**2**	**6**
1989-90	Meran	Italy	9	2	6	8	2	10	3	6	9	4
1990-91	**Detroit**	**NHL**	**65**	**2**	**14**	**16**	**24**	**3**	**0**	**0**	**0**	**0**
1991-92	**NY Islanders**	**NHL**	**4**	**0**	**0**	**0**	**0**	....	....	....	....	....
	NHL Totals		**845**	**43**	**220**	**263**	**588**	**100**	**3**	**16**	**19**	**73**

a OHA First All-Star Team (1976)
b OHA Outstanding Defenseman (1976)

Traded to **Montreal** by **Washington** with Ryan Walter for Brian Engblom, Rod Langway, Doug Jarvis and Craig Laughlin, September 9, 1982. Traded to **Detroit** by **Montreal** for Edmonton's fifth round choice (Brad Layzell – previously acquired by Detroit) in 1991 Entry Draft, June 15, 1990. Traded to **NY Islanders** by **Detroit** for Alan Kerr and future considerations, May 26, 1991.

GREEN, SHAYNE

Right wing. Shoots right. 6', 193 lbs. Born, Quesnel, B.C., August 13, 1971.
(Minnesota's 11th choice, 228th overall, in 1991 Entry Draft).

			Regular Season					Playoffs				
Season	Club	Lea	GP	G	A	TP	PIM	GP	G	A	TP	PIM
1988-89	Victoria	WHL	13	3	3	6	0	....	....	....	....	....
1989-90	Victoria	WHL	43	16	14	30	26	....	....	....	....	....
1990-91	Victoria	WHL	16	5	7	12	4	....	....	....	....	....
	Kamloops	WHL	32	15	15	30	43	12	4	8	12	14
1991-92	Kamloops	WHL	71	43	55	98	167	17	10	11	21	32

GREEN, TRAVIS

Center. Shoots right. 6', 195 lbs. Born, Creston, B.C., December 20, 1970.
(NY Islanders' 2nd choice, 23rd overall, in 1989 Entry Draft).

			Regular Season					Playoffs				
Season	Club	Lea	GP	G	A	TP	PIM	GP	G	A	TP	PIM
1986-87	Spokane	WHL	64	8	17	25	27	3	0	0	0	0
1987-88	Spokane	WHL	72	33	54	87	42	15	10	10	20	13
1988-89	Spokane	WHL	75	51	51	102	79	....	....	....	....	....
1989-90	Spokane	WHL	50	45	44	89	80	....	....	....	....	....
	Medicine Hat	WHL	25	15	24	39	19	3	0	0	0	2
1990-91	Capital Dist.	AHL	73	21	34	55	26	....	....	....	....	....
1991-92	Capital Dist.	AHL	71	23	27	50	10	7	0	4	4	21

GREENLAW, JEFF

Left wing. Shoots left. 6'1", 230 lbs. Born, Toronto, Ont., February 28, 1968.
(Washington's 1st choice, 19th overall, in 1986 Entry Draft).

			Regular Season					Playoffs				
Season	Club	Lea	GP	G	A	TP	PIM	GP	G	A	TP	PIM
1985-86	Cdn. Olympic	....	57	3	16	19	81	....	....	....	....	....
1986-87	**Washington**	**NHL**	**22**	**0**	**3**	**3**	**44**	....	....	....	....	....
	Binghamton	AHL	4	0	2	2	0	....	....	....	....	....
1987-88	Binghamton	AHL	56	8	7	15	142	1	0	0	0	2
	Washington	**NHL**	....	....	....	....	....	**1**	**0**	**0**	**0**	**19**
1988-89	Baltimore	AHL	55	12	15	27	115	....	....	....	....	....
1989-90	Baltimore	AHL	10	3	2	5	26	7	1	0	1	13
1990-91	**Washington**	**NHL**	**10**	**2**	**0**	**2**	**10**	**1**	**0**	**0**	**0**	**2**
	Baltimore	AHL	50	17	17	34	93	3	1	1	2	2
1991-92	**Washington**	**NHL**	**5**	**0**	**1**	**1**	**34**	....	....	....	....	....
	Baltimore	AHL	37	6	8	14	57	....	....	....	....	....
	NHL Totals		**37**	**2**	**4**	**6**	**88**	**2**	**0**	**0**	**0**	**21**

GREGG, RANDALL JOHN (RANDY)

Defense. Shoots left. 6'4", 215 lbs. Born, Edmonton, Alta., February 19, 1956.

			Regular Season					Playoffs				
Season	Club	Lea	GP	G	A	TP	PIM	GP	G	A	TP	PIM
1977-78	U. of Alberta	CWUAA	24	7	23	30	37	....	....	....	....	....
1978-79a	U. of Alberta	CWUAA	24	5	16	21	47	....	....	....	....	....
1979-80	Cdn. National	....	56	7	17	24	36	....	....	....	....	....
	Cdn. Olympic	....	6	1	1	2	2	....	....	....	....	....
1980-81	Kokuda	Japan	35	12	18	30	30	....	....	....	....	....
1981-82	Kokuda	Japan	36	12	20	32	25	....	....	....	....	....
	Edmonton	**NHL**	....	....	....	....	....	**4**	**0**	**0**	**0**	**0**
1982-83	**Edmonton**	**NHL**	**80**	**6**	**22**	**28**	**54**	**16**	**2**	**4**	**6**	**13**
1983-84	**Edmonton**	**NHL**	**80**	**13**	**27**	**40**	**56**	**19**	**3**	**7**	**10**	**21**
1984-85	**Edmonton**	**NHL**	**57**	**3**	**20**	**23**	**32**	**17**	**0**	**6**	**6**	**12**
1985-86	**Edmonton**	**NHL**	**64**	**2**	**26**	**28**	**47**	**10**	**1**	**0**	**1**	**12**
1986-87	**Edmonton**	**NHL**	**52**	**8**	**16**	**24**	**42**	**18**	**3**	**6**	**9**	**17**
1987-88	Cdn. National	....	37	2	6	8	37	....	....	....	....	....
	Cdn. Olympic	....	8	1	2	3	8	....	....	....	....	....
	Edmonton	**NHL**	**15**	**1**	**2**	**3**	**8**	**19**	**1**	**8**	**9**	**24**
1988-89	**Edmonton**	**NHL**	**57**	**3**	**15**	**18**	**28**	**7**	**1**	**0**	**1**	**4**
1989-90	**Edmonton**	**NHL**	**48**	**4**	**20**	**24**	**42**	**20**	**2**	**6**	**8**	**16**
1990-91						DID NOT PLAY						
1991-92	**Vancouver**	**NHL**	**21**	**1**	**4**	**5**	**24**	**7**	**0**	**1**	**1**	**8**
	NHL Totals		**474**	**41**	**152**	**193**	**333**	**137**	**13**	**38**	**51**	**127**

a CIAU Player of the Year (1979)

Signed as a free agent by **Edmonton**, October 18, 1982. Claimed by **Vancouver** in NHL Waiver Draft, October 1, 1990.

GREIG, MARK (GREG)

Right wing. Shoots right. 5'11", 190 lbs. Born, High River, Alta., January 25, 1970.
(Hartford's 1st choice, 15th overall, in 1990 Entry Draft).

			Regular Season					Playoffs				
Season	Club	Lea	GP	G	A	TP	PIM	GP	G	A	TP	PIM
1987-88	Lethbridge	WHL	65	9	18	27	38	....	....	....	....	....
1988-89	Lethbridge	WHL	71	36	72	108	113	8	5	5	10	16
1989-90a	Lethbridge	WHL	65	55	80	135	149	18	11	21	32	35
1990-91	**Hartford**	**NHL**	**4**	**0**	**0**	**0**	**0**	....	....	....	....	....
	Springfield	AHL	73	32	55	87	73	17	2	6	8	22
1991-92	**Hartford**	**NHL**	**17**	**0**	**5**	**5**	**6**	....	....	....	....	....
	Springfield	AHL	50	20	27	47	38	9	1	1	2	20
	NHL Totals		**21**	**0**	**5**	**5**	**6**	....	....	....	....	....

a WHL East First All-Star Team (1990)

GRETZKY, BRENT (GRETZ-kee)

Center. Shoots left. 5'10", 160 lbs. Born, Brantford, Ont., February 20, 1972.
(Tampa Bay's 3rd choice, 49th overall, in 1992 Entry Draft).

			Regular Season					Playoffs				
Season	Club	Lea	GP	G	A	TP	PIM	GP	G	A	TP	PIM
1989-90	Belleville	OHL	66	17	46	63	72	11	0	0	0	....
1990-91	Belleville	OHL	66	26	56	82	25	6	3	3	6	2
1991-92	Belleville	OHL	62	43	78	121	37	....	....	....	....	....

GRETZKY, WAYNE (GRETZ-kee)

Center. Shoots left. 6', 170 lbs. Born, Brantford, Ont., January 26, 1961.

			Regular Season					Playoffs				
Season	Club	Lea	GP	G	A	TP	PIM	GP	G	A	TP	PIM
1976-77	Peterborough	OHA	3	0	3	3	0	....	....	....	....	....
1977-78ab	S.S. Marie	OHA	64	70	112	182	14	13	6	20	26	0
1978-79	Indianapolis	WHA	8	3	3	6	0	....	....	....	....	....
cd	Edmonton	WHA	72	43	61	104	19	13	*10	10	*20	2
1979-80efg	**Edmonton**	**NHL**	**79**	**51**	***86**	***137**	**21**	**3**	**2**	**1**	**3**	**0**
1980-81ehijk	**Edmonton**	**NHL**	**80**	**55**	***109**	***164**	**28**	**9**	**7**	**14**	**21**	**4**
1981-82 ehijklmq	**Edmonton**	**NHL**	**80**	***92**	***120**	***212**	**26**	**5**	**5**	**7**	**12**	**8**
1982-83 ehijmnoq	**Edmonton**	**NHL**	**80**	***71**	***125**	***196**	**59**	**16**	**12**	***26**	***38**	**4**
1983-84 ehimq	**Edmonton**	**NHL**	**74**	***87**	***118**	***205**	**39**	**19**	**13**	***22**	***35**	**12**
1984-85 ehijmnopqr	**Edmonton**	**NHL**	**80**	***73**	***135**	***208**	**52**	**18**	**17**	***30**	***47**	**4**
1985-86 ehijkr	**Edmonton**	**NHL**	**80**	**52**	***163**	***215**	**46**	**10**	**8**	**11**	**19**	**2**
1986-87 ehimqr	**Edmonton**	**NHL**	**79**	***62**	***121**	***183**	**28**	**21**	**5**	***29**	***34**	**6**
1987-88gnp	**Edmonton**	**NHL**	**64**	**40**	***109**	**149**	**24**	**19**	**12**	***31**	***43**	**16**
1988-89egs	**Los Angeles**	**NHL**	**78**	**54**	***114**	**168**	**26**	**11**	**5**	**17**	**22**	**0**
1989-90gi	**Los Angeles**	**NHL**	**73**	**40**	***102**	***142**	**42**	**7**	**3**	**7**	**10**	**0**
1990-91fhi	**Los Angeles**	**NHL**	**78**	**41**	***122**	***163**	**16**	**12**	**4**	**11**	**15**	**2**
1991-92f	**Los Angeles**	**NHL**	**74**	**31**	***90**	**121**	**34**	**6**	**2**	**5**	**7**	**2**
	NHL Totals		**999**	**749**	***1514**	***2263**	**441**	**156**	***95**	***211**	***306**	**60**

a OHA Second All-Star Team (1978)
b Named OHA's Rookie of the Year (1978)
c WHA Second All-Star Team (1979)
d Named WHA's Rookie of the Year (1979)
e Won Hart Trophy (1980, 1981, 1982, 1983, 1984, 1985, 1986, 1987, 1989)
f Won Lady Byng Trophy (1980, 1991, 1992)
g NHL Second All-Star Team (1980, 1988, 1989, 1990)
h NHL First All-Star Team (1981, 1982, 1983, 1984, 1985, 1986, 1987, 1991)
i Won Art Ross Trophy (1981, 1982, 1983, 1984, 1985, 1986, 1987, 1990, 1991)
j NHL record for assists in regular season (1981, 1982, 1983, 1985, 1986)
k NHL record for points in regular season (1981, 1982, 1986)
l NHL record for goals in regular season (1982)
m Won Lester B. Pearson Award (1982, 1983, 1984, 1985, 1987)
n NHL record for assists in one playoff year (1983, 1985, 1988)
o NHL record for points in one playoff year (1983, 1985)
p Won Conn Smythe Trophy (1985, 1988)
q NHL Plus/Minus Leader (1982, 1983, 1984, 1985, 1987)
r Selected Chrysler-Dodge/NHL Performer of the Year (1985, 1986, 1987)
s Won Dodge Performance of the Year Award (1989)

Played in NHL All-Star Game (1980-1986, 1988-92)

Reclaimed by **Edmonton** as an under-age junior prior to Expansion Draft, June 9, 1979. Claimed as priority selection by **Edmonton**, June 9, 1979. Traded to **Los Angeles** by **Edmonton** with Mike Krushelnyski and Marty McSorley for Jimmy Carson, Martin Gelinas, Los Angeles' first round choices in 1989 (acquired by New Jersey, June 17, 1989. New Jersey selected Jason Miller), 1991 (Martin Rucinsky) and 1993 Entry Drafts and cash, August 9, 1988.

GREYERBIEHL, JASON

Left wing. Shoots left. 6', 175 lbs. Born, Bramalea, Ont., March 24, 1970.
(Chicago's 7th choice, 174th overall, in 1989 Entry Draft).

			Regular Season					Playoffs				
Season	Club	Lea	GP	G	A	TP	PIM	GP	G	A	TP	PIM
1988-89	Colgate	ECAC	31	6	9	15	15	....	....	....	....	....
1989-90	Colgate	ECAC	38	12	20	32	20	....	....	....	....	....
1990-91	Colgate	ECAC	30	7	14	21	12	....	....	....	....	....
1991-92	Colgate	ECAC	27	11	16	27	21	....	....	....	....	....

GRIEVE, BRENT

Left wing. Shoots left. 6'1", 202 lbs. Born, Oshawa, Ont., May 9, 1969.
(NY Islanders' 4th choice, 65th overall, in 1989 Entry Draft).

			Regular Season					Playoffs				
Season	Club	Lea	GP	G	A	TP	PIM	GP	G	A	TP	PIM
1986-87	Oshawa	OHL	60	9	19	28	102	24	3	8	11	22
1987-88	Oshawa	OHL	55	19	20	39	122	7	0	1	1	8
1988-89	Oshawa	OHL	49	34	33	67	105	6	4	3	7	4
1989-90	Oshawa	OHL	62	46	47	93	125	17	10	10	20	26
1990-91	Capital Dist.	AHL	61	14	13	27	80	....	....	....	....	....
	Kansas City	IHL	5	2	2	4	2	....	....	....	....	....
1991-92	Capital Dist.	AHL	74	34	32	66	84	7	3	1	4	16

GRILLO, DEAN

Right wing. Shoots right. 6'2", 210 lbs. Born, Bemidji, MN, December 8, 1972.
(San Jose's 9th choice, 155th overall, in 1991 Entry Draft).

			Regular Season					Playoffs				
Season	Club	Lea	GP	G	A	TP	PIM	GP	G	A	TP	PIM
1990-91	Warroad	HS	24	20	15	35	0	....	....	....	....	....
1991-92	Waterloo	USHL	48	27	38	65	42	....	....	....	....	....

GRIMSON, STU

Left wing. Shoots left. 6'5", 220 lbs. Born, Kamloops, B.C., May 20, 1965.
(Calgary's 8th choice, 143rd overall, in 1985 Entry Draft).

			Regular Season					Playoffs				
Season	Club	Lea	GP	G	A	TP	PIM	GP	G	A	TP	PIM
1982-83	Regina	WHL	48	0	1	1	105	5	0	0	0	14
1983-84	Regina	WHL	63	8	8	16	131	21	0	1	1	29
1984-85	Regina	WHL	71	24	32	56	248	8	1	2	3	14
1985-86	U. Manitoba	CWUAA	12	7	4	11	113	3	1	1	2	20
1986-87	U. Manitoba	CWUAA	29	8	8	16	67	14	4	2	6	28
1987-88	Salt Lake	IHL	38	9	5	14	268	....	....	....	....	....
1988-89	**Calgary**	**NHL**	**1**	**0**	**0**	**0**	**5**	....	....	....	....	....
	Salt Lake	IHL	72	9	18	27	397	14	2	3	5	86
1989-90	**Calgary**	**NHL**	**3**	**0**	**0**	**0**	**17**	....	....	....	....	....
	Salt Lake	IHL	62	8	8	16	319	4	0	0	0	8
1990-91	**Chicago**	**NHL**	**35**	**0**	**1**	**1**	**183**	**5**	**0**	**0**	**0**	**46**
1991-92	**Chicago**	**NHL**	**54**	**2**	**2**	**4**	**234**	**14**	**0**	**1**	**1**	**10**
	Indianapolis	IHL	5	1	1	2	17	....	....	....	....	....
	NHL Totals		**93**	**2**	**3**	**5**	**439**	**19**	**0**	**1**	**1**	**56**

Claimed by **Chicago** on conditional waivers, October 1, 1990.

GROLEAU, FRANCOIS

Defense. Shoots left. 6', 193 lbs. Born, Longueuil, Que., January 23, 1973.
(Calgary's 2nd choice, 41st overall, in 1991 Entry Draft).

			Regular Season					Playoffs				
Season	Club	Lea	GP	G	A	TP	PIM	GP	G	A	TP	PIM
1989-90ab	Shawinigan	QMJHL	65	11	54	65	80	6	0	1	1	12
1990-91	Shawinigan	QMJHL	70	9	60	69	70	6	0	3	3	2
1991-92c	Shawinigan	QMJHL	65	8	70	78	74	10	5	15	20	8

a QMJHL Defensive Rookie of the Year (1990)
b QMJHL Second All-Star Team (1990)
c QMJHL First All-Star Team (1992)

GRONMAN, THOMAS (GROHN-mahn)

Defense. Shoots left. 6'2", 190 lbs. Born, Viitasaari, Finland, March 22, 1974.
(Quebec's 3rd choice, 29th overall, in 1992 Entry Draft).

			Regular Season					Playoffs				
Season	Club	Lea	GP	G	A	TP	PIM	GP	G	A	TP	PIM
1990-91	Lukko	Fin. Jr.	40	15	20	35	60	....	....	....	....	....
1991-92	Tacoma	WHL	61	5	18	23	102	4	0	1	1	2

GRONVALL, JANNE (GROHN-vahl, YAH-neh)

Defense. Shoots left. 6'3", 187 lbs. Born, Rauma, Finland, July 17, 1973.
(Toronto's 5th choice, 101st overall, in 1992 Entry Draft).

			Regular Season					Playoffs				
Season	Club	Lea	GP	G	A	TP	PIM	GP	G	A	TP	PIM
1990-91	Lukko	Fin.	40	2	8	10	30	....	....	....	....	....
1991-92	Lukko	Fin.	42	2	6	8	40	2	0	0	0	2

GROSS, PAVEL (GROHSS)

Right wing. Shoots right. 6'3", 195 lbs. Born, Ustin Ogroh, Czechoslovakia, May 11, 1968.
(NY Islanders' 7th choice, 111th overall, in 1988 Entry Draft).

			Regular Season					Playoffs				
Season	Club	Lea	GP	G	A	TP	PIM	GP	G	A	TP	PIM
1987-88	Sparta Praha	Czech.	24	3	4	7	0	....	....	....	....	....
1988-89	Sparta Praha	Czech.	27	12	13	25	....	....	....	....	....	....
1989-90	Sparta Praha	Czech.	36	10	9	19	....	....	....	....	....	....
1990-91	Freiburg	Ger.	32	11	24	35	66	....	....	....	....	....
1991-92	Freiburg	Ger.	43	15	22	37	59	....	....	....	....	....

GROSSI, DINO

Right wing. Shoots right. 6', 195 lbs. Born, Toronto, Ont., June 25, 1970.
(Chicago's 10th choice, 247th overall, in 1990 Entry Draft).

			Regular Season					Playoffs				
Season	Club	Lea	GP	G	A	TP	PIM	GP	G	A	TP	PIM
1989-90	Northeastern	H.E.	31	6	9	15	43	....	....	....	....	....
1990-91	Northeastern	H.E.	34	11	11	22	70	....	....	....	....	....
1991-92	Northeastern	H.E.	31	15	11	26	50	....	....	....	....	....

GRUBA, ANTHONY

Right wing. Shoots right. 6', 205 lbs. Born, St. Paul, MN, August 23, 1972.
(Detroit's 8th choice, 171st overall, in 1990 Entry Draft).

			Regular Season					Playoffs				
Season	Club	Lea	GP	G	A	TP	PIM	GP	G	A	TP	PIM
1990-91	St. Cloud	WCHA	29	1	5	6	34	....	....	....	....	....
1991-92	St. Cloud	WCHA	37	14	22	36	76	....	....	....	....	....

GRUDEN, JOHN

Defense. Shoots left. 6', 180 lbs. Born, Hastings, MN, April 6, 1970.
(Boston's 7th choice, 168th overall, in 1990 Entry Draft).

			Regular Season					Playoffs				
Season	Club	Lea	GP	G	A	TP	PIM	GP	G	A	TP	PIM
1990-91	Ferris State	CCHA	37	4	11	15	27	....	....	....	....	....
1991-92	Ferris State	CCHA	37	9	14	23	24	....	....	....	....	....

GRUHL, SCOTT KENNETH (GROOL)

Left wing. Shoots left. 5'11", 185 lbs. Born, Port Colborne, Ont., September 13, 1959.

			Regular Season					Playoffs				
Season	Club	Lea	GP	G	A	TP	PIM	GP	G	A	TP	PIM
1978-79	Sudbury	OHA	68	35	49	94	78	10	5	7	12	15
1979-80	Binghamton	AHL	4	1	0	1	0	....	....	....	....	....
a	Saginaw	IHL	75	53	40	93	100	7	2	6	8	16
1980-81	Houston	CHL	4	0	0	0	0	....	....	....	....	....
	Saginaw	IHL	77	56	34	90	87	13	*11	8	*19	12
1981-82	**Los Angeles**	**NHL**	**7**	**2**	**1**	**3**	**2**	....	....	....	....	....
	New Haven	AHL	73	28	41	69	107	4	0	4	4	2
1982-83	**Los Angeles**	**NHL**	**7**	**0**	**2**	**2**	**4**	....	....	....	....	....
	New Haven	AHL	68	25	38	63	114	12	3	3	6	22
1983-84b	Muskegon	IHL	56	40	56	96	46	....	....	....	....	....
1984-85bc	Muskegon	IHL	82	62	64	126	102	17	7	16	23	25
1985-86a	Muskegon	IHL	82	*59	50	109	178	14	7	*13	20	22
1986-87	Muskegon	IHL	67	34	39	73	157	15	5	7	12	54
1987-88	**Pittsburgh**	**NHL**	**6**	**1**	**0**	**1**	**0**	....	....	....	....	....
	Muskegon	IHL	55	28	47	75	115	6	5	1	6	12
1988-89	Muskegon	IHL	79	37	55	92	163	14	8	11	19	37
1989-90	Muskegon	IHL	80	41	51	92	206	15	8	6	14	26
1990-91	Fort Wayne	IHL	59	23	47	70	109	19	4	6	10	39
1991-92a	Fort Wayne	IHL	78	44	61	105	196	6	2	2	4	48
	NHL Totals		**20**	**3**	**3**	**6**	**6**	....	....	....	....	....

a IHL Second All-Star Team (1980, 1986, 1992)
b IHL First All-Star Team (1984, 1985)
c Won James Gatschene Memorial Trophy (MVP-IHL) (1985)

Signed as a free agent by **Los Angeles**, October 11, 1979. Signed as a free agent by **Pittsburgh**, December 14, 1987.

GUAY, PAUL (GAY)

Right wing. Shoots right. 5'11", 185 lbs. Born, Providence, RI, September 2, 1963.
(Minnesota's 10th choice, 118th overall, in 1981 Entry Draft).

			Regular Season					Playoffs				
Season	Club	Lea	GP	G	A	TP	PIM	GP	G	A	TP	PIM
1981-82	Providence	ECAC	33	23	17	40	38	....	....	....	....	....
1982-83a	Providence	ECAC	42	34	31	65	83	....	....	....	....	....
1983-84	U.S. National	....	62	20	18	38	44	....	....	....	....	....
	U.S. Olympic	....	6	1	0	1	8	....	....	....	....	....
	Philadelphia	**NHL**	**14**	**2**	**6**	**8**	**14**	**3**	**0**	**0**	**0**	**4**
1984-85	**Philadelphia**	**NHL**	**2**	**0**	**1**	**1**	**0**	....	....	....	....	....
	Hershey	AHL	74	23	30	53	123	....	....	....	....	....
1985-86	**Los Angeles**	**NHL**	**23**	**3**	**3**	**6**	**18**	....	....	....	....	....
	New Haven	AHL	57	15	36	51	101	5	3	0	3	11
1986-87	**Los Angeles**	**NHL**	**35**	**2**	**5**	**7**	**16**	**2**	**0**	**0**	**0**	**0**
	New Haven	AHL	6	1	3	4	11	....	....	....	....	....
1987-88	**Los Angeles**	**NHL**	**33**	**4**	**4**	**8**	**40**	**4**	**0**	**1**	**1**	**8**
	New Haven	AHL	42	21	26	47	53	....	....	....	....	....
1988-89	**Los Angeles**	**NHL**	**2**	**0**	**0**	**0**	**2**	....	....	....	....	....
	New Haven	AHL	4	4	6	10	20	....	....	....	....	....
	Boston	**NHL**	**5**	**0**	**2**	**2**	**0**	....	....	....	....	....
	Maine	AHL	61	15	29	44	77	....	....	....	....	....
1989-90	Utica	AHL	75	25	30	55	103	5	2	2	4	13
1990-91	**NY Islanders**	**NHL**	**3**	**0**	**2**	**2**	**2**	....	....	....	....	....
	Capital Dist.	AHL	74	26	35	61	81	....	....	....	....	....
1991-92	Milwaukee	IHL	81	24	33	57	93	3	2	1	3	7
	NHL Totals		**117**	**11**	**23**	**34**	**92**	**9**	**0**	**1**	**1**	**12**

a ECAC Second All-Star Team (1983)

Rights traded to **Philadelphia** by **Minnesota** with Minnesota's third round choice in 1985 Entry Draft for Paul Holmgren, February 23, 1984. Traded to **Los Angeles** by **Philadelphia** with Philadelphia's fourth round choice (Sylvain Couturier) in 1986 Entry Draft for Steve Seguin and Los Angeles' second round choice (Jukka Seppo) in 1986 Entry Draft, October 11, 1985. Traded to **Boston** by **Los Angeles** for the rights to Dave Pasin, November 3, 1988. Signed as a free agent by **New Jersey**, August 14, 1989. Signed as a free agent by **NY Islanders**, August 13, 1990. Signed as a free agent by **Vancouver**, August 22, 1991.

GUERARD, DANIEL

Right wing. Shoots right. 6'4", 211 lbs. Born, LaSalle, Que., April 9, 1974.
(Ottawa's 5th choice, 98th overall, in 1992 Entry Draft).

			Regular Season					Playoffs				
Season	Club	Lea	GP	G	A	TP	PIM	GP	G	A	TP	PIM
1991-92	Victoriaville	QMJHL	31	5	16	21	66	....	....	....	....	....

GUERARD, STEPHANE

Defense. Shoots left. 6'2", 198 lbs. Born, Ste. Elizabeth, Que., April 12, 1968.
(Quebec's 3rd choice, 41st overall, in 1986 Entry Draft).

			Regular Season					Playoffs				
Season	Club	Lea	GP	G	A	TP	PIM	GP	G	A	TP	PIM
1985-86	Shawinigan	QMJHL	59	4	18	22	167	3	1	1	2	0
1986-87	Shawinigan	QMJHL	31	5	16	21	57	12	2	9	11	36
1987-88	**Quebec**	**NHL**	**30**	**0**	**0**	**0**	**34**	....	....	....	....	....
1988-89	Halifax	AHL	37	1	9	10	140	4	0	0	0	8
1989-90	**Quebec**	**NHL**	**4**	**0**	**0**	**0**	**6**	....	....	....	....	....
	Halifax	AHL	1	0	0	0	5	....	....	....	....	....
1990-91	Halifax	AHL				DID NOT PLAY						
	NHL Totals		**34**	**0**	**0**	**0**	**40**	....	....	....	....	....

Traded to **NY Rangers** by **Quebec** for Miloslav Horava, May 25, 1991. Traded to **Quebec** by **NY Rangers** for cash, September 3, 1991.

GUERIN, BILL (GAIR-ihn)

Center/Right wing. Shoots right. 6'2", 190 lbs. Born, Wilbraham, MA, November 9, 1970.
(New Jersey's 1st choice, 5th overall, in 1989 Entry Draft).

			Regular Season					Playoffs				
Season	Club	Lea	GP	G	A	TP	PIM	GP	G	A	TP	PIM
1989-90	Boston College	H.E.	39	14	11	25	54	....	....	....	....	....
1990-91	Boston College	H.E.	38	26	19	45	102	....	....	....	....	....
1991-92	U.S. National	....	46	12	15	27	67	....	....	....	....	....
	New Jersey	**NHL**	**5**	**0**	**1**	**1**	**9**	**6**	**3**	**0**	**3**	**4**
	Utica	AHL	22	13	10	23	6	4	1	3	4	14
	NHL Totals		**5**	**0**	**1**	**1**	**9**	**6**	**3**	**0**	**3**	**4**

GUILBERT, MICHAEL

Defense. Shoots left. 6'2", 195 lbs. Born, Manchester, NH, December 11, 1971.
(NY Islanders' 6th choice, 132nd overall, in 1990 Entry Draft).

			Regular Season					Playoffs				
Season	Club	Lea	GP	G	A	TP	PIM	GP	G	A	TP	PIM
1989-90	Gov. Dummer	HS	....	5	9	14	0	....	....	....	....	....
1990-91						UNAVAILABLE						
1991-92	N. Hampshire	H.E.	3	2	0	2	0	....	....	....	....	....

GUILLET, ROBERT

Right wing. Shoots right. 5'11", 189 lbs. Born, Montreal, Que., February 22, 1972.
(Montreal's 4th choice, 60th overall, in 1990 Entry Draft).

			Regular Season					Playoffs				
Season	Club	Lea	GP	G	A	TP	PIM	GP	G	A	TP	PIM
1989-90	Longueuil	QMJHL	69	32	40	72	132	7	2	1	3	15
1990-91a	Longueuil	QMJHL	69	55	32	87	96	8	4	7	11	27
1991-92b	Verdun	QMJHL	67	56	62	118	104	19	*14	11	*25	26

a QMJHL First All-Star Team (1991)
b QMJHL Second All-Star Team (1992)

GUSAROV, ALEXEI (goo-SAH-rahf)

Defense. Shoots left. 6'2", 183 lbs. Born, Leningrad, Soviet Union, July 8, 1964.
(Quebec's 11th choice, 213th overall, in 1988 Entry Draft).

			Regular Season					Playoffs				
Season	Club	Lea	GP	G	A	TP	PIM	GP	G	A	TP	PIM
1981-82	SKA Leningrad	USSR	20	1	2	3	16	....	....	....	....	....
1982-83	SKA Leningrad	USSR	42	2	1	3	32	....	....	....	....	....
1983-84	SKA Leningrad	USSR	43	2	3	5	32	....	....	....	....	....
1984-85	CSKA	USSR	36	3	2	5	26	....	....	....	....	....
1985-86	CSKA	USSR	40	3	5	8	30	....	....	....	....	....
1986-87	CSKA	USSR	38	4	7	11	24	....	....	....	....	....
1987-88	CSKA	USSR	39	3	2	5	28	....	....	....	....	....
1988-89	CSKA	USSR	42	5	4	9	37	....	....	....	....	....
1989-90	CSKA	USSR	42	4	7	11	42	....	....	....	....	....
1990-91	CSKA	USSR	15	0	0	0	12	....	....	....	....	....
	Quebec	**NHL**	**36**	**3**	**9**	**12**	**12**	....	....	....	....	....
	Halifax	AHL	2	0	3	3	2	....	....	....	....	....
1991-92	**Quebec**	**NHL**	**68**	**5**	**18**	**23**	**22**	....	....	....	....	....
	Halifax	AHL	3	0	0	0	0	....	....	....	....	....
	NHL Totals		**104**	**8**	**27**	**35**	**34**	....	....	....	....	....

GUY, KEVAN (GIGH)

Defense. Shoots right. 6'3", 202 lbs. Born, Edmonton, Alta., July 16, 1965.
(Calgary's 5th choice, 71st overall, in 1983 Entry Draft).

			Regular Season					Playoffs				
Season	Club	Lea	GP	G	A	TP	PIM	GP	G	A	TP	PIM
1982-83	Medicine Hat	WHL	69	7	20	27	89	5	0	3	3	16
1983-84	Medicine Hat	WHL	72	15	42	57	117	14	3	4	7	14
1984-85	Medicine Hat	WHL	31	7	17	24	46	10	1	2	3	2
1985-86	Moncton	AHL	73	4	20	24	56	10	0	2	2	6
1986-87	**Calgary**	**NHL**	**24**	**0**	**4**	**4**	**19**	**4**	**0**	**1**	**1**	**23**
	Moncton	AHL	46	2	10	12	38	....	....	....	....	....
1987-88	**Calgary**	**NHL**	**11**	**0**	**3**	**3**	**8**	....	....	....	....	....
	Salt Lake	IHL	61	6	30	36	51	19	1	6	7	26
1988-89	**Vancouver**	**NHL**	**45**	**2**	**2**	**4**	**34**	**1**	**0**	**0**	**0**	**0**
1989-90	**Vancouver**	**NHL**	**30**	**2**	**5**	**7**	**32**	....	....	....	....	....
	Milwaukee	IHL	29	2	11	13	33	....	....	....	....	....
1990-91	**Vancouver**	**NHL**	**39**	**1**	**6**	**7**	**39**	....	....	....	....	....
	Calgary	**NHL**	**4**	**0**	**0**	**0**	**4**	....	....	....	....	....
1991-92	**Calgary**	**NHL**	**3**	**0**	**0**	**0**	**2**	....	....	....	....	....
	Salt Lake	IHL	60	3	14	17	89	5	0	1	1	4
	NHL Totals		**156**	**5**	**20**	**25**	**138**	**5**	**0**	**1**	**1**	**23**

Traded to **Vancouver** by **Calgary** with Brian Bradley and Peter Bakovic for Craig Coxe, March 6, 1988. Traded to **Calgary** by **Vancouver** with Ron Stern and future considerations, March 5, 1991.

HAAPAKOSKI, MIKKO (HAH-puh-koh-skee)

Defense. Shoots left. 5'9", 172 lbs. Born, Oulu, Finland, January 19, 1967.
(Detroit's 10th choice, 179th overall, in 1987 Entry Draft).

			Regular Season					Playoffs				
Season	Club	Lea	GP	G	A	TP	PIM	GP	G	A	TP	PIM
1985-86	Karpat	Fin.	17	0	4	4	0	5	1	0	1	6
1986-87	Karpat	Fin.	41	13	15	28	18	9	1	1	2	4
1987-88	Karpat	Fin.	43	7	7	14	40	....	....	....	....	....
1988-89	Karpat	Fin.	40	7	18	25	20	5	1	1	2	2
1989-90	TPS	Fin.	44	4	10	14	14	9	0	1	1	16
1990-91	TPS	Fin.	40	9	12	21	10	9	1	4	5	4
1991-92	TPS	Fin.	43	11	13	24	18	1	0	0	0	0

HAAS, DAVID

Left wing. Shoots left. 6'2", 196 lbs. Born, Toronto, Ont., June 23, 1968.
(Edmonton's 5th choice, 105th overall, in 1986 Entry Draft).

			Regular Season					Playoffs				
Season	Club	Lea	GP	G	A	TP	PIM	GP	G	A	TP	PIM
1985-86	London	OHL	62	4	13	17	91	5	0	1	1	0
1986-87	London	OHL	5	1	0	1	5	....	....	....	....	....
	Kitchener	OHL	4	0	1	1	4	....	....	....	....	....
	Belleville	OHL	55	10	13	23	86	6	3	0	3	13
1987-88a	Windsor	OHL	63	60	47	107	246	11	9	11	20	50
1988-89	Cape Breton	AHL	61	9	9	18	325	....	....	....	....	....
1989-90	Cape Breton	AHL	53	6	12	18	230	4	2	2	4	15
1990-91	**Edmonton**	**NHL**	**5**	**1**	**0**	**1**	**0**	....	....	....	....	....
	Cape Breton	AHL	60	24	23	47	137	3	0	2	2	12
1991-92	Cape Breton	AHL	16	3	7	10	32	....	....	....	....	....
	New Haven	AHL	50	13	23	36	97	5	3	0	3	13
	NHL Totals		**5**	**1**	**0**	**1**	**0**	....	....	....	....	....

a OHL Second All-Star Team (1988)

HABSCHEID, MARC JOSEPH (HAB-shide)

Right wing/Center. Shoots right. 6', 185 lbs. Born, Swift Current, Sask., March 1, 1963.
(Edmonton's 6th choice, 113th overall, in 1981 Entry Draft).

			Regular Season					Playoffs				
Season	Club	Lea	GP	G	A	TP	PIM	GP	G	A	TP	PIM
1980-81	Saskatoon	WHL	72	34	63	97	50	....	....	....	....	....
1981-82	**Edmonton**	**NHL**	**7**	**1**	**3**	**4**	**2**	....	....	....	....	....
a	Saskatoon	WHL	55	64	87	151	74	5	3	4	7	4
	Wichita	CHL	....	....	....	....	....	3	0	0	0	0
1982-83	Kamloops	WHL	6	7	16	23	8	....	....	....	....	....
	Edmonton	**NHL**	**32**	**3**	**10**	**13**	**14**	....	....	....	....	....
1983-84	**Edmonton**	**NHL**	**9**	**1**	**0**	**1**	**6**	....	....	....	....	....
	Moncton	AHL	71	19	37	56	32	....	....	....	....	....
1984-85	**Edmonton**	**NHL**	**26**	**5**	**3**	**8**	**4**	....	....	....	....	....
	Nova Scotia	AHL	48	29	29	58	65	6	4	3	7	9
1985-86	**Minnesota**	**NHL**	**6**	**2**	**3**	**5**	**0**	**2**	**0**	**0**	**0**	**0**
	Springfield	AHL	41	18	32	50	21	....	....	....	....	....
1986-87	**Minnesota**	**NHL**	**15**	**2**	**0**	**2**	**2**	....	....	....	....	....
	Cdn. Olympic	....	51	29	32	61	70	....	....	....	....	....
1987-88	Cdn. National	....	61	19	34	53	42	....	....	....	....	....
	Cdn. Olympic	....	8	5	3	8	6	....	....	....	....	....
	Minnesota	**NHL**	**16**	**4**	**11**	**15**	**6**	....	....	....	....	....
1988-89	**Minnesota**	**NHL**	**76**	**23**	**31**	**54**	**40**	**5**	**1**	**3**	**4**	**13**
1989-90	**Detroit**	**NHL**	**66**	**15**	**11**	**26**	**33**	....	....	....	....	....
1990-91	**Detroit**	**NHL**	**46**	**9**	**8**	**17**	**22**	**5**	**0**	**0**	**0**	**0**
1991-92	**Calgary**	**NHL**	**46**	**7**	**11**	**18**	**42**	....	....	....	....	....
	NHL Totals		**345**	**72**	**91**	**163**	**171**	**12**	**1**	**3**	**4**	**13**

a WHL Second All-Star Team (1982)

Traded to **Minnesota** by **Edmonton** with Don Barber and Emanuel Viveiros for Gord Sherven and Don Biggs, December 20, 1985. Signed as a free agent by **Detroit**, June 9, 1989. Traded to **Calgary** by **Detroit** for Brian MacLellan, June 11, 1991.

HAGEN, GREG

Right wing. Shoots right. 5'11", 175 lbs. Born, St. Paul, MN, July 10, 1971.
(Pittsburgh's 11th choice, 205th overall, in 1989 Entry Draft).

			Regular Season					Playoffs				
Season	Club	Lea	GP	G	A	TP	PIM	GP	G	A	TP	PIM
1990-91	St. Cloud	WCHA	23	4	4	8	2	....	....	....	....	....
1991-92	St. Cloud	WCHA	34	10	8	18	28	....	....	....	....	....

HAGGERTY, RYAN

Center. Shoots left. 6'1", 185 lbs. Born, Rye, NY, May 2, 1973.
(Edmonton's 6th choice, 93rd overall, in 1991 Entry Draft).

			Regular Season					Playoffs				
Season	Club	Lea	GP	G	A	TP	PIM	GP	G	A	TP	PIM
1990-91	Westminster	HS	25	34	38	72	0	....	....	....	....	....
1991-92	Boston College	H.E.	34	12	5	17	16	....	....	....	....	....

HAKANSSON, MIKAEL

Center. Shoots left. 6'1", 180 lbs. Born, Stockholm, Sweden, March 31, 1974.
(Toronto's 7th choice, 125th overall, in 1992 Entry Draft).

			Regular Season					Playoffs				
Season	Club	Lea	GP	G	A	TP	PIM	GP	G	A	TP	PIM
1990-91	Nacka	Swe. Jr.	27	2	5	7	6	....	....	....	....	....
1991-92	Nacka	Swe. Jr.	29	3	15	18	24	....	....	....	....	....

HALKIDIS, BOB (hal-KEE-dihs)

Defense. Shoots left. 5'11", 200 lbs. Born, Toronto, Ont., March 5, 1966.
(Buffalo's 4th choice, 81st overall, in 1984 Entry Draft).

			Regular Season					Playoffs				
Season	Club	Lea	GP	G	A	TP	PIM	GP	G	A	TP	PIM
1983-84	London	OHL	51	9	22	31	123	8	0	2	2	27
1984-85ab	London	OHL	62	14	50	64	154	8	3	6	9	22
	Buffalo	**NHL**	....	....	....	....	....	**4**	**0**	**0**	**0**	**19**
1985-86	**Buffalo**	**NHL**	**37**	**1**	**9**	**10**	**115**	....	....	....	....	....
1986-87	**Buffalo**	**NHL**	**6**	**1**	**1**	**2**	**19**	....	....	....	....	....
	Rochester	AHL	59	1	8	9	144	8	0	0	0	43
1987-88	**Buffalo**	**NHL**	**30**	**0**	**3**	**3**	**115**	**4**	**0**	**0**	**0**	**22**
	Rochester	AHL	15	2	5	7	50	....	....	....	....	....
1988-89	**Buffalo**	**NHL**	**16**	**0**	**1**	**1**	**66**	....	....	....	....	....
	Rochester	AHL	16	0	6	6	64	....	....	....	....	....
1989-90	Rochester	AHL	18	1	13	14	70	....	....	....	....	....
	Los Angeles	**NHL**	**20**	**0**	**4**	**4**	**56**	....	....	....	....	....
	New Haven	AHL	30	3	17	20	67	....	....	....	....	....
1990-91	**Los Angeles**	**NHL**	**34**	**1**	**3**	**4**	**133**	**3**	**0**	**0**	**0**	**0**
	New Haven	AHL	7	1	3	4	10	....	....	....	....	....
	Phoenix	IHL	4	1	5	6	6	....	....	....	....	....
1991-92	**Toronto**	**NHL**	**46**	**3**	**3**	**6**	**145**	....	....	....	....	....
	NHL Totals		**189**	**6**	**24**	**30**	**649**	**11**	**0**	**0**	**0**	**41**

a Named Outstanding Defenseman in OHL (1985)
b OHL First All-Star Team (1985)

Traded to **Los Angeles** by **Buffalo** with future considerations for Dale DeGray and future considerations, November 24, 1989. Signed as a free agent by **Toronto**, July 24, 1991.

HALL, TODD

Defense. Shoots left. 6'1", 212 lbs. Born, Hamden, CT, January 22, 1973.
(Hartford's 3rd choice, 53rd overall, in 1991 Entry Draft).

			Regular Season					Playoffs				
Season	Club	Lea	GP	G	A	TP	PIM	GP	G	A	TP	PIM
1990-91	Hamden	HS	23	10	15	25	12	....	....	....	....	....
1991-92	Boston College	H.E.	33	2	10	12	14	....	....	....	....	....

HALLER, KEVIN

Defense. Shoots left. 6'2", 183 lbs. Born, Trochu, Alta., December 5, 1970.
(Buffalo's 1st choice, 14th overall, in 1989 Entry Draft).

			Regular Season					Playoffs				
Season	Club	Lea	GP	G	A	TP	PIM	GP	G	A	TP	PIM
1988-89	Regina	WHL	72	10	31	41	99	....	....	....	....	....
1989-90	**Buffalo**	**NHL**	**2**	**0**	**0**	**0**	**0**	....	....	....	....	....
a	Regina	WHL	58	16	37	53	93	11	2	9	11	16
1990-91	**Buffalo**	**NHL**	**21**	**1**	**8**	**9**	**20**	**6**	**1**	**4**	**5**	**10**
	Rochester	AHL	52	2	8	10	53	10	2	1	3	6
1991-92	**Buffalo**	**NHL**	**58**	**6**	**15**	**21**	**75**	....	....	....	....	....
	Rochester	AHL	4	0	0	0	18	....	....	....	....	....
	Montreal	**NHL**	**8**	**2**	**2**	**4**	**17**	**9**	**0**	**0**	**0**	**6**
	NHL Totals		**89**	**9**	**25**	**34**	**112**	**15**	**1**	**4**	**5**	**16**

a WHL East First All-Star Team (1990)

Traded to **Montreal** by **Buffalo** for Petr Svoboda, March 10, 1992.

HALVERSON, TREVOR

Left wing. Shoots left. 6'1", 195 lbs. Born, White River, Ont., April 6, 1971.
(Washington's 2nd choice, 21st overall, in 1991 Entry Draft).

			Regular Season					Playoffs				
Season	Club	Lea	GP	G	A	TP	PIM	GP	G	A	TP	PIM
1989-90	North Bay	OHL	54	22	20	42	172	2	2	1	3	2
1990-91a	North Bay	OHL	64	59	36	95	128	10	3	6	9	4
1991-92	Baltimore	AHL	74	10	11	21	181	....	....	....	....	....

a OHL First All-Star Team (1991)

HAMALAINEN, ERIK (HAH-muhl-ahy-nehn)

Defense. Shoots left. 6'1", 198 lbs. Born, Rauma, Finland, April 20, 1965.
(Detroit's 10th choice, 197th overall, in 1985 Entry Draft).

			Regular Season					Playoffs				
Season	Club	Lea	GP	G	A	TP	PIM	GP	G	A	TP	PIM
1985-86	Lukko	Fin.	31	13	6	19	32	....	....	....	....	....
1986-87	Lukko	Fin.	44	8	8	16	49	....	....	....	....	....
1987-88	Lukko	Fin.	44	8	4	12	52	8	0	3	3	2
1988-89	KalPa	Fin.	43	7	4	11	14	2	0	0	0	2
1989-90	KalPa	Fin.	44	9	20	29	32	....	....	....	....	....
1990-91	KalPa	Fin.	44	14	14	28	34	8	3	4	7	4
1991-92	KalPa	Fin.	44	12	21	33	22	....	....	....	....	....

HAMMOND, KEN

Defense. Shoots left. 6'1", 190 lbs. Born, Port Credit, Ont., August 22, 1963.
(Los Angeles' 8th choice, 152nd overall, in 1983 Entry Draft).

			Regular Season					Playoffs				
Season	Club	Lea	GP	G	A	TP	PIM	GP	G	A	TP	PIM
1982-83	RPI	ECAC	28	17	26	43	8	....	....	....	....	....
1983-84	RPI	ECAC	34	5	11	16	72	....	....	....	....	....
1984-85	**Los Angeles**	**NHL**	**3**	**1**	**0**	**1**	**0**	**3**	**0**	**0**	**0**	**4**
ab	RPI	ECAC	38	11	28	39	90	....	....	....	....	....
1985-86	**Los Angeles**	**NHL**	**3**	**0**	**1**	**1**	**2**	....	....	....	....	....
	New Haven	AHL	67	4	12	16	96	4	0	0	0	7
1986-87	**Los Angeles**	**NHL**	**10**	**0**	**2**	**2**	**11**	....	....	....	....	....
	New Haven	AHL	66	1	15	16	76	6	0	1	1	21
1987-88	**Los Angeles**	**NHL**	**46**	**7**	**9**	**16**	**69**	**2**	**0**	**0**	**0**	**4**
	New Haven	AHL	26	3	8	11	27	....	....	....	....	....
1988-89	**Edmonton**	**NHL**	**5**	**0**	**1**	**1**	**8**	....	....	....	....	....
	NY Rangers	**NHL**	**3**	**0**	**0**	**0**	**0**	....	....	....	....	....
	Denver	IHL	38	5	18	23	24	....	....	....	....	....
	Toronto	**NHL**	**14**	**0**	**2**	**2**	**12**	....	....	....	....	....
1989-90	Newmarket	AHL	75	9	45	54	106	....	....	....	....	....
1990-91	**Boston**	**NHL**	**1**	**1**	**0**	**1**	**2**	**8**	**0**	**0**	**0**	**10**
	Maine	AHL	80	10	41	51	159	2	0	1	1	16
1991-92	**San Jose**	**NHL**	**46**	**5**	**10**	**15**	**82**	....	....	....	....	....
	Vancouver	**NHL**	....	....	....	....	....	**2**	**0**	**0**	**0**	**6**
	NHL Totals		**131**	**14**	**25**	**39**	**186**	**15**	**0**	**0**	**0**	**24**

a ECAC First All-Star Team (1985)
b Named to NCAA All-American Team (1985)

Claimed by **Edmonton** in NHL Waiver Draft, October 3, 1988. Claimed by **NY Rangers** on waivers from **Edmonton**, November 1, 1988. Traded to **Toronto** by **NY Rangers** for Chris McRae, February 21, 1989. Traded to **Boston** by **Toronto** for cash, August 20, 1990. Signed as a free agent by **San Jose**, August 9, 1991. Traded to **Vancouver** by **San Jose** for Vancouver's eighth round choice (later traded to Detroit - C.J. Denomme) in 1992 Entry Draft, March 9, 1992. Claimed by **Ottawa** from **Vancouver** in Expansion Draft, June 18, 1992.

HAMR, RADEK (HAHM-er)

Defense. Shoots left. 5'11", 167 lbs. Born, Usti-Nad-Labem, Czech., June 15, 1974.
(Ottawa's 4th choice, 73rd overall, in 1992 Entry Draft).

			Regular Season					Playoffs				
Season	Club	Lea	GP	G	A	TP	PIM	GP	G	A	TP	PIM
1991-92	Sparta Praha	Czech.	3	0	0	0	....	....	....	....	....	....

HAMRLIK, MARTIN (HAHM-reh-lik)

Defense. Shoots right. 5'11", 176 lbs. Born, Zlin, Czechoslovakia, May 6, 1973.
(Hartford's 2nd choice, 31st overall, in 1991 Entry Draft).

			Regular Season					Playoffs				
Season	Club	Lea	GP	G	A	TP	PIM	GP	G	A	TP	PIM
1989-90	TJ Zlin	Czech.	12	2	0	2	....	....	....	....	....	....
1990-91	TJ Zlin	Czech.	50	8	14	22	44	....	....	....	....	....
1991-92	ZPS Zlin	Czech.	4	0	2	2	....	....	....	....	....	....

HAMRLIK, ROMAN (HAHM-reh-lik)

Defense. Shoots left. 6'2", 189 lbs. Born, Gottwaldov, Czech., April 12, 1974.
(Tampa Bay's 1st choice, 1st overall, in 1992 Entry Draft).

			Regular Season					Playoffs				
Season	Club	Lea	GP	G	A	TP	PIM	GP	G	A	TP	PIM
1990-91	ZPS Zlin	Czech.	14	2	2	4	18	....	....	....	....	....
1991-92	ZPS Zlin	Czech.	34	5	5	10	34	....	....	....	....	....

HANKINSON, BEN

Center. Shoots right. 6'2", 180 lbs. Born, Edina, MN, January 5, 1969.
(New Jersey's 5th choice, 107th overall, in 1987 Entry Draft).

			Regular Season					Playoffs				
Season	Club	Lea	GP	G	A	TP	PIM	GP	G	A	TP	PIM
1987-88	U. Minnesota	WCHA	24	4	7	11	36	....	....	....	....	....
1988-89	U. Minnesota	WCHA	43	7	11	18	115	....	....	....	....	....
1989-90a	U. Minnesota	WCHA	46	25	41	66	34	....	....	....	....	....
1990-91	U. Minnesota	WCHA	43	19	21	40	133	....	....	....	....	....
1991-92	Utica	AHL	77	17	16	33	186	4	3	1	4	2

a WCHA First All-Star Team (1990)

HANKINSON, PETER

Right wing. Shoots right. 5'9", 175 lbs. Born, Edina, MN, November 24, 1967.
(Winnipeg's 1st choice, 4th overall, in 1989 Supplemental Draft).

			Regular Season					Playoffs				
Season	Club	Lea	GP	G	A	TP	PIM	GP	G	A	TP	PIM
1986-87	U. Minnesota	WCHA	43	16	12	28	10	....	....	....	....	....
1987-88	U. Minnesota	WCHA	39	25	20	45	32	....	....	....	....	....
1988-89	U. Minnesota	WCHA	48	16	27	43	42	....	....	....	....	....
1989-90	U. Minnesota	WCHA	45	19	12	31	116	....	....	....	....	....
1990-91	Fort Wayne	IHL	10	1	2	3	4	....	....	....	....	....
	Moncton	AHL	47	2	14	16	10	4	0	0	0	0
1991-92	Fort Wayne	IHL	75	25	38	63	44	7	1	3	4	2

HANNAN, DAVID (DAVE)

Center. Shoots left. 5'10", 185 lbs. Born, Sudbury, Ont., November 26, 1961.
(Pittsburgh's 9th choice, 196th overall, in 1981 Entry Draft).

			Regular Season					Playoffs				
Season	**Club**	**Lea**	**GP**	**G**	**A**	**TP**	**PIM**	**GP**	**G**	**A**	**TP**	**PIM**
1979-80	S.S. Marie	OHA	28	11	10	21	31	....	....	....	....	....
	Brantford	OHA	25	5	10	15	26	....	....	....	....	....
1980-81	Brantford	OHA	56	46	35	81	155	6	2	4	6	20
1981-82	**Pittsburgh**	**NHL**	**1**	**0**	**0**	**0**	**0**	....	....	....	....	....
	Erie	AHL	76	33	37	70	129	....	....	....	....	....
1982-83	**Pittsburgh**	**NHL**	**74**	**11**	**22**	**33**	**127**	....	....	....	....	....
	Baltimore	AHL	5	2	2	4	13	....	....	....	....	....
1983-84	**Pittsburgh**	**NHL**	**24**	**2**	**3**	**5**	**33**	....	....	....	....	....
	Baltimore	AHL	47	18	24	42	98	10	2	6	8	27
1984-85	**Pittsburgh**	**NHL**	**30**	**6**	**7**	**13**	**43**	....	....	....	....	....
	Baltimore	AHL	49	20	25	45	91	....	....	....	....	....
1985-86	**Pittsburgh**	**NHL**	**75**	**17**	**18**	**35**	**91**	....	....	....	....	....
1986-87	**Pittsburgh**	**NHL**	**58**	**10**	**15**	**25**	**56**	....	....	....	....	....
1987-88	**Pittsburgh**	**NHL**	**21**	**4**	**3**	**7**	**23**	....	....	....	....	....
	Edmonton	**NHL**	**51**	**9**	**11**	**20**	**43**	**12**	**1**	**1**	**2**	**8**
1988-89	**Pittsburgh**	**NHL**	**72**	**10**	**20**	**30**	**157**	**8**	**0**	**1**	**1**	**4**
1989-90	**Toronto**	**NHL**	**39**	**6**	**9**	**15**	**55**	**3**	**1**	**0**	**1**	**4**
1990-91	**Toronto**	**NHL**	**74**	**11**	**23**	**34**	**82**	....	....	....	....	....
1991-92	**Toronto**	**NHL**	**35**	**2**	**2**	**4**	**16**	....	....	....	....	....
	Cdn. National	....	3	0	0	0	2	....	....	....	....	....
	Cdn. Olympic	....	8	3	5	8	8	....	....	....	....	....
	Buffalo	**NHL**	**12**	**2**	**4**	**6**	**48**	**7**	**2**	**0**	**2**	**2**
	NHL Totals		**566**	**90**	**137**	**227**	**774**	**30**	**4**	**2**	**6**	**18**

Traded to **Edmonton** by **Pittsburgh** with Craig Simpson, Moe Mantha and Chris Joseph for Paul Coffey, Dave Hunter and Wayne Van Dorp, November 24, 1987. Claimed by **Pittsburgh** in NHL Waiver Draft, October 3, 1988. Claimed by **Toronto** in NHL Waiver Draft, October 2, 1989. Traded to **Buffalo** by **Toronto** for future considerations, March 10, 1992.

HANSON, GREG

Defense. Shoots left. 6'3", 215 lbs. Born, Bloomington, MN, September 4, 1971.
(Philadelphia's 13th choice, 193rd overall, in 1990 Entry Draft).

			Regular Season					Playoffs				
Season	**Club**	**Lea**	**GP**	**G**	**A**	**TP**	**PIM**	**GP**	**G**	**A**	**TP**	**PIM**
1990-91	Dubuque	USHL	39	4	21	25	69	8	1	5	6	4
1991-92	Dubuque	USHL	39	4	21	25	69	....	....	....	....	....

HANUS, TIM

Left wing. Shoots left. 6'1", 185 lbs. Born, Minneapolis, MN, May 12, 1969.
(Quebec's 7th choice, 135th overall, in 1987 Entry Draft).

			Regular Season					Playoffs				
Season	**Club**	**Lea**	**GP**	**G**	**A**	**TP**	**PIM**	**GP**	**G**	**A**	**TP**	**PIM**
1988-89	St. Cloud	NCAA	33	13	22	35	31	....	....	....	....	....
1989-90	St. Cloud	NCAA	34	22	24	46	54	....	....	....	....	....
1990-91	St. Cloud	WCHA	40	21	26	47	26	....	....	....	....	....
1991-92	St. Cloud	WCHA	37	17	27	44	36	....	....	....	....	....

HARDING, MIKE

Right wing. Shoots right. 6'4", 221 lbs. Born, Edsow, Alta., February 24, 1971.
(Hartford's 6th choice, 119th overall, in 1991 Entry Draft).

			Regular Season					Playoffs				
Season	**Club**	**Lea**	**GP**	**G**	**A**	**TP**	**PIM**	**GP**	**G**	**A**	**TP**	**PIM**
1990-91	N. Michigan	WCHA				UNAVAILABLE						
1991-92	N. Michigan	WCHA	28	6	8	14	46	....	....	....	....	....

HARDY, MARK LEA

Defense. Shoots left. 5'11", 195 lbs. Born, Semaden, Switzerland, February 1, 1959.
(Los Angeles' 3rd choice, 30th overall, in 1979 Entry Draft).

			Regular Season					Playoffs				
Season	**Club**	**Lea**	**GP**	**G**	**A**	**TP**	**PIM**	**GP**	**G**	**A**	**TP**	**PIM**
1977-78	Montreal	QJHL	72	25	57	82	150	13	3	10	13	22
1978-79	Montreal	QJHL	67	18	52	70	117	11	5	8	13	40
1979-80	Binghamton	AHL	56	3	13	16	32	....	....	....	....	....
	Los Angeles	**NHL**	**15**	**0**	**1**	**1**	**10**	**4**	**1**	**1**	**2**	**9**
1980-81	**Los Angeles**	**NHL**	**77**	**5**	**20**	**25**	**77**	**4**	**1**	**2**	**3**	**4**
1981-82	**Los Angeles**	**NHL**	**77**	**6**	**39**	**45**	**130**	**10**	**1**	**2**	**3**	**9**
1982-83	**Los Angeles**	**NHL**	**74**	**5**	**34**	**39**	**101**	....	....	....	....	....
1983-84	**Los Angeles**	**NHL**	**79**	**8**	**41**	**49**	**122**	....	....	....	....	....
1984-85	**Los Angeles**	**NHL**	**78**	**14**	**39**	**53**	**97**	**3**	**0**	**1**	**1**	**2**
1985-86	**Los Angeles**	**NHL**	**55**	**6**	**21**	**27**	**71**	....	....	....	....	....
1986-87	**Los Angeles**	**NHL**	**73**	**3**	**27**	**30**	**120**	**5**	**1**	**2**	**3**	**10**
1987-88	**Los Angeles**	**NHL**	**61**	**6**	**22**	**28**	**99**	....	....	....	....	....
	NY Rangers	**NHL**	**19**	**2**	**2**	**4**	**31**	....	....	....	....	....
1988-89	**Minnesota**	**NHL**	**15**	**2**	**4**	**6**	**26**	....	....	....	....	....
	NY Rangers	**NHL**	**45**	**2**	**12**	**14**	**45**	**4**	**0**	**1**	**1**	**31**
1989-90	**NY Rangers**	**NHL**	**54**	**0**	**15**	**15**	**94**	**3**	**0**	**1**	**1**	**2**
1990-91	**NY Rangers**	**NHL**	**70**	**1**	**5**	**6**	**89**	**6**	**0**	**1**	**1**	**30**
1991-92	**NY Rangers**	**NHL**	**52**	**1**	**8**	**9**	**65**	**13**	**0**	**3**	**3**	**31**
	NHL Totals		**844**	**61**	**290**	**351**	**1177**	**52**	**4**	**14**	**18**	**128**

Traded to **NY Rangers** by **Los Angeles** for Ron Duguay, February 23, 1988. Traded to **Minnesota** by **NY Rangers** for future considerations (Louie Debrusk) June 13, 1988. Traded to **NY Rangers** by **Minnesota** for Larry Bernard and NY Rangers' fifth round choice (Rhys Hollyman) in 1989 Entry Draft, December 9, 1988.

HARKINS, BRETT

Left wing. Shoots left. 6'1", 170 lbs. Born, North Ridgeville, OH, July 2, 1970.
(NY Islanders' 9th choice, 133rd overall, in 1989 Entry Draft).

			Regular Season					Playoffs				
Season	**Club**	**Lea**	**GP**	**G**	**A**	**TP**	**PIM**	**GP**	**G**	**A**	**TP**	**PIM**
1989-90	Bowling Green	CCHA	41	11	43	54	45	....	....	....	....	....
1990-91	Bowling Green	CCHA	40	22	38	60	30	....	....	....	....	....
1991-92	Bowling Green	CCHA	34	8	39	47	32	....	....	....	....	....

HARKINS, TOD

Center. Shoots right. 6'3", 210 lbs. Born, Cleveland, OH, October 8, 1968.
(Calgary's 2nd choice, 42nd overall, in 1988 Entry Draft).

			Regular Season					Playoffs				
Season	**Club**	**Lea**	**GP**	**G**	**A**	**TP**	**PIM**	**GP**	**G**	**A**	**TP**	**PIM**
1987-88	Miami-Ohio	CCHA	34	9	7	16	133	....	....	....	....	....
1988-89	Miami-Ohio	CCHA	36	8	7	15	77	....	....	....	....	....
1989-90	Miami-Ohio	CCHA	40	27	17	44	78	....	....	....	....	....
1990-91	Salt Lake	IHL	79	15	27	42	113	3	0	0	0	0
1991-92	**Calgary**	**NHL**	**5**	**0**	**0**	**0**	**7**	....	....	....	....	....
	Salt Lake	IHL	72	32	30	62	67	5	1	1	2	6
	NHL Totals		**5**	**0**	**0**	**0**	**7**	....	....	....	....	....

HARLOCK, DAVID

Defense. Shoots left. 6'2", 195 lbs. Born, Toronto, Ont., March 16, 1971.
(New Jersey's 2nd choice, 24th overall, in 1990 Entry Draft).

			Regular Season					Playoffs				
Season	**Club**	**Lea**	**GP**	**G**	**A**	**TP**	**PIM**	**GP**	**G**	**A**	**TP**	**PIM**
1989-90	U. of Michigan	CCHA	42	2	13	15	44	....	....	....	....	....
1990-91	U. of Michigan	CCHA	39	2	8	10	70	....	....	....	....	....
1991-92	U. of Michigan	CCHA	44	1	6	7	80	....	....	....	....	....

HARPER, KELLY

Center. Shoots right. 6'2", 170 lbs. Born, Sudbury, Ont., May 9, 1972.
(Calgary's 8th choice, 151st overall, in 1991 Entry Draft).

			Regular Season					Playoffs				
Season	**Club**	**Lea**	**GP**	**G**	**A**	**TP**	**PIM**	**GP**	**G**	**A**	**TP**	**PIM**
1990-91	Michigan State	CCHA	34	1	8	9	21	....	....	....	....	....
1991-92	Michigan State	CCHA	33	4	4	8	2	....	....	....	....	....

HARRIS, TIM

Right wing. Shoots right. 6'2", 190 lbs. Born, Uxbridge, Ont., October 16, 1967.
(Calgary's 5th choice, 70th overall, in 1987 Entry Draft).

			Regular Season					Playoffs				
Season	**Club**	**Lea**	**GP**	**G**	**A**	**TP**	**PIM**	**GP**	**G**	**A**	**TP**	**PIM**
1987-88	Lake Superior	CCHA	43	8	10	18	79	....	....	....	....	....
1988-89	Lake Superior	CCHA	29	1	5	6	78	....	....	....	....	....
1989-90	Lake Superior	CCHA	39	6	17	23	71	....	....	....	....	....
1990-91	Lake Superior	CCHA	45	17	22	39	122	....	....	....	....	....
1991-92	Salt Lake	IHL	71	11	21	32	91	3	0	1	1	4

HARTJE, TOD

Center. Shoots left. 6'1", 180 lbs. Born, Anoka, MN, February 27, 1968.
(Winnipeg's 7th choice, 142nd overall, in 1987 Entry Draft).

			Regular Season					Playoffs				
Season	**Club**	**Lea**	**GP**	**G**	**A**	**TP**	**PIM**	**GP**	**G**	**A**	**TP**	**PIM**
1986-87	Harvard	ECAC	32	3	9	12	36	....	....	....	....	....
1987-88	Harvard	ECAC	32	5	17	22	40	....	....	....	....	....
1988-89	Harvard	ECAC	33	4	17	21	40	....	....	....	....	....
1989-90	Harvard	ECAC	28	6	10	16	29	....	....	....	....	....
1990-91	Sokol Kiev	USSR	32	2	4	6	18	....	....	....	....	....
	Fort Wayne	IHL	1	1	0	1	2	....	....	....	....	....
1991-92	Moncton	AHL	38	9	9	18	35	....	....	....	....	....

HARTMAN, MIKE

Left wing. Shoots left. 6', 190 lbs. Born, Detroit, MI, February 7, 1967.
(Buffalo's 8th choice, 131st overall, in 1986 Entry Draft).

			Regular Season					Playoffs				
Season	**Club**	**Lea**	**GP**	**G**	**A**	**TP**	**PIM**	**GP**	**G**	**A**	**TP**	**PIM**
1984-85	Belleville	OHL	49	13	12	25	119	....	....	....	....	....
1985-86	Belleville	OHL	4	2	1	3	5	....	....	....	....	....
	North Bay	OHL	53	19	16	35	205	10	2	4	6	34
1986-87	**Buffalo**	**NHL**	**17**	**3**	**3**	**6**	**69**	....	....	....	....	....
	North Bay	OHL	32	15	24	39	144	19	7	8	15	88
1987-88	**Buffalo**	**NHL**	**18**	**3**	**1**	**4**	**90**	**6**	**0**	**0**	**0**	**35**
	Rochester	AHL	57	13	14	27	283	4	1	0	1	22
1988-89	**Buffalo**	**NHL**	**70**	**8**	**9**	**17**	**316**	**5**	**0**	**0**	**0**	**34**
1989-90	**Buffalo**	**NHL**	**60**	**11**	**10**	**21**	**211**	**6**	**0**	**0**	**0**	**18**
1990-91	**Buffalo**	**NHL**	**60**	**9**	**3**	**12**	**204**	**2**	**0**	**0**	**0**	**17**
1991-92	**Winnipeg**	**NHL**	**75**	**4**	**4**	**8**	**264**	**2**	**0**	**0**	**0**	**2**
	NHL Totals		**300**	**38**	**30**	**68**	**1154**	**21**	**0**	**0**	**0**	**106**

Traded to **Winnipeg** by **Buffalo** with Darrin Shannon and Dean Kennedy for Dave McLlwain, Gord Donnelly, Winnipeg's fifth round choice (Yuri Khmylev) in 1992 Entry Draft and future considerations, October 11, 1991. Claimed by **Tampa Bay** from **Winnipeg** in Expansion Draft, June 18, 1992.

HARWELL, JOE

Defense. Shoots right. 6'3", 195 lbs. Born, Minneapolis, MN, November 21, 1968.
(Winnipeg's 6th choice, 121st overall, in 1987 Entry Draft).

			Regular Season					Playoffs				
Season	**Club**	**Lea**	**GP**	**G**	**A**	**TP**	**PIM**	**GP**	**G**	**A**	**TP**	**PIM**
1989-90	U. Wisconsin	WCHA	10	0	0	0	2	....	....	....	....	....
1990-91	U. Wisconsin	WCHA	42	3	5	8	44	....	....	....	....	....
1991-92	U. Wisconsin	WCHA	37	2	6	8	71	....	....	....	....	....

HASSELBLAD, PETER

Defense. Shoots right. 6'4", 195 lbs. Born, Orebro, Sweden, April 20, 1966.
(Calgary's 12th choice, 229th overall, in 1987 Entry Draft).

			Regular Season					Playoffs				
Season	**Club**	**Lea**	**GP**	**G**	**A**	**TP**	**PIM**	**GP**	**G**	**A**	**TP**	**PIM**
1989-90	Farjestad	Swe.	56	3	6	9	51	10	1	2	3	12
1990-91	Farjestad	Swe.	40	0	7	7	56	....	....	....	....	....
1991-92	Team Boro	Swe.2				UNAVAILABLE						

HATCHER, DERIAN

Defense. Shoots left. 6'5", 205 lbs. Born, Sterling Heights, MI, June 4, 1972.
(Minnesota's 1st choice, 8th overall, in 1990 Entry Draft).

			Regular Season					Playoffs				
Season	Club	Lea	GP	G	A	TP	PIM	GP	G	A	TP	PIM
1989-90	North Bay	OHL	64	14	38	52	81	5	2	3	5	8
1990-91a	North Bay	OHL	64	13	49	62	163	10	2	10	12	28
1991-92	**Minnesota**	**NHL**	**43**	**8**	**4**	**12**	**88**	**5**	**0**	**2**	**2**	**8**
	NHL Totals		**43**	**8**	**4**	**12**	**88**	**5**	**0**	**2**	**2**	**8**

a OHL Third All-Star Team (1991)

HATCHER, KEVIN

Defense. Shoots right. 6'4", 225 lbs. Born, Detroit, MI, September 9, 1966.
(Washington's 1st choice, 17th overall, in 1984 Entry Draft).

			Regular Season					Playoffs				
Season	Club	Lea	GP	G	A	TP	PIM	GP	G	A	TP	PIM
1983-84	North Bay	OHL	67	10	39	49	61	4	2	2	4	11
1984-85	**Washington**	**NHL**	**2**	**1**	**0**	**1**	**0**	**1**	**0**	**0**	**0**	**0**
a	North Bay	OHL	58	26	37	63	75	8	3	8	11	9
1985-86	**Washington**	**NHL**	**79**	**9**	**10**	**19**	**119**	**9**	**1**	**1**	**2**	**19**
1986-87	**Washington**	**NHL**	**78**	**8**	**16**	**24**	**144**	**7**	**1**	**0**	**1**	**20**
1987-88	**Washington**	**NHL**	**71**	**14**	**27**	**41**	**137**	**14**	**5**	**7**	**12**	**55**
1988-89	**Washington**	**NHL**	**62**	**13**	**27**	**40**	**101**	**6**	**1**	**4**	**5**	**20**
1989-90	**Washington**	**NHL**	**80**	**13**	**41**	**54**	**102**	**11**	**0**	**8**	**8**	**32**
1990-91	**Washington**	**NHL**	**79**	**24**	**50**	**74**	**69**	**11**	**3**	**3**	**6**	**8**
1991-92	**Washington**	**NHL**	**79**	**17**	**37**	**54**	**105**	**7**	**2**	**4**	**6**	**19**
	NHL Totals		**530**	**99**	**208**	**307**	**777**	**66**	**13**	**27**	**40**	**173**

a OHL Second All-Star Team (1985)

Played in NHL All-Star Game (1990, 1991, 1992)

HAUER, BRETT

Defense. Shoots right. 6'2", 190 lbs. Born, Edina, MN, July 11, 1971.
(Vancouver's 3rd choice, 71st overall, in 1989 Entry Draft).

			Regular Season					Playoffs				
Season	Club	Lea	GP	G	A	TP	PIM	GP	G	A	TP	PIM
1989-90	Minn.-Duluth	WCHA	37	2	6	8	44	....	....	....	....	....
1990-91	Minn.-Duluth	WCHA	30	1	7	8	54	....	....	....	....	....
1991-92	Minn.-Duluth	WCHA	33	8	14	22	40	....	....	....	....	....

HAWERCHUK, DALE (HOW-uhr-CHUHK)

Center. Shoots left. 5'11", 190 lbs. Born, Toronto, Ont., April 4, 1963.
(Winnipeg's 1st choice, 1st overall, in 1981 Entry Draft).

			Regular Season					Playoffs				
Season	Club	Lea	GP	G	A	TP	PIM	GP	G	A	TP	PIM
1979-80	Cornwall	QJHL	72	37	66	103	21	18	20	25	45	0
1980-81abc	Cornwall	QJHL	72	81	102	183	69	19	15	20	35	8
1981-82d	**Winnipeg**	**NHL**	**80**	**45**	**58**	**103**	**47**	**4**	**1**	**7**	**8**	**5**
1982-83	**Winnipeg**	**NHL**	**79**	**40**	**51**	**91**	**31**	**3**	**1**	**4**	**5**	**8**
1983-84	**Winnipeg**	**NHL**	**80**	**37**	**65**	**102**	**73**	**3**	**1**	**1**	**2**	**0**
1984-85e	**Winnipeg**	**NHL**	**80**	**53**	**77**	**130**	**74**	**3**	**2**	**1**	**3**	**4**
1985-86	**Winnipeg**	**NHL**	**80**	**46**	**59**	**105**	**44**	**3**	**0**	**3**	**3**	**0**
1986-87	**Winnipeg**	**NHL**	**80**	**47**	**53**	**100**	**52**	**10**	**5**	**8**	**13**	**4**
1987-88	**Winnipeg**	**NHL**	**80**	**44**	**77**	**121**	**59**	**5**	**3**	**4**	**7**	**16**
1988-89	**Winnipeg**	**NHL**	**75**	**41**	**55**	**96**	**28**	....	....	....	....	....
1989-90	**Winnipeg**	**NHL**	**79**	**26**	**55**	**81**	**60**	**7**	**3**	**5**	**8**	**2**
1990-91	**Buffalo**	**NHL**	**80**	**31**	**58**	**89**	**32**	**6**	**2**	**4**	**6**	**10**
1991-92	**Buffalo**	**NHL**	**77**	**23**	**75**	**98**	**27**	**7**	**2**	**5**	**7**	**0**
	NHL Totals		**870**	**433**	**683**	**1116**	**527**	**51**	**20**	**42**	**62**	**49**

a QMJHL First All-Star Team (1981)
b QMJHL Player of the Year (1981)
c Canadian Major Junior Player of the Year (1981)
d Won Calder Memorial Trophy (1982)
e NHL Second All-Star Team (1985)

Played in NHL All-Star Game (1982, 1985, 1986, 1988)

Traded to **Buffalo** by **Winnipeg** with Winnipeg's first round choice (Brad May) in 1990 Entry Draft and future considerations for Phil Housley, Scott Arniel, Jeff Parker and Buffalo's first round choice (Keith Tkachuk) in 1990 Entry Draft, June 16, 1990.

HAWGOOD, GREG

Left wing/Defense. Shoots left. 5'10", 190 lbs. Born, Edmonton, Alta., August 10, 1968.
(Boston's 9th choice, 202nd overall, in 1986 Entry Draft).

			Regular Season					Playoffs				
Season	Club	Lea	GP	G	A	TP	PIM	GP	G	A	TP	PIM
1983-84	Kamloops	WHL	49	10	23	33	39	....	....	....	....	....
1984-85	Kamloops	WHL	66	25	40	65	72	....	....	....	....	....
1985-86a	Kamloops	WHL	71	34	85	119	86	16	9	22	31	16
1986-87a	Kamloops	WHL	61	30	93	123	139	....	....	....	....	....
1987-88	**Boston**	**NHL**	**1**	**0**	**0**	**0**	**0**	**3**	**1**	**0**	**1**	**0**
ab	Kamloops	WHL	63	48	85	133	142	16	10	16	26	33
1988-89	**Boston**	**NHL**	**56**	**16**	**24**	**40**	**84**	**10**	**0**	**2**	**2**	**2**
	Maine	AHL	21	2	9	11	41	....	....	....	....	....
1989-90	**Boston**	**NHL**	**77**	**11**	**27**	**38**	**76**	**15**	**1**	**3**	**4**	**12**
1990-91	Asiago	Italy	2	3	0	3	9	....	....	....	....	....
	Edmonton	**NHL**	**6**	**0**	**1**	**1**	**6**	....	....	....	....	....
	Maine	AHL	5	0	1	1	13	....	....	....	....	....
	Cape Breton	AHL	55	10	32	42	73	4	0	3	3	23
1991-92	**Edmonton**	**NHL**	**20**	**2**	**11**	**13**	**22**	**13**	**0**	**3**	**3**	**23**
cd	Cape Breton	AHL	56	20	55	75	26	3	2	2	4	0
	NHL Totals		**160**	**29**	**63**	**92**	**188**	**41**	**2**	**8**	**10**	**39**

a WHL West All-Star Team (1986, 1987, 1988)
b WHL and Canadian Major Junior Defenseman of the Year (1988)
c AHL First All-Star Team (1992)
d Won Eddie Shore Plaque (Top Defenseman-AHL) (1992)

Traded to **Edmonton** by **Boston** for Vladimir Ruzicka, October 22, 1990.

HAWKINS, TODD

Left/Right wing. Shoots right. 6'1", 195 lbs. Born, Kingston, Ont., August 2, 1966.
(Vancouver's 10th choice, 217th overall, in 1986 Entry Draft).

			Regular Season					Playoffs				
Season	Club	Lea	GP	G	A	TP	PIM	GP	G	A	TP	PIM
1984-85	Belleville	OHL	58	7	16	23	117	12	1	0	1	10
1985-86	Belleville	OHL	60	14	13	27	172	24	9	7	16	60
1986-87	Belleville	OHL	60	47	40	87	187	6	3	5	8	16
1987-88	Flint	IHL	50	13	13	26	337	16	3	5	8	*174
	Fredericton	AHL	2	0	4	4	11	....	....	....	....	....
1988-89	**Vancouver**	**NHL**	**4**	**0**	**0**	**0**	**9**	....	....	....	....	....
	Milwaukee	IHL	63	12	14	26	307	9	1	0	1	33
1989-90	**Vancouver**	**NHL**	**4**	**0**	**0**	**0**	**6**	....	....	....	....	....
	Milwaukee	IHL	61	23	17	40	273	5	4	1	5	19
1990-91	Newmarket	AHL	22	2	5	7	66	....	....	....	....	....
	Milwaukee	IHL	39	9	11	20	134	....	....	....	....	....
1991-92	**Toronto**	**NHL**	**2**	**0**	**0**	**0**	**0**	....	....	....	....	....
	St. John's	AHL	66	30	27	57	139	7	1	0	1	10
	NHL Totals		**10**	**0**	**0**	**0**	**15**	....	....	....	....	....

Traded to **Toronto** by **Vancouver** for Brian Blad, January 22, 1991.

HAWLEY, JOE

Right wing. Shoots right. 5'10", 186 lbs. Born, Peterborough, Ont., March 13, 1971.
(St. Louis' 8th choice, 222nd overall, in 1990 Entry Draft).

			Regular Season					Playoffs				
Season	Club	Lea	GP	G	A	TP	PIM	GP	G	A	TP	PIM
1989-90	Peterborough	OHL	66	8	40	48	59	12	2	3	5	26
1990-91	Peterborough	OHL	63	17	47	64	70	4	2	3	5	11
1991-92	Peoria	IHL	40	6	7	13	42	....	....	....	....	....
	Dayton	ECHL	7	3	6	9	12	....	....	....	....	....

HEAPHY, SHAWN

Center. Shoots left. 5'8", 175 lbs. Born, Sudbury, Ont., November 27, 1968.
(Calgary's 1st choice, 26th overall, in 1989 Supplemental Draft).

			Regular Season					Playoffs				
Season	Club	Lea	GP	G	A	TP	PIM	GP	G	A	TP	PIM
1987-88	Michigan State	CCHA	44	19	24	43	48	....	....	....	....	....
1988-89	Michigan State	CCHA	47	26	17	43	80	....	....	....	....	....
1989-90	Michigan State	CCHA	45	28	31	59	54	....	....	....	....	....
1990-91	Michigan State	CCHA	39	30	19	49	57	....	....	....	....	....
	Salt Lake	IHL	....	....	....	....	....	1	0	0	0	0
1991-92	Salt Lake	IHL	76	41	36	77	85	5	2	2	4	2

HEDICAN, BRET

Left wing. Shoots left. 6'2", 188 lbs. Born, St. Paul, MN, August 10, 1970.
(St. Louis' 10th choice, 198th overall, in 1988 Entry Draft).

			Regular Season					Playoffs				
Season	Club	Lea	GP	G	A	TP	PIM	GP	G	A	TP	PIM
1988-89	St. Cloud	NCAA	28	5	3	8	28	....	....	....	....	....
1989-90	St. Cloud	NCAA	36	4	17	21	37	....	....	....	....	....
1990-91a	St. Cloud	WCHA	41	21	26	47	26	....	....	....	....	....
1991-92	U.S. National	....	54	1	8	9	59	....	....	....	....	....
	U.S. Olympic	....	8	0	0	0	4	....	....	....	....	....
	St. Louis	**NHL**	**4**	**1**	**0**	**1**	**0**	**5**	**0**	**0**	**0**	**0**
	NHL Totals		**4**	**1**	**0**	**1**	**0**	**5**	**0**	**0**	**0**	**0**

a WCHA First All-Star Team (1991)

HEDLUND, TODD

Right wing. Shoots right. 6'1", 177 lbs. Born, Roseau, MN, August 20, 1971.
(NY Rangers' 10th choice, 160th overall, in 1990 Entry Draft).

			Regular Season					Playoffs				
Season	Club	Lea	GP	G	A	TP	PIM	GP	G	A	TP	PIM
1989-90	Roseau	HS	28	16	12	28	....	....	....	....	....	....
1990-91	U. Wisconsin	WCHA			DID NOT PLAY							
1991-92	U. Wisconsin	WCHA	5	0	1	1	2	....	....	....	....	....

HEED, JONAS (HAD)

Defense. Shoots left. 6', 174 lbs. Born, Sodertalje, Sweden, January 3, 1967.
(Chicago's 6th choice, 116th overall, in 1985 Entry Draft).

			Regular Season					Playoffs				
Season	Club	Lea	GP	G	A	TP	PIM	GP	G	A	TP	PIM
1984-85	Sodertalje	Swe.	8	0	0	0	0	....	....	....	....	....
1985-86	Sodertalje	Swe.	17	3	2	5	6	....	....	....	....	....
1986-87	Sodertalje	Swe.	24	0	3	3	12	2	0	0	0	0
1987-88	Sodertalje	Swe.	26	1	4	5	12	....	....	....	....	....
1988-89	Sodertalje	Swe.	38	4	9	13	22	....	....	....	....	....
1989-90	Sodertalje	Swe.	36	7	4	11	28	2	0	0	0	0
1990-91	V. Frolunda	Swe.2	21	1	1	2	14	....	....	....	....	....
1991-92	V. Frolunda	Swe.	33	2	1	3	34	3	0	0	0	0

HEHR, JASON

Defense. Shoots left. 6'1", 193 lbs. Born, Medicine Hat, Alta., February 8, 1971.
(New Jersey's 12th choice, 253rd overall, in 1991 Entry Draft).

			Regular Season					Playoffs				
Season	Club	Lea	GP	G	A	TP	PIM	GP	G	A	TP	PIM
1990-91	Kelowna	BCJHL	55	18	46	64	89	....	....	....	....	....
1991-92	N. Michigan	WCHA	40	8	17	25	38	....	....	....	....	....

HEINZE, STEPHEN

Center. Shoots right. 5'11", 180 lbs. Born, Lawrence, MA, January 30, 1970.
(Boston's 2nd choice, 60th overall, in 1988 Entry Draft).

			Regular Season					Playoffs				
Season	Club	Lea	GP	G	A	TP	PIM	GP	G	A	TP	PIM
1988-89	Boston College	H.E.	36	26	23	49	26	....	....	....	....	....
1989-90ab	Boston College	H.E.	40	27	36	63	41	....	....	....	....	....
1990-91	Boston College	H.E.	35	21	26	47	35	....	....	....	....	....
1991-92	U.S. National	....	49	18	15	33	38	....	....	....	....	....
	U.S. Olympic	....	8	1	3	4	8	....	....	....	....	....
	Boston	**NHL**	**14**	**3**	**4**	**7**	**6**	**7**	**0**	**3**	**3**	**17**
	NHL Totals		**14**	**3**	**4**	**7**	**6**	**7**	**0**	**3**	**3**	**17**

a Hockey East First All-Star Team (1990)
b NCAA East First All-American Team (1990)

HELBER, MICHAEL

Center. Shoots right. 5'11", 175 lbs. Born, Ann Arbor, MI, June 23, 1970.
(Winnipeg's 11th choice, 178th overall, in 1988 Entry Draft).

			Regular Season					Playoffs				
Season	Club	Lea	GP	G	A	TP	PIM	GP	G	A	TP	PIM
1988-89	U. of Michigan	CCHA	35	8	10	18	15	....	....	....	....	....
1989-90	U. of Michigan	CCHA	20	3	2	5	8	....	....	....	....	....
1990-91	U. of Michigan	CCHA	37	15	22	37	45	....	....	....	....	....
1991-92	U. of Michigan	CCHA	43	8	13	21	26	....	....	....	....	....

HELGESON, JON

Center. Shoots left. 6'3", 205 lbs. Born, Roseau, MN, August 15, 1968.
(Vancouver's 6th choice, 133rd overall, in 1986 Entry Draft).

			Regular Season					Playoffs				
Season	Club	Lea	GP	G	A	TP	PIM	GP	G	A	TP	PIM
1987-88	U. Wisconsin	WCHA	5	0	2	2	2	....	....	....	....	....
1988-89	U. Wisconsin	WCHA	36	7	1	8	28	....	....	....	....	....
1989-90	U. Wisconsin	WCHA	18	2	2	4	12	....	....	....	....	....
1990-91	U. Wisconsin	WCHA	19	3	1	4	18	....	....	....	....	....
1991-92	U. Wisconsin	WCHA	37	5	6	11	64	....	....	....	....	....

HENDRICKSON, DARBY

Center. Shoots left. 6', 175 lbs. Born, Richfield, MN, August 28, 1972.
(Toronto's 3rd choice, 73rd overall, in 1990 Entry Draft).

			Regular Season					Playoffs				
Season	Club	Lea	GP	G	A	TP	PIM	GP	G	A	TP	PIM
1990-91	Richfield	HS	27	32	29	61	....	....	....	....	....	....
1991-92	U. Minnesota	WCHA	41	25	28	53	61	....	....	....	....	....

HENDRY, JOHN

Left wing. Shoots left. 6'1", 180 lbs. Born, Mississauga, Ont., May 15, 1970.
(Detroit's 11th choice, 234th overall, in 1990 Entry Draft).

			Regular Season					Playoffs				
Season	Club	Lea	GP	G	A	TP	PIM	GP	G	A	TP	PIM
1989-90	Lake Superior	CCHA	41	4	7	11	30	....	....	....	....	....
1990-91	Lake Superior	CCHA	44	7	10	17	42	....	....	....	....	....
1991-92	Lake Superior	CCHA	39	12	8	20	53	....	....	....	....	....

HENRICH, ED

Defense. Shoots left. 6'1", 192 lbs. Born, Buffalo, NY, February 4, 1971.
(Montreal's 10th choice, 209th overall, in 1989 Entry Draft).

			Regular Season					Playoffs				
Season	Club	Lea	GP	G	A	TP	PIM	GP	G	A	TP	PIM
1990-91	Clarkson	ECAC	37	4	23	27	22	....	....	....	....	....
1991-92	Clarkson	ECAC	28	2	11	13	22	....	....	....	....	....

HENTGES, MATHEW

Defense. Shoots left. 6', 220 lbs. Born, St. Paul, MN, December 19, 1969.
(Chicago's 8th choice, 176th overall, in 1988 Entry Draft).

			Regular Season					Playoffs				
Season	Club	Lea	GP	G	A	TP	PIM	GP	G	A	TP	PIM
1988-89	Merrimack	NCAA	33	0	16	16	22	....	....	....	....	....
1989-90	Merrimack	H.E.	33	1	2	3	40	....	....	....	....	....
1990-91	Merrimack	H.E.	32	0	7	7	24	....	....	....	....	....
1991-92	Merrimack	H.E.	8	0	0	0	6	....	....	....	....	....

HEROUX, YVES (ay-ROO, EEV)

Right wing. Shoots right. 5'11", 185 lbs. Born, Terrebonne, Que., April 27, 1965.
(Quebec's 1st choice, 32nd overall, in 1983 Entry Draft).

			Regular Season					Playoffs				
Season	Club	Lea	GP	G	A	TP	PIM	GP	G	A	TP	PIM
1982-83	Chicoutimi	QMJHL	70	41	40	81	44	5	0	4	4	8
1983-84	Chicoutimi	QMJHL	56	28	25	53	67	....	....	....	....	....
	Fredericton	AHL	4	0	0	0	0	....	....	....	....	....
1984-85	Chicoutimi	QMJHL	66	42	54	96	123	14	5	8	13	16
1985-86	Fredericton	AHL	31	12	10	22	42	2	0	1	1	7
	Muskegon	IHL	42	14	8	22	41	....	....	....	....	....
1986-87	**Quebec**	**NHL**	**1**	**0**	**0**	**0**	**0**	....	....	....	....	....
	Fredericton	AHL	37	8	6	14	13	....	....	....	....	....
	Muskegon	IHL	25	6	8	14	31	2	0	0	0	0
1987-88	Baltimore	AHL	5	0	2	2	2	....	....	....	....	....
1988-89	Flint	IHL	82	43	42	85	98	....	....	....	....	....
1989-90	Peoria	IHL	14	3	2	5	42	5	2	2	4	0
1990-91	Albany	IHL	45	22	18	40	46	....	....	....	....	....
	Peoria	IHL	33	16	8	24	26	17	4	4	8	16
1991-92	Peoria	IHL	80	41	36	77	72	8	5	1	6	6
	NHL Totals		**1**	**0**	**0**	**0**	**0**	....	....	....	....	....

Signed as a free agent by **St. Louis**, March 13, 1990. Signed as a free agent by **Minnesota**, August 10, 1992.

HERTER, JASON

Defense. Shoots right. 6'1", 190 lbs. Born, Hafford, Sask., October 2, 1970.
(Vancouver's 1st choice, 8th overall, in 1989 Entry Draft).

			Regular Season					Playoffs				
Season	Club	Lea	GP	G	A	TP	PIM	GP	G	A	TP	PIM
1988-89	North Dakota	WCHA	41	8	24	32	62	....	....	....	....	....
1989-90a	North Dakota	WCHA	38	11	39	50	40	....	....	....	....	....
1990-91a	North Dakota	WCHA	39	11	26	37	52	....	....	....	....	....
1991-92	Milwaukee	IHL	56	7	18	25	34	1	0	0	0	2

a WCHA Second All-Star Team (1990, 1991)

HERVEY, MATT

Defense. Shoots right. 5'11", 205 lbs. Born, Whittier, CA, May 16, 1966.

			Regular Season					Playoffs				
Season	Club	Lea	GP	G	A	TP	PIM	GP	G	A	TP	PIM
1983-84	Victoria	WHL	67	4	19	23	89	....	....	....	....	....
1984-85	Victoria	WHL	14	1	3	4	17	....	....	....	....	....
	Lethbridge	WHL	54	3	9	12	88	....	....	....	....	....
1985-86	Lethbridge	WHL	60	9	17	26	110	....	....	....	....	....
1986-87	Seattle	WHL	66	4	5	9	59	....	....	....	....	....
1987-88	Moncton	AHL	69	9	20	29	265	....	....	....	....	....
1988-89	**Winnipeg**	**NHL**	**2**	**0**	**0**	**0**	**4**	....	....	....	....	....
	Moncton	AHL	73	8	28	36	295	10	1	2	3	42
1989-90	Moncton	AHL	47	3	13	16	168	....	....	....	....	....
1990-91	Moncton	AHL	71	4	28	32	132	7	0	1	1	23
1991-92	**Boston**	**NHL**	**16**	**0**	**1**	**1**	**55**	**5**	**0**	**0**	**0**	**6**
	Maine	AHL	36	1	7	8	47	....	....	....	....	....
	NHL Totals		**18**	**0**	**1**	**1**	**59**	**5**	**0**	**0**	**0**	**6**

Signed as a free agent by **Winnipeg**, September 27, 1988. Signed as a free agent by **Boston**, August 15, 1991.

HEWARD, JAMIE

Right wing. Shoots right. 6'2", 183 lbs. Born, Regina, Sask., March 30, 1971.
(Pittsburgh's 1st choice, 16th overall, in 1989 Entry Draft).

			Regular Season					Playoffs				
Season	Club	Lea	GP	G	A	TP	PIM	GP	G	A	TP	PIM
1987-88	Regina	WHL	68	10	17	27	17	4	1	1	2	2
1988-89	Regina	WHL	52	31	28	59	29	....	....	....	....	....
1989-90	Regina	WHL	72	14	44	58	42	11	2	2	4	10
1990-91a	Regina	WHL	71	23	61	84	41	8	2	9	11	6
1991-92	Muskegon	IHL	54	6	21	27	37	14	1	4	5	4

a WHL East First All-Star Team (1991)

HEXTALL, DONEVAN

Left wing. Shoots left. 6'2", 192 lbs. Born, Wolseley, Sask., February 24, 1972.
(New Jersey's 3rd choice, 33rd overall, in 1991 Entry Draft).

			Regular Season					Playoffs				
Season	Club	Lea	GP	G	A	TP	PIM	GP	G	A	TP	PIM
1989-90	Weyburn	SJHL	63	23	45	68	127	....	....	....	....	....
	Prince Albert	WHL	7	1	2	3	4	....	....	....	....	....
1990-91	Prince Albert	WHL	70	30	59	89	55	3	1	3	4	0
1991-92a	Prince Albert	WHL	71	33	71	104	105	10	3	6	9	10

a WHL East Second All-Star Team (1992)

HILDITCH, TODD

Defense. Shoots right. 6'1", 200 lbs. Born, Vancouver, B.C., March 13, 1968.
(Washington's 9th choice, 162nd overall, in 1988 Entry Draft).

			Regular Season					Playoffs				
Season	Club	Lea	GP	G	A	TP	PIM	GP	G	A	TP	PIM
1988-89	RPI	ECAC	29	1	1	2	56	....	....	....	....	....
1989-90	RPI	ECAC	33	1	3	4	48	....	....	....	....	....
1990-91	RPI	ECAC	32	3	10	13	77	....	....	....	....	....
1991-92	RPI	ECAC	33	4	13	17	90	....	....	....	....	....

HILL, SEAN

Defense. Shoots right. 6', 195 lbs. Born, Duluth, MN, February 14, 1970.
(Montreal's 9th choice, 167th overall, in 1988 Entry Draft).

			Regular Season					Playoffs				
Season	Club	Lea	GP	G	A	TP	PIM	GP	G	A	TP	PIM
1988-89	U. Wisconsin	WCHA	45	2	23	25	69	....	....	....	....	....
1989-90a	U. Wisconsin	WCHA	42	14	39	53	78	....	....	....	....	....
1990-91ab	U. Wisconsin	WCHA	37	19	32	51	122	....	....	....	....	....
	Montreal	**NHL**	....	....	....	....	....	**1**	**0**	**0**	**0**	**0**
	Fredericton	AHL	....	....	....	....	....	3	0	2	2	2
1991-92	Fredericton	AHL	42	7	20	27	65	7	1	3	4	6
	U.S. National	....	12	4	3	7	16	....	....	....	....	....
	U.S. Olympic	....	8	2	0	2	6	....	....	....	....	....
	Montreal	**NHL**	....	....	....	....	....	**4**	**1**	**0**	**1**	**2**
	NHL Totals		....	....	....	....	....	**5**	**1**	**0**	**1**	**2**

a WCHA Second All-Star Team (1990, 1991)
b NCAA West Second All-American Team (1991)

HILLER, JIM

Right wing. Shoots right. 6', 190 lbs. Born, Port Alberni, B.C., May 15, 1969.
(Los Angeles' 10th choice, 207th overall, in 1989 Entry Draft).

			Regular Season					Playoffs				
Season	Club	Lea	GP	G	A	TP	PIM	GP	G	A	TP	PIM
1989-90	N. Michigan	WCHA	39	23	33	56	52	....	....	....	....	....
1990-91	N. Michigan	WCHA	43	22	41	63	59	....	....	....	....	....
1991-92ab	N. Michigan	WCHA	39	28	52	80	115	....	....	....	....	....

a NCAA West Second All-Star Team (1992)
b WCHA Second All-Star Team (1992)

HILLIER, RANDY GEORGE (HIHL-yuhr)

Defense. Shoots left. 6'1", 192 lbs. Born, Toronto, Ont., March 30, 1960.
(Boston's 4th choice, 102nd overall, in 1980 Entry Draft).

			Regular Season					Playoffs				
Season	Club	Lea	GP	G	A	TP	PIM	GP	G	A	TP	PIM
1978-79	Sudbury	OHA	61	8	25	33	173	10	2	5	7	21
1979-80	Sudbury	OHA	60	16	49	65	143	9	3	6	9	14
1980-81	Springfield	AHL	64	3	17	20	105	6	0	2	2	36
1981-82	Erie	AHL	35	6	13	19	52					
	Boston	NHL	25	0	8	8	29	8	0	1	1	16
1982-83	Boston	NHL	70	0	10	10	99	3	0	0	0	4
1983-84	Boston	NHL	69	3	12	15	125					
1984-85	Pittsburgh	NHL	45	2	19	21	56					
1985-86	Pittsburgh	NHL	28	0	3	3	53					
	Baltimore	AHL	8	0	5	5	14					
1986-87	Pittsburgh	NHL	55	4	8	12	97					
1987-88	Pittsburgh	NHL	55	1	12	13	144					
1988-89	Pittsburgh	NHL	68	1	23	24	141	9	0	1	1	49
1989-90	Pittsburgh	NHL	61	3	12	15	71					
1990-91	Pittsburgh	NHL	31	2	2	4	32	8	0	0	0	24
1991-92	NY Islanders	NHL	8	0	0	0	11					
	Buffalo	NHL	28	0	1	1	48					
	San Diego	IHL	6	0	2	2	4					
	NHL Totals		543	16	110	126	906	28	0	2	2	93

Traded to **Pittsburgh** by **Boston** for Pittsburgh's fourth round choice in 1985 Entry Draft (later traded to Quebec), October 15, 1984. Signed as a free agent by **NY Islanders**, June 30, 1991. Traded to **Buffalo** by **NY Islanders** with Pat Lafontaine, Randy Wood and future considerations for Pierre Turgeon, Uwe Krupp, Benoit Hogue and Dave McLlwain, October 25, 1991.

HLUSHKO, TODD

Left wing. Shoots left. 5'11", 180 lbs. Born, Toronto, Ont., February 7, 1970.
(Washington's 14th choice, 240th overall, in 1989 Entry Draft).

			Regular Season					Playoffs				
Season	Club	Lea	GP	G	A	TP	PIM	GP	G	A	TP	PIM
1988-89	Guelph	OHL	66	28	18	46	71	7	5	3	8	18
1989-90	Owen Sound	OHL	25	9	17	26	31					
	London	OHL	40	27	17	44	39	6	2	4	6	10
1990-91	Baltimore	AHL	66	9	14	23	55					
1991-92	Baltimore	AHL	74	16	35	51	113					

HOCKING, JUSTIN

Defense. Shoots right. 6'4", 205 lbs. Born, Stettler, Alta., January 9, 1974.
(Los Angeles' 1st choice, 39th overall, in 1992 Entry Draft).

			Regular Season					Playoffs				
Season	Club	Lea	GP	G	A	TP	PIM	GP	G	A	TP	PIM
1990-91	Fort Sask.	AJHL	38	4	6	10	84					
1991-92	Spokane	WHL	71	4	6	10	309	10	0	3	3	28

HODGE, DAN

Defense. Shoots right. 6'3", 205 lbs. Born, Melrose, MA, September 18, 1971.
(Boston's 8th choice, 194th overall, in 1991 Entry Draft).

			Regular Season					Playoffs				
Season	Club	Lea	GP	G	A	TP	PIM	GP	G	A	TP	PIM
1990-91	Merrimack	H.E.	11	2	3	5	4					
1991-92	Omaha	USHL	45	5	10	23	89					

HODGE, KENNETH DAVID (KEN)

Center/Right wing. Shoots left. 6'1", 200 lbs. Born, Windsor, Ont., April 13, 1966.
(Minnesota's 2nd choice, 46th overall, in 1984 Entry Draft).

			Regular Season					Playoffs				
Season	Club	Lea	GP	G	A	TP	PIM	GP	G	A	TP	PIM
1984-85	Boston College	H.E.	41	20	44	64	28					
1985-86	Boston College	H.E.	21	11	17	28	16					
1986-87	Boston College	H.E.	37	29	33	62	30					
1987-88	Kalamazoo	IHL	70	15	35	50	24					
1988-89	Minnesota	NHL	5	1	1	2	0					
	Kalamazoo	IHL	72	26	45	71	34	6	1	5	6	16
1989-90	Kalamazoo	IHL	68	33	53	86	19	10	5	13	18	2
1990-91a	Boston	NHL	70	30	29	59	20	15	4	6	10	6
	Maine	AHL	8	7	10	17	2					
1991-92	Boston	NHL	42	6	11	17	10					
	Maine	AHL	19	6	11	17	4					
	NHL Totals		117	37	41	78	30	15	4	6	10	6

a NHL/Upper Deck All-Rookie Team (1991)

Traded to **Boston** by **Minnesota** for future considerations, August 21, 1990.

HOFFMAN, MATT

Left wing. Shoots left. 6'2", 196 lbs. Born, Saginaw, MI, July 6, 1971.
(Calgary's 7th choice, 140th overall, in 1991 Entry Draft).

			Regular Season					Playoffs				
Season	Club	Lea	GP	G	A	TP	PIM	GP	G	A	TP	PIM
1990-91	Oshawa	OHL	66	41	58	99	93	16	9	8	17	23
1991-92	Oshawa	OHL	50	25	41	66	93	7	6	9	15	10

HOGAN, TIM

Defense. Shoots right. 6'2", 180 lbs. Born, Oshawa, Ont., January 7, 1974.
(Chicago's 5th choice, 113th overall, in 1992 Entry Draft).

			Regular Season					Playoffs				
Season	Club	Lea	GP	G	A	TP	PIM	GP	G	A	TP	PIM
1990-91	Wexford	Jr. B	33	5	19	24	46					
1991-92	Michigan	CCHA	34	2	8	10	34					

HOGUE, BENOIT (HOHG)

Center. Shoots left. 5'10", 190 lbs. Born, Repentigny, Que., October 28, 1966.
(Buffalo's 2nd choice, 35th overall, in 1985 Entry Draft).

			Regular Season					Playoffs				
Season	Club	Lea	GP	G	A	TP	PIM	GP	G	A	TP	PIM
1983-84	St-Jean	QMJHL	59	14	11	25	42					
1984-85	St-Jean	QMJHL	63	46	44	90	92					
1985-86	St-Jean	QMJHL	65	54	54	108	115	9	6	4	10	26
1986-87	Rochester	AHL	52	14	20	34	52	12	5	4	9	8
1987-88	Buffalo	NHL	3	1	1	2	0					
	Rochester	AHL	62	24	31	55	141	7	6	1	7	46
1988-89	Buffalo	NHL	69	14	30	44	120	5	0	0	0	17
1989-90	Buffalo	NHL	45	11	7	18	79	3	0	0	0	10
1990-91	Buffalo	NHL	76	19	28	47	76	5	3	1	4	10
1991-92	Buffalo	NHL	3	0	1	1	0					
	NY Islanders	NHL	72	30	45	75	67					
	NHL Totals		268	75	112	187	342	13	3	1	4	37

Traded to **NY Islanders** by **Buffalo** with Pierre Turgeon, Uwe Krupp and Dave McLlwain for Pat Lafontaine, Randy Hillier, Randy Wood and future considerations, October 25, 1991.

HOLDEMAN, TOM

Right wing. Shoots right. 6'2", 205 lbs. Born, Columbus, IN, November 8, 1970.
(Edmonton's 1st choice, 18th overall, in 1991 Supplemental Draft).

			Regular Season					Playoffs				
Season	Club	Lea	GP	G	A	TP	PIM	GP	G	A	TP	PIM
1989-90	Miami-Ohio	CCHA	28	3	1	4	8					
1990-91	Miami-Ohio	CCHA	28	2	2	4	42					
1991-92	W. Michigan	CCHA	DID NOT PLAY									

HOLDEN, PAUL

Defense. Shoots left. 6'3", 210 lbs. Born, Kitchener, Ont., March 15, 1970.
(Los Angeles' 2nd choice, 28th overall, in 1988 Entry Draft).

			Regular Season					Playoffs				
Season	Club	Lea	GP	G	A	TP	PIM	GP	G	A	TP	PIM
1987-88	London	OHL	65	8	12	20	87	12	1	1	2	10
1988-89	London	OHL	54	11	21	32	90	20	1	3	4	17
1989-90a	London	OHL	61	11	31	42	78	6	1	1	2	7
	New Haven	AHL	2	1	1	2	2					
1990-91	New Haven	AHL	59	2	8	10	23					
1991-92	Phoenix	IHL	47	3	3	6	63					

a OHL Second All-Star Team (1990)

HOLIK, ROBERT (BOBBY) (HOH-leek)

Left/Right wing. Shoots right. 6'3", 210 lbs. Born, Jihlava, Czechoslovakia, January 1, 1971.
(Hartford's 1st choice, 10th overall, in 1989 Entry Draft).

			Regular Season					Playoffs				
Season	Club	Lea	GP	G	A	TP	PIM	GP	G	A	TP	PIM
1987-88	Dukla Jihlava	Czech.	31	5	9	14	....					
1988-89	Dukla Jihlava	Czech.	24	7	10	17	....					
1989-90	Dukla Jihlava	Czech.	42	15	26	41	....					
1990-91	Hartford	NHL	78	21	22	43	113	6	0	0	0	7
1991-92	Hartford	NHL	76	21	24	45	44	7	0	1	1	6
	NHL Totals		154	42	46	88	157	13	0	1	1	13

HOLLAND, DENNIS

Center. Shoots left. 5'10", 165 lbs. Born, Vernon, B.C., January 30, 1969.
(Detroit's 4th choice, 52nd overall, in 1987 Entry Draft).

			Regular Season					Playoffs				
Season	Club	Lea	GP	G	A	TP	PIM	GP	G	A	TP	PIM
1986-87a	Portland	WHL	72	36	77	113	96	20	7	14	21	20
1987-88b	Portland	WHL	67	58	86	144	115					
1988-89bc	Portland	WHL	69	*82	85	*167	120	19	15	*22	*37	18
1989-90	Adirondack	AHL	78	19	34	53	53	6	1	1	2	10
1990-91	San Diego	IHL	45	25	30	55	129					
	Adirondack	AHL	28	8	7	15	31	2	0	0	0	4
1991-92	Fort Wayne	IHL	6	2	4	6	21					
	Salt Lake	IHL	73	20	25	45	102	4	0	2	2	2

a WHL Rookie of the Year (1987)
b WHL West All-Star Team (1988, 1989)
c WHL Player of the Year (1989)

Traded to **Calgary** by **Detroit** for future considerations, October 21, 1991.

HOLLINGER, TERRY

Defense. Shoots left. 6'1", 200 lbs. Born, Regina, Sask., February 24, 1971.
(St. Louis' 7th choice, 153rd overall, in 1991 Entry Draft).

			Regular Season					Playoffs				
Season	Club	Lea	GP	G	A	TP	PIM	GP	G	A	TP	PIM
1990-91	Regina	WHL	8	1	6	7	6					
	Lethbridge	WHL	62	9	32	41	113	16	3	14	17	22
1991-92	Lethbridge	WHL	65	23	62	85	155	5	1	2	3	13

HOLZINGER, BRIAN

Center. Shoots right. 5'11", 180 lbs. Born, Parma, OH, October 10, 1972.
(Buffalo's 7th choice, 124th overall, in 1991 Entry Draft).

			Regular Season					Playoffs				
Season	Club	Lea	GP	G	A	TP	PIM	GP	G	A	TP	PIM
1990-91	Detroit	US Jr.	37	45	41	86	16					
1991-92	Bowling Green	CCHA	30	14	8	22	36					

HOOVER, RON

Center. Shoots left. 6'1", 185 lbs. Born, Oakville, Ont., October 28, 1966.
(Hartford's 7th choice, 158th overall, in 1986 Entry Draft).

			Regular Season					Playoffs				
Season	Club	Lea	GP	G	A	TP	PIM	GP	G	A	TP	PIM
1985-86	W. Michigan	CCHA	43	10	23	33	36	....	....	....	....	....
1986-87	W. Michigan	CCHA	34	7	10	17	22	....	....	....	....	....
1987-88a	W. Michigan	CCHA	42	39	23	62	40	....	....	....	....	....
1988-89	W. Michigan	CCHA	42	32	27	59	66	....	....	....	....	....
1989-90	**Boston**	**NHL**	**2**	**0**	**0**	**0**	**0**	....	....	....	....	....
	Maine	AHL	75	28	26	54	57	....	....	....	....	....
1990-91	**Boston**	**NHL**	**15**	**4**	**0**	**4**	**31**	**8**	**0**	**0**	**0**	**18**
	Maine	AHL	62	28	16	44	40	....	....	....	....	....
1991-92	**St. Louis**	**NHL**	**1**	**0**	**0**	**0**	**0**	....	....	....	....	....
	Peoria	IHL	71	27	34	61	30	10	4	4	8	4
	NHL Totals		**18**	**4**	**0**	**4**	**31**	**8**	**0**	**0**	**0**	**18**

a CCHA Second All-Star Team (1988)

Signed as a free agent by **Boston**, September 1, 1989. Signed as a free agent by **St. Louis**, July 23, 1991.

HORACEK, TONY (HOHR-uh-chehk)

Left wing. Shoots left. 6'4", 210 lbs. Born, Vancouver, B.C., February 3, 1967.
(Philadelphia's 8th choice, 147th overall, in 1985 Entry Draft).

			Regular Season					Playoffs				
Season	Club	Lea	GP	G	A	TP	PIM	GP	G	A	TP	PIM
1984-85	Kelowna	WHL	67	9	18	27	114	6	0	1	1	11
1985-86	Spokane	WHL	64	19	28	47	129	9	4	5	9	29
1986-87	Spokane	WHL	64	23	37	60	177	5	1	3	4	18
	Hershey	AHL	....	....	....	....	....	1	0	0	0	0
1987-88	Hershey	AHL	1	0	0	0	0	....	....	....	....	....
	Spokane	WHL	24	17	23	40	63	....	....	....	....	....
	Kamloops	WHL	26	14	17	31	51	18	6	4	10	73
1988-89	Hershey	AHL	10	0	0	0	38	....	....	....	....	....
	Indianapolis	IHL	43	11	13	24	138	....	....	....	....	....
1989-90	**Philadelphia**	**NHL**	**48**	**5**	**5**	**10**	**117**	....	....	....	....	....
	Hershey	AHL	12	0	5	5	25	....	....	....	....	....
1990-91	**Philadelphia**	**NHL**	**34**	**3**	**6**	**9**	**49**	....	....	....	....	....
	Hershey	AHL	19	5	3	8	35	4	2	0	2	14
1991-92	**Philadelphia**	**NHL**	**34**	**1**	**3**	**4**	**51**	....	....	....	....	....
	Chicago	**NHL**	**12**	**1**	**4**	**5**	**21**	**2**	**1**	**0**	**1**	**2**
	NHL Totals		**128**	**10**	**18**	**28**	**238**	**2**	**1**	**0**	**1**	**2**

Traded to **Chicago** by **Philadelphia** for Ryan McGill, February 7, 1992.

HOSTAK, MARTIN (HOHS-tahk)

Center. Shoots left. 6'3", 198 lbs. Born, Hradec Kralove, Czech., November 11, 1967.
(Philadelphia's 3rd choice, 62nd overall, in 1987 Entry Draft).

			Regular Season					Playoffs				
Season	Club	Lea	GP	G	A	TP	PIM	GP	G	A	TP	PIM
1986-87	Sparta Praha	Czech.	34	6	2	8	....	....	....	....	....	....
1987-88	Sparta Praha	Czech.	26	8	9	17	....	....	....	....	....	....
1988-89	Sparta Praha	Czech.	35	11	15	26	....	....	....	....	....	....
1989-90	Sparta Praha	Czech.	44	26	27	53	....	11	4	7	11	....
1990-91	**Philadelphia**	**NHL**	**50**	**3**	**10**	**13**	**22**	....	....	....	....	....
	Hershey	AHL	11	6	2	8	2	3	1	0	1	0
1991-92	**Philadelphia**	**NHL**	**5**	**0**	**1**	**1**	**2**	....	....	....	....	....
	Hershey	AHL	63	27	36	63	77	6	1	2	3	2
	NHL Totals		**55**	**3**	**11**	**14**	**24**	....	....	....	....	....

HOUDA, DOUG (HOO-duh)

Defense. Shoots right. 6'2", 190 lbs. Born, Blairmore, Alta., June 3, 1966.
(Detroit's 2nd choice, 28th overall, in 1984 Entry Draft).

			Regular Season					Playoffs				
Season	Club	Lea	GP	G	A	TP	PIM	GP	G	A	TP	PIM
1982-83	Calgary	WHL	71	5	23	28	99	16	1	3	4	44
1983-84	Calgary	WHL	69	6	30	36	195	4	0	0	0	7
1984-85a	Calgary	WHL	65	20	54	74	182	8	3	4	7	29
1985-86	**Detroit**	**NHL**	**6**	**0**	**0**	**0**	**4**	....	....	....	....	....
	Calgary	WHL	16	4	10	14	60	....	....	....	....	....
	Medicine Hat	WHL	35	9	23	32	80	25	4	19	23	64
1986-87	Adirondack	AHL	77	6	23	29	142	11	1	8	9	50
1987-88	**Detroit**	**NHL**	**11**	**1**	**1**	**2**	**10**	....	....	....	....	....
b	Adirondack	AHL	71	10	32	42	169	11	0	3	3	44
1988-89	**Detroit**	**NHL**	**57**	**2**	**11**	**13**	**67**	**6**	**0**	**1**	**1**	**0**
	Adirondack	AHL	7	0	3	3	8	....	....	....	....	....
1989-90	**Detroit**	**NHL**	**73**	**2**	**9**	**11**	**127**	....	....	....	....	....
1990-91	**Detroit**	**NHL**	**22**	**0**	**4**	**4**	**43**	....	....	....	....	....
	Adirondack	AHL	38	9	17	26	67	....	....	....	....	....
	Hartford	**NHL**	**19**	**1**	**2**	**3**	**41**	**6**	**0**	**0**	**0**	**8**
1991-92	**Hartford**	**NHL**	**56**	**3**	**6**	**9**	**125**	**6**	**0**	**2**	**2**	**13**
	NHL Totals		**244**	**9**	**33**	**42**	**417**	**18**	**0**	**3**	**3**	**21**

a WHL Second All-Star Team, East Division (1985)
b AHL First All-Star Team (1988)

Traded to **Hartford** by **Detroit** for Doug Crossman, February 20, 1991.

HOUGH, MIKE (HUHF)

Left wing. Shoots left. 6'1", 192 lbs. Born, Montreal, Que., February 6, 1963.
(Quebec's 7th choice, 181st overall, in 1982 Entry Draft).

			Regular Season					Playoffs				
Season	Club	Lea	GP	G	A	TP	PIM	GP	G	A	TP	PIM
1981-82	Kitchener	OHL	58	14	24	38	172	14	4	1	5	16
1982-83	Kitchener	OHL	61	17	27	44	156	12	5	4	9	30
1983-84	Fredericton	AHL	69	11	16	27	142	1	0	0	0	7
1984-85	Fredericton	AHL	76	21	27	48	49	6	1	1	2	2
1985-86	Fredericton	AHL	74	21	33	54	68	6	0	3	3	8
1986-87	**Quebec**	**NHL**	**56**	**6**	**8**	**14**	**79**	**9**	**0**	**3**	**3**	**26**
	Fredericton	AHL	10	1	3	4	20	....	....	....	....	....
1987-88	**Quebec**	**NHL**	**17**	**3**	**2**	**5**	**2**	....	....	....	....	....
	Fredericton	AHL	46	16	25	41	133	15	4	8	12	55
1988-89	**Quebec**	**NHL**	**46**	**9**	**10**	**19**	**39**	....	....	....	....	....
	Halifax	AHL	22	11	10	21	87	....	....	....	....	....
1989-90	**Quebec**	**NHL**	**43**	**13**	**13**	**26**	**84**	....	....	....	....	....
1990-91	**Quebec**	**NHL**	**63**	**13**	**20**	**33**	**111**	....	....	....	....	....
1991-92	**Quebec**	**NHL**	**61**	**16**	**22**	**38**	**77**	....	....	....	....	....
	NHL Totals		**286**	**60**	**75**	**135**	**392**	**9**	**0**	**3**	**3**	**26**

HOULDER, BILL

Defense. Shoots left. 6'3", 218 lbs. Born, Thunder Bay, Ont., March 11, 1967.
(Washington's 4th choice, 82nd overall, in 1985 Entry Draft).

			Regular Season					Playoffs				
Season	Club	Lea	GP	G	A	TP	PIM	GP	G	A	TP	PIM
1984-85	North Bay	OHL	66	4	20	24	37	8	0	0	0	2
1985-86	North Bay	OHL	59	5	30	35	97	10	1	6	7	12
1986-87a	North Bay	OHL	62	17	51	68	68	22	4	19	23	20
1987-88	**Washington**	**NHL**	**30**	**1**	**2**	**3**	**10**	....	....	....	....	....
	Fort Wayne	IHL	43	10	14	24	32	....	....	....	....	....
1988-89	**Washington**	**NHL**	**8**	**0**	**3**	**3**	**4**	....	....	....	....	....
	Baltimore	AHL	65	10	36	46	50	....	....	....	....	....
1989-90	**Washington**	**NHL**	**41**	**1**	**11**	**12**	**28**	....	....	....	....	....
	Baltimore	AHL	26	3	7	10	12	7	0	2	2	2
1990-91	**Buffalo**	**NHL**	**7**	**0**	**2**	**2**	**4**	....	....	....	....	....
b	Rochester	AHL	69	13	53	66	28	15	5	13	18	4
1991-92	**Buffalo**	**NHL**	**10**	**1**	**0**	**1**	**8**	....	....	....	....	....
	Rochester	AHL	42	8	26	34	16	16	5	6	11	4
	NHL Totals		**96**	**3**	**18**	**21**	**54**	....	....	....	....	....

a OHL Third All-Star Team (1987)
b AHL First All-Star Team (1991)

Traded to **Buffalo** by **Washington** for Shawn Anderson, September 30, 1990.

HOUSE, BOBBY

Right wing. Shoots right. 6'1", 200 lbs. Born, Whitehorse, Yukon, January 7, 1973.
(Chicago's 4th choice, 66th overall, in 1991 Entry Draft).

			Regular Season					Playoffs				
Season	Club	Lea	GP	G	A	TP	PIM	GP	G	A	TP	PIM
1989-90	Spokane	WHL	64	18	16	34	74	5	0	0	0	6
1990-91	Spokane	WHL	38	11	19	30	63	....	....	....	....	....
	Brandon	WHL	23	18	7	25	14	....	....	....	....	....
1991-92	Brandon	WHL	71	35	42	77	133	....	....	....	....	....

HOUSE, KEN

Center. Shoots left. 6'1", 200 lbs. Born, Scarborough, Ont., November 3, 1969.
(Washington's 12th choice, 250th overall, in 1989 Entry Draft).

			Regular Season					Playoffs				
Season	Club	Lea	GP	G	A	TP	PIM	GP	G	A	TP	PIM
1988-89	Miami-Ohio	CCHA	38	19	14	33	18	....	....	....	....	....
1989-90	Miami-Ohio	CCHA	37	10	5	15	32	....	....	....	....	....
1990-91	Miami-Ohio	CCHA	34	13	11	24	20	....	....	....	....	....
1991-92	Miami-Ohio	CCHA	40	27	23	50	22	....	....	....	....	....

HOUSLEY, PHIL (HOWZ-lee)

Defense. Shoots left. 5'10", 179 lbs. Born, St. Paul, MN, March 9, 1964.
(Buffalo's 1st choice, 6th overall, in 1982 Entry Draft).

			Regular Season					Playoffs				
Season	Club	Lea	GP	G	A	TP	PIM	GP	G	A	TP	PIM
1981-82	South St. Paul	HS	22	31	34	65	18	....	....	....	....	....
1982-83a	**Buffalo**	**NHL**	**77**	**19**	**47**	**66**	**39**	**10**	**3**	**4**	**7**	**2**
1983-84	**Buffalo**	**NHL**	**75**	**31**	**46**	**77**	**33**	**3**	**0**	**0**	**0**	**6**
1984-85	**Buffalo**	**NHL**	**73**	**16**	**53**	**69**	**28**	**5**	**3**	**2**	**5**	**2**
1985-86	**Buffalo**	**NHL**	**79**	**15**	**47**	**62**	**54**	....	....	....	....	....
1986-87	**Buffalo**	**NHL**	**78**	**21**	**46**	**67**	**57**	....	....	....	....	....
1987-88	**Buffalo**	**NHL**	**74**	**29**	**37**	**66**	**96**	**6**	**2**	**4**	**6**	**6**
1988-89	**Buffalo**	**NHL**	**72**	**26**	**44**	**70**	**47**	**5**	**1**	**3**	**4**	**2**
1989-90	**Buffalo**	**NHL**	**80**	**21**	**60**	**81**	**32**	**6**	**1**	**4**	**5**	**4**
1990-91	**Winnipeg**	**NHL**	**78**	**23**	**53**	**76**	**24**	....	....	....	....	....
1991-92b	**Winnipeg**	**NHL**	**74**	**23**	**63**	**86**	**92**	**7**	**1**	**4**	**5**	**0**
	NHL Totals		**760**	**224**	**496**	**720**	**502**	**42**	**11**	**21**	**32**	**22**

a NHL All-Rookie Team (1983)
b NHL Second All-Star Team (1992)

Played in NHL All-Star Game (1984, 1989-92)

Traded to **Winnipeg** by **Buffalo** with Scott Arniel, Jeff Parker and Buffalo's first round choice (Keith Tkachuk) in 1990 Entry Draft for Dale Hawerchuk, Winnipeg's first round choice (Brad May) in 1990 Entry Draft and future considerations, June 16, 1990.

HOWE, MARK STEVEN

Defense. Shoots left. 5'11", 185 lbs. Born, Detroit, MI, May 28, 1955.
(Boston's 2nd choice, 25th overall, in 1974 Amateur Draft).

			Regular Season					Playoffs				
Season	Club	Lea	GP	G	A	TP	PIM	GP	G	A	TP	PIM
1972-73	Toronto	OMJHL	60	38	66	104	27	....	....	....	....	....
1973-74ab	Houston	WHA	76	38	41	79	20	14	9	10	19	4
1974-75	Houston	WHA	74	36	40	76	30	13	*10	12	*22	0
1975-76	Houston	WHA	72	39	37	76	38	17	6	10	16	18
1976-77a	Houston	WHA	57	23	52	75	46	10	4	10	14	2
1977-78	New England	WHA	70	30	61	91	32	14	8	7	15	18
1978-79c	New England	WHA	77	42	65	107	32	6	4	2	6	6
1979-80	**Hartford**	**NHL**	**74**	**24**	**56**	**80**	**20**	**3**	**1**	**2**	**3**	**2**
1980-81	**Hartford**	**NHL**	**63**	**19**	**46**	**65**	**54**	....	....	....	....	....
1981-82	**Hartford**	**NHL**	**76**	**8**	**45**	**53**	**18**	....	....	....	....	....
1982-83d	**Philadelphia**	**NHL**	**76**	**20**	**47**	**67**	**18**	**3**	**0**	**2**	**2**	**4**
1983-84	**Philadelphia**	**NHL**	**71**	**19**	**34**	**53**	**44**	**3**	**0**	**0**	**0**	**2**
1984-85	**Philadelphia**	**NHL**	**73**	**18**	**39**	**57**	**31**	**19**	**3**	**8**	**11**	**6**
1985-86de	**Philadelphia**	**NHL**	**77**	**24**	**58**	**82**	**36**	**5**	**0**	**4**	**4**	**0**
1986-87d	**Philadelphia**	**NHL**	**69**	**15**	**43**	**58**	**37**	**26**	**2**	**10**	**12**	**4**
1987-88	**Philadelphia**	**NHL**	**75**	**19**	**43**	**62**	**62**	**7**	**3**	**6**	**9**	**4**
1988-89	**Philadelphia**	**NHL**	**52**	**9**	**29**	**38**	**45**	**19**	**0**	**15**	**15**	**10**
1989-90	**Philadelphia**	**NHL**	**40**	**7**	**21**	**28**	**24**	....	....	....	....	....
1990-91	**Philadelphia**	**NHL**	**19**	**0**	**10**	**10**	**8**	....	....	....	....	....
1991-92	**Philadelphia**	**NHL**	**42**	**7**	**18**	**25**	**18**	....	....	....	....	....
	NHL Totals		**807**	**189**	**489**	**678**	**415**	**85**	**9**	**47**	**56**	**32**

a WHA Second All-Star Team (1974, 1977)
b Named WHA's Rookie of the Year (1974)
c WHA First All-Star Team (1979)
d NHL First All-Star Team (1983, 1986, 1987)
e NHL Plus/Minus Leader (1986)

Played in NHL All-Star Game (1981, 1983, 1986, 1988)

Reclaimed by **Boston** from **Hartford** prior to Expansion Draft, June 9, 1979. Claimed as priority selection by **Hartford**, June 9, 1979. Traded to **Philadelphia** by **Hartford** with Hartford's third round choice (Derrick Smith) in 1983 Entry Draft for Ken Linseman, Greg Adams and Philadelphia's first (David Jensen) and third round choices (Leif Karlsson) in the 1983 Entry Draft, August 19, 1982. Signed as a free agent by **Detroit**, July 7, 1992.

HRBEK, PETR (huhr-BEHK)

Right wing. Shoots right. 5'11", 180 lbs. Born, Prague, Czechoslovakia, April 3, 1969.
(Detroit's 4th choice, 59th overall, in 1988 Entry Draft).

			Regular Season					Playoffs				
Season	Club	Lea	GP	G	A	TP	PIM	GP	G	A	TP	PIM
1986-87	Sparta Praha	Czech.	11	2	0	2	....	....	....	....	....	....
1987-88	Sparta Praha	Czech.	31	13	9	22	....	....	....	....	....	....
1988-89	Sparta Praha	Czech.	41	10	13	23	....	....	....	....	....	....
1989-90	Dukla Jihlava	Czech.	32	12	7	19	....	....	....	....	....	....
1990-91	Sparta Praha	Czech.	39	20	17	37	14	....	....	....	....	....
1991-92	Sparta Praha	Czech.	46	33	20	53	....	....	....	....	....	....

HRDINA, JIRI (huhr-DEE-nuh)

Center. Shoots left. 6', 195 lbs. Born, Prague, Czech., January 5, 1958.
(Calgary's 8th choice, 159th overall, in 1984 Entry Draft).

			Regular Season					Playoffs				
Season	Club	Lea	GP	G	A	TP	PIM	GP	G	A	TP	PIM
1985-86	Sparta Praha	Czech.	44	18	19	37	30	....	....	....	....	....
1986-87	Sparta Praha	Czech.	31	18	18	36	24	....	....	....	....	....
1987-88	Sparta Praha	Czech.	22	7	15	22	0	....	....	....	....	....
	Czech Olympic	....	8	2	5	7	4	....	....	....	....	....
	Calgary	**NHL**	**9**	**2**	**5**	**7**	**2**	**1**	**0**	**0**	**0**	**0**
1988-89	**Calgary**	**NHL**	**70**	**22**	**32**	**54**	**26**	**4**	**0**	**0**	**0**	**0**
1989-90	**Calgary**	**NHL**	**64**	**12**	**18**	**30**	**31**	**6**	**0**	**1**	**1**	**2**
1990-91	**Calgary**	**NHL**	**14**	**0**	**3**	**3**	**4**	....	....	....	....	....
	Pittsburgh	**NHL**	**37**	**6**	**14**	**20**	**13**	**14**	**2**	**2**	**4**	**6**
1991-92	**Pittsburgh**	**NHL**	**56**	**3**	**13**	**16**	**16**	**21**	**0**	**2**	**2**	**16**
	NHL Totals		**250**	**45**	**85**	**130**	**92**	**46**	**2**	**5**	**7**	**24**

Traded to **Pittsburgh** by **Calgary** for Jim Kyte, December 13, 1990.

HRKAC, ANTHONY (TONY) (HUHR-kuhz)

Center. Shoots left. 5'11", 170 lbs. Born, Thunder Bay, Ont., July 7, 1966.
(St. Louis' 2nd choice, 32nd overall, in 1984 Entry Draft).

			Regular Season					Playoffs				
Season	Club	Lea	GP	G	A	TP	PIM	GP	G	A	TP	PIM
1984-85	North Dakota	WCHA	36	18	36	54	16	....	....	....	....	....
1985-86	Cdn. Olympic	....	62	19	30	49	36	....	....	....	....	....
1986-87abcd	North Dakota	WCHA	48	46	79	125	48	....	....	....	....	....
	St. Louis	**NHL**	....	....	....	....	....	**3**	**0**	**0**	**0**	**0**
1987-88	**St. Louis**	**NHL**	**67**	**11**	**37**	**48**	**22**	**10**	**6**	**1**	**7**	**4**
1988-89	**St. Louis**	**NHL**	**70**	**17**	**28**	**45**	**8**	**4**	**1**	**1**	**2**	**0**
1989-90	**St. Louis**	**NHL**	**28**	**5**	**12**	**17**	**8**	....	....	....	....	....
	Quebec	**NHL**	**22**	**4**	**8**	**12**	**2**	....	....	....	....	....
	Halifax	AHL	20	12	21	33	4	6	5	9	14	4
1990-91	**Quebec**	**NHL**	**70**	**16**	**32**	**48**	**16**	....	....	....	....	....
	Halifax	AHL	3	4	1	5	2	....	....	....	....	....
1991-92	**San Jose**	**NHL**	**22**	**2**	**10**	**12**	**4**	....	....	....	....	....
	Chicago	**NHL**	**18**	**1**	**2**	**3**	**6**	**3**	**0**	**0**	**0**	**2**
	NHL Totals		**297**	**56**	**129**	**185**	**66**	**20**	**7**	**2**	**9**	**6**

a WCHA First All-Star Team, Player of the Year (1987)
b NCAA West First All-American Team (1987)
c NCAA All-Tournament Team, Tournament MVP (1987)
d Winner of the 1987 Hobey Baker Memorial Trophy (Top U.S. Collegiate Player) (1987)

Traded to **Quebec** by **St. Louis** with Greg Millen for Jeff Brown, December 13, 1989. Traded to **San Jose** by **Quebec** for Greg Paslawski, May 31, 1991. Traded to **Chicago** by **San Jose** for future considerations, February 7, 1992.

HRSTKA, MARTIN (hurst-KAH)

Left wing. Shoots left. 6', 180 lbs. Born, Brno, Czechoslovakia, January 26, 1967.
(Vancouver's 6th choice, 109th overall, in 1985 Entry Draft).

			Regular Season					Playoffs				
Season	Club	Lea	GP	G	A	TP	PIM	GP	G	A	TP	PIM
1986-87	Dukla Trencin	Czech.	26	2	4	6	....	....	....	....	....	....
1987-88	Dukla Trencin	Czech.	22	5	6	11	....	....	....	....	....	....
1988-89	TJ Gottwaldov	Czech.	25	4	9	13	....	....	....	....	....	....
1989-90	TJ Gottwaldov	Czech.	39	8	7	15	....	....	....	....	....	....
1990-91	TJ Zlin	Czech.	41	11	19	30	20	....	....	....	....	....
1991-92	ZPS Zlin	Czech.	16	1	5	6	....	....	....	....	....	....

HUBER, PHIL

Center. Shoots left. 5'10", 194 lbs. Born, Calgary, Alta., January 10, 1969.
(NY Islanders' 8th choice, 149th overall, in 1989 Entry Draft).

			Regular Season					Playoffs				
Season	Club	Lea	GP	G	A	TP	PIM	GP	G	A	TP	PIM
1987-88	Kamloops	WHL	63	19	30	49	54	18	3	9	12	23
1988-89	Kamloops	WHL	72	54	68	122	103	16	18	13	31	48
1989-90a	Kamloops	WHL	72	63	89	152	176	17	12	11	23	44
1990-91	Capital Dist.	AHL	5	1	1	2	0	....	....	....	....	....
	Richmond	ECHL	56	32	40	72	87	4	1	3	4	4
1991-92	Capital Dist.	AHL	71	26	32	58	85	7	0	2	2	10

a WHL West First All-Star Team (1990)

HUDDY, CHARLES WILLIAM (CHARLIE)

Defense. Shoots left. 6', 210 lbs. Born, Oshawa, Ont., June 2, 1959.

			Regular Season					Playoffs				
Season	Club	Lea	GP	G	A	TP	PIM	GP	G	A	TP	PIM
1977-78	Oshawa	OHA	59	17	18	35	81	6	2	1	3	10
1978-79	Oshawa	OHA	64	20	38	58	108	5	3	4	7	12
1979-80	Houston	CHL	79	14	34	48	46	6	1	0	1	2
1980-81	**Edmonton**	**NHL**	**12**	**2**	**5**	**7**	**6**	....	....	....	....	....
	Wichita	CHL	47	8	36	44	71	17	3	11	14	10
1981-82	**Edmonton**	**NHL**	**41**	**4**	**11**	**15**	**46**	**5**	**1**	**2**	**3**	**14**
	Wichita	CHL	32	7	19	26	51	....	....	....	....	....
1982-83a	**Edmonton**	**NHL**	**76**	**20**	**37**	**57**	**58**	**15**	**1**	**6**	**7**	**10**
1983-84	**Edmonton**	**NHL**	**75**	**8**	**34**	**42**	**43**	**12**	**1**	**9**	**10**	**8**
1984-85	**Edmonton**	**NHL**	**80**	**7**	**44**	**51**	**46**	**18**	**3**	**17**	**20**	**17**
1985-86	**Edmonton**	**NHL**	**76**	**6**	**35**	**41**	**55**	**7**	**0**	**2**	**2**	**0**
1986-87	**Edmonton**	**NHL**	**58**	**4**	**15**	**19**	**35**	**21**	**1**	**7**	**8**	**21**
1987-88	**Edmonton**	**NHL**	**77**	**13**	**28**	**41**	**71**	**13**	**4**	**5**	**9**	**10**
1988-89	**Edmonton**	**NHL**	**76**	**11**	**33**	**44**	**52**	**7**	**2**	**0**	**2**	**4**
1989-90	**Edmonton**	**NHL**	**70**	**1**	**23**	**24**	**56**	**22**	**0**	**6**	**6**	**11**
1990-91	**Edmonton**	**NHL**	**53**	**5**	**22**	**27**	**32**	**18**	**3**	**7**	**10**	**10**
1991-92	**Los Angeles**	**NHL**	**56**	**4**	**19**	**23**	**43**	**6**	**1**	**1**	**2**	**10**
	NHL Totals		**750**	**85**	**306**	**391**	**543**	**144**	**17**	**62**	**79**	**115**

a NHL Plus/Minus Leader (1983)

Signed as a free agent by **Edmonton**, September 14, 1979. Claimed by **Minnesota** from **Edmonton** in Expansion Draft, May 30, 1991. Traded to **Los Angeles** by **Minnesota** with Randy Gilhen, Jim Thomson and NY Rangers' fourth round choice (previously acquired by Minnesota – Alexei Zhitnik) in 1991 Entry Draft for Todd Elik, June 22, 1991.

HUDSON, MIKE

Center/Left wing. Shoots left. 6'1", 185 lbs. Born, Guelph, Ont., February 6, 1967.
(Chicago's 6th choice, 140th overall, in 1986 Entry Draft).

			Regular Season					Playoffs				
Season	Club	Lea	GP	G	A	TP	PIM	GP	G	A	TP	PIM
1984-85	Hamilton	OHL	50	10	12	22	13	....	....	....	....	....
1985-86	Hamilton	OHL	7	3	2	5	4	....	....	....	....	....
	Sudbury	OHL	59	35	42	77	20	4	2	5	7	7
1986-87	Sudbury	OHL	63	40	57	97	18	....	....	....	....	....
1987-88	Saginaw	IHL	75	18	30	48	44	10	2	3	5	20
1988-89	**Chicago**	**NHL**	**41**	**7**	**16**	**23**	**20**	**10**	**1**	**2**	**3**	**18**
	Saginaw	IHL	30	15	17	32	10	....	....	....	....	....
1989-90	**Chicago**	**NHL**	**49**	**9**	**12**	**21**	**56**	**4**	**0**	**0**	**0**	**2**
1990-91	**Chicago**	**NHL**	**55**	**7**	**9**	**16**	**62**	**6**	**0**	**2**	**2**	**8**
	Indianapolis	IHL	3	1	2	3	0	....	....	....	....	....
1991-92	**Chicago**	**NHL**	**76**	**14**	**15**	**29**	**92**	**16**	**3**	**5**	**8**	**26**
	NHL Totals		**221**	**37**	**52**	**89**	**230**	**36**	**4**	**9**	**13**	**54**

HUFFMAN, KERRY

Defense. Shoots left. 6'2", 200 lbs. Born, Peterborough, Ont., January 3, 1968.
(Philadelphia's 1st choice, 20th overall, in 1986 Entry Draft).

			Regular Season					Playoffs				
Season	Club	Lea	GP	G	A	TP	PIM	GP	G	A	TP	PIM
1985-86	Guelph	OHL	56	3	24	27	35	20	1	10	11	10
1986-87	**Philadelphia**	**NHL**	**9**	**0**	**0**	**0**	**2**	....	....	....	....	....
	Hershey	AHL	3	0	1	1	0	4	0	0	0	0
a	Guelph	OHL	44	4	31	35	20	5	0	2	2	8
1987-88	**Philadelphia**	**NHL**	**52**	**6**	**17**	**23**	**34**	**2**	**0**	**0**	**0**	**0**
1988-89	**Philadelphia**	**NHL**	**29**	**0**	**11**	**11**	**31**	....	....	....	....	....
	Hershey	AHL	29	2	13	15	16	....	....	....	....	....
1989-90	**Philadelphia**	**NHL**	**43**	**1**	**12**	**13**	**34**	....	....	....	....	....
1990-91	**Philadelphia**	**NHL**	**10**	**1**	**2**	**3**	**10**	....	....	....	....	....
	Hershey	AHL	45	5	29	34	20	7	1	2	3	0
1991-92	**Philadelphia**	**NHL**	**60**	**14**	**18**	**32**	**41**	....	....	....	....	....
	NHL Totals		**203**	**22**	**60**	**82**	**152**	**2**	**0**	**0**	**0**	**0**

a OHL First All-Star Team (1987)

Traded to **Quebec** by **Philadelphia** with Peter Forsberg, Steve Duchesne, Mike Ricci, Ron Hextall, Chris Simon, Philadelphia's first choice in the 1993 and 1994 Entry Drafts and cash for Eric Lindros, June 30, 1992.

HUGHES, BRENT ALLEN

Left wing. Shoots left. 5'11", 185 lbs. Born, New Westminster, B.C., April 5, 1966.

			Regular Season					Playoffs				
Season	Club	Lea	GP	G	A	TP	PIM	GP	G	A	TP	PIM
1983-84	N. Westminster	WHL	67	21	18	39	133	9	2	2	4	27
1984-85	N. Westminster	WHL	64	25	32	57	135	11	2	1	3	37
1985-86	N. Westminster	WHL	71	28	52	80	180	....	....	....	....	....
1986-87	N. Westminster	WHL	8	5	4	9	22	....	....	....	....	....
	Victoria	WHL	61	38	61	99	146	5	4	1	5	8
1987-88	Moncton	AHL	73	13	19	32	206	....	....	....	....	....
1988-89	Winnipeg	NHL	28	3	2	5	82	....	....	....	....	....
	Moncton	AHL	54	34	34	68	286	10	9	4	13	40
1989-90	Winnipeg	NHL	11	1	2	3	33	....	....	....	....	....
	Moncton	AHL	65	31	29	60	277	....	....	....	....	....
1990-91	Moncton	AHL	63	21	22	43	144	3	0	0	0	7
1991-92	Baltimore	AHL	55	25	29	54	190	....	....	....	....	....
	Boston	NHL	8	1	1	2	38	10	2	0	2	20
	Maine	AHL	12	6	4	10	34	....	....	....	....	....
	NHL Totals		47	5	5	10	153	10	2	0	2	20

Signed as a free agent by **Winnipeg**, June 13, 1988. Traded to **Washington** by **Winnipeg** with Craig Duncanson and Simon Wheeldon for Bob Joyce, Tyler Larter and Kent Paynter, May 21, 1991. Traded to **Boston** by **Washington** with future considerations for John Byce and Dennis Smith, February 24, 1992.

HUGHES, RYAN

Center. Shoots left. 6'1", 180 lbs. Born, Montreal, Que., January 17, 1972.
(Quebec's 2nd choice, 22nd overall, in 1990 Entry Draft).

			Regular Season					Playoffs				
Season	Club	Lea	GP	G	A	TP	PIM	GP	G	A	TP	PIM
1989-90	Cornell	ECAC	27	7	16	23	35	....	....	....	....	....
1990-91	Cornell	ECAC	32	18	34	52	28	....	....	....	....	....
1991-92	Cornell	ECAC	27	8	13	21	36	....	....	....	....	....

HULBIG, JOE

Left wing. Shoots left. 6'3", 212 lbs. Born, Norwood, MA, September 29, 1973.
(Edmonton's 1st choice, 13th overall, in 1992 Entry Draft).

			Regular Season					Playoffs				
Season	Club	Lea	GP	G	A	TP	PIM	GP	G	A	TP	PIM
1990-91	St. Sebastians	HS	....	23	19	42	....	....	....	....	....	....
1991-92	St. Sebastians	HS	17	19	24	43	30	....	....	....	....	....

HULETT, DEAN

Right wing. Shoots right. 6'6", 210 lbs. Born, San Juan, Puerto Rico, July 25, 1971.
(Los Angeles' 7th choice, 154th overall, in 1990 Entry Draft).

			Regular Season					Playoffs				
Season	Club	Lea	GP	G	A	TP	PIM	GP	G	A	TP	PIM
1989-90	Lake Superior	CCHA	13	1	4	5	18	....	....	....	....	....
1990-91	Lake Superior	CCHA	36	5	8	13	52	....	....	....	....	....
1991-92	Lake Superior	CCHA	33	10	12	22	56	....	....	....	....	....

HULL, BRETT

Right wing. Shoots right. 5'10", 201 lbs. Born, Belleville, Ont., August 9, 1964.
(Calgary's 6th choice, 117th overall, in 1984 Entry Draft).

			Regular Season					Playoffs				
Season	Club	Lea	GP	G	A	TP	PIM	GP	G	A	TP	PIM
1984-85	Minn.-Duluth	WCHA	48	32	28	60	24	....	....	....	....	....
1985-86a	Minn.-Duluth	WCHA	42	52	32	84	46	....	....	....	....	....
	Calgary	NHL	....	....	....	....	....	2	0	0	0	0
1986-87	Calgary	NHL	5	1	0	1	0	4	2	1	3	0
bc	Moncton	AHL	67	50	42	92	16	3	2	2	4	2
1987-88	Calgary	NHL	52	26	24	50	12	....	....	....	....	....
	St. Louis	NHL	13	6	8	14	4	10	7	2	9	4
1988-89	St. Louis	NHL	78	41	43	84	33	10	5	5	10	6
1989-90def	St. Louis	NHL	80	*72	41	113	24	12	13	8	21	17
1990-91dfghi	St. Louis	NHL	78	*86	45	131	22	13	11	8	19	4
1991-92d	St. Louis	NHL	73	*70	39	109	48	6	4	4	8	4
	NHL Totals		379	302	200	502	143	57	42	28	70	35

a WCHA First All-Star Team (1986)
b AHL First All-Star Team (1987)
c Won Dudley "Red" Garrett Memorial Trophy (AHL's Top Rookie) (1987)
d NHL First All-Star Team (1990, 1991, 1992)
e Won Lady Byng Trophy (1990)
f Won Dodge Ram Tough Award (1990, 1991)
g Won Hart Memorial Trophy (1991)
h Won Lester B. Pearson Award (1991)
i Won ProSet/NHL Player of the Year Award (1991)

Played in NHL All-Star Game (1989, 1990, 1992)

Traded to **St. Louis** by **Calgary** with Steve Bozek for Rob Ramage and Rick Wamsley, March 7, 1988.

HULL, JODY

Right wing. Shoots right. 6'2", 200 lbs. Born, Cambridge, Ont., February 2, 1969.
(Hartford's 1st choice, 18th overall, in 1987 Entry Draft).

			Regular Season					Playoffs				
Season	Club	Lea	GP	G	A	TP	PIM	GP	G	A	TP	PIM
1985-86	Peterborough	OHL	61	20	22	42	29	16	1	5	6	4
1986-87	Peterborough	OHL	49	18	34	52	22	12	4	9	13	14
1987-88a	Peterborough	OHL	60	50	44	94	33	12	10	8	18	8
1988-89	Hartford	NHL	60	16	18	34	10	1	0	0	0	2
1989-90	Hartford	NHL	38	7	10	17	21	5	0	1	1	2
	Binghamton	AHL	21	7	10	17	6	....	....	....	....	....
1990-91	NY Rangers	NHL	47	5	8	13	10	....	....	....	....	....
1991-92	NY Rangers	NHL	3	0	0	0	2	....	....	....	....	....
	Binghamton	AHL	69	34	31	65	28	11	5	2	7	4
	NHL Totals		148	28	36	64	43	6	0	1	1	4

a OHL Second All-Star Team (1988)

Traded to **NY Rangers** by **Hartford** for Carey Wilson and NY Rangers' third round choice (Mikael Nylander) in the 1991 Entry Draft, July 9, 1990. Traded to **Ottawa** by **NY Rangers** for future considerations, July 28, 1992.

HULSE, CALE

Defense. Shoots right. 6'3", 205 lbs. Born, Edmonton, Alta., November 10, 1973.
(New Jersey's 3rd choice, 66th overall, in 1992 Entry Draft).

			Regular Season					Playoffs				
Season	Club	Lea	GP	G	A	TP	PIM	GP	G	A	TP	PIM
1990-91	Calgary	AJHL	49	3	23	26	220	....	....	....	....	....
1991-92	Portland	WHL	70	4	18	22	250	6	0	2	2	27

HULST, KENT

Center. Shoots left. 6', 180 lbs. Born, St. Thomas, Ont., April 8, 1968.
(Toronto's 4th choice, 69th overall, in 1986 Entry Draft).

			Regular Season					Playoffs				
Season	Club	Lea	GP	G	A	TP	PIM	GP	G	A	TP	PIM
1985-86	Belleville	OHL	43	6	17	23	20	....	....	....	....	....
	Windsor	OHL	17	6	10	16	9	....	....	....	....	....
1986-87	Windsor	OHL	37	18	20	38	49	....	....	....	....	....
	Belleville	OHL	27	13	10	23	17	6	1	1	2	0
1987-88	Belleville	OHL	66	42	43	85	48	6	3	1	4	7
1988-89	Belleville	OHL	45	21	41	62	43	....	....	....	....	....
	Flint	IHL	7	0	1	1	4	....	....	....	....	....
	Newmarket	AHL	....	....	....	....	....	2	1	1	2	2
1989-90	Newmarket	AHL	80	26	34	60	29	....	....	....	....	....
1990-91	Newmarket	AHL	79	28	37	65	57	....	....	....	....	....
1991-92	New Haven	AHL	80	21	39	60	59	5	2	2	4	0

HUMENIUK, SCOTT

Defense. Shoots right. 6', 190 lbs. Born, Saskatoon, Sask., September 10, 1969.

			Regular Season					Playoffs				
Season	Club	Lea	GP	G	A	TP	PIM	GP	G	A	TP	PIM
1986-87	Spokane	WHL	10	0	2	2	2	1	0	0	0	0
1987-88	Spokane	WHL	58	6	20	26	154	8	1	0	1	19
1988-89	Moose Jaw	WHL	56	18	39	57	159	7	5	0	5	32
1989-90	Moose Jaw	WHL	71	23	47	70	141	....	....	....	....	....
	Binghamton	AHL	4	0	1	1	11	....	....	....	....	....
1990-91	Springfield	AHL	57	6	17	23	69	14	2	2	4	18
1991-92	Springfield	AHL	28	2	3	5	27	....	....	....	....	....
	Louisville	ECHL	26	7	21	28	93	13	1	11	12	33

Signed as a free agent by **Hartford**, March, 1990.

HUNT, CURTIS

Defense. Shoots left. 6', 195 lbs. Born, North Battleford, Sask., January 28, 1967.
(Vancouver's 9th choice, 172nd overall, in 1985 Entry Draft).

			Regular Season					Playoffs				
Season	Club	Lea	GP	G	A	TP	PIM	GP	G	A	TP	PIM
1984-85	Prince Albert	WHL	64	2	13	15	61	13	0	3	3	24
1985-86	Prince Albert	WHL	72	5	29	34	108	18	2	8	10	28
1986-87	Prince Albert	WHL	47	6	31	37	101	8	1	3	4	4
1987-88	Flint	IHL	76	4	17	21	181	2	0	0	0	16
	Fredericton	AHL	1	0	0	0	2	....	....	....	....	....
1988-89	Milwaukee	IHL	65	3	17	20	226	11	1	2	3	43
1989-90	Milwaukee	IHL	69	8	25	33	237	3	0	1	1	4
1990-91	Albany	IHL	45	2	12	14	122	....	....	....	....	....
	Milwaukee	IHL	27	1	5	6	85	6	0	1	1	10
1991-92	St. John's	AHL	52	5	18	23	106	12	1	5	6	36

Signed as a free agent by **Toronto**, July 19, 1991.

HUNTER, DALE ROBERT

Center. Shoots left. 5'10", 198 lbs. Born, Petrolia, Ont., July 31, 1960.
(Quebec's 2nd choice, 41st overall, in 1979 Entry Draft).

			Regular Season					Playoffs				
Season	Club	Lea	GP	G	A	TP	PIM	GP	G	A	TP	PIM
1977-78	Kitchener	OHA	68	22	42	64	115	....	....	....	....	....
1978-79	Sudbury	OHA	59	42	68	110	188	10	4	12	16	47
1979-80	Sudbury	OHA	61	34	51	85	189	9	6	9	15	45
1980-81	Quebec	NHL	80	19	44	63	226	5	4	2	6	34
1981-82	Quebec	NHL	80	22	50	72	272	16	3	7	10	52
1982-83	Quebec	NHL	80	17	46	63	206	4	2	1	3	24
1983-84	Quebec	NHL	77	24	55	79	232	9	2	3	5	41
1984-85	Quebec	NHL	80	20	52	72	209	17	4	6	10	*97
1985-86	Quebec	NHL	80	28	42	70	265	3	0	0	0	15
1986-87	Quebec	NHL	46	10	29	39	135	13	1	7	8	56
1987-88	Washington	NHL	79	22	37	59	240	14	7	5	12	98
1988-89	Washington	NHL	80	20	37	57	219	6	0	4	4	29
1989-90	Washington	NHL	80	23	39	62	233	15	4	8	12	61
1990-91	Washington	NHL	76	16	30	46	234	11	1	9	10	41
1991-92	Washington	NHL	80	28	50	78	205	7	1	4	5	16
	NHL Totals		918	249	511	760	2676	120	29	56	85	564

Traded to **Washington** by **Quebec** with Clint Malarchuk for Gaetan Duchesne, Alan Haworth, and Washington's first round choice (Joe Sakic) in 1987 Entry Draft, June 13, 1987.

HUNTER, MARK

Right wing. Shoots right. 6', 200 lbs. Born, Petrolia, Ont., November 12, 1962.
(Montreal's 1st choice, 7th overall, in 1981 Entry Draft).

			Regular Season					Playoffs				
Season	Club	Lea	GP	G	A	TP	PIM	GP	G	A	TP	PIM
1979-80	Brantford	OHA	66	34	56	90	171	11	2	8	10	27
1980-81	Brantford	OHA	53	39	40	79	157	6	3	3	6	27
1981-82	**Montreal**	**NHL**	**71**	**18**	**11**	**29**	**143**	**5**	**0**	**0**	**0**	**20**
1982-83	**Montreal**	**NHL**	**31**	**8**	**8**	**16**	**73**	....	....	....	....	....
1983-84	**Montreal**	**NHL**	**22**	**6**	**4**	**10**	**42**	**14**	**2**	**1**	**3**	**69**
1984-85	**Montreal**	**NHL**	**72**	**21**	**12**	**33**	**123**	**11**	**0**	**3**	**3**	**13**
1985-86	**St. Louis**	**NHL**	**78**	**44**	**30**	**74**	**171**	**19**	**7**	**7**	**14**	**48**
1986-87	**St. Louis**	**NHL**	**74**	**36**	**33**	**69**	**167**	**5**	**0**	**3**	**3**	**10**
1987-88	**St. Louis**	**NHL**	**66**	**32**	**31**	**63**	**136**	**5**	**2**	**3**	**5**	**24**
1988-89	**Calgary**	**NHL**	**66**	**22**	**8**	**30**	**194**	**10**	**2**	**2**	**4**	**23**
1989-90	**Calgary**	**NHL**	**10**	**2**	**3**	**5**	**39**	....	....	....	....	....
1990-91	**Calgary**	**NHL**	**57**	**10**	**15**	**25**	**125**	....	....	....	....	....
	Hartford	**NHL**	**11**	**4**	**3**	**7**	**40**	**6**	**5**	**1**	**6**	**17**
1991-92	**Hartford**	**NHL**	**63**	**10**	**13**	**23**	**159**	**4**	**0**	**0**	**0**	**6**
	NHL Totals		**621**	**213**	**171**	**384**	**1412**	**79**	**18**	**20**	**38**	**230**

Played in NHL All-Star Game (1986)

Traded to **St. Louis** by **Montreal** with Michael Dark and Montreal's second (Herb Raglan); third (Nelson Emerson); fifth (Dan Brooks); and sixth (Rick Burchill) round choices in 1985 Entry Draft, for St. Louis' first (Jose Charbonneau); second (Todd Richard); fourth (Martin Desjardins); fifth (Tom Sagissor); and sixth (Don Dufresne) round choices in 1985 Entry Draft, June 15, 1985. Traded to **Calgary** by **St. Louis** with Doug Gilmour, Steve Bozek and Michael Dark for Mike Bullard, Craig Coxe and Tim Corkery, September 6, 1988. Traded to **Hartford** by **Calgary** for Carey Wilson, March 5, 1991. Traded to **Washington** by **Hartford** with future considerations (Yvon Corriveau) for Nick Kypreos, June 15, 1992.

HUNTER, TIMOTHY ROBERT (TIM)

Right wing. Shoots right. 6'2", 202 lbs. Born, Calgary, Alta., September 10, 1960.
(Atlanta's 4th choice, 54th overall, in 1979 Entry Draft).

			Regular Season					Playoffs				
Season	Club	Lea	GP	G	A	TP	PIM	GP	G	A	TP	PIM
1979-80	Seattle	WHL	72	14	53	67	311	12	1	2	3	41
1980-81	Birmingham	CHL	58	3	5	8	*236	....	....	....	....	....
	Nova Scotia	AHL	17	0	0	0	62	6	0	1	1	45
1981-82	**Calgary**	**NHL**	**2**	**0**	**0**	**0**	**9**	....	....	....	....	....
	Oklahoma City	CHL	55	4	12	16	222	....	....	....	....	....
1982-83	**Calgary**	**NHL**	**16**	**1**	**0**	**1**	**54**	**9**	**1**	**0**	**1**	***70**
	Colorado	CHL	46	5	12	17	225	....	....	....	....	....
1983-84	**Calgary**	**NHL**	**43**	**4**	**4**	**8**	**130**	**7**	**0**	**0**	**0**	**21**
1984-85	**Calgary**	**NHL**	**71**	**11**	**11**	**22**	**259**	**4**	**0**	**0**	**0**	**24**
1985-86	**Calgary**	**NHL**	**66**	**8**	**7**	**15**	**291**	**19**	**0**	**3**	**3**	**108**
1986-87	**Calgary**	**NHL**	**73**	**6**	**15**	**21**	***361**	**6**	**0**	**0**	**0**	**51**
1987-88	**Calgary**	**NHL**	**68**	**8**	**5**	**13**	**337**	**9**	**4**	**0**	**4**	**32**
1988-89	**Calgary**	**NHL**	**75**	**3**	**9**	**12**	***375**	**19**	**0**	**4**	**4**	**32**
1989-90	**Calgary**	**NHL**	**67**	**2**	**3**	**5**	**279**	**6**	**0**	**0**	**0**	**4**
1990-91	**Calgary**	**NHL**	**34**	**5**	**2**	**7**	**143**	**7**	**0**	**0**	**0**	**10**
1991-92	**Calgary**	**NHL**	**30**	**1**	**3**	**4**	**167**	....	....	....	....	....
	NHL Totals		**545**	**49**	**59**	**108**	**2405**	**86**	**5**	**7**	**12**	**352**

Claimed by **Tampa Bay** from **Calgary** in Expansion Draft, June 18, 1992. Traded to **Quebec** by **Tampa Bay** for future considerations, June 19, 1992.

HURD, KELLY

Right wing. Shoots right. 5'11", 170 lbs. Born, Castlegar, B.C., May 13, 1968.
(Detroit's 6th choice, 143rd overall, in 1988 Entry Draft).

			Regular Season					Playoffs				
Season	Club	Lea	GP	G	A	TP	PIM	GP	G	A	TP	PIM
1987-88	Michigan Tech	WCHA	41	18	22	40	34	....	....	....	....	....
1988-89	Michigan Tech	WCHA	42	18	14	32	36	....	....	....	....	....
1989-90	Michigan Tech	WCHA	37	12	13	25	50	....	....	....	....	....
1990-91a	Michigan Tech	WCHA	35	29	22	51	44	....	....	....	....	....
1991-92	Adirondack	AHL	36	9	7	16	16	8	1	4	5	2
	Fort Wayne	IHL	30	13	9	22	12	....	....	....	....	....

a WCHA Second All-Star Team (1991)

HURLBUT, MICHAEL (MIKE)

Defense. Shoots left. 6'2", 195 lbs. Born, Massena, NY, October 7, 1966.
(NY Rangers' 1st choice, 5th overall, in 1988 Supplemental Draft).

			Regular Season					Playoffs				
Season	Club	Lea	GP	G	A	TP	PIM	GP	G	A	TP	PIM
1985-86	St. Lawrence	ECAC	25	2	10	12	40	....	....	....	....	....
1986-87	St. Lawrence	ECAC	35	8	15	23	44	....	....	....	....	....
1987-88	St. Lawrence	ECAC	38	6	12	18	18	....	....	....	....	....
1988-89a	St. Lawrence	ECAC	36	8	25	33	30	....	....	....	....	....
	Denver	IHL	8	0	2	2	13	4	1	2	3	2
1989-90	Flint	IHL	74	3	34	37	38	3	0	1	1	2
1990-91	San Diego	IHL	2	1	0	1	0	....	....	....	....	....
	Binghamton	AHL	33	2	11	13	27	3	0	1	1	0
1991-92	Binghamton	AHL	79	16	39	55	64	11	2	7	9	8

a ECAC First All-Star Team (1989)

HUSCROFT, JAMIE

Defense. Shoots right. 6'2", 200 lbs. Born, Creston, B.C., January 9, 1967.
(New Jersey's 9th choice, 171st overall, in 1985 Entry Draft).

			Regular Season					Playoffs				
Season	Club	Lea	GP	G	A	TP	PIM	GP	G	A	TP	PIM
1983-84	Seattle	WHL	63	0	12	12	77	5	0	0	0	15
1984-85	Seattle	WHL	69	3	13	16	273	....	....	....	....	....
1985-86	Seattle	WHL	66	6	20	26	394	5	0	1	1	18
1986-87	Seattle	WHL	21	1	18	19	99	....	....	....	....	....
	Medicine Hat	WHL	35	4	21	25	170	20	0	3	3	*125
1987-88	Utica	AHL	71	5	7	12	316	....	....	....	....	....
	Flint	IHL	3	1	0	1	2	16	0	1	1	110
1988-89	**New Jersey**	**NHL**	**15**	**0**	**2**	**2**	**51**	....	....	....	....	....
	Utica	AHL	41	2	10	12	215	5	0	0	0	40
1989-90	**New Jersey**	**NHL**	**42**	**2**	**3**	**5**	**149**	**5**	**0**	**0**	**0**	**16**
	Utica	AHL	22	3	6	9	122	....	....	....	....	....
1990-91	**New Jersey**	**NHL**	**8**	**0**	**1**	**1**	**27**	**3**	**0**	**0**	**0**	**6**
	Utica	AHL	59	3	15	18	339	....	....	....	....	....
1991-92	Utica	AHL	50	4	7	11	224	....	....	....	....	....
	NHL Totals		**65**	**2**	**6**	**8**	**227**	**8**	**0**	**0**	**0**	**22**

Signed as a free agent by **Boston**, July 23, 1992.

HUSS, ANDERS (HUHS)

Center. Shoots right. 5'10", 183 lbs. Born, Gavle, Sweden, April 6, 1964.
(Washington's 8th choice, 225th overall, in 1983 Entry Draft).

			Regular Season					Playoffs				
Season	Club	Lea	GP	G	A	TP	PIM	GP	G	A	TP	PIM
1985-86	Brynas	Swe.	36	20	7	27	36	3	0	0	0	0
1986-87	Brynas	Swe.	33	12	13	25	40	....	....	....	....	....
1987-88	Brynas	Swe.	40	14	12	26	28	....	....	....	....	....
1988-89	Brynas	Swe.	40	22	17	39	26	....	....	....	....	....
1989-90	Brynas	Swe.	36	19	18	37	32	5	3	2	5	0
1990-91	Brynas	Swe.	35	9	5	14	30	....	....	....	....	....
1991-92	Brynas	Swe.	39	14	29	43	28	5	1	1	2	0

HUSSEY, MARC

Defense. Shoots right. 6'4", 182 lbs. Born, Chatam, N.B., January 22, 1974.
(Pittsburgh's 2nd choice, 43rd overall, in 1992 Entry Draft).

			Regular Season					Playoffs				
Season	Club	Lea	GP	G	A	TP	PIM	GP	G	A	TP	PIM
1990-91	Moose Jaw	WHL	68	5	8	13	67	8	2	2	4	7
1991-92	Moose Jaw	WHL	72	7	27	34	203	4	1	1	2	0

HUURA, PASI

Defense. Shoots left. 6'4", 220 lbs. Born, Tampere, Finland, March 23, 1966.
(Pittsburgh's 12th choice, 258th overall, in 1991 Entry Draft).

			Regular Season					Playoffs				
Season	Club	Lea	GP	G	A	TP	PIM	GP	G	A	TP	PIM
1989-90	Ilves	Fin.	39	2	6	8	50	....	....	....	....	....
1990-91	Ilves	Fin.	41	1	4	5	48	....	....	....	....	....
1991-92	Lukko	Fin.	44	1	5	6	40	....	....	....	....	....

HYNES, GORD

Defense. Shoots left. 6'1", 170 lbs. Born, Montreal, Que., July 22, 1966.
(Boston's 5th choice, 115th overall, in 1985 Entry Draft).

			Regular Season					Playoffs				
Season	Club	Lea	GP	G	A	TP	PIM	GP	G	A	TP	PIM
1983-84	Medicine Hat	WHL	72	5	14	19	39	14	0	0	0	0
1984-85	Medicine Hat	WHL	70	18	45	63	61	10	6	9	15	17
1985-86	Medicine Hat	WHL	58	22	39	61	45	25	8	15	23	32
1986-87	Moncton	AHL	69	2	19	21	21	4	0	0	0	2
1987-88	Maine	AHL	69	5	30	35	65	7	1	3	4	4
1988-89	Cdn. National	....	61	8	38	46	44	....	....	....	....	....
1989-90	Cdn. National	....	12	3	1	4	4	....	....	....	....	....
	Varese	Italy	29	13	36	49	16	3	3	3	6	0
1990-91	Cdn. National	....	57	12	30	42	62	....	....	....	....	....
1991-92	Cdn. National	....	48	12	22	34	50	....	....	....	....	....
	Cdn. Olympic	....	8	3	3	6	6	....	....	....	....	....
	Boston	**NHL**	**15**	**0**	**5**	**5**	**6**	**12**	**1**	**2**	**3**	**6**
	NHL Totals		**15**	**0**	**5**	**5**	**6**	**12**	**1**	**2**	**3**	**6**

HYNNES, CHRIS

Defense. Shoots left. 6', 185 lbs. Born, Thunder Bay, Ont., December 8, 1970.
(Quebec's 2nd choice, 8th overall, in 1991 Supplemental Draft).

			Regular Season					Playoffs				
Season	Club	Lea	GP	G	A	TP	PIM	GP	G	A	TP	PIM
1989-90	Colorado	WCHA	17	0	3	3	10	....	....	....	....	....
1990-91	Colorado	WCHA	40	8	18	26	64	....	....	....	....	....
1991-92ab	Colorado	WCHA	40	12	31	43	59	....	....	....	....	....

a NCAA West Second All-Star Team (1992)
b WCHA First All-Star Team (1992)

IAFRATE, AL (IGH-uh-FRAY-tee)

Defense. Shoots left. 6'3", 220 lbs. Born, Dearborn, MI, March 21, 1966.
(Toronto's 1st choice, 4th overall, in 1984 Entry Draft).

			Regular Season					Playoffs				
Season	Club	Lea	GP	G	A	TP	PIM	GP	G	A	TP	PIM
1983-84	U.S. National	....	55	4	17	21	26	....	....	....	....	....
	U.S. Olympic	....	6	0	0	0	2	....	....	....	....	....
	Belleville	OHL	10	2	4	6	2	3	0	1	1	5
1984-85	**Toronto**	**NHL**	**68**	**5**	**16**	**21**	**51**	....	....	....	....	....
1985-86	**Toronto**	**NHL**	**65**	**8**	**25**	**33**	**40**	**10**	**0**	**3**	**3**	**4**
1986-87	**Toronto**	**NHL**	**80**	**9**	**21**	**30**	**55**	**13**	**1**	**3**	**4**	**11**
1987-88	**Toronto**	**NHL**	**77**	**22**	**30**	**52**	**80**	**6**	**3**	**4**	**7**	**6**
1988-89	**Toronto**	**NHL**	**65**	**13**	**20**	**33**	**72**	....	....	....	....	....
1989-90	**Toronto**	**NHL**	**75**	**21**	**42**	**63**	**135**	....	....	....	....	....
1990-91	**Toronto**	**NHL**	**42**	**3**	**15**	**18**	**113**	....	....	....	....	....
	Washington	**NHL**	**30**	**6**	**8**	**14**	**124**	**10**	**1**	**3**	**4**	**22**
1991-92	**Washington**	**NHL**	**78**	**17**	**34**	**51**	**180**	**7**	**4**	**2**	**6**	**14**
	NHL Totals		**580**	**104**	**211**	**315**	**850**	**46**	**9**	**15**	**24**	**57**

Played in NHL All-Star Game (1988, 1990)

Traded to **Washington** by **Toronto** for Peter Zezel and Bob Rouse, January 16, 1991.

INTRANUOVO, RALPH

Center. Shoots left. 5'8", 170 lbs. Born, East York, Ont., December 11, 1973.
(Edmonton's 5th choice, 96th overall, in 1992 Entry Draft).

			Regular Season					Playoffs				
Season	**Club**	**Lea**	**GP**	**G**	**A**	**TP**	**PIM**	**GP**	**G**	**A**	**TP**	**PIM**
1990-91	S.S. Marie	OHL	63	25	42	67	22	14	7	13	20	17
1991-92	S.S. Marie	OHL	65	50	63	113	44	18	10	14	24	12

IOB, TONY

Left wing. Shoots left. 5'11", 202 lbs. Born, Renfrew, Ont., January 2, 1971.
(Buffalo's 10th choice, 189th overall, in 1991 Entry Draft).

			Regular Season					Playoffs				
Season	**Club**	**Lea**	**GP**	**G**	**A**	**TP**	**PIM**	**GP**	**G**	**A**	**TP**	**PIM**
1990-91	S.S. Marie	OHL	57	38	35	73	185	14	14	7	21	44
1991-92	S.S. Marie	OHL	42	28	34	62	157	19	17	17	34	45

JACKSON, DANE

Right wing. Shoots right. 6'1", 200 lbs. Born, Winnipeg, Man., May 17, 1970.
(Vancouver's 3rd choice, 44th overall, in 1988 Entry Draft).

			Regular Season					Playoffs				
Season	**Club**	**Lea**	**GP**	**G**	**A**	**TP**	**PIM**	**GP**	**G**	**A**	**TP**	**PIM**
1988-89	North Dakota	WCHA	30	4	5	9	33	....	....	....	....	....
1989-90	North Dakota	WCHA	44	15	11	26	56	....	....	....	....	....
1990-91	North Dakota	WCHA	37	17	9	26	79	....	....	....	....	....
1991-92	North Dakota	WCHA	39	23	19	42	81	....	....	....	....	....

JACKSON, JEFF

Left wing. Shoots left. 6'1", 195 lbs. Born, Dresden, Ont., April 24, 1965.
(Toronto's 2nd choice, 28th overall, in 1983 Entry Draft).

			Regular Season					Playoffs				
Season	**Club**	**Lea**	**GP**	**G**	**A**	**TP**	**PIM**	**GP**	**G**	**A**	**TP**	**PIM**
1982-83	Brantford	OHL	64	18	25	43	63	8	1	1	2	27
1983-84	Brantford	OHL	58	27	42	69	78	2	0	1	1	0
1984-85	**Toronto**	**NHL**	**17**	**0**	**1**	**1**	**24**	....	....	....	....	....
	Hamilton	OHL	20	13	14	27	51	17	8	12	20	26
1985-86	**Toronto**	**NHL**	**5**	**1**	**2**	**3**	**2**	....	....	....	....	....
	St. Catharines	AHL	74	17	28	45	122	13	5	2	7	30
1986-87	**Toronto**	**NHL**	**55**	**8**	**7**	**15**	**64**	....	....	....	....	....
	Newmarket	AHL	7	3	6	9	13	....	....	....	....	....
	NY Rangers	**NHL**	**9**	**5**	**1**	**6**	**15**	**6**	**1**	**1**	**2**	**16**
1987-88	**Quebec**	**NHL**	**68**	**9**	**18**	**27**	**103**	....	....	....	....	....
1988-89	**Quebec**	**NHL**	**33**	**4**	**6**	**10**	**28**	....	....	....	....	....
1989-90	**Quebec**	**NHL**	**65**	**8**	**12**	**20**	**71**	....	....	....	....	....
1990-91	**Quebec**	**NHL**	**10**	**3**	**1**	**4**	**4**	....	....	....	....	....
	Halifax	AHL	25	8	17	25	45	....	....	....	....	....
1991-92	**Chicago**	**NHL**	**1**	**0**	**0**	**0**	**2**	....	....	....	....	....
	Indianapolis	IHL	18	3	7	10	41	....	....	....	....	....
	New Haven	AHL	30	10	14	24	60	5	0	5	5	6
	NHL Totals		**263**	**38**	**48**	**86**	**313**	**6**	**1**	**1**	**2**	**16**

Traded to **NY Rangers** by **Toronto** with Toronto's third round choice (Rob Zamuner) in 1989 Entry Draft for Mark Osborne, March 5, 1987. Traded to **Quebec** by **NY Rangers** with Terry Carkner for John Ogrodnick and David Shaw, September, 30, 1987. Signed as a free agent by **Chicago**, February 19, 1992.

JAGR, JAROMIR (YAH-guhr)

Right wing. Shoots left. 6'2", 208 lbs. Born, Kladno, Czechoslovakia, February 15, 1972.
(Pittsburgh's 1st choice, 5th overall, in 1990 Entry Draft).

			Regular Season					Playoffs				
Season	**Club**	**Lea**	**GP**	**G**	**A**	**TP**	**PIM**	**GP**	**G**	**A**	**TP**	**PIM**
1988-89	Kladno	Czech.	39	8	10	18	....	....	....	....	....	....
1989-90	Kladno	Czech.	51	30	30	60	....	....	....	....	....	....
1990-91a	**Pittsburgh**	**NHL**	**80**	**27**	**30**	**57**	**42**	**24**	**3**	**10**	**13**	**6**
1991-92	**Pittsburgh**	**NHL**	**70**	**32**	**37**	**69**	**34**	**21**	**11**	**13**	**24**	**6**
	NHL Totals		**150**	**59**	**67**	**126**	**76**	**45**	**14**	**23**	**37**	**12**

a NHL/Upper Deck All-Rookie Team (1991)
Played in NHL All-Star Game (1992)

JANNEY, CRAIG

Center. Shoots left. 6'1", 190 lbs. Born, Hartford, CT, September 26, 1967.
(Boston's 1st choice, 13th overall, in 1986 Entry Draft).

			Regular Season					Playoffs				
Season	**Club**	**Lea**	**GP**	**G**	**A**	**TP**	**PIM**	**GP**	**G**	**A**	**TP**	**PIM**
1985-86	Boston College	H.E.	34	13	14	27	8	....	....	....	....	....
1986-87ab	Boston College	H.E.	37	26	55	81	6	....	....	....	....	....
1987-88	U.S. National	....	52	26	44	70	6	....	....	....	....	....
	U.S. Olympic	....	5	3	1	4	2	....	....	....	....	....
	Boston	**NHL**	**15**	**7**	**9**	**16**	**0**	**23**	**6**	**10**	**16**	**11**
1988-89	**Boston**	**NHL**	**62**	**16**	**46**	**62**	**12**	**10**	**4**	**9**	**13**	**21**
1989-90	**Boston**	**NHL**	**55**	**24**	**38**	**62**	**4**	**18**	**3**	**19**	**22**	**2**
1990-91	**Boston**	**NHL**	**77**	**26**	**66**	**92**	**8**	**18**	**4**	**18**	**22**	**11**
1991-92	**Boston**	**NHL**	**53**	**12**	**39**	**51**	**20**	....	....	....	....	....
	St. Louis	**NHL**	**25**	**6**	**30**	**36**	**2**	**6**	**0**	**6**	**6**	**0**
	NHL Totals		**287**	**91**	**228**	**319**	**46**	**75**	**17**	**62**	**79**	**45**

a Hockey East First All-Star Team (1987)
b NCAA East First All-American Team (1987)

Traded to **St. Louis** by **Boston** with Stephane Quintal for Adam Oates, February 7, 1992.

JANSSENS, MARK

Center. Shoots left. 6'3", 216 lbs. Born, Surrey, B.C., May 19, 1968.
(NY Rangers' 4th choice, 72nd overall, in 1986 Entry Draft).

			Regular Season					Playoffs				
Season	**Club**	**Lea**	**GP**	**G**	**A**	**TP**	**PIM**	**GP**	**G**	**A**	**TP**	**PIM**
1984-85	Regina	WHL	70	8	22	30	51	....	....	....	....	....
1985-86	Regina	WHL	71	25	38	63	146	9	0	2	2	17
1986-87	Regina	WHL	68	24	38	62	209	3	0	1	1	14
1987-88	**NY Rangers**	**NHL**	**1**	**0**	**0**	**0**	**0**	....	....	....	....	....
	Colorado	IHL	6	2	2	4	24	12	3	2	5	20
	Regina	WHL	71	39	51	90	202	4	3	4	7	6
1988-89	**NY Rangers**	**NHL**	**5**	**0**	**0**	**0**	**0**	....	....	....	....	....
	Denver	IHL	38	19	19	38	104	4	3	0	3	18
1989-90	**NY Rangers**	**NHL**	**80**	**5**	**8**	**13**	**161**	**9**	**2**	**1**	**3**	**10**
1990-91	**NY Rangers**	**NHL**	**67**	**9**	**7**	**16**	**172**	**6**	**3**	**0**	**3**	**6**
1991-92	**NY Rangers**	**NHL**	**4**	**0**	**0**	**0**	**5**	....	....	....	....	....
	Binghamton	AHL	55	10	23	33	109	....	....	....	....	....
	Minnesota	**NHL**	**3**	**0**	**0**	**0**	**0**	....	....	....	....	....
	Kalamazoo	IHL	2	0	0	0	2	11	1	2	3	22
	NHL Totals		**160**	**14**	**15**	**29**	**338**	**15**	**5**	**1**	**6**	**16**

Traded to **Minnesota** by **NY Rangers** for Mario Thyer and Minnesota's third round choice in 1993 Entry Draft, March 10, 1992.

JANTUNEN, MARKO (YAHN-tuh-nen)

Center. Shoots left. 5'10", 178 lbs. Born, Lahti, Finland, February 14, 1971.
(Calgary's 12th choice, 239th overall, in 1991 Entry Draft).

			Regular Season					Playoffs				
Season	**Club**	**Lea**	**GP**	**G**	**A**	**TP**	**PIM**	**GP**	**G**	**A**	**TP**	**PIM**
1990-91	Reipas	Fin.	39	9	20	29	20	....	....	....	....	....
1991-92	Reipas	Fin.	42	10	14	24	46	....	....	....	....	....

JAQUES, STEVE

Defense. Shoots left. 5'11", 180 lbs. Born, Burnaby, B.C., February 21, 1969.
(Los Angeles' 11th choice, 228th overall, in 1989 Entry Draft).

			Regular Season					Playoffs				
Season	**Club**	**Lea**	**GP**	**G**	**A**	**TP**	**PIM**	**GP**	**G**	**A**	**TP**	**PIM**
1987-88	N. Westminster	WHL	69	15	31	46	336	5	0	4	4	31
1988-89	Tri-Cities	WHL	61	18	34	52	233	2	0	0	0	9
1989-90a	Tri-Cities	WHL	64	20	64	84	185	6	1	2	3	55
1990-91	Phoenix	IHL	58	10	24	34	227	9	2	6	8	21
1991-92	Phoenix	IHL	13	2	4	6	69	....	....	....	....	....

a WHL West Second All-Star Team (1990)

JARDEMYR, DANIEL

Defense. Shoots left. 6'2", 183 lbs. Born, Uppsala, Sweden, May 28, 1971.
(Winnipeg's 7th choice, 119th overall, in 1990 Entry Draft).

			Regular Season					Playoffs				
Season	**Club**	**Lea**	**GP**	**G**	**A**	**TP**	**PIM**	**GP**	**G**	**A**	**TP**	**PIM**
1989-90	Uppsala	Swe.	27	5	9	14	32	....	....	....	....	....
1990-91	AIK	Swe.	27	1	2	3	41	....	....	....	....	....
1991-92	AIK	Swe.	24	2	1	3	12	....	....	....	....	....

JAX, FREDRIK

Right wing. Shoots left. 5'11", 165 lbs. Born, Leksand, Sweden, February 6, 1972.
(NY Rangers' 5th choice, 125th overall, in 1991 Entry Draft).

			Regular Season					Playoffs				
Season	**Club**	**Lea**	**GP**	**G**	**A**	**TP**	**PIM**	**GP**	**G**	**A**	**TP**	**PIM**
1990-91	Leksand	Swe.	29	3	2	5	2	....	....	....	....	....
1991-92	Leksand	Swe.	22	2	3	5	8	....	....	....	....	....

JELINEK, TOMAS

Right wing. Shoots left. 5'9", 189 lbs. Born, Prague, Czech., April 29, 1962.
(Ottawa's 11th choice, 242nd overall, in 1992 Entry Draft).

			Regular Season					Playoffs				
Season	**Club**	**Lea**	**GP**	**G**	**A**	**TP**	**PIM**	**GP**	**G**	**A**	**TP**	**PIM**
1989-90	Motor	Czech.	48	23	20	43	....	....	....	....	....	....
1990-91	Motor	Czech.	51	24	23	47	102	....	....	....	....	....
1991-92	HPK	Fin.	41	24	23	47	98	....	....	....	....	....

JENNINGS, GRANT

Defense. Shoots left. 6'3", 210 lbs. Born, Hudson Bay, Sask., May 5, 1965.

			Regular Season					Playoffs				
Season	**Club**	**Lea**	**GP**	**G**	**A**	**TP**	**PIM**	**GP**	**G**	**A**	**TP**	**PIM**
1983-84	Saskatoon	WHL	64	5	13	18	102	....	....	....	....	....
1984-85	Saskatoon	WHL	47	10	24	34	134	2	1	0	1	2
1985-86	Binghamton	AHL	51	0	4	4	109	....	....	....	....	....
1986-87	Fort Wayne	IHL	3	0	0	0	0	....	....	....	....	....
	Binghamton	AHL	47	1	5	6	125	13	0	2	2	17
1987-88	**Washington**	**NHL**	....	....	....	....	....	**1**	**0**	**0**	**0**	**0**
	Binghamton	AHL	56	2	12	14	195	3	1	0	1	15
1988-89	**Hartford**	**NHL**	**55**	**3**	**10**	**13**	**159**	**4**	**1**	**0**	**1**	**17**
	Binghamton	AHL	2	0	0	0	2	....	....	....	....	....
1989-90	**Hartford**	**NHL**	**64**	**3**	**6**	**9**	**171**	**7**	**0**	**0**	**0**	**13**
1990-91	**Hartford**	**NHL**	**44**	**1**	**4**	**5**	**82**	....	....	....	....	....
	Pittsburgh	**NHL**	**13**	**1**	**3**	**4**	**26**	**13**	**1**	**1**	**2**	**16**
1991-92	**Pittsburgh**	**NHL**	**53**	**4**	**5**	**9**	**104**	**10**	**0**	**0**	**0**	**12**
	NHL Totals		**229**	**12**	**28**	**40**	**542**	**35**	**2**	**1**	**3**	**58**

Signed as a free agent by **Washington**, June 25, 1985. Traded to **Hartford** by **Washington** with Ed Kastelic for Mike Millar and Neil Sheehy, July 6, 1988. Traded to **Pittsburgh** by **Hartford** with Ron Francis and Ulf Samuelsson for John Cullen, Jeff Parker and Zarley Zalapski, March 4, 1991.

JENNINGS, JASON

Right wing. Shoots right. 6', 190 lbs. Born, Vancouver, B.C., March 16, 1971.
(Winnipeg's 11th choice, 225th overall, in 1991 Entry Draft).

			Regular Season					Playoffs				
Season	**Club**	**Lea**	**GP**	**G**	**A**	**TP**	**PIM**	**GP**	**G**	**A**	**TP**	**PIM**
1989-90	W. Michigan	CCHA	28	3	1	4	50	....	....	....	....	....
1990-91	W. Michigan	CCHA	42	10	19	29	50	....	....	....	....	....
1991-92	W. Michigan	CCHA	35	8	9	17	52	....	....	....	....	....

JENSEN, CHRIS

Right wing. Shoots right. 5'11", 170 lbs. Born, Fort St. John, B.C., October 28, 1963.
(NY Rangers' 4th choice, 78th overall, in 1982 Entry Draft).

			Regular Season					Playoffs				
Season	Club	Lea	GP	G	A	TP	PIM	GP	G	A	TP	PIM
1982-83	North Dakota	WCHA	13	3	3	6	28	....	....	....	....	....
1983-84	North Dakota	WCHA	44	24	25	49	100	....	....	....	....	....
1984-85	North Dakota	WCHA	40	25	27	52	80	....	....	....	....	....
1985-86	North Dakota	WCHA	34	25	40	65	53	....	....	....	....	....
	NY Rangers	**NHL**	**9**	**1**	**3**	**4**	**0**	....	....	....	....	....
1986-87	**NY Rangers**	**NHL**	**37**	**6**	**7**	**13**	**21**	....	....	....	....	....
	New Haven	AHL	14	4	9	13	41	....	....	....	....	....
1987-88	**NY Rangers**	**NHL**	**7**	**0**	**1**	**1**	**2**	....	....	....	....	....
	Colorado	IHL	43	10	23	33	68	10	3	7	10	8
1988-89	Hershey	AHL	45	27	31	58	66	10	4	5	9	29
1989-90	**Philadelphia**	**NHL**	**1**	**0**	**0**	**0**	**0**	....	....	....	....	....
	Hershey	AHL	43	16	26	42	101	....	....	....	....	....
1990-91	**Philadelphia**	**NHL**	**18**	**2**	**1**	**3**	**2**	....	....	....	....	....
	Hershey	AHL	50	26	20	46	83	6	2	2	4	10
1991-92	**Philadelphia**	**NHL**	**2**	**0**	**0**	**0**	**0**	....	....	....	....	....
	Hershey	AHL	71	38	33	71	134	6	0	1	1	2
	NHL Totals		**74**	**9**	**12**	**21**	**25**	....	....	....	....	....

Traded to **Philadelphia** by **NY Rangers** for Michael Boyce, September 28, 1988.

JENSEN, CHRISTOPHER

Defense. Shoots right. 6'2", 190 lbs. Born, Wilmette, IL, June 29, 1968.
(Toronto's 8th choice, 154th overall, in 1987 Entry Draft).

			Regular Season					Playoffs				
Season	Club	Lea	GP	G	A	TP	PIM	GP	G	A	TP	PIM
1988-89	U. Wisconsin	WCHA	2	1	0	1	0	....	....	....	....	....
1989-90	N. Hampshire	H.E.				DID NOT PLAY						
1990-91	N. Hampshire	H.E.	5	0	3	3	2	....	....	....	....	....
1991-92	N. Hampshire	H.E.	25	1	1	2	10	....	....	....	....	....

JERRARD, PAUL

Right wing. Shoots right. 5'10", 185 lbs. Born, Winnipeg, Man., April 20, 1965.
(NY Rangers' 10th choice, 173rd overall, in 1983 Entry Draft).

			Regular Season					Playoffs				
Season	Club	Lea	GP	G	A	TP	PIM	GP	G	A	TP	PIM
1983-84	Lake Superior	CCHA	40	8	18	26	48	....	....	....	....	....
1984-85	Lake Superior	CCHA	43	9	25	34	61	....	....	....	....	....
1985-86	Lake Superior	CCHA	40	13	11	24	34	....	....	....	....	....
1986-87	Lake Superior	CCHA	35	10	19	29	56	....	....	....	....	....
1987-88	Colorado	IHL	77	20	28	48	182	11	2	4	6	40
1988-89	Denver	IHL	2	1	1	2	21	....	....	....	....	....
	Minnesota	**NHL**	**5**	**0**	**0**	**0**	**4**	....	....	....	....	....
	Kalamazoo	IHL	68	15	25	40	195	6	2	1	3	37
1989-90	Kalamazoo	IHL	60	9	18	27	134	7	1	1	2	11
1990-91	Albany	IHL	7	0	3	3	30	....	....	....	....	....
	Kalamazoo	IHL	62	10	23	33	111	7	0	0	0	13
1991-92	Kalamazoo	IHL	76	4	24	28	123	12	1	7	8	31
	NHL Totals		**5**	**0**	**0**	**0**	**4**	....	....	....	....	....

Traded to **Minnesota** by **NY Rangers** with Mark Tinordi, the rights to Bret Barnett and Mike Sullivan, and Los Angeles' third round choice (Murray Garbutt) in 1989 Entry Draft – acquired March 10, 1987 by Minnesota – for Brian Lawton, Igor Liba and the rights to Eric Bennett, October 11, 1988.

JESTADT, JEFF

Left wing. Shoots left. 6'1", 195 lbs. Born, Hinsdale, IL, September 6, 1970.
(Winnipeg's 2nd choice, 11th overall, in 1991 Supplemental Draft).

			Regular Season					Playoffs				
Season	Club	Lea	GP	G	A	TP	PIM	GP	G	A	TP	PIM
1989-90	Ferris State	CCHA	35	7	2	9	52	....	....	....	....	....
1990-91	Ferris State	CCHA	33	8	8	16	31	....	....	....	....	....
1991-92	Ferris State	CCHA	34	12	7	19	21	....	....	....	....	....

JIRANEK, MARTIN

Center. Shoots left. 5'11", 170 lbs. Born, Bashaw, Alta., October 3, 1969.
(Washington's 1st choice, 14th overall, in 1990 Supplemental Draft).

			Regular Season					Playoffs				
Season	Club	Lea	GP	G	A	TP	PIM	GP	G	A	TP	PIM
1988-89	Bowling Green	CCHA	41	9	18	27	36	....	....	....	....	....
1989-90	Bowling Green	CCHA	41	13	21	34	38	....	....	....	....	....
1990-91	Bowling Green	CCHA	39	31	23	54	33	....	....	....	....	....
1991-92a	Bowling Green	CCHA	34	25	28	53	46	....	....	....	....	....
	Baltimore	AHL	8	2	8	10	0	....	....	....	....	....

a CCHA Second All-Star Team (1992)

JOHANNSON, JAMES (JIM)

Center. Shoots right. 6'2", 200 lbs. Born, Rochester, MN, March 10, 1964.

			Regular Season					Playoffs				
Season	Club	Lea	GP	G	A	TP	PIM	GP	G	A	TP	PIM
1982-83	U. Wisconsin	WCHA	43	12	9	21	16	....	....	....	....	....
1983-84	U. Wisconsin	WCHA	35	17	21	38	52	....	....	....	....	....
1984-85	U. Wisconsin	WCHA	40	16	24	40	54	....	....	....	....	....
1985-86	U. Wisconsin	WCHA	30	18	13	31	44	....	....	....	....	....
1986-87	Landsberg	W.Ger.	57	46	56	102	90	....	....	....	....	....
1987-88	U.S. National	....	47	16	14	30	64	....	....	....	....	....
	U.S. Olympic	....	4	0	1	1	4	....	....	....	....	....
	Salt Lake	IHL	18	14	7	21	50	19	8	*15	23	55
1988-89	Salt Lake	IHL	82	35	40	75	87	13	2	5	7	13
1989-90	Indianapolis	IHL	82	22	41	63	74	14	1	4	5	6
1990-91	Indianapolis	IHL	82	28	41	69	116	7	1	2	3	8
1991-92	U.S. National	....	50	9	8	17	79	....	....	....	....	....
	U.S. Olympic	....	8	1	0	1	2	....	....	....	....	....
	Indianapolis	IHL	11	2	2	4	4	....	....	....	....	....

Signed as a free agent by **Calgary**, February 25, 1988. Signed as a free agent by **Chicago**, July 6, 1989.

JOHANSSON, ANDREAS

Center. Shoots left. 5'11", 198 lbs. Born, Falun, Sweden, May 19, 1973.
(NY Islanders' 7th choice, 136th overall, in 1991 Entry Draft).

			Regular Season					Playoffs				
Season	Club	Lea	GP	G	A	TP	PIM	GP	G	A	TP	PIM
1990-91	Falun	Swe.2	31	12	10	22	38	....	....	....	....	....
1991-92	Farjestad	Swe.	30	3	1	4	10	6	0	0	0	4

JOHANSSON, CALLE (yo-HAHN-suhn)

Defense. Shoots left. 5'11", 205 lbs. Born, Goteborg, Sweden, February 14, 1967.
(Buffalo's 1st choice, 14th overall, in 1985 Entry Draft).

			Regular Season					Playoffs				
Season	Club	Lea	GP	G	A	TP	PIM	GP	G	A	TP	PIM
1983-84	V. Frolunda	Swe.	28	4	4	8	10	....	....	....	....	....
1984-85	V. Frolunda	Swe.2	25	8	13	21	16	6	1	2	3	4
1985-86	Bjorkloven	Swe.	17	1	2	3	4	....	....	....	....	....
1986-87	Bjorkloven	Swe.	30	2	13	15	20	6	1	3	4	6
1987-88a	**Buffalo**	**NHL**	**71**	**4**	**38**	**42**	**37**	**6**	**0**	**1**	**1**	**0**
1988-89	**Buffalo**	**NHL**	**47**	**2**	**11**	**13**	**33**	....	....	....	....	....
	Washington	**NHL**	**12**	**1**	**7**	**8**	**4**	**6**	**1**	**2**	**3**	**0**
1989-90	**Washington**	**NHL**	**70**	**8**	**31**	**39**	**25**	**15**	**1**	**6**	**7**	**4**
1990-91	**Washington**	**NHL**	**80**	**11**	**41**	**52**	**23**	**10**	**2**	**7**	**9**	**8**
1991-92	**Washington**	**NHL**	**80**	**14**	**42**	**56**	**49**	**7**	**0**	**5**	**5**	**4**
	NHL Totals		**360**	**40**	**170**	**210**	**171**	**44**	**4**	**21**	**25**	**16**

a Named to NHL All-Rookie Team (1988)

Traded to **Washington** by **Buffalo** with Buffalo's second round choice (Byron Dafoe) in 1989 Entry Draft for Clint Malarchuk, Grant Ledyard and Washington's sixth round choice (Brian Holzinger) in 1991 Entry Draft, March 7, 1989.

JOHANSSON, MATHIAS

Center. Shoots left. 6'2", 187 lbs. Born, Okarshamn, Sweden, February 22, 1974.
(Calgary's 3rd choice, 54th overall, in 1992 Entry Draft).

			Regular Season					Playoffs				
Season	Club	Lea	GP	G	A	TP	PIM	GP	G	A	TP	PIM
1990-91	Farjestad	Swe.	3	0	0	0	0	....	....	....	....	....
1991-92	Farjestad	Swe.	16	0	0	0	2	1	0	0	0	0

JOHANSSON, MIKAEL

Center. Shoots left. 5'10", 176 lbs. Born, Stockholm, Sweden, December 6, 1966.
(Quebec's 7th choice, 134th overall, in 1991 Entry Draft).

			Regular Season					Playoffs				
Season	Club	Lea	GP	G	A	TP	PIM	GP	G	A	TP	PIM
1990-91	Djurgarden	Swe.	39	14	23	37	12	....	....	....	....	....
1991-92	Djurgarden	Swe.	30	15	21	36	12	9	1	5	6	4

JOHANSSON, ROGER (yo-HAHN-suhn)

Defense. Shoots left. 6'1", 185 lbs. Born, Ljungby, Sweden, April 17, 1967.
(Calgary's 5th choice, 80th overall, in 1985 Entry Draft).

			Regular Season					Playoffs				
Season	Club	Lea	GP	G	A	TP	PIM	GP	G	A	TP	PIM
1986-87	Farjestad	Swe.	31	6	11	17	20	7	1	1	2	8
1987-88	Farjestad	Swe.	24	3	11	14	20	....	....	....	....	....
1988-89	Farjestad	Swe.	40	5	15	20	36	....	....	....	....	....
1989-90	**Calgary**	**NHL**	**35**	**0**	**5**	**5**	**48**	....	....	....	....	....
1990-91	**Calgary**	**NHL**	**38**	**4**	**13**	**17**	**47**	....	....	....	....	....
1991-92	Leksand	Swe.	22	3	9	12	42	....	....	....	....	....
	NHL Totals		**73**	**4**	**18**	**22**	**95**	....	....	....	....	....

JOHNSON, CHAD

Center. Shoots left. 6', 175 lbs. Born, Grand Forks, ND, January 10, 1970.
(New Jersey's 7th choice, 117th overall, in 1988 Entry Draft).

			Regular Season					Playoffs				
Season	Club	Lea	GP	G	A	TP	PIM	GP	G	A	TP	PIM
1990-91	North Dakota	WCHA	37	2	5	7	30	....	....	....	....	....
1991-92	North Dakota	WCHA	32	0	6	6	41	....	....	....	....	....

JOHNSON, CRAIG

Left wing/Center. Shoots left. 6'2", 185 lbs. Born, St. Paul, MN, March 18, 1972.
(St. Louis' 1st choice, 33rd overall, in 1990 Entry Draft).

			Regular Season					Playoffs				
Season	Club	Lea	GP	G	A	TP	PIM	GP	G	A	TP	PIM
1990-91	U. Minnesota	WCHA	33	13	18	31	34	....	....	....	....	....
1991-92	U. Minnesota	WCHA	41	17	38	55	66	....	....	....	....	....

JOHNSON, ERIC

Right wing. Shoots right. 6'1", 196 lbs. Born, Minneapolis, MN, December 31, 1972.
(Vancouver's 8th choice, 161st overall, in 1991 Entry Draft).

			Regular Season					Playoffs				
Season	Club	Lea	GP	G	A	TP	PIM	GP	G	A	TP	PIM
1990-91	Armstrong	HS				UNAVAILABLE						
1991-92	St. Cloud	WCHA	20	0	2	2	8	....	....	....	....	....

JOHNSON, GREG

Center. Shoots left. 5'10", 173 lbs. Born, Thunder Bay, Ont., March 16, 1971.
(Philadelphia's 1st choice, 33rd overall, in 1989 Entry Draft).

			Regular Season					Playoffs				
Season	Club	Lea	GP	G	A	TP	PIM	GP	G	A	TP	PIM
1989-90	North Dakota	WCHA	44	17	38	55	11	....	....	....	....	....
1990-91ab	North Dakota	WCHA	38	18	*61	79	6	....	....	....	....	....
1991-92ac	North Dakota	WCHA	39	20	*54	74	8	....	....	....	....	....

a WCHA First All-Star Team (1991, 1992)
b NCAA West First All-American Team (1991)
c NCAA West Second All-Star Team (1992)

JOHNSON, JIM

Defense. Shoots left. 6'1", 190 lbs. Born, New Hope, MN, August 9, 1962.

			Regular Season					Playoffs				
Season	Club	Lea	GP	G	A	TP	PIM	GP	G	A	TP	PIM
1981-82	Minn.-Duluth	WCHA	40	0	10	10	62	....	....	....	....	....
1982-83	Minn.-Duluth	WCHA	44	3	18	21	118	....	....	....	....	....
1983-84	Minn.-Duluth	WCHA	43	3	13	16	116	....	....	....	....	....
1984-85	Minn.-Duluth	WCHA	47	7	29	36	49	....	....	....	....	....
1985-86	**Pittsburgh**	**NHL**	**80**	**3**	**26**	**29**	**115**	....	....	....	....	....
1986-87	**Pittsburgh**	**NHL**	**80**	**5**	**25**	**30**	**116**	....	....	....	....	....
1987-88	**Pittsburgh**	**NHL**	**55**	**1**	**12**	**13**	**87**	....	....	....	....	....
1988-89	**Pittsburgh**	**NHL**	**76**	**2**	**14**	**16**	**163**	**11**	**0**	**5**	**5**	**44**
1989-90	**Pittsburgh**	**NHL**	**75**	**3**	**13**	**16**	**154**	....	....	....	....	....
1990-91	**Pittsburgh**	**NHL**	**24**	**0**	**5**	**5**	**23**	....	....	....	....	....
	Minnesota	**NHL**	**44**	**1**	**9**	**10**	**100**	**14**	**0**	**1**	**1**	**52**
1991-92	**Minnesota**	**NHL**	**71**	**4**	**10**	**14**	**102**	**7**	**1**	**3**	**4**	**18**
	NHL Totals		**505**	**19**	**114**	**133**	**860**	**32**	**1**	**9**	**10**	**114**

Signed as a free agent by **Pittsburgh**, June 9, 1985. Traded to **Minnesota** by **Pittsburgh** with Chris Dahlquist for Larry Murphy and Peter Taglianetti, December 11, 1990.

JOHNSON, JOHN

Center. Shoots left. 5'10", 185 lbs. Born, Kirkfield, Ont., February 22, 1971.
(NY Islanders' 9th choice, 180th overall, in 1991 Entry Draft).

			Regular Season					Playoffs				
Season	Club	Lea	GP	G	A	TP	PIM	GP	G	A	TP	PIM
1990-91	Niagara Falls	OHL	54	38	56	94	21	13	8	5	13	4
1991-92	Niagara Falls	OHL	3	4	1	5	2	....	....	....	....	....
	Peterborough	OHL	52	45	39	84	24	10	2	7	9	15

JOHNSON, MICHAEL

Defense. Shoots left. 6'3", 172 lbs. Born, Halifax, N.S., May 29, 1974.
(Minnesota's 4th choice, 130th overall, in 1992 Entry Draft).

			Regular Season					Playoffs				
Season	Club	Lea	GP	G	A	TP	PIM	GP	G	A	TP	PIM
1990-91	Halifax	Midget	45	12	38	50	61	....	....	....	....	....
1991-92	Ottawa	OHL	63	1	8	9	49	11	1	0	1	14

JOHNSTON, GREG

Right wing. Shoots right. 6'1", 205 lbs. Born, Barrie, Ont., January 14, 1965.
(Boston's 2nd choice, 42nd overall, in 1983 Entry Draft).

			Regular Season					Playoffs				
Season	Club	Lea	GP	G	A	TP	PIM	GP	G	A	TP	PIM
1982-83	Toronto	OHL	58	18	19	37	58	4	1	0	1	4
1983-84	**Boston**	**NHL**	**15**	**2**	**1**	**3**	**2**	....	....	....	....	....
	Toronto	OHL	57	38	35	73	67	9	4	2	6	13
1984-85	**Boston**	**NHL**	**6**	**0**	**0**	**0**	**0**	....	....	....	....	....
	Hershey	AHL	3	1	0	1	0	....	....	....	....	....
	Toronto	OHL	42	22	28	50	55	5	1	3	4	4
1985-86	**Boston**	**NHL**	**20**	**0**	**2**	**2**	**0**	....	....	....	....	....
	Moncton	AHL	60	19	26	45	56	10	4	6	10	4
1986-87	**Boston**	**NHL**	**76**	**12**	**15**	**27**	**79**	**4**	**0**	**0**	**0**	**0**
1987-88	Maine	AHL	75	21	32	53	106	10	6	4	10	23
	Boston	**NHL**	....	....	....	....	....	**3**	**0**	**1**	**1**	**2**
1988-89	**Boston**	**NHL**	**57**	**11**	**10**	**21**	**32**	**10**	**1**	**0**	**1**	**6**
	Maine	AHL	15	5	7	12	31	....	....	....	....	....
1989-90	**Boston**	**NHL**	**9**	**1**	**1**	**2**	**6**	**5**	**1**	**0**	**1**	**4**
	Maine	AHL	52	16	26	42	45	....	....	....	....	....
1990-91	**Toronto**	**NHL**	**1**	**0**	**0**	**0**	**0**	....	....	....	....	....
	Newmarket	AHL	73	32	50	82	54	....	....	....	....	....
1991-92	**Toronto**	**NHL**	**3**	**0**	**1**	**1**	**5**	....	....	....	....	....
	St. John's	AHL	63	28	45	73	33	16	8	6	14	10
	NHL Totals		**187**	**26**	**30**	**56**	**124**	**22**	**2**	**1**	**3**	**12**

Traded to **NY Rangers** by **Boston** with future considerations for Chris Nilan, June 28, 1990. Traded to **Toronto** by **NY Rangers** for Tie Domi and Mark Laforest, June 28, 1990.

JOHNSTON, KARL

Defense. Shoots left. 6', 190 lbs. Born, Windsor, Ont., August 11, 1967.

			Regular Season					Playoffs				
Season	Club	Lea	GP	G	A	TP	PIM	GP	G	A	TP	PIM
1987-88	Lake Superior	CCHA	42	7	13	20	38	....	....	....	....	....
1988-89	Lake Superior	CCHA	43	7	19	26	38	....	....	....	....	....
1989-90	Lake Superior	CCHA	43	12	28	40	32	....	....	....	....	....
1990-91ab	Lake Superior	CCHA	45	14	36	50	86	....	....	....	....	....
1991-92	Springfield	AHL	34	1	11	12	17	....	....	....	....	....

a CCHA First All-Star Team (1991)
b NCAA West Second All-American Team (1991)

Signed as a free agent by **Hartford**, August 14, 1991.

JONES, BRAD

Left wing. Shoots left. 6', 195 lbs. Born, Sterling Heights, MI, June 26, 1965.
(Winnipeg's 8th choice, 156th overall, in 1984 Entry Draft).

			Regular Season					Playoffs				
Season	Club	Lea	GP	G	A	TP	PIM	GP	G	A	TP	PIM
1983-84	U. of Michigan	CCHA	37	8	26	34	32	....	....	....	....	....
1984-85	U. of Michigan	CCHA	34	21	27	48	66	....	....	....	....	....
1985-86a	U. of Michigan	CCHA	36	28	39	67	40	....	....	....	....	....
1986-87bc	U. of Michigan	CCHA	40	32	46	78	64	....	....	....	....	....
	Winnipeg	**NHL**	**4**	**1**	**0**	**1**	**0**	....	....	....	....	....
1987-88	**Winnipeg**	**NHL**	**19**	**2**	**5**	**7**	**15**	**1**	**0**	**0**	**0**	**0**
	U.S. National	....	50	27	23	50	59	....	....	....	....	....
1988-89	**Winnipeg**	**NHL**	**22**	**6**	**5**	**11**	**6**	....	....	....	....	....
	Moncton	AHL	44	20	19	39	62	7	0	1	1	22
1989-90	**Winnipeg**	**NHL**	**2**	**0**	**0**	**0**	**0**	....	....	....	....	....
	Moncton	AHL	15	5	6	11	47	....	....	....	....	....
	New Haven	AHL	36	8	11	19	71	....	....	....	....	....
1990-91	**Los Angeles**	**NHL**	**53**	**9**	**11**	**20**	**57**	**8**	**1**	**1**	**2**	**2**
1991-92	**Philadelphia**	**NHL**	**48**	**7**	**10**	**17**	**44**	....	....	....	....	....
	NHL Totals		**148**	**25**	**31**	**56**	**122**	**9**	**1**	**1**	**2**	**2**

a CCHA Second All-Star Team (1986)
b CCHA First All-Star Team (1987)
c NCAA West Second All-American Team (1987)

Traded to **Los Angeles** by **Winnipeg** for Phil Sykes, December 1, 1989. Signed as a free agent by **Philadelphia**, August 6, 1991.

JONES, KEITH

Right wing. Shoots right. 6'2", 190 lbs. Born, Brantford, Ont., November 8, 1968.
(Washington's 7th choice, 141st overall, in 1988 Entry Draft).

			Regular Season					Playoffs				
Season	Club	Lea	GP	G	A	TP	PIM	GP	G	A	TP	PIM
1988-89	W. Michigan	CCHA	37	9	12	21	51	....	....	....	....	....
1989-90	W. Michigan	CCHA	40	19	18	37	82	....	....	....	....	....
1990-91	W. Michigan	CCHA	41	30	19	49	106	....	....	....	....	....
1991-92a	W. Michigan	CCHA	35	25	31	56	77	....	....	....	....	....
	Baltimore	AHL	6	2	4	6	0	....	....	....	....	....

a CCHA First All-Star Team (1992)

JONSSON, STEFAN (YAHN-suhn)

Defense. Shoots left. 6'1", 194 lbs. Born, Sodertalje, Sweden, June 13, 1965.
(Calgary's 11th choice, 221st overall, in 1984 Entry Draft).

			Regular Season					Playoffs				
Season	Club	Lea	GP	G	A	TP	PIM	GP	G	A	TP	PIM
1987-88	Sodertalje	Swe.	36	4	6	10	24	2	0	0	0	8
1988-89	Sodertalje	Swe.	37	4	2	6	44	....	....	....	....	....
1989-90	Sodertalje	Swe.	37	5	10	15	62	2	0	1	1	0
1990-91	Sodertalje	Swe.	37	5	6	11	42	....	....	....	....	....
1991-92	Sodertalje	Swe.	22	2	3	5	20	....	....	....	....	....

JOSEPH, ANTHONY

Right wing. Shoots right. 6'4", 203 lbs. Born, Cornwall, Ont., March 1, 1969.
(Winnipeg's 5th choice, 94th overall, in 1988 Entry Draft).

			Regular Season					Playoffs				
Season	Club	Lea	GP	G	A	TP	PIM	GP	G	A	TP	PIM
1985-86	Oshawa	OHL	41	3	1	4	28	....	....	....	....	....
1986-87	Oshawa	OHL	44	2	5	7	93	....	....	....	....	....
1987-88	Oshawa	OHL	49	9	18	27	126	7	0	0	0	9
1988-89	**Winnipeg**	**NHL**	**2**	**1**	**0**	**1**	**0**	....	....	....	....	....
	Oshawa	OHL	52	20	16	36	105	6	4	2	6	22
1989-90	Moncton	AHL	61	9	9	18	74	....	....	....	....	....
1990-91	Moncton	AHL	16	4	2	6	79	8	0	1	1	31
1991-92	Kalamazoo	IHL	15	2	0	2	51	....	....	....	....	....
	Moncton	AHL	42	6	5	11	118	6	0	1	1	25
	NHL Totals		**2**	**1**	**0**	**1**	**0**	....	....	....	....	....

Traded to **Minnesota** by **Winnipeg** for Tyler Larter, October 15, 1991. Traded to **Winnipeg** by **Minnesota** for Warren Rychel, December 30, 1991.

JOSEPH, CHRIS

Defense. Shoots right. 6'2", 210 lbs. Born, Burnaby, B.C., September 10, 1969.
(Pittsburgh's 1st choice, 5th overall, in 1987 Entry Draft).

			Regular Season					Playoffs				
Season	Club	Lea	GP	G	A	TP	PIM	GP	G	A	TP	PIM
1985-86	Seattle	WHL	72	4	8	12	50	5	0	3	3	12
1986-87	Seattle	WHL	67	13	45	58	155	....	....	....	....	....
1987-88	**Pittsburgh**	**NHL**	**17**	**0**	**4**	**4**	**12**	....	....	....	....	....
	Seattle	WHL	23	5	14	19	49	....	....	....	....	....
	Edmonton	**NHL**	**7**	**0**	**4**	**4**	**6**	....	....	....	....	....
	Nova Scotia	AHL	8	0	2	2	8	4	0	0	0	9
1988-89	**Edmonton**	**NHL**	**44**	**4**	**5**	**9**	**54**	....	....	....	....	....
	Cape Breton	AHL	5	1	1	2	18	....	....	....	....	....
1989-90	**Edmonton**	**NHL**	**4**	**0**	**2**	**2**	**2**	....	....	....	....	....
	Cape Breton	AHL	61	10	20	30	69	6	2	1	3	4
1990-91	**Edmonton**	**NHL**	**49**	**5**	**17**	**22**	**59**	....	....	....	....	....
1991-92	**Edmonton**	**NHL**	**7**	**0**	**0**	**0**	**8**	**5**	**1**	**3**	**4**	**2**
	Cape Breton	AHL	63	14	29	43	72	5	0	2	2	8
	NHL Totals		**128**	**9**	**32**	**41**	**141**	**5**	**1**	**3**	**4**	**2**

Traded to **Edmonton** by **Pittsburgh** with Craig Simpson, Dave Hannan and Moe Mantha for Paul Coffey, Dave Hunter and Wayne Van Dorp, November 24, 1987.

JOSEPH, FABIAN

Center. Shoots left. 5'8", 170 lbs. Born, Sydney, N.S., December 5, 1965.
(Toronto's 5th choice, 109th overall, in 1984 Entry Draft).

			Regular Season					Playoffs				
Season	Club	Lea	GP	G	A	TP	PIM	GP	G	A	TP	PIM
1982-83	Victoria	WHL	69	42	48	90	50	12	4	7	11	9
1983-84	Victoria	WHL	72	52	75	127	27	....	....	....	....	....
1984-85	Toronto	OHL	60	32	43	75	16	5	2	4	6	14
1985-86	Cdn. Olympic	....	71	26	18	44	51	....	....	....	....	....
1986-87	Cdn. Olympic	....	74	15	30	45	26	....	....	....	....	....
1987-88	Nova Scotia	AHL	77	31	39	70	20	5	0	3	3	8
1988-89	Cape Breton	AHL	70	32	34	66	30	....	....	....	....	....
1989-90	Cape Breton	AHL	77	33	53	86	46	6	0	3	3	4
1990-91	Brunico	Italy	36	30	54	84	10	6	7	11	18	2
1991-92	Cdn. National	....	62	17	22	39	29	....	....	....	....	....
	Cdn. Olympic	....	8	2	1	3	2	....	....	....	....	....

Signed as a free agent by **Edmonton**, 1987.

JOYCE, DUANE

Defense. Shoots right. 6'2", 203 lbs. Born, Pembroke, MA, May 5, 1965.

			Regular Season					Playoffs				
Season	Club	Lea	GP	G	A	TP	PIM	GP	G	A	TP	PIM
1989-90	Kalamazoo	IHL	2	0	0	0	2	....	....	....	....	....
	Fort Wayne	IHL	66	10	26	36	53	....	....	....	....	....
	Muskegon	IHL	13	3	10	13	8	12	3	7	10	13
1990-91	Kalamazoo	IHL	80	12	32	44	53	11	0	3	3	6
1991-92	Kansas City	IHL	80	12	32	44	62	15	6	11	17	8

Signed as a free agent by **San Jose**, August 13, 1991.

JOYCE, JOHN

Center. Shoots right. 6'3", 185 lbs. Born, Wilbraham, MA, November 23, 1970.
(NY Islanders' 8th choice, 174th overall, in 1990 Entry Draft).

			Regular Season					Playoffs				
Season	Club	Lea	GP	G	A	TP	PIM	GP	G	A	TP	PIM
1990-91	Boston College	H.E.	18	1	4	5	6	....	....	....	....	....
1991-92	Boston College	H.E.	35	9	13	22	32	....	....	....	....	....

JOYCE, ROBERT THOMAS (BOB)

Left wing. Shoots left. 6'1", 195 lbs. Born, St. John, N.B., July 11, 1966.
(Boston's 4th choice, 82nd overall, in 1984 Entry Draft).

			Regular Season					Playoffs				
Season	Club	Lea	GP	G	A	TP	PIM	GP	G	A	TP	PIM
1984-85	North Dakota	WCHA	41	18	16	34	10	....	....	....	....	....
1985-86	North Dakota	WCHA	38	31	28	59	40	....	....	....	....	....
1986-87abc	North Dakota	WCHA	48	52	37	89	42	....	....	....	....	....
1987-88	Cdn. National	....	46	12	10	22	28	....	....	....	....	....
	Cdn. Olympic	....	4	1	0	1	0	....	....	....	....	....
	Boston	**NHL**	**15**	**7**	**5**	**12**	**10**	**23**	**8**	**6**	**14**	**18**
1988-89	**Boston**	**NHL**	**77**	**18**	**31**	**49**	**46**	**9**	**5**	**2**	**7**	**2**
1989-90	**Boston**	**NHL**	**23**	**1**	**2**	**3**	**22**	....	....	....	....	....
	Washington	**NHL**	**24**	**5**	**8**	**13**	**4**	**14**	**2**	**1**	**3**	**9**
1990-91	**Washington**	**NHL**	**17**	**3**	**3**	**6**	**8**	....	....	....	....	....
	Baltimore	AHL	36	10	8	18	14	6	1	0	1	4
1991-92	**Winnipeg**	**NHL**	**1**	**0**	**0**	**0**	**0**	....	....	....	....	....
	Moncton	AHL	66	19	29	48	51	10	0	5	5	9
	NHL Totals		**157**	**34**	**49**	**83**	**90**	**46**	**15**	**9**	**24**	**29**

a WCHA First All-Star Team (1987)
b NCAA West First All-American Team (1987)
c Named to NCAA All-Tournament Team (1987)

Traded to **Washington** by **Boston** for Dave Christian, December 13, 1989. Traded to **Winnipeg** by **Washington** with Tyler Larter and Kent Paynter for Craig Duncanson, Brent Hughes and Simon Wheeldon, May 21, 1991.

JUDSON, RICK

Left wing. Shoots left. 5'11", 180 lbs. Born, Toledo, OH, August 13, 1969.
(Detroit's 11th choice, 204th overall, in 1989 Entry Draft).

			Regular Season					Playoffs				
Season	Club	Lea	GP	G	A	TP	PIM	GP	G	A	TP	PIM
1988-89	Ill.-Chicago	CCHA	42	14	20	34	20	....	....	....	....	....
1989-90	Ill.-Chicago	CCHA	38	19	22	41	18	....	....	....	....	....
1990-91	Ill.-Chicago	CCHA	38	24	26	50	12	....	....	....	....	....
1991-92	Ill.-Chicago	CCHA	35	17	19	36	26	....	....	....	....	....
	Toledo	ECHL	2	1	0	1	2	....	....	....	....	....

JUHLIN, PATRIK (ew-LEEN)

Left wing. Shoots left. 6', 187 lbs. Born, Huddinge, Sweden, April 24, 1970.
(Philadelphia's 2nd choice, 34th overall, in 1989 Entry Draft).

			Regular Season					Playoffs				
Season	Club	Lea	GP	G	A	TP	PIM	GP	G	A	TP	PIM
1987-88	Vasteras	Swe.	28	25	10	35	....	....	....	....	....	....
1988-89	Vasteras	Swe.	30	29	13	42	....	....	....	....	....	....
1989-90	Vasteras	Swe.	35	10	13	23	18	2	0	0	0	0
1990-91	Vasteras	Swe.	40	13	9	22	24	....	....	....	....	....
1991-92	Vasteras	Swe.	39	15	12	27	40	....	....	....	....	....

JUNEAU, JOE

Center. Shoots right. 6', 175 lbs. Born, Pont-Rouge, Que., January 5, 1968.
(Boston's 3rd choice, 81st overall, in 1988 Entry Draft).

			Regular Season					Playoffs				
Season	Club	Lea	GP	G	A	TP	PIM	GP	G	A	TP	PIM
1987-88	RPI	ECAC	31	16	29	45	18	....	....	....	....	....
1988-89	RPI	ECAC	30	12	23	35	40	....	....	....	....	....
1989-90a	RPI	ECAC	34	18	*52	*70	31	....	....	....	....	....
1990-91bc	RPI	ECAC	29	23	40	63	68	....	....	....	....	....
	Cdn. National	....	7	2	3	5	0	....	....	....	....	....
1991-92	Cdn. National	....	60	20	49	69	35	....	....	....	....	....
	Cdn. Olympic	....	8	6	9	15	4	....	....	....	....	....
	Boston	**NHL**	**14**	**5**	**14**	**19**	**4**	**15**	**4**	**8**	**12**	**21**
	NHL Totals		**14**	**5**	**14**	**19**	**4**	**15**	**4**	**8**	**12**	**21**

a NCAA East First All-American Team (1990)
b ECAC Second All-Star Team (1991)
c NCAA East Second All-American Team (1991)

JUNKER, STEVE

Left wing. Shoots left. 6', 184 lbs. Born, Castlegar, B.C., June 26, 1972.
(NY Islanders' 5th choice, 92nd overall, in 1991 Entry Draft).

			Regular Season					Playoffs				
Season	Club	Lea	GP	G	A	TP	PIM	GP	G	A	TP	PIM
1990-91	Spokane	WHL	71	39	38	77	86	15	5	13	18	6
1991-92	Spokane	WHL	58	28	32	60	110	10	6	7	13	18

KACHOWSKI, MARK EDWARD

Left wing. Shoots left. 5'11", 200 lbs. Born, Edmonton, Alta., February 20, 1965.

			Regular Season					Playoffs				
Season	Club	Lea	GP	G	A	TP	PIM	GP	G	A	TP	PIM
1983-84	Kamloops	WHL	57	6	9	15	156	....	....	....	....	....
1984-85	Kamloops	WHL	68	22	15	37	185	....	....	....	....	....
1985-86	Kamloops	WHL	61	21	31	52	182	....	....	....	....	....
1986-87	Flint	IHL	75	18	13	31	273	6	1	1	2	21
1987-88	**Pittsburgh**	**NHL**	**38**	**5**	**3**	**8**	**126**	....	....	....	....	....
	Muskegon	IHL	25	3	6	9	72	5	0	2	2	11
1988-89	**Pittsburgh**	**NHL**	**12**	**1**	**1**	**2**	**43**	....	....	....	....	....
	Muskegon	IHL	57	8	8	16	167	8	1	2	3	17
1989-90	**Pittsburgh**	**NHL**	**14**	**0**	**1**	**1**	**40**	....	....	....	....	....
	Muskegon	IHL	61	23	8	31	129	12	2	4	6	21
1990-91	Muskegon	IHL	80	19	21	40	108	5	1	1	2	9
1991-92	Muskegon	IHL	6	0	0	0	9	4	2	0	2	16
	NHL Totals		**64**	**6**	**5**	**11**	**209**	....	....	....	....	....

Signed as a free agent by **Pittsburgh**, August 31, 1987.

KAISER, KEVIN

Left wing. Shoots left. 6', 185 lbs. Born, Winnipeg, Man., July 26, 1970.
(Quebec's 7th choice, 85th overall, in 1989 Entry Draft).

			Regular Season					Playoffs				
Season	Club	Lea	GP	G	A	TP	PIM	GP	G	A	TP	PIM
1988-89	Minn.-Duluth	WCHA	40	2	5	7	26	....	....	....	....	....
1989-90	Minn.-Duluth	WCHA	39	9	11	20	24	....	....	....	....	....
1990-91	Minn.-Duluth	WCHA	39	15	17	32	57	....	....	....	....	....
1991-92	Minn.-Duluth	WCHA	37	18	19	37	66	....	....	....	....	....

KAMENSKY, VALERI (kah-MEHN-skee)

Left wing. Shoots right. 6'2", 198 lbs. Born, Voskresensk, Soviet Union, April 18, 1966.
(Quebec's 8th choice, 129th overall, in 1988 Entry Draft).

			Regular Season					Playoffs				
Season	Club	Lea	GP	G	A	TP	PIM	GP	G	A	TP	PIM
1982-83	Khimik	USSR	5	0	0	0	0	....	....	....	....	....
1983-84	Khimik	USSR	20	2	2	4	6	....	....	....	....	....
1984-85	Khimik	USSR	45	9	3	12	24	....	....	....	....	....
1985-86	CSKA	USSR	40	15	9	24	8	....	....	....	....	....
1986-87	CSKA	USSR	37	13	8	21	16	....	....	....	....	....
1987-88	CSKA	USSR	51	26	20	46	40	....	....	....	....	....
1988-89	CSKA	USSR	40	18	10	28	30	....	....	....	....	....
1989-90	CSKA	USSR	45	19	18	37	40	....	....	....	....	....
1990-91	CSKA	USSR	46	20	26	46	66	....	....	....	....	....
1991-92	**Quebec**	**NHL**	**23**	**7**	**14**	**21**	**14**	....	....	....	....	....
	NHL Totals		**23**	**7**	**14**	**21**	**14**	....	....	....	....	....

KAMINSKI, KEVIN (kah-MIN-skee)

Center. Shoots left. 5'9", 170 lbs. Born, Churchbridge, Sask., March 13, 1969.
(Minnesota's 3rd choice, 48th overall, in 1987 Entry Draft).

			Regular Season					Playoffs				
Season	Club	Lea	GP	G	A	TP	PIM	GP	G	A	TP	PIM
1986-87	Saskatoon	WHL	67	26	44	70	325	11	5	6	11	45
1987-88	Saskatoon	WHL	55	38	61	99	247	10	5	7	12	37
1988-89	**Minnesota**	**NHL**	**1**	**0**	**0**	**0**	**0**	....	....	....	....	....
	Saskatoon	WHL	52	25	43	68	199	8	4	9	13	25
1989-90	**Quebec**	**NHL**	**1**	**0**	**0**	**0**	**0**	....	....	....	....	....
	Halifax	AHL	19	3	4	7	128	2	0	0	0	5
1990-91	Halifax	AHL	7	1	0	1	44	....	....	....	....	....
	Fort Wayne	IHL	56	9	15	24	*455	19	4	2	6	*169
1991-92	**Quebec**	**NHL**	**5**	**0**	**0**	**0**	**45**	....	....	....	....	....
	Halifax	AHL	63	18	27	45	329	....	....	....	....	....
	NHL Totals		**7**	**0**	**0**	**0**	**45**	....	....	....	....	....

Traded to **Quebec** by **Minnesota** for Gaetan Duchesne, June 19, 1989.

KAMINSKY, YAN

Left wing. Shoots left. 6'2", 176 lbs. Born, Penza, Soviet Union, July 28, 1971.
(Winnipeg's 6th choice, 99th overall, in 1991 Entry Draft).

			Regular Season					Playoffs				
Season	Club	Lea	GP	G	A	TP	PIM	GP	G	A	TP	PIM
1989-90	Moscow D'amo	USSR	6	1	0	1	4	....	....	....	....	....
1990-91	Moscow D'amo	USSR	25	10	5	15	2	....	....	....	....	....
1991-92	Moscow D'amo	CIS	35	8	7	15	22	....	....	....	....	....

KAMPERSAL, JEFFREY

Defense. Shoots right. 6'2", 190 lbs. Born, Beverly, MA, January 27, 1970.
(NY Islanders' 12th choice, 205th overall, in 1988 Entry Draft).

			Regular Season					Playoffs				
Season	Club	Lea	GP	G	A	TP	PIM	GP	G	A	TP	PIM
1988-89	Princeton	ECAC	26	0	3	3	32	....	....	....	....	....
1989-90	Princeton	ECAC	27	3	7	10	26	....	....	....	....	....
1990-91	Princeton	ECAC	27	5	7	12	14	....	....	....	....	....
1991-92	Princeton	ECAC	27	7	10	17	36	....	....	....	....	....

KANE, SHAUN

Defense. Shoots left. 6'3", 195 lbs. Born, Holyoke, MA, February 24, 1970.
(Minnesota's 3rd choice, 43rd overall, in 1988 Entry Draft).

			Regular Season					Playoffs				
Season	Club	Lea	GP	G	A	TP	PIM	GP	G	A	TP	PIM
1988-89	Providence	H.E.	37	2	9	11	54	....	....	....	....	....
1989-90	Providence	H.E.	31	9	8	17	46	....	....	....	....	....
1990-91a	Providence	H.E.	36	5	20	25	86	....	....	....	....	....
1991-92	Providence	H.E.	36	11	11	22	59	....	....	....	....	....

a Hockey East Second All-Star Team (1991)

Claimed by **San Jose** from **Minnesota** in Dispersal Draft, May 30, 1991.

KAPUSTA, THOMAS

Center. Shoots left. 6', 187 lbs. Born, Zlin, Czechoslovakia, February 23, 1967.
(Edmonton's 4th choice, 104th overall, in 1985 Entry Draft).

			Regular Season					Playoffs				
Season	Club	Lea	GP	G	A	TP	PIM	GP	G	A	TP	PIM
1988-89	Dukla Trencin	Czech.	44	8	25	33	....	....	....	....	....	....
1989-90	TJ Zlin	Czech.	16	9	5	14	....	....	....	....	....	....
	Cape Breton	AHL	55	12	37	49	56	6	2	7	9	4
1990-91	Cape Breton	AHL	73	21	46	67	47	4	0	2	2	21
1991-92	Cape Breton	AHL	67	18	33	51	55	5	1	2	3	2

KARABIN, LADISLAV (kar-ah-BIN)

Left wing. Shoots left. 6'1", 189 lbs. Born, Bratislava, Czechoslovakia, February 16, 1970.
(Pittsburgh's 11th choice, 173rd overall, in 1990 Entry Draft).

			Regular Season					Playoffs				
Season	Club	Lea	GP	G	A	TP	PIM	GP	G	A	TP	PIM
1990-91	Bratislava	Czech.	49	21	7	28	57	....	....	....	....	....
1991-92	Bratislava	Czech.	27	4	8	12	....	....	....	....	....	....

KARAMNOV, VITALI (kuh-RAHM-nov)

Left wing. Shoots left. 6'2", 185 lbs. Born, Moscow, Soviet Union, July 6, 1968.
(St. Louis' 2nd choice, 62nd overall, in 1992 Entry Draft).

			Regular Season					Playoffs				
Season	Club	Lea	GP	G	A	TP	PIM	GP	G	A	TP	PIM
1989-90	Torpedo-Yaro.	USSR	47	6	7	13	34	....	....	....	....	....
1990-91	Torpedo-Yaro.	USSR	44	14	8	22	32	....	....	....	....	....
1991-92	Moscow D'amo	CIS	40	13	19	32	25	....	....	....	....	....

KARJALAINEN, KYOSTI (kahr-ya-LAY-nehn)

Right wing. Shoots right. 6'1", 190 lbs. Born, Gavle, Sweden, June 19, 1967.
(Los Angeles' 6th choice, 132nd overall, in 1987 Entry Draft).

			Regular Season					Playoffs				
Season	Club	Lea	GP	G	A	TP	PIM	GP	G	A	TP	PIM
1986-87	Brynas	Swe.	11	3	2	5	0	....	....	....	....	....
1987-88	Brynas	Swe.	20	2	1	3	10	....	....	....	....	....
1988-89	Brynas	Swe.	39	20	17	37	16	....	....	....	....	....
1989-90	Brynas	Swe.	38	17	15	32	16	5	0	3	3	0
1990-91	Phoenix	IHL	70	14	35	49	10	6	2	3	5	6
1991-92	**Los Angeles**	**NHL**	**28**	**1**	**8**	**9**	**12**	**3**	**0**	**1**	**1**	**2**
	Phoenix	IHL	43	14	22	36	30	....	....	....	....	....
	NHL Totals		**28**	**1**	**8**	**9**	**12**	**3**	**0**	**1**	**1**	**2**

KARLSSON, LARS (KAHRL-suhn)

Left wing. Shoots left. 6'3", 194 lbs. Born, Karlstad, Sweden, August 18, 1966.
(Detroit's 7th choice, 152nd overall, in 1984 Entry Draft).

			Regular Season					Playoffs				
Season	Club	Lea	GP	G	A	TP	PIM	GP	G	A	TP	PIM
1986-87	Bjorkloven	Swe.	35	10	24	34	18	....	....	....	....	....
1987-88	Farjestad	Swe.	39	6	13	19	42	....	....	....	....	....
1988-89	Farjestad	Swe.	40	9	9	18	32	2	0	1	1	6
1989-90	Farjestad	Swe.	27	8	5	13	12	10	3	2	5	8
1990-91	Farjestad	Swe.	36	10	6	16	46	....	....	....	....	....
1991-92	Farjestad	Swe.	39	16	17	33	36	6	2	3	5	6

KARPA, DAVE

Defense. Shoots right. 6'1", 190 lbs. Born, Regina, Sask., May 7, 1971.
(Quebec's 4th choice, 68th overall, in 1991 Entry Draft).

			Regular Season					Playoffs				
Season	Club	Lea	GP	G	A	TP	PIM	GP	G	A	TP	PIM
1990-91	Ferris State	CCHA	41	6	19	25	109	....	....	....	....	....
1991-92	Ferris State	CCHA	34	7	12	19	124	....	....	....	....	....
	Quebec	**NHL**	**4**	**0**	**0**	**0**	**14**	....	....	....	....	....
	Halifax	AHL	2	0	0	0	4	....	....	....	....	....
	NHL Totals		**4**	**0**	**0**	**0**	**14**	....	....	....	....	....

KARPOVTSEV, ALEXANDER (kar-POV-tzev)

Defense. Shoots left. 6'2", 189 lbs. Born, Moscow, Soviet Union, April 7, 1970.
(Quebec's 7th choice, 158th overall, in 1990 Entry Draft).

			Regular Season					Playoffs				
Season	Club	Lea	GP	G	A	TP	PIM	GP	G	A	TP	PIM
1989-90	Moscow D'amo	USSR	35	1	1	2	27	....	....	....	....	....
1990-91	Moscow D'amo	USSR	40	0	5	5	15	....	....	....	....	....
1991-92	Moscow D'amo	CIS	35	4	2	6	26	....	....	....	....	....

KASATONOV, ALEXEI (kah-sah-TOH-nahf)

Defense. Shoots left. 6'1", 215 lbs. Born, Leningrad, Soviet Union, October 14, 1959.
(New Jersey's 10th choice, 225th overall, in 1983 Entry Draft).

			Regular Season					Playoffs				
Season	Club	Lea	GP	G	A	TP	PIM	GP	G	A	TP	PIM
1976-77	SKA Leningrad	USSR	7	0	0	0	0	....	....	....	....	....
1977-78	SKA Leningrad	USSR	35	4	7	11	15	....	....	....	....	....
1978-79	CSKA	USSR	40	5	14	19	30	....	....	....	....	....
1979-80a	CSKA	USSR	37	5	8	13	26	....	....	....	....	....
1980-81a	CSKA	USSR	47	10	12	22	38	....	....	....	....	....
1981-82a	CSKA	USSR	46	12	27	39	45	....	....	....	....	....
1982-83a	CSKA	USSR	44	12	19	31	37	....	....	....	....	....
1983-84a	CSKA	USSR	39	12	24	36	20	....	....	....	....	....
1984-85a	CSKA	USSR	40	18	18	36	26	....	....	....	....	....
1985-86a	CSKA	USSR	40	6	17	23	27	....	....	....	....	....
1986-87a	CSKA	USSR	40	13	17	30	16	....	....	....	....	....
1987-88a	CSKA	USSR	43	8	12	20	8	....	....	....	....	....
1988-89	CSKA	USSR	41	8	14	22	8	....	....	....	....	....
1989-90	CSKA	USSR	30	6	7	13	16	....	....	....	....	....
	New Jersey	**NHL**	**39**	**6**	**15**	**21**	**16**	**6**	**0**	**3**	**3**	**14**
	Utica	AHL	3	0	2	2	7	....	....	....	....	....
1990-91	**New Jersey**	**NHL**	**78**	**10**	**31**	**41**	**76**	**7**	**1**	**3**	**4**	**10**
1991-92	**New Jersey**	**NHL**	**76**	**12**	**28**	**40**	**70**	**7**	**1**	**1**	**2**	**12**
	NHL Totals		**193**	**28**	**74**	**102**	**162**	**20**	**2**	**7**	**9**	**36**

a Soviet National League All-Star Team (1980-88)

KASPARAITIS, DARIUS (kahs-pah-RIGH-tis, DAH-roos)

Defense. Shoots left. 5'11", 187 lbs. Born, Elektrenai, Soviet Union, October 16, 1972.
(NY Islanders' 1st choice, 5th overall, in 1992 Entry Draft).

			Regular Season					Playoffs				
Season	Club	Lea	GP	G	A	TP	PIM	GP	G	A	TP	PIM
1990-91	Moscow D'amo	USSR	17	0	1	1	10	....	....	....	....	....
1991-92	Moscow D'amo	CIS	31	2	10	12	14	....	....	....	....	....

KASPER, STEPHEN NEIL (STEVE)

Center. Shoots left. 5'8", 175 lbs. Born, Montreal, Que., September 28, 1961.
(Boston's 3rd choice, 81st overall, in 1980 Entry Draft).

			Regular Season					Playoffs				
Season	Club	Lea	GP	G	A	TP	PIM	GP	G	A	TP	PIM
1978-79	Verdun	QJHL	67	37	67	104	53	11	7	6	13	22
1979-80	Sorel	QJHL	70	57	65	122	117	....	....	....	....	....
1980-81	**Boston**	**NHL**	**76**	**21**	**35**	**56**	**94**	**3**	**0**	**1**	**1**	**0**
1981-82a	**Boston**	**NHL**	**73**	**20**	**31**	**51**	**72**	**11**	**3**	**6**	**9**	**22**
1982-83	**Boston**	**NHL**	**24**	**2**	**6**	**8**	**24**	**12**	**2**	**1**	**3**	**10**
1983-84	**Boston**	**NHL**	**27**	**3**	**11**	**14**	**19**	**3**	**0**	**0**	**0**	**7**
1984-85	**Boston**	**NHL**	**77**	**16**	**24**	**40**	**33**	**5**	**1**	**0**	**1**	**9**
1985-86	**Boston**	**NHL**	**80**	**17**	**23**	**40**	**73**	**3**	**1**	**0**	**1**	**4**
1986-87	**Boston**	**NHL**	**79**	**20**	**30**	**50**	**51**	**3**	**0**	**2**	**2**	**0**
1987-88	**Boston**	**NHL**	**79**	**26**	**44**	**70**	**35**	**23**	**7**	**6**	**13**	**10**
1988-89	**Boston**	**NHL**	**49**	**10**	**16**	**26**	**49**	....	....	....	....	....
	Los Angeles	**NHL**	**29**	**9**	**15**	**24**	**14**	**11**	**1**	**5**	**6**	**10**
1989-90	**Los Angeles**	**NHL**	**77**	**17**	**28**	**45**	**27**	**10**	**1**	**1**	**2**	**2**
1990-91	**Los Angeles**	**NHL**	**67**	**9**	**19**	**28**	**33**	**10**	**4**	**6**	**10**	**8**
1991-92	**Philadelphia**	**NHL**	**16**	**3**	**2**	**5**	**10**	....	....	....	....	....
	NHL Totals		**753**	**173**	**284**	**457**	**534**	**94**	**20**	**28**	**48**	**82**

a Won Frank J. Selke Trophy (1982)

Traded to **Los Angeles** by **Boston** for Bobby Carpenter, January 23, 1989. Traded to **Philadelphia** by **Los Angeles** with Steve Duchesne and Los Angeles' fourth round choice (Aris Brimanis) in 1991 Entry Draft for Jari Kurri and Jeff Chychrun, May 30, 1991.

KASTELIC, EDWARD (ED) (KAS-tuh-lihk)

Right/Left wing. Shoots right. 6'4", 215 lbs. Born, Toronto, Ont., January 29, 1964.
(Washington's 4th choice, 110th overall, in 1982 Entry Draft).

			Regular Season					Playoffs				
Season	Club	Lea	GP	G	A	TP	PIM	GP	G	A	TP	PIM
1981-82	London	OHL	68	5	18	23	63	4	0	1	1	4
1982-83	London	OHL	68	12	11	23	96	3	0	0	0	5
1983-84	London	OHL	68	17	16	33	218	8	0	2	2	41
1984-85	Moncton	AHL	62	5	11	16	187	....	....	....	....	....
	Binghamton	AHL	4	0	0	0	7	....	....	....	....	....
	Fort Wayne	IHL	5	1	0	1	37	....	....	....	....	....
1985-86	**Washington**	**NHL**	**15**	**0**	**0**	**0**	**73**	....	....	....	....	....
	Binghamton	AHL	23	7	9	16	76	....	....	....	....	....
1986-87	**Washington**	**NHL**	**23**	**1**	**1**	**2**	**83**	**5**	**1**	**0**	**1**	**13**
	Binghamton	AHL	48	17	11	28	124	....	....	....	....	....
1987-88	**Washington**	**NHL**	**35**	**1**	**0**	**1**	**78**	**1**	**0**	**0**	**0**	**19**
	Binghamton	AHL	6	4	1	5	6	....	....	....	....	....
1988-89	**Hartford**	**NHL**	**10**	**0**	**2**	**2**	**15**	....	....	....	....	....
	Binghamton	AHL	35	9	6	15	124	....	....	....	....	....
1989-90	**Hartford**	**NHL**	**67**	**6**	**2**	**8**	**198**	**2**	**0**	**0**	**0**	**0**
1990-91	**Hartford**	**NHL**	**45**	**2**	**2**	**4**	**211**	....	....	....	....	....
1991-92	**Hartford**	**NHL**	**25**	**1**	**3**	**4**	**61**	....	....	....	....	....
	NHL Totals		**220**	**11**	**10**	**21**	**719**	**8**	**1**	**0**	**1**	**32**

Traded to **Hartford** by **Washington** with Grant Jennings for Mike Millar and Neil Sheehy, July 6, 1988.

KAUTONEN, VELI-PEKKA (KAH-uh-toh-nehn)

Defense. Shoots right. 6'2", 200 lbs. Born, Helsinki, Finland, May 9, 1970.
(Calgary's 3rd choice, 50th overall, in 1989 Entry Draft).

			Regular Season					Playoffs				
Season	Club	Lea	GP	G	A	TP	PIM	GP	G	A	TP	PIM
1987-88	HIFK	Fin.	35	9	11	20	....	....	....	....	....	....
1988-89	HIFK	Fin.	36	4	5	9	....	....	....	....	....	....
1989-90	HIFK	Fin.	36	2	1	3	10	2	0	0	0	0
1990-91	SaiPa	Fin.	43	12	19	31	36	....	....	....	....	....
1991-92	Tappara	Fin.	44	6	12	18	30	....	....	....	....	....

KEANE, MIKE

Right wing. Shoots right. 5'10", 178 lbs. Born, Winnipeg, Man., May 29, 1967.

			Regular Season					Playoffs				
Season	Club	Lea	GP	G	A	TP	PIM	GP	G	A	TP	PIM
1984-85	Moose Jaw	WHL	65	17	26	43	141	....	....	....	....	....
1985-86	Moose Jaw	WHL	67	34	49	83	162	13	6	8	14	9
1986-87	Moose Jaw	WHL	53	25	45	70	107	9	3	9	12	11
	Sherbrooke	AHL	....	....	....	....	....	9	2	2	4	16
1987-88	Sherbrooke	AHL	78	25	43	68	70	6	1	1	2	18
1988-89	**Montreal**	**NHL**	**69**	**16**	**19**	**35**	**69**	**21**	**4**	**3**	**7**	**17**
1989-90	**Montreal**	**NHL**	**74**	**9**	**15**	**24**	**78**	**11**	**0**	**1**	**1**	**8**
1990-91	**Montreal**	**NHL**	**73**	**13**	**23**	**36**	**50**	**12**	**3**	**2**	**5**	**6**
1991-92	**Montreal**	**NHL**	**67**	**11**	**30**	**41**	**64**	**8**	**1**	**1**	**2**	**16**
	NHL Totals		**283**	**49**	**87**	**136**	**261**	**52**	**8**	**7**	**15**	**47**

Signed as a free agent by **Montreal**, September 25, 1985.

KEARNEY, FRANCIS (TOBY)

Left wing. Shoots left. 6'2", 185 lbs. Born, Newburyport, MA, September 2, 1970.
(Calgary's 7th choice, 105th overall, in 1989 Entry Draft).

			Regular Season					Playoffs				
Season	Club	Lea	GP	G	A	TP	PIM	GP	G	A	TP	PIM
1989-90	U. of Vermont	ECAC	25	2	3	5	24	....	....	....	....	....
1990-91	U. of Vermont	ECAC	33	8	11	19	16	....	....	....	....	....
1991-92	U. of Vermont	ECAC	31	6	11	17	56	....	....	....	....	....

KECZMER, DAN

Defense. Shoots left. 6'1", 190 lbs. Born, Mt. Clemens, MI, May 25, 1968.
(Minnesota's 11th choice, 201st overall, in 1986 Entry Draft).

			Regular Season					Playoffs				
Season	Club	Lea	GP	G	A	TP	PIM	GP	G	A	TP	PIM
1986-87	Lake Superior	CCHA	38	3	5	8	26	....	....	....	....	....
1987-88	Lake Superior	CCHA	41	2	15	17	34	....	....	....	....	....
1988-89	Lake Superior	CCHA	46	3	26	29	68	....	....	....	....	....
1989-90a	Lake Superior	CCHA	43	13	23	36	48	....	....	....	....	....
1990-91	**Minnesota**	**NHL**	**9**	**0**	**1**	**1**	**6**	....	....	....	....	....
	Kalamazoo	IHL	60	4	20	24	60	9	1	2	3	10
1991-92	U.S. National	....	51	3	11	14	56	....	....	....	....	....
	Hartford	**NHL**	**1**	**0**	**0**	**0**	**0**	....	....	....	....	....
	Springfield	AHL	18	3	4	7	10	4	0	0	0	6
	NHL Totals		**10**	**0**	**1**	**1**	**6**	....	....	....	....	....

a CCHA Second All-Star Team (1990)

Claimed by **San Jose** from **Minnesota** in Dispersal Draft, May 30, 1991. Traded to **Hartford** by **San Jose** for Dean Evason, October 2, 1991.

KEKALAINEN, JARMO (kee-kuh-LAY-nehn, YAHR-moh)

Left wing. Shoots right. 6', 190 lbs. Born, Tampere, Finland, July 3, 1966.

			Regular Season					Playoffs				
Season	Club	Lea	GP	G	A	TP	PIM	GP	G	A	TP	PIM
1987-88	Clarkson	ECAC	32	7	11	18	38	....	....	....	....	....
1988-89	Clarkson	ECAC	31	19	25	44	47	....	....	....	....	....
1989-90	**Boston**	**NHL**	**11**	**2**	**2**	**4**	**8**	....	....	....	....	....
	Maine	AHL	18	5	11	16	6	....	....	....	....	....
1990-91	**Boston**	**NHL**	**16**	**2**	**1**	**3**	**6**	....	....	....	....	....
	Maine	AHL	11	2	4	6	4	1	0	1	1	0
1991-92	KalPa	Fin.	24	2	8	10	24	....	....	....	....	....
	NHL Totals		**27**	**4**	**3**	**7**	**14**	....	....	....	....	....

Signed as a free agent by **Boston**, May 3, 1989.

KELLEY, ROBERT

Left wing. Shoots left. 6'2", 205 lbs. Born, Cambridge, MA, February 10, 1969.
(Montreal's 9th choice, 143rd overall, in 1987 Entry Draft).

			Regular Season					Playoffs				
Season	Club	Lea	GP	G	A	TP	PIM	GP	G	A	TP	PIM
1990-91	Merrimack	H.E.	7	1	1	2	12	....	....	....	....	....
1991-92	Merrimack	H.E.	27	10	7	17	30	....	....	....	....	....

KELLOGG, BOB

Defense. Shoots left. 6'4", 210 lbs. Born, Springfield, MA, February 16, 1971.
(Chicago's 3rd choice, 48th overall, in 1989 Entry Draft).

			Regular Season					Playoffs				
Season	Club	Lea	GP	G	A	TP	PIM	GP	G	A	TP	PIM
1989-90	Northeastern	H.E.	36	3	12	15	30	....	....	....	....	....
1990-91	Northeastern	H.E.	2	0	0	0	6	....	....	....	....	....
1991-92	Northeastern	H.E.	27	2	3	5	34	....	....	....	....	....

KENADY, CHRISTOPHER

Right wing. Shoots right. 6'2", 192 lbs. Born, Mound, MN, April 10, 1973.
(St. Louis' 8th choice, 175th overall, in 1991 Entry Draft).

			Regular Season					Playoffs				
Season	Club	Lea	GP	G	A	TP	PIM	GP	G	A	TP	PIM
1990-91	St. Paul	USHL	45	16	20	36	57	....	....	....	....	....
1991-92	U. of Denver	WCHA	36	8	5	13	56	....	....	....	....	....

KENNEDY, EDWARD (DEAN)

Defense. Shoots right. 6'2", 205 lbs. Born, Redvers, Sask., January 18, 1963.
(Los Angeles' 2nd choice, 39th overall, in 1981 Entry Draft).

			Regular Season					Playoffs				
Season	Club	Lea	GP	G	A	TP	PIM	GP	G	A	TP	PIM
1980-81	Brandon	WHL	71	3	29	32	157	5	0	2	2	7
1981-82	Brandon	WHL	49	5	38	43	103	....	....	....	....	....
1982-83	**Los Angeles**	**NHL**	**55**	**0**	**12**	**12**	**97**	....	....	....	....	....
	Brandon	WHL	14	2	15	17	22	....	....	....	....	....
	Saskatoon	WHL	....	....	....	....	....	4	0	3	3	0
1983-84	**Los Angeles**	**NHL**	**37**	**1**	**5**	**6**	**50**	....	....	....	....	....
	New Haven	AHL	26	1	7	8	23	....	....	....	....	....
1984-85	New Haven	AHL	76	3	14	17	104	....	....	....	....	....
1985-86	**Los Angeles**	**NHL**	**78**	**2**	**10**	**12**	**132**	....	....	....	....	....
1986-87	**Los Angeles**	**NHL**	**66**	**6**	**14**	**20**	**91**	**5**	**0**	**2**	**2**	**10**
1987-88	**Los Angeles**	**NHL**	**58**	**1**	**11**	**12**	**158**	**4**	**0**	**1**	**1**	**10**
1988-89	**NY Rangers**	**NHL**	**16**	**0**	**1**	**1**	**40**	....	....	....	....	....
	Los Angeles	**NHL**	**51**	**3**	**10**	**13**	**63**	**11**	**0**	**2**	**2**	**8**
1989-90	**Buffalo**	**NHL**	**80**	**2**	**12**	**14**	**53**	**6**	**1**	**1**	**2**	**12**
1990-91	**Buffalo**	**NHL**	**64**	**4**	**8**	**12**	**119**	**2**	**0**	**1**	**1**	**17**
1991-92	**Winnipeg**	**NHL**	**18**	**2**	**4**	**6**	**21**	**2**	**0**	**0**	**0**	**0**
	NHL Totals		**523**	**21**	**87**	**108**	**824**	**30**	**1**	**7**	**8**	**57**

Traded to **NY Rangers** by **Los Angeles** with Denis Larocque for Igor Liba, Michael Boyce, Todd Elik and future considerations, December 12, 1988. Traded to **Los Angeles** by **NY Rangers** for Los Angeles' fourth round choice – later traded to Minnesota (Cal McGowan) – in 1990 Entry Draft, February 3, 1989. Traded to **Buffalo** by **Los Angeles** for Buffalo's fourth round choice (Keith Redmond) in 1991 Entry Draft, October 4, 1989. Traded to **Winnipeg** by **Buffalo** with Darrin Shannon and Mike Hartman for Dave McLlwain, Gord Donnelly, Winnipeg's fifth round choice (Yuri Khmylev) in 1992 Entry Draft and future considerations, October 11, 1991.

KENNEDY, MIKE

Left wing. Shoots right. 6'1", 170 lbs. Born, Vancouver, B.C., April 13, 1972.
(Minnesota's 5th choice, 97th overall, in 1991 Entry Draft).

			Regular Season					Playoffs				
Season	Club	Lea	GP	G	A	TP	PIM	GP	G	A	TP	PIM
1989-90	U.B.C.	CIAU	9	5	7	12	0	....	....	....	....	....
1990-91	U.B.C.	CIAU	28	17	17	34	18	....	....	....	....	....
1991-92	Seattle	WHL	71	42	47	89	134	15	11	6	17	20

KENNEDY, SHELDON

Right wing. Shoots right. 5'11", 175 lbs. Born, Brandon, Man., June 15, 1969.
(Detroit's 5th choice, 80th overall, in 1988 Entry Draft).

			Regular Season					Playoffs				
Season	Club	Lea	GP	G	A	TP	PIM	GP	G	A	TP	PIM
1986-87	Swift Current	WHL	49	23	41	64	43	4	0	3	3	4
1987-88	Swift Current	WHL	59	53	64	117	45	10	8	9	17	12
1988-89	Swift Current	WHL	51	58	48	106	92	12	9	15	24	22
1989-90	**Detroit**	**NHL**	**20**	**2**	**7**	**9**	**10**	....	....	....	....	....
	Adirondack	AHL	26	11	15	26	35	....	....	....	....	....
1990-91	**Detroit**	**NHL**	**7**	**1**	**0**	**1**	**12**	....	....	....	....	....
	Adirondack	AHL	11	1	3	4	8	....	....	....	....	....
1991-92	**Detroit**	**NHL**	**27**	**3**	**8**	**11**	**24**	....	....	....	....	....
	Adirondack	AHL	46	25	24	49	56	16	5	9	14	12
	NHL Totals		**54**	**6**	**15**	**21**	**46**	....	....	....	....	....

KENNHOLT, KENNETH

Defense. Shoots right. 6'3", 191 lbs. Born, Stockholm, Sweden, January 13, 1965.
(Calgary's 13th choice, 252nd overall, in 1989 Entry Draft).

			Regular Season					Playoffs				
Season	Club	Lea	GP	G	A	TP	PIM	GP	G	A	TP	PIM
1988-89	Djurgarden	Swe.	34	6	10	16	30	....	....	....	....	....
1989-90	Djurgarden	Swe.	38	7	10	17	30	7	2	2	4	2
1990-91	Djurgarden	Swe.	39	9	13	22	30	....	....	....	....	....
1991-92	Djurgarden	Swe.	33	4	7	11	22	10	2	4	6	10

KERR, ALAN

Right wing. Shoots right. 5'11", 195 lbs. Born, Hazelton, B.C., March 28, 1964.
(NY Islanders' 4th choice, 84th overall, in 1982 Entry Draft).

			Regular Season					Playoffs				
Season	Club	Lea	GP	G	A	TP	PIM	GP	G	A	TP	PIM
1981-82	Seattle	WHL	68	15	18	33	107	10	6	6	12	32
1982-83	Seattle	WHL	71	38	53	91	183	4	2	3	5	0
1983-84a	Seattle	WHL	66	46	66	112	141	5	1	4	5	12
1984-85	**NY Islanders**	**NHL**	**19**	**3**	**1**	**4**	**24**	**4**	**1**	**0**	**1**	**4**
	Springfield	AHL	62	32	27	59	140	4	1	2	3	2
1985-86	**NY Islanders**	**NHL**	**7**	**0**	**1**	**1**	**16**	**1**	**0**	**0**	**0**	**0**
	Springfield	AHL	71	35	36	71	127	....	....	....	....	....
1986-87	**NY Islanders**	**NHL**	**72**	**7**	**10**	**17**	**175**	**14**	**1**	**4**	**5**	**25**
1987-88	**NY Islanders**	**NHL**	**80**	**24**	**34**	**58**	**198**	**6**	**1**	**0**	**1**	**14**
1988-89	**NY Islanders**	**NHL**	**71**	**20**	**18**	**38**	**144**	....	....	....	....	....
1989-90	**NY Islanders**	**NHL**	**75**	**15**	**21**	**36**	**129**	**4**	**0**	**0**	**0**	**10**
1990-91	**NY Islanders**	**NHL**	**2**	**0**	**0**	**0**	**5**	....	....	....	....	....
	Capital Dist.	AHL	43	11	21	32	131	....	....	....	....	....
1991-92	**Detroit**	**NHL**	**58**	**3**	**8**	**11**	**133**	**9**	**2**	**0**	**2**	**17**
	NHL Totals		**384**	**72**	**93**	**165**	**824**	**38**	**5**	**4**	**9**	**70**

a WHL First All-Star Team, West Division (1984)

Traded to **Detroit** by **NY Islanders** with future considerations for Rick Green, May 26, 1991.

KERR, TIM

Center/Right wing. Shoots right. 6'3", 230 lbs. Born, Windsor, Ont., January 5, 1960.

			Regular Season					Playoffs				
Season	Club	Lea	GP	G	A	TP	PIM	GP	G	A	TP	PIM
1978-79	Kingston	OHA	57	17	25	42	27	6	1	1	2	2
1979-80	Kingston	OHA	63	40	33	73	39	3	0	1	1	16
	Maine	AHL	7	2	4	6	2	....	....	....	....	....
1980-81	**Philadelphia**	**NHL**	**68**	**22**	**23**	**45**	**84**	**10**	**1**	**3**	**4**	**2**
1981-82	**Philadelphia**	**NHL**	**61**	**21**	**30**	**51**	**138**	**4**	**0**	**2**	**2**	**2**
1982-83	**Philadelphia**	**NHL**	**24**	**11**	**8**	**19**	**6**	**2**	**2**	**0**	**2**	**0**
1983-84	**Philadelphia**	**NHL**	**79**	**54**	**39**	**93**	**29**	**3**	**0**	**0**	**0**	**0**
1984-85	**Philadelphia**	**NHL**	**74**	**54**	**44**	**98**	**57**	**12**	**10**	**4**	**14**	**13**
1985-86	**Philadelphia**	**NHL**	**76**	**58**	**26**	**84**	**79**	**5**	**3**	**3**	**6**	**8**
1986-87a	**Philadelphia**	**NHL**	**75**	**58**	**37**	**95**	**57**	**12**	**8**	**5**	**13**	**2**
1987-88	**Philadelphia**	**NHL**	**8**	**3**	**2**	**5**	**12**	**6**	**1**	**3**	**4**	**4**
1988-89b	**Philadelphia**	**NHL**	**69**	**48**	**40**	**88**	**73**	**19**	**14**	**11**	**25**	**27**
1989-90	**Philadelphia**	**NHL**	**40**	**24**	**24**	**48**	**34**	....	....	....	....	....
1990-91	**Philadelphia**	**NHL**	**27**	**10**	**14**	**24**	**8**	....	....	....	....	....
1991-92	**NY Rangers**	**NHL**	**32**	**7**	**11**	**18**	**12**	**8**	**1**	**0**	**1**	**0**
	NHL Totals		**633**	**370**	**298**	**668**	**589**	**81**	**40**	**31**	**71**	**58**

a NHL Second All-Star Team (1987)
b Won Bill Masterton Award (1989)

Played in NHL All-Star Game (1984-86)

Signed as a free agent by **Philadelphia**, October 25, 1979. Claimed by **San Jose** from **Philadelphia** in Expansion Draft, May 30, 1991. Traded to **NY Rangers** by **San Jose** for Brian Mullen and future considerations, May 30, 1991. Traded to **Hartford** by **NY Rangers** for future considerations, July 9, 1992.

KESA, DANNY

Right wing. Shoots right. 5'11", 208 lbs. Born, Vancouver, B.C., November 23, 1971.
(Vancouver's 5th choice, 95th overall, in 1991 Entry Draft).

			Regular Season					Playoffs				
Season	Club	Lea	GP	G	A	TP	PIM	GP	G	A	TP	PIM
1990-91	Prince Albert	WHL	69	30	23	53	116	3	1	1	2	0
1991-92	Prince Albert	WHL	62	46	51	97	201	10	9	10	19	27

KESKINEN, ESA (KEHS-kee-nehn)

Center. Shoots right. 5'9", 191 lbs. Born, Ylojarvi, Finland, February 3, 1965.
(Calgary's 6th choice, 101st overall, in 1985 Entry Draft).

			Regular Season					Playoffs				
Season	Club	Lea	GP	G	A	TP	PIM	GP	G	A	TP	PIM
1986-87	TPS	Fin.	46	25	36	61	4	5	1	1	2	0
1987-88	TPS	Fin.	44	14	55	69	14	....	....	....	....	....
1988-89	Lukko	Fin.	41	24	46	70	12	....	....	....	....	....
1989-90	Lukko	Fin.	44	25	26	51	16	....	....	....	....	....
1990-91	Lukko	Fin.	44	17	51	68	14	....	....	....	....	....
1991-92	TPS	Fin.	44	24	45	69	12	3	1	1	2	0

KETTELHUT, MARK

Defense. Shoots left. 6', 195 lbs. Born, Duluth, MN, November 2, 1971.
(Montreal's 11th choice, 207th overall, in 1990 Entry Draft).

			Regular Season					Playoffs				
Season	Club	Lea	GP	G	A	TP	PIM	GP	G	A	TP	PIM
1989-90	Duluth East	HS	24	10	19	29	....	....	....	....	....	....
1990-91						DID NOT PLAY						
1991-92	St. Paul	USHL	40	9	6	15	93	....	....	....	....	....

KHARIN, SERGEI (HAH-reen)

Right wing. Shoots left. 5'11", 180 lbs. Born, Odintsovo, Soviet Union, February 20, 1963.
(Winnipeg's 15th choice, 240th overall, in 1989 Entry Draft).

			Regular Season					Playoffs				
Season	Club	Lea	GP	G	A	TP	PIM	GP	G	A	TP	PIM
1980-81	Soviet Wings	USSR	2	0	0	0	0	....	....	....	....	....
1981-82	Soviet Wings	USSR	34	4	3	7	10	....	....	....	....	....
1982-83	Soviet Wings	USSR	49	5	5	10	20	....	....	....	....	....
1983-84	Soviet Wings	USSR	33	5	3	8	18	....	....	....	....	....
1984-85	Soviet Wings	USSR	34	12	8	20	6	....	....	....	....	....
1985-86	Soviet Wings	USSR	38	15	14	29	19	....	....	....	....	....
1986-87	Soviet Wings	USSR	40	16	11	27	14	....	....	....	....	....
1987-88	Soviet Wings	USSR	45	17	13	30	20	....	....	....	....	....
1988-89	Soviet Wings	USSR	44	15	9	24	14	....	....	....	....	....
1989-90	Soviet Wings	USSR	47	12	5	17	28	....	....	....	....	....
1990-91	**Winnipeg**	**NHL**	**7**	**2**	**3**	**5**	**2**	....	....	....	....	....
	Moncton	AHL	66	22	18	40	38	5	1	0	1	2
1991-92	Halifax	AHL	40	10	12	22	15	....	....	....	....	....
	NHL Totals		**7**	**2**	**3**	**5**	**2**	....	....	....	....	....

Traded to **Quebec** by **Winnipeg** for Shawn Anderson, October 22, 1991.

KHMYLEV, YURI (kheh-meh-LUHV)

Left wing. Shoots right. 6'1", 196 lbs. Born, Moscow, Soviet Union, August 9, 1964.
(Buffalo's 7th choice, 108th overall, in 1992 Entry Draft).

			Regular Season					Playoffs				
Season	Club	Lea	GP	G	A	TP	PIM	GP	G	A	TP	PIM
1990-91	Soviet Wings	USSR	45	25	14	39	26	....	....	....	....	....
1991-92	Soviet Wings	CIS	42	19	17	36	20	....	....	....	....	....

KHOMUTOV, ANDREI (hoh-moo-TAHF)

Right wing. Shoots left. 5'10", 176 lbs. Born, Yaroslavl, Soviet Union, April 21, 1961.
(Quebec's 12th choice, 190th overall, in 1989 Entry Draft).

			Regular Season					Playoffs				
Season	Club	Lea	GP	G	A	TP	PIM	GP	G	A	TP	PIM
1979-80	CSKA	USSR	4	0	0	0	0	....	....	....	....	....
1980-81	CSKA	USSR	43	23	18	41	4	....	....	....	....	....
1981-82	CSKA	USSR	44	17	13	30	12	....	....	....	....	....
1982-83	CSKA	USSR	44	21	17	38	6	....	....	....	....	....
1983-84	CSKA	USSR	39	17	9	26	14	....	....	....	....	....
1984-85	CSKA	USSR	37	21	13	34	18	....	....	....	....	....
1985-86	CSKA	USSR	38	14	15	29	10	....	....	....	....	....
1986-87	CSKA	USSR	33	15	18	33	22	....	....	....	....	....
1987-88	CSKA	USSR	48	29	14	43	22	....	....	....	....	....
1988-89	CSKA	USSR	44	19	16	35	14	....	....	....	....	....
1989-90a	CSKA	USSR	47	21	14	35	16	....	....	....	....	....
1990-91	Fribourg	Switz.	36	39	43	82	....	....	13	12	25	....
1991-92	Fribourg	Switz.	35	32	47	79	34	....	....	....	....	....

a Soviet Player of the Year (1990)

KHRISTICH, DIMITRI (kris-tich)

Left wing/Center. Shoots right. 6'2", 195 lbs. Born, Kiev, Soviet Union, July 23, 1969.
(Washington's 6th choice, 120th overall, in 1988 Entry Draft).

			Regular Season					Playoffs				
Season	Club	Lea	GP	G	A	TP	PIM	GP	G	A	TP	PIM
1987-88	Sokol Kiev	USSR	37	9	1	10	18	....	....	....	....	....
1988-89	Sokol Kiev	USSR	42	17	10	27	15	....	....	....	....	....
1989-90	Sokol Kiev	USSR	47	14	22	36	32	....	....	....	....	....
1990-91	Sokol Kiev	USSR	28	10	12	22	20	....	....	....	....	....
	Washington	**NHL**	**40**	**13**	**14**	**27**	**21**	**11**	**1**	**3**	**4**	**6**
	Baltimore	AHL	3	0	0	0	0	....	....	....	....	....
1991-92	**Washington**	**NHL**	**80**	**36**	**37**	**73**	**35**	**7**	**3**	**2**	**5**	**15**
	NHL Totals		**120**	**49**	**51**	**100**	**56**	**18**	**4**	**5**	**9**	**21**

KIDD, IAN

Defense. Shoots right. 5'11", 195 lbs. Born, Gresham, OR, May 11, 1964.

			Regular Season					Playoffs				
Season	Club	Lea	GP	G	A	TP	PIM	GP	G	A	TP	PIM
1985-86	North Dakota	WCHA	37	6	16	22	65	....	....	....	....	....
1986-87	North Dakota	WCHA	47	13	47	60	58	....	....	....	....	....
1987-88	**Vancouver**	**NHL**	**19**	**4**	**7**	**11**	**25**	....	....	....	....	....
	Fredericton	AHL	53	1	21	22	70	12	0	4	4	22
1988-89	**Vancouver**	**NHL**	**1**	**0**	**0**	**0**	**0**	....	....	....	....	....
	Milwaukee	IHL	76	13	40	53	124	4	0	2	2	7
1989-90	Milwaukee	IHL	65	11	36	47	86	6	2	5	7	0
1990-91	Milwaukee	IHL	72	5	26	31	41	6	0	1	1	2
1991-92	Milwaukee	IHL	80	9	24	33	75	5	0	1	1	11
	NHL Totals		**20**	**4**	**7**	**11**	**25**	....	....	....	....	....

Signed as a free agent by **Vancouver**, July 30, 1987.

KIENASS, TORSTEN

Defense. Shoots left. 6'2", 175 lbs. Born, Berlin, East Germany, April 14, 1973.
(Boston's 11th choice, 260th overall, in 1991 Entry Draft).

			Regular Season					Playoffs				
Season	Club	Lea	GP	G	A	TP	PIM	GP	G	A	TP	PIM
1990-91	Dynamo Berlin	Ger.	27	1	1	2	19	....	....	....	....	....
1991-92	Dynamo Berlin	Ger.2	45	8	6	14	33	....	....	....	....	....

KIENE, CHRIS (KEEN)

Defense. Shoots left. 6'5", 220 lbs. Born, So. Windsor, CT, March 6, 1966.
(New Jersey's 12th choice, 231st overall, in 1984 Entry Draft).

			Regular Season					Playoffs				
Season	Club	Lea	GP	G	A	TP	PIM	GP	G	A	TP	PIM
1987-88	Merrimack	NCAA	40	6	34	40	72	....	....	....	....	....
1988-89	Merrimack	NCAA	32	3	25	28	76	....	....	....	....	....
1989-90	Utica	AHL	67	5	17	22	60	1	0	0	0	2
1990-91	Johnstown	ECHL	3	0	0	0	0	....	....	....	....	....
1991-92	Moncton	AHL	5	0	0	0	11	....	....	....	....	....

KILSTROM, MATS (CHEEL-struhm)

Defense. Shoots right. 6'2", 198 lbs. Born, Ludvika, Sweden, January 3, 1964.
(Calgary's 8th choice, 118th overall, in 1982 Entry Draft).

			Regular Season					Playoffs				
Season	Club	Lea	GP	G	A	TP	PIM	GP	G	A	TP	PIM
1981-82	Sodertalje	Swe.	25	2	3	5	20	....	....	....	....	....
1982-83	Sodertalje	Swe.	17	5	0	5	35	11	1	3	4	12
1983-84	Sodertalje	Swe.	25	4	3	7	25	3	1	0	1	0
1984-85	Brynas	Swe.	35	4	9	13	14	....	....	....	....	....
1985-86	Brynas	Swe.	35	3	8	11	48	3	1	0	1	4
1986-87	Sodertalje	Swe.	32	2	4	6	28	....	....	....	....	....
1987-88	Sodertalje	Swe.	37	5	7	12	36	2	0	2	2	0
1988-89	Sodertalje	Swe.	39	3	19	22	45	....	....	....	....	....
1989-90	Sodertalje	Swe.	37	7	16	23	26	2	0	1	1	5
1990-91	Sodertalje	Swe.	29	4	10	14	40	....	....	....	....	....
1991-92	Sodertalje	Swe.	19	1	4	5	10	....	....	....	....	....

KIMBLE, DARIN

Right wing. Shoots right. 6'2", 205 lbs. Born, Lucky Lake, Sask., November 22, 1968.
(Quebec's 5th choice, 66th overall, in 1988 Entry Draft).

			Regular Season					Playoffs				
Season	Club	Lea	GP	G	A	TP	PIM	GP	G	A	TP	PIM
1985-86	Calgary	WHL	37	14	8	22	93	....	....	....	....	....
	N. Westminster	WHL	11	1	1	2	22	....	....	....	....	....
	Brandon	WHL	15	1	6	7	39	....	....	....	....	....
1986-87	Prince Albert	WHL	68	17	13	30	190	....	....	....	....	....
1987-88	Prince Albert	WHL	67	35	36	71	307	10	3	2	5	4
1988-89	**Quebec**	**NHL**	**26**	**3**	**1**	**4**	**154**	....	....	....	....	....
	Halifax	AHL	39	8	6	14	188	....	....	....	....	....
1989-90	**Quebec**	**NHL**	**44**	**5**	**5**	**10**	**185**	....	....	....	....	....
	Halifax	AHL	18	6	6	12	37	6	1	1	2	61
1990-91	**Quebec**	**NHL**	**35**	**2**	**5**	**7**	**114**	....	....	....	....	....
	Halifax	AHL	7	1	4	5	20	....	....	....	....	....
	St. Louis	**NHL**	**26**	**1**	**1**	**2**	**128**	**13**	**0**	**0**	**0**	**38**
1991-92	**St. Louis**	**NHL**	**46**	**1**	**3**	**4**	**166**	**5**	**0**	**0**	**0**	**7**
	NHL Totals		**177**	**12**	**15**	**27**	**747**	**18**	**0**	**0**	**0**	**45**

Traded to **St. Louis** by **Quebec** for Herb Raglan, Tony Twist and Andy Rymsha, February 4, 1991. Traded to **Tampa Bay** by **St. Louis** with Pat Jablonski and Steve Tuttle for future considerations, June 19, 1992.

KING, DEREK

Left wing. Shoots left. 6'1", 203 lbs. Born, Hamilton, Ont., February 11, 1967.
(NY Islanders' 2nd choice, 13th overall, in 1985 Entry Draft).

			Regular Season					Playoffs				
Season	Club	Lea	GP	G	A	TP	PIM	GP	G	A	TP	PIM
1984-85a	S.S. Marie	OHL	63	35	38	73	106	16	3	13	16	11
1985-86	S.S. Marie	OHL	25	12	17	29	33	....	....	....	....	....
	Oshawa	OHL	19	8	13	21	15	6	3	2	5	13
1986-87	**NY Islanders**	**NHL**	**2**	**0**	**0**	**0**	**0**	....	....	....	....	....
b	Oshawa	OHL	57	53	53	106	74	17	14	10	24	40
1987-88	**NY Islanders**	**NHL**	**55**	**12**	**24**	**36**	**30**	**5**	**0**	**2**	**2**	**2**
	Springfield	AHL	10	7	6	13	6	....	....	....	....	....
1988-89	**NY Islanders**	**NHL**	**60**	**14**	**29**	**43**	**14**	....	....	....	....	....
	Springfield	AHL	4	4	0	4	0	....	....	....	....	....
1989-90	**NY Islanders**	**NHL**	**46**	**13**	**27**	**40**	**20**	**4**	**0**	**0**	**0**	**4**
	Springfield	AHL	21	11	12	23	33	....	....	....	....	....
1990-91	**NY Islanders**	**NHL**	**66**	**19**	**26**	**45**	**44**	....	....	....	....	....
1991-92	**NY Islanders**	**NHL**	**80**	**40**	**38**	**78**	**46**	....	....	....	....	....
	NHL Totals		**309**	**98**	**144**	**242**	**154**	**9**	**0**	**2**	**2**	**6**

a OHL Rookie of the Year (1985)
b OHL First All-Star Team (1987)

KING, KRIS

Left wing. Shoots left. 5'11", 210 lbs. Born, Bracebridge, Ont., February 18, 1966.
(Washington's 4th choice, 80th overall, in 1984 Entry Draft).

			Regular Season					Playoffs				
Season	Club	Lea	GP	G	A	TP	PIM	GP	G	A	TP	PIM
1983-84	Peterborough	OHL	62	13	18	31	168	8	3	3	6	14
1984-85	Peterborough	OHL	61	18	35	53	222	16	2	8	10	28
1985-86	Peterborough	OHL	58	19	40	59	254	8	4	0	4	21
1986-87	Binghamton	AHL	7	0	0	0	18	....	....	....	....	....
	Peterborough	OHL	46	23	33	56	160	12	5	8	13	41
1987-88	**Detroit**	**NHL**	**3**	**1**	**0**	**1**	**2**	....	....	....	....	....
	Adirondack	AHL	76	21	32	53	337	10	4	4	8	53
1988-89	**Detroit**	**NHL**	**55**	**2**	**3**	**5**	**168**	**2**	**0**	**0**	**0**	**2**
1989-90	**NY Rangers**	**NHL**	**68**	**6**	**7**	**13**	**286**	**10**	**0**	**1**	**1**	**38**
1990-91	**NY Rangers**	**NHL**	**72**	**11**	**14**	**25**	**154**	**6**	**2**	**0**	**2**	**36**
1991-92	**NY Rangers**	**NHL**	**79**	**10**	**9**	**19**	**224**	**13**	**4**	**1**	**5**	**14**
	NHL Totals		**277**	**30**	**33**	**63**	**834**	**31**	**6**	**2**	**8**	**90**

Signed as a free agent by **Detroit**, March 23, 1987. Traded to **NY Rangers** by **Detroit** for Chris McRae and Detroit's fifth round choice (Tony Burns) in 1990 Entry Draft which was previously acquired by NY Rangers, September 7, 1989.

KING, STEVE

Right wing. Shoots right. 6', 190 lbs. Born, Greenwich, RI, July 22, 1969.
(NY Rangers' 1st choice, 21st overall, in 1991 Supplemental Draft).

			Regular Season					Playoffs				
Season	Club	Lea	GP	G	A	TP	PIM	GP	G	A	TP	PIM
1989-90	Brown	ECAC	27	19	8	27	53	....	....	....	....	....
1990-91	Brown	ECAC	27	19	15	34	76	....	....	....	....	....
1991-92	Binghamton	AHL	66	27	15	42	56	10	2	0	2	14

KINISKY, AL

Left wing. Shoots left. 6'4", 220 lbs. Born, Port Coquitlam, B.C., May 31, 1972.
(Philadelphia's 8th choice, 52nd overall, in 1990 Entry Draft).

			Regular Season					Playoffs				
Season	Club	Lea	GP	G	A	TP	PIM	GP	G	A	TP	PIM
1989-90	Seattle	WHL	72	9	29	38	103	13	2	3	5	13
1990-91	Seattle	WHL	70	16	26	42	128	....	....	....	....	....
1991-92	Seattle	WHL	7	2	1	3	27	....	....	....	....	....
	Lethbridge	WHL	56	9	24	33	121	4	0	0	0	0

KIRTON, SCOTT

Right wing. Shoots right. 6'4", 215 lbs. Born, Penetanguishene, Ont., October 4, 1971.
(Chicago's 7th choice, 154th overall, in 1991 Entry Draft).

			Regular Season					Playoffs				
Season	Club	Lea	GP	G	A	TP	PIM	GP	G	A	TP	PIM
1990-91	Powell River	BCJHL	56	29	71	100	213	....	....	....	....	....
1991-92	North Dakota	WCHA	37	5	6	11	68	....	....	....	....	....

KISIO, KELLY

Center. Shoots right. 5'9", 183 lbs. Born, Peace River, Alta., September 18, 1959.

			Regular Season					Playoffs				
Season	Club	Lea	GP	G	A	TP	PIM	GP	G	A	TP	PIM
1978-79	Calgary	WHL	70	60	61	121	73	....	....	....	....	....
1979-80	Calgary	WHL	71	65	73	138	64	....	....	....	....	....
1980-81	Adirondack	AHL	41	10	14	24	43	....	....	....	....	....
	Kalamazoo	IHL	31	27	16	43	48	8	7	7	14	13
1981-82	Dallas	CHL	78	*62	39	101	59	16	*12	*17	*29	38
1982-83	Davos	Switz.	40	49	38	87	....	....	....	....	....	....
	Detroit	**NHL**	**15**	**4**	**3**	**7**	**0**	....	....	....	....	....
1983-84	**Detroit**	**NHL**	**70**	**23**	**37**	**60**	**34**	**4**	**1**	**0**	**1**	**4**
1984-85	**Detroit**	**NHL**	**75**	**20**	**41**	**61**	**56**	**3**	**0**	**2**	**2**	**2**
1985-86	**Detroit**	**NHL**	**76**	**21**	**48**	**69**	**85**	....	....	....	....	....
1986-87	**NY Rangers**	**NHL**	**70**	**24**	**40**	**64**	**73**	**4**	**0**	**1**	**1**	**2**
1987-88	**NY Rangers**	**NHL**	**77**	**23**	**55**	**78**	**88**	....	....	....	....	....
1988-89	**NY Rangers**	**NHL**	**70**	**26**	**36**	**62**	**91**	**4**	**0**	**0**	**0**	**9**
1989-90	**NY Rangers**	**NHL**	**68**	**22**	**44**	**66**	**105**	**10**	**2**	**8**	**10**	**8**
1990-91	**NY Rangers**	**NHL**	**51**	**15**	**20**	**35**	**58**	....	....	....	....	....
1991-92	**San Jose**	**NHL**	**48**	**11**	**26**	**37**	**54**	....	....	....	....	....
	NHL Totals		**620**	**189**	**350**	**539**	**644**	**25**	**3**	**11**	**14**	**25**

Signed as a free agent by **Detroit**, May 2, 1983. Traded to **NY Rangers** by **Detroit** with Lane Lambert and Jim Leavins for Glen Hanlon and New York's third round choices in 1987 (Dennis Holland) and 1988 (Guy Dupuis) Entry Drafts, July 29, 1986. Claimed by **Minnesota** from **NY Rangers** in Expansion Draft, May 30, 1991. Traded to **San Jose** by **Minnesota** for Shane Churla, June 3, 1991.

KITCHING, GARY

Center. Shoots left. 6'2", 190 lbs. Born, Thunder Bay, Ont., January 9, 1971.
(Edmonton's 8th choice, 166th overall, in 1991 Entry Draft).

			Regular Season					Playoffs				
Season	Club	Lea	GP	G	A	TP	PIM	GP	G	A	TP	PIM
1990-91	Thunder Bay	USHL	46	29	64	93	....	....	....	....	....	....
1991-92	Ferris State	CCHA	36	7	9	16	52	....	....	....	....	....

KIVI, KARRI

Defense. Shoots left. 6', 172 lbs. Born, Turku, Finland, January 31, 1970.
(Vancouver's 11th choice, 233rd overall, in 1990 Entry Draft).

			Regular Season					Playoffs				
Season	Club	Lea	GP	G	A	TP	PIM	GP	G	A	TP	PIM
1989-90	Ilves	Fin.	43	6	15	21	14	....	....	....	....	....
1990-91	Ilves	Fin.	43	2	9	11	18	....	....	....	....	....
1991-92	TPS	Fin.	33	3	1	4	14	3	0	0	0	0

KJELLBERG, PATRIK (CHEHL-buhrg)

Left wing. Shoots left. 6'2", 196 lbs. Born, Falun, Sweden, June 17, 1969.
(Montreal's 4th choice, 83rd overall, in 1988 Entry Draft).

			Regular Season					Playoffs				
Season	Club	Lea	GP	G	A	TP	PIM	GP	G	A	TP	PIM
1986-87	Falun	Swe.2	27	11	13	24	14	....	....	....	....	....
1987-88	Falun	Swe.2	29	15	10	25	18	....	....	....	....	....
1988-89	AIK	Swe.	25	7	9	16	8	....	....	....	....	....
1989-90	AIK	Swe.	33	8	16	24	6	3	1	0	1	0
1990-91	AIK	Swe.	38	4	11	15	18	....	....	....	....	....
1991-92	AIK	Swe.	40	20	13	33	16	3	1	0	1	2

KLASSEN, TODD

Defense. Shoots right. 6', 204 lbs. Born, Saskatoon, Sask., April 17, 1974.
(Pittsburgh's 4th choice, 91st overall, in 1992 Entry Draft).

			Regular Season					Playoffs				
Season	Club	Lea	GP	G	A	TP	PIM	GP	G	A	TP	PIM
1990-91	Tri-Cities	WHL	67	6	27	33	72	7	0	1	1	2
1991-92	Tri-Cities	WHL	69	23	42	65	60	5	0	0	0	2

KLATT, TRENT

Center. Shoots right. 6'1", 210 lbs. Born, Robbinsdale, MN, January 30, 1971.
(Washington's 5th choice, 82nd overall, in 1989 Entry Draft).

			Regular Season					Playoffs				
Season	Club	Lea	GP	G	A	TP	PIM	GP	G	A	TP	PIM
1989-90	U. Minnesota	WCHA	38	22	14	36	16	....	....	....	....	....
1990-91	U. Minnesota	WCHA	39	16	28	44	58	....	....	....	....	....
1991-92	U. Minnesota	WCHA	41	27	36	63	76	....	....	....	....	....
	Minnesota	**NHL**	**1**	**0**	**0**	**0**	**0**	**6**	**0**	**0**	**0**	**2**
	NHL Totals		**1**	**0**	**0**	**0**	**0**	**6**	**0**	**0**	**0**	**2**

Traded to **Minnesota** by **Washington** with Steve Maltais for Shawn Chambers, June 21, 1991.

KLEE, KEN

Defense. Shoots right. 6'1", 200 lbs. Born, Indianapolis, IN, April 24, 1971.
(Washington's 11th choice, 177th overall, in 1990 Entry Draft).

			Regular Season					Playoffs				
Season	Club	Lea	GP	G	A	TP	PIM	GP	G	A	TP	PIM
1989-90	Bowling Green	CCHA	39	0	5	5	52	....	....	....	....	....
1990-91	Bowling Green	CCHA	37	7	28	35	50	....	....	....	....	....
1991-92	Bowling Green	CCHA	10	0	1	1	14	....	....	....	....	....

KLEMM, JON

Defense. Shoots right. 6'3", 200 lbs. Born, Cranbrook, B.C., January 8, 1970.

			Regular Season					Playoffs				
Season	Club	Lea	GP	G	A	TP	PIM	GP	G	A	TP	PIM
1988-89	Seattle	WHL	2	1	1	2	0	....	....	....	....	....
	Spokane	WHL	66	6	34	40	42	....	....	....	....	....
1989-90	Spokane	WHL	66	3	28	31	100	....	....	....	....	....
1990-91	Spokane	WHL	72	7	58	65	65	15	3	6	9	8
1991-92	**Quebec**	**NHL**	**4**	**0**	**1**	**1**	**0**	....	....	....	....	....
	Halifax	AHL	70	6	13	19	40	....	....	....	....	....
	NHL Totals		**4**	**0**	**1**	**1**	**0**	....	....	....	....	....

Signed as a free agent by **Quebec**, May 14, 1991.

KLIMA, PETR (KLEE-muh)

Right/Left wing. Shoots right. 6', 190 lbs. Born, Chaomutov, Czech., December 23, 1964.
(Detroit's 5th choice, 86th overall, in 1983 Entry Draft).

			Regular Season					Playoffs				
Season	Club	Lea	GP	G	A	TP	PIM	GP	G	A	TP	PIM
1982-83	Czech. Jrs.	....	44	19	17	36	74	....	....	....	....	....
1983-84	Dukla Jihlava	Czech.	41	20	16	36	46	....	....	....	....	....
	Czech. Jrs.	....	7	6	5	11	....	....	....	....	....	....
1984-85	Dukla Jihlava	Czech.	35	23	22	45	....	....	....	....	....	....
	Czech. Nat'l	....	5	2	1	3	0	....	....	....	....	....
1985-86	**Detroit**	**NHL**	**74**	**32**	**24**	**56**	**16**	....	....	....	....	....
1986-87	**Detroit**	**NHL**	**77**	**30**	**23**	**53**	**42**	**13**	**1**	**2**	**3**	**4**
1987-88	**Detroit**	**NHL**	**78**	**37**	**25**	**62**	**46**	**12**	**10**	**8**	**18**	**10**
1988-89	**Detroit**	**NHL**	**51**	**25**	**16**	**41**	**44**	**6**	**2**	**4**	**6**	**19**
	Adirondack	AHL	5	5	1	6	4	....	....	....	....	....
1989-90	**Detroit**	**NHL**	**13**	**5**	**5**	**10**	**6**	....	....	....	....	....
	Edmonton	**NHL**	**63**	**25**	**28**	**53**	**66**	**21**	**5**	**0**	**5**	**8**
1990-91	**Edmonton**	**NHL**	**70**	**40**	**28**	**68**	**113**	**18**	**7**	**6**	**13**	**16**
1991-92	**Edmonton**	**NHL**	**57**	**21**	**13**	**34**	**52**	**15**	**1**	**4**	**5**	**8**
	NHL Totals		**483**	**215**	**162**	**377**	**385**	**85**	**26**	**24**	**50**	**65**

Traded to **Edmonton** by **Detroit** with Joe Murphy, Adam Graves and Jeff Sharples for Jimmy Carson, Kevin McClelland and Edmonton's fifth round choice (later traded to Montreal for Rick Green. Montreal selected Brad Layzell) in 1991 Entry Draft, November 2, 1989.

KLIMOVICH, SERGEI (klee-MOH-vich)

Center. Shoots right. 6'2", 189 lbs. Born, Novosibirsk, Soviet Union, May 8, 1974.
(Chicago's 3rd choice, 41st overall, in 1992 Entry Draft).

			Regular Season					Playoffs				
Season	Club	Lea	GP	G	A	TP	PIM	GP	G	A	TP	PIM
1991-92	Moscow D'amo	CIS	2	0	0	0	0	....	....	....	....	....

KLIMT, TOMAS

Center. Shoots left. 6'1", 183 lbs. Born, Plzen, Czech., December 26, 1973.
(NY Islanders' 3rd choice, 104th overall, in 1992 Entry Draft).

			Regular Season					Playoffs				
Season	Club	Lea	GP	G	A	TP	PIM	GP	G	A	TP	PIM
1990-91	Skoda Plzen	Czech. Jr.				UNAVAILABLE						
1991-92	Skoda Plzen	Czech.	40	3	6	9	0	....	....	....	....	....

KLIPPENSTEIN, WADE

Left wing. Shoots left. 6'3", 219 lbs. Born, Boissevain, Man., May 9, 1970.
(Quebec's 11th choice, 232nd overall, in 1990 Entry Draft).

			Regular Season					Playoffs				
Season	Club	Lea	GP	G	A	TP	PIM	GP	G	A	TP	PIM
1989-90	Alaska-Fair.	G.N.	37	17	14	31	....	....	....	....	....	....
1990-91	Alaska-Fair.	G.N.	35	22	11	33	32	....	....	....	....	....
1991-92	Alaska-Fair.	G.N.	33	12	13	25	108	....	....	....	....	....

KNUBLE, MICHAEL

Right wing. Shoots right. 6'3", 208 lbs. Born, Toronto, Ont., July 4, 1972.
(Detroit's 4th choice, 76th overall, in 1991 Entry Draft).

			Regular Season					Playoffs				
Season	Club	Lea	GP	G	A	TP	PIM	GP	G	A	TP	PIM
1990-91	Kalamazoo	US Jr.	36	16	17	33	46	....	....	....	....	....
1991-92	U. of Michigan	CCHA	43	7	8	15	48	....	....	....	....	....

KNUTSEN, ESPEN

Center. Shoots left. 5'11", 172 lbs. Born, Oslo, Norway, January 12, 1972.
(Hartford's 9th choice, 204th overall, in 1990 Entry Draft).

			Regular Season					Playoffs				
Season	Club	Lea	GP	G	A	TP	PIM	GP	G	A	TP	PIM
1989-90	Valerengen	Nor.	34	22	26	48	....	....	....	....	....	....
1990-91	Valerengen	Nor.	31	30	24	54	42	5	3	4	7	....
1991-92	Valerengen	Nor.	30	28	26	54	37	....	....	....	....	....

KOCH, PAUL

Defense. Shoots left. 6'3", 205 lbs. Born, St. Paul, MN, June 30, 1971.
(Quebec's 10th choice, 200th overall, in 1991 Entry Draft).

			Regular Season					Playoffs				
Season	Club	Lea	GP	G	A	TP	PIM	GP	G	A	TP	PIM
1990-91	Omaha	USHL	48	4	16	20	56	....	....	....	....	....
1991-92	U. of Denver	WCHA	36	4	13	17	48	....	....	....	....	....

KOCUR, JOEY (KOH-suhr)

Right wing. Shoots right. 6', 195 lbs. Born, Calgary, Alta., December 21, 1964.
(Detroit's 6th choice, 88th overall, in 1983 Entry Draft).

			Regular Season					Playoffs				
Season	Club	Lea	GP	G	A	TP	PIM	GP	G	A	TP	PIM
1982-83	Saskatoon	WHL	62	23	17	40	289	6	2	3	5	25
1983-84	Saskatoon	WHL	69	40	41	81	258	....	....	....	....	....
	Adirondack	AHL	....	....	....	....	....	5	0	0	0	20
1984-85	Detroit	NHL	17	1	0	1	64	3	1	0	1	5
	Adirondack	AHL	47	12	7	19	171	....	....	....	....	....
1985-86	Detroit	NHL	59	9	6	15	*377	....	....	....	....	....
	Adirondack	AHL	9	6	2	8	34	....	....	....	....	....
1986-87	Detroit	NHL	77	9	9	18	276	16	2	3	5	71
1987-88	Detroit	NHL	63	7	7	14	263	10	0	1	1	13
1988-89	Detroit	NHL	60	9	9	18	213	3	0	1	1	6
1989-90	Detroit	NHL	71	16	20	36	268	....	....	....	....	....
1990-91	Detroit	NHL	52	5	4	9	253	....	....	....	....	....
	NY Rangers	NHL	5	0	0	0	36	6	0	2	2	21
1991-92	NY Rangers	NHL	51	7	4	11	121	12	1	1	2	38
	NHL Totals		455	63	59	122	1871	50	4	8	12	154

Traded to **NY Rangers** by **Detroit** with Per Djoos for Kevin Miller, Jim Cummins and Dennis Vial, March 5, 1991.

KOCUR, KORY

Right wing. Shoots right. 5'11", 188 lbs. Born, Kelvington, Sask., March 6, 1969.
(Detroit's 1st choice, 17th overall, in 1988 Entry Draft).

			Regular Season					Playoffs				
Season	Club	Lea	GP	G	A	TP	PIM	GP	G	A	TP	PIM
1986-87	Saskatoon	WHL	62	13	17	30	98	4	0	0	0	7
1987-88	Saskatoon	WHL	69	34	37	71	95	10	5	4	9	18
1988-89	Saskatoon	WHL	66	45	57	102	111	8	7	11	18	15
1989-90	Adirondack	AHL	79	18	37	55	36	6	1	2	3	2
1990-91	Adirondack	AHL	65	8	13	21	83	2	0	0	0	12
1991-92	Fort Wayne	IHL	69	25	40	65	68	7	3	3	6	49

KOIVUNEN, PETRO

Right wing. Shoots right. 6', 180 lbs. Born, Espoo, Finland, May 30, 1970.
(Edmonton's 2nd choice, 39th overall, in 1988 Entry Draft).

			Regular Season					Playoffs				
Season	Club	Lea	GP	G	A	TP	PIM	GP	G	A	TP	PIM
1986-87	Espoo	Fin.	30	22	14	36	26	....	....	....	....	....
1987-88	Espoo	Fin.	31	27	31	58	38	....	....	....	....	....
1988-89	Espoo	Fin.	39	22	37	59	42	....	....	....	....	....
1989-90	Espoo	Fin.	39	24	35	59	28	....	....	....	....	....
1990-91	HIFK	Fin.	39	8	15	23	20	3	0	1	1	4
1991-92	HIFK	Fin.	41	11	3	14	0	8	0	0	0	2

KOLNIK, LUBOMIR (KOHL-neek)

Right wing. Shoots left. 5'11", 178 lbs. Born, Nitra, Czechoslovakia, January 23, 1968.
(New Jersey's 9th choice, 116th overall, in 1990 Entry Draft).

			Regular Season					Playoffs				
Season	Club	Lea	GP	G	A	TP	PIM	GP	G	A	TP	PIM
1989-90	Dukla Trencin	Czech.	53	37	25	62	....	....	....	....	....	....
1990-91	Dukla Trencin	Czech.	52	38	37	75	12	....	....	....	....	....
1991-92	Dukla Trencin	Czech.	49	26	23	49	....	....	....	....	....	....

KOLSTAD, DEAN

Defense. Shoots left. 6'6", 220 lbs. Born, Edmonton, Alta., June 16, 1968.
(Minnesota's 3rd choice, 33rd overall, in 1986 Entry Draft).

			Regular Season					Playoffs				
Season	Club	Lea	GP	G	A	TP	PIM	GP	G	A	TP	PIM
1985-86	N. Westminster	WHL	13	0	0	0	16	....	....	....	....	....
	Prince Albert	WHL	54	2	15	17	80	20	5	3	8	26
1986-87	Prince Albert	WHL	72	17	37	54	112	8	1	5	6	8
1987-88	Prince Albert	WHL	72	14	37	51	121	10	0	9	9	20
1988-89	Minnesota	NHL	25	1	5	6	42	....	....	....	....	....
	Kalamazoo	IHL	51	10	23	33	91	6	1	0	1	23
1989-90a	Kalamazoo	IHL	77	10	40	50	172	10	3	4	7	14
1990-91	Minnesota	NHL	5	0	0	0	15	....	....	....	....	....
	Kalamazoo	IHL	33	4	8	12	50	9	1	6	7	4
1991-92	Kansas City	IHL	74	9	20	29	83	15	3	6	9	8
	NHL Totals		30	1	5	6	57	....	....	....	....	....

a IHL Second All-Star Team (1990)

Claimed by **San Jose** from **Minnesota** in Dispersal Draft, May 30, 1991.

KONOWALCHUK, BRIAN

Center. Shoots left. 5'10", 178 lbs. Born, Prince Albert, Sask., October 14, 1971.
(San Jose's 1st choice, 3rd overall, in 1992 Supplemental Draft).

			Regular Season					Playoffs				
Season	Club	Lea	GP	G	A	TP	PIM	GP	G	A	TP	PIM
1990-91	U. of Denver	WCHA	38	8	19	27	40	....	....	....	....	....
1991-92	U. of Denver	WCHA	33	8	17	25	53	....	....	....	....	....

KONOWALCHUK, STEVE

Center. Shoots left. 6', 180 lbs. Born, Salt Lake City, UT, November 11, 1972.
(Washington's 5th choice, 58th overall, in 1991 Entry Draft).

			Regular Season					Playoffs				
Season	Club	Lea	GP	G	A	TP	PIM	GP	G	A	TP	PIM
1990-91	Portland	WHL	72	43	49	92	78	....	....	....	....	....
1991-92	Washington	NHL	1	0	0	0	0	....	....	....	....	....
	Baltimore	AHL	3	1	1	2	0	....	....	....	....	....
a	Portland	WHL	64	51	53	104	95	6	3	6	9	12

a WHL West First All-Star Team (1992)

KONROYD, STEPHEN MARK (STEVE) (KON-royd)

Defense. Shoots left. 6'1", 195 lbs. Born, Scarborough, Ont., February 10, 1961.
(Atlanta's 4th choice, 39th overall, in 1980 Entry Draft).

			Regular Season					Playoffs				
Season	Club	Lea	GP	G	A	TP	PIM	GP	G	A	TP	PIM
1979-80	Oshawa	OHA	62	11	23	34	133	7	0	2	2	14
1980-81	Calgary	NHL	4	0	0	0	4	....	....	....	....	....
a	Oshawa	OHA	59	19	47	68	232	11	3	11	14	35
1981-82	Calgary	NHL	63	3	14	17	78	3	0	0	0	12
	Oklahoma City	CHL	14	2	3	5	15	....	....	....	....	....
1982-83	Calgary	NHL	79	4	13	17	73	9	2	1	3	18
1983-84	Calgary	NHL	80	1	13	14	94	8	1	2	3	8
1984-85	Calgary	NHL	64	3	23	26	73	4	1	4	5	2
1985-86	Calgary	NHL	59	7	20	27	64	....	....	....	....	....
	NY Islanders	NHL	14	0	5	5	16	3	0	0	0	6
1986-87	NY Islanders	NHL	72	5	16	21	70	14	1	4	5	10
1987-88	NY Islanders	NHL	62	2	15	17	99	6	1	0	1	4
1988-89	NY Islanders	NHL	21	1	5	6	2	....	....	....	....	....
	Chicago	NHL	57	5	7	12	40	16	2	0	2	10
1989-90	Chicago	NHL	75	3	14	17	34	20	1	3	4	19
1990-91	Chicago	NHL	70	0	12	12	40	6	1	0	1	8
1991-92	Chicago	NHL	49	2	14	16	65	....	....	....	....	....
	Hartford	NHL	33	2	10	12	32	7	0	1	1	2
	NHL Totals		802	38	181	219	784	96	10	15	25	99

a OHA Second All-Star Team (1981)

Traded to **NY Islanders** by **Calgary** with Richard Kromm for John Tonelli, March 11, 1986. Traded to **Chicago** by **NY Islanders** with Bob Bassen for Marc Bergevin and Gary Nylund, November 25, 1988. Traded to **Hartford** by **Chicago** for Rob Brown, January 24, 1992.

KONSTANTINOV, VLADIMIR (kohn-stahn-TEE-nahf)

Defense. Shoots right. 5'11", 176 lbs. Born, Murmansk, Soviet Union, March 19, 1967.
(Detroit's 12th choice, 221st overall, in 1989 Entry Draft).

			Regular Season					Playoffs				
Season	Club	Lea	GP	G	A	TP	PIM	GP	G	A	TP	PIM
1984-85	CSKA	USSR	40	1	4	5	10	....	....	....	....	....
1985-86	CSKA	USSR	26	4	3	7	12	....	....	....	....	....
1986-87	CSKA	USSR	35	2	2	4	19	....	....	....	....	....
1987-88	CSKA	USSR	50	3	6	9	32	....	....	....	....	....
1988-89	CSKA	USSR	37	7	8	15	20	....	....	....	....	....
1989-90	CSKA	USSR	47	14	13	27	44	....	....	....	....	....
1990-91	CSKA	USSR	45	5	12	17	42	....	....	....	....	....
1991-92a	Detroit	NHL	79	8	26	34	172	11	0	1	1	16
	NHL Totals		79	8	26	34	172	11	0	1	1	16

a NHL/Upper Deck All-Rookie Team (1992)

KONTOS, CHRISTOPHER (CHRIS) (KONN-tohs)

Left wing/Center. Shoots left. 6'1", 195 lbs. Born, Toronto, Ont., December 10, 1963.
(NY Rangers' 1st choice, 15th overall, in 1982 Entry Draft).

			Regular Season					Playoffs				
Season	Club	Lea	GP	G	A	TP	PIM	GP	G	A	TP	PIM
1980-81	Sudbury	OHA	57	17	27	44	36	....	....	....	....	....
1981-82	Sudbury	OHL	12	6	6	12	18	....	....	....	....	....
	Toronto	OHL	59	36	56	92	68	10	7	9	16	2
1982-83	NY Rangers	NHL	44	8	7	15	33	....	....	....	....	....
	Toronto	OHL	28	21	33	54	23	....	....	....	....	....
1983-84	NY Rangers	NHL	6	0	1	1	8	....	....	....	....	....
	Tulsa	CHL	21	5	13	18	8	....	....	....	....	....
1984-85	NY Rangers	NHL	28	4	8	12	24	....	....	....	....	....
	New Haven	AHL	48	19	24	43	30	....	....	....	....	....
1985-86	Ilves	Fin.	36	16	15	31	30	....	....	....	....	....
	New Haven	AHL	21	8	15	23	12	5	4	2	6	4
1986-87	Pittsburgh	NHL	31	8	9	17	6	....	....	....	....	....
	New Haven	AHL	36	14	17	31	29	....	....	....	....	....
1987-88	Pittsburgh	NHL	36	1	7	8	12	....	....	....	....	....
	Muskegon	IHL	10	3	6	9	8	....	....	....	....	....
	Los Angeles	NHL	6	2	10	12	2	4	1	0	1	4
	New Haven	AHL	16	8	16	24	4	....	....	....	....	....
1988-89	EHC Kloten	Swiss	36	33	22	55	....	6	6	2	8	....
	Los Angeles	NHL	7	2	1	3	2	11	9	0	9	8
1989-90	Los Angeles	NHL	6	2	2	4	4	5	1	0	1	0
	New Haven	AHL	42	10	20	30	25	....	....	....	....	....
1990-91	Phoenix	IHL	69	26	36	62	19	11	9	12	21	0
1991-92	Cdn. National	....	25	10	10	20	16	....	....	....	....	....
	NHL Totals		164	27	45	72	91	20	11	0	11	12

Traded to **Pittsburgh** by **NY Rangers** for Ron Duguay, January 21, 1987. Traded to **Los Angeles** by **Pittsburgh** with Pittsburgh's sixth round choice in 1988 Entry Draft (Micah Aivazoff) for Bryan Erickson, February 5, 1988. Signed as a free agent by **Tampa Bay**, July 21, 1992.

KONTSEK, ROMAN (KON-chek)

Right wing. Shoots right. 5'11", 183 lbs. Born, Prague, Czechoslovakia, June 11, 1970.
(Washington's 8th choice, 135th overall, in 1990 Entry Draft).

			Regular Season					Playoffs				
Season	Club	Lea	GP	G	A	TP	PIM	GP	G	A	TP	PIM
1988-89	Dukla Trencin	Czech.	21	4	8	12	....	....	....	....	....	....
1989-90	Dukla Trencin	Czech.	21	8	7	15	....	....	....	....	....	....
1990-91	Dukla Trencin	Czech.	48	13	18	31	24	....	....	....	....	....
1991-92	Dukla Trencin	Czech.	35	5	6	11	....	....	....	....	....	....

KORDIC, DAN

Defense. Shoots left. 6'5", 220 lbs. Born, Edmonton, Alta., April 18, 1971.
(Philadelphia's 9th choice, 88th overall, in 1990 Entry Draft).

			Regular Season					Playoffs				
Season	Club	Lea	GP	G	A	TP	PIM	GP	G	A	TP	PIM
1988-89	Medicine Hat	WHL	70	1	13	14	190	....	....	....	....	....
1989-90	Medicine Hat	WHL	59	4	12	16	182	3	0	0	0	9
1990-91	Medicine Hat	WHL	67	8	15	23	150	12	2	6	8	42
1991-92	Philadelphia	NHL	46	1	3	4	126	....	....	....	....	....
	NHL Totals		46	1	3	4	126	....	....	....	....	....

KORDIC, JOHN

Right wing. Shoots right. 6'2", 210 lbs. Born, Edmonton, Alta., March 22, 1965.
(Montreal's 6th choice, 78th overall, in 1983 Entry Draft).

			Regular Season					Playoffs				
Season	Club	Lea	GP	G	A	TP	PIM	GP	G	A	TP	PIM
1982-83	Portland	WHL	72	3	22	25	235	14	1	6	7	30
1983-84	Portland	WHL	67	9	50	59	232	14	0	13	13	56
1984-85a	Seattle	WHL	46	17	36	53	154	....	....	....	....	....
	Portland	WHL	25	6	22	28	73	....	....	....	....	....
	Sherbrooke	AHL	4	0	0	0	4	4	0	0	0	11
1985-86	**Montreal**	**NHL**	**5**	**0**	**1**	**1**	**12**	**18**	**0**	**0**	**0**	**53**
	Sherbrooke	AHL	68	3	14	17	238	....	....	....	....	....
1986-87	**Montreal**	**NHL**	**44**	**5**	**3**	**8**	**151**	**11**	**2**	**0**	**2**	**19**
	Sherbrooke	AHL	10	4	4	8	49	....	....	....	....	....
1987-88	**Montreal**	**NHL**	**60**	**2**	**6**	**8**	**159**	**7**	**2**	**2**	**4**	**26**
1988-89	**Montreal**	**NHL**	**6**	**0**	**0**	**0**	**13**	....	....	....	....	....
	Toronto	**NHL**	**46**	**1**	**2**	**3**	**185**	....	....	....	....	....
1989-90	**Toronto**	**NHL**	**55**	**9**	**4**	**13**	**252**	**5**	**0**	**1**	**1**	**33**
1990-91	**Toronto**	**NHL**	**3**	**0**	**0**	**0**	**9**	....	....	....	....	....
	Newmarket	AHL	8	1	1	2	79	....	....	....	....	....
	Washington	**NHL**	**7**	**0**	**0**	**0**	**101**	....	....	....	....	....
1991-92	**Quebec**	**NHL**	**18**	**0**	**2**	**2**	**115**	....	....	....	....	....
	Cape Breton	AHL	12	2	1	3	141	5	0	1	1	53
	NHL Totals		**244**	**17**	**18**	**35**	**997**	**41**	**4**	**3**	**7**	**131**

a WHL Second All-Star Team, West Division (1985)

Traded to **Toronto** by **Montreal** with Montreal's sixth round choice (Michael Doers) in 1989 Entry Draft for Russ Courtnall, November 7, 1988. Traded to **Washington** by **Toronto** with Paul Fenton for Washington's fifth round choice (Alexei Kudashov) in 1991 Entry Draft, January 24, 1991. Signed as a free agent by **Quebec**, October 4, 1991.

Died August 8, 1992.

KOROLEV, IGOR (koh-roh-LEV)

Right wing. Shoots left. 6'1", 187 lbs. Born, Moscow, Soviet Union, September 6, 1970.
(St. Louis' 1st choice, 38th overall, in 1992 Entry Draft).

			Regular Season					Playoffs				
Season	Club	Lea	GP	G	A	TP	PIM	GP	G	A	TP	PIM
1990-91	Moscow D'amo	USSR	38	12	4	16	12	....	....	....	....	....
1991-92	Moscow D'amo	CIS	39	15	12	27	16	....	....	....	....	....

KOSKIMAKI, PETTERI (koz-kih-MAH-kee, PEH-ter-ee)

Center. Shoots left. 6'1", 180 lbs. Born, Helsinki, Finland, May 5, 1971.
(Pittsburgh's 10th choice, 152nd overall, in 1990 Entry Draft).

			Regular Season					Playoffs				
Season	Club	Lea	GP	G	A	TP	PIM	GP	G	A	TP	PIM
1988-89	HIFK	Fin.	31	11	17	28	2	....	....	....	....	....
1989-90	Boston U.	H.E.	44	12	12	24	15	....	....	....	....	....
1990-91	Boston U.	H.E.	37	16	22	38	12	....	....	....	....	....
1991-92	Boston U.	H.E.	32	19	18	37	12	....	....	....	....	....

KOSTICHKIN, PAVEL (kohs-TEECH-keen)

Center. Shoots left. 6', 189 lbs. Born, Moscow, Soviet Union, November 9, 1968.
(Winnipeg's 12th choice, 199th overall, in 1988 Entry Draft).

			Regular Season					Playoffs				
Season	Club	Lea	GP	G	A	TP	PIM	GP	G	A	TP	PIM
1985-86	CSKA	USSR	16	5	4	9	12	....	....	....	....	....
1986-87	CSKA	USSR	13	0	3	3	4	....	....	....	....	....
1987-88	CSKA	USSR	40	8	0	8	20	....	....	....	....	....
1988-89	CSKA	USSR	31	4	2	6	16	....	....	....	....	....
1989-90	CSKA	USSR	25	3	4	7	14	....	....	....	....	....
1990-91	CSKA	USSR	26	4	4	8	10	....	....	....	....	....
1991-92	CSKA	CIS	11	1	2	3	10	....	....	....	....	....

KOVACS, BILL

Left wing. Shoots left. 6'3", 224 lbs. Born, Hamilton, Ont., May 11, 1971.
(Washington's 12th choice, 256th overall, in 1991 Entry Draft).

			Regular Season					Playoffs				
Season	Club	Lea	GP	G	A	TP	PIM	GP	G	A	TP	PIM
1989-90	Hamilton	OHL	13	4	4	8	30	....	....	....	....	....
	Sudbury	OHL	47	4	14	18	63	....	....	....	....	....
1990-91	Sudbury	OHL	66	26	25	51	86	5	1	2	3	10
1991-92	Sudbury	OHL	5	3	4	7	8	....	....	....	....	....
	Guelph	OHL	55	35	38	73	61	....	....	....	....	....

KOVACS, FRANK

Left wing. Shoots left. 6'2", 205 lbs. Born, Regina, Sask., June 6, 1971.
(Minnesota's 4th choice, 71st overall, in 1990 Entry Draft).

			Regular Season					Playoffs				
Season	Club	Lea	GP	G	A	TP	PIM	GP	G	A	TP	PIM
1987-88	Regina	WHL	70	10	8	18	48	4	0	1	1	4
1988-89	Regina	WHL	70	16	27	43	90	....	....	....	....	....
1989-90	Regina	WHL	70	26	32	58	165	11	4	4	8	10
1990-91	Regina	WHL	72	50	51	101	148	8	10	3	13	15
1991-92	Regina	WHL	69	46	45	91	274	....	....	....	....	....

KOVALENKO, ANDREI

Right wing. Shoots left. 5'9", 161 lbs. Born, Gorky, Soviet Union, June 7, 1970.
(Quebec's 6th choice, 148th overall, in 1990 Entry Draft).

			Regular Season					Playoffs				
Season	Club	Lea	GP	G	A	TP	PIM	GP	G	A	TP	PIM
1989-90	CSKA	USSR	48	8	5	13	18	....	....	....	....	....
1990-91	CSKA	USSR	45	13	8	21	26	....	....	....	....	....
1991-92	CSKA	CIS	44	19	13	32	32	....	....	....	....	....

KOVALEV, ALEXEI

Right wing. Shoots left. 6'1", 189 lbs. Born, Togliatti, Soviet Union, February 24, 1973.
(NY Rangers' 1st choice, 15th overall, in 1991 Entry Draft).

			Regular Season					Playoffs				
Season	Club	Lea	GP	G	A	TP	PIM	GP	G	A	TP	PIM
1989-90	Moscow D'amo	USSR	1	0	0	0	0	....	....	....	....	....
1990-91	Moscow D'amo	USSR	16	1	2	3	4	....	....	....	....	....
1991-92	Moscow D'amo	CIS	33	16	9	25	20	....	....	....	....	....

KOVALEV, ANDREI

Right wing. Shoots right. 5'11", 189 lbs. Born, Minsk, Soviet Union, April 2, 1966.
(Washington's 7th choice, 114th overall, in 1990 Entry Draft).

			Regular Season					Playoffs				
Season	Club	Lea	GP	G	A	TP	PIM	GP	G	A	TP	PIM
1989-90	Moscow D'amo	USSR	41	10	8	18	8	....	....	....	....	....
1990-91	Moscow D'amo	USSR	43	17	8	25	18	....	....	....	....	....
1991-92	Minsk Dynamo	CIS	20	6	5	11	13	....	....	....	....	....
	New Haven	AHL	33	11	12	23	31	1	0	1	1	2

KOZLOV, VYACHESLAV

Center. Shoots left. 5'10", 172 lbs. Born, Voskresensk, Soviet Union, May 3, 1972.
(Detroit's 2nd choice, 45th overall, in 1990 Entry Draft).

			Regular Season					Playoffs				
Season	Club	Lea	GP	G	A	TP	PIM	GP	G	A	TP	PIM
1989-90	Khimik	USSR	45	14	12	26	38	....	....	....	....	....
1990-91	Khimik	USSR	45	11	13	24	46	....	....	....	....	....
1991-92	CSKA	CIS	11	6	5	11	12	....	....	....	....	....
	Detroit	**NHL**	**7**	**0**	**2**	**2**	**2**	....	....	....	....	....
	NHL Totals		**7**	**0**	**2**	**2**	**2**	....	....	....	....	....

KRAMER, BRADY

Center. Shoots left. 6'1", 155 lbs. Born, Philadelphia, PA, June 13, 1973.
(Montreal's 7th choice, 149th overall, in 1991 Entry Draft).

			Regular Season					Playoffs				
Season	Club	Lea	GP	G	A	TP	PIM	GP	G	A	TP	PIM
1990-91	Haverford	HS	....	....	....	....	....	....	....	....	....	....
1991-92	Providence	H.E.	36	11	10	21	47	....	....	....	....	....

KRAMER, TED

Right wing. Shoots right. 6', 190 lbs. Born, Findlay, OH, October 29, 1969.
(Los Angeles' 6th choice, 144th overall, in 1989 Entry Draft).

			Regular Season					Playoffs				
Season	Club	Lea	GP	G	A	TP	PIM	GP	G	A	TP	PIM
1988-89	U. of Michigan	CCHA	37	16	14	30	70	....	....	....	....	....
1989-90	U. of Michigan	CCHA	42	21	24	45	111	....	....	....	....	....
1990-91	U. of Michigan	CCHA	47	15	17	32	107	....	....	....	....	....
1991-92	U. of Michigan	CCHA	44	17	14	31	52	....	....	....	....	....

KRAVCHUK, IGOR (krahv-CHOOK)

Defense. Shoots left. 6'1", 200 lbs. Born, Ufa, Soviet Union, September 13, 1966.
(Chicago's 4th choice, 71st overall, in 1991 Entry Draft).

			Regular Season					Playoffs				
Season	Club	Lea	GP	G	A	TP	PIM	GP	G	A	TP	PIM
1990-91	CSKA	USSR	41	6	5	11	16	....	....	....	....	....
1991-92	CSKA	CIS	30	3	8	11	6	....	....	....	....	....
	CIS Olympic	....	8	3	2	5	6	....	....	....	....	....
	Chicago	**NHL**	**18**	**1**	**8**	**9**	**4**	**18**	**2**	**6**	**8**	**8**
	NHL Totals		**18**	**1**	**8**	**9**	**4**	**18**	**2**	**6**	**8**	**8**

KRAVETS, MIKHAIL

Right wing. Shoots left. 5'10", 182 lbs. Born, Leningrad, Soviet Union, November 12, 1963.
(San Jose's 12th choice, 243rd overall, in 1991 Entry Draft).

			Regular Season					Playoffs				
Season	Club	Lea	GP	G	A	TP	PIM	GP	G	A	TP	PIM
1988-89	SKA Leningrad	USSR 2	44	9	5	14	36	....	....	....	....	....
1989-90	SKA Leningrad	USSR 2	43	8	18	26	20	....	....	....	....	....
1990-91	SKA Leningrad	USSR	25	8	6	14	28	....	....	....	....	....
1991-92	**San Jose**	**NHL**	**1**	**0**	**0**	**0**	**0**	....	....	....	....	....
	Kansas City	IHL	74	10	32	42	172	15	6	8	14	12
	NHL Totals		**1**	**0**	**0**	**0**	**0**	....	....	....	....	....

KRISS, AARON

Defense. Shoots left. 6'2", 185 lbs. Born, Parma, OH, September 17, 1972.
(San Jose's 11th choice, 221st overall, in 1991 Entry Draft).

			Regular Season					Playoffs				
Season	Club	Lea	GP	G	A	TP	PIM	GP	G	A	TP	PIM
1990-91	Cranbrook	HS	24	14	21	35	95	....	....	....	....	....
1991-92	Lowell	H.E.	29	1	4	5	22	....	....	....	....	....

KRIVOKRASOV, SERGEI (kree-voh-KRAS-ohv)

Right wing. Shoots left. 5'10", 174 lbs. Born, Angarsk, Soviet Union, April 15, 1974.
(Chicago's 1st choice, 12th overall, in 1992 Entry Draft).

			Regular Season					Playoffs				
Season	Club	Lea	GP	G	A	TP	PIM	GP	G	A	TP	PIM
1990-91	CSKA	USSR	41	4	0	4	8	....	....	....	....	....
1991-92	CSKA	CIS	42	10	8	18	35	....	....	....	....	....

KROMM, RICHARD GORDON (RICH)

Left wing. Shoots left. 5'11", 180 lbs. Born, Trail, B.C., March 29, 1964.
(Calgary's 2nd choice, 37th overall, in 1982 Entry Draft).

			Regular Season					Playoffs				
Season	Club	Lea	GP	G	A	TP	PIM	GP	G	A	TP	PIM
1981-82	Portland	WHL	60	16	38	54	30	14	0	3	3	17
1982-83	Portland	WHL	72	35	68	103	64	14	7	13	20	12
1983-84	**Calgary**	**NHL**	**53**	**11**	**12**	**23**	**27**	**11**	**1**	**1**	**2**	**9**
	Portland	WHL	10	10	4	14	13	....	....	....	....	....
1984-85	**Calgary**	**NHL**	**73**	**20**	**32**	**52**	**32**	**3**	**0**	**1**	**1**	**4**
1985-86	**Calgary**	**NHL**	**63**	**12**	**17**	**29**	**31**	....	....	....	....	....
	NY Islanders	**NHL**	**14**	**7**	**7**	**14**	**4**	**3**	**0**	**1**	**1**	**0**
1986-87	**NY Islanders**	**NHL**	**70**	**12**	**17**	**29**	**20**	**14**	**1**	**3**	**4**	**4**
1987-88	**NY Islanders**	**NHL**	**71**	**5**	**10**	**15**	**20**	**5**	**0**	**0**	**0**	**5**
1988-89	**NY Islanders**	**NHL**	**20**	**1**	**6**	**7**	**4**	....	....	....	....	....
	Springfield	AHL	48	21	26	47	15	....	....	....	....	....
1989-90	Leksand	Swe.	40	8	16	24	28	3	3	1	4	0
	Springfield	AHL	9	3	4	7	4	16	1	5	6	4
1990-91	**NY Islanders**	**NHL**	**6**	**1**	**0**	**1**	**0**	....	....	....	....	....
	Capital Dist.	AHL	76	19	36	55	18	....	....	....	....	....
1991-92	**NY Islanders**	**NHL**	**1**	**0**	**0**	**0**	**0**	....	....	....	....	....
	Capital Dist.	AHL	76	16	39	55	36	7	2	3	5	6
	NHL Totals		**371**	**69**	**101**	**170**	**138**	**36**	**2**	**6**	**8**	**22**

Traded to **NY Islanders** by **Calgary** with Steve Konroyd for John Tonelli, March 11, 1986.

KRON, ROBERT (KROHN)

Left wing. Shoots left. 5'10", 174 lbs. Born, Brno, Czech., February 27, 1967.
(Vancouver's 5th choice, 88th overall, in 1985 Entry Draft).

			Regular Season					Playoffs				
Season	Club	Lea	GP	G	A	TP	PIM	GP	G	A	TP	PIM
1986-87	Zetor Brno	Czech.	28	14	11	25	....	....	....	....	....	....
1987-88	Zetor Brno	Czech.	32	12	6	18	....	....	....	....	....	....
1988-89	Zetor Brno	Czech.	43	28	19	47	....	....	....	....	....	....
1989-90	Dukla Trencin	Czech.	39	22	22	44	....	....	....	....	....	....
1990-91	Vancouver	NHL	76	12	20	32	21	....	....	....	....	....
1991-92	Vancouver	NHL	36	2	2	4	2	11	1	2	3	2
	NHL Totals		112	14	22	36	23	11	1	2	3	2

KRUMPSCHMID, NORM

Center. Shoots left. 5'11", 185 lbs. Born, Sudbury, Ont., December 13, 1969.
(Vancouver's 2nd choice, 7th overall, in 1990 Supplemental Draft).

			Regular Season					Playoffs				
Season	Club	Lea	GP	G	A	TP	PIM	GP	G	A	TP	PIM
1988-89	Ferris State	CCHA	35	5	7	12	40	....	....	....	....	....
1989-90	Ferris State	CCHA	36	6	14	20	22	....	....	....	....	....
1990-91	Ferris State	CCHA	38	7	22	29	16	....	....	....	....	....
1991-92	Ferris State	CCHA	37	11	18	29	26	....	....	....	....	....

KRUPP, UWE (KROOP, OO-VAY)

Defense. Shoots right. 6'6", 235 lbs. Born, Cologne, West Germany, June 24, 1965.
(Buffalo's 13th choice, 214th overall, in 1983 Entry Draft).

			Regular Season					Playoffs				
Season	Club	Lea	GP	G	A	TP	PIM	GP	G	A	TP	PIM
1983-84	KEC	W.Ger.	40	0	4	4	22	....	....	....	....	....
1984-85	KEC	W.Ger.	39	11	8	19	36	....	....	....	....	....
1985-86	KEC	W.Ger.	45	10	21	31	83	....	....	....	....	....
1986-87	Buffalo	NHL	26	1	4	5	23	....	....	....	....	....
	Rochester	AHL	42	3	19	22	50	17	1	11	12	16
1987-88	Buffalo	NHL	75	2	9	11	151	6	0	0	0	15
1988-89	Buffalo	NHL	70	5	13	18	55	5	0	1	1	4
1989-90	Buffalo	NHL	74	3	20	23	85	6	0	0	0	4
1990-91	Buffalo	NHL	74	12	32	44	66	6	1	1	2	6
1991-92	Buffalo	NHL	8	2	0	2	6	....	....	....	....	....
	NY Islanders	NHL	59	6	29	35	43	....	....	....	....	....
	NHL Totals		386	31	107	138	429	23	1	2	3	29

Played in NHL All-Star Game (1991)

Traded to **NY Islanders** by **Buffalo** with Pierre Turgeon, Benoit Hogue and Dave McLlwain for Pat Lafontaine, Randy Hillier, Randy Wood and future considerations, October 25, 1991.

KRUPPKE, GORD (KRUP-kee)

Defense. Shoots right. 6'1", 200 lbs. Born, Slave Lake, Alta., April 2, 1969.
(Detroit's 2nd choice, 32nd overall, in 1987 Entry Draft).

			Regular Season					Playoffs				
Season	Club	Lea	GP	G	A	TP	PIM	GP	G	A	TP	PIM
1985-86	Prince Albert	WHL	62	1	8	9	81	20	4	4	8	22
1986-87	Prince Albert	WHL	49	2	10	12	129	8	0	0	0	9
1987-88	Prince Albert	WHL	54	8	8	16	113	10	0	0	0	46
1988-89	Prince Albert	WHL	62	6	26	32	254	3	0	0	0	11
1989-90	Adirondack	AHL	59	2	12	14	103	....	....	....	....	....
1990-91	Detroit	NHL	4	0	0	0	0	....	....	....	....	....
	Adirondack	AHL	45	1	8	9	153	....	....	....	....	....
1991-92	Adirondack	AHL	65	3	9	12	208	16	0	1	1	52
	NHL Totals		4	0	0	0	0	....	....	....	....	....

KRUSE, PAUL

Left wing. Shoots left. 6', 202 lbs. Born, Merritt, B.C., March 15, 1970.
(Calgary's 6th choice, 83rd overall, in 1990 Entry Draft).

			Regular Season					Playoffs				
Season	Club	Lea	GP	G	A	TP	PIM	GP	G	A	TP	PIM
1988-89	Kamloops	WHL	68	8	15	23	209	....	....	....	....	....
1989-90	Kamloops	WHL	67	22	23	45	291	17	3	5	8	79
1990-91	Calgary	NHL	1	0	0	0	7	....	....	....	....	....
	Salt Lake	IHL	83	24	20	44	313	4	1	1	2	4
1991-92	Calgary	NHL	16	3	1	4	65	....	....	....	....	....
	Salt Lake	IHL	57	14	15	29	267	5	1	2	3	19
	NHL Totals		17	3	1	4	72	....	....	....	....	....

KRUSHELNYSKI, MICHAEL (MIKE) (KROO-shuhl-NIH-skee)

Left wing/Center. Shoots left. 6'2", 200 lbs. Born, Montreal, Que., April 27, 1960.
(Boston's 7th choice, 120th overall, in 1979 Entry Draft).

			Regular Season					Playoffs				
Season	Club	Lea	GP	G	A	TP	PIM	GP	G	A	TP	PIM
1978-79	Montreal	QJHL	46	15	29	44	42	11	3	4	7	8
1979-80	Montreal	QJHL	72	39	60	99	78	6	2	3	5	2
1980-81	Springfield	AHL	80	25	28	53	47	7	1	1	2	29
1981-82	Boston	NHL	17	3	3	6	2	1	0	0	0	2
	Erie	AHL	62	31	52	83	44	....	....	....	....	....
1982-83	Boston	NHL	79	23	42	65	43	17	8	6	14	12
1983-84	Boston	NHL	66	25	20	45	55	2	0	0	0	0
1984-85	Edmonton	NHL	80	43	45	88	60	18	5	8	13	22
1985-86	Edmonton	NHL	54	16	24	40	22	10	4	5	9	16
1986-87	Edmonton	NHL	80	16	35	51	67	21	3	4	7	18
1987-88	Edmonton	NHL	76	20	27	47	64	19	4	6	10	12
1988-89	Los Angeles	NHL	78	26	36	62	110	11	1	4	5	4
1989-90	Los Angeles	NHL	63	16	25	41	50	10	1	3	4	12
1990-91	Los Angeles	NHL	15	1	5	6	10	....	....	....	....	....
	Toronto	NHL	59	17	22	39	48	....	....	....	....	....
1991-92	Toronto	NHL	72	9	15	24	72	....	....	....	....	....
	NHL Totals		739	215	299	514	603	109	26	36	62	98

Played in NHL All-Star Game (1985)

Traded to **Edmonton** by **Boston** for Ken Linseman, June 21, 1984. Traded to **Los Angeles** by **Edmonton** with Wayne Gretzky and Marty McSorley for Jimmy Carson, Martin Gelinas, Los Angeles' first round choices in 1989 (acquired by New Jersey, June 17, 1989. New Jersey selected Jason Miller), 1991 (Martin Rucinsky) and 1993 Entry Drafts and cash, August 9, 1988. Traded to **Toronto** by **Los Angeles** for John McIntyre, November 9, 1990.

KRYGIER, TODD (KREE-guhr)

Left wing. Shoots left. 5'11", 180 lbs. Born, Northville, MI, October 12, 1965.
(Hartford's 1st choice, 16th overall, in 1988 Supplemental Draft).

			Regular Season					Playoffs				
Season	Club	Lea	GP	G	A	TP	PIM	GP	G	A	TP	PIM
1984-85	U. Connecticut	NCAA	14	14	11	25	12	....	....	....	....	....
1985-86	U. Connecticut	NCAA	32	29	27	56	46	....	....	....	....	....
1986-87	U. Connecticut	NCAA	28	24	24	48	44	....	....	....	....	....
1987-88	U. Connecticut	NCAA	27	32	39	71	28	....	....	....	....	....
	New Haven	AHL	13	1	5	6	34	....	....	....	....	....
1988-89	Binghamton	AHL	76	26	42	68	77	....	....	....	....	....
1989-90	Hartford	NHL	58	18	12	30	52	7	2	1	3	4
	Binghamton	AHL	12	1	9	10	16	....	....	....	....	....
1990-91	Hartford	NHL	72	13	17	30	95	6	0	2	2	0
1991-92	Washington	NHL	67	13	17	30	107	5	2	1	3	4
	NHL Totals		197	44	46	90	254	18	4	4	8	8

Traded to **Washington** by **Hartford** for future considerations, October 3, 1991.

KRYS, MARK

Defense. Shoots right. 6', 185 lbs. Born, Timmins, Ont., May 29, 1969.
(Boston's 6th choice, 165th overall, in 1988 Entry Draft).

			Regular Season					Playoffs				
Season	Club	Lea	GP	G	A	TP	PIM	GP	G	A	TP	PIM
1987-88	Boston U.	H.E.	34	0	6	6	40	....	....	....	....	....
1988-89	Boston U.	H.E.	35	0	7	7	54	....	....	....	....	....
1989-90	Boston U.	H.E.	30	0	4	4	34	....	....	....	....	....
1990-91	Boston U.	H.E.	36	1	9	10	18	....	....	....	....	....
1991-92	Maine	AHL	28	1	2	3	18	....	....	....	....	....
	Johnstown	ECHL	43	8	12	20	73	....	....	....	....	....

KUCERA, FRANTISEK (kuh-CHEH-rah)

Defense. Shoots right. 6'2", 205 lbs. Born, Prague, Czechoslovakia, February 3, 1968.
(Chicago's 3rd choice, 77th overall, in 1986 Entry Draft).

			Regular Season					Playoffs				
Season	Club	Lea	GP	G	A	TP	PIM	GP	G	A	TP	PIM
1986-87	Sparta Praha	Czech.	33	7	2	9	....	....	....	....	....	....
1987-88	Sparta Praha	Czech.	34	4	2	6	....	....	....	....	....	....
1988-89	Dukla Jihlava	Czech.	45	10	9	19	....	....	....	....	....	....
1989-90	Dukla Jihlava	Czech.	43	9	10	19	....	....	....	....	....	....
1990-91	Chicago	NHL	40	2	12	14	32	....	....	....	....	....
	Indianapolis	IHL	35	8	19	27	23	7	0	1	1	15
1991-92	Chicago	NHL	61	3	10	13	36	6	0	0	0	0
	Indianapolis	IHL	7	1	2	3	4	....	....	....	....	....
	NHL Totals		101	5	22	27	68	6	0	0	0	0

KUCERA, JIRI (kuh-CHEH-rah)

Center. Shoots left. 5'11", 180 lbs. Born, Plzen, Czechoslovakia, March 28, 1966.
(Pittsburgh's 8th choice, 152nd overall, in 1987 Entry Draft).

			Regular Season					Playoffs				
Season	Club	Lea	GP	G	A	TP	PIM	GP	G	A	TP	PIM
1987-88	Skoda Plzen	Czech.	32	19	11	30	....	....	....	....	....	....
1988-89	Skoda Plzen	Czech.	32	16	13	29	....	....	....	....	....	....
1989-90	Skoda Plzen	Czech.	47	10	24	34	....	....	....	....	....	....
1990-91	Tappara	Fin.	44	23	34	57	26	3	0	2	2	4
1991-92	Tappara	Fin.	44	22	20	42	8	....	....	....	....	....

KUCHARCIK, THOMAS

Center. Shoots left. 6'2", 200 lbs. Born, Mlada Boleslav, Czechoslovakia, May 10, 1970.
(Toronto's 11th choice, 167th overall, in 1991 Entry Draft).

			Regular Season					Playoffs				
Season	Club	Lea	GP	G	A	TP	PIM	GP	G	A	TP	PIM
1990-91	Dukla Jihlava	Czech.	23	7	6	13	6	....	....	....	....	....
1991-92	Dukla Jihlava	Czech.	37	13	17	30	....	....	....	....	....	....

KUCHYNA, PETR (kuh-HEE-nah)

Defense. Shoots right. 6'3", 180 lbs. Born, Jihlava, Czechoslovakia, January 14, 1970.
(New Jersey's 8th choice, 104th overall, in 1990 Entry Draft).

			Regular Season					Playoffs				
Season	Club	Lea	GP	G	A	TP	PIM	GP	G	A	TP	PIM
1989-90	Dukla Jihlava	Czech.	32	2	2	4	....	....	....	....	....	....
1990-91	Dukla Jihlava	Czech.	47	4	5	9	35	....	....	....	....	....
1991-92	Dukla Jihlava	Czech.	18	5	4	9	....	....	....	....	....	....
	Utica	AHL	53	3	6	9	22	4	0	0	0	2

KUDASHOV, ALEXEI (koo-dah-SHOV)

Center. Shoots right. 5'11", 183 lbs. Born, Elektrostal, Soviet Union, July 21, 1971.
(Toronto's 5th choice, 102nd overall, in 1991 Entry Draft).

			Regular Season					Playoffs				
Season	Club	Lea	GP	G	A	TP	PIM	GP	G	A	TP	PIM
1990-91	Soviet Wings	USSR	45	9	5	14	10	....	....	....	....	....
1991-92	Soviet Wings	CIS	36	8	16	24	12	....	....	....	....	....

KUDELSKI, BOB

Right wing. Shoots right. 6'1", 200 lbs. Born, Springfield, MA, March 3, 1964.
(Los Angeles' 1st choice, 2nd overall, in 1986 Supplemental Draft).

			Regular Season					Playoffs				
Season	Club	Lea	GP	G	A	TP	PIM	GP	G	A	TP	PIM
1983-84	Yale	ECAC	21	14	12	26	12	....	....	....	....	....
1984-85	Yale	ECAC	32	21	23	44	38	....	....	....	....	....
1985-86	Yale	ECAC	31	18	23	41	48	....	....	....	....	....
1986-87a	Yale	ECAC	30	25	22	47	34	....	....	....	....	....
1987-88	Los Angeles	NHL	26	0	1	1	8	....	....	....	....	....
	New Haven	AHL	50	15	19	34	41	....	....	....	....	....
1988-89	Los Angeles	NHL	14	1	3	4	17	....	....	....	....	....
	New Haven	AHL	60	32	19	51	43	17	8	5	13	12
1989-90	Los Angeles	NHL	62	23	13	36	49	8	1	2	3	2
1990-91	Los Angeles	NHL	72	23	13	36	46	8	3	2	5	2
1991-92	Los Angeles	NHL	80	22	21	43	42	6	0	0	0	0
	NHL Totals		254	69	51	120	162	22	4	4	8	4

a ECAC First All-Star Team (1987)

KULONEN, TIMO (KOO-loh-nehn)

Defense. Shoots right. 6'5", 220 lbs. Born, Forssa, Finland, November 1, 1967.
(Minnesota's 7th choice, 130th overall, in 1987 Entry Draft).

			Regular Season					Playoffs				
Season	Club	Lea	GP	G	A	TP	PIM	GP	G	A	TP	PIM
1986-87	KalPa	Fin.	39	2	8	10	20	....	....	....	....	....
1987-88	KalPa	Fin.	44	7	15	22	32	....	....	....	....	....
1988-89	KalPa	Fin.	40	9	16	25	18	2	0	1	1	0
1989-90	KalPa	Fin.	44	5	20	25	34	6	0	0	0	....
1990-91	KalPa	Fin.	42	1	10	11	16	8	0	2	2	4
1991-92	Lukko	Fin.	44	8	17	25	14	2	0	0	0	0

KUMMU, AL

Defense. Shoots right. 6'4", 195 lbs. Born, Kitchener, Ont., January 21, 1969.
(Philadelphia's 8th choice, 201st overall, in 1989 Entry Draft).

			Regular Season					Playoffs				
Season	Club	Lea	GP	G	A	TP	PIM	GP	G	A	TP	PIM
1989-90	RPI	ECAC	33	9	13	22	50	....	....	....	....	....
1990-91	RPI	ECAC	29	6	8	14	86	....	....	....	....	....
1991-92	RPI	ECAC	31	6	14	20	54	....	....	....	....	....

KUMPEL, MARK

Right wing. Shoots right. 6', 190 lbs. Born, Wakefield, MA, March 7, 1961.
(Quebec's 4th choice, 108th overall, in 1980 Entry Draft).

			Regular Season					Playoffs				
Season	Club	Lea	GP	G	A	TP	PIM	GP	G	A	TP	PIM
1979-80	U. of Lowell	ECAC	30	18	18	36	12	....	....	....	....	....
1980-81	U. of Lowell	ECAC	1	2	0	2	0	....	....	....	....	....
1981-82	U. of Lowell	ECAC	35	17	13	30	23	....	....	....	....	....
1982-83	U. of Lowell	ECAC	7	8	5	13	0	....	....	....	....	....
	U.S. National	....	30	14	18	32	6	....	....	....	....	....
1983-84	U.S. National	....	61	14	19	33	19	....	....	....	....	....
	U.S. Olympic	....	6	1	0	1	2	....	....	....	....	....
	Fredericton	AHL	16	1	1	2	5	3	0	0	0	15
1984-85	**Quebec**	**NHL**	**42**	**8**	**7**	**15**	**26**	**18**	**3**	**4**	**7**	**4**
	Fredericton	AHL	18	9	6	15	17	....	....	....	....	....
1985-86	**Quebec**	**NHL**	**47**	**10**	**12**	**22**	**17**	**2**	**1**	**0**	**1**	**0**
	Fredericton	AHL	7	4	2	6	4	....	....	....	....	....
1986-87	**Quebec**	**NHL**	**40**	**1**	**8**	**9**	**16**	....	....	....	....	....
	Detroit	**NHL**	**5**	**0**	**1**	**1**	**0**	**8**	**0**	**0**	**0**	**4**
	Adirondack	AHL	7	2	3	5	0	1	1	0	1	0
1987-88	**Detroit**	**NHL**	**13**	**0**	**2**	**2**	**4**	....	....	....	....	....
	Adirondack	AHL	4	5	0	5	2	....	....	....	....	....
	Winnipeg	**NHL**	**32**	**4**	**4**	**8**	**19**	**4**	**0**	**0**	**0**	**4**
1988-89	Moncton	AHL	53	22	23	45	25	10	3	4	7	0
1989-90	**Winnipeg**	**NHL**	**56**	**8**	**9**	**17**	**21**	**7**	**2**	**0**	**2**	**2**
1990-91	**Winnipeg**	**NHL**	**53**	**7**	**3**	**10**	**10**	....	....	....	....	....
1991-92	Moncton	AHL	41	11	18	29	12	2	0	0	0	0
	NHL Totals		**288**	**38**	**46**	**84**	**113**	**39**	**6**	**4**	**10**	**14**

Traded to **Detroit** by **Quebec** with Brent Ashton and Gilbert Delorme for Basil McRae, John Ogrodnick and Doug Shedden, January 17, 1987. Traded to **Winnipeg** by **Detroit** for Jim Nill, January 11, 1988.

KUNTOS, JIRI (KOON-tohsh)

Defense. Shoots left. 5'11", 187 lbs. Born, Jihlava, Czech., December 11, 1971.
(Buffalo's 9th choice, 162nd overall, in 1991 Entry Draft).

			Regular Season					Playoffs				
Season	Club	Lea	GP	G	A	TP	PIM	GP	G	A	TP	PIM
1990-91	Dukla Jihlava	Czech.	10	2	1	3	....	....	....	....	....	....
1991-92	Dukla Jihlava	Czech.	37	0	5	5	....	....	....	....	....	....

KURRI, JARI (KUHR-ree, YAH-ree)

Right wing. Shoots right. 6'1", 195 lbs. Born, Helsinki, Finland, May 18, 1960.
(Edmonton's 3rd choice, 69th overall, in 1980 Entry Draft).

			Regular Season					Playoffs				
Season	Club	Lea	GP	G	A	TP	PIM	GP	G	A	TP	PIM
1977-78	Jokerit	Fin.	29	2	9	11	12	....	....	....	....	....
1978-79	Jokerit	Fin.	33	16	14	30	12	....	....	....	....	....
1979-80	Jokerit	Fin.	33	23	16	39	22	6	7	2	9	13
1980-81	**Edmonton**	**NHL**	**75**	**32**	**43**	**75**	**40**	**9**	**5**	**7**	**12**	**4**
1981-82	**Edmonton**	**NHL**	**71**	**32**	**54**	**86**	**32**	**5**	**2**	**5**	**7**	**10**
1982-83	**Edmonton**	**NHL**	**80**	**45**	**59**	**104**	**22**	**16**	**8**	**15**	**23**	**8**
1983-84a	**Edmonton**	**NHL**	**64**	**52**	**61**	**113**	**14**	**19**	***14**	**14**	**28**	**13**
1984-85bc	**Edmonton**	**NHL**	**73**	**71**	**64**	**135**	**30**	**18**	***19**	**12**	**31**	**6**
1985-86a	**Edmonton**	**NHL**	**78**	***68**	**63**	**131**	**22**	**10**	**2**	**10**	**12**	**4**
1986-87c	**Edmonton**	**NHL**	**79**	**54**	**54**	**108**	**41**	**21**	***15**	**10**	**25**	**20**
1987-88	**Edmonton**	**NHL**	**80**	**43**	**53**	**96**	**30**	**19**	***14**	**17**	**31**	**12**
1988-89a	**Edmonton**	**NHL**	**76**	**44**	**58**	**102**	**69**	**7**	**3**	**5**	**8**	**6**
1989-90	**Edmonton**	**NHL**	**78**	**33**	**60**	**93**	**48**	**22**	**10**	**15**	**25**	**18**
1990-91	Milan	Italy	30	27	48	75	6	10	10	12	22	2
1991-92	**Los Angeles**	**NHL**	**73**	**23**	**37**	**60**	**24**	**4**	**1**	**2**	**3**	**4**
	NHL Totals		**827**	**497**	**606**	**1103**	**372**	**150**	**93**	**112**	**205**	**105**

a NHL Second All-Star Team (1984, 1986, 1989)
b Won Lady Byng Memorial Trophy (1985)
c NHL First All-Star Team (1985, 1987)

Played in NHL All-Star Game (1983, 1985, 1986, 1988-90)

Traded to **Philadelphia** by **Edmonton** with Dave Brown and Corey Foster for Craig Fisher, Scott Mellanby and Craig Berube, May 30, 1991. Traded to **Los Angeles** by **Philadelphia** with Jeff Chychrun for Steve Duchesne, Steve Kasper and Los Angeles' fourth round choice (Aris Brimanis) in 1991 Entry Draft, May 30, 1991.

KURVERS, TOM

Defense. Shoots left. 6'2", 195 lbs. Born, Minneapolis, MN, September 14, 1962.
(Montreal's 10th choice, 145th overall, in 1981 Entry Draft).

			Regular Season					Playoffs				
Season	Club	Lea	GP	G	A	TP	PIM	GP	G	A	TP	PIM
1980-81	Minn.-Duluth	WCHA	39	6	24	30	48	....	....	....	....	....
1981-82	Minn.-Duluth	WCHA	37	11	31	42	18	....	....	....	....	....
1982-83	Minn.-Duluth	WCHA	26	4	23	27	24	....	....	....	....	....
1983-84ab	Minn.-Duluth	WCHA	43	18	58	76	46	....	....	....	....	....
1984-85	**Montreal**	**NHL**	**75**	**10**	**35**	**45**	**30**	**12**	**0**	**6**	**6**	**6**
1985-86	**Montreal**	**NHL**	**62**	**7**	**23**	**30**	**36**	....	....	....	....	....
1986-87	**Montreal**	**NHL**	**1**	**0**	**0**	**0**	**0**	....	....	....	....	....
	Buffalo	**NHL**	**55**	**6**	**17**	**23**	**22**	....	....	....	....	....
1987-88	**New Jersey**	**NHL**	**56**	**5**	**29**	**34**	**46**	**19**	**6**	**9**	**15**	**38**
1988-89	**New Jersey**	**NHL**	**74**	**16**	**50**	**66**	**38**	....	....	....	....	....
1989-90	**New Jersey**	**NHL**	**1**	**0**	**0**	**0**	**0**	....	....	....	....	....
	Toronto	**NHL**	**70**	**15**	**37**	**52**	**29**	**5**	**0**	**3**	**3**	**4**
1990-91	**Toronto**	**NHL**	**19**	**0**	**3**	**3**	**8**	....	....	....	....	....
	Vancouver	**NHL**	**32**	**4**	**23**	**27**	**20**	**6**	**2**	**2**	**4**	**12**
1991-92	**NY Islanders**	**NHL**	**74**	**9**	**47**	**56**	**30**	....	....	....	....	....
	NHL Totals		**519**	**72**	**264**	**336**	**259**	**42**	**8**	**20**	**28**	**60**

a WCHA First All-Star Team (1984)
b Won Hobey Baker Memorial Trophy (1984)

Traded to **Buffalo** by **Montreal** for Buffalo's second round choice (Martin St. Amour) in 1988 Entry Draft, November 18, 1986. Traded to **New Jersey** by **Buffalo** for the rights to Detroit's third round choice (Andrew MacVicar) in 1987 Entry Draft previously acquired by New Jersey in Mel Bridgman deal, June 13, 1987. Traded to **Toronto** by **New Jersey** for Toronto's first round choice (Scott Niedermayer) in 1991 Entry Draft, October 16, 1989. Traded to **Vancouver** by **Toronto** for Brian Bradley, January 12, 1991. Traded to **Minnesota** by **Vancouver** for Dave Babych, June 22, 1991. Traded to **NY Islanders** by **Minnesota** for Craig Ludwig, June 22, 1991.

KUSHNER, DALE

Left wing. Shoots left. 6'1", 195 lbs. Born, Terrace, B.C., June 13, 1966.

			Regular Season					Playoffs				
Season	Club	Lea	GP	G	A	TP	PIM	GP	G	A	TP	PIM
1983-84	Prince Albert	WHL	1	2	0	2	5	....	....	....	....	....
1984-85	Prince Albert	WHL	2	0	0	0	2	....	....	....	....	....
	Moose Jaw	WHL	17	5	2	7	23	....	....	....	....	....
	Medicine Hat	WHL	48	23	17	40	173	10	3	3	6	18
1985-86	Medicine Hat	WHL	66	25	19	44	218	25	0	5	5	114
1986-87	Medicine Hat	WHL	63	34	34	68	250	20	8	13	21	57
1987-88	Springfield	AHL	68	13	23	36	201	....	....	....	....	....
1988-89	Springfield	AHL	45	5	8	13	132	....	....	....	....	....
1989-90	**NY Islanders**	**NHL**	**2**	**0**	**0**	**0**	**2**	....	....	....	....	....
	Springfield	AHL	45	14	11	25	163	7	2	3	5	61
1990-91	**Philadelphia**	**NHL**	**63**	**7**	**11**	**18**	**195**	....	....	....	....	....
	Hershey	AHL	5	3	4	7	14	....	....	....	....	....
1991-92	**Philadelphia**	**NHL**	**19**	**3**	**2**	**5**	**18**	....	....	....	....	....
	Hershey	AHL	46	9	7	16	98	6	0	2	2	23
	NHL Totals		**84**	**10**	**13**	**23**	**215**	....	....	....	....	....

Signed as a free agent by **NY Islanders**, April 7, 1987. Signed as a free agent by **Philadelphia**, July 31, 1990.

KUWABARA, RYAN

Right wing. Shoots right. 6', 205 lbs. Born, Hamilton, Ont., March 23, 1972.
(Montreal's 2nd choice, 39th overall, in 1990 Entry Draft).

			Regular Season					Playoffs				
Season	Club	Lea	GP	G	A	TP	PIM	GP	G	A	TP	PIM
1989-90	Ottawa	OHL	66	30	38	68	62	4	0	0	0	0
1990-91	Ottawa	OHL	64	34	38	72	67	17	12	15	27	25
1991-92	Ottawa	OHL	66	43	57	100	84	10	6	5	11	9

KUZMINSKY, ALEXANDER

Center. Shoots left. 5'11", 160 lbs. Born, Kiev, Soviet Union, July 12, 1972.
(Toronto's 7th choice, 120th overall, in 1991 Entry Draft).

			Regular Season					Playoffs				
Season	Club	Lea	GP	G	A	TP	PIM	GP	G	A	TP	PIM
1990-91	Sokol Kiev	USSR	34	2	0	2	10	....	....	....	....	....
1991-92	Sokol Kiev	CIS	23	1	3	4	8	....	....	....	....	....

KVARTALNOV, DMITRI (kvahr-TAHL-nov)

Left wing. Shoots left. 5'11", 180 lbs. Born, Voskresensk, Soviet Union, March 25, 1966.
(Boston's 1st choice, 16th overall, in 1992 Entry Draft).

			Regular Season					Playoffs				
Season	Club	Lea	GP	G	A	TP	PIM	GP	G	A	TP	PIM
1990-91	Khimik	USSR	42	12	10	22	18	....	....	....	....	....
1991-92abcd	San Diego	IHL	77	*60	58	*118	16	4	2	0	2	2

a Won James Gatschene Memorial Trophy (MVP–IHL) 1992
b Won Leo P. Lamoureaux Memorial Trophy (Top Scorer–IHL) 1992
c Won Garry F. Longman Memorial Trophy (Top Rookie–IHL) 1992
d IHL First All-Star Team (1992)

KYPREOS, NICHOLAS (NICK) (KIH-pree-ohz)

Left wing. Shoots left. 6', 195 lbs. Born, Toronto, Ont., June 4, 1966.

			Regular Season					Playoffs				
Season	Club	Lea	GP	G	A	TP	PIM	GP	G	A	TP	PIM
1983-84	North Bay	OHL	51	12	11	23	36	4	3	2	5	9
1984-85	North Bay	OHL	64	41	36	77	71	8	2	2	4	15
1985-86a	North Bay	OHL	64	62	35	97	112	....	....	....	....	....
1986-87	Hershey	AHL	10	0	1	1	4	....	....	....	....	....
b	North Bay	OHL	46	49	41	90	54	24	11	5	16	78
1987-88	Hershey	AHL	71	24	20	44	101	12	0	2	2	17
1988-89	Hershey	AHL	28	12	15	27	19	12	4	5	9	11
1989-90	**Washington**	**NHL**	**31**	**5**	**4**	**9**	**82**	**7**	**1**	**0**	**1**	**15**
	Baltimore	AHL	14	6	5	11	6	7	4	1	5	17
1990-91	**Washington**	**NHL**	**79**	**9**	**9**	**18**	**196**	**9**	**0**	**1**	**1**	**38**
1991-92	**Washington**	**NHL**	**65**	**4**	**6**	**10**	**206**	....	....	....	....	....
	NHL Totals		**175**	**18**	**19**	**37**	**484**	**16**	**1**	**1**	**2**	**53**

a OHL First All-Star Team (1986)
b OHL Second All-Star Team (1987)

Signed as a free agent by **Philadelphia**, September 30, 1984. Claimed by **Washington** in NHL Waiver Draft, October 2, 1989. Traded to **Hartford** by **Washington** for Mark Hunter and future considerations (Yvon Corriveau), June 15, 1992.

KYTE, JAMES (JIM) (KITE)

Defense. Shoots left. 6'5", 210 lbs. Born, Ottawa, Ont., March 21, 1964.
(Winnipeg's 1st choice, 12th overall, in 1982 Entry Draft).

			Regular Season					Playoffs				
Season	Club	Lea	GP	G	A	TP	PIM	GP	G	A	TP	PIM
1981-82	Cornwall	OHL	52	4	13	17	148	5	0	0	0	10
1982-83	Winnipeg	NHL	2	0	0	0	0	....	....	....	....	....
	Cornwall	OHL	65	6	30	36	195	8	0	2	2	24
1983-84	Winnipeg	NHL	58	1	2	3	55	3	0	0	0	11
1984-85	Winnipeg	NHL	71	0	3	3	111	8	0	0	0	14
1985-86	Winnipeg	NHL	71	1	3	4	126	3	0	0	0	12
1986-87	Winnipeg	NHL	72	5	5	10	162	10	0	4	4	36
1987-88	Winnipeg	NHL	51	1	3	4	128	....	....	....	....	....
1988-89	Winnipeg	NHL	74	3	9	12	190	....	....	....	....	....
1989-90	Pittsburgh	NHL	56	3	1	4	125	....	....	....	....	....
1990-91	Pittsburgh	NHL	1	0	0	0	2	....	....	....	....	....
	Muskegon	IHL	25	2	5	7	157	....	....	....	....	....
	Calgary	NHL	42	0	9	9	153	7	0	0	0	7
1991-92	Calgary	NHL	21	0	1	1	107	....	....	....	....	....
	Salt Lake	IHL	6	0	1	1	9	....	....	....	....	....
	NHL Totals		519	14	36	50	1159	31	0	0	0	80

Traded to **Pittsburgh** by **Winnipeg** with Andrew McBain and Randy Gilhen for Randy Cunnyworth, Rick Tabaracci and Dave McLlwain, June 17, 1989. Traded to **Calgary** by **Pittsburgh** for Jiri Hrdina, December 13, 1990.

LABELLE, MARC

Left wing. Shoots left. 6'1", 215 lbs. Born, Maniwaki, Que., December 20, 1969.

			Regular Season					Playoffs				
Season	Club	Lea	GP	G	A	TP	PIM	GP	G	A	TP	PIM
1987-88	Victoriaville	QMJHL	63	11	14	25	236	5	2	4	6	20
1988-89	Victoriaville	QMJHL	62	9	26	35	202	15	6	3	9	30
1989-90	Victoriaville	QMJHL	56	18	21	39	192	16	4	8	12	42
1990-91	Fredericton	AHL	25	1	4	5	95	4	0	2	2	25
	Richmond	ECHL	5	1	1	2	37	....	....	....	....	....
1991-92	Fredericton	AHL	62	7	10	17	238	3	0	0	0	6

Signed as a free agent by **Montreal**, January 21, 1991.

LACHANCE, BOB

Right wing. Shoots right. 5'11", 175 lbs. Born, Northampton, MA, February 1, 1974.
(St. Louis' 5th choice, 134th overall, in 1992 Entry Draft).

			Regular Season					Playoffs				
Season	Club	Lea	GP	G	A	TP	PIM	GP	G	A	TP	PIM
1991-92	Springfield	US Jr.	46	40	98	138	87	....	....	....	....	....

LACHANCE, SCOTT

Defense. Shoots left. 6'1", 197 lbs. Born, Charlottesville, VA, October 22, 1972.
(NY Islanders' 1st choice, 4th overall, in 1991 Entry Draft).

			Regular Season					Playoffs				
Season	Club	Lea	GP	G	A	TP	PIM	GP	G	A	TP	PIM
1989-90	Springfield	US Jr.	34	25	41	66	62	....	....	....	....	....
1990-91	Boston U.	H.E.	31	5	19	24	48	....	....	....	....	....
1991-92	U.S. National	....	36	1	10	11	34	....	....	....	....	....
	U.S. Olympic	....	8	0	1	1	6	....	....	....	....	....
	NY Islanders	NHL	17	1	4	5	9	....	....	....	....	....
	NHL Totals		17	1	4	5	9	....	....	....	....	....

LACOUTURE, DAVID

Right wing. Shoots right. 6'3", 205 lbs. Born, Framingham, MA, December 30, 1969.
(St. Louis' 5th choice, 105th overall, in 1988 Entry Draft).

			Regular Season					Playoffs				
Season	Club	Lea	GP	G	A	TP	PIM	GP	G	A	TP	PIM
1989-90	U. of Maine	H.E.	9	0	2	2	6	....	....	....	....	....
1990-91	U. of Maine	H.E.	40	7	9	16	33	....	....	....	....	....
1991-92	U. of Maine	H.E.	28	5	4	9	30	....	....	....	....	....

LACROIX, DANIEL (la-QUAH)

Left wing. Shoots left. 6'2", 188 lbs. Born, Montreal, Que., March 11, 1969.
(NY Rangers' 2nd choice, 31st overall, in 1987 Entry Draft).

			Regular Season					Playoffs				
Season	Club	Lea	GP	G	A	TP	PIM	GP	G	A	TP	PIM
1986-87	Granby	QMJHL	54	9	16	25	311	8	1	2	3	22
1987-88	Granby	QMJHL	58	24	50	74	468	5	0	4	4	12
1988-89	Granby	QMJHL	70	45	49	94	320	4	1	1	2	57
	Denver	IHL	2	0	1	1	0	2	0	1	1	0
1989-90	Flint	IHL	61	12	16	28	128	4	2	0	2	24
1990-91	Binghamton	AHL	54	7	12	19	237	5	1	0	4	24
1991-92	Binghamton	AHL	52	12	20	32	149	11	2	4	6	28

LACROIX, ERIC

Left wing. Shoots left. 6'1", 200 lbs. Born, Montreal, Que., July 15, 1971.
(Toronto's 6th choice, 136th overall, in 1990 Entry Draft).

			Regular Season					Playoffs				
Season	Club	Lea	GP	G	A	TP	PIM	GP	G	A	TP	PIM
1990-91	St. Lawrence	ECAC	35	13	11	24	35	....	....	....	....	....
1991-92	St. Lawrence	ECAC	34	11	20	31	40	....	....	....	....	....

LACROIX, MARTIN

Right wing. Shoots right. 5'11", 155 lbs. Born, Rosemere, Que., January 4, 1970.
(NY Islanders' 10th choice, 216th overall, in 1990 Entry Draft).

			Regular Season					Playoffs				
Season	Club	Lea	GP	G	A	TP	PIM	GP	G	A	TP	PIM
1988-89	St. Lawrence	ECAC	19	1	5	6	23	....	....	....	....	....
1989-90	St. Lawrence	ECAC	32	11	8	19	14	....	....	....	....	....
1990-91	St. Lawrence	ECAC	35	16	26	42	46	....	....	....	....	....
1991-92	St. Lawrence	ECAC	22	17	17	34	24	....	....	....	....	....

LADOUCEUR, RANDY (LAD-uh-SOOR)

Defense. Shoots left. 6'2", 220 lbs. Born, Brockville, Ont., June 30, 1960.

			Regular Season					Playoffs				
Season	Club	Lea	GP	G	A	TP	PIM	GP	G	A	TP	PIM
1978-79	Brantford	OHA	64	3	17	20	141	....	....	....	....	....
1979-80	Brantford	OHA	37	6	15	21	125	8	0	5	5	18
1980-81	Kalamazoo	IHL	80	7	30	37	52	8	1	3	4	10
1981-82	Adirondack	AHL	78	4	28	32	78	5	1	1	2	6
1982-83	Detroit	NHL	27	0	4	4	16	....	....	....	....	....
	Adirondack	AHL	48	11	21	32	54	....	....	....	....	....
1983-84	Detroit	NHL	71	3	17	20	58	4	1	0	1	6
	Adirondack	AHL	11	3	5	8	12	....	....	....	....	....
1984-85	Detroit	NHL	80	3	27	30	108	3	1	0	1	0
1985-86	Detroit	NHL	78	5	13	18	196	....	....	....	....	....
1986-87	Detroit	NHL	34	3	6	9	70	....	....	....	....	....
	Hartford	NHL	36	2	3	5	51	6	0	2	2	12
1987-88	Hartford	NHL	67	1	7	8	91	6	1	1	2	4
1988-89	Hartford	NHL	75	2	5	7	95	1	0	0	0	10
1989-90	Hartford	NHL	71	3	12	15	126	7	1	0	1	10
1990-91	Hartford	NHL	67	1	3	4	118	6	1	4	5	6
1991-92	Hartford	NHL	74	1	9	10	127	7	0	1	1	11
	NHL Totals		680	24	106	130	1056	40	5	8	13	59

Signed as a free agent by **Detroit**, November 1, 1979. Traded to **Hartford** by **Detroit** for Dave Barr, January 12, 1987.

LAFAYETTE, JUSTIN

Left wing. Shoots left. 6'6", 220 lbs. Born, Vancouver, B.C., January 23, 1970.
(Chicago's 5th choice, 113th overall, in 1988 Entry Draft).

			Regular Season					Playoffs				
Season	Club	Lea	GP	G	A	TP	PIM	GP	G	A	TP	PIM
1987-88	Ferris State	CCHA	34	1	2	3	20	....	....	....	....	....
1988-89	Ferris State	CCHA	36	3	4	7	59	....	....	....	....	....
1989-90	Ferris State	CCHA	34	4	5	9	38	....	....	....	....	....
1990-91	Ferris State	CCHA	39	11	9	20	74	....	....	....	....	....
1991-92	Indianapolis	IHL	51	7	10	17	37	....	....	....	....	....

LAFAYETTE, NATHAN

Center. Shoots right. 6'1", 194 lbs. Born, New Westminster, B.C., February 17, 1973.
(St. Louis' 3rd choice, 65th overall, in 1991 Entry Draft).

			Regular Season					Playoffs				
Season	Club	Lea	GP	G	A	TP	PIM	GP	G	A	TP	PIM
1989-90	Kingston	OHL	53	6	8	14	14	7	0	1	1	0
1990-91	Kingston	OHL	35	13	13	26	10	....	....	....	....	....
	Cornwall	OHL	28	16	22	38	25	....	....	....	....	....
1991-92a	Cornwall	OHL	66	28	45	73	26	6	2	5	7	15

a Canadian Major Junior Scholastic Player of the Year (1992)

LaFONTAINE, PAT

Center. Shoots right. 5'10", 177 lbs. Born, St. Louis, MO, February 22, 1965.
(NY Islanders' 1st choice, 3rd overall, in 1983 Entry Draft).

			Regular Season					Playoffs				
Season	Club	Lea	GP	G	A	TP	PIM	GP	G	A	TP	PIM
1982-83abcd	Verdun	QMJHL	70	*104	*130	*234	10	15	11	*24	*3	4
1983-84	U.S. National	....	58	56	55	111	22	....	....	....	....	....
	U.S. Olympic	....	6	5	5	10	0	....	....	....	....	....
	NY Islanders	NHL	15	13	6	19	6	16	3	6	9	8
1984-85	NY Islanders	NHL	67	19	35	54	32	9	1	2	3	4
1985-86	NY Islanders	NHL	65	30	23	53	43	3	1	0	1	0
1986-87	NY Islanders	NHL	80	38	32	70	70	14	5	7	12	10
1987-88	NY Islanders	NHL	75	47	45	92	52	6	4	5	9	8
1988-89	NY Islanders	NHL	79	45	43	88	26	....	....	....	....	....
1989-90e	NY Islanders	NHL	74	54	51	105	38	2	0	1	1	0
1990-91	NY Islanders	NHL	75	41	44	85	42	....	....	....	....	....
1991-92	Buffalo	NHL	57	46	47	93	98	7	8	3	11	4
	NHL Totals		587	333	326	659	407	57	22	24	46	34

a QMJHL First All-Star Team (1983)
b QMJHL Most Valuable Player (1983)
c QMJHL Most Valuable Player in Playoffs (1983)
d Canadian Major Junior Player of the Year (1983)
e Won Dodge Performer of the Year Award (1990)

Played in NHL All-Star Game (1988-91)

Traded to **Buffalo** by **NY Islanders** with Randy Hillier, Randy Wood and future considerations for Pierre Turgeon, Uwe Krupp, Benoit Hogue and Dave McLlwain, October 25, 1991.

LaFORGE, MARC

Left wing. Shoots left. 6'2", 210 lbs. Born, Sudbury, Ont., January 3, 1968.
(Hartford's 2nd choice, 32nd overall, in 1986 Entry Draft).

			Regular Season					Playoffs				
Season	Club	Lea	GP	G	A	TP	PIM	GP	G	A	TP	PIM
1984-85	Kingston	OHL	57	1	5	6	214	....	....	....	....	....
1985-86	Kingston	OHL	60	1	13	14	248	10	0	1	1	30
1986-87	Binghamton	AHL	....	....	....	....	....	4	0	0	0	7
	Kingston	OHL	53	2	10	12	224	12	1	0	1	79
1987-88	Sudbury	OHL	14	0	2	2	68	....	....	....	....	....
1988-89	Binghamton	AHL	38	2	2	4	179	....	....	....	....	....
	Indianapolis	IHL	14	0	2	2	138	....	....	....	....	....
1989-90	Hartford	NHL	9	0	0	0	43	....	....	....	....	....
	Binghamton	AHL	25	2	6	8	111	....	....	....	....	....
	Cape Breton	AHL	3	0	1	1	24	3	0	0	0	27
1990-91	Cape Breton	AHL	49	1	7	8	217	....	....	....	....	....
1991-92	Cape Breton	AHL	59	0	14	14	341	4	0	0	0	24
	NHL Totals		9	0	0	0	43	....	....	....	....	....

Traded to **Edmonton** by **Hartford** for the rights to Cam Brauer, March 6, 1990.

LAFRENIERE, JASON (LAH-frehn-YAIR)

Center. Shoots right. 5'11", 185 lbs. Born, St. Catharines, Ont., December 6, 1966.
(Quebec's 2nd choice, 36th overall, in 1985 Entry Draft).

			Regular Season					Playoffs				
Season	Club	Lea	GP	G	A	TP	PIM	GP	G	A	TP	PIM
1983-84	Brantford	OHL	70	24	57	81	4	6	2	4	6	2
1984-85	Hamilton	OHL	59	26	69	95	10	17	12	16	28	0
1985-86a	Hamilton	OHL	14	12	10	22	2	....	....	....	....	....
a	Belleville	OHL	48	37	73	110	2	23	10	*22	*32	6
1986-87	**Quebec**	**NHL**	**56**	**13**	**15**	**28**	**8**	**12**	**1**	**5**	**6**	**2**
	Fredericton	AHL	11	3	11	14	0	....	....	....	....	....
1987-88	**Quebec**	**NHL**	**40**	**10**	**19**	**29**	**4**	....	....	....	....	....
	Fredericton	AHL	32	12	19	31	38	....	....	....	....	....
1988-89	**NY Rangers**	**NHL**	**38**	**8**	**16**	**24**	**6**	**3**	**0**	**0**	**0**	**17**
	Denver	IHL	24	10	19	29	17	....	....	....	....	....
1989-90	Flint	IHL	41	9	25	34	34	....	....	....	....	....
	Phoenix	IHL	14	4	9	13	0	....	....	....	....	....
1990-91	Cdn. National	....	59	26	33	59	50	....	....	....	....	....
1991-92	Landshut	Ger.	23	7	22	29	16	....	....	....	....	....
	San Diego	IHL	5	1	2	3	2	....	....	....	....	....
	NHL Totals		**134**	**31**	**50**	**81**	**18**	**15**	**1**	**5**	**6**	**19**

a OHL First All-Star Team (1986)

Traded to **NY Rangers** by **Quebec** with Normand Rochefort for Bruce Bell, Jari Gronstrand, Walt Poddubny and NY Rangers' fourth round choice (Eric Dubois) in 1989 Entry Draft, August 1, 1988. Signed as a free agent by **Tampa Bay**, July 29, 1992.

LALONDE, CHRISTIAN

Left wing. Shoots left. 6'1", 210 lbs. Born, La Salle, Que., May 3, 1966.

			Regular Season					Playoffs				
Season	Club	Lea	GP	G	A	TP	PIM	GP	G	A	TP	PIM
1986-87	U. of Maine	H.E.	40	8	8	16	49	....	....	....	....	....
1987-88	U. of Maine	H.E.	44	20	31	51	40	....	....	....	....	....
1988-89	U. of Maine	H.E.	39	10	29	39	41	....	....	....	....	....
1989-90	U. of Maine	H.E.	41	2	13	15	44	....	....	....	....	....
	Newmarket	AHL	3	0	0	0	0	....	....	....	....	....
1990-91	Muskegon	IHL	33	1	4	5	25	....	....	....	....	....
	Albany	IHL	2	0	0	0	9	....	....	....	....	....
	Knoxville	ECHL	20	3	12	15	37	3	0	0	0	2
1991-92	Muskegon	IHL	3	0	3	3	0	....	....	....	....	....

Signed as a free agent by **Pittsburgh**, September 4, 1990.

LALOR, MIKE

Defense. Shoots left. 6', 200 lbs. Born, Buffalo, NY, March 8, 1963.

			Regular Season					Playoffs				
Season	Club	Lea	GP	G	A	TP	PIM	GP	G	A	TP	PIM
1981-82	Brantford	OHL	64	3	13	16	114	11	0	6	6	11
1982-83	Brantford	OHL	65	10	30	40	113	8	1	3	4	20
1983-84	Nova Scotia	AHL	67	5	11	16	80	12	0	2	2	13
1984-85	Sherbrooke	AHL	79	9	23	32	114	17	3	5	8	36
1985-86	**Montreal**	**NHL**	**62**	**3**	**5**	**8**	**56**	**17**	**1**	**2**	**3**	**29**
1986-87	**Montreal**	**NHL**	**57**	**0**	**10**	**10**	**47**	**13**	**2**	**1**	**3**	**29**
1987-88	**Montreal**	**NHL**	**66**	**1**	**10**	**11**	**113**	**11**	**0**	**0**	**0**	**11**
1988-89	**Montreal**	**NHL**	**12**	**1**	**4**	**5**	**15**	....	....	....	....	....
	St. Louis	**NHL**	**36**	**1**	**14**	**15**	**54**	**10**	**1**	**1**	**2**	**14**
1989-90	**St. Louis**	**NHL**	**78**	**0**	**16**	**16**	**81**	**12**	**0**	**2**	**2**	**31**
1990-91	**Washington**	**NHL**	**68**	**1**	**5**	**6**	**61**	**10**	**1**	**2**	**3**	**22**
1991-92	**Washington**	**NHL**	**64**	**5**	**7**	**12**	**64**	....	....	....	....	....
	Winnipeg	**NHL**	**15**	**2**	**3**	**5**	**14**	**7**	**0**	**0**	**0**	**19**
	NHL Totals		**458**	**14**	**74**	**88**	**505**	**80**	**5**	**8**	**13**	**155**

Signed as a free agent by **Montreal**, September, 1983. Traded to **St. Louis** by **Montreal** for the option (exercised by Montreal) to switch first round picks in 1990 Entry Draft and St. Louis' third round choice in the 1991 Entry Draft, January 16, 1989. Traded to **Washington** by **St. Louis** with Peter Zezel for Geoff Courtnall, July 13, 1990. Traded to **Winnipeg** by **Washington** for Paul MacDermid, March 2, 1992.

LAMB, MARK

Center. Shoots left. 5'9", 180 lbs. Born, Ponteix, Sask., August 3, 1964.
(Calgary's 5th choice, 72nd overall, in 1982 Entry Draft).

			Regular Season					Playoffs				
Season	Club	Lea	GP	G	A	TP	PIM	GP	G	A	TP	PIM
1981-82	Billings	WHL	72	45	56	101	46	5	4	6	10	4
1982-83	Nanaimo	WHL	30	14	37	51	16	....	....	....	....	....
	Medicine Hat	WHL	46	22	43	65	33	5	3	2	5	4
	Colorado	CHL	....	....	....	....	....	6	0	2	2	0
1983-84a	Medicine Hat	WHL	72	59	77	136	30	14	12	11	23	6
1984-85	Moncton	AHL	80	23	49	72	53	....	....	....	....	....
1985-86	**Calgary**	**NHL**	**1**	**0**	**0**	**0**	**0**	....	....	....	....	....
	Moncton	AHL	79	26	50	76	51	10	2	6	8	17
1986-87	**Detroit**	**NHL**	**22**	**2**	**1**	**3**	**8**	**11**	**0**	**0**	**0**	**11**
	Adirondack	AHL	49	14	36	50	45	....	....	....	....	....
1987-88	**Edmonton**	**NHL**	**2**	**0**	**0**	**0**	**0**	....	....	....	....	....
	Nova Scotia	AHL	69	27	61	88	45	5	0	5	5	6
1988-89	**Edmonton**	**NHL**	**20**	**2**	**8**	**10**	**14**	**6**	**0**	**2**	**2**	**8**
	Cape Breton	AHL	54	33	49	82	29	....	....	....	....	....
1989-90	**Edmonton**	**NHL**	**58**	**12**	**16**	**28**	**42**	**22**	**6**	**11**	**17**	**2**
1990-91	**Edmonton**	**NHL**	**37**	**4**	**8**	**12**	**25**	**15**	**0**	**5**	**5**	**20**
1991-92	**Edmonton**	**NHL**	**59**	**6**	**22**	**28**	**46**	**16**	**1**	**1**	**2**	**10**
	NHL Totals		**199**	**26**	**55**	**81**	**135**	**70**	**7**	**19**	**26**	**51**

a WHL First All-Star Team, East Division (1984)

Signed as a free agent by **Detroit**, July 28, 1986. Claimed by **Edmonton** in NHL Waiver Draft, October 5, 1987. Claimed by **Ottawa** from **Edmonton** in Expansion Draft, June 18, 1992.

LAMBERT, DAN

Defense. Shoots left. 5'8", 177 lbs. Born, St. Boniface, Man., January 12, 1970.
(Quebec's 8th choice, 106th overall, in 1989 Entry Draft).

			Regular Season					Playoffs				
Season	Club	Lea	GP	G	A	TP	PIM	GP	G	A	TP	PIM
1986-87	Swift Current	WHL	68	13	53	66	95	4	1	1	2	9
1987-88	Swift Current	WHL	69	20	63	83	120	10	2	10	12	45
1988-89ab	Swift Current	WHL	57	25	77	102	158	12	9	19	28	12
1989-90a	Swift Current	WHL	50	17	51	68	119	4	2	3	5	12
1990-91	**Quebec**	**NHL**	**1**	**0**	**0**	**0**	**0**	....	....	....	....	....
	Halifax	AHL	30	7	13	20	20	....	....	....	....	....
	Fort Wayne	IHL	49	10	27	37	65	19	4	10	14	20
1991-92	**Quebec**	**NHL**	**28**	**6**	**9**	**15**	**22**	....	....	....	....	....
	Halifax	AHL	47	3	28	31	33	....	....	....	....	....
	NHL Totals		**29**	**6**	**9**	**15**	**22**	....	....	....	....	....

a WHL East First All-Star Team (1989, 1990)
b WHL Best Defenseman (1989)

Traded to **Winnipeg** by **Quebec** for Dan Lambert, August 25, 1992.

LANG, ROBERT

Center. Shoots right. 6'2", 180 lbs. Born, Most, Czechoslovakia, December 19, 1970.
(Los Angeles' 6th choice, 133rd overall, in 1990 Entry Draft).

			Regular Season					Playoffs				
Season	Club	Lea	GP	G	A	TP	PIM	GP	G	A	TP	PIM
1989-90	Litvinov	Czech.	39	11	10	21	....	....	....	....	....	....
1990-91	Litvinov	Czech.	48	24	22	46	38	....	....	....	....	....
1991-92	Litvinov	Czech.	43	12	31	43	....	....	....	....	....	....

LANGILLE, DEREK

Defense. Shoots left. 6', 184 lbs. Born, Toronto, Ont., June 25, 1969.
(Toronto's 9th choice, 150th overall, in 1989 Entry Draft).

			Regular Season					Playoffs				
Season	Club	Lea	GP	G	A	TP	PIM	GP	G	A	TP	PIM
1986-87	Belleville	OHL	42	0	2	2	27	6	0	0	0	0
1987-88	Belleville	OHL	36	3	7	10	45	....	....	....	....	....
	Kingston	OHL	32	4	7	11	66	....	....	....	....	....
1988-89	North Bay	OHL	60	20	38	58	128	12	1	6	7	22
1989-90	Newmarket	AHL	64	5	12	17	75	....	....	....	....	....
1990-91	Newmarket	AHL	67	4	11	15	102	....	....	....	....	....
1991-92	Moncton	AHL	62	4	9	13	77	1	0	0	0	0

LANGWAY, ROD CORRY

Defense. Shoots left. 6'3", 218 lbs. Born, Maag, Formosa, May 3, 1957.
(Montreal's 3rd choice, 36th overall, in 1977 Amateur Draft).

			Regular Season					Playoffs				
Season	Club	Lea	GP	G	A	TP	PIM	GP	G	A	TP	PIM
1976-77	N. Hampshire	ECAC	34	10	43	53	52	....	....	....	....	....
1977-78	Hampton	AHL	30	6	16	22	50	....	....	....	....	....
	Birmingham	WHA	52	3	18	21	52	4	0	0	0	9
1978-79	**Montreal**	**NHL**	**45**	**3**	**4**	**7**	**30**	**8**	**0**	**0**	**0**	**16**
	Nova Scotia	AHL	18	6	13	19	29	....	....	....	....	....
1979-80	**Montreal**	**NHL**	**77**	**7**	**29**	**36**	**81**	**10**	**3**	**3**	**6**	**2**
1980-81	**Montreal**	**NHL**	**80**	**11**	**34**	**45**	**120**	**3**	**0**	**0**	**0**	**6**
1981-82	**Montreal**	**NHL**	**66**	**5**	**34**	**39**	**116**	**5**	**0**	**3**	**3**	**18**
1982-83ab	**Washington**	**NHL**	**80**	**3**	**29**	**32**	**75**	**4**	**0**	**0**	**0**	**0**
1983-84ab	**Washington**	**NHL**	**80**	**9**	**24**	**33**	**61**	**8**	**0**	**5**	**5**	**7**
1984-85c	**Washington**	**NHL**	**79**	**4**	**22**	**26**	**54**	**5**	**0**	**1**	**1**	**6**
1985-86	**Washington**	**NHL**	**71**	**1**	**17**	**18**	**61**	**9**	**1**	**2**	**3**	**6**
1986-87	**Washington**	**NHL**	**78**	**2**	**25**	**27**	**53**	**7**	**0**	**1**	**1**	**2**
1987-88	**Washington**	**NHL**	**63**	**3**	**13**	**16**	**28**	**6**	**0**	**0**	**0**	**8**
1988-89	**Washington**	**NHL**	**76**	**2**	**19**	**21**	**65**	**6**	**0**	**0**	**0**	**6**
1989-90	**Washington**	**NHL**	**58**	**0**	**8**	**8**	**39**	**15**	**1**	**4**	**5**	**12**
1990-91	**Washington**	**NHL**	**56**	**1**	**7**	**8**	**24**	**11**	**0**	**2**	**2**	**6**
1991-92	**Washington**	**NHL**	**64**	**0**	**13**	**13**	**22**	**7**	**0**	**1**	**1**	**2**
	NHL Totals		**973**	**51**	**278**	**329**	**829**	**104**	**5**	**22**	**27**	**96**

a Won James Norris Memorial Trophy (1983, 1984)
b NHL First All-Star Team (1983, 1984)
c NHL Second All-Star Team (1985)

Played in NHL All-Star Game (1981-86)

Claimed by **Montreal** as fill in Expansion Draft, June 13, 1979. Traded to **Washington** by **Montreal** with Doug Jarvis, Craig Laughlin and Brian Engblom for Ryan Walter and Rick Green, September 9, 1982.

LANZ, RICK ROMAN

Defense. Shoots right. 6'2", 203 lbs. Born, Karlouy Vary, Czech., September 16, 1961.
(Vancouver's 1st choice, 7th overall, in 1980 Entry Draft).

			Regular Season					Playoffs				
Season	Club	Lea	GP	G	A	TP	PIM	GP	G	A	TP	PIM
1978-79	Oshawa	OHA	65	12	47	59	88	5	1	3	4	14
1979-80a	Oshawa	OHA	52	18	38	56	51	7	2	3	5	6
1980-81	**Vancouver**	**NHL**	**76**	**7**	**22**	**29**	**40**	**3**	**0**	**0**	**0**	**4**
1981-82	**Vancouver**	**NHL**	**39**	**3**	**11**	**14**	**48**	....	....	....	....	....
1982-83	**Vancouver**	**NHL**	**74**	**10**	**38**	**48**	**46**	**4**	**2**	**1**	**3**	**0**
1983-84	**Vancouver**	**NHL**	**79**	**18**	**39**	**57**	**45**	**4**	**0**	**4**	**4**	**2**
1984-85	**Vancouver**	**NHL**	**57**	**2**	**17**	**19**	**69**	....	....	....	....	....
1985-86	**Vancouver**	**NHL**	**75**	**15**	**38**	**53**	**73**	**3**	**0**	**0**	**0**	**0**
1986-87	**Vancouver**	**NHL**	**17**	**1**	**6**	**7**	**10**	....	....	....	....	....
	Toronto	**NHL**	**44**	**2**	**19**	**21**	**32**	**13**	**1**	**3**	**4**	**27**
1987-88	**Toronto**	**NHL**	**75**	**6**	**22**	**28**	**65**	**1**	**0**	**0**	**0**	**2**
1988-89	**Toronto**	**NHL**	**32**	**1**	**9**	**10**	**18**	....	....	....	....	....
1989-90	Ambri-Piotta	Switz.	36	4	14	18	....	....	....	....	....	....
1990-91	Indianapolis	IHL	8	0	5	5	18	....	....	....	....	....
1991-92	**Chicago**	**NHL**	**1**	**0**	**0**	**0**	**2**	....	....	....	....	....
	Phoenix	IHL	38	7	14	21	21	....	....	....	....	....
	NHL Totals		**569**	**65**	**221**	**286**	**448**	**28**	**3**	**8**	**11**	**35**

a OHA Third All-Star Team (1980)

Traded to **Toronto** by **Vancouver** for Jim Benning and Dan Hodgson, December 2, 1986. Signed as a free agent by **Chicago**, August 13, 1990. Traded to **Los Angeles** by **Chicago** for cash, November 29, 1991.

LAPERRIERE, DANIEL

Defense. Shoots left. 6'1", 180 lbs. Born, Laval, Que., March 28, 1969.
(St. Louis' 4th choice, 93rd overall, in 1989 Entry Draft).

			Regular Season					Playoffs				
Season	Club	Lea	GP	G	A	TP	PIM	GP	G	A	TP	PIM
1988-89	St. Lawrence	ECAC	28	0	7	7	10	....	....	....	....	....
1989-90	St. Lawrence	ECAC	31	6	19	25	16	....	....	....	....	....
1990-91a	St. Lawrence	ECAC	34	7	31	38	18	....	....	....	....	....
1991-92bc	St. Lawrence	ECAC	32	8	*45	53	36	....	....	....	....	....

a ECAC Second All-Star Team (1991)
b ECAC First All-Star Team (1992)
c NCAA East First All-Star Team (1992)

LAPOINTE, CLAUDE

Center. Shoots left. 5'9", 173 lbs. Born, Lachine, Que., October 11, 1968.
(Quebec's 12th choice, 234th overall, in 1988 Entry Draft).

			Regular Season					Playoffs				
Season	Club	Lea	GP	G	A	TP	PIM	GP	G	A	TP	PIM
1986-87	Trois-Rivières	QMJHL	70	47	57	104	123	....	....	....	....	....
1987-88	Laval	QMJHL	69	37	83	120	143	13	2	17	19	53
1988-89	Laval	QMJHL	63	32	72	104	158	17	5	14	19	66
1989-90	Halifax	AHL	63	18	19	37	51	6	1	1	2	34
1990-91	**Quebec**	**NHL**	**13**	**2**	**2**	**4**	**4**	....	....	....	....	....
	Halifax	AHL	43	17	17	34	46	....	....	....	....	....
1991-92	**Quebec**	**NHL**	**78**	**13**	**20**	**33**	**86**	....	....	....	....	....
	NHL Totals		**91**	**15**	**22**	**37**	**90**	....	....	....	....	....

LAPOINTE, MARTIN

Right wing. Shoots right. 5'11", 200 lbs. Born, Lachine, Que., September 12, 1973.
(Detroit's 1st choice, 10th overall, in 1991 Entry Draft).

			Regular Season					Playoffs				
Season	Club	Lea	GP	G	A	TP	PIM	GP	G	A	TP	PIM
1989-90ab	Laval	QMJHL	65	42	54	96	77	14	8	17	25	54
1990-91c	Laval	QMJHL	64	44	54	98	66	13	7	14	21	26
1991-92	**Detroit**	**NHL**	**4**	**0**	**1**	**1**	**5**	**3**	**0**	**1**	**1**	**4**
	Laval	QMJHL	31	25	30	55	84	10	4	10	14	32
	NHL Totals		**4**	**0**	**1**	**1**	**5**	**3**	**0**	**1**	**1**	**4**

a QMJHL First All-Star Team (1990)
b QMJHL Offensive Rookie of the Year (1990)
c QMJHL Second All-Star Team (1991)

LAPOINTE, SYLVAIN

Defense. Shoots left. 6', 190 lbs. Born, Anjou, Que., March 14, 1973.
(Montreal's 4th choice, 83rd overall, in 1991 Entry Draft).

			Regular Season					Playoffs				
Season	Club	Lea	GP	G	A	TP	PIM	GP	G	A	TP	PIM
1990-91	Clarkson	ECAC	40	2	12	14	30	....	....	....	....	....
1991-92	Hull	QMJHL	67	0	11	11	65	6	1	1	2	10

LAPPIN, MICHAEL

Center. Shoots left. 5'10", 175 lbs. Born, Chicago, IL, January 1, 1969.
(Chicago's 12th choice, 239th overall, in 1987 Entry Draft).

			Regular Season					Playoffs				
Season	Club	Lea	GP	G	A	TP	PIM	GP	G	A	TP	PIM
1987-88	Boston U.	H.E.	34	12	15	27	40	....	....	....	....	....
1988-89	Boston U.	H.E.	27	11	16	27	43	....	....	....	....	....
1989-90			DID NOT PLAY									
1990-91	St. Lawrence	ECAC	35	27	42	69	36	....	....	....	....	....
1991-92ab	St. Lawrence	ECAC	33	*25	37	*62	20	....	....	....	....	....

a ECAC First All-Star Team (1992)
b NCAA East Second All-Star Team (1992)

LAPPIN, PETER

Right wing. Shoots right. 5'11", 180 lbs. Born, St. Charles, IL, December 31, 1965.
(Calgary's 1st choice, 24th overall, in 1987 Supplemental Draft).

			Regular Season					Playoffs				
Season	Club	Lea	GP	G	A	TP	PIM	GP	G	A	TP	PIM
1984-85	St. Lawrence	ECAC	32	10	12	22	22	....	....	....	....	....
1985-86	St. Lawrence	ECAC	30	20	26	46	64	....	....	....	....	....
1986-87ab	St. Lawrence	ECAC	35	34	24	58	32	....	....	....	....	....
1987-88cdef	St. Lawrence	ECAC	30	16	36	52	26	....	....	....	....	....
g	Salt Lake	IHL	3	1	1	2	0	17	*16	12	*28	11
1988-89	Salt Lake	IHL	81	48	42	90	50	14	*9	9	18	4
1989-90	**Minnesota**	**NHL**	**6**	**0**	**0**	**0**	**2**	....	....	....	....	....
h	Kalamazoo	IHL	74	45	35	80	42	8	5	2	7	4
1990-91	Kalamazoo	IHL	73	20	47	67	74	11	5	4	9	8
1991-92	**San Jose**	**NHL**	**1**	**0**	**0**	**0**	**0**	....	....	....	....	....
	Kansas City	IHL	78	28	30	58	41	4	2	1	3	0
	NHL Totals		**7**	**0**	**0**	**0**	**2**	....	....	....	....	....

a NCAA East Second All-American Team (1987)
b ECAC Second All-Star Team (1987)
c NCAA East First All-American Team (1988)
d NCAA All-Tournament Team (1988)
e ECAC Player of the Year (1988)
f ECAC First All-Star Team (1988)
g IHL Playoff MVP (1988)
h IHL Second All-Star Team (1990)

Traded to **Minnesota** by **Calgary** for Minnesota's second round choice in 1990 Entry Draft which was later transferred to New Jersey (Chris Gotziaman), September 5, 1989. Claimed by **San Jose** from **Minnesota** in Dispersal Draft, May 30, 1991.

LARIONOV, IGOR (LAIR-ee-AH-nohv)

Center. Shoots left. 5'9", 165 lbs. Born, Voskresensk, Soviet Union, December 3, 1960.
(Vancouver's 11th choice, 214th overall, in 1985 Entry Draft).

			Regular Season					Playoffs				
Season	Club	Lea	GP	G	A	TP	PIM	GP	G	A	TP	PIM
1977-78	Khimik	USSR	6	3	0	3	4	....	....	....	....	....
1978-79	Khimik	USSR	32	3	4	7	12	....	....	....	....	....
1979-80	Khimik	USSR	42	11	7	18	24	....	....	....	....	....
1980-81	Khimik	USSR	43	22	23	45	36	....	....	....	....	....
1981-82	CSKA	USSR	46	31	22	53	6	....	....	....	....	....
1982-83a	CSKA	USSR	44	20	19	39	20	....	....	....	....	....
1983-84	CSKA	USSR	43	15	26	41	30	....	....	....	....	....
1984-85	CSKA	USSR	40	18	28	46	20	....	....	....	....	....
1985-86a	CSKA	USSR	40	21	31	52	33	....	....	....	....	....
1986-87a	CSKA	USSR	39	20	26	46	34	....	....	....	....	....
1987-88ab	CSKA	USSR	51	25	32	57	54	....	....	....	....	....
1988-89	CSKA	USSR	31	15	12	27	22	....	....	....	....	....
1989-90	**Vancouver**	**NHL**	**74**	**17**	**27**	**44**	**20**	....	....	....	....	....
1990-91	**Vancouver**	**NHL**	**64**	**13**	**21**	**34**	**14**	**6**	**1**	**0**	**1**	**6**
1991-92	**Vancouver**	**NHL**	**72**	**21**	**44**	**65**	**54**	**13**	**3**	**7**	**10**	**4**
	NHL Totals		**210**	**51**	**92**	**143**	**88**	**19**	**4**	**7**	**11**	**10**

a Soviet National League All-Star (1983, 1985-88)
b Soviet Player of the Year (1988)

LARKIN, JAMES

Left wing. Shoots left. 6', 165 lbs. Born, Wallingford, VT, April 15, 1970.
(Los Angeles' 10th choice, 175th overall, in 1988 Entry Draft).

			Regular Season					Playoffs				
Season	Club	Lea	GP	G	A	TP	PIM	GP	G	A	TP	PIM
1988-89	U. of Vermont	ECAC	34	16	19	35	8	....	....	....	....	....
1989-90	U. of Vermont	ECAC	28	20	15	35	14	....	....	....	....	....
1990-91	U. of Vermont	ECAC	26	6	21	27	22	....	....	....	....	....
1991-92	U. of Vermont	ECAC	29	15	16	31	32	....	....	....	....	....

LARKIN, MIKE

Defense. Shoots right. 6'1", 180 lbs. Born, Boston, MA, March 15, 1973.
(Chicago's 11th choice, 242nd overall, in 1991 Entry Draft).

			Regular Season					Playoffs				
Season	Club	Lea	GP	G	A	TP	PIM	GP	G	A	TP	PIM
1990-91	Rice Memorial	HS	20	10	15	25	0	....	....	....	....	....
1991-92	U. of Vermont	ECAC	14	2	2	4	14	....	....	....	....	....

LARMER, STEVE DONALD

Right wing. Shoots left. 5'11", 189 lbs. Born, Peterborough, Ont., June 16, 1961.
(Chicago's 11th choice, 120th overall, in 1980 Entry Draft).

			Regular Season					Playoffs				
Season	Club	Lea	GP	G	A	TP	PIM	GP	G	A	TP	PIM
1977-78	Peterborough	OHA	62	24	17	41	51	18	5	7	12	27
1978-79	Niagara Falls	OHA	66	37	47	84	108	....	....	....	....	....
1979-80	Niagara Falls	OHA	67	45	69	114	71	10	5	9	14	15
1980-81	**Chicago**	**NHL**	**4**	**0**	**1**	**1**	**0**	....	....	....	....	....
a	Niagara Falls	OHA	61	55	78	133	73	12	13	8	21	24
1981-82	**Chicago**	**NHL**	**3**	**0**	**0**	**0**	**0**	....	....	....	....	....
b	New Brunswick	AHL	74	38	44	82	46	15	6	6	12	0
1982-83cd	**Chicago**	**NHL**	**80**	**43**	**47**	**90**	**28**	**11**	**5**	**7**	**12**	**8**
1983-84	**Chicago**	**NHL**	**80**	**35**	**40**	**75**	**34**	**5**	**2**	**2**	**4**	**7**
1984-85	**Chicago**	**NHL**	**80**	**46**	**40**	**86**	**16**	**15**	**9**	**13**	**22**	**14**
1985-86	**Chicago**	**NHL**	**80**	**31**	**45**	**76**	**47**	**3**	**0**	**3**	**3**	**4**
1986-87	**Chicago**	**NHL**	**80**	**28**	**56**	**84**	**22**	**4**	**0**	**0**	**0**	**2**
1987-88	**Chicago**	**NHL**	**80**	**41**	**48**	**89**	**42**	**5**	**1**	**6**	**7**	**0**
1988-89	**Chicago**	**NHL**	**80**	**43**	**44**	**87**	**54**	**16**	**8**	**9**	**17**	**22**
1989-90	**Chicago**	**NHL**	**80**	**31**	**59**	**90**	**40**	**20**	**7**	**15**	**22**	**2**
1990-91	**Chicago**	**NHL**	**80**	**44**	**57**	**101**	**79**	**6**	**5**	**1**	**6**	**4**
1991-92	**Chicago**	**NHL**	**80**	**29**	**45**	**74**	**65**	**18**	**8**	**7**	**15**	**6**
	NHL Totals		**807**	**371**	**482**	**853**	**427**	**103**	**45**	**63**	**108**	**69**

a OHA Second All-Star Team (1981)
b AHL Second All-Star Team (1982)
c Won Calder Trophy (1983)
d NHL All-Rookie Team (1983)

Played in NHL All-Star Game (1990, 1991)

LAROSE, GUY

Center. Shoots left. 5'9", 175 lbs. Born, Hull, Que., August 31, 1967.
(Buffalo's 11th choice, 224th overall, in 1985 Entry Draft).

			Regular Season					Playoffs				
Season	Club	Lea	GP	G	A	TP	PIM	GP	G	A	TP	PIM
1984-85	Guelph	OHL	58	30	30	60	63	....	....	....	....	....
1985-86	Guelph	OHL	37	12	36	48	55	....	....	....	....	....
	Ottawa	OHL	28	19	25	44	63	....	....	....	....	....
1986-87	Ottawa	OHL	66	28	49	77	77	11	2	8	10	27
1987-88	Moncton	AHL	77	22	31	53	127	....	....	....	....	....
1988-89	**Winnipeg**	**NHL**	**3**	**0**	**1**	**1**	**6**	....	....	....	....	....
	Moncton	AHL	72	32	27	59	176	10	4	4	8	37
1989-90	Moncton	AHL	79	44	26	70	232	....	....	....	....	....
1990-91	**Winnipeg**	**NHL**	**7**	**0**	**0**	**0**	**8**	....	....	....	....	....
	Moncton	AHL	35	14	10	24	60	....	....	....	....	....
	Binghamton	AHL	34	21	15	36	48	10	8	5	13	37
1991-92	Binghamton	AHL	30	10	11	21	36	....	....	....	....	....
	Toronto	**NHL**	**34**	**9**	**5**	**14**	**27**	....	....	....	....	....
	St. John's	AHL	15	7	7	14	26	....	....	....	....	....
	NHL Totals		**44**	**9**	**6**	**15**	**41**	....	....	....	....	....

Signed as a free agent by **Winnipeg**, July 16, 1987. Traded to **NY Rangers** by **Winnipeg** for Rudy Poeschek, January 22, 1991. Traded to **Toronto** by **NY Rangers** for Mike Stevens, December 26, 1991.

LAROUCHE, STEVE

Center. Shoots right. 5'11", 180 lbs. Born, Rouyn, Que., April 14, 1971.
(Montreal's 3rd choice, 41st overall, in 1989 Entry Draft).

			Regular Season					Playoffs				
Season	Club	Lea	GP	G	A	TP	PIM	GP	G	A	TP	PIM
1987-88	Trois-Rivières	QMJHL	66	11	29	40	25	....	....	....	....	....
1988-89	Trois-Rivières	QMJHL	70	51	102	153	53	4	4	2	6	6
1989-90a	Trois-Rivières	QMJHL	60	55	90	145	40	7	3	5	8	8
1990-91	Chicoutimi	QMJHL	45	35	41	76	64	17	*13	*20	*33	20
1991-92	Fredericton	AHL	74	21	35	56	41	7	1	0	1	0

a QMJHL Second All-Star Team (1990)

LARSON, DEAN

Center. Shoots left. 5'7", 160 lbs. Born, Calgary, Alta., June 4, 1969.
(Calgary's 1st choice, 25th overall, in 1991 Supplemental Draft).

			Regular Season					Playoffs				
Season	Club	Lea	GP	G	A	TP	PIM	GP	G	A	TP	PIM
1990-91	Alaska-Anch.	G.N.	33	13	30	43	14	....	....	....	....	....
1991-92	Alaska-Anch.	G.N.	31	20	28	48	30	....	....	....	....	....

LARSON, JON

Defense. Shoots left. 6'1", 190 lbs. Born, Roseau, MN, April 12, 1971.
(NY Islanders' 7th choice, 128th overall, in 1989 Entry Draft).

			Regular Season					Playoffs				
Season	Club	Lea	GP	G	A	TP	PIM	GP	G	A	TP	PIM
1989-90	North Dakota	WCHA	18	0	1	1	10	....	....	....	....	....
1990-91	North Dakota	WCHA	13	0	0	0	4	....	....	....	....	....
1991-92	North Dakota	WCHA	33	1	3	4	16	....	....	....	....	....

LARSSON, PETER (LAHR-suhn)

Center. Shoots left. 5'8", 176 lbs. Born, Sodertalje, Sweden, April 9, 1968.
(New Jersey's 10th choice, 236th overall, in 1989 Entry Draft).

			Regular Season					Playoffs				
Season	Club	Lea	GP	G	A	TP	PIM	GP	G	A	TP	PIM
1985-86	Sodertalje	Swe.	10	0	1	1	2	....	....	....	....	....
1986-87	Sodertalje	Swe.	26	3	4	7	8	....	....	....	....	....
1987-88	Sodertalje	Swe.	34	14	15	29	22	....	....	....	....	....
1988-89	Sodertalje	Swe.	40	20	17	37	26	....	....	....	....	....
1989-90	Sodertalje	Swe.	33	13	14	27	28	2	2	0	2	2
1990-91	Brynas	Swe.	40	13	12	25	12	....	....	....	....	....
1991-92	Brynas	Swe.	40	17	21	38	10	6	1	3	4	2

LARTER, TYLER

Center. Shoots left. 5'10", 185 lbs. Born, Charlottetown, P.E.I., March 12, 1968.
(Washington's 3rd choice, 78th overall, in 1987 Entry Draft).

			Regular Season					Playoffs				
Season	Club	Lea	GP	G	A	TP	PIM	GP	G	A	TP	PIM
1985-86	S.S. Marie	OHL	60	15	40	55	137	....	....	....	....	....
1986-87	S.S. Marie	OHL	59	34	59	93	122	4	0	2	2	8
1987-88	S.S. Marie	OHL	65	44	65	109	155	4	3	9	12	8
1988-89	Baltimore	AHL	71	9	19	28	189	....	....	....	....	....
1989-90	**Washington**	**NHL**	**1**	**0**	**0**	**0**	**0**	....	....	....	....	....
	Baltimore	AHL	79	31	36	67	104	12	5	6	11	57
1990-91	Baltimore	AHL	62	21	21	42	84	6	1	0	1	13
1991-92	Moncton	AHL	68	25	51	76	156	10	5	5	10	33
	Kalamazoo	IHL	3	0	2	2	4	....	....	....	....	....
	NHL Totals		**1**	**0**	**0**	**0**	**0**	....	....	....	....	....

Traded to **Winnipeg** by **Washington** with Bob Joyce and Kent Paynter for Craig Duncanson, Brent Hughes and Simon Wheeldon, May 21, 1991. Claimed by **Minnesota** from **Winnipeg** in Expansion Draft, May 30, 1991. Traded to **Winnipeg** by **Minnesota** for Tony Joseph, October 15, 1991.

LATTA, DAVID (LA-tuh)

Left wing. Shoots left. 6'1", 190 lbs. Born, Thunder Bay, Ont., January 3, 1967.
(Quebec's 1st choice, 15th overall, in 1985 Entry Draft).

			Regular Season					Playoffs				
Season	Club	Lea	GP	G	A	TP	PIM	GP	G	A	TP	PIM
1983-84	Kitchener	OHL	66	17	26	43	54	16	3	6	9	9
1984-85	Kitchener	OHL	52	38	27	65	26	4	2	4	6	4
1985-86	**Quebec**	**NHL**	**1**	**0**	**0**	**0**	**0**	....	....	....	....	....
	Fredericton	AHL	3	1	0	1	0	5	0	3	3	0
	Kitchener	OHL	55	36	34	70	60	5	7	1	8	15
1986-87a	Kitchener	OHL	50	32	46	78	46	4	0	3	3	2
1987-88	**Quebec**	**NHL**	**10**	**0**	**0**	**0**	**0**	....	....	....	....	....
	Fredericton	AHL	34	11	21	32	28	15	9	4	13	24
1988-89	**Quebec**	**NHL**	**24**	**4**	**8**	**12**	**4**	....	....	....	....	....
	Halifax	AHL	42	20	26	46	36	4	0	2	2	2
1989-90	Halifax	AHL	34	11	5	16	45	....	....	....	....	....
1990-91	**Quebec**	**NHL**	**1**	**0**	**0**	**0**	**0**	....	....	....	....	....
	Halifax	AHL	22	4	7	11	12	....	....	....	....	....
	Cdn. National	....	30	5	14	19	24	....	....	....	....	....
1991-92	New Haven	AHL	76	18	27	45	100	5	1	1	2	4
	NHL Totals		**36**	**4**	**8**	**12**	**4**	....	....	....	....	....

a OHL Third All-Star Team (1987)

LAUER, BRAD (LAU-er)

Left wing. Shoots left. 6', 195 lbs. Born, Humboldt, Sask., October 27, 1966.
(NY Islanders' 3rd choice, 34th overall, in 1985 Entry Draft).

			Regular Season					Playoffs				
Season	Club	Lea	GP	G	A	TP	PIM	GP	G	A	TP	PIM
1983-84	Regina	WHL	60	5	7	12	51	16	0	1	1	24
1984-85	Regina	WHL	72	33	46	79	57	8	6	6	12	9
1985-86	Regina	WHL	57	36	38	74	69	10	4	5	9	2
1986-87	**NY Islanders**	**NHL**	**61**	**7**	**14**	**21**	**65**	**6**	**2**	**0**	**2**	**4**
1987-88	**NY Islanders**	**NHL**	**69**	**17**	**18**	**35**	**67**	**5**	**3**	**1**	**4**	**4**
1988-89	**NY Islanders**	**NHL**	**14**	**3**	**2**	**5**	**2**	....	....	....	....	....
	Springfield	AHL	8	1	5	6	0	....	....	....	....	....
1989-90	**NY Islanders**	**NHL**	**63**	**6**	**18**	**24**	**19**	**4**	**0**	**2**	**2**	**10**
	Springfield	AHL	7	4	2	6	0	....	....	....	....	....
1990-91	**NY Islanders**	**NHL**	**44**	**4**	**8**	**12**	**45**	....	....	....	....	....
	Capital Dist.	AHL	11	5	11	16	14	....	....	....	....	....
1991-92	**NY Islanders**	**NHL**	**8**	**1**	**0**	**1**	**2**	....	....	....	....	....
	Chicago	**NHL**	**6**	**0**	**0**	**0**	**4**	**7**	**1**	**1**	**2**	**2**
	Indianapolis	IHL	57	24	30	54	46	....	....	....	....	....
	NHL Totals		**265**	**38**	**60**	**98**	**204**	**22**	**6**	**4**	**10**	**20**

Traded to **Chicago** by **NY Islanders** with Brent Sutter for Adam Creighton and Steve Thomas, October 25, 1991.

LAUKKANEN, JANNE

Defense. Shoots left. 6', 180 lbs. Born, Lahti, Finland, March 19, 1970.
(Quebec's 8th choice, 156th overall, in 1991 Entry Draft).

			Regular Season					Playoffs				
Season	Club	Lea	GP	G	A	TP	PIM	GP	G	A	TP	PIM
1990-91	Reipas	Fin.	44	8	14	22	56	....	....	....	....	....
1991-92	HPK	Fin.	43	5	14	19	62	....	....	....	....	....

LAUS, PAUL

Defense. Shoots right. 6'1", 212 lbs. Born, Beamsville, Ont., September 26, 1970.
(Pittsburgh's 2nd choice, 37th overall, in 1989 Entry Draft).

			Regular Season					Playoffs				
Season	Club	Lea	GP	G	A	TP	PIM	GP	G	A	TP	PIM
1987-88	Hamilton	OHL	56	1	9	10	171	14	0	0	0	28
1988-89	Niagara Falls	OHL	49	1	10	11	225	15	0	5	5	56
1989-90	Niagara Falls	OHL	60	13	35	48	231	16	6	16	22	71
1990-91	Albany	IHL	7	0	0	0	7	....	....	....	....	....
	Knoxville	ECHL	20	6	12	18	83	....	....	....	....	....
	Muskegon	IHL	35	3	4	7	103	4	0	0	0	13
1991-92	Muskegon	IHL	75	0	21	21	248	14	2	5	7	70

LAVIGNE, ERIC

Defense. Shoots left. 6'3", 195 lbs. Born, Victoriaville, Que., November 4, 1972.
(Washington's 3rd choice, 25th overall, in 1991 Entry Draft).

			Regular Season					Playoffs				
Season	Club	Lea	GP	G	A	TP	PIM	GP	G	A	TP	PIM
1989-90	Hull	QMJHL	69	7	11	18	203	11	0	0	0	32
1990-91	Hull	QMJHL	66	11	11	22	153	4	0	1	1	16
1991-92	Hull	QMJHL	46	4	17	21	101	6	0	0	0	32

LAVIOLETTE, PETER (LAH-vee-oh-LEHT)

Defense. Shoots left. 6'2", 200 lbs. Born, Norwood, MA, December 7, 1964.

			Regular Season					Playoffs				
Season	Club	Lea	GP	G	A	TP	PIM	GP	G	A	TP	PIM
1985-86	Westfield State	NCAA	19	12	8	20	44	....	....	....	....	....
1986-87	Indianapolis	IHL	72	10	20	30	146	....	....	....	....	....
1987-88	U.S. National	....	54	4	20	24	82	....	....	....	....	....
	U.S. Olympic	....	5	0	2	2	4	....	....	....	....	....
	Colorado	IHL	19	2	5	7	27	9	3	5	8	7
1988-89	**NY Rangers**	**NHL**	**12**	**0**	**0**	**0**	**6**	....	....	....	....	....
	Denver	IHL	57	6	19	25	120	3	0	0	0	4
1989-90	Flint	IHL	62	6	18	24	82	4	0	0	0	4
1990-91	Binghamton	AHL	65	12	24	36	72	10	2	7	9	30
1991-92	Binghamton	AHL	50	4	10	14	50	11	2	7	9	9
	NHL Totals		**12**	**0**	**0**	**0**	**6**	....	....	....	....	....

Signed as a free agent by **NY Rangers**, August 12, 1987.

LAVISH, JAMES

Right wing. Shoots right. 5'11", 175 lbs. Born, Albany, NY, October 13, 1970.
(Boston's 9th choice, 185th overall, in 1989 Entry Draft).

			Regular Season					Playoffs				
Season	Club	Lea	GP	G	A	TP	PIM	GP	G	A	TP	PIM
1989-90	Yale	ECAC	27	6	11	17	40	....	....	....	....	....
1990-91	Yale	ECAC	29	13	7	20	42	....	....	....	....	....
1991-92	Yale	ECAC	26	16	14	30	44	....	....	....	....	....

LAVOIE, DOMINIC

Defense. Shoots right. 6'2", 205 lbs. Born, Montreal, Que., November 21, 1967.

			Regular Season					Playoffs				
Season	Club	Lea	GP	G	A	TP	PIM	GP	G	A	TP	PIM
1985-86	St-Jean	QMJHL	70	12	37	49	99	10	2	3	5	20
1986-87	St-Jean	QMJHL	64	12	42	54	97	8	2	7	9	2
1987-88	Peoria	IHL	65	7	26	33	54	7	2	2	4	8
1988-89	**St. Louis**	**NHL**	**1**	**0**	**0**	**0**	**0**	....	....	....	....	....
	Peoria	IHL	69	11	31	42	98	4	0	0	0	4
1989-90	**St. Louis**	**NHL**	**13**	**1**	**1**	**2**	**16**	....	....	....	....	....
	Peoria	IHL	58	19	23	42	32	5	2	2	4	16
1990-91	**St. Louis**	**NHL**	**6**	**1**	**2**	**3**	**2**	....	....	....	....	....
a	Peoria	IHL	46	15	25	40	72	16	5	7	12	22
1991-92	**St. Louis**	**NHL**	**6**	**0**	**1**	**1**	**10**	....	....	....	....	....
b	Peoria	IHL	58	20	32	52	87	10	3	4	7	12
	NHL Totals		**26**	**2**	**4**	**6**	**28**	....	....	....	....	....

a IHL First All-Star Team (1991)
b IHL Second All-Star Team (1992)

Signed as a free agent by **St. Louis**, September 22, 1986. Claimed by **Ottawa** from **St. Louis** in Expansion Draft, June 18, 1992.

LAWRENCE, MARK

Right wing. Shoots right. 6'4", 212 lbs. Born, Burlington, Ont., January 27, 1972.
(Minnesota's 6th choice, 118th overall, in 1991 Entry Draft).

			Regular Season					Playoffs				
Season	Club	Lea	GP	G	A	TP	PIM	GP	G	A	TP	PIM
1988-89	Niagara Falls	OHL	63	9	27	36	142	....	....	....	....	....
1989-90	Niagara Falls	OHL	54	15	18	33	123	....	....	....	....	....
1990-91	Detroit	OHL	66	27	38	65	53	....	....	....	....	....
1991-92	Detroit	OHL	28	19	26	45	54	....	....	....	....	....
	North Bay	OHL	24	13	14	27	21	21	*23	12	35	36

LAWTON, BRIAN

Left wing. Shoots left. 6', 180 lbs. Born, New Brunswick, NJ, June 29, 1965.
(Minnesota's 1st choice, 1st overall, in 1983 Entry Draft).

			Regular Season					Playoffs				
Season	Club	Lea	GP	G	A	TP	PIM	GP	G	A	TP	PIM
1982-83	Mt. St. Charles	HS	23	40	43	83	....	....	....	....	....	....
1983-84	**Minnesota**	**NHL**	**58**	**10**	**21**	**31**	**33**	**5**	**0**	**0**	**0**	**10**
1984-85	**Minnesota**	**NHL**	**40**	**5**	**6**	**11**	**24**	....	....	....	....	....
	Springfield	AHL	42	14	28	42	37	4	1	1	2	2
1985-86	**Minnesota**	**NHL**	**65**	**18**	**17**	**35**	**36**	**3**	**0**	**1**	**1**	**2**
1986-87	**Minnesota**	**NHL**	**66**	**21**	**23**	**44**	**86**	....	....	....	....	....
1987-88	**Minnesota**	**NHL**	**74**	**17**	**24**	**41**	**71**	....	....	....	....	....
1988-89	**NY Rangers**	**NHL**	**30**	**7**	**10**	**17**	**39**	....	....	....	....	....
	Hartford	**NHL**	**35**	**10**	**16**	**26**	**28**	**3**	**1**	**0**	**1**	**0**
1989-90	**Hartford**	**NHL**	**13**	**2**	**1**	**3**	**6**	....	....	....	....	....
	Quebec	**NHL**	**14**	**5**	**6**	**11**	**10**	....	....	....	....	....
	Boston	**NHL**	**8**	**0**	**0**	**0**	**14**	....	....	....	....	....
	Maine	AHL	5	0	0	0	14	....	....	....	....	....
1990-91	Phoenix	IHL	63	26	40	66	108	11	4	9	13	40
1991-92	**San Jose**	**NHL**	**59**	**15**	**22**	**37**	**42**	....	....	....	....	....
	NHL Totals		**462**	**110**	**146**	**256**	**389**	**11**	**1**	**1**	**2**	**12**

Traded to **NY Rangers** by **Minnesota** with Igor Liba, and the rights to Eric Bennett for Paul Jerrard and Mark Tinordi, the rights to Bret Barnett and Mike Sullivan, and Los Angeles' third round choice (Murray Garbutt) in 1989 Entry Draft — acquired March 10, 1987 by Minnesota — October 11, 1988. Traded to **Hartford** by **NY Rangers** with Norm MacIver and Don Maloney for Carey Wilson and Hartford's fifth round choice (Lubos Rob) in 1990 Entry Draft, December 26, 1988. Claimed on waivers by **Quebec** from **Hartford**, December 1, 1989. Signed as a free agent by **Boston**, February 7, 1990. Signed as a free agent by **Los Angeles**, July 27, 1990. Signed as a free agent by **San Jose**, August 9, 1991.

LAXDAL, DEREK

Right wing. Shoots right. 6'1", 175 lbs. Born, St. Boniface, Man., February 21, 1966.
(Toronto's 7th choice, 151st overall, in 1984 Entry Draft).

			Regular Season					Playoffs				
Season	Club	Lea	GP	G	A	TP	PIM	GP	G	A	TP	PIM
1982-83	Portland	WHL	39	4	9	13	27	14	0	2	2	2
1983-84	Brandon	WHL	70	23	20	43	86	12	0	4	4	10
1984-85	**Toronto**	**NHL**	**3**	**0**	**0**	**0**	**6**	....	....	....	....	....
	Brandon	WHL	69	61	41	102	74	....	....	....	....	....
	St. Catharines	AHL	5	3	2	5	2	....	....	....	....	....
1985-86	Brandon	WHL	42	34	35	69	62	....	....	....	....	....
	N. Westminster	WHL	18	9	6	15	14	....	....	....	....	....
	St. Catharines	AHL	7	0	1	1	15	12	1	1	2	24
1986-87	**Toronto**	**NHL**	**2**	**0**	**0**	**0**	**7**	....	....	....	....	....
	Newmarket	AHL	78	24	20	44	69	....	....	....	....	....
1987-88	**Toronto**	**NHL**	**5**	**0**	**0**	**0**	**6**	....	....	....	....	....
	Newmarket	AHL	67	18	25	43	81	....	....	....	....	....
1988-89	**Toronto**	**NHL**	**41**	**9**	**6**	**15**	**65**	....	....	....	....	....
	Newmarket	AHL	34	22	22	44	53	2	0	2	2	5
1989-90	Newmarket	AHL	23	7	8	15	52	....	....	....	....	....
	NY Islanders	**NHL**	**12**	**3**	**1**	**4**	**6**	**1**	**0**	**2**	**2**	**2**
	Springfield	AHL	28	13	12	25	42	13	8	6	14	47
1990-91	**NY Islanders**	**NHL**	**4**	**0**	**0**	**0**	**0**	....	....	....	....	....
	Capital Dist.	AHL	65	14	25	39	75	....	....	....	....	....
1991-92	Capital Dist.	AHL	49	7	7	14	61	4	1	1	2	10
	NHL Totals		**67**	**12**	**7**	**19**	**90**	**1**	**0**	**2**	**2**	**2**

Traded to **NY Islanders** by **Toronto** with Jack Capuano and Paul Gagne for Mike Stevens and Gilles Thibaudeau, December 20, 1989.

LAYLIN, CORY

Left wing. Shoots left. 5'10", 170 lbs. Born, Minneapolis, MN, January 24, 1970.
(Pittsburgh's 11th choice, 214th overall, in 1988 Entry Draft).

			Regular Season					Playoffs				
Season	Club	Lea	GP	G	A	TP	PIM	GP	G	A	TP	PIM
1988-89	U. Minnesota	WCHA	47	14	10	24	24	....	....	....	....	....
1989-90	U. Minnesota	WCHA	39	13	14	27	31	....	....	....	....	....
1990-91	U. Minnesota	WCHA	40	12	13	25	24	....	....	....	....	....
1991-92	U. Minnesota	WCHA	41	19	12	31	44	....	....	....	....	....

LAYZELL, BRAD

Defense. Shoots left. 6'3", 200 lbs. Born, Beaconsfield, Que., March 15, 1972.
(Montreal's 5th choice, 100th overall, in 1991 Entry Draft).

			Regular Season					Playoffs				
Season	Club	Lea	GP	G	A	TP	PIM	GP	G	A	TP	PIM
1990-91	RPI	ECAC	24	1	2	3	28	....	....	....	....	....
1991-92	RPI	ECAC	31	1	8	9	46	....	....	....	....	....

LAZARO, JEFF

Left wing. Shoots left. 5'10", 180 lbs. Born, Waltham, MA, March 21, 1968.

			Regular Season					Playoffs				
Season	Club	Lea	GP	G	A	TP	PIM	GP	G	A	TP	PIM
1986-87	N. Hampshire	H.E.	38	7	14	21	38	....	....	....	....	....
1987-88	N. Hampshire	H.E.	30	4	13	17	48	....	....	....	....	....
1988-89	N. Hampshire	H.E.	31	8	14	22	38	....	....	....	....	....
1989-90	N. Hampshire	H.E.	39	16	19	35	34	....	....	....	....	....
1990-91	**Boston**	**NHL**	**49**	**5**	**13**	**18**	**67**	**19**	**3**	**2**	**5**	**30**
	Maine	AHL	26	8	11	19	18	....	....	....	....	....
1991-92	**Boston**	**NHL**	**27**	**3**	**6**	**9**	**31**	**9**	**0**	**1**	**1**	**2**
	Maine	AHL	21	8	4	12	32	....	....	....	....	....
	NHL Totals		**76**	**8**	**19**	**27**	**98**	**28**	**3**	**3**	**6**	**32**

Signed as a free agent by **Boston**, September 26, 1990. Claimed by **Ottawa** from **Boston** in Expansion Draft, June 18, 1992.

LEACH, JAMIE

Right wing. Shoots right. 6'1", 205 lbs. Born, Winnipeg, Man., August 25, 1969.
(Pittsburgh's 3rd choice, 47th overall, in 1987 Entry Draft).

			Regular Season					Playoffs				
Season	Club	Lea	GP	G	A	TP	PIM	GP	G	A	TP	PIM
1985-86	N. Westminster	WHL	58	8	7	15	20	....	....	....	....	....
1986-87	Hamilton	OHL	64	12	19	31	67	....	....	....	....	....
1987-88	Hamilton	OHL	64	24	19	43	79	14	6	7	13	12
1988-89a	Niagara Falls	OHL	58	45	62	107	47	17	9	11	20	25
1989-90	**Pittsburgh**	**NHL**	**10**	**0**	**3**	**3**	**0**	....	....	....	....	....
	Muskegon	IHL	72	22	36	58	39	15	9	4	13	14
1990-91	**Pittsburgh**	**NHL**	**7**	**2**	**0**	**2**	**0**	....	....	....	....	....
	Muskegon	IHL	43	33	22	55	26	....	....	....	....	....
1991-92	**Pittsburgh**	**NHL**	**38**	**5**	**4**	**9**	**8**	....	....	....	....	....
	Muskegon	IHL	3	1	1	2	2	....	....	....	....	....
	NHL Totals		**55**	**7**	**7**	**14**	**8**	....	....	....	....	....

a OHL Third All-Star Team (1989)

LEACH, STEPHEN

Right wing. Shoots right. 5'11", 200 lbs. Born, Cambridge, MA, January 16, 1966.
(Washington's 2nd choice, 34th overall, in 1984 Entry Draft).

			Regular Season					Playoffs				
Season	Club	Lea	GP	G	A	TP	PIM	GP	G	A	TP	PIM
1984-85	N. Hampshire	H.E.	41	12	25	37	53	....	....	....	....	....
1985-86	**Washington**	**NHL**	**11**	**1**	**1**	**2**	**2**	**6**	**0**	**1**	**1**	**0**
	N. Hampshire	H.E.	25	22	6	28	30	....	....	....	....	....
1986-87	**Washington**	**NHL**	**15**	**1**	**0**	**1**	**6**	....	....	....	....	....
	Binghamton	AHL	54	18	21	39	39	13	3	1	4	6
1987-88	**Washington**	**NHL**	**8**	**1**	**1**	**2**	**17**	**9**	**2**	**1**	**3**	**0**
	U.S. National	....	49	26	20	46	30	....	....	....	....	....
	U.S. Olympic	....	6	1	2	3	0	....	....	....	....	....
1988-89	**Washington**	**NHL**	**74**	**11**	**19**	**30**	**94**	**6**	**1**	**0**	**1**	**12**
1989-90	**Washington**	**NHL**	**70**	**18**	**14**	**32**	**104**	**14**	**2**	**2**	**4**	**8**
1990-91	**Washington**	**NHL**	**68**	**11**	**19**	**30**	**99**	**9**	**1**	**2**	**3**	**8**
1991-92	**Boston**	**NHL**	**78**	**31**	**29**	**60**	**147**	**15**	**4**	**0**	**4**	**10**
	NHL Totals		**324**	**74**	**83**	**157**	**469**	**59**	**10**	**6**	**16**	**38**

Traded to **Boston** by **Washington** for Randy Burridge, June 21, 1991.

LEASK, ROB

Defense. Shoots left. 6'2", 211 lbs. Born, Toronto, Ont., June 9, 1971.
(Washington's 10th choice, 209th overall, in 1991 Entry Draft).

			Regular Season					Playoffs				
Season	Club	Lea	GP	G	A	TP	PIM	GP	G	A	TP	PIM
1989-90	Hamilton	OHL	43	6	18	24	50	....	....	....	....	....
1990-91	Hamilton	OHL	62	11	27	38	85	4	1	2	3	2
1991-92	Guelph	OHL	7	0	1	1	15	....	....	....	....	....
	Oshawa	OHL	49	13	27	40	90	7	1	4	5	4

LEBEAU, PATRICK

Left wing. Shoots left. 5'10", 172 lbs. Born, St. Jerome, Que., March 17, 1970.
(Montreal's 8th choice, 167th overall, in 1989 Entry Draft).

			Regular Season					Playoffs				
Season	Club	Lea	GP	G	A	TP	PIM	GP	G	A	TP	PIM
1986-87	Shawinigan	QMJHL	66	26	52	78	90	13	2	6	8	17
1987-88	Shawinigan	QMJHL	53	43	56	99	116	11	3	9	12	16
1988-89	Shawinigan	QMJHL	17	19	17	36	18	....	....	....	....	....
	St-Jean	QMJHL	49	43	70	113	71	4	4	3	7	6
1989-90a	Victoriaville	QMJHL	72	68	*106	*174	109	16	7	15	22	12
1990-91	**Montreal**	**NHL**	**2**	**1**	**1**	**2**	**0**	....	....	....	....	....
bc	Fredericton	AHL	69	50	51	101	32	9	4	7	11	8
1991-92	Fredericton	AHL	55	33	38	71	48	7	4	5	9	10
	Cdn. National	....	7	4	1	5	6	....	....	....	....	....
	Cdn. Olympic	....	8	1	3	4	4	....	....	....	....	....
	NHL Totals		**2**	**1**	**1**	**2**	**0**	....	....	....	....	....

a QMJHL First All-Star Team (1990)
b AHL Second All-Star Team (1991)
c Won Dudley "Red" Garrett Memorial Trophy (Top Rookie – AHL) (1991)

LEBEAU, STEPHAN (leh-BOH)

Center. Shoots right. 5'10", 172 lbs. Born, St. Jerome, Que., February 28, 1968.

			Regular Season					Playoffs				
Season	Club	Lea	GP	G	A	TP	PIM	GP	G	A	TP	PIM
1984-85	Shawinigan	QMJHL	66	41	38	79	18	9	4	5	9	4
1985-86	Shawinigan	QMJHL	72	69	77	146	22	5	4	2	6	4
1986-87a	Shawinigan	QMJHL	65	77	90	167	60	14	9	20	29	20
1987-88a	Shawinigan	QMJHL	67	*94	94	188	66	11	17	9	26	10
	Sherbrooke	AHL	....	....	....	....	....	1	0	1	1	0
1988-89	**Montreal**	**NHL**	**1**	**0**	**1**	**1**	**2**	....	....	....	....	....
bcde	Sherbrooke	AHL	78	*70	64	*134	47	6	1	4	5	8
1989-90	**Montreal**	**NHL**	**57**	**15**	**20**	**35**	**11**	**2**	**3**	**0**	**3**	**0**
1990-91	**Montreal**	**NHL**	**73**	**22**	**31**	**53**	**24**	**7**	**2**	**1**	**3**	**2**
1991-92	**Montreal**	**NHL**	**77**	**27**	**31**	**58**	**14**	**8**	**1**	**3**	**4**	**4**
	NHL Totals		**208**	**64**	**83**	**147**	**51**	**17**	**6**	**4**	**10**	**6**

a QMJHL Second All-Star Team (1987, 1988)
b AHL First All-Star Team (1989)
c Won Dudley "Red" Garrett Memorial Trophy (Top Rookie-AHL) (1989)
d Won John B. Sollenberger Trophy (Top Scorer-AHL) (1989)
e Won Les Cunningham Trophy (MVP-AHL) (1989)

Signed as a free agent by **Montreal**, September 27, 1986.

LeBLANC, JOHN GLENN

Left wing. Shoots left. 6'1", 190 lbs. Born, Campbellton, N.B., January 21, 1964.

			Regular Season					Playoffs				
Season	Club	Lea	GP	G	A	TP	PIM	GP	G	A	TP	PIM
1983-84	Hull	QMJHL	69	39	35	74	32	....	....	....	....	....
1984-85	New Brunswick	AUAA	24	25	34	59	32	....	....	....	....	....
1985-86a	New Brunswick	AUAA	24	38	28	66	35	....	....	....	....	....
1986-87	**Vancouver**	**NHL**	**2**	**1**	**0**	**1**	**0**	....	....	....	....	....
	Fredericton	AHL	75	40	30	70	27	....	....	....	....	....
1987-88	**Vancouver**	**NHL**	**41**	**12**	**10**	**22**	**18**	....	....	....	....	....
	Fredericton	AHL	35	26	25	51	54	15	6	7	13	34
1988-89	Milwaukee	IHL	61	39	31	70	42	....	....	....	....	....
	Edmonton	**NHL**	**2**	**1**	**0**	**1**	**0**	**1**	**0**	**0**	**0**	**0**
	Cape Breton	AHL	3	4	0	4	0	....	....	....	....	....
1989-90	Cape Breton	AHL	77	*54	34	88	50	6	4	0	4	4
1990-91					DID NOT PLAY							
1991-92	**Winnipeg**	**NHL**	**16**	**6**	**1**	**7**	**6**	....	....	....	....	....
	Moncton	AHL	56	31	22	53	24	10	3	2	5	8
	NHL Totals		**61**	**20**	**11**	**31**	**24**	**1**	**0**	**0**	**0**	**0**

a Canadian University Player of the Year (1986)

Signed as a free agent by **Vancouver**, April 12, 1986. Traded to **Edmonton** by **Vancouver** with Vancouver's fifth round choice (Peter White) in 1989 Entry Draft for Doug Smith and Gregory C. Adams, March 7, 1989. Traded to **Winnipeg** by **Edmonton** with Edmonton's tenth round choice (Teemu Numminen) in 1992 Entry Draft for Winnipeg's fifth round choice (Ryan Haggerty) in 1991 Entry Draft, June 12, 1991.

LeBRUN, SEAN (luh-BRUN)

Left wing. Shoots left. 6'2", 200 lbs. Born, Prince George, B.C., May 2, 1969.
(NY Islanders' 3rd choice, 37th overall, in 1988 Entry Draft).

			Regular Season					Playoffs				
Season	Club	Lea	GP	G	A	TP	PIM	GP	G	A	TP	PIM
1985-86	Spokane	WHL	70	6	11	17	41	....	....	....	....	....
1986-87	Spokane	WHL	6	2	5	7	9	....	....	....	....	....
	N. Westminster	WHL	55	21	32	53	47	....	....	....	....	....
1987-88a	N. Westminster	WHL	72	36	53	89	59	5	1	3	4	2
1988-89	Tri-Cities	WHL	71	52	73	125	92	5	0	4	4	13
1989-90	Springfield	AHL	63	9	33	42	20	....	....	....	....	....
1990-91	Capital Dist.	AHL	56	14	26	40	35	....	....	....	....	....
1991-92	Richmond	ECHL	2	0	0	0	2	....	....	....	....	....
	Capital Dist.	AHL	14	0	2	2	15	....	....	....	....	....

a WHL West Division Second All-Star Team (1988)

LeCLAIR, JOHN

Left wing. Shoots left. 6'2", 205 lbs. Born, St. Albans, VT, July 5, 1969.
(Montreal's 2nd choice, 33rd overall, in 1987 Entry Draft).

			Regular Season					Playoffs				
Season	Club	Lea	GP	G	A	TP	PIM	GP	G	A	TP	PIM
1987-88	U. of Vermont	ECAC	31	12	22	34	62	....	....	....	....	....
1988-89	U. of Vermont	ECAC	18	9	12	21	40	....	....	....	....	....
1989-90	U. of Vermont	ECAC	10	10	6	16	38	....	....	....	....	....
1990-91a	U. of Vermont	ECAC	33	25	20	45	58	....	....	....	....	....
	Montreal	**NHL**	**10**	**2**	**5**	**7**	**2**	**3**	**0**	**0**	**0**	**0**
1991-92	**Montreal**	**NHL**	**59**	**8**	**11**	**19**	**14**	**8**	**1**	**1**	**2**	**4**
	Fredericton	AHL	8	7	7	14	10	2	0	0	0	4
	NHL Totals		**69**	**10**	**16**	**26**	**16**	**11**	**1**	**1**	**2**	**4**

a ECAC Second All-Star Team (1991)

LEDYARD, GRANT

Defense. Shoots left. 6'2", 195 lbs. Born, Winnipeg, Man., November 19, 1961.

			Regular Season					Playoffs				
Season	Club	Lea	GP	G	A	TP	PIM	GP	G	A	TP	PIM
1980-81	Saskatoon	WHL	71	9	28	37	148	....	....	....	....	....
1981-82	Fort Garry	MJHL	63	25	45	70	150	....	....	....	....	....
1982-83	Tulsa	CHL	80	13	29	42	115	....	....	....	....	....
1983-84a	Tulsa	CHL	58	9	17	26	71	9	5	4	9	10
1984-85	**NY Rangers**	**NHL**	**42**	**8**	**12**	**20**	**53**	**3**	**0**	**2**	**2**	**4**
	New Haven	AHL	36	6	20	26	18	....	....	....	....	....
1985-86	**NY Rangers**	**NHL**	**27**	**2**	**9**	**11**	**20**	....	....	....	....	....
	Los Angeles	**NHL**	**52**	**7**	**18**	**25**	**78**	....	....	....	....	....
1986-87	**Los Angeles**	**NHL**	**67**	**14**	**23**	**37**	**93**	**5**	**0**	**0**	**0**	**10**
1987-88	**Los Angeles**	**NHL**	**23**	**1**	**7**	**8**	**52**	....	....	....	....	....
	New Haven	AHL	3	2	1	3	4	....	....	....	....	....
	Washington	**NHL**	**21**	**4**	**3**	**7**	**14**	**14**	**1**	**0**	**1**	**30**
1988-89	**Washington**	**NHL**	**61**	**3**	**11**	**14**	**43**	....	....	....	....	....
	Buffalo	**NHL**	**13**	**1**	**5**	**6**	**8**	**5**	**1**	**2**	**3**	**2**
1989-90	**Buffalo**	**NHL**	**67**	**2**	**13**	**15**	**37**	....	....	....	....	....
1990-91	**Buffalo**	**NHL**	**60**	**8**	**23**	**31**	**46**	**6**	**3**	**3**	**6**	**10**
1991-92	**Buffalo**	**NHL**	**50**	**5**	**16**	**21**	**45**	....	....	....	....	....
	NHL Totals		**483**	**55**	**140**	**195**	**489**	**33**	**5**	**7**	**12**	**56**

a Won Bob Gassoff Trophy (CHL's Most Improved Defenseman) (1984)

Signed as a free agent by **NY Rangers**, July 7, 1982. Traded to **Los Angeles** by **NY Rangers** with Roland Melanson for Los Angeles' fourth round choice in 1987 Entry Draft (Michael Sullivan) and Brian MacLellan, December 7, 1985. Traded to **Washington** by **Los Angeles** for Craig Laughlin, February 9, 1988. Traded to **Buffalo** by **Washington** with Clint Malarchuk and Washington's sixth round choice (Brian Holzinger) in 1991 Entry Draft for Calle Johansson and Buffalo's second round choice (Byron Dafoe) in 1989 Entry Draft, March 7, 1989.

LEEMAN, GARY

Right wing. Shoots right. 5'11", 175 lbs. Born, Toronto, Ont., February 19, 1964.
(Toronto's 2nd choice, 24th overall, in 1982 Entry Draft).

			Regular Season					Playoffs				
Season	Club	Lea	GP	G	A	TP	PIM	GP	G	A	TP	PIM
1981-82	Regina	WHL	72	19	41	60	112	3	2	2	4	0
1982-83ab	Regina	WHL	63	24	62	86	88	5	1	5	6	4
	Toronto	**NHL**	....	....	....	....	....	**2**	**0**	**0**	**0**	**0**
1983-84	**Toronto**	**NHL**	**52**	**4**	**8**	**12**	**31**	....	....	....	....	....
1984-85	**Toronto**	**NHL**	**53**	**5**	**26**	**31**	**72**	....	....	....	....	....
	St. Catharines	AHL	7	2	2	4	11	....	....	....	....	....
1985-86	**Toronto**	**NHL**	**53**	**9**	**23**	**32**	**20**	**10**	**2**	**10**	**12**	**2**
	St. Catharines	AHL	25	15	13	28	6	....	....	....	....	....
1986-87	**Toronto**	**NHL**	**80**	**21**	**31**	**52**	**66**	**5**	**0**	**1**	**1**	**14**
1987-88	**Toronto**	**NHL**	**80**	**30**	**31**	**61**	**62**	**2**	**2**	**0**	**2**	**2**
1988-89	**Toronto**	**NHL**	**61**	**32**	**43**	**75**	**66**	....	....	....	....	....
1989-90	**Toronto**	**NHL**	**80**	**51**	**44**	**95**	**63**	**5**	**3**	**3**	**6**	**16**
1990-91	**Toronto**	**NHL**	**52**	**17**	**12**	**29**	**39**	....	....	....	....	....
1991-92	**Toronto**	**NHL**	**34**	**7**	**13**	**20**	**44**	....	....	....	....	....
	Calgary	**NHL**	**29**	**2**	**7**	**9**	**27**	....	....	....	....	....
	NHL Totals		**574**	**178**	**238**	**416**	**490**	**24**	**7**	**14**	**21**	**34**

a WHL First All-Star Team (1983)
b Named WHL's Top Defenseman (1983)

Played in NHL All-Star Game (1989)

Traded to **Calgary** by **Toronto** with Craig Berube, Alexander Godynyuk, Michel Petit and Jeff Reese for Doug Gilmour, Jamie Macoun, Ric Nattress, Rick Wamsley and Kent Manderville, January 2, 1992.

LEETCH, BRIAN

Defense. Shoots left. 5'11", 185 lbs. Born, Corpus Christi, TX, March 3, 1968.
(NY Rangers' 1st choice, 9th overall, in 1986 Entry Draft).

			Regular Season					Playoffs				
Season	Club	Lea	GP	G	A	TP	PIM	GP	G	A	TP	PIM
1986-87abcd	Boston College	H.E.	37	9	38	47	10	....	....	....	....	....
1987-88	U.S. National	....	50	13	61	74	38	....	....	....	....	....
	U.S. Olympic	....	6	1	5	6	4	....	....	....	....	....
	NY Rangers	**NHL**	**17**	**2**	**12**	**14**	**0**	....	....	....	....	....
1988-89ef	**NY Rangers**	**NHL**	**68**	**23**	**48**	**71**	**50**	**4**	**3**	**2**	**5**	**2**
1989-90	**NY Rangers**	**NHL**	**72**	**11**	**45**	**56**	**26**	....	....	....	....	....
1990-91g	**NY Rangers**	**NHL**	**80**	**16**	**72**	**88**	**42**	**6**	**1**	**3**	**4**	**0**
1991-92ij	**NY Rangers**	**NHL**	**80**	**22**	**80**	**102**	**26**	**13**	**4**	**11**	**15**	**4**
	NHL Totals		**317**	**74**	**257**	**331**	**144**	**23**	**8**	**16**	**24**	**6**

a Hockey East Player of the Year (1987)
b Hockey East Rookie of the Year (1987)
c Hockey East First All-Star Team (1987)
d NCAA East First All-American Team (1987)
e NHL All-Rookie Team (1989)
f Won Calder Memorial Trophy (1989)
g NHL Second All-Star Team (1991)
i Won James Norris Memorial Trophy (1992)
j NHL First All-Star Team (1992)

Played in NHL All-Star Game (1990-92)

LEFEBVRE, SYLVAIN

Defense. Shoots left. 6'2", 204 lbs. Born, Richmond, Que., October 14, 1967.

			Regular Season					Playoffs				
Season	Club	Lea	GP	G	A	TP	PIM	GP	G	A	TP	PIM
1984-85	Laval	QMJHL	66	7	5	12	31	....	....	....	....	....
1985-86	Laval	QMJHL	71	8	17	25	48	14	1	0	1	25
1986-87	Laval	QMJHL	70	10	36	46	44	15	1	6	7	12
1987-88	Sherbrooke	AHL	79	3	24	27	73	6	2	3	5	4
1988-89a	Sherbrooke	AHL	77	15	32	47	119	6	1	3	4	4
1989-90	**Montreal**	**NHL**	**68**	**3**	**10**	**13**	**61**	**6**	**0**	**0**	**0**	**2**
1990-91	**Montreal**	**NHL**	**63**	**5**	**18**	**23**	**30**	**11**	**1**	**0**	**1**	**6**
1991-92	**Montreal**	**NHL**	**69**	**3**	**14**	**17**	**91**	**2**	**0**	**0**	**0**	**2**
	NHL Totals		**200**	**11**	**42**	**53**	**182**	**19**	**1**	**0**	**1**	**10**

a AHL Second All-Star Team (1989)

Signed as a free agent by **Montreal**, September 24, 1986. Traded to **Toronto** by **Montreal** for Toronto's third round choice in 1994 Entry Draft, August 20, 1992.

LEGAULT, ALEXANDRE

Defense. Shoots right. 6'1", 205 lbs. Born, Chicoutimi, Que., December 27, 1971.
(Edmonton's 2nd choice, 38th overall, in 1990 Entry Draft).

			Regular Season					Playoffs				
Season	Club	Lea	GP	G	A	TP	PIM	GP	G	A	TP	PIM
1989-90	Boston U.	H.E.	43	9	21	30	54	....	....	....	....	....
1990-91	Boston U.	H.E.	19	2	9	11	30	....	....	....	....	....
	Drummondville	QMJHL	22	3	14	17	27	14	4	5	9	14
1991-92	Beauport	QMJHL	20	5	6	11	41	....	....	....	....	....
	Winston-Salem	ECHL	7	1	1	2	9	....	....	....	....	....

LEHOUX, GUY

Defense. Shoots left. 5'11", 205 lbs. Born, Disraeli, Que., October 19, 1971.
(Toronto's 9th choice, 179th overall, in 1991 Entry Draft).

			Regular Season					Playoffs				
Season	Club	Lea	GP	G	A	TP	PIM	GP	G	A	TP	PIM
1989-90	Drummondville	QMJHL	66	4	17	21	178	....	....	....	....	....
1990-91	Drummondville	QMJHL	63	8	26	34	107	14	1	7	8	24
1991-92	St. John's	AHL	67	1	7	8	134	....	....	....	....	....

LEHTINEN, JERE

Right wing. Shoots right. 6', 183 lbs. Born, Espoo, Finland, July 24, 1973.
(Minnesota's 3rd choice, 88th overall, in 1992 Entry Draft).

			Regular Season					Playoffs				
Season	Club	Lea	GP	G	A	TP	PIM	GP	G	A	TP	PIM
1990-91	Espoo	Fin.	32	15	9	24	12	....	....	....	....	....
1991-92	Espoo	Fin.2	43	32	17	49	6	....	....	....	....	....

LEHTO, JONI

Defense. Shoots left. 6', 175 lbs. Born, Turku, Finland, July 15, 1970.
(NY Islanders' 5th choice, 111th overall, in 1990 Entry Draft).

			Regular Season					Playoffs				
Season	Club	Lea	GP	G	A	TP	PIM	GP	G	A	TP	PIM
1988-89	Ottawa	OHL	63	9	25	34	26	....	....	....	....	....
1989-90a	Ottawa	OHL	60	17	55	72	58	....	....	....	....	....
1990-91	Ottawa	OHL	8	2	10	12	8	....	....	....	....	....
1991-92	Capital Dist.	AHL	26	2	5	7	6	....	....	....	....	....
	Richmond	ECHL	18	2	9	11	10	....	....	....	....	....

a OHL Second All-Star Team (1990)

LEMIEUX, CLAUDE (lehm-YOO)

Right wing. Shoots right. 6'1", 215 lbs. Born, Buckingham, Que., July 16, 1965.
(Montreal's 2nd choice, 26th overall, in 1983 Entry Draft).

			Regular Season					Playoffs				
Season	Club	Lea	GP	G	A	TP	PIM	GP	G	A	TP	PIM
1982-83	Trois-Rivières	QMJHL	62	28	38	66	187	4	1	0	1	30
1983-84	**Montreal**	**NHL**	**8**	**1**	**1**	**2**	**12**	....	....	....	....	....
	Verdun	QMJHL	51	41	45	86	225	9	8	12	20	63
	Nova Scotia	AHL	....	....	....	....	....	2	1	0	1	0
1984-85	**Montreal**	**NHL**	**1**	**0**	**1**	**1**	**7**	....	....	....	....	....
ab	Verdun	QMJHL	52	58	66	124	152	14	23	17	40	38
1985-86	**Montreal**	**NHL**	**10**	**1**	**2**	**3**	**22**	**20**	**10**	**6**	**16**	**68**
	Sherbrooke	AHL	58	21	32	53	145	....	....	....	....	....
1986-87	**Montreal**	**NHL**	**76**	**27**	**26**	**53**	**156**	**17**	**4**	**9**	**13**	**41**
1987-88	**Montreal**	**NHL**	**78**	**31**	**30**	**61**	**137**	**11**	**3**	**2**	**5**	**20**
1988-89	**Montreal**	**NHL**	**69**	**29**	**22**	**51**	**136**	**18**	**4**	**3**	**7**	**58**
1989-90	**Montreal**	**NHL**	**39**	**8**	**10**	**18**	**106**	**11**	**1**	**3**	**4**	**38**
1990-91	**New Jersey**	**NHL**	**78**	**30**	**17**	**47**	**105**	**7**	**4**	**0**	**4**	**34**
1991-92	**New Jersey**	**NHL**	**74**	**41**	**27**	**68**	**109**	**7**	**4**	**3**	**7**	**26**
	NHL Totals		**433**	**168**	**136**	**304**	**790**	**91**	**30**	**26**	**56**	**285**

a Named Most Valuable Player in QMJHL Playoffs (1985)
b QMJHL First All-Star Team (1985)

Traded to **New Jersey** by **Montreal** for Sylvain Turgeon, September 4, 1990.

LEMIEUX, JOCELYN (lehm-YOO)

Right wing. Shoots left. 5'10", 200 lbs. Born, Mont-Laurier, Que., November 18, 1967.
(St. Louis' 1st choice, 10th overall, in 1986 Entry Draft).

			Regular Season					Playoffs				
Season	Club	Lea	GP	G	A	TP	PIM	GP	G	A	TP	PIM
1984-85	Laval	QMJHL	68	13	19	32	92	....	....	....	....	....
1985-86a	Laval	QMJHL	71	57	68	125	131	14	9	15	24	37
1986-87	**St. Louis**	**NHL**	**53**	**10**	**8**	**18**	**94**	**5**	**0**	**1**	**1**	**6**
1987-88	**St. Louis**	**NHL**	**23**	**1**	**0**	**1**	**42**	**5**	**0**	**0**	**0**	**15**
	Peoria	IHL	8	0	5	5	35	....	....	....	....	....
1988-89	**Montreal**	**NHL**	**1**	**0**	**1**	**1**	**0**	....	....	....	....	....
	Sherbrooke	AHL	73	25	28	53	134	4	3	1	4	6
1989-90	**Montreal**	**NHL**	**34**	**4**	**2**	**6**	**61**	....	....	....	....	....
	Chicago	**NHL**	**39**	**10**	**11**	**21**	**47**	**18**	**1**	**8**	**9**	**28**
1990-91	**Chicago**	**NHL**	**67**	**6**	**7**	**13**	**119**	**4**	**0**	**0**	**0**	**0**
1991-92	**Chicago**	**NHL**	**78**	**6**	**10**	**16**	**80**	**18**	**3**	**1**	**4**	**33**
	NHL Totals		**295**	**37**	**39**	**76**	**443**	**50**	**4**	**10**	**14**	**82**

a QMJHL First All-Star Team (1986)

Traded to **Montreal** by **St. Louis** with Darrell May and St. Louis' second round choice (Patrice Brisebois) in the 1989 Entry Draft for Sergio Momesso and Vincent Riendeau, August 9, 1988. Traded to **Chicago** by **Montreal** for Chicago's third round choice (Charles Poulin) in 1990 Entry Draft, January 5, 1990.

LEMIEUX, MARIO (lehm-YOO)

Center. Shoots right. 6'4", 210 lbs. Born, Montreal, Que., October 5, 1965.
(Pittsburgh's 1st choice, 1st overall, in 1984 Entry Draft).

			Regular Season					Playoffs				
Season	Club	Lea	GP	G	A	TP	PIM	GP	G	A	TP	PIM
1981-82	Laval	QMJHL	64	30	66	96	22	18	5	9	14	31
1982-83a	Laval	QMJHL	66	84	100	184	76	12	14	18	32	18
1983-84bcd	Laval	QMJHL	70	*133	*149	*282	92	14	*29	*23	*52	29
1984-85ef	**Pittsburgh**	**NHL**	**73**	**43**	**57**	**100**	**54**	....	....	....	....	....
1985-86gh	**Pittsburgh**	**NHL**	**79**	**48**	**93**	**141**	**43**	....	....	....	....	....
1986-87g	**Pittsburgh**	**NHL**	**63**	**54**	**53**	**107**	**57**	....	....	....	....	....
1987-88 hijklm	**Pittsburgh**	**NHL**	**77**	***70**	**98**	***168**	**92**	....	....	....	....	....
1988-89jkmn	**Pittsburgh**	**NHL**	**76**	***85**	***114**	***199**	**100**	**11**	**12**	**7**	**19**	**16**
1989-90	**Pittsburgh**	**NHL**	**59**	**45**	**78**	**123**	**78**	....	....	....	....	....
1990-91o	**Pittsburgh**	**NHL**	**26**	**19**	**26**	**45**	**30**	**23**	**16**	***28**	***44**	**16**
1991-92gjop	**Pittsburgh**	**NHL**	**64**	**44**	**87**	***131**	**94**	**15**	***16**	**18**	***34**	**2**
	NHL Totals		**517**	**408**	**606**	**1014**	**548**	**49**	**44**	**53**	**97**	**34**

a QMJHL Second All-Star Team (1983)
b QMJHL First All-Star Team (1984)
c QMJHL Most Valuable Player (1984)
d Canadian Major Junior Player of the Year (1984)
e Won Calder Memorial Trophy (1985)
f NHL All-Rookie Team (1985)
g NHL Second All-Star Team (1986, 1987, 1992)
h Won Lester B. Pearson Award (1986, 1988)
i Won Hart Trophy (1988)
j Won Art Ross Trophy (1988, 1989, 1992)
k NHL First All-Star Team (1988, 1989)
l Won Dodge Performance of the Year Award (1988)
m Won Dodge Ram Tough Award (1989)
n Won Dodge Performer of the Year Award (1988, 1989)
o Won Conn Smythe Trophy (1991, 1992)
p Won ProSet/NHL Player of the Year Award (1992)

Played in NHL All-Star Game (1985, 1986, 1988-90, 1992)

LENARDON, TIM

Center/Left wing. Shoots left. 6'2", 185 lbs. Born, Trail, B.C., May 11, 1962.

			Regular Season					Playoffs				
Season	Club	Lea	GP	G	A	TP	PIM	GP	G	A	TP	PIM
1983-84	Brandon U.	CWUAA	24	22	21	43	....	....	....	....	....	....
1984-85	Brandon U.	CWUAA	24	21	39	60	....	....	....	....	....	....
1985-86a	Brandon U.	CWUAA	26	26	40	66	33	....	....	....	....	....
1986-87	**New Jersey**	**NHL**	**7**	**1**	**1**	**2**	**0**	....	....	....	....	....
	Maine	AHL	61	28	35	63	30	....	....	....	....	....
1987-88	Utica	AHL	79	38	53	91	72	....	....	....	....	....
1988-89	Utica	AHL	63	28	27	55	48	....	....	....	....	....
	Milwaukee	IHL	15	6	5	11	27	10	2	3	5	25
1989-90	**Vancouver**	**NHL**	**8**	**1**	**0**	**1**	**4**	....	....	....	....	....
	Milwaukee	IHL	66	32	36	68	134	6	1	1	2	4
1990-91	Fiemme	Italy	36	45	73	118	4	10	8	18	26	0
1991-92	Kalamazoo	IHL	73	27	24	51	37	12	5	5	10	4
	NHL Totals		**15**	**2**	**1**	**3**	**4**	....	....	....	....	....

a Canadian University Player of the Year (1986)

Signed as a free agent by **New Jersey**, August 6, 1986. Traded to **Vancouver** by **New Jersey** for Claude Vilgrain, March 7, 1989. Signed as a free agent by **Minnesota**, July 25, 1991.

LEROUX, FRANCOIS

Defense. Shoots left. 6'6", 225 lbs. Born, Ste.-Adele, Que., April 18, 1970.
(Edmonton's 1st choice, 19th overall, in 1988 Entry Draft).

			Regular Season					Playoffs				
Season	Club	Lea	GP	G	A	TP	PIM	GP	G	A	TP	PIM
1987-88	St-Jean	QMJHL	58	3	8	11	143	7	2	0	2	21
1988-89	**Edmonton**	**NHL**	**2**	**0**	**0**	**0**	**0**	....	....	....	....	....
	St-Jean	QMJHL	57	8	34	42	185	....	....	....	....	....
1989-90	**Edmonton**	**NHL**	**3**	**0**	**1**	**1**	**0**	....	....	....	....	....
	Victoriaville	QMJHL	54	4	33	37	169	....	....	....	....	....
1990-91	**Edmonton**	**NHL**	**1**	**0**	**2**	**2**	**0**	....	....	....	....	....
	Cape Breton	AHL	71	2	7	9	124	4	0	1	1	19
1991-92	**Edmonton**	**NHL**	**4**	**0**	**0**	**0**	**7**	....	....	....	....	....
	Cape Breton	AHL	61	7	22	29	114	5	0	0	0	8
	NHL Totals		**10**	**0**	**3**	**3**	**7**	....	....	....	....	....

LESCHYSHYN, CURTIS (lez-CHIH-shihn)

Defense. Shoots left. 6'1", 205 lbs. Born, Thompson, Man., September 21, 1969.
(Quebec's 1st choice, 3rd overall, in 1988 Entry Draft).

			Regular Season					Playoffs				
Season	Club	Lea	GP	G	A	TP	PIM	GP	G	A	TP	PIM
1986-87	Saskatoon	WHL	70	14	26	40	107	11	1	5	6	14
1987-88	Saskatoon	WHL	56	14	41	55	86	10	2	5	7	16
1988-89	**Quebec**	**NHL**	**71**	**4**	**9**	**13**	**71**	....	....	....	....	....
1989-90	**Quebec**	**NHL**	**68**	**2**	**6**	**8**	**44**	....	....	....	....	....
1990-91	**Quebec**	**NHL**	**55**	**3**	**7**	**10**	**49**	....	....	....	....	....
1991-92	**Quebec**	**NHL**	**42**	**5**	**12**	**17**	**42**	....	....	....	....	....
	Halifax	AHL	6	0	2	2	4	....	....	....	....	....
	NHL Totals		**236**	**14**	**34**	**48**	**206**	....	....	....	....	....

LESLIE, LEE J.

Left wing. Shoots left. 6'4", 191 lbs. Born, Prince George, B.C., August 15, 1972.
(St. Louis' 4th choice, 86th overall, in 1992 Entry Draft).

			Regular Season					Playoffs				
Season	Club	Lea	GP	G	A	TP	PIM	GP	G	A	TP	PIM
1989-90	Prince Albert	WHL	62	14	16	30	13	....	....	....	....	....
1990-91	Prince Albert	WHL	72	29	42	71	68	3	0	0	0	5
1991-92	Prince Albert	WHL	72	52	48	100	70	10	6	6	12	12

LESSARD, OWEN

Left wing. Shoots left. 6'1", 196 lbs. Born, Sudbury, Ont., January 11, 1970.
(Chicago's 7th choice, 184th overall, in 1990 Entry Draft).

			Regular Season					Playoffs				
Season	Club	Lea	GP	G	A	TP	PIM	GP	G	A	TP	PIM
1989-90	Owen Sound	OHL	46	22	33	55	77	12	5	2	7	26
1990-91	Indianapolis	IHL	73	8	14	22	52	1	0	0	0	0
1991-92	Indianapolis	IHL	41	3	2	5	53	....	....	....	....	....

LESSARD, RICK

Defense. Shoots left. 6'2", 206 lbs. Born, Timmins, Ont., January 9, 1968.
(Calgary's 6th choice, 142nd overall, in 1986 Entry Draft).

			Regular Season					Playoffs				
Season	Club	Lea	GP	G	A	TP	PIM	GP	G	A	TP	PIM
1985-86	Ottawa	OHL	64	1	20	21	231	....	....	....	....	....
1986-87	Ottawa	OHL	66	5	36	41	188	11	1	7	8	30
1987-88	Ottawa	OHL	58	5	34	39	210	16	1	0	1	31
1988-89	**Calgary**	**NHL**	**6**	**0**	**1**	**1**	**2**	....	....	....	....	....
a	Salt Lake	IHL	76	10	42	52	239	14	1	6	7	35
1989-90	Salt Lake	IHL	66	3	18	21	169	10	1	2	3	64
1990-91	**Calgary**	**NHL**	**1**	**0**	**1**	**1**	**0**	....	....	....	....	....
	Salt Lake	IHL	80	8	27	35	272	4	0	1	1	12
1991-92	**San Jose**	**NHL**	**8**	**0**	**2**	**2**	**16**	....	....	....	....	....
	Kansas City	IHL	46	3	16	19	117	3	0	0	0	2
	NHL Totals		**15**	**0**	**4**	**4**	**18**	....	....	....	....	....

a IHL First All-Star Team (1989)

Claimed by **San Jose** from **Calgary** in Expansion Draft, May 30, 1991.

LEVEQUE, GUY

Center. Shoots right. 5'11", 166 lbs. Born, Kingston, Ont., December 28, 1972.
(Los Angeles' 1st choice, 42nd overall, in 1991 Entry Draft).

			Regular Season					Playoffs				
Season	Club	Lea	GP	G	A	TP	PIM	GP	G	A	TP	PIM
1989-90	Cornwall	OHL	62	10	15	25	30	3	0	0	0	4
1990-91	Cornwall	OHL	66	41	56	97	34	....	....	....	....	....
1991-92	Cornwall	OHL	37	23	36	59	40	6	3	5	8	2

LEVINS, SCOTT

Center. Shoots right. 6'4", 210 lbs. Born, Spokane, WA, January 30, 1970.
(Winnipeg's 4th choice, 75th overall, in 1990 Entry Draft).

			Regular Season					Playoffs				
Season	Club	Lea	GP	G	A	TP	PIM	GP	G	A	TP	PIM
1989-90a	Tri-Cities	WHL	71	25	37	62	132	6	2	3	5	18
1990-91	Moncton	AHL	74	12	26	38	133	4	0	0	0	4
1991-92	Moncton	AHL	69	15	18	33	271	11	3	4	7	30

a WHL West Second All-Star Team (1990)

LIDSTER, DOUG

Defense. Shoots right. 6'1", 200 lbs. Born, Kamloops, B.C., October 18, 1960.
(Vancouver's 6th choice, 133rd overall, in 1980 Entry Draft).

			Regular Season					Playoffs				
Season	Club	Lea	GP	G	A	TP	PIM	GP	G	A	TP	PIM
1977-78	Seattle	WHL	2	0	0	0	0	....	....	....	....	....
1979-80	Colorado	WCHA	39	18	25	43	52	....	....	....	....	....
1980-81	Colorado	WCHA	36	10	30	40	54	....	....	....	....	....
1981-82	Colorado	WCHA	36	13	22	35	32	....	....	....	....	....
1982-83	Colorado	WCHA	34	15	41	56	30	....	....	....	....	....
1983-84	Cdn. Olympic	....	59	6	20	26	28	....	....	....	....	....
	Vancouver	**NHL**	**8**	**0**	**0**	**0**	**4**	**2**	**0**	**1**	**1**	**0**
1984-85	**Vancouver**	**NHL**	**78**	**6**	**24**	**30**	**55**	....	....	....	....	....
1985-86	**Vancouver**	**NHL**	**78**	**12**	**16**	**28**	**56**	**3**	**0**	**1**	**1**	**2**
1986-87	**Vancouver**	**NHL**	**80**	**12**	**51**	**63**	**40**	....	....	....	....	....
1987-88	**Vancouver**	**NHL**	**64**	**4**	**32**	**36**	**105**	....	....	....	....	....
1988-89	**Vancouver**	**NHL**	**63**	**5**	**17**	**22**	**78**	**7**	**1**	**1**	**2**	**9**
1989-90	**Vancouver**	**NHL**	**80**	**8**	**28**	**36**	**36**	....	....	....	....	....
1990-91	**Vancouver**	**NHL**	**78**	**6**	**32**	**38**	**77**	**6**	**0**	**2**	**2**	**6**
1991-92	**Vancouver**	**NHL**	**66**	**6**	**23**	**29**	**39**	**11**	**1**	**2**	**3**	**11**
	NHL Totals		**595**	**59**	**223**	**282**	**490**	**29**	**2**	**7**	**9**	**28**

LIDSTROM, NICKLAS (LID-struhm)

Defense. Shoots left. 6'2", 180 lbs. Born, Vasteras, Sweden, April 28, 1970.
(Detroit's 3rd choice, 53rd overall, in 1989 Entry Draft).

			Regular Season					Playoffs				
Season	Club	Lea	GP	G	A	TP	PIM	GP	G	A	TP	PIM
1988-89	Vasteras	Swe.	19	0	2	2	4	....	....	....	....	....
1989-90	Vasteras	Swe.	39	8	8	16	14	2	0	1	1	2
1990-91	Vasteras	Swe.	38	4	19	23	2	....	....	....	....	....
1991-92a	**Detroit**	**NHL**	**80**	**11**	**49**	**60**	**22**	**11**	**1**	**2**	**3**	**0**
	NHL Totals		**80**	**11**	**49**	**60**	**22**	**11**	**1**	**2**	**3**	**0**

a NHL/Upper Deck All-Rookie Team (1992)

LIEVERS, BRETT

Center. Shoots right. 6', 170 lbs. Born, Syracuse, NY, June 18, 1971.
(NY Rangers' 13th choice, 223rd overall, in 1990 Entry Draft).

			Regular Season					Playoffs				
Season	Club	Lea	GP	G	A	TP	PIM	GP	G	A	TP	PIM
1990-91	St. Cloud	WCHA	40	14	18	32	4	....	....	....	....	....
1991-92	St. Cloud	WCHA	16	2	10	12	2	....	....	....	....	....

LILLEY, JOHN

Center. Shoots right. 5'9", 170 lbs. Born, Wakefield, MA, August 3, 1972.
(Winnipeg's 8th choice, 140th overall, in 1990 Entry Draft).

			Regular Season					Playoffs				
Season	Club	Lea	GP	G	A	TP	PIM	GP	G	A	TP	PIM
1990-91	Cushing Aca.	HS	25	29	42	71	....	....	....	....	....	....
1991-92	Boston U.	H.E.	23	9	9	18	43	....	....	....	....	....

LILLIE, SHAWN

Left wing. Shoots left. 6', 180 lbs. Born, Sault Ste. Marie, Ont., August 13, 1967.
(Pittsburgh's 2nd choice, 9th overall, in 1988 Supplemental Draft).

			Regular Season					Playoffs				
Season	Club	Lea	GP	G	A	TP	PIM	GP	G	A	TP	PIM
1986-87	Colgate	ECAC	30	11	10	21	4	....	....	....	....	....
1987-88	Colgate	ECAC	32	12	22	34	12	....	....	....	....	....
1988-89	Colgate	ECAC	31	16	38	54	12	....	....	....	....	....
1989-90	Colgate	ECAC	38	17	22	39	32	....	....	....	....	....
1990-91	Richmond	ECHL	31	12	20	32	13	....	....	....	....	....
	Cincinnati	ECHL	14	2	7	9	2	3	1	0	1	0
1991-92	Knoxville	ECHL	39	15	28	43	6	....	....	....	....	....

LINDBERG, CHRIS

Left wing. Shoots left. 6'1", 190 lbs. Born, Fort Frances, Ont., April 16, 1967.

			Regular Season					Playoffs				
Season	Club	Lea	GP	G	A	TP	PIM	GP	G	A	TP	PIM
1987-88	Minn.-Duluth	WCHA	35	12	10	22	36	....	....	....	....	....
1988-89	Minn.-Duluth	WCHA	36	15	18	33	51	....	....	....	....	....
1989-90	Binghamton	AHL	32	4	4	8	36	....	....	....	....	....
	Virginia	ECHL	26	11	23	34	27	4	0	3	3	2
1990-91	Cdn. National	....	55	25	31	56	53	....	....	....	....	....
	Springfield	AHL	1	0	0	0	2	1	0	0	0	0
1991-92	Cdn. National	....	56	33	35	68	63	....	....	....	....	....
	Cdn. Olympic	....	8	1	4	5	4	....	....	....	....	....
	Calgary	**NHL**	**17**	**2**	**5**	**7**	**17**	....	....	....	....	....
	NHL Totals		**17**	**2**	**5**	**7**	**17**	....	....	....	....	....

Signed as a free agent by **Hartford**, March 17, 1989. Signed as a free agent by **Calgary**, August 2, 1991. Claimed by **Ottawa** from **Calgary** in Expansion Draft, June 18, 1992. Traded to **Calgary** by **Ottawa** for Mark Osiecki, June 22, 1992.

LINDEN, TREVOR

Center/Right wing. Shoots right. 6'4", 205 lbs. Born, Medicine Hat, Alta., April 11, 1970.
(Vancouver's 1st choice, 2nd overall, in 1988 Entry Draft).

			Regular Season					Playoffs				
Season	Club	Lea	GP	G	A	TP	PIM	GP	G	A	TP	PIM
1986-87	Medicine Hat	WHL	72	14	22	36	59	20	5	4	9	17
1987-88	Medicine Hat	WHL	67	46	64	110	76	16	*13	12	25	19
1988-89a	**Vancouver**	**NHL**	**80**	**30**	**29**	**59**	**41**	**7**	**3**	**4**	**7**	**8**
1989-90	**Vancouver**	**NHL**	**73**	**21**	**30**	**51**	**43**	....	....	....	....	....
1990-91	**Vancouver**	**NHL**	**80**	**33**	**37**	**70**	**65**	**6**	**0**	**7**	**7**	**2**
1991-92	**Vancouver**	**NHL**	**80**	**31**	**44**	**75**	**101**	**13**	**4**	**8**	**12**	**6**
	NHL Totals		**313**	**115**	**139**	**254**	**250**	**26**	**7**	**19**	**26**	**16**

a NHL All-Rookie Team (1989)

Played in NHL All-Star Game (1991, 1992)

LINDHOLM, MIKAEL (LIHND-hohlm)

Center. Shoots left. 6'1", 194 lbs. Born, Gavle, Sweden, December 19, 1964.
(Los Angeles' 10th choice, 237th overall, in 1987 Entry Draft).

			Regular Season					Playoffs				
Season	Club	Lea	GP	G	A	TP	PIM	GP	G	A	TP	PIM
1986-87	Brynas	Swe.	36	8	9	17	46	....	....	....	....	....
1987-88	Brynas	Swe.	38	9	8	17	56	....	....	....	....	....
1988-89	Brynas	Swe.	40	9	17	26	98	....	....	....	....	....
1989-90	**Los Angeles**	**NHL**	**18**	**2**	**2**	**4**	**2**	....	....	....	....	....
	New Haven	AHL	28	4	6	10	24	....	....	....	....	....
1990-91	Phoenix	IHL	70	16	45	61	92	11	0	12	12	14
1991-92	Brynas	Swe.	36	7	11	18	24	5	0	1	1	2
	NHL Totals		**18**	**2**	**2**	**4**	**2**	....	....	....	....	....

LINDMAN, MIKAEL (LIHND-mahn)

Defense. Shoots left. 6'1", 194 lbs. Born, Bolsaf, Sweden, May 15, 1967.
(Detroit's 12th choice, 239th overall, in 1985 Entry Draft).

			Regular Season					Playoffs				
Season	Club	Lea	GP	G	A	TP	PIM	GP	G	A	TP	PIM
1988-89	Skelleftea	Swe.	38	7	7	14	20	....	....	....	....	....
1989-90	Skelleftea	Swe.	28	2	5	7	8	5	0	0	0	0
1990-91	Brynas	Swe.	40	3	4	7	14	5	0	0	0	2

LINDQVIST, FREDRIK

Center. Shoots left. 5'11", 167 lbs. Born, Sadertalje, Sweden, June 21, 1973.
(New Jersey's 4th choice, 55th overall, in 1991 Entry Draft).

			Regular Season					Playoffs				
Season	Club	Lea	GP	G	A	TP	PIM	GP	G	A	TP	PIM
1989-90	Huddinge	Swe.	2	0	0	0	0	....	....	....	....	....
1990-91	Djurgarden	Swe.	28	6	4	10	0	....	....	....	....	....
1991-92	Djurgarden	Swe.	39	9	6	15	14	10	1	1	2	2

LINDROS, ERIC (LIHND-RAHZ)

Center. Shoots right. 6'4", 225 lbs. Born, London, Ont., February 28, 1973.
(Quebec's 1st choice, 1st overall, in 1991 Entry Draft).

			Regular Season					Playoffs				
Season	Club	Lea	GP	G	A	TP	PIM	GP	G	A	TP	PIM
1989-90	Det. Compuware	USHL	14	23	29	52	123	....	....	....	....	....
a	Oshawa	OHL	25	17	19	36	61	17	18	18	36	76
1990-91bc	Oshawa	OHL	57	*71	78	*149	189	16	*18	20	*38	*93
1991-92	Oshawa	OHL	13	9	22	31	54	....	....	....	....	....
	Cdn. National	....	24	19	16	35	34	....	....	....	....	....
	Cdn. Olympic	....	8	5	6	11	6	....	....	....	....	....

a Memorial Cup All-Star Team (1990)
b OHL First All-Star Team (1991)
c Canadian Major Junior Player of the Year (1991)

Traded to **Philadelphia** by **Quebec** for Peter Forsberg, Steve Duchesne, Kerry Huffman, Mike Ricci, Ron Hextall, Chris Simon, Philadelphia's first choice in the 1993 and 1994 Entry Drafts and cash, June 30, 1992.

LINDSAY, BILL

Left wing. Shoots left. 5'11", 185 lbs. Born, Big Fork, MT, May 17, 1971.
(Quebec's 6th choice, 103rd overall, in 1991 Entry Draft).

			Regular Season					Playoffs				
Season	Club	Lea	GP	G	A	TP	PIM	GP	G	A	TP	PIM
1990-91	Tri-Cities	WHL	63	46	47	93	151	5	3	6	9	10
1991-92	**Quebec**	**NHL**	**23**	**2**	**4**	**6**	**14**	....	....	....	....	....
	Tri-Cities	WHL	42	34	59	93	111	3	2	3	5	16
	NHL Totals		**23**	**2**	**4**	**6**	**14**	....	....	....	....	....

LINK, ANTHONY (TONY)

Defense. Shoots right. 6'2", 205 lbs. Born, Anchorage, AK, April 3, 1969.
(Philadelphia's 6th choice, 125th overall, in 1987 Entry Draft).

			Regular Season					Playoffs				
Season	Club	Lea	GP	G	A	TP	PIM	GP	G	A	TP	PIM
1988-89	U. of Maine	H.E.	22	0	3	3	12	....	....	....	....	....
1989-90	U. of Maine	H.E.	15	0	3	3	6	....	....	....	....	....
1990-91	U. of Maine	H.E.	40	0	5	5	30	....	....	....	....	....
1991-92	U. of Maine	H.E.	34	3	6	9	44	....	....	....	....	....

LINSEMAN, KEN (LIHNS-muhn)

Center. Shoots left. 5'11", 180 lbs. Born, Kingston, Ont., August 11, 1958.
(Philadelphia's 2nd choice, 7th overall, in 1978 Amateur Draft).

			Regular Season					Playoffs				
Season	Club	Lea	GP	G	A	TP	PIM	GP	G	A	TP	PIM
1975-76	Kingston	OHA	65	61	51	112	92	7	5	0	5	18
1976-77a	Kingston	OHA	63	53	74	127	210	10	9	12	21	54
1977-78	Birmingham	WHA	71	38	38	76	126	5	2	2	4	15
1978-79	**Philadelphia**	**NHL**	**30**	**5**	**20**	**25**	**23**	**8**	**2**	**6**	**8**	**22**
	Maine	AHL	38	17	22	39	106	....	....	....	....	....
1979-80	**Philadelphia**	**NHL**	**80**	**22**	**57**	**79**	**107**	**17**	**4**	***18**	**22**	**40**
1980-81	**Philadelphia**	**NHL**	**51**	**17**	**30**	**47**	**150**	**12**	**4**	**16**	**20**	**67**
1981-82	**Philadelphia**	**NHL**	**79**	**24**	**68**	**92**	**275**	**4**	**1**	**2**	**3**	**6**
1982-83	**Edmonton**	**NHL**	**72**	**33**	**42**	**75**	**181**	**16**	**6**	**8**	**14**	**22**
1983-84	**Edmonton**	**NHL**	**72**	**18**	**49**	**67**	**119**	**19**	**10**	**4**	**14**	**65**
1984-85	**Boston**	**NHL**	**74**	**25**	**49**	**74**	**126**	**5**	**4**	**6**	**10**	**8**
1985-86	**Boston**	**NHL**	**64**	**23**	**58**	**81**	**97**	**3**	**0**	**1**	**1**	**17**
1986-87	**Boston**	**NHL**	**64**	**15**	**34**	**49**	**126**	**4**	**1**	**1**	**2**	**22**
1987-88	**Boston**	**NHL**	**77**	**29**	**45**	**74**	**167**	**23**	**11**	**14**	**25**	**56**
1988-89	**Boston**	**NHL**	**78**	**27**	**45**	**72**	**164**	....	....	....	....	....
1989-90	**Boston**	**NHL**	**32**	**6**	**16**	**22**	**66**	....	....	....	....	....
	Philadelphia	**NHL**	**29**	**5**	**9**	**14**	**30**	....	....	....	....	....
1990-91	**Edmonton**	**NHL**	**56**	**7**	**29**	**36**	**94**	**2**	**0**	**1**	**1**	**0**
1991-92	**Toronto**	**NHL**	**2**	**0**	**0**	**0**	**2**	....	....	....	....	....
	Asiago	Italy	5	3	3	6	4	7	3	4	7	47
	NHL Totals		**860**	**256**	**551**	**807**	**1727**	**113**	**43**	**77**	**120**	**325**

a OHA Second All-Star Team (1977)

Traded to **Hartford** by **Philadelphia** with Greg Adams and Philadelphia's first (David Jensen) and third round choices (Leif Karlsson) in 1983 Entry Draft for Mark Howe and Hartford's third round choice (Derrick Smith) in the 1983 Entry Draft, August 19, 1982. Traded to **Edmonton** by **Hartford** with Don Nachbaur for Risto Siltanen and Brent Loney, August 19, 1982. Traded to **Boston** by **Edmonton** for Mike Krushelnyski, June 21, 1984. Traded to **Philadelphia** by **Boston** for Dave Poulin, January 16, 1990. Signed as a free agent by **Edmonton**, August 31, 1990. Traded to **Toronto** by **Edmonton** for cash, October 7, 1991.

LOACH, LONNIE

Left wing. Shoots left. 5'10", 181 lbs. Born, New Liskeard, Ont., April 14, 1968.
(Chicago's 4th choice, 98th overall, in 1986 Entry Draft).

			Regular Season					Playoffs				
Season	Club	Lea	GP	G	A	TP	PIM	GP	G	A	TP	PIM
1985-86a	Guelph	OHL	65	41	42	83	63	20	7	8	15	16
1986-87	Guelph	OHL	56	31	24	55	42	5	2	1	3	2
1987-88	Guelph	OHL	66	43	49	92	75	....	....	....	....	....
1988-89	Flint	IHL	41	22	26	48	30	....	....	....	....	....
	Saginaw	IHL	32	7	6	13	27	....	....	....	....	....
1989-90	Indianapolis	IHL	3	0	0	0	0	....	....	....	....	....
	Fort Wayne	IHL	54	15	33	48	40	5	4	2	6	15
1990-91bc	Fort Wayne	IHL	81	55	76	*131	45	19	5	11	16	13
1991-92	Adirondack	AHL	67	37	49	86	69	19	*13	4	17	10

a OHL Rookie of the Year (1986)
b IHL Second All-Star Team (1991)
c Won Leo P. Lamoureux Trophy (Leading Scorer – IHL) (1991)

Signed as a free agent by **Detroit**, June 7, 1991. Claimed by **Ottawa** from **Detroit** in Expansion Draft, June 18, 1992.

LOCKE, BRENDAN

Right wing. Shoots right. 6'4", 180 lbs. Born, Nahant, MA, May 31, 1970.
(Philadelphia's 2nd choice, 12th overall, in 1991 Supplemental Draft).

			Regular Season					Playoffs				
Season	Club	Lea	GP	G	A	TP	PIM	GP	G	A	TP	PIM
1989-90	Merrimack	H.E.	31	1	7	8	8	....	....	....	....	....
1990-91	Merrimack	H.E.	32	4	9	13	6	....	....	....	....	....
1991-92	Merrimack	H.E.	34	4	11	15	10	....	....	....	....	....

LOEWEN, DARCY

Left wing. Shoots left. 5'10", 185 lbs. Born, Calgary, Alta., February 26, 1969.
(Buffalo's 2nd choice, 55th overall, in 1988 Entry Draft).

			Regular Season					Playoffs				
Season	Club	Lea	GP	G	A	TP	PIM	GP	G	A	TP	PIM
1986-87	Spokane	WHL	68	15	25	40	129	5	0	0	0	16
1987-88	Spokane	WHL	72	30	44	74	231	15	7	5	12	54
1988-89	Spokane	WHL	60	31	27	58	194	....	....	....	....	....
	Cdn. National	....	2	0	0	0	0	....	....	....	....	....
1989-90	**Buffalo**	**NHL**	**4**	**0**	**0**	**0**	**4**	....	....	....	....	....
	Rochester	AHL	50	7	11	18	193	5	1	0	1	6
1990-91	**Buffalo**	**NHL**	**6**	**0**	**0**	**0**	**8**	....	....	....	....	....
	Rochester	AHL	71	13	15	28	130	15	1	5	6	14
1991-92	**Buffalo**	**NHL**	**2**	**0**	**0**	**0**	**2**	....	....	....	....	....
	Rochester	AHL	73	11	20	31	193	4	0	1	1	8
	NHL Totals		**12**	**0**	**0**	**0**	**14**	....	....	....	....	....

Claimed by **Ottawa** from **Buffalo** in Expansion Draft, June 18, 1992.

LOISELLE, CLAUDE (LWAH-ZEHL)

Center. Shoots left. 5'11", 195 lbs. Born, Ottawa, Ont., May 29, 1963.
(Detroit's 1st choice, 23rd overall, in 1981 Entry Draft).

			Regular Season					Playoffs				
Season	Club	Lea	GP	G	A	TP	PIM	GP	G	A	TP	PIM
1980-81	Windsor	OHA	68	38	56	94	103	11	3	3	6	40
1981-82	**Detroit**	**NHL**	**4**	**1**	**0**	**1**	**2**	....	....	....	....	....
	Windsor	OHL	68	36	73	109	192	9	2	10	12	42
1982-83	**Detroit**	**NHL**	**18**	**2**	**0**	**2**	**15**	....	....	....	....	....
	Adirondack	AHL	6	1	7	8	0	6	2	4	6	0
1983-84	**Detroit**	**NHL**	**28**	**4**	**6**	**10**	**32**	....	....	....	....	....
	Adirondack	AHL	29	13	16	29	59	....	....	....	....	....
1984-85	**Detroit**	**NHL**	**30**	**8**	**1**	**9**	**45**	**3**	**0**	**2**	**2**	**0**
	Adirondack	AHL	47	22	29	51	24	....	....	....	....	....
1985-86	**Detroit**	**NHL**	**48**	**7**	**15**	**22**	**142**	....	....	....	....	....
	Adirondack	AHL	21	15	11	26	32	16	5	10	15	38
1986-87	**New Jersey**	**NHL**	**75**	**16**	**24**	**40**	**137**	....	....	....	....	....
1987-88	**New Jersey**	**NHL**	**68**	**17**	**18**	**35**	**121**	**20**	**4**	**6**	**10**	**50**
1988-89	**New Jersey**	**NHL**	**74**	**7**	**14**	**21**	**209**	....	....	....	....	....
1989-90	**Quebec**	**NHL**	**72**	**11**	**14**	**25**	**104**	....	....	....	....	....
1990-91	**Quebec**	**NHL**	**59**	**5**	**10**	**15**	**86**	....	....	....	....	....
	Toronto	**NHL**	**7**	**1**	**1**	**2**	**2**	....	....	....	....	....
1991-92	**Toronto**	**NHL**	**64**	**6**	**9**	**15**	**102**	....	....	....	....	....
	NY Islanders	**NHL**	**11**	**1**	**1**	**2**	**13**	....	....	....	....	....
	NHL Totals		**558**	**86**	**113**	**199**	**1010**	**23**	**4**	**8**	**12**	**50**

Traded to **New Jersey** by **Detroit** for Tim Higgins, June 25, 1986. Traded to **Quebec** by **New Jersey** with Joe Cirella and New Jersey's eighth round choice (Alexander Karpovtsev) in 1990 Entry Draft for Walt Poddubny and Quebec's fourth round choice (Mike Bodnarchuk) in 1990 Entry Draft, June 17, 1989. Claimed on waivers by **Toronto**, March 5, 1991. Traded to **NY Islanders** by **Toronto** with Daniel Marois for Ken Baumgartner and Dave McLlwain, March 10, 1992.

LOMAKIN, ANDREI

Right wing. Shoots left. 5'10", 176 lbs. Born, Voskresensk, Soviet Union, April 3, 1964.
(Philadelphia's 7th choice, 138th overall, in 1991 Entry Draft).

			Regular Season					Playoffs				
Season	Club	Lea	GP	G	A	TP	PIM	GP	G	A	TP	PIM
1981-82	Khimik	USSR	8	1	1	2	2	....	....	....	....	....
1982-83	Khimik	USSR	56	15	8	23	32	....	....	....	....	....
1983-84	Khimik	USSR	44	10	8	18	26	....	....	....	....	....
1984-85	Khimik	USSR	52	13	10	23	34	....	....	....	....	....
1985-86						DID NOT PLAY						
1986-87	Moscow D'amo	USSR	40	15	14	29	30	....	....	....	....	....
1987-88	Moscow D'amo	USSR	45	10	15	25	24	....	....	....	....	....
1988-89	Moscow D'amo	USSR	44	9	16	25	22	....	....	....	....	....
1989-90	Moscow D'amo	USSR	48	11	15	26	36	....	....	....	....	....
1990-91	Moscow D'amo	USSR	45	16	17	33	22	....	....	....	....	....
1991-92	Moscow D'amo	CIS	2	1	3	4	2	....	....	....	....	....
	Philadelphia	**NHL**	**57**	**14**	**16**	**30**	**26**	....	....	....	....	....
	NHL Totals		**57**	**14**	**16**	**30**	**26**	....	....	....	....	....

LOMBARDI, STEPHEN

Left wing. Shoots left. 6'1", 180 lbs. Born, South Easton, MA, April 14, 1973.
(Boston's 10th choice, 238th overall, in 1991 Entry Draft).

			Regular Season					Playoffs				
Season	Club	Lea	GP	G	A	TP	PIM	GP	G	A	TP	PIM
1990-91	Deerfield	HS	20	15	15	30	0	....	....	....	....	....
1991-92	Yale	ECAC	14	2	3	5	2	....	....	....	....	....

LONEY, BRIAN

Right wing. Shoots right. 6'1", 195 lbs. Born, Winnipeg, Man., August 9, 1972.
(Vancouver's 6th choice, 110th overall, in 1992 Entry Draft).

			Regular Season					Playoffs				
Season	Club	Lea	GP	G	A	TP	PIM	GP	G	A	TP	PIM
1990-91	Notre Dame	SJHL	....	33	45	78	....	....	....	....	....	....
1991-92	Ohio State	CCHA	37	21	34	55	109	....	....	....	....	....

LONEY, TROY

Left wing. Shoots left. 6'3", 209 lbs. Born, Bow Island, Alta., September 21, 1963.
(Pittsburgh's 3rd choice, 52nd overall, in 1982 Entry Draft).

			Regular Season					Playoffs				
Season	Club	Lea	GP	G	A	TP	PIM	GP	G	A	TP	PIM
1980-81	Lethbridge	WHL	71	18	13	31	100	9	2	2	5	14
1981-82	Lethbridge	WHL	71	26	33	59	152	12	3	3	6	10
1982-83	Lethbridge	WHL	72	33	34	67	156	20	10	7	17	43
1983-84	**Pittsburgh**	**NHL**	**13**	**0**	**0**	**0**	**9**	....	....	....	....	....
	Baltimore	AHL	63	18	13	31	147	10	0	2	2	19
1984-85	**Pittsburgh**	**NHL**	**46**	**10**	**8**	**18**	**59**	....	....	....	....	....
	Baltimore	AHL	15	4	2	6	25	....	....	....	....	....
1985-86	**Pittsburgh**	**NHL**	**47**	**3**	**9**	**12**	**95**	....	....	....	....	....
	Baltimore	AHL	33	12	11	23	84	....	....	....	....	....
1986-87	**Pittsburgh**	**NHL**	**23**	**8**	**7**	**15**	**22**	....	....	....	....	....
	Baltimore	AHL	40	13	14	27	134	....	....	....	....	....
1987-88	**Pittsburgh**	**NHL**	**65**	**5**	**13**	**18**	**151**	....	....	....	....	....
1988-89	**Pittsburgh**	**NHL**	**69**	**10**	**6**	**16**	**165**	**11**	**1**	**3**	**4**	**24**
1989-90	**Pittsburgh**	**NHL**	**67**	**11**	**16**	**27**	**168**	....	....	....	....	....
1990-91	**Pittsburgh**	**NHL**	**44**	**7**	**9**	**16**	**85**	**24**	**2**	**2**	**4**	**41**
	Muskegon	IHL	2	0	0	0	5	....	....	....	....	....
1991-92	**Pittsburgh**	**NHL**	**76**	**10**	**16**	**26**	**127**	**21**	**4**	**5**	**9**	**32**
	NHL Totals		**450**	**64**	**84**	**148**	**881**	**56**	**7**	**10**	**17**	**97**

LONGO, CHRIS

Right wing. Shoots right. 5'10", 180 lbs. Born, Belleville, Ont., January 5, 1972.
(Washington's 3rd choice, 51st overall, in 1990 Entry Draft).

			Regular Season					Playoffs				
Season	Club	Lea	GP	G	A	TP	PIM	GP	G	A	TP	PIM
1989-90a	Peterborough	OHL	66	33	41	74	48	11	2	3	5	14
1990-91	Peterborough	OHL	64	30	38	68	68	4	1	0	1	0
1991-92	Peterborough	OHL	25	5	14	19	16	10	5	6	11	16

a OHL Rookie of the Year (1990)

LOSINGER, BRYAN

Defense. Shoots right. 6'2", 210 lbs. Born, Caldwell, NY, July 21, 1972.
(NY Rangers' 9th choice, 139th overall, in 1990 Entry Draft).

			Regular Season					Playoffs				
Season	Club	Lea	GP	G	A	TP	PIM	GP	G	A	TP	PIM
1991-92	Harvard	ECAC	19	1	5	6	4	....	....	....	....	....

LOVSIN, KEN

Defense. Shoots right. 6', 195 lbs. Born, Peace River, Alta., December 3, 1966.
(Hartford's 1st choice, 22nd overall, in 1987 Supplemental Draft).

			Regular Season					Playoffs				
Season	Club	Lea	GP	G	A	TP	PIM	GP	G	A	TP	PIM
1986-87	Saskatchewan	CWUAA	28	3	13	16	14	....	....	....	....	....
1987-88	Saskatchewan	CWUAA	28	14	24	38	20	....	....	....	....	....
1988-89	Cdn. National	....	59	0	10	10	59	....	....	....	....	....
1989-90	Cdn. National	....	66	7	15	22	80	....	....	....	....	....
1990-91	**Washington**	**NHL**	**1**	**0**	**0**	**0**	**0**	....	....	....	....	....
	Baltimore	AHL	79	8	28	36	54	6	1	1	2	2
1991-92	Baltimore	AHL	77	11	24	35	60	....	....	....	....	....
	NHL Totals		**1**	**0**	**0**	**0**	**0**	....	....	....	....	....

Signed as a free agent by **Washington**, July 3, 1990.

LOWE, KEVIN HUGH (LOH)

Defense. Shoots left. 6'2", 195 lbs. Born, Lachute, Que., April 15, 1959.
(Edmonton's 1st choice, 21st overall, in 1979 Entry Draft).

			Regular Season					Playoffs				
Season	Club	Lea	GP	G	A	TP	PIM	GP	G	A	TP	PIM
1977-78	Quebec	QJHL	64	13	52	65	86	4	1	2	3	6
1978-79a	Quebec	QJHL	68	26	60	86	120	6	1	7	8	36
1979-80	**Edmonton**	**NHL**	**64**	**2**	**19**	**21**	**70**	**3**	**0**	**1**	**1**	**0**
1980-81	**Edmonton**	**NHL**	**79**	**10**	**24**	**34**	**94**	**9**	**0**	**2**	**2**	**11**
1981-82	**Edmonton**	**NHL**	**80**	**9**	**31**	**40**	**63**	**5**	**0**	**3**	**3**	**0**
1982-83	**Edmonton**	**NHL**	**80**	**6**	**34**	**40**	**43**	**16**	**1**	**8**	**9**	**10**
1983-84	**Edmonton**	**NHL**	**80**	**4**	**42**	**46**	**59**	**19**	**3**	**7**	**10**	**16**
1984-85	**Edmonton**	**NHL**	**80**	**4**	**21**	**25**	**104**	**16**	**0**	**5**	**5**	**8**
1985-86	**Edmonton**	**NHL**	**74**	**2**	**16**	**18**	**90**	**10**	**1**	**3**	**4**	**15**
1986-87	**Edmonton**	**NHL**	**77**	**8**	**29**	**37**	**94**	**21**	**2**	**4**	**6**	**22**
1987-88	**Edmonton**	**NHL**	**70**	**9**	**15**	**24**	**89**	**19**	**0**	**2**	**2**	**26**
1988-89	**Edmonton**	**NHL**	**76**	**7**	**18**	**25**	**98**	**7**	**1**	**2**	**3**	**4**
1989-90bc	**Edmonton**	**NHL**	**78**	**7**	**26**	**33**	**140**	**20**	**0**	**2**	**2**	**10**
1990-91	**Edmonton**	**NHL**	**73**	**3**	**13**	**16**	**113**	**14**	**1**	**1**	**2**	**14**
1991-92	**Edmonton**	**NHL**	**55**	**2**	**8**	**10**	**107**	**11**	**0**	**3**	**3**	**16**
	NHL Totals		**966**	**73**	**296**	**369**	**1164**	**170**	**9**	**43**	**52**	**152**

a QMJHL Second All-Star Team (1979)
b Won Bud Man of the Year Award (1990)
c Won King Clancy Memorial Trophy (1990)

Played in NHL All-Star Game (1984-86, 1988-90)

LOWRY, DAVE

Left wing. Shoots left. 6'1", 195 lbs. Born, Sudbury, Ont., February 14, 1965.
(Vancouver's 6th choice, 110th overall, in 1983 Entry Draft).

			Regular Season					Playoffs				
Season	Club	Lea	GP	G	A	TP	PIM	GP	G	A	TP	PIM
1982-83	London	OHL	42	11	16	27	48	3	0	0	0	14
1983-84	London	OHL	66	29	47	76	125	8	6	6	12	41
1984-85a	London	OHL	61	60	60	120	94	8	6	5	11	10
1985-86	**Vancouver**	**NHL**	**73**	**10**	**8**	**18**	**143**	**3**	**0**	**0**	**0**	**0**
1986-87	**Vancouver**	**NHL**	**70**	**8**	**10**	**18**	**176**	....	....	....	....	....
1987-88	**Vancouver**	**NHL**	**22**	**1**	**3**	**4**	**38**	....	....	....	....	....
	Fredericton	AHL	46	18	27	45	59	14	7	3	10	72
1988-89	**St. Louis**	**NHL**	**21**	**3**	**3**	**6**	**11**	**10**	**0**	**5**	**5**	**4**
	Peoria	IHL	58	31	35	66	45	....	....	....	....	....
1989-90	**St. Louis**	**NHL**	**78**	**19**	**6**	**25**	**75**	**12**	**2**	**1**	**3**	**39**
1990-91	**St. Louis**	**NHL**	**79**	**19**	**21**	**40**	**168**	**13**	**1**	**4**	**5**	**35**
1991-92	**St. Louis**	**NHL**	**75**	**7**	**13**	**20**	**77**	**6**	**0**	**1**	**1**	**20**
	NHL Totals		**418**	**67**	**64**	**131**	**688**	**44**	**3**	**11**	**14**	**98**

a OHL First All-Star Team (1985)

Traded to **St. Louis** by **Vancouver** for Ernie Vargas, September 29, 1988.

LUDWIG, CRAIG LEE

Defense. Shoots left. 6'3", 222 lbs. Born, Rhinelander, WI, March 15, 1961.
(Montreal's 5th choice, 61st overall, in 1980 Entry Draft).

			Regular Season					Playoffs				
Season	Club	Lea	GP	G	A	TP	PIM	GP	G	A	TP	PIM
1979-80	North Dakota	WCHA	33	1	8	9	32	....	....	....	....	....
1980-81	North Dakota	WCHA	34	4	8	12	48	....	....	....	....	....
1981-82	North Dakota	WCHA	37	4	17	21	42	....	....	....	....	....
1982-83	**Montreal**	**NHL**	**80**	**0**	**25**	**25**	**59**	**3**	**0**	**0**	**0**	**2**
1983-84	**Montreal**	**NHL**	**80**	**7**	**18**	**25**	**52**	**15**	**0**	**3**	**3**	**23**
1984-85	**Montreal**	**NHL**	**72**	**5**	**14**	**19**	**90**	**12**	**0**	**2**	**2**	**6**
1985-86	**Montreal**	**NHL**	**69**	**2**	**4**	**6**	**63**	**20**	**0**	**1**	**1**	**48**
1986-87	**Montreal**	**NHL**	**75**	**4**	**12**	**16**	**105**	**17**	**2**	**3**	**5**	**30**
1987-88	**Montreal**	**NHL**	**74**	**4**	**10**	**14**	**69**	**11**	**1**	**1**	**2**	**6**
1988-89	**Montreal**	**NHL**	**74**	**3**	**13**	**16**	**73**	**21**	**0**	**2**	**2**	**24**
1989-90	**Montreal**	**NHL**	**73**	**1**	**15**	**16**	**108**	**11**	**0**	**1**	**1**	**16**
1990-91	**NY Islanders**	**NHL**	**75**	**1**	**8**	**9**	**77**	....	....	....	....	....
1991-92	**Minnesota**	**NHL**	**73**	**2**	**9**	**11**	**54**	**7**	**0**	**1**	**1**	**19**
	NHL Totals		**745**	**29**	**128**	**157**	**750**	**117**	**3**	**14**	**17**	**174**

Traded to **NY Islanders** by **Montreal** for Gerald Diduck, September 4, 1990. Traded to **Minnesota** by **NY Islanders** for Tom Kurvers, June 22, 1991.

LUDZIK, STEVE

Center. Shoots left. 5'11", 185 lbs. Born, Toronto, Ont., April 3, 1962.
(Chicago's 3rd choice, 28th overall, in 1980 Entry Draft).

			Regular Season					Playoffs				
Season	Club	Lea	GP	G	A	TP	PIM	GP	G	A	TP	PIM
1979-80	Niagara Falls	OHA	67	43	76	119	102	10	6	6	12	16
1980-81	Niagara Falls	OHA	58	50	92	142	108	12	5	9	14	40
1981-82	**Chicago**	**NHL**	**8**	**2**	**1**	**3**	**2**	....	....	....	....	....
	New Brunswick	AHL	73	21	41	62	142	15	3	7	10	6
1982-83	**Chicago**	**NHL**	**66**	**6**	**19**	**25**	**63**	**13**	**3**	**5**	**8**	**20**
1983-84	**Chicago**	**NHL**	**80**	**9**	**20**	**29**	**73**	**4**	**0**	**1**	**1**	**9**
1984-85	**Chicago**	**NHL**	**79**	**11**	**20**	**31**	**86**	**15**	**1**	**1**	**2**	**16**
1985-86	**Chicago**	**NHL**	**49**	**6**	**5**	**11**	**21**	**3**	**0**	**0**	**0**	**12**
1986-87	**Chicago**	**NHL**	**52**	**5**	**12**	**17**	**34**	**4**	**0**	**0**	**0**	**0**
1987-88	**Chicago**	**NHL**	**73**	**6**	**15**	**21**	**40**	**5**	**0**	**1**	**1**	**13**
1988-89	**Chicago**	**NHL**	**6**	**1**	**0**	**1**	**8**	....	....	....	....	....
	Saginaw	IHL	65	21	57	78	129	6	0	1	1	17
1989-90	**Buffalo**	**NHL**	**11**	**0**	**1**	**1**	**6**	....	....	....	....	....
	Rochester	AHL	54	25	29	54	71	16	5	6	11	57
1990-91	Rochester	AHL	65	22	29	51	137	8	3	5	8	6
1991-92	Rochester	AHL	45	6	22	28	88	14	2	1	3	8
	NHL Totals		**424**	**46**	**93**	**139**	**333**	**44**	**4**	**8**	**12**	**70**

Traded to **Buffalo** by **Chicago** with sixth round choice (Derek Edgerly) to complete earlier deal for Jacques Cloutier, September 28, 1989.

LUIK, SCOTT

Right wing. Shoots left. 6'1", 210 lbs. Born, Scarborough, Ont., January 15, 1970.
(New Jersey's 5th choice, 75th overall, in 1988 Entry Draft).

			Regular Season					Playoffs				
Season	Club	Lea	GP	G	A	TP	PIM	GP	G	A	TP	PIM
1987-88	Miami-Ohio	CCHA	34	4	10	14	47	....	....	....	....	....
1988-89	Miami-Ohio	CCHA	36	13	13	26	92	....	....	....	....	....
1989-90	Miami-Ohio	CCHA	16	4	7	11	32	....	....	....	....	....
	Oshawa	OHL	34	15	14	29	20	17	4	5	9	20
1990-91	Oshawa	OHL	56	26	51	77	74	16	6	11	17	25
1991-92	Cincinnati	ECHL	21	2	10	12	26	....	....	....	....	....
	Dayton	ECHL	13	5	7	12	14	3	0	1	1	4

LUMME, JYRKI (LOOM-meh)

Defense. Shoots left. 6'1", 205 lbs. Born, Tampere, Finland, July 16, 1966.
(Montreal's 3rd choice, 57th overall, in 1986 Entry Draft).

			Regular Season					Playoffs				
Season	Club	Lea	GP	G	A	TP	PIM	GP	G	A	TP	PIM
1984-85	KooVee	Fin.3	30	6	4	10	44	....	....	....	....	....
1985-86	Ilves	Fin.	31	1	4	5	4	....	....	....	....	....
1986-87	Ilves	Fin.	43	12	12	24	52	4	0	1	2	....
1987-88	Ilves	Fin.	43	8	22	30	75	....	....	....	....	....
1988-89	**Montreal**	**NHL**	**21**	**1**	**3**	**4**	**10**	....	....	....	....	....
	Sherbrooke	AHL	26	4	11	15	10	6	1	3	4	4
1989-90	**Montreal**	**NHL**	**54**	**1**	**19**	**20**	**41**	....	....	....	....	....
	Vancouver	**NHL**	**11**	**3**	**7**	**10**	**8**	....	....	....	....	....
1990-91	**Vancouver**	**NHL**	**80**	**5**	**27**	**32**	**59**	**6**	**2**	**3**	**5**	**0**
1991-92	**Vancouver**	**NHL**	**75**	**12**	**32**	**44**	**65**	**13**	**2**	**3**	**5**	**4**
	NHL Totals		**241**	**22**	**88**	**110**	**183**	**19**	**4**	**6**	**10**	**4**

Traded to **Vancouver** by **Montreal** for St. Louis' second round choice (Craig Darby) in 1991 Entry Draft (previously acquired by Vancouver), March 6, 1990.

LUND, WILLIAM

Center. Shoots left. 5'9", 165 lbs. Born, Roseau, MN, December 16, 1971.
(Philadelphia's 15th choice, 235th overall, in 1990 Entry Draft).

			Regular Season					Playoffs				
Season	Club	Lea	GP	G	A	TP	PIM	GP	G	A	TP	PIM
1989-90	Roseau	HS	28	36	50	86	....	....	....	....	....	....
1990-91	Minn.-Duluth	WCHA	20	0	2	2	8	....	....	....	....	....
1991-92	St. Paul	USHL	48	27	42	69	40	....	....	....	....	....

LUONGO, CHRISTOPHER (CHRIS) (loo-ON-go)

Defense. Shoots right. 6', 180 lbs. Born, Detroit, MI, March 17, 1967.
(Detroit's 5th choice, 92nd overall, in 1985 Entry Draft).

			Regular Season					Playoffs				
Season	Club	Lea	GP	G	A	TP	PIM	GP	G	A	TP	PIM
1985-86	Michigan State	CCHA	38	1	5	6	29	....	....	....	....	....
1986-87a	Michigan State	CCHA	27	4	16	20	38	....	....	....	....	....
1987-88	Michigan State	CCHA	45	3	15	18	49	....	....	....	....	....
1988-89b	Michigan State	CCHA	47	4	21	25	42	....	....	....	....	....
1989-90	Adirondack	AHL	53	9	14	23	37	3	0	0	0	0
	Phoenix	IHL	23	5	9	14	41	....	....	....	....	....
1990-91	**Detroit**	**NHL**	**4**	**0**	**1**	**1**	**4**	....	....	....	....	....
	Adirondack	AHL	76	14	25	39	71	2	0	0	0	7
1991-92	Adirondack	AHL	80	6	20	26	60	19	3	5	8	10
	NHL Totals		**4**	**0**	**1**	**1**	**4**	....	....	....	....	....

a Named to NCAA All-Tournament Team (1987)
b CCHA Second All-Star Team (1989)

LYONS, COREY

Right wing. Shoots left. 5'10", 186 lbs. Born, Calgary, Alta., June 13, 1970.
(Calgary's 4th choice, 63rd overall, in 1989 Entry Draft).

			Regular Season					Playoffs				
Season	Club	Lea	GP	G	A	TP	PIM	GP	G	A	TP	PIM
1987-88	Lethbridge	WHL	2	0	0	0	0	....	....	....	....	....
1988-89	Lethbridge	WHL	71	53	59	112	36	8	4	9	13	7
1989-90	Lethbridge	WHL	72	63	79	142	26	19	11	15	26	4
	Salt Lake	IHL	....	....	....	....	....	1	0	0	0	0
1990-91	Salt Lake	IHL	51	15	12	27	22	3	0	2	2	0
1991-92	Salt Lake	IHL	26	3	3	6	4	....	....	....	....	....
	Roanoke Valley	ECHL	22	10	13	23	13	7	4	3	7	4

MacARTHUR, KENNETH

Defense. Shoots left. 6'2", 185 lbs. Born, Rossland, B.C., March 15, 1968.
(Minnesota's 5th choice, 148th overall, in 1988 Entry Draft).

			Regular Season					Playoffs				
Season	Club	Lea	GP	G	A	TP	PIM	GP	G	A	TP	PIM
1987-88	U. of Denver	WCHA	38	6	16	22	69	....	....	....	....	....
1988-89	U. of Denver	WCHA	42	11	19	30	77	....	....	....	....	....
1989-90	U. of Denver	WCHA	38	12	29	41	96	....	....	....	....	....
	Cdn. National	....	13	2	1	3	14	....	....	....	....	....
1990-91	Cdn. National	....	59	4	11	15	34	....	....	....	....	....
1991-92	U. of Denver	WCHA	3	2	1	3	20	....	....	....	....	....

MacDERMID, PAUL

Right wing. Shoots right. 6'1", 205 lbs. Born, Chesley, Ont., April 14, 1963.
(Hartford's 2nd choice, 61st overall, in 1981 Entry Draft).

			Regular Season					Playoffs				
Season	Club	Lea	GP	G	A	TP	PIM	GP	G	A	TP	PIM
1980-81	Windsor	OHA	68	15	17	32	106	....	....	....	....	....
1981-82	Hartford	NHL	3	1	0	1	2	....	....	....	....	....
	Windsor	OHL	65	26	45	71	179	9	6	4	10	17
1982-83	Hartford	NHL	7	0	0	0	2	....	....	....	....	....
	Windsor	OHL	42	35	45	80	9	....	....	....	....	....
1983-84	Hartford	NHL	3	0	1	1	0	....	....	....	....	....
	Binghamton	AHL	70	31	30	61	130	....	....	....	....	....
1984-85	Hartford	NHL	31	4	7	11	29	....	....	....	....	....
	Binghamton	AHL	48	9	31	40	87	....	....	....	....	....
1985-86	Hartford	NHL	74	13	10	23	160	10	2	1	3	20
1986-87	Hartford	NHL	72	7	11	18	202	6	2	1	3	34
1987-88	Hartford	NHL	80	20	15	35	139	6	0	5	5	14
1988-89	Hartford	NHL	74	17	27	44	141	4	1	1	2	16
1989-90	Hartford	NHL	29	6	12	18	69	....	....	....	....	....
	Winnipeg	NHL	44	7	10	17	100	7	0	2	2	8
1990-91	Winnipeg	NHL	69	15	21	36	128	....	....	....	....	....
1991-92	Winnipeg	NHL	59	10	11	21	151	....	....	....	....	....
	Washington	NHL	15	2	5	7	43	7	0	1	1	22
	NHL Totals		560	102	130	232	1166	40	5	11	16	114

Traded to **Winnipeg** by **Hartford** for Randy Cunneyworth, December 13, 1989. Traded to **Washington** by **Winnipeg** for Mike Lalor, March 2, 1992.

MacDONALD, BRUCE

Defense. Shoots left. 6'1", 195 lbs. Born, Plaistow, NH, December 16, 1967.
(Philadelphia's 9th choice, 188th overall, in 1987 Entry Draft).

			Regular Season					Playoffs				
Season	Club	Lea	GP	G	A	TP	PIM	GP	G	A	TP	PIM
1987-88	N. Hampshire	H.E.	12	0	1	1	8	....	....	....	....	....
1988-89	N. Hampshire	H.E.	21	1	3	4	8	....	....	....	....	....
1989-90	N. Hampshire	H.E.	35	2	3	5	16	....	....	....	....	....
1990-91	N. Hampshire	H.E.	25	2	4	6	14	....	....	....	....	....
	Moncton	AHL	2	0	0	0	0	7	1	3	4	4
1991-92	Toledo	ECHL	42	29	26	55	32	5	0	4	4	22

MacDONALD, DOUG

Left wing. Shoots left. 6', 192 lbs. Born, Port Moody, B.C., February 8, 1969.
(Buffalo's 3rd choice, 77th overall, in 1989 Entry Draft).

			Regular Season					Playoffs				
Season	Club	Lea	GP	G	A	TP	PIM	GP	G	A	TP	PIM
1988-89	U. Wisconsin	WCHA	44	23	25	48	50	....	....	....	....	....
1989-90	U. Wisconsin	WCHA	44	16	35	51	52	....	....	....	....	....
1990-91	U. Wisconsin	WCHA	31	20	26	46	50	....	....	....	....	....
1991-92	U. Wisconsin	WCHA	29	14	25	39	58	....	....	....	....	....

MacDONALD, GARRETT

Defense. Shoots left. 6', 183 lbs. Born, Burnaby, B.C., January 12, 1971.
(Philadelphia's 1st choice, 7th overall, in 1992 Supplemental Draft).

			Regular Season					Playoffs				
Season	Club	Lea	GP	G	A	TP	PIM	GP	G	A	TP	PIM
1990-91	N. Michigan	WCHA	41	2	8	10	56	....	....	....	....	....
1991-92	N. Michigan	WCHA	34	0	5	5	39	....	....	....	....	....

MacDONALD, JASON

Right wing. Shoots right. 6', 195 lbs. Born, Charlottetown, P.E.I., April 1, 1974.
(Detroit's 5th choice, 142nd overall, in 1992 Entry Draft).

			Regular Season					Playoffs				
Season	Club	Lea	GP	G	A	TP	PIM	GP	G	A	TP	PIM
1990-91	North Bay	OHL	57	12	15	27	126	10	3	3	6	15
1991-92	North Bay	OHL	17	5	8	13	50	....	....	....	....	....
	Owen Sound	OHL	42	17	19	36	129	5	0	3	3	16

MacDONALD, SCOTT

Defense. Shoots right. 6'3", 202 lbs. Born, Brockton, MA, September 13, 1972.
(Chicago's 9th choice, 198th overall, in 1991 Entry Draft).

			Regular Season					Playoffs				
Season	Club	Lea	GP	G	A	TP	PIM	GP	G	A	TP	PIM
1990-91	Choate	HS	16	6	13	19	12	....	....	....	....	....
1991-92	U. of Vermont	ECAC	28	0	6	6	18	....	....	....	....	....

MACHANIC, COREY

Defense. Shoots right. 6'3", 197 lbs. Born, Rome, NY, September 26, 1972.
(NY Rangers' 5th choice, 96th overall, in 1991 Entry Draft).

			Regular Season					Playoffs				
Season	Club	Lea	GP	G	A	TP	PIM	GP	G	A	TP	PIM
1990-91	U. of Vermont	ECAC	31	0	8	8	30	....	....	....	....	....
1991-92	U. of Vermont	ECAC	30	3	8	11	24	....	....	....	....	....

MacINNIS, ALLAN (AL)

Defense. Shoots right. 6'2", 196 lbs. Born, Inverness, N.S., July 11, 1963.
(Calgary's 1st choice, 15th overall, in 1981 Entry Draft).

			Regular Season					Playoffs				
Season	Club	Lea	GP	G	A	TP	PIM	GP	G	A	TP	PIM
1980-81	Kitchener	OHA	47	11	28	39	59	18	4	12	16	20
1981-82	Calgary	NHL	2	0	0	0	0	....	....	....	....	....
a	Kitchener	OHL	59	25	50	75	145	15	5	10	15	44
1982-83	Calgary	NHL	14	1	3	4	9	....	....	....	....	....
a	Kitchener	OHL	51	38	46	84	67	8	3	8	11	9
1983-84	Calgary	NHL	51	11	34	45	42	11	2	12	14	13
	Colorado	CHL	19	5	14	19	22	....	....	....	....	....
1984-85	Calgary	NHL	67	14	52	66	75	4	1	2	3	8
1985-86	Calgary	NHL	77	11	57	68	76	21	4	*15	19	30
1986-87b	Calgary	NHL	79	20	56	76	97	4	1	0	1	0
1987-88	Calgary	NHL	80	25	58	83	114	7	3	6	9	18
1988-89bc	Calgary	NHL	79	16	58	74	126	22	7	*24	*31	46
1989-90d	Calgary	NHL	79	28	62	90	82	6	2	3	5	8
1990-91d	Calgary	NHL	78	28	75	103	90	7	2	3	5	8
1991-92	Calgary	NHL	72	20	57	77	83	....	....	....	....	....
	NHL Totals		678	174	512	686	794	82	22	65	87	131

a OHL First All-Star Team (1982, 1983)
b NHL Second All-Star Team (1987, 1989)
c Won Conn Smythe Trophy (1989)
d NHL First All-Star Team (1990, 1991)

Played in NHL All-Star Game (1985, 1988, 1990, 1991, 1992)

MacINTYRE, ANDY

Left wing. Shoots left. 6'1", 190 lbs. Born, Thunder Bay, Ont., April 16, 1974.
(Chicago's 4th choice, 89th overall, in 1992 Entry Draft).

			Regular Season					Playoffs				
Season	Club	Lea	GP	G	A	TP	PIM	GP	G	A	TP	PIM
1990-91	Seattle	WHL	71	16	13	29	52	4	0	0	0	2
1991-92	Seattle	WHL	12	6	2	8	18	....	....	....	....	....
	Saskatoon	WHL	55	22	13	35	66	....	....	....	....	....

MACIVER, NORM (mac-IGH-ver)

Defense. Shoots left. 5'11", 180 lbs. Born, Thunder Bay, Ont., September 8, 1964.

			Regular Season					Playoffs				
Season	Club	Lea	GP	G	A	TP	PIM	GP	G	A	TP	PIM
1982-83	Minn.-Duluth	WCHA	45	1	26	27	40	6	0	2	2	2
1983-84a	Minn.-Duluth	WCHA	31	13	28	41	28	8	1	10	11	8
1984-85bc	Minn.-Duluth	WCHA	47	14	47	61	63	10	3	3	6	6
1985-86bc	Minn.-Duluth	WCHA	42	11	51	62	36	4	2	3	5	2
1986-87	NY Rangers	NHL	3	0	1	1	0	....	....	....	....	....
	New Haven	AHL	71	6	30	36	73	7	0	0	0	9
1987-88	NY Rangers	NHL	37	9	15	24	14	....	....	....	....	....
	Colorado	IHL	27	6	20	26	22	....	....	....	....	....
1988-89	NY Rangers	NHL	26	0	10	10	14	....	....	....	....	....
	Hartford	NHL	37	1	22	23	24	1	0	0	0	2
1989-90	Binghamton	AHL	2	0	0	0	0	....	....	....	....	....
	Edmonton	NHL	1	0	0	0	0	....	....	....	....	....
	Cape Breton	AHL	68	13	37	50	55	6	0	7	7	10
1990-91	Edmonton	NHL	21	2	5	7	14	18	0	4	4	8
de	Cape Breton	AHL	56	13	46	59	60	....	....	....	....	....
1991-92	Edmonton	NHL	57	6	34	40	38	13	1	2	3	10
	NHL Totals		182	18	87	105	104	32	1	6	7	20

a WCHA Second All-Star Team (1984)
b WCHA First All-Star Team (1985, 1986)
c NCAA West First All-Star Team (1985, 1986)
d AHL First All-Star Team (1991)
e Won Eddie Shore Plaque (Top Defenseman – AHL) (1991)

Signed as a free agent by **NY Rangers**, September 8, 1986. Traded to **Hartford** by **NY Rangers** with Brian Lawton and Don Maloney for Carey Wilson and Hartford's fifth round choice (Lubos Rob) in 1990 Entry Draft, December 26, 1988. Traded to **Edmonton** by **Hartford** for Jim Ennis, October 10, 1989.

MacKENZIE, CHRIS

Left wing. Shoots left. 6', 195 lbs. Born, Toronto, Ont., September 16, 1971.
(St. Louis' 10th choice, 219th overall, in 1991 Entry Draft).

			Regular Season					Playoffs				
Season	Club	Lea	GP	G	A	TP	PIM	GP	G	A	TP	PIM
1990-91	Colgate	ECAC	22	1	7	8	8	....	....	....	....	....
1991-92	Colgate	ECAC	30	9	13	22	16	....	....	....	....	....

MACKEY, DAVID

Left wing. Shoots left. 6'4", 200 lbs. Born, Richmond, B.C., July 24, 1966.
(Chicago's 12th choice, 224th overall, in 1984 Entry Draft).

			Regular Season					Playoffs				
Season	Club	Lea	GP	G	A	TP	PIM	GP	G	A	TP	PIM
1982-83	Victoria	WHL	69	16	16	32	53	12	11	1	2	4
1983-84	Victoria	WHL	69	15	15	30	97	....	....	....	....	....
1984-85	Victoria	WHL	16	5	6	11	45	....	....	....	....	....
	Portland	WHL	56	28	32	60	122	6	2	1	3	13
1985-86	Kamloops	WHL	9	3	4	7	13	....	....	....	....	....
	Medicine Hat	WHL	60	25	32	57	167	25	6	3	9	72
1986-87	Saginaw	IHL	81	26	49	75	173	10	5	6	11	22
1987-88	Chicago	NHL	23	1	3	4	71	....	....	....	....	....
	Saginaw	IHL	62	29	22	51	211	10	3	7	10	44
1988-89	Chicago	NHL	23	1	2	3	78	....	....	....	....	....
	Saginaw	IHL	57	22	23	45	223	....	....	....	....	....
1989-90	Minnesota	NHL	16	2	0	2	28	....	....	....	....	....
1990-91	Milwaukee	IHL	82	28	30	58	226	6	7	2	9	6
1991-92	St. Louis	NHL	19	1	0	1	49	1	0	0	0	0
	Peoria	IHL	35	20	17	37	90	....	....	....	....	....
	NHL Totals		81	5	5	10	226	1	0	0	0	0

Claimed by **Minnesota** in NHL Waiver Draft, October 2, 1989. Traded to **Vancouver** by **Minnesota** for future considerations, September 7, 1990. Signed as a free agent by **St. Louis**, August 7, 1991.

MACKEY, JAMES

Defense. Shoots right. 6'4", 225 lbs. Born, Saratoga Springs, NY, January 20, 1972.
(Boston's 6th choice, 147th overall, in 1990 Entry Draft).

			Regular Season					Playoffs				
Season	Club	Lea	GP	G	A	TP	PIM	GP	G	A	TP	PIM
1990-91	Yale	ECAC	18	0	1	1	12	....	....	....	....	....
1991-92	Yale	ECAC	27	1	7	8	44	....	....	....	....	....

MacLEAN, JOHN

Right wing. Shoots right. 6', 200 lbs. Born, Oshawa, Ont., November 20, 1964.
(New Jersey's 1st choice, 6th overall, in 1983 Entry Draft).

			Regular Season					Playoffs				
Season	Club	Lea	GP	G	A	TP	PIM	GP	G	A	TP	PIM
1981-82	Oshawa	OHL	67	17	22	39	197	12	3	6	9	63
1982-83	Oshawa	OHL	66	47	51	98	138	17	*18	20	*38	35
1983-84	**New Jersey**	**NHL**	**23**	**1**	**0**	**1**	**10**	....	....	....	....	....
	Oshawa	OHL	30	23	36	59	58	7	2	5	7	18
1984-85	**New Jersey**	**NHL**	**61**	**13**	**20**	**33**	**44**	....	....	....	....	....
1985-86	**New Jersey**	**NHL**	**74**	**21**	**36**	**57**	**112**	....	....	....	....	....
1986-87	**New Jersey**	**NHL**	**80**	**31**	**36**	**67**	**120**	....	....	....	....	....
1987-88	**New Jersey**	**NHL**	**76**	**23**	**16**	**39**	**147**	**20**	**7**	**11**	**18**	**60**
1988-89	**New Jersey**	**NHL**	**74**	**42**	**45**	**87**	**122**	....	....	....	....	....
1989-90	**New Jersey**	**NHL**	**80**	**41**	**38**	**79**	**80**	**6**	**4**	**1**	**5**	**12**
1990-91	**New Jersey**	**NHL**	**78**	**45**	**33**	**78**	**150**	**7**	**5**	**3**	**8**	**20**
1991-92			DID NOT PLAY — INJURED									
	NHL Totals		**546**	**217**	**224**	**441**	**785**	**33**	**16**	**15**	**31**	**92**

Played in NHL All-Star Game (1989, 1991)

MacLELLAN, BRIAN

Left wing. Shoots left. 6'3", 220 lbs. Born, Guelph, Ont., October 27, 1958.

			Regular Season					Playoffs				
Season	Club	Lea	GP	G	A	TP	PIM	GP	G	A	TP	PIM
1978-79	Bowling Green	CCHA	44	34	29	63	94	....	....	....	....	....
1979-80	Bowling Green	CCHA	38	8	15	23	46	....	....	....	....	....
1980-81	Bowling Green	CCHA	37	11	14	25	96	....	....	....	....	....
1981-82	Bowling Green	CCHA	41	11	21	32	109	....	....	....	....	....
1982-83	**Los Angeles**	**NHL**	**8**	**0**	**3**	**3**	**7**	....	....	....	....	....
	New Haven	AHL	71	11	15	26	40	12	5	3	8	4
1983-84	**Los Angeles**	**NHL**	**72**	**25**	**29**	**54**	**45**	....	....	....	....	....
	New Haven	AHL	2	0	2	2	0	....	....	....	....	....
1984-85	**Los Angeles**	**NHL**	**80**	**31**	**54**	**85**	**53**	**3**	**0**	**1**	**1**	**0**
1985-86	**Los Angeles**	**NHL**	**27**	**5**	**8**	**13**	**19**	....	....	....	....	....
	NY Rangers	**NHL**	**51**	**11**	**21**	**32**	**47**	**16**	**2**	**4**	**6**	**15**
1986-87	**Minnesota**	**NHL**	**76**	**32**	**31**	**63**	**69**	....	....	....	....	....
1987-88	**Minnesota**	**NHL**	**75**	**16**	**32**	**48**	**74**	....	....	....	....	....
1988-89	**Minnesota**	**NHL**	**60**	**16**	**23**	**39**	**104**	....	....	....	....	....
	Calgary	**NHL**	**12**	**2**	**3**	**5**	**14**	**21**	**3**	**2**	**5**	**19**
1989-90	**Calgary**	**NHL**	**65**	**20**	**18**	**38**	**26**	**6**	**0**	**2**	**2**	**8**
1990-91	**Calgary**	**NHL**	**57**	**13**	**14**	**27**	**55**	**1**	**0**	**0**	**0**	**0**
1991-92	**Detroit**	**NHL**	**23**	**1**	**5**	**6**	**38**	....	....	....	....	....
	NHL Totals		**606**	**172**	**241**	**413**	**551**	**47**	**5**	**9**	**14**	**42**

Signed as a free agent by **Los Angeles,** May 12, 1982. Traded to **NY Rangers** by **Los Angeles** with Los Angeles' fourth round draft choice in 1987 (Michael Sullivan) for Roland Melanson and Grant Ledyard, December 9, 1985. Traded to **Minnesota** by **NY Rangers** for Minnesota's third round choice (Simon Gagne) in 1987 Entry Draft, September 8, 1986. Traded to **Calgary** by **Minnesota** with Minnesota's fourth round choice (Robert Reichel) in 1989 Entry Draft for Shane Churla and Perry Berezan, March 4, 1989. Traded to **Detroit** by **Calgary** for Marc Habscheid, June 11, 1991.

MacLEOD, PAT

Defense. Shoots left. 5'11", 190 lbs. Born, Melfort, Sask., June 15, 1969.
(Minnesota's 5th choice, 87th overall, in 1989 Entry Draft).

			Regular Season					Playoffs				
Season	Club	Lea	GP	G	A	TP	PIM	GP	G	A	TP	PIM
1987-88	Kamloops	WHL	50	13	33	46	27	18	2	7	9	6
1988-89	Kamloops	WHL	37	11	34	45	14	15	7	18	25	24
1989-90	Kalamazoo	IHL	82	9	38	47	27	10	1	6	7	2
1990-91	**Minnesota**	**NHL**	**1**	**0**	**1**	**1**	**0**	....	....	....	....	....
	Kalamazoo	IHL	59	10	30	40	16	11	1	2	3	5
1991-92	**San Jose**	**NHL**	**37**	**5**	**11**	**16**	**4**	....	....	....	....	....
	Kansas City	IHL	45	9	21	30	19	11	1	4	5	4
	NHL Totals		**38**	**5**	**12**	**17**	**4**	....	....	....	....	....

Claimed by **San Jose** from **Minnesota** in Dispersal Draft, May 30, 1991.

MACOUN, JAMIE (muh-KOW-uhn)

Defense. Shoots left. 6'2", 197 lbs. Born, Newmarket, Ont., August 17, 1961.

			Regular Season					Playoffs				
Season	Club	Lea	GP	G	A	TP	PIM	GP	G	A	TP	PIM
1980-81	Ohio State	CCHA	38	9	20	29	83	....	....	....	....	....
1981-82	Ohio State	CCHA	25	2	18	20	89	....	....	....	....	....
1982-83	Ohio State	CCHA	19	6	21	27	54	....	....	....	....	....
	Calgary	**NHL**	**22**	**1**	**4**	**5**	**25**	**9**	**0**	**2**	**2**	**8**
1983-84a	**Calgary**	**NHL**	**72**	**9**	**23**	**32**	**97**	**11**	**1**	**0**	**1**	**0**
1984-85	**Calgary**	**NHL**	**70**	**9**	**30**	**39**	**67**	**4**	**1**	**0**	**1**	**4**
1985-86	**Calgary**	**NHL**	**77**	**11**	**21**	**32**	**81**	**22**	**1**	**6**	**7**	**23**
1986-87	**Calgary**	**NHL**	**79**	**7**	**33**	**40**	**111**	**3**	**0**	**1**	**1**	**8**
1987-88			DID NOT PLAY — INJURED									
1988-89	**Calgary**	**NHL**	**72**	**8**	**19**	**27**	**76**	**22**	**3**	**6**	**9**	**30**
1989-90	**Calgary**	**NHL**	**78**	**8**	**27**	**35**	**70**	**6**	**0**	**3**	**3**	**10**
1990-91	**Calgary**	**NHL**	**79**	**7**	**15**	**22**	**84**	**7**	**0**	**1**	**1**	**4**
1991-92	**Calgary**	**NHL**	**37**	**2**	**12**	**14**	**53**	....	....	....	....	....
	Toronto	**NHL**	**39**	**3**	**13**	**16**	**18**	....	....	....	....	....
	NHL Totals		**625**	**65**	**197**	**262**	**682**	**84**	**6**	**19**	**25**	**87**

a NHL All-Rookie Team (1984)

Signed as a free agent by **Calgary**, January 30, 1983. Traded to **Toronto** by **Calgary** with Doug Gilmour, Ric Natress, Kent Manderville and Rick Wamsley for Gary Leeman, Alexander Godynyuk, Jeff Reese, Michel Petit and Craig Berube, January 2, 1992.

MacTAVISH, CRAIG

Center. Shoots left. 6'1", 195 lbs. Born, London, Ont., August 15, 1958.
(Boston's 9th choice, 153rd overall, in 1978 Amateur Draft).

			Regular Season					Playoffs				
Season	Club	Lea	GP	G	A	TP	PIM	GP	G	A	TP	PIM
1978-79	Lowell	ECAC	....	36	52	*88	....	....	....	....	....	....
1979-80	**Boston**	**NHL**	**46**	**11**	**17**	**28**	**8**	**10**	**2**	**3**	**5**	**7**
	Binghamton	AHL	34	17	15	32	29	....	....	....	....	....
1980-81	**Boston**	**NHL**	**24**	**3**	**5**	**8**	**13**	....	....	....	....	....
	Springfield	AHL	53	19	24	43	81	7	5	4	9	8
1981-82	**Boston**	**NHL**	**2**	**0**	**1**	**1**	**0**	....	....	....	....	....
	Erie	AHL	72	23	32	55	37	....	....	....	....	....
1982-83	**Boston**	**NHL**	**75**	**10**	**20**	**30**	**18**	**17**	**3**	**1**	**4**	**18**
1983-84	**Boston**	**NHL**	**70**	**20**	**23**	**43**	**35**	**1**	**0**	**0**	**0**	**0**
1984-85			DID NOT PLAY									
1985-86	**Edmonton**	**NHL**	**74**	**23**	**24**	**47**	**70**	**10**	**4**	**4**	**8**	**11**
1986-87	**Edmonton**	**NHL**	**79**	**20**	**19**	**39**	**55**	**21**	**1**	**9**	**10**	**16**
1987-88	**Edmonton**	**NHL**	**80**	**15**	**17**	**32**	**47**	**19**	**0**	**1**	**1**	**31**
1988-89	**Edmonton**	**NHL**	**80**	**21**	**31**	**52**	**55**	**7**	**0**	**1**	**1**	**8**
1989-90	**Edmonton**	**NHL**	**80**	**21**	**22**	**43**	**89**	**22**	**2**	**6**	**8**	**29**
1990-91	**Edmonton**	**NHL**	**80**	**17**	**15**	**32**	**76**	**18**	**3**	**3**	**6**	**20**
1991-92	**Edmonton**	**NHL**	**80**	**12**	**18**	**30**	**98**	**16**	**3**	**0**	**3**	**28**
	NHL Totals		**770**	**173**	**212**	**385**	**564**	**141**	**18**	**28**	**46**	**168**

Signed as a free agent by **Edmonton,** February 1, 1985.

MacWILLIAM, MICHAEL

Left wing. Shoots left. 6'1", 195 lbs. Born, Burnaby, B.C., February 14, 1967.

			Regular Season					Playoffs				
Season	Club	Lea	GP	G	A	TP	PIM	GP	G	A	TP	PIM
1990-91	Greensboro	ECHL	8	2	5	7	94	....	....	....	....	....
1991-92	St. John's	AHL	44	7	8	15	301	2	0	0	0	8

Signed as a free agent by **Toronto**, July 30, 1991.

MADILL, JEFF (muh-DILL)

Right wing. Shoots left. 5'11", 195 lbs. Born, Oshawa, Ont., June 21, 1965.
(New Jersey's 2nd choice, 7th overall, in 1987 Supplemental Draft).

			Regular Season					Playoffs				
Season	Club	Lea	GP	G	A	TP	PIM	GP	G	A	TP	PIM
1984-85	Ohio State	CCHA	12	5	6	11	18	....	....	....	....	....
1985-86	Ohio State	CCHA	41	32	25	57	65	....	....	....	....	....
1986-87	Ohio State	CCHA	43	38	32	70	139	....	....	....	....	....
1987-88	Utica	AHL	58	18	15	33	127	....	....	....	....	....
1988-89	Utica	AHL	69	23	25	48	225	4	1	0	1	35
1989-90	Utica	AHL	74	43	26	69	233	4	1	2	3	33
1990-91	**New Jersey**	**NHL**	**14**	**4**	**0**	**4**	**46**	**7**	**0**	**2**	**2**	**8**
a	Utica	AHL	54	42	35	77	151	....	....	....	....	....
1991-92	Kansas City	IHL	62	32	20	52	167	6	2	2	4	30
	NHL Totals		**14**	**4**	**0**	**4**	**46**	**7**	**0**	**2**	**2**	**8**

a AHL Second All-Star Team (1991)

Claimed by **San Jose** from **New Jersey** in Expansion Draft, May 30, 1991.

MAGNUSSON, STEVEN

Center. Shoots left. 5'11", 175 lbs. Born, Coon Rapids, MN, November 15, 1972.
(Calgary's 5th choice, 85th overall, in 1991 Entry Draft).

			Regular Season					Playoffs				
Season	Club	Lea	GP	G	A	TP	PIM	GP	G	A	TP	PIM
1990-91	Anoka	HS	23	37	35	72	40	....	....	....	....	....
1991-92	U. Minnesota	WCHA	38	9	21	30	54	....	....	....	....	....

MAGUIRE, DEREK

Defense. Shoots right. 6', 185 lbs. Born, Delbarton, NJ, December 9, 1971.
(Montreal's 10th choice, 186th overall, in 1990 Entry Draft).

			Regular Season					Playoffs				
Season	Club	Lea	GP	G	A	TP	PIM	GP	G	A	TP	PIM
1990-91	Harvard	ECAC	25	3	14	17	12	....	....	....	....	....
1991-92	Harvard	ECAC	25	1	16	17	16	....	....	....	....	....

MAGUIRE, KEVIN

Right Wing. Shoots right. 6'2", 200 lbs. Born, Toronto, Ont., January 5, 1963.

			Regular Season					Playoffs				
Season	Club	Lea	GP	G	A	TP	PIM	GP	G	A	TP	PIM
1983-84	Orilla	OPJHL	....	35	42	77	....	....	....	....	....	....
1984-85	St. Catharines	AHL	76	10	15	25	112	....	....	....	....	....
1985-86	St. Catharines	AHL	61	6	9	15	161	1	0	0	0	0
1986-87	**Toronto**	**NHL**	**17**	**0**	**0**	**0**	**74**	**1**	**0**	**0**	**0**	**0**
	Newmarket	AHL	51	4	2	6	131	....	....	....	....	....
1987-88	**Buffalo**	**NHL**	**46**	**4**	**6**	**10**	**162**	**5**	**0**	**0**	**0**	**50**
1988-89	**Buffalo**	**NHL**	**60**	**8**	**10**	**18**	**241**	**5**	**0**	**0**	**0**	**36**
1989-90	**Buffalo**	**NHL**	**61**	**6**	**9**	**15**	**115**	....	....	....	....	....
	Philadelphia	**NHL**	**5**	**1**	**0**	**1**	**6**	....	....	....	....	....
1990-91	**Toronto**	**NHL**	**63**	**9**	**5**	**14**	**180**	....	....	....	....	....
1991-92	**Toronto**	**NHL**	**8**	**1**	**0**	**1**	**4**	....	....	....	....	....
	St. John's	AHL	30	11	15	26	112	11	3	7	10	43
	NHL Totals		**260**	**29**	**30**	**59**	**782**	**11**	**0**	**0**	**0**	**6**

Signed as a free agent by**Toronto**, October 10, 1984. Claimed by **Buffalo** in NHL Waiver Draft, October 5, 1987. Traded to **Philadelphia** by **Buffalo** with Buffalo's second round choice (Mikael Renberg) in 1990 Entry Draft for Jay Wells and Philadelphia's fourth round choice (Peter Ambroziak) in 1991 Entry Draft, March 5, 1990. Traded to **Toronto** by **Philadelphia** with Philadelphia's eighth round choice (Dimitri Mironov) in 1991 Entry Draft for Toronto's third round choice (Al Kinisky) in 1990 Entry Draft, June 16, 1990.

MAHER, JIM

Defense. Shoots left. 6'1", 210 lbs. Born, Warren, MI, June 30, 1970.
(Los Angeles' 2nd choice, 81st overall, in 1989 Entry Draft).

			Regular Season					Playoffs				
Season	Club	Lea	GP	G	A	TP	PIM	GP	G	A	TP	PIM
1988-89	Ill.-Chicago	CCHA	31	1	5	6	40	....	....	....	....	....
1989-90	Ill.-Chicago	CCHA	38	4	12	16	64	....	....	....	....	....
1990-91	Ill.-Chicago	CCHA	37	6	8	14	49	....	....	....	....	....
1991-92	Ill.-Chicago	CCHA	34	5	9	14	52	....	....	....	....	....
	Phoenix	IHL	9	0	3	3	21	....	....	....	....	....

MAILLET, CLAUDE

Defense. Shoots right. 6'2", 200 lbs. Born, Memramcook, N.B., May 22, 1969.
(Chicago's 1st choice, 21st overall, in 1990 Supplemental Draft).

			Regular Season					Playoffs				
Season	Club	Lea	GP	G	A	TP	PIM	GP	G	A	TP	PIM
1988-89	Merrimack	NCAA	30	1	27	28	30	....	....	....	....	....
1989-90	Merrimack	H.E.	32	8	15	23	55	....	....	....	....	....
1990-91	Merrimack	H.E.	33	3	9	12	45	....	....	....	....	....
1991-92	Merrimack	H.E.	25	6	9	15	35	....	....	....	....	....

MAJIC, XAVIER

Center. Shoots left. 5'11", 185 lbs. Born, Fernie, B.C., March 10, 1973.
(Vancouver's 12th choice, 249th overall, in 1991 Entry Draft).

			Regular Season					Playoffs				
Season	Club	Lea	GP	G	A	TP	PIM	GP	G	A	TP	PIM
1990-91	RPI	ECAC	31	4	10	14	26	....	....	....	....	....
1991-92	RPI	ECAC	32	13	19	32	48	....	....	....	....	....

MAJOR, BRUCE

Center. Shoots left. 6'3", 180 lbs. Born, Vernon, B.C., January 3, 1967.
(Quebec's 6th choice, 99th overall, in 1985 Entry Draft).

			Regular Season					Playoffs				
Season	Club	Lea	GP	G	A	TP	PIM	GP	G	A	TP	PIM
1985-86	U. of Maine	H.E.	38	14	14	28	39	....	....	....	....	....
1986-87	U. of Maine	H.E.	37	14	10	24	12	....	....	....	....	....
1987-88	U. of Maine	H.E.	26	0	5	5	14	....	....	....	....	....
1988-89	U. of Maine	H.E.	42	13	11	24	22	....	....	....	....	....
1989-90	Halifax	AHL	32	5	6	11	23	....	....	....	....	....
	Greensboro	ECHL	12	4	3	7	6	10	2	2	4	12
1990-91	**Quebec**	**NHL**	**4**	**0**	**0**	**0**	**0**	....	....	....	....	....
	Halifax	AHL	9	2	0	2	9	....	....	....	....	....
	Fort Wayne	IHL	62	11	25	36	48	18	1	3	4	6
1991-92	Halifax	AHL	16	1	3	4	11	....	....	....	....	....
	NHL Totals		**4**	**0**	**0**	**0**	**0**	....	....	....	....	....

MAKAROV, SERGEI (mah-KAH-rahf)

Right wing. Shoots left. 5'11", 185 lbs. Born, Chelyabinsk, Soviet Union, June 19, 1958.
(Calgary's 14th choice, 231st overall, in 1983 Entry Draft).

			Regular Season					Playoffs				
Season	Club	Lea	GP	G	A	TP	PIM	GP	G	A	TP	PIM
1976-77	Chelyabinsk	USSR	11	1	0	1	4	....	....	....	....	....
1977-78	Chelyabinsk	USSR	36	18	13	31	10	....	....	....	....	....
1978-79a	CSKA	USSR	44	18	21	39	12	....	....	....	....	....
1979-80bc	CSKA	USSR	44	29	39	68	16	....	....	....	....	....
1980-81ab	CSKA	USSR	49	42	37	79	22	....	....	....	....	....
1981-82ab	CSKA	USSR	46	32	43	75	18	....	....	....	....	....
1982-83a	CSKA	USSR	30	25	17	42	6	....	....	....	....	....
1983-84ab	CSKA	USSR	44	36	37	73	28	....	....	....	....	....
1984-85abc	CSKA	USSR	40	26	39	65	28	....	....	....	....	....
1985-86ab	CSKA	USSR	40	30	32	62	28	....	....	....	....	....
1986-87ab	CSKA	USSR	40	21	32	53	26	....	....	....	....	....
1987-88ab	CSKA	USSR	51	23	45	68	50	....	....	....	....	....
1988-89bc	CSKA	USSR	44	21	33	54	42	....	....	....	....	....
1989-90de	**Calgary**	**NHL**	**80**	**24**	**62**	**86**	**55**	**6**	**0**	**6**	**6**	**0**
1990-91	**Calgary**	**NHL**	**78**	**30**	**49**	**79**	**44**	**3**	**1**	**0**	**1**	**0**
1991-92	**Calgary**	**NHL**	**68**	**22**	**48**	**70**	**60**	....	....	....	....	....
	NHL Totals		**226**	**76**	**159**	**235**	**159**	**9**	**1**	**6**	**7**	**0**

a Soviet National League All-Star (1981-88)
b Izvestia Trophy - leading scorer (1980-82, 1984-89)
c Soviet Player of the Year (1980, 1985, 1989)
d NHL All-Rookie Team (1990)
e Won Calder Memorial Trophy (1990)

MAKELA, MIKKO (MAK-uh-luh, MEE-koh)

Left wing. Shoots left. 6'2", 200 lbs. Born, Tampere, Finland, February 28, 1965.
(NY Islanders' 5th choice, 65th overall, in 1983 Entry Draft).

			Regular Season					Playoffs				
Season	Club	Lea	GP	G	A	TP	PIM	GP	G	A	TP	PIM
1983-84	Ilves	Fin.	35	17	11	28	26	2	0	1	1	0
1984-85a	Ilves	Fin.	36	34	25	59	24	9	4	7	11	10
1985-86	**NY Islanders**	**NHL**	**58**	**16**	**20**	**36**	**28**	....	....	....	....	....
	Springfield	AHL	2	1	1	2	0	....	....	....	....	....
1986-87	**NY Islanders**	**NHL**	**80**	**24**	**33**	**57**	**24**	**11**	**2**	**4**	**6**	**8**
1987-88	**NY Islanders**	**NHL**	**73**	**36**	**40**	**76**	**22**	**6**	**1**	**4**	**5**	**6**
1988-89	**NY Islanders**	**NHL**	**76**	**17**	**28**	**45**	**22**	....	....	....	....	....
1989-90	**NY Islanders**	**NHL**	**20**	**2**	**3**	**5**	**2**	....	....	....	....	....
	Los Angeles	**NHL**	**45**	**7**	**14**	**21**	**16**	**1**	**0**	**0**	**0**	**0**
1990-91	**Buffalo**	**NHL**	**60**	**15**	**7**	**22**	**25**	....	....	....	....	....
1991-92	TPS	Fin.	44	25	45	*70	38	3	2	3	5	0
	NHL Totals		**412**	**117**	**145**	**262**	**139**	**18**	**3**	**8**	**11**	**14**

a Finnish League First All-Star Team (1985)

Traded to **Los Angeles** by **NY Islanders** for Ken Baumgartner and Hubie McDonough, November 29, 1989. Traded to **Buffalo** by **Los Angeles** for Mike Donnelly, September 30, 1990.

MALAKHOV, VLADIMIR (mah-LAH-kahf)

Defense. 6'2", 207 lbs. Born, Sverdlovsk, Soviet Union, August 30, 1968.
(NY Islanders' 12th choice, 191st overall, in 1989 Entry Draft).

			Regular Season					Playoffs				
Season	Club	Lea	GP	G	A	TP	PIM	GP	G	A	TP	PIM
1986-87	Spartak	USSR	22	0	1	1	12	....	....	....	....	....
1987-88	Spartak	USSR	28	2	2	4	26	....	....	....	....	....
1988-89	CSKA	USSR	34	6	2	8	16	....	....	....	....	....
1989-90	CSKA	USSR	48	2	10	12	34	....	....	....	....	....
1990-91	CSKA	USSR	46	5	13	18	22	....	....	....	....	....
1991-92	CSKA	CIS	40	1	9	10	12	....	....	....	....	....

MALEY, DAVID

Left wing. Shoots left. 6'2", 195 lbs. Born, Beaver Dam, WI, April 24, 1963.
(Montreal's 4th choice, 33rd overall, in 1982 Entry Draft).

			Regular Season					Playoffs				
Season	Club	Lea	GP	G	A	TP	PIM	GP	G	A	TP	PIM
1982-83	U. Wisconsin	WCHA	47	17	23	40	24	....	....	....	....	....
1983-84	U. Wisconsin	WCHA	38	10	28	38	56	....	....	....	....	....
1984-85	U. Wisconsin	WCHA	38	19	9	28	86	....	....	....	....	....
1985-86	U. Wisconsin	WCHA	42	20	40	60	135	....	....	....	....	....
	Montreal	**NHL**	**3**	**0**	**0**	**0**	**0**	**7**	**1**	**3**	**4**	**2**
1986-87	**Montreal**	**NHL**	**48**	**6**	**12**	**18**	**55**	....	....	....	....	....
	Sherbrooke	AHL	11	1	5	6	25	12	7	7	14	10
1987-88	**New Jersey**	**NHL**	**44**	**4**	**2**	**6**	**65**	**20**	**3**	**1**	**4**	**80**
	Utica	AHL	9	5	3	8	40	....	....	....	....	....
1988-89	**New Jersey**	**NHL**	**68**	**5**	**6**	**11**	**249**	....	....	....	....	....
1989-90	**New Jersey**	**NHL**	**67**	**8**	**17**	**25**	**160**	**6**	**0**	**0**	**0**	**25**
1990-91	**New Jersey**	**NHL**	**64**	**8**	**14**	**22**	**151**	....	....	....	....	....
1991-92	**New Jersey**	**NHL**	**37**	**7**	**11**	**18**	**58**	....	....	....	....	....
	Edmonton	**NHL**	**23**	**3**	**6**	**9**	**46**	**10**	**1**	**1**	**2**	**4**
	NHL Totals		**354**	**41**	**68**	**109**	**784**	**43**	**5**	**5**	**10**	**111**

Traded to **New Jersey** by **Montreal** for New Jersey's third round choice (Mathieu Schneider) in 1987 Entry Draft, June 13, 1987. Traded to **Edmonton** by **New Jersey** for Troy Mallette, January 12, 1992.

MALKOC, DEAN

Defense. Shoots right. 6'3", 200 lbs. Born, Vancouver, B.C., January 26, 1970.
(New Jersey's 7th choice, 95th overall, in 1990 Entry Draft).

			Regular Season					Playoffs				
Season	Club	Lea	GP	G	A	TP	PIM	GP	G	A	TP	PIM
1989-90	Kamloops	WHL	48	3	18	21	209	17	0	3	3	56
1990-91	Kamloops	WHL	8	1	4	5	47	....	....	....	....	....
	Swift Current	WHL	56	10	23	33	248	3	0	2	2	5
	Utica	AHL	1	0	0	0	0	....	....	....	....	....
1991-92	Utica	AHL	66	1	11	12	274	4	0	2	2	6

MALLETTE, TROY

Left wing. Shoots left. 6'2", 210 lbs. Born, Sudbury, Ont., February 25, 1970.
(NY Rangers' 1st choice, 22nd overall, in 1988 Entry Draft).

			Regular Season					Playoffs				
Season	Club	Lea	GP	G	A	TP	PIM	GP	G	A	TP	PIM
1986-87	S.S. Marie	OHL	65	20	25	45	157	4	0	2	2	12
1987-88	S.S. Marie	OHL	62	18	30	48	186	6	1	3	4	12
1988-89	S.S. Marie	OHL	64	39	37	76	172	0	0	0	0	0
1989-90	**NY Rangers**	**NHL**	**79**	**13**	**16**	**29**	**305**	**10**	**2**	**2**	**4**	**81**
1990-91	**NY Rangers**	**NHL**	**71**	**12**	**10**	**22**	**252**	**5**	**0**	**0**	**0**	**18**
1991-92	**Edmonton**	**NHL**	**15**	**1**	**3**	**4**	**36**	....	....	....	....	....
	New Jersey	**NHL**	**17**	**3**	**4**	**7**	**43**	....	....	....	....	....
	NHL Totals		**182**	**29**	**33**	**62**	**636**	**15**	**2**	**2**	**4**	**99**

Acquired by **Edmonton** from **NY Rangers** as compensation for NY Rangers' signing of free agent Adam Graves, September 12, 1991. Traded to **New Jersey** by **Edmonton** for David Maley, January 12, 1992.

MALLGRAVE, MATTHEW

Right wing. Shoots right. 6', 180 lbs. Born, Washington, D.C., May 3, 1970.
(Toronto's 6th choice, 132nd overall, in 1988 Entry Draft).

			Regular Season					Playoffs				
Season	Club	Lea	GP	G	A	TP	PIM	GP	G	A	TP	PIM
1989-90	Harvard	ECAC	26	3	3	6	33	....	....	....	....	....
1990-91	Harvard	ECAC	25	5	14	19	14	....	....	....	....	....
1991-92	Harvard	ECAC	27	12	15	27	20	....	....	....	....	....

MALONE, SCOTT

Defense. Shoots left. 6', 180 lbs. Born, Boston, MA, January 16, 1971.
(Toronto's 10th choice, 220th overall, in 1990 Entry Draft).

			Regular Season					Playoffs				
Season	Club	Lea	GP	G	A	TP	PIM	GP	G	A	TP	PIM
1989-90	Northfield	HS	18	10	25	35	....					
1990-91	N. Hampshire	H.E.				DID NOT PLAY						
1991-92	N. Hampshire	H.E.	27	0	4	4	52	....	....	....	....	....

MALTAIS, STEVE (MAHL-tayz)

Left wing. Shoots left. 6'2", 210 lbs. Born, Arvida, Que., January 25, 1969.
(Washington's 2nd choice, 57th overall, in 1987 Entry Draft).

			Regular Season					Playoffs				
Season	Club	Lea	GP	G	A	TP	PIM	GP	G	A	TP	PIM
1986-87	Cornwall	OHL	65	32	12	44	29	5	0	0	0	2
1987-88	Cornwall	OHL	59	39	46	85	30	11	9	6	15	33
1988-89	Cornwall	OHL	58	53	70	123	67	18	14	16	30	16
	Fort Wayne	IHL	....	....	....	....	....	4	2	1	3	0
1989-90	**Washington**	**NHL**	**8**	**0**	**0**	**0**	**2**	**1**	**0**	**0**	**0**	**0**
	Baltimore	AHL	67	29	37	66	54	12	6	10	16	6
1990-91	**Washington**	**NHL**	**7**	**0**	**0**	**0**	**2**	....	....	....	....	....
	Baltimore	AHL	73	36	43	79	97	6	1	4	5	10
1991-92	**Minnesota**	**NHL**	**12**	**2**	**1**	**3**	**2**	....	....	....	....	....
	Kalamazoo	IHL	48	25	31	56	51	....	....	....	....	....
	Halifax	AHL	10	3	3	6	0	....	....	....	....	....
	NHL Totals		**27**	**2**	**1**	**3**	**6**	**1**	**0**	**0**	**0**	**0**

Traded to **Minnesota** by **Washington** with Trent Klatt for Shawn Chambers, June 21, 1991. Traded to **Quebec** by **Minnesota** for Kip Miller, March 8, 1992. Claimed by **Tampa Bay** from **Quebec** in Expansion Draft, June 18, 1992.

MALTBY, KIRK

Right wing. Shoots right. 6', 180 lbs. Born, Guelph, Ont., December 22, 1972.
(Edmonton's 4th choice, 65th overall, in 1992 Entry Draft).

			Regular Season					Playoffs				
Season	Club	Lea	GP	G	A	TP	PIM	GP	G	A	TP	PIM
1989-90	Owen Sound	OHL	61	12	15	27	90	....	....	....	....	....
1990-91	Owen Sound	OHL	66	34	32	66	100	....	....	....	....	....
1991-92	Owen Sound	OHL	66	50	41	91	99	5	3	3	6	18

MALYKHIN, IGOR (mahl-EE-khihn)

Defense. Shoots left. 6'1", 176 lbs. Born, Moscow, Soviet Union, June 6, 1969.
(Detroit's 6th choice, 142nd overall, in 1991 Entry Draft).

			Regular Season					Playoffs				
Season	Club	Lea	GP	G	A	TP	PIM	GP	G	A	TP	PIM
1990-91	CSKA	USSR	36	2	2	4	10	....	....	....	....	....
1991-92	CSKA	CIS	42	1	5	6	20	....	....	....	....	....

MANDERVILLE, KENT

Left wing. Shoots left. 6'3", 200 lbs. Born, Edmonton, Alta., April 12, 1971.
(Calgary's 1st choice, 24th overall, in 1989 Entry Draft).

			Regular Season					Playoffs				
Season	Club	Lea	GP	G	A	TP	PIM	GP	G	A	TP	PIM
1989-90a	Cornell	ECAC	26	11	15	26	28	....	....	....	....	....
1990-91	Cornell	ECAC	28	17	14	31	60	....	....	....	....	....
	Cdn. National	....	3	1	2	3	0	....	....	....	....	....
1991-92	Cdn. National	....	63	16	23	39	75	....	....	....	....	....
	Cdn. Olympic	....	8	1	2	3	0	....	....	....	....	....
	Toronto	**NHL**	**15**	**0**	**4**	**4**	**0**	....	....	....	....	....
	St. John's	AHL	....	....	....	....	....	12	5	9	14	14
	NHL Totals		**15**	**0**	**4**	**4**	**0**	....	....	....	....	....

a ECAC Rookie of the Year (1990)

Traded to **Toronto** by **Calgary** with Doug Gilmour, Jamie Macoun, Rick Wamsley and Ric Natress for Gary Leeman, Alexander Godynyuk, Jeff Reese, Michel Petit and Craig Berube, January 2, 1992.

MANSON, DAVE

Defense. Shoots left. 6'2", 202 lbs. Born, Prince Albert, Sask., January 27, 1967.
(Chicago's 1st choice, 11th overall, in 1985 Entry Draft).

			Regular Season					Playoffs				
Season	Club	Lea	GP	G	A	TP	PIM	GP	G	A	TP	PIM
1983-84	Prince Albert	WHL	70	2	7	9	233	5	0	0	0	4
1984-85	Prince Albert	WHL	72	8	30	38	247	13	1	0	1	34
1985-86	Prince Albert	WHL	70	14	34	48	177	20	1	8	9	63
1986-87	**Chicago**	**NHL**	**63**	**1**	**8**	**9**	**146**	**3**	**0**	**0**	**0**	**10**
1987-88	**Chicago**	**NHL**	**54**	**1**	**6**	**7**	**185**	**5**	**0**	**0**	**0**	**27**
	Saginaw	IHL	6	0	3	3	37	....	....	....	....	....
1988-89	**Chicago**	**NHL**	**79**	**18**	**36**	**54**	**352**	**16**	**0**	**8**	**8**	**84**
1989-90	**Chicago**	**NHL**	**59**	**5**	**23**	**28**	**301**	**20**	**2**	**4**	**6**	**46**
1990-91	**Chicago**	**NHL**	**75**	**14**	**15**	**29**	**191**	**6**	**0**	**1**	**1**	**36**
1991-92	**Edmonton**	**NHL**	**79**	**15**	**32**	**47**	**220**	**16**	**3**	**9**	**12**	**44**
	NHL Totals		**409**	**54**	**120**	**174**	**1395**	**66**	**5**	**22**	**27**	**247**

Played in NHL All-Star Game (1989)

Traded to **Edmonton** by **Chicago** with future considerations for Steve Smith, October 2, 1991.

MANTHA, MAURICE WILLIAM (MOE) (MAN-tha)

Defense. Shoots right. 6'2", 210 lbs. Born, Lakewood, OH, January 21, 1961.
(Winnipeg's 2nd choice, 23rd overall, in 1980 Entry Draft).

			Regular Season					Playoffs				
Season	Club	Lea	GP	G	A	TP	PIM	GP	G	A	TP	PIM
1978-79	Toronto	OHA	68	10	38	48	57	4	0	2	2	11
1979-80	Toronto	OHA	58	8	38	46	86	....	....	....	....	....
1980-81	**Winnipeg**	**NHL**	**58**	**2**	**23**	**25**	**35**	....	....	....	....	....
1981-82	**Winnipeg**	**NHL**	**25**	**0**	**12**	**12**	**28**	**4**	**1**	**3**	**4**	**16**
	Tulsa	CHL	33	8	15	23	56	....	....	....	....	....
1982-83	**Winnipeg**	**NHL**	**21**	**2**	**7**	**9**	**6**	**2**	**2**	**2**	**4**	**0**
	Sherbrooke	AHL	13	1	4	5	13	....	....	....	....	....
1983-84	**Winnipeg**	**NHL**	**72**	**16**	**38**	**54**	**67**	**3**	**1**	**0**	**1**	**0**
	Sherbrooke	AHL	7	1	1	2	10	....	....	....	....	....
1984-85	**Pittsburgh**	**NHL**	**71**	**11**	**40**	**51**	**54**	....	....	....	....	....
1985-86	**Pittsburgh**	**NHL**	**78**	**15**	**52**	**67**	**102**	....	....	....	....	....
1986-87	**Pittsburgh**	**NHL**	**62**	**9**	**31**	**40**	**44**	....	....	....	....	....
1987-88	**Pittsburgh**	**NHL**	**21**	**2**	**8**	**10**	**23**	....	....	....	....	....
	Edmonton	**NHL**	**25**	**0**	**6**	**6**	**26**	....	....	....	....	....
	Minnesota	**NHL**	**30**	**9**	**13**	**22**	**4**	....	....	....	....	....
1988-89	**Minnesota**	**NHL**	**16**	**1**	**6**	**7**	**10**	....	....	....	....	....
	Philadelphia	**NHL**	**30**	**3**	**8**	**11**	**33**	**1**	**0**	**0**	**0**	**0**
1989-90	**Winnipeg**	**NHL**	**73**	**2**	**26**	**28**	**28**	**7**	**1**	**5**	**6**	**2**
1990-91	**Winnipeg**	**NHL**	**57**	**9**	**15**	**24**	**33**	....	....	....	....	....
1991-92	U.S. National	....	13	0	2	2	29	....	....	....	....	....
	U.S. Olympic	....	8	1	1	2	4	....	....	....	....	....
	Winnipeg	**NHL**	**12**	**0**	**4**	**4**	**6**	....	....	....	....	....
	Philadelphia	**NHL**	**5**	**0**	**0**	**0**	**2**	....	....	....	....	....
	NHL Totals		**656**	**81**	**289**	**370**	**501**	**17**	**5**	**10**	**15**	**18**

Traded to **Pittsburgh** by **Winnipeg**, May 1, 1984 to complete deal of March 6, 1984 when Pittsburgh traded Randy Carlyle to Winnipeg. Traded to **Edmonton** by **Pittsburgh** with Craig Simpson, Dave Hannan, and Chris Joseph for Paul Coffey, Dave Hunter, and Wayne Van Dorp, November 24, 1987. Traded to **Minnesota** by **Edmonton** for Keith Acton, January 22, 1988. Traded to **Philadelphia** by **Minnesota** for Toronto's fifth round choice (Pat MacLeod) in 1989 Entry Draft, December 8, 1988. Claimed by **Winnipeg** in NHL Waiver Draft, October 2, 1989. Traded to **Philadelphia** by **Winnipeg** for future considerations, February 27, 1992.

MARCHMENT, BRYAN

Defense. Shoots left. 6'1", 198 lbs. Born, Scarborough, Ont., May 1, 1969.
(Winnipeg's 1st choice, 16th overall, in 1987 Entry Draft).

			Regular Season					Playoffs				
Season	Club	Lea	GP	G	A	TP	PIM	GP	G	A	TP	PIM
1985-86	Belleville	OHL	57	5	15	20	225	21	0	7	7	83
1986-87	Belleville	OHL	52	6	38	44	238	6	0	4	4	17
1987-88	Belleville	OHL	56	7	51	58	200	6	1	3	4	19
1988-89	**Winnipeg**	**NHL**	**2**	**0**	**0**	**0**	**2**	....	....	....	....	....
a	Belleville	OHL	43	14	36	50	118	5	0	1	1	12
1989-90	**Winnipeg**	**NHL**	**7**	**0**	**2**	**2**	**28**	....	....	....	....	....
	Moncton	AHL	56	4	19	23	217	....	....	....	....	....
1990-91	**Winnipeg**	**NHL**	**28**	**2**	**2**	**4**	**91**	....	....	....	....	....
	Moncton	AHL	33	2	11	13	101	....	....	....	....	....
1991-92	**Chicago**	**NHL**	**58**	**5**	**10**	**15**	**168**	**16**	**1**	**0**	**1**	**36**
	NHL Totals		**95**	**7**	**14**	**21**	**289**	**16**	**1**	**0**	**1**	**36**

a OHL Second All-Star Team (1989)

Traded to **Chicago** by **Winnipeg** with Chris Norton for Troy Murray and Warren Rychel, July 22, 1991.

MARCINYSHYN, DAVID (MAIR-sih-NIH-shuhn)

Defense. Shoots left. 6'3", 210 lbs. Born, Edmonton, Alta., February 4, 1967.

			Regular Season					Playoffs				
Season	Club	Lea	GP	G	A	TP	PIM	GP	G	A	TP	PIM
1985-86	Kamloops	WHL	57	2	7	9	111	16	1	3	4	12
1986-87	Kamloops	WHL	68	5	27	32	106	13	0	3	3	35
1987-88	Utica	AHL	73	2	7	9	179	....	....	....	....	....
	Flint	IHL	3	0	0	0	4	16	0	2	2	31
1988-89	Utica	AHL	74	4	14	18	101	5	0	0	0	13
1989-90	Utica	AHL	74	6	18	24	164	5	0	2	2	21
1990-91	**New Jersey**	**NHL**	**9**	**0**	**1**	**1**	**21**	....	....	....	....	....
	Utica	AHL	52	4	9	13	81	....	....	....	....	....
1991-92	**Quebec**	**NHL**	**5**	**0**	**0**	**0**	**26**	....	....	....	....	....
	Halifax	AHL	74	10	42	52	138	....	....	....	....	....
	NHL Totals		**14**	**0**	**1**	**1**	**47**	....	....	....	....	....

Signed as a free agent by **New Jersey**, September 26, 1986. Traded to **Quebec** by **New Jersey** for Brent Severyn, June 3, 1991.

MARINUCCI, CHRIS

Center. Shoots left. 6', 175 lbs. Born, Grand Rapids, MN, December 29, 1971.
(NY Islanders' 4th choice, 90th overall, in 1990 Entry Draft).

			Regular Season					Playoffs				
Season	Club	Lea	GP	G	A	TP	PIM	GP	G	A	TP	PIM
1990-91	Minn.-Duluth	WCHA	36	6	10	16	20	....	....	....	....	....
1991-92	Minn.-Duluth	WCHA	37	6	13	19	41	....	....	....	....	....

MARKOVICH, MICHAEL

Defense. Shoots left. 6'3", 200 lbs. Born, Grand Forks, ND, April 25, 1969.
(Pittsburgh's 6th choice, 121st overall, in 1989 Entry Draft).

			Regular Season					Playoffs				
Season	Club	Lea	GP	G	A	TP	PIM	GP	G	A	TP	PIM
1988-89	U. of Denver	WCHA	30	2	12	14	24	....	....	....	....	....
1989-90	U. of Denver	WCHA	42	4	17	21	34	....	....	....	....	....
1990-91	U. of Denver	WCHA	37	5	15	20	41	....	....	....	....	....
1991-92	U. of Denver	WCHA	3	0	1	1	10	....	....	....	....	....

MARKWART, NEVIN

Left wing. Shoots left. 5'10", 180 lbs. Born, Toronto, Ont., December 9, 1964.
(Boston's 1st choice, 21st overall, in 1983 Entry Draft).

			Regular Season					Playoffs				
Season	Club	Lea	GP	G	A	TP	PIM	GP	G	A	TP	PIM
1981-82	Regina	WHL	25	2	12	14	56	20	2	2	4	82
1982-83	Regina	WHL	43	27	39	66	91	1	0	0	0	0
1983-84	**Boston**	**NHL**	**70**	**14**	**16**	**30**	**121**	....	....	....	....	....
1984-85	**Boston**	**NHL**	**26**	**0**	**4**	**4**	**36**	**1**	**0**	**0**	**0**	**0**
	Hershey	AHL	38	13	18	31	79	....	....	....	....	....
1985-86	**Boston**	**NHL**	**65**	**7**	**15**	**22**	**207**	....	....	....	....	....
1986-87	**Boston**	**NHL**	**64**	**10**	**9**	**19**	**225**	**4**	**0**	**0**	**0**	**9**
	Moncton	AHL	3	3	3	6	11	....	....	....	....	....
1987-88	**Boston**	**NHL**	**25**	**1**	**12**	**13**	**85**	**2**	**0**	**0**	**0**	**2**
1988-89	Maine	AHL	1	0	1	1	0	....	....	....	....	....
1989-90	**Boston**	**NHL**	**8**	**1**	**2**	**3**	**15**	....	....	....	....	....
1990-91	**Boston**	**NHL**	**23**	**3**	**3**	**6**	**36**	**12**	**1**	**0**	**1**	**22**
	Maine	AHL	21	5	5	10	22	....	....	....	....	....
1991-92	**Boston**	**NHL**	**18**	**3**	**6**	**9**	**44**	....	....	....	....	....
	Maine	AHL	17	4	7	11	32	....	....	....	....	....
	Calgary	**NHL**	**10**	**2**	**1**	**3**	**25**	....	....	....	....	....
	NHL Totals		**309**	**41**	**68**	**109**	**794**	**19**	**1**	**0**	**1**	**33**

Claimed on waivers by **Calgary**, February 14, 1992.

MAROIS, DANIEL

Right wing. Shoots right. 6', 190 lbs. Born, Montreal, Que., October 3, 1968.
(Toronto's 2nd choice, 28th overall, in 1987 Entry Draft).

			Regular Season					Playoffs				
Season	Club	Lea	GP	G	A	TP	PIM	GP	G	A	TP	PIM
1985-86	Verdun	QMJHL	58	42	35	77	110	5	4	2	6	6
1986-87	Chicoutimi	QMJHL	40	22	26	48	143	16	7	14	21	25
1987-88	Verdun	QMJHL	67	52	36	88	153	....	....	....	....	....
	Newmarket	AHL	8	4	4	8	4	....	....	....	....	....
	Toronto	**NHL**	....	....	....	....	....	**3**	**1**	**0**	**1**	**0**
1988-89	**Toronto**	**NHL**	**76**	**31**	**23**	**54**	**76**	....	....	....	....	....
1989-90	**Toronto**	**NHL**	**68**	**39**	**37**	**76**	**82**	**5**	**2**	**2**	**4**	**12**
1990-91	**Toronto**	**NHL**	**78**	**21**	**9**	**30**	**112**	....	....	....	....	....
1991-92	**Toronto**	**NHL**	**63**	**15**	**11**	**26**	**76**	....	....	....	....	....
	NY Islanders	**NHL**	**12**	**2**	**5**	**7**	**18**	....	....	....	....	....
	NHL Totals		**297**	**108**	**85**	**193**	**364**	**8**	**3**	**2**	**5**	**12**

Traded to **NY Islanders** by **Toronto** with Claude Loiselle for Ken Baumgartner and Dave McLlwain, March 10, 1992.

MAROIS, MARIO (MAIR-wah)

Defense. Shoots right. 5'11", 190 lbs. Born, Quebec City, Que., December 15, 1957.
(NY Rangers' 5th choice, 62nd overall, in 1977 Amateur Draft).

			Regular Season					Playoffs				
Season	Club	Lea	GP	G	A	TP	PIM	GP	G	A	TP	PIM
1975-76	Quebec	QJHL	67	11	42	53	270	15	2	3	5	86
1976-77	Quebec	QJHL	72	17	67	84	239	14	1	17	18	75
1977-78	**NY Rangers**	**NHL**	**8**	**1**	**1**	**2**	**15**	**1**	**0**	**0**	**0**	**5**
	New Haven	AHL	52	8	23	31	147	12	5	3	8	31
1978-79	**NY Rangers**	**NHL**	**71**	**5**	**26**	**31**	**153**	**18**	**0**	**6**	**6**	**29**
1979-80	**NY Rangers**	**NHL**	**79**	**8**	**23**	**31**	**142**	**9**	**0**	**2**	**2**	**8**
1980-81	**NY Rangers**	**NHL**	**8**	**1**	**2**	**3**	**46**	....	....	....	....	....
	Vancouver	**NHL**	**50**	**4**	**12**	**16**	**115**	....	....	....	....	....
	Quebec	**NHL**	**11**	**0**	**7**	**7**	**20**	**5**	**0**	**1**	**1**	**6**
1981-82	**Quebec**	**NHL**	**71**	**11**	**32**	**43**	**161**	**13**	**1**	**2**	**3**	**44**
1982-83	**Quebec**	**NHL**	**36**	**2**	**12**	**14**	**108**	....	....	....	....	....
1983-84	**Quebec**	**NHL**	**80**	**13**	**36**	**49**	**151**	**9**	**1**	**4**	**5**	**6**
1984-85	**Quebec**	**NHL**	**76**	**6**	**37**	**43**	**91**	**18**	**0**	**8**	**8**	**12**
1985-86	**Quebec**	**NHL**	**20**	**1**	**12**	**13**	**42**	....	....	....	....	....
	Winnipeg	**NHL**	**56**	**4**	**28**	**32**	**110**	**3**	**1**	**4**	**5**	**6**
1986-87	**Winnipeg**	**NHL**	**79**	**4**	**40**	**44**	**106**	**10**	**1**	**3**	**4**	**23**
1987-88	**Winnipeg**	**NHL**	**79**	**7**	**44**	**51**	**111**	**5**	**0**	**4**	**4**	**6**
1988-89	**Winnipeg**	**NHL**	**7**	**1**	**1**	**2**	**17**	....	....	....	....	....
	Quebec	**NHL**	**42**	**2**	**11**	**13**	**101**	....	....	....	....	....
1989-90	**Quebec**	**NHL**	**67**	**3**	**15**	**18**	**104**	....	....	....	....	....
1990-91	**St. Louis**	**NHL**	**64**	**2**	**14**	**16**	**81**	**9**	**0**	**0**	**0**	**37**
1991-92	**St. Louis**	**NHL**	**17**	**0**	**1**	**1**	**38**	....	....	....	....	....
	Winnipeg	**NHL**	**34**	**1**	**3**	**4**	**34**	....	....	....	....	....
	NHL Totals		**955**	**76**	**357**	**433**	**1746**	**100**	**4**	**34**	**38**	**182**

Traded to **Vancouver** by **NY Rangers** with Jim Mayer for Jere Gillis and Jeff Bandura, November 11, 1980. Traded to **Quebec** by **Vancouver** for Garry Lariviere, March 10, 1981. Traded to **Winnipeg** by **Quebec** for Robert Picard, November 27, 1985. Traded to **Quebec** by **Winnipeg** for Gord Donnelly, December 6, 1988. Claimed by **St. Louis** in NHL Waiver Draft, October 1, 1990. Traded to **Winnipeg** by **St. Louis** for future considerations, November 26, 1991.

MARSH, CHARLES BRADLEY (BRAD)

Defense. Shoots left. 6'3", 220 lbs. Born, London, Ont., March 31, 1958.
(Atlanta's 1st choice, 11th overall, in 1978 Amateur Draft).

			Regular Season					Playoffs				
Season	Club	Lea	GP	G	A	TP	PIM	GP	G	A	TP	PIM
1976-77a	London	OHA	63	7	33	40	121	20	3	5	8	47
1977-78b	London	OHA	62	8	55	63	192	11	2	10	12	21
1978-79	**Atlanta**	**NHL**	**80**	**0**	**19**	**19**	**101**	**2**	**0**	**0**	**0**	**17**
1979-80	**Atlanta**	**NHL**	**80**	**2**	**9**	**11**	**119**	**4**	**0**	**1**	**1**	**2**
1980-81	**Calgary**	**NHL**	**80**	**1**	**12**	**13**	**87**	**16**	**0**	**5**	**5**	**8**
1981-82	**Calgary**	**NHL**	**17**	**0**	**1**	**1**	**10**	....	....	....	....	....
	Philadelphia	**NHL**	**66**	**2**	**22**	**24**	**106**	**4**	**0**	**0**	**0**	**2**
1982-83	**Philadelphia**	**NHL**	**68**	**2**	**11**	**13**	**52**	**2**	**0**	**1**	**1**	**0**
1983-84	**Philadelphia**	**NHL**	**77**	**3**	**14**	**17**	**83**	**3**	**1**	**1**	**2**	**2**
1984-85	**Philadelphia**	**NHL**	**77**	**2**	**18**	**20**	**91**	**19**	**0**	**6**	**6**	**65**
1985-86	**Philadelphia**	**NHL**	**79**	**0**	**13**	**13**	**123**	**5**	**0**	**0**	**0**	**2**
1986-87	**Philadelphia**	**NHL**	**77**	**2**	**9**	**11**	**124**	**26**	**3**	**4**	**7**	**16**
1987-88	**Philadelphia**	**NHL**	**70**	**3**	**9**	**12**	**57**	**7**	**1**	**0**	**1**	**8**
1988-89	**Toronto**	**NHL**	**80**	**1**	**15**	**16**	**79**	....	....	....	....	....
1989-90	**Toronto**	**NHL**	**79**	**1**	**13**	**14**	**95**	**5**	**1**	**0**	**1**	**2**
1990-91	**Toronto**	**NHL**	**22**	**0**	**0**	**0**	**15**	....	....	....	....	....
	Detroit	**NHL**	**20**	**1**	**3**	**4**	**16**	**1**	**0**	**0**	**0**	**0**
1991-92	**Detroit**	**NHL**	**55**	**3**	**4**	**7**	**53**	**3**	**0**	**0**	**0**	**0**
	NHL Totals		**1027**	**23**	**172**	**195**	**1211**	**97**	**6**	**18**	**24**	**124**

a OHA Third All-Star Team (1977)
b OHA First All-Star Team (1978)

Claimed by **Atlanta** as fill in Expansion Draft, June 13, 1979. Traded to **Philadelphia** by **Calgary** for Mel Bridgman, November 11, 1981. Claimed by **Toronto** in NHL Waiver Draft, October 3, 1988. Traded to **Detroit** by **Toronto** for Detroit's eighth round choice (Robb McIntyre) in 1991 Entry Draft, February 4, 1991. Traded to **Toronto** by **Detroit** for cash, June 10, 1992. Traded to **Ottawa** by **Toronto** for future considerations, July 20, 1992.

MARSHALL, BOBBY

Defense. Shoots left. 6'1", 190 lbs. Born, North York, Ont., April 11, 1972.
(Calgary's 6th choice, 129th overall, in 1991 Entry Draft).

			Regular Season					Playoffs				
Season	Club	Lea	GP	G	A	TP	PIM	GP	G	A	TP	PIM
1990-91	Miami-Ohio	CCHA	37	3	15	18	44	....	....	....	....	....
1991-92	Miami-Ohio	CCHA	40	5	20	25	48	....	....	....	....	....

MARSHALL, GRANT

Right wing. Shoots right. 6'1", 185 lbs. Born, Mississauga, Ont., June 9, 1973.
(Toronto's 2nd choice, 23rd overall, in 1992 Entry Draft).

			Regular Season					Playoffs				
Season	Club	Lea	GP	G	A	TP	PIM	GP	G	A	TP	PIM
1990-91	Ottawa	OHL	26	6	11	17	25	1	0	0	0	0
1991-92	Ottawa	OHL	64	34	100	134	70	11	6	11	17	11

MARSHALL, JASON

Defense. Shoots right. 6'2", 185 lbs. Born, Cranbrook, B.C., February 22, 1971.
(St. Louis' 1st choice, 9th overall, in 1989 Entry Draft).

			Regular Season					Playoffs				
Season	Club	Lea	GP	G	A	TP	PIM	GP	G	A	TP	PIM
1989-90	Cdn. National	....	72	1	11	12	57	....	....	....	....	....
1990-91	Tri-Cities	WHL	59	10	34	44	236	7	1	2	3	20
	Peoria	IHL	....	....	....	....	....	18	0	1	1	48
1991-92	**St. Louis**	**NHL**	**2**	**1**	**0**	**1**	**4**	....	....	....	....	....
	Peoria	IHL	78	4	18	22	178	10	0	1	1	16
	NHL Totals		**2**	**1**	**0**	**1**	**4**	....	....	....	....	....

MARSHALL, PAUL STEVEN

Defense. Shoots left. 6'2", 185 lbs. Born, Quincy, MA, October 22, 1966.
(Philadelphia's 5th choice, 84th overall, in 1985 Entry Draft).

			Regular Season					Playoffs				
Season	Club	Lea	GP	G	A	TP	PIM	GP	G	A	TP	PIM
1986-87	Boston College	H.E.	36	4	10	14	30	....	....	....	....	....
1987-88	Boston College	H.E.	34	12	23	35	50	....	....	....	....	....
1988-89	Boston College	H.E.	40	4	18	22	36	....	....	....	....	....
1989-90						DID NOT PLAY						
1990-91	San Diego	IHL	12	1	1	2	6	....	....	....	....	....
	Albany	AHL	22	4	10	14	6	....	....	....	....	....
1991-92	Kalamazoo	IHL	21	0	2	2	8	....	....	....	....	....
	Dayton	ECHL	36	19	29	48	32	3	1	3	4	20

Signed as a free agent by **Minnesota**, July 20, 1990.

MARTELL, STEVE

Right wing. Shoots right. 5'10", 185 lbs. Born, Sydney, N.S., March 3, 1970.
(Washington's 10th choice, 159th overall, in 1990 Entry Draft).

			Regular Season					Playoffs				
Season	Club	Lea	GP	G	A	TP	PIM	GP	G	A	TP	PIM
1988-89	London	OHL	65	9	17	26	59	21	2	5	7	18
1989-90	London	OHL	63	19	24	43	91	6	1	1	2	10
1990-91a	London	OHL	63	32	40	72	105	7	3	1	4	8
1991-92	Baltimore	AHL	42	5	7	12	120	....	....	....	....	....
	Hampton Rds.	ECHL	20	9	25	34	34	11	4	5	9	47

a OHL Third All-Star Team (1991)

MARTIN, CRAIG

Right wing. Shoots right. 6'2", 219 lbs. Born, Amherst, N.S., January 21, 1971.
(Winnipeg's 6th choice, 98th overall, in 1990 Entry Draft).

			Regular Season					Playoffs				
Season	Club	Lea	GP	G	A	TP	PIM	GP	G	A	TP	PIM
1989-90	Hull	QMJHL	66	14	31	45	299	11	2	1	3	65
1990-91	Hull	QMJHL	18	5	6	11	87	....	....	....	....	....
	St-Hyacinthe	QMJHL	36	8	9	17	166	....	....	....	....	....
1991-92	Moncton	AHL	11	1	1	2	70	....	....	....	....	....
	Fort Wayne	IHL	24	0	0	0	115	....	....	....	....	....

MARTIN, MATT

Defense. Shoots left. 6'3", 190 lbs. Born, Hamden, CT, April 30, 1971.
(Toronto's 4th choice, 66th overall, in 1989 Entry Draft).

			Regular Season					Playoffs				
Season	Club	Lea	GP	G	A	TP	PIM	GP	G	A	TP	PIM
1990-91	U. of Maine	H.E.	35	3	12	15	48	....	....	....	....	....
1991-92	U. of Maine	H.E.	30	4	14	18	46	....	....	....	....	....

MARTINI, DARCY

Defense. Shoots left. 6'4", 220 lbs. Born, Castlegar, B.C., January 30, 1969.
(Edmonton's 8th choice, 162nd overall, in 1989 Entry Draft).

			Regular Season					Playoffs				
Season	Club	Lea	GP	G	A	TP	PIM	GP	G	A	TP	PIM
1988-89	Michigan Tech	WCHA	35	1	2	3	103	....	....	....	....	....
1989-90	Michigan Tech	WCHA	36	3	6	9	151	....	....	....	....	....
1990-91	Michigan Tech	WCHA	38	4	7	11	52	....	....	....	....	....
1991-92	Michigan Tech	WCHA	17	5	13	18	58	....	....	....	....	....

MARTINSON, STEVEN

Left wing. Shoots left. 6'1", 205 lbs. Born, Minnetonka, MN, June 21, 1959.

			Regular Season					Playoffs				
Season	Club	Lea	GP	G	A	TP	PIM	GP	G	A	TP	PIM
1982-83	Toledo	IHL	32	9	10	19	111	....	....	....	....	....
	Birmingham	CHL	43	4	5	9	184	13	1	2	3	*80
1983-84	Tulsa	CHL	42	3	6	9	240	6	0	0	0	43
1984-85	Toledo	IHL	54	4	10	14	300	2	0	0	0	21
1985-86	Hershey	AHL	69	3	6	9	*432	3	0	0	0	56
1986-87	Hershey	AHL	17	0	3	3	85	....	....	....	....	....
	Adirondack	AHL	14	1	1	2	78	11	2	0	2	108
1987-88	**Detroit**	**NHL**	**10**	**1**	**1**	**2**	**84**	....	....	....	....	....
	Adirondack	AHL	32	6	8	14	146	6	1	2	3	66
1988-89	**Montreal**	**NHL**	**25**	**1**	**0**	**1**	**87**	**1**	**0**	**0**	**0**	**10**
	Sherbrooke	AHL	10	5	7	12	61	....	....	....	....	....
1989-90	**Montreal**	**NHL**	**13**	**0**	**0**	**0**	**64**	....	....	....	....	....
	Sherbrooke	AHL	37	6	20	26	113	....	....	....	....	....
1990-91	San Diego	IHL	53	16	24	40	268	....	....	....	....	....
1991-92	**Minnesota**	**NHL**	**1**	**0**	**0**	**0**	**9**	....	....	....	....	....
	San Diego	IHL	70	18	15	33	279	4	1	1	2	15
	NHL Totals		**49**	**2**	**1**	**3**	**244**	**1**	**0**	**0**	**0**	**10**

Signed as a free agent by **Philadelphia**, September 30, 1985. Signed as a free agent by **Detroit**, October 3, 1987. Signed as a free agent by **Montreal**, August 2, 1988. Signed as a free agent by **Winnipeg**, August 28, 1990. Signed as a free agent by **Minnesota**, October 1, 1991.

MARTINYUK, SERGEI (mar-tih-NYOOK)

Right wing. Shoots left. 6', 183 lbs. Born, Rybynsk, Soviet Union, January 30, 1971.
(Montreal's 13th choice, 249th overall, in 1990 Entry Draft).

			Regular Season					Playoffs				
Season	Club	Lea	GP	G	A	TP	PIM	GP	G	A	TP	PIM
1989-90	Torp. Jaroslav	USSR	40	5	1	6	8	....	....	....	....	....
1990-91	Torp. Jaroslav	USSR	37	7	11	18	52	....	....	....	....	....
1991-92	Torp. Jaroslav	CIS	29	12	5	17	32	....	....	....	....	....

MARTTILA, JUKKA (MAHR-tee-lah)

Defense. Shoots left. 6'1", 187 lbs. Born, Tampere, Finland, April 15, 1968.
(Winnipeg's 9th choice, 136th overall, in 1988 Entry Draft).

			Regular Season					Playoffs				
Season	Club	Lea	GP	G	A	TP	PIM	GP	G	A	TP	PIM
1986-87	Tappara	Fin.	33	4	1	5	18	....	....	....	....	....
1987-88	Tappara	Fin.	39	5	7	12	16	....	....	....	....	....
1988-89	Tappara	Fin.	43	11	20	31	32	....	....	....	....	....
1989-90	Tappara	Fin.	44	12	14	26	14	7	2	2	4	4
1990-91	Tappara	Fin.	42	10	21	31	32	3	0	0	0	0
1991-92	Tappara	Fin.	17	2	4	6	14	....	....	....	....	....

MASKARINEC, MARTIN (mahsh-KAH-ree-nehts)

Defense. Shoots left. 6'1", 185 lbs. Born, Prague, Czechoslovakia, February 3, 1969.
(Los Angeles' 9th choice, 186th overall, in 1989 Entry Draft).

			Regular Season					Playoffs				
Season	Club	Lea	GP	G	A	TP	PIM	GP	G	A	TP	PIM
1988-89	Sparta Praha	Czech.	31	3	1	4	....	....	....	....	....	....
1989-90	Sparta Praha	Czech.	46	3	11	14	....	....	....	....	....	....
1990-91	Dukla Trencin	Czech.	51	0	12	12	93	....	....	....	....	....
1991-92	Sparta Praha	Czech.	46	3	8	11	....	....	....	....	....	....

MATHIESON, JIM

Defense. Shoots left. 6'1", 209 lbs. Born, Kindersley, Sask., January 24, 1970.
(Washington's 3rd choice, 59th overall, in 1989 Entry Draft).

			Regular Season					Playoffs				
Season	Club	Lea	GP	G	A	TP	PIM	GP	G	A	TP	PIM
1986-87	Regina	WHL	40	0	9	9	40	3	0	1	1	2
1987-88	Regina	WHL	72	3	12	15	115	4	0	2	2	4
1988-89	Regina	WHL	62	5	22	27	151	....	....	....	....	....
1989-90	**Washington**	**NHL**	**2**	**0**	**0**	**0**	**4**	....	....	....	....	....
	Regina	WHL	67	1	26	27	158	11	0	7	7	16
	Baltimore	AHL	....	....	....	....	....	3	0	0	0	4
1990-91	Baltimore	AHL	65	3	5	8	168	4	1	0	1	6
1991-92	Baltimore	AHL	74	2	9	11	206	....	....	....	....	....
	NHL Totals		**2**	**0**	**0**	**0**	**4**	....	....	....	....	....

MATIKAINEN, PETRI (mah-tee-KAY-nehn)

Defense. Shoots left. 6', 189 lbs. Born, Savonlinna, Finland, January 7, 1967.
(Buffalo's 7th choice, 140th overall, in 1985 Entry Draft).

			Regular Season					Playoffs				
Season	Club	Lea	GP	G	A	TP	PIM	GP	G	A	TP	PIM
1984-85	SapKo	Fin.2	24	0	4	4	34	....	....	....	....	....
1985-86	Oshawa	OHL	53	14	42	56	27	....	....	....	....	....
1986-87	Oshawa	OHL	50	8	34	42	53	21	2	12	14	36
1987-88	Tappara	Fin.	41	5	1	6	58	1	0	2	2	4
1988-89	Tappara	Fin.	44	4	13	17	32	8	0	0	0	10
1989-90	JoKP	Fin.	44	6	8	14	34	....	....	....	....	....
1990-91	JoKP	Fin.	43	16	25	41	35	....	....	....	....	....
1991-92	JoKP	Fin.	42	4	8	12	38	....	....	....	....	....

MATILAINEN, ARI (mah-tee-LAY-nehn)

Left wing. Shoots left. 6'2", 198 lbs. Born, Pieksomaki, Finland, January 22, 1966.
(Minnesota's 7th choice, 190th overall, in 1988 Entry Draft).

			Regular Season					Playoffs				
Season	Club	Lea	GP	G	A	TP	PIM	GP	G	A	TP	PIM
1987-88	Assat	Fin.	44	15	23	38	40	....	....	....	....	....
1988-89	Karpat	Fin.	36	11	10	21	28	....	....	....	....	....
1989-90	Tappara	Fin.	28	8	7	15	30	7	1	4	5	22
1990-91	Tappara	Fin.	41	6	11	17	26	3	0	1	1	4
1991-92	Tappara	Fin.	40	8	7	15	12	....	....	....	....	....

MATTEAU, STEPHANE (mah-TOH)

Left wing. Shoots left. 6'3", 195 lbs. Born, Rouyn-Noranda, Que., September 2, 1969.
(Calgary's 2nd choice, 25th overall, in 1987 Entry Draft).

			Regular Season					Playoffs				
Season	Club	Lea	GP	G	A	TP	PIM	GP	G	A	TP	PIM
1985-86	Hull	QMJHL	60	6	8	14	19	4	0	0	0	0
1986-87	Hull	QMJHL	69	27	48	75	113	8	3	7	10	8
1987-88	Hull	QMJHL	57	17	40	57	179	18	5	14	19	94
1988-89	Hull	QMJHL	59	44	45	89	202	9	8	6	14	30
	Salt Lake	IHL	....	....	....	....	....	9	0	4	4	13
1989-90	Salt Lake	IHL	81	23	35	58	130	10	6	3	9	38
1990-91	**Calgary**	**NHL**	**78**	**15**	**19**	**34**	**93**	**5**	**0**	**1**	**1**	**0**
1991-92	**Calgary**	**NHL**	**4**	**1**	**0**	**1**	**19**	....	....	....	....	....
	Chicago	**NHL**	**20**	**5**	**8**	**13**	**45**	**18**	**4**	**6**	**10**	**24**
	NHL Totals		**102**	**21**	**27**	**48**	**157**	**23**	**4**	**7**	**11**	**24**

Traded to **Chicago** by **Calgary** for Trent Yawney, December 16, 1991.

MATTHEWS, JAMIE

Center. Shoots right. 6'1", 190 lbs. Born, Amherst, N.S., May 25, 1973.
(Chicago's 3rd choice, 44th overall, in 1991 Entry Draft).

			Regular Season					Playoffs				
Season	Club	Lea	GP	G	A	TP	PIM	GP	G	A	TP	PIM
1989-90	Sudbury	OHL	60	16	17	33	25	7	1	0	1	4
1990-91	Sudbury	OHL	66	14	38	52	41	5	3	5	8	8
1991-92	Sudbury	OHL	64	26	69	95	30	11	2	11	13	4

MATUSOVICH, SCOTT

Defense. Shoots left. 6'2", 205 lbs. Born, Southbury, CT, October 31, 1969.
(Calgary's 5th choice, 90th overall, in 1988 Entry Draft).

			Regular Season					Playoffs				
Season	Club	Lea	GP	G	A	TP	PIM	GP	G	A	TP	PIM
1988-89	Yale	ECAC	25	3	11	14	40	....	....	....	....	....
1989-90	Yale	ECAC	28	1	15	16	55	....	....	....	....	....
1990-91	Yale	ECAC	29	3	8	11	48	....	....	....	....	....
1991-92	Yale	ECAC	27	3	13	16	48	....	....	....	....	....

MATVICHUK, RICHARD

Defense. Shoots left. 6'2", 190 lbs. Born, Edmonton, Alta., February 5, 1973.
(Minnesota's 1st choice, 8th overall, in 1991 Entry Draft).

			Regular Season					Playoffs				
Season	Club	Lea	GP	G	A	TP	PIM	GP	G	A	TP	PIM
1989-90	Saskatoon	WHL	56	8	24	32	126	10	2	8	10	16
1990-91	Saskatoon	WHL	68	13	36	49	117	....	....	....	....	....
1991-92a	Saskatoon	WHL	58	14	40	54	126	....	....	....	....	....

a WHL East First All-Star Team (1992)

MAY, ALAN

Right wing. Shoots right. 6'1", 200 lbs. Born, Swan Hills, Alta., January 14, 1965.

			Regular Season					Playoffs				
Season	Club	Lea	GP	G	A	TP	PIM	GP	G	A	TP	PIM
1985-86	Medicine Hat	WHL	6	1	0	1	25	....	....	....	....	....
	N. Westminster	WHL	32	8	9	17	81	....	....	....	....	....
1986-87	Springfield	AHL	4	0	2	2	11	....	....	....	....	....
	Carolina	ACHL	42	23	14	37	310	5	2	2	4	57
1987-88	**Boston**	**NHL**	**3**	**0**	**0**	**0**	**15**	....	....	....	....	....
	Maine	AHL	61	14	11	25	257	....	....	....	....	....
	Nova Scotia	AHL	13	4	1	5	54	4	0	0	0	51
1988-89	**Edmonton**	**NHL**	**3**	**1**	**0**	**1**	**7**	....	....	....	....	....
	Cape Breton	AHL	50	12	13	25	214	....	....	....	....	....
	New Haven	AHL	12	2	8	10	99	16	6	3	9	*105
1989-90	**Washington**	**NHL**	**77**	**7**	**10**	**17**	**339**	**15**	**0**	**0**	**0**	**37**
1990-91	**Washington**	**NHL**	**67**	**4**	**6**	**10**	**264**	**11**	**1**	**1**	**2**	**37**
1991-92	**Washington**	**NHL**	**75**	**6**	**9**	**15**	**221**	**7**	**0**	**0**	**0**	**0**
	NHL Totals		**225**	**18**	**25**	**43**	**846**	**33**	**1**	**1**	**2**	**74**

Signed as a free agent by **Boston**, October 30, 1987. Traded to **Edmonton** by **Boston** for Moe Lemay, March 8, 1988. Traded to **Los Angeles** by **Edmonton** with Jim Wiemer for Brian Wilks and John English, March 7, 1989. Traded to **Washington** by **Los Angeles** for Washington's fifth round choice (Thomas Newman) in 1989 Entry Draft, June 17, 1989.

MAY, BRAD

Left wing. Shoots left. 6', 200 lbs. Born, Toronto, Ont., November 29, 1971.
(Buffalo's 1st choice, 14th overall, in 1990 Entry Draft).

			Regular Season					Playoffs				
Season	Club	Lea	GP	G	A	TP	PIM	GP	G	A	TP	PIM
1988-89	Niagara Falls	OHL	65	8	14	22	304	17	0	1	1	55
1989-90a	Niagara Falls	OHL	61	32	58	90	223	16	9	13	22	64
1990-91a	Niagara Falls	OHL	34	37	32	69	93	14	11	14	25	53
1991-92	**Buffalo**	**NHL**	**69**	**11**	**6**	**17**	**309**	**7**	**1**	**4**	**5**	**2**
	NHL Totals		**69**	**11**	**6**	**17**	**309**	**7**	**1**	**4**	**5**	**2**

a OHL Second All-Star Team (1990, 1991)

MAZUR, JAY

Center/Right wing. Shoots right. 6'2", 205 lbs. Born, Hamilton, Ont., January 22, 1965.
(Vancouver's 12th choice, 230th overall, in 1983 Entry Draft).

			Regular Season					Playoffs				
Season	Club	Lea	GP	G	A	TP	PIM	GP	G	A	TP	PIM
1983-84	Maine	H.E.	34	14	9	23	14	....	....	....	....	....
1984-85	Maine	H.E.	31	0	6	6	20	....	....	....	....	....
1985-86	Maine	H.E.	34	5	7	12	18	....	....	....	....	....
1986-87	Maine	H.E.	39	16	10	26	61	....	....	....	....	....
1987-88	Flint	IHL	39	17	11	28	28	....	....	....	....	....
	Fredericton	AHL	31	14	6	20	28	15	4	2	6	38
1988-89	**Vancouver**	**NHL**	**1**	**0**	**0**	**0**	**0**	....	....	....	....	....
	Milwaukee	IHL	73	33	31	64	86	11	6	5	11	2
1989-90	**Vancouver**	**NHL**	**5**	**0**	**0**	**0**	**4**	....	....	....	....	....
	Milwaukee	IHL	70	20	27	47	63	6	3	0	3	6
1990-91	**Vancouver**	**NHL**	**36**	**11**	**7**	**18**	**14**	**6**	**0**	**1**	**1**	**8**
	Milwaukee	IHL	7	2	3	5	21	....	....	....	....	....
1991-92	**Vancouver**	**NHL**	**5**	**0**	**0**	**0**	**2**	....	....	....	....	....
	Milwaukee	IHL	56	17	20	37	49	5	2	3	5	0
	NHL Totals		**47**	**11**	**7**	**18**	**20**	**6**	**0**	**1**	**1**	**8**

McALPINE, CHRIS

Defense. Shoots right. 6', 190 lbs. Born, Roseville, MN, December 1, 1971.
(New Jersey's 10th choice, 137th overall, in 1990 Entry Draft).

			Regular Season					Playoffs				
Season	Club	Lea	GP	G	A	TP	PIM	GP	G	A	TP	PIM
1990-91	U. Minnesota	WCHA	38	7	9	16	112	....	....	....	....	....
1991-92	U. Minnesota	WCHA	39	3	9	12	126	....	....	....	....	....

McAMMOND, DEAN

Center. Shoots left. 5'11", 185 lbs. Born, Grand Cache, Alta., June 15, 1973.
(Chicago's 1st choice, 22nd overall, in 1991 Entry Draft).

			Regular Season					Playoffs				
Season	Club	Lea	GP	G	A	TP	PIM	GP	G	A	TP	PIM
1989-90	Prince Albert	WHL	53	11	11	22	49	14	2	3	5	18
1990-91	Prince Albert	WHL	71	33	35	68	108	2	0	1	1	6
1991-92	**Chicago**	**NHL**	**5**	**0**	**2**	**2**	**0**	**3**	**0**	**0**	**0**	**2**
	Prince Albert	WHL	63	37	54	91	189	10	12	11	23	26
	NHL Totals		**5**	**0**	**2**	**2**	**0**	**3**	**0**	**0**	**0**	**2**

McBAIN, ANDREW

Right wing. Shoots right. 6'1", 205 lbs. Born, Scarborough, Ont., January 18, 1965.
(Winnipeg's 1st choice, 8th overall, in 1983 Entry Draft).

			Regular Season					Playoffs				
Season	Club	Lea	GP	G	A	TP	PIM	GP	G	A	TP	PIM
1981-82	Niagara Falls	OHL	68	19	25	44	35	5	0	3	3	4
1982-83a	North Bay	OHL	67	33	87	120	61	8	2	6	8	17
1983-84	**Winnipeg**	**NHL**	**78**	**11**	**19**	**30**	**37**	**3**	**2**	**0**	**2**	**0**
1984-85	**Winnipeg**	**NHL**	**77**	**7**	**15**	**22**	**45**	**7**	**1**	**0**	**1**	**0**
1985-86	**Winnipeg**	**NHL**	**28**	**3**	**3**	**6**	**17**	....	....	....	....	....
1986-87	**Winnipeg**	**NHL**	**71**	**11**	**21**	**32**	**106**	**9**	**0**	**2**	**2**	**10**
1987-88	**Winnipeg**	**NHL**	**74**	**32**	**31**	**63**	**145**	**5**	**2**	**5**	**7**	**29**
1988-89	**Winnipeg**	**NHL**	**80**	**37**	**40**	**77**	**71**	....	....	....	....	....
1989-90	**Pittsburgh**	**NHL**	**41**	**5**	**9**	**14**	**51**	....	....	....	....	....
	Vancouver	**NHL**	**26**	**4**	**5**	**9**	**22**	....	....	....	....	....
1990-91	**Vancouver**	**NHL**	**13**	**0**	**5**	**5**	**32**	....	....	....	....	....
	Milwaukee	IHL	47	27	24	51	69	6	2	5	7	12
1991-92	**Vancouver**	**NHL**	**6**	**1**	**0**	**1**	**0**	....	....	....	....	....
	Milwaukee	IHL	65	24	54	78	132	5	1	2	3	10
	NHL Totals		**494**	**111**	**148**	**259**	**526**	**24**	**5**	**7**	**12**	**39**

a OHL Second All-Star Team (1983)

Traded to **Pittsburgh** by **Winnipeg** with Jim Kyte and Randy Gilhen for Randy Cunnyworth, Rick Tabaracci and Dave McLlwain, June 17, 1989. Traded to **Vancouver** by **Pittsburgh** with Dave Capuano and Dan Quinn for Rod Buskas, Barry Pederson and Tony Tanti, January 8, 1990.

McBAIN, JASON

Defense. Shoots right. 6'2", 178 lbs. Born, Ilion, NY, April 12, 1974.
(Hartford's 5th choice, 81st overall, in 1992 Entry Draft).

			Regular Season					Playoffs				
Season	Club	Lea	GP	G	A	TP	PIM	GP	G	A	TP	PIM
1990-91	Lethbridge	WHL	52	2	7	9	39	1	0	0	0	0
1991-92	Lethbridge	WHL	13	0	1	1	12	....	....	....	....	....
	Portland	WHL	54	9	23	32	95	6	1	0	1	13

McBEAN, WAYNE

Defense. Shoots left. 6'2", 190 lbs. Born, Calgary, Alta., February 21, 1969.
(Los Angeles' 1st choice, 4th overall, in 1987 Entry Draft).

			Regular Season					Playoffs				
Season	Club	Lea	GP	G	A	TP	PIM	GP	G	A	TP	PIM
1985-86	Medicine Hat	WHL	67	1	14	15	73	25	1	5	6	36
1986-87a	Medicine Hat	WHL	71	12	41	53	163	20	2	8	10	40
1987-88	**Los Angeles**	**NHL**	**27**	**0**	**1**	**1**	**26**	....	....	....	....	....
	Medicine Hat	WHL	30	15	30	45	48	16	6	17	23	50
1988-89	**Los Angeles**	**NHL**	**33**	**0**	**5**	**5**	**23**	....	....	....	....	....
	New Haven	AHL	7	1	1	2	2	....	....	....	....	....
	NY Islanders	**NHL**	**19**	**0**	**1**	**1**	**12**	....	....	....	....	....
1989-90	**NY Islanders**	**NHL**	**5**	**0**	**1**	**1**	**2**	**2**	**1**	**1**	**2**	**0**
	Springfield	AHL	58	6	33	39	48	17	4	11	15	31
1990-91	**NY Islanders**	**NHL**	**52**	**5**	**14**	**19**	**47**	....	....	....	....	....
	Capital Dist.	AHL	22	9	9	18	19	....	....	....	....	....
1991-92	**NY Islanders**	**NHL**	**25**	**2**	**4**	**6**	**18**	....	....	....	....	....
	NHL Totals		**161**	**7**	**26**	**33**	**128**	**2**	**1**	**1**	**2**	**0**

a WHL East All-Star Team (1987)

Traded to **NY Islanders** by **Los Angeles** with Mark Fitzpatrick and future considerations (Doug Crossman acquired May 23, 1989) for Kelly Hrudey, February 22, 1989.

McCARTHY, BRIAN

Center. Shoots left. 6'2", 190 lbs. Born, Salem, MA, December 6, 1971.
(Buffalo's 2nd choice, 82nd overall, in 1990 Entry Draft).

			Regular Season					Playoffs				
Season	Club	Lea	GP	G	A	TP	PIM	GP	G	A	TP	PIM
1989-90	Pingree	HS	....	25	40	65	....	....	....	....	....	....
1990-91	Providence	H.E.	33	7	6	13	33	....	....	....	....	....
1991-92			DID NOT PLAY									

McCARTHY, JOE

Defense. Shoots left. 6'1", 200 lbs. Born, Bangor, ME, November 17, 1970.
(Toronto's 2nd choice, 9th overall, in 1991 Supplemental Draft).

			Regular Season					Playoffs				
Season	Club	Lea	GP	G	A	TP	PIM	GP	G	A	TP	PIM
1989-90	U. of Vermont	ECAC	31	2	1	3	21	....	....	....	....	....
1990-91	U. of Vermont	ECAC	33	3	7	10	16	....	....	....	....	....
1991-92	U. of Vermont	ECAC	26	2	7	9	21	....	....	....	....	....

McCARTHY, SANDY

Right wing. Shoots right. 6'3", 224 lbs. Born, Toronto, Ont., June 15, 1972.
(Calgary's 3rd choice, 52nd overall, in 1991 Entry Draft).

			Regular Season					Playoffs				
Season	Club	Lea	GP	G	A	TP	PIM	GP	G	A	TP	PIM
1989-90	Laval	QMJHL	65	10	11	21	269	13	6	5	11	67
1990-91	Laval	QMJHL	68	21	19	40	297	....	....	....	....	....
1991-92	Laval	QMJHL	62	39	51	90	326	8	4	5	9	81

McCARTY, DARREN

Right wing. Shoots right. 6'1", 214 lbs. Born, Burnaby, B.C., April 1, 1972.
(Detroit's 2nd choice, 46th overall, in 1992 Entry Draft).

			Regular Season					Playoffs				
Season	Club	Lea	GP	G	A	TP	PIM	GP	G	A	TP	PIM
1990-91	Belleville	OHL	60	30	37	67	151	6	2	2	4	13
1991-92	Belleville	OHL	65	*55	72	127	177	5	1	4	5	13

McCAULEY, WES

Defense. Shoots left. 6', 175 lbs. Born, Toronto, Ont., January 11, 1972.
(Detroit's 7th choice, 150th overall, in 1990 Entry Draft).

			Regular Season					Playoffs				
Season	Club	Lea	GP	G	A	TP	PIM	GP	G	A	TP	PIM
1989-90	Michigan State	CCHA	42	2	7	9	15	....	....	....	....	....
1990-91	Michigan State	CCHA	28	1	2	3	9	....	....	....	....	....
1991-92	Michigan State	CCHA	39	2	10	12	42	....	....	....	....	....

McCLELLAND, KEVIN WILLIAM

Right wing. Shoots right. 6'2", 205 lbs. Born, Oshawa, Ont., July 4, 1962.
(Hartford's 4th choice, 71st overall, in 1980 Entry Draft).

			Regular Season					Playoffs				
Season	Club	Lea	GP	G	A	TP	PIM	GP	G	A	TP	PIM
1980-81	Niagara Falls	OHA	68	36	72	108	186	12	8	13	21	42
1981-82	**Pittsburgh**	**NHL**	**10**	**1**	**4**	**5**	**4**	**5**	**1**	**1**	**2**	**5**
	Niagara Falls	OHL	46	36	47	83	184	....	....	....	....	....
1982-83	**Pittsburgh**	**NHL**	**38**	**5**	**4**	**9**	**73**	....	....	....	....	....
1983-84	**Pittsburgh**	**NHL**	**24**	**2**	**4**	**6**	**62**	....	....	....	....	....
	Baltimore	AHL	3	1	1	2	0	....	....	....	....	....
	Edmonton	**NHL**	**52**	**8**	**20**	**28**	**127**	**18**	**4**	**6**	**10**	**42**
1984-85	**Edmonton**	**NHL**	**62**	**8**	**15**	**23**	**205**	**18**	**1**	**3**	**4**	**75**
1985-86	**Edmonton**	**NHL**	**79**	**11**	**25**	**36**	**266**	**10**	**1**	**0**	**1**	**32**
1986-87	**Edmonton**	**NHL**	**72**	**12**	**13**	**25**	**238**	**21**	**2**	**3**	**5**	**43**
1987-88	**Edmonton**	**NHL**	**74**	**10**	**6**	**16**	**281**	**19**	**2**	**3**	**5**	**68**
1988-89	**Edmonton**	**NHL**	**79**	**6**	**14**	**20**	**161**	**7**	**0**	**2**	**2**	**16**
1989-90	**Edmonton**	**NHL**	**10**	**1**	**1**	**2**	**13**	....	....	....	....	....
	Detroit	**NHL**	**61**	**4**	**5**	**9**	**183**	....	....	....	....	....
1990-91	**Detroit**	**NHL**	**3**	**0**	**0**	**0**	**7**	....	....	....	....	....
	Adirondack	AHL	27	5	14	19	125	....	....	....	....	....
1991-92	**Toronto**	**NHL**	**18**	**0**	**1**	**1**	**33**	....	....	....	....	....
	St. John's	AHL	34	7	15	22	199	5	0	1	1	9
	NHL Totals		**582**	**68**	**112**	**180**	**1653**	**98**	**11**	**18**	**29**	**281**

Traded to **Pittsburgh** by **Hartford** with Pat Boutette as compensation for Hartford's signing of free agent goaltender Greg Millen, June 29, 1981. Traded to **Edmonton** by **Pittsburgh** with Pittsburgh's sixth round choice (Emanuel Viveiros) in 1984 Entry Draft for Tom Roulston, December 5, 1983. Traded to **Detroit** by **Edmonton** with Jimmy Carson and Edmonton's fifth round choice (later traded to Montreal for Rick Green. Montreal selected Brad Layzell) in 1991 Entry Draft for Petr Klima, Joe Murphy, Adam Graves and Jeff Sharples, November 2, 1989. Signed as a free agent by **Toronto**, September 2, 1991.

McCORMACK, BRIAN

Defense. Shoots right. 5'10", 170 lbs. Born, Bloomington, MN, November 11, 1969.
(Detroit's 7th choice, 164th overall, in 1988 Entry Draft).

			Regular Season					Playoffs				
Season	Club	Lea	GP	G	A	TP	PIM	GP	G	A	TP	PIM
1988-89	Harvard	ECAC	31	0	8	8	16	....	....	....	....	....
1989-90	Harvard	ECAC	27	2	3	5	36	....	....	....	....	....
1990-91	Harvard	ECAC	28	0	8	8	37	....	....	....	....	....
1991-92	Harvard	ECAC	26	0	5	5	24	....	....	....	....	....

McCOSH, SHAWN

Center. Shoots right. 6', 188 lbs. Born, Oshawa, Ont., June 5, 1969.
(Detroit's 5th choice, 95th overall, in 1989 Entry Draft).

			Regular Season					Playoffs				
Season	Club	Lea	GP	G	A	TP	PIM	GP	G	A	TP	PIM
1986-87	Hamilton	OHL	50	11	17	28	49	6	1	0	1	2
1987-88	Hamilton	OHL	64	17	36	53	96	14	6	8	14	14
1988-89	Niagara Falls	OHL	56	41	62	103	75	14	4	13	17	23
1989-90	Niagara Falls	OHL	9	6	10	16	24	....	....	....	....	....
	Hamilton	OHL	39	24	28	52	65	....	....	....	....	....
1990-91	New Haven	AHL	66	16	21	37	104	....	....	....	....	....
1991-92	**Los Angeles**	**NHL**	**4**	**0**	**0**	**0**	**4**	....	....	....	....	....
	Phoenix	IHL	71	21	32	53	118	....	....	....	....	....
	New Haven	AHL	....	....	....	....	....	5	0	1	1	0
	NHL Totals		**4**	**0**	**0**	**0**	**4**	....	....	....	....	....

Traded to **Los Angeles** by **Detroit** for future considerations, August 15, 1990.

McCRIMMON, BYRON (BRAD)

Defense. Shoots left. 5'11", 197 lbs. Born, Dodsland, Sask., March 29, 1959.
(Boston's 2nd choice, 15th overall, in 1979 Entry Draft).

			Regular Season					Playoffs				
Season	Club	Lea	GP	G	A	TP	PIM	GP	G	A	TP	PIM
1977-78ab	Brandon	WHL	65	19	78	97	245	8	2	11	13	20
1978-79a	Brandon	WHL	66	24	74	98	139	22	9	19	28	34
1979-80	Boston	NHL	72	5	11	16	94	10	1	1	2	28
1980-81	Boston	NHL	78	11	18	29	148	3	0	1	1	2
1981-82	Boston	NHL	78	1	8	9	83	2	0	0	0	2
1982-83	Philadelphia	NHL	79	4	21	25	61	3	0	0	0	4
1983-84	Philadelphia	NHL	71	0	24	24	76	1	0	0	0	4
1984-85	Philadelphia	NHL	66	8	35	43	81	11	2	1	3	15
1985-86	Philadelphia	NHL	80	13	43	56	85	5	2	0	2	2
1986-87	Philadelphia	NHL	71	10	29	39	52	26	3	5	8	30
1987-88cd	Calgary	NHL	80	7	35	42	98	9	2	3	5	22
1988-89	Calgary	NHL	72	5	17	22	96	22	0	3	3	30
1989-90	Calgary	NHL	79	4	15	19	78	6	0	2	2	8
1990-91	Detroit	NHL	64	0	13	13	81	7	1	1	2	21
1991-92	Detroit	NHL	79	7	22	29	118	11	0	1	1	8
	NHL Totals		969	75	291	366	1151	116	11	18	29	176

a WHL First All-Star Team (1978, 1979)
b Named WHL's Top Defenseman (1978)
c NHL Second All-Star Team (1988)
d NHL Plus/Minus Leader (1988)

Played in NHL All-Star Game (1988)

Traded to **Philadelphia** by **Boston** for Pete Peeters, June 9, 1982. Traded to **Calgary** by **Philadelphia** for Calgary's third round pick in 1988 Entry Draft (Dominic Roussel) and first round pick — acquired March 6, 1988 by Toronto — in 1989 Entry Draft, August 26, 1987. Toronto acquired Calgary's first round pick in 1989 Entry Draft from Philadelphia in deal for Ken Wregget, March 6, 1988. Toronto selected Steve Bancroft. Traded to **Detroit** by **Calgary** for Detroit's second round choice – later traded to New Jersey (David Harlock) – in 1990 Entry Draft, June 15, 1990.

McDONOUGH, HUBIE

Center. Shoots left 5'9", 180 lbs. Born, Manchester, NH, July 8, 1963.

			Regular Season					Playoffs				
Season	Club	Lea	GP	G	A	TP	PIM	GP	G	A	TP	PIM
1986-87	Flint	IHL	82	27	52	79	59	6	3	2	5	0
1987-88	New Haven	AHL	78	30	29	59	43	....	....	....	....	....
1988-89	Los Angeles	NHL	4	0	1	1	0	....	....	....	....	....
	New Haven	AHL	74	37	55	92	41	17	10	*21	*31	6
1989-90	Los Angeles	NHL	22	3	4	7	10	....	....	....	....	....
	NY Islanders	NHL	54	18	11	29	26	5	1	0	1	4
1990-91	NY Islanders	NHL	52	6	6	12	10	....	....	....	....	....
	Capital Dist.	AHL	17	9	9	18	4	....	....	....	....	....
1991-92	NY Islanders	NHL	33	7	2	9	15	....	....	....	....	....
	Capital Dist.	AHL	21	11	18	29	14	....	....	....	....	....
	NHL Totals		165	34	24	58	61	5	1	0	1	4

Signed as a free agent by **Los Angeles**, April 18, 1988. Traded to **NY Islanders** by **Los Angeles** with Ken Baumgartner for Mikko Makela, November 29, 1989.

McDOUGALL, WILLIAM HENRY

Center. Shoots right. 6', 185 lbs. Born, Mississauga, Ont., August 10, 1966.

			Regular Season					Playoffs				
Season	Club	Lea	GP	G	A	TP	PIM	GP	G	A	TP	PIM
1988-89	Pt. Basques	Sr.	26	20	41	61	129	....	....	....	....	....
1989-90abc	Erie	ECHL	57	80	68	148	226	7	5	5	10	20
	Adirondack	AHL	11	10	7	17	4	2	1	1	2	2
1990-91	Detroit	NHL	2	0	1	1	0	1	0	0	0	0
	Adirondack	AHL	71	47	52	99	192	2	1	2	3	2
1991-92	Adirondack	AHL	45	28	24	52	112	....	....	....	....	....
	Cape Breton	AHL	22	8	18	26	36	4	0	1	1	8
	NHL Totals		2	0	1	1	0	1	0	0	0	0

a Named ECHL Most Valuable Player (1990)
b Named ECHL Rookie of the Year (1990)
c ECHL First Team All-Star (1990)

Signed as a free agent by **Detroit**, January 9, 1990. Traded to **Edmonton** by **Detroit** for Max Middendorf, February 22, 1992.

McEACHERN, SHAWN

Center. Shoots left. 6'1", 180 lbs. Born, Waltham, MA, February 28, 1969.
(Pittsburgh's 6th choice, 110th overall, in 1987 Entry Draft).

			Regular Season					Playoffs				
Season	Club	Lea	GP	G	A	TP	PIM	GP	G	A	TP	PIM
1988-89	Boston U.	H.E.	36	20	28	48	32	....	....	....	....	....
1989-90a	Boston U.	H.E.	43	25	31	56	78	....	....	....	....	....
1990-91bc	Boston U.	H.E.	41	34	48	82	43	....	....	....	....	....
1991-92	U.S. National	....	57	26	23	49	38	....	....	....	....	....
	U.S. Olympic	....	8	1	0	1	10	....	....	....	....	....
	Pittsburgh	NHL	15	0	4	4	0	19	2	7	9	4
	NHL Totals		15	0	4	4	0	19	2	7	9	4

a Hockey East Second All-Star Team (1990)
b Hockey East First All-Star Team (1991)
c NCAA East First All-American Team (1991)

McFARLANE, SHANE

Center. Shoots left. 5'10", 165 lbs. Born, Warroad, MN, September 4, 1968.
(Buffalo's 1st choice, 24th overall, in 1990 Supplemental Draft).

			Regular Season					Playoffs				
Season	Club	Lea	GP	G	A	TP	PIM	GP	G	A	TP	PIM
1987-88	North Dakota	WCHA	27	0	1	1	8	....	....	....	....	....
1988-89	North Dakota	WCHA	30	1	4	5	8	....	....	....	....	....
1989-90	North Dakota	WCHA	22	3	2	5	10	....	....	....	....	....
1990-91	North Dakota	WCHA	1	0	0	0	2	....	....	....	....	....
1991-92	Erie	ECHL	36	10	18	28	29	....	....	....	....	....

McGEE, CHRIS

Center. Shoots right. 6'2", 175 lbs. Born, Pearl River, NY, April 18, 1970.
(St. Louis' 1st choice, 27th overall, in 1991 Supplemental Draft).

			Regular Season					Playoffs				
Season	Club	Lea	GP	G	A	TP	PIM	GP	G	A	TP	PIM
1989-90	Babson	NCAA	31	20	12	32	10	....	....	....	....	....
1990-91	Babson	NCAA	28	22	23	45	6	....	....	....	....	....
1991-92	Babson	NCAA	28	13	22	35	10	....	....	....	....	....

McGILL, ROBERT PAUL (BOB)

Defense. Shoots right. 6'1", 193 lbs. Born, Edmonton, Alta., April 27, 1962.
(Toronto's 2nd choice, 26th overall, in 1980 Entry Draft).

			Regular Season					Playoffs				
Season	Club	Lea	GP	G	A	TP	PIM	GP	G	A	TP	PIM
1979-80	Victoria	WHL	70	3	18	21	230	15	0	5	5	64
1980-81	Victoria	WHL	66	5	36	41	295	11	1	5	6	67
1981-82	Toronto	NHL	68	1	10	11	263	....	....	....	....	....
1982-83	Toronto	NHL	30	0	0	0	146	....	....	....	....	....
	St. Catharines	AHL	32	2	5	7	95	....	....	....	....	....
1983-84	Toronto	NHL	11	0	2	2	51	....	....	....	....	....
	St. Catharines	AHL	55	1	15	16	217	6	0	0	0	26
1984-85	Toronto	NHL	72	0	5	5	250	....	....	....	....	....
1985-86	Toronto	NHL	61	1	4	5	141	9	0	0	0	35
1986-87	Toronto	NHL	56	1	4	5	103	3	0	0	0	0
1987-88	Chicago	NHL	67	4	7	11	131	3	0	0	0	2
1988-89	Chicago	NHL	68	0	4	4	155	16	0	0	0	33
1989-90	Chicago	NHL	69	2	10	12	204	5	0	0	0	2
1990-91	Chicago	NHL	77	4	5	9	151	5	0	0	0	2
1991-92	San Jose	NHL	62	3	1	4	70	....	....	....	....	....
	Detroit	NHL	12	0	0	0	21	8	0	0	0	14
	NHL Totals		653	16	52	68	1686	49	0	0	0	88

Traded to **Chicago** by **Toronto** with Steve Thomas and Rick Vaive for Al Secord and Ed Olczyk, September 3, 1987. Claimed by **San Jose** from **Chicago** in Expansion Draft, May 30, 1991. Traded to **Detroit** by **San Jose** with Vancouver's eighth round choice - acquired in Ken Hammond trade. Detroit chose C.J. Denomme - in 1992 Entry Draft, March 10, 1992. Claimed by **Tampa Bay** from **Detroit** in Expansion Draft, June 18, 1992.

McGILL, RYAN

Defense. Shoots right. 6'2", 197 lbs. Born, Sherwood Park, Alta., February 28, 1969.
(Chicago's 2nd choice, 29th overall, in 1987 Entry Draft).

			Regular Season					Playoffs				
Season	Club	Lea	GP	G	A	TP	PIM	GP	G	A	TP	PIM
1985-86	Lethbridge	WHL	64	5	10	15	171	10	0	1	1	9
1986-87	Swift Current	WHL	72	12	36	48	226	4	1	0	1	9
1987-88	Medicine Hat	WHL	67	5	30	35	224	15	7	3	10	47
1988-89	Saginaw	IHL	8	2	0	2	12	6	0	0	0	42
	Medicine Hat	WHL	57	26	45	71	172	3	0	2	2	15
1989-90	Indianapolis	IHL	77	11	17	28	215	14	2	2	4	29
1990-91	Halifax	AHL	7	0	4	4	6	....	....	....	....	....
a	Indianapolis	IHL	63	11	40	51	200	....	....	....	....	....
1991-92	Chicago	NHL	9	0	2	2	20	....	....	....	....	....
	Indianapolis	IHL	40	7	19	26	170	....	....	....	....	....
	Hershey	AHL	17	3	5	8	67	6	1	1	2	4
	NHL Totals		9	0	2	2	20	....	....	....	....	....

a IHL Second All-Star Team (1991)

Traded to **Quebec** by **Chicago** with Mike McNeil for Paul Gillis and Dan Vincelette, March 5, 1991. Traded to **Chicago** by **Quebec** for Mike Dagenais, September 25, 1991. Traded to **Philadelphia** by **Chicago** for Tony Horacek, February 7, 1992.

McGOWAN, CAL

Center. Shoots left. 6'1", 185 lbs. Born, Sydney, N.S., June 19, 1970.
(Minnesota's 3rd choice, 70th overall, in 1990 Entry Draft).

			Regular Season					Playoffs				
Season	Club	Lea	GP	G	A	TP	PIM	GP	G	A	TP	PIM
1988-89	Kamloops	WHL	72	21	31	52	44	....	....	....	....	....
1989-90	Kamloops	WHL	71	33	45	78	76	17	4	5	9	42
1990-91a	Kamloops	WHL	71	58	81	139	147	12	7	7	14	24
1991-92	Kalamazoo	IHL	77	13	30	43	62	1	0	0	0	2

a WHL West First All-Star Team (1991)

McHUGH, MICHAEL (MIKE)

Left wing. Shoots left. 5'10", 190 lbs. Born, Bowdoin, MA, August 16, 1965.
(Minnesota's 1st choice, 1st overall, in 1988 Supplemental Draft).

			Regular Season					Playoffs				
Season	Club	Lea	GP	G	A	TP	PIM	GP	G	A	TP	PIM
1984-85	U. of Maine	H.E.	25	9	8	17	9	....	....	....	....	....
1985-86	U. of Maine	H.E.	38	9	10	19	24	....	....	....	....	....
1986-87	U. of Maine	H.E.	42	21	29	50	40	....	....	....	....	....
1987-88	U. of Maine	H.E.	44	29	37	66	90	....	....	....	....	....
1988-89	Minnesota	NHL	3	0	0	0	2	....	....	....	....	....
	Kalamazoo	IHL	70	17	29	46	89	6	3	1	4	17
1989-90	Minnesota	NHL	3	0	0	0	0	....	....	....	....	....
	Kalamazoo	IHL	73	14	17	31	96	10	0	6	6	16
1990-91	Minnesota	NHL	6	0	0	0	0	....	....	....	....	....
	Kalamazoo	IHL	69	27	38	65	82	11	3	8	11	6
1991-92	San Jose	NHL	8	1	0	1	14	....	....	....	....	....
	Springfield	AHL	70	23	31	54	51	11	4	7	11	25
	NHL Totals		20	1	0	1	16	....	....	....	....	....

Claimed by **San Jose** from **Minnesota** in Dispersal Draft, May 30, 1991. Traded to **Hartford** by **San Jose** for Paul Fenton, October 18, 1991.

McINNIS, MARTY

Center. Shoots right. 5'10", 165 lbs. Born, Weymouth, MA, June 2, 1970.
(NY Islanders' 10th choice, 163rd overall, in 1988 Entry Draft).

			Regular Season					Playoffs				
Season	Club	Lea	GP	G	A	TP	PIM	GP	G	A	TP	PIM
1988-89	Boston College	H.E.	39	13	19	32	8	....	....	....	....	....
1989-90	Boston College	H.E.	41	24	29	53	43	....	....	....	....	....
1990-91	Boston College	H.E.	38	21	36	57	40	....	....	....	....	....
1991-92	U.S. National	....	54	15	19	34	20	....	....	....	....	....
	U.S. Olympic	....	8	6	2	8	4	....	....	....	....	....
	NY Islanders	NHL	15	3	5	8	0	....	....	....	....	....
	NHL Totals		15	3	5	8	0	....	....	....	....	....

McINTYRE, IAN

Defense. Shoots left. 6', 184 lbs. Born, Montreal, Que., February 12, 1974.
(Quebec's 5th choice, 76th overall, in 1992 Entry Draft).

			Regular Season					Playoffs				
Season	Club	Lea	GP	G	A	TP	PIM	GP	G	A	TP	PIM
1990-91	Bourassa	Midget	40	9	32	41	29	....	....	....	....	....
1991-92	Beauport	QMJHL	63	29	32	61	250	....	....	....	....	....

McINTYRE, JOHN

Center. Shoots left. 6'1", 180 lbs. Born, Ravenswood, Ont., April 29, 1969.
(Toronto's 3rd choice, 49th overall, in 1987 Entry Draft).

			Regular Season					Playoffs				
Season	Club	Lea	GP	G	A	TP	PIM	GP	G	A	TP	PIM
1985-86	Guelph	OHL	30	4	6	10	25	20	1	5	6	31
1986-87	Guelph	OHL	47	8	22	30	95	....	....	....	....	....
1987-88	Guelph	OHL	39	24	18	42	109	....	....	....	....	....
1988-89	Guelph	OHL	52	30	26	56	129	7	5	4	9	25
	Newmarket	AHL	3	0	2	2	7	5	1	1	2	20
1989-90	**Toronto**	**NHL**	**59**	**5**	**12**	**17**	**117**	**2**	**0**	**0**	**0**	**2**
	Newmarket	AHL	6	2	2	4	12	....	....	....	....	....
1990-91	**Toronto**	**NHL**	**13**	**0**	**3**	**3**	**25**	....	....	....	....	....
	Los Angeles	**NHL**	**56**	**8**	**5**	**13**	**115**	**12**	**0**	**1**	**1**	**24**
1991-92	**Los Angeles**	**NHL**	**73**	**5**	**19**	**24**	**100**	**6**	**0**	**4**	**4**	**12**
	NHL Totals		**201**	**18**	**39**	**57**	**357**	**20**	**0**	**5**	**5**	**38**

Traded to **Los Angeles** by **Toronto** for Mike Krushelnyski, November 9, 1990.

McINTYRE, ROBB

Left wing. Shoots left. 6', 180 lbs. Born, Royal Oak, MI, April 27, 1972.
(Toronto's 10th choice, 164th overall, in 1991 Entry Draft).

			Regular Season					Playoffs				
Season	Club	Lea	GP	G	A	TP	PIM	GP	G	A	TP	PIM
1990-91	Dubuque	USHL	43	22	32	54	118	....	....	....	....	....
1991-92	Ferris State	CCHA	32	4	3	7	48	....	....	....	....	....

McKAY, RANDY

Right wing. Shoots right. 6'1", 185 lbs. Born, Montreal, Que., January 25, 1967.
(Detroit's 6th choice, 113th overall, in 1985 Entry Draft).

			Regular Season					Playoffs				
Season	Club	Lea	GP	G	A	TP	PIM	GP	G	A	TP	PIM
1984-85	Michigan Tech	WCHA	25	4	5	9	32	....	....	....	....	....
1985-86	Michigan Tech	WCHA	40	12	22	34	46	....	....	....	....	....
1986-87	Michigan Tech	WCHA	39	5	11	16	46	....	....	....	....	....
1987-88	Michigan Tech	WCHA	41	17	24	41	70	....	....	....	....	....
	Adirondack	AHL	10	0	3	3	12	6	0	4	4	0
1988-89	**Detroit**	**NHL**	**3**	**0**	**0**	**0**	**0**	**2**	**0**	**0**	**0**	**2**
	Adirondack	AHL	58	29	34	63	170	14	4	7	11	60
1989-90	**Detroit**	**NHL**	**33**	**3**	**6**	**9**	**51**	....	....	....	....	....
	Adirondack	AHL	36	16	23	39	99	6	3	0	3	35
1990-91	**Detroit**	**NHL**	**47**	**1**	**7**	**8**	**183**	**5**	**0**	**1**	**1**	**41**
1991-92	**New Jersey**	**NHL**	**80**	**17**	**16**	**33**	**246**	**7**	**1**	**3**	**4**	**10**
	NHL Totals		**163**	**21**	**29**	**50**	**480**	**14**	**1**	**4**	**5**	**53**

Acquired by **New Jersey** from **Detroit** with Dave Barr as compensation for Detroit's signing of free agent Troy Crowder, September 9, 1991.

McKEE, BRIAN

Defense. Shoots left. 5'11", 185 lbs. Born, Willowdale, Ont., December 13, 1964.

			Regular Season					Playoffs				
Season	Club	Lea	GP	G	A	TP	PIM	GP	G	A	TP	PIM
1988-89	Fort Wayne	IHL	47	8	22	30	42	....	....	....	....	....
1989-90	Fort Wayne	IHL				UNAVAILABLE						
1990-91	Fort Wayne	IHL	67	30	34	64	53	9	1	9	10	16
1991-92	Peoria	IHL	65	15	38	53	54	6	1	1	2	12

Signed as a free agent by **St. Louis**, August 7, 1991.

McKEE, MIKE

Defense. Shoots right. 6'3", 190 lbs. Born, Toronto, Ont., June 18, 1969.
(Quebec's 1st choice, 1st overall, in 1990 Supplemental Draft).

			Regular Season					Playoffs				
Season	Club	Lea	GP	G	A	TP	PIM	GP	G	A	TP	PIM
1988-89	Princeton	ECAC	16	2	1	3	14	....	....	....	....	....
1989-90a	Princeton	ECAC	26	7	18	25	18	....	....	....	....	....
1990-91	Princeton	ECAC	15	1	4	5	16	....	....	....	....	....
1991-92	Princeton	ECAC	27	12	17	29	34	....	....	....	....	....

a ECAC Second All-Star Team (1990)

McKEGNEY, ANTHONY SYIIYD (TONY) (ma-KEG-nee)

Left wing. Shoots left. 6'1", 200 lbs. Born, Montreal, Que., February 15, 1958.
(Buffalo's 2nd choice, 32nd overall, in 1978 Amateur Draft).

			Regular Season					Playoffs				
Season	Club	Lea	GP	G	A	TP	PIM	GP	G	A	TP	PIM
1974-75	Kingston	OMJHL	52	27	48	75	36	....	....	....	....	....
1975-76	Kingston	OHA	65	24	56	80	20	....	....	....	....	....
1976-77a	Kingston	OHA	66	58	77	135	30	14	13	10	23	14
1977-78b	Kingston	OHA	55	43	49	92	19	5	3	3	6	0
1978-79	**Buffalo**	**NHL**	**52**	**8**	**14**	**22**	**10**	**2**	**0**	**1**	**1**	**0**
	Hershey	AHL	24	21	18	39	4	1	0	0	0	0
1979-80	**Buffalo**	**NHL**	**80**	**23**	**29**	**52**	**24**	**14**	**3**	**4**	**7**	**2**
1980-81	**Buffalo**	**NHL**	**80**	**37**	**32**	**69**	**24**	**8**	**5**	**3**	**8**	**2**
1981-82	**Buffalo**	**NHL**	**73**	**23**	**29**	**52**	**41**	**4**	**0**	**0**	**0**	**2**
1982-83	**Buffalo**	**NHL**	**78**	**36**	**37**	**73**	**18**	**10**	**3**	**1**	**4**	**4**
1983-84	**Quebec**	**NHL**	**75**	**24**	**27**	**51**	**23**	**7**	**0**	**0**	**0**	**0**
1984-85	**Quebec**	**NHL**	**30**	**12**	**9**	**21**	**12**	....	....	....	....	....
	Minnesota	**NHL**	**27**	**11**	**13**	**24**	**4**	**9**	**8**	**6**	**14**	**0**
1985-86	**Minnesota**	**NHL**	**70**	**15**	**25**	**40**	**48**	**5**	**2**	**1**	**3**	**22**
1986-87	**Minnesota**	**NHL**	**11**	**2**	**3**	**5**	**16**	....	....	....	....	....
	NY Rangers	**NHL**	**64**	**29**	**17**	**46**	**56**	**6**	**0**	**0**	**0**	**12**
1987-88	**St. Louis**	**NHL**	**80**	**40**	**38**	**78**	**82**	**9**	**3**	**6**	**9**	**8**
1988-89	**St. Louis**	**NHL**	**71**	**25**	**17**	**42**	**58**	**3**	**0**	**1**	**1**	**0**
1989-90	**Detroit**	**NHL**	**14**	**2**	**1**	**3**	**8**	....	....	....	....	....
	Quebec	**NHL**	**48**	**16**	**11**	**27**	**45**	....	....	....	....	....
1990-91	**Quebec**	**NHL**	**50**	**17**	**16**	**33**	**44**	....	....	....	....	....
	Chicago	**NHL**	**9**	**0**	**1**	**1**	**4**	**2**	**0**	**0**	**0**	**4**
1991-92	Varese	Italy	16	15	13	28	70	6	8	2	10	12
	NHL Totals		**912**	**320**	**319**	**639**	**517**	**79**	**24**	**23**	**47**	**56**

a OHA First All-Star Team (1977)
b OHA Second All-Star Team (1978)

Traded to **Quebec** by **Buffalo** with Andre Savard, J.F. Sauve and Buffalo's third round choice (Iirvo Jarvi) in 1983 Entry Draft for Real Cloutier and Quebec's first round choice (Adam Creighton) in 1983 Entry Draft, June 8, 1983. Traded to **Minnesota** by **Quebec** with Bo Berglund for Brent Ashton and Brad Maxwell, December 14, 1984. Traded to **NY Rangers** by **Minnesota** with Curt Giles and Minnesota's second round choice (Troy Mallette) in 1988 Entry Draft for Bob Brooke and NY Rangers' rights to Minnesota's fourth round choice (Jeffery Stolp) in 1988 Entry Draft previously acquired by NY Rangers in Mark Pavelich deal, November 13, 1986. Traded to **St. Louis** by NY Rangers with Bob Whistle for Bruce Bell and future considerations, May 28, 1987. Traded to **Detroit** by St. Louis with Bernie Federko for Adam Oates and Paul MacLean, June 15, 1989. Traded to **Quebec** by **Detroit** for Robert Picard and Greg C. Adams, December 4, 1989. Traded to **Chicago** by **Quebec** for Jacques Cloutier, January 29, 1991.

McKENZIE, JIM

Left wing/Defense. Shoots left. 6'3", 205 lbs. Born, Gull Lake, Sask., November 3, 1969.
(Hartford's 3rd choice, 73rd overall, in 1989 Entry Draft).

			Regular Season					Playoffs				
Season	Club	Lea	GP	G	A	TP	PIM	GP	G	A	TP	PIM
1985-86	Moose Jaw	WHL	3	0	2	2	0	....	....	....	....	....
1986-87	Moose Jaw	WHL	65	5	3	8	125	9	0	0	0	7
1987-88	Moose Jaw	WHL	62	1	17	18	134	....	....	....	....	....
1988-89	Victoria	WHL	67	15	27	42	176	8	1	4	5	30
1989-90	**Hartford**	**NHL**	**5**	**0**	**0**	**0**	**4**	....	....	....	....	....
	Binghamton	AHL	56	4	12	16	149	....	....	....	....	....
1990-91	**Hartford**	**NHL**	**41**	**4**	**3**	**7**	**108**	**6**	**0**	**0**	**0**	**8**
	Springfield	AHL	24	3	4	7	102	....	....	....	....	....
1991-92	**Hartford**	**NHL**	**67**	**5**	**1**	**6**	**87**	....	....	....	....	....
	NHL Totals		**113**	**9**	**4**	**13**	**199**	**6**	**0**	**0**	**0**	**8**

McKIM, ANDREW HARRY

Center. Shoots right. 5'8", 175 lbs. Born, St. John, N.B., July 6, 1970.

			Regular Season					Playoffs				
Season	Club	Lea	GP	G	A	TP	PIM	GP	G	A	TP	PIM
1988-89	Verdun	QMJHL	68	50	56	106	36	....	....	....	....	....
1989-90ab	Hull	QMJHL	70	66	84	130	44	11	8	10	18	8
1990-91	Salt Lake	IHL	74	30	30	60	48	4	0	2	2	6
1991-92	St. John's	AHL	79	43	50	93	79	16	11	12	23	4

a QMJHL First All-Star Team (1990)
b QMJHL Player of the Year (1990)

Signed as a free agent by **Calgary**, October 5, 1990. Signed as a free agent by **Boston**, July 23, 1992.

McLAUGHLIN, MICHAEL

Left wing. Shoots right. 6'1", 175 lbs. Born, Longmeadow, MA, March 29, 1970.
(Buffalo's 7th choice, 118th overall, in 1988 Entry Draft).

			Regular Season					Playoffs				
Season	Club	Lea	GP	G	A	TP	PIM	GP	G	A	TP	PIM
1988-89	U. of Vermont	ECAC	32	5	6	11	12	....	....	....	....	....
1989-90	U. of Vermont	ECAC	29	11	12	23	37	....	....	....	....	....
1990-91	U. of Vermont	ECAC	32	12	14	26	34	....	....	....	....	....
1991-92	U. of Vermont	ECAC	30	9	9	18	34	....	....	....	....	....

McLAUGHLIN, PETER

Defense. Shoots left. 6'3", 190 lbs. Born, Norwood, MA, June 29, 1973.
(Pittsburgh's 8th choice, 170th overall, in 1991 Entry Draft).

			Regular Season					Playoffs				
Season	Club	Lea	GP	G	A	TP	PIM	GP	G	A	TP	PIM
1990-91	Belmont Hills	HS	28	12	18	30	8	....	....	....	....	....
1991-92	Belmont Hills	HS	22	22	18	40	24	....	....	....	....	....

McLEAN, JEFF

Center. Shoots left. 5'10", 185 lbs. Born, Port Moody, B.C., October 6, 1969.
(San Jose's 1st choice, 1st overall, in 1991 Supplemental Draft).

			Regular Season					Playoffs				
Season	Club	Lea	GP	G	A	TP	PIM	GP	G	A	TP	PIM
1989-90	North Dakota	WCHA	45	10	16	26	42	....	....	....	....	....
1990-91	North Dakota	WCHA	42	19	26	45	22	....	....	....	....	....
1991-92	North Dakota	WCHA	38	27	43	70	40	....	....	....	....	....

McLLWAIN, DAVE (MA-kuhl-WAYN)

Center/Right wing. Shoots left. 6', 190 lbs. Born, Seaforth, Ont., January 9, 1967.
(Pittsburgh's 9th choice, 172nd overall, in 1986 Entry Draft).

			Regular Season					Playoffs				
Season	Club	Lea	GP	G	A	TP	PIM	GP	G	A	TP	PIM
1984-85	Kitchener	OHL	61	13	21	34	29	....	....	....	....	....
1985-86	Kitchener	OHL	13	7	7	14	12	....	....	....	....	....
	North Bay	OHL	51	30	28	58	25	10	4	4	8	2
1986-87a	North Bay	OHL	60	46	73	119	35	24	7	18	25	40
1987-88	Pittsburgh	NHL	66	11	8	19	40	....	....	....	....	....
	Muskegon	IHL	9	4	6	10	23	6	2	3	5	8
1988-89	Pittsburgh	NHL	24	1	2	3	4	3	0	1	1	0
	Muskegon	IHL	46	37	35	72	51	7	8	2	10	6
1989-90	Winnipeg	NHL	80	25	26	51	60	7	0	1	1	2
1990-91	Winnipeg	NHL	60	14	11	25	46	....	....	....	....	....
1991-92	Winnipeg	NHL	3	1	1	2	2	....	....	....	....	....
	Buffalo	NHL	5	0	0	0	2	....	....	....	....	....
	NY Islanders	NHL	54	8	15	23	28	....	....	....	....	....
	Toronto	NHL	11	1	2	3	4	....	....	....	....	....
	NHL Totals		303	61	65	126	186	10	0	2	2	2

a OHL Second All-Star Team (1987)

Traded to **Winnipeg** by **Pittsburgh** with Randy Cunneyworth and Rick Tabaracci for Jim Kyte, Andrew McBain and Randy Gilhen, June 17, 1989. Traded to **Buffalo** by **Winnipeg** with Gord Donnelly, Winnipeg's fifth round choice (Yuri Khmylev) in 1992 Entry Draft and future considerations for Darrin Shannon, Mike Hartman and Dean Kennedy, October 11, 1991. Traded to **NY Islanders** by **Buffalo** with Pierre Turgeon, Uwe Krupp and Benoit Hogue for Pat Lafontaine, Randy Hillier, Randy Wood and future considerations, October 25, 1991. Traded to **Toronto** by **NY Islanders** with Ken Baumgartner for Daniel Marois and Claude Loiselle, March 10, 1992.

McNEILL, MICHAEL

Right wing. Shoots left. 6'1", 195 lbs. Born, Winona, MN, July 22, 1966.
(St. Louis' 1st choice, 14th overall, in 1988 Supplemental Draft).

			Regular Season					Playoffs				
Season	Club	Lea	GP	G	A	TP	PIM	GP	G	A	TP	PIM
1984-85	Notre Dame	NCAA	28	16	26	42	12	....	....	....	....	....
1985-86	Notre Dame	NCAA	34	18	29	47	32	....	....	....	....	....
1986-87	Notre Dame	NCAA	30	21	16	37	24	....	....	....	....	....
1987-88	Notre Dame	NCAA	32	28	44	72	12	....	....	....	....	....
1988-89	Moncton	AHL	1	0	0	0	0	....	....	....	....	....
	Fort Wayne	IHL	75	27	35	62	12	11	1	5	6	2
1989-90a	Indianapolis	IHL	74	17	24	41	10	14	6	4	10	21
1990-91	Chicago	NHL	23	2	2	4	6	....	....	....	....	....
	Indianapolis	IHL	33	16	9	25	19	....	....	....	....	....
	Quebec	NHL	14	2	5	7	4	....	....	....	....	....
1991-92	Quebec	NHL	26	1	4	5	8	....	....	....	....	....
	Halifax	AHL	30	10	8	18	20	....	....	....	....	....
	NHL Totals		63	5	11	16	18	....	....	....	....	....

a Won N.R. Poile Trophy (Playoff MVP–IHL) (1990)

Signed as a free agent by **Chicago**, September, 1989. Traded to **Quebec** by **Chicago** with Ryan McGill for Paul Gillis and Dan Vincelette, March 5, 1991.

McPHEE, MICHAEL JOSEPH (MIKE)

Left wing. Shoots left. 6'1", 203 lbs. Born, Sydney, N.S., July 14, 1960.
(Montreal's 8th choice, 124th overall, in 1980 Entry Draft).

			Regular Season					Playoffs				
Season	Club	Lea	GP	G	A	TP	PIM	GP	G	A	TP	PIM
1980-81	RPI	ECAC	29	28	18	46	22	....	....	....	....	....
1981-82	RPI	ECAC	6	0	3	3	4	....	....	....	....	....
1982-83	Nova Scotia	AHL	42	10	15	25	29	7	1	1	2	14
1983-84	Montreal	NHL	14	5	2	7	41	15	1	0	1	31
	Nova Scotia	AHL	67	22	33	55	101	....	....	....	....	....
1984-85	Montreal	NHL	70	17	22	39	120	12	4	1	5	32
1985-86	Montreal	NHL	70	19	21	40	69	20	3	4	7	45
1986-87	Montreal	NHL	79	18	21	39	58	17	7	2	9	13
1987-88	Montreal	NHL	77	23	20	43	53	11	4	3	7	8
1988-89	Montreal	NHL	73	19	22	41	74	20	4	7	11	30
1989-90	Montreal	NHL	56	23	18	41	47	9	1	1	2	16
1990-91	Montreal	NHL	64	22	21	43	56	13	1	7	8	12
1991-92	Montreal	NHL	78	16	15	31	63	8	1	1	2	4
	NHL Totals		581	162	162	324	581	125	26	26	52	191

Played in NHL All-Star Game (1989)

Traded to **Minnesota** by **Montreal** for Minnesota's fifth round choice in 1993 Entry Draft, August 17, 1992.

McRAE, BASIL PAUL

Left wing. Shoots left. 6'2", 205 lbs. Born, Beaverton, Ont., January 5, 1961.
(Quebec's 3rd choice, 87th overall, in 1980 Entry Draft).

			Regular Season					Playoffs				
Season	Club	Lea	GP	G	A	TP	PIM	GP	G	A	TP	PIM
1979-80	London	OHA	67	24	36	60	116	5	0	0	0	18
1980-81	London	OHA	65	29	23	52	266	....	....	....	....	....
1981-82	Quebec	NHL	20	4	3	7	69	9	1	0	1	34
	Fredericton	AHL	47	11	15	26	175	....	....	....	....	....
1982-83	Quebec	NHL	22	1	1	2	59	....	....	....	....	....
	Fredericton	AHL	53	22	19	41	146	12	1	5	6	75
1983-84	Toronto	NHL	3	0	0	0	19	....	....	....	....	....
	St. Catharines	AHL	78	14	25	39	187	6	0	0	0	40
1984-85	Toronto	NHL	1	0	0	0	0	....	....	....	....	....
	St. Catharines	AHL	72	30	25	55	186	....	....	....	....	....
1985-86	Detroit	NHL	4	0	0	0	5	....	....	....	....	....
	Adirondack	AHL	69	22	30	52	259	17	5	4	9	101
1986-87	Detroit	NHL	36	2	2	4	193	....	....	....	....	....
	Quebec	NHL	33	9	5	14	149	13	3	1	4	*99
1987-88	Minnesota	NHL	80	5	11	16	382	....	....	....	....	....
1988-89	Minnesota	NHL	78	12	19	31	365	5	0	0	0	58
1989-90	Minnesota	NHL	66	9	17	26	*351	7	1	0	1	24
1990-91	Minnesota	NHL	40	1	3	4	224	22	1	1	2	*94
1991-92	Minnesota	NHL	59	5	8	13	245	....	....	....	....	....
	NHL Totals		442	48	69	117	2061	56	6	2	8	309

Traded to **Toronto** by **Quebec** for Richard Turmel, August 12, 1983. Signed as a free agent by **Detroit**, July 17, 1985. Traded to **Quebec** by **Detroit** with John Ogrodnick and Doug Shedden for Brent Ashton, Gilbert Delorme and Mark Kumpel, January 17, 1987. Signed as a free agent by **Minnesota**, June 29, 1987. Claimed by **Tampa Bay** from **Minnesota** in Expansion Draft, June 18, 1992.

McRAE, CHRIS

Left wing. Shoots left. 6', 200 lbs. Born, Beaverton, Ont., August 26, 1965.

			Regular Season					Playoffs				
Season	Club	Lea	GP	G	A	TP	PIM	GP	G	A	TP	PIM
1983-84	Belleville	OHL	9	0	0	0	19	....	....	....	....	....
	Sudbury	OHL	53	14	31	45	120	....	....	....	....	....
1984-85	Sudbury	OHL	6	0	2	2	10	....	....	....	....	....
	Oshawa	OHL	43	8	7	15	118	5	0	1	1	2
	St. Catharines	AHL	6	4	3	7	24	....	....	....	....	....
1985-86	St. Catharines	AHL	59	1	1	2	233	11	0	1	1	65
1986-87	Newmarket	AHL	51	3	6	9	193	....	....	....	....	....
1987-88	Toronto	NHL	11	0	0	0	65	....	....	....	....	....
	Newmarket	AHL	34	7	6	13	165	....	....	....	....	....
1988-89	Toronto	NHL	3	0	0	0	12	....	....	....	....	....
	Newmarket	AHL	18	3	1	4	85	....	....	....	....	....
	Denver	IHL	23	1	4	5	121	2	0	0	0	20
1989-90	Detroit	NHL	7	1	0	1	45	....	....	....	....	....
	Adirondack	AHL	46	9	10	19	290	....	....	....	....	....
1990-91	Adirondack	AHL	23	2	3	5	109	2	0	0	0	11
1991-92	Fort Wayne	IHL	60	20	14	34	*413	5	1	0	1	44
	NHL Totals		21	1	0	1	122	....	....	....	....	....

Signed as a free agent by **Toronto**, October 16, 1985. Traded to **NY Rangers** by **Toronto** for Ken Hammond, February 21, 1989. Traded to **Detroit** by **NY Rangers** with Detroit's fifth round choice (Tony Burns) in 1990 Entry Draft which was previously acquired by NY Rangers for Kris King, September 7, 1989.

McRAE, KEN

Center. Shoots right. 6'1", 195 lbs. Born, Winchester, Ont., April 23, 1968.
(Quebec's 1st choice, 18th overall, in 1986 Entry Draft).

			Regular Season					Playoffs				
Season	Club	Lea	GP	G	A	TP	PIM	GP	G	A	TP	PIM
1985-86	Sudbury	OHL	66	25	49	74	127	4	2	1	3	12
1986-87	Sudbury	OHL	21	12	15	27	40	....	....	....	....	....
	Hamilton	OHL	20	7	12	19	25	7	1	1	2	12
1987-88	Quebec	NHL	1	0	0	0	0	....	....	....	....	....
	Hamilton	OHL	62	30	55	85	158	14	13	9	22	35
	Fredericton	AHL	....	....	....	....	....	3	0	0	0	8
1988-89	Quebec	NHL	37	6	11	17	68	....	....	....	....	....
	Halifax	AHL	41	20	21	41	87	....	....	....	....	....
1989-90	Quebec	NHL	66	7	8	15	191	....	....	....	....	....
1990-91	Quebec	NHL	12	0	0	0	36	....	....	....	....	....
	Halifax	AHL	60	10	36	46	193	....	....	....	....	....
1991-92	Quebec	NHL	10	0	1	1	31	....	....	....	....	....
	Halifax	AHL	52	30	41	71	184	....	....	....	....	....
	NHL Totals		126	13	20	33	326	....	....	....	....	....

Traded to **Toronto** by **Quebec** for Len Esau, July 21, 1992.

McREYNOLDS, BRIAN

Center. Shoots left. 6'1", 192 lbs. Born, Penetanguishene, Ont., January 5, 1965.
(NY Rangers' 6th choice, 112th overall, in 1985 Entry Draft).

			Regular Season					Playoffs				
Season	Club	Lea	GP	G	A	TP	PIM	GP	G	A	TP	PIM
1985-86	Michigan State	CCHA	45	14	24	38	78	....	....	....	....	....
1986-87	Michigan State	CCHA	45	16	24	40	68	....	....	....	....	....
1987-88	Michigan State	CCHA	43	10	24	34	50	....	....	....	....	....
1988-89	Cdn. National	....	58	5	25	30	59	....	....	....	....	....
1989-90	Winnipeg	NHL	9	0	2	2	4	....	....	....	....	....
	Moncton	AHL	72	18	41	59	87	....	....	....	....	....
1990-91	NY Rangers	NHL	1	0	0	0	0	....	....	....	....	....
	Binghamton	AHL	77	30	42	72	74	10	0	4	4	6
1991-92	Binghamton	AHL	48	19	28	47	22	7	2	2	4	12
	NHL Totals		10	0	2	2	4	....	....	....	....	....

Signed as a free agent by **Winnipeg**, June 20, 1989. Traded to **NY Rangers** by **Winnipeg** for Simon Wheeldon, July 10, 1990.

McSORLEY, MARTIN J. (MARTY)

Defense. Shoots right. 6'1", 235 lbs. Born, Hamilton, Ont., May 18, 1963.

			Regular Season					Playoffs				
Season	Club	Lea	GP	G	A	TP	PIM	GP	G	A	TP	PIM
1981-82	Belleville	OHL	58	6	13	19	234	....	....	....	....	....
1982-83	Belleville	OHL	70	10	41	51	183	4	0	0	0	7
	Baltimore	AHL	2	0	0	0	22	....	....	....	....	....
1983-84	**Pittsburgh**	**NHL**	**72**	**2**	**7**	**9**	**224**	....	....	....	....	....
1984-85	**Pittsburgh**	**NHL**	**15**	**0**	**0**	**0**	**15**	....	....	....	....	....
	Baltimore	AHL	58	6	24	30	154	14	0	7	7	47
1985-86	**Edmonton**	**NHL**	**59**	**11**	**12**	**23**	**265**	**8**	**0**	**2**	**2**	**50**
	Nova Scotia	AHL	9	2	4	6	34	....	....	....	....	....
1986-87	**Edmonton**	**NHL**	**41**	**2**	**4**	**6**	**159**	**21**	**4**	**3**	**7**	**65**
	Nova Scotia	AHL	7	2	2	4	48	....	....	....	....	....
1987-88	**Edmonton**	**NHL**	**60**	**9**	**17**	**26**	**223**	**16**	**0**	**3**	**3**	**67**
1988-89	**Los Angeles**	**NHL**	**66**	**10**	**17**	**27**	**350**	**11**	**0**	**2**	**2**	**33**
1989-90	**Los Angeles**	**NHL**	**75**	**15**	**21**	**36**	**322**	**10**	**1**	**3**	**4**	**18**
1990-91a	**Los Angeles**	**NHL**	**61**	**7**	**32**	**39**	**221**	**12**	**0**	**0**	**0**	**58**
1991-92	**Los Angeles**	**NHL**	**71**	**7**	**22**	**29**	**268**	**6**	**1**	**0**	**1**	**21**
	NHL Totals		**520**	**63**	**132**	**195**	**2047**	**84**	**6**	**13**	**19**	**312**

a Co-winner of Alka-Seltzer Plus Award with Theoren Fleury (1991)

Signed as a free agent by **Pittsburgh**, July 30, 1982. Traded to **Edmonton** by **Pittsburgh** with Tim Hrynewich for Gilles Meloche, September 12, 1985. Traded to **Los Angeles** by **Edmonton** with Wayne Gretzky and Mike Krushelnyski for Jimmy Carson, Martin Gelinas, Los Angeles' first round choices in 1989 (acquired by New Jersey, June 17, 1989. New Jersey selected Jason Miller), 1991 (Martin Rucinsky) and 1993 Entry Drafts and cash, August 9, 1988.

McSWEEN, DON

Defense. Shoots left. 5'11", 197 lbs. Born, Detroit, MI, June 9, 1964.
(Buffalo's 10th choice, 154th overall, in 1983 Entry Draft).

			Regular Season					Playoffs				
Season	Club	Lea	GP	G	A	TP	PIM	GP	G	A	TP	PIM
1983-84	Michigan State	CCHA	46	10	26	36	30	....	....	....	....	....
1984-85	Michigan State	CCHA	44	2	23	25	52	....	....	....	....	....
1985-86a	Michigan State	CCHA	45	9	29	38	18	....	....	....	....	....
1986-87abc	Michigan State	CCHA	45	7	23	30	34	....	....	....	....	....
1987-88	**Buffalo**	**NHL**	**5**	**0**	**1**	**1**	**6**	....	....	....	....	....
	Rochester	AHL	63	9	29	38	108	6	0	1	1	15
1988-89	Rochester	AHL	66	7	22	29	45	....	....	....	....	....
1989-90	**Buffalo**	**NHL**	**4**	**0**	**0**	**0**	**6**	....	....	....	....	....
d	Rochester	AHL	70	16	43	59	43	17	3	10	13	12
1990-91	Rochester	AHL	74	7	44	51	57	15	2	5	7	8
1991-92	Rochester	AHL	75	6	32	38	60	16	5	6	11	18
	NHL Totals		**9**	**0**	**1**	**1**	**12**	....	....	....	....	....

a CCHA First All-Star Team (1986, 1987)
b NCAA West Second All-American Team (1987)
c Named to NCAA All-Tournament Team (1987)
d AHL First All-Star Team (1990)

MEANY, SPENCER

Right wing. Shoots right. 6', 205 lbs. Born, Atikokan, Ont., April 8, 1971.
(Buffalo's 11th choice, 211th overall, in 1991 Entry Draft).

			Regular Season					Playoffs				
Season	Club	Lea	GP	G	A	TP	PIM	GP	G	A	TP	PIM
1990-91	St. Lawrence	ECAC	31	6	11	17	92	....	....	....	....	....
1991-92	St. Lawrence	ECAC	30	12	8	20	123	....	....	....	....	....

MEARS, GLEN

Defense. Shoots right. 6'3", 215 lbs. Born, Anchorage, AK, July 14, 1972.
(Calgary's 5th choice, 62nd overall, in 1990 Entry Draft).

			Regular Season					Playoffs				
Season	Club	Lea	GP	G	A	TP	PIM	GP	G	A	TP	PIM
1990-91	Bowling Green	CCHA	40	0	7	7	54	....	....	....	....	....
1991-92	Bowling Green	CCHA	32	1	2	3	38	....	....	....	....	....

MEEHAN, SCOTT

Defense. Shoots left. 6'1", 185 lbs. Born, Walpole, MA, November 27, 1970.
(Vancouver's 1st choice, 13th overall, in 1991 Supplemental Draft).

			Regular Season					Playoffs				
Season	Club	Lea	GP	G	A	TP	PIM	GP	G	A	TP	PIM
1989-90	Lowell	H.E.	24	0	0	0	16	....	....	....	....	....
1990-91	Lowell	H.E.	27	1	2	3	20	....	....	....	....	....
1991-92	Lowell	H.E.	34	0	2	2	28	....	....	....	....	....

MEJZLIK, ROMAN (MAIZ-lik)

Left wing/Center. Shoots left. 6'2", 198 lbs. Born, Trebic, Czechoslovakia, October 31, 1967.
(Edmonton's 8th choice, 164th overall, in 1990 Entry Draft).

			Regular Season					Playoffs				
Season	Club	Lea	GP	G	A	TP	PIM	GP	G	A	TP	PIM
1987-88	Dukla Jihlava	Czech.	39	12	10	22	30	....	....	....	....	....
1988-89	Dukla Jihlava	Czech.	43	4	14	18	24	....	....	....	....	....
1989-90	Dukla Jihlava	Czech.	44	3	11	14	....	7	4	5	9	....
1990-91	Dukla Jihlava	Czech.	48	9	9	18	30	7	1	4	5	....
1991-92	Dukla Jihlava	Czech.	43	5	17	22	....	....	....	....	....	....

MELANSON, DEAN

Defense. Shoots right. 5'11", 211 lbs. Born, Antigonish, N.S., November 19, 1973.
(Buffalo's 4th choice, 80th overall, in 1992 Entry Draft).

			Regular Season					Playoffs				
Season	Club	Lea	GP	G	A	TP	PIM	GP	G	A	TP	PIM
1990-91	St-Hyacinthe	QMJHL	69	10	17	27	110	4	0	1	1	2
1991-92	St-Hyacinthe	QMJHL	42	8	19	27	158	6	1	2	3	25

MELANSON, ROBERT

Defense. Shoots left. 6'1", 202 lbs. Born, Pomquet, N.S., March 5, 1971.
(Pittsburgh's 5th choice, 104th overall, in 1991 Entry Draft).

			Regular Season					Playoffs				
Season	Club	Lea	GP	G	A	TP	PIM	GP	G	A	TP	PIM
1990-91	Hull	QMJHL	66	1	8	9	210	6	0	1	1	34
1991-92	Knoxville	ECHL	49	0	11	11	186	....	....	....	....	....
	Muskegon	IHL	7	0	2	2	2	1	0	0	0	0

MELLANBY, SCOTT

Right wing. Shoots right. 6'1", 205 lbs. Born, Montreal, Que., June 11, 1966.
(Philadelphia's 2nd choice, 27th overall, in 1984 Entry Draft).

			Regular Season					Playoffs				
Season	Club	Lea	GP	G	A	TP	PIM	GP	G	A	TP	PIM
1984-85	U. Wisconsin	WCHA	40	14	24	38	60	....	....	....	....	....
1985-86	U. Wisconsin	WCHA	32	21	23	44	89	....	....	....	....	....
	Philadelphia	**NHL**	**2**	**0**	**0**	**0**	**0**	....	....	....	....	....
1986-87	**Philadelphia**	**NHL**	**71**	**11**	**21**	**32**	**94**	**24**	**5**	**5**	**10**	**46**
1987-88	**Philadelphia**	**NHL**	**75**	**25**	**26**	**51**	**185**	**7**	**0**	**1**	**1**	**16**
1988-89	**Philadelphia**	**NHL**	**76**	**21**	**29**	**50**	**183**	**19**	**4**	**5**	**9**	**28**
1989-90	**Philadelphia**	**NHL**	**57**	**6**	**17**	**23**	**77**	....	....	....	....	....
1990-91	**Philadelphia**	**NHL**	**74**	**20**	**21**	**41**	**155**	....	....	....	....	....
1991-92	**Edmonton**	**NHL**	**80**	**23**	**27**	**50**	**197**	**16**	**2**	**1**	**3**	**29**
	NHL Totals		**435**	**106**	**141**	**247**	**891**	**66**	**11**	**12**	**23**	**119**

Traded to **Edmonton** by **Philadelphia** with Craig Fisher and Craig Berube for Dave Brown, Corey Foster and Jari Kurri, May 30, 1991.

MELNYK, LARRY JOSEPH (MEHL-nihk)

Defense. Shoots left. 6', 195 lbs. Born, Saskatoon, Sask., February 21, 1960.
(Boston's 5th choice, 78th overall, in 1979 Entry Draft).

			Regular Season					Playoffs				
Season	Club	Lea	GP	G	A	TP	PIM	GP	G	A	TP	PIM
1978-79	N. Westminster	WHL	71	7	33	40	142	8	1	4	5	14
1979-80	N. Westminster	WHL	67	13	38	51	236	....	....	....	....	....
1980-81	**Boston**	**NHL**	**26**	**0**	**4**	**4**	**39**	....	....	....	....	....
	Springfield	AHL	47	1	10	11	109	1	0	0	0	0
1981-82	**Boston**	**NHL**	**48**	**0**	**8**	**8**	**84**	**11**	**0**	**3**	**3**	**40**
	Erie	AHL	10	0	3	3	36	....	....	....	....	....
1982-83	**Boston**	**NHL**	**1**	**0**	**0**	**0**	**0**	**11**	**0**	**0**	**0**	**9**
	Baltimore	AHL	72	2	24	26	215	....	....	....	....	....
1983-84	Hershey	AHL	50	0	18	18	156	....	....	....	....	....
	Moncton	AHL	14	0	3	3	17	....	....	....	....	....
	Edmonton	**NHL**	....	....	....	....	....	**6**	**0**	**1**	**1**	**0**
1984-85	**Edmonton**	**NHL**	**28**	**0**	**11**	**11**	**25**	**12**	**1**	**3**	**4**	**26**
	Nova Scotia	AHL	37	2	10	12	97	....	....	....	....	....
1985-86	**Edmonton**	**NHL**	**6**	**2**	**3**	**5**	**11**	....	....	....	....	....
	Nova Scotia	AHL	19	2	8	10	72	....	....	....	....	....
	NY Rangers	**NHL**	**46**	**1**	**8**	**9**	**65**	**16**	**1**	**2**	**3**	**46**
1986-87	**NY Rangers**	**NHL**	**73**	**3**	**12**	**15**	**182**	**6**	**0**	**0**	**0**	**4**
1987-88	**NY Rangers**	**NHL**	**14**	**0**	**1**	**1**	**34**	....	....	....	....	....
	Vancouver	**NHL**	**49**	**2**	**3**	**5**	**73**	....	....	....	....	....
1988-89	**Vancouver**	**NHL**	**74**	**3**	**11**	**14**	**82**	**4**	**0**	**0**	**0**	**2**
1989-90	**Vancouver**	**NHL**	**67**	**0**	**2**	**2**	**91**	....	....	....	....	....
1990-91						DID NOT PLAY						
1991-92						DID NOT PLAY						
	NHL Totals		**432**	**11**	**63**	**74**	**686**	**66**	**2**	**9**	**11**	**127**

Traded to **Edmonton** by **Boston** for John Blum, March 6, 1984. Traded to **NY Rangers** by **Edmonton** with Todd Strueby for Mike Rogers, December 20, 1985. Traded to **Vancouver** by **NY Rangers** with Willie Huber for Michel Petit, November 4, 1987.

MELROSE, KEVAN

Defense. Shoots left. 5'10", 185 lbs. Born, Calgary, Alta., March 28, 1966.
(Calgary's 7th choice, 138th overall in 1984 Entry Draft).

			Regular Season					Playoffs				
Season	Club	Lea	GP	G	A	TP	PIM	GP	G	A	TP	PIM
1986-87	Cdn. Olympic	....	8	1	0	1	4	....	....	....	....	....
	Red Deer	AJHL	29	15	15	30	171	19	8	16	24	60
1987-88	Harvard	ECAC	31	4	6	10	50	....	....	....	....	....
1988-89	Harvard	ECAC	32	2	13	15	126	....	....	....	....	....
1989-90	Harvard	ECAC	16	1	6	7	124	....	....	....	....	....
1990-91	Salt Lake	IHL	60	6	14	20	82	4	1	2	3	10
1991-92	Salt Lake	IHL	82	5	14	19	187	5	0	0	0	4

MELUZIN, ROMAN (MEH-loo-zin)

Right wing. Shoots right. 6', 174 lbs. Born, Brno, Czechoslovakia, June 17, 1972.
(Winnipeg's 3rd choice, 74th overall, in 1990 Entry Draft).

			Regular Season					Playoffs				
Season	Club	Lea	GP	G	A	TP	PIM	GP	G	A	TP	PIM
1989-90	Zetor Brno	Czech.	34	4	6	10	....	....	....	....	....	....
1990-91	Zetor Brno	Czech.	30	14	8	22	8	....	....	....	....	....
1991-92	Zetor Brno	Czech.	37	13	13	26	....	....	....	....	....	....

MENDEL, ROBERT (ROB)

Defense. Shoots left. 6'1", 195 lbs. Born, Los Angeles, CA, September 19, 1968.
(Quebec's 5th choice, 93rd overall, in 1987 Entry Draft).

			Regular Season					Playoffs				
Season	Club	Lea	GP	G	A	TP	PIM	GP	G	A	TP	PIM
1986-87	U. Wisconsin	WCHA	42	1	7	8	26	....	....	....	....	....
1987-88	U. Wisconsin	WCHA	40	0	7	7	22	....	....	....	....	....
1988-89	U. Wisconsin	WCHA	44	1	14	15	37	....	....	....	....	....
1989-90	U. Wisconsin	WCHA	44	1	13	14	30	....	....	....	....	....
1990-91	Baltimore	AHL	43	0	7	7	20	....	....	....	....	....
	Newmarket	AHL	13	1	0	1	6	....	....	....	....	....
	Hampton Rds.	ECHL	2	0	2	2	0	....	....	....	....	....
1991-92	St. John's	AHL	39	1	4	5	26	....	....	....	....	....
	Raleigh	ECHL	10	0	3	3	12	4	0	0	0	2

Signed as a free agent by **Washington**, May 24, 1990. Traded to **Toronto** by **Washington** for Bobby Reynolds, March 5, 1991.

MERKLER, KEITH

Left wing. Shoots left. 6'2", 205 lbs. Born, Syosset, NY, April 23, 1971.
(Toronto's 8th choice, 129th overall, in 1989 Entry Draft).

			Regular Season					Playoffs				
Season	Club	Lea	GP	G	A	TP	PIM	GP	G	A	TP	PIM
1989-90	Princeton	ECAC	8	0	0	0	4	....	....	....	....	....
1990-91	Princeton	ECAC	22	4	4	8	20	....	....	....	....	....
1991-92	Princeton	ECAC	13	2	2	4	14	....	....	....	....	....

MESSIER, JOBY

Defense. Shoots right. 6', 193 lbs. Born, Regina, Sask., March 2, 1970.
(NY Rangers' 7th choice, 118th overall, in 1989 Entry Draft).

			Regular Season					Playoffs				
Season	Club	Lea	GP	G	A	TP	PIM	GP	G	A	TP	PIM
1988-89	Michigan State	CCHA	39	2	10	12	66	....	....	....	....	....
1989-90	Michigan State	CCHA	42	1	11	12	58	....	....	....	....	....
1990-91	Michigan State	CCHA	39	5	11	16	71	....	....	....	....	....
1991-92ab	Michigan State	CCHA	41	13	15	28	81	....	....	....	....	....

a CCHA First All-Star Team (1992)
b NCAA West First All-Star Team (1992)

MESSIER, MARK DOUGLAS (MEHZ-yay)

Center. Shoots left. 6'1", 210 lbs. Born, Edmonton, Alta., January 18, 1961.
(Edmonton's 2nd choice, 48th overall, in 1979 Entry Draft).

			Regular Season					Playoffs				
Season	Club	Lea	GP	G	A	TP	PIM	GP	G	A	TP	PIM
1977-78	Portland	WHL	....	....	....	....	....	7	4	1	5	2
1978-79	Indianapolis	WHA	5	0	0	0	0	....	....	....	....	....
	Cincinnati	WHA	47	1	10	11	58	....	....	....	....	....
1979-80	**Edmonton**	**NHL**	**75**	**12**	**21**	**33**	**120**	**3**	**1**	**2**	**3**	**2**
	Houston	CHL	4	0	3	3	4	....	....	....	....	....
1980-81	**Edmonton**	**NHL**	**72**	**23**	**40**	**63**	**102**	**9**	**2**	**5**	**7**	**13**
1981-82a	**Edmonton**	**NHL**	**78**	**50**	**38**	**88**	**119**	**5**	**1**	**2**	**3**	**8**
1982-83a	**Edmonton**	**NHL**	**77**	**48**	**58**	**106**	**72**	**15**	**15**	**6**	**21**	**14**
1983-84bc	**Edmonton**	**NHL**	**73**	**37**	**64**	**101**	**165**	**19**	**8**	**18**	**26**	**19**
1984-85	**Edmonton**	**NHL**	**55**	**23**	**31**	**54**	**57**	**18**	**12**	**13**	**25**	**12**
1985-86	**Edmonton**	**NHL**	**63**	**35**	**49**	**84**	**68**	**10**	**4**	**6**	**10**	**18**
1986-87	**Edmonton**	**NHL**	**77**	**37**	**70**	**107**	**73**	**21**	**12**	**16**	**28**	**16**
1987-88	**Edmonton**	**NHL**	**77**	**37**	**74**	**111**	**103**	**19**	**11**	**23**	**34**	**29**
1988-89	**Edmonton**	**NHL**	**72**	**33**	**61**	**94**	**130**	**7**	**1**	**11**	**12**	**8**
1989-90ade	**Edmonton**	**NHL**	**79**	**45**	**84**	**129**	**79**	**22**	**9**	***22**	**31**	**20**
1990-91	**Edmonton**	**NHL**	**53**	**12**	**52**	**64**	**34**	**18**	**4**	**11**	**15**	**16**
1991-92ade	**NY Rangers**	**NHL**	**79**	**35**	**72**	**107**	**76**	**11**	**7**	**7**	**14**	**6**
	NHL Totals		**930**	**427**	**714**	**1141**	**1198**	**177**	**87**	**142**	**229**	**181**

a NHL First All-Star Team (1982, 1983, 1990, 1992)
b NHL Second All-Star Team (1984)
c Won Conn Smythe Trophy (1984)
d Won Hart Trophy (1990, 1992)
e Won Lester B. Pearson Award (1990, 1992)

Played in NHL All-Star Game (1982-86, 1988-92)

Traded to **NY Rangers** by **Edmonton** with future considerations for Bernie Nicholls, Steven Rice and Louie DeBrusk, October 4, 1991.

MESSIER, MITCH

Center. Shoots right. 6'2", 200 lbs. Born, Regina, Sask., August 21, 1965.
(Minnesota's 4th choice, 56th overall, in 1983 Entry Draft).

			Regular Season					Playoffs				
Season	Club	Lea	GP	G	A	TP	PIM	GP	G	A	TP	PIM
1983-84	Michigan State	CCHA	37	6	15	21	22	....	....	....	....	....
1984-85	Michigan State	CCHA	42	12	21	33	46	....	....	....	....	....
1985-86	Michigan State	CCHA	38	24	40	64	36	....	....	....	....	....
1986-87ab	Michigan State	CCHA	45	44	48	92	89	....	....	....	....	....
1987-88	**Minnesota**	**NHL**	**13**	**0**	**1**	**1**	**11**	....	....	....	....	....
	Kalamazoo	IHL	69	29	37	66	42	4	2	1	3	0
1988-89	**Minnesota**	**NHL**	**3**	**0**	**1**	**1**	**0**	....	....	....	....	....
	Kalamazoo	IHL	67	34	46	80	71	6	4	3	7	0
1989-90	**Minnesota**	**NHL**	**2**	**0**	**0**	**0**	**0**	....	....	....	....	....
	Kalamazoo	IHL	65	26	58	84	56	8	4	3	7	25
1990-91	**Minnesota**	**NHL**	**2**	**0**	**0**	**0**	**0**	....	....	....	....	....
	Kalamazoo	IHL	73	30	46	76	34	11	4	8	12	2
1991-92	Kalamazoo	IHL	77	43	33	76	42	12	3	3	6	25
	NHL Totals		**20**	**0**	**2**	**2**	**11**	....	....	....	....	....

a CCHA First All-Star Team (1987)
b NCAA West First All-American Team (1987)

METLYUK, DENIS (met-lee-OOK)

Center. Shoots left. 6'1", 183 lbs. Born, Togliatti, Soviet Union, January 30, 1972.
(Philadelphia's 3rd choice, 31st overall, in 1992 Entry Draft).

			Regular Season					Playoffs				
Season	Club	Lea	GP	G	A	TP	PIM	GP	G	A	TP	PIM
1991-92	Togliatti	CIS	26	0	1	1	6	....	....	....	....	....

MICHAYLUK, DAVID (DAVE) (muh-KIGH-luhk)

Left wing. Shoots left. 5'10", 189 lbs. Born, Wakaw, Sask., May 18, 1962.
(Philadelphia's 5th choice, 65th overall, in 1981 Entry Draft).

			Regular Season					Playoffs				
Season	Club	Lea	GP	G	A	TP	PIM	GP	G	A	TP	PIM
1980-81	Regina	WHL	72	62	71	133	39	11	5	12	17	8
1981-82	**Philadelphia**	**NHL**	**1**	**0**	**0**	**0**	**0**	....	....	....	....	....
a	Regina	WHL	72	62	111	172	128	12	16	24	*40	23
1982-83	**Philadelphia**	**NHL**	**13**	**2**	**6**	**8**	**8**	....	....	....	....	....
	Maine	AHL	69	32	40	72	16	8	0	2	2	0
1983-84	Springfield	AHL	79	18	44	62	37	4	0	0	0	2
1984-85	Hershey	AHL	3	0	2	2	2	....	....	....	....	....
b	Kalamazoo	IHL	82	*66	33	99	49	11	7	7	14	0
1985-86	Nova Scotia	AHL	3	0	1	1	0	....	....	....	....	....
	Muskegon	IHL	77	52	52	104	73	14	6	9	15	12
1986-87c	Muskegon	IHL	82	47	53	100	29	15	2	14	16	8
1987-88c	Muskegon	IHL	81	*56	81	137	46	6	2	0	2	18
1988-89cdef	Muskegon	IHL	80	50	72	*122	84	13	*9	12	*21	24
1989-90c	Muskegon	IHL	79	*51	51	102	80	15	8	*14	22	10
1990-91	Muskegon	IHL	83	40	62	102	16	5	2	2	4	4
1991-92b	Muskegon	IHL	82	39	63	102	154	13	9	8	17	4
	Pittsburgh	**NHL**	....	....	....	....	....	**7**	**1**	**1**	**2**	**0**
	NHL Totals		**14**	**2**	**6**	**8**	**8**	**7**	**1**	**1**	**2**	**0**

a WHL Second All-Star Team (1982)
b IHL Second All-Star Team (1985, 1992)
c IHL First All-Star Team (1987, 1988, 1989, 1990)
d IHL Playoff MVP (1989)
e Won James Gatschene Memorial Trophy (MVP-IHL) (1989)
f Won Leo P. Lamoureux Memorial Trophy (Top Scorer-IHL) (1989)

Signed as a free agent by **Pittsburgh**, May 24, 1989.

MICK, TROY

Left wing. Shoots left. 5'11", 192 lbs. Born, Burnaby, B.C., March 30, 1969.
(Pittsburgh's 6th choice, 130th overall, in 1988 Entry Draft).

			Regular Season					Playoffs				
Season	Club	Lea	GP	G	A	TP	PIM	GP	G	A	TP	PIM
1986-87	Portland	WHL	57	30	33	63	60	20	8	2	10	40
1987-88a	Portland	WHL	72	63	84	147	78	....	....	....	....	....
1988-89	Portland	WHL	66	49	*87	136	70	19	15	19	34	17
1989-90b	Regina	WHL	66	60	53	113	67	11	7	10	17	17
1990-91c	Knoxville	ECHL	38	35	48	83	24	....	....	....	....	....
	Albany	IHL	1	0	0	0	2	....	....	....	....	....
1991-92	Knoxville	ECHL	48	23	38	61	24	....	....	....	....	....

a WHL West All-Star Team (1988)
b WHL East First All-Star Team (1990)
c ECHL Second All-Star Team (1991)

MIDDENDORF, MAX

Right wing. Shoots right. 6'4", 210 lbs. Born, Syracuse, NY, August 18, 1967.
(Quebec's 3rd choice, 57th overall, in 1985 Entry Draft).

			Regular Season					Playoffs				
Season	Club	Lea	GP	G	A	TP	PIM	GP	G	A	TP	PIM
1984-85	Sudbury	OHL	63	16	28	44	106	....	....	....	....	....
1985-86	Sudbury	OHL	61	40	42	82	71	4	4	2	6	11
1986-87	**Quebec**	**NHL**	**6**	**1**	**4**	**5**	**4**	....	....	....	....	....
	Sudbury	OHL	31	31	29	60	7	....	....	....	....	....
	Kitchener	OHL	17	7	15	22	6	4	2	5	7	5
1987-88	**Quebec**	**NHL**	**1**	**0**	**0**	**0**	**0**	....	....	....	....	....
	Fredericton	AHL	38	11	13	24	57	12	4	4	8	18
1988-89	Halifax	AHL	72	41	39	80	85	4	1	2	3	6
1989-90	**Quebec**	**NHL**	**3**	**0**	**0**	**0**	**0**	....	....	....	....	....
	Halifax	AHL	48	20	17	37	60	....	....	....	....	....
1990-91	**Edmonton**	**NHL**	**3**	**1**	**0**	**1**	**2**	....	....	....	....	....
	Fort Wayne	IHL	15	9	11	20	12	....	....	....	....	....
	Cape Breton	AHL	44	14	21	35	82	4	0	1	1	6
1991-92	Cape Breton	AHL	51	20	19	39	108	....	....	....	....	....
	Adirondack	AHL	6	3	5	8	12	5	0	1	1	16
	NHL Totals		**13**	**2**	**4**	**6**	**6**	....	....	....	....	....

Traded to **Edmonton** by **Quebec** for Edmonton's ninth round choice (Brent Brekke) in 1991 Entry Draft, November 10, 1990. Traded to **Detroit** by **Edmonton** for Bill McDougall, February 22, 1992.

MIEHM, KEVIN (MEE-yuhm)

Centre. Shoots left. 6'2", 197 lbs. Born, Kitchener, Ont., September 10, 1969.
(St. Louis' 2nd choice, 54th overall, in 1987 Entry Draft).

			Regular Season					Playoffs				
Season	Club	Lea	GP	G	A	TP	PIM	GP	G	A	TP	PIM
1986-87	Oshawa	OHL	61	12	27	39	19	26	1	8	9	12
1987-88	Oshawa	OHL	52	16	36	52	30	7	2	5	7	0
1988-89a	Oshawa	OHL	63	43	79	122	19	6	6	6	12	0
	Peoria	IHL	3	1	1	2	0	4	0	2	2	0
1989-90	Peoria	IHL	76	23	38	61	20	3	0	0	0	4
1990-91	Peoria	IHL	73	25	39	64	14	16	5	7	12	2
1991-92	Peoria	IHL	66	21	53	74	22	10	3	4	7	2

a OHL Third All-Star Team (1989)

MILLEN, COREY

Center. Shoots right. 5'7", 168 lbs. Born, Cloquet, MN, April 29, 1964.
(NY Rangers' 3rd choice, 57th overall, in 1982 Entry Draft).

			Regular Season					Playoffs				
Season	Club	Lea	GP	G	A	TP	PIM	GP	G	A	TP	PIM
1982-83	U. Minnesota	WCHA	21	14	15	29	18	....	....	....	....	....
1983-84	U.S. Olympic	....	45	15	11	26	10	....	....	....	....	....
1984-85	U. Minnesota	WCHA	38	28	36	64	60	....	....	....	....	....
1985-86ab	U. Minnesota	WCHA	48	41	42	83	64	....	....	....	....	....
1986-87bc	U. Minnesota	WCHA	42	36	29	65	62	....	....	....	....	....
1987-88	U.S. National	....	47	41	43	84	26	....	....	....	....	....
	U.S. Olympic	....	6	6	5	11	4	....	....	....	....	....
1988-89	Ambri	Switz.	36	32	22	54	18	6	4	3	7	0
1989-90	**NY Rangers**	**NHL**	**4**	**0**	**0**	**0**	**2**	....	....	....	....	....
	Flint	IHL	11	4	5	9	2	....	....	....	....	....
1990-91	**NY Rangers**	**NHL**	**4**	**3**	**1**	**4**	**0**	**6**	**1**	**2**	**3**	**0**
	Binghamton	AHL	40	19	37	56	68	6	0	7	7	6
1991-92	**NY Rangers**	**NHL**	**11**	**1**	**4**	**5**	**10**	....	....	....	....	....
	Binghamton	AHL	15	8	7	15	44	....	....	....	....	....
	Los Angeles	**NHL**	**46**	**20**	**21**	**41**	**44**	**6**	**0**	**1**	**1**	**6**
	NHL Totals		**65**	**24**	**26**	**50**	**56**	**12**	**1**	**3**	**4**	**6**

a NCAA West Second All-American Team (1986)
b WCHA Second All-Star Team (1986, 1987)
c Named to NCAA All-Tournament Team (1987)

Traded to **Los Angeles** by **NY Rangers** for Randy Gilhen, December 23, 1991.

MILLER, AARON

Defense. Shoots right. 6'3", 197 lbs. Born, Buffalo, NY, August 11, 1971.
(NY Rangers' 6th choice, 88th overall, in 1989 Entry Draft).

			Regular Season					Playoffs				
Season	Club	Lea	GP	G	A	TP	PIM	GP	G	A	TP	PIM
1989-90	U. of Vermont	ECAC	31	1	15	16	24	....	....	....	....	....
1990-91	U. of Vermont	ECAC	30	3	7	10	22	....	....	....	....	....
1991-92	U. of Vermont	ECAC	31	3	16	19	28	....	....	....	....	....

Traded to **Quebec** by **NY Rangers** with NY Rangers' fifth round choice (Bill Lindsay) in 1991 Entry Draft for Joe Cirella, January 17, 1991.

MILLER, ANDREW

Right wing. Shoots right. 5'11", 200 lbs. Born, North York, Ont., January 20, 1971.
(Detroit's 10th choice, 252nd overall, in 1991 Entry Draft).

			Regular Season					Playoffs				
Season	Club	Lea	GP	G	A	TP	PIM	GP	G	A	TP	PIM
1990-91	Wexford	Jr. B	70	72	74	146	....	....	....	....	....	....
1991-92	Miami-Ohio	CCHA	40	9	16	25	34	....	....	....	....	....

MILLER, BRAD

Defense. Shoots left. 6'4", 220 lbs. Born, Edmonton, Alta., July 23, 1969.
(Buffalo's 2nd choice, 22nd overall, in 1987 Entry Draft).

			Regular Season					Playoffs				
Season	Club	Lea	GP	G	A	TP	PIM	GP	G	A	TP	PIM
1985-86	Regina	WHL	71	2	14	16	99	10	1	1	2	4
1986-87	Regina	WHL	67	10	38	48	154	3	0	0	0	6
1987-88	Rochester	AHL	3	0	0	0	4	2	0	0	0	2
	Regina	WHL	61	9	34	43	148	4	1	1	2	12
1988-89	**Buffalo**	**NHL**	7	0	0	0	6	....	....	....	....	....
	Regina	WHL	34	8	18	26	95	....	....	....	....	....
	Rochester	AHL	3	0	0	0	4	....	....	....	....	....
1989-90	**Buffalo**	**NHL**	1	0	0	0	0	....	....	....	....	....
	Rochester	AHL	60	2	10	12	273	8	1	0	1	52
1990-91	**Buffalo**	**NHL**	13	0	0	0	67	....	....	....	....	....
	Rochester	AHL	49	0	9	9	248	12	0	4	4	67
1991-92	**Buffalo**	**NHL**	42	1	4	5	192	....	....	....	....	....
	Rochester	AHL	27	0	4	4	113	11	0	0	0	61
	NHL Totals		63	1	4	5	265	....	....	....	....	....

Claimed by **Ottawa** from **Buffalo** in Expansion Draft, June 18, 1992.

MILLER, JASON

Center. Shoots left. 6'1", 190 lbs. Born, Edmonton, Alta., March 1, 1971.
(New Jersey's 2nd choice, 18th overall, in 1989 Entry Draft).

			Regular Season					Playoffs				
Season	Club	Lea	GP	G	A	TP	PIM	GP	G	A	TP	PIM
1987-88	Medicine Hat	WHL	71	11	18	29	28	15	0	1	1	2
1988-89	Medicine Hat	WHL	72	51	55	106	44	3	1	2	3	2
1989-90	Medicine Hat	WHL	66	43	56	99	40	3	3	2	5	0
1990-91	**New Jersey**	**NHL**	1	0	0	0	0	....	....	....	....	....
a	Medicine Hat	WHL	66	60	76	136	31	12	9	10	19	8
1991-92	Utica	AHL	71	23	32	55	31	4	1	3	4	0
	NHL Totals		4	0	0	0	0	....	....	....	....	....

a WHL East Second All-Star Team (1991)

MILLER, JAY

Left wing. Shoots left. 6'2", 210 lbs. Born, Wellesley, MA, July 16, 1960.
(Quebec's 2nd choice, 66th overall, in 1980 Entry Draft).

			Regular Season					Playoffs				
Season	Club	Lea	GP	G	A	TP	PIM	GP	G	A	TP	PIM
1981-82	N. Hampshire	ECAC	24	6	4	10	34	....	....	....	....	....
1982-83	N. Hampshire	ECAC	28	6	4	10	28	....	....	....	....	....
1983-84	Toledo	IHL	2	0	0	0	2	....	....	....	....	....
	Maine	AHL	15	1	1	2	27	....	....	....	....	....
	Mohawk Valley	ACHL	48	15	36	51	167	....	....	....	....	....
1984-85	Muskegon	IHL	56	5	29	34	177	17	1	1	2	56
1985-86	**Boston**	**NHL**	46	3	0	3	178	2	0	0	0	17
	Moncton	AHL	18	4	6	10	113	....	....	....	....	....
1986-87	**Boston**	**NHL**	55	1	4	5	208	....	....	....	....	....
1987-88	**Boston**	**NHL**	78	7	12	19	304	12	0	0	0	124
1988-89	**Boston**	**NHL**	37	2	4	6	168	....	....	....	....	....
	Los Angeles	**NHL**	29	5	3	8	133	11	0	1	1	63
1989-90	**Los Angeles**	**NHL**	68	10	2	12	224	10	1	1	2	10
1990-91	**Los Angeles**	**NHL**	66	8	12	20	259	8	0	0	0	17
1991-92	**Los Angeles**	**NHL**	67	4	7	11	249	5	1	1	2	12
	NHL Totals		446	40	44	84	1723	48	2	3	5	243

Signed as a free agent by **Boston**, October 1, 1985. Traded to **Los Angeles** by **Boston** for future considerations, January 22, 1989.

MILLER, KELLY

Left wing. Shoots left. 5'11", 197 lbs. Born, Lansing, MI, March 3, 1963.
(NY Rangers' 9th choice, 183rd overall, in 1982 Entry Draft).

			Regular Season					Playoffs				
Season	Club	Lea	GP	G	A	TP	PIM	GP	G	A	TP	PIM
1981-82	Michigan State	CCHA	38	11	18	29	17	....	....	....	....	....
1982-83	Michigan State	CCHA	36	16	19	35	12	....	....	....	....	....
1983-84	Michigan State	CCHA	46	28	21	49	12	....	....	....	....	....
1984-85ab	Michigan State	CCHA	43	27	23	50	21	....	....	....	....	....
	NY Rangers	**NHL**	5	0	2	2	2	3	0	0	0	2
1985-86	**NY Rangers**	**NHL**	74	13	20	33	52	16	3	4	7	4
1986-87	**NY Rangers**	**NHL**	38	6	14	20	22	....	....	....	....	....
	Washington	**NHL**	39	10	12	22	26	7	2	2	4	0
1987-88	**Washington**	**NHL**	80	9	23	32	35	14	4	4	8	10
1988-89	**Washington**	**NHL**	78	19	21	40	45	6	1	0	1	2
1989-90	**Washington**	**NHL**	80	18	22	40	49	15	3	5	8	23
1990-91	**Washington**	**NHL**	80	24	26	50	29	11	4	2	6	6
1991-92	**Washington**	**NHL**	78	14	38	52	49	7	1	2	3	4
	NHL Totals		552	113	178	291	309	79	18	19	37	51

a CCHA First All-Star Team (1985)
b Named to NCAA All-American Team (1985)

Traded to **Washington** by **NY Rangers** with Bob Crawford and Mike Ridley for Bob Carpenter and Washington's second round choice (Jason Prosofsky) in 1989 Entry Draft, January 1, 1987.

MILLER, KEVIN

Center. Shoots right. 5'11", 190 lbs. Born, Lansing, MI, September 9, 1965.
(NY Rangers' 10th choice, 202nd overall, in 1984 Entry Draft).

			Regular Season					Playoffs				
Season	Club	Lea	GP	G	A	TP	PIM	GP	G	A	TP	PIM
1984-85	Michigan State	CCHA	44	11	29	40	84	....	....	....	....	....
1985-86	Michigan State	CCHA	45	19	52	71	112	....	....	....	....	....
1986-87	Michigan State	CCHA	42	25	56	81	63	....	....	....	....	....
1987-88	U.S. National	....	48	31	32	63	33	....	....	....	....	....
	U.S. Olympic	....	5	1	3	4	4	....	....	....	....	....
	Michigan State	CCHA	9	6	3	9	18	....	....	....	....	....
1988-89	**NY Rangers**	**NHL**	24	3	5	8	2	....	....	....	....	....
	Denver	IHL	55	29	47	76	19	4	2	1	3	2
1989-90	**NY Rangers**	**NHL**	16	0	5	5	2	1	0	0	0	0
	Flint	IHL	48	19	23	42	41	....	....	....	....	....
1990-91	**NY Rangers**	**NHL**	63	17	27	44	63	....	....	....	....	....
	Detroit	**NHL**	11	5	2	7	4	7	3	2	5	20
1991-92	**Detroit**	**NHL**	80	20	26	46	53	9	0	2	2	4
	NHL Totals		194	45	65	110	124	17	3	4	7	24

Traded to **Detroit** by **NY Rangers** with Jim Cummins and Dennis Vial for Joey Kocur and Per Djoos, March 5, 1991. Traded to **Washington** by **Detroit** for Dino Ciccarelli, June 20, 1992.

MILLER, KIP

Center. Shoots left. 5'10", 160 lbs. Born, Lansing, MI, June 11, 1969.
(Quebec's 4th choice, 72nd overall, in 1987 Entry Draft).

			Regular Season					Playoffs				
Season	Club	Lea	GP	G	A	TP	PIM	GP	G	A	TP	PIM
1986-87	Michigan State	CCHA	41	20	19	39	92	....	....	....	....	....
1987-88	Michigan State	CCHA	39	16	25	41	51	....	....	....	....	....
1988-89ab	Michigan State	CCHA	47	32	45	77	94	....	....	....	....	....
1989-90abcd	Michigan State	CCHA	45	*48	53	*101	60	....	....	....	....	....
1990-91	**Quebec**	**NHL**	13	4	3	7	7	....	....	....	....	....
	Halifax	AHL	66	36	33	69	40	....	....	....	....	....
1991-92	**Quebec**	**NHL**	36	5	10	15	12	....	....	....	....	....
	Halifax	AHL	24	9	17	26	8	....	....	....	....	....
	Minnesota	**NHL**	3	1	2	3	2	....	....	....	....	....
	Kalamazoo	IHL	6	1	8	9	4	12	3	9	12	12
	NHL Totals		52	10	15	25	21	....	....	....	....	....

a CCHA First All-Star Team (1989, 1990)
b NCAA West First All-American Team (1989, 1990)
c CCHA Player of the Year (1990)
d Won Hobey Baker Memorial Award (Top U.S. Collegiate Player) (1990)

Traded to **Minnesota** by **Quebec** for Steve Maltais, March 8, 1992.

MILLER, KRIS

Defense. Shoots left. 6', 200 lbs. Born, Bemidji, MN, March 30, 1969.
(Montreal's 6th choice, 80th overall, in 1987 Entry Draft).

			Regular Season					Playoffs				
Season	Club	Lea	GP	G	A	TP	PIM	GP	G	A	TP	PIM
1987-88	Minn.-Duluth	WCHA	32	1	6	7	30	....	....	....	....	....
1988-89	Minn.-Duluth	WCHA	39	2	10	12	37	....	....	....	....	....
1989-90	Minn.-Duluth	WCHA	39	2	11	13	59	....	....	....	....	....
1990-91	Minn.-Duluth	WCHA	40	6	22	28	24	....	....	....	....	....
1991-92	Phoenix	IHL	16	1	2	3	17	....	....	....	....	....
	Utica	AHL	1	0	0	0	0	....	....	....	....	....
	Raleigh	ECHL	42	12	27	39	78	4	2	3	5	8

MILLER, KURTIS

Left wing. Shoots left. 5'11", 180 lbs. Born, Bemidji, MN, June 1, 1970.
(St. Louis' 4th choice, 117th overall, in 1990 Entry Draft).

			Regular Season					Playoffs				
Season	Club	Lea	GP	G	A	TP	PIM	GP	G	A	TP	PIM
1990-91	Lake Superior	CCHA	45	10	12	22	48	....	....	....	....	....
1991-92	Lake Superior	CCHA	15	6	7	13	32	....	....	....	....	....

MIRONOV, BORIS

Defense. Shoots right. 6'3", 196 lbs. Born, Moscow, Soviet Union, March 21, 1972.
(Winnipeg's 2nd choice, 27th overall, in 1992 Entry Draft).

			Regular Season					Playoffs				
Season	Club	Lea	GP	G	A	TP	PIM	GP	G	A	TP	PIM
1990-91	CSKA	USSR	36	1	5	6	16	....	....	....	....	....
1991-92	CSKA	CIS	36	2	1	3	22	....	....	....	....	....

MIRONOV, DMITRI

Defense. Shoots right. 6'2", 192 lbs. Born, Moscow, Soviet Union, December 25, 1965.
(Toronto's 9th choice, 160th overall, in 1991 Entry Draft).

			Regular Season					Playoffs				
Season	Club	Lea	GP	G	A	TP	PIM	GP	G	A	TP	PIM
1990-91	Soviet Wings	USSR	44	16	12	28	22	....	....	....	....	....
1991-92	Soviet Wings	CIS	35	15	16	31	62	....	....	....	....	....
	CIS Olympic	....	8	3	1	4	6	....	....	....	....	....
	Toronto	**NHL**	7	1	0	1	0	....	....	....	....	....
	NHL Totals		7	1	0	1	0	....	....	....	....	....

MISKOLCZI, TED

Right wing. Shoots right. 6'3", 180 lbs. Born, Port Colborne, Ont., August 5, 1970.
(Boston's 11th choice, 252nd overall, in 1990 Entry Draft).

			Regular Season					Playoffs				
Season	Club	Lea	GP	G	A	TP	PIM	GP	G	A	TP	PIM
1989-90	Belleville	OHL	68	34	27	61	89	11	4	4	8	26
1990-91	Belleville	OHL	14	6	11	17	19	....	....	....	....	....
	Owen Sound	OHL	53	44	35	79	70	....	....	....	....	....
1991-92	Johnstown	ECHL	38	25	15	40	71	4	0	1	1	2

MITCHELL, ROY

Defense. Shoots right. 6'1", 199 lbs. Born, Edmonton, Alta., March 14, 1969.
(Montreal's 9th choice, 188th overall, in 1989 Entry Draft).

			Regular Season					Playoffs				
Season	Club	Lea	GP	G	A	TP	PIM	GP	G	A	TP	PIM
1986-87	Portland	WHL	68	7	32	39	103	20	0	3	3	23
1987-88	Portland	WHL	72	5	42	47	219	....	....	....	....	....
1988-89	Portland	WHL	72	9	34	43	177	19	1	8	9	38
1989-90	Sherbrooke	AHL	77	5	12	17	98	12	0	2	2	31
1990-91	Fredericton	AHL	71	2	15	17	137	9	0	1	1	11
1991-92	Kalamazoo	IHL	69	3	26	29	102	11	1	4	5	18

Signed as a free agent by **Minnesota**, July 25, 1991.

MITROVIC, SAVO

Right wing. Shoots right. 5'11", 190 lbs. Born, Toronto, Ont., February 4, 1969.
(Pittsburgh's 2nd choice, 10th overall, in 1990 Supplemental Draft).

			Regular Season					Playoffs				
Season	Club	Lea	GP	G	A	TP	PIM	GP	G	A	TP	PIM
1988-89	N. Hampshire	H.E.	34	2	8	10	22	....	....	....	....	....
1989-90	N. Hampshire	H.E.	37	30	21	51	40	....	....	....	....	....
1990-91	N. Hampshire	H.E.	35	13	18	31	55	....	....	....	....	....
1991-92	N. Hampshire	H.E.	37	15	42	57	51	....	....	....	....	....

MODANO, MICHAEL (MIKE)

Center. Shoots left. 6'3", 190 lbs. Born, Livonia, MI, June 7, 1970.
(Minnesota's 1st choice, 1st overall, in 1988 Entry Draft).

			Regular Season					Playoffs				
Season	Club	Lea	GP	G	A	TP	PIM	GP	G	A	TP	PIM
1986-87	Prince Albert	WHL	70	32	30	62	96	8	1	4	5	4
1987-88	Prince Albert	WHL	65	47	80	127	80	9	7	11	18	18
1988-89a	Prince Albert	WHL	41	39	66	105	74	....	....	....	....	....
	Minnesota	**NHL**	....	....	....	....	....	**2**	**0**	**0**	**0**	**0**
1989-90b	**Minnesota**	**NHL**	**80**	**29**	**46**	**75**	**63**	**7**	**1**	**1**	**2**	**12**
1990-91	**Minnesota**	**NHL**	**79**	**28**	**36**	**64**	**65**	**23**	**8**	**12**	**20**	**16**
1991-92	**Minnesota**	**NHL**	**76**	**33**	**44**	**77**	**46**	**7**	**3**	**2**	**5**	**4**
	NHL Totals		**235**	**90**	**126**	**216**	**174**	**39**	**12**	**15**	**27**	**32**

a WHL East All-Star Team (1989)
b NHL All-Rookie Team (1990)

MODRY, JAROSLAV (MOHD-ree)

Defense. Shoots left. 6'2", 195 lbs. Born, Ceske-Budejovice, Czech., February 27, 1971.
(New Jersey's 11th choice, 179th overall, in 1990 Entry Draft).

			Regular Season					Playoffs				
Season	Club	Lea	GP	G	A	TP	PIM	GP	G	A	TP	PIM
1988-89	Budejovice	Czech.	28	0	1	1	....	....	....	....	....	....
1989-90	Budejovice	Czech.	41	2	2	4	....	....	....	....	....	....
1990-91	Dukla Trencin	Czech.	33	1	9	10	6	....	....	....	....	....
1991-92	Dukla Trencin	Czech.	18	0	4	4	....	....	....	....	....	....
	Budejovice	Czech.2	14	4	10	14	....	....	....	....	....	....

MOES, MICHAEL (MOOSE)

Center. Shoots left. 5'11", 185 lbs. Born, Burlington, Ont., March 30, 1967.
(Toronto's 2nd choice, 6th overall, in 1989 Supplemental Draft).

			Regular Season					Playoffs				
Season	Club	Lea	GP	G	A	TP	PIM	GP	G	A	TP	PIM
1986-87	U. of Michigan	CCHA	39	11	15	26	16	....	....	....	....	....
1987-88	U. of Michigan	CCHA	40	5	27	32	23	....	....	....	....	....
1988-89	U. of Michigan	CCHA	41	14	24	38	22	....	....	....	....	....
1989-90	U. of Michigan	CCHA	42	19	29	48	10	....	....	....	....	....
	Newmarket	AHL	8	2	1	3	2	....	....	....	....	....
1990-91	Newmarket	AHL	63	7	22	29	6	....	....	....	....	....
1991-92	St. John's	AHL	1	0	0	0	0	....	....	....	....	....

MOGER, SANDY

Right wing. Shoots right. 6'2", 187 lbs. Born, 100 Mile House, B.C., March 21, 1969.
(Vancouver's 7th choice, 176th overall, in 1989 Entry Draft).

			Regular Season					Playoffs				
Season	Club	Lea	GP	G	A	TP	PIM	GP	G	A	TP	PIM
1988-89	Lake Superior	CCHA	21	3	5	8	26	....	....	....	....	....
1989-90	Lake Superior	CCHA	46	17	15	32	76	....	....	....	....	....
1990-91	Lake Superior	CCHA	45	27	21	48	*172	....	....	....	....	....
1991-92a	Lake Superior	CCHA	38	24	24	48	93	....	....	....	....	....

a CCHA Second All-Star Team (1992)

MOGILNY, ALEXANDER (moh-GIHL-nee)

Right wing. Shoots left. 5'11", 187 lbs. Born, Khabarovsk, Soviet Union, February 18, 1969.
(Buffalo's 4th choice, 89th overall, in 1988 Entry Draft).

			Regular Season					Playoffs				
Season	Club	Lea	GP	G	A	TP	PIM	GP	G	A	TP	PIM
1986-87	CSKA	USSR	28	15	1	16	4	....	....	....	....	....
1987-88	CSKA	USSR	29	12	8	20	14	....	....	....	....	....
1988-89	CSKA	USSR	31	11	11	22	24	....	....	....	....	....
1989-90	**Buffalo**	**NHL**	**65**	**15**	**28**	**43**	**16**	**4**	**0**	**1**	**1**	**2**
1990-91	**Buffalo**	**NHL**	**62**	**30**	**34**	**64**	**16**	**6**	**0**	**6**	**6**	**2**
1991-92	**Buffalo**	**NHL**	**67**	**39**	**45**	**84**	**73**	**2**	**0**	**2**	**2**	**0**
	NHL Totals		**194**	**84**	**107**	**191**	**105**	**12**	**0**	**9**	**9**	**4**

Played in NHL All-Star Game (1992)

MOHNS, TROY

Defense. Shoots right. 6', 185 lbs. Born, Pembroke, Ont., April 20, 1971.
(Los Angeles' 11th choice, 238th overall, in 1990 Entry Draft).

			Regular Season					Playoffs				
Season	Club	Lea	GP	G	A	TP	PIM	GP	G	A	TP	PIM
1989-90	Colgate	ECAC	34	2	11	13	36	....	....	....	....	....
1990-91	Colgate	ECAC	21	0	0	0	10	....	....	....	....	....
1991-92	Colgate	ECAC	20	1	6	7	16	....	....	....	....	....

MOLLER, RANDY

Defense. Shoots right. 6'2", 207 lbs. Born, Red Deer, Alta., August 23, 1963.
(Quebec's 1st choice, 11th overall, in 1981 Entry Draft).

			Regular Season					Playoffs				
Season	Club	Lea	GP	G	A	TP	PIM	GP	G	A	TP	PIM
1980-81	Lethbridge	WHL	46	4	21	25	176	9	0	4	4	24
1981-82a	Lethbridge	WHL	60	20	55	75	249	12	4	6	10	65
	Quebec	**NHL**	....	....	....	....	....	**1**	**0**	**0**	**0**	**0**
1982-83	**Quebec**	**NHL**	**75**	**2**	**12**	**14**	**145**	**4**	**1**	**0**	**1**	**4**
1983-84	**Quebec**	**NHL**	**74**	**4**	**14**	**18**	**147**	**9**	**1**	**0**	**1**	**45**
1984-85	**Quebec**	**NHL**	**79**	**7**	**22**	**29**	**120**	**18**	**2**	**2**	**4**	**40**
1985-86	**Quebec**	**NHL**	**69**	**5**	**18**	**23**	**141**	**3**	**0**	**0**	**0**	**26**
1986-87	**Quebec**	**NHL**	**71**	**5**	**9**	**14**	**144**	**13**	**1**	**4**	**5**	**23**
1987-88	**Quebec**	**NHL**	**66**	**3**	**22**	**25**	**169**	....	....	....	....	....
1988-89	**Quebec**	**NHL**	**74**	**7**	**22**	**29**	**136**	....	....	....	....	....
1989-90	**NY Rangers**	**NHL**	**60**	**1**	**12**	**13**	**139**	**10**	**1**	**6**	**7**	**32**
1990-91	**NY Rangers**	**NHL**	**61**	**4**	**19**	**23**	**161**	**6**	**0**	**2**	**2**	**11**
1991-92	**NY Rangers**	**NHL**	**43**	**2**	**7**	**9**	**78**	....	....	....	....	....
	Binghamton	AHL	3	0	1	1	0	....	....	....	....	....
	Buffalo	**NHL**	**13**	**1**	**2**	**3**	**59**	**7**	**0**	**0**	**0**	**8**
	NHL Totals		**685**	**41**	**159**	**200**	**1439**	**71**	**6**	**14**	**20**	**189**

a WHL Second All-Star Team (1982)

Traded to **NY Rangers** by **Quebec** for Michel Petit, October 5, 1989. Traded to **Buffalo** by **NY Rangers** for Jay Wells, March 9, 1992.

MOMESSO, SERGIO (moh-MESS-oh)

Left wing. Shoots left. 6'3", 215 lbs. Born, Montreal, Que., September 4, 1965.
(Montreal's 3rd choice, 27th overall, in 1983 Entry Draft).

			Regular Season					Playoffs				
Season	Club	Lea	GP	G	A	TP	PIM	GP	G	A	TP	PIM
1982-83	Shawinigan	QMJHL	70	27	42	69	93	10	5	4	9	55
1983-84	**Montreal**	**NHL**	**1**	**0**	**0**	**0**	**0**	....	....	....	....	....
	Shawinigan	QMJHL	68	42	88	130	235	6	4	4	8	13
	Nova Scotia	AHL	....	....	....	....	....	8	0	2	2	4
1984-85a	Shawinigan	QMJHL	64	56	90	146	216	8	7	8	15	17
1985-86	**Montreal**	**NHL**	**24**	**8**	**7**	**15**	**46**	....	....	....	....	....
1986-87	**Montreal**	**NHL**	**59**	**14**	**17**	**31**	**96**	**11**	**1**	**3**	**4**	**31**
	Sherbrooke	AHL	6	1	6	7	10	....	....	....	....	....
1987-88	**Montreal**	**NHL**	**53**	**7**	**14**	**21**	**101**	**6**	**0**	**2**	**2**	**16**
1988-89	**St. Louis**	**NHL**	**53**	**9**	**17**	**26**	**139**	**10**	**2**	**5**	**7**	**24**
1989-90	**St. Louis**	**NHL**	**79**	**24**	**32**	**56**	**199**	**12**	**3**	**2**	**5**	**63**
1990-91	**St. Louis**	**NHL**	**59**	**10**	**18**	**28**	**131**	....	....	....	....	....
	Vancouver	**NHL**	**11**	**6**	**2**	**8**	**43**	**6**	**0**	**3**	**3**	**25**
1991-92	**Vancouver**	**NHL**	**58**	**20**	**23**	**43**	**198**	**13**	**0**	**5**	**5**	**30**
	NHL Totals		**397**	**98**	**130**	**228**	**953**	**58**	**6**	**20**	**26**	**189**

a QMJHL First All-Star Team (1985)

Traded to **St. Louis** by **Montreal** with Vincent Riendeau for Jocelyn Lemieux, Darrell May and St. Louis' second round choice (Patrice Brisebois) in the 1989 Entry Draft, August 9, 1988. Traded to **Vancouver** by **St. Louis** with Geoff Courtnall, Robert Dirk, Cliff Ronning and future considerations for Dan Quinn and Garth Butcher, March 5, 1991.

MONGEAU, MICHEL

Center. Shoots left. 5'9", 190 lbs. Born, Nun's Island, Que., February 9, 1965.

			Regular Season					Playoffs				
Season	Club	Lea	GP	G	A	TP	PIM	GP	G	A	TP	PIM
1983-84	Laval	QMJHL	60	45	49	94	30	....	....	....	....	....
1984-85	Laval	QMJHL	67	60	84	144	56	....	....	....	....	....
1985-86	Laval	QMJHL	72	71	109	180	45	....	....	....	....	....
1986-87	Saginaw	IHL	76	42	53	95	34	10	3	6	9	6
1987-88	France	....	30	31	21	52	....	....	....	....	....	....
1988-89	Flint	IHL	82	41	76	117	57	....	....	....	....	....
1989-90	**St. Louis**	**NHL**	**7**	**1**	**5**	**6**	**2**	**2**	**0**	**1**	**1**	**0**
abc	Peoria	IHL	73	39	*78	*117	53	5	3	4	7	6
1990-91	**St. Louis**	**NHL**	**7**	**1**	**1**	**2**	**0**	....	....	....	....	....
de	Peoria	IHL	73	41	65	106	114	19	10	*16	26	32
1991-92	**St. Louis**	**NHL**	**36**	**3**	**12**	**15**	**6**	....	....	....	....	....
	Peoria	IHL	32	21	34	55	77	10	5	14	19	8
	NHL Totals		**50**	**5**	**18**	**23**	**8**	**2**	**0**	**1**	**1**	**0**

a IHL First All-Star Team (1990)
b Won James Gatschene Memorial Trophy (MVP-IHL) (1990)
c Won Leo P. Lamoureux Memorial Trophy (Top Scorer-IHL) (1990)
d IHL Second All-Star Team (1991)
e Won N.R. Poile Trophy (MVP in Playoffs–IHL) (1991)

Signed as a free agent by **St. Louis**, August 21, 1989. Claimed by **Tampa Bay** from **St. Louis** in Expansion Draft, June 18, 1992.

MORAN, IAN

Defense. Shoots right. 5'11", 175 lbs. Born, Cleveland, OH, August 24, 1972.
(Pittsburgh's 6th choice, 107th overall, in 1990 Entry Draft).

			Regular Season					Playoffs				
Season	Club	Lea	GP	G	A	TP	PIM	GP	G	A	TP	PIM
1990-91	Belmont Hill	HS	23	7	44	51	12	....	....	....	....	....
1991-92	Boston College	H.E.	30	2	16	18	44	....	....	....	....	....

MORE, JAYSON

Defense. Shoots right. 6'1", 202 lbs. Born, Souris, Man., January 12, 1969.
(NY Rangers' 1st choice, 10th overall, in 1987 Entry Draft).

			Regular Season					Playoffs				
Season	Club	Lea	GP	G	A	TP	PIM	GP	G	A	TP	PIM
1984-85	Lethbridge	WHL	71	3	9	12	101	4	1	0	1	7
1985-86	Lethbridge	WHL	61	7	18	25	155	9	0	2	2	36
1986-87	Brandon	WHL	21	4	6	10	62	....	....	....	....	....
	N. Westminster	WHL	43	4	23	27	155	....	....	....	....	....
1987-88a	N. Westminster	WHL	70	13	47	60	270	5	0	2	2	26
1988-89	NY Rangers	NHL	1	0	0	0	0	....	....	....	....	....
	Denver	IHL	62	7	15	22	138	3	0	1	1	26
1989-90	Flint	IHL	9	1	5	6	41	....	....	....	....	....
	Minnesota	NHL	5	0	0	0	16	....	....	....	....	....
	Kalamazoo	IHL	64	9	25	34	316	10	0	3	3	13
1990-91	Kalamazoo	IHL	10	0	5	5	46	....	....	....	....	....
	Fredericton	AHL	57	7	17	24	152	9	1	1	2	34
1991-92	San Jose	NHL	46	4	13	17	85	....	....	....	....	....
	Kansas City	IHL	2	0	2	2	4	....	....	....	....	....
	NHL Totals		52	4	13	17	101	....	....	....	....	....

a WHL All-Star Team (1988)

Traded to **Minnesota** by **NY Rangers** for Dave Archibald, November 1, 1989. Traded to **Montreal** by **Minnesota** for Brian Hayward, November 7, 1990. Claimed by **San Jose** from **Montreal** in Expansion Draft, May 30, 1991.

MORIN, STEPHANE (mohr-AN)

Center. Shoots left. 6', 174 lbs. Born, Montreal, Que., March 27, 1969.
(Quebec's 3rd choice, 43rd overall, in 1989 Entry Draft).

			Regular Season					Playoffs				
Season	Club	Lea	GP	G	A	TP	PIM	GP	G	A	TP	PIM
1986-87	Shawinigan	QMJHL	65	9	14	23	28	....	....	....	....	....
1987-88	Chicoutimi	QMJHL	68	38	45	83	18	6	3	8	11	2
1988-89ab	Chicoutimi	QMJHL	70	77	*109	*186	71	....	....	....	....	....
1989-90	Quebec	NHL	6	0	2	2	2	....	....	....	....	....
	Halifax	AHL	65	28	32	60	60	6	3	4	7	6
1990-91	Quebec	NHL	48	13	27	40	30	....	....	....	....	....
	Halifax	AHL	17	8	14	22	18	....	....	....	....	....
1991-92	Quebec	NHL	30	2	8	10	14	....	....	....	....	....
	Halifax	AHL	30	17	13	30	29	....	....	....	....	....
	NHL Totals		84	15	37	52	46	....	....	....	....	....

a QMJHL First All-Star Team (1989)
b QMJHL Player of the Year (1989)

MORRIS, JON

Center. Shoots right. 6', 175 lbs. Born, Lowell, MA, May 6, 1966.
(New Jersey's 5th choice, 86th overall, in 1984 Entry Draft).

			Regular Season					Playoffs				
Season	Club	Lea	GP	G	A	TP	PIM	GP	G	A	TP	PIM
1984-85	Lowell	H.E.	42	29	31	60	16	....	....	....	....	....
1985-86	Lowell	H.E.	39	25	31	56	52	....	....	....	....	....
1986-87ab	Lowell	H.E.	35	28	33	61	48	....	....	....	....	....
1987-88	Lowell	H.E.	37	15	39	54	39	....	....	....	....	....
1988-89	New Jersey	NHL	4	0	2	2	0	....	....	....	....	....
1989-90	New Jersey	NHL	20	6	7	13	8	6	1	3	4	23
	Utica	AHL	49	27	37	64	6	....	....	....	....	....
1990-91	New Jersey	NHL	53	9	19	28	27	5	0	4	4	2
	Utica	AHL	6	4	2	6	5	....	....	....	....	....
1991-92	New Jersey	NHL	7	1	2	3	6	....	....	....	....	....
	Utica	AHL	7	1	4	5	0	....	....	....	....	....
	NHL Totals		84	16	30	46	41	11	1	7	8	25

a Hockey East First All-Star Team (1987)
b NCAA East Second All-American Team (1987)

MORRIS, KEITH

Center. Shoots left. 6'1", 185 lbs. Born, Winnipeg, Man., April 24, 1971.
(Winnipeg's 13th choice, 245th overall, in 1990 Entry Draft).

			Regular Season					Playoffs				
Season	Club	Lea	GP	G	A	TP	PIM	GP	G	A	TP	PIM
1989-90	Alaska-Anch.	G.N.	28	10	18	28	14	....	....	....	....	....
1990-91	Alaska-Anch.	G.N.	25	11	11	22	36	....	....	....	....	....
1991-92	Alaska-Anch.	G.N.	35	24	26	50	18	....	....	....	....	....

MORRISON, JUSTIN

Center. Shoots right. 5'10", 185 lbs. Born, Newmarket, Ont., February 9, 1972.
(Washington's 4th choice, 80th overall, in 1991 Entry Draft).

			Regular Season					Playoffs				
Season	Club	Lea	GP	G	A	TP	PIM	GP	G	A	TP	PIM
1989-90	Kingston	OHL	65	27	40	67	201	....	....	....	....	....
1990-91	Kingston	OHL	61	44	57	101	222	....	....	....	....	....
1991-92	Kingston	OHL	23	18	21	39	63	....	....	....	....	....
	Owen Sound	OHL	36	9	43	52	106	5	3	2	5	11

MORROW, SCOTT

Left wing. Shoots left. 6'1", 181 lbs. Born, Chicago, IL, June 18, 1969.
(Hartford's 4th choice, 95th overall, in 1988 Entry Draft).

			Regular Season					Playoffs				
Season	Club	Lea	GP	G	A	TP	PIM	GP	G	A	TP	PIM
1988-89	N. Hampshire	H.E.	19	6	7	13	14	....	....	....	....	....
1989-90	N. Hampshire	H.E.	29	10	11	21	35	....	....	....	....	....
1990-91	N. Hampshire	H.E.	31	11	11	22	52	....	....	....	....	....
1991-92a	N. Hampshire	H.E.	35	30	23	53	65	....	....	....	....	....
	Springfield	AHL	2	0	1	1	0	5	0	0	0	9

a Hockey East Second All-Star Team (1992)

MORROW, STEVEN

Defense. Shoots left. 6'2", 212 lbs. Born, Plano, TX, April 3, 1968.
(Philadelphia's 10th choice, 209th overall, in 1987 Entry Draft).

			Regular Season					Playoffs				
Season	Club	Lea	GP	G	A	TP	PIM	GP	G	A	TP	PIM
1988-89	N. Hampshire	H.E.	30	0	0	0	28	....	....	....	....	....
1989-90	N. Hampshire	H.E.	35	2	7	9	40	....	....	....	....	....
1990-91	N. Hampshire	H.E.	33	2	14	16	58	....	....	....	....	....
1991-92	Hershey	AHL	31	1	2	3	6	....	....	....	....	....

MOSER, JOHN (JAY)

Defense. Shoots left. 6'2", 170 lbs. Born, Cottage Grove, MN, December 26, 1972.
(Boston's 7th choice, 172nd overall, in 1991 Entry Draft).

			Regular Season					Playoffs				
Season	Club	Lea	GP	G	A	TP	PIM	GP	G	A	TP	PIM
1990-91	Park HS	HS	24	15	22	37	0	....	....	....	....	....
1991-92	St. Cloud	WCHA	35	3	9	12	40	....	....	....	....	....

MOTKOV, DMITRI (moht-KOHV)

Defense. Shoots left. 6'4", 178 lbs. Born, Moscow, Soviet Union, February 23, 1971.
(Detroit's 5th choice, 98th overall, in 1991 Entry Draft).

			Regular Season					Playoffs				
Season	Club	Lea	GP	G	A	TP	PIM	GP	G	A	TP	PIM
1990-91	CSKA	USSR	31	0	2	2	14	....	....	....	....	....
1991-92	CSKA	CIS	44	1	3	4	69	....	....	....	....	....

MUELLER, BRIAN

Defense. Shoots left. 5'11", 200 lbs. Born, Liverpool, NY, June 2, 1972.
(Hartford's 7th choice, 141st overall, in 1991 Entry Draft).

			Regular Season					Playoffs				
Season	Club	Lea	GP	G	A	TP	PIM	GP	G	A	TP	PIM
1990-91	S. Kent Prep.	HS	32	21	30	51	....	....	....	....	....	....
1991-92	Clarkson	ECAC	28	4	13	17	30	....	....	....	....	....

MULLEN, BRIAN

Right wing. Shoots left. 5'10", 180 lbs. Born, New York, NY, March 16, 1962.
(Winnipeg's 7th choice, 128th overall, in 1980 Entry Draft).

			Regular Season					Playoffs				
Season	Club	Lea	GP	G	A	TP	PIM	GP	G	A	TP	PIM
1980-81	U. Wisconsin	WCHA	38	11	13	24	28	....	....	....	....	....
1981-82	U. Wisconsin	WCHA	33	20	17	37	10	....	....	....	....	....
1982-83	Winnipeg	NHL	80	24	26	50	14	3	1	0	1	0
1983-84	Winnipeg	NHL	75	21	41	62	28	3	0	3	3	6
1984-85	Winnipeg	NHL	69	32	39	71	32	8	1	2	3	4
1985-86	Winnipeg	NHL	79	28	34	62	38	3	1	2	3	6
1986-87	Winnipeg	NHL	69	19	32	51	20	9	4	2	6	0
1987-88	NY Rangers	NHL	74	25	29	54	42	....	....	....	....	....
1988-89	NY Rangers	NHL	78	29	35	64	60	3	0	1	1	4
1989-90	NY Rangers	NHL	76	27	41	68	42	10	2	2	4	8
1990-91	NY Rangers	NHL	79	19	43	62	44	5	0	2	2	0
1991-92	San Jose	NHL	72	18	28	46	66	....	....	....	....	....
	NHL Totals		751	242	348	590	386	44	9	14	23	28

Played in NHL All-Star Game (1989)

Traded to **NY Rangers** by **Winnipeg** with Winnipeg's tenth round draft choice (Brett Barnett) in 1987 Entry Draft for NY Rangers' fifth round choice in 1988 Entry Draft (Benoit Lebeau) – acquired earlier by NY Rangers – and NY Rangers' third round choice – later traded to St. Louis (Denny Felsner) – in 1989 Entry Draft, June 8, 1987. Traded to **San Jose** by **NY Rangers** with future considerations for Tim Kerr, May 30, 1991. Traded to **NY Islanders** by **San Jose** for the rights to Marcus Thuresson, August 24, 1992.

MULLEN, JOE

Right wing. Shoots right. 5'9", 180 lbs. Born, New York, NY, February 26, 1957.

			Regular Season					Playoffs				
Season	Club	Lea	GP	G	A	TP	PIM	GP	G	A	TP	PIM
1977-78a	Boston College	ECAC	34	34	34	68	12	....	....	....	....	....
1978-79a	Boston College	ECAC	25	32	24	56	8	....	....	....	....	....
1979-80bc	Salt Lake	CHL	75	40	32	72	21	13	*9	11	20	0
	St. Louis	NHL	....	....	....	....	....	1	0	0	0	0
1980-81de	Salt Lake	CHL	80	59	58	*117	8	17	11	9	20	0
1981-82	St. Louis	NHL	45	25	34	59	4	10	7	11	18	4
	Salt Lake	CHL	27	21	27	48	12	....	....	....	....	....
1982-83	St. Louis	NHL	49	17	30	47	6	....	....	....	....	....
1983-84	St. Louis	NHL	80	41	44	85	19	6	2	0	2	0
1984-85	St. Louis	NHL	79	40	52	92	6	3	0	0	0	0
1985-86	St. Louis	NHL	48	28	24	52	10	....	....	....	....	....
	Calgary	NHL	29	16	22	38	11	21	*12	7	19	4
1986-87f	Calgary	NHL	79	47	40	87	14	6	2	1	3	0
1987-88	Calgary	NHL	80	40	44	84	30	7	2	4	6	10
1988-89fgh	Calgary	NHL	79	51	59	110	16	21	*16	8	24	4
1989-90	Calgary	NHL	78	36	33	69	24	6	3	0	3	0
1990-91	Pittsburgh	NHL	47	17	22	39	6	22	8	9	17	4
1991-92	Pittsburgh	NHL	77	42	45	87	30	9	3	1	4	4
	NHL Totals		770	400	449	849	176	112	55	41	96	30

a ECAC First All-Star Team (1978, 1979)
b CHL Second All-Star Team (1980)
c Won Ken McKenzie Trophy (CHL's Top Rookie) (1980)
d CHL First All-Star Team (1981)
e Won Tommy Ivan Trophy (CHL's Most Valuable Player) (1981)
f Won Lady Byng Trophy (1987, 1989)
g NHL First All-Star Team (1989)
h NHL Plus/Minus Leader (1989)

Played in NHL All-Star Game (1989, 1990)

Signed as a free agent by **St. Louis,** August 16, 1979. Traded to **Calgary** by **St. Louis** with Terry Johnson and Rik Wilson for Ed Beers, Charles Bourgeois and Gino Cavallini, February 1, 1986. Traded to **Pittsburgh** by **Calgary** for Pittsburgh's second round choice (Nicolas Perreault) in 1990 Entry Draft, June 16, 1990.

MULLER, KIRK

Left wing. Shoots left. 6', 205 lbs. Born, Kingston, Ont., February 8, 1966.
(New Jersey's 1st choice, 2nd overall, in 1984 Entry Draft).

			Regular Season					Playoffs				
Season	Club	Lea	GP	G	A	TP	PIM	GP	G	A	TP	PIM
1981-82	Kingston	OHL	67	12	39	51	27	4	5	1	6	4
1982-83ab	Guelph	OHL	66	52	60	112	41	....	....	....	....	....
1983-84b	Cdn. Olympic	....	21	4	3	7	6	....	....	....	....	....
	Guelph	OHL	49	31	63	94	27	....	....	....	....	....
1984-85	**New Jersey**	**NHL**	**80**	**17**	**37**	**54**	**69**	....	....	....	....	....
1985-86	**New Jersey**	**NHL**	**77**	**25**	**41**	**66**	**45**	....	....	....	....	....
1986-87	**New Jersey**	**NHL**	**79**	**26**	**50**	**76**	**75**	....	....	....	....	....
1987-88	**New Jersey**	**NHL**	**80**	**37**	**57**	**94**	**114**	**20**	**4**	**8**	**12**	**37**
1988-89	**New Jersey**	**NHL**	**80**	**31**	**43**	**74**	**119**	....	....	....	....	....
1989-90	**New Jersey**	**NHL**	**80**	**30**	**56**	**86**	**74**	**6**	**1**	**3**	**4**	**11**
1990-91	**New Jersey**	**NHL**	**80**	**19**	**51**	**70**	**76**	**7**	**0**	**2**	**2**	**10**
1991-92	**Montreal**	**NHL**	**78**	**36**	**41**	**77**	**86**	**11**	**4**	**3**	**7**	**31**
	NHL Totals		**634**	**221**	**376**	**597**	**658**	**44**	**9**	**16**	**25**	**89**

a OHL's Most Gentlemanly Player (1983)
b OHL Third All-Star Team (1983, 1984)

Played in NHL All-Star Game (1985, 1986, 1988, 1990, 1992)

Traded to **Montreal** by **New Jersey** with Roland Melanson for Stephane Richer and Tom Chorske, September 20, 1991.

MULLER, MIKE

Defense. Shoots left. 6'2", 205 lbs. Born, Fairview, MN, September 18, 1971.
(Winnipeg's 2nd choice, 35th overall, in 1990 Entry Draft).

			Regular Season					Playoffs				
Season	Club	Lea	GP	G	A	TP	PIM	GP	G	A	TP	PIM
1990-91	U. Minnesota	WCHA	33	4	4	8	44	....	....	....	....	....
1991-92	U. Minnesota	WCHA	41	4	12	16	52	....	....	....	....	....

MULVENNA, GLENN

Center. Shoots left. 5'11", 187 lbs. Born, Calgary, Alta., February 18, 1967.

			Regular Season					Playoffs				
Season	Club	Lea	GP	G	A	TP	PIM	GP	G	A	TP	PIM
1986-87	N. Westminster	WHL	53	24	44	68	43	....	....	....	....	....
	Kamloops	WHL	18	13	8	21	18	13	4	6	10	10
1987-88	Kamloops	WHL	38	21	38	59	35	....	....	....	....	....
1988-89	Flint	IHL	32	9	14	23	12	....	....	....	....	....
	Muskegon	IHL	11	3	2	5	0	....	....	....	....	....
1989-90	Muskegon	IHL	52	14	21	35	17	11	2	3	5	0
	Fort Wayne	IHL	6	2	5	7	2	....	....	....	....	....
1990-91	Muskegon	IHL	48	9	27	36	25	5	1	1	2	0
1991-92	**Pittsburgh**	**NHL**	**1**	**0**	**0**	**0**	**2**	....	....	....	....	....
	Muskegon	IHL	70	15	27	42	24	14	5	6	11	11
	NHL Totals		**1**	**0**	**0**	**0**	**2**	....	....	....	....	....

Signed as a free agent by **Pittsburgh**, December 3, 1987. Signed as a free agent by **Philadelphia**, July 11, 1992.

MUNI, CRAIG DOUGLAS (MYEW-nee)

Defense. Shoots left. 6'3", 200 lbs. Born, Toronto, Ont., July 19, 1962.
(Toronto's 1st choice, 25th overall, in 1980 Entry Draft).

			Regular Season					Playoffs				
Season	Club	Lea	GP	G	A	TP	PIM	GP	G	A	TP	PIM
1980-81	Kingston	OHA	38	2	14	16	65	....	....	....	....	....
	Windsor	OHA	25	5	11	16	41	11	1	4	5	14
	New Brunswick	AHL	....	....	....	....	....	2	0	1	1	10
1981-82	**Toronto**	**NHL**	**3**	**0**	**0**	**0**	**2**	....	....	....	....	....
	Windsor	OHL	49	5	32	37	92	9	2	3	5	16
	Cincinnati	CHL	....	....	....	....	....	3	0	2	2	2
1982-83	**Toronto**	**NHL**	**2**	**0**	**1**	**1**	**0**	....	....	....	....	....
	St. Catharines	AHL	64	6	32	38	52	....	....	....	....	....
1983-84	St. Catharines	AHL	64	4	16	20	79	7	0	1	1	0
1984-85	**Toronto**	**NHL**	**8**	**0**	**0**	**0**	**0**	....	....	....	....	....
	St. Catharines	AHL	68	7	17	24	54	....	....	....	....	....
1985-86	**Toronto**	**NHL**	**6**	**0**	**1**	**1**	**4**	....	....	....	....	....
	St. Catharines	AHL	73	3	34	37	91	13	0	5	5	16
1986-87	**Edmonton**	**NHL**	**79**	**7**	**22**	**29**	**85**	**14**	**0**	**2**	**2**	**17**
1987-88	**Edmonton**	**NHL**	**72**	**4**	**15**	**19**	**77**	**19**	**0**	**4**	**4**	**31**
1988-89	**Edmonton**	**NHL**	**69**	**5**	**13**	**18**	**71**	**7**	**0**	**3**	**3**	**8**
1989-90	**Edmonton**	**NHL**	**71**	**5**	**12**	**17**	**81**	**22**	**0**	**3**	**3**	**16**
1990-91	**Edmonton**	**NHL**	**76**	**1**	**9**	**10**	**77**	**18**	**0**	**3**	**3**	**20**
1991-92	**Edmonton**	**NHL**	**54**	**2**	**5**	**7**	**34**	**3**	**0**	**0**	**0**	**2**
	NHL Totals		**440**	**24**	**78**	**102**	**431**	**83**	**0**	**15**	**15**	**94**

Signed as a free agent by **Edmonton,** August 18, 1986. Sold to **Buffalo** by **Edmonton**, October 2, 1986. Traded to **Pittsburgh** by **Buffalo** for future considerations, October 3, 1986. Acquired by **Edmonton** from **Pittsburgh** to complete earlier trade for Gilles Meloche, October 6, 1986.

MURANO, ERIC

Center. Shoots right. 6', 200 lbs. Born, Montreal, Que., May 4, 1967.
(Vancouver's 4th choice, 91st overall, in 1986 Entry Draft).

			Regular Season					Playoffs				
Season	Club	Lea	GP	G	A	TP	PIM	GP	G	A	TP	PIM
1986-87	U. of Denver	WCHA	31	5	7	12	12	....	....	....	....	....
1987-88	U. of Denver	WCHA	37	8	13	21	26	....	....	....	....	....
1988-89	U. of Denver	WCHA	42	13	16	29	52	....	....	....	....	....
1989-90a	U. of Denver	WCHA	42	33	35	68	52	....	....	....	....	....
	Cdn. Olympic	....	6	1	0	1	4	....	....	....	....	....
1990-91	Milwaukee	IHL	63	32	35	67	63	3	0	1	1	4
1991-92	Milwaukee	IHL	80	35	48	83	61	5	3	4	7	0

a WCHA Second All-Star Team (1990)

MURPHY, DANIEL

Defense. Shoots left. 6'1", 185 lbs. Born, Needham, MA, May 13, 1970.
(Boston's 5th choice, 102nd overall, in 1988 Entry Draft).

			Regular Season					Playoffs				
Season	Club	Lea	GP	G	A	TP	PIM	GP	G	A	TP	PIM
1989-90	U. of Maine	H.E.	42	1	9	10	26	....	....	....	....	....
1990-91	U. of Maine	H.E.	42	1	5	6	26	....	....	....	....	....
1991-92	U. of Maine	H.E.	36	0	6	6	44	....	....	....	....	....

MURPHY, GORDON (GORD)

Defense. Shoots right. 6'2", 195 lbs. Born, Willowdale, Ont., March 23, 1967.
(Philadelphia's 10th choice, 189th overall, in 1985 Entry Draft).

			Regular Season					Playoffs				
Season	Club	Lea	GP	G	A	TP	PIM	GP	G	A	TP	PIM
1984-85	Oshawa	OHL	59	3	12	15	25	....	....	....	....	....
1985-86	Oshawa	OHL	64	7	15	22	56	6	1	1	2	6
1986-87	Oshawa	OHL	56	7	30	37	95	24	6	16	22	22
1987-88	Hershey	AHL	62	8	20	28	44	12	0	8	8	12
1988-89	**Philadelphia**	**NHL**	**75**	**4**	**31**	**35**	**68**	**19**	**2**	**7**	**9**	**13**
1989-90	**Philadelphia**	**NHL**	**75**	**14**	**27**	**41**	**95**	....	....	....	....	....
1990-91	**Philadelphia**	**NHL**	**80**	**11**	**31**	**42**	**58**	....	....	....	....	....
1991-92	**Philadelphia**	**NHL**	**31**	**2**	**8**	**10**	**33**	....	....	....	....	....
	Boston	**NHL**	**42**	**3**	**6**	**9**	**51**	**15**	**1**	**0**	**1**	**12**
	NHL Totals		**303**	**34**	**103**	**137**	**305**	**34**	**3**	**7**	**10**	**25**

Traded to **Boston** by **Philadelphia** with Brian Dobbin and Philadelphia's third round choice (Sergei Zholtok) in 1992 Entry Draft for Garry Galley, Wes Walz and future considerations, January 2, 1992.

MURPHY, JOE

Right wing. Shoots left. 6'1", 190 lbs. Born, London, Ont., October 16, 1967.
(Detroit's 1st choice, 1st overall, in 1986 Entry Draft).

			Regular Season					Playoffs				
Season	Club	Lea	GP	G	A	TP	PIM	GP	G	A	TP	PIM
1985-86	Cdn. Olympic	....	8	3	3	6	2	....	....	....	....	....
a	Michigan State	CCHA	35	24	37	61	50	....	....	....	....	....
1986-87	**Detroit**	**NHL**	**5**	**0**	**1**	**1**	**2**	....	....	....	....	....
	Adirondack	AHL	71	21	38	59	61	10	2	1	3	33
1987-88	**Detroit**	**NHL**	**50**	**10**	**9**	**19**	**37**	**8**	**0**	**1**	**1**	**6**
	Adirondack	AHL	6	5	6	11	4	....	....	....	....	....
1988-89	**Detroit**	**NHL**	**26**	**1**	**7**	**8**	**28**	....	....	....	....	....
	Adirondack	AHL	47	31	35	66	66	16	6	11	17	17
1989-90	**Detroit**	**NHL**	**9**	**3**	**1**	**4**	**4**	....	....	....	....	....
	Edmonton	**NHL**	**62**	**7**	**18**	**25**	**56**	**22**	**6**	**8**	**14**	**16**
1990-91	**Edmonton**	**NHL**	**80**	**27**	**35**	**62**	**35**	**15**	**2**	**5**	**7**	**14**
1991-92	**Edmonton**	**NHL**	**80**	**35**	**47**	**82**	**52**	**16**	**8**	**16**	**24**	**12**
	NHL Totals		**312**	**83**	**118**	**201**	**214**	**61**	**16**	**30**	**46**	**48**

a CCHA Rookie of the Year (1986)

Traded to **Edmonton** by **Detroit** with Petr Klima, Adam Graves and Jeff Sharples for Jimmy Carson, Kevin McClelland and Edmonton's fifth round choice (later traded to Montreal for Rick Green. Montreal selected Brad Layzell) in 1991 Entry Draft, November 2, 1989.

MURPHY, LAWRENCE THOMAS (LARRY)

Defense. Shoots right. 6'2", 210 lbs. Born, Scarborough, Ont., March 8, 1961.
(Los Angeles' 1st choice, 4th overall, in 1980 Entry Draft).

			Regular Season					Playoffs				
Season	Club	Lea	GP	G	A	TP	PIM	GP	G	A	TP	PIM
1978-79	Peterborough	OHA	66	6	21	27	82	19	1	9	10	42
1979-80a	Peterborough	OHA	68	21	68	89	88	14	4	13	17	20
1980-81	**Los Angeles**	**NHL**	**80**	**16**	**60**	**76**	**79**	**4**	**3**	**0**	**3**	**2**
1981-82	**Los Angeles**	**NHL**	**79**	**22**	**44**	**66**	**95**	**10**	**2**	**8**	**10**	**12**
1982-83	**Los Angeles**	**NHL**	**77**	**14**	**48**	**62**	**81**	....	....	....	....	....
1983-84	**Los Angeles**	**NHL**	**6**	**0**	**3**	**3**	**0**	....	....	....	....	....
	Washington	**NHL**	**72**	**13**	**33**	**46**	**50**	**8**	**0**	**3**	**3**	**6**
1984-85	**Washington**	**NHL**	**79**	**13**	**42**	**55**	**51**	**5**	**2**	**3**	**5**	**0**
1985-86	**Washington**	**NHL**	**78**	**21**	**44**	**65**	**50**	**9**	**1**	**5**	**6**	**6**
1986-87b	**Washington**	**NHL**	**80**	**23**	**58**	**81**	**39**	**7**	**2**	**2**	**4**	**6**
1987-88	**Washington**	**NHL**	**79**	**8**	**53**	**61**	**72**	**13**	**4**	**4**	**8**	**33**
1988-89	**Washington**	**NHL**	**65**	**7**	**29**	**36**	**70**	....	....	....	....	....
	Minnesota	**NHL**	**13**	**4**	**6**	**10**	**12**	**5**	**0**	**2**	**2**	**8**
1989-90	**Minnesota**	**NHL**	**77**	**10**	**58**	**68**	**44**	**7**	**1**	**2**	**3**	**31**
1990-91	**Minnesota**	**NHL**	**31**	**4**	**11**	**15**	**38**	....	....	....	....	....
	Pittsburgh	**NHL**	**44**	**5**	**23**	**28**	**30**	**23**	**5**	**18**	**23**	**44**
1991-92	**Pittsburgh**	**NHL**	**77**	**21**	**56**	**77**	**48**	**21**	**6**	**10**	**16**	**19**
	NHL Totals		**937**	**181**	**568**	**749**	**759**	**112**	**26**	**57**	**83**	**167**

a OHA First All-Star Team (1980)
b NHL Second All-Star Team (1987)

Traded to **Washington** by **Los Angeles** for Ken Houston and Brian Engblom, October 18, 1983. Traded to **Minnesota** by **Washington** with Mike Gartner for Dino Ciccarelli and Bob Rouse, March 7, 1989. Traded to **Pittsburgh** by **Minnesota** with Peter Taglianetti for Chris Dahlquist and Jim Johnson, December 11, 1990.

MURPHY, ROB

Left wing/Center. Shoots left. 6'3", 205 lbs. Born, Hull, Que., April 7, 1969.
(Vancouver's 1st choice, 24th overall, in 1987 Entry Draft).

			Regular Season					Playoffs				
Season	Club	Lea	GP	G	A	TP	PIM	GP	G	A	TP	PIM
1986-87	Laval	QMJHL	70	35	54	89	86	14	3	4	7	15
1987-88	**Vancouver**	**NHL**	**5**	**0**	**0**	**0**	**2**	....	....	....	....	....
	Laval	QMJHL	26	11	25	36	82	....	....	....	....	....
	Drummondville	QMJHL	33	16	28	44	41	17	4	15	19	45
1988-89	**Vancouver**	**NHL**	**8**	**0**	**1**	**1**	**2**	....	....	....	....	....
	Milwaukee	IHL	8	4	2	6	4	11	3	5	8	34
	Drummondville	QMJHL	26	13	25	38	16	4	1	3	4	20
1989-90	**Vancouver**	**NHL**	**12**	**1**	**1**	**2**	**0**	....	....	....	....	....
a	Milwaukee	IHL	64	24	47	71	87	6	2	6	8	12
1990-91	**Vancouver**	**NHL**	**42**	**5**	**1**	**6**	**90**	**4**	**0**	**0**	**0**	**2**
	Milwaukee	IHL	23	1	7	8	48	....	....	....	....	....
1991-92	**Vancouver**	**NHL**	**6**	**0**	**1**	**1**	**6**	....	....	....	....	....
	Milwaukee	IHL	73	26	38	64	141	5	0	3	3	2
	NHL Totals		**73**	**6**	**4**	**10**	**100**	**4**	**0**	**0**	**0**	**2**

a Won Garry F. Longman Memorial Trophy (Top Rookie-IHL) (1990)

Claimed by **Ottawa** from **Vancouver** in Expansion Draft, June 18, 1992.

MURRAY, GLEN

Right wing. Shoots right. 6'2", 200 lbs. Born, Halifax, N.S., November 1, 1972.
(Boston's 1st choice, 18th overall, in 1991 Entry Draft).

			Regular Season					Playoffs				
Season	Club	Lea	GP	G	A	TP	PIM	GP	G	A	TP	PIM
1989-90	Sudbury	OHL	62	8	28	36	17	7	0	0	0	4
1990-91	Sudbury	OHL	66	27	38	65	82	5	8	4	12	10
1991-92	**Boston**	**NHL**	**5**	**3**	**1**	**4**	**0**	**15**	**4**	**2**	**6**	**10**
	Sudbury	OHL	54	37	47	84	93	11	7	4	11	18
	NHL Totals		**5**	**3**	**1**	**4**	**0**	**15**	**4**	**2**	**6**	**10**

MURRAY, MICHAEL

Right wing. Shoots right. 6'1", 185 lbs. Born, Cumberland, RI, April 18, 1971.
(Calgary's 10th choice, 188th overall, in 1990 Entry Draft).

			Regular Season					Playoffs				
Season	Club	Lea	GP	G	A	TP	PIM	GP	G	A	TP	PIM
1990-91	Lowell	H.E.	30	5	8	13	18	....	....	....	....	....
1991-92	Lowell	H.E.	31	22	15	37	40	....	....	....	....	....

MURRAY, PAT

Left wing. Shoots left. 6'2", 185 lbs. Born, Stratford, Ont., August 20, 1969.
(Philadelphia's 2nd choice, 35th overall, in 1988 Entry Draft).

			Regular Season					Playoffs				
Season	Club	Lea	GP	G	A	TP	PIM	GP	G	A	TP	PIM
1987-88	Michigan State	CCHA	42	14	21	35	26	....	....	....	....	....
1988-89	Michigan State	CCHA	46	21	41	62	65	....	....	....	....	....
1989-90a	Michigan State	CCHA	45	24	60	84	36	....	....	....	....	....
1990-91	**Philadelphia**	**NHL**	**16**	**2**	**1**	**3**	**15**	....	....	....	....	....
	Hershey	AHL	57	15	38	53	8	7	5	2	7	0
1991-92	**Philadelphia**	**NHL**	**9**	**1**	**0**	**1**	**0**	....	....	....	....	....
	Hershey	AHL	69	19	43	62	25	6	1	2	3	0
	NHL Totals		**25**	**3**	**1**	**4**	**15**	....	....	....	....	....

a CCHA Second All-Star Team (1990)

MURRAY, RAYMOND (REM)

Left wing. Shoots left. 6'1", 178 lbs. Born, Stratford, Ont., October 9, 1972.
(Los Angeles' 5th choice, 135th overall, in 1992 Entry Draft).

			Regular Season					Playoffs				
Season	Club	Lea	GP	G	A	TP	PIM	GP	G	A	TP	PIM
1990-91	Stratford	Jr. B	48	39	59	98	22	....	....	....	....	....
1991-92	Michigan State	CCHA	41	12	36	48	16	....	....	....	....	....

MURRAY, ROB

Center. Shoots right. 6', 185 lbs. Born, Toronto, Ont., April 4, 1967.
(Washington's 3rd choice, 61st overall, in 1985 Entry Draft).

			Regular Season					Playoffs				
Season	Club	Lea	GP	G	A	TP	PIM	GP	G	A	TP	PIM
1984-85	Peterborough	OHL	63	12	9	21	155	17	2	7	9	45
1985-86	Peterborough	OHL	52	14	18	32	125	16	1	2	3	50
1986-87	Peterborough	OHL	62	17	37	54	204	3	1	4	5	8
1987-88	Fort Wayne	IHL	80	12	21	33	139	6	0	2	2	16
1988-89	Baltimore	AHL	80	11	23	34	235	....	....	....	....	....
1989-90	**Washington**	**NHL**	**41**	**2**	**7**	**9**	**58**	**9**	**0**	**0**	**0**	**18**
	Baltimore	AHL	23	5	4	9	63	....	....	....	....	....
1990-91	**Washington**	**NHL**	**17**	**0**	**3**	**3**	**19**	....	....	....	....	....
	Baltimore	AHL	48	6	20	26	177	4	0	0	0	12
1991-92	**Winnipeg**	**NHL**	**9**	**0**	**1**	**1**	**18**	....	....	....	....	....
	Moncton	AHL	60	16	15	31	247	8	0	1	1	56
	NHL Totals		**67**	**2**	**11**	**13**	**95**	**9**	**0**	**0**	**0**	**18**

Claimed by **Minnesota** from **Washington** in Expansion Draft, May 30, 1991. Traded to **Winnipeg** by **Minnesota** with future considerations for Winnipeg's seventh round choice (Geoff Finch) in 1991 Entry Draft and future considerations, May 31, 1991.

MURRAY, TROY NORMAN

Center. Shoots right. 6'1", 195 lbs. Born, Calgary, Alta., July 31, 1962.
(Chicago's 6th choice, 57th overall, in 1980 Entry Draft).

			Regular Season					Playoffs				
Season	Club	Lea	GP	G	A	TP	PIM	GP	G	A	TP	PIM
1980-81ab	North Dakota	WCHA	38	33	45	78	28	....	....	....	....	....
1981-82b	North Dakota	WCHA	26	13	17	30	62	....	....	....	....	....
	Chicago	**NHL**	**1**	**0**	**0**	**0**	**0**	**7**	**1**	**0**	**1**	**5**
1982-83	**Chicago**	**NHL**	**54**	**8**	**8**	**16**	**27**	**2**	**0**	**0**	**0**	**0**
1983-84	**Chicago**	**NHL**	**61**	**15**	**15**	**30**	**45**	**5**	**1**	**0**	**1**	**7**
1984-85	**Chicago**	**NHL**	**80**	**26**	**40**	**66**	**82**	**15**	**5**	**14**	**19**	**24**
1985-86c	**Chicago**	**NHL**	**80**	**45**	**54**	**99**	**94**	**2**	**0**	**0**	**0**	**2**
1986-87	**Chicago**	**NHL**	**77**	**28**	**43**	**71**	**59**	**4**	**0**	**0**	**0**	**5**
1987-88	**Chicago**	**NHL**	**79**	**22**	**36**	**58**	**96**	**5**	**1**	**0**	**1**	**8**
1988-89	**Chicago**	**NHL**	**79**	**21**	**30**	**51**	**113**	**16**	**3**	**6**	**9**	**25**
1989-90	**Chicago**	**NHL**	**68**	**17**	**38**	**55**	**86**	**20**	**4**	**4**	**8**	**2**
1990-91	**Chicago**	**NHL**	**75**	**14**	**23**	**37**	**74**	**6**	**0**	**1**	**1**	**12**
1991-92	**Winnipeg**	**NHL**	**74**	**17**	**30**	**47**	**69**	**7**	**0**	**0**	**0**	**2**
	NHL Totals		**728**	**213**	**317**	**530**	**745**	**89**	**15**	**25**	**40**	**92**

a WCHA Rookie of the Year (1981)
b WCHA Second All-Star Team (1981, 1982)
c Won Frank J. Selke Memorial Trophy (1986)

Traded to **Winnipeg** by **Chicago** with Warren Rychel for Bryan Marchment and Chris Norton, July 22, 1991.

MURZYN, DANA (MUR-zihn)

Defense. Shoots left. 6'2", 200 lbs. Born, Calgary, Alta., December 9, 1966.
(Hartford's 1st choice, 5th overall, in 1985 Entry Draft).

			Regular Season					Playoffs				
Season	Club	Lea	GP	G	A	TP	PIM	GP	G	A	TP	PIM
1983-84	Calgary	WHL	65	11	20	31	135	2	0	0	0	10
1984-85a	Calgary	WHL	72	32	60	92	233	8	1	11	12	16
1985-86b	**Hartford**	**NHL**	**78**	**3**	**23**	**26**	**125**	**4**	**0**	**0**	**0**	**10**
1986-87	**Hartford**	**NHL**	**74**	**9**	**19**	**28**	**95**	**6**	**2**	**1**	**3**	**29**
1987-88	**Hartford**	**NHL**	**33**	**1**	**6**	**7**	**45**	....	....	....	....	....
	Calgary	**NHL**	**41**	**6**	**5**	**11**	**94**	**5**	**2**	**0**	**2**	**13**
1988-89	**Calgary**	**NHL**	**63**	**3**	**19**	**22**	**142**	**21**	**0**	**3**	**3**	**20**
1989-90	**Calgary**	**NHL**	**78**	**7**	**13**	**20**	**140**	**6**	**2**	**2**	**4**	**2**
1990-91	**Calgary**	**NHL**	**19**	**0**	**2**	**2**	**30**	....	....	....	....	....
	Vancouver	**NHL**	**10**	**1**	**0**	**1**	**8**	**6**	**0**	**1**	**1**	**8**
1991-92	**Vancouver**	**NHL**	**70**	**3**	**11**	**14**	**147**	**1**	**0**	**0**	**0**	**15**
	NHL Totals		**466**	**33**	**98**	**131**	**826**	**49**	**6**	**7**	**13**	**97**

a WHL First All-Star Team, East Division (1985)
b NHL All-Rookie Team (1986)

Traded to **Calgary** by **Hartford** with Shane Churla for Neil Sheehy, Carey Wilson and the rights to Lane MacDonald, January 3, 1988. Traded to **Vancouver** by **Calgary** for Ron Stern, Kevan Guy and future considerations, March 5, 1991.

MUSIL, FRANTISEK (moo-SIHL)

Defense. Shoots left. 6'3", 205 lbs. Born, Pardubice, Czech., December 17, 1964.
(Minnesota's 3rd choice, 38th overall, in 1983 Entry Draft).

			Regular Season					Playoffs				
Season	Club	Lea	GP	G	A	TP	PIM	GP	G	A	TP	PIM
1985-86	Dukla Jihlava	Czech.	35	3	7	10	42	....	....	....	....	....
1986-87	**Minnesota**	**NHL**	**72**	**2**	**9**	**11**	**148**	....	....	....	....	....
1987-88	**Minnesota**	**NHL**	**80**	**9**	**8**	**17**	**213**	....	....	....	....	....
1988-89	**Minnesota**	**NHL**	**55**	**1**	**19**	**20**	**54**	**5**	**1**	**1**	**2**	**4**
1989-90	**Minnesota**	**NHL**	**56**	**2**	**8**	**10**	**109**	**4**	**0**	**0**	**0**	**14**
1990-91	**Minnesota**	**NHL**	**8**	**0**	**2**	**2**	**23**	....	....	....	....	....
	Calgary	**NHL**	**67**	**7**	**14**	**21**	**160**	**7**	**0**	**0**	**0**	**10**
1991-92	**Calgary**	**NHL**	**78**	**4**	**8**	**12**	**103**	....	....	....	....	....
	NHL Totals		**416**	**25**	**68**	**93**	**810**	**16**	**1**	**1**	**2**	**28**

Traded to **Calgary** by **Minnesota** for Brian Glynn, October 26, 1990.

MYHRES, BRANTT

Right wing. Shoots right. 6'3", 195 lbs. Born, Edmonton, Alta., March 18, 1974.
(Tampa Bay's 5th choice, 97th overall, in 1992 Entry Draft).

			Regular Season					Playoffs				
Season	Club	Lea	GP	G	A	TP	PIM	GP	G	A	TP	PIM
1990-91	Portland	WHL	59	2	7	9	125	....	....	....	....	....
1991-92	Portland	WHL	4	0	2	2	22	....	....	....	....	....
	Lethbridge	WHL	53	4	11	15	359	5	0	0	0	36

NAMESTNIKOV, YEVGENY (nah-MEST-nih-kov, yev-GAIN-ee)

Defense. Shoots right. 5'11", 193 lbs. Born, Novgorod, Soviet Union, October 9, 1971.
(Vancouver's 6th choice, 117th overall, in 1991 Entry Draft).

			Regular Season					Playoffs				
Season	Club	Lea	GP	G	A	TP	PIM	GP	G	A	TP	PIM
1990-91	Torpedo Niz.	USSR	45	1	2	3	47	....	....	....	....	....
1991-92	CSKA	CIS	34	1	0	1	37	....	....	....	....	....

NAPIERALA, JEFF

Right wing. Shoots right. 6'1", 195 lbs. Born, Muskegon, MI, February 27, 1968.
(Vancouver's 1st choice, 3rd overall, in 1989 Supplemental Draft).

			Regular Season					Playoffs				
Season	Club	Lea	GP	G	A	TP	PIM	GP	G	A	TP	PIM
1987-88	Lake Superior	CCHA	7	0	0	0	0	....	....	....	....	....
1988-89	Lake Superior	CCHA	43	17	9	26	22	....	....	....	....	....
1989-90	Lake Superior	CCHA	44	33	26	59	32	....	....	....	....	....
1990-91	Lake Superior	CCHA	45	30	27	57	70	....	....	....	....	....
1991-92	Maine	AHL	16	0	3	3	0	....	....	....	....	....
	Milwaukee	IHL	18	2	2	4	0	....	....	....	....	....
	Columbus	ECHL	13	7	6	13	10	....	....	....	....	....

NASLUND, MARKUS

Right wing. Shoots left. 5'11", 174 lbs. Born, Harnosand, Sweden, July 30, 1973.
(Pittsburgh's 1st choice, 16th overall, in 1991 Entry Draft).

			Regular Season					Playoffs				
Season	Club	Lea	GP	G	A	TP	PIM	GP	G	A	TP	PIM
1989-90	MoDo	Swe. Jr.	33	43	35	78	20	....	....	....	....	....
1990-91	MoDo	Swe.	32	10	9	19	14	....	....	....	....	....
1991-92	MoDo	Swe.	39	22	17	39	52	....	....	....	....	....

NATTRESS, ERIC (RIC)

Defense. Shoots right. 6'2", 210 lbs. Born, Hamilton, Ont., May 25, 1962.
(Montreal's 2nd choice, 27th overall, in 1980 Entry Draft).

			Regular Season					Playoffs				
Season	Club	Lea	GP	G	A	TP	PIM	GP	G	A	TP	PIM
1979-80	Brantford	OHA	65	3	21	24	94	11	1	6	7	38
1980-81	Brantford	OHA	51	8	34	42	106	6	1	4	5	19
1981-82	Brantford	OHL	59	11	50	61	126	11	3	7	10	17
	Nova Scotia	AHL	....	....	....	....	....	5	0	1	1	7
1982-83	**Montreal**	**NHL**	**40**	**1**	**3**	**4**	**19**	**3**	**0**	**0**	**0**	**10**
	Nova Scotia	AHL	9	0	4	4	16	....	....	....	....	....
1983-84	**Montreal**	**NHL**	**34**	**0**	**12**	**12**	**15**	....	....	....	....	....
1984-85	**Montreal**	**NHL**	**5**	**0**	**1**	**1**	**2**	**2**	**0**	**0**	**0**	**2**
	Sherbrooke	AHL	72	8	40	48	37	16	4	13	17	20
1985-86	**St. Louis**	**NHL**	**78**	**4**	**20**	**24**	**52**	**18**	**1**	**4**	**5**	**24**
1986-87	**St. Louis**	**NHL**	**73**	**6**	**22**	**28**	**24**	**6**	**0**	**0**	**0**	**2**
1987-88	**Calgary**	**NHL**	**63**	**2**	**13**	**15**	**37**	**6**	**1**	**3**	**4**	**0**
1988-89	**Calgary**	**NHL**	**38**	**1**	**8**	**9**	**47**	**19**	**0**	**3**	**3**	**20**
1989-90	**Calgary**	**NHL**	**49**	**1**	**14**	**15**	**26**	**6**	**2**	**0**	**2**	**0**
1990-91	**Calgary**	**NHL**	**58**	**5**	**13**	**18**	**63**	**7**	**1**	**0**	**1**	**2**
1991-92	**Calgary**	**NHL**	**18**	**0**	**5**	**5**	**31**	....	....	....	....	....
	Toronto	**NHL**	**36**	**2**	**14**	**16**	**32**	....	....	....	....	....
	NHL Totals		**492**	**22**	**125**	**147**	**348**	**67**	**5**	**10**	**15**	**60**

Rights sold to **St. Louis** by **Montreal**, October 7, 1985. Traded to **Calgary** by **St. Louis** for Calgary's fourth round choice (Andy Rymsha) in 1987 Entry Draft and fifth round choice (Dave Lacouture) in 1988 Entry Draft, June 13, 1987. Traded to **Toronto** by **Calgary** with Doug Gilmour, Jamie Macoun, Kent Manderville and Rick Wamsley for Gary Leeman, Alexander Godynyuk, Jeff Reese, Michel Petit and Craig Berube, January 2, 1992. Signed as a free agent by **Philadelphia**, August 20, 1992.

NAUSS, DARREN

Right wing. Shoots right. 5'11", 180 lbs. Born, Vancouver, B.C., March 19, 1967.
(Quebec's 11th choice, 198th overall, in 1987 Entry Draft).

			Regular Season					Playoffs				
Season	Club	Lea	GP	G	A	TP	PIM	GP	G	A	TP	PIM
1987-88	Minn.-Duluth	WCHA	41	8	13	21	24	....	....	....	....	....
1988-89	Minn.-Duluth	WCHA	40	10	4	14	40	....	....	....	....	....
1989-90	Minn.-Duluth	WCHA	37	21	17	38	24	....	....	....	....	....
1990-91	Minn.-Duluth	WCHA	39	7	13	20	43	....	....	....	....	....
	Halifax	AHL	4	0	0	0	0	....	....	....	....	....
1991-92	Greensboro	ECHL	8	0	3	3	0	....	....	....	....	....

NAZAROV, ANDREI (nah-ZAH-rohv)

Right wing. Shoots right. 6'4", 209 lbs. Born, Chelyabinsk, Soviet Union, May 22, 1974.
(San Jose's 2nd choice, 10th overall, in 1992 Entry Draft).

			Regular Season					Playoffs				
Season	Club	Lea	GP	G	A	TP	PIM	GP	G	A	TP	PIM
1991-92	Moscow D'amo	CIS	2	1	0	1	2	....	....	....	....	....

NEATON, PAT

Defense. Shoots left. 6', 180 lbs. Born, Redford, MI, May 21, 1971.
(Pittsburgh's 9th choice, 145th overall, in 1990 Entry Draft).

			Regular Season					Playoffs				
Season	Club	Lea	GP	G	A	TP	PIM	GP	G	A	TP	PIM
1989-90	U. of Michigan	CCHA	42	3	23	26	36	....	....	....	....	....
1990-91a	U. of Michigan	CCHA	44	15	28	43	78	....	....	....	....	....
1991-92	U. of Michigan	CCHA	43	10	20	30	62	....	....	....	....	....

a CCHA Second All-Star Team (1991)

NEDOMA, MILAN (neh-DOH-mah)

Defense. Shoots left. 5'10", 176 lbs. Born, Brno, Czech., March 29, 1972.
(Buffalo's 8th choice, 166th overall, in 1990 Entry Draft).

			Regular Season					Playoffs				
Season	Club	Lea	GP	G	A	TP	PIM	GP	G	A	TP	PIM
1991-92	Dukla Trencin	Czech.	47	5	7	12	....	....	....	....	....	....

NEDVED, PETR

Center. Shoots left. 6'3", 185 lbs. Born, Liberec, Czechoslovakia, December 9, 1971.
(Vancouver's 1st choice, 2nd overall, in 1990 Entry Draft).

			Regular Season					Playoffs				
Season	Club	Lea	GP	G	A	TP	PIM	GP	G	A	TP	PIM
1988-89	Litvinov	Czech.	20	32	19	51	12	....	....	....	....	....
1989-90a	Seattle	WHL	71	65	80	145	80	11	4	9	13	2
1990-91	**Vancouver**	**NHL**	**61**	**10**	**6**	**16**	**20**	**6**	**0**	**1**	**1**	**0**
1991-92	**Vancouver**	**NHL**	**77**	**15**	**22**	**37**	**36**	**10**	**1**	**4**	**5**	**16**
	NHL Totals		**138**	**25**	**28**	**53**	**56**	**16**	**1**	**5**	**6**	**16**

a WHL and CHL Rookie of the Year (1990)

NEEDHAM, MICHAEL

Right wing. Shoots right. 5'10", 185 lbs. Born, Calgary, Alta., April 4, 1970.
(Pittsburgh's 7th choice, 126th overall, in 1989 Entry Draft).

			Regular Season					Playoffs				
Season	Club	Lea	GP	G	A	TP	PIM	GP	G	A	TP	PIM
1986-87	Kamloops	WHL	3	1	2	3	0	11	2	1	3	5
1987-88	Kamloops	WHL	64	31	33	64	93	5	0	1	1	5
1988-89	Kamloops	WHL	49	24	27	51	55	16	2	9	11	13
1989-90a	Kamloops	WHL	60	59	66	125	75	17	11	13	24	10
1990-91	Muskegon	IHL	65	14	31	45	17	5	2	2	4	5
1991-92	Muskegon	IHL	80	41	37	78	83	8	4	4	8	6
	Pittsburgh	**NHL**	....	....	....	....	....	**5**	**1**	**0**	**1**	**2**
	NHL Totals		....	....	....	....	....	**5**	**1**	**0**	**1**	**2**

a WHL West First All-Star Team (1990)

NEELY, CAMERON MICHAEL (CAM)

Right wing. Shoots right. 6'1", 210 lbs. Born, Comox, B.C., June 6, 1965.
(Vancouver's 1st choice, 9th overall, in 1983 Entry Draft).

			Regular Season					Playoffs				
Season	Club	Lea	GP	G	A	TP	PIM	GP	G	A	TP	PIM
1982-83	Portland	WHL	72	56	64	120	130	14	9	11	20	17
1983-84	**Vancouver**	**NHL**	**56**	**16**	**15**	**31**	**57**	**4**	**2**	**0**	**2**	**2**
	Portland	WHL	19	8	18	26	29	....	....	....	....	....
1984-85	**Vancouver**	**NHL**	**72**	**21**	**18**	**39**	**137**	....	....	....	....	....
1985-86	**Vancouver**	**NHL**	**73**	**14**	**20**	**34**	**126**	**3**	**0**	**0**	**0**	**6**
1986-87	**Boston**	**NHL**	**75**	**36**	**36**	**72**	**143**	**4**	**5**	**1**	**6**	**8**
1987-88a	**Boston**	**NHL**	**69**	**42**	**27**	**69**	**175**	**23**	**9**	**8**	**17**	**51**
1988-89	**Boston**	**NHL**	**74**	**37**	**38**	**75**	**190**	**10**	**7**	**2**	**9**	**8**
1989-90a	**Boston**	**NHL**	**76**	**55**	**37**	**92**	**117**	**21**	**12**	**16**	**28**	**51**
1990-91a	**Boston**	**NHL**	**69**	**51**	**40**	**91**	**98**	**19**	**16**	**4**	**20**	**36**
1991-92	**Boston**	**NHL**	**9**	**9**	**3**	**12**	**16**	....	....	....	....	....
	NHL Totals		**573**	**281**	**234**	**515**	**1059**	**84**	**51**	**31**	**82**	**162**

a NHL Second All-Star Team (1988, 1990, 1991)

Played in NHL All-Star Game (1988-91)

Traded to **Boston** by **Vancouver** with Vancouver's first round choice in 1987 Entry Draft (Glen Wesley) for Barry Pederson, June 6, 1986.

NELSON, CHRISTOPHER

Defense. Shoots right. 6'2", 190 lbs. Born, Philadelphia, PA, February 12, 1969.
(New Jersey's 6th choice, 96th overall, in 1988 Entry Draft).

			Regular Season					Playoffs				
Season	Club	Lea	GP	G	A	TP	PIM	GP	G	A	TP	PIM
1988-89	U. Wisconsin	WCHA	21	1	4	5	24	....	....	....	....	....
1989-90	U. Wisconsin	WCHA	34	1	3	4	38	....	....	....	....	....
1990-91	U. Wisconsin	WCHA	42	5	12	17	48	....	....	....	....	....
1991-92	U. Wisconsin	WCHA	39	4	12	16	84	....	....	....	....	....

NELSON, JEFF

Center. Shoots left. 6', 180 lbs. Born, Prince Albert, Sask., December 18, 1972.
(Washington's 4th choice, 36th overall, in 1991 Entry Draft).

			Regular Season					Playoffs				
Season	Club	Lea	GP	G	A	TP	PIM	GP	G	A	TP	PIM
1989-90	Prince Albert	WHL	72	28	69	97	79	14	2	11	13	10
1990-91a	Prince Albert	WHL	72	46	74	120	58	3	1	1	2	4
1991-92a	Prince Albert	WHL	64	48	65	113	84	9	7	14	21	18

a WHL East Second All-Star Team (1991, 1992)

NELSON, TODD

Defense. Shoots left. 6', 201 lbs. Born, Prince Albert, Sask., May 15, 1969.
(Pittsburgh's 4th choice, 79th overall, in 1989 Entry Draft).

			Regular Season					Playoffs				
Season	Club	Lea	GP	G	A	TP	PIM	GP	G	A	TP	PIM
1985-86	Prince Albert	WHL	4	0	0	0	0	....	....	....	....	....
1986-87	Prince Albert	WHL	35	1	6	7	10	4	0	0	0	0
1987-88	Prince Albert	WHL	72	3	21	24	59	10	3	2	5	4
1988-89a	Prince Albert	WHL	72	14	45	59	72	4	1	3	4	4
1989-90a	Prince Albert	WHL	69	13	42	55	88	14	3	12	15	12
1990-91	Muskegon	IHL	79	4	20	24	32	3	0	0	0	4
1991-92	**Pittsburgh**	**NHL**	**1**	**0**	**0**	**0**	**0**	....	....	....	....	....
	Muskegon	IHL	80	6	35	41	46	14	1	11	12	4
	NHL Totals		**1**	**0**	**0**	**0**	**0**	....	....	....	....	....

a WHL East Second All-Star Team (1989, 1990)

NEMETH, TOM

Left wing. Shoots left. 6'2", 180 lbs. Born, St. Catharines, Ont., January 16, 1971.
(Minnesota's 10th choice, 206th overall, in 1991 Entry Draft).

			Regular Season					Playoffs				
Season	Club	Lea	GP	G	A	TP	PIM	GP	G	A	TP	PIM
1988-89	Cornwall	OHL	51	4	23	27	25	....	....	....	....	....
1989-90	Cornwall	OHL	41	12	15	27	14	....	....	....	....	....
1990-91	Cornwall	OHL	65	17	43	60	46	....	....	....	....	....
1991-92	Cornwall	OHL	66	25	49	74	33	6	3	2	5	4

NEMCHINOV, SERGEI

Center. Shoots left. 6', 183 lbs. Born, Moscow, Soviet Union, January 14, 1964.
(NY Rangers' 14th choice, 244th overall, in 1990 Entry Draft).

			Regular Season					Playoffs				
Season	Club	Lea	GP	G	A	TP	PIM	GP	G	A	TP	PIM
1981-82	Soviet Wings	USSR	15	1	0	1	0	....	....	....	....	....
1982-83	CSKA	USSR	11	0	0	0	2	....	....	....	....	....
1983-84	CSKA	USSR	20	6	5	11	4	....	....	....	....	....
1984-85	CSKA	USSR	31	2	4	6	4	....	....	....	....	....
1985-86	Soviet Wings	USSR	39	7	12	19	28	....	....	....	....	....
1986-87	Soviet Wings	USSR	40	13	9	22	24	....	....	....	....	....
1987-88	Soviet Wings	USSR	48	17	11	28	26	....	....	....	....	....
1988-89	Soviet Wings	USSR	43	15	14	29	28	....	....	....	....	....
1989-90	Soviet Wings	USSR	48	17	16	33	34	....	....	....	....	....
1990-91	Soviet Wings	USSR	46	21	24	45	30	....	....	....	....	....
1991-92	**NY Rangers**	**NHL**	**73**	**30**	**28**	**58**	**15**	**13**	**1**	**4**	**5**	**8**
	NHL Totals		**73**	**30**	**28**	**58**	**15**	**13**	**1**	**4**	**5**	**8**

NEUMEIER, TROY

Defense. Shoots left. 6'2", 195 lbs. Born, Langenburg, Sask., September 3, 1970.
(Vancouver's 9th choice, 191st overall, in 1990 Entry Draft).

			Regular Season					Playoffs				
Season	Club	Lea	GP	G	A	TP	PIM	GP	G	A	TP	PIM
1989-90	Prince Albert	WHL	72	8	26	34	73	14	3	5	8	12
1990-91a	Prince Albert	WHL	72	6	27	33	56	3	0	0	0	0
1991-92	Milwaukee	IHL	72	1	9	10	55	3	0	0	0	0

a WHL East First All-Star Team (1991)

NEURURER, PHILLIP

Defense. Shoots left. 6'2", 194 lbs. Born, Robbinsdale, MA, March 21, 1970.
(NY Islanders' 13th choice, 226th overall, in 1988 Entry Draft).

			Regular Season					Playoffs				
Season	Club	Lea	GP	G	A	TP	PIM	GP	G	A	TP	PIM
1988-89	N. Michigan	WCHA	23	0	1	1	12	....	....	....	....	....
1989-90	N. Michigan	WCHA	27	1	5	6	28	....	....	....	....	....
1990-91	N. Michigan	WCHA	11	1	2	3	6	....	....	....	....	....
1991-92	N. Michigan	WCHA	24	1	6	7	16	....	....	....	....	....

NICHOLLS, BERNIE IRVINE (NICK-els)

Center. Shoots right. 6'1", 185 lbs. Born, Haliburton, Ont., June 24, 1961.
(Los Angeles' 6th choice, 73rd overall, in 1980 Entry Draft).

			Regular Season					Playoffs				
Season	Club	Lea	GP	G	A	TP	PIM	GP	G	A	TP	PIM
1979-80	Kingston	OHA	68	36	43	79	85	3	1	0	1	10
1980-81	Kingston	OHA	65	63	89	152	109	14	8	10	18	17
1981-82	Los Angeles	NHL	22	14	18	32	27	10	4	0	4	23
	New Haven	AHL	55	41	30	71	31	....	....	....	....	....
1982-83	Los Angeles	NHL	71	28	22	50	124	....	....	....	....	....
1983-84	Los Angeles	NHL	78	41	54	95	83	....	....	....	....	....
1984-85	Los Angeles	NHL	80	46	54	100	76	3	1	1	2	9
1985-86	Los Angeles	NHL	80	36	61	97	78	....	....	....	....	....
1986-87	Los Angeles	NHL	80	33	48	81	101	5	2	5	7	6
1987-88	Los Angeles	NHL	65	32	46	78	114	5	2	6	8	11
1988-89a	Los Angeles	NHL	79	70	80	150	96	11	7	9	16	12
1989-90	Los Angeles	NHL	47	27	48	75	66	....	....	....	....	....
	NY Rangers	NHL	32	12	25	37	20	10	7	5	12	16
1990-91	NY Rangers	NHL	71	25	48	73	96	5	4	3	7	8
1991-92	NY Rangers	NHL	1	0	0	0	0	....	....	....	....	....
	Edmonton	NHL	49	20	29	49	60	16	8	11	19	25
	NHL Totals		**755**	**384**	**533**	**917**	**941**	**65**	**35**	**40**	**75**	**110**

a NHL Second All-Star Team (1989)

Played in NHL All-Star Game (1984, 1989, 1990)

Traded to **NY Rangers** by **Los Angeles** for Tomas Sandstrom and Tony Granato, January 20, 1990. Traded to **Edmonton** by **NY Rangers** with Steven Rice and Louie DeBrusk for Mark Messier and future considerations, October 4, 1991.

NIEDERMAYER, SCOTT

Defense. Shoots left. 6', 200 lbs. Born, Edmonton, Alta., August 31, 1973.
(New Jersey's 1st choice, 3rd overall, in 1991 Entry Draft).

			Regular Season					Playoffs				
Season	Club	Lea	GP	G	A	TP	PIM	GP	G	A	TP	PIM
1989-90	Kamloops	WHL	64	14	55	69	64	17	2	14	16	35
1990-91ab	Kamloops	WHL	57	26	56	82	52	....	....	....	....	....
1991-92	New Jersey	NHL	4	0	1	1	2	....	....	....	....	....
acd	Kamloops	WHL	35	7	32	39	61	17	9	14	23	28
	NHL Totals		**4**	**0**	**1**	**1**	**2**	....	....	....	....	....

a WHL West First All-Star Team (1991, 1992)
b Canadian Major Junior Scholastic Player of the Year (1991)
c Memorial Cup All-Star Team (1992)
d Won Stafford Smythe Memorial Trophy (Memorial Cup MVP) (1992)

NIELSON, JEFF

Right wing. Shoots right. 6', 170 lbs. Born, Grand Rapids, MN, September 20, 1971.
(NY Rangers' 4th choice, 69th overall, in 1990 Entry Draft).

			Regular Season					Playoffs				
Season	Club	Lea	GP	G	A	TP	PIM	GP	G	A	TP	PIM
1990-91	U. Minnesota	WCHA	45	11	14	25	50	....	....	....	....	....
1991-92	U. Minnesota	WCHA	41	14	14	28	70	....	....	....	....	....

NIEMAN, THOMAS

Right wing. Shoots right. 6', 183 lbs. Born, Winnetka, IL, January 22, 1970.
(Buffalo's 11th choice, 223rd overall, in 1988 Entry Draft).

			Regular Season					Playoffs				
Season	Club	Lea	GP	G	A	TP	PIM	GP	G	A	TP	PIM
1988-89	Dartmouth	ECAC	26	7	11	18	38	....	....	....	....	....
1989-90	Dartmouth	ECAC	26	6	3	9	16	....	....	....	....	....
1990-91	Dartmouth	ECAC	25	2	5	7	27	....	....	....	....	....
1991-92	Dartmouth	ECAC	25	5	3	8	38	....	....	....	....	....

NIEUWENDYK, JOE (NOO-ihn-DIGHK)

Center. Shoots left. 6'1", 175 lbs. Born, Oshawa, Ont., September 10, 1966.
(Calgary's 2nd choice, 27th overall, in 1985 Entry Draft).

			Regular Season					Playoffs				
Season	Club	Lea	GP	G	A	TP	PIM	GP	G	A	TP	PIM
1984-85a	Cornell	ECAC	23	18	21	39	20	....	....	....	....	....
1985-86bc	Cornell	ECAC	21	21	21	42	45	....	....	....	....	....
1986-87bcd	Cornell	ECAC	23	26	26	52	26	....	....	....	....	....
	Calgary	NHL	9	5	1	6	0	6	2	2	4	0
1987-88efg	Calgary	NHL	75	51	41	92	23	8	3	4	7	2
1988-89	Calgary	NHL	77	51	31	82	40	22	10	4	14	10
1989-90	Calgary	NHL	79	45	50	95	40	6	4	6	10	4
1990-91	Calgary	NHL	79	45	40	85	36	7	4	1	5	10
1991-92	Calgary	NHL	69	22	34	56	55	....	....	....	....	....
	NHL Totals		**388**	**219**	**197**	**416**	**194**	**49**	**23**	**17**	**40**	**26**

a ECAC Rookie of the Year (1985)
b NCAA East First All-American Team (1986, 1987)
c ECAC First All-Star Team (1986, 1987)
d ECAC Player of the Year (1987)
e Won Calder Memorial Trophy (1988)
f NHL All-Rookie Team (1988)
g Won Dodge Ram Tough Award (1988)

Played in NHL All-Star Game (1988-90)

NIKOLIC, ALEX

Left wing. Shoots left. 6'1", 200 lbs. Born, Sudbury, Ont., March 1, 1970.
(Calgary's 8th choice, 147th overall, in 1989 Entry Draft).

			Regular Season					Playoffs				
Season	Club	Lea	GP	G	A	TP	PIM	GP	G	A	TP	PIM
1988-89	Cornell	ECAC	13	0	3	3	31	....	....	....	....	....
1989-90	Cornell	ECAC	28	6	9	15	54	....	....	....	....	....
1990-91	Cornell	ECAC	15	4	3	7	16	....	....	....	....	....
1991-92	Cornell	ECAC	26	5	9	14	60	....	....	....	....	....

NIKOLISHIN, ANDREI (nee-koh-LEE-shin)

Left wing. Shoots left. 5'11", 189 lbs. Born, Vorkuta, Soviet Union, March 25, 1973.
(Hartford's 2nd choice, 47th overall, in 1992 Entry Draft).

			Regular Season					Playoffs				
Season	Club	Lea	GP	G	A	TP	PIM	GP	G	A	TP	PIM
1991-92	Moscow D'amo	CIS	18	1	0	1	4	....	....	....	....	....

NILAN, CHRISTOPHER JOHN (CHRIS) (NIGH-luhn)

Right wing. Shoots right. 6', 205 lbs. Born, Boston, MA, February 9, 1958.
(Montreal's 21st choice, 231st overall, in 1978 Amateur Draft).

			Regular Season					Playoffs				
Season	Club	Lea	GP	G	A	TP	PIM	GP	G	A	TP	PIM
1978-79	Northeastern	ECAC	32	9	17	26	....	....	....	....	....	....
1979-80	Montreal	NHL	15	0	2	2	50	5	0	0	0	2
	Nova Scotia	AHL	49	15	10	25	*304	....	....	....	....	....
1980-81	Montreal	NHL	57	7	8	15	262	2	0	0	0	0
1981-82	Montreal	NHL	49	7	4	11	204	5	1	1	2	22
1982-83	Montreal	NHL	66	6	8	14	213	3	0	0	0	5
1983-84	Montreal	NHL	76	16	10	26	*338	15	1	0	1	*81
1984-85	Montreal	NHL	77	21	16	37	*358	12	2	1	3	81
1985-86	Montreal	NHL	72	19	15	34	274	18	1	2	3	*141
1986-87	Montreal	NHL	44	4	16	20	266	17	3	0	3	75
1987-88	Montreal	NHL	50	7	5	12	209	....	....	....	....	....
	NY Rangers	NHL	22	3	5	8	96	....	....	....	....	....
1988-89	NY Rangers	NHL	38	7	7	14	177	4	0	1	1	38
1989-90	NY Rangers	NHL	25	1	2	3	59	4	0	1	1	19
1990-91	Boston	NHL	41	6	9	15	277	19	0	2	2	62
1991-92	Boston	NHL	39	5	5	10	186	....	....	....	....	....
	Montreal	NHL	17	1	3	4	74	7	0	1	1	15
	NHL Totals		**688**	**110**	**115**	**225**	**3043**	**111**	**8**	**9**	**17**	**541**

Traded to **NY Rangers** by **Montreal** for a switch of first round choices in 1989 Entry Draft, January 27, 1988. Traded to **Boston** by **NY Rangers** for Greg Johnston and future considerations, June 28, 1990. Claimed on waivers by **Montreal**, February 12, 1992.

NILSSON, FREDRIK (NEEL-suhn)

Center. Shoots left. 6'1", 198 lbs. Born, Vasteras, Sweden, April 16, 1971.
(San Jose's 7th choice, 111th overall, in 1991 Entry Draft).

			Regular Season					Playoffs				
Season	Club	Lea	GP	G	A	TP	PIM	GP	G	A	TP	PIM
1989-90	Vasteras	Swe.	23	1	1	2	4	1	0	0	0	0
1990-91	Vasteras	Swe.	35	13	7	20	20	....	....	....	....	....
1991-92	Vasteras	Swe.	40	5	14	19	40	....	....	....	....	....

NILSSON, STEFAN

Center. Shoots right. 5'11", 185 lbs. Born, Lulea, Sweden, April 5, 1968.
(Washington's 7th choice, 124th overall, in 1986 Entry Draft).

			Regular Season					Playoffs				
Season	Club	Lea	GP	G	A	TP	PIM	GP	G	A	TP	PIM
1985-86	Lulea	Swe.	4	0	0	0	0	....	....	....	....	....
1986-87	Lulea	Swe.	23	3	9	12	14	....	....	....	....	....
1987-88	Lulea	Swe.	31	10	10	20	24	....	....	....	....	....
1988-89	Lulea	Swe.	40	9	22	31	24	....	....	....	....	....
1989-90	Lulea	Swe.	38	11	26	37	32	5	0	0	0	4
1990-91	Lulea	Swe.	38	7	39	46	64	....	....	....	....	....
1991-92	Lulea	Swe.	37	7	*40	47	42	....	....	....	....	....
	Troja	Swe.2				UNAVAILABLE						
	Linkoping	Swe.3				UNAVAILABLE						

NOBILI, MARIO

Left wing. Shoots left. 6'1", 185 lbs. Born, Montreal, Que., February 16, 1971.
(Edmonton's 5th choice, 78th overall, in 1991 Entry Draft).

			Regular Season					Playoffs				
Season	Club	Lea	GP	G	A	TP	PIM	GP	G	A	TP	PIM
1988-89	Longueuil	QMJHL	61	8	6	14	32	....	....	....	....	....
1989-90	Longueuil	QMJHL	67	11	34	45	64	....	....	....	....	....
1990-91	Longueuil	QMJHL	70	33	52	85	115	8	4	7	11	20
1991-92	Verdun	QMJHL	52	27	48	75	184	18	6	9	15	10

NOLAN, OWEN

Right wing. Shoots right. 6'1", 194 lbs. Born, Belfast, Northern Ireland, February 12, 1972
(Quebec's 1st choice, 1st overall, in 1990 Entry Draft).

			Regular Season					Playoffs				
Season	Club	Lea	GP	G	A	TP	PIM	GP	G	A	TP	PIM
1988-89a	Cornwall	OHL	62	34	25	59	213	18	5	11	16	41
1989-90b	Cornwall	OHL	58	51	59	110	240	6	7	5	12	26
1990-91	Quebec	NHL	59	3	10	13	109	....	....	....	....	....
	Halifax	AHL	6	4	4	8	11	....	....	....	....	....
1991-92	Quebec	NHL	75	42	31	73	183	....	....	....	....	....
	NHL Totals		**134**	**45**	**41**	**86**	**292**	....	....	....	....	....

a OHL Rookie of the Year (1989)
b OHL First All-Star Team (1990)

Played in NHL All-Star Game (1992)

NOONAN, BRIAN

Right wing. Shoots right. 6'1", 180 lbs. Born, Boston, MA, May 29, 1965.
(Chicago's 10th choice, 179th overall, in 1983 Entry Draft).

			Regular Season					Playoffs				
Season	Club	Lea	GP	G	A	TP	PIM	GP	G	A	TP	PIM
1984-85	N. Westminster	WHL	72	50	66	116	76	11	8	7	15	4
1985-86	Nova Scotia	AHL	2	0	0	0	0	....	....	....	....	....
	Saginaw	IHL	76	39	39	78	69	11	6	3	9	6
1986-87	Nova Scotia	AHL	70	25	26	51	30	5	3	1	4	4
1987-88	**Chicago**	**NHL**	**77**	**10**	**20**	**30**	**44**	**3**	**0**	**0**	**0**	**4**
1988-89	**Chicago**	**NHL**	**45**	**4**	**12**	**16**	**28**	**1**	**0**	**0**	**0**	**0**
	Saginaw	IHL	19	18	13	31	36	1	0	0	0	0
1989-90	**Chicago**	**NHL**	**8**	**0**	**2**	**2**	**6**	....	....	....	....	....
a	Indianapolis	IHL	56	40	36	76	85	14	6	9	15	20
1990-91	**Chicago**	**NHL**	**7**	**0**	**4**	**4**	**2**	....	....	....	....	....
b	Indianapolis	IHL	59	38	53	91	67	7	6	4	10	18
1991-92	**Chicago**	**NHL**	**65**	**19**	**12**	**31**	**81**	**18**	**6**	**9**	**15**	**30**
	NHL Totals		**202**	**33**	**50**	**83**	**161**	**22**	**6**	**9**	**15**	**34**

a IHL Second All-Star Team (1990)
b IHL First All-Star Team (1991)

NORDMARK, ROBERT (NOORD-mahrk)

Defense. Shoots right. 6'1", 200 lbs. Born, Lulea, Sweden, August 20, 1962.
(St. Louis' 3rd choice, 59th overall, in 1987 Entry Draft).

			Regular Season					Playoffs				
Season	Club	Lea	GP	G	A	TP	PIM	GP	G	A	TP	PIM
1984-85	Lulea	Swe.	33	3	9	12	30	....	....	....	....	....
1985-86	Lulea	Swe.	35	9	15	24	48	....	....	....	....	....
1986-87	Lulea	Swe.	32	7	8	15	46	3	0	3	3	4
1987-88	**St. Louis**	**NHL**	**67**	**3**	**18**	**21**	**60**	....	....	....	....	....
1988-89	**Vancouver**	**NHL**	**80**	**6**	**35**	**41**	**97**	**7**	**3**	**2**	**5**	**8**
1989-90	**Vancouver**	**NHL**	**44**	**2**	**11**	**13**	**34**	....	....	....	....	....
1990-91	**Vancouver**	**NHL**	**45**	**2**	**6**	**8**	**63**	....	....	....	....	....
1991-92	Vasteras	Swe.	36	11	6	17	72	....	....	....	....	....
	NHL Totals		**236**	**13**	**70**	**83**	**254**	**7**	**3**	**2**	**5**	**8**

Traded to **Vancouver** by **St. Louis** for Dave Richter and Vancouver's second round choice in 1990 Entry Draft, September 6, 1988.

NOREN, DARRYL

Center. Shoots left. 5'10", 180 lbs. Born, Lavonia, MI, August 7, 1968.
(Quebecs's 2nd choice, 6th overall, in 1990 Supplemental Draft).

			Regular Season					Playoffs				
Season	Club	Lea	GP	G	A	TP	PIM	GP	G	A	TP	PIM
1988-89	Ill.-Chicago	CCHA	38	16	17	33	54	....	....	....	....	....
1989-90	Ill.-Chicago	CCHA	38	29	37	66	84	....	....	....	....	....
1990-91	Albany	IHL	7	0	0	0	2	....	....	....	....	....
	Greensboro	ECHL	43	27	23	50	29	13	2	5	7	18
1991-92	Halifax	AHL	3	0	0	0	0	....	....	....	....	....
	New Haven	AHL	34	11	9	20	22	....	....	....	....	....
	Greensboro	ECHL	37	36	52	88	48	....	....	....	....	....

NORRIS, CLAYTON

Right wing. Shoots right. 6'2", 205 lbs. Born, Edmonton, Alta., March 8, 1972.
(Philadelphia's 6th choice, 111th overall, in 1991 Entry Draft).

			Regular Season					Playoffs				
Season	Club	Lea	GP	G	A	TP	PIM	GP	G	A	TP	PIM
1990-91	Medicine Hat	WHL	71	26	27	53	165	12	5	4	9	41
1991-92	Medicine Hat	WHL	69	26	39	65	300	2	0	0	0	9

NORRIS, DWAYNE

Right wing. Shoots right. 5'10", 175 lbs. Born, St. John's, Nfld., January 8, 1970.
(Quebec's 5th choice, 127th overall, in 1990 Entry Draft).

			Regular Season					Playoffs				
Season	Club	Lea	GP	G	A	TP	PIM	GP	G	A	TP	PIM
1988-89	Michigan State	CCHA	40	16	21	37	32	....	....	....	....	....
1989-90	Michigan State	CCHA	33	18	25	43	30	....	....	....	....	....
1990-91	Michigan State	CCHA	40	26	25	51	60	....	....	....	....	....
1991-92ab	Michigan State	CCHA	41	40	38	78	58	....	....	....	....	....

a CCHA First All-Star Team (1992)
b NCAA West First All-Star Team (1992)

NORSTROM, MATTIAS

Defense. Shoots left. 6'1", 196 lbs. Born, Mora, Sweden, January 2, 1972.
(NY Rangers' 2nd choice, 48th overall, in 1992 Entry Draft).

			Regular Season					Playoffs				
Season	Club	Lea	GP	G	A	TP	PIM	GP	G	A	TP	PIM
1991-92	AIK	Swe.	39	4	4	8	28	3	0	2	2	2

NORTON, CHRIS

Defense. Shoots right. 6'2", 200 lbs. Born, Oakville, Ont., March 11, 1965.
(Winnipeg's 11th choice, 228th overall, in 1985 Entry Draft).

			Regular Season					Playoffs				
Season	Club	Lea	GP	G	A	TP	PIM	GP	G	A	TP	PIM
1984-85	Cornell	ECAC	29	4	19	23	34	....	....	....	....	....
1985-86a	Cornell	ECAC	21	8	15	23	56	....	....	....	....	....
1986-87	Cornell	ECAC	24	10	21	31	79	....	....	....	....	....
1987-88a	Cornell	ECAC	27	9	25	34	53	....	....	....	....	....
1988-89	Moncton	AHL	60	1	21	22	49	10	3	2	5	15
1989-90	Moncton	AHL	62	9	20	29	49	....	....	....	....	....
1990-91	Moncton	AHL	72	8	28	36	45	9	1	3	4	12
1991-92	Indianapolis	IHL	8	0	1	1	12	....	....	....	....	....
	Phoenix	IHL	62	12	14	26	44	....	....	....	....	....

a ECAC Second All-Star Team (1986, 1988)

Traded to **Chicago** by **Winnipeg** with Bryan Marchment for Troy Murray and Warren Rychel, July 22, 1991. Traded to **Los Angeles** by **Chicago** with future considerations for Rod Buskas, October 28, 1991.

NORTON, JEFF

Defense. Shoots left. 6'2", 195 lbs. Born, Acton, MA, November 25, 1965.
(NY Islanders' 3rd choice, 62nd overall, in 1984 Entry Draft).

			Regular Season					Playoffs				
Season	Club	Lea	GP	G	A	TP	PIM	GP	G	A	TP	PIM
1984-85	U. of Michigan	CCHA	37	8	16	24	103	....	....	....	....	....
1985-86	U. of Michigan	CCHA	37	15	30	45	99	....	....	....	....	....
1986-87a	U. of Michigan	CCHA	39	12	36	48	92	....	....	....	....	....
1987-88	U.S. National	....	54	7	22	29	52	....	....	....	....	....
	U.S. Olympic	....	6	0	4	4	4	....	....	....	....	....
	NY Islanders	**NHL**	**15**	**1**	**6**	**7**	**14**	**3**	**0**	**2**	**2**	**13**
1988-89	**NY Islanders**	**NHL**	**69**	**1**	**30**	**31**	**74**	....	....	....	....	....
1989-90	**NY Islanders**	**NHL**	**60**	**4**	**49**	**53**	**65**	**4**	**1**	**3**	**4**	**17**
1990-91	**NY Islanders**	**NHL**	**44**	**3**	**25**	**28**	**16**	....	....	....	....	....
1991-92	**NY Islanders**	**NHL**	**28**	**1**	**18**	**19**	**18**	....	....	....	....	....
	NHL Totals		**216**	**10**	**128**	**138**	**187**	**7**	**1**	**5**	**6**	**30**

a CCHA Second All-Star Team (1987)

NORTON, STEVE

Defense. Shoots left. 6'3", 210 lbs. Born, Mississauga, Ont., February 29, 1972.
(Boston's 9th choice, 216th overall, in 1991 Entry Draft).

			Regular Season					Playoffs				
Season	Club	Lea	GP	G	A	TP	PIM	GP	G	A	TP	PIM
1990-91	Michigan State	CCHA	39	1	4	5	42	....	....	....	....	....
1991-92	Michigan State	CCHA	41	0	6	6	36	....	....	....	....	....

NORWOOD, LEE CHARLES

Defense. Shoots left. 6'1", 198 lbs. Born, Oakland, CA, February 2, 1960.
(Quebec's 3rd choice, 62nd overall, in 1979 Entry Draft).

			Regular Season					Playoffs				
Season	Club	Lea	GP	G	A	TP	PIM	GP	G	A	TP	PIM
1978-79	Oshawa	OHA	61	23	38	61	171	5	2	2	4	17
1979-80	Oshawa	OHA	60	13	39	52	143	6	2	7	9	15
1980-81	**Quebec**	**NHL**	**11**	**1**	**1**	**2**	**9**	**3**	**0**	**0**	**0**	**2**
	Hershey	AHL	52	11	32	43	78	8	0	4	4	14
1981-82	**Quebec**	**NHL**	**2**	**0**	**0**	**0**	**2**	....	....	....	....	....
	Fredericton	AHL	29	6	13	19	74	....	....	....	....	....
	Washington	**NHL**	**26**	**7**	**10**	**17**	**125**	....	....	....	....	....
1982-83	**Washington**	**NHL**	**8**	**0**	**1**	**1**	**14**	....	....	....	....	....
	Hershey	AHL	67	12	36	48	90	5	0	1	1	2
1983-84	St. Catharines	AHL	75	13	46	59	91	7	0	5	5	31
1984-85ab	Peoria	IHL	80	17	60	77	229	18	1	11	12	62
1985-86	**St. Louis**	**NHL**	**71**	**5**	**24**	**29**	**134**	**19**	**2**	**7**	**9**	**64**
1986-87	**Detroit**	**NHL**	**57**	**6**	**21**	**27**	**163**	**16**	**1**	**6**	**7**	**31**
	Adirondack	AHL	3	0	3	3	0	....	....	....	....	....
1987-88	**Detroit**	**NHL**	**51**	**9**	**22**	**31**	**131**	**16**	**2**	**6**	**8**	**40**
1988-89	**Detroit**	**NHL**	**66**	**10**	**32**	**42**	**100**	**6**	**1**	**2**	**3**	**16**
1989-90	**Detroit**	**NHL**	**64**	**8**	**14**	**22**	**95**	....	....	....	....	....
1990-91	**Detroit**	**NHL**	**21**	**3**	**7**	**10**	**50**	....	....	....	....	....
	New Jersey	**NHL**	**28**	**3**	**2**	**5**	**87**	**4**	**0**	**0**	**0**	**18**
1991-92	**Hartford**	**NHL**	**6**	**0**	**0**	**0**	**16**	....	....	....	....	....
	St. Louis	**NHL**	**44**	**3**	**11**	**14**	**94**	**1**	**0**	**1**	**1**	**0**
	NHL Totals		**455**	**55**	**145**	**200**	**1020**	**65**	**6**	**22**	**28**	**171**

a Won Governors' Trophy (IHL's Top Defenseman) (1985)
b IHL First All-Star Team (1985)

Traded to **Washington** by **Quebec** for Tim Tookey and Washington's seventh round choice (Daniel Poudrier) in 1982 Entry Draft, February 1, 1982. Traded to **Toronto** by **Washington** for Dave Shand, October 6, 1983. Signed as a free agent by **St. Louis**, August 13, 1985. Traded to **Detroit** by **St. Louis** for Larry Trader, August 7, 1986. Traded to **New Jersey** by **Detroit** with future considerations for Paul Ysebaert, November 27, 1990. Traded to **Hartford** by **New Jersey** for future considerations, October 3, 1991. Traded to **St. Louis** by **Hartford** for future considerations, November 13, 1991.

NUMMINEN, TEPPO (NOO-mih-nehn)

Defense. Shoots right. 6'1", 190 lbs. Born, Tampere, Finland, July 3, 1968.
(Winnipeg's 2nd choice, 29th overall, in 1986 Entry Draft).

			Regular Season					Playoffs				
Season	Club	Lea	GP	G	A	TP	PIM	GP	G	A	TP	PIM
1985-86	Tappara	Fin.	31	2	4	6	6	8	0	0	0	0
1986-87	Tappara	Fin.	44	9	9	18	16	9	4	1	5	4
1987-88	Tappara	Fin.	40	10	10	20	29	10	6	6	12	6
1988-89	**Winnipeg**	**NHL**	**69**	**1**	**14**	**15**	**36**	....	....	....	....	....
1989-90	**Winnipeg**	**NHL**	**79**	**11**	**32**	**43**	**20**	**7**	**1**	**2**	**3**	**10**
1990-91	**Winnipeg**	**NHL**	**80**	**8**	**25**	**33**	**28**	....	....	....	....	....
1991-92	**Winnipeg**	**NHL**	**80**	**5**	**34**	**39**	**32**	**7**	**0**	**0**	**0**	**0**
	NHL Totals		**308**	**25**	**105**	**130**	**116**	**14**	**1**	**2**	**3**	**10**

NUUTINEN, SAMI

Defense. Shoots left. 6', 178 lbs. Born, Espoo, Finland, June 11, 1971.
(Edmonton's 11th choice, 248th overall, in 1990 Entry Draft).

			Regular Season					Playoffs				
Season	Club	Lea	GP	G	A	TP	PIM	GP	G	A	TP	PIM
1988-89	Espoo	Fin.	39	18	10	28	46	....	....	....	....	....
1989-90	Espoo	Fin.	40	8	15	23	....	....	....	....	....	....
1990-91	K-Kissat	Fin.	3	1	0	1	0	....	....	....	....	....
	HIFK	Fin.	27	1	3	4	6	3	0	0	0	0
1991-92	HIFK	Fin.	44	5	6	11	10	9	0	1	1	4

NYLANDER, MIKAEL (new-LAHN-der, mi-KIH-ehl)

Center. Shoots left. 5'11", 176 lbs. Born, Stockholm, Sweden, October 3, 1972.
(Hartford's 4th choice, 59th overall, in 1991 Entry Draft).

			Regular Season					Playoffs				
Season	Club	Lea	GP	G	A	TP	PIM	GP	G	A	TP	PIM
1989-90	Huddinge	Swe.	31	7	15	22	4	....	....	....	....	....
1990-91	Huddinge	Swe.	33	14	20	34	10	....	....	....	....	....
1991-92	AIK	Swe.	40	11	17	28	30	3	1	4	5	4

NYLUND, GARY (NIGH-lund)

Defense. Shoots left. 6'4", 210 lbs. Born, Surrey, B.C., October 28, 1963.
(Toronto's 1st choice, 3rd overall, in 1982 Entry Draft).

			Regular Season					Playoffs				
Season	Club	Lea	GP	G	A	TP	PIM	GP	G	A	TP	PIM
1979-80	Portland	WHL	72	5	21	26	59	8	0	1	1	2
1980-81a	Portland	WHL	70	6	40	46	186	9	1	7	8	17
1981-82bc	Portland	WHL	65	7	59	66	267	15	3	16	19	74
1982-83	**Toronto**	**NHL**	**16**	**0**	**3**	**3**	**16**	....	....	....	....	....
1983-84	**Toronto**	**NHL**	**47**	**2**	**14**	**16**	**103**	....	....	....	....	....
1984-85	**Toronto**	**NHL**	**76**	**3**	**17**	**20**	**99**	....	....	....	....	....
1985-86	**Toronto**	**NHL**	**79**	**2**	**16**	**18**	**180**	**10**	**0**	**2**	**2**	**25**
1986-87	**Chicago**	**NHL**	**80**	**7**	**20**	**27**	**190**	**4**	**0**	**2**	**2**	**11**
1987-88	**Chicago**	**NHL**	**76**	**4**	**15**	**19**	**208**	**5**	**0**	**0**	**0**	**10**
1988-89	**Chicago**	**NHL**	**23**	**3**	**2**	**5**	**63**	....	....	....	....	....
	NY Islanders	**NHL**	**46**	**4**	**8**	**12**	**74**	....	....	....	....	....
1989-90	**NY Islanders**	**NHL**	**64**	**4**	**21**	**25**	**144**	**5**	**0**	**2**	**2**	**17**
1990-91	**NY Islanders**	**NHL**	**72**	**2**	**21**	**23**	**105**	....	....	....	....	....
1991-92	**NY Islanders**	**NHL**	**7**	**0**	**1**	**1**	**10**	....	....	....	....	....
	Capital Dist.	AHL	4	0	0	0	0	....	....	....	....	....
	NHL Totals		**586**	**31**	**138**	**169**	**1192**	**24**	**0**	**6**	**6**	**63**

a WHL Second All-Star Team (1981)
b WHL First All-Star Team (1982)
c Named WHL's Top Defenseman (1982)

Signed as a free agent by **Chicago**, August 27, 1986. Traded to **NY Islanders** by **Chicago** with Marc Bergevin for Steve Konroyd and Bob Bassen, November 25, 1988.

OATES, ADAM

Center. Shoots right. 5'11", 189 lbs. Born, Weston, Ont., August 27, 1962.

			Regular Season					Playoffs				
Season	Club	Lea	GP	G	A	TP	PIM	GP	G	A	TP	PIM
1982-83	RPI	ECAC	22	9	33	42	8	....	....	....	....	....
1983-84	RPI	ECAC	38	26	57	83	15	....	....	....	....	....
1984-85ab	RPI	ECAC	38	31	60	91	29	....	....	....	....	....
1985-86	**Detroit**	**NHL**	**38**	**9**	**11**	**20**	**10**	....	....	....	....	....
	Adirondack	AHL	34	18	28	46	4	17	7	14	21	4
1986-87	**Detroit**	**NHL**	**76**	**15**	**32**	**47**	**21**	**16**	**4**	**7**	**11**	**6**
1987-88	**Detroit**	**NHL**	**63**	**14**	**40**	**54**	**20**	**16**	**8**	**12**	**20**	**6**
1988-89	**Detroit**	**NHL**	**69**	**16**	**62**	**78**	**14**	**6**	**0**	**8**	**8**	**2**
1989-90	**St. Louis**	**NHL**	**80**	**23**	**79**	**102**	**30**	**12**	**2**	**12**	**14**	**4**
1990-91c	**St. Louis**	**NHL**	**61**	**25**	**90**	**115**	**29**	**13**	**7**	**13**	**20**	**10**
1991-92	**St. Louis**	**NHL**	**54**	**10**	**59**	**69**	**12**	....	....	....	....	....
	Boston	**NHL**	**26**	**10**	**20**	**30**	**10**	**15**	**5**	**14**	**19**	**4**
	NHL Totals		**467**	**122**	**393**	**515**	**146**	**78**	**26**	**66**	**92**	**32**

a ECAC First All-Star Team (1985)
b Named to NCAA All-American Team (1985)
c NHL Second All-Star Team (1991)

Played in NHL All-Star Game (1991, 1992)

Signed as a free agent by **Detroit**, June 28, 1985. Traded to **St. Louis** by **Detroit** with Paul MacLean for Bernie Federko and Tony McKegney, June 15, 1989. Traded to **Boston** by **St. Louis** for Craig Janney and Stephane Quintal, February 7, 1992.

O'BRIEN, JAMES

Defense. Shoots left. 6', 190 lbs. Born, Stoney Creek, Ont., May 8, 1970.
(Calgary's 1st choice, 6th overall, in 1992 Supplemental Draft).

			Regular Season					Playoffs				
Season	Club	Lea	GP	G	A	TP	PIM	GP	G	A	TP	PIM
1989-90	Brown	ECAC	29	3	12	15	78	....	....	....	....	....
1990-91	Brown	ECAC	25	3	8	11	50	....	....	....	....	....
1991-92	Brown	ECAC	28	3	11	14	61	....	....	....	....	....

O'CONNOR, MYLES

Defense. Shoots left. 5'11", 165 lbs. Born, Calgary, Alta., April 2, 1967.
(New Jersey's 4th choice, 45th overall, in 1985 Entry Draft).

			Regular Season					Playoffs				
Season	Club	Lea	GP	G	A	TP	PIM	GP	G	A	TP	PIM
1985-86	U. of Michigan	CCHA	37	6	19	25	73	....	....	....	....	....
	Cdn. National	....	8	0	0	0	0	....	....	....	....	....
1986-87	U. of Michigan	CCHA	39	15	39	54	111	....	....	....	....	....
1987-88	U. of Michigan	CCHA	40	9	25	34	78	....	....	....	....	....
1988-89ab	U. of Michigan	CCHA	40	3	31	34	91	....	....	....	....	....
	Utica	AHL	1	0	0	0	0	....	....	....	....	....
1989-90	Utica	AHL	76	14	33	47	124	5	1	2	3	26
1990-91	**New Jersey**	**NHL**	**22**	**3**	**1**	**4**	**41**	....	....	....	....	....
	Utica	AHL	33	6	17	23	62	....	....	....	....	....
1991-92	**New Jersey**	**NHL**	**9**	**0**	**2**	**2**	**13**	....	....	....	....	....
	Utica	AHL	66	9	39	48	184	....	....	....	....	....
	NHL Totals		**31**	**3**	**3**	**6**	**54**	....	....	....	....	....

a CCHA First All-Star Team (1989)
b NCAA West First All-American Team (1989)

ODELEIN, LYLE (ah-duh-LEEN)

Defense. Shoots left. 5'10", 206 lbs. Born, Quill Lake, Sask., July 21, 1968.
(Montreal's 8th choice, 141st overall, in 1986 Entry Draft).

			Regular Season					Playoffs				
Season	Club	Lea	GP	G	A	TP	PIM	GP	G	A	TP	PIM
1985-86	Moose Jaw	WHL	67	9	37	46	117	13	1	6	7	34
1986-87	Moose Jaw	WHL	59	9	50	59	70	9	2	5	7	26
1987-88	Moose Jaw	WHL	63	15	43	58	166	....	....	....	....	....
1988-89	Sherbrooke	AHL	33	3	4	7	120	3	0	2	2	5
	Peoria	IHL	36	2	8	10	116	....	....	....	....	....
1989-90	**Montreal**	**NHL**	**8**	**0**	**2**	**2**	**33**	....	....	....	....	....
	Sherbrooke	AHL	68	7	24	31	265	12	6	5	11	79
1990-91	**Montreal**	**NHL**	**52**	**0**	**2**	**2**	**259**	**12**	**0**	**0**	**0**	**54**
1991-92	**Montreal**	**NHL**	**71**	**1**	**7**	**8**	**212**	**7**	**0**	**0**	**0**	**11**
	NHL Totals		**131**	**1**	**11**	**12**	**504**	**19**	**0**	**0**	**0**	**65**

ODGERS, JEFF

Right wing. Shoots right. 6', 195 lbs. Born, Spy Hill, Sask., May 31, 1969.

			Regular Season					Playoffs				
Season	Club	Lea	GP	G	A	TP	PIM	GP	G	A	TP	PIM
1988-89	Brandon	WHL	71	31	29	60	277	....	....	....	....	....
1989-90	Brandon	WHL	64	37	28	65	209	....	....	....	....	....
1990-91	Kansas City	IHL	77	12	19	31	318	....	....	....	....	....
1991-92	**San Jose**	**NHL**	**61**	**7**	**4**	**11**	**217**	....	....	....	....	....
	Kansas City	IHL	12	2	2	4	56	....	....	....	....	....
	NHL Totals		**61**	**7**	**4**	**11**	**217**	....	....	....	....	....

Signed as a free agent by **San Jose**, September 3, 1991.

ODJICK, GINO

Left wing. Shoots left. 6'3", 220 lbs. Born, Maniwaki, Que., September 7, 1970.
(Vancouver's 5th choice, 86th overall, in 1990 Entry Draft).

			Regular Season					Playoffs				
Season	Club	Lea	GP	G	A	TP	PIM	GP	G	A	TP	PIM
1988-89	Laval	QMJHL	50	9	15	24	278	16	0	9	9	129
1989-90	Laval	QMJHL	51	12	26	38	280	....	....	....	....	....
1990-91	**Vancouver**	**NHL**	**45**	**7**	**1**	**8**	**296**	....	....	....	....	....
	Milwaukee	IHL	17	7	3	10	102	....	....	....	....	....
1991-92	**Vancouver**	**NHL**	**65**	**4**	**6**	**10**	**348**	**4**	**0**	**0**	**0**	**6**
	NHL Totals		**110**	**11**	**7**	**18**	**644**	**4**	**0**	**0**	**0**	**6**

O'DONNELL, SEAN

Defense. Shoots left. 6'2", 214 lbs. Born, Ottawa, Ont., October 13, 1971.
(Buffalo's 6th choice, 123rd overall, in 1991 Entry Draft).

			Regular Season					Playoffs				
Season	Club	Lea	GP	G	A	TP	PIM	GP	G	A	TP	PIM
1990-91	Sudbury	OHL	66	8	23	31	114	5	1	4	5	10
1991-92	Rochester	AHL	73	4	9	13	193	16	1	2	3	21

O'DWYER, BILL

Center. Shoots left. 6', 190 lbs. Born, Boston, MA, January 25, 1960.
(Los Angeles' 10th choice, 157th overall, in 1980 Entry Draft).

			Regular Season					Playoffs				
Season	Club	Lea	GP	G	A	TP	PIM	GP	G	A	TP	PIM
1978-79	Boston College	ECAC	30	9	30	39	14	....	....	....	....	....
1979-80	Boston College	ECAC	33	20	22	42	22	....	....	....	....	....
1980-81	Boston College	ECAC	31	20	20	40	6	....	....	....	....	....
1981-82	Boston College	ECAC	30	15	26	41	10	....	....	....	....	....
1982-83	New Haven	AHL	77	24	23	47	29	11	3	4	7	9
1983-84	**Los Angeles**	**NHL**	**5**	**0**	**0**	**0**	**0**	....	....	....	....	....
	New Haven	AHL	58	15	42	57	39	....	....	....	....	....
1984-85	**Los Angeles**	**NHL**	**13**	**1**	**0**	**1**	**15**	....	....	....	....	....
	New Haven	AHL	46	19	24	43	27	....	....	....	....	....
1985-86	New Haven	AHL	41	10	15	25	41	5	0	1	1	2
1986-87	New Haven	AHL	65	22	42	64	74	3	0	0	0	14
1987-88	**Boston**	**NHL**	**77**	**7**	**10**	**17**	**83**	**9**	**0**	**0**	**0**	**0**
1988-89	**Boston**	**NHL**	**19**	**1**	**2**	**3**	**8**	....	....	....	....	....
1989-90	**Boston**	**NHL**	**6**	**0**	**1**	**1**	**7**	**1**	**0**	**0**	**0**	**2**
	Maine	AHL	71	26	45	71	56	....	....	....	....	....
1990-91	New Haven	AHL	6	2	1	3	2	....	....	....	....	....
	Phoenix	IHL	25	3	9	12	12	11	7	6	13	0
1991-92	Phoenix	IHL	39	9	17	26	12	....	....	....	....	....
	NHL Totals		**120**	**9**	**13**	**22**	**113**	**10**	**0**	**0**	**0**	**2**

Signed as a free agent by **NY Rangers**, July 13, 1985. Signed as a free agent by **Boston**, August 13, 1987. Signed as a free agent by **Los Angeles**, July 11, 1990.

OGRODNICK, JOHN ALEXANDER (oh-GRAHD-nik)

Left wing. Shoots left. 6', 204 lbs. Born, Ottawa, Ont., June 20, 1959.
(Detroit's 4th choice, 66th overall, in 1979 Entry Draft).

			Regular Season					Playoffs				
Season	Club	Lea	GP	G	A	TP	PIM	GP	G	A	TP	PIM
1977-78a	N. Westminster	WHL	72	59	29	88	47	21	14	7	21	14
1978-79	N. Westminster	WHL	72	48	36	84	38	6	2	0	2	4
1979-80	**Detroit**	**NHL**	**41**	**8**	**24**	**32**	**8**	....	....	....	....	....
	Adirondack	AHL	39	13	20	33	21	....	....	....	....	....
1980-81	**Detroit**	**NHL**	**80**	**35**	**35**	**70**	**14**	....	....	....	....	....
1981-82	**Detroit**	**NHL**	**80**	**28**	**26**	**54**	**28**	....	....	....	....	....
1982-83	**Detroit**	**NHL**	**80**	**41**	**44**	**85**	**30**	....	....	....	....	....
1983-84	**Detroit**	**NHL**	**64**	**42**	**36**	**78**	**14**	**4**	**0**	**0**	**0**	**0**
1984-85b	**Detroit**	**NHL**	**79**	**55**	**50**	**105**	**30**	**3**	**1**	**1**	**2**	**0**
1985-86	**Detroit**	**NHL**	**76**	**38**	**32**	**70**	**18**	....	....	....	....	....
1986-87	**Detroit**	**NHL**	**39**	**12**	**28**	**40**	**6**	....	....	....	....	....
	Quebec	**NHL**	**32**	**11**	**16**	**27**	**4**	**13**	**9**	**4**	**13**	**6**
1987-88	**NY Rangers**	**NHL**	**64**	**22**	**32**	**54**	**16**	....	....	....	....	....
1988-89	**NY Rangers**	**NHL**	**60**	**13**	**29**	**42**	**14**	**3**	**2**	**0**	**2**	**0**
	Denver	IHL	3	2	0	2	0	....	....	....	....	....
1989-90	**NY Rangers**	**NHL**	**80**	**43**	**31**	**74**	**44**	**10**	**6**	**3**	**9**	**0**
1990-91	**NY Rangers**	**NHL**	**79**	**31**	**23**	**54**	**10**	**4**	**0**	**0**	**0**	**0**
1991-92	**NY Rangers**	**NHL**	**55**	**17**	**13**	**30**	**22**	**3**	**0**	**0**	**0**	**0**
	NHL Totals		**909**	**396**	**419**	**815**	**258**	**40**	**18**	**8**	**26**	**6**

a Shared WHL Rookie of the Year Award with Keith Brown (Portland) (1978)
b NHL First All-Star Team (1985)

Played in NHL All-Star Game (1981, 1982, 1984-86)

Traded to **Quebec** by **Detroit** with Basil McRae and Doug Shedden for Brent Ashton, Gilbert Delorme and Mark Kumpel, January 17, 1987. Traded to **NY Rangers** by **Quebec** with David Shaw for Jeff Jackson and Terry Carkner, September 30, 1987.

OHMAN, PAUL

Defense. Shoots left. 6'1", 185 lbs. Born, Worcester, MA, July 30, 1969.
(Boston's 9th choice, 182nd overall, in 1987 Entry Draft).

			Regular Season					Playoffs				
Season	Club	Lea	GP	G	A	TP	PIM	GP	G	A	TP	PIM
1990-91	Brown	ECAC	13	0	0	0	6	....	....	....	....	....
1991-92	Brown	ECAC	16	0	0	0	14	....	....	....	....	....

OHMAN, ROGER (OH-mahn)

Defense. Shoots left. 6'3", 202 lbs. Born, Stockholm, Sweden, June 5, 1967.
(Winnipeg's 2nd choice, 39th overall, in 1985 Entry Draft).

			Regular Season					Playoffs				
Season	Club	Lea	GP	G	A	TP	PIM	GP	G	A	TP	PIM
1986-87	V. Frolunda	Swe.	26	4	10	14	16	2	0	1	1	0
1987-88	Moncton	AHL	67	11	17	28	38	....	....	....	....	....
1988-89	AIK	Swe.	36	11	8	19	20	....	....	....	....	....
1989-90	AIK	Swe.	39	8	17	25	22	3	0	0	0	0
1990-91	Malmo	Swe.	40	11	7	18	26	....	....	....	....	....
1991-92	Malmo	Swe.	40	11	19	30	22	10	3	1	4	6

OJANEN, JANNE (OY-uh-nehn, YAHN-ee)

Center. Shoots left. 6'2", 200 lbs. Born, Tampere, Finland, April 9, 1968.
(New Jersey's 3rd choice, 45th overall, in 1986 Entry Draft).

			Regular Season					Playoffs				
Season	Club	Lea	GP	G	A	TP	PIM	GP	G	A	TP	PIM
1985-86	Tappara	Fin. Jr.	14	5	17	22	14	5	2	3	5	8
	Tappara	Fin.	3	0	0	0	2	....	....	....	....	....
1986-87	Tappara	Fin.	40	18	13	31	16	9	4	6	10	2
1987-88	Tappara	Fin.	44	21	31	52	30	10	4	4	8	12
1988-89	**New Jersey**	**NHL**	**3**	**0**	**1**	**1**	**2**	....	....	....	....	....
	Utica	AHL	72	23	37	60	10	5	0	3	3	0
1989-90	**New Jersey**	**NHL**	**64**	**17**	**13**	**30**	**12**	....	....	....	....	....
1990-91	Tappara	Fin.	44	15	33	48	36	3	1	2	3	6
1991-92	Tappara	Fin.	44	21	27	48	24	....	....	....	....	....
	New Jersey	**NHL**	....	....	....	....	....	**3**	**0**	**2**	**2**	**0**
	NHL Totals		**67**	**17**	**14**	**31**	**14**	**3**	**0**	**2**	**2**	**0**

OKSYUTA, ROMAN (ohk-SEW-tah)

Right wing. Shoots left. 6'2", 213 lbs. Born, Murmansk, Soviet Union, August 21, 1970.
(NY Rangers' 11th choice, 202nd overall, in 1989 Entry Draft).

			Regular Season					Playoffs				
Season	Club	Lea	GP	G	A	TP	PIM	GP	G	A	TP	PIM
1987-88	Khimik	USSR	11	1	0	1	4	....	....	....	....	....
1988-89	Khimik	USSR	34	13	3	16	14	....	....	....	....	....
1989-90	Khimik	USSR	37	13	6	19	16	....	....	....	....	....
1990-91	Khimik	USSR	41	12	8	20	24	....	....	....	....	....
1991-92	Khimik	CIS	42	24	20	44	28	....	....	....	....	....

OLAUSSON, FREDRIK (OHL-AH-SUHN)

Defense. Shoots right. 6'2", 200 lbs. Born, Vaxsjo, Sweden, October 5, 1966.
(Winnipeg's 4th choice, 81st overall, in 1985 Entry Draft).

			Regular Season					Playoffs				
Season	Club	Lea	GP	G	A	TP	PIM	GP	G	A	TP	PIM
1984-85	Farjestad	Swe.	29	5	12	17	22	3	1	0	1	0
1985-86	Farjestad	Swe.	33	4	12	16	22	8	3	2	5	6
1986-87	**Winnipeg**	**NHL**	**72**	**7**	**29**	**36**	**24**	**10**	**2**	**3**	**5**	**4**
1987-88	**Winnipeg**	**NHL**	**38**	**5**	**10**	**15**	**18**	**5**	**1**	**1**	**2**	**0**
1988-89	**Winnipeg**	**NHL**	**75**	**15**	**47**	**62**	**32**	....	....	....	....	....
1989-90	**Winnipeg**	**NHL**	**77**	**9**	**46**	**55**	**32**	**7**	**0**	**2**	**2**	**2**
1990-91	**Winnipeg**	**NHL**	**71**	**12**	**29**	**41**	**24**	....	....	....	....	....
1991-92	**Winnipeg**	**NHL**	**77**	**20**	**42**	**62**	**34**	**7**	**1**	**5**	**6**	**4**
	NHL Totals		**410**	**68**	**203**	**271**	**164**	**29**	**4**	**11**	**15**	**10**

OLCZYK, ED (OHL-chehk)

Center. Shoots left. 6'1", 200 lbs. Born, Chicago, IL, August 16, 1966.
(Chicago's 1st choice, 3rd overall, in 1984 Entry Draft).

			Regular Season					Playoffs				
Season	Club	Lea	GP	G	A	TP	PIM	GP	G	A	TP	PIM
1983-84	U.S. Olympic	....	62	21	47	68	36	....	....	....	....	....
1984-85	**Chicago**	**NHL**	**70**	**20**	**30**	**50**	**67**	**15**	**6**	**5**	**11**	**11**
1985-86	**Chicago**	**NHL**	**79**	**29**	**50**	**79**	**47**	**3**	**0**	**0**	**0**	**0**
1986-87	**Chicago**	**NHL**	**79**	**16**	**35**	**51**	**119**	**4**	**1**	**1**	**2**	**4**
1987-88	**Toronto**	**NHL**	**80**	**42**	**33**	**75**	**55**	**6**	**5**	**4**	**9**	**2**
1988-89	**Toronto**	**NHL**	**80**	**38**	**52**	**90**	**75**	....	....	....	....	....
1989-90	**Toronto**	**NHL**	**79**	**32**	**56**	**88**	**78**	**5**	**1**	**2**	**3**	**14**
1990-91	**Toronto**	**NHL**	**18**	**4**	**10**	**14**	**13**	....	....	....	....	....
	Winnipeg	**NHL**	**61**	**26**	**31**	**57**	**69**	....	....	....	....	....
1991-92	**Winnipeg**	**NHL**	**64**	**32**	**33**	**65**	**67**	**6**	**2**	**1**	**3**	**4**
	NHL Totals		**610**	**239**	**330**	**569**	**590**	**39**	**15**	**13**	**28**	**35**

Traded to **Toronto** by **Chicago** with Al Secord for Rick Vaive, Steve Thomas and Bob McGill, September 3, 1987. Traded to **Winipeg** by **Toronto** with Mark Osborne for Dave Ellett and Paul Fenton, November 10, 1990.

O'LEARY, RYAN

Center. Shoots left. 6'1", 205 lbs. Born, Duluth, MN, June 8, 1971.
(Calgary's 6th choice, 84th overall, in 1989 Entry Draft).

			Regular Season					Playoffs				
Season	Club	Lea	GP	G	A	TP	PIM	GP	G	A	TP	PIM
1989-90	U. of Denver	WCHA	39	4	6	10	30	....	....	....	....	....
1990-91	U. of Denver	WCHA	38	3	6	9	40	....	....	....	....	....
1991-92	U. of Denver	WCHA	17	5	4	9	22	....	....	....	....	....

OLIMB, LAWRENCE

Defense. Shoots left. 5'10", 155 lbs. Born, Warroad, MN, August 11, 1969.
(Minnesota's 10th choice, 193rd overall, in 1987 Entry Draft).

			Regular Season					Playoffs				
Season	Club	Lea	GP	G	A	TP	PIM	GP	G	A	TP	PIM
1988-89	U. Minnesota	WCHA	47	10	29	39	50	....	....	....	....	....
1989-90	U. Minnesota	WCHA	46	6	36	42	44	....	....	....	....	....
1990-91a	U. Minnesota	WCHA	45	19	38	57	52	....	....	....	....	....
1991-92bc	U. Minnesota	WCHA	41	24	53	77	72	....	....	....	....	....

a WCHA Second All-Star Team (1991)
b WCHA First All-Star Team (1992)
c NCAA West Second All-Star Team (1992)

Claimed by **San Jose** from **Minnesota** in Dispersal Draft, May 30, 1991.

OLIVER, DAVID

Right wing. Shoots right. 5'11", 185 lbs. Born, Sechelt, B.C., April 17, 1971.
(Edmonton's 7th choice, 144th overall, in 1991 Entry Draft).

			Regular Season					Playoffs				
Season	Club	Lea	GP	G	A	TP	PIM	GP	G	A	TP	PIM
1990-91	U. of Michigan	CCHA	27	13	11	24	34	....	....	....	....	....
1991-92	U. of Michigan	CCHA	44	31	27	58	32	....	....	....	....	....

OLSEN, DARRYL

Defense. Shoots left. 6', 180 lbs. Born, Calgary, Alta., October 7, 1966.
(Calgary's 10th choice, 185th overall in 1985 Entry Draft).

			Regular Season					Playoffs				
Season	Club	Lea	GP	G	A	TP	PIM	GP	G	A	TP	PIM
1985-86	N. Michigan	WCHA	37	5	20	25	46	....	....	....	....	....
1986-87	N. Michigan	WCHA	37	5	20	25	96	....	....	....	....	....
1987-88	N. Michigan	WCHA	35	11	20	31	59	....	....	....	....	....
1988-89	Cdn. National	....	3	1	0	1	4	....	....	....	....	....
ab	N. Michigan	WCHA	45	16	26	42	88	....	....	....	....	....
1989-90	Salt Lake	IHL	72	16	50	66	90	11	3	6	9	2
1990-91	Salt Lake	IHL	76	15	40	55	89	4	1	5	6	2
1991-92	**Calgary**	**NHL**	**1**	**0**	**0**	**0**	**0**	....	....	....	....	....
	Salt Lake	IHL	59	7	33	40	80	5	2	1	3	4
	NHL Totals		**1**	**0**	**0**	**0**	**0**	....	....	....	....	....

a NCAA West Second All-American Team (1989)
b WCHA First All-Star Team (1989)

Signed as a free agent by **Boston**, July 23, 1992.

OLSSON, MATTIAS

Defense. Shoots left. 6'1", 183 lbs. Born, Stockholm, Sweden, April 1, 1971.
(Los Angeles' 10th choice, 218th overall, in 1991 Entry Draft).

			Regular Season					Playoffs				
Season	Club	Lea	GP	G	A	TP	PIM	GP	G	A	TP	PIM
1990-91	Farjestad	Swe.	36	3	7	10	22	....	....	....	....	....
1991-92	Farjestad	Swe.	40	5	11	16	28	6	0	0	0	4

O'ROURKE, CHRIS

Defense. Shoots right. 6'2", 195 lbs. Born, Sherwood Park, Alta., January 6, 1971.
(Toronto's 12th choice, 245th overall, in 1991 Entry Draft).

			Regular Season					Playoffs				
Season	Club	Lea	GP	G	A	TP	PIM	GP	G	A	TP	PIM
1990-91	Alaska-Fair.	G.N.	34	2	6	8	76	....	....	....	....	....
1991-92	Alaska-Fair.	G.N.	13	1	5	6	71	....	....	....	....	....

OSBORNE, KEITH

Right wing. Shoots right. 6'1", 188 lbs. Born, Toronto, Ont., April 2, 1969.
(St. Louis' 1st choice, 12th overall, in 1987 Entry Draft).

			Regular Season					Playoffs				
Season	Club	Lea	GP	G	A	TP	PIM	GP	G	A	TP	PIM
1986-87	North Bay	OHL	61	34	55	89	31	24	11	11	22	25
1987-88	North Bay	OHL	30	14	22	36	20	4	1	5	6	8
1988-89	North Bay	OHL	15	11	15	26	12	....	....	....	....	....
	Niagara Falls	OHL	50	34	49	83	45	17	12	12	25	36
1989-90	**St. Louis**	**NHL**	**5**	**0**	**2**	**2**	**8**	....	....	....	....	....
	Peoria	IHL	56	23	24	47	58	5	1	1	2	4
1990-91	Peoria	IHL	54	10	20	30	79	....	....	....	....	....
	Newmarket	AHL	12	0	3	3	6	....	....	....	....	....
1991-92	St. John's	AHL	53	11	16	27	21	4	0	1	1	2
	NHL Totals		**5**	**0**	**2**	**2**	**8**	....	....	....	....	....

Traded to **Toronto** by **St. Louis** for Darren Veitch and future considerations, March 5, 1991. Claimed by **Tampa Bay** from **Toronto** in Expansion Draft, June 18, 1992.

OSBORNE, MARK ANATOLE (AWS-born)

Left wing. Shoots left. 6'2", 205 lbs. Born, Toronto, Ont., August 13, 1961.
(Detroit's 2nd choice, 46th overall, in 1980 Entry Draft).

			Regular Season					Playoffs				
Season	Club	Lea	GP	G	A	TP	PIM	GP	G	A	TP	PIM
1979-80	Niagara Falls	OHA	52	10	33	43	104	10	2	1	3	23
1980-81	Niagara Falls	OHA	54	39	41	80	140	12	11	10	21	20
	Adirondack	AHL	....	....	....	....	....	13	2	3	5	2
1981-82	**Detroit**	**NHL**	**80**	**26**	**41**	**67**	**61**	....	....	....	....	....
1982-83	**Detroit**	**NHL**	**80**	**19**	**24**	**43**	**83**	....	....	....	....	....
1983-84	**NY Rangers**	**NHL**	**73**	**23**	**28**	**51**	**88**	**5**	**0**	**1**	**1**	**7**
1984-85	**NY Rangers**	**NHL**	**23**	**4**	**4**	**8**	**33**	**3**	**0**	**0**	**0**	**4**
1985-86	**NY Rangers**	**NHL**	**62**	**16**	**24**	**40**	**80**	**15**	**2**	**3**	**5**	**26**
1986-87	**NY Rangers**	**NHL**	**58**	**17**	**15**	**32**	**101**	....	....	....	....	....
	Toronto	**NHL**	**16**	**5**	**10**	**15**	**12**	**9**	**1**	**3**	**4**	**6**
1987-88	**Toronto**	**NHL**	**79**	**23**	**37**	**60**	**102**	**6**	**1**	**3**	**4**	**16**
1988-89	**Toronto**	**NHL**	**75**	**16**	**30**	**46**	**112**	....	....	....	....	....
1989-90	**Toronto**	**NHL**	**78**	**23**	**50**	**73**	**91**	**5**	**2**	**3**	**5**	**12**
1990-91	**Toronto**	**NHL**	**18**	**3**	**3**	**6**	**4**	....	....	....	....	....
	Winnipeg	**NHL**	**37**	**8**	**8**	**16**	**59**	....	....	....	....	....
1991-92	**Winnipeg**	**NHL**	**43**	**4**	**12**	**16**	**65**	....	....	....	....	....
	Toronto	**NHL**	**11**	**3**	**1**	**4**	**8**	....	....	....	....	....
	NHL Totals		**733**	**190**	**287**	**477**	**899**	**43**	**6**	**13**	**19**	**71**

Traded to **NY Rangers** by **Detroit** with Willie Huber and Mike Blaisdell for Ron Duguay, Eddie Mio and Eddie Johnstone, June 13, 1983. Traded to **Toronto** by **NY Rangers** for Jeff Jackson and Toronto's third round choice (Rod Zamuner) in 1989 Entry Draft, March 5, 1987. Traded to **Winnipeg** by **Toronto** with Ed Olcyk for Dave Ellett and Paul Fenton, November 10, 1990. Traded to **Toronto** by **Winnipeg** for Lucien Deblois, March 10, 1992.

O'SHEA, DAN

Right wing. Shoots right. 6'1", 177 lbs. Born, St. Cloud, MN, September 4, 1970.
(Minnesota's 1st choice, 14th overall, in 1991 Supplemental Draft).

			Regular Season					Playoffs				
Season	Club	Lea	GP	G	A	TP	PIM	GP	G	A	TP	PIM
1990-91	St. Cloud	WCHA	31	4	9	13	60	....	....	....	....	....
1991-92	St. Cloud	WCHA	35	10	14	24	65	....	....	....	....	....

OSIECKI, MARK

Defense. Shoots right. 6'2", 200 lbs. Born, St. Paul, MN, July 23, 1968.
(Calgary's 10th choice, 187th overall, in 1987 Entry Draft).

			Regular Season					Playoffs				
Season	Club	Lea	GP	G	A	TP	PIM	GP	G	A	TP	PIM
1986-87	U. Wisconsin	WCHA	8	0	1	1	4	....	....	....	....	....
1987-88	U. Wisconsin	WCHA	18	0	1	1	22	....	....	....	....	....
1988-89	U. Wisconsin	WCHA	44	1	3	4	56	....	....	....	....	....
1989-90a	U. Wisconsin	WCHA	46	5	38	43	78	....	....	....	....	....
1990-91	Salt Lake	IHL	75	1	24	25	36	4	2	0	2	2
1991-92	**Calgary**	**NHL**	**50**	**2**	**7**	**9**	**24**	....	....	....	....	....
	Salt Lake	IHL	1	0	0	0	0	....	....	....	....	....
	NHL Totals		**50**	**2**	**7**	**9**	**24**	....	....	....	....	....

a NCAA All-Tournament Team (1990)

Traded to **Ottawa** by **Calgary** for Chris Lindberg, June 22, 1992.

OSMAK, COREY

Center. Shoots left. 6'1", 180 lbs. Born, Edmonton, Alta., August 20, 1970.
(Hartford's 8th choice, 183rd overall, in 1990 Entry Draft).

			Regular Season					Playoffs				
Season	Club	Lea	GP	G	A	TP	PIM	GP	G	A	TP	PIM
1990-91	Minn.-Duluth	WCHA	22	3	0	3	34	....	....	....	....	....
1991-92	Minn.-Duluth	WCHA	26	1	4	5	58	....	....	....	....	....

O'SULLIVAN, CHRIS

Defense. Shoots left. 6'2", 180 lbs. Born, Dorchester, MA, May 15, 1974.
(Calgary's 2nd choice, 30th overall, in 1992 Entry Draft).

			Regular Season					Playoffs				
Season	Club	Lea	GP	G	A	TP	PIM	GP	G	A	TP	PIM
1990-91	Gov. Dummer	HS	24	8	18	26	25	....	....	....	....	....
1991-92	Catholic Mem.	HS	26	26	23	49	65	....	....	....	....	....

O'SULLIVAN, KEVIN

Defense. Shoots left. 6', 180 lbs. Born, Dorchester, MA, November 13, 1970.
(NY Islanders' 7th choice, 99th overall, in 1989 Entry Draft).

			Regular Season					Playoffs				
Season	Club	Lea	GP	G	A	TP	PIM	GP	G	A	TP	PIM
1989-90	Boston U.	H.E.	43	0	6	6	42	....	....	....	....	....
1990-91	Boston U.	H.E.	37	4	7	11	50	....	....	....	....	....
1991-92a	Boston U.	H.E.	32	3	18	21	62	....	....	....	....	....

a Hockey East Second All-Star Team (1992)

OTEVREL, JAROSLAV

Centre. Shoots left. 6'2", 185 lbs. Born, Gottwaldov, Czech., September 16, 1968.
(San Jose's 8th choice, 133rd overall, in 1991 Entry Draft).

			Regular Season					Playoffs				
Season	Club	Lea	GP	G	A	TP	PIM	GP	G	A	TP	PIM
1987-88	TJ Gottwaldov	Czech.	32	4	7	11	18	....	....	....	....	....
1988-89	TJ Zlin	Czech.	40	14	6	20	37	....	....	....	....	....
1989-90	Dukla Trencin	Czech.	43	7	10	17	20	....	....	....	....	....
1990-91	TJ Zlin	Czech.	49	24	26	50	105	....	....	....	....	....
1991-92	ZPS Zlin	Czech.	40	14	15	29	....	....	....	....	....	....

OTTO, JOEL STUART

Center. Shoots right. 6'4", 220 lbs. Born, Elk River, MN, October 29, 1961.

			Regular Season					Playoffs				
Season	Club	Lea	GP	G	A	TP	PIM	GP	G	A	TP	PIM
1980-81	Bemidji State	NCAA	23	5	11	16	10	....	....	....	....	....
1981-82	Bemidji State	NCAA	31	19	33	52	24	....	....	....	....	....
1982-83	Bemidji State	NCAA	37	33	28	61	68	....	....	....	....	....
1983-84	Bemidji State	NCAA	31	32	43	75	32	....	....	....	....	....
1984-85	**Calgary**	**NHL**	**17**	**4**	**8**	**12**	**30**	**3**	**2**	**1**	**3**	**10**
	Moncton	AHL	56	27	36	63	89	....	....	....	....	....
1985-86	**Calgary**	**NHL**	**79**	**25**	**34**	**59**	**188**	**22**	**5**	**10**	**15**	**80**
1986-87	**Calgary**	**NHL**	**68**	**19**	**31**	**50**	**185**	**2**	**0**	**2**	**2**	**6**
1987-88	**Calgary**	**NHL**	**62**	**13**	**39**	**52**	**194**	**9**	**3**	**2**	**5**	**26**
1988-89	**Calgary**	**NHL**	**72**	**23**	**30**	**53**	**213**	**22**	**6**	**13**	**19**	**46**
1989-90	**Calgary**	**NHL**	**75**	**13**	**20**	**33**	**116**	**6**	**2**	**2**	**4**	**2**
1990-91	**Calgary**	**NHL**	**76**	**19**	**20**	**39**	**183**	**7**	**1**	**2**	**3**	**8**
1991-92	**Calgary**	**NHL**	**78**	**13**	**21**	**34**	**161**	....	....	....	....	....
	NHL Totals		**527**	**129**	**203**	**332**	**1270**	**71**	**19**	**32**	**51**	**178**

Signed as a free agent by **Calgary**, September 11, 1984.

OUIMET, MARK

Center. Shoots left. 5'10", 165 lbs. Born, Poplar Hill, Ont., October 2, 1971.
(Washington's 6th choice, 94th overall, in 1990 Entry Draft).

			Regular Season					Playoffs				
Season	Club	Lea	GP	G	A	TP	PIM	GP	G	A	TP	PIM
1989-90	U. of Michigan	CCHA	38	15	32	47	14	....	....	....	....	....
1990-91	U. of Michigan	CCHA	46	18	32	50	22	....	....	....	....	....
1991-92	U. of Michigan	CCHA	40	10	19	29	30	....	....	....	....	....

OZOLNICH, SANDIS (oh-zohl-INSH)

Defense. Shoots left. 6'1", 189 lbs. Born, Riga, Soviet Union, August 3, 1972.
(San Jose's 3rd choice, 30th overall, in 1991 Entry Draft).

			Regular Season					Playoffs				
Season	Club	Lea	GP	G	A	TP	PIM	GP	G	A	TP	PIM
1990-91	Riga	USSR	44	0	3	3	49	....	....	....	....	....
1991-92	Riga	CIS	30	6	0	6	42	....	....	....	....	....
	Kansas City	IHL	34	6	9	15	20	15	2	5	7	22

PAEK, JIM (PAYK)

Defense. Shoots left. 6'1", 195 lbs. Born, Seoul, South Korea, April 7, 1967.
(Pittsburgh's 9th choice, 170th overall, in 1985 Entry Draft).

			Regular Season					Playoffs				
Season	Club	Lea	GP	G	A	TP	PIM	GP	G	A	TP	PIM
1984-85	Oshawa	OHL	54	2	13	15	57	5	1	0	1	9
1985-86	Oshawa	OHL	64	5	21	26	122	6	0	1	1	9
1986-87	Oshawa	OHL	57	5	17	22	75	26	1	14	15	43
1987-88	Muskegon	IHL	82	7	52	59	141	6	0	0	0	29
1988-89	Muskegon	IHL	80	3	54	57	96	14	1	10	11	24
1989-90	Muskegon	IHL	81	9	41	50	115	15	1	10	11	41
1990-91	Cdn. National	....	48	2	12	14	24	....	....	....	....	....
	Pittsburgh	**NHL**	**3**	**0**	**0**	**0**	**9**	**8**	**1**	**0**	**1**	**2**
1991-92	**Pittsburgh**	**NHL**	**49**	**1**	**7**	**8**	**36**	**19**	**0**	**4**	**4**	**6**
	NHL Totals		**52**	**1**	**7**	**8**	**45**	**27**	**1**	**4**	**5**	**8**

PALFFY, ZIGMUND

Left wing. Shoots left. 5'10", 169 lbs. Born, Skalica, Czechoslovakia, May 5, 1972.
(NY Islanders' 2nd choice, 26th overall, in 1991 Entry Draft).

			Regular Season					Playoffs				
Season	Club	Lea	GP	G	A	TP	PIM	GP	G	A	TP	PIM
1990-91	Nitra	Czech.	50	34	16	50	18	....	....	....	....	....
1991-92	Dukla Trencin	Czech.	45	41	33	74	....	....	....	....	....	....

PANTELEYEV, GRIGORY

Left wing. Shoots left. 5'9", 194 lbs. Born, Riga, Soviet Union, November 13, 1972.
(Boston's 5th choice, 136th overall, in 1992 Entry Draft).

			Regular Season					Playoffs				
Season	Club	Lea	GP	G	A	TP	PIM	GP	G	A	TP	PIM
1990-91	Riga	USSR	23	4	1	5	4	....	....	....	....	....
1991-92	Riga	CIS	26	4	8	12	4	....	....	....	....	....

PARKS, GREG

Center. Shoots right. 5'9", 180 lbs. Born, Edmonton, Alta., March 25, 1967.

			Regular Season					Playoffs				
Season	Club	Lea	GP	G	A	TP	PIM	GP	G	A	TP	PIM
1987-88	Bowling Green	CCHA	45	30	44	74	84	....	....	....	....	....
1988-89	Bowling Green	CCHA	47	32	42	74	98	....	....	....	....	....
1989-90	Springfield	AHL	49	22	32	54	30	18	9	13	22	22
	Johnstown	ECHL	8	5	9	14	7	....	....	....	....	....
1990-91	**NY Islanders**	**NHL**	**20**	**1**	**2**	**3**	**4**	....	....	....	....	....
	Capital Dist.	AHL	48	32	43	75	67	....	....	....	....	....
1991-92	**NY Islanders**	**NHL**	**1**	**0**	**0**	**0**	**2**	....	....	....	....	....
	Capital Dist.	AHL	70	36	57	93	84	7	5	8	13	4
	NHL Totals		**21**	**1**	**2**	**3**	**6**	....	....	....	....	....

Signed as a free agent by **NY Islanders**, August 13, 1990.

PARROTT, JEFF

Defense. Shoots right. 6'1", 195 lbs. Born, The Pas, Man., April 6, 1971.
(Quebec's 4th choice, 106th overall, in 1990 Entry Draft).

			Regular Season					Playoffs				
Season	Club	Lea	GP	G	A	TP	PIM	GP	G	A	TP	PIM
1989-90	Minn.-Duluth	WCHA	35	1	5	6	60	....	....	....	....	....
1990-91	Minn.-Duluth	WCHA	39	2	8	10	65	....	....	....	....	....
1991-92	Minn.-Duluth	WCHA	33	1	8	9	78	....	....	....	....	....

PASCALL, BRAD

Defense. Shoots left. 6'2", 192 lbs. Born, Coquitlam, B.C., July 29, 1970.
(Buffalo's 5th choice, 103rd overall, in 1990 Entry Draft).

			Regular Season					Playoffs				
Season	Club	Lea	GP	G	A	TP	PIM	GP	G	A	TP	PIM
1989-90	North Dakota	WCHA	45	1	9	10	98	....	....	....	....	....
1990-91	North Dakota	WCHA	38	1	4	5	81	....	....	....	....	....
1991-92	North Dakota	WCHA	28	0	7	7	85	....	....	....	....	....

PASCUCCI, RONALD

Defense. Shoots left. 6'1", 180 lbs. Born, North Andover, MA, June 9, 1970.
(Washington's 14th choice, 246th overall, in 1988 Entry Draft).

			Regular Season					Playoffs				
Season	Club	Lea	GP	G	A	TP	PIM	GP	G	A	TP	PIM
1989-90	Boston College	H.E.	37	0	6	6	12	....	....	....	....	....
1990-91	Boston College	H.E.	37	1	13	14	30	....	....	....	....	....
1991-92	Boston College	H.E.	35	2	6	8	30	....	....	....	....	....

PASLAWSKI, GREGORY STEPHEN (GREG) (pas-LAW-skee)

Right wing. Shoots right. 5'11", 190 lbs. Born, Kindersley, Sask., August 25, 1961.

			Regular Season					Playoffs				
Season	Club	Lea	GP	G	A	TP	PIM	GP	G	A	TP	PIM
1981-82	Nova Scotia	AHL	43	15	11	26	31	....	....	....	....	....
1982-83	Nova Scotia	AHL	75	46	42	88	32	6	1	3	4	8
1983-84	**Montreal**	**NHL**	**26**	**1**	**4**	**5**	**4**	....	....	....	....	....
	St. Louis	**NHL**	**34**	**8**	**6**	**14**	**17**	**9**	**1**	**0**	**1**	**2**
1984-85	**St. Louis**	**NHL**	**72**	**22**	**20**	**42**	**21**	**3**	**0**	**0**	**0**	**2**
1985-86	**St. Louis**	**NHL**	**56**	**22**	**11**	**33**	**18**	**17**	**10**	**7**	**17**	**13**
1986-87	**St. Louis**	**NHL**	**76**	**29**	**35**	**64**	**27**	**6**	**1**	**1**	**2**	**4**
1987-88	**St. Louis**	**NHL**	**17**	**2**	**1**	**3**	**4**	**3**	**1**	**1**	**2**	**2**
1988-89	**St. Louis**	**NHL**	**75**	**26**	**26**	**52**	**18**	**9**	**2**	**1**	**3**	**2**
1989-90	**Winnipeg**	**NHL**	**71**	**18**	**30**	**48**	**14**	**7**	**1**	**3**	**4**	**0**
1990-91	**Winnipeg**	**NHL**	**43**	**9**	**10**	**19**	**10**	....	....	....	....	....
	Buffalo	**NHL**	**12**	**2**	**1**	**3**	**4**	....	....	....	....	....
1991-92	**Quebec**	**NHL**	**80**	**28**	**17**	**45**	**18**	....	....	....	....	....
	NHL Totals		**562**	**167**	**161**	**328**	**155**	**54**	**16**	**13**	**29**	**25**

Signed as a free agent by **Montreal**, October 5, 1981. Traded to **St. Louis** by **Montreal** with Gilbert Delorme and Doug Wickenheiser for Perry Turnbull, December 21, 1983. Traded to **Winnipeg** by **St. Louis** with St. Louis' third round choice (Kris Draper) in 1989 Entry Draft for Winnipeg's third round choice (Denny Felsner) in 1989 Entry Draft and second round choice (Steve Staios) in 1991 Entry Draft, June 17, 1989. Traded to **Buffalo** by **Winnipeg** for future considerations, February 4, 1991. Claimed by **San Jose** from **Buffalo** in Expansion Draft, May 30, 1991. Traded to **Quebec** by **San Jose** for Tony Hrkac, May 31, 1991.

PASMA, ROD

Defense. Shoots left. 6'4", 207 lbs. Born, Brampton, Ont., February 26, 1972.
(Washington's 2nd choice, 30th overall, in 1990 Entry Draft).

			Regular Season					Playoffs				
Season	Club	Lea	GP	G	A	TP	PIM	GP	G	A	TP	PIM
1989-90	Cornwall	OHL	64	3	16	19	142	6	0	2	2	15
1990-91	Cornwall	OHL	33	3	9	12	64	....	....	....	....	....
	Kingston	OHL	31	1	9	10	39	....	....	....	....	....
1991-92	Kingston	OHL	23	2	1	3	68	....	....	....	....	....
	Windsor	OHL	27	3	4	7	59	7	0	1	1	18

PATERSON, JOSEPH (JOE)

Left wing. Shoots left. 6'2", 207 lbs. Born, Toronto, Ont., June 25, 1960.
(Detroit's 5th choice, 87th overall, in 1979 Entry Draft).

			Regular Season					Playoffs				
Season	Club	Lea	GP	G	A	TP	PIM	GP	G	A	TP	PIM
1978-79	London	OHA	59	22	19	41	158	7	2	3	5	13
1979-80	London	OHA	62	21	50	71	156	....	....	....	....	....
	Kalamazoo	IHL	4	1	2	3	2	3	2	1	3	11
1980-81	**Detroit**	**NHL**	**38**	**2**	**5**	**7**	**53**	....	....	....	....	....
	Adirondack	AHL	39	9	16	25	68	....	....	....	....	....
1981-82	**Detroit**	**NHL**	**3**	**0**	**0**	**0**	**0**	....	....	....	....	....
	Adirondack	AHL	74	22	28	50	132	5	1	4	5	6
1982-83	**Detroit**	**NHL**	**33**	**2**	**1**	**3**	**14**	....	....	....	....	....
	Adirondack	AHL	36	11	10	21	85	6	1	2	3	21
1983-84	**Detroit**	**NHL**	**41**	**2**	**5**	**7**	**148**	**3**	**0**	**0**	**0**	**7**
	Adirondack	AHL	20	10	15	25	43	....	....	....	....	....
1984-85	**Philadelphia**	**NHL**	**6**	**0**	**0**	**0**	**31**	**17**	**3**	**4**	**7**	**70**
	Hershey	AHL	67	26	27	53	173	....	....	....	....	....
1985-86	**Philadelphia**	**NHL**	**5**	**0**	**0**	**0**	**12**	....	....	....	....	....
	Hershey	AHL	20	5	10	15	68	....	....	....	....	....
	Los Angeles	**NHL**	**47**	**9**	**18**	**27**	**153**	....	....	....	....	....
1986-87	**Los Angeles**	**NHL**	**45**	**2**	**1**	**3**	**158**	**2**	**0**	**0**	**0**	**0**
1987-88	**Los Angeles**	**NHL**	**32**	**1**	**3**	**4**	**113**	....	....	....	....	....
	NY Rangers	**NHL**	**21**	**1**	**3**	**4**	**63**	....	....	....	....	....
1988-89	**NY Rangers**	**NHL**	**20**	**0**	**1**	**1**	**84**	....	....	....	....	....
	Denver	IHL	9	5	4	9	31	....	....	....	....	....
1989-90	Flint	IHL	69	21	26	47	198	4	0	1	1	2
1990-91	Binghamton	AHL	80	16	35	51	221	10	5	3	8	25
1991-92	Binghamton	AHL	49	7	10	17	115	5	0	0	0	4
	Phoenix	IHL	2	0	0	0	2	....	....	....	....	....
	NHL Totals		**291**	**19**	**37**	**56**	**829**	**22**	**3**	**4**	**7**	**77**

Traded to **Philadelphia** by **Detroit** with Murray Craven for Darryl Sittler, October 19, 1984. Traded to **Los Angeles** by **Philadelphia** for Philadelphia's fourth round choice (Mark Bar) — acquired earlier — in 1986 Entry Draft, December 18, 1985. Traded to **NY Rangers** by **Los Angeles** for Gordon Walker and Mike Siltala, January 21, 1988.

PATRICK, JAMES

Defense. Shoots right. 6'2", 204 lbs. Born, Winnipeg, Man., June 14, 1963.
(NY Rangers' 1st choice, 9th overall, in 1981 Entry Draft).

			Regular Season					Playoffs				
Season	Club	Lea	GP	G	A	TP	PIM	GP	G	A	TP	PIM
1981-82abc	North Dakota	WCHA	42	5	24	29	26	....	....	....	....	....
1982-83de	North Dakota	WCHA	36	12	36	48	29	....	....	....	....	....
1983-84	Cdn. Olympic	....	63	7	24	31	52	....	....	....	....	....
	NY Rangers	**NHL**	**12**	**1**	**7**	**8**	**2**	**5**	**0**	**3**	**3**	**2**
1984-85	**NY Rangers**	**NHL**	**75**	**8**	**28**	**36**	**71**	**3**	**0**	**0**	**0**	**4**
1985-86	**NY Rangers**	**NHL**	**75**	**14**	**29**	**43**	**88**	**16**	**1**	**5**	**6**	**34**
1986-87	**NY Rangers**	**NHL**	**78**	**10**	**45**	**55**	**62**	**6**	**1**	**2**	**3**	**2**
1987-88	**NY Rangers**	**NHL**	**70**	**17**	**45**	**62**	**52**	....	....	....	....	....
1988-89	**NY Rangers**	**NHL**	**68**	**11**	**36**	**47**	**41**	**4**	**0**	**1**	**1**	**2**
1989-90	**NY Rangers**	**NHL**	**73**	**14**	**43**	**57**	**50**	**10**	**3**	**8**	**11**	**0**
1990-91	**NY Rangers**	**NHL**	**74**	**10**	**49**	**59**	**58**	**6**	**0**	**0**	**0**	**6**
1991-92	**NY Rangers**	**NHL**	**80**	**14**	**57**	**71**	**54**	**13**	**0**	**7**	**7**	**12**
	NHL Totals		**605**	**99**	**339**	**438**	**478**	**63**	**5**	**26**	**31**	**62**

a WCHA Rookie of the Year (1982)
b WCHA Second All-Star Team (1982)
c Named to NCAA All-Tournament Team (1982)
d WCHA First All-Star Team (1983)
e NCAA All American (West) (1983)

PATTERSON, COLIN

Right/Left wing. Shoots right. 6'2", 195 lbs. Born, Rexdale, Ont., May 11, 1960.

			Regular Season					Playoffs				
Season	Club	Lea	GP	G	A	TP	PIM	GP	G	A	TP	PIM
1980-81	Clarkson	ECAC	34	20	31	51	8	....	....	....	....	....
1981-82	Clarkson	ECAC	34	21	31	52	32	....	....	....	....	....
1982-83	Clarkson	ECAC	31	23	29	52	30	....	....	....	....	....
	Colorado	CHL	7	1	1	2	0	3	0	0	0	15
1983-84	**Calgary**	**NHL**	**56**	**13**	**14**	**27**	**15**	**11**	**1**	**1**	**2**	**6**
	Colorado	CHL	6	2	3	5	9	....	....	....	....	....
1984-85	**Calgary**	**NHL**	**57**	**22**	**21**	**43**	**5**	**4**	**0**	**0**	**0**	**5**
1985-86	**Calgary**	**NHL**	**61**	**14**	**13**	**27**	**22**	**19**	**6**	**3**	**9**	**10**
1986-87	**Calgary**	**NHL**	**68**	**13**	**13**	**26**	**41**	**6**	**0**	**2**	**2**	**2**
1987-88	**Calgary**	**NHL**	**39**	**7**	**11**	**18**	**28**	**9**	**1**	**0**	**1**	**8**
1988-89	**Calgary**	**NHL**	**74**	**14**	**24**	**38**	**56**	**22**	**3**	**10**	**13**	**24**
1989-90	**Calgary**	**NHL**	**61**	**5**	**3**	**8**	**20**	....	....	....	....	....
1990-91	**Calgary**	**NHL**	....	....	....	....	....	**1**	**0**	**0**	**0**	**0**
1991-92	**Buffalo**	**NHL**	**52**	**4**	**8**	**12**	**30**	**5**	**1**	**0**	**1**	**0**
	NHL Totals		**468**	**92**	**107**	**199**	**217**	**77**	**12**	**16**	**28**	**55**

Signed as a free agent by **Calgary**, March 24, 1983. Traded to **Buffalo** by **Calgary** for future considerations, October 24, 1991.

PATTERSON, ED

Right wing. Shoots right. 6'2", 213 lbs. Born, Calgary, Alta., November 14, 1972.
(Pittsburgh's 7th choice, 148th overall, in 1991 Entry Draft).

			Regular Season					Playoffs				
Season	Club	Lea	GP	G	A	TP	PIM	GP	G	A	TP	PIM
1990-91	Swift Current	WHL	7	2	7	9	0	....	....	....	....	....
	Kamloops	WHL	55	14	33	47	134	5	0	0	0	7
1991-92	Kamloops	WHL	38	19	25	44	120	1	0	0	0	0

PAVELICH, MARK

Center. Shoots right. 5'8", 170 lbs. Born, Eveleth, MN, February 28, 1958.
(St. Louis' 5th choice, 117th overall, in 1980 Entry Draft).

			Regular Season					Playoffs				
Season	Club	Lea	GP	G	A	TP	PIM	GP	G	A	TP	PIM
1978-79a	Minn.-Duluth	WCHA	37	31	48	79	52	....	....	....	....	....
1979-80	U.S. National	....	53	15	30	45	12	....	....	....	....	....
	U.S. Olympic	....	7	1	6	7	2	....	....	....	....	....
1980-81	Lugano	Switz.	60	24	49	73	....	....	....	....	....	....
1981-82	**NY Rangers**	**NHL**	**79**	**33**	**43**	**76**	**67**	**6**	**1**	**5**	**6**	**0**
1982-83	**NY Rangers**	**NHL**	**78**	**37**	**38**	**75**	**52**	**9**	**4**	**5**	**9**	**12**
1983-84	**NY Rangers**	**NHL**	**77**	**29**	**53**	**82**	**96**	**5**	**2**	**4**	**6**	**0**
1984-85	**NY Rangers**	**NHL**	**48**	**14**	**31**	**45**	**29**	**3**	**0**	**3**	**3**	**2**
1985-86	**NY Rangers**	**NHL**	**59**	**20**	**20**	**40**	**82**	....	....	....	....	....
1986-87	**Minnesota**	**NHL**	**12**	**4**	**6**	**10**	**10**	....	....	....	....	....
1987-88	Davos	Switz.				UNAVAILABLE						
1988-89	Dundee	Brit.				UNAVAILABLE						
1989-90						DID NOT PLAY						
1990-91						DID NOT PLAY						
1991-92	**San Jose**	**NHL**	**2**	**0**	**1**	**1**	**4**	....	....	....	....	....
	NHL Totals		**355**	**137**	**192**	**329**	**340**	**23**	**7**	**17**	**24**	**14**

a WCHA First All-Star Team (1979)

Signed as a free agent by **NY Rangers**, June 5, 1981. Traded to **Minnesota** by **NY Rangers** for Minnesota's second round choice (Troy Mallette) in 1988 Entry Draft, October 24, 1986. Signed as a free agent by **San Jose**, August 9, 1991.

PAVLAS, PETR (PAHV-lahs)

Defense. Shoots left. 5'10", 172 lbs. Born, Olomouc, Czechoslovakia, February 4, 1968.
(Washington's 10th choice, 183rd overall, in 1988 Entry Draft).

			Regular Season					Playoffs				
Season	Club	Lea	GP	G	A	TP	PIM	GP	G	A	TP	PIM
1987-88	Dukla Trencin	Czech.	20	4	7	11	....	....	....	....	....	....
1988-89	Dukla Trencin	Czech.	31	14	15	29	....	....	....	....	....	....
1989-90	TJ Zlin	Czech.	51	13	15	28	....	....	....	....	....	....
1990-91	TJ Zlin	Czech.	48	14	20	34	16	....	....	....	....	....
1991-92	ZPS Zlin	Czech.	39	8	21	29	....	....	....	....	....	....

PAYNE, DAVIS

Left wing. Shoots left. 6'1", 190 lbs. Born, King City, Ont., October 24, 1970.
(Edmonton's 6th choice, 140th overall, in 1989 Entry Draft).

			Regular Season					Playoffs				
Season	Club	Lea	GP	G	A	TP	PIM	GP	G	A	TP	PIM
1988-89	Michigan Tech	WCHA	33	5	3	8	39	....	....	....	....	....
1989-90	Michigan Tech	WCHA	36	11	10	21	81	....	....	....	....	....
1990-91	Michigan Tech	WCHA	41	15	20	35	82	....	....	....	....	....
1991-92	Michigan Tech	WCHA	24	6	1	7	71	....	....	....	....	....

PAYNTER, KENT

Defense. Shoots left. 6', 183 lbs. Born, Summerside, P.E.I., April 17, 1965.
(Chicago's 9th choice, 159th overall, in 1983 Entry Draft).

			Regular Season					Playoffs				
Season	Club	Lea	GP	G	A	TP	PIM	GP	G	A	TP	PIM
1982-83	Kitchener	OHL	65	4	11	15	97	12	1	0	1	20
1983-84	Kitchener	OHL	65	9	27	36	94	16	4	9	13	18
1984-85	Kitchener	OHL	58	7	28	35	93	4	2	1	3	4
1985-86	Nova Scotia	AHL	23	1	2	3	36	....	....	....	....	....
	Saginaw	IHL	4	0	1	1	2	....	....	....	....	....
1986-87	Nova Scotia	AHL	66	2	6	8	57	2	0	0	0	0
1987-88	**Chicago**	**NHL**	**2**	**0**	**0**	**0**	**2**	....	....	....	....	....
	Saginaw	IHL	74	8	20	28	141	10	0	1	1	30
1988-89	**Chicago**	**NHL**	**1**	**0**	**0**	**0**	**2**	....	....	....	....	....
	Saginaw	IHL	69	12	14	26	148	6	2	2	4	17
1989-90	**Washington**	**NHL**	**13**	**1**	**2**	**3**	**18**	**3**	**0**	**0**	**0**	**10**
	Baltimore	AHL	60	7	20	27	110	11	5	6	1	34
1990-91	**Washington**	**NHL**	**1**	**0**	**0**	**0**	**15**	**1**	**0**	**0**	**0**	**0**
	Baltimore	AHL	43	10	17	27	64	6	2	1	3	8
1991-92	**Winnipeg**	**NHL**	**5**	**0**	**0**	**0**	**4**	....	....	....	....	....
	Moncton	AHL	62	3	30	33	71	11	2	6	8	25
	NHL Totals		**22**	**1**	**2**	**3**	**41**	**4**	**0**	**0**	**0**	**10**

Signed as a free agent by **Washington**, August 21, 1989. Traded to **Winnipeg** by **Washington** with Tyler Larter and Bob Joyce for Craig Duncanson, Brent Hughes and Simon Wheeldon, May 21, 1991. Claimed by **Ottawa** from **Winnipeg** in Expansion Draft, June 18, 1992.

PEACOCK, SHANE

Defense. Shoots right. 5'10", 198 lbs. Born, Edmonton, Alta., July 7, 1973.
(Pittsburgh's 3rd choice, 60th overall, in 1991 Entry Draft).

			Regular Season					Playoffs				
Season	Club	Lea	GP	G	A	TP	PIM	GP	G	A	TP	PIM
1989-90	Lethbridge	WHL	65	7	23	30	60	19	2	8	10	42
1990-91	Lethbridge	WHL	69	12	50	62	102	16	1	14	15	26
1991-92	Lethbridge	WHL	67	35	45	80	217	5	2	5	7	2

PEAKE, PAT

Center. Shoots right. 6', 195 lbs. Born, Rochester, MI, May 28, 1973.
(Washington's 1st choice, 14th overall, in 1991 Entry Draft).

			Regular Season					Playoffs				
Season	Club	Lea	GP	G	A	TP	PIM	GP	G	A	TP	PIM
1990-91	Detroit	OHL	63	39	51	90	54	....	....	....	....	....
1991-92	Detroit	OHL	53	41	52	93	44	7	8	9	17	10
	Baltimore	AHL	3	1	0	1	4	....	....	....	....	....

PEARCE, RANDY

Left wing. Shoots left. 5'11", 203 lbs. Born, Kitchener, Ont., February 23, 1970.
(Washington's 4th choice, 72nd overall, in 1990 Entry Draft).

			Regular Season					Playoffs				
Season	Club	Lea	GP	G	A	TP	PIM	GP	G	A	TP	PIM
1988-89	Kitchener	OHL	64	23	21	44	87	5	0	1	1	6
1989-90	Kitchener	OHL	62	31	34	65	139	17	8	15	23	42
1990-91					DID NOT PLAY - INJURED							
1991-92	Hampton Rds.	ECHL	55	32	46	78	134	11	5	9	14	56
	Baltimore	AHL	12	2	2	4	8	....	....	....	....	....

PEARSON, ROB

Right wing. Shoots right. 6'1", 185 lbs. Born, Oshawa, Ont., March 8, 1971.
(Toronto's 2nd choice, 12th overall, in 1989 Entry Draft).

			Regular Season					Playoffs				
Season	Club	Lea	GP	G	A	TP	PIM	GP	G	A	TP	PIM
1988-89	Belleville	OHL	26	8	12	20	51	....	....	....	....	....
1989-90	Belleville	OHL	58	48	40	88	174	11	5	5	10	26
1990-91	Belleville	OHL	10	6	3	9	27	....	....	....	....	....
a	Oshawa	OHL	41	57	52	109	76	16	16	17	33	39
	Newmarket	AHL	3	0	0	0	29	....	....	....	....	....
1991-92	**Toronto**	**NHL**	**47**	**14**	**10**	**24**	**58**	....	....	....	....	....
	St. John's	AHL	27	15	14	29	107	13	5	4	9	40
	NHL Totals		**47**	**14**	**10**	**24**	**58**	....	....	....	....	....

a OHL First All-Star Team (1991)

PEARSON, SCOTT

Left wing. Shoots left. 6'1", 205 lbs. Born, Cornwall, Ont., December 19, 1969.
(Toronto's 1st choice, 6th overall, in 1988 Entry Draft).

			Regular Season					Playoffs				
Season	Club	Lea	GP	G	A	TP	PIM	GP	G	A	TP	PIM
1986-87	Kingston	OHL	62	30	24	54	101	9	3	3	6	42
1987-88	Kingston	OHL	46	26	32	58	117	....	....	....	....	....
1988-89	**Toronto**	**NHL**	**9**	**0**	**1**	**1**	**2**	....	....	....	....	....
	Kingston	OHL	13	9	8	17	34	....	....	....	....	....
	Niagara Falls	OHL	32	26	34	60	90	17	14	10	24	53
1989-90	**Toronto**	**NHL**	**41**	**5**	**10**	**15**	**90**	**2**	**2**	**0**	**2**	**10**
	Newmarket	AHL	18	12	11	23	64	....	....	....	....	....
1990-91	**Toronto**	**NHL**	**12**	**0**	**0**	**0**	**20**	....	....	....	....	....
	Quebec	**NHL**	**35**	**11**	**4**	**15**	**86**	....	....	....	....	....
	Halifax	AHL	24	12	15	27	44	....	....	....	....	....
1991-92	**Quebec**	**NHL**	**10**	**1**	**2**	**3**	**14**	....	....	....	....	....
	Halifax	AHL	5	2	1	3	4	....	....	....	....	....
	NHL Totals		**107**	**17**	**17**	**34**	**212**	**2**	**2**	**0**	**2**	**10**

Traded to **Quebec** by **Toronto** with Toronto's second round choices in 1991 (later traded to Washington - Eric Lavigne) and 1992 Entry Drafts for Aaron Broten, Lucien Deblois and Michel Petit, November 17, 1990.

PECA, MICHAEL

Right wing. Shoots right. 5'11", 163 lbs. Born, North York, Ont., March 26, 1974.
(Vancouver's 2nd choice, 40th overall, in 1992 Entry Draft).

			Regular Season					Playoffs				
Season	Club	Lea	GP	G	A	TP	PIM	GP	G	A	TP	PIM
1990-91	Sudbury	OHL	62	14	27	41	24	5	1	0	1	7
1991-92	Sudbury	OHL	39	16	34	50	61	....	....	....	....	....
	Ottawa	OHL	27	8	17	25	32	11	6	10	16	6

PEDERSEN, ALLEN

Defense. Shoots left. 6'3", 210 lbs. Born, Fort Saskatchewan, Alta., January 13, 1965.
(Boston's 5th choice, 105th overall, in 1983 Entry Draft).

			Regular Season					Playoffs				
Season	Club	Lea	GP	G	A	TP	PIM	GP	G	A	TP	PIM
1982-83	Medicine Hat	WHL	63	3	10	13	49	5	0	0	0	7
1983-84	Medicine Hat	WHL	44	0	11	11	47	14	0	2	2	24
1984-85	Medicine Hat	WHL	72	6	16	22	66	10	0	0	0	9
1985-86	Moncton	AHL	59	1	8	9	39	3	0	0	0	0
1986-87	**Boston**	**NHL**	**79**	**1**	**11**	**12**	**71**	**4**	**0**	**0**	**0**	**4**
1987-88	**Boston**	**NHL**	**78**	**0**	**6**	**6**	**90**	**21**	**0**	**0**	**0**	**34**
1988-89	**Boston**	**NHL**	**51**	**0**	**6**	**6**	**69**	**10**	**0**	**0**	**0**	**2**
1989-90	**Boston**	**NHL**	**68**	**1**	**2**	**3**	**71**	**21**	**0**	**0**	**0**	**41**
1990-91	**Boston**	**NHL**	**57**	**2**	**6**	**8**	**107**	**8**	**0**	**0**	**0**	**10**
	Maine	AHL	15	0	6	6	18	2	0	1	1	2
1991-92	**Minnesota**	**NHL**	**29**	**0**	**1**	**1**	**10**	....	....	....	....	....
	NHL Totals		**362**	**4**	**32**	**36**	**418**	**64**	**0**	**0**	**0**	**91**

Claimed by **Minnesota** from **Boston** in Expansion Draft, May 30, 1991. Traded to **Hartford** by **Minnesota** for future considerations, June 15, 1992.

PEDERSON, BARRY ALAN (PEE-duhr-suhn)

Center. Shoots right. 5'11", 185 lbs. Born, Big River, Sask., March 13, 1961.
(Boston's 1st choice, 18th overall, in 1980 Entry Draft).

			Regular Season					Playoffs				
Season	Club	Lea	GP	G	A	TP	PIM	GP	G	A	TP	PIM
1978-79	Victoria	WHL	72	31	53	84	41	....	....	....	....	....
1979-80	Victoria	WHL	72	52	88	140	50	16	13	14	27	31
1980-81	**Boston**	**NHL**	**9**	**1**	**4**	**5**	**6**	....	....	....	....	....
a	Victoria	WHL	55	65	82	147	65	15	15	21	36	10
1981-82	**Boston**	**NHL**	**80**	**44**	**48**	**92**	**53**	**11**	**7**	**11**	**18**	**2**
1982-83	**Boston**	**NHL**	**77**	**46**	**61**	**107**	**47**	**17**	**14**	**18**	**32**	**21**
1983-84	**Boston**	**NHL**	**80**	**39**	**77**	**116**	**64**	**3**	**0**	**1**	**1**	**2**
1984-85	**Boston**	**NHL**	**22**	**4**	**8**	**12**	**10**	....	....	....	....	....
1985-86	**Boston**	**NHL**	**79**	**29**	**47**	**76**	**60**	**3**	**1**	**0**	**1**	**0**
1986-87	**Vancouver**	**NHL**	**79**	**24**	**52**	**76**	**50**	....	....	....	....	....
1987-88	**Vancouver**	**NHL**	**76**	**19**	**52**	**71**	**92**	....	....	....	....	....
1988-89	**Vancouver**	**NHL**	**62**	**15**	**26**	**41**	**22**	....	....	....	....	....
1989-90	**Vancouver**	**NHL**	**16**	**2**	**7**	**9**	**10**	....	....	....	....	....
	Pittsburgh	**NHL**	**38**	**4**	**18**	**22**	**29**	....	....	....	....	....
1990-91	**Pittsburgh**	**NHL**	**46**	**6**	**8**	**14**	**21**	....	....	....	....	....
1991-92	**Hartford**	**NHL**	**5**	**2**	**2**	**4**	**0**	....	....	....	....	....
	Boston	**NHL**	**32**	**3**	**6**	**9**	**8**	....	....	....	....	....
	Maine	AHL	14	5	13	18	6	....	....	....	....	....
	NHL Totals		**701**	**238**	**416**	**654**	**472**	**34**	**22**	**30**	**52**	**25**

a WHL First All-Star Team (1981)

Played in NHL All-Star Game (1983, 1984)

Traded to **Vancouver** by **Boston** for Cam Neely and Vancouver's first round choice in 1987 Entry Draft (Glen Wesley), June 6, 1986. Traded to **Pittsburgh** by **Vancouver** with Rod Buskas and Tony Tanti for Dave Capuano, Andrew McBain and Dan Quinn, January 8, 1990. Signed as a free agent by **Hartford**, September 5, 1991. Traded to **Boston** by **Hartford** for future considerations, November 14, 1991.

PEDERSON, MARK

Left wing. Shoots left. 6'2", 196 lbs. Born, Prelate, Sask., January 14, 1968.
(Montreal's 1st choice, 15th overall, in 1986 Entry Draft).

			Regular Season					Playoffs				
Season	Club	Lea	GP	G	A	TP	PIM	GP	G	A	TP	PIM
1984-85	Medicine Hat	WHL	71	42	40	82	63	10	3	2	5	0
1985-86	Medicine Hat	WHL	72	46	60	106	46	25	12	6	18	25
1986-87a	Medicine Hat	WHL	69	56	46	102	58	20	*19	7	26	14
1987-88	Medicine Hat	WHL	62	53	58	111	55	16	*13	6	19	16
1988-89	Sherbrooke	AHL	75	43	38	81	53	6	7	5	12	4
1989-90	**Montreal**	**NHL**	**9**	**0**	**2**	**2**	**2**	**2**	**0**	**0**	**0**	**0**
b	Sherbrooke	AHL	72	53	42	95	60	11	10	8	18	19
1990-91	**Montreal**	**NHL**	**47**	**8**	**15**	**23**	**18**	....	....	....	....	....
	Philadelphia	**NHL**	**12**	**2**	**1**	**3**	**5**	....	....	....	....	....
1991-92	**Philadelphia**	**NHL**	**58**	**15**	**25**	**40**	**22**	....	....	....	....	....
	NHL Totals		**126**	**25**	**43**	**68**	**47**	**2**	**0**	**0**	**0**	**0**

a WHL East All-Star Team (1987)
b AHL First All-Star Team (1990)

Traded to **Philadelphia** by **Montreal** for Philadelphia's second round choice (Jim Campbell) in 1991 Entry Draft, March 5, 1991.

PEDERSON, THOMAS

Defense. Shoots right. 5'9", 165 lbs. Born, Bloomington, MN, January 14, 1970.
(Minnesota's 12th choice, 217th overall, in 1989 Entry Draft).

			Regular Season					Playoffs				
Season	Club	Lea	GP	G	A	TP	PIM	GP	G	A	TP	PIM
1988-89	U. Minnesota	WCHA	36	4	20	24	40	....	....	....	....	....
1989-90	U. Minnesota	WCHA	43	8	30	38	58	....	....	....	....	....
1990-91	U. Minnesota	WCHA	36	12	20	32	46	....	....	....	....	....
1991-92	Kansas City	IHL	20	6	9	15	16	13	1	6	7	14

Claimed by **San Jose** from **Minnesota** in Dispersal Draft, May 30, 1991.

PELLERIN, BRIAN

Right wing. Shoots right. 5'10", 175 lbs. Born, Hinton, Alta., February 20, 1970.

			Regular Season					Playoffs				
Season	Club	Lea	GP	G	A	TP	PIM	GP	G	A	TP	PIM
1987-88	Prince Albert	WHL	62	6	2	8	113	10	0	0	0	17
1988-89	Prince Albert	WHL	60	17	16	33	216	3	0	1	1	27
1989-90	Prince Albert	WHL	53	6	15	21	175	10	1	3	4	26
1990-91a	Prince Albert	WHL	68	46	42	88	223	3	0	0	0	12
1991-92	Peoria	IHL	70	7	16	23	231	10	1	2	3	49

a WHL East First All-Star Team (1991)

Signed as a free agent by **St. Louis**, May 31, 1991.

PELLERIN, SCOTT

Left wing. Shoots left. 5'11", 180 lbs. Born, Shediac, N.B., January 9, 1970.
(New Jersey's 4th choice, 47th overall, in 1989 Entry Draft).

			Regular Season					Playoffs				
Season	Club	Lea	GP	G	A	TP	PIM	GP	G	A	TP	PIM
1988-89a	U. of Maine	H.E.	45	29	33	62	92	....	....	....	....	....
1989-90	U. of Maine	H.E.	42	22	34	56	68	....	....	....	....	....
1990-91	U. of Maine	H.E.	43	23	25	48	60	....	....	....	....	....
1991-92bcd	U. of Maine	H.E.	37	*32	25	57	54	....	....	....	....	....
	Utica	AHL	....	....	....	....	....	3	1	0	1	0

a Co-winner Hockey East Rookie of the Year (1989)
b Won Hobey Baker Memorial Award (Top U.S. Collegiate Player) (1992)
c Hockey East First All-Star Team (1992)
d NCAA East First All-Star Team (1992)

PELTOLA, PEKKA (PEHL-TUH-lah)

Right wing. Shoots left. 6'2", 194 lbs. Born, Helsinki, Finland, April 24, 1965.
(Winnipeg's 8th choice, 130th overall, in 1989 Entry Draft).

			Regular Season					Playoffs				
Season	Club	Lea	GP	G	A	TP	PIM	GP	G	A	TP	PIM
1988-89	HPK	Fin.	43	28	30	58	62	....	....	....	....	....
1989-90	HPK	Fin.	45	25	24	49	42	....	....	....	....	....
1990-91	HPK	Fin.	41	23	18	41	66	8	3	2	5	10
1991-92	HPK	Fin.	37	22	20	42	91	....	....	....	....	....

PELTOMAA, TIMO (PEHL-TUH-mah)

Right wing. Shoots right. 6'1", 194 lbs. Born, Tampere, Finland, July 26, 1968.
(Los Angeles' 9th choice, 154th overall, in 1988 Entry Draft).

			Regular Season					Playoffs				
Season	Club	Lea	GP	G	A	TP	PIM	GP	G	A	TP	PIM
1987-88	Ilves	Fin.	20	0	1	1	32	....	....	....	....	....
1988-89	Ilves	Fin.	23	4	0	4	16	....	....	....	....	....
1989-90	Ilves	Fin.	43	7	3	10	28	....	....	....	....	....
1990-91	Ilves	Fin.	44	8	16	24	63	....	....	....	....	....
1991-92	Ilves	Fin.	40	16	14	30	40	....	....	....	....	....

PELUSO, MIKE

Left wing/Defense. Shoots left. 6'4", 200 lbs. Born, Pengilly, MN, November 8, 1965.
(New Jersey's 10th choice, 190th overall, in 1984 Entry Draft).

			Regular Season					Playoffs				
Season	Club	Lea	GP	G	A	TP	PIM	GP	G	A	TP	PIM
1985-86	Alaska-Anch.	G.N.	32	2	11	13	59	....	....	....	....	....
1986-87	Alaska-Anch.	G.N.	30	5	21	26	68	....	....	....	....	....
1987-88	Alaska-Anch.	G.N.	35	4	33	37	76	....	....	....	....	....
1988-89	Alaska-Anch.	G.N.	33	10	27	37	75	....	....	....	....	....
1989-90	**Chicago**	**NHL**	**2**	**0**	**0**	**0**	**15**	....	....	....	....	....
	Indianapolis	IHL	75	7	10	17	279	14	0	1	1	58
1990-91	**Chicago**	**NHL**	**53**	**6**	**1**	**7**	**320**	**3**	**0**	**0**	**0**	**2**
	Indianapolis	IHL	6	2	1	3	21	5	0	2	2	40
1991-92	**Chicago**	**NHL**	**63**	**6**	**3**	**9**	***408**	**17**	**1**	**2**	**3**	**8**
	Indianapolis	IHL	4	0	1	1	15	....	....	....	....	....
	NHL Totals		**118**	**12**	**4**	**16**	**743**	**20**	**1**	**2**	**3**	**10**

Signed as a free agent by **Chicago**, September 7, 1989. Claimed by **Ottawa** from **Chicago** in Expansion Draft, June 18, 1992.

PENNEY, CHAD

Left wing. Shoots left. 6', 196 lbs. Born, Labrador City, Nfld., September 18, 1973.
(Ottawa's 2nd choice, 25th overall, in 1992 Entry Draft).

			Regular Season					Playoffs				
Season	Club	Lea	GP	G	A	TP	PIM	GP	G	A	TP	PIM
1990-91	North Bay	OHL	66	33	34	67	56	10	2	6	8	12
1991-92	North Bay	OHL	57	25	27	52	90	21	13	17	30	9

PERGOLA, DAVID

Right wing. Shoots right. 6'1", 185 lbs. Born, Waltham, MA, March 4, 1969.
(Buffalo's 5th choice, 85th overall, in 1987 Entry Draft).

			Regular Season					Playoffs				
Season	Club	Lea	GP	G	A	TP	PIM	GP	G	A	TP	PIM
1987-88	Boston College	H.E.	33	5	7	12	22	....	....	....	....	....
1988-89	Boston College	H.E.	39	12	9	21	16	....	....	....	....	....
1989-90	Boston College	H.E.	39	6	4	10	22	....	....	....	....	....
1990-91	Boston College	H.E.	35	8	12	20	24	....	....	....	....	....
1991-92	Erie	ECHL	43	19	18	37	44	4	1	0	1	2

PERREAULT, NICOLAS P.

Defense. Shoots left. 6'3", 200 lbs. Born, Loretteville, Que., April 24, 1972.
(Calgary's 2nd choice, 26th overall, in 1990 Entry Draft).

			Regular Season					Playoffs				
Season	Club	Lea	GP	G	A	TP	PIM	GP	G	A	TP	PIM
1990-91	Michigan State	CCHA	34	1	7	8	32	....	....	....	....	....
1991-92	Michigan State	CCHA	41	11	11	22	75	....	....	....	....	....

PERREAULT, YANIC

Center. Shoots left. 5'11", 182 lbs. Born, Sherbrooke, Que., April 4, 1971.
(Toronto's 1st choice, 47th overall, in 1991 Entry Draft).

			Regular Season					Playoffs				
Season	Club	Lea	GP	G	A	TP	PIM	GP	G	A	TP	PIM
1988-89	Trois-Rivières	QMJHL	70	53	55	108	48	....	....	....	....	....
1989-90	Trois-Rivières	QMJHL	63	51	63	114	75	7	6	5	11	19
1990-91a	Trois-Rivières	QMJHL	67	*87	98	*185	103	6	4	7	11	6
1991-92	St. John's	AHL	62	38	38	76	19	16	7	8	15	4

a QMJHL First All-Star Team (1991)

PERRY, JEFF

Left wing. Shoots left. 6', 192 lbs. Born, Sarnia, Ont., April 12, 1971.
(Toronto's 6th choice, 113th overall, in 1991 Entry Draft).

			Regular Season					Playoffs				
Season	Club	Lea	GP	G	A	TP	PIM	GP	G	A	TP	PIM
1990-91	Owen Sound	OHL	60	31	49	80	83	....	....	....	....	....
1991-92	Owen Sound	OHL	7	0	5	5	8	....	....	....	....	....
	St. John's	AHL	6	0	1	1	4	....	....	....	....	....
	Raleigh	ECHL	8	2	2	4	18	4	0	1	1	11

PERSSON, JOAKIM (PEHR-suhn)

Left wing. Shoots left. 5'8", 169 lbs. Born, Gavle, Sweden, May 15, 1966.
(Chicago's 10th choice, 195th overall, in 1984 Entry Draft).

			Regular Season					Playoffs				
Season	Club	Lea	GP	G	A	TP	PIM	GP	G	A	TP	PIM
1985-86	Stromsbro	Swe.	35	8	8	13	2	2	0	0	0	0
1986-87	Brynas	Swe.	34	9	8	17	10	....	....	....	....	....
1987-88	Stromsbro	Swe.	37	10	11	21	12	....	....	....	....	....
1988-89	Brynas	Swe.	39	7	10	17	22	....	....	....	....	....
1989-90	Brynas	Swe.	39	12	8	20	8	5	1	2	3	8
1990-91	Brynas	Swe.	40	3	4	7	18	....	....	....	....	....
1991-92	Brynas	Swe.	23	1	1	2	8	....	....	....	....	....

PERSSON, RICKARD

Defense. Shoots left. 6'2", 205 lbs. Born, Ostersund, Sweden, August 24, 1969.
(New Jersey's 2nd choice, 23rd overall, in 1987 Entry Draft).

			Regular Season					Playoffs				
Season	Club	Lea	GP	G	A	TP	PIM	GP	G	A	TP	PIM
1988-89	Leksand	Swe.	33	2	4	6	28	....	....	....	....	....
1989-90	Leksand	Swe.	43	9	10	19	62	....	....	....	....	....
1990-91	Leksand	Swe.	37	6	9	15	42	....	....	....	....	....
1991-92	Leksand	Swe.	21	0	7	7	28	....	....	....	....	....

PETERS, ROB

Defense. Shoots left. 6'6", 205 lbs. Born, North Tonowanda, NY, May 15, 1972.
(Hartford's 12th choice, 251st overall, in 1991 Entry Draft).

			Regular Season					Playoffs				
Season	Club	Lea	GP	G	A	TP	PIM	GP	G	A	TP	PIM
1990-91	Ohio State	CCHA	33	0	1	1	65	....	....	....	....	....
1991-92	Ohio State	CCHA	28	3	7	10	53	....	....	....	....	....

PETERSON, BRETT

Defense. Shoots right. 6'2", 195 lbs. Born, St. Paul, MN, February 1, 1969.
(Calgary's 9th choice, 189th overall, in 1988 Entry Draft).

			Regular Season					Playoffs				
Season	Club	Lea	GP	G	A	TP	PIM	GP	G	A	TP	PIM
1988-89	U. of Denver	WCHA	19	0	3	3	4	....	....	....	....	....
1989-90	U. of Denver	WCHA	34	3	6	9	23	....	....	....	....	....
1990-91	U. of Denver	WCHA	37	2	9	11	28	....	....	....	....	....
1991-92	U. of Denver	WCHA	36	3	5	8	30	....	....	....	....	....

PETERSON, ERIK

Center. Shoots left. 6', 185 lbs. Born, Boston, MA, March 31, 1972.
(Chicago's 8th choice, 205th overall, in 1990 Entry Draft).

			Regular Season					Playoffs				
Season	Club	Lea	GP	G	A	TP	PIM	GP	G	A	TP	PIM
1990-91	Providence	H.E.	34	8	4	12	12	....	....	....	....	....
1991-92	Providence	H.E.	32	9	5	14	26	....	....	....	....	....

PETIT, MICHEL (puh-TEE)

Defense. Shoots right. 6'1", 205 lbs. Born, St. Malo, Que., February 12, 1964.
(Vancouver's 1st choice, 11th overall, in 1982 Entry Draft).

			Regular Season					Playoffs				
Season	Club	Lea	GP	G	A	TP	PIM	GP	G	A	TP	PIM
1981-82a	Sherbrooke	QMJHL	63	10	39	49	106	22	5	20	25	24
1982-83	**Vancouver**	**NHL**	**2**	**0**	**0**	**0**	**0**	....	....	....	....	....
a	St-Jean	QMJHL	62	19	67	86	196	3	0	0	0	35
1983-84	Cdn. Olympic	....	19	3	10	13	58	....	....	....	....	....
	Vancouver	**NHL**	**44**	**6**	**9**	**15**	**53**	**1**	**0**	**0**	**0**	**0**
1984-85	**Vancouver**	**NHL**	**69**	**5**	**26**	**31**	**127**	....	....	....	....	....
1985-86	**Vancouver**	**NHL**	**32**	**1**	**6**	**7**	**27**	....	....	....	....	....
	Fredericton	AHL	25	0	13	13	79	....	....	....	....	....
1986-87	**Vancouver**	**NHL**	**69**	**12**	**13**	**25**	**131**	....	....	....	....	....
1987-88	**Vancouver**	**NHL**	**10**	**0**	**3**	**3**	**35**	....	....	....	....	....
	NY Rangers	**NHL**	**64**	**9**	**24**	**33**	**223**	....	....	....	....	....
1988-89	**NY Rangers**	**NHL**	**69**	**8**	**25**	**33**	**154**	**4**	**0**	**2**	**2**	**27**
1989-90	**Quebec**	**NHL**	**63**	**12**	**24**	**36**	**215**	....	....	....	....	....
1990-91	**Quebec**	**NHL**	**19**	**4**	**7**	**11**	**47**	....	....	....	....	....
	Toronto	**NHL**	**54**	**9**	**19**	**28**	**132**	....	....	....	....	....
1991-92	**Toronto**	**NHL**	**34**	**1**	**13**	**14**	**85**	....	....	....	....	....
	Calgary	**NHL**	**36**	**3**	**10**	**13**	**79**	....	....	....	....	....
	NHL Totals		**565**	**70**	**179**	**249**	**1308**	**5**	**0**	**2**	**2**	**27**

a QMJHL First All-Star Team (1982, 1983)

Traded to **NY Rangers** by **Vancouver** for Willie Huber and Larry Melnyk, November 4, 1987. Traded to **Quebec** by **NY Rangers** for Randy Moller, October 5, 1989. Traded to **Toronto** by **Quebec** with Aaron Broten and Lucien Deblois for Scott Pearson and Toronto's second round choices in 1991 (later traded to Washington - Eric Lavigne) and 1992 Entry Drafts, November 17, 1990. Traded to **Calgary** by **Toronto** with Craig Berube, Alexander Godynyuk, Gary Leeman and Jeff Reese for Doug Gilmour, Jamie Macoun, Ric Natress, Rick Wamsley and Kent Manderville, January 2, 1992.

PETROV, OLEG

Right wing. Shoots left. 5'9", 161 lbs. Born, Moscow, Soviet Union, April 18, 1971.
(Montreal's 6th choice, 127th overall, in 1991 Entry Draft).

			Regular Season					Playoffs				
Season	Club	Lea	GP	G	A	TP	PIM	GP	G	A	TP	PIM
1990-91	CSKA	USSR	43	7	4	11	8	....	....	....	....	....
1991-92	CSKA	CIS	34	8	13	21	6	....	....	....	....	....

PETROVICKY, ROBERT

Center. Shoots left. 5'11", 172 lbs. Born, Kosice, Czech., October 26, 1973.
(Hartford's 1st choice, 9th overall, in 1992 Entry Draft).

			Regular Season					Playoffs				
Season	Club	Lea	GP	G	A	TP	PIM	GP	G	A	TP	PIM
1990-91	Dukla Trencin	Czech.	33	9	14	23	12	....	....	....	....	....
1991-92	Dukla Trencin	Czech.	46	25	36	61	16	....	....	....	....	....

PICARD, MICHEL

Left wing. Shoots left. 5'11", 190 lbs. Born, Beauport, Que., November 7, 1969.
(Hartford's 8th choice, 178th overall, in 1989 Entry Draft).

			Regular Season					Playoffs				
Season	Club	Lea	GP	G	A	TP	PIM	GP	G	A	TP	PIM
1986-87	Trois-Rivières	QMJHL	66	33	35	68	53	....	....	....	....	....
1987-88	Trois-Rivières	QMJHL	69	40	55	95	71	....	....	....	....	....
1988-89	Trois-Rivières	QMJHL	66	59	81	140	170	4	1	3	4	2
1989-90	Binghamton	AHL	67	16	24	40	98	....	....	....	....	....
1990-91	**Hartford**	**NHL**	**5**	**1**	**0**	**1**	**2**	....	....	....	....	....
a	Springfield	AHL	77	*56	40	96	61	18	8	13	21	18
1991-92	**Hartford**	**NHL**	**25**	**3**	**5**	**8**	**6**	**7**	**0**	**0**	**0**	**0**
	Springfield	AHL	40	21	17	38	44	11	2	0	2	34
	NHL Totals		**30**	**4**	**5**	**9**	**8**	**7**	**0**	**0**	**0**	**0**

a AHL First All-Star Team (1991)

PILON, RICHARD

Defense. Shoots left. 6', 202 lbs. Born, Saskatoon, Sask., April 30, 1968.
(NY Islanders' 9th choice, 143rd overall, in 1986 Entry Draft).

			Regular Season					Playoffs				
Season	Club	Lea	GP	G	A	TP	PIM	GP	G	A	TP	PIM
1986-87	Prince Albert	WHL	68	4	21	25	192	7	1	6	7	17
1987-88	Prince Albert	WHL	65	13	34	47	177	9	0	6	6	38
1988-89	**NY Islanders**	**NHL**	**62**	**0**	**14**	**14**	**242**	....	....	....	....	....
1989-90	**NY Islanders**	**NHL**	**14**	**0**	**2**	**2**	**31**	....	....	....	....	....
1990-91	**NY Islanders**	**NHL**	**60**	**1**	**4**	**5**	**126**	....	....	....	....	....
1991-92	**NY Islanders**	**NHL**	**65**	**1**	**6**	**7**	**183**	....	....	....	....	....
	NHL Totals		**201**	**2**	**26**	**28**	**582**	....	....	....	....	....

PION, RICHARD

Right wing. Shoots right. 5'10", 180 lbs. Born, Montreal, Que., July 20, 1965.

			Regular Season					Playoffs				
Season	Club	Lea	GP	G	A	TP	PIM	GP	G	A	TP	PIM
1985-86	Merrimack	NCAA	14	9	13	22	10	....	....	....	....	....
1986-87	Merrimack	NCAA	37	31	33	64	46	....	....	....	....	....
1987-88	Merrimack	NCAA	40	35	40	75	58	4	3	3	6	....
1988-89	Merrimack	NCAA	34	28	42	70	34	....	....	....	....	....
1989-90	Peoria	IHL	69	10	21	31	58	5	0	0	0	0
1990-91	Peoria	IHL	76	14	24	38	113	17	3	5	8	36
1991-92	Peoria	IHL	82	21	50	71	173	9	3	1	4	30

Signed as a free agent by **St. Louis**, August 21, 1989.

PIVONKA, MICHAL (pih-VAHN-kuh)

Center. Shoots left. 6'2", 198 lbs. Born, Kladno, Czechoslovakia, January 28, 1966.
(Washington's 3rd choice, 59th overall, in 1984 Entry Draft).

			Regular Season					Playoffs				
Season	Club	Lea	GP	G	A	TP	PIM	GP	G	A	TP	PIM
1985-86	Dukla Jihlava	Czech.			UNAVAILABLE							
1986-87	**Washington**	**NHL**	**73**	**18**	**25**	**43**	**41**	**7**	**1**	**1**	**2**	**2**
1987-88	**Washington**	**NHL**	**71**	**11**	**23**	**34**	**28**	**14**	**4**	**9**	**13**	**4**
1988-89	**Washington**	**NHL**	**52**	**8**	**19**	**27**	**30**	**6**	**3**	**1**	**4**	**10**
	Baltimore	AHL	31	12	24	36	19	....	....	....	....	....
1989-90	**Washington**	**NHL**	**77**	**25**	**39**	**64**	**54**	**11**	**0**	**2**	**2**	**6**
1990-91	**Washington**	**NHL**	**79**	**20**	**50**	**70**	**34**	**11**	**2**	**3**	**5**	**8**
1991-92	**Washington**	**NHL**	**80**	**23**	**57**	**80**	**47**	**7**	**1**	**5**	**6**	**13**
	NHL Totals		**432**	**105**	**213**	**318**	**234**	**56**	**11**	**21**	**32**	**43**

PLAGER, KEVIN

Right wing. Shoots right. 5'11", 180 lbs. Born, St. Louis, MO, April 25, 1971.
(St. Louis' 8th choice, 156th overall, in 1989 Entry Draft).

			Regular Season					Playoffs				
Season	Club	Lea	GP	G	A	TP	PIM	GP	G	A	TP	PIM
1989-90	Kalamazoo	USHL	38	14	20	34	155	....	....	....	....	....
1990-91	Kalamazoo	USHL	45	10	12	22	20	....	....	....	....	....
1991-92	U. Wisc.-St. Pt.	NCAA			DID NOT PLAY							

PLANTE, DAN

Right wing. Shoots right. 5'11", 198 lbs. Born, St. Louis, MO, October 5, 1971.
(NY Islanders' 3rd choice, 48th overall, in 1990 Entry Draft).

			Regular Season					Playoffs				
Season	Club	Lea	GP	G	A	TP	PIM	GP	G	A	TP	PIM
1990-91	U. Wisconsin	WCHA	33	1	2	3	54	....	....	....	....	....
1991-92	U. Wisconsin	WCHA	36	13	13	26	107	....	....	....	....	....

PLANTE, DEREK

Center. Shoots left. 5'11", 160 lbs. Born, Duluth, MN, January 17, 1971.
(Buffalo's 7th choice, 161st overall, in 1989 Entry Draft).

			Regular Season					Playoffs				
Season	Club	Lea	GP	G	A	TP	PIM	GP	G	A	TP	PIM
1989-90	Minn.-Duluth	WCHA	28	10	11	21	12	....	....	....	....	....
1990-91	Minn.-Duluth	WCHA	36	23	20	43	6	....	....	....	....	....
1991-92a	Minn.-Duluth	WCHA	37	27	36	63	28	....	....	....	....	....

a WCHA Second All-Star Team (1992)

PLAQUIN, KEN

Defense. Shoots left. 6'2", 190 lbs. Born, Calgary, Alta., February 22, 1970.
(Pittsburgh's 8th choice, 131st overall, in 1990 Entry Draft).

			Regular Season					Playoffs				
Season	Club	Lea	GP	G	A	TP	PIM	GP	G	A	TP	PIM
1989-90	Michigan Tech	WCHA	33	2	13	15	20	....	....	....	....	....
1990-91	Michigan Tech	WCHA	37	3	6	9	8	....	....	....	....	....
1991-92	Michigan Tech	WCHA	32	3	7	10	10	....	....	....	....	....

PLAVSIC, ADRIEN

Defense. Shoots left. 6'1", 200 lbs. Born, Montreal, Que., January 13, 1970.
(St. Louis' 2nd choice, 30th overall, in 1988 Entry Draft).

			Regular Season					Playoffs				
Season	Club	Lea	GP	G	A	TP	PIM	GP	G	A	TP	PIM
1987-88	N. Hampshire	H.E.	30	5	6	11	45	....	....	....	....	....
1988-89	Cdn. National	....	62	5	10	15	25	....	....	....	....	....
1989-90	**St. Louis**	**NHL**	**4**	**0**	**1**	**1**	**2**	....	....	....	....	....
	Peoria	IHL	51	7	14	21	87	....	....	....	....	....
	Vancouver	**NHL**	**11**	**3**	**2**	**5**	**8**	....	....	....	....	....
	Milwaukee	IHL	3	1	2	3	14	6	1	3	4	6
1990-91	**Vancouver**	**NHL**	**48**	**2**	**10**	**12**	**62**	....	....	....	....	....
1991-92	Cdn. National	....	38	6	8	14	29	....	....	....	....	....
	Cdn. Olympic	....	8	0	2	2	0	....	....	....	....	....
	Vancouver	**NHL**	**16**	**1**	**9**	**10**	**14**	**13**	**1**	**7**	**8**	**4**
	NHL Totals		**79**	**6**	**22**	**28**	**86**	**13**	**1**	**7**	**8**	**4**

Traded to **Vancouver** by **St. Louis** with Montreal's first round choice (Shawn Antoski) – previously acquired by St. Louis – in 1990 Entry Draft and St. Louis' second round choice in 1991 Entry Draft for Rich Sutter, Harold Snepsts and St. Louis' second round choice (Craig Johnson) – previously acquired by Vancouver – in 1990 Entry Draft, March 6, 1990.

PLAYFAIR, JAMES (JIM)

Defense. Shoots left. 6'4", 200 lbs. Born, Fort St. James, B.C., May 22, 1964.
(Edmonton's 1st choice, 20th overall, in 1982 Entry Draft).

			Regular Season					Playoffs				
Season	Club	Lea	GP	G	A	TP	PIM	GP	G	A	TP	PIM
1981-82	Portland	WHL	70	4	13	17	121	15	1	2	3	21
1982-83	Portland	WHL	63	8	27	35	218	14	0	5	5	16
1983-84	**Edmonton**	**NHL**	**2**	**1**	**1**	**2**	**2**	....	....	....	....	....
	Portland	WHL	16	5	6	11	38	....	....	....	....	....
	Calgary	WHL	60	11	15	26	134	4	0	1	1	2
1984-85	Nova Scotia	AHL	41	0	4	4	107	....	....	....	....	....
1985-86	Nova Scotia	AHL	73	2	12	14	160	....	....	....	....	....
1986-87	Nova Scotia	AHL	60	1	21	22	82	....	....	....	....	....
1987-88	**Chicago**	**NHL**	**12**	**1**	**3**	**4**	**21**	....	....	....	....	....
	Saginaw	IHL	50	5	21	26	133	....	....	....	....	....
1988-89	**Chicago**	**NHL**	**7**	**0**	**0**	**0**	**28**	....	....	....	....	....
	Saginaw	IHL	23	3	6	9	73	6	0	2	2	20
1989-90	Indianapolis	IHL	67	7	24	31	137	14	1	5	6	24
1990-91	Indianapolis	IHL	23	3	4	7	31	....	....	....	....	....
1991-92	Indianapolis	IHL	23	1	1	2	53	....	....	....	....	....
	NHL Totals		**21**	**2**	**4**	**6**	**51**	....	....	....	....	....

Signed as a free agent by **Chicago**, July 31, 1987.

POCHIPINSKI, TREVOR

Defense. Shoots right. 6'2", 190 lbs. Born, Prince Albert, Sask., July 8, 1968.
(Los Angeles' 8th choice, 170th overall, in 1986 Entry Draft).

			Regular Season					Playoffs				
Season	Club	Lea	GP	G	A	TP	PIM	GP	G	A	TP	PIM
1987-88	Colorado	WCHA	37	2	6	8	91	....	....	....	....	....
1988-89	Colorado	WCHA	40	4	10	14	74	....	....	....	....	....
1989-90	Colorado	WCHA	40	5	13	18	54	....	....	....	....	....
1990-91	Colorado	WCHA	40	6	8	14	52	....	....	....	....	....
	New Haven	AHL	10	0	2	2	2	....	....	....	....	....
1991-92	Raleigh	ECHL	38	5	15	20	15	4	0	5	5	18
	New Haven	AHL	8	0	2	2	4	....	....	....	....	....

PODDUBNY, WALTER MICHAEL (WALT) (puh-DUHB-nee)

Left wing. Shoots left. 6'1", 210 lbs. Born, Thunder Bay, Ont., February 14, 1960.
(Edmonton's 4th choice, 90th overall, in 1980 Entry Draft).

			Regular Season					Playoffs				
Season	Club	Lea	GP	G	A	TP	PIM	GP	G	A	TP	PIM
1979-80	Kitchener	OHA	19	3	9	12	35	....	....	....	....	....
	Kingston	OHA	43	30	17	47	36	3	0	2	2	0
1980-81	Milwaukee	IHL	5	4	2	6	4	....	....	....	....	....
	Wichita	CHL	70	21	29	50	207	11	1	6	7	26
1981-82	**Edmonton**	**NHL**	**4**	**0**	**0**	**0**	**0**	....	....	....	....	....
	Wichita	CHL	60	35	46	81	79	....	....	....	....	....
	Toronto	**NHL**	**11**	**3**	**4**	**7**	**8**	....	....	....	....	....
1982-83	**Toronto**	**NHL**	**72**	**28**	**31**	**59**	**71**	**4**	**3**	**1**	**4**	**0**
1983-84	**Toronto**	**NHL**	**38**	**11**	**14**	**25**	**48**	....	....	....	....	....
1984-85	**Toronto**	**NHL**	**32**	**5**	**15**	**20**	**26**	....	....	....	....	....
	St. Catharines	AHL	8	5	7	12	10	....	....	....	....	....
1985-86	**Toronto**	**NHL**	**33**	**12**	**22**	**34**	**25**	**9**	**4**	**1**	**5**	**4**
	St. Catharines	AHL	37	28	27	55	52	....	....	....	....	....
1986-87	**NY Rangers**	**NHL**	**75**	**40**	**47**	**87**	**49**	**6**	**0**	**0**	**0**	**8**
1987-88	**NY Rangers**	**NHL**	**77**	**38**	**50**	**88**	**76**	....	....	....	....	....
1988-89	**Quebec**	**NHL**	**72**	**38**	**37**	**75**	**107**	....	....	....	....	....
1989-90	**New Jersey**	**NHL**	**33**	**4**	**10**	**14**	**28**	....	....	....	....	....
	Utica	AHL	2	1	2	3	0	....	....	....	....	....
1990-91	**New Jersey**	**NHL**	**14**	**4**	**6**	**10**	**10**	....	....	....	....	....
1991-92	**New Jersey**	**NHL**	**7**	**1**	**2**	**3**	**6**	....	....	....	....	....
	NHL Totals		**468**	**184**	**238**	**422**	**454**	**19**	**7**	**2**	**9**	**12**

Played in NHL All-Star Game (1989)

Traded to **Toronto** by **Edmonton** with Phil Drouilliard for Laurie Boschman, March 28, 1982. Traded to **NY Rangers** by **Toronto** for Mike Allison, August 18, 1986. Traded to **Quebec** by **NY Rangers** with Bruce Bell, Jari Gronstrand and NY Rangers' fourth round choice (Eric Dubois) in 1989 Entry Draft for Jason Lafreniere and Normand Rochefort, August 1, 1988. Traded to **New Jersey** by **Quebec** with Quebec's fourth round choice (Mike Bodnarchuk) in 1990 Entry Draft for Joe Cirella, Claude Loiselle and New Jersey's eighth round choice (Alexander Karpovtsev) in 1990 Entry Draft, June 17, 1989.

PODEIN, SHJON

Center. Shoots left. 6'2", 200 lbs. Born, Rochester, MN, March 5, 1968.
(Edmonton's 9th choice, 166th overall, in 1988 Entry Draft).

			Regular Season					Playoffs				
Season	Club	Lea	GP	G	A	TP	PIM	GP	G	A	TP	PIM
1987-88	Minn.-Duluth	WCHA	30	4	4	8	48	....	....	....	....	....
1988-89	Minn.-Duluth	WCHA	36	7	5	12	46	....	....	....	....	....
1989-90	Minn.-Duluth	WCHA	35	21	18	39	36	....	....	....	....	....
1990-91	Cape Breton	AHL	63	14	15	29	65	4	0	0	0	5
1991-92	Cape Breton	AHL	80	30	24	54	46	5	3	1	4	2

POESCHEK, RUDY (POH-shehk)

Right wing/Defense. Shoots right. 6'2", 210 lbs. Born, Kamloops, B.C., September 29, 1966.
(NY Rangers' 12th choice, 238th overall, in 1985 Entry Draft).

			Regular Season					Playoffs				
Season	Club	Lea	GP	G	A	TP	PIM	GP	G	A	TP	PIM
1983-84	Kamloops	WHL	47	3	9	12	93	8	0	2	2	7
1984-85	Kamloops	WHL	34	6	7	13	100	15	0	3	3	56
1985-86	Kamloops	WHL	32	3	13	16	92	16	3	7	10	40
1986-87	Kamloops	WHL	54	13	18	31	153	15	2	4	6	37
1987-88	**NY Rangers**	**NHL**	**1**	**0**	**0**	**0**	**2**	....	....	....	....	....
	Colorado	IHL	82	7	31	38	210	12	2	2	4	31
1988-89	**NY Rangers**	**NHL**	**52**	**0**	**2**	**2**	**199**	....	....	....	....	....
	Colorado	IHL	2	0	0	0	6	....	....	....	....	....
1989-90	**NY Rangers**	**NHL**	**15**	**0**	**0**	**0**	**55**	....	....	....	....	....
	Flint	IHL	38	8	13	21	109	4	0	0	0	16
1990-91	Binghamton	AHL	38	1	3	4	162	....	....	....	....	....
	Winnipeg	**NHL**	**1**	**0**	**0**	**0**	**5**	....	....	....	....	....
	Moncton	AHL	23	2	4	6	67	9	1	1	2	41
1991-92	**Winnipeg**	**NHL**	**4**	**0**	**0**	**0**	**17**	....	....	....	....	....
	Moncton	AHL	63	4	18	22	170	11	0	2	2	48
	NHL Totals		**73**	**0**	**2**	**2**	**278**	....	....	....	....	....

Traded to **Winnipeg** by **NY Rangers** for Guy Larose, January 22, 1991. Signed as a free agent by **Toronto**, August, 1992.

POHL, MICHAEL (POHL)

Center. Shoots left. 6'1", 163 lbs. Born, Rosenheim, West Germany, January 25, 1968.
(New Jersey's 14th choice, 243rd overall, in 1988 Entry Draft).

			Regular Season					Playoffs				
Season	Club	Lea	GP	G	A	TP	PIM	GP	G	A	TP	PIM
1987-88	Rosenheim	W.Ger.	44	7	9	16	32	....	....	....	....	....
1988-89	Rosenheim	W.Ger.	44	8	14	22	38	....	....	....	....	....
1989-90	Rosenheim	W.Ger.	38	10	11	21	28	....	....	....	....	....
1990-91	Rosenheim	Ger.	51	11	10	21	36	....	....	....	....	....
1991-92	Rosenheim	Ger.	49	3	8	11	30	....	....	....	....	....

POJAR, JAN

Left wing. Shoots left. 6'1", 190 lbs. Born, St. Paul, MN, May 5, 1970.
(Chicago's 8th choice, 155th overall, in 1988 Entry Draft).

			Regular Season					Playoffs				
Season	Club	Lea	GP	G	A	TP	PIM	GP	G	A	TP	PIM
1990-91	St. Cloud	WCHA	10	1	0	1	4	....	....	....	....	....
1991-92	St. Cloud	WCHA	31	4	5	9	24	....	....	....	....	....

POLASEK, LIBOR

Center. Shoots right. 6'3", 198 lbs. Born, Novy Jicin, Czech., April 22, 1974.
(Vancouver's 1st choice, 21st overall, in 1992 Entry Draft).

			Regular Season					Playoffs				
Season	Club	Lea	GP	G	A	TP	PIM	GP	G	A	TP	PIM
1991-92	TJ Vitkovice	Czech.	17	2	2	4	2	....	....	....	....	....

POMICHTER, MICHAEL

Center. Shoots left. 6'1", 200 lbs. Born, New Haven, CT, September 10, 1973.
(Chicago's 2nd choice, 39th overall, in 1991 Entry Draft).

			Regular Season					Playoffs				
Season	Club	Lea	GP	G	A	TP	PIM	GP	G	A	TP	PIM
1990-91	Springfield	USHL	38	61	64	125	22	....	....	....	....	....
1991-92	Boston U.	H.E.	34	11	27	38	14	....	....	....	....	....

POPOVIC, PETER

Defense. Shoots right. 6'5", 210 lbs. Born, Koping, Sweden, February 10, 1968.
(Montreal's 5th choice, 93rd overall, in 1988 Entry Draft).

			Regular Season					Playoffs				
Season	Club	Lea	GP	G	A	TP	PIM	GP	G	A	TP	PIM
1986-87	Vasteras	Swe.2	24	1	2	3	10	....	....	....	....	....
1987-88	Vasteras	Swe.2	28	3	17	20	16	....	....	....	....	....
1988-89	Vasteras	Swe.	44	3	8	11	68	....	....	....	....	....
1989-90	Vasteras	Swe.	30	2	10	12	24	2	0	1	1	2
1990-91	Vasteras	Swe.	40	3	2	5	54	....	....	....	....	....
1991-92	Vasteras	Swe.	34	7	10	17	30	....	....	....	....	....

PORKKA, TONI

Defense. Shoots right. 6'2", 190 lbs. Born, Rauma, Finland, February 4, 1970.
(Philadelphia's 12th choice, 172nd overall, in 1990 Entry Draft).

			Regular Season					Playoffs				
Season	Club	Lea	GP	G	A	TP	PIM	GP	G	A	TP	PIM
1989-90	Lukko	Fin.	41	0	3	3	18	....	....	....	....	....
1990-91	Lukko	Fin.	34	2	2	4	8	....	....	....	....	....
1991-92	Hershey	AHL	64	3	5	8	34	....	....	....	....	....

POTVIN, MARC (POT-vahn)

Right wing. Shoots right. 6'1", 200 lbs. Born, Ottawa, Ont., January 29, 1967.
(Detroit's 9th choice, 169th overall, in 1986 Entry Draft).

			Regular Season					Playoffs				
Season	Club	Lea	GP	G	A	TP	PIM	GP	G	A	TP	PIM
1986-87	Bowling Green	CCHA	43	5	15	20	74	....	....	....	....	....
1987-88	Bowling Green	CCHA	45	15	21	36	80	....	....	....	....	....
1988-89	Bowling Green	CCHA	46	23	12	35	63	....	....	....	....	....
1989-90	Bowling Green	CCHA	40	19	17	36	72	....	....	....	....	....
	Adirondack	AHL	5	2	1	3	9	4	0	1	1	23
1990-91	**Detroit**	**NHL**	**9**	**0**	**0**	**0**	**55**	**6**	**0**	**0**	**0**	**32**
	Adirondack	AHL	63	9	13	22	365	....	....	....	....	....
1991-92	**Detroit**	**NHL**	**5**	**1**	**0**	**1**	**52**	**1**	**0**	**0**	**0**	**0**
	Adirondack	AHL	51	13	16	29	314	19	5	4	9	57
	NHL Totals		**14**	**1**	**0**	**1**	**107**	**7**	**0**	**0**	**0**	**32**

POULIN, CHARLES

Center. Shoots left. 6', 172 lbs. Born, St. Jean d'Iberville, Que., July 27, 1972.
(Montreal's 3rd choice, 58th overall, in 1990 Entry Draft).

			Regular Season					Playoffs				
Season	Club	Lea	GP	G	A	TP	PIM	GP	G	A	TP	PIM
1989-90	St-Hyacinthe	QMJHL	65	39	45	84	132	11	5	8	13	47
1990-91	St-Hyacinthe	QMJHL	64	25	46	71	166	4	1	1	2	6
1991-92ab	St-Hyacinthe	QMJHL	68	38	*97	135	113	6	2	2	4	20

a QMJHL First All-Star Team (1992)
b Canadian Major Junior Player of the Year (1992)

POULIN, DAVID JAMES (DAVE) (POO-lihn)

Center. Shoots left. 5'11", 190 lbs. Born, Timmins, Ont., December 17, 1958.

			Regular Season					Playoffs				
Season	Club	Lea	GP	G	A	TP	PIM	GP	G	A	TP	PIM
1978-79	Notre Dame	WCHA	37	28	31	59	32	....	....	....	....	....
1979-80	Notre Dame	WCHA	24	19	24	43	46	....	....	....	....	....
1980-81	Notre Dame	WCHA	35	13	22	35	53	....	....	....	....	....
1981-82a	Notre Dame	CCHA	39	29	30	59	44	....	....	....	....	....
1982-83	Rogle	Swe.	32	35	27	62	64	....	....	....	....	....
	Philadelphia	**NHL**	**2**	**2**	**0**	**2**	**2**	**3**	**1**	**3**	**4**	**9**
	Maine	AHL	16	7	9	16	2	....	....	....	....	....
1983-84	**Philadelphia**	**NHL**	**73**	**31**	**45**	**76**	**47**	**3**	**0**	**0**	**0**	**2**
1984-85	**Philadelphia**	**NHL**	**73**	**30**	**44**	**74**	**59**	**11**	**3**	**5**	**8**	**6**
1985-86	**Philadelphia**	**NHL**	**79**	**27**	**42**	**69**	**49**	**5**	**2**	**0**	**2**	**2**
1986-87b	**Philadelphia**	**NHL**	**75**	**25**	**45**	**70**	**53**	**15**	**3**	**3**	**6**	**14**
1987-88	**Philadelphia**	**NHL**	**68**	**19**	**32**	**51**	**32**	**7**	**2**	**6**	**8**	**4**
1988-89	**Philadelphia**	**NHL**	**69**	**18**	**17**	**35**	**49**	**19**	**6**	**5**	**11**	**16**
1989-90	**Philadelphia**	**NHL**	**28**	**9**	**8**	**17**	**12**	....	....	....	....	....
	Boston	**NHL**	**32**	**6**	**19**	**25**	**12**	**18**	**8**	**5**	**13**	**8**
1990-91	**Boston**	**NHL**	**31**	**8**	**12**	**20**	**25**	**16**	**0**	**9**	**9**	**20**
1991-92	**Boston**	**NHL**	**18**	**4**	**4**	**8**	**18**	**15**	**3**	**3**	**6**	**22**
	NHL Totals		**548**	**179**	**268**	**447**	**358**	**112**	**28**	**39**	**67**	**103**

a CCHA Second All-Star Team (1982)
b Won Frank J. Selke Trophy (1987)

Played in NHL All-Star Game (1986, 1988)

Signed as a free agent by **Philadelphia**, March 8, 1983. Traded to **Boston** by **Philadelphia** for Ken Linseman, January 16, 1990.

POULIN, PATRICK (poo-LIHN)

Left wing. Shoots left. 6'1", 208 lbs. Born, Vanier, Que., April 23, 1973.
(Hartford's 1st choice, 9th overall, in 1991 Entry Draft).

			Regular Season					Playoffs				
Season	Club	Lea	GP	G	A	TP	PIM	GP	G	A	TP	PIM
1989-90	St-Hyacinthe	QMJHL	60	25	26	51	55	12	1	9	10	5
1990-91	St-Hyacinthe	QMJHL	56	32	38	70	82	4	0	2	2	23
1991-92	**Hartford**	**NHL**	**1**	**0**	**0**	**0**	**2**	**7**	**2**	**1**	**3**	**0**
	St-Hyacinthe	QMJHL	56	52	86	*138	58	5	2	2	4	4
	Springfield	AHL	....	....	....	....	....	1	0	0	0	0
	NHL Totals		**1**	**0**	**0**	**0**	**2**	**7**	**2**	**1**	**3**	**0**

PRAJSLER, PETR (PRAYS-luhr)

Defense. Shoots left. 6'2", 200 lbs. Born, Hradec Kralove, Czech., September 21, 1965.
(Los Angeles' 5th choice, 93rd overall, in 1985 Entry Draft).

			Regular Season					Playoffs				
Season	Club	Lea	GP	G	A	TP	PIM	GP	G	A	TP	PIM
1986-87	Pardubice	Czech.	41	3	4	7	....	....	....	....	....	....
1987-88	**Los Angeles**	**NHL**	**7**	**0**	**0**	**0**	**2**	....	....	....	....	....
	New Haven	AHL	41	3	8	11	58	....	....	....	....	....
1988-89	**Los Angeles**	**NHL**	**2**	**0**	**3**	**3**	**0**	**1**	**0**	**0**	**0**	**0**
	New Haven	AHL	43	4	6	10	96	16	3	3	6	34
1989-90	**Los Angeles**	**NHL**	**34**	**3**	**7**	**10**	**47**	**3**	**0**	**0**	**0**	**0**
	New Haven	AHL	6	1	7	8	2	....	....	....	....	....
1990-91	Phoenix	IHL	77	13	34	47	140	9	1	9	10	18
1991-92	**Boston**	**NHL**	**3**	**0**	**0**	**0**	**2**	....	....	....	....	....
	Maine	AHL	61	12	33	45	88	....	....	....	....	....
	NHL Totals		**46**	**3**	**10**	**13**	**51**	**4**	**0**	**0**	**0**	**0**

Signed as a free agent by **Boston**, August 1, 1991.

PRATT, JONATHAN

Center. Shoots left. 6'1", 195 lbs. Born, Danvers, MA, September 25, 1970.
(Minnesota's 9th choice, 154th overall, in 1989 Entry Draft).

			Regular Season					Playoffs				
Season	Club	Lea	GP	G	A	TP	PIM	GP	G	A	TP	PIM
1989-90	Boston U.	H.E.			DID NOT PLAY							
1990-91	Boston U.	H.E.	16	3	1	4	26	....	....	....	....	....
1991-92	Boston U.	H.E.	29	8	4	12	42	....	....	....	....	....

PRESLEY, WAYNE

Right wing. Shoots right. 5'11", 180 lbs. Born, Detroit, MI, March 23, 1965.
(Chicago's 2nd choice, 39th overall, in 1983 Entry Draft).

			Regular Season					Playoffs				
Season	Club	Lea	GP	G	A	TP	PIM	GP	G	A	TP	PIM
1982-83	Kitchener	OHL	70	39	48	87	99	12	1	4	5	9
1983-84a	Kitchener	OHL	70	63	76	139	156	16	12	16	28	38
1984-85	**Chicago**	**NHL**	**3**	**0**	**1**	**1**	**0**	....	....	....	....	....
	Kitchener	OHL	31	25	21	46	77	....	....	....	....	....
	S.S. Marie	OHL	11	5	9	14	14	16	13	9	22	13
1985-86	**Chicago**	**NHL**	**38**	**7**	**8**	**15**	**38**	**3**	**0**	**0**	**0**	**0**
	Nova Scotia	AHL	29	6	9	15	22	....	....	....	....	....
1986-87	**Chicago**	**NHL**	**80**	**32**	**29**	**61**	**114**	**4**	**1**	**0**	**1**	**9**
1987-88	**Chicago**	**NHL**	**42**	**12**	**10**	**22**	**52**	**5**	**0**	**0**	**0**	**4**
1988-89	**Chicago**	**NHL**	**72**	**21**	**19**	**40**	**100**	**14**	**7**	**5**	**12**	**18**
1989-90	**Chicago**	**NHL**	**49**	**6**	**7**	**13**	**69**	**19**	**9**	**6**	**15**	**29**
1990-91	**Chicago**	**NHL**	**71**	**15**	**19**	**34**	**122**	**6**	**0**	**1**	**1**	**38**
1991-92	**San Jose**	**NHL**	**47**	**8**	**14**	**22**	**76**	....	....	....	....	....
	Buffalo	**NHL**	**12**	**2**	**2**	**4**	**57**	**7**	**3**	**3**	**6**	**14**
	NHL Totals		**414**	**103**	**109**	**212**	**628**	**58**	**20**	**15**	**35**	**112**

a OHL First All-Star Team (1984)

Traded to **San Jose** by **Chicago** for San Jose's third round choice in 1993 Entry Draft, September 20, 1991. Traded to **Buffalo** by **San Jose** for Dave Snuggerud, March 9, 1992.

PRIESTLAY, KEN

Center. Shoots left. 5'10", 190 lbs. Born, Richmond, B.C., August 24, 1967.
(Buffalo's 5th choice, 98th overall, in 1985 Entry Draft).

			Regular Season					Playoffs				
Season	Club	Lea	GP	G	A	TP	PIM	GP	G	A	TP	PIM
1983-84	Victoria	WHL	55	10	18	28	31	....	....	....	....	....
1984-85	Victoria	WHL	50	25	37	62	48	....	....	....	....	....
1985-86	Victoria	WHL	72	73	72	145	45	....	....	....	....	....
	Rochester	AHL	4	0	2	2	0	....	....	....	....	....
1986-87	**Buffalo**	**NHL**	**34**	**11**	**6**	**17**	**8**	....	....	....	....	....
	Victoria	WHL	33	43	39	82	37	....	....	....	....	....
	Rochester	AHL	....	....	....	....	....	8	3	2	5	4
1987-88	**Buffalo**	**NHL**	**33**	**5**	**12**	**17**	**35**	**6**	**0**	**0**	**0**	**11**
	Rochester	AHL	43	27	24	51	47	....	....	....	....	....
1988-89	**Buffalo**	**NHL**	**15**	**2**	**0**	**2**	**2**	**3**	**0**	**0**	**0**	**2**
	Rochester	AHL	64	56	37	93	60	....	....	....	....	....
1989-90	**Buffalo**	**NHL**	**35**	**7**	**7**	**14**	**14**	**5**	**0**	**0**	**0**	**8**
	Rochester	AHL	40	19	39	58	46	....	....	....	....	....
1990-91	Cdn. National	....	40	20	26	46	34	....	....	....	....	....
	Pittsburgh	**NHL**	**2**	**0**	**1**	**1**	**0**	....	....	....	....	....
1991-92	**Pittsburgh**	**NHL**	**49**	**2**	**8**	**10**	**4**	....	....	....	....	....
	Muskegon	IHL	13	4	11	15	6	13	5	11	16	10
	NHL Totals		**168**	**27**	**34**	**61**	**63**	**14**	**0**	**0**	**0**	**21**

Traded to **Pittsburgh** by **Buffalo** for Tony Tanti, March 5, 1991.

PRIMEAU, KEITH

Center. Shoots left. 6'4", 225 lbs. Born, Toronto, Ont., November 24, 1971.
(Detroit's 1st choice, 3rd overall, in 1990 Entry Draft).

			Regular Season					Playoffs				
Season	Club	Lea	GP	G	A	TP	PIM	GP	G	A	TP	PIM
1987-88	Hamilton	OHL	47	6	6	12	69	....	....	....	....	....
1988-89	Niagara Falls	OHL	48	20	35	55	56	17	9	16	25	12
1989-90a	Niagara Falls	OHL	65	*57	70	*127	97	16	*16	17	*33	49
1990-91	**Detroit**	**NHL**	**58**	**3**	**12**	**15**	**106**	**5**	**1**	**1**	**2**	**25**
	Adirondack	AHL	6	3	5	8	8	....	....	....	....	....
1991-92	**Detroit**	**NHL**	**35**	**6**	**10**	**16**	**83**	**11**	**0**	**0**	**0**	**14**
	Adirondack	AHL	42	21	24	45	89	9	1	7	8	27
	NHL Totals		**93**	**9**	**22**	**31**	**189**	**16**	**1**	**1**	**2**	**39**

a OHL Second All-Star Team (1990)

PROBERT, BOB (PROH-buhrt)

Right wing. Shoots left. 6'3", 225 lbs. Born, Windsor, Ont., June 5, 1965.
(Detroit's 3rd choice, 46th overall, in 1983 Entry Draft).

			Regular Season					Playoffs				
Season	Club	Lea	GP	G	A	TP	PIM	GP	G	A	TP	PIM
1982-83	Brantford	OHL	51	12	16	28	133	8	2	2	4	23
1983-84	Brantford	OHL	65	35	38	73	189	6	0	3	3	16
1984-85	S.S. Marie	OHL	44	20	52	72	172	....	....	....	....	....
	Hamilton	OHL	4	0	1	1	21	....	....	....	....	....
1985-86	**Detroit**	**NHL**	**44**	**8**	**13**	**21**	**186**	....	....	....	....	....
	Adirondack	AHL	32	12	15	27	152	10	2	3	5	68
1986-87	**Detroit**	**NHL**	**63**	**13**	**11**	**24**	**221**	**16**	**3**	**4**	**7**	**63**
	Adirondack	AHL	7	1	4	5	15	....	....	....	....	....
1987-88	**Detroit**	**NHL**	**74**	**29**	**33**	**62**	***398**	**16**	**8**	**13**	**21**	**51**
1988-89	**Detroit**	**NHL**	**25**	**4**	**2**	**6**	**106**	....	....	....	....	....
1989-90	**Detroit**	**NHL**	**4**	**3**	**0**	**3**	**21**	....	....	....	....	....
1990-91	**Detroit**	**NHL**	**55**	**16**	**23**	**39**	**315**	**6**	**1**	**2**	**3**	**50**
1991-92	**Detroit**	**NHL**	**63**	**20**	**24**	**44**	**276**	**11**	**1**	**6**	**7**	**28**
	NHL Totals		**328**	**93**	**106**	**199**	**1523**	**49**	**13**	**25**	**38**	**192**

Played in NHL All-Star Game (1988)

PROCHAZKA, MARTIN (pro-HAHS-kah)

Center. Shoots right. 5'11", 176 lbs. Born, Slany, Czech., March 3, 1972.
(Toronto's 8th choice, 135th overall, in 1991 Entry Draft).

			Regular Season					Playoffs				
Season	Club	Lea	GP	G	A	TP	PIM	GP	G	A	TP	PIM
1990-91	Kladno	Czech.	50	19	10	29	21	....	....	....	....	....
1991-92	Dukla Jihlava	Czech.	36	13	10	23	....	....	....	....	....	....

PROKHOROV, VITALI (PROH-kohr-ohv)

Left wing. Shoots left. 5'9", 185 lbs. Born, Moscow, Soviet Union, December 25, 1966.
(St. Louis' 3rd choice, 64th overall, in 1992 Entry Draft).

			Regular Season					Playoffs				
Season	Club	Lea	GP	G	A	TP	PIM	GP	G	A	TP	PIM
1990-91	Spartak	USSR	43	21	10	31	29	....	....	....	....	....
1991-92	Spartak	CIS	32	12	16	28	54	....	....	....	....	....

PRONGER, SEAN

Center. Shoots left. 6'3", 195 lbs. Born, Thunder Bay, Ont., November 30, 1972.
(Vancouver's 3rd choice, 51st overall, in 1991 Entry Draft).

			Regular Season					Playoffs				
Season	Club	Lea	GP	G	A	TP	PIM	GP	G	A	TP	PIM
1990-91	Bowling Green	CCHA	40	3	7	10	30	....	....	....	....	....
1991-92	Bowling Green	CCHA	34	9	7	16	28	....	....	....	....	....

PROPP, BRIAN PHILIP

Left wing. Shoots left. 5'10", 195 lbs. Born, Lanigan, Sask., February 15, 1959.
(Philadelphia's 1st choice, 14th overall, in 1979 Entry Draft).

			Regular Season					Playoffs				
Season	Club	Lea	GP	G	A	TP	PIM	GP	G	A	TP	PIM
1976-77	Brandon	WHL	72	55	80	135	47	16	*14	12	26	5
1977-78a	Brandon	WHL	70	70	*112	*182	200	8	7	6	13	12
1978-79ab	Brandon	WHL	71	*94	*100	*194	127	22	15	23	*38	40
1979-80	**Philadelphia**	**NHL**	**80**	**34**	**41**	**75**	**54**	**19**	**5**	**10**	**15**	**29**
1980-81	**Philadelphia**	**NHL**	**79**	**26**	**40**	**66**	**110**	**12**	**6**	**6**	**12**	**32**
1981-82	**Philadelphia**	**NHL**	**80**	**44**	**47**	**91**	**117**	**4**	**2**	**2**	**4**	**4**
1982-83	**Philadelphia**	**NHL**	**80**	**40**	**42**	**82**	**72**	**3**	**1**	**2**	**3**	**8**
1983-84	**Philadelphia**	**NHL**	**79**	**39**	**53**	**92**	**37**	**3**	**0**	**1**	**1**	**6**
1984-85	**Philadelphia**	**NHL**	**76**	**43**	**53**	**96**	**43**	**19**	**8**	**10**	**18**	**6**
1985-86	**Philadelphia**	**NHL**	**72**	**40**	**57**	**97**	**47**	**5**	**0**	**2**	**2**	**4**
1986-87	**Philadelphia**	**NHL**	**53**	**31**	**36**	**67**	**45**	**26**	**12**	**16**	**28**	**10**
1987-88	**Philadelphia**	**NHL**	**74**	**27**	**49**	**76**	**76**	**7**	**4**	**2**	**6**	**8**
1988-89	**Philadelphia**	**NHL**	**77**	**32**	**46**	**78**	**37**	**18**	**14**	**9**	**23**	**14**
1989-90	**Philadelphia**	**NHL**	**40**	**13**	**15**	**28**	**31**	....	....	....	....	....
	Boston	**NHL**	**14**	**3**	**9**	**12**	**10**	**20**	**4**	**9**	**13**	**2**
1990-91	**Minnesota**	**NHL**	**79**	**26**	**47**	**73**	**58**	**23**	**8**	**15**	**23**	**28**
1991-92	**Minnesota**	**NHL**	**51**	**12**	**23**	**35**	**49**	**1**	**0**	**0**	**0**	**0**
	NHL Totals		**934**	**410**	**558**	**968**	**786**	**160**	**64**	**84**	**148**	**151**

a WHL First All-Star Team (1978, 1979)
b WHL Player of the Year (1979)

Played in NHL All-Star Game (1980, 1982, 1984, 1986, 1990)

Traded to **Boston** by **Philadelphia** for Boston's second round choice (Terran Sandwith) in 1990 Entry Draft, March 2, 1990. Signed as a free agent by **Minnesota**, July 25, 1990.

PROSOFSKY, JASON

Right wing. Shoots right. 6'4", 220 lbs. Born, Medicine Hat, Alta., May 4, 1971.
(NY Rangers' 2nd choice, 40th overall, in 1989 Entry Draft).

			Regular Season					Playoffs				
Season	Club	Lea	GP	G	A	TP	PIM	GP	G	A	TP	PIM
1987-88	Medicine Hat	WHL	47	6	1	7	94	14	0	0	0	20
1988-89	Medicine Hat	WHL	67	7	16	23	170	3	1	0	1	6
1989-90	Medicine Hat	WHL	71	12	13	25	153	3	0	0	0	8
1990-91	Medicine Hat	WHL	72	15	15	30	195	12	6	8	14	33
1991-92	Binghamton	AHL	4	0	0	0	5	....	....	....	....	....
	San Diego	IHL	31	0	0	0	111	....	....	....	....	....
	Erie	ECHL	7	2	2	4	28	4	1	2	3	18

PRPIC, TONY

Right wing. Shoots right. 6'4", 207 lbs. Born, Euclid, OH, June 16, 1973.
(Montreal's 5th choice, 105th overall, in 1991 Entry Draft).

			Regular Season					Playoffs				
Season	Club	Lea	GP	G	A	TP	PIM	GP	G	A	TP	PIM
1990-91	Culver Aca.	HS	25	25	17	42	37	....	....	....	....	....
1991-92	Sioux City	USHL	38	20	24	44	51	....	....	....	....	....

PUCHNIAK, ROB

Defense. Shoots left. 6'2", 204 lbs. Born, Winnipeg, Man., March 10, 1971.
(Washington's 11th choice, 234th overall, in 1991 Entry Draft).

			Regular Season					Playoffs				
Season	Club	Lea	GP	G	A	TP	PIM	GP	G	A	TP	PIM
1989-90	Brandon	WHL	56	2	3	5	81	....	....	....	....	....
1990-91	Brandon	WHL	49	2	10	12	137	....	....	....	....	....
	Lethbridge	WHL	23	1	6	7	80	15	0	2	2	63
1991-92	Brandon	WHL	71	1	18	19	303	....	....	....	....	....

PULLOLA, TOMMI (PUHL-loh-lah)

Center. Shoots left. 6'5", 202 lbs. Born, Vaasa, Finland, May 18, 1971.
(Chicago's 4th choice, 111th overall, in 1989 Entry Draft).

			Regular Season					Playoffs				
Season	Club	Lea	GP	G	A	TP	PIM	GP	G	A	TP	PIM
1988-89	Sport	Fin.	40	11	13	24	....	....	....	....	....	....
1989-90	Lukko	Fin.	40	7	9	16	8	....	....	....	....	....
1990-91	Lukko	Fin.	42	17	17	34	40	....	....	....	....	....
1991-92	Lukko	Fin.	44	15	9	24	36	2	1	0	1	2

PURVES, JOHN (PUR-vihs)

Right wing. Shoots right. 6'1", 201 lbs. Born, Toronto, Ont., February 12, 1968.
(Washington's 6th choice, 103rd overall, in 1986 Entry Draft).

			Regular Season					Playoffs				
Season	Club	Lea	GP	G	A	TP	PIM	GP	G	A	TP	PIM
1985-86	Belleville	OHL	16	3	9	12	6	....	....	....	....	....
	Hamilton	OHL	36	13	28	41	36	....	....	....	....	....
1986-87	Hamilton	OHL	28	12	11	23	37	9	2	0	2	12
1987-88	Hamilton	OHL	64	39	44	83	65	14	7	18	25	4
1988-89a	Niagara Falls	OHL	5	5	11	16	2	....	....	....	....	....
	North Bay	OHL	42	34	52	86	38	12	14	12	26	16
1989-90	Baltimore	AHL	75	29	35	64	12	9	5	7	12	4
1990-91	**Washington**	**NHL**	**7**	**1**	**0**	**1**	**0**	....	....	....	....	....
	Baltimore	AHL	53	22	29	51	27	6	2	3	5	0
1991-92	Baltimore	AHL	78	43	46	89	47	....	....	....	....	....
	NHL Totals		**7**	**1**	**0**	**1**	**0**	....	....	....	....	....

a OHL Second All-Star Team (1989)

PUSHOR, JAMIE

Defense. Shoots right. 6'3", 192 lbs. Born, Lethbridge, Alta., February 11, 1973.
(Detroit's 2nd choice, 32nd overall, in 1991 Entry Draft).

			Regular Season					Playoffs				
Season	Club	Lea	GP	G	A	TP	PIM	GP	G	A	TP	PIM
1989-90	Lethbridge	WHL	10	0	2	2	2	....	....	....	....	....
1990-91	Lethbridge	WHL	71	1	13	14	193	....	....	....	....	....
1991-92	Lethbridge	WHL	49	2	15	17	232	5	0	0	0	33

QUENNEVILLE, JOEL NORMAN (KWEHN-vihl)

Defense. Shoots left. 6'1", 200 lbs. Born, Windsor, Ont., September 15, 1958.
(Toronto's 1st choice, 21st overall, in 1978 Amateur Draft).

			Regular Season					Playoffs				
Season	Club	Lea	GP	G	A	TP	PIM	GP	G	A	TP	PIM
1975-76	Windsor	OHA	66	15	33	48	61	....	....	....	....	....
1976-77	Windsor	OHA	65	19	59	78	169	9	6	5	11	112
1977-78a	Windsor	OHA	66	27	76	103	114	6	2	3	5	17
1978-79	**Toronto**	**NHL**	**61**	**2**	**9**	**11**	**60**	**6**	**0**	**1**	**1**	**4**
	New Brunswick	AHL	16	1	10	11	10	....	....	....	....	....
1979-80	**Toronto**	**NHL**	**32**	**1**	**4**	**5**	**24**	....	....	....	....	....
	Colorado	**NHL**	**35**	**5**	**7**	**12**	**26**	....	....	....	....	....
1980-81	**Colorado**	**NHL**	**71**	**10**	**24**	**34**	**86**	....	....	....	....	....
1981-82	**Colorado**	**NHL**	**64**	**5**	**10**	**15**	**55**	....	....	....	....	....
1982-83	**New Jersey**	**NHL**	**74**	**5**	**12**	**17**	**46**	....	....	....	....	....
1983-84	**Hartford**	**NHL**	**80**	**5**	**8**	**13**	**95**	....	....	....	....	....
1984-85	**Hartford**	**NHL**	**79**	**6**	**16**	**22**	**96**	....	....	....	....	....
1985-86	**Hartford**	**NHL**	**71**	**5**	**20**	**25**	**83**	**10**	**0**	**2**	**2**	**12**
1986-87	**Hartford**	**NHL**	**37**	**3**	**7**	**10**	**24**	**6**	**0**	**0**	**0**	**0**
1987-88	**Hartford**	**NHL**	**77**	**1**	**8**	**9**	**44**	**6**	**0**	**2**	**2**	**2**
1988-89	**Hartford**	**NHL**	**69**	**4**	**7**	**11**	**32**	**4**	**0**	**3**	**3**	**4**
1989-90	**Hartford**	**NHL**	**44**	**1**	**4**	**5**	**34**	....	....	....	....	....
1990-91	**Washington**	**NHL**	**9**	**1**	**0**	**1**	**0**	....	....	....	....	....
	Baltimore	AHL	59	6	13	19	58	6	1	1	2	6
1991-92b	St. John's	AHL	73	7	23	30	58	16	0	1	1	10
	NHL Totals		**803**	**54**	**136**	**190**	**705**	**26**	**0**	**8**	**8**	**22**

a OHA Second All-Star Team (1978)
b AHL Second All-Star Team (1992)

Traded to **Colorado** by **Toronto** with Lanny McDonald for Pat Hickey and Wilf Paiement, December 29, 1979. Traded to **Calgary** by **New Jersey** with Steve Tambellini for Phil Russell and Mel Bridgman, June 20, 1983. Traded to **Hartford** by **Calgary** with Richie Dunn for Mickey Volcan, July 5, 1983. Traded to **Washington** by **Hartford** for cash, October 3, 1990.

QUINN, DAN

Center. Shoots left. 5'11", 182 lbs. Born, Ottawa, Ont., June 1, 1965.
(Calgary's 1st choice, 13th overall, in 1983 Entry Draft).

			Regular Season					Playoffs				
Season	Club	Lea	GP	G	A	TP	PIM	GP	G	A	TP	PIM
1981-82	Belleville	OHL	67	19	32	51	41	....	....	....	....	....
1982-83	Belleville	OHL	70	59	88	147	27	4	2	6	8	2
1983-84	**Calgary**	**NHL**	**54**	**19**	**33**	**52**	**20**	**8**	**3**	**5**	**8**	**4**
	Belleville	OHL	24	23	36	59	12	....	....	....	....	....
1984-85	**Calgary**	**NHL**	**74**	**20**	**38**	**58**	**22**	**3**	**0**	**0**	**0**	**0**
1985-86	**Calgary**	**NHL**	**78**	**30**	**42**	**72**	**44**	**18**	**8**	**7**	**15**	**10**
1986-87	**Calgary**	**NHL**	**16**	**3**	**6**	**9**	**14**	....	....	....	....	....
	Pittsburgh	**NHL**	**64**	**28**	**43**	**71**	**40**	....	....	....	....	....
1987-88	**Pittsburgh**	**NHL**	**70**	**40**	**39**	**79**	**50**	....	....	....	....	....
1988-89	**Pittsburgh**	**NHL**	**79**	**34**	**60**	**94**	**102**	**11**	**6**	**3**	**9**	**10**
1989-90	**Pittsburgh**	**NHL**	**41**	**9**	**20**	**29**	**22**	....	....	....	....	....
	Vancouver	**NHL**	**37**	**16**	**18**	**34**	**27**	....	....	....	....	....
1990-91	**Vancouver**	**NHL**	**64**	**18**	**31**	**49**	**46**	....	....	....	....	....
	St. Louis	**NHL**	**14**	**4**	**7**	**11**	**20**	**13**	**4**	**7**	**11**	**32**
1991-92	**Philadelphia**	**NHL**	**67**	**11**	**26**	**37**	**26**	....	....	....	....	....
	NHL Totals		**658**	**232**	**363**	**595**	**433**	**53**	**21**	**22**	**43**	**56**

Traded to **Pittsburgh** by **Calgary** for Mike Bullard, November 12, 1986. Traded to **Vancouver** by **Pittsburgh** with Dave Capuano and Andrew McBain for Rod Buskas, Barry Pederson and Tony Tanti, January 8, 1990. Traded to **St. Louis** by **Vancouver** with Garth Butcher for Geoff Courtnall, Robert Dirk, Sergio Momesso, Cliff Ronning and future considerations, March 5, 1991. Traded to **Philadelphia** by **St. Louis** with Rod Brind'Amour for Ron Sutter and Murray Baron, September 22, 1991.

QUINNEY, KEN (KWIH-nee)

Right wing. Shoots right. 5'10", 186 lbs. Born, New Westminster, B.C., May 23, 1965.
(Quebec's 9th choice, 203rd overall, in 1984 Entry Draft).

			Regular Season					Playoffs				
Season	Club	Lea	GP	G	A	TP	PIM	GP	G	A	TP	PIM
1981-82	Calgary	WHL	63	11	17	28	55	2	0	0	0	15
1982-83	Calgary	WHL	71	26	25	51	71	16	6	1	7	46
1983-84	Calgary	WHL	71	64	54	118	38	4	5	2	7	0
1984-85a	Calgary	WHL	56	47	67	114	65	7	6	4	10	15
1985-86	Fredericton	AHL	61	11	26	37	34	6	2	2	4	9
1986-87	**Quebec**	**NHL**	**25**	**2**	**7**	**9**	**16**	....	....	....	....	....
	Fredericton	AHL	48	14	27	41	20	....	....	....	....	....
1987-88	**Quebec**	**NHL**	**15**	**2**	**2**	**4**	**5**	....	....	....	....	....
b	Fredericton	AHL	58	37	39	76	39	13	3	5	8	35
1988-89	Halifax	AHL	72	41	49	90	65	4	3	0	3	0
1989-90	Halifax	AHL	44	9	16	25	63	2	0	0	0	2
1990-91	**Quebec**	**NHL**	**19**	**3**	**4**	**7**	**2**	....	....	....	....	....
	Halifax	AHL	44	20	20	40	76	....	....	....	....	....
1991-92	Adirondack	AHL	63	31	29	60	33	19	7	12	19	9
	NHL Totals		**59**	**7**	**13**	**20**	**23**	....	....	....	....	....

a WHL First All-Star Team, East Division (1985)
b Won Tim Horton Award (Most Three-Star Points-AHL) (1988)

Signed as a free agent by **Detroit**, August 12, 1991.

QUINTAL, STEPHANE (kihn-TAHL)

Defense. Shoots right. 6'3", 215 lbs. Born, Boucherville, Que., October 22, 1968.
(Boston's 2nd choice, 14th overall, in 1987 Entry Draft).

			Regular Season					Playoffs				
Season	Club	Lea	GP	G	A	TP	PIM	GP	G	A	TP	PIM
1985-86	Granby	QMJHL	67	2	17	19	144	....	....	....	....	....
1986-87a	Granby	QMJHL	67	13	41	54	178	8	0	9	9	10
1987-88	Hull	QMJHL	38	13	23	36	138	19	7	12	19	30
1988-89	**Boston**	**NHL**	**26**	**0**	**1**	**1**	**29**	....	....	....	....	....
	Maine	AHL	16	4	10	14	28	....	....	....	....	....
1989-90	**Boston**	**NHL**	**38**	**2**	**2**	**4**	**22**	....	....	....	....	....
	Maine	AHL	37	4	16	20	27	....	....	....	....	....
1990-91	**Boston**	**NHL**	**45**	**2**	**6**	**8**	**89**	**3**	**0**	**1**	**1**	**7**
	Maine	AHL	23	1	5	6	30	....	....	....	....	....
1991-92	**Boston**	**NHL**	**49**	**4**	**10**	**14**	**77**	....	....	....	....	....
	St. Louis	**NHL**	**26**	**0**	**6**	**6**	**32**	**4**	**1**	**2**	**3**	**6**
	NHL Totals		**184**	**8**	**25**	**33**	**249**	**7**	**1**	**3**	**4**	**13**

a QMJHL First All-Star Team (1987)

Traded to **St. Louis** by **Boston** with Craig Janney for Adam Oates, February 7, 1992.

QUINTIN, JEAN-FRANCOIS

Center. Shoots left. 6', 187 lbs. Born, St. Jean, Que., May 28, 1969.
(Minnesota's 4th choice, 75th overall, in 1989 Entry Draft).

			Regular Season					Playoffs				
Season	Club	Lea	GP	G	A	TP	PIM	GP	G	A	TP	PIM
1987-88	Shawinigan	QMJHL	70	28	70	98	143	11	5	8	13	26
1988-89	Shawinigan	QMJHL	69	52	100	152	105	10	9	15	24	16
1989-90	Kalamazoo	IHL	68	20	18	38	38	10	8	4	12	14
1990-91	Kalamazoo	IHL	78	31	43	74	64	9	1	5	6	11
1991-92	**San Jose**	**NHL**	**8**	**3**	**0**	**3**	**0**	....	....	....	....	....
	Kansas City	IHL	21	4	6	10	29	13	2	10	12	29
	NHL Totals		**8**	**3**	**0**	**3**	**0**	....	....	....	....	....

Claimed by **San Jose** from **Minnesota** in Dispersal Draft, May 30, 1991.

RACINE, YVES

Defense. Shoots left. 6', 200 lbs. Born, Matane, Que., February 7, 1969.
(Detroit's 1st choice, 11th overall, in 1987 Entry Draft).

			Regular Season					Playoffs				
Season	Club	Lea	GP	G	A	TP	PIM	GP	G	A	TP	PIM
1986-87	Longueuil	QMJHL	70	7	43	50	50	20	3	11	14	14
1987-88	Adirondack	AHL	....	....	....	....	....	9	4	2	6	2
a	Victoriaville	QMJHL	69	10	84	94	150	5	0	0	0	13
1988-89a	Victoriaville	QMJHL	63	23	85	108	95	16	3	*30	*33	41
	Adirondack	AHL	....	....	....	....	....	2	1	1	2	0
1989-90	**Detroit**	**NHL**	**28**	**4**	**9**	**13**	**23**	....	....	....	....	....
	Adirondack	AHL	46	8	27	35	31	....	....	....	....	....
1990-91	**Detroit**	**NHL**	**62**	**7**	**40**	**47**	**33**	**7**	**2**	**0**	**2**	**0**
	Adirondack	AHL	16	3	9	12	10	....	....	....	....	....
1991-92	**Detroit**	**NHL**	**61**	**2**	**22**	**24**	**94**	**11**	**2**	**1**	**3**	**10**
	NHL Totals		**151**	**13**	**71**	**84**	**150**	**18**	**4**	**1**	**5**	**10**

a QMJHL First-All Star Team (1988, 1989)

RAGLAN, HERB

Right wing. Shoots right. 6', 205 lbs. Born, Peterborough, Ont., August 5, 1967.
(St. Louis' 1st choice, 37th overall, in 1985 Entry Draft).

			Regular Season					Playoffs				
Season	Club	Lea	GP	G	A	TP	PIM	GP	G	A	TP	PIM
1984-85	Peterborough	OHL	58	20	22	42	166	....	....	....	....	....
1985-86	**St. Louis**	**NHL**	**7**	**0**	**0**	**0**	**5**	**10**	**1**	**1**	**2**	**24**
	Kingston	OHL	28	10	9	19	88	10	5	2	7	30
1986-87	**St. Louis**	**NHL**	**62**	**6**	**10**	**16**	**159**	**4**	**0**	**0**	**0**	**2**
1987-88	**St. Louis**	**NHL**	**73**	**10**	**15**	**25**	**190**	**10**	**1**	**3**	**4**	**11**
1988-89	**St. Louis**	**NHL**	**50**	**7**	**10**	**17**	**144**	**8**	**1**	**2**	**3**	**13**
1989-90	**St. Louis**	**NHL**	**11**	**0**	**1**	**1**	**21**	....	....	....	....	....
1990-91	**St. Louis**	**NHL**	**32**	**3**	**3**	**6**	**52**	....	....	....	....	....
	Quebec	**NHL**	**15**	**1**	**3**	**4**	**30**	....	....	....	....	....
1991-92	**Quebec**	**NHL**	**62**	**6**	**14**	**20**	**120**	....	....	....	....	....
	NHL Totals		**312**	**33**	**56**	**89**	**721**	**32**	**3**	**6**	**9**	**50**

Traded to **Quebec** by **St. Louis** with Tony Twist and Andy Rymsha for Darin Kimble, February 4, 1991.

RAGNARSSON, MARCUS

Defense. Shoots left. 6'1", 200 lbs. Born, Ostervala, Sweden, August 13, 1971.
(San Jose's 5th choice, 99th overall, in 1992 Entry Draft).

			Regular Season					Playoffs				
Season	Club	Lea	GP	G	A	TP	PIM	GP	G	A	TP	PIM
1990-91	Djurgarden	Swe.	35	4	1	5	12	....	....	....	....	....
1991-92	Djurgarden	Swe.	40	8	5	13	14	10	0	1	1	4

RAHN, NOEL

Center. Shoots left. 6', 155 lbs. Born, Edina, MN, February 6, 1971.
(Quebec's 14th choice, 232nd overall, in 1989 Entry Draft).

			Regular Season					Playoffs				
Season	Club	Lea	GP	G	A	TP	PIM	GP	G	A	TP	PIM
1989-90	U. Wisconsin	WCHA	4	0	0	0	0	....	....	....	....	....
1990-91	U. Wisconsin	WCHA			DID NOT PLAY							
1991-92	St. Cloud	WCHA	23	8	1	9	23	....	....	....	....	....

RAISKY, ANDREI (RIH-skee)

Center. Shoots left. 6'2", 185 lbs. Born, Ust-Kamenogorsk, Soviet Union, March 30, 1970.
(Winnipeg's 7th choice, 156th overall, in 1992 Entry Draft).

			Regular Season					Playoffs				
Season	Club	Lea	GP	G	A	TP	PIM	GP	G	A	TP	PIM
1990-91	Torpedo Ust	USSR	41	6	5	11	48	....	....	....	....	....
1991-92	Torpedo Ust	CIS	40	16	14	30	53	....	....	....	....	....

RAITANEN, RAULI

Center. Shoots left. 6'2", 183 lbs. Born, Pori, Finland, January 14, 1970.
(Winnipeg's 10th choice, 182nd overall, in 1990 Entry Draft).

			Regular Season					Playoffs				
Season	Club	Lea	GP	G	A	TP	PIM	GP	G	A	TP	PIM
1989-90	Assat	Fin.	41	17	44	61	20	....	....	....	....	....
1990-91	Assat	Fin.	43	6	16	22	14	....	....	....	....	....
1991-92	Assat	Fin.	41	12	22	34	34	8	1	5	6	2

RAITER, MARK

Defense. Shoots right. 6'4", 220 lbs. Born, Calgary, Alta., January 27, 1973.
(Toronto's 4th choice, 95th overall, in 1992 Entry Draft).

			Regular Season					Playoffs				
Season	Club	Lea	GP	G	A	TP	PIM	GP	G	A	TP	PIM
1990-91	Saskatoon	WHL	35	2	3	5	73	....	....	....	....	....
1991-92	Saskatoon	WHL	72	2	12	14	354	....	....	....	....	....

RAMAGE, GEORGE (ROB) (RAM-ihj)

Defense. Shoots right. 6'2", 200 lbs. Born, Byron, Ont., January 11, 1959.
(Colorado's 1st choice, 1st overall, in 1979 Entry Draft).

			Regular Season					Playoffs				
Season	Club	Lea	GP	G	A	TP	PIM	GP	G	A	TP	PIM
1975-76	London	OHA	65	12	31	43	113	5	0	1	1	11
1976-77a	London	OHA	65	15	58	73	177	20	3	11	14	55
1977-78b	London	OHA	59	17	48	65	162	11	4	5	9	29
1978-79	Birmingham	WHA	80	12	36	48	165	....	....	....	....	....
1979-80	**Colorado**	**NHL**	**75**	**8**	**20**	**28**	**135**	....	....	....	....	....
1980-81	**Colorado**	**NHL**	**79**	**20**	**42**	**62**	**193**	....	....	....	....	....
1981-82	**Colorado**	**NHL**	**80**	**13**	**29**	**42**	**201**	....	....	....	....	....
1982-83	**St. Louis**	**NHL**	**78**	**16**	**35**	**51**	**193**	**4**	**0**	**3**	**3**	**22**
1983-84	**St. Louis**	**NHL**	**80**	**15**	**45**	**60**	**121**	**11**	**1**	**8**	**9**	**32**
1984-85	**St. Louis**	**NHL**	**80**	**7**	**31**	**38**	**178**	**3**	**1**	**3**	**4**	**6**
1985-86	**St. Louis**	**NHL**	**77**	**10**	**56**	**66**	**171**	**19**	**1**	**10**	**11**	**66**
1986-87	**St. Louis**	**NHL**	**59**	**11**	**28**	**39**	**108**	**6**	**2**	**2**	**4**	**21**
1987-88	**St. Louis**	**NHL**	**67**	**8**	**34**	**42**	**127**	....	....	....	....	....
	Calgary	**NHL**	**12**	**1**	**6**	**7**	**37**	**9**	**1**	**3**	**4**	**21**
1988-89	**Calgary**	**NHL**	**68**	**3**	**13**	**16**	**156**	**20**	**1**	**11**	**12**	**26**
1989-90	**Toronto**	**NHL**	**80**	**8**	**41**	**49**	**202**	**5**	**1**	**2**	**3**	**20**
1990-91	**Toronto**	**NHL**	**80**	**10**	**25**	**35**	**173**	....	....	....	....	....
1991-92	**Minnesota**	**NHL**	**34**	**4**	**5**	**9**	**69**	....	....	....	....	....
	NHL Totals		**949**	**134**	**410**	**544**	**2064**	**77**	**8**	**42**	**50**	**214**

a OHA Third All-Star Team (1977)
b OHA First All-Star Team (1978)

Played in NHL All-Star Game (1981, 1984, 1986, 1988)

Traded to **St. Louis** by **New Jersey** for St. Louis' first round choice (Rocky Trottier) in 1982 Entry Draft and first round choice (John MacLean) in 1983 Entry Draft, June 9, 1982. Traded to **Calgary** by **St. Louis** with Rick Wamsley for Brett Hull and Steve Bozek, March 7, 1988. Traded to **Toronto** by **Calgary** for Toronto's second round choice (Kent Manderville) in 1989 Entry Draft, June 16, 1989. Claimed by **Minnesota** from **Toronto** in Expansion Draft, May 30, 1991. Claimed by **Tampa Bay** from **Minnesota** in Expansion Draft, June 18, 1992.

RAMSEY, MICHAEL ALLEN (MIKE)

Defense. Shoots left. 6'3", 195 lbs. Born, Minneapolis, MN, December 3, 1960.
(Buffalo's 1st choice, 11th overall, in 1979 Entry Draft).

			Regular Season					Playoffs				
Season	Club	Lea	GP	G	A	TP	PIM	GP	G	A	TP	PIM
1978-79	U. Minnesota	WCHA	26	6	11	17	30	....	....	....	....	....
1979-80	U.S. National	....	56	11	22	33	55	....	....	....	....	....
	U.S. Olympic	....	7	0	2	2	8	....	....	....	....	....
	Buffalo	**NHL**	**13**	**1**	**6**	**7**	**6**	**13**	**1**	**2**	**3**	**12**
1980-81	**Buffalo**	**NHL**	**72**	**3**	**14**	**17**	**56**	**8**	**0**	**3**	**3**	**20**
1981-82	**Buffalo**	**NHL**	**80**	**7**	**23**	**30**	**56**	**4**	**1**	**1**	**2**	**14**
1982-83	**Buffalo**	**NHL**	**77**	**8**	**30**	**38**	**55**	**10**	**4**	**4**	**8**	**15**
1983-84	**Buffalo**	**NHL**	**72**	**9**	**22**	**31**	**82**	**3**	**0**	**1**	**1**	**6**
1984-85	**Buffalo**	**NHL**	**79**	**8**	**22**	**30**	**102**	**5**	**0**	**1**	**1**	**23**
1985-86	**Buffalo**	**NHL**	**76**	**7**	**21**	**28**	**117**	....	....	....	....	....
1986-87	**Buffalo**	**NHL**	**80**	**8**	**31**	**39**	**109**	....	....	....	....	....
1987-88	**Buffalo**	**NHL**	**63**	**5**	**16**	**21**	**77**	**6**	**0**	**3**	**3**	**29**
1988-89	**Buffalo**	**NHL**	**56**	**2**	**14**	**16**	**84**	**5**	**1**	**0**	**1**	**11**
1989-90	**Buffalo**	**NHL**	**73**	**4**	**21**	**25**	**47**	**6**	**0**	**1**	**1**	**8**
1990-91	**Buffalo**	**NHL**	**71**	**6**	**14**	**20**	**46**	**5**	**1**	**0**	**1**	**12**
1991-92	**Buffalo**	**NHL**	**66**	**3**	**14**	**17**	**67**	**7**	**0**	**2**	**2**	**8**
	NHL Totals		**878**	**71**	**248**	**319**	**904**	**72**	**8**	**18**	**26**	**158**

Played in NHL All-Star Game (1982, 1983, 1985, 1986)

RANHEIM, PAUL

Left wing. Shoots right. 6', 195 lbs. Born, St. Louis, MO, January 25, 1966.
(Calgary's 3rd choice, 38th overall, in 1984 Entry Draft).

			Regular Season					Playoffs				
Season	Club	Lea	GP	G	A	TP	PIM	GP	G	A	TP	PIM
1984-85	U. Wisconsin	WCHA	42	11	11	22	40	....	....	....	....	....
1985-86	U. Wisconsin	WCHA	33	17	17	34	34	....	....	....	....	....
1986-87a	U. Wisconsin	WCHA	42	24	35	59	54	....	....	....	....	....
1987-88bc	U. Wisconsin	WCHA	44	36	26	62	63	....	....	....	....	....
1988-89	**Calgary**	**NHL**	**5**	**0**	**0**	**0**	**0**	....	....	....	....	....
def	Salt Lake	IHL	75	*68	29	97	16	14	5	5	10	8
1989-90	**Calgary**	**NHL**	**80**	**26**	**28**	**54**	**23**	**6**	**1**	**3**	**4**	**2**
1990-91	**Calgary**	**NHL**	**39**	**14**	**16**	**30**	**4**	**7**	**2**	**2**	**4**	**0**
1991-92	**Calgary**	**NHL**	**80**	**23**	**20**	**43**	**32**	....	....	....	....	....
	NHL Totals		**204**	**63**	**64**	**127**	**59**	**13**	**3**	**5**	**8**	**2**

a WCHA Second All-Star Team (1987)
b NCAA West First All-American Team (1988)
c WCHA First All-Star Team (1988)
d IHL Second All-Star Team (1989)
e Won Garry F. Longman Memorial Trophy (Top Rookie-IHL) (1989)
f Won Ken McKenzie Trophy (Outstanding U.S.-born Rookie-IHL) (1989)

RATHBONE, JASON

Right wing. Shoots right. 6', 210 lbs. Born, Brookline, MA, April 13, 1970.
(NY Islanders' 8th choice, 121st overall, in 1988 Entry Draft).

			Regular Season					Playoffs				
Season	Club	Lea	GP	G	A	TP	PIM	GP	G	A	TP	PIM
1988-89	Boston College	H.E.	21	0	3	3	10	....	....	....	....	....
1989-90	Boston College	H.E.	37	4	7	11	20	....	....	....	....	....
1990-91	Boston College	H.E.	31	0	1	1	16	....	....	....	....	....
1991-92	Boston College	H.E.	35	3	7	10	30	....	....	....	....	....

RATHJE, MIKE (RATH-gee)

Defense. Shoots left. 6'5", 205 lbs. Born, Mannville, Alta., May 11, 1974.
(San Jose's 1st choice, 3rd overall, in 1992 Entry Draft).

			Regular Season					Playoffs				
Season	Club	Lea	GP	G	A	TP	PIM	GP	G	A	TP	PIM
1990-91	Medicine Hat	WHL	64	1	16	17	28	12	0	4	4	2
1991-92	Medicine Hat	WHL	67	11	23	34	109	4	0	1	1	2

RATUSHNY, DAN

Defense. Shoots right. 6'1", 185 lbs. Born, Nepean, Ont., October 29, 1970.
(Winnipeg's 2nd choice, 25th overall, in 1989 Entry Draft).

			Regular Season					Playoffs				
Season	Club	Lea	GP	G	A	TP	PIM	GP	G	A	TP	PIM
1988-89	Cornell	ECAC	28	2	13	15	50	....	....	....	....	....
1989-90ab	Cornell	ECAC	26	5	14	19	54	....	....	....	....	....
1990-91ac	Cornell	ECAC	26	7	24	31	52	....	....	....	....	....
	Cdn. National	....	12	0	1	1	6	....	....	....	....	....
1991-92	Cdn. National	....	58	5	13	18	50	....	....	....	....	....
	Cdn. Olympic	....	8	0	0	0	4	....	....	....	....	....

a ECAC First All-Star Team (1990, 1991)
b NCAA East Second All-American Team (1990)
c NCAA East First All-American Team (1991)

RAY, ROBERT

Left wing. Shoots left. 6', 203 lbs. Born, Stirling, Ont., June 8, 1968.
(Buffalo's 5th choice, 97th overall, in 1988 Entry Draft).

			Regular Season					Playoffs				
Season	Club	Lea	GP	G	A	TP	PIM	GP	G	A	TP	PIM
1985-86	Cornwall	OHL	53	6	13	19	253	6	0	0	0	26
1986-87	Cornwall	OHL	46	17	20	37	158	5	1	1	2	16
1987-88	Cornwall	OHL	61	11	41	52	179	11	2	3	5	33
1988-89	Rochester	AHL	74	11	18	29	*446	....	....	....	....	....
1989-90	**Buffalo**	**NHL**	**27**	**2**	**1**	**3**	**99**	....	....	....	....	....
	Rochester	AHL	43	2	13	15	335	17	1	3	4	115
1990-91	**Buffalo**	**NHL**	**66**	**8**	**8**	**10**	***350**	**6**	**1**	**1**	**2**	**56**
	Rochester	AHL	8	1	1	2	15	....	....	....	....	....
1991-92	**Buffalo**	**NHL**	**63**	**5**	**3**	**8**	**354**	**7**	**0**	**0**	**0**	**2**
	NHL Totals		**156**	**15**	**12**	**27**	**803**	**13**	**1**	**1**	**2**	**58**

RECCHI, MARK

Right wing. Shoots left. 5'10", 185 lbs. Born, Kamloops, B.C., February 1, 1968.
(Pittsburgh's 4th choice, 67th overall, in 1988 Entry Draft).

			Regular Season					Playoffs				
Season	Club	Lea	GP	G	A	TP	PIM	GP	G	A	TP	PIM
1985-86	N. Westminster	WHL	72	21	40	61	55	....	....	....	....	....
1986-87	Kamloops	WHL	40	26	50	76	63	13	3	16	19	17
1987-88a	Kamloops	WHL	62	61	*93	154	75	17	10	*21	*31	18
1988-89	**Pittsburgh**	**NHL**	**15**	**1**	**1**	**2**	**0**	....	....	....	....	....
b	Muskegon	IHL	63	50	49	99	86	14	7	*14	*21	28
1989-90	**Pittsburgh**	**NHL**	**74**	**30**	**37**	**67**	**44**	....	....	....	....	....
	Muskegon	IHL	4	7	4	11	2	....	....	....	....	....
1990-91	**Pittsburgh**	**NHL**	**78**	**40**	**73**	**113**	**48**	**24**	**10**	**24**	**34**	**33**
1991-92c	**Pittsburgh**	**NHL**	**58**	**33**	**37**	**70**	**78**	....	....	....	....	....
c	**Philadelphia**	**NHL**	**22**	**10**	**17**	**27**	**18**	....	....	....	....	....
	NHL Totals		**247**	**114**	**165**	**279**	**188**	**24**	**10**	**24**	**34**	**33**

a WHL West All-Star Team (1988)
b IHL Second All-Star Team (1989)
c NHL Second All-Star Team (1992)

Played in NHL All-Star Game (1991)

Traded to **Philadelphia** by **Pittsburgh** with Brian Benning and Los Angeles' first round choice in 1992 Entry Draft (Jason Bowen) previously acquired by Pittsburgh in the Paul Coffey trade for Rick Tocchet, Kjell Samuelsson and Ken Wregget, February 19, 1992.

REDMOND, KEITH

Left wing. Shoots left. 6'3", 205 lbs. Born, Richmond Hill, Ont., October 25, 1972.
(Los Angeles' 4th choice, 79th overall, in 1991 Entry Draft).

			Regular Season					Playoffs				
Season	Club	Lea	GP	G	A	TP	PIM	GP	G	A	TP	PIM
1990-91	Bowling Green	CCHA	35	1	3	4	72	....	....	....	....	....
1991-92	Bowling Green	CCHA	8	0	0	0	14	....	....	....	....	....

REED, JACE

Defense. Shoots left. 6'3", 210 lbs. Born, Grand Rapids, MN, March 22, 1971.
(NY Islanders' 5th choice, 86th overall, in 1989 Entry Draft).

			Regular Season					Playoffs				
Season	Club	Lea	GP	G	A	TP	PIM	GP	G	A	TP	PIM
1989-90	North Dakota	WCHA	10	0	0	0	0	....	....	....	....	....
1990-91	North Dakota	WCHA	13	0	0	0	4	....	....	....	....	....
1991-92	North Dakota	WCHA	DID NOT PLAY – INJURED									

REEKIE, JOE

Defense. Shoots left. 6'3", 215 lbs. Born, Victoria, B.C., February 22, 1965.
(Buffalo's 6th choice, 119th overall, in 1985 Entry Draft).

			Regular Season					Playoffs				
Season	Club	Lea	GP	G	A	TP	PIM	GP	G	A	TP	PIM
1982-83	North Bay	OHL	59	2	9	11	49	8	0	1	1	11
1983-84	North Bay	OHL	9	1	0	1	18	....	....	....	....	....
	Cornwall	OHL	53	6	27	33	166	3	0	0	0	4
1984-85	Cornwall	OHL	65	19	63	82	134	9	4	13	17	18
1985-86	**Buffalo**	**NHL**	**3**	**0**	**0**	**0**	**14**	....	....	....	....	....
	Rochester	AHL	77	3	25	28	178	....	....	....	....	....
1986-87	**Buffalo**	**NHL**	**56**	**1**	**8**	**9**	**82**	....	....	....	....	....
	Rochester	AHL	22	0	6	6	52	....	....	....	....	....
1987-88	**Buffalo**	**NHL**	**30**	**1**	**4**	**5**	**68**	**2**	**0**	**0**	**0**	**4**
1988-89	**Buffalo**	**NHL**	**15**	**1**	**3**	**4**	**26**	....	....	....	....	....
	Rochester	AHL	21	1	2	3	56	....	....	....	....	....
1989-90	**NY Islanders**	**NHL**	**31**	**1**	**8**	**9**	**43**	....	....	....	....	....
	Springfield	AHL	15	1	4	5	24	....	....	....	....	....
1990-91	**NY Islanders**	**NHL**	**66**	**3**	**16**	**19**	**96**	....	....	....	....	....
	Capital Dist.	AHL	2	1	0	1	0	....	....	....	....	....
1991-92	**NY Islanders**	**NHL**	**54**	**4**	**12**	**16**	**85**	....	....	....	....	....
	Capital Dist.	AHL	3	2	2	4	2	....	....	....	....	....
	NHL Totals		**255**	**11**	**51**	**62**	**414**	**2**	**0**	**0**	**0**	**4**

Traded to **NY Islanders** by **Buffalo** for NY Islanders' sixth round choice (Bill Pye) in 1989 Entry Draft, June 17, 1989. Claimed by **Tampa Bay** from **NY Islanders** in Expansion Draft, June 18, 1992.

REEVES, KYLE

Right wing. Shoots right. 5'11", 190 lbs. Born, Stonewall, Man., May 12, 1971.
(St. Louis' 2nd choice, 64th overall, in 1991 Entry Draft).

			Regular Season					Playoffs				
Season	Club	Lea	GP	G	A	TP	PIM	GP	G	A	TP	PIM
1988-89	Swift Current	WHL	2	1	1	2	2	....	....	....	....	....
1989-90	Tri-Cities	WHL	67	67	36	103	94	7	2	1	3	8
1990-91a	Tri-Cities	WHL	63	*89	40	129	146	3	1	3	4	10
1991-92	Peoria	IHL	60	12	7	19	92	....	....	....	....	....

a WHL West Second All-Star Team (1991)

REICHEL, MARTIN (RIGH-khul)

Right wing. Shoots left. 6'1", 183 lbs. Born, Most, Czech., November 7, 1973.
(Edmonton's 2nd choice, 37th overall, in 1992 Entry Draft).

			Regular Season					Playoffs				
Season	Club	Lea	GP	G	A	TP	PIM	GP	G	A	TP	PIM
1990-91	Freiburg	Ger.	23	7	8	15	19	....	....	....	....	....
1991-92	Freiburg	Ger.	31	16	17	33	12	....	....	....	....	....

REICHEL, ROBERT (RIGH-khul)

Center. Shoots left. 5'11", 185 lbs. Born, Litvinov, Czechoslovakia, June 25, 1971.
(Calgary's 5th choice, 70th overall, in 1989 Entry Draft).

			Regular Season					Playoffs				
Season	Club	Lea	GP	G	A	TP	PIM	GP	G	A	TP	PIM
1988-89	Litvinov	Czech.	....	20	31	51	....	....	....	....	....	....
1989-90	Litvinov	Czech.	52	*49	34	*83	....	....	....	....	....	....
1990-91	**Calgary**	**NHL**	**66**	**19**	**22**	**41**	**22**	**6**	**1**	**1**	**2**	**0**
1991-92	**Calgary**	**NHL**	**77**	**20**	**34**	**54**	**32**	....	....	....	....	....
	NHL Totals		**143**	**39**	**56**	**95**	**54**	**6**	**1**	**1**	**2**	**0**

REID, DAVID

Left wing. Shoots left. 6'1", 205 lbs. Born, Toronto, Ont., May 15, 1964.
(Boston's 4th choice, 60th overall, in 1982 Entry Draft).

			Regular Season					Playoffs				
Season	Club	Lea	GP	G	A	TP	PIM	GP	G	A	TP	PIM
1981-82	Peterborough	OHL	68	10	32	42	41	9	2	3	5	11
1982-83	Peterborough	OHL	70	23	34	57	33	4	3	1	4	0
1983-84	**Boston**	**NHL**	**8**	**1**	**0**	**1**	**2**	....	....	....	....	....
	Peterborough	OHL	60	33	64	97	12	....	....	....	....	....
1984-85	**Boston**	**NHL**	**35**	**14**	**13**	**27**	**27**	**5**	**1**	**0**	**1**	**0**
	Hershey	AHL	43	10	14	24	6	....	....	....	....	....
1985-86	**Boston**	**NHL**	**37**	**10**	**10**	**20**	**10**	....	....	....	....	....
	Moncton	AHL	26	14	18	32	4	....	....	....	....	....
1986-87	**Boston**	**NHL**	**12**	**3**	**3**	**6**	**0**	**2**	**0**	**0**	**0**	**0**
	Moncton	AHL	40	12	22	34	23	5	0	1	1	0
1987-88	**Boston**	**NHL**	**3**	**0**	**0**	**0**	**0**	....	....	....	....	....
	Maine	AHL	63	21	37	58	40	10	6	7	13	0
1988-89	**Toronto**	**NHL**	**77**	**9**	**21**	**30**	**22**	....	....	....	....	....
1989-90	**Toronto**	**NHL**	**70**	**9**	**19**	**28**	**9**	**3**	**0**	**0**	**0**	**0**
1990-91	**Toronto**	**NHL**	**69**	**15**	**13**	**28**	**18**	....	....	....	....	....
1991-92	**Boston**	**NHL**	**43**	**7**	**7**	**14**	**27**	**15**	**2**	**5**	**7**	**4**
	Maine	AHL	12	1	5	6	4	....	....	....	....	....
	NHL Totals		**354**	**68**	**86**	**154**	**115**	**25**	**3**	**5**	**8**	**4**

Signed as a free agent by **Toronto**, June 23, 1988. Signed as a free agent by **Boston**, October, 1991.

REID, GRAYDEN

Center. Shoots left. 6', 185 lbs. Born, Mississauga, Ont., January 7, 1972.
(St. Louis' 4th choice, 87th overall, in 1991 Entry Draft).

			Regular Season					Playoffs				
Season	Club	Lea	GP	G	A	TP	PIM	GP	G	A	TP	PIM
1990-91	Owen Sound	OHL	66	23	74	97	58	....	....	....	....	....
1991-92	Owen Sound	OHL	8	2	10	12	4	....	....	....	....	....
	Ottawa	OHL	54	10	26	36	18	11	0	2	2	2

REID, JARRETT

Center. Shoots right. 5'10", 180 lbs. Born, Sault Ste. Marie, Ont., March 10, 1973.
(Hartford's 6th choice, 143rd overall, in 1992 Entry Draft).

			Regular Season					Playoffs				
Season	Club	Lea	GP	G	A	TP	PIM	GP	G	A	TP	PIM
1990-91	S.S. Marie	OHL	63	37	29	66	18	14	5	12	17	14
1991-92	S.S. Marie	OHL	61	53	40	93	67	19	5	13	18	17

REIGNER, CURT

Right wing. Shoots left. 6', 218 lbs. Born, Prince Albert, Sask., January 24, 1972.
(New Jersey's 6th choice, 121st overall, in 1991 Entry Draft).

			Regular Season					Playoffs				
Season	Club	Lea	GP	G	A	TP	PIM	GP	G	A	TP	PIM
1990-91	Prince Albert	WHL	69	20	39	59	40	3	2	2	4	6
1991-92	Prince Albert	WHL	58	30	42	72	98	10	1	9	10	2

REIMANN, DANIEL

Defense. Shoots left. 6'1", 190 lbs. Born, Fridley, MN, December 17, 1972.
(New Jersey's 9th choice, 187th overall, in 1991 Entry Draft).

			Regular Season					Playoffs				
Season	Club	Lea	GP	G	A	TP	PIM	GP	G	A	TP	PIM
1990-91	Anoka	HS	25	6	26	32	38	....	....	....	....	....
1991-92	Des Moines	USHL	47	6	14	20	78	....	....	....	....	....

REIRDEN, TODD

Defense. Shoots left. 6'4", 175 lbs. Born, Arlington Heights, IL, June 25, 1971.
(New Jersey's 14th choice, 242nd overall, in 1990 Entry Draft).

			Regular Season					Playoffs				
Season	Club	Lea	GP	G	A	TP	PIM	GP	G	A	TP	PIM
1990-91	Bowling Green	CCHA	28	1	5	6	22	....	....	....	....	....
1991-92	Bowling Green	CCHA	33	8	7	15	34	....	....	....	....	....

RENBERG, MIKAEL (REHN-buhrg)

Left wing. Shoots left. 6'2", 185 lbs. Born, Pitea, Sweden, May 5, 1972.
(Philadelphia's 3rd choice, 40th overall, in 1990 Entry Draft).

			Regular Season					Playoffs				
Season	Club	Lea	GP	G	A	TP	PIM	GP	G	A	TP	PIM
1988-89	Pitea	Swe.2	12	6	3	9	....	....	....	....	....	....
1989-90	Pitea	Swe.2	29	15	19	34	....	....	....	....	....	....
1990-91	Lulea	Swe.	29	11	6	17	12	....	....	....	....	....
1991-92	Lulea	Swe.	38	8	15	23	20	2	0	0	0	0

RICARD, ERIC

Defense. Shoots left. 6'4", 220 lbs. Born, St. Cesaire, Que., February 16, 1969.
(Los Angeles' 3rd choice, 102nd overall, in 1989 Entry Draft).

			Regular Season					Playoffs				
Season	Club	Lea	GP	G	A	TP	PIM	GP	G	A	TP	PIM
1988-89	Granby	QMJHL	68	5	31	36	213	4	1	1	2	21
1989-90	New Haven	AHL	28	1	1	2	55	....	....	....	....	....
1990-91	New Haven	AHL	35	1	4	5	65	....	....	....	....	....
	Phoenix	IHL	16	1	3	4	24	....	....	....	....	....
1991-92	New Haven	AHL	38	2	9	11	85	2	1	0	1	2

RICCI, MIKE (REECH-ee)

Center. Shoots left. 6', 190 lbs. Born, Scarborough, Ont., October 27, 1971.
(Philadelphia's 1st choice, 4th overall, in 1990 Entry Draft).

			Regular Season					Playoffs				
Season	Club	Lea	GP	G	A	TP	PIM	GP	G	A	TP	PIM
1987-88	Peterborough	OHL	41	24	37	61	20	....	....	....	....	....
1988-89a	Peterborough	OHL	60	54	52	106	43	17	19	16	35	18
1989-90bcd	Peterborough	OHL	60	52	64	116	39	12	5	7	12	26
1990-91	**Philadelphia**	**NHL**	**68**	**21**	**20**	**41**	**64**	....	....	....	....	....
1991-92	**Philadelphia**	**NHL**	**78**	**20**	**36**	**56**	**93**	....	....	....	....	....
	NHL Totals		**146**	**41**	**56**	**97**	**157**	....	....	....	....	....

a OHL Second All-Star Team (1989)
b Canadian Major Junior Player of the Year (1990)
c OHL First All-Star Team (1990)
d OHL Player of the Year (1990)

Traded to **Quebec** by **Philadelphia** with Peter Forsberg, Steve Duchesne, Kerry Huffman, Ron Hextall, Chris Simon, Philadelphia's first choice in the 1993 and 1994 Entry Drafts and cash for Eric Lindros, June 30, 1992.

RICCIARDI, JEFF

Defense. Shoots left. 5'10", 203 lbs. Born, Thunder Bay, Ont., June 22, 1971.
(Winnipeg's 8th choice, 159th overall, in 1991 Entry Draft).

			Regular Season					Playoffs				
Season	Club	Lea	GP	G	A	TP	PIM	GP	G	A	TP	PIM
1990-91	Ottawa	OHL	54	12	40	52	172	17	1	11	12	61
1991-92	Ottawa	OHL	61	15	41	56	220	11	3	8	11	45

RICE, STEVEN

Right wing. Shoots right. 6', 215 lbs. Born, Kitchener, Ont., May 26, 1971.
(NY Rangers' 1st choice, 20th overall, in 1989 Entry Draft).

			Regular Season					Playoffs				
Season	Club	Lea	GP	G	A	TP	PIM	GP	G	A	TP	PIM
1987-88	Kitchener	OHL	59	11	14	25	43	4	0	1	1	0
1988-89	Kitchener	OHL	64	36	30	66	42	5	2	1	3	8
1989-90ab	Kitchener	OHL	58	39	37	76	102	16	4	8	12	24
1990-91	**NY Rangers**	**NHL**	**11**	**1**	**1**	**2**	**4**	**2**	**2**	**1**	**3**	**6**
	Binghamton	AHL	8	4	1	5	12	5	2	0	2	2
c	Kitchener	OHL	29	30	30	60	43	6	5	6	11	2
1991-92	**Edmonton**	**NHL**	**3**	**0**	**0**	**0**	**2**	....	....	....	....	....
	Cape Breton	AHL	45	32	20	52	38	5	4	4	8	10
	NHL Totals		**14**	**1**	**1**	**2**	**6**	**2**	**2**	**1**	**3**	**6**

a OHL Third All-Star Team (1990)
b Memorial Cup All-Star Team (1990)
c OHL Second All-Star Team (1991)

Traded to **Edmonton** by **NY Rangers** with Bernie Nicholls and Louie DeBrusk for Mark Messier and future considerations, October 4, 1991.

RICHARD, JEAN-MARC

Defense. Shoots left. 5'11", 178 lbs. Born, St.-Raymond, Que., October 8, 1966.

			Regular Season					Playoffs				
Season	Club	Lea	GP	G	A	TP	PIM	GP	G	A	TP	PIM
1985-86a	Chicoutimi	QMJHL	72	20	87	107	111	9	3	5	8	14
1986-87a	Chicoutimi	QMJHL	67	21	81	102	105	16	6	25	31	28
1987-88	**Quebec**	**NHL**	**4**	**2**	**1**	**3**	**2**	....	....	....	....	....
	Fredericton	AHL	68	14	42	56	52	7	2	1	3	4
1988-89	Halifax	AHL	57	8	25	33	38	4	1	0	1	4
1989-90	**Quebec**	**NHL**	**1**	**0**	**0**	**0**	**0**	....	....	....	....	....
	Halifax	AHL	40	1	24	25	38	....	....	....	....	....
1990-91	Halifax	AHL	80	7	41	48	76	....	....	....	....	....
	Fort Wayne	IHL	1	0	0	0	0	19	3	9	12	8
1991-92bc	Fort Wayne	IHL	82	18	68	86	109	7	0	5	5	20
	NHL Totals		**5**	**2**	**1**	**3**	**2**	....	....	....	....	....

a QMJHL First All-Star Team (1986, 1987)
b Won Governors' Trophy (Top Defenseman-IHL) (1992)
c IHL First All-Star Team (1992)

Signed as a free agent by **Quebec**, April 13, 1987.

RICHARD, MICHAEL (MIKE)

Center. Shoots left. 5'10", 190 lbs. Born, Scarborough, Ont., July 9, 1966.

			Regular Season					Playoffs				
Season	Club	Lea	GP	G	A	TP	PIM	GP	G	A	TP	PIM
1983-84	Toronto	OHL	66	19	17	36	12	9	2	1	3	0
1984-85	Toronto	OHL	66	31	41	72	15	5	0	0	0	11
1985-86	Toronto	OHL	63	32	48	80	28	4	1	1	2	2
1986-87	Toronto	OHL	66	57	50	107	38	....	....	....	....	....
1987-88	**Washington**	**NHL**	**4**	**0**	**0**	**0**	**0**	....	....	....	....	....
a	Binghamton	AHL	72	46	48	94	23	4	0	3	3	4
1988-89	Baltimore	AHL	80	44	63	107	51	....	....	....	....	....
1989-90	**Washington**	**NHL**	**3**	**0**	**2**	**2**	**0**	....	....	....	....	....
b	Baltimore	AHL	53	41	42	83	14	11	4	*13	17	6
1990-91	Zurich	Switz.	36	28	23	51	....	....	1	3	4	....
1991-92	Milano	Italy	18	20	26	46	4	12	7	11	18	4
	NHL Totals		**7**	**0**	**2**	**2**	**0**	....	....	....	....	....

a Won Dudley "Red" Garrett Memorial Trophy (Top Rookie - AHL) (1988)
b AHL Second All-Star Team (1990)

Signed as a free agent by **Washington**, October 9, 1987.

RICHARDS, TODD

Defense. Shoots right. 6', 194 lbs. Born, Robindale, MN, October, 20, 1966.
(Montreal's 3rd choice, 33rd overall, in 1985 Entry Draft).

			Regular Season					Playoffs				
Season	Club	Lea	GP	G	A	TP	PIM	GP	G	A	TP	PIM
1985-86	U. Minnesota	WCHA	38	6	23	29	38	....	....	....	....	....
1986-87	U. Minnesota	WCHA	49	8	43	51	70	....	....	....	....	....
1987-88a	U. Minnesota	WCHA	34	10	30	40	26	....	....	....	....	....
1988-89abc	U. Minnesota	WCHA	46	6	32	38	60	....	....	....	....	....
1989-90	Sherbrooke	AHL	71	6	18	24	73	5	1	2	3	6
1990-91	Fredericton	AHL	3	0	1	1	2	....	....	....	....	....
	Hartford	**NHL**	**2**	**0**	**4**	**4**	**2**	**6**	**0**	**0**	**0**	**2**
	Springfield	AHL	71	10	41	51	62	14	2	8	10	2
1991-92	**Hartford**	**NHL**	**6**	**0**	**0**	**0**	**2**	**5**	**0**	**3**	**3**	**4**
	Springfield	AHL	43	6	23	29	33	11	0	3	3	2
	NHL Totals		**8**	**0**	**4**	**4**	**4**	**11**	**0**	**3**	**3**	**6**

a WCHA Second All-Star Team (1988, 1989)
b NCAA West Second All-American Team (1989)
c NCAA All-Tournament Team (1989)

Traded to **Hartford** by **Montreal** for future considerations, October 11, 1990.

RICHARDS, TRAVIS

Defense. Shoots left. 6'1", 185 lbs. Born, Crystal, MN, March 22, 1970.
(Minnesota's 6th choice, 169th overall, in 1988 Entry Draft).

			Regular Season					Playoffs				
Season	Club	Lea	GP	G	A	TP	PIM	GP	G	A	TP	PIM
1988-89	U. Minnesota	WCHA				DID NOT PLAY						
1989-90	U. Minnesota	WCHA	45	4	24	28	38	....	....	....	....	....
1990-91	U. Minnesota	WCHA	45	9	25	34	28	....	....	....	....	....
1991-92a	U. Minnesota	WCHA	41	10	22	32	65	....	....	....	....	....

a WCHA Second All-Star Team (1992)

RICHARDSON, LUKE

Defense. Shoots left. 6'4", 210 lbs. Born, Ottawa, Ont., March 26, 1969.
(Toronto's 1st choice, 7th overall, in 1987 Entry Draft).

			Regular Season					Playoffs				
Season	Club	Lea	GP	G	A	TP	PIM	GP	G	A	TP	PIM
1985-86	Peterborough	OHL	63	6	18	24	57	16	2	1	3	50
1986-87	Peterborough	OHL	59	13	32	45	70	12	0	5	5	24
1987-88	**Toronto**	**NHL**	**78**	**4**	**6**	**10**	**90**	**2**	**0**	**0**	**0**	**0**
1988-89	**Toronto**	**NHL**	**55**	**2**	**7**	**9**	**106**	....	....	....	....	....
1989-90	**Toronto**	**NHL**	**67**	**4**	**14**	**18**	**122**	**5**	**0**	**0**	**0**	**22**
1990-91	**Toronto**	**NHL**	**78**	**1**	**9**	**10**	**238**	....	....	....	....	....
1991-92	**Edmonton**	**NHL**	**75**	**2**	**19**	**21**	**118**	**16**	**0**	**5**	**5**	**45**
	NHL Totals		**353**	**13**	**55**	**68**	**674**	**23**	**0**	**5**	**5**	**67**

Traded to **Edmonton** by **Toronto** with Vincent Damphousse, Peter Ing, Scott Thornton, future considerations and cash for Grant Fuhr, Glenn Anderson and Craig Berube, September 19, 1991.

RICHER, STEPHANE J. G. (REE-shay)

Defense. Shoots right. 5'11", 190 lbs. Born, Hull, Que., April 28, 1966.

			Regular Season					Playoffs				
Season	Club	Lea	GP	G	A	TP	PIM	GP	G	A	TP	PIM
1986-87	Hull	QMJHL	33	6	22	28	74	8	3	4	7	17
1987-88	Baltimore	AHL	22	0	3	3	6	....	....	....	....	....
	Sherbrooke	AHL	41	4	7	11	46	5	1	0	1	10
1988-89	Sherbrooke	AHL	70	7	26	33	158	6	1	2	3	18
1989-90	Sherbrooke	AHL	60	10	12	22	85	12	4	9	13	16
1990-91	New Haven	AHL	3	0	1	1	0	....	....	....	....	....
	Phoenix	IHL	67	11	38	49	48	11	4	6	10	6
1991-92a	Fredericton	AHL	80	17	47	64	74	7	0	5	5	18

a AHL Second All-Star Team (1992)

Signed as a free agent by **Montreal**, January 9, 1988. Signed as a free agent by **Los Angeles**, July 11, 1990. Signed as a free agent by **Tampa Bay**, July 29, 1992.

RICHER, STEPHANE J. J. (REE-shay)

Right wing. Shoots right. 6'2", 200 lbs. Born, Ripon, Que., June 7, 1966.
(Montreal's 3rd choice, 29th overall, in 1984 Entry Draft).

			Regular Season					Playoffs				
Season	Club	Lea	GP	G	A	TP	PIM	GP	G	A	TP	PIM
1983-84a	Granby	QMJHL	67	39	37	76	58	3	1	1	2	4
1984-85	Granby	QMJHL	30	30	27	57	31	....	....	....	....	....
b	Chicoutimi	QMJHL	27	31	32	63	40	12	13	13	26	25
	Montreal	**NHL**	**1**	**0**	**0**	**0**	**0**	....	....	....	....	....
	Sherbrooke	AHL	....	....	....	....	....	9	6	3	9	10
1985-86	**Montreal**	**NHL**	**65**	**21**	**16**	**37**	**50**	**16**	**4**	**1**	**5**	**23**
1986-87	**Montreal**	**NHL**	**57**	**20**	**19**	**39**	**80**	**5**	**3**	**2**	**5**	**0**
	Sherbrooke	AHL	12	10	4	14	11	....	....	....	....	....
1987-88	**Montreal**	**NHL**	**72**	**50**	**28**	**78**	**72**	**8**	**7**	**5**	**12**	**6**
1988-89	**Montreal**	**NHL**	**68**	**25**	**35**	**60**	**61**	**21**	**6**	**5**	**11**	**14**
1989-90	**Montreal**	**NHL**	**75**	**51**	**40**	**91**	**46**	**9**	**7**	**3**	**10**	**2**
1990-91	**Montreal**	**NHL**	**75**	**31**	**30**	**61**	**53**	**13**	**9**	**5**	**14**	**6**
1991-92	**New Jersey**	**NHL**	**74**	**29**	**35**	**64**	**25**	**7**	**1**	**2**	**3**	**0**
	NHL Totals		**487**	**227**	**203**	**430**	**387**	**79**	**37**	**23**	**60**	**51**

a QMJHL Rookie of the Year (1984)
b QMJHL Second All-Star Team (1985)

Played in NHL All-Star Game (1990)

Traded to **New Jersey** by **Montreal** with Tom Chorske for Kirk Muller and Roland Melanson, September 20, 1991.

RICHTER, BARRY

Defense. Shoots left. 6'2", 185 lbs. Born, Madison, WI, September 11, 1970.
(Hartford's 2nd choice, 32nd overall, in 1988 Entry Draft).

			Regular Season					Playoffs				
Season	Club	Lea	GP	G	A	TP	PIM	GP	G	A	TP	PIM
1989-90	U. Wisconsin	WCHA	42	13	23	36	36	....	....	....	....	....
1990-91	U. Wisconsin	WCHA	43	15	20	35	42	....	....	....	....	....
1991-92a	U. Wisconsin	WCHA	39	10	25	35	62	....	....	....	....	....

a NCAA All-Tournament Team (1992)

RIDLEY, MIKE

Center. Shoots left. 6', 195 lbs. Born, Winnipeg, Man., July 8, 1963.

			Regular Season					Playoffs				
Season	Club	Lea	GP	G	A	TP	PIM	GP	G	A	TP	PIM
1983-84a	U. of Manitoba	GPAC	46	39	41	80	....	....	....	....	....	....
1984-85b	U. of Manitoba	GPAC	30	29	38	67	48	....	....	....	....	....
1985-86c	**NY Rangers**	**NHL**	**80**	**22**	**43**	**65**	**69**	**16**	**6**	**8**	**14**	**26**
1986-87	**NY Rangers**	**NHL**	**38**	**16**	**20**	**36**	**20**	....	....	....	....	....
	Washington	**NHL**	**40**	**15**	**19**	**34**	**20**	**7**	**2**	**1**	**3**	**6**
1987-88	**Washington**	**NHL**	**70**	**28**	**31**	**59**	**22**	**14**	**6**	**5**	**11**	**10**
1988-89	**Washington**	**NHL**	**80**	**41**	**48**	**89**	**49**	**6**	**0**	**5**	**5**	**2**
1989-90	**Washington**	**NHL**	**74**	**30**	**43**	**73**	**27**	**14**	**3**	**4**	**7**	**8**
1990-91	**Washington**	**NHL**	**79**	**23**	**48**	**71**	**26**	**11**	**3**	**4**	**7**	**8**
1991-92	**Washington**	**NHL**	**80**	**29**	**40**	**69**	**38**	**7**	**0**	**11**	**11**	**0**
	NHL Totals		**541**	**204**	**292**	**496**	**271**	**75**	**20**	**38**	**58**	**60**

a Canadian University Player of the Year; CIAU All-Canadian, GPAC MVP and First All-Star Team (1984)
b CIAU All-Canadian, GPAC First All-Star Team (1985)
c NHL All-Rookie Team (1986)

Played in NHL All-Star Game (1989)

Signed as a free agent by **NY Rangers**, September 26, 1985. Traded to **Washington** by **NY Rangers** with Bob Crawford and Kelly Miller for Bob Carpenter and Washington's second round choice (Jason Prosofsky) in 1989 Entry Draft, January 1, 1987.

RIEHL, KEVIN

Center. Shoots left. 5'7", 149 lbs. Born, Leader, Sask., March 11, 1971.
(New Jersey's 11th choice, 231st overall, in 1991 Entry Draft).

			Regular Season					Playoffs				
Season	Club	Lea	GP	G	A	TP	PIM	GP	G	A	TP	PIM
1990-91	Medicine Hat	WHL	72	66	50	116	43	....	....	....	....	....
1991-92	Medicine Hat	WHL	69	65	50	115	125	4	2	2	4	4

RIIHIJARVI, HEIKKI (ree-hee-YAHR-vee)

Defense. Shoots left. 6'5", 215 lbs. Born, Oulu, Finland, June 4, 1966.
(Edmonton's 8th choice, 147th overall, in 1984 Entry Draft).

			Regular Season					Playoffs				
Season	Club	Lea	GP	G	A	TP	PIM	GP	G	A	TP	PIM
1985-86	TPS	Fin. Jr.	25	6	8	14	12	....	....	....	....	....
1986-87	Karpat	Fin.	36	4	4	8	10	....	....	....	....	....
1987-88	Karpat	Fin.	21	0	5	5	0	....	....	....	....	....
1988-89	Karpat	Fin.	43	8	11	19	14	5	0	2	2	4
1989-90	Jokerit	Fin.	44	3	10	13	16	....	....	....	....	....
1990-91	Jokerit	Fin.	36	4	4	8	12	....	....	....	....	....
1991-92	Jokerit	Fin.	43	3	8	11	10	10	2	2	4	8

RIIHIJARVI, JUHA (ree-HEE-yahr-vee)

Right wing. Shoots right. 6'3", 196 lbs. Born, Salla, Finland, December 15, 1969.
(Edmonton's 11th choice, 254th overall, in 1991 Entry Draft).

			Regular Season					Playoffs				
Season	Club	Lea	GP	G	A	TP	PIM	GP	G	A	TP	PIM
1990-91	Karpat	Fin.2	42	29	41	70	34	....	....	....	....	....
1991-92	JyP HT	Fin.	38	29	33	62	37	10	4	4	8	10

RIVET, CRAIG

Defense. Shoots right. 6'1", 172 lbs. Born, North Bay, Ont., September 13, 1974.
(Montreal's 4th choice, 68th overall, in 1992 Entry Draft).

			Regular Season					Playoffs				
Season	Club	Lea	GP	G	A	TP	PIM	GP	G	A	TP	PIM
1990-91	Barrie	Jr. B	42	9	17	26	55	....	....	....	....	....
1991-92	Kingston	OHL	66	5	21	26	97	....	....	....	....	....

ROBERGE, MARIO (ro-BAIRZH)

Left wing. Shoots left. 5'11", 185 lbs. Born, Quebec City, Que., January 23, 1964.

			Regular Season					Playoffs				
Season	Club	Lea	GP	G	A	TP	PIM	GP	G	A	TP	PIM
1987-88	Pt. Basques	Sr.	35	25	64	89	152	....	....	....	....	....
1988-89	Sherbrooke	AHL	58	4	9	13	249	6	0	2	2	8
1989-90	Sherbrooke	AHL	73	13	27	40	247	12	5	2	7	53
1990-91	**Montreal**	**NHL**	**5**	**0**	**0**	**0**	**21**	**12**	**0**	**0**	**0**	**24**
	Fredericton	AHL	68	12	27	39	*365	2	0	2	2	5
1991-92	**Montreal**	**NHL**	**20**	**2**	**1**	**3**	**62**	....	....	....	....	....
	Fredericton	AHL	6	1	2	3	20	7	0	2	2	20
	NHL Totals		**25**	**2**	**1**	**3**	**83**	**12**	**0**	**0**	**0**	**24**

Signed as a free agent by **Montreal**, October 5, 1988.

ROBERGE, SERGE (ro-BAIRZH)

Right wing. Shoots right. 6'1", 195 lbs. Born, Quebec City, Que., March 31, 1965.

			Regular Season					Playoffs				
Season	Club	Lea	GP	G	A	TP	PIM	GP	G	A	TP	PIM
1984-85	Drummondville	QMJHL	45	8	19	27	299	....	....	....	....	....
1985-86						DID NOT PLAY						
1986-87	Virginia	ACHL	47	9	15	24	346	....	....	....	....	....
1987-88	Sherbrooke	AHL	30	0	1	1	130	5	0	0	0	21
1988-89	Sherbrooke	AHL	65	5	7	12	352	6	0	1	1	10
1989-90	Sherbrooke	AHL	66	8	5	13	343	12	2	0	2	44
1990-91	**Quebec**	**NHL**	**9**	**0**	**0**	**0**	**24**	....	....	....	....	....
	Halifax	AHL	52	0	5	5	152	....	....	....	....	....
1991-92	Halifax	AHL	66	2	8	10	319	....	....	....	....	....
	NHL Totals		**9**	**0**	**0**	**0**	**24**	....	....	....	....	....

Signed as a free agent by **Montreal**, January 25, 1988. Signed as a free agent by **Quebec**, December 28, 1990.

ROBERTS, DAVID

Left wing. Shoots left. 6', 185 lbs. Born, Alameda, CA, May 28, 1970.
(St. Louis' 5th choice, 114th overall, in 1989 Entry Draft).

			Regular Season					Playoffs				
Season	Club	Lea	GP	G	A	TP	PIM	GP	G	A	TP	PIM
1989-90a	U. of Michigan	CCHA	42	21	32	53	46	....	....	....	....	....
1990-91bc	U. of Michigan	CCHA	43	40	35	75	58	....	....	....	....	....
1991-92	U. of Michigan	CCHA	44	16	42	58	68	....	....	....	....	....

a CCHA Rookie of the Year (1990)
b CCHA Second All-Star Team (1991)
c NCAA West Second All-American Team (1991)

ROBERTS, GARY

Left wing. Shoots left. 6'1", 190 lbs. Born, North York, Ont., May 23, 1966.
(Calgary's 1st choice, 12th overall, in 1984 Entry Draft).

			Regular Season					Playoffs				
Season	Club	Lea	GP	G	A	TP	PIM	GP	G	A	TP	PIM
1982-83	Ottawa	OHL	53	12	8	20	83	5	1	0	1	19
1983-84	Ottawa	OHL	48	27	30	57	144	13	10	7	17	62
1984-85	Moncton	AHL	7	4	2	6	7	....	....	....	....	....
a	Ottawa	OHL	59	44	62	106	186	5	2	8	10	10
1985-86a	Ottawa	OHL	24	26	25	51	83	....	....	....	....	....
a	Guelph	OHL	23	18	15	33	65	20	18	13	31	43
1986-87	**Calgary**	**NHL**	**32**	**5**	**10**	**15**	**85**	**2**	**0**	**0**	**0**	**4**
	Moncton	AHL	38	20	18	38	72	....	....	....	....	....
1987-88	**Calgary**	**NHL**	**74**	**13**	**15**	**28**	**282**	**9**	**2**	**3**	**5**	**29**
1988-89	**Calgary**	**NHL**	**71**	**22**	**16**	**38**	**250**	**22**	**5**	**7**	**12**	**57**
1989-90	**Calgary**	**NHL**	**78**	**39**	**33**	**72**	**222**	**6**	**2**	**5**	**7**	**41**
1990-91	**Calgary**	**NHL**	**80**	**22**	**31**	**53**	**252**	**7**	**1**	**3**	**4**	**18**
1991-92	**Calgary**	**NHL**	**76**	**53**	**37**	**90**	**207**	....	....	....	....	....
	NHL Totals		**411**	**154**	**142**	**296**	**1298**	**46**	**10**	**18**	**28**	**149**

a OHL Second All-Star Team (1985, 1986)
Played in NHL All-Star Game (1992)

ROBERTS, GORDON (GORDIE)

Defense. Shoots left. 6'1", 195 lbs. Born, Detroit, MI, October 2, 1957.
(Montreal's 7th choice, 54th overall, in 1977 Amateur Draft).

			Regular Season					Playoffs				
Season	Club	Lea	GP	G	A	TP	PIM	GP	G	A	TP	PIM
1974-75	Victoria	WHL	53	19	45	64	145	12	1	9	10	42
1975-76	New England	WHA	77	3	19	22	102	17	2	9	11	36
1976-77	New England	WHA	77	13	33	46	169	5	2	2	4	6
1977-78	New England	WHA	78	15	46	61	118	14	0	5	5	29
1978-79	New England	WHA	79	11	46	57	113	10	0	4	4	10
1979-80	**Hartford**	**NHL**	**80**	**8**	**28**	**36**	**89**	**3**	**1**	**1**	**2**	**2**
1980-81	**Hartford**	**NHL**	**27**	**2**	**11**	**13**	**81**	....	....	....	....	....
	Minnesota	**NHL**	**50**	**6**	**31**	**37**	**94**	**19**	**1**	**5**	**6**	**17**
1981-82	**Minnesota**	**NHL**	**79**	**4**	**30**	**34**	**119**	**4**	**0**	**3**	**3**	**27**
1982-83	**Minnesota**	**NHL**	**80**	**3**	**41**	**44**	**103**	**9**	**1**	**5**	**6**	**14**
1983-84	**Minnesota**	**NHL**	**77**	**8**	**45**	**53**	**132**	**15**	**3**	**7**	**10**	**23**
1984-85	**Minnesota**	**NHL**	**78**	**6**	**36**	**42**	**112**	**9**	**1**	**6**	**7**	**6**
1985-86	**Minnesota**	**NHL**	**76**	**2**	**21**	**23**	**101**	**5**	**0**	**4**	**4**	**8**
1986-87	**Minnesota**	**NHL**	**67**	**3**	**10**	**13**	**68**	....	....	....	....	....
1987-88	**Minnesota**	**NHL**	**48**	**1**	**10**	**11**	**103**	....	....	....	....	....
	Philadelphia	**NHL**	**11**	**1**	**2**	**3**	**15**	....	....	....	....	....
	St. Louis	**NHL**	**11**	**1**	**3**	**4**	**25**	**10**	**1**	**2**	**3**	**33**
1988-89	**St. Louis**	**NHL**	**77**	**2**	**24**	**26**	**90**	**10**	**1**	**7**	**8**	**8**
1989-90	**St. Louis**	**NHL**	**75**	**3**	**14**	**17**	**140**	**10**	**0**	**2**	**2**	**26**
1990-91	**St. Louis**	**NHL**	**3**	**0**	**1**	**1**	**8**	....	....	....	....	....
	Peoria	IHL	6	0	8	8	4	....	....	....	....	....
	Pittsburgh	**NHL**	**61**	**3**	**12**	**15**	**70**	**24**	**1**	**2**	**3**	**63**
1991-92	**Pittsburgh**	**NHL**	**73**	**2**	**22**	**24**	**87**	**19**	**0**	**2**	**2**	**32**
	NHL Totals		**973**	**55**	**341**	**396**	**1437**	**137**	**10**	**46**	**56**	**259**

Claimed by **Hartford** from **Montreal** in 1979 Expansion Draft, June 22, 1979. Traded to **Minnesota** by **Hartford** for Mike Fidler, December 16, 1980. Traded to **Philadelphia** by **Minnesota** for future considerations, February 8, 1988. Traded to **St. Louis** by **Philadelphia** for future considerations, March 8, 1988. Traded to **Pittsburgh** by **St. Louis** for future considerations, October 27, 1990. Signed as a free agent by **Boston**, July 23, 1992.

ROBINSON, DOUGLAS (SCOTT)

Right wing. Shoots right. 6'2", 180 lbs. Born, 100 Mile House, B.C., March 29, 1964.

			Regular Season					Playoffs				
Season	Club	Lea	GP	G	A	TP	PIM	GP	G	A	TP	PIM
1986-87	U. of Calgary	CWUAA	19	12	14	26	95	....	....	....	....	....
1987-88	U. of Calgary	CWUAA	21	14	14	28	64	....	....	....	....	....
1988-89	Kalamazoo	IHL	49	14	17	31	129	....	....	....	....	....
1989-90	**Minnesota**	**NHL**	**1**	**0**	**0**	**0**	**2**	....	....	....	....	....
	Kalamazoo	IHL	47	13	12	25	97	....	....	....	....	....
1990-91	Kalamazoo	IHL	27	7	9	16	36	11	2	1	3	32
1991-92	Kalamazoo	IHL	78	29	27	56	58	11	2	6	8	86
	NHL Totals		**1**	**0**	**0**	**0**	**2**	....	....	....	....	....

Signed as a free agent by **Minnesota**, September 27, 1988.

ROBINSON, LARRY CLARK

Defense. Shots left. 6'4", 225 lbs. Born, Winchester, Ont., June 2, 1951.
(Montreal's 4th choice, 20th overall, in 1971 Amateur Draft).

			Regular Season					Playoffs				
Season	Club	Lea	GP	G	A	TP	PIM	GP	G	A	TP	PIM
1969-70	Brockville	OMJHL	40	22	29	51	74	....	....	....	....	....
1970-71	Kitchener	OMJHL	61	12	39	51	65	....	....	....	....	....
1971-72	Nova Scotia	AHL	74	10	14	24	54	15	2	10	12	31
1972-73	**Montreal**	**NHL**	**36**	**2**	**4**	**6**	**20**	**11**	**1**	**4**	**5**	**9**
	Nova Scotia	AHL	38	6	33	39	33	....	....	....	....	....
1973-74	**Montreal**	**NHL**	**78**	**6**	**20**	**26**	**66**	**6**	**0**	**1**	**1**	**26**
1974-75	**Montreal**	**NHL**	**80**	**14**	**47**	**61**	**76**	**11**	**0**	**4**	**4**	**27**
1975-76	**Montreal**	**NHL**	**80**	**10**	**30**	**40**	**59**	**13**	**3**	**3**	**6**	**10**
1976-77abc	**Montreal**	**NHL**	**77**	**19**	**66**	**85**	**45**	**14**	**2**	**10**	**12**	**12**
1977-78de	**Montreal**	**NHL**	**80**	**13**	**52**	**65**	**39**	**15**	**4**	***17**	***21**	**6**
1978-79b	**Montreal**	**NHL**	**67**	**16**	**45**	**61**	**33**	**16**	**6**	**9**	**15**	**8**
1979-80ab	**Montreal**	**NHL**	**72**	**14**	**61**	**75**	**39**	**10**	**0**	**4**	**4**	**2**
1980-81e	**Montreal**	**NHL**	**65**	**12**	**38**	**50**	**37**	**3**	**0**	**1**	**1**	**2**
1981-82	**Montreal**	**NHL**	**71**	**12**	**47**	**59**	**41**	**5**	**0**	**1**	**1**	**8**
1982-83	**Montreal**	**NHL**	**71**	**14**	**49**	**63**	**33**	**3**	**0**	**0**	**0**	**2**
1983-84	**Montreal**	**NHL**	**74**	**9**	**34**	**43**	**39**	**15**	**0**	**5**	**5**	**22**
1984-85	**Montreal**	**NHL**	**76**	**14**	**33**	**47**	**44**	**12**	**3**	**8**	**11**	**8**
1985-86e	**Montreal**	**NHL**	**78**	**19**	**63**	**82**	**39**	**20**	**0**	**13**	**13**	**22**
1986-87	**Montreal**	**NHL**	**70**	**13**	**37**	**50**	**44**	**17**	**3**	**17**	**20**	**6**
1987-88	**Montreal**	**NHL**	**53**	**6**	**34**	**40**	**30**	**11**	**1**	**4**	**5**	**4**
1988-89	**Montreal**	**NHL**	**74**	**4**	**26**	**30**	**22**	**21**	**2**	**8**	**10**	**12**
1989-90	**Los Angeles**	**NHL**	**64**	**7**	**32**	**39**	**34**	**10**	**2**	**3**	**5**	**10**
1990-91	**Los Angeles**	**NHL**	**62**	**1**	**22**	**23**	**16**	**12**	**1**	**4**	**5**	**15**
1991-92	**Los Angeles**	**NHL**	**56**	**3**	**10**	**13**	**37**	**2**	**0**	**0**	**0**	**0**
	NHL Totals		**1384**	**208**	**750**	**958**	**793**	**227**	**28**	**116**	**144**	**211**

a Won James Norris Memorial Trophy (1977, 1980)
b NHL First All-Star Team (1977, 1979, 1980)
c NHL Plus/Minus Leader (1977)
d Won Conn Smythe Trophy (1978)
e NHL Second All-Star Team (1978, 1981, 1986)
Played in NHL All-Star Game (1974, 1976-78, 1980, 1982, 1986, 1988, 1989, 1992)
Signed as a free agent by **Los Angeles**, July 26, 1989.

ROBINSON, ROBERT (ROB)

Defense. Shoots left. 6'1", 214 lbs. Born, St. Catharines, Ont., April 19, 1967.
(St. Louis' 6th choice, 117th overall, in 1987 Entry Draft).

			Regular Season					Playoffs				
Season	Club	Lea	GP	G	A	TP	PIM	GP	G	A	TP	PIM
1985-86	Miami-Ohio	CCHA	38	1	9	10	24	....	....	....	....	....
1986-87	Miami-Ohio	CCHA	33	3	5	8	32	....	....	....	....	....
1987-88	Miami-Ohio	CCHA	35	1	3	4	56	....	....	....	....	....
1988-89	Miami-Ohio	CCHA	30	3	4	7	42	....	....	....	....	....
	Peoria	IHL	11	2	0	2	6	....	....	....	....	....
1989-90	Peoria	IHL	60	2	11	13	72	5	0	1	1	10
1990-91a	Peoria	IHL	79	2	21	23	42	19	0	6	6	8
1991-92	**St. Louis**	**NHL**	**22**	**0**	**1**	**1**	**8**	....	....	....	....	....
	Peoria	IHL	35	1	10	11	29	10	0	2	2	12
	NHL Totals		**22**	**0**	**1**	**1**	**8**	....	....	....	....	....

a IHL Second All-Star Team (1991)

ROBISON, JEFF

Defense. Shoots left. 6'1", 175 lbs. Born, Wrentham, MA, June 3, 1970.
(Los Angeles' 5th choice, 91st overall, in 1988 Entry Draft).

			Regular Season					Playoffs				
Season	Club	Lea	GP	G	A	TP	PIM	GP	G	A	TP	PIM
1988-89	Providence	H.E.	41	0	5	5	36	....	....	....	....	....
1989-90	Providence	H.E.	35	2	8	10	16	....	....	....	....	....
1990-91	Providence	H.E.	36	3	8	11	34	....	....	....	....	....
1991-92	Providence	H.E.	33	0	3	3	20	....	....	....	....	....

ROBITAILLE, LUC (ROH-buh-tigh)

Left wing. Shoots left. 6'1", 190 lbs. Born, Montreal, Que., February 17, 1966.
(Los Angeles' 9th choice, 171st overall, in 1984 Entry Draft).

			Regular Season					Playoffs				
Season	Club	Lea	GP	G	A	TP	PIM	GP	G	A	TP	PIM
1983-84	Hull	QMJHL	70	32	53	85	48	....	....	....	....	....
1984-85a	Hull	QMJHL	64	55	94	149	115	5	4	2	6	27
1985-86bcd	Hull	QMJHL	63	68	123	191	91	15	17	27	44	28
1986-87ef	**Los Angeles**	**NHL**	**79**	**45**	**39**	**84**	**28**	**5**	**1**	**4**	**5**	**2**
1987-88g	**Los Angeles**	**NHL**	**80**	**53**	**58**	**111**	**82**	**5**	**2**	**5**	**7**	**18**
1988-89g	**Los Angeles**	**NHL**	**78**	**46**	**52**	**98**	**65**	**11**	**2**	**6**	**8**	**10**
1989-90g	**Los Angeles**	**NHL**	**80**	**52**	**49**	**101**	**38**	**10**	**5**	**5**	**10**	**10**
1990-91g	**Los Angeles**	**NHL**	**76**	**45**	**46**	**91**	**68**	**12**	**12**	**4**	**16**	**22**
1991-92f	**Los Angeles**	**NHL**	**80**	**44**	**63**	**107**	**95**	**6**	**3**	**4**	**7**	**12**
	NHL Totals		**473**	**285**	**307**	**592**	**376**	**49**	**25**	**28**	**53**	**74**

a QMJHL Second All-Star Team (1985)
b QMJHL First All-Star Team (1986)
c QMJHL Player of the Year (1986)
d Canadian Major Junior Player of the Year (1986)
e Won Calder Memorial Trophy (1987)
f NHL Second All-Star Team (1987, 1992)
g NHL First All-Star Team (1988, 1989, 1990, 1991)
Played in NHL All-Star Game (1988-92)

ROBITAILLE, MARTIN

Center. Shoots right. 5'10", 165 lbs. Born, St. Romuald, Que., March 17, 1969.
(Toronto's 1st choice, 15th overall, in 1990 Supplemental Draft).

			Regular Season					Playoffs				
Season	Club	Lea	GP	G	A	TP	PIM	GP	G	A	TP	PIM
1988-89	U. of Maine	H.E.	45	17	31	48	10	....	....	....	....	....
1989-90	U. of Maine	H.E.	46	24	28	52	24	....	....	....	....	....
1990-91	U. of Maine	H.E.	43	23	25	48	28	....	....	....	....	....
1991-92	U. of Maine	H.E.	31	5	22	27	8	....	....	....	....	....

ROCHEFORT, NORMAND (ROHSH-fohr)

Defense. Shoots left. 6'1", 214 lbs. Born, Trois-Rivières, Que., January 28, 1961.
(Quebec's 1st choice, 24th overall, in 1980 Entry Draft).

			Regular Season					Playoffs				
Season	Club	Lea	GP	G	A	TP	PIM	GP	G	A	TP	PIM
1978-79	Trois-Rivières	QJHL	72	17	57	74	30	13	3	11	14	17
1979-80	Trois-Rivières	QJHL	20	5	25	30	22	....	....	....	....	....
a	Quebec	QJHL	52	8	39	47	68	5	1	3	4	8
1980-81	**Quebec**	**NHL**	**56**	**3**	**7**	**10**	**51**	**5**	**0**	**0**	**0**	**4**
	Quebec	QJHL	9	2	6	8	14	....	....	....	....	....
1981-82	**Quebec**	**NHL**	**72**	**4**	**14**	**18**	**115**	**16**	**0**	**2**	**2**	**10**
1982-83	**Quebec**	**NHL**	**62**	**6**	**17**	**23**	**40**	**1**	**0**	**0**	**0**	**2**
1983-84	**Quebec**	**NHL**	**75**	**2**	**22**	**24**	**47**	**6**	**1**	**0**	**1**	**6**
1984-85	**Quebec**	**NHL**	**73**	**3**	**21**	**24**	**74**	**18**	**2**	**1**	**3**	**8**
1985-86	**Quebec**	**NHL**	**26**	**5**	**4**	**9**	**30**	....	....	....	....	....
1986-87	**Quebec**	**NHL**	**70**	**6**	**9**	**15**	**46**	**13**	**2**	**1**	**3**	**26**
1987-88	**Quebec**	**NHL**	**46**	**3**	**10**	**13**	**49**	....	....	....	....	....
1988-89	**NY Rangers**	**NHL**	**11**	**1**	**5**	**6**	**18**	....	....	....	....	....
1989-90	**NY Rangers**	**NHL**	**31**	**3**	**1**	**4**	**24**	**10**	**2**	**1**	**3**	**26**
	Flint	IHL	7	3	2	5	4	....	....	....	....	....
1990-91	**NY Rangers**	**NHL**	**44**	**3**	**7**	**10**	**35**	....	....	....	....	....
1991-92	**NY Rangers**	**NHL**	**26**	**0**	**2**	**2**	**31**	....	....	....	....	....
	NHL Totals		**592**	**39**	**119**	**158**	**560**	**69**	**7**	**5**	**12**	**82**

a QMJHL Second All-Star Team (1980)

Traded to **NY Rangers** by **Quebec** with Jason Lafreniere for Bruce Bell, Jari Gronstrand, Walt Poddubny and NY Rangers' fourth round choice (Eric Dubois) in 1989 Entry Draft, August 1, 1988.

RODERICK, JOHN

Defense. Shoots left. 6'2", 190 lbs. Born, Cambridge, MA, February 25, 1971.
(St. Louis' 9th choice, 177th overall, in 1989 Entry Draft).

			Regular Season					Playoffs				
Season	Club	Lea	GP	G	A	TP	PIM	GP	G	A	TP	PIM
1989-90	St. Lawrence	ECAC	16	0	1	1	20	....	....	....	....	....
1990-91	St. Lawrence	ECAC	21	0	2	2	20	....	....	....	....	....
1991-92	St. Lawrence	ECAC	28	1	1	2	40	....	....	....	....	....

ROENICK, JEREMY (ROH-nihk)

Center. Shoots right. 6', 170 lbs. Born, Boston, MA, January 17, 1970.
(Chicago's 1st choice, 8th overall, in 1988 Entry Draft).

			Regular Season					Playoffs				
Season	Club	Lea	GP	G	A	TP	PIM	GP	G	A	TP	PIM
1988-89a	Hull	QMJHL	28	34	36	70	14	....	....	....	....	....
	U.S. Jr. Nat'l.	....	11	8	8	16	0	....	....	....	....	....
	Chicago	**NHL**	**20**	**9**	**9**	**18**	**4**	**10**	**1**	**3**	**4**	**7**
1989-90	**Chicago**	**NHL**	**78**	**26**	**40**	**66**	**54**	**20**	**11**	**7**	**18**	**8**
1990-91	**Chicago**	**NHL**	**79**	**41**	**53**	**94**	**80**	**6**	**3**	**5**	**8**	**4**
1991-92	**Chicago**	**NHL**	**80**	**53**	**50**	**103**	**98**	**18**	**12**	**10**	**22**	**12**
	NHL Totals		**257**	**129**	**152**	**281**	**236**	**54**	**27**	**25**	**52**	**31**

a QMJHL Second All-Star Team (1989)

Played in NHL All-Star Game (1991, 1992)

ROHLIN, LEIF (roh-LEEN)

Defense. Shoots left. 6'1", 198 lbs. Born, Vasteras, Sweden, February 26, 1968.
(Vancouver's 2nd choice, 33rd overall, in 1988 Entry Draft).

			Regular Season					Playoffs				
Season	Club	Lea	GP	G	A	TP	PIM	GP	G	A	TP	PIM
1987-88	Vasteras	Swe.2	30	2	15	17	46	10	6	6	12	8
1988-89	Vasteras	Swe.	22	3	7	10	18	....	....	....	....	....
1989-90	Vasteras	Swe.	32	3	6	9	40	....	....	....	....	....
1990-91	Vasteras	Swe.	40	4	10	14	48	....	....	....	....	....
1991-92	Vasteras	Swe.	39	4	6	10	52	....	....	....	....	....

ROHLOFF, JON

Defense. Shoots right. 5'11", 200 lbs. Born, Mankato, MN, October 3, 1969.
(Boston's 7th choice, 186th overall, in 1988 Entry Draft).

			Regular Season					Playoffs				
Season	Club	Lea	GP	G	A	TP	PIM	GP	G	A	TP	PIM
1988-89	Minn.-Duluth	WCHA	39	1	2	3	44	....	....	....	....	....
1989-90	Minn.-Duluth	WCHA	5	0	1	1	6	....	....	....	....	....
1990-91	Minn.-Duluth	WCHA	32	6	11	17	38	....	....	....	....	....
1991-92	Minn.-Duluth	WCHA	27	9	9	18	48	....	....	....	....	....

ROHR, STEPHEN

Center. Shoots right. 6'3", 200 lbs. Born, Flint, MI, March 22, 1972.
(Montreal's 8th choice, 144th overall, in 1990 Entry Draft).

			Regular Season					Playoffs				
Season	Club	Lea	GP	G	A	TP	PIM	GP	G	A	TP	PIM
1990-91	Miami-Ohio	CCHA	26	6	6	12	8	....	....	....	....	....
1991-92	Miami-Ohio	CCHA	21	1	3	4	26	....	....	....	....	....

ROLFE, DANIEL

Defense. Shoots left. 6'4", 200 lbs. Born, Inglewood, CA, December 25, 1967.
(St. Louis' 12th choice, 222nd overall, in 1987 Entry Draft).

			Regular Season					Playoffs				
Season	Club	Lea	GP	G	A	TP	PIM	GP	G	A	TP	PIM
1987-88	Ferris State	CCHA	13	1	1	2	36	....	....	....	....	....
1988-89	Ferris State	CCHA	28	0	2	2	54	....	....	....	....	....
1989-90	Ferris State	CCHA	31	0	6	6	48	....	....	....	....	....
1990-91	Ferris State	CCHA	31	1	1	2	36	....	....	....	....	....
1991-92	Richmond	ECHL	11	1	1	2	29	....	....	....	....	....
	Nashville	ECHL	39	0	11	11	44	....	....	....	....	....

ROLSTON, BRIAN

Center. Shoots left. 6'1", 175 lbs. Born, Flint, MI, February 21,1973.
(New Jersey's 2nd choice, 11th overall, in 1991 Entry Draft).

			Regular Season					Playoffs				
Season	Club	Lea	GP	G	A	TP	PIM	GP	G	A	TP	PIM
1990-91	Detroit Jr. A	USHL	36	49	46	95	14	....	....	....	....	....
1991-92a	Lake Superior	CCHA	37	14	23	37	14	....	....	....	....	....

a NCAA All-Tournament Team (1992)

ROMANIUK, RUSSELL

Left wing. Shoots left. 6', 185 lbs. Born, Winnipeg, Man., June 9, 1970.
(Winnipeg's 2nd choice, 31st overall, in 1988 Entry Draft).

			Regular Season					Playoffs				
Season	Club	Lea	GP	G	A	TP	PIM	GP	G	A	TP	PIM
1988-89	North Dakota	WCHA	39	17	14	31	32	....	....	....	....	....
	Cdn. National	....	3	1	0	1	0	....	....	....	....	....
1989-90	North Dakota	WCHA	45	36	15	51	54	....	....	....	....	....
1990-91a	North Dakota	WCHA	39	40	28	68	30	....	....	....	....	....
1991-92	**Winnipeg**	**NHL**	**27**	**3**	**5**	**8**	**18**	....	....	....	....	....
	Moncton	AHL	45	16	15	31	25	10	5	4	9	19
	NHL Totals		**27**	**3**	**5**	**8**	**18**	....	....	....	....	....

a WCHA First All-Star Team (1991)

RONAN, EDWARD (ED)

Right wing. Shoots right. 6', 197 lbs. Born, Quincy, MA, March 21, 1968.
(Montreal's 13th choice, 227th overall, in 1987 Entry Draft).

			Regular Season					Playoffs				
Season	Club	Lea	GP	G	A	TP	PIM	GP	G	A	TP	PIM
1987-88	Boston U.	H.E.	31	2	5	7	20	....	....	....	....	....
1988-89	Boston U.	H.E.	36	4	11	15	34	....	....	....	....	....
1989-90	Boston U.	H.E.	44	17	23	40	50	....	....	....	....	....
1990-91	Boston U.	H.E.	41	16	19	35	38	....	....	....	....	....
1991-92	**Montreal**	**NHL**	**3**	**0**	**0**	**0**	**0**	....	....	....	....	....
	Fredericton	AHL	78	25	34	59	82	7	5	1	6	6
	NHL Totals		**3**	**0**	**0**	**0**	**0**	....	....	....	....	....

RONNING, CLIFF

Center. Shoots left. 5'8", 175 lbs. Born, Vancouver, B.C., October 1, 1965.
(St. Louis' 9th choice, 134th overall, in 1984 Entry Draft).

			Regular Season					Playoffs				
Season	Club	Lea	GP	G	A	TP	PIM	GP	G	A	TP	PIM
1983-84a	N. Westminster	WHL	71	69	67	136	10	9	8	13	21	10
1984-85bc	N. Westminster	WHL	70	*89	108	*197	20	11	10	14	24	4
1985-86	Cdn. Olympic	....	71	55	63	118	53	....	....	....	....	....
	St. Louis	**NHL**	....	....	....	....	....	**5**	**1**	**1**	**2**	**2**
1986-87	**St. Louis**	**NHL**	**42**	**11**	**14**	**25**	**6**	**4**	**0**	**1**	**1**	**0**
	Cdn. Olympic	....	26	16	16	32	12	....	....	....	....	....
1987-88	**St. Louis**	**NHL**	**26**	**5**	**8**	**13**	**12**	....	....	....	....	....
1988-89	**St. Louis**	**NHL**	**64**	**24**	**31**	**55**	**18**	**7**	**1**	**3**	**4**	**0**
	Peoria	IHL	12	11	20	31	8	....	....	....	....	....
1989-90	Asiago	Italy	36	67	49	116	25	6	7	12	19	4
1990-91	**St. Louis**	**NHL**	**48**	**14**	**18**	**32**	**10**	....	....	....	....	....
	Vancouver	**NHL**	**11**	**6**	**6**	**12**	**0**	**6**	**6**	**3**	**9**	**12**
1991-92	**Vancouver**	**NHL**	**80**	**24**	**47**	**71**	**42**	**13**	**8**	**5**	**13**	**6**
	NHL Totals		**271**	**84**	**124**	**208**	**88**	**35**	**16**	**13**	**29**	**20**

a WHL Rookie of the Year (1984)
b WHL First All-Star Team (1985)
c WHL Most Valuable Player (1985)

Traded to **Vancouver** by **St. Louis** with Geoff Courtnall, Robert Dirk, Sergio Momesso and future considerations for Dan Quinn and Garth Butcher, March 5, 1991.

ROONEY, LARRY

Defense. Shoots left. 5'11", 165 lbs. Born, Boston, MA, January 30, 1968.
(Buffalo's 6th choice, 89th overall, in 1986 Entry Draft).

			Regular Season					Playoffs				
Season	Club	Lea	GP	G	A	TP	PIM	GP	G	A	TP	PIM
1987-88	Providence	H.E.	33	1	9	10	34	....	....	....	....	....
1988-89	Providence	H.E	10	0	4	4	18	....	....	....	....	....
1989-90	Providence	H.E	33	7	12	19	34	....	....	....	....	....
1990-91	Providence	H.E.	35	8	18	26	24	....	....	....	....	....
1991-92	Richmond	ECHL	41	3	10	13	57	....	....	....	....	....
	Cincinnati	ECHL	20	0	10	10	16	9	2	6	8	6

ROSENBLATT, HOWARD DAVID

Defense. Shoots right. 6', 195 lbs. Born, Pawtucket, RI, January 3, 1969.
(Boston's 1st choice, 26th overall, in 1990 Supplemental Draft).

			Regular Season					Playoffs				
Season	Club	Lea	GP	G	A	TP	PIM	GP	G	A	TP	PIM
1987-88	Merrimack	NCAA	3	1	0	1	0	....	....	....	....	....
1988-89	Merrimack	NCAA	7	1	1	2	8	....	....	....	....	....
1989-90	Merrimack	H.E.	29	10	14	24	36	....	....	....	....	....
1990-91	Merrimack	H.E.	31	19	16	35	*118	....	....	....	....	....
1991-92	Cincinnati	ECHL	60	26	16	42	235	9	3	8	11	55
	Maine	AHL	2	0	0	0	9	....	....	....	....	....

ROSS, PATRIK

Right wing. Shoots left. 6'1", 185 lbs. Born, Jonkoping, Sweden, February 27, 1970.
(Los Angeles' 9th choice, 196th overall, in 1990 Entry Draft).

			Regular Season					Playoffs				
Season	Club	Lea	GP	G	A	TP	PIM	GP	G	A	TP	PIM
1989-90	HV-71	Swe.	37	14	7	21	0	....	....	....	....	....
1990-91	HV-71	Swe.	21	4	1	5	0	....	....	....	....	....
1991-92	HV-71	Swe.	37	8	5	13	10	3	0	0	0	4

ROUSE, ROBERT (BOB)

Defense. Shoots right. 6'1", 210 lbs. Born, Surrey, B.C., June 18, 1964.
(Minnesota's 3rd choice, 80th overall, in 1982 Entry Draft).

			Regular Season					Playoffs				
Season	Club	Lea	GP	G	A	TP	PIM	GP	G	A	TP	PIM
1980-81	Billings	WHL	70	0	13	13	116	5	0	0	0	2
1981-82	Billings	WHL	71	7	22	29	209	5	0	2	2	10
1982-83	Nanaimo	WHL	29	7	20	27	86	....	....	....	....	....
	Lethbridge	WHL	42	8	30	38	82	20	2	13	15	55
1983-84	Minnesota	NHL	1	0	0	0	0	....	....	....	....	....
a	Lethbridge	WHL	71	18	42	60	101	5	0	1	1	28
1984-85	Minnesota	NHL	63	2	9	11	113	....	....	....	....	....
	Springfield	AHL	8	0	3	3	6	....	....	....	....	....
1985-86	Minnesota	NHL	75	1	14	15	151	3	0	0	0	0
1986-87	Minnesota	NHL	72	2	10	12	179	....	....	....	....	....
1987-88	Minnesota	NHL	74	0	12	12	168	....	....	....	....	....
1988-89	Minnesota	NHL	66	4	13	17	124	....	....	....	....	....
	Washington	NHL	13	0	2	2	36	6	2	0	2	4
1989-90	Washington	NHL	70	4	16	20	123	15	2	3	5	47
1990-91	Washington	NHL	47	5	15	20	65	....	....	....	....	....
	Toronto	NHL	13	2	4	6	10	....	....	....	....	....
1991-92	Toronto	NHL	79	3	19	22	97	....	....	....	....	....
	NHL Totals		573	23	114	137	1066	24	4	3	7	53

a WHL First All-Star Team, East Division (1984)

Traded to **Washington** by **Minnesota** with Dino Ciccarelli for Mike Gartner and Larry Murphy, March 7, 1989. Traded to **Toronto** by **Washington** with Peter Zezel for Al Iafrate, January 16, 1991.

ROY, SIMON

Defense. Shoots left. 6'1", 177 lbs. Born, Montreal, Que., June 14, 1974.
(Edmonton's 3rd choice, 61st overall, in 1992 Entry Draft).

			Regular Season					Playoffs				
Season	Club	Lea	GP	G	A	TP	PIM	GP	G	A	TP	PIM
1990-91	Bourassa	Midget	37	3	14	17	18	....	....	....	....	....
1991-92	Shawinigan	QMJHL	63	3	24	27	24	10	1	4	5	9

RUBACHUK, BRAD

Center. Shoots left. 5'11", 185 lbs. Born, Winnipeg, Man., June 11, 1970.
(Buffalo's 11th choice, 250th overall, in 1990 Entry Draft).

			Regular Season					Playoffs				
Season	Club	Lea	GP	G	A	TP	PIM	GP	G	A	TP	PIM
1988-89	Lethbridge	WHL	66	19	13	32	161	6	3	1	4	25
1989-90	Lethbridge	WHL	67	37	36	73	179	16	3	7	10	51
1990-91	Lethbridge	WHL	70	64	68	132	237	16	*14	14	28	55
1991-92	Rochester	AHL	70	18	16	34	201	13	4	0	4	19

RUCHTY, MATTHEW

Left wing. Shoots left. 6'1", 210 lbs. Born, Kitchener, Ont., November 27, 1969.
(New Jersey's 4th choice, 65th overall, in 1988 Entry Draft).

			Regular Season					Playoffs				
Season	Club	Lea	GP	G	A	TP	PIM	GP	G	A	TP	PIM
1987-88	Bowling Green	CCHA	41	6	15	21	78	....	....	....	....	....
1988-89	Bowling Green	CCHA	43	11	21	32	110	....	....	....	....	....
1989-90	Bowling Green	CCHA	42	28	21	49	135	....	....	....	....	....
1990-91	Bowling Green	CCHA	38	13	18	31	147	....	....	....	....	....
1991-92	Utica	AHL	73	9	14	23	250	4	0	0	0	25

RUCINSKY, MARTIN

Left wing. Shoots left. 5'11", 178 lbs. Born, Most, Czechoslovakia, March 11, 1971.
(Edmonton's 2nd choice, 20th overall, in 1991 Entry Draft).

			Regular Season					Playoffs				
Season	Club	Lea	GP	G	A	TP	PIM	GP	G	A	TP	PIM
1989-90	CHZ Litvinov	Czech.	47	12	6	18	....	....	....	....	....	....
1990-91	CHZ Litvinov	Czech.	49	23	18	41	69	....	....	....	....	....
1991-92	Edmonton	NHL	2	0	0	0	0	....	....	....	....	....
	Cape Breton	AHL	35	11	12	23	34	....	....	....	....	....
	Quebec	NHL	4	1	1	2	2	....	....	....	....	....
	Halifax	AHL	7	1	1	2	6	....	....	....	....	....
	NHL Totals		6	1	1	2	2	....	....	....	....	....

Traded to **Quebec** by **Edmonton** for Ron Tugnutt and Brad Zavisha, March 10, 1992.

RUFF, JASON

Left wing. Shoots left. 6'2", 192 lbs. Born, Kelowna, B.C., January 27, 1970.
(St Louis' 3rd choice, 96th overall, in 1990 Entry Draft).

			Regular Season					Playoffs				
Season	Club	Lea	GP	G	A	TP	PIM	GP	G	A	TP	PIM
1989-90	Lethbridge	WHL	72	55	64	119	114	19	9	10	19	18
1990-91a	Lethbridge	WHL	66	61	75	136	154	16	12	17	29	18
1991-92	Peoria	IHL	67	27	45	72	148	10	7	7	14	19

a WHL East First All-Star Team (1991)

RUFF, LINDY CAMERON

Defense/Left wing. Shoots left. 6'2", 201 lbs. Born, Warburg, Alta., February 17, 1960.
(Buffalo's 2nd choice, 32nd overall, in 1979 Entry Draft).

			Regular Season					Playoffs				
Season	Club	Lea	GP	G	A	TP	PIM	GP	G	A	TP	PIM
1977-78	Lethbridge	WHL	66	9	24	33	219	8	2	8	10	4
1978-79	Lethbridge	WHL	24	9	18	27	108	6	0	1	1	0
1979-80	Buffalo	NHL	63	5	14	19	38	8	1	1	2	19
1980-81	Buffalo	NHL	65	8	18	26	121	6	3	1	4	23
1981-82	Buffalo	NHL	79	16	32	48	194	4	0	0	0	28
1982-83	Buffalo	NHL	60	12	17	29	130	10	4	2	6	47
1983-84	Buffalo	NHL	58	14	31	45	101	3	1	0	1	9
1984-85	Buffalo	NHL	39	13	11	24	45	5	2	4	6	15
1985-86	Buffalo	NHL	54	20	12	32	158	....	....	....	....	....
1986-87	Buffalo	NHL	50	6	14	20	74	....	....	....	....	....
1987-88	Buffalo	NHL	77	2	23	25	179	6	0	2	2	23
1988-89	Buffalo	NHL	63	6	11	17	86	....	....	....	....	....
	NY Rangers	NHL	13	0	5	5	31	2	0	0	0	17
1989-90	NY Rangers	NHL	56	3	6	9	80	8	0	3	3	12
1990-91	NY Rangers	NHL	14	0	1	1	27	....	....	....	....	....
1991-92	Rochester	AHL	62	10	24	34	110	13	0	4	4	18
	NHL Totals		691	105	195	300	1264	52	11	13	24	193

Traded to **NY Rangers** by **Buffalo** for NY Rangers' fifth round choice (Richard Smehlik) in 1990 Entry Draft, March 7, 1989.

RUMBLE, DARREN

Defense. Shoots left. 6'1", 200 lbs. Born, Barrie, Ont., January 23, 1969.
(Philadelphia's 1st choice, 20th overall, in 1987 Entry Draft).

			Regular Season					Playoffs				
Season	Club	Lea	GP	G	A	TP	PIM	GP	G	A	TP	PIM
1986-87	Kitchener	OHL	64	11	32	43	44	4	0	1	1	9
1987-88	Kitchener	OHL	55	15	50	65	64	....	....	....	....	....
1988-89	Kitchener	OHL	46	11	28	39	25	5	1	0	1	2
1989-90	Hershey	AHL	57	2	13	15	31	....	....	....	....	....
1990-91	Philadelphia	NHL	3	1	0	1	0	....	....	....	....	....
	Hershey	AHL	73	6	35	41	48	3	0	5	5	2
1991-92	Hershey	AHL	79	12	54	66	118	6	0	3	3	2
	NHL Totals		3	1	0	1	0	....	....	....	....	....

Claimed by **Ottawa** from **Philadelphia** in Expansion Draft, June 18, 1992.

RUOHO, DANIEL

Defense. Shoots left. 6'3", 220 lbs. Born, Madison, WI, June 22, 1970.
(Buffalo's 9th choice, 160th overall, in 1988 Entry Draft).

			Regular Season					Playoffs				
Season	Club	Lea	GP	G	A	TP	PIM	GP	G	A	TP	PIM
1989-90	N. Michigan	WCHA	18	2	4	6	26	....	....	....	....	....
1990-91	N. Michigan	WCHA	6	0	1	1	9	....	....	....	....	....
1991-92	N. Michigan	WCHA	10	2	2	4	26	....	....	....	....	....

RUSHFORTH, PAUL

Center. Shoots right. 6', 189 lbs. Born, Prince George, B.C., April 22, 1974.
(Buffalo's 8th choice, 131st overall, in 1992 Entry Draft).

			Regular Season					Playoffs				
Season	Club	Lea	GP	G	A	TP	PIM	GP	G	A	TP	PIM
1990-91	Ottawa	COJHL	38	14	16	30	58	....	....	....	....	....
1991-92	North Bay	OHL	65	8	11	19	24	19	0	2	2	6

RUSHIN, JOHN

Center. Shoots right. 6'5", 201 lbs. Born, Edina, MN, September 12, 1972.
(NY Rangers' 7th choice, 147th overall, in 1991 Entry Draft).

			Regular Season					Playoffs				
Season	Club	Lea	GP	G	A	TP	PIM	GP	G	A	TP	PIM
1990-91	Kennedy	HS	28	21	22	43	....	....	....	....	....	....
1991-92	Notre Dame	NCAA	17	8	2	10	30	....	....	....	....	....

RUSSELL, CAM

Defense. Shoots left. 6'4", 174 lbs. Born, Halifax, N.S., January 12, 1969.
(Chicago's 3rd choice, 50th overall, in 1987 Entry Draft).

			Regular Season					Playoffs				
Season	Club	Lea	GP	G	A	TP	PIM	GP	G	A	TP	PIM
1985-86	Hull	QMJHL	56	3	4	7	24	15	0	2	2	4
1986-87	Hull	QMJHL	66	3	16	19	119	8	0	1	1	16
1987-88a	Hull	QMJHL	53	9	18	27	141	19	2	5	7	39
1988-89	Hull	QMJHL	66	8	32	40	109	9	2	6	8	6
1989-90	Chicago	NHL	19	0	1	1	27	1	0	0	0	0
	Indianapolis	IHL	46	3	15	18	114	9	0	1	1	24
1990-91	Chicago	NHL	3	0	0	0	5	1	0	0	0	0
	Indianapolis	IHL	53	5	9	14	125	6	0	2	2	30
1991-92	Chicago	NHL	19	0	0	0	34	12	0	2	2	2
	Indianapolis	IHL	41	4	9	13	78	....	....	....	....	....
	NHL Totals		41	0	1	1	66	14	0	2	2	2

a QMJHL Third All-Star Team (1988)

RUSSELL, KERRY

Right wing. Shoots right. 5'11", 164 lbs. Born, Kamloops, B.C., June 23, 1969.
(Hartford's 6th choice, 137th overall, in 1988 Entry Draft).

			Regular Season					Playoffs				
Season	Club	Lea	GP	G	A	TP	PIM	GP	G	A	TP	PIM
1987-88	Michigan State	CCHA	46	16	23	39	50	....	....	....	....	....
1988-89	Michigan State	CCHA	46	5	23	28	50	....	....	....	....	....
1989-90	Michigan State	CCHA	45	15	12	27	62	....	....	....	....	....
1990-91	Michigan State	CCHA	39	20	28	48	36	....	....	....	....	....
1991-92	Springfield	AHL	47	10	14	24	44	5	1	1	2	2

RUUTTU, CHRISTIAN (ROO-TOO)

Center. Shoots left. 5'11", 194 lbs. Born, Lappeenranta, Finland, February 20, 1964.
(Buffalo's 9th choice, 134th overall, in 1983 Entry Draft).

			Regular Season					Playoffs				
Season	Club	Lea	GP	G	A	TP	PIM	GP	G	A	TP	PIM
1982-83	Assat	Fin.	36	15	18	33	34	....	....	....	....	....
1983-84	Assat	Fin.	37	18	42	60	72	9	2	5	7	12
1984-85	Assat	Fin.	32	14	32	46	34	8	1	6	7	8
1985-86	HIFK	Fin.	36	16	38	54	47	10	3	6	9	8
1986-87	**Buffalo**	**NHL**	**76**	**22**	**43**	**65**	**62**	....	....	....	....	....
1987-88	**Buffalo**	**NHL**	**73**	**26**	**45**	**71**	**85**	**6**	**2**	**5**	**7**	**4**
1988-89	**Buffalo**	**NHL**	**67**	**14**	**46**	**60**	**98**	**2**	**0**	**0**	**0**	**2**
1989-90	**Buffalo**	**NHL**	**75**	**19**	**41**	**60**	**66**	**6**	**0**	**0**	**0**	**4**
1990-91	**Buffalo**	**NHL**	**77**	**16**	**34**	**50**	**96**	**6**	**1**	**3**	**4**	**29**
1991-92	**Buffalo**	**NHL**	**70**	**4**	**21**	**25**	**76**	**3**	**0**	**0**	**0**	**6**
	NHL Totals		**438**	**101**	**230**	**331**	**483**	**23**	**3**	**8**	**11**	**45**

Played in NHL All-Star Game (1988)

Traded to **Winnipeg** by **Buffalo** with future considerations for Stephane Beauregard, June 15, 1992. Traded to **Chicago** by **Winnipeg** for Stephane Beauregard, August 10, 1992.

RUZICKA, VLADIMIR (ROO-zheech-kah)

Center. Shoots left. 6'3", 210 lbs. Born, Most, Czechoslovakia, June 6, 1963.
(Toronto's 5th choice, 73rd overall, in 1982 Entry Draft).

			Regular Season					Playoffs				
Season	Club	Lea	GP	G	A	TP	PIM	GP	G	A	TP	PIM
1986-87	CHZ Litvinov	Czech.	32	24	15	39	....	....	....	....	....	....
1987-88	Dukla Trencin	Czech.	34	32	21	53	....	....	....	....	....	....
1988-89	Dukla Trencin	Czech.	45	46	38	84	....	....	....	....	....	....
1989-90	CHZ Litvinov	Czech.	32	21	23	44	....	....	....	....	....	....
	Edmonton	**NHL**	**25**	**11**	**6**	**17**	**10**	....	....	....	....	....
1990-91	**Boston**	**NHL**	**29**	**8**	**8**	**16**	**19**	**17**	**2**	**11**	**13**	**0**
1991-92	**Boston**	**NHL**	**77**	**39**	**36**	**75**	**48**	**13**	**2**	**3**	**5**	**2**
	NHL Totals		**131**	**58**	**50**	**108**	**77**	**30**	**4**	**14**	**18**	**2**

Traded to **Edmonton** by **Toronto** for Edmonton's fourth round choice (Greg Walters) in 1990 Entry Draft, December 21, 1989. Traded to **Boston** by **Edmonton** for Greg Hawgood, October 22, 1990.

RYCHEL, WARREN (RIGH-kuhl)

Left wing. Shoots left. 6', 190 lbs. Born, Tecumseh, Ont., May 12, 1967.

			Regular Season					Playoffs				
Season	Club	Lea	GP	G	A	TP	PIM	GP	G	A	TP	PIM
1984-85	Sudbury	OHL	35	5	8	13	74	....	....	....	....	....
	Guelph	OHL	29	1	3	4	48	....	....	....	....	....
1985-86	Guelph	OHL	38	14	5	19	119	....	....	....	....	....
	Ottawa	OHL	29	11	18	29	54	....	....	....	....	....
1986-87	Ottawa	OHL	28	11	7	18	57	....	....	....	....	....
	Kitchener	OHL	21	5	5	10	39	4	0	0	0	9
1987-88	Peoria	IHL	7	2	1	3	7	....	....	....	....	....
	Saginaw	IHL	51	2	7	9	113	1	0	0	0	0
1988-89	**Chicago**	**NHL**	**2**	**0**	**0**	**0**	**17**	....	....	....	....	....
	Saginaw	IHL	50	15	14	29	226	6	0	0	0	51
1989-90	Indianapolis	IHL	77	23	16	39	374	14	1	3	4	64
1990-91	Indianapolis	IHL	68	33	30	63	338	5	2	1	3	30
	Chicago	**NHL**	....	....	....	....	....	**3**	**1**	**3**	**4**	**2**
1991-92	Moncton	AHL	36	14	15	29	211	....	....	....	....	....
	Kalamazoo	IHL	45	15	20	35	165	8	0	3	3	51
	NHL Totals		**2**	**0**	**0**	**0**	**17**	**3**	**1**	**3**	**4**	**2**

Signed as a free agent by **Chicago**, September 19, 1986. Traded to **Winnipeg** by **Chicago** with Troy Murray for Bryan Marchment and Chris Norton, July 22, 1991. Traded to **Minnesota** by **Winnipeg** for Tony Joseph, December 30, 1991.

RYDMARK, DANIEL (REWD-mahrk)

Center. Shoots left. 5'10", 169 lbs. Born, Vasteras, Sweden, February 23, 1970.
(Los Angeles' 5th choice, 123rd overall, in 1989 Entry Draft).

			Regular Season					Playoffs				
Season	Club	Lea	GP	G	A	TP	PIM	GP	G	A	TP	PIM
1989-90	Farjestad	Swe.	35	9	12	21	20	5	0	0	0	4
1990-91	Malmo	Swe.	39	14	14	28	34	....	....	....	....	....
1991-92	Malmo	Swe.	30	17	16	33	41	7	0	3	3	6

RYMSHA, ANDREW (ANDY)

Defense. Shoots left. 6'3", 210 lbs. Born, St. Catharines, Ont., December 10, 1968.
(St. Louis' 5th choice, 82nd overall, in 1987 Entry Draft).

			Regular Season					Playoffs				
Season	Club	Lea	GP	G	A	TP	PIM	GP	G	A	TP	PIM
1986-87	W. Michigan	CCHA	41	7	12	19	60	....	....	....	....	....
1987-88	W. Michigan	CCHA	42	5	6	11	114	....	....	....	....	....
1988-89	W. Michigan	CCHA	35	3	4	7	139	....	....	....	....	....
1989-90	W. Michigan	CCHA	37	1	10	11	108	....	....	....	....	....
1990-91	Halifax	AHL	12	1	2	3	22	....	....	....	....	....
	Peoria	IHL	45	2	9	11	64	....	....	....	....	....
1991-92	**Quebec**	**NHL**	**6**	**0**	**0**	**0**	**23**	....	....	....	....	....
	Halifax	AHL	44	4	7	11	54	....	....	....	....	....
	New Haven	AHL	16	0	5	5	20	....	....	....	....	....
	NHL Totals		**6**	**0**	**0**	**0**	**23**	....	....	....	....	....

Traded to **Quebec** by **St. Louis** with Herb Raglan and Tony Twist for Darin Kimble, February 4, 1991.

SABOL, SHAUN (SAY-buhl)

Defense. Shoots left. 6'3", 230 lbs. Born, Minneapolis, MN, July 13, 1966.
(Philadelphia's 9th choice, 209th overall, in 1986 Entry Draft).

			Regular Season					Playoffs				
Season	Club	Lea	GP	G	A	TP	PIM	GP	G	A	TP	PIM
1986-87	U. Wisconsin	WCHA	40	7	16	23	98	....	....	....	....	....
1987-88	U. Wisconsin	WCHA	8	4	3	7	10	....	....	....	....	....
	Hershey	AHL	51	1	9	10	66	2	0	0	0	5
1988-89	Hershey	AHL	58	7	11	18	134	12	0	2	2	35
1989-90	**Philadelphia**	**NHL**	**2**	**0**	**0**	**0**	**0**	....	....	....	....	....
	Hershey	AHL	46	6	16	22	49	....	....	....	....	....
1990-91	Hershey	AHL	59	6	13	19	136	7	0	1	1	34
1991-92	Binghamton	AHL	72	5	19	24	123	11	1	2	3	10
	NHL Totals		**2**	**0**	**0**	**0**	**0**	....	....	....	....	....

Traded to **NY Rangers** by **Philadelpia** for future considerations, August 5, 1991.

SABOURIN, KEN

Defense. Shoots left. 6'3", 205 lbs. Born, Scarborough, Ont., April 28, 1966.
(Calgary's 2nd choice, 33rd overall, in 1984 Entry Draft).

			Regular Season					Playoffs				
Season	Club	Lea	GP	G	A	TP	PIM	GP	G	A	TP	PIM
1982-83	S.S. Marie	OHL	58	0	8	8	90	10	0	0	0	14
1983-84	S.S. Marie	OHL	63	7	14	21	157	9	0	1	1	25
1984-85	S.S. Marie	OHL	63	5	19	24	139	16	1	4	5	10
1985-86	Moncton	AHL	3	0	0	0	0	6	0	1	1	2
	S.S. Marie	OHL	25	1	5	6	77	....	....	....	....	....
	Cornwall	OHL	37	3	12	15	94	6	1	2	3	6
1986-87	Moncton	AHL	75	1	10	11	166	6	0	1	1	27
1987-88	Salt Lake	IHL	71	2	8	10	186	16	1	6	7	57
1988-89	**Calgary**	**NHL**	**6**	**0**	**1**	**1**	**26**	**1**	**0**	**0**	**0**	**0**
	Salt Lake	IHL	74	2	18	20	197	11	0	1	1	26
1989-90	**Calgary**	**NHL**	**5**	**0**	**0**	**0**	**10**	....	....	....	....	....
	Salt Lake	IHL	76	5	19	24	336	11	0	2	2	40
1990-91	**Calgary**	**NHL**	**16**	**1**	**3**	**4**	**36**	....	....	....	....	....
	Salt Lake	IHL	28	2	15	17	77	....	....	....	....	....
	Washington	**NHL**	**28**	**1**	**4**	**5**	**81**	**11**	**0**	**0**	**0**	**34**
1991-92	**Washington**	**NHL**	**19**	**0**	**0**	**0**	**48**	....	....	....	....	....
	Baltimore	AHL	30	3	8	11	106	....	....	....	....	....
	NHL Totals		**74**	**2**	**8**	**10**	**201**	**12**	**0**	**0**	**0**	**34**

Traded to **Washington** by **Calgary** for Paul Fenton, January 24, 1991.

SACCO, DAVID

Defense. Shoots right. 6'1", 190 lbs. Born, Malden, MA, July 31, 1970.
(Toronto's 9th choice, 195th overall, in 1988 Entry Draft).

			Regular Season					Playoffs				
Season	Club	Lea	GP	G	A	TP	PIM	GP	G	A	TP	PIM
1988-89	Boston U.	H.E.	35	14	29	43	40	....	....	....	....	....
1989-90	Boston U.	H.E.	3	0	4	4	2	....	....	....	....	....
1990-91	Boston U.	H.E.	40	21	40	61	24	....	....	....	....	....
1991-92ab	Boston U.	H.E.	34	13	32	45	30	....	....	....	....	....

a NCAA East First All-Star Team (1992)
b Hockey East First All-Star Team (1992)

SACCO, JOSEPH (JOE)

Left wing. Shoots right. 6'1", 180 lbs. Born, Medford, MA, February 4, 1969.
(Toronto's 4th choice, 71st overall, in 1987 Entry Draft).

			Regular Season					Playoffs				
Season	Club	Lea	GP	G	A	TP	PIM	GP	G	A	TP	PIM
1987-88	Boston U.	H.E.	34	16	20	36	40	....	....	....	....	....
1988-89	Boston U.	H.E.	33	21	19	40	66	....	....	....	....	....
1989-90	Boston U.	H.E.	44	28	24	52	70	....	....	....	....	....
1990-91	**Toronto**	**NHL**	**20**	**0**	**5**	**5**	**2**	....	....	....	....	....
	Newmarket	AHL	49	18	17	35	24	....	....	....	....	....
1991-92	U.S. National	....	50	11	26	37	61	....	....	....	....	....
	U.S. Olympic	....	8	0	2	2	0	....	....	....	....	....
	Toronto	**NHL**	**17**	**7**	**4**	**11**	**4**	....	....	....	....	....
	St. John's	AHL	....	....	....	....	....	1	1	1	2	0
	NHL Totals		**37**	**7**	**9**	**16**	**6**	....	....	....	....	....

SAGISSOR, THOMAS (TOM)

Right wing. Shoots right. 5'11", 202 lbs. Born, Hastings, MN, September 12, 1967.
(Montreal's 7th choice, 96th overall, in 1985 Entry Draft).

			Regular Season					Playoffs				
Season	Club	Lea	GP	G	A	TP	PIM	GP	G	A	TP	PIM
1986-87	U. Wisconsin	WCHA	41	1	4	5	32	....	....	....	....	....
1987-88	U. Wisconsin	WCHA	38	4	5	9	65	....	....	....	....	....
1988-89	U. Wisconsin	WCHA	40	7	11	18	119	....	....	....	....	....
1989-90	U. Wisconsin	WCHA	43	19	28	47	122	....	....	....	....	....
1990-91	Fredericton	AHL	52	8	13	21	99	....	....	....	....	....
1991-92	Fredericton	AHL	57	12	15	27	111	3	0	2	2	2

SAILYNOJA, KEIJO

Left wing. Shoots left. 6'2", 187 lbs. Born, Vantaa, Finland, February 17, 1970.
(Edmonton's 6th choice, 122nd overall, in 1990 Entry Draft).

			Regular Season					Playoffs				
Season	Club	Lea	GP	G	A	TP	PIM	GP	G	A	TP	PIM
1989-90	Jokerit	Fin.	41	15	13	28	8	....	....	....	....	....
1990-91	Jokerit	Fin.	44	21	25	46	14	....	....	....	....	....
1991-92	Jokerit	Fin.	42	21	25	46	14	10	5	6	11	2

ST. AMOUR, MARTIN

Left wing. Shoots left. 6'3", 194 lbs. Born, Montreal, Que., January 30, 1970.
(Montreal's 2nd choice, 34th overall, in 1988 Entry Draft).

			Regular Season					Playoffs				
Season	Club	Lea	GP	G	A	TP	PIM	GP	G	A	TP	PIM
1987-88	Verdun	QMJHL	61	20	50	70	111	....	....	....	....	....
1988-89	Verdun	QMJHL	28	19	17	36	87	....	....	....	....	....
	Trois-Rivières	QMJHL	26	8	21	29	69	4	1	2	3	0
1989-90	Trois-Rivières	QMJHL	60	57	79	136	162	7	7	9	16	19
	Sherbrooke	AHL	....	....	....	....	....	1	0	0	0	0
1990-91	Fredericton	AHL	45	13	16	29	51	1	0	0	0	0
1991-92	Cincinnati	ECHL	60	44	44	88	183	9	4	9	13	18

ST. JACQUES, KEVIN

Left wing. Shoots right. 5'11", 190 lbs. Born, Edmonton, Alta., February 25, 1971.
(Chicago's 6th choice, 112th overall, in 1991 Entry Draft).

			Regular Season					Playoffs				
Season	Club	Lea	GP	G	A	TP	PIM	GP	G	A	TP	PIM
1990-91	Lethbridge	WHL	72	45	63	108	64	16	13	10	23	20
1991-92	Lethbridge	WHL	71	65	75	140	159	3	2	2	4	2

ST. LAURENT, JEFFREY

Right wing. Shoots right. 6'2", 175 lbs. Born, Sanford, ME, May 16, 1971.
(Toronto's 10th choice, 171st overall, in 1989 Entry Draft).

			Regular Season					Playoffs				
Season	Club	Lea	GP	G	A	TP	PIM	GP	G	A	TP	PIM
1989-90	N. Hampshire	H.E.				DID NOT PLAY						
1990-91	N. Hampshire	H.E.	5	0	1	1	4	....	....	....	....	....
1991-92						DID NOT PLAY						

ST. PIERRE, DAVID

Center. Shoots right. 6', 180 lbs. Born, Montreal, Que., March 22, 1972.
(Calgary's 9th choice, 173rd overall, in 1991 Entry Draft).

			Regular Season					Playoffs				
Season	Club	Lea	GP	G	A	TP	PIM	GP	G	A	TP	PIM
1990-91	Longueuil	QMJHL	66	34	45	79	51	8	4	4	8	8
1991-92	Verdun	QMJHL	69	40	55	95	98	15	3	6	9	15

SAKIC, BRIAN

Center. Shoots left. 5'10", 156 lbs. Born, Burnaby, B.C., September 4, 1971.
(Washington's 5th choice, 93rd overall, in 1990 Entry Draft).

			Regular Season					Playoffs				
Season	Club	Lea	GP	G	A	TP	PIM	GP	G	A	TP	PIM
1987-88	Swift Current	WHL	65	12	37	49	12	9	3	8	11	0
1988-89	Swift Current	WHL	71	36	64	100	28	12	9	9	18	8
1989-90a	Swift Current	WHL	8	6	7	13	4	....	....	....	....	....
a	Tri-Cities	WHL	58	47	92	139	8	....	....	....	....	....
1990-91	Tri-Cities	WHL	69	40	*122	162	19	5	2	3	5	4
1991-92	Tri-Cities	WHL	72	45	83	128	35	5	4	4	8	14

a WHL West Second All-Star Team (1990)

SAKIC, JOE (SA-kik)

Center. Shoots left. 5'11", 185 lbs. Born, Burnaby, B.C., July 7, 1969.
(Quebec's 2nd choice, 15th overall, in 1987 Entry Draft).

			Regular Season					Playoffs				
Season	Club	Lea	GP	G	A	TP	PIM	GP	G	A	TP	PIM
1986-87ab	Swift Current	WHL	72	60	73	133	31	4	0	1	1	0
1987-88acd	Swift Current	WHL	64	*78	82	*160	64	10	11	13	24	12
1988-89	**Quebec**	**NHL**	**70**	**23**	**39**	**62**	**24**	....	....	....	....	....
1989-90	**Quebec**	**NHL**	**80**	**39**	**63**	**102**	**27**	....	....	....	....	....
1990-91	**Quebec**	**NHL**	**80**	**48**	**61**	**109**	**24**	....	....	....	....	....
1991-92	**Quebec**	**NHL**	**69**	**29**	**65**	**94**	**20**	....	....	....	....	....
	NHL Totals		**299**	**139**	**228**	**367**	**95**	....	....	....	....	....

a WHL Player of the Year (1987, 1988)
b WHL Rookie of the Year (1987)
c Canadian Major Junior Player of the Year (1988)
d WHL East All-Star Team (1988)

Played in NHL All-Star Game (1990, 1991, 1992)

SALLE, JOHAN

Defense. Shoots left. 6'1", 187 lbs. Born, Orebro, Sweden, February 21, 1967.
(Philadelphia's 9th choice, 161st overall, in 1988 Entry Draft).

			Regular Season					Playoffs				
Season	Club	Lea	GP	G	A	TP	PIM	GP	G	A	TP	PIM
1987-88	Malmo	Swe.	36	9	4	13	48	....	....	....	....	....
1988-89	Malmo	Swe.	18	6	10	16	32	....	....	....	....	....
1989-90	Malmo	Swe.	32	12	16	28	98	....	....	....	....	....
1990-91	Malmo	Swe.	38	4	5	9	34	....	....	....	....	....
1991-92	Malmo	Swe.	29	2	5	7	62	10	2	0	2	12

SALMING, ANDERS BORJE (SAHL-mihng, BOHR-yuh)

Defense. Shoots left. 6'1", 193 lbs. Born, Kiruna, Sweden, April 17, 1951.

			Regular Season					Playoffs				
Season	Club	Lea	GP	G	A	TP	PIM	GP	G	A	TP	PIM
1970-71	Brynas	Swe.	27	2	6	8	22	....	....	....	....	....
1971-72	Brynas	Swe.	28	1	5	6	50	....	....	....	....	....
1972-73	Brynas	Swe.	26	5	4	9	34	....	....	....	....	....
1973-74	**Toronto**	**NHL**	**76**	**5**	**34**	**39**	**48**	**4**	**0**	**1**	**1**	**4**
1974-75a	**Toronto**	**NHL**	**60**	**12**	**25**	**37**	**34**	**7**	**0**	**4**	**4**	**6**
1975-76a	**Toronto**	**NHL**	**78**	**16**	**41**	**57**	**70**	**10**	**3**	**4**	**7**	**9**
1976-77b	**Toronto**	**NHL**	**76**	**12**	**66**	**78**	**46**	**9**	**3**	**6**	**9**	**6**
1977-78a	**Toronto**	**NHL**	**80**	**16**	**60**	**76**	**70**	**6**	**2**	**2**	**4**	**6**
1978-79a	**Toronto**	**NHL**	**78**	**17**	**56**	**73**	**76**	**6**	**0**	**1**	**1**	**8**
1979-80a	**Toronto**	**NHL**	**74**	**19**	**52**	**71**	**94**	**3**	**1**	**1**	**2**	**2**
1980-81	**Toronto**	**NHL**	**72**	**5**	**61**	**66**	**154**	**3**	**0**	**2**	**2**	**4**
1981-82	**Toronto**	**NHL**	**69**	**12**	**44**	**56**	**170**	....	....	....	....	....
1982-83	**Toronto**	**NHL**	**69**	**7**	**38**	**45**	**104**	**4**	**1**	**4**	**5**	**10**
1983-84	**Toronto**	**NHL**	**68**	**5**	**38**	**43**	**92**	....	....	....	....	....
1984-85	**Toronto**	**NHL**	**73**	**6**	**33**	**39**	**76**	....	....	....	....	....
1985-86	**Toronto**	**NHL**	**41**	**7**	**15**	**22**	**48**	**10**	**1**	**6**	**7**	**14**
1986-87	**Toronto**	**NHL**	**56**	**4**	**16**	**20**	**42**	**13**	**0**	**3**	**3**	**14**
1987-88	**Toronto**	**NHL**	**66**	**2**	**24**	**26**	**82**	**6**	**1**	**3**	**4**	**8**
1988-89	**Toronto**	**NHL**	**63**	**3**	**17**	**20**	**86**	....	....	....	....	....
1989-90	**Detroit**	**NHL**	**49**	**2**	**17**	**19**	**52**	....	....	....	....	....
1990-91	AIK	Swe.	36	4	8	12	46	....	....	....	....	....
1991-92	AIK	Swe.	38	6	14	20	100	....	....	....	....	....
	NHL Totals		**1148**	**150**	**637**	**787**	**1344**	**81**	**12**	**37**	**49**	**91**

a NHL Second All-Star Team (1975, 1976, 1978, 1979, 1980)
b NHL First All-Star Team (1977)

Played in NHL All-Star Game (1976-78)

Signed as a free agent by **Toronto**, May 12, 1973. Signed as a free agent by **Detroit**, June 12, 1989.

SALO, VESA (SAH-loh)

Defense. Shoots left. 6'3", 198 lbs. Born, Rauma, Finland, April 17, 1965.
(NY Rangers' 3rd choice, 49th overall, in 1983 Entry Draft).

			Regular Season					Playoffs				
Season	Club	Lea	GP	G	A	TP	PIM	GP	G	A	TP	PIM
1986-87	Luko	Fin.	44	4	22	26	34	....	....	....	....	....
1987-88	Ilves	Fin.	43	8	15	23	42	4	0	1	1	4
1988-89	Tappara	Fin.	42	7	14	21	46	8	0	2	2	8
1989-90	Tappara	Fin.	35	2	12	14	22	7	0	2	2	4
1990-91	Tappara	Fin.	44	9	16	25	32	3	0	3	3	6
1991-92	Tappara	Fin.	39	2	16	18	24	....	....	....	....	....

SAMUELSSON, KJELL (suh-MOO-ehl-suhn, SHELL)

Defense. Shoots right. 6'6", 235 lbs. Born, Tyngsryd, Sweden, October 18, 1958.
(NY Rangers' 5th choice, 119th overall, in 1984 Entry Draft).

			Regular Season					Playoffs				
Season	Club	Lea	GP	G	A	TP	PIM	GP	G	A	TP	PIM
1982-83	Tyngsryd	Swe.2	32	11	6	17	57	....	....	....	....	....
1983-84	Leksand	Swe.	36	6	7	13	59	....	....	....	....	....
1984-85	Leksand	Swe.	35	9	5	14	34	....	....	....	....	....
1985-86	**NY Rangers**	**NHL**	**9**	**0**	**0**	**0**	**10**	**9**	**0**	**1**	**1**	**8**
	New Haven	AHL	56	6	21	27	87	3	0	0	0	10
1986-87	**NY Rangers**	**NHL**	**30**	**2**	**6**	**8**	**50**	....	....	....	....	....
	Philadelphia	**NHL**	**46**	**1**	**6**	**7**	**86**	**26**	**0**	**4**	**4**	**25**
1987-88	**Philadelphia**	**NHL**	**74**	**6**	**24**	**30**	**184**	**7**	**2**	**5**	**7**	**23**
1988-89	**Philadelphia**	**NHL**	**69**	**3**	**14**	**17**	**140**	**19**	**1**	**3**	**4**	**24**
1989-90	**Philadelphia**	**NHL**	**66**	**5**	**17**	**22**	**91**	....	....	....	....	....
1990-91	**Philadelphia**	**NHL**	**78**	**9**	**19**	**28**	**82**	....	....	....	....	....
1991-92	**Philadelphia**	**NHL**	**54**	**4**	**9**	**13**	**76**	....	....	....	....	....
	Pittsburgh	**NHL**	**20**	**1**	**2**	**3**	**34**	**15**	**0**	**3**	**3**	**12**
	NHL Totals		**446**	**31**	**97**	**128**	**753**	**76**	**3**	**16**	**19**	**92**

Played in NHL All-Star Game (1988)

Traded to **Philadelphia** by **NY Rangers** with NY Rangers' second round choice (Patrik Juhlin) in 1989 Entry Draft for Bob Froese, December 18, 1986. Traded to **Pittsburgh** by **Philadelphia** with Rick Tocchet and Ken Wregget for Mark Recchi, Brian Benning and Los Angeles' first round choice in 1992 Entry Draft (Jason Bowen) previously acquired by Pittsburgh in the Paul Coffey trade, February 19, 1992.

SAMUELSSON, MORGAN (suh-MOO-ehl-suhn)

Left wing. Shoots left. 5'9", 169 lbs. Born, Boden, Sweden, April 6, 1968.
(Quebec's 7th choice, 123rd overall, in 1986 Entry Draft).

			Regular Season					Playoffs				
Season	Club	Lea	GP	G	A	TP	PIM	GP	G	A	TP	PIM
1988-89	Lulea	Swe.	36	14	19	33	14	....	....	....	....	....
1989-90	Lulea	Swe.	29	4	10	14	30	5	1	0	1	4
1990-91	Sodertalje	Swe.	40	23	15	38	14	....	....	....	....	....
1991-92	Sodertalje	Swe.	22	7	11	18	12	....	....	....	....	....

SAMUELSSON, ULF (suh-MOO-ehl-suhn)

Defense. Shoots left. 6'1", 195 lbs. Born, Fagersta, Sweden, March 26, 1964.
(Hartford's 4th choice, 67th overall, in 1982 Entry Draft).

			Regular Season					Playoffs				
Season	Club	Lea	GP	G	A	TP	PIM	GP	G	A	TP	PIM
1981-82	Leksand	Swe.	31	3	1	4	40	....	....	....	....	....
1982-83	Leksand	Swe.	33	9	6	15	72	....	....	....	....	....
1983-84	Leksand	Swe.	36	5	11	16	53	....	....	....	....	....
1984-85	**Hartford**	**NHL**	**41**	**2**	**6**	**8**	**83**	....	....	....	....	....
	Binghamton	AHL	36	5	11	16	92	....	....	....	....	....
1985-86	**Hartford**	**NHL**	**80**	**5**	**19**	**24**	**174**	**10**	**1**	**2**	**3**	**38**
1986-87	**Hartford**	**NHL**	**78**	**2**	**31**	**33**	**162**	**5**	**0**	**1**	**1**	**41**
1987-88	**Hartford**	**NHL**	**76**	**8**	**33**	**41**	**159**	**5**	**0**	**0**	**0**	**8**
1988-89	**Hartford**	**NHL**	**71**	**9**	**26**	**35**	**181**	**4**	**0**	**2**	**2**	**4**
1989-90	**Hartford**	**NHL**	**55**	**2**	**11**	**13**	**177**	**7**	**1**	**0**	**1**	**2**
1990-91	**Hartford**	**NHL**	**62**	**3**	**18**	**21**	**174**	....	....	....	....	....
	Pittsburgh	**NHL**	**14**	**1**	**4**	**5**	**37**	**20**	**3**	**2**	**5**	**34**
1991-92	**Pittsburgh**	**NHL**	**62**	**1**	**14**	**15**	**206**	**21**	**0**	**2**	**2**	**39**
	NHL Totals		**539**	**33**	**162**	**195**	**1353**	**72**	**5**	**9**	**14**	**166**

Traded to **Pittsburgh** by **Hartford** with Ron Francis and Grant Jennings for John Cullen, Jeff Parker and Zarley Zalapski, March 4, 1991.

SANDELIN, SCOTT (SAN-duh-lin)

Defense. Shoots right. 6', 200 lbs. Born, Hibbing, MN, August 8, 1964.
(Montreal's 5th choice, 40th overall, in 1982 Entry Draft).

			Regular Season					Playoffs				
Season	Club	Lea	GP	G	A	TP	PIM	GP	G	A	TP	PIM
1982-83	North Dakota	WCHA	21	0	4	4	10	....	....	....	....	....
1983-84	North Dakota	WCHA	41	4	23	27	24	....	....	....	....	....
1984-85	North Dakota	WCHA	38	4	17	21	30	....	....	....	....	....
1985-86ab	North Dakota	WCHA	40	7	31	38	38	....	....	....	....	....
	Sherbrooke	AHL	6	0	2	2	2	....	....	....	....	....
1986-87	**Montreal**	**NHL**	**1**	**0**	**0**	**0**	**0**	....	....	....	....	....
	Sherbrooke	AHL	74	7	22	29	35	16	2	4	6	2
1987-88	**Montreal**	**NHL**	**8**	**0**	**1**	**1**	**2**	....	....	....	....	....
	Sherbrooke	AHL	58	8	14	22	35	4	0	2	2	0
1988-89	Sherbrooke	AHL	12	0	9	9	8	....	....	....	....	....
	Hershey	AHL	39	6	9	15	38	8	2	1	3	4
1989-90	Hershey	AHL	70	4	27	31	38	....	....	....	....	....
1990-91	**Philadelphia**	**NHL**	**15**	**0**	**3**	**3**	**0**	....	....	....	....	....
	Hershey	AHL	39	3	10	13	21	7	1	2	3	0
1991-92	**Minnesota**	**NHL**	**1**	**0**	**0**	**0**	**0**	....	....	....	....	....
	Kalamazoo	IHL	49	3	18	21	32	11	1	1	2	2
	NHL Totals		**25**	**0**	**4**	**4**	**2**	....	....	....	....	....

a NCAA West Second All-Star Team (1986)
b WCHA First All-Star Team (1986)

Traded to **Philadelphia** by **Montreal** for the rights to J.J. Daigneault, November 7, 1988. Signed as a free agent by **Minnesota**, August 12, 1991.

SANDERSON, GEOFF

Center. Shoots left. 6', 185 lbs. Born, Hay River, N.W.T., February 1, 1972.
(Hartford's 2nd choice, 36th overall, in 1990 Entry Draft).

			Regular Season					Playoffs				
Season	Club	Lea	GP	G	A	TP	PIM	GP	G	A	TP	PIM
1988-89	Swift Current	WHL	58	17	11	28	16	12	3	5	8	6
1989-90	Swift Current	WHL	70	32	62	94	56	4	1	4	5	8
1990-91	**Hartford**	**NHL**	**2**	**1**	**0**	**1**	**0**	**3**	**0**	**0**	**0**	**0**
	Swift Current	WHL	70	62	50	112	57	3	1	2	3	4
	Springfield	AHL	....	....	....	....	....	1	0	0	0	2
1991-92	**Hartford**	**NHL**	**64**	**13**	**18**	**31**	**18**	**7**	**0**	**1**	**1**	**2**
	NHL Totals		**66**	**14**	**18**	**32**	**18**	**10**	**0**	**1**	**1**	**2**

SANDLAK, JIM

Right wing. Shoots right. 6'4", 219 lbs. Born, Kitchener, Ont., December 12, 1966.
(Vancouver's 1st choice, 4th overall, in 1985 Entry Draft).

			Regular Season					Playoffs				
Season	Club	Lea	GP	G	A	TP	PIM	GP	G	A	TP	PIM
1983-84	London	OHL	68	23	18	41	143	8	1	11	12	13
1984-85a	London	OHL	58	40	24	64	128	8	3	2	5	14
1985-86	**Vancouver**	**NHL**	**23**	**1**	**3**	**4**	**10**	**3**	**0**	**1**	**1**	**0**
	London	OHL	16	8	14	22	38	5	2	3	5	24
1986-87b	**Vancouver**	**NHL**	**78**	**15**	**21**	**36**	**66**	....	....	....	....	....
1987-88	**Vancouver**	**NHL**	**49**	**16**	**15**	**31**	**81**	....	....	....	....	....
	Fredericton	AHL	24	10	15	25	47	....	....	....	....	....
1988-89	**Vancouver**	**NHL**	**72**	**20**	**20**	**40**	**99**	**6**	**1**	**1**	**2**	**2**
1989-90	**Vancouver**	**NHL**	**70**	**15**	**8**	**23**	**104**	....	....	....	....	....
1990-91	**Vancouver**	**NHL**	**59**	**7**	**6**	**13**	**125**	....	....	....	....	....
1991-92	**Vancouver**	**NHL**	**66**	**16**	**24**	**40**	**176**	**13**	**4**	**6**	**10**	**22**
	NHL Totals		**417**	**90**	**97**	**187**	**661**	**22**	**5**	**8**	**13**	**24**

a OHL Third All-Star Team (1985)
b NHL All-Rookie Team (1987)

SANDSTROM, TOMAS (SAND-struhm)

Right wing. Shoots left. 6'2", 200 lbs. Born, Jakobstad, Finland, September 4, 1964.
(NY Rangers' 2nd choice, 36th overall, in 1982 Entry Draft).

			Regular Season					Playoffs				
Season	Club	Lea	GP	G	A	TP	PIM	GP	G	A	TP	PIM
1981-82	Fagersta	Swe.2	34	19	16	35	81	....	....	....	....	....
1982-83	Brynas	Swe.	36	22	14	36	50	....	....	....	....	....
1983-84	Brynas	Swe.	34	20	10	30	81	....	....	....	....	....
1984-85a	**NY Rangers**	**NHL**	**74**	**29**	**29**	**58**	**51**	**3**	**0**	**2**	**2**	**0**
1985-86	**NY Rangers**	**NHL**	**73**	**25**	**29**	**54**	**109**	**16**	**4**	**6**	**10**	**20**
1986-87	**NY Rangers**	**NHL**	**64**	**40**	**34**	**74**	**60**	**6**	**1**	**2**	**3**	**20**
1987-88	**NY Rangers**	**NHL**	**69**	**28**	**40**	**68**	**95**	....	....	....	....	....
1988-89	**NY Rangers**	**NHL**	**79**	**32**	**56**	**88**	**148**	**4**	**3**	**2**	**5**	**12**
1989-90	**NY Rangers**	**NHL**	**48**	**19**	**19**	**38**	**100**	....	....	....	....	....
	Los Angeles	**NHL**	**28**	**13**	**20**	**33**	**28**	**10**	**5**	**4**	**9**	**19**
1990-91	**Los Angeles**	**NHL**	**68**	**45**	**44**	**89**	**106**	**10**	**4**	**4**	**8**	**14**
1991-92	**Los Angeles**	**NHL**	**49**	**17**	**22**	**39**	**70**	**6**	**0**	**3**	**3**	**8**
	NHL Totals		**552**	**248**	**293**	**541**	**767**	**55**	**17**	**23**	**40**	**93**

a NHL All-Rookie Team (1985)
Played in NHL All-Star Game (1988, 1991)
Traded to **Los Angeles** by **NY Rangers** with Tony Granato for Bernie Nicholls, January 20, 1990.

SANDSTROM, ULF (SAND-struhm)

Right wing. Shoots right. 5'11", 178 lbs. Born, Fagerstad, Sweden, April 24, 1967.
(Chicago's 5th choice, 92nd overall, in 1987 Entry Draft).

			Regular Season					Playoffs				
Season	Club	Lea	GP	G	A	TP	PIM	GP	G	A	TP	PIM
1986-87	MoDo	Swe.	25	2	4	6	14	6	3	0	3	0
1987-88	MoDo	Swe.	38	26	9	35	12	....	....	....	....	....
1988-89	MoDo	Swe.	39	19	14	33	16	....	....	....	....	....
1989-90	MoDo	Swe.	18	6	4	10	2	....	....	....	....	....
1990-91	Lulea	Swe.	37	4	5	9	4	....	....	....	....	....
1991-92	Lulea	Swe.	40	4	4	8	8	2	0	0	0	0

SANDWITH, TERRAN

Defense. Shoots left. 6'4", 210 lbs. Born, Stoney Plain, Alta., April 17, 1972.
(Philadelphia's 4th choice, 42nd overall, in 1990 Entry Draft).

			Regular Season					Playoffs				
Season	Club	Lea	GP	G	A	TP	PIM	GP	G	A	TP	PIM
1988-89	Tri-Cities	WHL	31	0	0	0	29	6	0	0	0	4
1989-90	Tri-Cities	WHL	70	4	14	18	92	7	0	2	2	14
1990-91	Tri-Cities	WHL	46	5	17	22	132	7	1	0	1	14
1991-92	Brandon	WHL	41	6	14	20	145	....	....	....	....	....
	Saskatoon	WHL	18	2	5	7	53	....	....	....	....	....

SANGSTER, ROBERT (ROB)

Left wing. Shoots left. 6'2", 200 lbs. Born, Kitchener, Ont., May 2, 1969.
(Vancouver's 6th choice, 155th overall, in 1989 Entry Draft).

			Regular Season					Playoffs				
Season	Club	Lea	GP	G	A	TP	PIM	GP	G	A	TP	PIM
1987-88	Kitchener	OHL	58	2	7	9	196	4	0	1	1	12
1988-89	Kitchener	OHL	64	10	25	35	337	5	1	0	1	12
1989-90	Milwaukee	IHL	1	0	0	0	4	....	....	....	....	....
	Kitchener	OHL	24	6	18	24	151	....	....	....	....	....
	Ottawa	OHL	21	2	8	10	100	1	0	0	0	7
1990-91	Roanoke Valley	ECHL	38	2	6	8	331	....	....	....	....	....
1991-92	Columbus	ECHL	15	3	5	8	158	....	....	....	....	....

SANIPASS, EVERETT

Left wing. Shoots left. 6'2", 204 lbs. Born, Big Cove, N.B., February 13, 1968.
(Chicago's 1st choice, 14th overall, in 1986 Entry Draft).

			Regular Season					Playoffs				
Season	Club	Lea	GP	G	A	TP	PIM	GP	G	A	TP	PIM
1985-86	Verdun	QMJHL	67	23	66	89	320	5	0	2	2	16
1986-87	**Chicago**	**NHL**	**7**	**1**	**3**	**4**	**2**	....	....	....	....	....
a	Verdun	QMJHL	23	17	34	51	165	....	....	....	....	....
	Granby	QMJHL	12	17	14	31	55	8	6	4	10	48
1987-88	**Chicago**	**NHL**	**57**	**8**	**12**	**20**	**126**	**2**	**2**	**0**	**2**	**2**
1988-89	**Chicago**	**NHL**	**50**	**6**	**9**	**15**	**164**	**3**	**0**	**0**	**0**	**2**
	Saginaw	IHL	23	9	12	21	76	....	....	....	....	....
1989-90	**Chicago**	**NHL**	**12**	**2**	**2**	**4**	**17**	....	....	....	....	....
	Indianapolis	IHL	33	15	13	28	121	....	....	....	....	....
	Quebec	**NHL**	**9**	**3**	**3**	**6**	**8**	....	....	....	....	....
1990-91	**Quebec**	**NHL**	**29**	**5**	**5**	**10**	**41**	....	....	....	....	....
	Halifax	AHL	14	11	7	18	41	....	....	....	....	....
1991-92	Halifax	AHL	7	3	5	8	31	....	....	....	....	....
	NHL Totals		**164**	**25**	**34**	**59**	**358**	**5**	**2**	**0**	**2**	**4**

a QMJHL First All-Star Team (1987)
Traded to **Quebec** by **Chicago** with Mario Doyon and Dan Vincelette for Greg Millen, Michel Goulet and Quebec's sixth round choice (Kevin St. Jacques) in 1991 Entry Draft, March 5, 1990.

SARAULT, YVES

Left wing. Shoots left. 6'1", 170 lbs. Born, Valleyfield, Que., December 23, 1972.
(Montreal's 3rd choice, 61st overall, in 1991 Entry Draft).

			Regular Season					Playoffs				
Season	Club	Lea	GP	G	A	TP	PIM	GP	G	A	TP	PIM
1989-90	Victoriaville	QMJHL	70	12	28	40	140	16	0	3	3	26
1990-91	St-Jean	QMJHL	56	22	24	46	113	....	....	....	....	....
1991-92a	St-Jean	QMJHL	50	28	38	66	96	....	....	....	....	....
a	Trois-Rivières	QMJHL	18	15	14	29	12	15	10	10	20	18

a QMJHL Second All-Star Team (1992)

SATARDALEN, JEFF

Right wing. Shoots right. 6'1", 180 lbs. Born, Superior, WI, July 8, 1969.
(NY Islanders' 8th choice, 160th overall, in 1987 Entry Draft).

			Regular Season					Playoffs				
Season	Club	Lea	GP	G	A	TP	PIM	GP	G	A	TP	PIM
1988-89	St. Cloud	NCAA	35	17	19	36	22	....	....	....	....	....
1989-90	St. Cloud	NCAA	38	24	33	57	34	....	....	....	....	....
1990-91	St. Cloud	WCHA	38	21	20	41	24	....	....	....	....	....
1991-92	St. Cloud	WCHA	37	16	29	45	50	....	....	....	....	....

SAUNDERS, MATTHEW (MATT)

Left wing. Shoots left. 6', 180 lbs. Born, Ottawa, Ont., July 17, 1970.
(Chicago's 8th choice, 195th overall, in 1989 Entry Draft).

			Regular Season					Playoffs				
Season	Club	Lea	GP	G	A	TP	PIM	GP	G	A	TP	PIM
1988-89	Northeastern	H.E	26	8	9	17	14	....	....	....	....	....
1989-90	Northeastern	H.E	35	19	21	40	51	....	....	....	....	....
1990-91	Northeastern	H.E.	29	13	12	25	36	....	....	....	....	....
1991-92	Northeastern	H.E.	35	8	17	25	38	....	....	....	....	....

SAVAGE, BRIAN

Center. Shoots left. 6'1", 195 lbs. Born, Sudbury, Ont., February 24, 1971.
(Montreal's 8th choice, 171st overall, in 1991 Entry Draft).

			Regular Season					Playoffs				
Season	Club	Lea	GP	G	A	TP	PIM	GP	G	A	TP	PIM
1990-91	Miami-Ohio	CCHA	28	5	6	11	26	....	....	....	....	....
1991-92	Miami-Ohio	CCHA	40	24	16	40	43	....	....	....	....	....

SAVAGE, JOEL

Right wing. Shoots right. 5'11", 205 lbs. Born, Surrey, B.C., December 25, 1969.
(Buffalo's 1st choice, 13th overall, in 1988 Entry Draft).

			Regular Season					Playoffs				
Season	Club	Lea	GP	G	A	TP	PIM	GP	G	A	TP	PIM
1986-87	Victoria	WHL	68	14	13	27	48	5	2	0	2	0
1987-88	Victoria	WHL	69	37	32	69	73	....	....	....	....	....
1988-89	Victoria	WHL	60	17	30	47	95	6	1	1	2	8
1989-90	Rochester	AHL	43	6	7	13	39	5	0	1	1	4
1990-91	**Buffalo**	**NHL**	**3**	**0**	**1**	**1**	**0**	....	....	....	....	....
	Rochester	AHL	61	25	19	44	45	15	3	3	6	8
1991-92	Rochester	AHL	59	8	14	22	39	9	2	0	2	8
	NHL Totals		**3**	**0**	**1**	**1**	**0**	....	....	....	....	....

SAVAGE, REGINALD (REGGIE)

Center. Shoots left. 5'10", 187 lbs. Born, Montreal, Que., May 1, 1970.
(Washington's 1st choice, 15th overall, in 1988 Entry Draft).

			Regular Season					Playoffs				
Season	Club	Lea	GP	G	A	TP	PIM	GP	G	A	TP	PIM
1987-88	Victoriaville	QMJHL	68	68	54	122	77	5	2	3	5	8
1988-89	Victoriaville	QMJHL	54	58	55	113	178	16	15	13	28	52
1989-90	Victoriaville	QMJHL	63	51	43	94	79	16	13	10	23	40
1990-91	**Washington**	**NHL**	**1**	**0**	**0**	**0**	**0**	....	....	....	....	....
	Baltimore	AHL	62	32	29	61	10	6	1	1	2	6
1991-92	Baltimore	AHL	77	42	28	70	51	....	....	....	....	....
	NHL Totals		**1**	**0**	**0**	**0**	**0**	....	....	....	....	....

SAVARD, DENIS JOSEPH (sa-VARH, den-NY)

Center. Shoots right. 5'10", 175 lbs. Born, Pointe Gatineau, Que., February 4, 1961.
(Chicago's 1st choice, 3rd overall, in 1980 Entry Draft).

			Regular Season					Playoffs				
Season	Club	Lea	GP	G	A	TP	PIM	GP	G	A	TP	PIM
1978-79	Montreal	QJHL	70	46	*112	158	88	11	5	6	11	46
1979-80ab	Montreal	QJHL	72	63	118	181	93	10	7	16	23	8
1980-81	**Chicago**	**NHL**	**76**	**28**	**47**	**75**	**47**	**3**	**0**	**0**	**0**	**0**
1981-82	**Chicago**	**NHL**	**80**	**32**	**87**	**119**	**82**	**15**	**11**	**7**	**18**	**52**
1982-83c	**Chicago**	**NHL**	**78**	**35**	**86**	**121**	**99**	**13**	**8**	**9**	**17**	**22**
1983-84	**Chicago**	**NHL**	**75**	**37**	**57**	**94**	**71**	**5**	**1**	**3**	**4**	**9**
1984-85	**Chicago**	**NHL**	**79**	**38**	**67**	**105**	**56**	**15**	**9**	**20**	**29**	**20**
1985-86	**Chicago**	**NHL**	**80**	**47**	**69**	**116**	**111**	**3**	**4**	**1**	**5**	**6**
1986-87	**Chicago**	**NHL**	**70**	**40**	**50**	**90**	**108**	**4**	**1**	**0**	**1**	**12**
1987-88	**Chicago**	**NHL**	**80**	**44**	**87**	**131**	**95**	**5**	**4**	**3**	**7**	**17**
1988-89	**Chicago**	**NHL**	**58**	**23**	**59**	**82**	**110**	**16**	**8**	**11**	**19**	**10**
1989-90	**Chicago**	**NHL**	**60**	**27**	**53**	**80**	**56**	**20**	**7**	**15**	**22**	**41**
1990-91	**Montreal**	**NHL**	**70**	**28**	**31**	**59**	**52**	**13**	**2**	**11**	**13**	**35**
1991-92	**Montreal**	**NHL**	**77**	**28**	**42**	**70**	**73**	**11**	**3**	**9**	**12**	**8**
	NHL Totals		**883**	**407**	**735**	**1142**	**960**	**123**	**58**	**89**	**147**	**232**

a QMJHL First All-Star Team (1980)
b Named QMJHL's Most Valuable Player (1980)
c NHL Second All-Star Team (1983)

Played in NHL All-Star Game (1982-84, 1986, 1988, 1991)

Traded to **Montreal** by **Chicago** for Chris Chelios and Montreal's second round choice (Michael Pomichter) in 1991 Entry Draft, June 29, 1990.

SAWYER, DAN

Defense. Shoots left. 6'1", 210 lbs. Born, Denville, NJ, October 28, 1970.
(Calgary's 11th choice, 210th overall, in 1989 Entry Draft).

			Regular Season					Playoffs				
Season	Club	Lea	GP	G	A	TP	PIM	GP	G	A	TP	PIM
1989-90	Notre Dame	SJHL	33	12	10	22	68	....	....	....	....	....
1990-91			UNAVAILABLE									
1991-92	Notre Dame	NCAA	31	7	13	20	44	....	....	....	....	....

SCHAFHAUSER, PATRICK (PAT)

Defense. Shoots left. 6'1", 195 lbs. Born, St. Paul, MN, July 27, 1971.
(Pittsburgh's 8th choice, 142nd overall, in 1989 Entry Draft).

			Regular Season					Playoffs				
Season	Club	Lea	GP	G	A	TP	PIM	GP	G	A	TP	PIM
1989-90	Boston College	H.E.	39	1	6	7	30	....	....	....	....	....
1990-91	Boston College	H.E.	18	1	2	3	8					
1991-92	Zug	Switz.	34	1	1	2	16	....	....	....	....	....

SCHLEGEL, BRAD (shlay-GUHL)

Defense. Shoots right. 5'10", 188 lbs. Born, Kitchener, Ont., July 22, 1968.
(Washington's 8th choice, 144th overall, in 1988 Entry Draft).

			Regular Season					Playoffs				
Season	Club	Lea	GP	G	A	TP	PIM	GP	G	A	TP	PIM
1986-87	London	OHL	65	4	23	27	24	....	....	....	....	....
1987-88a	London	OHL	66	13	63	76	49	12	8	17	25	6
1988-89	Cdn. National	....	60	2	22	24	30	....	....	....	....	....
1989-90	Cdn. National	....	72	7	25	32	44	....	....	....	....	....
1990-91	Cdn. National	....	59	8	20	28	64	....	....	....	....	....
1991-92	Cdn. National	....	61	3	18	21	84	....	....	....	....	....
	Cdn. Olympic	....	8	1	2	3	4	....	....	....	....	....
	Washington	**NHL**	**15**	**0**	**1**	**1**	**0**	**7**	**0**	**1**	**1**	**2**
	Baltimore	AHL	2	0	1	1	0	....	....	....	....	....
	NHL Totals		**15**	**0**	**1**	**1**	**0**	**7**	**0**	**1**	**1**	**2**

a OHL Second All-Star Team (1988)

SCHNEIDER, MATHIEU

Defense. Shoots left. 5'11", 189 lbs. Born, New York, NY, June 12, 1969.
(Montreal's 4th choice, 44th overall, in 1987 Entry Draft).

			Regular Season					Playoffs				
Season	Club	Lea	GP	G	A	TP	PIM	GP	G	A	TP	PIM
1986-87	Cornwall	OHL	63	7	29	36	75	5	0	0	0	22
1987-88	**Montreal**	**NHL**	**4**	**0**	**0**	**0**	**2**	....	....	....	....	....
a	Cornwall	OHL	48	21	40	61	83	11	2	6	8	14
	Sherbrooke	AHL	....	....	....	....	....	3	0	3	3	12
1988-89	Cornwall	OHL	59	16	57	73	96	18	7	20	27	30
1989-90	**Montreal**	**NHL**	**44**	**7**	**14**	**21**	**25**	**9**	**1**	**3**	**4**	**31**
	Sherbrooke	AHL	28	6	13	19	20	....	....	....	....	....
1990-91	**Montreal**	**NHL**	**69**	**10**	**20**	**30**	**63**	**13**	**2**	**7**	**9**	**18**
1991-92	**Montreal**	**NHL**	**78**	**8**	**24**	**32**	**72**	**10**	**1**	**4**	**5**	**6**
	NHL Totals		**195**	**25**	**58**	**83**	**162**	**32**	**4**	**14**	**18**	**55**

a OHL First All-Star Team (1988)

SCHRINER, MARTY

Center. Shoots left. 5'11", 175 lbs. Born, Port Huron, MI, May 20, 1972.
(NY Islanders' 12th choice, 246th overall, in 1991 Entry Draft).

			Regular Season					Playoffs				
Season	Club	Lea	GP	G	A	TP	PIM	GP	G	A	TP	PIM
1990-91	North Dakota	WCHA	40	6	11	17	90	....	....	....	....	....
1991-92	North Dakota	WCHA	32	10	12	22	112	....	....	....	....	....

SCHULTE, PAXTON

Left wing. Shoots left. 6'2", 210 lbs. Born, Ionaway, Alta., July 16, 1972.
(Quebec's 7th choice, 124th overall, in 1992 Entry Draft).

			Regular Season					Playoffs				
Season	Club	Lea	GP	G	A	TP	PIM	GP	G	A	TP	PIM
1990-91	North Dakota	WCHA	38	2	4	6	32	....	....	....	....	....
1991-92	Spokane	WHL	70	42	42	84	222	10	2	8	10	48

SCISSONS, SCOTT

Center. Shoots left. 6'1", 201 lbs. Born, Saskatoon, Sask., October 29, 1971.
(NY Islanders' 1st choice, 6th overall, in 1990 Entry Draft).

			Regular Season					Playoffs				
Season	Club	Lea	GP	G	A	TP	PIM	GP	G	A	TP	PIM
1988-89	Saskatoon	WHL	71	30	56	86	65	7	0	4	4	16
1989-90	Saskatoon	WHL	61	40	47	87	81	10	3	8	11	6
1990-91	**NY Islanders**	**NHL**	**1**	**0**	**0**	**0**	**0**	....	....	....	....	....
	Saskatoon	WHL	57	24	53	77	61	....	....	....	....	....
1991-92			DID NOT PLAY – INJURED									
	NHL Totals		**1**	**0**	**0**	**0**	**0**	....	....	....	....	....

SCOTT, KEVIN

Center. Shoots left. 5'10", 170 lbs. Born, Vernon, B.C., November 3, 1967.
(Detroit's 9th choice, 158th overall, in 1987 Entry Draft).

			Regular Season					Playoffs				
Season	Club	Lea	GP	G	A	TP	PIM	GP	G	A	TP	PIM
1987-88	N. Michigan	WCHA	36	9	12	21	42	....	....	....	....	....
1988-89	N. Michigan	WCHA	40	11	14	25	36	....	....	....	....	....
1989-90	N. Michigan	WCHA	34	20	14	34	46	....	....	....	....	....
1990-91	N. Michigan	WCHA	47	27	30	57	42	....	....	....	....	....
1991-92	Fort Wayne	IHL	1	0	0	0	0	....	....	....	....	....
	Cincinnati	ECHL	61	35	41	76	69	9	5	2	7	17

SCREMIN, CLAUDIO

Defense. Shoots right. 6'2", 205 lbs. Born, Burnaby, B.C., May 28, 1968.
(Washington's 12th choice, 204th overall, in 1988 Entry Draft).

			Regular Season					Playoffs				
Season	Club	Lea	GP	G	A	TP	PIM	GP	G	A	TP	PIM
1986-87	U. of Maine	H.E.	15	0	1	1	2	....	....	....	....	....
1987-88	U. of Maine	H.E.	44	6	18	24	22	....	....	....	....	....
1988-89	U. of Maine	H.E.	45	5	24	29	42	....	....	....	....	....
1989-90	U. of Maine	H.E.	45	4	26	30	14	....	....	....	....	....
1990-91	Kansas City	IHL	77	7	14	21	60	....	....	....	....	....
1991-92	**San Jose**	**NHL**	**13**	**0**	**0**	**0**	**25**	....	....	....	....	....
	Kansas City	IHL	70	5	23	28	44	15	1	6	7	14
	NHL Totals		**13**	**0**	**0**	**0**	**25**	....	....	....	....	....

Traded to **Minnesota** by **Washington** for Don Beaupre, November 1, 1988. Signed as a free agent by **San Jose**, September 3, 1991.

SEARS, SVERRE

Defense. Shoots left. 6'2", 185 lbs. Born, Boston, MA, October 17, 1970.
(Philadelphia's 6th choice, 159th overall in 1989 Entry Draft).

			Regular Season					Playoffs				
Season	Club	Lea	GP	G	A	TP	PIM	GP	G	A	TP	PIM
1989-90	Princeton	ECAC	3	0	1	1	14	....	....	....	....	....
1990-91	Princeton	ECAC	27	2	9	11	56	....	....	....	....	....
1991-92	Princeton	ECAC	25	3	9	12	62	....	....	....	....	....

SEBASTIAN, JEFF

Defense. Shoots right. 6'2", 198 lbs. Born, Vancouver, B.C., November 21, 1971.
(Winnipeg's 6th choice, 115th overall, in 1991 Entry Draft).

			Regular Season					Playoffs				
Season	Club	Lea	GP	G	A	TP	PIM	GP	G	A	TP	PIM
1990-91	Seattle	WHL	59	9	30	39	105	6	2	2	4	10
1991-92	Seattle	WHL	72	15	33	48	144	15	3	7	10	40

SEFTEL, STEVE (SEFF-tuhl)

Left wing. Shoots left. 6'3", 200 lbs. Born, Kitchener, Ont., May 14, 1968.
(Washington's 2nd choice, 40th overall, in 1986 Entry Draft).

			Regular Season					Playoffs				
Season	Club	Lea	GP	G	A	TP	PIM	GP	G	A	TP	PIM
1985-86	Kingston	OHL	42	11	16	27	53	....	....	....	....	....
1986-87	Kingston	OHL	54	21	43	64	55	12	1	4	5	9
1987-88	Binghamton	AHL	3	0	0	0	2	....	....	....	....	....
	Kingston	OHL	66	32	43	75	51	....	....	....	....	....
1988-89	Baltimore	AHL	58	12	15	27	70	....	....	....	....	....
1989-90	Baltimore	AHL	74	10	19	29	52	12	4	3	7	10
1990-91	**Washington**	**NHL**	**4**	**0**	**0**	**0**	**2**	....	....	....	....	....
	Baltimore	AHL	66	22	22	44	46	6	0	0	0	14
1991-92	Baltimore	AHL	18	2	6	8	27	....	....	....	....	....
	NHL Totals		**4**	**0**	**0**	**0**	**2**	....	....	....	....	....

SEGUIN, BRETT

Center. Shoots left. 5'9", 199 lbs. Born, Rochester, NY, February 20, 1972.
(Los Angeles' 6th choice, 130th overall, in 1991 Entry Draft).

			Regular Season					Playoffs				
Season	Club	Lea	GP	G	A	TP	PIM	GP	G	A	TP	PIM
1989-90	Ottawa	OHL	63	28	*80	108	30	....	....	....	....	....
1990-91	Ottawa	OHL	63	24	*87	111	85	17	10	*25	35	21
1991-92	Ottawa	OHL	64	34	*100	134	70	11	8	10	18	16

SELANNE, TEEMU (SEH-lahn-nay, TEE-moo)

Right wing. Shoots right. 6', 181 lbs. Born, Helsinki, Finland, July 3, 1970.
(Winnipeg's 1st choice, 10th overall, in 1988 Entry Draft).

			Regular Season					Playoffs				
Season	Club	Lea	GP	G	A	TP	PIM	GP	G	A	TP	PIM
1987-88	Jokerit	Fin. Jr.	33	43	23	66	18	5	4	3	7	2
	Jokerit	Fin.2	5	1	1	2	0	....	....	....	....	....
1988-89	Jokerit	Fin.	34	35	33	68	12	5	7	3	10	4
1989-90	Jokerit	Fin.	11	4	8	12	0	....	....	....	....	....
1990-91	Jokerit	Fin.	42	33	25	58	12	....	....	....	....	....
1991-92	Jokerit	Fin.	44	*39	23	62	20	10	10	7	17	18

SELYANIN, SERGEI (sel-AN-in)

Defense. Shoots right. 6'2", 198 lbs. Born, Novosibirsk, Soviet Union, September 20, 1966.
(Winnipeg's 12th choice, 224th overall, in 1990 Entry Draft).

			Regular Season					Playoffs				
Season	Club	Lea	GP	G	A	TP	PIM	GP	G	A	TP	PIM
1985-86	CSKA	USSR	8	0	0	0	6	....	....	....	....	....
1986-87	CSKA	USSR	34	0	0	0	28	....	....	....	....	....
1987-88	CSKA	USSR	21	2	0	2	16	....	....	....	....	....
	Khimik	USSR	11	2	2	4	8	....	....	....	....	....
1988-89	Khimik	USSR	44	6	4	10	42	....	....	....	....	....
1989-90	Khimik	USSR	33	2	4	6	....	....	....	....	....	....
1990-91	Khimik	USSR	43	4	7	11	56	....	....	....	....	....
1991-92	Khimik	CIS	41	3	13	16	42	....	....	....	....	....

SEMAK, ALEXANDER (seh-MAHK)

Center. Shoots right. 5'10", 185 lbs. Born, Ufa, Soviet Union, February 11, 1966.
(New Jersey's 12th choice, 207th overall, in 1988 Entry Draft).

			Regular Season					Playoffs				
Season	Club	Lea	GP	G	A	TP	PIM	GP	G	A	TP	PIM
1987-88	Moscow D'amo	USSR	47	21	14	35	40	....	....	....	....	....
1988-89	Moscow D'amo	USSR	44	18	10	28	22	....	....	....	....	....
1989-90	Moscow D'amo	USSR	43	23	11	34	33	....	....	....	....	....
1990-91	Moscow D'amo	USSR	46	17	21	38	48	....	....	....	....	....
1991-92	Moscow D'amo	CIS	26	10	13	23	26	....	....	....	....	....
	New Jersey	**NHL**	**25**	**5**	**6**	**11**	**0**	**1**	**0**	**0**	**0**	**0**
	Utica	AHL	7	3	2	5	0	....	....	....	....	....
	NHL Totals		**25**	**5**	**6**	**11**	**0**	**1**	**0**	**0**	**0**	**0**

SEMCHUK, THOMAS (BRANDY)

Right wing. Shoots right. 6'1", 185 lbs. Born, Calgary, Alta., September 22, 1971.
(Los Angeles' 2nd choice, 28th overall, in 1990 Entry Draft).

			Regular Season					Playoffs				
Season	Club	Lea	GP	G	A	TP	PIM	GP	G	A	TP	PIM
1988-89	Cdn. National	....	42	11	11	22	60	....	....	....	....	....
1989-90	Cdn. National	....	55	10	15	25	40	....	....	....	....	....
1990-91	Lethbridge	WHL	14	9	8	17	10	15	8	5	13	18
	New Haven	AHL	21	1	4	5	6	....	....	....	....	....
1991-92	Phoenix	IHL	15	1	5	6	6	....	....	....	....	....
	Raleigh	ECHL	5	1	2	3	16	2	1	0	1	4

SEMENOV, ANATOLI (seh-MEH-nahf)

Center/Left wing. Shoots left. 6'2", 190 lbs. Born, Moscow, Soviet Union, March 5, 1962.
(Edmonton's 5th choice, 120th overall, in 1989 Entry Draft).

			Regular Season					Playoffs				
Season	Club	Lea	GP	G	A	TP	PIM	GP	G	A	TP	PIM
1979-80	Moscow D'amo	USSR	8	3	0	3	2	....	....	....	....	....
1980-81	Moscow D'amo	USSR	47	18	14	32	18	....	....	....	....	....
1981-82	Moscow D'amo	USSR	44	12	14	26	28	....	....	....	....	....
1982-83	Moscow D'amo	USSR	44	22	18	40	26	....	....	....	....	....
1983-84	Moscow D'amo	USSR	19	10	5	15	14	....	....	....	....	....
1984-85	Moscow D'amo	USSR	30	17	12	29	32	....	....	....	....	....
1985-86	Moscow D'amo	USSR	32	18	17	35	19	....	....	....	....	....
1986-87	Moscow D'amo	USSR	40	15	29	44	32	....	....	....	....	....
1987-88	Moscow D'amo	USSR	32	17	8	25	22	....	....	....	....	....
1988-89	Moscow D'amo	USSR	31	9	12	21	24	....	....	....	....	....
1989-90	Moscow D'amo	USSR	48	13	20	33	16	....	....	....	....	....
	Edmonton	**NHL**	....	....	....	....	....	**2**	**0**	**0**	**0**	**0**
1990-91	**Edmonton**	**NHL**	**57**	**15**	**16**	**31**	**26**	**12**	**5**	**5**	**10**	**6**
1991-92	**Edmonton**	**NHL**	**59**	**20**	**22**	**42**	**16**	**8**	**1**	**1**	**2**	**6**
	NHL Totals		**116**	**35**	**38**	**73**	**42**	**22**	**6**	**6**	**12**	**12**

Claimed by **Tampa Bay** from **Edmonton** in Expansion Draft, June 18, 1992.

SENTNER, PETER G.

Defense. Shoots left. 6'1", 200 lbs. Born, Boston, MA, June 13, 1969.
(Los Angeles' 1st choice, 12th overall, in 1990 Supplemental Draft).

			Regular Season					Playoffs				
Season	Club	Lea	GP	G	A	TP	PIM	GP	G	A	TP	PIM
1987-88	Lowell	ECAC	21	0	0	0	14	....	....	....	....	....
1988-89	Lowell	ECAC	34	6	20	26	46	....	....	....	....	....
1989-90	Lowell	ECAC	25	1	6	7	6	....	....	....	....	....
1990-91	New Haven	AHL	2	0	0	0	0	....	....	....	....	....
	Phoenix	IHL	8	0	0	0	0	....	....	....	....	....
	Roanoke Valley	ECHL	49	3	13	16	39	....	....	....	....	....
1991-92	Greensboro	ECHL	54	10	16	26	66	4	0	0	0	12

SEPPO, JUKKA PEKKA (SEHP-poh)

Center. Shoots left. 6'2", 198 lbs. Born, Vaasa, Finland, January 22, 1968.
(Philadelphia's 2nd choice, 23rd overall, in 1986 Entry Draft).

			Regular Season					Playoffs				
Season	Club	Lea	GP	G	A	TP	PIM	GP	G	A	TP	PIM
1986-87	Tappara	Fin.	39	11	16	27	50	....	....	....	....	....
1987-88	Sport	Fin.2	42	28	37	65	78	....	....	....	....	....
1988-89	HIFK	Fin.	35	7	13	20	28	....	....	....	....	....
1989-90	HIFK	Fin.	39	15	27	42	50	....	....	....	....	....
1990-91	HIFK	Fin.	35	17	22	39	81	3	1	0	1	2
1991-92	HIFK	Fin.	43	16	31	47	53	7	2	4	6	33

SEROWIK, JEFF (sir-OH-ik)

Defense. Shoots right. 6', 190 lbs. Born, Manchester, NH, October 1, 1967.
(Toronto's 5th choice, 85th overall, in 1985 Entry Draft).

			Regular Season					Playoffs				
Season	Club	Lea	GP	G	A	TP	PIM	GP	G	A	TP	PIM
1986-87	Providence	H.E.	33	3	8	11	22	....	....	....	....	....
1987-88	Providence	H.E.	33	3	9	12	44	....	....	....	....	....
1988-89	Providence	H.E.	35	3	14	17	48	....	....	....	....	....
1989-90a	Providence	H.E.	35	6	19	25	34	....	....	....	....	....
1990-91	**Toronto**	**NHL**	**1**	**0**	**0**	**0**	**0**	....	....	....	....	....
	Newmarket	AHL	60	8	15	23	45	....	....	....	....	....
1991-92	St. John's	AHL	78	11	34	45	60	16	4	9	13	22
	NHL Totals		**1**	**0**	**0**	**0**	**0**	....	....	....	....	....

a Hockey East Second All-Star Team (1990)

SEVERYN, BRENT

Left wing. Shoots left. 6'2", 210 lbs. Born, Vegreville, Alta., February 22, 1966.

			Regular Season					Playoffs				
Season	Club	Lea	GP	G	A	TP	PIM	GP	G	A	TP	PIM
1983-84	Seattle	WHL	72	14	22	36	49	....	....	....	....	....
1984-85	Seattle	WHL	38	8	32	40	54	....	....	....	....	....
	Brandon	WHL	26	7	16	23	57	....	....	....	....	....
1985-86	Seattle	WHL	33	11	20	31	164	....	....	....	....	....
	Saskatoon	WHL	9	1	4	5	38	....	....	....	....	....
1986-87	U. of Alberta	CWUAA	....	....	....	....	....	....	....	....	....	....
1987-88	U. of Alberta	CWUAA	46	21	29	50	178	....	....	....	....	....
1988-89	Halifax	AHL	47	2	12	14	141	....	....	....	....	....
1989-90	**Quebec**	**NHL**	**35**	**0**	**2**	**2**	**42**	....	....	....	....	....
	Halifax	AHL	43	6	9	15	105	6	1	2	3	49
1990-91	Halifax	AHL	50	7	26	33	202	....	....	....	....	....
1991-92	Utica	AHL	80	11	33	44	211	4	0	1	1	4
	NHL Totals		**35**	**0**	**2**	**2**	**42**	....	....	....	....	....

Signed as a free agent by **Quebec**, July 15, 1988. Traded to **New Jersey** by **Quebec** for Dave Marcinyshyn, June 3, 1991.

SEVIGNY, PIERRE (seh-VIH-nee)

Left wing. Shoots left. 6', 189 lbs. Born, Trois-Rivières, Que., September 8, 1971.
(Montreal's 4th choice, 51st overall, in 1989 Entry Draft).

			Regular Season					Playoffs				
Season	Club	Lea	GP	G	A	TP	PIM	GP	G	A	TP	PIM
1988-89	Verdun	QMJHL	67	27	43	70	88	....	....	....	....	....
1989-90a	St-Hyacinthe	QMJHL	67	47	72	119	205	12	8	8	16	42
1990-91a	St-Hyacinthe	QMJHL	60	36	46	82	203	....	....	....	....	....
1991-92	Fredericton	AHL	74	22	37	59	145	7	1	1	2	26

a QMJHL Second All-Star Team (1990, 1991)

SHANAHAN, BRENDAN

Right wing. Shoots right. 6'3", 215 lbs. Born, Mimico, Ont., January 23, 1969.
(New Jersey's 1st choice, 2nd overall, in 1987 Entry Draft).

			Regular Season					Playoffs				
Season	Club	Lea	GP	G	A	TP	PIM	GP	G	A	TP	PIM
1985-86	London	OHL	59	28	34	62	70	5	5	5	10	5
1986-87	London	OHL	56	39	53	92	92	....	....	....	....	....
1987-88	**New Jersey**	**NHL**	**65**	**7**	**19**	**26**	**131**	**12**	**2**	**1**	**3**	**44**
1988-89	**New Jersey**	**NHL**	**68**	**22**	**28**	**50**	**115**	....	....	....	....	....
1989-90	**New Jersey**	**NHL**	**73**	**30**	**42**	**72**	**137**	**6**	**3**	**3**	**6**	**20**
1990-91	**New Jersey**	**NHL**	**75**	**29**	**37**	**66**	**141**	**7**	**3**	**5**	**8**	**12**
1991-92	**St. Louis**	**NHL**	**80**	**33**	**36**	**69**	**171**	**6**	**2**	**3**	**5**	**14**
	NHL Totals		**361**	**121**	**162**	**283**	**695**	**31**	**10**	**12**	**22**	**90**

Signed as a free agent by **St. Louis**, July 25, 1991.

SHANK, DANIEL

Right wing. Shoots right. 5'10", 190 lbs. Born, Montreal, Que., May 12, 1967.

			Regular Season					Playoffs				
Season	Club	Lea	GP	G	A	TP	PIM	GP	G	A	TP	PIM
1985-86	Shawinigan	QMJHL	51	34	38	72	184	....	....	....	....	....
1986-87	Hull	QMJHL	46	26	43	69	325	....	....	....	....	....
1987-88	Hull	QMJHL	42	23	34	57	274	5	3	2	5	16
1988-89	Adirondack	AHL	42	5	20	25	113	17	11	8	19	102
1989-90	**Detroit**	**NHL**	**57**	**11**	**13**	**24**	**143**	....	....	....	....	....
	Adirondack	AHL	14	8	8	16	36	....	....	....	....	....
1990-91	**Detroit**	**NHL**	**7**	**0**	**1**	**1**	**14**	....	....	....	....	....
	Adirondack	AHL	60	26	49	75	278	....	....	....	....	....
1991-92	Adirondack	AHL	27	13	21	34	112	....	....	....	....	....
	Hartford	**NHL**	**13**	**2**	**0**	**2**	**18**	**5**	**0**	**0**	**0**	**22**
	Springfield	AHL	31	9	19	28	83	8	8	0	8	48
	NHL Totals		**77**	**13**	**14**	**27**	**175**	**5**	**0**	**0**	**0**	**22**

Signed as a free agent by **Detroit**, May 26, 1989. Traded to **Hartford** by **Detroit** for Chris Tancill, December 18, 1991.

SHANNON, DARRIN

Left wing. Shoots left. 6'2", 205 lbs. Born, Barrie, Ont., December 8, 1969.
(Pittsburgh's 1st choice, 4th overall, in 1988 Entry Draft).

			Regular Season					Playoffs				
Season	Club	Lea	GP	G	A	TP	PIM	GP	G	A	TP	PIM
1986-87	Windsor	OHL	60	16	67	83	116	14	4	6	10	8
1987-88	Windsor	OHL	43	33	41	74	49	12	6	12	18	9
1988-89	**Buffalo**	**NHL**	**3**	**0**	**0**	**0**	**0**	**2**	**0**	**0**	**0**	**0**
	Windsor	OHL	54	33	48	81	47	4	1	6	7	2
1989-90	**Buffalo**	**NHL**	**17**	**2**	**7**	**9**	**4**	**6**	**0**	**1**	**1**	**4**
	Rochester	AHL	50	20	23	43	25	9	4	1	5	2
1990-91	**Buffalo**	**NHL**	**34**	**8**	**6**	**14**	**12**	**6**	**1**	**2**	**3**	**4**
	Rochester	AHL	49	26	34	60	56	10	3	5	8	22
1991-92	**Buffalo**	**NHL**	**1**	**0**	**1**	**1**	**0**	....	....	....	....	....
	Winnipeg	**NHL**	**68**	**13**	**26**	**39**	**41**	**7**	**0**	**1**	**1**	**10**
	NHL Totals		**123**	**23**	**40**	**63**	**57**	**21**	**1**	**4**	**5**	**18**

Traded to **Buffalo** by **Pittsburgh** with Doug Bodger for Tom Barrasso and Buffalo's third round choice (Joe Dziedzic) in 1990 Entry Draft, November 12, 1988. Traded to **Winnipeg** by **Buffalo** with Mike Hartman and Dean Kennedy for Dave McLlwain, Gord Donnelly, Winnipeg's fifth round choice (Yuri Khmylev) in 1992 Entry Draft and future considerations, October 11, 1991.

SHANNON, DARRYL

Defense. Shoots left. 6'2", 195 lbs. Born, Barrie, Ont., June 21, 1968.
(Toronto's 2nd choice, 36th overall, in 1986 Entry Draft).

			Regular Season					Playoffs				
Season	Club	Lea	GP	G	A	TP	PIM	GP	G	A	TP	PIM
1985-86	Windsor	OHL	57	6	21	27	52	16	5	6	11	22
1986-87a	Windsor	OHL	64	23	27	50	83	14	4	8	12	18
1987-88b	Windsor	OHL	60	16	67	83	116	12	3	8	11	17
1988-89	**Toronto**	**NHL**	**14**	**1**	**3**	**4**	**6**	....	....	....	....	....
	Newmarket	AHL	61	5	24	29	37	5	0	3	3	10
1989-90	**Toronto**	**NHL**	**10**	**0**	**1**	**1**	**12**	....	....	....	....	....
	Newmarket	AHL	47	4	15	19	58	....	....	....	....	....
1990-91	**Toronto**	**NHL**	**10**	**0**	**1**	**1**	**0**	....	....	....	....	....
	Newmarket	AHL	47	2	14	16	51	....	....	....	....	....
1991-92	**Toronto**	**NHL**	**48**	**2**	**8**	**10**	**23**	....	....	....	....	....
	NHL Totals		**82**	**3**	**13**	**16**	**41**	....	....	....	....	....

a OHL Second All-Star Team (1987)
b OHL First All-Star Team, Defenseman of the Year (1988)

SHANTZ, JEFF

Center. Shoots right. 6', 184 lbs. Born, Duchess, Alta., October 10, 1973.
(Chicago's 2nd choice, 36th overall, in 1992 Entry Draft).

			Regular Season					Playoffs				
Season	Club	Lea	GP	G	A	TP	PIM	GP	G	A	TP	PIM
1990-91	Regina	WHL	69	16	21	37	22	8	2	2	4	2
1991-92	Regina	WHL	72	39	50	89	75	....	....	....	....	....

SHARPLES, JEFF

Defense. Shoots left. 6'1", 195 lbs. Born, Terrace, B.C., July 28, 1967.
(Detroit's 2nd choice, 29th overall, in 1985 Entry Draft).

			Regular Season					Playoffs				
Season	Club	Lea	GP	G	A	TP	PIM	GP	G	A	TP	PIM
1983-84	Kelowna	WHL	72	9	24	33	51	....	....	....	....	....
1984-85a	Kelowna	WHL	72	12	41	53	90	6	0	1	1	6
1985-86	Spokane	WHL	3	0	0	0	4	....	....	....	....	....
	Portland	WHL	19	2	6	8	44	15	2	6	8	6
1986-87	**Detroit**	**NHL**	**3**	**0**	**1**	**1**	**2**	**2**	**0**	**0**	**0**	**2**
	Portland	WHL	44	25	35	60	92	20	7	15	22	23
1987-88	**Detroit**	**NHL**	**56**	**10**	**25**	**35**	**42**	**4**	**0**	**3**	**3**	**4**
	Adirondack	AHL	4	2	1	3	4	....	....	....	....	....
1988-89	**Detroit**	**NHL**	**46**	**4**	**9**	**13**	**26**	**1**	**0**	**0**	**0**	**0**
	Adirondack	AHL	10	0	4	4	8	....	....	....	....	....
1989-90	Adirondack	AHL	9	2	5	7	6	....	....	....	....	....
	Cape Breton	AHL	38	4	13	17	28	....	....	....	....	....
	Utica	AHL	13	2	5	7	19	5	1	2	3	15
1990-91	Utica	AHL	64	16	29	45	42	....	....	....	....	....
1991-92	Capital Dist.	AHL	31	3	12	15	18	7	6	5	11	4
	NHL Totals		**105**	**14**	**35**	**49**	**70**	**7**	**0**	**3**	**3**	**6**

a WHL West Second All-Star Team (1985)

Traded to **Edmonton** by **Detroit** with Petr Klima, Joe Murphy and Adam Graves for Jimmy Carson, Kevin McClelland and Edmonton's fifth round choice (later traded to Montreal for Rick Green. Montreal selected Brad Layzell) in 1991 Entry Draft, November 2, 1989. Traded to **New Jersey** by **Edmonton** for Reijo Ruotsalainen, March 6, 1990.

SHAW, BRAD

Defense. Shoots right. 6', 190 lbs. Born, Cambridge, Ont., April 28, 1964.
(Detroit's 5th choice, 86th overall, in 1982 Entry Draft).

			Regular Season					Playoffs				
Season	Club	Lea	GP	G	A	TP	PIM	GP	G	A	TP	PIM
1981-82	Ottawa	OHL	68	13	59	72	24	15	1	13	14	4
1982-83	Ottawa	OHL	63	12	66	78	24	9	2	9	11	4
1983-84a	Ottawa	OHL	68	11	71	82	75	13	2	*27	29	9
1984-85	Binghamton	AHL	24	1	10	11	4	8	1	8	9	6
	Salt Lake	IHL	44	3	29	32	25	....	....	....	....	....
1985-86	**Hartford**	**NHL**	**8**	**0**	**2**	**2**	**4**	....	....	....	....	....
	Binghamton	AHL	64	10	44	54	33	5	0	2	2	6
1986-87	**Hartford**	**NHL**	**2**	**0**	**0**	**0**	**0**	....	....	....	....	....
bc	Binghamton	AHL	77	9	30	39	43	12	1	8	9	2
1987-88	**Hartford**	**NHL**	**1**	**0**	**0**	**0**	**0**	....	....	....	....	....
b	Binghamton	AHL	73	12	50	62	50	4	0	5	5	4
1988-89	Verese	Italy	35	10	30	40	44	11	4	8	12	13
	Cdn. National	....	4	1	0	1	2	....	....	....	....	....
	Hartford	**NHL**	**3**	**1**	**0**	**1**	**0**	**3**	**1**	**0**	**1**	**0**
1989-90d	**Hartford**	**NHL**	**64**	**3**	**32**	**35**	**30**	**7**	**2**	**5**	**7**	**0**
1990-91	**Hartford**	**NHL**	**72**	**4**	**28**	**32**	**29**	**6**	**1**	**2**	**3**	**2**
1991-92	**Hartford**	**NHL**	**62**	**3**	**22**	**25**	**44**	**3**	**0**	**1**	**1**	**4**
	NHL Totals		**212**	**11**	**84**	**95**	**107**	**19**	**4**	**8**	**12**	**6**

a OHL First All-Star Team (1984)
b AHL First All-Star Team (1987, 1988)
c Won Eddie Shore Plaque (AHL Outstanding Defenseman) (1987)
d NHL All-Rookie Team (1990)

Rights traded to **Hartford** by **Detroit** for Hartford's eighth round choice (Urban Nordin) in 1984 Entry Draft, May 29, 1984. Traded to **New Jersey** by **Hartford** for cash, June 13, 1992. Claimed by **Ottawa** from **New Jersey** in Expansion Draft, June 18, 1992.

SHAW, DAVID

Defense. Shoots right. 6'2", 204 lbs. Born, St. Thomas, Ont., May 25, 1964.
(Quebec's 1st choice, 13th overall, in 1982 Entry Draft).

			Regular Season					Playoffs				
Season	Club	Lea	GP	G	A	TP	PIM	GP	G	A	TP	PIM
1981-82	Kitchener	OHL	68	6	25	31	94	15	2	2	4	51
1982-83	**Quebec**	**NHL**	**2**	**0**	**0**	**0**	**0**	....	....	....	....	....
	Kitchener	OHL	57	18	56	74	78	12	2	10	12	18
1983-84	**Quebec**	**NHL**	**3**	**0**	**0**	**0**	**0**	....	....	....	....	....
a	Kitchener	OHL	58	14	34	48	73	16	4	9	13	12
1984-85	**Quebec**	**NHL**	**14**	**0**	**0**	**0**	**11**	....	....	....	....	....
	Fredericton	AHL	48	7	6	13	73	2	0	0	0	7
1985-86	**Quebec**	**NHL**	**73**	**7**	**19**	**26**	**78**	....	....	....	....	....
1986-87	**Quebec**	**NHL**	**75**	**0**	**19**	**19**	**69**	....	....	....	....	....
1987-88	**NY Rangers**	**NHL**	**68**	**7**	**25**	**32**	**100**	....	....	....	....	....
1988-89	**NY Rangers**	**NHL**	**63**	**6**	**11**	**17**	**88**	**4**	**0**	**2**	**2**	**30**
1989-90	**NY Rangers**	**NHL**	**22**	**2**	**10**	**12**	**22**	....	....	....	....	....
1990-91	**NY Rangers**	**NHL**	**77**	**2**	**10**	**12**	**89**	**6**	**0**	**0**	**0**	**11**
1991-92	**NY Rangers**	**NHL**	**10**	**0**	**1**	**1**	**15**	....	....	....	....	....
	Edmonton	**NHL**	**12**	**1**	**1**	**2**	**8**	....	....	....	....	....
	Minnesota	**NHL**	**37**	**0**	**7**	**7**	**49**	**7**	**2**	**2**	**4**	**10**
	NHL Totals		**456**	**25**	**103**	**128**	**529**	**17**	**2**	**4**	**6**	**51**

a OHL First All-Star Team (1984)

Traded to **NY Rangers** by **Quebec** with John Ogrodnick for Jeff Jackson and Terry Carkner, September 30, 1987. Traded to **Edmonton** by **NY Rangers** for Jeff Beukeboom, November 12, 1991. Traded to **Minnesota** by **Edmonton** for Brian Glynn, January 21, 1992.

SHEEHY, NEIL

Defense. Shoots right. 6'2", 214 lbs. Born, International Falls, MN, February 9, 1960.

			Regular Season					Playoffs				
Season	Club	Lea	GP	G	A	TP	PIM	GP	G	A	TP	PIM
1979-80	Harvard	ECAC	13	0	0	0	10	....	....	....	....	....
1980-81	Harvard	ECAC	26	4	8	12	22	....	....	....	....	....
1981-82	Harvard	ECAC	30	7	11	18	46	....	....	....	....	....
1982-83	Harvard	ECAC	34	5	13	18	48	....	....	....	....	....
1983-84	**Calgary**	**NHL**	**1**	**1**	**0**	**1**	**2**	**4**	**0**	**0**	**0**	**4**
	Colorado	CHL	74	5	18	23	151	....	....	....	....	....
1984-85	**Calgary**	**NHL**	**31**	**3**	**4**	**7**	**109**	....	....	....	....	....
	Moncton	AHL	34	6	9	15	101	....	....	....	....	....
1985-86	**Calgary**	**NHL**	**65**	**2**	**16**	**18**	**271**	**22**	**0**	**2**	**2**	**79**
	Moncton	AHL	4	1	1	2	21	....	....	....	....	....
1986-87	**Calgary**	**NHL**	**54**	**4**	**6**	**10**	**151**	**6**	**0**	**0**	**0**	**21**
1987-88	**Calgary**	**NHL**	**36**	**2**	**6**	**8**	**73**	....	....	....	....	....
	Hartford	**NHL**	**26**	**1**	**4**	**5**	**116**	**1**	**0**	**0**	**0**	**7**
1988-89	**Washington**	**NHL**	**72**	**3**	**4**	**7**	**179**	**6**	**0**	**0**	**0**	**19**
1989-90	**Washington**	**NHL**	**59**	**1**	**5**	**6**	**291**	**13**	**0**	**1**	**1**	**92**
1990-91	**Washington**	**NHL**	....	....	....	....	....	**2**	**0**	**0**	**0**	**19**
1991-92	**Calgary**	**NHL**	**35**	**1**	**2**	**3**	**119**	....	....	....	....	....
	Salt Lake	IHL	6	0	0	0	34	....	....	....	....	....
	NHL Totals		**379**	**18**	**47**	**65**	**1311**	**54**	**0**	**3**	**3**	**241**

Signed as a free agent by **Calgary**, August 16, 1983. Traded to **Hartford** by **Calgary** with Carey Wilson and the rights to Lane MacDonald for Dana Murzyn and Shane Churla, January 3, 1988. Traded to **Washington** by **Hartford** with Mike Millar for Grant Jennings and Ed Kastelic, July 6, 1988. Signed as a free agent by **Calgary**, September 3, 1991.

SHEPPARD, RAY

Right wing. Shoots right. 6'1", 190 lbs. Born, Pembroke, Ont., May 27, 1966.
(Buffalo's 3rd choice, 60th overall, in 1984 Entry Draft).

			Regular Season					Playoffs				
Season	Club	Lea	GP	G	A	TP	PIM	GP	G	A	TP	PIM
1983-84	Cornwall	OHL	68	44	36	80	69	....	....	....	....	....
1984-85	Cornwall	OHL	49	25	33	58	51	9	2	12	14	4
1985-86ab	Cornwall	OHL	63	*81	61	*142	25	6	7	4	11	0
1986-87	Rochester	AHL	55	18	13	31	11	15	12	3	15	2
1987-88c	**Buffalo**	**NHL**	**74**	**38**	**27**	**65**	**14**	**6**	**1**	**1**	**2**	**2**
1988-89	**Buffalo**	**NHL**	**67**	**22**	**21**	**43**	**15**	**1**	**0**	**1**	**1**	**0**
1989-90	**Buffalo**	**NHL**	**18**	**4**	**2**	**6**	**0**	....	....	....	....	....
	Rochester	AHL	5	3	5	8	2	17	8	7	15	9
1990-91	**NY Rangers**	**NHL**	**59**	**24**	**23**	**47**	**21**	....	....	....	....	....
1991-92	**Detroit**	**NHL**	**74**	**36**	**26**	**62**	**27**	**11**	**6**	**2**	**8**	**4**
	NHL Totals		**292**	**124**	**99**	**223**	**77**	**18**	**7**	**4**	**11**	**6**

a OHL Player of the Year (1986)
b OHL First All-Star Team (1986)
c NHL All-Rookie Team (1988)

Traded to **NY Rangers** by **Buffalo** for cash and future considerations, July 9, 1990. Signed as a free agent by **Detroit**, August 5, 1991.

SHEVALIER, JEFF

Left wing. Shoots left. 5'11", 178 lbs. Born, Mississauga, Ont., March 14, 1974.
(Los Angeles' 4th choice, 111th overall, in 1992 Entry Draft).

			Regular Season					Playoffs				
Season	Club	Lea	GP	G	A	TP	PIM	GP	G	A	TP	PIM
1990-91	Acton	Jr. C	28	29	31	60	62	....	....	....	....	....
1991-92	North Bay	OHL	64	28	29	57	26	21	5	11	16	25

SHIER, ANDREW

Center. Shoots right. 5'11", 165 lbs. Born, Lansing, MI, August 15, 1971.
(NY Islanders' 11th choice, 237th overall, in 1990 Entry Draft).

			Regular Season					Playoffs				
Season	Club	Lea	GP	G	A	TP	PIM	GP	G	A	TP	PIM
1990-91	U. Wisconsin	WCHA	20	4	9	13	28	....	....	....	....	....
1991-92	U. Wisconsin	WCHA	39	10	25	35	60	....	....	....	....	....

SHOEBOTTOM, BRUCE

Defense. Shoots left. 6'2", 200 lbs. Born, Windsor, Ont., August 20, 1965.
(Los Angeles' 1st choice, 47th overall, in 1983 Entry Draft).

			Regular Season					Playoffs				
Season	Club	Lea	GP	G	A	TP	PIM	GP	G	A	TP	PIM
1982-83	Peterborough	OHL	34	2	10	12	106	....	....	....	....	....
1983-84	Peterborough	OHL	16	0	5	5	73	....	....	....	....	....
1984-85	Peterborough	OHL	60	2	15	17	143	17	0	4	4	26
1985-86	New Haven	AHL	6	2	0	2	12	....	....	....	....	....
	Binghamton	AHL	62	7	5	12	249	....	....	....	....	....
1986-87	Fort Wayne	IHL	75	2	10	12	309	10	0	0	0	31
1987-88	**Boston**	**NHL**	**3**	**0**	**1**	**1**	**0**	**4**	**1**	**0**	**1**	**42**
	Maine	AHL	70	2	12	14	338	....	....	....	....	....
1988-89	**Boston**	**NHL**	**29**	**1**	**3**	**4**	**44**	**10**	**0**	**2**	**2**	**35**
	Maine	AHL	44	0	8	8	265	....	....	....	....	....
1989-90	**Boston**	**NHL**	**2**	**0**	**0**	**0**	**4**	....	....	....	....	....
	Maine	AHL	66	3	11	14	228	....	....	....	....	....
1990-91	**Boston**	**NHL**	**1**	**0**	**0**	**0**	**5**	....	....	....	....	....
	Maine	AHL	71	2	8	10	238	1	0	0	0	14
1991-92	Peoria	IHL	79	4	12	16	234	10	0	0	0	33
	NHL Totals		**35**	**1**	**4**	**5**	**53**	**14**	**1**	**2**	**3**	**77**

Traded to **Washington** by **Los Angeles** for Bryan Erickson, October 31, 1985. Signed as a free agent by **Boston**, July 20, 1987. Signed as a free agent by **St. Louis**, October 2, 1991.

SHUCHUK, GARY (SHOO-chuk)

Right wing. Shoots right. 5'10", 185 lbs. Born, Edmonton, Alta., February 17, 1967.
(Detroit's 1st choice, 22nd overall, in 1988 Supplemental Draft).

			Regular Season					Playoffs				
Season	Club	Lea	GP	G	A	TP	PIM	GP	G	A	TP	PIM
1986-87	U. Wisconsin	WCHA	42	19	11	30	72	....	....	....	....	....
1987-88	U. Wisconsin	WCHA	44	7	22	29	70	....	....	....	....	....
1988-89	U. Wisconsin	WCHA	46	18	19	37	102	....	....	....	....	....
1989-90abc	U. Wisconsin	WCHA	45	*41	39	*80	70	....	....	....	....	....
1990-91	**Detroit**	**NHL**	**6**	**1**	**2**	**3**	**6**	**3**	**0**	**0**	**0**	**0**
	Adirondack	AHL	59	23	24	47	32	....	....	....	....	....
1991-92	Adirondack	AHL	79	32	48	80	48	19	4	9	13	18
	NHL Totals		**6**	**1**	**2**	**3**	**6**	**3**	**0**	**0**	**0**	**0**

a WCHA First All-Star Team (1990)
b WCHA Player of the Year (1990)
c NCAA West First All-American Team (1990)

SHUTE, DAVID

Center. Shoots left. 5'11", 185 lbs. Born, Carlisle, PA, February 10, 1971.
(Pittsburgh's 9th choice, 163rd overall, in 1989 Entry Draft).

			Regular Season					Playoffs				
Season	Club	Lea	GP	G	A	TP	PIM	GP	G	A	TP	PIM
1988-89	Victoria	WHL	69	5	11	16	26	8	0	1	1	10
1989-90	Victoria	WHL	14	4	5	9	25	....	....	....	....	....
	Medicine Hat	WHL	48	13	15	28	56	....	....	....	....	....
1990-91	Medicine Hat	WHL	72	31	28	59	91	11	6	2	8	9
1991-92	Muskegon	IHL	7	1	2	3	6	....	....	....	....	....
	Knoxville	ECHL	57	18	35	53	91	....	....	....	....	....

SIDOROV, ANDREI (SEE-duh-rahf)

Left wing. Shoots right. 5'11", 174 lbs. Born, Kiev, Soviet Union, May 15, 1969.
(Washington's 10th choice, 229th overall, in 1989 Entry Draft).

			Regular Season					Playoffs				
Season	Club	Lea	GP	G	A	TP	PIM	GP	G	A	TP	PIM
1989-90	D'amo Kharkov	USSR	29	6	5	11	14	....	....	....	....	....
1990-91	Sokol Kiev	USSR	42	7	1	8	10	....	....	....	....	....
1991-92	Sokol Kiev	CIS	28	10	5	15	2	....	....	....	....	....

SILLINGER, MIKE

Center. Shoots right. 5'10", 191 lbs. Born, Regina, Sask., June 29, 1971.
(Detroit's 1st choice, 11th overall, in 1989 Entry Draft).

			Regular Season					Playoffs				
Season	Club	Lea	GP	G	A	TP	PIM	GP	G	A	TP	PIM
1987-88	Regina	WHL	67	18	25	43	17	4	2	2	4	0
1988-89	Regina	WHL	72	53	78	131	52	....	....	....	....	....
1989-90a	Regina	WHL	70	57	72	129	41	11	12	10	22	2
	Adirondack	AHL	....	....	....	....	....	1	0	0	0	0
1990-91	**Detroit**	**NHL**	**3**	**0**	**1**	**1**	**0**	**3**	**0**	**1**	**1**	**0**
b	Regina	WHL	57	50	66	116	42	8	6	9	15	4
1991-92	Adirondack	AHL	64	25	41	66	26	15	9	*19	*28	12
	Detroit	**NHL**	....	....	....	....	....	**8**	**2**	**2**	**4**	**2**
	NHL Totals		**3**	**0**	**1**	**1**	**0**	**11**	**2**	**3**	**5**	**2**

a WHL East Second All-Star Team (1990)
b WHL East First All-Star Team (1991)

SILVERMAN, ANDREW

Defense. Shoots left. 6'3", 210 lbs. Born, Beverly, MA, August 23, 1972.
(NY Rangers' 11th choice, 181st overall, in 1990 Entry Draft).

			Regular Season					Playoffs				
Season	Club	Lea	GP	G	A	TP	PIM	GP	G	A	TP	PIM
1990-91	Cushing Aca.	HS	25	8	26	34	84	....	....	....	....	....
1991-92	U. of Maine	H.E.	30	2	9	11	18	....	....	....	....	....

SIM, TREVOR

Right wing. Shoots left. 6'2", 192 lbs. Born, Calgary, Alta., June 9, 1970.
(Edmonton's 3rd choice, 53rd overall, in 1988 Entry Draft).

			Regular Season					Playoffs				
Season	Club	Lea	GP	G	A	TP	PIM	GP	G	A	TP	PIM
1987-88	Seattle	WHL	67	17	18	35	87	....	....	....	....	....
1988-89	Regina	WHL	21	4	8	12	48	....	....	....	....	....
	Swift Current	WHL	42	16	19	35	69	11	10	6	16	20
1989-90	**Edmonton**	**NHL**	**3**	**0**	**1**	**1**	**2**	....	....	....	....	....
	Swift Current	WHL	6	3	2	5	21	....	....	....	....	....
	Kamloops	WHL	43	27	35	62	53	17	3	13	16	28
1990-91	Cape Breton	AHL	62	20	9	29	39	2	0	0	0	0
1991-92	Cape Breton	AHL	2	0	1	1	0	....	....	....	....	....
	Winston-Salem	ECHL	53	25	29	54	110	5	7	2	9	4
	NHL Totals		**3**	**0**	**1**	**1**	**2**	....	....	....	....	....

SIMARD, MARTIN

Right wing. Shoots right. 6'3", 215 lbs. Born, Montreal, Que., June 25, 1966.

			Regular Season					Playoffs				
Season	Club	Lea	GP	G	A	TP	PIM	GP	G	A	TP	PIM
1984-85	Granby	QMJHL	58	22	31	53	78	8	3	7	10	21
1985-86	Granby	QMJHL	54	32	28	60	129	....	....	....	....	....
	Hull	QMJHL	14	8	8	16	55	14	8	19	27	19
1986-87	Granby	QMJHL	41	30	47	77	105	8	3	7	10	21
1987-88	Salt Lake	IHL	82	8	23	31	281	19	6	3	9	100
1988-89	Salt Lake	IHL	71	13	15	28	221	14	4	0	4	45
1989-90	Salt Lake	IHL	59	22	23	45	151	11	5	8	13	12
1990-91	**Calgary**	**NHL**	**16**	**0**	**2**	**2**	**53**	....	....	....	....	....
	Salt Lake	IHL	54	24	25	49	113	4	3	0	3	20
1991-92	**Calgary**	**NHL**	**21**	**1**	**3**	**4**	**119**	....	....	....	....	....
	Salt Lake	IHL	11	3	7	10	51	....	....	....	....	....
	Halifax	AHL	10	5	3	8	26	....	....	....	....	....
	NHL Totals		**37**	**1**	**5**	**6**	**172**	....	....	....	....	....

Signed as a free agent by **Calgary**, May 19, 1987. Traded to **Quebec** by **Calgary** for Greg Smyth, March 10, 1992.

SIMON, CHRIS

Left wing. Shoots left. 6'3", 230 lbs. Born, Wawa, Ont., January 30, 1972.
(Philadelphia's 2nd choice, 25th overall, in 1990 Entry Draft).

			Regular Season					Playoffs				
Season	Club	Lea	GP	G	A	TP	PIM	GP	G	A	TP	PIM
1988-89	Ottawa	OHL	36	4	2	6	31	....	....	....	....	....
1989-90	Ottawa	OHL	57	36	38	74	146	3	2	1	3	4
1990-91	Ottawa	OHL	20	16	6	22	69	17	5	9	14	59
1991-92	Ottawa	OHL	2	1	1	2	24	....	....	....	....	....
	S.S. Marie	OHL	31	19	25	44	143	11	5	8	13	49

Traded to **Quebec** by **Philadelphia** with Peter Forsberg, Steve Duchesne, Kerry Huffman, Mike Ricci, Ron Hextall, Philadelphia's first round choice in the 1993 and 1994 Entry Drafts and cash for Eric Lindros, June 30, 1992.

SIMON, DARCY

Defense. Shoots right. 6'1", 200 lbs. Born, North Battleford, Sask., January 21, 1970.

			Regular Season					Playoffs				
Season	Club	Lea	GP	G	A	TP	PIM	GP	G	A	TP	PIM
1987-88	Seattle	WHL	67	5	9	14	226	....	....	....	....	....
1988-89	Seattle	WHL	62	3	15	18	208	....	....	....	....	....
1989-90	Seattle	WHL	63	5	13	18	285	13	1	2	3	79
1990-91	Fredericton	AHL	29	0	3	3	183	9	2	0	2	45
1991-92	Fredericton	AHL	58	9	11	20	308	4	0	0	0	13

Signed as a free agent by **Montreal**, October 3, 1990.

SIMON, JASON

Left wing. Shoots left. 6'1", 190 lbs. Born, Sarnia, Ont., March 21, 1969.
(New Jersey's 9th choice, 215th overall, in 1989 Entry Draft).

			Regular Season					Playoffs				
Season	Club	Lea	GP	G	A	TP	PIM	GP	G	A	TP	PIM
1986-87	London	OHL	33	1	2	3	33	....	....	....	....	....
	Sudbury	OHL	26	2	3	5	50	....	....	....	....	....
1987-88	Sudbury	OHL	26	5	7	12	35	....	....	....	....	....
	Hamilton	OHL	29	5	13	18	124	11	0	2	2	15
1988-89	Windsor	OHL	62	23	39	62	193	4	1	4	5	13
1989-90	Utica	AHL	16	3	4	7	28	2	0	0	0	12
	Nashville	ECHL	13	4	3	7	81	5	1	3	4	17
1990-91	Utica	AHL	50	2	12	14	189	....	....	....	....	....
	Johnstown	ECHL	22	11	9	20	55	....	....	....	....	....
1991-92	Utica	AHL	1	0	0	0	12	....	....	....	....	....
	San Diego	IHL	13	1	4	5	45	3	0	1	1	9

SIMPSON, CRAIG

Left wing. Shoots right. 6'2", 195 lbs. Born, London, Ont., February 15, 1967.
(Pittsburgh's 1st choice, 2nd overall, in 1985 Entry Draft).

			Regular Season					Playoffs				
Season	Club	Lea	GP	G	A	TP	PIM	GP	G	A	TP	PIM
1983-84	Michigan State	CCHA	46	14	43	57	38	....	....	....	....	....
1984-85ab	Michigan State	CCHA	42	31	53	84	33	....	....	....	....	....
1985-86	**Pittsburgh**	**NHL**	**76**	**11**	**17**	**28**	**49**	....	....	....	....	....
1986-87	**Pittsburgh**	**NHL**	**72**	**26**	**25**	**51**	**57**	....	....	....	....	....
1987-88	**Pittsburgh**	**NHL**	**21**	**13**	**13**	**26**	**34**	....	....	....	....	....
	Edmonton	**NHL**	**59**	**43**	**21**	**64**	**43**	**19**	**13**	**6**	**19**	**26**
1988-89	**Edmonton**	**NHL**	**66**	**35**	**41**	**76**	**80**	**7**	**2**	**0**	**2**	**10**
1989-90	**Edmonton**	**NHL**	**80**	**29**	**32**	**61**	**180**	**22**	***16**	**15**	***31**	**8**
1990-91	**Edmonton**	**NHL**	**75**	**30**	**27**	**57**	**66**	**18**	**5**	**11**	**16**	**12**
1991-92	**Edmonton**	**NHL**	**79**	**24**	**37**	**61**	**80**	**1**	**0**	**0**	**0**	**0**
	NHL Totals		**528**	**211**	**213**	**424**	**589**	**67**	**36**	**32**	**68**	**56**

a CCHA First All-Star Team (1985)
b NCAA West First All-American Team (1985)

Traded to **Edmonton** by **Pittsburgh** with Dave Hannan, Moe Mantha and Chris Joseph for Paul Coffey, Dave Hunter and Wayne Van Dorp, November 24, 1987.

SIMPSON, GEOFF

Defense. Shoots right. 6'1", 180 lbs. Born, Victoria, B.C., March 6, 1969.
(Boston's 10th choice, 206th overall, in 1989 Entry Draft).

			Regular Season					Playoffs				
Season	Club	Lea	GP	G	A	TP	PIM	GP	G	A	TP	PIM
1989-90	N. Michigan	WCHA	39	4	19	23	40	....	....	....	....	....
1990-91	N. Michigan	WCHA	44	2	15	17	27	....	....	....	....	....
1991-92	N. Michigan	WCHA	25	1	3	4	20	....	....	....	....	....

SIMPSON, REID

Left wing. Shoots left. 6'1", 211 lbs. Born, Flin Flon, Man., May 21, 1969.
(Philadelphia's 3rd choice, 72nd overall, in 1989 Entry Draft).

			Regular Season					Playoffs				
Season	Club	Lea	GP	G	A	TP	PIM	GP	G	A	TP	PIM
1987-88	Prince Albert	WHL	72	13	14	27	164	10	1	0	1	43
1988-89	Prince Albert	WHL	59	26	29	55	264	4	2	1	3	30
1989-90	Prince Albert	WHL	29	15	17	32	121	14	4	7	11	34
	Hershey	AHL	28	2	2	4	175	....	....	....	....	....
1990-91	Hershey	AHL	54	9	15	24	183	1	0	0	0	0
1991-92	**Philadelphia**	**NHL**	**1**	**0**	**0**	**0**	**0**	....	....	....	....	....
	Hershey	AHL	60	11	7	18	145	....	....	....	....	....
	NHL Totals		**1**	**0**	**0**	**0**	**0**	....	....	....	....	....

SINCLAIR, AL

Defense. Shoots right. 6'3", 210 lbs. Born, Mississauga, Ont., April 3, 1973.
(Ottawa's 6th choice, 121st overall, in 1992 Entry Draft).

			Regular Season					Playoffs				
Season	Club	Lea	GP	G	A	TP	PIM	GP	G	A	TP	PIM
1990-91	Wexford	Jr. B	43	4	15	19	46	....	....	....	....	....
1991-92	U. of Michigan	CCHA	22	0	4	4	40	....	....	....	....	....

SINISALO, ILKKA (sin-i-SAL-oh)

Right wing. Shoots left. 6', 200 lbs. Born, Valeakoski, Finland, July 10, 1958.

			Regular Season					Playoffs				
Season	Club	Lea	GP	G	A	TP	PIM	GP	G	A	TP	PIM
1977-78	HIFK	Fin.	36	9	3	12	18	....	....	....	....	....
1978-79	HIFK	Fin.	30	6	4	10	16	6	0	5	5	25
1979-80	HIFK	Fin.	35	16	9	25	16	7	1	3	4	12
1980-81	HIFK	Fin.	36	27	17	44	14	6	5	3	8	4
1981-82	**Philadelphia**	**NHL**	**66**	**15**	**22**	**37**	**22**	**4**	**0**	**2**	**2**	**0**
1982-83	**Philadelphia**	**NHL**	**61**	**21**	**29**	**50**	**16**	**3**	**1**	**1**	**2**	**0**
1983-84	**Philadelphia**	**NHL**	**73**	**29**	**17**	**46**	**29**	**2**	**2**	**0**	**2**	**0**
1984-85	**Philadelphia**	**NHL**	**70**	**36**	**37**	**73**	**16**	**19**	**6**	**1**	**7**	**0**
1985-86	**Philadelphia**	**NHL**	**74**	**39**	**37**	**76**	**31**	**5**	**2**	**2**	**4**	**2**
1986-87	**Philadelphia**	**NHL**	**42**	**10**	**21**	**31**	**8**	**18**	**5**	**1**	**6**	**4**
1987-88	**Philadelphia**	**NHL**	**68**	**25**	**17**	**42**	**30**	**7**	**4**	**2**	**6**	**0**
1988-89	**Philadelphia**	**NHL**	**13**	**1**	**6**	**7**	**2**	**8**	**1**	**1**	**2**	**0**
1989-90	**Philadelphia**	**NHL**	**59**	**23**	**23**	**46**	**26**	....	....	....	....	....
1990-91	**Minnesota**	**NHL**	**46**	**5**	**12**	**17**	**24**	....	....	....	....	....
	Los Angeles	**NHL**	**7**	**0**	**0**	**0**	**2**	**2**	**0**	**1**	**1**	**0**
1991-92	**Los Angeles**	**NHL**	**3**	**0**	**1**	**1**	**2**	....	....	....	....	....
	Phoenix	IHL	42	19	21	40	32	....	....	....	....	....
	NHL Totals		**582**	**204**	**222**	**426**	**208**	**68**	**21**	**11**	**32**	**6**

Signed as a free agent by **Philadelphia**, February 14, 1981. Signed as a free agent by **Minnesota**, July 3, 1990. Traded to **Los Angeles** by **Minnesota** for Los Angeles' eighth round choice (Michael Burkett) in 1991 Entry Draft, March 5, 1991.

SIREN, VILLE (SIH-rihn)

Defense. Shoots left. 6'2", 191 lbs. Born, Tampere, Finland, February 11, 1964.
(Hartford's 3rd choice, 23rd overall, in 1983 Entry Draft).

			Regular Season					Playoffs				
Season	Club	Lea	GP	G	A	TP	PIM	GP	G	A	TP	PIM
1982-83	Ilves	Fin.	29	3	2	5	42	8	1	3	4	8
1983-84	Ilves	Fin.	36	1	10	11	40	2	0	0	0	2
	Fin. Olympic	....	2	0	0	0	0	....	....	....	....	....
1984-85	Ilves	Fin.	36	11	13	24	24	9	0	2	2	10
1985-86	**Pittsburgh**	**NHL**	**60**	**4**	**8**	**12**	**32**	....	....	....	....	....
1986-87	**Pittsburgh**	**NHL**	**69**	**5**	**17**	**22**	**50**	....	....	....	....	....
1987-88	**Pittsburgh**	**NHL**	**58**	**1**	**20**	**21**	**62**	....	....	....	....	....
1988-89	**Pittsburgh**	**NHL**	**12**	**1**	**0**	**1**	**14**	....	....	....	....	....
	Minnesota	**NHL**	**38**	**2**	**10**	**12**	**58**	**4**	**0**	**0**	**0**	**4**
1989-90	**Minnesota**	**NHL**	**53**	**1**	**13**	**14**	**60**	**3**	**0**	**0**	**0**	**2**
1990-91	HPK	Fin.	44	4	9	13	90	8	1	1	2	37
1991-92	Ilves	Fin.	43	8	14	22	88	....	....	....	....	....
	NHL Totals		**290**	**14**	**68**	**82**	**276**	**7**	**0**	**0**	**0**	**6**

Traded to **Pittsburgh** by **Hartford** for Pat Boutette, November 16, 1984. Traded to **Minnesota** by **Pittsburgh** with Steve Gotaas for Gord Dineen and Scott Bjugstad, December 17, 1988.

SIRKKA, JEFFREY

Defense. Shoots left. 6'1", 205 lbs. Born, Copper Cliff, Ont., June 17, 1968.

			Regular Season					Playoffs				
Season	Club	Lea	GP	G	A	TP	PIM	GP	G	A	TP	PIM
1986-87	Kingston	OHL	64	0	5	5	156	....	....	....	....	....
1987-88	Kingston	OHL	59	1	16	17	114	....	....	....	....	....
1988-89	North Bay	OHL	12	0	3	3	66	....	....	....	....	....
	Toronto	OHL	29	1	14	15	71	....	....	....	....	....
1989-90	Maine	AHL	56	0	9	9	110	....	....	....	....	....
1990-91	Indianapolis	IHL	69	6	12	18	203	6	0	0	0	6
1991-92	Indianapolis	IHL	71	3	17	20	146	....	....	....	....	....

Traded to **Hartford** by **Boston** for Steve Dykstra, March 3, 1990. Signed as a free agent by **Chicago**, September 20, 1990.

SITTLER, RYAN

Left wing. Shoots left. 6'2", 185 lbs. Born, London, Ont., January 28, 1974.
(Philadelphia's 1st choice, 7th overall, in 1992 Entry Draft).

			Regular Season					Playoffs				
Season	Club	Lea	GP	G	A	TP	PIM	GP	G	A	TP	PIM
1990-91	Nicholls	HS	7	8	9	17	8	....	....	....	....	....
	Buffalo Regals	Midget	20	25	34	59	26	....	....	....	....	....
1991-92	Nicholls	HS	21	19	29	48	....	....	....	....	....	....
	Buffalo Regals	Midget	30	39	54	93	....	....	....	....	....	....

SJODIN, TOMMY (SHOH-deen)

Defense. Shoots right. 5'11", 190 lbs. Born, Sundsvall, Sweden, August 13, 1965.
(Minnesota's 10th choice, 237th overall, in 1985 Entry Draft).

			Regular Season					Playoffs				
Season	Club	Lea	GP	G	A	TP	PIM	GP	G	A	TP	PIM
1987-88	Brynas	Swe.	40	6	9	15	28	....	....	....	....	....
1988-89	Brynas	Swe.	40	8	11	19	54	....	....	....	....	....
1989-90	Brynas	Swe.	40	14	14	28	46	5	0	0	0	2
1990-91	Brynas	Swe.	38	12	17	29	79	....	....	....	....	....
1991-92	Brynas	Swe.	40	6	16	22	46	5	0	3	3	4

SJOGREN, THOMAS (SHOH-gruhn)

Right wing. Shoots right. 5'9", 185 lbs. Born, Umea, Sweden, June 8, 1968.
(Washington's 7th choice, 162nd overall, in 1987 Entry Draft).

			Regular Season					Playoffs				
Season	Club	Lea	GP	G	A	TP	PIM	GP	G	A	TP	PIM
1987-88	V. Frolunda	Swe.2	36	36	27	63	42	10	6	6	12	8
1988-89	Sodertalje	Swe.	40	23	19	42	22	....	....	....	....	....
1989-90	Sodertalje	Swe.	33	7	8	15	14	2	0	1	1	0
1990-91	Baltimore	AHL	72	29	24	53	34	2	0	1	1	0
1991-92	V. Frolunda	Swe.	39	8	16	24	16	3	0	1	1	0

SKALDE, JARROD (SKAHL-day)

Center. Shoots left. 6', 170 lbs. Born, Niagara Falls, Ont., February 26, 1971.
(New Jersey's 3rd choice, 26th overall, in 1989 Entry Draft).

			Regular Season					Playoffs				
Season	Club	Lea	GP	G	A	TP	PIM	GP	G	A	TP	PIM
1987-88	Oshawa	OHL	60	12	16	28	24	7	2	1	3	2
1988-89	Oshawa	OHL	65	38	38	76	36	6	1	5	6	2
1989-90	Oshawa	OHL	62	40	52	92	66	17	10	7	17	6
1990-91	**New Jersey**	**NHL**	**1**	**0**	**1**	**1**	**0**	....	....	....	....	....
	Utica	AHL	3	3	2	5	0	....	....	....	....	....
	Oshawa	OHL	15	8	14	22	14	....	....	....	....	....
a	Belleville	OHL	40	30	52	82	21	6	9	6	15	10
1991-92	**New Jersey**	**NHL**	**15**	**2**	**4**	**6**	**4**	....	....	....	....	....
	Utica	AHL	62	20	20	40	56	4	3	1	4	8
	NHL Totals		**16**	**2**	**5**	**7**	**4**	....	....	....	....	....

a OHL Second All-Star Team (1991)

SKARDA, RANDY

Defense. Shoots right. 6'1", 205 lbs. Born, St. Paul, MN, May 5, 1968.
(St. Louis' 8th choice, 157th overall, in 1986 Entry Draft).

			Regular Season					Playoffs				
Season	Club	Lea	GP	G	A	TP	PIM	GP	G	A	TP	PIM
1986-87	U. Minnesota	WCHA	43	3	10	13	77	....	....	....	....	....
1987-88ab	U. Minnesota	WCHA	42	19	26	45	102	....	....	....	....	....
1988-89	U. Minnesota	WCHA	43	6	24	30	91	....	....	....	....	....
1989-90	**St. Louis**	**NHL**	**25**	**0**	**5**	**5**	**11**	....	....	....	....	....
	Peoria	IHL	38	7	17	24	40	4	0	0	0	0
1990-91	Peoria	IHL	78	8	34	42	126	19	3	5	8	22
1991-92	**St. Louis**	**NHL**	**1**	**0**	**0**	**0**	**0**	....	....	....	....	....
	Peoria	IHL	57	8	24	32	64	7	0	0	0	14
	NHL Totals		**26**	**0**	**5**	**5**	**11**	....	....	....	....	....

a NCAA West Second All-American Team (1988)
b WCHA First All-Star Team (1988)

SKRIKO, PETRI (SKREE-koh)

Left wing. Shoots left. 5'10", 175 lbs. Born, Lappeenranta, Finland, March 12, 1962.
(Vancouver's 7th choice, 157th overall, in 1981 Entry Draft).

			Regular Season					Playoffs				
Season	Club	Lea	GP	G	A	TP	PIM	GP	G	A	TP	PIM
1981-82	SaiPa	Fin.	33	19	27	46	24	....	....	....	....	....
1982-83	SaiPa	Fin.	36	23	12	35	12	....	....	....	....	....
1983-84	SaiPa	Fin.	32	25	26	51	13	....	....	....	....	....
	Fin. Olympic	....	7	1	1	2	0	....	....	....	....	....
1984-85	**Vancouver**	**NHL**	**72**	**21**	**14**	**35**	**10**	....	....	....	....	....
1985-86	**Vancouver**	**NHL**	**80**	**38**	**40**	**78**	**34**	**3**	**0**	**0**	**0**	**0**
1986-87	**Vancouver**	**NHL**	**76**	**33**	**41**	**74**	**44**	....	....	....	....	....
1987-88	**Vancouver**	**NHL**	**73**	**30**	**34**	**64**	**32**	....	....	....	....	....
1988-89	**Vancouver**	**NHL**	**74**	**30**	**36**	**66**	**57**	**7**	**1**	**5**	**6**	**0**
1989-90	**Vancouver**	**NHL**	**77**	**15**	**33**	**48**	**36**	....	....	....	....	....
1990-91	**Vancouver**	**NHL**	**20**	**4**	**4**	**8**	**8**	....	....	....	....	....
	Boston	**NHL**	**28**	**5**	**14**	**19**	**9**	**18**	**4**	**4**	**8**	**4**
1991-92	**Boston**	**NHL**	**9**	**1**	**0**	**1**	**6**	....	....	....	....	....
	Fin. Olympic	....	8	1	4	5	4	....	....	....	....	....
	Winnipeg	**NHL**	**15**	**2**	**3**	**5**	**4**	....	....	....	....	....
	NHL Totals		**524**	**179**	**219**	**398**	**240**	**28**	**5**	**9**	**14**	**4**

Traded to **Boston** by **Vancouver** for Boston's second round choice in the 1992 Entry Draft, January 16, 1991. Traded to **Winnipeg** by **Boston** for Brent Ashton, October 29, 1991.

SKRUDLAND, BRIAN (SKROOD-luhnd)

Center. Shoots left. 6', 196 lbs. Born, Peace River, Alta., July 31, 1963.

			Regular Season					Playoffs				
Season	Club	Lea	GP	G	A	TP	PIM	GP	G	A	TP	PIM
1980-81	Saskatoon	WHL	66	15	27	42	97	....	....	....	....	....
1981-82	Saskatoon	WHL	71	27	29	56	135	5	0	1	1	2
1982-83	Saskatoon	WHL	71	35	59	94	42	6	1	3	4	19
1983-84	Nova Scotia	AHL	56	13	12	25	55	12	2	8	10	14
1984-85	Sherbrooke	AHL	70	22	28	50	109	17	9	8	17	23
1985-86	**Montreal**	**NHL**	**65**	**9**	**13**	**22**	**57**	**20**	**2**	**4**	**6**	**76**
1986-87	**Montreal**	**NHL**	**79**	**11**	**17**	**28**	**107**	**14**	**1**	**5**	**6**	**29**
1987-88	**Montreal**	**NHL**	**79**	**12**	**24**	**36**	**112**	**11**	**1**	**5**	**6**	**24**
1988-89	**Montreal**	**NHL**	**71**	**12**	**29**	**41**	**84**	**21**	**3**	**7**	**10**	**40**
1989-90	**Montreal**	**NHL**	**59**	**11**	**31**	**42**	**56**	**11**	**3**	**5**	**8**	**30**
1990-91	**Montreal**	**NHL**	**57**	**15**	**19**	**34**	**85**	**13**	**3**	**10**	**13**	**42**
1991-92	**Montreal**	**NHL**	**42**	**3**	**3**	**6**	**36**	**11**	**1**	**1**	**2**	**20**
	NHL Totals		**452**	**73**	**136**	**209**	**537**	**101**	**14**	**37**	**51**	**261**

Signed as a free agent by **Montreal**, September 13, 1983.

SKRYPEC, GERRY

Defense. Shoots left. 5'11", 186 lbs. Born, Kitchener, Ont., June 21, 1974.
(Chicago's 6th choice, 137th overall, in 1992 Entry Draft).

			Regular Season					Playoffs				
Season	Club	Lea	GP	G	A	TP	PIM	GP	G	A	TP	PIM
1990-91	Ottawa	OHL	62	2	7	9	53	17	0	4	4	2
1991-92	Ottawa	OHL	65	6	21	27	105	5	0	1	1	8

SLANEY, JOHN

Defense. Shoots left. 6', 185 lbs. Born, St. John's, Nfld., February 7, 1972.
(Washington's 1st choice, 9th overall, in 1990 Entry Draft).

			Regular Season					Playoffs				
Season	Club	Lea	GP	G	A	TP	PIM	GP	G	A	TP	PIM
1988-89	Cornwall	OHL	66	16	43	59	23	18	8	16	24	10
1989-90ab	Cornwall	OHL	64	38	59	97	68	6	0	8	8	11
1990-91c	Cornwall	OHL	34	21	25	46	28	....	....	....	....	....
1991-92d	Cornwall	OHL	34	19	41	60	43	6	3	8	11	0
	Baltimore	AHL	6	2	4	6	0	....	....	....	....	....

a OHL First All-Star Team (1990)
b OHL and Canadian Major Junior Defenseman of the Year (1990)
c OHL Second All-Star Team (1991)
d OHL Third All-Star Team (1992)

SLANINA, PETER (slah-NEE-nah)

Defense. Shoots right. 6'1", 211 lbs. Born, Banska Bystrica, Czech., December 16, 1959.
(Toronto's 11th choice, 233rd overall, in 1984 Entry Draft).

			Regular Season					Playoffs				
Season	Club	Lea	GP	G	A	TP	PIM	GP	G	A	TP	PIM
1986-87	VSZ Kosice	Czech.	33	11	7	18	....	....	....	....	....	....
1987-88	VSZ Kosice	Czech.	34	7	15	22	....	....	....	....	....	....
1988-89	VSZ Kosice	Czech.	42	12	24	36	....	....	....	....	....	....
1989-90	KalPa	Fin.	39	12	17	29	45	6	0	0	0	4
1990-91	KalPa	Fin.	44	10	27	37	46	8	1	4	5	51
1991-92	KalPa	Fin.	43	8	16	24	36	....	....	....	....	....

SLEGR, JIRI (SHLEHGR)

Defense. Shoots left. 5'11", 190 lbs. Born, Litvinov, Czechoslovakia, May 30, 1971.
(Vancouver's 3rd choice, 23rd overall, in 1990 Entry Draft).

			Regular Season					Playoffs				
Season	Club	Lea	GP	G	A	TP	PIM	GP	G	A	TP	PIM
1988-89	Litvinov	Czech.	8	0	0	0	....	....	....	....	....	....
1989-90	Litvinov	Czech.	51	4	15	19	....	....	....	....	....	....
1990-91	Litvinov	Czech.	39	10	33	43	26	....	....	....	....	....
1991-92	Litvinov	Czech.	42	9	23	32	....	....	....	....	....	....

SMAIL, DOUGLAS (DOUG)

Left wing. Shoots left. 5'9", 175 lbs. Born, Moose Jaw, Sask., September 2, 1957.

			Regular Season					Playoffs				
Season	Club	Lea	GP	G	A	TP	PIM	GP	G	A	TP	PIM
1978-79	North Dakota	WCHA	35	24	34	58	46	....	....	....	....	....
1979-80ab	North Dakota	WCHA	40	43	44	87	70	....	....	....	....	....
1980-81	Winnipeg	NHL	30	10	8	18	45	....	....	....	....	....
1981-82	Winnipeg	NHL	72	17	18	35	55	4	0	0	0	0
1982-83	Winnipeg	NHL	80	15	29	44	32	3	0	0	0	6
1983-84	Winnipeg	NHL	66	20	17	37	62	3	0	1	1	7
1984-85	Winnipeg	NHL	80	31	35	66	45	8	2	1	3	4
1985-86	Winnipeg	NHL	73	16	26	42	32	3	1	0	1	0
1986-87	Winnipeg	NHL	78	25	18	43	36	10	4	0	4	10
1987-88	Winnipeg	NHL	71	15	16	31	34	5	1	0	1	22
1988-89	Winnipeg	NHL	47	14	15	29	52	....	....	....	....	....
1989-90	Winnipeg	NHL	79	25	24	49	63	5	1	0	1	0
1990-91	Winnipeg	NHL	15	1	2	3	10	....	....	....	....	....
	Minnesota	NHL	57	7	13	20	38	1	0	0	0	0
1991-92	Quebec	NHL	46	10	18	28	47	....	....	....	....	....
	NHL Totals		794	206	239	445	551	42	9	2	11	49

a WCHA Second All-Star Team (1980)
b Most Valuable Player, NCAA Tournament (1980)

Played in NHL All-Star Game (1990)

Signed as a free agent by **Winnipeg**, May 22, 1980. Traded to **Minnesota** by **Winnipeg** for Don Barber, November 7, 1990. Signed as a free agent by **Quebec**, August 30, 1991.

SMART, JASON

Center. Shoots left. 6'4", 212 lbs. Born, Prince George, B.C., January 23, 1970.
(Pittsburgh's 13th choice, 247th overall, in 1989 Entry Draft).

			Regular Season					Playoffs				
Season	Club	Lea	GP	G	A	TP	PIM	GP	G	A	TP	PIM
1986-87	Prince Albert	WHL	57	9	22	31	62	8	3	3	6	8
1987-88	Prince Albert	WHL	72	16	29	45	77	10	1	2	3	11
1988-89	Prince Albert	WHL	12	1	3	4	31	....	....	....	....	....
	Saskatoon	WHL	36	6	17	23	33	8	1	6	7	16
1989-90	Saskatoon	WHL	66	27	48	75	187	10	1	5	6	19
1990-91	Albany	IHL	15	4	2	6	28	....	....	....	....	....
	Muskegon	IHL	36	12	27	39	55	5	0	3	3	11
1991-92	Muskegon	IHL	45	10	14	24	49	....	....	....	....	....

SMEHLIK, RICHARD

Defense. Shoots left. 6'3", 208 lbs. Born, Ostrava, Czechoslovakia, January 23, 1970.
(Buffalo's 3rd choice, 97th overall, in 1990 Entry Draft).

			Regular Season					Playoffs				
Season	Club	Lea	GP	G	A	TP	PIM	GP	G	A	TP	PIM
1989-90	TJ Vitkovice	Czech.	43	4	3	7	....	....	....	....	....	....
1990-91	Dukla Jihlava	Czech.	51	4	2	6	22	....	....	....	....	....
1991-92	TJ Vitkovice	Czech.	47	9	10	19	....	....	....	....	....	....

SMITH, DENNIS

Defense. Shoots left. 5'11", 190 lbs. Born, Detroit, MI, July 27, 1964.

			Regular Season					Playoffs				
Season	Club	Lea	GP	G	A	TP	PIM	GP	G	A	TP	PIM
1981-82	Kingston	OHL	48	2	24	26	84	4	0	2	2	0
1982-83	Kingston	OHL	58	6	30	36	100	....	....	....	....	....
1983-84	Kingston	OHL	62	10	41	51	165	....	....	....	....	....
1984-85	Osby	Swe.	30	15	15	30	74	....	....	....	....	....
1985-86	Peoria	IHL	70	5	15	20	102	10	0	2	2	18
1986-87	Adirondack	AHL	64	4	24	28	120	6	0	0	0	8
1987-88	Adirondack	AHL	75	6	24	30	213	11	2	2	4	47
1988-89	Adirondack	AHL	75	5	35	40	176	17	1	6	7	47
1989-90	Washington	NHL	4	0	0	0	0	....	....	....	....	....
a	Baltimore	AHL	74	8	25	33	103	12	0	3	3	65
1990-91	Los Angeles	NHL	4	0	0	0	4	....	....	....	....	....
	New Haven	AHL	61	7	25	32	148	....	....	....	....	....
1991-92	Maine	AHL	59	2	32	34	63	....	....	....	....	....
	NHL Totals		8	0	0	0	4	....	....	....	....	....

a AHL Second All-Star Team (1990)

Signed as a free agent by **Detroit**, December 2, 1986. Signed as a free agent by **Washington**, July 25, 1989. Signed as a free agent by **Los Angeles**, September 28, 1990. Signed as a free agent by **Boston**, August 2, 1991. Traded to **Washington** by **Boston** with John Byce for Brent Hughes and future considerations in 1992 Entry Draft, February 24, 1992.

SMITH, DERRICK

Left wing. Shoots left. 6'2", 215 lbs. Born, Scarborough, Ont., January 22, 1965.
(Philadelphia's 2nd choice, 44th overall, in 1983 Entry Draft).

			Regular Season					Playoffs				
Season	Club	Lea	GP	G	A	TP	PIM	GP	G	A	TP	PIM
1982-83	Peterborough	OHL	70	16	19	35	47	....	....	....	....	....
1983-84	Peterborough	OHL	70	30	36	66	31	8	4	4	8	7
1984-85	Philadelphia	NHL	77	17	22	39	31	19	2	5	7	16
1985-86	Philadelphia	NHL	69	6	6	12	57	4	0	0	0	10
1986-87	Philadelphia	NHL	71	11	21	32	34	26	6	4	10	26
1987-88	Philadelphia	NHL	76	16	8	24	104	7	0	0	0	6
1988-89	Philadelphia	NHL	74	16	14	30	43	19	5	2	7	12
1989-90	Philadelphia	NHL	55	3	6	9	32	....	....	....	....	....
1990-91	Philadelphia	NHL	72	11	10	21	37	....	....	....	....	....
1991-92	Minnesota	NHL	33	2	4	6	33	7	1	0	1	9
	Kalamazoo	IHL	6	1	5	6	4	....	....	....	....	....
	NHL Totals		527	82	91	173	371	82	14	11	25	79

Claimed on waivers by **Minnesota**, October 26, 1991.

SMITH, GEOFF

Defense. Shoots left. 6'3", 200 lbs. Born, Edmonton, Alta., March 7, 1969.
(Edmonton's 3rd choice, 63rd overall, in 1987 Entry Draft).

			Regular Season					Playoffs				
Season	Club	Lea	GP	G	A	TP	PIM	GP	G	A	TP	PIM
1987-88	North Dakota	WCHA	42	4	12	16	34	....	....	....	....	....
1988-89	North Dakota	WCHA	9	0	1	1	8	....	....	....	....	....
	Kamloops	WHL	32	4	31	35	29	6	1	3	4	12
1989-90a	Edmonton	NHL	74	4	11	15	52	3	0	0	0	0
1990-91	Edmonton	NHL	59	1	12	13	55	4	0	0	0	0
1991-92	Edmonton	NHL	74	2	16	18	43	5	0	1	1	6
	NHL Totals		207	7	39	46	150	12	0	1	1	6

a NHL All-Rookie Team (1990)

SMITH, JAMES STEPHEN (STEVE)

Defense. Shoots left. 6'4", 215 lbs. Born, Glasgow, Scotland, April 30, 1963.
(Edmonton's 5th choice, 111th overall, in 1981 Entry Draft).

			Regular Season					Playoffs				
Season	Club	Lea	GP	G	A	TP	PIM	GP	G	A	TP	PIM
1980-81	London	OHA	62	4	12	16	141	....	....	....	....	....
1981-82	London	OHL	58	10	36	46	207	4	1	2	3	13
1982-83	Moncton	AHL	2	0	0	0	0	....	....	....	....	....
	London	OHL	50	6	35	41	133	3	1	0	1	10
1983-84	Moncton	AHL	64	1	8	9	176	....	....	....	....	....
1984-85	Edmonton	NHL	2	0	0	0	2	....	....	....	....	....
	Nova Scotia	AHL	68	2	28	30	161	5	0	3	3	40
1985-86	Edmonton	NHL	55	4	20	24	166	6	0	1	1	14
	Nova Scotia	AHL	4	0	2	2	11	....	....	....	....	....
1986-87	Edmonton	NHL	62	7	15	22	165	15	1	3	4	45
1987-88	Edmonton	NHL	79	12	43	55	286	19	1	11	12	55
1988-89	Edmonton	NHL	35	3	19	22	97	7	2	2	4	20
1989-90	Edmonton	NHL	75	7	34	41	171	22	5	10	15	37
1990-91	Edmonton	NHL	77	13	41	54	193	18	1	2	3	45
1991-92	Chicago	NHL	76	9	21	30	304	18	1	11	12	16
	NHL Totals		461	55	193	248	1384	105	11	40	51	232

Played in NHL All-Star Game (1991)

Traded to **Chicago** by **Edmonton** for Dave Manson and future considerations, October 2, 1991.

SMITH, JASON

Defense. Shoots right. 6'3", 183 lbs. Born, Calgary, Alta., November 2, 1973.
(New Jersey's 1st choice, 18th overall, in 1992 Entry Draft).

			Regular Season					Playoffs				
Season	Club	Lea	GP	G	A	TP	PIM	GP	G	A	TP	PIM
1990-91	Regina	WHL	2	0	0	0	7	4	0	0	0	2
1991-92	Regina	WHL	62	9	29	38	168	....	....	....	....	....

SMITH, MIKE

Defense. Shoots left. 6', 185 lbs. Born, Winnipeg, Man., January 17, 1971.
(Buffalo's 12th choice, 255th overall, in 1991 Entry Draft).

			Regular Season					Playoffs				
Season	Club	Lea	GP	G	A	TP	PIM	GP	G	A	TP	PIM
1990-91	Lake Superior	CCHA	43	5	29	34	30	....	....	....	....	....
1991-92	Lake Superior	CCHA	39	6	16	22	28	....	....	....	....	....

SMITH, RANDY

Center. Shoots left. 6'4", 200 lbs. Born, Saskatoon, Sask., July 7, 1965.

			Regular Season					Playoffs				
Season	Club	Lea	GP	G	A	TP	PIM	GP	G	A	TP	PIM
1983-84	Saskatoon	WHL	69	19	21	40	53	....	....	....	....	....
1984-85	Saskatoon	WHL	71	34	51	85	26	8	4	3	7	0
1985-86	**Minnesota**	**NHL**	**1**	**0**	**0**	**0**	**0**	....	....	....	....	....
	Saskatoon	WHL	70	60	86	146	44	9	4	9	13	4
1986-87	**Minnesota**	**NHL**	**2**	**0**	**0**	**0**	**0**	....	....	....	....	....
	Springfield	AHL	75	20	44	64	24	....	....	....	....	....
1987-88	Kalamazoo	IHL	77	13	43	56	54	6	0	8	8	2
1988-89	Maine	AHL	33	9	16	25	34	....	....	....	....	....
	Kalamazoo	IHL	23	4	9	13	2	....	....	....	....	....
1989-90	Kalamazoo	IHL	8	1	2	3	12	....	....	....	....	....
	Salt Lake	IHL	30	5	6	11	10	3	0	0	0	0
1990-91	Cdn. National	....	58	17	39	56	42	....	....	....	....	....
1991-92	Cdn. National	....	59	20	25	45	24	....	....	....	....	....
	Cdn. Olympic	....	8	1	7	8	4	....	....	....	....	....
	NHL Totals		**3**	**0**	**0**	**0**	**0**	....	....	....	....	....

Signed as a free agent by **Minnesota**, May 12, 1986.

SMITH, ROBERT DAVID (BOBBY)

Center. Shoots left. 6'4", 210 lbs. Born, North Sydney, N.S., February 12, 1958.
(Minnesota's 1st choice, 1st overall, in 1978 Amateur Draft).

			Regular Season					Playoffs				
Season	Club	Lea	GP	G	A	TP	PIM	GP	G	A	TP	PIM
1976-77a	Ottawa	OHA	64	*65	70	135	52	19	16	16	32	29
1977-78bc	Ottawa	OHA	61	69	*123	*192	44	16	15	15	30	10
1978-79d	**Minnesota**	**NHL**	**80**	**30**	**44**	**74**	**39**	....	....	....	....	....
1979-80	**Minnesota**	**NHL**	**61**	**27**	**56**	**83**	**24**	**15**	**1**	**13**	**14**	**9**
1980-81	**Minnesota**	**NHL**	**78**	**29**	**64**	**93**	**73**	**19**	**8**	**17**	**25**	**13**
1981-82	**Minnesota**	**NHL**	**80**	**43**	**71**	**114**	**82**	**4**	**2**	**4**	**6**	**5**
1982-83	**Minnesota**	**NHL**	**77**	**24**	**53**	**77**	**81**	**9**	**6**	**4**	**10**	**17**
1983-84	**Minnesota**	**NHL**	**10**	**3**	**6**	**9**	**9**	....	....	....	....	....
	Montreal	**NHL**	**70**	**26**	**37**	**63**	**62**	**15**	**2**	**7**	**9**	**8**
1984-85	**Montreal**	**NHL**	**65**	**16**	**40**	**56**	**59**	**12**	**5**	**6**	**11**	**30**
1985-86	**Montreal**	**NHL**	**79**	**31**	**55**	**86**	**55**	**20**	**7**	**8**	**15**	**22**
1986-87	**Montreal**	**NHL**	**80**	**28**	**47**	**75**	**72**	**17**	**9**	**9**	**18**	**19**
1987-88	**Montreal**	**NHL**	**78**	**27**	**66**	**93**	**78**	**11**	**3**	**4**	**7**	**8**
1988-89	**Montreal**	**NHL**	**80**	**32**	**51**	**83**	**69**	**21**	**11**	**8**	**19**	**46**
1989-90	**Montreal**	**NHL**	**53**	**12**	**14**	**26**	**35**	**11**	**1**	**4**	**5**	**6**
1990-91	**Minnesota**	**NHL**	**73**	**15**	**31**	**46**	**60**	**23**	**8**	**8**	**16**	**56**
1991-92	**Minnesota**	**NHL**	**68**	**9**	**37**	**46**	**109**	**7**	**1**	**4**	**5**	**6**
	NHL Totals		**1032**	**352**	**672**	**1024**	**907**	**184**	**64**	**96**	**160**	**245**

a OHA Second All-Star Team (1977)
b OHA First All-Star Team (1978)
c Named Canadian Major Junior Player of the Year (1978)
d Won Calder Memorial Trophy (1979)

Played in NHL All-Star Game (1981, 1982, 1989, 1991)

Traded to **Montreal** by **Minnesota** for Keith Acton, Mark Napier and Toronto's third round choice (Ken Hodge) in 1984 Entry Draft — Montreal's property via earlier deal — October 28, 1983. Traded to **Minnesota** by **Montreal** for Minnesota's fourth round choice (Louis Bernard) in the 1992 Entry Draft, August 7, 1990.

SMITH, SANDY

Right wing. Shoots right. 5'11", 200 lbs. Born, Brainerd, MN, October 23, 1967.
(Pittsburgh's 5th choice, 88th overall, in 1986 Entry Draft).

			Regular Season					Playoffs				
Season	Club	Lea	GP	G	A	TP	PIM	GP	G	A	TP	PIM
1986-87	Minn.-Duluth	WCHA	35	3	3	6	26	....	....	....	....	....
1987-88	Minn.-Duluth	WCHA	41	22	9	31	47	....	....	....	....	....
1988-89	Minn.-Duluth	WCHA	40	6	16	22	75	....	....	....	....	....
1989-90	Minn.-Duluth	WCHA	39	15	16	31	53	....	....	....	....	....
	Muskegon	IHL	3	1	0	1	0	....	....	....	....	....
1990-91	Muskegon	IHL	82	25	29	54	51	5	1	1	2	6
1991-92	Muskegon	IHL	64	15	18	33	109	14	7	2	9	4

SMOLINSKI, BRYAN

Center. Shoots right. 6'1", 195 lbs. Born, Toledo, OH, December 27, 1971.
(Boston's 1st choice, 21st overall, in 1990 Entry Draft).

			Regular Season					Playoffs				
Season	Club	Lea	GP	G	A	TP	PIM	GP	G	A	TP	PIM
1989-90	Michigan State	CCHA	35	9	13	22	34	....	....	....	....	....
1990-91	Michigan State	CCHA	35	9	12	21	24	....	....	....	....	....
1991-92	Michigan State	CCHA	41	28	33	61	55	....	....	....	....	....

SMYTH, GREG (SMIHTH)

Defense. Shoots right. 6'3", 212 lbs. Born, Oakville, Ont., April 23, 1966.
(Philadelphia's 1st choice, 22nd overall, in 1984 Entry Draft).

			Regular Season					Playoffs				
Season	Club	Lea	GP	G	A	TP	PIM	GP	G	A	TP	PIM
1983-84	London	OHL	64	4	21	25	252	6	1	0	1	24
1984-85	London	OHL	47	7	16	23	188	8	2	2	4	27
1985-86	Hershey	AHL	2	0	1	1	5	8	0	0	0	60
a	London	OHL	46	12	42	54	199	4	1	2	3	28
1986-87	**Philadelphia**	**NHL**	**1**	**0**	**0**	**0**	**0**	**1**	**0**	**0**	**0**	**2**
	Hershey	AHL	35	0	2	2	158	2	0	0	0	19
1987-88	**Philadelphia**	**NHL**	**48**	**1**	**6**	**7**	**192**	**5**	**0**	**0**	**0**	**38**
	Hershey	AHL	21	0	10	10	102	....	....	....	....	....
1988-89	**Quebec**	**NHL**	**10**	**0**	**1**	**1**	**70**	....	....	....	....	....
	Halifax	AHL	43	3	9	12	310	4	0	1	1	35
1989-90	**Quebec**	**NHL**	**13**	**0**	**0**	**0**	**57**	....	....	....	....	....
	Halifax	AHL	49	5	14	19	235	6	1	0	1	52
1990-91	**Quebec**	**NHL**	**1**	**0**	**0**	**0**	**0**	....	....	....	....	....
	Halifax	AHL	56	6	23	29	340	....	....	....	....	....
1991-92	**Quebec**	**NHL**	**29**	**0**	**2**	**2**	**138**	....	....	....	....	....
	Halifax	AHL	9	1	3	4	35	....	....	....	....	....
	Calgary	**NHL**	**7**	**1**	**1**	**2**	**15**	....	....	....	....	....
	NHL Totals		**109**	**2**	**10**	**12**	**472**	**6**	**0**	**0**	**0**	**40**

a OHL Second All-Star Team (1986)

Traded to **Quebec** by **Philadelphia** with Philadelphia's third round choice (John Tanner) in the 1989 Entry Draft for Terry Carkner, July 25, 1988. Traded to **Calgary** by **Quebec** for Martin Simard, March 10, 1992.

SMYTH, KEVIN

Left wing. Shoots left. 6'2", 217 lbs. Born, Banff, Alta., November 22, 1973.
(Hartford's 4th choice, 79th overall, in 1992 Entry Draft).

			Regular Season					Playoffs				
Season	Club	Lea	GP	G	A	TP	PIM	GP	G	A	TP	PIM
1990-91	Moose Jaw	WHL	66	30	45	75	96	6	1	1	2	0
1991-92	Moose Jaw	WHL	71	30	55	85	114	4	1	3	4	6

SNEDDON, KEVIN

Defense. Shoots left. 5'11", 170 lbs. Born, St. Catharines, Ont., April 23, 1970.
(Los Angeles' 12th choice, 249th overall, in 1989 Entry Draft).

			Regular Season					Playoffs				
Season	Club	Lea	GP	G	A	TP	PIM	GP	G	A	TP	PIM
1988-89	Harvard	ECAC	24	0	5	5	16	....	....	....	....	....
1989-90	Harvard	ECAC	26	0	8	8	18	....	....	....	....	....
1990-91	Harvard	ECAC	17	0	4	4	26	....	....	....	....	....
1991-92	Harvard	ECAC	17	2	3	5	10	....	....	....	....	....

SNELL, CHRIS

Defense. Shoots left. 5'10", 198 lbs. Born, Regina, Sask., May 12, 1971.
(Buffalo's 8th choice, 145th overall, in 1991 Entry Draft).

			Regular Season					Playoffs				
Season	Club	Lea	GP	G	A	TP	PIM	GP	G	A	TP	PIM
1989-90	Ottawa	OHL	63	18	62	80	36	3	2	4	6	4
1990-91	Ottawa	OHL	54	23	59	82	58	17	3	14	17	8
1991-92	Rochester	AHL	65	5	27	32	66	10	2	1	3	6

SNUGGERUD, DAVE

Right wing. Shoots left. 6', 190 lbs. Born, Minnetonka, MN, June 20, 1966.
(Buffalo's 1st choice, 1st overall, in 1987 Supplemental Draft).

			Regular Season					Playoffs				
Season	Club	Lea	GP	G	A	TP	PIM	GP	G	A	TP	PIM
1985-86	U. Minnesota	WCHA	42	14	18	32	47	....	....	....	....	....
1986-87	U. Minnesota	WCHA	39	30	29	59	38	....	....	....	....	....
1987-88	U.S. National	....	51	14	21	35	26	....	....	....	....	....
	U.S. Olympic	....	6	3	2	5	4	....	....	....	....	....
1988-89ab	U. Minnesota	WCHA	45	29	20	49	39	....	....	....	....	....
1989-90	**Buffalo**	**NHL**	**80**	**14**	**16**	**30**	**41**	**6**	**0**	**0**	**0**	**2**
1990-91	**Buffalo**	**NHL**	**80**	**9**	**15**	**24**	**32**	**6**	**1**	**3**	**4**	**4**
1991-92	**Buffalo**	**NHL**	**55**	**3**	**15**	**18**	**36**	....	....	....	....	....
	San Jose	**NHL**	**11**	**0**	**1**	**1**	**4**	....	....	....	....	....
	NHL Totals		**226**	**26**	**47**	**73**	**113**	**12**	**1**	**3**	**4**	**6**

a WCHA Second All-Star Team (1989)
b NCAA West Second All-American Team (1989)

Traded to **San Jose** by **Buffalo** for Wayne Presley, March 9, 1992.

SOCHA, GARY

Center. Shoots left. 6'4", 185 lbs. Born, North Attleboro, MA, December 30, 1969.
(Calgary's 3rd choice, 84th overall, in 1988 Entry Draft).

			Regular Season					Playoffs				
Season	Club	Lea	GP	G	A	TP	PIM	GP	G	A	TP	PIM
1989-90	Providence	H.E.	25	2	2	4	8	....	....	....	....	....
1990-91	Providence	H.E.	35	15	13	28	20	....	....	....	....	....
1991-92	Providence	H.E.	26	11	14	25	34	....	....	....	....	....

SOLLY, JIM

Center. Shoots left. 6'1", 180 lbs. Born, St. Catharines, Ont., March 19, 1970.
(Winnipeg's 10th choice, 151st overall, in 1989 Entry Draft).

			Regular Season					Playoffs				
Season	Club	Lea	GP	G	A	TP	PIM	GP	G	A	TP	PIM
1988-89	Bowling Green	CCHA	40	4	9	13	14	....	....	....	....	....
1989-90	Bowling Green	CCHA	44	9	11	20	14	....	....	....	....	....
1990-91	Bowling Green	CCHA	31	1	2	3	14	....	....	....	....	....
1991-92	Bowling Green	CCHA	34	10	11	21	45	....	....	....	....	....

SORENSEN, KELLY

Right wing. Shoots right. 5'11", 170 lbs. Born, Newmarket, Ont., June 11, 1970.
(Detroit's 1st choice, 16th overall, in 1991 Supplemental Draft).

			Regular Season					Playoffs				
Season	Club	Lea	GP	G	A	TP	PIM	GP	G	A	TP	PIM
1988-89	Ferris State	CCHA	29	1	3	4	5	....	....	....	....	....
1989-90	Ferris State	CCHA	37	7	12	19	48	....	....	....	....	....
1990-91	Ferris State	CCHA	37	8	15	23	42	....	....	....	....	....
1991-92	Ferris State	CCHA	38	7	14	21	59	....	....	....	....	....

SOROKIN, SERGEI

Defense. Shoots right. 5'11", 187 lbs. Born, Moscow, Soviet Union, October 2, 1969.
(Winnipeg's 12th choice, 247th overall, in 1991 Entry Draft).

			Regular Season					Playoffs				
Season	Club	Lea	GP	G	A	TP	PIM	GP	G	A	TP	PIM
1990-91	Moscow D'amo	USSR	41	4	5	9	20	....	....	....	....	....
1991-92	Moscow D'amo	CIS	35	6	9	15	28	....	....	....	....	....

SOULES, JASON

Defense. Shoots left. 6'2", 212 lbs. Born, Hamilton, Ont., March 14, 1971.
(Edmonton's 1st choice, 15th overall, in 1989 Entry Draft).

			Regular Season					Playoffs				
Season	Club	Lea	GP	G	A	TP	PIM	GP	G	A	TP	PIM
1987-88	Hamilton	OHL	19	1	1	2	56	4	0	0	0	13
1988-89	Niagara Falls	OHL	57	3	8	11	187	....	....	....	....	....
1989-90	Niagara Falls	OHL	9	2	8	10	20	....	....	....	....	....
	Hamilton	OHL	18	0	2	2	42	....	....	....	....	....
1990-91	Hamilton	OHL	25	3	16	19	50	....	....	....	....	....
	Belleville	OHL	37	5	26	31	94	6	1	2	3	4
	Cape Breton	AHL	1	0	0	0	0	....	....	....	....	....
1991-92	Cape Breton	AHL	51	0	9	9	44	....	....	....	....	....

SPARKS, TODD

Left wing. Shoots left. 6′, 187 lbs. Born, Edmundston, N.B., June 9, 1971.
(NY Islanders' 8th choice, 158th overall, in 1991 Entry Draft).

			Regular Season					Playoffs				
Season	**Club**	**Lea**	**GP**	**G**	**A**	**TP**	**PIM**	**GP**	**G**	**A**	**TP**	**PIM**
1990-91	Hull	QMJHL	70	35	52	87	109	6	3	5	8	34
1991-92	Hull	QMJHL	61	28	76	104	140	6	2	9	11	12

SPEER, MICHAEL

Defense. Shoots left. 6′2″, 202 lbs. Born, Toronto, Ont., March 26, 1971.
(Chicago's 2nd choice, 27th overall, in 1989 Entry Draft).

			Regular Season					Playoffs				
Season	**Club**	**Lea**	**GP**	**G**	**A**	**TP**	**PIM**	**GP**	**G**	**A**	**TP**	**PIM**
1987-88	Guelph	OHL	53	4	10	14	60	....	....	....	....	....
1988-89	Guelph	OHL	65	9	31	40	185	7	2	4	6	23
1989-90	Owen Sound	OHL	61	18	39	57	176	12	3	7	10	21
1990-91	Owen Sound	OHL	32	13	19	32	86	....	....	....	....	....
	Windsor	IHL	25	8	28	36	40	11	2	7	9	15
	Indianapolis	IHL	1	0	1	1	0	1	0	0	0	5
1991-92	Indianapolis	IHL	54	0	6	6	67	....	....	....	....	....

SPENRATH, GREG

Left wing. Shoots left. 6′1″, 212 lbs. Born, Edmonton, Alta., September 27, 1969.
(NY Rangers' 9th choice, 160th overall, in 1989 Entry Draft).

			Regular Season					Playoffs				
Season	**Club**	**Lea**	**GP**	**G**	**A**	**TP**	**PIM**	**GP**	**G**	**A**	**TP**	**PIM**
1987-88	N. Westminster	WHL	72	18	24	42	210	5	0	4	4	16
1988-89	Tri-Cities	WHL	64	26	35	61	213	7	4	2	6	23
1989-90	Tri-Cities	WHL	67	36	32	68	256	7	1	0	1	15
1990-91	Binghamton	AHL	2	0	0	0	14	....	....	....	....	....
	Erie	ECHL	61	29	36	65	*407	4	1	2	3	46
1991-92	Kalamazoo	IHL	69	4	7	11	237	....	....	....	....	....

Signed as a free agent by **Minnesota**, July 25, 1991.

SPROTT, JIM

Defense. Shoots left. 6′1″, 200 lbs. Born, Oakville, Ont., April 11, 1969.
(Quebec's 3rd choice, 51st overall, in 1987 Entry Draft).

			Regular Season					Playoffs				
Season	**Club**	**Lea**	**GP**	**G**	**A**	**TP**	**PIM**	**GP**	**G**	**A**	**TP**	**PIM**
1986-87	London	OHL	66	8	30	38	153	....	....	....	....	....
1987-88	London	OHL	65	8	23	31	211	12	1	6	7	8
1988-89a	London	OHL	64	15	42	57	236	21	4	17	21	68
1989-90	Halifax	AHL	22	2	1	3	103	....	....	....	....	....
1990-91	Halifax	AHL	9	0	2	2	17	....	....	....	....	....
	Fort Wayne	IHL	19	0	1	1	67	....	....	....	....	....
	Peoria	IHL	31	2	5	7	92	....	....	....	....	....
	Greensboro	ECHL	3	0	0	0	31	....	....	....	....	....
1991-92	New Haven	AHL	54	4	11	15	140	3	0	0	0	17

a OHL Second All-Star Team (1989)

SRSEN, TOMAS (suhz-SHEHN)

Right wing. Shoots left. 5′11″, 180 lbs. Born, Olomouc, Czechoslovakia, August 25, 1966.
(Edmonton's 7th choice, 147th overall, in 1987 Entry Draft).

			Regular Season					Playoffs				
Season	**Club**	**Lea**	**GP**	**G**	**A**	**TP**	**PIM**	**GP**	**G**	**A**	**TP**	**PIM**
1987-88	Zetor Brno	Czech.	34	14	5	19	....	....	....	....	....	....
1988-89	Zetor Brno	Czech.2	42	19	11	30	....	....	....	....	....	....
1989-90	Zetor Brno	Czech.	30	7	15	22	....	....	....	....	....	....
1990-91	**Edmonton**	**NHL**	**2**	**0**	**0**	**0**	**0**	....	....	....	....	....
	Cape Breton	AHL	72	32	26	58	100	4	3	1	4	6
1991-92	Cape Breton	AHL	68	19	27	46	79	5	2	2	4	4
	NHL Totals		**2**	**0**	**0**	**0**	**0**	....	....	....	....	....

STAIOS, STEVE

Defense. Shoots right. 6′, 183 lbs. Born, Hamilton, Ont., July 28, 1973.
(St. Louis' 1st choice, 27th overall, in 1991 Entry Draft).

			Regular Season					Playoffs				
Season	**Club**	**Lea**	**GP**	**G**	**A**	**TP**	**PIM**	**GP**	**G**	**A**	**TP**	**PIM**
1990-91	Niagara Falls	OHL	66	17	29	46	115	12	2	3	5	10
1991-92	Niagara Falls	OHL	65	11	42	53	122	17	7	8	15	27

STANTON, PAUL

Defense. Shoots right. 6′1″, 200 lbs. Born, Boston, MA, June 22, 1967.
(Pittsburgh's 8th choice, 149th overall, in 1985 Entry Draft).

			Regular Season					Playoffs				
Season	**Club**	**Lea**	**GP**	**G**	**A**	**TP**	**PIM**	**GP**	**G**	**A**	**TP**	**PIM**
1985-86	U. Wisconsin	WCHA	36	4	6	10	16	....	....	....	....	....
1986-87	U. Wisconsin	WCHA	41	5	17	22	70	....	....	....	....	....
1987-88ab	U. Wisconsin	WCHA	45	9	38	47	98	....	....	....	....	....
1988-89c	U. Wisconsin	WCHA	45	7	29	36	126	....	....	....	....	....
1989-90	Muskegon	IHL	77	5	27	32	61	15	2	4	6	21
1990-91	**Pittsburgh**	**NHL**	**75**	**5**	**18**	**23**	**40**	**22**	**1**	**2**	**3**	**24**
1991-92	**Pittsburgh**	**NHL**	**54**	**2**	**8**	**10**	**62**	**21**	**1**	**7**	**8**	**42**
	NHL Totals		**129**	**7**	**26**	**33**	**102**	**43**	**2**	**9**	**11**	**66**

a NCAA West First All-American Team (1988)
b WCHA Second All-Star Team (1988)
c WCHA First All-Star Team (1989)

STAPLETON, MIKE

Center. Shoots right. 5′10″, 183 lbs. Born, Sarnia, Ont., May 5, 1966.
(Chicago's 7th choice, 132nd overall, in 1984 Entry Draft).

			Regular Season					Playoffs				
Season	**Club**	**Lea**	**GP**	**G**	**A**	**TP**	**PIM**	**GP**	**G**	**A**	**TP**	**PIM**
1983-84	Cornwall	OHL	70	24	45	69	94	3	1	2	3	4
1984-85	Cornwall	OHL	56	41	44	85	68	9	2	4	6	23
1985-86	Cornwall	OHL	56	39	64	103	74	6	2	3	5	2
1986-87	**Chicago**	**NHL**	**39**	**3**	**6**	**9**	**6**	**4**	**0**	**0**	**0**	**2**
	Cdn. Olympic	....	21	2	4	6	4	....	....	....	....	....
1987-88	**Chicago**	**NHL**	**53**	**2**	**9**	**11**	**59**	....	....	....	....	....
	Saginaw	IHL	31	11	19	30	52	10	5	6	11	10
1988-89	**Chicago**	**NHL**	**7**	**0**	**1**	**1**	**7**	....	....	....	....	....
	Saginaw	IHL	69	21	47	68	162	6	1	3	4	4
1989-90	Indianapolis	IHL	16	5	10	15	6	13	9	10	19	38
1990-91	**Chicago**	**NHL**	**7**	**0**	**1**	**1**	**2**	....	....	....	....	....
	Indianapolis	IHL	75	29	52	81	76	7	1	4	5	0
1991-92	**Chicago**	**NHL**	**19**	**4**	**4**	**8**	**8**	....	....	....	....	....
	Indianapolis	IHL	59	18	40	58	65	....	....	....	....	....
	NHL Totals		**125**	**9**	**21**	**30**	**82**	**4**	**0**	**0**	**0**	**2**

STAROSTENKO, DMITRI (stahr-oh-STEN-koh)

Right wing. Shoots left. 6′, 185 lbs. Born, Minsk, Soviet Union, March 18, 1973.
(NY Rangers' 5th choice, 120th overall, in 1992 Entry Draft).

			Regular Season					Playoffs				
Season	**Club**	**Lea**	**GP**	**G**	**A**	**TP**	**PIM**	**GP**	**G**	**A**	**TP**	**PIM**
1990-91	CSKA	USSR	20	2	1	3	4	....	....	....	....	....
1991-92	CSKA	CIS	32	3	1	4	12	....	....	....	....	....

STASTNY, ANTON (STAHST-nee)

Left wing. Shoots left. 6′, 188 lbs. Born, Bratislava, Czechoslovakia, August 5, 1959.
(Quebec's 4th choice, 83rd overall, in 1979 Entry Draft).

			Regular Season					Playoffs				
Season	**Club**	**Lea**	**GP**	**G**	**A**	**TP**	**PIM**	**GP**	**G**	**A**	**TP**	**PIM**
1978-79	Slovan	Czech.	44	32	19	51	....	....	....	....	....	....
1979-80	Slovan	Czech.	40	30	30	60	....	....	....	....	....	....
	Czech. Oly.	....	6	4	4	8	2	....	....	....	....	....
1980-81	**Quebec**	**NHL**	**80**	**39**	**46**	**85**	**12**	**5**	**4**	**3**	**7**	**2**
1981-82	**Quebec**	**NHL**	**68**	**26**	**46**	**72**	**16**	**16**	**5**	**10**	**15**	**10**
1982-83	**Quebec**	**NHL**	**79**	**32**	**60**	**92**	**25**	**4**	**2**	**2**	**4**	**0**
1983-84	**Quebec**	**NHL**	**69**	**25**	**37**	**62**	**14**	**9**	**2**	**5**	**7**	**7**
1984-85	**Quebec**	**NHL**	**79**	**38**	**42**	**80**	**30**	**16**	**3**	**3**	**6**	**6**
1985-86	**Quebec**	**NHL**	**74**	**31**	**43**	**74**	**19**	**3**	**1**	**1**	**2**	**0**
1986-87	**Quebec**	**NHL**	**77**	**27**	**35**	**62**	**8**	**13**	**3**	**8**	**11**	**6**
1987-88	**Quebec**	**NHL**	**69**	**27**	**45**	**72**	**14**	....	....	....	....	....
1988-89	**Quebec**	**NHL**	**55**	**7**	**30**	**37**	**12**	....	....	....	....	....
	Halifax	AHL	16	9	5	14	4	....	....	....	....	....
1989-90	Gotteron	Switz.	36	25	22	47	....	....	....	....	....	....
1990-91	Olten	Switz.	36	26	14	40	....	....	....	....	....	....
1991-92	Olten	Switz.	33	20	19	39	66	....	....	....	....	....
	NHL Totals		**650**	**252**	**384**	**636**	**150**	**66**	**20**	**32**	**52**	**31**

STASTNY, PETER (STAHST-nee)

Center. Shoots left. 6′1″, 200 lbs. Born, Bratislava, Czechoslovakia, September 18, 1956.

			Regular Season					Playoffs				
Season	**Club**	**Lea**	**GP**	**G**	**A**	**TP**	**PIM**	**GP**	**G**	**A**	**TP**	**PIM**
1978-79	Slovan	Czech.	44	32	23	55	....	....	....	....	....	....
1979-80a	Slovan	Czech.	40	30	30	60	....	....	....	....	....	....
	Czech. Oly.	....	16	7	7	14	6	....	....	....	....	....
1980-81bcd	**Quebec**	**NHL**	**77**	**39**	**70**	**109**	**37**	**5**	**2**	**8**	**10**	**7**
1981-82	**Quebec**	**NHL**	**80**	**46**	**93**	**139**	**91**	**12**	**7**	**11**	**18**	**10**
1982-83	**Quebec**	**NHL**	**75**	**47**	**77**	**124**	**78**	**4**	**3**	**2**	**5**	**10**
1983-84	**Quebec**	**NHL**	**80**	**46**	**73**	**119**	**73**	**9**	**2**	**7**	**9**	**31**
1984-85	**Quebec**	**NHL**	**75**	**32**	**68**	**100**	**95**	**18**	**4**	**19**	**23**	**24**
1985-86	**Quebec**	**NHL**	**76**	**41**	**81**	**122**	**60**	**3**	**0**	**1**	**1**	**2**
1986-87	**Quebec**	**NHL**	**64**	**24**	**53**	**77**	**43**	**13**	**6**	**9**	**15**	**12**
1987-88	**Quebec**	**NHL**	**76**	**46**	**65**	**111**	**69**	....	....	....	....	....
1988-89	**Quebec**	**NHL**	**72**	**35**	**50**	**85**	**117**	....	....	....	....	....
1989-90	**Quebec**	**NHL**	**62**	**24**	**38**	**62**	**24**	....	....	....	....	....
	New Jersey	**NHL**	**12**	**5**	**6**	**11**	**16**	**6**	**3**	**2**	**5**	**2**
1990-91	**New Jersey**	**NHL**	**77**	**18**	**42**	**60**	**53**	**7**	**3**	**4**	**7**	**2**
1991-92	**New Jersey**	**NHL**	**66**	**24**	**38**	**62**	**42**	**7**	**3**	**7**	**10**	**19**
	NHL Totals		**892**	**427**	**754**	**1181**	**798**	**84**	**33**	**70**	**103**	**119**

a Czechoslovakian League Player of the Year (1980)
b Won Calder Memorial Trophy (1981)
c NHL record for assists by a rookie (1981)
d NHL record for points by a rookie (1981)

Played in NHL All-Star Game (1981, 1982-84, 1986, 1988)

Signed as a free agent by **Quebec**, August 26, 1980. Traded to **New Jersey** by **Quebec** for Craig Wolanin and future considerations (Randy Velischek), March 6, 1990.

STAUBER, PETE

Left wing. Shoots left. 5′11″, 185 lbs. Born, Duluth, MN, May 10, 1966.

			Regular Season					Playoffs				
Season	**Club**	**Lea**	**GP**	**G**	**A**	**TP**	**PIM**	**GP**	**G**	**A**	**TP**	**PIM**
1986-87	Lake Superior	CCHA	40	22	13	35	80	....	....	....	....	....
1987-88	Lake Superior	CCHA	45	25	33	58	103	....	....	....	....	....
1988-89	Lake Superior	CCHA	46	25	13	38	115	....	....	....	....	....
1989-90	Lake Superior	CCHA	46	25	31	56	90	....	....	....	....	....
1990-91	Adirondack	AHL	26	7	11	18	2	....	....	....	....	....
1991-92	Adirondack	AHL	25	2	5	7	14	....	....	....	....	....
	Toledo	ECHL	25	7	21	28	46	5	2	3	5	46

Signed as a free agent by **Detroit**, June 21, 1990.

STAVJANA, ANTONIN (stahv-YAH-nah)

Defense. Shoots left. 6', 187 lbs. Born, Gottwaldov, Czechoslovakia, February 10, 1963.
(Calgary's 11th choice, 247th overall, in 1986 Entry Draft).

			Regular Season					Playoffs				
Season	Club	Lea	GP	G	A	TP	PIM	GP	G	A	TP	PIM
1986-87	TJ Gottwaldov	Czech.	33	11	7	18	....	....	....	....	....	....
1987-88	TJ Gottwaldov	Czech.	28	5	11	16	....	....	....	....	....	....
1988-89	TJ Gottwaldov	Czech.	43	11	12	23	....	....	....	....	....	....
1989-90	TJ Zlin	Czech.	46	7	14	21	....	....	....	....	....	....
1990-91	JoKP	Fin.	42	13	35	48	10	....	....	....	....	....
1991-92	JoKP	Fin.	44	9	11	20	24	....	....	....	....	....

STEEN, THOMAS (STEEN)

Center. Shoots left. 5'10", 195 lbs. Born, Grums, Sweden, June 8, 1960.
(Winnipeg's 5th choice, 103rd overall, in 1979 Entry Draft).

			Regular Season					Playoffs				
Season	Club	Lea	GP	G	A	TP	PIM	GP	G	A	TP	PIM
1976-77	Leksand	Swe.	2	1	1	2	2	....	....	....	....	....
1977-78	Leksand	Swe.	35	5	6	11	30	....	....	....	....	....
1978-79	Leksand	Swe.	23	13	4	17	35	2	0	0	0	0
	Swe. National	....	2	0	0	0	0	....	....	....	....	....
1979-80	Leksand	Swe.	18	7	7	14	14	2	0	0	0	6
1980-81	Farjestad	Swe.	32	16	23	39	30	7	4	2	6	8
	Swe. National	....	19	2	5	7	12	....	....	....	....	....
1981-82	**Winnipeg**	**NHL**	**73**	**15**	**29**	**44**	**42**	**4**	**0**	**4**	**4**	**2**
1982-83	**Winnipeg**	**NHL**	**75**	**26**	**33**	**59**	**60**	**3**	**0**	**2**	**2**	**0**
1983-84	**Winnipeg**	**NHL**	**78**	**20**	**45**	**65**	**69**	**3**	**0**	**1**	**1**	**9**
1984-85	**Winnipeg**	**NHL**	**79**	**30**	**54**	**84**	**80**	**8**	**2**	**3**	**5**	**17**
1985-86	**Winnipeg**	**NHL**	**78**	**17**	**47**	**64**	**76**	**3**	**1**	**1**	**2**	**4**
1986-87	**Winnipeg**	**NHL**	**75**	**17**	**33**	**50**	**59**	**10**	**3**	**4**	**7**	**8**
1987-88	**Winnipeg**	**NHL**	**76**	**16**	**38**	**54**	**53**	**5**	**1**	**5**	**6**	**2**
1988-89	**Winnipeg**	**NHL**	**80**	**27**	**61**	**88**	**80**	....	....	....	....	....
1989-90	**Winnipeg**	**NHL**	**53**	**18**	**48**	**66**	**35**	**7**	**2**	**5**	**7**	**16**
1990-91	**Winnipeg**	**NHL**	**58**	**19**	**48**	**67**	**49**	....	....	....	....	....
1991-92	**Winnipeg**	**NHL**	**38**	**13**	**25**	**38**	**29**	**7**	**2**	**4**	**6**	**2**
	NHL Totals		**763**	**218**	**461**	**679**	**632**	**50**	**11**	**29**	**40**	**60**

STEER, JAMIE

Right wing. Shoots right. 5'11", 180 lbs. Born, Calgary, Alta., February 24, 1969.
(Buffalo's 1st choice, 19th overall, in 1991 Supplemental Draft).

			Regular Season					Playoffs				
Season	Club	Lea	GP	G	A	TP	PIM	GP	G	A	TP	PIM
1988-89	Michigan Tech	WCHA	42	13	16	29	22	....	....	....	....	....
1989-90	Michigan Tech	WCHA	40	21	21	42	26	....	....	....	....	....
1990-91	Michigan Tech	WCHA	39	14	14	28	20	....	....	....	....	....
1991-92	Michigan Tech	WCHA	39	26	24	50	30	....	....	....	....	....

STEINER, ONDREJ

Center. Shoots left. 6'1", 176 lbs. Born, Plzen, Czech., February 12, 1974.
(Buffalo's 3rd choice, 59th overall, in 1992 Entry Draft).

			Regular Season					Playoffs				
Season	Club	Lea	GP	G	A	TP	PIM	GP	G	A	TP	PIM
1991-92	Skoda Plzen	Czech. Jr.	4	0	1	1	0	....	....	....	....	....

STERN, RONALD (RONNIE)

Right wing. Shoots right. 6', 195 lbs. Born, Ste. Agathe, Que., January 11, 1967.
(Vancouver's 3rd choice, 70th overall, in 1986 Entry Draft).

			Regular Season					Playoffs				
Season	Club	Lea	GP	G	A	TP	PIM	GP	G	A	TP	PIM
1984-85	Longueuil	QMJHL	67	6	14	20	176	....	....	....	....	....
1985-86	Longueuil	QMJHL	70	39	33	72	317	....	....	....	....	....
1986-87	Longueuil	QMJHL	56	32	39	71	266	19	11	9	20	55
1987-88	**Vancouver**	**NHL**	**15**	**0**	**0**	**0**	**52**	....	....	....	....	....
	Fredericton	AHL	2	1	0	1	4	....	....	....	....	....
	Flint	IHL	55	14	19	33	294	16	8	8	16	94
1988-89	**Vancouver**	**NHL**	**17**	**1**	**0**	**1**	**49**	**3**	**0**	**1**	**1**	**17**
	Milwaukee	IHL	45	19	23	42	280	5	1	0	1	11
1989-90	**Vancouver**	**NHL**	**34**	**2**	**3**	**5**	**208**	....	....	....	....	....
	Milwaukee	IHL	26	8	9	17	165	....	....	....	....	....
1990-91	**Vancouver**	**NHL**	**31**	**2**	**3**	**5**	**171**	....	....	....	....	....
	Milwaukee	IHL	7	2	2	4	81	....	....	....	....	....
	Calgary	**NHL**	**13**	**1**	**3**	**4**	**69**	**7**	**1**	**3**	**4**	**14**
1991-92	**Calgary**	**NHL**	**72**	**13**	**9**	**22**	**338**	....	....	....	....	....
	NHL Totals		**182**	**19**	**18**	**37**	**887**	**10**	**1**	**4**	**5**	**31**

Traded to **Calgary** by **Vancouver** with Kevan Guy for Dana Murzyn, March 5, 1991.

STEVENS, JOHN

Defense. Shoots left. 6'1", 195 lbs. Born, Campbellton, N.B., May 4, 1966.
(Philadelphia's 5th choice, 47th overall, in 1984 Entry Draft).

			Regular Season					Playoffs				
Season	Club	Lea	GP	G	A	TP	PIM	GP	G	A	TP	PIM
1983-84	Oshawa	OHL	70	1	10	11	71	7	0	1	1	6
1984-85	Oshawa	OHL	44	2	10	12	61	5	0	2	2	4
	Hershey	AHL	3	0	0	0	0	....	....	....	....	....
1985-86	Kalamazoo	IHL	6	0	1	1	8	6	0	3	3	9
	Oshawa	OHL	65	1	7	8	146	6	0	2	2	14
1986-87	**Philadelphia**	**NHL**	**6**	**0**	**2**	**2**	**14**	....	....	....	....	....
	Hershey	AHL	63	1	15	16	131	3	0	0	0	7
1987-88	**Philadelphia**	**NHL**	**3**	**0**	**0**	**0**	**0**	....	....	....	....	....
	Hershey	AHL	59	1	15	16	108	....	....	....	....	....
1988-89	Hershey	AHL	78	3	13	16	129	12	1	1	2	29
1989-90	Hershey	AHL	79	3	10	13	193	....	....	....	....	....
1990-91	**Hartford**	**NHL**	**14**	**0**	**1**	**1**	**11**	....	....	....	....	....
	Springfield	AHL	65	0	12	12	139	18	0	6	6	35
1991-92	**Hartford**	**NHL**	**21**	**0**	**4**	**4**	**19**	....	....	....	....	....
	Springfield	AHL	45	1	12	13	73	11	1	3	4	27
	NHL Totals		**44**	**0**	**7**	**7**	**44**	....	....	....	....	....

Signed as a free agent by **Hartford**, July 30, 1990.

STEVENS, KEVIN

Left wing. Shoots left. 6'3", 217 lbs. Born, Brockton, MA, April 15, 1965.
(Los Angeles' 6th choice, 108th overall, in 1983 Entry Draft).

			Regular Season					Playoffs				
Season	Club	Lea	GP	G	A	TP	PIM	GP	G	A	TP	PIM
1983-84	Boston College	ECAC	37	6	14	20	36	....	....	....	....	....
1984-85	Boston College	H.E.	40	13	23	36	36	....	....	....	....	....
1985-86	Boston College	H.E.	42	17	27	44	56	....	....	....	....	....
1986-87ab	Boston College	H.E.	39	35	35	70	54	....	....	....	....	....
1987-88	U.S. National	....	44	22	23	45	52	....	....	....	....	....
	U.S. Olympic	....	5	1	3	4	2	....	....	....	....	....
	Pittsburgh	**NHL**	**16**	**5**	**2**	**7**	**8**	....	....	....	....	....
1988-89	**Pittsburgh**	**NHL**	**24**	**12**	**3**	**15**	**19**	**11**	**3**	**7**	**10**	**16**
	Muskegon	IHL	45	24	41	65	113	....	....	....	....	....
1989-90	**Pittsburgh**	**NHL**	**76**	**29**	**41**	**70**	**171**	....	....	....	....	....
1990-91c	**Pittsburgh**	**NHL**	**80**	**40**	**46**	**86**	**133**	**24**	***17**	**16**	**33**	**53**
1991-92d	**Pittsburgh**	**NHL**	**80**	**54**	**69**	**123**	**254**	**21**	**13**	**15**	**28**	**28**
	NHL Totals		**276**	**140**	**161**	**301**	**585**	**56**	**33**	**38**	**71**	**97**

a Hockey East First All-Star Team (1987)
b NCAA East Second All-American Team (1987)
c NHL Second All-Star Team (1991)
d NHL First All-Star Team (1992)

Played in NHL All-Star Game (1991, 1992)

Rights traded to **Pittsburgh** by **Los Angeles** for Anders Hakansson, September 9, 1983.

STEVENS, MIKE

Left wing. Shoots left. 5'11", 195 lbs. Born, Kitchener, Ont., December 30, 1965.
(Vancouver's 5th choice, 58th overall, in 1984 Entry Draft).

			Regular Season					Playoffs				
Season	Club	Lea	GP	G	A	TP	PIM	GP	G	A	TP	PIM
1982-83	Kitchener	OHL	13	0	4	4	16	12	0	1	1	9
1983-84	Kitchener	OHL	66	19	21	40	109	16	10	7	17	40
1984-85	**Vancouver**	**NHL**	**6**	**0**	**3**	**3**	**6**	....	....	....	....	....
	Kitchener	OHL	37	17	18	35	121	4	1	1	2	8
1985-86	Fredericton	AHL	79	12	19	31	208	6	1	1	2	35
1986-87	Fredericton	AHL	71	7	18	25	258	....	....	....	....	....
1987-88	**Boston**	**NHL**	**7**	**0**	**1**	**1**	**9**	....	....	....	....	....
	Maine	AHL	63	30	25	55	265	7	1	2	3	37
1988-89	**NY Islanders**	**NHL**	**9**	**1**	**0**	**1**	**14**	....	....	....	....	....
	Springfield	AHL	42	17	13	30	120	....	....	....	....	....
1989-90	Springfield	AHL	28	12	10	22	75	....	....	....	....	....
	Toronto	**NHL**	**1**	**0**	**0**	**0**	**0**	....	....	....	....	....
	Newmarket	AHL	46	16	28	44	86	....	....	....	....	....
1990-91	Newmarket	AHL	68	24	23	47	229	....	....	....	....	....
1991-92	St. John's	AHL	30	13	11	24	65	....	....	....	....	....
	Binghamton	AHL	44	15	15	30	87	11	7	6	13	45
	NHL Totals		**23**	**1**	**4**	**5**	**29**	....	....	....	....	....

Traded to **Boston** by **Vancouver** for cash, October 6, 1987. Signed as a free agent by **NY Islanders**, August 20, 1988. Traded to **Toronto** by **NY Islanders** with Gilles Thibaudeau for Jack Capuano, Paul Gagne and Derek Laxdal, December 20, 1989. Traded to **NY Rangers** by **Toronto** for Guy Larose, December 26, 1991.

STEVENS, SCOTT

Defense. Shoots left. 6'2", 215 lbs. Born, Kitchener, Ont., April 1, 1964.
(Washington's 1st choice, 5th overall, in 1982 Entry Draft).

			Regular Season					Playoffs				
Season	Club	Lea	GP	G	A	TP	PIM	GP	G	A	TP	PIM
1980-81	Kitchener	OPJHL	39	7	33	40	82	....	....	....	....	....
	Kitchener	OHA	1	0	0	0	0	....	....	....	....	....
1981-82	Kitchener	OHL	68	6	36	42	158	15	1	10	11	71
1982-83a	**Washington**	**NHL**	**77**	**9**	**16**	**25**	**195**	**4**	**1**	**0**	**1**	**26**
1983-84	**Washington**	**NHL**	**78**	**13**	**32**	**45**	**201**	**8**	**1**	**8**	**9**	**21**
1984-85	**Washington**	**NHL**	**80**	**21**	**44**	**65**	**221**	**5**	**0**	**1**	**1**	**20**
1985-86	**Washington**	**NHL**	**73**	**15**	**38**	**53**	**165**	**9**	**3**	**8**	**11**	**12**
1986-87	**Washington**	**NHL**	**77**	**10**	**51**	**61**	**283**	**7**	**0**	**5**	**5**	**19**
1987-88b	**Washington**	**NHL**	**80**	**12**	**60**	**72**	**184**	**13**	**1**	**11**	**12**	**46**
1988-89	**Washington**	**NHL**	**80**	**7**	**61**	**68**	**225**	**6**	**1**	**4**	**5**	**11**
1989-90	**Washington**	**NHL**	**56**	**11**	**29**	**40**	**154**	**15**	**2**	**7**	**9**	**25**
1990-91	**St. Louis**	**NHL**	**78**	**5**	**44**	**49**	**150**	**13**	**0**	**3**	**3**	**36**
1991-92c	**New Jersey**	**NHL**	**68**	**17**	**42**	**59**	**124**	**7**	**2**	**1**	**3**	**29**
	NHL Totals		**747**	**120**	**417**	**537**	**1902**	**87**	**11**	**48**	**59**	**245**

a NHL All-Rookie Team (1983)
b NHL First All-Star Team (1988)
c NHL Second All-Star Team (1992)

Played in NHL All-Star Game (1985, 1989, 1991, 1992)

Signed as a free agent by **St. Louis**, July 16, 1990. Acquired by **New Jersey** from **St. Louis** as compensation for St. Louis' signing of free agent Brendan Shanahan, September 3, 1991.

STEVENSON, JEREMY

Left wing. Shoots left. 6'1", 212 lbs. Born, San Bernadino, CA, June 28, 1974.
(Winnipeg's 3rd choice, 60th overall, in 1992 Entry Draft).

			Regular Season					Playoffs				
Season	Club	Lea	GP	G	A	TP	PIM	GP	G	A	TP	PIM
1990-91	Cornwall	OHL	58	13	20	33	124	....	....	....	....	....
1991-92	Cornwall	OHL	63	15	23	38	176	6	3	1	4	4

STEVENSON, SHAYNE

Right wing. Shoots right. 6'1", 190 lbs. Born, Newmarket, Ont., October 26, 1970.
(Boston's 1st choice, 17th overall, in 1989 Entry Draft).

			Regular Season					Playoffs				
Season	Club	Lea	GP	G	A	TP	PIM	GP	G	A	TP	PIM
1986-87	London	OHL	61	7	15	22	56	....	....	....	....	....
1987-88	London	OHL	36	14	25	39	56	....	....	....	....	....
	Kitchener	OHL	30	10	25	35	48	4	1	1	2	4
1988-89	Kitchener	OHL	56	25	50	75	86	5	2	3	5	4
1989-90	Kitchener	OHL	56	28	61	89	225	17	16	21	37	31
1990-91	**Boston**	**NHL**	**14**	**0**	**0**	**0**	**26**	....	....	....	....	....
	Maine	AHL	58	22	28	50	112	....	....	....	....	....
1991-92	**Boston**	**NHL**	**5**	**0**	**1**	**1**	**2**	....	....	....	....	....
	Maine	AHL	54	10	23	33	150	....	....	....	....	....
	NHL Totals		**19**	**0**	**1**	**1**	**28**	....	....	....	....	....

Claimed by **Tampa Bay** from **Boston** in Expansion Draft, June 18, 1992.

STEVENSON, TURNER

Right wing. Shoots right. 6'3", 200 lbs. Born, Prince George, B.C., May 18, 1972.
(Montreal's 1st choice, 12th overall, in 1990 Entry Draft).

			Regular Season					Playoffs				
Season	**Club**	**Lea**	**GP**	**G**	**A**	**TP**	**PIM**	**GP**	**G**	**A**	**TP**	**PIM**
1989-90	Seattle	WHL	62	29	32	61	276	....	....	....	....	....
1990-91	Seattle	WHL	57	36	27	63	222	6	1	5	6	15
1991-92	Seattle	WHL	58	20	32	52	304	15	9	3	12	55

STEWART, ALLAN

Left wing. Shoots left. 6', 195 lbs. Born, Fort St. John, B.C., January 31, 1964.
(New Jersey's 9th choice, 213th overall, in 1983 Entry Draft).

			Regular Season					Playoffs				
Season	**Club**	**Lea**	**GP**	**G**	**A**	**TP**	**PIM**	**GP**	**G**	**A**	**TP**	**PIM**
1982-83	Prince Albert	WHL	70	25	34	59	272	....	....	....	....	....
1983-84	Prince Albert	WHL	67	44	39	83	216	5	1	2	3	29
	Maine	AHL	....	....	....	....	....	3	0	0	0	0
1984-85	Maine	AHL	75	8	11	19	241	11	1	2	3	58
1985-86	**New Jersey**	**NHL**	**4**	**0**	**0**	**0**	**21**	....	....	....	....	....
	Maine	AHL	58	7	12	19	181	....	....	....	....	....
1986-87	**New Jersey**	**NHL**	**7**	**1**	**0**	**1**	**26**	....	....	....	....	....
	Maine	AHL	74	14	24	38	143	....	....	....	....	....
1987-88	**New Jersey**	**NHL**	**1**	**0**	**0**	**0**	**0**	....	....	....	....	....
	Utica	AHL	49	8	17	25	129	....	....	....	....	....
1988-89	**New Jersey**	**NHL**	**6**	**0**	**2**	**2**	**15**	....	....	....	....	....
	Utica	AHL	72	9	23	32	110	5	1	0	1	4
1989-90	Utica	AHL	....	....	....	....	....	1	0	0	0	11
1990-91	**New Jersey**	**NHL**	**41**	**5**	**2**	**7**	**159**	....	....	....	....	....
	Utica	AHL	9	2	0	2	9	....	....	....	....	....
1991-92	**New Jersey**	**NHL**	**1**	**0**	**0**	**0**	**5**	....	....	....	....	....
	Boston	**NHL**	**4**	**0**	**0**	**0**	**17**	....	....	....	....	....
	NHL Totals		**64**	**6**	**4**	**10**	**243**	....	....	....	....	....

Traded to **Boston** by **New Jersey** for future considerations, October 16, 1991.

STEWART, CAMERON

Center. Shoots left. 5'11", 190 lbs. Born, Kitchener, Ont., September 18, 1971.
(Boston's 2nd choice, 63rd overall, in 1990 Entry Draft).

			Regular Season					Playoffs				
Season	**Club**	**Lea**	**GP**	**G**	**A**	**TP**	**PIM**	**GP**	**G**	**A**	**TP**	**PIM**
1990-91	U. of Michigan	CCHA	44	8	24	32	122	....	....	....	....	....
1991-92	U. of Michigan	CCHA	44	13	15	28	106	....	....	....	....	....

STEWART, DAVE

Defense. Shoots right. 5'11", 195 lbs. Born, Norwood, Ont., January 11, 1972.

			Regular Season					Playoffs				
Season	**Club**	**Lea**	**GP**	**G**	**A**	**TP**	**PIM**	**GP**	**G**	**A**	**TP**	**PIM**
1990-91	Kingston	OHL	64	10	41	51	127	....	....	....	....	....
1991-92	Kingston	OHL	65	15	45	60	143	....	....	....	....	....

Signed as a free agent by **Los Angeles**, August 3, 1992.

STEWART, MICHAEL

Defense. Shoots left. 6'3", 210 lbs. Born, Calgary, Alta., May 30, 1972.
(NY Rangers' 1st choice, 13th overall, in 1990 Entry Draft).

			Regular Season					Playoffs				
Season	**Club**	**Lea**	**GP**	**G**	**A**	**TP**	**PIM**	**GP**	**G**	**A**	**TP**	**PIM**
1989-90	Michigan State	CCHA	40	2	6	8	39	....	....	....	....	....
1990-91	Michigan State	CCHA	37	3	12	15	58	....	....	....	....	....
1991-92	Michigan State	CCHA	8	1	3	4	6	....	....	....	....	....

STIENBURG, TREVOR

Right wing. Shoots right. 6'1", 200 lbs. Born, Kingston, Ont., May 13, 1966.
(Quebec's 1st choice, 15th overall, in 1984 Entry Draft).

			Regular Season					Playoffs				
Season	**Club**	**Lea**	**GP**	**G**	**A**	**TP**	**PIM**	**GP**	**G**	**A**	**TP**	**PIM**
1983-84	Guelph	OHL	65	33	18	51	104	....	....	....	....	....
1984-85	Guelph	OHL	18	7	12	19	38	....	....	....	....	....
	London	OHL	22	9	11	20	45	8	1	3	4	22
1985-86	**Quebec**	**NHL**	**2**	**1**	**0**	**1**	**0**	**1**	**0**	**0**	**0**	**0**
	London	OHL	31	12	18	30	88	5	0	0	0	20
1986-87	**Quebec**	**NHL**	**6**	**1**	**0**	**1**	**12**	....	....	....	....	....
	Fredericton	AHL	48	14	12	26	123	....	....	....	....	....
1987-88	**Quebec**	**NHL**	**8**	**0**	**1**	**1**	**24**	....	....	....	....	....
	Fredericton	AHL	55	12	24	36	279	13	3	3	6	115
1988-89	**Quebec**	**NHL**	**55**	**6**	**3**	**9**	**125**	....	....	....	....	....
1989-90	Halifax	AHL	11	3	3	6	36	....	....	....	....	....
1990-91	Halifax	AHL	41	16	7	23	190	....	....	....	....	....
1991-92	New Haven	AHL	66	17	22	39	201	1	0	0	0	2
	NHL Totals		**71**	**8**	**4**	**12**	**161**	**1**	**0**	**0**	**0**	**0**

Signed as a free agent by **Hartford**, July 21, 1992.

STICKNEY, BRETT

Center. Shoots left. 6'5", 205 lbs. Born, Hanover, NH, May 26, 1972.
(Chicago's 6th choice, 121st overall, in 1990 Entry Draft).

			Regular Season					Playoffs				
Season	**Club**	**Lea**	**GP**	**G**	**A**	**TP**	**PIM**	**GP**	**G**	**A**	**TP**	**PIM**
1990-91	St. Paul Prep.	HS	20	14	10	24	0	....	....	....	....	....
1991-92	Boston College	H.E.	29	1	2	3	10	....	....	....	....	....

STILLMAN, CORY

Center. Shoots left. 6', 174 lbs. Born, Peterborough, Ont., December 20, 1973.
(Calgary's 1st choice, 6th overall, in 1992 Entry Draft).

			Regular Season					Playoffs				
Season	**Club**	**Lea**	**GP**	**G**	**A**	**TP**	**PIM**	**GP**	**G**	**A**	**TP**	**PIM**
1990-91	Windsor	OHL	64	31	70	101	31	11	3	6	9	8
1991-92	Windsor	OHL	53	29	61	90	59	7	2	4	6	8

STIVER, DAN

Right wing. Shoots right. 6', 185 lbs. Born, Chicoutimi, Que., September 14, 1971.
(Toronto's 7th choice, 157th overall, in 1990 Entry Draft).

			Regular Season					Playoffs				
Season	**Club**	**Lea**	**GP**	**G**	**A**	**TP**	**PIM**	**GP**	**G**	**A**	**TP**	**PIM**
1989-90	U. of Michigan	CCHA	40	9	10	19	6	....	....	....	....	....
1990-91	U. of Michigan	CCHA	41	14	15	29	26	....	....	....	....	....
1991-92	U. of Michigan	CCHA	41	8	8	16	8	....	....	....	....	....

STOJANOV, ALEX

Right wing. Shoots left. 6'4", 220 lbs. Born, Windsor, Ont., April 25, 1973.
(Vancouver's 1st choice, 7th overall, in 1991 Entry Draft).

			Regular Season					Playoffs				
Season	**Club**	**Lea**	**GP**	**G**	**A**	**TP**	**PIM**	**GP**	**G**	**A**	**TP**	**PIM**
1989-90	Hamilton	OHL	37	4	4	8	91	....	....	....	....	....
1990-91	Hamilton	OHL	62	25	20	45	181	4	1	1	2	14
1991-92	Guelph	OHL	33	12	15	27	91	....	....	....	....	....

STOLK, DARREN

Defense. Shoots left. 6'4", 210 lbs. Born, Taber, Alta., July 22, 1968.
(Pittsburgh's 11th choice, 235th overall, in 1988 Entry Draft).

			Regular Season					Playoffs				
Season	**Club**	**Lea**	**GP**	**G**	**A**	**TP**	**PIM**	**GP**	**G**	**A**	**TP**	**PIM**
1986-87	Brandon	WHL	71	3	9	12	60	....	....	....	....	....
1987-88	Lethbridge	WHL	60	3	10	13	79	....	....	....	....	....
1988-89	Medicine Hat	WHL	65	8	31	39	141	3	0	0	0	2
1989-90	Muskegon	IHL	65	3	3	6	59	6	1	0	1	2
1990-91	Kansas City	IHL	23	2	10	12	36	....	....	....	....	....
	Muskegon	IHL	47	2	8	10	40	....	....	....	....	....
1991-92	Salt Lake	IHL	65	2	8	10	68	5	0	0	0	2

STONE, DONALD

Center. Shoots left. 5'11", 165 lbs. Born, Detroit, MI, May 6, 1969.
(Detroit's 11th choice, 248th overall, in 1988 Entry Draft).

			Regular Season					Playoffs				
Season	**Club**	**Lea**	**GP**	**G**	**A**	**TP**	**PIM**	**GP**	**G**	**A**	**TP**	**PIM**
1987-88	U. of Michigan	CCHA	38	18	19	37	22	....	....	....	....	....
1988-89	U. of Michigan	CCHA	40	24	17	41	19	....	....	....	....	....
1989-90	U. of Michigan	CCHA	42	20	24	44	12	....	....	....	....	....
1990-91	U. of Michigan	CCHA	47	21	27	48	20	....	....	....	....	....
1991-92	Toledo	ECHL	64	26	44	70	10	5	2	4	6	6

STORM, JIM

Left wing. Shoots left. 6'2", 200 lbs. Born, Milford, MI, February 5, 1971.
(Hartford's 5th choice, 75th overall, in 1991 Entry Draft).

			Regular Season					Playoffs				
Season	**Club**	**Lea**	**GP**	**G**	**A**	**TP**	**PIM**	**GP**	**G**	**A**	**TP**	**PIM**
1990-91	Michigan Tech	WCHA	36	16	18	34	46	....	....	....	....	....
1991-92	Michigan Tech	WCHA	39	25	33	58	12	....	....	....	....	....

STOTHERS, MICHAEL PATRICK (MIKE)

Defense. Shoots left. 6'4", 212 lbs. Born, Toronto, Ont., February 22, 1962.
(Philadelphia's 1st choice, 21st overall, in 1980 Entry Draft).

			Regular Season					Playoffs				
Season	**Club**	**Lea**	**GP**	**G**	**A**	**TP**	**PIM**	**GP**	**G**	**A**	**TP**	**PIM**
1979-80	Kingston	OHA	66	4	23	27	137	....	....	....	....	....
1980-81	Kingston	OHA	66	4	22	26	237	14	0	3	3	27
1981-82	Kingston	OHL	61	1	20	21	203	4	0	1	1	8
	Maine	AHL	5	0	0	0	4	1	0	0	0	0
1982-83	Maine	AHL	80	2	16	18	139	12	0	0	0	21
1983-84	Maine	AHL	61	2	10	12	109	17	0	1	1	34
1984-85	**Philadelphia**	**NHL**	**1**	**0**	**0**	**0**	**0**	....	....	....	....	....
	Hershey	AHL	60	8	18	26	142	....	....	....	....	....
1985-86	**Philadelphia**	**NHL**	**6**	**0**	**1**	**1**	**6**	**3**	**0**	**0**	**0**	**4**
	Hershey	AHL	66	4	9	13	221	13	0	3	3	88
1986-87	**Philadelphia**	**NHL**	**2**	**0**	**0**	**0**	**4**	**2**	**0**	**0**	**0**	**7**
	Hershey	AHL	75	5	11	16	283	5	0	0	0	10
1987-88	**Philadelphia**	**NHL**	**3**	**0**	**0**	**0**	**13**	....	....	....	....	....
	Hershey	AHL	13	3	2	5	55	....	....	....	....	....
	Toronto	**NHL**	**18**	**0**	**1**	**1**	**42**	....	....	....	....	....
	Newmarket	AHL	38	1	9	10	69	....	....	....	....	....
1988-89	Hershey	AHL	76	4	11	15	262	9	0	2	2	29
1989-90	Hershey	AHL	56	1	6	7	170	....	....	....	....	....
1990-91	Hershey	AHL	72	5	6	11	234	7	0	1	1	9
1991-92	Hershey	AHL	70	3	8	11	152	6	0	1	1	6
	NHL Totals		**30**	**0**	**2**	**2**	**65**	**5**	**0**	**0**	**0**	**11**

Traded to **Toronto** by **Philadelphia** for future considerations, December 4, 1987. Traded to **Philadelphia** by **Toronto** for Bill Root, June 21, 1988.

STRAKA, MARTIN

Center. Shoots left. 5'10", 178 lbs. Born, Plzen, Czech., September 3, 1972.
(Pittsburgh's 1st choice, 19th overall, in 1992 Entry Draft).

			Regular Season					Playoffs				
Season	**Club**	**Lea**	**GP**	**G**	**A**	**TP**	**PIM**	**GP**	**G**	**A**	**TP**	**PIM**
1990-91	Skoda Plzen	Czech.	47	7	24	31	6	....	....	....	....	....
1991-92	Skoda Plzen	Czech.	50	27	28	55	4	....	....	....	....	....

STRAUB, BRIAN

Defense. Shoots left. 6'2", 195 lbs. Born, Bozeman, MT, July 2, 1968.

			Regular Season					Playoffs				
Season	**Club**	**Lea**	**GP**	**G**	**A**	**TP**	**PIM**	**GP**	**G**	**A**	**TP**	**PIM**
1989-90	U. of Maine	H.E.	43	7	14	21	18	....	....	....	....	....
1990-91	U. of Maine	H.E.	42	6	25	31	14	....	....	....	....	....
1991-92	San Diego	IHL	43	3	16	19	75	....	....	....	....	....
	Kalamazoo	IHL	29	2	12	14	45	11	0	5	5	6

Signed as a free agent by **Minnesota**.

STROMBERG, MIKA

Defense. Shoots left. 5'11", 178 lbs. Born, Helsinki, Finland, February 28, 1970.
(Quebec's 10th choice, 211th overall, in 1990 Entry Draft).

			Regular Season					Playoffs				
Season	Club	Lea	GP	G	A	TP	PIM	GP	G	A	TP	PIM
1988-89	Jokerit	Fin.	39	6	12	18	....	....	....	....	....	....
1989-90	Jokerit	Fin.	42	2	15	17	....	....	....	....	....	....
1990-91	Jokerit	Fin.	44	4	16	20	38	....	....	....	....	....
1991-92	Jokerit	Fin.	36	7	14	21	32	9	2	3	5	16

STRUCH, DAVID

Center. Shoots left. 5'10", 180 lbs. Born, Calgary, Alta., February 11, 1971.
(Calgary's 10th choice, 195th overall, in 1991 Entry Draft).

			Regular Season					Playoffs				
Season	Club	Lea	GP	G	A	TP	PIM	GP	G	A	TP	PIM
1990-91	Saskatoon	WHL	72	45	57	102	69	....	....	....	....	....
1991-92	Saskatoon	WHL	47	29	26	55	34	....	....	....	....	....
	Salt Lake	IHL	12	4	1	5	8	....	....	....	....	....

STUMPEL, JOZEF (STUM-puhl)

Right wing. Shoots right. 6'1", 187 lbs. Born, Nitra, Czechoslovakia, June 20, 1972.
(Boston's 2nd choice, 40th overall, in 1991 Entry Draft).

			Regular Season					Playoffs				
Season	Club	Lea	GP	G	A	TP	PIM	GP	G	A	TP	PIM
1989-90	Nitra	Czech.	38	12	11	23	....	....	....	....	....	....
1990-91	Nitra	Czech.	49	23	22	45	14	....	....	....	....	....
1991-92	Koln	Ger.	37	20	19	39	35	....	....	....	....	....
	Boston	**NHL**	**4**	**1**	**0**	**1**	**0**	....	....	....	....	....
	NHL Totals		**4**	**1**	**0**	**1**	**0**	....	....	....	....	....

SUHY, ANDY

Defense. Shoots left. 6'1", 190 lbs. Born, Detroit, MI, March 9, 1970.
(Detroit's 8th choice, 158th overall, in 1989 Entry Draft).

			Regular Season					Playoffs				
Season	Club	Lea	GP	G	A	TP	PIM	GP	G	A	TP	PIM
1988-89	W. Michigan	CCHA	42	0	4	4	74	....	....	....	....	....
1989-90	W. Michigan	CCHA	34	3	5	8	52	....	....	....	....	....
1990-91	W. Michigan	CCHA	42	4	7	11	84	....	....	....	....	....
1991-92	W. Michigan	CCHA	36	3	9	12	89	....	....	....	....	....

SULLIVAN, BRIAN

Right wing. Shoots right. 6'4", 195 lbs. Born, South Windsor, CT, April 23, 1969.
(New Jersey's 3rd choice, 65th overall, in 1987 Entry Draft).

			Regular Season					Playoffs				
Season	Club	Lea	GP	G	A	TP	PIM	GP	G	A	TP	PIM
1987-88	Northeastern	H.E.	37	20	12	32	18	....	....	....	....	....
1988-89	Northeastern	H.E.	34	13	14	27	65	....	....	....	....	....
1989-90	Northeastern	H.E.	34	24	21	45	54	....	....	....	....	....
1990-91	Northeastern	H.E.	32	17	23	40	75	....	....	....	....	....
1991-92	Utica	AHL	70	23	24	47	58	4	0	4	4	6

SULLIVAN, MICHAEL (MIKE)

Center. Shoots left. 6'2", 193 lbs. Born, Marshfield, MA, February 27, 1968.
(NY Rangers' 4th choice, 69th overall, in 1987 Entry Draft).

			Regular Season					Playoffs				
Season	Club	Lea	GP	G	A	TP	PIM	GP	G	A	TP	PIM
1986-87	Boston U.	H.E.	37	13	18	31	18	....	....	....	....	....
1987-88	Boston U.	H.E.	30	18	22	40	30	....	....	....	....	....
1988-89	Boston U.	H.E.	36	19	17	36	30	....	....	....	....	....
1989-90	Boston U.	H.E.	38	11	20	31	26	....	....	....	....	....
1990-91	San Diego	IHL	74	12	23	35	27	....	....	....	....	....
1991-92	**San Jose**	**NHL**	**64**	**8**	**11**	**19**	**15**	....	....	....	....	....
	Kansas City	IHL	10	2	8	10	8	....	....	....	....	....
	NHL Totals		**64**	**8**	**11**	**19**	**15**	....	....	....	....	....

Rights traded to **Minnesota** by **NY Rangers** with Paul Jerrard, the rights to Bret Barnett, and Los Angeles' third round choice (Murray Garbutt) in 1989 Entry Draft — acquired March 10, 1987 by Minnesota — for Brian Lawton, Igor Liba and the rights to Eric Bennett, October 11, 1988. Signed as a free agent by **San Jose**, August 9, 1991.

SULLIVAN, MIKE

Center. Shoots left. 6'1", 190 lbs. Born, Woburn, MA, October 16, 1973.
(Detroit's 4th choice, 118th overall, in 1992 Entry Draft).

			Regular Season					Playoffs				
Season	Club	Lea	GP	G	A	TP	PIM	GP	G	A	TP	PIM
1991-92	Reading	HS	24	39	41	80	0	....	....	....	....	....

SUNDBLAD, NIKLAS

Right wing. Shoots right. 6'1", 196 lbs. Born, Stockholm, Sweden, January 3, 1973.
(Calgary's 1st choice, 19th overall, in 1991 Entry Draft).

			Regular Season					Playoffs				
Season	Club	Lea	GP	G	A	TP	PIM	GP	G	A	TP	PIM
1990-91	AIK	Swe.	39	1	3	4	14	....	....	....	....	....
1991-92	AIK	Swe.	33	9	2	11	24	3	3	1	4	0

SUNDIN, MATS (suhn-DEEN)

Center/Right wing. Shoots right. 6'2", 190 lbs. Born, Bromma, Sweden, February 13, 1971.
(Quebec's 1st choice, 1st overall, in 1989 Entry Draft).

			Regular Season					Playoffs				
Season	Club	Lea	GP	G	A	TP	PIM	GP	G	A	TP	PIM
1988-89	Nacka	Swe.	25	10	8	18	18	....	....	....	....	....
1989-90	Djurgarden	Swe.	34	10	8	18	16	8	7	0	7	4
1990-91	**Quebec**	**NHL**	**80**	**23**	**36**	**59**	**58**	....	....	....	....	....
1991-92	**Quebec**	**NHL**	**80**	**33**	**43**	**76**	**103**	....	....	....	....	....
	NHL Totals		**160**	**56**	**79**	**135**	**161**	....	....	....	....	....

SUNDSTROM, PATRIK (SUHND-struhm)

Center. Shoots left. 6'1", 200 lbs. Born, Skelleftea, Sweden, December 14, 1961.
(Vancouver's 8th choice, 175th overall, in 1980 Entry Draft).

			Regular Season					Playoffs				
Season	Club	Lea	GP	G	A	TP	PIM	GP	G	A	TP	PIM
1979-80	Bjorkloven	Swe.	26	5	7	12	20	3	1	0	1	4
1980-81	Bjorkloven	Swe.	36	10	18	28	30	3	1	0	1	4
	Swe. National	....	15	4	2	6	6	....	....	....	....	....
1981-82	Bjorkloven	Swe.	36	22	13	35	38	7	3	4	7	6
	Swe. National	....	36	17	7	24	24	....	....	....	....	....
1982-83	**Vancouver**	**NHL**	**74**	**23**	**23**	**46**	**30**	**4**	**0**	**0**	**0**	**2**
1983-84	**Vancouver**	**NHL**	**78**	**38**	**53**	**91**	**37**	**4**	**0**	**1**	**1**	**7**
1984-85	**Vancouver**	**NHL**	**71**	**25**	**43**	**68**	**46**	....	....	....	....	....
1985-86	**Vancouver**	**NHL**	**79**	**18**	**48**	**66**	**28**	**3**	**1**	**0**	**1**	**0**
1986-87	**Vancouver**	**NHL**	**72**	**29**	**42**	**71**	**40**	....	....	....	....	....
1987-88	**New Jersey**	**NHL**	**78**	**15**	**36**	**51**	**42**	**18**	**7**	**13**	**20**	**14**
1988-89	**New Jersey**	**NHL**	**65**	**28**	**41**	**69**	**36**	....	....	....	....	....
1989-90	**New Jersey**	**NHL**	**74**	**27**	**49**	**76**	**34**	**6**	**1**	**3**	**4**	**2**
1990-91	**New Jersey**	**NHL**	**71**	**15**	**31**	**46**	**48**	**2**	**0**	**0**	**0**	**0**
1991-92	**New Jersey**	**NHL**	**17**	**1**	**3**	**4**	**8**	....	....	....	....	....
	Utica	AHL	1	0	0	0	0	....	....	....	....	....
	NHL Totals		**679**	**219**	**369**	**588**	**349**	**37**	**9**	**17**	**26**	**25**

Traded to **New Jersey** by **Vancouver** with Vancouver's fourth round choice (Matt Ruchty) in 1988 Entry Draft for Kirk McLean and Greg Adams, September 15, 1987.

SUTER, GARY

Defense. Shoots left. 6', 190 lbs. Born, Madison, WI, June 24, 1964.
(Calgary's 9th choice, 180th overall, in 1984 Entry Draft).

			Regular Season					Playoffs				
Season	Club	Lea	GP	G	A	TP	PIM	GP	G	A	TP	PIM
1983-84	U. Wisconsin	WCHA	35	4	18	22	32	....	....	....	....	....
1984-85	U. Wisconsin	WCHA	39	12	39	51	110	....	....	....	....	....
1985-86ab	**Calgary**	**NHL**	**80**	**18**	**50**	**68**	**141**	**10**	**2**	**8**	**10**	**8**
1986-87	**Calgary**	**NHL**	**68**	**9**	**40**	**49**	**70**	**6**	**0**	**3**	**3**	**10**
1987-88c	**Calgary**	**NHL**	**75**	**21**	**70**	**91**	**124**	**9**	**1**	**9**	**10**	**6**
1988-89	**Calgary**	**NHL**	**63**	**13**	**49**	**62**	**78**	**5**	**0**	**3**	**3**	**10**
1989-90	**Calgary**	**NHL**	**76**	**16**	**60**	**76**	**97**	**6**	**0**	**1**	**1**	**14**
1990-91	**Calgary**	**NHL**	**79**	**12**	**58**	**70**	**102**	**7**	**1**	**6**	**7**	**12**
1991-92	**Calgary**	**NHL**	**70**	**12**	**43**	**55**	**128**	....	....	....	....	....
	NHL Totals		**511**	**101**	**370**	**471**	**740**	**43**	**4**	**30**	**34**	**54**

a Won Calder Memorial Trophy (1986)
b NHL All-Rookie Team (1986)
c NHL Second All-Star Team (1988)

Played in NHL All-Star Game (1986, 1988, 1989, 1991)

SUTTER, BRENT COLIN (SUH-tuhr)

Center. Shoots right. 5'11", 180 lbs. Born, Viking, Alta., June 10, 1962.
(NY Islanders' 1st choice, 17th overall, in 1980 Entry Draft).

			Regular Season					Playoffs				
Season	Club	Lea	GP	G	A	TP	PIM	GP	G	A	TP	PIM
1979-80	Red Deer	AJHL	59	70	101	171	....	....	....	....	....	....
	Lethbridge	WHL	5	1	0	1	2	....	....	....	....	....
1980-81	**NY Islanders**	**NHL**	**3**	**2**	**2**	**4**	**0**	....	....	....	....	....
	Lethbridge	WHL	68	54	54	108	116	9	6	4	10	51
1981-82	**NY Islanders**	**NHL**	**43**	**21**	**22**	**43**	**114**	**19**	**2**	**6**	**8**	**36**
	Lethbridge	WHL	34	46	33	79	162	....	....	....	....	....
1982-83	**NY Islanders**	**NHL**	**80**	**21**	**19**	**40**	**128**	**20**	**10**	**11**	**21**	**26**
1983-84	**NY Islanders**	**NHL**	**69**	**34**	**15**	**49**	**69**	**20**	**4**	**10**	**14**	**18**
1984-85	**NY Islanders**	**NHL**	**72**	**42**	**60**	**102**	**51**	**10**	**3**	**3**	**6**	**14**
1985-86	**NY Islanders**	**NHL**	**61**	**24**	**31**	**55**	**74**	**3**	**0**	**1**	**1**	**2**
1986-87	**NY Islanders**	**NHL**	**69**	**27**	**36**	**63**	**73**	**5**	**1**	**0**	**1**	**4**
1987-88	**NY Islanders**	**NHL**	**70**	**29**	**31**	**60**	**55**	**6**	**2**	**1**	**3**	**18**
1988-89	**NY Islanders**	**NHL**	**77**	**29**	**34**	**63**	**77**	....	....	....	....	....
1989-90	**NY Islanders**	**NHL**	**67**	**33**	**35**	**68**	**65**	**5**	**2**	**3**	**5**	**2**
1990-91	**NY Islanders**	**NHL**	**75**	**21**	**32**	**53**	**49**	....	....	....	....	....
1991-92	**NY Islanders**	**NHL**	**8**	**4**	**6**	**10**	**6**	....	....	....	....	....
	Chicago	**NHL**	**61**	**18**	**32**	**50**	**30**	**18**	**3**	**5**	**8**	**22**
	NHL Totals		**755**	**305**	**355**	**660**	**791**	**106**	**27**	**40**	**67**	**142**

Played in NHL All-Star Game (1985)

Traded to **Chicago** by **NY Islanders** with Brad Lauer for Adam Creighton and Steve Thomas, October 25, 1991.

SUTTER, RICHARD (RICH) (SUH-tuhr)

Right wing. Shoots right. 5'11", 188 lbs. Born, Viking, Alta., December 2, 1963.
(Pittsburgh's 1st choice, 10th overall, in 1982 Entry Draft).

			Regular Season					Playoffs				
Season	Club	Lea	GP	G	A	TP	PIM	GP	G	A	TP	PIM
1980-81	Lethbridge	WHL	72	23	18	41	255	9	3	1	4	35
1981-82	Lethbridge	WHL	57	38	31	69	263	12	3	3	6	55
1982-83	**Pittsburgh**	**NHL**	**4**	**0**	**0**	**0**	**0**	....	....	....	....	....
	Lethbridge	WHL	64	37	30	67	200	17	14	9	23	43
1983-84	**Pittsburgh**	**NHL**	**5**	**0**	**0**	**0**	**0**	....	....	....	....	....
	Baltimore	AHL	2	0	1	1	0	....	....	....	....	....
	Philadelphia	**NHL**	**70**	**16**	**12**	**28**	**93**	**3**	**0**	**0**	**0**	**15**
1984-85	**Philadelphia**	**NHL**	**56**	**6**	**10**	**16**	**89**	**11**	**3**	**0**	**3**	**10**
	Hershey	AHL	13	3	7	10	14	....	....	....	....	....
1985-86	**Philadelphia**	**NHL**	**78**	**14**	**25**	**39**	**199**	**5**	**2**	**0**	**2**	**19**
1986-87	**Vancouver**	**NHL**	**74**	**20**	**22**	**42**	**113**	....	....	....	....	....
1987-88	**Vancouver**	**NHL**	**80**	**15**	**15**	**30**	**165**	....	....	....	....	....
1988-89	**Vancouver**	**NHL**	**75**	**17**	**15**	**32**	**122**	**7**	**2**	**1**	**3**	**12**
1989-90	**Vancouver**	**NHL**	**62**	**9**	**9**	**18**	**133**	....	....	....	....	....
	St. Louis	**NHL**	**12**	**2**	**0**	**2**	**22**	**12**	**2**	**1**	**3**	**39**
1990-91	**St. Louis**	**NHL**	**77**	**16**	**11**	**27**	**122**	**13**	**4**	**2**	**6**	**16**
1991-92	**St. Louis**	**NHL**	**77**	**9**	**16**	**25**	**107**	**6**	**0**	**0**	**0**	**8**
	NHL Totals		**670**	**124**	**135**	**259**	**1165**	**57**	**13**	**4**	**17**	**119**

Traded to **Philadelphia** by **Pittsburgh** with Pittsburgh's second round (Greg Smyth) and third round (David McLay) choices in 1984 Entry Draft for Andy Brickley, Mark Taylor, Ron Flockhart, Philadelphia's first round (Roger Belanger) and third round (Mike Stevens — later transferred to Vancouver) choices in 1984 Entry Draft, October 23, 1983. Traded to **Vancouver** by **Philadelphia**, with Dave Richter and Vancouver's third round choice (Don Gibson) in 1986 Entry Draft — acquired earlier — for J.J. Daigneault and Vancouver's second round choice (Kent Hawley) in 1986 Entry Draft, June 6, 1986. Traded to **St Louis** by **Vancouver** with Harold Snepsts and St. Louis' second round choice (Craig Johnson) – previously acquired by Vancouver – in 1990 Entry Draft for Adrien Plavsic, Montreal's first round choice (Shawn Antoski) – previously acquired by St. Louis – in 1990 Entry Draft and St. Louis' second round choice in 1991 Entry Draft, March 6, 1990.

SUTTER, RONALD (RON) (SUH-tuhr)

Center. Shoots right. 6', 180 lbs. Born, Viking, Alta., December 2, 1963.
(Philadelphia's 1st choice, 4th overall, in 1982 Entry Draft).

			Regular Season					Playoffs				
Season	Club	Lea	GP	G	A	TP	PIM	GP	G	A	TP	PIM
1980-81	Lethbridge	WHL	72	13	32	45	152	9	2	5	7	29
1981-82	Lethbridge	WHL	59	38	54	92	207	12	6	5	11	28
1982-83	**Philadelphia**	**NHL**	**10**	**1**	**1**	**2**	**9**	....	....	....	....	....
	Lethbridge	WHL	58	35	48	83	98	20	*22	*19	*41	45
1983-84	**Philadelphia**	**NHL**	**79**	**19**	**32**	**51**	**101**	**3**	**0**	**0**	**0**	**22**
1984-85	**Philadelphia**	**NHL**	**73**	**16**	**29**	**45**	**94**	**19**	**4**	**8**	**12**	**28**
1985-86	**Philadelphia**	**NHL**	**75**	**18**	**42**	**60**	**159**	**5**	**0**	**2**	**2**	**10**
1986-87	**Philadelphia**	**NHL**	**39**	**10**	**17**	**27**	**69**	**16**	**1**	**7**	**8**	**12**
1987-88	**Philadelphia**	**NHL**	**69**	**8**	**25**	**33**	**146**	**7**	**0**	**1**	**1**	**26**
1988-89	**Philadelphia**	**NHL**	**55**	**26**	**22**	**48**	**80**	**19**	**1**	**9**	**10**	**51**
1989-90	**Philadelphia**	**NHL**	**75**	**22**	**26**	**48**	**104**	....	....	....	....	....
1990-91	**Philadelphia**	**NHL**	**80**	**17**	**28**	**45**	**92**	....	....	....	....	....
1991-92	**St. Louis**	**NHL**	**68**	**19**	**27**	**46**	**91**	**6**	**1**	**3**	**4**	**8**
	NHL Totals		**623**	**156**	**249**	**405**	**945**	**75**	**7**	**30**	**37**	**157**

Traded to **St. Louis** by **Philadelphia** with Murray Baron for Dan Quinn and Rod Brind'Amour, September 22, 1991.

SUTTON, KENNETH

Defense. Shoots left. 6', 198 lbs. Born, Edmonton, Alta., May 11, 1969.
(Buffalo's 4th choice, 98th overall, in 1989 Entry Draft).

			Regular Season					Playoffs				
Season	Club	Lea	GP	G	A	TP	PIM	GP	G	A	TP	PIM
1988-89	Saskatoon	WHL	71	22	31	53	104	8	2	5	7	12
1989-90	Rochester	AHL	57	5	14	19	83	11	1	6	7	15
1990-91	**Buffalo**	**NHL**	**15**	**3**	**6**	**9**	**13**	**6**	**0**	**1**	**1**	**2**
	Rochester	AHL	62	7	24	31	65	3	1	1	2	14
1991-92	**Buffalo**	**NHL**	**64**	**2**	**18**	**20**	**71**	**7**	**0**	**2**	**2**	**4**
	NHL Totals		**79**	**5**	**24**	**29**	**84**	**13**	**0**	**3**	**3**	**6**

SVEHLA, ROBERT (SCHVE-khlah)

Defense. Shoots right. 6', 185 lbs. Born, Martin, Czech., January 2, 1969.
(Calgary's 4th choice, 78th overall, in 1992 Entry Draft).

			Regular Season					Playoffs				
Season	Club	Lea	GP	G	A	TP	PIM	GP	G	A	TP	PIM
1990-91	Dukla Trencin	Czech.	52	14	8	22	62	....	....	....	....	....
1991-92	Dukla Trencin	Czech.	51	23	28	51	....	....	....	....	....	....

SVENSSON, MAGNUS (SVEHN-suhn)

Defense. Shoots left. 5'11", 180 lbs. Born, Leksand, Sweden, March 1, 1963.
(Calgary's 13th choice, 250th overall, in 1987 Entry Draft).

			Regular Season					Playoffs				
Season	Club	Lea	GP	G	A	TP	PIM	GP	G	A	TP	PIM
1983-84	Leksand	Swe.	35	3	8	11	20	....	....	....	....	....
1984-85	Leksand	Swe.	35	8	7	15	22	....	....	....	....	....
1985-86	Leksand	Swe.	36	6	9	15	62	....	....	....	....	....
1986-87	Leksand	Swe.	33	8	16	24	42	....	....	....	....	....
1987-88	Leksand	Swe.	40	12	11	23	20	....	....	....	....	....
1988-89	Leksand	Swe.	39	15	22	37	40	10	3	5	8	8
1989-90	Leksand	Swe.	26	11	12	23	60	1	0	0	0	0
1990-91	Lugano	Switz.	36	16	20	36	....	11	3	2	5	....
1991-92	Leksand	Swe.	22	4	10	14	32	....	....	....	....	....

SVOBODA, PETR (svah-BOH-duh)

Defense. Shoots left. 6'1", 174 lbs. Born, Most, Czechoslovakia, February 14, 1966.
(Montreal's 1st choice, 5th overall, in 1984 Entry Draft).

			Regular Season					Playoffs				
Season	Club	Lea	GP	G	A	TP	PIM	GP	G	A	TP	PIM
1983-84	Czech. Jrs.	....	40	15	21	36	14	....	....	....	....	....
1984-85	**Montreal**	**NHL**	**73**	**4**	**27**	**31**	**65**	**7**	**1**	**1**	**2**	**12**
1985-86	**Montreal**	**NHL**	**73**	**1**	**18**	**19**	**93**	**8**	**0**	**0**	**0**	**21**
1986-87	**Montreal**	**NHL**	**70**	**5**	**17**	**22**	**63**	**14**	**0**	**5**	**5**	**10**
1987-88	**Montreal**	**NHL**	**69**	**7**	**22**	**29**	**149**	**10**	**0**	**5**	**5**	**12**
1988-89	**Montreal**	**NHL**	**71**	**8**	**37**	**45**	**147**	**21**	**1**	**11**	**12**	**16**
1989-90	**Montreal**	**NHL**	**60**	**5**	**31**	**36**	**98**	**10**	**0**	**5**	**5**	**7**
1990-91	**Montreal**	**NHL**	**60**	**4**	**22**	**26**	**52**	**2**	**0**	**1**	**1**	**2**
1991-92	**Montreal**	**NHL**	**58**	**5**	**16**	**21**	**94**	....	....	....	....	....
	Buffalo	**NHL**	**13**	**1**	**6**	**7**	**52**	**7**	**1**	**4**	**5**	**6**
	NHL Totals		**547**	**40**	**196**	**236**	**813**	**79**	**3**	**32**	**35**	**86**

Traded to **Buffalo** by **Montreal** for Kevin Haller, March 10, 1992.

SWEENEY, DON

Defense. Shoots left. 5'11", 170 lbs. Born, St. Stephen, N.B., August 17, 1966.
(Boston's 8th choice, 166th overall, in 1984 Entry Draft).

			Regular Season					Playoffs				
Season	Club	Lea	GP	G	A	TP	PIM	GP	G	A	TP	PIM
1984-85	Harvard	ECAC	29	3	7	10	30	....	....	....	....	....
1985-86	Harvard	ECAC	31	4	5	9	12	....	....	....	....	....
1986-87	Harvard	ECAC	34	7	4	11	22	....	....	....	....	....
1987-88ab	Harvard	ECAC	30	6	23	29	37	....	....	....	....	....
	Maine	AHL	....	....	....	....	....	6	1	3	4	0
1988-89	**Boston**	**NHL**	**36**	**3**	**5**	**8**	**20**	....	....	....	....	....
	Maine	AHL	42	8	17	25	24	....	....	....	....	....
1989-90	**Boston**	**NHL**	**58**	**3**	**5**	**8**	**58**	**21**	**1**	**5**	**6**	**18**
	Maine	AHL	11	0	8	8	8	....	....	....	....	....
1990-91	**Boston**	**NHL**	**77**	**8**	**13**	**21**	**67**	**19**	**3**	**0**	**3**	**25**
1991-92	**Boston**	**NHL**	**75**	**3**	**11**	**14**	**74**	**15**	**0**	**0**	**0**	**10**
	NHL Totals		**246**	**17**	**34**	**51**	**219**	**55**	**4**	**5**	**9**	**53**

a NCAA East All-American Team (1988)
b ECAC First All-Star Team (1988)

SWEENEY, ROBERT (BOB)

Center/Right wing. Shoots right. 6'3", 200 lbs. Born, Concord, MA, January 25, 1964.
(Boston's 6th choice, 123rd overall, in 1982 Entry Draft).

			Regular Season					Playoffs				
Season	Club	Lea	GP	G	A	TP	PIM	GP	G	A	TP	PIM
1982-83	Boston College	ECAC	30	17	11	28	10	....	....	....	....	....
1983-84	Boston College	ECAC	23	14	7	21	10	....	....	....	....	....
1984-85a	Boston College	ECAC	44	32	32	64	43	....	....	....	....	....
1985-86	Boston College	H.E.	41	15	24	39	52	....	....	....	....	....
1986-87	**Boston**	**NHL**	**14**	**2**	**4**	**6**	**21**	**3**	**0**	**0**	**0**	**0**
	Moncton	AHL	58	29	26	55	81	4	0	2	2	13
1987-88	**Boston**	**NHL**	**80**	**22**	**23**	**45**	**73**	**23**	**6**	**8**	**14**	**66**
1988-89	**Boston**	**NHL**	**75**	**14**	**14**	**28**	**99**	**10**	**2**	**4**	**6**	**19**
1989-90	**Boston**	**NHL**	**70**	**22**	**24**	**46**	**93**	**20**	**0**	**2**	**2**	**30**
1990-91	**Boston**	**NHL**	**80**	**15**	**33**	**48**	**115**	**17**	**4**	**2**	**6**	**45**
1991-92	**Boston**	**NHL**	**63**	**6**	**14**	**20**	**103**	**14**	**1**	**0**	**1**	**25**
	Maine	AHL	1	1	0	1	0	....	....	....	....	....
	NHL Totals		**382**	**81**	**112**	**193**	**504**	**87**	**13**	**16**	**29**	**185**

a ECAC Second Team All-Star (1985)

SWEENEY, TIM

Left wing. Shoots left. 5'11", 180 lbs. Born, Boston, MA, April 12, 1967.
(Calgary's 7th choice, 122nd overall, in 1985 Entry Draft).

			Regular Season					Playoffs				
Season	Club	Lea	GP	G	A	TP	PIM	GP	G	A	TP	PIM
1985-86	Boston College	H.E.	32	8	4	12	8	....	....	....	....	....
1986-87	Boston College	H.E.	38	31	18	49	28	....	....	....	....	....
1987-88	Boston College	H.E.	18	9	11	20	18	....	....	....	....	....
1988-89ab	Boston College	H.E.	39	29	44	73	26	....	....	....	....	....
1989-90cd	Salt Lake	IHL	81	46	51	97	32	11	5	4	9	4
1990-91	**Calgary**	**NHL**	**42**	**7**	**9**	**16**	**8**	....	....	....	....	....
	Salt Lake	IHL	31	19	16	35	8	4	3	3	6	0
1991-92	U.S. National	....	21	9	11	20	10	....	....	....	....	....
	U.S. Olympic	....	8	3	4	7	6	....	....	....	....	....
	Calgary	**NHL**	**11**	**1**	**2**	**3**	**4**	....	....	....	....	....
	NHL Totals		**53**	**8**	**11**	**19**	**12**	....	....	....	....	....

a Hockey East First All-Star Team (1989)
b NCAA East Second All-American Team (1989)
c IHL Second All-Star Team (1990)
d Won Ken McKenzie Trophy (Outstanding U.S.-born rookie—IHL) (1990)

SYCHRA, MARTIN

Center. Shoots right. 6'1", 172 lbs. Born, Brno, Czech., June 19, 1974.
(Montreal's 8th choice, 140th overall, in 1992 Entry Draft).

			Regular Season					Playoffs				
Season	Club	Lea	GP	G	A	TP	PIM	GP	G	A	TP	PIM
1991-92	Zetor Brno	Czech.	14	2	2	4	....	....	....	....	....	....

SYDOR, DARRYL (CEE-der)

Defense. Shoots left. 6', 205 lbs. Born, Edmonton, Alta., May 13, 1972.
(Los Angeles' 1st choice, 7th overall, in 1990 Entry Draft).

			Regular Season					Playoffs				
Season	Club	Lea	GP	G	A	TP	PIM	GP	G	A	TP	PIM
1988-89	Kamloops	WHL	65	12	14	26	86	15	1	4	5	19
1989-90a	Kamloops	WHL	67	29	66	95	129	17	2	9	11	28
1990-91a	Kamloops	WHL	66	27	78	105	88	12	3	*22	25	10
1991-92	**Los Angeles**	**NHL**	**18**	**1**	**5**	**6**	**22**	....	....	....	....	....
a	Kamloops	WHL	29	9	39	48	43	17	3	15	18	18
	NHL Totals		**18**	**1**	**5**	**6**	**22**	....	....	....	....	....

a WHL West First All-Star Team (1990, 1991, 1992)

SYKES, PHIL

Left wing. Shoots left. 6', 175 lbs. Born, Dawson Creek, B.C., March 18, 1959.

			Regular Season					Playoffs				
Season	Club	Lea	GP	G	A	TP	PIM	GP	G	A	TP	PIM
1979-80	North Dakota	WCHA	37	22	27	49	34	....	....	....	....	....
1980-81	North Dakota	WCHA	38	28	34	62	22	....	....	....	....	....
1981-82abc	North Dakota	WCHA	37	22	27	49	34	....	....	....	....	....
1982-83	**Los Angeles**	**NHL**	**7**	**2**	**0**	**2**	**2**	....	....	....	....	....
	New Haven	AHL	71	19	26	45	111	12	2	2	4	21
1983-84	**Los Angeles**	**NHL**	**3**	**0**	**0**	**0**	**2**	....	....	....	....	....
	New Haven	AHL	77	29	37	66	101	....	....	....	....	....
1984-85	**Los Angeles**	**NHL**	**79**	**17**	**15**	**32**	**38**	**3**	**0**	**1**	**1**	**4**
1985-86	**Los Angeles**	**NHL**	**76**	**20**	**24**	**44**	**97**	....	....	....	....	....
1986-87	**Los Angeles**	**NHL**	**58**	**6**	**15**	**21**	**133**	**5**	**0**	**1**	**1**	**8**
1987-88	**Los Angeles**	**NHL**	**40**	**9**	**12**	**21**	**82**	**4**	**0**	**0**	**0**	**0**
1988-89	**Los Angeles**	**NHL**	**23**	**0**	**1**	**1**	**8**	**3**	**0**	**0**	**0**	**8**
	New Haven	AHL	34	9	17	26	23	....	....	....	....	....
1989-90	New Haven	AHL	25	3	12	15	32	....	....	....	....	....
	Winnipeg	**NHL**	**48**	**9**	**6**	**15**	**26**	**4**	**0**	**0**	**0**	**0**
	Moncton	AHL	5	0	1	1	20	....	....	....	....	....
1990-91	**Winnipeg**	**NHL**	**70**	**12**	**10**	**22**	**59**	....	....	....	....	....
1991-92	**Winnipeg**	**NHL**	**52**	**4**	**2**	**6**	**72**	**7**	**0**	**1**	**1**	**9**
	NHL Totals		**456**	**79**	**85**	**164**	**519**	**26**	**0**	**3**	**3**	**29**

a WCHA First All-Star Team (1982)
b Named WCHA Player of the Year (1982)
c Named Most Valuable Player, NCAA Tournament (1982)

Signed as a free agent by **Los Angeles**, April 5, 1982. Traded to **Winnipeg** by **Los Angeles** for Brad Jones, December 1, 1989.

SYKORA, MICHAL

Defense. Shoots left. 6'4", 198 lbs. Born, Pardubice, Czech., July 5, 1973.
(San Jose's 6th choice, 123rd overall, in 1992 Entry Draft).

			Regular Season					Playoffs				
Season	Club	Lea	GP	G	A	TP	PIM	GP	G	A	TP	PIM
1990-91	Pardubice	Czech.	40	17	26	43	45	....	....	....	....	....
1991-92	Tacoma	WHL	61	13	23	36	66	4	0	2	2	2

TAGLIANETTI, PETER

Defense. Shoots left. 6'2", 200 lbs. Born, Framingham, MA, August 15, 1963.
(Winnipeg's 4th choice, 43rd overall, in 1983 Entry Draft).

			Regular Season					Playoffs				
Season	Club	Lea	GP	G	A	TP	PIM	GP	G	A	TP	PIM
1981-82	Providence	ECAC	2	0	0	0	2	....	....	....	....	....
1982-83	Providence	ECAC	43	4	17	21	68	....	....	....	....	....
1983-84	Providence	ECAC	30	4	25	29	68	....	....	....	....	....
1984-85	**Winnipeg**	**NHL**	**1**	**0**	**0**	**0**	**0**	**1**	**0**	**0**	**0**	**0**
a	Providence	H.E.	35	6	18	24	32	....	....	....	....	....
1985-86	**Winnipeg**	**NHL**	**18**	**0**	**0**	**0**	**48**	**3**	**0**	**0**	**0**	**2**
	Sherbrooke	AHL	24	1	18	9	75	....	....	....	....	....
1986-87	**Winnipeg**	**NHL**	**3**	**0**	**0**	**0**	**12**	....	....	....	....	....
	Sherbrooke	AHL	54	5	14	19	104	10	2	5	7	25
1987-88	**Winnipeg**	**NHL**	**70**	**6**	**17**	**23**	**182**	**5**	**1**	**1**	**2**	**12**
1988-89	**Winnipeg**	**NHL**	**66**	**1**	**14**	**15**	**226**	....	....	....	....	....
1989-90	**Winnipeg**	**NHL**	**49**	**3**	**6**	**9**	**136**	**5**	**0**	**0**	**0**	**6**
	Moncton	AHL	3	0	2	2	2	....	....	....	....	....
1990-91	**Minnesota**	**NHL**	**16**	**0**	**1**	**1**	**14**	....	....	....	....	....
	Pittsburgh	**NHL**	**39**	**3**	**8**	**11**	**93**	**19**	**0**	**3**	**3**	**49**
1991-92	**Pittsburgh**	**NHL**	**44**	**1**	**3**	**4**	**57**	....	....	....	....	....
	NHL Totals		**306**	**14**	**49**	**63**	**768**	**33**	**1**	**4**	**5**	**69**

a Hockey East First All-Star Team (1985)

Traded to **Minnesota** by **Winnipeg** for future considerations, September 30, 1990. Traded to **Pittsburgh** by **Minnesota** with Larry Murphy for Chris Dahlquist and Jim Johnson, December 11, 1990. Claimed by **Tampa Bay** from **Pittsburgh** in Expansion Draft, June 18, 1992.

TAMER, CHRIS

Defense. Shoots left. 6'2", 185 lbs. Born, Dearborn, MI, November 17, 1970.
(Pittsburgh's 3rd choice, 68th overall, in 1990 Entry Draft).

			Regular Season					Playoffs				
Season	Club	Lea	GP	G	A	TP	PIM	GP	G	A	TP	PIM
1989-90	U. of Michigan	CCHA	42	2	7	9	147	....	....	....	....	....
1990-91	U. of Michigan	CCHA	45	8	19	27	130	....	....	....	....	....
1991-92	U. of Michigan	CCHA	43	4	15	19	125	....	....	....	....	....

TAMMINEN, JOE

Center. Shoots left. 6'1", 187 lbs. Born, Virginia, MN, January 23, 1973.
(Pittsburgh's 4th choice, 82nd overall, in 1991 Entry Draft).

			Regular Season					Playoffs				
Season	Club	Lea	GP	G	A	TP	PIM	GP	G	A	TP	PIM
1990-91	Virginia	HS	22	20	18	38	40	....	....	....	....	....
1991-92	Minn.-Duluth	WCHA	23	1	3	4	12	....	....	....	....	....

TANCILL, CHRIS (TAN-sihl)

Center. Shoots left. 5'10", 185 lbs. Born, Livonia, MI, February 7, 1968.
(Hartford's 1st choice, 15th overall, in 1989 Supplemental Draft).

			Regular Season					Playoffs				
Season	Club	Lea	GP	G	A	TP	PIM	GP	G	A	TP	PIM
1986-87	U. Wisconsin	WCHA	40	9	23	32	26	....	....	....	....	....
1987-88	U. Wisconsin	WCHA	44	13	14	27	48	....	....	....	....	....
1988-89	U. Wisconsin	WCHA	44	20	23	43	50	....	....	....	....	....
1989-90a	U. Wisconsin	WCHA	45	39	32	71	44	....	....	....	....	....
1990-91	**Hartford**	**NHL**	**9**	**1**	**1**	**2**	**4**	....	....	....	....	....
	Springfield	AHL	72	37	35	72	46	17	8	4	12	32
1991-92	**Hartford**	**NHL**	**10**	**0**	**0**	**0**	**2**	....	....	....	....	....
b	Springfield	AHL	17	12	7	19	20	....	....	....	....	....
	Detroit	**NHL**	**1**	**0**	**0**	**0**	**0**	....	....	....	....	....
	Adirondack	AHL	50	36	34	70	42	19	7	9	16	31
	NHL Totals		**20**	**1**	**1**	**2**	**6**	....	....	....	....	....

a NCAA All-Tournament Team, Tournament MVP (1990)
b AHL First All-Star Team (1992)

Traded to **Detroit** by **Hartford** for Daniel Shank, December 18, 1991.

TANGUAY, MARTIN

Center. Shoots left. 5'11", 185 lbs. Born, Ste-Julie, Que., January 12, 1973.
(Tampa Bay's 6th choice, 122nd overall, in 1992 Entry Draft).

			Regular Season					Playoffs				
Season	Club	Lea	GP	G	A	TP	PIM	GP	G	A	TP	PIM
1989-90	Longueuil	QMJHL	62	12	17	29	43	....	....	....	....	....
1990-91	Longueuil	QMJHL	69	27	34	61	14	8	3	4	7	6
1991-92	Verdun	QMJHL	67	41	50	91	117	19	8	13	21	32

TANTI, TONY (TAN-tee)

Right wing. Shoots left. 5'9", 180 lbs. Born, Toronto, Ont., September 7, 1963.
(Chicago's 1st choice, 12th overall, in 1981 Entry Draft).

			Regular Season					Playoffs				
Season	Club	Lea	GP	G	A	TP	PIM	GP	G	A	TP	PIM
1980-81a	Oshawa	OHA	67	81	69	150	197	11	7	8	15	41
1981-82	**Chicago**	**NHL**	**2**	**0**	**0**	**0**	**0**	....	....	....	....	....
b	Oshawa	OHL	57	62	64	126	138	12	14	12	26	15
1982-83	**Chicago**	**NHL**	**1**	**1**	**0**	**1**	**0**	....	....	....	....	....
	Oshawa	OHL	30	34	28	62	35	....	....	....	....	....
	Vancouver	**NHL**	**39**	**8**	**8**	**16**	**16**	**4**	**0**	**1**	**1**	**0**
1983-84	**Vancouver**	**NHL**	**79**	**45**	**41**	**86**	**50**	**4**	**1**	**2**	**3**	**0**
1984-85	**Vancouver**	**NHL**	**68**	**39**	**20**	**59**	**45**	....	....	....	....	....
1985-86	**Vancouver**	**NHL**	**77**	**39**	**33**	**72**	**85**	**3**	**0**	**1**	**1**	**11**
1986-87	**Vancouver**	**NHL**	**77**	**41**	**38**	**79**	**84**	....	....	....	....	....
1987-88	**Vancouver**	**NHL**	**73**	**40**	**37**	**77**	**90**	....	....	....	....	....
1988-89	**Vancouver**	**NHL**	**77**	**24**	**25**	**49**	**69**	**7**	**0**	**5**	**5**	**4**
1989-90	**Vancouver**	**NHL**	**41**	**14**	**18**	**32**	**50**	....	....	....	....	....
	Pittsburgh	**NHL**	**37**	**14**	**18**	**32**	**22**	....	....	....	....	....
1990-91	**Pittsburgh**	**NHL**	**46**	**6**	**12**	**18**	**44**	....	....	....	....	....
	Buffalo	**NHL**	**10**	**1**	**7**	**8**	**6**	**5**	**2**	**0**	**2**	**8**
1991-92	**Buffalo**	**NHL**	**70**	**15**	**16**	**31**	**100**	**7**	**0**	**3**	**3**	**4**
	NHL Totals		**697**	**287**	**273**	**560**	**661**	**30**	**3**	**12**	**15**	**27**

a OHA First All-Star Team (1981)
b OHL Second All-Star Team (1982)

Played in NHL All-Star Game (1986)

Traded to **Vancouver** by **Chicago** for Curt Fraser, January 6, 1983. Traded to **Pittsburgh** by **Vancouver** with Rod Buskas and Barry Pederson for Dave Capuano, Andrew McBain and Dan Quinn, January 8, 1990. Traded to **Buffalo** by **Pittsburgh** for Ken Priestlay, March 5, 1991.

TARDIF, PATRICE

Center. Shoots left. 6'2", 175 lbs. Born, Thetford Mines, Que., October 30, 1970.
(St. Louis' 2nd choice, 54th overall, in 1990 Entry Draft).

			Regular Season					Playoffs				
Season	Club	Lea	GP	G	A	TP	PIM	GP	G	A	TP	PIM
1990-91	U. of Maine	H.E.	36	13	12	25	18	....	....	....	....	....
1991-92	U. of Maine	H.E.	31	18	20	38	14	....	....	....	....	....

TATARINOV, MIKHAIL (tah-TAH-ree-nahf)

Defense. Shoots left. 5'10", 195 lbs. Born, Irkutsk, Soviet Union, July 16, 1966.
(Washington's 10th choice, 225th overall, in 1984 Entry Draft).

			Regular Season					Playoffs				
Season	Club	Lea	GP	G	A	TP	PIM	GP	G	A	TP	PIM
1983-84	Sokol Kiev	USSR	38	7	3	10	46	....	....	....	....	....
1984-85	Sokol Kiev	USSR	34	3	6	9	54	....	....	....	....	....
1985-86	Sokol Kiev	USSR	37	7	5	12	41	....	....	....	....	....
1986-87	Moscow D'amo	USSR	40	10	8	18	43	....	....	....	....	....
1987-88	Moscow D'amo	USSR	30	2	2	4	8	....	....	....	....	....
1988-89	Moscow D'amo	USSR	4	1	0	1	2	....	....	....	....	....
1989-90	Moscow D'amo	USSR	44	11	10	21	34	....	....	....	....	....
1990-91	Moscow D'amo	USSR	11	5	4	9	6	....	....	....	....	....
	Washington	**NHL**	**65**	**8**	**15**	**23**	**82**	....	....	....	....	....
1991-92	**Quebec**	**NHL**	**66**	**11**	**27**	**38**	**72**	....	....	....	....	....
	NHL Totals		**131**	**19**	**42**	**61**	**154**	....	....	....	....	....

Traded to **Quebec** by **Washington** for Toronto's second round choice (previously acquired by Quebec – Eric Lavigne) in 1991 Entry Draft, June 22, 1991.

TAYLOR, CHRIS

Center. Shoots left. 6', 185 lbs. Born, Stratford, Ont., March 6, 1972.
(NY Islanders' 2nd choice, 27th overall, in 1990 Entry Draft).

			Regular Season					Playoffs				
Season	Club	Lea	GP	G	A	TP	PIM	GP	G	A	TP	PIM
1988-89	London	OHL	62	7	16	23	52	15	0	2	2	15
1989-90	London	OHL	66	45	60	105	60	6	3	2	5	6
1990-91a	London	OHL	65	50	78	128	50	7	4	8	12	6
1991-92	London	OHL	66	48	74	122	57	10	8	16	24	9

a OHL Third All-Star Team (1991)

TAYLOR, DAVID ANDREW (DAVE)

Right wing. Shoots right. 6', 190 lbs. Born, Levack, Ont., December 4, 1955.
(Los Angeles' 14th choice, 210th overall, in 1975 Amateur Draft).

			Regular Season					Playoffs				
Season	Club	Lea	GP	G	A	TP	PIM	GP	G	A	TP	PIM
1975-76	Clarkson	ECAC	....	26	33	59	....	....	....	....	....	....
1976-77	Clarkson	ECAC	34	41	67	108	....	....	....	....	....	....
	Fort Worth	CHL	7	2	4	6	6	....	....	....	....	....
1977-78	Los Angeles	NHL	64	22	21	43	47	2	0	0	0	5
1978-79	Los Angeles	NHL	78	43	48	91	124	2	0	0	0	2
1979-80	Los Angeles	NHL	61	37	53	90	72	4	2	1	3	4
1980-81a	Los Angeles	NHL	72	47	65	112	130	4	2	2	4	10
1981-82	Los Angeles	NHL	78	39	67	106	130	10	4	6	10	20
1982-83	Los Angeles	NHL	46	21	37	58	76	....	....	....	....	....
1983-84	Los Angeles	NHL	63	20	49	69	91	....	....	....	....	....
1984-85	Los Angeles	NHL	79	41	51	92	132	3	2	2	4	8
1985-86	Los Angeles	NHL	76	33	38	71	110	....	....	....	....	....
1986-87	Los Angeles	NHL	67	18	44	62	84	5	2	3	5	6
1987-88	Los Angeles	NHL	68	26	41	67	129	5	3	3	6	6
1988-89	Los Angeles	NHL	70	26	37	63	80	11	1	5	6	19
1989-90	Los Angeles	NHL	58	15	26	41	96	6	4	4	8	2
1990-91bc	Los Angeles	NHL	73	23	30	53	148	12	2	1	3	12
1991-92	Los Angeles	NHL	77	10	19	29	63	6	1	1	2	20
	NHL Totals		1030	421	626	1047	1512	70	23	28	51	114

a NHL Second All-Star Team (1981)
b Won Bill Masterton Memorial Trophy (1991)
c Won King Clancy Memorial Trophy (1991)

Played in NHL All-Star Game (1981, 1982, 1986)

TAYLOR, TIM

Center. Shoots left. 6'1", 180 lbs. Born, Stratford, Ont., February 6, 1969.
(Washington's 2nd choice, 36th overall, in 1988 Entry Draft).

			Regular Season					Playoffs				
Season	Club	Lea	GP	G	A	TP	PIM	GP	G	A	TP	PIM
1986-87	London	OHL	34	7	9	16	11	....	....	....	....	....
1987-88	London	OHL	64	46	50	96	66	12	9	9	18	26
1988-89	London	OHL	61	34	80	114	93	21	*21	25	*46	58
1989-90	Baltimore	AHL	79	31	36	67	124	9	2	2	4	13
1990-91	Baltimore	AHL	79	25	42	67	75	5	0	1	1	4
1991-92	Baltimore	AHL	65	9	18	27	131	....	....	....	....	....

TEPPER, STEPHEN

Right wing. Shoots right. 6'4", 215 lbs. Born, Santa Ana, CA, March 10, 1969.
(Chicago's 7th choice, 134th overall, in 1987 Entry Draft).

			Regular Season					Playoffs				
Season	Club	Lea	GP	G	A	TP	PIM	GP	G	A	TP	PIM
1988-89	U. of Maine	H.E.	26	3	9	12	32	....	....	....	....	....
1989-90	U. of Maine	H.E.	41	10	6	16	68	....	....	....	....	....
1990-91	U. of Maine	H.E.	38	6	11	17	58	....	....	....	....	....
1991-92	U. of Maine	H.E.	16	0	3	3	20	....	....	....	....	....

THERIEN, CHRIS

Defense. Shoots left. 6'3", 205 lbs. Born, Ottawa, Ont., December 14, 1971.
(Philadelphia's 7th choice, 47th overall, in 1990 Entry Draft).

			Regular Season					Playoffs				
Season	Club	Lea	GP	G	A	TP	PIM	GP	G	A	TP	PIM
1990-91	Providence	H.E.	36	4	18	22	36	....	....	....	....	....
1991-92	Providence	H.E.	36	16	25	41	38	....	....	....	....	....

THIESSEN, TRAVIS

Defense. Shoots left. 6'3", 203 lbs. Born, North Battleford, Sask., July 11, 1972.
(Pittsburgh's 3rd choice, 67th overall, in 1992 Entry Draft).

			Regular Season					Playoffs				
Season	Club	Lea	GP	G	A	TP	PIM	GP	G	A	TP	PIM
1990-91	Moose Jaw	WHL	69	4	14	18	80	8	0	0	0	10
1991-92	Moose Jaw	WHL	72	9	50	59	112	4	0	2	2	8

THOMAS, JOHN (SCOTT)

Right wing. Shoots right. 6'2", 195 lbs. Born, Buffalo, NY, January 18, 1970.
(Buffalo's 2nd choice, 56th overall, in 1989 Entry Draft).

			Regular Season					Playoffs				
Season	Club	Lea	GP	G	A	TP	PIM	GP	G	A	TP	PIM
1989-90	Clarkson	ECAC	34	19	13	32	95	....	....	....	....	....
1990-91	Clarkson	ECAC	40	28	14	42	89	....	....	....	....	....
1991-92	Clarkson	ECAC	29	22	20	42	57	....	....	....	....	....
	Rochester	AHL	....	....	....	....	....	9	0	1	1	17

THOMAS, STEVE

Left wing. Shoots left. 5'11", 185 lbs. Born, Stockport, England, July 15, 1963.

			Regular Season					Playoffs				
Season	Club	Lea	GP	G	A	TP	PIM	GP	G	A	TP	PIM
1983-84	Toronto	OHL	70	51	54	105	77	....	....	....	....	....
1984-85	Toronto	NHL	18	1	1	2	2	....	....	....	....	....
ab	St. Catharines	AHL	64	42	48	90	56	....	....	....	....	....
1985-86	Toronto	NHL	65	20	37	57	36	10	6	8	14	9
	St. Catharines	AHL	19	18	14	32	35	....	....	....	....	....
1986-87	Toronto	NHL	78	35	27	62	114	13	2	3	5	13
1987-88	Chicago	NHL	30	13	13	26	40	3	1	2	3	6
1988-89	Chicago	NHL	45	21	19	40	69	12	3	5	8	10
1989-90	Chicago	NHL	76	40	30	70	91	20	7	6	13	33
1990-91	Chicago	NHL	69	19	35	54	129	6	1	2	3	15
1991-92	Chicago	NHL	11	2	6	8	26	....	....	....	....	....
	NY Islanders	NHL	71	28	42	70	71	....	....	....	....	....
	NHL Totals		463	179	210	389	578	64	20	26	46	86

a Won AHL Rookie of the Year (1985)
b AHL First All-Star Team (1985)

Signed as a free agent by **Toronto**, May 12, 1984. Traded to **Chicago** by **Toronto** with Rick Vaive and Bob McGill for Al Secord and Ed Olczyk, September 3, 1987. Traded to **NY Islanders** by **Chicago** with Adam Creighton for Brent Sutter and Brad Lauer, October 25, 1991.

THOMLINSON, DAVE

Left wing. Shoots left. 6'1", 196 lbs. Born, Edmonton, Alta., October 22, 1966.
(Toronto's 3rd choice, 43rd overall, in 1985 Entry Draft).

			Regular Season					Playoffs				
Season	Club	Lea	GP	G	A	TP	PIM	GP	G	A	TP	PIM
1984-85	Brandon	WHL	26	13	14	27	70	....	....	....	....	....
1985-86	Brandon	WHL	53	25	20	45	116	....	....	....	....	....
1986-87	Brandon	WHL	2	0	1	1	9	....	....	....	....	....
	Moose Jaw	WHL	70	44	36	80	117	9	7	3	10	19
1987-88	Peoria	IHL	74	27	30	57	56	7	4	3	7	11
1988-89	Peoria	IHL	64	27	29	56	154	3	0	1	1	8
1989-90	St. Louis	NHL	19	1	2	3	12	....	....	....	....	....
	Peoria	IHL	59	27	40	67	87	5	1	1	2	15
1990-91	St. Louis	NHL	3	0	0	0	0	9	3	1	4	4
	Peoria	IHL	80	53	54	107	107	11	6	7	13	28
1991-92	Boston	NHL	12	0	1	1	17	....	....	....	....	....
	Maine	AHL	25	9	11	20	36	....	....	....	....	....
	NHL Totals		34	1	3	4	29	9	3	1	4	4

Signed as a free agent by **St. Louis**, June 4, 1987. Signed as a free agent by **Boston**, July 30, 1991.

THOMPSON, BRENT

Defense. Shoots left. 6'2", 175 lbs. Born, Calgary, Alta., January 9, 1971.
(Los Angeles' 1st choice, 39th overall, in 1989 Entry Draft).

			Regular Season					Playoffs				
Season	Club	Lea	GP	G	A	TP	PIM	GP	G	A	TP	PIM
1988-89	Medicine Hat	WHL	72	3	10	13	160	3	0	0	0	2
1989-90	Medicine Hat	WHL	68	10	35	45	167	3	0	1	1	14
1990-91a	Medicine Hat	WHL	51	5	40	45	87	12	1	7	8	16
	Phoenix	IHL	....	....	....	....	....	4	0	1	1	6
1991-92	Los Angeles	NHL	27	0	5	5	89	4	0	0	0	4
	Phoenix	IHL	42	4	13	17	139	....	....	....	....	....
	NHL Totals		27	0	5	5	89	4	0	0	0	4

a WHL East Second All-Star Team (1991)

THOMPSON, MICHAEL

Right wing. Shoots right. 6', 202 lbs. Born, Montreal, Que., February 1, 1971.
(Pittsburgh's 13th choice, 215th overall, in 1990 Entry Draft).

			Regular Season					Playoffs				
Season	Club	Lea	GP	G	A	TP	PIM	GP	G	A	TP	PIM
1989-90	Michigan State	CCHA	17	4	4	8	4	....	....	....	....	....
1990-91	Michigan State	CCHA	15	1	3	4	8	....	....	....	....	....
1991-92	Michigan State	CCHA	14	1	1	2	10	....	....	....	....	....

THOMSON, JIM

Right wing. Shoots right. 6'1", 205 lbs. Born, Edmonton, Alta., December 30, 1965.
(Washington's 8th choice, 185th overall, in 1984 Entry Draft).

			Regular Season					Playoffs				
Season	Club	Lea	GP	G	A	TP	PIM	GP	G	A	TP	PIM
1983-84	Toronto	OHL	60	10	18	28	68	9	1	0	1	26
1984-85	Toronto	OHL	63	23	28	51	122	5	3	1	4	25
	Binghamton	AHL	4	0	0	0	2	....	....	....	....	....
1985-86	Binghamton	AHL	59	15	9	24	195	....	....	....	....	....
1986-87	Washington	NHL	10	0	0	0	35	....	....	....	....	....
	Binghamton	AHL	57	13	10	23	360	10	0	1	1	40
1987-88	Binghamton	AHL	25	8	9	17	64	4	1	2	3	7
1988-89	Washington	NHL	14	2	0	2	53	....	....	....	....	....
	Baltimore	AHL	41	25	16	41	129	....	....	....	....	....
	Hartford	NHL	5	0	0	0	14	....	....	....	....	....
1989-90	Binghamton	AHL	8	1	2	3	30	....	....	....	....	....
	New Jersey	NHL	3	0	0	0	31	....	....	....	....	....
	Utica	AHL	60	20	23	43	124	4	1	0	1	19
1990-91	Los Angeles	NHL	8	1	0	1	19	....	....	....	....	....
	New Haven	AHL	27	5	8	13	121	....	....	....	....	....
1991-92	Los Angeles	NHL	45	1	2	3	162	....	....	....	....	....
	Phoenix	IHL	2	1	0	1	0	....	....	....	....	....
	NHL Totals		85	4	2	6	314	....	....	....	....	....

Traded to **Hartford** by **Washington** for Scot Kleinendorst, March 6, 1989. Traded to **New Jersey** by **Hartford** for Chris Cichocki, October 31, 1989. Signed as a free agent by **Los Angeles**, July 2, 1990. Claimed by **Minnesota** from **Los Angeles** in Expansion Draft, May 30, 1991. Traded to **Los Angeles** by **Minnesota** with Randy Gilhen, Charlie Huddy and NY Rangers' fourth round choice (previously acquired by Minnesota - Alexei Zhitnik) in 1991 Entry Draft for Todd Elik, June 22, 1991. Claimed by **Ottawa** from **Los Angeles** in Expansion Draft, June 18, 1992.

THORNTON, SCOTT

Center. Shoots left. 6'2", 200 lbs. Born, London, Ont., January 9, 1971.
(Toronto's 1st choice, 3rd overall, in 1989 Entry Draft).

			Regular Season					Playoffs				
Season	Club	Lea	GP	G	A	TP	PIM	GP	G	A	TP	PIM
1987-88	Belleville	OHL	62	11	19	30	54	6	0	1	1	2
1988-89	Belleville	OHL	59	28	34	62	103	5	1	1	2	6
1989-90	Belleville	OHL	47	21	28	49	91	11	2	10	12	15
1990-91	Toronto	NHL	33	1	3	4	30	....	....	....	....	....
	Newmarket	AHL	5	1	0	1	4	....	....	....	....	....
	Belleville	OHL	3	2	1	3	2	6	0	7	7	14
1991-92	Edmonton	NHL	15	0	1	1	43	1	0	0	0	0
	Cape Breton	AHL	49	9	14	23	40	5	1	0	1	8
	NHL Totals		48	1	4	5	73	1	0	0	0	0

Traded to **Edmonton** by **Toronto** with Vincent Damphousse, Peter Ing, Luke Richardson, future considerations and cash for Grant Fuhr, Glenn Anderson and Craig Berube, September 19, 1991.

THURESSON, MARCUS

Center. Shoots left. 6'1", 183 lbs. Born, Vasteras, Sweden, May 31, 1971.
(NY Islanders' 11th choice, 224th overall, in 1991 Entry Draft).

			Regular Season					Playoffs				
Season	Club	Lea	GP	G	A	TP	PIM	GP	G	A	TP	PIM
1990-91	Leksand	Swe.	38	8	8	16	14	....	....	....	....	....
1991-92	Leksand	Swe.	21	2	4	6	22	....	....	....	....	....

Rights traded to **San Jose** by **NY Islanders** for Brian Mullen, August 24, 1992.

THYER, MARIO

Center. Shoots left. 5'11", 170 lbs. Born, Montreal, Que., September 29, 1966.

			Regular Season					Playoffs				
Season	Club	Lea	GP	G	A	TP	PIM	GP	G	A	TP	PIM
1987-88	U. of Maine	H.E.	44	24	42	66	4	....	....	....	....	....
1988-89	U. of Maine	H.E.	9	9	7	16	0	....	....	....	....	....
1989-90	Minnesota	NHL	5	0	0	0	0	1	0	0	0	2
	Kalamazoo	IHL	68	19	42	61	12	10	2	6	8	4
1990-91	Kalamazoo	IHL	75	15	51	66	15	10	4	5	9	2
1991-92	Kalamazoo	IHL	46	17	28	45	0	....	....	....	....	....
	NHL Totals		5	0	0	0	0	1	0	0	0	2

Signed as a free agent by **Minnesota**, July 12, 1989. Traded to **NY Rangers** by **Minnesota** with Minnesota's third round choice in 1992 Entry Draft for Mark Janssens, March 10, 1992. Traded to **Minnesota** by **NY Rangers** for future considerations, July 16, 1992.

TICHY, MILAN (TEE-hee)

Defense. Shoots left. 6'3", 198 lbs. Born, Plzen, Czechoslovakia, September 22, 1969.
(Chicago's 6th choice, 153rd overall, in 1989 Entry Draft).

			Regular Season					Playoffs				
Season	Club	Lea	GP	G	A	TP	PIM	GP	G	A	TP	PIM
1988-89	Skoda Plzen	Czech.	36	1	12	13	44	....	....	....	....	....
1989-90	Dukla Trencin	Czech.	51	14	8	22	....	....	....	....	....	....
1990-91	Dukla Trencin	Czech.	39	9	11	20	72	....	....	....	....	....
1991-92	Indianapolis	IHL	49	6	23	29	28	....	....	....	....	....

TIKKANEN, ESA (TEE-kuh-nehn)

Left wing. Shoots left. 6'1", 200 lbs. Born, Helsinki, Finland, January 25, 1965.
(Edmonton's 4th choice, 80th overall, in 1983 Entry Draft).

			Regular Season					Playoffs				
Season	Club	Lea	GP	G	A	TP	PIM	GP	G	A	TP	PIM
1981-82	Regina	SJHL	59	38	37	75	216	....	....	....	....	....
	Regina	WHL	2	0	0	0	0	....	....	....	....	....
1982-83	HIFK	Fin. Jr.	30	34	31	65	104	4	4	3	7	10
	HIFK	Fin.	....	....	....	....	....	1	0	0	0	2
1983-84	HIFK	Fin. Jr.	6	5	9	14	13	4	4	3	7	8
	HIFK	Fin.	36	19	11	30	30	2	0	0	0	0
1984-85	HIFK	Fin.	36	21	33	54	42	....	....	....	....	....
	Edmonton	NHL	....	....	....	....	....	3	0	0	0	2
1985-86	Edmonton	NHL	35	7	6	13	28	8	3	2	5	7
	Nova Scotia	AHL	15	4	8	12	17	....	....	....	....	....
1986-87	Edmonton	NHL	76	34	44	78	120	21	7	2	9	22
1987-88	Edmonton	NHL	80	23	51	74	153	19	10	17	27	72
1988-89	Edmonton	NHL	67	31	47	78	92	7	1	3	4	12
1989-90	Edmonton	NHL	79	30	33	63	161	22	13	11	24	26
1990-91	Edmonton	NHL	79	27	42	69	85	18	12	8	20	24
1991-92	Edmonton	NHL	40	12	16	28	44	16	5	3	8	8
	NHL Totals		456	164	239	403	683	114	51	46	97	173

TILEY, BRAD

Defense. Shoots left. 6'1", 185 lbs. Born, Markdale, Ont., July 5, 1971.
(Boston's 4th choice, 84th overall, in 1991 Entry Draft).

			Regular Season					Playoffs				
Season	Club	Lea	GP	G	A	TP	PIM	GP	G	A	TP	PIM
1990-91	S.S. Marie	OHL	66	11	55	66	29	14	4	15	19	12
1991-92	Maine	AHL	62	7	22	29	36	....	....	....	....	....

TILLEY, TOM

Defense. Shoots right. 6', 189 lbs. Born, Trenton, Ont., March 28, 1965.
(St. Louis' 13th choice, 196th overall, in 1984 Entry Draft).

			Regular Season					Playoffs				
Season	Club	Lea	GP	G	A	TP	PIM	GP	G	A	TP	PIM
1984-85	Michigan State	CCHA	37	1	5	6	58	....	....	....	....	....
1985-86	Michigan State	CCHA	42	9	25	34	48	....	....	....	....	....
1986-87	Michigan State	CCHA	42	7	14	21	48	....	....	....	....	....
1987-88a	Michigan State	CCHA	46	8	18	26	44	....	....	....	....	....
1988-89	St. Louis	NHL	70	1	22	23	47	10	1	2	3	17
1989-90	St. Louis	NHL	34	0	5	5	6	....	....	....	....	....
	Peoria	IHL	22	1	8	9	13	....	....	....	....	....
1990-91	St. Louis	NHL	22	2	4	6	4	....	....	....	....	....
b	Peoria	IHL	48	7	38	45	53	13	2	9	11	25
1991-92	Milano	Italy	18	7	13	20	12	12	5	12	17	10
	NHL Totals		126	3	31	34	57	10	1	2	3	17

a CCHA First All-Star Team (1988)
b IHL Second All-Star Team (1991)

TINORDI, MARK

Defense. Shoots left. 6'4", 205 lbs. Born, Red Deer, Alta., May 9, 1966.

			Regular Season					Playoffs				
Season	Club	Lea	GP	G	A	TP	PIM	GP	G	A	TP	PIM
1982-83	Lethbridge	WHL	64	0	4	4	50	20	1	1	2	6
1983-84	Lethbridge	WHL	72	5	14	19	53	5	0	1	1	7
1984-85	Lethbridge	WHL	58	10	15	25	134	4	0	2	2	12
1985-86	Lethbridge	WHL	58	8	30	38	139	8	1	3	4	15
1986-87	Calgary	WHL	61	29	37	66	148	....	....	....	....	....
	New Haven	AHL	2	0	0	0	2	2	0	0	0	0
1987-88	NY Rangers	NHL	24	1	2	3	50	....	....	....	....	....
	Colorado	IHL	41	8	19	27	150	11	1	5	6	31
1988-89	Minnesota	NHL	47	2	3	5	107	5	0	0	0	0
	Kalamazoo	IHL	10	0	0	0	35	....	....	....	....	....
1989-90	Minnesota	NHL	66	3	7	10	240	7	0	1	1	16
1990-91	Minnesota	NHL	69	5	27	32	189	23	5	6	11	78
1991-92	Minnesota	NHL	63	4	24	28	179	7	1	2	3	11
	NHL Totals		269	15	63	78	765	42	6	9	15	105

Played in NHL All-Star Game (1992)

Signed as a free agent by **NY Rangers**, January 4, 1987. Traded to **Minnesota** by **NY Rangers** with Paul Jerrard, the rights to Bret Barnett and Mike Sullivan, and Los Angeles' third round choice (Murray Garbutt) in 1989 Entry Draft — acquired March 10, 1987 by Minnesota — for Brian Lawton, Igor Liba and the rights to Eric Bennett, October 11, 1988.

TIPPETT, DAVE (TIP-it)

Left wing. Shoots left. 5'10", 180 lbs. Born, Moosomin, Sask., August 25, 1961.

			Regular Season					Playoffs				
Season	Club	Lea	GP	G	A	TP	PIM	GP	G	A	TP	PIM
1981-82	North Dakota	WCHA	43	13	28	41	20	....	....	....	....	....
1982-83	North Dakota	WCHA	36	15	31	46	24	....	....	....	....	....
1983-84	Cdn. Olympic	....	66	14	19	33	24	....	....	....	....	....
	Hartford	NHL	17	4	2	6	2	....	....	....	....	....
1984-85	Hartford	NHL	80	7	12	19	12	....	....	....	....	....
1985-86	Hartford	NHL	80	14	20	34	18	10	2	2	4	4
1986-87	Hartford	NHL	80	9	22	31	42	6	0	2	2	4
1987-88	Hartford	NHL	80	16	21	37	32	6	0	0	0	2
1988-89	Hartford	NHL	80	17	24	41	45	4	0	1	1	0
1989-90	Hartford	NHL	66	8	19	27	32	7	1	3	4	2
1990-91	Washington	NHL	61	6	9	15	24	10	2	3	5	8
1991-92	Washington	NHL	30	2	10	12	16	7	0	1	1	0
	Cdn. National	....	1	0	0	0	4	....	....	....	....	....
	Cdn. Olympic	....	7	1	2	3	10	....	....	....	....	....
	NHL Totals		574	83	139	222	223	50	5	12	17	20

Signed as a free agent by **Hartford**, February 29, 1984. Traded to **Washington** by **Hartford** for future considerations, September 30, 1990.

TIRKKONEN, PEKKA (TEER-kuh-nehn)

Center. Shoots left. 6'1", 194 lbs. Born, Savonlinna, Finland, July 17, 1968.
(Boston's 2nd choice, 34th overall, in 1986 Entry Draft).

			Regular Season					Playoffs				
Season	Club	Lea	GP	G	A	TP	PIM	GP	G	A	TP	PIM
1987-88	TPS	Fin.	44	11	12	23	4	....	....	....	....	....
1988-89	TPS	Fin.	42	11	15	26	8	10	1	2	3	0
1989-90	TPS	Fin.	41	17	11	28	0	9	3	4	7	0
1990-91	TPS	Fin.	44	9	23	32	10	9	4	2	6	0
1991-92	KalPa	Fin.	29	5	7	12	6	....	....	....	....	....

TKACHUK, KEITH (kuh-CHUK)

Left wing. Shoots left. 6'2", 200 lbs. Born, Melrose, MA, March 28, 1972.
(Winnipeg's 1st choice, 19th overall, in 1990 Entry Draft).

			Regular Season					Playoffs				
Season	Club	Lea	GP	G	A	TP	PIM	GP	G	A	TP	PIM
1990-91	Boston U.	H.E.	36	17	23	40	70	....	....	....	....	....
1991-92	U.S. National	....	45	10	10	20	141	....	....	....	....	....
	U.S. Olympic	....	8	1	1	2	12	....	....	....	....	....
	Winnipeg	NHL	17	3	5	8	28	7	3	0	3	30
	NHL Totals		17	3	5	8	28	7	3	0	3	30

TOCCHET, RICK (TOK-iht)

Right wing. Shoots right. 6', 205 lbs. Born, Scarborough, Ont., April 9, 1964.
(Philadelphia's 5th choice, 121st overall, in 1983 Entry Draft).

			Regular Season					Playoffs				
Season	Club	Lea	GP	G	A	TP	PIM	GP	G	A	TP	PIM
1981-82	S.S. Marie	OHL	59	7	15	22	184	11	1	1	2	28
1982-83	S.S. Marie	OHL	66	32	34	66	146	16	4	13	17	67
1983-84	S.S. Marie	OHL	64	44	64	108	209	16	*22	14	*36	41
1984-85	Philadelphia	NHL	75	14	25	39	181	19	3	4	7	72
1985-86	Philadelphia	NHL	69	14	21	35	284	5	1	2	3	26
1986-87	Philadelphia	NHL	69	21	26	47	288	26	11	10	21	72
1987-88	Philadelphia	NHL	65	31	33	64	301	5	1	4	5	55
1988-89	Philadelphia	NHL	66	45	36	81	183	16	6	6	12	69
1989-90	Philadelphia	NHL	75	37	59	96	196	....	....	....	....	....
1990-91	Philadelphia	NHL	70	40	31	71	150	....	....	....	....	....
1991-92	Philadelphia	NHL	42	13	16	29	102	....	....	....	....	....
	Pittsburgh	NHL	19	14	16	30	49	14	6	13	19	24
	NHL Totals		550	229	263	492	1734	85	28	39	67	318

Played in NHL All-Star Game (1989-91)

Traded to **Pittsburgh** by **Philadelphia** with Kjell Samuelsson and Ken Wregget for Mark Recchi, Brian Benning and Los Angeles' first round choice in 1992 Entry Draft (Jason Bowen) previously acquired by Pittsburgh in the Paul Coffey trade, February 19, 1992.

TODD, KEVIN

Center. Shoots left. 5'10", 175 lbs. Born, Winnipeg, Man., May 4, 1968.
(New Jersey's 7th choice, 129th overall, in 1986 Entry Draft).

			Regular Season					Playoffs				
Season	Club	Lea	GP	G	A	TP	PIM	GP	G	A	TP	PIM
1985-86	Prince Albert	WHL	55	14	25	39	19	20	7	6	13	29
1986-87	Prince Albert	WHL	71	39	46	85	92	8	2	5	7	17
1987-88	Prince Albert	WHL	72	49	72	121	83	10	8	11	19	27
1988-89	New Jersey	NHL	1	0	0	0	0	....	....	....	....	....
	Utica	AHL	78	26	45	71	62	4	2	0	2	6
1989-90	Utica	AHL	71	18	36	54	72	5	2	4	6	2
1990-91	New Jersey	NHL	1	0	0	0	0	1	0	0	0	6
abc	Utica	AHL	75	37	*81	*118	75	....	....	....	....	....
1991-92d	New Jersey	NHL	80	21	42	63	69	7	3	2	5	8
	NHL Totals		82	21	42	63	69	8	3	2	5	14

a AHL First All-Star Team (1991)
b Won Les Cunningham Plaque (MVP - AHL) (1991)
c Won John B. Sollenberger Trophy (Leading Scorer - AHL) (1991)
d NHL/Upper Deck All-Rookie Team (1992)

TOIVOLA, TERO (TOHI-voh-lah)

Right wing. Shoots left. 5'10", 191 lbs. Born, Tampere, Finland, July 22, 1968.
(Washington's 10th choice, 187th overall, in 1986 Entry Draft).

			Regular Season					Playoffs				
Season	Club	Lea	GP	G	A	TP	PIM	GP	G	A	TP	PIM
1987-88	Tappara	Fin.	31	6	8	14	18	7	0	1	1	12
1988-89	Tappara	Fin.	32	7	14	21	16	5	2	1	3	4
1989-90	KooKoo	Fin.	42	14	32	46	41	....	....	....	....	....
1990-91	SaiPa	Fin.	44	12	11	23	28	....	....	....	....	....
1991-92	Tappara	Fin.	42	14	15	29	26	....	....	....	....	....

TOK, CHRIS

Defense. Shoots left. 6'1", 185 lbs. Born, Grand Rapids, MN, March 19, 1973.
(Pittsburgh's 10th choice, 214th overall, in 1991 Entry Draft).

			Regular Season					Playoffs				
Season	Club	Lea	GP	G	A	TP	PIM	GP	G	A	TP	PIM
1990-91	Greenway	HS	19	2	17	19	34	....	....	....	....	....
1991-92	U. Wisconsin	WCHA	19	0	2	2	8	....	....	....	....	....

TOMBERLIN, JUSTIN

Center. Shoots left. 6', 191 lbs. Born, Grand Rapids, MN, November 15, 1970.
(Toronto's 11th choice, 192nd overall, in 1989 Entry Draft).

			Regular Season					Playoffs				
Season	Club	Lea	GP	G	A	TP	PIM	GP	G	A	TP	PIM
1989-90	U. of Maine	H.E.	35	10	7	17	6	....	....	....	....	....
1990-91	U. of Maine	H.E.	26	8	5	13	10	....	....	....	....	....
1991-92			DID NOT PLAY									

TOMILIN, VITALI

Left wing. Shoots left. 6', 183 lbs. Born, Elektrostal, Soviet Union, January 15, 1974.
(New Jersey's 4th choice, 90th overall, in 1992 Entry Draft).

			Regular Season					Playoffs				
Season	Club	Lea	GP	G	A	TP	PIM	GP	G	A	TP	PIM
1990-91	Soviet Wings	USSR	1	0	0	0	0	....	....	....	....	....
1991-92	Soviet Wings	CIS	37	1	1	2	8	....	....	....	....	....

TOMLAK, MIKE

Center/Left wing. Shoots left. 6'3", 205 lbs. Born, Thunder Bay, Ont., October 17, 1964.
(Toronto's 10th choice, 208th overall, in 1983 Entry Draft).

			Regular Season					Playoffs				
Season	Club	Lea	GP	G	A	TP	PIM	GP	G	A	TP	PIM
1982-83	Cornwall	OHL	70	18	49	67	26	....	....	....	....	....
1983-84	Cornwall	OHL	64	24	64	88	21	....	....	....	....	....
1984-85	Cornwall	OHL	66	30	70	100	9	....	....	....	....	....
1985-86	Western Ont.	OUAA	38	28	20	48	45	....	....	....	....	....
1986-87	Western Ont.	OUAA	38	16	30	46	10	....	....	....	....	....
1987-88	Western Ont.	OUAA	39	24	52	76	....	....	....	....	....	....
1988-89	Western Ont.	OUAA	35	16	34	50	....	....	....	....	....	....
1989-90	**Hartford**	**NHL**	**70**	**7**	**14**	**21**	**48**	**7**	**0**	**1**	**1**	**2**
1990-91	**Hartford**	**NHL**	**64**	**8**	**8**	**16**	**55**	**3**	**0**	**0**	**0**	**2**
	Springfield	AHL	15	4	9	13	15	....	....	....	....	....
1991-92	**Hartford**	**NHL**	**6**	**0**	**0**	**0**	**0**	....	....	....	....	....
	Springfield	AHL	39	16	21	37	24	....	....	....	....	....
	NHL Totals		**140**	**15**	**22**	**37**	**103**	**10**	**0**	**1**	**1**	**4**

Signed as a free agent by **Hartford**, June, 1989.

TOMLINSON, DAVE

Center. Shoots left. 5'11", 177 lbs. Born, North Vancouver, B.C., May 8, 1969.
(Toronto's 1st choice, 3rd overall, in 1989 Supplemental Draft).

			Regular Season					Playoffs				
Season	Club	Lea	GP	G	A	TP	PIM	GP	G	A	TP	PIM
1987-88	Boston U.	H.E.	34	16	20	36	28	....	....	....	....	....
1988-89	Boston U.	H.E.	34	16	30	46	40	....	....	....	....	....
1989-90	Boston U.	H.E.	43	15	22	37	53	....	....	....	....	....
1990-91	Boston U.	H.E.	41	30	30	60	55	....	....	....	....	....
1991-92	**Toronto**	**NHL**	**3**	**0**	**0**	**0**	**2**	....	....	....	....	....
	St. John's	AHL	75	23	34	57	75	12	4	5	9	6
	NHL Totals		**3**	**0**	**0**	**0**	**2**	....	....	....	....	....

TONELLI, JOHN (tah-NEL-ee)

Left wing. Shoots left. 6'1", 200 lbs. Born, Milton, Ont., March 23, 1957.
(NY Islanders' 2nd choice, 33rd overall, in 1977 Amateur Draft).

			Regular Season					Playoffs				
Season	Club	Lea	GP	G	A	TP	PIM	GP	G	A	TP	PIM
1973-74	Toronto	OMJHL	69	18	37	55	62	....	....	....	....	....
1974-75a	Toronto	OMJHL	70	49	86	135	85	....	....	....	....	....
1975-76	Houston	WHA	79	17	14	31	66	17	7	7	14	18
1976-77	Houston	WHA	80	24	31	55	109	11	3	4	7	12
1977-78	Houston	WHA	65	23	41	64	103	6	1	3	4	8
1978-79	**NY Islanders**	**NHL**	**73**	**17**	**39**	**56**	**44**	**10**	**1**	**6**	**7**	**0**
1979-80	**NY Islanders**	**NHL**	**77**	**14**	**30**	**44**	**49**	**21**	**7**	**9**	**16**	**18**
1980-81	**NY Islanders**	**NHL**	**70**	**20**	**32**	**52**	**57**	**16**	**5**	**8**	**13**	**16**
1981-82b	**NY Islanders**	**NHL**	**80**	**35**	**58**	**93**	**57**	**19**	**6**	**10**	**16**	**18**
1982-83	**NY Islanders**	**NHL**	**76**	**31**	**40**	**71**	**55**	**20**	**7**	**11**	**18**	**20**
1983-84	**NY Islanders**	**NHL**	**73**	**27**	**40**	**67**	**66**	**17**	**1**	**3**	**4**	**31**
1984-85b	**NY Islanders**	**NHL**	**80**	**42**	**58**	**100**	**95**	**10**	**1**	**8**	**9**	**10**
1985-86	**NY Islanders**	**NHL**	**65**	**20**	**41**	**61**	**50**	....	....	....	....	....
	Calgary	**NHL**	**9**	**3**	**4**	**7**	**10**	**22**	**7**	**9**	**16**	**49**
1986-87	**Calgary**	**NHL**	**78**	**20**	**31**	**51**	**72**	**3**	**0**	**0**	**0**	**4**
1987-88	**Calgary**	**NHL**	**74**	**17**	**41**	**58**	**84**	**6**	**2**	**5**	**7**	**8**
1988-89	**Los Angeles**	**NHL**	**77**	**31**	**33**	**64**	**110**	**6**	**0**	**0**	**0**	**8**
1989-90	**Los Angeles**	**NHL**	**73**	**31**	**37**	**68**	**62**	**10**	**1**	**2**	**3**	**6**
1990-91	**Los Angeles**	**NHL**	**71**	**14**	**16**	**30**	**49**	**12**	**2**	**4**	**6**	**12**
1991-92	**Chicago**	**NHL**	**33**	**1**	**7**	**8**	**37**	....	....	....	....	....
	Quebec	**NHL**	**19**	**2**	**4**	**6**	**14**	....	....	....	....	....
	NHL Totals		**1028**	**325**	**511**	**836**	**911**	**172**	**40**	**75**	**115**	**200**

a OMJHL First All-Star Team (1975)
b NHL Second All-Star Team (1982, 1985)

Played in NHL All-Star Game (1982, 1985)

Traded to **Calgary** by **NY Islanders** for Richard Kromm and Steve Konroyd, March 11, 1986. Signed as a free agent by **Los Angeles**, June 29, 1988. Signed as a free agent by **Chicago**, June 30, 1991. Traded to **Quebec** by **Chicago** for future considerations, February 18, 1992.

TOOKEY, TIMOTHY RAYMOND (TIM)

Center. Shoots left. 5'11", 185 lbs. Born, Edmonton, Alta., August 29, 1960.
(Washington's 4th choice, 88th overall, in 1979 Entry Draft).

			Regular Season					Playoffs				
Season	Club	Lea	GP	G	A	TP	PIM	GP	G	A	TP	PIM
1977-78	Portland	WHL	72	16	15	31	55	8	2	2	4	5
1978-79	Portland	WHL	56	33	47	80	55	25	6	14	20	6
1979-80	Portland	WHL	70	58	83	141	55	8	2	5	7	4
1980-81	**Washington**	**NHL**	**29**	**10**	**13**	**23**	**18**	....	....	....	....	....
	Hershey	AHL	47	20	38	58	129	....	....	....	....	....
1981-82	**Washington**	**NHL**	**28**	**8**	**8**	**16**	**35**	....	....	....	....	....
	Hershey	AHL	14	4	9	13	10	....	....	....	....	....
	Fredericton	AHL	16	6	10	16	16	....	....	....	....	....
1982-83	**Quebec**	**NHL**	**12**	**1**	**6**	**7**	**4**	....	....	....	....	....
	Fredericton	AHL	53	24	43	67	24	9	5	4	9	0
1983-84	**Pittsburgh**	**NHL**	**8**	**0**	**2**	**2**	**2**	....	....	....	....	....
	Baltimore	AHL	58	16	28	44	25	8	1	1	2	2
1984-85	Baltimore	AHL	74	25	43	68	74	15	8	10	18	13
1985-86ab	Hershey	AHL	69	35	*62	97	66	18	*11	8	19	10
1986-87	**Philadelphia**	**NHL**	**2**	**0**	**0**	**0**	**0**	**10**	**1**	**3**	**4**	**2**
cde	Hershey	AHL	80	51	*73	*124	45	5	5	4	9	0
1987-88	**Los Angeles**	**NHL**	**20**	**1**	**6**	**7**	**8**	....	....	....	....	....
	New Haven	AHL	11	6	7	13	2	....	....	....	....	....
1988-89	**Los Angeles**	**NHL**	**7**	**2**	**1**	**3**	**4**	....	....	....	....	....
	New Haven	AHL	33	11	18	29	30	....	....	....	....	....
	Muskegon	IHL	18	7	14	21	7	8	2	9	11	4
1989-90	Hershey	AHL	42	18	22	40	28	....	....	....	....	....
1990-91	Hershey	AHL	51	17	42	59	43	5	0	5	5	0
1991-92a	Hershey	AHL	80	36	69	105	63	6	4	2	6	4
	NHL Totals		**106**	**22**	**36**	**58**	**71**	**10**	**1**	**3**	**4**	**2**

a AHL Second All-Star Team (1986, 1992)
b AHL Playoff MVP (1986)
c AHL First All-Star Team (1987)
d Won Les Cunningham Plaque (MVP-AHL) (1987)
e Won John B. Sollenberger Trophy (Top Scorer–AHL) (1987)

Traded to **Quebec** by **Washington** with Washington's seventh round choice (Daniel Poudrier) in 1982 Entry Draft for Lee Norwood and Quebec's sixth round choice (Mats Kihlstron) —later transferred to Calgary— in 1982 Entry Draft, February 1, 1982. Signed as a free agent by **Pittsburgh**, September 12, 1983. Signed as a free agent by **Philadelphia**, July 23, 1985. Claimed by **Los Angeles** in NHL Waiver Draft, October 5, 1987. Traded to **Pittsburgh** by **Los Angeles** for Patrick Mayer, March 7, 1989. Signed as a free agent by **Philadelphia**, June 30, 1989.

TOPOROWSKI, KERRY

Defense. Shoots right. 6'2", 213 lbs. Born, Paddockwood, Sask., April 9, 1971.
(San Jose's 5th choice, 67th overall, in 1991 Entry Draft).

			Regular Season					Playoffs				
Season	Club	Lea	GP	G	A	TP	PIM	GP	G	A	TP	PIM
1989-90	Spokane	WHL	65	1	13	14	384	6	0	0	0	37
1990-91	Spokane	WHL	65	11	16	27	*505	15	2	2	4	*108
1991-92	Indianapolis	IHL	18	1	2	3	206	....	....	....	....	....

Traded to **Chicago** by **San Jose** with San Jose's second round choice in 1992 Entry Draft (later traded to Winnipeg - Boris Mironov), September 6, 1991.

TORREL, DOUGLAS

Center. Shoots right. 6'2", 180 lbs. Born, Hibbing, MN, April 29, 1969.
(Vancouver's 3rd choice, 66th overall, in 1987 Entry Draft).

			Regular Season					Playoffs				
Season	Club	Lea	GP	G	A	TP	PIM	GP	G	A	TP	PIM
1988-89	Minn.-Duluth	WCHA	40	4	6	10	36	....	....	....	....	....
1989-90	Minn.-Duluth	WCHA	39	11	11	22	48	....	....	....	....	....
1990-91	Minn.-Duluth	WCHA	40	17	18	35	78	....	....	....	....	....
1991-92	Minn.-Duluth	WCHA	37	22	22	44	84	....	....	....	....	....

TORREY, JEFF

Right wing. Shoots right. 6', 190 lbs. Born, Syracuse, NY, March 6, 1970.
(Montreal's 1st choice, 23rd overall, in 1991 Supplemental Draft).

			Regular Season					Playoffs				
Season	Club	Lea	GP	G	A	TP	PIM	GP	G	A	TP	PIM
1988-89	Clarkson	ECAC	32	6	6	12	20	....	....	....	....	....
1989-90	Clarkson	ECAC	26	4	8	12	24	....	....	....	....	....
1990-91	Clarkson	ECAC	40	10	21	31	36	....	....	....	....	....
1991-92	Clarkson	ECAC	32	6	16	22	26	....	....	....	....	....

TOUPAL, RADEK

Center. Shoots right. 5'11", 185 lbs. Born, Pisek, Czechoslovakia, August 16, 1966.
(Edmonton's 6th choice, 126th overall, in 1987 Entry Draft).

			Regular Season					Playoffs				
Season	Club	Lea	GP	G	A	TP	PIM	GP	G	A	TP	PIM
1982-83	Motor	Czech.	3	1	0	1	0	....	....	....	....	....
1983-84	Motor	Czech.	6	0	2	2	0	....	....	....	....	....
1984-85	Motor	Czech.	40	8	10	18	16	....	....	....	....	....
1985-86	Motor	Czech.	43	21	14	35	....	....	....	....	....	....
1986-87	Motor	Czech.	35	16	14	30	20	....	....	....	....	....
1987-88	Motor	Czech.	31	16	17	33	10	....	....	....	....	....
1988-89	Motor	Czech.	43	29	29	58	10	....	....	....	....	....
1989-90	Motor	Czech.	47	23	27	50	....	....	....	....	....	....
1990-91	Motor	Czech.	8	0	0	0	0	....	....	....	....	....
	Dukla Trencin	Czech.	50	22	54	76	32	....	....	....	....	....
1991-92	HPK	Fin.	44	17	29	46	10	....	....	....	....	....

TOWNSHEND, GRAEME

Right wing. Shoots right. 6'2", 225 lbs. Born, Kingston, Jamaica, October 2, 1965.

			Regular Season					Playoffs				
Season	Club	Lea	GP	G	A	TP	PIM	GP	G	A	TP	PIM
1985-86	RPI	ECAC	29	1	7	8	52	....	....	....	....	....
1986-87	RPI	ECAC	29	6	1	7	50	....	....	....	....	....
1987-88	RPI	ECAC	32	6	14	20	64	....	....	....	....	....
1988-89	Maine	AHL	5	2	1	3	11	....	....	....	....	....
	RPI	ECAC	31	6	16	22	50	....	....	....	....	....
1989-90	**Boston**	**NHL**	**4**	**0**	**0**	**0**	**7**	....	....	....	....	....
	Maine	AHL	64	15	13	28	162	....	....	....	....	....
1990-91	**Boston**	**NHL**	**18**	**2**	**5**	**7**	**12**	....	....	....	....	....
	Maine	AHL	46	16	10	26	119	2	2	0	2	4
1991-92	**NY Islanders**	**NHL**	**7**	**1**	**2**	**3**	**0**	....	....	....	....	....
	Capital Dist.	AHL	61	14	23	37	94	4	0	2	2	0
	NHL Totals		**29**	**3**	**7**	**10**	**19**	....	....	....	....	....

Signed as a free agent by **Boston**, May 12, 1989. Signed as a free agent by **NY Islanders**, September 3, 1991.

TRAVERSE, PATRICK

Defense. Shoots left. 6'3", 173 lbs. Born, Montreal, Que., March 14, 1974.
(Ottawa's 3rd choice, 50th overall, in 1992 Entry Draft).

			Regular Season					Playoffs				
Season	Club	Lea	GP	G	A	TP	PIM	GP	G	A	TP	PIM
1990-91	Bourassa	Midget	42	4	19	23	10	....	....	....	....	....
1991-92	Shawinigan	QMJHL	69	3	11	14	12	10	0	0	0	4

TREBIL, DANIEL

Defense. Shoots right. 6'3", 185 lbs. Born, Edina, MN, April 10, 1974.
(New Jersey's 7th choice, 138th overall, in 1992 Entry Draft).

			Regular Season					Playoffs				
Season	Club	Lea	GP	G	A	TP	PIM	GP	G	A	TP	PIM
1991-92	Jefferson	HS	28	7	26	33	6	....	....	....	....	....

TRESL, LADISLAV (TREHSHL)

Center. Shoots left. 6'1", 170 lbs. Born, Brno, Czechoslovakia, July 30, 1961.
(Quebec's 10th choice, 183rd overall, in 1987 Entry Draft).

			Regular Season					Playoffs				
Season	Club	Lea	GP	G	A	TP	PIM	GP	G	A	TP	PIM
1986-87	Zetor Brno	Czech.	33	13	11	24	....	....	....	....	....	....
1987-88	Fredericton	AHL	30	6	16	22	16	....	....	....	....	....
1988-89	Halifax	AHL	67	24	35	59	28	4	0	1	1	4
1989-90	Halifax	AHL	66	35	39	74	64	6	3	2	5	6
1990-91	New Haven	AHL	77	25	42	67	59	....	....	....	....	....
1991-92	Milwaukee	IHL	48	15	28	43	64	5	1	1	2	6

TRETOWICZ, DAVID

Defense. Shoots left. 5'11", 190 lbs. Born, Liverpool, NY, March 15, 1969.
(Calgary's 11th choice, 231st overall, in 1988 Entry Draft).

			Regular Season					Playoffs				
Season	Club	Lea	GP	G	A	TP	PIM	GP	G	A	TP	PIM
1987-88	Clarkson	ECAC	35	8	14	22	28	....	....	....	....	....
1988-89	Clarkson	ECAC	32	6	17	23	22	....	....	....	....	....
1989-90a	Clarkson	ECAC	35	15	24	39	34	....	....	....	....	....
1990-91b	Clarkson	ECAC	40	4	32	36	18	....	....	....	....	....
1991-92	U.S. National	....	57	1	7	8	4	....	....	....	....	....
	U.S. Olympic	....	8	0	0	0	0	....	....	....	....	....
	Phoenix	IHL	16	3	2	5	14	....	....	....	....	....

a ECAC Second All-Star Team (1990)
b ECAC First All-Star Team (1991)

TROMBLEY, DAVE

Center. Shoots left. 5'11", 178 lbs. Born, Toronto, Ont., August 11, 1968.
(Quebec's 1st choice, 2nd overall, in 1991 Supplemental Draft).

			Regular Season					Playoffs				
Season	Club	Lea	GP	G	A	TP	PIM	GP	G	A	TP	PIM
1988-89	Clarkson	ECAC	32	10	29	39	28	....	....	....	....	....
1989-90	Clarkson	ECAC	34	15	27	42	44	....	....	....	....	....
1990-91	Clarkson	ECAC	36	31	38	69	42	....	....	....	....	....
1991-92	New Haven	AHL	4	0	0	0	0	....	....	....	....	....

TROTTIER, BRYAN JOHN (TRAH-chay)

Center. Shoots left. 5'11", 195 lbs. Born, Val Marie, Sask., July 17, 1956.
(NY Islanders' 2nd choice, 22nd overall, in 1974 Amateur Draft).

			Regular Season					Playoffs				
Season	Club	Lea	GP	G	A	TP	PIM	GP	G	A	TP	PIM
1972-73	Swift Current	WHL	67	16	29	45	10	....	....	....	....	....
1973-74	Swift Current	WHL	68	41	71	112	76	13	7	8	15	8
1974-75ab	Lethbridge	WHL	67	46	*98	144	103	6	2	5	7	14
1975-76c	**NY Islanders**	**NHL**	**80**	**32**	**63**	**95**	**21**	**13**	**1**	**7**	**8**	**8**
1976-77	**NY Islanders**	**NHL**	**76**	**30**	**42**	**72**	**34**	**12**	**2**	**8**	**10**	**2**
1977-78d	**NY Islanders**	**NHL**	**77**	**46**	***77**	**123**	**46**	**7**	**0**	**3**	**3**	**4**
1978-79defg	**NY Islanders**	**NHL**	**76**	**47**	***87**	***134**	**50**	**10**	**2**	**4**	**6**	**13**
1979-80h	**NY Islanders**	**NHL**	**78**	**42**	**62**	**104**	**68**	**21**	***12**	**17**	***29**	**16**
1980-81	**NY Islanders**	**NHL**	**73**	**31**	**72**	**103**	**74**	***18**	**11**	***18**	**29**	**34**
1981-82i	**NY Islanders**	**NHL**	**80**	**50**	**79**	**129**	**88**	**19**	**6**	***23**	***29**	**40**
1982-83	**NY Islanders**	**NHL**	**80**	**34**	**55**	**89**	**68**	**17**	**8**	**12**	**20**	**18**
1983-84i	**NY Islanders**	**NHL**	**68**	**40**	**71**	**111**	**59**	**21**	**8**	**6**	**14**	**49**
1984-85	**NY Islanders**	**NHL**	**68**	**28**	**31**	**59**	**47**	**10**	**4**	**2**	**6**	**8**
1985-86	**NY Islanders**	**NHL**	**78**	**37**	**59**	**96**	**72**	**3**	**1**	**1**	**2**	**2**
1986-87	**NY Islanders**	**NHL**	**80**	**23**	**64**	**87**	**50**	**14**	**8**	**5**	**13**	**12**
1987-88j	**NY Islanders**	**NHL**	**77**	**30**	**52**	**82**	**48**	**6**	**0**	**0**	**0**	**10**
1988-89k	**NY Islanders**	**NHL**	**73**	**17**	**28**	**45**	**44**	....	....	....	....	....
1989-90	**NY Islanders**	**NHL**	**59**	**13**	**11**	**24**	**29**	**4**	**1**	**0**	**1**	**4**
1990-91	**Pittsburgh**	**NHL**	**52**	**9**	**19**	**28**	**24**	**23**	**3**	**4**	**7**	**49**
1991-92	**Pittsburgh**	**NHL**	**63**	**11**	**18**	**29**	**54**	**21**	**4**	**3**	**7**	**8**
	NHL Totals		**1238**	**520**	**890**	**1410**	**876**	**219**	**71**	**113**	**184**	**277**

a WHL Most Valuable Player (1975)
b WHL First All-Star Team (1975)
c Won Calder Memorial Trophy (1976)
d NHL First All-Star Team (1978, 1979)
e Won Art Ross Trophy (1979)
f Won Hart Trophy (1979)
g NHL Plus/Minus Leader (1979)
h Won Conn Smythe Trophy (1980)
i NHL Second All-Star Team (1982, 1984)
j Named Budweiser/NHL Man of the Year (1988)
k Won King Clancy Memorial Trophy (1989)

Played in NHL All-Star Game (1976, 1978, 1980, 1982, 1983, 1985, 1986, 1992)

Signed as a free agent by **Pittsburgh**, July 20, 1990.

TRUE, SOREN

Left wing. Shoots left. 6'1", 180 lbs. Born, Aarhus, Denmark, February 9, 1968.
(NY Rangers' 12th choice, 240th overall, in 1986 Entry Draft).

			Regular Season					Playoffs				
Season	Club	Lea	GP	G	A	TP	PIM	GP	G	A	TP	PIM
1989-90	Flint	IHL	54	15	17	32	49	4	0	1	1	2
1990-91	Albany	IHL	55	15	16	31	40	....	....	....	....	....
	San Diego	IHL	19	7	4	11	18	....	....	....	....	....
1991-92	Phoenix	IHL	21	3	3	6	12	....	....	....	....	....
	San Diego	IHL	45	18	19	37	31	....	....	....	....	....

Traded to **Los Angeles** by **NY Rangers** for future considerations, January 31, 1992.

TSCHUPP, CHRIS

Center. Shoots left. 6'2", 180 lbs. Born, Toms River, NJ, April 6, 1971.
(Calgary's 7th choice, 125th overall, in 1990 Entry Draft).

			Regular Season					Playoffs				
Season	Club	Lea	GP	G	A	TP	PIM	GP	G	A	TP	PIM
1990-91	Notre Dame	NCAA	33	1	6	7	26	....	....	....	....	....
1991-92	Notre Dame	NCAA	13	1	3	4	8	....	....	....	....	....

TUCKER, CHRIS

Center. Shoots left. 5'11", 183 lbs. Born, White Plains, NY, February 9, 1972.
(Chicago's 3rd choice, 79th overall, in 1990 Entry Draft).

			Regular Season					Playoffs				
Season	Club	Lea	GP	G	A	TP	PIM	GP	G	A	TP	PIM
1990-91	U. Wisconsin	WCHA	35	5	6	11	6	....	....	....	....	....
1991-92	U. Wisconsin	WCHA	34	12	8	20	23	....	....	....	....	....

TUCKER, JOHN

Center. Shoots right. 6', 200 lbs. Born, Windsor, Ont., September 29, 1964.
(Buffalo's 4th choice, 31st overall, in 1983 Entry Draft).

			Regular Season					Playoffs				
Season	Club	Lea	GP	G	A	TP	PIM	GP	G	A	TP	PIM
1981-82	Kitchener	OHL	67	16	32	48	32	15	2	3	5	2
1982-83	Kitchener	OHL	70	60	80	140	33	11	5	9	14	10
1983-84	**Buffalo**	**NHL**	**21**	**12**	**4**	**16**	**4**	**3**	**1**	**0**	**1**	**0**
ab	Kitchener	OHL	39	40	60	100	25	12	12	18	30	8
1984-85	**Buffalo**	**NHL**	**64**	**22**	**27**	**49**	**21**	**5**	**1**	**5**	**6**	**0**
1985-86	**Buffalo**	**NHL**	**75**	**31**	**34**	**65**	**39**	....	....	....	....	....
1986-87	**Buffalo**	**NHL**	**54**	**17**	**34**	**51**	**21**	....	....	....	....	....
1987-88	**Buffalo**	**NHL**	**45**	**19**	**19**	**38**	**20**	**6**	**7**	**3**	**10**	**18**
1988-89	**Buffalo**	**NHL**	**60**	**13**	**31**	**44**	**31**	**3**	**0**	**3**	**3**	**0**
1989-90	**Buffalo**	**NHL**	**8**	**1**	**2**	**3**	**2**	....	....	....	....	....
	Washington	**NHL**	**38**	**9**	**19**	**28**	**10**	**12**	**1**	**7**	**8**	**4**
1990-91	**Buffalo**	**NHL**	**18**	**1**	**3**	**4**	**4**	....	....	....	....	....
	NY Islanders	**NHL**	**20**	**3**	**4**	**7**	**4**	....	....	....	....	....
1991-92	Asiago	Italy	18	16	21	37	6	11	7	13	20	15
	NHL Totals		**403**	**128**	**177**	**305**	**156**	**29**	**10**	**18**	**28**	**22**

a OHL First All-Star Team (1984)
b OHL Player of the Year (1984)

Traded to **Washington** by **Buffalo** for future considerations, January 5, 1990. Traded to **Buffalo** by **Washington** for cash, July 3, 1990. Traded to **NY Islanders** by **Buffalo** for future considerations, January 21, 1991. Signed as a free agent by **Tampa Bay**, August 5, 1992.

TUCKER, TRAVIS

Defense. Shoots right. 6'4", 205 lbs. Born, Hartford, CT, March 15, 1971.
(Detroit's 9th choice, 192nd overall, in 1990 Entry Draft).

			Regular Season					Playoffs				
Season	Club	Lea	GP	G	A	TP	PIM	GP	G	A	TP	PIM
1990-91	Lowell	H.E.	22	0	0	0	40	....	....	....	....	....
1991-92	Lowell	H.E.	32	1	7	8	77	....	....	....	....	....

TULLY, BRENT

Defense. Shoots right. 6'3", 184 lbs. Born, Peterborough, Ont., March 26, 1974.
(Vancouver's 5th choice, 93rd overall, in 1992 Entry Draft).

			Regular Season					Playoffs				
Season	Club	Lea	GP	G	A	TP	PIM	GP	G	A	TP	PIM
1990-91	Peterborough	OHL	45	3	5	8	35	2	0	0	0	0
1991-92	Peterborough	OHL	65	9	23	32	65	10	0	0	0	2

TURCOTTE, DARREN

Center. Shoots left. 6', 185 lbs. Born, Boston, MA, March 2, 1968.
(NY Rangers' 6th choice, 114th overall, in 1986 Entry Draft).

			Regular Season					Playoffs				
Season	Club	Lea	GP	G	A	TP	PIM	GP	G	A	TP	PIM
1984-85	North Bay	OHL	62	33	32	65	28	....	....	....	....	....
1985-86	North Bay	OHL	62	35	37	72	35	10	3	4	7	8
1986-87	North Bay	OHL	55	30	48	78	20	18	12	8	20	6
1987-88	North Bay	OHL	32	30	33	63	16	4	3	0	3	4
	Colorado	IHL	8	4	3	7	9	6	2	6	8	8
1988-89	**NY Rangers**	**NHL**	**20**	**7**	**3**	**10**	**4**	**1**	**0**	**0**	**0**	**0**
	Denver	IHL	40	21	28	49	32	....	....	....	....	....
1989-90	**NY Rangers**	**NHL**	**76**	**32**	**34**	**66**	**32**	**10**	**1**	**6**	**7**	**4**
1990-91	**NY Rangers**	**NHL**	**74**	**26**	**41**	**67**	**37**	**6**	**1**	**2**	**3**	**0**
1991-92	**NY Rangers**	**NHL**	**71**	**30**	**23**	**53**	**57**	**8**	**4**	**0**	**4**	**6**
	NHL Totals		**241**	**95**	**101**	**196**	**130**	**25**	**6**	**8**	**14**	**10**

Played in NHL All-Star Game (1991)

TURGEON, PIERRE

Center. Shoots left. 6'1", 202 lbs. Born, Rouyn, Que., August 28, 1969.
(Buffalo's 1st choice, 1st overall, in 1987 Entry Draft).

			Regular Season					Playoffs				
Season	Club	Lea	GP	G	A	TP	PIM	GP	G	A	TP	PIM
1985-86	Granby	QMJHL	69	47	67	114	31	....	....	....	....	....
1986-87	Granby	QMJHL	58	69	85	154	8	7	9	6	15	15
1987-88	**Buffalo**	**NHL**	**76**	**14**	**28**	**42**	**34**	**6**	**4**	**3**	**7**	**4**
1988-89	**Buffalo**	**NHL**	**80**	**34**	**54**	**88**	**26**	**5**	**3**	**5**	**8**	**2**
1989-90	**Buffalo**	**NHL**	**80**	**40**	**66**	**106**	**29**	**6**	**2**	**4**	**6**	**2**
1990-91	**Buffalo**	**NHL**	**78**	**32**	**47**	**79**	**26**	**6**	**3**	**1**	**4**	**6**
1991-92	**Buffalo**	**NHL**	**8**	**2**	**6**	**8**	**4**	....	....	....	....	....
	NY Islanders	**NHL**	**69**	**38**	**49**	**87**	**16**	....	....	....	....	....
	NHL Totals		**391**	**160**	**250**	**410**	**135**	**23**	**12**	**13**	**25**	**14**

Played in NHL All-Star Game (1990)

Traded to **NY Islanders** by **Buffalo** with Uwe Krupp, Benoit Hogue and Dave McLlwain for Pat Lafontaine, Randy Hillier, Randy Wood and future considerations, October 25, 1991.

TURGEON, SYLVAIN

Left wing. Shoots left. 6', 200 lbs. Born, Noranda, Que., January 17, 1965.
(Hartford's 1st choice, 2nd overall, in 1983 Entry Draft).

			Regular Season					Playoffs				
Season	Club	Lea	GP	G	A	TP	PIM	GP	G	A	TP	PIM
1981-82	Hull	QMJHL	57	33	40	73	78	14	11	11	22	16
1982-83a	Hull	QMJHL	67	54	109	163	103	7	8	7	15	10
1983-84b	**Hartford**	**NHL**	**76**	**40**	**32**	**72**	**55**	....	....	....	....	....
1984-85	**Hartford**	**NHL**	**64**	**31**	**31**	**62**	**67**	....	....	....	....	....
1985-86	**Hartford**	**NHL**	**76**	**45**	**34**	**79**	**88**	**9**	**2**	**3**	**5**	**4**
1986-87	**Hartford**	**NHL**	**41**	**23**	**13**	**36**	**45**	**6**	**1**	**2**	**3**	**4**
1987-88	**Hartford**	**NHL**	**71**	**23**	**26**	**49**	**71**	**6**	**0**	**0**	**0**	**4**
1988-89	**Hartford**	**NHL**	**42**	**16**	**14**	**30**	**40**	**4**	**0**	**2**	**2**	**4**
1989-90	**New Jersey**	**NHL**	**72**	**30**	**17**	**47**	**81**	**1**	**0**	**0**	**0**	**0**
1990-91	**Montreal**	**NHL**	**19**	**5**	**7**	**12**	**20**	**5**	**0**	**0**	**0**	**2**
1991-92	**Montreal**	**NHL**	**56**	**9**	**11**	**20**	**39**	**5**	**1**	**0**	**1**	**4**
	NHL Totals		**517**	**222**	**185**	**407**	**506**	**36**	**4**	**7**	**11**	**22**

a QMJHL First All-Star Team (1983)
b NHL All-Rookie Team (1984)

Played in NHL All-Star Game (1986)

Traded to **New Jersey** by **Hartford** for Pat Verbeek, June 17, 1989. Traded to **Montreal** by **New Jersey** for Claude Lemieux, September 4, 1990. Claimed by **Ottawa** from **Montreal** in Expansion Draft, June 18, 1992.

TURNER, BART

Left wing. Shoots left. 6'3", 200 lbs. Born, Beaverton, OR, January 11, 1972.
(Detroit's 9th choice, 230th overall, in 1991 Entry Draft).

			Regular Season					Playoffs				
Season	Club	Lea	GP	G	A	TP	PIM	GP	G	A	TP	PIM
1990-91	Michigan State	CCHA	21	3	1	4	4	....	....	....	....	....
1991-92	Michigan State	CCHA	41	8	7	15	36	....	....	....	....	....

TURNER, BRAD

Defense. Shoots right. 6'2", 205 lbs. Born, Winnipeg, Man., May 25, 1968.
(Minnesota's 6th choice, 58th overall, in 1986 Entry Draft).

			Regular Season					Playoffs				
Season	Club	Lea	GP	G	A	TP	PIM	GP	G	A	TP	PIM
1986-87	U. of Michigan	CCHA	40	3	10	13	40	....	....	....	....	....
1987-88	U. of Michigan	CCHA	39	3	11	14	52	....	....	....	....	....
1988-89	U. of Michigan	CCHA	33	3	8	11	38	....	....	....	....	....
1989-90	U. of Michigan	CCHA	32	8	9	17	34	....	....	....	....	....
1990-91	Capital Dist.	AHL	31	1	2	3	8	....	....	....	....	....
	Richmond	ECHL	40	16	25	41	31	....	....	....	....	....
1991-92	**NY Islanders**	**NHL**	**3**	**0**	**0**	**0**	**0**	....	....	....	....	....
	Capital Dist.	AHL	35	3	6	9	17	....	....	....	....	....
	New Haven	AHL	32	6	11	17	58	....	....	....	....	....
	NHL Totals		**3**	**0**	**0**	**0**	**0**	....	....	....	....	....

TUTT, BRIAN

Defense. Shoots left. 6'1", 195 lbs. Born, Swalwell, Alta., June 9, 1962.
(Philadelphia's 6th choice, 126th overall, in 1980 Entry Draft).

			Regular Season					Playoffs				
Season	Club	Lea	GP	G	A	TP	PIM	GP	G	A	TP	PIM
1979-80	Calgary	WHL	2	0	0	0	2	4	0	1	1	6
1980-81	Calgary	WHL	72	10	41	51	111	22	3	11	14	30
1981-82	Calgary	WHL	40	2	16	18	85	9	2	2	4	22
1982-83	Maine	AHL	31	0	0	0	28	....	....	....	....	....
	Toledo	IHL	23	5	10	15	26	11	1	7	8	16
1983-84	Springfield	AHL	1	0	0	0	2	....	....	....	....	....
a	Toledo	IHL	82	7	44	51	79	13	0	6	6	16
1984-85	Hershey	AHL	3	0	0	0	8	....	....	....	....	....
a	Kalamazoo	IHL	80	8	45	53	62	11	2	4	6	19
1985-86	Kalamazoo	IHL	82	11	39	50	129	6	1	6	7	11
1986-87	Maine	AHL	41	6	15	21	19	....	....	....	....	....
	Kalamazoo	IHL	19	2	7	9	10	....	....	....	....	....
1987-88	New Haven	AHL	32	1	12	13	33	....	....	....	....	....
1988-89	Baltimore	AHL	6	1	5	6	6	....	....	....	....	....
	Cdn. National	....	63	0	19	19	87	....	....	....	....	....
1989-90	**Washington**	**NHL**	**7**	**1**	**0**	**1**	**2**	....	....	....	....	....
	Baltimore	AHL	67	2	13	15	80	9	1	0	1	4
1990-91	Cdn. National	....	10	4	3	7	14	....	....	....	....	....
1991-92	Cdn. National	....	6	0	1	1	6	....	....	....	....	....
	Cdn. Olympic	....	8	0	0	0	4	....	....	....	....	....
	NHL Totals		**7**	**1**	**0**	**1**	**2**	....	....	....	....	....

a IHL Second All-Star Team (1984, 1985)

Signed as a free agent by **Washington**, July 25, 1989.

TUTTLE, STEVE

Right wing. Shoots right. 6'1", 197 lbs. Born, Vancouver, B.C., January 5, 1966.
(St. Louis' 8th choice, 113th overall, in 1984 Entry Draft).

			Regular Season					Playoffs				
Season	Club	Lea	GP	G	A	TP	PIM	GP	G	A	TP	PIM
1984-85	U. Wisconsin	WCHA	28	3	4	7	0	....	....	....	....	....
1985-86	U. Wisconsin	WCHA	32	2	10	12	2	....	....	....	....	....
1986-87	U. Wisconsin	WCHA	42	31	21	52	14	....	....	....	....	....
1987-88ab	U. Wisconsin	WCHA	45	27	39	66	18	....	....	....	....	....
1988-89	**St. Louis**	**NHL**	**53**	**13**	**12**	**25**	**6**	**6**	**1**	**2**	**3**	**0**
1989-90	**St. Louis**	**NHL**	**71**	**12**	**10**	**22**	**4**	**5**	**0**	**1**	**1**	**2**
1990-91	**St. Louis**	**NHL**	**20**	**3**	**6**	**9**	**2**	**6**	**0**	**3**	**3**	**0**
	Peoria	IHL	42	24	32	56	8	....	....	....	....	....
1991-92c	Peoria	IHL	71	43	46	89	22	10	4	8	12	4
	NHL Totals		**144**	**28**	**28**	**56**	**12**	**17**	**1**	**6**	**7**	**2**

a NCAA West Second All-American Team (1988)
b WCHA Second All-Star Team (1988)
c IHL First All-Star Team (1992)

Traded to **Tampa Bay** by **St. Louis** with Pat Jablonski and Darin Kimble for future considerations, June 19, 1992.

TWIST, ANTHONY (TONY)

Left wing/Defense. Shoots left. 6'1", 212 lbs. Born, Sherwood Park, Alta., May 9, 1968.
(St. Louis' 9th choice, 177th overall, in 1988 Entry Draft).

			Regular Season					Playoffs				
Season	Club	Lea	GP	G	A	TP	PIM	GP	G	A	TP	PIM
1987-88	Saskatoon	WHL	55	1	8	9	226	10	1	1	2	6
1988-89	Peoria	IHL	67	3	8	11	312	....	....	....	....	....
1989-90	**St. Louis**	**NHL**	**28**	**0**	**0**	**0**	**124**	....	....	....	....	....
	Peoria	IHL	36	1	5	6	200	5	0	1	1	8
1990-91	Peoria	IHL	38	2	10	12	244	....	....	....	....	....
	Quebec	**NHL**	**24**	**0**	**0**	**0**	**104**	....	....	....	....	....
1991-92	**Quebec**	**NHL**	**44**	**0**	**1**	**1**	**164**	....	....	....	....	....
	NHL Totals		**96**	**0**	**1**	**1**	**392**	....	....	....	....	....

Traded to **Quebec** by **St. Louis** with Herb Raglan and Andy Rymsha for Darin Kimble, February 4, 1991.

ULANOV, IGOR (oo-LAH-nov)

Defense. Shoots right. 6'2", 202 lbs. Born, Krasnokamsk, Soviet Union, October 1, 1969.
(Winnipeg's 10th choice, 203rd overall, in 1991 Entry Draft).

			Regular Season					Playoffs				
Season	Club	Lea	GP	G	A	TP	PIM	GP	G	A	TP	PIM
1990-91	Khimik	USSR	41	2	2	4	52	....	....	....	....	....
1991-92	Khimik	CIS	27	1	4	5	24	....	....	....	....	....
	Winnipeg	**NHL**	**27**	**2**	**9**	**11**	**67**	**7**	**0**	**0**	**0**	**39**
	NHL Totals		**27**	**2**	**9**	**11**	**67**	**7**	**0**	**0**	**0**	**39**

UNIAC, JOHN

Defense. Shoots right. 5'11", 210 lbs. Born, Stratford, Ont., March 29, 1971.
(Montreal's 12th choice, 228th overall, in 1990 Entry Draft).

			Regular Season					Playoffs				
Season	Club	Lea	GP	G	A	TP	PIM	GP	G	A	TP	PIM
1988-89	Sudbury	OHL	20	1	6	7	13	....	....	....	....	....
	Kitchener	OHL	45	5	13	18	32	5	0	2	2	0
1989-90	Kitchener	OHL	57	9	35	44	38	14	1	1	2	2
1990-91	Kitchener	OHL	58	12	59	71	53	6	0	3	3	8
1991-92	Winston-Salem	ECHL	38	4	16	20	39	5	0	2	2	2

USTORF, STEFAN

Center. Shoots left. 5'11", 172 lbs. Born, Kaufbeuren, Germany, January 3, 1974.
(Washington's 3rd choice, 53rd overall, in 1992 Entry Draft).

			Regular Season					Playoffs				
Season	Club	Lea	GP	G	A	TP	PIM	GP	G	A	TP	PIM
1991-92	Kaufbeuren	Ger.	46	4	29	33	52	....	....	....	....	....

UVAYEV, VJATESLAV (oo-VIH-ev)

Defense. Shoots left. 5'11", 189 lbs. Born, Moscow, Soviet Union, April 15, 1966.
(NY Rangers' 9th choice, 191st overall, in 1991 Entry Draft).

			Regular Season					Playoffs				
Season	Club	Lea	GP	G	A	TP	PIM	GP	G	A	TP	PIM
1990-91	Spartak	USSR	45	1	10	11	44	....	....	....	....	....
1991-92	Spartak	CIS	36	0	7	7	6	....	....	....	....	....

VACHON, NICK

Center. Shoots left. 5'10", 190 lbs. Born, Montreal, Que., July 20, 1972.
(Toronto's 11th choice, 241st overall, in 1990 Entry Draft).

			Regular Season					Playoffs				
Season	Club	Lea	GP	G	A	TP	PIM	GP	G	A	TP	PIM
1990-91	Boston U.	H.E.	8	0	1	1	4	....	....	....	....	....
1991-92	Boston U.	H.E.	16	6	7	13	10	....	....	....	....	....
	Portland	WHL	25	9	19	28	46	6	0	3	3	14

VAIVE, RICHARD CLAUDE (RICK) (VIGHV)

Right wing. Shoots right. 6'1", 198 lbs. Born, Ottawa, Ont., May 14, 1959.
(Vancouver's 1st choice, 5th overall, in 1979 Entry Draft).

			Regular Season					Playoffs				
Season	Club	Lea	GP	G	A	TP	PIM	GP	G	A	TP	PIM
1976-77	Sherbrooke	QJHL	67	51	59	110	91	18	10	13	23	78
1977-78	Sherbrooke	QJHL	68	76	79	155	199	9	8	4	12	38
1978-79	Birmingham	WHA	75	26	33	59	*248	....	....	....	....	....
1979-80	**Vancouver**	**NHL**	**47**	**13**	**8**	**21**	**111**	....	....	....	....	....
	Toronto	**NHL**	**22**	**9**	**7**	**16**	**77**	**3**	**1**	**0**	**1**	**11**
1980-81	**Toronto**	**NHL**	**75**	**33**	**29**	**62**	**229**	**3**	**1**	**0**	**1**	**4**
1981-82	**Toronto**	**NHL**	**77**	**54**	**35**	**89**	**157**	....	....	....	....	....
1982-83	**Toronto**	**NHL**	**78**	**51**	**28**	**79**	**105**	**4**	**2**	**5**	**7**	**6**
1983-84	**Toronto**	**NHL**	**76**	**52**	**41**	**93**	**114**	....	....	....	....	....
1984-85	**Toronto**	**NHL**	**72**	**35**	**33**	**68**	**112**	....	....	....	....	....
1985-86	**Toronto**	**NHL**	**61**	**33**	**31**	**64**	**85**	**9**	**6**	**2**	**8**	**9**
1986-87	**Toronto**	**NHL**	**73**	**32**	**34**	**66**	**61**	**13**	**4**	**2**	**6**	**23**
1987-88	**Chicago**	**NHL**	**76**	**43**	**26**	**69**	**108**	**5**	**6**	**2**	**8**	**38**
1988-89	**Chicago**	**NHL**	**30**	**12**	**13**	**25**	**60**	....	....	....	....	....
	Buffalo	**NHL**	**28**	**19**	**13**	**32**	**64**	**5**	**2**	**1**	**3**	**8**
1989-90	**Buffalo**	**NHL**	**70**	**29**	**19**	**48**	**74**	**6**	**4**	**2**	**6**	**6**
1990-91	**Buffalo**	**NHL**	**71**	**25**	**27**	**52**	**74**	**6**	**1**	**2**	**3**	**6**
1991-92	**Buffalo**	**NHL**	**20**	**1**	**3**	**4**	**14**	....	....	....	....	....
	Rochester	AHL	12	4	9	13	4	16	4	4	8	10
	NHL Totals		**876**	**441**	**347**	**788**	**1445**	**54**	**27**	**16**	**43**	**111**

Played in NHL All-Star Game (1982-84)

Traded to **Toronto** by **Vancouver** with Bill Derlago for Dave Williams and Jerry Butler, February 18, 1980. Traded to **Chicago** by **Toronto** with Steve Thomas and Bob McGill for Al Secord and Ed Olczyk, September 3, 1987. Traded to **Buffalo** by **Chicago** for Adam Creighton, December 26, 1988.

VALICEVIC, ROBERT

Right wing. Shoots right. 6'2", 197 lbs. Born, Detroit, MI, January 6, 1971.
(NY Islanders' 6th choice, 114th overall, in 1991 Entry Draft).

			Regular Season					Playoffs				
Season	Club	Lea	GP	G	A	TP	PIM	GP	G	A	TP	PIM
1990-91	Detroit	USHL	39	31	44	75	54	....	....	....	....	....
1991-92	Lake Superior	CCHA	32	8	4	12	12	....	....	....	....	....

VALILA, MIKA

Center. Shoots left. 6', 172 lbs. Born, Sodertalje, Sweden, February 20, 1970.
(Pittsburgh's 7th choice, 130th overall, in 1990 Entry Draft).

			Regular Season					Playoffs				
Season	Club	Lea	GP	G	A	TP	PIM	GP	G	A	TP	PIM
1989-90	Tappara	Fin.	44	8	16	24	16	7	2	2	4	4
1990-91	Tappara	Fin.	41	10	9	19	16	3	0	1	1	0
1991-92	Jokerit	Fin.	30	4	3	7	4	8	1	1	2	2

VALIMONT, CARL

Defense. Shoots left. 6'1", 200 lbs. Born, Southington, CT, March 1, 1966.
(Vancouver's 10th choice, 193rd overall, in 1985 Entry Draft).

			Regular Season					Playoffs				
Season	Club	Lea	GP	G	A	TP	PIM	GP	G	A	TP	PIM
1984-85	U. of Lowell	H.E.	40	4	11	15	24	....	....	....	....	....
1985-86	U. of Lowell	H.E.	26	1	9	10	12	....	....	....	....	....
1986-87	U. of Lowell	H.E.	36	8	9	17	36	....	....	....	....	....
1987-88a	U. of Lowell	H.E.	38	6	26	32	59	....	....	....	....	....
1988-89	Milwaukee	IHL	79	4	33	37	56	11	2	8	10	12
1989-90	Milwaukee	IHL	78	13	28	41	48	3	0	1	1	6
1990-91	Milwaukee	IHL	80	10	21	31	66	6	2	1	3	2
1991-92	Milwaukee	IHL	71	14	31	45	81	5	0	2	2	4

a Hockey East Second All-Star Team (1988)

VALK, GARRY

Left wing. Shoots left. 6'1", 205 lbs. Born, Edmonton, Alta., November 27, 1967.
(Vancouver's 5th choice, 108th overall, in 1987 Entry Draft).

			Regular Season					Playoffs				
Season	Club	Lea	GP	G	A	TP	PIM	GP	G	A	TP	PIM
1987-88	North Dakota	WCHA	38	23	12	35	64	....	....	....	....	....
1988-89	North Dakota	WCHA	40	14	17	31	71	....	....	....	....	....
1989-90	North Dakota	WCHA	43	22	17	39	92	....	....	....	....	....
1990-91	**Vancouver**	**NHL**	**59**	**10**	**11**	**21**	**67**	**5**	**0**	**0**	**0**	**20**
	Milwaukee	IHL	10	12	4	16	13	3	0	0	0	2
1991-92	**Vancouver**	**NHL**	**65**	**8**	**17**	**25**	**56**	**4**	**0**	**0**	**0**	**5**
	NHL Totals		**124**	**18**	**28**	**46**	**123**	**9**	**0**	**0**	**0**	**25**

VALLIS, LINDSAY

Right wing. Shoots right. 6'3", 207 lbs. Born, Winnipeg, Man., January 12, 1971.
(Montreal's 1st choice, 13th overall, in 1989 Entry Draft).

			Regular Season					Playoffs				
Season	Club	Lea	GP	G	A	TP	PIM	GP	G	A	TP	PIM
1987-88	Seattle	WHL	68	31	45	76	65	....	....	....	....	....
1988-89	Seattle	WHL	63	21	32	53	48	....	....	....	....	....
1989-90	Seattle	WHL	65	34	43	77	68	13	6	5	11	14
1990-91	Seattle	WHL	72	41	38	79	119	6	1	3	4	17
	Fredericton	AHL	....	....	....	....	....	7	0	0	0	6
1991-92	Fredericton	AHL	71	10	19	29	84	4	0	1	1	7

VAN ALLEN, SHAUN

Center. Shoots left. 6'1", 200 lbs. Born, Shaunavon, Sask., August 29,1967.
(Edmonton's 5th choice, 105th overall, in 1987 Entry Draft).

			Regular Season					Playoffs				
Season	Club	Lea	GP	G	A	TP	PIM	GP	G	A	TP	PIM
1984-85	Swift Current	WHL	61	12	20	32	136	....	....	....	....	....
1985-86	Saskatoon	WHL	55	12	11	23	43	13	4	8	12	28
1986-87	Saskatoon	WHL	72	38	59	97	116	11	4	6	10	24
1987-88	Milwaukee	IHL	40	14	28	42	34	....	....	....	....	....
	Nova Scotia	AHL	19	4	10	14	17	4	1	1	2	4
1988-89	Cape Breton	AHL	76	32	42	74	81	....	....	....	....	....
1989-90	Cape Breton	AHL	61	25	44	69	83	4	0	2	2	8
1990-91	**Edmonton**	**NHL**	**2**	**0**	**0**	**0**	**0**	....	....	....	....	....
a	Cape Breton	AHL	76	25	75	100	182	4	0	1	1	8
1991-92bc	Cape Breton	AHL	77	29	*84	*113	80	5	3	7	10	14
	NHL Totals		**2**	**0**	**0**	**0**	**0**	....	....	....	....	....

a AHL Second All-Star Team (1991)
b Won John B. Sollenberger Trophy (Top Scorer-AHL) (1992)
c AHL First All-Star Team (1992)

VAN DORP, WAYNE

Left wing. Shoots left. 6'4", 225 lbs. Born, Vancouver, B.C., May 19, 1961.

			Regular Season					Playoffs				
Season	Club	Lea	GP	G	A	TP	PIM	GP	G	A	TP	PIM
1979-80	Seattle	WHL	68	8	13	21	195	12	3	1	4	33
1980-81	Seattle	WHL	63	22	30	52	242	5	1	0	1	10
1981-82	Heerenveen	Neth.	22	11	7	18	44	12	1	4	5	34
1982-83	Heerenveen	Neth.	23	7	12	19	40	15	4	5	9	20
1984-85	GIJS Groningen	Neth.	29	38	46	84	112	6	6	2	8	23
	Erie	ACHL	7	9	8	17	21	10	0	2	6	2
1985-86a	GIJS Groningen	Neth.	29	19	24	43	81	8	9	*12	21	6
1986-87	Rochester	AHL	47	7	3	10	192	....	....	....	....	....
	Edmonton	**NHL**	**3**	**0**	**0**	**0**	**25**	**3**	**0**	**0**	**0**	**2**
	Nova Scotia	AHL	11	2	3	5	37	5	0	0	0	56
1987-88	**Pittsburgh**	**NHL**	**25**	**1**	**3**	**4**	**75**	....	....	....	....	....
	Nova Scotia	AHL	12	2	2	4	87	....	....	....	....	....
1988-89	Rochester	AHL	28	3	6	9	202	....	....	....	....	....
	Chicago	**NHL**	**8**	**0**	**0**	**0**	**23**	**16**	**0**	**1**	**1**	**17**
	Saginaw	IHL	11	4	3	7	60	....	....	....	....	....
1989-90	**Chicago**	**NHL**	**61**	**7**	**4**	**11**	**303**	**8**	**0**	**0**	**0**	**23**
1990-91	**Quebec**	**NHL**	**4**	**1**	**0**	**1**	**30**	....	....	....	....	....
1991-92	**Quebec**	**NHL**	**24**	**3**	**5**	**8**	**109**	....	....	....	....	....
	Halifax	AHL	15	5	5	10	54	....	....	....	....	....
	NHL Totals		**125**	**12**	**12**	**24**	**565**	**27**	**0**	**1**	**1**	**42**

a Named playoff MVP (1986)

Traded to **Edmonton** by **Buffalo** with Normand Lacombe and future consideration for Lee Fogolin and Mark Napier, March 6, 1987. Traded to **Pittsburgh** by **Edmonton** with Paul Coffey and Dave Hunter for Craig Simpson, Dave Hannan, Moe Mantha, and Chris Joseph, November 24, 1987. Traded to **Buffalo** by **Pittsburgh** for future considerations, September 30, 1988. Traded to **Chicago** by **Buffalo** for Chicago's seventh round choice (Viktor Gordijuk) in 1990 Entry Draft, February 16, 1989. Claimed by **Quebec** in NHL Waiver Draft, October 1, 1990.

VAN KESSEL, JOHN

Right wing. Shoots right. 6'4", 193 lbs. Born, Bridgewater, N.S., December 19, 1969.
(Los Angeles' 3rd choice, 49th overall, in 1988 Entry Draft).

			Regular Season					Playoffs				
Season	Club	Lea	GP	G	A	TP	PIM	GP	G	A	TP	PIM
1986-87	Belleville	OHL	61	1	10	11	58	....	....	....	....	....
1987-88	North Bay	OHL	50	13	16	29	214	4	1	1	2	16
1988-89	North Bay	OHL	50	7	13	20	218	11	2	4	6	31
1989-90	New Haven	AHL	6	1	1	2	9	....	....	....	....	....
	North Bay	OHL	40	7	21	28	127	5	0	3	3	16
1990-91	Phoenix	IHL	65	15	15	30	246	3	1	1	2	16
1991-92	Phoenix	IHL	44	2	6	8	247	....	....	....	....	....

Claimed by **Ottawa** from **Los Angeles** in Expansion Draft, June 18, 1992.

VARGA, JOHN

Left wing. Shoots left. 5'9", 172 lbs. Born, Chicago, IL, January 31, 1974.
(Washington's 5th choice, 119th overall, in 1992 Entry Draft).

			Regular Season					Playoffs				
Season	Club	Lea	GP	G	A	TP	PIM	GP	G	A	TP	PIM
1990-91	Chicago Y.A.	Midget	54	50	40	90	117	....	....	....	....	....
1991-92	Tacoma	WHL	72	25	34	59	93	4	1	2	3	0

VARVIO, JARKKO (VAHR-vee-oh, YAHR-koh)

Right wing. Shoots right. 5'9", 172 lbs. Born, Tampere, Finland, April 28, 1972.
(Minnesota's 1st choice, 34th overall, in 1992 Entry Draft).

			Regular Season					Playoffs				
Season	Club	Lea	GP	G	A	TP	PIM	GP	G	A	TP	PIM
1990-91	Ilves	Fin.	37	10	7	17	6	....	....	....	....	....
1991-92	HPK	Fin.	41	25	9	34	6	....	....	....	....	....

VARY, JOHN

Defense. Shoots right. 6'1", 207 lbs. Born, Owen Sound, Ont., February 11, 1972.
(NY Rangers' 3rd choice, 55th overall, in 1990 Entry Draft).

			Regular Season					Playoffs				
Season	Club	Lea	GP	G	A	TP	PIM	GP	G	A	TP	PIM
1988-89	North Bay	OHL	45	2	7	9	38	3	0	0	0	0
1989-90	North Bay	OHL	59	7	39	46	79	5	0	2	2	8
1990-91	North Bay	OHL	39	5	21	26	108	....	....	....	....	....
	Kingston	OHL	31	5	15	20	16	....	....	....	....	....
1991-92	Kingston	OHL	54	11	38	49	102	....	....	....	....	....
	Binghamton	AHL	1	0	0	0	0	....	....	....	....	....

VASKE, DENNIS (VAS-kee)

Defense. Shoots left. 6'2", 210 lbs. Born, Rockford, IL, October 11, 1967.
(NY Islanders' 2nd choice, 38th overall, in 1986 Entry Draft).

			Regular Season					Playoffs				
Season	Club	Lea	GP	G	A	TP	PIM	GP	G	A	TP	PIM
1986-87	Minn.-Duluth	WCHA	33	0	2	2	40	....	....	....	....	....
1987-88	Minn.-Duluth	WCHA	39	1	6	7	90	....	....	....	....	....
1988-89	Minn.-Duluth	WCHA	37	9	19	28	86	....	....	....	....	....
1989-90	Minn.-Duluth	WCHA	37	5	24	29	72	....	....	....	....	....
1990-91	NY Islanders	NHL	5	0	0	0	2	....	....	....	....	....
	Capital Dist.	AHL	67	10	10	20	65	....	....	....	....	....
1991-92	NY Islanders	NHL	39	0	1	1	39	....	....	....	....	....
	NHL Totals		44	0	1	1	41	....	....	....	....	....

VEILLEUX, STEVE

Defense. Shoots right. 6', 190 lbs. Born, Lachenaie, Que., March 9, 1969.
(Vancouver's 2nd choice, 45th overall, in 1987 Entry Draft).

			Regular Season					Playoffs				
Season	Club	Lea	GP	G	A	TP	PIM	GP	G	A	TP	PIM
1985-86	Trois-Rivières	QMJHL	67	1	20	21	132	5	0	0	0	13
1986-87	Trois-Rivières	QMJHL	62	6	22	28	227	....	....	....	....	....
1987-88a	Trois-Rivières	QMJHL	63	7	25	32	150	....	....	....	....	....
1988-89a	Trois-Rivières	QMJHL	49	5	28	33	149	4	0	0	0	10
	Milwaukee	IHL	1	0	0	0	0	4	0	0	0	13
1989-90	Milwaukee	IHL	76	4	12	16	195	2	0	0	0	2
1990-91	Milwaukee	IHL	58	0	9	9	152	....	....	....	....	....
	Indianapolis	IHL	11	1	3	4	30	7	0	3	3	13
1991-92	Fredericton	AHL	53	3	7	10	122	....	....	....	....	....

a QMJHL Second All-Star Team (1988, 1989)

Signed as a free agent by **Montreal**, August 6, 1991.

VELISCHEK, RANDY (VEHL-ih-shehk)

Defense. Shoots left. 6', 200 lbs. Born, Montreal, Que., February 10, 1962.
(Minneota's 3rd choice, 53rd overall, in 1980 Entry Draft).

			Regular Season					Playoffs				
Season	Club	Lea	GP	G	A	TP	PIM	GP	G	A	TP	PIM
1979-80	Providence	ECAC	31	5	5	10	20	....	....	....	....	....
1980-81	Providence	ECAC	33	3	12	15	26	....	....	....	....	....
1981-82a	Providence	ECAC	33	1	14	15	38	....	....	....	....	....
1982-83bc	Providence	ECAC	41	18	34	52	50	....	....	....	....	....
	Minnesota	NHL	3	0	0	0	2	9	0	0	0	0
1983-84	Minnesota	NHL	33	2	2	4	10	1	0	0	0	0
	Salt Lake	CHL	43	7	21	28	54	5	0	3	3	2
1984-85	Minnesota	NHL	52	4	9	13	26	9	2	3	5	8
	Springfield	AHL	26	2	7	9	22	....	....	....	....	....
1985-86	New Jersey	NHL	47	2	7	9	39	....	....	....	....	....
	Maine	AHL	21	0	4	4	4	....	....	....	....	....
1986-87	New Jersey	NHL	64	2	16	18	52	....	....	....	....	....
1987-88	New Jersey	NHL	51	3	9	12	66	19	0	2	2	20
1988-89	New Jersey	NHL	80	4	14	18	70	....	....	....	....	....
1989-90	New Jersey	NHL	62	0	6	6	72	6	0	0	0	4
1990-91	Quebec	NHL	79	2	10	12	42	....	....	....	....	....
1991-92	Quebec	NHL	38	2	3	5	22	....	....	....	....	....
	Halifax	AHL	16	3	6	9	0	....	....	....	....	....
	NHL Totals		509	21	76	97	401	44	2	5	7	32

a ECAC Second All-Star Team (1982)
b ECAC First All-Star Team (1983)
c Named ECAC Player of the Year (1983)

Claimed by **New Jersey** from **Minnesota** in NHL Waiver Draft, October 7, 1985. Traded to **Quebec** by **New Jersey** as future considerations with Craig Wolanin to complete March 6, 1990 Peter Stastny deal, August 13, 1990.

VERBEEK, PATRICK (PAT) (vuhr-BEEK)

Right/Left wing. Shoots right. 5'9", 190 lbs. Born, Sarnia, Ont., May 24, 1964.
(New Jersey's 3rd choice, 43rd overall, in 1982 Entry Draft).

			Regular Season					Playoffs				
Season	Club	Lea	GP	G	A	TP	PIM	GP	G	A	TP	PIM
1981-82	Sudbury	OHL	66	37	51	88	180	....	....	....	....	....
1982-83	New Jersey	NHL	6	3	2	5	8	....	....	....	....	....
	Sudbury	OHL	61	40	67	107	184	....	....	....	....	....
1983-84	New Jersey	NHL	79	20	27	47	158	....	....	....	....	....
1984-85	New Jersey	NHL	78	15	18	33	162	....	....	....	....	....
1985-86	New Jersey	NHL	76	25	28	53	79	....	....	....	....	....
1986-87	New Jersey	NHL	74	35	24	59	120	....	....	....	....	....
1987-88	New Jersey	NHL	73	46	31	77	227	20	4	8	12	51
1988-89	New Jersey	NHL	77	26	21	47	189	....	....	....	....	....
1989-90	Hartford	NHL	80	44	45	89	228	7	2	2	4	26
1990-91	Hartford	NHL	80	43	39	82	246	6	3	2	5	40
1991-92	Hartford	NHL	76	22	35	57	243	7	0	2	2	12
	NHL Totals		699	279	270	549	1660	40	9	14	23	129

Played in NHL All-Star Game (1991)

Traded to **Hartford** by **New Jersey** for Sylvain Turgeon, June 17, 1989.

VERMETTE, MARK

Right wing. Shoots right. 6'1", 203 lbs. Born, Cochenour, Ont., October 3, 1967.
(Quebec's 8th choice, 134th overall, in 1986 Entry Draft).

			Regular Season					Playoffs				
Season	Club	Lea	GP	G	A	TP	PIM	GP	G	A	TP	PIM
1985-86	Lake Superior	CCHA	32	1	4	5	7	....	....	....	....	....
1986-87	Lake Superior	CCHA	38	19	17	36	59	....	....	....	....	....
1987-88abc	Lake Superior	CCHA	46	*45	30	75	154	....	....	....	....	....
1988-89	Quebec	NHL	12	0	4	4	7	....	....	....	....	....
	Halifax	AHL	52	12	16	28	30	1	0	0	0	0
1989-90	Quebec	NHL	11	1	5	6	8	....	....	....	....	....
	Halifax	AHL	47	20	17	37	44	6	1	5	6	6
1990-91	Quebec	NHL	34	3	4	7	10	....	....	....	....	....
	Halifax	AHL	46	26	22	48	37	....	....	....	....	....
1991-92	Quebec	NHL	10	1	0	1	8	....	....	....	....	....
	Halifax	AHL	44	21	18	39	39	....	....	....	....	....
	NHL Totals		67	5	13	18	33	....	....	....	....	....

a NCAA West All-American Team (1988)
b CCHA Player of the Year (1988)
c CCHA First All-Star Team (1988)

VESEY, JIM

Center/Right wing. Shoots right. 6'1", 202 lbs.. Born, Columbus, MA, October 29, 1965.
(St. Louis' 11th choice, 155th overall, in 1984 Entry Draft).

			Regular Season					Playoffs				
Season	Club	Lea	GP	G	A	TP	PIM	GP	G	A	TP	PIM
1984-85	Merrimack	NCAA	33	19	11	30	28	....	....	....	....	....
1985-86	Merrimack	NCAA	32	29	32	61	67	....	....	....	....	....
1986-87	Merrimack	NCAA	35	22	36	58	57	....	....	....	....	....
1987-88	Merrimack	NCAA	33	33	50	83	....	....	....	....	....	....
1988-89	St. Louis	NHL	5	1	1	2	7	....	....	....	....	....
a	Peoria	IHL	76	47	46	93	137	4	1	2	3	6
1989-90	St. Louis	NHL	6	0	1	1	0	....	....	....	....	....
	Peoria	IHL	60	47	44	91	75	5	1	3	4	21
1990-91	Peoria	IHL	58	32	41	73	69	19	4	14	18	26
1991-92	Boston	NHL	4	0	0	0	0	....	....	....	....	....
	Maine	AHL	10	6	7	13	13	....	....	....	....	....
	NHL Totals		15	1	2	3	7	....	....	....	....	....

a IHL First All-Star Team (1989)

Traded to **Winnipeg** by **St. Louis** (future consideration in trade which sent Tom Draper to St. Louis on February 28, 1991) May 24, 1991. Traded to **Boston** by **Winnipeg** for future considerations, June 20, 1991.

VIAL, DENNIS (vee-AHL)

Defense. Shoots left. 6'1", 215 lbs. Born, Sault Ste. Marie, Ont., April 10, 1969.
(NY Rangers' 5th choice, 110th overall, in 1988 Entry Draft).

			Regular Season					Playoffs				
Season	Club	Lea	GP	G	A	TP	PIM	GP	G	A	TP	PIM
1985-86	Hamilton	OHL	31	1	1	2	66	....	....	....	....	....
1986-87	Hamilton	OHL	53	1	8	9	194	8	0	0	0	8
1987-88	Hamilton	OHL	52	3	17	20	229	13	2	2	4	49
1988-89	Niagara Falls	OHL	50	10	27	37	227	15	1	7	8	44
1989-90	Flint	IHL	79	6	29	35	351	4	0	0	0	10
1990-91	NY Rangers	NHL	21	0	0	0	61	....	....	....	....	....
	Binghamton	AHL	40	2	7	9	250	....	....	....	....	....
	Detroit	NHL	9	0	0	0	16	....	....	....	....	....
1991-92	Detroit	NHL	27	1	0	1	72	....	....	....	....	....
	Adirondack	AHL	20	2	4	6	107	17	1	3	4	43
	NHL Totals		57	1	0	1	149	....	....	....	....	....

Traded to **Detroit** by **NY Rangers** with Kevin Miller and Jim Cummins for Joey Kocur and Per Djoos, March 5, 1991. Traded to **Quebec** by **Detroit** with Doug Crossman for cash, June 15, 1992.

VILGRAIN, CLAUDE

Right wing. Shoots right. 6'1", 205 lbs. Born, Port-au-Prince, Haiti, March 1, 1963.
(Detroit's 6th choice, 107th overall, in 1982 Entry Draft).

			Regular Season					Playoffs				
Season	Club	Lea	GP	G	A	TP	PIM	GP	G	A	TP	PIM
1983-84	U. of Moncton	AUAA	20	11	20	31	8	....	....	....	....	....
1984-85	U. of Moncton	AUAA	24	35	28	63	20	....	....	....	....	....
1985-86	U. of Moncton	AUAA	19	17	20	37	25	....	....	....	....	....
1986-87	Cdn. Olympic	....	78	28	42	70	38	....	....	....	....	....
1987-88	Cdn. National	....	61	21	20	41	41	....	....	....	....	....
	Cdn. Olympic	....	6	0	0	0	0	....	....	....	....	....
	Vancouver	NHL	6	1	1	2	0	....	....	....	....	....
1988-89	Milwaukee	IHL	23	9	13	22	26	....	....	....	....	....
	Utica	AHL	55	23	30	53	41	5	0	2	2	2
1989-90	New Jersey	NHL	6	1	2	3	4	4	0	0	0	0
	Utica	AHL	73	37	52	89	32	....	....	....	....	....
1990-91	Utica	AHL	59	32	46	78	26	....	....	....	....	....
1991-92	New Jersey	NHL	71	19	27	46	74	7	1	1	2	17
	NHL Totals		83	21	30	51	78	11	1	1	2	17

Signed as a free agent by **Vancouver**, June 18, 1987. Traded to **New Jersey** by **Vancouver** for Tim Lenardon, March 7, 1989.

VINCELETTE, DANIEL

Left wing. Shoots left. 6'2", 202 lbs. Born, Verdun, Que., August 1, 1967.
(Chicago's 3rd choice, 74th overall, in 1985 Entry Draft).

			Regular Season					Playoffs				
Season	Club	Lea	GP	G	A	TP	PIM	GP	G	A	TP	PIM
1984-85	Drummondville	QMJHL	64	11	24	35	124	12	0	1	1	11
1985-86	Drummondville	QMJHL	70	37	47	84	234	22	11	14	25	40
1986-87	Drummondville	QMJHL	50	34	35	69	288	8	6	5	11	17
	Chicago	NHL	....	....	....	....	....	3	0	0	0	0
1987-88	Chicago	NHL	69	6	11	17	109	4	0	0	0	0
1988-89	Chicago	NHL	66	11	4	15	119	5	0	0	0	4
	Saginaw	IHL	2	0	0	0	14	....	....	....	....	....
1989-90	Chicago	NHL	2	0	0	0	4	....	....	....	....	....
	Indianapolis	IHL	49	16	13	29	262	....	....	....	....	....
	Quebec	NHL	11	0	1	1	25	....	....	....	....	....
1990-91	Quebec	NHL	16	0	1	1	38	....	....	....	....	....
	Halifax	AHL	24	4	9	13	85	....	....	....	....	....
	Indianapolis	IHL	15	5	3	8	51	7	2	1	3	62
1991-92	Chicago	NHL	29	3	5	8	56	....	....	....	....	....
	Indianapolis	IHL	16	5	3	8	84	....	....	....	....	....
	NHL Totals		193	20	22	42	351	12	0	0	0	4

Traded to **Quebec** by **Chicago** with Mario Doyon and Everett Sanipass for Greg Millen, Michel Goulet and Quebec's sixth round choice (Kevin St. Jacques) in 1991 Entry Draft, March 5, 1990. Traded to **Chicago** by **Quebec** with Paul Gillis for Ryan McGill and Mike McNeil, March 5, 1991. Claimed by **Tampa Bay** from **Chicago** in Expansion Draft, June 18, 1992.

VIRTA, HANNU (VIR-ta, HAN-oo)

Defense. Shoots left. 5'11", 180 lbs. Born, Turku, Finland, March 22, 1963.
(Buffalo's 2nd choice, 38th overall, in 1981 Entry Draft).

			Regular Season					Playoffs				
Season	Club	Lea	GP	G	A	TP	PIM	GP	G	A	TP	PIM
1980-81a	TPS	Fin.	1	0	1	1	0	4	0	1	1	4
1981-82b	TPS	Fin.	36	5	12	17	6	7	1	1	2	2
	Buffalo	**NHL**	**3**	**0**	**1**	**1**	**4**	**4**	**0**	**1**	**1**	**0**
1982-83	**Buffalo**	**NHL**	**74**	**13**	**24**	**37**	**18**	**10**	**1**	**2**	**3**	**4**
1983-84	**Buffalo**	**NHL**	**70**	**6**	**30**	**36**	**12**	**3**	**0**	**0**	**0**	**2**
1984-85	**Buffalo**	**NHL**	**51**	**1**	**23**	**24**	**16**	....	....	....	....	....
1985-86	**Buffalo**	**NHL**	**47**	**5**	**23**	**28**	**16**	....	....	....	....	....
1986-87c	TPS	Fin.	41	13	30	43	20	5	0	3	3	2
1987-88	TPS	Fin.	44	10	28	38	20	....	....	....	....	....
1988-89	TPS	Fin.	43	7	25	32	30	10	1	7	8	0
1989-90	TPS	Fin.	41	7	19	26	14	9	0	6	6	10
1990-91	TPS	Fin.	43	4	16	20	40	9	4	2	6	4
1991-92	TPS	Fin.	43	6	22	28	32	3	1	4	5	0
	NHL Totals		**245**	**25**	**101**	**126**	**66**	**17**	**1**	**3**	**4**	**6**

a Named to All-Star Team, 1981 European Junior Championships
b Named Rookie of the Year in Finnish National League (1982)
c Finnish League First All-Star Team (1987)

VISHEAU, MARK

Defense. Shoots right. 6'4", 197 lbs. Born, Burlington, Ont., June 27, 1973.
(Winnipeg's 4th choice, 84th overall, in 1992 Entry Draft).

			Regular Season					Playoffs				
Season	Club	Lea	GP	G	A	TP	PIM	GP	G	A	TP	PIM
1990-91	London	OHL	59	4	11	15	40	7	0	1	1	6
1991-92	London	OHL	66	5	31	36	104	10	0	4	4	27

VITAKOSKI, VESA

Left wing. Shoots left. 6'2", 205 lbs. Born, Lappeenranta, Finland, February 13, 1971.
(Calgary's 3rd choice, 32nd overall, in 1990 Entry Draft).

			Regular Season					Playoffs				
Season	Club	Lea	GP	G	A	TP	PIM	GP	G	A	TP	PIM
1989-90	SaiPa	Fin.	44	24	10	34	....	....	....	....	....	....
1990-91	Tappara	Fin.	41	17	23	40	14	....	....	....	....	....
1991-92	Tappara	Fin.	44	19	19	38	39	....	....	....	....	....

VITOLINSH, HARIJS (VEE-toh-leensh)

Center. Shoots left. 6'3", 205 lbs. Born, Riga, Soviet Union, April 30, 1968.
(Montreal's 10th choice, 188th overall, in 1988 Entry Draft).

			Regular Season					Playoffs				
Season	Club	Lea	GP	G	A	TP	PIM	GP	G	A	TP	PIM
1987-88	Dynamo Riga	USSR	30	3	3	6	27	....	....	....	....	....
1988-89	Dynamo Riga	USSR	36	3	2	5	16	....	....	....	....	....
1989-90	Dynamo Riga	USSR	45	7	6	13	18	....	....	....	....	....
1990-91	Dynamo Riga	USSR	46	12	19	31	22	....	....	....	....	....
1991-92	Riga	CIS	30	12	5	17	10	....	....	....	....	....

VIVEIROS, EMANUEL (VEE-VEH-ROHZ)

Defense. Shoots left. 6', 175 lbs. Born, St. Albert, Alta., January 8, 1966.
(Edmonton's 6th choice, 106th overall, in 1984 Entry Draft).

			Regular Season					Playoffs				
Season	Club	Lea	GP	G	A	TP	PIM	GP	G	A	TP	PIM
1982-83	Prince Albert	WHL	59	6	26	32	55	....	....	....	....	....
1983-84	Prince Albert	WHL	67	15	94	109	48	2	0	3	3	6
1984-85a	Prince Albert	WHL	68	17	71	88	94	13	2	9	11	14
1985-86	**Minnesota**	**NHL**	**4**	**0**	**1**	**1**	**0**	....	....	....	....	....
bc	Prince Albert	WHL	57	22	70	92	30	20	4	24	28	4
1986-87	**Minnesota**	**NHL**	**1**	**0**	**1**	**1**	**0**	....	....	....	....	....
	Springfield	AHL	76	7	35	42	38	....	....	....	....	....
1987-88	**Minnesota**	**NHL**	**24**	**1**	**9**	**10**	**6**	....	....	....	....	....
	Kalamazoo	IHL	57	15	48	63	41	....	....	....	....	....
1988-89	Kalamazoo	IHL	54	11	29	40	37	....	....	....	....	....
1989-90	Kaufberer	W.Ger.	8	2	7	9	8	....	....	....	....	....
1990-91	Albany	IHL	14	3	7	10	6	....	....	....	....	....
	Springfield	AHL	48	2	22	24	29	7	0	2	2	4
	NHL Totals		**29**	**1**	**11**	**12**	**6**	....	....	....	....	....

a WHL Second All-Star Team, East Division (1985)
b WHL East All-Star Team (1986)
c WHL Player of the Year (1986)

Traded to **Minnesota** by **Edmonton** with Marc Habscheid and Don Barber for Gord Sherven and Don Biggs, December 20, 1985. Signed as a free agent by **Hartford**, February 9, 1990.

VLACH, ROSTISLAV (VLAKH)

Center/Left wing. Shoots left. 6', 170 lbs. Born, Gottwaldov, Czech., July 3, 1962.
(Los Angeles' 9th choice, 216th overall, in 1987 Entry Draft).

			Regular Season					Playoffs				
Season	Club	Lea	GP	G	A	TP	PIM	GP	G	A	TP	PIM
1987-88	TJ Gottwaldov	Czech.	30	15	14	29	4	....	....	....	....	....
1988-89	TJ Gottwaldov	Czech.	41	20	18	38	83	....	....	....	....	....
1989-90	TJ Zlin	Czech.	51	16	24	40	....	....	....	....	....	....
1990-91	JoKP	Fin.	44	33	48	81	83	....	....	....	....	....
1991-92	JoKP	Fin.	37	9	9	18	70	....	....	....	....	....

VOLEK, DAVID (VOH-lehk)

Left/Right wing. Shoots left. 6', 185 lbs. Born, Prague, Czechoslovakia, June 18, 1966.
(NY Islanders' 11th choice, 208th overall, in 1984 Entry Draft).

			Regular Season					Playoffs				
Season	Club	Lea	GP	G	A	TP	PIM	GP	G	A	TP	PIM
1986-87	Sparta Praha	Czech.	39	27	25	52	....	....	....	....	....	....
1987-88	Sparta Praha	Czech.	30	18	12	30	....	....	....	....	....	....
1988-89a	**NY Islanders**	**NHL**	**77**	**25**	**34**	**59**	**24**	....	....	....	....	....
1989-90	**NY Islanders**	**NHL**	**80**	**17**	**22**	**39**	**41**	**5**	**1**	**4**	**5**	**0**
1990-91	**NY Islanders**	**NHL**	**77**	**22**	**34**	**56**	**57**	....	....	....	....	....
1991-92	**NY Islanders**	**NHL**	**74**	**18**	**42**	**60**	**35**	....	....	....	....	....
	NHL Totals		**308**	**82**	**132**	**214**	**157**	**5**	**1**	**4**	**5**	**0**

a NHL All-Rookie Team (1989)

VOLKOV, MIKHAIL (vohl-KOHV)

Right wing. Shoots right. 5'10", 174 lbs. Born, Voronezh, Soviet Union, March 9, 1972.
(Buffalo's 11th choice, 233rd overall, in 1991 Entry Draft).

			Regular Season					Playoffs				
Season	Club	Lea	GP	G	A	TP	PIM	GP	G	A	TP	PIM
1990-91	Soviet Wings	USSR	40	8	4	12	8	....	....	....	....	....
1991-92	Soviet Wings	CIS	37	3	6	9	16	....	....	....	....	....

VON STEFENELLI, PHILIP

Defense. Shoots left. 6'1", 195 lbs. Born, Vancouver, B.C., April 10, 1969.
(Vancouver's 5th choice, 122nd overall, in 1988 Entry Draft).

			Regular Season					Playoffs				
Season	Club	Lea	GP	G	A	TP	PIM	GP	G	A	TP	PIM
1987-88	Boston U.	H.E.	34	3	13	16	38	....	....	....	....	....
1988-89	Boston U.	H.E.	33	2	6	8	34	....	....	....	....	....
1989-90	Boston U.	H.E.	44	8	20	28	40	....	....	....	....	....
1990-91	Boston U.	H.E.	41	7	23	30	32	....	....	....	....	....
1991-92	Milwaukee	IHL	80	2	34	36	40	5	1	2	3	2

VOPAT, JAN (VOH-paht)

Defense. Shoots left. 6', 198 lbs. Born, Most, Czech., March 22, 1973.
(Hartford's 3rd choice, 57th overall, in 1992 Entry Draft).

			Regular Season					Playoffs				
Season	Club	Lea	GP	G	A	TP	PIM	GP	G	A	TP	PIM
1990-91	Litvinov	Czech.	25	1	4	5	4	....	....	....	....	....
1991-92	Litvinov	Czech.	46	4	2	6	0	....	....	....	....	....

VUJTEK, VLADIMIR (VOI-tek)

Left wing. Shoots left. 5'11", 175 lbs. Born, Ostrava, Czech., February 17, 1972.
(Montreal's 4th choice, 73rd overall, in 1991 Entry Draft).

			Regular Season					Playoffs				
Season	Club	Lea	GP	G	A	TP	PIM	GP	G	A	TP	PIM
1990-91	Tri-Cities	WHL	37	26	18	44	25	7	2	3	5	4
1991-92	**Montreal**	**NHL**	**2**	**0**	**0**	**0**	**0**	....	....	....	....	....
	Tri-Cities	WHL	53	41	61	102	114	....	....	....	....	....
	NHL Totals		**2**	**0**	**0**	**0**	**0**	....	....	....	....	....

VUKONICH, MICHAEL

Center. Shoots left. 6'1", 190 lbs. Born, Duluth, MN, May 11, 1968.
(Los Angeles' 4th choice, 90th overall, in 1987 Entry Draft).

			Regular Season					Playoffs				
Season	Club	Lea	GP	G	A	TP	PIM	GP	G	A	TP	PIM
1987-88	Harvard	ECAC	32	9	14	23	24	....	....	....	....	....
1988-89	Harvard	ECAC	27	11	8	19	12	....	....	....	....	....
1989-90a	Harvard	ECAC	27	22	29	51	18	....	....	....	....	....
1990-91b	Harvard	ECAC	27	31	23	54	28	....	....	....	....	....
1991-92	Phoenix	IHL	68	17	11	28	21	....	....	....	....	....

a ECAC First All-Star Team (1990)
b ECAC Second All-Star Team (1991)

VUKOTA, MICK

Right wing. Shoots right. 6'2", 195 lbs. Born, Saskatoon, Sask., September 14, 1966.

			Regular Season					Playoffs				
Season	Club	Lea	GP	G	A	TP	PIM	GP	G	A	TP	PIM
1983-84	Winnipeg	WHL	3	1	1	2	10	....	....	....	....	....
1984-85	Kelowna	WHL	66	10	6	16	247	....	....	....	....	....
1985-86	Spokane	WHL	64	19	14	33	369	9	6	4	10	68
1986-87	Spokane	WHL	61	25	28	53	*337	4	0	0	0	40
1987-88	**NY Islanders**	**NHL**	**17**	**1**	**0**	**1**	**82**	**2**	**0**	**0**	**0**	**23**
	Springfield	AHL	52	7	9	16	375	....	....	....	....	....
1988-89	**NY Islanders**	**NHL**	**48**	**2**	**2**	**4**	**237**	....	....	....	....	....
	Springfield	AHL	3	1	0	1	33	....	....	....	....	....
1989-90	**NY Islanders**	**NHL**	**76**	**4**	**8**	**12**	**290**	**1**	**0**	**0**	**0**	**17**
1990-91	**NY Islanders**	**NHL**	**60**	**2**	**4**	**6**	**238**	....	....	....	....	....
	Capital Dist.	AHL	2	0	0	0	9	....	....	....	....	....
1991-92	**NY Islanders**	**NHL**	**74**	**0**	**6**	**6**	**293**	....	....	....	....	....
	NHL Totals		**275**	**9**	**20**	**29**	**1140**	**3**	**0**	**0**	**0**	**40**

Signed as a free agent by **NY Islanders**, March 2, 1987.

VYKOUKAL, JIRI (vee-KOH-uh-kahl)

Defense. Shoots right. 5'11", 176 lbs. Born, Olomouc, Czechoslovakia, March 11, 1971.
(Washington's 9th choice, 208th overall, in 1989 Entry Draft).

			Regular Season					Playoffs				
Season	Club	Lea	GP	G	A	TP	PIM	GP	G	A	TP	PIM
1989-90	Sparta Praha	Czech.	47	5	12	17	....	....	....	....	....	....
1990-91	Baltimore	AHL	60	4	22	26	41	....	....	....	....	....
1991-92	Baltimore	AHL	56	1	21	22	47	....	....	....	....	....
	Hampton Rds.	ECHL	9	3	9	12	12	....	....	....	....	....

WALTER, RYAN WILLIAM

Center/Left wing. Shoots left. 6', 200 lbs. Born, New Westminster, B.C., April 23, 1958.
(Washington's 1st choice, 2nd overall, in 1978 Amateur Draft).

			Regular Season					Playoffs				
Season	Club	Lea	GP	G	A	TP	PIM	GP	G	A	TP	PIM
1974-75	Kamloops	WHL	9	8	4	12	2	2	1	1	2	2
1975-76	Kamloops	WHL	72	35	49	84	96	12	3	9	12	10
1976-77	Kamloops	WHL	71	41	58	99	100	5	1	3	4	11
1977-78abc	Seattle	WHL	62	54	71	125	148	....	....	....	....	....
1978-79	**Washington**	**NHL**	**69**	**28**	**28**	**56**	**70**	....	....	....	....	....
1979-80	**Washington**	**NHL**	**80**	**24**	**42**	**66**	**106**	....	....	....	....	....
1980-81	**Washington**	**NHL**	**80**	**24**	**44**	**68**	**150**	....	....	....	....	....
1981-82	**Washington**	**NHL**	**78**	**38**	**49**	**87**	**142**	....	....	....	....	....
1982-83	**Montreal**	**NHL**	**80**	**29**	**46**	**75**	**40**	**3**	**0**	**0**	**0**	**11**
1983-84	**Montreal**	**NHL**	**73**	**20**	**29**	**49**	**83**	**15**	**2**	**1**	**3**	**4**
1984-85	**Montreal**	**NHL**	**72**	**19**	**19**	**38**	**59**	**12**	**2**	**7**	**9**	**13**
1985-86	**Montreal**	**NHL**	**69**	**15**	**34**	**49**	**45**	**5**	**0**	**1**	**1**	**2**
1986-87	**Montreal**	**NHL**	**76**	**23**	**23**	**46**	**34**	**17**	**7**	**12**	**19**	**10**
1987-88	**Montreal**	**NHL**	**61**	**13**	**23**	**36**	**39**	**11**	**2**	**4**	**6**	**6**
1988-89	**Montreal**	**NHL**	**78**	**14**	**17**	**31**	**48**	**21**	**3**	**5**	**8**	**6**
1989-90	**Montreal**	**NHL**	**70**	**8**	**16**	**24**	**59**	**11**	**0**	**2**	**2**	**0**
1990-91	**Montreal**	**NHL**	**25**	**0**	**1**	**1**	**12**	**5**	**0**	**0**	**0**	**2**
1991-92d	**Vancouver**	**NHL**	**67**	**6**	**11**	**17**	**49**	**13**	**0**	**3**	**3**	**8**
	NHL Totals		**978**	**261**	**382**	**643**	**936**	**113**	**16**	**35**	**51**	**62**

a WHL Most Valuable Player (1978)
b WHL Player of the Year (1978)
c WHL First All-Star Team (1978)
d Won Bud Light/NHL Man of the Year Award (1992)

Played in NHL All-Star Game (1983)

Traded to **Montreal** by **Washington** with Rick Green for Rod Langway, Brian Engblom, Doug Jarvis and Craig Laughlin, September 9, 1982. Signed as a free agent by **Vancouver**, July 26, 1991.

WALTERS, GREG

Center. Shoots right. 6'1", 195 lbs. Born, Calgary, Alta., August 12, 1970.
(Toronto's 4th choice, 80th overall, in 1990 Entry Draft).

			Regular Season					Playoffs				
Season	Club	Lea	GP	G	A	TP	PIM	GP	G	A	TP	PIM
1989-90	Ottawa	OHL	63	36	54	90	57	....	....	....	....	....
1990-91	Newmarket	AHL	54	7	14	21	58	....	....	....	....	....
1991-92	St. John's	AHL	10	0	2	2	20	....	....	....	....	....
	Raleigh	ECHL	18	9	13	22	30	4	1	2	3	8

WALZ, WES

Center. Shoots right. 5'10", 180 lbs. Born, Calgary, Alta., May 15, 1970.
(Boston's 3rd choice, 57th overall, in 1989 Entry Draft).

			Regular Season					Playoffs				
Season	Club	Lea	GP	G	A	TP	PIM	GP	G	A	TP	PIM
1988-89a	Lethbridge	WHL	63	29	75	104	32	8	1	5	6	6
1989-90	**Boston**	**NHL**	**2**	**1**	**1**	**2**	**0**	....	....	....	....	....
b	Lethbridge	WHL	56	54	86	140	69	19	13	*24	*37	33
1990-91	**Boston**	**NHL**	**56**	**8**	**8**	**16**	**32**	**2**	**0**	**0**	**0**	**0**
	Maine	AHL	20	8	12	20	19	2	0	0	0	21
1991-92	**Boston**	**NHL**	**15**	**0**	**3**	**3**	**12**	....	....	....	....	....
	Maine	AHL	21	13	11	24	38	....	....	....	....	....
	Philadelphia	**NHL**	**2**	**1**	**0**	**1**	**0**	....	....	....	....	....
	Hershey	AHL	41	13	28	41	37	6	1	2	3	0
	NHL Totals		**75**	**10**	**12**	**22**	**44**	**2**	**0**	**0**	**0**	**0**

a WHL Rookie of the Year (1989)
b WHL East First All-Star Team (1990)

Traded to **Philadelphia** by **Boston** with Garry Galley and future considerations for Gord Murphy, Brian Dobbin and Philadelphia's third round choice (Sergei Zholtok) in 1992 Entry Draft, January 2, 1992.

WARD, AARON

Defense. Shoots right. 6'2", 200 lbs. Born, Windsor, Ont., January 17, 1973.
(Winnipeg's 1st choice, 5th overall, in 1991 Entry Draft).

			Regular Season					Playoffs				
Season	Club	Lea	GP	G	A	TP	PIM	GP	G	A	TP	PIM
1990-91	U. of Michigan	CCHA	46	8	11	19	126	....	....	....	....	....
1991-92	U. of Michigan	CCHA	42	7	12	19	64	....	....	....	....	....

WARD, DIXON

Right wing. Shoots right. 6', 195 lbs. Born, Leduc, Alta., September 23, 1968.
(Vancouver's 6th choice, 128th overall, in 1988 Entry Draft).

			Regular Season					Playoffs				
Season	Club	Lea	GP	G	A	TP	PIM	GP	G	A	TP	PIM
1988-89	North Dakota	WCHA	37	8	9	17	26	....	....	....	....	....
1989-90	North Dakota	WCHA	45	35	34	69	44	....	....	....	....	....
1990-91a	North Dakota	WCHA	43	34	35	69	84	....	....	....	....	....
1991-92a	North Dakota	WCHA	38	33	31	64	90	....	....	....	....	....

a WCHA Second All-Star Team (1991, 1992)

WARD, EDWARD

Right wing. Shoots right. 6'3", 190 lbs. Born, Edmonton, Alta., November 10, 1969.
(Quebec's 7th choice, 108th overall, in 1988 Entry Draft).

			Regular Season					Playoffs				
Season	Club	Lea	GP	G	A	TP	PIM	GP	G	A	TP	PIM
1987-88	N. Michigan	WCHA	25	0	2	2	40	....	....	....	....	....
1988-89	N. Michigan	WCHA	42	5	15	20	36	....	....	....	....	....
1989-90	N. Michigan	WCHA	39	5	11	16	77	....	....	....	....	....
1990-91	N. Michigan	WCHA	46	13	18	31	109	....	....	....	....	....
1991-92	Greensboro	ECHL	12	4	8	12	21	....	....	....	....	....
	Halifax	AHL	51	7	11	18	65	....	....	....	....	....

WARE, MICHAEL

Right wing. Shoots right. 6'5", 216 lbs. Born, York, Ont., March 22, 1967.
(Edmonton's 3rd choice, 62nd overall, in 1985 Entry Draft).

			Regular Season					Playoffs				
Season	Club	Lea	GP	G	A	TP	PIM	GP	G	A	TP	PIM
1984-85	Hamilton	OHL	57	4	14	18	225	12	0	1	1	29
1985-86	Hamilton	OHL	44	8	11	19	155	....	....	....	....	....
1986-87	Cornwall	OHL	50	5	19	24	173	5	0	1	1	10
1987-88	Nova Scotia	AHL	52	0	8	8	253	3	0	0	0	16
1988-89	**Edmonton**	**NHL**	**2**	**0**	**1**	**1**	**11**	....	....	....	....	....
	Cape Breton	AHL	48	1	11	12	317	....	....	....	....	....
1989-90	**Edmonton**	**NHL**	**3**	**0**	**0**	**0**	**4**	....	....	....	....	....
	Cape Breton	AHL	54	6	13	19	191	6	0	3	3	29
1990-91	Cape Breton	AHL	43	4	8	12	176	3	0	0	0	4
1991-92			DID NOT PLAY — INJURED									
	NHL Totals		**5**	**0**	**1**	**1**	**15**	....	....	....	....	....

WARRINER, TODD

Left wing. Shoots left. 6'1", 172 lbs. Born, Blenheim, Ont., January 3, 1974.
(Quebec's 1st choice, 4th overall, in 1992 Entry Draft).

			Regular Season					Playoffs				
Season	Club	Lea	GP	G	A	TP	PIM	GP	G	A	TP	PIM
1990-91	Windsor	OHL	57	36	28	64	26	11	5	6	11	12
1991-92	Windsor	OHL	50	41	41	82	64	7	5	4	9	6

WASLEY, CHARLIE

Defense. Shoots left. 6'2", 173 lbs. Born, Minneapolis, MN, April 4, 1974.
(Quebec's 6th choice, 100th overall, in 1992 Entry Draft).

			Regular Season					Playoffs				
Season	Club	Lea	GP	G	A	TP	PIM	GP	G	A	TP	PIM
1991-92	St. Paul	USHL	44	3	6	9	144	....	....	....	....	....

WATTERS, TIMOTHY J. (TIM)

Defense. Shoots left. 5'11", 185 lbs. Born, Kamloops, B.C., July 25, 1959.
(Winnipeg's 6th choice, 124th overall, in 1979 Entry Draft).

			Regular Season					Playoffs				
Season	Club	Lea	GP	G	A	TP	PIM	GP	G	A	TP	PIM
1978-79	Michigan Tech	WCHA	38	6	21	27	48	....	....	....	....	....
1979-80	Cdn. National	....	56	8	21	29	43	....	....	....	....	....
	Cdn. Olympic	....	6	1	1	2	0	....	....	....	....	....
1980-81ab	Michigan Tech	WCHA	43	12	38	50	36	....	....	....	....	....
1981-82	Tulsa	CHL	5	1	2	3	0	....	....	....	....	....
	Winnipeg	**NHL**	**69**	**2**	**22**	**24**	**97**	**4**	**0**	**1**	**1**	**8**
1982-83	**Winnipeg**	**NHL**	**77**	**5**	**18**	**23**	**98**	**3**	**0**	**0**	**0**	**2**
1983-84	**Winnipeg**	**NHL**	**74**	**3**	**20**	**23**	**169**	**3**	**1**	**0**	**1**	**2**
1984-85	**Winnipeg**	**NHL**	**63**	**2**	**20**	**22**	**74**	**8**	**0**	**1**	**1**	**16**
1985-86	**Winnipeg**	**NHL**	**56**	**6**	**8**	**14**	**97**	....	....	....	....	....
1986-87	**Winnipeg**	**NHL**	**63**	**3**	**13**	**16**	**119**	**10**	**0**	**0**	**0**	**21**
1987-88	Cdn. National	....	8	0	1	1	2	....	....	....	....	....
	Cdn. Olympic	....	2	0	2	2	0	....	....	....	....	....
	Winnipeg	**NHL**	**36**	**0**	**0**	**0**	**106**	**4**	**0**	**0**	**0**	**4**
1988-89	**Los Angeles**	**NHL**	**76**	**3**	**18**	**21**	**168**	**11**	**0**	**1**	**1**	**6**
1989-90	**Los Angeles**	**NHL**	**62**	**1**	**10**	**11**	**92**	**4**	**0**	**0**	**0**	**6**
1990-91	**Los Angeles**	**NHL**	**45**	**0**	**4**	**4**	**92**	**7**	**0**	**0**	**0**	**12**
1991-92	**Los Angeles**	**NHL**	**37**	**0**	**7**	**7**	**92**	**6**	**0**	**0**	**0**	**8**
	Phoenix	IHL	5	0	3	3	6	....	....	....	....	....
	NHL Totals		**658**	**25**	**140**	**165**	**1204**	**60**	**1**	**3**	**4**	**85**

a WCHA First All-Star Team (1981)
b Named to NCAA All-Tournament Team (1981)

Signed as a free agent by **Los Angeles**, June 27, 1988.

WEIGHT, DOUG

Center. Shoots left. 5'11", 185 lbs. Born, Warren, MI, January 21, 1971.
(NY Rangers' 2nd choice, 34th overall, in 1990 Entry Draft).

			Regular Season					Playoffs				
Season	Club	Lea	GP	G	A	TP	PIM	GP	G	A	TP	PIM
1989-90	Lake Superior	CCHA	46	21	48	69	44	....	....	....	....	....
1990-91ab	Lake Superior	CCHA	42	29	46	75	86	....	....	....	....	....
	NY Rangers	**NHL**	....	....	....	....	....	**1**	**0**	**0**	**0**	**0**
1991-92	**NY Rangers**	**NHL**	**53**	**8**	**22**	**30**	**23**	**7**	**2**	**2**	**4**	**0**
	Binghamton	AHL	9	3	14	17	2	4	1	4	5	6
	NHL Totals		**53**	**8**	**22**	**30**	**23**	**8**	**2**	**2**	**4**	**0**

a CCHA First All-Start Team (1991)
b NCAA West Second All-American Team (1991)

WEINRICH, ALEXANDER

Defense. Shoots right. 6', 180 lbs. Born, Lewiston, ME, March 12, 1969.
(Toronto's 12th choice, 238th overall, in 1987 Entry Draft).

			Regular Season					Playoffs				
Season	Club	Lea	GP	G	A	TP	PIM	GP	G	A	TP	PIM
1990-91	Merrimack	H.E.	38	2	12	14	16	....	....	....	....	....
1991-92	Merrimack	H.E.	34	2	18	20	40	....	....	....	....	....

WEINRICH, ERIC (WIGHN-rick)

Defense. Shoots left. 6'1", 210 lbs. Born, Roanoke, VA, December 19, 1966.
(New Jersey's 3rd choice, 32nd overall, in 1985 Entry Draft).

			Regular Season					Playoffs				
Season	Club	Lea	GP	G	A	TP	PIM	GP	G	A	TP	PIM
1985-86	U. of Maine	H.E.	34	0	15	15	26	....	....	....	....	....
1986-87ab	U. of Maine	H.E.	41	12	32	44	59	....	....	....	....	....
1987-88	U. of Maine	H.E.	8	4	7	11	22	....	....	....	....	....
	U.S. National	....	38	3	9	12	24	....	....	....	....	....
	U.S. Olympic	....	3	0	0	0	0	....	....	....	....	....
1988-89	**New Jersey**	**NHL**	**2**	**0**	**0**	**0**	**0**	....	....	....	....	....
	Utica	AHL	80	17	27	44	70	5	0	1	1	4
1989-90	**New Jersey**	**NHL**	**19**	**2**	**7**	**9**	**11**	**6**	**1**	**3**	**4**	**17**
cd	Utica	AHL	57	12	48	60	38	....	....	....	....	....
1990-91e	**New Jersey**	**NHL**	**76**	**4**	**34**	**38**	**48**	**7**	**1**	**2**	**3**	**6**
1991-92	**New Jersey**	**NHL**	**76**	**7**	**25**	**32**	**55**	**7**	**0**	**2**	**2**	**4**
	NHL Totals		**173**	**13**	**66**	**79**	**114**	**20**	**2**	**7**	**9**	**27**

a Hockey East First All-Star Team (1987)
b NCAA East Second All-American Team (1987)
c AHL First All-Star Team (1990)
d Won Eddie Shore Plaque (Outstanding Defenseman-AHL) (1990)
e NHL/Upper Deck All-Rookie Team (1991)

WEINRICH, JASON

Defense. Shoots right. 6'2", 189 lbs. Born, Lewiston, ME, February 13, 1972.
(NY Rangers' 8th choice, 118th overall, in 1990 Entry Draft).

			Regular Season					Playoffs				
Season	Club	Lea	GP	G	A	TP	PIM	GP	G	A	TP	PIM
1990-91	U. of Maine	H.E.	14	1	1	2	4	....	....	....	....	....
1991-92	U. of Maine	H.E.	36	1	15	16	18	....	....	....	....	....

WEISBROD, JOHN

Center. Shoots right. 6'3", 215 lbs. Born, Syosset, NY, October 8, 1968.
(Minnesota's 4th choice, 73rd overall, in 1987 Entry Draft).

			Regular Season					Playoffs				
Season	Club	Lea	GP	G	A	TP	PIM	GP	G	A	TP	PIM
1987-88	Harvard	ECAC	22	8	11	19	16	....	....	....	....	....
1988-89	Harvard	ECAC	31	22	13	35	61	....	....	....	....	....
1989-90	Harvard	ECAC	27	11	21	32	62	....	....	....	....	....
1990-91	Harvard	ECAC	5	2	8	10	8	....	....	....	....	....
1991-92			DID NOT PLAY – INJURED									

Claimed by **San Jose** from **Minnesota** in Dispersal Draft, May 30, 1991.

WELLS, GORDON (JAY)

Defense. Shoots left. 6'1", 210 lbs. Born, Paris, Ont., May 18, 1959.
(Los Angeles' 1st choice, 16th overall, in 1979 Entry Draft).

			Regular Season					Playoffs				
Season	Club	Lea	GP	G	A	TP	PIM	GP	G	A	TP	PIM
1977-78	Kingston	OHA	68	9	13	22	195	5	1	2	3	6
1978-79a	Kingston	OHA	48	6	21	27	100	11	2	7	9	29
1979-80	**Los Angeles**	**NHL**	**43**	**0**	**0**	**0**	**113**	**4**	**0**	**0**	**0**	**11**
	Binghamton	AHL	28	0	6	6	48	....	....	....	....	....
1980-81	**Los Angeles**	**NHL**	**72**	**5**	**13**	**18**	**155**	**4**	**0**	**0**	**0**	**27**
1981-82	**Los Angeles**	**NHL**	**60**	**1**	**8**	**9**	**145**	**10**	**1**	**3**	**4**	**41**
1982-83	**Los Angeles**	**NHL**	**69**	**3**	**12**	**15**	**167**	....	....	....	....	....
1983-84	**Los Angeles**	**NHL**	**69**	**3**	**18**	**21**	**141**	....	....	....	....	....
1984-85	**Los Angeles**	**NHL**	**77**	**2**	**9**	**11**	**185**	**3**	**0**	**1**	**1**	**0**
1985-86	**Los Angeles**	**NHL**	**79**	**11**	**31**	**42**	**226**	....	....	....	....	....
1986-87	**Los Angeles**	**NHL**	**77**	**7**	**29**	**36**	**155**	**5**	**1**	**2**	**3**	**10**
1987-88	**Los Angeles**	**NHL**	**58**	**2**	**23**	**25**	**159**	**5**	**1**	**2**	**3**	**21**
1988-89	**Philadelphia**	**NHL**	**67**	**2**	**19**	**21**	**184**	**18**	**0**	**2**	**2**	**51**
1989-90	**Philadelphia**	**NHL**	**59**	**3**	**16**	**19**	**129**	....	....	....	....	....
	Buffalo	**NHL**	**1**	**0**	**1**	**1**	**0**	**6**	**0**	**0**	**0**	**12**
1990-91	**Buffalo**	**NHL**	**43**	**1**	**2**	**3**	**86**	**1**	**0**	**1**	**1**	**0**
1991-92	**Buffalo**	**NHL**	**41**	**2**	**9**	**11**	**157**	....	....	....	....	....
	NY Rangers	**NHL**	**11**	**0**	**0**	**0**	**24**	**13**	**0**	**2**	**2**	**10**
	NHL Totals		**826**	**42**	**190**	**232**	**2026**	**69**	**3**	**13**	**16**	**183**

a OHA First All-Star Team (1979)

Traded to **Philadelphia** by **Los Angeles** for Doug Crossman, September 29, 1988. Traded to **Buffalo** by **Philadelphia** with Philadelphia's fourth round choice (Peter Ambroziak) in 1991 Entry Draft for Kevin Maguire and Buffalo's second round choice (Mikael Renberg) in 1990 Entry Draft, March 5, 1990. Traded to **NY Rangers** by **Buffalo** for Randy Moller, March 9, 1992.

WERENKA, BRAD

Defense. Shoots left. 6'2", 205 lbs. Born, Two Hills, Alta., February 12, 1969.
(Edmonton's 2nd choice, 42nd overall, in 1987 Entry Draft).

			Regular Season					Playoffs				
Season	Club	Lea	GP	G	A	TP	PIM	GP	G	A	TP	PIM
1986-87	N. Michigan	WCHA	30	4	4	8	35	....	....	....	....	....
1987-88	N. Michigan	WCHA	34	7	23	30	26	....	....	....	....	....
1988-89	N. Michigan	WCHA	28	7	13	20	16	....	....	....	....	....
1989-90	N. Michigan	WCHA	8	2	5	7	8	....	....	....	....	....
1990-91abc	N. Michigan	WCHA	47	20	43	63	36	....	....	....	....	....
1991-92	Cape Breton	AHL	66	6	21	27	95	5	0	3	3	6

a WCHA First All-Star Team (1991)
b NCAA West First All-American Team (1991)
c NCAA Final Four All-Tournament Team (1991)

WERENKA, DARCY

Defense. Shoots right. 6'1", 210 lbs. Born, Edmonton, Alta., May 13, 1973.
(NY Rangers' 2nd choice, 37th overall, in 1991 Entry Draft).

			Regular Season					Playoffs				
Season	Club	Lea	GP	G	A	TP	PIM	GP	G	A	TP	PIM
1990-91	Lethbridge	WHL	72	13	37	50	39	16	1	7	8	4
1991-92	Lethbridge	WHL	69	17	58	75	56	5	2	1	3	0

WESLEY, GLEN

Defense. Shoots left. 6'1", 195 lbs. Born, Red Deer, Alta., October 2, 1968.
(Boston's 1st choice, 3rd overall, in 1987 Entry Draft).

			Regular Season					Playoffs				
Season	Club	Lea	GP	G	A	TP	PIM	GP	G	A	TP	PIM
1983-84	Portland	WHL	3	1	2	3	0	....	....	....	....	....
1984-85	Portland	WHL	67	16	52	68	76	6	1	6	7	8
1985-86a	Portland	WHL	69	16	75	91	96	15	3	11	14	29
1986-87a	Portland	WHL	63	16	46	62	72	20	8	18	26	27
1987-88b	**Boston**	**NHL**	**79**	**7**	**30**	**37**	**69**	**23**	**6**	**8**	**14**	**22**
1988-89	**Boston**	**NHL**	**77**	**19**	**35**	**54**	**61**	**10**	**0**	**2**	**2**	**4**
1989-90	**Boston**	**NHL**	**78**	**9**	**27**	**36**	**48**	**21**	**2**	**6**	**8**	**36**
1990-91	**Boston**	**NHL**	**80**	**11**	**32**	**43**	**78**	**19**	**2**	**9**	**11**	**19**
1991-92	**Boston**	**NHL**	**78**	**9**	**37**	**46**	**54**	**15**	**2**	**4**	**6**	**16**
	NHL Totals		**392**	**55**	**161**	**216**	**310**	**88**	**12**	**29**	**41**	**97**

a WHL West All-Star Team (1986, 1987)
b NHL All-Rookie Team (1988)

Played in NHL All-Star Game (1989)

WETHERILL, DARREN

Defense. Shoots left. 6', 180 lbs. Born, Regina, Sask., January 28, 1970.
(Boston's 8th choice, 189th overall, in 1990 Entry Draft).

			Regular Season					Playoffs				
Season	Club	Lea	GP	G	A	TP	PIM	GP	G	A	TP	PIM
1990-91	Lake Superior	CCHA	26	0	6	6	14	....	....	....	....	....
1991-92	Lake Superior	CCHA	27	1	4	5	42	....	....	....	....	....

WHEELDON, SIMON

Center. Shoots left. 5'11", 170 lbs. Born, Vancouver, B.C., August 30, 1966.
(Edmonton's 11th choice, 229th overall, in 1984 Entry Draft).

			Regular Season					Playoffs				
Season	Club	Lea	GP	G	A	TP	PIM	GP	G	A	TP	PIM
1983-84	Victoria	WHL	56	14	24	38	43	....	....	....	....	....
1984-85a	Victoria	WHL	67	50	76	126	78	....	....	....	....	....
	Nova Scotia	AHL	4	0	1	1	0	1	0	0	0	0
1985-86	Victoria	WHL	70	61	96	157	85	....	....	....	....	....
1986-87	Flint	IHL	41	17	53	70	20	....	....	....	....	....
	New Haven	AHL	38	11	28	39	39	5	0	0	0	6
1987-88	**NY Rangers**	**NHL**	**5**	**0**	**1**	**1**	**4**	....	....	....	....	....
b	Colorado	IHL	69	45	54	99	80	13	8	11	19	12
1988-89	**NY Rangers**	**NHL**	**6**	**0**	**1**	**1**	**2**	....	....	....	....	....
b	Denver	IHL	74	50	56	106	77	4	0	2	2	6
1989-90	Flint	IHL	76	34	49	83	61	4	1	2	3	2
1990-91	**Winnipeg**	**NHL**	**4**	**0**	**0**	**0**	**4**	....	....	....	....	....
	Moncton	AHL	66	30	38	68	38	8	4	3	7	2
1991-92	Baltimore	AHL	78	38	53	91	62	....	....	....	....	....
	NHL Totals		**15**	**0**	**2**	**2**	**10**	....	....	....	....	....

a WHL Second All-Star Team, West Division (1985)
b IHL Second All-Star Team (1988, 1989)

Signed as a free agent by **NY Rangers**, September 8, 1986. Traded to **Winnipeg** by **NY Rangers** for Brian McReynolds, July 9, 1990. Traded to **Washington** by **Winnipeg** with Craig Duncanson and Brent Hughes for Bob Joyce, Tyler Larter and Kent Paynter, May 21, 1991.

WHITE, PETER

Left wing. Shoots left. 5'11", 200 lbs. Born, Montreal, Que., March 15, 1969.
(Edmonton's 4th choice, 92nd overall, in 1989 Entry Draft).

			Regular Season					Playoffs				
Season	Club	Lea	GP	G	A	TP	PIM	GP	G	A	TP	PIM
1988-89	Michigan State	CCHA	46	20	33	53	17	....	....	....	....	....
1989-90	Michigan State	CCHA	45	22	40	62	6	....	....	....	....	....
1990-91	Michigan State	CCHA	37	7	31	38	28	....	....	....	....	....
1991-92	Michigan State	CCHA	41	26	49	75	32	....	....	....	....	....

WHITNEY, RAY

Center. Shoots right. 5'9", 160 lbs. Born, Edmonton, Alta., May 8, 1972.
(San Jose's 2nd choice, 23rd overall, in 1991 Entry Draft).

			Regular Season					Playoffs				
Season	Club	Lea	GP	G	A	TP	PIM	GP	G	A	TP	PIM
1988-89	Spokane	WHL	71	17	33	50	16	....	....	....	....	....
1989-90	Spokane	WHL	71	57	56	113	50	6	3	4	7	6
1990-91abc	Spokane	WHL	72	67	118	*185	36	15	13	18	*31	12
1991-92	Koln	Ger.	10	3	6	9	4	....	....	....	....	....
	San Diego	IHL	63	36	54	90	12	4	0	0	0	0
	San Jose	**NHL**	**2**	**0**	**3**	**3**	**0**	....	....	....	....	....
	NHL Totals		**2**	**0**	**3**	**3**	**0**	....	....	....	....	....

a WHL West First All-Star Team (1991)
b Memorial Cup All-Star Team (1991)
c Won George Parsons Trophy (Memorial Cup Most Sportsmanlike Player) (1991)

WHYTE, SEAN

Right wing. Shoots right. 6', 198 lbs. Born, Sudbury, Ont., May 4, 1970.
(Los Angeles' 7th choice, 165th overall, in 1989 Entry Draft).

			Regular Season					Playoffs				
Season	Club	Lea	GP	G	A	TP	PIM	GP	G	A	TP	PIM
1986-87	Guelph	OHL	41	1	3	4	13	....	....	....	....	....
1987-88	Guelph	OHL	62	6	22	28	71	....	....	....	....	....
1988-89	Guelph	OHL	53	20	44	64	57	....	....	....	....	....
1989-90	Owen Sound	OHL	54	23	30	53	90	3	0	1	1	10
1990-91	Phoenix	IHL	60	18	17	35	61	4	1	0	1	2
1991-92	**Los Angeles**	**NHL**	**3**	**0**	**0**	**0**	**0**	....	....	....	....	....
	Phoenix	IHL	72	24	30	54	113	....	....	....	....	....
	NHL Totals		**3**	**0**	**0**	**0**	**0**	....	....	....	....	....

WIDMEYER, STEVE

Right wing. Shoots right. 6'2", 200 lbs. Born, Waterloo, Ont., September 29, 1970.
(St. Louis' 7th choice, 201st overall, in 1990 Entry Draft).

			Regular Season					Playoffs				
Season	Club	Lea	GP	G	A	TP	PIM	GP	G	A	TP	PIM
1989-90	U. of Maine	H.E.	26	5	1	6	30	....	....	....	....	....
1990-91	U. of Maine	H.E.	25	4	2	6	61	....	....	....	....	....
1991-92	U. of Maine	H.E.	23	1	2	3	20	....	....	....	....	....

WIEMER, JAMES DUNCAN (JIM) (WEE-muhr)

Defense. Shoots left. 6'4", 210 lbs. Born, Sudbury, Ont., January 9, 1961.
(Buffalo's 5th choice, 83rd overall, in 1980 Entry Draft).

			Regular Season					Playoffs				
Season	Club	Lea	GP	G	A	TP	PIM	GP	G	A	TP	PIM
1978-79	Peterborough	OHA	61	15	12	27	50	18	4	4	8	15
1979-80	Peterborough	OHA	53	17	32	49	63	14	6	9	15	19
1980-81	Peterborough	OHA	65	41	54	95	102	5	1	2	3	15
1981-82	Rochester	AHL	74	19	26	45	57	9	0	4	4	2
1982-83	Rochester	AHL	74	15	44	59	43	15	5	15	20	22
	Buffalo	**NHL**	....	....	....	....	....	**1**	**0**	**0**	**0**	**0**
1983-84	**Buffalo**	**NHL**	**64**	**5**	**15**	**20**	**48**	....	....	....	....	....
	Rochester	AHL	12	4	11	15	11	18	3	13	16	20
1984-85	**Buffalo**	**NHL**	**10**	**3**	**2**	**5**	**4**	....	....	....	....	....
	Rochester	AHL	13	1	9	10	24	....	....	....	....	....
	NY Rangers	**NHL**	**22**	**4**	**3**	**7**	**30**	**1**	**0**	**0**	**0**	**0**
	New Haven	AHL	33	9	27	36	39	....	....	....	....	....
1985-86	**NY Rangers**	**NHL**	**7**	**3**	**0**	**3**	**2**	**8**	**1**	**0**	**1**	**6**
ab	New Haven	AHL	73	24	49	73	108	....	....	....	....	....
1986-87	New Haven	AHL	6	0	7	7	6	....	....	....	....	....
	Nova Scotia	AHL	59	9	25	34	72	5	0	4	4	2
1987-88	**Edmonton**	**NHL**	**12**	**1**	**2**	**3**	**15**	**2**	**0**	**0**	**0**	**2**
	Nova Scotia	AHL	57	11	32	43	99	5	1	1	2	14
1988-89	Cape Breton	AHL	51	12	29	41	80	....	....	....	....	....
	Los Angeles	**NHL**	**9**	**2**	**3**	**5**	**20**	**10**	**2**	**1**	**3**	**19**
	New Haven	AHL	3	1	1	2	2	7	2	3	5	2
1989-90	**Boston**	**NHL**	**61**	**5**	**14**	**19**	**63**	**8**	**0**	**1**	**1**	**4**
	Maine	AHL	6	3	4	7	27	....	....	....	....	....
1990-91	**Boston**	**NHL**	**61**	**4**	**19**	**23**	**62**	**16**	**1**	**3**	**4**	**14**
1991-92	**Boston**	**NHL**	**47**	**1**	**8**	**9**	**84**	**15**	**1**	**3**	**4**	**14**
	Maine	AHL	3	0	1	1	4	....	....	....	....	....
	NHL Totals		**293**	**28**	**66**	**94**	**328**	**61**	**5**	**8**	**13**	**59**

a AHL First All-Star Team (1986)
b AHL Defenseman of the Year (1986)

Traded to **NY Rangers** by **Buffalo** with Steve Patrick for Dave Maloney and Chris Renaud, December 6, 1984. Traded to **Edmonton** by **NY Rangers** with Reijo Ruotsalainen, Clark Donatelli and Ville Kentala for Don Jackson, Mike Golden, Miloslav Horvava and future considerations, October 23, 1986. Traded to **Los Angeles** by **Edmonton** with Alan May for Brian Wilks and John English, March 7, 1989. Signed as a free agent by **Boston**, July 6, 1989.

WILKIE, BOB

Defense. Shoots right. 6'2", 200 lbs. Born, Calgary, Alta., February 11, 1969.
(Detroit's 3rd choice, 41st overall, in 1987 Entry Draft).

			Regular Season					Playoffs				
Season	Club	Lea	GP	G	A	TP	PIM	GP	G	A	TP	PIM
1985-86	Calgary	WHL	63	8	19	27	56	....	....	....	....	....
1986-87	Swift Current	WHL	65	12	38	50	50	4	1	3	4	2
1987-88	Swift Current	WHL	67	12	68	80	124	10	4	12	16	8
1988-89	Swift Current	WHL	62	18	67	85	89	12	1	11	12	47
1989-90	Adirondack	AHL	58	5	33	38	64	6	1	4	5	2
1990-91	**Detroit**	**NHL**	**8**	**1**	**2**	**3**	**2**	....	....	....	....	....
	Adirondack	AHL	43	6	18	24	71	2	1	0	1	2
1991-92	Adirondack	AHL	7	1	4	5	6	16	2	5	7	12
	NHL Totals		**8**	**1**	**2**	**3**	**2**	....	....	....	....	....

WILKIE, DAVID

Defense. Shoots right. 6'1", 202 lbs. Born, Ellensburgh, WA, May 30, 1974.
(Montreal's 1st choice, 20th overall, in 1992 Entry Draft).

			Regular Season					Playoffs				
Season	Club	Lea	GP	G	A	TP	PIM	GP	G	A	TP	PIM
1990-91	Seattle	WHL	25	1	1	2	22	....	....	....	....	....
1991-92	Kamloops	WHL	71	12	28	40	153	16	6	5	11	19

WILKINSON, NEIL

Defense. Shoots right. 6'3", 180 lbs. Born, Selkirk, Man., August 15, 1967.
(Minnesota's 2nd choice, 30th overall, in 1986 Entry Draft).

			Regular Season					Playoffs				
Season	Club	Lea	GP	G	A	TP	PIM	GP	G	A	TP	PIM
1986-87	Michigan State	CCHA	19	3	4	7	18	....	....	....	....	....
1987-88	Medicine Hat	WHL	55	11	21	32	157	5	1	0	1	2
1988-89	Kalamazoo	IHL	39	5	15	20	96	....	....	....	....	....
1989-90	**Minnesota**	**NHL**	**36**	**0**	**5**	**5**	**100**	**7**	**0**	**2**	**2**	**11**
	Kalamazoo	IHL	20	6	7	13	62	....	....	....	....	....
1990-91	**Minnesota**	**NHL**	**50**	**2**	**9**	**11**	**117**	**22**	**3**	**3**	**6**	**12**
	Kalamazoo	IHL	10	0	3	3	38	....	....	....	....	....
1991-92	**San Jose**	**NHL**	**60**	**4**	**15**	**19**	**107**	....	....	....	....	....
	NHL Totals		**146**	**6**	**29**	**35**	**324**	**29**	**3**	**5**	**8**	**23**

Claimed by **San Jose** from **Minnesota** in Dispersal Draft, May 30, 1991.

WILLIAMS, DARRYL

Left wing. Shoots left. 5'11", 185 lbs. Born, Mt. Pearl, Nfld., February 9, 1968.

			Regular Season					Playoffs				
Season	Club	Lea	GP	G	A	TP	PIM	GP	G	A	TP	PIM
1986-87	Belleville	OHL	58	9	10	19	108	....	....	....	....	....
1987-88	Belleville	OHL	63	29	39	68	169	....	....	....	....	....
1988-89	Belleville	AHL	46	24	21	45	137	....	....	....	....	....
	New Haven	AHL	15	5	5	10	24	....	....	....	....	....
1989-90	New Haven	AHL	51	9	13	22	124	....	....	....	....	....
1990-91	New Haven	AHL	57	14	11	25	278	....	....	....	....	....
	Phoenix	IHL	12	1	2	3	53	7	1	0	1	12
1991-92	Phoenix	IHL	48	8	19	27	219	....	....	....	....	....
	New Haven	AHL	13	0	2	2	69	....	....	....	....	....

Signed as a free agent by **Los Angeles**, September, 1989.

WILLIAMS, DAVID

Defense. Shoots right. 6'2", 195 lbs. Born, Plainfield, NJ, August 25, 1967.
(New Jersey's 12th choice, 234th overall, in 1985 Entry Draft).

			Regular Season					Playoffs				
Season	Club	Lea	GP	G	A	TP	PIM	GP	G	A	TP	PIM
1986-87	Dartmouth	ECAC	23	2	19	21	20	....	....	....	....	....
1987-88	Dartmouth	ECAC	25	8	14	22	30	....	....	....	....	....
1988-89ab	Dartmouth	ECAC	25	4	11	15	28	....	....	....	....	....
1989-90	Dartmouth	ECAC	26	3	12	15	32	....	....	....	....	....
1990-91	Muskegon	IHL	14	1	2	3	4	....	....	....	....	....
	Knoxville	ECHL	38	12	15	27	40	3	0	0	0	4
1991-92	**San Jose**	**NHL**	**56**	**3**	**25**	**28**	**40**	....	....	....	....	....
	Kansas City	IHL	18	2	3	5	22	....	....	....	....	....
	NHL Totals		**56**	**3**	**25**	**28**	**40**	....	....	....	....	....

a ECAC First All-Star Team (1989)
b NCAA East Second All-American Team (1989)

Signed as a free agent by **San Jose**, August 9, 1991.

WILLIAMS, SEAN

Center. Shoots left. 6'1", 182 lbs. Born, Oshawa, Ont., January 28, 1968.
(Chicago's 11th choice, 245th overall, in 1986 Entry Draft).

			Regular Season					Playoffs				
Season	Club	Lea	GP	G	A	TP	PIM	GP	G	A	TP	PIM
1984-85	Oshawa	OHL	40	6	7	13	28	5	1	0	1	0
1985-86	Oshawa	OHL	55	15	23	38	23	6	2	3	5	4
1986-87	Oshawa	OHL	62	21	23	44	32	25	7	5	12	19
1987-88a	Oshawa	OHL	65	*58	65	123	38	7	3	3	6	6
1988-89	Saginaw	IHL	77	32	27	59	75	6	0	3	3	0
1989-90	Indianapolis	IHL	78	21	37	58	25	14	8	5	13	12
1990-91	Indianapolis	IHL	82	46	52	98	59	7	1	2	3	12
1991-92	**Chicago**	**NHL**	**2**	**0**	**0**	**0**	**4**	....	....	....	....	....
	Indianapolis	IHL	79	29	36	65	89	....	....	....	....	....
	NHL Totals		**2**	**0**	**0**	**0**	**4**	....	....	....	....	....

a OHL First All-Star Team (1988)

WILLIS, RICK

Left wing. Shoots left. 6', 190 lbs. Born, Lynn, MA, January 12, 1972.
(NY Rangers' 5th choice, 76th overall, in 1990 Entry Draft).

			Regular Season					Playoffs				
Season	Club	Lea	GP	G	A	TP	PIM	GP	G	A	TP	PIM
1990-91	Northwood	HS	....	....	....	32	....	....	....	....	....	....
1991-92	U. of Michigan	CCHA	32	1	4	5	42	....	....	....	....	....

WILLNER, BRADLEY

Defense. Shoots right. 6'3", 191 lbs. Born, Edina, MN, January 6, 1973.
(New Jersey's 4th choice, 77th overall, in 1991 Entry Draft).

			Regular Season					Playoffs				
Season	Club	Lea	GP	G	A	TP	PIM	GP	G	A	TP	PIM
1990-91	Richfield	HS	25	7	18	25	24	....	....	....	....	....
1991-92	Lake Superior	CCHA	16	0	0	0	10	....	....	....	....	....

WILSON, CAREY

Center. Shoots right. 6'2", 195 lbs. Born, Winnipeg, Man., May 19, 1962.
(Chicago's 8th choice, 67th overall, in 1980 Entry Draft).

			Regular Season					Playoffs				
Season	Club	Lea	GP	G	A	TP	PIM	GP	G	A	TP	PIM
1979-80	Dartmouth	ECAC	31	16	22	38	20	....	....	....	....	....
1980-81	Dartmouth	ECAC	24	9	13	22	52	....	....	....	....	....
1981-82	HIFK	Fin.	29	15	17	32	58	7	1	4	5	6
1982-83	HIFK	Fin.	36	16	24	40	62	9	1	3	4	12
1983-84	Cdn. Olympic	....	56	19	24	43	34	....	....	....	....	....
	Calgary	**NHL**	**15**	**2**	**5**	**7**	**2**	**6**	**3**	**1**	**4**	**2**
1984-85	**Calgary**	**NHL**	**74**	**24**	**48**	**72**	**27**	**4**	**0**	**0**	**0**	**0**
1985-86	**Calgary**	**NHL**	**76**	**29**	**29**	**58**	**24**	**9**	**0**	**2**	**2**	**2**
1986-87	**Calgary**	**NHL**	**80**	**20**	**36**	**56**	**42**	**6**	**1**	**1**	**2**	**6**
1987-88	**Calgary**	**NHL**	**34**	**9**	**21**	**30**	**18**	....	....	....	....	....
	Hartford	**NHL**	**36**	**18**	**20**	**38**	**22**	**6**	**2**	**4**	**6**	**2**
1988-89	**Hartford**	**NHL**	**34**	**11**	**11**	**22**	**14**	....	....	....	....	....
	NY Rangers	**NHL**	**41**	**21**	**34**	**55**	**45**	**4**	**1**	**2**	**3**	**2**
1989-90	**NY Rangers**	**NHL**	**41**	**9**	**17**	**26**	**57**	**10**	**2**	**1**	**3**	**0**
1990-91	**Hartford**	**NHL**	**45**	**8**	**15**	**23**	**16**	....	....	....	....	....
	Calgary	**NHL**	**12**	**3**	**3**	**6**	**2**	**7**	**2**	**2**	**4**	**0**
1991-92	**Calgary**	**NHL**	**42**	**11**	**12**	**23**	**37**	....	....	....	....	....
	NHL Totals		**530**	**165**	**251**	**416**	**306**	**52**	**11**	**13**	**24**	**14**

Rights traded to **Calgary** by **Chicago** for Denis Cyr November 8, 1982. Traded to **Hartford** by **Calgary** with Neil Sheehy and the rights to Lane MacDonald for Dana Murzyn and Shane Churla, January 3, 1988. Traded to **NY Rangers** by **Hartford** with Hartford's fifth round choice (Lubos Rob) in 1990 Entry Draft for Brian Lawton, Norm MacIver and Don Maloney, December 26, 1988. Traded to **Hartford** by **NY Rangers** with NY Rangers' third round choice (Mikael Nylander) in 1991 Entry Draft for Jody Hull, July 9, 1990. Traded to **Calgary** by **Hartford** for Mark Hunter, March 5, 1991.

WILSON, DOUGLAS, JR. (DOUG)

Defense. Shoots left. 6'1", 187 lbs. Born, Ottawa, Ont., July 5, 1957.
(Chicago's 1st choice, 6th overall, in 1977 Amateur Draft).

			Regular Season					Playoffs				
Season	Club	Lea	GP	G	A	TP	PIM	GP	G	A	TP	PIM
1975-76	Ottawa	OHA	58	26	62	88	142	12	5	10	15	24
1976-77a	Ottawa	OHA	43	25	54	79	85	19	4	20	24	34
1977-78	**Chicago**	**NHL**	**77**	**14**	**20**	**34**	**72**	**4**	**0**	**0**	**0**	**0**
1978-79	**Chicago**	**NHL**	**56**	**5**	**21**	**26**	**37**	....	....	....	....	....
1979-80	**Chicago**	**NHL**	**73**	**12**	**49**	**61**	**70**	**7**	**2**	**8**	**10**	**6**
1980-81	**Chicago**	**NHL**	**76**	**12**	**39**	**51**	**80**	**3**	**0**	**3**	**3**	**2**
1981-82bc	**Chicago**	**NHL**	**76**	**39**	**46**	**85**	**54**	**15**	**3**	**10**	**13**	**32**
1982-83	**Chicago**	**NHL**	**74**	**18**	**51**	**69**	**58**	**13**	**4**	**11**	**15**	**12**
1983-84	**Chicago**	**NHL**	**66**	**13**	**45**	**58**	**64**	**5**	**0**	**3**	**3**	**2**
1984-85d	**Chicago**	**NHL**	**78**	**22**	**54**	**76**	**44**	**12**	**3**	**10**	**13**	**12**
1985-86	**Chicago**	**NHL**	**79**	**17**	**47**	**64**	**80**	**3**	**1**	**1**	**2**	**2**
1986-87	**Chicago**	**NHL**	**69**	**16**	**32**	**48**	**36**	**4**	**0**	**0**	**0**	**0**
1987-88	**Chicago**	**NHL**	**27**	**8**	**24**	**32**	**28**	....	....	....	....	....
1988-89	**Chicago**	**NHL**	**66**	**15**	**47**	**62**	**69**	**4**	**1**	**2**	**3**	**0**
1989-90d	**Chicago**	**NHL**	**70**	**23**	**50**	**73**	**40**	**20**	**3**	**12**	**15**	**18**
1990-91	**Chicago**	**NHL**	**51**	**11**	**29**	**40**	**32**	**5**	**2**	**1**	**3**	**2**
1991-92	**San Jose**	**NHL**	**44**	**9**	**19**	**28**	**26**	....	....	....	....	....
	NHL Totals		**982**	**234**	**573**	**807**	**790**	**95**	**19**	**61**	**80**	**88**

a OHA First All-Star Team (1977)
b Won James Norris Memorial Trophy (1982)
c NHL First All-Star Team (1982)
d NHL Second All-Star Team (1985, 1990)

Played in NHL All-Star Game (1982-86, 1990, 1992)

Traded to **San Jose** by **Chicago** for Kerry Toporowski and San Jose's second round choice in 1992 Entry Draft (later traded to Winnipeg - Boris Mironov), September 6, 1991.

WILSON, RONALD LEE (RON)

Center. Shoots left. 5'9", 180 lbs. Born, Toronto, Ont., May 13, 1956.
(Montreal's 15th choice, 133rd overall, in 1976 Amateur Draft).

			Regular Season					Playoffs				
Season	Club	Lea	GP	G	A	TP	PIM	GP	G	A	TP	PIM
1974-75	Toronto	OMJHL	16	6	12	18	6	23	9	17	26	6
1975-76	St. Catharines	OHA	64	37	62	99	44	4	1	6	7	7
1976-77	Nova Scotia	AHL	67	15	21	36	18	6	0	0	0	0
1977-78	Nova Scotia	AHL	59	15	25	40	17	11	4	4	8	9
1978-79	Nova Scotia	AHL	77	33	42	75	91	10	5	6	11	14
1979-80	**Winnipeg**	**NHL**	**79**	**21**	**36**	**57**	**28**	....	....	....	....	....
1980-81	**Winnipeg**	**NHL**	**77**	**18**	**33**	**51**	**55**	....	....	....	....	....
1981-82	**Winnipeg**	**NHL**	**39**	**3**	**13**	**16**	**49**	....	....	....	....	....
	Tulsa	CHL	41	20	38	58	22	3	1	0	1	2
1982-83	**Winnipeg**	**NHL**	**12**	**6**	**3**	**9**	**4**	**3**	**2**	**2**	**4**	**2**
	Sherbrooke	AHL	65	30	55	85	71	....	....	....	....	....
1983-84	**Winnipeg**	**NHL**	**51**	**3**	**12**	**15**	**12**	....	....	....	....	....
	Sherbrooke	AHL	22	10	30	40	16	....	....	....	....	....
1984-85	**Winnipeg**	**NHL**	**75**	**10**	**9**	**19**	**31**	**8**	**4**	**2**	**6**	**2**
1985-86	**Winnipeg**	**NHL**	**54**	**6**	**7**	**13**	**16**	**1**	**0**	**0**	**0**	**0**
	Sherbrooke	AHL	10	9	8	17	9	....	....	....	....	....
1986-87	**Winnipeg**	**NHL**	**80**	**3**	**13**	**16**	**13**	**10**	**1**	**2**	**3**	**0**
1987-88	**Winnipeg**	**NHL**	**69**	**5**	**8**	**13**	**28**	**1**	**0**	**0**	**0**	**2**
1988-89a	Moncton	AHL	80	31	61	92	110	8	1	4	5	20
1989-90	Moncton	AHL	47	16	37	53	39	....	....	....	....	....
	St. Louis	**NHL**	**33**	**3**	**17**	**20**	**23**	**12**	**3**	**5**	**8**	**18**
1990-91	**St. Louis**	**NHL**	**73**	**10**	**27**	**37**	**54**	**7**	**0**	**0**	**0**	**28**
1991-92	**St. Louis**	**NHL**	**64**	**12**	**17**	**29**	**46**	**6**	**0**	**1**	**1**	**0**
	NHL Totals		**706**	**100**	**195**	**295**	**359**	**48**	**10**	**12**	**22**	**52**

a AHL Second All-Star Team (1989)

Sold to **Winnipeg** by **Montreal**, October 4, 1979. Traded to **St. Louis** by **Winnipeg** for Doug Evans, January 22, 1990.

WILSON, ROSS

Right wing. Shoots right. 6'3", 197 lbs. Born, The Pas, Man., June 26, 1969.
(Los Angeles' 3rd choice, 43rd overall, in 1987 Entry Draft).

			Regular Season					Playoffs				
Season	Club	Lea	GP	G	A	TP	PIM	GP	G	A	TP	PIM
1986-87	Peterborough	OHL	66	28	11	39	91	12	3	5	8	16
1987-88	Peterborough	OHL	66	29	30	59	114	12	2	9	11	15
1988-89	Peterborough	OHL	64	48	41	89	90	15	10	13	23	23
1989-90	New Haven	AHL	61	19	14	33	39	....	....	....	....	....
1990-91	New Haven	AHL	68	29	17	46	28	....	....	....	....	....
1991-92	Phoenix	IHL	28	9	9	18	81	....	....	....	....	....
	Kalamazoo	IHL	31	18	6	24	38	11	9	1	10	6

WINCH, JASON

Left wing. Shoots left. 6'1", 203 lbs. Born, Listowel, Ont., May 23, 1971.
(Buffalo's 8th choice, 187th overall, in 1990 Entry Draft).

			Regular Season					Playoffs				
Season	Club	Lea	GP	G	A	TP	PIM	GP	G	A	TP	PIM
1988-89	Toronto	OHL	66	33	50	83	8	6	3	3	6	0
1989-90	Niagara Falls	OHL	64	31	63	94	23	16	9	12	21	4
1990-91	Niagara Falls	OHL	66	40	82	122	16	14	14	12	26	6
1991-92	Rochester	AHL	73	23	35	58	24	12	2	6	8	0

WINNES, CHRISTOPHER (CHRIS)

Right wing. Shoots right. 6', 170 lbs. Born, Ridgefield, CT, February 12, 1968.
(Boston's 9th choice, 161st overall, in 1987 Entry Draft).

			Regular Season					Playoffs				
Season	Club	Lea	GP	G	A	TP	PIM	GP	G	A	TP	PIM
1987-88	N. Hampshire	H.E.	30	17	19	36	28	....	....	....	....	....
1988-89	N. Hampshire	H.E.	30	11	20	31	22	....	....	....	....	....
1989-90	N. Hampshire	H.E.	24	10	13	23	12	....	....	....	....	....
1990-91	N. Hampshire	H.E.	33	15	16	31	24	....	....	....	....	....
	Maine	AHL	7	3	1	4	0	1	0	2	2	0
	Boston	**NHL**	....	....	....	....	....	**1**	**0**	**0**	**0**	**0**
1991-92	**Boston**	**NHL**	**24**	**1**	**3**	**4**	**6**	....	....	....	....	....
	Maine	AHL	45	12	35	47	30	....	....	....	....	....
	NHL Totals		**24**	**1**	**3**	**4**	**6**	**1**	**0**	**0**	**0**	**0**

WISEMAN, BRIAN

Center. Shoots left. 5'6", 175 lbs. Born, Chatham, Ont., July 13, 1971.
(NY Rangers' 12th choice, 257th overall, in 1991 Entry Draft).

			Regular Season					Playoffs				
Season	Club	Lea	GP	G	A	TP	PIM	GP	G	A	TP	PIM
1990-91	U. of Michigan	CCHA	47	25	33	58	58	....	....	....	....	....
1991-92	U. of Michigan	CCHA	44	27	44	71	38	....	....	....	....	....

WITKOWSKI, BYRON

Left wing. Shoots left. 6'3", 197 lbs. Born, Edenwold, Sask., November 20, 1969.
(Quebec's 13th choice, 211th overall, in 1989 Entry Draft).

			Regular Season					Playoffs				
Season	Club	Lea	GP	G	A	TP	PIM	GP	G	A	TP	PIM
1989-90	W. Michigan	CCHA	36	1	2	3	36	....	....	....	....	....
1990-91	W. Michigan	CCHA	31	10	4	14	66	....	....	....	....	....
1991-92	W. Michigan	CCHA	34	9	9	18	36	....	....	....	....	....

WOLANIN, CHRISTOPHER

Defense. Shoots left. 6'2", 205 lbs. Born, Detroit, MI, September 12, 1968.
(Vancouver's 10th choice, 212th overall, in 1988 Entry Draft).

			Regular Season					Playoffs				
Season	Club	Lea	GP	G	A	TP	PIM	GP	G	A	TP	PIM
1987-88	Ill.-Chicago	CCHA	37	1	6	7	38	....	....	....	....	....
1988-89	Ill.-Chicago	CCHA	30	1	9	10	33	....	....	....	....	....
1989-90	Ill.-Chicago	CCHA	34	1	6	7	116	....	....	....	....	....
1990-91	Ill.-Chicago	CCHA	37	4	13	17	104	....	....	....	....	....
1991-92	Greensboro	ECHL	61	5	10	15	127	11	0	3	3	12

WOLANIN, CRAIG (wuh-LAN-ihn)

Defense. Shoots left. 6'3", 205 lbs. Born, Grosse Pointe, MI, July 27, 1967.
(New Jersey's 1st choice, 3rd overall, in 1985 Entry Draft).

			Regular Season					Playoffs				
Season	Club	Lea	GP	G	A	TP	PIM	GP	G	A	TP	PIM
1984-85	Kitchener	OHL	60	5	16	21	95	4	1	1	2	2
1985-86	**New Jersey**	**NHL**	**44**	**2**	**16**	**18**	**74**	....	....	....	....	....
1986-87	**New Jersey**	**NHL**	**68**	**4**	**6**	**10**	**109**	....	....	....	....	....
1987-88	**New Jersey**	**NHL**	**78**	**6**	**25**	**31**	**170**	**18**	**2**	**5**	**7**	**51**
1988-89	**New Jersey**	**NHL**	**56**	**3**	**8**	**11**	**69**	....	....	....	....	....
1989-90	**New Jersey**	**NHL**	**37**	**1**	**7**	**8**	**47**	....	....	....	....	....
	Utica	AHL	6	2	4	6	2	....	....	....	....	....
	Quebec	**NHL**	**13**	**0**	**3**	**3**	**10**	....	....	....	....	....
1990-91	**Quebec**	**NHL**	**80**	**5**	**13**	**18**	**89**	....	....	....	....	....
1991-92	**Quebec**	**NHL**	**69**	**2**	**11**	**13**	**80**	....	....	....	....	....
	NHL Totals		**445**	**23**	**89**	**112**	**648**	**18**	**2**	**5**	**7**	**51**

Traded to **Quebec** by **New Jersey** with future considerations (Randy Velischek) for Peter Stastny, March 6, 1990.

WOLANSKI, PAUL

Defense. Shoots right. 6', 212 lbs. Born, Kitchener, Ont., March 22, 1971.
(New Jersey's 8th choice, 165th overall, in 1991 Entry Draft).

			Regular Season					Playoffs				
Season	Club	Lea	GP	G	A	TP	PIM	GP	G	A	TP	PIM
1990-91	Niagara Falls	OHL	66	14	47	61	76	14	5	12	17	12
1991-92	Niagara Falls	OHL	3	0	0	0	0	....	....	....	....	....
	London	OHL	44	11	35	46	57	10	4	6	10	10

WOOD, DODY

Center. Shoots left. 5'11", 181 lbs. Born, Chetwynd, B.C., March 10, 1972.
(San Jose's 4th choice, 45th overall, in 1991 Entry Draft).

			Regular Season					Playoffs				
Season	Club	Lea	GP	G	A	TP	PIM	GP	G	A	TP	PIM
1989-90	Ft. St. John	Tier II	44	51	73	124	270	....	....	....	....	....
	Seattle	WHL	....	....	....	....	....	5	0	0	0	2
1990-91	Seattle	WHL	69	28	37	65	272	6	0	1	1	2
1991-92	Seattle	WHL	37	13	19	32	232	....	....	....	....	....
	Swift Current	WHL	3	0	2	2	14	7	2	1	3	37

WOOD, RANDY

Left wing/Center. Shoots left. 6', 195 lbs. Born, Princeton, NJ, October 12, 1963.

			Regular Season					Playoffs				
Season	Club	Lea	GP	G	A	TP	PIM	GP	G	A	TP	PIM
1982-83	Yale	ECAC	26	5	14	19	10	....	....	....	....	....
1983-84	Yale	ECAC	18	7	7	14	10	....	....	....	....	....
1984-85a	Yale	ECAC	32	25	28	53	23	....	....	....	....	....
1985-86bc	Yale	ECAC	31	25	30	55	26	....	....	....	....	....
1986-87	**NY Islanders**	**NHL**	**6**	**1**	**0**	**1**	**4**	**13**	**1**	**3**	**4**	**14**
	Springfield	AHL	75	23	24	47	57	....	....	....	....	....
1987-88	**NY Islanders**	**NHL**	**75**	**22**	**16**	**38**	**80**	**5**	**1**	**0**	**1**	**6**
	Springfield	AHL	1	0	1	1	0	....	....	....	....	....
1988-89	**NY Islanders**	**NHL**	**77**	**15**	**13**	**28**	**44**	....	....	....	....	....
	Springfield	AHL	1	1	1	2	0	....	....	....	....	....
1989-90	**NY Islanders**	**NHL**	**74**	**24**	**24**	**48**	**39**	**5**	**1**	**1**	**2**	**4**
1990-91	**NY Islanders**	**NHL**	**76**	**24**	**18**	**42**	**45**	....	....	....	....	....
1991-92	**NY Islanders**	**NHL**	**8**	**2**	**2**	**4**	**21**	....	....	....	....	....
	Buffalo	**NHL**	**70**	**20**	**16**	**36**	**65**	**7**	**2**	**1**	**3**	**6**
	NHL Totals		**386**	**108**	**89**	**197**	**298**	**30**	**5**	**5**	**10**	**30**

a ECAC Second All-Star Team (1985)
b ECAC First All-Star Team (1986)
c NCAA East Second All-Star Team (1986)

Signed as a free agent by **NY Islanders**, September 17, 1986. Traded to **Buffalo** by **NY Islanders** with Pat Lafontaine, Randy Hillier and future considerations for Pierre Turgeon, Uwe Krupp, Benoit Hogue and Dave McLlwain, October 25, 1991.

WOODCROFT, CRAIG

Left wing. Shoots left. 6'1", 185 lbs. Born, Toronto, Ont., December 3, 1969.
(Chicago's 6th choice, 134th overall, in 1988 Entry Draft).

			Regular Season					Playoffs				
Season	Club	Lea	GP	G	A	TP	PIM	GP	G	A	TP	PIM
1987-88	Colgate	ECAC	29	7	10	17	28	....	....	....	....	....
1988-89	Colgate	ECAC	29	20	29	49	62	....	....	....	....	....
	Cdn. National	....	2	0	0	0	4	....	....	....	....	....
1989-90	Colgate	ECAC	37	20	26	46	108	....	....	....	....	....
1990-91	Colgate	ECAC	32	26	30	56	52	....	....	....	....	....
1991-92	Indianapolis	IHL	75	21	17	38	67	....	....	....	....	....

WOODWARD, ROBERT (ROB)

Left wing. Shoots left. 6'4", 225 lbs. Born, Evanston, IL, January 15, 1971.
(Vancouver's 2nd choice, 29th overall, in 1989 Entry Draft).

			Regular Season					Playoffs				
Season	Club	Lea	GP	G	A	TP	PIM	GP	G	A	TP	PIM
1989-90	Michigan State	CCHA	37	17	9	26	8	....	....	....	....	....
1990-91	Michigan State	CCHA	32	5	13	18	16	....	....	....	....	....
1991-92	Michigan State	CCHA	40	14	15	29	60	....	....	....	....	....

WOOLF, MARK

Right wing. Shoots right. 5'11", 200 lbs. Born, Brandon, Man., September 30, 1970.
(Boston's 5th choice, 126th overall, in 1990 Entry Draft).

			Regular Season					Playoffs				
Season	Club	Lea	GP	G	A	TP	PIM	GP	G	A	TP	PIM
1989-90	Spokane	WHL	68	52	52	104	73	6	2	1	3	9
1990-91	Spokane	WHL	67	41	49	90	96	13	8	6	14	14
1991-92	Salt Lake	IHL	1	0	0	0	0	....	....	....	....	....
	Roanoke Valley	ECHL	63	50	51	101	93	7	2	8	10	10

WOOLLEY, JASON

Defense. Shoots left. 6', 186 lbs. Born, Toronto, Ont., July 27, 1969.
(Washington's 4th choice, 61st overall, in 1989 Entry Draft).

			Regular Season					Playoffs				
Season	Club	Lea	GP	G	A	TP	PIM	GP	G	A	TP	PIM
1988-89	Michigan State	CCHA	47	12	25	37	26	....	....	....	....	....
1989-90	Michigan State	CCHA	45	10	38	48	26	....	....	....	....	....
1990-91ab	Michigan State	CCHA	40	15	44	59	24	....	....	....	....	....
1991-92	Cdn. National	....	60	14	30	44	36	....	....	....	....	....
	Cdn. Olympic	....	8	0	5	5	4	....	....	....	....	....
	Washington	**NHL**	**1**	**0**	**0**	**0**	**0**	....	....	....	....	....
	Baltimore	AHL	15	1	10	11	6	....	....	....	....	....
	NHL Totals		**1**	**0**	**0**	**0**	**0**	....	....	....	....	....

a CCHA First All-Star Team (1991)
b NCAA West First All-American Team (1991)

WORTMAN, KEVIN

Defense. Shoots right. 6', 200 lbs. Born, Sagus, MA, February 22, 1969.
(Calgary's 9th choice, 168th overall, in 1989 Entry Draft).

			Regular Season					Playoffs				
Season	Club	Lea	GP	G	A	TP	PIM	GP	G	A	TP	PIM
1990-91	American Int'l	NCAA	28	21	25	46	6	....	....	....	....	....
1991-92	Salt Lake	IHL	82	12	34	46	34	5	1	0	1	0

WRIGHT, TYLER

Center. Shoots right. 5'11", 175 lbs. Born, Canora, Sask., April 6, 1973.
(Edmonton's 1st choice, 12th overall, in 1991 Entry Draft).

			Regular Season					Playoffs				
Season	Club	Lea	GP	G	A	TP	PIM	GP	G	A	TP	PIM
1989-90	Swift Current	WHL	67	14	18	32	139	4	0	0	0	12
1990-91	Swift Current	WHL	66	41	51	92	157	3	0	0	0	6
1991-92	Swift Current	WHL	63	36	46	82	295	8	2	5	7	16

YAKE, TERRY

Center. Shoots right. 5'11", 185 lbs. Born, New Westminster, B.C., October 22, 1968.
(Hartford's 3rd choice, 81st overall, in 1987 Entry Draft).

			Regular Season					Playoffs				
Season	Club	Lea	GP	G	A	TP	PIM	GP	G	A	TP	PIM
1984-85	Brandon	WHL	11	1	1	2	0	....	....	....	....	....
1985-86	Brandon	WHL	72	26	26	52	49	....	....	....	....	....
1986-87	Brandon	WHL	71	44	58	102	64	....	....	....	....	....
1987-88	Brandon	WHL	72	55	85	140	59	3	4	2	6	7
1988-89	**Hartford**	**NHL**	**2**	**0**	**0**	**0**	**0**	....	....	....	....	....
	Binghamton	AHL	75	39	56	95	57	....	....	....	....	....
1989-90	**Hartford**	**NHL**	**2**	**0**	**1**	**1**	**0**	....	....	....	....	....
	Binghamton	AHL	77	13	42	55	37	....	....	....	....	....
1990-91	**Hartford**	**NHL**	**19**	**1**	**4**	**5**	**10**	**6**	**1**	**1**	**2**	**16**
	Springfield	AHL	60	35	42	77	56	15	9	9	18	10
1991-92	**Hartford**	**NHL**	**15**	**1**	**1**	**2**	**4**	....	....	....	....	....
	Springfield	AHL	53	21	34	55	63	8	3	4	7	2
	NHL Totals		**38**	**2**	**6**	**8**	**14**	**6**	**1**	**1**	**2**	**16**

YAKUBOV, RAVIL (yah-KOO-bohv, rah-VEEL)

Center. Shoots left. 6'1", 187 lbs. Born, Moscow, Soviet Union, July 26, 1970.
(Calgary's 6th choice, 126th overall, in 1992 Entry Draft).

			Regular Season					Playoffs				
Season	Club	Lea	GP	G	A	TP	PIM	GP	G	A	TP	PIM
1990-91	Moscow D'amo	USSR	31	4	4	8	6	....	....	....	....	....
1991-92	Moscow D'amo	CIS	32	11	2	13	18	....	....	....	....	....

YASHIN, ALEXEI (YAH-shin)

Center. Shoots right. 6'2", 196 lbs. Born, Sverdlovsk, Soviet Union, November 5, 1973.
(Ottawa's 1st choice, 2nd overall, in 1992 Entry Draft).

			Regular Season					Playoffs				
Season	Club	Lea	GP	G	A	TP	PIM	GP	G	A	TP	PIM
1990-91	Sverdlovsk	USSR 2	26	2	1	3	10	....	....	....	....	....
1991-92	Moscow D'amo	CIS	35	7	5	12	19	....	....	....	....	....

YAWNEY, TRENT

Defense. Shoots left. 6'3", 192 lbs. Born, Hudson Bay, Sask., September 29, 1965.
(Chicago's 2nd choice, 45th overall, in 1984 Entry Draft).

			Regular Season					Playoffs				
Season	Club	Lea	GP	G	A	TP	PIM	GP	G	A	TP	PIM
1982-83	Saskatoon	WHL	59	6	31	37	44	6	0	2	2	0
1983-84	Saskatoon	WHL	73	13	46	59	81	....	....	....	....	....
1984-85	Saskatoon	WHL	72	16	51	67	158	3	1	6	7	7
1985-86	Cdn. Olympic	....	73	6	15	21	60	....	....	....	....	....
1986-87	Cdn. Olympic	....	51	4	15	19	37	....	....	....	....	....
1987-88	Cdn. National	....	60	4	12	16	81	....	....	....	....	....
	Cdn. Olympic	....	8	1	1	2	6	....	....	....	....	....
	Chicago	**NHL**	**15**	**2**	**8**	**10**	**15**	**5**	**0**	**4**	**4**	**8**
1988-89	**Chicago**	**NHL**	**69**	**5**	**19**	**24**	**116**	**15**	**3**	**6**	**9**	**20**
1989-90	**Chicago**	**NHL**	**70**	**5**	**15**	**20**	**82**	**20**	**3**	**5**	**8**	**27**
1990-91	**Chicago**	**NHL**	**61**	**3**	**13**	**16**	**77**	**1**	**0**	**0**	**0**	**0**
1991-92	**Calgary**	**NHL**	**47**	**4**	**9**	**13**	**45**	....	....	....	....	....
	Indianapolis	IHL	9	2	3	5	12	....	....	....	....	....
	NHL Totals		**262**	**19**	**64**	**83**	**335**	**41**	**6**	**15**	**21**	**55**

Traded to **Calgary** by **Chicago** for Stephane Matteau, December 16, 1991.

YLONEN, JUHA (YOU-leh-nin, YOU-hah)

Center. Shoots left. 6'1", 178 lbs. Born, Helsinki, Finland, February 13, 1972.
(Winnipeg's 5th choice, 91st overall, in 1991 Entry Draft).

			Regular Season					Playoffs				
Season	Club	Lea	GP	G	A	TP	PIM	GP	G	A	TP	PIM
1990-91	Espoo	Fin.2	40	12	21	33	4	....	....	....	....	....
1991-92	HPK	Fin.	43	7	11	18	8	....	....	....	....	....

YORK, JASON

Defense. Shoots right. 6'1", 192 lbs. Born, Ottawa, Ont., May 20, 1970.
(Detroit's 6th choice, 129th overall, in 1990 Entry Draft).

			Regular Season					Playoffs				
Season	Club	Lea	GP	G	A	TP	PIM	GP	G	A	TP	PIM
1989-90	Windsor	OHL	39	9	30	39	38	....	....	....	....	....
	Kitchener	OHL	25	11	25	36	17	17	3	19	22	10
1990-91a	Windsor	OHL	66	13	80	93	40	11	3	10	13	12
1991-92	Adirondack	AHL	49	4	20	24	32	5	0	1	1	0

a OHL Third All-Star Team (1991)

YOUNG, BARRY

Defense. Shoots left. 6'2", 202 lbs. Born, Belfast, Northern Ireland, August 7, 1972.
(NY Rangers' 6th choice, 128th overall, in 1991 Entry Draft).

			Regular Season					Playoffs				
Season	Club	Lea	GP	G	A	TP	PIM	GP	G	A	TP	PIM
1990-91	Sudbury	OHL	59	1	14	15	93	5	0	2	2	8
1991-92	Sudbury	OHL	60	6	19	25	110	11	2	0	2	27

YOUNG, C.J.

Right wing. Shoots right. 5'10", 180 lbs. Born, Waban, MA, January 1, 1968.
(New Jersey's 1st choice, 5th overall, in 1989 Supplemental Draft).

			Regular Season					Playoffs				
Season	Club	Lea	GP	G	A	TP	PIM	GP	G	A	TP	PIM
1986-87	Harvard	ECAC	34	17	12	29	30	....	....	....	....	....
1987-88	Harvard	ECAC	28	13	16	29	40	....	....	....	....	....
1988-89a	Harvard	ECAC	36	20	31	51	36	....	....	....	....	....
1989-90bc	Harvard	ECAC	28	21	28	49	32	....	....	....	....	....
1990-91	Salt Lake	IHL	80	31	36	67	43	4	1	2	3	2
1991-92	U.S. National	....	49	17	17	34	38	....	....	....	....	....
	U.S. Olympic	....	8	1	3	4	4	....	....	....	....	....
	Salt Lake	IHL	9	2	2	4	2	5	0	1	1	4

a ECAC Second All-Star Team (1989)
b ECAC First All-Star Team (1990)
c NCAA East Second All-American Team (1990)

Signed as a free agent by **Calgary**, October 5, 1990.

YOUNG, JASON

Left wing. Shoots left. 5'10", 197 lbs. Born, Sudbury, Ont., December 16, 1972.
(Buffalo's 3rd choice, 57th overall, in 1991 Entry Draft).

			Regular Season					Playoffs				
Season	Club	Lea	GP	G	A	TP	PIM	GP	G	A	TP	PIM
1989-90	Sudbury	OHL	62	26	47	73	64	7	3	2	5	8
1990-91	Sudbury	OHL	37	21	38	59	22	5	0	4	4	10
1991-92	Sudbury	OHL	55	26	56	82	49	11	3	2	5	14

YOUNG, SCOTT

Right wing. Shoots right. 6', 190 lbs. Born, Clinton, MA, October 1, 1967.
(Hartford's 1st choice, 11th overall, in 1986 Entry Draft).

			Regular Season					Playoffs				
Season	Club	Lea	GP	G	A	TP	PIM	GP	G	A	TP	PIM
1985-86a	Boston U.	H.E.	38	16	13	29	31	....	....	....	....	....
1986-87	Boston U.	H.E.	33	15	21	36	24	....	....	....	....	....
1987-88	U.S. National	....	56	11	47	58	31	....	....	....	....	....
	U.S. Olympic	....	6	2	6	8	4	....	....	....	....	....
	Hartford	**NHL**	**7**	**0**	**0**	**0**	**2**	**4**	**1**	**0**	**1**	**0**
1988-89	**Hartford**	**NHL**	**76**	**19**	**40**	**59**	**27**	**4**	**2**	**0**	**2**	**4**
1989-90	**Hartford**	**NHL**	**80**	**24**	**40**	**64**	**47**	**7**	**2**	**0**	**2**	**2**
1990-91	**Hartford**	**NHL**	**34**	**6**	**9**	**15**	**8**	....	....	....	....	....
	Pittsburgh	**NHL**	**43**	**11**	**16**	**27**	**33**	**17**	**1**	**6**	**7**	**2**
1991-92	Bolzano	Italy	18	22	17	39	6	5	4	3	7	7
	U.S. National	....	10	2	4	6	21	....	....	....	....	....
	U.S. Olympic	....	8	2	1	3	2	....	....	....	....	....
	NHL Totals		**240**	**60**	**105**	**165**	**117**	**32**	**6**	**6**	**12**	**8**

a Hockey East Rookie of the Year (1986)

Traded to **Pittsburgh** by **Hartford** for Rob Brown, December 21, 1990. Traded to **Quebec** by **Pittsburgh** for Bryan Fogarty, March 10, 1992.

YSEBAERT, PAUL (IGHS-BAHRT)

Center. Shoots left. 6'1", 190 lbs. Born, Sarnia, Ont., May 15, 1966.
(New Jersey's 4th choice, 74th overall, in 1984 Entry Draft).

			Regular Season					Playoffs				
Season	Club	Lea	GP	G	A	TP	PIM	GP	G	A	TP	PIM
1984-85	Bowling Green	CCHA	42	23	32	55	54	....	....	....	....	....
1985-86a	Bowling Green	CCHA	42	23	45	68	50	....	....	....	....	....
1986-87a	Bowling Green	CCHA	45	27	58	85	44	....	....	....	....	....
	Cdn. Olympic	....	5	1	0	1	4	....	....	....	....	....
1987-88	Utica	AHL	78	30	49	79	60	....	....	....	....	....
1988-89	**New Jersey**	**NHL**	**5**	**0**	**4**	**4**	**0**	....	....	....	....	....
	Utica	AHL	56	36	44	80	22	5	0	1	1	4
1989-90	**New Jersey**	**NHL**	**5**	**1**	**2**	**3**	**0**	....	....	....	....	....
bcd	Utica	AHL	74	53	52	*105	61	5	2	4	6	0
1990-91	**New Jersey**	**NHL**	**11**	**4**	**3**	**7**	**6**	....	....	....	....	....
	Detroit	**NHL**	**51**	**15**	**18**	**33**	**16**	**2**	**0**	**2**	**2**	**0**
1991-92e	**Detroit**	**NHL**	**79**	**35**	**40**	**75**	**55**	**10**	**1**	**0**	**1**	**10**
	NHL Totals		**151**	**55**	**67**	**122**	**77**	**12**	**1**	**2**	**3**	**10**

a CCHA Second All-Star Team (1986, 1987)
b AHL First All-Star Team (1990)
c Won John B. Sollenberger Trophy (Top Scorer-AHL) (1990)
d Won Les Cunningham Trophy (MVP-AHL) (1990)
e Won Alka-Seltzer Plus Award (1992)

Traded to **Detroit** by **New Jersey** for Lee Norwood and future considerations, November 27, 1990.

YUDIN, ALEXANDER (EW-din)

Defense. Shoots left. 6'1", 191 lbs. Born, Minsk, Soviet Union, April 1, 1969.
(Calgary's 12th choice, 231st overall, in 1989 Entry Draft).

			Regular Season					Playoffs				
Season	Club	Lea	GP	G	A	TP	PIM	GP	G	A	TP	PIM
1986-87	Dynamo Minsk	USSR 2	35	0	4	4	36	....	....	....	....	....
1987-88	Dynamo Minsk	USSR 2	33	2	7	9	28	....	....	....	....	....
1988-89	Moscow D'amo	USSR	21	2	2	4	27	....	....	....	....	....
1989-90	Moscow D'amo	USSR	36	4	5	9	36	....	....	....	....	....
1990-91	Moscow D'amo	USSR	36	1	7	8	78	....	....	....	....	....
1991-92	Moscow D'amo	CIS	30	7	7	14	22	....	....	....	....	....

YULE, STEVE

Defense. Shoots right. 6', 210 lbs. Born, Gleichen, Alta., May 27, 1972.
(Hartford's 8th choice, 163rd overall, in 1991 Entry Draft).

			Regular Season					Playoffs				
Season	Club	Lea	GP	G	A	TP	PIM	GP	G	A	TP	PIM
1990-91	Kamloops	WHL	66	7	16	23	141	6	0	1	1	8
1991-92	Kamloops	WHL	61	7	10	17	257	17	2	1	3	37

YUSHKEVICH, DIMITRI (yoush-KAY-vich)

Defense. Shoots left. 5'11", 187 lbs. Born, Cherepovets, Soviet Union, November 19, 1971.
(Philadelphia's 6th choice, 122nd overall, in 1991 Entry Draft).

			Regular Season					Playoffs				
Season	Club	Lea	GP	G	A	TP	PIM	GP	G	A	TP	PIM
1990-91	Torpedo Yaro.	USSR	41	10	4	14	22	....	....	....	....	....
1991-92	Moscow D'amo	CIS	35	5	7	12	14	....	....	....	....	....

YZERMAN, STEVE (IGH-zuhr-muhn)

Center. Shoots right. 5'11", 185 lbs. Born, Cranbrook, B.C., May 9, 1965.
(Detroit's 1st choice, 4th overall, in 1983 Entry Draft).

			Regular Season					Playoffs				
Season	Club	Lea	GP	G	A	TP	PIM	GP	G	A	TP	PIM
1981-82	Peterborough	OHL	58	21	43	64	65	6	0	1	1	16
1982-83	Peterborough	OHL	56	42	49	91	33	4	1	4	5	0
1983-84a	**Detroit**	**NHL**	**80**	**39**	**48**	**87**	**33**	**4**	**3**	**3**	**6**	**0**
1984-85	**Detroit**	**NHL**	**80**	**30**	**59**	**89**	**58**	**3**	**2**	**1**	**3**	**2**
1985-86	**Detroit**	**NHL**	**51**	**14**	**28**	**42**	**16**	....	....	....	....	....
1986-87	**Detroit**	**NHL**	**80**	**31**	**59**	**90**	**43**	**16**	**5**	**13**	**18**	**8**
1987-88	**Detroit**	**NHL**	**64**	**50**	**52**	**102**	**44**	**3**	**1**	**3**	**4**	**6**
1988-89b	**Detroit**	**NHL**	**80**	**65**	**90**	**155**	**61**	**6**	**5**	**5**	**10**	**2**
1989-90	**Detroit**	**NHL**	**79**	**62**	**65**	**127**	**79**	....	....	....	....	....
1990-91	**Detroit**	**NHL**	**80**	**51**	**57**	**108**	**34**	**7**	**3**	**3**	**6**	**4**
1991-92	**Detroit**	**NHL**	**79**	**45**	**58**	**103**	**64**	**11**	**3**	**5**	**8**	**12**
	NHL Totals		**673**	**387**	**516**	**903**	**432**	**50**	**22**	**33**	**55**	**34**

a NHL All-Rookie Team (1984)
b Won Lester B. Pearson Award (1989)

Played in NHL All-Star Game (1984, 1988-92)

ZALAPSKI, ZARLEY

Defense. Shoots left. 6'1", 211 lbs. Born, Edmonton, Alta., April 22, 1968.
(Pittsburgh's 1st choice, 4th overall, in 1986 Entry Draft).

			Regular Season					Playoffs				
Season	Club	Lea	GP	G	A	TP	PIM	GP	G	A	TP	PIM
1985-86	Cdn. Olympic	....	59	22	37	59	56	....	....	....	....	....
1986-87	Cdn. Olympic	....	74	11	29	40	28	....	....	....	....	....
1987-88	Cdn. National	....	47	3	13	16	32	....	....	....	....	....
	Cdn. Olympic	....	8	1	3	4	2	....	....	....	....	....
	Pittsburgh	**NHL**	**15**	**3**	**8**	**11**	**7**	....	....	....	....	....
1988-89a	**Pittsburgh**	**NHL**	**58**	**12**	**33**	**45**	**57**	**11**	**1**	**8**	**9**	**13**
1989-90	**Pittsburgh**	**NHL**	**51**	**6**	**25**	**31**	**37**	....	....	....	....	....
1990-91	**Pittsburgh**	**NHL**	**66**	**12**	**36**	**48**	**59**	....	....	....	....	....
	Hartford	**NHL**	**11**	**3**	**3**	**6**	**6**	**6**	**1**	**3**	**4**	**8**
1991-92	**Hartford**	**NHL**	**79**	**20**	**37**	**57**	**120**	**7**	**2**	**3**	**5**	**6**
	NHL Totals		**280**	**56**	**142**	**198**	**286**	**24**	**4**	**14**	**18**	**27**

a NHL All-Rookie Team (1989)

Traded to **Hartford** by **Pittsburgh** with John Cullen and Jeff Parker for Ron Francis, Grant Jennings and Ulf Samuelsson, March 4, 1991.

ZAMUNER, ROB (ZAM-un-uhr)

Center. Shoots left. 6'2", 202 lbs. Born, Oakville, Ont., September 17, 1969.
(NY Rangers' 3rd choice, 45th overall, in 1989 Entry Draft).

			Regular Season					Playoffs				
Season	Club	Lea	GP	G	A	TP	PIM	GP	G	A	TP	PIM
1986-87	Guelph	OHL	62	6	15	21	8	....	....	....	....	....
1987-88	Guelph	OHL	58	20	41	61	18	....	....	....	....	....
1988-89a	Guelph	OHL	66	46	65	111	38	7	5	5	10	9
1989-90	Flint	IHL	77	44	35	79	32	4	1	0	1	6
1990-91	Binghamton	AHL	80	25	58	83	50	9	7	6	13	35
1991-92	**NY Rangers**	**NHL**	**9**	**1**	**2**	**3**	**2**	....	....	....	....	....
	Binghamton	AHL	61	19	53	72	42	11	8	9	17	8
	NHL Totals		**9**	**1**	**2**	**3**	**2**	....	....	....	....	....

a OHL Third All-Star Team (1989)

Signed as a free agent by **Tampa Bay**, July 13, 1992.

ZAVISHA, BRAD

Left wing. Shoots left. 6'2", 205 lbs. Born, Hines Creek, Alta., January 4, 1972.
(Quebec's 3rd choice, 43rd overall, in 1990 Entry Draft).

			Regular Season					Playoffs				
Season	Club	Lea	GP	G	A	TP	PIM	GP	G	A	TP	PIM
1988-89	Seattle	WHL	52	8	13	21	43	....	....	....	....	....
1989-90	Seattle	WHL	69	22	38	60	124	13	1	6	7	16
1990-91	Seattle	WHL	24	15	12	27	40	....	....	....	....	....
	Portland	WHL	48	25	22	47	41	....	....	....	....	....
1991-92a	Portland	WHL	11	7	4	11	18	....	....	....	....	....
	Lethbridge	WHL	59	44	40	84	160	5	3	1	4	18

a WHL East First All-Star Team (1992)

Traded to **Edmonton** by **Quebec** with Ron Tugnutt for Martin Ruchinsky, March 10, 1992.

ZELEPUKIN, VALERI (zeh-leh-POO-kin)

Left wing. Shoots left. 5'11", 180 lbs. Born, Voskresensk, Soviet Union, September 17, 1968.
(New Jersey's 13th choice, 221st overall, in 1990 Entry Draft).

			Regular Season					Playoffs				
Season	Club	Lea	GP	G	A	TP	PIM	GP	G	A	TP	PIM
1984-85	Khimik	USSR	5	0	0	0	2	....	....	....	....	....
1985-86	Khimik	USSR	33	2	2	4	10	....	....	....	....	....
1986-87	Khimik	USSR	19	1	0	1	4	....	....	....	....	....
1987-88	SKA MVO	USSR	18	18	6	24	....	....	....	....	....	....
	CSKA	USSR	19	3	1	4	8	....	....	....	....	....
1988-89	CSKA	USSR	17	2	3	5	2	....	....	....	....	....
1989-90	Khimik	USSR	46	17	14	31	26	....	....	....	....	....
1990-91	Khimik	USSR	46	12	19	31	22	....	....	....	....	....
1991-92	**New Jersey**	**NHL**	**44**	**13**	**18**	**31**	**28**	**4**	**1**	**1**	**2**	**2**
	Utica	AHL	22	20	9	29	8	....	....	....	....	....
	NHL Totals		**44**	**13**	**18**	**31**	**28**	**4**	**1**	**1**	**2**	**2**

ZEMLAK, RICHARD ANDREW

Right wing. Shoots right. 6'2", 190 lbs. Born, Wynard, Sask., March 3, 1963.
(St. Louis' 9th choice, 209th overall, in 1981 Entry Draft).

			Regular Season					Playoffs				
Season	Club	Lea	GP	G	A	TP	PIM	GP	G	A	TP	PIM
1980-81	Spokane	WHL	72	19	19	38	132	4	1	1	2	6
1981-82	Spokane	WHL	26	9	20	29	113	....	....	....	....	....
	Winnipeg	WHL	2	1	2	3	0	....	....	....	....	....
	Medicine Hat	WHL	41	11	20	31	70	....	....	....	....	....
	Salt Lake	CHL	6	0	0	0	2	1	0	0	0	0
1982-83	Medicine Hat	WHL	51	20	17	37	119	....	....	....	....	....
	Nanaimo	WHL	18	2	8	10	50	....	....	....	....	....
1983-84	Montana	CHL	14	2	2	4	17	....	....	....	....	....
	Toledo	IHL	45	8	19	27	101	....	....	....	....	....
1984-85	Muskegon	IHL	64	19	18	37	223	17	5	4	9	68
	Fredericton	AHL	16	3	4	7	59	....	....	....	....	....
1985-86	Fredericton	AHL	58	6	5	11	305	3	0	0	0	49
	Muskegon	IHL	3	1	2	3	36	....	....	....	....	....
1986-87	**Quebec**	**NHL**	**20**	**0**	**2**	**2**	**47**	....	....	....	....	....
	Fredericton	AHL	29	9	6	15	201	....	....	....	....	....
1987-88	**Minnesota**	**NHL**	**54**	**1**	**4**	**5**	**307**	....	....	....	....	....
1988-89	**Minnesota**	**NHL**	**3**	**0**	**0**	**0**	**13**	....	....	....	....	....
	Kalamazoo	IHL	2	1	3	4	22	....	....	....	....	....
	Pittsburgh	**NHL**	**31**	**0**	**0**	**0**	**135**	**1**	**0**	**0**	**0**	**10**
	Muskegon	IHL	18	5	4	9	55	8	1	1	2	35
1989-90	**Pittsburgh**	**NHL**	**19**	**1**	**5**	**6**	**43**	....	....	....	....	....
	Muskegon	IHL	61	17	39	56	263	14	3	4	7	105
1990-91	Salt Lake	IHL	59	14	20	34	194	3	0	1	1	14
1991-92	**Calgary**	**NHL**	**5**	**0**	**1**	**1**	**42**	....	....	....	....	....
	Salt Lake	IHL	60	5	14	19	204	3	0	0	0	0
	NHL Totals		**132**	**2**	**12**	**14**	**587**	**1**	**0**	**0**	**0**	**10**

Rights sold to **Quebec** by **St. Louis** with rights to Dan Wood and Roger Hagglund, June 22, 1984. Claimed by **Minnesota** in NHL Waiver Draft, October 5, 1987. Traded to **Pittsburgh** by **Minnesota** for the rights to Rob Gaudreau, November 1, 1988. Signed as a free agent by **Calgary**, November 8, 1990.

ZEMLICKA, RICHARD (zhem-LEECH-kah)

Right/Left wing. Shoots left. 6'1", 189 lbs. Born, Czechoslovakia, April 13, 1964.
(Edmonton's 9th choice, 185th overall, in 1990 Entry Draft).

			Regular Season					Playoffs				
Season	Club	Lea	GP	G	A	TP	PIM	GP	G	A	TP	PIM
1987-88	Sparta Praha	Czech.	44	8	10	18	32	....	....	....	....	....
1988-89	Sparta Praha	Czech.	42	20	17	37	40	....	....	....	....	....
1989-90	Sparta Praha	Czech.	45	15	14	29	....	....	....	....	....	....
1990-91	Sparta Praha	Czech.	51	22	30	52	99	....	....	....	....	....
1991-92	Sparta Praha	Czech.	27	14	23	37	....	....	....	....	....	....
	TPS	Fin.	15	5	9	14	6	3	2	1	3	0

ZENT, JASON

Left wing. Shoots left. 5'11", 180 lbs. Born, Buffalo, NY, April 15, 1971.
(NY Islanders' 3rd choice, 44th overall, in 1989 Entry Draft).

			Regular Season					Playoffs				
Season	Club	Lea	GP	G	A	TP	PIM	GP	G	A	TP	PIM
1990-91	U. Wisconsin	WCHA	39	19	18	37	51	....	....	....	....	....
1991-92a	U. Wisconsin	WCHA	39	22	17	39	128	....	....	....	....	....

a NCAA All-Tournament Team (1992)

ZETTLER, ROB

Defense. Shoots left. 6'3", 195 lbs. Born, Sept Iles, Que., March 8, 1968.
(Minnesota's 5th choice, 55th overall, in 1986 Entry Draft).

			Regular Season					Playoffs				
Season	Club	Lea	GP	G	A	TP	PIM	GP	G	A	TP	PIM
1985-86	S.S. Marie	OHL	57	5	23	28	92	....	....	....	....	....
1986-87	S.S. Marie	OHL	64	13	22	35	89	4	0	0	0	0
1987-88	Kalamazoo	IHL	2	0	1	1	0	7	0	2	2	2
	S.S. Marie	OHL	64	7	41	48	77	6	2	2	4	9
1988-89	**Minnesota**	**NHL**	**2**	**0**	**0**	**0**	**0**	....	....	....	....	....
	Kalamazoo	IHL	80	5	21	26	79	6	0	1	1	26
1989-90	**Minnesota**	**NHL**	**31**	**0**	**8**	**8**	**45**	....	....	....	....	....
	Kalamazoo	IHL	41	6	10	16	64	7	0	0	0	6
1990-91	**Minnesota**	**NHL**	**47**	**1**	**4**	**5**	**119**	....	....	....	....	....
	Kalamazoo	IHL	1	0	0	0	2	....	....	....	....	....
1991-92	**San Jose**	**NHL**	**74**	**1**	**8**	**9**	**99**	....	....	....	....	....
	NHL Totals		**154**	**2**	**20**	**22**	**263**	....	....	....	....	....

Claimed by **San Jose** from **Minnesota** in Dispersal Draft, May 30, 1991.

ZEZEL, PETER (ZEH-zuhl)

Center. Shoots left. 5'11", 200 lbs. Born, Toronto, Ont., April 22, 1965.
(Philadelphia's 1st choice, 41st overall, in 1983 Entry Draft).

			Regular Season					Playoffs				
Season	Club	Lea	GP	G	A	TP	PIM	GP	G	A	TP	PIM
1982-83	Toronto	OHL	66	35	39	74	28	4	2	4	6	0
1983-84	Toronto	OHL	68	47	86	133	31	9	7	5	12	4
1984-85	**Philadelphia**	**NHL**	**65**	**15**	**46**	**61**	**26**	**19**	**1**	**8**	**9**	**28**
1985-86	**Philadelphia**	**NHL**	**79**	**17**	**37**	**54**	**76**	**5**	**3**	**1**	**4**	**4**
1986-87	**Philadelphia**	**NHL**	**71**	**33**	**39**	**72**	**71**	**25**	**3**	**10**	**13**	**10**
1987-88	**Philadelphia**	**NHL**	**69**	**22**	**35**	**57**	**42**	**7**	**3**	**2**	**5**	**7**
1988-89	**Philadelphia**	**NHL**	**26**	**4**	**13**	**17**	**15**	....	....	....	....	....
	St. Louis	**NHL**	**52**	**17**	**36**	**53**	**27**	**10**	**6**	**6**	**12**	**4**
1989-90	**St. Louis**	**NHL**	**73**	**25**	**47**	**72**	**30**	**12**	**1**	**7**	**8**	**4**
1990-91	**Washington**	**NHL**	**20**	**7**	**5**	**12**	**10**	....	....	....	....	....
	Toronto	**NHL**	**32**	**14**	**14**	**28**	**4**	....	....	....	....	....
1991-92	**Toronto**	**NHL**	**64**	**16**	**33**	**49**	**26**	....	....	....	....	....
	NHL Totals		**551**	**170**	**305**	**475**	**327**	**78**	**17**	**34**	**51**	**57**

Traded to **St. Louis** by **Philadelphia** for Mike Bullard, November 29, 1988. Traded to **Washington** by **St. Louis** with Mike Lalor for Geoff Courtnall, July 13, 1990. Traded to **Toronto** by **Washington** with Bob Rouse for Al Iafrate, January 16, 1991.

ZHAMNOV, ALEXEI (zham-NOV)

Center. Shoots left. 6'1", 187 lbs. Born, Moscow, Soviet Union, October 1, 1970.
(Winnipeg's 5th choice, 77th overall, in 1990 Entry Draft).

			Regular Season					Playoffs				
Season	Club	Lea	GP	G	A	TP	PIM	GP	G	A	TP	PIM
1989-90	Moscow D'amo	USSR	43	11	6	17	21	....	....	....	....	....
1990-91	Moscow D'amo	USSR	46	16	12	28	24	....	....	....	....	....
1991-92	Moscow D'amo	CIS	39	15	21	36	28	....	....	....	....	....

ZHITNIK, ALEXEI (ZHIT-nik)

Defense. Shoots left. 5'10", 178 lbs. Born, Kiev, Soviet Union, October 10, 1972.
(Los Angeles' 4th choice, 81st overall, in 1991 Entry Draft).

			Regular Season					Playoffs				
Season	Club	Lea	GP	G	A	TP	PIM	GP	G	A	TP	PIM
1990-91	Sokol Kiev	USSR	40	1	4	5	46	....	....	....	....	....
1991-92	CSKA	CIS	36	2	7	9	48	....	....	....	....	....

ZHOLTOK, SERGEI (ZHOL-tok)

Left wing. Shoots right. 6', 185 lbs. Born, Riga, Soviet Union, December 2, 1972.
(Boston's 2nd choice, 55th overall, in 1992 Entry Draft).

			Regular Season					Playoffs				
Season	Club	Lea	GP	G	A	TP	PIM	GP	G	A	TP	PIM
1990-91	Dynamo Riga	USSR	4	0	4	4	16	....	....	....	....	....
1991-92	Riga	CIS	27	6	3	9	6	....	....	....	....	....

ZMOLEK, DOUG

Defense. Shoots left. 6'1", 195 lbs. Born, Rochester, MN, November 3, 1970.
(Minnesota's 1st choice, 7th overall, in 1989 Entry Draft).

			Regular Season					Playoffs				
Season	Club	Lea	GP	G	A	TP	PIM	GP	G	A	TP	PIM
1989-90	U. Minnesota	WCHA	40	1	10	11	52	....	....	....	....	....
1990-91	U. Minnesota	WCHA	34	11	6	17	38	....	....	....	....	....
1991-92ab	U. Minnesota	WCHA	41	6	20	26	84	....	....	....	....	....

a WCHA Second All-Star Team (1992)
b NCAA West Second All-Star Team (1992)

Claimed by **San Jose** from **Minnesota** in Dispersal Draft, May 30, 1991.

ZOLOTOV, SERGEI (ZOH-loh-tov)

Left wing. Shoots left. 5'10", 172 lbs. Born, Moscow, Soviet Union, January 27, 1971.
(Calgary's 11th choice, 219th overall, in 1991 Entry Draft).

			Regular Season					Playoffs				
Season	Club	Lea	GP	G	A	TP	PIM	GP	G	A	TP	PIM
1990-91	Soviet Wings	USSR	42	9	6	15	12	....	....	....	....	....
1991-92	Soviet Wings	CIS	32	10	5	15	2	....	....	....	....	....

ZOMBO, RICHARD (RICK)

Defense. Shoots right. 6'1", 195 lbs. Born, Des Plaines, IL, May 8, 1963.
(Detroit's 6th choice, 149th overall, in 1981 Entry Draft).

			Regular Season					Playoffs				
Season	Club	Lea	GP	G	A	TP	PIM	GP	G	A	TP	PIM
1981-82	North Dakota	WCHA	45	1	15	16	31	....	....	....	....	....
1982-83	North Dakota	WCHA	35	5	11	16	41	....	....	....	....	....
1983-84	North Dakota	WCHA	34	7	24	31	40	....	....	....	....	....
1984-85	**Detroit**	**NHL**	**1**	**0**	**0**	**0**	**0**	....	....	....	....	....
	Adirondack	AHL	56	3	32	35	70	....	....	....	....	....
1985-86	**Detroit**	**NHL**	**14**	**0**	**1**	**1**	**16**	....	....	....	....	....
	Adirondack	AHL	69	7	34	41	94	17	0	4	4	40
1986-87	**Detroit**	**NHL**	**44**	**1**	**4**	**5**	**59**	**7**	**0**	**1**	**1**	**9**
	Adirondack	AHL	25	0	6	6	22	....	....	....	....	....
1987-88	**Detroit**	**NHL**	**62**	**3**	**14**	**17**	**96**	**16**	**0**	**6**	**6**	**55**
1988-89	**Detroit**	**NHL**	**75**	**1**	**20**	**21**	**106**	**6**	**0**	**1**	**1**	**16**
1989-90	**Detroit**	**NHL**	**77**	**5**	**20**	**25**	**95**	....	....	....	....	....
1990-91	**Detroit**	**NHL**	**77**	**4**	**19**	**23**	**55**	**7**	**1**	**0**	**1**	**10**
1991-92	**Detroit**	**NHL**	**3**	**0**	**0**	**0**	**15**	....	....	....	....	....
	St. Louis	**NHL**	**64**	**3**	**15**	**18**	**46**	**6**	**0**	**2**	**2**	**12**
	NHL Totals		**417**	**17**	**93**	**110**	**488**	**42**	**1**	**10**	**11**	**102**

Traded to **St. Louis** by **Detroit** for Vincent Riendeau, October 18, 1991.

ZUBOV, SERGEI (ZOO-bahf)

Defense. Shoots right. 6', 187 lbs. Born, Moscow, Soviet Union, July 22, 1970.
(NY Rangers' 6th choice, 85th overall, in 1990 Entry Draft).

			Regular Season					Playoffs				
Season	Club	Lea	GP	G	A	TP	PIM	GP	G	A	TP	PIM
1988-89	CSKA	USSR	29	1	4	5	10	....	....	....	....	....
1989-90	CSKA	USSR	48	6	2	8	16	....	....	....	....	....
1990-91	CSKA	USSR	41	6	5	11	12	....	....	....	....	....
1991-92	CSKA	CIS	44	4	7	11	8	....	....	....	....	....

ZYGULSKI, SCOTT

Defense. Shoots right. 6'1", 190 lbs. Born, South Bend, IN, April 11, 1970.
(Detroit's 7th choice, 137th overall, in 1989 Entry Draft).

			Regular Season					Playoffs				
Season	Club	Lea	GP	G	A	TP	PIM	GP	G	A	TP	PIM
1989-90	Boston College	H.E.	14	0	1	1	6	....	....	....	....	....
1990-91	Boston College	H.E.	25	0	5	5	2	....	....	....	....	....
1991-92	Boston College	H.E.	32	0	4	4	24	....	....	....	....	....

Late Additions to Player and Goaltender Registers

Marc Bergevin signed as a free agent by Tampa Bay, July 9, 1992.

David Marcinyshyn signed as a free agent by NY Rangers, August 5, 1992.

Jim Benning signed as a free agent by Tampa Bay, August 11, 1992.

Petri Skriko signed as a free agent by San Jose, August 27, 1992.

Shayne Corson, **Brent Gilchrist** and **Vladimir Vujtek** traded to Edmonton by Montreal for **Vincent Damphousse** and Edmonton's fourth round choice in 1993 Entry Draft, August 27, 1992.

Sean Burke and **Eric Weinrich** traded to Hartford by New Jersey for **Bobby Holik**, Hartford's second round choice in 1993 Entry Draft and future considerations, August 28, 1992.

Hubie McDonough traded to San Jose by NY Islanders for cash, August 28, 1992.

Brian Bellows traded to Montreal by Minnesota for **Russ Courtnall**, August 31, 1992.

Phil Bourque signed as a free agent by NY Rangers, August 31, 1992.

David Shaw traded to Boston by Minnesota for future considerations, September 2, 1992.

James Black traded to Minnesota by Hartford for **Mark Janssens**, September 3, 1992.

Neil Brady traded to Ottawa by New Jersey for future considerations, September 3, 1992.

Pat Conacher traded to Los Angeles by New Jersey for future considerations, September 3, 1992.

Matt Hervey and **Ken Hodge** traded to Tampa Bay by Boston for **Darin Kimble** and future considerations, September 4, 1992.

Retired NHL Player Index

Abbreviations: Teams/Cities: — **Atl.** – Atlanta, **Bos.** – Boston; **Bro.** – Brooklyn; **Buf.** – Buffalo; **Cal.** – California; **Cgy.** – Calgary; **Chi.** – Chicago; **Cle.** – Cleveland; **Col.** – Colorado; **Det.** – Detroit; **Edm.** – Edmonton; **Ham.** – Hamilton; **Hfd.** – Hartford; **K.C.** – Kansas City; **L.A.** – Los Angeles; **Min.** – Minnesota; **Mtl.** – Montreal; **Mtl.M.** – Montreal Maroons; **Mtl.W.** – Montreal Wanderers; **N.J.** – New Jersey; **NYA** – NY Americans; **NYI** – New York Islanders; **NYR** – New York Rangers; **Oak.** – Oakland; **Ott.** – Ottawa; **Phi.** – Philadelphia; **Pit.** – Pittsburgh; **Que.** – Quebec; **St.L.** – St. Louis; **Tor.** – Toronto; **Van.** – Vancouver; **Wpg.** – Winnipeg; **Wsh.** – Washington.

Total seasons are rounded off to the nearest full season. **A** – assists; **G** – goals; **GP** – games played; **PIM** – penalties in minutes; **TP** – total points. * – deceased. Assists not recorded during 1917-18 season.

Fred Ahern

Syl Apps

Al Arbour

Don Awrey

			Regular Schedule					Playoffs					NHL	First	Last
Name	NHL Teams	NHL Seasons	GP	G	A	TP	PIM	GP	G	A	TP	PIM	Cup Wins	NHL Season	NHL Season
A															
Abbott, Reg	Mtl.	1	3	0	0	0	0	....	....	....	....	....		1952-53	1952-53
* Abel, Clarence	NYR, Chi.	8	333	18	18	36	359	38	1	1	2	58	2	1926-27	1933-34
Abel, Gerry	Det.	1	1	0	0	0	0	....	....	....	....	....		1966-67	1966-67
Abel, Sid	Det., Chi.	14	613	189	283	472	376	96	28	30	58	77	3	1938-39	1953-54
Abgrall, Dennis	L.A.	1	13	0	2	2	4	....	....	....	....	....		1975-76	1975-76
Abrahamsson, Thommy	Hfd.	1	32	6	11	17	16	....	....	....	....	....		1980-81	1980-81
Achtymichuk, Gene	Mtl., Det.	4	32	3	5	8	2	....	....	....	....	....		1951-52	1958-59
Acomb, Doug	Tor.	1	2	0	1	1	0	....	....	....	....	....		1969-70	1969-70
Adam, Douglas	NYR	1	4	0	1	1	0	....	....	....	....	....		1949-50	1949-50
Adam, Russ	Tor.	1	8	1	2	3	11	....	....	....	....	....		1982-83	1982-83
Adams, Greg C.	Phi., Hfd., Wsh., Edm., Van., Que., Det.	10	545	84	143	227	1173	43	2	11	13	153		1980-81	1989-90
* Adams, Jack J.	Tor., Ott.	7	173	82	29	111	307	10	3	0	3	12	2	1917-18	1926-27
Adams, Jack	Mtl.	1	42	6	12	18	11	3	0	0	0	0		1940-41	1940-41
Adams, Stewart	Chi., Tor.	4	106	9	26	35	60	11	3	3	6	14		1929-30	1932-33
Adduono, Rick	Bos., Atl.	2	4	0	0	0	2	....	....	....	....	....		1975-76	1979-80
Affleck, Bruce	St.L., Van., NYI	7	280	14	66	80	86	8	0	0	0	0		1974-75	1983-84
Ahern, Fred	Cal., Cle., Col.	4	146	31	30	61	130	2	0	1	1	2		1974-75	1977-78
Ahlin	Chi.	1	1	0	0	0	0	....	....	....	....	....		1937-38	1937-38
Ahrens, Chris	Min.	6	52	0	3	3	14	1	0	0	0	0		1973-74	1977-78
Ailsby, Lloyd	NYR	1	3	0	0	0	2	....	....	....	....	....		1951-52	1951-52
Albright, Clint	NYR	1	59	14	5	19	19	....	....	....	....	....		1948-49	1948-49
Aldcorn, Gary	Tor., Det., Bos.	5	226	41	56	97	78	6	1	2	3	4		1956-57	1960-61
Alexander, Claire	Tor., Van.	4	155	18	47	65	36	16	2	4	6	4		1974-75	1977-78
Alexandre, Art	Mtl.	2	11	0	2	2	8	4	0	0	0	0		1931-32	1932-33
Allen, George	NYR, Chi., Mtl.	8	339	82	115	197	179	41	9	10	19	32		1938-39	1946-47
Allen, Jeff	Cle.	1	4	0	0	0	2	....	....	....	....	....		1977-78	1977-78
Allen, Keith	Det.	2	28	0	4	4	8	5	0	0	0	0	1	1953-54	1954-55
Allen, Viv	NYA	1	6	0	1	1	0	....	....	....	....	....		1940-41	1940-41
Alley, Steve	Hfd.	2	15	3	3	6	11	3	0	1	1	0		1979-80	1980-81
Allison, Dave	Mtl.	1	3	0	0	0	12	....	....	....	....	....		1983-84	1983-84
Allison, Mike	NYR, Tor., L.A.	10	499	102	166	268	630	82	9	17	26	135		1980-81	1989-90
Allison, Ray	Hfd., Phi.	7	238	64	93	157	223	12	2	3	5	20		1979-80	1986-87
Allum, Bill	NYR	1	1	0	1	1	0	....	....	....	....	....		1940-41	1940-41
Amadio, Dave	Det., L.A.	3	125	5	11	16	163	16	1	2	3	18		1957-58	1968-69
Amodeo, Mike	Wpg.	1	19	0	0	0	2	....	....	....	....	....		1979-80	1979-80
Anderson, Bill	Bos.	1	....	....	....	....	....	1	0	0	0	0		1942-43	1942-43
Anderson, Dale	Det.	1	13	0	0	0	6	2	0	0	0	0		1956-57	1956-57
Anderson, Doug	Mtl.	1	....	....	....	....	....	2	0	0	0	0	1	1952-53	1952-53
Anderson, Earl	Det., Bos.	3	109	19	19	38	22	5	0	1	1	0		1974-75	1976-77
Anderson, Jim	L.A.	1	7	1	2	3	2	....	....	....	....	....		1967-68	1967-68
Anderson, Murray	Wsh.	1	40	0	1	1	68	....	....	....	....	....		1974-75	1974-75
Anderson, Ron C.	Det., L.A., St.L., Buf.	5	251	28	30	58	146	5	0	0	0	4		1967-68	1971-72
Anderson, Ron H.	Wsh.	1	28	9	7	16	8	....	....	....	....	....		1974-75	1974-75
Anderson, Russ	Pit., Hfd., L.A.	10	519	22	99	121	1086	10	0	3	3	28		1976-77	1984-85
Anderson, Tom	Det., NYA, Bro.	8	319	62	127	189	190	16	2	7	9	62		1934-35	1941-42
Andersson, Kent-Erik	Min., NYR	7	456	72	103	175	78	50	4	11	15	4		1977-78	1983-84
Andersson, Peter	Wsh., Que.	3	172	10	41	51	80	7	0	2	2	2		1983-84	1985-86
Andrascik, Steve	NYR	1	....	....	....	....	....	1	0	0	0	0		1971-72	1971-72
Andrea, Paul	NYR, Pit., Cal., Buf.	4	150	31	49	80	12	....	....	....	....	....		1965-66	1970-71
Andrews, Lloyd	Tor.	4	53	8	5	13	10	7	2	0	2	5		1921-22	1924-25
Andruff, Ron	Mtl., Col.,	5	153	19	36	55	54	2	0	0	0	0		1974-75	1978-79
Angotti, Lou	NYR, Chi., Phi., Pit., St.L.	10	653	103	186	289	228	65	8	8	16	17		1964-65	1973-74
Anholt, Darrel	Chi.	1	1	0	0	0	0	....	....	....	....	....		1983-84	1983-84
Anslow, Bert	NYR	1	2	0	0	0	0	....	....	....	....	....		1947-48	1947-48
Antonovich, Mike	Min., Hfd., N.J.	5	87	10	15	25	37	....	....	....	....	....		1975-76	1983-84
Apps, Syl (Jr.)	NYR, Pit., L.A.	10	727	183	423	606	311	23	5	5	10	23		1970-71	1979-80
Apps, Syl (Sr.)	Tor.	10	423	201	231	432	56	69	25	28	53	16	3	1936-37	1947-48
Arbour, Al	Det., Chi., Tor., St.L.	14	626	12	58	70	617	86	1	8	9	92	3	1953-54	1970-71
* Arbour, Amos	Mtl., Ham., Tor.	6	109	51	13	64	66	....	....	....	....	....		1918-19	1923-24
Arbour, Jack	Det., Tor.	2	47	5	1	6	56	....	....	....	....	....		1926-27	1928-29
Arbour, John	Bos., Pit., Van., St.L.	5	106	1	9	10	149	5	0	0	0	0		1965-66	1971-72
Arbour, Ty	Pit., Chi.	5	207	28	28	56	112	11	2	0	2	6		1926-27	1930-31
Archambault, Michel	Chi.	1	3	0	0	0	0	....	....	....	....	....		1976-77	1976-77
Archibald, Jim	Min.	3	16	1	2	3	45	....	....	....	....	....		1984-85	1986-87
Areshenkoff, Ronald	Edm.	1	4	0	0	0	0	....	....	....	....	....		1979-80	1979-80
* Armstrong, Bob	Bos.	12	542	13	86	99	671	42	1	7	8	28		1950-51	1961-62
Armstrong, George	Tor.	21	1187	296	417	713	721	110	26	34	60	88	4	1949-50	1970-71
Armstrong, Murray	Tor., NYA, Bro., Det.	8	270	67	121	188	62	30	4	6	10	2		1937-38	1945-46
Armstrong, Red	Tor.	1	7	1	1	2	2	....	....	....	....	....		1962-63	1962-63
Armstrong, Tim	Tor.	1	11	1	0	1	6	....	....	....	....	....		1988-89	1988-89
Arnason, Chuck	Mtl., Atl., Pit., K.C., Col., Cle., Min., Wsh.	8	401	109	90	199	122	9	2	4	6	4		1971-72	1978-79
Arthur, Fred	Hfd., Phi.	3	80	1	8	9	49	4	0	0	0	2		1980-81	1982-83
Arundel, John	Tor.	1	3	0	0	0	0	....	....	....	....	....		1949-50	1949-50
* Ashbee, Barry	Bos., Phi.	5	284	15	70	85	291	17	0	4	4	22	1	1965-66	1973-74
* Ashby, Don	Tor., Col., Edm.	6	188	40	56	96	40	12	1	0	1	4		1975-76	1980-81
Ashworth, Frank	Chi.	1	18	5	4	9	2	....	....	....	....	....		1946-47	1946-47
Asmundson, Oscar	NYR, Det., St.L., NYA, Mtl.	5	112	11	23	34	30	9	0	2	2	4	1	1932-33	1937-38
Atanas, Walt	NYR	1	49	13	8	21	40	....	....	....	....	....		1944-45	1944-45
Atkinson, Steve	Bos., Buf., Wsh.	6	302	60	51	111	104	1	0	0	0	0		1968-69	1974-75
Attwell, Bob	Col.	2	22	1	5	6	0	....	....	....	....	....		1979-80	1980-81
Attwell, Ron	St.L., NYR	1	21	1	7	8	8	....	....	....	....	....		1967-68	1967-68
Aubin, Norm	Tor.	2	69	18	13	31	30	1	0	0	0	0		1981-82	1982-83
Aubry, Pierre	Que., Det.	5	202	24	26	50	133	20	1	1	2	32		1980-81	1984-85
Aubuchon, Ossie	Bos., NYR	2	50	19	12	31	4	6	1	0	1	0		1942-43	1943-44
Auge, Les	Col.	1	6	0	3	3	4	....	....	....	....	....		1980-81	1980-81
* Aurie, Larry	Det.	12	489	147	129	276	279	24	6	9	15	10	2	1927-28	1938-39
Awrey, Don	Bos., St.L., Mtl., Pit., NYR, Col.	16	979	31	158	189	1065	71	0	18	18	150	2	1963-64	1978-79
Ayres, Vern	NYA, Mtl.M., St.L., NYR	6	211	6	14	20	350	....	....	....	....	....		1930-31	1935-36
B															
Babando, Pete	Bos., Det., Chi., NYR	6	351	86	73	159	194	17	3	3	6	6	1	1947-48	1952-53
Babe, Warren	Min.	3	21	2	5	7	23	2	0	0	0	0		1987-88	1990-91
Babin, Mitch	St.L.	1	8	0	0	0	0	....	....	....	....	....		1975-76	1975-76
Baby, John	Cle., Min.	2	26	2	8	10	26	....	....	....	....	....		1977-78	1978-79
Babych, Wayne	St.L., Pit., Que., Hfd.	9	519	192	246	438	498	41	7	9	16	25		1978-79	1986-87
Backman, Mike	NYR	3	18	1	6	7	18	10	2	2	4	2		1981-82	1983-84
Backor, Peter	Tor.	1	36	4	5	9	6	....	....	....	....	....	1	1944-45	1944-45
Backstrom, Ralph	Mtl., L.A., Chi.	17	1032	278	361	639	386	116	27	32	59	68	6	1956-57	1972-73

Frank Bathe

Jean Beliveau

Red Berenson

Gregg Boddy

Name	NHL Teams	NHL Seasons	Regular Schedule GP	G	A	TP	PIM	Playoffs GP	G	A	TP	PIM	NHL Cup Wins	First NHL Season	Last NHL Season
Bailey, Ace (G.)	Bos., Det., St.L., Wsh.	10	568	107	171	278	633	15	2	4	6	28	1	1968-69	1977-78
* Bailey, Ace (I.)	Tor.	8	314	111	82	193	472	20	3	4	7	12	1	1926-27	1933-34
Bailey, Bob	Tor., Det., Chi.	4	150	15	21	36	207	15	0	4	4	22		1953-54	1957-58
Bailey, Reid	Phi., Tor., Hfd.	4	40	1	3	4	105	16	0	2	2	25		1980-81	1983-84
Baillargeon, Joel	Wpg., Que.	3	20	0	2	2	31	....	....	....	....	....		1986-87	1988-89
Baird, Ken	Cal.	1	10	0	2	2	15	....	....	....	....	....		1971-72	1971-72
Baker, Bill	Mtl., Col., St.L., NYR	3	143	7	25	32	175	6	0	0	0	0		1980-81	1982-83
Bakovic, Peter	Van.	1	10	2	0	2	48	....	....	....	....	....		1987-88	1987-88
Balderis, Helmut	Min.	1	26	3	6	9	2	....	....	....	....	....		1989-90	1989-90
Baldwin, Doug	Tor., Det., Chi.	3	24	0	1	1	8	....	....	....	....	....		1945-46	1947-48
Balfour, Earl	Tor., Chi.	7	288	30	22	52	78	26	0	3	3	4	1	1951-52	1960-61
* Balfour, Murray	Mtl., Chi., Bos.	8	306	67	90	157	393	40	9	10	19	45	1	1956-57	1964-65
Ball, Terry	Phi., Buf.	4	74	7	19	26	26	....	....	....	....	....		1967-68	1971-72
Balon, Dave	NYR, Mtl., Min., Van.	14	776	192	222	414	607	78	14	21	35	109	2	1959-60	1972-73
Baltimore, Byron	Edm.	1	2	0	0	0	4	....	....	....	....	....		1979-80	1979-80
Baluik, Stanley	Bos.	1	7	0	0	0	2	....	....	....	....	....		1959-60	1959-60
Bandura, Jeff	NYR	1	2	0	1	1	0	....	....	....	....	....		1980-81	1980-81
Barbe, Andy	Tor.	1	1	0	0	0	2	....	....	....	....	....		1950-51	1950-51
Barber, Bill	Phi.	12	903	420	463	883	623	129	53	55	108	109	2	1972-73	1984-85
* Barilko, Bill	Tor.	5	252	26	36	62	456	47	5	7	12	104	4	1946-47	1950-51
Barkley, Doug	Chi., Det.	6	253	24	80	104	382	30	0	9	9	63		1957-58	1965-66
Barlow, Bob	Min.	2	77	16	17	33	10	6	2	2	4	6		1969-70	1970-71
Barnes, Blair	L.A.	1	1	0	0	0	0	....	....	....	....	....		1982-83	1982-83
Barnes, Norm	Phi., Hfd.	4	156	6	38	44	178	12	0	0	0	8		1976-77	1981-82
Baron, Normand	Mtl., St.L.	2	27	2	0	2	51	3	0	0	0	22		1983-84	1985-86
Barrett, Fred	Min., L.A.	13	745	25	123	148	671	44	0	2	2	60		1970-71	1983-84
Barrett, John	Det., Wsh., Min.	8	488	20	77	97	604	16	2	2	4	50		1980-81	1987-88
Barrie, Doug	Pit., Buf., L.A.	3	158	10	42	52	268	....	....	....	....	....		1968-69	1971-72
Barry, Ed	Bos.	1	19	1	3	4	2	....	....	....	....	....		1946-47	1946-47
* Barry, Marty	NYA, Bos., Det., Mtl.	12	509	195	192	387	231	43	15	18	33	34	2	1927-28	1939-40
Barry, Ray	Bos.	1	18	1	2	3	6	....	....	....	....	....		1951-52	1951-52
Bartel, Robin	Cgy., Van.	2	41	0	1	1	14	6	0	0	0	16		1985-86	1986-87
Bartel, Robin	Cgy., Van.	2	41	0	1	1	14	6	0	0	0	0		1985-86	1986-87
Bartlett, Jim	Mtl., NYR, Bos.	5	191	34	23	57	273	2	0	0	0	0		1954-55	1960-61
Barton, Cliff	Pit., Phi., NYR	3	85	10	9	19	22	....	....	....	....	....		1929-30	1939-40
Bathe, Frank	Det., Phi.	9	224	3	28	31	542	27	1	3	4	42		1974-75	1983-84
Bathgate, Andy	NYR, Tor., Det., Pit.	17	1069	349	624	973	624	54	21	14	35	76	1	1952-53	1970-71
Bathgate, Frank	NYR	1	2	0	0	0	2	....	....	....	....	....		1952-53	1952-53
* Bauer, Bobby	Bos.	10	327	123	137	260	36	48	11	8	19	6	2	1935-36	1951-52
Baumgartner, Mike	K.C.	1	17	0	0	0	0	....	....	....	....	....		1974-75	1974-75
Baun, Bob	Tor., Oak., Det.	17	964	37	187	224	1493	96	3	12	15	171	4	1956-57	1972-73
Baxter, Paul	Que., Pit., Cgy.	8	472	48	121	169	1564	40	0	5	5	162		1979-80	1986-87
Beadle, Sandy	Wpg.	1	6	1	0	1	2	....	....	....	....	....		1980-81	1980-81
Beaton, Frank	NYR	2	25	1	1	2	43	....	....	....	....	....		1978-79	1979-80
Beattie, Red	Bos., Det., NYA	9	335	62	85	147	137	22	4	2	6	6		1930-31	1938-39
Beaudin, Norm	St.L., Min.	2	25	1	2	3	4	....	....	....	....	....		1967-68	1970-71
Beaudoin, Serge	Atl.	1	3	0	0	0	0	....	....	....	....	....		1979-80	1979-80
Beaudoin, Yves	Wsh.	3	11	0	0	0	5	....	....	....	....	....		1985-86	1987-88
Beck, Barry	Col., NYR, L.A.	10	615	104	251	355	1016	51	10	23	33	77		1977-78	1989-90
Beckett, Bob	Bos.	4	68	7	6	13	18	....	....	....	....	....		1956-57	1963-64
Bedard, James	Chi.	2	22	1	1	2	8	....	....	....	....	....		1949-50	1950-51
Bednarski, John	NYR, Edm.	4	100	2	18	20	114	1	0	0	0	0		1974-75	1979-80
Beers, Eddy	Cgy., St.L.	5	250	94	116	210	256	41	7	10	17	47		1981-82	1985-86
Behling, Dick	Det.	2	5	1	0	1	2	....	....	....	....	....		1940-41	1942-43
Beisler, Frank	NYA	2	2	0	0	0	0	....	....	....	....	....		1936-37	1939-40
Belanger, Alain	Tor.	1	9	0	1	1	6	....	....	....	....	....		1977-78	1977-78
Belanger, Roger	Pit.	1	44	3	5	8	32	....	....	....	....	....		1984-85	1984-85
Belisle, Danny	NYR	1	4	2	0	2	0	....	....	....	....	....		1960-61	1960-61
Beliveau, Jean	Mtl.	20	1125	507	712	1219	1029	162	79	97	176	211	10	1950-51	1970-71
* Bell, Billy	Mtl.W, Mtl., Ott.	6	61	3	1	4	4	9	0	0	0	0	1	1917-18	1923-24
Bell, Harry	NYR	1	1	0	1	1	0	....	....	....	....	....		1946-47	1946-47
Bell, Joe	NYR	2	62	8	9	17	18	....	....	....	....	....		1942-43	1946-47
Belland, Neil	Van., Pit.	6	109	13	32	45	54	21	2	9	11	23		1981-82	1986-87
Bellefeuille, Pete	Tor., Det.	4	92	26	4	30	58	....	....	....	....	....		1925-26	1929-30
Bellemer, Andy	Mtl.M.	1	15	0	0	0	0	....	....	....	....	....		1932-33	1932-33
Bend, Lin	NYR	1	8	3	1	4	2	....	....	....	....	....		1942-43	1942-43
Bennett, Bill	Bos., Hfd.	2	31	4	7	11	65	....	....	....	....	....		1978-79	1979-80
Bennett, Curt	St.L., NYR, Atl.	10	580	152	182	334	347	21	1	1	2	57		1970-71	1979-80
Bennett, Frank	Det.	1	7	0	1	1	2	....	....	....	....	....		1943-44	1943-44
Bennett, Harvey	Pit., Wsh., Phi., Min., St.L.	5	268	44	46	90	347	4	0	0	0	2		1974-75	1978-79
Bennett, Max	Mtl.	1	1	0	0	0	0	....	....	....	....	....		1935-36	1935-36
Benoit, Joe	Mtl.	5	185	75	69	144	94	11	6	3	9	11	1	1940-41	1946-47
Benson, Bill	NYA, Bro.	2	67	11	25	36	35	....	....	....	....	....		1940-41	1941-42
Benson, Bobby	Bos.	1	8	0	1	1	4	....	....	....	....	....		1924-25	1924-25
* Bentley, Doug	Chi., NYR	13	566	219	324	543	217	23	9	8	17	8		1939-40	1953-54
* Bentley, Max	Chi., Tor., NYR	12	646	245	299	544	179	52	18	27	45	14	3	1940-41	1953-54
Bentley, Reggie	Chi.	1	11	1	2	3	2	....	....	....	....	....		1942-43	1942-43
Berenson, Red	Mtl., NYR, St.L., Det.	17	987	261	397	658	305	85	23	14	37	49	2	1961-62	1977-78
Bergdinon, Fred	Bos.	1	2	0	0	0	0	....	....	....	....	....		1925-26	1925-26
Bergen, Todd	Phi.	1	14	11	5	16	4	17	4	9	13	8		1984-85	1984-85
Berger, Mike	Min.	2	30	3	1	4	67	....	....	....	....	....		1987-88	1988-89
Bergeron, Michel	Det., NYI, Wsh.	5	229	80	58	138	165	....	....	....	....	....		1974-75	1978-79
Bergeron, Yves	Pit.	2	3	0	0	0	0	....	....	....	....	....		1974-75	1976-77
Bergloff, Bob	Min.	1	2	0	0	0	5	....	....	....	....	....		1982-83	1982-83
Berglund, Bo	Que., Min., Phi.	3	130	28	39	67	40	9	2	0	2	6		1983-84	1985-86
Bergman, Gary	Det., Min., K.C.	12	838	68	299	367	1249	21	0	5	5	20		1964-65	1975-76
Bergman, Thommie	Det.	6	246	21	44	65	243	7	0	2	2	2		1972-73	1979-80
Bergqvist, Jonas	Cgy.	1	22	2	5	7	10	....	....	....	....	....		1989-90	1989-90
* Berlinquette, Louis	Mtl., Mtl.M., Pit.	8	193	44	29	73	111	16	1	1	2	0		1917-18	1925-26
Bernier, Serge	Phi., L.A., Que.	7	302	78	119	197	234	5	1	1	2	0		1968-69	1980-81
Berry, Bob	Mtl., L.A.	8	541	159	191	350	344	26	2	6	8	6		1968-69	1976-77
Berry, Doug	Col.	2	121	10	33	43	25	....	....	....	....	....		1979-80	1980-81
Berry, Fred	Det.	1	3	0	0	0	0	....	....	....	....	....		1976-77	1976-77
Berry, Ken	Edm., Van.	4	55	8	10	18	30	....	....	....	....	....		1981-82	1988-89
Besler, Phil	Bos., Chi., Det.	2	30	1	4	5	18	....	....	....	....	....		1935-36	1938-39
Bessone, Pete	Det.	1	6	0	1	1	6	....	....	....	....	....		1937-38	1937-38
Bethel, John	Wpg.	1	17	0	2	2	4	....	....	....	....	....		1979-80	1979-80
Bettio, Sam	Bos.	1	44	9	12	21	32	....	....	....	....	....		1949-50	1949-50
Beverley, Nick	Bos., Pit., NYR, Min., L.A., Col.	11	502	18	94	112	156	7	0	1	1	0		1966-67	1979-80
Bialowas, Dwight	Atl., Min.	4	164	11	46	57	46	....	....	....	....	....		1973-74	1976-77
Bianchin, Wayne	Pit., Edm.	7	276	68	41	109	137	3	0	1	1	6		1973-74	1979-80
Bidner, Todd	Wsh.	1	12	2	1	3	7	....	....	....	....	....		1981-82	1981-82
Biggs, Don	Min.	1	1	0	0	0	0	....	....	....	....	....		1984-85	1984-85
Bignell, Larry	Pit.	2	20	0	3	3	2	3	0	0	0	2		1973-74	1974-75
Bilodeau, Gilles	Que.	1	9	0	1	1	25	....	....	....	....	....		1979-80	1979-80
Bionda, Jack	Tor., Bos.	4	93	3	9	12	113	11	0	1	1	14		1955-56	1958-59
Black, Stephen	Det., Chi.	2	113	11	20	31	77	13	0	0	0	13	1	1949-50	1950-51
Blackburn, Bob	NYR., Pit.	3	135	8	12	20	105	6	0	0	0	4		1968-69	1970-71
Blackburn, Don	Bos., Phi., NYR, NYI, Min.	6	185	23	44	67	87	12	3	0	3	10		1962-63	1972-73
Blade, Hank	Chi.	2	24	2	3	5	2	....	....	....	....	....		1946-47	1947-48
Bladon, Tom	Phi., Pit., Edm., Wpg., Det.	9	610	73	197	270	392	86	8	29	37	70	2	1972-73	1980-81
Blaine, Gary	Mtl.	1	1	0	0	0	0	....	....	....	....	....		1954-55	1954-55
Blair, Andy	Tor., Chi.	9	402	74	86	160	323	38	6	6	12	32	1	1928-29	1936-37
Blair, Chuck	Tor.	2	3	0	0	0	0	....	....	....	....	....		1948-49	1950-51
Blair, George	Tor.	1	2	0	0	0	0	....	....	....	....	....		1950-51	1950-51
Blaisdell, Mike	Det., NYR, Pit., Tor.	9	343	70	84	154	166	....	....	....	....	....		1980-81	1988-89
Blake, Mickey	St.L., Bos., Tor.	2	16	1	1	2	4	....	....	....	....	....		1934-35	1935-36
Blake, Toe	Mtl.M., Mtl.	15	578	235	292	527	272	57	25	37	62	23	3	1932-33	1947-48
Blight, Rick	Van., L.A.	7	326	96	125	221	170	5	0	5	5	2		1975-76	1982-83
Blinco, Russ	Mtl.M, Chi.	6	268	59	66	125	24	19	3	3	6	4	1	1933-34	1938-39
Block, Ken	Van.	1	1	0	0	0	0	....	....	....	....	....		1970-71	1970-71
Blomqvist, Timo	Wsh., N.J.	5	243	4	53	57	293	13	0	0	0	24		1981-82	1986-87
Bloom, Mike	Wsh., Det.	3	201	30	47	77	215	....	....	....	....	....		1974-75	1976-77
Bodak, Bob	Cgy., Hfd.	2	4	0	0	0	29	....	....	....	....	....		1987-88	1989-90
Boddy, Gregg	Van.	5	273	23	44	67	263	3	0	0	0	0		1971-72	1975-76

Name	NHL Teams	NHL Seasons	Regular Schedule GP	G	A	TP	PIM	Playoffs GP	G	A	TP	PIM	NHL Cup Wins	First NHL Season	Last NHL Season
Bodnar, Gus	Tor., Chi., Bos.	12	667	142	254	396	207	32	4	3	7	10	2	1943-44	1954-55
Boehm, Ron	Oak.	1	16	2	1	3	10	....	....	....	....	....		1967-68	1967-68
Boesch, Garth	Tor.	4	197	9	28	37	205	34	2	5	7	18	3	1946-47	1949-50
Boh, Rick	Min.	1	8	2	1	3	4	....	....	....	....	....		1987-88	1987-88
Boileau, Marc	Det.	1	54	5	6	11	8	....	....	....	....	....		1961-62	1961-62
Boileau, Rene	NYA	1	7	0	0	0	0	....	....	....	....	....		1925-26	1925-26
Boimistruck, Fred	Tor.	2	83	4	14	18	45	....	....	....	....	....		1981-82	1982-83
Boisvert, Serge	Tor., Mtl.	5	46	5	7	12	8	23	3	7	10	4	1	1982-83	1987-88
Boivin, Leo	Tor., Bos., Det., Pit., Min.	19	1150	72	250	322	1192	54	3	10	13	59		1951-52	1969-70
Boland, Mike A.	Phi.	1	2	0	0	0	0	....	....	....	....	....		1974-75	1974-75
Boland, Mike J.	K.C., Buf.	2	23	1	2	3	29	3	1	0	1	2		1974-75	1978-79
Boldirev, Ivan	Bos., Cal., Chi., Atl., Van., Det.	15	1052	361	505	866	507	48	13	20	33	14		1970-71	1984-85
Bolduc, Danny	Det., Cgy.	3	102	22	19	41	33	1	0	0	0	0		1978-79	1983-84
Bolduc, Michel	Que.	2	10	0	0	0	6	....	....	....	....	....		1981-82	1982-83
Boll, Buzz	Tor., NYA, Bro., Bos.	11	436	133	130	263	148	29	7	3	10	13		1933-34	1943-44
Bolonchuk, Larry	Van., Wsh.	4	74	3	9	12	97	....	....	....	....	....		1972-73	1977-78
Bolton, Hughie	Tor.	8	235	10	51	61	221	17	0	5	5	14		1949-50	1956-57
Bonar, Dan	L.A.	3	170	25	39	64	208	14	3	4	7	22		1980-81	1982-83
Bonin, Marcel	Det., Bos., Mtl.	9	454	97	175	272	336	50	11	14	25	51	4	1952-53	1961-62
Boo, Jim	Min.	1	6	0	0	0	22	....	....	....	....	....		1977-78	1977-78
Boone, Buddy	Bos.	2	34	5	3	8	28	22	2	1	3	25		1956-57	1957-58
Boothman, George	Tor.	2	58	17	19	36	18	5	2	1	3	2		1942-43	1943-44
Bordeleau, Chris.	Mtl., St.L., Chi.,	4	205	38	65	103	82	19	4	7	11	17	1	1968-69	1971-72
Bordeleau, J. P.	Chi.	10	519	97	126	223	143	48	3	6	9	12		1969-70	1979-80
Bordeleau, Paulin	Van.	3	183	33	56	89	47	5	2	1	3	0		1973-74	1975-76
Borotsik, Jack	St.L.	1	1	0	0	0	0	....	....	....	....	....		1974-75	1974-75
Bossy, Mike	NYI	10	752	573	553	1126	210	129	85	75	160	38	4	1977-78	1986-87
Bostrom, Helge	Chi.	4	96	3	3	6	58	13	0	0	0	16		1929-30	1932-33
Botell, Mark	Phi.	1	32	4	10	14	31	....	....	....	....	....		1981-82	1981-82
Bothwell, Tim	NYR, St.L., Hfd.	11	502	28	93	121	382	49	0	3	3	56		1978-79	1988-89
Botting, Cam	Atl.	1	2	0	1	1	0	....	....	....	....	....		1975-76	1975-76
Boucha, Henry	Det., Min., K.C., Col.	6	247	53	49	102	157	....	....	....	....	....		1971-72	1976-77
Bouchard, Dick	NYR	1	1	0	0	0	0	....	....	....	....	....		1954-55	1954-55
Bouchard, Edmond	Mtl., Ham., NYA, Pit.	8	223	19	20	39	105	....	....	....	....	....		1921-22	1928-29
Bouchard, Emile (Butch)	Mtl.	15	785	49	144	193	863	113	11	21	32	121	4	1941-42	1955-56
Bouchard, Pierre	Mtl., Wsh.	12	595	24	82	106	433	76	3	10	13	56	5	1970-71	1981-82
* Boucher, Billy	Mtl., Bos., NYA	7	213	93	35	128	391	21	9	3	12	35	1	1921-22	1927-28
* Boucher, Frank	Ott., NYR	14	557	161	262	423	119	56	16	18	34	12	2	1921-22	1943-44
* Boucher, George	Ott., Mtl.M, Chi.	15	457	122	62	184	712	44	11	4	15	84	4	1917-18	1931-32
Boucher, Robert	Mtl.	1	12	0	0	0	0	....	....	....	....	....	1	1923-24	1923-24
Boudrias, Andre	Mtl., Min., Chi., St.L., Van.	12	662	151	340	491	218	34	6	10	16	12		1963-64	1975-76
Boughner, Barry	Oak., Cal.	2	20	0	0	0	11	....	....	....	....	....		1969-70	1970-71
Bourbonnais, Dan	Hfd.	2	59	3	25	28	11	....	....	....	....	....		1981-82	1983-84
Bourbonnais, Rick	St.L.	3	71	9	15	24	29	4	0	1	1	0		1975-76	1977-78
Bourcier, Conrad	Mtl.	1	6	0	0	0	0	....	....	....	....	....		1935-36	1935-36
Bourcier, Jean	Mtl.	1	9	0	1	1	0	....	....	....	....	....		1935-36	1935-36
Bourgeault, Leo	Tor. NYR, Ott., Mtl.	8	307	24	20	44	269	24	1	1	2	18	1	1926-27	1934-35
Bourgeois, Charlie	Cgy., St.L., Hfd.	7	290	16	54	70	788	40	2	3	5	194		1981-82	1987-88
Bourne, Bob	NYI, L.A.	14	964	258	324	582	605	139	40	56	96	108	4	1974-75	1987-88
Boutette, Pat	Tor., Hfd., Pit.	10	756	171	282	453	1354	46	10	14	24	109		1975-76	1984-85
Boutilier, Paul	NYI, Bos., Min., NYR, Wpg.	8	288	27	83	110	358	41	1	9	10	45		1981-82	1988-89
Bowcher, Clarence	NYA	2	47	2	2	4	110	....	....	....	....	....		1926-27	1927-28
Bowman, Kirk	Chi.	3	88	11	17	28	19	7	1	0	1	0		1976-77	1978-79
Bowman, Ralph	Ott., St.L., Det.	7	274	8	17	25	260	22	2	2	4	6	2	1933-34	1939-40
Bownass, Jack	Mtl., NYR	4	80	3	8	11	58	....	....	....	....	....		1957-58	1961-62
Bowness, Rick	Atl., Det., St. L, Wpg.	7	173	18	37	55	191	5	0	0	0	2		1975-76	1981-82
Boyd, Bill	NYR, NYA	4	138	15	7	22	72	9	0	0	0	2	1	1926-27	1929-30
Boyd, Irwin	Bos., Det.	4	97	18	19	37	51	15	0	1	1	4		1931-32	1943-44
Boyd, Randy	Pit., Chi., NYI, Van.	8	257	20	67	87	328	13	0	2	2	26		1981-82	1988-89
Boyer, Wally	Tor., Chi., Oak. Pit.	7	365	54	105	159	163	15	1	3	4	0		1965-66	1971-72
Boyko, Darren	Wpg.	1	1	0	0	0	0	....	....	....	....	....		1988-89	1988-89
Brackenborough, John	Bos.	1	7	0	0	0	0			....	....	....		1925-26	1925-26
Brackenbury, Curt	Que., Edm., St.L.	4	141	9	17	26	226	2	0	0	0	0		1979-80	1982-83
Bradley, Barton	Bos.	1	1	0	0	0	0	....	....	....	....	....		1949-50	1949-50
Bradley, Lyle	Cal. Cle.	2	6	1	0	1	2	....	....	....	....	....		1973-74	1976-77
Bragnalo, Rick	Wsh.	4	145	15	35	50	46	....	....	....	....	....		1975-76	1978-79
Brannigan, Andy	NYA, Bro.	2	26	1	2	3	31	....	....	....	....	....		1940-41	1941-42
Brasar, Per-Olov	Min., Van.	5	348	64	142	206	33	13	1	2	3	0		1977-78	1981-82
Brayshaw, Russ	Chi.	1	43	5	9	14	24	....	....	....	....	....		1944-45	1944-45
Breitenbach, Ken	Buf.	3	68	1	13	14	49	8	0	1	1	4		1975-76	1978-79
Brennan, Dan	L.A.	2	8	0	1	1	9	....	....	....	....	....		1983-84	1985-86
Brennan, Doug	NYR	3	123	9	7	16	152	16	1	0	1	21	1	1931-32	1933-34
Brennan, Tom	Bos.	2	22	2	2	4	2	....	....	....	....	....		1943-44	1944-45
Brenneman, John	Chi., NYR, Tor., Det., Oak.	5	152	21	19	40	46	....	....	....	....	....		1964-65	1968-69
Bretto, Joe	Chi.	1	3	0	0	0	4	....	....	....	....	....		1944-45	1944-45
Brewer, Carl	Tor., Det., St.L.	12	604	25	198	223	1037	72	3	17	20	146	3	1957-58	1979-80
Briden, Archie	Det., Pit.	2	72	9	5	14	56	....	....	....	....	....		1926-27	1929-30
Bridgman, Mel	Phi., Cgy., N.J., Det., Van.	14	977	252	449	701	1625	125	28	39	67	298		1975-76	1988-89
* Briere, Michel	Pit.	1	76	12	32	44	20	10	5	3	8	17		1969-70	1969-70
Brindley, Doug	Tor.	1	3	0	0	0	0	....	....	....	....	....		1970-71	1970-71
Brink, Milt	Chi.	1	5	0	0	0	0	....	....	....	....	....		1936-37	1936-37
Brisson, Gerry	Mtl.	1	4	0	2	2	4	....	....	....	....	....		1962-63	1962-63
Britz, Greg	Tor., Hfd.	3	8	0	0	0	4	....	....	....	....	....		1983-84	1986-87
* Broadbent, Harry	Ott. Mt.M, NYA	11	302	122	45	167	553	41	13	3	16	69	4	1918-19	1928-29
Brochu, Stephane	NYR	1	1	0	0	0	0	....	....	....	....	....		1988-89	1988-89
Broden, Connie	Mtl.	3	6	2	1	3	2	7	0	1	1	0	2	1955-56	1957-58
Brooke, Bob	NYR, Min., N.J.	7	447	69	97	166	520	34	9	9	18	59		1983-84	1989-90
Brooks, Gord	St.L., Wsh.	3	70	7	18	25	37	....	....	....	....	....		1971-72	1974-75
Brophy, Bernie	Mtl.M, Det.	3	62	4	4	8	25	2	0	0	0	2	1	1925-26	1929-30
Brossart, Willie	Phi., Tor., Wsh.	6	129	1	14	15	88	1	0	0	0	0		1970-71	1975-76
* Brown, Adam	Det. Chi. Bos.	10	391	104	113	217	358	26	2	14	6	14	1	1941-42	1951-52
Brown, Arnie	Tor. NYR, Det., NYI, Atl.	12	681	44	141	185	738	22	0	6	6	23		1961-62	1973-74
Brown, Connie	Det.	5	91	15	24	39	12	14	2	3	5	0		1938-39	1942-43
Brown, Fred	Mtl.M	1	19	1	0	1	0	9	0	0	0	0		1927-28	1927-28
Brown, George	Mtl.	3	79	6	22	28	34	7	0	0	0	2		1936-37	1938-39
Brown, Gerry	Det.	2	23	4	5	9	2	12	2	1	3	4		1941-42	1945-46
Brown, Harold	NYR	1	13	2	1	3	2	....	....	....	....	....		1945-46	1945-46
Brown, Jim	L.A.	1	3	0	1	1	5	....	....	....	....	....		1982-83	1982-83
Brown, Larry	NYR, Det., Phi., L.A.	9	455	7	53	60	180	35	0	4	4	10		1969-70	1977-78
Brown, Stan	NYR, Det.	2	48	8	2	10	18	2	0	0	0	0		1926-27	1927-28
Brown, Wayne	Bos.	1	....	....	....	....	....	4	0	0	0	2		1953-54	1953-54
Browne, Cecil	Chi.	1	13	2	0	2	4	....	....	....	....	....		1927-28	1927-28
Brownschidle, Jack	St.L., Hfd.	9	494	39	162	201	151	26	0	5	5	18		1977-78	1985-86
Brownschidle, Jeff	Hfd.	2	7	0	1	1	2	....	....	....	....	....		1981-82	1982-83
Brubaker, Jeff	Hfd., Mtl., Cgy., Tor., Edm., NYR, Det.	8	178	16	9	25	512	2	0	0	0	27		1979-80	1988-89
Bruce, Gordie	Bos.	3	28	4	9	13	13	7	2	3	5	4		1940-41	1945-46
Bruce, Morley	Ott.	4	72	8	1	9	27	12	0	0	0	3	2	1917-18	1921-22
Brumwell, Murray	Min., N.J.,	7	128	12	31	43	70	2	0	0	0	2		1980-81	1987-88
Bruneteau, Eddie	Det.	7	180	40	42	82	35	26	7	6	13	0		1940-41	1948-49
Bruneteau, Mud	Det.	11	411	139	138	277	80	77	23	14	37	22	3	1935-36	1945-46
* Brydge, Bill	Tor., Det., NYA	9	368	26	52	78	506	2	0	0	0	4		1926-27	1935-36
Brydges, Paul	Buf.	1	15	2	2	4	6	....	....	....	....	....		1986-87	1986-87
Brydson, Glenn	Mtl.M, St.L., NYR, Chi.	8	299	56	79	135	203	11	0	0	0	8		1930-31	1937-38
Brydson, Gord	Tor	1	8	0	0	0	0	....	....	....	....	....		1929-30	1929-30
Bubla, Jiri	Van.	5	256	17	101	118	202	6	0	0	0	7		1981-82	1985-86
Buchanan, Al	Tor.	2	4	0	1	1	2	....	....	....	....	....		1948-49	1949-50
Buchanan, Bucky	NYR	1	2	0	0	0	0	....	....	....	....	....		1948-49	1948-49
Buchanan, Mike	Chi.	1	1	0	0	0	0	....	....	....	....	....		1951-52	1951-52
Buchanan, Ron	Bos., St.L.	2	5	0	0	0	0	....	....	....	....	....		1966-67	1969-70
Bucyk, John	Det., Bos.,	23	1540	556	813	1369	497	124	41	62	103	42	2	1955-56	1977-78
Bucyk, Randy	Mtl., Cgy.	2	19	4	2	6	8	2	0	0	0	0		1985-86	1987-88
Buhr, Doug	K.C.	1	6	0	2	2	4	....	....	....	....	....		1974-75	1974-75
Bukovich, Tony	Det.	2	44	7	3	10	6	6	0	1	1	0		1943-44	1944-45
* Buller, Hy	Det., NYR	5	188	22	58	80	215	....	....	....	....	....		1943-44	1953-54
Bulley, Ted	Chi., Wsh., Pit.	8	414	101	113	214	704	29	5	5	10	24		1976-77	1983-84

Ivan Boldirev

Marcel Bonin

Wally Boyer

Mel Bridgman

Bill Carroll

Name	NHL Teams	NHL Seasons	Regular Schedule GP	G	A	TP	PIM	Playoffs GP	G	A	TP	PIM	NHL Cup Wins	First NHL Season	Last NHL Season
* Burch, Billy	Ham., NYA, Bos., Chi.	11	390	137	53	190	251	2	0	0	0	0		1922-23	1932-33
Burchell, Fred	Mtl.	2	4	0	0	0	2	....	....	....	....	....		1950-51	1953-54
Burdon, Glen	K.C.	1	11	0	2	2	0	....	....	....	....	....		1974-75	1974-75
Burega, Bill	Bos.	1	4	0	1	1	4	....	....	....	....	....		1955-56	1955-56
Burke, Eddie	Bos., NYA	4	106	29	20	49	55	....	....	....	....	....		1931-32	1934-35
Burke, Marty	Mtl., Pit., Ott., Chi.	11	494	19	47	66	560	31	2	4	6	44	2	1927-28	1937-38
Burmeister, Roy	NYA	3	67	4	3	7	2	....	....	....	....	....		1929-30	1931-32
Burnett, Kelly	NYR	1	3	1	0	1	0	....	....	....	....	....		1952-53	1952-53
Burns, Bobby	Chi.	3	20	1	0	1	8	....	....	....	....	....		1927-28	1929-30
Burns, Charlie	Det., Bos., Oak., Pit., Min.	11	749	106	198	304	252	31	5	4	9	4		1958-59	1972-73
Burns, Gary	NYR	2	11	2	2	4	18	5	0	0	0	6		1980-81	1981-82
Burns, Norm	NYR	1	11	0	4	4	2	....	....	....	....	....		1941-42	1941-42
Burns, Robin	Pit., K.C.	5	190	31	38	69	139	....	....	....	....	....		1970-71	1975-76
Burrows, Dave	Pit., Tor.	10	724	29	135	164	377	29	1	5	6	25		1971-72	1980-81
Burry, Bert	Ott.	1	4	0	0	0	0	....	....	....	....	....		1932-33	1932-33
Burton, Cummy	Det.	3	43	0	2	2	21	3	0	0	0	0		1955-56	1958-59
Burton, Nelson	Wsh.	2	8	1	0	1	21	....	....	....	....	....		1977-78	1978-79
Bush, Eddie	Det.	2	27	4	6	10	50	12	1	6	7	23		1938-39	1941-42
Busniuk, Mike	Phi.	2	143	3	23	26	297	25	2	5	7	34		1979-80	1980-81
Busniuk, Ron	Buf.	2	6	0	3	3	4	....	....	....	....	....		1972-73	1973-74
Buswell, Walt	Det., Mtl.	8	368	10	40	50	164	24	2	1	3	10		1932-33	1939-40
Butler, Dick	Chi.	1	7	2	0	2	0	....	....	....	....	....		1947-48	1947-48
Butler, Jerry	NYR, St.L., Tor., Van., Wpg.	11	641	99	120	219	515	48	3	3	6	79		1972-73	1982-83
Butters, Bill	Min.	2	72	1	4	5	77	....	....	....	....	....		1977-78	1978-79
Buttrey, Gord	Chi.	1	10	0	0	0	0	10	0	0	0	0		1943-44	1943-44
Buynak, Gordon	St. L	1	4	0	0	0	2	....	....	....	....	....		1974-75	1974-75
Byers, Gord	Bos.	1	1	0	1	1	0	....	....	....	....	....		1949-50	1949-50
Byers, Jerry	Min., Atl, NYR	4	43	3	4	7	10	....	....	....	....	....		1972-73	1977-78
Byers, Mike	Tor., Phi., Buf., L.A.	4	166	42	34	76	39	4	0	1	1	0		1967-68	1971-72

C

Wayne Cashman

Blair Chapman

Guy Charron

Name	NHL Teams	NHL Seasons	Regular Schedule GP	G	A	TP	PIM	Playoffs GP	G	A	TP	PIM	NHL Cup Wins	First NHL Season	Last NHL Season
Caffery, Jack	Tor., Bos.	3	57	3	2	5	22	10	1	0	1	4		1954-55	1957-58
Caffery, Terry	Chi., Min.	2	14	0	0	0	0	1	0	0	0	0		1969-70	1970-71
* Cahan, Larry	Tor., NYR, Oak., L.A.	13	665	38	92	130	700	29	1	1	2	38		1954-55	1970-71
Cahill, Chuck	Bos.	2	32	0	1	1	4	....	....	....	....	....		1925-26	1926-27
Cain, Herbert	Mtl.M, Mtl., Bos.	13	571	206	194	400	178	64	16	13	29	13	2	1933-34	1945-46
Cain, Jim	Mtl.M, Tor.	2	61	4	0	4	35	....	....	....	....	....	1	1924-25	1925-26
Cairns, Don	K.C., Col.	2	9	0	1	1	2	....	....	....	....	....		1975-76	1976-77
Calder, Eric	Wsh.	2	2	0	0	0	0	....	....	....	....	....		1981-82	1982-83
Calladine, Norm	Bos.	3	63	19	29	48	8	....	....	....	....	....		1942-43	1944-45
Callander, Drew	Phi., Van.	4	39	6	2	8	7	....	....	....	....	....		1976-77	1979-80
Callighen, Brett	Edm.	3	160	56	89	145	132	14	4	6	10	8		1979-80	1981-82
Callighen, Patsy	NYR	1	36	0	0	0	32	9	0	0	0	0	1	1927-28	1927-28
Camazzola, James	Chi.	2	3	0	0	0	0	....	....	....	....	....		1983-84	1986-87
Camazzola, Tony	Wsh.	1	3	0	0	0	4	....	....	....	....	....		1981-82	1981-82
* Cameron, Al	Det., Wpg.	6	282	11	44	55	356	7	0	1	1	2		1975-76	1980-81
Cameron, Billy	Mtl., NYA	2	39	0	0	0	2	6	0	0	0	0	1	1923-24	1925-26
Cameron, Craig	Det., St.L., Min., NYI	9	552	87	65	152	202	27	3	1	4	17		1966-67	1975-76
Cameron, Dave	Col., N.J.	3	168	25	28	53	238	....	....	....	....	....		1981-82	1983-84
* Cameron, Harry	Tor., Ott., Mtl.	6	127	90	27	117	120	20	7	3	10	29	3	1917-18	1922-23
Cameron, Scotty	NYR	1	35	8	11	19	0	....	....	....	....	....		1942-43	1942-43
Campbell, Bryan	L.A., Chi.	5	260	35	71	106	74	22	3	4	7	2		1967-68	1971-72
Campbell, Colin	Pit., Col., Edm., Van., Det.	11	636	25	103	128	1292	45	4	10	14	181		1974-75	1984-85
* Campbell, Dave	Mtl.	1	3	0	0	0	0	....	....	....	....	....		1920-21	1920-21
Campbell, Don	Chi.	1	17	1	3	4	8	....	....	....	....	....		1943-44	1943-44
Campbell, Scott	Wpg., St.L.	3	80	4	21	25	243	....	....	....	....	....		1979-80	1981-82
Campbell, Spiff	Ott., NYA	3	77	5	1	6	12	2	0	0	0	0		1923-24	1925-26
Campbell, Wade	Wpg., Bos.	6	213	9	27	36	305	10	0	0	0	20		1982-83	1987-88
Campeau, Tod	Mtl.	3	42	5	9	14	16	1	0	0	0	0		1943-44	1948-49
Campedelli, Dom	Mtl.	1	2	0	0	0	0	....	....	....	....	....		1985-86	1985-86
Carbol, Leo	Chi.	1	6	0	1	1	4	....	....	....	....	....		1942-43	1942-43
Cardin, Claude	St.L.	1	1	0	0	0	0	....	....	....	....	....		1967-68	1967-68
Cardwell, Steve	Pit.	3	53	9	11	20	35	4	0	0	0	2		1970-71	1972-73
* Carey, George	Que, Ham., Tor.	5	72	22	8	30	14	....	....	....	....	....		1919-20	1923-24
Carleton, Wayne	Tor., Bos., Cal.	7	278	55	73	128	172	18	2	4	6	14	1	1965-66	1971-72
Carlin, Brian	L.A.	1	5	1	0	1	0	....	....	....	....	....		1971-72	1971-72
Carlson, Jack	Min., St.L.	6	236	30	15	45	417	25	1	2	3	72		1978-79	1986-87
Carlson, Kent	Mtl., St.L., Wsh.	5	113	7	11	18	148	8	0	0	0	13		1983-84	1988-89
Carlson, Steve	L.A.	1	52	9	12	21	23	4	1	1	2	7		1979-80	1979-80
Carlsson, Anders	N.J.	3	104	7	26	33	34	3	1	0	1	2		1986-87	1988-89
* Caron, Alain	Oak., Mtl.	2	60	9	13	22	18	....	....	....	....	....		1967-68	1968-69
* Carpenter, Eddie	Que, Ham.	2	44	10	4	14	23	....	....	....	....	....		1919-20	1920-21
Carr, Al	Tor.	1	5	0	1	1	4	....	....	....	....	....		1943-44	1943-44
Carr, Gene	St.L., NYR, L.A., Pit., Atl.	8	465	79	136	215	365	35	5	8	13	66		1971-72	1978-79
Carr, Lorne	NYR, NYA, Tor.	13	580	204	222	426	132	53	10	9	19	13	1	1933-34	1945-46
Carriere, Larry	Buf. Atl, Van., L.A., Tor.	7	366	16	74	90	463	27	0	3	3	42		1972-73	1979-80
Carrigan, Gene	NYR, StL, Det.	3	37	2	1	3	13	4	0	0	0	0		1930-31	1934-35
Carroll, Billy	NYI, Edm., Det.	7	322	30	54	84	113	71	6	12	18	18	4	1980-81	1986-87
Carroll, George	Mtl.M, Bos.	1	15	0	0	0	9	....	....	....	....	....		1924-25	1924-25
Carroll, Greg	Wsh., Det., Hfd.	2	131	20	34	54	44	....	....	....	....	....		1978-79	1979-80
Carruthers, Dwight	Det. Phi.	2	2	0	0	0	0	....	....	....	....	....		1965-66	1967-68
Carse, Bill	NYR, Chi.	4	124	28	43	71	38	16	3	2	5	0		1938-39	1941-42
Carse, Bob	Chi., Mtl.	5	167	32	55	87	52	10	0	2	2	2		1939-40	1947-48
Carson, Bill	Tor., Bos.	4	159	54	24	78	156	11	3	0	3	14	1	1926-27	1929-30
Carson, Frank	Mtl.M., NYA, Det.	7	248	42	48	90	166	22	0	2	2	9	1	1925-26	1933-34
Carson, Gerry	Mtl., NYR, Mtl.M.	6	261	12	11	23	205	22	0	0	0	12	1	1928-29	1936-37
Carson, Lindsay	Phi., Hfd.	7	373	66	80	146	524	49	4	10	14	56		1981-82	1987-88
Carter, Billy	Mtl., Bos.	3	16	0	0	0	6	....	....	....	....	....		1957-58	1961-62
Carter, Ron	Edm.	1	2	0	0	0	0	....	....	....	....	....		1979-80	1979-80
Carveth, Joe	Det., Bos., Mtl.	11	504	150	189	339	81	69	21	16	37	28	2	1940-41	1950-51
Cashman, Wayne	Bos.	17	1027	277	516	793	1041	145	31	57	88	250	2	1964-65	1982-83
Cassidy, Bruce	Chi.	6	36	4	13	17	10	1	0	0	0	0		1983-84	1989-90
Cassidy, Tom	Pit.	1	26	3	4	7	15	....	....	....	....	....		1977-78	1977-78
Cassolato, Tony	Wsh.	3	23	1	6	7	4	....	....	....	....	....		1979-80	1981-82
Ceresino, Ray	Tor.	1	12	1	1	2	2	....	....	....	....	....		1948-49	1948-49
Cernik, Frantisek	Det.	1	49	5	4	9	13	....	....	....	....	....		1984-85	1984-85
Chad John	Chi.	3	80	15	22	37	29	10	0	1	1	2		1939-40	1945-46
Chalmers, Bill	NYR	1	1	0	0	0	0	....	....	....	....	....		1953-54	1953-54
Chalupa, Milan	Det.	1	14	0	5	5	6	....	....	....	....	....		1984-85	1984-85
Chamberlain, Murph	Tor., Mtl., Bro., Bos.	12	510	100	175	275	769	66	14	17	31	96	2	1937-38	1948-49
Champagne, Andre	Tor.	1	2	0	0	0	0	....	....	....	....	....		1962-63	1962-63
* Chapman, Art	Bos., NYA	10	438	62	176	238	140	25	1	5	6	9		1930-31	1939-40
Chapman, Blair	Pit., St.L.	7	402	106	125	231	158	25	4	6	10	15		1976-77	1982-83
Charlebois, Bob	Min.	1	7	1	0	1	0	....	....	....	....	....		1967-68	1967-68
Charlesworth, Todd	Pit., NYR	6	93	3	9	12	47	....	....	....	....	....		1983-84	1989-90
Charron, Guy	Mtl., Det., K.C., Wsh.	12	734	221	309	530	146	....	....	....	....	....		1969-70	1980-81
Chartier, Dave	Wpg.	1	1	0	0	0	0	....	....	....	....	....		1980-81	1980-81
Chartraw, Rick	Mtl., L.A., NYR, Edm.	10	420	28	64	92	399	75	7	9	16	80	4	1974-75	1983-84
Check, Lude	Det., Chi.	2	27	6	2	8	4	....	....	....	....	....		1943-44	1944-45
Chernoff, Mike	Min.	1	1	0	0	0	0	....	....	....	....	....		1968-69	1968-69
Cherry, Dick	Bos., Phi.	3	145	12	10	22	45	4	1	0	1	4		1956-57	1969-70
Cherry, Don	Bos.	1	....	....	....	....	....	1	0	0	0	0		1954-55	1954-55
Chevrefils, Real	Bos., Det.	8	387	104	97	201	185	30	5	4	9	20		1951-52	1958-59
Chicoine, Dan	Cle. Min.	3	31	1	2	3	12	1	0	0	0	0		1977-78	1979-80
Chinnick, Rick	Min.	2	4	0	2	2	0	....	....	....	....	....		1973-74	1974-75
Chipperfield, Ron	Edm., Que.,	2	83	22	24	46	34	....	....	....	....	....		1979-80	1980-81
Chisholm, Art	Bos.	1	3	0	0	0	0	....	....	....	....	....		1960-61	1960-61
Chisholm, Colin	Min.	1	1	0	0	0	0	....	....	....	....	....		1986-87	1986-87
Chisholm, Lex	Tor.	2	54	10	8	18	19	3	1	0	1	0		1939-40	1940-41
Chorney, Marc	Pit. L.A.	4	210	8	27	35	209	7	0	1	1	2		1980-81	1983-84
Chouinard, Gene	Ott.	1	8	0	0	0	0	....	....	....	....	....		1927-28	1927-28
Chouinard, Guy	Atl, Cgy., St.L.	10	578	205	370	575	120	46	9	28	37	12		1974-75	1983-84

Name	NHL Teams	NHL Seasons	Regular Schedule GP	G	A	TP	PIM	Playoffs GP	G	A	TP	PIM	NHL Cup Wins	First NHL Season	Last NHL Season
Christie, Mike	Cal., Cle., Col., Van.	7	412	15	101	116	550	2	0	0	0	0		1974-75	1980-81
Christoff, Steve	Min. Cgy., L.A.	5	248	77	64	141	108	35	16	12	28	25		1979-80	1983-84
Chrystal, Bob	NYR	2	132	11	14	25	112	....	....	....	....	....		1953-54	1954-55
Church, Jack	Tor., Bro., Bos.	6	145	5	22	27	164	25	1	1	2	18		1938-39	1945-46
* Ciesla, Hank	Chi., NYR	4	269	26	51	77	87	6	0	2	2	0		1955-56	1958-59
Clackson, Kim	Pit., Que.	2	106	0	8	8	370	8	0	0	0	70		1979-80	1980-81
* Clancy, Francis (King)	Ott., Tor.	16	592	137	143	280	904	61	9	8	17	92	3	1921-22	1936-37
Clancy, Terry	Oak., Tor.	4	93	6	6	12	39	....	....	....	....	....		1967-68	1972-73
* Clapper, Dit	Bos.	20	833	228	246	474	462	86	13	17	30	50	3	1927-28	1946-47
Clark, Andy	Bos.	1	5	0	0	0	0	....	....	....	....	....		1927-28	1927-28
Clark, Dan	NYR	1	4	0	1	1	6	....	....	....	....	....		1978-79	1978-79
Clark, Dean	Edm.	1	1	0	0	0	0	....	....	....	....	....		1983-84	1983-84
Clark, Gordie	Bos.	2	8	0	1	1	0	1	0	0	0	0		1974-75	1975-76
Clarke, Bobby	Phi.	15	1144	358	852	1210	1453	136	42	77	119	152	2	1969-70	1983-84
* Cleghorn, Odie	Mtl., Pit.	10	180	95	29	124	147	23	9	2	11	2	1	1918-19	1927-28
* Cleghorn, Sprague	Ott. Tor. Mtl., Bos.	10	256	84	39	123	489	37	7	8	15	48	3	1918-19	1927-28
Clement, Bill	Phi., Wsh., Atl., Cgy.	11	719	148	208	356	383	50	5	3	8	26	2	1971-72	1981-82
Cline, Bruce	NYR	1	30	2	3	5	10	....	....	....	....	....		1956-57	1956-57
Clippingdale, Steve	L.A., Wsh.	2	19	1	2	3	9	1	0	0	0	0		1976-77	1979-80
Cloutier, Real	Que. Buf.	6	317	146	198	344	119	25	7	5	12	20		1979-80	1984-85
Cloutier, Rejean	Det.	2	5	0	2	2	2	....	....	....	....	....		1979-80	1981-82
Cloutier, Roland	Det., Que.	3	34	8	9	17	2	....	....	....	....	....		1977-78	1979-80
Clune, Wally	Mtl.	1	5	0	0	0	6	....	....	....	....	....		1955-56	1955-56
Coalter, Gary	Cal., K.C.	2	34	2	4	6	2	....	....	....	....	....		1973-74	1974-75
Coates, Steve	Det.	1	5	1	0	1	24	....	....	....	....	....		1976-77	1976-77
Cochrane, Glen	Phi., Van., Chi., Edm.	10	411	17	72	89	1556	18	1	1	2	31		1978-79	1988-89
Coflin, Hughie	Chi.	1	31	0	3	3	33	....	....	....	....	....		1950-51	1950-51
Colley, Tom	Min.	1	1	0	0	0	2	....	....	....	....	....		1974-75	1974-75
Collings, Norm	Mtl.	1	1	0	1	1	0	....	....	....	....	....		1934-35	1934-35
Collins, Bill	Min., Mtl., Det., St. L, NYR, Phi., Wsh.	11	768	157	154	311	415	18	3	5	8	12		1967-68	1977-78
Collins, Gary	Tor.	1	....	....	....	....	....	2	0	0	0	0		1958-59	1958-59
Collyard, Bob	St.L.	1	10	1	3	4	4	....	....	....	....	....		1973-74	1973-74
Colville, Mac	NYR	9	353	71	104	175	130	40	9	10	19	14	1	1935-36	1946-47
Colville, Neil	NYR	12	464	99	166	265	213	46	7	19	26	33	1	1935-36	1948-49
Colwill, Les	NYR	1	69	7	6	13	16	....	....	....	....	....		1958-59	1958-59
Comeau, Rey	Mtl., Atl, Col.	9	564	98	141	239	175	9	2	1	3	8		1971-72	1979-80
Conacher, Brian	Tor., Det.	5	154	28	28	56	84	12	3	2	5	21	1	1961-62	1971-72
* Conacher, Charlie	Tor., Det., NYA	12	460	225	173	398	523	49	17	18	35	53	1	1929-30	1940-41
Conacher, Jim	Det., Chi., NYR	8	328	85	117	202	91	19	5	2	7	4		1945-46	1952-53
* Conacher, Lionel	Pit., NYA, Mtl.M., Chi.	12	500	80	105	185	882	35	2	2	4	34	2	1925-26	1936-37
Conacher, Pete	Chi., NYR, Tor.	6	229	47	39	86	57	7	0	0	0	0		1951-52	1957-58
Conacher, Roy	Bos., Det., Chi.	11	490	226	200	426	90	42	15	15	30	14	2	1938-39	1951-52
Conn, Hugh	NYA	2	96	9	28	37	22	....	....	....	....	....		1933-34	1934-35
Connelly, Wayne	Mtl., Bos., Min., Det., St. L, Van.	10	543	133	174	307	156	24	11	7	18	4		1960-61	1971-72
Connolly, Bert	NYR, Chi.	3	87	13	15	28	37	14	1	0	1	0	1	1934-35	1937-38
Connor, Cam	Mtl., Edm., NYR	5	89	9	22	31	256	20	5	0	5	6	1	1978-79	1982-83
Connor, Harry	Bos., NYA, Ott.	4	134	16	5	21	139	10	0	0	0	2		1927-28	1930-31
Connors, Bobby	NYA, Det.	3	78	17	10	27	110	2	0	0	0	10		1926-27	1929-30
Contini, Joe	Col., Min.	3	68	17	21	38	34	2	0	0	0	0		1977-78	1980-81
* Convey, Eddie	NYR	3	36	1	1	2	33	....	....	....	....	....		1930-31	1932-33
* Cook, Bill	NYR	11	452	229	138	367	386	46	13	12	25	66	2	1926-27	1936-37
Cook, Bob	Van., Det., NYI, Min.	4	72	13	9	22	22	....	....	....	....	....		1970-71	1974-75
Cook, Bud	Bos., Ott., St.L.	3	51	5	4	9	22	....	....	....	....	....		1931-32	1934-35
Cook, Bun	NYR, Bos.	11	473	158	144	302	449	46	15	3	18	57	2	1926-27	1936-37
Cook, Lloyd	Bos.	1	4	1	0	1	0	....	....	....	....	....		1924-25	1924-25
* Cook, Tom	Chi., Mtl.M.	8	311	77	98	175	184	24	2	4	6	17	1	1929-30	1937-38
* Cooper, Carson	Bos., Mtl., Det.	8	278	110	57	167	111	4	0	0	0	2		1924-25	1931-32
Cooper, Ed	Col.	2	49	8	7	15	46	....	....	....	....	....		1980-81	1981-82
Cooper, Hal	NYR	1	8	0	0	0	2	....	....	....	....	....		1944-45	1944-45
Cooper, Joe	NYR, Chi.	11	420	30	66	96	442	32	3	5	8	6		1935-36	1946-47
Copp, Bob	Tor.	2	40	3	9	12	26	....	....	....	....	....		1942-43	1950-51
* Corbeau, Bert	Mtl., Ham., Tor.,	10	257	64	31	95	501	14	2	0	2	10		1917-18	1926-27
Corbett, Michael	L.A.	1	....	....	....	....	....	2	0	1	1	2		1967-68	1967-68
Corcoran, Norm	Bos., Det., Chi.	4	29	1	3	4	21	4	0	0	0	6		1949-50	1955-56
Cormier, Roger	Mtl.	1	0	0	0	0	0	....	....	....	....	....		1925-26	1925-26
Corrigan, Charlie	Tor., NYA	2	19	2	2	4	2	....	....	....	....	....		1937-38	1940-41
Corrigan, Mike	L.A., Van., Pit.	10	594	152	195	347	698	17	2	3	5	20		1967-68	1977-78
Corriveau, Andre	Mtl.	1	3	0	1	1	0	....	....	....	....	....		1953-54	1953-54
Cory, Ross	Wpg.	2	51	2	10	12	41	....	....	....	....	....		1979-80	1980-81
Cossete, Jacques	Pit.	3	64	8	6	14	29	3	0	1	1	4		1975-76	1978-79
Costello, Les	Tor.	3	15	2	3	5	11	6	2	2	4	2	1	1947-48	1949-50
Costello, Murray	Chi., Bos., Det.	4	162	13	19	32	54	5	0	0	0	2		1953-54	1956-57
Costello, Rich	Tor.	2	12	2	2	4	2	....	....	....	....	....		1983-84	1985-86
Cotch, Charlie	Ham.	1	11	1	0	1	0	....	....	....	....	....		1924-25	1924-25
Cote, Alain	Que.	10	696	103	190	293	383	67	9	15	24	44		1979-80	1988-89
Cote, Ray	Edm.	3	15	0	0	0	4	14	3	2	5	0		1982-83	1984-85
* Cotton, Baldy	Pit., Tor., NYA	12	500	101	103	204	419	43	4	9	13	46	1	1925-26	1936-37
* Coughlin, Jack	Tor., Que, Mtl., Ham.	3	19	2	0	2	0	....	....	....	....	....	1	1917-18	1920-21
Coulis, Tim	Wsh., Min.	4	47	4	5	9	138	3	1	0	1	2		1979-80	1985-86
Coulson, D'arcy	Phi.	1	28	0	0	0	103	....	....	....	....	....		1930-31	1930-31
Coulter, Art	Chi., NYR	11	465	30	82	112	543	49	4	5	9	61	2	1931-32	1941-42
Coulter, Neal	NYI	3	26	5	5	10	11	1	0	0	0	0		1985-86	1987-88
Coulter, Tommy	Chi.	1	2	0	0	0	0	....	....	....	....	....		1933-34	1933-34
Cournoyer, Yvan	Mtl.	16	968	428	435	863	255	147	64	63	127	47	10	1963-64	1978-79
Courteau, Yves	Cgy., Hfd.	3	22	2	5	7	4	1	0	0	0	0		1984-85	1986-87
* Couture, Billy	Mtl., Ham., Bos.	10	239	33	18	51	350	32	2	0	2	42	1	1917-18	1926-27
Couture, Gerry	Det., Mtl., Chi.,	10	385	86	70	156	89	45	9	7	16	4	1	1944-45	1953-54
Couture, Rosie	Chi., Mtl.	8	304	48	56	104	184	23	1	5	6	15		1928-29	1935-36
Cowan, Tommy	Phi.	1	1	0	0	0	0	....	....	....	....	....		1930-31	1930-31
Cowick, Bruce	Phi., Wsh., St.L.	3	70	5	6	11	43	8	0	0	0	9	1	1973-74	1975-76
Cowley, Bill	St.L., Bos.	13	549	195	353	548	143	64	13	33	46	22	2	1934-35	1946-47
Cox, Danny	Tor., Ott., Det., NYR, St.L.	9	329	47	49	96	110	10	0	1	1	6		1926-27	1934-35
Crashley, Bart	Det., K.C., L.A.	6	140	7	36	43	50	....	....	....	....	....		1965-66	1975-76
Crawford, Bob	St.L., Hfd., NYR, Wsh.	7	246	71	71	142	72	11	0	1	1	8		1979-80	1986-87
Crawford, Bobby	Col., Det.	2	16	1	3	4	6	....	....	....	....	....		1980-81	1982-83
* Crawford, John	Bos.	13	547	38	140	178	202	66	4	13	17	36	2	1937-38	1949-50
Crawford, Marc	Van.	6	176	19	31	50	229	20	1	2	3	44		1981-82	1986-87
* Crawford, Rusty	Ott., Tor.,	2	38	10	3	13	51	2	2	1	3	0	1	1917-18	1918-19
Creighton, Dave	Bos., Chi., Tor., NYR	12	615	140	174	314	223	51	11	13	24	20		1948-49	1959-60
Creighton, Jimmy	Det.,	1	11	1	0	1	2	....	....	....	....	....		1930-31	1930-31
Cressman, Dave	Min.	2	85	6	8	14	37	....	....	....	....	....		1974-75	1975-76
Cressman, Glen	Mtl.	1	4	0	0	0	2	....	....	....	....	....		1956-57	1956-57
Crisofoli, Ed	Mtl.	1	9	0	1	1	4	....	....	....	....	....		1989-90	1989-90
Crisp, Terry	Bos., St.L., Phi., NYI	11	536	67	134	201	135	110	15	28	43	40	2	1965-66	1976-77
Croghen, Maurice	Mtl.M.	1	16	0	0	0	4	....	....	....	....	....		1937-38	1937-38
Crombeen, Mike	Cle., St.L., Hfd.	8	475	55	68	123	218	27	6	2	8	32		1977-78	1984-85
Crossett, Stan	Phi.,	1	21	0	0	0	10	....	....	....	....	....		1930-31	1930-31
Croteau, Gary	L.A., Det., Cal., K.C., Col.	12	684	144	175	319	143	11	3	2	5	8		1968-69	1979-80
Crowder, Bruce	Bos., Pit.	4	243	47	51	98	156	31	8	4	12	41		1981-82	1984-85
Crowder, Keith	Bos., L.A.	10	662	223	271	494	1346	85	14	22	36	218		1980-81	1989-90
Crozier, Joe	Tor.,	1	5	0	3	3	2	....	....	....	....	....		1959-60	1959-60
Crutchfield, Nels	Mtl.	1	41	5	5	10	20	2	0	1	1	22		1934-35	1934-35
Culhane, Jim	Hfd.	1	6	0	1	1	4	....	....	....	....	....		1989-90	1989-90
Cullen, Barry	Tor., Det.	5	219	32	52	84	111	6	0	0	0	2		1955-56	1959-60
Cullen, Brian	Tor., NYR	7	326	56	100	156	92	19	3	0	3	2		1954-55	1960-61
Cullen, Ray	NYR, Det., Min., Van.	6	313	92	123	215	120	20	3	10	13	2		1965-66	1970-71
Cummins, Barry	Cal.	1	36	1	2	3	39	....	....	....	....	....		1973-74	1973-74
Cunningham, Bob	NYR	2	4	0	1	1	0	....	....	....	....	....		1960-61	1961-62
Cunningham, Jim	Phi.	1	1	0	0	0	4	....	....	....	....	....		1977-78	1977-78
Cunningham, Les	NYA, Chi.	2	60	7	19	26	21	1	0	0	0	2		1936-37	1939-40
Cupolo, Bill	Bos.	1	47	11	13	24	10	7	1	2	3	0		1944-45	1944-45
Currie, Glen	Wsh., L.A.	8	326	39	79	118	100	12	1	3	4	4		1979-80	1987-88
Currie, Hugh	Mtl.	1	1	0	0	0	0	....	....	....	....	....		1950-51	1950-51
Currie, Tony	St.L., Hfd., Van.	8	290	92	119	211	73	16	4	12	16	14		1977-78	1984-85
Curry, Floyd	Mtl.	11	601	105	99	204	147	91	23	17	40	38	4	1947-48	1957-58

Bobby Clarke

Lionel Conacher

Jacques Cossette

Yvan Cournoyer

Bob Dailey

Dan Daoust

Michel Deziel

Cy Denneny

Name	NHL Teams	NHL Seasons	Regular Schedule GP	G	A	TP	PIM	Playoffs GP	G	A	TP	PIM	NHL Cup Wins	First NHL Season	Last NHL Season
Curtale, Tony	Cgy.	1	2	0	0	0	0	....	....	....	....	....		1980-81	1980-81
Curtis, Paul	Mtl., L.A., St.L.	4	185	3	34	37	151	5	0	0	0	2		1969-70	1972-73
Cushenan, Ian	Chi., Mtl., NYR, Det.	5	129	3	11	14	134	....	....	....	....	....		1956-57	1963-64
Cusson, Jean	Oak.	1	2	0	0	0	0	....	....	....	....	....		1967-68	1967-68
Cyr, Denis	Cgy., Chi., St.L.	6	193	41	43	84	36	4	0	0	0	0		1980-81	1985-86
D															
Dahlin, Kjell	Mtl.	3	166	57	59	116	10	35	6	11	17	6	1	1985-86	1987-88
Dahlstrom, Cully	Chi.	8	342	88	118	206	52	29	6	8	14	4	1	1937-38	1944-45
Daigle, Alain	Chi.	6	389	56	50	106	122	17	0	1	1	0		1974-75	1979-80
Dailey, Bob	Van., Phi.	9	561	94	231	325	814	63	12	34	46	106		1973-74	1981-82
Daley, Frank	Det.	1	5	0	0	0	0	2	0	0	0	0		1928-29	1928-29
Daley, Pat	Wpg.	2	12	1	0	1	13	....	....	....	....	....		1979-80	1980-81
Dallman, Marty	Tor.	2	6	0	1	1	0	....	....	....	....	....		1987-88	1988-89
Dame, Bunny	Mtl.	1	34	2	5	7	4	....	....	....	....	....		1941-42	1941-42
Damore, Hank	NYR	1	4	1	0	1	2	....	....	....	....	....		1943-44	1943-44
Daoust, Dan	Mtl., Tor.	8	522	87	167	254	544	32	7	5	12	83		1982-83	1989-90
Dark, Michael	St.L.	2	43	5	6	11	14	....	....	....	....	....		1986-87	1987-88
Darragh, Harry	Pit., Phi., Bos., Tor.	8	308	68	49	117	50	16	1	3	4	4	1	1925-26	1932-33
* Darragh, Jack	Ott.	6	120	68	21	89	84	21	14	2	16	7	3	1917-18	1923-24
David, Richard	Que.	3	31	4	4	8	10	1	0	0	0	0		1979-80	1982-83
Davidson, Bob	Tor.,	12	491	94	160	254	398	82	5	17	22	79	2	1934-35	1945-46
Davidson, Gord	NYR	2	51	3	6	9	8	....	....	....	....	....		1942-43	1943-44
Davie, Bob	Bos.	3	41	0	1	1	25	....	....	....	....	....		1933-34	1935-36
Davies, Ken	NYR	1	....	....	....	....	....	1	0	0	0	0		1947-48	1947-48
Davis, Bob	Det.	1	3	0	0	0	0	....	....	....	....	....		1932-33	1932-33
Davis, Kim	Pit., Tor.	4	36	5	7	12	12	4	0	0	0	0		1977-78	1980-81
Davis, Lorne	Mtl., Chi., Det., Bos.	6	95	8	12	20	20	18	3	1	4	10	1	1951-52	1959-60
Davis, Mal	Det., Buf.	5	100	31	22	53	34	7	1	0	1	0		1980-81	1985-86
Davison, Murray	Bos.	1	1	0	0	0	0	....	....	....	....	....		1965-66	1965-66
Dawes, Robert	Tor., Mtl.	4	32	2	7	4	6	10	0	0	0	2	1	1946-47	1950-51
* Day, Hap	Tor., NYA	14	581	86	116	202	601	53	4	7	11	56	1	1924-25	1937-38
Dea, Billy	Chi., NYR, Det., Pit.	8	397	67	54	121	44	11	2	0	2	6		1953-54	1970-71
Deacon, Don	Det.	3	30	6	4	10	6	2	2	1	3	0		1936-37	1939-40
Deadmarsh, Butch	Buf., ATL, K.C.	5	137	12	5	17	155	4	0	0	0	17		1970-71	1974-75
Dean, Barry	Col., Phi.	3	165	25	56	81	146	....	....	....	....	....		1976-77	1978-79
Debenedet, Nelson	Det., Pit.	2	46	10	4	14	13	....	....	....	....	....		1973-74	1974-75
Debol, David	Hfd.	2	92	26	26	52	4	3	0	0	0	0		1979-80	1980-81
Defazio, Dean	Pit.	1	22	0	2	2	28	....	....	....	....	....		1983-84	1983-84
DeGray, Dale	Cgy., Tor. L.A., Buf.	5	153	18	47	65	195	13	1	3	4	28		1985-86	1989-90
Delmonte, Armand	Bos.	1	1	0	0	0	0	....	....	....	....	....		1945-46	1945-46
Delorme, Ron	Col., Van.	9	524	83	83	166	667	25	1	2	3	59		1976-77	1984-85
Delory, Valentine	NYR	1	0	0	0	0	0	....	....	....	....	....		1948-49	1948-49
Delparte, Guy	Col.	1	48	1	8	9	18	....	....	....	....	....		1976-77	1976-77
Delvecchio, Alex	Det.	24	1549	456	825	1281	383	121	35	69	104	29	3	1950-51	1973-74
DeMarco, Ab	Chi., Tor., Bos., NYR	7	209	72	93	165	53	11	3	0	3	2		1938-39	1946-47
DeMarco, Albert	NYR, St.L., Pit., Van., L.A., Bos.	9	344	44	80	124	75	25	1	2	3	17		1969-70	1978-79
DeMeres, Tony	Mtl., NYR	6	83	20	22	42	23	3	0	0	0	0		1937-38	1943-44
Denis, Johnny	NYR	2	10	0	2	2	2	....	....	....	....	....		1946-47	1949-50
Denis, Lulu	Mtl.	2	3	0	1	1	0	....	....	....	....	....		1949-50	1950-51
* Denneny, Corbett	Tor., Ham., Chi.	9	175	99	29	128	130	15	7	4	11	6	2	1917-18	1927-28
* Denneny, Cy	Ott., Bos.	12	326	246	69	315	176	37	18	3	21	31	5	1917-18	1928-29
Dennis, Norm	St.L.	4	12	3	0	3	11	5	0	0	0	2		1968-69	1971-72
Denoird, Gerry	Tor.	1	15	0	0	0	0	....	....	....	....	....		1922-23	1922-23
Derlago, Bill	Van., Bos., Wpg., Que., Tor.	9	555	189	227	416	247	13	5	0	5	8		1978-79	1986-87
Desaulniers, Gerard	Mtl.	3	8	0	2	2	4	....	....	....	....	....		1950-51	1953-54
Desilets, Joffre	Mtl., Chi.	5	192	37	45	82	57	7	1	0	1	7		1935-36	1939-40
Desjardins, Vic	Chi., NYR	2	87	6	15	21	27	16	0	0	0	0		1930-31	1931-32
Deslauriers, Jacques	Mtl.	1	2	0	0	0	0	....	....	....	....	....		1955-56	1955-56
Devine, Kevin	NYI	1	2	0	1	1	8	....	....	....	....	....		1982-83	1982-83
Dewar, Tom	NYR	1	9	0	2	2	4	....	....	....	....	....		1943-44	1943-44
Dewsbury, Al	Det., Chi.	9	347	30	78	108	365	14	1	5	6	60	1	1946-47	1955-56
Deziel, Michel	Buf.	1	....	....	....	....	....	1	0	0	0	0		1974-75	1974-75
Dheere, Marcel	Mtl.	1	11	1	2	3	2	5	0	0	0	6		1942-43	1942-43
Diachuk, Edward	Det.	1	12	0	0	0	19	....	....	....	....	....		1960-61	1960-61
Dick, Harry	Chi.	1	12	0	1	1	12	....	....	....	....	....		1946-47	1946-47
Dickens, Ernie	Tor., Chi.	6	278	12	44	56	48	13	0	0	0	4	1	1941-42	1950-51
Dickenson, Herb	NYR	2	48	18	17	35	10	....	....	....	....	....		1951-52	1952-53
Dietrich, Don	Chi., N.J.	2	28	0	7	7	10	....	....	....	....	....		1983-84	1985-86
Dill, Bob	NYR	2	76	15	15	30	135	....	....	....	....	....		1943-44	1944-45
Dillabough, Bob	Det., Bos., Pit., Oak.	7	283	32	54	86	76	17	3	0	3	0		1961-62	1969-70
Dillon, Cecil	NYR, Det.	10	453	167	131	298	105	43	14	9	23	14	1	1930-31	1939-40
Dillon, Gary	Col.	1	13	1	1	2	29	....	....	....	....	....		1980-81	1980-81
Dillon, Wayne	NYR, Wpg.	4	229	43	66	109	60	3	0	1	1	0		1975-76	1979-80
Dineen, Bill	Det., Chi.	5	323	51	44	95	122	37	1	1	2	18	2	1953-54	1957-58
Dineen, Gary	Min.	1	4	0	1	1	0	....	....	....	....	....		1968-69	1968-69
Dineen, Peter	L.A., Det.	2	13	0	2	2	13	0	0	0	0	0		1986-87	1989-90
Dinsmore, Chuck	Mtl.M	4	100	6	2	8	44	12	1	0	1	6	1	1924-25	1929-30
Dionne, Marcel	Det., L.A., NYR	18	1348	731	1040	1771	600	49	21	24	45	17		1971-72	1988-89
Doak, Gary	Det., Bos., Van., NYR	16	789	23	107	130	908	78	2	4	6	121	1	1965-66	1980-81
Dobson, Jim	Min., Col.	3	11	0	0	0	6	....	....	....	....	....		1979-80	1981-82
* Doherty, Fred	Mtl.	1	3	0	0	0	0	....	....	....	....	....		1918-19	1918-19
Donaldson, Gary	Chi.	1	1	0	0	0	0	....	....	....	....	....	2	1973-74	1973-74
Donnelly, Babe	Mtl.M.	1	34	0	1	1	14	2	0	0	0	0		1926-27	1926-27
Donnelly, Dave	Bos., Chi., Edm.	5	137	15	24	39	150	5	0	0	0	0		1983-84	1987-88
Doran, Red (J.)	NYA., Det., Mtl.	5	98	5	10	15	110	3	0	0	0	0		1933-34	1939-40
Doran, Red (I.)	Det.	1	24	3	2	5	10	....	....	....	....	....		1946-47	1946-47
Doraty, Ken	Chi., Tor., Det.	5	103	15	26	41	24	15	7	2	9	2		1926-27	1937-38
Dore, Andre	NYR, St.L., Que.	7	257	14	81	95	261	23	1	2	3	32		1978-79	1984-85
Dorey, Jim	Tor., NYR	4	232	25	74	99	553	11	0	2	2	40		1968-69	1971-72
Dorion, Dan	N.J.	2	4	1	1	2	2	....	....	....	....	....		1985-86	1987-88
Dornhoefer, Gary	Bos., Phi.	14	787	214	328	542	1291	80	17	19	36	203	2	1963-64	1977-78
Dorohoy, Eddie	Mtl.	1	16	0	0	0	6	....	....	....	....	....		1948-49	1948-49
Douglas, Jordy	Hfd., Min., Wpg.	6	268	76	62	138	160	6	0	0	0	4		1979-80	1984-85
Douglas, Kent	Tor., Oak., Det.	7	428	33	115	148	631	19	1	3	4	33	1	1962-63	1968-69
Douglas, Les	Det.	4	52	6	12	18	8	10	3	2	5	0	1	1940-41	1946-47
Downie, Dave	Tor.	1	11	0	1	1	2	....	....	....	....	....		1932-33	1932-33
* Draper, Bruce	Tor.	1	1	0	0	0	0	....	....	....	....	....		1962-63	1962-63
* Drillon, Gordie	Tor., Mtl.	7	311	155	139	294	56	50	26	15	41	10	1	1936-37	1942-43
Driscoll, Pete	Edm.	2	60	3	8	11	97	3	0	0	0	0		1979-80	1980-81
Drolet, Rene	Phi., Det.	2	2	0	0	0	0	....	....	....	....	....		1971-72	1974-75
Drouillard, Clarence	Det.	1	10	0	1	1	0	....	....	....	....	....		1937-38	1937-38
Drouin, Jude	Mtl., Min., NYI, Wpg.	12	666	151	305	456	346	72	27	41	68	33		1968-69	1980-81
Drouin, Polly	Mtl.	6	173	23	50	73	80	5	0	1	1	5		1935-36	1940-41
Drummond, John	NYR	1	2	0	0	0	0	....	....	....	....	....		1944-45	1944-45
Drury, Herb	Pit., Phi.	6	213	24	13	37	203	4	1	1	2	0		1925-26	1930-31
Dube, Gilles	Mtl.., Det.	2	12	1	2	3	2	2	0	0	0	0	1	1949-50	1953-54
Dube, Norm	K.C.	2	57	8	10	18	54	....	....	....	....	....		1974-75	1975-76
Dudley, Rick	Buf., Wpg.	6	309	75	99	174	292	25	7	2	9	69		1972-73	1980-81
Duff, Dick	Tor., NYR, Mtl., L.A., Buf.	18	1030	283	289	572	743	114	30	49	79	78	6	1954-55	1971-72
Dufour, Luc	Bos., Que., St.L.	3	167	23	21	44	199	18	1	0	1	32		1982-83	1984-85
Dufour, Marc	NYR, L.A.	3	14	1	0	1	2	....	....	....	....	....		1963-64	1968-69
Duggan, Jack	Ott.	1	27	0	0	0	0	2	0	0	0	0		1925-26	1925-26
Duggan, Ken	Min.	1	1	0	0	0	0	....	....	....	....	....		1987-88	1987-88
Duguid, Lorne	Mtl.M, Det., Bos.	6	135	9	15	24	57	2	0	0	0	4		1931-32	1936-37
Dumart, Woody	Bos.	16	771	211	218	429	99	82	12	15	27	23	2	1935-36	1953-54
Dunbar, Dale	Van., Bos.	2	2	0	0	0	2	....	....	....	....	....		1985-86	1988-89
Duncan, Art	Det., Tor.	5	156	18	16	34	225	5	0	0	0	4		1926-27	1930-31
Dundas, Rocky	Tor.	1	5	0	0	0	14	....	....	....	....	....		1989-90	1989-90
Dunlap, Frank	Tor.	1	15	0	1	1	2	....	....	....	....	....		1943-44	1943-44
Dunlop, Blake	Min., Phi., St.L., Det.	11	550	130	274	404	172	40	4	10	14	18		1973-74	1983-84
Dunn, Dave	Van., Tor.	3	184	14	41	55	313	10	1	1	2	41		1973-74	1975-76

Name	NHL Teams	NHL Seasons	Regular Schedule GP	G	A	TP	PIM	Playoffs GP	G	A	TP	PIM	NHL Cup Wins	First NHL Season	Last NHL Season
Dunn, Richie	Buf., Cgy., Hfd.	12	483	36	140	176	314	36	3	15	18	24		1977-78	1988-89
Dupere, Denis	Tor., Wsh., St.L., K.C., Col.	8	421	80	99	179	66	16	1	0	1	0		1970-71	1977-78
Dupont, Andre	NYR, St.L., Phi., Que.	13	810	59	185	244	1986	140	14	18	32	352	2	1970-71	1982-83
Dupont, Jerome	Chi., Tor.	6	214	7	29	36	468	20	0	2	2	56		1981-82	1986-87
Dupont, Norm	Mtl., Wpg., Hfd.	5	256	55	85	140	52	13	4	2	6	0		1979-80	1983-84
Durbano, Steve	St.L., Pit., K.C., Col.	6	220	13	60	73	1127	5	0	2	2	8		1972-73	1978-79
Duris, Vitezslav	Tor.	2	89	3	20	23	62	3	0	1	1	2		1980-81	1982-83
Dussault, Norm	Mtl.	4	206	31	62	93	47	7	3	1	4	0		1947-48	1950-51
Dutkowski, Duke	Chi., NYA, NYR	5	200	16	30	46	172	6	0	0	0	6		1926-27	1933-34
* Dutton, Red	Mtl.M, NYA	10	449	29	67	96	871	18	1	0	1	33		1926-27	1935-36
Dvorak, Miroslav	Phi.	3	193	11	74	85	51	18	0	2	2	6		1982-83	1984-85
Dwyer, Mike	Col., Cgy.	4	31	2	6	8	25	1	1	0	1	0		1978-79	1981-82
Dyck, Henry	NYR	1	1	0	0	0	0	....	....	....	....	....		1943-44	1943-44
* Dye, Babe	Tor., Ham., Chi., NYA	11	271	202	41	243	205	15	11	2	13	11	1	1919-20	1930-31
Dykstra, Steven	Buf., Edm., Pit., Hfd.	5	217	8	32	40	545	1	0	0	0	2		1985-86	1989-90
Dyte, John	Chi.	1	27	1	0	1	31	....	....	....	....	....		1943-44	1943-44

E

Name	NHL Teams	NHL Seasons	Regular Schedule GP	G	A	TP	PIM	Playoffs GP	G	A	TP	PIM	NHL Cup Wins	First NHL Season	Last NHL Season
Eakin, Bruce	Cgy., Det.	4	13	2	2	4	4	....	....	....	....	....		1981-82	1985-86
Eatough, Jeff	Buf.	1	1	0	0	0	0	....	....	....	....	....		1981-82	1981-82
Eaves, Mike	Min., Cgy.	8	324	83	143	226	80	43	7	10	17	14		1978-79	1985-86
Eaves, Murray	Wpg., Det.	8	57	4	13	17	9	4	0	1	1	2		1980-81	1989-90
Ecclestone, Tim	St.L., Det., Tor., Atl.	11	692	126	233	359	346	48	6	11	17	76		1967-68	1977-78
Edberg, Rolf	Wsh.	3	184	45	58	103	24	....	....	....	....	....		1978-79	1980-81
* Eddolls, Frank	Mtl., NYR	8	317	23	43	66	114	31	0	2	2	10	1	1944-45	1951-52
Edestrand, Darryl	St.L., Phi., Pit., Bos., L.A.	10	455	34	90	124	404	42	3	9	12	57		1967-68	1978-79
Edmundson, Garry	Mtl., Tor.	3	43	4	6	10	49	11	0	1	1	8		1951-52	1960-61
Edur, Tom	Col., Pit	2	158	17	70	87	67	....	....	....	....	....		1976-77	1977-78
Egan, Pat	Bro., Det., Bos., NYR	11	554	77	153	230	776	44	9	4	13	44		1939-40	1950-51
Egers, Jack	NYR, St.L., Wsh.	7	284	64	69	133	154	32	5	6	11	32		1969-70	1975-76
Ehman, Gerry	Bos., Det., Tor., Oak, Cal.	9	429	96	118	214	100	41	10	10	20	12	1	1957-58	1970-71
Eldebrink, Anders	Van., Que.	2	55	3	11	14	29	14	0	0	0	0		1981-82	1982-83
Elik, Boris	Det.	1	3	0	0	0	0	....	....	....	....	....		1962-63	1962-63
Elliot, Fred	Ott.	1	43	2	0	2	6	....	....	....	....	....		1928-29	1928-29
Ellis, Ron	Tor.	16	1034	332	308	640	207	70	18	8	26	20	1	1963-64	1980-81
Eloranta, Kari	Cgy., St.L.	5	267	13	103	116	155	26	1	7	8	19		1981-82	1986-87
Emberg, Eddie	Mtl.	1	....	....	....	....	....	2	1	0	1	0		1944-45	1944-45
* Emms, Hap	Mtl.M, NYA, Det., Bos.	10	320	36	53	89	311	14	0	0	0	12		1926-27	1937-38
Engblom, Brian	Mtl., Wsh., L.A., Buf., Cgy.	11	659	29	177	206	599	48	3	9	12	43	3	1976-77	1986-87
Engele, Jerry	Min.	3	100	2	13	15	162	2	0	1	1	0		1975-76	1977-78
English, John	L.A.	1	3	1	3	4	4	1	0	0	0	0		1987-88	1987-88
Ennis, Jim	Edm.	1	5	1	0	1	10	....	....	....	....	....		1987-88	1987-88
Erickson, Aut	Bos., Chi., Oak., Tor.	7	227	7	84	31	182	7	0	0	0	2	1	1959-60	1969-70
Erickson, Grant	Bos., Min.	2	6	1	0	1	4	....	....	....	....	....		1968-69	1969-70
Eriksson, Peter	Edm.	1	20	3	3	6	24	....	....	....	....	....		1989-90	1989-90
Eriksson, Rolie	Min., Van.	3	193	48	95	143	26	2	1	0	1	0		1976-77	1978-79
Eriksson, Thomas	Phi.	5	208	22	76	98	107	19	0	3	3	6		1980-81	1985-86
Esposito, Phil	Chi., Bos., NYR	18	1282	717	873	1590	910	130	61	76	137	137	2	1963-64	1980-81
Evans, Chris	Tor., Buf., St.L., Det., K.C.	5	241	19	42	61	143	12	1	1	2	8		1969-70	1974-75
Evans, Daryl	L.A., Wsh., Tor.	6	113	22	30	52	25	11	5	8	13	12		1981-82	1986-87
Evans, Jack	NYR, Chi.	14	752	19	80	99	989	56	2	2	4	97	1	1948-49	1962-63
Evans, John	Phi.	3	103	14	25	39	34	1	0	0	0	0		1978-79	1982-83
Evans, Paul	Tor.	2	11	1	1	2	21	2	0	0	0	0		1976-77	1977-78
Evans, Stewart	Det., Mtl.M., Mtl.	8	367	28	49	77	425	26	0	0	0	20	1	1930-31	1938-39
Ezinicki, Bill	Tor., Bos., NYR	9	368	79	105	184	713	40	5	8	13	87	3	1944-45	1954-55

F

Name	NHL Teams	NHL Seasons	Regular Schedule GP	G	A	TP	PIM	Playoffs GP	G	A	TP	PIM	NHL Cup Wins	First NHL Season	Last NHL Season
Fahoy, Trovor	NYR	1	1	0	0	0	0	....	....	....	....	....		1964-65	1964-65
Fairbairn, Bill	NYR, Min. St.L.	11	658	162	261	423	173	54	13	22	35	42		1968-69	1978-79
Falkenberg, Bob	Det.	5	54	1	5	6	26	....	....	....	....	....		1966-67	1971-72
Farrant, Walt	Chi.	1	1	0	0	0	0	....	....	....	....	....		1943-44	1943-44
Farrish, Dave	NYR, Que, Tor.	7	430	17	110	127	440	14	0	2	2	24		1976-77	1983-84
Fashoway, Gordie	Chi.	1	13	3	2	5	14	....	....	....	....	....		1950-51	1950-51
Faubert, Mario	Pit.	7	231	21	90	111	292	10	2	2	4	6		1974-75	1981-82
Faulkner, Alex	Tor., Det.	3	101	15	17	32	15	12	5	0	5	2		1961-62	1963-64
Fauss, Ted	Tor.	2	28	0	2	2	15	....	....	....	....	....		1986-87	1987-88
Feamster, Dave	Chi.	4	169	13	24	37	155	33	3	5	8	61		1981-82	1984-85
Featherstone, Tony	Oak., Cal., Min.	3	130	17	21	38	65	2	0	0	0	0		1969-70	1973-74
Federko, Bernie	St.L., Det.	14	1000	369	761	1130	487	91	35	66	101	83		1976-77	1989-90
Felix, Chris	Wsh.	4	35	1	12	13	10	2	0	1	1	0		1987-88	1990-91
Feltrin, Tony	Pit., NYR	4	48	3	3	6	65	....	....	....	....	....		1980-81	1985-86
Ferguson	Chi.	1	1	0	0	0	0	....	....	....	....	....		1939-40	1939-40
Ferguson, George	Tor., Pit, Min	12	797	160	238	398	431	86	14	23	37	44		1972-73	1983-84
Ferguson, John	Mtl.	8	500	145	158	303	1214	85	20	18	38	260	5	1963-64	1970-71
Ferguson, Lorne	Bos., Det., Chi.	8	422	82	80	162	193	31	6	3	9	24		1949-50	1958-59
Ferguson, Norm	Oak., Cal.	4	279	73	66	139	72	10	1	4	5	7		1968-69	1971-72
Ferner, Mark	Buf.	1	13	0	3	3	9	....	....	....	....	....		1986-87	1986-87
Fidler, Mike	Cle., Min, Hfd., Chi.	7	271	84	97	181	124	....	....	....	....	....		1976-77	1982-83
Field, Wilf	Bro., Mtl., Chi.	6	218	17	25	42	151	3	0	0	0	0		1936-37	1944-45
Fielder, Guyle	Det., Chi.	4	36	0	0	0	2	6	0	0	0	2		1950-51	1957-58
Fillion, Bob	Mtl.	7	327	42	61	103	84	33	7	4	11	10	2	1943-44	1949-50
Fillion, Marcel	Bos.	1	1	0	0	0	0	....	....	....	....	....		1944-45	1944-45
Filmore, Tommy	Det., NYA, Bos.	4	116	15	12	27	33	....	....	....	....	....		1930-31	1933-34
Finkbeiner, Lloyd	NYA	1	1	0	0	0	0	....	....	....	....	....		1940-41	1940-41
Finney, Sid	Chi.	3	59	10	7	17	4	7	0	0	0	2		1951-52	1953-54
Finnigan, Ed	Bos.	1	3	0	0	0	0	....	....	....	....	....		1935-36	1935-36
* Finnigan, Frank	Ott., Tor., St.L.	14	555	115	88	203	405	39	6	9	15	22	2	1923-24	1936-37
Fischer, Ron	Buf.	2	18	0	7	7	6	....	....	....	....	....		1981-82	1982-83
Fisher, Alvin	Tor.	1	9	1	0	1	4	....	....	....	....	....		1924-25	1924-25
Fisher, Dunc	NYR, Bos., Det.	7	275	45	70	115	104	21	4	4	8	14		1947-48	1958-59
Fisher, Joe	Det.	4	66	8	12	20	13	15	2	1	3	6	1	1939-40	1942-43
Fitchner, Bob	Que	2	78	12	20	32	59	3	0	0	0	10		1979-80	1980-81
Fitzpatrick, Ross	Phi.	4	20	5	2	7	0	....	....	....	....	....		1982-83	1985-86
Fitzpatrick, Sandy	NYR, Min.	2	22	3	6	9	8	12	0	0	0	0		1964-65	1967-68
Flaman, Fern	Bos., Tor.	17	910	34	174	208	1370	63	4	8	12	93	1	1944-45	1960-61
Fleming, Reggie	Mtl., Chi., Bos., NYR, Phi., Buf.	12	749	108	132	240	1468	50	3	6	9	106	1	1959-60	1970-71
Flesch	Ham.	1	1	0	0	0	0	....	....	....	....	....		1920-21	1920-21
Flesch, John	Min, Pit, Col.	4	124	18	23	41	117	....	....	....	....	....		1974-75	1979-80
Fletcher, Steven	Mtl., Wpg.	2	3	0	0	0	5	1	0	0	0	5		1987-88	1988-89
Flett, Bill	L.A., Phi., Tor., Atl, Edm.	11	689	202	215	417	501	52	7	16	23	42	1	1967-68	1979-80
Flichel, Todd	Wpg.	4	6	0	1	1	4	....	....	....	....	....		1987-88	1989-90
Flockhart, Rob	Van., Min	5	55	2	5	7	14	1	1	0	1	2		1976-77	1980-81
Flockhart, Ron	Phi., Pit., Mtl., St.L., Bos.	9	453	145	183	328	208	29	11	18	29	16		1980-81	1988-89
Floyd, Larry	N.J.	2	12	2	3	5	9	....	....	....	....	....		1982-83	1983-84
Floyd, Larry	N.J.	2	12	2	3	5	9	....	....	....	....	....		1982-83	1983-84
Fogolin, Lee	Buf., Edm.	13	924	44	195	239	1318	108	5	19	24	173	2	1974-75	1986-87
Fogolin, Lidio (Lee)	Det., Chi.	9	427	10	48	58	575	28	0	2	2	30	1	1947-48	1955-56
Folco, Peter	Van.	1	2	0	0	0	0	....	....	....	....	....		1973-74	1973-74
Foley, Gerry	Tor., NYR, L.A.	4	142	9	14	23	99	9	0	1	1	2		1954-55	1968-69
Foley, Rick	Chi., Phi., Det.	3	67	11	26	37	180	4	0	1	1	4		1970-71	1973-74
Folk, Bill	Det.	2	12	0	0	0	4	....	....	....	....	....		1951-52	1952-53
Fontaine, Len	Det.	2	46	8	11	19	10	....	....	....	....	....		1972-73	1973-74
Fontas, Jon	Min.	2	2	0	0	0	0	....	....	....	....	....		1979-80	1980-81
Fonteyne, Val	Det., NYR, Pit.	13	820	75	154	229	26	59	3	10	13	8		1959-60	1971-72
Fontinato, Louie	NYR, Mtl.	9	535	26	78	104	1247	21	0	2	2	42		1954-55	1962-63
Forbes, Dave	Bos., Wsh.	6	363	64	64	128	341	45	1	4	5	13		1973-74	1978-79
Forbes, Mike	Bos., Edm.	3	50	1	11	12	41	....	....	....	....	....		1977-78	1981-82
Forey, Connie	St.L.	1	4	0	0	0	2	....	....	....	....	....		1973-74	1973-74
Forsey, Jack	Tor.	1	19	7	9	16	10	3	0	1	1	0		1942-43	1942-43
Forslund, Gus	Ott.	1	48	4	9	13	2	....	....	....	....	....		1932-33	1932-33

Richie Dunn

Steve Durbano

Ron Ellis

Fern Flaman

Dan Frawley

Bob Gainey

Paul Gardner

Bernie Geoffrion

			Regular Schedule					Playoffs					NHL	First	Last
Name	NHL Teams	NHL Seasons	GP	G	A	TP	PIM	GP	G	A	TP	PIM	Cup Wins	NHL Season	NHL Season
Forsyth, Alex	Wsh.	1	1	0	0	0	0	....	....	....	....	....		1976-77	1976-77
Fortier, Charles	Mtl.	1	1	0	0	0	0	....	....	....	....	....	1	1923-24	1923-24
Fortier, Dave	Tor., NYI, Van.	4	205	8	21	29	335	20	0	2	2	33		1972-73	1976-77
Fortin, Ray	St.L.	3	92	2	6	8	33	6	0	0	0	8		1967-68	1969-70
Foster, Dwight	Bos., Col., N.J., Det.	10	541	111	163	274	420	35	5	12	17	4		1977-78	1986-87
Foster, Harry	NYR, Bos., Det.	4	83	3	2	5	32	....	....	....	....	....		1929-31	1934-35
Foster, Herb	NYR	2	5	1	0	1	5	....	....	....	....	....		1940-41	1947-48
Fotiu, Nick	NYR, Hfd., Cgy., Phi., Edm.	13	646	60	77	137	1362	38	0	4	4	67		1976-77	1988-89
Fowler, Jimmy	Tor.	3	135	18	29	47	39	18	0	3	3	2		1936-37	1938-39
Fowler, Tom	Chi.	1	24	0	1	1	18	....	....	....	....	....		1946-47	1946-47
Fox, Greg	Atl, Chi., Pit.	8	494	14	92	106	637	44	1	9	10	67		1977-78	1984-85
Fox, Jim	L.A.	10	578	186	293	479	143	22	4	8	12	0		1980-81	1989-90
* Foyston, Frank	Det.	2	64	17	7	24	32	....	....	....	....	....		1926-27	1927-28
Frampton, Bob	Mtl.	1	2	0	0	0	0	3	0	0	0	0		1949-50	1949-50
Francis, Bobby	Det.	1	14	2	0	2	0	....	....	....	....	....		1982-83	1982-83
Fraser, Archie	NYR	1	3	0	1	1	0	....	....	....	....	....		1943-44	1943-44
Fraser, Curt	Van., Chi., Min.	12	704	193	240	433	1306	65	15	18	33	198		1978-79	1989-90
Fraser, Gord	Chi., Det., Mtl., Pit., Phi.	5	144	24	12	36	224	2	1	0	1	6		1926-27	1930-31
Fraser, Harry	Chi.	1	21	5	4	9	0	....	....	....	....	....		1944-45	1944-45
Fraser, Jack	Ham.	1	1	0	0	0	0	....	....	....	....	....		1923-24	1923-24
Frawley, Dan	Chi., Pit.	6	273	37	40	77	674	1	0	0	0	0		1983-84	1988-89
* Frederickson, Frank	Det., Bos., Pit.	5	165	39	34	73	207	10	2	5	7	26	1	1926-27	1930-31
Frew, Irv	Mtl.M, St.L., Mtl.	3	95	2	5	7	146	4	0	0	0	6		1933-34	1935-36
Friday, Tim	Det.	1	23	0	3	3	6	....	....	....	....	....		1985-86	1985-86
Fridgen, Dan	Hfd.	2	13	2	3	5	2	....	....	....	....	....		1981-82	1982-83
Friest, Ron	Min.	3	64	7	7	14	191	6	1	0	1	7		1980-81	1982-83
Frig, Len	Chi., Cal., Cle., St.L.	7	311	13	51	64	479	14	2	1	3	0		1972-73	1979-80
Frost, Harry	Bos.	1	3	0	0	0	0	1	0	0	0	0		1938-39	1938-39
Frycer, Miroslav	Que., Tor., Det., Edm.	8	415	147	183	330	486	17	3	8	11	16		1981-82	1988-89
Fryday, Bob	Mtl.	2	5	1	0	1	0	....	....	....	....	....		1949-50	1951-52
Ftorek, Robbie	Det., Que, NYR	8	334	77	150	227	262	19	9	6	15	28		1972-73	1984-85
Fullan, Lawrence	Wsh.	1	4	1	0	1	0	....	....	....	....	....		1974-75	1974-75
Fusco, Mark	Hfd.	2	80	3	12	15	42	....	....	....	....	....		1983-84	1984-85

G

Name	NHL Teams	NHL Seasons	GP	G	A	TP	PIM	GP	G	A	TP	PIM	Cup Wins	First NHL Season	Last NHL Season
Gadsby, Bill	Chi., NYR, Det.	20	1248	130	437	567	1539	67	4	23	27	92		1946-47	1965-66
Gagne, Art	Mtl., Bos., Ott., Det.	6	228	67	33	100	257	11	2	1	3	20		1926-27	1931-32
Gagne, Paul	Col., N.J., Tor., NYI	8	400	11	101	211	127	....	....	....	....	....		1980-81	1989-90
Gagne, Pierre	Bos.	1	2	0	0	0	0	....	....	....	....	....		1959-60	1959-60
Gagnon, Germaine	Mtl., NYI, Chi., K.C.	5	259	40	101	141	72	19	2	3	5	2		1971-72	1975-76
* Gagnon, Johnny	Mtl., Bos., NYA	10	454	120	141	261	295	32	12	12	24	37	1	1930-31	1939-40
Gainey, Bob	Mtl.	16	1160	239	262	501	585	182	25	48	73	151	5	1973-74	1988-89
Gainor, Dutch	Bos., NYR, Ott., Mtl.M	7	243	51	56	107	129	25	2	1	3	14	2	1927-28	1934-35
Galarneau, Michel	Hfd.	3	78	7	10	17	34	....	....	....	....	....		1980-81	1982-83
* Galbraith, Percy	Bos., Ott.	8	347	29	31	60	223	31	4	7	11	24		1926-27	1933-34
Gallagher, John	Mtl.M, Det., NYA	7	204	14	19	33	153	22	2	3	5	27	1	1930-31	1938-39
Gallimore, Jamie	Min.	1	2	0	0	0	0	....	....	....	....	....		1977-78	1977-78
Gallinger, Don	Bos.	5	222	65	88	153	89	23	5	5	10	19		1942-43	1947-48
Gamble, Dick	Mtl., Chi., Tor.	8	195	41	41	82	66	14	1	2	3	4	2	1950-51	1966-67
Gambucci, Gary	Min.	2	51	2	7	9	9	....	....	....	....	....		1971-72	1973-74
Gans, Dave	L.A.	2	6	0	0	0	2	....	....	....	....	....		1982-83	1985-86
* Gardiner, Herb	Mtl., Chi.	3	101	10	9	19	52	7	0	1	1	14		1926-27	1928-29
Gardner, Bill	Chi., Hfd.	9	380	73	115	188	68	45	3	8	11	17		1980-81	1988-89
Gardner, Cal	NYR, Tor., Chi., Bos.	12	696	154	238	392	517	61	7	10	17	20	2	1945-46	1956-57
Gardner, Dave	Mtl., St.L., Cal., Cle., Phi.	7	350	75	115	190	41	....	....	....	....	....		1972-73	1979-80
Gardner, Paul	Col., Tor., Pit., Wsh., Buf.	7	447	201	201	402	207	16	2	6	8	14		1976-77	1985-86
Gare, Danny	Buf., Det., Edm.	13	827	354	331	685	1285	64	25	21	46	195		1974-75	1986-87
Gariepy, Ray	Bos., Tor.	2	36	1	6	7	43	....	....	....	....	....		1953-54	1955-56
* Garland, Scott	Tor., L.A.	3	91	13	24	37	115	7	1	2	3	35		1975-76	1978-79
Garner, Bob	Pit.	1	1	0	0	0	0	....	....	....	....	....		1982-83	1982-83
Garrett, Red	NYR	1	23	1	1	2	18	....	....	....	....	....		1942-43	1942-43
* Gassoff, Bob	St.L.	4	245	11	47	58	866	9	0	1	1	16		1973-74	1976-77
Gassoff, Brad	Van.	4	122	19	17	36	163	3	0	0	0	0		1975-76	1978-79
Gatzos, Steve	Pit.	4	89	15	20	35	83	1	0	0	0	0		1981-82	1984-85
Gaudreault, Armand	Bos.	1	44	15	9	24	27	7	0	2	2	8		1944-45	1944-45
Gaudreault, Leo	Mtl.	3	67	8	4	12	30	....	....	....	....	....		1927-28	1932-33
Gaulin, Jean-Marc	Que.	4	26	4	3	7	8	1	0	0	0	0		1982-83	1985-86
Gaume, Dallas	Hfd.	1	4	1	1	2	0	....	....	....	....	....		1988-89	1988-89
Gauthier, Art	Mtl.	1	13	0	0	0	0	1	0	0	0	0		1926-27	1926-27
Gauthier, Fern	NYR, Mtl., Det.	6	229	46	50	96	35	22	5	1	6	7		1943-44	1948-49
Gauthier, Jean	Mtl., Phi., Bos.	10	166	6	29	35	150	14	1	3	4	22	1	1960-61	1969-70
Gauvreau, Jocelyn	Mtl.	1	2	0	0	0	0	....	....	....	....	....		1983-84	1983-84
Geale, Bob	Pit.	1	1	0	0	0	2	....	....	....	....	....		1984-85	1984-85
* Gee, George	Chi., Det.	9	551	135	183	318	345	41	6	13	19	32	1	1945-46	1953-54
Geldart, Gary	Min.	1	4	0	0	0	5	....	....	....	....	....		1970-71	1970-71
Gendron, Jean-Guy	NYR, Mtl., Bos., Phi.	14	863	182	201	383	701	42	7	4	11	47		1955-56	1971-72
Geoffrion, Bernie	Mtl., NYR	16	883	393	429	822	689	132	58	60	118	88	6	1950-51	1967-68
Geoffrion, Danny	Mtl., Wpg.	3	111	20	32	52	99	2	0	0	0	7		1979-80	1981-82
Geran, Gerry	Mtl.W., Bos.	2	37	5	1	6	6	....	....	....	....	....		1917-18	1925-26
* Gerard, Eddie	Ott.	6	128	50	30	80	94	26	7	3	10	51	4	1917-18	1922-23
Getliffe, Ray	Bos., Mtl.	10	393	136	137	273	260	45	9	10	19	30	2	1935-36	1944-45
Giallonardo, Mario	Col.	2	23	0	3	3	6	....	....	....	....	....		1979-80	1980-81
Gibbs, Barry	Bos., Min., Atl., St.L., L.A.	13	797	58	224	282	945	36	4	2	6	67		1967-68	1979-80
Gibson, Doug	Bos., Wsh.	3	63	9	19	28	0	1	0	0	0	0		1973-74	1977-78
Gibson, John	L.A., Tor., Wpg.	3	48	0	2	2	120	....	....	....	....	....		1980-81	1983-84
Giesebrecht, Gus	Det.	4	135	27	51	78	13	17	2	3	5	0		1938-39	1941-42
Giffin, Lee	Pit.	2	27	1	3	4	9	....	....	....	....	....		1986-87	1987-88
Gilbert, Ed	K.C., Pit.	3	166	21	31	52	22	....	....	....	....	....		1974-75	1976-77
Gilbert, Jean	Bos.	2	9	0	0	0	4	....	....	....	....	....		1962-63	1964-65
Gilbert, Rod	NYR	18	1065	406	615	1021	508	79	34	33	67	43		1960-61	1977-78
Gilbertson, Stan	Cal., St.L., Wsh., Pit.	6	428	85	89	174	148	3	1	1	2	2		1971-72	1976-77
Gillen, Don	Phi., Hfd.	2	35	2	4	6	22	....	....	....	....	....		1979-80	1981-82
Gillie, Ferrand	Det.	1	1	0	0	0	0	....	....	....	....	....		1928-29	1928-29
Gillies, Clark	NYI, Buf.	14	958	319	378	697	1023	164	47	47	94	287	4	1974-75	1987-88
Gillis, Jere	Que., Buf., Phi., Van., NYR	9	386	78	95	173	230	19	4	7	11	9		1977-78	1986-87
Gillis, Mike	Col., Bos.	6	246	33	43	76	186	27	2	5	7	10		1978-79	1983-84
Gingras, Gaston	Mtl., Tor., St.L.	10	476	61	174	235	161	52	6	18	24	20	1	1979-80	1988-89
Girard, Bob	Cal., Cle., Wsh.	5	305	45	69	114	140	....	....	....	....	....		1975-76	1979-80
Girard, Kenny	Tor.	3	7	0	1	1	2	....	....	....	....	....		1956-57	1959-60
Giroux, Art	Mtl., Bos., Det.	3	54	6	4	10	14	2	0	0	0	0		1932-33	1935-36
Giroux, Larry	St.L., K.C., Det., Hfd.	7	274	15	74	89	333	5	0	0	0	4		1973-74	1979-80
Giroux, Pierre	L.A.	1	6	1	0	1	17	....	....	....	....	....		1982-83	1982-83
Gladney, Bob	L.A., Pit.	2	14	1	5	6	4	....	....	....	....	....		1982-83	1983-84
Gladu, Jean	Bos.	1	40	6	14	20	2	7	2	2	4	0		1944-45	1944-45
Glennie, Brian	Tor., L.A.	10	572	14	100	114	621	32	0	1	1	66		1969-70	1978-79
Gloeckner, Lorry	Det.	1	13	0	2	2	6	....	....	....	....	....		1978-79	1978-79
Gloor, Dan	Van.	1	2	0	0	0	0	....	....	....	....	....		1973-74	1973-74
Glover, Fred	Det., Chi.	4	92	13	11	24	62	3	0	0	0	0		1948-49	1952-53
Glover, Howie	Chi., Det., NYR, Mtl.	5	144	29	17	46	101	11	1	2	3	2		1958-59	1968-69
Godden, Ernie	Tor.	1	5	1	1	2	6	....	....	....	....	....		1981-82	1981-82
Godfrey, Warren	Bos., Det.	16	786	32	125	157	752	52	1	4	5	42		1952-53	1967-68
Godin, Eddy	Wsh.	2	27	3	6	9	12	....	....	....	....	....		1977-78	1978-79
Godin, Sammy	Ott., Mtl.	3	83	4	3	7	36	....	....	....	....	....		1927-28	1933-34
Goegan, Peter	Det., NYR, Min.	11	383	19	67	86	365	33	1	3	4	61		1957-58	1967-68
Goertz, Dave	Pit.	1	2	0	0	0	2	....	....	....	....	....		1987-88	1987-88
Goldham, Bob	Tor., Chi., Det.	12	650	28	143	171	400	66	3	14	17	53	4	1941-42	1955-56
Goldsworthy, Bill	Bos., Min., NYR	14	771	283	258	541	793	40	18	19	37	30		1964-65	1977-78
Goldsworthy, Leroy	NYR, Det., Chi., Mtl., Bos., NYA	9	337	66	57	123	79	22	1	0	1	4	1	1929-30	1938-39
Goldup, Glenn	Mtl., L.A.	9	291	52	67	119	303	16	4	3	7	22		1973-74	1981-82
Goldup, Hank	Tor., NYR	6	181	63	80	143	97	26	5	1	6	6	1	1939-40	1945-46
Gooden, Bill	NYR	2	53	9	11	20	15	....	....	....	....	....		1942-43	1943-44
Goodenough, Larry	Phi., Van.	6	242	22	77	99	179	22	3	15	18	10	1	1974-75	1979-80

			Regular Schedule					Playoffs							
Name	NHL Teams	NHL Seasons	GP	G	A	TP	PIM	GP	G	A	TP	PIM	NHL Cup Wins	First NHL Season	Last NHL Season
* Goodfellow, Ebbie	Det.	14	554	134	190	324	511	45	8	8	16	65	3	1929-30	1942-43
Gordon, Fred	Det., Bos.	2	77	8	7	15	68	1	0	0	0	0		1926-27	1927-28
Gordon, Jackie	NYR	3	36	3	10	13	0	9	1	1	2	7		1948-49	1950-51
Gorence, Tom	Phi., Edm.	6	303	58	53	111	89	37	9	6	15	47		1978-79	1983-84
Goring, Butch	L.A., NYI, Bos.	16	1107	375	513	888	102	134	38	50	88	32	4	1969-70	1984-85
Gorman, Dave	Atl.	1	3	0	0	0	0	....	....	....	....	....		1979-80	1979-80
* Gorman, Ed	Ott., Tor.	4	111	14	5	19	108	8	0	0	0	2	1	1924-25	1927-28
Gosselin, Benoit	NYR	1	7	0	0	0	33	....	....	....	....	....		1977-78	1977-78
Gottselig, Johnny	Chi.	16	589	176	195	371	203	43	13	13	26	20	2	1928-29	1944-45
Gould, Bobby	Atl., Cgy., Wsh., Bos.	11	697	145	159	304	572	78	15	13	28	58		1979-80	1989-90
Gould, John	Buf., Van., Atl.	9	504	131	138	269	113	14	3	2	5	4		1971-72	1979-80
Gould, Larry	Van.	1	2	0	0	0	0	....	....	....	....	....		1973-74	1973-74
Goupille, Red	Mtl.	8	222	12	28	40	256	8	2	0	2	6		1935-36	1942-43
Goyer, Gerry	Chi.	1	40	1	2	3	4	3	0	0	0	2		1967-68	1967-68
Goyette, Phil	Mtl., NYR, St.L., Buf.	16	941	207	467	674	131	94	17	29	46	26	4	1956-57	1971-72
Graboski, Tony	Mtl.	3	66	6	10	16	18	2	0	0	0	0		1940-41	1942-43
* Gracie, Bob	Tor., Bos., NYA, Mtl.M., Mtl., Chi.	9	378	82	109	191	204	33	4	7	11	4	2	1930-31	1938-39
Gradin, Thomas	Van., Bos.	9	677	209	384	593	298	42	17	25	42	20		1978-79	1986-87
* Graham, Leth	Ott., Ham.	6	26	3	0	3	0	1	0	0	0	0	1	1920-21	1925-26
Graham, Pat	Pit., Tor.	3	103	11	17	28	136	4	0	0	0	2		1981-82	1983-84
Graham, Rod	Bos.	1	14	2	1	3	7	....	....	....	....	....		1974-75	1974-75
Graham, Ted	Chi., Mtl.M., Det., St.L., Bos., NYA	9	343	14	25	39	300	23	3	1	4	34		1927-28	1936-37
Grant, Danny	Mtl., Min., Det., L.A.	13	736	263	273	536	239	43	10	14	24	19	1	1965-66	1978-79
Gratton, Dan	L.A.	1	7	1	0	1	5	....	....	....	....	....		1987-88	1987-88
Gratton, Norm	NYR, Atl., Buf., Min.	5	201	39	44	83	64	6	0	1	1	2		1971-72	1975-76
Gravelle, Leo	Mtl., Det.	5	223	44	34	78	42	17	4	1	5	2		1946-47	1950-51
Graves, Hilliard	Cal., Atl., Van., Wpg.	9	556	118	163	281	209	2	0	0	0	0		1970-71	1979-80
Gray, Alex	NYR, Tor.	2	50	7	0	7	30	13	1	0	1	0	1	1927-28	1928-29
Gray, Terry	Bos., Mtl., L.A., St.L.	6	147	26	28	54	64	35	5	5	10	22		1961-62	1970-71
Green	Det.	1	2	0	0	0	0	....	....	....	....	....		1928-29	1928-29
Green, Red	Ham., NYA, Bos.	6	195	59	13	72	261	....	....	....	....	....	1	1923-24	1928-29
Green, Ted	Bos.	11	620	48	206	254	1029	31	4	8	12	54	1	1960-61	1971-72
* Green, Wilf	Ham., NYA	4	103	33	8	41	151	....	....	....	....	....		1923-24	1926-27
Greig, Bruce	Cal.	2	9	0	1	1	46	....	....	....	....	....		1973-74	1974-75
Grenier, Lucien	Mtl., L.A.	4	151	14	14	28	18	2	0	0	0	0	1	1968-69	1971-72
Grenier, Richard	NYI	1	10	1	1	2	2	....	....	....	....	....		1972-73	1972-73
Greschner, Ron	NYR	16	982	179	431	610	1226	84	17	32	49	106		1974-75	1989-90
Grigor, George	Chi.	1	2	1	0	1	0	1	0	0	0	0		1943-44	1943-44
Grisdale, John	Tor., Van.	6	250	4	39	43	346	10	0	1	1	15		1972-73	1978-79
Gronsdahl, Lloyd	Bos.	1	10	1	2	3	0	....	....	....	....	....		1941-42	1941-42
Gronstrand, Jari	Min., NYR, Que., NYI	5	185	8	26	34	135	3	0	0	0	4		1986-87	1990-91
Gross, Llyod	Tor., NYA, Bos., Det.	3	62	11	5	16	20	1	0	0	0	0		1926-27	1934-35
Grosso, Don	Det., Chi., Bos.	9	334	87	117	204	90	50	14	12	26	46	1	1938-39	1946-47
Grosvenar, Len	Ott., NYA, Mtl.	6	147	9	11	20	78	4	0	0	0	2		1927-28	1932-33
Groulx, Wayne	Que.	1	1	0	0	0	0	....	....	....	....	....		1984-85	1984-85
Gruen, Danny	Det., Col.	3	49	9	13	22	19	....	....	....	....	....		1972-73	1976-77
Gryp, Bob	Bos., Wsh.	3	74	11	13	24	33	....	....	....	....	....		1973-74	1975-76
Guay, Francois	Buf.	1	117	11	23	34	92	9	0	1	1	12		1989-90	1989-90
Guevremont, Jocelyn	Van., Buf., NYR	9	571	84	223	307	319	40	4	17	21	18		1971-72	1979-80
Guidolin, Aldo	NYR	4	182	9	15	24	117	....	....	....	....	....		1952-53	1955-56
Guidolin, Bep	Bos., Det., Chi.	9	519	107	171	278	606	24	5	7	12	35		1942-43	1951-52
Guindon, Bobby	Wpg.	1	6	0	1	1	0	....	....	....	....	....		1979-80	1979-80
Gustafsson, Bengt	Wsh.	9	629	196	359	555	196	32	9	19	28	16		1979-80	1988-89
Gustavsson, Peter	Col.	1	2	0	0	0	0	....	....	....	....	....		1981-82	1981-82

H

Name	NHL Teams	NHL Seasons	GP	G	A	TP	PIM	GP	G	A	TP	PIM	NHL Cup Wins	First NHL Season	Last NHL Season
Haanpaa, Ari	NYI	3	60	6	11	17	37	6	0	0	0	10		1985-86	1987-88
Hachborn, Len	Phi., L.A.	3	102	20	39	59	29	7	0	3	3	7		1983-84	1985-86
Haddon, Lloyd	Det.	1	8	0	0	0	2	1	0	0	0	0		1959-60	1959-60
Hadfield, Vic	NYR, Pit.	16	1002	323	389	712	1154	73	27	21	48	117		1961-62	1976-77
Haggarty, Jim	Mtl.	1	5	1	1	2	0	3	2	1	3	0		1941-42	1941-42
Hagglund, Roger	Que.	1	3	0	0	0	0	....	....	....	....	....		1984-85	1984-85
Hagman, Matti	Bos., Edm.	4	237	56	89	145	36	20	5	2	7	6		1976-77	1981-82
Haidy, Gord	Det.	1	....	....	....	....	....	1	0	0	0	0	1	1949-50	1949-50
Hajdu, Richard	Buf.	2	5	0	0	0	4	....	....	....	....	....		1985-86	1986-87
Hajt, Bill	Buf.	14	854	42	202	244	43	80	2	16	18	70		1973-74	1986-87
Hakansson, Anders	Min., Pit., L.A.	5	330	52	46	98	141	6	0	0	0	2		1981-82	1985-86
Halderson, Slim	Det., Tor.	1	44	3	2	5	65	....	....	....	....	....	1	1926-27	1926-27
Hale, Larry	Phi.	4	196	5	37	42	90	8	0	0	0	12		1968-69	1971-72
Haley, Len	Det.	2	30	2	2	4	14	6	1	3	4	6		1959-60	1960-61
Hall, Bob	NYA	1	8	0	0	0	0	....	....	....	....	....		1925-26	1925-26
Hall, Del	Cal.	3	9	2	0	2	2	....	....	....	....	....		1971-72	1973-74
* Hall, Joe	Mtl.	2	37	15	1	16	85	12	0	2	2	0		1917-18	1918-19
Hall, Murray	Chi., Det., Min., Van.	9	164	35	48	83	46	6	0	0	0	0		1961-62	1971-72
Hall, Taylor	Van., Bos.	5	41	7	9	16	29	....	....	....	....	....		1983-84	1987-88
Hall, Wayne	NYR	1	4	0	0	0	0	....	....	....	....	....		1960-61	1960-61
Halliday, Milt	Ott.	3	67	1	0	1	6	6	0	0	0	0	1	1926-27	1928-29
Hallin, Mats	NYI, Min.	5	152	17	14	31	193	15	1	0	1	13	1	1982-83	1986-87
Halward, Doug	Bos., L.A., Van., Det., Edm.	14	653	69	224	293	774	47	7	10	17	113		1975-76	1988-89
Hamel, Gilles	Buf., Wpg., L.A.	9	519	127	147	274	276	27	4	5	9	10		1980-81	1988-89
Hamel, Herb	Tor.	1	2	0	0	0	14	....	....	....	....	....		1930-31	1930-31
Hamel, Jean	St.L., Det., Que., Mtl.	12	699	26	95	121	766	33	0	2	2	44		1972-73	1983-84
Hamill, Red	Bos., Chi.	12	418	128	94	222	160	13	1	2	3	12	2	1937-38	1950-51
Hamilton, Al	NYR, Buf., Edm.	7	257	10	78	88	258	7	0	0	0	2		1965-66	1979-80
Hamilton, Chuck	Mtl., St.L.	2	4	0	2	2	2	....	....	....	....	....		1961-62	1972-73
Hamilton, Jack	Tor.	3	138	31	48	79	76	11	2	1	3	0		1942-43	1945-46
Hamilton, Jim	Pit.	8	95	14	18	32	28	6	3	0	3	0		1977-78	1984-85
Hamilton, Reg	Tor., Chi.	12	387	21	87	108	412	64	6	6	12	54	2	1935-36	1946-47
Hammarstrom, Inge	Tor., St.L.	6	427	116	123	239	86	13	2	3	5	4		1973-74	1978-79
Hampson, Gord	Cgy.	1	4	0	0	0	5	....	....	....	....	....		1982-83	1982-83
Hampson, Ted	Tor., NYR, Det., Oak., Cal., Min.	12	676	108	245	353	94	35	7	10	17	2		1959-60	1971-72
Hampton, Rick	Cal., Cle., L.A.	6	337	59	113	172	147	2	0	0	0	0		1974-75	1979-80
Hamway, Mark	NYI	3	53	5	13	18	9	1	0	0	0	0		1984-85	1986-87
Handy, Ron	NYI, St.L.	2	14	0	3	3	0	....	....	....	....	....		1984-85	1987-88
Hangsleben, Al	Hfd., Wsh., L.A.	3	185	21	48	69	396	....	....	....	....	....		1979-80	1981-82
Hanna, John	NYR, Mtl., Phi.	5	198	6	26	32	206	....	....	....	....	....		1958-59	1967-68
* Hannigan, Gord	Tor.	4	161	29	31	60	117	9	2	0	2	8		1952-53	1955-56
Hannigan, Pat	Tor., NYR, Phi.	5	182	30	39	69	116	11	1	2	3	11		1959-60	1968-69
Hannigan, Ray	Tor.	1	3	0	0	0	2	....	....	....	....	....		1948-49	1948-49
Hansen, Ritchie	NYI, St.L.	4	20	2	8	10	6	....	....	....	....	....		1976-77	1981-82
Hanson, Dave	Det., Min.	2	33	1	1	2	65	....	....	....	....	....		1978-79	1979-80
Hanson, Emil	Det.	1	7	0	0	0	6	....	....	....	....	....		1932-33	1932-33
Hanson, Keith	Cgy.	1	25	0	2	2	77	....	....	....	....	....		1983-84	1983-84
Hanson, Ossie	Chi.	1	7	0	0	0	0	....	....	....	....	....		1937-38	1937-38
Harbaruk, Nick	Pit., St.L.	5	364	45	75	120	273	14	3	1	4	20		1969-70	1973-74
Harding, Jeff	Phi.	2	15	0	0	0	47	....	....	....	....	....		1988-89	1989-90
Hardy, Joe	Oak., Cal.	2	63	9	14	23	51	4	0	0	0	0		1969-70	1970-71
Hargreaves, Jim	Van.	2	66	1	7	8	105	....	....	....	....	....		1970-71	1972-73
Harlow, Scott	St.L.	1	1	0	1	1	0	....	....	....	....	....		1987-88	1987-88
Harmon, Glen	Mtl.	9	452	50	96	146	334	53	5	10	15	37	2	1942-43	1950-51
Harms, John	Chi.	2	44	5	5	10	21	3	3	0	3	2		1943-44	1944-45
Harnott, Happy	Bos.	1	6	0	0	0	6	....	....	....	....	....		1933-34	1933-34
Harper, Terry	Mtl., L.A., Det., St.L., Col.	19	1066	35	221	256	1362	112	4	13	17	140	5	1962-63	1980-81
Harrer, Tim	Cgy.	1	3	0	0	0	2	....	....	....	....	....		1982-83	1982-83
Harrington, Hago	Bos., Mtl.	3	72	9	3	12	15	4	1	0	1	2		1925-26	1932-33
Harris, Billy	Tor., Det., Oak., Cal., Pit.	12	769	126	219	345	205	62	8	10	18	30	3	1955-56	1968-69
Harris, Billy	NYI, L.A., Tor.	12	897	231	327	558	394	71	19	19	38	48		1972-73	1983-84
Harris, Duke	Min., Tor.	1	26	1	4	5	4	....	....	....	....	....		1967-68	1967-68
Harris, Hugh	Buf.	1	60	12	26	38	17	3	0	0	0	0		1972-73	1972-73
Harris, Ron	Det., Oak., Atl., NYR	12	476	20	91	111	484	28	4	3	7	33		1962-63	1975-76
Harris, Smokey	Bos.	2	40	5	5	10	28	2	0	0	0	0		1924-25	1930-31
Harris, Ted	Mtl., Min., Det., St.L., Phi.	12	788	30	168	198	1000	100	1	22	23	230	5	1963-64	1974-75

Ron Greschner

Bengt Gustaffson

Ari Haanpaa

Craig Hartsburg

Buster Harvey

Tim Horton

Harry Howell

Bobby Hull

Name	NHL Teams	NHL Seasons	Regular Schedule GP	G	A	TP	PIM	Playoffs GP	G	A	TP	PIM	NHL Cup Wins	First NHL Season	Last NHL Season
Harrison, Ed	Bos., NYR	4	194	27	24	51	53	9	1	0	1	2		1947-48	1950-51
Harrison, Jim	Bos., Tor., Chi., Edm.	8	324	67	86	153	435	13	1	1	2	43		1968-69	1979-80
Hart, Gerry	Det., NYI, Que., St.L.	15	730	29	150	179	1240	78	3	12	15	175		1968-69	1982-83
* Hart, Gizzy	Det., Mtl.	3	100	6	8	14	12	8	0	1	1	0	1	1926-27	1932-33
Hartsburg, Craig	Min.	10	570	98	315	413	818	61	15	27	42	70		1979-80	1988-89
* Harvey, Doug	Mtl., NYR, Det., St.L.	20	1113	88	452	540	1216	137	8	64	72	152	6	1947-48	1968-69
Harvey, Fred	Min., Atl., K.C., Det.	7	407	90	118	208	131	14	0	2	2	8		1970-71	1976-77
Harvey, Hugh	K.C.	2	18	1	1	2	4	....	....	....	....	....		1974-75	1975-76
Hassard, Bob	Tor., Chi.	5	126	9	28	37	22	....	....	....	....	....		1949-50	1954-55
Hatoum, Ed	Det., Van.	3	47	3	6	9	25	....	....	....	....	....		1968-69	1970-71
Haworth, Alan	Buf., Wsh., Que.	8	524	189	211	400	425	42	12	16	28	28		1980-81	1987-88
Haworth, Alan	Buf., Wsh., Que.	8	524	189	211	400	425	42	12	16	28	28		1980-81	1987-88
Haworth, Gord	NYR	1	2	0	1	1	0	....	....	....	....	....		1952-53	1952-53
Hawryliw, Neil	NYI	1	1	0	0	0	0	....	....	....	....	....		1981-82	1981-82
Hay, Billy	Chi.	8	506	113	273	386	244	67	15	21	36	62		1959-60	1966-67
* Hay, George	Chi., Det.	7	242	74	60	134	84	8	2	3	5	14		1926-27	1933-34
Hay, Jim	Det.	3	75	1	5	6	22	9	1	0	1	2	1	1952-53	1954-55
Hayek, Peter	Min.	1	1	0	0	0	0	....	....	....	....	....		1981-82	1981-82
Hayes, Chris	Bos.	1	....	....	....	....	....	1	0	0	0	0	1	1971-72	1971-72
Haynes, Paul	Mtl.M., Bos., Mtl.	11	390	61	134	195	164	25	2	8	10	13		1930-31	1940-41
Hayward, Rick	L.A.	1	4	0	0	0	5	....	....	....	....	....		1990-91	1990-91
Hazlett, Steve	Van.	1	1	0	0	0	0	....	....	....	....	....		1979-80	1979-80
Head, Galen	Det.	1	1	0	0	0	0	....	....	....	....	....		1967-68	1967-68
Headley, Fern	Bos., Mtl.	1	27	1	1	2	6	5	0	0	0	0		1924-25	1924-25
Healey, Dick	Det.	1	1	0	0	0	2	....	....	....	....	....		1960-61	1960-61
Heaslip, Mark	NYR, L.A.	3	117	10	19	29	110	5	0	0	0	2		1976-77	1978-79
Heath, Randy	NYR	2	13	2	4	6	15	....	....	....	....	....		1984-85	1985-86
Hebenton, Andy	NYR, Bos.	9	630	189	202	391	83	22	6	5	11	8		1955-56	1963-64
Hedberg, Anders	NYR	7	465	172	225	397	144	58	22	24	46	31		1978-79	1984-85
* Heffernan, Frank	Tor.	1	17	0	0	0	4	....	....	....	....	....		1919-20	1919-20
Heffernan, Gerry	Mtl.	3	83	33	35	68	27	11	3	3	6	8	1	1941-42	1943-44
Heidt, Mike	L.A.	1	6	0	1	1	7	....	....	....	....	....		1983-84	1983-84
Heindl, Bill	Min., NYR	3	18	2	1	3	0	....	....	....	....	....		1970-71	1972-73
Heinrich, Lionel	Bos.	1	35	1	1	2	33	....	....	....	....	....		1955-56	1955-56
Heiskala, Earl	Phi.	3	127	13	11	24	294	....	....	....	....	....		1968-69	1970-71
Helander, Peter	L.A.	1	7	0	1	1	0	....	....	....	....	....		1982-83	1982-83
* Heller, Ott.	NYR	15	647	55	176	231	465	61	6	8	14	61	2	1931-32	1945-46
Helman, Harry	Ott.	3	42	1	0	1	7	5	0	0	0	0	1	1922-23	1924-25
Helminen, Raimo	NYR, Min., NYI	3	117	13	46	59	16	2	0	0	0	0		1985-86	1988-89
Hemmerling, Tony	NYA	2	24	3	3	6	4	....	....	....	....	....		1935-36	1936-37
Henderson, Archie	Wsh., Min., Hfd.	3	23	3	1	4	92	....	....	....	....	....		1980-81	1982-83
Henderson, Murray	Bos.	8	405	24	62	86	305	41	2	3	5	23		1944-45	1951-52
Henderson, Paul	Det., Tor., Atl.	13	707	236	241	477	304	56	11	14	25	28		1962-63	1979-80
Hendrickson, John	Det.	3	5	0	0	0	4	....	....	....	....	....		1957-58	1961-62
Henning, Lorne	NYI	9	544	73	111	184	102	81	7	7	14	8	2	1972-73	1980-81
Henry, Camille	NYR, Chi., St.L.	14	727	279	249	528	88	47	6	12	18	7		1953-54	1969-70
Henry, Dale	NYI	6	132	13	26	39	263	....	....	....	....	....		1984-85	1989-90
Hepple, Alan	N.J.	3	3	0	0	0	7	....	....	....	....	....		1983-84	1985-86
Hepple, Alan	N.J.	3	3	0	0	0	7	....	....	....	....	....		1983-84	1985-86
* Herberts, Jimmy	Bos., Tor., Det.	6	206	83	29	112	250	9	3	0	3	35		1924-25	1929-30
Herchenratter, Art	Det.	1	10	1	2	3	2	....	....	....	....	....		1940-41	1940-41
Hergerts, Fred	NYA	2	19	2	4	6	2	....	....	....	....	....		1934-35	1935-36
Hergesheimer, Philip	Chi., Bos.	4	125	21	41	62	19	7	0	0	0	2		1939-40	1942-43
Hergesheimer, Wally	NYR, Chi.	7	351	114	85	199	106	5	1	0	1	0		1951-52	1958-59
Heron, Red	Tor., Bro., Mtl.	4	106	21	19	40	38	16	2	2	4	55		1938-39	1941-42
Hess, Bob	St.L., Buf., Hfd.	8	329	27	95	122	178	4	1	1	2	2		1974-75	1983-84
Heximer, Orville	NYR, Bos., NYA	3	85	13	7	20	28	5	0	0	0	2		1929-30	1934-35
Hextall, Bryan Jr.	NYR, Pit., Atl., Det., Min.	8	549	99	161	260	738	18	0	4	4	59		1962-63	1975-76
* Hextall, Bryan Sr.	NYR	11	447	187	175	362	227	37	8	9	17	19	1	1936-37	1947-48
Hextall, Dennis	NYR, L.A., Cal., Min., Det., Wsh.	13	681	153	350	503	1398	22	3	3	6	45		1968-69	1979-80
Heyliger, Vic	Chi.	2	34	2	3	5	2	....	....	....	....	....		1937-38	1943-44
Hicke, Bill	Mtl., NYR, Oak.	14	729	168	234	402	395	42	3	10	13	41	2	1958-59	1971-72
Hicke, Ernie	Cal., Atl., NYI, Min., L.A.	8	520	132	140	272	407	2	1	0	1	0		1970-71	1977-78
Hickey, Greg	NYR	1	1	0	0	0	0	....	....	....	....	....		1977-78	1977-78
Hickey, Pat	NYR, Col., Tor., Que., St.L.	10	646	192	212	404	351	55	5	11	16	37		1975-76	1984-85
Hicks, Doug	Min., Chi., Edm., Wsh.	9	561	37	131	168	442	....	....	....	....	....		1974-75	1982-83
Hicks, Glenn	Det.	2	108	6	12	18	127	....	....	....	....	....		1979-80	1980-81
* Hicks, Hal	Mtl.M., Det.	3	110	7	2	9	72	....	....	....	....	....		1928-29	1930-31
Hicks, Wayne	Chi., Bos., Mtl., Phi., Pit.	5	115	13	23	36	22	2	0	1	1	2	1	1959-60	1967-68
Hidi, Andre	Wsh.	2	7	2	1	3	9	2	0	0	0	0		1983-84	1984-85
Hiemer, Uli	N.J.	3	143	19	54	73	176	....	....	....	....	....		1984-85	1986-87
Higgins, Paul	Tor.	2	25	0	0	0	152	1	0	0	0	0		1981-82	1982-83
Higgins, Tim	Chi., N.J., Det.	11	706	154	198	352	719	65	5	8	13	77		1978-79	1988-89
Hildebrand, Ike	NYR, Chi.	2	41	7	11	18	16	....	....	....	....	....		1953-54	1954-55
Hill, Al	Phi.	8	221	40	55	95	227	51	8	11	19	43		1976-77	1987-88
Hill, Brian	Hfd.	1	19	1	1	2	4	....	....	....	....	....		1979-80	1979-80
Hill, Mel	Bos., Bro., Tor.	9	323	89	109	198	138	43	12	7	19	18	3	1937-38	1945-46
Hiller, Dutch	NYR, Det., Bos., Mtl.	9	385	91	113	204	163	48	9	8	17	21	2	1937-38	1945-46
Hillman, Floyd	Bos.	1	6	0	0	0	10	....	....	....	....	....		1956-57	1956-57
Hillman, Larry	Det., Bos., Tor., Min., Mtl., Phi., L.A., Buf.	19	790	36	196	232	579	74	2	9	11	30	4	1954-55	1972-73
* Hillman, Wayne	Chi., NYR, Min., Phi.	13	691	18	86	104	534	28	0	3	3	19	1	1960-61	1972-73
Hilworth, John	Det.	3	57	1	1	2	89	....	....	....	....	....		1977-78	1979-80
Himes, Normie	NYA	9	402	106	113	219	127	2	0	0	0	0		1926-27	1934-35
Hindmarch, Dave	Cgy.	4	99	21	17	38	25	10	0	0	0	6		1980-81	1983-84
Hinse, Andre	Tor.	1	4	0	0	0	0	....	....	....	....	....		1967-68	1967-68
Hinton, Dan	Chi.	1	14	0	0	0	16	....	....	....	....	....		1976-77	1976-77
Hirsch, Tom	Min.	3	31	1	7	8	30	12	0	0	0	6		1983-84	1987-88
Hirschfeld, Bert	Mtl.	2	33	1	4	5	2	5	1	0	1	0		1949-50	1950-51
Hislop, Jamie	Que., Cgy.	5	345	75	103	178	86	28	3	2	5	11		1979-80	1983-84
Hitchman, Lionel	Ott., Bos.	12	413	28	33	61	523	40	4	1	5	77	2	1922-23	1933-34
Hlinka, Ivan	Van.	2	137	42	81	123	28	16	3	10	13	8		1981-82	1982-83
Hodge, Ken	Chi., Bos., NYR	13	881	328	472	800	779	97	34	47	81	120		1965-66	1977-78
Hodgson, Dan	Tor., Van.	4	114	29	45	74	64	....	....	....	....	....		1985-86	1988-89
Hodgson, Rick	Hfd.	1	6	0	0	0	6	1	0	0	0	0		1979-80	1979-80
Hodgson, Ted	Bos.	1	4	0	0	0	0	....	....	....	....	....		1966-67	1966-67
Hoekstra, Cecil	Mtl.	1	4	0	0	0	0	....	....	....	....	....		1959-60	1959-60
Hoekstra, Ed	Phi.	1	70	15	21	36	6	7	0	1	1	0		1967-68	1967-68
Hoene, Phi.	L.A.	3	37	2	4	6	22	....	....	....	....	....		1972-73	1974-75
Hoffinger, Vic	Chi.	2	28	0	1	1	30	....	....	....	....	....		1927-28	1928-29
Hoffman, Mike	Hfd.	3	9	1	3	4	2	....	....	....	....	....		1982-83	1985-86
Hoffmeyer, Bob	Chi., Phi., N.J.	6	198	14	52	66	325	3	0	1	1	25		1977-78	1984-85
Hofford, Jim	Buf., L.A.	3	18	0	0	0	47	....	....	....	....	....		1985-86	1988-89
Hogaboam, Bill	Atl., Det., Min.	8	332	80	109	189	100	2	0	0	0	0		1972-73	1979-80
Hoganson, Dale	L.A., Mtl., Que.	7	343	13	77	90	186	11	0	3	3	12		1969-70	1981-82
Holbrook, Terry	Min.	2	43	3	6	9	4	6	0	0	0	0		1972-73	1973-74
Holland, Jerry	NYR	2	37	8	4	12	6	....	....	....	....	....		1974-75	1975-76
Hollett, Frank	Tor., Ott., Bos., Det.	13	565	132	181	313	358	79	8	26	34	38	2	1933-34	1945-46
* Hollingworth, Gord	Chi., Det.	4	163	4	14	18	201	3	0	0	0	2		1954-55	1957-58
Holloway, Bruce	Van.	1	2	0	0	0	0	....	....	....	....	....		1984-85	1984-85
Holmes, Bill	Mtl., NYA.	2	51	6	4	10	35	....	....	....	....	....		1925-26	1929-30
Holmes, Chuck	Det.	2	23	1	3	4	10	....	....	....	....	....		1958-59	1961-62
Holmes, Lou	Chi.	2	59	1	4	5	6	2	0	0	0	2		1931-32	1932-33
Holmes, Warren	L.A.	3	45	8	18	26	7	....	....	....	....	....		1981-82	1983-84
Holmgren, Paul	Phi., Min.	10	527	144	179	323	1684	82	19	32	51	195		1975-76	1984-85
Holota, John	Det.	2	15	2	0	2	0	....	....	....	....	....		1942-43	1945-46
Holst, Greg	NYR	3	11	0	0	0	0	....	....	....	....	....		1975-76	1977-78
Holt, Gary	Cal., Clev., St.L.	5	101	13	11	24	183	....	....	....	....	....		1973-74	1977-78
Holt, Randy	Chi., Clev., Van., L.A., Cgy., Wsh., Phi.	10	395	4	37	41	1438	21	2	3	5	83		1974-75	1983-84
Holway, Albert	Tor., Mtl.M., Pit.	5	117	7	2	9	48	8	0	0	0	2	1	1923-24	1928-29
Homenuke, Ron	Van.	1	1	0	0	0	0	....	....	....	....	....		1972-73	1972-73
Hopkins, Dean	L.A., Edm.	5	218	23	49	72	302	18	1	5	6	29		1979-80	1985-86
Hopkins, Dean	L.A., Edm., Que.	6	223	23	51	74	306	18	1	5	6	29		1979-80	1988-89
Hopkins, Larry	Tor., Wpg.	4	60	13	16	29	26	6	0	0	0	2		1977-78	1982-83
Horava, Miloslav	NYR	3	80	5	17	22	38	2	0	1	1	0		1988-89	1990-91
Horbul, Doug	K.C.	1	4	1	0	1	2	....	....	....	....	....		1974-75	1974-75

Name	NHL Teams	NHL Seasons	Regular Schedule GP	G	A	TP	PIM	Playoffs GP	G	A	TP	PIM	NHL Cup Wins	First NHL Season	Last NHL Season
Hordy, Mike	NYI	2	11	0	0	0	7	....	....	....	....	....		1978-79	1979-80
Horeck, Pete	Chi., Det., Bos.	8	426	106	118	224	340	34	6	8	14	43		1944-45	1951-52
Horne, George	Mtl.M, Tor.	3	54	9	3	12	34	4	0	0	0	4	1	1925-26	1928-29
Horner, Red	Tor.	12	490	42	110	152	1264	71	7	10	17	166	1	1928-29	1939-40
Hornung, Larry	St.L.	2	48	2	9	11	10	11	0	2	2	2		1970-71	1971-72
* Horton, Tim	Tor., NYR, Buf., Pit.	24	1446	115	403	518	1611	126	11	39	50	183	4	1949-50	1973-74
Horvath, Bronco	NYR, Mtl., Bos., Chi., Tor., Min.	9	434	141	185	326	319	36	12	9	21	18		1955-56	1967-68
Hospodar, Ed	NYR, Hfd., Phi., Min., Buf.	9	450	17	51	68	1314	44	4	1	5	206		1979-80	1987-88
Hotham Greg	Tor., Pit.	6	230	15	74	89	139	5	0	3	3	6		1979-80	1984-85
Houck, Paul	Min.	3	16	1	2	3	2	....	....	....	....	....		1985-86	1987-88
Houde, Claude	K.C.	2	59	3	6	9	40	....	....	....	....	....		1974-75	1975-76
Houle, Rejean	Mtl.	11	635	161	247	408	395	90	14	34	48	66	5	1969-70	1982-83
Houston, Ken	Atl., Cgy., Wsh., L.A.	9	570	161	167	328	624	35	10	9	19	66		1975-76	1983-84
Howard, Frank	Tor.	1	2	0	0	0	0	....	....	....	....	....		1936-37	1936-37
Howatt, Garry	NYI, Hfd., N.J.	12	720	112	156	268	1836	87	12	14	26	289	2	1972-73	1983-84
Howe, Gordie	Det., Hfd.	26	1767	801	1049	1850	1685	157	68	92	160	220	4	1946-47	1979-80
Howe, Marty	Hfd., Bos.	6	197	2	29	31	99	15	1	2	3	9		1979-80	1984-85
* Howe, Syd	Ott., Phi., Tor., St.L., Det.	17	691	237	291	528	212	70	17	27	44	10	3	1929-30	1945-46
Howe, Vic	NYR	3	33	3	4	7	10	....	....	....	....	....		1950-51	1954-55
Howell, Harry	NYR, Oak., L.A.	21	1411	94	324	418	1298	38	3	3	6	32		1952-53	1972-73
Howell, Ron	NYR	2	4	0	0	0	4	....	....	....	....	....		1954-55	1955-56
Howse, Don	L.A.	1	33	2	5	7	6	2	0	0	0	0		1979-80	1979-80
Howson, Scott	NYI	2	18	5	3	8	4	....	....	....	....	....		1984-85	1985-86
Hoyda, Dave	Phi., Wpg.	4	132	6	17	23	299	12	0	0	0	17		1977-78	1980-81
Hrechkosy, Dave	Cal., St.L.	4	140	42	24	66	41	3	1	0	1	2		1973-74	1976-77
Hrycuik, Jim	Wsh.	1	21	5	5	10	12	....	....	....	....	....		1974-75	1974-75
Hrymnak, Steve	Chi., Det.	2	18	2	1	3	4	2	0	0	0	0		1951-52	1952-53
Hrynewich, Tim	Pit.	2	55	6	8	14	82	....	....	....	....	....		1982-83	1983-84
Huard, Rolly	Tor.	1	1	1	0	1	0	....	....	....	....	....		1930-31	1930-31
Huber, Willie	Det., NYR, Van., Phi.	10	655	104	217	321	950	33	5	5	10	35		1978-79	1987-88
Hubick, Greg	Tor., Van.	2	77	6	9	15	10	....	....	....	....	....		1975-76	1979-80
Huck, Fran	Mtl., St.L.	3	94	24	30	54	38	11	3	4	7	2		1969-70	1972-73
Hucul, Fred	Chi., St.L.	5	164	11	30	41	113	6	1	0	1	10		1950-51	1967-68
Hudson, Dave	NYI, K.C., Col.	6	409	59	124	183	89	2	1	1	2	0		1972-73	1977-78
Hudson, Lex	Pit.	1	2	0	0	0	0	2	0	0	0	0		1978-79	1978-79
Hudson, Ron	Det.	2	34	5	2	7	2	....	....	....	....	....		1937-38	1939-40
Huggins, Al	Mtl.M	1	20	1	1	2	2	....	....	....	....	....		1930-31	1930-31
Hughes, Al	NYA	2	60	6	8	14	22	....	....	....	....	....		1930-31	1931-32
Hughes, Brent	L.A., Phi., St.L., Det., K.C.	8	435	15	117	132	440	22	1	3	4	53		1967-68	1974-75
Hughes, Frank	Cal.	1	5	0	0	0	0	....	....	....	....	....		1971-72	1971-72
Hughes, Howie	L.A.	3	168	25	32	57	30	14	2	0	2	2		1967-68	1969-70
Hughes, Jack	Col.	2	46	2	5	7	104	....	....	....	....	....		1980-81	1981-82
Hughes, John	Van., Edm., NYR	3	70	2	14	16	211	7	0	1	1	16		1979-80	1980-81
Hughes, Pat	Mtl., Pit., Edm., Buf., St.L., Hfd.	10	573	130	128	258	646	71	8	25	33	77	3	1977-78	1986-87
Hughes, Rusty	Det.	1	40	0	1	1	48	....	....	....	....	....		1929-30	1929-30
Hull, Bobby	Chi., Wpg., Hfd.	16	1063	610	560	1170	640	119	62	67	129	102	1	1957-58	1979-80
Hull, Dennis	Chi., Det.	14	959	303	351	654	261	104	33	34	67	30		1964-65	1977-78
* Hunt, Fred	NYA, NYR	2	59	15	14	29	6	....	....	....	....	....		1940-41	1944-45
Hunter, Dave	Edm., Pit., Wpg.	10	746	133	190	323	918	105	16	24	40	211	3	1979-80	1988-89
Huras, Larry	NYR	1	1	0	0	0	0	....	....	....	....	....		1976-77	1976-77
Hurlburt, Bob	Van.	1	1	0	0	0	2	....	....	....	....	....		1974-75	1974-75
Hurley, Paul	Bos.	1	1	0	1	1	0	....	....	....	....	....		1968-69	1968-69
Hurst, Ron	Tor.	2	64	9	7	16	7	3	0	2	2	4		1955-56	1956-57
Huston, Ron	Cal.	2	79	15	31	46	8	....	....	....	....	....		1973-74	1974-75
Hutchinson, Ronald	NYR	1	9	0	0	0	0	....	....	....	....	....		1960-61	1960-61
Hutchison, Dave	L.A., Tor., Chi., N.J.	10	584	19	97	116	1550	48	2	12	14	149		1974-75	1983-84
* Hutton, William	Bos., Ott., Phi.	2	64	3	2	5	8	2	0	0	0	0		1929-30	1930-31
* Hyland, Harry	Mtl.W, Ott.	1	16	14	0	14	0	....	....	....	....	....		1917-18	1917-18
Hynes, Dave	Bos.	2	22	4	0	4	2	....	....	....	....	....		1973-74	1974-75

I

Name	NHL Teams	NHL Seasons	Regular Schedule GP	G	A	TP	PIM	Playoffs GP	G	A	TP	PIM	NHL Cup Wins	First NHL Season	Last NHL Season
Ihnacak, Miroslav	Tor., Det.	3	56	8	9	17	39	1	0	0	0	0		1985-86	1988-89
Ihnacak, Peter	Tor.	8	417	102	165	267	175	28	4	10	14	25		1982-83	1989-90
Imlach, Brent	Tor.	2	3	0	0	0	2	....	....	....	....	....		1965-66	1966-67
Ingarfield, Earl Jr.	Atl., Cgy., Det.	2	39	4	4	8	22	2	0	1	1	0		1979-80	1980-81
Ingarfield, Earl	NYR, Pit., Oak., Cal.	13	746	179	226	405	239	21	9	8	17	10		1958-59	1970-71
Inglis, Bill	L.A., Buf.	3	36	1	3	4	4	11	1	2	3	4		1967-68	1970-71
Ingoldsby, Johnny	Tor.	2	29	5	1	6	15	....	....	....	....	....		1942-43	1943-44
Ingram, Frank	Bos., Chi.	4	102	24	16	40	69	11	0	1	1	2		1924-25	1931-32
Ingram, Ron	Chi., Det., NYR	4	114	5	15	20	81	2	0	0	0	0		1956-57	1964-65
* Irvin, Dick	Chi.	3	94	29	23	52	76	2	2	0	2	4		1926-27	1928-29
Irvine, Ted	Bos., L.A., NYR, St.L.	11	724	154	177	331	657	83	16	24	40	115		1963-64	1976-77
Irwin, Ivan	Mtl., NYR	5	155	2	27	29	214	5	0	0	0	8		1952-53	1957-58
Isaksson, Ulf	L.A.	1	50	7	15	22	10	....	....	....	....	....		1982-83	1982-83
Issel, Kim	Edm.	1	4	0	0	0	0	....	....	....	....	....		1988-89	1988-89

J

Name	NHL Teams	NHL Seasons	Regular Schedule GP	G	A	TP	PIM	Playoffs GP	G	A	TP	PIM	NHL Cup Wins	First NHL Season	Last NHL Season
Jackson, Art	Bos., Tor.	11	466	123	178	301	144	51	8	12	20	27	2	1934-35	1944-45
Jackson, Don	Min., Edm., NYR	10	311	16	52	68	640	53	4	5	9	147	2	1977-78	1986-87
Jackson, Hal	Chi., Det.	8	222	17	34	51	208	31	1	2	3	33	2	1936-37	1946-47
* Jackson, Harvey	Tor., Bos., NYA	15	636	241	234	475	437	71	18	12	30	53	1	1929-30	1943-44
Jackson, Jim	Cgy., Buf.	4	112	17	30	47	20	14	3	2	5	6		1982-83	1987-88
Jackson, John	Chi.	1	48	2	5	7	38	....	....	....	....	....		1946-47	1946-47
Jackson, Lloyd	NYA	1	14	1	1	2	0	....	....	....	....	....		1936-37	1936-37
Jackson, Stan	Tor., Bos., Ott.	5	84	9	4	13	74	....	....	....	....	....	1	1921-22	1926-27
Jackson, Walt	NYA	3	82	16	11	27	18	....	....	....	....	....		1932-33	1934-35
* Jacobs, Paul	Tor.	1	1	0	0	0	0	....	....	....	....	....		1918-19	1918-19
Jacobs, Tim	Cal.	1	46	0	10	10	35	....	....	....	....	....		1975-76	1975-76
Jalo, Risto	Edm.	1	3	0	3	3	0	....	....	....	....	....		1985-86	1985-86
Jalonen, Kari	Cgy., Edm.	2	37	9	6	15	4	5	1	0	1	0		1982-83	1983-84
James, Gerry	Tor.	5	149	14	26	40	257	15	1	0	1	8		1954-55	1959-60
James, Val	Buf., Tor.	2	11	0	0	0	30	....	....	....	....	....		1981-82	1986-87
Jamieson, Jim	NYR	1	1	0	1	1	0	....	....	....	....	....		1943-44	1943-44
Jankowski, Lou	Det., Chi.	4	127	19	18	37	15	1	0	0	0	0		1950-51	1954-55
Jarrett, Doug	Chi., NYR	13	775	38	182	220	631	99	7	16	23	82		1964-65	1976-77
Jarrett, Gary	Tor., Det., Oak., Cal.	7	341	72	92	164	131	11	3	1	4	9		1960-61	1971-72
Jarry, Pierre	NYR, Tor., Det., Min.	7	344	88	117	205	142	5	0	1	1	0		1971-72	1977-78
Jarvenpaa, Hannu	Wpg.	3	114	11	26	37	83	....	....	....	....	....		1986-87	1988-89
Jarvi, Iiro	Que.	2	116	18	43	61	58	....	....	....	....	....		1988-89	1989-90
Jarvis, Doug	Mtl., Wsh., Hfd.	13	964	139	264	403	263	105	14	27	41	42	4	1975-76	1987-88
Jarvis, Jim	Pit., Phi., Tor.	3	108	17	15	32	62	....	....	....	....	....		1929-30	1936-37
Jarvis, Wes	Wsh., Min., L.A., Tor.	8	237	31	55	86	98	2	0	0	0	2		1979-80	1987-88
Javanainen, Arto	Pit.	1	14	4	1	5	2	....	....	....	....	....		1984-85	1984-85
Jeffrey, Larry	Det., Tor., NYR	8	368	39	62	101	293	38	4	10	14	42	1	1961-62	1968-69
Jenkins, Dean	L.A.	1	5	0	0	0	2	....	....	....	....	....		1983-84	1983-84
Jenkins, Roger	Tor., Chi., Mtl., Bos., Mtl.M., NYA	8	328	15	39	54	279	25	1	7	8	12	2	1930-31	1938-39
Jennings, Bill	Det., Bos.	5	108	32	33	65	45	20	4	4	8	6		1940-41	1944-45
Jensen, David H.	Min.	3	18	0	2	2	11	....	....	....	....	....		1983-84	1985-86
Jensen, David A.	Hfd., Wsh.	4	69	9	13	22	22	11	0	0	0	2		1983-84	1987-88
Jensen, Steve	Min., L.A.	7	438	113	107	220	318	12	0	3	3	9		1975-76	1981-82
* Jeremiah, Ed	NYA, Bos.	1	15	0	1	1	0	....	....	....	....	....		1931-32	1931-32
Jerwa, Frank	Bos.	1	28	4	5	9	12	....	....	....	....	....		1931-32	1931-32
Jerwa, Joe	NYR, Bos., St.L., NYA	9	293	36	69	105	338	17	2	3	5	20		1930-31	1938-39
Jirik, Jaroslav	St.L.	1	3	0	0	0	0	....	....	....	....	....		1969-70	1969-70
Joanette, Rosario	Mtl.	1	2	0	1	1	4	....	....	....	....	....		1944-45	1944-45
Jodzio, Rick	Col., Clev.	1	70	2	8	10	71	....	....	....	....	....		1977-78	1977-78
Johannesen, Glenn	NYI	1	2	0	0	0	0	....	....	....	....	....		1985-86	1985-86
Johannson, John	N.J.	1	5	0	0	0	0	....	....	....	....	....		1983-84	1983-84
Johansen, Trevor	Tor., Col., L.A.	5	286	11	46	57	282	13	0	3	3	21		1977-78	1981-82
Johansson, Bjorn	Clev.	2	15	1	1	2	10	....	....	....	....	....		1976-77	1977-78

Peter Ihnacak

Doug Jarvis

Tomas Jonsson

Forbes Kennedy

Dave Keon

Veli-Pekka Ketola

Guy Lafleur

Pierre Larouche

Name	NHL Teams	NHL Seasons	Regular Schedule GP	G	A	TP	PIM	Playoffs GP	G	A	TP	PIM	NHL Cup Wins	First NHL Season	Last NHL Season
Johns, Don	NYR, Mtl., Min.	6	153	2	21	23	76	....	....	....	....	....		1960-61	1967-68
Johnson, Al	Mtl., Det.	4	105	21	28	49	30	11	2	2	4	6		1956-57	1962-63
Johnson, Brian	Det.	1	3	0	0	0	5	....	....	....	....	....		1983-84	1983-84
Johnson, Danny	Tor., Van., Det.	3	121	18	19	37	24	....	....	....	....	....		1969-70	1971-72
Johnson, Earl	Det.	1	1	0	0	0	0	....	....	....	....	....		1953-54	1953-54
* Johnson, Ivan	NYR, NYA	12	435	38	48	86	808	60	5	2	7	161	2	1926-27	1937-38
Johnson, Jim	NYR, Phi., L.A.	8	302	75	111	186	73	7	0	2	2	2		1964-65	1971-72
Johnson, Mark	Pit., Min., Hfd., St.L., N.J.	11	669	203	305	508	260	37	16	12	28	10		1979-80	1989-90
Johnson, Norm	Bos., Chi.	3	61	5	20	25	41	14	4	0	4	6		1957-58	1959-60
Johnson, Terry	Que., St.L., Cgy., Tor.	9	285	3	24	27	580	38	0	4	4	118		1979-80	1987-88
Johnson, Tom	Mtl., Bos.	17	978	51	213	264	960	111	8	15	23	109	6	1947-48	1964-65
Johnson, Virgil	Chi.	3	75	2	9	11	27	19	0	3	3	4	1	1937-38	1944-45
Johnson, William	Tor.	1	1	0	0	0	0	....	....	....	....	....		1949-50	1949-50
Johnston, Bernie	Hfd.	2	57	12	24	36	44	3	0	1	1	0		1979-80	1980-81
Johnston, George	Chi.	4	58	20	12	32	2	....	....	....	....	....		1941-42	1946-47
Johnston, Jay	Wsh.	2	8	0	0	0	13	....	....	....	....	....		1980-81	1981-82
Johnston, Joey	Min., Cal., Chi.	6	332	85	106	191	320	....	....	....	....	....		1968-69	1975-76
Johnston, Larry	L.A., Det., K.C., Col.	7	320	9	64	73	580	....	....	....	....	....		1967-68	1976-77
Johnston, Marshall	Min., Cal.	7	251	14	52	66	58	6	0	0	0	2		1967-68	1973-74
Johnston, Randy	NYI	1	4	0	0	0	4	....	....	....	....	....		1979-80	1979-80
Johnstone, Eddie	NYR, Det.	10	426	122	136	258	375	55	13	10	23	83		1975-76	1986-87
Johnstone, Ross	Tor.	2	42	5	4	9	14	3	0	0	0	0	1	1943-44	1944-45
* Joliat, Aurel	Mtl.	16	654	270	190	460	757	54	14	19	33	89	3	1922-23	1937-38
Joliat, Bobby	Mtl.	1	1	0	0	0	0	....	....	....	....	....		1924-25	1924-25
Joly, Greg	Wsh., Det.	9	365	21	76	97	250	5	0	0	0	8		1974-75	1982-83
Joly, Yvan	Mtl.	3	2	0	0	0	0	10	0	0	0	0		1979-80	1982-83
Jonathon, Stan	Bos., Pit.	8	411	91	110	201	751	63	8	4	12	137		1975-76	1982-83
Jones, Bob	NYR	1	2	0	0	0	0	....	....	....	....	....		1968-69	1968-69
Jones, Buck	Det., Tor.	4	50	2	2	4	36	12	0	1	1	18		1938-39	1942-43
Jones, Jim	Cal.	1	2	0	0	0	0	....	....	....	....	....		1971-72	1971-72
Jones, Jimmy	Tor.	3	148	13	18	31	68	19	1	5	6	11		1977-78	1979-80
Jones, Ron	Bos., Pit., Wsh.	5	54	1	4	5	31	....	....	....	....	....		1971-72	1975-76
Jonsson, Tomas	NYI	8	552	85	259	344	482	80	11	26	37	97	2	1981-82	1988-89
Joyal, Eddie	Det., Tor., L.A., Phi.	9	466	128	134	262	103	50	11	8	19	18		1962-63	1971-72
Juckes, Bing	NYR	2	16	2	1	3	6	....	....	....	....	....		1947-48	1949-50
Julien, Claude	Que.	2	14	0	1	1	25	....	....	....	....	....		1984-85	1985-86
Jutila, Timo	Buf.	1	10	1	5	6	13	....	....	....	....	....		1984-85	1984-85
Juzda, Bill	NYR, Tor.	9	393	14	54	68	398	42	0	3	3	46	2	1940-41	1951-52

K

Name	NHL Teams	NHL Seasons	Regular Schedule GP	G	A	TP	PIM	Playoffs GP	G	A	TP	PIM	NHL Cup Wins	First NHL Season	Last NHL Season
Kabel, Bob	NYR	2	48	5	13	18	34	....	....	....	....	....		1959-60	1960-61
Kachur, Ed	Chi.	2	96	10	14	24	35	....	....	....	....	....		1956-57	1957-58
Kaese, Trent	Buf.	1	1	0	0	0	0	....	....	....	....	....		1988-89	1988-89
Kaiser, Vern	Mtl.	1	50	7	5	12	33	2	0	0	0	0		1950-51	1950-51
Kalbfleish, Walter	Ott., St.L., NYA, Bos.	4	36	0	4	4	32	5	0	0	0	2		1933-34	1936-37
Kaleta, Alex	Chi., NYR	7	387	92	121	213	190	17	1	6	7	2		1941-42	1950-51
Kallur, Anders	NYI	6	383	101	110	211	149	78	12	23	35	32	4	1979-80	1984-85
* Kaminsky, Max	Ott., St.L., Bos., Mtl.M.	4	130	22	34	56	38	4	0	0	0	0		1933-34	1936-37
Kampman, Bingo	Tor.	5	189	14	30	44	287	47	1	4	5	38	1	1937-38	1941-42
Kane, Frank	Det.	1	2	0	0	0	0	....	....	....	....	....		1943-44	1943-44
Kannegiesser, Gord	St.L.	2	23	0	1	1	15	....	....	....	....	....		1967-68	1971-72
Kannegiesser, Sheldon	Pit., NYR, L.A., Van.	8	366	14	67	81	292	18	0	2	2	10		1970-71	1977-78
Karlander, Al	Det.	4	212	36	56	92	70	4	0	1	1	0		1969-70	1972-73
Kaszycki, Mike	NYI, Wsh., Tor.	5	226	42	80	122	108	19	2	6	8	10		1977-78	1982-83
Kea, Ed	Atl., St.L.	10	583	30	145	175	508	32	2	4	6	39		1973-74	1982-83
Kearns, Dennis	Van.	10	677	31	290	321	386	11	1	2	3	8		1971-72	1980-81
* Keating, Jack	NYA	2	35	5	5	10	17	....	....	....	....	....		1931-32	1932-33
Keating, John	Det.	2	11	2	1	3	4	....	....	....	....	....		1938-39	1939-40
Keating, Mike	NYR	1	1	0	0	0	0	....	....	....	....	....		1977-78	1977-78
* Keats, Duke	Det., Chi.	3	80	3	19	49	113	....	....	....	....	....		1926-27	1928-29
* Keeling, Butch	Tor., NYR	12	528	157	63	220	331	47	11	11	22	32	1	1926-27	1937-38
Keenan, Larry	Tor., St.L., Buf., Phi.	6	233	38	64	102	28	46	15	16	31	12		1961-62	1971-72
Kehoe, Rick	Tor., Pit.	14	906	371	396	767	120	39	4	17	21	4		1971-72	1984-85
Keller, Ralph	NYR	1	3	1	0	1	6	....	....	....	....	....		1962-63	1962-63
Kellgren, Christer	Col.	1	5	0	0	0	0	....	....	....	....	....		1981-82	1981-82
Kelly, Bob	St.L., Pit., Chi.	6	425	87	109	196	687	23	6	3	9	40		1973-74	1978-79
Kelly, Bob	Phi., Wsh.	12	837	154	208	362	1454	101	9	14	23	172	2	1970-71	1981-82
Kelly, Dave	Det.	1	16	2	0	2	4	....	....	....	....	....		1976-77	1976-77
Kelly, John Paul	L.A.	7	400	54	70	124	366	18	1	1	2	41		1979-80	1985-86
Kelly, Pete	St.L., Det., NYA, Bro.	7	180	21	38	59	68	19	3	1	4	8	2	1934-35	1941-42
Kelly, Red	Det., Tor.	20	1316	281	542	823	327	164	33	59	92	51	8	1947-48	1966-67
* Kelly, Reg	Tor., Chi., Bro.	8	289	74	53	127	105	39	7	6	13	10		1934-35	1941-42
Kemp, Kevin	Hfd.	1	3	0	0	0	4	....	....	....	....	....		1980-81	1980-81
Kemp, Stan	Tor.	1	1	0	0	0	2	....	....	....	....	....		1948-49	1948-49
Kendall, William	Chi., Tor.	5	132	16	10	26	28	5	0	0	0	0	1	1933-34	1937-38
Kennedy, Forbes	Chi., Det., Bos., Phi., Tor.	11	603	70	108	178	988	12	2	4	6	64		1956-57	1968-69
Kennedy, Ted	Tor.	14	696	231	329	560	432	78	29	31	60	32	5	1942-43	1956-57
Kenny, Eddie	NYR, Chi.	2	11	0	0	0	18	....	....	....	....	....		1930-31	1934-35
Keon, Dave	Tor., Hfd.	18	1296	396	590	986	117	92	32	36	68	6	4	1960-61	1981-82
Kerr, Reg	Cle., Chi., Edm.	6	263	66	94	160	169	7	1	0	1	7		1977-78	1983-84
Kessell, Rick	Pit., Cal.	5	135	4	24	28	6	....	....	....	....	....		1969-70	1973-74
Ketola, Veli-Pekka	Col.	1	44	9	5	14	4	....	....	....	....	....		1981-82	1981-82
Ketter, Kerry	Atl.	1	41	0	2	2	58	....	....	....	....	....		1972-73	1972-73
Kiessling, Udo	Min.	1	1	0	0	0	2	....	....	....	....	....		1981-82	1981-82
Kilrea, Brian	Det., L.A.	2	26	3	5	8	12	....	....	....	....	....		1957-58	1967-68
Kilrea, Hec	Ott., Det., Tor.	15	633	167	129	296	438	48	8	7	15	18	3	1925-26	1939-40
Kilrea, Ken	Det.	5	88	16	23	39	8	10	2	2	4	4		1938-39	1943-44
Kilrea, Wally	Ott., Phi., NYA, Mtl.M., Det.	9	315	35	58	93	87	25	2	4	6	6		1929-30	1937-38
Kindrachuk, Orest	Phi., Pit., Wsh.	10	508	118	261	379	648	76	20	20	40	53	2	1972-73	1981-82
King, Frank	Mtl.	1	10	1	0	1	2	....	....	....	....	....		1950-51	1950-51
King, Wayne	Cal.	3	73	5	18	23	34	....	....	....	....	....		1973-74	1975-76
Kinsella, Brian	Wsh.	2	10	0	1	1	0	....	....	....	....	....		1975-76	1976-77
Kinsella, Ray	Ott.	1	14	0	0	0	0	....	....	....	....	....		1930-31	1930-31
Kirk, Bobby	NYR	1	39	4	8	12	14	....	....	....	....	....		1937-38	1937-38
Kirkpatrick, Bob	NYR	1	49	12	12	24	6	....	....	....	....	....		1942-43	1942-43
Kirton, Mark	Tor., Det., Van.	6	266	57	56	113	121	4	1	2	3	7		1979-80	1984-85
Kitchen, Bill	Mtl., Tor.	4	41	1	4	5	40	3	0	1	1	0		1981-82	1984-85
Kitchen, Hobie	Mtl.M., Det.	2	47	5	4	9	58	....	....	....	....	....		1925-26	1926-27
Kitchen, Mike	Col., N.J.	8	474	12	62	74	370	2	0	0	0	2		1976-77	1983-84
Klassen, Ralph	Cal., Clev., Col., St.L.	9	497	52	93	145	120	26	4	2	6	12		1975-76	1983-84
Klein, Jim	Bos., NYA	8	169	30	24	54	68	5	0	0	0	2	1	1928-29	1937-38
Kleinendorst, Scot	NYR, Hfd., Wsh.	8	281	12	46	58	452	26	2	7	9	40		1982-83	1989-90
Klingbeil, Ike	Chi.	1	5	1	2	3	2	....	....	....	....	....		1936-37	1936-37
Klukay, Joe	Tor., Bos.	11	566	109	127	236	189	71	13	10	23	23	4	1942-43	1955-56
Kluzak, Gord	Bos.	7	299	25	98	123	543	46	6	13	19	129		1982-83	1990-91
Knibbs, Bill	Bos.	1	53	7	10	17	4	....	....	....	....	....		1964-65	1964-65
Knott, Nick	Bro.	1	14	3	1	4	9	....	....	....	....	....		1941-42	1941-42
Knox, Paul	Tor.	1	1	0	0	0	0	....	....	....	....	....		1954-55	1954-55
Komadoski, Neil	L.A., St.L.	8	502	16	76	92	632	23	0	2	2	47		1972-73	1979-80
Konik, George	Pit.	1	52	7	8	15	26	....	....	....	....	....		1967-68	1967-68
Kopak, Russ	Bos.	1	24	7	9	16	0	....	....	....	....	....		1943-44	1943-44
Korab, Jerry	Chi., Van., Buf., L.A.	15	975	114	341	455	1629	93	8	18	26	201		1970-71	1984-85
Korn, Jim	Det., Tor., Buf., N.J., Cgy.	10	597	66	122	188	1801	16	1	2	3	109		1979-80	1989-80
Korney, Mike	Det., NYR	4	77	9	10	19	59	....	....	....	....	....		1973-74	1978-79
Koroll, Cliff	Chi.	11	814	208	254	462	376	85	19	29	48	67		1969-70	1979-80
Kortko, Roger	NYI	2	79	7	17	24	28	10	0	3	3	17		1984-85	1985-86
Kostynski, Doug	Bos.	2	15	3	1	4	4	....	....	....	....	....		1983-84	1984-85
Kotanen, Dick	Det., NYR	2	2	0	1	1	0	....	....	....	....	....		1948-49	1950-51
Kotsopoulos, Chris	NYR, Hfd.,Tor., Det.	10	479	44	109	153	827	31	1	3	4	91		1980-81	1989-90
Kowal, Joe	Buf.	2	22	0	5	5	13	2	0	0	0	0		1976-77	1977-78
Kozak, Don	L.A., Van.	7	437	96	86	182	480	29	7	2	9	69		1972-73	1978-79
Kozak, Les	Tor.	1	12	1	0	1	2	....	....	....	....	....		1961-62	1961-62

Name	NHL Teams	NHL Seasons	Regular Schedule GP	G	A	TP	PIM	Playoffs GP	G	A	TP	PIM	NHL Cup Wins	First NHL Season	Last NHL Season
Kraftcheck, Stephen	Bos., NYR, Tor.	4	157	11	18	29	83	6	0	0	0	7		1950-51	1958-59
Krake, Skip	Bos., L.A., Buf.	7	249	23	40	63	182	10	1	0	1	17		1963-64	1970-71
Krentz, Dale	Det.	3	30	5	3	8	9	2	0	0	0	0		1986-87	1988-89
Krol, Joe	NYR, Bro.	3	26	10	4	14	8	....	....	....	....	....		1936-37	1941-42
Krook, Kevin	Col.	1	3	0	0	0	2	....	....	....	....	....		1978-79	1978-79
Krulicki, Jim	NYR, Det.	1	41	0	3	3	6	....	....	....	....	....		1970-71	1970-71
Krutov, Vladimir	Van.	1	61	11	23	34	20	....	....	....	....	....		1989-90	1989-90
Kryskow, Dave	Chi., Wsh., Det., Atl.	4	231	33	56	89	174	12	2	0	2	4		1972-73	1975-76
Kryznowski, Edward	Bos., Chi.	5	237	15	22	37	65	18	0	1	1	4		1948-49	1952-53
Kuhn, Gord	NYA	1	12	1	1	2	4	....	....	....	....	....		1932-33	1932-33
Kukulowicz, Adolph	NYR	2	4	1	0	1	0	....	....	....	....	....		1952-53	1953-54
Kulak, Stu	Van., Edm., NYR, Que., Wpg.	4	90	8	4	12	130	3	0	0	0	2		1982-83	1988-89
Kullman, Arnie	Bos.	2	13	0	1	1	11	....	....	....	....	....		1947-48	1949-50
Kullman, Eddie	NYR	6	343	56	70	126	298	6	1	0	1	2		1947-48	1953-54
Kuntz, Alan	NYR	2	45	10	12	22	12	6	1	0	1	2		1941-42	1945-46
Kuntz, Murray	St.L.	1	7	1	2	3	0	....	....	....	....	....		1974-75	1974-75
Kurtenbach, Orland	NYR, Bos., Tor., Van.	13	639	119	213	332	628	19	2	4	6	70		1960-61	1973-74
Kuryluk, Mervin	Chi.	1	....	....	....	....	....	2	0	0	0	0		1961-62	1961-62
Kuzyk, Ken	Clev.	2	41	5	9	14	8	....	....	....	....	....		1976-77	1977-78
Kwong, Larry	NYR	1	1	0	0	0	0	....	....	....	....	....		1947-48	1947-48
Kyle, Bill	NYR	2	3	0	3	3	0	....	....	....	....	....		1949-50	1950-51
Kyle, Gus	NYR, Bos.	3	203	6	20	26	362	14	1	2	3	34		1949-50	1951-52
Kyllonen, Marku	Wpg.	1	9	0	2	2	2	....	....	....	....	....		1988-89	1988-89

L

Name	NHL Teams	NHL Seasons	Regular Schedule GP	G	A	TP	PIM	Playoffs GP	G	A	TP	PIM	NHL Cup Wins	First NHL Season	Last NHL Season
Labadie, Mike	NYR	1	3	0	0	0	0	....	....	....	....	....		1952-53	1952-53
Labatte, Neil	St.L.	2	26	0	2	2	19	....	....	....	....	....		1978-79	1981-82
L'abbe, Moe	Chi.	1	5	0	1	1	0	....	....	....	....	....		1972-73	1972-73
Labine, Leo	Bos., Det.	11	643	128	193	321	730	60	11	12	23	82		1951-52	1961-62
Labossierre, Gord	NYR, L.A., Min.	6	215	44	62	106	75	10	2	3	5	28		1963-64	1971-72
Labovitch, Max	NYR	1	5	0	0	0	4	....	....	....	....	....		1943-44	1943-44
Labraaten, Dan	Det., Cgy.	4	268	71	73	144	47	5	1	0	1	4		1978-79	1981-82
Labre, Yvon	Pit., Wsh.	9	371	14	87	101	788	....	....	....	....	....		1970-71	1980-81
Labrie, Guy	Bos., NYR	2	42	4	9	13	16	....	....	....	....	....		1943-44	1944-45
Lach, Elmer	Mtl.	14	664	215	408	623	478	76	19	45	64	36	3	1940-41	1953-54
Lachance, Earl	Mtl.	1	1	0	0	0	0	....	....	....	....	....		1926-27	1926-27
Lachance, Michel	Col.	1	21	0	4	4	22	....	....	....	....	....		1978-79	1978-79
Lacombe, Francois	Oak., Buf., Que.	4	78	2	17	19	54	3	1	0	1	0		1968-69	1979-80
Lacombe, Normand	Buf., Edm., Phi	7	319	53	62	115	196	26	5	1	6	49	1	1984-85	1990-91
Lacroix, Andre	Phi., Chi., Hfd.	6	325	79	119	198	44	16	2	5	7	0		1967-68	1979-80
Lacroix, Pierre	Que., Hfd.	4	274	24	108	132	197	8	0	2	2	10		1979-80	1982-83
Lafleur, Guy	Mtl., NYR, Que.	17	1126	560	793	1353	399	128	58	76	134	67	5	1971-72	1990-91
Lafleur, Rene	Mtl.	1	0	0	0	0	0	....	....	....	....	....		1924-25	1924-25
Laforce, Ernie	Mtl.	1	0	0	0	0	0	....	....	....	....	....		1942-43	1942-43
LaForest, Bob	L.A.	1	5	1	0	1	2	....	....	....	....	....		1983-84	1983-84
Laforge, Claude	Mtl., Det., Phi.	8	192	24	33	57	82	5	1	2	3	15		1957-58	1968-69
Laframboise, Pete	Cal., Wsh., Pit.	4	227	33	55	88	70	9	1	0	1	0		1971-72	1974-75
Lafrance, Adie	Mtl.	1	3	0	0	0	2	2	0	0	0	0		1933-34	1933-34
Lafrance, Leo	Mtl., Chi.	2	33	2	0	2	6	....	....	....	....	....		1926-27	1927-28
Lafreniere, Roger	Det., St.L.	2	13	0	0	0	4	....	....	....	....	....		1962-63	1972-73
Lagace, Jean-Guy	Pit., Buf., K.C.	6	187	9	39	48	251	....	....	....	....	....		1968-69	1975-76
Laidlaw, Tom	NYR, L.A.	10	705	25	139	164	717	69	4	17	21	78		1980-81	1989-90
Laird, Robbie	Min.	1	1	0	0	0	0	....	....	....	....	....		1979-80	1979-80
Lajeunesse, Serge	Det., Phi.	5	103	1	4	5	103	7	1	2	3	4		1970-71	1974-75
Lalande, Hec	Chi., Det.	4	151	21	39	60	120	....	....	....	....	....		1953-54	1957-58
Lalonde, Bobby	Van., Atl., Bos., Cgy.	11	641	124	210	334	298	16	4	2	6	6		1971-72	1981-82
* Lalonde, Edouard	Mtl., NYA	6	99	124	27	151	122	12	22	1	23	0	1	1917-18	1926-27
Lalonde, Ron	Pit., Wsh.	7	397	45	78	123	106	....	....	....	....	....		1972-73	1978-79
Lamb, Joe	Mtl.M., Ott., NYA, Bos., Mtl., St.L., Det.	11	444	108	101	209	601	18	1	1	2	51		1927-28	1937-38
Lambert, Lane	Det., NYR, Que.	6	283	58	66	124	521	17	2	4	6	40		1983-84	1988-89
Lambert, Yvon	Mtl., Buf.	10	683	206	273	479	340	90	27	22	49	67	4	1972-73	1981-82
Lamby, Dick	St.L.	3	22	0	5	5	22	....	....	....	....	....		1978-79	1980-81
* Lamirande, Jean-Paul	NYR, Mtl.	4	49	5	5	10	26	8	0	0	0	4		1946-47	1954-55
* Lamoureux, Leo	Mtl.	6	235	19	79	98	175	28	1	6	7	16	2	1941-42	1946-47
Lamoureux, Mitch	Pit., Phi.	3	73	11	9	20	59	....	....	....	....	....		1983-84	1987-88
Lampman, Mike	St.L., Van., Wsh.	4	96	17	20	37	34	....	....	....	....	....		1972-73	1976-77
Lancien, Jack	NYR	4	63	1	5	6	35	6	0	1	1	2		1946-47	1950-51
Landon, Larry	Mtl., Tor.	2	9	0	0	0	2	....	....	....	....	....		1983-84	1984-85
Lane, Gord	Wsh., NYI	10	539	19	94	113	1228	75	3	14	17	214	4	1975-76	1984-85
* Lane, Myles	NYR, Bos.	3	60	4	1	5	41	10	0	0	0	0	1	1928-29	1933-34
Langdon, Steve	Bos.	3	7	0	1	1	2	4	0	0	0	2		1974-75	1977-78
Langelle, Pete	Tor.	4	137	22	51	73	11	41	5	9	14	4	1	1938-39	1941-42
Langevin, Chris	Buf.	2	22	3	1	4	22	....	....	....	....	....		1983-84	1985-86
Langevin, Dave	NYI, Min., L.A.	8	513	12	107	119	530	87	2	15	17	106	4	1979-80	1986-87
Langlais, Alain	Min.	2	25	4	4	8	10	....	....	....	....	....		1973-74	1974-75
Langlois, Al	Mtl., NYR, Det., Bos.	9	448	21	91	112	488	53	1	5	6	60	3	1957-58	1965-66
Langlois, Charlie	Ham., NYA., Pit., Mtl.	4	151	22	3	25	201	2	0	0	0	0		1924-25	1927-28
Lanthier, Jean-Marc	Van.	4	105	16	16	32	29	....	....	....	....	....		1983-84	1987-88
Lanyon, Ted	Pit.	1	5	0	0	0	4	....	....	....	....	....		1967-68	1967-68
Laperriere, Jacques	Mtl.	12	691	40	242	282	674	88	9	22	31	101	6	1962-63	1973-74
Lapointe, Guy	Mtl., St.L., Bos.	16	884	171	451	622	893	123	26	44	70	138	6	1968-69	1983-84
Lapointe, Rick	Det., Phi., St.L., Que., L.A.	11	664	44	176	220	831	46	2	7	9	64		1975-76	1985-86
Laprade, Edgar	NYR	10	501	108	172	280	42	18	4	9	13	4		1945-46	1954-55
LaPrairie, Ben	Chi.	1	7	0	0	0	0	....	....	....	....	....		1936-37	1936-37
Lariviere, Garry	Que., Edm.	4	219	6	57	63	167	14	0	5	5	8		1979-80	1982-83
Larmer, Jeff	Col., N.J., Chi.	5	158	37	51	88	57	5	1	0	1	2		1981-82	1985-86
* Larochelle, Wildor	Mtl., Chi.	12	474	92	74	166	211	34	6	4	10	24	2	1925-26	1936-37
Larocque, Denis	L.A.	1	8	0	1	1	18	....	....	....	....	....		1987-88	1987-88
Larose, Charles	Bos.	1	6	0	0	0	0	....	....	....	....	....		1925-26	1925-26
Larose, Claude	NYR	2	25	4	7	11	2	2	0	0	0	0		1979-80	1981-82
Larose, Claude	Mtl., Min., St.L.	16	943	226	257	483	887	97	14	18	32	143	5	1962-63	1977-78
Larouche, Pierre	Pit., Mtl., Hfd., NYR	14	812	395	427	822	237	64	20	34	54	16	1	1974-75	1987-88
Larson, Norman	NYA., Bro., NYR	3	89	25	18	43	12	....	....	....	....	....		1940-41	1946-47
Larson, Reed	Det., Bos., Edm., NYI, Min., Buf.	14	904	222	463	685	1391	32	4	7	11	63		1976-77	1989-90
Latal, Jiri	Phi.	2	92	12	36	48	24	....	....	....	....	....		1989-90	1990-91
Latos, James	NYR	1	1	0	0	0	0	....	....	....	....	....		1988-89	1988-89
Latreille, Phil	NYR	1	4	0	0	0	2	....	....	....	....	....		1960-61	1960-61
Lauder, Marty	Bos.	1	3	0	0	0	2	....	....	....	....	....		1927-28	1927-28
Lauen, Mike	Wpg.	1	3	0	1	1	0	....	....	....	....	....		1983-84	1983-84
Laughlin, Craig	Mtl., Wsh., L.A., Tor.	8	549	136	205	341	364	33	6	6	12	20		1981-82	1988-89
Laughton, Mike	Oak., Cal.	4	189	39	48	87	101	11	2	4	6	0		1967-68	1970-71
Laurence, Red	Atl., St.L.	2	79	15	22	37	14	....	....	....	....	....		1978-79	1979-80
LaVallee, Kevin	Cgy., L.A., St.L., Pit.	7	366	110	125	235	85	32	5	8	13	24		1980-81	1986-87
Lavarre, Mark	Chi.	3	78	9	16	25	58	1	0	0	0	2		1985-86	1987-88
Lavender, Brian	St.L., NYI, Det., Cal.	4	184	16	26	42	174	3	0	0	0	2		1971-72	1974-75
* Laviolette, Jack	Mtl.	1	18	2	0	2	0	2	0	0	0	0		1917-18	1917-18
Lawless, Paul	Hfd., Phi., Van., Tor.	7	239	49	77	126	54	3	0	2	2	2		1982-83	1989-90
Lawson, Danny	Det., Min., Buf.	5	219	28	29	57	61	16	0	1	1	2		1967-68	1971-72
Laycoe, Hal	NYR, Mtl., Bos.	11	531	25	77	102	292	40	2	5	7	39		1945-46	1955-56
Leach, Larry	Bos.	3	126	13	29	42	91	7	1	1	2	8		1958-59	1961-62
Leach, Reggie	Bos., Cal., Phi., Det.	13	934	381	285	666	387	94	47	22	69	22	1	1970-71	1982-83
Leavins, Jim	Det., NYR	2	41	2	12	14	30	....	....	....	....	....		1985-86	1986-87
Leavins, Jim	Det., NYR	2	41	2	12	14	30	....	....	....	....	....		1985-86	1986-87
LeBlanc, Fern	Det.	3	34	5	6	11	0	....	....	....	....	....		1976-77	1978-79
LeBlanc, J.P.	Chi., Det.	5	153	14	30	44	87	2	0	0	0	0		1968-69	1978-79
LeBrun, Al	NYR	2	6	0	2	2	4	....	....	....	....	....		1960-61	1965-66
Lecaine, Bill	Pit.	1	4	0	0	0	0	....	....	....	....	....		1968-69	1968-69
Leclair, Jackie	Mtl.,	3	160	20	40	60	56	20	6	0	7	6	1	1954-55	1956-57
Leclerc, Rene	Det.	2	87	10	11	21	105	....	....	....	....	....		1968-69	1970-71
Lecuyer, Doug	Chi., Wpg., Pit.	4	126	11	31	42	178	7	4	0	4	15		1978-79	1982-83
Ledingham, Walt	Chi., NYI	3	15	0	2	2	4	....	....	....	....	....		1972-73	1976-77
LeDuc, Albert	Mtl., Ott., NYR	10	383	57	35	92	614	31	5	6	11	32	2	1925-26	1934-35

Paul Lawless

Roger Lemelin

Nick Libett

Ed Litzenberger

Hakan Loob

Al MacAdam

Lowell MacDonald

Keith Magnuson

Name	NHL Teams	NHL Seasons	Regular Schedule					Playoffs					NHL Cup Wins	First NHL Season	Last NHL Season
			GP	G	A	TP	PIM	GP	G	A	TP	PIM			
LeDuc, Rich	Bos., Que.	4	130	28	38	66	55	5	0	0	0	9		1972-73	1980-81
Lee, Bobby	Mtl.	1	1	0	0	0	0	....	....	....	....	....		1942-43	1942-43
Lee, Edward	Que.	1	2	0	0	0	5	....	....	....	....	....		1984-85	1984-85
Lee, Peter	Pit.	6	431	114	131	245	257	19	0	8	8	4		1977-78	1982-83
Lefley, Bryan	N.Y.I., K.C., Col.	5	228	7	29	36	101	2	0	0	0	0		1972-73	1977-78
Lefley, Chuck	Mtl., St.L.	9	407	128	164	292	137	29	5	8	13	10		1970-71	1980-81
* Leger, Roger	NYR, Mtl.	5	187	18	53	71	71	20	0	7	7	14		1943-44	1949-50
Legge, Barry	Que., Wpg.	3	107	1	11	12	144	....	....	....	....	....		1979-80	1981-82
Legge, Randy	NYR	1	12	0	2	2	2	....	....	....	....	....		1972-73	1972-73
Lehmann, Tommy	Bos., Edm.	3	36	5	5	10	16	....	....	....	....	....		1987-88	1989-90
Lehto, Petteri	Pit.	1	6	0	0	0	4	....	....	....	....	....		1984-85	1984-85
Lehtonen, Antero	Wsh.	1	65	9	12	21	14	....	....	....	....	....		1979-80	1979-80
Lehvonen, Henri	K.C.	1	4	0	0	0	0	....	....	....	....	....		1974-75	1974-75
Leier, Edward	Chi.	2	16	2	1	3	2	....	....	....	....	....		1949-50	1950-51
Leinonen, Mikko	NYR, Wsh.	4	162	31	78	109	71	20	2	11	13	28		1981-82	1984-85
Leiter, Bobby	Bos., Pit., Atl.	10	447	98	126	224	144	8	3	0	3	2		1962-63	1975-76
Leiter, Ken	NYI, Min.	5	143	14	36	50	62	15	0	6	6	8		1984-85	1989-90
Lemaire, Jacques	Mtl.	12	853	366	469	835	217	145	61	78	139	63	8	1967-68	1978-79
Lemay, Moe	Van., Edm., Bos., Wpg.	8	317	72	94	166	442	28	6	3	9	55	1	1981-82	1988-89
Lemelin, Roger	K.C., Col.	4	36	1	2	3	27	....	....	....	....	....		1974-75	1977-78
Lemieux, Alain	St.L., Que., Pit.	6	119	28	44	72	38	19	4	6	10	0		1981-82	1986-87
Lemieux, Bob	Oak.	1	19	0	1	1	12	....	....	....	....	....		1967-68	1967-68
Lemieux, Jacques	L.A.	2	19	0	4	4	8	1	0	0	0	0		1967-68	1969-70
Lemieux, Jean	L.A., Atl., Wsh.	6	204	23	63	86	39	3	1	1	2	0		1969-70	1977-78
* Lemieux, Real	Det., L.A., NYR, Buf.	7	381	40	75	115	184	18	2	4	6	10		1966-67	1973-74
Lemieux, Richard	Van., St.L., K.C., Atl.	5	274	39	82	121	132	2	0	0	0	0		1971-72	1975-76
Lepine, Hec	Mtl.	1	33	5	2	7	2	....	....	....	....	....		1925-26	1925-26
* Lepine, Pit	Mtl.	13	526	143	98	241	392	41	7	5	12	26	2	1925-26	1937-38
Leroux, Gaston	Mtl.	1	2	0	0	0	0	....	....	....	....	....		1935-36	1935-36
Lesieur, Art	Mtl., Chi.	4	100	4	2	6	50	14	0	0	0	4	1	1928-29	1935-36
Lesuk, Bill	Bos., Phi., L.A., Wsh., Wpg.	8	388	44	63	107	368	9	1	0	1	12	1	1968-69	1979-80
Leswick, Jack	Chi.	1	47	1	7	8	16	....	....	....	....	....	1	1933-34	1933-34
Leswick, Peter	NYA, Bos.	2	3	1	0	1	0	....	....	....	....	....		1936-37	1944-45
Leswick, Tony	NYR, Det., Chi.	12	740	165	159	324	900	59	13	10	23	91	3	1945-46	1957-58
Levandoski, Joseph	NYR	1	8	1	1	2	0	....	....	....	....	....		1946-47	1946-47
Leveille, Norm	Bos.	2	75	17	25	42	49	....	....	....	....	....		1981-82	1982-83
Lever, Don	Van., Atl., Cgy., Col., N.J., Buf.	15	1020	313	367	680	593	30	7	10	17	26		1972-73	1986-87
Levie, Craig	Wpg., Min., Van., St.L.	6	183	22	53	75	177	16	2	3	5	32		1981-82	1986-87
Levinsky, Alex	Tor., Chi., NYR	9	367	19	49	68	307	34	2	1	3	2	2	1930-31	1938-39
Levo, Tapio	Col., N.J.,	2	107	16	53	69	36	....	....	....	....	....		1981-82	1982-83
Lewicki, Danny	Tor., NYR, Chi.	9	461	105	135	240	177	28	0	4	4	8	1	1950-51	1958-59
Lewis, Bob	NYR	1	8	0	0	0	0	....	....	....	....	....		1975-76	1975-76
Lewis, Dave	NYI, L.A., N.J., Det.	15	1008	36	187	223	953	91	1	20	21	143		1973-74	1987-88
Lewis, Douglas	Mtl..	1	3	0	0	0	0	....	....	....	....	....		1946-47	1946-47
* Lewis, Herbie	Det.	11	483	148	161	309	248	38	13	10	23	6	2	1928-29	1938-39
Ley, Rick	Tor., Hfd.	6	310	12	72	84	528	14	0	2	2	20		1968-69	1980-81
Liba, Igor	NYR, L.A.	1	37	7	18	25	36	2	0	0	0	2		1988-89	1988-89
Libett, Nick	Det., K.C., Pit.	14	982	237	268	505	472	16	6	2	8	2		1967-68	1980-81
Licari, Anthony	Det.	1	9	0	1	1	0	....	....	....	....	....		1946-47	1946-47
Liddington, Bob	Tor.	1	11	0	1	1	2	....	....	....	....	....		1970-71	1970-71
Lindgren, Lars	Van., Min.	6	394	25	113	138	325	40	5	6	11	20		1978-79	1983-84
Lindsay, Ted	Det., Chi.	17	1068	379	472	851	1808	133	47	49	96	194	4	1944-45	1964-65
Lindstrom, Willy	Wpg., Edm., Pit.	8	582	161	162	323	200	57	14	18	32	24	2	1979-80	1986-87
Liscombe, Carl	Det.	9	383	137	140	277	117	59	22	19	41	20	1	1937-38	1945-46
Litzenberger, Ed	Mtl., Chi., Det., Tor.	12	618	178	238	416	283	40	5	13	18	34	4	1952-53	1963-64
Locas, Jacques	Mtl..	2	59	7	8	15	66	....	....	....	....	....		1947-48	1948-49
Lochead, Bill	NYR, Det., Col.	6	330	69	62	131	180	7	3	0	3	6		1974-75	1979-80
Locking, Norm	Chi.	2	48	2	6	8	26	1	0	0	0	0		1934-35	1935-36
Lofthouse, Mark	Wsh., Det.	6	181	42	38	80	73	....	....	....	....	....		1977-78	1982-83
Logan, Dave	Chi., Van.	6	218	5	29	34	470	12	0	0	0	10		1975-76	1980-81
Logan, Robert	Buf., L.A.	3	42	10	5	15	0	....	....	....	....	....		1986-87	1988-89
Long, Barry	L.A., Det., Wpg.	5	280	11	68	79	250	5	0	1	1	18		1972-73	1981-82
Long, Stanley	Mtl..	1	....	....	....	....	....	3	0	0	0	0		1951-52	1951-52
Lonsberry, Ross	Phi., Pit., Bos., L.A.	15	968	256	310	566	806	100	21	25	46	87	2	1966-67	1980-81
Loob, Hakan	Cgy.	6	450	193	236	429	189	73	26	28	54	16	1	1983-84	1988-89
Loob, Peter	Que.	1	8	1	2	3	0	....	....	....	....	....		1984-85	1984-85
Lorentz, Jim	NYR, Buf., Bos., St.L.	10	659	161	238	399	208	54	12	10	22	30	1	1968-69	1977-78
Lorimer, Bob	NYI, Col., N.J.	10	529	22	90	112	431	49	3	10	13	83	2	1976-77	1985-86
Lorraine, Rod	Mtl..	6	179	28	39	67	30	11	0	3	3	0		1935-36	1941-42
Loughlin, Clem	Det., Chi.	3	101	8	6	14	77	....	....	....	....	....		1926-27	1928-29
Loughlin, Wilf	Tor.	1	14	0	0	0	2	....	....	....	....	....		1923-24	1923-24
Lowdermilk, Dwayne	Wsh.	1	2	0	1	1	2	....	....	....	....	....		1980-81	1980-81
Lowe, Darren	Pit.	1	8	1	2	3	0	....	....	....	....	....		1983-84	1983-84
Lowe, Norm	NYR	2	4	1	1	2	0	....	....	....	....	....		1948-49	1949-50
* Lowe, Ross	Bos., Mtl..	3	77	6	8	14	82	2	0	0	0	0		1949-50	1951-52
Lowery, Fred	Mtl.M., Pit.	2	54	1	0	1	10	2	0	0	0	6	1	1924-25	1925-26
* Lowrey, Eddie	Ott., Ham.	3	24	2	0	2	3	....	....	....	....	....		1917-18	1920-21
Lowrey, Gerry	Chi., Ott., Tor., Phi., Pit.	6	209	48	48	96	168	2	1	0	1	2		1927-28	1932-33
Lucas, Danny	Phi.	1	6	1	0	1	0	....	....	....	....	....		1978-79	1978-79
Lucas, Dave	Det.	1	1	0	0	0	0	....	....	....	....	....		1962-63	1962-63
Luce, Don	NYR, Det., Buf., L.A., Tor.	13	894	225	329	554	364	71	17	22	39	52		1969-70	1981-82
Ludvig, Jan	N.J., Buf.	7	314	54	87	141	418	....	....	....	....	....		1982-83	1988-89
Lukowich, Bernie	Pit., St.L.	2	79	13	15	28	34	2	0	0	0	0		1973-74	1974-75
Lukowich, Morris	Wpg., Bos., L.A.	8	582	199	219	418	584	11	0	2	2	24		1979-80	1986-87
Luksa, Charlie	Hfd.	1	8	0	1	1	4	....	....	....	....	....		1979-80	1979-80
Lumley, Dave	Mtl., Edm., Hfd.	9	437	98	160	258	680	61	6	8	14	131	2	1978-79	1986-87
Lund, Pentti	NYR, Bos.	7	259	44	55	99	40	18	7	5	12	0		1946-47	1952-53
Lundberg, Brian	Pit.	1	1	0	0	0	2	....	....	....	....	....		1982-83	1982-83
Lunde, Len	Min., Van., Det., Chi.	8	321	39	83	122	75	20	3	2	5	2		1958-59	1970-71
Lundholm, Bengt	Wpg.	5	275	48	95	143	72	14	3	4	7	14		1981-82	1985-86
Lundrigan, Joe	Tor., Wsh.	2	52	2	8	10	22	....	....	....	....	....		1972-73	1974-75
Lundstrom, Tord	Det.	1	11	1	1	2	0	....	....	....	....	....		1973-74	1973-74
Lundy, Pat	Det. Chi.	5	150	37	32	69	31	9	1	1	2	2		1945-46	1950-51
Lupien, Gilles	Mtl., Pit., Hfd.	5	226	5	25	30	416	25	0	0	0	21	2	1977-78	1981-82
Lupul, Gary	Van.	7	293	70	75	145	243	25	4	7	11	11		1979-80	1985-86
Lyle, George	Det., Hfd.	4	99	24	38	62	51	....	....	....	....	....		1979-80	1982-83
Lynch, Jack	Pit., Det., Wsh.	7	382	24	106	130	336	....	....	....	....	....		1972-73	1978-79
Lynn, Vic	Det., Mtl., Tor., Bos., Chi.	10	326	49	76	125	274	47	7	10	17	46	3	1943-44	1953-54
Lyon, Steve	Pit.	1	3	0	0	0	2	....	....	....	....	....		1976-77	1976-77
Lyons, Ron	Bos., Phi.	1	36	2	4	6	29	5	0	0	0	0		1930-31	1930-31
Lysiak, Tom	Atl., Chi.	13	919	292	551	843	567	78	25	38	63	49		1973-74	1985-86
M															
MacAdam, Al	Phi., Cal., Cle., Min., Van.	12	864	240	351	591	509	64	20	24	44	21	1	1973-74	1984-85
MacDonald, Blair	Edm., Van.	4	219	91	100	191	65	11	0	6	6	2		1979-80	1982-83
MacDonald, Brett	Van.	1	1	0	0	0	0	....	....	....	....	....		1987-88	1987-88
MacDonald, Kilby	NYR	4	151	36	34	70	47	15	1	2	3	4	1	1939-40	1944-45
MacDonald, Lowell	Det., L.A., Pit.	13	506	180	210	390	92	30	11	11	22	12		1961-62	1977-78
MacDonald, Parker	Tor., NYR, Det., Bos., Min.	14	676	144	179	323	253	75	14	14	28	20		1952-53	1968-69
MacDougall, Kim	Min.	1	1	0	0	0	0	....	....	....	....	....		1974-75	1974-75
MacEachern, Shane	St.L.	1	1	0	0	0	0	....	....	....	....	....		1987-88	1987-88
Macey, Hubert	NYR, Mtl.	3	30	6	9	15	0	8	0	0	0	0		1941-42	1946-47
MacGregor, Bruce	Det., NYR	14	893	213	257	470	217	107	19	28	47	44		1960-61	1973-74
MacGregor, Randy	Hfd.	1	2	1	1	2	2	....	....	....	....	....		1981-82	1981-82
MacGuigan, Garth	NYI	1	2	0	0	0	0	....	....	....	....	....		1979-80	1979-80
MacIntosh, Ian	NYR	1	4	0	0	0	4	....	....	....	....	....		1952-53	1952-53
MacIver, Don	Wpg.	1	6	0	0	0	2	....	....	....	....	....		1979-80	1979-80
MacKasey, Blair	Tor.	1	1	0	0	0	2	....	....	....	....	....		1976-77	1976-77
Mackay, Dave	Chi.	1	29	3	0	3	26	5	0	1	1	2		1940-41	1940-41
MacKay, Calum	Det., Mtl.	8	237	50	55	105	214	38	5	13	18	20	1	1946-47	1954-55
* MacKay, Mickey	Chi., Pit., Bos.	4	151	44	19	63	79	11	0	0	0	6	1	1926-27	1929-30
MacKay, Murdo	Mtl.	3	19	0	3	3	0	15	1	2	3	0		1945-46	1947-48

			Regular Schedule					Playoffs					NHL	First	Last
Name	NHL Teams	NHL Seasons	GP	G	A	TP	PIM	GP	G	A	TP	PIM	Cup Wins	NHL Season	NHL Season
Mackell, Fleming	Tor., Bos.	13	665	149	220	369	562	80	22	41	63	75	2	1947-48	1959-60
MacKenzie, Barry	Min.	1	6	0	1	1	6	....	....	....	....	....		1968-69	1968-69
MacKenzie, Bill	Chi., Mtl.(M),Mtl., NYR	7	266	15	14	29	133	19	1	1	2	11	1	1932-33	1939-40
MacKey, Reggie	NYR	1	34	0	0	0	16	1	0	0	0	0		1926-27	1926-27
Mackie, Howie	Det.	2	20	1	0	1	4	8	0	0	0	0	1	1936-37	1937-38
MacKinnon, Paul	Wsh.	5	147	5	23	28	91	....	....	....	....	....		1979-80	1983-84
MacLean, Paul	St.L., Wpg., Det.	11	719	324	349	673	968	53	21	14	35	104		1980-81	1990-91
MacLeish, Rick	Phi., Hfd., Pit., Det.	14	846	349	410	759	434	114	54	53	107	38	2	1970-71	1983-84
MacMillan, Billy	Tor., Atl., NYI	7	446	74	77	151	184	53	6	6	12	40		1970-71	1976-77
MacMillan, Bob	NYR, St.L., Atl., Cgy., Col., N.J., Chi.	11	753	228	349	577	260	31	8	11	19	16		1974-75	1984-85
MacMillan, John	Tor., Det.	5	104	5	10	15	32	12	0	1	1	2	2	1960-61	1964-65
MacNeil, Al	Tor., Mtl., Chi., NYR, Pit.	11	524	17	75	92	617	37	0	4	4	67		1955-56	1967-68
MacNeil, Bernie	St.L.	1	4	0	0	0	0	....	....	....	....	....		1973-74	1973-74
MacPherson, Bud	Mtl.	7	259	5	33	38	233	29	0	3	3	21	1	1948-49	1956-57
MacSweyn, Ralph	Phi.	5	47	0	5	5	10	8	0	0	0	6		1967-68	1971-72
Madigan, Connie	St.L.	1	20	0	3	3	25	5	0	0	0	4		1972-73	1972-73
Magee, Dean	Min.	1	7	0	0	0	4	....	....	....	....	....		1977-78	1977-78
Maggs, Daryl	Chi., Cal., Tor.	3	135	14	19	33	54	4	0	0	0	0		1971-72	1979-80
Magnan, Marc	Tor.	1	4	0	1	1	5	....	....	....	....	....		1982-83	1982-83
Magnuson, Keith	Chi.	11	589	14	125	139	1442	68	3	9	12	164		1969-70	1979-80
Mahaffy, John	Mtl., NYR	3	37	11	25	36	4	1	0	1	1	0		1942-43	1944-45
Mahovlich, Frank	Tor., Det., Mtl.	18	1181	533	570	1103	1056	137	51	67	118	163	6	1956-57	1973-74
Mahovlich, Pete	Det., Mtl., Pit.	16	884	288	485	773	916	88	30	42	72	134	4	1965-66	1980-81
Mailhot, Jacques	Que.	1	5	0	0	0	33	....	....	....	....	....		1988-89	1988-89
Mailley, Frank	Mtl.	1	1	0	0	0	0	....	....	....	....	....		1942-43	1942-43
Mair, Jim	Phi., NYI, Van.	5	76	4	15	19	49	3	1	2	3	4		1970-71	1974-75
Majeau, Fern	Mtl.	2	56	22	24	46	43	1	0	0	0	0	1	1943-44	1944-45
Maki, Chico	Chi.	15	841	143	292	435	345	113	17	36	53	43	1	1960-61	1975-76
* Maki, Wayne	Chi., St.L., Van.	6	246	57	79	136	184	2	1	0	1	2		1967-68	1972-73
Makkonen, Karl	Edm.	1	9	2	2	4	0	....	....	....	....	....		1979-80	1979-80
Malinowski, Merlin	Col., N.J., Hfd.	5	282	54	111	165	121	....	....	....	....	....		1978-79	1982-83
Malone, Cliff	Mtl.	1	3	0	0	0	0	....	....	....	....	....		1951-52	1951-52
Malone, Greg	Pit., Hfd., Que.	11	704	191	310	501	661	20	3	5	8	32		1976-77	1986-87
* Malone, Joe	Mtl., Que., Ham.	7	125	146	21	167	23	9	5	0	5	0	1	1917-18	1923-24
Maloney, Dan	Chi., L.A., Det., Tor.	11	737	192	259	451	1489	40	4	7	11	35		1970-71	1981-82
Maloney, Dave	NYR, Buf.	11	657	71	246	317	1154	49	7	17	24	91		1974-75	1984-85
Maloney, Don	NYR, Hfd., NYI	13	765	214	350	564	815	94	22	35	57	101		1978-79	1990-91
Maloney, Phi.	Bos., Tor., Chi.	5	158	28	43	71	16	6	0	0	0	0		1949-50	1959-60
Maluta, Ray	Bos.	2	25	2	3	5	6	2	0	0	0	0		1975-76	1976-77
Manastersky, Tom	Mtl.	1	6	0	0	0	11	....	....	....	....	....		1950-51	1950-51
Mancuso, Gus	Mtl., NYR	4	42	7	9	16	17	....	....	....	....	....		1937-38	1942-43
Mandich, Dan	Min.	4	111	5	11	16	303	7	0	0	0	2		1982-83	1985-86
Manery, Kris	Van., Wpg., Clev., Min.	4	250	63	64	127	91	....	....	....	....	....		1977-78	1980-81
Manery, Randy	L.A., Det., Atl.	10	582	50	206	256	415	13	0	2	2	12		1970-71	1979-80
Mann, Jack	NYR	2	9	3	4	7	0	....	....	....	....	....		1943-44	1944-45
Mann, Jimmy	Wpg., Que., Pit.	8	293	10	20	30	895	22	0	0	0	89		1979-80	1987-88
Mann, Ken	Det.	1	1	0	0	0	0	....	....	....	....	....		1975-76	1975-76
Mann, Norm	Tor.	2	31	0	3	3	4	1	0	0	0	0		1938-39	1940-41
Manners, Rennison	Pit., Phi.	2	37	3	2	5	14	....	....	....	....	....		1929-30	1930-31
Manno, Bob	Van., Tor., Det.	8	371	41	131	172	274	17	2	4	6	12		1976-77	1984-85
Manson, Ray	Bos., NYR	2	2	0	1	1	0	....	....	....	....	....		1947-48	1948-49
Mantha, Georges	Mtl..	13	498	89	102	181	148	36	6	2	8	16	2	1928-29	1940-41
* Mantha, Sylvio	Mtl., Bos.	14	543	63	72	135	667	46	5	4	9	66	3	1923-24	1936-37
Maracle, Buddy	NYR	1	11	1	3	4	4	4	0	0	0	0		1930-31	1930-31
Marcetta, Milan	Tor., Min.	3	54	7	15	22	10	17	7	7	14	4	1	1966-67	1968-69
March, Mush	Chi.	17	758	153	230	383	540	48	12	15	27	41	2	1928-29	1944-45
Marchinko, Brian	Tor., NYI	4	47	2	6	8	0	....	....	....	....	....		1970-71	1973-74
Marcon, Lou	Det.	3	70	0	4	4	42	....	....	....	....	....		1958-59	1962-63
Marcotte, Don	Bos.	15	868	230	255	485	317	132	34	27	61	81	2	1965-66	1981-82
Marini, Hector	NYI, N.J.	5	154	27	46	73	246	10	3	6	9	14	2	1978-79	1983-84
Mario, Frank	Bos.	2	53	9	19	28	24	....	....	....	....	....		1941-42	1944-45
* Mariucci, John	Chi.	5	223	11	34	45	308	8	0	3	3	26		1940-41	1947-48
Mark, Gordon	N.J.	2	55	3	7	10	109	....	....	....	....	....		1986-87	1987-88
Markell, John	Wpg.	2	52	11	10	21	36	....	....	....	....	....		1979-80	1980-81
Marker, Gus	Det., Mtl.M., Tor., Bro.	10	336	64	69	133	133	45	6	8	14	36	1	1932-33	1941-42
Markham, Ray	NYR	1	14	1	1	2	21	7	1	0	1	24		1979-80	1979-80
Markle, Jack	Tor.	1	8	0	1	1	0	....	....	....	....	....		1935-36	1935-36
* Marks, Jack	Mtl.W, Tor., Que.	2	7	0	0	0	4	....	....	....	....	....	1	1917-18	1919-20
Marks, John	Chi.	10	657	112	163	275	330	57	5	9	14	60		1972-73	1981-82
Marotte, Gilles	Bos., Chi., L.A., NYR, St.L.	12	808	56	265	321	872	29	3	3	6	26		1965-66	1976-77
Marquess, Mark	Bos.	1	27	5	4	9	27	4	0	0	0	0		1946-47	1946-47
Marsh, Gary	Det., Tor.	2	7	1	3	4	4	....	....	....	....	....		1967-68	1968-69
Marsh, Peter	Wpg., Chi.	5	278	48	71	119	224	26	1	5	6	33		1979-80	1983-84
Marshall, Bert	Det., Oak., Cal., NYR, NYI	14	868	17	181	198	926	72	4	22	26	99		1965-66	1978-79
Marshall, Don	Mtl., NYR, Buf., Tor.	19	1176	265	324	589	127	94	8	15	23	14	5	1951-52	1971-72
Marshall, Paul	Pit., Tor., Hfd.	4	95	15	18	33	17	1	0	0	0	0		1979-80	1982-83
Marshall, Willie	Tor.	4	33	1	15	16	2	....	....	....	....	....		1952-53	1958-59
Marson, Mike	Wsh., L.A.	6	196	24	24	48	233	....	....	....	....	....		1974-75	1979-80
Martin, Clare	Bos., Det., Chi., NYR	6	237	12	28	40	78	22	0	2	2	6	1	1941-42	1951-52
Martin, Frank	Bos., Chi.	6	282	11	46	57	122	10	0	1	1	2		1952-53	1957-58
Martin, Grant	Van., Wsh.	4	44	0	4	4	55	1	1	0	1	2		1983-84	1986-87
Martin, Jack	Tor.	1	1	0	0	0	0	....	....	....	....	....		1960-61	1960-61
Martin, Pit	Det., Bos., Chi., Van.	17	1101	324	485	809	609	100	27	31	58	56		1961-62	1978-79
Martin, Rick	Buf., L.A.	11	685	384	317	701	477	63	24	29	53	74		1971-72	1981-82
Martin, Ron	NYA	2	94	13	16	29	36	....	....	....	....	....		1932-33	1933-34
Martin, Terry	Buf., Que., Tor., Edm., Min.	10	479	104	101	205	202	21	4	2	6	26		1975-76	1984-85
Martin, Tom	Tor.	1	3	1	0	1	0	....	....	....	....	....		1967-68	1967-68
Martineau, Don	Atl., Min., Det.	4	90	6	10	16	63	....	....	....	....	....		1973-74	1976-77
Maruk, Dennis	Cal., Clev., Min., Wsh.	14	888	356	522	878	761	34	14	22	36	26		1975-76	1988-89
Masnick, Paul	Mtl., Chi., Tor.	6	232	18	41	59	139	33	4	5	9	27	1	1950-51	1957-58
Mason, Charley	NYR, NYA, Det., Chi.	4	95	7	18	25	44	4	0	1	1	0		1934-35	1938-39
Massecar, George	NYA	3	100	12	11	23	46	....	....	....	....	....		1929-30	1931-32
Masters, Jamie	St.L.	3	33	1	13	14	2	2	0	0	0	0		1975-76	1978-79
* Masterton, Bill	Min.	1	38	4	8	12	4	....	....	....	....	....		1967-68	1967-68
Mathers, Frank	Tor.	3	23	1	3	4	4	....	....	....	....	....		1948-49	1951-52
Mathiasen, Dwight	Pit.	3	33	1	7	8	18	....	....	....	....	....		1985-86	1987-88
* Matte, Joe	Tor., Ham., Bos., Mtl.	4	64	18	14	32	43	....	....	....	....	....		1919-20	1925-26
Matte, Joe	Chi.	1	12	0	1	1	0	....	....	....	....	....		1942-43	1942-43
Matte, Roland	Det.	1	12	0	1	1	0	....	....	....	....	....		1929-30	1929-30
Mattiussi, Dick	Pit., Oak., Cal.	4	200	8	31	39	124	8	0	1	1	6		1967-68	1970-71
Matz, Johnny	Mtl.	1	30	3	2	5	0	5	0	0	0	2		1924-25	1924-25
Maxner, Wayne	Bos.	2	62	8	9	17	48	....	....	....	....	....		1964-65	1965-66
Maxwell, Brad	Min., Que., Tor., Van., NYR	10	612	98	270	368	1292	79	12	49	61	178		1977-78	1986-87
Maxwell, Bryan	Min., St.L., Wpg., Pit.	8	331	18	77	95	745	15	1	1	2	86		1977-78	1984-85
Maxwell, Kevin	Min., Col., N.J.	3	66	6	15	21	61	16	3	4	7	24		1980-81	1983-84
Maxwell, Wally	Tor.	1	2	0	0	0	0	....	....	....	....	....		1952-53	1952-53
Mayer, Jim	NYR	1	4	0	0	0	0	....	....	....	....	....		1979-80	1979-80
Mayer, Pat	Pit.	1	1	0	0	0	4	....	....	....	....	....		1987-88	1987-88
Mayer, Shep	Tor.	1	12	1	2	3	4	....	....	....	....	....		1942-43	1942-43
Mazur, Eddie	Mtl., Chi.	6	107	8	20	28	120	25	4	5	9	22	1	1950-51	1956-57
McAdam, Gary	Buf., Pit., Det., Cal., Wsh., N.J., Tor.	11	534	96	132	228	243	30	6	5	11	16		1975-76	1985-86
McAdam, Sam	NYR	1	5	0	0	0	0	....	....	....	....	....		1930-31	1930-31
McAndrew, Hazen	Bro.	1	7	0	1	1	6	....	....	....	....	....		1941-42	1941-42
McAneeley, Ted	Cal.	3	158	8	35	43	141	....	....	....	....	....		1972-73	1974-75
McAtee, Jud	Det.	3	46	15	13	28	6	14	2	1	3	0		1942-43	1944-45
McAtee, Norm	Bos.	1	13	0	1	1	0	....	....	....	....	....		1946-47	1946-47
McAvoy, George	Mtl.	1	....	....	....	....	....	4	0	0	0	0		1954-55	1954-55
McBride, Cliff	Mtl.M., Tor.	2	2	0	0	0	0	....	....	....	....	....		1928-29	1929-30
McBurney, Jim	Chi.	1	1	0	1	1	0	....	....	....	....	....		1952-53	1952-53
McCabe, Stan	Det., Mtl.M.	4	78	9	4	13	49	....	....	....	....	....		1929-30	1933-34
McCaffrey, Bert	Tor., Pit., Mtl.	7	260	42	30	72	202	8	2	1	3	12		1924-25	1930-31
McCahill, John	Col.	1	1	0	0	0	0	....	....	....	....	....		1977-78	1977-78
McCaig, Douglas	Det., Chi.	7	263	8	21	29	255	17	0	1	1	8		1941-42	1950-51
McCallum, Dunc	NYR, Pit.	5	187	14	35	49	230	10	1	2	3	12		1965-66	1970-71
McCalmon, Eddie	Chi., Phi.	2	39	5	0	5	14	....	....	....	....	....		1927-28	1930-31

Frank Mahovlich

Joe Malone

Hector Marini

Gilles Marotte

Denis Maruk

Walt McKechnie

Stan Mikita

Hartland Monahan

Name	NHL Teams	NHL Seasons	Regular Schedule GP	G	A	TP	PIM	Playoffs GP	G	A	TP	PIM	NHL Cup Wins	First NHL Season	Last NHL Season
McCann, Rick	Det.	6	43	1	4	5	6	....	....	....	....	....		1967-68	1974-75
McCarthy, Dan	NYR	1	5	4	0	4	4	....	....	....	....	....		1980-81	1980-81
McCarthy, Kevin	Phi., Van., Pit.	10	537	67	191	258	527	21	2	3	5	20		1977-78	1986-87
* McCarthy, Tom	Que., Ham.	2	34	19	3	22	10	....	....	....	....	....		1919-20	1920-21
McCarthy, Tom	Det., Bos.	4	60	8	9	17	8	....	....	....	....	....		1956-57	1960-61
McCarthy, Tom	Min., Bos.	9	460	178	221	399	330	68	12	26	38	67		1979-80	1987-88
McCartney, Walt	Mtl.	1	2	0	0	0	0	....	....	....	....	....		1932-33	1932-33
McCaskill, Ted	Min.	1	4	0	2	2	0	....	....	....	....	....		1967-68	1967-68
McClanahan, Rob	Buf., Hfd., NYR	5	224	38	63	101	126	34	4	12	16	31		1979-80	1983-84
McCord, Bob	Bos., Det., Min., St.L.	7	316	58	68	126	262	14	2	5	7	10		1963-64	1972-73
McCord, Dennis	Van.	1	3	0	0	0	0	....	....	....	....	....		1973-74	1973-74
McCormack, John	Tor., Mtl., Chi.	8	311	25	49	74	35	22	1	1	2	0	1	1947-48	1954-55
McCourt, Dale	Det., Buf., Tor.	7	532	194	284	478	124	21	9	7	16	6		1977-78	1983-84
McCreary, Bill	Tor.	1	12	1	0	1	4	....	....	....	....	....		1980-81	1980-81
McCreary, Bill E.	NYR, Det., Mtl., St.L.	10	309	53	62	115	108	48	6	16	22	14		1953-54	1970-71
McCreary, Keith	Mtl., Pit., Atl.	10	532	131	112	243	294	16	0	4	4	6		1961-62	1974-75
McCreedy, Johnny	Tor.	2	64	17	12	29	25	21	4	3	7	16	2	1941-42	1944-45
McCrimmon, Jim	St.L.	1	2	0	0	0	0	....	....	....	....	....		1974-75	1974-75
McCulley, Bob	Mtl.	1	1	0	0	0	0	....	....	....	....	....		1934-35	1934-35
McCurry, Duke	Pit.	4	148	21	11	32	119	4	0	2	2	4		1925-26	1928-29
McCutcheon, Brian	Det.	3	37	3	1	4	7	....	....	....	....	....		1974-75	1976-77
McCutheon, Darwin	Tor.	1	1	0	0	0	0	....	....	....	....	....		1981-82	1981-82
McDill, Jeff	Chi.	1	1	0	0	0	0	....	....	....	....	....		1976-77	1976-77
McDonagh, Bill	NYR	1	4	0	0	0	2	....	....	....	....	....		1949-50	1949-50
McDonald, Ab	Mtl., Chi., Bos., Det., Pit., St.L.	15	762	182	248	430	200	84	21	29	50	42	4	1957-58	1971-72
McDonald, Brian	Chi., Buf.	2	12	0	0	0	29	8	0	0	0	2		1967-68	1970-71
McDonald, Bucko	Det., Tor., NYR	11	448	35	88	123	206	63	6	1	7	24	3	1934-35	1944-45
McDonald, Butch	Det., Chi.	2	66	8	20	28	2	5	0	2	2	10		1939-40	1944-45
McDonald, Gerry	Hfd.	1	3	0	0	0	0	....	....	....	....	....		1981-82	1981-82
McDonald, Jack	Mtl.W, Mtl., Que., Tor.	5	73	27	11	38	13	12	2	0	2	0		1917-18	1921-22
McDonald, John	NYR	1	43	10	9	19	6	....	....	....	....	....		1943-44	1943-44
McDonald, Lanny	Tor., Col., Cgy.	16	1111	500	506	1006	899	117	44	40	84	120	1	1973-74	1988-89
McDonald, Robert	NYR	1	1	0	0	0	0	....	....	....	....	....		1943-44	1943-44
McDonald, Terry	K.C.	1	8	0	1	1	6	....	....	....	....	....		1975-76	1975-76
McDonnell, Joe	Van., Pit.	3	50	2	10	12	34	....	....	....	....	....		1981-82	1985-86
* McDonnell, Moylan	Ham.	1	20	1	1	2	0	....	....	....	....	....		1920-21	1920-21
McDonough, Al	L.A., Pit., Atl., Det.	5	237	73	88	161	73	8	0	1	1	2		1970-71	1977-78
McDougal, Mike	NYR, Hfd.	4	61	8	10	18	43	....	....	....	....	....		1978-79	1982-83
McElmury, Jim	Min., K.C., Col.	5	180	14	47	61	49	....	....	....	....	....		1972-73	1977-78
McEwen, Mike	NYR, Col., NYI, L.A., Wsh., Det., Hfd.	12	716	108	296	404	460	78	12	36	48	48	3	1976-77	1987-88
McFadden, Jim	Det., Chi.	7	412	100	126	226	89	49	10	9	19	30	1	1947-48	1953-54
McFadyen, Don	Chi.	4	179	12	33	45	77	12	2	2	4	5	1	1932-33	1935-36
McFall, Dan	Wpg.	2	9	0	1	1	0	....	....	....	....	....		1984-85	1985-86
McFarland, George	Chi.	1	2	0	0	0	0	....	....	....	....	....		1926-27	1926-27
McGeough, Jim	Wsh., Pit.	4	57	7	10	17	32	....	....	....	....	....		1981-82	1986-87
McGibbon, John	Mtl.	1	1	0	0	0	2	....	....	....	....	....		1942-43	1942-43
McGill, Jack G.	Bos.	4	97	23	36	59	42	27	7	4	11	17		1941-42	1946-47
McGill, Jack	Mtl.	3	134	27	10	37	71	3	2	0	2	0		1934-35	1936-37
McGregor, Sandy	NYR	1	2	0	0	0	2	....	....	....	....	....		1963-64	1963-64
McGuire, Mickey	Pit.	2	36	3	0	3	6	....	....	....	....	....		1926-27	1927-28
McIlhargey, Jack	Phi., Van., Hfd.	8	393	11	36	47	1102	27	0	3	3	68		1974-75	1981-82
McInenly, Bert	Det., NYA, Ott., Bos.	6	166	19	15	34	144	4	0	0	0	2		1930-31	1935-36
McIntosh, Bruce	Min.	1	2	0	0	0	0	....	....	....	....	....		1972-73	1972-73
McIntosh, Paul	Buf.	2	48	0	0	2	66	2	0	0	0	7		1974-75	1975-76
McIntyre, Jack	Bos., Chi., Det.	11	499	109	102	211	173	29	7	6	13	4		1949-50	1959-60
McIntyre, Larry	Tor.	2	41	0	3	3	26	....	....	....	....	....		1969-70	1972-73
McKay, Doug	Det.	1	....	....	....	....	....	1	0	0	0	0	1	1949-50	1949-50
McKay, Ray	Chi., Buf., Cal.	6	140	2	16	18	102	....	....	....	....	....		1968-69	1973-74
McKechnie, Walt	Min., Cal., Bos., Det., Wsh., Clev., Tor., Col.	16	955	214	392	606	469	15	7	5	12	9		1967-68	1982-83
McKegney, Ian	Chi.	1	3	0	0	0	2	....	....	....	....	....		1976-77	1976-77
* McKell, Jack	Ott.	2	42	4	1	5	42	9	0	0	0	0	1	1919-20	1920-21
McKendry, Alex	NYI, Cgy.	4	46	3	6	9	21	6	2	2	4	0	1	1977-78	1980-81
McKenna, Sean	Buf., L.A., Tor.	9	414	82	80	162	181	15	1	2	3	2		1981-82	1989-90
McKenney, Don	Bos., NYR, Tor., Det., St.L.	13	798	237	345	582	211	58	18	29	47	10	1	1954-55	1967-68
McKenny, Jim	Tor., Min.	14	604	82	247	329	294	37	7	9	16	10		1965-66	1978-79
McKenzie, Brian	Pit.	1	6	1	1	2	4	....	....	....	....	....		1971-72	1971-72
McKenzie, John	Chi., Det., NYR, Bos.	12	691	206	268	474	917	69	15	32	47	133	2	1958-59	1971-72
McKinnon, Alex	Ham., NYA, Chi.	5	194	19	10	29	235	....	....	....	....	....		1924-25	1928-29
McKinnon, Bob	Chi.	1	2	0	0	0	0	....	....	....	....	....		1928-29	1928-29
McKinnon, John	Mtl., Pit., Phi.	6	218	28	11	39	224	2	0	0	0	4		1925-26	1930-31
McLean, Don	Wsh.	1	9	0	0	0	6	....	....	....	....	....		1975-76	1975-76
* McLean, Fred	Que., Ham.	2	9	0	0	0	2	....	....	....	....	....		1919-20	1920-21
McLean, Jack	Tor.	3	67	14	24	38	76	13	2	2	4	8	1	1942-43	1944-45
* McLellan, John	Tor.	1	2	0	0	0	0	....	....	....	....	....		1951-52	1951-52
McLellan, Scott	Bos.	1	2	0	0	0	0	....	....	....	....	....		1982-83	1982-83
McLellan, Todd	NYI	1	5	1	1	2	0	....	....	....	....	....		1987-88	1987-88
McLenahan, Roly	Det.	1	9	2	1	3	10	2	0	0	0	0		1945-46	1945-46
McLeod, Al	Det.	1	26	2	2	4	24	....	....	....	....	....		1973-74	1973-74
McLeod, Jackie	NYR	5	106	14	23	37	12	7	0	0	0	0		1949-50	1954-55
McMahon, Mike C.	Mtl., Bos.	3	57	7	18	25	102	13	1	2	3	30	1	1942-43	1945-46
McMahon, Mike	NYR, Min., Chi., Det., Pit., Buf.	8	224	15	68	83	171	14	3	7	10	4		1963-64	1971-72
McManama, Bob	Pit.	3	99	11	25	36	28	8	0	1	1	6		1973-74	1975-76
McManus, Sammy	Mtl.M., Bos.	2	26	0	1	1	8	1	0	0	0	0	1	1934-35	1936-37
McMurchy, Tom	Chi., Edm.	4	55	8	4	12	65	....	....	....	....	....		1983-84	1987-88
McNab, Max	Det.	4	128	16	19	35	24	25	1	0	1	4	1	1947-48	1950-51
McNab, Peter	Buf., Bos., Van., N.J.	14	954	363	450	813	179	107	40	42	82	20		1973-74	1986-87
McNabney, Sid	Mtl.	1	....	....	....	....	....	5	0	1	1	2		1950-51	1950-51
* McNamara, Howard	Mtl.	1	11	1	0	1	2	....	....	....	....	....		1919-20	1919-20
* McNaughton, George	Que.B.	1	1	0	0	0	0	....	....	....	....	....		1919-20	1919-20
McNeill, Billy	Det.	6	257	21	46	67	142	4	1	1	2	4		1956-57	1963-64
McNeill, Stu	Det.	3	10	1	1	2	2	....	....	....	....	....		1957-58	1959-60
McPhee, George	NYR, N.J.	7	115	24	25	49	257	29	5	3	8	69		1982-83	1988-89
McReavy, Pat	Bos., Det.	4	55	5	10	15	4	20	3	3	6	9	1	1938-39	1941-42
McSheffrey, Bryan	Van., Buf.	3	90	13	7	20	44	....	....	....	....	....		1972-73	1974-75
McTaggart, Jim	Wsh.	2	71	3	10	13	205	....	....	....	....	....		1980-81	1981-82
McTavish, Gordon	St.L., Wpg.	2	11	1	3	4	2	....	....	....	....	....		1978-79	1979-80
McVeigh, Charley	Chi., NYA	9	397	84	88	172	138	4	0	0	0	2		1926-27	1934-35
McVicar, Jack	Mtl.M.	2	88	2	4	6	63	2	0	0	0	2		1930-31	1931-32
Meagher, Rick	Mtl., Hfd., N.J., St.L.	12	691	144	165	309	383	62	8	7	15	41		1979-80	1990-91
Meehan, Gerry	Tor., Phi., Buf., Van., Atl., Wsh.	10	670	180	243	423	111	10	0	1	1	0		1968-69	1978-79
Meeke, Brent	Cal., Clev.	5	75	9	22	31	8	....	....	....	....	....		1972-73	1976-77
Meeker, Howie	Tor.	8	346	83	102	185	329	42	6	9	15	50	3	1946-47	1953-54
Meeker, Mike	Pit.	1	4	0	0	0	5	....	....	....	....	....		1978-79	1978-79
* Meeking, Harry	Tor., Det., Bos.	3	63	18	3	21	42	14	4	2	6	0	1	1917-18	1926-27
Meger, Paul	Mtl.	6	212	39	52	91	112	35	3	8	11	16	1	1949-50	1954-55
Meighan, Ron	Min., Pit.	2	48	3	7	10	18	....	....	....	....	....		1981-82	1982-83
Meissner, Barrie	Min.	2	6	0	1	1	4	....	....	....	....	....		1967-68	1968-69
Meissner, Dick	Bos., NYR	5	171	11	15	26	37	....	....	....	....	....		1959-60	1964-65
Melametsa, Anssi	Wpg.	1	27	0	3	3	2	....	....	....	....	....		1985-86	1985-86
Melin, Roger	Min.	2	3	0	0	0	0	....	....	....	....	....		1980-81	1981-82
Mellor, Tom	Det.	2	26	2	4	6	25	....	....	....	....	....		1973-74	1974-75
Melnyk, Gerry	Det., Chi., St.L.	6	269	39	77	116	34	53	6	6	12	6		1955-56	1967-68
Melrose, Barry	Wpg., Tor., Det.	6	300	10	23	33	728	7	0	2	2	38		1979-80	1985-86
Menard, Hillary	Chi.	1	1	0	0	0	0	....	....	....	....	....		1953-54	1953-54
Menard, Howie	Det., L.A., Chi., Oak.	4	151	23	42	65	87	19	3	7	10	36		1963-64	1969-70
Mercredi, Vic	Atl.	1	2	0	0	0	0	....	....	....	....	....		1974-75	1974-75
Meredith, Greg	Cgy.	2	38	6	4	10	8	5	3	1	4	4		1980-81	1982-83
Merkosky, Glenn	Hfd., N.J., Det.	4	63	5	12	17	22	....	....	....	....	....		1981-82	1985-86
Merkosky, Glenn	Hfd., N.J., Det.	5	66	5	12	17	22	....	....	....	....	....		1981-82	1989-90
Meronek, Bill	Mtl.	2	19	5	8	13	0	1	0	0	0	0		1939-40	1942-43
Merrick, Wayne	St.L., Cal., Clev., NYI	12	774	191	265	456	303	102	19	30	49	30	4	1972-73	1983-84
* Merrill, Horace	Ott.	2	11	0	0	0	0	....	....	....	....	....	1	1917-18	1919-20
Messier, Paul	Col.	1	9	0	0	0	4	....	....	....	....	....		1978-79	1978-79
Metcalfe, Scott	Edm., Buf.	3	19	1	2	3	18	....	....	....	....	....		1987-88	1989-90

Name	NHL Teams	NHL Seasons	Regular Schedule GP	G	A	TP	PIM	Playoffs GP	G	A	TP	PIM	NHL Cup Wins	First NHL Season	Last NHL Season
Metz, Don	Tor.	8	172	20	35	55	42	47	7	8	15	10	5	1939-40	1948-49
* Metz, Nick	Tor.	12	518	131	119	250	149	76	19	20	39	31	4	1934-35	1947-48
Michaluk, Art	Chi.	1	5	0	0	0	0	....	....	....	....	....		1947-48	1947-48
Michaluk, John	Chi.	1	1	0	0	0	0	....	....	....	....	....		1950-51	1950-51
Michayluk, Dave	Phi.	2	14	2	6	8	8	....	....	....	....	....		1981-82	1982-83
Micheletti, Pat	Min.	1	12	2	0	2	8	....	....	....	....	....		1987-88	1987-88
Micheletti, Joe	St.L., Col.	3	158	11	60	71	114	11	1	11	12	10		1979-80	1981-82
* Mickey, Larry	Chi., NYR., Tor., Mtl., L.A., Phi., Buf.	11	292	39	53	92	160	9	1	0	1	10		1964-65	1974-75
Mickoski, Nick	NYR, Chi., Det., Bos.	13	703	158	184	342	319	18	1	6	7	6		1947-48	1959-60
Middleton, Rick	NYR, Bos.	14	1005	448	540	988	157	114	45	55	100	19		1974-75	1987-88
Migay, Rudy	Tor.	10	418	59	92	151	293	15	1	0	1	20		1949-50	1959-60
Mikita, Stan	Chi.	22	1394	541	926	1467	1270	155	59	91	150	169	1	1958-59	1979-80
Mikkelson, Bill	L.A., N.Y.I., Wsh.	4	147	4	18	22	105	....	....	....	....	....		1971-72	1976-77
Mikol, Jim	Tor., NYR	2	34	1	4	5	8	....	....	....	....	....		1962-63	1964-65
Milbury, Mike	Bos.	12	754	49	189	238	1552	86	4	24	28	219		1975-76	1986-87
Milks, Hib	Pit., Phi., NYR, Ott.	8	314	87	41	128	179	10	0	0	0	2		1925-26	1932-33
Millar, Hugh	Det.	1	4	0	0	0	0	1	0	0	0	0		1946-47	1946-47
Millar, Mike	Hfd., Wsh., Bos., Tor.	5	78	18	18	36	12	....	....	....	....	....		1986-87	1990-91
Miller, Bill	Mtl.M., Mtl.	3	95	7	3	10	16	12	0	0	0	0	1	1934-35	1936-37
Miller, Bob	Bos., Col., L.A.	6	404	75	119	194	220	36	4	7	11	27		1977-78	1984-85
Miller, Earl	Chi., Tor.	5	116	19	14	33	124	10	1	0	1	6	1	1927-28	1931-32
Miller, Jack	Chi.	2	17	0	0	0	4	....	....	....	....	....		1949-50	1950-51
Miller, Paul	Col.	1	3	0	3	3	0	....	....	....	....	....		1981-82	1981-82
Miller, Perry	Det.	4	217	10	51	61	387	....	....	....	....	....		1977-78	1980-81
Miller, Tom	Det., NYI	4	118	16	25	41	34	....	....	....	....	....		1970-71	1974-75
Miller, Warren	NYR, Hfd.	4	262	40	50	90	137	6	1	0	1	0		1979-80	1982-83
Miner, John	Edm.	1	14	2	3	5	16	....	....	....	....	....		1987-88	1987-88
Minor, Gerry	Van.	5	140	11	21	32	173	12	1	3	4	25		1979-80	1983-84
Miszuk, John	Det., Chi., Phi., Min.	6	237	7	39	46	232	19	0	3	3	19		1963-64	1969-70
Mitchell, Bill	Det.	1	1	0	0	0	0	....	....	....	....	....		1963-64	1963-64
Mitchell, Herb	Bos.	2	53	6	0	6	38	....	....	....	....	....		1924-25	1925-26
Mitchell, Red	Chi.	3	83	4	5	9	67	....	....	....	....	....		1941-42	1944-45
Moe, Billy	NYR	5	261	11	42	53	163	1	0	0	0	0		1944-45	1948-49
Moffat, Lyle	Tor., Wpg.	3	97	12	16	28	51	....	....	....	....	....		1972-73	1979-80
Moffat, Ron	Det.	3	36	1	1	2	8	7	0	0	0	0		1932-33	1934-35
Moher, Mike	N.J.	1	9	0	1	1	28	....	....	....	....	....		1982-83	1982-83
Mohns, Doug	Bos., Chi., Min., Atl., Wsh.	22	1390	248	462	710	1250	94	14	36	50	122		1953-54	1974-75
Mohns, Lloyd	NYR	1	1	0	0	0	0	....	....	....	....	....		1943-44	1943-44
Mokosak, Carl	Cgy., L.A., Phi., Pit., Bos.	6	83	11	15	26	170	1	0	0	0	0		1981-82	1988-89
Mokosak, John	Det.	2	41	0	2	2	96	....	....	....	....	....		1988-89	1989-90
Molin, Lars	Van.	3	172	33	65	98	37	19	2	9	11	7		1981-82	1983-84
Moller, Mike	Buf., Edm.	7	134	15	28	43	41	3	0	1	1	0		1980-81	1986-87
Molloy, Mitch	Buf.	1	2	0	0	0	10	....	....	....	....	....		1989-90	1989-90
Molyneaux, Larry	NYR	2	45	0	1	1	20	3	0	0	0	8		1937-38	1938-39
Monahan, Garry	Mtl., Det., L.A., Tor., Van.	12	748	116	169	285	484	22	3	1	4	13		1967-68	1978-79
Monahan, Hartland	Cal., NYR, Wsh., Pit., L.A., St.L.	7	334	61	80	141	163	6	0	0	0	4		1973-74	1980-81
Mondou, Armand	Mtl.	12	385	47	71	118	99	35	3	5	8	12	2	1928-29	1939-40
Mondou, Pierre	Mtl.	9	548	194	262	456	179	69	17	28	45	26	3	1976-77	1984-85
Mongrain, Bob	Buf., L.A.	6	83	13	14	27	14	11	1	2	3	2		1979-80	1985-86
Monteith, Hank	Det.	3	77	5	12	17	6	4	0	0	0	0		1968-69	1970-71
Moore, Dickie	Mtl., Tor., St.L.	14	719	261	347	608	652	135	46	64	110	122	6	1951-52	1967-68
Moran, Amby	Mtl., Chi.	2	35	1	1	2	24	....	....	....	....	....		1926-27	1927-28
* Morenz, Howie	Mtl., Chi., NYR	14	550	273	197	470	563	47	21	11	32	68	3	1923-24	1936-37
Moretto, Angelo	Clev.	1	5	1	2	3	2	....	....	....	....	....		1976-77	1976-77
Morin, Pete	Mtl.	1	31	10	12	22	7	1	0	0	0	0		1941-42	1941-42
Morris, Bernie	Bos.	1	6	2	0	2	0	....	....	....	....	....		1924-25	1924-25
Morris, Elwyn	Tor., NYR	4	135	13	29	42	58	18	4	2	6	16	1	1943-44	1948-49
Morrison, Dave	L.A., Van.	4	39	3	3	6	4	....	....	....	....	....		1980-81	1984-85
Morrison, Don	Det., Chi.	3	112	18	28	46	12	3	0	1	1	0		1947-48	1950-51
Morrison, Doug	Bos.	4	23	7	3	10	15	....	....	....	....	....		1979-80	1984-85
Morrison, Gary	Phi.	3	43	1	15	16	70	5	0	1	1	2		1979-80	1981-82
Morrison, George	St.L.	2	115	17	21	38	13	3	0	0	0	0		1970-71	1971-72
Morrison, Jim	Bos., Tor., Det., NYR, Pit.	12	704	40	160	200	542	36	0	12	12	38		1951-52	1970-71
Morrison, John	NYA	1	18	0	0	0	0	....	....	....	....	....		1925-26	1925-26
Morrison, Kevin	Col.	1	41	4	11	15	23	....	....	....	....	....		1979-80	1979-80
Morrison, Lew	Phi., Atl., Wsh., Pit.	9	564	39	52	91	107	17	0	0	0	2		1969-70	1977-78
Morrison, Mark	NYR	2	10	1	1	2	0	....	....	....	....	....		1981-82	1983-84
Morrison, Roderick	Det.	1	34	8	7	15	4	3	0	0	0	0		1947-48	1947-48
Morrow, Ken	NYI	10	550	17	88	105	309	127	11	22	33	97	4	1979-80	1988-89
Morton, Dean	Det.	1	1	1	0	1	2	....	....	....	....	....		1989-90	1989-90
Mortson, Gus	Tor., Chi., Det.	13	797	46	152	198	1380	54	5	8	13	68	4	1946-47	1958-59
Mosdell, Kenny	Bro., Mtl., Chi.	16	693	141	168	309	475	79	16	13	29	48	4	1941-42	1958-59
Mosienko, Bill	Chi.	14	711	258	282	540	117	22	10	4	14	15		1941-42	1954-55
Mott, Morris	Cal.	3	199	18	32	50	49	....	....	....	....	....		1972-73	1974-75
Motter, Alex	Bos., Det.	8	267	39	64	103	135	40	3	9	12	41	1	1934-35	1942-43
Moxey, Jim	Cal., Clev., L.A.	3	127	22	27	49	59	....	....	....	....	....		1974-75	1976-77
Mulhern, Richard	Atl., L.A., Tor., Wpg.	6	303	27	93	120	217	7	0	3	3	5		1975-76	1980-81
Muloin, Wayne	Det., Oak., Cal., Min.	3	147	3	21	24	93	11	0	0	0	2		1963-64	1970-71
Mulvey, Grant	Chi., N.J.	10	586	149	135	284	816	42	10	5	15	70		1974-75	1983-84
Mulvey, Paul	Wsh., Pit., L.A.	4	225	30	51	81	613	....	....	....	....	....		1978-79	1981-82
* Mummery, Harry	Tor., ue., Mtl., Ham.	6	106	33	13	46	161	7	1	4	5	0		1917-18	1922-23
* Munro, Dunc	Mtl.	8	239	28	18	46	170	25	3	2	5	24	1	1924-25	1931-32
Munro, Gerry	Mtl., Tor.	2	33	1	0	1	22	....	....	....	....	....		1924-25	1925-26
Murdoch, Bob L.	Cal., Clev., St.L.	4	260	72	85	157	127	....	....	....	....	....		1975-76	1978-79
Murdoch, Bob J.	Mtl., L.A., Atl., Cgy.	12	757	60	218	278	764	69	4	18	22	92	2	1970-71	1981-82
Murdoch, Don	NYR, Edm., Det.		320	121	117	238	155	24	10	8	18	16		1976-77	1981-82
Murdoch, Murray	NYR	11	507	84	108	192	197	55	9	12	21	28		1926-27	1936-37
Murphy, Brian	Det.	1	1	0	0	0	0	....	....	....	....	....		1974-75	1974-75
Murphy, Mike	St.L. NYR, L.A.	12	831	238	318	556	514	66	13	23	36	54		1971-72	1982-83
Murphy, Ron	NYR, Chi., Det., Bos.	18	889	205	274	479	460	53	7	8	15	26	1	1952-53	1969-70
Murray, Allan	NYA	7	277	5	9	14	163	14	0	0	0	8		1933-34	1939-40
Murray, Bob F.	Chi.	15	1008	132	382	514	873	112	19	37	56	....		1975-76	1989-90
Murray, Bob J.	Atl., Van.	4	194	6	16	22	98	9	1	1	2	15		1973-74	1976-77
Murray, Jim	L.A.	1	30	0	2	2	14	....	....	....	....	....		1967-68	1967-68
Murray, Ken	Tor., N.Y.I., Det., K.C.	5	106	1	10	11	135	....	....	....	....	....		1969-70	1975-76
Murray, Leo	Mtl.	1	6	0	0	0	2	....	....	....	....	....		1932-33	1932-33
Murray, Mike	Phi.	1	1	0	0	0	0	....	....	....	....	....		1987-88	1987-88
Murray, Randy	Tor.	1	3	0	0	0	2	....	....	....	....	....		1969-70	1969-70
Murray, Terry	Cal., Phi., Det., Wsh.	8	302	4	76	80	199	18	2	2	4	10		1972-73	1981-82
Myers, Hap	Buf.	1	13	0	0	0	6	....	....	....	....	....		1970-71	1970-71
Myles, Vic	NYR	1	45	6	9	15	57	....	....	....	....	....		1942-43	1942-43

N

Name	NHL Teams	NHL Seasons	Regular Schedule GP	G	A	TP	PIM	Playoffs GP	G	A	TP	PIM	NHL Cup Wins	First NHL Season	Last NHL Season
Nachbaur, Don	Hfd., Edm., Phi.	8	223	23	46	69	465	11	1	1	2	24		1980-81	1989-90
Nahrgang, Jim	Det.	3	57	5	12	17	34	....	....	....	....	....		1974-75	1976-77
Nanne, Lou	Min.	11	635	68	157	225	356	32	4	10	14	9		1967-68	1977-78
Nantais, Richard	Min.	3	63	5	4	9	79	....	....	....	....	....		1974-75	1976-77
Napier, Mark	Mtl., Min., Edm., Buf.	11	767	235	306	541	157	82	18	24	42	11	1	1978-79	1988-89
Naslund, Mats	Mtl.	8	617	243	369	612	107	97	34	57	91	33	1	1982-83	1989-90
Nattrass, Ralph	Chi.	4	223	18	38	56	308	....	....	....	....	....		1946-47	1949-50
Natyshak, Mike	Que.	1	4	0	0	0	0	....	....	....	....	....		1987-88	1987-88
Nechaev, Victor	L.A.	1	3	1	0	1	0	....	....	....	....	....		1982-83	1982-83
Nedomansky, Vaclav	Det., NYR, St.L.	6	421	122	156	278	88	7	3	5	8	0		1977-78	1982-83
Neely, Bob	Tor., Col.	5	283	39	59	98	266	26	5	7	12	15		1973-74	1977-78
Neilson, Jim	NYR, Cal., Clev.	16	1023	69	299	368	904	65	1	17	18	61		1962-63	1977-78
Nelson, Gordie	Tor.	1	3	0	0	0	11	....	....	....	....	....		1969-70	1969-70
Nemeth, Steve	NYR	1	12	2	0	2	2	....	....	....	....	....		1987-88	1987-88
Nesterenko, Eric	Tor., Chi.	21	1219	250	324	574	1273	124	13	24	37	127	1	1951-52	1971-72
Nethery, Lance	NYR, Edm.	2	41	11	14	25	14	14	5	3	8	9		1980-81	1981-82
Neufeld, Ray	Hfd., Win., Bos.	11	595	157	200	357	816	28	8	6	14	55		1979-80	1989-90
* Neville, Mike	Tor., NYA	4	62	6	3	9	14	2	0	0	0	0	1	1917-18	1930-31
Nevin, Bob	Tor., NYR, Min., L.A.	18	1128	307	419	726	211	84	16	18	34	24	2	1957-58	1975-76

Ken Morrow

Bob Murray

Jim Neilson

Bob Nevin

John Paddock

Jim Peplinski

Gil Perreault

Denis Potvin

Name	NHL Teams	NHL Seasons	Regular Schedule GP	G	A	TP	PIM	Playoffs GP	G	A	TP	PIM	NHL Cup Wins	First NHL Season	Last NHL Season
Newberry, John	Mtl., Hfd.	4	22	0	4	4	6	2	0	0	0	0		1982-83	1985-86
Newell, Rick	Det.	2	7	0	0	0	0	....	....	....	....	....		1972-73	1973-74
Newman, Dan	NYR, Mtl., Edm.	4	126	17	24	41	63	3	0	0	0	4		1976-77	1979-80
Newman, John	Det.	1	8	1	1	2	0	....	....	....	....	....		1930-31	1930-31
Nicholson, Al	Bos.	2	19	0	1	1	4	....	....	....	....	....		1955-56	1956-57
Nicholson, Edward	Det.	1	1	0	0	0	0	....	....	....	....	....		1947-48	1947-48
Nicholson, Graeme	Bos., Col., NYR	3	52	2	7	9	60	....	....	....	....	....		1978-79	1982-83
Nicholson, John	Chi.	1	2	1	0	1	0	....	....	....	....	....		1937-38	1937-38
Nicholson, Neil	Oak., N.Y.I.	4	39	3	1	4	23	2	0	0	0	0		1969-70	1977-78
Nicholson, Paul	Wsh.	3	62	4	8	12	18	....	....	....	....	....		1974-75	1976-77
Niekamp, Jim	Det.	2	29	0	2	2	27	....	....	....	....	....		1970-71	1971-72
Nienhui, Kraig	Bos.	3	87	20	16	36	39	2	0	0	0	14		1985-86	1987-88
* Nighbor, Frank	Ott., Tor.	13	348	136	60	196	241	36	11	9	20	27	4	1917-18	1929-30
Nigro, Frank	Tor.	2	68	8	18	26	39	3	0	0	0	2		1982-83	1983-84
Nill, Jim	St.L., Van., Bos., Wpg., Det.	9	524	58	87	145	854	59	10	5	15	203		1981-82	1989-90
Nilsson, Kent	Atl., Cgy., Min., Edm.	8	547	263	422	685	116	59	11	41	52	14	1	1979-80	1986-87
Nilsson, Ulf	NYR	4	170	57	112	169	85	25	8	14	22	27		1978-79	1982-83
Nistico, Lou	Col.	1	3	0	0	0	0	....	....	....	....	....		1977-78	1977-78
* Noble, Reg	Tor., Mtl.M., Det.	16	526	167	79	246	807	32	4	5	9	39	3	1917-18	1932-33
Noel, Claude	Wsh.	1	7	0	0	0	0	....	....	....	....	....		1979-80	1979-80
Nolan, Pat	Tor.	1	2	0	0	0	0	....	....	....	....	....	1	1921-22	1921-22
Nolan, Ted	Det., Pit.	3	78	6	16	22	105	....	....	....	....	....		1981-82	1985-86
Nolet, Simon	Phi., K.C., Pit., Col.	10	562	150	182	332	187	34	6	3	9	8	1	1967-68	1976-77
Noris, Joe	Pit., St.L., Buf.	3	55	2	5	7	22	....	....	....	....	....		1971-72	1973-74
Norrish, Rod	Min.	2	21	3	3	6	2	....	....	....	....	....		1973-74	1974-75
Northcott, Baldy	Mtl.M., Chi.	11	446	133	112	245	273	31	8	5	13	14	1	1928-29	1938-39
Norwich, Craig	Wpg., St.L., Col.	2	104	17	58	75	60	....	....	....	....	....		1979-80	1980-81
Novy, Milan	Wsh.	1	73	18	30	48	16	2	0	0	0	0		1982-83	1982-83
Nowak, Hank	Pit., Det., Bos.	4	180	26	29	55	161	3	1	0	1	8		1973-74	1976-77
Nykoluk, Mike	Tor.	1	32	3	1	4	20	....	....	....	....	....		1956-57	1956-57
Nyrop, Bill	Mtl., Min.	4	207	12	51	63	101	35	1	7	8	22	3	1975-76	1981-82
Nystrom, Bob	NYI	14	900	235	278	513	1248	157	39	44	83	236	4	1972-73	1985-86
O															
* Oatman, Russell	Det., Mtl.M., NYR	3	124	20	9	29	100	17	1	0	1	18		1926-27	1928-29
O'Brien, Dennis	Min., Col., Clev., Bos.	10	592	31	91	122	1017	34	1	2	3	101		1970-71	1979-80
O'Brien, Obie	Bos.	1	2	0	0	0	0	....	....	....	....	....		1955-56	1955-56
O'Callahan, Jack	Chi., N.J.	7	389	27	104	131	541	32	4	11	15	41		1982-83	1988-89
O'Connell, Mike	Chi., Bos., Det.	13	860	105	334	439	605	82	8	24	32	64		1977-78	1989-90
* O'Connor, Buddy	Mtl., NYR	10	509	140	257	397	34	53	15	21	36	6	2	1941-42	1950-51
Oddleifson, Chris	Bos., Van.	9	524	95	191	286	464	14	1	6	7	8		1972-73	1980-81
Odelin, Selmar	Edm.	3	18	0	2	2	35	....	....	....	....	....		1985-86	1988-89
O'Donnell Fred	Bos.	2	115	15	11	26	98	5	0	1	1	5		1972-73	1973-74
O'Donoghue, Don	Oak., Cal.	3	125	18	17	35	35	3	0	0	0	0		1969-70	1971-72
Odrowski, Gerry	Det., Oak., St.L.	6	299	12	19	31	111	30	0	1	1	16		1960-61	1971-72
O'Flaherty, Gerry	Tor., Van., Atl.	8	438	99	95	194	168	7	2	2	4	6		1971-72	1978-79
O'Flaherty, John	NYA, Bro.	2	21	5	1	6	0	....	....	....	....	....		1940-41	1941-42
Ogilvie, Brian	Chi., St.L.	6	90	15	21	36	29	....	....	....	....	....		1972-73	1978-79
O'Grady, George	Mtl.M.	1	4	0	0	0	0	....	....	....	....	....		1917-18	1917-18
Okerlund, Todd	NYI	1	4	0	0	0	2	....	....	....	....	....		1987-88	1987-88
* Oliver, Harry	Bos., NYA	11	473	127	85	212	147	35	10	6	16	22	1	1926-27	1936-37
Oliver, Murray	Det., Bos., Tor., Min.	17	1127	274	454	728	319	35	9	16	25	10		1957-58	1974-75
Olmstead, Bert	Chi., Mtl., Tor.	14	848	181	421	602	884	115	16	42	58	01	5	1948-49	1961-62
Olson, Dennis	Det.	1	4	0	0	0	0	....	....	....	....	....		1957-58	1957-58
O'Neil, Paul	Van., Bos.	2	6	0	0	0	0	....	....	....	....	....		1973-74	1975-76
O'Neill, Jim	Bos., Mtl.	6	165	6	30	36	109	11	1	1	2	13		1933-34	1941-42
* O'Neill, Tom	Tor.	2	66	10	12	22	53	4	0	0	0	6	1	1943-44	1944-45
Orban, Bill	Chi., Min.	3	114	8	15	23	673	3	0	0	0	0		1967-68	1969-70
O'Ree, Willie	Bos.	2	45	4	10	14	26	....	....	....	....	....		1957-58	1960-61
O'Regan, Tom	Pit.	3	60	5	12	17	10	....	....	....	....	....		1983-84	1985-86
O'Reilly, Terry	Bos.	14	891	204	402	606	2095	108	25	42	67	335		1971-72	1984-85
Orlando, Gaetano	Buf.	3	98	18	26	44	51	5	0	4	4	14		1984-85	1986-87
Orlando, Jimmy	Det.	6	200	7	24	31	375	36	0	9	9	105	1	1936-37	1942-43
Orleski, Dave	Mtl.	2	2	0	0	0	0	....	....	....	....	....		1980-81	1981-82
Orr, Bobby	Bos., hi.	12	657	270	645	915	953	74	26	66	92	107	2	1966-67	1978-79
Osburn, Randy	Tor., Phi.	2	27	0	2	2	0	....	....	....	....	....		1972-73	1974-75
O'Shea, Danny	Min., Chi., St.L.	5	369	64	115	179	265	39	3	7	10	62		1968-69	1972-73
O'Shea, Kevin	Buf., St.L.	3	134	13	18	31	85	12	2	1	3	10		1970-71	1972-73
Ouelette, Eddie	Chi.	1	43	3	2	5	11	1	0	0	0	0		1935-36	1935-36
Ouelette, Gerry	Bos.	1	34	5	4	9	0	....	....	....	....	....		1960-1	1960-61
Owchar, Dennis	Pit., Col.	6	288	30	85	115	200	10	1	1	2	8		1974-75	1979-80
* Owen, George	Bos.	5	192	44	33	77	151	21	2	5	7	25	1	1928-29	1932-33
P															
Pachal, Clayton	Bos., Col.	3	35	2	3	5	95	....	....	....	....	....		1976-77	1978-79
Paddock, John	Wsh., Phi., Que.	5	87	8	14	22	86	5	2	0	2	0		1975-76	1982-83
Paiement, Rosaire	Phi., Van.	5	190	48	52	100	343	3	3	0	3	0		1967-68	1971-72
Paiement, Wilf	K.C. Col., Tor., Que., NYR, Buf., Pit.	14	946	356	458	814	1757	69	18	17	35	185		1974-75	1987-88
Palangio, Peter	Mtl., Det., Chi.	5	71	13	10	23	28	7	0	0	0	0	1	1926-27	1937-38
Palazzari, Aldo	Bos., NYR	1	35	8	3	11	4	....	....	....	....	....		1943-44	1943-44
Palazzari, Doug	St.L.	4	108	18	20	38	23	2	0	0	0	0		1974-75	1978-79
Palmer, Brad	Min., Bos.	3	168	32	38	70	58	29	9	5	14	16		1980-81	1982-83
Palmer, Rob H.	Chi.	3	16	0	3	3	2	....	....	....	....	....		1973-74	1975-76
Palmer, Rob R.	L.A., N.J.		320	9	101	110	115	8	1	2	3	6		1977-78	1983-84
Panagabko, Ed	Bos.	2	29	0	3	3	38	....	....	....	....	....		1955-56	1956-57
Papike, Joe	Chi.	3	21	3	3	6	4	5	0	2	2	0		1940-41	1944-45
Pappin, Jim	Tor., Chi., Cal., Clev.	14	767	278	295	573	667	92	33	34	67	101	2	1963-64	1976-77
Paradise, Bob	Min., Atl., Pit., Wsh.	8	368	8	54	62	393	12	0	1	1	19		1971-72	1978-79
Pargeter, George	Mtl.	1	4	0	0	0	0	....	....	....	....	....		1946-47	1946-47
Parise, J.P.	Bos., Tor., Min., NYI, Clev.	14	890	238	356	594	706	86	27	31	58	87		1965-66	1978-79
Parizeau, Michel	St.L., Phi.	1	58	3	14	17	18	....	....	....	....	....		1971-72	1971-72
Park, Brad	NYR, Bos., Det.	17	1113	213	683	896	1429	161	35	90	125	217		1968-69	1984-85
Parker, Jeff	Buf., Hfd.	5	141	16	19	35	163	5	0	0	0	26		1986-87	1990-91
Parkes, Ernie	Mtl.M.	1	17	0	0	0	2	....	....	....	....	....		1924-25	1924-25
Parsons, George	Tor.	3	64	12	13	25	17	7	3	2	5	11		1936-37	1938-39
Pasek, Dusan	Min.	1	48	4	10	14	30	2	1	0	1	0		1988-89	1988-89
Pasin, Dave	Bos., L.A.	2	76	18	19	37	50	3	0	1	1	0		1985-86	1988-89
Paterson, Mark	Hfd.	4	29	3	3	6	33	....	....	....	....	....		1982-83	1985-86
Paterson, Rick	Chi.	9	430	50	43	93	136	61	7	10	17	51		1978-79	1986-87
Patey, Doug	Wsh.	3	45	4	2	6	8	....	....	....	....	....		1976-77	1978-79
Patey, Larry	Cal., St.L., NYR	12	717	153	163	316	631	40	8	10	18	57		1973-74	1984-85
Patrick, Craig	Cal., St.L., K.C., Min. Wsh.	8	401	72	91	163	61	2	0	1	1	0		1971-72	1978-79
Patrick, Glenn	St.L., Cal., Clev.	3	38	2	3	5	72	....	....	....	....	....		1973-74	1976-77
* Patrick, Lester	NYR	1	1	0	0	0	2	....	....	....	....	....		1926-27	1926-27
* Patrick, Lynn	NYR	10	455	145	190	335	240	44	10	6	16	22	1	1934-35	1945-46
Patrick, Muzz	NYR	5	166	5	26	31	133	25	4	0	4	34	1	1937-38	1945-46
Patrick, Steve	Buf., NYR, Que.	6	250	40	68	108	242	12	0	1	1	12		1980-81	1985-86
Patterson, Dennis	K.C., Phi.	3	138	6	22	28	67	....	....	....	....	....		1974-75	1979-80
Patterson, George	Bos., Det., St.L., Tor., Mtl., NYA	9	289	51	27	78	218	3	0	0	0	2		1926-27	1934-35
Paul, Butch	Det.	1	3	0	0	0	0	....	....	....	....	....		1964-65	1964-65
Paulus, Rollie	Mtl.	1	33	0	0	0	0	....	....	....	....	....		1925-26	1925-26
Pavelich, Mark	NYR, Min.	6	353	137	191	328	336	23	7	17	24	14		1981-82	1986-87
Pavelich, Marty	Det.	10	634	93	159	252	454	91	13	15	28	74	4	1947-48	1956-57
Pavese, Jim	St.L., NYR, Det., Hfd.	8	328	13	44	57	689	34	0	6	6	81		1981-82	1988-89
* Payer, Evariste	Mtl.	1	1	0	0	0	0	....	....	....	....	....		1917-18	1917-18
Payne, Steve	Min.	10	613	228	238	466	435	71	35	35	70	60		1978-79	1987-88
Pearson, Mel	NYR, Pit.	5	38	2	6	8	25	....	....	....	....	....		1949-50	1967-68
Peer, Bert	Det.	1	1	0	0	0	0	....	....	....	....	....		1939-40	1939-40
Peirson, Johnny	Bos.	11	545	153	173	326	315	49	9	17	26	26		1946-47	1957-58
Pelensky, Perry	Chi.	1	4	0	0	0	5	....	....	....	....	....		1983-84	1983-84

Name	NHL Teams	NHL Seasons	Regular Schedule GP	G	A	TP	PIM	Playoffs GP	G	A	TP	PIM	NHL Cup Wins	First NHL Season	Last NHL Season
Pelletier, Roger	Phi.	1	1	0	0	0	0	....	....	....	....	....		1967-68	1967-68
Peloffy, Andre	Wsh.	1	9	0	0	0	2	....	....	....	....	....		1974-75	1974-75
Pelyk, Mike	Tor.	9	441	26	88	114	566	40	0	3	3	41		1967-68	1977-78
Pennington, Cliff	Mtl., Bos.	3	101	17	42	59	6	....	....	....	....	....		1960-61	1962-63
Peplinski, Jim	Cgy.	10	705	161	262	423	1456	99	15	31	46	382	1	1980-81	1989-90
Perlini, Fred	Tor.	2	8	2	3	5	0	....	....	....	....	....		1981-82	1983-84
Perreault, Fern	NYR	2	3	0	0	0	0	....	....	....	....	....		1947-48	1949-50
Perreault, Gilbert	Buf.	17	1191	512	814	1326	500	90	33	70	103	44		1970-71	1986-87
Perry, Brian	Oak., Buf.	3	96	16	29	45	24	8	1	1	2	4		1968-69	1970-71
Persson, Stefan	NYI	9	622	52	317	369	574	102	7	50	57	69	4	1977-78	1985-86
Pesut, George	Cal.	2	92	3	22	25	130	....	....	....	....	....		1974-75	1975-76
Peters, Frank	NYR	1	43	0	0	0	59	4	0	0	0	2		1930-31	1930-31
Peters, Garry	Mtl., NYR, Phi., Bos.	8	331	34	34	68	261	9	2	2	4	31	1	1964-65	1971-72
Peters, Jim	Det., Chi., Mtl., Bos.	9	574	125	150	275	186	60	5	9	14	22	3	1945-46	1953-54
Peters, Jimy	Det., L.A.	9	309	37	36	73	48	11	0	2	2	2		1964-65	1974-75
Peters, Steve	Col.	1	2	0	1	1	0	....	....	....	....	....		1979-80	1979-80
Peterson, Brent	Det., Buf., Van., Hfd.	10	620	72	141	213	484	31	4	4	8	65		1979-80	1988-89
Pettersson, Jorgen	St.L., Hfd., Wsh.	6	435	174	192	366	117	44	15	12	27	4		1980-81	1985-86
Pettinger, Eric	Ott., Bos., Tor.	3	97	7	12	19	83	4	1	0	1	8		1928-29	1930-31
Pettinger, Gord	Det., NYR, Bos.	8	292	42	74	116	77	49	4	5	9	11	4	1932-33	1939-40
Phair, Lyle	L.A.	3	48	6	7	13	12	1	0	0	0	0		1985-86	1987-88
Phillipoff, Harold	Atl., Chi.,	3	141	26	57	83	267	6	0	2	2	9		1977-78	1979-80
Phillips, Bat	Mtl.M.	1	27	1	1	2	6	4	0	0	0	2		1929-30	1929-30
Phillips, Bill	Mtl.M., NYA.	8	302	52	31	83	232	28	6	2	8	19	1	1925-26	1932-33
Phillips, Charlie	Mtl.	1	17	0	0	0	6	....	....	....	....	....		1942-43	1942-43
Picard, Noel	Atl., Mtl., St.L.	7	335	12	63	75	616	50	2	11	13	167	1	1964-65	1972-73
Picard, Robert	Wsh. Tor., Mtl., Wpg., Que., Det.	13	899	104	319	423	1025	36	5	15	20	39		1977-78	1989-90
Picard, Roger	St.L.	1	15	2	2	4	21	....	....	....	....	....		1967-68	1967-68
Pichette, Dave	Que., St.L., N.J., NYR	7	322	41	140	181	348	28	3	7	10	54		1980-81	1987-88
Picketts, Hal	NYA.	1	48	3	1	4	32	....	....	....	....	....		1933-34	1933-34
Pidhirny, Harry	Bos.	1	2	0		0	0	....	....	....	....	....		1957-58	1957-58
Pierce, Randy	Col., N.J., Hfd.	8	277	62	76	138	223	2	0	0	0	0		1977-78	1984-85
Pike, Alf	NYR	6	234	42	77	119	145	21	4	2	6	12	1	1939-40	1946-47
Pilote, Pierre	Chi., Tor.	14	890	80	418	498	1251	86	8	53	61	102	1	1955-56	1968-69
Pinder, Gerry	Chi., Cal.	3	223	55	69	124	135	17	0	4	4	6		1969-70	1971-72
Pirus, Alex	Min., Det.	4	159	30	28	58	94	2	0	1	1	2		1976-77	1979-80
* Pitre, Didier	Mtl.	6	127	64	17	81	50	14	2	2	4	0		1917-18	1922-23
* Plager, Barclay	St.L.	10	614	44	187	231	1115	68	3	20	23	182		1967-68	1976-77
Plager, Bob	NYR, St.L.	14	644	20	126	146	802	74	2	17	19	195		1964-65	1977-78
Plager, William	Min., St.L., Atl.	9	263	4	34	38	292	31	0	2	2	26		1967-68	1975-76
Plamondon, Gerry	Mtl.	5	74	7	13	20	10	11	5	2	7	2	1	1945-46	1950-51
Plante, Cam	Tor.	1	2	0	0	0	0	....	....	....	....	....		1984-85	1984-85
Plante, Pierre	NYR, Que., Phi., St.L., Chi.	9	599	125	172	297	599	33	2	6	8	51		1971-72	1979-80
Plantery, Mark	Wpg.	1	25	1	5	6	14	....	....	....	....	....		1980-81	1980-81
Plaxton, Hugh	Mtl.M.	1	15	1	2	3	4	....	....	....	....	....		1932-33	1932-33
Playfair, Larry	Buf., L.A.	12	688	26	94	120	1812	43	0	6	6	111		1978-79	1989-90
Pleau, Larry	Mtl.	3	94	9	15	24	27	4	0	0	0	0		1969-70	1971-72
Plett, Willi	Atl., Cgy., Min., Bos.	13	834	222	215	437	2572	83	24	22	46	466		1975-76	1987-88
Plumb, Rob	Det.	1	7	2	1	3	0	....	....	....	....	....		1977-78	1977-78
Plumb, Ron	Hfd.	1	26	3	4	7	14	....	....	....	....	....		1979-80	1979-80
Pocza, Harvie	Wsh.	2	3	0	0	0	0	....	....	....	....	....		1979-80	1981-82
Podloski, Ray	Bos.	1	8	0	1	1	2	....	....	....	....	....		1988-89	1988-89
Podolsky, Nels	Det.	1	1	0	0	0	0	7	0	0	0	4		1948-49	1948-49
Poeta, Anthony	Chi.	1	1	0	0	0	0	....	....	....	....	....		1951-52	1951-52
Poile, Bud	NYR, Bos., Det., Tor., Chi.,	7	311	107	122	229	91	23	4	4	8	8	1	1942-43	1949-50
Poile, Don	Det.	2	66	7	9	16	12	4	0	0	0	0		1954-55	1957-58
Poirer, Gordie	Mtl.	1	10	0	1	1	0	....	....	....	....	....		1939-40	1939-40
Polanic, Tom	Min.	2	19	0	2	2	53	5	1	1	2	4		1969-70	1970-71
Polich, John	NYR	2	3	0	1	1	0	....	....	....	....	....		1939-40	1940-41
Polich, Mike	Mtl., Min.	5	226	24	29	53	7	23	2	1	3	2	1	1976-77	1980-81
Polis, Greg	Pit., St.L., NYR, Wsh.	10	615	174	169	343	391	7	0	2	2	6		1970-71	1979-80
Poliziani, Daniel	Bos.	1	1	0	0	0	0	3	0	0	0	0		1958-59	1958-59
Polonich, Dennis	Dot.	8	390	59	82	141	1242	7	1	0	1	19		1974-75	1982-83
Pooley, Paul	Wpg.	2	15	0	3	3	0	....	....	....	....	....		1984-85	1985-86
Popein, Larry	NYR, Oak.	8	449	80	141	221	162	16	1	4	5	6		1954-55	1967-68
Popiel, Paul	Bos., .A., Det., Van., Edm.	7	224	13	41	54	210	4	1	0	1	4		1965-66	1979-80
Portland, Jack	Chi., Mtl., Bos.	10	381	15	56	71	323	33	1	3	4	25	1	1933-34	1942-43
Porvari, Jukka	Col., N.J.	2	39	3	9	12	4	....	....	....	....	....		1981-82	1982-83
Posa, Victor	Chi.	1	2	0	0	0	2	....	....	....	....	....		1985-86	1985-86
Posavad, Mike	St.L.	2	8	0	0	0	0	....	....	....	....	....		1985-86	1986-87
Potvin, Denis	NYI	15	1060	310	742	1052	1356	185	56	108	164	253	4	1973-74	1987-88
Potvin, Jean	L.A., Min., Phi., NYI, Cle.	11	613	63	224	287	478	39	2	9	11	17	1	1970-71	1980-81
Poudrier, Daniel	Que.	1	25	1	5	6	10	....	....	....	....	....		1985-86	1987-88
Poulin, Dan	Min., Phi.	2	5	3	1	4	4	....	....	....	....	....		1981-82	1982-83
Pouzar, Jaroslav	Edm.	4	186	34	48	82	135	29	6	4	10	16	3	1982-83	1986-87
Powell, Ray	Chi.	1	31	7	15	22	2	....	....	....	....	....		1950-51	1950-51
Powis, Geoff	Chi.	1	2	0	0	0	0	....	....	....	....	....		1967-68	1967-68
Powis, Lynn	Chi., K.C.	2	130	19	33	52	25	1	0	0	0	0		1973-74	1974-75
* Pratt, Babe	Bos., NYR, Tor.	12	517	83	209	292	473	63	12	17	29	90	2	1935-36	1946-47
Pratt, Jack	Bos.	2	37	2	0	2	42	4	0	0	0	0		1930-31	1931-32
Pratt, Kelly	Pit.	1	22	0	6	6	15	....	....	....	....	....		1974-75	1974-75
Pratt, Tracy	Van., Col., Buf., Pit. Tor., Oak.	10	580	17	97	114	1026	25	0	1	1	62		1967-68	1976-77
Prentice, Dean	Pit., Min., Det., NYR, Bos.	22	1378	391	469	860	484	54	13	17	30	38		1952-53	1973-74
Prentice, Eric	Tor.	1	5	0	0	0	4	....	....	....	....	....		1943-44	1943-44
Preston, Rich	Chi., N.J.	8	580	127	164	291	348	47	4	18	22	56		1979-80	1986-87
Preston, Yves	Phi.	2	28	7	3	10	4	....	....	....	....	....		1978-79	1980-81
Priakin, Sergei	Cgy.	3	46	3	8	11	2	1	0	0	0	0		1988-89	1990-91
* Price, Bob	Ott.	1	1	0	0	0	0	....	....	....	....	....		1919-20	1919-20
Price, Jack	Chi.	3	57	4	6	10	24	4	0	0	0	0		1951-52	1953-54
Price, Noel	Pit., L.A., Det., Tor., NYR, Mtl., Atl.	14	499	14	114	128	333	12	0	1	1	8	1	1957-58	1975-76
Price, Pat	NYI, Edm., Pit., Que., NYR, Min.	13	726	43	218	261	1456	74	2	10	12	195		1975-76	1987-88
Price, Tom	Cal., Clev., Pit.	5	29	0	2	2	12	....	....	....	....	....		1974-75	1978-79
* Primeau, Joe	Tor.	9	310	66	177	243	105	38	5	18	23	12	1	1927-28	1935-36
Primeau, Kevin	Van.	1	2	0	0	0	4	....	....	....	....	....		1980-81	1980-81
Pringle, Ellie	NYA	1	6	0	0	0	0	....	....	....	....	....		1930-31	1930-31
* Prodgers, Goldie	Tor., Ham.	6	110	63	22	85	33	....	....	....	....	....		1919-20	1924-25
Pronovost, Andre	Det., Min., Mtl., Bos.	10	556	94	104	198	408	70	11	11	22	58	4	1956-57	1967-68
Pronovost, Jean	Wsh., Pit., Atl.	14	998	391	383	774	413	35	11	9	20	14		1968-69	1981-82
Pronovost, Marcel	Det., Tor.	21	1206	88	257	345	851	134	8	23	31	104	5	1950-51	1969-70
* Provost, Claude	Mtl.	15	1005	254	335	589	469	126	25	38	63	86	9	1955-56	1969-70
Pryor, Chris	Min., NYI	6	82	1	4	5	122	....	....	....	....	....		1984-85	1989-90
Prystai, Metro	Chi., Det.	11	674	151	179	330	231	43	12	14	26	8	2	1947-48	1957-58
Pudas, Al	Tor.	1	3	0	0	0	0	....	....	....	....	....		1926-27	1926-27
Pulford, Bob	Tor., L.A.	16	1079	281	362	643	792	89	25	26	51	126	4	1956-57	1971-72
Pulkkinen, Dave	NYI	1	2	0	0	0	0	....	....	....	....	....		1972-73	1972-73
Purpur, Cliff	Det., Chi., St.L.	5	144	26	34	60	46	16	1	2	3	4		1934-35	1944-45
* Pusie, Jean	Mtl., NYR, Bos.	5	61	1	4	5	28	7	0	0	0	0	1	1930-31	1935-36
Pyatt, Nelson	Det., Wsh., Col.	7	296	71	63	134	69	....	....	....	....	....		1973-74	1979-80

Q

Name	NHL Teams	NHL Seasons	Regular Schedule GP	G	A	TP	PIM	Playoffs GP	G	A	TP	PIM	NHL Cup Wins	First NHL Season	Last NHL Season
Quackenbush, Bill	Det., Bos.	14	774	62	222	284	95	79	2	19	21	8		1942-43	1955-56
Quackenbush, Max	Bos., Chi.,	2	61	4	7	11	30	6	0	0	0	4		1950-51	1951-52
Quenneville, Leo	NYR	1	25	0	3	3	10	3	0	0	0	0		1929-30	1929-30
Quilty, John	Mtl., Bos.	4	125	36	34	70	81	13	3	5	8	9		1940-41	1947-48
Quinn, Pat	Tor., Van., Atl.	9	606	18	113	131	950	11	0	1	1	21		1968-69	1976-77

R

Name	NHL Teams	NHL Seasons	Regular Schedule GP	G	A	TP	PIM	Playoffs GP	G	A	TP	PIM	NHL Cup Wins	First NHL Season	Last NHL Season
Radley, Yip	NYA, Mtl.M.	2	18	0	1	1	13	....	....	....	....	....		1930-31	1936-37
Raglan, Clare	Det., Chi.	3	100	4	9	13	52	3	0	0	0	0		1950-51	1952-53
Raleigh, Don	NYR	10	535	101	219	320	96	18	6	5	11	6		1943-44	1955-56

Claude Provost

Bob Pulford

Bill Quackenbush

Earl Reibel

Paul Reinhart

Rene Robert

Darcy Rota

Terry Ruskowski

Name	NHL Teams	NHL Seasons	Regular Schedule GP	G	A	TP	PIM	Playoffs GP	G	A	TP	PIM	NHL Cup Wins	First NHL Season	Last NHL Season
* Ramsay, Beattie	Tor.,	1	43	0	2	2	10	....	....	....	....	....		1927-28	1927-28
Ramsay, Craig	Buf.	14	1070	252	420	672	201	89	17	31	48	27		1971-72	1984-85
Ramsay, Wayne	Buf.	1	2	0	0	0	0	....	....	....	....	....		1977-78	1977-78
Ramsey, Les	Chi.	1	11	2	2	4	2	....	....	....	....	....		1944-45	1944-45
* Randall, Ken	Tor., Ham., NYA	10	217	67	28	95	360	13	3	1	4	19	2	1917-18	1926-27
Ranieri, George	Bos.	1	2	0	0	0	0	....	....	....	....	....		1956-57	1956-57
Ratelle, Jean	NYR, Bos.	21	1281	491	776	1267	276	123	32	66	98	24		1960-61	1980-81
Rathwell, John	Bos.	1	1	0	0	0	0	....	....	....	....	....		1974-75	1974-75
Rausse, Errol	Wsh.	3	31	7	3	10	0	....	....	....	....	....		1979-80	1981-82
Rautakallio, Pekka	Atl., Cgy.	3	235	33	121	154	122	23	2	5	7	8		1979-80	1981-82
Ravlich, Matt	Bos., Chi., Det., L.A.	9	410	12	78	90	364	24	1	5	6	16		1962-63	1972-73
Raymond, Armand	Mtl.	2	22	0	2	2	10	....	....	....	....	....		1937-38	1939-40
Raymond, Paul	Mtl.	4	76	2	3	5	6	5	0	0	0	2		1932-33	1937-38
Read, Mel	NYR	1	1	0	0	0	0	....	....	....	....	....		1946-47	1946-47
Reardon, Ken	Mtl.	7	341	26	96	122	604	31	2	5	7	62	1	1940-41	1949-50
Reardon, Terry	Bos., Mtl.	7	193	47	53	100	73	30	8	10	18	12	1	1938-39	1946-47
Reaume, Marc	Tor., Det., Mtl., Van.	9	344	8	43	51	273	21	0	2	2	8		1954-55	1970-71
Reay, Billy	Det., Mtl.	10	479	105	162	267	202	63	13	16	29	43	2	1943-44	1952-53
Redahl, Gord	Bos.	1	18	0	1	1	2	....	....	....	....	....		1958-59	1958-59
Redding, George	Bos.	2	35	3	2	5	10	....	....	....	....	....		1924-25	1925-26
Redmond, Craig	L.A., Edm.	5	191	16	68	84	134	3	1	0	1	2		1984-85	1988-89
Redmond, Dick	Min., Cal., Chi., St.L., Atl., Bos.	13	771	133	312	445	504	66	9	22	31	27		1969-70	1981-82
Redmond, Mickey	Mtl., Det.	9	538	233	195	428	219	16	2	3	5	2	2	1967-68	1975-76
Reeds, Mark	St.L., Hfd.	8	365	45	114	159	135	53	8	9	17	23		1981-82	1988-89
Regan, Bill	NYR, NYA	3	67	3	2	5	67	8	0	0	0	2		1929-30	1932-33
Regan, Larry	Bos., Tor.,	5	280	41	95	136	71	42	7	14	21	18		1956-57	1960-61
Regier, Darcy	Clev., NYI	3	26	0	2	2	35	....	....	....	....	....		1977-78	1983-84
Reibel, Earl	Det., Chi., Bos.	6	409	84	161	245	75	39	6	14	20	4	2	1953-54	1958-59
Reid, Dave	Tor.	3	7	0	0	0	0	....	....	....	....	....		1952-53	1955-56
Reid, Gerry	Det.	1	....	....	....	....	....	2	0	0	0	2		1948-49	1948-49
Reid, Gordie	NYA	1	1	0	0	0	2	....	....	....	....	....		1936-37	1936-37
Reid, Reg	Tor.	2	40	2	0	2	4	2	0	0	0	0		1924-25	1925-26
Reid, Tom	Chi., Min.	11	701	17	113	130	654	42	1	13	14	49		1967-68	1977-78
Reierson, Dave	Cgy.	1	2	0	0	0	2	....	....	....	....	....		1988-89	1988-89
Reigle, Ed	Bos.	1	17	0	2	2	25	....	....	....	....	....		1950-51	1950-51
Reinhart, Paul	Atl., Cgy., Van.	11	648	133	426	559	277	83	23	54	77	42		1979-80	1989-90
Reinikka, Ollie	NYR	1	16	0	0	0	0	....	....	....	....	....		1926-27	1926-27
Reise, Leo Sr.	Ham., NYA, NYR	8	199	36	29	65	177	6	0	0	0	16		1920-21	1929-30
Reise, Leo Jr.	Chi., Det., NYR	9	494	28	81	109	399	52	8	5	13	68	2	1945-46	1953-54
Renaud, Mark	Hfd., Buf.	5	152	6	50	56	86	....	....	....	....	....		1979-80	1983-84
Reynolds, Bobby	Tor.	1	7	1	1	2	0	....	....	....	....	....		1989-90	1989-90
Ribble, Pat	Atl., Chi., Tor., Wsh., Cgy.	8	349	19	60	79	365	8	0	1	1	12		1975-76	1982-83
Richard, Henri	Mtl.	20	1256	358	688	1046	928	180	49	80	129	181	11	1955-56	1974-75
Richard, Jacques	Alt., Buf., Que.	10	556	160	187	347	307	35	5	5	10	34		1972-73	1982-83
Richard, Maurice	Mtl.	18	978	544	421	965	1285	133	82	44	126	188	8	1942-43	1959-60
Richardson, Dave	NYR, Chi., Det.	4	45	3	2	5	27	....	....	....	....	....		1963-64	1967-68
Richardson, Glen	Van.	1	24	3	6	9	19	....	....	....	....	....		1975-76	1975-76
Richardson, Ken	St.L.	3	49	8	13	21	16	....	....	....	....	....		1974-75	1978-79
Richer, Bob	Buf.	1	3	0	0	0	0	....	....	....	....	....		1972-73	1972-73
Richmond, Steve	NYR, Det., N.J., L.A.	5	159	4	23	27	514	4	0	0	0	12		1983-84	1988-89
Richter, Dave	Min., Phi., Van., St.L.	9	365	9	40	49	1030	22	1	0	1	80		1981-82	1989-90
Riley, Bill	sh., Wpg.	5	139	31	30	61	320	....	....	....	....	....		1974-75	1979-80
Riley, Jack	Det., Mtl., Bos.,	4	104	10	22	32	8	4	0	3	3	0		1932-33	1935-36
Riley, Jim	Det.	1	17	0	2	2	14	....	....	....	....	....		1926-27	1926-27
Riopellie, Howard	Mtl.	3	169	27	16	43	73	8	1	1	2	2		1947-48	1949-50
Rioux, Gerry	Wpg.	1	8	0	0	0	6	....	....	....	....	....		1979-80	1979-80
Rioux, Pierre	Cgy.	1	14	1	2	3	4	....	....	....	....	....		1982-83	1982-83
Ripley, Vic	Chi., Bos., NYR, St.L.	7	278	51	49	100	173	20	4	1	5	10		1928-29	1934-35
Risebrough, Doug	Mtl., Cgy.	14	740	185	286	471	1542	124	21	37	58	238	4	1974-75	1986-87
Rissling, Gary	Wsh., Pit.	7	221	23	30	53	1008	5	0	1	1	4		1978-79	1984-85
Ritchie, Bob	Phi., Det.	2	29	8	4	12	10	....	....	....	....	....		1976-77	1977-78
* Ritchie, Dave	Mtl.W, Ott., Tor., Que., Mtl.	6	54	15	3	18	27	1	0	0	0	0		1917-18	1925-26
Ritson, Alex	NYR	1	1	0	0	0	0	....	....	....	....	....		1944-45	1944-45
Rittinger, Alan	Bos.	1	19	3	7	10	0	....	....	....	....	....		1943-44	1943-44
Rivard, Bob	Pit.	1	27	5	12	17	4	....	....	....	....	....		1967-68	1967-68
Rivers, Gus	Mtl.	3	88	4	5	9	12	16	2	0	2	2	2	1929-30	1931-32
Rivers, Wayne	Det., Bos., St.L., NYR	7	108	15	30	45	94	....	....	....	....	....		1961-62	1968-69
Rizzuto, Garth	Van.	1	37	3	4	7	16	....	....	....	....	....		1970-71	1970-71
* Roach, Mickey	Tor., Ham., NYA	8	209	75	27	102	41	....	....	....	....	....		1919-20	1926-27
Robert, Claude	Mtl.	1	23	1	0	1	9	....	....	....	....	....		1950-51	1950-51
Robert, Rene	Tor., Pit., Buf., Col.	12	744	284	418	702	597	50	22	19	41	73		1970-71	1981-82
* Robert, Sammy	Ott.	1	1	0	0	0	0	....	....	....	....	....		1917-18	1917-18
Roberto, Phil	Mtl., St.L., Det., K.C., Col., Clev.	8	385	75	106	181	464	31	9	8	17	69	1	1969-70	1976-77
Roberts, Doug	Det., Dak., Cal., Bos.	10	419	43	104	147	342	16	2	3	5	46		1965-66	1974-75
Roberts, Jim	Mtl., St.L.	15	1006	126	194	320	621	153	20	16	36	160	5	1963-64	1977-78
Roberts, Jimmy	Min.	3	106	17	23	40	33	2	0	0	0	0		1976-77	1978-79
Robertson, Fred	Tor., Det.,	2	34	1	0	1	35	7	0	0	0	0	1	1931-32	1933-34
Robertson, Geordie	Buf.	1	5	1	2	3	7	....	....	....	....	....		1982-83	1982-83
Robertson, George	Mtl.	2	31	2	5	7	6	....	....	....	....	....		1947-48	1948-49
Robertson, Torrie	Wsh., Hfd., Det.	10	442	49	99	148	1751	22	2	1	3	90		1980-81	1989-90
Robidoux, Florent	Chi.	3	52	7	4	11	75	....	....	....	....	....		1980-81	1983-84
Robinson, Doug	Chi., NYR, L.A.	7	239	44	67	111	34	11	4	3	7	0		1963-64	1970-71
Robinson, Douglas	Min.	1	1	0	0	0	2	....	....	....	....	....		1989-90	1989-90
Robinson, Earl	Mtl.M., Chi., Mtl.	11	418	83	98	181	123	25	5	4	9	0	1	1928-29	1939-40
Robinson, Moe	Mtl	1	1	0	0	0	0	....	....	....	....	....		1979-80	1979-80
Robitaille, Mike	NYR, Det., Buf., Van.	8	382	23	105	128	280	13	0	1	1	4		1969-70	1976-77
* Roche, Earl	Mtl.M., Bos., Ott., St.L., Det.	4	146	25	27	52	48	2	0	0	0	0		1930-31	1934-35
Roche, Ernest	Mtl.	1	4	0	0	0	2	....	....	....	....	....		1950-51	1950-51
Roche, Michel	Mtl.M., Ott., St.L., Mtl., Det.	4	112	20	18	38	44	....	....	....	....	....		1930-31	1934-35
Rochefort, Dave	Det	1	1	0	0	0	0	....	....	....	....	....		1966-67	1966-67
Rochefort, Leon	NYR, Mtl., Phi., L.A., Det., Atl., Van.	15	617	121	147	268	93	39	4	4	8	16	2	1960-61	1975-76
Rockburn, Harvey	Det., Ott.	3	94	4	2	6	254	....	....	....	....	....		1929-30	1932-33
Rodden, Eddie	Chi., Tor., Bos., NYR	4	98	6	14	20	152	2	0	1	1	0	1	1926-27	1930-31
Rogers, Alfred	Min.	2	14	2	4	6	0	....	....	....	....	....		1973-74	1974-75
Rogers, Mike	Hfd., NYR, Edm.	7	484	202	317	519	184	17	1	13	14	6		1979-80	1985-86
Rohlicek, Jeff	Van.	2	9	0	0	0	8	....	....	....	....	....		1987-88	1988-89
Rolfe, Dale	Bos., L.A., Det., NYR	9	509	25	125	150	556	71	5	24	29	89		1959-60	1974-75
Romanchych, Larry	Chi., Atl	6	298	68	97	165	102	7	2	2	4	4		1970-71	1976-77
Rombough, Doug	Buf., NYI, Min.	4	150	24	27	51	80	....	....	....	....	....		1972-73	1975-76
* Romnes, Doc	Chi., Tor., NYA	10	359	68	136	204	42	43	7	18	25	4	2	1930-31	1939-40
* Ronan, Skene	Ott.	1	11	0	0	0	0	....	....	....	....	....		1918-19	1918-19
Ronson, Len	NYR, Oak.	2	18	2	1	3	10	....	....	....	....	....		1960-61	1968-69
Ronty, Paul	Bos., NYR, Mtl.	8	488	101	211	312	103	21	1	7	8	6		1947-48	1954-55
Rooney, Steve	Mtl., Wpg., N.J.	5	154	15	13	28	496	25	3	2	5	86	1	1984-85	1988-89
Root, Bill	Mtl., Tor., St.L., Phi.	6	247	11	23	34	180	22	1	2	3	25		1982-83	1987-88
* Ross, Art	Mtl.W	1	3	1	0	1	0	....	....	....	....	....		1917-18	1917-18
Ross, Jim	NYR	2	62	2	11	13	29	....	....	....	....	....		1951-52	1952-53
Rossignol, Roland	Det., Mtl.	3	14	3	5	8	6	1	0	0	0	2		1943-44	1945-46
Rota, Darcy	Chi., Atl., Van.	11	794	256	239	495	973	60	14	7	21	147		1973-74	1983-84
Rota, Randy	Mtl., L.A., K.C., Col.	5	212	38	39	77	60	5	0	1	1	0		1972-73	1976-77
Rothschild, Sam	Mtl.M., NYA	4	99	8	6	14	24	10	0	0	0	0	1	1924-25	1927-28
Roulston, Rolly	Det.	3	24	0	6	6	10	....	....	....	....	....	1	1935-36	1937-38
Roulston, Tom	Edm., Pit.	6	195	47	49	96	74	21	2	2	4	2		1980-81	1985-86
Roupe, Magnus	Phi.	2	40	3	5	8	42	....	....	....	....	....		1987-88	1988-89
Rousseau, Bobby	Mtl., Min., NYR	15	942	245	458	703	359	128	27	57	84	69	4	1960-61	1974-75
Rousseau, Guy	Mtl.	2	4	0	1	1	0	....	....	....	....	....		1954-55	1956-57
Rousseau, Roland	Mtl.	1	2	0	0	0	0	....	....	....	....	....		1952-53	1952-53
Routhier, Jean-Marc	Que.	1	8	0	0	0	9	....	....	....	....	....		1989-90	1989-90
Rowe, Bobby	Bos.	1	4	1	0	1	0	....	....	....	....	....		1924-25	1924-25
Rowe, Mike	Pit.	3	11	0	0	0	11	....	....	....	....	....		1984-85	1986-87
Rowe, Ron	NYR	1	5	1	0	1	0	....	....	....	....	....		1947-48	1947-48
Rowe, Tom	Wsh., Hfd., Det.	7	357	85	100	185	615	3	2	0	2	0		1976-77	1982-83
Roy, Stephane	Min.	1	12	1	0	1	0	....	....	....	....	....		1987-88	1987-88
Rozzini, Gino	Bos.	1	31	5	10	15	20	6	1	2	3	6		1944-45	1944-45
Rucinski, Mike	Chi.	2	1	0	0	0	0	2	0	0	0	0		1987-88	1988-89

Name	NHL Teams	NHL Seasons	Regular Schedule					Playoffs					NHL Cup Wins	First NHL Season	Last NHL Season
			GP	G	A	TP	PIM	GP	G	A	TP	PIM			
Ruelle, Bernard	Det.	1	2	1	0	1	0	....	....	....	....	....		1943-44	1943-44
Ruhnke, Kent	Bos.	1	2	0	1	1	0	....	....	....	....	....		1975-76	1975-76
Rundqvist, Thomas	Mtl.	1	2	0	1	1	0	....	....	....	....	....		1984-85	1984-85
Runge, Paul	Bos., Mtl.M., Mtl.	7	143	18	22	40	57	7	0	0	0	6		1930-31	1937-38
Ruotsalainen, Reijo	NYR, Edm., N.J.	7	446	107	237	344	180	86	15	32	47	44	2	1981-82	1989-90
Ruotsalinen, Reijo	NYR, Edm.	6	405	104	225	329	160	64	13	21	34	32	2	1981-82	1986-87
Rupp, Duane	NYR, Tor., Min., Pit.	10	374	24	93	117	220	10	2	2	4	8		1962-63	1972-73
Ruskowski, Terry	Chi., L.A., Pit., Min.	10	630	113	313	426	1354	21	1	6	7	86		1979-80	1988-89
Russell, Churchill	NYR	3	90	20	16	36	12	....	....	....	....	....		1945-46	1947-48
Russell, Phil	Chi., Atl., Cgy., N.J., Buf.	15	1016	99	325	424	2038	73	4	22	26	202		1972-73	1986-87

Borje Salming

S

Name	NHL Teams	NHL Seasons	GP	G	A	TP	PIM	GP	G	A	TP	PIM	NHL Cup Wins	First NHL Season	Last NHL Season
Saarinen, Simo	NYR	1	8	0	0	0	0	....	....	....	....	....		1984-85	1984-85
Sabourin, Bob	Tor.	1	1	0	0	0	2	....	....	....	....	....		1951-52	1951-52
Sabourin, Gary	St.L., Tor., Cal., Clev.	10	627	169	188	357	397	62	19	11	30	58		1967-68	1976-77
Sacharuk, Larry	NYR, St.L.	5	151	29	33	62	42	2	1	1	2	2		1972-73	1976-77
Saganiuk, Rocky	Tor., Pit.	6	259	57	65	122	201	6	1	0	1	15		1978-79	1983-84
Saleski, Don	Phi., Col.	9	543	128	125	253	629	82	13	17	30	131	2	1971-72	1979-80
Salovaara, John	Det.	2	90	2	13	15	70	....	....	....	....	....		1974-75	1975-76
Salvian, Dave	NYI	1	....	0	1	1	2	1	0	1	1	2		1976-77	1976-77
Samis, Phi.	Tor.	2	2	0	0	0	0	5	0	1	1	2	1	1947-48	1949-50
Sampson, Gary	Wsh.	4	105	13	22	35	25	12	1	0	1	0		1983-84	1986-87
Sanderson, Derek	Bos., NYR, St.L., Van., Pit.	13	598	202	250	452	911	56	18	12	30	187	2	1965-66	1977-78
Sandford, Ed	Bos., Det., Chi.	9	502	106	145	251	355	42	12	11	24	27		1947-48	1955-56
Sands, Charlie	Tor., Bos., Mtl., NYR	12	432	99	109	208	58	44	6	6	12	4	1	1932-33	1943-44
Sargent, Gary	L.A., Min.	8	402	61	161	222	273	20	5	7	12	8		1975-76	1982-83
Sarner, Craig	Bos.	1	7	0		0	0	....	....	....	....	....		1974-75	1974-75
Sarrazin, Dick	Phi.	3	100	20	35	55	22	4	0	0	0	0		1968-69	1971-72
Saskamoose, Fred	Chi.	1	11	0	0	0	6	....	....	....	....	....		1953-54	1953-54
Sasser, Grant	Pit.	1	3	0	0	0	0	....	....	....	....	....		1983-84	1983-84
Sather, Glen	Bos., Pit., NYR, St.L., Mtl., Min.	10	658	80	113	193	724	72	1	5	6	86		1966-67	1975-76
Saunders, Bernie	Que.	2	10	0	1	1	8	....	....	....	....	....		1979-80	1980-81
Saunders, Bud	Ott.	1	19	1	3	4	4	....	....	....	....	....		1933-34	1933-34
Saunders, David	Van.	1	56	7	13	20	10	....	....	....	....	....		1987-88	1987-88
Sauve, Jenn F.	Buf., Que.	7	290	65	138	203	117	36	9	12	21	10		1980-81	1986-87
Savage, Tony	Bos., Mtl.	1	49	1	5	6	6	2	0	0	0	0		1934-35	1934-35
Savard, Andre	Bos., Buf., Que.	12	790	211	271	482	411	85	13	18	31	77		1973-74	1984-85
Savard, Jean	Chi, Hfd.	3	43	7	12	19	29	....	....	....	....	....		1977-78	1979-80
Savard, Serge	Mtl., Wpg.	17	1040	106	333	439	592	130	19	49	68	88	7	1966-67	1982-83
Scamurra, Peter	Wsh.	4	132	8	25	33	59	....	....	....	....	....		1975-76	1979-80
Sceviour, Darin	Chi.	1	1	0	0	0	0	....	....	....	....	....		1986-87	1986-87
Schaeffer, Butch	Chi.,	1	5	0	0	0	6	....	....	....	....	....		1936-37	1936-37
Schamehorn, Kevin	Det., L.A.	3	10	0	0	0	17	....	....	....	....	....		1976-77	1980-81
Schella, John	Van.	2	115	2	18	20	224	....	....	....	....	....		1970-71	1971-72
Scherza, Chuck	Bos., NYR	2	56	6	6	12	35	....	....	....	....	....		1943-44	1944-45
Schinkel, Ken	NYR, Pit.	12	636	127	198	325	163	19	7	2	9	4		1959-60	1972-73
Schliebener, Andy	Van.	3	84	2	11	13	74	6	0	0	0	0		1981-82	1984-85
Schmautz, Bobby	Chi., Bos., Edm., Col., Van.	13	764	271	286	557	988	73	28	33	61	92		1967-68	1980-81
Schmautz, Cliff	Buf., Phi.	1	56	13	19	32	33	....	....	....	....	....		1970-71	1970-71
Schmidt, Clarence	Bos.,	1	7	1	0	1	2	....	....	....	....	....		1943-44	1943-44
Schmidt, Jackie	Bos.	1	45	6	7	13	6	5	0	0	0	0		1942-43	1942-43
Schmidt, Joseph	Bos.	1	2	0	0	0	0	....	....	....	....	....		1943-44	1943-44
Schmidt, Milt	Bos.	16	778	229	346	575	466	86	24	25	49	60	2	1936-37	1954-55
Schmidt, Norm	Pit.	4	125	23	33	56	73	....	....	....	....	....		1983-84	1987-88
Schnarr, Werner	Bos.	2	25	0	0	0	0	....	....	....	....	....		1924-25	1925-26
Schock, Danny	Bos., Phi.	2	20	1	2	3	0	1	0	0	0	0	1	1969-70	1970-71
Schock, Ron	Bos., St.L., Pit., Buf.	15	909	166	351	517	260	55	4	16	20	29		1963-64	1977-78
Schoenfeld, Jim	Buf., Det., Bos.	13	719	51	204	255	1132	75	3	13	16	151		1972-73	1984-85
Schofield, Dwight	Det., Mtl., St.L., Wsh., Pit., Wpg.	7	211	8	22	30	631	9	0	0	0	55		1976-77	1987-88
Schreiber, Wally	Min.	2	41	0	10	10	12	....	....	....	....	....		1987-88	1988-89
* Schriner, Sweeny	NYA, Tor.	11	484	201	204	405	148	60	18	11	29	54	2	1934-35	1945-46
Schultz, Dave	Phi., L.A., Pit., Buf.	9	535	79	121	200	2294	73	8	12	20	412	2	1971-72	1979-80
Schurman, Maynard	Hfd.	1	7	0	0	0	0	....	....	....	....	....		1979-80	1979-80
Schutt, Rod	Mtl., Pit., Tor.	8	286	77	92	169	177	22	8	6	14	26		1977-78	1985-86
Sclisizzi, Enio	Det., Chi.	6	81	12	11	23	26	13	0	0	0	6		1946-47	1952-53
Scott, Ganton	Tor., Ham., Mtl.M.	3	53	1	1	2	0	....	....	....	....	....		1922-23	1924-25
Scott, Laurie	NYA, NYR	2	62	6	3	9	28	....	....	....	....	....	1	1926-27	1927-28
Scruton, Howard	L.A.	1	4	0	4	4	9	....	....	....	....	....		1982-83	1982-83
Seabrooke, Glen	Phi.	3	19	1	6	7	4	....	....	....	....	....		1986-87	1988-89
Secord, Al	Bos., Chi., Tor, Phi.	12	766	273	222	495	2093	102	21	34	55	382		1978-79	1989-90
Sedlbauer, Ron	Van., Chi., Tor.	7	430	143	86	229	210	19	1	3	4	27		1974-75	1980-81
Seguin, Dan	Min., Van.	2	37	2	6	8	50	....	....	....	....	....		1970-71	1973-74
Seguin, Steve	L.A.	1	5	0	0	0	9	....	....	....	....	....		1984-85	1984-85
* Seibert, Earl	NYR, Chi., Det.	15	652	89	187	276	768	11	8	9	19	66	2	1931-32	1945-46
Seiling, Ric	Buf., Det.	10	738	179	208	387	573	62	14	14	28	36		1977-78	1986-87
Seiling, Rod	Tor., NYR, Wsh., St.L., Atl.	17	979	62	269	331	603	77	4	8	12	55		1962-63	1978-79
Sejba, Jiri	Buf.	1	11	0	2	2	8	....	....	....	....	....		1990-91	1990-91
Selby, Brit	Tor., Phi., St.L.	8	350	55	62	117	163	16	1	1	2	8		1964-65	1971-72
Self, Steve	Wsh.	1	3	0	0	0	0	....	....	....	....	....		1976-77	1976-77
Selwood, Brad	Tor., L.A.	3	163	7	40	47	153	6	0	0	0	4		1970-71	1979-80
Semenko, Dave	Edm., Hfd., Tor.	9	575	65	88	153	1175	73	6	6	12	208	2	1979-80	1987-88
Senick, George	NYR	1	13	2	3	5	8	....	....	....	....	....		1952-53	1952-53
Seppa, Jyrki	Wpg.	1	13	0	2	2	6	....	....	....	....	....		1983-84	1983-84
Serafini, Ron	Cal.	1	2	0	0	0	2	....	....	....	....	....		1973-74	1973-74
Servinis, George	Min.	1	5	0	0	0	0	....	....	....	....	....		1987-88	1987-88
Sevcik, Jaroslav	Que.	1	13	0	2	2	2	....	....	....	....	....		1989-90	1989-90
Shack, Eddie	NYR, Tor., Bos., L.A., Buf., Pit.	17	1047	239	226	465	1437	74	6	7	13	151	4	1958-59	1974-75
Shack, Joe	NYR	2	70	23	13	36	20	....	....	....	....	....		1942-43	1944-45
Shakes, Paul	Cal.	1	21	0	4	4	12	....	....	....	....	....		1973-74	1973-74
Shanahan, Sean	Mtl., Col., Bos.	3	40	1	3	4	47	....	....	....	....	....		1975-76	1977-78
Shand, Dave	Atl., Tor., Wsh.	8	421	19	84	103	544	26	1	2	3	83		1976-77	1984-85
Shannon, Charles	NYA	1	4	0	0	0	2	....	....	....	....	....		1939-40	1939-40
Shannon, Gerry	Ott., St.L., Bos., Mtl.M.	5	183	23	29	52	121	9	0	1	1	2		1933-34	1937-38
Sharpley, Glen	Min., Chi.	6	389	117	161	278	199	27	7	11	18	24		1976-77	1981-82
Shaunessy, Scott	Que.	1	3	0	0	0	7	....	....	....	....	....		1986-87	1986-87
Shaunessy, Scott	Que.	2	7	0	0	0	23	....	....	....	....	....		1986-87	1988-89
Shay, Norman	Bos., Tor.	2	53	5	2	7	34	....	....	....	....	....		1924-25	1925-26
Shea, Pat	Chi.	1	14	0	1	1	0	....	....	....	....	....		1931-32	1931-32
Shedden, Doug	Pit., Det., Que., Tor.	8	416	139	186	325	176	....	....	....	....	....		1981-82	1990-91
Sheehan, Bobby	Mtl., Cal., Chi., Det., NYR, Col., L.A.	9	310	48	63	111	50	25	4	3	7	8	1	1969-70	1981-82
Sheehy, Tim	Det., Hfd.	2	27	2	1	3	0	....	....	....	....	....		1977-78	1979-80
Shelton, Doug	Chi.	1	5	0	1	1	0	....	....	....	....	....		1967-68	1967-68
Sheppard, Frank	Det.	1	8	1	1	2	0	....	....	....	....	....		1927-28	1927-28
Sheppard, Gregg	Bos., Pit.	10	657	205	293	498	243	92	32	40	72	31		1972-73	1981-82
Sheppard, Johnny	Det., NYA, Bos., Chi.	8	311	68	58	126	224	10	0	0	0	0	1	1926-27	1933-34
Sherf, John	Det.	5	19	0	0	0	8	8	0	1	1	2	1	1935-36	1943-44
* Shero, Fred	NYR	3	145	6	14	20	137	13	0	2	2	8		1947-48	1949-50
Sherritt, Gordon	Det.	1	8	0	0	0	12	....	....	....	....	....		1943-44	1943-44
Sherven, Gord	Edm., Min., Hfd.	5	97	13	22	35	33	3	0	0	0	0		1983-84	1987-88
Shewchuck, Jack	Bos.	6	187	9	19	28	160	20	0	1	1	19	1	1938-39	1944-45
Shibicky, Alex	NYR	8	317	110	91	201	159	40	12	12	24	12	1	1935-36	1945-46
Shields, Al	Ott., Phi., NYA, Mtl.M., Bos.	11	460	42	46	88	637	17	0	1	1	14	1	1927-28	1937-38
Shill, Bill	Bos.	3	79	21	13	34	18	7	1	2	3	2		1942-43	1946-47
Shill, Jack	Tor., Bos., NYA, Chi.	6	163	15	20	35	70	27	1	6	7	13	1	1933-34	1938-39
Shinske, Rick	Clev., St.L.	3	63	5	16	21	10	....	....	....	....	....		1976-77	1978-79
Shires, Jim	Det., St.L., Pit.	3	56	3	6	9	32	....	....	....	....	....		1970-71	1972-73
Shmyr, Paul	Chi., Cal., Min., Hfd.	7	343	13	72	85	528	34	3	3	6	44		1968-69	1981-82
* Shore, Eddie	Bos., NYA	14	553	105	179	284	1047	55	6	13	19	187	2	1926-27	1939-40
Shore, Hamby	Ott.	1	18	3	0	3	0	....	....	....	....	....		1917-18	1917-18
Shores, Aubry	Phi.	1	1	0	0	0	0	....	....	....	....	....		1930-31	1930-31
Short, Steve	L.A., Det.	2	6	0	0	0	2	....	....	....	....	....		1977-78	1978-79
Shudra, Ron	Edm.	1	10	0	5	5	6	....	....	....	....	....		1987-88	1987-88

Ron Shock

Jim Schoenfeld

Darryl Sittler

Tod Sloan

Pete Stemkowski

Doug Sulliman

Duane Sutter

Name	NHL Teams	NHL Seasons	Regular Schedule					Playoffs					NHL Cup Wins	First NHL Season	Last NHL Season
			GP	G	A	TP	PIM	GP	G	A	TP	PIM			
Shutt, Steve	Mtl., L.A.	13	930	424	393	817	410	99	50	48	98	65	5	1972-73	1984-85
Siebert, Babe	Mtl.M., NYR, Bos., Mtl.	14	593	140	156	296	982	54	8	7	15	62	2	1925-26	1938-39
Silk, Dave	NYR, Bos., Wpg., Det.	7	249	54	59	113	271	13	2	4	6	13		1979-80	1985-86
Siltala, Mike	Wsh., NYR	3	7	1	0	1	2	....	....	....	....	....		1981-82	1987-88
Siltanen, Risto	Edm., Hfd., Que.	8	562	90	265	355	266	32	6	12	18	30		1979-80	1986-87
Simmer, Charlie	Cal., Cle., L.A., Bos., Pit.	14	712	342	369	711	544	24	9	9	18	32		1974-75	1987-88
Simmons, Al	Cal., Bos.	3	11	0	1	1	21	1	0	0	0	0		1971-72	1975-76
Simon, Cully	Det., Chi.	3	130	4	11	15	121	14	0	1	1	6	1	1942-43	1944-45
Simon, Thain	Det.	1	3	0	0	0	0	....	....	....	....	....		1946-47	1946-47
Simonetti, Frank	Bos.	4	115	5	8	13	76	12	0	1	1	8		1984-85	1987-88
Simpson, Bobby	Atl., St.L., Pit.	5	175	35	29	64	98	6	0	1	1	2		1976-77	1982-83
Simpson, Cliff	Det.	2	6	0	1	1	0	2	0	0	0	0		1946-47	1947-48
* Simpson, Joe	NYA	6	228	21	19	40	156	2	0	0	0	0		1925-26	1930-31
Sims, Al	Bos., Hfd., L.A.	10	475	49	116	165	286	41	0	2	2	14		1973-74	1982-83
Sinclair, Reg	NYR, Det.	3	208	49	43	92	139	3	1	0	1	0		1950-51	1952-53
Singbush, Alex	Mtl.	1	32	0	5	5	15	3	0	0	0	4		1940-41	1940-41
Siren, Ville	Pit., Min.	5	290	14	68	82	276	7	0	0	0	6		1985-86	1989-90
Sirois, Bob	Phi., Wsh.	6	286	92	120	212	42	....	....	....	....	....		1974-75	1979-80
Sittler, Darryl	Tor., Phi., Det.	15	1096	484	637	1121	948	76	29	45	74	137		1970-71	1984-85
* Sjoberg, Lars-Erik	Wpg.	1	79	7	27	34	48	....	....	....	....	....		1979-80	1979-80
Skaare, Bjorne	Det.	1	1	0	0	0	0	....	....	....	....	....		1978-79	1978-79
* Skilton, Raymie	Mtl.W	1	1	1	0	1	0	....	....	....	....	....		1917-18	1917-18
* Skinner, Alf	Tor., Bos., Mtl.M., Pit.	4	70	26	4	30	56	7	8	1	9	0	1	1917-18	1925-26
Skinner, Larry	Col.	4	47	10	12	22	8	2	0	0	0	0		1976-77	1979-80
Skov, Glen	Det., Chi., Mtl.	12	650	106	136	242	413	53	7	7	14	48	3	1949-50	1960-61
Sleaver, John	Chi.	2	24	2	0	2	6	....	....	....	....	....		1953-54	1956-57
Sleigher, Louis	Que., Bos.	6	194	46	53	99	146	17	1	1	2	64		1979-80	1985-86
Sloan, Tod	Tor., Chi.	13	745	220	262	482	781	47	9	12	21	47	2	1947-48	1960-61
Slobodzian, Peter	NYA	1	41	3	2	5	54	....	....	....	....	....		1940-41	1940-41
Slowinski, Eddie	NYR	6	291	58	74	132	63	16	2	6	8	6		1947-48	1952-53
Sly, Darryl	Tor., Min., Van.	4	79	1	2	3	20	....	....	....	....	....		1965-66	1970-71
Smart, Alex	Mtl.	1	8	3	5	8	0	....	....	....	....	....		1942-43	1942-43
Smedsmo, Dale	Tor.	1	4	0	0	0	0	....	....	....	....	....		1972-73	1972-73
Smillie, Don	Bos.	1	12	2	2	4	4	....	....	....	....	....		1933-34	1933-34
* Smith, Alex	Ott., Det., Bos., NYA	11	443	41	50	91	643	19	0	2	2	40	1	1924-25	1934-35
Smith, Arthur	Tor., Ott.	4	137	15	10	25	249	4	1	1	2	8		1927-28	1930-31
Smith, Barry	Bos., Col.	3	114	7	7	14	10	....	....	....	....	....		1975-76	1980-81
Smith, Brad	Van., Atl., Cgy., Det., Tor.	9	222	28	34	62	591	20	3	3	6	49		1978-79	1986-87
Smith, Brian D.	L.A., Min.	2	67	10	10	20	33	7	0	0	0	0		1967-68	1968-69
Smith, Brian S.	Det.	3	61	2	8	10	12	5	0	0	0	0		1957-58	1960-61
Smith, Carl	Det.	1	7	1	1	2	2	....	....	....	....	....		1943-44	1943-44
Smith, Clint	NYR, Chi.	11	483	161	236	397	24	44	10	14	24	2	1	1936-37	1946-47
Smith, Dallas	Bos., NYR	16	890	55	252	307	959	86	3	29	32	128	2	1959-60	1977-78
Smith, Dalton	NYA, Det.	2	11	1	2	3	0	....	....	....	....	....		1936-37	1943-44
Smith, Derek	Buf., Det.	8	335	78	116	194	60	30	9	14	23	13		1975-76	1982-83
Smith, Des	Mtl.M., Mtl., Chi., Bos.	5	195	22	25	47	236	25	1	4	5	18	1	1937-38	1941-42
* Smith, Don	Mtl.	1	10	1	0	1	4	....	....	....	....	....		1919-20	1919-20
Smith, Don A.	NYR	1	11	1	1	2	0	1	0	0	0	0		1949-50	1949-50
Smith, Doug	L.A., Buf., Edm., Van., Pit.	9	535	115	138	253	624	....	....	....	....	....		1981-82	1989-90
Smith, Floyd	Bos., NYR, Det., Tor., Buf.	13	616	129	178	307	207	48	12	11	23	16		1954-55	1971-72
Smith, George	Tor.	1	9	0	0	0	0	....	....	....	....	....		1921-22	1921-22
Smith, Glen	Chi.	1	2	0	0	0	0	....	....	....	....	....		1950-51	1950-51
Smith, Glenn	Tor.	1	9	0	0	0	0	....	....	....	....	....		1922-23	1922-23
Smith, Gord	Wsh., Wpg.	6	299	9	30	39	284	....	....	....	....	....		1974-75	1979-80
Smith, Greg	Cal., Clev., Min., Det., Wsh.	13	829	56	232	288	1110	63	4	7	11	106		1975-76	1987-88
* Smith, Hooley	Ott., Mtl.M., Bos., NYA	17	715	200	215	415	1013	54	11	8	19	109	2	1924-25	1940-41
Smith, Kenny	Bos.	7	331	78	93	171	49	30	8	13	21	6		1944-45	1950-51
Smith, Randy	Min.	2	3	0	0	0	0	....	....	....	....	....		1985-86	1986-87
Smith, Rick	Bos., Cal., St.L., Det., Wsh.	11	687	52	167	219	560	78	3	23	26	73	1	1968-69	1980-81
Smith, Roger	Pit., Phi.	6	210	20	4	24	172	4	3	0	3	0		1925-26	1930-31
Smith, Ron	NYI	1	11	1	1	2	14	....	....	....	....	....		1972-73	1972-73
Smith, Sid	Tor.	12	601	186	183	369	94	44	17	10	27	2	3	1946-47	1957-58
Smith, Stan	NYR	2	9	2	1	3	0	....	....	....	....	....	1	1939-40	1940-41
Smith, Steve	Phi., Buf.	6	17	0	1	1	15	....	....	....	....	....		1981-82	1988-89
Smith, Stu E.	Mtl.	2	17	2	4	6	2	....	....	....	....	....		1940-41	1941-42
Smith, Stu G.	Hfd.	4	77	2	10	12	95	....	....	....	....	....		1979-80	1982-83
* Smith, Tommy	Que.B.	1	10	0	0	0	9	....	....	....	....	....		1919-20	1919-20
Smith, Vern	NYI	1	1	0	0	0	0	....	....	....	....	....		1984-85	1984-85
Smith, Wayne	Chi.	1	2	1	1	2	2	1	0	0	0	0		1966-67	1966-67
Smrke, John	St.L., Que.	3	103	11	17	28	33	....	....	....	....	....		1977-78	1979-80
Smrke, Stan	Mtl.	2	9	0	3	3	0	....	....	....	....	....		1956-57	1957-58
Smyl, Stan	Van.	13	896	262	411	673	1556	41	16	17	33	64		1978-79	1990-91
* Smylie, Rod	Tor., Ott.	6	76	4	1	5	10	9	1	2	3	2	1	1920-21	1925-26
Snell, Ron	Pit.	2	7	3	2	5	6	....	....	....	....	....		1968-69	1969-70
Snell, Ted	Pit., K.C., Det.	2	104	7	18	25	22	....	....	....	....	....		1973-74	1974-75
Snepsts, Harold	Van., Min., Det., St.L.	17	1033	38	195	223	2009	93	1	14	15	231		1974-75	1990-91
Snow, Sandy	Det.	1	3	0	0	0	2	....	....	....	....	....		1968-69	1968-69
Sobchuk, Denis	Det., Que.	2	35	5	6	11	2	....	....	....	....	....		1979-80	1982-83
Sobchuk, Gene	Van.	1	1	0	0	0	0	....	....	....	....	....		1973-74	1973-74
Solheim, Ken	Chi., Min., Det., Edm.	5	135	19	20	39	34	3	1	1	2	2		1980-81	1985-86
Solinger, Bob	Tor., Det.	5	99	10	11	21	19	....	....	....	....	....		1951-52	1959-60
* Somers, Art	Chi., NYR	6	222	33	56	89	189	30	1	5	6	20	1	1929-30	1934-35
Sommer, Roy	Edm.	1	3	1	0	1	7	....	....	....	....	....		1980-81	1980-81
Songin, Tom	Bos.	3	43	5	5	10	22	....	....	....	....	....		1978-79	1980-81
Sonmor, Glen	NYR	2	28	2	0	2	21	....	....	....	....	....		1953-54	1954-55
Sorrell, John	Det., NYA	11	490	127	119	246	100	42	12	15	27	10	2	1930-31	1940-41
Sparrow, Emory	Bos.	1	6	0	0	0	4	....	....	....	....	....		1924-25	1924-25
Speck, Fred	Det., Van.	3	28	1	2	3	2	....	....	....	....	....		1968-69	1971-72
Speer, Bill	Pit., Bos.	4	130	5	20	25	79	8	1	0	1	4	1	1967-68	1970-71
Speers, Ted	Det.	1	4	1	1	2	0	....	....	....	....	....		1985-86	1985-86
* Spencer, Brian	Tor., NYI, Buf., Pit.	10	553	80	143	223	634	37	1	5	6	29		1969-70	1978-79
Spencer, Irv	NYR, Bos., Det.	8	230	12	38	50	127	16	0	0	0	8		1959-60	1967-68
Speyer, Chris	Tor., NYA	3	14	0	0	0	0	....	....	....	....	....		1923-24	1933-34
Spring, Don	Wpg.	4	259	1	52	55	80	6	0	0	0	10		1980-81	1983-84
Spring, Frank	Bos., St.L., Cal., Clev.	5	61	14	20	34	12	....	....	....	....	....		1969-70	1976-77
Spring, Jesse	Ham., Pit., Tor., NYA	6	137	11	2	13	62	2	0	2	2	2		1923-24	1929-30
Spruce, Andy	Van., Col.	3	172	31	42	73	111	2	0	2	2	2		1976-77	1978-79
St. Laurent, Andre	NYI, Det., L.A., Pit.	11	644	129	187	316	749	59	8	12	20	48		1973-74	1983-84
St. Laurent, Dollard	Mtl., Chi.	12	652	29	133	162	496	92	2	22	24	87	5	1950-51	1961-62
St. Marseille, Frank	St.L., L.A.	10	707	140	285	425	242	88	20	25	45	18		1967-68	1976-77
St. Sauveur, Claude	Atl.	1	79	24	24	48	23	2	0	0	0	0		1975-76	1975-76
Stackhouse, Ron	Cal., Det., Pit.	12	889	87	372	459	824	32	5	8	13	38		1970-71	1981-82
Stackhouse, Ted	Tor.	1	12	0	0	0	2	5	0	0	0	0	1	1921-22	1921-22
Stahan, Butch	Mtl.	1	....	....	....	....	....	3	0	1	1	2		1944-45	1944-45
Staley, Al	NYR	1	1	0	1	1	0	....	....	....	....	....		1948-49	1948-49
Stamler, Lorne	L.A., Tor., Wpg.	4	116	14	11	25	16	....	....	....	....	....		1976-77	1979-80
Standing, George	Min.	1	2	0	0	0	0	....	....	....	....	....		1967-68	1967-68
Stanfield, Fred	Chi., Bos., Min., Buf.	14	914	211	405	616	134	106	21	35	56	10	2	1964-65	1977-78
Stanfield, Jack	Chi.	1	....	....	....	....	....	1	0	0	0	0		1965-66	1965-66
Stanfield, Jim	L.A.	3	7	0	1	1	0	....	....	....	....	....		1969-70	1971-72
Stankiewicz, Edward	Det.	2	6	0	0	0	2	....	....	....	....	....		1953-54	1955-56
Stankiewicz, Myron	St.L., Phi.	1	35	0	7	7	36	1	0	0	0	0		1968-69	1968-69
Stanley, Allan	NYR, Chi., Bos., Tor., Phi.	21	1244	100	333	433	792	109	7	36	43	80	4	1948-49	1968-69
* Stanley, Barney	Chi.	1	1	0	0	0	0	....	....	....	....	....		1927-28	1927-28
Stanley, Daryl	Phi., Van.	6	189	8	17	25	408	17	0	0	0	30		1983-84	1989-90
Stanowski, Wally	Tor., NYR	10	428	23	88	111	160	60	3	14	17	13	4	1939-40	1950-51
Stapleton, Brian	Wsh.	1	1	0	0	0	0	....	....	....	....	....		1975-76	1975-76
Stapleton, Pat	Bos., Chi.	10	635	43	294	337	353	65	10	39	49	38		1961-62	1972-73
Starikov, Sergei	N.J.	1	16	0	1	1	8	....	....	....	....	....		1989-90	1989-90
Starr, Harold	Ott., Mtl.M., Mtl., NYR	7	203	6	5	11	186	17	1	0	1	2		1929-30	1935-36
Starr, Wilf	NYA, Det.	4	89	8	6	14	25	7	0	2	2	2	1	1932-33	1935-36
Stasiuk, Vic	Chi., Det., Bos.	14	745	183	254	437	669	69	16	18	34	40	2	1949-50	1962-63
Stastny, Marian	Que., Tor.	5	322	121	173	294	110	32	5	17	22	7		1981-82	1985-86
Staszak, Ray	Det.	1	4	0	1	1	7	....	....	....	....	....		1985-86	1985-86
Steele, Frank	Det.	1	1	0	0	0	0	....	....	....	....	....		1930-31	1930-31

Name	NHL Teams	NHL Seasons	Regular Schedule					Playoffs					NHL Cup Wins	First NHL Season	Last NHL Season
			GP	G	A	TP	PIM	GP	G	A	TP	PIM			
Steen, Anders	Wpg.	1	42	5	11	16	22	....	....	....	....	....		1980-81	1980-81
Stefaniw, Morris	Atl.	1	13	1	1	2	2	....	....	....	....	....		1972-73	1972-73
Stefanski, Bud	NYR	1	1	0	0	0	0	....	....	....	....	....		1977-78	1977-78
Stemkowski, Pete	Tor., Det., NYR, L.A.	15	967	206	349	555	866	83	25	29	54	136	1	1963-64	1977-78
Stenlund, Vern	Clev.	1	4	0	0	0	0	....	....	....	....	....		1976-77	1976-77
* Stephens, Phil	Mtl.W, Mtl.	2	8	1	0	1	0	....	....	....	....	....		1917-18	1921-22
Stephenson, Bob	Hfd., Tor.	1	18	2	3	5	4	....	....	....	....	....		1979-80	1979-80
Sterner, Ulf	NYR	1	4	0	0	0	0	....	....	....	....	....		1964-65	1964-65
Stevens, Paul	Bos.	1	17	0	0	0	0	....	....	....	....	....		1925-26	1925-26
Stewart, Bill	Buf., St.L., Tor., Min.	8	261	7	64	71	424	13	1	3	4	11		1977-78	1985-86
Stewart, Blair	Det., Wsh., Que.	7	229	34	44	78	326	....	....	....	....	....		1973-74	1979-80
Stewart, Gaye	Tor., Chi., Det., NYR, Mtl.	11	502	185	159	344	274	25	2	9	11	16	2	1941-42	1953-54
* Stewart, Jack	Det., Chi.	12	565	31	84	115	765	80	5	14	19	143	2	1938-39	1951-52
Stewart, John	Pit., Atl., Cal., Que.	6	260	58	60	118	158	4	0	0	0	10		1970-71	1979-80
Stewart, Ken	Chi.	1	6	1	1	2	2	....	....	....	....	....		1941-42	1941-42
* Stewart, Nels	Mtl.M., Bos., NYA	15	651	324	191	515	953	54	15	13	28	61	1	1925-26	1939-40
Stewart, Paul	Que.	1	21	2	0	2	74	....	....	....	....	....		1979-80	1979-80
Stewart, Ralph	Van., NYI	7	252	57	73	130	28	19	4	4	8	2		1970-71	1977-78
Stewart, Robert	Bos., Cal., Clev., St.L., Pit.	9	510	27	101	128	809	5	1	1	2	2		1971-72	1979-80
Stewart, Ron	Tor., Bos., St.L., NYR, Van., NYI	21	1353	276	253	529	560	119	14	21	35	60	3	1952-53	1972-73
Stewart, Ryan	Wpg.	1	3	1	0	1	0	....	....	....	....	....		1985-86	1985-86
Stiles, Tony	Cgy.	1	30	2	7	9	20	....	....	....	....	....		1983-84	1983-84
Stoddard, Jack	NYR	2	80	16	15	31	31	....	....	....	....	....		1951-52	1952-53
Stoltz, Roland	Wsh.	1	14	2	2	4	14	....	....	....	....	....		1981-82	1981-82
Stone, Steve	Van.	1	2	0	0	0	0	....	....	....	....	....		1973-74	1973-74
Stoughton, Blaine	Pit., Tor., Hfd., NYR	8	526	258	191	449	204	8	4	2	6	2		1973-74	1983-84
Stoyanovich, Steve	Hfd.	1	23	3	5	8	11	....	....	....	....	....		1983-84	1983-84
Strain, Neil	NYR	1	52	11	13	24	12	....	....	....	....	....		1952-53	1952-53
Strate, Gord	Det.	3	61	0	0	0	34	....	....	....	....	....		1956-57	1958-59
Stratton, Art	NYR, Det., Chi., Pit., Phi.	4	95	18	33	51	24	5	0	0	0	0		1959-60	1967-68
Strobel, Art	NYR	1	7	0	0	0	0	....	....	....	....	....		1943-44	1943-44
Strong, Ken	Tor.	3	15	2	2	4	6	....	....	....	....	....		1982-83	1984-85
Strueby, Todd	Edm.	3	5	0	1	1	2	....	....	....	....	....		1981-82	1983-84
* Stuart, Billy	Tor., Bos.	7	193	30	17	47	145	17	1	0	1	12	1	1920-21	1926-27
Stumpf, Robert	St.L., Pit.	1	10	1	1	2	20	....	....	....	....	....		1974-75	1974-75
Sturgeon, Peter	Col.	2	6	0	1	1	2	....	....	....	....	....		1979-80	1980-81
Suikkanen, Kai	Buf.	2	2	0	0	0	0	....	....	....	....	....		1981-82	1982-83
Sulliman, Doug	NYR, Hfd., N.J., Phi.	11	631	160	168	328	175	16	1	3	4	2		1979-80	1989-90
Sullivan, Barry	Det.	1	1	0	0	0	0	....	....	....	....	....		1947-48	1947-48
Sullivan, Bob	Hfd.	1	62	18	19	37	18	....	....	....	....	....		1982-83	1982-83
Sullivan, Frank	Tor., Chi.	4	8	0	0	0	2	....	....	....	....	....		1949-50	1955-56
Sullivan, Peter	Wpg.	2	126	28	54	82	40	....	....	....	....	....		1979-80	1980-81
Sullivan, Red	Bos., Chi., NYR	11	557	107	239	346	441	18	1	2	3	7		1949-50	1960-61
Summanen, Raimo	Edm., Van.	5	151	36	40	76	35	10	2	5	7	0		1983-84	1987-88
Summerhill, Bill	Mtl., Bro.	3	72	14	17	31	70	3	0	0	0	2		1938-39	1941-42
Sundstrom, Peter	NYR, Wsh., N.J.	6	679	219	369	588	349	37	9	17	26	25		1983-84	1989-90
Suomi, Al	Chi.	1	5	0	0	0	0	....	....	....	....	....		1936-37	1936-37
Sutherland, Bill	Mtl., Phi., Tor., St.L., Det.	6	250	70	58	128	99	14	2	4	6	0		1962-63	1971-72
Sutherland, Ron	Bos.	1	2	0	0	0	0	....	....	....	....	....		1931-32	1931-32
Sutter, Brian	St.L.	12	779	303	333	636	1786	65	21	21	42	249		1976-77	1987-88
Sutter, Darryl	Chi.	8	406	161	118	279	288	51	24	19	43	26		1979-80	1986-87
Sutter, Duane	NYI, Chi.	11	731	139	203	342	1333	161	26	32	58	405		1979-80	1989-90
Suzor, Mark	Phi., Col.	2	64	4	16	20	60	....	....	....	....	....		1976-77	1977-78
Svensson, Leif	Wsh.	2	121	6	40	46	49	....	....	....	....	....		1978-79	1979-80
Swain, Garry	Pit.	1	9	1	1	2	0	....	....	....	....	....		1968-69	1968-69
Swarbrick, George	Oak., Pit., Phi.	4	132	17	25	42	173	....	....	....	....	....		1967-68	1970-71
Sweeny, Bill	NYR	1	4	1	0	1	0	....	....	....	....	....		1959-60	1959-60
Sykes, Bob	Tor.	1	2	0	0	0	0	....	....	....	....	....		1974-75	1974-75
Szura, Joe	Oak.	2	90	10	15	25	30	7	2	3	5	2		1967-68	1968-69

T

Name	NHL Teams	NHL Seasons	GP	G	A	TP	PIM	GP	G	A	TP	PIM	NHL Cup Wins	First NHL Season	Last NHL Season
Taft, John	Det.	1	15	0	2	2	4	....	....	....	....	....		1978-79	1978-79
Talafous, Dean	Atl., Min., NYR	8	497	104	154	258	163	21	4	7	11	11		1974-75	1981-82
Talakoski, Ron	NYR	2	9	0	1	1	33	....	....	....	....	....		1986-87	1987-88
Talbot, Jean-Guy	Mtl., Min., Det., St.L., Buf.	17	1056	43	242	285	1006	150	4	26	30	142	7	1954-55	1970-71
Tallon, Dale	Van., Chi., Pit.	10	642	98	238	336	568	33	2	10	12	45		1970-71	1979-80
Tambellini, Steve	NYI, Col., N.J., Cgy., Van.	10	553	160	150	310	105	2	0	1	1	0	1	1978-79	1987-88
Tanguay, Chris	Que.	1	2	0	0	0	0	....	....	....	....	....		1981-82	1981-82
Tannahill, Don	Van.	2	111	30	33	63	25	....	....	....	....	....		1972-73	1973-74
Tardif, Marc	Mtl., Que.	8	517	194	207	401	443	62	13	15	28	75	2	1969-70	1982-83
Taylor, Billy	Tor., Det., Bos., NYR	7	323	87	180	267	120	33	6	18	24	13	1	1939-40	1947-48
* Taylor, Billy	NYR	1	2	0	0	0	0	....	....	....	....	....		1964-65	1964-65
Taylor, Bob	Bos.	1	8	0	0	0	6	....	....	....	....	....		1929-30	1929-30
Taylor, Harry	Tor., Chi.	3	66	5	10	15	30	1	0	0	0	0	1	1946-47	1951-52
Taylor, Mark	Phi., Pit., Wsh.	5	209	42	68	110	73	6	0	0	0	0		1981-82	1985-86
Taylor, Ralph	Chi., NYR	3	99	4	1	5	169	4	0	0	0	10		1927-28	1929-30
Taylor, Ted	NYR, Det., Min., Van.	6	166	23	35	58	181	....	....	....	....	....		1964-65	1971-72
Teal, Jeff	Mtl.	1	6	0	1	1	0	....	....	....	....	....		1984-85	1984-85
Teal, Skip	Bos.	1	1	0	0	0	0	....	....	....	....	....		1954-55	1954-55
Teal, Victor	NYI	1	1	0	0	0	0	....	....	....	....	....		1973-74	1973-74
Tebbutt, Greg	Que., Pit.	2	26	0	3	3	35	....	....	....	....	....		1979-80	1983-84
Terbenche, Paul	Chi., Buf.	5	189	5	26	31	28	12	0	0	0	0		1967-68	1973-74
Terrion, Greg	L.A., Tor.	8	561	93	150	243	339	35	2	9	11	41		1980-81	1987-88
Terry, Bill	Min.	1	5	0	0	0	0	....	....	....	....	....		1987-88	1987-88
Tessier, Orval	Mtl., Bos.	3	59	5	7	12	6	....	....	....	....	....		1954-55	1960-61
Thatchell, Spence	NYR	1	1	0	0	0	0	....	....	....	....	....		1942-43	1942-43
Theberge, Greg	Wsh.	5	153	15	63	78	73	4	0	1	1	0		1979-80	1983-84
Thelin, Mats	Bos.	3	163	8	19	27	107	5	0	0	0	6		1984-85	1986-87
Thelven, Michael	Bos.	5	207	20	80	100	217	34	4	10	14	34		1985-86	1989-90
Therrien, Gaston	Que.	3	22	0	8	8	12	9	0	1	1	4		1980-81	1982-83
Thibaudeau, Gilles	Mtl., NYI, Tor.	5	119	25	37	62	40	8	3	3	6	2		1986-87	1990-91
Thibeault, Laurence	Det., Mtl.	2	5	0	2	2	0	....	....	....	....	....		1944-45	1945-46
Thiffault, Leo	Min.	1	....	....	....	....	....	5	0	0	0	0		1967-68	1967-68
Thomas, Cy	Chi., Tor.	1	14	2	2	4	12	....	....	....	....	....		1947-48	1947-48
Thomas, Reg	Que.	1	39	9	7	16	6	....	....	....	....	....		1979-80	1979-80
Thompson, Cliff	Bos.	2	13	0	1	1	2	....	....	....	....	....		1941-42	1948-49
Thompson, Errol	Tor., Det., Pit.	10	599	208	185	393	184	34	7	5	12	11		1970-71	1980-81
* Thompson, Kenneth	Mtl.W	1	1	0	0	0	0	....	....	....	....	....		1917-18	1917-18
Thompson, Paul	NYR, Chi.	13	586	153	179	332	336	48	11	11	22	54	3	1926-27	1938-39
Thoms, Bill	Tor., Chi., Bos.	13	549	135	206	341	172	44	6	10	16	6		1932-33	1944-45
Thomson, Bill	Det., Chi.	2	10	2	2	4	0	2	0	0	0	0		1938-39	1943-44
Thomson, Floyd	St.L.	8	411	56	97	153	341	10	0	2	2	6		1971-72	1979-80
Thomson, Jack	NYA	3	15	1	1	2	0	2	0	0	0	0		1938-39	1940-41
* Thomson, Jimmy	Tor., Chi.	13	787	19	215	234	920	63	2	13	15	135	4	1945-46	1957-58
* Thomson, Rhys	Mtl., Tor.	2	25	0	2	2	38	....	....	....	....	....		1939-40	1942-43
Thornbury, Tom	Pit.	1	14	1	8	9	16	....	....	....	....	....		1983-84	1983-84
Thorsteinson, Joe	NYA	1	4	0	0	0	0	....	....	....	....	....		1932-33	1932-33
Thurier, Fred	NYA, Bro., NYR	3	80	25	27	52	18	....	....	....	....	....		1940-41	1944-45
Thurlby, Tom	Oak.	1	20	1	2	3	4	....	....	....	....	....		1967-68	1967-68
Tidey, Alex	Buf., Edm.	3	9	0	0	0	8	2	0	0	0	0		1976-77	1979-80
Timgren, Ray	Tor., Chi.	6	251	14	44	58	70	30	3	9	12	6	2	1948-49	1954-55
Titanic, Morris	Buf.	2	19	0	0	0	0	....	....	....	....	....		1974-75	1975-76
Tkaczuk, Walt	NYR	14	945	227	451	678	556	93	19	32	51	119		1967-68	1980-81
Toal, Mike	Edm.	1	3	0	0	0	0	....	....	....	....	....		1979-80	1979-80
Tomalty, Glenn	Wpg.	1	1	0	0	0	0	....	....	....	....	....		1979-80	1979-80
Tomlinson, Kirk	Min.	1	1	0	0	0	0	....	....	....	....	....		1987-88	1987-88
Toomey, Sean	Min.	1	1	0	0	0	0	....	....	....	....	....		1986-87	1986-87
Toppazzini, Jerry	Bos., Chi., Det.	12	783	163	244	407	436	40	13	9	22	13		1952-53	1963-64
Toppazzini, Zellio	Bos., NYR, Chi.	5	123	21	22	43	49	2	0	0	0	0		1948-49	1956-57
Torkki, Jari	Chi.	1	4	1	0	1	0	....	....	....	....	....		1988-89	1988-89
Touhey, Bill	Mtl.M., Ott., Bos.	7	280	65	40	105	107	2	1	0	1	0		1927-28	1933-34
Toupin, Jaques	Chi.	1	8	1	2	3	0	4	0	0	0	0		1943-44	1943-44

Jean Guy Talbot

Paul Terbenche

Errol Thompson

Ian Turnbull

Darren Veitch

Steve Vickers

Joe Watson

Doug Wickenheiser

Name	NHL Teams	NHL Seasons	Regular Schedule					Playoffs					NHL Cup Wins	First NHL Season	Last NHL Season
			GP	G	A	TP	PIM	GP	G	A	TP	PIM			
Townsend, Art	Chi.	1	5	0	0	0	0	....	....	....	....	....		1926-27	1926-27
Trader, Larry	Det., St.L., Mtl.	4	91	5	13	18	74	3	0	0	0	0		1982-83	1987-88
Trainor, Wes	NYR	1	17	1	2	3	6	....	....	....	....	....		1948-49	1948-49
Trapp, Bobby	Chi.	2	82	4	4	8	129	2	0	0	0	4		1926-27	1927-28
Trapp, Doug	Buf.	1	2	0	0	0	0	....	....	....	....	....		1986-87	1986-87
Traub, Percy	Chi., Det.	3	130	3	3	6	214	4	0	0	0	6		1926-27	1928-29
Tredway, Brock	L.A.	1	....	....	....	....	....	1	0	0	0	0		1981-82	1981-82
Tremblay, Brent	Wsh.	2	10	1	0	1	6	....	....	....	....	....		1978-79	1979-80
Tremblay, Gilles	Mtl.	9	509	168	162	330	161	48	9	14	23	4	2	1960-61	1968-69
Tremblay, J.C.	Mtl.	13	794	57	306	363	204	108	14	51	65	58	5	1959-60	1971-72
Tremblay, Marcel	Mtl.	1	10	0	2	2	0	....	....	....	....	....		1938-39	1938-39
Tremblay, Mario	Mtl.	12	852	258	326	584	1043	100	20	29	49	187	5	1974-75	1985-86
Tremblay, Nels	Mtl.	2	3	0	1	1	0	2	0	0	0	0		1944-45	1945-46
Trimper, Tim	Chi., Wpg., Min.	6	190	30	36	66	153	2	0	0	0	2		1979-80	1984-85
* Trottier, Dave	Mtl.M., Det.	11	446	121	113	234	517	31	4	3	7	41	1	1928-29	1938-39
Trottier, Guy	NYR, Tor.	3	115	28	17	45	37	9	1	0	1	16		1968-69	1971-72
Trottier, Rocky	N.J.	2	38	6	4	10	2	....	....	....	....	....		1983-84	1984-85
Trudel, Louis	Chi., Mtl.	8	306	49	69	118	122	24	1	3	4	6	2	1933-34	1940-41
Trudell, Rene	NYR	3	129	24	28	52	72	5	0	0	0	2		1945-46	1947-48
Tudin, Connie	Mtl.	1	4	0	1	1	4	....	....	....	....	....		1941-42	1941-42
Tudor, Rob	Van., St.L.	3	28	4	4	8	19	3	0	0	0	0		1978-79	1982-83
Tuer, Allan	L.A., Min., Hfd.	4	57	1	1	2	208	....	....	....	....	....		1985-86	1989-90
Turcotte, Alfie	Mtl., Wpg., Wsh.	7	112	17	29	46	49	5	0	0	0	0		1983-84	1990-91
Turlick, Gord	Bos.	1	2	0	0	0	2	....	....	....	....	....		1959-60	1959-60
Turnbull, Ian	Tor., L.A., Pit.	10	628	123	317	440	736	55	13	32	45	94		1973-74	1982-83
Turnbull, Perry	St.L., Mtl., Wpg.	9	608	188	163	351	1245	34	6	7	13	86		1979-80	1987-88
Turnbull, Randy	Cgy.	1	1	0	0	0	2	....	....	....	....	....		1981-82	1981-82
Turner, Bob	Mtl., Chi.	8	478	19	51	70	307	68	1	4	5	44	5	1955-56	1962-63
Turner, Dean	NYR, Col., L.A.	4	35	1	0	1	59	....	....	....	....	....		1978-79	1982-83
Tustin, Norman	NYR	1	18	2	4	6	0	....	....	....	....	....		1941-42	1941-42
Tuten, Audley	Chi.	2	39	4	8	12	48	....	....	....	....	....		1941-42	1942-43

UV

Name	NHL Teams	NHL Seasons	GP	G	A	TP	PIM	GP	G	A	TP	PIM	NHL Cup Wins	First NHL Season	Last NHL Season
Ubriaco, Gene	Pit., Oak., Chi.	3	177	39	35	74	50	11	2	0	2	4		1967-68	1969-70
Ullman, Norm	Det., Tor.	20	1410	490	739	1229	712	106	30	53	83	67		1955-56	1974-75
Unger, Garry	Tor., Det., St.L., Atl., L.A., Edm.	16	1105	413	391	804	1075	52	12	18	30	105		1967-68	1982-83
Vadnais, Carol	Mtl., Oak., Cal., Bos., NYR, N.J.	17	1087	169	418	587	1813	106	10	40	50	185	2	1966-67	1982-83
Vail, Eric	Atl, Cgy., Det.	9	591	216	260	476	281	20	5	6	11	6		1973-74	1981-82
Vail, Melville	NYR	2	50	4	1	5	18	10	0	0	0	2		1928-29	1929-30
Valentine, Chris	Wsh.	3	105	43	52	95	127	2	0	0	0	4		1981-82	1983-84
Valiquette, Jack	Tor., Col.	7	350	84	134	218	79	23	3	6	9	4		1974-75	1980-81
Van Boxmeer, John	Mtl., Col., Buf., Que.	11	588	84	274	358	465	38	5	15	20	37		1973-74	1983-84
Van Impe, Ed	Chi., Phi., Pit.	11	700	27	126	153	1025	66	1	12	13	131	2	1966-67	1976-77
Vasko, Elmer	Chi., Min.	13	786	34	166	200	719	78	2	7	9	73	1	1956-57	1969-70
Vasko, Rick	Det.	3	31	3	7	10	29	....	....	....	....	....		1977-78	1980-81
Vautour, Yvon	NYI, Col., N.J., Que.	6	204	26	33	59	401	....	....	....	....	....		1979-80	1984-85
Vaydik, Greg	Chi.	1	5	0	0	0	0	....	....	....	....	....		1976-77	1976-77
Veitch, Darren	Wsh., Det., Tor.	10	511	48	209	257	296	33	4	11	15	33		1980-81	1990-91
Venasky, Vic	L.A.	7	430	61	101	162	66	21	1	5	6	12		1972-73	1978-79
Veneruzzo, Gary	St.L.	2	7	1	1	2	0	9	0	2	2	2		1967-68	1971-72
Verret, Claude	Buf.	2	14	2	5	7	2	....	....	....	....	....		1983-84	1984-85
Verstraete, Leigh	Tor.	3	8	0	1	1	14	....	....	....	....	....		1982-83	1987-88
Ververgaert, Dennis	Van., Phi., Wsh.	8	583	176	216	392	247	8	1	2	3	6		1973-74	1980-81
Veysey, Sid	Van.	1	1	0	0	0	0	....	....	....	....	....		1977-78	1977-78
Vickers, Steve	NYR	10	698	246	340	586	330	68	24	25	49	58		1972-73	1981-82
Vigneault, Alain	St.L.	2	42	2	5	7	82	4	0	1	1	26		1981-82	1982-83
Vipond, Pete	Cal.	1	3	0	0	0	0	....	....	....	....	....		1972-73	1972-73
Vokes, Ed	Chi.	1	5	0	0	0	0	....	....	....	....	....		1930-31	1930-31
Volcan, Mickey	Hfd., Cgy.	4	162	8	33	41	146	....	....	....	....	....		1980-81	1983-84
Volmar, Doug	Det., L.A.	4	62	13	8	21	26	2	1	0	1	0		1969-70	1972-73
Voss, Carl	Tor., NYR, Det., Ott., St.L., Mtl.M., NYA, Chi.	8	261	34	70	104	50	24	5	3	8	0		1926-27	1937-38
Vyazmikin, Igor	Edm.	1	4	1	0	1	0	....	....	....	....	....		1990-91	1990-91

W

Name	NHL Teams	NHL Seasons	GP	G	A	TP	PIM	GP	G	A	TP	PIM	NHL Cup Wins	First NHL Season	Last NHL Season
Waddell, Don	L.A.	1	1	0	0	0	0	....	....	....	....	....		1980-81	1980-81
Waite, Frank	NYR	1	17	1	3	4	4	....	....	....	....	....		1930-31	1930-31
Walker, Gord	NYR, L.A.	4	31	3	4	7	23	....	....	....	....	....		1986-87	1989-90
Walker, Howard	Wsh., Cal.	3	83	2	13	15	133	....	....	....	....	....		1980-81	1982-83
* Walker, Jack	Det.	2	80	5	8	13	18	....	....	....	....	....		1926-27	1927-28
Walker, Kurt	Tor.	3	71	4	5	9	152	16	0	0	0	34		1975-76	1977-78
Walker, Russ	L.A.	2	17	1	0	1	41	....	....	....	....	....		1976-77	1977-78
Wall, Bob	Det., L.A., St.L.	8	322	30	55	85	155	22	0	3	3	2		1964-65	1971-72
Wallin, Peter	NYR	2	52	3	14	17	14	14	2	6	8	6		1980-81	1981-82
Walsh, Jim	Buf.	1	4	0	1	1	4	....	....	....	....	....		1981-82	1981-82
Walsh, Mike	NYI	2	14	2	0	2	4	....	....	....	....	....		1987-88	1988-89
Walton, Bobby	Mtl.	1	4	0	0	0	0	....	....	....	....	....		1943-44	1943-44
Walton, Mike	Tor., Bos., Van., Chi., St.L.	12	588	201	247	448	357	47	14	10	24	45	2	1965-66	1978-79
Wappel, Gord	Atl., Cgy.	3	20	1	1	2	10	2	0	0	0	4		1979-80	1981-82
Ward, Don	Chi., Bos.	2	34	0	1	1	16	....	....	....	....	....		1957-58	1959-60
Ward, Jimmy	Mtl.M., Mtl.	12	532	147	127	274	465	31	4	4	8	18	1	1927-28	1938-39
Ward, Joe	Col.	1	4	0	0	0	2	....	....	....	....	....		1980-81	1980-81
Ward, Ron	Tor., Van.,	2	89	2	5	7	6	....	....	....	....	....		1969-70	1971-72
Wares, Eddie	NYR, Det., Chi.	9	291	60	102	162	161	45	5	7	12	34	1	1936-37	1946-47
Warner, Bob	Tor.	2	10	1	1	2	4	4	0	0	0	0		1975-76	1976-77
Warner, Jim	Hfd.	1	32	0	3	3	10	....	....	....	....	....		1979-80	1979-80
Warwick, Bill	NYR	2	14	3	3	6	16	....	....	....	....	....		1942-43	1943-44
Warwick, Grant	NYR, Bos., Mtl.	9	395	147	142	289	220	16	2	4	6	6		1941-42	1949-50
Wasnie, Nick	Chi., Mtl., NYA, Ott., St.L.	7	248	57	34	91	176	14	6	3	9	20	2	1927-28	1934-35
Watson, Bill	Chi.	4	115	23	36	59	12	6	0	2	2	0		1985-86	1988-89
Watson, Bryan	Mtl., Oak., Pit., Det., St.L., Wsh.	16	878	17	135	152	2212	32	2	0	2	70		1963-64	1978-79
Watson, Dave	Col.	2	18	0	1	1	10	....	....	....	....	....		1979-80	1980-81
* Watson, Harry	Bro., Det., Tor., Chi.	14	805	236	207	443	150	62	16	9	25	27	5	1941-42	1956-57
Watson, Jim	Det., Buf.	7	221	4	19	23	345	....	....	....	....	....		1963-64	1971-72
Watson, Jimmy	Phi.	10	613	38	148	186	492	101	5	34	39	89	2	1972-73	1981-82
Watson, Joe	Bos., Phi., Col.	14	835	38	178	216	447	84	3	12	15	82	2	1964-65	1978-79
* Watson, Phil	NYR, Mtl.	13	590	144	265	409	542	45	10	25	35	67	2	1935-36	1947-48
Watts, Brian	Det.	1	4	0	0	0	0	....	....	....	....	....		1975-76	1975-76
Webster, Aubrey	Phi., Mtl.M.	2	5	0	0	0	0	....	....	....	....	....		1930-31	1934-35
Webster, Don	Tor.	1	27	7	6	13	28	5	0	0	0	12		1943-44	1943-44
Webster, John	NYR	1	14	0	0	0	4	....	....	....	....	....		1949-50	1949-50
Webster, Tom	Bos., Det., Cal.	5	102	33	42	75	61	1	0	0	0	0		1968-69	1979-80
* Weiland, Cooney	Bos., Ott., Det.	11	508	173	160	333	147	45	12	10	22	12		1928-29	1938-39
Weir, Stan	Cal., Tor., Edm., Col., Det.	10	642	139	207	346	183	37	6	5	11	4		1972-73	1982-83
Weir, Wally	Que., Hfd., Pit.	6	320	21	45	66	625	23	0	1	1	96		1979-80	1984-85
* Wellington, Duke	Que.	1	1	0	0	0	0	....	....	....	....	....		1919-20	1919-20
Wensink, John	Bos., Que., Col., N.J., St.L.	8	403	70	68	138	840	43	2	6	8	86		1973-74	1982-83
Wentworth, Cy	Chi., Mtl.M., Mtl.	13	578	39	68	107	355	35	5	6	11	22	1	1927-28	1939-40
Wesley, Blake	Phi., Hfd., Que., Tor.	7	298	18	46	64	486	19	2	2	4	30		1979-80	1985-86
Westfall, Ed	Bos., NYI	18	1227	231	394	625	544	95	22	37	59	41	2	1961-62	1978-79
Wharram, Kenny	Chi.	14	766	252	281	533	222	80	16	27	43	38	1	1951-52	1968-69
Wharton, Len	NYR	1	1	0	0	0	0	....	....	....	....	....		1944-45	1944-45
Wheldon, Donald	St.L.	1	2	0	0	0	0	....	....	....	....	....		1974-75	1974-75
Whelton, Bill	Wpg.	1	2	0	0	0	0	....	....	....	....	....		1980-81	1980-81
Whistle, Rob	NYR, St.L.	2	51	7	5	12	16	4	0	0	0	2		1985-86	1987-88
White, Bill	L.A., Chi.	9	604	50	215	265	495	91	7	32	39	76		1967-68	1975-76
White, Moe	Mtl.	1	4	0	1	1	2	....	....	....	....	....		1945-46	1945-46
White, Sherman	NYR	2	4	0	2	2	0	....	....	....	....	....		1946-47	1949-50
White, Tex	Pit., NYA, Phi.	6	203	33	12	45	141	4	0	0	0	2		1925-26	1930-31
White, Tony	Wsh., Min.	5	164	37	28	65	104	....	....	....	....	....		1974-75	1979-80

			Regular Schedule					Playoffs							
Name	NHL Teams	NHL Seasons	GP	G	A	TP	PIM	GP	G	A	TP	PIM	NHL Cup Wins	First NHL Season	Last NHL Season
Whitelaw, Bob	Det.	2	32	0	2	2	2	8	0	0	0	0		1940-41	1941-42
Whitlock, Bob	Min.	1	1	0	0	0	0	....	....	....	....	....		1969-70	1969-70
Wickenheiser, Doug	Mtl., St.L., Van., NYR, Wsh.	19	556	111	165	276	286	....	....	....	....	....		1980-81	1989-90
* Widing, Juha	NYR, L.A., Clev.	8	575	144	226	370	208	8	1	2	3	2		1969-70	1976-77
Wiebe, Art	Chi.	11	411	14	27	41	209	31	1	3	4	8	1	1932-33	1943-44
Wilcox, Archie	Mtl.M., Bos., St.L.	6	212	8	14	22	158	12	1	0	1	10		1929-30	1934-35
Wilcox, Barry	Van.	2	33	3	2	5	15	....	....	....	....	....		1972-73	1974-75
Wilder, Arch	Det.	1	18	0	2	2	2	....	....	....	....	....		1940-41	1940-41
Wiley, Jim	Pit., Van.	5	63	4	10	14	8	....	....	....	....	....		1972-73	1976-77
Wilkins, Barry	Bos., Van., Pit.	9	418	27	125	152	663	6	0	1	1	4		1966-67	1975-76
Wilkinson, John	Bos.	1	9	0	0	0	3	....	....	....	....	....		1943-44	1943-44
Wilks, Brian	L.A.	4	48	4	8	12	27	....	....	....	....	....		1984-85	1988-89
Willard, Rod	Tor.	1	1	0	0	0	0	....	....	....	....	....		1982-83	1982-83
Williams, Burr	Det., St.L., Bos.	3	19	0	1	1	28	2	0	0	0	8		1933-34	1936-37
Williams, Dave	Tor., Van., Det., L.A., Hfd.	14	962	241	272	513	3966	83	12	23	35	455		1974-75	1987-88
Williams, Fred	Det.	1	44	2	5	7	10	....	....	....	....	....		1976-77	1976-77
Williams, Gord	Phi.	2	2	0	0	0	2	....	....	....	....	....		1981-82	1982-83
* Williams, Tom	Bos., Min., Cal., Wsh.	13	663	161	269	430	177	10	2	5	7	2		1961-62	1975-76
Williams, Tommy	NYR, L.A.	8	397	115	138	253	73	29	8	7	15	4		1971-72	1978-79
Williams, Warren	St.L., Cal.	3	108	14	35	49	131	....	....	....	....	....		1973-74	1975-76
Willson, Don	Mtl.	2	22	2	7	9	0	3	0	0	0	0		1937-38	1938-39
Wilson, Behn	Phi., Chi.	9	601	98	260	358	1480	67	12	29	41	190		1978-79	1987-88
* Wilson, Bert	NYR, L.A., St.L., Cgy.	8	478	37	44	81	646	21	0	2	2	42		1973-74	1980-81
Wilson, Bob	Chi.	1	1	0	0	0	0	....	....	....	....	....		1953-54	1953-54
Wilson, Cully	Tor., Mtl., Ham., Chi.	5	125	60	23	83	232	2	1	0	1	6		1919-20	1926-27
Wilson, Gord	Bos.	1	....	....	....	....	....	2	0	0	0	0		1954-55	1954-55
Wilson, Hub	NYA	1	2	0	0	0	0	....	....	....	....	....		1931-32	1931-32
Wilson, Jerry	Mtl.	1	3	0	0	0	2	....	....	....	....	....		1956-57	1956-57
Wilson, Johnny	Det., Chi., Tor., NYR	13	688	161	171	332	190	66	14	13	27	11	4	1949-50	1961-62
* Wilson, Larry	Det., Chi.	6	152	21	48	69	75	4	0	0	0	0	1	1949-50	1955-56
Wilson, Mitch	N.J., Pit.	2	26	2	3	5	104	....	....	....	....	....		1984-85	1986-87
Wilson, Murray	Mtl., L.A.	7	386	94	95	189	162	53	5	14	19	32	3	1972-73	1978-79
Wilson, Rick	Mtl., St.L., Det.	4	239	6	26	32	165	3	0	0	0	0		1973-74	1976-77
Wilson, Rik	St.L., Cgy., Chi.	6	251	25	65	90	220	22	0	4	4	23		1981-82	1987-88
Wilson, Roger	Chi.	1	7	0	2	2	6	....	....	....	....	....		1974-75	1974-75
Wilson, Ron	Tor., Min.	7	177	26	67	93	68	20	4	13	17	8		1977-78	1987-88
Wilson, Wally	Bos.	1	53	11	8	19	18	1	0	0	0	0		1947-48	1947-48
Wing, Murray	Det.	1	1	0	1	1	0	....	....	....	....	....		1973-74	1973-74
Wiseman, Eddie	Det., NYA, Bos.	10	454	115	164	279	137	45	10	10	20	16	1	1932-33	1941-42
Wiste, Jim	Chi., Van.	3	52	1	10	11	8	....	....	....	....	....		1968-69	1970-71
Witherspoon, Jim	L.A.	1	2	0	0	0	0	....	....	....	....	....		1975-76	1975-76
Witiuk, Steve	Chi.	1	33	3	8	11	14	....	....	....	....	....		1951-52	1951-52
Woit, Benny	Det., Chi.	7	334	7	26	33	170	41	2	6	8	18	3	1950-51	1956-57
Wojciechowski, Steven	Det.	2	54	19	20	39	17	6	0	1	1	0		1944-45	1946-47
Wolf, Bennett	Pit.	3	30	0	1	1	133	....	....	....	....	....		1980-81	1982-83
Wong, Mike	Det.	1	22	1	1	2	12	....	....	....	....	....		1975-76	1975-76
Wood, Robert	NYR	1	1	0	0	0	0	....	....	....	....	....		1950-51	1950-51
Woodley, Dan	Van.	1	5	2	0	2	17	....	....	....	....	....		1987-88	1987-88
Woods, Paul	Det.	7	501	72	124	196	276	7	0	5	5	4		1977-78	1983-84
Woytowich, Bob	Bos., Min., Pit., L.A.	8	503	32	126	158	352	24	1	3	4	20		1964-65	1971-72
Wright, John	Van., St.L., K.C.	3	127	16	36	52	67	....	....	....	....	....		1972-73	1974-75
Wright, Keith	Phi.	1	1	0	0	0	0	....	....	....	....	....		1967-68	1967-68
Wright, Larry	Phi., Cal., Det.	5	106	4	8	12	19	....	....	....	....	....		1971-72	1977-78
Wycherley, Ralph	NYA, Bro.	2	28	4	7	11	6	....	....	....	....	....		1940-41	1941-42
Wylie, Duane	Chi.	2	14	3	3	6	2	....	....	....	....	....		1974-75	1976-77
Wylie, William	NYR	1	1	0	0	0	0	....	....	....	....	....		1950-51	1950-51
Wyrozub, Randy	Buf.	4	100	8	10	18	10	....	....	....	....	....		1970-71	1973-74

YZ

Name	NHL Teams	NHL Seasons	GP	G	A	TP	PIM	GP	G	A	TP	PIM	NHL Cup Wins	First NHL Season	Last NHL Season
Yackel, Ken	Bos.	1	6	0	0	0	2	2	0	0	0	0		1958-59	1958-59
Yaremchuk, Gary	Tor.	4	34	1	4	5	28	....	....	....	....	....		1981-82	1984-85
Yaremchuk, Ken	Chi., Tor.	6	235	36	56	92	106	31	6	8	14	49		1983-84	1988-89
Yates, Ross	Hfd.	1	7	1	1	2	4	....	....	....	....	....		1983-84	1983-84
Young, Brian	Chi.	1	8	0	2	2	6	....	....	....	....	....		1980-81	1980-81
Young, Douglas	Mtl., Det.	10	391	35	45	80	303	28	1	5	6	16	2	1931-32	1940-41
Young, Howie	Det., Chi., Van.	8	336	12	62	74	851	19	2	4	6	46		1960-61	1970-71
Young, Tim	Min., Wpg., Phi.	10	628	195	341	536	438	36	7	24	31	27		1975-76	1984-85
Young, Warren	Min., Pit., Det.	7	236	72	77	149	472	....	....	....	....	....		1981-82	1987-88
Younghans, Tom	Min., NYR	6	429	44	41	85	373	24	2	1	3	21		1976-77	1981-82
Zabroski, Marty	Chi.	1	1	0	0	0	0	....	....	....	....	....		1944-45	1944-45
Zaharko, Miles	Atl., Chi.	4	129	5	32	37	84	3	0	0	0	0		1977-78	1981-82
Zaine, Rod	Pit., Buf.	2	61	10	6	16	25	....	....	....	....	....		1970-71	1971-72
Zanussi, Joe	NYR, Bos., St.L.	3	87	1	13	14	46	4	0	1	1	2		1974-75	1976-77
Zanussi, Ron	Min., Tor.	5	299	52	83	135	373	17	0	4	4	17		1977-78	1981-82
Zeidel, Larry	Det., Chi., Phi.	5	158	3	16	19	198	12	0	1	1	12	1	1951-52	1968-69
Zeniuk, Ed	Det.	1	2	0	0	0	0	....	....	....	....	....		1954-55	1954-55
Zetterstrom, Lars	Van.	1	14	0	1	1	2	....	....	....	....	....		1978-79	1978-79
Zuke, Mike	St.L., Hfd.	8	455	86	196	282	220	26	6	6	12	12		1978-79	1985-86
Zunich, Ruby	Det.	1	2	0	0	0	2	....	....	....	....	....		1943-44	1943-44

Retired Players and Goaltenders Research Project

THROUGHOUT THE RETIRED PLAYERS AND RETIRED GOALTENDERS SECTIONS OF this book, you will notice many players with an asterisk (*) by their names. These players, according to our records, are deceased. The editors recognize that our information on the death dates of former NHLers is incomplete. If you have documented information on the passing of any player not marked with an asterisk (*) in this edition, we would like to hear from you. Please send this information to:

Retired Player Research Project
c/o NHL Publishing
194 Dovercourt Road
Toronto, Ontario
M6J 3C8 Canada

fax: 416/531-3939

All contributors will be acknowledged in next year's *Official Guide & Record Book.*

Special thanks to Peter Fillman of Toronto for initial research on this project.

Tommy Williams

Paul Woods

Tom Younghans

Notes

Vancouver's Kirk McLean led all NHL goaltenders with 38 wins in 1991-92.

1992-93 Goaltender Register

Note: The 1992-93 Goaltender Register lists every goaltender who appeared in an NHL game in the 1991-92 season, every goaltender drafted in the first six rounds of the 1992 Entry Draft, every goaltender drafted in the first three rounds of the 1991 Entry Draft and other goaltenders on NHL Reserve Lists.

Trades and roster changes are current as of August 25, 1992.

To calculate a goaltender's goals-against-per-game average **(Avg)**, divide goals against **(GA)** by minutes played **(Mins)** and multiply this result by **60**.

Abbreviations: A list of league names can be found at the beginning of the Player Register. **Avg** – goals against per game average; **GA** – goals against; **GP** – games played; **L** – losses; **Lea** – league; **SO** – shutouts; **T** – ties; **W** – wins.

Player Register begins on page 221.

ALLAN, SANDY

Goaltender. Catches left. 6', 175 lbs. Born, Nassau, Bahamas, January 22, 1974.
(Los Angeles' 2nd choice, 63rd overall, in 1992 Entry Draft).

			Regular Season								Playoffs						
Season	Club	Lea	GP	W	L	T	Mins	GA	SO	Avg	GP	W	L	Mins	GA	SO	Avg
1991-92	North Bay	OHL	34	18	5	4	1747	112	0	3.85	3	0	0	18	2	0	6.67

ANDERSON, DEAN

Goaltender. Catches left. 5'10", 175 lbs. Born, Oshawa, Ont., July 14, 1966.
(Toronto's 1st choice, 11th overall, in 1988 Supplemental Draft).

			Regular Season								Playoffs						
Season	Club	Lea	GP	W	L	T	Mins	GA	SO	Avg	GP	W	L	Mins	GA	SO	Avg
1984-85	U. Wisconsin	WCHA	36	21	13	0	2072	148	0	4.29	....	....	....	....	....	....	....
1985-86	U. Wisconsin	WCHA	20	13	6	0	1128	80	0	4.25	....	....	....	....	....	....	....
1986-87	U. Wisconsin	WCHA	9	4	2	0	409	27	0	3.96	....	....	....	....	....	....	....
1987-88a	U. Wisconsin	WCHA	45	30	13	2	2718	148	2	3.27	....	....	....	....	....	....	....
1988-89	Newmarket	AHL	2	0	1	0	38	4	0	6.32	1	0	1	30	1	0	2.00
	Flint	IHL	16	1	12	0	770	82	1	6.39	....	....	....	....	....	....	....
1989-90	Knoxville	ECHL	17	6	8	3	997	73	0	4.39	....	....	....	....	....	....	....
1990-91	Newmarket	AHL	3	1	2	0	180	16	0	5.33	....	....	....	....	....	....	....
b	Knoxville	ECHL	29	*23	3	2	1625	80	*3	*2.95	3	0	3	187	10	0	3.20
1991-92	Knoxville	ECHL	37	9	20	5	2004	188	0	5.63	....	....	....	....	....	....	....

a WCHA Second All-Star Team (1988)
b ECHL First All-Star Team (1991)

BAILEY, SCOTT

Goaltender. Catches left. 6', 195 lbs. Born, Calgary, Alta., May 2, 1972.
(Boston's 3rd choice, 112th overall, in 1992 Entry Draft).

			Regular Season								Playoffs						
Season	Club	Lea	GP	W	L	T	Mins	GA	SO	Avg	GP	W	L	Mins	GA	SO	Avg
1990-91	Spokane	WHL	46	33	11	0	2537	157	*4	3.71	....	....	....	....	....	....	....
1991-92	Spokane	WHL	65	34	23	5	3798	206	1	3.30	10	5	5	605	43	0	4.26

BALES, MICHAEL

Goaltender. Catches left. 6'1", 180 lbs. Born, Prince Albert, Sask., August 6, 1971.
(Boston's 4th choice, 105th overall, in 1990 Entry Draft).

			Regular Season								Playoffs						
Season	Club	Lea	GP	W	L	T	Mins	GA	SO	Avg	GP	W	L	Mins	GA	SO	Avg
1989-90	Ohio State	CCHA	21	6	13	2	1117	95	0	5.11	....	....	....	....	....	....	....
1990-91	Ohio State	CCHA	*39	11	24	3	*2180	184	0	5.06	....	....	....	....	....	....	....
1991-92	Ohio State	CCHA	36	11	20	5	2060	180	0	5.24	....	....	....	....	....	....	....

BARRASSO, TOM (buh-RAH-soh)

Goaltender. Catches right. 6'3", 211 lbs. Born, Boston, MA, March 31, 1965.
(Buffalo's 1st choice, 5th overall, in 1983 Entry Draft).

			Regular Season								Playoffs						
Season	Club	Lea	GP	W	L	T	Mins	GA	SO	Avg	GP	W	L	Mins	GA	SO	Avg
1982-83	Acton-Boxboro	HS	23	....	....	....	1035	17	10	0.73	....	....	....	....	....	....	....
1983-84																	
abcd	**Buffalo**	**NHL**	**42**	**26**	**12**	**3**	**2475**	**117**	**2**	**2.84**	**3**	**0**	**2**	**139**	**8**	**0**	**3.45**
1984-85ef	**Buffalo**	**NHL**	**54**	**25**	**18**	**10**	**3248**	**144**	***5**	***2.66**	**5**	**2**	**3**	**300**	**22**	**0**	**4.40**
	Rochester	AHL	5	3	1	1	267	6	1	1.35	....	....	....	....	....	....	....
1985-86	**Buffalo**	**NHL**	**60**	**29**	**24**	**5**	**3561**	**214**	**2**	**3.61**	....	....	....	....	....	....	....
1986-87	**Buffalo**	**NHL**	**46**	**17**	**23**	**2**	**2501**	**152**	**2**	**3.65**	....	....	....	....	....	....	....
1987-88	**Buffalo**	**NHL**	**54**	**25**	**18**	**8**	**3133**	**173**	**2**	**3.31**	**4**	**1**	**3**	**224**	**16**	**0**	**4.29**
1988-89	**Buffalo**	**NHL**	**10**	**2**	**7**	**0**	**545**	**45**	**0**	**4.95**	....	....	....	....	....	....	....
	Pittsburgh	**NHL**	**44**	**18**	**15**	**7**	**2406**	**162**	**0**	**4.04**	**11**	**7**	**4**	**631**	**40**	**0**	**3.80**
1989-90	**Pittsburgh**	**NHL**	**24**	**7**	**12**	**3**	**1294**	**101**	**0**	**4.68**	....	....	....	....	....	....	....
1990-91	**Pittsburgh**	**NHL**	**48**	**27**	**16**	**3**	**2754**	**165**	**1**	**3.59**	**20**	**12**	**7**	**1175**	**51**	***1**	***2.60**
1991-92	**Pittsburgh**	**NHL**	**57**	**25**	**22**	**9**	**3329**	**196**	**1**	**3.53**	***21**	***16**	**5**	***1233**	**58**	**1**	**2.82**
	NHL Totals		**439**	**201**	**167**	**50**	**25246**	**1469**	**15**	**3.49**	**64**	**38**	**24**	**3702**	**195**	**2**	**3.16**

a NHL First All-Star Team (1984)
b Won Vezina Trophy (1984)
c Won Calder Memorial Trophy (1984)
d NHL All-Rookie Team (1984)
e NHL Second All-Star Team (1985)
f Shared William Jennings Trophy with Bob Sauve (1985)

Played in NHL All-Star Game (1985)

Traded to **Pittsburgh** by **Buffalo** with Buffalo's third round choice (Joe Dziedzic) in 1990 Entry Draft for Doug Bodger and Darrin Shannon, November 12, 1988.

BEAUPRE, DONALD WILLIAM (DON) (boh-PRAY)

Goaltender. Catches left. 5'10", 172 lbs. Born, Waterloo, Ont., September 19, 1961.
(Minnesota's 2nd choice, 32nd overall, in 1980 Entry Draft).

			Regular Season								Playoffs						
Season	Club	Lea	GP	W	L	T	Mins	GA	SO	Avg	GP	W	L	Mins	GA	SO	Avg
1978-79	Sudbury	OHA	54	....	....	....	3248	260	2	4.78	10	....	....	600	44	0	4.20
1979-80a	Sudbury	OHA	59	28	29	2	3447	248	0	4.32	9	5	4	552	38	0	4.13
1980-81	**Minnesota**	**NHL**	**44**	**18**	**14**	**11**	**2585**	**138**	**0**	**3.20**	**6**	**4**	**2**	**360**	**26**	**0**	**4.33**
1981-82	**Minnesota**	**NHL**	**29**	**11**	**8**	**9**	**1634**	**101**	**0**	**3.71**	**2**	**0**	**1**	**60**	**4**	**0**	**4.00**
	Nashville	CHL	5	2	3	0	299	25	0	5.02	....	....	....	....	....	....	....
1982-83	**Minnesota**	**NHL**	**36**	**19**	**10**	**5**	**2011**	**120**	**0**	**3.58**	**4**	**2**	**2**	**245**	**20**	**0**	**4.90**
	Birmingham	CHL	10	8	2	0	599	31	0	3.11	....	....	....	....	....	....	....
1983-84	**Minnesota**	**NHL**	**33**	**16**	**13**	**2**	**1791**	**123**	**0**	**4.12**	**13**	**6**	**7**	**782**	**40**	**1**	**3.07**
	Salt Lake	CHL	7	2	5	0	419	30	0	4.30	....	....	....	....	....	....	....
1984-85	**Minnesota**	**NHL**	**31**	**10**	**17**	**3**	**1770**	**109**	**1**	**3.69**	**4**	**1**	**1**	**184**	**12**	**0**	**3.91**
1985-86	**Minnesota**	**NHL**	**52**	**25**	**20**	**6**	**3073**	**182**	**1**	**3.55**	**5**	**2**	**3**	**300**	**17**	**0**	**3.40**
1986-87	**Minnesota**	**NHL**	**47**	**17**	**20**	**6**	**2622**	**174**	**1**	**3.98**	....	....	....	....	....	....	....
1987-88	**Minnesota**	**NHL**	**43**	**10**	**22**	**3**	**2288**	**161**	**0**	**4.22**	....	....	....	....	....	....	....
1988-89	**Minnesota**	**NHL**	**1**	**0**	**1**	**0**	**59**	**3**	**0**	**3.05**	....	....	....	....	....	....	....
	Kalamazoo	IHL	3	1	2	0	179	9	1	3.02	....	....	....	....	....	....	....
	Washington	**NHL**	**11**	**5**	**4**	**0**	**578**	**28**	**1**	**2.91**	....	....	....	....	....	....	....
	Baltimore	AHL	30	14	12	2	1715	102	0	3.57	....	....	....	....	....	....	....
1989-90	**Washington**	**NHL**	**48**	**23**	**18**	**5**	**2793**	**150**	**2**	**3.22**	**8**	**4**	**3**	**401**	**18**	**0**	**2.69**
1990-91	**Washington**	**NHL**	**45**	**20**	**18**	**3**	**2572**	**113**	***5**	**2.64**	**11**	**5**	**5**	**624**	**29**	***1**	**2.79**
	Baltimore	AHL	2	2	0	0	120	3	0	1.50	....	....	....	....	....	....	....
1991-92	**Washington**	**NHL**	**54**	**29**	**17**	**6**	**3108**	**166**	**1**	**3.20**	**7**	**3**	**4**	**419**	**22**	**0**	**3.15**
	Baltimore	AHL	3	1	1	1	184	10	0	3.26	....	....	....	....	....	....	....
	NHL Totals		**474**	**203**	**182**	**59**	**26884**	**1568**	**12**	**3.50**	**60**	**27**	**27**	**3375**	**188**	**2**	**3.34**

a OHA First All-Star Team (1980)

Played in NHL All-Star Game (1981, 1992)

Traded to **Washington** by **Minnesota** for rights to Claudio Scremin, November 1, 1988.

BEAUREGARD, STEPHANE

Goaltender. Catches right. 5'11", 188 lbs. Born, Cowansville, Que., January 10, 1968.
(Winnipeg's 3rd choice, 52nd overall, in 1988 Entry Draft).

			Regular Season								Playoffs						
Season	Club	Lea	GP	W	L	T	Mins	GA	SO	Avg	GP	W	L	Mins	GA	SO	Avg
1986-87	St-Jean	QMJHL	13	6	7	0	785	58	0	4.43	5	1	3	260	26	0	6.00
1987-88ab	St-Jean	QMJHL	66	38	20	3	3766	229	2	3.65	7	3	4	423	34	0	4.82
1988-89	Moncton	AHL	15	4	8	2	824	62	0	4.51	....	....	....	....	....	....	....
	Fort Wayne	IHL	16	9	5	0	830	43	0	3.10	9	4	4	484	21	*1	*2.60
1989-90	**Winnipeg**	**NHL**	**19**	**7**	**8**	**3**	**1079**	**59**	**0**	**3.28**	**4**	**1**	**3**	**238**	**12**	**0**	**3.03**
	Fort Wayne	IHL	33	20	8	3	1949	115	0	3.54	....	....	....	....	....	....	....
1990-91	**Winnipeg**	**NHL**	**16**	**3**	**10**	**1**	**836**	**55**	**0**	**3.95**	....	....	....	....	....	....	....
	Moncton	AHL	9	3	4	1	504	20	1	2.38	1	1	0	60	1	0	1.00
	Fort Wayne	IHL	32	14	13	2	1761	109	0	3.71	*19	*10	9	*1158	57	0	2.95
1991-92	**Winnipeg**	**NHL**	**26**	**6**	**8**	**6**	**1267**	**61**	**2**	**2.89**	....	....	....	....	....	....	....
	NHL Totals		**61**	**16**	**26**	**10**	**3182**	**175**	**2**	**3.30**	**4**	**1**	**3**	**238**	**12**	**0**	**3.03**

a QMJHL First All-Star Team (1988)
b QMJHL and Canadian Major Junior Goaltender of the year (1988)

Traded to **Buffalo** by **Winnipeg** for Christian Ruuttu and future considerations, June 15, 1992. Traded to **Chicago** by **Buffalo** for Dominik Hasek and future considerations, August 7, 1992. Traded to **Winnipeg** by **Chicago** for Christian Ruuttu, August 10, 1992.

BELFOUR, ED

Goaltender. Catches left. 5'11", 182 lbs. Born, Carman, Man., April 21, 1965.

			Regular Season								Playoffs						
Season	Club	Lea	GP	W	L	T	Mins	GA	SO	Avg	GP	W	L	Mins	GA	SO	Avg
1986-87a	North Dakota	WCHA	34	29	4	0	2049	81	3	2.43	....	....	....	....	....	....	....
1987-88bc	Saginaw	IHL	61	32	25	0	*3446	183	3	3.19	9	4	5	561	33	0	3.53
1988-89	**Chicago**	**NHL**	**23**	**4**	**12**	**3**	**1148**	**74**	**0**	**3.87**	....	....	....	....	....	....	....
	Saginaw	IHL	29	12	10	0	1760	92	0	3.10	5	2	3	298	14	0	2.82
1989-90	Cdn. National	....	33	13	12	6	1808	93	0	3.08	....	....	....	....	....	....	....
	Chicago	**NHL**	....	....	....	....	....	....	....	....	**9**	**4**	**2**	**409**	**17**	**0**	**2.49**
1990-91																	
defghi	**Chicago**	**NHL**	***74**	***43**	**19**	**7**	***4127**	**170**	**4**	***2.47**	**6**	**2**	**4**	**295**	**20**	**0**	**4.07**
1991-92	**Chicago**	**NHL**	**52**	**21**	**18**	**10**	**2928**	**132**	***5**	**2.70**	**18**	**12**	**4**	**949**	**39**	**1**	***2.47**
	NHL Totals		**149**	**68**	**49**	**20**	**8203**	**376**	**9**	**2.75**	**33**	**18**	**10**	**1653**	**76**	**1**	**2.76**

a WCHA First All-Star Team (1987)
b IHL First All-Star Team (1988)
c Shared Garry F. Longman Memorial Trophy (Top Rookie - IHL) (1988)
d NHL First All-Star Team (1991)
e Won Vezina Trophy (1991)
f Won Calder Memorial Trophy (1991)
g Won William M. Jennings Trophy (1991)
h Won Trico Goaltender Award (1991)
i NHL/Upper Deck All-Rookie Team (1991)

Played in NHL All-Star Game (1992)

Signed as a free agent by **Chicago**, September 25, 1987.

BELLEY, ROCH

Goaltender. Catches left. 5'10", 170 lbs. Born, Hull, Que., August 12, 1971.
(Chicago's 8th choice, 176th overall, in 1991 Entry Draft).

			Regular Season								Playoffs						
Season	Club	Lea	GP	W	L	T	Mins	GA	SO	Avg	GP	W	L	Mins	GA	SO	Avg
1990-91	Niagara Falls	OHL	45	26	8	7	2499	151	1	3.68	14	7	5	743	49	....	3.96
1991-92	Indianapolis	IHL	25	4	12	3	1270	88	0	4.16	....	....	....	....	....	....	....

BERGERON, JEAN-CLAUDE

Goaltender. Catches left. 6'2", 192 lbs. Born, Hauterive, Que., October 14, 1968.
(Montreal's 6th choice, 104th overall, in 1988 Entry Draft).

			Regular Season								Playoffs						
Season	Club	Lea	GP	W	L	T	Mins	GA	SO	Avg	GP	W	L	Mins	GA	SO	Avg
1987-88	Verdun	QMJHL	49	13	31	3	2715	265	0	5.86	....	....	....	....	....	....	....
1988-89	Verdun	QMJHL	44	8	34	1	2417	199	0	4.94	....	....	....	....	....	....	....
	Sherbrooke	AHL	5	4	1	0	302	18	0	3.58	....	....	....	....	....	....	....
1989-90abc	Sherbrooke	AHL	40	21	8	7	2254	103	2	*2.74	9	6	2	497	28	0	3.38
1990-91	**Montreal**	**NHL**	**18**	**7**	**6**	**2**	**941**	**59**	**0**	**3.76**	....	....	....	....	....	....	....
	Fredericton	AHL	18	12	6	0	1083	59	1	3.27	10	5	5	546	32	0	3.52
1991-92	Fredericton	AHL	13	5	7	1	791	57	0	4.32	....	....	....	....	....	....	....
	Peoria	IHL	27	14	9	3	1632	96	1	3.53	6	3	3	352	24	0	4.09
	NHL Totals		**18**	**7**	**6**	**2**	**941**	**59**	**0**	**3.76**	....	....	....	....	....	....	....

a AHL First All-Star Team (1990)
b Shared Harry "Hap" Holmes Trophy (fewest goals-against-AHL) with Andre Racicot (1990)
c Won Baz Bastien Award (Top Goaltender-AHL) (1990)

Traded to **Tampa Bay** by **Montreal** for Frederic Chabot, June 19, 1992.

BERTHIAUME, DANIEL (bair-TYOHM)

Goaltender. Catches left. 5'9", 150 lbs. Born, Longueuil, Que., January 26, 1966.
(Winnipeg's 3rd choice, 60th overall, in 1985 Entry Draft).

			Regular Season								Playoffs						
Season	Club	Lea	GP	W	L	T	Mins	GA	SO	Avg	GP	W	L	Mins	GA	SO	Avg
1984-85	Chicoutimi	QMJHL	59	40	11	2	2177	149	0	4.11	14	8	6	770	51	0	3.97
1985-86	Chicoutimi	QMJHL	66	34	29	3	3718	286	1	4.62	9	4	5	580	36	0	3.72
	Winnipeg	**NHL**	....	....	....	....	....	....	....	....	**1**	**0**	**1**	**68**	**4**	**0**	**3.53**
1986-87	**Winnipeg**	**NHL**	**31**	**18**	**7**	**3**	**1758**	**93**	**1**	**3.17**	**8**	**4**	**4**	**439**	**21**	**0**	**2.87**
	Sherbrooke	AHL	7	4	3	0	420	23	0	3.29	....	....	....	....	....	....	....
1987-88	**Winnipeg**	**NHL**	**56**	**22**	**19**	**7**	**3010**	**176**	**2**	**3.51**	**5**	**1**	**4**	**300**	**25**	**0**	**5.00**
1988-89	**Winnipeg**	**NHL**	**9**	**0**	**8**	**0**	**443**	**44**	**0**	**5.96**	....	....	....	....	....	....	....
	Moncton	AHL	21	6	9	2	1083	76	0	4.21	3	1	2	180	11	0	3.67
1989-90	**Winnipeg**	**NHL**	**24**	**10**	**11**	**3**	**1387**	**86**	**1**	**3.72**	....	....	....	....	....	....	....
	Minnesota	**NHL**	**5**	**1**	**3**	**0**	**240**	**14**	**0**	**3.50**	....	....	....	....	....	....	....
1990-91	**Los Angeles**	**NHL**	**37**	**20**	**11**	**4**	**2119**	**117**	**1**	**3.31**	....	....	....	....	....	....	....
1991-92	**Los Angeles**	**NHL**	**19**	**7**	**10**	**1**	**979**	**66**	**0**	**4.04**	....	....	....	....	....	....	....
	Boston	**NHL**	**8**	**1**	**4**	**2**	**399**	**21**	**0**	**3.16**	....	....	....	....	....	....	....
	NHL Totals		**189**	**79**	**73**	**20**	**10335**	**617**	**5**	**3.58**	**14**	**5**	**9**	**807**	**50**	**0**	**3.72**

Traded to **Minnesota** by **Winnipeg** for future considerations, January 22, 1990. Traded to **Los Angeles** by **Minnesota** for Craig Duncanson, September 6, 1990. Traded to **Boston** by **Los Angeles** for future considerations, January 18, 1992. Traded to **Winnipeg** by **Boston** for Doug Evans, June 10, 1992.

BESTER, ALLAN J.

Goaltender. Catches left. 5'7", 155 lbs. Born, Hamilton, Ont., March 26, 1964.
(Toronto's 3rd choice, 48th overall, in 1983 Entry Draft).

			Regular Season								Playoffs						
Season	Club	Lea	GP	W	L	T	Mins	GA	SO	Avg	GP	W	L	Mins	GA	SO	Avg
1981-82	Brantford	OHL	19	4	11	0	970	68	0	4.21	....	....	....	....	....	....	....
1982-83a	Brantford	OHL	56	29	21	3	3210	188	0	3.51	8	3	3	480	20	*1	*2.50
1983-84	**Toronto**	**NHL**	**32**	**11**	**16**	**4**	**1848**	**134**	**0**	**4.35**	....	....	....	....	....	....	....
	Brantford	OHL	23	12	9	1	1271	71	1	3.35	1	0	1	60	5	0	5.00
1984-85	**Toronto**	**NHL**	**15**	**3**	**9**	**1**	**767**	**54**	**1**	**4.22**	....	....	....	....	....	....	....
	St. Catharines	AHL	30	9	18	1	1669	133	0	4.78	....	....	....	....	....	....	....
1985-86	**Toronto**	**NHL**	**1**	**0**	**0**	**0**	**20**	**2**	**0**	**6.00**	....	....	....	....	....	....	....
	St. Catharines	AHL	50	23	23	3	2855	173	1	3.64	11	7	3	637	27	0	2.54
1986-87	**Toronto**	**NHL**	**36**	**10**	**14**	**3**	**1808**	**110**	**2**	**3.65**	**1**	**0**	**0**	**39**	**1**	**0**	**1.54**
	Newmarket	AHL	3	1	0	0	190	6	0	1.89	....	....	....	....	....	....	....
1987-88	**Toronto**	**NHL**	**30**	**8**	**12**	**5**	**1607**	**102**	**2**	**3.81**	**5**	**2**	**3**	**253**	**21**	**0**	**4.98**
1988-89	**Toronto**	**NHL**	**43**	**17**	**20**	**3**	**2460**	**156**	**2**	**3.80**	....	....	....	....	....	....	....
1989-90	**Toronto**	**NHL**	**42**	**20**	**16**	**0**	**2206**	**165**	**0**	**4.49**	**4**	**0**	**3**	**196**	**14**	**0**	**4.29**
	Newmarket	AHL	5	2	1	1	264	18	0	4.09	....	....	....	....	....	....	....
1990-91	**Toronto**	**NHL**	**6**	**0**	**4**	**0**	**247**	**18**	**0**	**4.37**	....	....	....	....	....	....	....
	Newmarket	AHL	19	7	8	4	1157	58	1	3.01	....	....	....	....	....	....	....
	Detroit	**NHL**	**3**	**0**	**3**	**0**	**178**	**13**	**0**	**4.38**	**1**	**0**	**0**	**20**	**1**	**0**	**3.00**
1991-92	**Detroit**	**NHL**	**1**	**0**	**0**	**0**	**31**	**2**	**0**	**3.87**	....	....	....	....	....	....	....
b	Adirondack	AHL	22	13	8	0	1268	78	0	3.69	*19	*14	5	1174	50	*1	*2.56
	NHL Totals		**209**	**69**	**94**	**16**	**11172**	**756**	**7**	**4.06**	**11**	**2**	**6**	**508**	**37**	**0**	**4.37**

a OHL First All-Star Team (1983)
b Won Jack Butterfield Trophy (Playoff MVP-AHL) (1992)

Traded to **Detroit** by **Toronto** for Detroit's sixth round choice (Alexander Kuzminsky) in 1991 Entry Draft, March 5, 1991.

BILLINGTON, CRAIG

Goaltender. Catches left. 5'10", 170 lbs. Born, London, Ont., September 11, 1966.
(New Jersey's 2nd choice, 23rd overall, in 1984 Entry Draft).

			Regular Season								Playoffs						
Season	Club	Lea	GP	W	L	T	Mins	GA	SO	Avg	GP	W	L	Mins	GA	SO	Avg
1983-84	Belleville	OHL	44	20	19	0	2335	162	1	4.16	1	0	0	30	3	0	6.00
1984-85a	Belleville	OHL	47	26	19	0	2544	180	1	4.25	14	7	5	761	47	1	3.71
1985-86	**New Jersey**	**NHL**	**18**	**4**	**9**	**1**	**901**	**77**	**0**	**5.13**	....	....	....	....	....	....	....
	Belleville	OHL	3	2	1	0	180	11	0	3.67	20	9	6	1133	68	0	3.60
1986-87	**New Jersey**	**NHL**	**22**	**4**	**13**	**2**	**1114**	**89**	**0**	**4.79**	....	....	....	....	....	....	....
	Maine	AHL	20	9	8	2	1151	70	0	3.65	....	....	....	....	....	....	....
1987-88	Utica	AHL	*59	22	27	8	*3404	208	1	3.67	....	....	....	....	....	....	....
1988-89	**New Jersey**	**NHL**	**3**	**1**	**1**	**0**	**140**	**11**	**0**	**4.71**	....	....	....	....	....	....	....
	Utica	AHL	41	17	18	6	2432	150	2	3.70	4	1	3	220	18	0	4.91
1989-90	Utica	AHL	38	20	13	1	2087	138	0	3.97	....	....	....	....	....	....	....
1990-91	Cdn. National	....	34	17	14	2	1879	110	2	3.51	....	....	....	....	....	....	....
1991-92	**New Jersey**	**NHL**	**26**	**13**	**7**	**1**	**1363**	**69**	**2**	**3.04**	....	....	....	....	....	....	....
	NHL Totals		**69**	**22**	**30**	**4**	**3518**	**246**	**2**	**4.20**	....	....	....	....	....	....	....

a OHL First All-Star Team (1985)

BLUE, JOHN

Goaltender. Catches left. 5'10", 190 lbs. Born, Huntington Beach, CA, February 19, 1966.
(Winnipeg's 9th choice, 197th overall, in 1986 Entry Draft).

			Regular Season								Playoffs						
Season	Club	Lea	GP	W	L	T	Mins	GA	SO	Avg	GP	W	L	Mins	GA	SO	Avg
1984-85	U. Minnesota	WCHA	34	23	10	0	1964	111	2	3.39	....	....	....	....	....	....	....
1985-86a	U. Minnesota	WCHA	29	20	6	0	1588	80	2	3.02	....	....	....	....	....	....	....
1986-87	U. Minnesota	WCHA	33	21	9	1	1889	99	3	3.14	....	....	....	....	....	....	....
1987-88	Kalamazoo	IHL	15	3	8	4	847	65	0	4.60	1	0	1	40	6	0	9.00
	U.S. National	....	13	3	4	1	588	33	0	3.37	....	....	....	....	....	....	....
1988-89	Kalamazoo	IHL	17	8	6	0	970	69	0	4.27	....	....	....	....	....	....	....
	Virginia	ECHL	10	....	....	....	570	38	0	4.00	....	....	....	....	....	....	....
1989-90	Phoenix	IHL	19	5	10	3	986	92	0	5.65	....	....	....	....	....	....	....
	Knoxville	ECHL	19	6	10	1	1000	85	0	5.15	....	....	....	....	....	....	....
	Kalamazoo	IHL	4	2	1	1	232	18	0	4.65	....	....	....	....	....	....	....
1990-91	Maine	AHL	10	3	4	2	545	22	0	2.42	1	0	1	40	7	0	10.50
	Albany	IHL	19	11	6	0	1077	71	0	3.96	....	....	....	....	....	....	....
	Kalamazoo	IHL	1	1	0	0	64	2	0	1.88	....	....	....	....	....	....	....
	Peoria	IHL	4	4	0	0	240	12	0	3.00	....	....	....	....	....	....	....
	Knoxville	ECHL	3	1	1	0	149	13	0	5.23	....	....	....	....	....	....	....
1991-92	Maine	AHL	43	11	23	6	2168	165	1	4.57	....	....	....	....	....	....	....

a WCHA First All-Star Team (1986)

Traded to **Minnesota** by **Winnipeg** for Winnipeg's seventh round choice in 1988 Entry Draft (Markus Akerblom), March 7, 1988. Signed as a free agent by **Boston**, August 1, 1991.

BRADLEY, JOHN

Goaltender. Catches left. 6', 165 lbs. Born, Pawtucket, RI, February 6, 1968.
(Buffalo's 4th choice, 84th overall, in 1987 Entry Draft).

			Regular Season								Playoffs						
Season	Club	Lea	GP	W	L	T	Mins	GA	SO	Avg	GP	W	L	Mins	GA	SO	Avg
1987-88	Boston U.	H.E.	9	4	4	0	528	40	0	4.53	....	....	....	....	....	....	....
1988-89	Boston U.	H.E.	11	5	4	1	584	53	0	5.45	....	....	....	....	....	....	....
1989-90	Boston U.	H.E.	7	2	3	1	377	20	1	3.18	....	....	....	....	....	....	....
1990-91	Boston U.	H.E.	20	14	4	1	1177	62	*3	3.16	....	....	....	....	....	....	....
1991-92	Rochester	AHL	6	2	2	1	248	13	1	3.15	1	0	0	20	2	0	6.00
	Erie	ECHL	15	6	4	2	810	59	0	4.37	....	....	....	....	....	....	....

BRODEUR, MARTIN

Goaltender. Catches left. 6'1", 190 lbs. Born, Montreal, Que., May 6, 1972.
(New Jersey's 1st choice, 20th overall, in 1990 Entry Draft).

			Regular Season								Playoffs						
Season	Club	Lea	GP	W	L	T	Mins	GA	SO	Avg	GP	W	L	Mins	GA	SO	Avg
1989-90	St-Hyacinthe	QMJHL	42	23	13	2	2333	156	0	4.01	12	5	7	678	46	0	4.07
1990-91	St-Hyacinthe	QMJHL	52	22	24	4	2946	162	2	3.30	4	0	4	232	16	0	4.14
1991-92	**New Jersey**	**NHL**	**4**	**2**	**1**	**0**	**179**	**10**	**0**	**3.35**	**1**	**0**	**1**	**32**	**3**	**0**	**5.63**
a	St-Hyacinthe	QMJHL	48	27	16	4	2846	161	2	3.39	5	2	3	317	14	0	2.65
	NHL Totals		**4**	**2**	**1**	**0**	**179**	**10**	**0**	**3.35**	**1**	**0**	**1**	**32**	**3**	**0**	**5.63**

a QMJHL Second All-Star Team (1992)

BROWN, CRAIG

Goaltender. Catches left. 5'11", 170 lbs. Born, Scarborough, Ont., February 29, 1972.
(Los Angeles' 9th choice, 196th overall, in 1991 Entry Draft).

			Regular Season								Playoffs						
Season	Club	Lea	GP	W	L	T	Mins	GA	SO	Avg	GP	W	L	Mins	GA	SO	Avg
1990-91	W. Michigan	CCHA	33	17	13	2	1898	111	0	3.51	....	....	....	....	....	....	....
1991-92	W. Michigan	CCHA	28	13	10	5	1668	89	0	3.20	....	....	....	....	....	....	....

BRUNETTA, MARIO

Goaltender. Catches left. 6'3", 180 lbs. Born, Quebec City, Que., January 25, 1967.
(Quebec's 9th choice, 162nd overall, in 1985 Entry Draft).

			Regular Season								Playoffs						
Season	Club	Lea	GP	W	L	T	Mins	GA	SO	Avg	GP	W	L	Mins	GA	SO	Avg
1984-85	Quebec	QMJHL	45	20	21	1	2255	192	0	5.11	2	0	2	120	13	0	6.50
1985-86	Laval	QMJHL	63	30	25	1	3383	279	0	4.95	14	9	5	834	60	0	4.32
1986-87	Laval	QMJHL	59	27	25	4	3469	261	1	4.51	14	8	6	820	63	0	4.61
1987-88	**Quebec**	**NHL**	**29**	**10**	**12**	**1**	**1550**	**96**	**0**	**3.72**	....	....	....	....	....	....	....
	Fredericton	AHL	5	4	1	0	300	24	0	4.80	....	....	....	....	....	....	....
1988-89	**Quebec**	**NHL**	**5**	**1**	**3**	**0**	**226**	**19**	**0**	**5.04**	....	....	....	....	....	....	....
	Halifax	AHL	36	14	14	5	1898	124	0	3.92	3	0	2	142	12	0	5.07
1989-90	**Quebec**	**NHL**	**6**	**1**	**2**	**0**	**191**	**13**	**0**	**4.08**	....	....	....	....	....	....	....
	Halifax	AHL	24	8	14	2	1444	99	0	4.11	....	....	....	....	....	....	....
1990-91	Asiago	Italy	42	....	....	....	2446	160	3	3.92	....	....	....	....	....	....	....
1991-92	Asiago	Italy	29	....	....	....	1746	116	1	3.98	11	....	....	668	43	1	3.86
	NHL Totals		**40**	**12**	**17**	**1**	**1967**	**128**	**0**	**3.90**	....	....	....	....	....	....	....

BURKE, SEAN

Goaltender. Catches left. 6'4", 210 lbs. Born, Windsor, Ont., January 29, 1967.
(New Jersey's 2nd choice, 24th overall, in 1985 Entry Draft).

			Regular Season								Playoffs						
Season	Club	Lea	GP	W	L	T	Mins	GA	SO	Avg	GP	W	L	Mins	GA	SO	Avg
1984-85	Toronto	OHL	49	25	21	3	2987	211	0	4.24	5	1	3	266	25	0	5.64
1985-86	Toronto	OHL	47	16	27	3	2840	233	0	4.92	4	0	4	238	24	0	6.05
1986-87	Cdn. National	....	42	27	13	2	2550	130	0	3.05	....	....	....	....	....	....	....
1987-88	Cdn. National	....	37	19	9	2	1962	92	1	2.81	....	....	....	....	....	....	....
	Cdn. Olympic	....	4	1	2	1	238	12	0	3.02	....	....	....	....	....	....	....
	New Jersey	**NHL**	**13**	**10**	**1**	**0**	**689**	**35**	**1**	**3.05**	**17**	**9**	**8**	**1001**	**57**	***1**	**3.42**
1988-89	**New Jersey**	**NHL**	**62**	**22**	**31**	**9**	**3590**	**230**	**3**	**3.84**	....	....	....	....	....	....	....
1989-90	**New Jersey**	**NHL**	**52**	**22**	**22**	**6**	**2914**	**175**	**0**	**3.60**	**2**	**0**	**2**	**125**	**8**	**0**	**3.84**
1990-91	**New Jersey**	**NHL**	**35**	**8**	**12**	**8**	**1870**	**112**	**0**	**3.59**	....	....	....	....	....	....	....
1991-92	Cdn. National	....	31	18	6	4	1721	75	1	2.61	....	....	....	....	....	....	....
	Cdn. Olympic	....	7	....	....	....	429	17	0	2.37	....	....	....	....	....	....	....
	San Diego	IHL	7	4	2	1	424	17	0	2.41	3	0	3	160	13	0	4.88
	NHL Totals		**162**	**62**	**66**	**23**	**9063**	**552**	**4**	**3.65**	**19**	**9**	**10**	**1126**	**65**	**1**	**3.46**

Played in NHL All-Star Game (1989)

BUTLER, JEROME

Goaltender. Catches left. 5'11", 155 lbs. Born, Roseau, MN, December 14, 1972.
(Calgary's 6th choice, 107th overall, in 1991 Entry Draft).

			Regular Season								Playoffs						
Season	Club	Lea	GP	W	L	T	Mins	GA	SO	Avg	GP	W	L	Mins	GA	SO	Avg
1990-91	Roseau	HS	18	14	4	0	....	....	....	1.96	....	....	....	....	....	....	....
1991-92	Minn.-Duluth	WCHA	22	9	11	2	1325	91	0	4.12	....	....	....	....	....	....	....

CALLINAN, JEFF

Goaltender. Catches left. 5'10", 169 lbs. Born, Minneapolis, MN, January 6, 1973.
(St. Louis' 5th choice, 109th overall, in 1991 Entry Draft).

			Regular Season								Playoffs						
Season	Club	Lea	GP	W	L	T	Mins	GA	SO	Avg	GP	W	L	Mins	GA	SO	Avg
1990-91	Minnetonka	HS	20	....	....	....	900	62	2	3.10	....	....	....	....	....	....	....
1991-92	U. Minnesota	WCHA	6	2	1	0	209	15	0	4.32	....	....	....	....	....	....	....

CAPPRINI, JOSEPH

Goaltender. Catches left. 5'10", 165 lbs. Born, Pingree, MA, February 26, 1968.
(NY Islanders' 14th choice, 247th overall, in 1988 Entry Draft).

			Regular Season								Playoffs						
Season	Club	Lea	GP	W	L	T	Mins	GA	SO	Avg	GP	W	L	Mins	GA	SO	Avg
1987-88	Babson	NCAA	21	14	5	0	1260	53	0	2.76	....	....	....	....	....	....	....
1988-89	Babson	NCAA	28	17	10	1	1680	71	0	2.60	....	....	....	....	....	....	....
1989-90	Babson	NCAA	19	11	2	5	1140	41	0	2.27	....	....	....	....	....	....	....
1990-91	Babson	NCAA	24	15	6	0	1440	55	0	2.58	....	....	....	....	....	....	....
1991-92	Capital Dist.	AHL	2	0	0	1	77	5	0	3.90	....	....	....	....	....	....	....
	Richmond	ECHL	4	2	1	0	195	15	0	4.62	....	....	....	....	....	....	....

CAREY, JIM

Goaltender. Catches left. 6'2", 190 lbs. Born, Dorchester, MA, May 31, 1974.
(Washington's 2nd choice, 32nd overall, in 1992 Entry Draft).

			Regular Season								Playoffs						
Season	Club	Lea	GP	W	L	T	Mins	GA	SO	Avg	GP	W	L	Mins	GA	SO	Avg
1990-91	Catholic Mem.	HS	12	....	....	....	180	20	....	1.66	....	....	....	....	....	....	....
1991-92	Catholic Mem.	HS	16	....	....	....	240	27	....	1.67	....	....	....	....	....	....	....

CASEY, DENIS

Goaltender. Catches left. 5'10", 180 lbs. Born, Kelowna, B.C., March 5, 1971.
(Pittsburgh's 6th choice, 110th overall, in 1990 Entry Draft).

			Regular Season								Playoffs						
Season	Club	Lea	GP	W	L	T	Mins	GA	SO	Avg	GP	W	L	Mins	GA	SO	Avg
1989-90	Colorado	WCHA	19	7	9	1	1059	75	1	4.15	....	....	....	....	....	....	....
1990-91	Colorado	WCHA	11	3	7	0	607	43	0	4.25	....	....	....	....	....	....	....
1991-92	Colorado	WCHA	12	6	4	1	664	44	0	3.97	....	....	....	....	....	....	....

CASEY, JON

Goaltender. Catches left. 5'10", 155 lbs. Born, Grand Rapids, MN, March 29, 1962.

			Regular Season								Playoffs						
Season	Club	Lea	GP	W	L	T	Mins	GA	SO	Avg	GP	W	L	Mins	GA	SO	Avg
1980-81	North Dakota	WCHA	5	3	1	0	300	19	0	3.80	....	....	....	....	....	....	....
1981-82	North Dakota	WCHA	18	15	3	0	1038	48	1	2.77	....	....	....	....	....	....	....
1982-83	North Dakota	WCHA	17	9	6	2	1020	42	0	2.51	....	....	....	....	....	....	....
1983-84	North Dakota	WCHA	37	25	10	2	2180	115	2	3.13	....	....	....	....	....	....	....
	Minnesota	**NHL**	**2**	**1**	**0**	**0**	**84**	**6**	**0**	**4.29**	....	....	....	....	....	....	....
1984-85ab	Baltimore	AHL	46	30	11	4	2646	116	*4	*2.63	*13	8	3	689	38	0	3.31
1985-86	**Minnesota**	**NHL**	**26**	**11**	**11**	**1**	**1402**	**91**	**0**	**3.89**	....	....	....	....	....	....	....
	Springfield	AHL	9	4	3	1	464	30	0	3.88	....	....	....	....	....	....	....
1986-87	Springfield	AHL	13	1	8	0	770	56	0	4.36	....	....	....	....	....	....	....
	Indianapolis	IHL	31	14	15	0	1794	133	0	4.45	....	....	....	....	....	....	....
1987-88	**Minnesota**	**NHL**	**14**	**1**	**7**	**4**	**663**	**41**	**0**	**3.71**	....	....	....	....	....	....	....
	Kalamazoo	IHL	42	24	13	5	2541	154	2	3.64	7	3	3	382	26	0	4.08
1988-89	**Minnesota**	**NHL**	**55**	**18**	**17**	**12**	**2961**	**151**	**1**	**3.06**	**4**	**1**	**3**	**211**	**16**	**0**	**4.55**
1989-90	**Minnesota**	**NHL**	**61**	***31**	**22**	**4**	**3407**	**183**	**3**	**3.22**	**7**	**3**	**4**	**415**	**21**	**1**	**3.04**
1990-91	**Minnesota**	**NHL**	**55**	**21**	**20**	**11**	**3185**	**158**	**3**	**2.98**	***23**	***14**	**7**	***1205**	**61**	***1**	**3.04**
1991-92	**Minnesota**	**NHL**	**52**	**19**	**23**	**5**	**2911**	**165**	**2**	**3.40**	**7**	**3**	**4**	**437**	**22**	**0**	**3.02**
	NHL Totals		**265**	**102**	**100**	**37**	**14613**	**795**	**9**	**3.26**	**41**	**21**	**18**	**2268**	**120**	**2**	**3.17**

a Won Baz Bastien Trophy (AHL Most Valuable Goaltender) (1985)
b AHL First All-Star Team (1985)

Signed as a free agent by **Minnesota**, April 1, 1984.

CASHMAN, SCOTT

Goaltender. Catches left. 6'2", 186 lbs. Born, Ottawa, Ont., September 20, 1969.
(Minnesota's 8th choice, 112th overall, in 1989 Entry Draft).

			Regular Season								Playoffs						
Season	Club	Lea	GP	W	L	T	Mins	GA	SO	Avg	GP	W	L	Mins	GA	SO	Avg
1989-90ab	Boston U.	H.E.	*39	*23	14	1	*2277	122	*2	3.27	....	....	....	....	....	....	....
1990-91	Boston U.	H.E.	22	14	7	1	1307	79	0	3.58	....	....	....	....	....	....	....
1991-92	Boston U.	H.E.	20	12	5	2	1149	73	0	3.81	....	....	....	....	....	....	....

a Hockey East Rookie of the Year (1990)
b Hockey East Second All-Star Team (1990)

Claimed by **San Jose** from **Minnesota** in Dispersal Draft, May 30, 1991.

CHABOT, FREDERIC (shah-BOH)

Goaltender. Catches right. 5'11", 177 lbs. Born, Hebertville-Station, Que., February 12, 1968.
(New Jersey's 10th choice, 192nd overall, in 1986 Entry Draft).

			Regular Season								Playoffs						
Season	Club	Lea	GP	W	L	T	Mins	GA	SO	Avg	GP	W	L	Mins	GA	SO	Avg
1986-87	Drummondville	QMJHL	62	31	29	0	3508	293	1	5.01	8	2	6	481	40	0	4.99
1987-88	Drummondville	QMJHL	58	27	24	4	3276	237	1	4.34	16	10	6	1019	56	*1	*3.30
1988-89a	Prince Albert	WHL	54	21	29	0	2957	202	2	4.10	4	1	1	199	16	0	4.82
1989-90	Sherbrooke	AHL	2	1	1	0	119	8	0	4.03	....	....	....	....	....	....	....
	Fort Wayne	IHL	23	6	13	3	1208	87	1	4.32	....	....	....	....	....	....	....
1990-91	**Montreal**	**NHL**	**3**	**0**	**0**	**1**	**108**	**6**	**0**	**3.33**	....	....	....	....	....	....	....
	Fredericton	AHL	35	9	15	5	1800	122	0	4.07	....	....	....	....	....	....	....
1991-92	Fredericton	AHL	30	17	9	4	1761	79	2	*2.69	7	3	4	457	20	0	2.63
	Winston-Salem	ECHL	24	15	7	2	1449	71	0	*2.94	....	....	....	....	....	....	....
	NHL Totals		**3**	**0**	**0**	**1**	**108**	**6**	**0**	**3.33**	....	....	....	....	....	....	....

a WHL East All-Star Team (1989)

Signed as a free agent by **Montreal**, January 16, 1990. Claimed by **Tampa Bay** from **Montreal** in Expansion Draft, June 18, 1992. Traded to **Montreal** by **Tampa Bay** for J.C. Bergeron, June 19, 1992.

CHEVELDAE, TIM (SHE-vehl-day)

Goaltender. Catches left. 5'10", 175 lbs. Born, Melville, Sask., February 15, 1968.
(Detroit's 4th choice, 64th overall, in 1986 Entry Draft).

			Regular Season								Playoffs						
Season	Club	Lea	GP	W	L	T	Mins	GA	SO	Avg	GP	W	L	Mins	GA	SO	Avg
1985-86	Saskatoon	WHL	36	21	10	3	2030	165	0	4.88	8	6	2	480	29	0	3.63
1986-87	Saskatoon	WHL	33	20	11	0	1909	133	2	4.18	5	4	1	308	20	0	3.90
1987-88a	Saskatoon	WHL	66	44	19	3	3798	235	1	3.71	6	4	2	364	27	0	4.45
1988-89	**Detroit**	**NHL**	**2**	**0**	**2**	**0**	**122**	**9**	**0**	**4.43**	....	....	....	....	....	....	....
	Adirondack	AHL	30	20	8	0	1694	98	1	3.47	2	1	0	99	9	0	5.45
1989-90	**Detroit**	**NHL**	**28**	**10**	**9**	**8**	**1600**	**101**	**0**	**3.79**	....	....	....	....	....	....	....
	Adirondack	AHL	31	17	8	6	1848	116	0	3.77	....	....	....	....	....	....	....
1990-91	**Detroit**	**NHL**	**65**	**30**	**26**	**5**	**3615**	**214**	**2**	**3.55**	**7**	**3**	**4**	**398**	**22**	**0**	**3.32**
1991-92	**Detroit**	**NHL**	***72**	***38**	**23**	**9**	***4236**	**226**	**2**	**3.20**	**11**	**3**	**7**	**597**	**25**	***2**	**2.51**
	NHL Totals		**167**	**78**	**60**	**22**	**9573**	**550**	**4**	**3.45**	**18**	**6**	**11**	**995**	**47**	**2**	**2.83**

a WHL East All-Star Team (1988)

Played in NHL All-Star Game (1992)

CLIFFORD, CHRIS

Goaltender. Catches left. 5'9", 167 lbs. Born, Kingston, Ont., May 26, 1966.
(Chicago's 6th choice, 111th overall, in 1984 Entry Draft).

			Regular Season								Playoffs						
Season	Club	Lea	GP	W	L	T	Mins	GA	SO	Avg	GP	W	L	Mins	GA	SO	Avg
1983-84	Kingston	OHL	50	16	28	0	2808	229	2	4.89	....	....	....	....	....	....	....
1984-85	**Chicago**	**NHL**	**1**	**0**	**0**	**0**	**20**	**0**	**0**	**0.00**	....	....	....	....	....	....	....
	Kingston	OHL	52	15	34	0	2768	241	0	5.22	....	....	....	....	....	....	....
1985-86	Kingston	OHL	50	26	21	3	2988	178	1	3.57	10	5	5	564	31	1	3.30
1986-87	Kingston	OHL	44	18	25	0	2596	191	1	4.41	12	6	6	730	42	0	3.45
1987-88	Saginaw	IHL	22	9	7	2	1146	80	0	4.19	....	....	....	....	....	....	....
1988-89	**Chicago**	**NHL**	**1**	**0**	**0**	**0**	**4**	**0**	**0**	**0.00**	....	....	....	....	....	....	....
	Saginaw	IHL	7	4	2	0	321	23	0	4.30	....	....	....	....	....	....	....
1989-90	Muskegon	IHL	23	17	4	1	1352	77	0	3.42	6	3	3	360	24	0	4.01
	Virginia	ECHL	10	7	1	0	547	16	0	1.75	....	....	....	....	....	....	....
1990-91	Muskegon	IHL	*56	24	26	4	*3247	215	1	3.97	5	1	4	299	20	0	4.01
1991-92	Fort Wayne	IHL	2	2	0	0	120	4	0	2.00	....	....	....	....	....	....	....
	Louisville	ECHL	*56	29	19	6	*3151	223	0	4.25	13	7	6	780	53	0	4.08
	NHL Totals		**2**	**0**	**0**	**0**	**24**	**0**	**0**	**0.00**	....	....	....	....	....	....	....

Signed as a free agent by **Pittsburgh**, September 6, 1989.

CLOUTIER, JACQUES (clootz-YAY)

Goaltender. Catches left. 5'7", 168 lbs. Born, Noranda, Que., January 3, 1960.
(Buffalo's 4th choice, 55th overall, in 1979 Entry Draft).

			Regular Season								Playoffs						
Season	Club	Lea	GP	W	L	T	Mins	GA	SO	Avg	GP	W	L	Mins	GA	SO	Avg
1977-78	Trois-Rivières	QJHL	71	....	....	....	4134	240	*4	3.48	13	....	....	779	40	1	3.08
1978-79a	Trois-Rivières	QJHL	72	....	....	....	4168	218	*3	*3.14	13	....	....	780	36	0	*2.77
1979-80	Trois-Rivières	QJHL	55	27	20	7	3222	231	2	4.30	7	3	4	420	33	0	4.71
1980-81	Rochester	AHL	*61	27	27	6	*3478	209	1	3.61	....	....	....	....	....	....	....
1981-82	**Buffalo**	**NHL**	**7**	**5**	**1**	**0**	**311**	**13**	**0**	**2.51**	....	....	....	....	....	....	....
	Rochester	AHL	23	14	7	2	1366	64	0	2.81	....	....	....	....	....	....	....
1982-83	**Buffalo**	**NHL**	**25**	**10**	**7**	**6**	**1390**	**81**	**0**	**3.50**	....	....	....	....	....	....	....
	Rochester	AHL	13	7	3	1	634	42	0	3.97	16	12	4	992	47	0	2.84
1983-84	Rochester	AHL	*51	26	22	1	*2841	172	1	3.63	*18	9	9	*1145	68	0	3.56
1984-85	**Buffalo**	**NHL**	**1**	**0**	**0**	**1**	**65**	**4**	**0**	**3.69**	....	....	....	....	....	....	....
	Rochester	AHL	14	10	2	1	803	36	0	2.69	....	....	....	....	....	....	....
1985-86	**Buffalo**	**NHL**	**15**	**5**	**9**	**1**	**872**	**49**	**1**	**3.37**	....	....	....	....	....	....	....
	Rochester	AHL	14	10	2	2	835	38	1	2.73	....	....	....	....	....	....	....
1986-87	**Buffalo**	**NHL**	**40**	**11**	**19**	**5**	**2167**	**137**	**0**	**3.79**	....	....	....	....	....	....	....
1987-88	**Buffalo**	**NHL**	**20**	**4**	**8**	**2**	**851**	**67**	**0**	**4.72**	....	....	....	....	....	....	....
1988-89	**Buffalo**	**NHL**	**36**	**15**	**14**	**0**	**1786**	**108**	**0**	**3.63**	**4**	**1**	**3**	**238**	**10**	**1**	**2.52**
	Rochester	AHL	11	2	7	0	527	41	0	4.67	....	....	....	....	....	....	....
1989-90	**Chicago**	**NHL**	**43**	**18**	**15**	**2**	**2178**	**112**	**2**	**3.09**	**4**	**0**	**2**	**175**	**8**	**0**	**2.74**
1990-91	**Chicago**	**NHL**	**10**	**2**	**3**	**0**	**403**	**24**	**0**	**3.57**	....	....	....	....	....	....	....
	Quebec	**NHL**	**15**	**3**	**8**	**2**	**829**	**61**	**0**	**4.41**	....	....	....	....	....	....	....
1991-92	**Quebec**	**NHL**	**26**	**6**	**14**	**3**	**1345**	**88**	**0**	**3.93**	....	....	....	....	....	....	....
	NHL Totals		**238**	**79**	**98**	**22**	**12197**	**744**	**3**	**3.66**	**8**	**1**	**5**	**413**	**18**	**1**	**2.62**

a QMJHL First All-Star Team (1979)

Traded to **Chicago** by **Buffalo** for future considerations, September 28, 1989. Traded to **Quebec** by **Chicago** for Tony McKegney, January 29, 1991.

COLE, THOMAS

Goaltender. Catches left. 6', 185 lbs. Born, Woburn, MA, February 18, 1969.
(Edmonton's 10th choice, 187th overall, in 1988 Entry Draft).

			Regular Season								Playoffs						
Season	Club	Lea	GP	W	L	T	Mins	GA	SO	Avg	GP	W	L	Mins	GA	SO	Avg
1988-89	Northeastern	H.E.	6	2	4	0	319	30	0	5.64	....	....	....	....	....	....	....
1989-90	Northeastern	H.E.	25	10	12	2	1412	106	0	4.51	....	....	....	....	....	....	....
1990-91	Northeastern	H.E.	*31	8	18	1	*1583	137	1	5.19	....	....	....	....	....	....	....
1991-92	Northeastern	H.E.	22	10	9	0	1139	92	0	4.85	....	....	....	....	....	....	....

COUSINEAU, MARCEL

Goaltender. Catches left. 5'9", 180 lbs. Born, Delson, Que., April 30, 1973.
(Boston's 3rd choice, 62nd overall, in 1991 Entry Draft).

			Regular Season								Playoffs						
Season	Club	Lea	GP	W	L	T	Mins	GA	SO	Avg	GP	W	L	Mins	GA	SO	Avg
1990-91	Beauport	QMJHL	49	13	29	3	2739	196	1	4.29	....	....	....	....	....	....	....
1991-92	Beauport	QMJHL	*67	26	32	5	*3673	241	0	3.94	....	....	....	....	....	....	....

COWLEY, WAYNE

Goaltender. Catches left. 6', 185 lbs. Born, Scarborough, Ont., December 4, 1964.

			Regular Season								Playoffs						
Season	Club	Lea	GP	W	L	T	Mins	GA	SO	Avg	GP	W	L	Mins	GA	SO	Avg
1985-86	Colgate	ECAC	7	2	2	0	313	23	1	4.42	....	....	....	....	....	....	....
1986-87	Colgate	ECAC	31	21	8	1	1805	106	0	3.52	....	....	....	....	....	....	....
1987-88	Colgate	ECAC	20	11	7	1	1162	58	1	2.99	....	....	....	....	....	....	....
1988-89	Salt Lake	IHL	29	17	7	1	1423	94	0	3.96	2	1	0	69	6	0	5.22
1989-90	Salt Lake	IHL	36	15	12	5	2009	124	1	3.70	3	0	0	118	6	0	3.05
1990-91	Salt Lake	IHL	7	3	4	0	377	23	1	3.66	....	....	....	....	....	....	....
a	Cincinnati	ECHL	30	19	9	2	1680	108	1	3.85	4	1	3	249	13	*1	3.13
1991-92	Cape Breton	AHL	11	6	5	0	644	45	0	3.53	1	0	1	61	3	0	2.95
	Raleigh	ECHL	38	16	18	2	2213	137	0	3.71	....	....	....	....	....	....	....

a ECHL Second All-Star Team (1991)

Signed as a free agent by **Calgary**, May 1, 1988.

CURRIE, JASON

Goaltender. Catches right. 5'10", 170 lbs. Born, Brampton, Ont., April 26, 1972.
(Hartford's 10th choice, 207th overall, in 1991 Entry Draft).

			Regular Season								Playoffs						
Season	Club	Lea	GP	W	L	T	Mins	GA	SO	Avg	GP	W	L	Mins	GA	SO	Avg
1990-91	Clarkson	ECAC	21	11	3	2	968	58	0	3.59	....	....	....	....	....	....	....
1991-92	Clarkson	ECAC	18	11	6	1	965	42	2	2.61	....	....	....	....	....	....	....

DAFOE, BYRON

Goaltender. Catches left. 5'11", 175 lbs. Born, Sussex, England, February 25, 1971.
(Washington's 2nd choice, 35th overall, in 1989 Entry Draft).

			Regular Season								Playoffs						
Season	Club	Lea	GP	W	L	T	Mins	GA	SO	Avg	GP	W	L	Mins	GA	SO	Avg
1988-89	Portland	WHL	59	29	24	3	3279	291	1	5.32	*18	10	8	*1091	81	*1	4.45
1989-90	Portland	WHL	40	14	21	3	2265	193	0	5.11	....	....	....	....	....	....	....
1990-91	Portland	WHL	8	1	5	1	414	41	0	5.94	....	....	....	....	....	....	....
	Prince Albert	WHL	32	13	12	4	1839	124	0	4.05	....	....	....	....	....	....	....
1991-92	New Haven	AHL	7	3	2	1	364	22	0	3.63	....	....	....	....	....	....	....
	Baltimore	AHL	33	12	16	4	1847	119	0	3.87	....	....	....	....	....	....	....
	Hampton Rds.	ECHL	10	6	4	0	562	26	0	2.78	....	....	....	....	....	....	....

D'ALESSIO, CORRIE

Goaltender. Catches left. 5'11", 155 lbs. Born, Cornwall, Ont., September 9, 1969.
(Vancouver's 4th choice, 107th overall, in 1988 Entry Draft).

			Regular Season								Playoffs						
Season	Club	Lea	GP	W	L	T	Mins	GA	SO	Avg	GP	W	L	Mins	GA	SO	Avg
1987-88a	Cornell	ECAC	25	17	8	0	1457	67	0	2.76	....	....	....	....	....	....	....
1988-89	Cornell	ECAC	29	15	13	1	1684	96	1	3.42	....	....	....	....	....	....	....
1989-90	Cornell	ECAC	16	6	7	2	887	50	0	3.38	....	....	....	....	....	....	....
1990-91	Cornell	ECAC	24	10	8	3	1160	67	0	3.47	....	....	....	....	....	....	....
1991-92	Milwaukee	IHL	27	9	14	2	1435	96	0	4.01	2	0	2	119	12	0	6.05

a ECAC All-Rookie Team (1988)

D'AMOUR, MARC (dah-MOHR)

Goaltender. Catches left. 5'9", 190 lbs. Born, Sudbury, Ont., May 29, 1961.

			Regular Season								Playoffs						
Season	Club	Lea	GP	W	L	T	Mins	GA	SO	Avg	GP	W	L	Mins	GA	SO	Avg
1979-80	S.S. Marie	OHA	33	16	15	0	1429	117	0	4.91	....	....	....	....	....	....	....
1980-81	S.S. Marie	OHA	16	7	1	1	653	38	0	3.49	14	5	4	683	41	0	3.60
1981-82a	S.S. Marie	OHL	41	28	12	1	3284	130	1	*3.27	10	3	2	504	30	0	3.57
1982-83	Colorado	CHL	42	16	21	2	2373	153	1	3.87	1	....	....	59	4	0	4.08
1983-84	Colorado	CHL	36	18	12	1	1917	131	0	4.10	1	0	0	20	0	0	0.00
1984-85	Moncton	AHL	37	18	14	2	2051	115	0	3.36	....	....	....	....	....	....	....
	Salt Lake	IHL	12	7	2	2	694	33	0	2.85	....	....	....	....	....	....	....
1985-86	**Calgary**	**NHL**	**15**	**2**	**4**	**2**	**560**	**32**	**0**	**3.43**	....	....	....	....	....	....	....
	Moncton	AHL	21	6	9	3	1129	72	0	3.83	5	1	4	296	20	0	4.05
1986-87	Binghamton	AHL	8	5	3	0	461	30	0	3.90	....	....	....	....	....	....	....
	Salt Lake	IHL	10	3	6	0	523	37	0	4.24	....	....	....	....	....	....	....
	Cdn. Olympic	....	1	0	0	0	30	4	0	8.00	....	....	....	....	....	....	....
1987-88	Salt Lake	IHL	*62	26	19	5	3245	177	0	3.27	*19	*12	7	*1123	67	0	3.58
1988-89	**Philadelphia**	**NHL**	**1**	**0**	**0**	**0**	**19**	**0**	**0**	**0.00**	....	....	....	....	....	....	....
	Hershey	AHL	39	19	13	3	2174	127	0	3.51	....	....	....	....	....	....	....
	Indianapolis	IHL	6	2	3	0	324	20	0	3.70	....	....	....	....	....	....	....
1989-90	Hershey	AHL	43	15	20	6	2505	148	2	3.54	....	....	....	....	....	....	....
1990-91	Hershey	AHL	28	10	8	4	1331	80	0	3.61	2	0	1	80	5	0	3.75
	Fort Wayne	IHL	3	1	0	0	136	9	0	3.97	....	....	....	....	....	....	....
1991-92	Hershey	AHL	21	9	8	2	1073	79	0	4.42	....	....	....	....	....	....	....
	NHL Totals		**16**	**2**	**4**	**2**	**579**	**32**	**0**	**3.32**	....	....	....	....	....	....	....

a OHL First All-Star Team (1982)

Signed as a free agent by **Calgary**, June 7, 1982. Signed as a free agent by **Philadelphia**, September 30, 1988.

DEGRACE, YANICK

Goaltender. Catches left. 5'11", 167 lbs. Born, Lameque, N.B., April 16, 1971.
(Philadelphia's 5th choice, 94th overall, in 1991 Entry Draft).

			Regular Season								Playoffs						
Season	Club	Lea	GP	W	L	T	Mins	GA	SO	Avg	GP	W	L	Mins	GA	SO	Avg
1990-91	Trois-Rivières	QMJHL	33	13	11	2	1726	97	1	3.37	4	1	0	129	11	0	5.12
1991-92	Hull	QMJHL	35	18	9	3	1970	112	0	3.41	2	0	2	31	4	0	7.64

DelGUIDICE, MATT (del-GOO-dis)

Goaltender. Catches right. 5'9", 170 lbs. Born, West Haven, CT, March 5, 1967.
(Boston's 5th choice, 77th overall, in 1987 Entry Draft).

			Regular Season								Playoffs						
Season	Club	Lea	GP	W	L	T	Mins	GA	SO	Avg	GP	W	L	Mins	GA	SO	Avg
1988-89	U. of Maine	H.E.	20	16	4	0	1090	57	1	*3.14	....	....	....	....	....	....	....
1989-90	U. of Maine	H.E.	23	16	4	0	1257	68	0	3.25	....	....	....	....	....	....	....
1990-91	**Boston**	**NHL**	**1**	**0**	**0**	**0**	**10**	**0**	**0**	**0.00**	....	....	....	....	....	....	....
	Maine	AHL	52	23	18	9	2893	160	2	3.32	2	1	1	82	5	0	3.66
1991-92	**Boston**	**NHL**	**10**	**2**	**5**	**1**	**424**	**28**	**0**	**3.96**	....	....	....	....	....	....	....
	Maine	AHL	25	5	15	0	1369	101	0	4.43	....	....	....	....	....	....	....
	NHL Totals		**11**	**2**	**5**	**1**	**434**	**28**	**0**	**3.87**	....	....	....	....	....	....	....

DERKSEN, DUANE

Goaltender. Catches left. 6'1", 180 lbs. Born, St. Boniface, Man., July 7, 1968.
(Washington's 4th choice, 57th overall, in 1988 Entry Draft).

			Regular Season								Playoffs						
Season	Club	Lea	GP	W	L	T	Mins	GA	SO	Avg	GP	W	L	Mins	GA	SO	Avg
1988-89	U. Wisconsin	WCHA	11	4	5	0	561	37	1	3.96	....	....	....	....	....	....	....
1989-90ab	U. Wisconsin	WCHA	*41	*31	8	1	*2345	133	*2	*3.40	....	....	....	....	....	....	....
1990-91a	U. Wisconsin	WCHA	*42	24	15	3	*2474	133	3	3.23	....	....	....	....	....	....	....
1991-92cd	U. Wisconsin	WCHA	31	18	11	2	1825	100	0	3.29	....	....	....	....	....	....	....

a WCHA Second All-Star Team (1990, 1991)
b NCAA All-Tournament Team, Tournament Top Goaltender (1990)
c NCAA West Second All-Star Team (1992)
d WCHA First All-Star Team (1992)

DEROUVILLE, PHILIPPE

Goaltender. Catches left. 6'1", 183 lbs. Born, Victoriaville, Que., August 7, 1974.
(Pittsburgh's 5th choice, 115th overall, in 1992 Entry Draft).

			Regular Season								Playoffs						
Season	Club	Lea	GP	W	L	T	Mins	GA	SO	Avg	GP	W	L	Mins	GA	SO	Avg
1990-91	Longueuil	QMJHL	20	13	6	0	1030	50	0	2.91	....	....	....	....	....	....	....
1991-92	Verdun	QMJHL	34	20	6	3	1854	99	2	3.20	11	7	3	593	28	1	2.83

DONEGHEY, MICHAEL

Goaltender. Catches left. 6', 165 lbs. Born, Boston, MA, July 28, 1970.
(Chicago's 10th choice, 237th overall, in 1989 Entry Draft).

			Regular Season								Playoffs						
Season	Club	Lea	GP	W	L	T	Mins	GA	SO	Avg	GP	W	L	Mins	GA	SO	Avg
1989-90	Merrimack	H.E.	9	3	5	0	424	36	1	5.09	....	....	....	....	....	....	....
1990-91	Merrimack	H.E.	12	2	4	1	557	48	0	4.90	....	....	....	....	....	....	....
1991-92	Merrimack	H.E.	3	1	2	0	233	18	0	4.64	....	....	....	....	....	....	....

DOPSON, ROBERT

Goaltender. Catches left. 6', 200 lbs. Born, Smiths Falls, Ont., August 21, 1967.

			Regular Season								Playoffs						
Season	Club	Lea	GP	W	L	T	Mins	GA	SO	Avg	GP	W	L	Mins	GA	SO	Avg
1989-90	Wilfred Laurier	OUAA	22	....	....	....	1319	57	0	2.59	....	....	....	....	....	....	....
1990-91	Muskegon	IHL	24	10	10	0	1243	90	0	4.34	....	....	....	....	....	....	....
1991-92	Muskegon	IHL	28	13	12	2	1655	90	4	3.26	....	....	....	....	....	....	....

Signed as a free agent by **Pittsburgh**, July 6, 1991.

DRAPER, TOM

Goaltender. Catches left. 5'11", 185 lbs. Born, Outremont, Que., November 20, 1966.
(Winnipeg's 8th choice, 165th overall, in 1985 Entry Draft).

			Regular Season								Playoffs						
Season	Club	Lea	GP	W	L	T	Mins	GA	SO	Avg	GP	W	L	Mins	GA	SO	Avg
1983-84	U. of Vermont	ECAC	20	8	12	0	1205	82	0	4.08	....	....	....	....	....	....	....
1984-85	U. of Vermont	ECAC	24	5	17	0	1316	90	0	4.11	....	....	....	....	....	....	....
1985-86	U. of Vermont	ECAC	29	15	12	1	1697	87	1	3.08	....	....	....	....	....	....	....
1986-87a	U. of Vermont	ECAC	29	16	13	0	1662	96	2	3.47	....	....	....	....	....	....	....
1987-88	Tappara	Fin.	28	16	3	9	1619	87	0	3.22	....	....	....	....	....	....	....
1988-89	**Winnipeg**	**NHL**	**2**	**1**	**1**	**0**	**120**	**12**	**0**	**6.00**	....	....	....	....	....	....	....
b	Moncton	AHL	*54	27	17	5	*2962	171	2	3.46	7	5	2	419	24	0	3.44
1989-90	**Winnipeg**	**NHL**	**6**	**2**	**4**	**0**	**359**	**26**	**0**	**4.35**	....	....	....	....	....	....	....
	Moncton	AHL	51	20	24	3	2844	167	1	3.52	....	....	....	....	....	....	....
1990-91	Moncton	AHL	30	15	13	2	1779	95	1	3.20	....	....	....	....	....	....	....
	Fort Wayne	IHL	10	5	3	1	564	32	0	3.40	....	....	....	....	....	....	....
	Peoria	IHL	10	6	3	1	584	36	0	3.70	4	2	1	214	10	0	2.80
1991-92	**Buffalo**	**NHL**	**26**	**10**	**9**	**5**	**1403**	**75**	**1**	**3.21**	**7**	**3**	**4**	**433**	**19**	**1**	**2.63**
	Rochester	AHL	9	4	3	2	531	28	0	3.16	....	....	....	....	....	....	....
	NHL Totals		**34**	**13**	**14**	**5**	**1882**	**113**	**1**	**3.60**	**7**	**3**	**4**	**433**	**19**	**1**	**2.63**

a ECAC First All-Star Team (1987)
b AHL Second All-Star Team (1989)

Traded to **St. Louis** by **Winnipeg** for future considerations (Jim Vesey - May 24, 1991), February 28, 1991. Traded to **Winnipeg** by **St. Louis** for future considerations, May 24, 1991. Traded to **Buffalo** by **Winnipeg** for future considerations, June 22, 1991.

DUFFUS, PARRIS

Goaltender. Catches left. 6'2", 192 lbs. Born, Denver, CO, January 27, 1970.
(St. Louis' 6th choice, 180th overall, in 1990 Entry Draft).

			Regular Season								Playoffs						
Season	Club	Lea	GP	W	L	T	Mins	GA	SO	Avg	GP	W	L	Mins	GA	SO	Avg
1990-91	Cornell	ECAC	4	0	0	0	37	3	0	4.86	....	....	....	....	....	....	....
1991-92ab	Cornell	ECAC	28	14	11	3	1677	74	1	2.65	....	....	....	....	....	....	....

a NCAA East First All-Star Team (1992)
b ECAC Second All-Star Team (1992)

DUNHAM, MICHAEL

Goaltender. Catches left. 6'2", 170 lbs. Born, Johnson City, NY, June 1, 1972.
(New Jersey's 4th choice, 53rd overall, in 1990 Entry Draft).

			Regular Season								Playoffs						
Season	Club	Lea	GP	W	L	T	Mins	GA	SO	Avg	GP	W	L	Mins	GA	SO	Avg
1990-91	U. of Maine	H.E.	23	14	5	2	1275	63	0	*2.96	....	....	....	....	....	....	....
1991-92	U. of Maine	H.E.	7	6	0	0	382	14	1	2.20	....	....	....	....	....	....	....
	U.S. National	....	3	0	1	1	157	10	0	3.82	....	....	....	....	....	....	....

DYCK, LARRY

Goaltender. Catches left. 5'11", 180 lbs. Born, Winkler, Man., December 15, 1965.

			Regular Season								Playoffs						
Season	Club	Lea	GP	W	L	T	Mins	GA	SO	Avg	GP	W	L	Mins	GA	SO	Avg
1986-87	U. Manitoba	CWUAA	18	....	....	....	1019	61	*3	3.59	....	....	....	....	....	....	....
1987-88	U. Manitoba	CWUAA	19	....	....	....	1118	87	0	4.78	....	....	....	....	....	....	....
1988-89	Kalamazoo	IHL	42	17	20	2	2308	168	0	4.37	....	....	....	....	....	....	....
1989-90	Kalamazoo	IHL	36	20	12	0	1959	116	0	3.55	7	2	3	353	22	0	3.74
	Knoxville	ECHL	3	1	1	1	184	12	0	3.91	....	....	....	....	....	....	....
1990-91	Kalamazoo	IHL	38	21	15	0	2182	133	1	3.66	1	0	1	60	6	0	6.00
1991-92	Kalamazoo	IHL	*56	25	23	6	*3305	195	0	3.54	12	5	7	690	43	0	3.74

Signed as a free agent by **Minnesota**, November 10, 1988.

ELO, HANS-GORAN

Goaltender. Catches left. 6'2", 202 lbs. Born, Stockholm, Sweden, June 27, 1966.
(Winnipeg's 11th choice, 247th overall, in 1987 Entry Draft).

			Regular Season								Playoffs						
Season	Club	Lea	GP	W	L	T	Mins	GA	SO	Avg	GP	W	L	Mins	GA	SO	Avg
1990-91	Hammarby	Swe.2	24	....	....	....	1440	89	0	3.71	....	....	....	....	....	....	....
1991-92	Hammarby	Swe.2						UNAVAILABLE									

ERICKSON, CHAD

Goaltender. Catches right. 5'9", 175 lbs. Born, Minneapolis, MN, August 21, 1970.
(New Jersey's 8th choice, 138th overall, in 1988 Entry Draft).

			Regular Season								Playoffs						
Season	Club	Lea	GP	W	L	T	Mins	GA	SO	Avg	GP	W	L	Mins	GA	SO	Avg
1988-89	Minn.-Duluth	WCHA	15	5	7	1	821	49	0	3.58	....	....	....	....	....	....	....
1989-90ab	Minn.-Duluth	WCHA	39	19	19	1	2301	141	0	3.68	....	....	....	....	....	....	....
1990-91	Minn.-Duluth	WCHA	40	14	19	7	2393	159	0	3.99	....	....	....	....	....	....	....
1991-92	**New Jersey**	**NHL**	**2**	**1**	**1**	**0**	**120**	**9**	**0**	**4.50**	....	....	....	....	....	....	....
	Utica	AHL	43	18	19	3	2341	147	2	3.77	2	0	2	127	11	0	5.20
	NHL Totals		**2**	**1**	**1**	**0**	**120**	**9**	**0**	**4.50**	....	....	....	....	....	....	....

a WCHA Second All-Star Team (1990)
b NCAA West First All-American Team (1990)

ESSENSA, BOB (EH-sehn-sah)

Goaltender. Catches left. 6', 180 lbs. Born, Toronto, Ont., January 14, 1965.
(Winnipeg's 5th choice, 69th overall, in 1983 Entry Draft).

			Regular Season								Playoffs						
Season	Club	Lea	GP	W	L	T	Mins	GA	SO	Avg	GP	W	L	Mins	GA	SO	Avg
1983-84	Michigan State	CCHA	17	11	4	0	946	44	2	2.79	....	....	....	....	....	....	....
1984-85	Michigan State	CCHA	18	15	2	0	1059	29	2	1.64	....	....	....	....	....	....	....
1985-86a	Michigan State	CCHA	23	17	4	1	1333	74	1	3.33	....	....	....	....	....	....	....
1986-87	Michigan State	CCHA	25	19	3	1	1383	64	2	2.78	....	....	....	....	....	....	....
1987-88	Moncton	AHL	27	7	11	1	1287	100	1	4.66	....	....	....	....	....	....	....
1988-89	**Winnipeg**	**NHL**	**20**	**6**	**8**	**3**	**1102**	**68**	**1**	**3.70**	....	....	....	....	....	....	....
	Fort Wayne	IHL	22	14	7	0	1287	70	0	3.26	....	....	....	....	....	....	....
1989-90b	**Winnipeg**	**NHL**	**36**	**18**	**9**	**5**	**2035**	**107**	**1**	**3.15**	**4**	**2**	**1**	**206**	**12**	**0**	**3.50**
	Moncton	AHL	6	3	3	0	358	15	0	2.51	....	....	....	....	....	....	....
1990-91	**Winnipeg**	**NHL**	**55**	**19**	**24**	**6**	**2916**	**153**	**4**	**3.15**	....	....	....	....	....	....	....
	Moncton	AHL	2	1	0	1	125	6	0	2.88	....	....	....	....	....	....	....
1991-92	**Winnipeg**	**NHL**	**47**	**21**	**17**	**6**	**2627**	**126**	***5**	**2.88**	**1**	**0**	**0**	**33**	**3**	**0**	**5.45**
	NHL Totals		**158**	**64**	**58**	**20**	**8680**	**454**	**11**	**3.14**	**5**	**2**	**1**	**239**	**15**	**0**	**3.77**

a CCHA Second All-Star Team (1986)
b NHL All-Rookie Team (1990)

FERNANDEZ, EMMANUEL

Goaltender. Catches left. 6', 173 lbs. Born, Etobicoke, Ont., August 27, 1974.
(Quebec's 4th choice, 52nd overall, in 1992 Entry Draft).

			Regular Season								Playoffs						
Season	Club	Lea	GP	W	L	T	Mins	GA	SO	Avg	GP	W	L	Mins	GA	SO	Avg
1991-92	Laval	QMJHL	31	14	13	2	1593	99	1	3.73	9	3	5	468	39	0	5.00

FINCH, GEOFF

Goaltender. Catches left. 6', 178 lbs. Born, Oshawa, Ont., April 8, 1972.
(Minnesota's 7th choice, 137th overall, in 1991 Entry Draft).

			Regular Season								Playoffs						
Season	Club	Lea	GP	W	L	T	Mins	GA	SO	Avg	GP	W	L	Mins	GA	SO	Avg
1990-91	Brown	ECAC	22	9	9	1	1203	78	1	3.89	....	....	....	....	....	....	....
1991-92	Brown	ECAC	15	4	7	2	815	65	0	4.79	....	....	....	....	....	....	....

FISET, STEPHANE (fih-SET)

Goaltender. Catches left. 6', 175 lbs. Born, Montreal, Que., June 17, 1970.
(Quebec's 3rd choice, 24th overall, in 1988 Entry Draft).

			Regular Season								Playoffs						
Season	Club	Lea	GP	W	L	T	Mins	GA	SO	Avg	GP	W	L	Mins	GA	SO	Avg
1987-88	Victoriaville	QMJHL	40	15	17	4	2221	146	1	3.94	2	0	2	163	10	0	3.68
1988-89a	Victoriaville	QMJHL	43	25	14	0	2401	138	1	*3.45	12	*9	2	711	33	0	*2.78
1989-90	**Quebec**	**NHL**	**6**	**0**	**5**	**1**	**342**	**34**	**0**	**5.96**	....	....	....	....	....	....	....
	Victoriaville	QMJHL	24	14	6	3	1383	63	1	*2.73	*14	7	6	*790	49	0	3.72
1990-91	**Quebec**	**NHL**	**3**	**0**	**2**	**1**	**186**	**12**	**0**	**3.87**	....	....	....	....	....	....	....
	Halifax	AHL	36	10	15	8	1902	131	0	4.13	....	....	....	....	....	....	....
1991-92	**Quebec**	**NHL**	**23**	**7**	**10**	**2**	**1133**	**71**	**1**	**3.76**	....	....	....	....	....	....	....
	Halifax	AHL	29	8	14	6	1675	110	*3	3.94	....	....	....	....	....	....	....
	NHL Totals		**32**	**7**	**17**	**4**	**1661**	**117**	**1**	**4.23**	....	....	....	....	....	....	....

a QMJHL First All-Star Team (1989)

FITZPATRICK, MARK

Goaltender. Catches left. 6'2", 190 lbs. Born, Toronto, Ont., November 13, 1968.
(Los Angeles' 2nd choice, 27th overall, in 1987 Entry Draft).

			Regular Season								Playoffs						
Season	Club	Lea	GP	W	L	T	Mins	GA	SO	Avg	GP	W	L	Mins	GA	SO	Avg
1985-86	Medicine Hat	WHL	41	26	6	1	2074	99	1	2.86	19	12	5	986	58	0	3.53
1986-87	Medicine Hat	WHL	50	31	11	4	2844	159	4	3.35	20	12	8	1224	71	1	3.48
1987-88	Medicine Hat	WHL	63	36	15	6	3600	194	2	3.23	16	12	4	959	52	*1	*3.25
1988-89	**Los Angeles**	**NHL**	**17**	**6**	**7**	**3**	**957**	**64**	**0**	**4.01**	....	....	....	....	....	....	....
	New Haven	AHL	18	10	5	1	980	54	1	3.31	....	....	....	....	....	....	....
	NY Islanders	**NHL**	**11**	**3**	**5**	**2**	**627**	**41**	**0**	**3.92**	....	....	....	....	....	....	....
1989-90	**NY Islanders**	**NHL**	**47**	**19**	**19**	**5**	**2653**	**150**	**3**	**3.39**	**4**	**0**	**2**	**152**	**13**	**0**	**5.13**
1990-91	**NY Islanders**	**NHL**	**2**	**1**	**1**	**0**	**120**	**6**	**0**	**3.00**	....	....	....	....	....	....	....
	Capital Dist.	AHL	12	3	7	2	734	47	0	3.84	....	....	....	....	....	....	....
1991-92	**NY Islanders**	**NHL**	**30**	**11**	**13**	**5**	**1743**	**93**	**0**	**3.20**	....	....	....	....	....	....	....
	Capital Dist.	AHL	14	6	5	1	782	39	0	2.99	....	....	....	....	....	....	....
	NHL Totals		**107**	**40**	**45**	**15**	**6100**	**354**	**3**	**3.48**	**4**	**0**	**2**	**152**	**13**	**0**	**5.13**

Traded to **NY Islanders** by **Los Angeles** with Wayne McBean and future considerations (Doug Crossman, acquired May 23, 1989) for Kelly Hrudey, February 22, 1989.

FITZSIMMONS, JASON

Goaltender. Catches left. 5'10", 180 lbs. Born, Regina, Sask., June 3, 1971.
(Vancouver's 11th choice, 227th overall, in 1991 Entry Draft).

			Regular Season								Playoffs						
Season	Club	Lea	GP	W	L	T	Mins	GA	SO	Avg	GP	W	L	Mins	GA	SO	Avg
1990-91	Moose Jaw	WHL	44	15	23	2	2170	179	0	4.95	8	4	4	481	27	....	3.37
1991-92	Moose Jaw	WHL	60	29	28	1	3286	222	0	4.05	4	0	4	186	27	0	8.71

FLAHERTY, WADE

Goaltender. Catches right. 6', 170 lbs. Born, Terrace, B.C., January 11, 1968.
(Buffalo's 10th choice, 181st overall, in 1988 Entry Draft).

			Regular Season								Playoffs						
Season	Club	Lea	GP	W	L	T	Mins	GA	SO	Avg	GP	W	L	Mins	GA	SO	Avg
1988-89	Victoria	WHL	42	21	19	0	2408	180	4	4.49	....	....	....	....	....	....	....
1989-90	Greensboro	ECHL	27	12	10	0	1308	96	0	4.40	....	....	....	....	....	....	....
1990-91	Kansas City	IHL	56	16	31	4	2990	224	0	4.49	....	....	....	....	....	....	....
1991-92	Kansas City	IHL	43	26	14	3	2603	140	1	3.23	1	0	0	1	0	0	0.00

Signed as a free agent by **San Jose**, September 3, 1991.

FLETCHER, JOHN

Goaltender. Catches right. 5'7", 165 lbs. Born, Holden, MA, October 14, 1967.
(Vancouver's 9th choice, 192nd overall, in 1987 Entry Draft).

			Regular Season								Playoffs						
Season	Club	Lea	GP	W	L	T	Mins	GA	SO	Avg	GP	W	L	Mins	GA	SO	Avg
1986-87a	Clarkson	ECAC	23	11	8	1	1240	62	4	2.99	....	....	....	....	....	....	....
1987-88bc	Clarkson	ECAC	33	16	11	3	1820	97	1	3.19	....	....	....	....	....	....	....
1988-89	Clarkson	ECAC	23	9	8	2	1146	79	0	4.13	....	....	....	....	....	....	....
1989-90	Clarkson	ECAC	34	20	11	3	1900	89	0	3.13	....	....	....	....	....	....	....
1990-91	Winston-Salem	ECHL	11	0	8	0	534	57	0	6.40	....	....	....	....	....	....	....
	Cincinnati	ECHL	14	3	8	1	783	71	0	5.44	....	....	....	....	....	....	....
1991-92	Johnstown	ECHL	6	3	2	0	318	13	0	2.45	....	....	....	....	....	....	....
	Knoxville	ECHL	2	0	1	0	79	10	0	7.59	....	....	....	....	....	....	....
	Nashville	ECHL	11	3	7	1	583	54	0	5.56	....	....	....	....	....	....	....

a ECAC Rookie of the Year (1987)
b ECAC First All-Star Team (1988)
c NCAA East Second All-American Team (1988)

FOSTER, NORM

Goaltender. Catches left. 5'9", 175 lbs. Born, Vancouver, B.C., February 10, 1965.
(Boston's 11th choice, 222nd overall, in 1983 Entry Draft).

			Regular Season								Playoffs						
Season	Club	Lea	GP	W	L	T	Mins	GA	SO	Avg	GP	W	L	Mins	GA	SO	Avg
1984-85	Michigan State	CCHA	26	22	4	0	1531	67	0	2.63	....	....	....	....	....	....	....
1985-86	Michigan State	CCHA	24	17	5	1	1414	87	0	3.69	....	....	....	....	....	....	....
1986-87	Michigan State	CCHA	24	14	7	1	1383	90	1	3.90	....	....	....	....	....	....	....
1987-88	Milwaukee	IHL	38	10	22	1	2001	170	0	5.10	....	....	....	....	....	....	....
1988-89	Maine	AHL	47	16	17	6	2411	156	1	3.88	....	....	....	....	....	....	....
1989-90	Maine	AHL	*64	23	28	10	*3664	217	3	3.55	....	....	....	....	....	....	....
1990-91	**Boston**	**NHL**	**3**	**2**	**1**	**0**	**184**	**14**	**0**	**4.57**	....	....	....	....	....	....	....
	Maine	AHL	2	1	1	0	122	7	0	3.44	....	....	....	....	....	....	....
	Cape Breton	AHL	40	15	14	7	2207	135	1	3.67	2	0	2	128	8	0	3.75
1991-92	**Edmonton**	**NHL**	**10**	**5**	**3**	**0**	**439**	**20**	**0**	**2.73**	....	....	....	....	....	....	....
	Cape Breton	AHL	29	15	13	1	1699	119	0	4.20	3	1	2	193	14	0	4.35
	NHL Totals		**13**	**7**	**4**	**0**	**623**	**34**	**0**	**3.27**	....	....	....	....	....	....	....

Traded to **Edmonton** by **Boston** for future considerations, September 11, 1991.

FOUNTAIN, MIKE

Goaltender. Catches left. 6', 176 lbs. Born, North York, Ont., January 26, 1972.
(Vancouver's 4th choice, 69th overall, in 1992 Entry Draft).

			Regular Season								Playoffs						
Season	Club	Lea	GP	W	L	T	Mins	GA	SO	Avg	GP	W	L	Mins	GA	SO	Avg
1990-91	S.S. Marie	OHL	7	5	2	0	380	19	....	3.00	....	....	....	....	....	....	....
	Oshawa	OHL	30	17	5	1	1483	84	....	3.40	8	1	4	292	26	0	5.34
1991-92	Oshawa	OHL	40	18	13	6	2260	149	1	3.96	7	3	4	429	26	0	3.64

FUHR, GRANT (FYOOR)

Goaltender. Catches right. 5'10", 186 lbs. Born, Spruce Grove, Alta., September 28, 1962.
(Edmonton's 1st choice, 8th overall, in 1981 Entry Draft).

			Regular Season								Playoffs						
Season	Club	Lea	GP	W	L	T	Mins	GA	SO	Avg	GP	W	L	Mins	GA	SO	Avg
1979-80ab	Victoria	WHL	43	30	12	0	2488	130	2	3.14	8	5	3	465	22	0	2.84
1980-81a	Victoria	WHL	59	48	9	1	3448	160	*4	*2.78	15	12	3	899	45	*1	*3.00
1981-82c	**Edmonton**	**NHL**	**48**	**28**	**5**	**14**	**2847**	**157**	**0**	**3.31**	**5**	**2**	**3**	**309**	**26**	**0**	**5.05**
1982-83	**Edmonton**	**NHL**	**32**	**13**	**12**	**5**	**1803**	**129**	**0**	**4.29**	**1**	**0**	**0**	**11**	**0**	**0**	**0.00**
	Moncton	AHL	10	4	5	1	604	40	0	3.98	....	....	....	....	....	....	....
1983-84	**Edmonton**	**NHL**	**45**	**30**	**10**	**4**	**2625**	**171**	**1**	**3.91**	**16**	**11**	**4**	**883**	**44**	**1**	**2.99**
1984-85	**Edmonton**	**NHL**	**46**	**26**	**8**	**7**	**2559**	**165**	**1**	**3.87**	***18**	***15**	**3**	**1064**	**55**	**0**	**3.10**
1985-86	**Edmonton**	**NHL**	**40**	**29**	**8**	**0**	**2184**	**143**	**0**	**3.93**	**9**	**5**	**4**	**541**	**28**	**0**	**3.11**
1986-87	**Edmonton**	**NHL**	**44**	**22**	**13**	**3**	**2388**	**137**	**0**	**3.44**	**19**	**14**	**5**	**1148**	**47**	**0**	**2.46**
1987-88de	**Edmonton**	**NHL**	***75**	***40**	**24**	**9**	***4304**	**246**	***4**	**3.43**	***19**	***16**	**2**	***1136**	**55**	**0**	**2.90**
1988-89	**Edmonton**	**NHL**	**59**	**23**	**26**	**6**	**3341**	**213**	**1**	**3.83**	**7**	**3**	**4**	**417**	**24**	**1**	**3.45**
1989-90	**Edmonton**	**NHL**	**21**	**9**	**7**	**3**	**1081**	**70**	**1**	**3.89**	....	....	....	....	....	....	....
	Cape Breton	AHL	2	2	0	0	120	6	0	3.01	....	....	....	....	....	....	....
1990-91	**Edmonton**	**NHL**	**13**	**6**	**4**	**3**	**778**	**39**	**1**	**3.01**	**17**	**8**	**7**	**1019**	**51**	**0**	**3.00**
	Cape Breton	AHL	4	2	2	0	240	17	0	4.25	....	....	....	....	....	....	....
1991-92	**Toronto**	**NHL**	**66**	**25**	**33**	**5**	**3774**	**230**	**2**	**3.66**	....	....	....	....	....	....	....
	NHL Totals		**489**	**251**	**150**	**59**	**27684**	**1700**	**11**	**3.68**	**111**	**74**	**32**	**6528**	**330**	**2**	**3.03**

a WHL First All-Star Team (1980, 1981)
b WHL Rookie of the Year (1980)
c NHL Second All-Star Team (1982)
d NHL First All-Star Team (1988)
e Won Vezina Trophy (1988)

Played in NHL All-Star Game (1982, 1984-86, 1988-89)

Traded to **Toronto** by **Edmonton** with Glenn Anderson and Craig Berube for Vincent Damphousse, Peter Ing, Scott Thornton, Luke Richardson, future considerations and cash, September 19, 1991.

GAGE, JOAQUIN

Goaltender. Catches left. 6', 200 lbs. Born, Vancouver, B.C., October 19, 1973.
(Edmonton's 6th choice, 109th overall, in 1992 Entry Draft).

			Regular Season								Playoffs						
Season	Club	Lea	GP	W	L	T	Mins	GA	SO	Avg	GP	W	L	Mins	GA	SO	Avg
1990-91	Portland	WHL	3	0	3	0	180	17	0	5.70	....	....	....	....	....	....	....
1991-92	Portland	WHL	63	27	30	4	3635	269	2	4.44	6	2	4	366	28	0	4.59

GAGNON, DAVID

Goaltender. Catches left. 6', 185 lbs. Born, Windsor, Ont., October 31, 1967.

			Regular Season								Playoffs						
Season	Club	Lea	GP	W	L	T	Mins	GA	SO	Avg	GP	W	L	Mins	GA	SO	Avg
1987-88	Colgate	ECAC	13	6	4	2	743	43	1	3.47	....	....	....	....	....	....	....
1988-89	Colgate	ECAC	28	17	9	2	1622	102	0	3.77	....	....	....	....	....	....	....
1989-90ab	Colgate	ECAC	33	28	3	1	1986	93	0	2.88	....	....	....	....	....	....	....
1990-91	**Detroit**	**NHL**	**2**	**0**	**1**	**0**	**35**	**6**	**0**	**10.29**	....	....	....	....	....	....	....
	Adirondack	AHL	24	8	8	5	1356	94	0	4.16	....	....	....	....	....	....	....
c	Hampton Rds.	ECHL	10	7	1	2	606	26	2	2.57	11	*10	1	696	27	0	*2.32
1991-92	Fort Wayne	IHL	2	2	0	0	125	7	0	3.36	....	....	....	....	....	....	....
	Toledo	ECHL	7	4	2	0	354	18	0	3.05	....	....	....	....	....	....	....
	NHL Totals		**2**	**0**	**1**	**0**	**35**	**6**	**0**	**10.29**	....	....	....	....	....	....	....

a ECAC First All-Star Team (1990)
b ECAC Player of the Year (1990)
c MVP in Playoffs — ECHL (Shared with Dave Flanagan) (1991)

Signed as a free agent by **Detroit**, June 11, 1990.

GAMBLE, TROY

Goaltender. Catches left. 5'11", 195 lbs. Born, New Glasgow, N.S., April 7, 1967.
(Vancouver's 2nd choice, 25th overall, in 1985 Entry Draft).

			Regular Season								Playoffs						
Season	Club	Lea	GP	W	L	T	Mins	GA	SO	Avg	GP	W	L	Mins	GA	SO	Avg
1984-85a	Medicine Hat	WHL	37	27	6	2	2095	100	3	2.86	2	1	1	120	9	0	4.50
1985-86	Medicine Hat	WHL	45	28	11	0	2264	142	0	3.76	11	5	4	530	31	0	3.51
1986-87	**Vancouver**	**NHL**	**1**	**0**	**1**	**0**	**60**	**4**	**0**	**4.00**	....	....	....	....	....	....	....
	Medicine Hat	WHL	11	7	3	0	646	46	0	4.27	....	....	....	....	....	....	....
	Spokane	WHL	38	17	17	1	2155	163	0	4.54	5	0	5	298	35	0	7.05
1987-88b	Spokane	WHL	67	36	26	1	3824	235	0	3.69	15	7	8	875	56	1	3.84
1988-89	**Vancouver**	**NHL**	**5**	**2**	**3**	**0**	**302**	**12**	**0**	**2.38**	....	....	....	....	....	....	....
	Milwaukee	IHL	42	23	9	0	2198	138	0	3.77	11	5	5	640	35	0	3.28
1989-90	Milwaukee	IHL	*56	22	21	4	2779	160	2	4.21	5	2	2	216	19	0	5.28
1990-91	**Vancouver**	**NHL**	**47**	**16**	**16**	**6**	**2433**	**140**	**1**	**3.45**	**4**	**1**	**3**	**249**	**16**	**0**	**3.86**
1991-92	**Vancouver**	**NHL**	**19**	**4**	**9**	**3**	**1009**	**73**	**0**	**4.34**	....	....	....	....	....	....	....
	Milwaukee	IHL	9	2	4	2	521	31	0	3.57	....	....	....	....	....	....	....
	NHL Totals		**72**	**22**	**29**	**9**	**3804**	**229**	**1**	**3.61**	**4**	**1**	**3**	**249**	**16**	**0**	**3.86**

a WHL First All-Star Team, East Division (1985)
b WHL First All-Star Team, West Division (1988)

GAUTHIER, SEAN

Goaltender. Catches left. 5'11", 202 lbs. Born, Sudbury, Ont., March 28, 1971.
(Winnipeg's 9th choice, 181st overall, in 1991 Entry Draft).

			Regular Season								Playoffs						
Season	Club	Lea	GP	W	L	T	Mins	GA	SO	Avg	GP	W	L	Mins	GA	SO	Avg
1990-91	Kingston	OHL	59	16	36	3	3200	282	0	5.29	....	....	....	....	....	....	....
1991-92	Moncton	AHL	25	8	10	5	1415	88	1	3.73	2	0	0	26	2	0	4.62

GILMORE, MIKE

Goaltender. Catches left. 5'10", 173 lbs. Born, Detroit, MI, March 11, 1968.
(NY Rangers' 1st choice, 18th overall, in 1990 Supplemental Draft).

			Regular Season								Playoffs						
Season	Club	Lea	GP	W	L	T	Mins	GA	SO	Avg	GP	W	L	Mins	GA	SO	Avg
1988-89	Michigan State	CCHA	3	1	0	0	74	5	0	4.04	....	....	....	....	....	....	....
1989-90	Michigan State	CCHA	12	9	1	0	638	29	0	2.73	....	....	....	....	....	....	....
1990-91a	Michigan State	CCHA	22	9	8	3	1218	54	*2	2.66	....	....	....	....	....	....	....
1991-92	Michigan State	CCHA	33	14	9	7	1831	95	0	3.11	....	....	....	....	....	....	....

a CCHA Second All-Star Team (1991)

GILMOUR, DARRYL

Goaltender. Catches left. 6', 171 lbs. Born, Winnipeg, Man., February 13, 1967.
(Philadelphia's 3rd choice, 48th overall, in 1985 Entry Draft).

			Regular Season								Playoffs						
Season	Club	Lea	GP	W	L	T	Mins	GA	SO	Avg	GP	W	L	Mins	GA	SO	Avg
1984-85	Moose Jaw	WHL	58	15	35	0	3004	297	0	5.93	....	....	....	....	....	....	....
1985-86a	Moose Jaw	WHL	62	19	34	3	3482	276	1	4.76	9	4	4	490	48	0	5.88
1986-87	Moose Jaw	WHL	31	14	13	2	1776	123	2	4.16	....	....	....	....	....	....	....
	Portland	WHL	24	15	7	1	1460	111	0	4.56	19	12	7	1167	83	1	4.27
1987-88	Hershey	AHL	25	14	7	0	1273	78	1	3.68	....	....	....	....	....	....	....
1988-89	Hershey	AHL	38	16	14	5	2093	144	0	4.13	....	....	....	....	....	....	....
1989-90	New Haven	AHL	23	10	11	2	1356	85	0	3.76	....	....	....	....	....	....	....
	Nashville	ECHL	10	6	3	0	529	43	0	4.87	....	....	....	....	....	....	....
1990-91	New Haven	AHL	26	5	14	3	1375	90	1	3.93	....	....	....	....	....	....	....
	Phoenix	IHL	4	2	0	0	180	13	0	4.33	....	....	....	....	....	....	....
1991-92	Phoenix	IHL	30	10	15	3	1774	120	0	4.06	....	....	....	....	....	....	....

a WHL First All-Star Team, East Division (1986)

Signed as a free agent by **Los Angeles**, December 15, 1989.

GORDON, SCOTT

Goaltender. Catches left. 5'10", 175 lbs. Born, Brockton, MA, February 6, 1963.

			Regular Season								Playoffs						
Season	Club	Lea	GP	W	L	T	Mins	GA	SO	Avg	GP	W	L	Mins	GA	SO	Avg
1982-83	Boston College	ECAC	9	3	3	0	371	15	0	2.43	....	....	....	....	....	....	....
1983-84	Boston College	ECAC	35	21	13	0	2034	127	1	3.75	....	....	....	....	....	....	....
1984-85	Boston College	H.E.	36	23	11	2	2179	131	1	3.61	....	....	....	....	....	....	....
1985-86a	Boston College	H.E.	32	17	8	1	1852	112	2	3.63	....	....	....	....	....	....	....
1986-87	Fredericton	AHL	32	9	12	2	1616	120	0	4.46	....	....	....	....	....	....	....
1987-88	Baltimore	AHL	34	7	17	3	1638	145	0	5.31	....	....	....	....	....	....	....
1988-89	Halifax	AHL	2	0	2	0	116	10	0	5.17	....	....	....	....	....	....	....
	Johnstown	ECHL	31	....	....	....	1839	117	2	3.82	....	....	....	....	....	....	....
1989-90	**Quebec**	**NHL**	**10**	**2**	**8**	**0**	**597**	**53**	**0**	**5.33**	....	....	....	....	....	....	....
	Halifax	AHL	48	28	16	3	2851	158	0	3.33	6	2	4	340	28	0	4.94
1990-91	**Quebec**	**NHL**	**13**	**0**	**8**	**0**	**485**	**48**	**0**	**5.94**	....	....	....	....	....	....	....
	Halifax	AHL	24	12	10	2	1410	87	2	3.70	....	....	....	....	....	....	....
1991-92	U.S. National	....	29	13	12	3	1666	112	0	4.03	....	....	....	....	....	....	....
	U.S. Olympic	....	1	....	....	....	17	2	0	6.97	....	....	....	....	....	....	....
	Halifax	AHL	7	3	3	1	424	27	0	3.82	....	....	....	....	....	....	....
	New Haven	AHL	4	3	1	0	239	11	0	2.76	2	0	2	119	9	0	4.54
	NHL Totals		**23**	**2**	**16**	**0**	**1082**	**101**	**0**	**5.60**	....	....	....	....	....	....	....

a Hockey East First All-Star Team (1986)

Signed as a free agent by **Quebec**, October 2, 1986.

GOSSELIN, MARIO

Goaltender. Catches left. 5'8", 160 lbs. Born, Thetford Mines, Que., June 15, 1963.
(Quebec's 3rd choice, 55th overall, in 1982 Entry Draft).

			Regular Season								Playoffs						
Season	Club	Lea	GP	W	L	T	Mins	GA	SO	Avg	GP	W	L	Mins	GA	SO	Avg
1980-81	Shawinigan	QMJHL	21	4	9	0	907	75	0	4.96	1	0	0	20	2	0	6.00
1981-82a	Shawinigan	QMJHL	60	....	....	....	3404	230	0	4.05	14	....	....	788	58	0	4.42
1982-83	Shawinigan	QMJHL	46	32	9	1	2496	133	3	3.12	8	5	3	457	29	0	3.81
1983-84	Cdn. Olympic	....	36	....	....	....	2007	126	0	3.77	....	....	....	....	....	....	....
	Quebec	**NHL**	**3**	**2**	**0**	**0**	**148**	**3**	**1**	**1.21**	....	....	....	....	....	....	....
1984-85	**Quebec**	**NHL**	**35**	**19**	**10**	**3**	**1960**	**109**	**1**	**3.34**	**17**	**9**	**8**	**1059**	**54**	**0**	**3.06**
1985-86	**Quebec**	**NHL**	**31**	**14**	**14**	**1**	**1726**	**111**	**2**	**3.86**	**1**	**0**	**1**	**40**	**5**	**0**	**7.50**
	Fredericton	AHL	5	2	2	1	304	15	0	2.96	....	....	....	....	....	....	....
1986-87	**Quebec**	**NHL**	**30**	**13**	**11**	**1**	**1625**	**86**	**0**	**3.18**	**11**	**7**	**4**	**654**	**37**	**0**	**3.39**
1987-88	**Quebec**	**NHL**	**54**	**20**	**28**	**4**	**3002**	**189**	**2**	**3.78**	....	....	....	....	....	....	....
1988-89	**Quebec**	**NHL**	**39**	**11**	**19**	**3**	**2064**	**146**	**0**	**4.24**	....	....	....	....	....	....	....
	Halifax	AHL	3	3	0	0	183	9	0	2.95	....	....	....	....	....	....	....
1989-90	**Los Angeles**	**NHL**	**26**	**7**	**11**	**1**	**1226**	**79**	**0**	**3.87**	**3**	**0**	**2**	**63**	**3**	**0**	**2.90**
1990-91	Phoenix	IHL	46	24	15	4	2673	172	1	3.86	11	7	4	670	43	0	3.83
1991-92	Springfield	AHL	47	28	11	5	2606	142	0	3.27	6	1	4	319	18	0	3.39
	NHL Totals		**218**	**86**	**93**	**13**	**11751**	**723**	**6**	**3.69**	**32**	**16**	**15**	**1815**	**99**	**0**	**3.27**

a QMJHL Second All-Star Team (1982)

Played in NHL All-Star Game (1986)

Signed as a free agent by **Los Angeles**, June 14, 1989. Signed as a free agent by **Hartford**, September 4, 1991.

GOVERDE, DAVID

Goaltender. Catches right. 6', 210 lbs. Born, Toronto, Ont., April 9, 1970.
(Los Angeles' 4th choice, 91st overall, in 1990 Entry Draft).

			Regular Season								Playoffs						
Season	Club	Lea	GP	W	L	T	Mins	GA	SO	Avg	GP	W	L	Mins	GA	SO	Avg
1989-90	Sudbury	OHL	52	28	12	7	2941	182	0	3.71	7	3	3	394	25	0	3.81
1990-91	Phoenix	IHL	40	11	19	5	2007	137	0	4.10	....	....	....	....	....	....	....
1991-92	**Los Angeles**	**NHL**	**2**	**1**	**1**	**0**	**120**	**9**	**0**	**4.50**	....	....	....	....	....	....	....
	Phoenix	IHL	35	11	19	3	1951	129	1	3.97	....	....	....	....	....	....	....
	NHL Totals		**2**	**1**	**1**	**0**	**120**	**9**	**0**	**4.50**	....	....	....	....	....	....	....

GRAVISTIN, SHAUN

Goaltender. Catches left. 5'7", 150 lbs. Born, Calgary, Alta., November 17, 1970.
(Hartford's 1st choice, 15th overall, in 1991 Supplemental Draft).

			Regular Season								Playoffs						
Season	Club	Lea	GP	W	L	T	Mins	GA	SO	Avg	GP	W	L	Mins	GA	SO	Avg
1989-90	Alaska-Anch.	G.N.	2	1	0	0	81	3	0	2.22	....	....	....	....	....	....	....
1990-91	Alaska-Anch.	G.N.	8	4	2	1	425	20	0	2.82	....	....	....	....	....	....	....
1991-92	Alaska-Anch.	G.N.	9	8	0	1	524	30	0	3.44	....	....	....	....	....	....	....

GREENLAY, MIKE

Goaltender. Catches left. 6'3", 200 lbs. Born, Vitoria, Brazil, September 15, 1968.
(Edmonton's 9th choice, 189th overall, in 1986 Entry Draft).

			Regular Season								Playoffs						
Season	Club	Lea	GP	W	L	T	Mins	GA	SO	Avg	GP	W	L	Mins	GA	SO	Avg
1986-87	Lake Superior	CCHA	17	7	5	0	744	44	0	3.54	....	....	....	....	....	....	....
1987-88	Lake Superior	CCHA	19	10	3	3	1023	57	0	3.34	....	....	....	....	....	....	....
1988-89	Saskatoon	WHL	20	10	8	1	1128	86	0	4.57	6	2	0	174	16	0	5.52
	Lake Superior	CCHA	2	1	1	0	85	6	0	4.23	....	....	....	....	....	....	....
1989-90	**Edmonton**	**NHL**	**2**	**0**	**0**	**0**	**20**	**4**	**0**	**12.00**	....	....	....	....	....	....	....
	Cape Breton	AHL	46	19	18	5	2595	146	2	3.38	5	1	3	306	26	0	5.09
1990-91	Cape Breton	AHL	11	5	2	0	493	33	0	4.02	....	....	....	....	....	....	....
	Knoxville	ECHL	29	17	9	2	1725	108	2	3.75	....	....	....	....	....	....	....
1991-92	Cape Breton	AHL	3	1	1	1	144	12	0	5.00	....	....	....	....	....	....	....
	Knoxville	ECHL	27	8	12	2	1415	113	0	4.79	....	....	....	....	....	....	....
	NHL Totals		**2**	**0**	**0**	**0**	**20**	**4**	**0**	**12.00**	....	....	....	....	....	....	....

Signed as a free agent by **Tampa Bay**, July 29, 1992.

GUENETTE, STEVE (guh-NEHT)

Goaltender. Catches left. 5'10", 175 lbs. Born, Gloucester, Ont., November 13, 1965.

			Regular Season								Playoffs						
Season	Club	Lea	GP	W	L	T	Mins	GA	SO	Avg	GP	W	L	Mins	GA	SO	Avg
1983-84	Guelph	OHL	38	9	18	2	1808	155	0	5.14	....	....	....	....	....	....	....
1984-85	Guelph	OHL	47	16	22	4	2593	200	1	4.63	....	....	....	....	....	....	....
1985-86a	Guelph	OHL	48	26	20	1	2908	165	*3	3.40	20	15	3	1167	54	1	2.77
1986-87	**Pittsburgh**	**NHL**	**2**	**0**	**2**	**0**	**113**	**8**	**0**	**4.25**	....	....	....	....	....	....	....
	Baltimore	AHL	54	21	23	0	3035	157	5	3.10	....	....	....	....	....	....	....
1987-88	**Pittsburgh**	**NHL**	**19**	**12**	**7**	**0**	**1092**	**61**	**1**	**3.35**	....	....	....	....	....	....	....
bc	Muskegon	IHL	33	23	4	5	1943	91	*4	*2.81	....	....	....	....	....	....	....
1988-89	**Pittsburgh**	**NHL**	**11**	**5**	**6**	**0**	**574**	**41**	**0**	**4.29**	....	....	....	....	....	....	....
	Muskegon	IHL	10	6	4	0	597	39	0	*3.92	....	....	....	....	....	....	....
c	Salt Lake	IHL	30	24	5	0	1810	82	2	*2.72	*13	*8	5	*782	44	0	3.38
1989-90	**Calgary**	**NHL**	**2**	**1**	**1**	**0**	**119**	**8**	**0**	**4.03**	....	....	....	....	....	....	....
	Salt Lake	IHL	47	22	21	4	2779	160	0	3.45	*10	4	4	545	35	*1	3.85
1990-91	**Calgary**	**NHL**	**1**	**1**	**0**	**0**	**60**	**4**	**0**	**4.00**	....	....	....	....	....	....	....
	Salt Lake	IHL	43	*26	13	4	2521	137	2	3.26	2	0	1	59	9	0	9.15
1991-92	Kalamazoo	IHL	21	7	9	3	1094	70	1	3.84	....	....	....	....	....	....	....
	NHL Totals		**35**	**19**	**16**	**0**	**1958**	**122**	**1**	**3.74**	....	....	....	....	....	....	....

a OHL Second All-Star Team (1986)
b Won James Norris Memorial Trophy (IHL Top Goaltender) (1988, 1989)
c IHL Second All-Star Team (1988, 1989)

Signed as a free agent by **Pittsburgh**, April 6, 1985. Traded to **Calgary** by **Pittsburgh** for Calgary's sixth round choice (Mike Needham) in 1989 Entry Draft, January 9, 1989. Traded to **Minnesota** by **Calgary** for Minnesota's seventh round choice (Matt Hoffman) in 1991 Entry Draft, May 30, 1991.

HACKETT, JEFF

Goaltender. Catches left. 6'1", 180 lbs. Born, London, Ont., June 1, 1968.
(NY Islanders' 2nd choice, 34th overall, in 1987 Entry Draft).

			Regular Season								Playoffs						
Season	Club	Lea	GP	W	L	T	Mins	GA	SO	Avg	GP	W	L	Mins	GA	SO	Avg
1986-87	Oshawa	OHL	31	18	9	2	1672	85	2	3.05	15	8	7	895	40	0	2.68
1987-88a	Oshawa	OHL	53	30	21	2	3165	205	0	3.89	7	3	4	438	31	0	4.25
1988-89	**NY Islanders**	**NHL**	**13**	**4**	**7**	**0**	**662**	**39**	**0**	**3.53**	....	....	....	....	....	....	....
	Springfield	AHL	29	12	14	2	1677	116	0	4.15	....	....	....	....	....	....	....
1989-90b	Springfield	AHL	54	24	25	3	3045	187	1	3.68	*17	*10	5	934	60	0	3.85
1990-91	**NY Islanders**	**NHL**	**30**	**5**	**18**	**1**	**1508**	**91**	**0**	**3.62**	....	....	....	....	....	....	....
1991-92	**San Jose**	**NHL**	**42**	**11**	**27**	**1**	**2314**	**148**	**0**	**3.84**	....	....	....	....	....	....	....
	NHL Totals		**85**	**20**	**52**	**2**	**4484**	**278**	**0**	**3.72**	....	....	....	....	....	....	....

a OHL Third All-Star Team (1988)
b Won Jack Butterfield Trophy (Playoff MVP-AHL) (1990)

Claimed by **San Jose** from **NY Islanders** in Expansion Draft, May 30, 1991.

HARVEY, CHRIS

Goaltender. Catches left. 6'1", 180 lbs. Born, Cambridge, MA, December 8, 1967.
(Boston's 1st choice, 23rd overall, in 1988 Supplemental Draft).

			Regular Season								Playoffs						
Season	Club	Lea	GP	W	L	T	Mins	GA	SO	Avg	GP	W	L	Mins	GA	SO	Avg
1986-87	Brown	ECAC	22	9	13	0	1241	88	0	4.26	....	....	....	....	....	....	....
1987-88	Brown	ECAC	21	3	17	1	1235	104	0	5.05	....	....	....	....	....	....	....
1988-89	Brown	ECAC	23	1	22	0	1327	131	0	5.92	....	....	....	....	....	....	....
1989-90ab	Brown	ECAC	28	10	15	3	1646	107	0	3.90	....	....	....	....	....	....	....
1990-91	Maine	AHL	3	1	1	0	149	8	0	3.22	....	....	....	....	....	....	....
	Johnstown	ECHL	31	11	13	2	1606	113	1	4.22	2	0	0	68	8	0	7.05
1991-92	Johnstown	ECHL	4	2	2	0	193	12	0	4.04	....	....	....	....	....	....	....
	Nashville	ECHL	20	5	6	2	956	68	0	4.27	....	....	....	....	....	....	....
	Raleigh	ECHL	5	3	2	0	305	24	0	4.72	4	1	3	249	17	0	4.10

a ECAC Second All-Star Team (1990)
b NCAA East Second All-American Team (1990)

HASEK, DOMINIK (HAH-shehk)

Goaltender. Catches left. 5'11", 165 lbs. Born, Pardubice, Czechoslovakia, January 29, 1965.
(Chicago's 11th choice, 199th overall, in 1983 Entry Draft).

			Regular Season								Playoffs						
Season	Club	Lea	GP	W	L	T	Mins	GA	SO	Avg	GP	W	L	Mins	GA	SO	Avg
1981-82	Pardubice	Czech.	12	....	....	....	661	34	....	3.09	....	....	....	....	....	....	....
1982-83	Pardubice	Czech.	42	....	....	....	2358	105	....	2.67	....	....	....	....	....	....	....
1983-84	Pardubice	Czech.	40	....	....	....	2304	108	....	2.81	....	....	....	....	....	....	....
1984-85	Pardubice	Czech.	42	....	....	....	2419	131	....	3.25	....	....	....	....	....	....	....
1985-86a	Pardubice	Czech.	45	....	....	....	2689	138	....	3.08	....	....	....	....	....	....	....
1986-87ab	Pardubice	Czech.	43	....	....	....	2515	103	....	2.46	....	....	....	....	....	....	....
1987-88ac	Pardubice	Czech.	31	....	....	....	2265	98	....	2.60	....	....	....	....	....	....	....
1988-89abc	Pardubice	Czech.	42	....	....	....	2507	114	....	2.73	....	....	....	....	....	....	....
1989-90abc	Dukla Jihlava	Czech.	40	....	....	....	2251	80	....	2.13	....	....	....	....	....	....	....
1990-91	**Chicago**	**NHL**	**5**	**3**	**0**	**1**	**195**	**8**	**0**	**2.46**	**3**	**0**	**0**	**69**	**3**	**0**	**2.61**
d	Indianapolis	IHL	33	20	11	1	1903	80	*5	*2.52	1	1	0	60	3	0	3.00
1991-92e	**Chicago**	**NHL**	**20**	**10**	**4**	**1**	**1014**	**44**	**1**	**2.60**	**3**	**0**	**2**	**158**	**8**	**0**	**3.04**
	Indianapolis	IHL	20	7	10	3	1162	69	1	3.56	....	....	....	....	....	....	....
	NHL Totals		**25**	**13**	**4**	**2**	**1209**	**52**	**1**	**2.58**	**6**	**0**	**2**	**227**	**11**	**0**	**2.91**

a Czechoslovakian Goaltender-of-the-Year (1986, 1987, 1988, 1989, 1990)
b Czechoslovakian Player-of-the-Year (1987, 1989, 1990)
c Czechoslovakian First-Team All-Star (1988, 1989, 1990)
d IHL First All-Star Team (1991)
e NHL/Upper Deck All-Rookie Team (1992)

Traded to **Buffalo** by **Chicago** for Stephane Beauregard and future considerations, August 7, 1992.

HAYWARD, BRIAN

Goaltender. Catches left. 5'10", 180 lbs. Born, Toronto, Ont., June 25, 1960.

			Regular Season								Playoffs						
Season	Club	Lea	GP	W	L	T	Mins	GA	SO	Avg	GP	W	L	Mins	GA	SO	Avg
1978-79	Cornell	ECAC	25	18	6	0	1469	95	0	3.88	3	2	1	179	14	0	4.66
1979-80	Cornell	ECAC	12	2	7	0	508	52	0	6.02	....	....	....	....	....	....	....
1980-81	Cornell	ECAC	19	11	4	1	967	58	1	3.54	4	2	1	181	18	0	4.50
1981-82ab	Cornell	ECAC	22	11	10	1	1320	68	0	3.09	....	....	....	....	....	....	....
1982-83	**Winnipeg**	**NHL**	**24**	**10**	**12**	**2**	**1440**	**89**	**1**	**3.71**	**3**	**0**	**3**	**160**	**14**	**0**	**5.24**
	Sherbrooke	AHL	22	6	11	3	1208	89	1	4.42	....	....	....	....	....	....	....
1983-84	**Winnipeg**	**NHL**	**28**	**7**	**18**	**2**	**1530**	**124**	**0**	**4.86**	....	....	....	....	....	....	....
	Sherbrooke	AHL	15	4	8	0	781	69	0	5.30	....	....	....	....	....	....	....
1984-85	**Winnipeg**	**NHL**	**61**	**33**	**17**	**7**	**3436**	**220**	**0**	**3.84**	**6**	**2**	**4**	**309**	**23**	**0**	**4.47**
1985-86	**Winnipeg**	**NHL**	**52**	**13**	**28**	**5**	**2721**	**217**	**0**	**4.79**	**2**	**0**	**1**	**68**	**6**	**0**	**5.29**
	Sherbrooke	AHL	3	2	0	1	185	5	0	1.62	....	....	....	....	....	....	....
1986-87c	**Montreal**	**NHL**	**37**	**19**	**13**	**4**	**2178**	**102**	**1**	***2.81**	**13**	**6**	**5**	**708**	**32**	**0**	**2.71**
1987-88c	**Montreal**	**NHL**	**39**	**22**	**10**	**4**	**2247**	**107**	**2**	**2.86**	**4**	**2**	**2**	**230**	**9**	**0**	**2.35**
1988-89c	**Montreal**	**NHL**	**36**	**20**	**13**	**3**	**2091**	**101**	**1**	**2.90**	**2**	**1**	**1**	**124**	**7**	**0**	**3.39**
1989-90	**Montreal**	**NHL**	**29**	**10**	**12**	**6**	**1674**	**94**	**1**	**3.37**	**1**	**0**	**0**	**33**	**2**	**0**	**3.64**
1990-91	**Minnesota**	**NHL**	**26**	**6**	**15**	**3**	**1473**	**77**	**2**	**3.14**	**6**	**0**	**2**	**171**	**11**	**0**	**3.86**
	Kalamazoo	IHL	2	2	0	0	120	5	0	2.50	....	....	....	....	....	....	....
1991-92	**San Jose**	**NHL**	**7**	**1**	**4**	**0**	**305**	**25**	**0**	**4.92**	....	....	....	....	....	....	....
	Kansas City	IHL	2	1	1	0	119	3	1	1.51	....	....	....	....	....	....	....
	NHL Totals		**339**	**141**	**142**	**36**	**19095**	**1156**	**8**	**3.63**	**37**	**11**	**18**	**1803**	**104**	**0**	**3.46**

a ECAC First All-Star Team (1982)
b NCAA All-American Team (1982)
c Shared William Jennings Trophy with Patrick Roy (1987, 1988, 1989)

Signed as a free agent by **Winnipeg**, May 5, 1982. Traded to **Montreal** by **Winnipeg** for Steve Penney and the rights to Jan Ingman, August 19, 1986. Traded to **Minnesota** by **Montreal** for Jayson More, November 7, 1990. Claimed by **San Jose** from **Minnesota** in Dispersal Draft, May 30, 1991.

HEALY, GLENN

Goaltender. Catches left. 5'10", 183 lbs. Born, Pickering, Ont., August 23, 1962.

			Regular Season								Playoffs						
Season	Club	Lea	GP	W	L	T	Mins	GA	SO	Avg	GP	W	L	Mins	GA	SO	Avg
1981-82	W. Michigan	CCHA	27	7	19	1	1569	116	0	4.44	....	....	....	....	....	....	....
1982-83	W. Michigan	CCHA	30	8	19	2	1732	116	0	4.01	....	....	....	....	....	....	....
1983-84	W. Michigan	CCHA	38	19	16	3	2241	146	0	3.90	....	....	....	....	....	....	....
1984-85	W. Michigan	CCHA	37	21	14	2	2171	118	0	3.26	....	....	....	....	....	....	....
1985-86	**Los Angeles**	**NHL**	**1**	**0**	**0**	**0**	**51**	**6**	**0**	**7.06**	....	....	....	....	....	....	....
	New Haven	AHL	43	21	15	4	2410	160	0	3.98	2	0	2	49	11	0	5.55
1986-87	New Haven	AHL	47	21	15	0	2828	173	1	3.67	7	3	4	427	19	0	2.67
1987-88	**Los Angeles**	**NHL**	**34**	**12**	**18**	**1**	**1869**	**135**	**1**	**4.33**	**4**	**1**	**3**	**240**	**20**	**0**	**5.00**
1988-89	**Los Angeles**	**NHL**	**48**	**25**	**19**	**2**	**2699**	**192**	**0**	**4.27**	**3**	**0**	**1**	**97**	**6**	**0**	**3.71**
1989-90	**NY Islanders**	**NHL**	**39**	**12**	**19**	**6**	**2197**	**128**	**2**	**3.50**	**4**	**1**	**2**	**166**	**9**	**0**	**3.25**
1990-91	**NY Islanders**	**NHL**	**53**	**18**	**24**	**9**	**2999**	**166**	**0**	**3.32**	....	....	....	....	....	....	....
1991-92	**NY Islanders**	**NHL**	**37**	**14**	**16**	**4**	**1960**	**124**	**1**	**3.80**	....	....	....	....	....	....	....
	NHL Totals		**212**	**81**	**96**	**22**	**11775**	**751**	**4**	**3.83**	**11**	**2**	**6**	**503**	**35**	**0**	**4.18**

Signed as a free agent by **Los Angeles**, June 13, 1985. Signed as a free agent by **NY Islanders**, August 16, 1989.

HEBERT, GUY (HEE-buhrt, GIGH)

Goaltender. Catches left. 5'11", 180 lbs. Born, Troy, NY, January 7, 1967.
(St. Louis' 8th choice, 159th overall, in 1987 Entry Draft).

			Regular Season								Playoffs						
Season	Club	Lea	GP	W	L	T	Mins	GA	SO	Avg	GP	W	L	Mins	GA	SO	Avg
1986-87	Hamilton Coll.	NCAA	18	12	5	0	1070	40	0	2.19	....	....	....	....	....	....	....
1987-88	Hamilton Coll.	NCAA	8	5	3	0	450	19	0	2.53	....	....	....	....	....	....	....
1988-89	Hamilton Coll.	NCAA	25	18	7	0	1453	62	0	2.56	....	....	....	....	....	....	....
1989-90	Peoria	IHL	30	7	13	7	1706	124	1	4.36	2	0	1	76	5	0	3.95
1990-91a	Peoria	IHL	36	24	10	1	2093	100	2	2.87	8	3	4	458	32	0	4.19
1991-92	**St. Louis**	**NHL**	**13**	**5**	**5**	**1**	**738**	**36**	**0**	**2.93**	....	....	....	....	....	....	....
	Peoria	IHL	29	20	9	0	1731	98	0	3.40	4	3	1	239	9	0	2.26
	NHL Totals		**13**	**5**	**5**	**1**	**738**	**36**	**0**	**2.93**	....	....	....	....	....	....	....

a IHL Second All-Star Team (1991)

HEINKE, MICHAEL

Goaltender. Catches left. 5'11", 165 lbs. Born, Denville, NY, January 11, 1971.
(New Jersey's 5th choice, 89th overall, in 1989 Entry Draft).

			Regular Season								Playoffs						
Season	Club	Lea	GP	W	L	T	Mins	GA	SO	Avg	GP	W	L	Mins	GA	SO	Avg
1990-91	Providence	H.E.	14	8	7	1	923	74	0	4.81	....	....	....	....	....	....	....
1991-92	Providence	H.E.	16	10	4	0	816	48	*2	3.53	....	....	....	....	....	....	....

HENDERSON, TODD

Goaltender. Catches left. 6'1", 155 lbs. Born, Sault Ste. Marie, Ont., March 8, 1969.
(Buffalo's 11th choice, 224th overall, in 1989 Entry Draft).

			Regular Season								Playoffs						
Season	Club	Lea	GP	W	L	T	Mins	GA	SO	Avg	GP	W	L	Mins	GA	SO	Avg
1990-91	Alaska-Fair.	G.N.	20	10	9	1	1155	74	0	3.85	....	....	....	....	....	....	....
1991-92	Alaska-Fair.	G.N.	20	8	12	0	1111	80	0	4.32	....	....	....	....	....	....	....

HERLOFSKY, DEREK

Goaltender. Catches left. 6', 160 lbs. Born, Minneapolis, MN, October 1, 1971.
(Minnesota's 9th choice, 184th overall, in 1991 Entry Draft).

			Regular Season								Playoffs						
Season	Club	Lea	GP	W	L	T	Mins	GA	SO	Avg	GP	W	L	Mins	GA	SO	Avg
1990-91	St. Paul	USHL	33	18	12	2	1930	113	0	3.51	....	....	....	....	....	....	....
1991-92	Boston U.	H.E.	9	7	1	1	537	22	0	2.46	....	....	....	....	....	....	....

HEXTALL, RON

Goaltender. Catches left. 6'3", 192 lbs. Born, Brandon, Man., May 3, 1964.
(Philadelphia's 6th choice, 119th overall, in 1982 Entry Draft).

			Regular Season								Playoffs						
Season	Club	Lea	GP	W	L	T	Mins	GA	SO	Avg	GP	W	L	Mins	GA	SO	Avg
1981-82	Brandon	WHL	30	12	11	0	1398	133	0	5.71	3	0	2	103	16	0	9.32
1982-83	Brandon	WHL	44	13	30	0	2589	249	0	5.77	....	....	....	....	....	....	....
1983-84	Brandon	WHL	46	29	13	2	2670	190	0	4.27	10	5	5	592	37	0	3.75
1984-85	Hershey	AHL	11	4	6	0	555	34	0	3.68	....	....	....	....	....	....	....
	Kalamazoo	IHL	19	6	11	1	1103	80	0	4.35	....	....	....	....	....	....	....
1985-86ab	Hershey	AHL	*53	30	19	2	*3061	174	*5	3.41	13	5	7	780	42	*1	3.23
1986-87cdef	**Philadelphia**	**NHL**	***66**	**37**	**21**	**6**	***3799**	**190**	**1**	**3.00**	***26**	**15**	**11**	***1540**	**71**	***2**	**2.77**
1987-88g	**Philadelphia**	**NHL**	**62**	**30**	**22**	**7**	**3560**	**208**	**0**	**3.50**	**7**	**2**	**4**	**379**	**30**	**0**	**4.75**
1988-89h	**Philadelphia**	**NHL**	***64**	**30**	**28**	**6**	***3756**	**202**	**0**	**3.23**	**15**	**8**	**7**	**886**	**49**	**0**	**3.32**
1989-90	**Philadelphia**	**NHL**	**8**	**4**	**2**	**1**	**419**	**29**	**0**	**4.15**	....	....	....	....	....	....	....
	Hershey	AHL	1	1	0	0	49	3	0	3.67	....	....	....	....	....	....	....
1990-91	**Philadelphia**	**NHL**	**36**	**13**	**16**	**5**	**2035**	**106**	**0**	**3.13**	....	....	....	....	....	....	....
1991-92	**Philadelphia**	**NHL**	**45**	**16**	**21**	**6**	**2668**	**151**	**3**	**3.40**	....	....	....	....	....	....	....
	NHL Totals		**281**	**130**	**110**	**31**	**16237**	**886**	**4**	**3.27**	**48**	**25**	**22**	**2805**	**150**	**2**	**3.21**

a AHL First All-Star Team (1986)
b AHL Rookie of the Year (1986)
c NHL First All-Star Team (1987)
d Won Vezina Trophy (1987)
e Won Conn Smythe Trophy (1987)
f NHL All-Rookie Team (1987)
g Scored a goal vs. Boston, December 8, 1987
h Scored a goal in playoffs vs. Washington, April 11, 1989

Played in NHL All-Star Game (1988)

Traded to **Quebec** by **Philadelphia** with Peter Forsberg, Steve Duchesne, Kerry Huffman, Mike Ricci, Chris Simon, Philadelphia's first choice in the 1993 and 1994 Entry Drafts and cash for Eric Lindros, June 30, 1992.

HILLEBRANDT, JON

Goaltender. Catches left. 5'10", 160 lbs. Born, Cottage Grove, WI, December 18, 1971.
(NY Rangers' 12th choice, 202nd overall, in 1990 Entry Draft).

			Regular Season								Playoffs						
Season	Club	Lea	GP	W	L	T	Mins	GA	SO	Avg	GP	W	L	Mins	GA	SO	Avg
1990-91	Madison	USHL	28	10	14	3	1631	111	0	4.08	....	....	....	....	....	....	....
1991-92a	Ill.-Chicago	CCHA	31	7	19	....	1754	121	0	4.14	....	....	....	....	....	....	....

a CCHA Second All-Star Team (1992)

HIRSCH, COREY

Goaltender. Catches left. 5'9", 150 lbs. Born, Medicine Hat, Alta., July 1, 1972.
(NY Rangers' 8th choice, 169th overall, in 1991 Entry Draft).

			Regular Season								Playoffs						
Season	Club	Lea	GP	W	L	T	Mins	GA	SO	Avg	GP	W	L	Mins	GA	SO	Avg
1989-90	Kamloops	WHL	*63	*48	13	0	3608	230	*3	3.82	*17	*14	3	*1043	60	0	*3.45
1990-91	Kamloops	WHL	38	26	7	1	1970	100	3	*3.05	11	5	6	623	42	....	4.04
1991-92a	Kamloops	WHL	48	35	10	2	2732	124	5	*2.72	*16	*11	5	954	35	*2	*2.20

a WHL and Canadian Major Junior Goaltender of the Year (1992)

HNILICKA, MILAN (hih-LEECH-kah, MEE-lahn)

Goaltender. Catches left. 6', 180 lbs. Born, Kladno, Czech., June 25, 1973.
(NY Islanders' 4th choice, 70th overall, in 1991 Entry Draft).

			Regular Season								Playoffs						
Season	Club	Lea	GP	W	L	T	Mins	GA	SO	Avg	GP	W	L	Mins	GA	SO	Avg
1990-91	Kladno	Czech.	35	....	....	....	2122	98	0	2.80	....	....	....	....	....	....	....
1991-92	Kladno	Czech.	30	....	....	....	1788	107	0	3.59	....	....	....	....	....	....	....

HOFFORT, BRUCE

Goaltender. Catches left. 5'10", 185 lbs. Born, North Battleford, Sask., July 30, 1966.

			Regular Season								Playoffs						
Season	Club	Lea	GP	W	L	T	Mins	GA	SO	Avg	GP	W	L	Mins	GA	SO	Avg
1987-88ab	Lake Superior	CCHA	31	23	4	3	1787	79	2	2.65	....	....	....	....	....	....	....
1988-89ac	Lake Superior	CCHA	44	27	10	5	2595	117	0	2.71	....	....	....	....	....	....	....
1989-90	**Philadelphia**	**NHL**	**7**	**3**	**0**	**2**	**329**	**19**	**0**	**3.47**	....	....	....	....	....	....	....
	Hershey	AHL	40	16	18	4	2284	139	1	3.65	....	....	....	....	....	....	....
1990-91	**Philadelphia**	**NHL**	**2**	**1**	**0**	**1**	**39**	**3**	**0**	**4.62**	....	....	....	....	....	....	....
	Hershey	AHL	18	3	12	1	913	74	0	4.86	....	....	....	....	....	....	....
	Kansas City	IHL	18	6	7	0	883	68	0	4.62	....	....	....	....	....	....	....
1991-92	San Diego	IHL	26	11	9	4	1474	89	0	3.62	....	....	....	....	....	....	....
	NHL Totals		**9**	**4**	**0**	**3**	**368**	**22**	**0**	**3.59**	....	....	....	....	....	....	....

a CCHA First All-Star Team (1988, 1989)
b NCAA All-Tournament Team (1988)
c CCHA Player of the Year (1989)

Signed as a free agent by **Philadelphia**, June 30, 1989.

HORYNA, ROBERT (hohr-EE-nah)

Goaltender. Catches left. 5'11", 185 lbs. Born, Hradec Kralove, Czech., September 10, 1970.
(Toronto's 8th choice, 178th overall, in 1990 Entry Draft).

			Regular Season								Playoffs						
Season	Club	Lea	GP	W	L	T	Mins	GA	SO	Avg	GP	W	L	Mins	GA	SO	Avg
1989-90	Dukla Jihlava	Czech.	13	....	....	....	710	41	....	3.46	....	....	....	....	....	....	....
1990-91	Newmarket	AHL	22	8	10	2	1162	81	0	4.18	....	....	....	....	....	....	....
1991-92	St. John's	AHL	7	1	2	0	220	17	0	4.64	....	....	....	....	....	....	....

HOUK, ROD

Goaltender. Catches left. 5'8", 170 lbs. Born, Regina, Sask., February 2, 1968.
(Minnesota's 1st choice, 13th overall, in 1990 Supplemental Draft).

			Regular Season								Playoffs						
Season	Club	Lea	GP	W	L	T	Mins	GA	SO	Avg	GP	W	L	Mins	GA	SO	Avg
1987-88	Regina	WHL	58	29	20	3	3072	200	2	3.91	....	....	....	....	....	....	....
1988-89	Regina	WHL	59	20	30	6	3466	248	0	4.29	....	....	....	....	....	....	....
1989-90	U. of Regina	CWUAA	18	7	9	1	1064	58	1	3.27	....	....	....	....	....	....	....
1990-91	U. of Regina	CWUAA	28	13	14	1	1671	111	1	3.99	....	....	....	....	....	....	....
1991-92	San Diego	IHL	2	0	1	0	80	6	0	4.5	....	....	....	....	....	....	....
	Kalamazoo	IHL	4	2	1	0	199	10	0	3.02	3	0	0	41	3	0	4.39
	Dayton	ECHL	33	16	12	1	1775	130	0	4.39	2	0	2	69	10	0	8.70

HRIVNAK, JIM (riv-NAK)

Goaltender. Catches left. 6'2", 195 lbs. Born, Montreal, Que., May 28, 1968.
(Washington's 4th choice, 61st overall, in 1986 Entry Draft).

			Regular Season								Playoffs						
Season	Club	Lea	GP	W	L	T	Mins	GA	SO	Avg	GP	W	L	Mins	GA	SO	Avg
1985-86	Merrimack	NCAA	21	12	8	0	1230	75	0	3.66	....	....	....	....	....	....	....
1986-87	Merrimack	NCAA	34	27	7	0	1618	58	3	2.14	....	....	....	....	....	....	....
1987-88	Merrimack	NCAA	37	31	6	0	2119	84	4	2.38	....	....	....	....	....	....	....
1988-89	Merrimack	NCAA	22	....	....	....	1295	52	4	2.41	....	....	....	....	....	....	....
	Baltimore	AHL	10	1	8	0	502	55	0	6.57	....	....	....	....	....	....	....
1989-90	**Washington**	**NHL**	**11**	**5**	**5**	**0**	**609**	**36**	**0**	**3.55**	....	....	....	....	....	....	....
a	Baltimore	AHL	47	24	19	2	2722	139	*4	3.06	6	4	2	360	19	0	3.17
1990-91	**Washington**	**NHL**	**9**	**4**	**2**	**1**	**432**	**26**	**0**	**3.61**	....	....	....	....	....	....	....
	Baltimore	AHL	42	20	16	6	2481	134	1	3.24	6	2	3	324	21	0	3.89
1991-92	**Washington**	**NHL**	**12**	**6**	**3**	**0**	**605**	**35**	**0**	**3.47**	....	....	....	....	....	....	....
	Baltimore	AHL	22	10	8	3	1303	73	0	3.36	....	....	....	....	....	....	....
	NHL Totals		**32**	**15**	**10**	**1**	**1646**	**97**	**0**	**3.54**	....	....	....	....	....	....	....

a AHL Second All-Star Team (1990)

HRUDEY, KELLY STEPHEN (ROO-dee)

Goaltender. Catches left. 5'10", 189 lbs. Born, Edmonton, Alta., January 13, 1961.
(NY Islanders' 2nd choice, 38th overall, in 1980 Entry Draft).

			Regular Season								Playoffs						
Season	Club	Lea	GP	W	L	T	Mins	GA	SO	Avg	GP	W	L	Mins	GA	SO	Avg
1978-79	Medicine Hat	WHL	57	12	34	7	3093	318	0	6.17	....	....	....	....	....	....	....
1979-80	Medicine Hat	WHL	57	25	23	4	3049	212	1	4.17	13	6	6	638	48	0	4.51
1980-81a	Medicine Hat	WHL	55	32	19	1	3023	200	4	3.97	4	....	....	244	17	0	4.18
	Indianapolis	CHL	....	....	....	....	....	....	....	....	2	....	....	135	8	0	3.56
1981-82bc	Indianapolis	CHL	51	27	19	4	3033	149	1	*2.95	13	11	2	842	34	*1	*2.42
1982-83bcd	Indianapolis	CHL	47	*26	17	1	2744	139	2	3.04	10	*7	3	*637	28	0	*2.64
1983-84	**NY Islanders**	**NHL**	**12**	**7**	**2**	**0**	**535**	**28**	**0**	**3.14**	....	....	....	....	....	....	....
	Indianapolis	CHL	6	3	2	1	370	21	0	3.40	....	....	....	....	....	....	....
1984-85	**NY Islanders**	**NHL**	**41**	**19**	**17**	**3**	**2335**	**141**	**2**	**3.62**	**5**	**1**	**3**	**281**	**8**	**0**	**1.71**
1985-86	**NY Islanders**	**NHL**	**45**	**19**	**15**	**8**	**2563**	**137**	**1**	**3.21**	**2**	**0**	**2**	**120**	**6**	**0**	**3.00**
1986-87	**NY Islanders**	**NHL**	**46**	**21**	**15**	**7**	**2634**	**145**	**0**	**3.30**	**14**	**7**	**7**	**842**	**38**	**0**	**2.71**
1987-88	**NY Islanders**	**NHL**	**47**	**22**	**17**	**5**	**2751**	**153**	**3**	**3.34**	**6**	**2**	**4**	**381**	**23**	**0**	**3.62**
1988-89	**NY Islanders**	**NHL**	**50**	**18**	**24**	**3**	**2800**	**183**	**0**	**3.92**	....	....	....	....	....	....	....
	Los Angeles	**NHL**	**16**	**10**	**4**	**2**	**974**	**47**	**1**	**2.90**	**10**	**4**	**6**	**566**	**35**	**0**	**3.71**
1989-90	**Los Angeles**	**NHL**	**52**	**22**	**21**	**6**	**2860**	**194**	**2**	**4.07**	**9**	**4**	**4**	**539**	**39**	**0**	**4.34**
1990-91	**Los Angeles**	**NHL**	**47**	**26**	**13**	**6**	**2730**	**132**	**3**	**2.90**	**12**	**6**	**6**	**798**	**37**	**0**	**2.78**
1991-92	**Los Angeles**	**NHL**	**60**	**26**	**17**	**13**	**3509**	**197**	**1**	**3.37**	**6**	**2**	**4**	**355**	**22**	**0**	**3.72**
	NHL Totals		**416**	**190**	**145**	**53**	**23691**	**1357**	**13**	**3.44**	**64**	**26**	**36**	**3882**	**208**	**0**	**3.21**

a WHL Second All-Star Team (1981)
b CHL First All-Star Team (1982, 1983)
c Shared Terry Sawchuk Trophy (CHL's Leading Goaltender) with Rob Holland (1982, 1983)
d Won Tommy Ivan Trophy (CHL's Most Valuable Player) (1983)

Traded to **Los Angeles** by **NY Islanders** for Mark Fitzpatrick, Wayne McBean and future considerations (Doug Crossman, acquired May 23, 1989) February 22, 1989.

HUGHES, CHARLES

Goaltender. Catches right. 5'8", 165 lbs. Born, Quincy, MA, January 30, 1970.
(New Jersey's 13th choice, 222nd overall, in 1988 Entry Draft).

			Regular Season								Playoffs						
Season	Club	Lea	GP	W	L	T	Mins	GA	SO	Avg	GP	W	L	Mins	GA	SO	Avg
1988-89	Harvard	ECAC	17	15	1	0	990	46	1	2.79	....	....	....	....	....	....	....
1989-90	Harvard	ECAC	11	5	5	1	669	43	0	3.86	....	....	....	....	....	....	....
1990-91	Harvard	ECAC	12	5	4	1	622	39	0	3.95	....	....	....	....	....	....	....
1991-92	Harvard	ECAC	12	5	3	4	739	38	0	3.09	....	....	....	....	....	....	....

ING, PETER

Goaltender. Catches left. 6'2", 170 lbs. Born, Toronto, Ont., April 28, 1969.
(Toronto's 3rd choice, 48th overall, in 1988 Entry Draft).

			Regular Season								Playoffs						
Season	Club	Lea	GP	W	L	T	Mins	GA	SO	Avg	GP	W	L	Mins	GA	SO	Avg
1986-87	Windsor	OHL	28	13	11	3	1615	105	0	3.90	5	4	0	161	9	0	3.35
1987-88	Windsor	OHL	43	30	7	1	2422	125	2	3.10	3	2	0	225	7	0	1.87
1988-89	Windsor	OHL	19	7	7	3	1043	76	*1	4.37	....	....	....	....	....	....	....
a	London	OHL	32	18	11	2	1848	104	*2	3.38	21	11	9	1093	82	0	4.50
1989-90	**Toronto**	**NHL**	**3**	**0**	**2**	**1**	**182**	**18**	**0**	**5.93**	....	....	....	....	....	....	....
	Newmarket	AHL	48	16	19	12	2829	184	0	3.90	....	....	....	....	....	....	....
	London	OHL	8	6	2	0	480	27	0	3.38	....	....	....	....	....	....	....
1990-91	**Toronto**	**NHL**	**56**	**16**	**29**	**8**	**3126**	**200**	**1**	**3.84**	....	....	....	....	....	....	....
1991-92	**Edmonton**	**NHL**	**12**	**3**	**4**	**0**	**463**	**33**	**0**	**4.28**	....	....	....	....	....	....	....
	Cape Breton	AHL	24	9	10	4	1411	92	0	3.91	1	0	1	60	9	0	9.00
	NHL Totals		**71**	**19**	**35**	**9**	**3771**	**251**	**1**	**3.99**	....	....	....	....	....	....	....

a OHL Third All-Star Team (1989)

Traded to **Edmonton** by **Toronto** with Vincent Damphousse, Scott Thornton, Luke Richardson, future considerations and cash for Grant Fuhr, Glenn Anderson and Craig Berube, September 19, 1991.

IRBE, ARTURS (EER-bay, AHR-turs)

Goaltender. Catches left. 5'7", 180 lbs. Born, Riga, Soviet Union, February 2, 1967.
(Minnesota's 11th choice, 196th overall, in 1989 Entry Draft).

			Regular Season								Playoffs						
Season	Club	Lea	GP	W	L	T	Mins	GA	SO	Avg	GP	W	L	Mins	GA	SO	Avg
1986-87	Dynamo Riga	USSR	2	....	....	....	27	1	0	2.22	....	....	....	....	....	....	....
1987-88a	Dynamo Riga	USSR	34	....	....	....	1870	84	4	2.69	....	....	....	....	....	....	....
1988-89	Dynamo Riga	USSR	40	....	....	....	2460	116	4	2.85	....	....	....	....	....	....	....
1989-90	Dynamo Riga	USSR	48	....	....	....	2880	115	2	2.42	....	....	....	....	....	....	....
1990-91	Dynamo Riga	USSR	46	....	....	....	2713	133	5	2.94	....	....	....	....	....	....	....
1991-92	**San Jose**	**NHL**	**13**	**2**	**6**	**3**	**645**	**48**	**0**	**4.47**	....	....	....	....	....	....	....
bc	Kansas City	IHL	32	24	7	1	1955	80	0	2.46	15	12	3	914	44	0	2.89
	NHL Totals		**13**	**2**	**6**	**3**	**645**	**48**	**0**	**4.47**	....	....	....	....	....	....	....

a Soviet National League Rookie-of-the-Year (1988)
b IHL First All-Star Team (1992)
c Won James Norris Memorial Trophy (Top Goaltender-IHL) (1992)

Claimed by **San Jose** from **Minnesota** in Dispersal Draft, May 30, 1991.

JABLONSKI, PAT

Goaltender. Catches right. 6', 178 lbs. Born, Toledo, OH, June 20, 1967.
(St. Louis' 6th choice, 138th overall, in 1985 Entry Draft).

			Regular Season								Playoffs						
Season	Club	Lea	GP	W	L	T	Mins	GA	SO	Avg	GP	W	L	Mins	GA	SO	Avg
1985-86	Windsor	OHL	29	6	16	4	1600	119	1	4.46	6	0	3	263	20	0	4.56
1986-87	Windsor	OHL	41	22	14	2	2328	128	*3	3.30	12	8	4	710	38	0	3.21
1987-88	Peoria	IHL	5	2	2	1	285	17	0	3.58	....	....	....	....	....	....	....
	Windsor	OHL	18	14	3	0	994	48	2	*2.90	9	*8	0	537	28	0	3.13
1988-89	Peoria	IHL	35	11	20	0	2051	163	1	4.77	3	0	2	130	13	0	6.00
1989-90	**St. Louis**	**NHL**	**4**	**0**	**3**	**0**	**208**	**17**	**0**	**4.90**	....	....	....	....	....	....	....
	Peoria	IHL	36	14	17	4	2023	165	0	4.89	4	1	3	223	19	0	5.11
1990-91	**St. Louis**	**NHL**	**8**	**2**	**3**	**3**	**492**	**25**	**0**	**3.05**	**3**	**0**	**0**	**90**	**5**	**0**	**3.33**
	Peoria	IHL	29	23	3	2	1738	87	0	3.00	10	7	2	532	23	0	2.59
1991-92	**St. Louis**	**NHL**	**10**	**3**	**6**	**0**	**468**	**38**	**0**	**4.87**	....	....	....	....	....	....	....
	Peoria	IHL	8	6	1	1	493	29	1	3.53	....	....	....	....	....	....	....
	NHL Totals		**22**	**5**	**12**	**3**	**1168**	**80**	**0**	**4.11**	**3**	**0**	**0**	**90**	**5**	**0**	**3.33**

Traded to **Tampa Bay** by **St. Louis** with Steve Tuttle and Darin Kimble for future considerations, June 19, 1992.

JAKS, PAULI (YAHKS, POW-lee)

Goaltender. Catches left. 6', 191 lbs. Born, Schaffhausen, Switzerland, January 25, 1972.
(Los Angeles' 5th choice, 108th overall, in 1991 Entry Draft).

			Regular Season								Playoffs						
Season	Club	Lea	GP	W	L	T	Mins	GA	SO	Avg	GP	W	L	Mins	GA	SO	Avg
1990-91	Ambri-Piotta	Switz.	22	....	....	....	1247	100	0	4.81	....	....	....	....	....	....	....
1991-92	Ambri-Piotta	Switz.	33	25	7	1	1890	97	2	2.93	....	....	....	....	....	....	....

JOSEPH, CURTIS

Goaltender. Catches left. 5'10", 182 lbs. Born, Keswick, Ont., April 29, 1967.

			Regular Season								Playoffs						
Season	Club	Lea	GP	W	L	T	Mins	GA	SO	Avg	GP	W	L	Mins	GA	SO	Avg
1988-89abc	U. Wisconsin	WCHA	38	21	11	5	2267	94	1	2.49	....	....	....	....	....	....	....
1989-90	**St. Louis**	**NHL**	**15**	**9**	**5**	**1**	**852**	**48**	**0**	**3.38**	**6**	**4**	**1**	**327**	**18**	**0**	**3.30**
	Peoria	IHL	23	10	8	2	1241	80	0	3.87	....	....	....	....	....	....	....
1990-91	**St. Louis**	**NHL**	**30**	**16**	**10**	**2**	**1710**	**89**	**0**	**3.12**	....	....	....	....	....	....	....
1991-92	**St. Louis**	**NHL**	**60**	**27**	**20**	**10**	**3494**	**175**	**2**	**3.01**	**6**	**2**	**4**	**379**	**23**	**0**	**3.64**
	NHL Totals		**105**	**52**	**35**	**13**	**6056**	**312**	**2**	**3.09**	**12**	**6**	**5**	**706**	**41**	**0**	**3.48**

a WCHA First All-Star Team (1989)
b WCHA Player of the Year (1989)
c WCHA Rookie of the Year (1989)

Signed as a free agent by **St. Louis**, June 16, 1989.

KETTERER, MARKUS

Goaltender. Catches left. 5'11", 165 lbs. Born, Helsinki, Finland, August 23, 1967.
(Buffalo's 6th choice, 107th overall, in 1992 Entry Draft).

			Regular Season								Playoffs						
Season	Club	Lea	GP	W	L	T	Mins	GA	SO	Avg	GP	W	L	Mins	GA	SO	Avg
1991-92	Jokerit	Fin.	37	....	....	....	2128	97	0	2.73	10	7	3	634	20	3	1.89

KIDD, TREVOR

Goaltender. Catches left. 6'2", 185 lbs. Born, Dugald, Man., March 29, 1972.
(Calgary's 1st choice, 11th overall, in 1990 Entry Draft).

			Regular Season								Playoffs						
Season	Club	Lea	GP	W	L	T	Mins	GA	SO	Avg	GP	W	L	Mins	GA	SO	Avg
1988-89	Brandon	WHL	32	....	....	....	1509	102	0	4.06	....	....	....	....	....	....	....
1989-90a	Brandon	WHL	*63	24	32	2	*3676	254	2	4.15	....	....	....	....	....	....	....
1990-91	Brandon	WHL	30	10	19	1	1730	117	0	4.06	....	....	....	....	....	....	....
	Spokane	WHL	14	8	3	0	749	44	0	3.52	15	*14	1	926	32	2	*2.07
1991-92	Cdn. National	....	28	18	4	4	1349	79	2	3.51	....	....	....	....	....	....	....
	Cdn. Olympic	....	1	1	0	0	60	0	1	0.00	....	....	....	....	....	....	....
	Calgary	**NHL**	**2**	**1**	**1**	**0**	**120**	**8**	**0**	**4.00**	....	....	....	....	....	....	....
	NHL Totals		**2**	**1**	**1**	**0**	**120**	**8**	**0**	**4.00**	....	....	....	....	....	....	....

a WHL East First All-Star Team (1990)

KING, SCOTT

Goaltender. Catches left. 6'1", 185 lbs. Born, Thunder Bay, Ont., June 25, 1967.
(Detroit's 10th choice, 190th overall, in 1986 Entry Draft).

			Regular Season								Playoffs						
Season	Club	Lea	GP	W	L	T	Mins	GA	SO	Avg	GP	W	L	Mins	GA	SO	Avg
1986-87	U. of Maine	H.E.	21	11	6	1	1111	58	0	3.13	....	....	....	....	....	....	....
1987-88a	U. of Maine	H.E.	33	25	5	1	1761	91	0	3.10	....	....	....	....	....	....	....
1988-89a	U. of Maine	H.E.	27	13	8	0	1394	83	0	3.57	....	....	....	....	....	....	....
1989-90b	U. of Maine	H.E.	29	17	7	2	1526	67	1	2.63	....	....	....	....	....	....	....
1990-91	**Detroit**	**NHL**	**1**	**0**	**0**	**0**	**45**	**2**	**0**	**2.67**	....	....	....	....	....	....	....
	Adirondack	AHL	24	8	10	2	1287	91	0	4.24	1	0	0	32	4	0	7.50
	Hampton Rds.	ECHL	15	8	4	1	819	57	0	4.17	....	....	....	....	....	....	....
1991-92	**Detroit**	**NHL**	**1**	**0**	**0**	**0**	**16**	**1**	**0**	**3.75**	....	....	....	....	....	....	....
	Adirondack	AHL	33	14	14	3	1904	112	0	3.53	....	....	....	....	....	....	....
	Toledo	ECHL	7	4	2	1	424	25	0	3.54	....	....	....	....	....	....	....
	NHL Totals		**2**	**0**	**0**	**0**	**61**	**3**	**0**	**2.95**	....	....	....	....	....	....	....

a Hockey East Second All-Star Team (1988, 1989)
b Hockey East First All-Star Team (1990)

KNICKLE, RICHARD (RICK)

Goaltender. Catches left. 5'10", 155 lbs. Born, Chatham, N.B., February 26, 1960.
(Buffalo's 7th choice, 116th overall, in 1979 Entry Draft).

			Regular Season								Playoffs						
Season	Club	Lea	GP	W	L	T	Mins	GA	SO	Avg	GP	W	L	Mins	GA	SO	Avg
1977-78	Brandon	WHL	49	34	5	7	2806	182	0	3.89	8	....	....	450	36	0	4.82
1978-79a	Brandon	WHL	38	26	3	8	2240	118	1	*3.16	16	12	3	886	41	*1	*2.78
1979-80	Brandon	WHL	33	11	14	1	1604	125	0	4.68	....	....	....	....	....	....	....
	Muskegon	IHL	16	....	....	....	829	52	0	3.76	3	....	....	156	17	0	6.54
1980-81b	Erie	EHL	43	....	....	....	2347	125	1	*3.20	8	....	....	446	14	0	*1.88
1981-82	Rochester	AHL	31	10	12	5	1753	108	1	3.70	3	0	2	125	7	0	3.37
1982-83	Flint	IHL	27	....	....	....	1638	92	2	3.37	3	....	....	193	10	0	3.11
	Rochester	AHL	4	....	....	....	143	11	0	4.64	....	....	....	....	....	....	....
1983-84c	Flint	IHL	60	32	21	5	3518	203	3	3.46	8	8	0	480	24	0	3.00
1984-85	Sherbrooke	AHL	14	7	6	0	780	53	0	4.08	....	....	....	....	....	....	....
	Flint	IHL	36	18	11	3	2018	115	2	3.42	7	3	4	401	27	0	4.04
1985-86	Saginaw	IHL	39	16	15	0	2235	135	2	3.62	3	2	1	193	12	0	3.73
1986-87	Saginaw	IHL	26	9	13	0	1413	113	0	4.80	5	1	4	329	21	0	3.83
1987-88	Flint	IHL	1	0	1	0	60	4	0	4.00	....	....	....	....	....	....	....
	Peoria	IHL	13	2	8	1	705	58	0	4.94	6	3	3	294	20	....	4.08
1988-89de	Fort Wayne	IHL	47	22	16	0	2716	141	1	*3.11	4	1	2	173	15	0	5.20
1989-90	Flint	IHL	55	25	24	1	2998	210	1	4.20	2	0	2	101	13	0	7.72
1990-91	Albany	IHL	14	4	6	2	679	52	0	4.59	....	....	....	....	....	....	....
	Springfield	AHL	9	6	0	2	509	28	0	3.30	....	....	....	....	....	....	....
1991-92c	San Diego	IHL	46	*28	13	4	2686	155	0	3.46	2	0	1	78	3	0	2.31

a WHL First All-Star Team (1979)
b EHL First All-Star Team (1981)
c IHL Second All-Star Team (1984, 1992)
d IHL First All-Star Team (1989)
e Won James Norris Memorial Trophy (Top Goaltender-IHL) (1989)

Signed as a free agent by **Montreal**, February 8, 1985.

KOLZIG, OLAF

Goaltender. Catches left. 6'3", 205 lbs. Born, Johannesburg, South Africa, April 9, 1970.
(Washington's 1st choice, 19th overall, in 1989 Entry raft).

			Regular Season								Playoffs						
Season	Club	Lea	GP	W	L	T	Mins	GA	SO	Avg	GP	W	L	Mins	GA	SO	Avg
1987-88	N. Westminster	WHL	15	6	5	0	650	48	1	4.43	3	....	....	149	11	0	4.43
1988-89	Tri-Cities	WHL	30	16	10	2	1671	97	1	*3.48	....	....	....	....	....	....	....
1989-90	**Washington**	**NHL**	**2**	**0**	**2**	**0**	**120**	**12**	**0**	**6.00**	....	....	....	....	....	....	....
	Tri-Cities	WHL	48	27	27	3	2504	250	1	4.38	6	4	0	318	27	0	5.09
1990-91	Baltimore	AHL	26	10	12	1	1367	72	0	3.16	....	....	....	....	....	....	....
	Hampton Rds.	ECHL	21	11	9	1	1248	71	2	3.41	3	1	2	180	14	0	4.66
1991-92	Baltimore	AHL	28	5	17	2	1503	105	1	4.19	....	....	....	....	....	....	....
	Hampton Rds.	ECHL	14	11	3	0	847	41	0	2.9	....	....	....	....	....	....	....
	NHL Totals		**2**	**0**	**2**	**0**	**120**	**12**	**0**	**6.00**	....	....	....	....	....	....	....

KRAKE, PAUL

Goaltender. Catches left. 6', 175 lbs. Born, Lloydminster, Sask., March 25, 1969.
(Quebec's 10th choice, 148th overall, in 1989 Entry Draft).

			Regular Season								Playoffs						
Season	Club	Lea	GP	W	L	T	Mins	GA	SO	Avg	GP	W	L	Mins	GA	SO	Avg
1988-89	Alaska-Anch.	G.N.	19	....	....	....	1111	75	0	4.05	....	....	....	....	....	....	....
1989-90	Alaska-Anch.	G.N.	18	8	6	2	937	58	0	3.87	....	....	....	....	....	....	....
1990-91	Alaska-Anch.	G.N.	37	18	15	3	2183	123	4	3.38	....	....	....	....	....	....	....
1991-92	Alaska-Anch.	G.N.	27	19	7	0	1587	87	0	3.29	....	....	....	....	....	....	....

KRUHLAK, ROB

Goaltender. Catches left. 5'11", 170 lbs. Born, Calgary, Alta., April 18, 1970.
(New Jersey's 1st choice, 17th overall, in 1991 Supplemental Draft).

			Regular Season								Playoffs						
Season	Club	Lea	GP	W	L	T	Mins	GA	SO	Avg	GP	W	L	Mins	GA	SO	Avg
1989-90	N. Michigan	WCHA	9	1	4	0	357	22	0	3.69	....	....	....	....	....	....	....
1990-91	N. Michigan	WCHA	11	5	2	0	428	18	0	*2.52	....	....	....	....	....	....	....
1991-92	N. Michigan	WCHA	7	2	2	2	367	30	0	4.90	....	....	....	....	....	....	....

KUNTAR, LES

Goaltender. Catches left. 6'2", 195 lbs. Born, Elma, NY, July 28, 1969.
(Montreal's 8th choice, 122nd overall, in 1987 Entry Draft).

			Regular Season								Playoffs						
Season	Club	Lea	GP	W	L	T	Mins	GA	SO	Avg	GP	W	L	Mins	GA	SO	Avg
1987-88	St. Lawrence	ECAC	10	6	1	0	488	27	0	3.31	....	....	....	....	....	....	....
1988-89	St. Lawrence	ECAC	14	11	2	0	786	31	0	2.37	....	....	....	....	....	....	....
1989-90	St. Lawrence	ECAC	20	7	11	1	1136	80	0	4.23	....	....	....	....	....	....	....
1990-91ab	St. Lawrence	ECAC	*33	*19	11	1	*1797	97	*1	*3.24	....	....	....	....	....	....	....
1991-92	Fredericton	AHL	11	7	3	0	638	26	0	2.45	....	....	....	....	....	....	....

a ECAC First All-Star Team (1991)
b NCAA East First All-American Team (1991)

LABRECQUE, PATRICK

Goaltender. Catches left. 6', 187 lbs. Born, Laval, Que., March 6, 1971.
(Quebec's 5th choice, 90th overall, in 1991 Entry Draft).

			Regular Season								Playoffs						
Season	Club	Lea	GP	W	L	T	Mins	GA	SO	Avg	GP	W	L	Mins	GA	SO	Avg
1990-91	St-Jean	QMJHL	59	17	34	6	3375	216	1	3.84	....	....	....	....	....	....	....
1991-92	Halifax	AHL	29	5	12	8	1570	114	0	4.36	....	....	....	....	....	....	....

LaFOREST, MARK ANDREW

Goaltender. Catches left. 5'11", 190 lbs. Born, Welland, Ont., July 10, 1962.

			Regular Season								Playoffs						
Season	Club	Lea	GP	W	L	T	Mins	GA	SO	Avg	GP	W	L	Mins	GA	SO	Avg
1981-82	Niagara Falls	OHL	24	10	13	1	1365	105	1	4.62	5	1	2	300	19	0	3.80
1982-83	North Bay	OHL	54	34	17	1	3140	195	0	3.73	8	4	4	474	31	0	3.92
1983-84	Adirondack	AHL	7	3	3	1	351	29	0	4.96	....	....	....	....	....	....	....
	Kalamazoo	IHL	13	4	5	2	718	48	1	4.01	....	....	....	....	....	....	....
1984-85	Adirondack	AHL	11	2	3	1	430	35	0	4.88	....	....	....	....	....	....	....
1985-86	**Detroit**	**NHL**	**28**	**4**	**21**	**0**	**1383**	**114**	**1**	**4.95**	....	....	....	....	....	....	....
	Adirondack	AHL	19	13	5	1	1142	57	0	2.99	*17	*12	5	*1075	58	0	3.24
1986-87	**Detroit**	**NHL**	**5**	**2**	**1**	**0**	**219**	**12**	**0**	**3.29**	....	....	....	....	....	....	....
a	Adirondack	AHL	37	23	8	0	2229	105	*3	2.83	....	....	....	....	....	....	....
1987-88	**Philadelphia**	**NHL**	**21**	**5**	**9**	**2**	**972**	**60**	**1**	**3.70**	**2**	**1**	**0**	**48**	**1**	**0**	**1.25**
	Hershey	AHL	5	2	1	2	309	13	0	2.52	....	....	....	....	....	....	....
1988-89	**Philadelphia**	**NHL**	**17**	**5**	**7**	**2**	**933**	**64**	**0**	**4.12**	....	....	....	....	....	....	....
	Hershey	AHL	3	2	0	0	185	9	0	2.92	12	7	5	744	27	1	2.18
1989-90	**Toronto**	**NHL**	**27**	**9**	**14**	**0**	**1343**	**87**	**0**	**3.89**	....	....	....	....	....	....	....
	Newmarket	AHL	10	6	4	0	604	33	1	3.28	....	....	....	....	....	....	....
1990-91ab	Binghamton	AHL	45	25	14	2	2452	129	0	3.16	9	3	4	442	28	1	3.80
1991-92	Binghamton	AHL	43	25	15	3	2559	146	1	3.42	11	7	4	662	34	0	3.08
	NHL Totals		**98**	**25**	**52**	**4**	**4850**	**337**	**2**	**4.17**	**2**	**1**	**0**	**48**	**1**	**0**	**1.25**

a Won Baz Bastien Trophy (Top Goalie - AHL) (1987, 1991)
b AHL Second All-Star Team (1991)

Signed as a free agent by **Detroit**, April 29, 1983. Traded to **Philadelphia** by **Detroit** for Philadelphia's second round choice (Bob Wilkie) in 1987 Entry Draft, June 13, 1987. Traded to **Toronto** by **Philadelphia** for Toronto's sixth round choice in 1991 Entry Draft and its seventh round choice in 1991 Entry Draft (previously obtained from Philadelphia), September 8, 1989. Traded to **NY Rangers** by **Toronto** with Tie Domi for Greg Johnston, June 28, 1990. Claimed by **Ottawa** from **NY Rangers** in Expansion Draft, June 18, 1992.

LAGRAND, SCOTT

Goaltender. Catches left. 6', 165 lbs. Born, Potsdam, NY, February 11, 1970.
(Philadelphia's 5th choice, 77th overall, in 1988 Entry Draft).

			Regular Season								Playoffs						
Season	Club	Lea	GP	W	L	T	Mins	GA	SO	Avg	GP	W	L	Mins	GA	SO	Avg
1989-90	Boston College	H.E.	24	17	4	0	1268	57	0	2.70	....	....	....	....	....	....	....
1990-91a	Boston College	H.E.	12	7	2	0	557	39	2	4.20	....	....	....	....	....	....	....
1991-92b	Boston College	H.E.	30	11	16	2	1750	108	1	3.70	....	....	....	....	....	....	....

a Hockey East First All-Star Team (1991)
b NCAA East Second All-Star Team (1992)

LAMOTHE, MARC

Goaltender. Catches left. 6'1", 186 lbs. Born, New Liskeard, Ont., February 27, 1974.
(Montreal's 6th choice, 92nd overall, in 1992 Entry Draft).

			Regular Season								Playoffs						
Season	Club	Lea	GP	W	L	T	Mins	GA	SO	Avg	GP	W	L	Mins	GA	SO	Avg
1990-91	Ottawa	COJHL	25	....	....	....	1220	82	1	4.03	....	....	....	....	....	....	....
1991-92	Kingston	OHL	42	10	25	2	2378	189	1	4.77	....	....	....	....	....	....	....

LEBLANC, RAYMOND

Goaltender. Catches right. 5'10", 170 lbs. Born, Fitchburg, MA, October 24, 1964.

			Regular Season								Playoffs						
Season	Club	Lea	GP	W	L	T	Mins	GA	SO	Avg	GP	W	L	Mins	GA	SO	Avg
1983-84	Kitchener	OHL	54	....	....	....	2965	185	1	3.74			....	....	....	....	....
1984-85	Pinebridge	ACHL	40	....	....	....	2178	150	0	4.13	....	....	....	....	....	....	....
1985-86	Carolina	ACHL	42	....	....	....	2505	133	3	3.19	....	....	....	....	....	....	....
1986-87	Flint	IHL	64	....	....	....	3417	222	0	3.90	....	....	....	....	....	....	....
1987-88	Flint	IHL	62	27	19	8	3269	239	1	4.39	16	10	6	925	55	1	3.57
1988-89	Flint	IHL	15	5	9	0	852	67	0	4.72	....	....	....	....	....	....	....
	Saginaw	IHL	29	19	7	2	1655	99	0	3.59	1	0	1	5	9	0	3.05
1989-90	Indianapolis	IHL	23	15	6	2	1334	71	2	3.19	....	....	....	....	....	....	....
	New Haven	AHL	1	0	0	0	20	3	0	9.00	....	....	....	....	....	....	....
	Fort Wayne	IHL	15	3	3	3	680	44	0	3.88	3	0	2	139	11	0	4.75
1990-91	Fort Wayne	IHL	21	10	8	0	1072	69	0	3.86	....	....	....	....	....	....	....
	Indianapolis	IHL	3	2	0	0	145	7	0	2.90	1	0	0	19	1	0	3.20
1991-92	U.S. National	....	17	5	10	1	891	54	0	3.63	....	....	....	....	....	....	....
	U.S. Olympic	....	8	....	....	....	463	17	2	2.20	....	....	....	....	....	....	....
	Chicago	**NHL**	**1**	**1**	**0**	**0**	**60**	**1**	**0**	**1.00**	....	....	....	....	....	....	....
	NHL Totals		**1**	**1**	**0**	**0**	**60**	**1**	**0**	**1.00**	....	....	....	....	....	....	....

Signed as a free agent by **Chicago**, September, 1989.

LEHKONEN, TIMO (LEH-koh-nehn)

Goaltender. Catches left. 5'11", 183 lbs. Born, Helsinki, Finland, January 8, 1966.
(Chicago's 4th choice, 90th overall, in 1984 Entry Draft).

			Regular Season								Playoffs						
Season	Club	Lea	GP	W	L	T	Mins	GA	SO	Avg	GP	W	L	Mins	GA	SO	Avg
1983-84	Jokerit	Fin.	1	....	....	....	60	7	0	7.00	....	....	....	....	....	....	....
1984-85	Toronto	OHL	16	....	....	....	821	64	0	4.68	1	....	....	34	4	0	7.06
1985-86	Jokerit	Fin.	2	....	....	....	57	9	0	9.47	....	....	....	....	....	....	....
1986-87	Jokerit	Fin.	13	....	....	....	679	66	0	5.83	....	....	....	....	....	....	....
1987-88	TPS	Fin.	17	....	....	....	910	60	2	3.96	....	....	....	....	....	....	....
1988-89	TPS	Fin.	12	8	4	0	644	25	3	2.33	8	....	....	459	14	1	1.91
1989-90	HPK	Fin.	35	18	13	4	2032	123	0	3.63	....	....	....	....	....	....	....
1990-91	HPK	Fin.	37	...	....	....	....	123	....	....	8	....	....	440	26	....	3.55
1991-92	HPK	Fin.	43	....	....	....	2493	164	....	3.95	....	....	....	....	....	....	....

LEMBKE, JEFF

Goaltender. Catches left. 5'11", 170 lbs. Born, Pembina, ND, November 29, 1972.
(Pittsburgh's 9th choice, 192nd overall, in 1991 Entry Draft).

			Regular Season								Playoffs						
Season	Club	Lea	GP	W	L	T	Mins	GA	SO	Avg	GP	W	L	Mins	GA	SO	Avg
1990-91	Omaha	USHL	28	16	9	1	....	....	....	3.65	....	....	....	....	....	....	....
1991-92	North Dakota	WCHA	10	3	3	0	412	41	0	5.97	....	....	....	....	....	....	....

LEMELIN, REJEAN (REGGIE) (LEHM-uh-lihn)

Goaltender. Catches left. 5'11", 170 lbs. Born, Quebec City, Que., November 19, 1954.
(Philadelphia's 6th choice, 125th overall, in 1974 Amateur Draft).

			Regular Season								Playoffs						
Season	Club	Lea	GP	W	L	T	Mins	GA	SO	Avg	GP	W	L	Mins	GA	SO	Avg
1972-73	Sherbrooke	QJHL	28	....	....	....	1681	146	0	5.21	2	....	....	120	12	0	6.00
1973-74	Sherbrooke	QJHL	35	....	....	....	2061	158	0	4.60	1	....	....	60	3	0	3.00
1974-75	Philadelphia	NAHL	43	....	....	....	2277	131	3	3.45	....	....	....	....	....	....	....
1975-76	Philadelphia	NAHL	29	....	....	....	1601	97	1	3.63	3	....	....	171	15	0	5.26
1976-77	Springfield	AHL	3	2	1	0	180	10	0	3.33	....	....	....	....	....	....	....
	Philadelphia	NAHL	51	26	19	1	2763	170	1	3.61	3	....	....	191	14	0	4.40
1977-78a	Philadelphia	AHL	60	31	21	7	3585	177	4	2.96	2	0	2	119	12	0	6.05
1978-79	**Atlanta**	**NHL**	**18**	**8**	**8**	**1**	**994**	**55**	**0**	**3.32**	**1**	**0**	**0**	**20**	**0**	**0**	**0.00**
	Philadelphia	AHL	13	3	9	1	780	36	0	2.77	....	....	....	....	....	....	....
1979-80	**Atlanta**	**NHL**	**3**	**0**	**2**	**0**	**150**	**15**	**0**	**6.00**	....	....	....	....	....	....	....
	Birmingham	CHL	38	13	21	2	2188	137	0	3.76	2	0	1	79	5	0	3.80
1980-81	**Calgary**	**NHL**	**29**	**14**	**6**	**7**	**1629**	**88**	**2**	**3.24**	**6**	**3**	**3**	**366**	**22**	**0**	**3.61**
	Birmingham	CHL	13	3	8	2	757	56	0	4.44	....	....	....	....	....	....	....
1981-82	**Calgary**	**NHL**	**34**	**10**	**5**	**6**	**1866**	**135**	**0**	**4.34**	....	....	....	....	....	....	....
1982-83	**Calgary**	**NHL**	**39**	**16**	**12**	**8**	**2211**	**133**	**0**	**3.61**	**7**	**3**	**3**	**327**	**27**	**0**	**4.95**
1983-84	**Calgary**	**NHL**	**51**	**21**	**12**	**9**	**2568**	**150**	**0**	**3.50**	**8**	**4**	**4**	**448**	**32**	**0**	**4.29**
1984-85	**Calgary**	**NHL**	**56**	**30**	**12**	**10**	**3176**	**183**	**1**	**3.46**	**4**	**1**	**3**	**248**	**15**	**1**	**3.63**
1985-86	**Calgary**	**NHL**	**60**	**29**	**24**	**4**	**3369**	**229**	**1**	**4.08**	**3**	**0**	**1**	**109**	**7**	**0**	**3.85**
1986-87	**Calgary**	**NHL**	**34**	**16**	**9**	**1**	**1735**	**94**	**2**	**3.25**	**2**	**0**	**1**	**101**	**6**	**0**	**3.56**
1987-88	**Boston**	**NHL**	**49**	**24**	**17**	**6**	**2828**	**138**	**3**	**2.93**	**17**	**11**	**6**	**1027**	**45**	***1**	***2.63**
1988-89	**Boston**	**NHL**	**40**	**19**	**15**	**6**	**2392**	**120**	**0**	**3.01**	**4**	**1**	**3**	**252**	**16**	**0**	**3.81**
1989-90b	**Boston**	**NHL**	**43**	**22**	**15**	**2**	**2310**	**108**	**2**	**2.81**	**3**	**0**	**1**	**135**	**13**	**0**	**5.78**
1990-91	**Boston**	**NHL**	**33**	**17**	**10**	**3**	**1829**	**111**	**1**	**3.64**	**2**	**0**	**0**	**32**	**0**	**0**	**0.00**
1991-92	**Boston**	**NHL**	**8**	**5**	**1**	**0**	**407**	**23**	**0**	**3.39**	**2**	**0**	**0**	**54**	**3**	**0**	**3.33**
	NHL Totals		**497**	**231**	**148**	**63**	**27464**	**1582**	**12**	**3.46**	**59**	**23**	**25**	**3119**	**186**	**2**	**3.58**

a AHL First All-Star Team (1978)
b Shared William Jennings Trophy with Andy Moog (1990)

Played in NHL All-Star Game (1989)

Signed as a free agent by **Atlanta**, August 17, 1978. Signed as a free agent by **Boston**, August 13, 1987.

LENARDUZZI, MIKE

Goaltender. Catches left. 6'1", 165 lbs. Born, London, Ont., September 14, 1972.
(Hartford's 3rd choice, 57th overall, in 1990 Entry Draft).

			Regular Season								Playoffs						
Season	Club	Lea	GP	W	L	T	Mins	GA	SO	Avg	GP	W	L	Mins	GA	SO	Avg
1989-90	Oshawa	OHL	12	6	3	1	444	32	0	4.32	....	....	....	....	....	....	....
1990-91a	S.S. Marie	OHL	35	19	8	3	1966	107	0	3.27	5	3	1	268	13	*1	2.91
1991-92	S.S. Marie	OHL	9	5	3	0	486	33	0	4.07	....	....	....	....	....	....	....
	Ottawa	OHL	18	5	12	1	986	60	1	3.65	....	....	....	....	....	....	....
	Sudbury	OHL	22	11	5	4	1201	84	2	4.20	11	4	7	651	38	0	3.50
	Springfield	AHL	....	....	....	....	....	....	....	....	1	0	0	39	2	0	3.08

a OHL Third All-Star Team (1991)

LETOURNEAU, RAYMOND GEORGE (RAY)

Goaltender. Catches left. 5'11", 185 lbs. Born, Penacook, NH, January 14, 1969.
(Philadelphia's 2nd choice, 9th overall, in 1990 Supplemental Draft).

			Regular Season								Playoffs						
Season	Club	Lea	GP	W	L	T	Mins	GA	SO	Avg	GP	W	L	Mins	GA	SO	Avg
1987-88	Yale	ECAC	4	0	3	0	175	24	0	8.21	....	....	....	....	....	....	....
1988-89	Yale	ECAC	7	1	5	0	378	42	0	6.66	....	....	....	....	....	....	....
1989-90	Yale	ECAC	28	8	19	1	1631	125	0	4.59	....	....	....	....	....	....	....
1990-91	Yale	ECAC	27	11	14	2	1572	106	0	4.05	....	....	....	....	....	....	....
1991-92	Hershey	AHL	15	4	8	1	791	67	0	5.08	....	....	....	....	....	....	....
	Roanoke Valley	ECHL	5	2	3	0	245	33	0	8.80	....	....	....	....	....	....	....

LEVY, JEFF

Goaltender. Catches left. 5'11", 160 lbs. Born, Salt Lake City, UT, December 9, 1970.
(Minnesota's 7th choice, 134th overall, in 1990 Entry Draft).

			Regular Season								Playoffs						
Season	Club	Lea	GP	W	L	T	Mins	GA	SO	Avg	GP	W	L	Mins	GA	SO	Avg
1990-91abc	N. Hampshire	H.E.	24	15	7	2	1490	80	0	3.22	....	....	....	....	....	....	....
1991-92	N. Hampshire	H.E.	6	2	2	0	191	14	0	4.40	....	....	....	....	....	....	....

a Hockey East Rookie of the Year (1991)
b Hockey East Second All-Star Team (1991)
c NCAA East Second All-American Team (1991)

LIBERTUCCI, ANGELO

Goaltender. Catches left. 5'10", 165 lbs. Born, Toronto, Ont., January 3, 1970.
(Philadelphia's 1st choice, 6th overall, in 1991 Supplemental Draft).

			Regular Season								Playoffs						
Season	Club	Lea	GP	W	L	T	Mins	GA	SO	Avg	GP	W	L	Mins	GA	SO	Avg
1989-90	Bowling Green	CCHA	28	16	10	1	1591	107	0	4.03	....	....	....	....	....	....	....
1990-91	Bowling Green	CCHA	29	12	15	1	1594	124	1	4.67	....	....	....	....	....	....	....
1991-92	Bowling Green	CCHA	18	3	8	4	1002	81	0	4.85	....	....	....	....	....	....	....

LINDFORS, SAKARI (LIHND-fohrs)

Goaltender. Catches left. 5'7", 150 lbs. Born, Helsinki, Finland, April 27, 1966.
(Quebec's 9th choice, 150th overall, in 1988 Entry Draft).

			Regular Season								Playoffs						
Season	Club	Lea	GP	W	L	T	Mins	GA	SO	Avg	GP	W	L	Mins	GA	SO	Avg
1988-89	HIFK	Fin.	24	11	11	2	1433	89	1	3.75	....	....	....	....	....	....	....
1989-90	HIFK	Fin.	42	23	15	4	2518	146	2	3.48	....	....	....	....	....	....	....
1990-91	HIFK	Fin.	41	....	....	....	1492	137	0	5.61	3	....	....	180	14	0	4.67
1991-92	HIFK	Fin.	38	....	....	....	2222	127	0	3.43	....	....	....	....	....	....	....

LITTLE, NEIL

Goaltender. Catches left. 6'1", 170 lbs. Born, Medicine Hat, Alta., December 18, 1971.
(Philadelphia's 11th choice, 226th overall, in 1991 Entry Draft).

			Regular Season								Playoffs						
Season	Club	Lea	GP	W	L	T	Mins	GA	SO	Avg	GP	W	L	Mins	GA	SO	Avg
1990-91	RPI	ECAC	18	9	8	0	1032	71	0	4.13	....	....	....	....	....	....	....
1991-92	RPI	ECAC	28	11	11	3	1532	96	0	3.76	....	....	....	....	....	....	....

LITTMAN, DAVID

Goaltender. Catches left. 6', 183 lbs. Born, Cranston, RI, June 13, 1967.
(Buffalo's 12th choice, 211th overall, in 1987 Entry Draft).

			Regular Season								Playoffs						
Season	Club	Lea	GP	W	L	T	Mins	GA	SO	Avg	GP	W	L	Mins	GA	SO	Avg
1985-86	Boston College	H.E.	7	4	0	1	312	18	0	3.46	....	....	....	....	....	....	....
1986-87	Boston College	H.E.	21	15	5	0	1182	68	0	3.45	....	....	....	....	....	....	....
1987-88a	Boston College	H.E.	30	11	16	2	1726	116	0	4.03	....	....	....	....	....	....	....
1988-89bc	Boston College	H.E.	*32	19	9	4	*1945	107	0	3.30	....	....	....	....	....	....	....
1989-90	Rochester	AHL	14	5	6	1	681	37	0	3.26	....	....	....	....	....	....	....
	Phoenix	IHL	18	8	7	2	1047	64	0	3.67	....	....	....	....	....	....	....
1990-91	**Buffalo**	**NHL**	**1**	**0**	**0**	**0**	**36**	**3**	**0**	**5.00**	....	....	....	....	....	....	....
d	Rochester	AHL	*56	*33	13	5	*3155	160	3	3.04	8	4	2	378	16	0	2.54
1991-92	**Buffalo**	**NHL**	**1**	**0**	**1**	**0**	**60**	**4**	**0**	**4.00**	....	....	....	....	....	....	....
ef	Rochester	AHL	*61	*29	20	9	*3558	174	*3	2.93	15	8	7	879	43	*1	2.94
	NHL Totals		**2**	**0**	**1**	**0**	**96**	**7**	**0**	**4.38**	....	....	....	....	....	....	....

a Hockey East Second All-Star Team (1988)
b Hockey East First All-Star Team (1989)
c NCAA East Second All-American Team (1989)
d AHL First All-Star Team (1991)
e Won Harry "Hap" Holmes Memorial Trophy (Leading Goaltender-AHL) (1992)
f AHL Second All-Star Team (1992)

LIUT, MICHAEL (MIKE) (lee-OOT)

Goaltender. Catches left. 6'2", 195 lbs. Born, Weston, Ont., January 7, 1956.
(St. Louis' 5th choice, 56th overall, in 1976 Amateur Draft).

			Regular Season								Playoffs						
Season	Club	Lea	GP	W	L	T	Mins	GA	SO	Avg	GP	W	L	Mins	GA	SO	Avg
1973-74	Bowling Green	CCHA	24	10	12	0	1272	88	1	4.15	....	....	....	....	....	....	....
1974-75	Bowling Green	CCHA	20	12	6	1	1174	78	0	3.99	....	....	....	....	....	....	....
1975-76	Bowling Green	CCHA	21	13	5	0	1171	50	2	2.56	....	....	....	....	....	....	....
1976-77	Bowling Green	CCHA	24	18	4	0	1346	61	2	2.72	....	....	....	....	....	....	....
1977-78	Cincinnati	WHA	27	8	12	0	1215	86	0	4.25	....	....	....	....	....	....	....
1978-79	Cincinnati	WHA	54	23	27	4	3181	184	*3	3.47	3	1	2	179	12	0	4.02
1979-80	**St. Louis**	**NHL**	**64**	**32**	**23**	**9**	**3661**	**194**	**2**	**3.18**	**3**	**0**	**3**	**193**	**12**	**0**	**3.73**
1980-81ab	**St. Louis**	**NHL**	**61**	**33**	**14**	**13**	**3570**	**199**	**1**	**3.34**	**11**	**5**	**6**	**685**	**50**	**0**	**4.38**
1981-82	**St. Louis**	**NHL**	***64**	**28**	**28**	**7**	***3691**	**250**	**2**	**4.06**	**10**	**5**	**3**	**494**	**27**	**0**	**3.28**
1982-83	**St. Louis**	**NHL**	***68**	**21**	**27**	**13**	***3794**	**235**	**1**	**3.72**	**4**	**1**	**3**	**240**	**15**	**0**	**3.75**
1983-84	**St. Louis**	**NHL**	**58**	**25**	**29**	**4**	**3425**	**197**	**3**	**3.45**	**11**	**6**	**5**	**714**	**29**	**1**	**2.44**
1984-85	**St. Louis**	**NHL**	**32**	**12**	**12**	**6**	**1869**	**119**	**1**	**3.82**	....	....	....	....	....	....	....
	Hartford	**NHL**	**12**	**4**	**7**	**1**	**731**	**36**	**1**	**2.95**	....	....	....	....	....	....	....
1985-86	**Hartford**	**NHL**	**57**	**27**	**23**	**4**	**3282**	**198**	**2**	**3.62**	**8**	**5**	**2**	**441**	**14**	***1**	***1.90**
1986-87c	**Hartford**	**NHL**	**59**	**31**	**22**	**5**	**3476**	**187**	***4**	**3.23**	**6**	**2**	**4**	**332**	**25**	**0**	**4.52**
1987-88	**Hartford**	**NHL**	**60**	**25**	**28**	**5**	**3532**	**187**	**2**	**3.18**	**3**	**1**	**1**	**160**	**11**	**0**	**4.13**
1988-89	**Hartford**	**NHL**	**35**	**13**	**19**	**1**	**2006**	**142**	**1**	**4.25**	....	....	....	....	....	....	....
1989-90	**Hartford**	**NHL**	**29**	**15**	**12**	**1**	**1683**	**74**	***3**	***2.64**	....	....	....	....	....	....	....
	Washington	**NHL**	**8**	**4**	**4**	**0**	**478**	**17**	***1**	***2.13**	**9**	**4**	**4**	**507**	**28**	**0**	**3.31**
1990-91	**Washington**	**NHL**	**35**	**13**	**16**	**3**	**1834**	**114**	**0**	**3.73**	**2**	**0**	**1**	**48**	**4**	**0**	**5.00**
1991-92	**Washington**	**NHL**	**21**	**10**	**7**	**2**	**1123**	**70**	**1**	**3.74**	....	....	....	....	....	....	....
	NHL Totals		**663**	**293**	**271**	**74**	**38155**	**2219**	**25**	**3.49**	**67**	**29**	**32**	**3814**	**215**	**2**	**3.38**

a NHL First All-Star Team (1981)
b Won Lester B. Pearson Award (1981)
c NHL Second All-Star Team (1987)

Played in NHL All-Star Game (1981)

Reclaimed by **St. Louis** from Cincinnati (WHA) prior to Expansion Draft, June 9, 1979. Traded to **Hartford** by **St. Louis** with Jorgen Pettersson for Mark Johnson and Greg Millen, February 21, 1985. Traded to **Washington** by **Hartford** for Yvon Corriveau, March 6, 1990.

LOEWEN, JAMIE

Goaltender. Catches left. 5'10", 165 lbs. Born, Vancouver, B.C., September 23, 1968.
(Minnesota's 1st choice, 12th overall, in 1989 Supplemental Draft).

			Regular Season								Playoffs						
Season	Club	Lea	GP	W	L	T	Mins	GA	SO	Avg	GP	W	L	Mins	GA	SO	Avg
1988-89	Alaska-Fair.	G.N.	24	....	....	....	1501	84	0	3.48	....	....	....	....	....	....	....
1989-90	Alaska-Fair.	G.N.	17	5	12	0	1023	101	0	5.94	....	....	....	....	....	....	....
1990-91	Alaska-Fair.	G.N.	15	7	7	1	938	52	1	3.33	....	....	....	....	....	....	....
1991-92	Alaska-Fair.	G.N.	14	8	4	0	816	52	0	3.83	....	....	....	....	....	....	....

LORENZ, DANNY

Goaltender. Catches left. 5'10", 183 lbs. Born, Murrayville, B.C., December 12, 1969.
(NY Islanders' 4th choice, 58th overall, in 1988 Entry Draft).

			Regular Season								Playoffs						
Season	Club	Lea	GP	W	L	T	Mins	GA	SO	Avg	GP	W	L	Mins	GA	SO	Avg
1986-87	Seattle	WHL	38	12	21	2	2103	199	0	5.68	....	....	....	....	....	....	....
1987-88	Seattle	WHL	62	20	37	2	3302	314	0	5.71	....	....	....	....	....	....	....
1988-89	Springfield	AHL	4	2	1	0	210	12	0	3.43	....	....	....	....	....	....	....
a	Seattle	WHL	*68	31	33	4	*4003	240	*3	3.60	....	....	....	....	....	....	....
1989-90a	Seattle	WHL	56	37	15	2	3226	221	0	4.11	13	6	7	751	40	0	3.21
1990-91	**NY Islanders**	**NHL**	**2**	**0**	**1**	**0**	**80**	**5**	**0**	**3.75**	....	....	....	....	....	....	....
	Capital Dist.	AHL	17	5	9	2	940	70	0	4.47	....	....	....	....	....	....	....
	Richmond	ECHL	20	6	9	2	1020	75	0	4.41	....	....	....	....	....	....	....
1991-92	**NY Islanders**	**NHL**	**2**	**0**	**2**	**0**	**120**	**10**	**0**	**5.00**	....	....	....	....	....	....	....
	Capital Dist.	AHL	53	22	22	7	3050	181	2	3.56	7	3	4	442	25	0	3.39
	NHL Totals		**4**	**0**	**3**	**0**	**200**	**15**	**0**	**4.50**	....	....	....	....	....	....	....

a WHL West First All-Star Team (1989, 1990)

LOUDER, GREG

Goaltender. Catches left. 6'1", 185 lbs. Born, Concord, MA, November 16, 1971.
(Edmonton's 5th choice, 101st overall, in 1990 Entry Draft).

			Regular Season								Playoffs						
Season	Club	Lea	GP	W	L	T	Mins	GA	SO	Avg	GP	W	L	Mins	GA	SO	Avg
1990-91	Notre Dame	NCAA	33	16	5	2	1958	134	1	4.11	....	....	....	....	....	....	....
1991-92	Notre Dame	NCAA	18	5	13	0	1055	88	0	5.00	....	....	....	....	....	....	....

LUKOWSKI, BRIAN

Goaltender. Catches left. 5'9", 170 lbs. Born, Buffalo, NY, January 8, 1971.
(St. Louis' 11th choice, 219th overall, in 1989 Entry Draft).

			Regular Season								Playoffs						
Season	Club	Lea	GP	W	L	T	Mins	GA	SO	Avg	GP	W	L	Mins	GA	SO	Avg
1989-90	Lake Superior	CCHA	4	1	0	0	114	8	0	4.20	....	....	....	....	....	....	....
1990-91	Lake Superior	CCHA	4	3	0	0	200	8	0	2.40	....	....	....	....	....	....	....
1991-92	Lake Superior	CCHA	1	0	0	0	30	2	0	4.00	....	....	....	....	....	....	....

MADELY, DARRIN

Goaltender. Catches left. 5'11", 165 lbs. Born, Holland Landing, Ont., February 25, 1968.

			Regular Season								Playoffs						
Season	Club	Lea	GP	W	L	T	Mins	GA	SO	Avg	GP	W	L	Mins	GA	SO	Avg
1989-90	Lake Superior	CCHA	30	21	7	1	....	68	....	2.42	....	....	....	....	....	....	....
1990-91a	Lake Superior	CCHA	36	29	3	3	....	93	....	2.61	....	....	....	....	....	....	....
1991-92abc	Lake Superior	CCHA	36	23	6	4	....	69	....	2.05	....	....	....	....	....	....	....

a NCAA West First All-American Team (1991, 1992)
b NCAA All-Tournament Team (1992)
c CCHA First All-Star Team (1992)

Signed as a free agent by **Ottawa**, June 20, 1992.

MALARCHUK, CLINT

Goaltender. Catches left. 6', 185 lbs. Born, Grande Prairie, Alta., May 1, 1961.
(Quebec's 3rd choice, 74th overall, in 1981 Entry Draft).

			Regular Season								Playoffs						
Season	Club	Lea	GP	W	L	T	Mins	GA	SO	Avg	GP	W	L	Mins	GA	SO	Avg
1979-80	Portland	WHL	37	21	10	0	1948	147	0	4.53	1	0	0	40	3	0	4.50
1980-81	Portland	WHL	38	28	8	0	2235	142	3	3.81	4	....	....	307	21	0	4.10
1981-82	**Quebec**	**NHL**	**2**	**0**	**1**	**1**	**120**	**14**	**0**	**7.00**	....	....	....	....	....	....	....
	Fredericton	AHL	51	15	34	2	2906	247	0	5.10	....	....	....	....	....	....	....
1982-83	**Quebec**	**NHL**	**15**	**8**	**5**	**2**	**900**	**71**	**0**	**4.73**	....	....	....	....	....	....	....
	Fredericton	AHL	25	....	....	....	1506	78	0	3.11	....	....	....	....	....	....	....
1983-84	**Quebec**	**NHL**	**23**	**10**	**9**	**2**	**1215**	**80**	**0**	**3.95**	....	....	....	....	....	....	....
	Fredericton	AHL	11	5	5	1	663	40	0	3.62	....	....	....	....	....	....	....
1984-85	Fredericton	AHL	*56	26	25	4	*3347	198	2	3.55	6	2	4	379	20	0	3.17
1985-86	**Quebec**	**NHL**	**46**	**26**	**12**	**4**	**2657**	**142**	**4**	**3.21**	**3**	**0**	**2**	**143**	**11**	**0**	**4.62**
1986-87	**Quebec**	**NHL**	**54**	**18**	**26**	**9**	**3092**	**175**	**1**	**3.40**	**3**	**0**	**2**	**140**	**8**	**0**	**3.43**
1987-88	**Washington**	**NHL**	**54**	**24**	**20**	**4**	**2926**	**154**	***4**	**3.16**	**4**	**0**	**2**	**193**	**15**	**0**	**4.66**
1988-89	**Washington**	**NHL**	**42**	**16**	**18**	**7**	**2428**	**141**	**1**	**3.48**	**1**	**0**	**1**	**59**	**5**	**0**	**5.08**
	Buffalo	**NHL**	**7**	**3**	**1**	**1**	**326**	**13**	**1**	**2.39**	....	....	....	....	....	....	....
1989-90	**Buffalo**	**NHL**	**29**	**14**	**11**	**2**	**1596**	**89**	**0**	**3.35**	....	....	....	....	....	....	....
1990-91	**Buffalo**	**NHL**	**37**	**12**	**14**	**10**	**2131**	**119**	**1**	**3.35**	**4**	**2**	**2**	**246**	**17**	**0**	**4.15**
1991-92	**Buffalo**	**NHL**	**29**	**10**	**13**	**3**	**1639**	**102**	**0**	**3.73**	....	....	....	....	....	....	....
	Rochester	AHL	2	2	0	0	120	3	1	1.50	....	....	....	....	....	....	....
	NHL Totals		**338**	**141**	**130**	**45**	**19030**	**1100**	**12**	**3.47**	**15**	**2**	**9**	**781**	**56**	**0**	**4.30**

Traded to **Washington** by **Quebec** with Dale Hunter for Gaetan Duchesne, Alan Haworth and Washington's first round choice (Joe Sakic) in 1987 Entry Draft, June 13, 1987. Traded to **Buffalo** by **Washington** with Grant Ledyard and Washington's sixth round choice (Brian Holzinger) in 1991 Entry Draft for Calle Johansson and Buffalo's second round choice (Byron Dafoe) in 1989 Entry Draft, March 7, 1989.

MANELUK, GEORGE

Goaltender. Catches left. 5'11", 185 lbs. Born, Winnipeg, Man., July 25, 1967.
(NY Islanders' 4th choice, 76th overall, in 1987 Entry Draft).

			Regular Season								Playoffs						
Season	Club	Lea	GP	W	L	T	Mins	GA	SO	Avg	GP	W	L	Mins	GA	SO	Avg
1986-87	Brandon	WHL	58	16	35	4	3258	315	0	5.80	....	....	....	....	....	....	....
1987-88	Brandon	WHL	64	24	33	3	3651	297	0	4.88	4	1	3	271	22	0	4.87
	Springfield	AHL	2	0	1	1	125	9	0	4.32	....	....	....	....	....	....	....
	Peoria	IHL	3	1	2	0	148	14	0	5.68	1	0	1	60	5	0	5.00
1988-89	Springfield	AHL	24	7	13	0	1202	84	0	4.19	....	....	....	....	....	....	....
1989-90	Springfield	AHL	27	11	9	1	1382	94	1	4.08	4	2	1	174	9	0	3.10
	Winston-Salem	ECHL	3	2	0	0	140	11	0	4.71	....	....	....	....	....	....	....
1990-91	**NY Islanders**	**NHL**	**4**	**1**	**1**	**0**	**140**	**15**	**0**	**6.43**	....	....	....	....	....	....	....
	Capital Dist.	AHL	29	10	14	1	1524	103	1	4.06	....	....	....	....	....	....	....
1991-92	New Haven	AHL	54	25	22	0	2863	175	1	3.67	3	1	2	216	13	0	3.61
	NHL Totals		**4**	**1**	**1**	**0**	**140**	**15**	**0**	**6.43**	....	....	....	....	....	....	....

MASON, BOB

Goaltender. Catches right. 6'1", 180 lbs. Born, International Falls, MN, April 22, 1961.

			Regular Season								Playoffs						
Season	Club	Lea	GP	W	L	T	Mins	GA	SO	Avg	GP	W	L	Mins	GA	SO	Avg
1981-82	Minn.-Duluth	WCHA	26	....	....	....	1401	115	0	4.45	....	....	....	....	....	....	....
1982-83	Minn.-Duluth	WCHA	43	....	....	....	2593	151	1	3.49	....	....	....	....	....	....	....
1983-84	U.S. National	....	33	....	....	....	1895	89	0	2.82	....	....	....	....	....	....	....
	U.S. Olympic	....	3	....	....	....	160	10	0	3.75	....	....	....	....	....	....	....
	Washington	**NHL**	**2**	**2**	**0**	**0**	**120**	**3**	**0**	**1.50**	....	....	....	....	....	....	....
	Hershey	AHL	5	1	4	0	282	26	0	5.53	....	....	....	....	....	....	....
1984-85	**Washington**	**NHL**	**12**	**8**	**2**	**1**	**661**	**31**	**1**	**2.81**	....	....	....	....	....	....	....
	Binghamton	AHL	20	10	6	1	1052	58	1	3.31	....	....	....	....	....	....	....
1985-86	**Washington**	**NHL**	**1**	**1**	**0**	**0**	**16**	**0**	**0**	**0.00**	....	....	....	....	....	....	....
	Binghamton	AHL	34	20	11	2	1940	126	0	3.90	3	1	1	124	9	0	4.35
1986-87	**Washington**	**NHL**	**45**	**20**	**18**	**5**	**2536**	**137**	**0**	**3.24**	**4**	**2**	**2**	**309**	**9**	**1**	**1.75**
	Binghamton	AHL	2	1	1	0	119	4	0	2.02	....	....	....	....	....	....	....
1987-88	**Chicago**	**NHL**	**41**	**13**	**18**	**8**	**2312**	**160**	**0**	**4.15**	**1**	**0**	**1**	**60**	**3**	**0**	**3.00**
1988-89	**Quebec**	**NHL**	**22**	**5**	**14**	**1**	**1168**	**92**	**0**	**4.73**	....	....	....	....	....	....	....
	Halifax	AHL	23	11	7	1	1278	73	1	3.43	2	0	2	97	9	0	5.57
1989-90	**Washington**	**NHL**	**16**	**4**	**9**	**1**	**822**	**48**	**0**	**3.50**	....	....	....	....	....	....	....
	Baltimore	AHL	13	9	2	2	770	44	0	3.43	6	2	4	373	20	0	3.22
1990-91	**Vancouver**	**NHL**	**6**	**2**	**4**	**0**	**353**	**29**	**0**	**4.93**	....	....	....	....	....	....	....
	Milwaukee	IHL	22	8	12	1	1199	82	0	4.10	....	....	....	....	....	....	....
1991-92	Milwaukee	IHL	51	27	18	4	3024	171	1	3.39	3	1	2	179	15	0	5.03
	NHL Totals		**145**	**55**	**65**	**16**	**7988**	**500**	**1**	**3.76**	**5**	**2**	**3**	**369**	**12**	**1**	**1.95**

Signed as a free agent by **Washington**, February 21, 1984. Signed as a free agent by **Chicago**, June 12, 1987. Traded to **Quebec** by **Chicago** for Mike Eagles, July 5, 1988. Traded to **Washington** by **Quebec** for future considerations, June 17, 1989. Signed as a free agent by **Vancouver**, November, 1990.

MAY, DARRELL

Goaltender. Catches left. 6', 175 lbs. Born, Edmonton, Alta., March 6, 1962.
(Vancouver's 4th choice, 91st overall, in 1980 Entry Draft).

			Regular Season								Playoffs						
Season	Club	Lea	GP	W	L	T	Mins	GA	SO	Avg	GP	W	L	Mins	GA	SO	Avg
1978-79	Portland	WHL	21	12	2	2	1113	64	0	3.45	2	1	0	80	7	0	5.25
1979-80	Portland	WHL	43	32	8	1	2416	143	1	3.55	8	3	5	439	27	0	3.69
1980-81	Portland	WHL	36	28	7	1	2128	122	3	3.44	4	....	....	243	21	0	5.19
1981-82	Portland	WHL	52	31	20	2	3097	226	0	4.38	15	....	....	851	59	0	4.16
1982-83	Fort Wayne	IHL	46	....	....	....	2584	177	0	4.11	2	....	....	120	13	0	6.50
1983-84	Erie	ACHL	43	21	16	2	2404	163	1	4.07	....	....	....	....	....	....	....
1984-85	Peoria	IHL	19	13	4	2	1133	56	1	2.97	10	6	4	609	33	0	3.25
1985-86	**St. Louis**	**NHL**	**3**	**1**	**2**	**0**	**184**	**13**	**0**	**4.24**	....	....	....	....	....	....	....
	Peoria	IHL	56	33	21	0	3321	179	1	3.23	11	6	5	634	38	1	3.60
1986-87a	Peoria	IHL	58	26	31	1	3420	214	2	3.75	....	....	....	....	....	....	....
1987-88	**St. Louis**	**NHL**	**3**	**0**	**3**	**0**	**180**	**18**	**0**	**6.00**	....	....	....	....	....	....	....
	Peoria	IHL	48	22	19	5	2754	162	....	3.53	....	....	....	....	....	....	....
1988-89	Peoria	IHL	52	20	22	0	2908	202	0	4.17	2	0	2	137	13	0	5.69
1989-90								DID NOT PLAY									
1990-91								DID NOT PLAY									
1991-92								DID NOT PLAY									
	NHL Totals		**6**	**1**	**5**	**0**	**364**	**31**	**0**	**5.11**	....	....	....	....	....	....	....

a IHL First All-Star Team (1987)

Traded to **Montreal** by **St. Louis** with Jocelyn Lemieux and St. Loius' second round choice (Patrice Brisebois) in the 1989 Entry Draft for Sergio Momesso and Vincent Riendeau, August 9, 1988. Signed as a free agent by **St. Louis**, May 26, 1991.

MAZZOLI, PAT

Goaltender. Catches left. 5'10", 172 lbs. Born, Toronto, Ont., March 16, 1970.
(Quebec's 8th choice, 169th overall, in 1990 Entry Draft).

			Regular Season								Playoffs						
Season	Club	Lea	GP	W	L	T	Mins	GA	SO	Avg	GP	W	L	Mins	GA	SO	Avg
1990-91	Ferris State	CCHA	22	13	8	1	1265	66	0	3.13	....	....	....	....	....	....	....
1991-92	Ferris State	CCHA	18	5	7	3	939	71	0	4.54	....	....	....	....	....	....	....

McGARRY, PAT

Goaltender. Catches left. 6'2", 185 lbs. Born, Ottawa, Ont., November 3, 1970.
(Toronto's 1st choice, 3rd overall, in 1991 Supplementary Draft).

			Regular Season								Playoffs						
Season	Club	Lea	GP	W	L	T	Mins	GA	SO	Avg	GP	W	L	Mins	GA	SO	Avg
1990-91	Dalhousie	AUAA	....	....	....	....	990	60	0	3.63	....	....	....	....	....	....	....
1991-92	Dalhousie	AUAA	....	....	....	....	806	49	0	3.65	....	....	....	....	....	....	....

McKERSIE, JOHN

Goaltender. Catches left. 6', 210 lbs. Born, Madison, WI, January 23, 1972.
(Minnesota's 12th choice, 239th overall, in 1990 Entry Draft).

			Regular Season								Playoffs						
Season	Club	Lea	GP	W	L	T	Mins	GA	SO	Avg	GP	W	L	Mins	GA	SO	Avg
1991-92	Boston U.	H.E.	8	3	2	1	396	23	1	3.48	....	....	....	....	....	....	....

McLEAN, KIRK

Goaltender. Catches left. 6', 195 lbs. Born, Willowdale, Ont., June 26, 1966.
(New Jersey's 6th choice, 107th overall, in 1984 Entry Draft).

			Regular Season								Playoffs						
Season	Club	Lea	GP	W	L	T	Mins	GA	SO	Avg	GP	W	L	Mins	GA	SO	Avg
1983-84	Oshawa	OHL	17	5	9	0	940	67	0	4.28	....	....	....	....	....	....	....
1984-85	Oshawa	OHL	47	23	17	2	2581	143	1	*3.32	5	1	3	271	21	0	4.65
1985-86	**New Jersey**	**NHL**	**2**	**1**	**1**	**0**	**111**	**11**	**0**	**5.95**	....	....	....	....	....	....	....
	Oshawa	OHL	51	24	21	2	2830	169	1	3.58	4	1	2	201	18	0	5.37
1986-87	**New Jersey**	**NHL**	**4**	**1**	**1**	**0**	**160**	**10**	**0**	**3.75**	....	....	....	....	....	....	....
	Maine	AHL	45	15	23	4	2606	140	1	3.22	....	....	....	....	....	....	....
1987-88	**Vancouver**	**NHL**	**41**	**11**	**27**	**3**	**2380**	**147**	**1**	**3.71**	....	....	....	....	....	....	....
1988-89	**Vancouver**	**NHL**	**42**	**20**	**17**	**3**	**2477**	**127**	**4**	**3.08**	**5**	**2**	**3**	**302**	**18**	**0**	**3.58**
1989-90	**Vancouver**	**NHL**	***63**	**21**	**30**	**10**	***3739**	**216**	**0**	**3.47**	....	....	....	....	....	....	....
1990-91	**Vancouver**	**NHL**	**41**	**10**	**22**	**3**	**1969**	**131**	**0**	**3.99**	**2**	**1**	**1**	**123**	**7**	**0**	**3.41**
1991-92a	**Vancouver**	**NHL**	**65**	***38**	**17**	**9**	**3852**	**176**	***5**	**2.74**	**13**	**6**	**7**	**785**	**33**	***2**	**2.52**
	NHL Totals		**258**	**102**	**115**	**28**	**14688**	**818**	**10**	**3.34**	**20**	**9**	**11**	**1210**	**58**	**2**	**2.88**

a NHL Second All-Star Team (1992)

Played in NHL All-Star Game (1990, 1992)

Traded to **Vancouver** by **New Jersey** with Greg Adams for Patrik Sundstrom and Vancouver's fourth round choice (Matt Ruchty) in 1988 Entry Draft, September 15, 1987.

McLENNAN, JAMIE

Goaltender. Catches left. 6', 190 lbs. Born, Edmonton, Alta., June 30, 1971.
(NY Islanders' 3rd choice, 48th overall, in 1991 Entry Draft).

			Regular Season								Playoffs						
Season	Club	Lea	GP	W	L	T	Mins	GA	SO	Avg	GP	W	L	Mins	GA	SO	Avg
1989-90	Lethbridge	WHL	34	20	4	2	1690	110	1	3.91	13	6	5	677	44	0	3.90
1990-91a	Lethbridge	WHL	56	32	18	4	3230	205	0	3.81	*16	8	8	*970	56	0	3.46
1991-92	Capital Dist.	AHL	18	4	10	2	952	60	1	3.78	....	....	....	....	....	....	....
	Richmond	ECHL	32	16	12	2	1837	114	0	3.72	....	....	....	....	....	....	....

a WHL East First All-Star Team (1991)

MELANSON, ROLAND JOSEPH (ROLLIE) (mel-AWN-son)

Goaltender. Catches left. 5'10", 185 lbs. Born, Moncton, N.B., June 28, 1960.
(NY Islanders' 4th choice, 59th overall, in 1979 Entry Draft).

			Regular Season								Playoffs						
Season	Club	Lea	GP	W	L	T	Mins	GA	SO	Avg	GP	W	L	Mins	GA	SO	Avg
1978-79a	Windsor	OHA	58	....	....	....	3468	258	1	4.41	7	....	....	392	31	0	4.75
1979-80	Windsor	OHA	22	11	8	0	1099	90	0	4.91	....	....	....	....	....	....	....
	Oshawa	OHA	38	26	12	0	2240	136	3	3.64	7	3	4	420	32	0	4.57
1980-81	NY Islanders	NHL	11	8	1	1	620	32	0	3.10	3	1	0	92	6	0	3.91
bc	Indianapolis	CHL	52	31	16	3	3056	131	2	*2.57	....	....	....	....	....	....	....
1981-82	NY Islanders	NHL	36	22	7	6	2115	114	0	3.23	3	0	1	64	5	0	4.69
1982-83de	NY Islanders	NHL	44	24	12	5	2460	109	1	2.66	5	2	2	238	10	0	2.52
1983-84	NY Islanders	NHL	37	20	11	2	2019	110	0	3.27	6	0	1	87	5	0	3.45
1984-85	NY Islanders	NHL	8	3	3	0	425	35	0	4.94	....	....	....	....	....	....	....
	Minnesota	NHL	20	5	10	3	1142	78	0	4.10	....	....	....	....	....	....	....
1985-86	Minnesota	NHL	6	2	1	2	325	24	0	4.43	....	....	....	....	....	....	....
	Los Angeles	NHL	22	4	16	1	1246	87	0	4.19	....	....	....	....	....	....	....
	New Haven	AHL	3	1	2	0	179	13	0	4.36	....	....	....	....	....	....	....
1986-87	Los Angeles	NHL	46	18	21	6	2734	168	1	3.69	5	1	4	260	24	0	5.54
1987-88	Los Angeles	NHL	47	17	20	7	2676	195	2	4.37	1	0	1	60	9	0	9.00
1988-89	Los Angeles	NHL	4	1	1	0	178	19	0	6.40	....	....	....	....	....	....	....
	New Haven	AHL	29	11	15	3	1734	106	1	3.67	*17	9	8	*1019	74	1	4.36
1989-90	Utica	AHL	48	24	19	3	2737	167	1	3.66	5	1	4	298	20	0	4.03
1990-91	New Jersey	NHL	1	0	0	0	20	2	0	6.00	....	....	....	....	....	....	....
	Utica	AHL	54	23	28	1	3058	208	0	4.08	....	....	....	....	....	....	....
1991-92	Montreal	NHL	9	5	3	0	492	22	2	2.68	....	....	....	....	....	....	....
	NHL Totals		291	129	106	33	16452	995	6	3.63	23	4	9	801	59	0	4.42

a OHA Second All-Star Team (1979)
b CHL First All-Star Team (1981)
c Won Ken McKenzie Trophy (CHL's Rookie of the Year) (1981)
d Shared William Jennings Trophy with Billy Smith (1983)
e NHL Second All-Star Team (1983)

Traded to **Minnesota** by **NY Islanders** for Minnesota's first round choice in 1985 Entry Draft (Brad Dalgarno), November 19, 1984. Traded to **NY Rangers** by **Minnesota** for New York's second round draft choice in 1986 (Neil Wilkinson) and fourth round choice in 1987 (John Weisbrod), December 9, 1985. Traded to **Los Angeles** by **NY Rangers** with Grant Ledyard for Brian MacLellan and Los Angeles' fourth round draft choice in 1987 (Michael Sullivan), December 9, 1985. Signed as a free agent by **New Jersey**, August 10, 1989. Traded to **Montreal** by **New Jersey** with Kirk Muller for Stephane Richer and Tom Chorske, September 20, 1991.

MILLEN, GREG H.

Goaltender. Catches right. 5'9", 175 lbs. Born, Toronto, Ont., June 25, 1957.
(Pittsburgh's 4th choice, 102nd overall, in 1977 Amateur Draft).

			Regular Season								Playoffs						
Season	Club	Lea	GP	W	L	T	Mins	GA	SO	Avg	GP	W	L	Mins	GA	SO	Avg
1976-77	Peterborough	OHA	59	....	....	....	3457	244	0	4.23	4	....	....	240	23	0	5.75
1977-78	Kalamazoo	IHL	3	....	....	....	180	14	0	4.67	....	....	....	....	....	....	....
	S.S. Marie	OHA	25	....	....	....	1449	105	1	4.29	13	....	....	774	61	0	4.73
1978-79	Pittsburgh	NHL	28	14	11	1	1532	86	2	3.37	....	....	....	....	....	....	....
1979-80	Pittsburgh	NHL	44	18	18	7	2586	157	2	3.64	5	2	3	300	21	0	4.20
1980-81	Pittsburgh	NHL	63	25	27	10	3721	258	0	4.16	5	2	3	325	19	0	3.51
1981-82	Hartford	NHL	55	11	30	12	3201	229	0	4.29	....	....	....	....	....	....	....
1982-83	Hartford	NHL	60	14	38	6	3520	282	1	4.81	....	....	....	....	....	....	....
1983-84	Hartford	NHL	*60	21	30	9	*3583	221	2	3.70	....	....	....	....	....	....	....
1984-85	Hartford	NHL	44	16	22	6	2659	187	1	4.22	....	....	....	....	....	....	....
	St. Louis	NHL	10	2	7	1	607	35	0	3.46	1	0	1	60	2	0	2.00
1985-86	St. Louis	NHL	36	14	16	6	2168	129	1	3.57	10	6	3	586	29	0	2.97
1986-87	St. Louis	NHL	42	15	18	9	2482	146	0	3.53	4	1	3	250	10	0	2.40
1987-88	St. Louis	NHL	48	21	19	7	2854	167	1	3.51	10	5	5	600	38	0	3.80
1988-89	St. Louis	NHL	52	22	20	7	3019	170	*6	3.38	10	5	5	649	34	0	3.14
1989-90	St. Louis	NHL	21	11	7	3	1245	61	1	2.94	....	....	....	....	....	....	....
	Quebec	NHL	18	3	14	1	1080	95	0	5.28	....	....	....	....	....	....	....
	Chicago	NHL	10	5	4	1	575	32	0	3.34	14	6	6	613	40	0	3.92
1990-91	Chicago	NHL	3	0	1	0	58	4	0	4.14	....	....	....	....	....	....	....
1991-92	Detroit	NHL	10	3	2	3	487	22	0	2.71	....	....	....	....	....	....	....
	Maine	AHL	11	2	5	2	599	37	0	3.71	....	....	....	....	....	....	....
	San Diego	IHL	5	2	3	0	296	20	0	4.05	....	....	....	....	....	....	....
	NHL Totals		604	215	284	89	35377	2281	17	3.87	59	27	29	3383	193	0	3.42

Signed as a free agent by **Hartford**, June 15, 1981. As compensation, **Pittsburgh** received Pat Boutette and the rights to Kevin McLelland, June 29, 1981. Traded to **St. Louis** by **Hartford** with Mark Johnson for Mike Liut and Jorgen Pettersson, February 21, 1985. Traded to **Quebec** by **St. Louis** with Tony Hrkac for Jeff Brown, December 13, 1989. Traded to **Chicago** by **Quebec** with Michel Goulet and Quebec's sixth round choice (Kevin St. Jacques) in 1991 Entry Draft for Mario Doyon, Everett Sanipass and Dan Vincelette, March 5, 1990. Traded to **NY Rangers** by **Chicago** for future considerations, September 24, 1991. Traded to **Detroit** by **NY Rangers** for future considerations, December 26, 1991.

MOOG, DONALD ANDREW (ANDY) (MOHG)

Goaltender. Catches left. 5'8", 170 lbs. Born, Penticton, B.C., February 18, 1960.
(Edmonton's 6th choice, 132nd overall, in 1980 Entry Draft).

			Regular Season								Playoffs						
Season	Club	Lea	GP	W	L	T	Mins	GA	SO	Avg	GP	W	L	Mins	GA	SO	Avg
1978-79	Billings	WHL	26	13	5	4	1306	90	4	4.13	5	1	3	229	21	0	5.50
1979-80a	Billings	WHL	46	23	14	1	2435	149	1	3.67	3	2	1	190	10	0	3.16
1980-81	Edmonton	NHL	7	3	3	0	313	20	0	3.83	9	5	4	526	32	0	3.65
	Wichita	CHL	29	14	13	1	1602	89	0	3.33	5	3	2	300	16	0	3.20
1981-82	Edmonton	NHL	8	3	5	0	399	32	0	4.81	....	....	....	....	....	....	....
b	Wichita	CHL	40	23	13	3	2391	119	1	2.99	7	3	4	434	23	0	3.18
1982-83	Edmonton	NHL	50	33	8	7	2833	167	1	3.54	16	11	5	949	48	0	3.03
1983-84	Edmonton	NHL	38	27	8	1	2212	139	1	3.77	7	4	0	263	12	0	2.74
1984-85	Edmonton	NHL	39	22	9	3	2019	111	1	3.30	2	0	0	20	0	0	0.00
1985-86	Edmonton	NHL	47	27	9	7	2664	164	1	3.69	1	1	0	60	1	0	1.00
1986-87	Edmonton	NHL	46	28	11	3	2461	144	0	3.51	2	2	0	120	8	0	4.00
1987-88	Cdn. National	....	27	10	7	5	1438	86	0	3.58	....	....	....	....	....	....	....
	Cdn. Olympic	....	4	4	0	0	240	9	1	2.25	....	....	....	....	....	....	....
	Boston	NHL	6	4	2	0	360	17	1	2.83	7	1	4	354	25	0	4.24
1988-89	Boston	NHL	41	18	14	8	2482	133	1	3.22	6	4	2	359	14	0	2.34
1989-90c	Boston	NHL	46	24	10	7	2536	122	3	2.89	20	13	7	1195	44	*2	*2.21
1990-91	Boston	NHL	51	25	13	9	2844	136	4	2.87	19	10	9	1133	60	0	3.18
1991-92	Boston	NHL	62	28	22	9	3640	196	1	3.23	15	8	7	866	46	1	3.19
	NHL Totals		441	242	114	54	24763	1381	14	3.35	104	59	38	5845	290	3	2.98

a WHL Second All-Star Team (1980)
b CHL Second All-Star Team (1982)
c Shared William Jennings Trophy with Rejean Lemelin (1990)

Played in NHL All-Star Game (1985, 1986, 1991)

Traded to **Boston** by **Edmonton** for Geoff Courtnall, Bill Ranford and Boston's second choice (Petro Koivunen) in 1988 Entry Draft, March 8, 1988.

MORISSETTE, ALAIN

Goaltender. Catches left. 5'9", 165 lbs. Born, Rimouski, Que., August 26, 1969.

			Regular Season								Playoffs						
Season	Club	Lea	GP	W	L	T	Mins	GA	SO	Avg	GP	W	L	Mins	GA	SO	Avg
1988-89	Trois-Rivières	QMJHL	46	25	16	2	2360	167	1	4.25	4	0	4	243	18	0	4.44
1989-90	Trois-Rivières	QMJHL	49	31	16	0	2674	166	1	3.72	5	2	3	297	28	0	5.66
1990-91	Fredericton	AHL	14	2	6	3	709	43	0	3.64	2	0	0	17	1	0	3.53
	Winston-Salem	ECHL	23	10	13	0	1222	99	0	4.86	....	....	....	....	....	....	....
1991-92	Muskegon	IHL	31	15	6	8	1796	100	1	3.34	2	0	1	97	9	0	5.57
	Knoxville	ECHL	1	0	0	1	65	5	0	4.62	....	....	....	....	....	....	....

Signed as a free agent by **Montreal**, October 15, 1990.

MULLAHY, BRAD

Goaltender. Catches left. 5'10", 180 lbs. Born, North Easton, MA, February 12, 1970.
(Winnipeg's 1st choice, 5th overall, in 1991 Supplemental Draft).

			Regular Season								Playoffs						
Season	Club	Lea	GP	W	L	T	Mins	GA	SO	Avg	GP	W	L	Mins	GA	SO	Avg
1989-90	Providence	H.E.	5	2	1	0	207	13	0	3.77	....	....	....	....	....	....	....
1990-91	Providence	H.E.	22	14	5	1	1257	65	0	3.10	....	....	....	....	....	....	....
1991-92	Providence	H.E.	22	11	9	2	1291	80	2	3.72	....	....	....	....	....	....	....

MURRAY, SHAWN

Goaltender. Catches left. 5'9", 160 lbs. Born, St. Paul, MN, September 3, 1971.
(Calgary's 9th choice, 167th overall, in 1990 Entry Draft).

			Regular Season								Playoffs						
Season	Club	Lea	GP	W	L	T	Mins	GA	SO	Avg	GP	W	L	Mins	GA	SO	Avg
1990-91	Colgate	ECAC	6	2	2	0	311	21	0	4.06	....	....	....	....	....	....	....
1991-92	Colgate	ECAC	15	7	7	0	904	71	0	4.71	....	....	....	....	....	....	....

MUZZATTI, JASON

Goaltender. Catches left. 6'1", 190 lbs. Born, Toronto, Ont., February 3, 1970.
(Calgary's 1st choice, 21st overall, in 1988 Entry Draft).

			Regular Season								Playoffs						
Season	Club	Lea	GP	W	L	T	Mins	GA	SO	Avg	GP	W	L	Mins	GA	SO	Avg
1987-88a	Michigan State	CCHA	33	19	9	3	1915	109	0	3.41	....	....	....	....	....	....	....
1988-89	Michigan State	CCHA	42	32	9	1	2515	127	3	*3.03	....	....	....	....	....	....	....
1989-90bc	Michigan State	CCHA	33	*24	6	0	1976	99	0	3.01	....	....	....	....	....	....	....
1990-91	Michigan State	CCHA	22	8	10	2	1204	75	1	3.74	....	....	....	....	....	....	....
1991-92	Salt Lake	IHL	52	24	22	5	3033	167	2	3.30	4	1	3	247	18	0	4.37

a CCHA Second All-Star Team (1988)
b CCHA First All-Star Team (1990)
c NCAA West Second All-American Team (1990)

MYLLYS, JARMO (MEE-lus, YAR-moh)

Goaltender. Catches left. 5'8", 160 lbs. Born, Savonlinna, Finland, May 29, 1965.
(Minnesota's 9th choice, 172nd overall, in 1987 Entry Draft).

			Regular Season								Playoffs						
Season	Club	Lea	GP	W	L	T	Mins	GA	SO	Avg	GP	W	L	Mins	GA	SO	Avg
1987-88	Lukko	Fin.	43	....	....	....	2580	160	....	3.72	....	....	....	....	....	....	....
1988-89	Minnesota	NHL	6	1	4	0	238	22	0	5.55	....	....	....	....	....	....	....
	Kalamazoo	IHL	28	13	8	4	1523	93	0	3.66	6	2	4	419	22	0	3.15
1989-90	Minnesota	NHL	4	0	3	0	156	16	0	6.15	....	....	....	....	....	....	....
a	Kalamazoo	IHL	49	31	9	3	2715	159	1	3.51	5	4	0	258	11	0	2.56
1990-91	Minnesota	NHL	2	0	2	0	78	8	0	6.15	....	....	....	....	....	....	....
	Kalamazoo	IHL	38	24	13	1	2278	144	1	3.79	10	6	4	600	26	0	*2.60
1991-92	San Jose	NHL	27	3	18	1	1374	115	0	5.02	....	....	....	....	....	....	....
	Kansas City	IHL	5	5	0	0	307	15	0	2.93	....	....	....	....	....	....	....
	NHL Totals		39	4	27	1	1846	161	0	5.23	....	....	....	....	....	....	....

a IHL Second All-Star Team (1990)

Claimed by **San Jose** from **Minnesota** in Disersal Draft, May 30, 1991. Traded to **Toronto** by **San Jose** for cash, June 15, 1992.

NEWMAN, THOMAS

Goaltender. Catches left. 6'1", 185 lbs. Born, Golden Valley, MN, February 23, 1971.
(Los Angeles' 4th choice, 103rd overall, in 1989 Entry Draft).

			Regular Season								Playoffs						
Season	Club	Lea	GP	W	L	T	Mins	GA	SO	Avg	GP	W	L	Mins	GA	SO	Avg
1989-90	U. Minnesota	WCHA	35	19	13	2	1982	127	0	3.84	....	....	....	....	....	....	....
1990-91	U. Minnesota	WCHA	22	12	2	2	942	54	2	3.44	....	....	....	....	....	....	....
1991-92	U. Minnesota	WCHA	11	5	1	0	399	15	0	2.26	....	....	....	....	....	....	....

O'NEILL, MICHAEL (MIKE)

Goaltender. Catches left. 5'7", 160 lbs. Born, LaSalle, Que., November 3, 1967.
(Winnipeg's 1st choice, 15th overall, in 1988 Supplemental Draft).

			Regular Season								Playoffs						
Season	Club	Lea	GP	W	L	T	Mins	GA	SO	Avg	GP	W	L	Mins	GA	SO	Avg
1985-86	Yale	ECAC	6	3	1	0	389	17	0	3.53	....	....	....	....	....	....	....
1986-87a	Yale	ECAC	16	9	6	1	964	55	2	3.42	....	....	....	....	....	....	....
1987-88	Yale	ECAC	24	6	17	0	1385	101	0	4.37	....	....	....	....	....	....	....
1988-89ab	Yale	ECAC	25	10	14	1	1490	93	0	3.74	....	....	....	....	....	....	....
1989-90	Tappara	Fin.	41	23	13	5	2369	127	2	3.22	....	....	....	....	....	....	....
1990-91	Fort Wayne	IHL	8	5	2	1	490	31	0	3.80	....	....	....	....	....	....	....
	Moncton	AHL	30	13	7	6	1613	84	0	3.12	8	3	4	435	29	0	4.00
1991-92	Winnipeg	NHL	1	0	0	0	13	1	0	4.62	....	....	....	....	....	....	....
	Moncton	AHL	32	14	16	2	1902	108	1	3.41	11	4	7	670	43	*1	3.85
	Fort Wayne	IHL	33	22	6	3	1858	97	*4	3.13	....	....	....	....	....	....	....
	NHL Totals		1	0	0	0	13	1	0	4.62	....	....	....	....	....	....	....

a ECAC First All-Star Team (1987, 1989)
b NCAA East First All-American Team (1989)

OSGOOD, CHRIS

Goaltender. Catches left. 5'10", 156 lbs. Born, Peace River, Alta., November 26, 1972.
(Detroit's 3rd choice, 54th overall, in 1991 Entry Draft).

			Regular Season								Playoffs						
Season	Club	Lea	GP	W	L	T	Mins	GA	SO	Avg	GP	W	L	Mins	GA	SO	Avg
1989-90	Medicine Hat	WHL	57	24	28	2	3094	228	0	4.42	3	0	3	173	17	0	5.91
1990-91a	Medicine Hat	WHL	46	23	18	3	2630	173	2	3.95	12	7	5	712	42	0	3.54
1991-92	Medicine Hat	WHL	15	10	3	0	819	44	0	3.22	....	....	....	....	....	....	....
	Brandon	WHL	16	3	10	1	890	60	1	4.04	....	....	....	....	....	....	....
	Seattle	WHL	21	12	7	1	1217	65	1	3.20	15	9	6	904	51	0	3.38

a WHL East Second All-Star Team (1991)

PARSON, MIKE

Goaltender. Catches left. 6', 170 lbs. Born, Listowel, Ont., March 12, 1970.
(Boston's 2nd choice, 38th overall, in 1989 Entry Draft).

			Regular Season								Playoffs						
Season	Club	Lea	GP	W	L	T	Mins	GA	SO	Avg	GP	W	L	Mins	GA	SO	Avg
1987-88	Guelph	OHL	31	9	17	2	1703	135	0	4.76	....	....	....	....	....	....	....
1988-89	Guelph	OHL	*53	25	22	5	*3047	194	0	3.82	7	3	4	421	29	0	4.13
1989-90	Owen Sound	OHL	29	21	21	4	2750	207	1	4.52	12	5	7	722	61	0	4.24
1990-91	Maine	AHL	24	6	10	1	1154	79	0	4.11	....	....	....	....	....	....	....
	Johnstown	ECHL	6	4	2	0	333	23	0	4.14	....	....	....	....	....	....	....
1991-92	Maine	AHL	12	5	4	1	645	37	0	3.44	....	....	....	....	....	....	....
	Johnstown	ECHL	17	6	7	3	994	61	0	3.68	5	2	1	224	15	0	4.02

PIETRANGELO, FRANK (PEE-tuhr-AN-jehl-oh)

Goaltender. Catches left. 5'10", 185 lbs. Born, Niagara Falls, Ont., December 17, 1964.
(Pittsburgh's 4th choice, 63rd overall, in 1983 Entry Draft).

			Regular Season								Playoffs						
Season	Club	Lea	GP	W	L	T	Mins	GA	SO	Avg	GP	W	L	Mins	GA	SO	Avg
1982-83	U. Minnesota	WCHA	25	15	6	1	1348	80	1	3.55	....	....	....	....	....	....	....
1983-84	U. Minnesota	WCHA	20	13	7	0	1141	66	0	3.47	....	....	....	....	....	....	....
1984-85	U. Minnesota	WCHA	17	8	3	3	912	52	0	3.42	....	....	....	....	....	....	....
1985-86	U. Minnesota	WCHA	23	15	7	0	1284	76	0	3.55	....	....	....	....	....	....	....
1986-87	Muskegon	IHL	35	23	11	0	2090	119	2	3.42	15	10	4	923	46	0	2.99
1987-88	**Pittsburgh**	**NHL**	**21**	**9**	**11**	**0**	**1207**	**80**	**1**	**3.98**	....	....	....	....	....	....	....
	Muskegon	IHL	15	11	3	1	868	43	2	2.97	....	....	....	....	....	....	....
1988-89	**Pittsburgh**	**NHL**	**15**	**5**	**3**	**0**	**669**	**45**	**0**	**4.04**	....	....	....	....	....	....	....
	Muskegon	IHL	13	10	1	0	760	38	1	3.00	9	*8	1	566	29	0	3.07
1989-90	**Pittsburgh**	**NHL**	**21**	**8**	**6**	**2**	**1066**	**77**	**0**	**4.33**	....	....	....	....	....	....	....
	Muskegon	IHL	12	9	2	1	691	38	0	3.30	....	....	....	....	....	....	....
1990-91	**Pittsburgh**	**NHL**	**25**	**10**	**11**	**1**	**1311**	**86**	**0**	**3.94**	**5**	**4**	**1**	**288**	**15**	***1**	**3.13**
1991-92	**Pittsburgh**	**NHL**	**5**	**2**	**1**	**0**	**225**	**20**	**0**	**5.33**	....	....	....	....	....	....	....
	Hartford	**NHL**	**5**	**3**	**1**	**1**	**306**	**12**	**0**	**2.35**	**7**	**3**	**4**	**425**	**19**	**0**	**2.68**
	NHL Totals		**92**	**37**	**33**	**4**	**4784**	**320**	**1**	**4.01**	**12**	**7**	**5**	**713**	**34**	**1**	**2.86**

Traded to **Hartford** by **Pittsburgh** for future considerations, March 10, 1992.

POTVIN, FELIX

Goaltender. Catches left. 6'1", 183 lbs. Born, Anjou, Que., June 23, 1971.
(Toronto's 2nd choice, 31st overall, in 1990 Entry Draft).

			Regular Season								Playoffs						
Season	Club	Lea	GP	W	L	T	Mins	GA	SO	Avg	GP	W	L	Mins	GA	SO	Avg
1988-89	Chicoutimi	QMJHL	*65	25	31	1	*3489	271	*2	4.66	....	....	....	....	....	....	....
1989-90a	Chicoutimi	QMJHL	*62	*31	26	2	*3478	231	*2	3.99	....	....	....	....	....	....	....
1990-91bcde	Chicoutimi	QMJHL	54	33	15	4	3216	145	*6	*2.71	*16	*11	5	*992	46	0	*2.78
1991-92	**Toronto**	**NHL**	**4**	**0**	**2**	**1**	**210**	**8**	**0**	**2.29**	....	....	....	....	....	....	....
fgh	St. John's	AHL	35	10	6	1	2070	101	2	2.93	11	7	4	642	41	0	3.83
	NHL Totals		**4**	**0**	**2**	**1**	**210**	**8**	**0**	**2.29**	....	....	....	....	....	....	....

a QMJHL Second All-Star Team (1990)
b QMJHL First All-Star Team (1991)
c Canadian Major Junior Goaltender of the Year (1991)
d Memorial Cup All-Star Team (1991)
e Won Hap Emms Memorial Trophy (Memorial Cup Top Goalie) (1991)
f Won Baz Bastien Trophy (Top Goalie-AHL) (1992)
g Won Dudley "Red" Garrett Memorial Trophy (Top Rookie-AHL) (1992)
h AHL First All-Star Team (1992)

PUPPA, DAREN (POO-puh)

Goaltender. Catches right. 6'3", 205 lbs. Born, Kirkland Lake, Ont., March 23, 1965.
(Buffalo's 6th choice, 74th overall, in 1983 Entry Draft).

			Regular Season								Playoffs						
Season	Club	Lea	GP	W	L	T	Mins	GA	SO	Avg	GP	W	L	Mins	GA	SO	Avg
1983-84	RPI	ECAC	32	24	6	0	....	....	....	2.94	....	....	....	....	....	....	....
1984-85	RPI	ECAC	32	31	1	0	1830	78	0	2.56	....	....	....	....	....	....	....
1985-86	**Buffalo**	**NHL**	**7**	**3**	**4**	**0**	**401**	**21**	**1**	**3.14**	....	....	....	....	....	....	....
	Rochester	AHL	20	8	11	0	1092	79	0	4.34	....	....	....	....	....	....	....
1986-87	**Buffalo**	**NHL**	**3**	**0**	**2**	**1**	**185**	**13**	**0**	**4.22**	....	....	....	....	....	....	....
a	Rochester	AHL	57	*33	14	0	3129	146	1	2.80	*16	*10	6	*944	48	*1	3.05
1987-88	**Buffalo**	**NHL**	**17**	**8**	**6**	**1**	**874**	**61**	**0**	**4.19**	**3**	**1**	**1**	**142**	**11**	**0**	**4.65**
	Rochester	AHL	26	14	8	2	1415	65	2	2.76	2	0	1	108	5	0	2.78
1988-89	**Buffalo**	**NHL**	**37**	**17**	**10**	**6**	**1908**	**107**	**1**	**3.36**	....	....	....	....	....	....	....
1989-90b	**Buffalo**	**NHL**	**56**	***31**	**16**	**6**	**3241**	**156**	**1**	**2.89**	**6**	**2**	**4**	**370**	**15**	**0**	**2.43**
1990-91	**Buffalo**	**NHL**	**38**	**15**	**11**	**6**	**2092**	**118**	**2**	**3.38**	**2**	**0**	**1**	**81**	**10**	**0**	**7.41**
1991-92	**Buffalo**	**NHL**	**33**	**11**	**14**	**4**	**1757**	**114**	**0**	**3.89**	....	....	....	....	....	....	....
	NHL Totals		**191**	**85**	**63**	**24**	**10458**	**590**	**5**	**3.38**	**11**	**3**	**6**	**593**	**36**	**0**	**3.64**

a AHL First All-Star Team (1987)
b NHL Second All-Star Team (1990)

Played in NHL All-Star Game (1990)

PYE, BILL

Goaltender. Catches left. 5'9", 180 lbs. Born, Canton, MI, April 9, 1969.
(Buffalo's 5th choice, 107th overall, in 1989 Entry Draft).

			Regular Season								Playoffs						
Season	Club	Lea	GP	W	L	T	Mins	GA	SO	Avg	GP	W	L	Mins	GA	SO	Avg
1987-88	N. Michigan	WCHA	13	....	....	....	654	49	0	4.49	....	....	....	....	....	....	....
1988-89	N. Michigan	WCHA	43	26	15	2	2533	133	1	3.15	....	....	....	....	....	....	....
1989-90	N. Michigan	WCHA	36	20	14	1	2035	149	1	4.39	....	....	....	....	....	....	....
1990-91abc	N. Michigan	WCHA	39	*32	3	4	2300	109	*4	2.84	....	....	....	....	....	....	....
1991-92	Rochester	AHL	7	0	4	0	272	13	0	2.87	1	1	0	60	2	0	2.00
	New Haven	AHL	4	0	3	1	200	19	0	5.70	....	....	....	....	....	....	....
	Fort Wayne	IHL	8	5	2	1	451	29	0	3.86	....	....	....	....	....	....	....
	Erie	ECHL	5	5	0	0	310	22	0	4.26	4	1	3	220	15	0	4.09

a WCHA First All-Star Team (1991)
b NCAA West Second All-American Team (1991)
c NCAA Final Four All-Tournament Team (1991)

RACICOT, ANDRÉ

Goaltender. Catches left. 5'11", 165 lbs. Born, Rouyn-Noranda, Que., June 9, 1969.
(Montreal's 5th choice, 83rd overall, in 1989 Entry Draft).

			Regular Season								Playoffs						
Season	Club	Lea	GP	W	L	T	Mins	GA	SO	Avg	GP	W	L	Mins	GA	SO	Avg
1986-87	Longueuil	QMJHL	3	1	2	0	180	19	0	6.33	....	....	....	....	....	....	....
1987-88	Granby	QMJHL	30	15	11	1	1547	105	1	4.07	5	1	4	298	23	0	4.63
1988-89a	Granby	QMJHL	54	22	24	3	2944	198	0	4.04	4	0	4	218	18	0	4.95
1989-90	**Montreal**	**NHL**	**1**	**0**	**0**	**0**	**13**	**3**	**0**	**13.85**	....	....	....	....	....	....	....
b	Sherbrooke	AHL	33	19	11	2	1948	97	1	2.99	5	0	4	227	18	0	4.76
1990-91	**Montreal**	**NHL**	**21**	**7**	**9**	**2**	**975**	**52**	**1**	**3.20**	**2**	**0**	**1**	**12**	**2**	**0**	**10.00**
	Fredericton	AHL	22	13	8	1	1252	60	1	2.88	....	....	....	....	....	....	....
1991-92	**Montreal**	**NHL**	**9**	**0**	**3**	**3**	**436**	**23**	**0**	**3.17**	**1**	**0**	**0**	**1**	**0**	**0**	**0.00**
	Fredericton	AHL	28	14	8	5	1666	86	0	3.10	....	....	....	....	....	....	....
	NHL Totals		**31**	**7**	**12**	**5**	**1424**	**78**	**1**	**3.29**	**3**	**0**	**0**	**13**	**2**	**0**	**9.23**

a QMJHL Second All-Star Team (1989)
b Shared Harry "Hap" Holmes Trophy (fewest goals-against-AHL) with J.C. Bergeron (1990)

RACINE, BRUCE

Goaltender. Catches left. 6', 178 lbs. Born, Cornwall, Ont., August 9, 1966.
(Pittsburgh's 3rd choice, 58th overall, in 1985 Entry Draft).

			Regular Season								Playoffs						
Season	Club	Lea	GP	W	L	T	Mins	GA	SO	Avg	GP	W	L	Mins	GA	SO	Avg
1984-85	Northeastern	H.E.	26	11	14	1	1615	103	1	3.83	....	....	....	....	....	....	....
1985-86	Northeastern	H.E.	32	17	14	1	1920	147	0	4.56	....	....	....	....	....	....	....
1986-87ab	Northeastern	H.E.	33	12	18	3	1966	133	0	4.06	....	....	....	....	....	....	....
1987-88b	Northeastern	H.E.	30	15	11	4	1808	108	1	3.58	....	....	....	....	....	....	....
1988-89	Muskegon	IHL	51	*37	11	0	*3039	184	*3	3.63	5	4	1	300	15	0	3.00
1989-90	Muskegon	IHL	49	29	15	4	2911	182	1	3.75	9	5	4	566	32	1	3.34
1990-91	Albany	IHL	29	7	18	1	1567	104	0	3.98	....	....	....	....	....	....	....
	Muskegon	IHL	9	4	4	1	516	40	0	4.65	....	....	....	....	....	....	....
1991-92	Muskegon	IHL	27	13	10	3	1559	91	1	3.50	1	0	1	60	6	0	6.00

a Hockey East First All-Star Team (1987)
b NCAA East First All-American Team (1987, 1988)

RANFORD, BILL

Goaltender. Catches left. 5'10", 170 lbs. Born, Brandon, Man., December 14, 1966.
(Boston's 2nd choice, 52nd overall, in 1985 Entry Draft).

			Regular Season								Playoffs						
Season	Club	Lea	GP	W	L	T	Mins	GA	SO	Avg	GP	W	L	Mins	GA	SO	Avg
1983-84	N. Westminster	WHL	27	10	14	0	1450	130	0	5.38	1	0	0	27	2	0	4.44
1984-85	N. Westminster	WHL	38	19	17	0	2034	142	0	4.19	7	2	3	309	26	0	5.05
1985-86	**Boston**	**NHL**	**4**	**3**	**1**	**0**	**240**	**10**	**0**	**2.50**	**2**	**0**	**2**	**120**	**7**	**0**	**3.50**
	N. Westminster	WHL	53	17	29	1	2791	225	0	4.84	....	....	....	....	....	....	....
1986-87	**Boston**	**NHL**	**41**	**16**	**20**	**2**	**2234**	**124**	**3**	**3.33**	**2**	**0**	**2**	**123**	**8**	**0**	**3.90**
	Moncton	AHL	3	3	0	0	180	6	0	2.00	....	....	....	....	....	....	....
1987-88	Maine	AHL	51	27	16	6	2856	165	1	3.47	....	....	....	....	....	....	....
	Edmonton	**NHL**	**6**	**3**	**0**	**2**	**325**	**16**	**0**	**2.95**	....	....	....	....	....	....	....
1988-89	**Edmonton**	**NHL**	**29**	**15**	**8**	**2**	**1509**	**88**	**1**	**3.50**	....	....	....	....	....	....	....
1989-90a	**Edmonton**	**NHL**	**56**	**24**	**16**	**9**	**3107**	**165**	**1**	**3.19**	***22**	***16**	**6**	***1401**	**59**	**0**	**2.53**
1990-91	**Edmonton**	**NHL**	**60**	**27**	**27**	**3**	**3415**	**182**	**0**	**3.20**	**3**	**1**	**2**	**135**	**8**	**0**	**3.56**
1991-92	**Edmonton**	**NHL**	**67**	**27**	**26**	**10**	**3822**	**228**	**1**	**3.58**	**16**	**8**	**8**	**909**	**51**	***2**	**3.37**
	NHL Totals		**263**	**115**	**98**	**28**	**14652**	**813**	**6**	**3.33**	**45**	**25**	**20**	**2688**	**133**	**2**	**2.97**

a Won Conn Smythe Trophy (1990)

Played in NHL All-Star Game (1991)

Traded to **Edmonton** by **Boston** with Geoff Courtnall and future considerations for Andy Moog, March 8, 1988.

RAM, JAMIE

Goaltender. Catches left. 5'11", 164 lbs. Born, Scarborough, Ont., January 18, 1971.
(NY Rangers' 10th choice, 213th overall, in 1991 Entry Draft).

			Regular Season								Playoffs						
Season	Club	Lea	GP	W	L	T	Mins	GA	SO	Avg	GP	W	L	Mins	GA	SO	Avg
1990-91	Michigan Tech	WCHA	14	5	9	0	826	57	0	4.14	....	....	....	....	....	....	....
1991-92	Michigan Tech	WCHA	23	9	9	1	1144	83	0	4.35	....	....	....	....	....	....	....

RAYMOND, ALAIN

Goaltender. Catches left. 5'10", 180 lbs. Born, Rimouski, Que., June 24, 1965.
(Washington's 7th choice, 215th overall, in 1983 Entry Draft).

			Regular Season								Playoffs						
Season	Club	Lea	GP	W	L	T	Mins	GA	SO	Avg	GP	W	L	Mins	GA	SO	Avg
1983-84	Trois-Rivières	QMJHL	53	18	25	0	2725	223	3	4.91	....	....	....	....	....	....	....
1984-85a	Trois-Rivières	QMJHL	58	29	26	1	3295	220	2	4.01	7	3	5	438	32	0	4.38
1985-86	Cdn. National	....	46	25	18	3	2571	151	4	3.52	....	....	....	....	....	....	....
1986-87b	Fort Wayne	IHL	45	23	16	0	2433	134	1	*3.30	6	2	3	320	23	0	4.31
1987-88	**Washington**	**NHL**	**1**	**0**	**1**	**0**	**40**	**2**	**0**	**3.00**	....	....	....	....	....	....	....
	Fort Wayne	IHL	40	20	15	3	2271	142	2	3.75	2	0	1	67	7	0	6.27
1988-89	Baltimore	AHL	41	14	22	2	2301	162	0	4.22	....	....	....	....	....	....	....
1989-90	Baltimore	AHL	11	4	5	2	612	34	0	3.33	....	....	....	....	....	....	....
	Hampton Rds.	ECHL	31	17	12	1	2048	123	0	3.60	5	2	3	302	24	0	4.77
1990-91	Peoria	IHL	5	1	3	1	304	22	0	4.34	....	....	....	....	....	....	....
	Nashville	ECHL	43	21	18	3	2508	189	1	4.52	....	....	....	....	....	....	....
1991-92	Peoria	IHL	6	1	3	2	370	27	0	4.38	....	....	....	....	....	....	....
	NHL Totals		**1**	**0**	**1**	**0**	**40**	**2**	**0**	**3.00**	....	....	....	....	....	....	....

a QMJHL Second All-Star Team (1985)
b Shared James Norris Memorial Trophy (IHL's Top Goaltender) with Michel Dufour (1987)

Signed as a free agent by **St. Louis**, September 12, 1990.

REAUGH, DARYL (RAY)

Goaltender. Catches left. 5'8", 175 lbs. Born, Prince George, B.C., February 13, 1965.
(Edmonton's 2nd choice, 42nd overall, in 1984 Entry Draft).

			Regular Season								Playoffs						
Season	Club	Lea	GP	W	L	T	Mins	GA	SO	Avg	GP	W	L	Mins	GA	SO	Avg
1983-84	Kamloops	WHL	55				2748	199	1	4.34	17			972	57	0	3.52
1984-85	**Edmonton**	**NHL**	**1**	**0**	**1**	**0**	**60**	**5**	**0**	**5.00**							
a	Kamloops	WHL	49				2749	170	2	3.71	14			787	56	0	4.27
1985-86	Nova Scotia	AHL	38	15	18	4	2205	156	0	4.24							
1986-87	Nova Scotia	AHL	46	19	22	0	2637	163	1	3.71	2	0	2	120	13	0	6.50
1987-88	**Edmonton**	**NHL**	**6**	**1**	**1**	**0**	**176**	**14**	**0**	**4.77**							
	Nova Scotia	AHL	8	2	5	0	443	33	0	4.47							
	Milwaukee	IHL	9	0	8	0	493	44	0	5.35							
1988-89	Cape Breton	AHL	13	3	10	0	778	72	0	5.55							
	Karpat	Fin.	13	7	5	1	756	46	2	3.65							
1989-90	Binghamton	AHL	52	8	31	6	2375	192	0	4.21							
1990-91	**Hartford**	**NHL**	**20**	**7**	**7**	**1**	**1010**	**53**	**1**	**3.15**							
	Springfield	AHL	16	7	6	3	912	55	0	3.62							
1991-92	Springfield	AHL	22	3	12	2	1005	63	0	3.76	1	0	0	39	1	0	1.54
	NHL Totals		**27**	**8**	**9**	**1**	**1246**	**72**	**1**	**3.47**							

a WHL First All-Star Team, West Division (1985)

Signed as a free agent by **Hartford**, October 9, 1989.

REDDICK, ELDON

Goaltender. Catches left. 5'8", 170 lbs. Born, Halifax, N.S., October 6, 1964.

			Regular Season								Playoffs						
Season	Club	Lea	GP	W	L	T	Mins	GA	SO	Avg	GP	W	L	Mins	GA	SO	Avg
1982-83	Nanaimo	WHL	66	19	38	1	3549	383	0	6.46							
1983-84	N. Westminster	WHL	50	24	22	2	2930	215	0	4.40	9	4	5	542	53	0	5.87
1984-85	Brandon	WHL	47	14	30	1	2585	243	0	5.64							
1985-86	Fort Wayne	IHL	29	15	11	0	1674	86	*3	3.00							
1986-87	**Winnipeg**	**NHL**	**48**	**21**	**21**	**4**	**2762**	**149**	**0**	**3.24**	**3**	**0**	**2**	**166**	**10**	**0**	**3.61**
1987-88	**Winnipeg**	**NHL**	**28**	**9**	**13**	**3**	**1487**	**102**	**0**	**4.12**							
	Moncton	AHL	9	2	6	1	545	26	0	2.86							
1988-89	**Winnipeg**	**NHL**	**41**	**11**	**17**	**7**	**2109**	**144**	**0**	**4.10**							
1989-90	**Edmonton**	**NHL**	**11**	**5**	**4**	**2**	**604**	**31**	**0**	**3.08**	**1**	**0**	**0**	**2**	**0**	**0**	**0.00**
	Cape Breton	AHL	15	9	4	1	821	54	0	3.95							
	Phoenix	IHL	3	2	1	0	185	7	0	2.27							
1990-91	**Edmonton**	**NHL**	**2**	**0**	**2**	**0**	**120**	**9**	**0**	**4.50**							
	Cape Breton	AHL	31	19	10	0	1673	97	2	3.48	2	0	2	124	10	0	4.84
1991-92	Cape Breton	AHL	16	5	3	3	765	45	0	3.53							
	Fort Wayne	IHL	14	6	5	2	787	40	1	3.05	7	3	4	369	18	0	2.93
	NHL Totals		**130**	**46**	**57**	**16**	**7082**	**435**	**0**	**3.69**	**4**	**0**	**2**	**168**	**10**	**0**	**3.57**

Signed as a free agent by **Winnipeg**, September 27, 1985. Traded to **Edmonton** by **Winnipeg** for future considerations, September 28, 1989.

REESE, JEFF

Goaltender. Catches left. 5'9", 170 lbs. Born, Brantford, Ont., March 24, 1966.
(Toronto's 3rd choice, 67th overall, in 1984 Entry Draft).

			Regular Season								Playoffs						
Season	Club	Lea	GP	W	L	T	Mins	GA	SO	Avg	GP	W	L	Mins	GA	SO	Avg
1983-84	London	OHL	43	18	19	0	2308	173	0	4.50	6	3	3	327	27	0	4.95
1984-85	London	OHL	50	31	15	1	2878	186	1	3.88	8	5	2	440	20	1	2.73
1985-86	London	OHL	57	25	26	3	3281	215	0	3.93	5	0	4	299	25	0	5.02
1986-87	Newmarket	AHL	50	11	29	0	2822	193	1	4.10							
1987-88	**Toronto**	**NHL**	**5**	**1**	**2**	**1**	**249**	**17**	**0**	**4.10**							
	Newmarket	AHL	28	10	14	3	1587	103	0	3.89							
1988-89	**Toronto**	**NHL**	**10**	**2**	**6**	**1**	**486**	**40**	**0**	**4.94**							
	Newmarket	AHL	37	17	14	3	2072	132	0	3.82							
1989-90	**Toronto**	**NHL**	**21**	**9**	**6**	**3**	**1101**	**81**	**0**	**4.41**	**2**	**1**	**1**	**108**	**6**	**0**	**3.33**
	Newmarket	AHL	7	3	2	1	431	29	0	4.04							
1990-91	**Toronto**	**NHL**	**30**	**6**	**13**	**3**	**1430**	**92**	**1**	**3.86**							
	Newmarket	AHL	3	2	1	0	180	7	0	2.33							
1991-92	**Toronto**	**NHL**	**8**	**1**	**5**	**1**	**413**	**20**	**1**	**2.91**							
	Calgary	**NHL**	**12**	**3**	**2**	**2**	**587**	**37**	**0**	**3.78**							
	NHL Totals		**86**	**22**	**34**	**11**	**4266**	**287**	**2**	**4.04**	**2**	**1**	**1**	**108**	**6**	**0**	**3.33**

Traded by **Calgary** to **Toronto** with Craig Berube, Alexander Godynyuk, Gary Leeman and Michel Petit for Doug Gilmour, Jamie Macoun, Ric Nattress, Rick Wamsley and Kent Manderville, January 2, 1992.

REIMER, MARK (RIGH-muhr)

Goaltender. Catches left. 5'11", 170 lbs. Born, Calgary, Alta., March 23, 1967.
(Detroit's 5th choice, 74th overall, in 1987 Entry Draft).

			Regular Season								Playoffs						
Season	Club	Lea	GP	W	L	T	Mins	GA	SO	Avg	GP	W	L	Mins	GA	SO	Avg
1984-85	Saskatoon	WHL	2	2	0	0	120	7	0	3.50							
1985-86	Saskatoon	WHL	41	17	18	3	2362	192	0	4.88	5			300	25	0	5.00
1986-87	Saskatoon	WHL	42	24	15	2	2442	141	1	3.46	6			360	20	0	3.33
1987-88	Portland	WHL	38	13	23	2	2268	208	0	5.50							
	Flint	IHL	5	0	3	0	169	22	0	7.86							
	Adirondack	AHL	8	6	1	0	459	24	0	3.14	1	0	0	20	0	0	0.00
1988-89	Adirondack	AHL	18	5	6	3	900	64	0	4.27							
	Flint	IHL	17	5	8	0	1022	83	0	4.87							
1989-90	Adirondack	AHL	36	14	17	3	2092	131	0	3.76							
1990-91	Adirondack	AHL	19	6	9	2	1019	71	0	4.18							
	San Diego	IHL	14	3	6	3	688	51	0	4.45							
	Erie	ECHL									4	2	2	240	13	0	3.25
1991-92	Adirondack	AHL	25	11	13	1	1459	99	0	4.07							
	Indianapolis	IHL	6	2	3	1	369	21	0	3.41							
	Toledo	ECHL	2	1	1	0	119	6	0	3.03	4	1	3	249	17	0	4.10

RHODES, DAMIAN

Goaltender. Catches left. 6', 165 lbs. Born, St. Paul, MN, May 28, 1969.
(Toronto's 6th choice, 112th overall, in 1987 Entry Draft).

			Regular Season								Playoffs						
Season	Club	Lea	GP	W	L	T	Mins	GA	SO	Avg	GP	W	L	Mins	GA	SO	Avg
1987-88	Michigan Tech	WCHA	29	16	10	1	1625	114	0	4.20							
1988-89	Michigan Tech	WCHA	37	15	22	0	2216	163	0	4.41							
1989-90	Michigan Tech	WCHA	25	6	17	0	1358	119	0	6.26							
1990-91	**Toronto**	**NHL**	**1**	**1**	**0**	**0**	**60**	**1**	**0**	**1.00**							
	Newmarket	AHL	38	8	24	3	2154	144	1	4.01							
1991-92	St. John's	AHL	43	20	16	5	2454	148	0	3.62	6	4	1	331	16	0	2.90
	NHL Totals		**1**	**1**	**0**	**0**	**60**	**1**	**0**	**1.00**							

RICHARDS, MARK A.

Goaltender. Catches left. 5'8", 179 lbs. Born, Jamison, PA, July 24, 1969.
(Winnipeg's 1st choice, 19th overall, in 1990 Supplemental Draft).

			Regular Season								Playoffs						
Season	Club	Lea	GP	W	L	T	Mins	GA	SO	Avg	GP	W	L	Mins	GA	SO	Avg
1988-89	Lowell	H.E.	18	1	12	1	918	83	0	5.42							
1989-90	Lowell	H.E.	32	11	19	2	1773	149	0	5.04							
1990-91	Lowell	H.E.	22	5	13	1	1149	91	0	4.75							
1991-92a	Lowell	H.E.	23	8	11	4	1393	97	0	4.18							

a Hockey East First All-Star Team (1992)

RICHTER, MIKE

Goaltender. Catches left. 5'10", 185 lbs. Born, Abington, PA, September 22, 1966.
(NY Rangers' 2nd choice, 28th overall, in 1985 Entry Draft).

			Regular Season								Playoffs						
Season	Club	Lea	GP	W	L	T	Mins	GA	SO	Avg	GP	W	L	Mins	GA	SO	Avg
1985-86a	U. Wisconsin	WCHA	24	14	9	0	1394	92	1	3.96							
1986-87b	U. Wisconsin	WCHA	36	19	16	1	2136	126	0	3.54							
1987-88	Colorado	IHL	22	16	5	0	1298	68	1	3.14	10	5	3	536	35	0	3.92
	U.S. National	....	29	17	7	2	1559	86	0	3.31							
	U.S. Olympic	....	4	2	2	0	230	15	0	3.91							
1988-89	Denver	IHL	*57	23	26	0	3031	217	1	4.30	4	0	4	210	21	0	6.00
	NY Rangers	**NHL**									**1**	**0**	**1**	**58**	**4**	**0**	**4.14**
1989-90	**NY Rangers**	**NHL**	**23**	**12**	**5**	**5**	**1320**	**66**	**0**	**3.00**	**6**	**3**	**2**	**330**	**19**	**0**	**3.45**
	Flint	IHL	13	7	4	2	782	49	0	3.76							
1990-91	**NY Rangers**	**NHL**	**45**	**21**	**13**	**7**	**2596**	**135**	**0**	**3.12**	**6**	**2**	**4**	**313**	**14**	***1**	**2.68**
1991-92	**NY Rangers**	**NHL**	**41**	**23**	**12**	**2**	**2298**	**119**	**3**	**3.11**	**7**	**4**	**2**	**412**	**24**	**1**	**3.50**
	NHL Totals		**109**	**56**	**30**	**14**	**6214**	**320**	**3**	**3.09**	**20**	**9**	**9**	**1113**	**61**	**2**	**3.29**

a WCHA Rookie of the Year (1986)
b WCHA Second All-Star Team (1987)

Played in NHL All-Star Game (1992)

RIENDEAU, VINCENT (ree-EHN-doh)

Goaltender. Catches left. 5'10", 181 lbs. Born, St. Hyacinthe, Que., April 20, 1966.

			Regular Season								Playoffs						
Season	Club	Lea	GP	W	L	T	Mins	GA	SO	Avg	GP	W	L	Mins	GA	SO	Avg
1985-86a	Drummondville	QMJHL	57	33	20	3	3336	215	2	3.87	23	10	13	1271	106	1	5.00
1986-87b	Sherbrooke	AHL	41	25	14	0	2363	114	2	2.89	13	8	5	742	47	0	3.80
1987-88	**Montreal**	**NHL**	**1**	**0**	**0**	**0**	**36**	**5**	**0**	**8.33**							
cd	Sherbrooke	AHL	44	27	13	3	2521	112	*4	*2.67	2	0	2	127	7	0	3.31
1988-89	**St. Louis**	**NHL**	**32**	**11**	**15**	**5**	**1842**	**108**	**0**	**3.52**							
1989-90	**St. Louis**	**NHL**	**43**	**17**	**19**	**5**	**2551**	**149**	**1**	**3.50**	**8**	**3**	**4**	**397**	**24**	**0**	**3.63**
1990-91	**St. Louis**	**NHL**	**44**	**29**	**9**	**6**	**2671**	**134**	**3**	**3.01**	**13**	**6**	**7**	**687**	**35**	***1**	**3.06**
1991-92	**St. Louis**	**NHL**	**3**	**1**	**2**	**0**	**157**	**11**	**0**	**4.20**							
	Detroit	**NHL**	**2**	**2**	**0**	**0**	**87**	**2**	**0**	**1.38**	**2**	**1**	**0**	**73**	**4**	**0**	**3.29**
	Adirondack	AHL	3	2	1	0	179	8	0	2.68							
	NHL Totals		**125**	**60**	**45**	**16**	**7344**	**409**	**4**	**3.34**	**23**	**10**	**11**	**1157**	**63**	**1**	**3.27**

a QMJHL Second All-Star Team (1986)
b Won Harry "Hap" Holmes Memorial Trophy (AHL Leading Goaltender) (1987)
c Shared Harry "Hap" Holmes Memorial Trophy (AHL Leading Goaltender) with Jocelyn Perreault (1988)
d AHL Second All-Star Team (1988)

Signed as a free agent by **Montreal**, October 9, 1985. Traded to **St. Louis** by **Montreal** with Sergio Momesso for Jocelyn Lemieux, Darrell May and St. Louis' second round choice (Patrice Brisebois) in 1989 Entry Draft, August 9, 1988. Traded to **Detroit** by **St. Louis** for Rick Zombo, October 18, 1991.

ROMAINE, MARK

Goaltender. Catches left. 5'9", 160 lbs. Born, Sharon, MA, October 25, 1968.
(New Jersey's 2nd choice, 10th overall, in 1989 Supplemental Draft).

			Regular Season								Playoffs						
Season	Club	Lea	GP	W	L	T	Mins	GA	SO	Avg	GP	W	L	Mins	GA	SO	Avg
1986-87	Providence	H.E.	5				289	25	0	5.19							
1987-88	Providence	H.E.	19				883	60	0	4.08							
1988-89	Providence	H.E.	29				1536	95	1	3.71							
1989-90	Providence	H.E.	19	12	5	1	1023	52	1	3.05							
1990-91	Utica	AHL	35	13	14	1	1710	125	0	4.39							
1991-92	Cincinnati	ECHL	27	11	8	5	1544	124	0	4.82							
	Columbus	ECHL	7	1	3	2	309	34	0	6.60							
	Raleigh	ECHL	1	0	1	0	60	5	0	5.00							
	Toledo	ECHL	3	1	1	0	140	11	0	4.71							

ROSATI, MICHAEL

Goaltender. Catches left. 5'10", 170 lbs. Born, Toronto, Ont., January 7, 1968.
(NY Rangers' 6th choice, 131st overall, in 1988 Entry Draft).

			Regular Season								Playoffs						
Season	Club	Lea	GP	W	L	T	Mins	GA	SO	Avg	GP	W	L	Mins	GA	SO	Avg
1986-87	Hamilton	OHL	26				1334	85	1	3.82							
1987-88	Hamilton	OHL	62	29	25	3	3468	233	1	4.03	14	8	6	833	66	0	4.75
1988-89	Niagara Falls	OHL	52	*28	15	2	2339	174	1	4.46	16	10	4	861	62	0	4.32
1989-90	Erie	ECHL	18	12	5	0	1056	73	0	4.14							
1990-91	Bolzano	Italy	46				2700	212	0	4.71							
1991-92	Bolzano	Italy	18	11	6	1	1022	58	2	3.22	7	5	2	409	30	0	4.28

ROUSSEL, DOMINIC (roo-SEHL)

Goaltender. Catches left. 6'1", 185 lbs. Born, Hull, Que., February 22, 1970.
(Philadelphia's 4th choice, 63rd overall, in 1988 Entry Draft).

			Regular Season								Playoffs						
Season	Club	Lea	GP	W	L	T	Mins	GA	SO	Avg	GP	W	L	Mins	GA	SO	Avg
1987-88	Trois-Rivières	QMJHL	51	18	25	4	2905	251	0	5.18							
1988-89	Shawinigan	QMJHL	46	24	15	2	2555	171	0	4.02	10	6	4	638	36	0	3.39
1989-90	Shawinigan	QMJHL	37	20	14	1	1985	133	0	4.02	2	1	1	120	12	0	6.00
1990-91	Hershey	AHL	45	20	14	7	2507	151	1	3.61	7	3	4	366	21	0	3.44
1991-92	**Philadelphia**	**NHL**	**17**	**7**	**8**	**2**	**922**	**40**	**1**	**2.60**							
	Hershey	AHL	35	15	11	6	2040	121	1	3.56							
	NHL Totals		**17**	**7**	**8**	**2**	**922**	**40**	**1**	**2.60**							

ROUSSON, BORIS

Goaltender. Catches left. 6'2", 195 lbs. Born, Val D'or, Que., June 14, 1970.

			Regular Season								Playoffs						
Season	Club	Lea	GP	W	L	T	Mins	GA	SO	Avg	GP	W	L	Mins	GA	SO	Avg
1988-89	Laval	QMJHL	22	12	7	0				4.44							
1989-90	Granby	QMJHL	39	10	26	0				4.56							
1990-91	Granby	QMJHL	*63	28	25	6	*3693	190	0	3.09							
1991-92	Binghamton	AHL	38	16	15	6	2261	123	1	3.26							

Signed as a free agent by **NY Rangers**, March 31, 1991.

ROY, ALLAIN

Goaltender. Catches left. 5'10", 170 lbs. Born, Campbellton, N.B., February 6, 1970.
(Winnipeg's 6th choice, 69th overall, in 1989 Entry Draft).

			Regular Season								Playoffs						
Season	Club	Lea	GP	W	L	T	Mins	GA	SO	Avg	GP	W	L	Mins	GA	SO	Avg
1988-89	Harvard	ECAC	16	14	2	0	952	40	0	2.46	....	....	....	....	....	....	....
1989-90	Harvard	ECAC	15	7	8	0	867	54	1	3.74	....	....	....	....	....	....	....
1990-91	Harvard	ECAC	14	7	5	2	821	45	*1	3.29	....	....	....	....	....	....	....
1991-92	Harvard	ECAC	15	9	4	2	919	39	1	*2.55	....	....	....	....	....	....	....

ROY, PATRICK (WAH)

Goaltender. Catches left. 6', 182 lbs. Born, Quebec City, Que., October 5, 1965.
(Montreal's 4th choice, 51st overall, in 1984 Entry Draft).

			Regular Season								Playoffs						
Season	Club	Lea	GP	W	L	T	Mins	GA	SO	Avg	GP	W	L	Mins	GA	SO	Avg
1982-83	Granby	QMJHL	54	....	....	....	2808	293	0	6.26	....	....	....	....	....	....	....
1983-84	Granby	QMJHL	61	29	29	1	3585	265	0	4.44	4	0	4	244	22	0	5.41
1984-85	**Montreal**	**NHL**	**1**	**1**	**0**	**0**	**20**	**0**	**0**	**0.00**	....	....	....	....	....	....	....
	Granby	QMJHL	44	16	25	1	2463	228	0	5.55	....	....	....	....	....	....	....
	Sherbrooke	AHL	1	1	0	0	60	4	0	4.00	13	10	3	*769	37	0	*2.89
1985-86ab	**Montreal**	**NHL**	**47**	**23**	**18**	**3**	**2651**	**148**	**1**	**3.35**	**20**	***15**	**5**	**1218**	**39**	***1**	**1.92**
1986-87c	**Montreal**	**NHL**	**46**	**22**	**16**	**6**	**2686**	**131**	**1**	**2.93**	**6**	**4**	**2**	**330**	**22**	**0**	**4.00**
1987-88cd	**Montraal**	**NHL**	**45**	**23**	**12**	**9**	**2586**	**125**	**3**	**2.90**	**8**	**3**	**4**	**430**	**24**	**0**	**3.35**
1988-89cefg	**Montreal**	**NHL**	**48**	**33**	**5**	**6**	**2744**	**113**	**4**	***2.47**	**19**	**13**	**6**	**1206**	**42**	**2**	***2.09**
1989-90efg	**Montreal**	**NHL**	**54**	***31**	**16**	**5**	**3173**	**134**	**3**	***2.53**	**11**	**5**	**6**	**641**	**26**	**1**	**2.43**
1990-91d	**Montreal**	**NHL**	**48**	**25**	**15**	**6**	**2835**	**128**	**1**	**2.71**	**13**	**7**	**5**	**785**	**40**	**0**	**3.06**
1991-92efh	**Montreal**	**NHL**	**67**	**36**	**22**	**8**	**3935**	**155**	**5**	**2.36**	**11**	**4**	**7**	**686**	**30**	**1**	**2.62**
	NHL Totals		**356**	**194**	**104**	**43**	**20630**	**934**	**18**	**2.72**	**88**	**51**	**35**	**5296**	**223**	**5**	**2.53**

a Won Conn Smythe Trophy (1986)
b NHL All-Rookie Team (1986)
c Shared William Jennings Trophy with Brian Hayward (1987, 1988, 1989)
d NHL Second All-Star Team (1988, 1991)
e Won Vezina Trophy (1989, 1990, 1992)
f NHL First All-Star Team (1989, 1990, 1992)
g Won Trico Goaltending Award (1989, 1990)
h Won William M. Jennings Award (1992)

Played in NHL All-Star Game (1988, 1990-92)

RYDER, DAN

Goaltender. Catches left. 6'1", 184 lbs. Born, Kitchener, Ont., October 24, 1972.
(San Jose's 5th choice, 89th overall, in 1991 Entry Draft).

			Regular Season								Playoffs						
Season	Club	Lea	GP	W	L	T	Mins	GA	SO	Avg	GP	W	L	Mins	GA	SO	Avg
1990-91	Hamilton	OHL	1	0	0	0	40	1	0	1.50	....	....	....	....	....	....	....
	Sudbury	OHL	37	18	9	4	2089	126	....	3.62	2	0	0	26	1	0	2.31
1991-92	Sudbury	OHL	23	9	11	1	1157	91	0	4.72	....	....	....	....	....	....	....
	Ottawa	OHL	24	16	6	0	1380	55	3	*3.29	11	5	6	625	38	0	3.64

ST. LAURENT, SAM (sa-luh-RAH)

Goaltender. Catches left. 5'10", 190 lbs. Born, Arvida, Que., February 16, 1959.

			Regular Season								Playoffs						
Season	Club	Lea	GP	W	L	T	Mins	GA	SO	Avg	GP	W	L	Mins	GA	SO	Avg
1977-78	Chicoutimi	QJHL	60	....	....	....	3251	351	0	6.46	....	....	....	....	....	....	....
1978-79	Chicoutimi	QJHL	70	....	....	....	3806	290	0	4.57	1	....	....	47	8	0	10.21
1979-80	Maine	AHL	5	2	1	0	229	17	0	4.45	....	....	....	....	....	....	....
	Toledo	IHL	38	....	....	....	2143	138	2	3.86	4	....	....	239	24	0	6.03
1980-81	Maine	AHL	7	3	3	0	363	28	0	4.63	....	....	....	....	....	....	....
	Toledo	IHL	30	....	....	....	1614	113	1	4.20	....	....	....	....	....	....	....
1981-82	Toledo	IHL	4	....	....	....	248	11	0	2.66	....	....	....	....	....	....	....
	Maine	AHL	25	15	7	1	1396	76	0	3.27	4	1	3	240	18	0	4.50
1982-83	Maine	AHL	30	....	....	....	1739	109	0	3.76	*17	....	....	*1012	54	0	3.20
1983-84	Maine	AHL	38	14	18	4	2158	145	0	4.03	12	9	2	708	32	*1	*2.71
1984-85a	Maine	AHL	55	26	22	7	3245	168	4	3.11	10	5	5	656	45	0	4.12
1985-86	**New Jersey**	**NHL**	**4**	**2**	**1**	**0**	**188**	**13**	**1**	**4.15**	....	....	....	....	....	....	....
	Maine	AHL	50	24	20	4	2862	161	1	3.38	....	....	....	....	....	....	....
1986-87	**Detroit**	**NHL**	**6**	**1**	**2**	**2**	**342**	**16**	**0**	**2.81**	....	....	....	....	....	....	....
	Adirondack	AHL	25	7	13	0	1397	98	1	4.21	3	0	2	105	10	0	5.71
1987-88	**Detroit**	**NHL**	**6**	**2**	**2**	**0**	**294**	**16**	**0**	**3.27**	**1**	**0**	**0**	**10**	**1**	**0**	**6.00**
	Adirondack	AHL	32	12	14	4	1826	104	2	3.42	1	0	1	59	6	0	6.10
1988-89	**Detroit**	**NHL**	**4**	**0**	**1**	**1**	**141**	**9**	**0**	**3.83**	....	....	....	....	....	....	....
b	Adirondack	AHL	34	20	11	3	2054	113	0	3.30	16	*11	5	956	47	*2	*2.95
1989-90	**Detroit**	**NHL**	**14**	**2**	**6**	**1**	**607**	**38**	**0**	**3.76**	....	....	....	....	....	....	....
	Adirondack	AHL	13	10	2	1	785	40	0	3.06	....	....	....	....	....	....	....
1990-91	Binghamton	AHL	45	19	16	4	2379	138	1	3.48	3	1	2	160	11	0	4.13
1991-92	Cdn. National	....	1	0	1	0	60	3	0	3.00	....	....	....	....	....	....	....
	Binghamton	AHL	1	0	0	0	20	2	0	6.00	....	....	....	....	....	....	....
	NHL Totals		**34**	**7**	**12**	**4**	**1572**	**92**	**1**	**3.51**	**1**	**0**	**0**	**10**	**1**	**0**	**6.00**

a AHL Second All-Star Team (1985)
b Won Jack Butterfield Trophy (Playoff MVP-AHL) (1989)

Signed as a free agent by **Philadelphia**, October 10, 1979. Traded to **New Jersey** by **Philadelphia** for future considerations, August, 1984. Traded to **Detroit** by **New Jersey** for Steve Richmond, August 18, 1986. Traded to **NY Rangers** by **Detroit** for cash, June 26, 1990.

SARJEANT, GEOFF

Goaltender. Catches left. 5'9", 175 lbs. Born, Newmarket, Ont., November 30, 1969.
(St. Louis' 1st choice, 17th overall, in 1990 Supplemental Draft).

			Regular Season								Playoffs						
Season	Club	Lea	GP	W	L	T	Mins	GA	SO	Avg	GP	W	L	Mins	GA	SO	Avg
1988-89	Michigan Tech	WCHA	6	0	3	2	329	22	0	4.01	....	....	....	....	....	....	....
1989-90	Michigan Tech	WCHA	19	4	13	0	1043	94	0	5.41	....	....	....	....	....	....	....
1990-91	Michigan Tech	WCHA	23	5	15	3	1540	97	0	3.78	....	....	....	....	....	....	....
1991-92	Michigan Tech	WCHA	23	7	13	0	1201	90	1	4.50	....	....	....	....	....	....	....

SAURDIFF, CORWIN

Goaltender. Catches left. 5'11", 168 lbs. Born, Warroad, MN, October 17, 1972.
(San Jose's 9th choice, 177th overall, in 1991 Entry Draft).

			Regular Season								Playoffs						
Season	Club	Lea	GP	W	L	T	Mins	GA	SO	Avg	GP	W	L	Mins	GA	SO	Avg
1990-91	Waterloo	USHL	44	15	27	2	2484	170	0	4.10	....	....	....	....	....	....	....
1991-92	N. Michigan	WCHA	34	22	9	1	1926	110	0	3.43	....	....	....	....	....	....	....

SCHOEN, BRYAN

Goaltender. Catches left. 6'2", 180 lbs. Born, St. Paul, MN, September 9, 1971.
(Minnesota's 6th choice, 91st overall, in 1989 Entry Draft).

			Regular Season								Playoffs						
Season	Club	Lea	GP	W	L	T	Mins	GA	SO	Avg	GP	W	L	Mins	GA	SO	Avg
1989-90	U. of Denver	WCHA	18	8	9	0	1040	81	0	4.67	....	....	....	....	....	....	....
1990-91	U. of Denver	WCHA	19	4	13	2	1103	94	0	5.11	....	....	....	....	....	....	....
1991-92	U. of Denver	WCHA	36	9	25	2	2039	167	0	4.91	....	....	....	....	....	....	....

Claimed by **San Jose** from **Minnesota** in Dispersal Draft, May 30, 1991.

SCHWAB, COREY

Goaltender. Catches left. 6', 180 lbs. Born, Battleford, Sask., November 4, 1970.
(New Jersey's 12th choice, 200th overall, in 1990 Entry Draft).

			Regular Season								Playoffs						
Season	Club	Lea	GP	W	L	T	Mins	GA	SO	Avg	GP	W	L	Mins	GA	SO	Avg
1988-89	Seattle	WHL	10	2	2	0	386	31	0	4.82	....	....	....	....	....	....	....
1989-90	Seattle	WHL	27	15	2	1	1150	69	0	3.60	....	....	....	....	....	....	....
1990-91	Seattle	WHL	*58	32	18	3	*3289	224	0	4.09	6	1	5	382	25	0	3.93
1991-92	Utica	AHL	24	9	12	1	1322	95	0	4.31	....	....	....	....	....	....	....
	Cincinnati	ECHL	8	6	0	1	450	31	0	4.13	9	6	3	540	29	0	3.22

SHARPLES, SCOTT

Goaltender. Catches left. 6', 180 lbs. Born, Montreal, Que., March 1, 1968.
(Calgary's 8th choice, 184th overall, in 1986 Entry Draft).

			Regular Season								Playoffs						
Season	Club	Lea	GP	W	L	T	Mins	GA	SO	Avg	GP	W	L	Mins	GA	SO	Avg
1986-87	U. of Michigan	CCHA	32	12	16	1	1720	148	1	5.14	....	....	....	....	....	....	....
1987-88	U. of Michigan	CCHA	33	18	15	0	1930	132	0	4.10	....	....	....	....	....	....	....
1988-89	U. of Michigan	CCHA	33	17	11	2	1887	116	0	3.69	....	....	....	....	....	....	....
1989-90	U. of Michigan	CCHA	*39	20	10	0	*2165	117	0	3.24	....	....	....	....	....	....	....
	Salt Lake	IHL	3	0	3	0	178	13	0	4.38	....	....	....	....	....	....	....
1990-91	Salt Lake	IHL	37	21	11	1	2097	124	2	3.55	4	0	3	188	14	0	4.47
1991-92	**Calgary**	**NHL**	**1**	**0**	**0**	**1**	**65**	**4**	**0**	**3.69**	....	....	....	....	....	....	....
	Salt Lake	IHL	35	9	18	4	1936	121	0	3.75	1	0	1	60	7	0	7.00
	NHL Totals		**1**	**0**	**0**	**1**	**65**	**4**	**0**	**3.69**	....	....	....	....	....	....	....

SHIELDS, STEVE

Goaltender. Catches left. 6'3", 210 lbs. Born, Toronto, Ont., July 19, 1972.
(Buffalo's 5th choice, 101st overall, in 1991 Entry Draft).

			Regular Season								Playoffs						
Season	Club	Lea	GP	W	L	T	Mins	GA	SO	Avg	GP	W	L	Mins	GA	SO	Avg
1990-91	U. of Michigan	CCHA	37	26	6	3	1963	106	0	3.24	....	....	....	....	....	....	....
1991-92	U. of Michigan	CCHA	*37	*27	7	2	*2090	99	1	2.84	....	....	....	....	....	....	....

SHULMISTRA, RICHARD

Goaltender. Catches right. 6'2", 186 lbs. Born, Sudbury, Ont., April 1, 1971.
(Quebec's 1st choice, 4th overall, in 1992 Supplemental Draft).

			Regular Season								Playoffs						
Season	Club	Lea	GP	W	L	T	Mins	GA	SO	Avg	GP	W	L	Mins	GA	SO	Avg
1990-91	Miami-Ohio	CCHA	20	2	12	2	920	80	0	5.21	....	....	....	....	....	....	....
1991-92	Miami-Ohio	CCHA	19	3	5	2	850	67	0	4.72	....	....	....	....	....	....	....

SIDORKIEWICZ, PETER (sih-DOHR-kuh-vihch)

Goaltender. Catches left. 5'9", 180 lbs. Born, Dabrowa Bialostocka, Poland, June 29, 1963.
(Washington's 5th choice, 91st overall, in 1981 Entry Draft).

			Regular Season								Playoffs						
Season	Club	Lea	GP	W	L	T	Mins	GA	SO	Avg	GP	W	L	Mins	GA	SO	Avg
1980-81	Oshawa	OHA	7	3	3	0	308	24	0	4.68	5	2	2	266	20	0	4.52
1981-82	Oshawa	OHL	29	14	11	1	1553	123	*2	4.75	1	0	0	13	1	0	4.62
1982-83	Oshawa	OHL	60	36	20	3	3536	213	0	3.61	17	15	1	1020	60	0	3.53
1983-84a	Oshawa	OHL	52	28	21	1	2966	250	1	4.15	7	3	4	420	27	*1	3.86
1984-85	Binghamton	AHL	45	31	9	5	2691	137	3	3.05	8	4	4	481	31	0	3.87
	Fort Wayne	IHL	10	4	4	2	590	43	0	4.37	....	....	....	....	....	....	....
1985-86	Binghamton	AHL	49	21	22	3	2819	150	2	*3.19	4	1	3	235	12	0	3.06
1986-87b	Binghamton	AHL	57	23	16	0	3304	161	4	2.92	13	6	7	794	36	0	*2.72
1987-88	**Hartford**	**NHL**	**1**	**0**	**1**	**0**	**60**	**6**	**0**	**6.00**	....	....	....	....	....	....	....
	Binghamton	AHL	42	19	17	3	2345	144	0	3.68	3	0	2	147	8	0	3.27
1988-89c	**Hartford**	**NHL**	**44**	**22**	**18**	**4**	**2635**	**133**	**4**	**3.03**	**2**	**0**	**2**	**124**	**8**	**0**	**3.87**
1989-90	**Hartford**	**NHL**	**46**	**19**	**19**	**7**	**2703**	**161**	**1**	**3.57**	**7**	**3**	**4**	**429**	**23**	**0**	**3.22**
1990-91	**Hartford**	**NHL**	**52**	**21**	**22**	**7**	**2953**	**164**	**1**	**3.33**	**6**	**2**	**4**	**359**	**24**	**0**	**4.01**
1991-92	**Hartford**	**NHL**	**35**	**9**	**19**	**6**	**1995**	**111**	**2**	**3.34**	....	....	....	....	....	....	....
	NHL Totals		**178**	**71**	**79**	**24**	**10346**	**575**	**8**	**3.33**	**15**	**5**	**10**	**912**	**55**	**0**	**3.62**

a OHL Third All-Star Team (1984)
b AHL Second All-Star Team (1987)
c NHL All-Rookie Team (1989)

Traded to **Hartford** by **Washington** with Dean Evason for David Jensen, March 12, 1985. Claimed by **Ottawa** from **Hartford** in Expansion Draft, June 18, 1992.

SNOW, GARTH

Goaltender. Catches left. 6'3", 200 lbs. Born, Wrentham, MA, July 28, 1969.
(Quebec's 6th choice, 114th overall, in 1987 Entry Draft).

			Regular Season								Playoffs						
Season	Club	Lea	GP	W	L	T	Mins	GA	SO	Avg	GP	W	L	Mins	GA	SO	Avg
1988-89	U. of Maine	H.E.	5	2	2	0	241	14	1	3.49	....	....	....	....	....	....	....
1989-90	DID NOT PLAY																
1990-91	U. of Maine	H.E.	25	*18	4	0	1290	64	2	2.98	....	....	....	....	....	....	....
1991-92a	U. of Maine	H.E.	31	*25	4	2	1792	73	*2	*2.44	....	....	....	....	....	....	....

a Hockey East Second All-Star Team (1992)

SODERSTROM, TOMMY (SOH-der-strom)

Goaltender. Catches left. 5'9", 165 lbs. Born, Stockholm, Sweden, July 17, 1969.
(Philadelphia's 14th choice, 214th overall, in 1990 Entry Draft).

			Regular Season								Playoffs						
Season	Club	Lea	GP	W	L	T	Mins	GA	SO	Avg	GP	W	L	Mins	GA	SO	Avg
1989-90	Djurgarden	Swe.	4	....	....	....	240	14	0	3.50	....	....	....	....	....	....	....
1990-91	Djurgarden	Swe.	39	....	....	....	2340	104	3	2.67	7	....	....	420	10	....	1.43
1991-92	Djurgarden	Swe.	39	....	....	....	2340	109	4	2.79	10	....	....	635	26	0	2.65

STAUBER, ROBB

Goaltender. Catches left. 5'11", 180 lbs. Born, Duluth, MN, November 25, 1967.
(Los Angeles' 5th choice, 107th overall, in 1986 Entry Draft).

			Regular Season								Playoffs						
Season	Club	Lea	GP	W	L	T	Mins	GA	SO	Avg	GP	W	L	Mins	GA	SO	Avg
1986-87	U. Minnesota	WCHA	20	13	5	0	1072	63	0	3.53	....	....	....	....	....	....	....
1987-88abcd	U. Minnesota	WCHA	44	34	10	0	2621	119	5	2.72	....	....	....	....	....	....	....
1988-89e	U. Minnesota	WCHA	34	26	8	0	2024	82	0	2.43	....	....	....	....	....	....	....
1989-90	**Los Angeles**	**NHL**	**2**	**0**	**1**	**0**	**83**	**11**	**0**	**7.95**	....	....	....	....	....	....	....
	New Haven	AHL	14	6	6	2	851	43	0	3.03	5	2	3	302	24	0	4.77
1990-91	New Haven	AHL	33	13	16	4	1882	115	1	3.67	....	....	....	....	....	....	....
	Phoenix	IHL	4	1	2	0	160	11	0	4.13	....	....	....	....	....	....	....
1991-92	Phoenix	IHL	22	8	12	1	1242	80	0	3.86	....	....	....	....	....	....	....
	NHL Totals		**2**	**0**	**1**	**0**	**83**	**11**	**0**	**7.95**	....	....	....	....	....	....	....

a Won Hobey Baker Memorial Award (Top U.S. Collegiate Player) (1988)
b NCAA West First All-American Team (1988)
c WCHA Player of the Year (1988)
d WCHA First All-Star Team (1988)
e WCHA Second All-Star Team (1989)

STOLP, JEFFREY

Goaltender. Catches left. 6', 180 lbs. Born, Nashwauk, MN, June 20, 1970.
(Minnesota's 4th choice, 64th overall, in 1988 Entry Draft).

			Regular Season								Playoffs						
Season	Club	Lea	GP	W	L	T	Mins	GA	SO	Avg	GP	W	L	Mins	GA	SO	Avg
1988-89	U. Minnesota	WCHA	16	7	2	3	742	45	0	3.64	....	....	....	....	....	....	....
1989-90	U. Minnesota	WCHA	10	5	1	0	417	33	1	4.75	....	....	....	....	....	....	....
1990-91	U. Minnesota	WCHA	32	18	8	3	1766	82	2	2.79	....	....	....	....	....	....	....
1991-92a	U. Minnesota	WCHA	33	25	7	0	1858	88	0	2.84	....	....	....	....	....	....	....

a WCHA Second All-Star Team (1992)

TABARACCI, RICHARD (RICK)

Goaltender. Catches left. 5'11", 179 lbs. Born, Toronto, Ont., January 2, 1969.
(Pittsburgh's 2nd choice, 26th overall, in 1987 Entry Draft).

			Regular Season								Playoffs						
Season	Club	Lea	GP	W	L	T	Mins	GA	SO	Avg	GP	W	L	Mins	GA	SO	Avg
1986-87	Cornwall	OHL	59	23	32	3	3347	290	1	5.20	5	1	4	303	26	0	3.17
1987-88a	Cornwall	OHL	58	*33	18	6	3448	200	*3	3.48	11	5	6	642	37	0	3.46
	Muskegon	IHL	....	....	....	....	....	....	....	....	1	0	0	13	1	0	4.62
1988-89	**Pittsburgh**	**NHL**	**1**	**0**	**0**	**0**	**33**	**4**	**0**	**7.27**	....	....	....	....	....	....	....
b	Cornwall	OHL	50	24	20	5	2974	210	1	4.24	18	10	8	1080	65	*1	3.61
1989-90	Moncton	AHL	27	10	15	2	1580	107	2	4.06	....	....	....	....	....	....	....
	Fort Wayne	IHL	22	8	9	1	1064	73	0	4.12	3	1	2	159	19	0	7.17
1990-91	**Winnipeg**	**NHL**	**24**	**4**	**9**	**4**	**1093**	**71**	**1**	**3.90**	....	....	....	....	....	....	....
	Moncton	AHL	11	4	5	2	645	41	0	3.81	....	....	....	....	....	....	....
1991-92	**Winnipeg**	**NHL**	**18**	**6**	**7**	**3**	**966**	**52**	**0**	**3.23**	**7**	**3**	**4**	**387**	**26**	**0**	**4.03**
	Moncton	AHL	23	10	11	1	1313	80	0	3.66	....	....	....	....	....	....	....
	NHL Totals		**43**	**10**	**16**	**7**	**2092**	**127**	**1**	**3.64**	**7**	**3**	**4**	**387**	**26**	**0**	**4.03**

a OHL First All-Star Team (1988)
b OHL Second All-Star Team (1989)

Traded to **Winnipeg** by **Pittsburgh** with Randy Cunneyworth and Dave McLlwain for Jim Kyte, Andrew McBain and Randy Gilhen, June 17, 1989.

TAKKO, KARI (TAH-koh)

Goaltender. Catches left. 6'2", 185 lbs. Born, Uusikaupunki, Finland, June 23, 1962.
(Minnesota's 5th choice, 97th overall, in 1984 Entry Draft).

			Regular Season								Playoffs						
Season	Club	Lea	GP	W	L	T	Mins	GA	SO	Avg	GP	W	L	Mins	GA	SO	Avg
1978-79	Assat	Fin.	2	....	....	....	....	2	....	....	....	....	....	....	....	....	....
1979-80	Assat	Fin.	2	....	....	....	....	8	....	....	....	....	....	....	....	....	....
1980-81	Assat	Fin.	4	....	....	....	....	16	....	....	....	....	....	....	....	....	....
1981-82	Assat	Fin.	14	....	....	....	....	60	....	....	....	....	....	....	....	....	....
1982-83	Assat	Fin.	21	....	....	....	....	77	0	....	....	....	....	....	....	....	....
1983-84	Assat	Fin.	32	....	....	....	....	102	3	....	9	....	....	....	37	0	....
1984-85	Assat	Fin.	35	....	....	....	....	123	3	....	8	....	....	....	32	0	....
1985-86	**Minnesota**	**NHL**	**1**	**0**	**1**	**0**	**60**	**3**	**0**	**3.00**	....	....	....	....	....	....	....
	Springfield	AHL	43	18	19	3	2286	161	1	4.05	....	....	....	....	....	....	....
1986-87	**Minnesota**	**NHL**	**38**	**13**	**18**	**4**	**2075**	**119**	**0**	**3.44**	....	....	....	....	....	....	....
	Springfield	AHL	5	3	2	0	300	16	1	3.20	....	....	....	....	....	....	....
1987-88	**Minnesota**	**NHL**	**37**	**8**	**19**	**6**	**1919**	**143**	**1**	**4.47**	....	....	....	....	....	....	....
1988-89	**Minnesota**	**NHL**	**32**	**8**	**15**	**4**	**1603**	**93**	**0**	**3.48**	**3**	**0**	**1**	**105**	**7**	**0**	**4.00**
1989-90	Kalamazoo	IHL	1	0	1	0	59	5	0	5.08	....	....	....	....	....	....	....
	Minnesota	**NHL**	**21**	**4**	**12**	**0**	**1012**	**68**	**0**	**4.03**	**1**	**0**	**0**	**4**	**0**	**0**	**0.00**
1990-91	**Minnesota**	**NHL**	**2**	**0**	**2**	**0**	**119**	**12**	**0**	**6.05**	....	....	....	....	....	....	....
	Kalamazoo	IHL	5	4	1	0	300	10	1	2.00	....	....	....	....	....	....	....
	Edmonton	**NHL**	**11**	**4**	**4**	**0**	**529**	**37**	**0**	**4.20**	....	....	....	....	....	....	....
1991-92	Assat	Fin.	28	....	....	....	1628	98	....	3.61	....	....	....	....	....	....	....
	NHL Totals		**142**	**37**	**71**	**14**	**7317**	**475**	**1**	**3.90**	**4**	**0**	**1**	**109**	**7**	**0**	**3.85**

Traded to **Edmonton** by **Minnesota** for Bruce Bell, November 22, 1990.

TANNER, JOHN

Goaltender. Catches left. 6'3", 182 lbs. Born, Cambridge, Ont., March 17, 1971.
(Quebec's 4th choice, 54th overall, in 1989 Entry Draft).

			Regular Season								Playoffs						
Season	Club	Lea	GP	W	L	T	Mins	GA	SO	Avg	GP	W	L	Mins	GA	SO	Avg
1987-88a	Peterborough	OHL	26	18	4	3	1532	88	0	3.45	2	1	0	98	3	0	1.84
1988-89	Peterborough	OHL	34	22	10	0	1923	107	2	*3.34	8	4	3	369	23	0	3.74
1989-90	**Quebec**	**NHL**	**1**	**0**	**1**	**0**	**60**	**3**	**0**	**3.00**	....	....	....	....	....	....	....
	Peterborough	OHL	18	6	8	2	1037	70	0	4.05	....	....	....	....	....	....	....
	London	OHL	19	12	5	1	1097	53	1	2.90	6	2	4	341	24	0	4.22
1990-91	**Quebec**	**NHL**	**6**	**1**	**3**	**1**	**228**	**16**	**0**	**4.21**	....	....	....	....	....	....	....
	London	OHL	7	3	3	1	427	29	0	4.07	....	....	....	....	....	....	....
	Sudbury	OHL	19	10	8	0	1043	60	0	3.45	5	1	4	274	21	0	4.60
1991-92	**Quebec**	**NHL**	**14**	**1**	**7**	**4**	**796**	**46**	**1**	**3.47**	....	....	....	....	....	....	....
	Halifax	AHL	12	6	5	1	672	29	2	2.59	....	....	....	....	....	....	....
	New Haven	AHL	16	7	6	2	908	57	0	3.77	....	....	....	....	....	....	....
	NHL Totals		**21**	**2**	**11**	**5**	**1084**	**65**	**1**	**3.60**	....	....	....	....	....	....	....

a Won Dave Pinkney Trophy (Top Team Goaltending, OHL) shared with Todd Bojcun (1989)

TERRERI, CHRIS

Goaltender. Catches left. 5'8", 155 lbs. Born, Providence, RI, November 15, 1964.
(New Jersey's 3rd choice, 87th overall, in 1983 Entry Draft).

			Regular Season								Playoffs						
Season	Club	Lea	GP	W	L	T	Mins	GA	SO	Avg	GP	W	L	Mins	GA	SO	Avg
1982-83	Providence	ECAC	11	7	1	0	528	17	2	1.93	....	....	....	....	....	....	....
1983-84	Providence	ECAC	10	4	2	0	391	20	0	3.07	....	....	....	....	....	....	....
1984-85abc	Providence	H.E.	33	15	13	5	1956	116	1	3.35	....	....	....	....	....	....	....
1985-86	Providence	H.E.	22	6	16	0	1320	84	0	3.74	....	....	....	....	....	....	....
1986-87	**New Jersey**	**NHL**	**7**	**0**	**3**	**1**	**286**	**21**	**0**	**4.41**	....	....	....	....	....	....	....
	Maine	AHL	14	4	9	1	765	57	0	4.47	....	....	....	....	....	....	....
1987-88	Utica	AHL	7	5	1	0	399	18	0	2.71	....	....	....	....	....	....	....
	U.S. National	....	26	17	7	2	1430	81	0	3.40	....	....	....	....	....	....	....
	U.S. Olympic	....	3	1	1	0	128	14	0	6.56	....	....	....	....	....	....	....
1988-89	**New Jersey**	**NHL**	**8**	**0**	**4**	**2**	**402**	**18**	**0**	**2.69**	....	....	....	....	....	....	....
	Utica	AHL	39	20	15	3	2314	132	0	3.42	2	0	1	80	6	0	4.50
1989-90	**New Jersey**	**NHL**	**35**	**15**	**12**	**3**	**1931**	**110**	**0**	**3.42**	**4**	**2**	**2**	**238**	**13**	**0**	**3.28**
1990-91	**New Jersey**	**NHL**	**53**	**24**	**21**	**7**	**2970**	**144**	**1**	**2.91**	**7**	**3**	**4**	**428**	**21**	**0**	**2.94**
1991-92	**New Jersey**	**NHL**	**54**	**22**	**22**	**10**	**3186**	**169**	**1**	**3.18**	**7**	**3**	**3**	**386**	**23**	**0**	**3.58**
	NHL Totals		**157**	**61**	**62**	**23**	**8775**	**462**	**2**	**3.16**	**18**	**8**	**9**	**1052**	**57**	**0**	**3.25**

a Hockey East All-Star Team (1985)
b Hockey East Player of the Year (1985)
c NCAA All-American Team (1985)

TORCHIA, MIKE (TOR-chee-ah)

Goaltender. Catches left. 5'11", 215 lbs. Born, Toronto, Ont., February 23, 1972.
(Minnesota's 2nd choice, 74th overall, in 1991 Entry Draft).

			Regular Season								Playoffs						
Season	Club	Lea	GP	W	L	T	Mins	GA	SO	Avg	GP	W	L	Mins	GA	SO	Avg
1988-89	Kitchener	OHL	30	14	9	4	1472	102	0	4.02	2	0	2	126	8	0	3.81
1989-90a	Kitchener	OHL	40	25	11	2	2280	136	1	3.58	*17	*11	6	*1023	60	0	3.52
1990-91	Kitchener	OHL	57	25	24	7	*3317	219	0	3.95	6	2	4	382	30	0	4.71
1991-92	Kitchener	OHL	55	25	24	3	3042	203	1	4.00	14	7	7	900	47	0	3.13

a Memorial Cup All-Star Team, Top Goaltender (1990)

TREFILOV, ANDREI (treh-FEE-lohv)

Goaltender. Catches left. 6', 174 lbs. Born, Kirovo-Chepetsk, Soviet Union, August 31, 1969.
(Calgary's 14th choice, 261st overall, in 1991 Entry Draft).

			Regular Season								Playoffs						
Season	Club	Lea	GP	W	L	T	Mins	GA	SO	Avg	GP	W	L	Mins	GA	SO	Avg
1990-91	Moscow D'amo	USSR	20	....	....	....	1070	36	0	2.01	....	....	....	....	....	....	....
1991-92	Moscow D'amo	CIS	28	....	....	....	1326	35	0	1.58	....	....	....	....	....	....	....

TUGNUTT, RON

Goaltender. Catches left. 5'11", 155 lbs. Born, Scarborough, Ont., October 22, 1967.
(Quebec's 4th choice, 81st overall, in 1986 Entry Draft).

			Regular Season								Playoffs						
Season	Club	Lea	GP	W	L	T	Mins	GA	SO	Avg	GP	W	L	Mins	GA	SO	Avg
1984-85	Peterborough	OHL	18	7	4	2	938	59	0	3.77	....	....	....	....	....	....	....
1985-86	Peterborough	OHL	26	18	7	0	1543	74	1	2.88	3	2	0	133	6	0	2.71
1986-87a	Peterborough	OHL	31	21	7	2	1891	88	2	*2.79	6	3	3	374	21	1	3.37
1987-88	**Quebec**	**NHL**	**6**	**2**	**3**	**0**	**284**	**16**	**0**	**3.38**	....	....	....	....	....	....	....
	Fredericton	AHL	34	20	9	4	1964	118	1	3.60	4	1	2	204	11	0	3.24
1988-89	**Quebec**	**NHL**	**26**	**10**	**10**	**3**	**1367**	**82**	**0**	**3.60**	....	....	....	....	....	....	....
	Halifax	AHL	24	14	7	2	1368	79	1	3.46	....	....	....	....	....	....	....
1989-90	**Quebec**	**NHL**	**35**	**5**	**24**	**3**	**1978**	**152**	**0**	**4.61**	....	....	....	....	....	....	....
	Halifax	AHL	6	1	5	0	366	23	0	3.77	....	....	....	....	....	....	....
1990-91	**Quebec**	**NHL**	**56**	**12**	**29**	**10**	**3144**	**212**	**0**	**4.05**	....	....	....	....	....	....	....
	Halifax	AHL	2	0	1	0	100	8	0	4.80	....	....	....	....	....	....	....
1991-92	**Quebec**	**NHL**	**30**	**6**	**17**	**3**	**1583**	**106**	**1**	**4.02**	....	....	....	....	....	....	....
	Edmonton	**NHL**	**3**	**1**	**1**	**0**	**124**	**10**	**0**	**4.84**	**2**	**0**	**0**	**60**	**3**	**0**	**3.00**
	NHL Totals		**156**	**36**	**84**	**19**	**8480**	**578**	**1**	**4.09**	**2**	**0**	**0**	**60**	**3**	**0**	**3.00**

a OHL First All-Star Team (1987)

Traded to **Edmonton** by **Quebec** with Brad Zavisha for Martin Ruchinsky, March 10, 1992.

TUREK, ROMAN (TOOR-ehk)

Goaltender. Catches left. 6'3", 190 lbs. Born, Pisek, Czechoslovakia, May 21, 1970.
(Minnesota's 6th choice, 113th overall, in 1990 Entry Draft).

			Regular Season								Playoffs						
Season	Club	Lea	GP	W	L	T	Mins	GA	SO	Avg	GP	W	L	Mins	GA	SO	Avg
1990-91	Motor	Czech.	21	....	....	....	1244	98	0	4.70	....	....	....	....	....	....	....
1991-92	Motor	Czech.2	....	....	....	....	1629	62	....	2.28	....	....	....	....	....	....	....

VANBIESBROUCK, JOHN (van-BEES-bruhk)

Goaltender. Catches left. 5'8", 172 lbs. Born, Detroit, MI, September 4, 1963.
(NY Rangers' 5th choice, 72nd overall, in 1981 Entry Draft).

			Regular Season								Playoffs						
Season	Club	Lea	GP	W	L	T	Mins	GA	SO	Avg	GP	W	L	Mins	GA	SO	Avg
1980-81a	S.S. Marie	OHA	56	31	16	1	2941	203	0	4.14	11	3	3	457	24	1	3.15
1981-82	**NY Rangers**	**NHL**	**1**	**1**	**0**	**0**	**60**	**1**	**0**	**1.00**	....	....	....	....	....	....	....
	S.S. Marie	OHL	31	12	12	2	1686	102	0	3.62	7	1	4	276	20	0	4.35
1982-83b	S.S. Marie	OHL	62	33	21	1	3471	209	0	3.61	16	7	6	944	56	*1	3.56
1983-84	**NY Rangers**	**NHL**	**3**	**2**	**1**	**0**	**180**	**10**	**0**	**3.33**	**1**	**0**	**0**	**1**	**0**	**0**	**0.00**
cde	Tulsa	CHL	37	20	13	2	2153	124	*3	3.46	4	4	0	240	10	0	*2.50
1984-85	**NY Rangers**	**NHL**	**42**	**12**	**24**	**3**	**2358**	**166**	**1**	**4.22**	**1**	**0**	**0**	**20**	**0**	**0**	**0.00**
1985-86fg	**NY Rangers**	**NHL**	**61**	***31**	**21**	**5**	**3326**	**184**	**3**	**3.32**	**16**	**8**	**8**	**899**	**49**	***1**	**3.27**
1986-87	**NY Rangers**	**NHL**	**50**	**18**	**20**	**5**	**2656**	**161**	**0**	**3.64**	**4**	**1**	**3**	**195**	**11**	**1**	**3.38**
1987-88	**NY Rangers**	**NHL**	**56**	**27**	**22**	**7**	**3319**	**187**	**2**	**3.38**	....	....	....	....	....	....	....
1988-89	**NY Rangers**	**NHL**	**56**	**28**	**21**	**4**	**3207**	**197**	**0**	**3.69**	**2**	**0**	**1**	**107**	**6**	**0**	**3.36**
1989-90	**NY Rangers**	**NHL**	**47**	**19**	**19**	**7**	**2734**	**154**	**1**	**3.38**	**6**	**2**	**3**	**298**	**15**	**0**	**3.02**
1990-91	**NY Rangers**	**NHL**	**40**	**15**	**18**	**6**	**2257**	**126**	**3**	**3.35**	**1**	**0**	**0**	**52**	**1**	**0**	**1.15**
1991-92	**NY Rangers**	**NHL**	**45**	**27**	**13**	**3**	**2526**	**120**	**2**	**2.85**	**7**	**2**	**5**	**368**	**23**	**0**	**3.75**
	NHL Totals		**401**	**180**	**159**	**40**	**22623**	**1306**	**12**	**3.46**	**38**	**13**	**20**	**1940**	**105**	**2**	**3.25**

a OHA Third All-Star Team (1981)
b OHL Second All-Star Team (1983)
c CHL First All-Star Team (1984)
d Shared Terry Sawchuk Trophy (CHL's Leading Goaltender) with Ron Scott (1984)
e Shared Tommy Ivan Trophy (CHL's Most Valuable Player) with Bruce Affleck of Indianapolis (1984)
f Won Vezina Trophy (1986)
g NHL First All-Star Team (1986)

VEISOR, MIKE

Goaltender. Catches right. 6'2", 190 lbs. Born, Dallas, TX, December 7, 1972.
(St. Louis' 12th choice, 263rd overall, in 1991 Entry Draft).

			Regular Season								Playoffs						
Season	Club	Lea	GP	W	L	T	Mins	GA	SO	Avg	GP	W	L	Mins	GA	SO	Avg
1990-91	Springfield	US Jr.	36	....	....	....	....	....	....	3.75	....	....	....	....	....	....	....
1991-92	Springfield	US Jr.	46	....	....	....	2226	153	0	4.12	....	....	....	....	....	....	....

VERNER, ANDREW

Goaltender. Catches left. 6', 194 lbs. Born, Weston, Ont., November 20, 1972.
(Edmonton's 3rd choice, 34th overall, in 1991 Entry Draft).

			Regular Season								Playoffs						
Season	Club	Lea	GP	W	L	T	Mins	GA	SO	Avg	GP	W	L	Mins	GA	SO	Avg
1989-90	Peterborough	OHL	13	7	3	0	624	38	1	3.65	....	....	....	....	....	....	....
1990-91a	Peterborough	OHL	46	22	14	7	2523	148	0	3.52	3	0	3	185	15	0	4.86
1991-92a	Peterborough	OHL	53	*34	13	6	3123	190	1	3.65	10	5	5	539	30	0	3.34

a OHL Second All-Star Team (1991, 1992)

VERNON, MICHAEL (MIKE)

Goaltender. Catches left. 5'9", 155 lbs. Born, Calgary, Alta., February 24, 1963.
(Calgary's 2nd choice, 56th overall, in 1981 Entry Draft).

			Regular Season								Playoffs						
Season	Club	Lea	GP	W	L	T	Mins	GA	SO	Avg	GP	W	L	Mins	GA	SO	Avg
1980-81	Calgary	WHL	59	33	17	1	3154	198	1	3.77	22	....	....	1271	82	1	3.87
1981-82ab	Calgary	WHL	42	22	14	2	2329	143	3	3.68	9	....	....	527	30	0	3.42
	Oklahoma City	CHL	....	....	....	....	....	....	....	....	1	0	1	70	4	0	3.43
1982-83	Calgary	NHL	2	0	2	0	100	11	0	6.59	....	....	....	....	....	....	....
ab	Calgary	WHL	50	19	18	2	2856	155	3	3.26	16	9	7	925	60	0	3.89
1983-84	Calgary	NHL	1	0	1	0	11	4	0	22.22	....	....	....	....	....	....	....
c	Colorado	CHL	46	30	13	2	2648	148	1	*3.35	6	2	4	347	21	0	3.63
1984-85	Moncton	AHL	41	10	20	4	2050	134	0	3.92	....	....	....	....	....	....	....
1985-86	Calgary	NHL	18	9	3	3	921	52	1	3.39	*21	12	*9	1229	60	0	2.93
	Moncton	AHL	6	3	1	2	374	21	0	3.37	....	....	....	....	....	....	....
	Salt Lake	IHL	10	....	....	....	600	34	1	3.40	....	....	....	....	....	....	....
1986-87	Calgary	NHL	54	30	21	1	2957	178	1	3.61	5	2	3	263	16	0	3.65
1987-88	Calgary	NHL	64	39	16	7	3565	210	1	3.53	9	4	4	515	34	0	3.96
1988-89d	Calgary	NHL	52	*37	6	5	2938	130	0	2.65	*22	*16	5	*1381	52	*3	2.26
1989-90	Calgary	NHL	47	23	14	9	2795	146	0	3.13	6	2	3	342	19	0	3.33
1990-91	Calgary	NHL	54	31	19	3	3121	172	1	3.31	7	3	4	427	21	0	2.95
1991-92	Calgary	NHL	63	24	30	9	3640	217	0	3.58	....	....	....	....	....	....	....
	NHL Totals		355	193	112	33	20048	1120	4	3.35	70	39	28	4157	202	0	2.92

a WHL First All-Star Team (1982, 1983)
b WHL Most Valuable Player (1982, 1983)
c CHL Second All-Star Team (1984)
d NHL Second All-Star Team (1989)

Played in NHL All-Star Game (1988-91)

WAITE, JIMMY

Goaltender. Catches left. 6'1", 182 lbs. Born, Sherbrooke, Que., April 15, 1969.
(Chicago's 1st choice, 8th overall, in 1987 Entry Draft).

			Regular Season								Playoffs						
Season	Club	Lea	GP	W	L	T	Mins	GA	SO	Avg	GP	W	L	Mins	GA	SO	Avg
1986-87a	Chicoutimi	QMJHL	50	23	17	3	2569	209	2	4.48	11	4	6	576	54	1	5.63
1987-88	Chicoutimi	QMJHL	36	17	16	1	2000	150	0	4.50	4	1	2	222	17	0	4.59
1988-89	Chicago	NHL	11	0	7	1	494	43	0	5.22	....	....	....	....	....	....	....
	Saginaw	IHL	5	3	1	0	304	10	0	1.97	....	....	....	....	....	....	....
1989-90	Chicago	NHL	4	2	0	0	183	14	0	4.59	....	....	....	....	....	....	....
bc	Indianapolis	IHL	54	*34	14	5	*3207	135	*5	*2.53	*10	*9	1	*602	19	*1	*1.89
1990-91	Chicago	NHL	1	1	0	0	60	2	0	2.00	....	....	....	....	....	....	....
	Indianapolis	IHL	49	*26	18	4	2888	167	3	3.47	6	2	4	369	20	0	3.25
1991-92	Chicago	NHL	17	4	7	4	877	54	0	3.69	....	....	....	....	....	....	....
	Indianapolis	IHL	13	4	7	1	702	53	0	4.53	....	....	....	....	....	....	....
	Hershey	AHL	11	6	4	1	631	44	0	4.18	6	2	4	360	19	0	3.17
	NHL Totals		33	7	14	5	1614	113	0	4.20	....	....	....	....	....	....	....

a QMJHL Second All-Star Team (1987)
b IHL First All-Star Team (1990)
c Won James Norris Memorial Trophy (Top Goaltender-IHL) (1990)

WAKALUK, DARCY (WAHK-uh-luhk)

Goaltender. Catches left. 5'11", 180 lbs. Born, Pincher Creek, Alta., March 14, 1966.
(Buffalo's 7th choice, 144th overall, in 1984 Entry Draft).

			Regular Season								Playoffs						
Season	Club	Lea	GP	W	L	T	Mins	GA	SO	Avg	GP	W	L	Mins	GA	SO	Avg
1983-84	Kelowna	WHL	31	....	....	....	1555	163	0	6.29	....	....	....	....	....	....	....
1984-85	Kelowna	WHL	54	19	30	4	3094	244	0	4.73	5	1	4	282	22	0	4.68
1985-86	Spokane	WHL	47	21	22	1	2562	224	1	5.25	7	3	4	419	37	0	5.30
1986-87	Rochester	AHL	11	2	2	0	545	26	0	2.86	5	2	0	141	11	0	4.68
1987-88	Rochester	AHL	55	27	16	3	2763	159	0	3.45	6	3	3	328	22	0	4.02
1988-89	Buffalo	NHL	6	1	3	0	214	15	0	4.21	....	....	....	....	....	....	....
	Rochester	AHL	33	11	14	0	1566	97	1	3.72	....	....	....	....	....	....	....
1989-90	Rochester	AHL	56	31	16	4	3095	173	2	3.35	*17	*10	6	*1001	50	0	*3.01
1990-91	Buffalo	NHL	16	4	5	3	630	35	0	3.33	2	0	1	37	2	0	3.24
	Rochester	AHL	26	10	10	3	1363	68	4	*2.99	9	6	3	544	30	0	3.31
1991-92	Minnesota	NHL	36	13	19	1	1905	104	1	3.28	....	....	....	....	....	....	....
	Kalamazoo	IHL	1	1	0	0	60	7	0	7.00	....	....	....	....	....	....	....
	NHL Totals		58	18	27	4	2749	154	1	3.36	2	0	1	37	2	0	3.24

Traded to **Minnesota** by **Buffalo** for Minnesota's eighth round choice (Jiri Kuntos) in 1991 Entry Draft, May 26, 1991.

WAMSLEY, RICHARD (RICK) (WAHMS-lee)

Goaltender. Catches left. 5'11", 185 lbs. Born, Simcoe, Ont., May 25, 1959.
(Montreal's 5th choice, 58th overall, in 1979 Entry Draft).

			Regular Season								Playoffs						
Season	Club	Lea	GP	W	L	T	Mins	GA	SO	Avg	GP	W	L	Mins	GA	SO	Avg
1977-78	Hamilton	OHA	25	....	....	....	1495	74	2	2.97	....	....	....	....	....	....	....
1978-79	Brantford	OHA	24	....	....	....	1444	128	0	5.32	....	....	....	....	....	....	....
1979-80	Nova Scotia	AHL	40	19	16	2	2305	125	2	3.25	3	1	1	143	12	0	5.03
1980-81	Montreal	NHL	5	3	0	1	253	8	1	1.90	....	....	....	....	....	....	....
	Nova Scotia	AHL	43	17	19	3	2372	155	0	3.92	4	2	1	199	6	*1	1.81
1981-82a	Montreal	NHL	38	23	7	7	2206	101	2	2.75	5	2	3	300	11	0	*2.20
1982-83	Montreal	NHL	46	27	12	5	2583	151	0	3.51	3	0	3	152	7	0	2.77
1983-84	Montreal	NHL	42	19	17	3	2333	144	2	3.70	1	0	0	32	0	0	0.00
1984-85	St. Louis	NHL	40	23	12	5	2319	126	0	3.26	2	0	2	120	7	0	3.50
1985-86	St. Louis	NHL	42	22	16	3	2517	144	1	3.43	10	4	6	569	37	0	3.90
1986-87	St. Louis	NHL	41	17	15	6	2410	142	0	3.54	2	1	1	120	5	0	2.50
1987-88	St. Louis	NHL	31	13	16	1	1818	103	2	3.40	....	....	....	....	....	....	....
	Calgary	NHL	2	1	0	0	73	5	0	4.11	1	0	1	33	2	0	3.64
1988-89	Calgary	NHL	35	17	11	4	1927	95	2	2.96	1	0	1	20	2	0	6.00
1989-90	Calgary	NHL	36	18	8	6	1969	107	2	3.26	1	0	1	49	9	0	11.02
1990-91	Calgary	NHL	29	14	7	5	1670	85	0	3.05	1	0	0	2	1	0	30.00
1991-92	Calgary	NHL	9	3	4	0	457	34	0	4.46	....	....	....	....	....	....	....
	Toronto	NHL	8	4	3	0	428	27	0	3.79	....	....	....	....	....	....	....
	NHL Totals		404	204	128	46	22963	1272	12	3.32	27	7	18	1397	81	0	3.48

a Shared Williams Jennings Trophy with Denis Herron (1982)

Traded to **St. Louis** by **Montreal** with Hartford's second round choice (Brian Benning) — Montreal property via earlier deal — Montreal's second round choice (Tony Hrkac) and third round choice (Robert Dirk), all in the 1984 Entry Draft, for St. Louis' first (Shayne Corson) and second round (Stephane Richer) choices in the 1984 Entry Draft, June 9, 1984. Traded to **Calgary** by **St. Louis** with Rob Ramage for Brett Hull and Steve Bozek, March 7, 1988. Traded to **Toronto** by **Calgary** with Doug Gilmour, Jamie Macoun, Kent Manderville and Ric Natress for Gary Leeman, Alexander Godynyuk, Jeff Reese, Michel Petit and Craig Berube, January 2, 1992.

WEEKS, STEPHEN (STEVE)

Goaltender. Catches left. 5'11", 170 lbs. Born, Scarborough, Ont., June 30, 1958.
(NY Rangers' 12th choice, 176th overall, in 1978 Amateur Draft).

			Regular Season								Playoffs						
Season	Club	Lea	GP	W	L	T	Mins	GA	SO	Avg	GP	W	L	Mins	GA	SO	Avg
1977-78	N. Michigan	CCHA	19	....	....	....	1015	56	1	3.31	....	....	....	....	....	....	....
1978-79	N. Michigan	CCHA	25	....	....	....	1437	82	0	3.42	....	....	....	....	....	....	....
1979-80	N. Michigan	CCHA	36	29	6	1	2133	105	0	2.95	....	....	....	....	....	....	....
1980-81	NY Rangers	NHL	1	0	1	0	60	2	0	2.00	1	0	0	14	1	0	4.29
	New Haven	AHL	36	14	17	3	2065	142	1	4.04	....	....	....	....	....	....	....
1981-82	NY Rangers	NHL	49	23	16	9	2852	179	1	3.77	4	1	2	127	9	0	4.25
1982-83	NY Rangers	NHL	18	9	5	3	1040	68	0	3.92	....	....	....	....	....	....	....
	Tulsa	CHL	19	8	10	0	1116	60	0	3.23	....	....	....	....	....	....	....
1983-84	NY Rangers	NHL	26	10	11	2	1361	90	0	3.97	....	....	....	....	....	....	....
	Tulsa	CHL	3	3	0	0	180	7	0	2.33	....	....	....	....	....	....	....
1984-85	Hartford	NHL	24	10	12	2	1457	93	2	3.82	....	....	....	....	....	....	....
	Binghamton	AHL	5	5	0	0	303	13	0	2.57	....	....	....	....	....	....	....
1985-86	Hartford	NHL	27	13	13	0	1544	99	1	3.85	3	1	2	169	8	0	2.84
1986-87	Hartford	NHL	25	12	8	2	1367	78	1	3.42	1	0	0	36	1	0	1.67
1987-88	Hartford	NHL	18	6	7	2	918	55	0	3.59	....	....	....	....	....	....	....
	Vancouver	NHL	9	4	3	2	550	31	0	3.38	....	....	....	....	....	....	....
1988-89	Vancouver	NHL	35	11	19	5	2056	102	0	2.98	3	1	1	140	8	0	3.43
1989-90	Vancouver	NHL	21	4	11	4	1142	79	0	4.15	....	....	....	....	....	....	....
1990-91	Vancouver	NHL	1	0	1	0	59	6	0	6.10	....	....	....	....	....	....	....
	Milwaukee	IHL	37	16	19	0	2014	127	0	3.78	3	1	2	210	13	0	3.71
1991-92	NY Islanders	NHL	23	9	4	2	1032	62	0	3.60	....	....	....	....	....	....	....
	Los Angeles	NHL	7	1	3	0	252	17	0	4.05	....	....	....	....	....	....	....
	NHL Totals		284	112	114	35	15690	961	5	3.67	12	3	5	486	27	0	3.33

Traded to **Vancouver** by **Hartford** for Richard Brodeur, March 8, 1988. Traded to **Buffalo** by **Vancouver** for future considerations, March 5, 1991. Signed as a free agent by **NY Islanders**, September 16, 1991. Traded to **Los Angeles** by **NY Islanders** for Los Angeles' seventh round choice (Steve O'Rourke) in 1992 Entry Draft, February 18, 1992. Signed as a free agent by **Washington**, June 16, 1992. Traded to **Ottawa** by **Washington** for future considerations, August 13, 1992.

WHITMORE, KAY

Goaltender. Catches left. 5'11", 175 lbs. Born, Sudbury, Ont., April 10, 1967.
(Hartford's 2nd choice, 26th overall, in 1985 Entry Draft).

			Regular Season								Playoffs						
Season	Club	Lea	GP	W	L	T	Mins	GA	SO	Avg	GP	W	L	Mins	GA	SO	Avg
1983-84	Peterborough	OHL	29	17	8	0	1471	110	0	4.49	....	....	....	....	....	....	....
1984-85a	Peterborough	OHL	53	*35	16	2	3077	172	*2	3.35	17	10	4	1020	58	0	3.41
1985-86b	Peterborough	OHL	41	27	12	2	2467	114	*3	*2.77	14	8	5	837	40	0	2.87
1986-87	Peterborough	OHL	36	14	17	5	2159	118	1	3.28	7	3	3	366	17	1	2.79
1987-88	Binghamton	AHL	38	17	15	4	2137	121	*3	3.40	2	0	2	118	10	0	5.08
1988-89	Hartford	NHL	3	2	1	0	180	10	0	3.33	2	0	2	135	10	0	4.44
	Binghamton	AHL	*56	21	29	4	*3200	241	1	4.52	....	....	....	....	....	....	....
1989-90	Hartford	NHL	9	4	2	1	442	26	0	3.53	....	....	....	....	....	....	....
	Binghamton	AHL	24	3	19	2	1386	109	0	4.72	....	....	....	....	....	....	....
1990-91	Hartford	NHL	18	3	9	3	850	52	0	3.67	....	....	....	....	....	....	....
c	Springfield	AHL	33	22	9	1	1916	98	1	3.07	*15	*11	4	*926	37	0	*2.40
1991-92	Hartford	NHL	45	14	21	6	2567	155	3	3.62	1	0	0	19	1	0	3.16
	NHL Totals		75	23	34	11	4039	243	3	3.61	3	0	2	154	11	0	4.29

a OHL Third All-Star Team (1985)
b OHL First All-Star Team (1986)
c Won Jack A. Butterfield Trophy (MVP in Playoffs - AHL) (1991)

WILLIAMS, MIKE

Goaltender. Catches left. 6', 185 lbs. Born, Woodhaven, MI, April 16, 1967.
(Quebec's 12th choice, 219th overall, in 1987 Entry Draft).

			Regular Season								Playoffs						
Season	Club	Lea	GP	W	L	T	Mins	GA	SO	Avg	GP	W	L	Mins	GA	SO	Avg
1986-87	Ferris State	CCHA	17	4	9	0	846	65	0	4.61	....	....	....	....	....	....	....
1987-88	Ferris State	CCHA	30	11	11	5	1671	122	0	4.38	....	....	....	....	....	....	....
1988-89	Ferris State	CCHA	25	6	13	5	1394	84	0	3.62	....	....	....	....	....	....	....
1989-90	Ferris State	CCHA	31	9	16	3	1697	138	0	4.88	....	....	....	....	....	....	....
1990-91	Nashville	ECHL	3	1	1	0	121	12	0	5.95	....	....	....	....	....	....	....
	Cincinnati	ECHL	12	6	6	0	671	58	0	5.18	....	....	....	....	....	....	....
1991-92	Toledo	ECHL	44	*32	8	2	2490	158	0	3.81	1	0	1	59	6	0	6.10

WREGGET, KEN

Goaltender. Catches left. 6'1", 195 lbs. Born, Brandon, Man., March 25, 1964.
(Toronto's 4th choice, 45th overall, in 1982 Entry Draft).

			Regular Season								Playoffs						
Season	**Club**	**Lea**	**GP**	**W**	**L**	**T**	**Mins**	**GA**	**SO**	**Avg**	**GP**	**W**	**L**	**Mins**	**GA**	**SO**	**Avg**
1981-82	Lethbridge	WHL	36	19	12	0	1713	118	0	4.13	3	....	....	84	3	0	2.14
1982-83	Lethbridge	WHL	48	26	17	1	2696	157	0	3.49	20	14	5	1154	58	1	3.02
1983-84	**Toronto**	**NHL**	**3**	**1**	**1**	**1**	**165**	**14**	**0**	**5.09**	....	....	....	....	....	....	....
a	Lethbridge	WHL	53	32	20	0	3053	161	0	*3.16	4	1	3	210	18	0	5.14
1984-85	**Toronto**	**NHL**	**23**	**2**	**15**	**3**	**1278**	**103**	**0**	**4.84**	....	....	....	....	....	....	....
	St. Catharines	AHL	12	2	8	1	688	48	0	4.19	....	....	....	....	....	....	....
1985-86	**Toronto**	**NHL**	**30**	**9**	**13**	**4**	**1566**	**113**	**0**	**4.33**	**10**	**6**	**4**	**607**	**32**	***1**	**3.16**
	St. Catharines	AHL	18	8	9	0	1058	78	1	4.42	....	....	....	....	....	....	....
1986-87	**Toronto**	**NHL**	**56**	**22**	**28**	**3**	**3026**	**200**	**0**	**3.97**	**13**	**7**	**6**	**761**	**29**	**1**	**2.29**
1987-88	**Toronto**	**NHL**	**56**	**12**	**35**	**4**	**3000**	**222**	**2**	**4.44**	**2**	**0**	**1**	**108**	**11**	**0**	**6.11**
1988-89	**Toronto**	**NHL**	**32**	**9**	**20**	**2**	**1888**	**139**	**0**	**4.42**	....	....	....	....	....	....	....
	Philadelphia	**NHL**	**3**	**1**	**1**	**0**	**130**	**13**	**0**	**6.00**	**5**	**2**	**2**	**268**	**10**	**1**	**2.24**
1989-90	**Philadelphia**	**NHL**	**51**	**22**	**24**	**3**	**2961**	**169**	**0**	**3.42**	....	....	....	....	....	....	....
1990-91	**Philadelphia**	**NHL**	**30**	**10**	**14**	**3**	**1484**	**88**	**0**	**3.56**	....	....	....	....	....	....	....
1991-92	**Philadelphia**	**NHL**	**23**	**9**	**8**	**3**	**1259**	**75**	**0**	**3.57**	....	....	....	....	....	....	....
	Pittsburgh	**NHL**	**9**	**5**	**3**	**0**	**448**	**31**	**0**	**4.15**	**1**	**0**	**0**	**40**	**4**	**0**	**6.00**
	NHL Totals		**316**	**102**	**162**	**26**	**17205**	**1167**	**2**	**4.07**	**31**	**15**	**13**	**1784**	**86**	**3**	**2.89**

a WHL First All-Star Team, East Division (1984)

Traded to **Philadelphia** by **Toronto** for Philadelphia's first round choice (Rob Pearson) and Calgary's first round choice (Steve Bancroft) — acquired by Philadelphia in the Brad McCrimmon trade — in 1989 Entry Draft, March 6, 1989. Traded to **Pittsburgh** by **Philadelphia** with Rick Toccket and Kjell Samuelsson for Mark Recchi, Brian Benning and Los Angeles' first round choice (Jason Bowen) in 1992 Entry Draft previously acquired by Pittsburgh in the Paul Coffey trade, February 19, 1992.

YOUNG, WENDELL

Goaltender. Catches left. 5'9", 181 lbs. Born, Halifax, N.S., August 1, 1963.
(Vancouver's 3rd choice, 73rd overall, in 1981 Entry Draft).

			Regular Season								Playoffs						
Season	**Club**	**Lea**	**GP**	**W**	**L**	**T**	**Mins**	**GA**	**SO**	**Avg**	**GP**	**W**	**L**	**Mins**	**GA**	**SO**	**Avg**
1980-81	Kitchener	OHA	42	19	15	0	2215	164	1	4.44	14	9	1	800	42	*1	3.15
1981-82	Kitchener	OHL	60	38	17	2	3470	195	1	3.37	15	12	1	900	35	*1	*2.33
1982-83a	Kitchener	OHL	61	41	19	0	3611	231	1	3.84	12	6	5	720	43	0	3.58
1983-84	Fredericton	AHL	11	7	3	0	569	39	1	4.11	....	....	....	....	....	....	....
	Milwaukee	IHL	6	....	....	....	339	17	0	3.01	....	....	....	....	....	....	....
	Salt Lake	CHL	20	11	6	0	1094	80	0	4.39	4	0	2	122	11	0	5.42
1984-85	Fredericton	AHL	22	7	11	3	1242	83	0	4.01	....	....	....	....	....	....	....
1985-86	**Vancouver**	**NHL**	**22**	**4**	**9**	**3**	**1023**	**61**	**0**	**3.58**	**1**	**0**	**1**	**60**	**5**	**0**	**5.00**
	Fredericton	AHL	24	12	8	4	1457	78	0	3.21	....	....	....	....	....	....	....
1986-87	**Vancouver**	**NHL**	**8**	**1**	**6**	**1**	**420**	**35**	**0**	**5.00**	....	....	....	....	....	....	....
	Fredericton	AHL	30	11	16	0	1676	118	0	4.22	....	....	....	....	....	....	....
1987-88	**Philadelphia**	**NHL**	**6**	**3**	**2**	**0**	**320**	**20**	**0**	**3.75**	....	....	....	....	....	....	....
bcd	Hershey	AHL	51	*33	15	1	2922	135	1	2.77	12	*12	0	*767	28	*1	*2.19
1988-89	**Pittsburgh**	**NHL**	**22**	**12**	**9**	**0**	**1150**	**92**	**0**	**4.80**	**1**	**0**	**0**	**39**	**1**	**0**	**1.54**
	Muskegon	IHL	2	....	....	....	125	7	0	3.36	....	....	....	....	....	....	....
1989-90	**Pittsburgh**	**NHL**	**43**	**16**	**20**	**3**	**2318**	**161**	**1**	**4.17**	....	....	....	....	....	....	....
1990-91	**Pittsburgh**	**NHL**	**18**	**4**	**6**	**2**	**773**	**52**	**0**	**4.04**	....	....	....	....	....	....	....
1991-92	**Pittsburgh**	**NHL**	**18**	**7**	**6**	**0**	**838**	**53**	**0**	**3.79**	....	....	....	....	....	....	....
	NHL Totals		**137**	**47**	**58**	**9**	**6842**	**474**	**1**	**4.16**	**2**	**0**	**1**	**99**	**6**	**0**	**3.64**

a OHL Third All-Star Team (1983)
b AHL First All-Star Team (1988)
c Won Baz Bastien Award (AHL Most Valuable Goaltender) (1988)
d Won Jack Butterfield Trophy (AHL Playoff MVP) (1988)

Traded to **Philadelphia** by **Vancouver** with Vancouver's third round choice (Kimbi Daniels) in 1990 Entry Draft for Daryl Stanley, August 28, 1987. Traded to **Pittsburgh** by **Philadelphia** with Philadelphia's seventh round choice (Mika Valila) in 1990 Entry Draft for Pittsburgh's third round choice (Chris Therien) in 1990 Entry Draft, Steptember 1, 1988. Claimed by **Tampa Bay** from **Pittsburgh** in Expansion Draft, June 18, 1992.

Notes

Action from the 1953 Stanley Cup semi-finals. Terry Sawchuk, who is the NHL's all-time leader in wins and shutouts, searches for a puck pinned beneath defenseman Marcel Pronovost. Boston captain Milt Schmidt looks for a rebound. Note the wire mesh above the boards. Protective glass first appeared in Maple Leaf Gardens in 1947-48, but some NHL buildings stayed with the old-style mesh until the early 1960s.

Michel Belhumeur

Tony Esposito

Gilles Meloche

Turk Broda

Frank Caprice

Jacques Plante

Gerry Cheevers

Glenn Hall

Chuck Rayner

Gerry Desjardins

Charlie Hodge

Gilles Villemure

Retired NHL Goaltender Index

Abbreviations: Teams/Cities:—**Atl.**-Atlanta; **Bos.**-Boston; **Bro.**-Brooklyn; **Buf.**-Buffalo; **Cal.**-California; **Cgy.**-Calgary; **Chi.**-Chicago; **Cle.**-Cleveland; **Col.**-Colorado; **Det.**-Detroit; **Edm.**-Edmonton; **Ham.**-Hamilton; **Hfd.**-Hartford; **K.C.**-Kansas City; **L.A.**-Los Angeles; **Min.**-Minnesota; **Mtl.**-Montreal; **Mtl. M.**-Montreal Maroons; **Mtl. W.**-Montreal Wanderers; **N.J.**-New Jersey; **NY**-New York; **NYA**-NY Americans; **NYI**-New York Islanders; **NYR**-New York Rangers; **Oak.**-Oakland; **Ott.**-Ottawa; **Phi.**-Philadelphia; **Pit.**-Pittsburgh; **Que.**-Quebec; **St. L.**-St. Louis; **Tor.**-Toronto; **Van.**-Vancouver; **Wpg.**-Winnipeg; **Wsh.**-Washington.

Avg – goals against per 60 minutes played; **GA** – goals against; **GP** – games played; **Mins** – minutes played; **SO** – shutouts.

			Regular Schedule								Playoffs										
Name	NHL Teams	NHL Seasons	GP	W	L	T	Mins	GA	SO	Avg	GP	W	L	T	Mins	GA	SO	Avg	NHL Cup Wins	First NHL Season	Last NHL Season
Abbott, George	Bos.	1	1	0	1	0	60	7	0	7.00	....	....	....	....	....	....	....	....		1943-44	1943-44
Adams, John	Bos., Wsh.	2	22	9	10	1	1180	85	1	4.32	....	....	....	....	....	....	....	....		1972-73	1974-75
Aiken, Don	Mtl.	1	1	0	1	0	34	6	0	10.59	....	....	....	....	....	....	....	....		1957-58	1957-58
Aitkenhead, Andy	NYR	3	106	47	43	16	6570	257	11	2.35	10	6	3	1	608	15	3	1.48	1	1932-33	1934-35
Almas, Red	Det., Chi.	3	3	0	2	1	180	13	0	4.33	5	1	3	....	263	13	0	2.97		1946-47	1952-53
Anderson, Lorne	NYR	1	3	1	2	0	180	18	0	6.00	....	....	....	....	....	....	....	....		1951-52	1951-52
Astrom, Hardy	NYR, Col.	3	83	17	44	12	4456	278	0	3.74	....	....	....	....	....	....	....	....		1977-78	1980-81
Baker, Steve	NYR	4	57	20	20	11	3081	190	3	3.70	14	7	7	....	826	55	0	4.00		1979-80	1982-83
Bannerman, Murray	Van., Chi.	8	289	116	125	33	16470	1051	8	3.83	40	20	18	....	2322	165	0	4.26		1977-78	1986-87
Baron, Marco	Bos., L.A., Edm.	6	86	34	39	9	4822	292	1	3.63	1	0	1	....	20	3	0	9.00		1979-80	1984-85
Bassen, Hank	Chi., Det., Pit.	9	157	47	66	31	8829	441	5	2.99	5	1	4	....	274	11	0	2.41		1954-55	1967-68
* Bastien, Baz	Tor.	1	5	0	4	1	300	20	0	4.00	....	....	....	....	....	....	....	....		1945-46	1945-46
Bauman, Gary	Mtl., Min.	3	35	6	18	6	1718	102	0	3.56	....	....	....	....	....	....	....	....		1966-67	1968-69
Bedard, Jim	Wsh.	2	73	17	40	13	4232	278	1	3.94	....	....	....	....	....	....	....	....		1977-78	1978-79
Behrend, Marc	Wpg.	3	38	12	19	3	1991	164	1	4.94	7	1	3	....	312	19	0	3.65		1983-84	1985-86
Belanger, Yves	St.L., Atl., Bos.	6	78	27	36	6	4134	259	2	3.76	....	....	....	....	....	....	....	....		1974-75	1979-80
Belhumeur, Michel	Phi., Wsh.	3	65	9	36	7	3306	254	0	4.61	1	0	0	....	10	1	0	6.00		1972-73	1975-76
Bell, Gordie	Tor., NYR	2	8	3	5	0	480	31	0	3.88	2	1	1	....	120	9	0	4.50		1945-46	1955-56
* Benedict, Clint	Ott., Mtl.M.	13	362	190	43	28	22321	863	57	2.32	48	25	18	4	2907	87	15	1.80	4	1917-18	1929-30
Bennett, Harvey	Bos.	1	24	10	12	2	1470	103	0	4.20	....	....	....	....	....	....	....	....		1944-45	1944-45
Bernhardt, Tim	Cgy., Tor.	4	67	17	36	2	3748	267	0	4.27	....	....	....	....	....	....	....	....		1982-83	1986-87
Beveridge, Bill	Det., Ott., St.L., Mtl.M., NYR	9	297	87	166	42	18375	879	18	2.87	5	2	3	....	300	11	0	2.20		1929-30	1942-43
* Bibeault, Paul	Mtl., Tor., Bos., Chi.	7	214	68	82	21	12890	785	10	3.65	20	6	14	....	1237	71	2	3.44		1940-41	1946-47
Binette, Andre	Mtl.	1	1	1	0	0	60	4	0	4.00	....	....	....	....	....	....	....	....		1954-55	1954-55
Binkley, Les	Pit.	5	196	58	94	34	11046	575	11	3.12	7	5	2	....	428	15	0	2.10		1967-68	1971-72
Bittner, Richard	Bos.	1	1	0	0	1	60	3	0	3.00	....	....	....	....	....	....	....	....		1949-50	1949-50
Blake, Mike	L.A.	3	40	13	5	15	2117	150	0	4.25	....	....	....	....	....	....	....	....		1981-82	1983-84
Boisvert, Gilles	Det.	1	3	0	3	0	180	9	0	3.00	....	....	....	....	....	....	....	....		1959-60	1959-60
Bouchard, Dan	Atl., Cgy., Que., Wpg.	14	655	286	232	113	37919	2061	27	3.26	43	13	30	....	2549	147	1	3.46		1972-73	1985-86
Bourque, Claude	Mtl., Det.	2	62	16	38	8	3830	192	5	3.01	3	1	2	....	188	8	1	2.55		1938-39	1939-40
Boutin, Rollie	Wsh.	3	22	7	10	1	1137	75	0	3.96	....	....	....	....	....	....	....	....		1978-79	1980-81
Bouvrette, Lionel	NYR	1	1	0	1	0	60	6	0	6.00	....	....	....	....	....	....	....	....		1942-43	1942-43
Bower, Johnny	NYR, Tor.	15	552	251	196	90	32077	1347	37	2.52	74	34	35	....	4350	184	5	2.54	4	1953-54	1969-70
Brannigan, Andy	NYA	1	1	0	0	0	7	0	0	0.00	....	....	....	....	....	....	....	....		1940-41	1940-41
Brimsek, Frank	Bos., Chi.	10	514	252	182	80	31210	1404	40	2.70	68	32	36	....	4365	186	2	2.56	2	1938-39	1949-50
* Broda, Turk	Tor.	14	629	302	224	101	38173	1609	62	2.53	101	58	42	1	6389	211	13	1.98	5	1936-37	1951-52
Broderick, Ken	Min., Bos.	3	27	11	12	1	1464	74	2	3.03	....	....	....	....	....	....	....	....		1969-70	1974-75
Broderick, Len	Mtl.	1	1	1	0	0	60	2	0	2.00	....	....	....	....	....	....	....	....		1957-58	1957-58
Brodeur, Richard	NYI, Van., Hfd.	9	385	131	176	62	21968	1410	6	3.85	33	13	20	....	2009	111	1	3.32		1979-80	1987-88
Bromley, Gary	Buf., Van.	6	136	54	44	28	7427	425	7	3.43	7	2	5	....	360	25	0	4.17		1973-74	1980-81
* Brooks, Arthur	Tor.	1	4	2	1	0	220	23	0	5.75	....	....	....	....	....	....	....	....		1917-18	1917-18
Brooks, Ross	Bos.	3	54	37	7	6	3047	134	4	2.64	1	0	0	....	20	3	0	9.00		1972-73	1974-75
* Brophy, Frank	Que.	1	21	3	18	0	1247	148	0	7.05	....	....	....	....	....	....	....	....		1919-20	1919-20
Brown, Andy	Det., Pit.	3	62	22	26	9	3373	213	1	3.79	....	....	....	....	....	....	....	....		1971-72	1973-74
Brown, Ken	Chi.	1	1	0	0	0	18	1	0	3.33	....	....	....	....	....	....	....	....		1970-71	1970-71
Bullock, Bruce	Van.	3	16	3	9	3	927	74	0	4.79	....	....	....	....	....	....	....	....		1972-73	1976-77
Buzinski, Steve	NYR	1	9	2	6	1	560	55	0	5.89	....	....	....	....	....	....	....	....		1942-43	1942-43
Caley, Don	St.L.	1	1	0	0	0	30	3	0	6.00	....	....	....	....	....	....	....	....		1967-68	1967-68
Caprice, Frank	Van.	6	102	31	40	11	5589	391	1	4.20	....	....	....	....	....	....	....	....		1982-83	1987-88
Caron, Jacques	L.A., St.L., Van.	5	72	24	29	11	3846	211	2	3.29	12	4	7	....	639	34	0	3.19		1967-68	1973-74
Carter, Lyle	Cal.	1	15	4	7	0	721	50	0	4.16	....	....	....	....	....	....	....	....		1971-72	1971-72
* Chabot, Lorne	NYR, Tor., Mtl., Chi., Mtl.M., NYA	11	411	206	140	65	25309	861	73	2.04	37	13	17	6	2558	64	5	1.50	2	1926-27	1936-37
Chadwick, Ed	Tor., Bos.	6	184	57	92	35	10980	551	14	3.01	....	....	....	....	....	....	....	....		1955-56	1961-62
Champoux, Bob	Det., Cal.	2	17	2	11	3	923	80	0	5.20	1	0	0	....	55	4	0	4.36		1963-64	1973-74
Cheevers, Gerry	Tor., Bos.	13	418	230	94	74	24394	1175	26	2.89	88	47	35	....	5396	242	8	2.69	2	1961-62	1979-80
Chevrier, Alain	N.J., Wpg., Chi., Pit., Det.	6	234	91	100	14	12202	845	2	4.16	16	9	7	....	1013	44	0	2.61		1985-86	1990-91
Clancy, Frank	Tor.	1	1	0	0	0	1	0	0	0.00	....	....	....	....	....	....	....	....		1931-32	1931-32
Cleghorn, Odie	Pit.	1	1	1	0	0	60	2	0	2.00	....	....	....	....	....	....	....	....		1925-26	1925-26
Colvin, Les	Bos.	1	1	0	1	0	60	4	0	4.00	....	....	....	....	....	....	....	....		1948-49	1948-49
Conacher, Charlie	Tor., Det.	13	3	0	0	0	9	0	0	0.00	....	....	....	....	....	....	....	....		1929-30	1940-41
* Connell, Alex	Ott., Det., NYA, Mtl.M.	12	417	199	155	59	26030	830	81	1.91	21	9	5	7	1309	26	4	1.19	2	1924-25	1936-37
Corsi, Jim	Edm.	1	26	8	14	3	1366	83	0	3.65	....	....	....	....	....	....	....	....		1979-80	1979-80
Courteau, Maurice	Bos.	1	6	2	4	0	360	33	0	5.50	....	....	....	....	....	....	....	....		1943-44	1943-44
Cox, Abbie	Mtl.M., Det., NYA, Mtl.	3	5	1	1	2	263	11	0	2.51	....	....	....	....	....	....	....	....		1929-30	1935-36
Craig, Jim	Atl., Bos., Min.	3	30	11	10	7	1588	100	0	3.78	....	....	....	....	....	....	....	....		1979-80	1983-84
Crha, Jiri	Tor.	2	69	28	27	11	3942	261	0	3.97	5	0	4	....	186	21	0	6.77		1979-80	1980-81
Crozier, Roger	Det., Buf., Wsh.	14	518	206	197	74	28567	1446	30	3.04	31	14	15	....	1769	82	1	2.78		1963-64	1976-77
Cude, Wilf	Phi., Bos., Chi., Det., Mtl.	10	282	100	129	49	17486	796	24	2.73	19	7	11	1	1317	51	1	2.32		1930-31	1940-41
Cutts, Don	Edm.	1	6	1	2	1	269	16	0	3.57	....	....	....	....	....	....	....	....		1979-80	1979-80
Cyr, Claude	Mtl.	1	1	0	0	0	20	1	0	3.00	....	....	....	....	....	....	....	....		1958-59	1958-59
Dadswell, Doug	Cgy.	2	27	8	8	3	1346	99	0	4.41	....	....	....	....	....	....	....			1986-87	1987-88
Daley, Joe	Pit., Buf., Det.	4	105	34	44	19	5836	326	3	3.35	....	....	....	....	....	....	....	....		1968-69	1971-72
Damore, Nick	Bos.	1	1	0	1	0	60	3	0	3.00	....	....	....	....	....	....	....	....		1941-42	1941-42
Daskalakis, Cleon	Bos.	3	12	3	4	1	506	41	0	4.86	....	....	....	....	....	....	....			1984-85	1986-87
Davidson, John	St.L., NYR	10	301	123	124	39	17109	1004	7	3.52	31	16	14	....	1862	77	1	2.48		1973-74	1982-83
Decourcy, Robert	NYR	1	1	0	1	0	29	6	0	12.41	....	....	....	....	....	....	....	....		1947-48	1947-48
Defelice, Norman	Bos.	1	10	3	5	2	600	30	0	3.00	....	....	....	....	....	....	....	....		1956-57	1956-57
DeJordy, Denis	Chi., L.A., Mtl., Det.	11	316	124	127	51	17798	929	15	3.13	18	6	9	....	946	55	0	3.49		1962-63	1973-74
Desjardins, Gerry	L.A., Chi., NYI, Buf.	10	331	122	153	44	19014	1042	12	3.29	35	15	15	....	1874	108	0	3.46		1968-69	1977-78
Dickie, Bill	Chi.	1	1	1	0	0	60	3	0	3.00	....	....	....	....	....	....	....	....		1941-42	1941-42
Dion, Connie	Det.	2	38	23	11	4	2280	119	0	3.13	5	1	4	....	300	17	0	3.40		1943-44	1944-45
Dion, Michel	Que., Wpg., Pit.	6	227	60	118	32	12695	898	2	4.24	5	2	3	....	304	22	0	4.34		1979-80	1984-85
Dolson, Clarence	Det.	3	93	35	44	13	5820	192	16	1.98	2	0	2	....	120	7	0	3.50		1928-29	1930-31
Dowie, Bruce	Tor.	1	2	0	1	0	72	4	0	3.33	....	....	....	....	....	....	....	....		1983-84	1983-84
Dryden, Dave	NYR, Chi., Buf., Edm.	9	203	48	57	24	10424	555	9	3.19	3	0	2	....	133	9	0	4.06		1961-62	1979-80
Dryden, Ken	Mtl.	8	397	258	57	74	23352	870	46	2.24	112	80	32	....	6846	274	10	2.40	6	1970-71	1978-79
Dumas, Michel	Chi.	2	8	2	1	2	362	24	0	3.98	1	0	0	....	19	1	0	3.16		1974-75	1976-77
Dupuis, Bob	Edm.	1	1	0	1	0	60	4	0	4.00	....	....	....	....	....	....	....	....		1979-80	1979-80
* Durnan, Bill	Mtl.	7	383	208	112	62	22945	901	34	2.36	45	27	18	....	2851	99	2	2.08	2	1943-44	1949-50
Dyck, Ed	Van.	3	49	8	28	5	2453	178	1	4.35	....	....	....	....	....	....	....	....		1971-72	1973-74
Edwards, Don	Buf., Cgy., Tor.	10	459	208	155	77	26181	1449	16	3.32	42	16	21	....	2302	132	1	3.44		1976-77	1985-86
Edwards, Gary	St.L., L.A., Clev., Min., Edm., Pit.	13	286	88	125	43	16002	973	10	3.65	11	5	4	....	537	34	0	3.80		1968-69	1981-82
Edwards, Marv	Pit., Tor., Cal.	4	61	15	34	7	3467	218	2	3.77	....	....	....	....	....	....	....	....		1968-69	1973-74
Edwards, Roy	Det., Pit.	7	236	92	88	38	13109	637	12	2.92	4	0	3	....	206	11	0	3.20		1967-68	1973-74
Eliot, Darren	L.A., Det., Buf.	5	89	25	41	12	4931	377	1	4.59	1	0	0	....	40	7	0	10.50		1984-85	1988-89
Ellacott, Ken	Van.	1	12	2	3	4	555	41	0	4.43	....	....	....	....	....	....	....	....		1982-83	1982-83
Esposito, Tony	Mtl., Chi.	16	886	423	307	151	52585	2563	76	2.92	99	45	53	....	6017	308	6	3.09	1	1968-69	1983-84
Evans, Claude	Mtl., Bos.	2	5	2	2	1	280	16	0	3.43	....	....	....	....	....	....	....	....		1954-55	1957-58
Exelby, Randy	Mtl., Edm.	2	2	0	1	0	63	5	0	4.76	....	....	....	....	....	....	....	....		1988-89	1989-90
Farr, Rocky	Buf.	3	19	2	6	3	722	42	0	3.49	....	....	....	....	....	....	....	....		1972-73	1974-75
Favell, Doug	Phi., Tor., Col.	12	373	123	153	69	20771	1096	18	3.17	21	5	16	....	1270	66	1	3.12		1967-68	1978-79
* Forbes, Jake	Tor., Ham., NYA, Phi.	13	210	84	114	11	12922	594	19	2.76	2	0	2	....	120	7	0	3.50		1919-20	1932-33

Name	NHL Teams	NHL Seasons	Regular Schedule								Playoffs								NHL Cup Wins	First NHL Season	Last NHL Season
			GP	W	L	T	Mins	GA	SO	Avg	GP	W	L	T	Mins	GA	SO	Avg			
Ford, Brian	Que., Pit.	2	11	3	7	0	580	61	0	6.31	....	....	....	....	....	....	....	....		1983-84	1984-85
Fowler, Hec	Bos.	1	7	1	6	0	420	43	0	6.14	....	....	....	....	....	....	....	....		1924-25	1924-25
Francis, Emile	Chi., NYR	6	95	31	52	11	5660	355	1	3.76	....	....	....	....	....	....	....	....		1946-47	1951-52
Franks, Jim	Det., NYR, Bos.	4	43	12	23	7	2580	185	1	4.30	1	0	1	....	30	2	0	4.00	1	1936-37	1943-44
Frederick, Ray	Chi.	1	5	0	4	1	300	22	0	4.40	....	....	....	....	....	....	....	....		1954-55	1954-55
Friesen, Karl	N.J.	1	4	0	2	1	130	16	0	7.38	....	....	....	....	....	....	....	....		1986-87	1986-87
Froese, Bob	Phi., NYR	9	242	128	72	20	13451	694	13	3.10	18	3	9	830	55	0	3.98	....		1982-83	1990-91
* Gamble, Bruce	NYR, Bos., Tor., Phi.	10	327	109	139	47	18442	992	22	3.23	5	0	4	....	206	25	0	7.28		1958-59	1971-72
Gardiner, Bert	NYR, Mtl., Chi., Bos.	6	144	49	68	27	8760	554	3	3.79	9	4	5	....	647	20	0	1.85		1935-36	1943-44
* Gardiner, Chuck	Chi.	7	316	112	152	52	19687	664	42	2.02	21	12	6	3	1532	35	5	1.37	1	1927-28	1933-34
Gardner, George	Det., Van.	5	66	16	30	6	3313	207	0	3.75	....	....	....	....	....	....	....	....		1965-66	1971-72
Garrett, John	Hfd., Que., Van.	6	207	68	91	37	11763	837	1	4.27	9	4	3	....	461	33	0	4.30		1979-80	1984-85
Gatherum, Dave	Det.	1	3	2	0	1	180	3	1	1.00	....	....	....	....	....	....	....	....		1953-54	1953-54
Gauthier, Paul	Mtl.	1	1	0	0	1	70	2	0	1.71	....	....	....	....	....	....	....	....		1937-38	1937-38
Gelineau, Jack	Bos., Chi.	4	143	46	64	33	8580	447	7	3.13	4	2	2	....	260	7	1	1.62		1948-49	1953-54
Giacomin, Ed	NYR, Det.	13	610	289	206	97	35693	1675	54	2.82	65	29	35	....	3834	180	1	2.82		1965-66	1977-78
Gilbert, Gilles	Min., Bos., Det.	14	416	182	148	60	23677	1290	18	3.27	32	17	15	....	1919	97	3	3.03		1969-70	1982-83
Gill, Andre	Bos.	1	5	3	2	0	270	13	1	2.89	....	....	....	....	....	....	....	....		1967-68	1967-68
Goodman, Paul	Chi.	3	52	23	20	9	3240	117	6	2.17	3	0	3	....	187	10	0	3.21	1	1937-38	1940-41
Grahame, Ron	Bos., L.A., Que.	4	114	50	43	15	6472	409	5	3.79	4	2	1	....	202	7	0	2.08		1977-78	1980-81
Grant, Ben	Tor., NYA., Bos.	6	50	17	26	4	2990	188	4	3.77	....	....	....	....	....	....	....	....		1928-29	1943-44
Grant, Doug	Det., St.L.	7	77	27	34	8	4199	280	2	4.00	....	....	....	....	....	....	....	....		1973-74	1979-80
Gratton, Gilles	St.L., NYR	2	47	13	18	9	2299	154	0	4.02	....	....	....	....	....	....	....	....		1975-76	1976-77
Gray, Gerry	Det., NYI	2	8	1	5	1	440	35	0	4.77	....	....	....	....	....	....	....	....		1970-71	1972-73
Gray, Harrison	Det.		1	1	0	0	0	40	5	0	730.	....	....	....	....	....	....	....		1963-64	1963-64
* Hainsworth, George	Mtl., Tor.	11	465	246	145	74	29415	937	94	1.91	52	21	26	5	3486	112	8	1.93	2	1926-27	1936-37
Hall, Glenn	Det., Chi., St.L.	18	906	407	327	165	53484	2239	84	2.51	115	49	65	....	6899	321	6	2.79	1	1952-53	1970-71
Hamel, Pierre	Tor., Wpg.	4	69	13	41	7	3766	276	0	4.40	....	....	....	....	....	....	....	....		1974-75	1980-81
Hanlon, Glen	Van., St.L., NYR, Det.	14	477	167	202	61	26037	1561	13	3.60	35	11	15	1756	92	4	3.14	....		1977-78	1990-91
Harrison, Paul	Min., Tor., Pit., Buf.	7	109	28	53	8	5806	408	2	4.22	4	0	1	....	157	9	0	3.44		1975-76	1981-82
Head, Don	Bos.	1	38	9	26	3	2280	161	2	4.24	....	....	....	....	....	....	....	....		1961-62	1961-62
* Hebert, Sammy	Tor., Ott.	2	4	1	3	0	200	19	0	5.70	....	....	....	....	....	....	....	....	1	1917-18	1923-24
Heinz, Rick	St.L., Van.	5	49	14	19	5	2356	159	2	4.05	1	0	0	....	8	1	0	7.50		1980-81	1984-85
Henderson, John	Bos.	2	46	15	15	15	2700	113	5	2.51	2	0	2	....	120	8	0	4.00		1954-55	1955-56
Henry, Gord	Bos.	4	3	1	2	0	180	5	1	1.67	5	0	4	....	283	21	0	4.45		1948-49	1952-53
Henry, Jim	NYR, Chi., Bos.	9	404	159	178	67	24240	1166	28	2.88	29	11	18	....	1741	81	2	2.79		1941-42	1954-55
Herron, Denis	Pit., K.C., Mtl.	14	462	146	203	76	25608	1579	10	3.70	15	5	10	....	901	50	0	3.33		1972-73	1985-86
Highton, Hec	Chi.	1	24	10	14	0	1440	108	0	4.50	....	....	....	....	....	....	....	....		1943-44	1943-44
Himes, Normie	NYA	2	2	0	0	1	79	3	0	2.28	....	....	....	....	....	....	....	....		1927-28	1928-29
Hodge, Charlie	Mtl., Oak., Van.	13	358	152	124	60	20593	927	24	2.70	16	6	8	....	803	32	2	2.39	1	1954-55	1970-71
Hoganson, Paul	Pit.	1	2	0	1	0	57	7	0	7.37	....	....	....	....	....	....	....	....		1970-71	1970-71
Hogosta, Goran	NYI, Que.	2	22	5	12	3	1208	83	1	4.12	....	....	....	....	....	....	....	....		1977-78	1979-80
Holden, Mark	Mtl., Wpg.	4	8	2	2	1	372	25	0	4.03	....	....	....	....	....	....	....	....		1981-82	1984-85
Holland, Ken	Hfd.	1	1	0	1	0	60	7	0	7.00	....	....	....	....	....	....	....	....		1980-81	1980-81
Holland, Robbie	Pit.	2	44	11	22	9	2513	171	1	4.06	....	....	....	....	....	....	....	....		1979-80	1980-81
* Holmes, Harry	Tor., Det.	4	105	41	54	10	6510	264	17	2.43	7	4	3	....	420	26	0	3.71		1917-18	1927-28
Horner, Red	Tor.	1	1	0	0	0	1	1	0	60.00	....	....	....	....	....	....	....	....		1932-33	1932-33
Inness, Gary	Pit., Phi., Wsh.	7	162	58	61	27	8710	494	2	3.40	9	5	4	....	540	24	0	2.67		1973-74	1980-81
Ireland, Randy	Buf.	1	2	0	0	0	30	3	0	6.00	....	....	....	....	....	....	....	....		1978-79	1978-79
Irons, Robbie	St.L.	1	1	0	0	0	3	0	0	0.00	....	....	....	....	....	....	....	....		1968-69	1968-69
Ironstone, Joe	NYA, Tor.	2	2	1	1	0	110	3	0	1.64	....	....	....	....	....	....	....	....		1925-26	1927-28
Jackson, Doug	Chi.	1	6	2	3	1	360	42	0	7.00	....	....	....	....	....	....	....	....		1947-48	1947-48
Jackson, Percy	Bos., NYA, NYR	4	7	1	3	1	392	26	0	3.98	....	....	....	....	....	....	....	....		1931-32	1935-36
Janaszak, Steve	Min., Col.	2	3	0	1	1	160	15	0	5.63	....	....	....	....	....	....	....	....		1979-80	1981-82
Janecyk, Bob	Chi., L.A.	6	110	43	47	13	6250	432	2	4.15	3	0	3	....	184	10	0	3.26		1983-84	1988-89
Jenkins, Roger	NYA	1	1	0	1	0	30	7	0	14.00	....	....	....	....	....	....	....	....		1938-39	1938-39
Jensen, Al	Det., Wsh., L.A.	7	179	95	53	18	9974	557	8	3.35	12	5	5	....	598	32	0	3.21		1980-81	1986-87
Jensen, Darren	Phi.	2	30	15	10	1	1496	95	2	3.81	....	....	....	....	....	....	....	....		1984-85	1985-86
Johnson, Bob	St.L., Pit.	2	24	9	9	1	1059	66	0	3.74	....	....	....	....	....	....	....	....		1972-73	1974-75
Johnston, Eddie	Bos., Tor., St.L., Chi.	16	592	236	256	87	34209	1855	32	3.25	18	7	10	....	1023	57	1	3.34	2	1962-63	1977-78
Junkin, Joe	Bos.	1	1	0	0	0	8	0	0	0.00	....	....	....	....	....	....	....	....		1968-69	1968-69
Kaarela, Jari	Col.	1	5	2	2	0	220	22	0	6.00	....	....	....	....	....	....	....	....		1980-81	1980-81
Kampurri, Hannu	N.J.	1	13	1	10	1	645	54	0	5.02	....	....	....	....	....	....	....	....		1984-85	1984-85
* Karakas, Mike	Chi., Mtl.	8	336	114	169	53	20616	1002	28	2.92	23	11	12	....	1434	72	3	3.01	1	1935-36	1945-46
Keans, Doug	L.A., Bos.	9	210	96	64	26	11388	666	4	3.51	9	2	6		432	34	0	4.72		1979-80	1987-88
Keenan, Don	Bos.	1	1	0	1	0	60	4	0	4.00	....	....	....	....	....	....	....	....		1958-59	1958-59
* Kerr, Dave	Mtl.M., NYA, NYR	11	426	203	148	75	26519	960	51	2.17	40	18	19	3	2616	76	8	1.74	1	1930-31	1940-41
Kleisinger, Terry	NYR	1	4	0	2	0	191	14	0	4.40	....	....	....	....	....	....	....	....		1985-86	1985-86
Klymkiw, Julian	NYR	1	1	0	0	0	19	2	0	6.32	....	....	....	....	....	....	....	....		1958-59	1958-59
Kurt, Gary	Cal.	1	16	1	7	5	838	60	0	4.30	....	....	....	....	....	....	....	....		1971-72	1971-72
Lacroix, Al	Mtl.	1	5	1	4	0	280	16	0	3.20	....	....	....	....	....	....	....	....		1925-26	1925-26
LaFerriere, Rick	Col.	1	1	0	0	0	20	1	0	3.00	....	....	....	....	....	....	....	....		1981-82	1981-82
* Larocque, Michel	Mtl., Tor., Phi., St.L.	11	312	160	89	45	17615	978	17	3.33	14	6	6	....	759	37	1	2.92	4	1973-74	1983-84
Laskowski, Gary	L.A.	2	59	19	27	5	2942	228	0	4.65	....	....	....	....	....	....	....	....		1982-83	1983-84
Laxton, Gord	Pit.	4	17	4	9	0	800	74	0	5.55	....	....	....	....	....	....	....	....		1975-76	1978-79
LeDuc, Albert	Mtl.	1	1	0	0	0	2	1	0	30.00	....	....	....	....	....	....	....	....		1931-32	1931-32
Legris, Claude	Det.	2	4	0	1	1	91	4	0	2.64	....	....	....	....	....	....	....	....		1980-81	1981-82
* Lehman, Hugh	Chi.	2	48	20	24	4	3047	136	6	2.68	2	0	1	1	120	10	0	5.00		1926-27	1927-28
Lessard, Mario	L.A.	6	240	92	97	39	13529	843	9	3.74	20	6	12	....	1136	83	0	4.38		1978-79	1983-84
Levasseur, Louis	Min.	1	1	0	1	0	60	7	0	7.00	....	....	....	....	....	....	....	....		1979-80	1979-80
Levinsky, Alex	Tor.	1	1	0	0	0	1	1	0	60.00	....	....	....	....	....	....	....	....		1932-33	1932-33
* Lindbergh, Pelle	Phi.	5	157	87	49	15	9151	503	7	3.30	23	12	10	....	1214	63	3	3.11		1981-82	1985-86
* Lindsay, Bert	Mtl.W., Tor.	2	20	6	14	0	2219	118	0	3.19	....	....	....	....	....	....	....	....		1917-18	1918-19
Lockett, Ken	Van.	2	55	13	15	8	2348	131	2	3.35	1	0	1	....	60	6	0	6.00		1974-75	1975-76
* Lockhart, Howie	Tor., Que., Ham., Bos.	5	57	17	39	0	3371	282	1	5.02	....	....	....	....	....	....	....	....		1919-20	1924-25
LoPresti, Pete	Min., Edm.	6	175	43	102	20	9858	668	5	4.07	2	0	2	....	77	6	0	4.68		1974-75	1980-81
* LoPresti, Sam	Chi.	2	74	30	38	6	4530	236	4	3.13	8	3	5	....	530	17	1	1.92		1940-41	1941-42
Loustel, Ron	Wpg.	1	1	0	1	0	60	10	0	10.00	....	....	....	....	....	....	....	....		1980-81	1980-81
Low, Ron	Tor., Wsh., Det., Que., Edm., NJ	11	382	102	203	37	20502	1463	4	4.28	7	1	6	....	452	29	0	3.85		1972-73	1984-85
Lozinski, Larry	Det.	1	30	6	11	7	1459	105	0	4.32	....	....	....	....	....	....	....	....		1980-81	1980-81
Lumley, Harry	Det., NYR, Chi., Tor., Bos.	16	804	332	324	143	48107	2210	71	2.76	76	29	47	....	4759	199	7	2.51	1	1943-44	1959-60
MacKenzie, Shawn	N.J.	1	4	0	1	0	130	15	0	6.92	....	....	....	....	....	....	....	....		1982-83	1982-83
Maniago, Cesare	Tor., Mtl., NYR, Min., Van.	15	568	189	261	96	32570	1774	30	3.27	36	15	21	....	2245	100	3	2.67		1960-61	1977-78
Marios, Jean	Tor., Chi.	2	3	1	2	0	180	15	0	5.00	....	....	....	....	....	....	....	....		1943-44	1953-54
Martin, Seth	St.L.	1	30	8	10	7	1552	67	1	2.59	2	0	0	....	73	5	0	4.11		1967-68	1967-68
Mattson, Markus	Wpg., Min., L.A.	4	92	21	46	14	5007	343	6	4.11	....	....	....	....	....	....	....	....		1979-80	1983-84
Mayer, Gilles	Tor.	4	9	1	7	1	540	25	0	2.78	....	....	....	....	....	....	....	....		1949-50	1955-56
McAuley, Ken	NYR	2	96	17	64	15	5740	537	1	5.61	....	....	....	....	....	....	....	....		1943-44	1944-45
McCartan, Jack	NYR	2	12	3	7	2	680	43	1	3.79	....	....	....	....	....	....	....	....		1959-60	1960-61
McCool, Frank	Tor.	2	72	34	31	7	4320	242	4	3.36	13	8	5	....	807	30	4	2.23	1	1944-45	1945-46
McDuffe, Pete	St.L., NYR, K.C., Det.	5	57	11	36	6	3207	218	0	4.08	1	0	1	....	60	7	0	7.00		1971-72	1975-76
McGrattan, Tom	Det.	1	1	0	0	0	8	0	0	0.00	....	....	....	....	....	....	....	....		1947-48	1947-48
McKay, Ross	NYI	1	1	0	0	0	35	3	0	5.14	....	....	....	....	....	....	....	....		1990-91	1990-91
McKenzie, Bill	Det., K.C., Col.	6	91	18	49	13	4776	326	2	4.10	....	....	....	....	....	....	....	....		1973-74	1979-80
McKichan, Steve	Van.	1	1	0	0	0	20	2	0	6.00	....	....	....	....	....	....	....	....		1990-91	1990-91
McLachlan, Murray	Tor.	1	2	0	1	0	25	4	0	9.60	....	....	....	....	....	....	....	....		1970-71	1970-71
McLelland, Dave	Van.	1	2	1	1	0	120	10	0	5.00	....	....	....	....	....	....	....	....		1972-73	1972-73
McLeod, Don	Det., Phi.	2	18	3	10	1	879	74	0	5.05	....	....	....	....	....	....	....	....		1970-71	1971-72
McLeod, Jim	St.L.	1	16	6	6	4	880	44	0	3.00	....	....	....	....	....	....	....	....		1971-72	1971-72
McNamara, Gerry	Tor.	2	7	2	2	1	323	15	0	2.79	....	....	....	....	....	....	....	....		1960-61	1969-70
McNeil, Gerry	Mtl.	7	276	119	105	52	16535	650	28	2.36	35	17	18	....	2284	72	5	1.89	1	1947-48	1956-57
McRae, Gord	Tor.	5	71	21	32	10	3799	221	1	3.49	8	2	5	....	454	22	0	2.91		1972-73	1977-78
Meloche, Gilles	Chi., Cal., Cle., Min., Pit.	18	788	270	351	131	45401	2756	20	3.64	45	21	19	....	2464	143	2	3.48		1970-71	1987-88
Micalef, Corrado	Det.	5	113	26	59	15	5794	409	2	4.24	3	0	0	....	49	8	0	9.80		1981-82	1985-86
Middlebrook, Lindsay	Wpg., Min., N.J., Edm.	4	37	3	23	6	1845	152	0	4.94	....	....	....	....	....	....	....	....		1979-80	1982-83

Name	NHL Teams	NHL Seasons	Regular Schedule GP	W	L	T	Mins	GA	SO	Avg	Playoffs GP	W	L	T	Mins	GA	SO	Avg	NHL Cup Wins	First NHL Season	Last NHL Season
Millar, Joe	Bos.	1	6	1	3	2	360	25	0	4.17	....	....	....	....	....	....	....	....		1957-58	1957-58
Miller, Joe	NYA, Pit., Phi.	4	130	24	90	16	7981	386	16	2.90	3	2	1	....	180	3	1	1.00		1927-28	1930-31
Mio, Eddie	Edm., NYR, Det.	7	192	83	85	31	12299	822	6	4.01	17	9	7	....	986	63	0	3.83		1979-80	1985-86
* Mitchell, Ivan	Tor.	3	21	11	9	0	1232	93	0	4.53	....	....	....	....	....	....	....	....	1	1919-20	1921-22
Moffatt, Mike	Bos.	3	19	7	7	2	979	70	0	4.29	11	6	5	....	663	38	0	3.44		1981-82	1983-84
Moore, Alfie	NYA, Det., Chi.,	4	21	7	14	0	1290	81	1	3.77	3	1	2	....	180	7	0	2.33	1	1936-37	1939-40
Moore, Robbie	Phi., Wsh.	2	6	3	1	1	257	8	2	1.87	5	3	2	....	268	18	0	4.03		1978-79	1982-83
Morisette, Jean	Mtl.	1	1	0	1	0	36	4	0	6.67	....	....	....	....	....	....	....	....		1963-64	1963-64
Mowers, Johnny	Det.	4	152	65	55	25	9350	399	15	2.56	32	19	13	....	2000	85	2	2.55	1	1940-41	1946-47
Mrazek, Jerry	Phi.	1	1	0	0	0	6	1	0	10.00	....	....	....	....	....	....	....	....		1975-76	1975-76
* Mummery, Harry	Que., Ham.	2	4	2	1	0	191	20	0	6.28	....	....	....	....	....	....	....	....		1919-20	1921-22
Murphy, Hal	Mtl.	1	1	1	0	0	60	4	0	4.00	....	....	....	....	....	....	....	....		1952-53	1952-53
Murray, Tom	Mtl.	1	1	0	1	0	60	4	0	4.00	....	....	....	....	....	....	....	....		1929-30	1929-30
Mylnikov, Sergei	Que.	1	10	1	7	2	568	47	0	4.96	....	....	....	....	....	....	....	....		1989-90	1989-90
Myre, Phil	Mtl., Atl., St.L., Phi., Col., Buf.	14	439	149	198	76	25220	1482	14	3.53	12	6	5	....	747	41	1	3.29		1969-70	1982-83
Newton, Cam	Pit.	2	16	4	7	1	814	51	0	3.76	....	....	....	....	....	....	....	....		1970-71	1972-73
Norris, Jack	Bos., Chi., L.A.	4	58	19	26	4	3119	202	2	3.89	....	....	....	....	....	....	....	....		1964-65	1970-71
Oleschuk, Bill	K.C., Col.	4	55	7	28	10	2835	188	1	3.98	....	....	....	....	....	....	....	....		1975-76	1979-80
Olesevich, Dan	NYR	1	1	0	0	1	40	2	0	3.00	....	....	....	....	....	....	....	....		1961-62	1961-62
Ouimet, Ted	St.L.	1	1	0	1	0	60	2	0	2.00	....	....	....	....	....	....	....	....		1968-69	1968-69
Pageau, Paul	L.A.	1	1	0	1	0	60	8	0	8.00	....	....	....	....	....	....	....	....		1980-81	1980-81
Paille, Marcel	NYR	7	107	33	52	21	6342	362	2	3.42	....	....	....	....	....	....	....	....		1957-58	1964-65
Palmateer, Mike	Tor., Wsh.	8	356	149	138	52	20131	1183	17	3.53	29	12	17	....	1765	89	2	3.03		1976-77	1983-84
Pang, Darren	Chi.	3	81	27	35	7	4252	287	0	4.05	6	1	3	....	250	18	0	4.32		1984-85	1988-89
Parent, Bernie	Bos., Tor., Phi.	13	608	270	197	121	35136	1493	55	2.55	71	38	33	....	4302	174	6	2.43	2	1965-66	1978-79
Parent, Bob	Tor.	2	3	0	2	0	160	15	0	5.63	....	....	....	....	....	....	....	....		1981-82	1982-83
Parro, Dave	Wsh.	4	77	21	36	10	4015	274	2	4.09	....	....	....	....	....	....	....	....		1980-81	1983-84
Patrick, Lester	NYR	....	....	....	....	....	....	....	....	....	1	1	0	0	46	1	0	1.30		1927-28	1927-28
Peeters, Pete	Phi., Bos., Wsh.	13	489	246	155	51	27699	1424	21	3.08	71	35	35	4200	232	2	3.31	....		1978-79	1990-91
Pelletier, Marcel	Chi., NYR	2	8	1	6	1	395	33	0	5.01	....	....	....	....	....	....	....	....		1950-51	1962-63
Penney, Steve	Mtl., Wpg.	5	91	35	38	12	5194	313	1	3.62	27	15	12	....	1604	72	4	2.69		1983-84	1987-88
Perreault, Robert	Mtl., Det., Bos.	3	31	8	16	6	1833	106	2	3.47	....	....	....	....	....	....	....	....		1955-56	1962-63
Pettie, Jim	Bos.	3	21	9	7	2	1157	71	1	3.68	....	....	....	....	....	....	....	....		1976-77	1978-79
Plante, Jacques	Mtl., NYR, St.L., Tor., Bos.	18	837	434	246	137	49553	1965	82	2.38	112	71	37	....	6651	241	15	2.17	6	1952-53	1972-73
Plasse, Michel	St.L., Mtl., K.C., Pit., Col., Que.	11	299	92	136	54	16760	1058	2	3.79	4	1	2	....	195	9	1	2.77	1	1970-71	1981-82
Plaxton, Hugh	Mtl.M.	1	1	0	1	0	59	5	0	5.08	....	....	....	....	....	....	....	....		1932-33	1932-33
Pronovost, Claude	Bos., Mtl.	2	3	1	1	0	120	7	1	3.50	....	....	....	....	....	....	....	....		1955-56	1958-59
Pusey, Chris	Det.	1	1	0	0	0	40	3	0	4.50	....	....	....	....	....	....	....	....		1985-86	1985-86
Rayner, Chuck	NYA, Bro., NYR	10	424	138	209	77	25491	1294	25	3.05	18	9	9	....	1134	46	1	2.43		1940-41	1952-53
Redquest, Greg	Pit.	1	1	0	0	0	13	3	0	13.85	....	....	....	....	....	....	....	....		1977-78	1977-78
Reece, Dave	Bos.	1	14	7	5	2	777	43	2	3.32	....	....	....	....	....	....	....	....		1975-76	1975-76
Resch, Glenn	NYI, Col., N.J., Phi.	14	571	231	224	82	32279	1761	26	3.27	41	17	17	....	2044	85	2	2.50	1	1973-74	1986-87
Rheaume, Herb	Mtl.	1	31	10	19	1	1889	92	0	2.97	....	....	....	....	....	....	....	....		1925-26	1925-26
Ricci, Nick	Pit.	4	19	7	12	0	1087	79	0	4.36	....	....	....	....	....	....	....	....		1979-80	1982-83
Richardson, Terry	Det., St.L.	5	20	3	11	0	906	85	0	5.63	....	....	....	....	....	....	....	....		1973-74	1978-79
Ridley, Curt	NYR, Van., Tor.	6	104	27	47	16	5498	355	1	3.87	2	0	2	....	120	8	0	4.00		1974-75	1980-81
Riggin, Denis	Det.	2	18	5	10	2	985	54	1	3.29	....	....	....	....	....	....	....	....		1959-60	1962-63
Riggin, Pat	Atl., Cgy., Wsh., Bos., Pit.	9	350	153	120	52	19872	1135	11	3.43	25	8	13	....	1336	72	0	3.23		1979-80	1987-88
Ring, Bob	Bos.	1	1	0	0	0	34	4	0	7.06	....	....	....	....	....	....	....	....		1965-66	1965-66
Rivard, Fern	Min.	4	55	9	20	7	2865	190	2	3.98	....	....	....	....	....	....	....	....		1968-69	1974-75
Roach, John	Tor., NYR, Det.	14	491	218	204	69	30423	1246	58	2.46	34	15	16	3	2206	69	8	1.88	1	1921-22	1934-35
Roberts, Moe	Bos., NYA, Chi.	4	10	2	5	0	506	31	0	3.68	....	....	....	....	....	....	....	....		1925-26	1951-52
Robertson, Earl	NYA, Bro., Det.	6	190	60	95	34	11820	575	16	2.92	15	6	7	....	995	29	2	1.75	1	1936-37	1941-42
Rollins, Al	Tor., Chi., NYR	9	430	138	205	84	25717	1196	28	2.79	13	6	7	....	755	30	0	2.38	1	1949-50	1959-60
Romano, Roberto	Pit., Bos.	5	125	45	64	7	7046	474	4	4.04	....	....	....	....	....	....	....	....		1982-83	1986-87
Rupp, Pat	Det.	1	1	0	1	0	60	4	0	4.00	....	....	....	....	....	....	....	....		1963-64	1963-64
Rutherford, Jim	Dot., Pit., Tor., L.A.	13	457	150	227	59	25895	1576	14	3.65	8	2	5	....	440	28	0	3.82		1970-71	1982-83
Rutledge, Wayne	L.A.	3	82	22	30	5	4325	241	2	3.34	8	2	2	....	378	20	0	3.17		1967-68	1969-70
St.Croix, Rick	Phi., Tor.	8	129	49	54	18	7275	450	2	3.71	11	4	6	....	562	29	1	3.10		1977-78	1984-85
Sands, Charlie	Mtl.	1	1	0	0	0	25	5	0	12.00	....	....	....	....	....	....	....	....		1939-40	1939-40
Sands, Mike	Min.	2	6	0	5	0	302	26	0	5.17	....	....	....	....	....	....	....	....		1984-85	1986-87
Sauve, Bob	Buf., Det., Chi., N.J.	12	405	178	149	53	22991	1321	8	3.45	34	15	16		1850	95	4	3.08		1976-77	1987-88
* Sawchuk, Terry	Det., Bos., Tor., L.A., NYR	21	971	435	337	188	57205	2401	103	2.52	106	54	48	....	6291	267	12	2.64	4	1949-50	1969-70
Schaefer, Joe	NYR	2	2	0	1	0	86	8	0	5.58	....	....	....	....	....	....	....	....		1959-60	1960-61
Scott, Ron	NYR, L.A.	5	28	8	13	4	1450	91	0	3.77	1	0	0	32	4	0	7.50	....		1983-84	1989-90
Sevigny, Richard	Mtl., Que.	8	176	90	44	20	9485	507	5	3.21	6	0	3	....	208	13	0	3.75	1	1979-80	1986-87
Shields, Al	NYA	1	2	0	0	0	41	9	0	13.17	....	....	....	....	....	....	....	....		1931-32	1931-32
Simmons, Don	Bos., Tor., NYR	11	247	100	104	39	14436	705	20	2.93	24	13	11	....	1436	64	3	2.67	1	1956-57	1968-69
Simmons, Gary	Cal., Clev., L.A.	4	107	30	57	15	6162	366	5	3.56	1	0	0	....	20	1	0	3.00		1974-75	1977-78
Skidmore, Paul	St.L.	1	2	1	1	0	120	6	0	3.00	....	....	....	....	....	....	....	....		1981-82	1981-82
Skorodenski, Warren	Chi., Edm.	5	35	12	11	4	1732	100	2	3.46	2	0	0	....	33	6	0	10.91		1981-82	1987-88
Smith, Al	Tor., Pit., Det., Buf., Hfd., Col.	10	233	68	99	36	12752	735	10	3.46	6	1	4	....	317	21	0	3.97		1965-66	1980-81
Smith, Billy	L.A., NYI	18	680	305	233	105	38431	2031	22	3.17	132	88	36		7645	348	5	2.73	4	1971-72	1988-89
Smith, Gary	Tor., Oak., Cal., Chi., Van., Min., Wsh., Wpg.	14	532	152	237	67	29619	1675	26	3.39	20	5	13	....	1153	62	1	3.23		1965-66	1979-80
Smith, Norman	Mtl.M., Det.	8	199	81	83	35	12297	475	17	2.32	12	9	2	....	880	18	3	1.23	2	1931-32	1944-45
Sneddon, Bob	Cal.	1	5	0	2	0	225	21	0	5.60	....	....	....	....	....	....	....	....		1970-71	1970-71
Soetaert, Doug	NYR, Wpg., Mtl.	12	284	110	103	44	15583	1030	6	3.97	5	1	2	....	180	14	0	4.67	1	1975-76	1986-87
Spooner, Red	Pit.	1	1	0	1	0	60	6	0	6.00	....	....	....	....	....	....	....	....		1929-30	1929-30
Staniowski, Ed	St.L., Wpg., Hfd.	10	219	67	104	21	12075	818	2	4.06	8	1	6	....	428	28	0	3.92		1975-76	1984-85
Starr, Harold	Mtl.M.	1	1	0	0	0	3	0	0	0.00	....	....	....	....	....	....	....	....		1931-32	1931-32
Stefan, Greg	Det.	9	299	115	127	30	16333	1068	5	3.92	30	12	17	1681	99	1	3.53	....		1981-82	1989-90
Stein, Phil	Tor.	1	1	0	0	1	70	2	0	1.71	....	....	....	....	....	....	....	....		1939-40	1939-40
Stephenson, Wayne	St.L., Phi., Wsh.	10	328	146	93	46	18343	937	14	3.06	26	11	12	....	1522	79	2	3.11	1	1971-72	1980-81
Stevenson, Doug	NYR, Chi.	2	8	2	6	0	480	39	0	4.88	....	....	....	....	....	....	....	....		1944-45	1945-46
Stewart, Charles	Bos.	3	77	31	41	5	4737	194	10	2.46	....	....	....	....	....	....	....	....		1924-25	1926-27
Stewart, Jim	Bos.	1	1	0	1	0	20	5	0	15.00	....	....	....	....	....	....	....	....		1979-80	1979-80
Stuart, Herb	Det.	1	3	0	1	0	180	5	0	1.67	....	....	....	....	....	....	....	....		1926-27	1926-27
Sylvestri, Don	Bos.	1	3	0	0	2	102	6	0	3.53	....	....	....	....	....	....	....	....		1984-85	1984-85
Tataryn, Dave	NYR	1	2	1	1	0	80	10	0	7.50	....	....	....	....	....	....	....	....		1976-77	1976-77
Taylor, Bobby	Phi., Pit.	5	46	15	17	6	2268	155	0	4.10	....	....	....	....	....	....	....	....	1	1971-72	1975-76
Teno, Harvey	Det.	1	5	2	3	0	3.00	15	0	3.00	....	....	....	....	....	....	....	....		1938-39	1938-39
Thomas, Wayne	Mtl., Tor., NYR	8	243	103	93	34	13768	766	10	3.34	15	6	8	....	849	50	1	3.53		1972-73	1980-81
Thompson, Tiny	Bos., Det.	12	553	284	194	75	34174	1183	81	2.08	44	20	22	....	2970	93	7	1.88	1	1928-29	1939-40
Tremblay, Vince	Tor., Pit.	5	58	12	26	8	2785	223	1	4.80	....	....	....	....	....	....	....	....		1979-80	1983-84
Tucker, Ted	Cal.	1	5	1	1	1	177	10	0	3.39	....	....	....	....	....	....	....	....		1973-74	1973-74
Turner, Joe	Det.	1	1	0	0	1	60	3	0	3.00	....	....	....	....	....	....	....	....		1941-42	1941-42
Vachon, Rogatien	Mtl., L.A., Det., Bos.	16	795	355	291	115	46298	2310	51	2.99	48	23	23	....	2876	133	2	2.77	3	1966-67	1981-82
Veisor, Mike	Chi., Hfd., Wpg.	10	139	41	62	26	7806	532	5	4.09	4	0	2	....	180	15	0	5.00		1973-74	1983-84
Vezina, Georges	Mtl.	9	191	105	80	5	11564	633	13	3.28	26	19	6	....	1596	74	4	2.78	2	1917-18	1925-26
Villemure, Gilles	NYR, Chi.	10	205	98	65	27	11581	542	13	2.81	14	5	5	....	656	32	0	2.93		1963-64	1976-77
Wakely, Ernie	Mtl., St.L.	5	113	41	42	17	6344	290	8	2.79	10	2	6	....	509	37	1	4.36		1962-63	1971-72
Walsh, James	Mtl.M., NYA	7	108	48	43	16	6461	250	12	2.32	8	2	4	2	570	16	2	1.68		1926-27	1932-33
Watt, Jim	St.L.	1	1	0	0	0	20	2	0	6.00	....	....	....	....	....	....	....	....		1973-74	1973-74
Wetzel, Carl	Det., Min.	2	7	1	3	1	302	22	0	4.37	....	....	....	....	....	....	....	....		1964-65	1967-68
Wilson, Dunc	Phi., Van., Tor., NYR, Pit.	10	287	80	150	33	15851	988	8	3.74	....	....	....	....	....	....	....	....		1969-70	1978-79
Wilson, Lefty	Det., Tor., Bos.	3	3	0	0	1	85	1	0	0.71	....	....	....	....	....	....	....	....		1953-54	1957-58
Winkler, Hal	NYR, Bos.	2	75	35	26	14	4739	126	21	1.60	10	2	3	5	640	18	2	1.69		1926-27	1927-28
Wolfe, Bernie	Wsh.	4	120	20	61	21	6104	424	1	4.17	....	....	....	....	....	....	....	....		1975-76	1978-79
Woods, Alec	NYA	1	1	0	1	0	70	3	0	2.57	....	....	....	....	....	....	....	....		1936-37	1936-37
Worsley, Gump	NYR, Mtl., Min.	21	862	335	353	150	50232	2432	43	2.90	70	41	25	....	4081	192	5	2.82	4	1952-53	1973-74
Worters, Roy	Pit., NYA, Mtl.	12	484	171	233	68	30175	1143	66	2.27	11	3	6	2	690	24	3	2.09		1925-26	1936-37
Worthy, Chris	Oak., Cal.	3	26	5	10	4	1326	98	0	4.43	....	....	....	....	....	....	....	....		1968-69	1970-71
Young, Doug	Det.	1	1	0	0	0	21	1	0	2.86	....	....	....	....	....	....	....	....		1933-34	1933-34
Zanier, Mike	Edm.	1	3	1	1	1	185	12	0	3.89	....	....	....	....	....	....	....	....		1984-85	1984-85

THREE STAR SELECTION...

NHL PUBLISHING IS PLEASED TO OFFER THREE OF THE GAME'S LEADING ANNUAL PUBLICATIONS

1. The NHL Official Guide & Record Book

is the NHL's authoritative information source. 61st year in print. 424 pages. The "Bible of Hockey". Read worldwide.

2. The NHL Yearbook

Offered here for the first time. 200-page, full- color magazine with features on each club. Award winners, All-Stars and special statistics.

3. The NHL Rule Book & Schedule

Complete playing rules, including all changes for 1992-93.

Order 1992-93 books today or ensure prompt delivery next fall by placing your order for 1993-94.

CREDIT CARD HOLDERS CAN ORDER BY FAX: 416/531-3939, 24 HOURS (PLEASE INCLUDE EXPIRY DATE)

NHL PUBLISHING ORDER FORM

Please send

☐ copies of next year's *NHL Guide & Record Book/93-94 (available Sept. 93)*

☐ copies of this year's *NHL Guide & Record Book/92-93 (available now)*

☐ copies of next year's *NHL Yearbook 1994 magazine (available Sept. 93)*

☐ copies of this year's *NHL Yearbook 1993 magazine (available now)*

☐ copies of the *NHL Rule Book and Schedule*

PRICES:	CANADA	U.S.A.	OVERSEAS
Guide & Record Book	$ 17.95	$ 16.95	$ 17.95 CDN
Handling (per copy)	$ 3.00	$ 4.50	$ 7.50 CDN
7% GST	$ 1.47	—	—
Total (per copy)	**$ 22.42**	**$ 19.95**	**$ 25.45** CDN
Extra for Airmail	$ 8.00	$ 9.00	$ 14.00 CDN
Yearbook	$ 6.95	$ 6.95	$ 6.95 CDN
Handling (per copy)	$ 2.35	$ 3.50	$ 5.00 CDN
7% GST	$ .65	—	—
Total (per copy)	**$ 9.95**	**$ 10.45**	**$ 11.95** CDN
Rule Book	$ 5.00	$ 5.00	$ 5.00 CDN
Handling (per copy)	$ 1.75	$ 2.50	$ 3.00 CDN
7% GST	$ .47	—	—
Total (per copy)	**$ 7.22**	**$ 7.50**	**$ 8.00** CDN

☐ Enclosed is my cheque or money order.

Charge my ☐ Mastercard ☐ Visa ☐ Am Ex

Credit card #   Expiry Date

Signature

Name

Address

Province/State   Zip/Postal Code

IN CANADA
Mail completed form to:
NHL Publishing
194 Dovercourt Rd.
Toronto, Ontario
M6J 3C8

IN U.S.A.
Mail completed form to:
NHL Publishing
194 Dovercourt Rd.
Toronto, Ontario
M6J 3C8
Remit in U.S. funds

OVERSEAS
Mail completed form to:
NHL Publishing
194 Dovercourt Rd.
Toronto, Ontario
CANADA M6J 3C8
Money order or
credit card only

Please allow up to five weeks for delivery.

Notes

1991-92 Transactions

June, 1991

20 - **Jim Vesey** traded from Winnipeg to Boston for future considerations.

21 - **Steve Maltais** and **Trent Klatt** traded from Washington to Minnesota for **Shawn Chambers**.

21 - **Randy Burridge** traded from Boston to Washington for **Stephen Leach**.

22 - **Dave Babych** traded from Minnesota to Vancouver for **Tom Kurvers**.

June – continued

22 - **Craig Ludwig** traded from NY Islanders to Minnesota for **Tom Kurvers**.

22 - **Randy Gilhen, Charlie Huddy** and **Jim Thomson** and the NY Rangers' 4th round choice in 1991 Entry Draft (previously acquired – **Alexei Zhitnik**) traded from Minnesota to Los Angeles for **Todd Elik**.

22 - **Mikhail Tatarinov** traded from Washington to Quebec for Toronto's 2nd round choice in 1991 Entry Draft (previously acquired – **Eric Lavigne**).

22 - **Tom Draper** traded from Winnipeg to Buffalo for future considerations.

July

22 - **Bryan Marchment** and **Chris Norton** traded from Winnipeg to Chicago for **Troy Murray** and **Warren Rychel**.

26 - **Mike Bullard** traded from Philadelphia to Toronto for future considerations.

31 - **Robin Bawa** traded from Washington to Vancouver for cash.

August

5 - **Shaun Sabol** traded from Philadelphia to NY Rangers for future considerations.

8 - **Don Biggs** traded from Philadelphia to NY Rangers for future considerations.

9 - **Jim Nesich** traded from Montreal to Minnesota for cash.

26 - **Paul Fenton** traded from Calgary to Hartford for Hartford's 6th round choice in 1992 Entry Draft (**Joel Bouchard**).

September

3 - **Stephane Guerard** traded from NY Rangers to Quebec for cash.

6 - **Doug Wilson** traded from Chicago to San Jose for **Kerry Toporowski** and San Jose's 2nd round choice in 1992 Entry Draft, later traded to Winnipeg (**Boris Mironov**).

8 - **Sylvain Cote** traded from Hartford to Washington for Washington's 2nd round choice in 1992 Entry Draft (**Andrei Nikolishin**).

11 - **Norm Foster** traded from Boston to Edmonton for future considerations.

17 - **Andrew Cassels** traded from Montreal to Hartford for Hartford's 2nd round draft choice in 1992 Entry Draft.

19 - **Vincent Damphousse, Peter Ing, Scott Thornton, Luke Richardson**, future considerations and cash traded from Toronto to Edmonton for **Grant Fuhr, Glenn Anderson** and **Craig Berube**.

20 - **Wayne Presley** traded from Chicago to San Jose for San Jose's 3rd round draft choice in 1993 Entry Draft.

20 - **Stephane Richer** and **Tom Chorske** traded from Montreal to New Jersey for **Kirk Muller** and **Roland Melanson**.

22 - **Dan Quinn** and **Rod Brind'Amour** traded from St. Louis to Philadelphia for **Ron Sutter** and **Murray Baron.**

24 - **Greg Millen** traded from Chicago to NY Rangers for future considerations.

25 - **Ryan McGill** traded from Quebec to Chicago for **Mike Dagenais**.

October

2 - **Dan Keczmer** traded from San Jose to Hartford for Dean Evason.

2 - Dave Manson **and future considerations traded from Chicago to Edmonton for Steve Smith**.

3 - **Todd Krygier** traded from Hartford to Washington for future considerations.

3 - **Lee Norwood** traded from New Jersey to Hartford for future considerations.

4 - **Mark Messier** and future considerations traded from Edmonton to NY Rangers for **Bernie Nicholls, Steve Rice** and **Louis DeBrusk**.

7 - **Ken Linseman** traded from Edmonton to Toronto for cash.

11 - **Dave McLlwain, Gord Donnelly**, Winnipeg's 5th round choice in 1992 Entry Draft (**Yuri Khmylev**) and future considerations traded from Winnipeg to Buffalo for **Darrin Shannon, Mike Hartman** and **Dean Kennedy**.

15 - **Tony Joseph** traded from Winnipeg to Minnesota for **Tyler Larter**.

16 - **Alan Stewart** traded from New Jersey to Boston for future considerations.

18 - **Vincent Riendeau** traded from St. Louis to Detroit for **Rick Zombo**.

October – continued

18 - **Mike McHugh** traded from San Jose to Hartford for **Paul Fenton**.

21 - **Dennis Holland** traded from Detroit to Calgary for future considerations.

22 - **Sergei Kharin** traded from Winnipeg to Quebec for **Shawn Anderson**.

23 - **Shawn Anderson** traded from Winnipeg to Washington for future considerations.

24 - **Colin Patterson** traded from Calgary to Buffalo for future considerations.

25 - **Brent Sutter** and **Brad Lauer** traded from NY Islanders to Chicago for **Adam Creighton** and **Steve Thomas**.

25 - **Pat LaFontaine, Randy Hillier, Randy Wood** and future considerations traded from NY Islanders to Buffalo for **Pierre Turgeon, Uwe Krupp, Benoit Hogue** and **Dave McLlwain**.

28 - **Chris Norton** and future considerations traded from Chicago to Los Angeles for **Rod Buskas**.

29 - **Brent Ashton** traded from Winnipeg to Boston for **Petri Skriko**.

November

12 - **Jeff Beukeboom** traded from Edmonton to NY Rangers for **David Shaw**.

13 - **Murray Craven** and future considerations traded from Philadelphia to Hartford for **Kevin Dineen**.

13 - **Lee Norwood** traded from Hartford to St. Louis for future considerations.

14 - **Barry Pederson** traded from Hartford to Boston for future considerations.

22 - **Scott Arniel** traded from Winnipeg to Boston for future considerations.

26 - **Mario Marois** traded from St. Louis to Winnipeg for future considerations.

29 - **Rick Lanz** traded from Chicago to Los Angeles for cash.

December

16 - **Stephane Matteau** traded from Calgary to Chicago for **Trent Yawney**.

18 - **Daniel Shank** traded from Detroit to Hartford for **Chris Tancill**.

18 - **Tom Fergus** traded from Toronto to Vancouver for cash.

23 - **Randy Gilhen** traded from Los Angeles to NY Rangers for **Corey Millen**.

26 - **Greg Millen** traded from NY Rangers to Detroit for future considerations.

26 - **Guy Larose** traded from NY Rangers to Toronto for **Mike Stevens**.

30 - **Warren Rychel** traded from Winnipeg to Minnesota for **Tony Joseph** and future considerations.

January, 1992

2 - **Craig Berube, Alexander Godynyuk, Gary Leeman, Michel Petit** and **Jeff Reese** traded from Toronto to Calgary for **Doug Gilmour, Jamie Macoun, Ric Nattress, Rick Wamsley** and **Kent Manderville**.

2 - **Garry Galley, Wes Walz** and future considerations traded from Boston to Philadelphia for **Gord Murphy, Brian Dobbin** and Philadelphia's 3rd round choice in 1992 Entry Draft.

9 - **Steve Bancroft** and Boston's 11th round choice in 1993 Entry Draft traded from Boston to Chicago for Chicago's 11th round choice in 1992 Entry Draft and 12th round choice in 1993 Entry Draft.

12 - **David Maley** traded from New Jersey to Edmonton for **Troy Mallette**.

15 - **Todd Gillingham** traded from Calgary to Toronto for cash.

18 - **Daniel Berthiaume** traded from Los Angeles to Boston for future considerations.

21 - **Brian Glynn** traded from Minnesota to Edmonton for **David Shaw**.

24 - **Rob Brown** traded from Hartford to Chicago for **Steve Konroyd**.

27 - **Paul Gillis** traded from Chicago to Hartford for future considerations.

31 - **Søren True** traded from NY Rangers to Los Angeles for future considerations.

February

7 - **Tony Hrkac** traded from San Jose to Chicago for future considerations.

7 - **Ryan McGill** traded from Chicago to Philadelphia for **Tony Horacek**.

7 - **Adam Oates** traded from St. Louis to Boston for **Craig Janney** and **Stephane Quintal**.

18 - **Steve Weeks** traded from NY Islanders to Los Angeles for Los Angeles' 7th round choice in 1992 Entry Draft (**Steve O'Rourke**).

February – continued

18 - **John Tonelli** traded from Chicago to Quebec for future considerations.

19 - **Jeff Chychrun, Brian Benning** and Los Angeles' 1st round choice in 1992 Entry Draft – later traded to Philadelphia (**Jason Bowen**) – traded from Los Angeles to Pittsburgh for **Paul Coffey**.

19 - **Rick Tocchet, Kjell Samuelsson** and **Ken Wregget** traded from Philadelphia to Pittsburgh for **Mark Recchi, Brian Benning** and Los Angeles' 1st round choice in 1992 Entry Draft acquired earlier by Pittsburgh (**Jason Bowen**).

22 - **Bill McDougall** traded from Detroit to Edmonton for **Max Middendorf**.

24 - **John Byce** and **Dennis Smith** traded from Boston to Washington for **Brent Hughes**.

27 - **Moe Mantha** traded from Winnipeg to Philadelphia for future considerations.

27 - **Mark Ferner** traded from Washington to Toronto for future considerations.

March

2 - **Paul MacDermid** traded from Winnipeg to Washington for **Mike Lalor**.

7 - **Murray Garbutt** traded from San Jose to Quebec for **Don Barber**.

8 - **Kip Miller** traded from Quebec to Minnesota for **Steve Maltais**.

9 - **Randy Moller** traded from NY Rangers to Buffalo for **Jay Wells**.

9 - **Wayne Presley** traded from San Jose to Buffalo for **Dave Snuggerud**.

9 - **Ken Hammond** traded from San Jose to Vancouver for Vancouver's 8th round choice in 1992 Entry Draft – later traded to Detroit (**C.J. Denomme**).

10 - **Johan Garpenlov** traded from Detroit to San Jose for **Bob McGill** and Vancouver's 8th round choice in 1992 Entry Draft previously acquired by Detroit (**C.J. Denomme**).

10 - **Bobby Reynolds** traded from Washington to Minnesota for future considerations.

10 - **Petr Svoboda** traded from Montreal to Buffalo for **Kevin Haller**.

10 - **Dave Hannan** traded from Toronto to Buffalo for future considerations.

10 - **Daniel Marois** and **Claude Loiselle** traded from Toronto to NY Islanders for **Ken Baumgartner** and **Dave McLlwain**.

10 - **Martin Rucinsky** traded from Edmonton to Quebec for **Ron Tugnutt** and **Brad Zavisha**.

10 - **Mark Janssens** traded from NY Rangers to Minnesota for **Mario Thyer** and Minnesota's 3rd round choice in 1993 Entry Draft.

10 - **Martin Simard** traded from Calgary to Quebec for **Greg Smyth**.

10 - **Bryan Fogarty** traded from Quebec to Pittsburgh for **Scott Young**.

10 - **Frank Pietrangelo** traded from Pittsburgh to Hartford for future considerations.

10 - **Mark Osborne** traded from Winnipeg to **Toronto** for **Lucien DeBlois**.

June

2 - **Todd Gillingham** traded from Toronto to Calgary for cash.

10 - **Brad Marsh** traded from Detroit to Toronto for cash.

10 - **Doug Evans** traded from Winnipeg to Boston for **Daniel Berthiaume**.

13 - **Brad Shaw** traded from Hartford to New Jersey for future considerations.

15 - **Jarmo Myllys** traded from San Jose to Toronto for cash.

15 - **Nick Kypreos** traded from Washington to Hartford for **Mark Hunter** and future considerations (**Yvon Corriveau**).

15 - **Dennis Vial** and **Doug Crossman** traded from Detroit to Quebec for cash.

15 - **Christian Ruuttu** and future considerations traded from Buffalo to Winnipeg for **Stephane Beauregard**.

15 - **Allen Pedersen** traded from Minnesota to Hartford for future considerations.

19 - **Danton Cole** traded from Winnipeg to Tampa Bay for future considerations.

19 - **J.C. Bergeron** traded from Montreal to Tampa Bay for **Frederic Chabot**.

19 - **Pat Jablonski, Steve Tuttle** and **Darin Kimble** traded from St. Louis to Tampa Bay for future considerations.

19 - **Rob Robinson** traded from St. Louis to Tampa Bay for Tampa Bay's 6th round choice in 1996 Entry Draft.

June – continued

19 - **Tim Hunter** traded from Tampa Bay to Quebec for future considerations.

19 - **NHL Supplemental Draft**

Tampa Bay	**Cory Cross** (U. of Alta.)
Ottawa	**Steve Flomenhoft** (Harvard)
San Jose	**Brian Konawalchuk** (U. of Denver)
Quebec	**Rich Shulmistra** (Miami-Ohio)
Toronto	**Nick Wohlers** (St. Thomas)
Calgary	**James O'Brien** (Brown)
Philadelphia	**Garrett MacDonald** (N. Michigan)
NY Islanders	**Chris Foy** (Northeastern)

20 - Winnipeg's 1st round choice in 1992 Entry Draft (**Sergei Krivokrasov**) traded from Winnipeg to Chicago for Chicago's 1st round choice in 1992 Entry Draft (**Sergei Bautin**).

20 - Winnipeg's 2nd round choice in 1992 Entry Draft (**Jeff Shantz**) traded from Winnipeg to Chicago for San Jose's 2nd round choice in 1992 Entry Draft – previously acquired by Chicago (**Boris Mironov**).

20 - Winnipeg's 11th round choice in 1993 Entry Draft traded from Winnipeg to St. Louis for St. Louis' 11th round choice in 1992 Entry Draft (**Ivan Vologzhaninov**).

20 - **Dino Ciccarelli** traded from Washington to Detroit for **Kevin Miller**.

20 - Toronto's 1st round choice in 1992 Entry Draft (**Darius Kasparaitis**) traded from Toronto to NY Islanders for NY Islanders' 1st round choice (**Brandon Convery**) and 2nd round choice (later traded to Washington) in 1992 Entry Draft.

20 - Washington's 1st and 4th round choices in 1992 Entry Draft (**Grant Marshall** and **Mark Raiter**) traded from Washington to Toronto for NY Islanders' 2nd round choice in 1992 Entry Draft – previously acquired by Toronto (**Jim Carey**), Toronto's 3rd round choice in 1992 Entry Draft (**Stefan Ustorf**) and 4th round choice in 1993 Entry Draft.

20 - Edmonton's 4th round choice in 1992 Entry Draft (**Chris Ferraro**) traded from Edmonton to NY Rangers for NY Rangers' 4th round choice in 1992 Entry Draft (**Ralph Intranuovo**) and Detroit's 8th round choice in 1992 Entry Draft – previously acquired by NY Rangers (**Colin Schmidt**).

20 - NY Rangers' 11th round choice in 1992 Entry Draft (**Petter Ronnqvist**) traded from NY Rangers to Ottawa for future considerations.

22 - **Mark Osiecki** traded from Calgary to Ottawa for **Chris Lindberg**.

30 - **Steve Duchesne, Peter Forsberg, Ron Hextall, Kerry Huffman, Mike Ricci, Chris Simon** and Philadelphia's 1st round choice in 1993 and 1994 Entry Draft, cash and future considerations traded from Philadelphia to Quebec for **Eric Lindros**.

July

9 - **Tim Kerr** traded from NY Rangers to Hartford for future considerations.

16 - **Mario Thyer** traded from NY Rangers to Minnesota for future considerations.

20 - **Brad Marsh** traded from Toronto to Ottawa for future considerations.

21 - **Ken McRae** traded from Quebec to Toronto for **Len Esau**.

28 - **Jody Hull** traded from NY Rangers to Ottawa for future considerations.

August

4 - **Collin Bauer** traded from Edmonton to Minnesota for future considerations.

7 - **Dominik Hasek** traded from Chicago to Buffalo for **Stephane Beauregard** and future considerations.

10 - **Christian Ruuttu** traded from Winnipeg to Chicago for **Stephane Beauregard**.

13 - **Steve Weeks** traded from Washington to Ottawa for future considerations.

14- **Mike McPhee** traded from Montreal to Minnesota for Minnesota's fifth round choice in 1993 Entry Draft.

20 - **Sylvain Lefebvre** traded from Montreal to Toronto for Toronto's 3rd round choice in 1994 Entry Draft.

20 - **Yvon Corriveau** traded from Hartford to Washington to complete earlier transaction.

24 - **Brian Mullen** traded from San Jose to NY Islanders for the rights to **Marcus Thuresson**.

25 - **Shawn Cronin** traded from Winnipeg to Quebec for **Dan Lambert**.

NHL Schedule 1992-93 *continued from inside front cover*

Visitor	Home
Sun. Nov. 29	
BUF	OTT
Mon. Nov. 30	
BOS	QUE
BUF	MTL
MIN	NYR
WSH	DET
Tue. Dec. 1	
HFD	ST.L.
MIN	OTT
PIT	NYI
TOR	N.J.
L.A.	CHI
at Milwaukee, WI	
EDM	S.J.
Wed. Dec. 2	
DET	NYR
WPG	CGY
Thur. Dec. 3	
MTL	BOS
HFD	S.J.
N.J.	OTT
QUE	PHI
PIT	L.A.
TOR	CHI
MIN	DET
EDM	VAN
Fri. Dec. 4	
NYI	BUF
NYR	WSH
ST.L.	CGY
Sat. Dec. 5	
* BOS	N.J.
HFD	L.A.
PHI	OTT
MTL	WPG
MIN	QUE
WSH	NYI
* PIT	S.J.
CHI	TOR
DET	T.B.
ST.L.	EDM
Sun. Dec. 6	
BOS	PHI
N.J.	BUF
MTL	CHI
TOR	NYR
Mon. Dec. 7	
BUF	QUE
WSH	OTT
NYI	T.B.
ST.L.	VAN
EDM	CGY
Tue. Dec. 8	
MTL	L.A.
at Phoenix, AZ	
WPG	PIT
CHI	DET
CGY	EDM
Wed. Dec. 9	
BOS	BUF
OTT	HFD
T.B.	NYR
at Miami, FL	
WSH	N.J.
DET	TOR
S.J.	VAN
Thur. Dec. 10	
OTT	BOS
QUE	L.A.
NYI	CHI
ST.L.	S.J.
EDM	MIN
Fri. Dec. 11	
HFD	BUF
NYR	T.B.
PIT	N.J.
PHI	DET
WPG	WSH
CGY	TOR
Sat. Dec. 12	
BOS	MTL
BUF	HFD
CGY	OTT
QUE	S.J.
WPG	NYI
N.J.	PIT
WSH	PHI
EDM	T.B.
CHI	MIN
ST.L.	L.A.
Sun. Dec. 13	
MTL	NYR
QUE	VAN
EDM	NYI
at Oklahoma City, OK	
Mon. Dec. 14	
BUF	BOS
CGY	DET
Tue. Dec. 15	
DET	OTT
NYI	ST.L.
at Dallas, TX	
CGY	NYR
N.J.	WPG
PHI	PIT
TOR	MIN
T.B.	L.A.
Wed. Dec. 16	
WSH	HFD
QUE	MTL
T.B.	S.J.
VAN	EDM
Thur. Dec. 17	
OTT	NYI
MTL	QUE
NYR	ST.L.
PIT	PHI
WPG	CHI
Fri. Dec. 18	
BOS	DET
HFD	WSH
N.J.	T.B.
L.A.	EDM
S.J.	VAN
Sat. Dec. 19	
WSH	BOS
NYR	HFD
BUF	MTL
OTT	TOR
* NYI	PIT
* CHI	PHI
DET	MIN
WPG	ST.L.
L.A.	CGY
VAN	S.J.
Sun. Dec. 20	
TOR	BUF
* NYI	QUE
PHI	T.B.
MIN	CHI
Mon. Dec. 21	
HFD	MTL
WSH	OTT
QUE	PIT
NYR	N.J.
S.J.	WPG
EDM	CGY
Tue. Dec. 22	
T.B.	BOS
TOR	DET
ST.L.	MIN
VAN	L.A.
Wed. Dec. 23	
T.B.	HFD
WSH	BUF
CHI	OTT
NYI	MTL
N.J.	NYR
PIT	PHI
CGY	WPG
S.J.	EDM
Sat. Dec. 26	
BOS	HFD
OTT	QUE
NYR	NYI
PHI	WSH
DET	TOR
ST.L.	CHI
WPG	MIN
L.A.	S.J.
Sun. Dec. 27	
BOS	NYR
HFD	N.J.
* PIT	BUF
QUE	OTT
MTL	VAN
TOR	ST.L.
DET	CHI
MIN	WPG
CGY	EDM
Tue. Dec. 29	
BOS	WPG
ST.L.	HFD
*at Birmingham, AL***	
MTL	EDM
N.J.	QUE
TOR	NYI
NYR	WSH
PHI	L.A.
CHI	DET
S.J.	VAN
Wed. Dec. 30	
PHI	S.J.
Thur. Dec. 31	
BOS	MIN
QUE	HFD
NYR	BUF
OTT	DET
MTL	CGY
NYI	ST.L.
TOR	PIT
T.B.	CHI
* EDM	WPG
L.A.	VAN
Fri. Jan. 1	
* N.J.	WSH
Sat. Jan. 2	
HFD	BOS
BUF	OTT
MTL	L.A.
DET	QUE
MIN	NYI
NYR	PIT
WPG	N.J.
PHI	CGY
* CHI	WSH
ST.L.	TOR
T.B.	EDM
VAN	S.J.
Sun. Jan. 3	
MIN	HFD
ST.L.	BUF
PHI	EDM
T.B.	VAN
WPG	CHI
Mon. Jan. 4	
S.J.	MTL
at Sacramento, CA	
N.J.	NYR
TOR	DET
Tue. Jan. 5	
BOS	PIT
MTL	S.J.
QUE	NYI
EDM	ST.L.
WPG	CGY
Wed. Jan. 6	
BUF	HFD
OTT	NYR
MIN	N.J.
VAN	TOR
T.B.	L.A.
Thur. Jan. 7	
QUE	BOS
WSH	PHI
MIN	PIT
EDM	CHI
CGY	ST.L.
Fri. Jan. 8	
NYI	BUF
OTT	N.J.
S.J.	TOR
VAN	DET
L.A.	WPG
Sat. Jan. 9	
N.J.	BOS
QUE	HFD
TOR	MTL
VAN	NYI
* NYR	PHI
* CGY	PIT
EDM	WSH
T.B.	MIN
CHI	ST.L.
Sun. Jan. 10	
MTL	HFD
CGY	BUF
* S.J.	OTT
EDM	PHI
PIT	WPG
L.A.	CHI
Mon. Jan. 11	
VAN	NYR
T.B.	TOR
ST.L.	DET
Tue. Jan. 12	
BUF	BOS
L.A.	OTT
CGY	NYI
VAN	N.J.
CHI	MIN
S.J.	WPG
Wed. Jan. 13	
HFD	MTL
WSH	NYR
ST.L.	TOR
T.B.	DET
WPG	EDM
Thur. Jan. 14	
PIT	BOS
ST.L.	OTT
MTL	QUE
WSH	NYI
L.A.	N.J.
CGY	PHI
MIN	CHI
Fri. Jan. 15	
HFD	EDM
BUF	VAN
S.J.	DET
Sat. Jan. 16	
PHI	BOS
HFD	VAN
OTT	PIT
NYR	MTL
S.J.	QUE
NYI	N.J.
CHI	TOR
ST.L.	T.B.
CGY	MIN
WPG	L.A.
Sun. Jan. 17	
BUF	EDM
NYI	OTT
DET	PHI
WSH	T.B.
TOR	CHI
Mon. Jan. 18	
* S.J.	BOS
HFD	WPG
at Saskatoon, Sask.	
Tue. Jan. 19	
BOS	NYI
BUF	CGY
QUE	OTT
NYR	DET
PIT	VAN
TOR	ST.L.
MIN	T.B.
CHI	WPG
L.A.	EDM
Wed. Jan. 20	
N.J.	MTL
Thur. Jan. 21	
BOS	PHI
S.J.	HFD
OTT	MIN
WSH	CHI
TOR	T.B.
ST.L.	DET
VAN	L.A.
Fri. Jan. 22	
QUE	BUF
MTL	N.J.
PIT	EDM
WPG	CGY
Sat. Jan. 23	
N.J.	BOS
* CHI	HFD
BUF	QUE
OTT	WSH
MTL	TOR
PHI	NYI
NYR	L.A.
PIT	CGY
DET	ST.L.
S.J.	T.B.
* VAN	MIN
EDM	WPG
Sun. Jan. 24	
HFD	PHI
MIN	T.B.
VAN	CHI
Mon. Jan. 25	
BOS	MTL
Tue. Jan. 26	
BOS	QUE
BUF	PHI
OTT	ST.L.
N.J.	NYI
WSH	PIT
MIN	TOR
DET	CGY
S.J.	L.A.
Wed. Jan. 27	
HFD	MTL
WSH	BUF
WPG	NYR
DET	EDM
CHI	VAN
Thur. Jan. 28	
WPG	BOS
HFD	OTT
QUE	PHI
NYI	PIT
N.J.	MIN
ST.L.	T.B.
CGY	L.A.
Fri. Jan. 29	
NYR	BUF
QUE	WSH
CHI	S.J.
Sat. Jan. 30	
BOS	NYI
WPG	HFD
* OTT	MTL
NYR	TOR
N.J.	ST.L.
* PHI	PIT
DET	VAN
T.B.	MIN
CHI	L.A.
CGY	S.J.
Sun. Jan. 31	
* EDM	BUF
* PHI	MTL
* PIT	WSH
Mon. Feb. 1	
WPG	OTT
NYR	NYI
TOR	ST.L.
T.B.	S.J.
MIN	VAN
Tue. Feb. 2	
EDM	BOS
L.A.	QUE
CGY	WSH
Wed. Feb. 3	
BOS	QUE
HFD	BUF
EDM	OTT
L.A.	MTL
NYI	TOR
PHI	NYR
CGY	N.J.
CHI	DET
T.B.	VAN
ST.L.	WPG
MIN	S.J.
Sat. Feb. 6	
All-Star Game	
at Montreal, Que.	
Mon. Feb. 8	
BOS	PIT
at Atlanta, GA	
BUF	OTT
NYR	N.J.
Tue. Feb. 9	
BOS	ST.L.
OTT	PHI
MTL	NYI
VAN	QUE
N.J.	DET
WSH	MIN
TOR	T.B.
EDM	L.A.
Wed. Feb. 10	
BUF	WPG
PIT	NYR
S.J.	CGY
Thur. Feb. 11	
BOS	CHI
MTL	PHI
WSH	ST.L.
VAN	TOR
DET	L.A.
MIN	T.B.
Fri. Feb. 12	
HFD	WPG
VAN	BUF
QUE	CGY
NYI	NYR
S.J.	EDM
Sat. Feb. 13	
HFD	CGY
MTL	OTT
NYR	NYI
* PHI	N.J.
* CHI	PIT
WSH	L.A.
MIN	TOR
DET	ST.L.

*** Subject to change*

** AFTERNOON GAME*